COMMUNICATION FOR SOCIAL CHANGE
ANTHOLOGY

CFSC

COMMUNICATION FOR
SOCIAL CHANGE
CONSORTIUM

Published by Communication for Social Change Consortium, Inc.

PUBLISHER: Denise Gray-Felder
PRODUCTION EDITOR: Susan Mach
COPY EDITORS: Denise Gray-Felder, Laurence Mach, Susan Mach
BOOK AND COVER DESIGN: © Emerson Wajdowicz Studios / www.DesignEWS.com

LIBRARY OF CONGRESS CONTROL NUMBER: 2006931661

Manufactured in the United States of America

For information on the Communication for Social Change Consortium visit our website:
www.communicationforsocialchange.org or write:
  14 South Orange Avenue, Suite 2F
  South Orange, New Jersey 07079
  United States
  Phone: 1-973-763-1115
  Fax: 1-973-762-8257

ISBN: 0-9770357-9-4

COMMUNICATION FOR SOCIAL CHANGE

ANTHOLOGY: HISTORICAL AND CONTEMPORARY READINGS

Edited by Alfonso Gumucio-Dagron and Thomas Tufte

CFSC

COMMUNICATION FOR
SOCIAL CHANGE
CONSORTIUM

TABLE OF CONTENTS

1927
1960
1963
1964
1967
1969
1970
1971
1972
1973
1974
1975
1976
1977
1978
1979
1980
1981
1982
1983
1984
1985
1986
1987
1988
1989
1990
1991
1992
1993
1994
1995
1996
1997
1998
1999
2000
2001
2002
2003
2004
2005
2006

1927
1960
1963
1964
1967
1969
1970
1971
1972
1973
1974
1975
1976
1977
1978
1979
1980
1981
1982
1983
1984
1985
1986
1987
1988
1989
1990
1991
1992
1993
1994
1995
1996
1997
1998
1999
2000
2001
2002
2003
2004
2005
2006

1927
1960
1963
1964
1967
1969
1970
1971
1972
1973
1974
1975
1976
1977
1978
1979
1980
1981
1982
1983
1984
1985
1986
1987
1988
1989
1990
1991
1992
1993
1994
1995
1996
1997
1998
1999
2000
2001
2002
2003
2004
2005
2006

FOREWORD

By The Honourable Vida Yeboah (d.2006)

Vida Yeboah was the founding president and chief executive officer of the Forum for African Women Educationalists (FAWE) Ghana Chapter. She was formerly minister of tourism for her native Ghana and a deputy minister of education who led, for eight years, the implementation of Ghana's Educational Reforms which sought to increase access and make education relevant and functional for self and national development. Mrs. Yeboah also was an elected member of Ghana's legislature for two consecutive terms of eight years.

A well-respected educator, politician, civic leader and advocate for girls' education in Africa, Mrs. Yeboah was an inaugural member of the pan-African International FAWE Executive Committee, serving for six years.

Working for social and political justice and equity has been a central focus in my life, whether fighting for national sovereignty and human rights in Africa or raising awareness of gender and health inequities that plague women and children throughout the world. In working for change, it is crucial to ensure that we see and hear the voices and stories of the people and communities with whom we work. All too often we make the mistake of assuming viewpoints, needs and solutions on behalf of others. Yet long experience has shown that the people who are best able to push the need for change and identify the most effective solutions, are those who are most directly affected by the injustice, poverty and discrimination we seek to eradicate.

There can be little argument about the importance of communication in the modern world—including the power of mass media, the ubiquity of telephones and the immediate international connections provided through Internet communication.

Yet in the majority of villages and communities of the world, voice and listening is the day-to-day means of reaching out to others—of making human connection. It is the way our children learn how to be good people. It is the way we learn about our local traditions and operate within our native cultures. It is the way we learn of the values and morals of our forebears.

Perhaps less well known outside of the African continent is the history of, and the value placed on oral communication in moving communities and nations forward: the griot traditions, storytelling, drama, dance and song. In southern Africa, dialogue circles have prospered for more than 2000 years as ways for villages to make collective decisions. In West Africa, durbars announce news and visitors through song, dance and the spoken word. Women gather at marketplaces across the continent every day bringing news and stories that are important to the greater community. We are a verbal people and a community-based people who live the principles of communication for social change daily.

Change happens in many ways, but sustained social change relies upon people to endure: the power of people to advocate for the change that will benefit them, the power of people to negotiate through their differences, and the power of people to come together, to form social movements, in order to demand their rights. Communication for Social Change is a way of developing and strengthening people's confidence and skills to tell their own stories, explain their needs, and advocate for the kind of change they want.

Academic scholarship on communication often focuses on communication technology or the impact of media. This anthology is groundbreaking in that it spotlights first and foremost dialogue, listening and collective action. The writers included paint an interesting portrait of ideas about the history of participatory, community-based approaches. I can only hope that students of communication for social change will appreciate the rich foundation—evolving heavily from value systems with their base in Africa, Latin America and parts of Asia—analysed within these pages.

Arguing powerfully that the global community can use communication more effectively to save lives and improve our world, this is an important piece of work for communication scholars and professionals as well as development specialists and social activists.

1927
1960
1963
1964
1967
1969
1970
1971
1972
1973
1974
1975
1976
1977
1978
1979
1980
1981
1982
1983
1984
1985
1986
1987
1988
1989
1990
1991
1992
1993
1994
1995
1996
1997
1998
1999
2000
2001
2002
2003
2004
2005

2006

NOTE FROM THE PUBLISHER

Denise Gray-Felder
President, Communication for Social Change Consortium

Thanks to the mission of the Communication for Social Change Consortium, I now truly understand the meaning of the words "love your work, live your passion." This anthology, the Consortium's fourth publication since our inception, reflects the commitment and passion of all the talented people in our worldwide network; people who dedicate their lives to helping move people out of poverty. With this book, like all our other efforts, we are able to demonstrate a love of humanity as well as a passion for our profession and craft.

Three years ago, Alfonso Gumucio had a vision that the Consortium should produce a signature contribution to the development field—an anthology that would trace the evolution of communication for social change thinking and practice. It is safe to say that none of us at that time had a realistic picture of what a daunting task this would be. But we did know that there was not only a need—but also a demand—for such a reference to illustrate the deep, historical roots of participatory communication as well as to demonstrate the heritage of communication for social change within the social science fields. We also wanted a book that connects, in multidisciplinary ways, contemporary academic thinking between scholars from rich countries with those from less economically rich countries.

Alfonso recruited Thomas Tufte of Roskilde University as co-editor. Off they went on an intellectual scavenger hunt for the most reflective and stimulating texts, looking as far back as the 1920s. The Consortium brought together an editorial advisory team to help make initial recommendations and to create the list of core writings that should be included in the book. For a week at the Rockefeller Foundation Study and Conference Centre in Bellagio, Italy, we pored over more than 200 manuscripts, arguing about intent and impact. Following that, Alfonso and Thomas read and considered hundreds more famous and not-so-famous documents, debating the ideas included within them, in order to determine just which are the most instructive from among hundreds of seminal manuscripts.

The book before you will never be finished. I suspect that each reader will find a favoured scholar missing, or that you might question the inclusion of others. Following CFSC principles, we used an inclusive process in producing this book. We wanted to provide a broad array of opinions and perspectives. Several of the texts "dialogue" with each other: ideas are presented and then "responded to" with accompanying manuscripts. In this regard, the writers "talk to each other" in ways that illustrate, instruct and innovate.

You may be surprised to find several writers who are not household names. This is deliberate: we sought to give increased visibility to those scholars who are less well known in global fora, constrained simply because they write in a language other than English.

Every writer, in her or his own way, contributes to the foundation of the CFSC "building." They illustrate that communication for social change, in some ways, has always been around. CFSC is a process of public and private dialogue through which people define who they are, what they want and need, and how they will work together to get what they need to improve their lives. It uses open and democratic dialogue that leads to community-based problem identification, decision-making and implementation of solutions to development issues.

Put another way, this type of communication process honours culture and tradition; respect for the power of local decision-making power; the dialogue involving external information and traditional knowledge; and dialogue between development specialists and communities. CFSC is about engaging people to want to change and to help them define the change and necessary actions to achieve their goals. The ultimate goal should always be self-renewing societies.

We learn from within these pages that as practitioners and scholars, if we keep the intended beneficiaries in the forefront of our work, we will be continually motivated and inspired.

ACKNOWLEDGEMENTS

We gratefully acknowledge the contributions of the authors and publishers who contributed to this text. A complete list of them is included in the Permissions section.

In addition, this book would not be possible without the engagement of numerous communication scholars, practitioners and development professionals including those who participated in an editorial advisory capacity: CFSC Consortium board members Maria Celeste Cadiz, Warren Feek and Denise Gray-Felder; James Deane, Ailish Byrne, Rosa Maria Alfaro, Silvia Balit, Luis Ramiro Beltrán, John Downing, Cees Hamelink, Jim Hunt, Tom Jacobson, Chris Kamlongera, Alfred Opubor, Will Parks, Daniel Prieto Castillo, Clemencia Rodriguez, Jan Servaes, Pradip Thomas, Ruth Teer Tomaselli, Keyan Tomaselli, Robert White and Karin Gwinn Wilkins. We were also honoured to have the early and ongoing involvement in the Consortium's work of two true communication pioneers, George Gerbner and Everett Rogers.

We dedicate this book to George, Everett and to Juan Jamias, all who passed away before seeing the finished product. Our professional lives and knowledge were enriched by their contributions and our hearts were touched by calling each of them "friend."

Many contributions were received from people working in communication or in development in general. A key part of this process was ably facilitated by the Communication Initiative, and we thank the CI staff and people in their network, and especially for their help in locating hundreds of authors and references. We ultimately reviewed more than 1,000 texts, from which we selected the most representative. While we relied heavily on suggestions made by an editorial review board of experts from universities in Asia, Latin America, North America, Africa, the Pacific region and Europe, the final selections were ours. So the fault for any errors and omissions lies at our feet.

New translations were provided by the extraordinarily talented Paul Keller, plus Esther Gomez Babin, Florencia Enghel, Sheila Wilkins and A&A translations. Throughout the process we had numerous assistants: Maider Iriarte, Rocio Cajías, Ana Luisa Néca, Alejandra Gumucio, Janne Juul Sørensen and Amelia Morales Navarro. Special thanks to the editorial support team in the United States: Diana Burke and Jackie Bivens. We must give special recognition to Vivian James who kept all the files, kept track of details, and compiled thousands of changes from reviewers and proofreaders.

We owe a huge debt to our life partners—Katherine Grigsby and Pernille Tufte,—who forfeited weekends, holidays and social events while we were fixated on our computer screens.

To the Rockefeller Foundation staff, thank you for your core support which allows us to distribute copies of this book free of charge to institutions in poorer countries.

And finally, we'd like to recognize *our* talented editors: Denise Gray-Felder and Susan Mach, who read every word with precision and oversaw every detail of the production process with keen eyes. They too gave up weekends, holidays and celebrations with their families and spouses, Donald Felder and Larry Mach, for this effort. They shared our vision and persistence in making this book the best it can be, and we're proud to have worked with you.

We cannot end without giving special acknowledgement to the contributors whose ideas, thinking and vision has so clarified our own scholarship and practice. And to the people living and working in villages, districts and towns across the globe whose innovative use of communication as a way to improve lives continually inspires us. Without you, this book would not have been. Thank you.

Alfonso Gumucio-Dagron
Thomas Tufte
July 2006

1927
1960
1963
1964
1967
1969
1970
1971
1972
1973
1974
1975
1976
1977
1978
1979
1980
1981
1982
1983
1984
1985
1986
1987
1988
1989
1990
1991
1992
1993
1994
1995
1996
1997
1998
1999
2000
2001
2002
2003
2004
2005
2006

ROOTS AND RELEVANCE: INTRODUCTION TO THE CFSC ANTHOLOGY

This introductory chapter explains the organization of the book and the rationale for selections. We summarize many of the key points during the evolution of CFSC thinking, and, as such, this chapter serves as the roadmap to volumes one and two.

After many years studying, teaching, discussing, writing, practicing and analyzing the field of work known as Communication for Social Change (CFSC), we at the Communication for Social Change Consortium realized a gaping hole remains in the compilation of literature on this subject. Because the field has evolved from the work of numerous scholars and practitioners from varied backgrounds and disciplines, there has been no central reference where people can go to learn about the theoretical evolution of this field.

We wanted to fill the void. We spent two years looking at the evolution of CFSC, reviewing the literature and answering the question: "Which thinkers and writers contributed to the formation of the key ideas and ideals of CFSC?" Early on, we formed an editorial advisory committee, which met at the Bellagio Study and Conference Centre, in Italy, to plan the scope of work. We came up with initial suggestions of seminal thinkers and, following that meeting, dozens of leading communication academics worldwide added their own suggestions.

For the first time, we have in one place a picture of how CFSC-type thinking was born, how the discipline has matured, which disciplines contributed to CFSC theory and how these contributions have influenced current thinking and practice.

Producing this book was an inclusive, participatory effort by many scholars from five continents. We worked hard to find the writings and work of authors who may not be particularly well known in English-speaking countries or in the industrialised world. Whereas they might have been considered "fringe" to students and teachers in rich industrialised countries, many of these people are renowned among academia in Latin America, Africa or Asia.

The writing of the more than 150 authors form this book's collage of ideas. The diversity of styles, opinions and backgrounds is deliberate: we have retained as much of the original styles and formatting as is practical.

This is in keeping with the key values of communication for social change: valuing all voices and giving people the space to tell their own stories in their own ways. No one approach or theory dominates: the reader is exposed to a wide variety of thinking from which he or she must form his or her own beliefs.

As CFSC proponents, we believe that this approach must be mirrored in development. No longer should experts from outside of communities dictate predetermined solutions to pressing social needs. Most people—with the chance to come together and discuss problems, determine solutions together and plan ways to address their problems—can come up with workable answers. For the most part, communication processes which allow people themselves to define who they are, what they want and need, and how they will work together to improve their lives are more appropriate ways to address complex social issues.

Dialogue is at the heart of communication for social change. It gives people from diverse backgrounds the chance to share ideas, inform others, persuade some —and first and foremost to listen. This book, therefore, offers the reader a rich mixture of ideas to consider. We offer a broad array of concepts to demonstrate CFSC's dominant attributes, how they evolved, how useful and applicable they are—and to illustrate the interdisciplinary nature of this work.

It is an academic book, but not only for the academic world. We want to acknowledge the importance of practice as inspiration for theoretical work. Many people contribute important and interesting experiences by working in development and by perfecting principles of communication for social change, often without labelling them as such. We've chosen to produce a book based on theory, yet we wanted also to make it important reading for CFSC practitioners, aid workers and policymakers.

We were particularly keen to select texts that advance the critical values of communication for social change and share the beliefs that participatory communication is essential to developing societies. Many of the authors we selected may not use these words, but, when assembled together, their writings have a central focus.

You will find within these pages ideas current today—even though they were written in the 1950s, 1960s or 1970s. We expect that their inclusion will spark reflection, discourse and debate about voice, participation, and democratic principles and their value to current development thinking.

This anthology has two sections: historical perspectives and contemporary readings. Beginning in 1927 with Bertolt Brecht's piece "The Radio as an Apparatus of Communication," the first section of the book reveals the historical roots of CFSC principles and pioneering thinking. One sees quite clearly the significant contributions from Asia and Latin America in the earliest years of communication for development. Despite such contributions, the dominant voices in the earliest years came from North American and European scholars, in no small part due to their ability to write in English, the language used by faculty at the largest and best-funded universities of the time.

For the first time here, a number of key texts have been translated into English. While academics and students in non-English speaking nations have read classic communication texts by scholars in the United States from the beginning, authors from developing regions were often overlooked. We believe this book, by translating into English many of these authors, minimizes that imbalance and takes a more enlightened, equitable approach.

The second section showcases texts published since 1995, covering 10-plus years of intensive contributions to the new field of communication for social change. The 80 or so works included in this section are organised thematically:

Paradigms in Communication for Development
Popular Culture and Identity
Social Movements and Community Participation
Power, Media and the Public Sphere
Information Society and Communication Rights

ROOTS: HISTORICAL READINGS

A Walk Through the Looking Glass of Paradigms

It is important to describe the context in which the various paradigms of communication for development and social change have evolved since the 1960s in order to better understand the cyclical nature of current debate. While this is not a literature review, we've included selections of innovative thinking to illustrate the evolution of concepts such as participatory communication and social change. Many of the writers broke new ground in the earlier years; those who followed later also added new insights.

The systematic use of communication tools in development programmes started after the Second World War and developed in different directions according to the various geographic, cultural, social and economic contexts. Development communication models have been around since the 1950s, some as a result of academic study and others inspired by fieldwork. Models often developed concurrently and in parallel with each other, with marked and irreconcilable differences. We have seen recently more of a tendency to close the gaps and foster convergence of previously divergent models and approaches.

1927
1960
1963
1964
1967
1969
1970
1971
1972
1973
1974
1975
1976
1977
1978
1979
1980
1981
1982
1983
1984
1985
1986
1987
1988
1989
1990
1991
1992
1993
1994
1995
1996
1997
1998
1999
2000
2001
2002
2003
2004
2005
2006

Two main threads dominate five decades of development communication. The first is modernisation. Communication models inspired by modernisation theories developed primarily as information strategies, first used by the U.S. Government during the Second World War and then by an industrial sector struggling to position its post-war products. The second thread is dependency. Dependency theory-based models of communication emerged in the heat of the social and political struggles against colonial and dictatorial powers in Third World [developing] countries.

Models based on modernisation theories support the expansion of markets for products and the assimilation of large numbers of marginalised people. Persuasion, information dissemination, and diffusion of innovation and technologies are most often used. These are generally vertical approaches, mostly generated in the research laboratories of private corporations, marketing agencies and university departments. The main premise of these approaches is that information and knowledge, *per se*, generate development. In this view, local culture and traditions are "barriers" for Third World countries to reach levels of development similar to those of industrialised countries. Perhaps due to their funding by U.S. government agencies, they appear to be linked to U.S. foreign policy. Such modernisation approaches have dominated international cooperation for several decades.

Conversely, the approaches that emerged from the independence struggles in Africa, Asia and Latin America are intimately linked to political and social events, and in a larger sense, to values and expressions of cultural identity. Their main premise is that the underlying causes of underdevelopment are structural and have to do with land tenure, lack of collective civil liberties, oppression of indigenous cultures, and social inequity, among other political and social challenges. These communication models promote social change rather than individual behaviour change. They suggest actions that emerge *from* the communities and not just *for* the communities. The involvement of local stakeholders is considered essential in the entire spectrum of such alternative, horizontal and participatory communication models. The right to communicate and the ownership of the communication process are at the heart of these approaches.

Modernisation Theories and Models

Based on their technological and economic supremacy, industrialised countries promulgated, for many years, the belief that the poorest nations are somehow responsible for their fate. Models based on modernisation theories—dominant even today in many development organisations—suggest that local traditions prevent developing nations from leapfrogging towards modernity. Such theories suggest implicitly that every poor country should aspire to achieve materially, as has been the case with industrialised countries. To do so, developing countries must shed beliefs and cultural practices that hinder modernisation.

Such models attach foremost importance to economic and technological progress; they advocate that a better life is the corollary of increased agricultural and industrial productivity. Therefore, the introduction of new technologies and knowledge will help poor, illiterate and "ignorant" peasants to modernise. This premise suggests that knowledge is a privilege of rich countries—and that poor nations lack it; that transfer of information will improve the lives of the poor. The underlying assumption is that "information-poor" people are poor because of a knowledge deficit. If only development strategists could massively provide the world's poor people essential information, such people would be able to produce more, boost family incomes, integrate better into the society and be happier.

This concept of massively sharing innovations, called diffusion theory—from knowledge centres in the United States and Europe with less-advanced rural populations in Asia, Africa and Latin America—generated one of the most lasting communication paradigms in development. Everett Rogers, often referred to as a communication pioneer, was a key proponent for much of his career. Later in his life, Rogers reevaluated his positions and began to write and promote participatory approaches as well as diffusion theory.

The diffusion of innovation model was first applied to agriculture in the 1960s, when donor agencies believed that increasing agricultural productivity was the development priority. Increasing crop production by introducing new technologies would curb hunger in the Third World. Surplus food produced in developing countries could also supply food markets in industrialised countries with cheap agricultural products. What we now term "banana republic," implying economic, social and political dysfunction, is an expression of this conceptualization.

In some cases, powerful media strategies were used with overt political aims. Guatemala is a good example. The U.S. intervention in 1951 promoted a military coup against the elected government of Jacobo Arbenz. New measures were established to stop land reform and facilitate the concentration of productive land in the hands of a small sector of the white minority, leaving the majority of the indigenous population landless. Since then, 65 percent of productive land is in the hands of 2.1 percent of Guatemalans. In an attempt to validate the process of counter-reform in the eyes of the general population, the US Information Agency (USIA) used all possible means—radio, television, film, posters, brochures and interpersonal communication—to persuade the Mayan majority to accept the measures dictated by the U.S.-backed military dictatorship.

Widely adopted throughout Latin America, the dissemination of innovation model ended up benefiting large *terratenientes* [landowners] far more than poor peasants. History has shown that development is accelerated not so much by the acquisition of information, but rather is dependent upon structural issues such as land ownership and human rights. Even armed with useful information, poor peasants usually do not break the vicious cycles of social injustice and exploitation.

Diffusion of innovation led to social marketing, which is widely embraced today. Proponents argue that the approach originated in an attempt by industry and academia to be more sensitive to social issues. In the political context of the late 1960s, characterised by demonstrations against the Vietnam war, against racism and for civil liberties, both the U.S. administration and the private sector recognised the need to respond to a demanding social agenda.

Today, social marketing has its most fervent proponents within the health sector, mirroring the affection the agriculture sector had with diffusion of innovation theory. Social marketing is frequently favoured by development professionals interested in supporting policy agendas of the world's power brokers: the G-8 nations primarily. Even before AIDS erupted as the world's major health priority, health workers were using social marketing techniques to promote family planning and reproductive health behaviours.

Population explosion was considered a catastrophe for this planet. Rising birth rates, especially among people living in poverty, is a threat to rich countries, which see their borders invaded by huge numbers of immigrants from the South seeking work. For 50 years, social marketing programs have addressed family planning and population growth; today social marketing is applied to the AIDS pandemic, with very limited success. Such initiatives promote condom use and safe sex absent consideration of the social conditions in which people are making decisions.

Mass media are essential to social marketing campaigns. With strong roots in commercial marketing and advertising, radio and televisions campaigns are used to "sell" a version of harmony and happiness worldwide. Product marketing strategies, such as those used to sell Coca Cola, are exported by social marketing aficionados to convince people to buy the latest icon of safety and good health: a condom. Attractive messages, often featuring famous role models, use state-of-the-art technology to persuade rather than to educate.

Individual behaviour change is the goal of social marketing. Implicit is the belief that traditions and cultural patterns of behaviour in poor countries prevent people from living better lives. Local cultures are seen as barriers to modernisation, and collective cohesion delays changes in attitudes, which is why

1927
1960
1963
1964
1967
1969
1970
1971
1972
1973
1974
1975
1976
1977
1978
1979
1980
1981
1982
1983
1984
1985
1986
1987
1988
1989
1990
1991
1992
1993
1994
1995
1996
1997
1998
1999
2000
2001
2002
2003
2004
2005
2006

the individual is targeted as a "champion" of change within his/her own community. Too often, social marketing campaigns are conducted by people from commercial advertising agencies. This trend is alien to social development and perhaps more effective with urban "clients" than with people living in poor rural communities.

Planners who lack knowledge and sensitivity to the local context have, at times, inadvertently made bad situations worse. In the 1970s, a worldwide boycott was sparked due to promotion of infant formulas in poor regions of the developing world. Responding to the marketing goals of a multinational corporation, promoting infant formula actually worsened the plight of poor people. The campaigns persuaded mothers that mixable formula was as good as breast milk. Yet families lacking access to clean water and proper refrigeration actually made their babies sick when using local water supplies to mix the formulas. It took years to turn around this disaster and to encourage some mothers in poorer countries to begin breast feeding their babies again.[†]

Health promotion, often a variation of behavioural change strategies, emphasizes the role of health workers in the health education process. Despite sometimes using innovative interpersonal communication, health promotion primarily focuses on disease, not on communication about health. Issues of poverty, discrimination or social inequity are not factors.

By the late 1970s, we began to see proponents of dissemination, diffusion, social marketing and health promotion approaches reviewing their assumptions, especially looking for ways to account for the influence of culture and tradition on social change. Some communication theorists acknowledged that their original models were based more on psychology of individuals than on political and socio-cultural factors. Thus in some ways we were witnessing validation of the criticisms levelled by proponents of participatory approaches.

[†] The Nestle boycott.

The marriage between social marketing and entertainment gave rise to the edutainment approach. Because of its flexibility and capacity for adaptation to local cultural contexts, edutainment has been very successful in some countries. Edutainment applies techniques of the spectacle to awareness raising and education, using dramatic radio or TV soap operas, pop songs, theatre, print stories and attractive posters to impart socially relevant messages and to spark communication.

The experience of South Africa's "Soul City" is perhaps the best-known example of large-scale edutainment. The priorities are decided locally, as well as the communication tools. Mass media are a means to spark community-level dialogue and understanding, yet they are never considered "silver bullets."

Some of the most valuable outgrowths of the edutainment approach are the networks and social organizations of people who come together because of their shared interest in a particular social issue highlighted in a programme or song.

Dependency Theories and Approaches to Communication

Since the 1940s, Third World countries have experienced liberation and anti-colonial struggles in Africa and anti-dictatorship movements in Latin America and Asia. With the struggles for liberation and independence, intellectuals emerged who asserted that underdevelopment and poverty are not merely the result of ancestral cultural defects. They have resulted due to a system of exploitation of poor nations by rich ones and of enormous social inequalities between rich and poor people within each nation.

Structural reasons—political, economic, social, cultural and legal explain the causes of underdevelopment and poverty. Social and political action led to the emergence of countless experiences of alternative and participatory communication within marginalised communities, urban as well as rural. These experiences sought to claim spaces for expression and to empower collective voices. They grew without relying on any existing communication models, and, in fact, the theory grew out of the practice. Such participatory ways of working are known by various names including popular, horizontal, dialogical, alternative, participatory or endogenous communication. All involve principles critical to what we now know as communication for social change.

In 1980, UNESCO released *Many Voices, One World,* known as the MacBride report. (Excerpts from the conclusions are in this anthology). The report revealed alarming data about control of information on a global scale. Just two United States-based print news agencies at that time controlled two-thirds of the world's news and information flow. There were no national or regional news agencies in Africa, Asia or Latin America offering alternative perspectives. Large media conglomerates—which, today, are even larger—monopolised daily and weekly publications, as well as radio and television stations. The report sparked much debate about the influence of rich countries on the hearts and minds of the world's people. Political debate about the implications of the report, and the actions termed the New World Information and Communication Order contributed to the United States and the United Kingdom withdrawing as UNESCO members. [The United Kingdom rejoined UNESCO in 1997, and the United States rejoined in 2003.]

Development communication prospered beginning around 1970, especially within key U.N. agencies, such as the Food and Agriculture Organization (FAO). Development communication and the diffusion of innovations theory are complementary. Both are used effectively in rural settings and both promote the introduction of new technology for improving agricultural and livestock production. Development communication emphasizes the need to establish two-way knowledge flow and information exchange between rural communities and technocrats, rather than one-way "transfer of knowledge." Development communication not only values local knowledge, but it also promotes the strengthening of traditional forms of social organization in which communication is empowering, and it respects local cultures.

Alternative communication, also known as radical media, emerged as a number of unconnected experiences throughout the world. Seen as nonconformist efforts, alternative communication promotes the right to communicate and taking possession of communication space in neocolonial, neoliberal and repressive societies. Alternative communication media spring up, as peasants, workers, students, miners, women, youth, indigenous people and other politically marginalised people develop their own communication tools, since they have no possibility of accessing the State's or the private sector's mass media. Social groups—who share ideology, needs and a desire to raise their voices—establish community radio stations, popular journals, street theatre troupes and sometimes local television channels. Often, because they upset the dominant private media and conservative governments, they are victims of repression.

Bolivia's miners' radio is a paradigmatic example. The fundamental aspect of alternative communication is the appropriation of communication tools for the benefit of marginalised people. The concept goes beyond the ownership of media and technology; it is not simply a matter of owning the tools, e.g., a radio station, a newspaper or a television channel, but also a question of gaining a piece of, or appropriating, the communication process, including content design, management and decision-making.

Evolution of Communication for Social Change

Communication for social change is a way of thinking and practice that puts people in control of the means and content of communication processes. Based on dialogue and collective action, CFSC is a process of public and private dialogue through which people determine who they are, what they need and what they want in order to improve their lives. It has at its heart the assumption that affected people understand their realities better than any "experts" from outside their society, and that they can become the drivers of their own change.

1927
1960
1963
1964
1967
1969
1970
1971
1972
1973
1974
1975
1976
1977
1978
1979
1980
1981
1982
1983
1984
1985
1986
1987
1988
1989
1990
1991
1992
1993
1994
1995
1996
1997
1998
1999
2000
2001
2002
2003
2004
2005
2006

The CFSC Consortium, among others, has been refining the assumptions and practice of CFSC, looking at how CFSC is taught and learned, how thinking has evolved, where and why communication for social change works, how to monitor and assess impact and effectiveness, and how to document social change within social groupings or communities. Principles underlying CFSC ways of working include voice and participation, unleashing unheard or marginalised voices, equity and justice. The theoretical formulation continues to evolve, but finds supportive theory within anthropology, social justice and community building fields.

With communication for social change the process is key: it highlights the critical two-way nature of communication during which people and communities come together in dialogue, listening and responding. The products, or dissemination of messages, are merely by-products of the communication process. Like participatory communication, CFSC attaches importance to the appropriation of the communication process, not just the content of the information. Communication for social change builds upon local knowledge and traditions, basing the communication process on the societal realities in place within an affected community.

The driving forces of communication for social change can be synthesized as follows:
■ Social change can be sustained if individuals and communities affected own the means, content and methods of communication.
■ Communication for social change is horizontal and strengthens community bonds by amplifying the voices of the people who are poorest.
■ People within poor communities must be the protagonists for their own change and manage their own communication tools.
■ Rather than focusing on persuasion and information dissemination, communication for social change promotes dialogue among equal voices, and debate and negotiation within communities.
■ The results of the communication for social change process go beyond individual behaviour and con-sider the influence of social norms, values, current policies, culture and the overall development context.
■ Communication for social change strives to strengthen cultural identity, trust, commitment, voice, ownership, community engagement and empowerment.
■ CFSC rejects the linear model of information transmission from a central sender to an individual receiver, and relies instead on a cyclical process of interactions focused on shared knowledge and collective action.

Communication for social change is a living process, one that's highly dependent upon context, conditions and the culture within which it evolves. Essential characteristics include:

1. COMMUNITY PARTICIPATION AND OWNERSHIP
Far too many communication projects in the context of development fail due to lack of participation and commitment of the subjects/agents of change. Access to information and to media is insufficient.

2. LANGUAGE AND CULTURAL RELEVANCE
For decades development programmes and communication strategies forced on Third World nations were designed in laboratories of industrialised countries. Models, messages, formats and techniques are applied, without adaptations to different cultures or circumstances. Cultural interaction is healthy when it happens within a framework of equity and respect, through dialogue, debate and solidarity. When power dynamics within societies make one culture dominant over others, true dialogue between cultures is limited. Communication for social change addresses the imbalance by supporting marginalised voices and promoting dialogue across differences.

3. CREATING LOCAL CONTENT
Vertical models of communication for development assume poor communities in developing nations lack knowledge. The communication for social change process acknowledges the specificity of each culture and language; moreover, it supports local knowledge as a way of gaining legitimacy. While access to information generated in industrialised countries is often

seen as a silver bullet, communication for social change reinforces creation of local content and revival of traditional, indigenous knowledge.

4. USING APPROPRIATE TECHNOLOGY

Fascination with technological innovation, often presented as the *sine qua non* condition for development, can lead towards greater dependency. Many projects fail because they are reliant on technology that people are unable to pay for, to renew or to control. Communication for social change promotes processes, not technologies. When in use, technology must meet the real needs of the people who are affected, and it must be owned or controlled by them.

5. NETWORK AND CONVERGENCE

Once people in a community use dialogue processes and collective action to address their concerns and come up with solutions to their development challenges, it is important that they apply what they've learned to new situations and share their learning among networks of people with similar concerns.

Theoretical Analysis

Communication for development is often used as the umbrella term which covers all communication approaches aimed at reaching people living in poverty or in developing countries in order to address pressing social issues. Several of the writers included in this anthology take a comprehensive look at the evolution of this field since 1960: José Cisneros, Silvio Waisbord, Nancy Morris and Erick Torrico Villanueva.

Others analyse communication work along specific themes such as health (Airhihenbuwa, & Obregón 2000, Pereira & Cardozo 2003) or rural development (Cimadevilla 1997); or from a regional perspective (Sonderling 1997, Nyamnjoh 2000).

Erick Torrico Villanueva (2004) writes about four periods in the evolution of communication theory: diffusionist (1927-1963), critical (1947-1987), culturalist (1987-2001) and the current period (2001 onward). These timeframes correspond to four periods of world political and economic events: capitalist expansion (1919-1946); the Cold War (1946-1991); globalisation (1991-2001), and what he calls the period of "global hegemonic unbinding," starting in 2001.

Writers representing each period are included in this book. Because it is important to include a diversity of voices, we've included modernists with dependency theorists. Those known as "pioneers" are here (Wilbur Schramm and Everett Rogers)[††] along with lesser-known writers whose works have rarely been published but whose ideas have reinforced the backbone of CFSC theory and practice.

While not included here, Lerner's *The Passing of Traditional Society: Modernizing the Middle East* is worth mentioning, as it is thought by some to be a pioneering work. Published in 1958, the book was among the first to discuss communication, culture and development in that region.

We believe that Lerner's Anglo-centralist approach is overestimated; it does not significantly contribute to communication for development and social change theory. The case study "The Grocer and the Chief: A Parable," a cornerstone of his hypothesis and blown-up into theory, relates a few visits he made to the village of Balgat, in Turkey. He asserts that to be part of the modern world, rural and suburban communities in developing nations must leave their traditions behind and embrace Western mass media and new technology.

For years Lerner's name has been grouped with Schramm and Rogers as being a communication pioneer. But when we read Lerner critically, we don't agree.

Schramm's and Rogers' contributions are far greater to communication for social change ideology. Rogers, in particular, never stopped learning and evolving. It is not common in the academic world for a scholar to admit his or her mistakes in earlier years, as Everett

---

[††] Daniel Lerner, Wilbur Schramm and Everett Rogers are considered by many to be the founding fathers of communication for development. The editors believe that the contributions of Schramm and Rogers far exceed those of Lerner.

1927
1960
1963
1964
1967
1969
1970
1971
1972
1973
1974
1975
1976
1977
1978
1979
1980
1981
1982
1983
1984
1985
1986
1987
1988
1989
1990
1991
1992
1993
1994
1995
1996
1997
1998
1999
2000
2001
2002
2003
2004
2005
2006

Rogers did in 1976 when he wrote about "the passing of the dominant paradigm" in reference to Lerner but also to his own pivotal work, *Diffusion of Innovations* (1962). He stayed in close touch with developing countries, continuing to research and implement projects in Latin America, Africa and Asia until his health no longer allowed it. In one of his last interviews (published in *Mazi,* the CFSC Consortium electronic report) before his death in late 2004, Rogers reflected on how his thinking had changed.*

Wilbur Schramm also made early contributions to communication for social change theory. In spite of being optimistic about the role of mass media as "agents of social change," he introduced the issues of cultural linkages, group relationships and participation in decision-making to theoretical discourse.

Perhaps less popular but influential nevertheless was David Berlo. As early as 1960, Berlo described communication as a "process" and outlined key principles of a dialogical approach: "Communication theory reflects a process point of view. A communication theorist rejects the possibility that nature consists of events or ingredients that are separable from all other events." He argues that one cannot talk about the beginning or the end of communication or say that a particular idea came from one specific source, that communication occurs in only one way, and so on.

Parallel with modernisation thinking, theories of dependency began to influence communication thinking in the early 1960s. However, since the majority of theoretical discussions took place in Latin America and in Spanish, few of these discussions affected thinking elsewhere until the 1970s. One good example is Antonio Pasquali's "Communication Theory: The Sociological Implications of Information on Mass Culture" (1963).

Key proponents of dependency theories were Brazilian scholars Celso Furtado, Fernando Henrique Cardoso (who later became president of Brazil), Darcy Ribero,

Maria da Conceicao Tavares and Theotonio dos Santos, author of *The Theory of Dependency*. They opposed the vertical approach and patronising way of seeing development once prominent in Europe and the United States. Dependency theories never caught on with academics in the North. Perhaps dos Santos was right when he argued that Latin American ideas on the economy were excluded from academia and had no real impact on the global mechanism of dependency.

The earliest voices proposing a different paradigm of communication, more related to culture and development, came from Latin America. Venezuela-born Pasquali wrote about deconstructing the sender/receiver model. The depth of his thinking and his broad cultural knowledge make this text a penetrating analysis of dominant communication models. Pasquali describes the "deaf sender" and the "mute receiver" who are unable to establish dialogue, the real basis for communication.

Pasquali breaks down the differences between information and communication, something that is still not clear in many academic texts today. He analyses the relation of information where the allocution or unilateral discourse "does not admit a reply" and attempts to "subtract, to diminish, to take over and to alienate" the receiver. "Every receiver becomes a violated non-deliberative subject." The so-publicized freedom of information is," according to Pasquali, "an ironic *contradicto in adjecto,* since it only denotes the freedom of who informs." His work predicted today's discourse on the right to communicate in the context of freedom of information demands.

In Pasquali's terms, communication defines society. "Society, *mitsein* or living-together, only exists where shared knowledge takes place, and shared-knowledge only exists where communication forms have developed."

Dialogue is a central thesis of Brazilian educator Paulo Freire. Nourished through his life-long practice, Freire's reflection on education and communication has influenced several generations of writers and

---

* www.communicationforsocialchange.org/php/mazi/archives

development practitioners. From 1967 onwards, each book by Paulo Freire, particularly *Pedagogy of the Oppressed* (1970), greatly influenced scholarship on education as a process of liberation. Several aspects of Paulo Freire's work have particular significance for communication for social change theory.

First and foremost is Freire's emphasis on dialogue, derived from his experience in popular and informal education. His concept of dialogue involves respect; it is not one person acting on others, but rather people relating with each other as equals. Another important element of Freire's theory was raising collective consciousness to build the power to transform reality. Freire insisted on approaching education within the lived experience of participants and suggested the use of key words that would have the effect of generating new ways of naming the world and acting as agents of change.

Bolivian communication specialist Luis Ramiro Beltrán has been a proponent of communication for social change for five decades. His initial work, influenced by modernisation theories, deals with applications of communication for development in rural areas. By 1967, he had departed from supporting mass media-driven, vertical approaches in favour of a participatory paradigm, suggesting that development should be guided by "universal participation in decision-making on matters of public interest and in the process of implementing national goals."

As early as 1969, Beltrán argued for the need for developing countries to design their own communication strategies for development and their own information policies. He pointed to the "lack of effective and independent national information agencies and, especially, of such an agency Latin American in scope; this permits a virtual monopoly of the international news flow by extra-regional news services which neither inform the region objectively about world events nor report fairly about events in the region." These ideals were at the heart of UNESCO's MacBride commission, formed in the late 1970s.

In 1973, Frank Gerace, with Hernando Lazaro, produced a small book that made waves in Latin America. Modestly printed in Lima, *La Comunicación Horizontal* is a reflection on communication for social change from the perspective of hands-on practice working within rural communities. The book was never reprinted, but portions of it are translated in this anthology for the first time.

Gerace was motivated to write the book when he noticed that the field of communication for development as applied in rural Latin America was being invaded by "mechanical" theories imported from the United States. He writes about the centrality of ethics and other human values, while rejecting "technicist proselitism" [technical proselytism] of diffusion of innovations and proposes "commitment with peoples' liberation struggle" as a condition to practice horizontal communication." Participation and dialogue are two key concepts in the text. As with Beltrán, their ideas influenced the MacBride report: "The owners of the information industry became the moguls of cultural industries. The Third World has no freedom of choice. Mass media come to us charged of ideology. …"

Gerace, along with Pasquali and other Latin American authors who published in the 1960s and 1970s, were pioneers in revealing the imbalances in global information and communication flows. Their pioneering scholarship signalled years before today's current debates the criticality of communication for social change to development progress.

Other disciplines that contributed to communication for social change theory were politics and art. During times of political turmoil and U.S.-backed military intervention in several Latin American countries, artists and political activists from the region, such as Octavio Getino and Fernando Solanas from the Argentinean Cine Liberación Group (directors of the documentary "The Hour of Furnaces,"), issued a manifesto for the Third Cinema, including principles of voice and participation in the communication process (in this case through cinema). Similarly, Brazilian theatre director Augusto Boal argued in favour

1927
1960
1963
1964
1967
1969
1970
1971
1972
1973
1974
1975
1976
1977
1978
1979
1980
1981
1982
1983
1984
1985
1986
1987
1988
1989
1990
1991
1992
1993
1994
1995
1996
1997
1998
1999
2000
2001
2002
2003
2004
2005
2006

of a "theatre of the oppressed"—a clear reference to Paulo Freire—based on dialogue and debate. Despite repressive politics and governments, the ground was fertile for innovation and new ideas for social change.

Nora Quebral, of the Philippines, was among the first scholars in Asia to analyse critically the dominant models of communication for development. In 1971, although still influenced by the ideas of individual behaviour change, she underlined the educational value of communication to "stimulate public awareness and understanding." In 1971, Quebral questions the dominant paradigm in her paper "Development Communication":

> What makes development communication different are the purpose it serves and the venue of its action. Advertising, public relations, propaganda and even agricultural extension are Western institutions. They took root and matured in the West in answer to the special needs of that society [those societies]. While viable on other soils, they tend to retain their native assumptions and methodology. But development communication is no transplant. Given our definition, it can only be a Third World phenomenon. So, accept it or not, it is our responsibility to explore its dimensions, cultivate it and above all, use it. Communication scientists and practitioners from developed countries can help us with the first two endeavours. But in the final analysis, only we can have the gut determination to make development communication work.

Quebral writes that development communication "is no transplant," meaning that communication models developed in North America or Europe are not automatic solutions for Third World countries. Consistent with communication work emerging at the same time in Latin America, Quebral links communication with education efforts, and she touches upon issues of democratisation and civic participation in the decision-making process. It is interesting that the bibliographic references included with Quebral's text are mainly authors who support dominant paradigms,

such as Schramm and Lerner. This suggests that only Quebral's own experience and reflection influenced her thinking opposing modernisation theory.

As its former dean, Quebral has influenced several generations of students and faculty at the College of Development Communication of the University of The Philippines at Los Baños. This institution is one of the oldest academic centres in the world specialising in development communication, and most of the Filipino authors in this anthology gravitated to it at different times. Other important Filipino contributions to communication for social change came from Juan Jamias, Gloria Feliciano and Florangel Rosario-Braid, and early in the 1980s, from Victor Valbuena, Karina David and Mina Ramirez.

It is worth noting that women scholars made many of the most significant contributions during those years. Feliciano's approach to development communication is also influenced by the diffusionist model, which was very influential in the Philippines. Juan F. Jamias, along with Quebral, was among those who wrote about the need for new paradigms. Curiously enough, in his text titled *The Philosophy of Development Communication,* Jamias (1975) questions the use of the term social change as too neutral to define the communication process accurately. He advocates for "development communication" as more appropriate.

Most Filipino authors learned through personal field experience that vertical models that don't take into consideration the voices and culture of people are not sustainable. They preferred, for the most part, interpersonal communication to mass media. Some, like Valbuena, Bonifacio and Mercado, added to the discourse analysis of indigenous forms of communication, such as traditional Filipino theatre performances, as "viable channels for development communication: drama, the *zarzuela,* the *cancionan,* the *balagtasan,* the *balitao,* the *banatayonon,* and the puppet theatre." (Victor Valbuena is one of the Asian communication specialists who questions new communication technologies that "have concentrated their focus mainly on the delivery system, and may have, wittingly or unwittingly, disregarded the cultural contexts in which they may have to operate.")

Wang and Dissanayake (1982) and H.K. Ranganath (1980), among other scholars, analysed participatory approaches through community theatre, puppets and other traditional media in the context of development programmes.

In 1980, at the same time that Valbuena was writing, Brazilian Luiz Beltrao completed his analysis of the importance of folk media in development. His text on the "system of *folkcomunicação*" is illustrative of a worldwide growing trend in communication studies that valued the role of culture and tradition. This discussion was taken further in the 1990s by such authors as Néstor García Canclini, Armand Mattelart, Héctor Schmucler and Rosa María Alfaro.

During the 1970s and 1980s, Asian, Latin American and African scholars were refining development in ways that moved beyond the modernisation paradigm. In 1984, Wimal Dissanayake and Georgette Wang wrote:

> Development is a process of social change that has as its goal the improvement in the quality of life of all or the majority of the people without doing violence to the natural and cultural environment in which they exist, and which seeks to involve the majority of the people as closely as possible in this enterprise, making them the masters of their own destiny.

Parallels can be found in Africa. As early as 1972, Frank Ugboajah analysed the role of traditional communication in development, providing a wealth of examples from various West African countries on the use of drums, dancing, masks, piercing and scars as forms of communication. By 1985, Ugboajah coined the term "oramedia" to refer to those manifestations of cultural traditions that play a role in community development:

> Oramedia or folk media are grounded on indigenous culture produced and consumed by members of a group. They reinforce the values of the group. They are visible cultural features,

often strictly conventional, by which social relationships and a worldview are maintained and defined. They take on many forms and are rich in symbolism.

Other authors who made important contributions to the African view are Joseph Ascroft (1974) and Andreas Fuglesang (1982), who questioned the role of technical experts within communities. They argued for respect towards cultural differences, pleaded for "tact and humility" (Ascroft) and shedding development myths. (Fuglesang)

Joseph Ascroft, Robert Agunga and Sipho Masilela strongly argue for participatory approaches to development, including during the decision-making process. Ascroft epitomizes the international hands-on consultant who approaches development with an open mind. Development communication consultants from Europe or North America working for the United Nations or for bilateral agencies seemed to have a more respectful approach to other cultures and traditional settings. Their contact with communities in Africa or Asia encouraged them to reflect on their own role as development experts and what they could learn from the communities in which they worked.

To contribute to the development process, Ascroft acknowledges he had to switch from the conventional and uninspired approach of an evaluator, to one that was more a listener of what local people had to say. He narrates how a FAO project, well thought-out and well developed by six experts in Rome, was irrelevant to the reality of the communities it was supposed to help, and so unsustainable. At the time, Ascroft was a consultant, but his critical remarks may have helped move FAO closer to participatory development in the coming years. Reading his *A Conspiracy of Courtesy* (1974), one wonders why, 30 years later, we still see so much vertical planning for development and so little real community participation.

In many ways, few things have really changed. Still today, very little value is given to communication that helps to bring out the knowledge that people have on

1927
1960
1962
1964
1967
1969
1970
1971
1972
1973
1974
1975
1976
1977
1978
1979
1980
1981
1982
1983
1984
1985
1986
1987
1988
1989
1990
1991
1992
1993
1994
1995
1996
1997
1998
1999
2000
2001
2002
2003
2004
2005
2006

development issues that affect them. Ascroft points to the pervasive influence of development agencies using younger generations of Africans to antagonise the moral authority and to challenge the knowledge of the elders in their communities. He asks for a more tactful, respectful approach to local culture and communities, using interpersonal communication based on dialogue and listening, not imposing alien ideas and techniques.

During this period, authors/practitioners like Mario Kaplún, Pierre de Zutter, Manuel Calvelo and Juan Diaz Bordenave were simultaneously walking similar paths in Latin America, questioning overuse of technical approaches and promoting horizontal forms of dialogue within rural communities. Daniel Prieto Castillo and Francisco Gutierrez, both inspired by Freire, developed new insights into the inseparable tandem of education and communication.

MacBride Report Poses Challenges

By the time the UNESCO MacBride Report was published, many authors had contributed to discussions about the need to establish national policies of information and communication. Among those involved were Fernando Reyes Matta, Juan Somavia, Rafael Roncagliolo, Luis Ramiro Beltrán, and Oswaldo Capriles from Latin America, and Herbert Schiller and Kaarle Nordenstreng. Some of these writers participated in international and regional conferences that provided input to the MacBride Report.

The call for a broader participation of people in the communication process came from two ends: the "upper" governance level, where developing nations demanded a balanced international flow of information and more space to access information as well as generate it; and from the "lower" community level, where principles of local ownership (and not simply access) and ethical approaches to participation were promoted. Authors from all regions, but mostly those with first-hand experience in developing countries, urged participatory approaches, the use of new technologies, and the role of culture in communication for development.

Many other authors included in this anthology made similar calls, including L. David Brown, Shirley White, Robert Huesca, Emile McAnany, Robert Hornik, Jesús Martin-Barbero, Orlando Fals Borda and Pilar Riaño; Jan Servaes, Niels Röling, Göran Hedebro, Erskine Childers, Silvia Balit, Robert White, Ullamaija Kivikuru, Colin Fraser, Alfred Opubor, Robert Agunga, Stefan Sonderling, Andrew Moemeka, Srinivas Melkote, Pradip Thomas, Neville Jayaweera and Maria Celeste Habito-Cadiz.

Erskine Childers did not publish text on communication for development during his career with the United Nations; however, his reports and recommendations helped convince officials to include communication in U.N. development programmes. He worked to convince U.N. managers to use communication-planning tools adapted to the sociocultural context of development.

Childers died in 1996, and that same year Royal Colle published an article about the contributions of Childers and his wife, Mallica Vajrathan, to communication for development, mainly through creation of the Development Support Communications Service (DSCS), a unit in Bangkok that operated under the United Nations Development Programme (UNDP). Childers' legacy was honoured in subsequent years, when FAO, UNESCO and UNICEF created development support communication programmes and became lead organisations, during the 1970s, in proposing a communication for development approach that clearly broke from the modernisation model.

RELEVANCE: INTRODUCTION TO CONTEMPORARY READINGS

Five Pathways to Contemporary Discourse

By the mid 1990s, a number of events, technological developments and theoretical advancements together created a new momentum in thinking about development and social change. Such thinking, in turn, influenced the practice of communication for social change. This momentum, which has set the agenda for the contemporary debate about communication, development and social change, evolved at one time both as an academic critique of, and a deliberate rupture with, past thinking about core concepts. This trend was increasingly evident with the publication of a number of major academic books in the mid-1990s, and within a series of U.N. summits held between 1992 and 1997.

These international meetings and critical thinking about current practice in development affected scholarship on communication for development and social change. A rethinking of core concepts occurred, primarily leading to renewed foci on issues of human rights, gender equity, sustainability, participatory processes, good governance and social justice. At the same time, technological advancements forced re-examination. The development of the World Wide Web, combined with deregulation of the media and liberalisation of media markets, all contributed to the rapidly accepted notion that the mediated public sphere must serve as a forum for negotiation and for the struggle of ideas and opinions. Such momentum has gathered force, voice and visibility since the mid 1990s.

We suggest there have been five core pathways or perspectives on communication for social change since 1995 which affect both scholarship and practice:
- Paradigms in development, and paradigms in communication for development and social change;
- Popular culture, narrative and identity;
- Social movements and community participation;
- Power, media and the public sphere and
- Information society and communication rights.

These five pathways form the outline of the Contemporary Readings section of this book. Most often, a single text covers more than one of these five themes. Yet for ease of organisation, each manuscript has been placed under one of these perspectives. The point is to demonstrate how each writer contributed to contemporary debate surrounding each of the themes.

In addition to the five thematic areas, writers included in this Contemporary Readings section offer three levels of reflection: theoretical, specific and grounded (on-the-ground), or how the subject is addressed in different parts of the world.

Paradigms in Communication for Development

Within the scientific discipline of development studies, 1995 is marked by the publication of the Colombian anthropologist Arturo Escobar's *Encountering Development: The Making and Unmaking of the Third World,* which became a milestone in the post-colonial critique of the dominant discourses in development. Voices from former European colonies and countries in the so-called developing world increasingly contested both the discursive dominance of the debate by scholars and voices from the so-called developed world as well as the fundamental definitions of the problems and challenges in the field of development. Escobar's text marks a paradigmatic change in the conceptualization of development problems, in who is voicing what concerns, and in which agendas are brought to bear. Such post-colonial critique and other more recent critical voices continue and are even increasing in scope and intensity.

The World Social Forum in Porto Alegre, Brazil, together with the anti-globalisation movement protesting the World Trade Organization meeting in Hong Kong (both in 2005), combined with increased transnational networks, point to growing governmental and nongovernmental preoccupation with how to conceptualise development.

If we look back, contemporary debate about the development paradigm, which also informs thinking about communication for social change, began after the fall of the Berlin Wall in 1989 and the collapse of the Soviet Union. These events, on one hand, helped pave the ideological way for the proliferation of market-driven development as the key principle for development. This became the centrepiece in World Bank principles of development and was reflected in structural

1927
1960
1963
1964
1967
1969
1970
1971
1972
1973
1974
1975
1976
1977
1978
1979
1980
1981
1982
1983
1984
1985
1986
1987
1988
1989
1990
1991
1992
1993
1994
1995
1996
1997
1998
1999
2000
2001
2002
2003
2004
2005
2006

adjustment programs and privatisation of large state companies in many developing countries. It resonated within media development with privatisation of state media, deregulation and liberalisation of media flow.

However, parallel to the free market mantra was a growing concern with the narrow focus on economic development and the lack of results of development efforts over past decades. Broader perspectives and new strategies were desperately needed to counter many problems of development. It was in this context that the postcolonial critique grew more compelling.

In the world of development institutions, a key step forward in nuancing the understanding of development came from debates that emerged around United Nations conferences held throughout the 1990s. In 1991 UNDP launched their innovative Human Development Index (HDI) as a tool to capture and thus measure some of the broader and "softer" dimensions of development, such as health and education. This concept profoundly challenged the otherwise very economically focused indices for the measurement of development, and it contributed, together with some of the larger U.N summits that followed—such as the 1992 Rio Summit on Sustainable Development, the 1994 Cairo Conference on Population and Reproductive Health, the 1995 Beijing Women's Conference and the 1995 Copenhagen Social Summit—to a profound, conceptual expansion of the notion of development.

In the academic world, British scholar Robert Chambers was a forerunner and inspiration for some of the institutional debate, when, in 1983, his book *Putting People First* elaborated the notion of participation and argued strongly for a poverty-focused participatory development agenda. Policy-wise, this came to the forefront of the global development agenda 12 years later during the UN Social Summit in Copenhagen in March 1995, to which Chambers contributed one of the key background papers.

With the dawn of the 1990s, the field of development began "relooks" at what were historically considered development issues. For instance, UNAIDS was established in 1995 as the joint office of the U.N. system to combat HIV/AIDS. The establishment of this coordinating agency constituted an expansion in the conceptualization of HIV/AIDS from a health problem under the auspices of the World Health Organisation to becoming a broader issue that all U.N. agencies must deal with. The conceptual broadening of this major development challenge, HIV/AIDS, marks a notable trend in the development debate: broader-based thematic approaches to development challenges, a conceptual change we're now seeing across sectors, from agriculture to sustainable development, from gender equity to human rights. With HIV/AIDS it's the recognition of the pandemic's moving from being exclusively a health problem to being a broad and complex development challenge.

The theoretical level of debate focuses on core concepts and approaches recurrent in the contemporary discourse about communication for social change. These texts suggest perspectives, theories and approaches relevant to building the conceptual field of communication for social change. While many of the texts may not explicitly use the words communication for social change, we have selected those pieces whose principles are in keeping with CFSC theory and which contribute to the contemporary debate.

James Deane begins this section with a review of recurrent critiques of the emerging field of communication for social change. He looks at four arguments:

- Participatory people-centred communication has been central to most of the mainstream communication thinking and practice for many years;
- Artificial boundaries are being created between different approaches within the academic discipline of communication;
- Principles of communication for social change need more rigorous academic analysis to back their arguments, and
- CFSC principles must be strengthened in practice.

Since this piece was written, the field has advanced considerably as reflected in the writings which follow his.

In the assessment of how communication for social change relates to mainstream communication thinking, the focus on planned and/or strategic use of communication comes through as an emerging principle, however challenged by the horizontal approach not just to communication but to decision making, which is known from participatory development theory.

Another element is the relation between research and action. Stated bluntly, communication for social change has for many been seen as an action-driven process, in which the role of research has been viewed as marginal. Sandra Massoni's text argues for action-driven research, and thus relates to the point about the academic boundaries of the discipline and about how theory and practice relate to each other. Her view is to suggest a cross-disciplinary approach to communication, maintaining a strategic and action-driven research agenda somewhat similar to Fals-Borda's early ideas about action research. Research—and, thus, academia—becomes an integral element in a communication for social change process, and vice versa.

Massoni's model is based on an epistemology of complexity, derived from Edgar Morin. It relates well with the call in CFSC debates to contemplate multiple contexts of communication.

Adding to the layers of complexity Robert Huesca summarizes key advances in the field—pointing towards a needed move from Freire's "naming of the world" to a call for a stronger theorizing of Freire's principle. At this overall level of reflection, we also find Jesus Galindo's ambitious attempt to formulate a "communicology," a theory about communication, an endeavour we could see as an attempt to do today what Pasquali did more than 40 years ago; assess the very nature and explore the possibilities and limitations of communication, taking current theoretical and technological development into consideration.

The second entry level to the debate lies in discussing communication for development and social change from both regional and conceptual perspectives. On one hand, South African scholar Stefan Sonderling

delivers a critical assessment of development support communication, and on the other, Cortés delivers a harsh critique of the "campaign mantra."

An important step in the conceptual building of the discipline of communication for social change lies in the convergence of theory and practice. For example, Silvio Waisbord's text** is an overview of key lines of inquiry and debate within development communication, seeking the points of convergence between what previously were very separate spheres of thinking and practice in development communication. Others highlight alternative dimensions: For example, Huesca's insistence on viewing communication as process and, Fraser's and Restrepo's retrieving of core issues learned from social marketing. Their perspective is again contrasted by Cortés' critical assessment of social marketing.

The third level moves into a more grounded assessment of how communication for development and social change is perceived in different parts of the world: Writers Cimadevilla (Latin America), Nyamnjoh (Africa) and Hemant Shah with Karin Wilkins (Middle East/United States) offer perspectives based on regional experiences—as well as different thematic perspectives including sustainable development (Bedregal and Bornenave) and health communication (Obregón and Airhihenbuwa).

What characterizes this overall debate around communication, development and social change seems to be that communication for social change has emerged as a key site of theoretical encounter and convergence. CFSC reflects recognized limitations in traditionally separate schools of thought within the field of communication for development and serves as the forum for debate of the new voices and the re-articulation of long-standing concepts of participation, dialogue and horizontal communication. These processes of convergence and encounter of ideas bring together what currently is developing gradually into a stronger call

** Waisbord's paper was commissioned by the Rockefeller Foundation as part of its early exploration into the field of communication for social change. These inquiries and subsequent research and explorations led to the formation of the Communication for Social Change Consortium in 2003.

1927
1960
1963
1964
1967
1969
1970
1971
1972
1973
1974
1975
1976
1977
1978
1979
1980
1981
1982
1983
1984
1985
1986
1987
1988
1989
1990
1991
1992
1993
1994
1995
1996
1997
1998
1999
2000
2001
2002
2003
2004
2005
2006

for a social change-oriented communication practice guided by the principles outlined earlier.

Popular Culture, Narrative and Identity

The increased focus on the role of popular culture in processes of development emerged in Latin America during the 1980s with articles highlighting the Latin American debate about media, popular culture and identity in relation to development of the region. However, they only gained broad international circulation with their English versions in the mid-1990s. This is the case of Colombian Jesús Martin-Barbero's *De los Medios a las Mediaciones* published first in Spanish in 1987 and in English in 1993. It is also the case with Argentinean-Mexican Nestor Garcia-Canclini's book *Cultural Híbridas* published in Spanish in 1989 and in English in 1995.

Pioneers like Peruvian Rosa María Alfaro's work on popular culture, gender and the public sphere, was written and published in Spanish throughout the 1980s and early 1990s. Other pioneers included Mexican scholars Jorge González, Guillermo Orozco and Rossana Reguillo. However, for many of these scholars, because their work was published only in Spanish, in most cases, circulation of their ideas has been limited.

Parallel to this Latin American development, British cultural studies grew as a discipline within sociology, media studies, education and other social and human sciences. A re-orientation within communication studies from critical content analysis to audience studies, with particular emphasis on qualitative audience studies, is noteworthy, and seen in the works of reception analysts David Morley, Janice Radway, Ien Ang and many others. A similar re-orientation was seen in the Nordic countries, with a strong emergence of qualitative audience studies by scholars like Klaus Bruhn Jensen, Kim Schrøder, Kirsten Drotner and Birgitta Højer. However, compared to their Latin American colleagues, the North Europeans have a more limited link to debates about development and social change, although social and

policy critique does come through in some of the British scholarship. However, Northern Europe and Latin America—supplemented by early poles of similar academic attention in South Africa and Australia—together became forerunners to the growing inter-national focus on popular culture, narrative and identity formation, not least the growing attention seen in the United States and Canada in the 1990s.

What jointly characterises the writing of these authors is their re-assessment of the role of popular culture, storytelling and everyday life in processes of sense-making. The Latin Americans linked their focus on popular culture to the political agenda of cultural policy and other development issues. Ignoring popular culture—omitting cultural diversity, cultural resistance and cultural rights for so many years of development thinking—radically changed due to the influence of some of the Latin American thinkers included here.

In the world of development institutions, UNESCO has had the key role of integrating communication and culture into the development agenda. From 1988 to 1997 UNESCO actually headed, on behalf of the U.N. system, what resulted in a quite sleepy World Decade for Culture and Development. In the course of this decade, the World Commission on Culture and Development did produce a final report, "Our Creative Diversity," which, in assessing the role of communication in relation to culture and development, was innovative. In the assessment of the state-of-the-art of the world's cultural diversity, the report attributes to cultural diversity, for the first time ever, a central and integral role for communication.

The report's media chapter, co-authored by anthropologist Nestor García-Canclini, is intended as important input into formulating national cultural policies. It is important in the sense that it describes a broad concept of culture wherein communication, and increasingly, mediated communication, plays a part.

UNESCO has traditionally kept its mandate for culture and communication separate. In times of cultural globalisation and strong international and transnational media development, this must change. In the aftermath of the World Decade for Culture and Development, UNESCO passed the Declaration on Cultural Diversity in 2001, a declaration that—again, in 2005—was contested because of the growing discussions about whether to consider media flow and culture productions as commercial products included in trade agreements. This schism pinpoints the dilemma between the "softer" issues in the development debate—culture and communication, as opposed to the "harder" issues of economy and trade. In our view of the role of communication in articulating social change, it is essential to clarify the manifold aspects of culture, communication and development.

As one of the most prominent post-colonial thinkers on cultural globalisation, Indian anthropologist Arjun Appadurai introduces the Popular Culture and Identity section with an excerpt from his 1996 book describing his "theory of rupture." Appadurai's epistemological interest is in exploring the relation between globalisation and modernity.

Appadurai argues that the electronic media "offer new resources and new disciplines for the construction of imagined selves and imagined worlds." Juxtaposed with both voluntary and forced mass migrations, the result, he argues, is "a new order of instability in the production of modern subjectivities." In this way, Appadurai argues for the centrality of media and communication, and, implicitly, popular culture and narrative, in forming identity in times of globalisation.

Many of the issues Appadurai highlights are grounded theoretically in Latin American cultural studies. Jesús Martin-Barbero's work is important in showing how the genres in the mass media are in cultural synch with oral storytelling and popular cultural traditions, issues also highlighted by the works of Chilean communication researchers Maria Helena Hermosilla and Valerio Fuenzalida.

Explored as a potential for articulating social change—seen both in Argentina's *cultura piquetera* and Mexico's *cultura zapatista*—popular cultural traditions have merely in their day-to-day existence created spaces of resistance and change. From this point of departure, Mexican Rossana Reguillo rightly asks: *'En qué medida y hasta dónde la 'cultural piquetera', la 'cultura zapatista' o 'la cultura antiglobalización', es capaz de desestabilizar no sólo los símbolos consagrados sino además las estructuras de la vida cotidiana y hacer posible desde ahí una subjetividad distinta'?* (Reguillo, 2004)

['To what extent are the 'cultural piquetera', the 'culture zapatista' or 'the culture anti-globalisation' advocates capable of destabilizing not only the consecrated symbols but also the structures of everyday life, making it possible to make a real distinction? (Reguillo, 2004)]

Also focusing on popular culture, South African Charles Malan and Indian Pradip Thomas write about the role of folk media in development. From a theoretical perspective, they both write about contemporary rapid change, globalisation and cultural hybridity, fine-tuning Valbuena and Beltráo's earlier thinking. Valbuena and Beltráo write on folk media's contributions to the expression of cultural resistance and to social critique and political activism.

Canclini (Latin America) and Gilroy (British Cultural Studies) both write on the crosscutting importance of "cultural hybridity" as contemporaries of Martin-Barbero's scholarship on *cultural mestizaje,* conditions of everyday life and production of meaning. The cultural fusions of everyday practices, rituals, habits, values and cultural traditions can fuse both rural and urban, or pre-modern and modern cultural practices. This often occurs in contested and conflicting manners, and at the price of some forms of expression gaining dominance and others subordinated. Argentinean Gustavo Cimadevilla also brings to our attention the need to reflect the role of "new ruralities" in times when the process of development and modernisation seems synonymous with urbanisation. With both academic and civil society institutions interested in understanding the potential of modernisation and urbanisation on cultural transformation, scholars are beginning to recognize culture as a key mediator in development and social change.

1927
1960
1963
1964
1967
1969
1970
1971
1972
1973
1974
1975
1976
1977
1978
1979
1980
1981
1982
1983
1984
1985
1986
1987
1988
1989
1990
1991
1992
1993
1994
1995
1996
1997
1998
1999
2000
2001
2002
2003
2004
2005
2006

Within the communication practice, notions of culture and recognition of its force have now become critical. While the tradition of entertainment-education (edutainment or EE) has long existed as an approach used by social marketers, during the past 10 years the EE perspective has expanded both in its theoretical basis and as a communication strategy. This is seen in Douglas Storey's inspiration from Bakthin in the conceptual development of EE, as well as in Valerio Fuenzalida's work on social protagonists in his soap opera projects for Chilean television. Tufte summarises the new developments by outlining three core directions within contemporary entertainment-education. Thematically, one of the development challenges employing popular cultural narrative formats most frequently is the fight against HIV/AIDS.

In leading her search for "new communication utopias" Rosa María Alfaro assesses current communication thinking and practice and outlines transitions necessary to transform popular communication to a more civic one:

- From recovery of cultures and popular memory to participation in universal cultural production;
- From explaining innovative ideas or blasting hegemonic ones to furthering deliberative and propositional culture change, and
- From visibility of the popular word to the concept of influencing decisions or empowerment.

Social Movements and Community Participation

An increasingly significant dimension of the development processes of the mid 1990s is the growth and articulation of transnational civil society movements. These social movements are possibly the result of expanded connections between countries brought about by increased international mobility, both physical and symbolic. Technological development is an important factor facilitating both physical and symbolic mobility. Symbolic mobility encompasses the growing circulation of media and cultural products worldwide.

Swedish anthropologist Ulf Hannerz deals with these issues in his 1996 book *Trans-national Connections.*

Physically, transnational connections can be seen as an outcome of growing economic globalisation. Yet, while international and transnational networks grow, national platforms for the expression of social demands are weakening. The opportunity for communication for social change, as a result, is increasingly on a transnational level.

Combined with technological developments—mainly the World Wide Web, E-mail, and satellite, cable media and cable communications—a transnational platform was born *de facto*. In relation to communication for social change, this resulted in configuring new and more dynamic transnational opportunities for people within civil society to voice their concerns on a global level.

One example is the Zapatista uprising in southern Mexico, which began on January 1, 1994. Local social protests of Mexico's Indian people broke through in a major way in the international mediated public sphere, via the Web, becoming a symbol of all the oppressed people of the world.

In the world of international development organisations, the operation of transnational platforms for voicing civil society concerns was first seen at the 1992 Summit on Sustainable Development in Rio de Janeiro. This U.N. summit attracted a huge number of representatives from international nongovernmental organisations, community based organisations, and other social organisations to the parallel forum for civil society. The number of organisations represented was unprecedented. Using these U.N. summits as a transnational platform for social mobilisation grew and became significant around the Cairo Conference in 1994, the Social Summit in Copenhagen in 1995 and the Women's Conference in Beijing, also in 1995. Most recently, the World Summit for Information Society (WSIS) in Geneva, in 2003, and in Tunis, in 2005, were marked by strong articulation of civil society.

The transnational connections outlined above facilitated international articulation of voice and protest. Transnationalism, as a core dimension of civil society's expression of issues, was born as a platform of social protest and voice, questioning development and change processes, thus adding a new layer to levels of social movement and participation.

The anti-globalisation movement picked up speed in the late 1990s, marked by protests at the World Trade Organisation meetings in Seattle (1999), Geneva (2000) and Göteborg (2001). These encounters provided powerful claims for citizen participation in cultural, political and economic processes impacting globalisation. Combining public demonstrations and acts of civil disobedience with strategic use of the Internet as a communication tool, these protests garnered high media visibility.

Communication-wise, many social movements and transnational encounters use the type of horizontal communication Frank Gerace and Luiz Ramiro Beltrán advocated as far back as 1970. Insisting on participating in international decision-making processes affecting large global constituencies and world development (Van Pieterse 2001) is now a hallmark of international development cooperation and an important use by civil society of transnational communication for social change.

The texts in this section focus on understanding the characteristics of new social movements emerging in light of recent economic, political and cultural globalisation. When describing new social movements, Robert Huesca defines social change as "emerging from coordinated action occurring outside of formal institutions like political parties and labour unions." The newness, according to Huesca, lies in "their attention to identity formation as a locus of coordinated action and their de-emphasis of group access to institutional resources or adherence to overarching ideologies that guided mobilisation."

We open this section with Huesca's piece highlighting how social movements are bottom-up responses to globalisation processes imposed from above. He writes that social movements are "globalisation from below," representing various issues but similarly focused on justice and social equity during times of fundamental changes in society. As Huesca states: "Indeed, new social movements, often diverse and focused on identity formation, have arisen in this rich, contradictory context and may post the most significant challenge in the global struggle for democratic guarantees and the provision of social services."

While one focus of this section is on social movements, another focus is on the role of communication and the media in contemporary change processes. Clemencia Rodriguez writes on citizens movements' use of the media to pursue their goals. She urges closer examination of community media: "While cultural studies seem to be concerned with the media texts of the dominant and how audiences interact with them, the media texts of ordinary citizens have not achieved status as objects of study." To capture the lived experiences of alternative media, Rodriguez suggests a theoretical framework drawing on Mouffe and McClure's theory of radical democracy. Based on analysis of conceptions of citizenship, Rodriguez's most important conceptual contribution is her suggestion of a new marker to substitute alternative media, namely the concept of citizen's media.

The term citizens' media implies that a collective citizenry actively intervenes and transforms the established media landscape; these media contest social codes, legitimised identities and institutionalised social relations; and communication practices empower the community involved, to the point where social transformation and change are possible.

Other writers included in this section reflect on concepts of participation (Cleaver), community media (Opubor, Peruzzo, Yoon and Bessette) as well as debate the requirements of communicators within a communication for social change framework (Gumucio-Dagron). Development of community radio provides new opportunities for local participation though public debate via the media. Peruzzo, Roncagliolo and Opoku-Mensah all write about this. One of the founding fathers of alternative media, John Downing, offers the concept of "radical media" which, together with Clemencia Rodriguez's article on citizens' media,

1927
1960
1963
1964
1967
1969
1970
1971
1972
1973
1974
1975
1976
1977
1978
1979
1980
1981
1982
1983
1984
1985
1986
1987
1988
1989
1990
1991
1992
1993
1994
1995
1996
1997
1998
1999
2000
2001
2002
2003
2004
2005
2006

proves a useful point of departure in discussing notions of community media. To each of the texts in this section we might apply Alfred Opubor's words: "If Community Media is the Answer, What is the Question?"

Power, Media and the Public Sphere

During the mid 1990s increased focus was put on the concept of power and power relations in development. Tied to this focus is the role of the public sphere in development. While the New World Information and Communication Order (NWICO) debate of the 1980s focused on access to the public sphere, the focus by the mid-1990s was more on the character and nature of the changing public sphere. Growing attention was given to how unequal power relations impede some social groups, be they women or people living with HIV/AIDS—from gaining both access to, and visibility in, the mediated public sphere.

Following the 1989 translation to English of German social scientist Jürgen Habermas' book *The Structural Transformation of the Public Sphere*, the Anglo-Saxon debate about the public sphere was reignited. Sociologist John B. Thompson, in *Media and Society: A Social Theory of the Media* (1995) critiques Habermas' conceptualisation and reassesses the mediated public sphere as the core forum for democratic debate. Peruvian feminist and media scholar Rosa María Alfaro formulates her critique of the public sphere from the activist perspective, arguing for grassroots-driven rights to access, representation and voice in the mediated public sphere.

For media institutions, the 1990s witnessed the combination of several developments contributing to the reconfiguration of the public sphere into several sub-scenarios. On one hand, we see an increasingly commercialised, privatised and mediated public sphere at national levels, driven by market logic and focused on ratings. It is hard for ordinary citizens to access media as a result. This is primarily the profile of media in the Americas, reinforced in recent years. In Africa, the media are less developed, but the obstacles are the same. Civil society's response has been

to professionalize their communication and media strategies hoping to gain better access to the privately-controlled mediated public spheres. In so doing, they focus on events and actions designed to attract media attention. The downside is that presentation of causes, ideals, messages and arguments are overly simplified.

Another sub-scenario of how the public sphere is developing lies in the proliferation of channels of communication and the lowering of prices of information and communication technologies. In Africa, liberalisation and deregulation processes lead to a proliferation of community media—commercial, state-owned and community radio—many driven by nongovernmental organisations, community-based organisations and churches. To keep up, civil society must acquire their own channels of communication particularly due to the increased difficulty in accessing larger, mainstream media.

Together, the development of media and the development of an increasingly mediated public sphere points to polarisation between citizens' media, (local or transnational), on one side, and on the other, an increasingly privatised public sphere of all major media and communication networks. New social movements, almost by definition, will have difficulty voicing their concerns within larger, privatised communication networks. They are left with more marginal, often smaller, community-oriented media. This is where Ignacio Ramonet's arguments for a fifth power seem to come in as a thought-provoking, necessary way forward:

> Globalisation now also means the globalisation of the mass media and the communications-information companies. These big companies are preoccupied with growth, which means that they have to develop relations with the other estates in society, so they no longer claim to act as a fourth estate with a civic objective and a commitment to denouncing human rights abuses. They are not interested in correcting the malfunctions of democracy and creating a better political system. They have no interest in being a fourth

estate and even less in acting as a countervailing power. And even when they do constitute a fourth estate, that estate is just an adjunct to the existing political and economic estates and operates as a supplementary, media power to crush people.

How do we react to all of this? How can we defend ourselves? How can we resist the offensive of this new power that has betrayed society and gone over to the enemy? The answer is simple. We have to create a new estate, a fifth estate that will let us pit a civic force against this new coalition of rulers. A fifth estate to denounce the hyper-power of the media conglomerates which are complicit in, and diffusers of, neo-liberal globalisation.

The texts in this section explain the problems and relationships of media in modern democratic societies. Armand Mattelart reinforces Ramonet's critical stance and call for a fifth estate. Mattelart criticises the lack of democracy in development during a time of technological euphoria, when democracy is market-driven. Instead of assessing communication as a public good, he sees it as something that should be regulated and decided upon by consumers. Mattelart finds it problematic, arguing that: "For me, both communication, education, health and the environment are indispensable public rights (public goods)."

South Africa's Ruth Teer-Tomaselli reaffirms that the communication and information sector constitutes "both sites and instruments of change" and brings to our attention the current crisis in public service broadcasting.

Other articles in this section further analyse what Martin-Barbero calls "the crisis of representation" in the public sphere, which is echoed—focusing on discourses of development—in Escobar's analysis of the "unmaking of development." He characterises this unmaking as a slow and painful process. However, in calling for the end of discursive practices of the past 40 years of development—a call echoed by Karin Wilkins from a gender perspective—Escobar does open a window of hope and optimism by stating: "although always partial, disconnection not infrequently presents attractive opportunities from poor people's perspectives." Alfaro's contribution here is a thorough deconstruction of the concept of public sphere, suggesting, from a participatory and action-oriented stance, pathways ahead. Spanish media scholar Alejandro Barranquero also pursues the theoretical exploration of communication for social change by analysing the complementarities of Freire and Habermas.

Finally, Khotari analyses the concept of power in relation to the development of participatory strategies within development policy and practice. Jan Servaes provides a critical assessment of evaluation in communication research, and Nurit Guttmann provides an equally critical assessment of the use of campaigns in health information and communication. Warren Feek completes this section by suggesting a simple way to analyse the role of communication and media in achieving sustainable impact.

Information Society and Communication Rights

The final pathway to new momentum in contemporary debate about communication for social change is the networked society. In 1995 Google was registered on the New York Stock Exchange, marking a technological climax in the establishment of a networked global society. Conceptually, and in relation to communication for social change, sociologist Manuel Castells of Spain and the United States makes an important contribution with *The Rise of the Network Society*. This work contributes much to the conceptualisation and understanding of how new technology, and the Internet in particular, impacts social development and change. Arguing that a new socio-economic organisation has emerged, Castells says: "this is a brand of capitalism that is at the same time very old and fundamentally new. It is old because it appeals to relentless competition in the pursuit of profit, and new because it is tooled by new information and communication technologies that are at the roots of new productivity sources, new organisational forms, and of the formation of a global economy."

1927
1960
1963
1964
1967
1969
1970
1971
1972
1973
1974
1975
1976
1977
1978
1979
1980
1981
1982
1983
1984
1985
1986
1987
1988
1989
1990
1991
1992
1993
1994
1995
1996
1997
1998
1999
2000
2001
2002
2003
2004
2005
2006

The Internet has become a social, cultural and economic phenomenon that is profoundly challenging forms of communication and the general organisation of society. What remains unsolved is the social and geographical imbalance in the development of the network society. Castells highlights some of the consequences, including individualization, exploitation of the labour force, social exclusion and social underdevelopment. In other words, poverty, inequality, misery and social exclusion also are consequences of the rise of the network society.

We also see a new form of struggle emerging: the questioning of the social consequences of the new global economy and the way information and communication technologies serve essentially commercial purposes. In this context, euphoria surrounding the visionary and democratic potential of technological development is challenged, most concretely during the World Summits for Information Society (Geneva, in 2003; Tunis, in 2005).

One of the critical voices questioning the euphoria about the development of a network society based on information and knowledge is that of Dutch media scholar Cees Hamelink. He writes, "There is abundant empirical evidence to support the importance of information and knowledge sharing. We should, however, assure that all the present emphasis on information and knowledge does not obscure the insight that at the heart of social development is communication in the form of dialogue. Since this is a complex and difficult, the development community should make it its principle challenge for the early 21st century." Eric Kluitenberg agrees, arguing "the networked environment should primarily be seen as a social space, in which active relationships are pursued and deployed."

A key question is: To what degree can global media be controlled, and by whom? Much of the debate at the WSIS summits dealt with concerns about global media governance and the principles and guidelines set by the World Trade Organisation regime. A number of the texts included here address the need for a global regulatory mechanism, arguing that is it not enough to develop national-level regulations, given the transnational character of the networks at stake.

Irish media scholar Seán Ó Siochrú outlines four points of concern. First, he worries about the growing failure of media in the public sphere, flagging the risk of the public sphere becoming distorted or controlled by narrow commercial interests. Second, he is concerned with the propagation of a single worldview, that of "individualist consumerism," in which all human relationships end up mediated through the market. Third, Ó Siochrú is concerned with corralling knowledge and the issue of copyright and the public domain. And fourthly, Ó Siochrú's concern is the possible erosion of civil rights in electronic communication, highlighting the increase in recent levels of surveillance since September 11, 2001. He suggests that civil society will need a transnational advocacy network to resolve these issues.

Along the lines of Ó Siochrú, Alfonso Gumucio-Dagron outlines five essential, non-negotiable conditions of ICT for development, including community ownership and local content on the Web. Gumucio says this is the most important condition as it can make the Web a more relevant tool for people.

And, finally, let us say that many of the contributions in this final section of the book focus on potential communication obstacles to truly democratic societies. Several of the writers argue that clearer principles and better strategies are needed to ensure that democratic societies, with the right for everyone to communicate, become real. As Hamelink writes: "The international recognition of a right to communicate is an essential step towards the development of communication societies in which social development equals people's empowerment to manage and control their own lives."

This is the underlying doctrine of communication for social change.

The Editors
July 2006

1927

9271960196319641967196971
7019711972197319741975191
6197719781979198019811198
1983198419851986198719888

HISTORICAL READINGS
VOLUME ❶

98919901991199219931994
95199619971998199920003
012002200320042005006

1994

THE RADIO AS AN APPARATUS OF COMMUNICATION

By Bertolt Brecht

1927 In our society one can invent and perfect discoveries that still have to conquer their market and justify their existence; in other words discoveries that have not been called for. Thus there was a moment when technology was advanced enough to produce the radio and society was not yet advanced enough to accept it. The radio was then in its first phase of being a substitute: a substitute for theatre, opera, concerts, lectures, cafe music, local newspapers and so forth. This was the patient's period of halcyon youth. I am not sure if it is finished yet, but if so then this stripling who needed no certificate of competence to be born will have to start looking retrospectively for an object in life. Just as a man will begin asking at a certain age when his first innocence has been lost, what he is supposed to be doing in the world.

As for the radio's object, I don't think it can consist simply in prettifying public life. Nor is radio in my view an adequate means of bringing back cosiness to the home and making family life bearable again. But quite apart from the dubiousness of its functions, radio is one-sided when it should be two. It is purely an apparatus for distribution, for mere sharing out. So here is a positive suggestion: change this apparatus over from distribution to communication. The radio would be the finest possible communication apparatus in public life, a vast network of pipes. That is to say, it would be if it knew how to receive as well as to transmit, how to let the listener speak as well as hear, how to bring him into a relationship instead of isolating him. On this principle the radio should step out of the supply business and organize its listeners as suppliers. Any attempt by the radio to give a truly public character to public occasions is a step in the right direction.

Whatever the radio sets out to do it must strive to combat that lack of consequences which makes such asses of almost all our public institutions. We have a literature without consequences, which not only itself sets out to lead nowhere, but does all it can to neutralize its readers by depicting each object and situation stripped of the consequences to which they lead. We have educational establishments without consequences, working frantically to hand on an education that leads nowhere and has come from nothing.

The slightest advance in this direction is bound to succeed far more spectacularly than any performance of a culinary kind. As for the technique that needs to be developed for all such operations, it must follow the prime objective of turning the audience not only into pupils but into teachers. It is the radio's formal task to give these educational operations an interesting turn, i.e., to ensure that these interest people. Such an attempt by the radio to put its instruction into an artistic form would link up with the efforts of modern artists to give art an instructive character. As an example or model of the exercises possible along these lines let me repeat the explanation of *Der Flug der Lindberghs* that I gave at the Baden-Baden music festival of 1929.

[Brecht repeats here the second, third and fifth paragraphs of "An Example of Pedagogics"]

> In obedience to the principle that the State shall be rich and man shall be poor, that the State shall be obliged to have many possibilities and man shall be allowed to have few possibilities, where music is concerned the State shall furnish whatever needs special apparatus and special abilities; the individual, however, shall furnish an exercise. Free-roaming feelings aroused by music, special thoughts such as may be entertained when listening to music, physical exhaustion such as easily arises just from listening to music, are all distractions from music. To avoid these distractions the individual shares in the music, thus obeying the

principle that doing is better than feeling, by following the music with his eyes as printed, and contributing the parts and places reserved for him by singing them for himself or in conjunction with others (school class).

Der Flug der Lindberghs is not intended to be of use to the present-day radio but to alter it. The increasing concentration of mechanical means and the increasingly specialized training—tendencies that should be accelerated—call for a kind of resistance by the listener, and for his mobilization and redrafting as a producer.

This exercise is an aid to discipline, which is the basis of freedom. The individual will reach spontaneously for a means to pleasure, but not for an object of instruction that offers him neither profit nor social advantages. Such exercises only serve the individual in so far as they serve the State, and they only serve a State that wishes to serve all men equally. Thus *Der Flug der Lindberghs* has no aesthetic and no revolutionary value independent of its application, and only the State can organize this. Its proper application, however, makes it so "revolutionary" that the present-day State has no interest in sponsoring such exercises.

This is an innovation, a suggestion that seems utopian and that I myself admit to be utopian. When I say that the radio or the theatre "could" do so-and-so I am aware that these vast institutions cannot do all they "could," and not even all they want.

But it is not at all our job to renovate ideological institutions on the basis of the existing social order by means of innovations. Instead our innovations must force them to surrender that basis. So: For innovations, against renovation!

Published as "Der Rundfunk als Kommunikationsapparat" in the *Berliner Börsen-Courier*, December 25, 1927.

A MODEL OF THE COMMUNICATION PROCESS

Excerpt from: Process of Communication

By David Berlo

1960 Every communication situation differs, in some ways, from every other. Yet we can attempt to isolate certain elements that all communication situations share in common. It is these ingredients and their interrelationships that we consider when we try to construct a general model of communication.

We attach the word "process" to our discussion of communication. The concept of process is itself complex. If we begin to discuss a model of the communication process without a common meaning for the word "process," our discussion might result in distorted views about communication.

The Concept of Process

At least one dictionary defines "process" as "any phenomenon which shows a continuous change in time," or "any continuous operation or treatment."

If we accept the concept of process, we view events and relationships as dynamic, on-going, ever-changing, continuous. When we label something as a process, we also mean that it does not have a beginning, an end, or a fixed sequence of events. It is not static, at rest. ...The ingredients within a process interact; each affects all the others.

The concept of process is inextricably woven into the contemporary view of science and physical reality. If we analyze the work of physical scientists, up to and including Isaac Newton, we do not find a comprehensive analysis of process. It was believed that the world could be divided into "things" and

1927
1960
1963
1964
1967
1969
1970
1971
1972
1973
1974
1975
1976
1977
1978
1979
1980
1981
1982
1983
1984
1985
1986
1987
1988
1989
1990
1991
1992
1993
1994
1995
1996
1997
1998
1999
2000
2001
2002
2003
2004
2005
2006

"processes." It was believed also that things existed, that they were static entities, that their existence was independent of the existence or operations of other "things."

The crisis and revolution in scientific philosophy brought about by the work of Einstein, Russell, Whitehead and others denied both these beliefs in two ways. First, the concept of relativity suggested that any given object or event could be analyzed or described only in light of other events that were related to it; other operations were involved in observing it. Second, the availability of more powerful observational techniques led to the demonstration that something as static or stable as a table, a chair, could be looked on as a constantly changing phenomenon, acting upon and being acted upon by all other objects in its environment, changing just as the person who observed it changes. The traditional division between things was questioned. The traditional distinction between things and processes was broken down. An entirely different way of looking at the world had to be developed—a process view of reality.

Communication theory reflects a process point of view. A communication theorist rejects the possibility that nature comprises events or ingredients that are separable from all other events. He argues that you cannot talk about the beginning or the end of communication or say that a particular idea came from one specific source, that communication occurs in only one way, and so on.

The basis for the concept of process is the belief that the structure of physical reality cannot be discovered by man; it must be created by man. In "constructing" reality, the theorist chooses to organize his perception in one way or another. He may choose to say that we can call certain things "elements" or "ingredients." In doing this, he realizes that he has not discovered anything, he has created a set of tools which may or may not be useful in analyzing or describing the world. He recognizes that certain things may precede others, but that in many cases the order of precedence

will vary from situation to situation. This is not to say that we can place no order on events. The dynamic of process has limitations; nevertheless, there is more than one dynamic that can be developed for nearly any combination of events.

When we try to talk or write about a process, such as communication, we face at least two problems. First, we must arrest the dynamic of the process, in the same way that we arrest motion when we take a still picture with a camera. We can make useful observations from photographs, but we err if we forget that the camera is not a complete reproduction of the objects photographed. The interrelationships among elements are obliterated, the fluidity of motion, the dynamics, are arrested. The picture is a representation of the event, it is not the event. As Hayakawa has put it, the word is not the thing, it is merely a map that we can use to guide us in exploring the territories of the world.

A second problem in describing a process derives from the necessity for the use of language. Language itself, as used by people over time, is a process. It too, is changing, on-going; however, the process of language is lost when we write it. Marks on paper are a recording of language, a picture of language. They are fixed, permanent, static. Even spoken language, over a short period of time, is relatively static.

In using language to describe a process, we must choose certain words, we must freeze the physical world in a certain way. Furthermore, we must put some words first, others last. Western languages go from left to right, top to bottom. All languages go from front to back. Beginning to end—even though we are aware that the process we are describing may not have a left and right, a top and a bottom, a beginning and an end.

We have no alternative if we are to analyze and communicate about a process. The important point is that we must remember that we are not including everything in our discussion. The things we talk about do not have to exist in exactly the ways we talk about them, and they certainly do not have to operate in the order in which we talk about them. Objects we separate may not always be separable, and they never operate independently—each affects and interacts with the others.

Berlo, David. "A Model of the Communication Process," New York: Holt, Rinehart, and Winston, 1960. Excerpt from *Process of Communication* 1st edition by BERLO, D. © 1960. Reprinted with permission of Wadsworth, a division of Thomson Learning: www.thomsonrights.com. Fax 800 730-2215

1927
1960
1963
1964
1967
1969
1970
1971
1972
1973
1974
1975
1976
1977
1978
1979
1980
1981
1982
1983
1984
1985
1986
1987
1988
1989
1990
1991
1992
1993
1994
1995
1996
1997
1998
1999
2000
2001
2002
2003
2004
2005
2006

COMMUNICATION THEORY: THE SOCIOLOGICAL IMPLICATIONS OF INFORMATION ON MASS CULTURE

Excerpt from: Communication and Culture of the Masses

By Antonio Pasquali

1963 Only in true speech is true silence possible... Being silent, however, is not the same as being speechless. (Heidegger: *Being and Time*.)

The form and level of culture that social groups manifest are a function of the medium they employ to communicate knowledge: The less developed a culture, the more causal is the nature of that relation. Due to the specialization involved in present-day communications media, knowledge is transmitted by a small nucleus of sending agents. These serve as "experts" within or acting on behalf of pressure groups that operate outside of the cultural sphere, channeling and transmitting this knowledge to an expanded arena of individual recipients. When the increasing disproportion between sending agents and recipients reaches such a point that the bilateral nature of true intercommunication atrophies irreversibly—with the professionalization of the sending group, which assumes the monopolizing role of "informer," and the concurrent reduction of the receiving group's role to that of the "informed"—then the expansive and self-creating force of knowledge is diminished, and its mass dissemination is reduced to a unilateral relationship between an informing oligarchy, which has become an elite, and an undifferentiated population of recipients, which has become a mass.

Exploiting the most astute intuitions of cultural sociology (which postulates that knowledge-in-common is the constituent, not the superstructure, of the social), it becomes clear that the existence of the communications media does not depend on a given body of knowledge, which would be the epiphenomenon of a pre-existing social substance. Rather, the society-knowledge-communication relationship operates in much the reverse fashion. A society's type is determined by a body of knowledge, which in turn is dictated by the society's communications media. Social structures do not, a posteriori, engender a body of knowledge from which communications media emanate; rather, the media shape and constrain the forms of knowledge that determine and characterize a social group. The function determines, or at least "configures," the organ—just as virtuous acts create virtue, not the reverse. Philosophy has always, for good reason, rejected "incommunicable knowledge" (such as that derived from mystical experience), or has posited from the outset that the incommunicable is the unknowable, and that the unknowable is not, since we assume that the inexpressible is alogical, and that the alogical is an agnoia, or not-knowing.

The degree and mode of its communicability, then, defines a body of knowledge, as the knowledge defines its social plexus. The direct inference, from a sociological perspective, is that a mutual dialectical inherence obtains between the media employed for communicating knowledge and the social group to which they pertain. Society (*Mitsein* or being-with) exists only where there is co-knowledge, and co-knowledge exists only where there are forms of communication. The functional relationship between society and the means-of-communication-of-knowledge implies that the nature of the latter is determinative for the former, at least to the extent to which the reverse relationship has always been considered valid. However, no simple cause-effect, part-all or super/infrastructure

relationship exists between communications media and total social reality. Rather, there is a dialectical inherence or mutual immanence. Such axioms open up a new methodological horizon, allowing the degree of culture to be inferred from the inter-relationship between a society and its communications media. For example, a judgment of cultural underdevelopment could be based on a finding of communicational atrophy—as, indeed, will be attempted here.

The full demonstration of this thesis requires a new sociological categorization of the relationship. The definitions offered below attempt to address the need for new dynamic categories. Their novelty lies in the effort to assimilate whatever scientific suggestions can be drawn from modern scientific attempts to formalize the problem of communication (specifically, information theory). While there is certainly no attempt to extend the logical/mathematical formulations of this discipline to the entire anthropological area, a new conceptual systematization of the fundamental nature of social relations, from the scientific perspective of information theory, can at least be attempted, albeit with a healthy recognition of the attendant risks and difficulties. This, indirectly, is an indication of the limitations and problems involved in attempting a strictly social application. The rationale and foundation for this risky undertaking are based on the assumption that the most immediate implications and repercussions of information theory are less semiotic, psychological, esthetic and historical than sociological—though the latter elements have received the least attention from social philosophers.

In this essay, communication or communicational relationship, is used to signify that relationship which produces (and at the same time presupposes) an interaction involving co-knowledge, this being possible only when a law of bivalence governs the two poles of the sender-receiver relational structure, such that any sender may be a receiver, and any receiver may be a sender. There is neither "communication" nor any other type of dialectical relationship with nature

1927
1960
1963
1964
1967
1969
1970
1971
1972
1973
1974
1975
1976
1977
1978
1979
1980
1981
1982
1983
1984
1985
1986
1987
1988
1989
1990
1991
1992
1993
1994
1995
1996
1997
1998
1999
2000
2001
2002
2003
2004
2005
2006

or raw materials, but rather some other form of mon-ovalent relationship: utilitarian, energetic, etc., since in this case the pole of the relationship is a pure object of knowledge or action, a pure, essentially mute *res extensa* that, strictly speaking, does not even necessarily act as a receiver, since it lacks any knowledge of receptivity. In the case of the machine, the work of art, and the artifact in general, there is at most an indirect communication with the "other" through an interposed artifice, which exceeds the limits of communication, as such: neither attaining the state of a pure informational relationship nor receding to the status of a mere energy relationship of spirit to matter. The only entities capable of provoking authentic communication and social forms of behavior—not mere mechanical exchange of information and stimuli—are rational beings that are depositories of co-knowledge—beings with the capacity to send/receive at the sensory and intellectual levels. Hence the man as zoon logon exon, the speaking and dialoguing animal (with or without the use of artificial channels of communication), which is therefore the zoon politikon, or coexisting animal.

Humanity, generically speaking, is the principal specific element in co-knowledge (of which self-consciousness is a secondary moment)—i.e., conscious co-presence in communication. The term communication, then, applies to dialogic relationships between human beings, or ethically autonomous persons, and points precisely to the fundamental ethical connection with an "other" with whom "I need to communicate" [Wiener]. This in turn implies an "open state," an openness or discovery-acceptance of otherness in dialogue and, by reflection, consciousness of self. There is a double dialectical tension in this situation, though this will not be discussed in detail here. One of the tensions—external and secondary—is a function of the role-switching potential of the sender/receiver, and of the phenomenon of two well-defined poles with mutual absorptive capacity facing each other. The other—intrinsic and primary—reflects a contradictory situation within the communicator. One of the

moments of communication—which is not the same as communing, fusing with another, or becoming alienated—implies a transcendent impulse to objectify, to place the other as other, as otherness linked to a subject that does not become alienated in this operation. Communication (which does not place the other as other) rests entirely, then, on the subject's preserving this non-fusing transcendence, or maintaining this distanced presence or presence-absence. To the extent that such an attraction-repulsion equilibrium is relaxed, otherness ceases to be simple heteronomy, and assumes an autonomy that is pure negation or indifference. The other becomes a hostile monad, transcendent and closed, and incommunicability or alienation of one from the other emerges. Thus, it is communicability itself—which only subsists as a harmonic tension between two poles—that dialectically encompasses the seeds of incommunicability.

Authentic communication, then, is only that which is based on a symmetric relational scheme, with parity of conditions between sender and receiver, and the possibility of one hearing or giving ear to the other [Heidegger], as a mutual will to understand one another. This latter is the basic and indispensable condition of non-contradiction in any relationship of communication (which we call dialogue), since even if I accepted the request of the other to make an effort not to understand him, I would fall into a contradiction, since that very act would reflect an understanding of him [Calogero]. In the experience of dialogue, a common territory between the other and myself is constituted; his thought and mine intertwine in a single fabric… inserting itself in a common operation of which neither is the creator. There is one dual being… we are reciprocal collaborators under perfectly equal conditions, our perspectives fade into each other, and we coexist through a common world. [Merleau-Ponty]. A relation of dialogue or authentic communication is recognized in that the person who is the object of discursive address "talks back" by virtue of a coherent and irresistible impulse (which Renouvier would have called "normal vertigo") that tends to reduce the alien logos to dia-logos between equals, and bring it to realization.

The multiplicity of communicating channels, along with the enormous expansion they produce within the old molds of co-knowledge and co-existence, suggests that a theory of communication will soon occupy an important place alongside theories of knowledge. It will be based on semiotics on the one hand, and the mathematical sciences on the other, with major ramifications in the areas of sociology, psychology and, more generally, the moral sciences.

The term communication theory—not information theory—is employed here, out of a belief that the concept of information developed in recent years lacks any logical univocality, precisely because of its enormous and still unexplored richness. Its most common use, indeed, suggests the presence of a receiving pole constituted by a rational interpretant, when we know that the reception of information can also be accomplished by any machine equipped for interpreting, storing and creating messages (in the sense of stimuli or "programs" that provoke responses through "effector" mechanisms). It remains, then, to clearly and definitively differentiate between cybernetic information and anthropological information. However, the principal axiomatic and categorical results of information theory to date—namely, the quantification of information as unpredictability, and the definition of its loss as greater probability (information loss is also the progressive "obsolescence" or "entropy" of messages degraded by their banality or repetition), as well as the concepts of redundancy and noise, esthetic and semantic segments, etc.— become meaningful only in an informational context in which the receiving pole is a res cogitans, since such structural factors in information are part of the unavoidable functional perspective created by an interpretant or non-mechanical receiver. Indeed, a machine designed to receive information can never measure the loss of information in a message; differentiate the semantic, quantifiable and encodable element from the

esthetic; or increase the informational coefficent as a function of its unpredictability, etc.

Thus, a system that proposes to conceive of communicational processes anthropologically must create a categorical distinction that eliminates the equivocal nature of the term information. Given the primary importance, for present purposes, of the sociological implications being considered, what is proposed here is a distinction between types of interrelationship, depending on the coefficient of communicability of the poles present, which would mean that information can be taken as a species within the genus communication. "Coefficient of communicability" here means the potential sender-receiver charge present at each pole of the relational field, a charge that should be describable and even quantifiable. (A potential sender, for example, may "self-materialize" in the presence of a specific receiver, in the presence of n receivers of identical characteristics, or in the presence of one or n receivers of unlike characteristics; or he may switch solely in the direction of the receiver/sender from whom a message was previously received, function as a relay, etc. A potential receiver can thus "self-materialize" in the presence of a specific sender, or of n equal or unlike senders, or exchange messages with a previously agreed sender/receiver, etc.). The primary distinction, in any case, will be based on these three basic coefficients of communicability:

- S (sender only);
- R (receiver only);
- S/R (sender-receiver).

This typology has the advantage of applying equally to "communication" of a completely mechanical type, and to communication of a totally thinking type, as well as to all intermediate cases. However, it excludes any possibility of applying the concept of communication to cybernetic relationships (where there can only be information/stimulus reciprocity, but no "dialogue"), while it allows for the use of the terms communicate and inform when bipolarity is established between thinking, non-mechanical entities. Between such thinking beings, communication will define the exchange of messages with a possibility of non-mechanical return between poles with the same coefficient of communicability (R-T), and information will define the sending of messages without possibility of non-mechanical return between a T pole and a peripheral and only afferent R pole. In this way, the term information would connote the principal distinctive feature of communication, which is a relationship between poles with low coefficients of communicability. An anthropological information theory would thus form part of a general theory of communication, as it would be the important part designed to analyze transmission of messages that are unilateral, or without return channels, between thinking and/or artificial entities.

This, in addition to molding itself docilely to a technological reality that has decreed the predominance of unilateral means of transmission, opens a new perspective on the entire sphere of co-knowledge. In the long term, this general theory of communication could formalize and bring together basic elements of co-existence that can no longer be kept apart (the educational group elements, as well as the moral, informational, and advertising elements; the human-relations elements and the elements pertaining to the sociology of knowledge; those involving comprehension of a work of art, and political ones; etc.), becoming the metalanguage of all sciences whose object is man as a dialoguing and social entity.

The following definitions would broaden the sociological perspectives of this first, substantial distinction between communicating and informing. When one refers to communications media, one is referring less to the basic symbols adopted by man to signify, express and communicate knowledge (language), but rather to the specific artificial channels used as vehicles for transmitting such language between thinking sending/receiving beings. Communications media in the broadest sense, then, are all signifying languages (most of which are currently conventional, rather than artificial), and in general any sign capable of exciting a receiver by carrying a meaning or significance: the means of spoken language, visual language, etc. However, the primary function of any sign or signifier is to "make reference to" a signified concept, and then, subsidiarily, to communicate it. A medium of communication, on the other hand, has no function but to materially "transport" signs previously agreed upon in a symbolic context that precedes the selection of the communicating medium. The expressions medium of communication and communications media do not attempt, in principle, to usurp semantic territory, but connote those artificial channels of transmission that man has invented to send a receiver meaningful messages of any nature, expressed in any system of symbols in the qualitatively and numerically most efficient form.

If the word, for example, is the key sign designated to evoke by association, for a receiver, the meaning that the sender wishes to communicate, then any one or more of numerous media—telephone, radio, cinema, oscilloscope, television, telegraphy, etc.—could serve as the optimal means of conveying the key sign to the receiver. All of these channels are artificial, because (a) the term "natural" must be reserved for those afferent-efferent organs of the body that always occupy the extremes of a communicational relationship, even when there are innumerable artificial channels in between; and (b) all imply a commuting of the original sign into a key (mechanical, chemical, electrical, etc.) as an indispensable condition for its transport over a distance. An SOS sent by relay through smoke signals, talking drums, a messenger who communicates a message telephonically to a telegraph station, and finally a radio broadcast, will have been transposed to different keys by each of the artificial channels employed in communicating it (optics, acoustics, wire, radio, etc.), but will always involve (a) the inalterability of the original meaning sent through different systems of signifying signs; and (b) an initial natural "converter" channel in the sender, and a natural "interpreting" channel in the (final or intermediate) receiver. The signs or signifiers

1927
1960
1963
1964
1967
1969
1970
1971
1972
1973
1974
1975
1976
1977
1978
1979
1980
1981
1982
1983
1984
1985
1986
1987
1988
1989
1990
1991
1992
1993
1994
1995
1996
1997
1998
1999
2000
2001
2002
2003
2004
2005
2006

are direct carriers of meanings; the media of communication are their secondary carriers. It is hoped that, in this way, confusion can be avoided in the use of the terms (strictly speaking, there is no "language" of radio, cinema, etc., but a language of sounds, images, etc., transported and therefore syntactically coordinated through the radio, cinema, etc.). However, this in turn means that some semiotic principles should, analogously, be applied to the study of communications media, since this second level of transport is able to produce profound syntactic transformations, thus expanding the signifying function of the signs transported, rather than simply facilitating their dissemination. The combination of iconographic signs that film, for example, has made possible, does not follow the rules of any syntax—musical, poetic, stained glass, fold-out pamphlets, etc., or the sum of all of these—as the first theorists of the cinema dreamed. The emergence of a new communications medium can only bring a revolution in the syntactic coordinates of a basic system of signs by increasing and differentiating their signifying function.

Since film entered the scene, we "say" more with images (since they "say" and mean more in this new diachronic context) than we have at any other time, even though the sign used is essentially the same one known to people in the seventeenth century, medieval man and even the humans of Lascaux and Altamira. The possibilities, limits and peculiarities typical of a channel turn back syntactically on the signifying contexts for which they are vehicles. The process of "embodying" information in a channel (knowing beforehand which channel one is going to use) affects the "encryption" or significant encoding of the message. In the most extreme case, it may impose itself on the same source of meaning from which the raw material of the expressible emanates. Stated simply: the old hypothesis that "the limits of my expressive arsenal translate into limitations in my thinking capacity" must be expanded, in terms of the whole that is meaning-signified-communicated. It is now the limits and prerogatives of the medium of communication that

begin the series of retroactive prefigurations, which determine the channel, the code, the type of encryption or signifying expression of the message—an operation which, in turn, may predetermine the nature and scope of the expressible. In this sense, at least, the "neutrality" of the communications media vis-à-vis the meaning or content of a message seems arguable. Thus, it is clear that, though by communications media we refer to the material or artificial substrate used to transport signs preconceived by human beings, it must not be forgotten that the use of such means, by expanding the syntactic coefficient, turns back on the totality of signifying processes (which is possibly the most important novelty that semiotic parameters contribute to an analysis of communication).

Thus, a communications medium transports a language, but in doing so can admit a change in its syntax, thus increasing its signifying power. Therefore, not every message or set of meanings can be encoded or put in material form for any of the available channels, since the cipher or sign is not invariant in relation to what is thought, experienced, etc., in its expressional phase.

The elements addressed here relate to the communicating function in general, i.e., both the communicational relationship as such (communication in the narrow sense) and information. In fact, all the means of relation currently available to humanity can be used either to communicate or to inform—categories that are defined in the subsequent paragraphs.

The expression informational relationship (as proposed here) is reserved to refer to those relations in which the sender and receiver lose the ambivalence proper to communication, replacing dialogue with allocution or "pareresis." Allocution here refers to the unilateral discourse that produces an informational relationship, which is an ordered utterance allowing for no possible reply by the receiver [Kafka and Heidegger's *Ermittelung*, or notification]. Pareresis, which is taken here from the Greek *paraireo*, very precisely (to the point of justifying the idiomatic license) connotes the most peculiar feature of allocution: the attempt to take away, make smaller, appropriate and alienate (the receiver) as a basic function of an ordered utterance that admits of no response. The dialectical complementarity between the two poles of the communicational relationship—which generates new forms of co-knowledge through a process of synthesis—withdraws now to an asymmetrical and pre-dialectical configuration that is not even *antinomy*, but merely a relationship of opposites in which one of the parts always denies the other without denying itself. "Without reciprocity there is no alter ego, since the world of oneself then includes the other, so that one of the two feels alienated in favor of the other" [Merleau-Ponty: *Phénoménologie de la Perception*]. The receiver (specifically, a receiver of messages sent by the mass media) finds him/herself, here, in a situation in which it is impossible to directly or indirectly become a sender in a dialogued reply. The sender thus experiences a gradual sterilization of his/her receptive potential. Hence the everyday factum of the information media which, by their very nature, fail to use the dual nature implicit in each pole of the relation: of the two alternative possibilities in communication, only one, and the same one, is always realized—and, necessarily, as information—while the other is relegated to the sphere of impossibility, or of possibilities with no future. In that instant, one of the poles always acts as sender, the other as receiver.

This impossibility of immediate reversal of poles, typical of, and constraining to, the informational relationship, so reduces the possibility of rebuilding the dual relation on new foundations, that the channel employed ends up functioning with a diode, a rigidly irreversible convector. The spontaneous impulse of the one spoken to, namely, to change the discourse of the interlocutor (Logos) into a dual discourse or dialogue, is frustrated. The "will to understand," imposed unilaterally now on the receiver, is transformed from an agreement into a command. All that remains is, on the one hand, someone who makes himself heard, without having to hear the other (a deaf sender) and, on

the other, someone who must only hear without being heard (a dumb receiver)—and this not as a result of voluntary renunciation, but because his possibilities have been renounced for him. The receiver becomes pure absorbing consciousness "in a dumbness that is, nonetheless, recognized as dumbness" [Sartre]. If nature is spontaneously knowable… and in its totality cannot be silent, people, in contrast, either can be silent and hide their thoughts, and this is something distinct from mere speech… it is an active manner of behaving"… [Scheler], or they can be silent and become purely passive and unknowing from which communication is impossible.

The silence thus produced is inauthentic, since it is compelled by the notifying pareresis. It is no longer the silence of one who is really in communication and hence able to convert the alien "logos" into "dialogue" but prefers not to. Only in true speech is true silence possible… "Being silent, however, is not the same as being speechless" [Heidegger]. Of the one who does not dialogue, it has been said that he can never apply the logic of *yes* and *no*, and this is precisely the case of the receiver of information. The sender, conscious of the privileges that accompany his functions as constitutive informer, assumes the arrogant posture of one who says something but knows that his pareretic utterance is a "command to silence" that artificially reduces the receiver's coefficient of communicability, thus alienating his expressive functions and enormously increasing his receptive ones. "Behind the mask of "one for the other" acts a "one against the other" [Heidegger]. Now the receiver is a purely afferent system, something thought, and his receptive and interpretive faculties suffer from elephantiasis, as compensation for the not-being-able-to-say-anything state that he is compelled to accept. Each time a means of information contacts and subjugates us, we are in the presence of an utterance that silences us. ("Don't think," said Karl, "that I am completely in your power; I could even start to scream. And I could cover your mouth… Your hopes are unfounded…" Kafka, *America*). This is the health of the sender through the

1927
1960
1963
1964
1967
1969
1970
1971
1972
1973
1974
1975
1976
1977
1978
1979
1980
1981
1982
1983
1984
1985
1986
1987
1988
1989
1990
1991
1992
1993
1994
1995
1996
1997
1998
1999
2000
2001
2002
2003
2004
2005
2006

muting and annihilation of the receiver, the leaden freight of forms of knowledge manipulated and sent by one-way channels that block the impulse to dialogue. The hyperinterpretive capacity, the almost magical auscultation of pareresis, and the conjectural hysterical hypertrophy (so perfectly symbolized by Kafka's K in *The Castle*) are highly symptomatic of the social structures in which information takes precedence over communication or dialogue. Bilateralness allows mutual selection and control of a communications medium in a relationship of communication. In a unilateral relationship of informational transmission, on the other hand, the control, selection and use of the means of information become the absolute prerogative of the sending agent, who has become an institutionalized elite for the performance of that function.

Many still undefined aspects of our conception of contemporary man, many obscure elements of his behavioral patterns, may be conceptualized by using categories such as communication and information. The latter, which, as we have seen, can spawn concepts such as allocution, pareresis, notification, communicational unilateralness, silencing of the receiver, etc., seems, despite its apparent simplicity, to be sufficiently fertile to become one of the more important categories for the understanding of many contemporary social phenomena.

The only possible transmission of messages between mechanical or electronic complexes is transmission of pure "epitactic" or causative information in the lowest sense. Each pole is previously prepared to send a number of rigidly encoded messages, in the pure sense of the word, or to receive and interpret the key to stimulus/information designed to trigger a mechanical response as the only "conditioned reflex" possible. A scientist or thinker does not establish a relationship of communication, let alone of information, with the mute object (whether concrete or abstract) of his research, but rather a parsimonious relationship of knowledge. When the other pole of the relation is an interlocutor, the pole never informs, but communicates, essentially under conditions of equality. The purely informational level is only reached when the receiver, though theoretically preserving his potential as an interlocutor, loses it in practice due to the presence of means that technically prevent its actualization. Here, one should emphasize the receiver's maintaining the ability to dialogue as a pure possibility never made reality (as a co-possibility with no possible future, in indeterministic terms). This feature, which could be expressed by the symbol (S)-R, prevents confusing the energy relationship man-nature with informational relationships. In the former, the object/receiver is essentially deprived of sending power; in the latter, he is theoretically provided with it, but effectively prevented from actualizing it. That does not prevent every informational relationship from hiding, within it, an outburst of the sender designed to leave the petrified receiver in a reified state, and to make every allocution a more or less successful attempt to become the instrument of a relationship more utilitarian and energetic than communicational, at the expense of the receiver.

The receiver of information does not limit his passivity to automatically registering the message received. Despite the more or less vague awareness of this that he may have, from the moral perspective, the situation creates a context of involuntary action, both because of the alienation of the efficient and final cause and because the means are predetermined. A receiver is compelled by the sender, willy-nilly, to enter into an informational relationship and to be grafted, despite himself, onto a teleological structure with which he does not necessarily agree. ("Freedom of information" is an ironic contradiction in terms, since it refers only to the freedom of the informer.) The receiver is obliged to submit to the use of informational means chosen beyond his ability to deliberate or exert influence. Such means are imposed, in the abstract, by principles of economy in the subdivision of labor, but are, in fact, concretely chosen and manipulated by the sending agent. The receiver is invited to a spurious banquet of intercommunication, but is forced to

1927
1960
1963
1964
1967
1969
1970
1971
1972
1973
1974
1975
1976
1977
1978
1979
1980
1981
1982
1983
1984
1985
1986
1987
1988
1989
1990
1991
1992
1993
1994
1995
1996
1997
1998
1999
2000
2001
2002
2003
2004
2005
2006

play the role of the stone guest. All of this occurs in the context of a strict social determinism in which the idea (held by some) that it is still feasible for us to withdraw from the informational relationship in order to preserve our calm and self-sufficiency is an illusion. Coercion, necessariness, compulsion and power make every mass-human a receiver of information, and every receiver a non-deliberating and violated subject. Ethically, this involuntariness is independent of whether the individual receiver acts without awareness, or seeks subjection and massification.

Psychologically, the passivity of the information receiver reflects all the syndromes of frustration. When a content involving "dissemination" predominates in the unilateral relation—i.e., when it carries the product of a relationship of knowledge (scientific or poetic)—the situation does not produce the need for immediate reply in the receiver, and occurs without major consequences. The receiver here expects to receive and be silent. If the information relation does not contain predominant elements of dissemination, if it functions doxastically, imposing opinions, interpretations, news, etc., of which we vaguely intuit the motivating role, its contents arouse intense desires to enter into immediate dialogue. Such desires are soon smothered in the receiver, leading to the frustration associated with muteness. In more culturally and politically developed societies, these frustrations may not produce profound collective repression. The informational relationship is not predominant there, or else it allows individuals from different sectors of society to have free access to it. In the latter case, different reactions and insights will be normal escape valves for many impulses to create the conditions for, or reestablish, even indirectly, the bilateral function of the communicational arrangement.

In culturally underdeveloped societies that are subject to a hybrid economic-political monopoly of the information media, no one has the legitimate and free right to appeal (or, for the person who succeeds in obtaining it, a curtain of silence makes his/her efforts inoperative), leading to enormous collective frustration and repression. Messages that should flow to a receiver through normal channels of communication and dialogue may be forced to go through unilateral and information-promoting channels, in the most subtle of communicational immoralities. (For example, a political "dialogue" among the members of a governing elite, televised for the benefit of a population more or less deprived of its political rights, is a grotesque ersatz of the communicational relationship, an illusory escape valve used by those who have blocked the true channels of communication, leading to massive collective frustration.) In the long run, such palliatives can only fuel the repression that may contain traumatic feelings until they reach the point of explosion. The information receiver's frustration, caused by his muteness, is fundamental. From this flow all of the features described in the scientific literature under the heading of "psychological idiocy": thinking and action based on stereotypes, drooling admiration of the exponents of the informing elite or of their mythology, adoption of a prescribed personality or of certain aspirations, "tranquilizers" to avoid dealing with muteness, etc.

What is the role today, in the intercommunication of knowledge, of the basic forms of communication in the strict sense (dialogue, paideia, school, etc., with all the means of communication they entail), and what is the role of the information media, especially the audiovisual media? Which of these communicational schemes is currently most operative, especially in the broad, quantitative sense of popular culture, or in relation to specific phenomena such as collective ideologies, public opinion and behavior patterns? In this communication-dissemination-information scheme (which may be equated to the dialogue-book-television configuration) there are complex and obscure problems that need to be addressed by semiotics, psychology, sociology, ethics and other disciplines concerned with co-knowledge. In any case, there is a clear descending relationship of distance between sender and receiver, which goes from the nonexistence of intermediate artificial channels (personal dialogue) to the maximum currently admissible use of them (in which the information is subject to a greater number of communications, and directed impersonally to the masses). Hence, there is a progressive transformation of dialogue into pareresis, of bilateral communication into unilateral information. This in turn produces a progressive loss of the possibility of obtaining new forms of knowledge by synthesis, since in its lower layers the dialectical confrontation is brusquely interrupted, and knowledge is channeled in only one direction. The scheme may represent a hierarchy of values: more quality and specialization but less reach in the upper layer; less quality but greater reach in the lower; and a descending degree of irrationality with an ascending degree of rationality, as well as progressive nuances of univocal/equivocal, sincere-sophisticated and altruistic/egotistical. The basic question here, however, regards the function of each communications medium in creating a popular or mass culture. If spontaneous dialogue and, strictly speaking, all means for the dissemination of knowledge, continue functioning as basic mechanisms in the creation of knowledge by negation, contribution, synthesis, etc., among the cultural elites, would not massification of ideologies apply solely to those media that renounced bilateralness for the sake of multiplying and leveling the receiving pole? With this question, a new concept in need of definition enters the picture, namely, the masses.

To derive the definition of mass media and masses (sociological concepts) from the communicational categories set forth above, one must fully acknowledge the basic postulate that there is a functional interrelationship between a society's dominant communications media and its overall social reality. From this flows the possibility of sociologically and culturally describing a collectivity in terms of the degree of development (or atrophy) of the communications media available to it for the transmission of knowledge. The methodological novelty here lies in the attempt to derive sociological categories from communicational concepts and forms. If one wishes to do this, and if, by

the term "masses," one refers to a social structure, then one must conclude that a "mass society" emerges from the predominance (whether spontaneous or imposed) of one type of communication of knowledge over another. The predominant reality here is undoubtedly the informational relationship. It functionalizes a social structure, in the sense of massification. Hence a mass society is one in which informational relationships predominate among members, to the detriment of communicational relationships. Here, then, is the sociological implication sought: The predominance of unilateral communication (information) shapes the massification of the receivers. The sender's silencing allocution or "view" is not limited to changing the receiver into a for-the-other and alienating him from his world. By cutting off his potential for dialogue and silencing him as an interlocutor, it can also direct itself indifferently to one or "n" receivers. By establishing equal treatment, by being one-for-all, it tends to produce uniformity in a temporal dimension, to alienate and massify. Mutual convergence toward a single vertex (the notifying sender) produces horizontal relations of equality among receivers as a reflection, each of whom is atomistically converted into a unified unit, into one-of-so-many, whose value no longer depends on qualitative criteria, but on statistical and probabilistic ones. "They formed a sort of block, in which one could not have been destroyed without destroying the others. ("They formed a cohesiveness that is generally nearly impossible to obtain except with dead material." Kafka, *The Trial*). If the communicating and dialoguing relationship preserves and celebrates personal diversity among receivers, the informational relationship tends to eliminate it, petrifying and massifying the receivers. ("Frieda again raised the whip. (In the name of Klamm)," she exclaimed, "to the stable, to the stable, all!" Kafka, *The Castle*.)

Strictly speaking, then, only in the context of the informational relationship can one speak of mass media, since only where relationships of information are predominant does massification occur. The communicational relationship, limited as it is to dialogue between bivalent poles, finds the use of such an expression repugnant. Information and mass media, on the other hand, are functionally intertwined. If the presence of one or "*n*" receivers is a matter of indifference in the unilateral informational relationship, gravity will dictate a mechanical law of least action, which will translate into a constant attempt by the sending agent to reach the entire mass of receivers with each allocution.

Mass information media, accordingly, will be the artificial channels of communication when they carry in unilateral fashion allocutions or messages of an omnibus nature. If all information is massifying, it is because its freight of meanings tends to stabilize at the level of one-for-all (omnibus). In other words, it becomes impersonal in its content to avoid the need for being selective in its reach. Since the receiver is not now an interlocutor, but one-of-many mute listeners and watchers, there is no need for him/her to be selected by persons, partial social structures, levels and spheres of culture, places or situations, as always and necessarily occurs with communication and the dissemination of knowledge. The informational allocution shoots without aiming, because it will always hit the target. It is the message *urbi et orbi,* whose other important distinctive feature is mediocrity of content and form, which is necessary it if is to be susceptible of interpretation by all. This averageness or mediocrity takes place on various levels: in the content, which reshapes all forms of knowledge on the Procrustean bed of the all-understandable; in the impairment of the receiver by weakening or deactivating the selective function in him; in the degradation and vulgarization of the sublime by excessive dissemination, irreverent use and wear; in the dizzying rhythm and scansion imposed on messages, which create in the receiver a progressive loss of sensitivity accompanied by an obsessive erethism around novelty (which reflexively produces what some writers call the obsolescence of all values due to progressive stimulus saturation in which stimuli lose their power, etc.). However, this mediocrity of the for-all in no way resembles "objectivity." The latter term, which

with suspicious frequency is supplied as a garnish for the word "information," is the false connotation under which a mass culture hides the interested subjectivism of the sending agent. An authentic objectivity, such as the objectivity of knowing how to speak and knowing how to listen, would be a mortal dart aimed at the very essence of unilateral information (which is always doxastic), and would be suicidal for the sender. The wrapping of digestive "objectivity," which covers the allocution, hides the ingredients of a partiality that cannot be contested by the mute receiver, but that is highly beneficial to the informer. "False objectivity is no more than the self-defense of the egotistical empirical existence. Its apparent objectivity becomes radical subjectivity" (Jaspers).

The expression "mass communications media" contains a flagrant contradiction in terms and should be banished. Either we are in the presence of means used for communication, in which case the receiving pole is never a "mass," or we are in the presence of the same means used for information, in which case it is redundant to specify "mass." All the artificial channels used today for "communication" with the masses, by virtue of their very structure, silence the receiving subject and block his/her interlocutory capacity, for they inherently promote the informational relationship, while being entirely inadequate instruments for communication in the real sense. Moreover, there exists no mass relationship of communication. The expression could nevertheless subsist if the term communication clearly alluded to the general sense of the term, connoting the entire region that is the object of a theory of communication (both in the narrow sense as well as in the sense of information). As it is used, however, it lends itself, instead, to numerous ambiguities. Once the distinction between "communicate" and "inform" has been made, it could even be interpreted as a hypocritical disguising of the source of information under the mantle of an ennobling term.

Thus, mass must be understood as the social totality receiving omnibus messages, e.g., the social structure

1927
1960
1963
1964
1967
1969
1970
1971
1972
1973
1974
1975
1976
1977
1978
1979
1980
1981
1982
1983
1984
1985
1986
1987
1988
1989
1990
1991
1992
1993
1994
1995
1996
1997
1998
1999
2000
2001
2002
2003
2004
2005
2006

whose knowledge-transfer schemes are characterized by a predominance of information over communication. The mass is the sum of the already enunciated descriptive and explicative characteristics of the receiver immersed in the informational relationship. A more explicit sociological characterization emerges from comparing the social structure and the masses. If, by this term, one means the group receiving the predominant information, how should one describe the set of receivers/senders linked by the media employed? Sociology offers two terms: community and public. Here, preference is given to the latter, for historical reasons and reasons of meaning unnecessary to detail here. Better than anyone, C. Wright Mills has defined a public society as one that can be recognized by the presence of rational free discussion, individualism and an elite that is responsible to the people and does not subjugate them. These are undoubtedly some of the consequences that sociology can draw from an analysis of the communicational relationship. The others, which correspond to the informational relationship, or mass society, are the contraction of free discussion to a privileged group, the presence of standardized schemes of behavior with an elite of "experts" lacking contact with the masses and playing an interventionist role, while evincing no responsibility to the people. Mills himself, who is far from developing a theory of communication, does recognize that it is "easy to distinguish the public from the masses by its dominant means of communication" (the power elite), thus intuiting the existence of implications between the communicational and social levels. All the differentiating features that he then proposes for distinguishing between public and masses can easily be derived from the features of the communicational and informational relationship, of the sender as interlocutor and notified, etc., without the communicationally defined features failing at any moment to correspond to the sociologically-defined ones.

The uniformly alienated group of receivers or organized nonresponsible individuals that constitute mass society presents very peculiar behavioral features in connection with the production and consumption of goods. Here, the for-the-other is dramatically evident. Both material and cultural goods have their source of production in sectors that transcend the masses, from which they later emanate in the form already indicated. When such goods are cultural in nature, the informer is the visible vehicle for them, shaping what has properly been called a mass culture.

Mass culture is the residue of all the omnibus messages carried by senders of information, which form a sediment at the receiving pole, which is composed of a mass society. Where communicational relationships predominate, there is, properly speaking, no mass culture, but only *culture tout court* in its different degrees of development. The most characteristic feature of mass culture is its sterility for the purposes of authentic co-knowledge, since, as we are experiencing, what is involved are channels without return, which dialectically turn back on the sending pole. Its other features may be inferred by analogy from the respective attributes assigned to the elements of the informer-allocution-informed series. It has been stated here that allocution is a "pareresis" or ordered utterance of an alienating, not selective, type: one-for-all. Mass culture will be precisely the sedimentation of forms of knowledge, patterns of behavior, ideologies and motivations deposited in the consciousness of mass humanity by the omnipresent allocution, and whatever does not correspond to the features of that allocution will not leave social residues that can be grouped under the heading of mass culture. If one accepts the distinction proposed by Scheler, between traditional, semi-conscious, insignificant, and static forms of knowing (the collective soul) and rational, changing, superior and dynamic forms of knowing (the collective spirit), the massification of a collection of receivers of omnibus information can only be equivalent to the exaltation and universalization of the static components of knowledge, i.e., to a reiteration, in a vicious circle, of the objectifications of the collective soul (expressive automatisms, myths, popular language and customs, etc.) at the expense of a freezing or "coagulation" of the creative dynamic proper to the collective spirit (cultured language, law, art, philosophy, science, politics, etc.). In this sense of a progressive fossilization that nuances the dynamic layer of the spirit to coarsen the region of the culturally static, mass culture must be understood as a euphemism designed to signal the stagnation traditionally connected with the stages of civilization. This mass culture today configures one of the largest cyclical movements of regressive metamorphosis that equally affect ways of life and forms of knowing. In this metamorphosis of a culture (or of a collective spirit) into a civilization of "mass culture" (collective soul) there is as much regressiveness to more static stages as in the great mythological metamorphoses of the human to the animal or vegetable, or in actual geological mutation by reabsorption of the biosphere in the lithosphere. From the point of view of cultural becoming, the massification of a culture thus represents a moment of directed involutive metamorphosis whose hypothetical and adialectical end would be that absolute cultural entropy into which the agents of massification aspire to precipitate mass humanity, in order to hypostasize his dialogic impotence.

Vehicles for a mass culture are not, in the end, either those of communication or dissemination, but more parsimoniously those of the omnibus type, because of the universal interpretability of their meanings—i.e., the press rather than literary or scientific work; radio and television in their pure "informative" use rather than the concert, theatre or speech (directed at a simple, present mass); film and comics rather than the exhibit, teaching or any other form of knowing that requires an effort of understanding. If allocution massifies by its mediocrity, which is adaptable to any mental age, level of knowledge, etc., and if a mass society is characterized by the use of standardized consumer goods (both material and cultural)—a mass culture, which is the sedimentation of messages pre-tailored for all—there will be a subsequent standardization of the uniform, or a synthesis of the commonplaces of the collectivity.

One thing should be clear. No aspect of this irreversible "quotidienneté" (determined by new communications technologies) would have sufficient specific mass to provoke a sociological or moral problem, if it were a matter of an unavoidable and accidental historical contingency, an innocent tithe paid by contemporary man to the technification of co-existence and, above all, if it were a matter of pure, anonymous spontaneity of the being-with, without identifiable causal agents or institutionalized informers. Cybernetics insists that an aligning of human with machine is theoretically possible by virtue of a common denominator, "negentropy," or resistance of equal sign that both oppose to disorganization, since both are creators and receivers of information, and hence causers of increasing organization (if only regional), which can be translated into terms of progress. It is precisely this cybernetic perspective that underlies a substantial anthropological problem. It can reasonably be predicted (despite other, more fatalistic predictions) that in regard to artifacts and information constituting programmed "food" for machines, man, as a being able to learn, fabricate instruments and create teleological order, can indefinitely continue exercising his primary functions of governing and controlling the artifacts subject to his designs, as numerous and complex as they may be, and even under the hypothesis already advanced, by some, of a possible "machine society" parallel to human society.

Sectoral governing and control by machines will exalt, rather than degrade, the imperative and governing functions of man over nature and the mediating instrument. However, has not this "ophelimatic" energy relationship (or relation of pure utilitarian advantage with the machine and the inanimate), mediatized by rigorous control of information and "orders," extended progressively into the sphere of human interaction, precisely because of the progressive establishment of informational relationships, i.e., by an instrumentalization of man by man, and a strict unilateral control of information/order? Everyday experience shows that modern communications technology has installed humanity in a universe in which

1927
1960
1963
1964
1967
1969
1970
1971
1972
1973
1974
1975
1976
1977
1978
1979
1980
1981
1982
1983
1984
1985
1986
1987
1988
1989
1990
1991
1992
1993
1994
1995
1996
1997
1998
1999
2000
2001
2002
2003
2004
2005
2006

the dominance of information over biunivocal communication is more and more in evidence, where the statistical increase of epitactic messages is hypostasizing the hegemonic powers of the informer, where a subtle "cybernetization" or technification of mass man, thanks to the imposition of patterns, the coagulation of the receiver into afferent dumbness, and the "feeding" of individuals by programs designed to obtain yields, is progressing at a rapid pace. Thus, the predominant use of technically more-advanced means of communication for unilateral, informational use does not seem to produce a simple and inconsequential "quotidienneté" of a new type, since they have in fact created an enormous predominance of information in human relations. This Copernican revolution is not such that it can be regarded with indifference by the sciences of man. As an example, let us say that the episodes of a radio that saves shipwrecked people, that educates, that creates currents of sympathy among men and nations, etc., belong to the romantic oleography of the medium, because radio, statistically and regionally, is today often a unilateral channel of coercion and massification hegemonically exploited by its controllers —an instrument of cultural entropy rather than of organization and process.

If, in any energy relationship, the controller is at the same time the efficient and final cause (producer and collector of the yield), and if the dominance of information tends to "cyberneticize" human co-existence, then here, too, it should be possible to indicate the agents and final causes of an instrumentalization that has become massification. The social sciences cannot gainsay the basic fact that an increase in the coefficient of information in the anthropological sphere, though in one sense (precisely the cybernetic sense) it constitutes an increase of organization "negentropy," simultaneously produces a dissolution or entropy of human co-existence, of mutual tensions, of harmony between co-existers from a communicational and sociocultural perspective. If the humanistic and teleological point of view is not totally bankrupt, such sciences will be compelled to pose questions regarding

the opportunity and dénouement of the instrumental hyperorganization of man, which is, at the same time, an increase of cultural or moral disorganization. The question that demands the attention of the sciences of man, then, is: "Is this revolutionary process really the result of a spontaneous social dynamic that is neither institutionalized nor directed, that is irreversible, natural and not teleologically preordained?"

A certain philosophy and social psychology have considered it so, putting the problem in metaphysical terms, or basing it on concepts that, frankly, have been left behind. In reality, any anthropological concern would be the product of a false analogy with mechanical schemes if certain propositions proved valid—e.g., the philosopheme according to which a phenomenon like massification pertains to the pure existential spontaneity of social facts (without visible responsible parties), and the sociological affirmation that the problems of mass culture are a part of the limited perspective of the man-after-work or of the leisure culture. This second hypothesis, which is frequently encountered in studies (and studies of great rigor, let it be said) may even prove dangerous because of its ingenuousness, for it assumes the dualism of alienation caused by work, alongside a possible dealienation through leisure, as though a social process like massification allowed for such a radical discontinuity and could, for instance, be interrupted voluntarily each time one leaves the office or turns off the television. (This would reduce the problem to dimensions so trivial and casuistic that even an advisor in the pages of popular magazines could solve it on a case by case basis.)

Supporters of the former hypothesis (spontaneous massification) claim not to know that the advantages of the informational and massifying relationship are systematically preordained and exploited by extremely specific sending agents, according to principles that no self-respecting science of man could vouch for a priori. Here, too, many scholars of the State—particularly those interested in the triumph of the inductive, empirical and anti-finalist (that of the social status quo)—have been supporting, albeit in incoherent fits of abstraction, the philosophers who advise against moralistically freighting the search for "he who holds the reins." If their attitude were objectively scientific and disinterested, they would notice that, just as no ignorance or blindness goes unexploited by someone, history holds forth no mass society exempt from exploitive elites. Certainly, the informational relationship mutes, coerces, frustrates, alienates and massifies in favor of the active subject or sending agent. Hence, mass culture, wherever it manifests itself, is an instrumental creation of the elite, of its informers/formers. Thus, one arrives at a dual conclusion: (1) No discontinuity or oscillation is possible in the massification process within a social structure; the problems thus provoked are unsolvable, given their ineluctable nature; and (2) cultural interventionism as a current form of alienation, theoretically implied in a description of the informational phenomenon, acquires, in social reality, the specific name of the pressure groups that control the major channels of information and use them for the massive instrumentalization of the people.

Here, the similarity between ontological-existential analysis and sociological-communicational analysis begins to take on more the appearance of discord. Formulating the question as does Merleau-Ponty (Phénonénologie de la Perception): "How can a human action or thought take the form of 'one,' given that, by principle, it is a first-person operation, inseparable from an I?" Heidegger expressly affirms that the ontological exegesis of the Dasein must not cover aspirations associated with a philosophy of culture. However, in claiming to indicate who rules and dominates in the co-existence, he wants to locate in an impersonal and anodyne "one" a sort of evanescent spontaneous public opinion that springs from the being as ungraspable as the interventionist phenomenon. The "who" is neither this one nor that, not oneself, and neither some others nor the sum of others. The "who" is anyone, "one." And this is enough

for one to close one's eyes in Olympic fashion to historical concreteness and plenitude, inspiring though they may be; to ignore the existence of a "who" really holding the reins, in the name of an ontology that no longer functions in relation to specific reality. Jaspers and Scheler, who take different paths to the concept of a community with a personalist foundation, do not pose the problem when they are closest to it. Witness descriptive premises such as "What is not realized in communication does not exist… In communication I manifest myself to myself in the other person" (Jaspers). Or, "the knowledge of being members of a society is not an empirical but an a priori knowledge, and genetically precedes the degrees of so-called self-awareness" (Scheler). Premises of this sort led to important explanatory consequences by acting as a sort of trait d'union, an analysis of the modes and degrees of such communication, its traumas and contradictions. What is found in the work of these authors, on the other hand, is a vague and hurried social questioning of the masses as "herd," the lower, first step of the ladder of co-existence, of which we are meant to see the supposed genetic moment in a sort of unspecified imitative contagion, an endogenous deformation of the being, without even suspecting the presence of deliberative attitudes that tend, selfishly, to massify the social group.

In ethical, sociological or historical plenitude, the who is always and necessarily a this one or that one, a someone or the sum of "others," even when a literary or existential view sees only something indistinct and undefinable. It is the massifying and monopolizing elite of the information media, it is interventionism, the efficient and final causes of which can and must be uncovered and examined by a sociology of knowledge, and whose experts and functionaries can be named and confronted face to face.

With the path now cleared for a search for "he who holds the reins" (fully justified sociologically and politically), the first, and disconcerting, contradiction appears: for between the two terms that should be

1927
1960
1963
1964
1967
1969
1970
1971
1972
1973
1974
1975
1976
1977
1978
1979
1980
1981
1982
1983
1984
1985
1986
1987
1988
1989
1990
1991
1992
1993
1994
1995
1996
1997
1998
1999
2000
2001
2002
2003
2004
2005
2006

logically implicit in the creation of a mass culture—namely, its senders/creators and cultural elites—there appears, in many cases, to be not the slightest relationship. Among the elites that possess the possibility of creating a mass culture, channels of information (under capitalism) share at least four estates (though with different compositions): the military, the economic, the political and the religious. Missing are authentic representatives of the cultural. However, it is those power groups, not the knowledge elites, that create and manipulate the mass culture.

One constraint, associated with the necessary mediocrity of the allocution, is that the creating agents of mass culture must exhibit the same degree of underdevelopment as their product. Thus, the content of the omnibus message emanates from none of the levels of authentic knowledge, but from the interests of the group. From a cultural point of view, this more than justifies the search for the *cui prodest* (the one benefited) in manipulating the instruments seized for the purpose of communication and the dissemination of knowledge. Of all the sectors theoretically interested in managing a popular culture, only the excluded, i.e., the cultural as such, could ensure the transmission of knowledge that is sufficient unto itself, valuable in itself and fertile—i.e., neither massifying nor alienating, but capable of germination and developing. In engendering a mass culture, the military, economic, political and religious elites can only act *pro domo sua*, giving rise to a "culture" that consists of alienating culture in favor of power, religious, economic and political interests, etc. Only in those exceptional cases where there is either a confrontation between power groups at the vertex, or where they are totally dismembered by some act of the people, are the ironclad unilateral ties between the old elite and the masses momentarily upset, and the informational relationship immediately replaced by the communicational one. Once the structure has been rebuilt, the elite-mass information system again functions with all its notifying force, and new forces of alienation materialize pursuant to the interests of the elite currently in power.

Other important features are needed in order for a definition of mass culture to be beneficial in terms of specific applications. First, as precise as possible an answer should be given to the question: Which of the pressure groups in a given social structure plays the role of the informing elite? Everything would seem to indicate that, in the overwhelming majority of cases, it is the State and the economic sectors that contend for control of the information media—witness the great struggle between the State and free enterprise for control of the mass media. The military and religious sectors are somewhat on the sidelines in this conflict, except when the primary groups intervene on their behalf. Of the two contending sectors, it is unquestionably the State that could still, in theory at least, ensure that the cultural elites are reincorporated in the senders' circle, provided that it has not been totally reshaped by private-sector forces and is still capable of keeping the most transitory political/governmental interests in their place, rather than confusing them with its high governing mission. (A political force in power that allows itself to be corrupted by oligarchical pressures, or that implicitly respects the principle of *l'état c'est moi*, is in a poor position to guarantee the reincorporation of the most select cultural elites.)

As for the economic pressure group, it is, by virtue of its ideological cast and class composition, totally opposed to this reincorporation. It makes use of culture where low-quality products require misleadingly luxurious packaging, or to scientifically coordinate the motivational work of alienating mass humanity. The only possibility for the economic information elite, if it wants to possess culture, is to prostitute it, since an unprostituted culture will always tend to reject the elite—or even try it for rape. Unprostitutable culture, on its side, will be ostracized and subject to a conspiracy of silence, like Kafka's Amalia—the only one who did not want to let herself be raped by the masters of the Castle. Political sociology has pointed to the contamination, at the highest levels of power and action, between the economic and the political/professional sectors. The triumphant businessperson, a living illustration that "it is the rich who know," tends, as an "expert," to displace the political professional from all positions of command. The personnel list of the large private firms replaces party members when political elites are chosen. The management offices of the private sector thus replace the steering committees of political groups. The most influential support for this absorption of the political elite by the economic consists of the prior massive muting accomplished by the informer. A previously "notified" collectivity, silenced and anesthetized by the dominant information emanating from the economic sphere, can hardly regard as illicit the assault or power perpetrated by the masters of its conscience, nor find that they are acting officiously. ["Have you forgotten, Mr. K… that whoever we are, we represent, at least at this moment, for you, free men, and that is not a contemptible superiority." Kafka, *The Trial*.] A collectivity of this nature will find it perfectly normal for figures that are nothing but political anodynes, but have great entrepreneurial pasts, to occupy key posts in public administration— even in the educational area—since massification desensitizes people and makes the normal, sensible use of values difficult. One of the great symptoms of the massification of a culture, then, is that all power over information slides from the arenas of culture and State into the economic sphere, as a prelude to the same process in all branches of the State's activity.

The dominance of pareretic and massifying relational schemes is equally patent, thanks to the rationale employed by its sending agents, in which it is easy to find circular reasoning. Each time that the mass media go beyond their proper area in a way that provokes protest, the sender's justification is that he is giving the public what the public asks for. The pharisaical nature of this response not only reveals a determination to definitively silence mass humanity in its last fits of consciousness, but to transpose to the cultural sphere a typical argument of mercantile thinking. The sender confesses that he acts with a salesman's mentality, showing and sending only what, according to him, the client is requesting. This reasoning

alone is supposed to be sufficient to demonstrate that, in such circumstances, it is an economic elite that dominates and manipulates the information media. A state, as dissolute as it may be, could never put forth this argument. In practice, it is de rigueur for states that exercise controls over the mass media not to give in to absolutist arguments of that type. Countries whose governments provide high-level "third programs" on the radio, or require educational use of television, promote quality film, or limit audiovisual propaganda to a few minutes a day, may not be giving any sector of the collectivity (and surely not the most parasitic) what it would like. What is certain is that such governments act on the basis of higher collective interests, and the means thus used perform, at least partially, a healthier and more honorable role as disseminators of knowledge.

Another important implicit element of the sender's self-justification is that with the sophistic argument of "I'm giving them what they ask for," the informing agent of the economic elite is protesting his innocence. However, in doing so, he is confirming his unshakable faith in the most skeptical and negating notions of human progress. For he does not limit himself to treating the receiver/slave as a child and in an interventionist fashion, but also attempts to escape all judgment, placing the blame on an unavoidable human evil of which he is but a neutral exponent. The informer from the economic sphere takes for granted the great Kafkan human-to-beast metamorphosis— with the human beast devoting itself only to satisfying its basic instincts. When he affirms that he only gives the masses what they ask for, he rejects responsibility for the mediocrity and perversion of taste, as though he were not the very demiurge that ushered these vices into existence. The makers of mass culture base their operation on the execrable empirical criterion of human non-perfectibility or, at best, on the belief that if man is perfectible it is not the informer's function to promote such a process. "Giving them what they ask for" is the eternal argument with which mass-culture businesspeople (film producers, managers of radio

1927
1960
1963
1964
1967
1969
1970
1971
1972
1973
1974
1975
1976
1977
1978
1979
1980
1981
1982
1983
1984
1985
1986
1987
1988
1989
1990
1991
1992
1993
1994
1995
1996
1997
1998
1999
2000
2001
2002
2003
2004
2005
2006

and television stations, advertising agency folks, etc.) have successfully defended their interests, especially in those societies most massified by the economic elite. The circular reasoning implicit in their arguments consists in assuming agreement on an inherent human evil and imperfectability that actually remains to be proven, and for whose forcible hypostasis they are most directly responsible. The silencing of mass humanity, as has been seen here, does not consist simply in short-circuiting his sending faculty, but rather in preparing him to believe that he wants what the informer wants him to want (metamorphosis).

Circe brings up her victims with porcine thinking, having previously transformed them into swine. Thus, the economic elites that manipulate the information, after coercing, frustrating, alienating and massifying the individual, toss him the feed of irrational slaves. And in the solace of the receiver, who believes his tastes satisfied, shines the sad contentment of a metamorphosed being. Notions of knowledge as dialectical and intellectually rigorous progress then disappear, as they must when personality is lost. Everything must be adjusted to the level of the allocutional and notifying mediocritas—the great Procrustean bed that everyone must accept, giving up any aspiration to dealienation. Submerged in that conservatist atmosphere of pure passive reception, where the individual is reduced to his physical dimension—with only unthinking thought afloat in the mind, wafted by the whims of the wind—power's contempt for and desire to destroy its betters finds shelter in the impotent mass, which offers up deafness to knowledge, marginalization of cultural elites, and the all too familiar divorce of people and culture. Thus are the interventionist elites able to reaffirm and practice with impunity the techniques designed to keep the masses atomized and constrained within their insuperable limits. A typical example of the reality of a culture totally informed by the economic elites (which, as we have seen, have the greatest power to massify) is the following: No one in these elites has an organ of dissemination tailored to his own aspirations. Rather, the organs of dissemination are tailored to the desires of the conservative right, i.e., the power elite that manufactures the alienated mediocrity (a distinctly non-accidental case in underdeveloped or semi-colonial countries). Another significant detail is that public organizations and institutions designed to defend collective interests that are not purely material, or that are not protected by government, are either nonexistent or die of starvation shortly after they are spawned. Thus, many countries lack voluntary associations for the protection of cultural interests (e.g., radio listeners' and television watchers' associations). This is a symptom of the total starvation that defines highly massified societies that exist as a notifying elite.

Another case, even more symptomatic of mass culture, is the success of the so-called "vocational trick." (The information experts, for example, do not manifest culture, but rather "vocation.") The unified unit that is mass humanity is led to think that it can freely choose a life project, though this choice is actually coerced by the marketized and massified environment in which the individual is immersed. The vocation is the nominal vestige of a freedom already lost to alienation. However, its exaltation is a subtle expedient with which, once more, mass humanity is led to believe that it wanted what the imperatives of the mass culture obligated it to want. Once motivated to desire, the individual may select what he most likes, but all vocational projects will function as alternatives in the ancient dilemma whose answers always favor the Sphinx. In this case, it is the power elite that, by sponsoring "freedom of vocation," gathers the fruits of an individualistic fragmentation that lacks any awareness of its power as a collective entity. The vocational trick in effect favors the status quo of a massified social structure, paralyzes functional progress and blocks higher social mechanisms. Thanks to it, a society that needs agronomists or veterinarians will continue to produce lawyers; when there is an urgent need for vocational decentralization it will continue to concentrate jobs in urban areas, etc.

It must be admitted that many exponents of unalienated culture for its own sake unconsciously fall into the same circular reasoning as the great rationalizing sophism—namely, those intellectuals who fear a relationship of dialogue and hesitate to raise their voices, so to speak, in their thinking or presentations, or in communicating or disseminating their knowledge in any way. By lowering the level and rigor of their intellectual activity so that all can understand them, these victims of massification end up thinking at a low level and without rigor—also a reflexive result of the fact that they have joined in the production of a massifying knowledge of pure information. In this way, they lend their support to mediocrity and corroborate the thesis of human imperfectability. A vigorous and dense tone is dealienating for some. A banal tone is always massifying for all. It is strangely similar to the omnibus message of the informing allocution, and sets the collective mediocrity without favoring the germination of co-knowledge. From the quantity of such collaborators one may also infer a culture's degree of massification. They contaminate all spheres of communication and all dissemination of knowledge with these vices of the informational relationship. They are the writers and essayists who think only of the mediocre reader, the professor who prepares his presentations with the worst of his students in mind, the architect who prostitutes himself to satisfy the bad taste of his client, the political leader who, in the guise of satisfying all, satisfies no one. They are the addicts of compromise and chicanery, the timid who are fearful of the intellectual aristocracy because they do not belong to it, who are unable to think in finalist categories or assign a clear function to their knowledge, tired coryphaei of a mass culture whose secret prototype will continue to be the propertied informer, "the one who truly knows"—i.e., the rich.

If there is hope of giving life to a purely formal scheme that can later be used to specifically define mass culture in different social structures, one must not limit oneself to explaining the causal factors (the *cui prodest*) or, through the mercantilist sophism ("I give them what they want") to unmask the informational dominance of the economic elites. One must show equal interest in a final, fundamental, but difficult question. Does the web of implications cited above—between types of co-existence and means of communicating knowledge—extend to every last specific difference, until the web becomes a pure causal relationship? In other words, will a given type of dominant mass media engender a particular type of massification? Can this question be explored on the basis of the difference between logical and alogical information?

Mention has been made of the dialectical implications linking the informational relationship with mass culture. The appearance of a specific difference between media that carry "logical" messages composed of verbal or discursive signs, and "alogical" media that carry audiovisual or presentational signs was then demonstrated. Is it feasible—and this is where the previous question points—without altering the basic characteristics of an informational relationship, to subsequently differentiate between processes of massification with "logical" information and processes in which alogical information predominates? A purely deductive answer would only be possible using premises that are equally purely hypothetical, thus creating the risk of drawing questionable conclusions. Strictly speaking, it is impossible to infer the existence of different types of masses that have similar specific differences between verbal and audiovisual allocution, since this difference between the verbal and the audiovisual, though it may be objectively demonstrated in a semiotic context based on the distinction between signs, is not equally demonstrable in its subjective aspects (i.e., level of interpretation and comprehension). To differentiate sociologically among different types of masses on the basis of the subjective characteristics of the massifying information, one would have to demonstrate that: (1) the verbal and audiovisual channels always carry different signifying messages; (2) they give rise, in the receiver/interpretant, to processes of perception and comprehension that are essentially differentiated; and (3) each type of comprehension, provoked by

1927
1960
1963
1964
1967
1969
1970
1971
1972
1973
1974
1975
1976
1977
1978
1979
1980
1981
1982
1983
1984
1985
1986
1987
1988
1989
1990
1991
1992
1993
1994
1995
1996
1997
1998
1999
2000
2001
2002
2003
2004
2005
2006

specifically distinct stimuli, subsequently spawns essentially differentiated cultures and social dynamics. The first proposition has been demonstrated. However, the legitimacy of the conclusion depends entirely on the verifiability of the minor premise, which is given here only as a postulate. What it expresses is almost certainly true, and its definitive experimental verification would confirm that the relationships linking types of society with their knowledge-communicating media extend to the last possible implications. However, logical arguments to prove this must await the scientific confirmation that only psychology can provide. It is not relevant, in the context of this set of definitions, to examine the theorems that support the thesis of the minor premise, for it would take the reader too far from the sociological purposes at hand. Such arguments, in short, aim to demonstrate that verbal signs induce a primary interpretation of a rational nature (since "rational" means extracting the meaning that is enclosed in the sign/word), while iconographic signs—film being the optimal example—induce a primary comprehension of an affective nature in the interpretant. (This is the case since the rational operation of extraction lapses in the face of the image, which presents the sign/signified block on a single plane of patency; on the other hand, the special situation in which the iconographic context is read can also exist without any active participation—participation that may, nonetheless, be evoked. Thus, reactions and responses of all kinds result—producing a discharge of the dual rational/voluntary inhibition through the emotional.)

This situation, contemplated but unproven, does not support the deduction that there is a simple parallel between mass societies and different types of information. If such a parallel could be demonstrated, one could at once conclude that logical massification and emotional or irrational massification are distinct phenomena. Meanwhile, the inductive path seems to have similar obstacles. We do not have sufficient experimental evidence of specific differences between the interpretation, comprehension, response time, setting of content, etc., related to signifying stimuli of a verbal nature and those of an audiovisual nature. Pedagogical experiments conducted in this connection must be taken with the greatest of caution, for their results regarding the communication and dissemination of knowledge, though not in regard to the informational relationship within the informer/masses scheme, are, at most, suggestive. Experiments on larger partial social structures are far less numerous, and almost always tend to focus on aspects that do not center on the specific differences that are of interest here. Proof regarding overall social structure has certainly never been produced. Hence one cannot state, with any rigorous basis in experimental findings, whether there is a difference between the cultural residues subjected to predominantly verbal information, and those of a culture predominantly subjected to audiovisual information.

While mutual dialectical implications between information and massification of culture are clearly demonstrable, a single and more specific implication linking types of mass structures and types of information is less so, whether based on deduction or on observation. Nonetheless, intuition dictates (for the present) that such a difference must exist; that there must be a major difference between massification by the word and massification by sight and sound; that there may not even be any true massification through logical channels, but only through the alogical channel of audiovisual information; that he who reads thinks, and he who thinks remains awake and remains one, while the watcher and listener only sense and passively feel, etc. As has been shown here, the choice of a communicating channel turns back on the syntactic coefficient of the message carried, modulating it after its own fashion. This second difference, objective in nature, is the initial logical basis for the hypothesis of a final specific implication between the medium used and the type of massification produced in the receiver. It makes no difference, in principle, to the ordered utterance whether it flows through verbal or audiovisual information channels. However, it is also clear that the verbum, in its all-signifying power, can encompass all that which can be thought, while the visual covers only the sphere of the sensorially intuitable. Thus, here, too, the differentiation has some logical justification, for if the logical allocution is multifaceted and the alogical monodic, the predominance of the latter should necessarily deposit in the receivers types of knowledge with more limited content circumscribed by the expressive and communicative possibilities of the visual. The proposition espoused here is that the intentionality of consciousness exposed to verbal signs is not structurally the same as it is when exposed to visual signs. If the word "rose," as a word, is a total abstraction whose significatum can be deduced only through rational processes, its image, as image, is the "specter of a rose"—its double or ghost. Hence rational implications here are at least partially replaced by unconscious, fetishistic, and generally emotional functional factors. These three arguments, then, should support the thesis of a sociological differentiation among masses according to the information channel employed in the massification process.

The foregoing leads to a reasonably realistic assumption that audiovisual information is the most irrational and irrationalizing producer of massification in the social context, i.e., the most operative massifying medium of all, since it is not directed at the receiver as a rational and therefore diversified entity, but to the mass receiver and his/her irrational agglutinating agents: the instinctive and affective, the collective unconscious, etc. Hence, audiovisual information should be capable of making the coercion, frustration, alienation and massification that are implicit in all informational relationships more acute and rapid. This difference (one of degree, if not type) should therefore be directly deducible from the preceding points. It is clear that the worldwide dissemination of instruments for the multiplication of informational relationships of an audiovisual nature, involving alogical or presentational means (screens, radios and televisions) has for some years been numerically greater than the dissemination of vehicles for the transmission of logical information (newspapers and omnibus print media,

in general). In culturally underdeveloped countries, this disproportion is especially marked, since the high illiteracy rate and deficiency of communications infrastructure make it difficult for print information to reach all of its potential recipients—problems that radio, film and television scarcely confront, either objectively or subjectively.

If this conclusion is deemed to be realistic (i.e., that audiovisual information media accelerate social massification), and if there is a real predominance of audiovisual media in the culturally underdeveloped countries, then the grave consequence (which must be accepted as a first therapeutic step toward dealienation) is that such societies are the most enslaved and the most massified in the world.

Pasquali, Antonio. "Communication Theory: The Sociological Implications of Information on Mass Culture." Excerpt from: *Comunicación y Cultura de Masas*, Caracas, Venezuela: Monte Avila Editores, 1963. Reprinted with permission of copyright holder.

1927
1960
1963
1964
1967
1969
1970
1971
1972
1973
1974
1975
1976
1977
1978
1979
1980
1981
1982
1983
1984
1985
1986
1987
1988
1989
1990
1991
1992
1993
1994
1995
1996
1997
1998
1999
2000
2001
2002
2003
2004
2005
2006

WHAT MASS COMMUNICATION CAN DO, AND WHAT IT CAN 'HELP' TO DO, IN NATIONAL DEVELOPMENT

Excerpt from: Mass Media and National Development

By Wilbur Schramm

1964

How Social Change Occurs

Increasing the number of radios, newspapers and cinemas will not necessarily bring about a corresponding increase in the rate of social change. Merely multiplying messages and channels is not enough. For instance, several countries have found that adding a farm radio program has not by itself appeared to accomplish much in the adoption of new practices.[1] Yet, a question-and-answer program on farm practices in Jordan has proved to be very useful, and the combination of radio broadcasts with group discussion in rural forums has been very helpful in bringing about change.[2] Radio has not generally proved useful in literacy training, but in schools it has been highly useful.[3] It is obvious from examples like these that there are some tasks the mass media can and some they can't do and some they can do better than others, and that "how" they are used has much to do with their effectiveness. Therefore, we shall need to look at some of the evidence on how the mass media may be used effectively in the service of national development.

In the service of national development, the mass media are agents of social change. The specific kind of social change they are expected to help accomplish is the transition to new customs and practices and, in some cases, to different social relationships. Behind such changes in behavior must necessarily lie substantial changes in attitudes, beliefs, skills and social norms.

How do changes like these occur? They may come about slowly, in the ordinary course of history, by continuing contact with another culture that leads to the borrowing of customs and beliefs. They may come about more quickly (although perhaps less permanently) by force—for example, when a conqueror or ruler "imposes" new patterns of behavior. The kind of change most developing countries are seeking today is neither of these. It is intended to be faster than the measured rhythm of historical change, less violent than the process of enforced change. It aims at voluntary development in which many people will participate, and the better informed will assist the less. In place of force, it prefers persuasion and the provision of opportunity; in place of the usual rhythm of acculturation, a heightened flow of information.

Basically the mechanism of such a change is simple. First, the populace must become aware of a need which is not satisfied by present customs and behavior. Second, they must invent or borrow behavior that comes closer to meeting the need. A nation that will try to make its people more widely and quickly aware of needs, and of the opportunities for meeting them, will facilitate the decision process, and will help the people put the new practices smoothly and swiftly into effect.

Superficially, therefore, the process is simple. Actually, it is far from that.

Cultural Linkage

One reason why it is not simple is that any custom or practice that is to be replaced or introduced will be closely linked with other customs and beliefs. Social organization is an interrelated whole; a change in any

---

1   For example, see Dube, *India's Changing Villages*, 114-15.
2   See Schramm and Winfield; also Mathur and Neurath.
3   See, for example, Xoomsai and Ratamangkala.

part of it will be felt in other parts, and a change in any aspects of man's behavior will be reflected in other aspects of his behavior. Therefore, when we think of social change, we must think of it in terms of the change it will bring about in the "whole society" and the "whole man."...The practical import of cultural linkage is, therefore, that any item of social change must be considered on a very broad basis, in order to anticipate the secondary effects and the resistances, take advantage of relationships where possible, and smooth the transition. To be able to do that, it is necessary to know the culture well, and to understand the whole pattern of life of which the proposed change is a part. What would such a change "mean" to the people who are being asked to change? That is the pertinent question.

Group Relationships

Another reason why social change is complicated is that group relationships must always be taken into account. It is individuals who must change, but these individuals live in groups, work and play in groups, enjoy many of their most cherished experiences in groups. Many of the beliefs and values they hold most strongly are group norms—commonly held, and mutually defended. It is very difficult for an individual to turn against a strong group norm, for in that case either the whole group must change or he must find a new group.

Practically, this means that social change is much easier if it is not contrary to group norms. But many of the group norms in almost all traditional societies are inimical to modernization. Among such norms are the religious beliefs about fatalism and man's inability to do anything about nature; the taboos against killing living things no matter how dangerous to health and crops; the belief that hard work is demeaning; and the custom of going deeply into debt for weddings and dowries. It is impossible, in the process of modernizing, to avoid some confrontations with group norms. The question is how to confront them. ...

Bringing about "understanding participation" in the decision-making on social change, then, is one way in which an effective program can take account of group relationships. A second is making use of the channels of communication and influence that exist in a community where change is desired. It is axiomatic that a change agent begins to work with leadership. Dube tells how agricultural workers in an Indian village made the mistake of working with the elected political officials, who responded enthusiastically but had no particular influence over agricultural practices. The agricultural leaders, as the visitors later found out, were entirely different people from the political officials.[4] In the village, there are many levels and specialized functions of leadership, and to work efficiently in that culture these must be understood and utilized.

Furthermore, it is obvious that many kinds of social change are threatening to old social relationships and positions of authority. The extended family, for instance, is threatened when the young men go into industry or move to the city. Young, educated men tend to be impatient with the traditional leaders. Technical skills and a money economy offer the people occupational alternatives and, consequently, a degree of self-determination they have not had before. As a result, new concentrations of power, new leaders and new work groups challenge old leaders and old patterns of relationship. There is always a certain degree of social ferment connected with economic and social development.

Practically, this means that just as one must understand the cultural linkages, so also must one understand the social relationships, if the objective is to speed and smooth social change in the culture.

Modernizing Skills

Another thing that complicates social change is that changes in many instances require people to learn new skills. When development that would ordinarily take centuries is compressed into a few decades, and particularly when a society is moving into technology, as the developing countries are today, it is often

---

4 Dube, "Some Problems of Communication in Rural Community Development."

1927
1960
1963
1964
1967
1969
1970
1971
1972
1973
1974
1975
1976
1977
1978
1979
1980
1981
1982
1983
1984
1985
1986
1987
1988
1989
1990
1991
1992
1993
1994
1995
1996
1997
1998
1999
2000
2001
2002
2003
2004
2005
2006

difficult to teach skills soon enough. If a small factory were built in a village of Africa or Asia tomorrow, the skilled workers would not be on hand to operate it. When radios are distributed in villages, there are no technicians locally available to repair them; and if a tube or condenser goes bad, they may rest in peace and silence forever.

Therefore, any social change in the direction of modernization requires a program in teaching the necessary skills. Some of these are general skills; for example, no society will modernize very far until a substantial proportion of the population can read and count. Others are quite specific—for example, repairing radios and farm machinery, operating machine tools, bookkeeping, surveying, medicine and pharmacy. Almost invariably, skills like these are in short supply when development begins, and one of the great tasks of smoothing social change is to make technical skills and technical development march at the same pace, so that technology does not wait for workers, nor skilled workers for machines and jobs.

Implications for the Mass Media

For one thing, it is clear that they risk being ineffective—indeed, being counterproductive—if they are used without adequate knowledge of the local culture where they are going to be received. This is true of any communication, mass or interpersonal, but it is particularly true of the mass media because they cover larger areas, operate from a distance and get less feedback from their audiences. A village-level worker, talking to a cultivator about contour ploughing, can tell at once whether he is being understood; the same village-level worker, speaking over the radio to several hundred villages, many of which he has never seen, may never know whether his listeners have understood, and certainly he will not learn in time to make a change in the talk he is broadcasting. Therefore, an efficient use of the mass media for economic and social development implies that they should be as "local" as possible. Their programs should originate

no farther than necessary from their audiences, the programs should be prepared by persons who understand the cultures to which they are speaking, and means should be available for the audiences to report back to the media. …

The communication tasks behind the social changes of national development are of three kinds. In the first place, the populace must have "information" about national development: Their attention must be focused on the need of change; the opportunities inviting change; the methods and means of change; and, if possible, their aspirations for themselves and their country must be raised. In the second place, there must be opportunity to participate intelligently in the "decision process": The dialogue must be broadened to include all those who must decide to change; the leaders must have an opportunity to lead and the common people to be heard; the issues of change must be made clear and the alternatives discussed; and information must flow both up and down the hierarchy. And third, the needed "skills must be taught": Adults must be taught to read; children must be educated; farmers must learn the methods of modern farming, etc. …

If these three groups of communication tasks correspond to the three basic functions of communication —the watchman, decision-maker and teacher functions—it is no accident. These are the fundamental tasks of communication within society, whether it is traditional society or modernizing society. The only difference is that when a society is in the ferment of rapid social and economic change, all the needs are intensified.

Which of these tasks can the mass media do by themselves, and which can they only help to do? On the basis of what we now know about the media in developing countries, we can say this.

The first group of tasks—the watchman, the informing functions—are well within the capability of the media to handle directly. In fact, without the media it would be impossible to handle them on any such timetable as the developing countries propose.

The second group—the decision-making functions—are, for the most part, jobs the mass media can only help to do. These require, in many cases, group decision; they require the changing of strongly held attitudes, beliefs and social norms; and, therefore, the mechanisms of interpersonal communication are the key ones. It goes without saying that the mass media can be of great help by feeding information into the discussion, by carrying the word of the leaders and by making the issues clear. But theirs is still a supportive role.

The third group of tasks—the teaching function—can be handled directly in part, and partly in combination with interpersonal communicators. For example, the media are perhaps best used in education when they can be employed in a classroom as part of a total educational experience under the guidance of a classroom teacher; but where teachers or schools are not available, or insufficiently trained, the media can fill in. Likewise, it is very hard for radio (to take the most common example) to do the job a skilled demonstration agent would do in teaching a new agricultural skill, but once the skill is learned, radio can be of great help by supplying additional information, answering questions, reporting results and the like. …

What the Mass Media Can Do

The media as watchmen. People who live in societies where the mass media are common sometimes forget how much they learn from the media. … Wherever newspapers have been available, they have become the chief reporters on the environment beyond the reach of one's own senses; indeed, whole generations of people have formed their ideas of the non-local world largely on what they have learned from newspapers (and more recently from radio, films, television and news magazines). Everyone who has experienced motion pictures and printed fiction has noticed the extraordinarily long-lasting

memory traces of those media. Scenes, characters, plots, phrases still remain vivid, sharp and clear, a part of one's usable resources, many years after they are first read or seen. Parents note, not always approvingly, how children learn "singing commercials," slogans, vocabulary and customs from television, without trying to, without even realizing they are learning. In other words, all our experience with the mass media illustrates how easy it is, voluntarily or involuntarily, to learn from them.[5]

Because the media have this ability to report and inform so effectively, we can say with great confidence that they can perform certain essential services for a developing country.

The mass media can widen horizons. Many people in a traditional society correctly perceive a quality of magic in the media when they first encounter them. They are magic, a wise African said to this writer, because they can "take a man up to a hill higher than any we can see on the horizon and let him look beyond." They are magic because they can "let a man see and hear where he has never been and know people he has never met." And even after the aura of magic has dissipated, still they can help people in a developing country to understand how other people live and, consequently, to look at their own lives with new insight. They are a liberating force because they can break the bonds of distance and isolation and transport people from a traditional society to "The Great Society," where all eyes are on the future and the faraway—as Pool puts it, "where every business firm must anticipate the wants of unknown clients, every politician those of unknown voters; where planning takes place for a vastly changed future; where the actions of people in quite different cultures may affect one daily."[6]

5 For evidence, see Waples, Berelson and Bradshaw. See also Hovland, "Mass Communication," and Schramm, *An Annotated Bibliography of the Research on Programmed Instruction.* On how much is remembered from radio newcasts, see Harrell, Brown and Schramm. On learning from entertainment films, see P. W. Holaday and G. D. Stoddard, *Getting Ideas From the Movies,* New York: Macmillan, 1933. On remembering arguments from mass media, see Douglas Waples and Bernard Berelson, "Public Communication and Public Opinion," reported in R. D. Leigh, "The Conceptual Framework of Public Communication," mimeo, New York, 1954.
6   Pool, 249; "The Great Society," of course, is Graham Wallas' phrase.

1927
1960
1963
1964
1967
1969
1970
1971
1972
1973
1974
1975
1976
1977
1978
1979
1980
1981
1982
1983
1984
1985
1986
1987
1988
1989
1990
1991
1992
1993
1994
1995
1996
1997
1998
1999
2000
2001
2002
2003
2004
2005
2006

One reason why this is important for any developing country is that it helps to develop the quality of empathy. Daniel Lerner, who has written better than anyone else about this matter, considers empathy the basic and fundamental quality which the people of a developing nation must have. This, he says, is because it:

> … enables newly mobile persons to operate efficiently in a changing world. Empathy, to simplify the matter, is the capacity to see oneself in the other fellow's situation. This is an indispensable skill for people moving out of traditional settings. Ability to empathize may make all the difference, for example, when the newly mobile persons are villagers who grew up knowing all the extant individuals, roles and relationships in their environment. Outside his village or tribe, each must meet new individuals, recognize new roles and learn new relationships involving himself. [High empathic capacity] is the predominant personal style only in modern society which is distinctively industrial, urban, literate and participant. Traditional society is nonparticipant— it deploys people by kinship into communities isolated from each other and from a centre; without an urban-rural division of labour, it develops few needs requiring economic interdependence; lacking the bonds of interdependence, people's horizons are limited by locale and their decisions involve other known people in known situations. Hence there is no need for … a national 'ideology' which enables persons unknown to each other to achieve 'consensus' by comparing their opinions.

But modern society is participant in that it functions by "consensus"—individuals making personal decisions on public issues must concur often enough with other individuals they do not know to make possible a stable common governance. Among the marks of this historic achievement in social organization, which we call Participant Society, are that most people go through school, read newspapers, receive cash payments in jobs they are legally free to change, buy goods for cash in an open market, vote in elections which actually decide among competing candidates

and express opinions on many matters which are not their personal business. Especially important, for the Participant Style, is the enormous proportion of people who are expected to "have opinions" on public matters—and the corollary expectation of these people that their opinions will matter.[7]

Thus the media, by bringing what is distant near and making what is strange understandable, can help to bridge the transition between traditional and modern society.

The mass media can focus attention. In modern society, much of our picture of distant environment comes from the mass media. As traditional society moves towards modernity, it too begins to depend on the mass media. Consequently, a large share of the ideas as to who is important, who is dangerous, what is interesting and so forth necessarily derives from the media. The newspaper, radio, magazine—serving as watchmen on the hill—must decide what to report back. This act of choice—choosing whom to write about, whom to focus the camera on, whom to quote, what events to record—determines in large degree what people know and talk about.

Thus, for example, in countries where the media are common, a political candidate has little chance unless the people have become well acquainted with him through the media. Where political campaigns have been studied intensively, the general conclusion is that the media do not directly change the voting decision of any large proportion of the electorate, but do have a lot to do with what issues or individuals are talked about during the campaign.[8] By focusing attention on certain topics rather than others, they are able to make these topics play a larger part in the campaign. Many advertising campaigns also are intended to focus attention on one brand or product. This is particularly true in cases where there is little difference except brand name between competing products. In such cases, advertising

---

7   Lerner, 49-51
8   See Pool, 250. In more detail, see Lazarsfeld, Berelson and Gaudet; also Berelson, Lazarsfeld and McPhee.

has proved the power of the media to keep public attention on one brand name rather than others.[9]

This is a significant matter for the developing countries because it means that public attention can be kept on development. From time to time, interest can be directed to a new custom, a new behavior, a new health or agricultural practice, a reward to be gained by modernizing or something that needs to be changed. By directing attention to given topics or issues of this kind, the media can also control some of the topics of interpersonal communication. The leaders of a developing country would personally go, if they could, to every small group in the country and put in their minds a development problem or an idea or opportunity to think about or discuss. They cannot go personally to many villages or many groups. But they can plant ideas and topics widely through the mass media.

The mass media can raise aspirations. The history of advertising, the success of mail-order catalogues and the many cases in which families have worked hard to reach a standard of life they have seen others enjoy, or to acquire an article they have only read or heard about or seen pictures of, encourages us to believe that the mass media may be able to raise their audiences' aspirations in developing cultures, as well as in highly developed ones.

If true, this is a matter of great importance to the developing countries. They face the need to rouse their people from fatalism and a fear of change. They need to encourage both personal and national aspirations. Individuals must come to desire a better life than they have and to be willing to work for it. As citizens they must aspire to national strength and greatness. …

"Thus, the mass media can create a climate for development." We can sum up by saying that the mass media can contribute substantially to the amount and kinds of information available to the people of a developing country. They can widen horizons and thus help to build empathy; they can focus attention on problems and goals of development; they can raise personal and national aspirations; and all this they can do largely themselves and directly. This amounts to creating an informational "climate" in which development is stimulated. By showing modern equipment and life in economically well-developed societies, by disseminating news of development from far away, by carrying political, economic, social and cultural reports from elsewhere in the country and the world, the media can create an intellectual climate which stimulates people to take another look at their own current practices and future perspectives.[10]

The media in the decision process. The mass media can help only indirectly to change strongly held attitudes or valued practices. Mass communication has never proved very effective in attacking attitudes, values or social customs that are deep-set or strongly held. One reason why they are strongly held is that for a very long time they have been found rewarding. Furthermore, they are usually socially anchored in approval by family or other groups which are important to the individual; to go against such attitudes means that the individual must go against groups in which he values membership. The individual usually feels personally involved in such attitudes and customs; to change them would cause personal anguish and alienation from the life and companions he has become used to. Therefore, such positions are strongly defended.

How firmly they are defended we can judge from the studies showing that the human psyche will go to almost any length to repel an attack on strong beliefs and attitudes. People select news or broadcasts or articles that support their strong beliefs and reject or forget what does not.[11] If they do come into contact with mass media information unfavorable to their strong beliefs, they often misread or distort it. This is wholly irrational; they are not "deliberately" distorting: Their belief structure is merely acting to preserve

---

9 See Lucas and Britt.

10 Some of these phrases are borrowed, with permission, from a personal communication from Dr. Henry Cassirer.
11 See Festinger; also Lazarsfeld, Berelson and Gaudet; and Berelson, Lazarsfeld and McPhee.

1927
1960
1963
1964
1967
1969
1970
1971
1972
1973
1974
1975
1976
1977
1978
1979
1980
1981
1982
1983
1984
1985
1986
1987
1988
1989
1990
1991
1992
1993
1994
1995
1996
1997
1998
1999
2000
2001
2002
2003
2004
2005
2006

itself. In the research literature, there are case studies of whole campaigns that have failed because their meaning has been completely misread by the persons whose attitudes they were supposed to change. For example, there was a famous campaign in which cartoons of a "Mr. Biggott" were used to pour ridicule on racial prejudice.[12] But prejudiced people interpreted these cartoons as "supporting" the idea of racial prejudice. As a result, such people became more prejudiced than ever.

Direct social control over attitudes is exerted mostly by group relationships—by persons one admires or respects, or by groups one belongs to or aspires to belong to. In a group, an individual learns to play a certain role and to follow certain norms. Role and norm understandings help to make life comfortable and pleasant in the group. A member does not have constantly to review what is proper for him to do, and he can understand and predict what other group members will be doing.

In major decisions … the channels of interpersonal communication and influence are far more effective than the mass media. The media can be helpful, but only indirectly. Some of the indirect ways in which the media can enter into the decision process are suggested in the following pages.

The mass media can feed the interpersonal channels. The influential persons whose advice and viewpoints bulk large in the interpersonal decision process of society are typically heavy users of the mass media.[13] For example, the man who is influential with the farmers in a given area usually reads more or hears more broadcasts about farming than does the average farmer. The man whose advice about politics is respected usually makes an abnormally high use of the political media. This is important to developing countries because it means that it is possible through the mass media to feed the channels of interpersonal influence. When agricultural information is carried in the mass media, there is a very high chance that this same information will be picked up and repeated by the agricultural "influentials." When information on child care is carried, there is a good chance that the women whose advice on child care is important will pick the information up and repeat it. And so on.

We must add: "Other things being equal." If the influential spokesmen have no access to the media—if, for instance, they are illiterate, and they have no radios—they are not likely to pick up information from the mass media. If they hold attitudes violently opposed to those expressed or implied by mass communication, they are very likely to reject or distort the mass media message. But if they are not basically opposed, if they have ready access to the media, then there is no good reason why the media should not supply information to interpersonal channels.

In some cases, mass communication is the most effective way to conduct point-to-point communication. For example, there is the problem of reaching, informing and updating community or extension workers. Some developing countries have many thousands of such workers in agriculture, health or community development. These are typically scattered far and wide. Often there has not been time to train them adequately, and they are still in need of information and assistance. In this case, it has been found useful to use the radio—and sometimes film and print—to upgrade and update the extension workers. Sometimes it is possible to reach both the worker and the public at the same time—that is to broadcast, show a film or produce some printed material which the extension agent can read, so to speak, over the shoulders of the villager, and which he can then help the villager to understand and apply. The same tactics have been used in assisting and upgrading teachers.

It should be noted that in certain situations the mass media can take over some of the usually interpersonal channels of leadership. The radio addresses of Winston Churchill, during the war of 1939-45, were examples of personal leadership exerted most effectively through

---

12 See Cooper and Jahoda; also Kendall and Wolf.
13 The most complete treatment of "influentials" is to be found in Katz and Lazarsfeld. There is a somewhat later review of the literature by Katz in "The Two-Step Flow of Communication."

the mass media. The leaders of many developing countries have also learned to use the radio effectively.

The mass media can confer status. It helps an individual's reputation, of course, to be endorsed or praised by a well-regarded newspaper or radio. In fact, merely to be "noticed" by the media contributes to the status of an individual.[14] This somewhat puzzling ability of the media to confer status has been described by Lazarsfeld and Merton in these words:

> The mass media bestow prestige and enhance the authority of individuals and groups by legitimatizing their status. Recognition by the press or radio or magazines or newsreels testifies that one has arrived, that one is important enough to have been singled out from the large anonymous masses, that one's behaviour and opinions are significant enough to require public notice.[15]

In a developing country where the media are relatively scarce and the stream of names in the news is smaller, this power of the media may be even greater than it is in economically developed countries and may provide a way to build leadership.

14 Many a political figure has said that he would willingly give up the editorial endorsement of a newspaper if he could frequently make news that appeared on the news pages. One political figure who expressed himself in that way was Franklin D. Roosevelt, who was elected to four terms in the United States presidency despite editorial opposition by a great majority of newspapers.

15 Lazarsfeld and Merton, in Schramm, *Mass Communications,* 498. They add to what we have already quoted: "The operation of this status conferral function may be witnessed most vividly in the advertising pattern of testimonials to a product by 'prominent people.' Within wide circles of the population (though not within certain selected social strata), such testimonials not only enhance the prestige of the product but also reflect prestige on the person who provides the testimonials. They give public notice that the large and powerful world of commerce regards him as possessing sufficiently high status for his opinion to count with many people. In a word, his testimonial is a testimonial to his own status. The ideal, if homely, embodiment of this circular prestige pattern is to be found in the Lord Calvert series of advertisements centred on 'Men of Distinction.' The commercial firm and the commercialized witness to the merit of the product engage in an unending series of reciprocal pats on the back. In effect, a distinguished man congratulates a distinguished whisky which, through the manufacturer, congratulates the man of distinction on his being so distinguished as to be sought out for a testimonial to the distinction of the product. The workings of this mutual admiration society may be as nonlogical as they are effective. The audiences of mass media apparently subscribe to the circular belief: 'If you really matter, you will be at the focus of mass attention and, if you are at the focus of mass attention, then surely you must really matter.' "

Most national political leaders in developing countries have long since discovered the status-conferral power of the mass media, but the local leader often needs additional status. We mean not only the elected leaders but also the community development workers, the agricultural advisers and other people who are in an advisory or instructive capacity with the villagers. Their voices on radio, their pictures or their words in print, are real contributions to their local standing and their visibility in the community. Similarly, it is helpful to give status and visibility to certain persons or acts that deserve emulation. The Soviet and East European mass media have perhaps done the best job of this—in publicizing heroes of labour, productivity records, successful collectives and other exemplary models for developmental activity. Undoubtedly, the whole movement of national development can be given status through attention by the mass media. This will attract people to participate in development who by their participation will give it further status and so on, through the spiral we described earlier.

The mass media can broaden the policy dialogue. In the village, the people concerned with local policy matters are close enough to talk about them face to face if they want to and if custom permits. So far as the traditional village is concerned, this is usually sufficient, because the village is usually not much interested in policy at higher levels, and the higher levels are not much interested in sharing policy with the village. But when a country begins to develop, it has an urgent need to widen the theatre of political discussion and policymaking. The ordinary people need to overhear the national policy debates so that they can form opinions and, at the proper time, act on their opinions. The policymakers need to understand, more clearly than before, the needs and wishes of the villages, so that they can take account of them in making their larger policies. To accomplish these things in a nation of any size, without the mass media, would be almost out of the question.[16]

16 For an illustration of mass media dialogue in one country, see Kraus.

1927
1960
1963
1964
1967
1969
1970
1971
1972
1973
1974
1975
1976
1977
1978
1979
1980
1981
1982
1983
1984
1985
1986
1987
1988
1989
1990
1991
1992
1993
1994
1995
1996
1997
1998
1999
2000
2001
2002
2003
2004
2005
2006

As a country develops, the mass media begin to cover news, local problems, local spokesmen. The more the local press and radio develop, the better the coverage. These items are seen or heard by audiences in other parts of the country and by the national policymakers. At the same time, the media cover the national news, the national problems and the statements and arguments of leaders as to what policies should be adopted. Thus the theatre of policy discussion is widened until it begins to be as large as the nation. As this happens, during development, the conditions of national participation are set up, national empathy is encouraged and all the requirements for developing "as a nation" are brought within reach.

The mass media can enforce social norms. … In modern society the job of carrying the public announcements has been given, in large part, to the mass media. Their job is to make serious deviations known. If the norms are not universally known, as they are unlikely to be in a developing society, then part of the job of the media is to publicize the norms.

Thus it is possible through the media to establish in the public mind norms for development behaviour and to police deviations from those norms. In a sense, this is the other side of the status-conferral coin. Just as some developing countries have conferred status on their best farmers and labourers, so also they have not hesitated to denounce laziness, inefficiency and corruption. Once out in the open, these deviations can be socially punished, and individuals warned away from them.

The mass media can help form tastes. Within limits, people learn to like what they hear and see. This is true notably in the area of music and art. In some highly developed countries, the success of popular songs and dances depends largely on their being introduced and made familiar by the mass media. Throughout history, there have been repeated instances when new music or new paintings have been rejected because they were unfamiliar, although later they have become great "classics." The particular power of the mass media is to speed up this familiarization process, and thus to have an effect on the forming of taste.

To a developing country this has significance quite apart from the matter of "plugging" popular songs or introducing new kinds of painting. Culture is one of the best bridges between peoples. If People A like the music or the dances or the graphic art of People B, they are predisposed to like People B. If Peoples A and B like each other's art, they are predisposed to feel a bond between them and to understand each other better. Developing countries can use this powerful mechanism to build the sense of "nation-ness" many of them need so badly. If a "national" art or music or dance exists, it can be emphasized as a rallying point for all the nation's people. With or without a national art, the folk art of different parts of the country can be used to bring those subgroups psychologically closer together. Something like this is what the Soviet Union has done by publicizing the folk dances and music of the many peoples within its borders.

The mass media can affect attitudes lightly held, and slightly canalize stronger attitudes. As we have indicated, mass communication is not very effective by itself in changing attitudes that are strongly held and deeply anchored. But it is quite possible through mass communication to have some effect on positions that are not strongly defended, or on new questions concerning which there has been neither time nor information to build up strong attitudes. …

It is clear that the mass media can be of great use in the decision making that must accompany economic and social development. But their usefulness does not lie in frontal attacks on strongly held attitudes or long-valued customs. These strongly held positions are in the domain of personal influence and group norms. If changes are made in stoutly defended customs and beliefs, interpersonal communication is usually required, and group change is usually involved. In such major decisions, therefore, the mass media can help only "indirectly." They can feed information into the channels of interpersonal influence. They can confer status and enforce norms. They can broaden the policy dialogue. They can help form tastes. Where there are no strong attitudes, or where the only change desired is a slight canalization of an existing attitude, they can be directly effective. But for the most part, in the area of entrenched belief and behaviour, they can only help.

The mass media as teachers. In a cogent article prepared for the *World Radio Handbook*, Cassirer specifies some of the tasks which information can perform for the people of developing countries. For one thing, he says, it enables the individual to see himself in the context of national unity and worldwide inter-relation. It creates the climate in which adoption of new technological practices and new attitudes becomes possible. It enables the citizen to play his part in the nation. But this "awareness through information" is bound to be inadequate "as long as the individual is insufficiently educated to master new skills and new knowledge."[17]

This is the skills barrier which we have mentioned before. In the process of economic and social development, it is not sufficient merely to know the need for change or even to decide for change. Before substantial amounts of change can occur, new skills must be spread throughout the population. This requires a nationwide programme of education and training. Therefore, it is of the greatest importance to developing countries that we can say confidently:

The mass media can help substantially in all types of education and training. They have proved themselves under many different conditions in and out of schools. They have proved their ability to supplement and enrich school work. Where teachers and schools are scarce, they have proved able to carry a very large part of the instructional task themselves. They have proved to be of great help in adult education and literacy training. And they have been *very* helpful in training for industry and technical services, and for the in-service training of teachers.

These facts are important because, as we know, teachers and schools *are* scarce, and many of the available teachers are trained for yesterday's rather than today's teaching job. Technical skills *are* in short supply. There *are* 70 million illiterate adults in the world. Throughout the developing regions there *are* great needs for learning new agricultural skills and practices. …

We have said that the media can "help" in education and training, and have thus distinguished what they can do in these fields from what they can do in imparting information. In other words, we have said that the media can do the watchman's and reporter's job unaided, but that they can only "help" the teacher. This is because education and training are more than the transmission of information. They require a purposeful growth, a learning of skills, a systematic building of knowledge, a preparation for action. This is accomplished best when there is an interpersonal link in the process—a teacher to work with the pupil, a discussion group to help decide what new techniques and customs a community shall absorb into its life, or at least a monitor to coordinate some of the studying and provide or get help for the student when he needs it. In a secondary school science class, a teacher *and* a television lesson or film will probably be more effective than either alone. In literacy training, a monitor or teacher has proved necessary at the student-end of a broadcast. In industrial training, films can greatly speed up learning, but ordinarily cannot do the whole job. In community adult education, discussion groups and local field staffs have contributed greatly to the effectiveness of radio. "Two-way" communication is needed somewhere in the process—someone to guide, react, answer questions, discuss. The "combination" of mass media and interpersonal instruction—expert instruction from the media and two-way interaction with a teacher—are thus extraordinarily powerful.

W. Schramm. *Mass Media and National Development.* Stanford, Calif.: Stanford University Press, 1964. Copyright © 1964, UNESCO. Reprinted with permission of the publisher.

17 Henry B. Cassirer, "Radio and Television in the Service of Information and Education in Developing Countries," for *World Radio Handbook,* 1963.

1927
1960
1963
1964
1967
1969
1970
1971
1972
1973
1974
1975
1976
1977
1978
1979
1980
1981
1982
1983
1984
1985
1986
1987
1988
1989
1990
1991
1992
1993
1994
1995
1996
1997
1998
1999
2000
2001
2002
2003
2004
2005
2006

EXCERPT FROM:

COMMUNICATION: FORGOTTEN TOOL OF NATIONAL DEVELOPMENT

By Luis Ramiro Beltrán

1967 In fact, it is possible to infer the level of a country's *general* development from its level of *communication* development. There can hardly be a well-developed country with poor communications. The correlation explains itself easily. Development implies interaction, massive mobilization, universal participation in decision making on matters of public interest and in the process of implementing national goals. And interaction, mobilization and participation cannot occur without communication.

Blocked Communication

Almost all underdeveloped countries show a pattern of blocked communication. Most obviously, lack of records and transportation limit communication. But the absence of opportunity for people to "talk" to each other, to get to know one another within the country, is perhaps more dramatic. Social relations are restricted to a few contacts within the immediate circle of acquaintances. People in one province do not know what is going on in the capital city or in the other provinces. Each small community regards the other as foreign. Indifference, suspicion and isolation prevail over mutual understanding and cooperation. Governments do not have adequate channels to transmit development messages to the population; field agents can reach only minimal numbers of people in a few regions. People have no way to express their wishes to the government and little opportunity to check the behavior of the official agencies. Indeed, in most cases, the majority do not even vote to form government. Save minor exceptions, mass media—where they exist at all—are actually elite media since they only reach the minority of urban dwellers.

Among the explanations for this are illiteracy, low buying power of the people, lack of roads and electrification, insufficient qualified communication personnel, and the high cost of installation and operation of communication equipment.

Given such characteristics, a true nation—an integrated social system comprising interacting members who freely share needs, goals, means, efforts and benefits—can hardly be thought to exist. And when some such articulation comes close to existing, when the country somehow approaches a form of national unity for development, that existence is tragically weak and precarious.

This reality is so self-evident that there should be little need for promoting the importance of communication in national development. Unfortunately, perhaps because communication—the "cobweb of society"—is so obvious that it can be taken for granted, few developing countries have cared to properly organize it in the service of development. It would seem they think communication is there, somehow automatically; nothing needs to be done to bring it about. *Talking is equated with persuading, and hearing with understanding and accepting.*

Such a serious misconception of communication—the fundamental social process and the art and science of engineering change in human behavior—has led most governments of the developing countries to neglect almost completely neglect communication in planning and implementing development. They may perceive communication development as a product of economic development but they fail to see it as an antecedent. Plans do attribute importance to the need for educating the masses. Policy makers do speak about the necessity for diffusion of technology and are increasingly coming to accept the notion that popular adult education as an investment for development. But, when it comes to action, virtually no one seems concerned with allocating funds specifically for communication development.

Development Hinges on Communication

Therefore, the global strategy for national development excludes the particular strategy for communication development that should be its main operational support and instrument. For it is only through people communicating (efficiently and effectively) that any development can occur. It is man who must change in order for things to be changed by him. And changing man—manipulating his social environment so as to modify, in multiple directions and ways, feelings, thoughts and behaviors of millions of distinct human beings to a point that they become autonomously innovative—is a far more difficult endeavor than changing the course of rivers, the composition of soils and the performance of plants and animals.

It follows that, as long as the development of organized communication is kept out of overall planning for change, the very success of national development is at stake.

Suggestions for Action

What can the developing countries do to correct this? There are, of course, no universal formulas. Yet, a few basic suggestions for action may prove useful.

- Incorporate communication development into the master national development plan so that it serves all other development activities.
- Include funds in the national budget to promote communication development in a proportion correspondent to the communication needs of other development projects.
- Promote, intensely and systematically, awareness in the public administration and among the entire population of the significance of communication improvement in the service of national development.
- Induce and help universities and other top-level educational institutions to establish, on a national scale, professional training in communication principles and techniques for specialists and technical field agents.

- Organize and foster research in communication so that planners have reliable information about *which* developmental messages, transmitted through *which* channels, are more likely to be effective with *which* audiences.
- Produce, in the language of the country, the essential literature needed for communication training.
- Provide the field workers with the communication aids (verbal, written and visual) that they must have to make their personal contacts effective.
- Use traditional modes of communication to spur innovation.
- Promote the growth and expansion of privately owned mass media so that they reach the rural audience.
- Establish communication institutions that combine mass media with interpersonal communication strategies, such as farm radio forums.

Beltrán, Luis Ramiro. "Communication: Forgotten Tool of National Development." In *International Agricultural Development*, Communications Issue, October 1967, No. 36. Reprinted with permission of the author.

1927
1960
1963
1964
1967
1969
1970
1971
1972
1973
1974
1975
1976
1977
1978
1979
1980
1981
1982
1983
1984
1985
1986
1987
1988
1989
1990
1991
1992
1993
1994
1995
1996
1997
1998
1999
2000
2001
2002
2003
2004
2005
2006

ANATOMY OF INCOMMUNICATION
Excerpt from: 'Communication and Modernization: The Case of Latin America'
By Luis Ramiro Beltrán

1969

In spite of all the appreciable progress and meritorious efforts which have been reviewed, many problems still raise huge barriers for communication practitioners with crucial challenges. It is thus unavoidable to pay also attention to their ugly side of the coin.

Some of Latin America's most serious problems of social communication in relation to the needs of national development are the following:

1. A marked lack of awareness, on the part of policy-makers and development strategists, of the significance and functions of communication in modernization.
2. An assignment of very low priority to communication work in government plans, and, thus, an inadequate allotment of funds for it in the national budgets.
3. A virtually complete inarticulation between general development strategies and specific communication strategies for that development.
4. An insufficient availability of government-owned mass media needed to establish and maintain an efficient two-way communication system between the public officers and the broad population, as well as among the different sectors of that population.
5. An exaggerated preference, on the part of government agencies, for one kind of content—institutional publicity, i.e., political propaganda, as well as for one kind of channel, the printed word (which is easiest and perhaps cheapest to use but reaches only a minimum of people).
6. An unduly pronounced concentration, on the part of government agencies, on an unplanned production of messages, at the expense of tasks such as proper distribution, research, evaluation, training, and promotion, which are at least as important as production.
7. A prevalence of deficiencies in physical infrastructure, such as lack of roads, lack of electricity, and lack of modern communication equipment, which makes the existence of a truly national network of social communication extremely difficult.
8. A high level of illiteracy which, coupled with the poverty of the majority of the people and aggravated in some cases by the existence of languages other than Spanish or Portuguese, imposes heavy restrictions on the use of the printed media.
9. An absence of motivation on the part of the mass media institutions—most of which are privately owned—to actually reach the broad masses and, particularly, the rural masses; they remain content with reaching the elite and the upper middle classes in the cities.
10. An insufficient growth of national and regional associations of professional communicators, such as journalists, audio-visual specialists, agricultural editors, and the like.
11. A lack of effective and independent national information agencies and, especially, of such an agency that is Latin American in scope; this permits a virtual monopoly of the international news flow by regional news services [external to the region] that neither inform the region objectively about world events nor report fairly about events in the region.
12. A weakness of the national private advertising firms that allows extra-regional [externally based] advertising consortiums to control much of the internal advertising market of the countries.

The problems that have merely been listed above are, certainly, not exclusively Latin American. They are common to very many of the countries of lesser development, with differences only of intensity.

What is behind those shortcomings? Where do they originate? Are there any basic factors—in addition to intrinsic communication deficiencies—which explain these problems of communication for modernization?

Presentation at the Eleventh World Conference of the Society for International Development, New Delhi, India, November 14-17, 1969. Copyright © 1969, Luis Ramiro Beltrán. Reprinted with permission of copyright holder.

EXCERPT FROM:

EDUCATION FOR CRITICAL CONSCIOUSNESS

By Paulo Freire

1969 My concern for the democratisation of culture, within the context of fundamental democratisation, required special attention to the quantitative and qualitative deficits in our education. In 1964, approximately 4 million school-age children lacked schools; there were 16 million illiterates 14 years and older. These truly alarming deficits constituted obstacles to the development of the country and to the creation of a democratic mentality.

For more than 15 years, I had been accumulating experiences in the field of adult education, in urban and rural proletarian and subproletarian areas. Urban dwellers showed a surprising interest in education, associated directly to the transitivity of their consciousness; the inverse was true in rural areas. (Today, in some areas, that situation is already changing.) I had experimented with—and abandoned—various methods and processes of communication. Never, however, had I abandoned the conviction that only by working with the people could I achieve anything authentic on their behalf. Never had I believed that the democratisation of culture meant either its vulgarisation or simply passing on to the people prescriptions formulated in the teacher's office. I agreed with Mannheim that "as democratic processes become widespread, it becomes more and more difficult to permit the masses to remain in a state of ignorance."[1] Mannheim would not restrict his definition of ignorance to illiteracy, but would include the masses' lack of experience at participating and intervening in the historical process.

My experiences as the Coordinator of the Adult Education Project of the Movement of Popular Culture

in Recife led to the maturing of my early educational convictions.

Through this project, we launched a new institution of popular culture, a "culture circle," since among us a school was a traditionally passive concept. Instead of a teacher, we had a coordinator; instead of lectures, dialogue; instead of pupils, group participants; instead of alienating syllabi, compact programs that were "broken down" and "codified" into learning units.

In the culture circles, we attempted through group debate either to clarify situations or to seek action rising from that clarification. The topics for these debates were offered us by the groups themselves. Nationalism, profit remittances abroad, the political evolution of Brazil, development, illiteracy, the vote for illiterates, democracy, were some of the themes repeated from group to group. These subjects and others were schematised as far as possible and presented to the groups with visual aids in the form of dialogue. We were amazed by the results.

After six months of experience with the culture circles, we asked ourselves if it would not be possible to do something in the field of adult literacy which would give us similar results to those we were achieving in the analysis of aspects of Brazilian reality. We started with some data and added more, aided by the Service of Cultural Extension of the University of Recife, which I directed at the time, and under whose auspices the experiment was conducted.

The first literacy attempt took place in Recife, with a group of five illiterates, two of whom dropped out on the second or third day. The participants, who had migrated from rural areas, revealed a certain fatalism and apathy in regard to their problems. They were totally illiterate. At the 20th meeting, we gave progress tests. To achieve greater flexibility, we used an epidiascope. We projected a slide on which two kitchen containers appeared. "Sugar" was written on one, "poison" on the other. And underneath the caption: "Which of the two would you use in your orangeade?" We asked the

---

1 Karl Mannheim, *Freedom, Power, and Democratic Planning*, New York: Oxford University Press, 1950.

1927
1960
1963
1964
1967
1969
1970
1971
1972
1973
1974
1975
1976
1977
1978
1979
1980
1981
1982
1983
1984
1985
1986
1987
1988
1989
1990
1991
1992
1993
1994
1995
1996
1997
1998
1999
2000
2001
2002
2003
2004
2005
2006

group to try to read the question and to give the answer orally. They answered, laughing, after several seconds, "Sugar." We followed the same procedure with other tests, such as recognizing bus lines and public buildings. During the 21st hour of study, one of the participants wrote, confidently, "I am amazed at myself."

From the beginning, we rejected the hypothesis of a purely mechanistic literacy program and considered the problem of teaching adults how to read in relation to the awakening of their consciousness. We wished to design a project in which we would attempt to move from naiveté to a critical attitude, at the same time as we taught reading. We wanted a literacy program which would be an introduction to the democratisation of culture, a program with men as its subjects rather than as patient recipients,[2] a program which itself would be an act of creation, capable of releasing other creative acts, one in which students would develop the impatience and vivacity which characterise search and invention.

We began with the conviction that the role of man was not only to be in the world, but to engage in relations with the world—that through acts of creation and re-creation—man makes cultural reality and thereby adds to the natural world, which he did not make. We were certain that man's relation to reality, expressed as a subject to an object, results in knowledge man could express through language.

This relation, as is already clear, is carried out by men whether or not they are literate. It is sufficient to be a person to perceive the data of reality, to be capable of knowing, even if this knowledge is mere opinion. There is no such thing as absolute ignorance or absolute wisdom.[3] But men do not perceive those data

in a pure form. As they apprehend a phenomenon or a problem, they also apprehend its causal links. The more accurately men grasp true causality, the more critical their understanding of reality will be. Their understanding will be magical to the degree that they fail to grasp causality. Further, critical consciousness always submits that causality to analysis; what is true today may not be so tomorrow. Naive consciousness sees causality as a static, established fact, and thus is deceived in its perception.

Critical consciousness represents "things and facts as they exist empirically, in their causal and circumstantial correlations … naive consciousness considers itself superior to facts, in control of facts, and thus free to understand them as it pleases."[4]

Magic consciousness, in contrast, simply apprehends facts and attributes to them a superior power by which it is controlled and to which it must therefore submit. Magic consciousness is characterised by fatalism, which leads men to fold their arms, resigned to the impossibility of resisting the power of facts.

Critical consciousness is integrated with reality; naive consciousness superimposes itself on reality; and fanatical consciousness, whose pathological naiveté leads to the irrational, adapts to reality.

It so happens that to every understanding, sooner or later an action corresponds. Once man perceives a challenge, understands it and recognises the possibilities of response, he acts. The nature of that action corresponds to the nature of his understanding. Critical understanding leads to critical action; magic understanding to magic response.

We wanted to offer the people the means by which they could supersede their magic or naive perception of reality by one that was predominantly critical,

---

2   In most reading programs, the students must endure an abysm between their own experience and the contents offered for them to learn. It requires patience indeed, after the hardships of a day's work (or of a day without work), to tolerate lessons dealing with "wing." "Johnny saw the wing." "The wing is on the bird." Lessons talking of Graces and grapes to men who never knew a Grace and never ate a grape. "Grace saw the grape."
3   No one ignores everything, just as no one knows everything. The dominating consciousness absolutises ignorance in order to manipulate the so-called "uncultured." If some men are "totally ignorant," they will

be incapable of managing themselves, and will need the orientation, the "direction," "the leadership" of those who consider themselves to be "cultured" and "superior."
4   Alvaro Vieira Pinto, *Consciência e Realidade Nacional*, Rio de Janeiro, Brazil:1961.

so that they could assume positions appropriate to the dynamic climate of the transition. This meant that we must take the people at the point of emergence and, by helping them move from naive to critical transitivity, facilitate their intervention in the historical process.

But how could this be done?

The answer seemed to lie:

a. in an active, dialogical, critical and criticism-stimulating method;
b. in changing the program content of education;
c. in the use of techniques like thematic "breakdown" and "codification."[5]

Our method, then, was to be based on dialogue, which is a horizontal relationship between persons.

Born of a critical matrix, dialogue creates a critical attitude (Jaspers). It is nourished by love, humility, hope, faith and trust. When the two "poles" of the dialogue are thus linked by love, hope and mutual trust, they can join in critical search for something. Only dialogue truly communicates.

[According to Karl Jaspers] dialogue is the only way, not only in the vital questions of the political order, but in all the expressions of our being. Only by virtue of faith, however, does dialogue have power and meaning: by faith in man and his possibilities, by the faith that I can only become truly myself when other men also become themselves.

And so we set dialogue in opposition with the anti-dialogue, which was so much a part of our historical-cultural formation and is so present in the climate of transition.

It involves vertical relationships between persons. It lacks love, is therefore a-critical, and cannot create a critical attitude. It is self-sufficient and hopelessly

---

5 "Breakdown": a splitting of themes into their fundamental nuclei. See *Pedagogy of the Oppressed*, p.113 ff. "Codification": the representation of a theme in the form of an existential situation. See *Pedagogy*, pp. 106-107 and pp.114-115 (Translator's note).

arrogant. In anti-dialogue, the relation of empathy between the "poles" is broken. Thus, anti-dialogue does not communicate, but rather issues communiqués, [according to Jaspers].

Whoever enters into dialogue does so with someone about something; and that something ought to constitute the new content of our proposed education. We felt that even before teaching someone to read, we could help him to overcome his magical or naive understanding and to develop an increasingly critical understanding. Towards this end, the first dimension of our new program content would be the anthropological concept of culture—that is, the distinction between the world of nature and the world of culture; the active role of men "in" and "with" their reality; the role of mediation nature plays in relationships and communication among men; culture as the addition made by men to a world they did not make; culture as the result of men's labour, of their efforts to create, and re-create; the transcendental meaning of human relationships; the humanist dimension of culture; culture as a systematic acquisition of human experience (but as creative assimilation, not as information-storing); the democratisation of culture; the learning of reading and writing as a key to the world of written communication. In short, the role of man as subject in the world and with the world.

From that point of departure, the illiterate person would begin to effect a change in his former attitudes, by discovering himself to be a maker of the world of culture, by discovering that he, as well as the literate person, has a creative and re-creative impulse. He would discover that culture is just as much a clay doll made by artists who are his peers as it is the work of a great sculptor, a great painter, a great mystic or a great philosopher; that culture is the poetry of lettered poets and also the poetry of his own popular songs—that culture is all human creation.

To introduce the concept of culture, first we "broke down" this concept into its fundamental aspects. Then, on the basis of this breakdown, we "codified,"

1927
1960
1963
1964
1967
1969
1970
1971
1972
1973
1974
1975
1976
1977
1978
1979
1980
1981
1982
1983
1984
1985
1986
1987
1988
1989
1990
1991
1992
1993
1994
1995
1996
1997
1998
1999
2000
2001
2002
2003
2004
2005
2006

i.e., represented visually, 10 existential situations. … Each representation contained a number of elements to be "decoded" by the group participants, with the help of the coordinator. Francisco Brenand, one of the greatest contemporary Brazilian artists, painted these codifications, perfectly integrating education and art.

It is remarkable to see with what enthusiasm these illiterates engage in debate and with what curiosity they respond to questions implicit in the codifications. In the words of Odilon Ribeiro Coutinho, "These detemporalised men begin to integrate themselves in time." As the dialogue intensifies, a "current" is established among the participants, dynamic to the degree that the content of the codifications corresponds to the existential reality of the groups.

Many participants during these debates affirm happily and self-confidently that they are not being shown "anything new, just remembering."

"I make shoes," said one, "and now I see that I am worth as much as the Ph.D. who writes books."

"Tomorrow," said a street-sweeper in Brasília, "I'm going to go to work with my head high." He had discovered the value of his person.

"I know now that I am cultured," an elderly peasant said emphatically. And when he was asked how it was that now he knew himself to be cultured; he answered with the same emphasis, "Because I work, and working, I transform the world."[6]

Once the group has perceived the distinction between the two worlds—nature and culture—and recognized man's role in each, the coordinator presents situations focusing on or expanding other aspects of culture.

The participants go on to discuss culture as a systematic acquisition of human experience and to discover that in a lettered culture this acquisition is not limited to oral transmission, as is the case in unlettered cultures which lack graphic signs. They conclude by debating the democratisation of culture, which opens the perspective of acquiring literacy.

All these discussions are critical, stimulating and highly motivating. The illiterate person perceives critically that it is necessary to learn to read and write and prepares himself to become the agent of this learning.

To acquire literacy is more than to psychologically and mechanically dominate reading and writing techniques. It is to dominate these techniques in terms of consciousness; to understand what one reads and to write what one understands; it is to "communicate" graphically. Acquiring literacy does not involve memorising sentences, words or syllables—lifeless objects unconnected to an existential universe—but rather an attitude of creation and re-creation, a self-transformation producing a stance of intervention in one's context.

Thus, the educator's role, fundamentally, is to enter into dialogue with the illiterate about concrete situations and simply to offer him the instruments with which he can teach himself to read and write. This teaching cannot be done from the top down, but only from the inside out, by the illiterate himself, with the collaboration of the educator. That is why we searched for a method which would be the instrument of the learner as well as of the educator, and which, in the lucid observation of a young Brazilian sociologist,[7] "would identify learning 'content' with the learning process."

Hence, we mistrust primers,[8] which set up a certain grouping of graphic signs as a gift, casting the illiterate person in the role of the "object" rather than the "subject" of his learning. Primers, even when they try to avoid this pitfall, end up giving people who are illiterate words and sentences that really should result from his own creative effort. We opted instead for the

---

6 Similar responses were evoked by the programs in Chile.

7 Celso Beisegel, in an unpublished work.
8 I am not opposed to reading texts, which are in fact indispensable to developing the visual-graphic channel of communication and which in great part should be elaborated by the participants themselves. I should add that our experience is based on the use of multiple channels of communication.

use of "generative words," those words whose syllabic elements offer, through recombination, the creation of new words. Teaching men how to read and write a syllabic language like Portuguese means showing them how to grasp, critically, the way its words are formed, so that they themselves can carry out the creative play of combinations. Fifteen or eighteen words seemed sufficient to present the basic phonemes of the Portuguese language.

Freire, Paulo. *Extensión o Comunicación*. Santiago, Chile: ICIRA, 1969. Original publication. Excerpt from *Education for Critical Consciousness*, Paulo Freire. Reprinted by permission of The Continuum International Publishing Group.

CINEMA-ACTION

Excerpt from: Towards a Third Cinema: Notes and Experiences for the Development of a Cinema of Liberation in the Third World

By Octavio Getino and Fernando E. Solanas

1969 There is no possibility of access to the knowledge of a given reality as long as there is no action addressing that reality, as long as action aiming to transform the reality in question from each battlefront is not undertaken. The widely known saying by Marx deserves to be repeated at each and every moment: Interpreting the world is not enough; it is now a matter of transforming it.

From this perspective, it is up to the moviemaker to discover his own language, the one arising from his militant and transforming vision and from the nature of the subject at hand. In this regard we must point out that old dogmatic positions that expect from the moviemaker or artist only an apologetic version of reality can still be found among certain political cadres, more in accordance with what "would be wished" ideally, than with what actually "is." These positions which, deep down, hide a lack of trust in the possibilities of reality itself, have led in certain cases to use the language of filmmaking as a mere idealized illustration of fact: to want to strip reality of its deep contradictions, its dialectic richness, which is what can give a film beauty and efficacy. The reality of revolutionary processes around the world, despite its confusing and negative aspects, has a dominant line, a synthesis rich and stimulating enough not to be reduced to partial or sectarian visions.

Pamphlet movies, didactic movies, report movies, essay movies, testimonial movies, every militant form

1927
1960
1963
1964
1967
1969
1970
1971
1972
1973
1974
1975
1976
1977
1978
1979
1980
1981
1982
1983
1984
1985
1986
1987
1988
1989
1990
1991
1992
1993
1994
1995
1996
1997
1998
1999
2000
2001
2002
2003
2004
2005
2006

of expression is valid, and it would be absurd to set aesthetic work rules. Giving people the best, or as Che [Guevara] would say, respecting the people by giving them quality. It is advisable to bear this in mind against those tendencies, always latent in the revolutionary artist, towards reducing the study and language of a subject matter to some sort of neopopulism; to levels that, although they may well be those in which the masses move, do not help them get rid of the remnants left behind by imperialism. The power of the best works of militant filmmaking show that layers of the population considered to be in an inferior situation are well able to grasp the exact sense of a metaphor made of images, of an editing effect, of any linguistic experimentation based on a specific idea.

On the other hand, revolutionary cinema is not fundamentally one that illustrates and documents, or passively fixes, a situation, but one that tries to influence it as a driving or rectifying element. It is not just testimonial cinema, or communicational cinema, but prominently action-cinema.

Hacia un Tercer Cine: Apuntes y Experiencias Para El Desarrollo de un Cinde de Liberación en el Tercer Mundo was first published in Tricontinental, Paris, October 1969. Also Cine Club, año I, núm. 1, México, Octubre de 1970, and in Octavio Getino and Fernando Solanas, *Cine, Cultura y Descolonización,* Buenos Aires, Argentina: Siglo XXI, 1973. Reprinted with permission of author and publisher.

EXCERPT FROM:

PEDAGOGY OF THE OPPRESSED

By Paulo Freire

1970 As we attempt to analyze dialogue as a human phenomenon, we discover something that is the essence of dialogue itself: *the word.* But the word is more than just an instrument that makes dialogue possible; accordingly, we must seek its constitutive elements. Within the word, we find two dimensions, reflection and action, in such radical interaction that if one is sacrificed—even in part—the other immediately suffers. There is no true word that is not at the same time a praxis.[1] Thus, to speak a true word is to transform the world.[2]

On the other hand, if action is emphasized exclusively, to the detriment of reflection, the word is converted into *activism.* The latter—action for action's sake—negates the true praxis and makes dialogue impossible. Either dichotomy, by creating unauthentic forms of existence, creates also unauthentic forms of thought, which reinforce the original dichotomy.

Human existence cannot be silent, nor can it be nourished by false words but only by true words, with which men and women transform the world. To exist, humanly, is to *name* the world, to change it. Once named, the world in its turn reappears to the namers as a problem and requires of them a new *naming.* Human beings are not built in silence,[3] but in word, in work, in action-reflection.

---

1 Action Reflection } word = work = praxis
Sacrifice of action = verbalism
Sacrifice of reflection = activism
2 Some of these reflections emerged as a result of conversations with Professor Ernani Maria Fiori.
3 I obviously do not refer to the silence of profound meditation, in which men only apparently leave the world, withdrawing from it in order to consider it in its totality and thus remaining with it. But this type of retreat is authentic only when the mediator is "bathed" in reality, not when the retreat signifies contempt for the world and flight from it, in a type of "historical schizophrenia."

But while to say the true word—which is work, which is praxis—is to transform the world, saying that word is not the privilege of some few persons, but the right of everyone. Consequently, no one can say a true word alone—nor can she say it *for* another, in a prescriptive act which robs others of their words.

Dialogue is the encounter between men, mediated by the world, in order to name the world. Hence, dialogue cannot occur between those who want to name the world and those who do not wish this naming—between those who deny others the right to speak their word and those whose right to speak has been denied them. Those who have been denied their primordial right to speak their word must first reclaim this right and prevent the continuation of this dehumanizing aggression.

If it is in speaking their word that people, by naming the world, transform it, dialogue imposes itself as the way by which they achieve significance as human beings. Dialogue is thus an existential necessity. And since dialogue is the encounter in which the united reflection and action of the dialoguers are addressed to the world that is to be transformed and humanized, this dialogue cannot be reduced to the act of one person's "depositing" ideas in another, nor can it become a simple exchange of ideas to be "consumed" by the discussants. Nor is it a hostile, polemical argument between those who are committed neither to the naming of the world nor to the search for truth but rather to the imposition of their own truth. Because dialogue is an encounter among women and men who name the world, it must not be a situation where some name on behalf of others. It is an act of creation; it must not serve as a crafty instrument for the domination of one person by another. The domination implicit in dialogue is that of the world by the dialoguers; it is conquest of the world for the liberation of humankind.

Dialogue cannot exist, however, in the absence of a profound love for the world and for people. The naming of the world, which is an act of creation and re-creation, is not possible if it is not infused with love.[4] Love is at the same time the foundation of dialogue and dialogue itself. It is thus necessarily the task of responsible subjects and cannot exist in a relation of domination. Domination reveals the pathology of love: sadism in the dominator and masochism in the dominated. Because love is an act of courage, not of fear, love is commitment to others. No matter where the oppressed are found, the act of love is commitment to their cause—the cause of liberation. And this commitment, because it is loving, is dialogical. As an act of bravery, love cannot be sentimental; as an act of freedom, it must not serve as a pretext for manipulation. It must generate other acts of freedom; otherwise, it is not love. Only by abolishing the situation of oppression is it possible to restore the love which that situation made impossible. If I do not love the world—if I do not love life—if I do not love people—I cannot enter into dialogue.

On the other hand, dialogue cannot exist without humility. The naming of the world, through which people constantly re-create that world, cannot be an act of arrogance. Dialogue, as the encounter of those addressed to the common task of learning and acting, is broken if the parties (or one of them) lack humility. How can I dialogue if I always project ignorance onto others and never perceive my own? How can I dialogue if I regard myself as a case apart from others—mere "its" in whom I cannot recognize other "I"s? How can I dialogue if I consider myself a member of the in-group of "pure" men, the owners of truth and knowledge,

---

4 I am more and more convinced that true revolutionaries must perceive the revolution, because of its creative and liberating nature, as an act of love. For me, the revolution, which is not possible without a theory of revolution—and therefore science—is not irreconcilable with love. On the contrary; the revolution is made by people to achieve their humanization. What, indeed, is the deeper reason that moves individuals to become revolutionaries? It's the dehumanization of people. The distortion imposed on the word "love" by the capitalist world cannot prevent the revolution from being essentially loving in character, nor can it prevent the revolutionaries from affirming their love of life. Guevara (while admitting the "risk of seeming ridiculous") was not afraid to affirm it: "Let me say, with the risk of appearing ridiculous, that the true revolutionary is guided by strong feelings of love. It is impossible to think of an authentic revolutionary without this quality." *Venceremos—The Speeches and Writings of Che Guevara*, edited by John Gerassi (New York, 1969), p. 398.

1927
1960
1963
1964
1967
1969
1970
1971
1972
1973
1974
1975
1976
1977
1978
1979
1980
1981
1982
1983
1984
1985
1986
1987
1988
1989
1990
1991
1992
1993
1994
1995
1996
1997
1998
1999
2000
2001
2002
2003
2004
2005
2006

for whom all nonmembers are "these people" or "the great unwashed"? How can I dialogue if I start from the premise that naming the world is the task of an elite and that the presence of the people in history is a sign of deterioration, thus to be avoided? How can I dialogue if I am closed to—and even offended by—the contribution of others? How can I dialogue if I am afraid of being displaced, the mere possibility causing me torment and weakness? Self-sufficiency is incompatible with dialogue. Men and women who lack humility (or have lost it) cannot come to the people, cannot be their partners in naming the world. Someone who cannot acknowledge himself to be a mortal as everyone else is still has a long way to go before he can reach the point of encounter. At the point of encounter, there are neither utter ignoramuses nor perfect sages; there are only people who are attempting, together, to learn more than they now know.

Dialogue further requires an intense faith in humankind; faith in people's power to make and remake, to create and re-create; faith in their vocation to be more fully human (which is not the privilege of an elite, but the birthright of all). Faith in people is an *a priori* requirement for dialogue; the "dialogical man" believes in others even before he meets them face-to-face. His faith, however, is not naïve. The "dialogical man" is critical and knows that although it is within the power of humans to create and transform, in a concrete situation of alienation individuals may be impaired in the use of that power. Far from destroying his faith in the people, however, this possibility strikes him as a challenge to which he must respond. He is convinced that the power to create and transform, even when thwarted in concrete situations, tends to be reborn. And that rebirth can occur—not gratuitously, but in and through the struggle for liberation—in the supersedence of slave labor by emancipated labor, which gives zest to life. Without this faith in people, dialogue is a farce that inevitably degenerates into paternalistic manipulation.

Founding itself upon love, humility and faith, dialogue becomes a horizontal relationship in which

mutual trust between the dialoguers is the logical consequence. It would be a contradiction in terms if dialogue—loving, humble, and full of faith—did not produce this climate of mutual trust, which leads the dialoguers into ever closer partnership in the naming of the world. Conversely, such trust is obviously absent in the anti-dialogics of the banking method of education. Whereas faith in humankind is an *a priori* requirement for dialogue, trust is established by dialogue. Should it flounder, it will be seen that the preconditions were lacking. False love, false humility, and feeble faith in others cannot create trust. Trust is contingent on the evidence which one party provides the others of his true, concrete intentions; it cannot exist if that party's words do not coincide with their actions. To say one thing and do another—to take one's own word lightly—cannot inspire trust. To glorify democracy and to silence the people is a farce; to discourse on humanism and to negate people is a lie.

Nor yet can dialogue exist without hope. Hope is rooted in men's incompletion, from which they move out in constant search—a search which can be carried out only in communion with others. Hopelessness is a form of silence, of denying the world and fleeing from it. The dehumanization resulting from an unjust order is not a cause for despair but for hope, leading to the incessant pursuit of the humanity denied by injustice. Hope, however, does not consist in crossing one's arms and waiting. As long as I fight, I am moved by hope; and if I fight with hope, then I can wait. As the encounter of women and men seeking to be more fully human, dialogue cannot be carried on in a climate of hopelessness. If the dialoguers expect nothing to come of their efforts, their encounter will be empty and sterile, bureaucratic and tedious.

Finally, true dialogue cannot exist unless the dialoguers engage in critical thinking—thinking that discerns an indivisible solidarity between the world and the people and admits of no dichotomy between them—thinking that perceives reality as process, as transformation, rather than as a static entity—thinking that does not separate itself from action but constantly immerses itself in temporality without fear of the risks involved. Critical thinking contrasts with naïve thinking, which sees "historical time as a weight, a stratification of the acquisitions and experience of the past,"[5] from which the present should emerge normalized and "well-behaved." For the naïve thinker, the important thing is accommodation to this normalized "today." For the critic, the important thing is the continuing transformation of reality, on behalf of the continuing humanization of men. In the words of Pierre Furter:

> The goal will no longer be to eliminate the risks of temporality by clutching the guaranteed space, but rather to temporalize space…The universe is revealed to me not as space, imposing a massive presence to which I can but adapt, but as a scope, a domain which takes shape as I act upon it.[6]

For naïve thinking, the goal is precisely to hold fast to this guaranteed space and adjust to it. By thus denying temporality, it denies itself as well.

Only dialogue, which requires critical thinking, is also capable of generating critical thinking. Without dialogue there is no communication, and without communication, there cannot be true education. Education that is able to resolve the contradiction between teacher and student takes place in a situation in which both address their act of cognition to the object by which they are mediated. Thus, the dialogical character of education as the practice of freedom does not begin when the teacher-student meets with the students-teachers in a pedagogical situation, but rather when the former first asks herself or himself *what* she or he will dialogue with the latter *about*. And preoccupation with the content of dialogue is really preoccupation with the program content of education.

For the anti-dialogical banking educator, the question of content simply concerns the program about which he will discourse to his students; and he answers his own question, by organizing his own program.

For the dialogical, problem-posing teacher-student, the program content of education is neither a gift nor an imposition—bits of information to be deposited in the students—but rather the organized, systematized, and developed "re-presentation" to individuals of the things about which they want to know more.[7]

Authentic education is not carried on by "A" *for* "B" or by "A" *about* "B," but rather by "A" *with* "B," mediated by the world—a world that impresses and challenges both parties, giving rise to views or opinions about it. These views, impregnated with anxieties, doubts, hopes or hopelessness, imply significant themes on the basis of which the program content of education can be built. In its desire to create an ideal model of the "good man", a naïvely conceived humanism often overlooks the concrete, existential, present situation of real people. Authentic humanism, in Pierre Furter's words, "consists in permitting the emergence of the awareness of our full humanity, as a condition and as an obligation, as a situation and as a project."[8] We simply cannot go to the laborers—urban or peasant[9]—in the banking style, to give them "knowledge" or to impose upon them the model of the "good man" contained in a program whose content we have ourselves organized. Many political and educational plans have failed because their authors designed them according to their own personal views of reality, never once taking into account (except as mere objects of their actions) the men-in-a-situation to whom their program was ostensibly directed.

For the truly humanist educator and the authentic revolutionary, the object of action is the reality to be transformed by them together with other people—not other men and women themselves. The oppressors

---

5 From the letter of a friend.
6 Pierre Furter, *Educação e Vida* (Rio, 1966), 26-27.
7 In a long conversation with Malraux, Mao Tse-Tung declared, "You know I've proclaimed for a long time: we must teach the masses clearly what we have received from them confusedly." André Malraux, *Anti-Memoirs*, New York, 1968, 361-362. This affirmation contains an entire dialogical theory of how to construct the program content of education, which cannot be elaborated according to what the *educator* thinks best for the *students*.
8 Furter, op. cit., 165.
9 The latter, usually submerged in a colonial context, are almost umbilically linked to the world of nature, in relation to which they feel themselves to be component parts rather than shapers.

1927
1960
1963
1964
1967
1969
1970
1971
1972
1973
1974
1975
1976
1977
1978
1979
1980
1981
1982
1983
1984
1985
1986
1987
1988
1989
1990
1991
1992
1993
1994
1995
1996
1997
1998
1999
2000
2001
2002
2003
2004
2005
2006

are the ones who act upon the people to indoctrinate them and adjust them to a reality which must remain untouched. Unfortunately, however, in their desire to obtain the support of the people for revolutionary action, revolutionary leaders often fall for the banking line of planning program content from the top down. They approach the peasant or urban masses with projects which may correspond to their own view of the world, but not to that of the people.[10] They forget that their fundamental objective is to fight alongside the people for the recovery of the people's stolen humanity, not to "win the people over" to their side. Such a phrase does not belong in the vocabulary of revolutionary leaders, but in that of the oppressor. The revolutionary's role is to liberate, and be liberated with, the people—not to win them over.

In their political activity, the dominant elites utilize the banking concept to encourage passivity in the oppressed, corresponding with the latter's "submerged" state of consciousness, and take advantage of that passivity to "fill" that consciousness with slogans which create even more fear of freedom. This practice is incompatible with a truly liberating course of action, which, by presenting the oppressors' slogans as a problem, helps the oppressed to "eject" those slogans from within themselves. After all, the task of the humanists is surely not that of pitting their slogans against the slogans of the oppressors, with the oppressed as the testing ground, "housing" the slogans of first one group and then the other. On the contrary,

the task of the humanists is to see that the oppressed become aware of the fact that as dual beings, "housing" the oppressors within themselves, they cannot be truly human.

This task implies that revolutionary leaders do not go to the people in order to bring them a message of "salvation," but to come to know through dialogue with them both their *objective situation* and their *awareness* of that situation—the various levels of perception of themselves and of the world in which and with which they exist. One cannot expect positive results from an educational or political action program which fails to respect the particular view of the world held by the people. Such a program constitutes cultural invasion, good intentions notwithstanding.

Freire, Paulo. *Pedagogia do Oprimido*. Rio de Janeiro, Brasil: Edições Paz e Terra, 1970. Original publication. Excerpts from Chapter 3 of *Pedagogy of the Oppressed*, Paulo Freire, 1970. Reprinted by Permission of The Continuum International Publishing Group.

10 "Our cultural workers must serve the people with great enthusiasm and devotion, and they must link themselves with the masses, not divorce themselves from the masses. In order to do so, they must act in accordance with the needs and wishes of the masses. All work done for the masses must start from their needs and not from the desire of any individual, however well-intentioned. It often happens that objectively the masses need a certain change, but subjectively they are not yet conscious of the need, not yet willing or determined to make the change. In such cases, we should wait patiently. We should not make the change until, through our work, most of the masses have become conscious of the need and are willing and determined to carry it out. Otherwise we shall isolate ourselves from the masses... There are two principles here: one is the actual needs of the masses rather than what we fancy they need, and the other is the wishes of the masses, who must make up their own minds instead of our making up their minds for them." From the *Selected Works of Mao Tse-Tung*, Vol. III, "The United Front in Cultural Work" (October 30, 1944) (Peking, 1967), 186-187.

1927
1960
1963
1964
1967
1969
1970

EXCERPT FROM:

HOW TO READ DONALD DUCK: IMPERIALIST IDEOLOGY IN THE DISNEY COMIC

By Ariel Dorfman and Armand Mattelart

1971 The formal breakdown of the Disney world into fragments (a mechanism characteristic of capitalist life in general), into different comic strips, serves to deceive the reader, who is but another little wheel in the great grinding mill of consumption.

Boredom and fear of change is held at bay by the physical mobility of the characters. But not only in their epileptic daily activity, in their perpetual traveling and in their constant decamping from their homes.

They also are allowed to cross over from their preassigned sector to meet other members of the Disney reality, like the figures dressed as Disney characters who patrol the streets of Disneyland, California, lending cohesion to the crowd of visitors. Madame Mim and Goofy visit Scrooge. Big Bad Wolf converses with the duckling. Mickey helps out Grandma Duck. In this fake tower of Babel, where all speak the same language of the established repressive order, the ingredients are always thrown together to concoct the same old mental potion: curiosity. How will Snow White react toward Mickey? Familiarity is preserved through the maintenance of the traditional character traits. The reader, who is attracted by the adventure, does not notice that beneath the novelty of the encounter, the characters are continually repeating themselves.

1971
1972
1973
1974
1975
1976
1977
1978
1979
1980
1981
1982
1983
1984
1985
1986
1987
1988
1989
1990
1991
1992
1993
1994
1995
1996
1997
1998
1999
2000
2001
2002
2003
2004
2005
2006

Excerpt from: *"How to read Donald Duck"*
By Armand Mattelart & Ariel Dorfman

Attacking Disney is no novelty; he has often been exposed as the traveling salesman of the imagination, the propagandist of the "American Way of Life", and a spokesman of "unreality." But true as it is, such criticism misses the true impulse behind the manufacture of the Disney characters, and the true danger they represent to dependent countries like Chile. The threat derives not so much from their embodiment of the "American Way of Life", as that of the "American Dream of Life." It is the manner in which the United States. dreams and redeems itself, and then imposes that dream upon others for its own salvation, which poses the danger for the dependent countries. It forces us Latin Americans to see ourselves as they see us.

Any social reality may be defined as the incessant dialectical interaction between a material base and the superstructure which reflects it and anticipates it in the human mind. From the moment people find themselves involved in a certain social system that is, from conception and birth it is impossible for their consciousness to develop without being based on concrete material conditions. In a society where one class controls the means of economic production, that class also controls the means of intellectual production; ideas; feelings, intuitions, in short—the very meaning of life. To capture the true message of Disney, we must reflect upon these two components [material base and the superstructure] in his fantasy world to understand precisely in what way he represents reality, and how his fantasy may relate to concrete social existence, that is, the immediate historical conditions. The way Disney conceives the relationship between base and superstructure is comparable to the way the bourgeoisie conceive this relationship in the real life of the dependent countries (as well as their own). Once we have analyzed the structural differences and similarities, we will be better able to judge the effects of Disney-type magazines on the condition of underdevelopment.

Editors' Note: We have included two excerpts from this 1970s classic; the excerpts are not necessarily sequential in the Dorfman/Mattelart book.

The characters are overactive and appear flexible; the magic wand sends off a lot of sparks, but despite all the magic they still remain straight and rigid. There is an unholy terror of change. Trapped in the strict limitations of the personality drawn for him—a catalog assortment with very few entries—anytime a character tries to articulate himself differently, he is doomed to stupendous failure. Donald is under constant attack for his forgetfulness, but as soon as Gyro transplants the memory of an elephant into his brain, the world around him begins to break up (DD 7/67).

Almost immediately, everyone—and Donald especially—demands that he be returned to his original state, the good old Donald we all love. The same happens when Uncle Scrooge uses a magic ink to shame his nephew into paying a debt. It works not only on Donald but on Scrooge as well, so that he feels ashamed of himself and heaps costly gifts on Donald. Better not change another person's habitual psychological mechanisms; it is better to be satisfied with the way one is. Great danger lurks behind very sudden changes. Although usually provoked by some microbe or magical device, changes such as revolutions, which pose external threats to a personality structure, and individual psychological disturbances, which threaten a character's escape from his past and present stereotype, also pose a threat. Disney subjects his characters to a relentless slimming course: They pedal away on fixed bicycles, shed a pound, gain a pound, but the same old skeleton remains under the New You. If this remedy seems directed only to the privileged classes who can indulge in such sport, it is equally mandatory for the savages, both good and bad.

In any individual hero, it is the tentacles of competition which provoke these formal paroxysms. In 90 percent of our sample, the explicit theme is a race to get to some place or object in the shortest possible (and therefore, most frantic) time. In this (always public) contest, this obstacle race and test of athletic prowess, the goal is usually money ("Time Is Money," as the title of one story tells us). But not always: Sometimes it is a

hankering for prestige, and to stand out from the common herd. Not only because this automatically means dollars, and women to admire and cater to the winner, but also because it represents the happy conclusion to the suffering, the "work" leading to the halls of fame.

Fame is being able to enjoy, in leisure, all the benefits of productive work. The image radiating from the celebrity assures his livelihood; he can sell himself forever. It is like having found the gold of personality. Converting fame itself into a source of income, it is the business of selling one's own super self.

But the prerequisite to all this is to have become a news item, broadcast by the mass media and recognized by "public opinion." To the Disney hero, the adventure in and of itself is not sufficient reward. Without an audience it makes no sense, for the hero must play to the gallery. The importance of the exploit is measured by the degree to which others know that he has surpassed them. Thus, from the television, radio and newspaper he is able to impress other people of his importance and dominate them. A powerful figure may be able to help them become famous themselves. On one occasion (D 443, CS 2/61), Donald is worried because he seems to be one of those people "just born to be nobodies," and wants to do something about it. He asks an actor how he started on the road to fame. Reply: "I was playing golf and made a hole-in-one…. A rich producer saw me do it, and he was so impressed he made me a star."

Donald tries the same but fails because the television cameras were aimed at someone else: "I would hit a hole-in-one as everybody turned to watch Brigitte van Doren walking by." A politico tells Donald how he found the way to make people notice him. So Donald twice climbs a flagpole but falls down each time without getting his photograph taken. Finally, he succeeds by accident. "Success did not come easily, but it came," he says to the ducklings. "With this start, "Unca" Donald, you can become a movie star or a Senator . . . or even President!" But the newspaper ("Tripe") misspells the name under the photograph: Ronald Dunk. Final and total defeat.

It is not truth, but appearance, that matters. The hero's reputation rests entirely upon the gossip column. When his party is a flop (also D 443), Donald says, "I can only hope that no reporter gets to hear about this. An article on that party would finish me for good." But naturally there was a reporter there, and the owner and social editor (of the *Evening Tattler*) as well.

With this obsession for the successful propagation of one's own image, it is not surprising that a common trick for getting an episode going is by means of a photograph album. If there is no evidence, it never happened. Every adventure is viewed by its protagonist as a photograph in an album, in a kind of *self-tourism*. The camera is only a means to can and preserve the past. When the photo fails to come out (D 440), it is a disaster, for the guarantee of self-reproduction (in the mass media) has been lost, the bridge of memory has been broken. Immortality has been forfeited; indeed, history itself has been mislaid.

But there is something even better than a photograph: a statue. If a character can get a statue made of himself, immortality is his. Statue. Statute. Status. Static. Time and time again, someone is rewarded with the prize of a statue standing in a public place or museum. "The secret ambition of Donald: to be the local hero, with a right to a statue in the park." (D 441, DD 7/68). This he achieves by defeating the Martians (sic): "We are thinking of hiring a famous sculptor, so that your likeness may stand among the other 'greats' in the city park!" Every corner is a record of the climactic moment of personal past histories. Time, far from being a curse, as in the Bible, is stopped, turned to stone and made immortal.

But the family photograph and the statue are not only "souvenirs" brought back from a "tour" of the past. They also validate the past and present importance of one's ancestors and guarantee their future importance. King Michael the First, "except for the moustache" (D 433), is just like Mickey. The fame of the multitude of uncle ducks can only be proven through the image which they leave behind. Fear of time and competition come

to an end when a consensus is reached over an individual's reputation: "I am leaving before they have time to change their opinion of me," explains Goofy (TB 99).

Fame and prize-winning turn an individual into a product—that is, in the etymological sense of the word, a finished object, cut off from any other productive process, ready to be consumed or consummated.

Once again, change leads to immobility.

We have seen that the same static relationships occurred in the supposed conflict between adults and youngsters. The poles were apparently in opposition, divided and mobile. But in reality (whether expressed negatively or positively), they were turning around the same central standard and constantly switching roles; two masks over the same face. In fusing father and son with the same ideals, the adult projects into his offspring the perpetuation of his own values, so that he can pass the baton to himself. The movement generated from the confrontation between the two people, or strata, was tautological and illusory. The antagonism disappeared as soon as the two agreed on the rules, which put one on top and the other below. Each was himself and his double.

This false dialogue, which is the monologue of the dominant class and its taped playback, is repeated at all levels of the socially stratified cast of characters. Here the age-old concept of twins enters the picture. This folk-motif, which also figures prominently in elite literature (for example, in the work of Poe, Dostoevsky, Cortázar), is often used to express the contradiction people suffer inside their own personality; that is to say, against the rebellious and demonical layer of their being; as in that ambiguous part of them which threatens established order, saving their souls and destroying their lives. The cultural monopolists have flattened and exploited this duality in which one is both commended and condemned, and served it up in simplified form as the collective vision to all the people.

In the two levels in Disney—the dominators, most of the little denizens of Duckburg and, in the dominated,

1927
1960
1963
1964
1967
1969
1970
1971
1972
1973
1974
1975
1976
1977
1978
1979
1980
1981
1982
1983
1984
1985
1986
1987
1988
1989
1990
1991
1992
1993
1994
1995
1996
1997
1998
1999
2000
2001
2002
2003
2004
2005
2006

the noble savages and the delinquents—this duality is present on both sides, but is conveyed in a most symbolic manner. In folklore, as we all know, one twin is good and the other bad, with nothing in between. Similarly, among the *dominated* of Disney there are those who happily accept their innocent and subject condition (good guys) and those who attack their bosses' property (bad guys).

The sharpness of the division, and the lack of mobility from one side to the other, is absolute. The bad guys run around crazily within the prison of their stereotype, with no chance of ever escaping into the realm of the good guys. To such an extent that in one episode, when disguised as (neutral and passive) natives, the bad guys are still punished by having to pick up Uncle Scrooge's money for him. The noble savages, for their part, have to stay quietly *in situ*, so as not to risk being cheated in the city. Each stratum of the dominated is frozen in its goodness or wickedness, for apparently in the plains of the people there are no communication channels between the two.

There is no way to be both good *and* attack property. There is no way to be bad if you obey the rules. "Become what you are" goes an old popular saying, coined by the bourgeoisie. Change is prohibited in these sectors. The noble savage cannot become a criminal, and the criminal cannot become innocent. So whether they be actively wicked or passively virtuous, the role of the dominated is fixed, and history, it seems, is made somewhere else.

Contrast this with the dynamism of the dominant classes, where mobility reigns and anything is possible. There are rich and poor within the same family. Among friends, one is lucky, the other not. Among the rich, there are good and bad, and intelligent and stupid. The captivating and craggy land of the dominant tolerates discordance and dilemma. There are no 100 percenters, that is, completely polarized characters. Donald tends to lose, but he wins 20 percent of the time. Uncle Scrooge is often defeated. Even Mickey occasionally behaves like a coward (in D 401 the children frighten

him and supplant him. Says Minnie: "You really are sometimes worse than the children. I don't know what to do with you. The children are right." And Mickey replies: "Those doggone kids always get the best of it."). Gladstone Gander is not always the winner, and the Boy Scout ducklings sometime slip up. Only the prodigy Little Wolf escapes this rule, but he needs to, with such a rotten, stupidly wicked father. The realm of the dominant Duckburgers is one of refined nuances and marked by small contradictions. Over the mass, sunk in its collective determinism (that's the way it is; whether you like it or not, you get screwed), rises the dominant personality who can "freely" choose and determine his course in life.

His liberty lies in having a personality, in flourishing through statuary, in holding a monopoly over the voice of history.

Once the adversary is disqualified in advance (and that disqualification is systematic), he is then beaten in a race that he cannot even run. History acquires the face that the dominant class chooses to give it.

Need we stress further how closed and suffocating this world of Disney really is?

Just as the subject classes are deprived of voice and face, and the possibility to open the prison door (notice how easy it is to eliminate them when production is performed magically and they are not needed), so the past is deprived of its real character and is made to appear the same as the present. Past history in its entirety is colonized by the anxieties and values of the present moment. Historical experience is a huge treasure chest full of hallowed moral tags and recipes, of the same old standards and doctrines, all defending the same old thesis of domination. Donald is suspicious of Uncle Scrooge's preoccupation with money, but the miser can always demonstrate that his fortune was justly acquired, since it is liable suddenly to disappear and is subject to potential disasters. For which a historical precedent from ancient Greece is adduced (F 174): King Dionysus spins his servant Damocles the same yarn.

This analogy underlines the repetitive character of history in Disney. A history in which any earlier epoch is seen as the pioneer of present-day morality. To see the world as a ceaseless prefiguration of Disney you just look back. It may not be true, but at least chronology is protected.

In reality, the past is known through (and in) the present, and as such it exists as a function of the present, as a support for prevailing ideas. Disney's mutilation of the relationship between the past and present accounts for his schematization and moralization of Third World history. Many years ago the conquistadors (like the Beagle Boys) tried to take away the property of the Aztec natives (ducks) who hid it. History is portrayed as a self-repeating, constantly renascent adventure, in which the bad guys try, unsuccessfully, to steal from the good guys (D 432, DD 9/65). The pattern is repeated in many other episodes in which the struggles of contemporary Duckburg are projected onto the history of past cultures. From time to time the heroes are transported, by a dream, hypnosis or time machine, into another era. Old California (D 357) is the scene of the well-worn formula: the search for gold with hardship, the struggle between cops and robbers and then the return to leisure and order. The same thing happens in their journeys to ancient Rome, Babylon and prehistory. There are also micro-ducks who come from outer space (TR 96, US 9/66), with traumatic adventures identical to those of our heroes. It's a sure bet that the "future time and infinite space" market will be cornered and colonialized by Disney.

By invading the past (and the future) with the structures of the present, Disney takes possession of the whole of human history. In Egypt there is a sphinx with the face of Uncle Scrooge (D 422, DD 3/64): "When he discovered the Sphinx some years back, it didn't have a face, so he put his on it." It is only proper that the face of McDuck should be transposable everywhere. It is the trademark of U.S. history. It fits everywhere. At the end of the above story, he adds his likeness to the giant sculptures of Washington, Lincoln, etc., on Mount Rushmore—now called Mount Duckmore. Thus Scrooge joins the Founding Fathers. His statue is even in outer space (TR 48).

The comic-as-history turns the unforeseeable into a foregone conclusion. It translates the painful course of time into eternal and premature old age. The causes of the present are not to be sought in the past; just consult Donald Duck, trouble-shooting ambassador-at-large. …

The visa of the past for entry into the future through Disneyland Customs and Immigration (and Interpol) is stamped with exoticism and folklore. History becomes a marketplace where ancient civilizations pass by the plebiscite of purchase. The only difference among past civilizations lies in the extent of their value today as entertainment and sensation. …

Disney approaches an individual existence in the same spirit as he does a foreign civilization, and both compete for success and the propagation of their petrified image. This is suggested in a story where Donald is the night watchman in a wax museum (D 436, CS 12/59). One night, while he is at work, a costume ball takes place in the house opposite the museum. The same historical figures (with the same clothes, faces and expressions, etc.) are present at the ball as are petrified in the wax museum. Inevitably, Donald falls asleep, and upon awakening mistakes the moving live figures for the wax ones. He concludes that while he was asleep a "revolution" took place. Apparently, there can be no other explanation for this movement of history. … (Donald cannot accept any movement of history, real or imaginary.)

When he awakes he desperately tries to control the real figures with rope and stop the "revolution," yelling that "Queen Elizabeth, Joan of Arc, Attila the Hun, the whole museum, is walking around in the street." All this happened because the guests at the costume ball had used as models the same historical figures as are in the museum, turning the past into an oasis of entertainment and tourism. Although it was not his

1927
1960
1963
1964
1967
1969
1970
1971
1972
1973
1974
1975
1976
1977
1978
1979
1980
1981
1982
1983
1984
1985
1986
1987
1988
1989
1990
1991
1992
1993
1994
1995
1996
1997
1998
1999
2000
2001
2002
2003
2004
2005
2006

fault, the episode makes Donald a celebrity, and he is rewarded for his work as guardian of the past. He seems to prefer the profession of guardian of the past in the interests of the iron-hard present. "Months have passed, and Unca Donald is making so much money he doesn't need to work anymore," say the youngsters. "Yes, he's a famous character now . . . so famous that he gets paid just for allowing his wax dummy to be exhibited at the museum. . . . Our own Unca Donald has caused the greatest commotion in the whole history of Duckburg!"

Donald has realized his dreams: easy, well-paid and undemanding work. Any civilization, ancient or modern, can model itself on him. Just write Walt Disney Productions.

Dorfman, Ariel and Armand Mattelart. *How to Read Donald Duck: Imperialist Ideology in the Disney Comic*. New York: International General, 1971. Reprinted with permission of author.

DEVELOPMENT COMMUNICATION IN THE AGRICULTURAL CONTEXT

By Nora C. Quebral

1971 (This paper was updated by the author in 2005)

If I were pressed for a definition o development communication, I would say that it is the art and science of human communication applied to the speedy transformation of a country and the mass of its people from poverty to a dynamic state of economic growth that makes possible greater social equality and the larger fulfillment of the human potential.

Or similar words to that effect.

The reason for my having to coin my own definition is that development communication is still very much in the evolutionary stage so that no one is quite prepared to be pinned down to an exact definition of it. The evolving concept of development communication, for the most part, remains the preoccupation of the social scientists. The only action organization I know that has put down on paper some pertinent ideas on the subject is the United Nations, whose specialized agencies have had long experience with field projects in developing countries.

In most of the developing world itself, if the Philippines is representative, not many professional communicators are willing at this point to grant development communication legitimacy of existence, much less of purpose. Two international meetings held in Manila in the past two years, while posing a changed role for the Asian press as the main issue, either refrained or were prevented from getting down to specifics. In the One Asia Assembly convened by press people themselves, only the delegates from India spoke of the electronic media and only they related these newer media to the development of people. In the ASEAN seminar on "The Role of the Mass Media in the Development of Southeast Asia" organized by government men and academicians, the maverick participants from the Philippine press, judging from newspaper accounts, were suspicious, belligerent and frustrated by turns. They saw themselves as being conned into a role distasteful to them because alien to their training.

The systematic use of the art and science of human communication to persuade specified groups of people to change their habits, lifestyle or ways of thought is by no means new. It is what advertising is all about. Public relations and propaganda are no strangers to the discipline. Indeed, it might well be the self-serving element commonly associated with these subjects that has made persuasive communication the object of some distrust. To cite an example from a more disinterested sector, agricultural extension—a kindred although earlier development—is beginning to find the terminology of communication quite descriptive of its essential nature.

What makes development communication different are the purpose it serves and the venue of its action. Advertising, public relations, propaganda and even agricultural extension are Western institutions. They took root and matured in the West in answer to the special needs of that society. While viable in other soils, they tend to retain their native assumptions and methodology. But development communication is no transplant. Given our definition, it can only be a Third World phenomenon. So that accept it or not, it is our responsibility to explore its dimensions, cultivate it and, above all, use it. Communication scientists and practitioners from developed countries can help us with the first two endeavors, but in the final analysis, only we can have the gut determination to make development communication work.

The purpose of development communication is to advance development. Development requires that a mass of people with a low rate of literacy and income, and the socio-economic attributes that go with it, first of all be informed about and motivated to accept and use a sizeable body of hitherto unfamiliar ideas and skills in very much less time than that process would normally take. This then is the job of development communication: to inform and motivate at the national, sectoral and project levels. Stated in these terms, the job of development communication is the process of development itself.

The breakthroughs in the social sciences are not material objects that can be seen or grasped. They are chiefly ideas and concepts that are not easy to appreciate until translated into action. Development communication is one of them. Like other breakthroughs, it is an innovation that must be made known and accepted before it can come into use, in this case as a carrier of other breakthroughs. Unlike other breakthroughs, it is most useable not by the end audience of development but by administrators, policymakers and professionals who, however, can be just as resistant to change and as traditional in their ways of thought. It follows that the first job of the development communicator is to win over this group.

Motivation is a key element in development communication. Experience has shown that the success of communication programs depends no less on the amount of information disseminated as on motivating people to want to act on the information. This is particularly true of the unsophisticated audience served by development communication. Indeed, in its concern for motivation, development communication recognizes basic linkages with education. Like education, it starts with objectives and lays great store on methods.

To explain development communication a bit more, let us first establish what it is not. It is not publicity per se, or getting the maximum media exposure for something or someone for the sake of image-building. The development communicator may use the same media as the publicist does, but his aim is to

1927
1960
1963
1964
1967
1969
1970
1971
1972
1973
1974
1975
1976
1977
1978
1979
1980
1981
1982
1983
1984
1985
1986
1987
1988
1989
1990
1991
1992
1993
1994
1995
1996
1997
1998
1999
2000
2001
2002
2003
2004
2005
2006

stimulate public awareness and understanding of planned change, and of the agency that is promoting it, so as to create a climate of acceptance under which that agency can do its appointed work.

It is not mass communication alone. It will use any and all communication channels that will achieve its goals. The channel may be an entire extension service serving a population sector, the low-keyed and casual conversation within a family, a demonstration plot, a course curriculum, a stage play. Many times the mediated channels only repeat or reinforce the spoken word.

It is more than a slide set, a leaflet or a seminar. It is basically an approach or a point of view that sizes up a problem in the light of people to be reached and of overcoming or side-stepping the barriers in the way of reaching them.

It is audience-oriented, its main target being rural and farm folks whose characteristics point to an affinity with oral and pictorial communication.

It is not non-purposive chronicling of facts. It is communicating with the intent of promoting development in all aspects and at all levels.

In the Philippines, it was probably first applied in agriculture, chiefly at Los Baños. It is off to a fresh start on the problems of forest conservation, of population and, lately, of environmental pollution. Other themes of development await its ministration.

Like advertising, it seeks to influence and persuade. Indeed, in its use of audience studies and the science of human behavior, its reliance on planned campaigns, and its attention to proper budgeting, advertising is way ahead of development communication and can teach it a thing or two. Development communication, on the other hand, does not advocate only one course of action. It presents several alternatives and points the way to a decision based on rational thinking. It considers the socio-economic environment in relation to an innovation and will help alter the environment if the technology so demands.

Let us look at some of the ways that development communication can be made to work at the national, sectoral and project levels.

It is an axiom of development that government is the chief designer and administrator of the master plan. But only you and I and the rest of the people can execute the nuts and bolts of nation-building. Assuming our democratic political framework, persuasive communication then becomes terribly important. Government must convince all of us that the task is worth making sacrifices for, and one way of doing this is by keeping before our eyes the goals, mechanics and progress of development.

Development planners who contemplate the awesome task of lifting a nation by its bootstraps may muse on the merits of a more authoritarian form of government that can cut through indifference, sloth and indecision. They merely indulge in wishful thinking, however, for our history and accumulated values have already set our political course for us. There is no other recourse for a democratic government that sincerely wants development except to inform and motivate the citizenry, and thereby mobilize the popular commitment that it must have.

Assuming, too, the free-enterprise nature of our communication system, government has no other recourse except to co-opt privately owned media to carry the bulk of its development message to all corners of the nation. Here lies the ostensible reason for the tug-of-war between government and our professional communicators. The more analytical of the latter have begun to block out the terms under which a rapprochement is possible. Mochtar Lubis poses two: a government committed to both economic and democratic development, and a press also committed to economic and democratic development (1971).

Leaving out the credibility and sincerity of government for the present, all of us—the press included—must take a hard look at our hierarchy of values in the light of our circumstances. Media owners and practitioners must make up their minds soon whether or not to loosen their ties from what are essentially Western concepts of the press and work out modifications that reflect our struggles and answer our exigencies. It will not be an easy nor painless process, but change never is. The context in which our communication system operates is simply not the highly individualistic, Liberal milieu that produced such concepts as "freedom of the press" or "laissez-faire economics." To cleave to the original tenets of Liberalism is in truth an inconsistent posture for an institution that has exposed vestiges of colonialism in other institutions of our society.

Until our professional communicators put behind them their version of the Establishment and carve out a more innovative role for our communication system, our media will remain irrelevant and sway its audience to remain irrelevant. Our newspapers, for one thing, will continue to have compartmentalized inside pages on advances in the world of agriculture, business, science and progress while reserving the front pages for the foot-in-mouth clichés of politicians or the latest shootout in Makati.

I shall not dwell overlong on communication within the agricultural sector beyond mentioning the inadequacy of its communication infrastructure. Communication within our agricultural system, the most populous sector in the society, is fragmented, slow, and often unreliable. Few channels for interaction exist that link the components within the system, and these do not work at high efficiency. A continuous flow of accurate two-way information as a basis for decision-making loses its currency under these circumstances.

At the project level is where development communication must come to grips with live people over specific issues. To paraphrase President Harry Truman, the project level is where the buck ends. Let me give you an illustration of how the communication approach was used to analyze one agricultural project (1971). The case in point is the government project on grain processing whose training phase is based at the Department of Agricultural Engineering.

The rationale for the project was the need to modernize the grain processing system of the country which the rice yields of 1968, the year when the Philippines experienced a brief rice bonanza, had proved highly outmoded and inadequate. The tons of grain coming in from the fields were held up in the threshing, drying, storage and milling stages so that rice distribution was uneven and prices beneficial neither to the producer nor to the consumer.

Government policymakers ruled that integrated grain processing plants would have to be set up if the country was to get the full benefits of the high-yielding grain varieties. A World Bank loan for $14.3 million was arranged to sub-finance private entrepreneurs in the grain installation business. And since grain centrals need competent technicians to run them, a training program was deemed necessary insurance for the loan. Almost as an afterthought, the idea of regional demonstration centers was appended to the plan of operations, which made it logical to train extension technicians too. The project was labeled Training of Technicians for Grain Industries and turned over to UP at Los Baños for implementation.

On closer scrutiny, the project was not as simplistic as the title suggested. Using the communication approach to put the project in focus revealed other ramifications that would be needed to link the training and demonstration phases and to achieve the large goals assigned to the project, which are to improve the quality of processed grain in the Philippines and to cut down on economic and physical losses due to improper processing.

Once these objectives are accepted as valid, the project takes on new dimensions. It will have to do something about three main groups of people: the farmers—the big and small producers of the grain whose harvest will start the processing chain; the processors—the owners and operators of already existing and proposed grain centrals, as well as the owners and operators of the traditional kiskisan and cono mills; the consumers, whose claims to quantity, quality and reasonable price should be reflected in the growth of the grain industries.

1927
1960
1963
1964
1967
1969
1970
1971
1972
1973
1974
1975
1976
1977
1978
1979
1980
1981
1982
1983
1984
1985
1986
1987
1988
1989
1990
1991
1992
1993
1994
1995
1996
1997
1998
1999
2000
2001
2002
2003
2004
2005
2006

Surrounding and intermingling with these core groups are subsidiary groups who also need to be informed and motivated because some time during the life of the project and afterwards, they are going to make decisions that will affect the course of grain processing in the country. Some of them are:

1. Bank appraisers who will assess loan applications for the new centrals and for other processing loans.
2. Legislators who will draw up bills on quality control and other subjects that touch on grain processing.
3. Professional communicators who can help create public awareness of the value of good processing.
4. Present and future donors of the project.
5. People in some way related to the project, such as its steering committee, its resource persons, the staff of the UP at Los Baños.
6. Landlords.
7. Farmers' families.
8. In-school youth who will be grain producers and processors before long.
9. Barrio influentials and opinion leaders.
10. Processing machinery designers and manufacturers.

In other words, a lot more people than the technicians for whom the project was originally conceived.

With the project objectives always as the referral point, identifying the target audiences is the first step in a communication analysis of the project. Such an analysis can best be outlined by this question adapted from Childers and Vajrathon (1969): 'To what groups of people; where; with what existing state of awareness of improved grain processing; what indigenous leadership/communication structures; what available material resources plus planned project inputs; and what existing socio-economic practices; must what new ideas, attitudes, and specific techniques on improved grain processing be conveyed; when in relation to the project's target phases; by whom and using what media?

Studying the personal, social and economic characteristics of the audiences in their environments is plainly the second step in the analysis. Identifying the set of messages

for each group is the third step. Only with ample understanding of the audience groups and of the technology of improved grain processing can suitable strategies be devised that are likely to convince people to adopt, or make it easy for others to adopt, the recommendations of the project. We are now ready to plan what to say to whom and by whom; how to say it and when.

It further becomes evident from our analysis that the two principal methods of extending information—the training program and the regional demonstration centers—must be supplemented by others that will cater to originally unplanned-for audiences. The most obvious one is diversified communication through the mass media channels.

The analysis also suggests certain strategies. The grain processing technology is a whole complex of practices that is not expected to take quickly in the barrios for a number of reasons:

1. It requires a shift to mechanization to a lesser or greater degree.
2. The cost of processing equipment is relatively high.
3. The recommended practices come up against institutionalized work habits and patterns. In Laguna, for example, the practice is for the farmer to contract a group of workers to weed, harvest, and thresh his crop in return for a share of the harvest in kind. If he uses a mechanical thresher, he will have no one to weed or harvest his field.
4. At the barrio level the problem is still the old one of increasing production. The national concept of second-generation problems loses some of its validity in the face of this local fact.
5. Introducing machines at this time will displace people who have no alternate sources of income.

These conditions confirm the soundness of the proposed strategy to use farmers' associations as a key communication channel for the grain processing technology. Another strategy suggested by the analysis is not propagating the processing technology all at once in its entirety or in its chronological sequence in the barrios.

1927
1960
1963
1964
1967
1969
1970
1971
1972
1973
1974

The best move appears to be to identify the processing aspect most needed in an area and to begin from there. The other aspects can be emphasized as the barrio people themselves begin to see the need for them in relation to the first aspect, begin to be dissatisfied with the old methods, and as the situational factors change.

Mechanized threshing, for example, is not considered a necessity in Laguna because present practices suffice for the existing socio-economic environment. But the Laguna farmers readily appreciate the need for more efficient drying methods in the wet season. The drying technology could then be the foot in the door, so to speak, for the whole body of recommended processing techniques.

In summary, development communication in the grain processing project means the communication strategies and materials that will be needed to support its objectives. More than this, it means the idea of planning the materials and strategies in advance for certain well-thought-out purposes, for specified groups of people, at certain time phases. It includes the motivational research that will be called for and the evaluation of effectiveness of the communication materials and strategies. Most of all, it is viewing the project as a multi-level communication campaign that will teach people new skills about grain processing, create receptive attitudes to the processing innovations, and spread knowledge on all aspects of processing throughout the country. With the communication approach, we translate the objectives of the project in terms of people who are, after all, the real target of development.

One other thing needs to be said. If our analysis is not to remain an academic exercise, the communication dimension added to the project must be given proper staffing and financing. With the present leadership of the project, prospects are bright that this will indeed come to pass.

Quebral, Nora Cruz. "Development Communication in the Agricultural Context." Paper presented at the symposium on the theme 'In Search of Breakthroughs in Agricultural Development' held in honor of Dr. Dioscoro L. Umali, December 9–10, 1971, College, Laguna; published as 'Development Communication', in Solidarity, 7(6), 1972, pp. 39–44 and reprinted as "What Do We Mean by 'Development Communication,'" International Development Review, 15(2), 1973/1972, pp. 25–28. This paper was updated by the author in 2005. Reprinted with permission of the author.

EXCERPT FROM:

TRADITIONAL URBAN MEDIA MODEL: STOCKTAKING FOR AFRICAN DEVELOPMENT

Role of Traditional Communication

By Frank Okwu Ugboajah

1972 In the traditional societies of Africa, communication uses more informal than formal mechanisms. The Amhara of Ethiopia is a rumour monger, the Tiv of Nigeria an orator, the Yoruba of Nigeria a poet who is noted for his artistry of greeting known personalities with appropriate songs, in distinctive quality of tone produced by mere voice.

To Africans, dancing is a means of informal communication; hence he dances "for joy, for grief, for love, for hate, for prosperity, for religion, for pastime." Singing accompanies his normal work activity, improving team work and promoting coordination in manual communal work. Music, as Hailey points out, infuses all the activities of the African from the cradle to the grave.

Written scripts had existed in Africa before the Europeans arrived. The Vai and the Mum of West Africa communicated formerly among themselves by written script, while the Bantus communicated through symbols and cult scripts.

Permanent records were also kept in the people's memories or on mnemonic or mechanical devices. Doob notes that he has learnt to trust men "in the bust" more than most metropolitan tabloids in the United States.

The drum in traditional Africa operates as an unmuffled extending medium and communicates either by "signature" or by "talking." African languages are tonal, so the drums are technically built to reproduce tonal patterns of sentences through pitch, timber and volume.

1975
1976
1977
1978
1979
1980
1981
1982
1983
1984
1985
1986
1987
1988
1989
1990
1991
1992
1993
1994
1995
1996
1997
1998
1999
2000
2001
2002
2003
2004
2005
2006

The Mbutu of the Congo imitate songs of birds or cries of beasts simply by blowing upon a pipe. This conveys a message to hunters in the chase. A special form of "tonography" can be coded by shouting experts to send messages to hilly villages. Such messages are decoded and onwardly similarly retransmitted to other neighbouring villages.

The linguist plays a prominent role in information interpretation and dissemination. He acts as a messenger among the Amhara of Ethiopia and is taught secret musical notes in order to establish the authenticity of written notes. Among the Mossi of Mali, he acts as an intermediary between audience and oracle and in courtship and marriage.

Scars and taboos identify cult and ethnic belonging of the wearer and also give social prestige. Ornaments, charms and insignia serve both aesthetic and communicative functions, providing, in some cases, information about the wearer's status. The Mende who wears a leopard's tooth is from a royal family.

Masks camouflage the wearer and portray a different being. The Igbo of Nigeria believe the dead communicated with the living through masks. Masks are spirits of benign ancestors to the Dan of Ivory Coast. Masks generally symbolize important ceremonies, such as funerals, new yam festivals, installation of a chief and cult ceremonies.

Market-goers in Africa are essentially communicators who receive and disseminate information from market centres. Apart from being a centre for buying, selling and/or bartering commercial items, market centres serve the social function of a place for meeting friends and participating in market-day festivities. Important communication between families and distant friends and relatives is likely to take place on a market day, at the dinner table or in the drinking party which follows afterward.

Communication plays an important role in the cohesiveness among Africa's traditional peoples. Stability among the Igbo of Nigeria is evident in the system of their tribal government, which fosters considerable informal communication through a group system of village social structure, title and secret societies, exogamous marriage structure and cult oracles.

For Africans in traditional society, law cannot be differentiated from custom. The rule of law is therefore guided by sanctions made up from "a body of (informally and formally communicative) rules regulating rights and imposing correlative duties." Social disapproval means a withdrawal of communication or using communication to punish.

The most important thing about Africa's traditional communication is that the audience has learned to attach great significance to it. Traditional media have force and credibility. They put stability into Africa's indigenous institutions.

Colonial Africa and Communication

With this traditional backdrop, it is appropriate here to share insights into colonial Africa and investigate the part communication played or failed to play.

Both the cultural and commercial glory of Africa and her communication systems were struck a deadening blow in the 16th century, when the Portuguese intruded into the continent. They and other European powers that followed succeeded in "cutting off the flow of commerce and struck heavily on the economic life of a large portion of Africa."

The slave trade that resulted drained both human and economic resources of Africa. An alien culture was superimposed, and by the 19th century, the cultural and communication breakdown was of an unprecedented nature.

The earlier commercial barons who first came into contact with Africa may not have contemplated colonization, but foreign consuls in African posts had entertained ambitions of higher status and administrative glory. The British consul in Fernando Po, for example, persuaded the British government in 1861 to forgo anti-colonial policy and permit him to occupy

Lagos, Nigeria. That same year, Lagos was declared a British colony, its king subjugated and a governor appointed to impose British rule on African peoples and institutions.

The European had little understanding of the African's simple way of life and the generation of experience that backed it up. This hindered sympathetic understanding of African practices and social organization.

Colonialism was confused for commerce by the ignorant African who attempted to change some part of his traditional way of life. This change further encouraged European misjudgement and a tendency to judge African mores by their "worst" features.

Agriculture, which is a total life pattern of the African, which according to Shalaby "is a highly integrated way of life…involving emotional expression, family ties, religious sentiments, social intercourse and established habits of behaviour," received little European empathy and was positioned against deep-rooted attitudes.

Colonial powers imposed inflexible monoculture on various African nations to meet home-government needs. For example, Ashanti farmers cultivated cocoa to meet British beverage and confectionary needs; Nigeria met the rubber needs of her war factories; Kenya's maize met the breeding of white settlers; Tanzania's cotton paid off British losses in India.

Counterproductive Education System
Colonial education was geared toward meeting the narrow needs for clerks and semi-skilled assistants. The school system was planned against the creation of modern agriculture needed for resolving primary economic problems. Colonial schools emphasized rote memorization and literacy on the humanities and classics which were foreign to African culture. Technical education was ignored and teaching the social and natural sciences was delayed until very late.

Brewster found in a study that colonial educational planning gave little priority to mass communication,

engineering and agriculture. Of the 7,894 students enrolled in the universities in tropical Africa, he found that between 1958 and 1959, 4 percent were taking courses in agriculture, 7 percent in engineering, 20 percent in the humanities, 20 percent in the natural sciences, 14 percent in the social sciences, 12 percent in law, 11 percent in education, 8 percent in medicine and 4 percent in fine arts.

The Christian missionary who accompanied the territorial and economic-minded European did not attempt to redefine his "win converts" goal, even when feedback revealed this goal inefficient. The missionary adhered rigidly to Western forms within the Church. "We expect our converts," declared one missionary, "to conform to our mode of life, to adopt our form of ritual and to take over our architecture, our music and even perhaps our language."

Doob notes that the missionary entrenched unchanged music and words which communicated little to African audience. He forgot that African music is devoid of metrical forms of Western music, that Western melodies ignore the imitation of the rhythm of speech and of the intonation of words, that African music required drums instead of organ or piano, that Africans prefer dancing to nodding of the head.

The African deity Oluadah Equiano,[1] an Igbo slave boy-turned-minister, described as "governor of all events, especially our deaths or captivity," was dismissed by the missionary as non-Christian and therefore a dispensable belief. Thus, Christianity operated as an adjunct to colonial imperialism and showed little mercy to existing African religious and cultural institutions.

---

1 Oluadah Equiano was kidnapped as a little boy from his village in Igboland, the East Central State of Nigeria, in the 18th century and sold as slave to Virginia in the USA. He was later resold to Britain, where he grew up, worked hard and rebought his liberty. Equiano became a minister of religion and married an English girl. He gave his whole life to work and preaching against slave trade. In his memoirs, he gave the first account outside Africa about life in Igboland. He reminisced that 'the Ibo believes in one Creator of all things, who lives in the Sun and is girded round with a belt, never drinks but smokes a pipe'. Op. cit, Hatch, p. 86.

1927
1960
1963
1964
1967
1969
1970
1971
1972
1973
1974
1975
1976
1977
1978
1979
1980
1981
1982
1983
1984
1985
1986
1987
1988
1989
1990
1991
1992
1993
1994
1995
1996
1997
1998
1999
2000
2001
2002
2003
2004
2005
2006

Works Cited

Allot, A. N. 'Customary Law of the Akan People,' *African Studies*, Vol. 12, No. 1 p. 26-30. March 1953.

Beier, H. U. 'Yoruba Vocal Music,' *Africa Music,* Vol. 1, pp. 23–28. 1956.

Doob, Leonard. Communication in Africa, A Search for Boundaries, p. 6. Yale University Press, 1961.

Hailey, Lord. *An African Survey: A Study of Problems Arising in Africa South of the Sahara*, p. 67. London: Oxford University Press, 1957.

Hatch, John. Nigeria: *The Seeds of Disaster*, p. 142. Henry Regnery Company, 1970.

Liebenow, Gus J. *Agriculture, Education and Rural Transformation*, p. 16. 1969.

Shalaby, Mohamed M. *Rural Reconstruction in Egypt*, p. 7.

Smith, Brewster. 'Foreign vs. Indigenous Education' in Don C. Piper and Taylor Cole (editors), *Post-Primary Education and Political and Economic Development*, p. 57.

Ugboajah, Frank Okwu. Traditional-Urban Media Model: Stocktaking for African Development, SAGE, *Gazette*. Vol. VIII, No. 2. 1972.

PARTICIPATION
AND COMMUNICATION
Excerpt from: Comunicación Horizontal

By Frank Gerace, in Collaboration with Hernando Lázaro

1973 Participation is currently a topic of much discussion, with politicians holding out promises of greater participation in the conduct of governmental affairs. While the concept of participation is fundamental to the idea of democracy, it is clear that, in the modern world, grassroots participation is not a major component of human activity.

It is precisely people's increasing awareness of being excluded from decisions vital to their well-being that has given the word and the concept new vigor. Despite renewed interest in the idea, however, participation remains largely a slogan. While there is hardly a government without its proposals for increased citizen participation, actual practice of the principle is rare.

This gap between proclamation and practice is attributable to a number of factors. It is interesting to note the disparate reasons cited by those at the top and those at the bottom of the societal spectrum, with the former accusing the populace at large of apathy, and the latter blaming their plight on the authoritarianism of politicians. Some politicians even make the claim that efforts to hasten greater popular participation would interfere with their ability to successfully address the urgent tasks at hand.

Thus, the question is which should take precedence: the achievement of specific goals or a deepening of the process involved in achieving these goals. In short, the issue is one of priorities.

In any enterprise, whether it be a government or a corporation, certain people place more importance on performing tasks, while others emphasize the process and experience involved in seeking the goal. It is the goal-oriented mindset that gives rise to impatience in the face of ineptitude or apathy—real or imagined. Such a mentality, rather than risking delays or changes in achieving goals, is content to sacrifice the participation of the masses.

The Priority of Process

What is posited here is that a mentality that values process is best suited to promoting community participation [participation in common projects.] Later in this work, when a model for participatory communication is proposed, the objections—including the issue of urgency—will be addressed.

For the moment, let it be clear that the authors, having posed the problem of participation in terms of meta-process, come down squarely on the side of process as the most deserving of priority treatment. There are two reasons for this.

First is the need to counter a perennial tendency among those who hold power, namely, that of being paternalistic or, worse, authoritarian. Greater attention to community participation and decision-making provides a check on abuse. (The inevitably positive contribution of those at the bottom of society will be addressed below.)

Second is the need to combat a tendency on the part of the populace at large to "fear freedom." Without introducing people gradually to the concept of responsibility, the clamor for more participation is doomed to remain mere rhetoric, since humankind is inclined to follow the path of least resistance.

For people to participate, they must become conscious of their own dignity. This in turn means that they must express themselves and be given the opportunity to have their say, based on the individual reality that infuses each person's life.

The Experience of the People

Often, the routine or challenges of life, in combination with factors such as education, propaganda and conditioning, make reflection on that life impossible.

No human being can endure being bombarded by experiences without being affected by them. The experiences that shape people's realities are economic, social, religious and political. Any program, whether governmental or voluntary, aiming to touch the lives of people—be it in important or in modest ways—must wrestle with the raw material of people's lives and experience, not merely with figures and statistics. For such programs to be successful, the people themselves must participate in the research, planning and execution.

Who, however, listens to the people? Are their voices heard when surveys are conducted and meetings are held? No matter how capable and honest a survey's subjects, their sociocultural condition exert an inescapable influence and shapes the ultimate results.[1]

Is the populace at large heard through its "appointed spokespersons" or leaders? And who appoints these individuals to speak for the people?

To continue with the main conceptual thread: How can the people participate in shaping the decisions that affect them? As has been pointed out, in order for people to participate, they must overcome the fear of freedom, gain awareness of the value of their experience and have the freedom to express themselves. This leads us to suggest that the problem of participation is one of communication.

Admittedly, merely stating this bypasses numerous steps in the argument. There are multiple ways of achieving the consciousness required in order for this process to advance. Sometimes this occurs suddenly. Other times it is achieved through discussion groups. Conscientization always, however, implies critical thinking achieved through a dialogic situation.

---

1   Participatory surveys attempt to overcome this difficulty by maximizing the participation of the subjects as they reveal and diagnose their own problems, and by reducing the role of technicians to a minimum. In this research model, it is not the sociologist who conducts the research, but the people, who are themselves living the reality being studied.

1927
1960
1963
1964
1967
1969
1970
1971
1972
1973
1974
1975
1976
1977
1978
1979
1980
1981
1982
1983
1984
1985
1986
1987
1988
1989
1990
1991
1992
1993
1994
1995
1996
1997
1998
1999
2000
2001
2002
2003
2004
2005
2006

Communication

What is of interest here is the role of communication and of the communications media in the very process of communication. While communication clearly includes far more than the so-called communications media, there are a number of reasons for focusing on the media as the frame of reference in examining popular participation.

First, the authors' professional experience lies in the areas of radio, television and film. If the media are to somehow serve the people, this will be accomplished only through the willingness of people to break away from professional hermeticism and share knowledge of the instruments of communication—instruments as important in today's world as were the pen and the book in an earlier time.

Another reason for studying the relation between participation and the media is the conviction that the communications industry today is fraught with abuse. The suggestion offered here—that modern media, in the form of dialogue, be employed in seeking horizontal communication alternatives—is based on the observation that the commercial industry and, to a great extent, vertical activities of the State (imitating the modus operandi of commercial production) are almost irremediably distorted.

Considering the relationships between different communications media, centers of banking, and commercial and agribusiness power in Latin America, it is clear that, based on the interests already invested in disseminating certain points of view through media, the people at large will find little room for free expression.

Even in the few circumstances in which oligarchic domination has been limited (e.g., in some cooperative newspapers and broadcast operations; in countries where the State has assumed majority positions in the management of TV stations, etc.), many of the same mechanisms are still at work.

One reason for this is the mindset of the journalists and artists who continue to shape their information to reach conclusions at odds with the interests of the people.

Another reason is the atmosphere created by commercial advertising, which unfailingly sets forth, as ideals, the bourgeois values of the consumer society. Given the bombardment by alienating stimuli from middle-class comedies, humor, situations, values and products, any measures that seize profits from the hands of the entrenched rulers of the culture industry are doomed to insignificance.

The business profits reaped from people's eagerness to consume products so skillfully inculcated in their consciousness more than counterbalances the modest advertising losses incurred as a result of new and stricter laws. Thus, far from ceasing to mine the wealth of the communications media, business continues to place its bourgeois stamp on every product that passes through its doors.

Vertical Communication

A final reason for examining participation in the communication process is the dangers inherent in the improper use of the mass media by private institutions and government.

The danger of the media in the quest for liberation and conscientization of the people lies not only in the potential for anti-national ideologies, alienating values, and control by big business, but also in the massification of the public, and in vertical propaganda that is antipathetic to dialogue—a type of propaganda that inevitably holds allure for those who, with the best of intentions, use the media to reach the people. This, then, is the crux of the problem, the point of convergence for the different conceptual strands presented above: Should the goals-based or the process-based approach prevail?

Centralized programming designed to encourage participation and conscientization is an alarming prospect when shaped by ideologues, produced by professionals, and transmitted by technicians.

must be respected, and that opportunity must be provided for their voices to be heard. The imposition of slogans and programs will have some value as topics for reflection, but thinking is internalized only by active subjects, never by passive receivers. The problem is one of methodology—i.e., how to turn the receiver into an active participant.

Some examples of participatory production may be of interest here. Among many possible examples is the use of comics, radio and video.

If, for example, the goal is to prepare a message using the popular form of comics, the target group can be incorporated in every level of the production process. This requires that the project's ideological leaders work jointly with the people's representatives to choose the subjects on which to focus, while at the same time enlisting the cooperative effort of the artists and the group in preparing sketches. It should be noted that in projects where participation is the primary goal, there is no such thing as a definitively "finished" work.

The entire goal-oriented mindset—as exemplified in publication of a comic dealing with land reform—must change. What is needed is the unfolding of a process, not the achievement of a goal. The production team must engage in dialogue sessions, using materials adapted to the people's linguistic and cultural realities.

Another way of encouraging active participation in any regional development process is through satellite centers for dialogue, coordinated by a central entity. Each satellite group (union, neighborhood council, indigenous community, etc.) would have a cassette recorder. Each group of people would record material on its concerns. The recorded cassettes would pass from group to group, creating closer links of solidarity between them, while encouraging each group to critique the views of the others. Periodically, representatives of the different groups would meet at a central facility to synthesize, collate and critique the views of each satellite group.

Infinite variations of this model are possible. It is not necessary to limit the groups' contributions to social commentary. There may be a mutual sharing of artistic expression, for example. Moreover, a statement from the informal chain of horizontal communications can, from time to time, be transmitted by the mass media, though this is not the principal purpose of the process.

The decentralized recording process can be organized with minimal training, with relatively little work required to enlist people's participation. In this scenario, rather than being sold another project, people are being offered tools for improving communication. Existing human links are used, without the need for bosses or bureaucracies.

This model, of different groups creating materials in coordination with a cooperative center, is not limited to the sound recording format. Indeed, using the same principles, projects employing videotape can be even more successful, though the equipment and materials are more expensive. One interesting use of videotape is in popular participation projects designed to resolve operational or ideological conflicts. Mediation via videotape is already a well-developed approach. Where tension exists between two groups, one group records interviews expressing its point of view, its grievances, etc., and the tape is then played for the other group, which in turn records its reactions, and so forth. Commonly, a dynamic emerges in which each group gains a deeper understanding of the other's perspective than would be likely to occur in the heat of personal encounters and confrontations. Moreover, the unforgiving light of the recorded medium, in which each group views itself, can foster self-criticism.

While these brief examples of horizontal communication relate to local organizations and processes, they can also be adapted to national programs. In the description above, for instance, the brain that gathers stimuli from the ganglia—i.e., the cooperative coordination center that organizes and synthesizes the work of the satellite groups—can be a national entity providing materials and advice for the informational,

1927
1960
1963
1964
1967
1969
1970
1971
1972
1973
1974
1975
1976
1977
1978
1979
1980
1981
1982
1983
1984
1985
1986
1987
1988
1989
1990
1991
1992
1993
1994
1995
1996
1997
1998
1999
2000
2001
2002
2003
2004
2005
2006

political and artistic content from different regional and local centers. This model is suitable for any national dissemination plan. The role of the national entity, rather than being one of creating content, is to coordinate contributions from the people.

Whether at a local or central level—using theater, puppets, radio, TV, etc.—any attempt to encourage popular participation using the communications media must be governed by a vision encompassing participation throughout all phases of the process.

Objections

Despite its benefits, objections to horizontal communication schemes always arise. The most common are the following:

1. The people are ignorant and have nothing to contribute: what they need is to be taught.
2. Even if people did have something to say, they would be unable to navigate the technology of the communications media.
3. While there is value in having people express themselves, and though they have the ability to handle simplified technology, one cannot risk potential infiltration by negative elements, e.g., political agitators monopolizing, for their own ends, use of the public's channel of expression).
4. While there is value in having people express themselves, and though they have the ability to handle simplified technology, and though the democratic risks of free expression are acceptable, society cannot afford the luxury of participatory communication, given the urgency of education, development, etc.

All of these objections demonstrate a lack of faith in the people, and reflect a strongly goal-oriented, as opposed to process-oriented, mentality. Moreover, all four objections are inconsistent with the declared intention to encourage participation.

The first two show the vestiges of a culture of classism, which will never bring itself to encourage the true

1973

FIVE STRATEGIES TO USE
Excerpt from: 'Radio's Role in Development'
By Emile McAnany

A final conclusion from all the evidence is that these projects lack both planning and careful administrative follow-through. Too little attention seems to be paid to the determination and definition of goals and too much to simply getting a project operational; too little to an evaluation of results and an ability to change or even cease operation and too much to the virtue of sheer self-preservation. A lack of coordination between radio projects and other development efforts in rural areas is endemic to most of the cases reviewed. Better planning and more attention given to management would be of great benefit.

Radio has been widely used by developing nations for a variety of tasks, although this application of radio has been sporadic and poorly planned and the medium's potential poorly exploited. Nevertheless, radio is the most promising mass medium for rural development in the next decade if only because it alone reaches the rural audience. Despite suggestive ideas about television's role in rural areas (Bourret 1971) and increasing use of video tape recorders for community development (Gwyn 1972), the cost-effectiveness of radio is still more promising in comparison.

What role should radio play in the next ten years and how might this role be fostered by those interested in education and social change in the rural areas? The following recommendations are tentative outcroppings of this review:

1. Better efforts to get costs of the different radio strategies should he undertaken. This should be in two phases: first, some costs of ongoing projects should be gathered to examine empirically what different projects spend their money on; second, costs should be kept on projects just beginning. Out of this should grow some consideration

of where expenditures should be made, what percentages of budgets should be allocated to various parts of a radio project according to the different strategies.

2. The promotion of new projects should place an emphasis on careful planning and clear definition of objectives. An understanding of what development problem is being attacked and the assumptions which underlie the approach taken must he developed. In the more community oriented strategies of rural forums, radio schools and animation, this demands coordination with existing rural agencies to tie development activities into a common effort. In instructional radio, careful planning of curriculum is an essential but neglected aspect of most projects in the past. A small amount of effort in this area would increase effectiveness of this strategy greatly.

3. New radio projects should be tied into a multiple media approach, especially with simply printed materials (much in the way Acción Cultural Popular (ACPO) [Popular Cultural Action] ACPO has been promoted in Colombia), so that appropriate reading matter is provided for new literates. This material should be practical to the needs of rural life regarding family, agriculture and health.

4. New radio projects in all of the strategics, except for open broadcasting, should allocate a significant amount of time, money and effort to the training of monitors and field supervisors since these are often the key elements in both learning and social change. It is clear that radio projects will cost more, the more field support they provide, yet a great deal of evidence points to the critical role the monitor, group leader or animator plays in rural development.

5. New radio projects should attempt to evoke as much local participation as possible. A mechanism for allowing feedback should be planned for each project. Moreover, radio should allow the group leader to localize the message and elicit response from the audience.

6. New radio projects might be chosen for those areas in a country that have shown signs of increased awareness. This recommendation recognizes the role of radio as accelerating social change and development rather than beginning the process. Too frequently in the past we have experimented with technique and forgotten the crucial social context into which the technique must fit. If there is general apathy and nothing is done by governments to develop rural areas, radio, however well planned and financed, cannot change this situation.

7. More research is needed in radio strategies. This research might take two broad lines: careful evaluation of a few small projects that are already operating to estimate costs and effectiveness; and evaluations of several pilot projects in the three strategies, an open broadcast case, an instructional radio case, and perhaps a case combining the best features of rural forums, radio schools and animation.

8. Training of technical production people should emphasize basic skills and a simplicity of method so that rural people themselves can become involved.

9. New radio projects should examine the possibilities of coordinating the political necessity for more locally controlled projects with the economic necessity for larger-scale uses of technology.

References

Bourret, P. 1971. Television in rural areas: a low cost alternative. Menlo Park, Calif.: International Educational Development (mimeo).

Gwyn, S. "Cinema as Catalyst: Film, Video Tape and Social Change", a report on a seminar. Memorial Univ. of Newfoundland (St. Johns, Newfoundland), March, 1972.

McAnany, Emile G. 1973. "Radio's Role in Development: Five Strategies of Use." Information Bulletin Number Four, Information Centre on Instructional Technology, Academy for Educational Development (AED), Washington D.C. Reprinted with permission of the author and the publisher.

1927
1960
1963
1964
1967
1969
1970
1971
1972
1973
1974
1975
1976
1977
1978
1979
1980
1981
1982
1983
1984
1985
1986
1987
1988
1989
1990
1991
1992
1993
1994
1995
1996
1997
1998
1999
2000
2001
2002
2003
2004
2005
2006

ascent of the masses. The second two objections reveal an inclination to mystify technology, but a latent developmentism [paternalism] that will never be capable of exploiting the rich human resources of people prepared to take in new horizons.

Following is a critique of each of the four points:

1. As to the ignorance of the people, it should be emphasized that there can be no development without first enveloping the unique cultural heritage of the people. All liberation pedagogy, as well as anthropological and ethnological research, shows that people know their own culture and that the life of a nation consists of the life of its people. The only way cultural revolution can occur is if it springs from the idiosyncratic values of a human group.

2. The notion that the people are incapable of mastering communications media technology overlooks a central fact: although all development entails modernization, not all modernization constitutes development. The argument set forth here obviates the second objection, since it rejects macro-technology for participatory communication. Admittedly, the technology of vertical mass media excludes the people from the communication process, which is precisely why it is proposed here that more flexible technology is the most appropriate vehicle for horizontal communication.

3. The third objection haunts many who are involved in the urgent work of restructuring society and asks whether the lack of time and the urgency of the task at hand are conducive to dialogue on important issues such as land reform. To this, the only possible response is to note that a people's history, its attitudes, and its habitual ways of doing things—particularly in the case of non-technical people—are the result of historical processes and do not change overnight. The moment of decision for decision-makers bears no relation to the personal history of those affected by the decisions; the effective date of a law does not enter into the chronology of the people. What is real to the people is the materialization of the law, not its promulgation: legislation must go through the same process of assimilation as other elements of popular culture.

Given the space constraints of this brief essay, the interested reader will do well to consult anthropological investigations of popular learning. Popular wisdom counsels that "going slow will take you far." In the history of the Catholic missions of the *altiplano*, [highlands], it is striking that, even after 400 years of catechism, Andean values remain firmly in place.

4. The fourth objection—that the horizontal communication process will be infiltrated by disruptive elements—expresses a very real danger. Obviously, the populace is not an ideological virgin. Suffice it to note that the only way to entirely eliminate negative activity is through repression.

The more participatory the communication, the greater is the chance that people will be called upon to distinguish propaganda contrary to their true interests. One essential element of the communication models proposed here is the element of continual review by the people themselves. The purpose of the process is not so much to communicate with other groups, but rather to maximize internal communication. In many cases, partisan perspectives, emanating from a context alien to the real situation of the people, will be refuted when expressed. Even if people are mystified and deceived, the experience of confronting these contradictory realities does much to develop the vital element of critical judgment.[3]

---

3   The intervention of political interest groups serves the process. On one hand, it is important to avoid naiveté, to be aware of the existence of people working against popular interests, whether consciously or unconsciously. However, where the process has gone astray, this may foster self-criticism. No process is perfect, and some aspects of it may—as it unfolds—prove to be contrary to the interests of the people. Another positive aspect of the intervention of political groups with contrarian interests is that it serves as a control. The opposition, even when there is no intrinsic merit in their claims, will attack the weakest points. Moreover, any mature process must accept plurality.

Meanwhile, other entities, working within the central coordinating entity, whether governmental or voluntary, will continue the work of disseminating orthodox ideas.

In summary, in order to address the objections to participatory communication effectively, the purpose of the activity involved must be clarified. All depends on expectation. One must decide whether to opt for a goals-based or process-based orientation, i.e., whether to choose propaganda or conscientization. In the authors' view, if conscientization or education is the goal, some form of horizontal communication is essential. Despite the hazards posed by potential political motives intrinsic to the process of horizontal communication, the process must be left to operate freely. ...

Balance

The great challenge of our era is to strike a balance between planning and pluralism.

One final objection to the models of communication presented here, and to the concept of test tube situations for addressing conflict, is that they may be overly utopian. This characterization is a valid one: Only utopian visions are free of dogmatism. There is a close relationship between free communication and freedom, between propaganda and oppression. The task of building a new society is, indeed, a utopian one. There are no available models with 100 percent success rates. Nevertheless, the effort to find ways of fostering greater participation in society continues.

Gerace, Frank (1973) *Comunicación Horizontal,* Editorial Universo, Lima, Peru. Reprinted with permission of the author.

A CONSPIRACY OF COURTESY

By Joseph Ascroft

1974 Courtesy requires that honoured guests in African countries not be criticized; the result is a lack of communication between technical assistance personnel and local nationals who can seriously hamper development projects.

I have just completed a special mission to Africa to visit a particular country. My assignment was to look into the need for setting up rural communications training workshops for rural development workers. The unusual nature of my status—a "local boy" turned international consultant—brought an uncommon twist to my findings.

Initially, I used the typical, rather uninspired approach of examining existing training facilities, curricula and programmes, looking for the short-comings and gaps which at least in theory were deserving of workshop attention. This approach did not pay off very well, principally because the many nationals I talked with, including the rank and file of government, had a more compelling story to tell.

Let me illustrate this with a brief episode recounted to me by a high-ranking civil servant commenting about a development project that seemed to be fairly well-esteemed in the country.

Six Food and Agriculture Organisation (FAO) experts showed up with a project already worked out in Rome. They came to create a community of horticulturists to supply the nearby towns. They negotiated with the chief in the area, thinking they were talking to the people. He gave them land and helped them with recruitment by giving them not his first-class farm families but the chronically shiftless hard cases he wanted to get rid of. Additionally, the project was only half-filled

1927
1960
1963
1964
1967
1969
1970
1971
1972
1973
1974
1975
1976
1977
1978
1979
1980
1981
1982
1983
1984
1985
1986
1987
1988
1989
1990
1991
1992
1993
1994
1995
1996
1997
1998
1999
2000
2001
2002
2003
2004
2005
2006

with farmers and these were mostly commuters whose permanent homes were elsewhere because to them this was only a place to work, not to live. But these experts didn't know this. They thought they were succeeding in establishing a permanent residential community here. But if the experts were to leave today, the project and its community would die tomorrow. And what was being said about the project by the local people? "Agricultural economists! What do they know about transplanting people, about community development, about our customs and traditions? Just look, they say this is a permanent community, but there is no cemetery, here!"

This was the point. Indeed there was no cemetery, nor had any been contemplated or even imagined to be necessary. Yet we all know that, in these parts, there can be no permanent home for the living unless there is also a permanent home for the dead. It seems so simple and reasonable a requirement. Yet, incredibly, development projects, so fastidiously detailed in technical planning, fail utterly to have any means of guarding against such fundamental oversights. And still, we consistently overlook the need to tell the experts about their shortcomings.

I say "we" even though I, too, am an FAO expert, albeit only on a short-term assignment in this country. But my own homeland neighbours this country and shares much in common with it, including language. To a large extent, therefore, I know and appreciate many of the local customs and traditions.

And this was the twist. It turned out that my respondents, especially the nationals, were far more eager to talk to me about what goes on in the field than about what goes on in the classroom and about the failures in rural development projects past, present and proposed.

This can be rather traumatic for an academician, but the nationals had a point which could not be denied expression. Sometimes individually, sometimes in groups, the nationals talked vehemently and indignantly about present field practices which precondition project failure. They seemed, without premeditation, to be seizing an opportunity to place on some authoritative record their opinions and suggestions of what ought to be going on in the field to increase the chances of project success. My local-boy-turned-international-consultant status provided them with the opportunity. They used it with a passion. It was so rare an event that no one could recall its precedent. Given my occidental name and my somewhat esoteric area of expertise—communications—no one expected an African to show up.

Silent Treatment

It was thus interesting in the way my unmasking occurred. The interview, especially with nationals, would begin in a formal way. Then several minutes into the interview, I would reveal my nationality and a dramatic change would take place, from deferential formality to confidential familiarity. The viewpoint expressed to me before my identity became known seldom corresponded with what followed. For instance, the individual who made the indignant remarks contained in the episode recounted earlier began by praising the project. It was as though he had two mutually inconsistent viewpoints: one reserved for aliens and the other for allies and, by some circumstantial peculiarity, I was getting both treatments.

To understand what was happening, one must realize that alien technical assistance personnel are treated like honoured house guests in African countries. The local customs dictate that one does not criticize one's house guest to his face, nor does one tell tales to some of one's guests about one's other guests. It is up to the guest himself to know he is violating expectations, when he is exceeding the bounds of good taste, judgement or behaviour. But if the guest is an alien, he may never know, without being told to his face, what these violations and excesses are, or when he is committing any of them. The result is a seemingly unsolvable problem where one party doesn't know and the other daren't tell.

By way of example, there was, at the time of my visit, a major development project being planned. Its aim was to intensify rural development by dividing the country into zones and concentrating government services and investment resources in a few of them at a time, instead of spreading the same resources too thinly and thus ineffectually across the whole country.

The project, suggested by the president of the country met, in principle, with widespread approval. Yet I was unable to find a single national who was happy with the way it was developing. Even its home-grown chairman was privately sceptical and filled with pessimistic foreboding about its chances. For the most part, seasoned rural development workers, grown adept through experience at reading the signs of doom, were forecasting outright failure. Yet despite this, no one was raising a voice in meaningful dissent. The project, apparently, was being allowed to grow and gather momentum unimpeded by any realistic intervention from even those local officials who, in private, protested most strongly that it was heading inexorably toward disaster. The problem, of course, is that the project has been adopted as a *cause celebre* by eager-to-help, well-intentioned international agencies and bilateral aid donors. And financing from them requires a plan of operations which they apparently believe only their own agents are capable of constructing. So part of the aid comes in the form of technical assistance personnel. These technical experts usually take to development projects with missionary zeal, systematising, organising, rationalising and even proselytising with commendable energy and enthusiasm.

Verbal Wizardry

At first, the technical experts' attentions are welcome because they have more time to devote to the project than the local officials who are endlessly plagued by ongoing duties of other kinds. Thus, the experts are allowed to take the project into a sort of protective custody. But it doesn't stop there. The experts quietly annex de facto leadership and control and gradually

the project begins to develop and be directed almost entirely from within the ranks of the experts.

Soon a bulging document of formidable technicality is ready. This is the vaunted plan of operations which proposes a complex framework for undertaking integrated rural development on an intensified scale. It also places the project beyond the intellectual grasp of the majority of the local officials. Out of touch now with developments in the project and unable to match the verbal wizardry of the project's new technocratic leaders, the local originators of the project suddenly find themselves powerless to even infiltrate practical ideas and suggestions into the now official plan.

And this is the depressing part of it all. The locals have many practical ideas and suggestions, especially with regard to project implementation, i.e., field operations. They argue that the technical assistance personnel, while admittedly experts in their substantive areas, frequently turn out to be grossly inexperienced amateurs in the actual on-the-job practice of rural development. Most of them bring with them either only book knowledge or field experience gained in noncomparable situations. Furthermore, many of the experts approach rural development in the spirit of well-meaning pioneers embarking for the first time upon an exploration of an as yet "uncharted" domain. Thus, they ignore the lessons learnt from previous explorations, even those of their most immediate predecessors. The lessons they fail to learn include particularly the dangers of impatience wherein experts with short-term contracts cannot spare the time to plant and nurture an acorn to produce a sturdy oak. Instead, they try to transplant the full-grown tree, spending the rest of their time frantically shoring and propping it up until they leave, after which it collapses for lack of support.

A striking example of this proclivity toward short-term projects concerns an impressive network of radio farm forums assembled by an international expert whose contract terminated the month before I arrived. When I got there, I learnt that, since he left, the network was

1927
1960
1963
1964
1967
1969
1970
1971
1972
1973
1974
1975
1976
1977
1978
1979
1980
1981
1982
1983
1984
1985
1986
1987
1988
1989
1990
1991
1992
1993
1994
1995
1996
1997
1998
1999
2000
2001
2002
2003
2004
2005
2006

already in rapid decline. Half of the forums in some areas had ceased to function. In terms of leadership and control, it had been a one-man show. When that man left, the show folded.

Experts have technical skills and planning know-how which local officials may not have. This is one blade of the scissors. But the same experts seem to lack the practical field experience, the operational know-how, the communicative skills and long-term continuity that the local officials claim to have. And this is the other blade of the scissors.

Many of the locals are indeed veterans of former projects directed by widely varied assemblages of international experts. The locals thus believe themselves to be the experts, not so much in designing and preparing projects but in implementing them. Among the older hands, when they talk about the subject, there is never any shortage of highly plausible and feasible ideas. But the foreign experts seem to regard local offerings as quaint, simplistic inconsequentialities that tend to confound their sophisticated economic formulae and development models. The local is reduced to the status of a bystander observing the patently futile antics of the technical experts, wondering no doubt when his international partner is going to learn the value of a two-bladed scissors. In the meantime, locals suffer their frustration silently, prisoners of their own outdated customs denying themselves, at their own expense, the right to discipline their house guests in a firm, no-nonsense way.

Most of the experienced local officials tend, in the final analysis, to reduce the problem of abortive rural development to difficulties arising from ineffective styles of rural communication. Foreigners, they say, have neither the innate cultural knowledge nor the native vernacular ability to communicate effectively with rural people in Africa.

The Young Teach the Old

Yet, foreign experts do not generally look upon this shortcoming as serious. The reason, say the more seasoned officials, is that foreigners tend to rely heavily on the more youthful, better-trained and-educated nationals, not only because they have more in common with them in terms of level of sophistication and general outlook but also because today's youth are not so dogmatically bound by tradition and, hence, not squeamish about riding roughshod over a few customs to save time when the need arises.

Herein lies the crux of the problem. This reliance upon an increasingly elite youth to serve as extension linkages between project designers and the rural folk themselves accounts, in the eyes of many Africans I have talked with, for the high rate of project failure in Africa. It is a problem peculiar to these times, one which may not have existed in any significant degree a generation ago and one which may no longer obtain a generation hence.

It is only in the past decade or so that much of Africa has become independent. It is in even more recent times that the emphasis has switched increasingly to rural development. Until now, there has been no steady pressure on rural folk to radicalize their styles of farming, nutrition and hygiene. This burden has fallen upon the present owners and farmers of land. Whatever new ways of living they decide to adopt will automatically become the ways by which future generations will have to abide. The problem, however, is that the person who needs to be convinced now, the one who must decide on behalf of his family and farm, is not the rural youth, but the more traditional, difficult-to-change rural elders.

It has, however, long been the custom in Africa that the old are the teachers of the young in all the ways of life: in farming, building houses, preparing food, marrying, having children and raising families in the venerated tradition of generations before them. Now this tradition has been shattered. The elders of today, who once sat and learned at the feet of their fathers, find themselves still sitting and learning, only now at the feet of their own children. Worse, these children are openly discrediting, ridiculing and making a mockery of tradition. How can they expect their parents to swallow this bitter pill without resistance?

None of the training institutions I visited seems to have taken any special pains to study this problem, perhaps because institutional staff are largely expatriate and, hence, ignorant of its importance. Therefore, none of the young men and women interested in teaching new ways of living to their elders has been especially equipped with communication strategies to handle so delicate and loaded a situation with tact, good taste and, above all, with professionalism.

It is disheartening to visit a farmer-training centre and observe an authoritarian youth arrogantly berating his elders in a manner redolent of colonial times. It is apparent he has not been taught how to teach adults. Instead, he relies upon the only models of teaching he has in his experience, namely, his own teachers. But he forgets in the process that when he was being trained, his teachers were, in fact, his elders. So, without premeditation, this young man makes himself thoroughly obnoxious to his elders by treating them like his subordinates. He is rejected and, with him, all those grandiose ideas and projects he has been trying to promote.

In a nutshell, there is an unintended conspiracy of courtesy on the part of local nationals, preventing crucial communication between them and alien experts from occurring freely. On another plane, there is an equally unintended manifestation of discourtesy on the part of the young, nullifying crucial communication between them and their rural elders. Together these negative elements act to frustrate the best-laid plans.

Tact and Humility

I found these arguments to be so compelling that I spent my assignment listening to them being repeated by different people in different walks of life and in different circumstances and with different emphases and examples. Consequently, I have been led to change my whole approach on this assignment from a theoretical consideration of what is missing in existing project curricula, facilities and equipment geared towards training in communication arts, to an essentially pragmatic concern for what is missing in the existing practice of rural development.

It would seem, on the surface, that what is needed is: (a) to get an honest dialogue going between alien technical experts and local experienced officials, and (b) to infuse at least some tact and humility into the communication approaches of the young change agents so that they can work more effectively with their elders. However, to the professional specialist in communication, there is nothing simple about training people to question their own deep-seated beliefs and values, let alone training others to train still others to question and give up the customs and traditions of generations gone by. Not a simple problem perhaps, but certainly not an insoluble one. The techniques and technologies of the professional communicator for handling these problems are considerably more developed than is widely supposed to be the case in developing countries.

From the 1974/1 issue of *Ceres, The FAO Review*, later reprinted as Ascroft, Joseph. (1978). "A Conspiracy of Courtesy." *International Development Review*, 3, the valedictory issue. Reprinted with permission of the author and the publisher.

1927
1960
1963
1964
1967
1969
1970
1971
1972
1973
1974
1975
1976
1977
1978
1979
1980
1981
1982
1983
1984
1985
1986
1987
1988
1989
1990
1991
1992
1993
1994
1995
1996
1997
1998
1999
2000
2001
2002
2003
2004
2005
2006

RURAL DEVELOPMENT AND SOCIAL COMMUNICATION: RELATIONSHIPS AND STRATEGIES

Excerpt from: Communication Strategies for Rural Development

By Luis Ramiro Beltrán

1974 The developed world has produced several major conceptions of the nature of national development. With a few exceptions, however, most of the prevailing conceptualizations—be they capitalist or socialist—tend to have common detectable elements to a degree that they may be subsumed into…the "classical materialistic model."

The central features of that model can be summarized as follows: National development is fundamentally a process—spontaneous or induced—of economic growth; economic growth generates the material advancement or physical improvement of a country; material advancement, in turn, makes possible improvements in the general well-being of the population; material advancement producing well-being may by itself lead to social justice, cultural freedom, and political democracy. In light of those premises, the chief goals of development-seeking efforts according to the model are: to increase production of goods and services; to facilitate the widespread distribution of them; to expand their consumption; to save and invest at continuously increasing rates.

Consequently, increased financial investments and improved technological inputs, along with better marketing structures and techniques, become the key tools to attain these goals. …

Model Has Many Faults

Development policies, strategies, plans and projects are usually patterned after such a philosophy of man's life and societal progress. What is wrong with such a model, so long in practice in the world's most developed countries and eagerly adopted by so many underdeveloped ones? "Nothing", many would say. "Almost everything", a few would contend.[1] I tend to join the latter. In doing so, I would like to recruit some authoritative assistance. In support of my position, I will cite a few leading specialists.

Economist Robert Heilbroner contends "Economic development is not primarily an economic but a political and social process. Thus we deceive ourselves when we think of economic development in pallid terms of economics alone."

Economist-development planner Roberto de Oliveira Campos provides a Latin American corroboration:

> There is indeed the implicit assumption that the problem of development is primarily economic. In fact however it may well be said that crucial issues of Latin American development are *motivational* and *political* in nature. …

In summary, the "classical materialistic model" of national development is objectionable on many serious grounds. It entails a dehumanized vision of progress which stems from the eminently mercantile mentality that rules much of life in the nations which have reached the highest levels of advancement. It equates having more with being better. It does indeed confuse means with ends, sacrificing the highest values of human beings—dignity, justice and freedom—to abundance and prosperity at any price … for the privileged minorities. It wrongly regards as accessory and derivative the reorganization of society in terms of changes in the distribution of power and wealth as well as in the democratic expansion of social and cultural opportunities.

---

1   Among the studies analyzing the case of the Latin American country which has applied to a great extent the classical model, three are readily available: C. Furtado, *Análise do modelo brasileiro*, 2d. ed. (Rio de Janeiro: Civilicao Brasileira, 1972); R. Ghioldi, et. al. *El modelo brasileño*, (Buenos Aires: Centro de Estudios, 1972); M. Melo Filho, *El desafío brasileño*, (Buenos Aires: Pomaire, 1972).

No wonder, then, that the efforts of the "First Decade of Development" have mostly brought further stagnation, increased concentration of income and of decision making and an acute shortage of food production to the majority of the so-called "developing" countries.

New Model Needed

It follows that a new conceptual model of national development is urgently required before it is too late. Certainly, I do not pretend to have one ready now. But my hope is that when such a model becomes finally available through the effort of highly qualified designers, it may be described … somewhat as follows:

National development is a directed and widely participatory process of deep and accelerated socio-political change geared towards producing substantial changes in the economy, the technology, the ecology and the overall culture of a country, so that the moral and material advancement of the majority of its population can be obtained within conditions of generalized equality, dignity, justice and liberty.

This model would be a humanized, democratic, structural and integral conception of a nation's development based on a reverent vision of man's life and destiny. No matter how schematic it may yet be, I confess to be…a subscriber.

What Is Communication?

It must be acknowledged, once again, that also in the case of "communication" there are numerous and diverse conceptualizations of that process. Again too, however, some features will easily be found to be central to many of the varying definitions. And, just as in the case of the concept of "development", the prevailing one of "communication" appears to have been born in the world's most advanced countries and then adopted, rather indiscriminately, by those not so advanced. The autocratic, elitist and materialistic characteristics of the classical "development" concept are not at all alien to what I should call the "classical mechanic-vertical model of communication."

The model's key features can be synthesized in three premises: (1) social communication is a process of transmission of modes of thinking, feeling and behaving from one or more persons to another person or persons; (2) the paramount goal of communication is persuasion, so that the "transmitting" person, or persons, will obtain from the "receiving" person, or persons, given intended behaviors; and (3) two-way communication through "feedback" is important chiefly as a message-adjusting devise enabling the "transmitter" to secure the performance of the expected response from the "receiver".

Upper-Class Orientation

What is wrong with this model that we have embraced and put into practice for so long most everywhere in the world? Plenty. … When observing, in every-day life, the consequences of the application of the classical communication model, one finds indications that it stems essentially from an upper-class orientation, a will of political domination and the interests of industrialists and merchants.

In fact, as the late C. Wright Mills once contended, in societies where the voice of individual and democratic groups does not count, the communication media facilitate a sort of "psychological illiteracy" in the service of subtle but strong manipulation of the people by power elites.

Mills saw the mass media as performing the following functions in the interest of those elites:

1. To tell the man in the mass who he is—give him identity.
2. To tell him what he wants to be—give him aspirations.
3. To tell him how to get to be that way—give him techniques.
4. To tell him how to feel that he is that way even when he is not—give him—escape.

Was he wrong or was he at least exaggerating?

1927
1960
1963
1964
1967
1969
1970
1971
1972
1973
1974
1975
1976
1977
1978
1979
1980
1981
1982
1983
1984
1985
1986
1987
1988
1989
1990
1991
1992
1993
1994
1995
1996
1997
1998
1999
2000
2001
2002
2003
2004
2005
2006

What often takes place under the label of communication is little more than a dominating monologue in the interest of the starter of the process. Feedback is not employed to provide an opportunity for genuine dialogue. The receiver of the messages is passive and subdued…obeying.

Such a vertical, asymmetric and quasi-authoritarian social relationship constitutes, in my view, an undemocratic instance of communication. Those few who concentrate in their hands financial, cultural, social and political power concentrate also the message-emitting opportunities. And the many that are low in income, education, status and power are condemned to be only receivers … if and when someone really cares to reach them. Indeed, as David K. Berlo asserts: "… nearly everything we do now is couched in terms of how a small number of people can get the rest of the people to do what the small number wants—whether it is in the interest of the large number or not."

Moral Implications

Is that what we wish to keep on doing as professional communicators? Are we no more than signal-generating technicians who could serve equally well any type of interests? Are we conscious enough to the fact that, while technically it may be the same to sell bread as to sell poison, ethically it is not? Can we indefinitely help sell dogmas, abuse and oppression to the masses? Are we in reality so ideologically aseptic—as perhaps dentists or carpenters can afford to be—that we do not care what we are helping someone to communicate for?

I resist the belief we are so. I prefer to think that what happens is that we are barely beginning to understand some disquieting moral implications of our profession. And I hope that, once we have found ourselves doing wrong, we will have the courage to stop it. Thus I join Berlo in feeling that:

> We need now to concentrate on the functions of communication, on ways in which people use messages—not, as we have in the past, on the

effect of communication, on ways in which messages can use people.

In other words, just as in the case of development, we must first be able to build a new concept of communication—a humanized, non-elitist, democratic and non-mercantile model. It is no small challenge but I have faith that it will be met soon.

To stress just a few of the principal components of this sketchy attempt at reaching a new definition of communication, let me point out that it implies a horizontal social relationship based on genuine dialogue, involves a free and proportioned opportunity for persons to exert mutual influences, and denies that persuasion is the chief aim of the sociocultural transaction.

Development and Communication: Their Relation

At three levels of analysis, research has found substantive evidence in many countries of the world that development and communication are strongly correlated.

At the individual level, there are many factor-analytic studies—including two in Latin America—showing communication variables to be in a significant interplay with development variables in general.

At the village level, Rao/9 found, in a comparative study of two Indian villages, clear correlations between communication and social, economic and political development. So did Frey/10 in a survey of nearly 460 villages of Turkey.

At the national level, several multinational studies came up with similar correlations. One of the earliest was that of Lerner who found, in more than 50 countries, media participation highly correlated with urbanization (including industrialization), literacy and political participation. He also found that the degree of change in communication behavior appears to correlate significantly with other behavioral changes. An index of communication development was found by Cutright highly correlated with indices of political development, economic growth, education and urbanization in more than 70 countries. A UNESCO study concentrated in the underdeveloped countries of Latin America, Africa, the Middle East and Southeast Asia, found a strong correlation between mass media factors and economic factors in general development. Similar findings were reported by, among others, Schramm and Carter for 100 countries and by Farace for more than 50 countries, as well as by Schrone and Deutschmann and McNelly.

Hence, as Fagen concludes: "Although the correlations themselves tell us nothing about causality, it is clear that the mass media have been both cause and effect, both mover and moved, in the complex interplay of factors which we call the modernization process."

It is, of course, useful to count on reliable evidence of such correlation. However, for the underdeveloped countries, what is most important is to find the specific circumstances contributing to make social communication an impactful stimulator and accelerator of national development.

Direction of Inquiries

Research exploring all major aspects of communication's contribution to development is not comprehensive yet, and it has not been sufficiently accompanied with inquiry in a critical reverse direction—the influence of the social structure on the communication process. Nevertheless, certain studies have led some researchers to formulate a series of plausible propositions on the roles of communication in development. Distinguished among these are the works of scholars such as Lerner, Schramm, Pye, Pool, Frey and Rao, along with the many studies pertaining to the diffusion of agricultural innovations school represented by researchers such as Rogers. To summarize in some detail the findings of all those researchers is a task outside the scope of this paper. Here it should be sufficient to say that the main prospectors of the relationship of interest appear convinced that the roles of communication in the service of development are numerous and of decisive influence. ... With few exceptions, they

seem to attribute to mass media so much and so great an ability to help generate national advancement. ...

Hoping that such judgment is wrong one cannot avoid going back to the crucial question: What kind of "communication" in the service of which type of "development?" A nation is not developed when minorities in it can afford to squander fortunes on superfluous articles when majorities can barely buy bread. A person is not modern just because he is led to feel an urge to enjoy washing machines, have a bigger car than his neighbor's, or vacation in Acapulco. That is the kind of "development" to which the "developing" countries have no reason to subscribe. And mercantilist and undemocratic persuasion is not the type of communication from which those countries may profit most.

I acknowledge with pleasure the existence of a promising correlation between communication and development in general. I also share the faith that the former may indeed contribute much to the latter—under given circumstances. ...

Latin America: Communication and Rural Development

What, in essence, is the nature of Latin America's overall communication system? What are the chief characteristics of the communication process in relation to the region's rural population? How do the system and process of communication appear to be related to the rural development process?[2]

A system of communication is a defined set of interrelated social entities—public, private, and mixed—specializing in serving as mediators among people participating in the communication process. The systems usually understood to be composed of three

2   The volume of data available today on this subject is more than one would suspect. Those interested in an extensive treatment of it may wish to see this author's "Communication in Latin America: Persuasion for Status Quo or for National Development" (Ph.D. Dissertation, Michigan State University, East Lansing, Michigan, 1970) and, for a relatively extensive summary, his *La Problemática de la Comunicación para el Desarrollo Rural en America Latina*, 1972, Buenos Aires, Argentina, AIBDA, and also El Sistema y el *Proceso de Comunicación Social en Latinoamérica y su Relación con el Desarrollo Rural*, 1973, Cusco, Peru, UNESCO.

1927
1960
1963
1964
1967
1969
1970
1971
1972
1973
1974
1975
1976
1977
1978
1979
1980
1981
1982
1983
1984
1985
1986
1987
1988
1989
1990
1991
1992
1993
1994
1995
1996
1997
1998
1999
2000
2001
2002
2003
2004
2005
2006

major subsystems: interpersonal, impersonal or massive, and a mixed one resulting from stable combinations of the former two.

Given the insufficient degree of integration among the three subsystems, Latin America's communication system can be taken as an imperfect one. In fact, while the interpersonal sub-system can be seen in operation throughout the whole society, it is characteristic of the rural segment and shows minimal connection with the other two sub-systems. On the other hand, the impersonal subsystem is characteristic of the situation in the urban sector. And the mixed sub-system is mostly, though minimally, operating in the rural society. Important as the interpersonal and mixed systems are, I shall concentrate on describing the impersonal one. ...

Mass Media Availability

In 1961 UNESCO set minimum desirable standards of mass media availability for each 100 inhabitants of the underdeveloped countries. They were the following: 10 newspaper copies, 5 radio receivers, 2 television receivers, and 2 cinema seats.

Latin America's figures for 1961 were: 7.4 newspaper copies, 9.8 radio receivers, 1.5 television receivers, and 3.5 cinema seats. The Latin American figures were, in the aggregate, higher than those for equivalent regions of Asia and Africa.

In 1971 the figures for Latin America had become the following: 7.5 newspaper copies, 11.3 radio receivers, 5.7 television receivers and 2.7 cinema seats.

The first survey showed that Latin America then had mass media availability levels which were either clearly above UNESCO's minimum standards or only a little below them.

The second survey showed also that half the total population was still left without access even to the most diffused medium, radio. Nevertheless, it is evident that the advancements in mass media availability have been, as a whole, impressive in this region in the last decade. However, before one jubilantly raises hands

to applaud, an important question must be poised: Available to whom?

Access to Mass Media Messages

Availability of mass media is not necessarily equal to access or exposure of people to messages. As a rule, the distribution of those messages in Latin America is uneven within groups of countries, within each country, and within each of the cities in them.

Research has found urban concentration of mass media messages to be particularly high in the larger cities, especially in the case of television and press; concentration is appreciably less acute for radio and somewhat less acute for the cinema. For the most part, mass media do not reach the masses in rural Latin America. Communication in this region is but one more privilege enjoyed by the ruling urban elite.

Within each city, a minority of the population has far more access to mass media messages than the majority. And, within the rural areas, even smaller minorities have the privilege of access to those messages.

In general, then, the distribution of mass communication opportunities in Latin America follows the steep pattern of stratification that characterized the socio-economic structure prevailing in the region. The higher the income, education and status, the higher the level of access to mass media messages. People in the intermediate brackets of the scale have intermediate level of access. And the great majority of the population—low class urbanities and the peasantry—have as low levels of access to communication as to food, shelter and education.

The rural population's access to mass media messages reaches such extremely low levels that most peasants can be said to be virtually outside the communication system.

Selected from among several studies, a few illustrations should suffice to document the point. Take one channel: the press. And one country: Colombia. We find that 83 percent of the circulation of 800,000 daily copies of 32 newspapers is found in the three largest cities—Bogota, Medellin and Cali. The difference goes to the rest of the cities and to the rural areas.

Of Mexico City's six largest newspapers' total daily circulation—665,000 copies—80 percent is sold within that city itself, the rest being distributed in all other cities and in rural areas. Moreover, the daily average of copies sold per one thousand inhabitants reaches as high as 160 in the large commercial farming states of the North while in the Southern subsistence agriculture states the figure is a low as 9.

Take another channel—radio which is supposed to reach "everybody" thanks to the transistor—and another country—Brazil—and you will find that the case is not very different from those of the press in Mexico and Colombia.

Let's move to Peru and find, with Mejía, some exposure figures for three channels in two small rural towns and two large farms (haciendas). None of the peasants (peones) in those haciendas saw movies or read newspapers and 85 percent did not listen to radio. But in the towns 20 percent of the independent small-land holders read newspapers, 50 percent listened to radio and 13 percent sometimes went to the movies. As this study, and those of Canizales and Myren in Mexico and of Blair in Brazil show, communication is indeed more markedly stratified in rural than in urban areas of Latin America. …

Brazilian peasants living more than two hours from a large city acceptably endowed with mass media were once interviewed to find out their information level on matters which were often treated by those mass media. These were some of the results: 95 percent of the peasants did not know that coffee was the chief export product of their country; 80 percent of them had no meaning for the word "democracy"; and 48 percent did not know the name of the President of the Republic. Other studies in Brazil itself, as well as in Mexico and Chile, found comparable results, verifying the acute state of sub-information in which the peasantry lives.

Compare that situation again with the one prevailing in the cities. A study obtained mass media consumption data of a "sub-elite" (professionals with studies in foreign countries) sampled from 14 Latin American countries and contrasted them with those pertinent to an equivalent U.S. sample. The Latin Americans not only were found to have, in general, as good standards as their U.S. counterparts but fared better in figures for books and radio.

Lack of roads and electricity, poverty and illiteracy are often stressed as explanations for the lack of access of realties in this region to mass media messages. Those factors have, indeed, a limiting influence, but one may ask why it is, in the first place, that peasants are deprived of education, income and facilities such as roads and electricity. At any rate, those barriers are not always and necessarily adequate explanations. For, sometimes, even in the uncommon cases where peasant illiteracy is low and transportation and access to mass media is good, peasants say they do not buy newspapers or pay much attention to radio messages. This is precisely what Gutierrez and McNamara found in a Colombian village well linked to the country's second largest city. Could it be that peasants find nothing for them in those channels?

Content of Mass Media Messages

Within the classical model of development the Latin American peasants do not constitute a "public" as they are clearly marginal to the "market." Concomitantly, within the classical model of communication, these peasants do not constitute an "audience" as little can be done to persuade them to buy—in terms of consumption.

In terms of production, however, peasants may, up to a point, be regarded as a "public" and an "audience" within those models. But the task of communicating with them is not directly or immediately lucrative. Therefore, the private mass media institutions leave it altogether to government rural education efforts.

1927
1960
1963
1964
1967
1969
1970
1971
1972
1973
1974
1975
1976
1977
1978
1979
1980
1981
1982
1983
1984
1985
1986
1987
1988
1989
1990
1991
1992
1993
1994
1995
1996
1997
1998
1999
2000
2001
2002
2003
2004
2005
2006

Research already exists to demonstrate that the mass media are oriented, eminently and not accidentally, to the urban audiences that constitute the market. Therefore, sad as it may be, it is logical not to expect their content to include materials of interest for peasants—except in the cases of agricultural mass media or of farming sections of the general-audience media. …

Gutierrez-Sanchez analyzed three months' content of the weekly agricultural pages of five Bogota dailies and sampled materials from a national weekly rural newspaper, measuring volumes for ten categories. He found that the dailies gave first priority to meetings and organizational activities of large farmers (ranked sixth by the weekly), while the weekly gave most emphasis to public programs to aid agriculture. For both the dailies and the weekly, two of the top three categories were national government programs and foreign trade, and crops. News of rural education needs and other peasant community programs were ranked lowest, along with fishing, by both the dailies and the weekly. …

A more complex and recent study, also conducted in Colombia, corroborated those findings. Fifty one editions of farm pages in eight dailies were content-analyzed over a period of eight years. On a scale of seven content categories, land reform was found to be the last. And, with a slight tendency of regional newspapers to publish rural educational materials, the dailies showed an exclusive preference for purely informative and promotional items. Felstehausen found comparable results for radio in a region of Colombia.

Brazilian, Chilean and Mexican studies, including that of Ruanova on farm magazines, produced similar results. And Cordero/36 found that in Costa Rica, a country whose livelihood is eminently based on agriculture, the dailies assign minimal importance to it. In fact, his content analysis revealed that the categories of agriculture, animal husbandry, rural community development, land reform, and agricultural economy occupied intermediate and low places on the scale. The lowest categories were conservation of natural resources and reforestation. The first category (occupying most of the space) in the farm supplements was commercial farm advertising.

This may be so not only in the commercial domain but also in the political sphere. It is something which communication research in Latin America has not yet empirically verified at the level of the rural society. There is, however, a very suggestive study conducted in Peru by Roca. He hypothesized that the interests of owners of daily newspapers in Lima influence content orientation in them, especially when such interests are threatened.

The researcher content-analyzed six dailies for the six-week period of 1963 during which peasant invasions of large farm states constituted a serious threat for the land-monopolizing interests in the country. Of the 391 items of news, editorials and advertisements analyzed, 290 were in favor of the large landowners, 39 for the peasants and the balance were neutral. News content, in particular, markedly favored the landlords.

While those results were not surprising, their importance was raised when the researcher also found that the ownership of three of the six dailies studied was clearly related to ownership of large farm states; and, as hypothesized, they accounted for 184 of the total of 290 items against the peasants. …

Code of Mass Media Messages

We find here again the same situation: given that mass media are strongly urban-oriented, they codify their messages in styles corresponding to the urban audience. Thus, the rural population is ignored not only in terms of content but also in those of code. And this does not happen only in the case of private mass media but also in that of government-produced massive agricultural communication materials.

Perhaps the earliest scientific verification of that problem was that conducted by Spaulding/38 in Mexico and Costa Rica. He tested how understandable were the visual illustrations in a series of fundamental education booklets. He found that effectiveness was dependent upon: (1) how well the booklets fit the intended audience's experience; (2) keeping the number of objects in each illustration to a minimum; (3) keeping also to a minimum the number of separate actions necessary to correct interpretation of the message; (4) using color realistically and functionally; and (5) portraying objects and inferred actions in a realistic and unambiguous way.

A later and more complex study in rural Brazil provided similar but richer evidence. This study probably constitutes a pioneer case of inquiry on the semantics and semiotics of non-verbal communication for rural development.

Comparable studies for radio, television and film messages are so far unavailable in Latin America. For press, however, there are several.

Using Spaulding's readability formula, Ruanova evaluated seven of Mexico's fourteen agricultural magazines and found them beyond the understanding of most of that country's farmers. Amaya analyzed a Spanish-language farm magazine by means of re-writing several articles in it and then testing the original and the simplified versions; she found the former located in the "extremely difficult" and "difficult" categories of comprehension. Comparable results were obtained by Magdub in measuring, mostly by the Cloze procedure, technical and extension agriculture publications and one grammar school textbook. And his analysis of 122 articles of the agricultural pages of four dailies and one rural weekly in Colombia, led Gutierrez-Sanchez to conclude "… that which may be of direct value in improving agriculture is beyond the comprehension of those who could best use the information."

Evidently, then, even in communication materials aimed at the rural audience, the code being used is one pertaining to urban culture and alien to the peasantry. Why? Is it accidental or deliberate?

Simmons and others have proposed, in the case of dailies, this explanation: "Even in developing nations, journalists seldom make great concessions in their level of presentation for the poorly educated or otherwise culturally deprived." It is not only journalists, however, who seem to behave in that manner; writers, illustrators and other communicators in rural development government agencies also seem often unaware that they are actually writing, painting, photographing or speaking in terms understandable only by urbanites. For some analysts this is just another expression of the domination that rural people suffer under the imposition of the urban culture. Research has yet to go into verifying hypotheses as important as this one. …

Communication Strategies for Rural Development

I can now venture into discussing strategies. First, let's consider the definitions:

A strategy is a behavioral design involving decisions on how to use power and resources to attain given goals through certain instrumental actions.

A national development strategy is a statement of collective goals and implementing procedures to effect given changes in man and nature's behavior in the direction of given kinds and levels of improvement and growth identified with a certain state and type of modernity.

A communication strategy is a set of decisions on who is to communicate what to whom, what for, when and how.

A developmental communication strategy is a set of decisions concerning communication behaviors directly instrumental to the attainment of a nation's development as conceived in the broader strategy.

Rural development[3] is a subset of overall national development. "Rural communication" is a subset of communication in general. Therefore, strategies for each need to be defined separately here.

---

3   It implies far more than agricultural growth. We see rural development as "a process in which a nation's agriculture becomes a continually more productive and rationally organized component of an emerging modern industrial state with the changes in the social and political structure, productive processes and values that this implies."

1927
1960
1963
1964
1967
1969
1970
1971
1972
1973
1974
1975
1976
1977
1978
1979
1980
1981
1982
1983
1984
1985
1986
1987
1988
1989
1990
1991
1992
1993
1994
1995
1996
1997
1998
1999
2000
2001
2002
2003
2004
2005
2006

The View From Inside

Strategic communication behavior, i.e., rational, organized, efficient, in the service of rural development is still yet more the exception than the rule. I do not know how true this may be in the totality of underdeveloped countries. But I feel quite sure that the assertion holds well for those of Latin America. These are some indicators of it:

1. As a rule, there are no overall yearly plans of communication in the service of rural development. (Initial attempts at formulating them have been recorded in Peru, Brazil, Chile, Colombia and Argentina).[4] In the absence of such plans, communication activities support rural development actions on an insufficient, erratic and unbalanced basis.

2. Sometimes rural communication organs tend to operate by themselves; that is, with little regard for the requisites of the population to be reached and without proper adjustment to institutional objectives and demands of field personnel.[5]

3. There is lack of coordination among the different organizations carrying developmental messages to the rural areas; duplication of efforts and even competitive rivalry are not necessarily strange phenomena.

4. Functional priorities are set in arbitrary manners. Characteristically, and virtually without exception, the production function is assigned the highest priority.[6] The simplest inspection of operations, staff and budgets makes this evident. Most human and financial resources are spent in producing messages without a worry as to their utilization and actual effectiveness. Only minimal energy is assigned to the distribution and evaluation functions and practically no resources go to the research and training functions. The materialistic vision of development and of communication accounts for the expenditure of large sums in communication equipment, buildings and vehicles while basic non-hardware needs are grossly neglected.

5. Media selection is equally arbitrary. For instance, an unduly high proportion of production resources is spent in printed messages in flagrant contrast with the high indices of illiteracy prevailing in rural areas. Mass channels are often blindly preferred by rural communication specialists while extension agents exaggerate their preference for the impersonal ones.

6. Messages are geared almost exclusively to assisting the farmers with technological information for production purposes, thus disregarding the sociocultural dimensions of the development effort. In addition, messages are couched in terms of the urban culture, as previously shown.

7. Political convenience and lack of comprehension of the nature of developmental communication often leads rural development agencies to spend much of their communication resources in public relations tasks. Important as those activities are for these institutions, they are also alien to the needs and interests of the peasantry.

---

4   The most comprehensive is probably that of Peru (Ministerio de Agricultura, "Plan Nacional de Comunicación Agraria, 1972", Peru). The Colombian attempt seems barely starting, and Argentina's efforts have been mostly at the level of extension projects. In a recent international meeting of experts a recommendation was approved in favor of the formulation of communication policies and plans in support of those of rural development. At a broader level, UNESCO has produced a basic guidance document for the formulation of overall communication policies for national development (United Nations Educational, Scientific and Cultural Organization, *Report of the Meeting of Experts on Communication Policies and Planning*. Paris, France: UNESCO, 1972), and will conduct in July 1974 a Latin American experts meeting on the subject in Colombia.

5   The content of educational publications of the Instituto Colombiano Agropecuario for three years was found not to be "… in complete conformity with the priorities of the Ministry of Agriculture …" (A. R. and V. Alba Robayo and B. Novoa, *Analisis de Contenido de las Publicaciones Divulgativas del ICA y su relación con los planes del Ministerio de Agricultura, 1970.* Bogotá, Instituto Colombiano Agropecuario). Similar findings have emerged in studies of farm pages in daily newspapers, and other media of agricultural communication.

6   An appraisal of communication planning in a rural development organization in Colombia, performed exclusively on the basis of production analysis, showed the following: (1) more unprogrammed than programmed activities were conducted; (2) communication materials were required by the field project managers without adjustment to objectives, priorities, time or resources; (3) of all forms of communication utilized, publications showed the highest volume; and (4) the need for a system of control, evaluation and follow-up was made evident. (Novoa y Vejarano, 1973).

There are several other similar shortcomings. But these suffice to indicate that, rigorously speaking, we cannot yet talk in Latin America of the existence of communication strategies for rural development. Improvisation and arbitrariness still take much precedence over planning and rationality.

If this view is accepted, then it should be evident that it is not possible to tell here what the actual contribution of communication strategies to rural development strategies might be—at least not in reference to Latin America. Why is that so?

First, let me put the blame on ourselves—the specialists in rural development communication. Our fault is, however, one of immaturity only. Young as our sub-discipline is, we have not grown yet to the level of strategists. For about twenty years, we remained content with being able practitioners of media handling and message production. Then, starting some ten years ago, a few of Latin America's "agricultural communication specialists" became social scientists and started looking critically at communication as a process. The conjunction of art and science in our profession has meant, no doubt, a net gain. But we still have to make a third major move upwards: to learn how to use optimally our art and our science in the service of human and democratic rural development.[7]

Faith and enthusiasm will not be sufficient for the success of such a novel endeavor. We must become knowledgeable in the nature of underdevelopment in our society so as to be able to contribute to its real development. And the latter is something that we may never be able to accomplish unless, in addition to mastering communication, we train ourselves in the infant art of democratic planning[8] and apply it to our field.

The time available to do that is not ample. Social communication efficiently organized to help generate deep and accelerated societal change is the only alternative to abrupt and violent transformation to be fully useful to the attainment of their ends. For we have no ends of our own. Communication is indeed vital to the development of a nation. But it is only an instrument. It may be mighty but it is not magic: it cannot generate development by itself.

The View from Outside

Unfortunately, the importance of communication has not been properly understood yet either by political leaders or general development strategists. Most of them seem not to have a proper understanding of it. Even more so, they fail to perceive what communication can do to help them obtain development. Thus, our first practical duty is to attain successful communication with those decision-makers.

On the other hand, it is not sensible to expect communication specialists to grow to the stature of development communication strategists in situations where integral development strategies, strictly speaking, do not exist either. ...

It is a rare event to find a country in this region in which rural development is given a top priority within the overall development strategy along with an adequate proportion of the national budget. And it is equally unusual to find a country in the area having a complete, solid, coherent and durable policy for rural development. In the absence of it, what can communication strategists do?

Low priority, ill-financed, contingent and partial rural development plans do exist in many Latin American countries. Many of them fail to involve systematically the totality of agricultural development agencies, particularly the mushrooming specialized autonomous ones. And some of those plans also fail to reach an acceptable degree of articulation with the overall development scheme. It is small wonder, then, that social communication is far from integrated to rural development.... .

---

7   An insightful analysis of the evolution of the profession in Latin America has been done by Diaz-Bordenave. ("*New approaches to Communication Training for Developing Countries*", 1972. Baton Rouge, Louisiana).

8   A valuable contribution towards this end has been made by Carvalho (*Comunicacao e o Processo de Planejamento*, 1972. Brasilia, Ministerio de Agricultura). (Textos Técnicos).

1927
1960
1963
1964
1967
1969
1970
1971
1972
1973
1974
1975
1976
1977
1978
1979
1980
1981
1982
1983
1984
1985
1986
1987
1988
1989
1990
1991
1992
1993
1994
1995
1996
1997
1998
1999
2000
2001
2002
2003
2004
2005
2006

Looking Ahead

A general strategy of development rural communication cannot be formulated in a vacuum. It has to be derived from an overall rural development strategy and be subservient to it. Improvements of the formulation of the latter must be effected in the countries, therefore, as a prerequisite for designing the one on communication.

Let us be optimistic about the likelihood of those improvements since the region counts on a number of competent rural development experts and since development planning would appear to be starting, at long last, to take a direction more concerned with human beings than with input-output ratios. Let us, therefore, assume that we shall soon have in a country a sound general strategy for rural development. Will we, the communicators, be ready and able then to derive from it a sound general communication strategy?

I honestly believe that, once we are able to help at least one country to devise and successfully utilize the strategy in question, then we might, as true communication strategists, earn inclusion in propositions such as the following of economist-planner Roberto de Oliveira Campos:

> Although there is no immediate danger that the economists will join the army of the unemployed, it is quite clear that they have left precious little that is new or unsaid on the mechanics of development. The floor must be given to social psychologists and the political scientists.

Works/Authors Cited

1. R. L. Heilbroner, *The Great Ascent; the Struggle for Economic Development in our Time* (New York: Harper and Row, 1963).

2. D. Rockefeller, "Lessons of the '60s, Challenges of the '70s," War on Hunger 3 (November 1969): 1-2.

3. Norman Uphoff, "Rural Development; Social and Political Aspects of Agrarian Reform, Some Propositions on the Political Economy of Rural Development," 1973, San José, Costa Rica, Society for International Development. (Mimeographed).

4. R. de O. Campos, *Reflections on Latin American Development*. 2nd ed. (Austin, Texas: University of Texas, 1969).

5. Ministerio de Agricultura, Colombia, "Programas Agrícolas 1973; Evaluación 1971-72, Programación 1973, Proyecciones 1974-75," 1972, Bogotá, Oficina de Planeamiento del Sector Agropecuario.

6. C. Wright Mills, *The Power Elite* (New York: Oxford University, 1959).

7. David K. Berlo, "Given Development, What Role for Communication," 1970, Mexico, National Advertising Council, summary of a presentation at the First World Conference on Social Communication for Development.

8. Ibid.

9. Y. V. Laksmana Rao, *Communication and Development; a Study of Two Indian Villages* (Minneapolis, Minnesota: University of Minnesota, 1966).

10. F. W. Frey, *The Mass Media and Rural Development in Turkey* (Cambridge, Massachusetts: Massachusetts Institute of Technology, Center for International Studies, 1966).

11. D. Lerner, *The Passing of the Traditional Society* (Glencoe, Illinois: Free Press, 1958).

12. P. Cutright, "National Political Development; Measurement and Analysis," *American Sociological Review* 28 (1963): 253-264.

13. United Nations Educational, Scientific and Cultural Organization, *Mass Media in the Developing Countries* (Paris, France: UNESCO, 1961).

14. R. F. Carter and W. Schramm, "Scales for Describing National Communication Systems," 1969, Stanford, California, Institute for Communication Research. (Mimeographed).

15. V. R. Farace, "Mass Communication, Political Participation and Other National Characteristics: A Factor Analytic Investigation," 1965, Lincoln, Nebraska.

16. L. F. Schrone, "The Statistical Measurement of Urbanization and Economic Development," *Land Economics* 37 (1961): 229-245.

17. P. J. Deutschmann and J. T. McNelly, "Media Use and Socio-economic Status in a Latin American Capital," 1964, East Lansing, Michigan State University, (Series No. 3).

18. R. R. Fagen, *Politics and Communication* (Boston, Mass: Little, Brown, 1966).

19. UNESCO, *Mass Media in the Developing Countries*.

20. M. Kaplun, "Los Medios de Comunicación Social en América Latina," 1971, Distrito Federal, Mexico.

21. Deutschmann and McNelly, "Media Use and Socio-economic Status in a L.A. Capital."

22. A. García, "El Problema Agrario en América Latina y los Medios de Información Colectiva," 1966, Quito, Ecuador, Centro Internacional de Estudios Superiores en Periodismo para América Latina.

23. Ibid.

24. L. R. Bostian and F. C. Oliveira, "Relationships of Literacy and Education to Communication and Social Conditions on Small Farms in two Municipios of Southern Brazil," *Rural Sociological Society* (1965).

25. P. Mejía, "Dominación y Reacciones a la Reforma Agraria," *Desarrollo Rural en las Américas* (Colombia) 3(3) (1971): 35-42.

26. J. A. Canizales and D. T. Myren, "Difusión de la Información Agrícola en el Valle del Yaqui," 1976, Distrito Federal, México, Secretaría de Agricultura y Ganadería, Instituto Nacional de Investigaciones Agrícolas.

27. T. L. Blair, "Social Structures and Information Exposure in Rural Brazil," Rural Sociology, XXV (1), (1960): 65-75.

28. United States Information Agency, *The General Pattern of Exposure to Mass Media in Seven Latin American Countries* (Washington, D.C., USIA, 1961). (Research and Reference Service Survey Research Studies, Program and Media Series No. 58).

29. J. Diaz-Bordenave, "New Approaches to Communication Training for Developing Countries," 1972, Baton Rouge, Louisiana.

30. P. J. Deutschmann, H. Ellingsworth and J. T. McNelly, "Mass Media Use by Sub-elites in Latin American Countries," *Journalism Quarterly* 38 (1961): 460-472.

31. R. L. McNamara and J. Gutierrez Sanchez, "Algunos Factores que Afectan el Proceso de Comunicación en una Vereda Colombiana," *Revista ICA* (Colombia) 3 (1968).

32. Gutierrez Sanchez, "Content Analysis and Readability Study of the Agricultural Pages in Five Colombian Newspapers," (M.S. Thesis, University of Wisconsin, Madison, Wisconsin, 1966).

33. E. DeVries and J. Medina Echavarría, *Social Aspects of Economic Development* in *Latin America*, 2 vols. (Tournai, Belgica: UNESCO, 1967).

34. H. Felstehausen, "Economic Knowledge, Participation and Farmer Decision Making in a Developed and Underdeveloped Country," *International Journal of Agrarian Affairs* 5(7) (1968): 263-281.

35. H. A. Ruanova, "Content and Readability for Some Latin American Agricultural Magazines," (M.A. Thesis, University of Wisconsin, Madison, Wisconsin, 1958).

36. M. Cordero Rodriguez, "Análisis de Contenido de los Suplementos Agropecuarios de dos Periódicos de Costa Rica," (Tesis, Universidad de Costa Rica, Escuela de Periodismo, San José, Costa Rica, 1973).

37. L. Roca, "Los intereses Económicos y la Orientación de Noticias sobre el Movimiento Campesino," *Campesino* 1(1) (1969): 37-52.

38. S. Spaulding, "A Spanish Readability Formula," *The Modern Language Journal* 40 (1956): 433-441.

39. L. Fonseca and B. Kearl, "Comprehension of Pictorial Symbols; an Experiment in Rural Brazil," 1960, Madison, Wisconsin, University of Wisconsin, Department of Agicultural Journalism.

40. Ruanova, "Content and Readability of Some L.A. Ag. Magazines."

41. S. Amaya, "A Plan for Empirical Testing of the Spaulding Readability Formula for Colombian Agricultural Publications," (M.S. Thesis, University of Wisconsin, Madison, Wisconsin, 1959). (Abstract).

42. A. Magdub, "Cloze Procedure; its Application as a Tool for Measuring Readability in Spanish Agricultural Information," (M.S. Thesis, University of Wisconsin, Madison, Wisconsin, 1966). (Abstract).

43. Gutierrez-Sanchez, "Content Analysis & Readability Study of the Agricultural Pages in Five Colombian Newspapers."

44. K. Kent, V. M. Mishra, and R. Simmons, "Media and Development News in Slums of Ecuador and India," *Journalism Quarterly* 45, (1968): 698-705.

Communication Strategies for Rural Development: Proceedings of the Cornell-CIAT International Symposium; 1974 March 17-22; Cali, Colombia, S.A. Ithaca, NY : Cornell University, 1974. pp. 11-27. Reprinted with permission of the author.

EXCERPT FROM:

THEATER OF THE OPPRESSED

By Augusto Boal

1974 The first word of the theatrical vocabulary is the human body, the main source of sound and movement. Therefore, to control the means of theatrical production, man must, first of all, control his own body; know his own body, to be capable of making it more expressive. Then he will be able to practice theatrical forms, in which by stages, he frees himself from his condition of spectator and becomes the actor. He ceases to be an object and becomes a subject. …

Transforming the spectator into actor can be systematized in the following outline:

First stage: Knowing the body: a series of exercises in which one gets to know one's body. …

Second stage: Making the body expressive: a series of games in which one begins to express one's self through the body. …

Third stage: The theater as language: One begins to practice theater as a language that is living and present, not as a finished product. …

- First degree: Simultaneous dramaturgy: The spectators "write" simultaneously with the acting of the actors;
- Second degree: Image theater: The spectators intervene directly, "speaking" through images made with the actors' bodies;
- Third degree: Forum theater: The spectators intervene directly in the dramatic action and act.

Fourth stage: The theater as discourse: simple forms in which the spectator-actor creates "spectacles" according to his need to discuss certain themes or rehearse certain actions.

1927
1960
1963
1964
1967
1969
1970
1971
1972
1973
1974
1975
1976
1977
1978
1979
1980
1981
1982
1983
1984
1985
1986
1987
1988
1989
1990
1991
1992
1993
1994
1995
1996
1997
1998
1999
2000
2001
2002
2003
2004
2005
2006

Examples:

1. Newspaper theater
2. Invisible theater
3. Photo-romance theater
4. Breaking of repression
5. Myth theater
6. Trial theater
7. Masks and Rituals

First stage: Knowing the body

The initial contact with a group of peasants, workers or villagers—if they are confronted with the proposal to put on a theatrical performance—can be extremely difficult. They have quite likely never heard of theater, and if they have heard of it, their conception of it will probably have been distorted by television, with its emphasis on sentimentality, or by some traveling circus group. It is also very common for those people to associate theater with leisure or frivolity. Thus caution is required even when the contact takes place through an educator who belongs to the same class as the illiterates or semi-illiterates, even if he lives among them in a shack and shares their comfortless life. The very fact that the educator comes with the mission of eradicating illiteracy, which presupposes a coercive, forceful action, is itself alienating. … The theatrical experience should not begin with something alien to the people.

To clarify this point: Compare the muscular structure of a typist with that of the night watchman of a factory. The first performs his or her work seated in a chair: From the waist down the body becomes, during working hours, a kind of pedestal, while arms and fingers are active. The watchman, on the other hand, must walk continually during his eight-hour shift and consequently will develop muscular structures that facilitate walking. The bodies of both become alienated in accordance with their respective types of work.

The same is true of any person whatever the work or social status. The combination of roles that a person must perform imposes on him a "mask" of behavior. This is why those who perform the same roles

end up resembling one another: artists, soldiers, clergymen, teachers, workers, peasants, landlords, decadent noblemen, etc.

The exercises of this first stage are designed to "undo" the muscular structures of the participants. That is, to take them apart, to study and analyze them. Not to weaken or destroy them, but to raise them to the level of consciousness—so that each worker, each peasant, understands, sees and feels to what point his body is governed by his work.

If one is able in this way to disjoint one's own muscular structures, one will surely be able to assemble structures characteristic of other professions and social classes; that is, one will be able to physically "interpret" characters different from oneself.

All the exercises of this series are designed to disjoint. I offer the following examples:

1. Slow-motion race. The participants are invited to run a race with the aim of losing: The last one is the winner. Moving in slow motion, the body will find its center of gravity dislocated at each successive moment and so must find again a new muscular structure, which will maintain its balance. The participants must never interrupt the motion or stand still; also, they must take the longest step they can and their feet must rise above knee level. In this exercise, a 10-meter run can be more tiring than a conventional 500-meter run, for the effort needed to keep one's balance in each new position is intense.
2. Cross-legged race. The participants form pairs, embrace each other and intertwine their legs (the left of one with the right of the other, and vice versa). In the race, each pair acts as if it were a single person and each person acts as if his mate were his leg. The "leg" doesn't move alone: It must be put in motion by its mate!
3. Monster race. "Monsters" of four legs are formed: Each person embraces the thorax of his mate but in reverse position; so the legs of one fit around the

actors. All the solutions, suggestions and opinions are revealed in theatrical form. The discussion itself need not simply take the form of words, but rather should be effected through all the other elements of theatrical expression as well.

Here's an example of how simultaneous dramaturgy works. In a barrio of San Hilarión, in Lima, a woman proposed a controversial theme. Her husband, some years before, had told her to keep some "documents" which, according to him, were extremely important. The woman—who happened to be illiterate—put them away without suspicion. One day they had a fight for one reason or another and, remembering the documents, the woman decided to find out what they were all about, since she was afraid they had something to do with the ownership of their small house. Frustrated by her inability to read, she asked a neighbor to read the documents to her. The lady next door kindly made haste to read the documents, which, to the surprise and amusement of the whole barrio, were not documents at all but rather love letters written by the mistress of the poor woman's husband. Now this betrayed and illiterate woman wanted revenge. The actors improvised the scenes until the moment when the husband returns home at night, after his wife has uncovered the mystery of the letters. The woman wants revenge: How is she to get it? Here the action was interrupted and the participant interpreting the woman asked the others what should be her attitude in relation to her husband.

All the women of the audience entered into a lively exchange of views. The actors listened to the different suggestions and acted them out according to instructions given by the audience. All the possibilities were tried. Here are some of the suggested solutions in this particular case:

1. To cry a lot in order to make him feel guilty. One young woman suggested that the betrayed woman start to cry a lot so that the husband might feel bad about his own behavior. The actress carried out this suggestion: She cried a lot, the husband consoled her, and when the crying was over, he asked

POETICS OF THE OPPRESSED
Excerpt from: *Theater of the Oppressed*
By Augusto Boal

In the beginning the theater was the dithyrambic song: free people singing in the open air. The carnival. The feast.

Later, the ruling classes took possession of the theater and built their dividing walls. First, they divided the people, separating actors from spectators, people who act and people who watch. The party was over! Second, among the actors, they separated the protagonists from the masses. Coercive indoctrination began!

Now the oppressed people are themselves liberated and, once more, are making the theater their own. The walls must be torn down. First, the spectator starts acting again: invisible theater, forum theater, image theater, etc. Second, it is necessary to eliminate the private property of the characters by the individual actors.

(Translated from the Spanish by Charles A. and Maria-Odilia Leal McBride.)

Boal, Augusto. *Teatro del Oprimido y Otras Poéticas Políticas*. Buenos Aires, Argentina: Ediciones La Flor, 1974. *Theater of the Oppressed*. New York: Theater Communications Group, Inc., 1979. Copyright © 1979 Theater Communications Group. Reprinted with permission of TCG.

her to serve his dinner; and everything remained as it was before. The husband assured her that he had already forgotten the mistress, that he loved only his wife, etc., etc. The audience did not accept this solution.

2. To abandon the house, leaving her husband alone as a punishment. The actress carried out this suggestion and, after reproaching her husband for his wicked behavior, grabbed her things, put them in a bag and left him alone, very lonely, so that he would learn a lesson. But upon leaving the house (that is, her own house), she asked the

1927
1960
1963
1964
1967
1969
1970
1971
1972
1973
1974
1975
1976
1977
1978
1979
1980
1981
1982
1983
1984
1985
1986
1987
1988
1989
1990
1991
1992
1993
1994
1995
1996
1997
1998
1999
2000
2001
2002
2003
2004
2005
2006

public about what she should do next. In punishing her husband, she ended up punishing herself. Where would she go now? Where could she live? This punishment positively was not good since it turned against the punisher herself.

3. To lock the house so that the husband would have to go away. This variation was also rehearsed. The husband repeatedly begged to be let in, but the wife steadfastly refused. After several attempts, the husband commented: Very well, I'll go away. They paid me my salary today, so I'll take the money and go live with my mistress and you can just get by the best way you can." And he left. The actress commented that she did not like this solution, since her husband went to live with the other woman, and what about the wife? How is she going to live now? The poor woman does not make enough money to support herself and cannot get along without her husband.

4. The last solution was presented by a large, exuberant woman; it was the solution accepted unanimously by the entire audience, men and women. She said, "Do it like this: Let him come in, get a really big stick, and hit him with all your might—give him a good beating. After you've beat him enough for him to feel repentant, put the stick away, serve him his dinner with affection and forgive him."

The actress performed this version, after overcoming the natural resistance of the actor who was playing the husband, and after a barrage of blows—to the amusement of the audience—the two of them sat at the table, ate and discussed the latest measures taken by the government, which happened to be the nationalization of American companies.

This form of theater creates great excitement among the participants and starts to demolish the wall that separates actors from spectators. Some "write" and others act almost simultaneously. The spectators feel that they can intervene in the action. The action ceases to be presented in a deterministic manner, as something inevitable, as Fate. Man is man's fate. Thus man

the spectator is the creator of man the character. Everything is subject to criticism, to rectification. All can be changed, and at a moment's notice: The actors must always be ready to accept, without protest, any proposed action; they must simply act it out, to give a live view of its consequences and drawbacks. Any spectator, by virtue of being a spectator, has the right to try his version—without censorship. The actor does not change his main function: He goes on being the interpreter. What changes is the object of his interpretation. If formerly he interpreted the solitary author locked in his study, to whom divine inspiration dictated a finished text, here, on the contrary, he must interpret the mass audience, assembled in their local committees, societies of "friends of the barrio," groups of neighbors, schools, unions, peasant leagues or whatever; he must give expression to the collective thought of men and women. The actor ceases to interpret the individual and starts to interpret the group, which is much more difficult and much more creative.

Second degree: Image theater. Here the spectator has to participate more directly. He is asked to express his views on a certain theme of common interest that the participants wish to discuss. The theme can be far-reaching, abstract—as, for example, imperialism—or it can be a local problem such as the lack of water, a common occurrence in almost all the barrios. The participant is asked to express his opinion but without speaking, using only the bodies of the other participants and "sculpting" with them a group of statues, in such a way that his opinions and feelings become evident. The participant is to use the bodies of the others as if he were a sculptor and the others were made of clay: He must determine the position of each body down to the most minute details of facial expression. He is not allowed to speak under any circumstances. The most that is permitted to him is to show with his own facial expressions what he wants the statue-spectator to do. After organizing this group of statues he is allowed to enter into a discussion with the other participants in order to determine if all agree with his "sculpted" opinion. Modifications can be rehearsed: The spectator has the right to modify the statues in their totality or in some detail. When finally an image is arrived at that is the most acceptable to all, the spectator-sculptor is asked to show the way he would like the given theme to be; that is, in the first grouping the actual image is shown, in the second the ideal image. Finally he is to show a transitional image to show how it would be possible to pass from one reality to the other—in other words, how to carry out the change, the transformation, the revolution or whatever term one wishes to use. Thus, starting with a grouping of "statues" accepted by all as representative of a real situation, each one is asked to propose ways of changing it.

Once again, a concrete example can best clarify the matter. A young woman, a literacy agent who lived in the village of Otuzco, was asked to explain, through a grouping of live images, what her hometown was like. In Otuzco, before the present revolutionary government[1], there was a peasant rebellion; the landlords (which no longer exist in Peru) imprisoned the leader of the rebellion, took him to the main square and, in front of everyone, castrated him. The young woman from Otuzco composed the image of the castration, placing one of the participants on the ground while another pretended to be castrating him and still another held him from behind. Then at one side she placed a woman praying, on her knees, and at the other side a group of five men and women, also on their knees, with hands tied behind their backs. Behind the man being castrated, the young woman placed another participant in a position obviously suggestive of power and violence and, behind him, two armed men pointing their guns at the prisoner.

This was the image that person had of her village. A terrible, pessimistic, defeatist image but also a true reflection of something that had actually taken place. Then the young woman was asked to show what she would want her village to be like. She modified

completely the "statues" of the group and regrouped them as people who worked in peace and loved each other—in short, a happy and contented, ideal Otuzco. Then came the third, and most important, part of this form of theater: How can one, starting with the actual image, arrive at the ideal image? How to bring about the change, the transformation, the revolution?

Here it was a question of giving an opinion but without words. Each participant had the right to act as a "sculptor" and to show how the grouping, or organization, could be modified through a reorganization of forces for the purpose of arriving at an ideal image. Each one expressed his opinion through imagery. Lively discussions arose, but without words. When one would exclaim, "It's not possible like this; I think that…," he was immediately interrupted: "Don't say what you think; come and show it to us." The participant would go and demonstrate physically, visually, his thought, and the discussion would continue. In this particular case the following variations were observed:

1. When a young woman from the interior was asked to form the image of change, she would never change the image of the kneeling woman, signifying clearly that she did not see in that woman a potential force for revolutionary change. The young women naturally identified themselves with that feminine figure, and, since they could not perceive themselves as possible protagonists of the revolution, they left unmodified the image of the kneeling woman. On the other hand, when the same thing was asked of a girl from Lima, she, being more "liberated," would start off by changing precisely that image with which she identified herself. This experiment was repeated many times and always produced the same results, without variation. Undoubtedly the different patterns of action represent not chance occurrence but the sincere, visual expression of the ideology and psychology of the participants. The young women from Lima always modified the image: Some would make the woman clasp the figure of the castrated man, others

---

1   The government established after the October 1968 revolution and headed by President Juan Velasco Alvarado (replaced in August 1975 by Francisco Morales Bermúdez). (Translators' note.)

1927
1960
1963
1964
1967
1969
1970
1971
1972
1973
1974
1975
1976
1977
1978
1979
1980
1981
1982
1983
1984
1985
1986
1987
1988
1989
1990
1991
1992
1993
1994
1995
1996
1997
1998
1999
2000
2001
2002
2003
2004
2005
2006

would prompt the woman to fight against the castrator, etc. Those from the interior did little more than allow the woman to lift her hands in prayer.

2. All the participants who believed in the revolutionary government would start by modifying the armed figures in the background. They changed the two men who were aiming their guns at the victim so that they would then aim at the powerful figure in the center or at the castrators themselves. On the other hand, when a participant did not have the same faith in his government, he would alter all figures except the armed ones.

3. The people who believed in magical solutions or in a "change of conscience" on the part of the exploiting classes would start by modifying the castrators— viewing them in effect as changing of their own volition—as well as the powerful figure in the center, who would become regenerated. By contrast, those who did not believe in this form of social change would first alter the kneeling men, making them assume a fighting posture, attacking the oppressors.

4. One of the young women, besides showing the transformations to be the work of the kneeling men—who would free themselves, attack their torturers and imprison them—also had one of the figures representing the people address the other participants, clearly expressing her opinion that social changes are made by the people as a whole and not only by their vanguard.

5. Another young woman made all kinds of changes, leaving untouched only the five persons with their hands tied. This girl belonged to the upper-middle class. When she showed signs of nervousness for not being able to imagine any further changes, someone suggested to her the possibility of changing the group of tied figures; the girl looked at them in surprise and exclaimed, "The truth is that those people didn't fit in …" It was the truth. The people did not fit into her view of the scheme of things, and she had never before been able to see it.

This form of image theater is without doubt one of the most stimulating, because it is so easy to practice and because of its extraordinary capacity for making thought *visible*. This happens because use of the language idiom is avoided. Each word has a denotation that is the same for all, but it also has a connotation that is unique for each individual. If I utter the word "revolution," obviously everyone will realize that I am talking about a radical change, but at the same time each person will think of his or her "own" revolution, a personal conception of revolution. But if I have to arrange a group of statues that will signify "my revolution," here there will be no denotation-connotation dichotomy. The image synthesizes the individual connotation and the collective denotation. In my arrangement signifying revolution, what are the statues doing? Do they have weapons in their hands, or do they have ballots? Are the figures of the people united in a fighting posture against the figures representing the common enemies; or are the figures of the people dispersed, or showing disagreement among themselves? My conception of "revolution" will become clear if, instead of speaking, I show with images what I think.

I remember that in a session of psychodrama a girl spoke repeatedly of the problems she had with her boyfriend, and she always started with more or less the same phrase: "He came in, embraced me and then…" Each time we heard this opening phrase we understood that they did in fact embrace; that is, we understood what the word "embrace" denotes. Then one day she showed by acting how their meetings were: He approached, she crossed her arms over her breasts as if protecting herself; he took hold of her and hugged her tightly, while she continued to keep her hands closed, defending herself. That was clearly a particular connotation for the word "embrace." When we understood her "embrace," we were finally able to understand her problems with her boyfriend.

In image theater other techniques can be used:

1. Each participant transformed into a statue is allowed one movement or gesture, and only one, each time a signal (such as clapping of hands) is

given. In this case the arrangement of images will change according to the individual desire of each participant.

2. The participants are first asked to memorize the ideal image, then to return to the original, actual image, and finally to make the movements necessary to arrive again at the ideal image—thus showing the group of images in motion and allowing the analysis of the feasibility of the proposed transitions. One will then be able to see if change occurs by the grace of God or if it is brought about by the opposing forces operating within the very core of the group.

3. The sculptor-participant, once his work is finished, is asked to try to place himself in the group he has created. This sometimes helps the person to realize that his own vision of reality is a cosmic one, as if he were a part of that reality.

The game of images offers many other possibilities. The important thing is always to analyze the feasibility of the change.

Third degree: Forum theater. This is the last degree, and here the participant has to intervene decisively in the dramatic action and change it. The procedure is as follows: First, the participants are asked to tell a story containing a political or social problem of difficult solution. Then a 10- or 15-minute skit portraying that problem and the solution intended for discussion is improvised or rehearsed and subsequently presented. When the skit is over, the participants are asked if they agree with the solution presented. At least some will say no. At this point it is explained that the scene will be performed once more, exactly as it was the first time. But now any participant in the audience has the right to replace any actor and lead the action in the direction that seems to him most appropriate. The displaced actor steps aside but remains ready to resume action the moment the participant considers his own intervention to be terminated. The other actors have to face the newly created situation, responding instantly to all the possibilities that it may present.

The participants who choose to intervene must continue the physical actions of the replaced actors; they are not allowed to come on the stage and talk, talk, talk: They must carry out the same type of work or activities performed by the actors who were in their place. The theatrical activity must go on in the same way, on the stage. Anyone may propose any solution, but it must be done on the stage, working, acting, doing things, and not from the comfort of his seat. Often a person is very revolutionary when in a public forum he envisages and advocates revolutionary and heroic acts; on the other hand, he often realizes that things are not so easy when he himself has to practice what he suggests.

An example: An 18-year-old man worked in the city of Chimbote, one of the world's most important fishing ports. There are in that city a great number of factories of fish meal, a principal export product of Peru. Some factories are very large, while others have only eight or nine employees. Our young man worked for one of the latter. The boss was a ruthless exploiter and forced his employees to work from eight o'clock in the morning to eight at night, or vice versa—twelve consecutive hours of work. Thus the problem was how to combat this inhuman exploitation. Each participant had a proposal: One of them was, for example, "operation turtle," which consists in working very slowly, especially when the boss is not looking. One young man had a brilliant idea: to work faster and fill the machine with so much fish that it would break with the excessive weight, requiring two or three hours to fix it. During this time the workers could rest. There was the problem, the employer's exploitation; and there was one solution, invented by native ingenuity. But would that be the best solution?

The scene was performed in the presence of all the participants. Some actors represented the workers, another represented the boss, another the foreman, another a "stool pigeon." The stage was converted into a fish-meal factory: one worker unloading the fish, another weighing the bags of fish, another carrying the bags to the machines, another tending the machine, while still others performed other pertinent tasks.

1927
1960
1963
1964
1967
1969
1970
1971
1972
1973
1974
1975
1976
1977
1978
1979
1980
1981
1982
1983
1984
1985
1986
1987
1988
1989
1990
1991
1992
1993
1994
1995
1996
1997
1998
1999
2000
2001
2002
2003
2004
2005
2006

While they worked, they kept up a dialogue, proposing solutions and discussing them until they came to accept the solution proposed by the young man and broke the machine; the boss came and the workers rested while the engineer repaired the machine. When the repair was done, they went back to work.

The scene was staged for the first time and the question was raised: Were all in agreement? No, definitely not. On the contrary, they disagreed. Each one had a different proposal: to start a strike, throw a bomb at the machine, start a union, etc.

Then the technique of forum theater was applied: The scene would be staged exactly as it had been the first time, but now each spectator-participant would have the right to intervene and change the action, trying out his proposal. The first to intervene was the one who'd suggested the use of a bomb. He got up, replaced the actor who was portraying the young man and made his bomb-throwing proposal. Of course, all the other actors argued against it since that would mean the destruction of the factory and therefore the source of work. What would become of so many workers if the factory closed up? Disagreeing, the man decided to throw the bomb himself, but soon realized that he did not know how to manufacture a bomb nor even how to throw it. Many people who in theoretical discussions advocate throwing bombs would not know what to do in reality, and would probably be the first to perish in the explosion. After trying his bomb solution, the man returned to his place and the actor replaced him until a second person came to try his solution, the strike. After much argument with the others he managed to convince them to stop working and walk out, leaving the factory abandoned. In this case, the owner, the foreman, and the "stool pigeon," who had remained in the factory, went to the town square (among the audience) to look for other workers to replace the strikers (there is mass unemployment in Chimbote). This spectator-participant tried his solution, the strike, and realized its impracticability; with so much unemployment the bosses would always be able to find workers

hungry enough and with little enough political consciousness to replace the strikers.

The third attempt was to form a small union for the purpose of negotiating the workers' demands, politicizing the employed workers as well as the unemployed, setting up mutual funds, etc. In this particular session of forum theater, this was the solution judged to be the best by the participants. In the forum theater, no idea is imposed: The audience, the people, have the opportunity to try out all their ideas, to rehearse all the possibilities, and to verify them in practice, that is, in theatrical practice. If the audience had come to the conclusion that it was necessary to dynamite all the fish-meal factories in Chimbote, this would also be right from their point of view. It is not the place of the theater to show the correct path but only to offer the means by which all possible paths may be examined.

Maybe the theater in itself is not revolutionary, but these theatrical forms are without a doubt a *rehearsal of revolution*. The truth of the matter is that the spectator-actor practices a real act even though he does it in a fictional manner. While he rehearses throwing a bomb onstage, he is concretely rehearsing the way a bomb is thrown; acting out his attempt to organize a strike, he is concretely organizing a strike. Within its fictitious limits, the experience is a concrete one.

Here the cathartical effect is entirely avoided. We are used to plays in which the characters make the revolution onstage and the spectators in their seats feel themselves to be triumphant revolutionaries. Why make a revolution in reality if we have already made it in the theater? But that does not happen here: The rehearsal stimulates the practice of the act in reality. Forum theater, as well as these other forms of a people's theater, instead of taking something away from the spectator evoke in him a desire to practice in reality the act he has rehearsed in the theater. The practice of these theatrical forms creates a sort of uneasy sense of incompleteness that seeks fulfillment through real action.

Fourth Stage: The Theater as Discourse

George Ikishawa used to say that the bourgeois theater is the finished theater. The bourgeoisie already knows what the world is like, *their* world, and is able to present images of this complete, finished world. The bourgeoisie presents the spectacle. On the other hand, the proletariat and the oppressed classes do not know yet what their world will be like; consequently, their theater will be the rehearsal, not the finished spectacle. This is quite true, though it is equally true that the theater can present images of transition.

I have been able to observe the truth of this view during all my activities in the people's theater of so many and such different countries of Latin America. Popular audiences are interested in experimenting, in rehearsing, and they abhor the "closed" spectacles. In those cases they try to enter into a dialogue with the actors, to interrupt the action, to ask for explanations without waiting politely for the end of the play. Contrary to the bourgeois code of manners, the people's code allows and encourages the spectator to ask questions, to dialogue, to participate.

All the methods that I have discussed are forms of a rehearsal theater, not a spectacle theater. One knows how these experiments will begin but not how they will end, because the spectator is freed from his chains, finally acts and becomes a protagonist. Because they respond to the real needs of a popular audience they are practiced with success and joy.

But nothing in this prohibits a popular audience from practicing also more "finished" forms of theater. In Peru many forms previously developed in other countries, especially Brazil and Argentina, were also utilized and with great success. Some of these forms were:

1. NEWSPAPERS THEATER

It was initially developed by the Nucleus Group of the Arena Theater of Sao Paulo, of which I was the artistic director until forced to leave Brazil[2]. It consists of several simple techniques for transforming daily news items, or any other nondramatic material, into theatrical performances:

a. Simple reading: The news item is read detached from the context of the newspaper, from the format that makes it false or tendentious.

b. Crossed reading: Two news items are read in crossed (alternating) form, one throwing light on the other, explaining it, giving it a new dimension.

c. Complementary reading: Data and information generally omitted by the newspapers of the ruling classes are added to the news.

d. Rhythmical reading: As a musical commentary, the news is read to the rhythm of the samba, tango, Gregorian chant, etc., so that the rhythm functions as a critical "filter" of the news, revealing its true content, which is obscured in the newspaper.

e. Parallel action: The actors mime parallel actions while the news is read, showing the context in which the reported event really occurred; one hears the news and sees something else that complements it visually.

f. Improvisation: The news is improvised onstage to exploit all its variants and possibilities.

g. Historical: Data or scenes showing the same event in other historical moments, in other countries, or in other social systems, are added to the news.

h. Reinforcement: The news is read or sung with the aid or accompaniment of slides, jingles, songs or publicity materials.

i. Concretion of the abstract: That which the news often hides in its purely abstract information is made concrete on the stage: torture, hunger, unemployment, etc., are shown concretely, using graphic images, real or symbolic.

---

2   Under the author's leadership the Arena Theater developed into one of Brazil's—indeed, one of Latin America's—most outstanding theaters. After 1964, when military rule was established in that country, Boal's work continued, though hampered by censorship and other restrictions imposed by the government. His outspoken position against the authoritarian regime led to his imprisonment and torture in 1971. Released after three months and acquitted of all charges, he was, nevertheless, compelled to leave Brazil in order to insure the safety of himself and his family. After political circumstances also forced him to leave Buenos Aires, Argentina, he took up residence in Portugal.

1927
1960
1963
1964
1967
1969
1970
1971
1972
1973
1974
1975
1976
1977
1978
1979
1980
1981
1982
1983
1984
1985
1986
1987
1988
1989
1990
1991
1992
1993
1994
1995
1996
1997
1998
1999
2000
2001
2002
2003
2004
2005
2006

j. Text out of context: The news is presented out of the context in which it was published; for example, an actor gives the speech about austerity previously delivered by the Minister of Economics while he devours an enormous dinner. The real truth behind the minister's words becomes demystified—he wants austerity for the people but not for himself.

2. INVISIBLE THEATER

It consists of the presentation of a scene in an environment other than the theater, before people who are not spectators. The place can be a restaurant, a sidewalk, a market, a train, a line of people, etc. The people who witness the scene are those who are there by chance. During the spectacle, these people must not have the slightest idea that it is a "spectacle," for this would make them "spectators."

The invisible theater calls for the detailed preparation of a skit with a complete text or a simple script, but it is necessary to rehearse the scene sufficiently so that the actors are able to incorporate into their acting and their actions the intervention of the spectators. During the rehearsal it is also necessary to include every imaginable intervention from the spectators; these possibilities will form a kind of optional text.

The invisible theater erupts in a location chosen as a place where the public congregates. All the people who are near become involved in the eruption, and the effects of it last long after the skit is ended. …

Several presentations of invisible theater were made in different locations in Peru. Particularly interesting is what happened at the Carmen Market, in the barrio of Comas, some 14 kilometers from downtown Lima. Two actresses were protagonists in a scene enacted at a vegetable stand. One of them, who was pretending to be illiterate, insisted that the vendor was cheating her, taking advantage of the fact that she did not know how to read; the other actress checked the figures, finding them to be correct, and advised the "illiterate" one to register in one of ALFIN's literacy courses. After some discussion about the best age to start one's

studies, about what to study and with whom, the first actress kept on insisting that she was too old for those things. It was then that a little old woman, leaning on her cane, very indignantly shouted:

"My dears, that's not true! For learning and making love one is never too old!"

Everyone witnessing the scene broke into laughter at the old woman's amorous outburst, and the actresses were unable to continue the scene.

3. PHOTO-ROMANCE

In many Latin American countries there is a genuine epidemic of photo-romances, sub-literature on the lowest imaginable level, which furthermore always serves as a vehicle for the ruling classes' ideology. The technique here consists in reading to the participants the general lines in the plot of a photo-romance without telling them the source of this plot. The participants are asked to act out the story. Finally, the acted-out story is compared to the story as it is told in the photo-romance, and the differences are discussed.

For example: A rather stupid story taken from Corín Tellado, the worst author of this brutalizing genre, started like this:

A woman is waiting for her husband in the company of another woman who is helping her with the housework. …

The participants acted according to their customs: A woman at home expecting her husband will naturally be preparing the meal; the one helping her is a neighbor, who comes to chat about various things; the husband comes home tired after a long day's work; the house is a one-room shack, etc., etc. In Corín Tellado, on the contrary, the woman is dressed in a long evening gown, with pearl necklaces, etc.; the woman who is helping her is a black maid who says no more than "Yes, ma'am"; "The dinner is served, ma'am"; "Very well, ma'am"; "Here comes Mr. X, ma'am," and nothing else. The house is a marble palace; the husband comes home after a day's work in his factory, where he had an argument with the workers because they, "not understanding the crisis we are all living through, wanted an increase in salaries . . ." and continues in this vein.

This particular story was sheer trash, but at the same time it served as a magnificent example of ideological insight. The well-dressed woman received a letter from an unknown woman, went to visit her, and discovered her to be a former mistress of her husband; the mistress stated that the husband had left her because he wanted to marry the factory owner's daughter—that is, the well-dressed woman. To top it all, the mistress exclaimed:

"Yes, he betrayed me, deceived me. But I forgive him because, after all, he has always been very ambitious, and he knew very well that with me he could not climb very high. On the other hand, with you he can go very far indeed!"

That is to say, the former mistress forgave her lover because he had in the highest degree that capitalistic eagerness to possess everything. The desire to be a factory owner is presented as something so noble that even a few betrayals on the way up are to be forgiven.

And the young wife, not to be outdone, pretends to be ill so that he will have to remain at her side, and so that, as a result of this trick, he will finally fall in love with her. What an ideology! This love story is crowned with a happy ending rotten to the core. Of course the story, when told without the dialogue, and acted out by peasants, takes on an entirely different meaning. When at the end of the performance, the participants are told the origin of the plot they have just acted out, they experience a shock. And this must be understood: When they read Corín Tellado they immediately assume the passive role of "spectators," but if they first of all have to act out a story themselves; afterward, when they do read Corin Tellado's version, they will no longer assume a passive, expectant attitude but instead a critical, comparative one. They will look at the lady's house and compare it with their own, at the husband's or wife's attitudes

and compare them with those of their own spouses, etc. And they will be prepared to detect the poison infiltrating the pages of those photo-stories, or the comics and other forms of cultural and ideological domination.

I was overjoyed when, months after the experiments with the educators, back in Lima, I was informed that the residents of several barrios were using that same technique to analyze television programs, an endless source of poison directed against the people.

4. BREAKING OF REPRESSION
The dominant classes crush the dominated ones through repression; the old crush the young through repression; certain races subjugate certain others through repression. Never through a cordial understanding, through an honest interchange of ideas, through criticism and autocriticism. No. The ruling classes, the old, the "superior" races, or the masculine sex, have their sets of values and impose them by force, by unilateral violence, upon the oppressed classes, the young, the races they consider inferior, or women.

The capitalist does not ask the working man if he agrees that the capital should belong to one and the labor to another; he simply places an armed policeman at the factory door, and that is that—private property is decreed.

The dominated class, race, sex or age group suffers the most constant, daily and omnipresent repression. The ideology becomes concrete in the figure of the dominated person. The proletariat is exploited through the domination exerted on all proletarians. Sociology becomes psychology. There is not an oppression by the masculine sex in general of the feminine sex in general: What exists is the concrete oppression that men (individuals) direct against women (individuals).

The technique of breaking repression consists in asking a participant to remember a particular moment when he felt especially repressed, accepted that repression and began to act in a manner contrary to his own desires. That moment must have deep personal meaning: I, a proletarian, am oppressed; we proletarians are

1927
1960
1963
1964
1967
1969
1970
1971
1972
1973
1974
1975
1976
1977
1978
1979
1980
1981
1982
1983
1984
1985
1986
1987
1988
1989
1990
1991
1992
1993
1994
1995
1996
1997
1998
1999
2000
2001
2002
2003
2004
2005
2006

oppressed; therefore the proletariat is oppressed; it is necessary to pass from the particular to the general, not vice versa, and to deal with something that has happened to someone in particular but which at the same time is typical of what happens to others.

The person who tells the story also chooses from among the rest of the participants all the other characters who will participate in the reconstruction of the incident. Then, after receiving the information and directions provided by the protagonist, the participants and the protagonist act out the incident just as it happened in reality—recreating the same scene, the same circumstances and the same original feelings.

Once the "reproduction" of the actual event is over, the protagonist is asked to repeat the scene but this time without accepting the repression, fighting to impose his will, his ideas, his wishes. The other participants are urged to maintain the repression as in the first performance. The clash that results helps to measure the possibility one often has to resist and yet fails to do so; it helps to measure the true strength of the enemy. It also gives the protagonist the opportunity of trying once more and carrying out, in fiction, what he had not been able to do in reality. But we have already seen that this is not cathartic: The fact of having rehearsed a resistance to oppression will prepare him to resist effectively in a future reality, when the occasion presents itself once more.

On the other hand, it is necessary to take care that the generic nature of the particular case under study be understood. In this type of theatrical experiment the particular instance must serve as the point of departure, but it is indispensable to reach the general. ...

5. MYTH THEATER

It is simply a question of discovering the obvious behind the myth: to logically tell a story, revealing its evident truths.

In a place called Motupe there was a hill, almost a mountain, with a narrow road that led through the trees to the top; halfway to the top stood a cross. One could go as far as that cross: To go beyond it was dangerous; it inspired fear, and the few who had tried had never returned. It was believed that some sanguinary ghosts inhabited the top of the mountain. But the story is also told of a brave young man who armed himself and climbed to the top, where he found the "ghosts." They were in reality some Americans who owned a gold mine located precisely on the top of that mountain.

Another legend is that of the lagoon of Cheken. It is said that there was no water there and that all the peasants, having to travel for several kilometers to get a glass of water, were dying of thirst. Today a lagoon exists there, the property of a local landowner. How did that lagoon spring up and how did it become the property of one man? The legend explains it. When there was still no water, one day of intense heat all the villagers were lamenting and praying to God to grant then even a tiny stream of water. But God did not have pity on that arid village. At midnight of the same day, however, a man dressed in a long black poncho and riding a black horse arrived and addressed the landowner, who was then only a poor peasant like the others:

"I will give a lagoon for all of you, but you, friend, must give me your most precious possession."

The poor man, very distressed, moaned:

"But I have nothing; I am very poor. We all here suffer from the lack of water, live in miserable shacks, suffer from the most terrible hunger. We have nothing precious, not even our lives. And myself in particular, my only precious possession is my three daughters, nothing else."

"And of the three," responded the stranger, "the oldest is the most beautiful. I will give you a lagoon filled with the freshest water of all Peru; but in exchange you will give me your oldest daughter so that I may marry her."

The future landlord thought for a long while, cried a lot, and asked this frightened eldest daughter if she would accept such an unusual marriage proposal. The obedient daughter expressed herself in this way:

> If it is for the salvation of all, so that the thirst and hunger of all the peasants will come to an end, if it is so that you may have a lagoon with the freshest water of all Peru, if it is so that that lagoon will belong to you alone and bring you personal prosperity and riches—for you will be able to sell this wonderful water to the peasants, who will find it cheaper to buy from you than to travel so many kilometers—if it is for all this, tell the gentleman in the black poncho, astride his black horse, that I will go with him, even if in my heart I am suspicious of his true identity and of the places he will take me.

Happy and content, and of course somewhat tearful, the kind father went to inform the man in black of the decision, meanwhile asking the daughter to make some little signs showing the price of a liter of water, in order to expedite the work. The man in black undressed the girl, for he did not want to take anything from that house besides the girl herself, and placed her on his horse, which set off at a gallop toward a great depression in the plains. Then an enormous explosion was heard, and a large cloud of smoke remained in the very place where the horse, horseman and naked girl had disappeared. From the huge hole that had been made in the ground, a spring started to flow and formed the lagoon with the freshest water of all Peru.

This myth no doubt hides a truth: The landlord took possession of what did not belong to him. If formerly the noblemen attributed to God the granting of their property and rights, today explanations no less magical are still used. In this case, the property of the lagoon was explained by the loss of the eldest daughter, the landlord's most precious possession—a transaction took place! And serving as a reminder of that, the legend said that on the nights of the new moon one could hear the girl singing at the bottom of the lagoon, still naked and combing her long hair with a beautiful golden comb. Yes, the truth is that, for the landlord, the lagoon was like gold.

The myths told by the people should be studied and analyzed and their hidden truths revealed. In this task the theater can be extraordinarily useful.

6. ANALYTICAL THEATER

A story is told by one of the participants and immediately the actors improvise it. Afterward each character is broken down into all his social roles and the participants are asked to choose a physical object to symbolize each role. For example, a policeman killed a chicken thief. The policeman is analyzed:

a. He is a worker because he rents his labor power; symbol: a pair of overalls.
b. He is a bourgeois because he protects private property and values it more than human life; symbol: a necktie, or a top hat, etc.
c. He is a repressive agent because he is a policeman; symbol: a revolver.

This is continued until the participants have analyzed all his roles: head of a family (symbol: the wallet, for example), member of a fraternal order, etc., etc. It is important that the symbols be chosen by the participants present and that they not be imposed "from above." For a particular community the symbol for the head of the family might be a wallet, because he is the person who controls the household finances and in this way controls the family. For another community this symbol may not communicate anything, that is, it may not be a symbol; then an armchair may be chosen…

Having analyzed the character or characters (it is advisable to limit this operation to the central characters only, for simplicity and clarity), a fresh attempt to tell the story is made, while also taking away some of the symbols from each character, and consequently, some social roles as well. Would the story be exactly the same if:

a. The policeman did not have the top hat or the necktie?
b. The robber had a top hat or necktie?
c. The robber had a revolver?
d. The policeman and the robber both had the same symbol for the fraternal order?

1927
1960
1963
1964
1967
1969
1970
1971
1972
1973
1974
1975
1976
1977
1978
1979
1980
1981
1982
1983
1984
1985
1986
1987
1988
1989
1990
1991
1992
1993
1994
1995
1996
1997
1998
1999
2000
2001
2002
2003
2004
2005
2006

The participants are asked to make varying combinations, and the proposed combinations must be performed by the actors and criticized by all those present. In this way they will realize that human actions are not the exclusive and primordial result of individual psychology: Almost always, though, the individual speaks his class!

7. RITUALS AND MASKS

The relations of production (infrastructure) determine the culture of a society (superstructure).

Sometimes the infrastructure changes but the superstructure for a while remains the same. In Brazil, the landlords would not allow the peasants to look them in the face while talking with them: This would mean lack of respect. The peasants were accustomed to talking with the landlords only while staring at the ground and murmuring: "Yes, sir; yes, sir; yes, sir." When the government decreed an agrarian reform (before 1964, date of the fascist coup d'etat), its emissaries went to the fields to tell the peasants that now they could become landowners. The peasants, staring at the ground, murmured: "Yes, friend; yes, friend; yes, friend." A feudalistic culture had totally permeated their lives. The relationships of the peasant with the landlord were entirely different from those with the agent of the Institute of Agrarian Reform, but the ritual remained unchanged.

This particular technique of a people's theater ("rituals and masks") consists precisely in revealing the superstructures, the rituals which reify all human relationships, and the masks of behavior that those rituals impose on each person according to the roles he plays in society and the rituals he must perform.

A very simple example: A man goes to a priest to confess his sins. How will he do it? Of course, he will kneel, confess his sins, hear the penitence, cross himself and leave. But do all men confess always in the same way before all priests? Who is the man, and who is the priest?

In this case we need two versatile actors to stage the same confession four times:

First scene: The priest and the parishioner are landlords.
Second scene: The priest is a landlord and the parishioner is a peasant.
Third scene: The priest is a peasant and the parishioner is a landlord.
Fourth scene: The priest and the parishioner are peasants.

The ritual is the same in each instance, but the different social masks will cause the four scenes to be different also.

This is an extraordinarily rich technique which has countless variants: the same ritual changing masks; the same ritual performed by people of one social class, and later by people of another class; exchange of masks within the same ritual, etc., etc.

Conclusion: "Spectator," a Bad Word!

Yes, this is without a doubt the conclusion: "Spectator" is a bad word! The spectator is less than a man and it is necessary to humanize him, to restore to him his capacity for action in all its fullness. He too must be a subject, an actor on an equal plane with those generally accepted as actors, who must also be spectators. All these experiments of a people's theater have the same objective—the liberation of the spectator, on whom the theater has imposed finished visions of the world.

Perhaps the theater is not revolutionary in itself; but have no doubt: It is a rehearsal of revolution!

(Translated from the Spanish by Charles A. and Maria-Odilia Leal McBride.)

Boal, Augusto. Originally published as *Teatro del Oprimido*. *Theater of the Oppressed*. New York: Theatre Communications Group, Inc., 1979. Copyright © 1979 Theatre Communications Group. Reprinted with permission of TCG.

COMMUNICATION STRATEGIES FOR RURAL DEVELOPMENT

By Gloria D. Feliciano

1974 A great number of the studies dealing with the process and effects of communication have been conducted for the most part in relation to agricultural development. Done mostly in Korea, India and the Philippines, these studies focus on the dissemination of new farming practices and others related to rural community development.[1]

The passing of traditional, antiquated farming practices in the above countries of the subregion may partly be attributed to the diffusion of new farming methods by various types of rural communication channels. This is one of the main findings of much of the village research on the communication process done in the area during the last two decades. The research has dealt for the most part with sources or communicators of new farming technology, as well as the recipients of this type of agricultural information.

The great bulk of this research has been done on the macro level, utilizing data obtained from sample surveys, with the farmers and village elders usually serving as the respondents. Some examples are: agricultural innovation in Indian villages, agro-information flow at the village level, the human variable in farm practice adoption in Philippine villages, and knowledge and practice of new farming methods. Those conducted at the micro level have dealt with an analysis of "cases," i.e., particular agro-cultural innovations such as high-yielding rice and corn varieties, fertilizers, pesticides and other innovations in a few villages ranging from one to fewer than five per study. The experimental studies have centered on the comparative effectiveness of various communications media and change approaches or strategies.[2] The studies have been undertaken by individual researchers or groups of researchers in communication institutions based mostly in privately owned universities. Further, the researchers usually have had training and experience in North American schools, which have a strong program in diffusion research.

The Field Worker

The research findings have identified the field worker (or extension worker in some countries) as the central character in the drama of change in the villages of the sub-region that are covered by extension programs. The great majority of these field workers come from the ministry/department of agriculture and its subsidiary agencies. The rest are from national, private institutions or from voluntary organizations affiliated with international community development or rural reconstruction movements, e.g., Thailand Rural Reconstruction Movement, Philippine Rural Reconstruction Movement, etc. In some countries, these workers are college degree holders, whereas in others they are high school graduates with training in vocational agriculture.

The positive response of the rural folk to farming innovations has been due to a large extent to these field workers. Their success in convincing farmers to adopt the new farming practices has been attributed to their knowledge of new agricultural technology, their oral communication skills, their competence in demonstrating the effectiveness of the innovations, their social stature in the village community and their "smooth, interpersonal relations" with the village constituency, in general.[3]

Rural Communication Network

The extension worker, however, is only one of several key individuals and groups in Asian rural communication

1   Gloria D. Feliciano, *An Overview of Communication Research in Asia: Status, Problems and Needs,* East-West Communication Institute, East-West Center, Honolulu, Hawaii, June 1973.

2   Asian Mass Communication Institutions – Teaching, Training and Research – A Directory, Asian Mass Communication Research and Information Centre, Singapore, 1973.

3   Gloria D. Feliciano, *The Farm and Home Development Project: An Evaluation,* Community Development Research Council, University of the Philippines, Diliman, Quezon City, 1969.

1927
1960
1963
1964
1967
1969
1970
1971
1972
1973
1974
1975
1976
1977
1978
1979
1980
1981
1982
1983
1984
1985
1986
1987
1988
1989
1990
1991
1992
1993
1994
1995
1996
1997
1998
1999
2000
2001
2002
2003
2004
2005
2006

network, which plays a significant role in the diffusion and adoption of farming innovations. The others are the village elders, the farmer and his wife, neighbors, relatives and friends, religious leaders, community leaders (often the village council members), formal and informal groups and various types of traditional/ folk media.

The village elders are the venerable old men who are highly respected by the village folk because of their age, wisdom and experience and have a large following in the community. They often endorse the innovation and, in some countries of the sub-region, the village elders also function as opinion leaders or "influence" persons. In other countries, these rural influentials may include the elective village council members, the land proprietors (where agrarian reform has not been implemented), religious leaders and the professionals. This group has been identified in some studies as legitimizers of the farming innovations, particularly where the effectiveness of the new technology has been amply demonstrated. In a number of cases, they have been shown to exert social pressure on farmers, thus facilitating the adoption of the innovation.[4]

The farmer has played a dual role in village change. He not only receives agricultural information but also acts as source and as channel, relaying the information he gets to others if he deems it important and useful. Studies in Japan, India, Pakistan, Korea, Taiwan and the Philippines have shown the farmer as information seeker and information giver of farming and related data. The situation, however, is characteristic more of the modernizing villages.

In the isolated, tradition-bound villages, farmers who obtain new technological information from initial sources, such as extension workers, tend to hold on to the information rather than pass it on the others. This behavior is due to one or more of the following: (1) the farmer is not prone to risk-taking; he cannot take the risk of being embarrassed or ridiculed if the new

practice fails; (2) he is skeptical; he doubts the efficacy of the practice until he has tried it and proven its effectiveness; (3) he is not adequately motivated on the merits of innovation so that he cannot recognize its significance until he has tried it and succeeds and sees to other farmers' favorable reaction to his success; and (4) he feels it's his good fortune to get the information and that other farmers will have their own chance at one time or another.

On the other hand, the farmer's wife, in some Southeast Asian countries, has functioned as initiator of homemaking innovations, such as new ways of preparing food (where no shortage exists), food preservation, needlecraft and handicraft, new kitchen layout, household gadgets, frontyard or backyard gardening, home planning and building sanitary privies. In a few countries she provides social support to agricultural innovations, thereby facilitating their legitimation. The rural housewife also shares decision making with her husband with regard to the adoption of modern agricultural technology.[5]

Village studies in Thailand, Malaysia, Korea and the Philippines have revealed the exogamous character of village marriages as evidenced by the observation that often neighbors and friends are also relatives. This is specially true in villages that have relatively less exposure to urbanizing influences. Although kinfolk sometimes live in non-mutual obligations and the sharing of mutual benefits. In this process, the spread of new technology, especially on their means of livelihood, usually farming, is facilitated through these functional relationships and filial ties.

In countries where villages are governed by groups usually called councils comprising of elective officials, new farming technology is often channeled through these institutionalized groups. Because of their advantages in terms of greater and prior exposure to modern practices and sometimes higher socioeconomic status, the council members are often the

---

4   *Ibid.*

5   *Ibid.*

early adoptors of farming and related innovations. They also help legitimize these innovations by initiating group discussions, encouraging greater interaction and leading in field demonstrations to test their effectiveness and adaptability to the village situation.

These formal groupings that help in the dissemination of new agricultural practices include, as previously mentioned, the village councils, the parent-teacher associations, the farmers' cooperative and credit organizations, farmers' marketing associations, homemakers' clubs and youth clubs. In countries like India and the Philippines, one finds rural media groupings as well as the radio forums and the teleclubs.

There are also the small, informal groups, such as neighborhood associations that meet irregularly. These groups are usually preferred to formal groups, which do not allow the free flow of information due to the observance of protocol and the stratification between the leaders and the followers. The venues for these informal encounters are the house of the chieftain, the village store, the village's place of worship where such exists, and by the cool river banks and roadsides fringed with shady trees.

The Mass Media

Available agricultural communication studies have established the fact that the personal channels at the village level that have just been discussed are more effective than the mass media in the adoption of farming innovations. However, low economic and literacy levels have made their reach in Asia's villages much too limited to leave the communication support to agricultural development entirely to them.

With the exception of radio, the mass media and mass media aids—newspapers, radio, television, film, magazines, leaflets, pamphlets, posters, comics, etc.—have not filtered down to the grassroots to any appreciable degree. This is due to the inaccessibility of many villages resulting from inadequate transportation facilities and also to poor distribution procedures and practices. ...

For purposes of rural development, study findings on rural audience deserve close scrutiny by development strategists. Available studies in this field have focused on target audiences as groups with reference to their socioeconomic attributes, attitudes, value orientations, motivations and aspirations, media preferences, reactions to media messages, as well as the effects these messages have had on them, in terms of changes in levels of awareness and knowledge and, to a limited extent, attitudes and behavior vis-à-vis selected agricultural innovations.

Insofar as these variables are concerned, the findings exhibit a variance not just between countries of the subregion, but also within countries. In addition, for several of the less-developed countries, the audience studies were undertaken as part of benchmark surveys for development, such as agrarian reform and allied projects, such as cooperatives, statistical surveys of households, advertising and marketing studies and pre-election pools. Those not included in this classification were mostly exploratory studies with very limited area coverage, small samples and nonrigorous research methods. All these factors militate against their use in policy and planning for rural development on a large and meaningful scale.[6]

There is a need to do in-depth studies of the process of adoption vis-à-vis agriculture, nutrition and family planning in the Asian setting. These studies need to take into account the factors that impinge on the process—as facilitators or deterrents—particularly communication and related socio-psychological and socio-cultural elements.

The many day-to-day operational or logistics problems of the agricultural, nutrition, or family planning administrator that have some bearing on the communication process also need to be studied. For instance, what type of communication materials for which groups should one have at the family planning clinic, a farm demonstration area or an agricultural

---

6   Gloria D. Feliciano, *An overview... op. cit.*

1927
1960
1963
1964
1967
1969
1970
1971
1972
1973
1974
1975
1976
1977
1978
1979
1980
1981
1982
1983
1984
1985
1986
1987
1988
1989
1990
1991
1992
1993
1994
1995
1996
1997
1998
1999
2000
2001
2002
2003
2004
2005
2006

extension office? What type of incentive schemes should one consider for field motivators? What motivational strategies will work for specific situations? What type of reporting forms will provide a valid measure for program accomplishment? What other feedback mechanism will adequately measure program effectiveness?

Conference Paper. In Robert H. Crawford and William B. Ward (eds.), *Communication Strategies for Rural Development*. Proceedings of the Cornell-CIAT international symposium, Cali, Colombia, March 17-22, 1974. Cornell University, Ithaca, NY.

THE PHILOSOPHY OF DEVELOPMENT COMMUNICATION

Excerpt from: Readings in Development Communication

By Juan F. Jamias

1975 Development communication is evolving its own philosophy and guiding principles. The purpose here is to state categorically the major ideas that underpin development communication as a field of study.

1. In the development context, communication is viewed as purposive. It is to be noted that other communication scholars hold that communication is, and should be "ethically" non-purposive.

2. In the development context, a tacit positive value is assumed for what one espouses, what one communicates about. Thus, the high yielding varieties of rice are justifiably worth promoting to farmers, population control is a key to the decent survival of mankind, land reform is a must for social justice.

3. The third conceptual thrust of development communication is its pragmatism. This idea emphasizes that development communication is to be judged by its results. The results in turn are determined by the specific behavioural objectives of the communicator. What does the communicator want to happen as a result of speaking, writing, visualizing or simply doing none of these?

Excerpt from *Readings in Development Communication*, Juan F. Jamias, ed. Department of Development Communication, College of Agriculture, University of the Philippines at Los Baños, 1975. Reprinted with permission of Estrella Jamias.

EXCERPT FROM:

THE APPEARANCE OF
NATIONAL COMMUNICATION POLICIES:
A NEW ARENA FOR SOCIAL STRUGGLE

By Herbert I. Schiller

1975 Modern mind management, employing information, imagery, education and technology, pose new problems to dominated people—both inside the core, industrialized countries and in the peripheral, dependent regions.

Class conflict historically has been seen as an economic battle, a conflict between contending groups, the working class against the property-owning class: In the near term, for a larger share of the immediate (annual) product; ultimately, for the control and direction of the production system. Now, however, in the major industrialized, capitalist nations of Western Europe, in North America and Japan, a new element has entered the confrontation: utilization to the hilt by the dominating class of an enormously expanded and totally penetrative informational apparatus. In the still unindustrialized countries, struggling to overcome their economic dependency, national independence and social transformation are blocked to the extent that the communications system is controlled by, or represents, the dominating class, externally or internally based.

Accordingly, class conflict has now moved into the communications-cultural sphere in an explicit way; and the emergence of national communication policies is the reflection of generally still unresolved battles between contradictory interests and demand in the cultural informational sector. Yet this is not secondary level of conflict. The communications cultural component has been enjoying a continuous expansion in all market economies. It seems likely to become, both absolutely (in terms of workers employed, capital invested, value of output, etc.) and qualitatively (in terms of decisive influence), a critical, if not the central, locus of the future struggle within and against capitalism. Examples of growing class and national concern with the forces that create and shape individual and group beliefs and outlooks are numerous and multiplying.

Schiller, Herbert I. (1975). *The Appearance of National Communication Policies: A New Arena for Social Struggle*. Vol. 21, No. 2, Gazette, Amsterdam. Copyright © 1975, Sage Publications. Reprinted with the permission of the copyright holder.

1927
1960
1963
1964
1967
1969
1970
1971
1972
1973
1974
1975
1976
1977
1978
1979
1980
1981
1982
1983
1984
1985
1986
1987
1988
1989
1990
1991
1992
1993
1994
1995
1996
1997
1998
1999
2000
2001
2002
2003
2004
2005
2006

THE NEED FOR NEW MODELS
Excerpt from: *Communication of Agricultural Innovations in Latin America: The Need for New Models*
By Juan Díaz Bordenave

We stated earlier that technification of Latin American agriculture should occur as part of a more general process of gaining independence from foreign economic masters. Intellectual independence may also be needed in diffusion research. Until now, most of the studies conducted in Latin America carry the imprint of the U.S. "classical" diffusion model. Latin American communication scholars must overcome their mental compulsion to perceive their own reality through foreign concepts and ideologies, and they must learn to look at the communication and adoption of innovations from their own perspective. Indeed, because the classical diffusion model was formulated under significantly different socioeconomic conditions and in agreement with an ideological stance not compatible with the Latin American reality, the types of research questions that were asked by Latin American researchers who used that diffusion model unquestioningly do not get to the real issues affecting rural development.

Let us compare the type of questions emanating from the classical model with some questions that should be asked by Latin American scholars. Havens (1972) listed the following questions as typical of the "diffusionist approach" to the study of development:

1. Which innovations are available (in the technological inventory)?
2. Who uses the technological innovations?
3. How are they diffused?
4. What are the differences between users and nonusers of the innovations (a) in personal characteristics, and (b) in social characteristics?
5. Which groups orient individual behavior toward the innovations?
6. How do individuals feel deprivation, and what attitude do they take in order to reduce it?
7. Which are the pertinent social codes and norms for innovation?

8. How do values affect individual or group behavior regarding innovation?

In order to decide which research questions should be asked to better understand the communication and adoption of agricultural innovations in Latin America, let us imagine ourselves as government planners of a nation which is transforming its agriculture and rural life to secure a more just social structure and a solid national development. Here are some questions that might occur to the government planners:

1. How autonomous or independent is the country from external forces which affect its economy and its political decisions?
2. How is the rural social structure organized, and what influence does it exert over individual decision-making? What is the historical genesis of this situation?
3. Do the majority of the farmers own their land, either individually or cooperatively? Do they own their agricultural tools?
4. Who controls the economic institutions, particularly the market, credit, and input supply organizations?
5. Who decides what kinds of innovations should be diffused and developed?
6. Are the farmers consulted and are their needs for innovation ascertained?
7. What criteria are used to guide the choice of innovations for diffusion—(a) the common welfare, (b) the increase of production for export, (c) the maintenance of low prices for the urban consumers, (d) the profit of big commercial farmers and landowners?
8. What effects will the adoption of certain innovations be likely to have on individual and family welfare? On regional and national development in the short, medium and long range? Will they promote employment or unemployment, fixation of the rural population or migration to the

cities, enrichment of the already rich or better income distribution?

9. Do the innovations take into account regional and local differences in ecology, economy, farming habits and cultural norms?

10. Is there any degree of coercion necessary for the adoption of an innovation, either by the market situation, the credit institutions, the government, or the landlords?

11. What is the role of mass-media advertising? Is it persuading farmers to adopt innovations that they really need or that they do not need?

12. How appropriate and well-proven are the products and techniques being diffused? Are they adequate to the stage of technological, economic and social development in the nation?

13. What kind of living and learning adjustments do the innovations require from the farmers? Do they require the establishment of new systems of credit, land tenure, technical assistance, marketing and insurance?

14. Who controls the sources and channels of communication for the innovations? Is there communication monopoly, censorship, blockage or distortion?

15. How adequate are the communication channels' content and treatment of the innovation in relation to the needs of the farmers? Are they at the service of all the farmers or mainly at the service of the government, the input industries, the buyers of farm products, the larger farmers, the consumer groups?

16. What are the feedback possibilities and channels for the farmers to communicate their needs and results to the innovation sources and policy-makers?

17. Are farmers organized in pressure groups that can exert influence on the social structure of land tenure, on the production infrastructure, and on the marketing system so as to facilitate the diffusion of appropriate innovations?

18. How adequate are the change agents or extension-service personnel as a two-way communication channel? Are they technically competent,

ideologically oriented to the welfare of the farmers, methodologically adequate?

19. Which are the institutions that directly or indirectly transfer technology to the farmers? What are the present relationships between the processes of conscientization, formal education, organization, politization and technification of the rural population?

20. Is technification promoted and executed without efforts for simultaneous conscientization?

21. How do farmers diagnose and solve their problems? How do they search for extracommunity resources and help? How well developed is their communication ability? What are the personal and group roles in farmers' problem-solving?

This list may be accused of being more of a political program than a research perspective. It should be. Because if there is one thing we are learning in Latin America, it is that studies of the communication of innovations cannot exist as ideologically free and politically neutral research. The scientist who says that he wants to do research without committing himself to any of the ways of changing rural society is, in fact, as ideologically committed as the one who believes in research as a tool for forging his chosen path to human and social change. Education, technological progress and political action should not be separated in Latin America, because they are various aspects of the total system.

In summary, the classic diffusion model was mostly concerned with what happens to the innovation in the process of diffusion and adoption. Needed are models concerned with what happens to the person who adopts an innovation and to his society.

References

Havens, E. "Methodological Issues in the Study of Development." Sociologia Ruralis, 1972, 12: 252-272.

1927
1960
1963
1964
1967
1969
1970
1971
1972
1973
1974
1975
1976
1977
1978
1979
1980
1981
1982
1983
1984
1985
1986
1987
1988
1989
1990
1991
1992
1993
1994
1995
1996
1997
1998
1999
2000
2001
2002
2003
2004
2005
2006

COMMUNICATION AND DEVELOPMENT: THE PASSING OF THE DOMINANT PARADIGM

Excerpt from: Communication Research

By Everett M. Rogers

1976 The most influential book about communication and development is probably Wilbur Schramm's *Mass Media and National Development*. When it appeared in 1964, social scientists thought they understood the nature of development and the role of communication in development. The ensuing decade shows us that our conception of development was rather limited and perhaps not entirely correct. Today we see that past notions do not entirely fit the reality and potential of the contemporary scene.

In this paper, I shall (1) describe the old concept of development and contrast it with some emerging alternatives, and (2) set forth our previous conception of communication in development and contrast it with some of the roles of communication in the emerging models of development.

The Dominant Paradigm of Development[1]

Through the late 1960s, a dominant paradigm ruled intellectual definitions and discussions of development and guided national development programs. This concept of development grew out of certain historical events, such as the industrial revolution in Europe and the United States; the colonial experience in Latin America, Africa and Asia; the quantitative empiricism of North American social science; and

capitalistic economic/political philosophy. Implicit in the ruling paradigm were numerous assumptions which were generally thought to be valid, or at least were not widely questioned, until about the 1970s.

Definitions of development centered around the criterion of the rate of economic growth. The level of national development at any given point in time was the gross national product (GNP) or, when divided by the total population in a nation, per capita income. Although there was a certain amount of intellectual discomfort with per capita income as the main index of development, especially among non-economists, alternative measures and definitions of development had relatively few proponents.

What were the major academic and historical influences on the old conception of development?

1. *The Industrial Revolution*, usually accompanied by foreign colonization and domestic urbanization, during the latter 1800s. The rapid economic growth of this period in Europe and the United States (and again in post–World War II Europe) implied that such growth was development, or at least was the driving engine of development. Industrialization was seen as the main route to development. And so less-developed countries (they were often called "underdeveloped" in the 1950s and 1960s) were advised by development planners to industrialize.

The old paradigm stressed economic growth through industrialization as the key to development. At the heart of industrialization were technology and capital, which substituted for labor. This simple synthesis of development may have been a fairly correct lesson from the experience of the industrial revolution in Western Europe and North America. Whether it could be applied adequately and successfully to very different sociocultural settings, such as the developing nations where labor was generally not in short supply, seemed a likely hypothesis in the 1950s, and it was certainly tested on a mammoth scale.

---

1   The following section is adapted from Rogers (1975)

What has happened in Western nations regarding their pathways to development is not necessarily an accurate predictor of the process in non-Western states. For instance, European nations were often greatly aided in their socioeconomic transformation by their exploitation of colonies. Obviously, the contemporary states of Latin America, Africa and Asia do not have colonies (although they may have an interior region or regions that act as economic colonies for another part of their nation).

2. Capital-intensive technology. More-developed nations possessed such technology. Less-developed nations had less of it. So the implication seemed plain: Introduce the technology to the less-developed countries and they would become relatively more developed, too. It was assumed that appropriate social technology would appear to accompany the externally introduced material technology. When the needed social structures did not always materialize in less-developed countries, the fault was accorded to "traditional" ways of thinking, beliefs and social values. Social-science research was aimed at identifying the individual variables in which rapid change was needed, and the modernization of traditional individuals became a priority task of various government agencies, an activity in which the mass media were widely utilized.

Capital was required, of course, for the high-capital technology, to be provided by national governments, by local entrepreneurs, by international loans and through the activities of multinational firms (usually owned and controlled by the industrially advanced nations). Gradually the newly independent nations

THE FREIRE REVOLUTION
Excerpt from: *Communication of Agricultural Innovations in Latin America: The Need for New Models*
By Juan Díaz Bordenave

In essence, what Paulo Freire proposed was the abolition of the "transmission mentality" in education and communication, and its replacement with a more liberating type of communication education that would contain more dialogue and would be both more receiver-centered and more conscious of social structure.

Let us explain by contrasting the difference between these two options. In the transmission mentality, called "banking education" by Freire (1970), the contents are deposited into a passive "receiver," thus establishing a marked difference in status and roles between the receiver and the source. Freire proposed that the distinction between "giver" and "receiver" be abolished inasmuch as they are both "learners." Of course, they are both learners only if an alternative model, called "problematizing" or "liberating" education by Freire, is adopted. Essentially, this model may be described as follows: The learner is given an opportunity to look at the problem to be studied with his own fresh eyes.

He is helped to penetrate the "ideological mist" imposed by the dominant class which blinds his eyes, and to see the existential situation in which the structure and culture of his society keep him from self-realization and participation. This process is called "conscientization." Through this process he learns that "culture" (what man can do with the world) is superior to "nature" (what the world gives man). The learner then "problematizes" his situation and naturally looks for a way out. This he finds through association with others and through the use of "cultural tools" for "liberation" such as political participation, social-class organization, literacy, school and the cooperative.

References

Freire, Paulo. *Pedagogy of the Oppressed.* New York: Herder and Herder, 1970.

Díaz Bordenave, Juan. "Communication of Agricultural Innovations in Latin America: The Need for New Models." SAGE, *Communication Research*, 1976, Vol. 3, No. 2: 135-154. Copyright © 1976, Sage Publications. Reprinted with permission of the publisher.

1927
1960
1963
1964
1967
1969
1970
1971
1972
1973
1974
1975
1976
1977
1978
1979
1980
1981
1982
1983
1984
1985
1986
1987
1988
1989
1990
1991
1992
1993
1994
1995
1996
1997
1998
1999
2000
2001
2002
2003
2004
2005
2006

began to realize that political freedom was a different matter than economic independence. The end of colonialism did not necessarily mark the end of financial dependence on the industrially advanced countries. Often it increased such dependency. And capital-intensive technology, including military armaments, was one reason.

3. Economic growth. It was assumed that "man" (all men, actually) was economic, that he would respond rationally to economic incentives, that the profit motive would be sufficient to motivate the widespread and large-scale behavior changes required for development to occur. Economists were firmly in the driver's seat of development programs. They defined the problem of underdevelopment largely in economic terms, and in turn this perception of the problem as predominantly economic in nature helped to put and to keep economists in charge.

Central economic planning of development was widely accepted as a legitimate and reasonable means by which a nation should seek development goals.[2] Almost every country in Asia, Africa and Latin America established a national development commission during the 1950s and 1960s. Bankers and economists were usually appointed to such commissions. Five-year development plans were produced to serve as a guide to the economic-development activities of national governments. When invited, international agencies provided technical assistance to such planners. The focus on economic growth carried with it an "aggregate bias" about development: that it had to be planned and executed by national governments. Local communities of course, would be changed eventually by such development, but their advance was thought to depend upon the provision of information and resource inputs from higher levels. Autonomous self-development was considered unlikely or impossible. In any event it seemed too slow.

Further, growth was thought to be infinite. Those rare observers who pointed out that known supplies of coal or oil or some other resource would run out in so many years were considered alarmists, and they were told that new technology would be invented to compensate for future shortages. More and bigger was better. It was not until the early 1970s that the book by Meadows et al. *The Limits to Growth* (1972) appeared to challenge the infinite-growth enthusiasts and the proponents of no-growth policies became heard.

4. Quantification. One reason for reliance on per capita income as the main index of development was its deceitful simplicity of measurement. The expression "quality of life" was seldom heard until the very late 1960s. (I cannot actually remember ever hearing it until then in the context of development.) It seemed reasonable that if some dimension of development could not be measured and quantified in numbers, then it probably did not exist. Even if it did, it must not be very important. Or so it seemed prior to the Stockholm Conference on the Human Environment in 1972.

Further, the qualification of development invoked a very short-range perspective of 10 or 20 or 25 years at most. Development was today. It was facile to forget that India, China, Persia and Egypt were old, old centers of civilization, that their rich cultures had in fact provided the basis for contemporary Western cultures. Such old cultures were now poor (in a cash sense), and even if their family life displayed a warmer intimacy and their artistic triumphs were greater, that was not development. It could not be measured in dollars and cents.

The drive for the quantification of development—an outgrowth and extension of North American social-science empiricism—helped define what development was and was not. Material well-being could be measured. Such values as dignity, justice and freedom did not fit on a dollars-and-cents yardstick. And so the meaning of development began to have

---

2   A critique of centralized economic planning of development in light of actual accomplishments appeared in a chapter by Caiden and Wildavsky (1974: 264-292) with the charming title: "Planning Is Not the Solution: It's Part of the Problem."

a somewhat dehumanized nature. Political stability and unity were thought to be necessary for continued economic growth, and authoritarian leadership increasingly emerged, often in the form of military dictatorships. And in the push for government stability, individual freedoms often were trampled.

Further, *what* was quantified about development was usually just growth, measured in the aggregate or on a per capita basis. Development policies of the 1950s and 1960s paid little attention to the *equality* of development benefits. The "growth-first-and-let-equality-come-later" mentality often was justified by the trickle-down theory—that leading sectors, once advanced, would then spread their advantage to the lagging sectors. Anyway, income disparities were thought to provide incentives for hard work and sacrifice and to act as a motivating force for individuals to invest in a lengthy formal education for themselves or for their children.

It was not until much later, in the 1970s, that the focus of quantification began to shift to measures of the equality of distribution. Gini ratios. Unemployment rates. Consideration of widening gaps.

Criticisms of the Dominant Paradigm of Development

In short, the old paradigm implied that poverty was equivalent to underdevelopment. And the obvious way for less-developed countries to develop was for them to become more like the developed countries.[3]

It was less obvious that the industrially advanced nations largely controlled the "rules of the game" of development. Most of the scholars writing about development were Westerners. That balances of payment and monetary exchange rates were largely determined in New York, London and Washington. And the international technical-assistance programs sponsored by the rich nations, unfortunately, made the recipients even more dependent on the donors. These gradual lessons took some time to emerge and to sink into intellectual thought.

INTELLECTUAL ETHNOCENTRISM

Theoretical writings about modernization in this period after World War II generally followed an "individual-blame" logic and may have been overly narrow and ethnocentric in a cultural sense. Examples are the works of Walt Rostow (1961), Everett Hagen (1962) and David McClelland (1961), all drawing more or less on the earlier writings of Max Weber. The leading theorists were Westerners, and there often was a rather inadequate database to support their conceptualizations. Portes (1973) criticized this Western and person-blame bias: "There is, I believe, a profoundly ethnocentric undercurrent in characterizations of modern men in underdeveloped countries. An invariably positive description obviously has something to do with similarity of these individuals with the self-images and values of researchers." Many economists insisted that their discipline

---

Excerpt from: Communication of Agricultural Innovations in Latin America: The Need for New Models
By Juan Díaz Bordenave

Just as aeronautical science evolved from the linear-engine concept to the idea of the circular combustion engine, then the turbo-propeller and recently to the era of the jet, communication science has also evolved from a simple linear concept of information and influence to a more complex view of communication as a dynamic social component.

---

3   Karl Marx in *Das Kapital* stated: "The country that is more developed industrially shows only, to the less developed, the image of its own future." Lerner (1967: 115) stated: "Indeed, the Western model is virtually an inevitable baseline for Asian development planning because there is no other model which can serve this purpose." This predominance of the Western paradigm of development was probably correct at the time of Lerner's writing.

1927
1960
1963
1964
1967
1969
1970
1971
1972
1973
1974
1975
1976
1977
1978
1979
1980
1981
1982
1983
1984
1985
1986
1987
1988
1989
1990
1991
1992
1993
1994
1995
1996
1997
1998
1999
2000
2001
2002
2003
2004
2005
2006

consisted of a universally valid body of theory applicable to both. One might ask rhetorically how different economic theory would be if Adam Smith had been Chinese or a Sikh. "Economic theorists, more than other social scientists, have long been disposed to arrive at general propositions and then postulate them as valid for every time, place and culture" (Myrdal, 1968: 16).

After reviewing the history and nature of the dominant paradigm and contrasting it with the reality of Asian development, Inayatullah (1975, 1976) concludes: "The Western development theory … is not an adequate intellectual framework … as it suffers from an overemphasis on the role of factors internal to Asian societies as causes of underdevelopment to the exclusion of external factors."

Continuing underdevelopment was attributed to "traditional" ways of thinking and acting of the mass of individuals in developing nations. The route to modernization was to transform the people, to implant new values and beliefs.

The dominant paradigm sought to explain the transition from traditional to modern societies. In the 1950s, the traditional systems were the nations of Latin American, Africa and Asia. All were relatively poor, with GNPs averaging about one-fifth or less of those of the developed nations of Europe and North America. Almost all were former colonies (the African and Asian nations more recently so), and most were still highly dependent on the developed nations for trade, capital technology and, in many cases, for their national language, dress, institutions and other cultural items. It seemed that the developing nations were less able to control their environment and were more likely to be influenced by unexpected perturbations in their surroundings. In these several respects the developing countries seemed to be somehow "inferior" to the developed nations, but of course with the hoped-for potential of catching up in their overall development. The developed nations of the West were taken as the ideal toward which the developing states should aspire.[4] The development of traditional societies into modern ones was a contemporary intellectual extension of social Darwinian evolution.

REDEFINING THE CAUSES OF UNDERDEVELOPMENT

Western models of development assumed that the main causes of underdevelopment lay within the underdeveloped nation rather than external to it. The causes were thought to be (1) of an individual-blame nature[5] (peasants were traditional, fatalistic and generally unresponsive to technological innovation) and/or (2) of a social-structural nature within the nation (for example, a tangled government bureaucracy, a top-heavy land-tenure system and so on). Western intellectual models of development, and Euro-American technical-assistance programs based on such models, were less likely to recognize the importance of external constraints on a nation's development: international terms of trade, the economic imperialism of international corporations, and the vulnerability and dependence of the recipients of technical-assistance programs. The dominant paradigm put the blame for underdevelopment on the developing nations rather than on the developed countries, or even jointly on both parties.

During the 1950s and 1960s, this assumption of blame was widely accepted not only in Euro-America but also by most government leaders and by many social scientists in Latin America, Africa and Asia. Many of the latter were educated in the United States or Europe, or at least their teachers and professors had been. And the power elites of developing countries were often co-opted to accept "within-blame" assumption by international technical-assistance agencies or by multinational corporations.

---

4   An assumption criticized by Portes (1973): "Modernity as a consequence of Western structural transformations may have little to do with, or be in fact detrimental to, causes of development in Third World nations."
5   Caplan and Nelson (1973) argue that social scientists are more likely to accept an individual-blame definition of a social problem that they investigate than a system-blame definition. For instance, unemployment and poverty are considered to be due to laziness, not to the unavailability of work and to blocked opportunities.

International power in the 1950-to-1970 era was concentrated in the hands of the United States, and this helped lead international efforts in the development field to follow a within-blame causal attribution and to reinforce it as an assumption. As the U.S. corner on world power began to crack in the 1970s (at least in the U.N. General Assembly), so did faith in the dominant paradigm of development. The "oil blackmail" of Euro-America following the Yom Kippur War in 1973 not only redistributed millions of dollars from developed to certain developing countries, but it dramatically demonstrated that developing countries could redefine the social situation of international finance. Then why not redefine the definition of the causes of underdevelopment? Starting at the Stockholm Conference on the Human Environment in 1972 and carried forward at the Bucharest World Population Conference and the Rome Conference on Food in 1974, the delegates from developing nations began to collaborate in redefining the problem of underdevelopment, so that the causes of underdevelopment were seen as external to developing nations *as well as within them.*

SMALL TECHNOLOGY AND RADICAL ECONOMISTS

"Westerners as well as Western-trained planners in the poor countries have been taught to think of small-scale, labor-intensive operations as inefficient, as a type of investment that retards economic growth" (Owens and Shaw, 1974: 2). But these prior assumptions of the dominant paradigm about the centrality of technology also began to be questioned. In China, for example, the Maoist philosophy is "not to allow the machines and their incumbent bureaucracies to control the men, but to insist that technology serve and be controlled by the people" (Rifkin, 1975). The Green Revolution was originally expected to represent a kind of ultimate in the use of technical solutions to human social problems. Indeed, it led to impressive increases in wheat and rice yields in Pakistan, India and the Philippines. But the Green Revolution also widened the socio-economic gap between smaller and larger farmers and between the government and the public. Many tenants and landless farm laborers were displaced by the tractors and farm machines which the larger farmers began to buy. Where could these rural poor go? Only to already-overcrowded cities. So the Green Revolution helped demonstrate that "improved seeds cannot solve the problem of unimproved farmers" (Owens and Shaw: p. 72).

Economists in the 1970s engaged in a critique of the dominant paradigm, especially its assumption of "a linear theory of missing components" (like capital, foreign exchange, skills or management) such as had been promoted by Rostow (1961). Many of these economist-critics advocated some version of a neocolonialist/cultural-imperialism theory of underdevelopment accompanied by a questioning of what constitutes the meaning and measure of development.

Most influential among the radical economists is André Gunder Frank, who centers on capitalism as the main cause of exploitation, inequality and generally of underdevelopment: "It is capitalism, world and national, which produced underdevelopment in the past and still generates underdevelopment in the present" (Frank, 1971: 1). By leading the academic charge against the prior paradigm of development, and by proposing "dependency theory" (that is, the dependency of poor countries on the rich, and "internal colonies" on their urban imperialists) in its place as an explanation of underdevelopment, Frank caused considerable academic rethinking about development.

Alternative Pathways to Development

In the very late 1960s and the 1970s, several world events combined with the intellectual critiques just described and began to crack the prior credibility of the dominant paradigm.

1. The ecological disgust with environmental pollution in the developed nations led to questioning whether they were, after all, such ideal models for development. Pollution problems and overpopulation pressures on available resources helped

1927
1960
1963
1964
1967
1969
1970
1971
1972
1973
1974
1975
1976
1977
1978
1979
1980
1981
1982
1983
1984
1985
1986
1987
1988
1989
1990
1991
1992
1993
1994
1995
1996
1997
1998
1999
2000
2001
2002
2003
2004
2005
2006

create doubts about whether unending economic growth was possible or desirable, and whether high technology was the most appropriate engine for development.

2. The world oil crisis demonstrated that certain developing countries could make their own rules of the international game and produced some suddenly rich developing nations. Their escape from national poverty, even though in part at the expense of other developed countries, was a lesson to their neighbors in Latin America, Asia and Africa. No longer were these nations willing to accept prior assumptions that the causes of underdevelopment were mainly internal.

3. The sudden opening of international relations with the People's Republic of China allowed the rest of the world to learn details of her pathway to development. Here was one of the poorest countries, and the largest, that in two decades had created a miracle of modernization including a public-health and family-planning system that was envied by the richest nations. Well-fed and-clothed citizens. Increasing equality. And all this was accomplished with very little foreign assistance and presumably without much capitalistic competition. China, and to a lesser extent Cuba, Tanzania and Chile (in the early 1970s), suggested that there must be alternatives to the dominant paradigm.

4. Finally, and perhaps most convincing of all, was the discouraging realization that development was not going very well in the developing countries that had closely followed the paradigm. However one might measure development in most of the nations of Latin America, Africa and Asia in the past 25 years, not much had occurred. Instead, most "development" efforts brought further stagnation, a greater concentration of income and power, high unemployment and food shortages in these nations. If these past development programs represented any kind of test of the intellectual paradigm on which they were based, the model was found to be rather seriously wanting.

Elements in the New Development

From these events grew the conclusion that there are many alternative pathways to development. While their exact combination would be somewhat different in every nation, some of the main elements in this newer conception began to emerge.

1. *The equality of distribution of information, socioeconomic benefits and so forth.* This new emphasis in development led to the realization that villagers and urban poor should be the priority audience for development programs and, more generally, that the closing of socioeconomic gaps by bringing up the lagging sectors was a priority task in many nations.

2. *Popular participation in self-development planning and execution, usually accompanied by the decentralization of certain of these activities to the village level.* Development came to be less a mere function of what national governments did to villagers, although it was recognized that perhaps some government assistance was necessary even in local self-development. An example is the "group planning of births" at the village level in the People's Republic of China, where the villagers decide how many babies they should have each year and who should have them. Another illustration of decentralized development was occurring in Tanzania, where social-mobilization activities by the political party, the army and by radio-listening groups help provide mass motivation for local participation in development activities. As President Julius K. Nyerere stated: "If development is to benefit the people, the people must participate in considering, planning and implementing their development plans" (Tanganyika African National Union, 1971). People cannot be developed; they can only develop themselves. And this realization was demonstrated not only in communist and socialist nations but also in such capitalistic settings as Korea and Taiwan.

3. *Self-reliance and independence in development, with an emphasis upon the potential of local resources.* Mao Tse-tung's conception of national

self-development in China is an illustration of this viewpoint, including the rejection of foreign aid (after some years of such assistance from Russia), as well as the decentralization of certain types of development to the village level (as mentioned previously). Not only may international and binational technical assistance be rejected, but so too are most external models of development—leading to a viewpoint that every nation, and perhaps each village, may develop in its own way. If this occurs, of course, standardized indexes of the rate of development become inappropriate and largely irrelevant.

4. *Integration of traditional with modern systems, so that modernization is a syncretization of old and new ideas, with the exact mixture somewhat different in each locale.* The integration of Chinese medicine with Western scientific medicine in contemporary China is an example of this approach to development. Acupuncture and antibiotics mix quite well in the people's minds as shown by this experience. Such attempts to overcome the "empty-vessels fallacy" remind us that tradition is really yesterday's modernity. Until the 1970s, development thinking implied that traditional institutions would have to be entirely replaced by their modern counterparts. Belatedly, it was recognized that these traditional forms could contribute directly to development. "African countries should not imitate the patterns of development of the industrialized countries, but adopt development patterns suited to African indigenous traditional and cultural patterns" (Omo-Fadaka, 1974).

By the mid-1970s it seemed safe to conclude that the dominant paradigm had passed, or at least had passed as the main model for development in Latin America, Africa and Asia. Of course, it would still be followed enthusiastically in some nations, but even then with certain important modifications. The Chinese model, or at least particular components, had been (and were being) adopted elsewhere when nations were willing to forgo certain advantages of liberal democracy for the tighter government control that they thought to be necessary to maintain nationhood over tribal, religious or regional factions. While Cambodia, Vietnam and perhaps Tanzania were influenced by the Chinese route to development, they seem far from very exact replicas. So multiple and varied models of development were now in style.

What Is Development?

Out of the various criticisms of the dominant paradigm of development grew a questioning of the concept of development from one that had centered on materialistic, economic growth to a definition that implied such other valued ends as social advancement, equality and freedom. These valued qualities should be determined by the people themselves through a widely participatory process. Thus, each nation might pursue a somewhat different pathway to development, depending on exactly what style of development was desired. In this sense, development is simply a powerful change toward the kind of social and economic system that a country decides it needs (Schramm and Lerner, 1976). Development is change toward patterns of society that allow better realization of human values, that allow a society greater control over its environment and over its own political destiny, and that enables its individuals to gain increased control over themselves (Inayatullah, 1967: 101).

We summarize these newer conceptions of development by defining development as *a widely participatory process of social change in a society, intended to bring about both social and material advancement (including greater equality, freedom and other valued qualities) for the majority of the people through their gaining greater control over their environment* (Rogers, 1975b).[6]

---

6 Note how my thinking has changed as to the definition of development in the past seven years: "Development is a type of social change in which new ideas are introduced into a social system in order to produce higher per capita incomes and levels of living through more modern production methods and improved social organization" (Rogers with Svenning, 1969).

1927
1960
1963
1964
1967
1969
1970
1971
1972
1973
1974
1975
1976
1977
1978
1979
1980
1981
1982
1983
1984
1985
1986
1987
1988
1989
1990
1991
1992
1993
1994
1995
1996
1997
1998
1999
2000
2001
2002
2003
2004
2005
2006

Thus the concept of development has been expanded and made much more flexible, and, at the same time more humanitarian, in its implications.

Communication in Development

The rise of alternatives to the old paradigm of development implied that the role of communication in development must also change. Previously, mass communication had been considered to play an important role in development, especially in conveying informative and persuasive messages from a government to the public in a downward, hierarchical way.

A decade or so ago, mass communication was often thought to be a very powerful and direct force for development. "It was the pressure of communications which brought about the downfall of traditional societies" (Pye, 1963: 3–4). And there was some support for this position from communication research. An early and influential study of modernization in the Middle East by Lerner (1958) led communication scholars to expect the mass media to be a kind of magic multiplier for development in other developing nations. This period was characterized by considerable optimism about the potential contribution of communication to development, one that was consistent with the general upbeat opinion about the possibilities for rapid development.

Certainly, the media were expanding during the 1950s and 1960s. Literacy was becoming more widespread in most developing nations, leading to greater print-media exposure. Transistor radios were penetrating every village. A predominantly one-way flow of communication from government development agencies to the people was implied by the dominant paradigm. And the mass media seemed ideally suited to this role. They could rapidly reach large audiences with informative and persuasive messages about the details of development.

A series of communication research projects were launched in various developing nations which showed that mass-media exposure was highly correlated with individual modernization variables. Undoubtedly, however, some of the most solid evidence for the impact of the mass media on modernization came from the six-nation investigation by Inkeles and Smith (1974: 146), who concluded: "The mass media were in the front rank, along with the school and the factory, as inculcators of individual modernization."[7]

In the early 1960s … the relative power of the mass media in leading to development was mainly assumed rather than proven. Certainly, determining the effects of the media in development is a complicated affair. The audience surveys of communication effects and the field experiments were actually small in number and size; and in the face of this lack of firm evidence on the point, there was a tendency to assume a powerful mass-media role in development. Actually, this "oversold position" bore a similarity close to the hypodermic-needle model of media effects in the United States—an overly enthusiastic position which eventually succumbed to empirically oriented communication research (Rogers and Shoemaker, 1971).

Gradually, it was realized that the role of mass communication in facilitating development was often indirect and only contributory, rather than direct and powerful. But this varied depending on such circumstances as the media, the messages, the audience and the nature of the intended effects.[8]

Criticisms of Communication in Development

By the late 1960s and the 1970s a number of critical evaluations were being made of the mass-communication role in development. Some scholars, especially in Latin America, perceived the mass media in their nations as an extension of exploitive relationships with U.S.-based multinational corporations, especially through the advertising of commercial products.

---

7   In these investigations, modernization was considered as the individual-level manifestations of development: "Modern man is an informed participant citizen, has a marked sense of personal efficacy, is highly independent and autonomous, and he is ready for new experiences and ideas" (Inkeles and Smith, 1974: 290).

8   A much-quoted list of what the mass media can and cannot do in development was provided by Schramm (1964).

Further, questions were asked about the frequent patterns of elite ownership and control of mass-media institutions in Latin America and the influence of such ownership on the media content. The 1965–1975 decade saw a rising number of military dictatorships in Latin America, Africa and Asia, and these governments stressed the media's propaganda role, decreasing the public's trust in mass communication.

Communication researchers also began to question some of their prior assumptions, becoming especially critical of earlier inattention to (1) the content of the mass media, (2) the need for social-structural changes in addition to communication if development were to occur and (3) the shortcomings of the classical diffusion-of-innovations viewpoint, which had become an important explanation of microlevel development.

Inattention to Media Content

We showed previously that mass-media exposure on the part of individuals in developing nations was highly correlated with their modernization, as expressed by their exhibiting modern attitudes and behavior. This seemed logical because the mass media were thought to carry generally pro-development messages (Rogers and Svenning, 1969).

However, a strange anomaly was encountered. When individuals in developing nations who had adopted an innovation like a weed spray, a new crop variety or family planning were asked of the sources/channels through which they had learned about the new idea, the mass media were almost never reported. Interpersonal channels with peers totally predominated in diffusing the innovation. A possible explanation of this anomaly seemed to lie in the contents of the media messages, which investigation showed seldom to carry specific messages about the innovation (such as what it is, where to obtain it and at what cost and how to use it), even though there was much content promoting national development in a general sense (such as news of a new highway being constructed, appointment of a new minister of

agriculture, and so on). So when the media content was analyzed it was found to contain very little attention to the technological innovations that were diffusing; they spread most frequently through interpersonal communication (1) from government development workers to their clients; and (2) among peers in the mass audience.

Barghouti (1974) in a content analysis of the print and electronic media of Jordan found that "agricultural news occupies an insignificant place among other categories of the content of the mass media."[9] In contrast, there is much political news in the media. Surveys of a sample of Jordanian farmers showed that only 9 percent mentioned the mass media as their source of agricultural information, but 88 percent received their political information from the media. Barghouti's study indicates the advantage of combining content analysis of the media with an audience survey and suggests the need for much more content analysis of the media messages in developing nations if we are to understand more fully the media's role in development.[10]

Need for Structural Change as Well as Communication

Even in the days of the dominant paradigm, it was realized that the contribution of mass communication to development was often limited by the social structure, by the unavailability of resource inputs and the like. There was much more, of course, to development than just communication and information. But there was at least some hope that by raising the public's aspirations for modernization, pressure was created to change some of the limiting factors on development.

By the 1970s, it was becoming apparent that the social-structural restraints on development were often unyielding to the indirect influences of the media or even to more direct intervention. Under these conditions, it was realized that mass communication's role

9   Similar conclusions about the lack of agricultural content in the mass media in Latin America were cited by Luis Beltrán.
10   This point is also made by Golding (1974).

1927
1960
1963
1964
1967
1969
1970
1971
1972
1973
1974
1975
1976
1977
1978
1979
1980
1981
1982
1983
1984
1985
1986
1987
1988
1989
1990
1991
1992
1993
1994
1995
1996
1997
1998
1999
2000
2001
2002
2003
2004
2005
2006

in development might be much more diminished than previously thought. And communication research was designed to determine just how limiting the structure might be on the development effects of mass communication. Illustrative of such researches is Grunig's (1971) investigation among Colombian farmers; he concluded that "communication is a complementary factor to modernization and development … It can have little effect unless structural changes come first to initiate the development process." Such studies helped to modify the previously enthusiastic statements by communication scholars about the power of the media.

Diffusion of Innovations and Development

One of the most frequent types of communication research in developing nations dealt with the diffusion of innovations (as noted earlier). In such research, an idea perceived as new by the receiver—an innovation—is traced as it spreads through a system (Rogers and Shoemaker, 1971). The innovation is usually a technological idea, and thus one can see that past diffusion research fits well with the dominant paradigm's focus on technology and on its top-down communication to the public.

During the 1960s, there was a tremendous increase in the number of diffusion studies in developing countries; such research was especially concerned with the spread of agricultural innovations and of family-planning methods. In fact, there were about 500 family-planning diffusion studies in India alone (Rogers, 1973). Many of them left much to be desired in scientific rigor or in the originality of their design.

A number of criticisms of the assumptions and directions of diffusion research appeared in the 1970s: Marceau (1972), Grunig (1971), Golding (1974), Havens (1972) and Beltrán (1975), as well as the articles by Diaz Bordenave and Röling, et al. These critiques centered on the pro-innovation bias of such research and on the propensity for diffusion to widen the socioeconomic gaps in a rural audience. Out of such

frank criticism came a number of modifications in the classical diffusion model and in the research designs utilized (such as more field experiments and network analysis), and these newer approaches are now being tried (Rogers, 1973, 1976).

After a tour of 20 U.S. communication-research centers, Nordenstreng (1968) criticized North American scholars for their "hyperscience," which he explains as due to the fact that "American communication research has grown up in an atmosphere of behaviorism and operationalism, which has made it correct in technical methodology but poor in conceptual productivity." This comment on communication research in the United States may also apply to diffusion research. Such inquiry often sided unduly with the source "against" the receiver, perhaps a reflection of the one-way linear model of communication and of the mechanistic/atomistic components approach of much communication research. So the needed alterations in the classical diffusion model, such as a greater concern with communication-effects gaps and the importance of audience participation in the diffusion process, may also hold implications for the entire field of communication.

Alternative Conceptions of Communication in Development

In this section we describe some of the directions under way in newer conceptions of development communication: self-development, the communication-effects gap and new communication technology.

SELF-DEVELOPMENT

Most nations in the past have implicitly defined development in terms of what government does to (and for) the people. Decisions about needed development were made by the national government in the capital city and then implemented through development programs carried out by government employees who contacted the public (at the operational level) in order to inform and persuade them to change some aspect of their behavior. This top-down approach to development implied a one-way role for communication: The sources were government officials seeking to inform and persuade a mass audience of receivers.

In recent years, several nations (examples are the People's Republic of China, Tanzania, the Republic of Korea and Taiwan) have recognized the importance of self-development at the village and urban-neighborhood level. In this approach, some type of small group at the local level (mothers' clubs in Korea, farmers' associations in Taiwan, radio-listening clubs in Tanzania and communes and/or work brigades in China) takes primary responsibility (1) for deciding exactly what type of development is most needed in their village or neighborhood; (2) for planning how to achieve this development goal; and (3) for obtaining whatever government or nongovernment resources may be necessary, and (4) for carrying out their own development activities. The advantages of such a self-development approach are that the rate of accomplishment is often higher than in the case of top-down development by government; the cost to government, which often lacks sufficient resources in most poor countries, is much less and more likely to be affordable; and the nature of development activities is more flexible and more appropriate to changing local needs because of the decentralization of planning, decision-making and execution.

Naturally, self-development implies a completely different role for communication than in the usual top-down development approach of the past. Technical information about development problems and possibilities and about appropriate innovations is sought by local systems from the central government, so that the role of government development agencies is mainly to communicate in answer to these locally initiated requests rather than to design and conduct top-down communication campaigns. The mass media may be used to feed local groups with information of a background nature about their expressed needs and to disseminate innovations that may meet certain of these needs.

This communication function is illustrated in the radio-listening group campaigns for public health and for food/agriculture that were conducted in Tanzania in 1974 and 1976, respectively. The later campaign of a month's duration achieved participation in the radio groups of 2.5 million villagers, nearly 40 percent of the adult population of Tanzania, while the earlier public-health campaign reached 2 million people (Hall, 1975; Dodds and Hall, 1974).

Both campaigns led to a great deal of village-level self-development. For example, in the health campaign, the radio forums decided to build latrines, sweep village streets and paths, dig wells and adopt other sanitation and preventive health measures. Although the radio programs (and related print materials) focused national attention on health problems and provided information about certain ways of solving them, each of the approximately 100,000 radio forums discussed these mass-media messages, applied them to local conditions, decided which health activities they wished to conduct (if any), and then did so with little direct assistance from the Ministry of Public Health. So the role of mass communication in self-development is more permissive and supportive than in the usual top-down development approach, where local citizens are told what their problems are and persuaded to follow certain specific lines of action to solve them, usually involving a good deal of dependence on government.

Mass communication may be even less directive in assisting the self-development activities of village groups in Korea and China. Mothers' clubs in the Republic of Korea are organized in about 24,000 villages; originally, the government assisted their initiation in 1968 to promote family-planning diffusion and to deliver contraceptives to adopters. Typically, after several meetings, a mothers' club would begin to pursue whatever types of group activity it felt was needed: improved nutrition, food production and preservation, sanitation, child health, cooperative savings, female equality and so on. A monthly

1927
1960
1963
1964
1967
1969
1970
1971
1972
1973
1974
1975
1976
1977
1978
1979
1980
1981
1982
1983
1984
1985
1986
1987
1988
1989
1990
1991
1992
1993
1994
1995
1996
1997
1998
1999
2000
2001
2002
2003
2004
2005
2006

magazine sent to each mothers' club leader describes the self-development accomplishments of certain exemplary clubs and thus inspires others to greater development efforts (Kincaid et al., 1973; Park and others, 1974; Rogers, 1975a).

Somewhat similarly, in the People's Republic of China mass communication circulates information about the self-development accomplishments of a particular village to other such local systems. For example, the idea of the "group planning of births" (in which all of the members of a commune or labor brigade or urban-neighborhood committee meet annually to assess their demographic situation and to decide their fertility goals for the year ahead, including which parents are to have a baby and which are not) began in one local system in about 1971 (Chen with Miller, 1975). This innovative approach to population planning was featured in radio and newspaper messages, and the idea quickly spread throughout China and is now widely adopted.

Key elements of self-development approaches are participation, mass mobilization and group efficacy, with the main responsibility for development planning and execution at the local level. The main roles of mass communication in such self-development may be summarized as (1) providing technical information about development problems and possibilities, and about appropriate innovations, in answer to local requests, and (2) circulating information about the self-development accomplishments of local groups so that other such groups may profit from others' experience and perhaps be challenged to achieve a similar performance.

THE COMMUNICATION-EFFECTS GAP

Needed are more appropriate and adequate means for testing the communication-gap hypothesis. This hypothesis was originally stated by Tichenor, et al. (1970) to imply that one effect of mass communication is to widen the gap in knowledge between two categories of receivers (high and low in socio-

economic status). It often has been overlooked that the "gap" was originally proposed only as a hypothesis rather than a proven fact. I feel that several important changes must first be made in the statement of the gap hypothesis before it can be adequately tested.

1. It should deal with the attitudinal and overt behavioral effects of communication as well as just "knowledge"; thus, I propose calling it the "communication-effects gap" hypothesis.
2. The hypothesis should not be limited to mass-media efforts alone but should include also the differential effects of interpersonal communication and the joint effects of mass media plus interpersonal communication, as measured by network analysis.
3. There need not be just two categories of receivers, nor must the gap be found only on the basis of a socioeconomic-status variable.

Past research on the communication-effects gap hypothesis, while notable for its pioneering nature, has suffered somewhat from the fact that the hypothesis usually was imposed on the data after they were gathered for another purpose. Ideally, in order to test the communication-effects gap hypothesis, one would prefer:

1. That data were gathered before and after a communication event (like a campaign) in a field experiment rather than mainly using correlational analysis of one-shot survey data as has sometimes been done in the past;
2. That the "after" data might be gathered at several points in time to determine whether or not the gap is only a short-term phenomenon;
3. That a control group be included in the design in order to remove the effects of a growing gap due to other (than communication) causes; and
4. That the interpersonal communication channels linking the receiver categories be measured and network-analyzed so as to determine the effect of such audience interconnectedness in modifying or magnifying the gap effects of the main

communication event studied. Essentially, the network analysis seeks to explore whether or not a "trickle down" occurs from one of the two receiver categories to the other, and how soon.

Probably the reasons why methodological considerations such as these have not already been utilized in testing the communication-gap hypothesis are the relatively high cost and the length of time that would be required. But these problems can be overcome.

One important function of improved research is the light that it may be able to shed on why the communication-effects gap generally occurs. A possible explanation, in many cases, is that the "ups," perhaps as an artifact of gaining their original superior status, possess greater receptivity to the change-oriented communication messages and hence show greater response to them than the "downs." Also the "ups" may possess greater slack resources which can be utilized for innovation—larger farmers responded first by adopting the miracle seeds of the Green Revolution. Furthermore, the sources or producers of the change-oriented messages are usually more homophilous with the "ups" than with the "downs," and hence these messages have relatively greater effects on the "ups." Finally, the lack of integration of the "downs," in interpersonal-communication networks means they are not even reached through a trickle-down.

If more equitable distribution of socioeconomic benefits were indeed a paramount goal of development activities, the following communication strategies might be considered in developing nations:

1. Use the traditional mass media as credible channels to reach the most disadvantaged audiences.
2. Identify the opinion leaders among the disadvantaged segment of the total audience, and concentrate development efforts on them.
3. Use change-agent aides who are selected from among the disadvantaged to work for development agencies in contacting their homophilous peers.
4. Provide means for the disadvantaged audience

to participate in the planning and execution of development activities and in the setting of development priorities.
5. Establish special development agencies that work only with the disadvantaged audiences. An example is the Small Farmers Development Agency in India, founded in 1970 to provide agricultural information and credit only to small-size farmers.
6. Produce and disseminate communication messages that are redundant to the "ups" because of their ceiling effect, but which are of need and interest to the "downs."

Much further research is needed on the communication-effects gap; this work has only begun. But at least we are beginning to realize that the gap is not always inevitable.

NEW COMMUNICATION TECHNOLOGY AND DEVELOPMENT

What is the potential of new communication technology, such as satellite broadcasting, cable television and computers for facilitating the process of development in Latin America, Africa and Asia? At least in the immediate future of the next 10 years it will probably be fairly limited, although satellite-television broadcasting is in operation at present in India on an experimental basis, and nationwide satellite-television-broadcasting systems are soon to be launched in Iran and Indonesia.

But what is really new about communication technology is not the technology per se as much as the *social technology* of how the new communication devices are organized and used. Much of the total effect of a communication system rests on the program or software aspects, on how the audience is organized to receive and discuss the messages and how feedback is conveyed to the communicators.

Directions for Communication Research

The newer paradigms for development pose certain implications for communication research as well as for communication activities.

1927
1960
1963
1964
1967
1969
1970
1971
1972
1973
1974
1975
1976
1977
1978
1979
1980
1981
1982
1983
1984
1985
1986
1987
1988
1989
1990
1991
1992
1993
1994
1995
1996
1997
1998
1999
2000
2001
2002
2003
2004
2005
2006

THE ROLE OF RESEARCH IN CHANGE AND DEVELOPMENT

Mass-media institutions may tend to side with the "establishment" in most nations; hence, the content of most mass-media messages is seldom designed to radically alter the existing social structure in a society. Mass communication in development usually espouses an incremental-change approach in which change is promoted within the existing structure rather than directly seeking to alter structural constraints to development.

Some radical critics of communication research feel that it also tends to side with the existing social structure and to reflect mainly an incremental-change position. Most present-day communication research requires a team of research assistants, considerable data-gathering costs and a sizable budget for computer-dependent data analysis. The relatively high price of most contemporary communication research may influence the nature of such research. Research funds for investigations of communication in development usually are provided by national governments, foundations, large corporations or universities. Seldom do the funds come from urban poor or villagers, the main targets of development efforts. So the sponsorship of communication research tends to influence it to concentrate on studying a range of problems that reflect the priority concern of government rather than that of the public, of elites, rather than the mass audience, of communication sources rather than communication receivers, of the establishment rather than revolutionary attempts to alter the social structure.

Certain communication scholars have become aware of this possible bias in their research and have sought to launch research projects that deal with topics of special benefit to those sectors of society that cannot sponsor research themselves. Ultimately, this approach amounts to greater effort (than in the past) to free the selection of what is studied from the influence of those who sponsor communication inquiry.

One means of doing so is to seek to design research that is very low-cost in nature so as to free it from possible sponsorship influences.

A successful illustration is Prakash Shingi and Bella Mody's report on a field experiment on agricultural television's ability to close the communication-effects gap between advantaged and disadvantaged farmers in India. Shingi and Mody designed a "natural experiment" in which the treatment (two television programs) was produced at no cost to their study. The database is rather modest (farmers in only three villages), and the authors gathered their own data through personal interviews with the farmers before and after the television broadcasts.

The total budget for the Shingi-Mody field experiment was only about $70 (U.S.). While there may be additional hidden costs (their salaries, for example), this experiment is probably one of the lower-priced research studies in the field of development communication, where big budgets are generally the rule. Another example of low-cost communication research is Granovetter's (1974: 141) study of job information in a Boston suburb, where his total budget was about $900.

FIELD EXPERIMENTS AND CURRENT PRACTICE

In addition to the cost and the sponsorship of communication research, the type of research design that is employed may also affect how directly the research results can contribute to social change versus reifying the existing social structure. Niels Röling and others argue for field experimental designs rather than surveys, if diffusion research is to influence development policies in the direction of gap-narrowing communication strategies. In an era when important changes are occurring in our definition and understanding of the concept of development, and when accompanying changes are being made to the communication aspects of development, we expect that field experimental approaches will become more common than they have been in past communication research.

FOCUS ON INTERPERSONAL NETWORKS

Network analysis is a type of research in which relational data about communication flows or patterns are analyzed by using interpersonal relationships as the units of analysis (Rogers, 1976). The advantage of network analysis in comparison to the more usual monadic analysis (where the individual is the unit of analysis) is that the social structure can be overlayed on the communication flows in order to improve the scientific understanding of both the structure and the message flows.

Past communication research has frequently identified opinion leaders in a mass audience and investigated their role in the interpersonal transmission of mass-media messages. But until network analysis began to be utilized in such research, little of an exact nature could be learned about where the opinion leaders obtained the message, and specifically, to whom each such opinion leader disseminated the message.

Thus, we see that the passing of the dominant paradigm of development led to new and wider roles for communication in development. The exact nature of such newer conceptions will become clear only in the years ahead, as communication research helps illuminate the new pathways to development.

References

Barghouti, S. M. "The Role of Communication in Jordan's Rural Development." *Journalism Quarterly*, 1974, 51: 418-424.

Beltran, S., L. R. "Research Ideologies in Conflict." *Journal of Communication*, 1975, 25: 187-193.

Chen, P. "China's Population Program at the Grass-Roots Level." *Studies in Family Planning*, 1973, 4: 219-227.

Chen, P., with A. E. Miller. "Lessons From the Chinese Experience: China's Planned Birth Program and Its Transferability." *Studies in Family Planning*, 1975, 6, 10: 354-366.

Frank, A. G. *Capitalism and Underdevelopment in Latin America*. London: Penguin, 1971.

Golding, P. "Media Role in National Development: Critique of a Theoretical Orthodoxy." *Journal of Communication*, 1974, 24: 39-53.

Granovetter, M. S. *Getting a Job: A Study of Contacts and Careers*. Cambridge: Harvard University Press, 1974.

Grunig, J. E. "Communication and the Economic Decision-Making Processes of Colombian Peasants." *Econony, Development & Cultural Change*, 1971, 18: 580-597.

Havens, A. E. "Methodological Issues in the Study of Development." *Sociologia Ruralis*, 1972, 12: 252-272.

Inayatullah. "Western, Asian, or Global Model of Development." In W. Schramm and D. Lerner, eds., *Communication and Change in the Developing Countries: Ten Years After*. Honolulu: University of Hawaii/East-West Center Press, 1976.

—. *Transfer of Western Development Model to Asia and Its Impact*. Kuala Lumpur: Asian Centre for Development Administration, report, 1975.

—. "Toward a Non-Western Model of Development." In D. Lerner and W. Schramm, eds., *Communication and Change in the Developing Countries*. Honolulu: University of Hawaii/East-West Center Press, 1967.

Kincaid, D. L., et al. Mothers' Clubs and Family Planning in Rural Korea: The Case of Oryu Li. Honolulu: *East-West Communication Institute Report*, 1973.

Lerner, D. "International Cooperation and Communication in National Development." In D. Lerner and W. Schramm, eds., *Communication and Change in the Developing Countries*. Honolulu: University of Hawaii/East-West Center Press, 1967.

—. *The Passing of Traditional Society: Modernizing the Middle East*. New York: Free Press, 1958.

Marceau, F. J. "Communication and Development: A Reconsideration." *Public Opinion Quarterly*, 1972, 36: 235-245.

Meadows, P., et al. *The Limits to Growth*. Cambridge: MIT Press, 1972.

Myrdal, G. *Asian Drama*. New York: Pantheon, 1968.

Neurath, P. M. "Radio Rural Forum as a Tool of Change in Indian Villages." *Economy. Development & Cultural Change*, 1962, 10: 275-283.

Nordenstreng, K. "Communication Research in the United States: A Critical Perspective." *Gazette*, 1968, 14: 207-216.

Nove, A. "On Reading Andre Gunder Frank." *Journal of Developing Studies*, 1974, 10: 445-455.

Omo-Fadaka, J. "Develop Your Own Way." *Development Forum* 2, 1974.

Owens, E., and R. Shaw. *Development Reconsidered: Bridging the Gap Between Government and the People*. Lexington, Mass.: Lexington Books, 1974.

Oxaal, I., et al. *Beyond the Sociology of Development: Economy and Society in Latin America and Africa*. London: Routledge & Kegan Paul, 1975.

Portes, A. "The Factorial Structure of Modernity: Empirical Replications and a Critique." *American Journal of Sociology*, 1973, 79: 15-44.

Pye, L. *Communications and Political Development*. Princeton, N.J.: Princeton University Press, 1963.

Rifkin, S. B. "The Chinese Model for Science and Technology: Its Relevance for Other Developing Countries." *Development and Change*, 1975, 6: 23-40.

Rogers, E. M. "Where We Are in Understanding the Diffusion of Innovations." In W. Schramm and D. Lerner, eds., *Communication and Change in the Developing Countries: Ten Years After*. Honolulu: University of Hawaii/East-West Center Press, 1976.

—. "Network Analysis of the Diffusion of Innovations." Presented at the Mathematical Social Science Board Symposium on Social Networks. Dartmouth, New Hampshire, 1975a.

—. "The Anthropology of Modernization and the Modernization of Anthropology." *Reviews in Anthropology*, 1975b, 2: 345-358.

—. *Communication Strategies for Family Planning*. New, York: Free Press, 1973.

— "Mass Media Exposure and Modernization Among Colombian Peasants." *Public Opinion Quarterly*, 1965, 29: 614-625.

1927
1960
1963
1964
1967
1969
1970
1971
1972
1973
1974
1975
1976
1977
1978
1979
1980
1981
1982
1983
1984
1985
1986
1987
1988
1989
1990
1991
1992
1993
1994
1995
1996
1997
1998
1999
2000
2001
2002
2003
2004
2005
2006

—, with F. F. Shoemaker. *Communication of Innovations: A Cross-Cultural Approach.* New York: Free Press, 1971.

—, with L. Svenning. *Modernization Among Peasants: The Impact of Communications.* New York: Holt, Rinehart & Winston, 1969.

Rostow, W. W. *The Stages of Economic Growth.* New York: Cambridge University Press, 1961.

Schramm, W. *Mass Media and National Development.* Stanford, California: Stanford University Press, 1964.

—, and D. Lerner, eds. *Communication and Change in the Developing Countries: Ten Years After.* Honolulu: University of Hawaii/East-West Center Press, 1976.

Schumacher, E. F. *Small Is Beautiful: Economics as if People Mattered.* New York: Harper & Row, 1973.

Seers, D. "The Limitations of the Special Case." *Bulletin of the Oxford Institute of Economics and Statistics,* 1963, 25: 77-98.

—, and L. Joy, eds. *Development in a Divided World.* London: Penguin, 1971.

Tanganyika African National Union. *TANU Guidelines, 1971.* Dar es Salaam: Government Printer, 1971.

Tichenor, P. J., et al. "Mass Media Flow, and Differential Growth in Knowledge." *Public Opinion Quarterly,* 1970, 34: 159-170.

THE EFFECTS GAP HYPOTHESIS

Excerpt from: The Communication Effects Gap: A Field Experiment in TV and Agricultural Ignorance

By Prakash M. Shingi and Bella Mody

1976 An underlying assumption of much communication research and practice is that information exposure and gain is always a desirable effect, and that a maximum effect of communication is a desired state. However, in recent years it has been realized that the mass media can be responsible for creating widening gaps in a system between the advantaged and disadvantaged segments of the audience. Especially in certain developing countries where equality is considered one dimension of development, such widened gaps are considered undesirable by stability-oriented governments. This discrepancy in knowledge between the better-off and worse-off segments of society was termed a "knowledge gap" by Tichenor and others (1970).

Although even early pioneers in communication research showed an implicit awareness of the gaps idea, Tichenor, et al. (1970) first proposed this knowledge-gap hypothesis as the result of their perception of an implicit assumption, throughout the literature on mass-communication effects, that education is a powerful correlate with the acquisition of knowledge from the media about public affairs, science and other content. They define the process giving rise to this gap by referring to a cumulative social-change model: "Because certain subsystems within any total social system have patterns of behavior and values conducive to change, gaps tend to appear between subgroups already experiencing change [rather] than those that are stagnant or slower in initiating change" (Tichenor, et al., 1970). They further propose that "as the infusion of mass-media information into a social system increases, segments of the population with higher socioeconomic status tend to acquire this information at a faster rate than the lower-status segments, so that the gap in knowledge between these segments tends to increase rather than decrease.

The existence of this gap does not mean, however, that the lower-status population remains completely uninformed or even *absolutely* worse off in knowledge, but rather that they become *relatively* lower in knowledge—thus the "gap." Tichenor and others (1970) also state that their hypothesis only concerns print media on subjects of low salience to individuals, and therefore the results may not apply to learning from television or other electronic media.

The predominant question asked by communication researchers over the past 25 years has been what effects a particular source, channel, message or combination of such elements has on a specific audience of receivers. This effects-oriented inquiry, however, has focused mainly on the first dimension of communication effects by pursuing such queries as: Has the communication activity had any effect? Only occasionally has communication research sought to determine a second dimension of communication effects by asking: Has the communication attempt had a relatively greater (or different) effect on certain receivers than on others? Why? Whereas the first question asks about the level (or degree) of communication effects, the second question directs communication research to the distribution of such effects and to the concern with gaps (Rogers and Danziger, 1975: 225).

We feel it is theoretically and pragmatically fruitful to generalize the knowledge-gap hypothesis into a broader form: *Attempts at change-oriented communication over time tend to widen the gap in effects variables between the audience segments high and low in socioeconomic status* (Rogers, 1974).

Thus, we posit a "communication-effects-gap" hypothesis that is limited neither to any particular mass medium nor just to knowledge effects. Perhaps it need not even be limited to socioeconomic status:

Alternative variables might be literacy; racial, ethnic or religious-minority membership; rural-urban residence; and subsistence/commercial farming (although there is probably an overlap of each of these variables with socioeconomic status).

It is important to remember that the communication-effects-gap hypothesis is still just a hypothesis, rather than a proven principle. The evidence presented by Tichenor and others (1970) is rather tentative and limited, although consistent across several researches. A more adequate set of data would come from a benchmark/follow-up experimental design with a control group, which would indicate how much the effects gap would have widened even if the attempt at change-oriented communication had not occurred (Galloway, 1974).

References

Cook, T. D., et al. "'Sesame Street' Revisited." New York: Russell Sage Foundation, 1975.

Donohue, G. A., et al. "Mass Media and the Knowledge Gas: A Hypothesis Reconsidered." *Communication Research*, 1975, 2: 3-23.

Galloway, J. J. "Substructural Rates of Change, and Adoption and Knowledge Gaps in the Diffusion of Innovations." Ph.D. dissertation, Michigan State University, 1975.

Hornik, R. C. "Television, Background Characteristics, and Learning in El Salvador's Educational Reform." *Instructional Science*, 1975, 4: 293-302.

Katzman, N. "The Impact of the Communication Technology: Some Theoretical Premises and Their Implications." Ekistics, 1974a, 225: 125-130.

—. "The Impact of Communication Technology: Promises and Prospects." *Journal of Communication*, 1974b, 24: 47-58.

McNelly, J. T., and J. R. Molina. "Communication, Stratification, and International Affairs Information in a Developing Urban Society." *Journalism Quarterly*, 1972, 49: 316-326, 339.

Operations Research Group. Media Scene in India: Highlights from the National Readership Survey. Baroda, India: ORG report, 1971.

Rogers, E. M. "Social Structure and Communication Strategies in Rural Development: The Communications Effects Gap and the Second Dimension of Development." In Cornell-CIAT International Symposium on Communication Strategies for Rural Development. Ithaca, N.Y.: Cornell University, Institute for International Agriculture, 1974.

— and S. Danziger. "Nonformal Education and Communication Technology: The Second Dimension of Development and the Little Media." In T. J. La Belle, ed., *Educational Alternatives in Latin America: Social Change and Social Stratification*. Los Angeles: UCLA Latin American Center, 1975.

Rogers, E. M., with F. F. Shoemaker. *Communication of Innovations: A Cross-Cultural Approach*. New York: Free Press, 1971.

Roy, P., et. al. *The Impact of Communication on Rural Development: An Investigation in Costa Rica and India*. Paris: UNESCO, 1969.

1927
1960
1963
1964
1967
1969
1970
1971
1972
1973
1974
1975
1976
1977
1978
1979
1980
1981
1982
1983
1984
1985
1986
1987
1988
1989
1990
1991
1992
1993
1994
1995
1996
1997
1998
1999
2000
2001
2002
2003
2004
2005
2006

Shingi, P. M., and B. Mody. *Farmers' Ignorance and the Role of Television.* Ahmedabad: Indian Institute of Management, Centre for Management in Agriculture, report, 1974.

Tichenor, P. J., et. al. "Mass Media Flow and Differential Growth in Knowledge." *Public Opinion Quarterly*, 1970, 34: 159-170.

Werner, A. "A Case of Sec and Class Socialization." *Journal of Communication*, 1975, 25: 45-50.

Shingi, P., and Mody B. The Communication Effects Gap: A Field Experiment in TV and Agricultural Ignorance in India. *Communication Research*, Vol. 3,2, April 1976. Copyright © 1976, Rowman and Littlefield Publishers. Reprinted with permission of the publisher.

EXCERPT FROM:

THE COMMUNICATION EFFECTS GAP: A FIELD EXPERIMENT IN TV AND AGRICULTURAL IGNORANCE

By Prakash M. Shingi and Bella Mody

1976 Why do gaps occur? The explanations include (1) differential levels of communication skills between segments of the total audience; (2) amounts of stored information, that is, existing levels of knowledge, resulting from prior exposure to the topic: such receivers of communication would be better prepared to understand the next communication; (3) relevant social contact; there may be a greater number of people in the reference groups of the more advantaged segment, and these receivers may have more interpersonal contact with other information-rich individuals; and (4) selective exposure, acceptance and retention of information. Thus, to the extent that communication skills, prior knowledge, social contact or attitudinal selectivity is engaged, the gap should widen as heavy mass-media flow continues.

In developing countries like India, most development benefits have tended to accrue to better-off segments rather than to the downtrodden for whom they may ostensibly have been intended. A much-discussed case in point is the so-called Green Revolution that benefited the larger farmers and widened existing socioeconomic gaps. Given their higher levels of knowledge, capital and social contract, it is not surprising that the "haves" achieve greater effects from exposure to most interpersonal and mass-media information sources.

Those media (radio, press, private TV, cinema) that demand education and/or income for ownership and exposure naturally reinforce knowledge inequities, particularly in developing societies characterized by a lopsided distribution of both education and income. As in many other nations, exposure to all of the mass media in India is concentrated in urban areas.

Shingi, P., and Mody B. "The Communication Effects Gap: A Field Experiment in TV and Agricultural Ignorance in India," *Communication Research*, Vol. 3, No. 2, April 1976. Copyright © 1976, Rowman and Littlefield Publishers. Reprinted with permission of the publisher.

EXCERPT FROM:

COMMUNICATION RECOMMENDATIONS ISSUED 1976–1980

By UNESCO

1976 In 1972, at the XVII Session of the General Conference of UNESCO, the idea of a Declaration of the Fundamental Principles Governing the Use of the Mass Media with a View to Strengthening Peace and Understanding and Combating War Propaganda, Racialism and Apartheid was first officially expressed. Parallel to this, the debate over Direct Broadcast Satellite (DBS) began to intensify as the Soviet Union introduced a proposal to the United Nations General Assembly for "a binding convention of principles for television transmission from satellites." In essence, this was a call for a more "regulatory" response to DBS than previous policies, which had been characterized by a Western laissez-faire attitude. Some delegations considered this necessary, since the Outer Space Treaty had not dealt with outer-space activities the direct effects of which would be essentially earthbound (such as direct television broadcasting from space, which appeared to have very definite political implications)"[1]. ...

By a vote of 102 to 1, with the United States the lone no vote, the United Nations General Assembly called upon CUPUOS to "elaborate principles governing the use by States of artificial earth satellites for direct television broadcasting with a view toward concluding an international agreement or agreements."

1973: Fourth Conference of Heads of State or Government of Non-Aligned Countries (Algiers) which is considered as the beginning of the nonaligned

---

[1] *The United States and the Debate on the World "Information Order,"* USICA, Washington, D.C., 1979, pp. 20-21.

1927
1960
1963
1964
1967
1969
1970
1971
1972
1973
1974
1975
1976
1977
1978
1979
1980
1981
1982
1983
1984
1985
1986
1987
1988
1989
1990
1991
1992
1993
1994
1995
1996
1997
1998
1999
2000
2001
2002
2003
2004
2005
2006

countries' involvement in the information-communication area in a more organized way. In items xiii and xiv of the Action Programme for Economic Cooperation, which was adopted by the conference (attended by 75 member states, 24 observers and three guest countries), the following is stated:

Developing countries should take concerted action in the field of mass communications on the following lines in order to promote a greater interchange of ideas among themselves:

a. Reorganization of existing communication channels which are the legacy of the colonial past and which have hampered free, direct and fast communication between them.
b. Initiate joint action for the revision of existing multilateral agreements with a view to reviewing press cable rates and facilitating faster and cheaper intercommunication.
c. Take urgent steps to expedite the process of collective ownership of communication satellite and evolve a code of conduct for directing their use.
d. Promote increased contact between the mass media, universities, libraries, planning and research bodies and other institutions so as to enable developing countries to exchange experience and expertise and share ideas. ...[2]"

1976: Fifth Conference of Heads of State or Government of the Non-Aligned Countries (Colombo) at which heads of state of 84 participating countries endorsed these declarations and recommendations, adopting as part of the Conference's Political Declaration the following wording:

160. A new international order in the fields of information and mass communications is as vital as a new international economic order.

161. Nonaligned countries noted with concern the vast and ever-growing gap between communication capacities in nonaligned countries and in the advanced countries which is a legacy of their colonial past. This has created a situation of dependence and domination in which the majority of countries are reduced to being passive recipients of biased, inadequate and distorted information. The fuller identification and affirmation of their national and cultural identity thus required them to rectify this serious imbalance and to take urgent steps to provide greater momentum in this new area of mutual cooperation.

162. The emancipation and development of national information media is an integral part of the overall struggle for political, economic and social independence for a large majority of the peoples of the world who should not be denied the right to inform and to be informed objectively and correctly. Self-reliance in *sources* of information is as important as technological self-reliance since dependence in the field of information in turn retards the very achievement of political and economic growth.

163. Nonaligned countries must achieve these objectives through their own efforts as well as by more active cooperation on a bilateral, regional as well as inter-regional basis and by coordinating their activities in the United Nations and other international fora. It is particularly necessary for nonaligned countries to strengthen their existing infrastructures and to take full advantage of the scientific and technological breakthroughs already made in this field. This would facilitate more complete dissemination of objective information amongst their own public as well as in the world at large about developments in nonaligned countries in the social, economic, cultural and other fields and their growing role in the international community.[3]

1976 July: Intergovernmental Conference on Communication Policies in Latin America and the Caribbean (San Jose, Costa Rica) initiated by UNESCO.

---

2 Documents of the Fourth Conference of Non-Aligned Countries, Algiers, 1973, Action Programme for Economic Cooperation.

3 Documents of the Fifth Conference of Heads of State or Government of the Non-Aligned Countries (Colombo, 1976), Political Declaration.

The importance of this conference is considerable.[4]

In terms of the development of the concept of a new international/world information-communication order, the following ideas expressed in the recommendations of this conference deserve particular mention:

- The conference recognized that "a balanced flow of messages must be one of the factors directly operative in bringing about the new economic and social order to which our countries aspire."
- It also recognized "the need for new national policies for the sovereign determination of respective needs and priorities with regard to the international flow of messages;
- "That the principle of the 'free flow of information' will not be applicable unless all our countries have equal access to all the sources of information and take part on an equal footing in the control over and use of international channels of dissemination." In this respect, seven proposals addressed to member states of the region were formulated in recommendation no. 1; point 4 states "[Member States need to] define and implement policies, plans and laws that will make

---

4 For more insight into its content, see: the final report of the conference, UNESCO document COM/MD/38, Paris, October 1976. The nature of the political pressure which manifested itself in regard to this conference can be detected from Rosemary Righter's account: "These meetings (preparatory meetings in Bogotá and Quito) and the Costa Rica Conference were explicitly intended to set the pattern for UNESCO's long-term plans to promote national communications which, in the words of its Costa Rica working paper, would 'strengthen national sovereignty in all its aspects, particularly with regard to culture.' ... Quito was also to have been the site for the Inter-Governmental Conference. But as the reports of the two preparatory meetings circulated, and when the provisional agenda for the Quito Conference was issued in March 1976, the Inter-American Press Association and other organizations launched a campaign against UNESCO's policies and the conference itself. The Inter-American Broadcasters' Association and IAPA issued a joint statement on 27 April that the conference was contrary both to UNESCO's constitution and that of many of the participating countries. Ecuador withdrew its invitation, and the conference was switched to San José." Rosemary Righter, *Whose News?* London: Burnett Books, 1978, pp.153-154.) See also: Raquel Salinas Bascur, "New Agencies and the New Information Order" (The Associated Press coverage of the Intergovernmental Conference on Communication Policies in Latin America and the Caribbean held in Costa Rica, July 1976), in "International News and the New Information Order" by Tapio Varis, Raquel Salinas and Renny Jokelin, *Institute of Journalism and Mass Communication Reports* No. 39, Tampere, 1977. An account of what happened as a response to the Bogota and Quito meetings as well as at San José is given also in Thomas L. McPhail, op. cit., pp.95-98.

possible the advent of more balanced communication relations at both the national and international levels. Furthermore, in Recommendation no. 6 it says:

- "...the development of communication and information systems is one of the essential requirements for the achievement of integral economic, social and cultural development at both the national and regional levels."

1979 February: Intergovernmental Conference on Communication Policies in Asia and Oceania,

(Kuala Lumpur, Malaysia) adopted 51 important recommendations on various aspects of communication policies, ranging from national to regional and international level. These, as well as the Declaration of the Conference, reflect the evolution which the notion of a new international/world information-communication order had undergone since the San José Conference. Thus the Kuala Lumpur Declaration states, among other things:

- "... Since each nation has the right to determine its own communication policies, we call for the elaboration, by States and citizens together, of comprehensive national policies and programmes based on a global vision of communication and on the goals of economic and social development. Countries planning the implementation of these policies and programmes should do it as an integral part of overall national planning.
- ... [there must be a call for] greater participation of people and individuals in the communication process and for more freedom and autonomy for and the assumption of greater social responsibility by mass-information media and at the same time for greater individual responsibility by and protection of those who run the media and prepare messages for circulation. ...
- every effort must be made to eliminate the many obstacles impeding the exchange and circulation of information. ...
- [the need to develop] greater awareness on the part of communication media of their potential as catalyst of socioeconomic progress and reform.

1927
1960
1963
1964
1967
1969
1970
1971
1972
1973
1974
1975
1976
1977
1978
1979
1980
1981
1982
1983
1984
1985
1986
1987
1988
1989
1990
1991
1992
1993
1994
1995
1996
1997
1998
1999
2000
2001
2002
2003
2004
2005
2006

- A new, more just and more effective world information and communication order, the basis of good neighbourliness, demands in turn an opening to the world. Professional, cultural and scientific collaboration between groups, nations and regions must be a vital element of the order we seek to establish.

- We urge the United Nations system as a whole, and more specifically UNESCO, to support these objectives, promote various forms of regional and international cooperation and thus pave the way for a new, more just and more effective world communication and information order which is an integral part of the efforts to achieve a new international economic order. We believe that such a new communication and information order would be one of the most vivid contemporary manifestations of the ideals of justice, independence and equality between men and nations."[5]

Among the recommendations of the Conference, particular mention should be made of Recommendation No.8, which says:

> Considering that planning is an essential process for the achievement of planned and desired social and economic growth, recognizing that communication plays a vital role to inform, educate and motivate the people in achieving the goals of planned development, (The Conference) Recommends to Member States of Asia and Oceania that they treat the communication sector not only as a support to development but as an integral part of the development plan itself, and provide necessary resources for the planned development of the communication sector with a view to fully realizing the fruits of the overall development plan.[6]

1980: First Intergovernmental Conference on Communication Policies in Africa, (Yaoundé, Cameroon).

Declaration:

- "...the solution of communication problems cannot be reduced simply to the transfer of technology or the mere redistribution of resources, although both for Africa and for the world these measures are an essential part of a new information and communication order. The solution of our problems remains intimately bound up with the defence of the fundamental freedoms of individuals and peoples—all peoples, and especially those who still remain the most underprivileged."

- "The success of development in African countries will increasingly depend on the practice of collective self-reliance. This policy, based on increased confidence in inner resources and their capacity for innovation, is the only one calculated to reduce excessive dependence on the outside world. This is true in politics as in culture, in economics as in communication."[7]

1980: UNESCO General Conference (Belgrade) at which the Final Report of the International Commission for the Study of Communication Problems (the "MacBride Commission") was presented and the notion of a new world information-communication order given further impetus.

a. This new world information and communication order could be based, among other considerations, on:

i.   elimination of the imbalances and inequalities which characterize the present situation;

ii. elimination of the negative effects of certain monopolies, public or private, and excessive concentrations;

iii. removal of the internal and external obstacles to a free-flow and wider-and better-balanced dissemination of information and ideas;

iv. plurality of sources and channels of information;

v.   freedom of the press and information;

vi. the freedom of journalists and all professionals in the communication media, a freedom inseparable from responsibility;

vii. the capacity of developing countries to achieve improvement of their own situations, notably by providing their own equipment, by training their

5   Final Report, UNESCO document CC/MD/42, Paris, June 1979, pp.31-34.
6   Ibid., pp.38-39.
7   The Yaoundé Declaration, articles V and VI, 1980.

personnel, by improving their infrastructures and by making their information and communication means suitable to their needs and aspirations;

viii. the sincere will of developed countries to help them attain these objectives ;

ix. respect for each people's cultural identity and the right of each nation to inform the world public about its interests, its aspirations and its social and cultural values;

x. respect for the right of all peoples to participate in international exchanges of information on the basis of equality, justice and mutual benefit;

xi. respect for the right of the public, of ethnic and social groups and of individuals to have access to information sources and to participate actively in the communication process;

b. This new world information and communication order should be based on the fundamental principles of international law, as laid down in the United Nations Charter."

Excerpt from: Breda Pavlic and Cees J. Hamelink, *The New International Economic Order: Links between Economics and Communications*, UNESCO, Paris, 1985. Copyright © 1985, UNESCO. Reprinted with permission of the publisher.

1927
1960
1963
1964
1967
1969
1970
1971
1972
1973
1974
1975
1976
1977

COMMUNICATION THEORY AND RURAL DEVELOPMENT: A BRIEF REVIEW

Excerpt from: Communication and Rural Development

By Juan Diaz Bordenave

1977 Any attempt to use mass communication for rural development can be said to have a theoretical foundation. That is, it is based on certain assumptions about how people acquire and accept or reject information, ideas and beliefs—and how they use their knowledge and act on the basis of their convictions.

Similarly, every such effort also presupposes a concept of development. For example, for some, development is handing over technology to the unskilled so that they can become more productive; for others, it is awakening the intellectual and decision-making potential of rural people so that they themselves can change the very structure of society.

These two underlying concepts—one regarding the nature of communication, and the other the nature of development—are closely related.

The theoretical study of communication's role in rural development has advanced with the growth of empirical knowledge, a result of finding out what works and what does not. New approaches have been devised to overcome perceived weaknesses in previous efforts, and attempts have been made to explain why some approaches fail and others succeed.

The theoretical study of rural-development communication has also been influenced by the evolution of accepted ideas about development. It has not only been concerned with how communication contributes to bringing about change and why; it has also

1978
1979
1980
1981
1982
1983
1984
1985
1986
1987
1988
1989
1990
1991
1992
1993
1994
1995
1996
1997
1998
1999
2000
2001
2002
2003
2004
2005
2006

had to consider shifts in thinking about what kinds of changes rural development should foster.

Thus, although theoreticians tend to state their views in absolute terms, there are no absolutely "right" or "wrong" theoretical models for rural-development communication. A model that seems to work in one kind of development situation may not be suitable for another. Today theoreticians know much more about communication in rural settings than they did 10 or 20 years ago; tomorrow they will need to know even more.

At the risk of oversimplification, we will attempt here a brief historical review of theoretical approaches to communication. We deliberately ascribe no dates to the various concepts described, nor do we attempt to document statements about them.

From Source to Receiver: A One-Way Road

Up until the Renaissance, the central concern in communication was "content," or "ideas." The form in which ideas were presented and the means of diffusion were considered less important than the ideas themselves.

With the invention of the printing press by Gutenberg, the number of people who could be reached and influenced by ideas increased considerably. This fact drew attention to channels of communication, particularly to books and, later, journals. Books were banned, smuggled and even burnt. Journalism acquired prestige as a political tool and eventually became a full-fledged profession. Faced with a large audience instead of a privileged few, communicators refined the art of message elaboration and simplified the pompous and erudite language previously used in order to facilitate the public's acceptance of their ideas.

Communication became the object of scientific study only when electronic media were invented and adopted. It was no coincidence that the first formal model of the communication process originated with electrical engineers and mathematicians (Fig. 1).

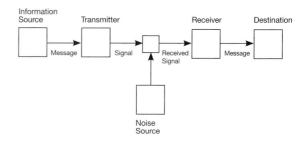

Fig. 1. The Telecommunication Model

Many key concepts—for example, "signal," "sign," "code," "message," "source," "destination," "channel," "information," "encoding" and "decoding"—were first made explicit by this model.

The authors of the telecommunication model were not concerned with the human aspects of communication, whether face-to-face or through the mass media. Perhaps for this reason, most of the thinking and research on communication that followed was based on a rather simple, mechanistic view of communication as a process of message transmission.

During the Second World War, all forms of communication received a great deal of attention. Signals and codes took on military importance, and communication was vital to propaganda and psychological warfare. For these reasons, the dominant concept became that of communication as persuasion.

What was learned about communication during this period was transferred to various fields of activity, particularly advertising and technological change, which acquired considerable importance after the Second World War. In both fields, communication as transmission of information and communication as persuasion were the orientations adopted. Within a short time, people engaged in such professions as public relations, agricultural extension, health education and so on began to show interest in these applications of communication.

The basic characteristic of the communication approaches used in advertising and in promoting technical change was a preoccupation with effects: the purchase of a given product, the adoption of a given attitude, the acceptance of a farm practice, the modification of a nutritional habit. Comparing the marketing model and the agricultural-extension model shows their common orientation (Figs. 2 and 3).

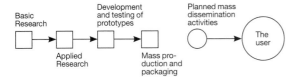

Fig. 2. The Marketing Model

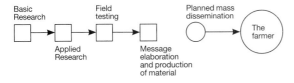

Fig. 3. The Agricultural-extension Model

The preoccupation with results increased when concern with economic development spread to the developing countries. The essence of economic development was seen to be a rapid growth in economic productivity. Inasmuch as such an increase requires considerable human change, and communication was perceived as an agent of change, communication was considered, at least by communicators, a key instrument for development.

The pressures of economic-development goals, the size and dispersion of target audiences in developing areas, the availability of modern communication technology and an interest in selling expensive communication equipment all worked to make the media an important element in rural-development programmes. Development personnel strived to use the latest gadgets ("hardware") in carrying out aggressive multimedia campaigns. As a consequence, the relevance and accuracy of content were often neglected, and slowly, more profound approaches to education were discarded. There was, however, a positive effect:

Many technicians in developing countries were trained in the use of media.

Communication Theory Turns to the Social Sciences

A significant enrichment of development-communication theory occurred when communicators applied the idea of process, acquired from the philosophical and scientific thinking of the times, to communication. A view of communication as a process takes into account the infinite number of variables involved in any communication act: the image the sender has of the receiver, and vice versa; the personal experiences, values of meaning that symbols and situations can have; the many and varying aspects of the cultural context, and so on. In this view, communication participates in the complexity of life itself and is no longer seen as a purely mechanistic phenomenon. John Ball says: [1]

> "It is the concept of process that prevents our supplying easy formulas for communication and that permits us instead to promise an approach that is realistic and based firmly on current knowledge in a range of scientific fields."

Gradually, communicators began to take more aspects of the communication situation into account, and to approach it in a relativistic frame of mind. It became accepted that a thing can be perceived differently by different persons, and that "reality" is not that objective and absolute. The expression "meanings are not in words but in people" became a cliché. This new orientation meant a revolution for many change agents who previously had believed that a technically correct message should be universally accepted just because it was "correct."

The process idea led communication experts to extract specialized knowledge about variables affecting the communication process from the reservoir of social-science disciplines, such as anthropology,

1 John Ball, "The Conceptual Basis for Communication," *Research, Principle and Practices in Visual Communication*, East Lansing, Michigan: National Project in Agricultural Communications, 1960.

1927
1960
1963
1964
1967
1969
1970
1971
1972
1973
1974
1975
1976
1977
1978
1979
1980
1981
1982
1983
1984
1985
1986
1987
1988
1989
1990
1991
1992
1993
1994
1995
1996
1997
1998
1999
2000
2001
2002
2003
2004
2005
2006

sociology, social psychology, psychology, political science and economics.

From sociology, to mention but one case, communication borrowed two ideas that attracted the interest of scholars and practitioners for a while: the concepts of social systems and of diffusion of innovations.

Social systems were said to be any interactive social structure (a family, a church congregation, a rural community and so on) having ends or objectives, norms, status roles, power, social rank, sanctions, facilities and territoriality. The life of social systems occurred through several important processes, such as communication, decision-making, boundary maintenance and social-cultural linkage. Communication was defined as [2] the process by which information, decisions and directives pass through a social system, and the ways in which knowledge, opinions and attitudes are formed or modified.

The social-system concept made communicators aware of how organically and intimately communication is related to other elements and processes of society. Nevertheless, its contribution to a theoretical understanding of development communication was limited because the social-system model explained social conflict and social change essentially in terms of a search for equilibrium. Such a search does not characterize the developing countries. Thus, the concept was eventually replaced by the more general idea of "systems" (see below).

The ideas and research generated by study of the diffusion of innovations grew out of the concern with technological change, seen as a key element in economic development. North American rural sociologists, and later their colleagues in Europe and Latin America, concentrated their attention on such aspects of the diffusion of innovations as: (a) the personal antecedents favouring the adoption and diffusion of a new idea; (b) the social characteristics of individuals

and communities influencing the adoption and diffusion of practices; (c) the behaviour stages the farmer undergoes from the time he meets a new idea until he adopts it (awareness, interest, evaluation, trial and decision); (d) the characteristics of a new idea or practice that make it more or less adoptable (compatibility, divisibility, complexity, communicability, etc.); (e) the personal roles intervening in the diffusion of an innovation within a given community (innovator, opinion leader, laggard, etc.).

Among the various applications of the concept, an important one for communication was the discovery of the different usefulness of impersonal and personal channels (mass media versus friends and neighbours) at different stages of the adoption process. The diffusion mentality also generated a great deal of enthusiasm for the use of opinion leaders as channels of information and influence. This, in turn, produced a search for reliable techniques to spot such leaders.

Among the many criticisms thrown at the diffusion model were that it does not take account of the constraints imposed by social structures in the developing countries; it pays insufficient attention to the quality of the practices to be diffused and to the competency of adoption agents; and it relies on a "dripping-down" view of development communication, which fails to provide for feedback and communication from farmers to the sources of innovations. The diffusionist models were, it seems, conceived to explain what happens in the more developed countries, where the farmer may be considered a decision-making unit. But this is hardly the case in the developing countries, where most farmers are subject to social and economic constraints of all kinds.

Two more recent ideas have enriched theoretical views of communication significantly: those of communication functions and social structure.

The idea of function grew out of the observation that people use communication because it accomplishes certain functions for them. They listen to the radio,

---

2   J. Allan Beegle and Charles P. Loomis, *Rural Sociology, the Strategy of Change,* Englewood Cliffs, N.J.: Prentice-Hall, 1957.

read the newspapers, attend meetings and so on not because an external source wants to communicate something to them but because they themselves feel the media satisfy some of their needs. Obviously, communication performs different functions for different people. One person may listen to the radio to obtain useful information, while another mainly cherishes the feeling of companionship the speaker's voice provides.

The idea of communication functions led to a distinction between instrumental and consumatory communication. Instrumental communication refers to content the receiver may apply to a utilitarian end. Consumatory communication refers to content that reduces tension or produces pleasure. …In practice, however, the distinction between the two is not so sharp.

Daniel Lerner, in *The Passing of Traditional Society*,[3] contributed a fresh viewpoint to thinking about the communication process—the idea of "empathy." Empathy refers to a person's ability to put himself in the place of another, to see the world as the other person does. According to Lerner, this ability is essential for development since it is only by assuming the viewpoint of more "modern" persons that a peasant can desire to change his life.

The analysis of the functions that communication fulfils in people's lives led to another important observation: Not only do people like to receive communication from others, they also like to communicate what they think and feel to others. Thus, to the concept of communication were added such notions as *expression, relationship* and *participation.*

An interesting manifestation of the attention paid to the receiver in the study of the communication process is the concept of "co-orientation," which has become popular in the United States recently. The idea behind this concept is that two persons can have similar perceptions and interpretations of the same object, and the greater the similarity (co-orientation), the more

efficient will be the flow of communication between the persons. Conversely, an intense flow of communication may increase co-orientation. The concept of co-orientation, an extension of the concept of empathy, may help improve the relationship between communication-change agents and their audiences. Co-orientation can also be used as a didactic tool to increase receiver orientation among communicators.

The persuasion-for-effect mentality is so dominant among development planners and change agents, however, that the human needs for expression, relationship and participation stressed in the theories outlined above were often not adequately valued in themselves. Instead, knowledge about them has been used to improve techniques of persuading and manipulating people. Thus, the discovery that people accept an innovation more easily if they first discuss it among themselves and then collectively decide to adopt it has been widely utilized to justify coupling the practice of group dynamics with persuasive efforts. Similarly, findings on the important role of the intermediary receiver-transmitter, or opinion leader, were used by effect-oriented communicators to design better strategies of mass persuasion and not necessarily to satisfy people's need for co-orientation and co-operative problem solving.

During the 1940s and 1950s, the community-development movement acquired importance in the Western countries providing technical assistance to developing regions of the world. Communication then entered a stage in which receivers were seen not as isolated individuals but as members of global human communities, with problems that could only be solved collectively. The awareness of the community's potential to diagnose, articulate and mobilize resources to solve its problems enriched communication; it demonstrated the close relationship that must exist between messages and community decision making, thus engaging communication's involvement in such activities as: (a) encouraging diagnosis by the community of its own situation and problem; (b) providing access

---

3 Glencoe, Illinois: Free Press, 1958.

1927
1960
1963
1964
1967
1969
1970
1971
1972
1973
1974
1975
1976
1977
1978
1979
1980
1981
1982
1983
1984
1985
1986
1987
1988
1989
1990
1991
1992
1993
1994
1995
1996
1997
1998
1999
2000
2001
2002
2003
2004
2005
2006

to all relevant information on alternatives; (c) organizing the people; (d) aiding the community to obtain means and resources—that is, power; (e) creating suitable institutions for community decision making and collective action.

Communication Theory Discovers Social Structure

Not all communities are alike, however; nor, it became apparent, is each community a homogeneous unit. The concept of social structure views society as a network of statuses and roles in which some persons occupy more privileged positions of power and control than others.

If a given social structure is such that most of a person's decisions are influenced or thwarted by external forces, we can be sure that his access to information and communication will also be limited. …

In recent years a number of studies have been made of the relationship between social structure and the role of communication. To summarize the viewpoint and findings of these studies, let us take the case of a typical hierarchical social structure, one consisting of a small group of ruling elites, a larger middle class, and a popular mass that constitutes the majority. (In developing countries there may also be foreign groups, situated even higher in the hierarchy than the ruling elites, which are able to impose their decisions, values and strategies.)

In such a system, the lower strata attempt to identify with the elites, adopting their perceptions of the world, their values, their ways of relating to others—in short, their ideology. This is partly because to survive within the society the communication media must act as vehicles of this ideology. The population does not perceive that, along with news, technical information and entertainment provided through various channels (newspapers, magazines, television and radio programming, advertisements, etc.), it is absorbing the ideology of the dominant elites. In fact, it can even internalize beliefs and values antagonistic to its own interests.

In this kind of system, communication serves the establishment and the social status quo. Most dissident ideas not approved by the elites are ignored by the media because they are also a threat to their interests. Others are picked up by the media and returned to the audience in a distorted form less disturbing to the established order.

An awareness of the ideological influences exerted through the mass media in many societies has led several researchers to investigate the content of media (newspapers, comic books, radio and television soap operas and so on) from this viewpoint. They discovered that in some developing countries the mass media do in fact often transmit certain values and beliefs that may be detrimental to national development—for example, consumerism, exaggerated individuality, the cult of violence, elitism. The discovery of the subliminal influence of mass media on the formation of national attitudes has enriched the understanding of communication; most significantly, it has shown that many messages supposedly supporting national development may in fact be aiming only at "Westernization," and even at perpetuating anachronistic social structures.

A rigid class structure is not the only factor cutting off the great mass of the population in developing countries from the communication media. Other studies of access to information by the rural populations of these countries have revealed the disadvantaged situation of rural people as far as the media are concerned. Content analyses of mass media have shown that most messages are urban-oriented and thus largely irrelevant for rural people. Moreover, the media penetrate very insignificantly into some rural areas. As for the print media, their diffusion is necessarily limited where illiteracy is rampant. While this is not the case for radio and television, the commercial interests that often control these channels find it more profitable to aim their broadcast at the richer urban consumers. Thus, in many areas the only channels open for peasant communication are the interpersonal channels; indeed, most studies demonstrate the predominance of personal contacts in diffusing messages in rural areas.

Communication as a System; Communication in Systems

A relatively recent approach that has enriched thinking about communication considerably is the concept of "systems." A system is any set of interacting parts that maintains its boundaries while exchanging influences with its environment. Inputs are the influences received from the environment; through various processes the system transforms these into outputs. Outputs are the products, services and influences delivered by the system with the aim of transforming its environment (Fig. 4). …

A communication programme is a goal-establishing system because those responsible for it formulate a set of objectives they can change as the programme proceeds. They can also choose and adapt the means to achieve these objectives.

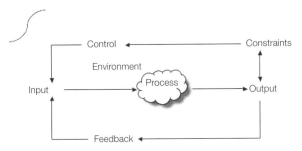

Fig. 4. System components

A close look at how human systems work has shown that communication is the very essence of these systems: It supplies information about environmental needs and conditions; facilitates internal interaction and coordination through information exchange; channels—through outgoing messages—the system's influences on the environment; and brings back—through feedback—information about the environment's reactions and its changing needs.

While the idea of "reaction" or "response" is not new, it was the concepts of systems that revealed the full

importance of this element of communication, now known as "feedback." In the past, feedback was considered useful for determining audience reaction or the effects of a message. Currently, feedback is considered an integral component, not only of a communication system but of any kind of reactive system, inasmuch as it triggers corrective mechanisms that keep the system working toward its established goal, as shown in Figure 5.

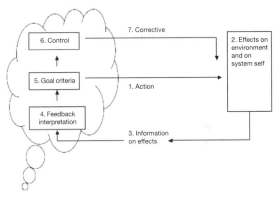

Fig. 5. How a system Works Toward a Goal

The theory of systems and the systems approach have not completely banished the "transmission-persuasion" tradition in development communication. In fact, in the hands of development technocrats the systems concept can become a straitjacket, discouraging human individuality and originality just because these upset the neat goal-seeking design of the system.

Nevertheless, introducing the systems concept into the theoretical study of development communication has had several positive consequences. For one, viewing events systemically reveals how the various aspects of rural development are interrelated. Low productivity, for instance, is seen as organizations. As a result, communicators having a systemic viewpoint tend to approach development problems with a broader, more inclusive outlook and thus make a more useful contribution to integrated programmes and projects.

For another, the attention to objectives inherent in the systems approach has made for a more careful analysis of problems at the planning stage of development-

1927
1960
1963
1964
1967
1969
1970
1971
1972
1973
1974
1975
1976
1977
1978
1979
1980
1981
1982
1983
1984
1985
1986
1987
1988
1989
1990
1991
1992
1993
1994
1995
1996
1997
1998
1999
2000
2001
2002
2003
2004
2005
2006

communication programmes. It has also led planners to pay more attention to matching the media used in a programme. ...

In addition, the concept of systems leads to awareness of the fact that development programmes and institutions are but subsystems within larger systems, and, therefore, their goals must be consistent with and support the goals of the larger system.

At the same time, important byproducts of the systems approach are having a deep and beneficial effect on development communication.

For example, one very important trend growing out of this approach is an interest in formulating overall communication policies and plans. In other words, the more careful analysis that the systems approach has promoted in designing given development communication programmes has an analogue in the examination of the totality of communication activities—what they are now and what they should be.

To formulate communication policies and plans, it is necessary to study the norms in society that govern assumptions about communication and communication practices. From the results of such a study, one can elicit general principles for action. ...

Communication planning seeks to make an inventory of all communication resources and to use these resources in the most effective way possible in line with set objectives. Since in the developing countries these objectives usually concern the orientation of society toward development, and since communication resources are scarce, communication planning can contribute to ensuring that resources in these countries will be used to promote all forms of development, including rural development. Communication planning on a national level is receiving growing attention both from national governments and from international agencies.

The systems approach has also inspired research in other associated disciplines, which has important implications for development communications. One of these disciplines is educational technology. Some results of the research done on the use of new methods and materials in formal (school) education have been shown to have application to nonformal (out-of-school, developmental) education. This fertilization from one field to the other has become more intense as UNESCO, the Food and Agricultural Organization and bilateral and other international aid agencies and research organizations have grown more interested in the areas of out-of-school education and rural development. It is not only a question of transferring the use of certain methods and materials (though this is important) but, even more significant, of adopting a new approach to the study of learning and communication. Present-day innovative educational technology is above all a discipline of synthesis, and a trend toward synthesis is what seems very much required. ...

Communication as an Instrument for Changing Society

The various concepts enriching our knowledge of the role of communication in rural development summarized above did not significantly alter the generally accepted view of communication as a means of transmitting information in order to persuade. On the whole, the behaviour of communicators—teachers, change agents, advertising experts, politicians and so on—has revealed an orientation that is essentially vertical, directive, aimed at manipulation and indoctrination.

This orientation seems a natural consequence of a view of development that stresses "modernization." According to this view, "backward" countries should adopt the values, the social organization and the technology of the more advanced countries. Also communication should serve to promote these values, this organization and this technology.

However, in recent years this concept of development has been challenged as a result of repeated failures, and a new notion of development, more centralized on the people concerned, has been proposed. At the same time, the "modernization" orientation of development communication has begun to be criticized and modified.

Credit for explaining the weaknesses of the traditional view of development communication belongs to many thinkers and practitioners. Probably best known among them is Paulo Freire, a Brazilian educator who has vividly described present communication and education systems as tools for the domination and domestication of the masses. Freire points out that merely transferring content from a knowledgeable and authoritative source to a passive receiver does nothing to promote the receiver's growth as a person with an autonomous and critical conscience capable of contributing to and influencing his society.

Thus, Freire proposes transforming what he calls "banking education" into "pedagogy" based on the following principles:

- Faith in the people's ability to learn, to change and to liberate themselves from oppressive conditions of ignorance, poverty and exploitation.
- Direct contact of the learners with their own reality and its problems; analysis of the constraints imposed on them by social structure and official "ideology."
- Elimination of the differences between "educator" and "educate," in so far as they are both "learners."
- Free dialogue.
- Participation in liberating action.

Under the influence of Freire, Ivan Illich and others, many communicators have come to think of communication as a process that is inseparable from the other social and political processes necessary for national development and independence. The numerous failures and frustrations met by modernization efforts have shown that communication, to be really effective, must be organically integrated with such processes as conscientization, organization, politicization and technification.

The argument goes as follows: If the transfer of technology to the rural population is promoted unilaterally within a social structure containing large commercial farmers with big landholdings, family farmers with medium-sized farms, and landless agricultural workers, benefits are likely to be concentrated in the hands of the most privileged, those with better access to resources, instruction, credit, influence and power.

To provide more equal access to the benefits of development, therefore, it is necessary to foster grassroots organization of the least favoured aimed at forming pressure groups and facilitating collective action. However, in order to organize effectively people must become conscious of their rights and their potential. Conscientization alone, though, may lead to frustration and repression if, at the same time, the people do not attain a degree of *politicization,* giving them not only a reason to change but also the decision-making and leadership abilities necessary to achieve power.

It is evident that communication can be an important means for achieving conscientization, organization, politicization and technification. However, for communication to play this role a coherent communication philosophy and methodology must be accepted by all institutions involved. This is possible only in countries that have adopted a development model calling for popular participation in social and political transformation at all levels. ...

1927
1960
1963
1964
1967
1969
1970
1971
1972
1973
1974
1975
1976
1977
1978
1979
1980
1981
1982
1983
1984
1985
1986
1987
1988
1989
1990
1991
1992
1993
1994
1995
1996
1997
1998
1999
2000
2001
2002
2003
2004
2005
2006

EXCERPT FROM:

COMMUNICATIONS: BLINDSPOT OF WESTERN MARXISM

By Dallas W. Smythe

1977 At the root of a Marxist view of capitalism is the necessity to seek an objective reality, which means, in this case, an objective definition of the commodities produced by capitalism. What is the commodity form of mass-produced, advertiser-supported communications? This is the threshold question. The bourgeois idealist view of the reality of the communication commodity is "messages," "information," "images," "meaning," "entertainment," "orientation," "education" and "manipulation." All of these concepts are subjective mental entities, and all deal with superficial appearances. Nowhere do the theorists who adopt this worldview deal with the commodity form of mass communications under monopoly capitalism on which exist parasitically a host of submarkets dealing with cultural industry, e.g., the markets for "news" and "entertainment." Tacitly, this idealist theory of the communications commodity appears to have been held by most Western Marxists after Marx as well as by bourgeois theorists: Lenin,[1] Veblen, Marcuse, Adorno, Baran and Sweezy, for example, as well as Galbraith and orthodox economists. So, too, for those who take a more or less Marxist view of communications (Nordenstreng, Enzensberger, Hamelink, Schiller,[2] Burdock and Golding,[3] and me until now), as well as the conventional writers exemplified in the *Sage Annual Review of Communications Research*.[4]

Also included in the idealist camp are those apologists who dissolve the reality of communications under the appearance of the "medium," such as Marshall McLuhan.[5] No wonder, as Livant says, that "the field of communications is a jungle of idealism."[6] I submit that the materialist answer to the question -- What is the commodity form of mass-produced, advertiser-supported communications under monopoly capitalism? -- is audiences and readerships, hereafter referred to for simplicity as audiences. The material reality under monopoly capitalism is that all nonsleeping time of most of the population is work time. This work time is devoted to the production of commodities in general (both where people get paid for their work and as members of audiences) and to the production and reproduction of labour power (the pay for which is subsumed in their income). Of the off-the-job work time, the largest single block is audience time sold to advertisers. It is not sold by workers but by the mass media of communications. Who produces this commodity? The mass media of communications do, by the mix of explicit and hidden advertising and "programme" material, the markets that preoccupy the bourgeois communication theorists.[7]

---

2 *The Mind Managers*, Boston: Beacon Press, 1973.

3 "For a Political Economy of Mass Communications," The Socialist Register, 1973.

4 Beverly Hills, Calif.: Sage Publications.

5 See Sidney Finkelstein, *Sense and Nonsense of McLuhan*, New York: International Publishers, 1968; Donald Theall, *The Medium is the Rear View Mirror*, Montreal: McGill/Queen's University Press, 1971; and my review of the latter in Queen's Quarterly, Summer, 1971.

6 I am indebted to Professor William Livant, University of Regina, for much hard criticism, which he formulated in a critique of a draft of this paper in December 1975.

7 The objective reality is that the ostensible advertisements and the material which comes between them, whether in the print or electronic media, have a common purpose of producing the audience. It is an interesting consequence of the idealist perspective that in most liberal analysis, the "advertising" is considered to be separate from the "news," "entertainment," "educational material" which is interlarded between the advertisements.

---

1 Lenin held a manipulative theory of the mass media and admitted naiveté in this respect. "What was the fate of the decree establishing a state monopoly of private advertising issued in the first weeks of the Soviet government? … It is amusing to think how naive we were. …The enemy, i.e., the capitalist class, retaliated to this decree of the state power by completely repudiating that state power." "Report on the New Economic Policy," Seventh Moscow Gubernia Conference of the Russian Communist Party, October 21, 1921, in *Lenin About the Press*, Prague: International Organization of Journalists, 1972, 203. Lenin's Imperialism is devoid of recognition of the relation of advertising to monopoly capitalism and imperialism.

But although the mass media play the leading role on the production side of the consciousness industry, the people in the audiences pay directly much more for the privilege of being in those audiences than do the mass media. In Canada, in 1975, audience members directly bore about three times as large a cost as did the broadcasters and cable TV operators, combined.[8] In "their" time, which is sold to advertisers, workers (a) perform essential marketing functions for the producers of consumers' goods, and (b) work at the production and reproduction of labour power. This joint process, as shall be noted, embodies a principal contradiction. If this analytical sketch is valid, serious problems for Marxist theory emerge. Among them is the apparent fact that while the superstructure is not ordinarily thought of as being itself engaged in infrastructural productive activity, mass media communications are simultaneously in the superstructure and engaged indispensably in the last stage of infrastructural production, in which demand is produced and satisfied by purchases of consumer goods.

8   The annual cost to audience members of providing their own broadcast receivers (and paying for cable TV), consisting of depreciation, interest on investment, maintenance and electric power, amounted to slightly more than $1.8 billion, while the over-the-air broadcasters' (Canadian Broadcasting Corporation plus private broadcasters) and cable TV operators' costs were about $631 million.

EXCERPT FROM:

COMMUNICATIONS: BLINDSPOT OF WESTERN MARXISM

By Dallas W. Smythe

1977 The mass media institutions in monopoly capitalism developed the equipment, workers and organization to produce audiences for the purposes of the system between about 1875 and 1950. The prime purpose of the mass media is to produce people in audiences who work at learning the theory and practice of consumerism for civilian goods and who support (with taxes and votes) the military demand management system. The second principal purpose is to produce audiences whose theory and practice confirms the ideology of monopoly capitalism (possessive individualism in an authoritarian political system). The third principal purpose is to produce public opinion supportive of the strategic and tactical policies of the state, e.g., presidential candidates, support of Indochinese military adventures, space race, detente with the Soviet Union, rapprochement with China and ethnic and youth dissent. Necessarily in the monopoly capitalist system, the fourth purpose of the mass media complex is to operate itself so profitably as to ensure unrivalled respect for its economic importance in the system. It has been quite successful in achieving all four purposes.

If we recognize the reality of monopoly capitalism's buying audiences to complete the mass marketing of mass-produced consumer goods and services, much further analysis is needed of the implications of this "principal and decisive" integration of superstructure and base which reality presents. First, the contradictions produced within the audience commodity should be understood more clearly. I refer to the contradiction between audience members serving as producers' goods in the marketing of mass produced consumer goods and their work in producing and reproducing labour power. I think that the consciousness industry, through advertising-supported mass media, produces three kinds of alienation for the members of the audience commodity: (1) alienation from the result of their work "on the job," (2) alienation from the commodities-in-general, which they participate in marketing to themselves; and (3) alienation from the labour power they produce and reproduce in themselves and their children. It would seem that the theory of work needs reconsideration.

Then connections to other areas need to be examined. Among such connections, there come to mind those to Marxist theory about social consciousness (and false consciousness), to theory about the nature of the class struggle, the nature of the proletariat under monopoly capitalism and sex chauvinism, and to theories of the state. The last of these seems obvious if this analysis is considered in connection with the articles by Gold, Lo and Wright.[1] The role of the mass media and the consciousness industry in producing the audience commodity, both as commodity in general and peculiar commodity, might provide the real sinews to the structural-Marxist model of the state of [Nicos] Poulantzas and to the theoretical initiatives of Claus Offe in seeking the processes within the state that "guarantee" its class character.

The connection to the work of de Bord[2] regarding consciousness is proximate. The relation of industrially produced images to the "real" world of nutrition, clothing, housing, birth and death is dialectical. The mass media are the focus of production of images of popular culture under monopoly capitalism, both through the explicit advertising and the "free lunch" which hook and hold people in audiences. Because the consciousness industry produces consumable, saleable spectacles, its product treats both past and future like the present -- as blended in the eternal present of a system which was never created and will never end. The society of the spectacle, however, cannot be abstractly contrasted with the "real" world of actual people and things. The two interact. The spectacle inverts the real and is itself produced and is real. Hence, as de Bord says, objective reality is present on both sides. But because the society of the spectacle is a system that really stands the world on its head, the truth in it is a moment of the false. Because the spectacle monopolizes the power to make mass appearance, it demands and gets passive acceptance by the "real" world. And because it is undeniably real (as well as false), it has the persuasive power of the most effective propaganda.[3]

Finally, another example of necessary connections is that to the theory of imperialism and socialism in the present stage of monopoly capitalism. There are many ways by which a theory of commodity production through mass communications would strengthen the analysis, for example, of Samir Amin.[4] The coca-colonisation of the dependent and peripheral countries cannot be grounded in Marxist theory without attention to the production of audience commodities in the interest of multinational corporations. It would link Amin's theory to Herbert Schiller's work on the relation of the mass media to the American empire.[5] And, when linked with analysis of the ideological aspects of science and "technology," it could strengthen the development of a noneconomistic, nonpositive, non-Eurocentered Marxism. Analysis of such connections is inviting but beyond the scope of the present essay.

1   David A. Gold, Clarence Y. H. Lo, and Erik Olin Wright, "Recent Developments in Marxist Theories of the Capitalist State," Monthly Review, October 1975, 29-43; November 1975, 36-52.
2   Guy de Bord, "The Society of the Spectacle," Detroit, Black and Red, Box 9546, 1970.
3   Ibid., 6-9.
4   Samir Amin, "Accumulation on a World Scale," New York, Monthly Review Press, 1974; and "Toward a Structural Crisis of World Capitalism," Socialist Revolution, April 1975, 9-44.
5   Herbert I. Schiller, Mass Communications and American Empire, Critical Studies in Communication and in the Cultural Industries, New York: A. Kelley, 1969.

THE TRANSNATIONAL POWER STRUCTURE AND INTERNATIONAL INFORMATION

Excerpt from: Information in the New International Order

By Juan Somavia

1977 Most Third World countries are part of an international system, the rationality of which inevitably operates in favor of developed countries. The roots of this system lie in diverse forms of colonial domination and exploitation that have historically characterized the relationships between center and periphery. At present the system operates according to a set of practices and principles that arose after World War II, in regional and international organizations created during that time, with the explicit or tacit approval of a small number of countries that by then made up the "international community." This has all been fine-tuned and adjusted during the last 30 years to form a coherent whole from which the key instrument of domination clearly emerges—the transnational power structure, itself, acting internationally and operating in practically all Third World countries.

The transnational power structure expresses itself through functionally differentiated working patterns which, taken as a whole, represent a complex set of tools with the central aim of consolidating and expanding its action and influence throughout the world. To introduce itself, it uses a set of values and aspirations supposedly representing political stability, economic efficiency, technological creativity, market "logic," the benefits of consumerism, the defense of liberty and others.

Experience demonstrates that the real behavior of the transnational power structure manifests in terms very different from those supposedly intended. In the name of political stability, it defends the status quo and those more conservative regimes, guaranteeing a lack of deep structural changes in Third World societies. In the name of efficiency, it promotes the expansion of multinational companies that originate within it, as a "technically" ideal solution to the problems of growth and economic development, promoting a "homogenization" of consumption patterns that frequently neglect basic needs and local cultural realities. In the name of technological creativity, it concentrates huge resources in research and development efforts linked to its industrial-military apparatus and the interests of its multinational companies, which have little to do with the real needs of Third World peoples. In the name of market-"logic," it advocates governments' abdication from their fundamental responsibility, to define and guide national development in favor of majorities, instead promoting forms of social organization that leave decisions about what, how much, how and for whom to produce in the hands of large private companies. In the name of the benefits of consumerism, it focuses production only toward those who effectively have the ability to obtain an income, thus consolidating development styles that benefit the most favored sectors of society and marginalize economic and social processes that would benefit the national majorities of the Third World. Finally, in the name of liberty, it blocks, intervenes and destabilizes the actions, policies and programs of progressive governments, weakening or replacing them and instead supporting and aiding regimes characterized by systematic repression and the violation of human rights.

To achieve these objectives it has an array of different complementary instruments that reflect the diverse dimensions of the transnational power structure.

a. The political/military/intelligence services dimension: NATO, SEATO, TIAR[1], and links between intelligence services. As well, it expresses itself through open and veiled threats to use force; attempts to promote changes favorable to its interests, and to prevent modifications against them in the power

---

1 Translator's note: Tratado Interamericano de Asistencia Recíproca, or Inter-American Treaty of Reciprocal Assistance.

1927
1960
1963
1964
1967
1969
1970
1971
1972
1973
1974
1975
1976
1977
1978
1979
1980
1981
1982
1983
1984
1985
1986
1987
1988
1989
1990
1991
1992
1993
1994
1995
1996
1997
1998
1999
2000
2001
2002
2003
2004
2005
2006

relationships in Third World countries; different forms of military intervention and political penetration; and policies of international isolation applied to certain progressive governments.

b. The economic/industrial/trade dimension: promotion of multinational companies; reinforcement of structures and agreements favorable to the system such as the IMF, World Bank, GATT; efforts to weaken instruments that question aspects of the system, such as UNCTAD, producers' associations; measures to control multinational companies and regional cooperation and integration organizations; stimuli for the implantation of "imitation" development models; use of economic instruments to block and weaken the policies of progressive governments.

Only recently, has the *communications/advertising/culture dimension* begun to emerge clearly as an integral part of the transnational set of instruments. It is increasingly evident that the transnational communications system has been developed with the support and at the service of that international power structure. It is an integral part of the system, through which the fundamental instrument that information constitutes in contemporary society is controlled. It is vehicle for the transmission of values and lifestyles to Third World countries, stimulating the type of consumption and the type of society required by the overall system. Politically, the status quo is defended when it supports the above interests; economically, conditions are created for the transnational expansion of capital. If the transnational system lost its control of communication structures, it would loose one of its most powerful weapons; hence the difficulty of bringing about change.

The transnational communications system constitutes a whole: it includes news agencies, advertising companies and data banks, and the provision of information retrieval services, radio and television programs, films, radiophotographs, magazines, books and comics with international circulation. Its different components, which originate mainly in industrialized countries,

reinforce one another, stimulating as a whole consumer aspirations to reach forms of social organization and lifestyles that imitate those of industrialized capitalist countries. Experience has shown that these can only be reproduced in Third World countries characterized by a high and growing concentration of income in a few hands, and on unacceptable social inequalities.

At the same time, the "pressure of information" emanating from so many different sources, seemingly unrelated but substantially coherent, gradually eliminates the ability to react to messages, and, therefore, the receiver progressively becomes a passive element, with no capacity for critical judgment. The communication process then becomes something similar to a theater where people watch but do not participate. Under these conditions, the audience gradually convinces itself of the fact that the transnational made of consumption and development is historically inevitable. Thus, the communications system fulfills its primary function: culturally penetrating the human being to condition him in such a way that he will accept the political, economic and cultural values of the transnational power structure.

That is the reason why communication policies are an integral part of development policies. If information is communicated in the interest and at the service of the transnational power system, the sovereign ability to decide and execute national development policies is hampered, since the international communication structure conditions and directly determines individual and social reactions within each country.

Notes

1. Al Hester, "International News Agencies." In Alan Wells (ed.), *Mass Communication: A World View*, Edited by Allan Wells, page 208.

2. Resolution 24 was passed in December 1970, and it has thus far been the political backbone of the Andean Group. At present, it is enduring intense attacks from conservative elements related to the transnational power structure in the Andean region.

3. Herbert Schiller, "La livre circulation de l'information et la domination mondiale," Le Monde Diplomatique, September 1975.

First published in: Fernando Reyes Matta (ed.) 1977. *La información en el nuevo orden internacional*. Instituto Latinoamericano de Estudios Transnacionales (ILET): México. Reprinted with permission of F. Reyes Matta.

WHY EDUCATE?

Excerpt from: Radio Program Production: Realizing the Script

By Mario Kaplún

1978 The question is not only how much can be accomplished, but how we should set about accomplishing it. …Radio techniques, practices and production techniques are of little use without a theoretical basis. This is especially true of radio as an end in itself when no educational purpose is set forth. It is impossible to approach an educational task, in any medium, without first clarifying what type of pedagogy is to be adopted and what function the educational task is intended to serve.

Three Educational Options

Here, the well-designed scheme of Juan Díaz Bordenave[1] will be followed, distinguishing three types of education.

As Bordenave points out, in the real world none of the three is to be found in a pure state but, rather, intermixed—present in different proportions in different educational schemes. Thus, three educational models can be distinguished:

1. Education that emphasizes content.
2. Education that emphasizes results.
3. Education that emphasizes process.

---

1 Juan Diaz Bordenave: "Las nuevas pedagogías y tecnologías de comunicación: sus implicaciones para la investigación" [New communication pedagogies and technologies: implications for research]. Paper for the *Reunión de Consulta sobre Investigación en Comunicación para el Desarrollo Rural* [Consultative Meeting on Research in Communication for Rural Development] (Latin America, organized by CIID, Cali, Colombia, 1976). Bordenave is an OAS communications expert and graduate-studies Professor of Communication and Popular Education at the University of Brasilia. Here, his invaluable analysis is summarized, while glossing and broadening it with the author's own comments and with quotes from a number of other writers. The goal is to apply the concepts, using various examples, to the author's specific field of expertise—radio. To the extent possible, there has been an effort to clearly identify where Professor Bordenave's thoughts leave off and the author's begin. However, it should be understood that, while acknowledging his valuable contributions, the author assumes sole responsibility for any statements made here in this connection.

In the inevitably simplified form that space imposes here, making it necessary to accentuate certain features at the risk of neglecting others, an attempt will be made to describe and schematically characterize each of these three types.

FIRST TYPE: EDUCATION EMPHASIZING CONTENT

"This is traditional education, based essentially on the transmission of knowledge and values from one generation to another, from teacher to student, from the elite to the masses." It tends to be vertical, is generally authoritarian and often paternalistic, and assigns clear roles to the teacher and the taught—those who "know" and those who are "ignorant."

This, as the reader will have recognized, is the type of education referred to by one of its most ardent critics, Paulo Freire, as the "banking" model of education. In it, the educator deposits knowledge in the mind of the student. The point is to inculcate knowledge, introducing it into the memory of the student, who is seen as the receptacle and depository of information. Traditional schools have repeatedly been criticized for their tendency to confuse authentic education with mere instruction, which, as has also been pointed out, informs rather than forms.

While this type of education is prevalent in the conventional school system, it has an even more dominant place in radio-based education, where, because of the limitations of the medium itself, the student is absent and is therefore reduced to silence and passivity. The student can only listen, repeat what the radio teacher says, and "learn" it. Many of Latin America's admirable "radio schools" for educating adult *campesinos* have taken up a healthy opposition to this passive approach, rejecting it—often with unquestionable sincerity. Their postulates today include the principles of a "liberating" and "personalizing" education. However, having discovered no alternative method of radio-based teaching and having, therefore, developed no other ways of producing educational programs, their broadcasts continue to follow the mechanistic scheme of the teacher who "teaches" and the student who "learns."

The methodological features of this type of education are well known. Díaz Bordenave points, for example, to the fact that "the teacher and the text are the basis for the method (in the case of radio education, the 'text' is the textbook given to the students, who are expected to strictly follow its lessons and exercises); the curricula are packed with material based on the concepts and data that the teacher or communicator considers important. Little importance is placed on dialogue and feedback. Retention of content, i.e., memorization, is rewarded, and unfaithful or overly original reproduction of the materials is punished." The consequences of this approach are not difficult to infer. "The student (listener, audience) becomes accustomed to passivity, and does not develop the ability to think independently or critically; a difference in status is established between professor and student; a mental structure of respecting authority is promoted, since the student 'internalizes' the superiority and authority of the teacher; and the student acquires a 'closed' or dogmatic mindset, incapable of assessing received messages on their own merits, regardless of the authority of the source." They become simplistic, and experience the need for everything to be either totally white or totally black. They evince an anxiety for formulas, organizational structures and discipline, showing little tolerance for ambiguity or critical analysis.

SECOND TYPE: EDUCATION EMPHASIZING RESULTS

This is the type of education that has most influenced the field of communication. Almost all communication manuals employed as textbooks in Latin American countries are explicitly or implicitly built on the principles of this form of education. Hence the importance of analyzing it carefully.

This educational model emerged in Latin America as an initial response to the problem of underdevelopment. Modernization was thought to be the solution to the poverty in which the countries of the region were immersed. This translated to a desire to adopt the features and production methods of the so-called developed countries. Production and productivity were to be increased rapidly, thus requiring the introduction of new, modern technologies. Technological innovation capable of engendering spectacular progress was viewed as the panacea for all the ills of Latin America.

Education was to serve these goals. For example, it was to be used to persuade "backward" *campesinos* to abandon their primitive agricultural methods and quickly learn new methods. The communications media were to be used to promote these changes, playing an ongoing, penetrating and persuasive role. Understandably, this development model assigned great importance to communication techniques.

For these new educators and communicators of the "development decade"—whose good faith and sincere cooperative spirit are beyond question—the problem consisted in finding the quickest and most effective ways to encourage the region's "primitive and backward" people to accept change, consent to modify their traditional habits and customs, and adopt the new technologies. How, then, was one to set about changing people? What techniques of persuasion were to be used, what psychological principles employed?

Thus, the so-called behavioral engineering approach emerged. In the communication texts of the late 1950s, one finds enlightening definitions such as the following: "The communicator is a sort of architect of human conduct, a behavioral engineer whose function is to induce the population to adopt given forms of thinking, feeling and acting that will allow it to increase its production and productivity and to improve its standard of living and habits." Or, again, "Communicating is not only the act of transmitting messages or signals, or of using media or channels. Communicating is the art of creating meanings and producing behavior; it provokes changes in the thinking, feeling and actions of human beings. Communicating consists of transmitting messages with the well-defined intention of leading people to behave in a certain way.

More precisely, it produces these behaviors through the transmission of messages."

Another typical expression of this "vertical/persuasive/disseminationist" education is the concept of "attitudinal change," construed as replacing traditional habits by ones that favor the new technologies. Formulations such as the following make clear the extent to which this type of education emphasizes results: "When we learn to express our message as a function of specific responses on the part of those who receive them, we take the first step toward efficient and effective communication… When confronted with a proposal for change—an attempt at communication—the subject's reaction may be positive or negative. For example, when our educational campaign proposes to *campesinos* that they adopt a new chemical product to combat a particular pest, they may accept or reject the proposal. If they accept it, there is communication… If the desired change does not take place, if the desired response to the stimulus employed does not occur, the communication can be considered to have failed. Or, more radically yet, it may be said, technically, that communication has not occurred."

The point is not that this type of education does not "take people into account." Indeed, there is a vast body of psychological study devoted to serving this approach. However, it is not a psychology designed to promote the full, autonomous development of the individual personality. Rather, it is concerned with mechanisms to "persuade" the individual and "lead" him or her more effectively, with shaping-behavior based on predetermined objectives. This is the "behavioral" psychology approach founded on the stimuli and rewards principle, of which Skinner is the figurehead.

In this connection, the theories of the American communications scientist, David Berlo, are well known. He assigns habit a major role in communication. By "habit" he refers to the relation between a stimulus and the response a person makes, as a result of which he receives a reward, a principle evidently very similar to Pavlov's conditioned reflex theory. Thus, for Berlo,

the reward plays an essential role in communication techniques, since it is the reward that shapes new habits in the individual, as well as the pace and extent of learning. The greater the reward offered, and the more quickly given, the more effective will be the action in producing the desired response to the stimulus, and the more the new habit will develop, strengthen, and replace the old. In accordance with these precepts, Berlo recommends that communicators always offer their public an incentive, a reward associated with each message, and that the reward be quickly achievable: "Study what can quickly move your audience to action."

Perhaps these educational theories are responsible for the fact that, in many Latin American development plans, communications deemed necessary for the success of the plan are not placed in the hands of communicators and educators, but rather of advertising agencies. These experts, responsible for the mass campaigns that guide the public's purchasing and consumption of particular products, are presumed to know best how to marshal the mechanisms, techniques and resources involved in the play of stimulus and response.

It is striking that this type of educational communication, when employing radio, opts for "mass campaigns" based on 10- second or 20-second messages repeated insistently, rather than on 15- minute or 30-minute programs where the foundations and objectives of the proposed behavior could be explained and the thinking behind them laid out.

As Díaz Bordenave points out in his study, in terms of effectiveness and efficiency, this type of education offers obvious advantages over the "banking" education described earlier. However, critics have raised serious doubts, such as the following:

> With the objectives specifically and rather rigidly established by the teacher, instructor or communicator, the student becomes accustomed to being guided by others. If, in addition, the rewards or reinforcements are established by

1927
1960
1963
1964
1967
1969
1970
1971
1972
1973
1974
1975
1976
1977
1978
1979
1980
1981
1982
1983
1984
1985
1986
1987
1988
1989
1990
1991
1992
1993
1994
1995
1996
1997
1998
1999
2000
2001
2002
2003
2004
2005
2006

others, the student becomes used to shaping his or her life according to the support and approval of outside forces.

Moreover, mercantile or utilitarian values are inculcated, including material success as the criterion for personal realization, and personal economic gain as a basic objective in life, along with consumption, individualism, competition, profit, etc. (The very notion of personal "reward" is consubstantial with these values.) On the other hand, cooperative activity and the values of solidarity and community, "so indispensable for an underdeveloped continent whose power is based on the union of the weak," are left by the wayside.

Furthermore—and, this, perhaps, is one of the most important criticisms:

> The method does not place emphasis on the development of intelligence in and of itself, which occurs only as a secondary effect. Only predetermined objectives matter, thus it is doubtful that this type of education contributes to developing creativity, originality or critical awareness. Nor will it be easy for it to promote an attitude of interrelationship with the natural and social surroundings, or to foster a comprehensive integration of the knowledge acquired.

> Communication is assigned an instrumental and persuasive function, leaving aside other important functions such as self-knowledge, self-expression, mutual relationship, social participation, and the development of the population's social awareness and critical consciousness.

Even in terms of mere efficacy, this education is questionable, since, in the opinion of many analysts, the results produced are counterproductive to the objectives. According to these analysts, communication applied to the transfer of agricultural technology, for instance, has largely resulted in the users rejecting the messages.

It is increasingly clear that no development is possible—even in the sense of mere economic growth—without people's active participation, and without their creativity, initiative and autonomous decision making. This is due, among other factors, to the fact that the development of the region's countries cannot offer immediate individual "rewards," but requires, on the contrary, a spirit of struggle, of freely assumed sacrifice and community cooperation.

THIRD TYPE: EDUCATION EMPHASIZING PROCESS

This type of education, as described by Díaz Bordenave, emphasizes the importance of the process of personal and community change. It is not as concerned with the material to be communicated, or with the resulting behavior, as with the dialectical interaction between people and their reality, and the development of intellectual capacity and social awareness.

It is not that this type of education denies or ignores the needs and requirements of development. However, it begins with a different concept of development, based on the integral development of the person, in which the aim is not to simply have more, but to be more. It is based on the belief that, even in terms of purely quantitative and material development goals, a deep transformation in the education of the people is necessary—one that produces thinking individuals capable of participating actively in the process, with an enhanced sense of responsibility and creativity.

This model, like the preceding one, is designed to achieve a certain "attitudinal change," though not associated principally with the adoption of new technologies. The fundamental change here consists in the change from an uncritical to a critical individual; from persons made passive, conformist and fatalistic by the conditioning of their surroundings, to individuals who take responsibility for their own destiny—people capable of overcoming their egoistical and individualistic tendencies and opening themselves to the values of solidarity and community.

If the first type of education can be schematically described as one where the subject *learns*, and the second as one that seeks to make the subject *do*, the third, then, can be described as one whose aim is to have the individual *think*.

As Paulo Freire says:

> If man's ontological vocation is to be a subject and not an object, it can only be developed to the extent that, reflecting on his temporal-spatial conditions, he inserts himself in them critically. The more he is led to reflect on his situation, on his temporal-spatial grounding, the more he will emerge from it consciously "freighted" with commitment to his reality, in which, because he is a subject, he must not be a mere spectator, but must increasingly intervene.[2]

Thus, this type of education is problem-based. The first methodological consequence of this model, as Díaz Bordenave points out, is that "the object of communication and education is to help the person wrestle with his reality, both natural and social. It seeks to stimulate the growth of intelligence, in the sense of becoming structurally more complex, and more rapid and flexible in its functioning." Here, what matters is that, more than learning *things*, the subject learns to learn, to become capable of thinking autonomously, of "overcoming the purely empirical and immediate findings of observed facts, and developing individual deductive abilities." What the uneducated adult needs, more than knowledge, is tools for thinking: It is not so much the lack of data or ideas as the unexercised state of his thinking faculties that constrains him, limiting him to what he is capable of perceiving, what is in his immediate environment, what he can actually touch.

As O'Sullivan-Ryan so aptly expresses it, this type of education promotes "the cultivation of the intelligence more than of the memory. It focuses on learning and the learning process more than on memory—on learning to learn—and considers vital the activity of the intelligence and the will to achieve precisely a liberating education that gives man back his own humanity."[3]

Along with developing intelligence, this type of education develops awareness. It promotes a process of questioning, and works to change the "tranquilist" and fatalistic worldview that keeps the Latin American masses in a state of lethargy, representing an acutely paralyzing obstacle to authentic development. This is the process that Freire refers to when he distinguishes different phases of awareness and speaks of the passage from magical thinking to naïve thinking, and then to critical thinking.

For Díaz Bordenave, however, "The main triumph of this type of education is that it creates an awareness of the subject's own dignity and value as a person, of man's essential freedom to fully realize himself … and of his free commitment to other men."

"Clearly, this type of education involves participation and prepares for it. Popular education must create the pedagogical conditions for the practice of participation."[4] As applied to the medium of radio, this is an excellent formulation. In an understandable and healthy reaction (albeit an exaggerated one, in the author's view) to the verticalism that reigns in traditional types of communication, an approach has arisen in which communication is considered valid only if it is "horizontal" and participatory. Thus, only radio programs

---

2   Though this type of education has much in common with Freire's philosophical postulates, it should not be taken as identical to "conscientization," which is a particular method with its own characteristics and precise methodological steps. Freire himself has insistently protested against what he considers the abusive use of the term—which he coined to describe a specific method—and has demanded that the term be used exclusively to designate the method he created. Thus, a type of education—which is what Díaz Bordenave describes here—should not be confused with a specific methodology. The former is much broader, and may include a range of methodologies—"conscientization" and others—leading to the same end and sharing the same educational philosophy. Moreover, here, when dealing with the example of radio, such a distinction is particularly important, since Freire's method is exclusively interpersonal, or face to face, and does not include the use of collective means of communication.

3   Jeremiah O'Sullivan-Ryan: Pedagogia de los medios [Pedagogy of Media]. Paper for the Seminar on the Pedagogy of Radiophonic Education, held by ISI (Konrad Adenauer Foundation) and the Asociación Latinoamericana de Educación Radiofónica (ALER) [Latin American Radio Education Association]. Santiago de los Caballeros, Dominican Republic, April 1975. The author is a professor at Stanford University.

4   Aida Bezerra and Pedro Garcia Ramirez: Consideracões sobre Avaliação em Educação Popular [Observations on the Evaluation of Popular Education]. Lecture given at the graduate communications program (specifically, in the field of Communication and Popular Education) at the University of Brasilia. June 1975. Quoted by Juan Díaz Bordenave, op. cit.

1927
1960
1963
1964
1967
1969
1970
1971
1972
1973
1974
1975
1976
1977
1978
1979
1980
1981
1982
1983
1984
1985
1986
1987
1988
1989
1990
1991
1992
1993
1994
1995
1996
1997
1998
1999
2000
2001
2002
2003
2004
2005
2006

in which the people express themselves directly, "without intermediaries," and where they cease to be listeners and "hear their own voice," are recognized as valid instruments of popular education.

Though this model of communication is valuable, and is important in programming, not every radio program must—or can—follow this model. What is important is that participation be encouraged and prepared for, and that, as Bezerra and García Ramírez suggest, "the pedagogical conditions for participation" be created. A radio program can do much to promote—and can be an effective and valid element in—popular communication if it is based on the concrete social reality of the human group to which it is directed; if it helps the group gain awareness of, and responsibility for, this reality; and if it associates its educational activities with the social interests of the group. Participatory practices consist of more than "the people speaking, through radio." Participation is broader and more encompassing, and can occur through a variety of actions and grassroots organizations. The contribution of a radio program may very well be to prepare the way by removing cultural obstacles internalized in the listener, etc.[5]

In sum, Díaz Bordenave lists the following imperatives of such a pedagogy:

1. Facilitate the observation of reality and problem-posing, such that people seek solutions adapted to their individual situations.
2. Facilitate dialogue, participation and cooperation, such that individuals learn to live together, articulate common problems and resolve them cooperatively.
3. Stimulate the development of intelligence, thinking and awareness, such that each individual learns to think, make his own decisions and plan his behavior in a mature, autonomous fashion.

4. Promote the acquisition of an integrated, encompassing view of reality.
5. Facilitate access to the reception and expression of all inhabitants of a nation, such that communication and education do not become the privilege of a few.

Consequences for Latin American Radio

Radio alone is insufficient to accomplish this educational objective. However, it can contribute to, and be an instrument in, the process.

Following is a list of some of the characteristics that would be desirable elements of radio programs, based on this educational approach:

1. Programs should stimulate a process in the listeners, rather than inculcate knowledge or seek immediate practical results.
2. They should help listeners gain an awareness of the reality surrounding them (both natural and social), become integrally part of that reality, and be based on issues specific to them and to their living situation.
3. They should facilitate the elements needed to understand and address the problems of everyday reality: They should be problem-posing programs.
4. They should stimulate intelligence, encourage reasoning, provoke listeners to think, and lead to reflection.
5. They should associate themselves with the needs and interests of the community to which they are directed, and help it identify its own needs and interests.
6. They should stimulate dialogue and participation. In some cases, this will take the form of direct participation, but generally they will "create the pedagogical conditions for the development of participatory practice." They should emphasize the values of solidarity and community, and promote unity and cooperation.
7. They should stimulate critical awareness, as well as autonomous, mature, responsible decision making.

---

5 The author is well aware of the simplified and limited presentation, given here, of new themes, involving major issues of communication. Because of the nature of this book, as well as space limitations, these issues could not be covered with as much breadth as might otherwise be desirable.

Communicators educated in the second type of education face what is termed "resistance to change" when working with techniques to achieve modernization and bring about an "attitudinal change." This resistance consists of beliefs, myths, judgments, customs, prejudices, superstitions and attitudes of a social, esthetic, economic and religious, etc., nature. They form and shape individual behavior and can be an obstacle to acceptance of the new technology being presented. For example, if a new method of growing corn—one considered more productive and rational—is to be introduced, but the target community continues following traditional ancestral growing practices for which it feels a deep connection, the proposed change will most likely encounter resistance.

To overcome this resistance, the guideline for persuasion-based communication is to avoid conflict. In other words, proposals for change must be formulated so as not to conflict with existing social values. According to this view, to change something, one need not point out its defects. It is better to skillfully and insistently emphasize the advantages of the new thing being proposed. When the message conflicts with the values of the social environment in which the target audience lives, all references to the contradiction should be omitted.

This technique is consistent with a pedagogy concerned above all, as has been pointed out, with achieving a result: It is less concerned with encouraging people to think and make free, autonomous decisions or adopt the desired change. Hence its solution of keeping the problem out of view by eliminating any reference to the contradiction. In such a scenario, the attempt is to lead listeners to accept change without their ever realizing that it goes against their traditional social and cultural values.

The methods of a communicator who subscribes to the type of education being proposed in this paper will be fundamentally different. Rather than setting as a priority the goal that the person (or, better, the group) adopt the innovation, the point is rather that that

person or group should know why he or it is doing so, and embrace it as a personal, free and conscious act.

A communicator of this type will know that the introduction of new and strange technologies has led, in many cases, to profound cultural backwardness: Instead of achieving the intended goal, the individual or group, on the contrary, undergoes a profound loss of identity, a depersonalizing conflict between its most treasured and deeply-rooted traditions and the new practices imported from outside. This invasion of foreign technological practices has often done more harm than good and, rather than promoting development, has been an obstacle to it. Even in terms of pure economic growth, it is not profitable to introduce tractors at the expense of the personality of those who are to drive the tractors. Hence, if the introduction of the new technology is deemed necessary and appropriate, it should be done employing a pedagogy that takes account of the social and cultural costs of the operation, one that respects the people.

The communicator will also have to determine whether the "resistance to change" is unfounded, irrational and merely the result of prejudice, as is likely to be assumed by the modernizing technician. In many cases, results have shown that supposedly backward *campesinos* knew much more about the specific conditions of their land and about effective ways of cultivating it than did the technician, and they had sound reasons to defend their traditional practices and resist innovation. One need merely contemplate the grave ecological imbalances produced (previously and currently) by the irrational introduction of certain chemical pesticides, excessively intensive exploitation of agricultural land, and other practices.

However, once the communicator becomes convinced that the proposed practice is genuinely good and necessary, and that the resistance it generates in the group is, in fact, the product of unfounded, irrational prejudice—which may certainly be the case— then he must choose the elusive path of ensuring that the problem maintains a low profile, following the

1927
1960
1963
1964
1967
1969
1970
1971
1972
1973
1974
1975
1976
1977
1978
1979
1980
1981
1982
1983
1984
1985
1986
1987
1988
1989
1990
1991
1992
1993
1994
1995
1996
1997
1998
1999
2000
2001
2002
2003
2004
2005
2006

procedure mentioned above; or, alternatively, confront the *campesinos* with the truth, acknowledging openly the contradiction such change poses to traditional values, and allowing them to make a free decision.

A communicator whose action is consistent with the type of education proposed here will certainly choose the second option: not only because it is more respectful of the person, but because it is the only truly effective course.

If prejudices do not rise to the surface and find expression, they will remain latent at the preconscious level or in the profound layers of the human being, generating in the person or group a conflict between the new practice and the most intimate level of feeling, resulting in anguish, tension, uprooting and a sense of guilt over having violated tradition. At any moment, those latent prejudices may appear again in some form, provoking a violent, closed-minded rejection of innovation.

First, then, the communicator/educator will make certain that the reasons for the resistance to the proposed change are explicitly expressed, so that the group becomes aware of them. A survey, sociodrama, interview program, rural forum, radio theatre, etc., can usefully serve this purpose.

Then, in the same broadcast or series of broadcasts, the communicator will ensure that any other potentially problematic group beliefs and traditions are brought to the fore and expressed, causing the group's members to begin a process of reflection as to whether the proposed change may, indeed, be of value. It must be remembered that traditional cultures are not monolithic. Some react negatively to change, leading to tranquilist, static, closed attitudes. However, every group has traditions that also hold the potential for more dynamic and open attitudes, ones more conducive to change.

By way of example: The communicator may demonstrate that the group's ancestors often adopted, or even devised, new techniques: Thus, to accept an innovation does not represent a betrayal of, but instead is consonant with, the spirit of those ancestors. Another possibility is to show that by increasing the land's yield and thus improving the living conditions of the family and community, they are fostering a value rooted in traditions of love and loyalty to one's own—a value perhaps even more important than the one creating the resistance to the new technique.

In this way, a situation that would otherwise produce a violent cultural upheaval can be experienced by the group as a form of cultural continuity.

Finally, the communicator who adheres to the third type of education will allow the community to make a decision freely. If it chooses to adopt the new technique, the choice will be a thoughtful, mature and autonomous one, with a far better chance of lasting and being incorporated by the community—experienced not as the imposition of an outside force but, rather, as something freely accepted and linked with tradition.

It is also clear that the behaviorist stimulus/reward methodology generally appeals to individualistic and competitive motivations—the desire for greater gain in order to stand out and possess more than does one's neighbors. The communicator/educator, in contrast, will present innovation as beneficial for the entire community, presenting it in terms of union and cooperation. In both cases, technology transfer will occur, but the educational effects will be very different.

Kaplún, Mario (1978). *Producción de programas de radio. El guio—la realización*. Colección Intiyan, Ediciones CIESPAL. Quito, Ecuador. Reprinted with permission of Gabriel Kaplún.

A FAREWELL TO ARISTOTLE: 'HORIZONTAL' COMMUNICATION

By Luis Ramiro Beltrán

1979

That which is utopian
is not that which is unattainable;
it is not idealism;
it is a dialectic process of
denouncing and announcing;
denouncing the dehumanizing structure
and announcing the humanizing structure.

—Paulo Freire

International communication used to be, for the most part, a territory of quiet waters. Not any more. In the present decade it has become a center of major, and often heated, controversy as a part of a broader and increasing confrontation between developed and developing countries. Militant discomfort between them existed already. …What is rather a new event is the full realization that the situation of dependence is also true in the cultural sphere—and the acknowledgement—[in] this decade—that communication does much in the service of all three types of neocolonial domination.[1]

Third World countries are not only struggling today to bring about a real end to colonialism by obtaining fair treatment in trade and aid. They are simultaneously and relatedly pursuing the establishment of a *"New International Economic Order"*[2] and a *"New International Information Order."* As both these attempts are being actively resisted by most developed countries, communication has now come to lie neatly in the domain of international conflict.

Manifestations of the conflict occur at different levels and in many places, mostly through public discussion, which, since the middle of the decade, often reaches combustive characteristics. One illustration was an intergovernmental conference on national communication policies in Latin America held under UNESCO's sponsorship in Costa Rica in 1976. This meeting included recommendations to achieve balance in the international flow of information and to endow the region with an independent news agency capable of at least alleviating the consequences of the quasi-monopoly exercised by UPI and AP. From inception to conclusions, the meeting was the object of a concerted and virulent attack by international communication organizations that regarded it as a threat to freedom of information.[3] Another illustration of the conflict is the recent approval by UNESCO's General Conference of a declaration on international communication.[4] This compromise statement is the final product of a years-long fierce and noisy battle between those considering it an expression of intent of totalitarian control of communication and those perceiving it, on the contrary, as an expression of the will for genuinely democratizing it.

…The conflict embraces several major areas of concern. Political leaders, development strategists, researchers, and communication practitioners in developing countries are on the one hand questioning the structure, operations, financing, ideology, and influence of certain mighty international communication organizations. On the other hand, they are challenging many of the traditional concepts of communication born in developed countries and not too long ago accepted also in the rest of the world.

In the former area the role of international news agencies, TV and film exporters, and transnational advertisers is being condemned as a key tool for external domination. In the latter area, the classical concepts of press freedom, communication rights, and free flow of information, as well as the standard definition of news itself, are also rated instrumental for domination. Even the alien influences on the orientation and conduct of research[5] and training in communication are subject to critical assessment.

1927
1960
1963
1964
1967
1969
1970
1971
1972
1973
1974
1975
1976
1977
1978
1979
1980
1981
1982
1983
1984
1985
1986
1987
1988
1989
1990
1991
1992
1993
1994
1995
1996
1997
1998
1999
2000
2001
2002
2003
2004
2005
2006

Finally, the very conceptualization of the nature of communication, as coming from developed countries, is today being contested in developing ones.

…Attempts at defining communication can be traced back to Aristotle, who saw rhetoric as composed of three elements: *the speaker, the speech, and the listener* and perceived the aim of it as "the search for all possible means of persuasion." Centuries later, and with many more minds working on the matter, this classical definition seems …the root of almost all prevailing conceptualizations.

Lasswell: Communicators after Effects

Indeed, the most widely accepted definition of our age is that of Lasswell,[6] who essentially advanced Aristotle's proposition by adding two elements to it. Whereas Aristotle had identified the *who*, *what*, and *to whom* of communication, Lasswell refined the scheme by stipulating the *how* and making explicit the *what for* as follows:

A convenient way to describe an act of communication is to answer the following questions:

- Who
- Says What
- In Which Channel
- To Whom
- With What Effect?

Lasswell saw communication as performing three functions: *surveillance* of the environment, *correlation* of the components of society, and cultural *transmission* between generations. In doing so, according to De Fleur,[7] Lasswell was attempting to temper the mechanistic influence of the classical stimulus-response theory. He was taking into account contextual or situational variables stressed as intervening between "S" and "R" by the social categories and individual differences theories. His basic paradigm generated prompt and widespread following. His attention to some sociostructural considerations did not.

Transmission and Influence

From Lasswell on, the notion of *transfer* was to characterize many derived conceptualizations of communication. Such was the case, for instance, of an also extensively used definition provided by Berelson and Steiner.[8]

> The transmission of information, ideas, emotions, skills, etc. by use of symbols-words, pictures, figures, graphs, etc. It is the act or process of transmission that is usually called communication.

Similarly, the notion of influence (through persuasion) as the central goal of communication was to be included in several subsequent definitions, such as this one by Osgood.[9]

> In the most general sense, we have communication whenever one system, a source, influences another, the destination, by manipulation of alternative signals which can be transferred over the channel connecting them.

Also staying with Lasswell's paradigm, Nixon[10] stressed two ingredients of the process: *the intentions of the communicator* and *the conditions under which the message is received.*

From Electronics: Sources and Receivers

Then, engineers Shannon and Weaver[11] came up with a mathematical theory of communication, the presentation of which they made with the following statement:

> The word communication will be used here in a very broad sense to include all of the procedures by which one mind may affect another.

Shannon and Weaver[12] conceive of a general communication system as composed of five essential parts (plus "noise"):

1. An *information source* which produces a message or sequence of messages to be communicated to the receiving terminal…
2. A *transmitter* which operates on the message in some way to produce a signal suitable of transmission over the channel…

3. The *channel* is merely the medium used to transmit the signal from transmitter to receiver...

4. The *receiver* ordinarily performs the inverse operation of that done by the transmitter, reconstructing the message from the signal...

5. The *destination* is the person (or thing) for whom the message is intended.

Schramm[13] adapted this model, essentially constructed to describe electromechanic communication, to human communication, emphasizing the signal (message) encoding-decoding functions of the mind. Defining communication as *the sharing of information, ideas, or attitudes* and stressing with different terms the Aristotelian principle that communication always requires at least three elements: *source, message, and destination,* he played up in the scheme the *encoder* and *decoder* components, noted Schramm.[14] Substitute "microphone" for encoder, and "earphone" for decoder and you are talking about electronic communication. Consider that the source and encoder are one person, decoder and destination are another, and the signal is language, and you are talking about human communication.

Berlo[15] significantly contributed also to the analysis of encoding-decoding operations in human communication, suggesting the convenience of distinguishing source from encoder and decoder from receiver. Furthermore, Berlo advocated perceiving communication as a process.[16]

> If we accept the concept of process, we view the events and relationships as dynamic, on-going, ever-changing, continuous ... The ingredients within a process interact; each affects all of the others. ...Communication theory reflects a process point of view. ...

From Cybernetics: Feedback for Control

Cybernetics added one more factor to the description of the process: *feedback*. It refers to control mechanisms enabling organisms to adjust automatically to behavioural goals. These are essentially communication mechanisms. In fact, as Wiener[17] understands cybernetics, "It is the study of messages, and in particular of effective message control…"

Although these concepts were intended to apply basically to the engineering and physiological domains, several theoreticians of human communication accepted them as useful also to describe the process of this latter. For, if sources were to attain, through their messages, the effects they intended over the receivers, they had to get back, from these latter, reactive clues as to the effectiveness of their persuasive attempts and, accordingly, adjust their messages to those goals. One example of such assimilation is found in the model proposed by Westley and McLean.[18]

The Endurable Scheme: S-M-C-R

Finally, the human or social communication model derived from the concatenated conceptualizations reviewed here came to include the following elements as fundamental: *Source—Encoder—Message—Channel—Decoder—Receiver—Effect.* And its paramount purpose –persuasion – was stressed: "When people control one another, they do so primarily through communication."[19]

The basic definitions and general schemes so far inventoried in this paper permeated the scientific literature pertinent to communication, reproducing their key elements in several more specialized definitions. For instance, Hovland[20] understood *interpersonal communication* as an interacting situation in which an individual (the communicator) transmits stimuli (usually verbal symbols) to modify the behaviour of other individuals in a face-to-face setting. Comparably, *mass communication* has been perceived as follows: "Every mass-communicated act can be broken down into five elements: *communicators* who transmit a given *message* through a *channel* to an *audience* with some kind of *effect*." [21] Likewise, *nonverbal communication* was defined as "the transfer of meaning, involving the absence of symbolic sound representations."[22]

In summary, the traditional definition of communication is one depicting it as the act or process of transmission of messages from sources to receivers through the exchange of symbols (pertaining to codes shared by them) by means of signal-carrying channels. In this classical paradigm, the chief aim of communication is the communicator's intent to affect in given directions the behaviour of the communicateees.… .

Early Criticisms of Traditional Conceptualizations

Definitions are the product of reflections about experience and, in turn, at least to some extent, they orient practice. Basically, the traditional conceptualization of communication and the classical paradigm of it were the result of experience with communication in the United States of America and Western Europe. The model then reflected back on the subsequent practice of communication (production, teaching, research, etc.) and not only in those countries but most everywhere else in the world. Its impact proved particularity strong on communication training and research, activities started some 40 years ago.

No Transmission and No Act

…Nevertheless, the pattern did not remain unchallenged for too long, although its influence was to show strength and penetration so remarkable that it survives to this day. From different standpoints a few precursors began questioning some aspects of the traditional model. Toch and MacLean were among them, but a scholar who articulated and propagated a major early criticism was David K. Berlo, chairman of the Department of Communication at Michigan State University. Berlo[23] argued against what he labelled the "bucket" theory of communication as follows:

> This viewpoint assumes that meanings are to be found in words or other symbols and that communication consists of the transmission of ideas from one individual to another through the use of symbols. This can be characterized as a process of dumping ideas from the source into a bucket—such as a film, a lecture, a book, a television program or what-have-you and shipping the bucket over to the receiver and dumping the contents into his head … The communication position is that meanings are not contained in the symbols used but are found in the people who produce and receive those symbols. There are no right meanings for a symbol. There only are whatever meanings people have. Correspondingly, communication is not viewed as the transmission of ideas or information through the use of a message-media vehicle. Rather it is considered as the selection and transmission of symbols *which have a probability of eliciting the intended meaning from the receiver* [emphasis added].

Two basic assumptions of the traditional conceptualization were being questioned here. On the one hand, the mechanical notion of knowledge transfer from one mind to another by means of signals transported by channels was being replaced by one arguing that symbols were only stimuli exerted by the source on the receiver with the expectation that they would make the latter retrieve from his experience the meanings involved and thus, probably, obtain from him the behavioral responses intended. In a certain sense, this implied a non-passive role by the receiver. And thus, on the other hand, the reformulation involved a relationship of interaction rather than one in which the action was only performed by the source/emitter of the stimuli. This, in turn, was rooted in the perception of communication as a process that Berlo had proposed. Moreover, with communication being perceived as interactive and a process, the concept of feedback had to gain in relevance. Its bidirectionality was now played up conceptually. Later, some of the most distinguished academic leaders of the profession came to share this acknowledgement, as can be seen in the following statement of Daniel Lerner[24]:

> We have studied communication as a linear operation in which a certain sender uses a certain channel to deliver a message to a receiver (an audience) who then is affected in some way by that message … Today, even sober professionals like

ourselves recognize that two-way interaction and feedback are essential concepts in our thinking about communication and its future.

Referring to the traditional models of communication, Wilbur Schramm[25] himself admitted: "They all were built upon the idea of something being transferred from a sender to a receiver. I am going to ask whether this is any longer the most fruitful way to look at communication." And, in assessing models somewhat more socially oriented, he added: "Their essential element is not something passing from sender to receiver, like a baseball from pitcher to catcher (perhaps with a batter between them to represent noise) but rather a *relationship*."

The partial amendment of the transmission concept, as well as its interaction-process corollary, were evidently not resisted at the conceptual level. In fact, several scholars sincerely shared them as is seen, for instance, in Gerbner's[26] definition of communication as social interaction through the exchange of messages involving cultural sharing. Models developed by Newcomb, Westley and MacLean,[27] and Schramm[28] emphasized the audience as an active component of the process, so active, in fact, that was now called "obstinate."[29]

Practice Betrays Theory

At the operational level, however, the established concepts had—and still have—but negligible application to every-day practice. For the most part, communication training appears still based today on the notion of transmission. And in the research activity, many—such as, Brooks and Scheidel,[30] Smith,[31] and Arundale[32] —have noted that the majority of studies are in fact still conducted taking communication as a static phenomenon while the academic community verbally professes adherence to the notion of process. Bauer,[29] on the other hand, demonstrated how communication research was limited by the transmission paradigm. And Kumata[33] explained that adherence to old concepts and methods had produced unidimensional communication research unable to cope with complex and dynamic social realities.

Similarly, although professional discourse does acknowledge widely the two-way nature of communication, the practice of it still conforms predominantly to the unilinear S-M-C-R traditional paradigm.

Katz and Lazarsfeld[34] demonstrated that the "hypodermic effect" of the mass media on the isolated individual in the lonely crowd was actually mediated by reference groups and through influentials in a two-step flow fashion. This gave opportunities for paying attention to social interaction considerations.

Nevertheless, "what they described as interaction between the receiver and his social communication network is generally still a one-way model" (Harms and Richstad).[35] Indeed, as Coleman[36] noted, communication researchers placed exaggerated emphasis on the individual as the unit of analysis, neglecting the *relationship* between sources and receivers. The strong influence of social psychology on communication research provided later another set of opportunities for perceiving communication as affected by the structure containing it. And so did the concomitant research based upon the very popular model of diffusion of innovations. However, on the former, Zires de Janka[37] pointed out that "…. the basic framework of the scheme was neither altered nor questioned." And, on the latter, several critics have noted that, in spite of its attention to some sociocultural variables, it failed to grasp the determinant influence that archaic social structures exert on communication (Cuellar and Gutierrez).[38] Admitting, these and other shortcomings, Rogers[39] strongly advocated for research methodologies tapping *relationships*, such as network analysis.

Research is not the only area of activity where the traditional model exhibits stubborn endurance. The practice of international communication constitutes an eloquent example of how also at the level of nations communication essentially occurs in a unilinear direction from the developed countries to the

1927
1960
1963
1964
1967
1969
1970
1971
1972
1973
1974
1975
1976
1977
1978
1979
1980
1981
1982
1983
1984
1985
1986
1987
1988
1989
1990
1991
1992
1993
1994
1995
1996
1997
1998
1999
2000
2001
2002
2003
2004
2005
2006

underdeveloped ones. As has been extensively verified, U. S. transnational news agencies and advertising firms control the great majority of the respective businesses almost all over the world. And what was for years proclaimed as "the free flow of information" has been found by research to be pretty much a one-way flow and not exactly free, especially in view of propaganda uses of news and ads addressed at manipulating public opinion.[40, 41, 42]

Information: Not Equal to Communication

Another line of criticism focused on the confusion between information and communication resulting also from the traditional schemes. An Argentinian analyst argued about the nature of communication as follows:

> Communication is not an act but a process by which an individual enters into mental co-operation with another individual until they come to constitute a common conscience… Information, instead, is just a unilateral translation of a message from an emitter to a receiver… The radiation, from centralized informants, of messages without dialogical return, cannot be identified with the intersubjective co-activity of which communication consists.[43]

Likewise, a Peruvian scholar, Rafael Roncagliolo[44] contended that "we are witnessing a reduction in human communication—a concept that implies reciprocity—in favor of information and dissemination; that is, of all the modern forms of imposition by transmitters upon receivers that we erroneously continue to call mass communication."[45] European scholars concur:

> To communicate refers to a two-way process, which has emotional as well as cognitive elements and which takes place in non-verbal as well as verbal forms. To inform on the other hand refers to a one-way process of predominantly knowledge oriented, verbal communication.

And an analyst of communication rights, Jean D'Arcy[46] predicts that: "The time will come when the Universal Declaration of Human Rights will have to encompass a more extensive right than man's right to information, first laid down (in 1948) in Article 19. This is the right of man to communicate."

The criticisms so far reviewed in this paper can be summarized in the following manner: (1) Traditional definitions and models are unilinear, wrongly postulating a mechanical notion of communication as the transmission of information from active sources to passive receivers. Actually, there is no transmission; there is only elicitation of meanings which already exist in people and who, in decoding symbols, become actively involved. (2) Those models, moreover, are based on the erroneous notion that communication is an act, a static phenomenon privileging the source; communication is really a process where all elements operate dynamically. Thus it is eminently a case of social relationships, a phenomenon of multiple exchange of experiences, and not a unilateral exercise of individual influence. (3) The models, finally, induce a confusion between information, which can be transferred, by a one-way act, and communication, which is different and broader than information as its two-way nature necessarily involves interaction, seeking commonality of meanings or conscience.

Recent Criticisms: Different Concerns

Most of the criticisms of the traditional definitions and models of communication surfaced within the very society that had generated these latter: the United States of America. Thus, understandably, those criticisms included aspects of interest to that society and excluded others which were not of its concern. One in the latter category has been, most evidently, persuasion. With very few exceptions, objections to persuasion as the central aim of communication were not raised in the United States.[47] Behavioural manipulation of people through the means of communication appeared to be natural and legitimate in that country. Already in 1957 Merton[48] had asked: "How can we analyze propaganda, films, radio, and print in such a way that we can determine what is likely to *produce given effects*?" (Emphasis added.) For many years, many people concentrated on seeking answers:

> The all-consuming question that has dominated research and the development of contemporary theory in the study of the mass media can be summed up in simple terms, namely, 'What has been their effect?'....Persuasion is only one possible "effect" among many, but upon which great attention has been focused. It has been assumed that an effective persuasive message is one which has properties capable of altering the psychological functioning of the individual in such a way that he will respond overtly (toward the item which is the object of persuasion) in modes desired or suggested by the communicator.[49]

On the other hand, when attention was granted to sociocultural variables affecting communication behaviour, this seemed essentially motivated by persuaders having learned that individuals could not be most effectively influenced if taken as detached from their societal context. Basically, the challenge then became how to best use the social environment to help attain audience responses fitting with the purposes of communicators, or how to secure individual compliance with the norms and values of their social structure.

...Evidently, the classical paradigm had steered researchers to concentrate their studies on the persuasibility of the receiver, as an individual and as member of social groupings, so as to be able to help control his behavior. "If from time to time attention has been given to some other aspect of the media, for example, to the nature of the communicator, the structure of media content, or the nature of the audiences, the ultimate purpose was to see how variations in these factors have influenced the kinds of responses that have resulted from exposure to the media."[50] Not surprisingly, research on the source was especially neglected.[51, 52]

Persuasion: A Tool for the Status Quo

The classical paradigm also lead researchers to focus on mass communication *functions* in society, which had been expanded beyond Lasswell's basic propositions by Lazarsfeld and Merton,[53] Wright,[54] and others.

Whereas *the effects orientation* sought to find out what media do *to* people, the *functions orientation* aimed at finding what media do *for* people.

It was in Latin America, where objections to both orientations were probably first made. In 1970, Armand Mattelart[55] argued:

> The study of effects indicates the therapeutic and operative nature of this sociology whose aim is to improve the relationship between a given audience and a message-emitting commercial firm. ... The analysis of functions indicates the preoccupation of this sociology with the receiver's motivation. ... Now, if we look for the common point between these observations, we shall see that neither of the two is conceivable without the researcher implicitly endorsing the extant social system."

The analyst explained his assessment of functionalism as a pro-status quo orientation by stressing "... the fact that the indicator of a rupture with the system (the dysfunction) is never considered in its prospective or transformational aspect. ... The dysfunction is never explicitly regarded as the fundament for another system."[56]

Facilitating Mercantilism and Propaganda

The presence of a conservative bias in persuasion operations may not constitute a substantive preoccupation in societies such as the United States of America. But it is a matter of serious concern for societies such as those of Latin America, especially in terms of international communication. Thus, naturally, several Latin Americans shared the early criticisms of the traditional paradigm, such as the one on mechanism. They, however, contended, that acknowledging the fact that communication is a process falls short of divesting the scheme from its authoritarian affiliation.[57]

...Because of a long experience, Latin Americans questioned them as instrumental for mercantilism,

1927
1960
1963
1964
1967
1969
1970
1971
1972
1973
1974
1975
1976
1977
1978
1979
1980
1981
1982
1983
1984
1985
1986
1987
1988
1989
1990
1991
1992
1993
1994
1995
1996
1997
1998
1999
2000
2001
2002
2003
2004
2005
2006

propaganda, and alienation. They saw them as components of both U. S. external domination and of that internally exerted in each of the region's countries by power elites over the masses.

Latin American analysts recalled that propaganda had been deemed a necessity by the founding fathers of communication science, such as Lasswell, who regarded propaganda as the "new hammer and anvil of social solidarity."[58] They were aware that World War II was the origin of mass communication theory, research, and modern practice."[59] And they had reasons to feel that the traditional paradigm was well suited to the United States and Western European postwar purposes of overseas economic, political, and cultural empire-like expansion that keeps countries such as those of Latin America in a situation of underdevelopment resembling colonial days."[60]

Such preoccupations were substantiated by evidence of quasi-monopolistic control of international news, advertising, and film and television materials by the United States, as well as of related investments and policies of this country abroad.[61] The analysts also expressed alarm when the United States Congress investigations revealed that, beyond the overt propaganda activities of the United States Information Agency (USIA), covert United States government activities in communication in and on Latin America had taken place not only to discredit but even to help overthrow some change-oriented and legitimately established governments of Latin America.[62] And they noted that all such operations were instances of communication practice congenial with the undemocratic, unilinear transmission and persuasion mentality.

On the other hand, Latin Americans do not celebrate feedback as understood in the classical paradigm. They feel it expresses a privilege of sources to allow their receivers to respond to the initiatives of those controlling the media. They also point out that feedback is exclusively used to make sure that the message is adjusted to the receiver in such a manner that he will understand it and comply with the communicator's requests.[63, 64]

Alienation: Imposing an Ideology

We Latin Americans are quite emphatic about the alienating influences of mass communication. Research has extensively documented the overwhelming influence of United States orientation, content, and financing on the mass media of the region. Several studies have uncovered the inculcation of a series of alien values and norms amounting to the promotion of a whole way of life: the capitalist ideology. This takes place through virtually all media but appears more pronounced via television, specialized magazines (including comics), transnational advertising in general, and foreign news.[65]

In being worried about the consequences of such media content, the Latin Americans object also to certain nontraditional conceptualizations of communication such as those of Marshall McLuhan.[66] For instance, Antonio Pasquali,[67] a Venezuelan philosopher and researcher of communication, rejects as conservative the postulate that "the medium is the message." This objection is not meant to deny that today's ubiquitous presence of the mass media must have, per se, some influence on people. It is addressed at preventing such conformist statements from throwing a veil over the reality of the impact of noxious messages carried by the media. These viewpoints are shared by other Latin Americans, such as Diaz Bordenave.[68] "In spite of whatever Marshall McLuhan may argue, the content of social communication media is relevant for the development of persons and thus for national development." Latin Americans are not too sure that the world has become a "global village" since millions of them, to start with, have no access whatever to any mass media. And, if the magic of electronics is indeed bringing all of humanity together, they fear the "village" will be run, more than ever before in history, by the few and the mighty. On the other hand, Latin Americans are not alone in suspecting that, for all his shocking originality, McLuhan is not really too far apart from the classical conservative mentality in that—as pointed out by Finkelstein[69]—he can be regarded as the foremost spokesman of the corporate establishment.

Vertical Communication

"We cannot conceive of the exercise of power by individual A over individual B without some communication from A to B."[70] Latin America is a most clear example of the appropriateness of such statement. A sheer minority of its population exerts power over the vast majority so as to secure overall domination. To do so, the oligarchic elites' recourse to mass communication is a tool for keeping the situation unchanged. This use of communication is often done in such an undemocratic manner that leads to calling it "vertical communication," as Pasquali, Freire and Gerace did. And this which happens between social classes within each Latin American country also happens between all of them—a dependent society—and the United States of America, its external dominator. In both cases, the powerful subordinate the powerless with the assistance of communication.

The situation neatly fits with the linearity of the classical paradigm, which does not favour democratic communication behaviour, as the following observation suggests:

> What often takes place under the label of communication is little more than a dominating monologue in the interest of the starter of the process. Feedback is not employed to provide an opportunity for genuine dialogue. The receiver of the messages is passive and subdued, as he is hardly ever given proportionate opportunities to act concurrently also as a true and free emitter; his essential role is that of listening and obeying. [71]

Many in Latin America agree with such statements. Gerace[72] feels that it is urgent to conceive other communication theories more in accordance with this region and with the Third World in general. And a Paraguayan scholar puts it this way:

> We must overcome our mental compulsion to perceive our own reality through foreign concepts and ideologies and learn to look at communication and adoption from a new perspective.[73]

The Freirean Perspective: A Landmark

New perspectives emerged in the early part of the 1960s, thanks to a Brazilian Catholic teacher and philosopher of education, Paulo Freire. His view of education as a tool of liberation of the masses from oppression by the elites earned him exile from his country at the middle of the decade. Since then, writing first from Chile, and later from Geneva, he has seen his ideas spread internationally and put into experimentation even in Africa. ...

Education for Oppression

Freire[74] launched a major critique of traditional education as a tool for cultural domination of the majorities by the conservative elites. Just as Berlo had called the traditional transmission scheme "bucket" theory of communication, Freire called classical pedagogy "banking" education. "Bankers" (teachers) are those representing the "rich" in knowledge (the members of the power elites who monopolize information along with most everything else of value in society) who make "deposits" in the minds of the "poor" (ignorant), the students, who are to receive passively the "wealth" so transferred to them. The "deposits" contain the set of norms, myths, and values of the oppressors of humanity. If the oppressed learn them well, they can hope to move up in the socio-economic, political and cultural structure presided over by the oppressors. That is, they can "cash in" one day the deposits for the material goods that the bankers are willing to paternalistically grant them as a reward for conforming to their ideology and not upsetting the established order. In doing so, most of the oppressed tend to become oppressors since, although some may wish to act differently, they are "afraid of freedom." In this manner the exploited masses themselves are used to help secure the perpetuation of the system. And as Gerace[75] pointed out: "Perhaps the worst oppression is that which grabs the soul of man, turning him into the shadow of his oppressor."

Thus Freire[76] warns that: "No pedagogy that is truly liberating can remain distant from the oppressed by

1927
1960
1963
1964
1967
1969
1970
1971
1972
1973
1974
1975
1976
1977
1978
1979
1980
1981
1982
1983
1984
1985
1986
1987
1988
1989
1990
1991
1992
1993
1994
1995
1996
1997
1998
1999
2000
2001
2002
2003
2004
2005
2006

treating them as unfortunates and *by presenting for their emulation models from among the oppressors. The oppressed must be their own example in the struggle for their redemption."*

How is Truth Propagated?

Behind "banking education" lies—Pinto[77] argues—a theory of knowledge that defines the relationships prevailing between a subject who knows and a reality-object which is known. Such reality is understood as something static and finished. And both the subject who knows and the known object are regarded as metaphysical entities as well as fixed and distinct units. This accounts for making very difficult the subject-object relationship. It is hard for the subject to comprehend the object. When eventually he manages to comprehend it, what is born is a relationship of ownership between the former and the latter. Here comes in, adds Pinto, the notion of truth as the possession of the subject. Pinto concludes:

> It is then generated between educator and learner, a totally vertical social relationship: the educator-subject, owner of absolute truth, deposits it (imposes) into the intelligence of the learner, who receives it passively (memorizes)... This verticality implies an intellectual domination of the educator over the learner, which is supported by a system of disciplinary sanctions so that the truth shall always be accepted without contestation.[78]

Domestication Instead of Liberation

Such an authoritarian relationship, Freire feels, is manipulative of persons, who are treated as things or animals. Regardless of how much this may be disguised at times by apparently non-ruthless teaching devices, it constitutes an offence to human dignity and freedom. Such "domestication" is only possible because the teacher, instead of helping the student to demystify reality, contributes to the further mystification of it. Thus the student is not allowed to discover that culture is superior to nature, that man is a historical being able to constantly transform its physical

and social reality, and that the oppressed, rather than accepting such reality fatalistically, are capable of freeing themselves from it and constructing a different one. ...Freire stresses:[79]

> This is why, to us, education as the practice of freedom, is not the transfer or transmission of wisdom or culture, it is not the extension of technical knowledge, it is not the act of depositing reports or facts in learners, it is not the "perpetuation of the values of a given culture," it is not "the effort of adaptation of the learner to his milieu.

In addition to submissiveness and passivity, lack of creativity is seen as one consequence of the "banking" type of education. Prevented from reasoning critically, the person is inhibited from developing his imagination; his consciousness about nature and social existence remains naive and often [perceived as] magic, as the rulers prefer it to be. This may also foster selfish individualism and competitiveness among the oppressed rather than solidarity and co-operation. Thus society remains as if narcotized to serve the ends of the minorities controlling education and communication.

The Media: Agents of Subjugation

Freire regarded mass communication media as propagators of the myths, norms and values of the oligarchic minorities and, as such, vertical and alienating communication tools in charge of helping attain the subjugation of the oppressed. And referring to the interpersonal adult education format known as agricultural extension, established in Latin America through U. S. [foreign] aid, the Brazilian scholar attacked it as the opposite of true communication since to educate is not to extend something from the "seat of wisdom" to the "seat of ignorance."

> For us, education as the practice of freedom is, above and before all, a truly agnostic situation, that in which the act of knowing does not end in the object to be known since it gets in communication with other subjects that are also knowledgeable.[79]

Towards Democratic Communication

With very few exceptions, early critics of the traditional conceptualisations of communication did not reach deep enough into the roots of what they criticized: economy and politics, the power game. One of those exceptions was the late C. Wright Mills,"[80] who denounced the mass media as promoters of a psychological illiteracy among the masses addressed at favouring the hegemony of the power elites. Recently, Rogers[81] claimed that the linear models imply an autocratic, one-sided view of human relationships and rated the classical pattern a "passing paradigm." And Professor Lasswell himself, in prospecting in 1972 the future of world communication as related to the development of nations, came to anticipate two contrasting paradigms. He labelled one the "oligarchic model" serving the aims of transnational power centers: "In striving to consolidate an oligarchic world public order, the instruments of communication are used to indoctrinate and distract." Lasswell labelled the alternative a "participatory model," under which he sees that "… mass media provide attention opportunities that generate and re-edit common maps of man's past, present, and future and strengthen a universal and differentiated sense of identity and common interest.[82] To Harms and Richstad[83] the oligarchic model "is seen as parallel to the linear, one-way transmission communication model that has been employed in the study of mass communication and other source-controlled systems."

To a large extent, however, it has been Latin American perspectives which uncovered the roots of the classical transmission/persuasion pro status quo paradigm: the undemocratic nature of social relationships within nations and between them. Indeed virtually all Latin American criticisms are well condensed in the expression "vertical communication"; that is, from the top down, domineering, imposing, monological and manipulatory: in short, not democratic.

So perceived, communication is not a technical question to be antiseptically dealt with in isolation from the economic, political and cultural structure of society. It is a political matter largely determined by this structure and, in turn, contributes to the perpetuation of it. Thus, the search for a way out of such a situation is addressed in moving from vertical/undemocratic communication to horizontal/democratic communication. …

Theoretical and Practical Advances

In diverse parts of the world, but especially in the less developed countries, and notoriously in those of Latin America, horizontal communication technologies are being experimented with. They are face-to-face communication procedures, such as Freire's conscientization, special combinations of mass media with group techniques, or group communication formats built around modern audio-visual instruments. In Peru, for instance, mobile videotape units are being used for rural nonformal education in a way that gives peasants opportunities for being not only receivers but also emitters of messages.[84, 85] In the same country a large effort with simple media, such as community newspapers and loudspeaker systems, is turning slum people into active and autonomous communicators.[86] And in Uruguay, audio-cassette units provided with recording facilities are making cooperative farmers share in a nationwide teleforum whose contents they determine.[87] UNESCO is sponsoring studies, bibliographies, and publications in this area of "mini-media" or "intermediate" communication technologies. International meetings directly and exclusively addressed at participatory communication have recently taken place in Yugoslavia and Ecuador.[88, 89]

Several authors have contributed to the reformulation of the concept of communication. Few, however, concentrated on this task sufficiently to arrive at a systematic design of models of democratic communication. By 1967, Moles[90] had offered the notion of "cultural cycle" involving creator, micromedia, mass media and macromedia. In 1970 Schaeffer[91] proposed the communication triangle with the mediator as central. Concurrently, Williams[92] urged researchers to study communication as a relational phenomenon of transaction.

1927
1960
1963
1964
1967
1969
1970
1971
1972
1973
1974
1975
1976
1977
1978
1979
1980
1981
1982
1983
1984
1985
1986
1987
1988
1989
1990
1991
1992
1993
1994
1995
1996
1997
1998
1999
2000
2001
2002
2003
2004
2005
2006

At the onset of the present decade, Johannesen[93] produced a valuable analytical summary of conceptualizations of "communication as dialogue." In critically analysing communication as related to the mass culture, Pasquali[94] provided some basis for horizontal communication thought. Díaz Bordenave[95] perceptively evaluated the initial evolution of the concept of communication towards a democratic model, which had been highly stimulated by Freire's thinking. Then Cloutier[96] formulated the "EMIREC" scheme, which attempted to bring together emitter and receiver. And, elaborating on Freire's education for liberation proposal as well as capitalizing on pioneer experiences in Bolivia and Perú, Gerace[97] explored further the nature of horizontal communication, and Gutierrez[98] wrote on the notion of "total language." Almost invariably across these and other similar works, dialogue was played up as the crucial agent of democratic communication.…

A more recent and methodical proposition is that of Fernando Reyes Matta,[99] who developed in considerable detail a macro-operative "model of communication with active social participation." More than explicitly attempting to redefine communication, this Latin American analyst postulated a broad pragmatic blueprint of institutional organization to make possible horizontal communication. Although concepts such as communication rights, access, and participation appeared not to have been sufficiently defined, Reyes Matta sought to utilize them in interrelated ways. Other recent contributions to conceptualizing horizontal communication are those of Azcueta,[103] Diaz Bordenave,[104] Jouet,[105,106] and Pinto.[107] CIESPAL[108] has published a preliminary report of its 1978 Quito meeting on participatory communication.

Finally, two United States researchers—L.S. Harms[100, 101] and Jim Richstad[102]—conducted pioneer systematic efforts to interrelate the notions of communication rights, resources, and needs. They arrived at an interchange model of human communication which, in spite of limitations such as its purely dyadic nature, offers democratizing insights and shows considerable heuristic power. This model did not attempt to integrate communication rights-needs-resources with access-dialogue-participation in communication. And neither the model of Reyes Matta nor that of Harms and Richstad deals specifically with communication purposes, such as persuasion.

The Nature of Horizontal Communication

In light of the criticisms reviewed, the innovative propositions just summarized and other related considerations, the following definition is now proposed for discussion:[109]

> Communication is the process of democratic social interaction, based upon exchange of symbols, by which human beings voluntarily share experiences under conditions of free and egalitarian access, dialogue, and participation. Everyone has the right to communicate in order to satisfy communication needs by enjoying communication resources.[110]

Human beings communicate with multiple purposes. The exertion of influence on the behavior of others is not the main one.

Access is the effective exercise of the right to receive messages.

Dialogue is the effective exercise of the right to concurrently receive and emit messages.

Participation is the effective exercise of the right to emit messages.

Communication right is the natural entitlement of every human being to emit and receive messages, intermittently or concurrently.

Communication need is both a natural individual demand and a requirement of social existence to use communication resources in order to engage in the sharing of experiences through symbol-mediated interaction.

Communication resource is any energy/matter element—cognitive, affective or physical—usable to make possible the exchange of symbols among human beings.

Freedom is a relative concept. Absolute freedom is neither desirable nor viable. Each individual's freedom is limited by the freedom of the others, the restriction being the product of a social responsibility agreement in the service of common good. Each society's freedom is relative to the freedom of other societies.

Egalitarianism is a relative concept. Absolute equality is not possible. Total symmetry in the distribution of opportunities for emitting and receiving messages is unattainable. Comparable opportunities are possible inasmuch as expanding the receiving opportunities is possible and inasmuch as significantly reducing the concentration of emitting opportunities may not be impossible. Thus, a fair balance of proportions is sought; mathematical equivalence is not.

Exerting behavioural influence is a licit communication purpose on condition that it is not unilateral, authoritarian or manipulatory. That is to say, persuasion that at least potentially is mutual and which in effect respects human dignity needs not be dismissed as an aim of communication. Even in such cases, however, persuasion is but one among the many and diverse goals of communication and should not be deemed the most important.

A Few Operative Considerations

1. The free and egalitarian access-dialogue-participation process of communication is based upon the rights-needs-resources structure and is addressed to the fulfillment of multiple purposes.
2. Access is a precondition for horizontal communication since, without comparable opportunities for all persons to receive messages, there can be, to start with, no democratic social interaction.
3. Dialogue is the axis of horizontal communication for, if genuine democratic interaction is to take place, each person should have comparable opportunities for emitting and receiving messages so as to preclude monopolization of the word through monologue. Given that, under such perspective, these opposite roles are subsumed into a constant

and balanced dual performance, all participants in the communication process should be identified as *"communicators,"* as Harms-Richstad correctly proposed. Thus the differentiation between the two separate options—"source" and "receiver"— becomes no longer appropriate.

The conviction that dialogue—conversation – is at the heart of true human communication is held not only by educators like Freire. The philosopher Buber[111] is a strong advocate of it. And so are psychiatrists and psychologists such as Carl Rogers[112] and Eric Fromm.[113] Dialogue makes possible a cultural environment favorable to freedom and creativity of the type deemed most conducive to full growth of intelligence by biologist Jean Piaget.[114]

4. Participation is the culmination of horizontal communication because without comparable opportunities for all persons to emit messages the process would remain governed by the few.
5. From a perspective of practical viability, access-dialogue-participation constitutes a probabilistic sequence. This is to say that, in terms of degree of difficulty of attainment, access is at a low level, dialogue at an intermediate one, and participation at a high level. Getting more people to receive messages is deemed easier than building circumstances that would make dialogue possible and doing this latter is regarded as more feasible than effectively turning every person into a significant emitter.
6. Access is essentially a quantitative matter. Dialogue is eminently a qualitative matter. And participation is a qualitative/quantitative matter.
7. Access, dialogue and participation are the key components of the systemic process of horizontal communication. They have a relationship of interdependence. Namely, (a) the more the access, the higher the probabilities of dialogue and participation; (b) the better the dialogue, the more the usefulness of access and the greater the impact of participation; and (c) the more and better the participation, the more the probabilities

1927
1960
1963
1964
1967
1969
1970
1971
1972
1973
1974
1975
1976
1977
1978
1979
1980
1981
1982
1983
1984
1985
1986
1987
1988
1989
1990
1991
1992
1993
1994
1995
1996
1997
1998
1999
2000
2001
2002
2003
2004
2005
2006

of occurrence of dialogue and access. All together, the more access, dialogue and participation there is, the more communication needs will be satisfied and communication rights will be effective, and the more and better will communication resources be used.

8. Self-management, illustrated by the outstanding Yugoslavian experience with communication enterprises which are neither private nor governmental but communitarian, is deemed the most advanced and wholistic form of participation since it allows the citizenry to decide on policy, plans and actions.[115]

9. Feedback is a positive key feature of dialogue when it operates in a balanced multidirectional way by which each and every person involved in a communication situation gives it and receives it in comparable proportions. Feedback is contrary to dialogue when it is unidirectional, for it serves dependence, not balanced interdependence.

10. The practice of horizontal communication is more viable in the case of interpersonal formats (individual and group) than in the case of impersonal (mass) formats. An obvious technical explanation for it is the intrinsic difficulty of attaining feedback in mass communication. But the main explanation is political: the fact that the means of mass communication, for the most part, are entrenched tools of the conservative and mercantilistic forces controlling the means of production nationally and internationally.

A Word of Caution and a Word of Hope

Restraint is indispensable. Horizontal communication is, conceptually, the exact opposite of vertical communication. But, realistically, the former should not be regarded necessarily as a substitute for the latter. Under given circumstances, it can be such. Under different circumstances, it can be a co-existing alternative. As Buber[116] pointed out, dialogue is not always possible. And, it can be added, monologue is often not avoidable and sometimes it turns even necessary,

THE POPULAR AND THE MASS
Excerpt from: *Cuadernos de Comunicación*
By Jesús Martín Barbero

It is time to break from the cybernetic model of sender-message-receiver, etc. The break must be a radical one, since this model prevents us from thinking "domination," or from knowing how the dominated decipher the messages of the communications media. Such a break involves a double displacement. First, the processes and products of mass culture must be placed historically; second, they must be placed within the context of the other fields and spheres in which culture is produced today. What is vital in this historical placement is to abandon the idealism that causes us to believe that the cultural muck that surrounds us can be blamed on marketers, or that the monster we call "the system" can be faulted for everything that goes wrong—or that we consider wrong.

Martín Barbero, Jesús (1979). "Lo popular y lo masivo," *Cuadernos de Comunicación* No. 62, Mexico City. Reprinted with permission of the author.

depending on varying aims and circumstances. They may be viewed, Johannesen[117] suggests, as extremes on a continuum. Ideally, all communication should be horizontal. Practically, this is not always possible nor, perhaps, even desirable. Thus, if vertical communication has to remain on the scene, to some extent, what should not at any rate happen is that it be manipulatory, deceiving, exploitative and coercive.

Notes and References:

1. Luis Ramiro Beltrán S., Communication Between the United States and Latin America: A Case of Cultural Domination. Paper presented to the World Media Conference, sponsored by The News World, New York City, October 19-22, 1978.

2. Jonathan F. Gunter, "An Introduction to a Great Debate," *Journal of Communication*, Vol. 28 (Autumn 1978), pp. 142-155.

3. UNESCO, Conferencia Intergubernamental sobre Políticas de Comunicación en América Latina y el Caribe, San José, Costa Rica, 12-21 de julio; informe final, 1976 (COM/MD/38).

4. UNESCO, General Conference, Twentieth Session, Draft Declaration on Fundamental Principles concerning the Contribution of the Mass Media to Strengthening Peace and International Understanding, the Promotion of Human Rights and to countering Racialism, Apartheid, and Incitement to War; compromise text proposed by the Director-General with a view to consensus, Paris, 1978 (UNESCO 20 C/20 Rev.).

5. Everett M. Rogers, ed., *Communication and Development: Critical Perspectives* (London: Sage Publications, 1976).

6. Harold D. Lasswell, "The Structure and Function of Communication in Society," in *The Communication of Ideas,* ed. L. Bryson (New York: Harper and Row, 1948), pp. 37-51.

7. Melvin L. De Fleur, Theories of Mass Communication (New York: David McKay Company, Inc., 1968).

8. Bernard Berelson and Gary Steiner, *Human Behavior* (New York; Harcourt, Brace and World, Inc., 1964), p. 527.

9. Charles E. Osgood, *Some Terms and Associated Measures for Talking About Communication* (Urbana, Illinois: Institute for Communication Research, 196 1), p. 48.

10. Raymond Nixon, Investigaciones sobre Comunicación Colectiva Quito; Ediciones CIESPAL, 1963).

11. Claude E. Shannon and Warren Weaver, *The Mathematical Theory of Communication* (Urbana: University of Illinois Press, 19 7 1), p. 4

12. Ibid., pp. 33-34.

13. Wilbur Schramm, "How Communication Works" in *The Process and Effects of Mass Communication (*Urbana: University of Illinois Press 1961), pp. 4-26.

14. Ibid., p. 4.

15. David K. Berlo, *The Process of Communication* (New York. Holt, Rinehart and Winston, 1960), p. 30.

16. Ibid., p. 24

17. Norbert Wiener, *The Human Use of Human Beings: Cybernetics and Society* (Boston; Houghton Mifflin Co., 1950).

18. Bruce H. Westley and Malcolm S. MacLean, "A Conceptual Model for Communication Research," *Journalism Quarterly,* Vol. 34 (195 7), pp. 31-38

19. Alfred B. Smith, *Communication and Culture* (New York; Holt, Rinehart, and Winston, 1966).

20. C.I. Hovland, "Social Communication," Proceedings of the American Philosophical Society, Vol. 92 (1948), pp. 371-375.

21. Reed H. Blake and Edwin O. Haroldsen, A Taxonomy of Concepts in Communication (New York: Hastings House, 1975).

22. Ibid., p. 43.

23. David K. Berlo, Communication Theory and Audiovisual Instruction, Keynote Address to the National Convention of the Department of Audiovisual Instruction, National Education Association, Denver, April 23, 1963.

24. Daniel Lerner, in *World Communication, Population Communication, Communication Technology, Communication in the Future,* eds. Jim Richstad and L. S. Harms (Honolulu: Speech-Communication Association, 1973).

25. Wilbur Schramm, Toward a General Theory of Human Communication, Lecture presented at the University of Texas.

26. George Gerbner, "Content Analysis and Critical Research in Mass Communication," A V, *Communications Review,* Vol. 6 (Spring 1958), pp. 85-108.

27. T. M. Newcomb, "An Approach to the Study of Communicative Acts," Psychological Review, Vol. 60 (1953), pp. 393-404.

28. Wilbur Schramm, *Men, Messages, and Media: A Look at Human Communication* (New York: Harper and Row, 1973).

29. R. Bauer, "The Obstinate Audience," *American Psychologist,* Vol. 19 (1964), pp. 319-328.

30. Robert D. Brooks and Thomas M. Scheidel, "Speech as Process: A Case Study," SM, Vol. 35 (March 1968).

31. David H. Smith, "Communication Research and the Idea of Process," Speech Monographs, Vol. 39 (1972), pp. 174-182.

32. R. B. Arundale, The Concept of Process in Human Communication Research, Ph.D. Dissertation, Michigan State University, 1971.

33. H. Kumata, in *World Communication….* n. 24.

34. E. Katz and P. Lazarsfeld, *Personal Influence: The Part Played by People in the Flow of Mass Communications* (New York: Free Press, 1955).

35. L. S. Harms and Jim Richstad, *An Interchange Model of Communicatio*n, Honolulu: no date, p. 10.

36. J. S. Coleman, "Relational Analysis: A study of Social Organization with Survey Methods," *Human Organization,* Vol. 17 (1958), pp. 28-36.

37. M. Zires de Janka, Mass Communication in the Context of Development with special reference to Latin America. Research Paper for Diploma in International and National Development. The Hague: Netherlands Institute of Social Studies, 1973, p. 6.

38. G. D. Cuellar and J. Gutiérrez, Análisis de la Investigación y de la Aplicación del Difusionismo. Documento presentado en la Segunda Reunión Anual de Comunicadores Rurales, Cali: 1971.

39. Everett M. Rogers, "Where We Are in Understanding Diffusion of Innovations," in Communication and Change in Developing Countries: Ten Years After, eds. Wilbur Schramm and Daniel Lerner (Honolulu: University of Hawaii/East-West Center Press, 1975).

40. Armand Mattelart, "Criticas a la Communication Research;" in Cuadernos de la Realidad Nacional, edición especial (1970), pp. 11-22.

41. Juan Somavia, "The Transnational Power Structure and International Information: Elements of a Third World Policy for Transnational News Agencies," *Development Dialogue,* No. 2 (1976), pp. 15-28.

42. Fernando Reyes Matta, "The Information Bedazzlement of Latin America: A Study of World News in the Region," *Development Dialogue,* No. 2 (1976), pp. 29-42.

43. Ricardo C. Noseda, Definición y Deslinde Conceptual de la Comunicación. Documento presentado a la IX Asamblea y Congreso de la Asociación Internacional de Investigación en Comunicación de Masas, Buenos Aires: 1972, pp. 6-8.

44. Rafael Roncagliolo, Communication: Social Change and the Need for a New Conceptual Framework. Document prepared to be presented to the Seminar on International Communications and Third World Participation: A Conceptual and Practical Framework, Amsterdam: September 5 -8, 1977, p. 1.

45. Kjell Nowak, Karl Erik Rosengren, and Bengt Sigurd, "Communication Privilege and the Realization of Human Values," in Communication, Social Organization, Human Resources (MIKS Project) (Stockholm: Committee for Future Oriented Research, 1977), p. 1.

46. Jean D'Arcy, Direct Broadcast Satellites and the Right to Communicate, *EBU Review,* 118 (1969).

1927
1960
1963
1964
1967
1969
1970
1971
1972
1973
1974
1975
1976
1977
1978
1979
1980
1981
1982
1983
1984
1985
1986
1987
1988
1989
1990
1991
1992
1993
1994
1995
1996
1997
1998
1999
2000
2001
2002
2003
2004
2005
2006

47. David K. Berlo, "Given Development, What Role for Communication?" Document presented to the National Advertising Council, México City, 1969, p. 14.

48. R. K. Merton, "The Sociology of Knowledge of Mass Communications," in *Social Theory and Social Structure*, ed. R. K. Merton (Glencoe; Free Press, 1957).

49. M. DeFleur, n. 7, pp. 118-123.

50. Idid., p. 118.

51. Hugo Assman, Evaluación de Algunos Estudios Latinoameicanos sobre Comunicación Masiva, con especial referencia a los escritos de Armand Mattelart. Documento presentado al Congreso Latinoamericano de Sociología, San José, Costa Rica: 1973.

52. James D. Halloran, *Mass Media and Society: The Challenge of Research* (Leicester; Leicester University Press, 19 74).

53. Paul Lazarsfeld and Robert Merton, "Mass Communication, Popular Taste, and Organized Social Action," in The Communication of Ideas, ed. L. Bryson, (New York: Harper, 1948).

54. Charles R. Wright, Mass Communication: A Sociological Perspective (New York: Random House, 1959).

55. Armand Mattelart, n. 40, pp. 11-22.

56. Ibid., p. 19.

57. Frank Gerace, *Comunicación Horizontal* (Lima: Librería Studium, 1973).

58. Harold D. Lasswell, *Propaganda Technique in the World War* (New York: Alfred A. Knopf, 1927), pp. 220-221.

59. Luis Ramiro Beltrán S., "Alien Premises, Objects, and Methods in Latin American Communication Research," in Communication and Development: Critical Perspectives, ed. Everett M. Rogers (London: Sage Publications, 1976), pp. 15-42.

60. James D. Cockroft, André Gunder Frank, and Dale Johnson, *Dependence and Underdevelopment: Latin America's Political Economy* (Garden City: Anchor Books/Doubleday, 1972).

61. Luis Ramiro Beltrán S. and Elizabeth Fox de Cardona, "Flaws in the Free Flow of Information," in Conference on Fair Communication Policy for the International Exchange of Information, Communication Report, ed. Jim Richstad, Honolulu: East-West Communication Institute, East-West Center, 1977, pp. 85-127.

62. Bernardo A. Carvalho, The CIA and the Press, Freedom of Information Center Report No. 382 (Columbia: University of Missouri School of journalism, 1977).

63. Richard L. Johannesen, "The Emerging Concept of Communication as Dialogue," *The Quarterly Journal of Speech*, Vol. 15 (December 1971), pp. 373-382.

64. Luis Ramiro Beltrán S., "Rural Development and Social Communication: Relationships and Strategies," in Cornell-CIAT International Symposium on Communication Strategies for Rural Development, Cali, Columbia: March 17-22, 1974; proceedings (Ithaca, N.Y.: Cornell University, 1974), pp. 11-27.

65. Luis Ramiro Beltrán S., "TV Etchings in the Minds of Latin Americans: Conservatism, Materialism, and Conformism, "Gazette, Vol. 24 (1978), pp. 61-85.

66. Marshall McLuhan, *Understanding Media: The Extensions of Man* (New York: McGraw-Hill, 1964).

67. Antonio Pasquali, Comunicación y Cultura de Masas (Caracas: Monte Avila, 1972).

68. Juan Diaz Bordenave, Comunicación y Desarrollo, Barquisimeto, Septiembre 8-9, 1974, p. 2.

69. Sidney Finkelstein, *Sense and Nonsense of McLuhan* (New York: International Publishers, 1969).

70. Richard R. Fagen, *Politics and Communication* (Boston: Little, Brown, 1966), p. 5.

71. L. R. Beltrán S., n. 64, pp. 14-15.

72. F. Gerace, n. 57, p. 25.

73. Juan Diaz Bordenave, "Communication and Adoption of Agricultural innovations in Latin America," in Cornell-CIAT International Symposium on Communication Strategies for Rural Development, Cali., Columbia: March 17-22, 1974; proceedings (Ithaca, N. Y.: Cornell University, 1974)p.208.

74. Paulo Freire, *Pedagogy of the Oppressed* (New York: Herder & Herder, 1970).

75. F. Gerace, n. 57, p. 66.

76. P. Freire, n. 74, p. 39.

77. Joao Bosco Pinto, Subdesarrollo, Medios de Educación de Masa y Educación, Curso Regional Andino sobre Educación Campesina Extraescolar. Bogota, Colombia: Instituto Interamericano de Ciencias Agrícolas de la OEA, Marzo 6-Abril 14, 1972).

78. Ibid., p. 14.

79. Paulo Freire, *¿Extensión o Comunicación?* (Santiago de Chile: ICIRA, 1969), p. 59

80. C. Wright Mills, *The Power Elite* (New York: Oxford University Press, 1956).

81. Everett M. Rogers, "Social Structure and Communication Strategies in Rural Development," in Cornell-CIAT International Symposium on Communication Strategies for Rural Development, Cali., Columbia: March 17-22, 1974; proceedings (Ithaca, N. Y.: Cornell University, 1974), pp. 51-52.

82. Harold D. Lasswell, *The Future of World Communication: Quality and Style of Life*, EWCI Lecture in International Communication. Honolulu: East-West Communication Institute, East-West Center, September 1972, pp. 16-17.

83. L. S. Harms and J. Richstad, n. 35.

84. Manuel Calvelo Ríos, Tecnología de Capacitación Masiva Audiovisual: Un Caso de Aplicación a la Capacitación Campesina, Documento presentado al Primer Seminario Latinoamericano de Comunicación Participatoria, Quito, Ecuador: CIESPAL, Noviembre de 1978.

85. Manuel Calvelo Ríos, "Mass Communication Technology: A Case Study in Training Campesinos," Development Communication Report, No. 25 (January 1979), p. 4.

86. María C. Mata, Dora Montesinos Mertz, y Graciela Solezzi, Evaluación del Centro de Comunicación Popular de Villa El Salvador (Lima: Centro de Teleducación, Universidad Católica del Perú, 1976).

87. Mario Kaplun, Cassette- Foro: Un Sistema de Comunicación Participatoria. Documento presentado al Primer Seminario Latinoamericano de Comunicación Participatoria, Quito: CIESPAL, Noviembre de 1978.

88. Frank Gerace, Cinco Experiencias de Comunicación Participatoria. Documento presentado al Primer Seminario Latinoamericano de Comunicación Participatoria, Quito: CIESPAL, Noviembre de 1978.

89. Colin Fraser, Technology for Participatory Communication. Document submitted to the First Latin American Seminar on Participatory Communication, Quito: CIESPAL, November, 1978.

90. Abraham Moles, *Sociodynamique de la Culture* (Paris: 1967).

91. P. Schaeffer, *Machines d Communiquer* (Paris: Seuil, 1970).

92. Keneth R. Williams, "Speech Communication Research: One World or Two?" *Central States Speech Journal*, Vol. 21 (Fall 19 70), pp. 1 76-178.

93. R. L. Johannesen, n. 63.

94. A. Pasquali, n. 67.

95. Juan Diaz Bordenave, New Approaches to Communication Training for Developing Countries. Paper presented at the Section of Information and Communication Problems in Development at the Third World Congress of Rural Sociology, Baton Rouge, Louisiana: August 21-27, 1972.

96. Jean Cloutier, La Communication Audio-Scripto-Visuelle (Montreal: Presses Universitaires, 1973).

97. F. Gerace, n. 57.

98. Francisco Gutiérrez, El Lenguaje Total: *Una Pedagogía de los Medios de Comunicación* (Buenos Aires: Editorial Humanitas, 1973).

99. Fernando Reyes Matta, From Right to Praxis: A Model of Communications with Active Social Participation. Paper prepared to be presented to the Seminar on International Communications and Third World Participation: A Conceptual and Practical Framework, Amsterdam: September 5-8, 1977.

100. Miguel Azcueta, Comunicación de Masas y Cultura Popular. Documento presentado al Primer Seminario Latinoamericano de Comunicación Cooperativa. Garanhuns, Brasil: Septiembre 17-23, 1978.

101. Juan Díaz Bordenave, Aspectos Políticos e Implicaciones Políticas de la Comunicación Participatoria. Documento presentado al Primer Seminario Latinoamericano de Comunicación Participatoria, Quito: CIESPAL, Noviembre de 1978.

102. Josiane Jouet, Community Media and Development: Problems of Adaptation. Working paper prepared for UNESCO's Meeting on Self-Management, Access, and Participation in Communication, Belgrade: October 18-21, 1977.

103. Josiane Jouet, Participatory Communication in the Third World: A Critical Outlook. Paper presented at the First Latin American Seminar on Participatory Communication, Quito: CIESPAL, November, 1978.

104. Joao Bosco Pinto, La Comunicación Participatoria como Pedagogía del Cambio: Fundamentos Epistemológicos. Documento presentado al Primer Seminario Latinoamericano de Comunicación Participatoria, Quito: Noviembre de 1978.

105. CIESPAL, Informe Preliminar de los Grupos de Trabajo, Primer Seminario Latinoamericano de Comunicación Participatoria, Quito: Noviembre de 1978.

106. L. S. Harms, Towards a Shared Paradigm for Communication: An Emerging Foundation for the New Communication Policy and Communication Planning Sciences. In Syed A. Rahim and John Middleton (eds.), Perspectives in Communication Policy and Planning, (Honolulu: East West Communication Institute, 19 77), pp. 77-99.

107. L. S. Harms, To Achieve the Right to Communicate, Issues in Communication, 2:55-60, 1978 (London: International Institute of Communications.)

108. L. S. Harms and J. Richstad, n. 35.

109. UNESCO, Reunión sobre la Autogestión, el Acceso y la Participación en Materia de Comunicación; informe final, Belgrado: Octubre 18-21, 1977.

110. L. S. Harms, n. 100.

111. Martin Buber, *I and Thou* (New York: Scribner's, 1958).

112. Carl Rogers, *Freedom to Learn* (Columbus: Charles Merrill, 1969).

113. Eric Fromm, *The Art of Loving* (New York: Harper, 1956).

114. Jean Piaget, Seis Estudos de Psicología (Río de Janeiro: Fundo de Cultura, 1961).

115. UNESCO, n. 109.

116. Martin Buber, *Between Man and Man* (New York: Macmillan, 1965).

117. R. L. Johannesen, n. 63, p. 379.

1927
1960
1963
1964
1967
1969
1970
1971
1972
1973
1974
1975
1976
1977
1978
1979
1980
1981
1982
1983
1984
1985
1986
1987
1988
1989
1990
1991
1992
1993
1994
1995
1996
1997
1998
1999
2000
2001
2002
2003
2004
2005
2006

TOWARDS A THEORY OF COMMUNICATION AND SOCIAL CHANGE

Excerpt from: Communication and Social Change in Developing Nations: A Critical View

By Göran Hedebro

1979 The basic idea is that when a change is made in, say, the legal relation between landowner and tenants—e.g., a new law is passed increasing the rights of the tiller—this must be made public. At least, it has to become known by those affected. The landowner will most surely learn about it. But for those working in the fields, this is far from certain. Information explaining and interpreting the provisions of the law must be brought to them. This is the meaning of the complementary role of communication.

This particular function of communication has been treated by the United Nations Development Program and has been given a special label — "development support communication." It refers to the use of communication in aid projects to explain the aims of the project to the people the project will affect. The hope is that this will improve the chances of success of such programs. The idea is well founded, but since it in practice means only information *from* the authorities to the "grassroots," it can only bring about very limited improvements. It amounts to an extension of the dominant top-down development thinking and gives people little chance to work out suitable projects themselves.

In a more general sense, however, the complementary function is extremely important—not least in its negative form. Consider the hypothetical situation in which government is trying to improve material conditions for the poor, while privately owned mass media campaign against the measures proposed. Here we have not "support communication" but a case of *hostile* complementary communication. The record shows that the vested interests behind such hostile media campaigns may be so influential as to be able to pigeonhole bills and block the implementation of legislation.

Summary and Conclusions

In this excerpt some basic ingredients of a theory of communication and social change have been put forward. In short, the following points have been underlined:

■ Communication is basic to all human life; it is an absolutely necessary prerequisite. Man gains his identity by relating himself to others through the exchange of messages and meanings.

■ Communication is indispensable to all forms of social change, but it's not the prime mover. Historical, economic and political conditions are.

■ Communication has an *overall* influence on the direction social development takes through its function as a producer of ideology. This sets the bounds within which change is possible. The groups which control the media exercise decisive influence over the change process.

■ Communication activities can never act as substitutes for structural changes. Only when the real problem consists of disseminating some particular knowledge or message should the mass media and other communication channels be employed.

■ Communication in the teaching function outside the school is a form of nonformal education. When the mass media alone are used, the effects seem to be small. When personal contacts are also involved, the chances are better. The media should be seen as a *potential* which, if properly used, can result in the learning of specific skills and ideas. But successful teaching is no guarantee for improved living conditions. The overall development philosophy determines what the social benefits for the society as a whole will be.

■ Communication can serve as a complement to other changes. Often this function can determine the whole outcome of the measure itself.

These points concern the overall perspective of communication and social change.

Hedebro, Göran. "Communication and Social Change in Developing Nations: A Critical View," *Studies in Economic Psychology, 110*. Stockholm School of Economics, 1979. Reprinted with permission of the author and the publisher.

COMMUNICATION IN THE PEDAGOGY OF PAULO FREIRE

Excerpt from: Brazilian Communicational Thinking

By José Marques de Melo

1979

1. The pedagogy of Paulo Freire is a pedagogy of communication

When, at the beginning of his first book, PF [Paolo Freire] states that "man is a being of relationships rather than solely of contacts, he is not merely in the world, but with the world" (EPL, 39), he made the framework of his pedagogy quite clear.

This idea helps us to understand that he bases his educational proposal on a "world of communication,"[1] in which man is at its center and relates to other men and nature. He is also in "connection" with the Creator; hence his notion of religion—*religare*—which embodies the "transcendental sense of human relationships" and, by its very essence, must never be understood as a relationship of "domination or domestication" but rather as an instrument of "liberation" (EPL, 40).

Man's relationship with the world introduces him to the domain of history ("inheriting acquired experience") and culture ("creating and re-creating, integrating himself into the conditions of his context") (EPL, 41).

In relating to the world, man integrates himself into it ("ability to adapt himself to reality, in addition to transforming it, as well as the ability to choose, the basic feature of which is criticality"). For this reason, he goes beyond contact (which involves the aspect of massification [becoming part of a popular mass] and

"uprooting"). Man in contact with the world is man "accommodated to the adjustments" imposed upon him "without the right to discuss them;" man who sacrifices his "creative capacity," that is, his capacity for transformation (EPL, 42).

Man integrated into his world makes culture. "Based on man's relationship with reality, resulting from being with it and in it, through acts of creation, re-creation, and decision, he is able to dynamize his world" (EPL, 43). A contrary position is that of the massified [part of a popular mass] man, in contact with reality, but not integrated into it. Therefore he is "dominated by the force of myths and controlled by organized advertising" and "without knowing it, he increasingly abandons his ability to decide" (EPL, 43).

To integrate himself into society, man must "use increasingly more intellectual functions and increasingly fewer purely instinctive and emotional functions" (EPL, 44).

The massified man is inclined toward gregariousness, which implies a "fear of solitude, which may be extended to mean a fear of freedom, in the juxtaposition of individuals who lack a critical and love-centered link" (EPL, 45).

Consequently, in order to develop a system[2] capable of stimulating the use of man's "intellectual functions,"

---

1 In the interview granted to Ligia Moraes Leite, PF confirms that his educational concerns, initially self-taught, and afterwards learning from his wife Elza's experience as a "gartener" (a kindergarten and child literacy teacher), led him one day to "address the problem of communication." See: LEITE, Ligia Chiappini Moraes – *Encontro com Paulo Freire* [Meeting with Paulo Freire], *Educação & Sociedade* [Education & Society], (3), p. 53. São Paulo, Cortez & Moraes, 1979.

2 Paulo Freire's contribution to adult education became popularly known as the "Paulo Freire Method." However, his primary intent was to formulate not a "method," but rather a "system of adult education." Aurenice Cardoso, a member of the original team that collaborated with PF at the Federal University of Pernambuco, explains the conceptual differences between method and system. "When method, processes, and technique are synthesized in a set of principles and consequences, singly and organically, we have a system. Because it is broader, the system must be characterized by its functional character. This allows us to analyze the Brazilian educational system, which is considered organic. First, however, we would raise some questions: Has the Brazilian educational system been operational? Has it led us to examine our problems? To what extent does it integrate Brazilian man into his reality?" And she adds: "Research of this kind led Prof. Paulo Freire to develop not merely an active method, but rather a system of adult education, which leads illiterates not only to become literate, but also to develop an awareness of their social and political responsibility. The system provides man with much more than mere literacy, since the discussion of local, regional, and national problems makes him more critical and subsequently leads him to become aware and political." See: Aurenice Cardoso, *Conscientização e Alfabetização—uma visão prática do Sistema Paulo Freire* [Awareness and Literacy – A Practical View of the Paulo Freire System], Estudos Universitários (4), Recife, Universidade do Recife, pp. 71-72, 1963.

1927
1960
1963
1964
1967
1969
1970
1971
1972
1973
1974
1975
1976
1977
1978
1979
1980
1981
1982
1983
1984
1985
1986
1987
1988
1989
1990
1991
1992
1993
1994
1995
1996
1997
1998
1999
2000
2001
2002
2003
2004
2005
2006

PF thinks of a "Pedagogy of Communication," as something that would establish "dialogue" and provide a "new programmatic content for education." The key to this system would not actually be in "literacy," but prior, in overcoming man's magical or ingenuous understanding of the world, in developing a critical understanding (EPL, 106/108).

The formulation of this pedagogy is based on the anthropological notion of culture, in which communication plays a fundamental role.[3] As noted by Jarbas Maciel, a former collaborator of the Pernambucan master: "The fundamental category within which the Paulo Freire System of Education is immersed, is the sociological and anthropo-cultural category of communication." Describing the anthropological notion of culture, as outlined by PF, Maciel says that the key issue is that initial idea: "Man is a being of relationships." And he explains:

> Now, man is a being of relationships. Placed before nature, which he knows, man is placed before other men with whom he communicates. However, he does not merely know nature but also reacts to it, dialectically, transforming it, conquering it through work. From there the sphere of culture arises. …
> In turn, the sphere of culture dialectically reacts to conscience through work, expanding, challenging, stimulating, moving, and instrumentalizing it, and thus developing within man his second signaling system. It is through work that man sharpens and perfects his understanding. Alone, man would still not be making culture. Placed before other men with whom he is in relation, man communicates the transformation he effected on nature, and only then, as of that moment, does he make culture, as it were. Without communication between human beings, there can be no culture. Communication is the breath that gives life to culture.

Along this line of interpretation, Maciel adds that one must distinguish objective knowledge from subjective knowledge. And this distinction is made by the unleashing of a process of communication.

> Placed in isolation before objective reality and other men, man knows: this is subjective knowledge. By communicating this knowledge, which is also a way of transforming nature — i.e., nature turning in on itself through conscience — man engages in education. Knowledge after communication becomes objective knowledge and is also culture. Subjective knowledge, typical of the attitude of man isolated before external reality, is not truly culture, since communication with other human beings has not yet occurred. Transferring objective knowledge from man to man, over time, from generation to generation, i.e., transmitting culture, is engaging in education.[4]

Based on this notion, PF offers his proposal for a new content for education, which firstly involves understanding the limits between the worlds of nature and culture.

> We required a pedagogy of communication with which we could conquer the acritical dislike of anti-dialogue. There is more. Whoever engages in dialogue does so with someone, about something. This was to be the new programmatic content of the education we would call for. And it seemed to us that the first aspect of this new content with which we would help the illiterate, even before initiating his literacy education, in overcoming his magical comprehension as naive, and in developing increasing criticality, would be the anthropological notion of culture. The distinction between two worlds: that of nature and that of culture. The active role of man in and with his reality. Nature's sense of mediation of relationships and communications between men. Culture such as the additions man contributes to a world he did

---

3   This perspective, which PF uses to analyze the phenomenon of culture, had already been detected and analyzed in our *"Comunicação: conceitos e estrutura"* [Communication: Concepts and Structure] essay. See: José Marques de Melo, *Comunicação Social: Teoria e Pesquisa* [Social Communication: Theory and Research] (Petrópolis, Vozes, 1971), pp. 22-23.

4   Jarbas Maciel, *A fundamentação teórica do Sistema Paulo Freire de Educação* [The Theoretical Foundations of the Paulo Freire System of Education], Estudos Universitários (4), (Recife, Universidade do Recife, 1963), p. 23.

---

not make. Culture as the result of his work. Of his creative and re-creative effort. The transcendental sense of his relationships. The human dimension of culture. Culture as a systematic acquisition of the human experience. As an incorporation, one that is therefore critical and creative, and not as a juxtaposition of 'donated' reports or recommendations. The democratization of culture – an aspect of fundamental democratization. Learning to write and read as a key with which the illiterate would initiate his own introduction to the world of written communication. Man finally in the world and with the world. His role as subject and not merely and purely as object. From there, the illiterate would begin to change his prior attitudes. He would discover himself, critically, as a maker of this world of culture (EPL, 108/109).

2. A pedagogy rooted in the world of Brazilian man

PF's pedagogy is the product of his reflection on Brazilian society; of his concern with our democratic inexperience, and, therefore, our non-communication. With what he calls the "mutism" of Brazilian man.

To understand the transition process that the country's current historic moment represents, it is indispensable, according to PF, to review its past and those characteristics that made Brazilian society a "closed society"— colonial, slavocratic, without a people, reflexive, anti-democratic. And within this framework, to identify "our democratic inexperience."

Citing de Toqueville, PF says that every democratic experience is made feasible as a work of society by the very hands of its people, i.e., with the participation of its people. The essence of democracy lies in people's participation, in their power to decide or choose.

In Brazil, we have never experienced "self-government." During the colonial phase, we had a government imposed by the metropolis. As an independent country, the government was forged by the national elites, similar to that of the metropolis.

THE POPULAR AND THE MASS
Excerpt from: *Cuadernos de Comunicación*
By Jesús Martín Barbero

Put another way, the bourgeoisie is obliged, if it wishes to produce a culture, to produce two: one for itself and one for the working class. While the culture it produces for itself will present the individual subject as the focus of historical change (as do the great bourgeois novels, from Balzac to Flaubert), popular culture, rather than portraying individuals and focusing on them as transformative agents of history, will portray a collectivity relegated by destiny to the social—or, more precisely, a collectivity that experiences the social, and the social order, as destiny. As will be seen, this hypothesis proposed by Del Grosso opens the door to a profound understanding of the way in which the popular texts of the 19th century were created. This process occurred at the end of the 18th century and the beginning of the 19th, when the bourgeoisie, having assumed economic power, was able to begin producing what is called an ideology, i.e., a mode of apprehending and interpreting reality.

A second element deserves emphasis at the outset: This new popular culture was to be characterized by a new and strange intermingling of the real and the imaginary, a marriage of what one might term the informational and the fictional sphere, two realms that became inextricably intertwined.

Martín Barbero, Jesús (1979). "Lo popular y lo masivo," *Cuadernos de Comunicación* No. 62, Mexico City. Reprinted with permission of the author.

Democratic inexperience results from inexperience in communication, among other factors. "Brazil was born and grew without experience in dialogue. Head down, in fear of the Crown. Without a press. Without relationships. Without schools. Ill. Without authentic speech" (EPL, 66). PF points to this phenomenon of

1927
1960
1963
1964
1967
1969
1970
1971
1972
1973
1974
1975
1976
1977
1978
1979
1980
1981
1982
1983
1984
1985
1986
1987
1988
1989
1990
1991
1992
1993
1994
1995
1996
1997
1998
1999
2000
2001
2002
2003
2004
2005
2006

colonial non-communication as something that Vieira himself broached in his sermons.

Thus, one of the features of national life is mutism.

> Societies that are denied dialogue—communication—and instead are offered communiqués, resulting from compulsion or gift, are rendered preponderantly mute. Mutism is not precisely the absence of response. It is a response that lacks a markedly critical content (EPL, 69).

PF warns against the potential error of confusing the softening of relationships with authentic communication, dialogue. "Even when human relationships are, in a way, softened, between masters and slaves, between nobles and plebeians, there is no dialogue under tight control. There is paternalism."

Therefore, his conclusion is emphatic: "Among us… what predominated was man's mutism. It was his non-participation in resolving common problems. In fact, we lacked… community experience" (EPL, 70).

This social non-communication was aggravated by spatial non-communication. Brazilian society settled like an archipelago consisting of culturally and economically isolated islands.

> Thus we lived our entire period of colonial life. Constantly pressured. Almost always prohibited from speaking. The only voice heard, in the silence to which we were subjected, was the one coming from the pulpit. The restrictions on our relationships, even internal, were most drastic. Relationships that would undoubtedly have opened up other possibilities of indispensable exchanges of the experience with which human groups perfect themselves and grow. Relationships that lead human groups through mutual observation, to correct themselves and follow examples. Only the isolation imposed on the Colony, closed within itself, and charged with fulfilling the increasingly greedy needs and interests of the Metropolis, clearly revealed the Court's verticality and anti-democratic impermeability (EPL, 74/75).

3. Culture of silence, a common phenomenon among colonized peoples

Upon reflecting on the problem of non-communication, PF clearly and naturally situates himself within the framework of domination peculiar to colonialism. But in his first book, which was completed in exile but structured while still living and working in Brazil, one notes a certain reductionism of the phenomenon to the national environment. This horizon is expanded in subsequent works, where he demonstrates a more universal understanding, to which his harsh and intense experience of exile and direct contact with the neocolonial problem certainly contributed in a crucial way.

Thus, the expression "mutism of Brazilian man" gives way, in PF's analysis, to the development of the term "culture of silence." Imposing and reproducing oppression, the "culture of silence" is a characteristic of all colonized peoples and is rooted in the secular practice of non-communication.

> This type of culture is a superstructural expression that conditions a special form of conscience. The culture of silence overdetermines the infrastructure from which it springs… It is not possible to understand the culture of silence unless it is viewed as a totality forming part of a greater whole… It is true that the infrastructure, created in the relationships by which man's work transforms the world, gives rise to the superstructure. But it is also true that the latter, mediated by men who assimilate their myths, turns toward the infrastructure and over-determines it… Hence the dualism of a dependent society, its ambiguity, its being and not being itself… Dependent society is by definition a silent society. Its voice is not an authentic voice but rather a mere echo of the voice of the metropolis (CTPL, 63/65).

It is not hard to establish an immediate conclusion: The colonized are silent, they lack their own voice, they speak through the speech of the oppressor.

This is why PF does not hesitate to say that his pedagogy is also a "pedagogy of the oppressed."

His starting point for the theoretical substantiation of the pedagogy of the oppressed is the dramatic challenge men currently face. This challenge means that "men propose themselves as a problem," they discover how little they know of themselves, and become concerned with knowing more. They inquire, they respond, "and their responses lead them to new questions" (PO, 29).

Thus, the problem of communication is inevitably at the core of the book *Pedagogy of the Oppressed*: the man who discovers his own humanity when communicating with nature, himself and other men. To know himself, in his contextualization, means to discover himself as oppressed.

The pedagogy of the oppressed is part of the struggle of man for his own humanization. For this reason, it is a pedagogy forged with man, and not for man. It is a pedagogy that "will make and re-make itself" (PO, 32).

PF then further explains the nature of his pedagogy of communication: Implying a communion between teacher and student, it is presented as an open pedagogy, in constant re-development. The more intense the communication, the richer the interaction among the participants.

It is also a liberating pedagogy. Through communication, it leads to freedom. "Freedom is acquired by conquest, not by gift. It must be pursued constantly… It is rather the indispensable condition for the quest for human completion" (PO, 35).

Communication and freedom are co-inciding phenomena. Not dichotomized. Communication occurs automatically only with freedom. In turn, freedom is conquered only through communication.

Often, "touched by fear of freedom," men avoid communication. They prefer gregariousness to authentic co-existence. They prefer adaptation to creative communion.

What is this, if not the syndrome of oppression? It is a specific situation of man subjected to injustice, especially in his speech. The oppressed is someone who does not communicate. He receives communiqués. The greatest oppression is perhaps his silence, since when he speaks, it is to reproduce the speech of his oppressor.

A situation of oppression does not vanish, however, with recognition of it. A radical requirement identified by PF is the "transformation of the specific situation that causes the oppression" (PO, 38). Thus, the pedagogy of the oppressed is also a pedagogy of praxis. "Praxis is the reflection and action of men on the world to transform it" (PO, 40).

It is, therefore, a communicative praxis: Acting on and thinking about the world, with other men, is how one discerns paths for transformation. "In dialectical thought, world and action are intimately interdependent. But action is human only when it is not merely an occupation but also a preoccupation, that is, when it is not dichotomized from reflection" (PO, 42).

The basic focus of the book *Pedagogy of the Oppressed* "is not simply explaining to the masses, but engaging in dialogue with them on their actions." That means its main function is to break and dismantle the "culture of silence."

4. The "culture of silence" is reproduced through "banking education," which is antidialogue

To the extent that the "culture of silence" is the "echo of the voice of the metropolis," it is reproduced not only through mutism, but especially through the information process implicit in current education, which PF labels "banking education."

In banking education, there is no place for communication, since teacher-student relationships are fundamentally narrative and formal.

That means the teacher (narrator) is the subject and the students are patient, listening objects. The narration encompasses "something completely alien to the experience of the students" or presents "reality

1927
1960
1963
1964
1967
1969
1970
1971
1972
1973
1974
1975
1976
1977
1978
1979
1980
1981
1982
1983
1984
1985
1986
1987
1988
1989
1990
1991
1992
1993
1994
1995
1996
1997
1998
1999
2000
2001
2002
2003
2004
2005
2006

as if it were motionless, static, compartmentalized, and predictable" (PO, 65). Thus, the words "are emptied of their concreteness." They become hollow. And therefore, it leads students to the mechanical memorization of the narrated content.

In the banking concept of education, the teacher, rather than communicating, deposits pre-established content into the student. Education becomes the act of depositing, of transmitting values and knowledge.

Banking education takes place within a "culture of silence," i.e., of non-communication. Why? Because the interests of the oppressors lie in "changing the consciousness of the oppressed, not the situation that oppresses them, for the more the oppressed can be led to adapt to that situation, the more easily they can be dominated" (PO, 69). …

[Freire] lament[s]:

> We needed a pedagogy of communication with which to conquer the dislike inherent in anti-dialogue. Unfortunately, for a number of reasons, this position—antidialogue—has been the most common one in Latin America. Education that kills the creative power not only of the student but also of the teacher, as the latter is transformed into someone who imposes or, at best, into a giver of formulas and communiqués, which are received passively by his students. He who imposes does not create, nor do those who receive; both atrophy, and education is no longer education (EM, 69).

5. The Pedagogy of Communication as problem-posing education

Fully aware that "education reflects the power structure" and recognizing that banking education is the oppressors' instrument of power, PF inquires whether it is possible to practice dialogue-centered education in a society whose power rejects dialogue. Recognizing the difficulty of an act of this nature, he suggests that "nevertheless, something fundamental may be done: dialoguing about the negation of dialogue itself" (PO, 71).

In other words: the basic requirement for establishing a pedagogy of communication is to resolve "the teacher-student contradiction." Overcoming this leads to "problem-posing education," which "rejects communiqués and embodies communication" (PO, 77).

Student and teacher would cease to have strict roles, and would perform both roles simultaneously. "The teacher is no longer merely the-one-who-teaches, but one who is himself taught in dialogue with the students, who in turn while being taught also teach. They become jointly responsible for a process in which all grow" (PO, 78). In summary, "people teach each other, mediated by the world" (PO, 79), since "the teacher's thinking is authenticated only by the authenticity of the students' thinking, both of them mediated by reality, therefore, in inter-communication" (PO, 73). …

6. The search for popular communication

The strategy used to achieve that transformation [from real awareness to possible awareness] is based on the process of capturing the limiting situations that, when converted to visual and verbal codes, might motivate students to overcome the inhibiting forces that often lead to a negation of concrete reality.

To this end, an ongoing process of communication with students is essential, so the teacher may grasp their reality in order to properly codify it and then provide a "re-reading" of the world in which the students live.

This does not involve the vocabulary universe alone but rather a search for new content to be incorporated into the educational process. To PF, this initial search is the teacher's "decoding" live reality with the decisive participation of the students. It is nothing more than an attempt to recover "popular communication," to use it as the common sign between teacher and student."

The next stage, after "reducing" the topic being researched, is the "codification" stage of the educational content, i.e., that of "choosing the best channel of communication," which depends "not only on the material to be codified but also on whether or not the individuals with whom one wishes to communicate are literate."

PF suggests a multiplicity of visual, pictorial, graphic, auditive [audio], and tangible channels.

> In preparing this material, the team may propose some themes or aspects of some themes, and if, when, and where possible, using recorders, offer them to specialists as topics for interviews to be conducted with one of the team members... Some themes or nuclei may be presented by means of brief dramatizations, containing the theme only—no "solutions"! The dramatization acts as a codification, as a problem-posing situation to be discussed. Another didactic resource, within a problem-posing... approach to education — is the reading and discussion of magazine articles, newspapers, and book chapters (PO, 138/139). ...

7. Can mass media contribute to problem-posing education?

In analyzing the development process of Brazilian society, PF specifically considered the role of mass media in its conversion from a "closed society" to an "open society."

On the one hand, he calls attention to the "massifying" [popularizing for the masses] function of these vehicles, which contribute to alienating citizens, stimulating them to adopt an acritical attitude toward life. "Excluded from the orbit of decision-making, increasingly restricted to small minorities, citizens are controlled by the advertising media to such an extent that they trust or believe in nothing if not heard on the radio or television, or not read in the newspapers" (EPL, 90/91).

He also acknowledges that such vehicles, in the situation experienced by Brazil prior to 1964, when conditions were appropriate for a democratic transition in the country's political life, were also bearers of "influences," that radiated from large and medium-sized centers to smaller and more backward centers (EPL, 91).

Certainly that is why PF recommends the use of messages disseminated by the mass media as additional resources in the process of popular education. He states:

> It seems indispensable to analyze the contents of newspaper editorials following any given event: 'Why do different newspapers express different opinions about the same event?' Then let people develop a sense of critique, so that they may react to newspapers they read or news broadcasts they hear on the radio not as passive objects of the "communiqués" prescribed to them, but rather as a consciousness seeking to be free (PO, 139). ...

8. The opposition between communication and propaganda

A rather peculiar characteristic of PF is the constant explanation or even re-elaboration of his thought. Insofar as his educational ideas and proposals always take communication as a fundamental element, he attempts a conceptual redundancy, which is often significant for understanding what he really means.

Thus, when proposing the practice of communication as a way to overcome the "culture of silence" and "banking education," PF not only wants to avoid the understanding of communication for the sake of communication (dialogue stripped of its liberating content, problem-posing, the presence of the contradictions of society represented by limiting situations), but also, insofar as communication is a revolutionary act, to prevent it from being confused with propaganda, as has been used by the populist movements.

According to him, propaganda is an instrument of domination, of domestication, and its ideological framework is the indoctrination of men to accommodate them to the world of oppression. For this reason, PF does not approve of true revolutionaries using the methods of propaganda and slogans, which correspond, on a higher level, to the concept of banking education. He even suggests that if a revolutionary society continues with propaganda, it is because it is mistaken, or has lost its trust and belief in men.

1927
1960
1963
1964
1967
1969
1970
1971
1972
1973
1974
1975
1976
1977
1978
1979
1980
1981
1982
1983
1984
1985
1986
1987
1988
1989
1990
1991
1992
1993
1994
1995
1996
1997
1998
1999
2000
2001
2002
2003
2004
2005
2006

Explaining his concept of true revolutionary communication, PF does a "reading" of Leninist speeches on the relationships between revolutionary theory and revolutionary movement. He suggests how it might be possible to make the communication of revolutionary theory to an oppressed people dialogue-centered, and therefore more efficient.

> A revolution is achieved with neither verbalism nor activism, but rather with praxis, that is, with reflection and action directed at the structures to be transformed. The revolutionary effort to transform these structures radically cannot designate its leaders as its thinkers and the oppressed as mere doers... Leaders who deny praxis to the oppressed thereby invalidate their own praxis. By imposing their word on others, they falsify that word, making it dominant by nature (PO, 146).

PF emphatically concluded that:

> Dialogue with the people is radically necessary to every authentic revolution. This is what makes it a revolution.. The earlier dialogue begins, the more truly revolutionary will the movement be. The dialogue which is radically necessary to revolution corresponds to another radical need: that of women and men as beings who cannot be truly human apart from communication, for they are essentially communicative creatures. To impede communication is to reduce men to the status of "things" – and this is a job for oppressors, not for revolutionaries (PO, 149).

9. Rural extension as a form of manipulation and cultural invasion

Just as domination exists in the vertical relationship between revolutionary leadership and the people, there is manipulation and cultural invasion in the action of technicians who seek to offer workers knowledge that may improve their productive activity.

PF deals specifically with this issue, considering the problem of agricultural modernization in Chile, as part of the land reform process unleashed by the Frei Government.

Agricultural technicians charged with disseminating processes to speed up the agrarian activity revisited the method used until then, which was a set of techniques originating in the United States and known as rural extension. Invited to collaborate in this change of action for the purpose of transforming Chilean agriculture, PF reflected on rural extension, basing himself on the premises already discussed with regard to propaganda, and taking them further by linking them to the set of behavior manipulation techniques.[5]

That reflection by PF is basic to an understanding of his concept of communication.

"Communication implies reciprocity that cannot be broken." Thus, "there are no passive subjects in communication" (EC, 66/67).

What characterizes communication, therefore, is dialogue. This relationship between dialogue and communication implies an agreement between the subjects with respect to signs—i.e., an agreement about the dual dimension of the sign, the signifier and the signified, mediated by the reference (object).

Now, in order for this agreement to hold, a permanent articulation of the subjects in communication becomes indispensable, so the content of the communication may be understood.

In a typical situation of communication between agronomist and farmer, we see that the main resource used is the presentation. PF shows that the presentation is an inadequate resource for communication, since it is a monologue. It is an instrument of extension – transfer of knowledge. He recommends problem-posing dialogue as a more appropriate resource that enables reduction of the distance between the technician's signifying expression and the peasants' perception of the signified. This would result in ad-

---

5   In this regard, it is interesting to note the suggestive essay by Antônio Cerveira de Moura, 'A Comunicação segundo Paulo Freire' [Communication According to Paulo Freire], published in the Comunicação e Sociedade [Communication and Society] magazine, nº 1 (São Paulo, Cortez & Moraes, 1979), pp. 31-38.

miration of the knowledge (communication), promoting co-participation in the act of understanding the signification of the signified, which would be a critical attitude.

This search for the signification is not limited merely to the objective (real, palpable) and subjective (mental, i.e., convictions) worlds. Communication will only be complete if the interlocutors can agree to the understanding of the meaning of the object and the reconstitution of the convictions that guide the process of understanding one another.

In other words, the process of human communication cannot be immune to socio-cultural conditionings. I can only obtain full communication to the extent that I am capable of placing myself empathetically before my interlocutor's socio-cultural conditionings, and vice-versa.

If "education is communication, dialogue, insofar as it is not the transfer of knowledge" (EC, 69), it is natural that PF denies to rural extension "the connotations of truly educational thinking, which are found in the concept of communication" (EC, 74). And he does not hesitate to denounce: "the trend of extensionism is to fall easily into the use of propaganda and persuasion techniques," and therefore, to unleash "acts of cultural invasion and manipulation." PF explains that rural extension technicians, "upon first sensing difficulty in their attempt to communicate with the peasants, do not realize that these difficulties stem from, among other causes, the following: the process of human communication cannot be immune to socio-cultural conditionings. So, rather than taking this truth into account and reflecting on the peasants' socio-cultural conditionings, which are not theirs, they simplify the question, and conclude that the peasants are incapable of dialogue" (EC, 72/73).

THE POPULAR AND THE MASS
Excerpt from: *Cuadernos de Comunicación*
By Jesús Martín Barbero

Any history of the popular would first require a dialectical shift—both an affirmation and a negation of the popular. First, one would have to place oneself in an anthropological opposition. On one side would be popular culture, comprised of oral and visual elements, with the oral encompassing popular sayings, proverbs, storytelling, and the songs that preserve and condense an entire memory of that map; characterized by mockery, exaggeration and authorlessness. On the opposite side would be literary culture, i.e., written culture, the culture of the elite—a culture characterized by refinement, measure and control, whose products are invariably signed by an author. This opposition between an oral/visual culture and a written, literary one began to dissolve between the end of the 18th and mid-19th centuries, only to reappear as a fusion. This fusion first showed itself in the serial—one in which the oral culture yet to come (which had already appeared in the form

of hawkers' tales in English Gothic novels) merged with the literary phenomenon of the great bourgeois novel. The serial represents a fascinating mix, combining popular subjects with forms taken from the bourgeois novel, posing for the first time the problem of popular genres, and even prefiguring what was to be our present-day radio and television serials. That initial 19th-century fusion of oral and literary culture was succeeded by a coupling, so familiar to modern audiences, that joined oral/literary culture with popular visual culture—principally in the form of film, comics, photoromances and television soap operas. This map makes no attempt to establish a noble origin for mass culture but rather to shed light on the historical materialization of processes that are not only economic and political, but also cultural, in nature.

Martín Barbero, Jesús (1979). "Lo popular y lo masivo," *Cuadernos de Comunicación* No. 62, Mexico City. Reprinted with permission of the author.

1979

1927
1960
1963
1964
1967
1969
1970
1971
1972
1973
1974
1975
1976
1977
1978
1979
1980
1981
1982
1983
1984
1985
1986
1987
1988
1989
1990
1991
1992
1993
1994
1995
1996
1997
1998
1999
2000
2001
2002
2003
2004
2005
2006

Thus, according to PF, there is a great difference between rural extension and communication. In extension, someone comes before another or before the community as a mere issuer of communiqués, molding their behavior. However, a humanistic attitude predominates in communication, rejecting all forms of manipulation, seeking to achieve the comprehension of the objects that are targeted by the communicative relationship, and establish an understanding. This attitude is based on the "belief that men can do and re-do things; they can transform the world" (EC, 74).

10. Foundations of the concept of communication in Paulo Freire …

When he [Freire] originally developed the concept of communication and pointed to dialogue as its main characteristic, PF was inspired by Jasper. "And what is dialogue? It is a horizontal relationship of A and B. It is born from a critical matrix and generates criticality (Jaspers). It is nursed on love, humility, hope, faith, trust. For this reason, there is communication only in dialogue. And when the two extremes of the dialogue are thus linked, with love, hope, and faith in one another, they become critics in search of something. A relationship of sympathy is then established between both. Only then is there communication" (EPL, 107).

However, the framework of transcendentalism becomes more explicit when PF says that dialogue is not reduced to a connection between men, but rather between them and the Creator.

> Existing surpasses living because it is more than being in the world. It is being in it and with it. It is that capacity or possibility of communicative connection between the existing and the objective world, contained in the very etymology of the word, which incorporates into existing the sense of criticality that is absent in simply living. Transcending, discerning, dialoguing (communicating and participating) are exclusive to existing. Existing is individual, however it is only carried out in relation to other existings, and in communication with them (EPL, 40/41). …

When PF notes that the human world is a "world of communication," the argument he uses reflects the transcendentalist mode of analysis of the communicative phenomenon.

> The thinking subject cannot think alone; he cannot think without the co-participation of other subjects in the act of thinking about the object. There is no "I think," but rather a "we think." It is the "we think" that establishes the "I think," not the other way around. This co-participation in the act of thinking occurs in communication. For this very reason, the object is not the terminative incidence of the thought of a subject, but rather the mediator of communication. Hence, as the content of communication, it cannot be communicated from one subject to another (EC, 66). It is an analytical perspective similar to that proposed for direct cognition.

However, upon examining the role of linguistic signs in the dialogical-communicative relationship, PF applies Adam Schaff's Marxist interpretation. Defending the theory that communication is divided into two distinct types, meanings and convictions, Schaff suggests that this distinction can only be made through the mediation of the "world of labor" (context or reality). PF fully incorporates this analytical position: "efficient communication requires that the interlocutory subjects focus their admiration on a single object; that they express it through linguistic signs belonging to a universe common to both, in order to thereby understand, in similar fashion, the object of the communication, which takes place through words, as the thought-language-context or reality relationship cannot be broken" (EC, 70).

When he revisits the question of the notion of communication (dialogue), in *Pedagogia do Oprimido* [Pedagogy of the Oppressed], PF gives a more prominent presence to Marxist categories of analysis. The sense that Marx and Engels attribute to communication is implicit there, not as a mere instrument of sociability (sheep or flock consciousness) but as an instrument of labor leading to socialization.

It is not in silence that men are made, but in words, in labor, in action-reflection. But if speaking the true word, which is labor, which is praxis, is transforming the world, speaking the word is not the privilege of a few, but the right of all men. …

(Translated by Myra Bergman Ramos)

References

Works by Paulo Freire

Conscientização e alfabetização. Uma nova visão do Processo. [Awareness and Literacy. A New View of the Process] Estudos Universitários (4). Recife: Universidade do Recife, 1963, pp. 5-23.

Educação como prática da liberdade [Education as the Practice of Liberty]. Rio de Janeiro: Paz e Terra, 1967.

Extensão ou Comunicação? [Extension or Communication?] Rio de Janeiro: Paz e Terra, 1971.

Ação cultural para a liberdade [Cultural Action for Freedom]. Rio de Janeiro: Paz e Terra, 1976.

Cartas a Guiné-Bissau [Letters to Guinea Bissau]. Rio de Janeiro: Paz e Terra, 1977.

Pedagogia do oprimido [Pedagogy of the Oppressed]. 6th ed., Rio de Janeiro: Paz e Terra, 1979.

Conscientização, teoria e prática da libertação [Awareness, Theory and Practice of Liberation]. São Paulo: Cortez & Moraes, 1979.

Educação e Mudança [Education and Change]. Rio de Janeiro: Paz e Terra, 1979.

Works about Paulo Freire

COSTA, Aurenice Cardoso da. *Conscientização e alfabetização. Uma Visão Prática do Sistema Paulo Freire* [Awareness and Literacy. A Practical View of the Paulo Freire System], Estudos Universitários (4) Recife: Universidade do Recife, 1963, pp. 71-80.

MACIEL, Jarbas. A fundamentação teórica do sistema Paulo Freire [The Theoretical Foundations of the Paulo Freire System], Estudos Universitários (4), Recife: Universidade do Recife, 1963, pp. 25-70.

MOURA, Antônio Cerveira de. *A comunicação segundo Paulo Freire* [Communication According to Paulo Freire], *Comunicação & Sociedade* [Communication & Society] (1). São Paulo: Cortez & Moraes, 1979, pp. 31-38.

LEITE, Ligia Chiappini Moraes. '*Encontro com Paulo Freire*' [Meeting with Paulo Freire]. *Educação & Sociedade* [Education & Society] (3). São Paulo: Cortez & Moraes, 1979, pp. 47-75.

TORRES, Carlos Alberto. *Diálogo com Paulo Freire* [Dialogue with Paulo Freire], São Paulo: Loyola, 1979.

JORGE, J. Simões. *A ideologia de Paulo Freire* [The Ideology of Paulo Freire]. São Paulo, Loyola, 1979.

OLABUENAGA, J. I. Ruiz; Morales, P., and Marroquina, M., Paulo Freire, *Conscientização y Andragogia* [Awareness and Andragogia]. Buenos Aires: Paidós, 1975.

Source: Marques de Melo, José & Castelo Branco, Samantha (orgs.) *Pensamento Comunicacional Brasileiro* [Brazilian Communicational Thought]. The São Bernardo Group (1978-1998). São Bernardo do Campo: Umesp, 1999, p. 225-246.

This work constitutes a new version, with slight additions and changes, of the work presented to the interdisciplinary seminar on communications in the thinking of Paulo Freire, which was held in the second half of 1979 by the Post-Graduate Center of the Methodist Advanced Education Institute, in São Bernardo do Campo, SP. The didactic form of presentation was completely maintained in this text. That is why we systematically cite the works of Paulo Freire, as a way to enliven the argument. To avoid unnecessary repetition of the titles of the cited works, we have adopted the following codes: EPL = *Educação como Prática da Liberdade* [Education as the Practice of Liberty]; PO = *Pedagogia do Oprimido* [Pedagogy of the Oppressed]; EC = *Extensão ou Comunicação?* [Extension or Communication?]; ACL = *Ação Cultural para a Liberdade* [Cultural Action for Freedom]; CGB = *Cartas à Guiné Bissau* [Letters to Guinea Bissau]; CTPL = *Conscientização, Teoria e Prática da Libertação* [Awareness, Theory, and Practice of Liberation]; EM = *Educação e Mudança* [Education and Change]. We did the same for Paulo Freire's name, which is represented solely by the initials PF. Used with permission of the author.

1927
1960
1963
1964
1967
1969
1970
1971
1972
1973
1974
1975
1976
1977
1978
1979
1980
1981
1982
1983
1984
1985
1986
1987
1988
1989
1990
1991
1992
1993
1994
1995
1996
1997
1998
1999
2000
2001
2002
2003
2004
2005
2006

EXCERPT FROM:

COMMUNICATION AND DAILY LIFE

By Daniel Prieto Castillo

1979 In no way do messages determine everyday life. (For example, advertising does not produce consumption). In any case, they reinforce patterns, forms of existence already active. Messages do not alienate anyone. The presence of alienating forms and contents is a sign of previously alienated consumers. It is always prevailing social relationships that result in alienation.

There is enough proof of this. The most helpless social groups tend to consume a higher quantity of messages (for example, children, the elderly, outcasts, construction workers who spend most of their time at work). As a form of leisure, the consumption of messages replaces other ways of using free time (creativity, sports, etc.)

There is no mystery in the case of advertising or magazines with more than a million copies of weekly circulation. Their success is secured in advance by prevailing social relationships. We have known for some time that messages do not directly produce violence. If a child throws himself out of a window believing he is a superhero, it is not because he saw one or many programs on TV. His attitude originates in family relationships or relationships with other groups that have prevailed throughout his existence.

Still, however, millions keep being spent on advertising, and there is wide controversy surrounding the new international information order.

It is through messages that there is a tendency to reinforce an everyday life that favors the status quo. Stereotypes are reinforced, and versions that circulate around the globe over and over again are asserted.

What is important about alienated everyday life (important for those who benefit from it) is people's being

in it without becoming aware. Reinforcement means the constant issuing of versions that favor the conceptions, assessments and perceptions that dominate. All formal elements of the message must strictly follow a rigid rule: Don't make the receiver uncomfortable. This implies guaranteeing a degree of confidence in the message, a degree of entertainment, a degree of comfort when it comes to understanding on the part of the receiver. A minimum degree that is, at the same time, a maximum degree. That is, all dominating messages must be inserted within that narrow range. The message/everyday life relationship is in no way symmetrical. In any event, this tends to be true of certain groups. Symmetry begins to take place when what the version offers literally concurs with the consumer's life. And this happens with the social sectors that benefit more directly from the status quo. That is, symmetry exists when messages have nothing to hide, when they speak in a positive tone, of clothes, of intellectual and social circles, of objects already part of the existence of those who consume them. Messages turn out to be functional for an everyday life that is functional within the prevailing system; integrated, without much trauma, satisfied with its share in the social hierarchy. There is an attempt here to reinforce functionality. However, it so happens that the whole population does not enjoy a similar existence, even less when we talk about our Latin American countries. For the great majority, everyday life is not functional simply because there are enormous differences in the distribution of wealth, which manifest themselves in all fields (food, housing, clothing, education…). Here, McLuhan's speculations about a "global village," or those of Moles regarding the integration of men with men on a large scale, have no value whatsoever. This is false to the extent that "man" does not exist, but instead very concrete beings exist in very concrete social relations.

The everyday life of the great majority in our countries is dysfunctional, plagued with catastrophes, poverty and deficiencies. If an individual must walk everyday for more than three kilometers to obtain water, if he constantly lacks his daily bread (*quotidianem panem da nobis* reads a wall in a Mexican monastery), if he does not possess the basic objects that could ease his relationship with his environment, he will hardly be able to have a functional everyday life.

Messages are also directed at him, this time not to establish a symmetric reaffirmation, but to try to seal the wound, to hide everyday problems from the eyes of those who are suffering. This is done by reducing facts to anecdotes, by psychologizing conflict, by disseminating stereotypes that tend to order reality, so as to ensure the mental order of those who will share such messages.

And since messages are less than reality, they certainly do not fully occupy the dysfunctional everyday life of our large majority. Something is always left out.

No message can hide the death of a son due to lack of medicine or hunger; no message can solve the catastrophes that destroy whole families. Conscience is not interwoven from the outside; it is the result of daily experience and not of messages or total manipulation.

From *Diseño y comunicación*, Mexico, Ed. Coyoacán, 1994. Originally circulated as *Vida cotidiana y comunicación*, written for a discussion meeting at the Department of Design, Unidad Azcapotzalco, Universidad Autónoma Metropolitana, Mexico, 1979. Reprinted with permission of the author.

THE POPULAR AND THE MASS
Excerpt from: *Cuadernos de Comunicación*
By Jesús Martín Barbero

Popular culture is intermixed with mass culture—confused with it, trapped within its forms, and compelled to seek expression through it. An illustration will suffice. When I was viewing the film, "La Ley del Monte" ["The Law of the Mountain"], the women and men beside me cried from beginning to end. Something in the film was capable of drawing tears from people who, by no means mentally retarded, simply lived in another culture, in a realm of experience quite foreign to the ideological and semiological decoding I undertook as I watched the film. Around the same time, I received the proceedings of a conference on alternative communication processes, held in Barcelona the year before, which included presentations by participants ranging from PLO members to Red Brigade sympathizers, as well as other presenters coming from alternative experiences. The author of the introduction to the proceedings wrote as follows:

> The popular is the cornerstone of all alternative discourse. That which is alternative is either

popular or has been degraded into a toy, a machine for domination. "Popular" refers to that which makes possible collective aspirations and expectations for and by grassroots social groups, both majorities and minorities. I am referring, here, to the type of movements represented, for example, by homosexual groups, patients' groups agitating for empowerment in hospitals, movements of prisoners battling for power within prisons—all the movements one sees reported in the press.

Popular communication alternatives are not free of the fundamental contradiction of the social, namely, the contradiction between the right of the majority to direct and that of the minority to participate, the contradiction between pluralism and efficacy, between spontaneity and organization.

Martín Barbero, Jesús (1979). "Lo popular y lo masivo," *Cuadernos de Comunicación* No. 62, Mexico City. Reprinted with permission of the author.

EXCERPT FROM:

A USER-ORIENTED
COMMUNICATION STRATEGY
Communication and Development

By Florangel Rosario-Braid

1979 Early communication theorists[1] have underscored the functions of communication in development as those of "promoting a climate of acceptance," "agenda-setting," "raising aspirations," "surveying new environment," "socialization" and "establishing nationness."[2] Communication is so basic to development that it has been stated that a direct relationship exists between a country's underdevelopment and the state of its communication system.[3] The need for a global framework for development has surfaced because of the inadequacies of the old models to explain and guide the development process in most of the developing countries. The transfer of experiences from the technologically advanced countries to the less-developing countries (LDCs) has not been too successful and has led to a questioning of the applicability of the old paradigm. The new definition of development through creation of a self-reliant base at the grassroots levels would bring about a spirit of cooperation and unity among the poor, raise social and political consciousness, and ensure a more equitable redistribution of existing resources.

Recently, the term "development communication" has been used to describe any form of communication that supports development. For example, Quebral states that the purpose of development communication is to "advance development." This refers to the "speedy transformation of a country and the mass of its people from poverty to a dynamic state of economic growth that makes possible greater equality and the larger fulfillment of the human potential."[4] Woods views development communication as an element of the management process in the overall planning and implementation of development programmes. It is, in a broad sense, the "identification and utilization of appropriate expertise in the development process that will assist in increasing participation of intended beneficiaries at the grassroots level."[5] According to him, development communication is a process, not a technique, that is problem-oriented and requires a multidisciplinary approach. ...

Castro defines development journalism as being "largely rural-based, popular rather than elitist, practical rather than theoretical and esoteric; and service-oriented. ... It is involved in the community's growth rather than detached from or above it."[6]

Another viewpoint on the role of communication in helping people adapt to changes in their environment is that given by Tuluhungwa, who sees social-development communication as a "catalytic process by which human beings share information, knowledge, experience, ideas and motivations. From this sharing can come a collective need for changes."[7]

The concept of development had changed from that of a "linear" process to a continuing interaction or dialectic. It was assumed in the linear model that there is a central source of technology, primarily in the urban area, and a concentric flow of knowledge and information. This view was disputed in the late 1960s, when scholars started to conceptualize communication differently. Knowledge, resources and innovations do not necessarily have to originate from external sources. On the contrary, communication is now being encouraged to help examine existing resources, develop indigenous technology and encourage bottom-up planning and participation. The redefinition of communication operates within the framework of the new development philosophy, which encourages labor-intensive industries, participatory planning and new learning delivery systems.

Experiments are being conducted in the use of the dialectic approach to problems and needs identification. The new approach departs from the traditional change agent–client or interviewer-respondent relationships.[8] The dialectic approach is also an improvement to the "feedback-feedforward" concept, which is based on the traditional approach and involves the client merely as a reactor to ideas. The dialectic approach suggests mechanisms by which the client is able to ask questions and articulate his needs instead of merely responding to external stimuli. The Freire[9] approach to creative communication, which encourages frequent interaction between planners and people, has found its way into some change strategies. The approach suggests that learning is maximized when the content of message is laden with emotionally charged stimuli, which awakens and mobilizes people to participate and act. The Freire approach suggests the development of a user-oriented research methodology. Because this approach advocates the need to engage the respondent-client in critical thinking through dialogue, it could serve as a useful framework in developing research techniques that are able to:

a. elicit honest response from the respondent;
b. encourage him to think about the problem instead of merely selecting from alternatives;
c. articulate aspirations and distinguish between "wants" and needs;
d. organize units of analysis and group respondents so that one is able to match various groups' perceptions of problems; and
e. encourage openness between the interactors.

Theory in Development Strategy Planning

In developing objectives and strategies, planners start by using knowledge of the social categories in the community. One may assume that people who have a number of similar characteristics will have similar communication orientations. The *social categories* theory is a descriptive formula that serves as a basis for predicting mass-media behavior. It is difficult,

---

ALTERNATIVE COMMUNICATION
Excerpt from: *Communication and Daily Life*
By Daniel Prieto Castillo

Finally, the social relationships that I am so worried about will not necessarily change when the general structure changes. Authoritarianism does not magically disappear; it does not vanish as a consequence of eating more or providing more information. I remain quite aware, as an example, of Agnes Heller's statement about a young woman she met in a socialist country. "She woke up at six a.m. to prepare her kids' breakfast, saw them off to school, left lunch ready, went to work and typed until three p.m., returned home, fed the children, cleaned the kitchen, kept track of her young ones' homework duties, took care of her sick mother, fixed dinner and ironed clothes. At midnight she got into bed and her husband, who was a pig, got furious when she refused to make love".

Nobody is trying to characterize a socialist country through this example, but it should not be ignored either, pretending it does not exist. Nobody intends to have

erased objections with this answer. Personally, I believe that objections are useful to somehow set things in place. Because when it comes to communication, what happens is the same as in that famous sentence: "The bourgeois are the others". Or, likewise, I acknowledge social problems beyond myself and beyond those who are around me, I speak about and for society because it is sick, I am not sick.

Alternative communication starts with oneself and one's immediate relationships. There is no use theorizing about the goodness of the valid path for humanity if, when the time comes for intimacy, for coexistence, such good purposes are contradicted.

From *Diseño y comunicación*, Mexico, Ed. Coyoacán, 1994. Originally circulated as "Vida cotidiana y comunicación," written for a discussion meeting at the Department of Design, Unidad Azcapotzalco, Universidad Autónoma Metropolitana, Mexico, 1979. Copyright © 1979, Daniel Prieto Castillo. Reprinted with permission of the copyright holder.

1927
1960
1963
1964
1967
1969
1970
1971
1972
1973
1974
1975
1976
1977
1978
1979
1980
1981
1982
1983
1984
1985
1986
1987
1988
1989
1990
1991
1992
1993
1994
1995
1996
1997
1998
1999
2000
2001
2002
2003
2004
2005
2006

however, to use this formula in many Asian societies that are undergoing many rapid changes.

At every stage of the development process, the need for people's participation is paramount. Techniques for encouraging articulation of problems and needs are dependent on the *human dialogue* approach, where communication occurs in the context of openness, trust and authenticity.

In the implementation of a project, one seeks support from legitimators or influentials who are able to facilitate adoption of new ideas. Thus, credible leaders provide sanction to the idea either by interpreting it to others or communicatiing it to a larger group. The *social-relationships* theory, or *two-step flow of communication,* shows how information flows first to a few people who are better informed and who then pass on the information to others, usually though interpersonal channels. Sometimes, this may occur in a multistep process. In a campaign, one considers the selection and filtering that occurs in the flow of information. Thus, a radio listener, or newspaper reader, normally listens or attends to information that tends to confirm his own beliefs. The theory of *cognitive dissonance* explains how this type of selective retention and recall alters the content of information that is passed on.

In participatory planning, a certain filtering of messages takes place. There is often a tendency to send messages that enhance the sender's status, and thus there is a greater tendency for upward communication.

In communicating for social action, there is a need for information about the innovation—on where to obtain services and information—that reassures and provides moral support. The theory of persuasion is expressed in such concepts as *two-sided vs. one-sided* information, source credibility, and fear and threat appeals. It is also shown through utilization of communication strategies that show the advantages of practice that provide both positive and negative information about an innovation, and messages that counteract fear and threat. Likewise, indirect persuasion is

ALTERNATIVE COMMUNICATION
Excerpt from: '*Vida cotidiana y comunicación*'
[Communication and Daily Life]
By Daniel Prieto Castillo

Alternative communication is not explained in relation to communication itself, but in relation to alternative social relationships. The notion of 'alternative' must be understood in connection with the breaking down of authoritarianism. If the key to authoritarianism is found not only in what is general, but also and fundamentally in the structure of everyday life, thought of an individual, interpersonal and group terms, *alternative communication will be valid, will only be such, if it reclaims that very same everyday life from authoritarianism, in its individual, interpersonal and group instances*.

From *Diseño y comunicación*, Mexico, Ed. Coyoacán, 1994. Originally circulated as "Vida cotidiana y comunicación," written for a discussion meeting at the Department of Design, Unidad Azcapotzalco, Universidad Autónoma Metropolitana, Mexico, 1979. Reprinted with permission of the author.

more effective than direct or "hard-sell" persuasion, and learning or retention occurs when the source is credible. *Learning theories* may help us to understand attitudes and motivations—why we readily adopt certain forms of behavior and not others.

The mobilization of leaders and people on a common community project requires careful preplanning of activities. The *theory of organizational or administrative communication* is defined in terms of concepts such as openness of organizations to change, willingness of leaders to allow information or new ideas to spread to a wider group of people, and politics of development. The latter will determine whether the doors of a local government office will be open to the change agent or whether the project is provided local counterpart support and is implemented within a reasonable timeframe. Success in communication is also seen in terms of the willingness of people to share information and power with others, so that integration may take place much more easily.

The impact of communication on community life can be seen by understanding people's perception of media and how they are used. Thus, if media are primarily regarded as entertainment and dependent on advertising, they would be used to sell goods and services. The effect of minority programming such as agricultural and other educational programs is often mitigated by the heavy volume of entertainment that dominates the airwaves and drives out other programs.

A development-support communication project emphasizes use of interactive mechanisms utilizing both the mass media and interpersonal networks to provide dialogue between people and planners. A communication strategy is successful when a system of feedback occurs between the two groups. However, one must guard against the tendencies of certain groups in the community to interfere in the process by selecting or editing information sent upward or downward.

Development communication is [purposeful]; that is, there is a deliberate intent to communicate with a purpose. Usually, the message focuses on the goals of a five-year national development-program plan or adoption of farm and home technologies. A strategy that takes the *systems* approach shows the interdependence of various parts of the system.

It is important to understand people's values and beliefs before the introduction of change. Cultural communication focuses on building effective relationships through a better understanding of differences in verbal and nonverbal communication patterns and developing strategies which use this knowledge.

Endnotes

1. Schramm, in D. Lerner and W., Schramm, *Communication and Change in the Developing Countries,* Honolulu: East-West Center, 1967, described the process thus: "Communication is deeply integrated into society. It has little life of its own. It is something people do—the fundamental social process. When we study it, we are really studying people and societies… Whenever change occurs in human society, there communication flows." Lerner, in W. Schramm and D. Lerner, *Communication and Change, the Last Ten Years and*

the Next, Honolulu: East-West Center, 1976 (1977), defines communication as a "general process of attitude formation and attitude change by which a society is shaped."

Milikan, in Schramm and Lerner, 1977, states, "…of all the technological changes which have been sweeping through the traditional societies of the under-developed world during the decade, the most fundamental and pervasive in their effect on human society have been changes in communication."

Pye Lucian [Lucian Pye] *Communication, Institution-Building and the Reach of Authority,* in Lerner and Schramm, 1967, states that the basic problems of political modernization and national development can be conceived of as problems in communication.

2. Lerner and Schramm, 1967, op. cit.

3. John A. R. Lee, *Towards Realistic Communication Policies: Recent Trends and Ideas Compiled and Analyzed,* Reports and Papers on Mass Communication, Paris: UNESCO, 1976, 8.

4. Nora Quebral, "Development Communication," in J. Jamais, ed., *Readings in Development Communication,* University of the Philippines at Los Baños, 1975, 2.

5. John Woods, "Development and Communication—Bringing Them Closer Together Through Training," paper prepared for a colloquium on Training in Development Training and Communication Planning, UNDP, 1977.

6. Jose Luna Castro, "Development Communications," Publishers Association of the Philippines, Inc., Seminar, Dec. 9, 1977 (mimeo), 3.

7. R. R. Tuluhungwa, "What is Social Development Communication?" Communication Newsletter, February 1978, Vol. 1.

8. See Sagasti H. E. Perrett, *Communication With the Rural Poor: An Action Approach,* Vol. II, Academy for Educational Development, 1975, 4. The author cites observations on present approaches to development communication such as (1) an approach to rural people as an essentially passive "target" of development programs, (2) a focus on the role of communication as broadly educational and only indirectly related to action, and (3) a definition of the communication specialist as essentially a technician, expert in the use of certain mechanical communication instruments to transmit messages. The main point that emerges from discussion on this topic, he says, is that knowledge about communication technology and about communication process is considerable; where we fail is in our understanding of the human element."

9. The Freire approach departs from the "banking" concept that characterizes many of our teaching and change strategies. In the latter, the teacher or change agent deposits knowledge in the minds of the students/clients instead of creating an interaction situation where each learns from the other. The Freire approach assumes that the peasant, no matter how illiterate, is capable of looking critically at the world. Information provides the tools needed in interaction. Dialogue can only happen if there is perception of one another as equal; and if there is humility, love and faith in man and hope that things can change.

Rosario-Braid, Florangel. "A User-Oriented Communication Strategy." In F. Rosario-Braid, ed., *Communication Strategy for Productivity Improvement.* Tokyo: Asian Productivity Organization, 1979, 27-46. Copyright © 1979, APO. Reprinted with permission of copyright holder.

1927
1960
1963
1964
1967
1969
1970
1971
1972
1973
1974
1975
1976
1977
1978
1979
1980
1981
1982
1983
1984
1985
1986
1987
1988
1989
1990
1991
1992
1993
1994
1995
1996
1997
1998
1999
2000
2001
2002
2003
2004
2005
2006

THE FOLK-COMMUNICATION SYSTEM

Excerpt from: Folkcomunicação: A Comunicação dos Marginalizados

By Luiz Beltrão

1980 Research into the nature, elements and structure, the agents and users, and the process, modes, and effects of folk communication is an absolute necessity. This is particularly so in countries such as ours, which have high illiteracy rates, irregular patterns of population distribution, demonstrably uneven income distribution, and high levels of poverty. And so, as a result of these and other factors, countries like ours are characterized by frequent institutional crises that lead inevitably to political instability.

To reduce these ills, everyone's collaboration is required. Surprisingly, the transmission of messages intended to build a unity of purpose is entrusted almost solely to conventional communications through mass media, which are beyond the reach of vast segments of the audience as a whole, when we do not truly know even those we use in our day-to-day discourse.

Nature, Structure and Process

In a folk-communication system, notwithstanding the existence and use, in certain cases, of indirect and industrialized modes and channels (such as TV sports broadcasts, recorded songs, or messages printed in brochures and flyers), messages are produced, above all, through the craft of the communicator-agent. The dissemination process is horizontal, with typical users receiving messages through their own intermediary in one of the multiple stages of dissemination. Reception without such an intermediary occurs only when the recipient has mastered the coding and technique and has the ability and opportunity to use them in response to, or in the transmission of, original messages.

In other words, folk-communication is, by its nature and structure, a horizontal process based on craft, similar in essence to interpersonal types of communication since its messages are developed, codified, and transmitted in languages and channels that are familiar to the audience, which in turn is familiar to the communicator, both psychologically and experientially, even if it is scattered.

The case of radio, undoubtedly the most common means of mass communication among the popular masses, especially since the invention of the transistor, might serve as an example. The majority of the folk audience receives clearly, interprets, and reacts to soccer-related messages, thanks to the generalized knowledge not only of the rules of the game but also of the terms and expressions, even technical ones, used by the announcer, whose delivery is as simple as possible and laden with enthusiasm—a type of eloquence much appreciated by the masses. The same may be said of religious programs, particularly those of the Afro-Brazilian religions, or broadcasts of Brazilian country music. However, messages dealing with economic, political, or administrative affairs, broadcasts of classical music, or even specialized technical courses (except when intermediaries are used, as on educational radio) hit a wall of incomprehension, even when they are heard by groups of interested listeners, as was the case with the Ministry of Agriculture's Rural Radio broadcasts. It is curious to note that this incomprehension affects people who, because of their educational level or the position they hold in the community, are part of the system of social communication: journalist-announcer Meira Filho, from Brasília, who produced a very popular morning show for one of the local radio stations, addressing complaints or playing song requests from listeners, and was also one of the newscasters for the national radio news program, recounted how, during a Sunday visit, a friend who was a local legislator in a city near the capital criticized him for being two-faced—correct in the morning, when criticizing the government, but a true sycophant in the evening … For this and other reasons, Zita de Andrade, in her manual—*Princípios e Técnica de Radiojornalismo* [Principles and Techniques of Radio Journalism]—published as a monograph by ICINFORM's *Comunicação & Problemas* [Communication & Problems] magazine in Brasília in 1970, and elsewhere, defends the concept of regional radio as a true path to properly informing and educating an audience.

Transposition of the message from one system of communication to another, in order to reach the desired whole, is based on research carried out particularly in the United States, which raised the aforementioned questions regarding the omnipotence of mass media. These arose from the failure or minimal results of political and advertising campaigns that were ineffective in driving radical changes in the audience's behavior despite the investment of millions of dollars.

It is true that there changes occurred, but these were superficial and faddish in nature, like changes in cigarette or soap brands, or the replacement of obsolete models of household appliances for more advanced ones. There was success also when the content was absolutely new and most of the audience had not yet formed an opinion on it. But in the case of messages touching upon deeply held convictions, recipients turned a deaf ear, particularly to public affairs.

In addition, in the few cases of conversion, i.e., of acceptance of solutions presented by the mass communicator, this occurred as a result of the advice of friends, relatives, or study and work groups to which the recipient belonged, rather than the guidance of the unapproachable and dogmatic monopolizer of the discourse on the microphone or printed paper.

The influence of mass media is exercised not directly, but rather through groups included among recipients who are part of the audience, because of their dispersed and disorganized nature. (The root of the confusion lies precisely in identifying an x number of recipients for a mass message—for example, the audience at a movie viewing—out of all those at whom the message is aimed and might possibly reach, as it is transmitted by a multiplier and/or universal reach medium.) Moreover, the audience receiving the mass message is heterogeneous, particularly with regard to culture; thus, a significant portion of the audience, lacking the common experience required for the synthesis between communicator and recipient, fails to capture the underlying content of the communication.

Unlike the direct interpersonal/intergroup dialogue process, the industrialization of the mass message does not permit immediate correction, reformulation, or adaptation to the recipient's ability to receive. Which leads him, particularly when he does not know the "language" and is situated within a "universe of discourse" different from that of the communicator, to seek clarification from the group or groups with which he is related, whether family, ideological, or professional.

These considerations inspired Schramm[1] to construct a model for the dissemination of mass communications, represented by a tuba, according to which the communicator (publisher, radio or TV broadcaster, film producer, etc.) sends identical messages through an appropriate medium. The recipients are individuals, each one decoding, interpreting, retransmitting, and discussing the information with his group, resulting in reinterpretation and production of a group opinion and, perhaps, of a return communication act (feedback) that will promote dialogue with the source entity.

1 Schramm, Wilbur, *Mecanismos de la Comunicación* [Mechanisms of Communication], in "Proceso y Efectos de la Comunicación Coletiva" [Process and Effects of Collective Communication], CIESPAL, Quito [Ecuador], 1964.

1927
1960
1963
1964
1967
1969
1970
1971
1972
1973
1974
1975
1976
1977
1978
1979
1980
1981
1982
1983
1984
1985
1986
1987
1988
1989
1990
1991
1992
1993
1994
1995
1996
1997
1998
1999
2000
2001
2002
2003
2004
2005
2006

In concluding that the main influence of mass communications is secondary, since it results from a discussion of the message within a group, pre-eminent figures in the field of Communications Theory stand out, such as Lazarsfeld, Berelson and Gaudet,[2] in a study carried out during a presidential election in the United States; Merton,[3] evaluating types of interpersonal influence in communications within a community; Katz, also in partnership with Lazarsfeld, in a now-classic work on the importance of personal influence,[4] as well as other social scientists, such as Lerner, De Fleur, Dood, Coleman, and Bryce, whose research in communities of several countries resulted in a consolidation of the process known as two-stage flow of communications, i.e., from the media to the leaders and from these to their closest friends.

In general, they have confirmed that:

1. The influence of other people on specific decisions tends to be more frequent—and certainly more effective—than that of the mass media;
2. Influencers and those who are influenced maintain close relations, and consequently, tend to share the same characteristics of social status: it is very rare for a person of high social status to influence those of low status, and vice versa;
3. Closely related individuals tend to have common opinions and attitudes and are reluctant to diverge from the group consensus, even if the arguments of the mass media seem appealing to them;
4. There is specialization among "opinion leadership." For example: a woman might have influence over shopping decisions, but probably will not with regard to fashions;
5. Even if influence is exerted by the most onto the least interested, the latter must have sufficient interest as to be susceptible; there are no leaders without partisans, and partisanship requires interest;
6. "Opinion leaders" tend to be more exposed to mass media, particularly those that are most relevant to their spheres of influence."[5]

Leader-Communicators

Although the relationships under study pertained to the system of social communications, the identification of an opinion leader as an agent-communicator of the folk-communication system was the starting point for the work carried out by all who sought to identify and analyze the agents and users of the process, the modes, and the accomplishments of the major parallel flow of messages that will provide knowledge about the expressions of popular thinking, their exchange of ideas and, ultimately, the attempts at co-existence, if not integration, between groups so fundamentally different. Lazarsfeld, in discussing the conclusions of the research in which he participated, detected four main characteristics in opinion leaders:

1. They personified specific interests—for example, young single women became fashion leaders because of the importance their group attributed to ways of dressing;
2. They occupied positions considered to be favorable for promoting high levels of competence in the area in question: Thus, elderly women with large families were considered as shopping advisors, because of their greater experience;
3. They were accessible and extroverted individuals, with many relationships ….
4. They had access to relevant information from outside their immediate circle … due either to frequent visits to other cities, or else to uncommon attention to mass media—newspapers, magazines, and radio … with a particular inclination to expose themselves to media …appropriate to their spheres of influence," whether in fashion, cinema, politics,

2   Lazarsfeld, Paul *et al.*, *The People's Choice.* Columbia University Press, New York, 1948.
3   Merton, Robert K. "Patterns of influence: a study of interpersonal influence and communication behavior in a local community." In *Communications Research*. Harper and Bros., New York, 1948/1949.
4   Katz, Elihu and Lazarsfeld, Paul. *Personal influence*. The Free Press, Glencoe, Ill., 1958.

5   Katz, Elihu and Lazarsfeld, Paul. *Op. Cit.*

etc. Moreover, politically and ideologically, they were "the greatest defenders of their factions' attitudes in all possible matters. They also belonged to the greatest number of associations; knew members of their party ... showed greater tendency to seek advice and information from other people."[6]

It fell to French sociologist Dumazedier,[7] in evaluating the role of the opinion leader, to lay out a basic structure, showing the relationship between the mass communicator, who uses mechanical and electronic means to disseminate messages, and the audience (R), with the leader in the center of the dialogue.

However, by emphasizing the incidence of situations involving direct communication from the medium to the public, particularly in areas relating to entertainment, or in external aspects of religion or politics, he includes media other than mass media in his structure, which the leader uses to become informed. More recent research has expanded the hypothesis of the flow of communications: It is not merely a two-stage dissemination, from the media, through the leaders, and to the public under their influence, but rather involves multiple stages, including media, leaders with their closest group, leaders with other leaders, and finally, with the great folk audience.

The correlation between the two systems may be seen in the proposed diagram, which shows the mass communicator—the basic element in the social communication system—as the main source of information. His message, when disseminated throughout the dispersed audience, finds a special recipient—the folk communicator, the opinion leader of the social groups from which the language and deepest meaning of the transmitted information escape.

Through his leadership characteristics and ability to interpret information, this distinguished recipient

becomes (often after consulting other sources, leaders and media) a communicator for an audience who seeks him out and understands him, since he uses vehicles (folk media) that, despite their massive nature (such as radio and printed brochures or flyers), are accessible and familiar to them.

One clear example of this process is the production of messages through Cordel (folk poetry). The folk communicator is one of the countless viewers of the film "The Lost Weekend," produced in Hollywood, which focuses on the issue of alcoholism. Since his audience does not go to movies and is unfamiliar with at least their language, he—the poet of the people—turns the plot into a verse brochure, disguising the characters as people of his own world and sometimes publishing it with manual typesetters and printing presses and, not rarely, with the collaboration of popular xylographers who fortunately still exist in the world of Brazilian Cordel.

The folk communicator has the characteristic personality of opinion leaders, which is observed (and perhaps even more acutely in him) among his colleagues in the social communications system:

1. *prestige in the community, regardless of social or economic position, due to his level of knowledge on specific issues and his sharp perception of their reflections in the life* and customs of his people;
2. *exposure to the messages from the social communication system*, as part of the mass media audience, but filtering the contents through his group's ideas, principles and norms;
3. *frequent contact with authorized external sources of information*, with which he discusses or supplements the information he has collected;
4. *mobility*, making contact with various groups with which he exchanges knowledge and receives valuable assistance; and finally,
5. *deep-rooted philosophical convictions*, based on his traditional beliefs and customs, and the culture of the group to which he belongs, to which he submits ideas and innovations before accepting

6   Lazarsfeld, Paul. "Mass Media and Personal Influence," *Voice of America*, Washington, s/d.
7   Dumazedier, Joffre. *De la sociologia de la comunicación colectiva a la sociologia del desarrollo cultural* [From a collective communication sociology to a cultural development sociology]. CIESPAL, Quito, 1966.

1927
1960
1963
1964
1967
1969
1970
1971
1972
1973
1974
1975
1976
1977
1978
1979
1980
1981
1982
1983
1984
1985
1986
1987
1988
1989
1990
1991
1992
1993
1994
1995
1996
1997
1998
1999
2000
2001
2002
2003
2004
2005
2006

and disseminating them, in order to introduce the changes he deems beneficial to his community's procedure of existence.

While within the social communications system, opinion leaders are often political, scientific, artistic, or economic authorities, in folk-communication there is greater elasticity in their identification: leading folk agent-communicators apparently are not always recognized authorities, but have some kind of charisma, attracting listeners, readers, admirers, and followers, and in general, achieving the position of advisors or guides for the audience without full awareness of the role they play.

In research we conducted in Luziânia, a city in the state of Goiás, which is transitioning from a predominantly rural to an industrially focused community, as a result of its proximity to Brasília, we adopted the snowball technique to find people of extremely low status who had become agents influencing public opinion. In one curious case, the vast majority of local prostitutes identified an elderly gentleman as an advisor on matters of finances, health, social relations, and family (children's education and future). We sought to find and interview him, and discovered that he was a now retired former chief of police: His prestige originated not from any remaining political power, but from the fact that he had treated the prostitutes as human beings while on active duty, never punishing them for their excesses or violations, but rather seeking to understand and help them with guidance.

It should be noted, however, that other such leaders are not only aware of their position but act, sometimes even abusively, to maintain or expand it. Consciously, and in a constructive sense, preachers such as Father Cícero and Friar Damião, songsters and guitarists, pamphlet poets and commentators, popular composers such as Luiz (Lua) Gonzaga and the samba musicians on the hills in Rio de Janeiro, journalists and announcers for small radio stations of the interior have developed and are developing their leadership abilities.

On the other hand, exploiting the credulity and fighting spirit of the public, there still are false preachers, psychics, seers, and religious fanatics, as well as the vast legion of cunning executives and political demagogues who, to the detriment of the communities, took over positions of municipal command from the "colonels," whose political-social performance was admirably set in fiction and as intensely studied by Brazilian sociologists.[8]

The rise to leadership is intimately linked to the credibility that the agent-communicator acquires in his environment, and to his ability to codify the message at his audience's level of understanding. As a result of the discriminatory social structure maintained in nations such as ours, the mass of peasants, the marginalized urban populations, and even the extensive areas of proletarians or the underemployed communicate with one another with a limited vocabulary, organized around the group's own functional meanings.

When the intent is to transmit a message to these individuals, and especially when the contents introduce a new system of values and concepts, as in the case of campaigns to promote change, it is necessary to "translate" the idea for them, adapting it to the recipients' normal value structures. The folk leader-communicator is a translator who knows how to use not only words but also arguments capable of

---

8   In literature, we need only recall the José Lins do Rego novels about the sugar cane cycle, the writings of Jorge Amado about the cacao period, and *O coronel e o lobisomem* [The Colonel and the Werewolf], by José Cândido de Carvalho, some of which have already been transferred to the movies and television. In this latter medium, one cannot ignore the role of "Colonel" Odorico, in *O Bem-Amado* [The Beloved], an adaptation of a play by Dias Gomes. In terms of essays on the topic, we might point out the study by Marcos Vinícius Vilaça and Roberto C. de Albuquerque: *Coronel, Coronéis* [Colonel, Colonels], published by Tempo Brasileiro, of Rio de Janeiro, in 1965, in which the authors analyze the phenomenon, in the entire process of economic, social, and political domination, its development and decline, through the actions of four famous "colonels" from Pernambuco. The book is rich with extensive photographic documentation, maps, statistical tables, and transcriptions of depositions, flyers, and letters.

reaching the pre-logical forms that, according to Levy Bruhl, Bastide, Malinowsky, and other social scientists, characterize thinking and dictate the behavior of these groups.[9]

The Folk-Communication Audience

We have identified the user audiences of folk-communication systems as marginalized, and both the derived expressions and the phenomenon of marginality are susceptible to the widest range of meanings and specific connotations, both in common usage and in the social sciences. In her study on the slums and politics of Rio de Janeiro,[10] Perlmann offers a succinct but clear and orderly explanation of the theory of marginality, identifying the attributes of the marginal status of migrants living in urban slums in their social, cultural, economic, and political dimensions, and constructing an ideal type or paradigm that served as the basis for her research and conclusions. In contrast, Paoli, in a sociological research work,[11] focuses on the role performed by religion and the world of the imaginary, largely disseminated by mass media and often transposed into the folk media, in maintaining dominant relationships imposed by elites on subordinate layers of society, through the symbolic integration caused by these magical experiences. The aforementioned works were the primary source for the basic elements we used in this step, to characterize the folk-communication audience.

The term "marginal" appears in the scientific literature for the first time in 1928, in an article by Robert Park on human migrations, published in the *American Journal of Sociology*. There, the migrant is defined as a "cultural hybrid," a "marginal," who, though he shares the cultural life and traditions of two different peoples, "never decides to break with his past and traditions, even if permitted to do so, and, because of racial prejudice, (is) never completely accepted in the new society in which he seeks to find a place."

Obviously the author refers to the situation of the foreign migrant; however, both the essence of the underlined characteristics (opposition to change/prejudice) and the typification below are consistent with our purpose: "He is an individual at the margin of two cultures and two societies that never completely penetrate and meld with each other." (Emphasis added.) The term subsequently gained a pejorative meaning, with a marginal considered to be a dangerous element, linked to crime, an outlaw, a vagabond, violent, a man or woman who lives on alcohol, drugs, prostitution and theft. By extension, it was applied "to the poor in general, unemployed, migrants, members of other subcultures, racial and ethnic minorities, and deviants of any kind" (Perlmann). The same author notes, among the important points relating to the rise and characterization of marginality that are of particular interest to us, the influence of foreign invasions, as occurred in Latin America, where "the process of colonization involved not only conquest and invasion, but cultural contact and daily manipulation of the indigenous population," which placed existing cultures in a marginal situation; as well as the absence of this phenomenon in tribal or feudal systems, since the former "did not harbor a notion of superiority" and, in the latter, "there was tacit acceptance of one's position and the hierarchical nature of society."

The phenomenon of marginality came about after the bourgeois revolution and its ideology, and worsened with the Industrial Revolution, the conceptual and formal origin of mass society. The upper layers—the economic and political elite—that establish the levels of civilization and goals for development, including sociocultural development, contrast with individuals and groups lacking in the conditions (or to whom the conditions are always denied) for achieving

---

9   See, on this topic: Levy Bruhl., L., *Les fonctions Mentales dans les Societés Inferieures* [Mental Functions in Inferior Societies], Alcan, Paris, 1910; Bastide, Roger: *Sociologie et Psychanalyse* [Sociology and Psychoanalysis], Puf, Paris, 1950; Malinowsky, B., *Estudios de Psicologia Primitiva* [Studies in Primitive Psychology], Paidós, Buenos Aires, 1949.

10 Perlmann, Janice E., *O mito da marginalidade* [The Myth of Marginality], Paz e Terra, Rio de Janeiro, 1977.

11 Paoli, Maria Célia Pinheiro Machado, *Desenvolvimento e marginalidade* [Development and Marginality], Pioneira, São Paulo, 1977.

1927
1960
1963
1964
1967
1969
1970
1971
1972
1973
1974
1975
1976
1977
1978
1979
1980
1981
1982
1983
1984
1985
1986
1987
1988
1989
1990
1991
1992
1993
1994
1995
1996
1997
1998
1999
2000
2001
2002
2003
2004
2005
2006

them, because of their poverty, traditional cultures, geographic, rural, or urban isolationism, and low intellectual level, or their active and conscious non-conformity with the dominant philosophy and/or social structure.

A survey and analysis of these conditions, on which we have focused our studies, resulted in the identification and classification of groups of users of folk communication, through which these are understood to be the marginalized, (and not the marginal, an expression we avoid in order to distance ourselves from its negative connotation), since they are excluded from, not only the political but also the social communication system, both of which are oriented toward preserving the status quo defined by the ideology and planned actions of the governing groups.

Under the adopted criteria, we may distinguish in the folk-communication audience (users) three major groups, to which we will dedicate, as research models, the remaining parts of this essay:

1. Marginalized rural groups, particularly because of their geographic isolationism, economic hardship, and low intellectual level.
2. Marginalized urban groups, comprising individuals situated in the lower strata of society, consisting of the subordinate classes, the disadvantaged, the under-informed, and those with minimal access.
3. Culturally marginalized groups, whether urban or rural, who contest current principles, morals, or social structure.

Since in folk communications, each environment generates its own vocabulary and own syntax, and each agent-communicator employs the channel at hand, which he knows how to operate the best in order for his public to see its way of life, needs, and aspirations reflected in the message, the characterization of any segment of the community as part of one of these groups depends primarily upon researching the specific languages used by the individuals comprising it and the means of expression they use.

It must not be forgotten that while social communication discourses are aimed at the world, folk-communication ones are intended for a world in which words, graphic signs, gestures, attitudes, lines, and shapes are very tenuously linked to the language, writing, dance, rituals, plastic arts, work and leisure, and ultimately, the behavior of the integrated classes of society. These links are similar in their depth to those that exist between Latin and the language spoken in Brazil, or between Catholic doctrine and morals and Umbandist syncretism and ethics. Nevertheless, as we will show below, the rich system we studied contains a trace of universality, possibly more vigorous than the other, which comes from its foundations in folklore, since authentic popular culture has roots, a trunk, and branches so deeply ingrained in human nature that their manifestations seem to derive from a single seed, regardless of race and latitude.

THE MACBRIDE REPORT:
CONCLUSIONS
AND RECOMMENDATIONS

Excerpt from: Many Voices, One World: The MacBride Report

By Sean MacBride

1980

1. Our review of communication the world over reveals a variety of solutions adopted in different countries—in accordance with diverse traditions, patterns of social, economic and cultural life, needs and possibilities. This diversity is valuable and should be respected; there is no place for the universal application of preconceived models. Yet it should be possible to establish, in broad outline, common aims and common values in the sphere of communication, based on common interests in a world of interdependence. The whole human race is threatened by the arms race and by the persistence of unacceptable global inequalities, both of which generate tensions and which jeopardize its future and even its survival. The contemporary situation demands A BETTER, MORE JUST AND MORE DEMOCRATIC SOCIAL ORDER, AND THE REALIZATION OF FUNDAMENTAL HUMAN RIGHTS. These goals can be achieved only through understanding and tolerance, gained in large part by free, open and balanced communications.

2. The review has also shown that the utmost importance should be given to eliminating imbalances and disparities in communication and its structures, and particularly in information flows. Developing countries need to reduce their dependence, and claim a new, more just and more equitable order in the field of communication. This issue has been fully debated in various settings; the time has now come to move from principles to substantive reforms and concrete action.

3. Our conclusions are founded on the firm conviction that communication is a basic individual right, as well as a collective one required by all communities and nations. Freedom of information—and, more specifically the right to seek, receive and impart information—is a fundamental human right; indeed, a prerequisite for many others. The inherent nature of communication means that its fullest possible exercise and potential depend on the surrounding political, social and economic conditions, the most vital of these being democracy within countries and equal, democratic relations between them. It is in this context that the democratization of communication at national and international levels, as well as the larger role of communication in democratizing society, acquires utmost importance.

4. For these purposes, it is essential to develop comprehensive national communication policies linked to overall social, cultural and economic development objectives. Such policies should evolve from broad consultations with all sectors concerned and adequate mechanisms for wide participation of organized social groups in their definition and implementation. National governments as much as the international community should recognize the urgency of according communications higher priority in planning and funding. Every country should develop its communication patterns in accordance with its own conditions, needs and traditions, thus strengthening its integrity, independence and self-reliance.

5. The basic considerations which are developed at length in the body of our Report are intended to provide a framework for the development of a new information and communication order. We see its implementation as an on-going process of change in the nature of relations between and within nations in the field of communications. Imbalances in national information and communication systems are as disturbing and unacceptable as social, economic, cultural and technological,

1927
1960
1963
1964
1967
1969
1970
1971
1972
1973
1974
1975
1976
1977
1978
1979
1980
1981
1982
1983
1984
1985
1986
1987
1988
1989
1990
1991
1992
1993
1994
1995
1996
1997
1998
1999
2000
2001
2002
2003
2004
2005
2006

both national and international disparities. Indeed, rectification of the latter is inconceivable in any true or lasting sense without elimination of the former. Crucial decisions concerning communication development need to be taken urgently, at both national and international levels. These decisions are not merely the concern of professionals, researchers or scholars, nor can they be the sole prerogative of those holding political or economic power. The decision-making process has to involve social participation at all levels. This calls for new attitudes for overcoming stereotyped thinking and to promote more understanding of diversity and plurality, with full respect for the dignity and equality of peoples living in different conditions and acting in different ways.

Thus our call for reflection and action is addressed broadly to governments and international organizations, to policy-makers and planners, to the media and professional organizations, to researchers, communication practitioners, to organized social groups and the public at large.

THE ROLE OF INFORMATION IN COMMUNICATING WITH THE RURAL POOR: SOME REFLECTIONS

Excerpt from: An Alternative Pattern of Basic Education: Radio Santa Maria

By Emile G. McAnany

1980 During the past several years, the nonaligned nations have held several symposia concerning the flow of information among different countries of the world. They confirmed, not surprisingly, that they were informationally, as well as economically, dependent upon advanced countries especially the United States. To promote a new economic order, they agreed, first, to take control of their information systems, both to stem the tide of one-sided news, cultural programs and other kinds of information coming from advanced capitalist countries and to turn their information resources internally toward promoting the social and economic welfare of their own people, especially the masses of poor people in rural areas (for example, Ma Ekonzo and Basri 1976).

Not many years before, the U.S. Congress had directed the Department of State (U.S. Congress 1975) to create a priority in foreign assistance for the poorest countries and the poor majority in these countries. A similar priority was proposed in 1973 by Robert McNamara of the World Bank, the development assistance loans of that reached a record of nearly $9 billion in 1978 (World Bank 1978). A significant amount of money from the World Bank has been spent on rural development to help raise productivity of small farmers and to meet basic human needs for food, shelter, education and health services.

One point of convergence among both nonaligned countries and international aid agencies is a growing belief in the importance of information, education and communication (IEC) to promote goals of increased material welfare and improved social services for the rural poor of low-income countries. It is not enough to create more schools or even adult, nonformal education schemes if the immediate needs of people for information in their everyday lives are not met by access to this information through some kind of communication system. ...

Some Basic Assumptions About Information's Role

In The Design of Rural Development (1975), World Bank economist Uma Lele designates a number of key areas where improvement would impact on the productivity and income of farmers—the backbone of most Third World countries. These are agricultural extension, local farmer participation, credit, marketing, social services, project administration and training.

If these areas are analysed carefully, in each activity is found an information component that is assumed by the author but is hardly touched upon in the text. In extension, for example, the agent is basically the source of new information. In most of the Third World, these agents are in such short supply that they reach only a fraction of the farmers, yet there may be other ways, such as mass media, of diffusing the same information to a much larger portion of the target population. Local participation, when it is a built-in goal of a project, can be promoted by both interpersonal and mediated communication. It also depends upon a feedback mechanism, so that information flows in both directions.

Credit is obviously a resource; but it is also often an underused service in rural areas, because the poor, isolated farmers may not know about it. Information about the availability of credit could change this. Marketing depends, in an intimate way, on information, and if the communication system is strictly a proprietary one, its benefits go to those who control it. A more open market information system, on radio perhaps, would help to promote equity. Social services in rural areas are a mix of material resources and information, whether they are concerned with adult education, health, family planning, and nutrition or community development. Administration of rural services also heavily depends on communication. For example, a two-way communication system, often missing entirely in rural areas, could keep field personnel in touch with central project leaders. Finally, training is obviously a largely information-based activity.

What this brief exercise is meant to illustrate is that almost every activity considered vital to rural development is information related or information dependent in some way. The argument for paying increased attention to this aspect of rural development should not be taken to mean that communication can be substituted completely for other resources, but only that a better mix of material and information resources can achieve a better result, perhaps at less cost.

There are a number of assumptions about information's role that need to be carefully examined within the context of the new approach, alluded to above, in which governments are placing more emphasis on mobilizing national information resources for national development goals, especially regarding the poor, rural majority. The author will identify and discuss briefly some of the more important assumptions in the following paragraph.

Equity

There are two assumptions about the equity properties of information that need careful scrutiny in a Third World context. The first characteristic of information that seems to promote equity is that, unlike material resources, information (or education) is not a zero-sum phenomenon. Giving it to others does not take it away from another. But information that has any potential for economic impact is assimilated immediately into the prevailing economic structure. Information concerning manufacturing processes, or even management know-how, is proprietary and

1927
1960
1963
1964
1967
1969
1970
1971
1972
1973
1974
1975
1976
1977
1978
1979
1980
1981
1982
1983
1984
1985
1986
1987
1988
1989
1990
1991
1992
1993
1994
1995
1996
1997
1998
1999
2000
2001
2002
2003
2004
2005
2006

sold to Third World customers like any other commodity (Goulet 1977; Oettinger 1977). Information, if not "owned" by someone, is often available to those in power to serve their own economic interests. Third World government officials can use their knowledge of international aid to help direct these resources to areas of the country where they own or can acquire property. Information too widely diffused can lose its economic value, just as too many primary school degrees can devalue the education investment of many Third World people.

The second assumption about equity that needs to be questioned is that public information with potential value reaches everyone. The rural poor are isolated from such public information that could be useful by a series of filters that makes reaching them more difficult than reaching other groups. Thus, they are often physically isolated, illiterate, perhaps speaking the dominant language poorly, if at all, without a radio, and suspicious of information coming from a government long exploitative, or at least negligent, of their needs.

Cost Efficiency

It is assumed, often correctly so, that technologies such as radio or print can provide massive public information in substitution, for example, of human information carriers, such as social service agents. Thus, insofar as radio can substitute for or complement the work of an agricultural extension agent, it can reach more people at a lower cost than the agent alone. What needs careful review, however, is whether it is the information that most small farmers lack or the resources needed to put the information into practice (Grunig 1971).

Feasibility

Governments often assume that a plan on paper can be translated directly and easily into action, with all of the promised benefits of increased information and education, through the media. This overlooks the historical record of the success/failure rate of such projects and does not take seriously the constraints to implementation that limit impact. Thus, planners often point to a few examples of relative success without carefully specifying the particular factors in these cases that may have contributed to the success (McAnany 1978b).

Change Model

There is often an assumption that the problems of the rural poor are of a technical, rather than political, nature and that with sufficient care in planning and resource input they can be resolved on a technical level. Unless all the structural limitations are considered within the political context of their origin and continuation, the role of information and its impact will be judged only as a technical matter. Examples of information used to mobilize masses of the rural poor in Tanzania (Hall 1978) or Cuba (Fagen 1969), for example, can be found that are heavily political in their contents, yet practical in their outcomes for health or adult literacy. One fundamental assumption in any program is the extent to which the government is willing to make political choices to bring about this change (for example, land tenure policies that are highly controversial in nature). All of this argues for the dual nature of the problem as being both political and technical.

Change Rates

There are always constraints, both internal and external, to a project that limits the impact of information or education to ensure maximum potential change possible in the given environment. The ratio of maximum change is often unspecified in projects for the rural poor or based on unfounded positive assumptions. Thus, for example, more information, training and credit for small farmers with only one or two acres of land may have a maximum of, say, a 6 percent increase in income, even if everything works perfectly in a project to help these farmers. Because they already may be working at almost maximum efficiency on their small plots of land, they cannot significantly change their productivity or their income without major changes either in land tenure or cropping patterns and market structures. The question here is not whether some, but how much, change is possible. There is an additional question of whether a little change may not be counterproductive by delaying recognition of the need for more fundamental structural change.

Unless these assumptions are carefully examined, there is a danger of misleading people with the promise of significant benefits from investing in information for the rural poor. This danger holds even for those countries in the Third World that have managed to gain control of their national information system and have turned off much of the "free flow" of information from outside.

The Information Environment of the Rural Poor

If the postindustrial society in the most advanced nations is being referred to as an information society in which information replaces energy as the basic economic component (Parker 1976), by contrast, the least developed sectors of the Third World are those least rich in the kind of information likely to have direct economic impact. We know very little about the information environment of the rural poor of the Third World. Our knowledge is often fragmented, according to the disciplinary interests of those researching the question.

There is a good deal of research in the area of agricultural economics and economic anthropology concerning how small farmers or others involved in rural marketing get information and make decisions (for example, Myren 1970); there is an extensive literature on the diffusion of innovations among farmers and other Third World groups (Rogers and Shoemaker 1971); and there are studies, among anthropologists especially, of how traditional communication systems work through such channels as plays, mimes and town criers.

Some sociologists and political scientists, studying the media's role in the Third World, find that consumerist messages from commercial media are more powerful to persuade the poor to purchase Coca Cola or powdered milk than to adopt more positive nutritional behaviours (Wells 1972; Beltran 1976b).

There is, however, very little good descriptive evidence of the comprehensive information environment of the rural poor, nor even a good description of the process of the penetration of the mass media into rural areas. We know, for example, even from national statistics (UNESCO 1978), that both radio and television have grown exponentially over the last two decades in all Third World countries. Partial evidence also permits us to assume that some of this growth, especially in radio, has taken place in rural areas. But there is only scattered empirical evidence concerning the exposure of rural audiences, what the content of the media messages are (Seya and Yao 1977), and how they might affect the quality of users' lives (Contreras 1979).

To pursue an examination of the role of information for improving the quality of life of the rural poor, a hypothetical taxonomy of the information environment in which they live must be proposed.

Among the interpersonal forms of communication through which rural people will be likely to receive and give information are the family and neighbourhood, markets and washing areas and festival gatherings for the village. Institutional networks would involve the church or religious network, the administrative structure, the political party, the school, police or army and such government service agencies as agricultural extension, health and family planning among others that might operate in the village.

For the mediated forms of mass communication, there are radio, film, posters, printed materials (such as newspapers and pamphlets) and television. Among the person-to-person media there are the telephone, telex or telegraph and mail systems.

There are two sets of questions concerning these forms of communicating information in the rural environment. What functions do the various kinds of media perform in different rural environments, and how widespread are the various communication structures? There is no empirical evidence to make any

1927
1960
1963
1964
1967
1969
1970
1971
1972
1973
1974
1975
1976
1977
1978
1979
1980
1981
1982
1983
1984
1985
1986
1987
1988
1989
1990
1991
1992
1993
1994
1995
1996
1997
1998
1999
2000
2001
2002
2003
2004
2005
2006

useful generalizations about either of the questions, so the form information takes in rural environments must be speculative, for the most part.

On the interpersonal level, communication of a variety of information can be traced through social networks. The role of networks in the study of communication is increasingly recognized by scholars (Rogers 1977). A number of social networks—such as neighbourhoods, traditional markets and wandering merchants or performers—are part of the traditional structure of rural communications and still function, for the most part, as they always have. They serve as communication networks for the kinds of content that usually flow in each neighbourhood, such as news and gossip, cultural information reinforcing traditional values and price information on local goods. Although such networks, as well as folk media, could be used to transmit other kinds of development information, no successful formula has yet been devised to tap into this potentially rich resource on a large scale.

The social and political institutions typically serving rural areas have important communication functions to perform. Usually, the information serves to promote the continuation of the structures of society (one thinks of such institutions as schools, churches, armies and political administrations in many rural areas). However, there are some types of information that directly benefit people—as, for example, information to farmers concerning available credit, or to rural women concerning health or nutritional practices.

The mass medium that one is most likely to encounter among poor rural people is radio. There may be a few printed materials, such as the Bible or the Koran and perhaps a pamphlet or two. It is unlikely that newspapers come regularly to the isolated village, at least to more than a few households; nor is it likely that there is a cinema, television, posters, telegraph or telephone available (although some form of mail service may bring letters to local officials).

Looking at the hypothetical rural information environment, then, one can conclude that probably there are not many channels functioning to bring development information to rural people. There are a number of traditional networks, but these function for traditional purposes. Modern media, with the exception of radio, are almost nonexistent. This leads analysts to one of several strategies in efforts to help the rural poor: (1) an attempt to use traditional media and networks to introduce new information and behavioural change; (2) an attempt to place more information agents in the service institutions of agriculture, health, education and community development; and/ or (3) an attempt to increase the availability of information through radio or other mass media, if they can be more widely and equitably distributed.

Constraints on an Information / Communication Approach

The problems or constraints that face attempts to improve the economic and social levels of the rural poor are numerous. Only a few of the more general ones can be alluded to here.

POLITICAL CONSTRAINTS

One very good indicator of a government's priority for a social program is the size of the budget it allocates to the effort. The rural poor are not often high on anyone's priority list, but when they are, they are so numerous that projects, which are often pilot programs, have little impact on the overall problem. They are, by definition, that proportion (whatever the percentage one wishes to choose—30, 50, 70 or 90 percent) of the population that is the hardest to reach and has the least education, the worst health conditions, the least cash income and the least number of material resources, such as land. This immediately makes it not only much more difficult to communicate with the rural poor but also—though politicians often do not wish to recognize it—much more costly. For most governments, the first problem encountered in serving the rural poor is the dilemma of cost. Communication projects for these people may promise to save money, but often these costs are based upon comparisons with delivering information to urban audiences or the highly motivated rural elite, not to the hard-to-reach mass of rural people.

The second problem is knowing how much difference information can make on the structural constraints of rural areas. Agricultural knowledge, as has been mentioned, may not be able to make any significant impact on the productivity of very small farm holdings, already at almost a maximum of efficiency (Daines 1975; O'Sullivan 1978b). Another structural problem related to land tenure is the increasing number of landless labourers in rural areas. For them, much information concerning agriculture may be useless. They are not needed on very small farms, where the owner and family do the work; and they cannot be absorbed into larger farms, where investment is in more technology rather than more labour. Even if they are not pushed towards the city, the usual kind of agricultural information is irrelevant because any increased productivity that may result from applying new knowledge will go to their employer, not to themselves.

The third problem is that of the credibility of the source of information. If the poor are at the bottom of the social system, they will have a built-in bias against information from a government source, unless that government has taken some clear steps to improve their situation. The danger that the poor may see in government information is that it can be self-serving and political and may simply be a device to substitute words for concrete actions in helping rural people.

These first three constraints suggest that the approach to a "solution" to the problem of the rural poor is a political one, rooted in the history of the country and the structures that continue to support the status quo; however, the political solution is not the only aspect of importance, and a look at the technical constraints must be considered as well. How much of a technical solution is possible within a given set of political constraints is what has been referred to above under the assumption of the change ratio, how much room for manoeuvre is there in a situation?

TECHNICAL CONSTRAINTS

If it is correct to assume that the government is willing to invest a reasonable amount of money in rural areas, but is unable or unwilling to make basic structural changes, there are some technical constraints that can hinder even the relative amount of change possible. These constraints are primarily internal to the project and concern the efficiency and effectiveness of its operation, whereas the constraints discussed above are external and concern not the short-term objectives but the longer-term goals of projects.

At the level of planning, development communication projects often ignore the most elementary principles in defining their goals as based on the objective needs of the people. Moreover, the goals are often unrealistic in their ambitions. There are often a series of empirical assumptions underlying the ultimate goal of a project for which there is little empirical evidence. Thus, a radio project in agriculture may assume that the rural poor own sufficient radios to listen in great numbers to radio messages, that most people speak the language of broadcast well enough to receive the messages or that the information, once applied, can lead to increased productivity regardless of the land size of most of the farms in the area. With careful planning, many of these assumptions can be checked before going ahead with implementation, but such planning research is frequently not done.

Lack of significant leadership within a project may be an important constraint hindering both planning and implementation. One project in Guatemala, which lost its original leader, failed for two years to clearly decide on the objectives it wished to pursue. In contrast, the success of Columbia's Acción Cultural Popular (ACPO) radio project during the 30 years of its existence is in large part due to the leadership of its founder.

At the institutional level, communication projects often cut across a number of rival bureaucracies—such as broadcasting, education, agriculture and health, to mention only the most common. Attempts to get coordination have not worked *well* in rural

1927
1960
1963
1964
1967
1969
1970
1971
1972
1973
1974
1975
1976
1977
1978
1979
1980
1981
1982
1983
1984
1985
1986
1987
1988
1989
1990
1991
1992
1993
1994
1995
1996
1997
1998
1999
2000
2001
2002
2003
2004
2005
2006

education in projects in Brazil and Guatemala (McAnany and Oliveira, forthcoming; O'Sullivan 1977) and in the Ivory Coast (Lenglet 1976). It seems easier to define goals narrowly under the jurisdiction of one institution than to broaden the scope of rural communication and risk the problems caused by shared responsibility and bureaucratic rivalries. Yet, the integrated approach to rural development could have important benefits if institutional constraints could be overcome. Some small, self-contained private groups often can achieve a more integrated approach, although on a more limited scale (White 1976).

Carefully planned and executed teaching/learning strategies that have had success in formal schooling have not had comparable development for rural adults in the less formal learning areas of agriculture, health, nutrition and the like. There are questions of sequential versus nonsequential programming, organized versus open audiences, motivational versus didactic approaches and active versus passive response modes of reception, that all need testing among rural adult audiences.

How best to organize the audience for reception and follow-up action is both an obvious need, in most cases, and a basic constraint. Esman (1974) sees the organization of small farmers into cooperative groups as an essential element in successfully helping them to increase their agricultural productivity. But organizing the rural poor runs into the technical problems of creating a structure, where none has existed, and financing it, as well as winning the trust and loyalty of persons long suspicious of external agencies. But there is also a major political problem in organizing a group: The rural majority, who are very sensitive. There is a fear of widespread mobilization of the rural poor. Elliot (1974) speaks of the difficulty that creating animation groups in the rural Ivory Coast caused the government, and of their eventual elimination.

Many rural projects are constrained by a lack not only of leadership but also of trained persons in such areas as educational planning and broadcast production and evaluation. This is in part due to the general scarcity of trained persons for any kind of rural development project and, in part, to the specialized skills in broadcasting and communications that are demanded in this case. Once people have received some training in these areas, they often are hired away by the private sector or other government agencies. It is also clear that unless people are personally committed to the work, they are less likely to want to stay in rural, rather than urban-oriented, projects.

The bureaucratic constraint is a significant one for the administration of *rural* projects and may account for a large part of the inefficiency and failure that is reported in the literature of rural development projects. How this might be avoided or improved has no easy answers. The size of the project may be one aspect of the problem, but commitment to a set of common goals may be a significant element as well. Such commitment is rare across government bureaucratic structures.

A final constraint is one already touched upon above but worth mentioning separately; this concerns the participation of rural people in projects directed towards them. There are a number of policy statements by lending institutions, as well as by politicians from Third World governments, concerning participation of rural people in their own development. There are many meanings and degrees of participation and ways to measure it, but the basic starting point concerns who and how many of the target audience take part in the project.

Many rural projects simply have reached too few of the right people to have made any significant impact on the problems of the rural poor. Self-selection is the problem with most projects of this kind. Where information is available, those who are most likely to take advantage of it are the relatively better off. This phenomenon is clear in communication projects where information or education may be freely available to all, but taken advantage of by few; the result is a widening of a knowledge gap among different social classes. The same thing happens in other kinds of interventions where services or other public goods are offered, as in the adoption of innovations (Rolling, Ascroft, and Chege 1976). Unless some way is found to overcome the structural bias against participation of the rural poor, by some carefully planned strategy to diminish the self-selection bias, the result of programs for the rural poor will be not only unsuccessful but often even counterproductive, making the poor relatively worse off than before. …

Impact of Information: Potential and Real

Education is sometimes thought of as training in how to process a wider spectrum of information. One problem with simply making more information available in rural areas is that the rural poor are generally illiterate or without much formal education, and their ability to take advantage of new information may be limited. With the spread of the nonprint mass media, such as radio and television, however, information can be made more accessible in verbal and audiovisualbased messages, instead of those coded in printed language.

A second consideration is the possibility of substituting mass media for expensive extension agents in rural areas. Agricultural productivity, for example, could be significantly improved by the regular visits of an extension agent to farmers; but when the agent can visit only a small fraction of the potential clientele, as often happens, radio might provide the information more widely. In health or nutrition education, information vital for preventive medicine may be substituted for health educators, who are in chronic short supply. The same analysis can be made for nutrition, education and community development.

As a support to field agents, information in the form of nonformal didactic messages, appropriately organized and presented, can supplement a poorly trained group leader or field agent. This is especially true in educational programs where a teacher's skills may be limited yet the teacher can guide the students in a form of self-education that can be quite effective.

These two strategies of substitution for development agents or support of development agents with added media messages are important to consider seriously, because their successful application could mean a substantial saving in the cost, as well as in the improved effectiveness, of rural projects.

It must be asked what evidence there is, or might be developed, to test the validity of either of the two strategies of substitution or supplementation suggested above. In agricultural productivity, we find in Lockheed, Jamison and Lau (forthcoming) and Ashby et al. (1977) evidence that there is a consistent, although small, positive relationship between education and agricultural productivity. The same is true, to a lesser degree, for information, extension agent visits and some forms of nonformal education (for example, literacy). If projects can massively provide appropriate agricultural information via radio to a significant number of rural listeners, then some benefits may accrue from this exposure. Some evidence for this appears in a rural project in Guatemala (Academy for Educational Development 1978).

In the field of health care, health and nutrition education and family planning, there is much less evidence, although the potential would seem greater than for agriculture. This is true because health practices may be adopted without as many resource inputs as in agriculture, where results depend not just on practice but resources (credit) to buy fertilizers, seeds, pesticides, tools and the like. White (1977), for example, found that in a group of Honduran villages that received health and agricultural information from a local radio station, the health practices were employed significantly more often than were the agricultural practices—presumably, as the author believes, because it cost little or nothing to adopt the health practices.

Nutrition and environment education (concerning latrines, water supply and the like) are two high-potential areas where slight improvements would have much wider consequences on the quality of life than may appear. Improved nutrition practice may have an indirect but significant impact on size, mortality and cognitive growth of children, while improved water and latrinization can help improve health, as

1927
1960
1963
1964
1967
1969
1970
1971
1972
1973
1974
1975
1976
1977
1978
1979
1980
1981
1982
1983
1984
1985
1986
1987
1988
1989
1990
1991
1992
1993
1994
1995
1996
1997
1998
1999
2000
2001
2002
2003
2004
2005
2006

well as raise agricultural productivity and the level of employment. Hall (1978) provides a case study of a massive mobilization of almost two million rural people in Tanzania for a public health radio campaign, the short-term benefits of which included an estimated 750,000 latrines built. Experimental efforts to use radio spot announcements in several Third World countries (that is, Ecuador, the Philippines and Nicaragua) to get mothers to adopt simple nutritional practices also seem to have had some success (Cooke and Romweber 1977).

Finally, in the area of nonformal education for agriculture, health, literacy and the like, we come closer to a relatively information-weighted practice. There have been a number of efforts to use low-cost communication technologies, especially radio, in the education of rural people (Spain, Jamison and McAnany 1977; Jamison and McAnany 1978). There are several examples in the Dominican Republic (White 1976), Nicaragua (Suppes, Searle and Friend 1979) and Tanzania (Hall 1978) where results have been encouraging.

Some examples of rural projects have been mentioned that have had success in providing better information to rural areas, but there is a need to review the circumstances of each project carefully and to estimate the potential impact it has for improving the lives of the rural poor. The structural context is something that enters into the outcome of any communication strategy and considerably modifies the potential benefit of most projects. For example, Spain (1977) argues that even if we could educate rural children in Mexico to finish primary school, the rural environment would not provide employment for those graduates. The positive impact of education and information on agricultural productivity may be considerably lessened when we look at traditional subsistence farms separately and not lump together large and middle-sized farms with very small plots. Mexican researchers found that in a second trial of the impact of their version of "Sesame Street" in rural Mexico, there was no replication of the positive findings among the poor

of Mexico City (Diaz-Guerrero et al. 1976). Grunig (1971) found—among Colombian peasants—that although information can help an individual adapt to a changing situation, "it can do little to change the situation." The small subsistence farmers may not lack for information but often cannot use it in any productive way because of structural constraints such as land size or lack of credit. The principle for planning information strategies that pay off for the poor seems to be a careful estimate of the ratio for potential change in the target area of each project.

Policy Alternatives For Information's Role

There are two ways to analyse the problems of the rural poor—a political analysis of the factors that have caused and continue to help keep the poor "in their place" and an analysis of the problem that looks for a technical solution to the situation. In neither case is the author satisfied with the solution offered in isolation from the other. It has been suggested that both kinds of analysis be made and that, ultimately, the problem demands an integrated solution, both political and technical.

Thus, for countries that, politically, have made serious choices to put equity into practice, the technical analysis may be a help in carrying out such a development goal more effectively. Tanzania, for example, has tried to further the benefits of its equity principle for the rural masses through radio mobilization campaigns. For those countries that do not put priority on equity, there may be some benefit for the rural poor in a careful technical approach to an information strategy. Thus, at given historical moments, even status quo-oriented governments may allow their own agencies or private groups to promote programs that try to mobilize rural people for development. But content of the campaign may make political differences, so that a rural health and nutrition education campaign might clash less with vested interests in rural areas than an agricultural campaign that may arrive at the fundamental necessity for land reform.

There are two sets of policy recommendations that must be briefly mentioned in this context—those that help ensure IEC prospects of benefiting the right people in rural areas (that is, the poor and the relatively better-off farmers), and those that ensure IEC projects achieve a more effective outcome, regardless of selection.

At the political and administrative level should be placed certain preconditions for the planning of IEC projects:

1. There should be a serious political commitment of the government to improve the conditions of the rural poor (an important but not exclusive measure is the budget commitment).
2. The project should not be a pilot project, but involve enough people so that it will be more difficult, if the project succeeds, for a future government to cut it off.
3. There should be a clear-cut mechanism for involving the target audience itself (participation in planning, implementation, definition of needs and sharing in benefits).
4. There should be an integrated approach covering several areas of rural need (for example, health education, agricultural practice, nutrition education, environmental hygiene), so that a broader participation of rural people is encouraged.

All of these provisions are applicable to governments that have sought political and technical solutions to rural poverty and those that seek only a technical solution. At the technical planning level, there are several recommendations to be made:

1. There should be an analysis of different substantive areas for rural change projects (for example, health and nutrition, agriculture, literacy, small industry and the like) in which the physical resource/information trade-off is most clear.
2. There should be a careful task analysis within those areas that hold the most promise....

3. There should be a study of the self-selection mechanisms of rural audiences and a subsequent monitoring of the information/resource delivery, to assure the project planners that not only the right people are selected but also that they continue to receive the services.
4. There should be a policy study to decide whether investment in a greater number of smaller, private projects or in fewer, large-scale government projects in rural development would be more beneficial.
5. There should be an evaluation not only of the shorter- but also of the longer-term benefits of IEC projects for their impact on rural equity.

Currently, there is much attention being given to the question of a now international economic order and to a new information world order. If Third World countries succeed in freeing their communication systems from undue influence and control by metropolitan countries, they face the vital stage of transforming their communication infrastructure into a system that will, in turn, help to create a better economic base for their people. A major task that confronts most countries is to try to equalize the difference between their urban and rural populations.

The role that information might play in this task of helping rural people to lead more productive, healthy lives depends not only on political decisions concerning the struggle to eliminate structural blocks to growth, but also on a decision to use their own information resources in the most appropriate way in that struggle.

References

Academy fo Educational Development. 1978. "The Basic Village Education Project, Guatemala: Final Report." Washington, D.C.: AED.

Ashby, J., S. Klees, D. Pachico, and S. Wells. 1977. Agricultural Development and Human Capital: The Impact of Education and Communications. Palo Alto, Calif. :EDUTEL.

Beltran, L. 1976. "TV Etchings in the Minds of Latin Americans: Conservatisms, Materialism and Communism." Paper read at the conference of the International Association of Mass Communication Research, Leicester, United Kingdom.

1927
1960
1963
1964
1967
1969
1970
1971
1972
1973
1974
1975
1976
1977
1978
1979
1980
1981
1982
1983
1984
1985
1986
1987
1988
1989
1990
1991
1992
1993
1994
1995
1996
1997
1998
1999
2000
2001
2002
2003
2004
2005
2006

Contreras, E. 1979. "Communication, Rural Modernity and Structural Constraints." Ph.D. Dissertation, Stanford University.

Cooke, T., and S. Romweber. 1977. Radio Advertising Techniques and Nutrituion Education: A Summary of Field Experiments in the Phillippines and Nicaragua. New York: Manoff International.

Daines, S., and H. Howell. 1975. Guatemala Farm Policy Analysis. Washington, D.C.: Agency for International Development, Latin American Bureau.

Elliot, H. 1974. "Animation Rural and Encadrement Technique in the Ivory Coast." Discussion Paper no. 40. Ann Arbor: University of Michigan, Center for Research on Economic Development.

Esman, M. 1974. "Popular Participation and Feedback Systems in Rural Development." In Communication Strategies for Rural Development: Proceedings of the Cornell-DIAT Symposium. Ithaca, N.Y.: Cornell University Press.

Fagen, R. 1969. The Transformation of Political Culture in Cuba. Stanford, Calif.: Stanford University Press.

Goulet, D. 1977. The Uncertain Promise: Value Conflicts in Technology Transfer. New York: IDOC/North America.

Grunig, J. 1971. Communications and Economic Decision Making of Columbian Peasants. Economic Development and Cultural Change. 18: 580-97.

Hall, B. 1978. Mt Ni Afya: Tanzania's Health Campaign. Washington, D.D. Academy for International Development.

Lele, U. 1975. The Design of Rural Development: Lessons from Africa. Baltimore: Johns Hopkins University Press.

Lenglet, F. 1978. "Out of School Educational Television in the Ivory Coast: Its Effectiveness in Rural Development." Ph.D. Dissertation, Stanford University.

Lockheed, M., D. Jamison, and L. Lau. Forthcoming. "Farmer Education and Farm Efficiency: A Survey." Economic Development and Cultural Change.

Ma Ekonzo, E., and T. Baari. 1976. "Final Report of the Second Committee: Role of Information in Consolidating Economic and Social Cooperation among Nonaligned Nations." Report of the Symposium of the Nonaligned Nations on Information, Tunis, March.

Rolling, N., J. Ascroft, and F. Chege. 1978. "Success or Failure of Communication Technology in the Third Word: By What Criteria Shall We Judge?" Paper read at the United Nations Educational, Scientific and Cultural Organization conference on Economic Analysis for Educational Technology Decisions, Dijon, France.

McAnany, E., and J. Oliveira. Forthcoming. The SACI/EXERN Project in Brazil: An Analytical Case Study. Paris: United Nations Educational, Scientific and Cultural Organization, Reports and Papers on Mass Communication.

Myren, D., ed. 1970. "Strategies for Increasing Agricultural Productivity on Small Holdings." Mexico City: International Maize and Wheat Improvement Center.

Oettinger, A., and J. Legates. 1977. "International Formation and Communication Issues: An Overview and International Security." In Congressional Record, vol. 123, no. 101, S, 9534-9537, June 13, 1977.

O'Sullivan, J. 1978. "Rural Development Programs among Marginal Farmers in the Western Highlands of Guatemala." Stanford, Calif.; Stanford University, Institute for Communication Research.

O'Sullivan, J. 1977. Personal Communication

Parker, E. 1976. "Social Implications of Computer/Telecommunications Systems." In OECD Informative Study: Conference on Computer/ Telecommunications. Paris: Organization for Economic Cooperation and Development.

Rogers, E. 1977. "Network Analysis of Diffusion of Family Planning Innovations." In Social Networks: Surveys, Advances and Commentaries, edited by P.W. Holland and S. Leinhardt, New York: Academic Press.

Rolling, N., J. Ascroft, and F. Chege. 1976. "The Diffusion of Innovations and the Issue of Equity in Rural Development. " Communication Research 3, no. 2: 155-70.

Seyr, P., and F. Yao. 1977. Television for the Rural African Village: Studies of Audiences and Impact in the Ivory Coast. Washington, D.C.: Academy for Educational Development.

Shore, I. 1978. "Mass Media for Development: A Reexamination of Access, Exposure and Impact." In Communication with the Rural Poor of the Third World: Does Information Make a Difference?, edited by E. McAnany. Stanford, Calif.: Stanford University, Institute for Communication Research.

United Nations Educational, Scientific and Cultural Organization. 1978. UNESCO Statistical Yearbook, 1976. Paris: UNESCO.

U.S., Congress. Committee on International Relations. 1975. Implementation of "New Directions in Development Assistance. Report prepared by the Agency for International Development, 94th Cong., 1st sess., July 22, 1975.

Wells, A. 1972. Picture-Tube Imperialism? The Impact of U.S. Television in Latin America. Maryknoll, NY. Orbis Books.

White, R. 1977. "Mass Communication and the Popular Promotion Strategy of Rural Development in Honduras." In Radio for Education and Development: Case Studies, edited by P. Spain, D. Jamison, and E. McAnany. Working Paper 266. 2 vols. Washington, D.C.: World Bank.

White, R. 1976. "An Alternative Pattern of Basic Education: Radio Santa Maria." Series No. 30. United Nations Educational, Scientific and Cultural Organization. Institute for Education, Experiments and Innovations in Education.

PHILIPPINE THEATRE ARTS AS DEVELOPMENT COMMUNICATION

Excerpt from: Continuity and Change in Communication Systems: An Asian Perspective

By Victor Valbuena

1980

"One of the main functions of the arts as communication is to transmit and reinforce beliefs, customs and values. In some art traditions this function may be extended to instruction or propaganda." —*Ralph L. Beals*

With the change in the political structure of the Philippines in 1972 came a change in the communication system, particularly in the operation and utilization of the various communication media. An ideology was imposed on the communication system, leading to a redirection of the media from predominantly entertainment to information, education and propaganda, as well. This ideology demanded the effective marshalling of all available resources and services in support of the country's development plans. Local development planners recognized that communication, as an intensified and organized activity, is a resource with great potential to rally popular support and positive action toward national development goals. Therefore, a policy of communication for national development must be the main thrust of the country's communication network if it is to be relevant in shaping the Philippine future.

The *theatre arts,* as a medium and as part of the total communication system, must assume a larger dimension and play a more challenging role, directed toward a more meaningful realization of its potential.

Conceptual Framework

The concept of using theatre arts as a channel for development-oriented communication derives from a synthesis of the basic philosophy of development communication as stated by Quebral (1972), Jamias (1973–1975), Mercado (1976) and Braid (1979). Quebral defines development communication as the "art and sciences of human communication applied to the speedy transformation of a country and the mass of its people from poverty to a dynamic state of economic growth that makes possible equality and the larger fulfillment of the human potential." Jamias categorically states the major ideas that characterized development communication: It is purposive, value-laden and pragmatic. Thus, the results of development communication should be judged by criteria determined by the communicator according to specific behavioral objectives.

Mercado defines development communication as an "incremental process which starts with the diffusion of new information and technology which stimulate people to bring about conditions in the environment favorable to maximum productivity and the improvement of general well-being." Braid says that development communication requires communication personnel to go beyond their traditional roles: "The communicator's role will be that of enabling people to express their aspirations through available media and to assist them in attaining greater productivity."

Common to all of these definitions is the purposive nature of communication—its intent to influence knowledge, attitude and behavior with the goal of improving the quality of human life. It is assumed that information, instruction and persuasive or motivations communication are carefully planned inputs of development. Invariably, a multichannel approach is employed with the various forms of theatre arts fitting into the whole scheme of communication strategy. Theatre can be utilized as a medium for transmitting and reinforcing messages to specific groups of audiences, so that they learn to consciously and actively

1927
1960
1963
1964
1967
1969
1970
1971
1972
1973
1974
1975
1976
1977
1978
1979
1980
1981
1982
1983
1984
1985
1986
1987
1988
1989
1990
1991
1992
1993
1994
1995
1996
1997
1998
1999
2000
2001
2002
2003
2004
2005
2006

participate in the attainment of national development objectives that contribute to their general well-being and the improvement of their environment.

Theatre Arts as Development Communication

In 1979, the present author conducted a study (Valbuena, 1980), demonstrating that, during the period between 1972 and 1979, the various forms of theatre arts were used extensively as a development communication channel in the Philippines. Specifically, the study sought to answer the following questions:

1. What forms of theatre arts have been utilized as channels for development communication in the Philippines?
2. What has been the extent of utilization? Have these forms been integrated with and/or extended through other communication media to support national development programs?
3. What has been the impact on the achievement of national development goals?
4. What are the prospects for further development of these theatre art forms to fully maximize their value in national development?

The study was based on surveys, case studies, documents analysis and participant observation. It led to the conclusion that, indeed, over the past eight years, there has been extensive utilization of various forms of theatre arts in the Philippines as a channel for development communication. The effectiveness of individual agencies varied, but the overall influence was extensive.

Between 1972 and 1979 at least seven existing forms of theatre arts in the Philippines were demonstrated as viable channels for development communication: drama, the *zarzuela,* the *cancionan,* the *balagtasan,* the *balitao,* the *bantayonon* and the puppet theatre.

Drama. Performances of one-act plays, usually of the soap-opera type, are standard offerings in many Philippine town fiestas. Plays with moral lessons are favorites of Filipino audiences, especially in the rural areas.

Drama has a more serious function than mere entertainment in the Philippines. Watching a drama presentation is an opportunity for gaining new insights into life, for learning lessons about man's relationships and their implications for personal as well as communal welfare. Thus, standard plots of many Philippine dramas revolve around a wayward youth who returns to his family; a philandering husband who returns to his wife and family; a rich landlord and the poor, exploited tenant. There is conflict between the young and the old, between new, emerging values and age-old, traditional behavior patterns.

A performance provides an opportunity for the audience to hear the message of the playwright, who assumes the important social role of critic and teacher (Bonifacio, 1976).

Zarzuela. The *zarzuela* is a musical play similar to light opera. The Filipino *zarzuela* has its roots in the Spanish *zarzuelas*—simple, comic operas dealing with manners, customs and foibles of different segments of Spanish society. The *zarzuela* is always accompanied by dances and songs, making the play a type of musical.

The main appeal of the *zarzuela* lies in the satire and the biting social criticism underlying the sharp, witty, humorous and often earthy language of the dialogue. "The musical score and the lyrics give flavor to the *zarzuela,* so much so that the songwriter or composer is as important as the playwright, if he is not himself both; and a script is often built around a musical score" (Coseteng and Nernenzo, 1975).

The homespun wisdom, common problems, catchy tunes, lively dances and attractive sets immediately involve the audience in the *zarzuela.* There is instant rapport, something not as possible with more sophisticated dramas and audiences.

The *zarzuela* has built-in originality and versatility. It is a flexible and dynamic dramatic form with local situations and issues, ordinary characters, familiar problems and native songs and dances. The acceptability and versatility of the *zarzuela* as propaganda in drama form were apparent during the revolution against Spain in 1896 and against the United States in 1898, and in the struggle against the American occupation at the turn of the century (Bonifacio, 1972). The *zarzuela* is easily updated, and the form can just as easily clothe the theme.

Although retaining the basic elements of the Spanish model, the Filipino *zarzuela* has developed into a full-blown, three-act melodrama. It may border on sentimentality, but it is complex in theme, plot and characterization.

The play centers mainly on the family, and the conflict is usually due to familial and social relationships, romantic love or economic difficulties. The values, morals and social traditions of the middle class prevail in spite of all the action. The Filipino *zarzuela* has a variety of topics: dowry, capital and labor, cockfighting, the trade monopoly of the Chinese, the corruption of native politicians, and native customs (Edades, 1956). Its themes include: relationships between husband and wife and between in-laws; the love between young master and servant girl, between rich boy and poor girl, and vice versa; and the conflict between young and old. All these are favorite topics of the *zarzuela*.

Cancionan. Very popular in the Ilocoa region, the *cancionan* is a form of argumentation in song and verse. It is a usual feature in town fiestas, a contest that pits male against female in argument on any topic. In many instances, it appears as a double bill or an intermission number in *zarzuela* presentations. The *cancionan* uses wit, humor, irony and satire as natural components, preventing it from becoming a dull musical contest. It has remained a popular medium because it lends itself to any topic and provokes the audience to take sides.

Balagtasan. This is a poetic debate between two protagonists using rhythmic, colorful language, with humor, satire and irony. It is a popular form in the Tagalog region. The balagtasan can provoke, not only arguments, but it also generates thinking and influence, for the audience has to make a choice. The emotion

that the *balagtasan* arouses is very much a part of the reaction of the audience.

Balagtasan can lend itself to any topic, issue, idea or sentiment, provided an opposing view (or several opposing views) exists, as it invariably does. Romantic, domestic, religious, ethical, political or economic matters can be taken up in a *balagtasan*. Subjects range from ordinary, everyday problems to leftist sentiments and most controversial topics. In fact, the strength of the *balagtasan* is in argument and thought, giving it a directness which the *zarzuela* or the conventional drama could not approach.

Although the *balagtasan* is essentially a debate, it is invested with a sense of drama because of the fast and sharp exchange in the arguments between the protagonists that gives it an impression of a dialogue, perhaps planned, certainly well structured, compact and rich. It is the kind of dialogue that demands the full concentration of the audience, broken only when the audience responds by applauding a protagonist who has won a point during the course of the argument or who has parried a counterargument with a quick turn of wit and speech (Coseteng and Nemenzo, 1975).

Balitao. The *balitao* is a courtship debate in song and dance, almost always extemporaneously performed by a man and a woman. The man presses his suit, and the woman, out of modesty, declines his advances and offers resistance to his sweet songs by singing and dancing her objections. In times past, at the end of a hard day's work in the fields—especially during the planting or harvest season—the young men and women would gather and perform the *balitao* to entertain themselves. They would either divide into two groups, male and female, and sing the debate in chorus; or select a boy and a girl who would play the *balitao* to the cheers and clapping of hands and laughter of the audience whenever one contestant had made a verbal thrust or a sharp retort.

According to Coseteng and Nemenzo (1975), although the subject matter of the *balitao* is mainly

1927
1960
1963
1964
1967
1969
1970
1971
1972
1973
1974
1975
1976
1977
1978
1979
1980
1981
1982
1983
1984
1985
1986
1987
1988
1989
1990
1991
1992
1993
1994
1995
1996
1997
1998
1999
2000
2001
2002
2003
2004
2005
2006

love and courtship, it may have variations which are interspersed with other topics. The elaborations and digressions of the debate involve the ability, intelligence and wit of the performers, and how well and fast they can construct short verses for repartee. Tradition, history, religion, customs and sociocultural values can all be used in advancing an argument, pressing a point or challenging or warding off an opponent's argument. At the end, resolution may come when the girl accepts the suitor's proposal but with the promises she has exacted. Because of the girl's ability and wit, she may succeed at other times in warding off the suitor and win the argument. The audience and the occasion may decide the subject matter of a *balitao*.

Fortunately, the *balitao* has retained its abundance of wit, quick repartee and humor reflecting traditional beliefs and practices. It also contains the omnipresent moral lessons. Allusions, suggestions, comparisons and other figures of speech are used often in appeals to both the emotions and the intellect. Strong sexual connotations bordering on the lewd and obscene are usually present, depending on the audience (Gutierrez, 1961).

Bantayonon. Another poetic debate form found in the Christian areas of Mindanao, the *bantayonon* usually focuses on love, courtship and marriage. Today, however, public affairs and other popular current issues are integrated into the *bantayonon*.

Puppet Theatre. Puppetry is a prevalent art form in Asia. At one time there was a type of shadow-puppet play in the Philippines called *carillos,* akin to the Indonesian *wayang*. Over the years, however, the tradition of the *carillos* was lost. In its place came the more colorful and popular hand or rod puppets now used in the development-communication activities of at least four nationwide institutions in the country.

Forms of Theatre Arts Used. Organizations seem to prefer the use of drama and musical plays in their communication campaigns. For example, the Commission on Population and the University of the Philippines are noted for their pioneering efforts in using the Ilocano *cancionan,* the Tagalog *balagtasan* and the Visayan *balitao* to support popular education and promote family planning. The Mindanao State University Sining Kambayoka uses the Maranao *bayok* in its theatrical productions. The Ministry of Public Information encourages the use of the *bantayonon* as part of its theatre activities in Mindanao. The Nation Media Production Center and Catholic Relief Service are proponents of puppet theatre in development.

References

Bonifacio, Amelia L. *The Seditious Tagalog Playwrights: Early American Occupation.* Manila: Zarzuela Foundation of the Philippines, 1972.

Bonifacio, Amelia L. "The Social Role of Theater in Asia." In *Literature and Society: Cross Cultural Perspectives.* Los Baños, Philippines: The Proceedings of the Eleventh American Studies Seminar, October 1976.

Braid, Florangel Rosario. *Communication Strategies for Productivity Improvement.* Tokyo: Asian Productivity Organization, 1979.

Coseteng, Alicia M. L. and Gemma A. Nemenzo. *Folk Media in the Philippines: Their Extension and Integration With the Mass Media for Family Planning.* Quezon City: University of the Philippines Institute of Mass Communication, 1975.

Edades, Jean. "The Zarzuela and Propaganda." Sunday Times Magazine (Manila), May 20, 1956: 30-31.

Gutierrez, Maria Colina. "The Cebuano Balitao and How It Mirrors Culture and Folklife." Cebu City: University of San Carlos, 1961.

Jamias, Juan. "The Philosophy of Development Communication." Solidarity (Manila), 1973, 8 (5): 29-34.

Jamias, Juan. "Development Communication." Concept paper (mimeographed). Los Baños: University of the Philippines, 1975.

Mercado, Cesar M. "Communication for Human Development: Theory and Practice." Concept paper (typescript). Quezon City: Institute of Mass Communication, University of the Philippines, Diliman, 1976.

Quebral, Nora. "Development Communication." Concept paper (mimeographed). Los Baños: University of the Philippines, 1972.

Valbuena, Victor T. "Philippine Theatre Arts as Development Communication": Perspectives and Prospects." Ph.D. dissertation. Manila: Centro Escolar University, 1980.

HOW TO COMMUNICATE WITH RURAL PEASANTS

By Pierre de Zutter

1980 A refrain heard not infrequently from campesinos [rural peasants] goes as follows: "First we need land, loans, food, health, education, houses. Then we'll see about communication." Institutions have their own refrain: "We have our hands full carrying out our various activities and completing our important projects—projects that will develop not only the rural environment but the country as a whole. Things like communication are add-ons that will come later." Given this state of affairs, communication in Latin America appears to be a luxury reserved for urban areas or countries with higher economic levels. The rural world—"backward" as it is—has other priorities. In today's environment, insisting on the importance of accelerating efforts at communication places one at risk of being regarded as merely another specialist, obsessed with defending and expanding one's own field of work.

Communication, however, is one of the cornerstones of any development process. Alone, it does not resolve social, economic, cultural or political contradictions and conflicts. Nevertheless, no formula or system can be effective without adequate communication. And it is safe to say that, managed poorly—or absent altogether—it can be one (though certainly not the only) cause of the failures and partial failures of so many development, education and rural education programs. What, then, can be done to provide a better understanding of what we are about?

Let us start by considering the problem in reverse. Who would deny that current relations between rural and urban, the State and the campesino, political

parties and the great rural masses, institutions (public or private) and campesinos, are characterized by a lack of communication? What does a person feel, arriving for the first time in a rural area? Distrust. What does a city dweller feel upon entering a community; an institutional worker or political party member when attending a meeting of campesinos? Incomprehension. What does the campesino feel, arriving in the city to live, or on some errand? Rejection and contempt, if not hatred. All of this distrust and confrontation are the result of the conspicuous differences between two worlds—with distrust and confrontation magnified, however, by the barrier of noncommunication between the two.

Why do so many rural development projects and efforts fail? Among many other reasons, because there is no true dialogue between the project heads and implementers on one side, and the campesinos who are the supposed beneficiaries on the other. This leads the former to attempt to impose their own solutions and prescriptions for what they suppose to be the needs of the campesinos, while the latter adopt a negative or passive attitude, interrupted from time to time by the promise of an immediate benefit. The failures are often due to the fact that communication occurs only *between* the two sides: the outside promoters and the individual campesinos. Without communication and debate *within* the campesino group the project is intended to benefit, there can be no collective appropriation of the project by the group—a circumstance that diminishes the chance of its success.

Cases in Point

1. IRRIGATION

One instance of this situation is the productive investments made by institutions in rural areas, with irrigation being a classic example. There is concern, throughout Latin America, over the failure of irrigation projects. Though they require massive levels of funding, many governments are forced to undertake them due to national or regional political pressures. By embarking on a long-desired irrigation project, presented

1927
1960
1963
1964
1967
1969
1970
1971
1972
1973
1974
1975
1976
1977
1978
1979
1980
1981
1982
1983
1984
1985
1986
1987
1988
1989
1990
1991
1992
1993
1994
1995
1996
1997
1998
1999
2000
2001
2002
2003
2004
2005
2006

as the salvation for a given area, the loyalty of the local population can, in large measure, be secured. Nevertheless, plans for inhabiting the land and making it profitable are so seldom realized that a 50 percent success rate is considered good. Why is this the case? Admittedly, technical errors—in connection with mistaken assessments of water supplies, locating irrigation canals on useless land, etc.—are sometimes at fault. The principal problem in most cases, however, is that the so-called beneficiaries do not take full advantage of the available water, and do not bother to maintain the infrastructure. Again, one may well ask "why?" The explanation is that these beneficiaries of works—projects planned and executed by others—do not have a full understanding of the projects, their implications and requirements. They have not assimilated the task at that level and are not motivated to look beyond their own immediate interests. They remain incommunicado with respect to aspects such as irrigation infrastructure, loan services, provision of inputs, etc.

In stark contrast are irrigation projects whose conception, planning and execution are undertaken at the initiative of the interested groups (whether communities or associations of small and medium producers), under their own control and with their participation. These projects are generally far more successful, assuming that the group is not manipulated by a local *cacique* [local boss], since the participants know each other and can cooperatively address problems that arise, alternatives for improvement, better formulas for distribution and use of the water, and ways of obtaining other elements necessary for the success of the project—in short, as a result of better communication. The circulation of information, the motivation of the participants, the dialogue and debate concerning the irrigation problem, all of these factors permit the group, as a group, to assume responsibility for, and take an active role in advancing, the work at hand.

2. BASIC SERVICES

Similar observations may be made regarding investments in basic services. Slogans are in ample supply: "Literacy is a must!" "Preventive health must be improved!" "Potable water must be provided." Public entities and private institutions adopt such slogans and embark on works and training projects. However, the region is full of the traces of abandoned efforts: water tanks rusted due to community neglect following the initial contribution—made by some international organization whose acronym appears shamelessly on the rusted ruins; latrines half disassembled and unused because the inhabitants, reluctant to refuse the supply of excellent materials, "accepted" the project, but without an understanding or appreciation of the need for latrines; people like the one who explained: "I don't have a head for these things. I went a couple times to some classes they gave, but I didn't understand anything. The instructors finally left because nobody was coming to the classes."

In all of these cases, lack of communication constitutes a barrier to success. On the other hand, basic service projects that involve discussion among the populace itself, and between the people and the outside promoters, almost always produce superior results. Better communication, with dialogue between the two parties, gives the institutions an appreciation for people's real needs, impelling them to seek solutions adapted to the local realities. At the same time, the campesinos reflect on the implications of their various customs, analyze certain factors or gain knowledge they previously lacked, and reach a decision based on their own priorities. If that decision is to go ahead, one can be certain that it is not the work itself that is the focus of the endorsement, but rather the service that it will provide. Communication is the indispensable pillar of this reflective, analytical and decision-making process—communication within the campesino group, as well as between the group and the institution involved.

3. EDUCATION

The same phenomenon often occurs in the area of rural education or training. Institutions arrive with their programs and materials, created by their experts, and the campesino must adapt to these if he or she wishes to "learn." Worse yet are those educational formulas based on texts that deal with realities totally foreign to the rural reality, or ones that impose subjects holding no interest for the rural population. Students who stay with the program generally do so because of the prospects of better jobs or upward social mobility, based on the piece of paper they will receive—the certificate or diploma. Even in the case of institutions motivated by the best of intentions, however, there is a high dropout rate: The campesino becomes bored with words that, inspiring as they may be, have no immediate personal benefit—teaching him how to write his name or compose a letter to his girlfriend when she leaves to work in the sugar or coffee harvest. Moreover, the technical courses suffer a fate nearly as bleak: In a course providing people training to operate tractors, the five top students in a class of 20, instead of returning to their communities and cooperatives, go to work for a nearby highway construction firm, or move to the city to make use of their newly gained knowledge. Lack of communication breeds failure. One party seeks to educate, while all the other wants is a piece of paper. One party attempts integral education through literacy, while the other's interest in literacy relates to more immediate, concrete needs. One party aspires to provide communities and cooperatives with individuals trained in certain skills, while the other wants simply the chance to escape to more alluring horizons.

The Search for Solutions

The ideas presented here are nothing new: For the most part, institutions have been aware of these realities for some time. Where there has perhaps been a lack of awareness among these institutions is in the diagnostic phase. They began by ascertaining that the perpetual errors—in conception, planning and realizing rural programs—could be attributed to the gap between the nature of the programs and the reality of the rural world, with its own forms of work, organization, values and attitudes. In response, planners and project designers decided to surround themselves with sociologists, anthropologists and specialists from the social sciences. Research—aimed at gaining a better understanding of that little-known reality and determining how to have a more effective impact on it—became the catchword of the hour. Despite all the studies and the intelligence devoted to it, however, another novelty emerged: Participation of the people turned out to be an essential component of success. Thus began the frenzied competition between one model of participation and another, each more original than the last, each specialist more innovate than his colleague.

The inadequacy of the specialists' reports, and the practical difficulties in applying them, like the numerous failed attempts to elicit the participation of campesinos, suggest the need to reformulate the problem from the perspective of communication. What, after all, is research if not a unilateral attempt to communicate, to know by observing... Is not communication the foundation of any participatory experience? Is today's research hobbled by its own communicational concepts and methods? Are the difficulties in achieving participation a result of conceptual, attitudinal and methodological errors in the communication so integral to this process? Answers to these questions reveal the importance of communication, not for its own sake, but as a fundamental and little known component of most activities involving rural development and education.

Research = Communication

What do rural planners and project creators do? First, they commission major studies to familiarize themselves with the area, population, resources, etc. The experts go in with their investigations, analyzing existing documents, conducting interviews and filling out questionnaires, processing the data, interpreting it, and then presenting their learned conclusions. They begin, in other words, by gathering information, and then organize it into what seems required by the institutions that hire them. The major problem with this procedure is that it is based on attitudes, as well as instruments of communication, that are both narrow

1927
1960
1963
1964
1967
1969
1970
1971
1972
1973
1974
1975
1976
1977
1978
1979
1980
1981
1982
1983
1984
1985
1986
1987
1988
1989
1990
1991
1992
1993
1994
1995
1996
1997
1998
1999
2000
2001
2002
2003
2004
2005
2006

and unilateral. The questionnaires and interviews are a form of communication, but a distorted, falsified and restricted one, one in which the interviewee is allowed to discuss only what interests the interviewer, and only in the form determined by the interviewer, with the interviewee knowing that his participation will end when the interview ends and that he will be judged by what he says, with no possibility of intervening later to correct or amplify his statements. Thus, he is compelled to either remain silent or distort his responses. This, in short, is a form of communication in which the campesino is allowed only minimal opportunity to express himself. The prescribed form of this expression is usually oral (or, on occasion, written), never with any provision for other forms of expression—ones that may, in fact, be more explicit and richer in meaning: silence, drawing, gesture, attitude, etc.

The deficiencies in handling communication lead to incomplete, erroneous studies, of remarkably little utility considering the amount of effort invested in them. Many responses of campesinos are predetermined by the questions; often interviewees say what they suppose the institution wishes to hear; some take advantage of the opportunity to ask the institution for what they imagine "can be gotten" out of the situation, even though it is not something of real importance to them. Others feel inhibited by the examination environment, omitting much that they would like to make known were the circumstances different.

Moreover, this process holds no benefit for the campesino, who only vaguely, at best, has a sense of the purpose or ultimate use of the research. The subjects are offered no opportunity to enhance their knowledge of their own reality, to discuss the proposed projects or unite around them. Instead, what often happens is that the subjects of the questionnaires and interviews begin to react negatively to the outsiders, while those not consulted feel excluded and thus predisposed to criticize and oppose the project.

One can only imagine how much better the studies would be if the researchers dedicated themselves to analyzing and processing the information that emerges in the communications exchanged among the inhabitants themselves; if the researchers were to join in the discussion, offering ideas, explaining the intentions and experiences that inspired the proposed project; if they were able to observe the reactions—positive and negative—that their ideas elicited. To say nothing of the benefits to be gained if the initial results of the research were made known to, and discussed by, the people themselves. The resulting data would be far richer and more reliable, and the local population, motivated by the experience, would adopt creative and positive attitudes toward development projects. The same dynamic of dialogue would create ongoing debate, information and adjustment throughout the various phases of planning, execution and use. In short, inasmuch as a major component of research consists of communication, the endeavor needs to be re-evaluated from the perspective of communication.

Participation = Communication

Communication plays a major and obvious role in participation itself. To participate in something, one must be familiar with that something, i.e., obtain the relevant information. To participate is also to have the opportunity to express oneself, communicate and debate opinions and ideas, and take part in the decision-making process. For if these elements are not part of the process, how can it be said to involve participation? Thus, if participation is the objective, it is essential to create an entire communicational dynamic within the base population, and between that group and the institution involved.

Many institutions believe that it is sufficient to invite a few representatives of the population to participate, in the form of speaking and voting in meetings held by the technical personnel. This formula may be useful, but only if the representative is a true delegate of his community, i.e., when the local population has engaged in a process of information and debate to define its positions, and has made the delegate its spokesperson and intermediary with the institution. How many representatives fulfill these conditions? How often does the delegate limit himself to reporting to his people what occurred at the meetings, without the opportunity for the people to debate the issues and have their views expressed? And how often does the representative fail even to report back to his community? Representation of this type may be useful in terms of seeking legitimacy vis-à-vis the local population. However, if true participation is to be achieved, much more is needed—namely, communication. Without good communication, there is no participation.

Communication, the Lifeblood of Society

With this, we come back to the point of departure. The two major advances to be made by planners and project designers—namely, carrying out social science research and gaining the participation of local populations—depend, in terms of their quality, on the type of communication involved. This—after a moment's reflection—will be recognized as natural and obvious. Communication is the essence, the lifeblood, of organized life, of any society, small or large, of family or tribe—life at the national or international level. The dynamic stability of any society (for no society is static) depends in large part on how successfully it handles communication: whether it controls it, prevents certain information flows, and limits communication to an informational, often unilateral, role; or whether instead it promotes dialogue and debate at all levels and between all members of the society.

Contrary to common belief, even with the benefit of a broad theoretical approach, communication is more than an instrument of development: It is a consequence, and foundation, of a society's organized life. A group's language is not a simple tool that permits the group to function more or less harmoniously ("language" here, is used to mean not only the word, but also other forms of expression: graphic and gestural, attitudes, even clothing, hair styles and other customs sometimes rich with significance). Language is also one of the major factors in the cohesion or divisiveness of the group. It is a vital element of group identity, whether through integration with, or self-isolation from, the larger society. Thus, any development policy should include an appropriate communication policy based on respect for, and strengthening of, communication. This should include the creation, reinforcement or energizing of the group's own communication (in accordance with the group's degree of acculturation, or of cultural paralysis or isolation), while at the same time helping it familiarize itself with the attitudes and forms of communication of the rest of the society (interpreting and using outside messages, modes of expression, encoding of their own messages). Without this strengthening of communication at different levels, it is impossible for the social group to achieve the integration and cohesion that are essential, or to participate in the national dialogue that makes democracy viable.

Communication in Rural Development

Will improving communication overcome all of the barriers to rural development? To believe it capable of this would be a concession to simplistic thinking. However, new attention to the problem of communication is indispensable, and a refined approach, combined with an improved work methodology, can help resolve many of today's problems, bringing clarity to situations of incomprehension and confrontation, and fostering dialogue and participation. For while communication is important to a society's functioning, it is even more vital when the society is in the midst of change and development. Indirect confirmation of this can be gleaned from an example, namely, the behavior of many large land owners in the Andes some years back. These land holders, in order to prevent change and maintain their domination, did their utmost to prohibit the populations under their control from interrelating with other social groups or communicating with the society at large. Thus, they prevented their populations from learning to read and write, to sell independently, etc. The land owners themselves, however, endeavored to become

1927
1960
1963
1964
1967
1969
1970
1971
1972
1973
1974
1975
1976
1977
1978
1979
1980
1981
1982
1983
1984
1985
1986
1987
1988
1989
1990
1991
1992
1993
1994
1995
1996
1997
1998
1999
2000
2001
2002
2003
2004
2005
2006

part of the local traditional channels and forms of communication (indigenous language, *compadrazgo* or godparent relationships, etc.), in an effort to increase their manipulative capacities.

Learning to handle communication more effectively is an essential condition for achieving harmonious, integral rural development—unless, of course, one prefers to rely on domination and authoritarianism to produce a form of mere economic growth that fragments and destroys rural populations.

Zutter, Pierre de (1980) *¿Cómo comunicarse con los campesinos?* Editorial Horizonte, Lima (Peru). Reprinted with permission of the author.

THE ROOTS OF THE VERB 'COMMUNICATE'

Excerpt from: ¿Cómo Comunicarse con los Campesinos? How to Comunícate with Rural Peasants

By Pierre de Zutter •

1980 — "What do you do for a living?"
—"I am a communicator. I write the communiqués at the Ministry, the Minister's speeches, responses to questions posed by the news magazines."

It could, indeed, be maintained that writing communiqués qualifies one as a communicator. Beyond simplistic formulations, however, consensus must be reached on what is meant by communication, on the ways we interpret the word, and on the different attitudes and concerns that come into play in communication.

For the present purposes, the verb "communicate" has two principal meanings. The first—and, today, more usual one—is not unlike inform, disseminate or broadcast. The second, and older, meaning is more along the lines of "to be in relation with" or "to have in common with"—older in that it is the meaning of the Latin word *communicare*, from which communicate derives. Indeed, the medieval Church borrowed the term to express the idea of communion. Thus, *communicate* and *communion* share the same root. The current predominance of the first meaning (disseminate, broadcast) reveals much about the evolution of modern society, which featured, along with economic, political and cultural centralization, a centralization of the word, of expression. These two dimensions of the word are vastly different: one restrictive, the other much broader, more open.

Two Conceptions of Society and Humanity

Exploring the roots of the word communicate is more than an idle exercise. Though it may seem academic, it has utility, for behind the two interpretations of communication lie the realities of two antagonistic concepts of life, two different philosophies of man and society. This opposition may be explored further by tracing its presence in the educational process. Communication is a pillar of the educational process, a process that is fundamentally one of communication. There are, of course, opposing forms of education: On one hand, education is seen as a transfer of knowledge and techniques; on the other, as a process of integral formation designed to develop the attitudes and abilities needed for people to think, analyze and act so as to influence their local and national realities. In one case, the starting point is the conviction that absolute, universal knowledge is a tangible commodity, and that the entire problem of education is to acquire, store, and manage it. In the other, the idea is to prepare human beings to adapt as effectively as possible to their environment, comprised of both their social and natural surroundings.

Behind these two approaches to education, two totally opposing views of society and humanity can be discerned. The champions of knowledge tend to assign to humanity the grandiose mission of conquering the universe and mastering the laws governing nature. They tend, however, to assign the flesh-and-blood individual a far less important role: as efficient cog in a worldwide machine directed by economic, scientific and political elites. Hence, they favor a type of education concerned with the simple task of preparing human beings for the roles they are to perform in this undertaking. The fundamental objective, therefore, is not the human being's ability to think and make decisions to guide social group and self, but rather the ability to accomplish the circumscribed task assigned to the individual—except, of course, in the case of those who demonstrate superior intelligence and can be incorporated into the nucleus of thinking elites.

Advocates of the second type of education see humanity as composed of beings seeking to develop and realize themselves as individuals and as a society. Accordingly, they view education as an apprenticeship for active and creative participation in society, and for acting upon nature in accordance with both human needs and the possibilities that nature provides. Such education cannot, obviously, be a simple transfer of knowledge and techniques, but must concern itself with increasing the ability to understand and interpret social and ecological reality and to participate responsibly in it.

This presentation of the two attitudes is far from definitive, since there are infinite gradations between the two poles. Moreover, political and ideological discourse tends to blanket everything with words that, though much repeated, are difficult to interpret: democracy, progress, socialism, etc. Our intention here is not to enter into a philosophical debate on those subjects, but merely to establish a basis on which to analyze where the two interpretations of the word communication lead. Communicational needs will appear very different, indeed, depending on which of the two views one adopts.

Communication as Transmission: Advertising and the Remodeling of Man?

What is the major concern of those who believe in the need to effectively transfer a body of knowledge? It is, of course, to improve the impact of their teaching messages, so that people understand, memorize and apply them. For this they require communication—in the sense of information, dissemination and transmission, if not outright imposition. This is precisely the dominant trend in today's society. Therefore, most of the efforts in the area of communication are designed to improve systems for the coding of messages to make them more persuasive, and to advance the technology of the communications media in order to continually enhance their ability to predispose the public to look favorably on the messages they send.

In the field, planners and project designers with this mentality seek to pave the way for the objectives,

1927
1960
1963
1964
1967
1969
1970
1971
1972
1973
1974
1975
1976
1977
1978
1979
1980
1981
1982
1983
1984
1985
1986
1987
1988
1989
1990
1991
1992
1993
1994
1995
1996
1997
1998
1999
2000
2001
2002
2003
2004
2005
2006

goals, methods, information, knowledge and techniques that interest them. Their priority is on implementing good communications infrastructure, using media capable of reaching the greatest possible number of people with the greatest impact—media that will then be managed by the project or institution. Experts are hired to create the messages in a form such that the people will more easily digest them and more faithfully obey them. Rural educators with this mindset seek ways of handling communication that allow them to increase individuals' capacity to absorb educational content and put it into practice.

Those who adopt this approach would seem to be committing an obvious error in hiring journalists or communicators to produce their messages and manage their media. Would they not be wiser to seek the services of advertising professionals? For no body of experts is better equipped to make the least attractive message interesting, the least useful thing indispensable. Experts in advertising are more skilled than simple journalists at selling an image or political measure, since they know far better how to create impact. In place of the vast array of boring messages generated by development projects, there would be an agreeable bombardment of sex, fear, laughter, vanity, envy, etc., all deftly aimed at our feelings and institutions. Researchers and scientists in many countries have, in fact, begun to offer new, more advanced technologies in the art of persuading and guiding the population: different forms of behavior control and human remodeling, including behavioral conditioning, brain surgery, electrical and chemical stimulation, intelligence transplants, genetic modification of fetuses, etc., techniques that ardent futurists are perfecting in order to create a more knowledgeable, less conflict-prone and more docile human being.

Thus, one sees an evolution perfectly consistent with certain ideas about what type of development, society and humanity is desirable. The classroom of tomorrow could be a laboratory with its educational content hermetically packaged and ready to be grafted to the students with the aid of machines and drugs. The teacher would be primarily a mechanic or pharmacist with the expertise needed to provide the doses required by each individual. The promoter or trainer in a development institution could walk through the countryside with a tool which, using an unconscious mechanism, would convince campesinos that they should use fertilizer X, begin planting on the 7th of the month rather than on the 15th, change their choice of crops, etc. Obviously, in this case, communication would be unnecessary, except among the small number of wise individuals directing the country (or directing humanity as a whole), who would determine which directions to pursue. The problem of dissemination and transmission would be solved.

Communication as Dialogue and Sharing: Mistakes and Constraints

In contrast, advocates of the second attitude described above need to develop people's capacity to think, analyze and act on the basis of knowledge and techniques drawn, above all, from their own reality, and then placed in relation with the rest of society. This requires a type of communication that consists of both information/dissemination and communion/mutuality, and involves not only improving the ability to send messages, but, most importantly, developing the capacity to express and listen, and to create and put into place channels for sharing and dialogue.

However, there are numerous limitations and errors in the way the advocates of this second group approaches communication. Almost all tend still to limit the role of communication in any process involving change and learning. They are less than fully aware of the importance of developing communicational attitudes and abilities in the formation of the human being, and as one of the requisites for functioning in any society. Moreover, when these experts do manage to gain a slightly clearer view of the problem, they fail in the process of transferring it to the practical level, due to a lack of strategies and fieldwork methodologies. Many also confuse training in communication with, on the one hand, learning to increase expressive ability and, on the other, the mere ability to interpret and decode the messages of the mass media. They neglect learning concerned with interpersonal communication. Others, meanwhile, laudably follow one of the basic principles of communication—the need to begin with the interests and needs of the group with which one wishes to communicate—but, when it comes time to put principle into practice, themselves decide what those interests and needs are, how to address them, the order in which to address them, etc.

Communicators as Media Intermediaries and Media Propagandists

What about the communicators themselves? What is their position on communication? The very concept of communicators is problematic. Do they actually exist? One can certainly find radio or print journalists, filmmakers, creators of drawings, and an endless list of specialists in the use of one or another means of communication. There are also numerous communications analysts and theorists with doctorates from the top universities. It is more difficult to find true communicators, i.e., individuals who help people and groups communicate among themselves. Such individuals do, however, exist.

Specialists in handling any given communications medium generally play the role of intermediaries in the communication process. Many cling to that role, speaking, writing and drawing for others because it is their livelihood, or because their primary interest is in the artistic dimension and the formal quality of their messages. In turn, those who wish to directly help people communicate, while themselves disappearing as irreplaceable intermediaries, often display a highly dangerous deformation, for they establish a hierarchy of the different communications media and dedicate themselves to trying to convince others that the medium in which they work is the most effective. Thus, fashions sweep over Latin America, overlapping and provoking confrontations. The last two or three decades were dominated by the vogue of radio and radio education. This was gradually challenged by the comics, and is now being severely threatened by closed-circuit television—which, in turn, is vulnerable to the invasion of super-8 film. Meanwhile, advocates of written media, theater, puppets, etc., are being left in the dust. For many of these communicators, the most important motivation is not so much that of seeking the most appropriate form of communication but, rather, that of defending their medium and increasing its potential, since that is what they know and like.

A Question of Attitude

In all of these cases, the most serious problem is the lack of clarity among all of these groups and experts with respect to what communication consists of, and what its use is or should be. People working in this field need to reflect on, and define for themselves, what type of communication, society and humanity is to be the goal, and then reconsider methods of working with communication based on that definition. Those who interpret communication as a simple tool for dissemination and transmission would increase their efforts to master techniques for achieving the greater impact, so that their messages, persuasive techniques, control and reshaping of the human being will be successful. For those who choose to view humans as responsible, creative, thinking beings, it will be essential to re-analyze communication, first in terms of attitude, then in terms of skills.

Why do we speak of attitudes in connection with communication? Why is communication, in the sense of dialogue and sharing, a question of attitude first and foremost? By way of answer, other questions need to be posed: What is the use of so many techniques and methods without the proper attitude? And can there be dialogue if a listening attitude is not present? Can there be sharing if there is no attitude of contributing or taking account of the contributions of others? That is precisely what is missing in the great majority of institutions working in rural education and development: an attitude of communication. This is perfectly understandable, for this would require changing

1927
1960
1963
1964
1967
1969
1970
1971
1972
1973
1974
1975
1976
1977
1978
1979
1980
1981
1982
1983
1984
1985
1986
1987
1988
1989
1990
1991
1992
1993
1994
1995
1996
1997
1998
1999
2000
2001
2002
2003
2004
2005
2006

nearly all aspects of current fieldwork—planning and execution, assessment of the ultimate utility of the various activities—because an attitude of communication is incompatible with the vertical, imposed management that is the norm. If, however, these institutions are genuinely interested in overcoming the difficulties and moving beyond the failures that are so prevalent, they will have no choice but to initiate themselves in an attitude of communication, learn about authentic communication and follow that road to the end.

Zutter, Pierre de (1980) ¿Cómo comunicarse con los campesinos? Editorial Horizonte, Lima (Peru). Copyright © 1980, Editorial Horizonte. Reprinted with permission of the author.

EXCERPT FROM:

ALTERNATIVE COMMUNICATION FOR SOCIAL CHANGE IN LATIN AMERICA

By Fernando Reyes Matta

1981 It has been said repeatedly, but it must be emphasized: The journalist is a professional mediator and, as such, he appears situated in the middle of the information process, shaping the background that energizes a society's internal dialogue.

A. The Journalist in the Context of Political-Social Structure

The thesis of journalism situated on some sort of "balcony" or "lighthouse" observing reality—a mere chronicler detached from struggles and aspirations—has served as an ideological platform for the expansion of the industrial forms of communication advocated by capitalism. It is from such a position that the principle of "freedom of the press" is supported, conceived as an autonomous task whereby a company grants itself the prerogative of owning, in the name of society, the right to information that belongs to all. It concentrates power, determines content and imposes an agenda on public opinion, and in all of these instances its own interests dominate, reflecting the economic power structure in which such company is embedded.

However, this industrial journalism—tied to transnational interests and information systems—posits itself as neutral, objective, factual. It has developed a broad thesis on the value of "facts," a central element of its informative speech. The presentation of these in a model that claims to be constantly seeking the articulation delivery of both sides of the coin, to deliver reality's black and white, constitutes its calling card, one that disqualifies ideological and opinion journalism.

Naturally, there are several fallacies in that position. The first is the fact that this industrial journalism constructed by powerful minorities in Latin American countries is partial, distorting, mercantile, highly superficial and atomizing of reality; but at the same time, a firm supporter of an "order" within which its interests are satisfied. It is the bearer of an ideology that is not introduced openly, but which constitutes the permanent manipulation of a rhetoric in which what is false and what is partial are situated in a specific succession of facts inscribed in the framework of what is "normal." Journalism that involves expressing an opinion, which is critical and orienting, bears ideas, and appears as the journalism of "disorder", and of what's "abnormal" for our societies.

This in turn forces us to point out another one of the fallacies hidden in the above statement. The dominant industrial journalism has come to impose the idea that what is customary, what is natural in Latin America, what has always been there, is supposedly neutral and matter-of-fact journalism. Hidden in this attitude is the essentially ideological, contesting and critical nature that Latin American journalism has had since its origins, bound to struggles for independence. In each of our countries, there are categorical examples of that perspective given to journalistic work. Such attitude appears full of symbolism in Bolivar, who travels throughout Latin America carrying with him a small print mounted on top of a mule, while he keeps stating that "the press is the artillery of thought."

Where and how does that characteristic of Latin American journalism go astray? The answer is directly tied to the evolution witnessed in the make-up of Latin American society and the formation of classes within it. While national bourgeoisies settle, oligarchies are formed in connection with the exploitation of land, and power groups related to industrial, mining and financial exploitation emerge, conditions for the emergence of the "great press" linked to this social sector. At the end of the past century, this so-called "great press" (*El Mercurio* in Chile, *La Prensa* in Buenos Aires, *La Prensa* in Lima, to give some examples) established a relationship with the North American model of industrial exploitation of information. Pulitzer's and Hertz's battles to dominate the market using the rotative printing press, which allowed large print runs to sell copies for one penny, create a journalistic style, and a system of exploitation of current events, in which the liaison between information and advertising imposes itself as an expression of the system.

The functional circle thus created by the makers of the industrial capitalist information system remains valid, and each media venture aspires to consolidate itself in the following scheme:

a. Producing impressive, sensationalist information, with the highest universal interest possible and in massive runs;
b. Getting that information to reach high circulation in the market, through the maintenance and intensification of the sensationalistic style, uncommitted in terms of social conflict;
c. Becoming advertising's preferred instrument, achieving an increase in advertisements even at the expense of informative space, thus establishing a financial dependence on advertising;
d. Maintaining high impact, universal, alienating content to sustain high circulation and receive continuous support from advertising.

The Latin American press evolved according to this model in the two first decades of the century, while radio joined the model from the 1920s and television during so in the 1950s. This makes Latin America the only region in the world, except for the United States— and obviously leaving Cuba out of this description— where all of the media is private property, operates by responding to market interests, and are the principle agent, in terms of mobilizing advertising. Since all media is in private hands, virtually always linked to national bourgeoisies and the main capital in the region, they remain situated within a transnational system with a structure such that national bourgeoisies and minority power groups become dependent on,

1927
1960
1963
1964
1967
1969
1970
1971
1972
1973
1974
1975
1976
1977
1978
1979
1980
1981
1982
1983
1984
1985
1986
1987
1988
1989
1990
1991
1992
1993
1994
1995
1996
1997
1998
1999
2000
2001
2002
2003
2004
2005
2006

and promoters of, the penetration of transnational corporations and their development model.

It is within this framework that most journalists are forced to perform their job. That reality limits their potential, not only as mediators who are expert in shaping information, but also as agents for social change. For this reason, it is relevant to highlight the analysis a group of Mexican journalists:

> His [the journalist's] task is indispensable mainly in the stages of searching, elaborating and channeling newsworthy materials. However, his participation in the decision-making process in terms of the selection of sources, use of news concepts and message dissemination policy is limited by a broad spectrum of factors. These encompass the media private property system's interests, political pressure and advertising's influence. It is therefore legitimate to distinguish between the journalist's performance—subject to restrictions—and the behavior of private media businessmen.

The quality of being a wage-earner intellectual puts journalists in a situation in which it is impossible to use the product of their work freely, a fact that could turn into an outrage for the individual's consciousness; in the broader framework, this situation constitutes a negative factor for the social goals of journalism. We must also point out that journalistic work has witnessed in the last years, especially in countries with oppressive regimes, persecution, jail, expatriation, and sometimes even the journalist's death, making this profession one of the most hard hit on the continent[1].

These situations take place precisely when the journalist decides to leave that neutral and uncommitted situation that the system seeks for him as part of an industrial process and instead, to situate himself in the trenches of ideas that stand for a democratic, fair coexistence in solidarity with others.

In this process of journalism's workers becoming aware, understanding the information phenomenon as a whole, in all the dimensions it shows in its current configuration, is especially important. Informative issues—and in consequence, formative issues—do not only involve a news program or the news section of a daily newspaper. Everything that constitutes a message—be it music, advertisement, entertainment, "fill-up" commentary during transmission—bear ideas that promote a specific attitude. Prohibiting a certain kind of music can turn that music into a communicative message such that merely hearing it transmits many signs beyond those posed by its lyrics and melody. If that music comes to be granted a certain space in specific radios, it turns those stations into the expression of a medium defying or nonconforming to the system. It is amidst this informative universe of multiple messages that the journalist's action expresses itself.

This overall vision is necessary because the system acts in an integrated and articulated manner. Its reality in Latin America responds to the transnational expansion initiated at the end of World War II, as the contemporary phase of capitalism, breaking in to search for markets throughout the countries of the underdeveloped periphery. That expansion process coincided with the solidification of North American capitalism and the domination of its consortiums over the rest of the Western capitalist system. Economic expansion takes place leaning on the military and political apparatus, but also, constantly and increasingly on the ideological-cultural apparatuses that shape a model of development with demands, such that multinational companies arise as the natural response to them. The 1970s have allowed us to confirm this view economic multinational expansion requires informational transnational expansion. This trend took place based on the principles of "free flow of information" and "freedom of expression," vigorously posed by the United States between 1946 and 1950, which served

---

1 Informe de la Reunión de Trabajo de Periodistas Latinoamericanos sobre Nuevo Orden Informativo Internacional. Proyecto RLA/77/007. ILET, México, may1979.

to concentrate informational power in a few corporations that decide, advocate and promote what is seen and heard in the world.

Towards the end of such a dramatic decade on the continent, and moving on to the century's penultimate decade, Latin American journalists cannot ignore this structural reality or fail to acknowledge that change towards a free, participatory, social interest journalism is not achieved merely through professional assertion. It's achieved, rather, in the context of major changes in society, based on political principles that can mobilize the neglected majority.

B. Multinational Companies as a Central Factor of the Structure

In mid-1974, at the sixth United Nations General Assembly Extraordinary Session, when the declaration on the New International Economic Order was approved, it was said that, among other reasons, "Neocolonialism in all its forms continues to be among the great obstacles to the complete emancipation and progress of developing countries and their peoples," To the extent that the analysis identifies *all* forms of colonialism, evidence arises of the role played by information as a neocolonial mechanism in contemporary society. Neocolonial expression is based largely on expanding transnational power.

The transnational communications system, as Juan Somavia has said, is a whole: It includes news agencies, advertising companies, databanks and information retrieval services, radio and television programs, films, radiophotographs, magazines, books, comic strips of international circulation. Its different components, mainly originating in industrialized countries, reinforce one another, stimulating as a whole the consumer's aspiration to reach forms of social organization and lifestyles imitative of the industrialized capitalist countries. These, as proven through experience, can be reproduced only in Third World countries on the basis of a high and increasing concentration of income in a few hands, and of unacceptable social inequalities.

At the same time, the pressure of information coming from several different origins, apparently unrelated but substantially coherent, progressively eliminates the ability to react *vis-à-vis* the message; and, in turn, the receiver becomes passive and incapable of critical judgment. Thus, for people, the communication process becomes something similar to theatre: You watch, but you do not participate.

Under such conditions, the audience convinces itself that the transnational model of consumption and development is historically inevitable. Thus, the communications system complies with its main function: to permeate the human being culturally in order to condition him in such a way that he will accept the political, economic and cultural values of the transnational power structure[2].

2 "La estructura transnacional de poder y la información internacional", Juan Somavia, in *La Información en el Nuevo Orden Internacional,* Fernando Reyes Matta (Comp.), ILET, México, 1977

1927
1960
1963
1964
1967
1969
1970
1971
1972
1973
1974
1975
1976
1977
1978
1979
1980
1981
1982
1983
1984
1985
1986
1987
1988
1989
1990
1991
1992
1993
1994
1995
1996
1997
1998
1999
2000
2001
2002
2003
2004
2005
2006

EXCERPT FROM:

COMMUNICATION AND CIVIL SOCIETY: AN EMERGING THEME

By Elizabeth Fox

1982 ...Little is known concerning the subject of communication and civil society. While different aspects of the issue have been examined—such as the impact of mass communications on the population and the structure of the media—the significance of communication within, and as a part of, civil society has seldom been addressed. The topic has been studied even less in relation to the State, and issues relating to today's information and communication technologies remain relatively unexamined in this context.

Although research and thinking remain in their early stages, there is a long tradition, in the region [Latin America], of viewing the two subjects—communication and society—separately. Thus, bridges between the two have not yet been built. This means, on one hand, putting an end to many of the stereotypes regarding communication processes in society and, on the other, posing new questions on the topic.

...In both sets of areas—communication and democracy, and communication and civil society—knowledge is still in an embryonic state, both in terms of volume of work and the need to identify specific areas for study. No clear definitions exist.

Fox, Elizabeth (1982) Comunicación y Sociedad Civil: Una Temática Incipiente, in *Comunicación y Sociedad* No. 7. Telemetric y Sociedad, Buenos Aires, Argentina. Reprinted with permission of the author.

EXCERPT FROM:

INFORMATION IS THE OPPOSITE OF UNCERTAINTY

By Andreas Fuglesang

1982 Information is not communication. Information is only potential communication. We must use information in the right way, in the right social context, for communication to occur. Communication between people thrives not on the ability to talk fast, as some mass-media prophets seem to think, but on the ability to listen well. We do not communicate by cramming an enormous quantity of information bits together into a monologue, but by being socially intelligent and capable of listening to what the other person has in mind before we respond. It is so simple, and yet we fail continuously in our attempt to communicate because of an egocentric attitude.

In *About Understanding: Ideas and Observations on Cross-Cultural Communication*", Decade Media Books, Inc. New York, USA, 1982. Reprinted with permission of the author.

THE NEED FOR DEMYSTIFYING OUR WORDS

Excerpt from: About Understanding: Ideas and Observations on Cross-Cultural Communication

By Andreas Fuglesang

1982

"Why do you Mzungu [white person] not try to understand the minds of Africans more than their ability to work? You people do not understand your words do not belong to our mind." —*Mukahamubwatu, an old village woman, Mapanza, Zambia*

"….A main source of our failure to understand is that we do not command a clear view of the use of our words." —*Ludwig Wittgenstein*

The Virtue of Exactness

Our language is a technique of communication we learn to master from our social environment. The words we learn have cultural connotations and reflect the prejudices, preferences, sympathies, aversions, superstitions, taboos or myths of that social environment. Mastering a language also means subjecting oneself to verbal habits and value judgements. We commit ourselves in casual, everyday use to meanings of words which, in more thoughtful moments, we may not want the words to have.

For example, the word "exact" has a connotation of something virtuous and, conversely, "in-exact" has a connotation of something reproachable. From this arises the myth that the footnotes, references and verbal mannerisms of the academic are a more exact, and therefore more valuable, means of communication than the gutsy remarks of the man in the street or the proverbs of the elders under the village tree. We disregard the fact that these people and the academic do not necessarily have the same measurement of exactness. There is no single ideal of exactness.

Distrust in People

The myth sustains other strange illusions; for example, a judgement of reality made by a technical expert is more trusted than a judgement by a village farmer. We disrespect the ideas and opinions of people who happen to have their knowledge from sources other than books. Such misconceptions are also rampant in other connections. The notion that there is only one single correct way of talking and writing a language, that some dialects within a language are inferior, and that some languages have more sophisticated and expressive qualities than others are examples.

This leads to the idea that a foreign language represents colonial oppression or cultural domination or to the idea that a community will only safeguard its cultural identity by retaining its tribal language. The exponents of such ideas are all yielding to the same myth of paternalism, the general distrust in people's ability to cope with their lives. They are unaware that people develop the language they require; people learn a skill or acquire knowledge when they perceive it as a priority.

The Myth of Logical Necessity

A halo of superstitions and value judgements surrounds the concepts of *logic* and *logical necessity*. In the European culture, we consider more or less explicitly that it is desirable to be logical and, conversely, that it is undesirable to be illogical. To be very logical is even admirable! We attach universality to the concept of logical necessity and talk about "the logical universe," "the world of pure reason," "a contradiction-free system," i.e. the negation, stone/not stone. In doing so, we overlook the simple circumstance that the universality is not a fact in reality, but only a feature in the linguistic picture we are using.

Necessity may be defined as a state where all alternatives except one are excluded—that is, excluded in the picture. The circumstance is really very simple and that is probably why we do not see it clearly! The only thing corresponding to a "logical necessity" in our language is an arbitrary rule. The concept of "logical

1927
1960
1963
1964
1967
1969
1970
1971
1972
1973
1974
1975
1976
1977
1978
1979
1980
1981
1982
1983
1984
1985
1986
1987
1988
1989
1990
1991
1992
1993
1994
1995
1996
1997
1998
1999
2000
2001
2002
2003
2004
2005
2006

necessity" in the Aristotelian syllogism or other logical mechanisms is simply a linguistic/social convention. Hence it is valid only for those who adhere to that convention. Consequently, to say a person from another culture has made an "illogical statement" is really to express a racist attitude in the world of logic. That the language of formal logic is useful in some situations is another matter.

Ludwig Wittgenstein has illustrated so lucidly this conception of what "logical necessity" is. We can only understand it by understanding the way we use our language (1).

The Myth of Technology

Let us turn to other words which typically mystify and obscure our view of the way we use our language. *Technology is* one such word. A dominant myth emanates from the connotation that modern technology is for the good of mankind. It is desirable, clean, apolitical and efficient, in the long run cheap—and, above all, *technology is necessary.* Mass media and our modern social environment have propagandized the above connotations so effectively that they have become synonymous with the word "technology." In our sub-conscious, these connotations are the "meaning of the word." This is what we "see" and by seeing this—perhaps because technology itself is so conspicuous—we overlook the fact that technology is a manifestation of a specific political system, namely a society based on capitalist principles, whether it is private or state capitalism is of minor importance in that connection. The shrewdness of the myth is demonstrated by the fact that we throw the blame for environmental pollution on the technology, whereas the real culprit is the political system. A world without modern technology is clearly thinkable and possible. We may even say with some justification that technology is not necessary.

The Myth of Development

Another myth in our language is projected through the word *development.* Intertwined with the myth of

"technology," it has many of the same connotations. In addition, its general use implies a value judgement, i.e., that good, desirable social development is synonymous with economic growth, a linear process of social change ending in the model of the modern western consumer society. The myth is that this is the only thinkable and possible direction of social development. The myth is also that the peoples of the Third World, in the serfdom of national debts, trade deficits and cultural oppression, have the freedom to define the direction of this development. This myth is sustained particularly by the North-South flow from the information monopolies.

The myth of development has devastating effects at the local, human level. Use of such terms as undeveloped and underdeveloped is outrageous. Those who have worked closely with people in the Third World cannot avoid seeing how it hurts to be called underdeveloped, to be told—explicitly or implicitly—that what you do is a mistake, that what you have done is inferior, and that you do not really know what you should do.

There is No Primitive Mind

Another mystification is represented in the word *primitive.* The word carries a disparaging implication and connotes a past stage in mankind's development or a stage from which society should progress. In general, it is used to indicate something of inferior quality: "They live in a rather primitive house" or "This institution has a primitive administration." And then, of course, primitive is used as a characterization of Third World societies. The myth of "the primitive mind" has been a particularly tenacious concept. It has been nurtured by "the civilized citizen" since the days of Rome's battles with the barbarians and elevated by the romanticists since Rousseau. The myth of "the primitive mind" gained momentum through the Freudian school of psychoanalysis and proliferates today in the much extolled educational psychology of J. Piaget (2).

It is essential to realize that the phenomenon of a primitive mind does not exist. This notion is a verbal tool of oppression deftly applied by the privileged under the cloak of scholarship. The thought processes of all people are functionally equivalent and can be inferred from people's linguistic behaviour (3). There is no such thing as a stage of mental development which is "lower" than that of an educated person. The notion that being "illiterate" is something less desirable, less valuable than being literate derives from our misuse of language. People's thought processes are not different, but the classification systems they use to describe reality may be different.

This premise is fundamental to understanding and solving the problems of cross-cultural communication.

The Myth of Social Institutions

Let us take a closer look at the mythical connotations of social institutions such as the church, civil service, government, national defence forces, trade unions, industry, medical establishment, business community, finance, educational system, family and mass media. These institutions have specialized, complex functions, often incomprehensible and unexplained to the common man. Interlocked in an intricate interaction process, these institutions preserve and perpetuate the overall social system of which they are a part. This does not exclude the continuous power struggle between them. The common myth pervasively reinforced by the action of these institutions is that they are irreplaceable and irreproachable. Furthermore, they represent social respectability and common sense, law and order, the ethical standard, etc.

They have a history as long as settled man himself. They direct the process of social development through an agenda defined *for their actions*. Their pomp and power is awe-inspiring, but in the perspective of the universe, they are, indeed, little more than the faintly discernible patterns of interactions in an ant-hill.

Clusters of Social Habits

We may command a clearer view of the words we use for social institutions by perceiving them simply as structured clusters of social habits. Institutions are social habits, i.e. systematic and perpetuated relationships and interactions between people (4). We can also add that they are networks of vested interests with a potential for exploitation.

The Myth of the Educational System

In coping with the question of cross-cultural communication, we are dealing particularly with adult education, primary health care, nutrition, agriculture and similar issues. It is necessary, therefore, to devote more time to one of the social institutions of special significance, *the educational system*, often referred to as the formal and non-formal educational system.

The concept of this institution requires demystifying and placing in alternative perspectives. The formal educational system is primarily concerned with instructing the next generation in the techniques and values of the dominant social system, thereby preserving and perpetuating a power structure. There is no reason to believe that the motivations and inventions of the educational system are of a nobler nature than those of other institutions. I am deeply suspicious of the professional attitudes and value judgements made by educators with particular reference to the educational system in the Third World. The educational elite is surviving its own ineptness by enlarging frenetically the bulwarks of its professed professionalism. Whose privilege is it to define the learning needs of the deprived and the poor? For too long, the educators have betrayed people with their professionalism. People are neither objects to be formed nor cases of ignorance to be treated. It is the thoughtfulness and creativity of the people which is the ultimate resource of any social development. It is not the privilege of the educator to list requirements in terms of knowledge and skills which are supposed to define an educated person. The educator behaves as if he were listing empirical facts when he is, in reality, uttering a series of value judgements.

In itself, it is an extremely dubious endeavour to assess people's learning needs from an outsider's perception of the social situation of others—and yet, educational

1927
1960
1963
1964
1967
1969
1970
1971
1972
1973
1974
1975
1976
1977
1978
1979
1980
1981
1982
1983
1984
1985
1986
1987
1988
1989
1990
1991
1992
1993
1994
1995
1996
1997
1998
1999
2000
2001
2002
2003
2004
2005
2006

programmes in health care, nutrition, family planning, etc, are continuously defined according to alien objectives and attitudes and launched in the villages. To formulate a definition of competence, the design of curricula and the development of course plans in this way is unrealistic, unviable and culturally oppressive. Extension workers and adult educators in the field are slow to realize that youngsters and adults alike may have priorities other than the educational priorities espoused by the educators. No learning experience will work unless the priorities of the people themselves are an integral part of a programme developed for their benefit.

There is a poisonous myth permeating our professional thinking. Our educators are taught-and teach-that ignorance is the cause of poverty. This sustains the deception that a structural change in society to eliminate the deeper causes is not necessary.

The Educated: A Negative Contribution to Development?

Education has been promulgated as the key to modernization and development. Over the last two decade, in Third World countries, this has led to an enormous growth in allocations to educational systems. Many countries now set aside 20-25 percent of the national budget for educational expenditures. The idea, conceived and maintained by the educationists, that a correlation exists between the stock of educated manpower and the rate of economic growth has not been borne out. It remains another myth.

In fact, the evidence now seems to indicate that education, and in particular higher education, has reached a point in many Third World countries where it is making a negative contribution to their development (5). The products of the educational system, the school leavers, are finding it difficult to secure employment, By and large, the unemployed are the educated and there are considerable differences in the rates of unemployment among labour force groups with different levels of education—with particularly low unemployment rates among the illiterate urban

population (6). The Indian Educational Commission was already concerned with this problem in the early sixties, and stated: '. . . The educated elite thus become largely parasitical in character and the real productive workers are the unlettered peasants and artisans (7).

In view of this, we should perhaps agree that there are new dimensions to consider in the eulogy of education and the disrespect of the illiterate. A deeper understanding of the functions of educational institutions and the educational process itself is essential. By simplifying the concepts currently in vogue when describing this part of reality and by neutralizing the prevalent mythical terminology, a clearer view may be achieved.

Simply Social Formations

In the following pages, we shall look at social institutions and systems in their various configurations and with their various traditions as *social formations*. An insurance company is a specialized social formation. A village community is a social formation of a more general nature. A group of farmers who collaborate to build a storage house for their grain, or who meet simply to discuss new methods, is a social formation, although it may be of short duration or weak cohesion. The Catholic Church is a social formation of long duration and strong cohesion.

As previously indicated, social formations can be considered patterned ways of behaviour, clusters of social habits which are structured in various ways and for various purposes and which exhibit various degrees of duration and cohesion. This simple definition may lead to more fruitful thinking.

All too often, we ask the wrong questions. It serves no purpose to ask: "What is a social formation?" Rather, we should look at its function. What is the purpose of a social formation such as a women's club, a stock exchange, a university, a Freemason lodge, a group of tribesmen chasing a boar? All these formations have very specialized agendas for their activities and their members act in accordance with specialized codes of behaviour. What are the common features which allow us to classify them as social formations?

Processing of Information

One answer to the question may be that social formations *process information*. The attempt to qualify this view for our understanding of different social realities and the issue of cross-cultural communication will occupy the rest of this book.

It is reasonably clear that information processing is a common characteristic of social formations such as the British Broadcasting Corporation, Harvard University or the Adult Literacy Class in Mutondo Village. It is less clear, perhaps, in formations which have a conspicuous agenda or physical output such as the armed forces, an automobile manufacturing plant or a farmers' cooperative, which purchases fertilizer and seeds and organizes the storage and sale of the maize crop.

In what sense do such formations process information? A closer look reveals that they are, indeed, involved in a whole spectrum of information activities. They collect information; they record and store information; they have various systems for retrieving and presenting information; and they transmit information to other social formations.

For the farmers' cooperative, information processing ranges from collection of data on fertilizer prices and distribution of the data to members to records of membership fees, quantities of maize delivered by each member, and distribution of the yearly accounts and report to members.

Social Formations—and Transformations

As mentioned, social formations vary in duration. A hunting party of tribesmen is transient; once the hunt is over, the group changes form. Institutions such as the church or the government, however, convey a feeling of longevity and permanence. This derives from the time perspective of the observation. In the time perspective of the universe there are no social formations, there are only social transformations.

This concept carries a very specific definition. To transform means "to make change in form" and *transformation* means "a change in form." Such a "new" change in the form of a social formation is no more permanent than the "old" form. Transformation, therefore, really comes to mean "the process of change," the continuous change of form which takes place.

It is important to note that the concept of the transformation is concerned with *what* happens, not with *why* it happens (8). *Panta rei*—or everything is in flux. When we say that change occurs continuously, we encounter problems with our language. No words are available to describe what happens inside a continuum except the notion of "the infinite step." This is cumbersome and, for some of us, mentally unhealthy. We shall, therefore, think of social transformation as happening in finite steps. Although we know there is a continuum of social transformation, we choose to say that at any definite point in time there are social formations which can be observed and described. Being clusters of social habits, these formations carry with them a notion of predictability, a potential for forecasting social behaviour. Among other things, social habits are the tracks through which information is processed. It can be posited that people who have acquired a certain type of education have really just established a certain type of habitual social behaviour.

Directed and Non-directed Social Transformation

Social transformation is a passionless word. It does not have the same halo of mystification as the word development. The word development is therefore deleted from the vocabulary in this book and it is considered more clear and fruitful to describe reality in terms of social transformation. However, we are not satisfied with this expression alone. …We want to control, manage, steer or direct social transformation. That is the goal of all governments and the intention of governments in the Third World particularly. Although we try, we do not really control social

1927
1960
1963
1964
1967
1969
1970
1971
1972
1973
1974
1975
1976
1977
1978
1979
1980
1981
1982
1983
1984
1985
1986
1987
1988
1989
1990
1991
1992
1993
1994
1995
1996
1997
1998
1999
2000
2001
2002
2003
2004
2005
2006

transformation. Therefore, we cannot talk about controlled social transformation. On the other hand, there is social transformation which occurs without the interventions of government. It appears that the terms directed social transformation and *nondirected social transformation* can be used productively. Directed social transformation may naturally be attempted also by other agents than government officials, for example missionaries or local politicians. The concept of *nondirected transformation* has much of the connotation of the word spontaneous. Transformation is on-going. At best, we can influence its direction. Today's societies are in a more tumultuous process of transformation than ever before and we find ourselves unsuccessful in directing events. We do not quite understand what is happening to us. The chaos arises because we do not command a clear view of the words we use. We do not process information well.

Maybe the solution is simpler than we think. You cannot wait for others to save the world. You must do it yourself.

Notes

1. Wittgenstein, Ludwig, *Philosophical Investigations,* Blackwells, Oxford, 1958.

2. Wharf, B. Lee, *Language, Thought and Reality,* MIT Press, Cambridge, Mass., 1974.

3. Cole, A., Gay, G., Click, J., Sharp, D., *Thinking,* Basic Books, New York, 1971.

4. Smythe, Dallas W., "The Role of Mass Media and Popular Culture in Defining Development," Paper for the International Scientific Conference *The Cultural Context of Learning and* on Mass Communication and Social Consciousness in a Changing World, Leipzig, September 1974.

5. Bacchus, M.K., "Structural Change and Transformation-Education and Development," Lead Paper, Commonwealth Conference on Non Formal Education for Development, New Delhi, January 1979.

6. Turnham, D., *Empirical Evidence of Open Unemployment in Developing Countries, Third World Employment*, Penguin Books, London, 1973.

7. Government of India, *Report of the Education Commission, 1964-66,* New Delhi, 1967.

8. Ashby, W. Ross, *An Introduction to Cybernetics,* Methuen & Co., London, 1976.

9. Smedslund, J., *Psykologi,* Universitetsforlaget, Oslo, 1967 (Norwegian).

10. *Ibid*.

11. Whorf, B. Lee, *op. cit.*

12. Wober, M., *Psychology in Africa,* International African Institute, London, 1975 and Mbiti, John S., *African religions and philosophy,* Heinemann, London, 1969.

13. Whorf, B. Lee, *op. cit.*

14. Stanner, W.E.H., "The Dreaming," *Australian Signpost,* Sidney, 1956.

15. Whorf, B. Lee, *op. cit.*

16. Schmandt-Besserat, Denise, "An Archaic Recording System and the Origin of Writing," *Syro-Mesopotamian Studies, Vol. 1,* Issue 2, Undena Publications, Basel, 1977.

17. Oppenheim, 0. Leo, "An Operational Device in Mesopotamian Bureaucracy," *Journal of Near Eastern Studies,* 17, 121-28, Chicago, 1958.

18. Amiet, Pierre, "11 y a 5,000 ans les Elamites inventaient l'icriture," *Archéologia,* 12, 20-22, Paris, 1966.

19. Schmandt-Besserat, Denise, *op. cit.*

20. *Ibid*.

21. *Ibid*.

22. Piaget, J. and Inhelder, B., *La Psychologie de L'Enfant,* Presses Universitaires. Paris, 1967.

23. Fuglesang, A., *Applied Communication in Developing Countries,* Dag Banmarskjöld Foundation, Uppsala, 1973.

24. Whorf, B. Lee, *op. cit.*

25. *Ibid*.

26. Wittgenstein, Ludwig, *op. cit.*

27. *Ibid*.

28. Katz, D., *Gestaltpsychologie,* Benno Schwabe & Co., Basel. 194L

29. Smedslund, J., *op. cit.*

30. Raum, 0.1., *Chaga Childhood,* Oxford University Preps. London. 1967

31. Whorf, B. Lee, *op. cit.*

32. Egudu, R. and Nwoga, D., *Igbo Traditional Verse,* Heinemann. London, 1973

33. *Ibid*.

34. Bateson, G., *Steps to an Ecology of Mind,* Paladin Books, London, 1978

In *About Understanding: Ideas and Observations on Cross-Cultural Communication*, Decade Media Books, Inc. New York, U.S.A., 1982. Reprinted with permission of Minou Fuglesang.

WHOSE PRIORITIES?

Excerpt from: Rural Development: Putting the Last First

By Robert Chambers

1983 In trying to see what to do, non-rural outsiders are trapped by core-periphery perception and thinking. Looking outwards and downwards towards the remote and powerless, their vision is blurred. They see most clearly what is close by; they see action starting from where they are. The very words reflect the problem: "Remote" means remote from urban and administrative centres, from where most of the outsiders are; and "what to do" implies initiatives taken by them in the centres of power. However much the rhetoric changes to "participation," "participatory research," "community involvement" and the like, at the end of the day there is still an outsider seeking to change things. Marxist, socialist, capitalist, Muslim, Christian, Hindu, Buddhist, humanist, male, female, young, old, national, foreigner, black, brown, white—who the outsider is may change, but the relation is the same. A stronger person wants to change things for a person who is weaker.

From this paternal trap there is no complete escape. A decision not to act is itself an action. A person who withdraws or who abstains from intervening is by that withdrawal or abstention still intervening by default. The weaker person is affected by what does not happen but which might have happened. There is, however, a partial remedy. Respect for the poor and what they want offsets paternalism. The reversal this implies is that outsiders should start not with their own priorities but with those of the poor, although however much self-insight they have, outsiders will still project their own values and priorities. In what follows, I too am trapped, an outsider asking what poor people want. All one can hope is that the effort of trying to find out, of asking again and again and doubting the outcomes, will check some of the worse effects of core-periphery paternalism, and that the more the priorities of the poor are known, the easier it will be to see what it is best to do.

Priorities and Strategies of the Poor

For those who are neither rural nor poor to know the priorities of those who are both is not as easy as it sounds. The rural poor are dispersed, isolated, uncommunicative, rarely asked their views, frequently masked by others, selectively perceived, deferential. The silent cannot be heard. Direct approaches distort impressions: Replies in interviews notoriously mislead, especially when respondents believe that their replies may bring benefits. An indirect approach may help, drawing on social-science research, especially case studies of social anthropologists and social workers, and agricultural economists' understanding of the behaviour of poor farmers. On the basis of such evidence something can be said about what poor people want, inferring their priorities from what they do as much as, or even more than, from what they say.

1927
1960
1963
1964
1967
1969
1970
1971
1972
1973
1974
1975
1976
1977
1978
1979
1980
1981
1982
1983
1984
1985
1986
1987
1988
1989
1990
1991
1992
1993
1994
1995
1996
1997
1998
1999
2000
2001
2002
2003
2004
2005
2006

OBJECTIVES FOR OUTSIDERS

Excerpt from: Rural Development: Putting the Last First

By Robert Chambers

1983 Objectives for outsiders can, then, be expressed as a reversal, putting first the wishes of the poor themselves. But this cannot be all. Dilemmas remain: from conflicting values and objectives; from times when outsiders' knowledge is believed to be more valid than rural people's knowledge for achieving what poor people want; from trade-offs between short- and long-term costs and benefits; and from outsiders' need to be true to themselves. The question whether to give medical treatment against a patient's wishes, but in order to save her or his life, is an example of the more general problem of power and paternalism. I see no universal solution to this. But for practical purposes in rural development, a partial answer is to concentrate on those aspects of life where outsiders and the rural poor agree. Peter Berger ends his book *Pyramids of Sacrifice* with an appeal for people of different ideologies to find common ground by looking at specific situations to which there will be a common "no." Outsiders and the rural poor may agree in saying "no" to children dying, to preventable disease, to famine, to the poor becoming poorer,

---

Excerpt from: *The Popular as Dimension: Place, Rhetoric and Issues of Reception*
By Beatriz Sarlo

The other issue in regard to receiving cultural messages concerns the skills needed to deal with texts and artifacts that are aesthetically complex and ideologically/morally problematic. Both the production and reception of messages of this type require a set of acquired attitudes and skills that, along the lines of Bourdieu, one might refer to as *habitus*. The leisure required for intellectual activity and aesthetic enjoyment, the symbolic—and, specifically, educational—capital available and invested in the process of receiving cultural goods, the degree of access people have to such goods, the abundance or scarcity of these goods, etc., all represent objective and subjective prerequisites to dealing with discourses that contain varying degrees of complexity. In this respect, economic and social inequalities act as a cleaving force. It follows, then, that the audience is not composed of readers cut to a single mold, but rather is fragmented and culturally stratified.

Furthermore, these different groups of readers within the society do not establish unvarying relationships with discourse and objects in the world of culture. The cultured reader engages in a range of types of reading, which must not be conflated. This range includes the aesthetic pleasures that may be involved in reception, the recognition of influences, the operation of a vast and complex register of formal and ideological systems, and a knowledge of preceding forms, lineages, additions, quotations, parodies, stylizations, etc. Similarly, there is unlikely to be a single type of reading or reception on the part of the popular classes. Culture is not always consumed in the same way, and the popular audience, like the cultured, has different experiences of objects and discourse that it recognizes as different, ranging from an eminently political reading of cultural messages to the discovery of critical keys contained in stories based entirely, it seems, on travel and adventure; from the happy passivity of identification with a hero to the intellectual operations that are needed to follow the plot of a whodunit, dismiss false clues, respond to narrative tensions, and interpret (and take pleasure in) the multiple meanings of figurative discourse.

Sarlo, Beatriz (1983). *Lo popular como dimensión: tópica, retórica y problemática de la recepción*. Serie Documentos. Pontificia Universidad Javeriana, Facultad de Comunicación Social, no. 842. September 1983, Bogotá, Colombia. Reprinted with permission of the author.

1927
1960
1963
1964
1967
1969
1970
1971
1972
1973
1974
1975
1976
1977
1978
1979
1980
1981
1982
1983
1984
1985
1986
1987
1988
1989
1990
1991
1992
1993
1994
1995
1996
1997
1998
1999
2000
2001
2002
2003
2004
2005
2006

to exploitation of the poor by the rich. Agreement on points such as these can provide a moral foundation for the next steps, to see what outsiders should do.

But outsiders think they know best. Some will say that the rural poor do not know what is in their interests; or that with greater awareness (which is liable to mean by agreeing with the outsider), they would have other priorities; or that they should confront their powerlessness by organizing against their rich exploiters; or that they should be encouraged to have longer time horizons; or that they must be enabled to see what they would want if they knew what they really wanted. But if vulnerable people have short time horizons, who is justified in imposing long ones on them? If they have low-risk strategies, who is justified in thrusting upon them strategies with high risks? It is safer and more humane to proceed by short steps into what can be foreseen than by long leaps into the unknown, in the meantime gaining experience on the way. Changing power relations and the distribution of wealth may often be a necessary condition for major improvement.

Chambers, Robert. *Rural Development: Putting the Last First*. Essex, England: Longman Scientific & Technical, Longman Group U.K., Ltd., Longman House, 1983. Copyright © 1983, Robert Chambers. Used with permission of the author.

EXCERPT FROM:
COMMUNITY ORGANIZATION AND PEOPLE'S PARTICIPATION

By Karina C. David

1984 Like the much-abused word "development," the terms "people's participation" and "community organization" today no longer inspire easy confidence and automatic trust. Their meaning now, more than ever, resides in the context of their actual use and, indeed, in the identity of their users.

…This phenomenon—the appropriation of radical and populist concepts and methodologies and the evacuation of their original value premises as they are harnessed by planners, technocrats and development experts for their own ends—has become a notable feature of development policies of the Third World. The old vocabulary of paternal planning by government agencies and aid-giving institutions has been adequately refurbished and enriched through the clever appropriation of progressive language. But what is even more important is that the very process of political subjugation and pacification itself need no longer be seen for what it is. Today, entire communities can be led into captivity under the banner of people's participation.

Today's mobilization campaigns launched by Third World authoritarian governments are seldom sponsored by cold and mindless bureaucrats. The developmentalist governments have learned their lessons well. They are now among the most avid clients of community-organizing experts. They too speak the language of participation and of popular leadership—but only for as long as the realities dealt with do not go beyond the local community level. The situation is such that one may well accurately speak of the "absorption" of people's participation or its repressive incorporation into the machinery of domination.

The First Meanings of the Words

…It has become very urgent to restate the first meanings of these terms as they are understood in nongovernmental popular settings. …

While many groups and individuals claim to be community organizers, it is immediately apparent that apart from the fact that they operate within the community setting, there does not seem to be any recognizable thread in their activities that would point to a holistic and common framework upon which their activities rest. Analytically, based on their perspective of society and its concomitant implications in practice, three types of community organizers can be distinguished—the apologetic, the liberal and the liberative.

Apologetic Community Organizers

The apologetic community organizer accepts the essential viability of the existing system. To him, the societal order is based on consensus and cooperation, where the various sectors of society relate through reciprocity and interdependence. The state represents the will of the people, is generally responsive and promotes the common good. Such a perspective views economic differentiation and even inequality as social necessities which must be harnessed in order that development can be achieved. Since the state represents the people, then the direction of development is clearly laid out and what remains is to convince people to participate wholeheartedly in such undertakings.

STRENGTHENING THE SYSTEM

Within this perspective, the role of the community organizer is limited to that of working to strengthen the system. Thus the organizer is a tool toward the realization of the plans of both local and national leadership. As such, the organizer operates as the intermediary between national policies and their implementation by the people. Since such policies and thrusts are unquestioningly accepted, the organizer becomes a conduit who possesses some skills to ensure acceptance of such policies by the people. Within such a perspective,

the organizer can only view the masses in a condescending manner. He, thus, very easily becomes prescriptive and even dictatorial, reflecting the same authoritarian attitudes as those who hold the reins of political power. …Very often, such organizers confine themselves to the distribution of dole-outs, encouraging people to intervene only in the implementation of ready-made programs…cultivating an unquestioning obedience to the state or its local representatives.

ULTIMATELY ANTI-PARTICIPATIVE

Apologetic community organizers—the family-planning agent whose basic function is to fulfill his acceptor quota, the extension worker whose intervention remains on the level of telling the people what to do, the other state bureaucrats—can only be techno-fascists who wittingly or unwittingly deny the people their right to participation. Unfortunately, because of the structures that such states perpetuate, community organizing, or what masquerades as such, is ultimately anti-participative.

It must be noted that in recent years, this sinister appropriation of the techniques of community organization has taken up a large portion of the budgets of most ministries of government.

Liberal Community Organizers

The liberal community organizer, on the other hand, sees the necessity of altering certain aspects of the system. He accepts the role that conflict and exploitation play in the society. While accepting the essential viability of the system, he clearly sees that there are certain systemic aberrations. Very often, the liberal organizer accounts for these by attacking three basic areas: the fact that leadership both at the local and at the national level is not responsive to the needs of the majority; the fact that social inequalities and exploitation are too grave; and the fact that the people are not organized enough to act as a countervailing force. Thus, the liberal organizer is trapped within the confines of the existing structure and yet aims at resolving issues that are actually structurally generated.

REFORMISTS WHO HOPE

Because of such a perspective that realizes the manifestations but refuses to recognize the structural causes, liberal community organizers are usually torn between the pull of the apologists and the attraction of the more radical organizers. Ultimately, liberal organizers end up by tinkering with the system, instituting structural improvements without actually confronting the root causes of such problems. In a very real sense, such organizers are reformists who hope vainly that an aroused citizenry can overcome problems which the organizer refuses to recognize as basically structural. The liberal organizer, then, sees the process of organizing as an end in itself, where some structural improvements can be accomplished, inequality lessened and leadership made more responsive because the people are organized.

But such a conception of organizing implies a particular approach. Since the primary aim is to develop the necessary conditions so that people's power can emerge, much of the emphasis is placed on the locality and the issues that directly confront the people in the area. Apart from being localist, the organizer relies very heavily on the people. Because the organizer's vision is limited to a romantic ideal of militant communities that can stand up against the powerful forces that threaten them—no matter that these forces are not analyzed from a holistic perspective—the organizer confronts problems on an issue-to-issue basis, hoping for a time in the future when there are no more issues to confront. And yet knowing that many of these problems are generated by conditions beyond the confines of the community, the organizer falls short of any intervention that links up community issues with larger social, economic and political problems.

PROCESS-CENTERED ACTIVITIES

Lacking a vision upon which to anchor change, the organizer just tails the limited perceptions of the people. As such, he is very often confined to tactic- and process-centered activities aimed generally at obtaining welfare gains for the community. Liberal organizers enhance participation among the people to a level of participation where they can deal with issues whose roots go beyond the community.

The standard response of such organizers to the question of direction is that the people know best. The people initially appreciate the entrance of liberal organizers but ultimately wonder where all the activities are leading to.

Liberative Community Organizers

The liberative organizer views the society as having a system which is woven around the exploitation of the majority. As such, the existing leadership cannot be responsive to the needs of the people. In fact, liberative organizers accept that the people confront not only private oppressors but the forces of the state itself. In the Third World, what people face are states that have found common cause with the agencies of the world capitalist system. Under this arrangement, the state plays the role of foreman of its people to facilitate their exploitation and the plunder of the country's resources by world capitalism. In exchange, regimes that have long lost whatever shred of legitimacy they might have started with are kept in power.

RESTRUCTURING THE SYSTEM

Liberative organizers, therefore, aim at restructuring the system, using community organization as the initial step in developing a people who react to local conditions within the perspective of the larger national context. Thus, emphasis is placed on consciousness-raising and politicization, building upon local and sectoral struggles to create an appreciation of the root causes of these problems. Such struggles are always situated within the context of historical forces and a vision of an alternative social order. It is the liberative community organizer that most Third World countries have to develop because such organizers not only encourage people's participation but lay the groundwork for the conditions that will allow such forms of participation to flourish.

1927
1960
1963
1964
1967
1969
1970
1971
1972
1973
1974
1975
1976
1977
1978
1979
1980
1981
1982
1983
1984
1985
1986
1987
1988
1989
1990
1991
1992
1993
1994
1995
1996
1997
1998
1999
2000
2001
2002
2003
2004
2005
2006

The Communities We Face

While people's participation remains the foremost goal as well as the primary process of any genuine community organization effort, the results have been varied. On the one hand, organizers have surrendered by concluding that certain communities are not ready for organizing efforts. Very often organizers have accounted for this defeat in terms of what they perceive to be the almost insurmountable apathy and indifference of the people. On the extreme are numerous examples of successful experiments where whole communities have actively taken their destinies into their own hands, even to the extent of laying down their lives for the causes they believed in.

What types of communities do we generally face in most Third World countries?

These are communities which have been marginalized by societal forces beyond their control, people who have accepted their fate as that of simple recipients of national and international developments.

Because of the demand for particular commodities such as bananas and pineapples, rice-growing communities which could at least survive because they produced their own staple food, have been enticed to shift to export crops. Without understanding the vagaries of the market, these communities find themselves powerless when the market dries up and they cannot sell their crops. Unfortunately, realizing this does not enable them to return to growing rice since the nutrients of the land have been destroyed as a result of the years of fertilizers and other inputs used for export crops.

We face communities and people who are capable only of reacting to conditions which threaten them. Their reactions are nothing more than grumbling about issues and ultimately simply finding ways of individually coping with such situations.

Because of state policies, increases in the prices of farm inputs, consumer items, and the overall standard of living as a result of the devaluation of the local currency are perceived as situations beyond their control. The usual reaction is to tighten belts; to look for new sources of income, which are generally absent; even to mercilessly compete against each other for the few scarce resources. This reaction simply points to the acceptance of a fate of powerlessness, and people hardly ever consider the option that they themselves can collectively do something about such situations.

We face communities that have an almost total lack of understanding of the structures that determine their lives.

Urban poor communities faced by the prospects of demolition and forced relocation find it hard to comprehend why lands they have improved for years are now being claimed by both the government and wealthy individuals. While these communities see immediate causes—the need to beautify the city for the First Lady's caprices, the need to artificially erase all manifestations of poverty so that tourists and foreign funders believe we are developing—it is rare that such communities can relate such problems to structures of oppression in society. Very often, the explanations that are given only reach the level of misdirected priorities and the lack of a conscience of those in power.

We face people who, through generations, have accepted powerlessness as a permanent feature of their lives and are thus unable to even perceive reality as problematic. Above all, we face people who have forfeited the right to intervene in decisions and policies that determine the quality of their lives.

For most people, especially in rural areas, the entry of community organizers is greeted with hope. However, faced with questions that try to ascertain whether they perceive the necessity of actively involving themselves in a process of change, they usually react by surrendering this option to standard leaders. Realizing in the process that such leaders will not help them solve their problems, they rationalize their poverty and exploitation as being God-given. In fact, it is not uncommon to hear people argue that there are certain advantages in their style of life that even the wealthy do not possess.

Factors That Have Contributed To The State Of The Community

THE LEGACY OF COLONIALISM

Most countries whose historical development was aborted by the intervention of colonial powers have developed a people whose initiative and sense of potency have been systematically and consistently killed by the overpowering force of colonialism. Through both repression and ideological mechanisms, the people were led to believe in their inferiority, on the one hand, and the benevolence of those in power, on the other. For those who chose to assert their rights, outright repression was the answer. Slowly, through successive generations, the people were taught to accept their fate as passive objects of forces they could not understand.

CLASS-DIVIDED SOCIETIES

Because these societies and these communities are divided into classes with necessarily different access to both wealth and power, the majority of the people have been relegated to positions of absolute powerlessness. Because the upper classes have more resources, because they are more articulate, because they deceive the masses by ostensibly speaking and acting on their behalf, because they ultimately control the life chances of the people, the masses are caught in a bind. On the one hand, they are more easily manipulated because they cannot grasp the total situation and thus trust that their self-appointed leaders are indeed on their side. On the other, even if some them saw through these machinations, they could not possibly contest the power of those whose lands they till, those to whom they owe money, those who control middle-man operations, those who have access to centers of power beyond their own reach.

DIRECT STATE INTERVENTION

In many countries, even participation has been pre-empted by the state. Issues that should be objects of decision-making have been removed from the realm of public debate, and in their place the state has introduced forms of co-optive participation. Decisions are made by the state, and people are given a taste of participation only on matters of implementation. Thus politics have been absorbed by central authorities as well as by local leaders. Finally, it is not uncommon to hear of state repression when communities are belligerent in asserting their right to politics.

LACK OF INFORMATION

In class-divided societies, especially those under authoritarian governments, information is kept safely away from the masses through various means. First, by sheer lack of resources, the people are effectively cut off from even ordinary information sources. The media are beyond their reach; they are confined to very limited areas and cannot get any exposure to developments in other areas; information is actually withheld through censorship; and, perhaps most significantly, the channels of information are clogged with trivia and noise that have a numbing effect upon the intellect. This lack of information on the one hand, and overdose of garbage on the other, paralyzes the people in such a way that they are robbed even of a concept of reality and a vision of a better life.

PRESSURES OF A HAND-TO-MOUTH EXISTENCE

When people are preoccupied with their own physical survival, there is very little chance for reflection. People are reduced to day-to-day activities and unable to consider what is happening around them. For those who take the effort to reflect upon their conditions, these thoughts, limited as they are by all the previously mentioned factors, cannot be shared by others, much less can they become the objects of collective scrutiny. This isolation necessarily detracts from the possibility that collective discussions can lead to clearer conceptions and consequently determine actions to deal with their situations. People are thus consigned to pre-political states because they are not even granted the option of meaningful nonparticipation. What emerges is an apparent apathy and indifference among the masses.

1927
1960
1963
1964
1967
1969
1970
1971
1972
1973
1974
1975
1976
1977
1978
1979
1980
1981
1982
1983
1984
1985
1986
1987
1988
1989
1990
1991
1992
1993
1994
1995
1996
1997
1998
1999
2000
2001
2002
2003
2004
2005
2006

Liberative Community Organization As The Initial Step Towards National Transformation

Community organizers must always be conscious of the role they play in the national context. Because of the type of communities we face in most Third World countries, it is community organizing that can effect the initial breakthrough. Faced with communities that have accepted powerlessness as a way of life, participation in the shaping of a national future can only be accomplished in stages. The first stage is learning to confront reality at close range, in the immediate milieu one belongs to. But at the same time, knowing that community organization is just a step toward more basic changes, the organizer must continuously view local issues within the context of the larger social structure.

There is another function of community organization which organizers must strive toward. Much of the experimentation at the local community level must be geared toward trying out new forms of social arrangements that are practical applications of relationships expected in a transformed social order. Community organization must be a venue through which the national vision can be fleshed out.

Experiments with communal farms, various forms of cooperatives, alternative leadership patterns and the like serve not only to effect meaningful changes in communities, but also to set the stage for forms of social relationships that could be viable in a transformed society. What are tested out in such cases are not only principles and visions but actual forms of organization. These should become the blueprints for an alternative future.

It is not enough for organizers to cling to the vague vision of a potent people collectively pursuing their interests. The organizer must clarify the larger purpose within which organized, participative and militant communities can have some instrumental meaning. Organizing without a concrete model of an alternative future can only lead to superficial and directionless actions that end in frustration and a further feeling of powerlessness among the people. ...

THE END GOAL: DETERMINATION TO ACT

...Action must not only be determined, it must always be organized and collective. The people must see, through experience in small, concrete struggles, that their collective strength is effective. From minor actions and victories, the people can then start to challenge reality. ...

David, Karina C. "Community Organization and People's Participation." Lambatlaya, Third and Fourth Quarters, 1984. This paper was presented at the Conference on Methods and Media in Community Participation held in Uppsala, Sweden, May 1984. Used with permission of the author.

EXCERPT FROM:

A BUDDHIST APPROACH TO
DEVELOPMENT:
A SRI LANKAN ENDEAVOR

By Wimal Dissanayake

1984 Communication is the veritable lifeblood of human society—no society can possibly function without it. Therefore, we must pay very close attention to the role of communication in any development effort. One of the major weaknesses of early development plans of developing countries was the insignificant role assigned to communication. Lucien W. Pye's observation (1963) is relevant in this regard:

> Communication is the web of human society. The structure of a communication system with its more or less well-defined channels is in a sense the skeleton of the social body which envelops it. The content of communication is of course the very substance of human intercourse. The flow of communication determines the direction and the pace of dynamic social development. (p. 4).

I will now outline the four main approaches to development. The first approach was popular in the 1950s and 1960s. It emphasized industrialization, capital-intensive technology and centralized planning. Advocates claimed that developing countries could progress only by following the lead given by industrially advanced countries. Rostow's (1960) book *The Stages of Economic Growth: A Non–Communist Manifesto* had a profound impact on this mode of thinking.

Communication scholars like Schramn (1964), Lerner (1964) and Pye (1963) endorsed this approach to development. They expressed the view that mass media can play a highly significant role in creating the climate for development. This approach stressed the need for increased productivity through speedy industrialization. It was said that productivity is the key to development and that the most productive sector of

modern society is the industrial sector. Communication efforts inclined in this direction.

This approach to development generated a great deal of optimism. However, by the 1970s, it was clear that the strategy advocated in this approach to development had failed to deliver the goods. Although the gross national product (GNP) had increased and exports were up, many existing problems such as the increase of unemployment and underemployment and urban congestion were aggravated in the process. Proponents maintained that the benefits accruing through this approach would have a "trickle down" effect. This, too, failed to materialize. Actually, the gap between rich and poor in the developing countries widened appreciably.

By the 1970s, many development communication scholars began to find fault with this approach. Four counterarguments are particularly relevant. First, it was ethnocentric and held up the Western experience as a model to be imitated by developing countries, without paying adequate attention to questions of historical background, uniqueness of cultural context, etc. Second, it posited a unilinear view of history. Critics argued that there was not one, but several paths to development, and that the historical route taken by developed countries was not the only one available to developing nations. Third, it concentrated on only exogenous factors of development, to the exclusion of endogenous factors. Fourth, it placed too much emphasis on the individual and laid the blame at his door without taking into sufficient consideration effects of the social structure. Adherents of the first approach often accused the peasants in developed countries of being too traditional, superstitious, fatalistic, etc., and of not being motivated by the "Protestant work ethic." Critics countered that these claims totally ignored the effect of the social structure, which would otherwise explain more cogently some of these features (Rogers, 1976, pp. 121-148).

The second approach to development is a reaction to the first. Rogers (1976), closely associated with the first

1927
1960
1963
1964
1967
1969
1970
1971
1972
1973
1974
1975
1976
1977
1978
1979
1980
1981
1982
1983
1984
1985
1986
1987
1988
1989
1990
1991
1992
1993
1994
1995
1996
1997
1998
1999
2000
2001
2002
2003
2004
2005
2006

approach, has pointed out the central concerns of the second approach very lucidly. He designates one as the "old" paradigm and the other as the "new" paradigm.

The first approach emphasized economic growth, industrialization, centralized planning and exogenous factors of development. On the contrary, the second approach underlined income distribution, decentralized planning, labor-intensive technology and endogenous as well as exogenous factors in development. This shift in emphasis was accompanied by a related effort calling attention to the quality of life, the need to blend modern and traditional media of communication, appropriate technology and a popular participation in the decision-making process.

The proponents of the second approach focused their attention on such questions as: How can distributive justice be achieved? How can the ideals of self-reliance and self-management be realized? How can the old and the new media of communication be integrated productively? How can culture best be employed as a mediator and facilitator of development? How can one construct more history-conscious and society-specific models of development communication? How can one bring social-structural factors impending development into the equation?

This shift in the meaning of development was accompanied by a parallel shift regarding the meaning of communication. The old mechanistic, linear, one-way communicator-based model of communication gave way to a more organic, interactive, two-way model. Communication scholars like Berlo (1977) pointed out the process-like and interactive nature of communication.

This new approach to development communication represents a potentially more rewarding perception of development and communication. Many of its strengths can be seen as efforts to remedy the defects of the older approach. However, several contradictions remain. It does not emerge from a consistent social philosophy, as does the first, and it seems to incorporate many conflicting trends of thought. Indeed this new paradigm or approach manifests not one, but many, paradigms. On the one hand, it talks of the interdependence of the developed and on the other hand, much is made of the notions of self-management and self-reliance. But these ideas are not developed in a sufficiently comprehensive manner enabling us to comprehend their full implications and to take cognizance of their conflicting demands.

This leads to what I term the third approach to development. It is characterized by insistence on the interdependence of developed and developing countries and the need to make this relationship a central concern. However, one has to bear in mind that when the spokesmen for this approach employ the term "interdependence," they are talking of a viciously asymmetrical relationship in which developed countries thrive at the expense of developing countries. Therefore, they believe that a basic precondition for development is the elimination of this asymmetrical relationship.

The advocates of the third approach to development stress the futility of discussing communication and development in a national setting without examining the historical evolution of each society and the way in which the world economic system conditions and regulates its development. Nordenstreng and Schiller (1979), while complimenting the spokesmen for the second approach, observe that the old paradigm has not been entirely abandoned. They maintain that the notion, developing according to conditions determined mainly within that society, remains largely unexamined and that this is a fundamental issue which should not be ignored. Nordenstreng and Schiller argue that while advocates of the second approach to development and communication talk of external courses of development and dependence theory, such notions do not appear to significantly influence their conceptualization.

The colonial experience of less developed countries is crucial to this mode of argument. The factors which brought about the growth of industrially advanced countries also brought about the conditions of poverty existing in Third World countries. Obtaining political independence from foreign domination does not appear to have appreciably altered the picture. Scholars like Galtung (1980) express the view that colonial structures still persist, but with the systems of control exercised in a subtler fashion. Economic aid, transnational corporations and the international monetary institutions are cited as examples of newer and subtler modes of imperialism. Scholars argue that this imperialism is found not only in economics but also in the political, military, communications and cultural domains. According to this approach, then, unless there is a structural rearrangement in international relationships, less developed countries are unlikely to make much progress.

Finally, the fourth approach to development and communication is currently gaining wide recognition. It is characterized by a strong emphasis on self-reliance. This approach to development brings together a number of ideas that have surfaced in recent times, including integrated village development, popular participation in decision-making processes, grass-roots development, productive use of local resources, fulfillment of basic needs, maintenance of the ecological balance, popular definition of development problems and culture as a mediating force in development.

Galtung (1980) lucidly presents the essence of the strategy of self-reliance in the development process:

> Self-reliance is a dynamic movement from the periphery, at all levels—individual, local, regional. It is not something done for the periphery. Thus, control over the economic machinery of a country by national and even by local, state or private capitalists in order to produce for the satisfaction of basic needs is not self-reliance. It may be 'serve the people,' but is not to 'trust the people'—to use the Chinese jargon. Self-reliance ultimately means that the society is organized in such a way that the masses arrive at self-fulfillment though self-reliance—in participation with others in the same situation." (p.401).

This, undoubtedly, is an idealistic proposition. Galtung himself has pointed out that there is as much economics as there is psycho-politics involved. This fourth approach to development discourages the widespread tendency in developing countries to imitate the goals and strategies of Western countries and to engage in the impossible task of catching up. Instead, it urges a rethinking of the issues and implications of development.

References

Ahmed, M. "Introduction in the Sarvodaya Movement: Self-help Rural Development in Sri Lanka." In M. H. Coombs, ed., *Meeting the Basic Needs of the Rural Poor.* New York: Pergamon, 1980.

Aristotle. *Rhetoric.* Translated by R. W. Roberts. New York: Random House Inc., 1954.

Ariyaratne, A.. T. *Collected Works,* Vol.1. Colombo: Sarvodaya Research Centre, no date.

Berlo, David K. "Communication as Process: Review and Commentary." Communication Yearbook, 1977, 1, 11-27.

Galtung, J. *The True Worlds: A Transnational Perspective.* New York: Free Press, 1980.

Kantowsky, D. *Sarvodaya: The Other Development.* New Delhi: Vikas Publishing House, 1980.

Lerner, David. *The Passing of Traditional Society.* New York: Free Press, 1964.

Nordenstreng, Kaarle, and Herbert I. Shiller. *National Sovereignty and International Communication.* Norwood: Ablex, 1979.

The Progress Report of the Sarvodaya Movement, 1978.

Pye, Lucian W. *Communication and Political Development.* Princeton: Princeton University Press, 1963.

Ratnapala, N. *Study Service in Sarvodaya.* Colombo: Sarvodaya Research Centre, no date.

Rogers, Everett M. *Communication and Development.* Beverly Hills: Sage, 1976.

Rogers, Everett M., and F. F. Shoemaker. *Communication of Innovations: A Cross-Cultural Approach.* New York: Free Press, 1971.

Rostow, W. W. *The Stages of Economic Growth: A Non-Communist Manifesto.* New York: Cambridge University Press, 1960.

Schramm, Wilbur. *Mass Media and National Development.* Stanford: Stanford University Press, 1964.

Seers, D. "The Meaning of Development." *International Development Review,* 1969. 11 (4), 2-6.

1927
1960
1963
1964
1967
1969
1970
1971
1972
1973
1974
1975
1976
1977
1978
1979
1980
1981
1982
1983
1984
1985
1986
1987
1988
1989
1990
1991
1992
1993
1994
1995
1996
1997
1998
1999
2000
2001
2002
2003
2004
2005
2006

NATIONAL INFORMATION POLICIES:
A PLEA FOR DISSOCIATION

Excerpt from: Cultural Autonomy in Global Communications: Planning National Information Policy

By Cees J. Hamelink

1984 From a review of the still-inchoate and scattered efforts to resist dependency in the field of international information, it is evident that we must search for a more adequate response to cultural synchronization. The key question is how the Third World can develop *effective* policies to maintain and strengthen its cultural autonomy.

In the international discussions that have evolved over the past decade, the question of information and cultural autonomy, is intimately linked with the need for a new international economic order.

The New International Economic Order and the New International Information Order

"Sometimes education can start announcing the new society. But in order that the announcement become concrete, it is absolutely necessary for the infrastructure of society to change." —*Mario Cabral, Minister of Education. Guinea Bissau*

Two concepts have increasingly become the major focuses of international debates and negotiations: the new international economic order and the new international information order.

In September 1975, the Dag Hammarskjöld Third World Journalists' Seminar (which met during the 7th Special Session of the United Nations General Assembly) stated:

For the new international economic order to emerge, people of both industrialized and Third World countries must be given the opportunity of understanding that they share a common

interest in creating international conditions that will permit another development of societies in all parts of the world.[1]

The Rio Report, coordinated by Nobel laureate Jan Tinbergen, insisted that the widening of the capacity to inform must be viewed as an essential component of attempts to create a new international order and, as such, the monopolistic and discriminatory practices inherent in current international information dissemination must be deemed as one of the worst, though subtle, characteristics of the present system.[2]

In 1976, the summit meeting in Colombo, Sri Lanka, of the nonaligned countries declared: "A new international order in the field of information and mass communications is as vital as a new international economic order."[3] In these positions bringing about a new information order is seen as an essential contribution to the advent of a new economic order. As former Venezuelan President Carlos Andrés Peréz stated succinctly, "There will never be a new economic international order without the liberation of the information order."[4]

There can be little doubt, indeed, that reshaping the international order will demand a fundamental replacement of the stereotyped, alienating and discriminatory sets of ideas that current communications structures perpetuate. The transformation of present global inequalities and injustices requires another type of information, "one which will fight preconceived ideas, ignorance and alienation" and facilitate the conscientization of citizens to ensure their control over decision making."[5]

A basic element in the process of restructuring international relations will be international public opinion. As the Rio Report rightly claims:

Public opinion in the industrialized countries will not have real access to full information on the Third World, its demands, aspirations and needs, until such time as information and communication patterns are liberated from the market-oriented sensationalism and news presentations which characterize them at present and until they are consciously of ethnocentric prejudices.[6]

This demands that the present information order move "from an unidirectional to a multidirectional structure, from an ethnocentric to a culturally pluralistic and multidimensional perspective, from the receiver's passivity to active participation, from dominant transnational influences to a multinational balance."[7]

International information processes will have to be liberated from their "monopolistic and discriminatory practices":

- to present a realistic picture of existing economic power relations;
- to contribute to the insight that dependency relations ought to disappear; and
- to make cultural autonomy possible.

However, the problem is that these international information processes are an integral part of the dependency relations that determine the economic, political and cultural organization of the current international order. The international relations stem from the development of Western editorial and economic expansion that was consolidated in the 19th century with the internalization of industrial capitalism. In conjunction with this expansion, Western techniques, symbols and social patterns were exported to the colonized territories.[8]

As indicated before, it is only in the second half of the 20th century that this occurs on such a massive scale and, at the same time, so subtly that one can describe it as transnational cultural synchronization. Moreover, despite the fact that the new nations have achieved independence as sovereign states, they are still confronted with an international order controlled by their former colonial metropolitan powers.

Thus, drastic changes in the current international order are necessary if a new information order is to come about. The two aspects of a new international order are linked together in a dialectical way, so that not only will fundamental economic changes have to support changes in the information order but changes in the informational structures will also support basic economic transformation. To paraphrase Mario Cabral, international information can start announcing the new international order; but for that announcement to become concrete, it is absolutely necessary that the economic order change.

These dialectics make it meaningful and possible to develop proposals for the new international information order based on the perspective of the new international economic order. The cohesive element in this relation is the conception of information as a "resource."[9]

On the world market, information—in all of its ramifications—is a resource that is collected, processed and marketed, just like all other economic commodities. As with other resources, the control over its production and distribution is grossly maldistributed among the nations of the world. Yet information as a resource offers opportunities to dependent countries which are more readily accessible than are other resources, such as mineral or agricultural resources. Unlike other resources, information can be collected, processed and marketed many times over. The national exploitation of the information resource can, therefore, be embarked upon without the immediate nationalization of foreign industries and a complicated protective legislation, which may take years to design and many more to be implemented.

Moreover, the exploitation of the resource information can be done with more indigenous capabilities and less transfer of capital and technology than is the case with many other resources.

Information as a national resource is a liberating force in the economic and cultural emancipation of a country, if its exploitation is guided by the principles upon which a new ordering of international economic relations should be based.

1927
1960
1963
1964
1967
1969
1970
1971
1972
1973
1974
1975
1976
1977
1978
1979
1980
1981
1982
1983
1984
1985
1986
1987
1988
1989
1990
1991
1992
1993
1994
1995
1996
1997
1998
1999
2000
2001
2002
2003
2004
2005
2006

The New International Economic Order

The international economic order that emerged after World War II was designed in its general dimensions by the 1943-1944 Bretton Woods Conference held in New Hampshire in the United States. With almost no involvement of the Third World, the basis was established for such institutions as the International Monetary Fund, the World Bank and the General Agreement on Trade and Tariffs (GATT). These institutions offered a development model to the Third World in which the growth of developing countries would be intimately linked with the existing colonial metropolis-satellite structure. The model projected a type of industrial development in the Third World nations that would be strongly oriented toward markets in the metropolitan countries. It was assumed that with the growth of metropolitan markets, the demand for goods produced in developing countries would also vastly increase. Many of the developing countries would have a very weak industrial base, but by their using the comparative advantage of cheap labor, a certain type of labor-intensive industry could be established which would allow them some participation in the international trade of manufactured goods.

Instead of forcefully encouraging receiving countries to build up their own infrastructure of finance and technology, new industries would be established with the support of large financial and technological transfers form the metropolis, especially through the emerging economic structure of the transnational corporation. Industrially less-developed countries would thus become better integrated into the world economy, and the increased employment that the new industrialization offered would at least lead to higher national incomes.

After World War II, and especially since the mid-1960s, many developing countries indeed experienced an industrialization process but one that had a strong external dependence on the markets of the wealthy, industrially advanced, countries. Such export-linked production has generally become part of the vertically integrated manufacturing structure of the transnational corporation.

However, this model did not generate the kinds of improved economic conditions in the satellite countries that were expected. Whereas during the 1960s the market economies of the metropolitan countries enjoyed an unprecedented growth, the countries with a dependent industrialization experienced an increasing economic lag, and the international development efforts that were highly touted in such plans as the First United Nations Development Decade met with almost total failure.

Serious questions were thus raised about the validity of a model that was still based essentially on a colonial structure; and its fundamental assumptions increasingly came under fire from political leaders as well as economists in academic circles. In the late 1960s and early 1970s, the questioning brought about proposals for alternative development models based on concepts such as self-reliance, basic needs and a new international economic order.

Since 1974, the basic principles of a new international economic order have been formulated in a number of declarations and programs of action. Most were proposed by Third World countries and have met with approval from a majority in the international community.[10]

The key principles are:

- the sovereignty and equality of states;
- the full and effective participation of all states in international decision making;
- the right of all states to adopt appropriate economic, political and cultural systems;
- the full, permanent sovereignty over national resources;
- the right to regulate the activities of foreign entities, such as transnational corporations, in concurrence with national goals and priorities;
- the right to formulate a model of autonomous development geared toward the basic needs of the population, and

- the right to pursue progressive social transformation that enables the full participation of the population in the development process.

With these principles, some basic assumptions of the present economic order have been questioned in a fundamental way. These assumptions are:

- The present economic system is fundamentally sound social and the crisis that we are faced with is only of a temporary nature.
- The present economic order is in the interest of both the industrialized and the Third World countries.
- Poor countries will be able to develop as long as rich countries remain rich and let their affluence trickle down to the poor.
- The model of development applied in the rich countries is also the best possible model for the poor countries.

Confronting these assumptions, the new economic order claims:

- Since the beginning of the 1970s, the economic crisis is the result of the fundamental breakdown of traditional economic mechanisms.
- The present economic order is incompatible with the Third World ambition of total emancipation; since this order is rooted in colonial exploitation, it can operate only against the interest of the Third World.
- The trickle-down effect does not work in the relation between rich and poor countries; moreover, the development of the international community has to depend on the development of *all* its members, who decide on an equal footing about economic developments.
- Development in Third World countries cannot be an imitation of Western models; the purpose is not to catch up with the rich countries. The development in the Third World that must take place will respect national sovereignty and limit the influence of decisions taken elsewhere.

In the proposals for the new international economic order, the crucial concept is *sovereignty*. But one should not confound sovereignty with a concept of

nationalism as we know it from European history. It had an extraterritorial meaning that could often cause armed conflicts as the national proprietary rights were extended to include other countries. In the new economic order, sovereignty pertains to the national territory itself; it implies protection of whatever national resources a nation has. The core of the concept of sovereignty is that of making self-reliant development possible. The new economic order in this respect differs from earlier development strategies that often stressed the integration of Third World countries into the international economic system. Opposing the integration into an international system that continues economic dependence, the new economic order designs an independent development as the basis of an international system in which states participate on an equal footing.

Such a reordering implies that Third World countries must decide autonomously about their own social arrangements. A self-reliant development does require decisive social transformations. This points to a close connection between the international and the national orders. Changes in the international order cannot be achieved without related changes in the national order. The international order has to create the necessary space for national sovereignty; the national order has to translate this space into effective policy.

Despite the wide discussion of these principles for a new international economic order, especially from 1974 onward, there has still been relatively little improvement achieved in the economic relations of the Third World with the advanced industrial countries. Much of this may be owing to the rigidity of present economic structures. But one must also question the shortcomings and inconsistencies implicit in many of the proposals for a new international economic order.

A fundamental premise of many of these proposals is a claim of sovereign control over a nation's resources. But this control does not automatically make a country less dependent if in its international relations it

1927
1960
1963
1964
1967
1969
1970
1971
1972
1973
1974
1975
1976
1977
1978
1979
1980
1981
1982
1983
1984
1985
1986
1987
1988
1989
1990
1991
1992
1993
1994
1995
1996
1997
1998
1999
2000
2001
2002
2003
2004
2005
2006

does not have the power to bargain with its national resources. Bargaining strength presupposes building some form of countervailing power by developing countries. Such power would make it possible for developing countries to enter into international trade and other negotiations with reasonable chances of equitable exchange. Apart from the oil producers' cartel, no effective bargaining power has been created among less-developed countries during the past decade.

Underlying this failure to build countervailing power is a crucial inconsistency in the proposals: Despite their demand for autonomous development at the level of policy discussions, these countries remain more oriented toward the metropolis than toward each other. As a consequence, they have concentrated very little on formulating common, mutually complementing national policies and have not directed much attention toward strengthening horizontal linkages among themselves.

This inconsistency between the demand for national autonomy and the continued linkage with current international relations is particularly evident in the emphasis on a strategy of interdependence, which is so central to much of the debate on the new international economic order.

In the present structure of international political-economic relations, interdependence is virtually equated with a hierarchical dependency relation between powerful and powerless countries. In such a process of interaction between parties of unequal strength, it is illusory to think that through a joint effort the weaker nations will develop an economic system which responds primarily to the needs of its own people. In the interchange, nations with a more developed technological base will instead tend to hold the margin of advantage, and the more powerful the nation, the more it will exploit the interdependent relation to its own benefit. Furthermore, the greater the volume of economic interchange between unequal parties, the greater will be the disadvantages of the powerless.

Some suggest that in trade relations, satellite and metropolitan countries are mutually dependent, but such a concept is very deceptive if one considers the technological advantage of the latter. Can one really argue that the leading industrialized countries are dependent upon the Third World for their development? What is the significance of the often proclaimed dependence of the industrialized nations if they can substitute the Third World's cheap labor force with automated machinery, if they increasingly protect their markets against products from Third World countries and if, as a final recourse, they are ready to secure their access to Third World resources militarily with rapid deployment forces?

The thesis of interdependence has found strong support from the protagonists of the new realism. This stand of development thinking has gained strength in the member countries of the Organization for Economic Cooperation and Development (OECD), especially since 1978. It emphasizes that aid to developing countries will increase their potential for buying products on metropolitan markets and that such improved trading relations will be in the enlightened self-interest of the industrialized countries.

Aid, however, tends to flow mainly to the so-called middle-income countries. According to the *1981 World Development Report* of the World Bank, the 36 poorest countries receive only 37 percent of the total development aid.

In reality, the aid-trade model tends to focus the interdependent relations upon countries that are the most promising trading partners, integrating them more firmly into the existing international economic order. This inevitably further undermines the chance for autonomous development in the Third World.

In the current international order, the concept of interdependence represents an unequal relation between sovereign but *dependent* states. The *new* international economic order, however, would have to establish a relation between states that is based on sovereignty and *equality* for all. A concept more appropriate for this relation would be *interindependence*.

On the basis of the principles and concepts elaborated so far, the new international economic order could be defined in the following way:

> An organization of international economic relations in which states, by developing their economic system in an autonomous way and with complete sovereign control of resources, fully and effectively participate as independent members of the international community.

The Thesis of Dieter Senghaas

In an important contribution to the international debate on development, Dieter Senghaas has proposed the thesis of "dissociation."[11] He claims that dissociation from the metropolis-centered economy offers the only way toward an adequate development process in Third World countries. Such a development process would have to be achieved through a variety of measures, such as:

- an increase in agricultural productivity;
- an increase of nonexport-oriented industrial production of mass consumption goods, rather than fancy, luxury goods for middle and upper classes;
- establishment of facilities that create independent means of production;
- development of adequate infrastructures for collective needs; and
- full exploitation of available human and natural resources.

The present asymmetrically structured international economy makes such a development process impossible. Third World countries generally have at their disposal most of the resources that they need for their development. Their chances of developing their economies cooperatively are optimal, however, only if they dissociate themselves from the conditions that govern the structure of the world market. At present, the most powerful parties active in the market determine these conditions primarily in terms of *their own needs*.

Only dissociation will make the satisfaction of Third World countries basic needs possible. If they do not choose this option, Third World countries will only become more dependent.

Dissociation should be an essential component in the proposals for a new international economic order. Without dissociation, all the proposals—for enlarged transfer of technology, finances and other resources, for the improvement of trade conditions and better regulation of markets for raw materials—will make the satellite countries even more dependent.

Dissociation and Self-Reliance

Dissociation, or "de-linking," as it is sometimes referred to, does not necessarily find support in all Third World countries at present. Resistance is particularly strong where the governing elite has a strong cultural and political orientation toward the metropolitan countries. Consequently, in these countries industrialization tends to follow the metropolitan model, and trade relations are largely oriented toward the metropolitan export markets.

But without dissociation, action programs for a new economic order are merely "new wine in old vessels." As Senghaas puts it, the new order could easily end up being a mere conflict over the distribution of resources between the metropolis and the Third World social classes that have been integrated into the international economy.[12] It is precisely these social classes, the political and economic elites and the privileged classes of the Third World, who will be inclined to choose according to their own interests, that is, against dissociation and for integration.

However, the integrationists have built up their close linkages with the metropolitan economies largely on the basis of the rapid growth and affluence of the North Atlantic nations in the 1960s. Since the mid-1970s, economic growth in these countries has been slowing down, and without the prospect of limitless growth of markets, the association may no longer be so attractive to the dependent countries.

1927
1960
1963
1964
1967
1969
1970
1971
1972
1973
1974
1975
1976
1977
1978
1979
1980
1981
1982
1983
1984
1985
1986
1987
1988
1989
1990
1991
1992
1993
1994
1995
1996
1997
1998
1999
2000
2001
2002
2003
2004
2005
2006

The decision on a national policy of dissociation may be a direct challenge to the interests of a traditional governing elite. It often implies profound structural changes and a transition to a new political leadership with a broad popular democratic base within a country.

Where social structures are rigid and power is largely concentrated in the hands of the leading elite, the risks are high. On the one hand, the political leadership emerging from the radical social transformation through which dissociation is achieved may maintain itself only at the cost of strong internal controls. On the other hand, as the case of Chile indicates, where dissociation is attempted through a careful process of social change, it can be subverted by combined internal and external pressures. In order to be successful, dissociation has to combine resistance to external synchronization with internal equality.

It is important to note that the dissociation proposed by Senghaas is not identical with autarchy.[13] International exchange will continue to take place but on conditions that were described above as interindependence. This implies that in international cultural, economic and political exchanges, the sovereign states will select what promotes self-reliant development. Indeed, the concept of self-reliance is central to the strategy of dissociation.

This principle of self-reliant development has been increasingly stressed in the past decade. An important example of this thinking is the statement of the Cocoyoc Declaration drawn up by participants in the 1974 symposium on Patterns of Resource Use, Environment and Development Strategies. In this statement, self-reliance could "imply a temporary detachment from the present economic system; it is impossible to develop self-reliance through full participation in a system that perpetuates economic dependence."

Self-reliance can be defined as the domestic determination of development objectives and the self-confident use of local resources. Self-reliance represents an alternative development model that moves away from emphasis on linkage with the metropolitan countries and that concentrates on the exploitation of indigenous resources for the benefit of the indigenous population. Self-reliance as a strategy "requires, in its collective dimension, that the political, economic and sociocultural structures created to link colonies to metropolitan countries (in a status of dependence) be altered to link developing countries to each other."[14]

With self-reliance as the objective, dissociation means the conscious choice against the delusory offer of integration in an international order which appears to respond to all the interests of the developing countries, but which, in fact, represents almost exclusively the interests of the powerful. Dissociation demands a questioning of all international relations of interdependence between metropolitan and satellite countries and developing a strategy of relations in terms of the concept of interindependence. It also demands the abandonment or reformulation of exogenously defined objectives, priorities and cultural images and ideals. Taken in a strict sense, dissociation means the development of a distinct personality—a political, economic and cultural personality which is not imitative. As Frantz Fanon wrote during the Algerian liberation struggle, "We today can do everything, so long as we do not imitate Europe, so long as we are not obsessed by the desire to catch up with Europe. … European achievements, European style ought no longer to tempt us and throw us off our balance."[15] The rejection of imitation is absolutely crucial in a strategy of dissociation. This reliance on indigenous, creative resources for the generation of an alternative development model requires not only economic but also cultural dissociation.

Cultural Dissociation

To move to the central theme, the plea for cultural dissociation is based essentially on the thesis of Senghaas, as elaborated above. Applying this thesis to cultural development implies that cultural emancipation of satellite countries will be possible only through dissociation from the existing metropolis-dominated relations. Without cultural dissociation, all proposals for cultural emancipation are bound to remain new wine in old vessels. This is implicitly true as well for the new international information order. If the search for this order is not complemented with a plea for cultural dissociation, inevitably the choice is made for the integration model. This model might bring minor marginal improvements, but it will integrate Third World countries in an international system that operates against their very interests, impedes their emancipation, consolidates existing dependency relations and both creates and legitimizes cultural synchronization.

In the current political debate, the new international information order is discussed mainly from the perspective of integration, which is the case for representatives of both industrialized and Third World countries. The integration model proposes that the satellite countries be enabled to participate more fully in an information exchange designed and controlled by the metropolis, to take place through the greater transfer of funds to establish, for example, national news agencies, technology for the technical infrastructure for such agencies, and expertise for the training of journalists.

In such a transfer, the organization and professional standards of metropolitan information media are decisive. When Third World countries are lured into accepting such offers, which are often highly attractive, they are involved in a perpetual catching-up strategy. If one examines closely the process of transfer of advanced information technology, it is clear that this is an utterly senseless objective. The technological level of metropolitan countries is moving so fast that the satellite countries can only race after them breathlessly. Even if catching up were possible, one would still wonder what meaning this could have for an independent national development. For independent development, it is not decisive whether all countries participate in the international system with equal

levels of volume and sophistication in technical advances; it is crucial, however, whether the scope, volume and technical design of their contributions are determined by their own political, economic and cultural priorities. Whether or not the exchange is exactly balanced is of secondary importance.

In this respect, the emphasis in the present international debate on the concept of balance is somewhat misleading. The new international information order stands for an information exchange in which all parties participate with inputs and outputs that are appropriate to their particular situations and not necessarily balanced in quantity or quality with the inputs and outputs of the others. The new international information order stands for a system of nonhierarchical relations between the participating nation states, whereas a balanced system is not necessarily nonhierarchical.

One could imagine situations in which exporting information is very important for country A but less important for country B. In a certain phase of its development process, a country could feel the necessity to isolate itself from the international information exchange, precisely in view of its cultural emancipation.

The integration model is the very opposite of the dissociation model. The central argument of the latter is that an interindependent international system requires states to develop self-reliantly, which necessitates sovereign control of resources, including information. Only in this way can a state become independent not only *culturally* but also *economically* and *politically*.

For the development of an autonomous *cultural* system, it is essential that instrumental, symbolic and social adaptive mechanisms be maintained and/or designed so that they are adequate vis-à-vis the specific environment. In order to achieve economic liberation, it is vital that Third World countries present their own version of their development problems and independently provide information about raw materials, import-export relations, technology, labor conditions, activities of transnational corporations, etc.

1927
1960
1963
1964
1967
1969
1970
1971
1972
1973
1974
1975
1976
1977
1978
1979
1980
1981
1982
1983
1984
1985
1986
1987
1988
1989
1990
1991
1992
1993
1994
1995
1996
1997
1998
1999
2000
2001
2002
2003
2004
2005
2006

Moreover, controlling the export of crucial economic information is necessary if a country wants to make national decisions without foreign influence. This has become very critical with advances in the international computer data traffic and satellite telecommunication channels.[16]

Sovereign control of production and distribution of information is also pertinent for *political* emancipation. Activating the total population to participate in the national development inevitably demands important contributions from the national information system.

Cultural dissociation, like economic dissociation, cannot be equated with total autarchy. The main goal is autonomous and self-reliant development; consequently, a task with high priority is that of liberating the country from the conditions that were designed to meet the needs of the metropolis. Dissociation is meant to create the necessary space to take inventory of national resources according to one's own concept of development and to exploit these independently. Dissociation is a prerequisite for the active social involvement of the people in national independence movements. Otherwise, to use the phrase of Gandhi, the people will be "blown off their feet" in the fragile beginnings of independence by the overwhelming presence of the powerful metropolis. As in the case of the feminist liberation movement, this implies that there is a decision to engage in struggle under rules that are not set by the opponent but are determined autonomously.

The concrete realization of dissociation may differ according to the various stages of development in which dependent parties find themselves. The different types of metropolis-satellite relations may also require quite different processes of dissociation. In all cases, however, it is of crucial importance to accept dissociation as the guiding principle.

This proposal for cultural dissociation may be summarized in terms of five major points:

1. It is a process in which a country chooses to disengage and de-link itself from international relations that hinder its autonomous development.

2. It is an active choice *against* imitation of foreign cultural systems and *for* design of a cultural system adequate for a country's specific environment.

3. It is a series of strategies which will counterbalance the dimensions of cultural synchronization and which imply precisely the opposite of the tendencies toward cultural synchronization.

4. A key requirement in the process of cultural dissociation is a national information policy which establishes a new pattern of international information relations. The national policies which imply interdependence in unequal relations and a type of technology transfer which is a perpetual catching up are rejected in favor of policies of interindependence. A country starts with the principle of self-reliance and selects elements that are conducive to long-range cultural autonomy. National information policy may be looked on as the cornerstone of cultural dissociation because information flows and information technologies influence so profoundly cultural development.

5. Finally, cultural dissociation demands four crucial components in a national information policy that halt the process of cultural synchronization: autonomous definition of a country's fundamental needs; formulation of policy principles based on these needs; translation of these principles into concrete planning; and mobilization of indigenous resources.

It is a fundamental premise of this study that the movement toward a new international information order can contribute to real Third World autonomy in global communications only in the degree that national information policies incorporate these principles of cultural dissociation. In the perspective of dissociation, a new international information order can be defined as an international exchange of information in which states that develop their cultural system in an autonomous way and with complete sovereign control.

Resources fully and effectively participate as independent members of the international community.

The first and decisive step toward a new international information order has to be the Third World countries' choice for their own independent information policy. National policies must also plan regional forms of cooperation so that the mutual support of a block of countries will provide a stronger base of information exchange and stop the divide-and-conquer strategy of the more industrialized countries.

National Information Policy

At the beginning of the 1980s, many Third World nations were beginning to be aware of the need to design and implement national information policies.[17] As the International Commission for the Study of Communication Problems (the MacBride Commission) has recommended in its report, "It is essential to develop comprehensive national communication policies linked to overall social, cultural and economic development objectives."[18] The commission has stressed as essential for policymaking the democratic participation of all social groups concerned. Moreover, as the commission states, "every country should develop its communication patterns in accordance with is own conditions, needs and traditions, thus strengthening its integrity, independence and self-reliance."[19]

In the analysis of the present study, the concept of cultural dissociation fulfills most of the conditions as a guiding principle for the development of a self-reliant information system.

In general, this study prefers the phrase national *information* policy to that used by the MacBride Commission, national *communication* policy. Although no fundamental differences are implied, the concept of information is used for the following reasons. First, it corresponds better with the formula of a new international information order. Second, and more important, communication tends to be associated with mass communication only. In this study, the proposed policymaking has to be comprehensive, encompassing

also point-to-point forms of information transfer, as, for example, in informatics. Moreover, such policymaking should address not only problems of infrastructure but also those relating to the information contents that these infrastructures carry.

In establishing a national information policy, the following elements appear to be essential:

- definition of the *function* of the information system;
- *resource inventory*;
- *design of the structure* of a national information system; and
- *control*, that is, the rules and mechanisms by which the internal and external functioning of the system can be controlled.

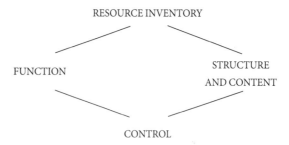

Figure 1 The Elements Necessary for Establishing a National Information Policy

These elements are all interrelated, as Figure 1 shows. This is a schematic model, to be interpreted as a prescriptive plan to be applied exactly in the form of the model. It is important, however, that all the elements be taken into consideration in any plan so that each factor reinforces the others. In the formulation of the information policy, objectives have to be clearly defined. Resources necessary for the achievement of these objectives have to be carefully analyzed. Resources and policy objectives have to be matched in light of overall developmental goals and principles. In the implementation of the information policy, resources will have to be deployed so as to create infrastructures and information policy. Some form of monitoring has to be established through which corrections and adjustments are made possible.

1927
1960
1963
1964
1967
1969
1970
1971
1972
1973
1974
1975
1976
1977
1978
1979
1980
1981
1982
1983
1984
1985
1986
1987
1988
1989
1990
1991
1992
1993
1994
1995
1996
1997
1998
1999
2000
2001
2002
2003
2004
2005
2006

Function

Every society has to define, in one way or another, the crucial functions of information processes in the society as well as a description of the function of social institutions that carry these information processes. This is all the more urgent in Third World societies because of the severe problems that jeopardize the development processes both internally and externally.

Information processes often critically hamper autonomous development by introducing inadequate forms of adaptation to the environment. Early in the planning process, it is important to examine carefully how information processes contribute to the shaping of techniques, symbols and social patterns that enable a society to adapt to the needs of its particular environment.

For example, in many Third World countries, information processes, such as advertising, carry messages that induce people to acquire goods and services which bear no relation to real needs. Think of the many luxury articles pushed by advertising throughout the Third World. These goods and services often take on an added value beyond their intrinsic exchange value. They symbolize a status that people aspire to, and in almost magical fashion, they promise to fulfill dreams that many people could never realize through their own efforts.[20] As symbols, these goods and services satisfy real psychological and social needs. For example, a Mexican household may save a whole week in order to enable the father to drink Coca-Cola during the weekend. This is important because Coke has become a symbol that satisfies a genuine need for status and identity.

Such intangible needs are important in the lives of all persons, and it is therefore perhaps preferable to look for products that can satisfy these needs and at the same time bring substantial benefits. For example, fruit juice might well be a more nutritious refreshment and also be given a symbolic meaning that is associated with status and identity. Such is the case if the native drink comes to symbolize the resistance to cultural annihilation and the search for Mexican identity.

The general function of the information processes—achieving adequate adaptive relations —has three important dimensions: political participation, autonomy of minorities and national integration.

Political Participation

The design of any national policy must begin by asking, "What kind of society do we want and how do we want to achieve this?" The answer will be decisive in defining the contribution to be expected from information processes.

Deciding on the most desirable societal structure must also take into consideration the existing political, economic and cultural structures of the country. Usually some national political goals will have been formulated already and a specific type of economic system will be functioning. At times, a country may have a heavy overlay of imposed foreign culture, especially in Westernized urban enclaves; in most countries, however, more or less adequate cultural adaptive relations have evolved and have been sustained. In general, such political goals, economic systems and cultural adaptive relations have been determined without a decentralized process of decision making which permits a wide base of popular participation.

Paulo Freire observed that development cannot be realized in conditions of "silence."[21] This suggests that a plan for national development can be meaningful only if decisions about the distribution and execution of goods and services, and the development of adequate techniques, symbols and social patterns, have been reached with extensive participation.

For any development process, it is vital to have horizontal information channels that activate all sectors of the population and that facilitate access to decision making for otherwise excluded sectors. The strategy regarding the national economic organization will have to be guided by what the people themselves indicate as their basic needs.[22]

In most Third World countries, the current economic organization certainly is not geared to these basic needs. An essential function of information processes is to make people conscious of this fact and to point to alternatives.

CULTURAL AUTONOMY FOR MINORITIES

...Some forms of liberation from dependence only install within a country another dominant elite who imposes a condition of dependency on minorities. For this reason, it was stressed that national liberation movements are completed not simply with the removal of external dependency but simultaneously with a process of eliminating internal inequalities. As a country achieves self-reliance, there must also be the flexibility that allows different social groups to develop their specific adaptive relations.

Therefore, in the formulation of policy, a pertinent question is whether the efforts to achieve national cultural autonomy may jeopardize the cultural expression of regional or ethnic groups. Can national information policy sufficiently take into account the needs and aspirations of national minorities—the Fourth World within the Third World? This is a particularly difficult question, since national information policy will also have to take seriously the objectives of national integration.

NATIONAL INTEGRATION

Encouraging the use of information processes for the expression of strongly contradictory interests may very well be a luxury that only highly developed and socially integrated nations can afford.

Many new nations have recently been formed that contained quite disparate ethnic and language groups, many of which have been geographically isolated from one another and for a long time have had separate cultural identities. The lack of a communication and transportation infrastructure, a condition typical of many underdeveloped countries, tends to reinforce such cultural isolation. Governments in these nations must seek a delicate balance between bringing these groups into a unity and at the same time respecting their minority cultures. Vital for such unity is the mobilization of all available resources and equitable distribution of them among all social groups. In a country which has a low level of developed resources to distribute in the first place and must carefully motivate a people to exert a coordinated effort, open encouragement of rancorous debate needlessly exacerbates divisions and courts disaster. At such a point the developing country finds itself in a situation significantly different from that of the advanced industrial state. The laborious and delicate process or development can afford only a minimum of internal contradictions to retain some potential for warding off the external pressures.

The more power that developing nations can exert in international relations, for example, through coordination with other nations in movements, such as the nonaligned countries, the greater the flexibility in allowing internal minority autonomy. But when a nation has little power and is experiencing debilitating internal conflict, it is vulnerable to external intervention and consolidation of external dependencies.

Internal contradictions impede the development process and invite external intervention, which, in turn, reinforces the transnational cultural synchronization that hampers self-reliance and aggravates national disintegration.

National information policy has to promote national integration—not at the cost of monopoly by certain social classes but through balanced participation of all social sectors.

Taking Inventory of National Resources

Before translating the functions of a national information system into a concrete organization, technical infrastructure and content, it is necessary to analyze both the availability and the form of adaptation of resources. When cultural autonomy is a major criterion, it is methodologically important to consider resources in terms of three categories: resources which are an

1927
1960
1963
1964
1967
1969
1970
1971
1972
1973
1974
1975
1976
1977
1978
1979
1980
1981
1982
1983
1984
1985
1986
1987
1988
1989
1990
1991
1992
1993
1994
1995
1996
1997
1998
1999
2000
2001
2002
2003
2004
2005
2006

integral part of the national context; resources already imported and adaptable to the national needs; and foreign resources which must still be imported.

National Resources

The way in which the critical functions described above can be implemented in specific national contexts depends very much on the nature and availability of existing resources—both physical and cultural—or resources that the country can at least produce within its limits.

If functions such as participation and autonomy are to be respected, it is important to consider whether elements from the indigenous national tradition can be exploited as contributions to an adequate adaptation to the environment. Traditional social values and institutions which underlie the cultural patterns of a country can often be most effective in the national development process, especially for gaining participation of large groups of the indigenous population. In the highland areas of Peru, for example, institutions rooted in the Inca past were revived to provide the organizational basis of a socialist society. In some countries there have been attempts to re-introduce traditional technologies which are better adapted and more economical in their specific situation. An example is the return to certain Indian medical practices in Mexico or the integration of folk doctors in the modern health-care system of Zimbabwe. Another example is the study of the application of Inca irrigation systems on the upland plains of Peru.

For planning information processes, a key factor to take into account is that the basic resource, information, is already present within the national system and is controlled by the people themselves. This cultural resource is built out of the knowledge, experience, events and historical developments present in every society. Every society also already possesses a great variety of traditional cultural symbols through which information can be expressed and exchanged in ways especially meaningful and comprehensible to the people of

that country or region. This information exchange is supported by traditional techniques and communication channels which may be especially effective for the massive distribution of information precisely because they exist at the level of local communities throughout the country and because the people know how to use them without special training.

In many Third World countries these traditional forms are the living carriers of the cultural system that contributes in a relevant way to national consciousness. These are often more effective and more credible than are the modern information media because they are part of the native culture and use the language of the people. These traditional media often demand more active participation than do the modern mass media, facilitate interaction and feedback and are more economical.

In some cases these can be very successfully combined with modern media. In Thailand, for example, the folk opera singers (maulum) maintain an important national tradition through their stories and songs on radio and television.

Attempts to combine traditional and modern forms, however, raise the question of whether these expressions, which often have a sacred or literary context, can be tastefully and effectively used for contemporary social and political goals. In India, for example, villagers were enraged when the text of religious Yellama songs were adapted as a form of education for birth control.

A combination of old and new is feasible when the traditional form is flexible and open to improvisation. Examples are the Wajang Kulit performance in Indonesia, the clowns in the Nautanki play in India, the Indian storytelling (Katha) and puppet theater (Kathputli), the puppet show of Iran, the Egyptian ballads (cham soun), the comic stage play in Ghana (Kakaku), the folk music of Mexico (canción popular) and the calypso of the West Indies. These are all information processes that are readily available and embedded in a national cultural tradition. They must be considered important elements of an effective and authentic national information system.

Finally, in all Third World countries, the most important resource—human labor—abounds. In capital-short conditions, people can be engaged in achieving national information processes in place of expensive and often ill-adapted equipment.

Professional personnel should be local people who understand their indigenous audience well. Their training, insofar as is possible, should be planned and executed by local people in accordance with the level of expertise available in the country. For most of the information processes, Third World countries can train their own personnel with their own methods, professional norms and social priorities.

It is often claimed that Third World countries would have too little program material and too few competent personnel to fill their media. This claim is deceptive, because it is based on the demands imposed by the arbitrary norms of more developed countries. A shortage of material and personnel is a problem only if one feels it is necessary to program more broadcast hours than the available material and personnel permit. Thailand provides a good example. When television was introduced in the late 1950s, Thai television broadcasting time was very limited. There were no problems in producing sufficient programs with talented local dancers, singers, performers and puppet players. Only when commercial interests forced an extension of television broadcast time were material and personnel in short supply. In order to fill the approximately 70 hours of programming per week, it became necessary to import programs from the United States and West Germany.

As these cases show, an essential condition for autonomy is the tailoring of demands upon the information media to fit the available resources.

Adapting Resources of Foreign Origin

Most Third World countries have a colonial or foreign-dominated past, and much of the initial organization or technology for information processing was introduced during this period of heavy foreign influence. If a country wishes to adopt a policy of cultural autonomy, then it faces the question of adapting the policy to present national goals. A decisive criterion is whether the foreign elements are inherently linked with dependence or are open to often radical transformations.

For example, the question Mexican and Algerian television producers have posed is whether television drama, a form imported from the United States, can express the ideals of the country's national independence movements or will it be a negative influence on national loyalties? Or the question from Mozambiquans: How can the colonizers' language be used to support national liberation?

Techniques introduced under colonial rule can be exploited for national revolutionary goals. Radio in Algeria is an example. In the early 1950s, Radio Alger was *the* symbol of French colonialism and an instrument for the synchronization of Algerian culture with the French model. For the Algerians, radio was "Frenchmen talking to Frenchmen." After 1956 this changed radically. Radio became *the* means of communication for the revolution. The Voice of Algeria quickly changed the Algerians' attitudes regarding radio and led in a short time to technical control for the medium. Radio was no longer part of the colonial oppression; it became a symbol of liberation.[23]

Another example of the adaptation of techniques imported during the colonial period and now available in Third World countries is the printing press. Many countries have access to small- and medium-sized local printing shops that have come to play an important role in national information processes.

Some Third World countries have also embarked upon the production of their own broadcasting equipment. They have developed the expertise to adapt previously imported technology and have then exploited this with local people and materials. In Pakistan, for example, transmitters for medium-wave broadcasting and control systems for radio studios are manufactured by the Pakistan broadcasting corporation. The transmitters meet international quality standards and the cost is half that of formerly imported equipment.

Importing New Technology

For most of their more advanced communication technology, developing countries must go abroad. Vendors of this technology argue that new technology will enable developing countries to cut costs and accomplish in a few decades what it has taken Western developed countries generations to achieve in communication infrastructures. For countries in a hurry to develop, this argument is an attractive one. Seldom, however, do they question sufficiently whether this technology developed primarily for an urban industrial society is relevant or adaptable to the often vastly different conditions of their lands. In the decision on the import of foreign technology, a major criterion should be whether this technology can contribute to autonomous development.

From the perspective of autonomous development, importation of television and even radio has often been questionable. These are one-way traffic media which do not encourage an active participation of their audience and which are unable to take into account with some seriousness the local needs and problems.

In searching for an adequate technology, it may even be more meaningful to choose more advanced media in some circumstances. New mobile mini-equipment can be far more adequate than that of current television and film techniques. The cases of Tanzania and of India described earlier are examples of this. In 1974 and 1975, attention in India was directed toward an experiment with educational programs by satellite. A project with a very cheap, small-scale technique located in Uttar Pradesh was hardly noticed. A system of portable video equipment was designed to improve the information exchange between villagers.[24] In contrast with radio and television, this was a medium the villagers could manage themselves and through

which they could express their own local problems. They quickly became accustomed to the technical requirements of the equipment, decided themselves upon the program content and used the programs to discuss their real problems. Interest in the commercial films that were initially shown on the monitor slowly disappeared and gave way to a keen appreciation for the locally produced programs.

In terms of professional television standards, their programs may have been of lower quality, but as channels for public information exchange they were highly relevant.

Scientific research methods could play an important role in the inventory of national resources. Research is presently primarily concerned with problems, concepts, methods and techniques designed in the metropolis. Moreover, social research, including media research, has become a carrier of cultural synchronization.[25] Third World countries will have to gain independence in this field through their own initiative. They will have to ask their own questions and find relevant answers through their own methods of research.

The Structure and Content of Information Processes

STRUCTURE

This structure of a national information system will have to be designed in relation to the critical functions and the available resources described above. Consequently, structure must take into consideration four aspects:

- national control;
- decentralization;
- avoidance of control by professional elite; and
- a diachronic mode of information exchange.

NATIONAL CONTROL

In current international relations, national control over a country's information system is an absolute prerequisite for national sovereignty. As a highly integrated system of global communications develops, a clear plan for keeping within the country control of information systems becomes more urgent. At stake is a vital resource for national development that must be exploited in accordance with a country's own goals. Sovereign control of the resource information means that a society maintains its autonomy in decisions regarding the processing, use and export of information. To maintain this national autonomy, it is possible to employ many different forms of ownership and administration. A country must decide whether information systems should be fully nationalized or whether different media and different types of services require different kinds of control structures.

In Nigeria, for example, there are three different categories of proprietary control. In category I—involving radio, television, newspapers, advertising agencies, cinemas and film distribution—full ownership by nationals is obligatory. In the case of category II, affecting the printing of books and the publishing of books and magazines, 60 percent of the ownership must be national. Category III requires 40 percent Nigerian ownership. This includes the industrial manufacture of parts for computers, radios and television sets and the production of motion pictures for theaters and television.[26]

Other aspects of national control to be considered are decisions regarding allocation of public funds for the development of facilities for information production, fiscal policy: For example, taxation of information flows) toward foreign companies, price policy for information services, PTT tariffs on television and telecommunication and regulation of information imports and exports.

Given the expected functions of information systems mentioned above, national control implies both wide public participation and benefits for all social sectors, because the development of the total society is at stake.

In the past several years, sufficient empirical evidence has been collected to support the observation that in Third World countries the free-market mechanisms for the production and distribution of information have not been able to satisfy the basic needs of these countries.

Systems of ownership, administration, regulation, etc., must respect this public and social purpose of information in order to fulfill the people's right to inform and to be informed, and to avoid serving the needs of only the privileged classes of society. Information processes in Third World countries are an important form of public service, comparable to the educational facilities. Society can delegate this service to specific social institutions, but it retains the right to regulate the execution of the service.

It should be clear that in this reasoning, national *control* does not mean that a governing elite has exclusive power over the operations of an information system. In any discussion of the forms of control over the means of production, it is important to make a distinction between allocative and operational control—that is, the difference between the *ownership* of the means of production (including the long-range allocation of resources) and the *execution* of the daily production operations. In the Netherlands, for example, there is an editorial statute that attempts to maintain a clear separation between the two forms of control, that is, between owners and directors and editors and journalists. One could conceive of a system in which the state would have allocative control of the information media, with various social groups having the operational control.

This position evidently begs quite a few questions. Information systems under national control are prone to abuse; evidence of this abounds in many Third World countries. It is not unusual to find a type of government-controlled development journalism that is virtually propaganda for the governing elite and its projects. Here the viewpoint of Third World spokespeople often creates confusion when they strongly emphasize the need to receive good press coverage in the North. It should be clear from this analysis that such coverage is certainly not a priority and possibly may even be threatening for national development.

In the international debate much attention is paid to such phenomena; some even see them as the core of

1927
1960
1963
1964
1967
1969
1970
1971
1972
1973
1974
1975
1976
1977
1978
1979
1980
1981
1982
1983
1984
1985
1986
1987
1988
1989
1990
1991
1992
1993
1994
1995
1996
1997
1998
1999
2000
2001
2002
2003
2004
2005
2006

the problem. In particular, those who limit the discussion to the problems of international newsgathering and distribution contend that most difficulties would be solved if in Third World countries no more journalists were censored, jailed or expelled. Problems of censorship, detention and expulsion have to be confronted and should not be minimized. It is important, however, to place this question in a more balanced perspective.

1. The problems of censorship, detention and expulsion are not exclusive to Third World countries; they occur everywhere and are not "inherently" linked with certain types of ownership structure of the information media. Abuse of information processes under national control is not an *inevitability*. It is rather a consequence of the level of national development; the dominant political structure; the economic organization; the state of the population's political consciousness; and the degree of external political, economic and cultural pressure.

2. One must also take into consideration that many problems accompanying present political institutions have their roots in the colonial or neocolonial dependency situation. This is not to sanction these abuses in any way. But it must be pointed out that critical analysis has to focus on structures that cause the problems with the freedom of information in Third World countries. Criticism of Third World governments is often also offered by defenders of Western liberties who were very silent at the time these very governments were installed by Western interests.

3. In cases of censorship, detention or expulsion, the governments concerned are not automatically violating the freedom of the press. In many Third World counties, Western journalists either have collaborated with intelligence services, irresponsibly and carelessly reported or exported data which indeed should have been protected. One example of inaccurate reporting relates to Cambodia. In early 1977, international media such as *Newsweek, Time* and *The Washington Post* published pictures

of executions and forced labor under the Red Khmer regime. Different sources (among them the U.S. State Department) identified these pictures as fakes that were stage-managed in Thailand. It has also become known that some media e.g., *The Washington Post* and *Time,* knew this before they decided to publish. Such behavior can hardly promote the case for press freedom in Third World countries. In some cases the individual journalist has gotten into difficulties through personal and irresponsible behavior, for which any government can expel even diplomats.

However important the preceding discussion may be, it does not touch upon the core of the problem: the inability of national governing elite to develop adequate cultural systems. The decisive question is thus: Which social classes control decision making? This, then, leads to the second characteristic of the structure—decentralization.

DECENTRALIZATION AND PARTICIPATION

To prevent monopolization of information systems by a small but articulate and educated elite, the structure of information systems requires a broader and more democratic form of control. Public and social control of information processes demands a fully decentralized form of decision making that allows the whole population to participate, at least in some way. The public media have an important role in political consciousness raising (conscientization), which fosters the active involvement of all sectors of society and a more critical judgment about national developments.

AVOIDING CONTROL BY MEDIA PROFESSIONALS

In the evolution of the public media over the past century or more, the ordinary citizens have come to think of themselves simply as passive observers. The media are seen as the private domain of a small group of stars and professional producers.

One of the central proposals of the new information order challenges this form of the public media not only in the developing but also in the more developed countries. Structural decentralization in the information system means that the ordinary person sees his or her participation as a form of public service. It also signifies taking exclusive control of the information processes out of the hands of a professional elite.

The administration and operation of a national information system require recruiting and training individuals who have special talents for such jobs. However, once information is defined as the unique capacity of an elite group—separated from the rest of society even by its lifestyle—then the very structure of the information system gives a few specialists the exclusive right to inform nonspecialists.

Deprofessionalization means making an effort to guarantee everybody's right to inform and to be informed. It comes closest to the learning situation proposed by Paulo Freire. In his thinking, the conventional separation between instructor-specialist and pupil must be abolished. He assumes that everyone has knowledge and information about a part of reality and he advocates a situation in which everyone can contribute. In this perspective, the discovery of our reality can come about only through a creative process of co-learning.

INTRODUCING A DIACHRONIC MODE OF INFORMATION EXCHANGE

Every society is characterized by a complexity of information processes and by the exchange of an immense variety of messages through such processes. In a very real sense, the processes of information exchange constitute society and faithfully reflect its power relations.

Those with a higher socio-economic status, education, etc., tend to have a more central position within information exchanges and are more likely to receive more information—especially more *strategically* important information. Their more central access to channels also gives them a better chance to decide which messages will be exchanged, because they decide on the agenda. More importantly, they determine which contributions in the exchange will be decisive. Many information processes are related to situations

in which decisions have to be taken and choices have to be made from various possibilities. The positions of the participants in such situations will largely determine which alternatives are taken seriously.

Insofar as information processes are a reflection of existing power relations, they will in general follow a synchronic mode. In this mode, there is a great distance between sender and receiver; the receiver is supposed to synchronize with the input from the sender. The sender becomes the specialist who alone can select, process and distribute the messages. Messages are "prescribed" to the passive receiver who is expected to register and store them in his *archives*.[27]

In the synchronic mode, there is no dialogue that can possibly make the receiver an active participant in the process or enable him to question the messages and search for ways to relate the messages to everyday reality.

This synchronic mode is totally inadequate for a decentralized structure of information processes. The emancipation of individuals and social groups demands a diachronic mode for information processes. In such a mode, the distance between sender and receiver is reduced to the minimum. Messages from all participants in the process are pooled in order to come to grips with reality jointly.

The diachronic mode implies a series of characteristics in the pattern of information process:

- The information is organized in such a way as to make visible the structural relations of reality.
- There exists a clear relation between the information and the contextual situation of the participants in the process of exchange.
- All participants have access to the facilities for input and correction.
- Information and social action are integrally linked.

CONTENT

The general criteria that guide content decisions in a national information system are suggested, in the

1927
1960
1963
1964
1967
1969
1970
1971
1972
1973
1974
1975
1976
1977
1978
1979
1980
1981
1982
1983
1984
1985
1986
1987
1988
1989
1990
1991
1992
1993
1994
1995
1996
1997
1998
1999
2000
2001
2002
2003
2004
2005
2006

first place, by function, resources and structural characteristics. Since the underlying criterion for these dimensions of information systems is national autonomy, this will ultimately influence the choice of content most significantly.

Self-reliant development presupposes liberation not only from external oppression but also from the "mentality of the colonized." For the oppressed, paradoxically, to be human is to be an oppressor: The oppressor has become the model of humanity.[28]

At the same time, the oppressed looks at himself through the eyes of the oppressor and depreciates himself. "Self-depreciation is another characteristic of the oppressed, which derives from their internalization of the opinion the oppressors hold of them."[29]

In the process of liberation from these alienating images, information processes play an important role. Their content has to be oriented toward a liberation which leads to an authentic self-image.

If information processes are to contribute to liberated and self-confident acting, the implication for content is that:

■ It facilitates the understanding of the environment in which people live ("What is your own life situation?").
■ The mechanisms which determine and maintain the environment become transparent ("How is your own life situation structured?").
■ Alternatives are offered for action leading to change ("How can your life situation be changed?").

As an example of how the content of information processes contributes to a more adequate understanding of the environment and greater freedom of choice, we can take the problem of hunger, which afflicts so many millions of poor in the Third World.[30]

Information on food problems in Third World countries could concentrate on the following:

1. Discovering with those concerned (especially the rural population) how their present situation is controlled by inaccurate *presuppositions* (such as the belief that hunger is caused simply by scarcity of food or by there being too many people).

2. Exploring how *real problems* are obscured through these inaccurate presuppositions. (For example, the problem of exporting too much of food produced in the country, control of land resources by a small group that has no interest in feeding the whole population or the import of modern agricultural techniques that benefit only a tiny elite).

3. Analyzing which *structural* causes underlie these problems: For example, the control of the national bureaucratic decision making by an elite that resists basic land reform, or the control of food production and distribution by a small number of large producers.

4. Designing *alternative* courses of action: For example, each country has the resources to minimize or solve the hunger problems of its population, or the food production has to be directed primarily toward the population's own needs.

In the case of hunger, such information content is contributing to a more adequate adaptation to the environment and thus to cultural autonomy of the nation.

CONTROL

The final dimension to be considered in planning a national information system is control of that system in accordance with national goals. Controlling the functioning of an information system is a universal characteristic of all societies regardless of the political-economic system or guiding philosophy. It will be found in free or totalitarian, developed or underdeveloped societies. It is simply an aspect of the general social controls that reflect the dominant cultural value orientations of a society. Every society has laws and rules to protect itself against the production and distribution of information that violates the moral and public order, state security and national social institutions.

Again, the basic criterion of control is national autonomy, as well as respect for the culture of minorities and the right of the individual to be informed and to inform.

Such control mechanisms can be internal as well as external. International regulation determines whether the functions that are defined for the information system are indeed met. External regulation includes a variety of international agreements that have an impact on the national information system, such as telecommunication tariffs and frequency allocations. A combination of internal and external regulations is found in cases where rules for the national system are expected to have validity for the international system as well. In Mexico since the beginning of 1978, the international information flow is subject to all national laws regulating the domestic information flow.

Regulations and mechanisms for sanctions can be voluntarily imposed by those directly responsible for information processes: for example, through journalistic professional codes and press councils. Another possibility is for the state to legislate norms and check on their implementation. Finally, the audience itself can organize in consumer unions and take action.

In the international debate it is fashionable to criticize Third World countries for excessive controls that violate the right to know and to inform. It would only be fair to add that the industrialized countries themselves have not found satisfactory solutions to this problem. The freedom of information only too frequently is used by professionals in the information field without sufficient responsibility. The influence of the state is often indirect and ambiguous. Critical consumer actions in the information field are weak or are easily thwarted by powerful political and/or economic interests.

For Third World countries, the key issue once again will be that of determining which rules and sanctions are adequate from the perspective of their own priorities and sanctions. It is essential that the national information system meet its functions as defined. A society has to be able to judge and correct this.

The opportunity to participate in this should be open to all social groups concerned.

Controls will also be applicable to the foreigners who participate in the national information system. They will at least be required not to disrupt the national development process.[31] Inherent in the right of a nation to its cultural autonomy is also the right to expect respect for the rules a nation designs to realize this autonomy.

A sovereign state will also want to design rules for the regulation of the international information traffic.[32] Codes of conduct will have to be developed to regulate the activities of both governments and private corporations.

In the next two decades, more detailed and careful planning of national information systems may well become as central in the development strategies of most countries as is economic planning now. It has been the thesis here that an information policy guiding this planning must be built around a choice for cultural dissociation. Otherwise, the worldwide tendency toward cultural synchronization will increasingly threaten cultural autonomy.

Now we will examine the main considerations for the application of the dissociation policy in the case of one of the most important new computer-like information developments—informatics.

INFORMATICS AS A CASE STUDY OF NATIONAL INFORMATION POLICY

The previous section outlined a general model for a national information policy. The broad guidelines were suggested in terms of four dimensions: function, resource inventory, content and control. The basic criterion is achieving and maintaining cultural autonomy through a strategy of cultural dissociation. Underlying this strategy of cultural dissociation is the need for a parallel economic dissociation. This reflects the intimate relation that the international discussions have seen between the new international order and the new international economic order.

1927
1960
1963
1964
1967
1969
1970
1971
1972
1973
1974
1975
1976
1977
1978
1979
1980
1981
1982
1983
1984
1985
1986
1987
1988
1989
1990
1991
1992
1993
1994
1995
1996
1997
1998
1999
2000
2001
2002
2003
2004
2005
2006

All this has been presented at a relatively abstract level, however. The implementation of this in concrete circumstances will vary a great deal in different societies and at different stages of social and economic development. A universally valid blueprint cannot be given.

It is possible, though, to point to the concrete questions that a Third World country confronts in formulating national information policy. Computer communication, or informatics, offers a good case study for a number of reasons:

■ In present international relations, computer communication plays a significant role in cultural synchronization and poses a serious threat to national sovereignty.[33]

■ Third World countries are at present confronted with highly attractive possibilities for becoming integrated in the international computer traffic. The Carter administration, for example, studied a plan to provide Third World countries with access to United States data banks. The costs involved for telecommunication channels and terminals would be covered by the United States.[34]

■ The capacities of the advanced computer, especially through microelectronics, promise to make an impressive contribution to development processes.

■ The applications of computers are manifold, which makes a selective policy possible. In India, for example, the computer is used as a "people supplement" where there is not sufficient labor. In sectors where labor is abundant, as in the case of banking, there is no electronic equipment: For example, no online banking.

■ The computer can be very efficiently used in an extremely centralized system. At the same time, however, it can be adapted to specific personal and cultural characteristics: For example, learning speed or language and thereby facilitate the participation of many people in decision-making procedures.

■ The computer industry consists of various sectors, such as design and manufacture of equipment, maintenance and development, application of the uses of

the equipment and design of systems and programs. This also opens up the possibility of a selective policy.

■ The case of the computer demonstrates that a self-reliant development does not necessarily imply exclusive interest for small-scale, indigenous techniques.

■ The computer performs many functions at high speed, thus raising a question relevant to cultural values: How important is speed?

Taking computer communications (informatics) as a case study of national information policy is especially pertinent, because this is a new and vulnerable area of information flow. The dialectics between international economic and informational structures in the field of informatics deserve special attention.

Until recently, informatics and information have usually been dealt with as separate entities. Technological developments, however, make this separation obsolete. In a general way, information and informatics intersect at the point where informatics provides an increasing number of support services in newspaper mailing rooms. In a more specific way, the fields are related in a number of media applications of informatics, as Table 5 indicates.

The linking of information and informatics has many important implications:

Information	Informatics
Newspaper	Word processing and text composition Home-terminal publishing
Magazine	Online editing
Television	Computer-generated video Viewdata
Film	Graphics produced via computer
Radio and television	Computer-steered satellite transmissions
Educational publishing	Computer-assisted instruction packages
Telephone	Computer voice recognition
Telegraph	Data networks

Table 5.

- Information becomes strongly personalized ("atomization of information consumption"), i.e., due to increasing miniaturization.
- Information dissemination media become information retrieval systems.
- Computers become information/communication media.

The crucial element in the integrative process is the expected digitalizing of all types of information, which will make technical distinctions between data flows and information flows obsolete. Computer data and journalistic information alike will be transmitted across borders in digital form.

MEDIA APPLICATIONS OF INFORMATICS

The change from analog to digital form will have far-reaching consequences for the storage capacity and the transmission speed of information as well as for its accessibility and manipulation.

If present developments continue, the informatics-information link may well provide the vital stronghold for consolidating the power of the present international order. This may be particularly so in an application, sometimes described as "telematics," which links advanced telecommunications technology with electronic data processing. It has greatly facilitated the development of transborder computer-communication systems. These systems carry increasing volumes of information across national borders: medical, employment, criminal and credit records of private citizens; credit data about commercial firms and information about national economic developments. In fact, such transborder data flows have become the backbone of international business and banking.

Almost exclusively in control of this computer communications system are a small number of United States electronics corporations that have access to the technology that enables the collecting, processing, transmitting and storing of enormous volumes of data. For many Third World countries this signifies that an important basis for national decision making is now located extraterritorially with some private corporation.

A spectacular element in this field is remote sensing by photo satellites. The "spy-in-the-sky" satellites can remotely sense the Earth's surface in a country and by so doing "impede the exercise of the sovereignty of any state over its natural resources."[35]

Data extracted by these satellite explorations are processed by computer systems and stored in data banks, all controlled by the major Western transnational corporation. As Louis Joinet of France's Ministry of Justice stated in a speech to the Organisation of Economic Cooperation and Development (OECD):

Information is power, and economic information is economic power. Information has an economic value, and the ability to store and process certain types of data may well give one country political and technological advantage over other countries. This, in turn, may lead to a loss of national sovereignty through supranational data flows.[36]

The dependent nations will find that even if they achieve significant progress in redressing inequality in international news exchange but do not gain self-reliance and sovereign control in the informatics field, equality and independence will remain empty diplomatic phrases.

The inclusion of information in programs of research and action related to a new international order is essential. The case of informatics provides an important illustration of both the necessity and the feasibility of a new international order.

The necessity is demonstrated by the fact that informatics in its present form constitutes a basic infrastructural component of the international economic and information order. The informatics industry is among the world's largest industries and is almost totally controlled by a few corporations located in the heart of the Western industrialized nations. Geared to the needs of these nations, it puts dependent,

1927
1960
1963
1964
1967
1969
1970
1971
1972
1973
1974
1975
1976
1977
1978
1979
1980
1981
1982
1983
1984
1985
1986
1987
1988
1989
1990
1991
1992
1993
1994
1995
1996
1997
1998
1999
2000
2001
2002
2003
2004
2005
2006

developing nations at a considerable economic and informational disadvantage.

Informatics opens up the feasibility of the new order in that it represents at the same time both the power and the vulnerability of the controlling nations. The business community of the industrialized world has become increasingly dependent upon telematics both for its information flows and its economic performance. Third World countries, apart from being potentially important informatics markets in the next decade, could seriously affect the economy of the industrialized world if they restricted transborder data flows, imposed taxes on these flows or indigenized informatics facilities.

These observations suggest a series of questions that a Third World country should ask when designing a national information policy:

■ How does informatics contribute to the functioning of an information system? Will it further national disintegration? Will it introduce inadequate techniques, symbols and social patterns? Will potential short-term benefits be outweighed by long-term deleterious effects?
■ How will informatics relate to resources? Are they to be imported? Will this jeopardize national self-reliance? Can investments be brought in line with overall development priorities and needs? What does this mean, in terms of the present allocation of human and financial resources?
■ How will informatics be structured? Can a *national* production structure be organized? Will this contribute to self-reliant development? Will a strengthening of domestic informatics facilities lead to an improvement of international bargaining positions?
■ How will informatics be controlled? Can the import and export of computer data be regulated? Can taxes be imposed on data flows?

These questions suggest that the design of a national policy for the informatics field should focus on the following elements:

■ Since information technology is often introduced without specification of the objectives to be achieved by it, a priority would be the precise definition of a country's information needs.
■ Technologies that are currently offered to Third World countries have to be carefully analyzed and matched against stated developmental objectives and information needs.
■ Since information policymakers have often concentrated on the procurement of hardware only, careful analysis and projection ought to be made regarding the secondary impact of information technology, in terms of the distribution of political, economic and cultural benefits.
■ Careful attention has to be given to the institutional context within which the technology is applied. It will have to be studied whether present infrastructural arrangements are sufficiently solid to monitor and control the applications.
■ Careful evaluation of the physical and human resources is needed to determine which resources can be developed independently, which can be mobilized

collectively through regional cooperation and which must be imported from developed countries with a minimum of external dependence.

As has been stressed throughout here, delinking or dissociation, although central, is but one side of the coin in national information policy and planning. It must be complemented by building a new pattern of regional, horizontal linkages among developing countries.

Endnotes

1. *Development Dialogue* (Uppsala), 1976, Vol. 2: 9.

2. Jan Tinbergen, et al., *Reshaping the International Order*, New York: Dutton, 1976, 111.

3. Jörg Becker, ed., *Free Flow of Information*, Frankfurt: Gemeinschaftswerk der Evangelischen Publiczistik, 1979, 215.

4. *Inter Press Service Newsletter*, January 1979.

5. Editorial comment in *Development Dialogue*, op. cit., 10.

6. Tinbergen, *Reshaping the International Order*, op. cit., 111.

7. Ibid.

8. R. D. Curtin, *The Image of África,* Madison, Wisconson: University of Wisconsin Press, 1963.

9. The Information Industry Association, representing the major information industries in the United States, defines information as a "resource" in its report to President Carter 15 July 1977: "It [information] is the raw material of knowledge ... it has a central role in the market place as a commodity." Information Industry Association, Bethesda, Maryland: 1977.

10. Documentation for these principles has been derived from: *Cocoyoc Declaration*, October 1975, Mexico; United Nations, General Assembly, 6th Special Session, May 1974, *Declaration and Action—Program on the Establishment of a New International Economic Order*, Resolutions 3201 and 3202; United Nations, General Assembly, December 1974, *Charter of Economic Rights and Duties of States, Resolution 3281; Dakar Declaration and Action Program of the Conference of Developing Countries on Raw Materials*, 1975. These documents can be found in G. F. Erb and V. Kallb, eds., *Beyond Dependency*, New York: Praeger, Appendix B, 185-250.

11. *Weltwirtschaftsordnung und Entwicklungspolitik*, Frankfort: Surhkamp, 1977.

12. Ibid., 215.

13. Ibid., 277.

14. Karl P Sauvant and H. Hasenpflug, eds., *The New International Economic Order*, Frankfurt: Campus Verlag, 1977, 5.

15. Frantz Fanon, *The Wretched of the Earth*, Baltimore, Maryland: Penguin, 1967, 252.

16. See A. Gotlieb, et al., "The Transborder .Transfer of Information by Communications and Computer Systems," *The American Journal of International Law*, 1974, Vol. 68, No. 1: 227-257.

17. E. Lloyd Sommerlad, *National Communication Systems*, Paris: UNESCO, 1975; John A. R. Lee, *Towards Realistic Communication Policies,* Paris: UNESCO, 1976; Raquel Salinas, *Communication Policies: The Case of Latin America*, Stockholm: Institute of Latin American Studies, 1978.

18. Sean MacBride, et al., *Many Voices, One World: Communication and Society Today and Tomorrow,* Paris: UNESCO, 1980, 254.

19. Ibid.

20. "The fetishism of commodities lies in their prestige-value, in their ability as 'signs' to command respect, authority, deference." John P. Digging, "Reification and the Cultural Hegemony of Capitalism," Social Research, 1977, Vol. 44, No. 2: 365.

21. Paolo Freire, *Cultural Action for Freedom*, Baltimore, Maryland: Penguin, 1972, 17.

22. The concept of basic needs can be used as a paternalistic instrument in north-south negotiations in cases where the north defines for the South which these are. It can also be exclusively focused on national situations as a means of avoiding any structural changes in the international order. "Basic needs" in this study is used as a strategic concept for a developmental process in which needs are primarily and autonomously defined by the people concerned themselves; and the international order is structured in such a way as to make this possible.

23. Frantz Fanon, *A Dying Colonialism*, Baltimore, Maryland: Penguin, 1970, 67.

24. Centre for Development of Instructional Technology (CENDIT) in New Delhi.

25. Cees J. Hamelink, ed., *Communication Research in the Third World,* Geneva: Lutheran World Federation, 1976; Phillip Elliott and Peter Golding, "Mass Communication and Social Change: The Imagery of Development and the Development of Imagery," in E. de Kadt and G. Williams, eds., *Sociology and Development*, London: Tavistock, 1974, 229-254.

26. *Nigerian Enterprises Promotion Decree*, Lagos, Nigeria: Government Publishing, 13 January 1977.

27. Cees J. Hamelink, "An Alternative to News," *Journal of Communication*, 1976, Vol. 26, No. 4: 120-123.

28. Paolo Freire, *Cultural Action for Freedom*, op. cit., 22.

29. Ibid., 38.

30. Frances M. Lappe and J. Collins, *Food First*, Boston: Houghton Mifflin, 1977.

31. Recall the role of foreign media in Chile during the Allende government. NACLA, Latin America Report, 1974, Vol. 8, No. 6; Herbert I. Schiller, *Communication and Cultural Domination*, New York: International Arts and Sciences Press, 1976.

32. Such rules have been accepted by the states that signed the Final Act of the Helsinki conference on Security and Cooperation in Europe in 1975.

33. Butt Nanus, "The Social Implication of the Use of Computers Across National Boundaries," New Jersey: American Federation of Information Processing Societies, 1973.

34. "Global Net May Serve Third World," *Computerworld*, 26 June 1978.

35. U.N. Resolution 626, VII.

36. Given at the OECD Symposium on Transborder Data Flows and the Protection of Privacy, Vienna: October 1977.

Hammelink, Cees J. *Cultural Autonomy in Global Communications: Planning National Information Policy*. New York and London: Longman, 1984. Reprinted with permission of the author.

1927
1960
1963
1964
1967
1969
1970
1971
1972
1973
1974
1975
1976
1977
1978
1979
1980
1981
1982
1983
1984
1985
1986
1987
1988
1989
1990
1991
1992
1993
1994
1995
1996
1997
1998
1999
2000
2001
2002
2003
2004
2005
2006

COMMUNICATION PLANNING AND PARTICIPATORY PROJECTS

By Luiz Gonzaga Motta

1984 What is the role of the external agent in a participatory communication project? In matters of work with popular groups, only practice will teach the more adequate ways. Beyond professional training, the work in popular communication and education is, and will always be, a contradictory and conflictive activity of relationships among different actors. Trial and error and the experience lived by each one are important elements of a necessarily difficult and slow learning process. Many times, badly prepared to carry out his new tasks, the communicator and the popular educator end up resorting to their traditional behaviorist methods and repeat methodological errors that annul the good intentions. Other times, the agents completely lose the professional references and a methodological void is left. The most common consequence is professional, ethical and personal ambiguity, which only makes the agent's practice more difficult. Whenever the communication schools introduce in their programs the methodology of popular education, the problems may get smaller.

However, some recent experiences have accumulated certain knowledge that we must take in. Evidently, the appropriation of this knowledge and its application in diverse situations does not guarantee the success of the task. Experimentation and confrontation must be carried out by each one in every situation, carefully and skillfully. Additionally, the points that we are going to include here are not obviously new and cannot be assumed as work rules. In work with popular groups,

the only rule is that there are no rules. Here we simply expose seven points for discussion and confrontation. They might, at least in part, decrease the methodological ambiguities. They can be viewed as preconditions for participative planning.

1. Working with and from professional knowledge: A first source of ambiguity is derived from the fact that, to be equal to popular groups and create a relationship in dialogue with them, the external agent ignored his technical knowledge, spoke like a peasant, dressed as a workman. There is nothing more false. The external agent must not "be ashamed" of his professional technical knowledge. Nor should he worry too much about his "technical-professional influence" on people. The relationship between the agent and the popular groups will always be a relationship among different actors. Each one of them has a different life story and experience that cannot be hidden or deleted by words or appearances. Their roles are quite different. Additionally, professional knowledge is useful and necessary. There is no "equality" in these terms. That is, to achieve communication in dialogue with the popular groups, it is not necessary or recommendable to "hide" class status or professional condition. Establishing a relationship in dialogue is not caricaturizing the process. It is achieving a relationship of mutual confidence, contributing each to the growth of the other.

2. Making contradictions a pedagogical factor: This point is derived from the previous question. If the relationship between the agent and the popular groups is a relationship between different actors, it is best to lay out, without exaggeration, the different roles for each one from the beginning and make this fact a component of the pedagogical process. That is, the agent must be clear on what kind of contribution he wants or can give. And what are the limits of this contribution. He must get rid of the myth, without destroying or abandoning it, of technical-professional knowledge, without exaggerations. If the group he is going to work with understands his own role clearly and that of the agent and assimilates the

differences in common work, the ambiguities will be smaller and the tasks at hand will be easier.

3. Working with social movements: The specific needs of the poor man (hunger, housing, sickness, unemployment, low salaries and other human needs) and the correlation of political forces (degree of organization and mobilization, degree of repression, etc.) are the real factors that condition the life practices of popular groups, independently from any external immediate action. That is, the popular classes create and recreate their lives and their social practices on a daily basis. The state of social organization in these groups varies in each case. In some, the social situation can be found in a moment that is still primary, of self-defense and self-conservation. In others, the groups may be more organized. In any situation these actions have an existential functionality for these groups; they reflect specific needs, imply priorities and degrees of motivation for people to get involved. Therefore, the external agents may identify themselves with these needs and work with them, offering their technical, logistical, economic, legal and political support to the social movement, contributing to its dynamic evolution. Thus, their work will certainly be more productive and less ambiguous. There is no room for artificial needs.

4. Always work with groups that already exist: The work in communication and popular education cannot be developed through isolated individuals. Inversely, the work method must be collective; it must…gather people around common objectives, and it must stimulate debate and participation. For this reason, it is important to work with groups but not with just any group but with already-existing groups. If there are formal organized and active groups, it is better to work with them; if there aren't any, then with the informal ones that exist in any social situation. Proposing, from the beginning of the work, the creation of new groups around matters artificially created by agents means introducing matters from outside the communities. This will only make work harder.

5. Working with immediate benefits, bearing in mind the long-range pedagogical process: Any educational work must be carried out in relation to gaining some specific benefit for the group. This benefit—better agricultural productivity, better transportation or better housing, better health, better salaries, etc.—is what motivates people to participate. However, these benefits are only means through which the educational action, the main goal, is developed. We must not fall into the trap of immediacy that only creates relationships of barter and interest exchange. In these cases, the only participation is to obtain a reward. The retribution is undoubtedly important, but the pedagogical action surpasses immediate material victories with an educational and political character that is much more ample and permanent.

6. Working with the everyday life of the popular classes: The means-benefit of the pedagogical action must be related to the daily life of popular groups and translate to very specific needs, such as unemployment; work; salary; social security; the cost of life, housing and urban transportation; the ownership of the land where they live or work; education; nutrition; health, etc. The resolution of these needs has many more possibilities to motivate the people because they need these benefits, they worry about them directly. These problems are generally common and can be solved only through collective actions. For the agent, this means that he must identify himself and link himself with popular fights, supporting them. The external agent must not simply propose, as happens many times, the simple adhesion of the group to his wishes or his own political principles, assuming the role of "political vanguard."

7. Working in no hurry: Structural, institutional, professional and personal difficulties and obstacles in the work with popular groups are immense. There are a number of inhibiting factors: available time, beliefs and individual values, institutional and personal resistances, repressive forces, lack of resources, etc. The elimination of these obstacles is impossible the

1927
1960
1963
1964
1967
1969
1970
1971
1972
1973
1974
1975
1976
1977
1978
1979
1980
1981
1982
1983
1984
1985
1986
1987
1988
1989
1990
1991
1992
1993
1994
1995
1996
1997
1998
1999
2000
2001
2002
2003
2004
2005
2006

agent, in most occasions. All of this makes it very hard to achieve benefits and develop the educational process, implying delays and dispersion. The agent must consider and assess from the beginning all these matters and understand that they will influence the rhythm of the work and the response of the groups. There is a need for a lot of patience and perseverance. It is not worth trying to solve everything at once. This would only mean that the agent is advancing himself, trying to solve issues by himself that need to be decided and executed collectively. We can never forget the pedagogical action.... .

In addition to these seven points on the individual action of the agent—preconditions of participative planning—it is important to define clearly and honestly the objectives and the methods of work of the supporting institution, discuss them with the groups that we are intended to work with, to specify what kind of support they need. The decision-making power must be transferred to the communitarian collective. They must define the problems, identify priorities, formulate objectives, alternatives, specify the means to achieve them and decide on the kind and degree of support they need. Having defined the dimension and quality of the support, the external agency must transform itself into a supporting and work-stimulation entity. A certain degree of direction may be unavoidable at some stages. It would be naive to intend total abstention. But the leading action must be reduced to the minimum or annulled, whenever possible.

In fact, the external agent representative of an institution (social entertainer or worker, educator, planner, etc.) must always intervene and contribute for more intelligent decisions. However, the final word must always lie with the communitarian group, even when to the technician's discern the decision is not so rational. The external agent, technically more informed, may on many occasions influence the group. However, to the extent that he has more power, individual opinions will adjust to his. In addition, when the community is actually the one identifying its problems, defining what it wants and selecting alternatives, it tends

to collectively compromise to achieve objectives and depend less upon external orientation and help.

Participative planning is, thus, an educational and productive activity at the same time. During the process there is an active learning practice while working, simultaneously, for the achievement of collectively established goals...

EXCERPT FROM:

CONTINUITY AND CHANGE IN COMMUNICATION SYSTEMS: AN ASIAN PERSPECTIVE

By Georgette Wang and Wimal Dissanayake

1984 The study of "modernization" and "development" has been a cross-disciplinary subject, as well as an international concern, since the Second World War. The reasons these two concepts attract so much academic attention are easy to identify; they involve changes in almost every society in the world and the scope of the changes touches on everything.

Seldom has the study of change taken a bird's-eye view. Frequently, one or two of the major aspects of change have been singled out to formulate theories, and these theories have then been used to explain, predict or prescribe overall changes. Of course, many prior theories have been important. However, their weaknesses became apparent as reality deviated from, or even ran counter to, what the theories stated.

The purpose of this paper is not to formulate another "universally applicable" theory, but to point out the importance of one major factor which has not been given due attention in the study of development and change: the role of culture. Because misconceptions regarding culture and development account for part of the failure of the "old paradigm of development," culture, as one variable in the process of change, certainly deserves attention in the search for a "new paradigm." We propose to look at development as a dynamic process in which culture actively accepts, rejects and directs change, while at the same time retaining a certain degree of continuity. But before there can be meaningful discussions on this subject, definitions of key concepts are both helpful and necessary.

Intrinsically, culture is difficult to define. In 1952, two anthropologists undertook this seemingly simple task. Kroeber and Kluckhohn (1952) found 154 different definitions, and countless incomplete definitions of, or statements about, culture. Since then, more definitions have been generated in various social-science fields. The number reflects the elusive nature of culture as a concept in scientific research. Feibleman has described the problem (1968, p. 170):

> They [cultures] do not always have abrupt beginnings and endings; when flourishing, they have indistinct peripheries; and they shade off into one another in a quite indefinite way. We do not always recognize a culture when we see one.

Culture can be defined as social heritage, customs or traditions. It can also refer to the way of behaving and thinking with or without the function of providing problem-solving mechanisms. It can even include "all non-genetically produced means of adjustment" or "the sum total of all that is artificial" (Kroeber and Kluckhohn, 1952, pp. 139, 125). Each definition of culture has strengths and weaknesses because the concept is so complex. For the purpose of this discussion, we would like to point out three important features of culture. First, culture has a memory manifested in traditions, customs and beliefs. This memory of the past often serves to direct reaction and responses to present stimuli. The result is a degree of cultural continuity in most aspects of life. Second, culture is an open system. Constant interaction of elements within the system and interaction with the outside environment brings stimuli to change, and the extent of change varies. Third, through values, norms and sanctioned behavioral patterns, a culture manages to keep its integrity by exercising a certain degree of authority over its members. At the same time, it acts to accept, integrate or reject stimuli for change. Therefore, culture changes, but the presence of one or two manipulated stimuli does not always bring the desired change.

Given the above, a working definition of culture might include manifestations of man's attempt to

1927
1960
1963
1964
1967
1969
1970
1971
1972
1973
1974
1975
1976
1977
1978
1979
1980
1981
1982
1983
1984
1985
1986
1987
1988
1989
1990
1991
1992
1993
1994
1995
1996
1997
1998
1999
2000
2001
2002
2003
2004
2005
2006

relate meaningfully to his environment. Hence it encompasses artifacts as well as values, beliefs and behavioral patterns which all tend to change with a certain degree of continuity. Culture is, therefore, much more than a static entity of spirit and practice accumulated in the past.

"Development" is no less ambiguous a concept. The term has often been confused with "Westernization," "industrialization" and "modernization." Each of these concepts should be distinguished from the other.

"Westernization" refers to the process of becoming like Western nations, but does not specify either which Western nation is considered the model or at what point in time. "Industrialization" emphasizes the growth and expansion of industry and the related social changes. "Modernization" essentially carries a meaning which includes both of the above terms. It refers to a process of social change brought by a change in the economic structure. The eventual product is expected to be something close to what Western nations are.

Over the years, the definition of "development" has undergone some changes. In its earlier stage of conceptualization, it resembled "modernization." For example, Rogers and Shoemaker (1971, p. 4) thought of development as "a type of social change in which new ideas are introduced into a social system in order to produce higher per capita income and levels of living through more modern production methods and improved social organization. Development is modernization at the social level."

In recent years, scholars and policymakers in many Third World nations began to challenge such an orientation and its meaning has taken a more humanistic flavor. In this paper, the concept of "development" is defined as, "a process of social change which has as its goal the improvement in the quality of life of all or the majority of the people without doing violence to the natural and cultural environment in which they exist, and which seeks to involve the majority of the people

as closely as possible in this enterprise, making them the masters of their own destiny."

Over three decades have now gone by since what is commonly considered the initial phase of development. A look at the current world situation indicates that, in spite of the great outlay of capital, more is needed.

From 1968 to 1977, economic assistance to the Third World nations from major international financial institutions[1] totaled over 10 billion dollars (Kurian, 1978). The expenditure of the United Nations Development Programme, one of the major international development agencies, reached $839.5 million in 1980. United States economic aid to other nations from 1946 to 1979 totaled $134,181 million (Statistic Abstract of the United States, 1980). Even more impressive is the constant and steady increase in aid to developing nations. Within a span of nine years, for example, assistance from international banks increased fivefold. Due to structural weaknesses in the Third World economy, continued dependence on international finance institutions is forecasted (World Bank Annual Report, 1981).

Although some success has resulted from the investment of money and manpower, two striking gaps remain: the gap between the rich and the poor in developing nations, and the gap between the developed and the developing nations in the world. For example, the gross per capita national income in North America was over $8,510 in 1978. However, it was $600 in Africa, $800 in East and Southeast Asia (except for Japan), $2,060 in the Middle East and $1,390 is Latin America (United Nations, 1980). Approximately three-fourths of the population in developing nations receive a little over one-fifth of the total world income (Starr and Ritterbush, 1980). Per capita energy use in various regions also differs a great deal, and there will probably be little change in the future. It has been predicted that per capita energy use in Africa in the year 2000 will increase from 0.3 metric tons of coal equivalent in 1965 to 0.9;

---

1   Including World Bank, International Development Association, International American Development Bank, Asian Development Bank and others.

Asia, from 0.4 to 1.5; and the figure for North America will double from 10 to 20. The United States, with six percent of the world's population, uses 33 percent of the available energy (Galtung, 1980). The illiteracy rate has decreased from 44.3 percent in 1950 to 34.2 percent in 1970 (Galtung, 1980), but, in absolute numbers, illiterate adults are now more numerous because of steady population growth.

The gap between rich and poor in developing societies is equally problematic. Because the sociocultural structure in developing nations is not usually considered where new technology is introduced, technology transfer has often served the privileged. The urban centers attract a surplus of labor to big cities and the result is a new class of city poor.

The international one-way flow of information and technology has raised concern because of a prospective loss of cultural identity in developing nations. Statistics give a grim picture. For example, 80 percent of the television programs presented in Latin America are produced in the United States, leading commentators to predict that viewers will abandon their traditional values and absorb the telecasted foreign stereotypes and prejudices (Dagnino, 1973). Researchers such as Nordenstreng (Nordenstreng and Varis, 1974), Varis (1974) and Schiller (1969, 1973, 1976) have shown how this phenomenon is related to global patterns of domination and dependence. This fear of cultural imperialism undoubtedly hampers the development effort.

These facts and figures demonstrate that development programs have failed to bridge the gap between rich and poor. Poverty still exists in large parts of the world and it is complicated by other problems. The dismal outlook for the future has fostered a serious reconsideration of development strategies and policy directions on both practical and theoretical levels.

References

Dagnino, E. "Cultural and Ideological Dependence: Building a Theoretical Framework." In P. Bonilla and R. Girling, eds., *Struggle of Dependency*. Stanford, California: Stanford University Press, 1973.

Feibleman, James. *The Theory of Human Culture.* New York: Humanities Press, 1968.

Galtung, Johan. *The True Worlds.* New York: The Free Press, 1980.

Kroeber, Alfred L., and Clyde Kluckhohn. *Culture.* New York: Vintage Books, 1952.

Kurian, George T. *Encyclopedia of the Third World.* New York: Facts on File, 1978.

Leed, E. J. "Communications revolutions and the enactment of culture." *Communication Research 5*, 305-319. 1978 July

Nordenstreng, Kaarle, and Tapio Varis. "Television Traffic—A One-Way Street." *Reports and Papers on Mass Communication,* No. 70. Paris: UNESCO, 1974.

Rogers, Everett M., and F. F. Shoemaker. *Communication of Innovations.* New York: The Free Press, 1971.

Schiller, Herbert I. *Mass Communications and American Empire.* New York: A. M. Kelley, 1969.

Schiller, Herbert I. *The Mind Managers.* Boston: Beacon Press, 1973.

Schiller, Herbert I. *Communication and Cultural Domination.* New York: International Arts & Sciences Press, 1976.

Starr, Chauncey, and Philip C. Ritterbush, eds. *Science, Technology, and Human Prospect.* New York: Pergamon, 1980.

Statistic Abstract of the United States. Washington, D.C.: U.S. Department of Commerce, 1980.

World Bank Annual Report. Washington, D.C.: World Bank, 1981.

Wang, Georgette, and Wimal Dissanayake. *Continuity and Change in Communication Systems: An Asian Perspective.* New Jersey: Ablex Publishing Corporation, 1984. Copyright © 1984, Ablex Publishing Corporation. Reproduced with permission of Greenwood Publishing Group, Inc., Westport, Conn.

1927
1960
1963
1964
1967
1969
1970
1971
1972
1973
1974
1975
1976
1977
1978
1979
1980
1981
1982
1983
1984
1985
1986
1987
1988
1989
1990
1991
1992
1993
1994
1995
1996
1997
1998
1999
2000
2001
2002
2003
2004
2005
2006

PEOPLE-CENTERED DEVELOPMENT AND PARTICIPATORY RESEARCH

By L. David Brown

1985 Theories and strategies of development have historically focused on expanding production of physical and economic resources (Nugent and Yotopoulos, 1984). More recently, theorists have challenged this overemphasis on production from a variety of perspectives (Lehman, 1979). Proponents of "people-centered development" have emphasized human development, equitable distribution of resources and long-term ecological sustainability as central concerns of development strategy (Gran, 1983; Korten and Klaus, 1984). The tools of this type of development contrast sharply with those of production-centered development: organizational self-regulation instead of regulation by hierarchical command; interactive social learning instead of expert-dominated positivist social research; and political and economic analyses that treat people and environments as primary rather than as secondary concerns (Korten, 1984).

People-centered development strategies place a high premium on the development of human resources and social systems. Education is potentially central to planning and implementing those strategies. Although education has been an important consideration in the development strategies of many countries for years, its record as a catalyst for development is mixed at best. Investments in formal education systems were expected to fuel rapid economic development, promote equitable distributions of resources and provide the human base for political and social as well as economic development. The actual outcome has been disappointing. Expanded formal education has not been consistently related to expanded economic production (Walters, 1981) and appears to be largely irrelevant to reductions in economic inequalities

(Fry, 1981). A formal educational system appears to be more of a consequence than a cause of the political economies in which it operates, a dependent rather than an independent variable (Bowles, 1980).

These results have raised serious questions about the roles education and educators play in the task of development (Simmons, 1980). For example, if expanding educational systems—widely undertaken in the last two decades—do not have the expected developmental impacts, how can renewed emphasis on expanding human resources be a credible development strategy? The answer, for many, is that education will not contribute much to people-centered development unless it differs fundamentally from the formal education of the past.

Formal education in most countries, both developed and developing, has grown out of production-centered logic, preparing students to work in hierarchical organizations, teaching principles and methods of physical scientific inquiry, and emphasizing techniques and skills rather than the human or ecological consequences of decisions (Bowles, 1980; Korten, 1984). In contrast, people-centered development calls for educational processes that emphasize self-regulating organizations, interactive learning that empowers both learners and teachers, and decisions that contribute to human development and ecological sustainability, as well as economic productivity. Participatory research is a people-centered learning process that can transform local patterns of awareness, equalize distributions of power and resources and increase participation in development activity.

Participatory Research: Description and Example

Participatory research has emerged from work with oppressed peoples in many developing areas. Paulo Freire and his colleagues in Latin America, for example, have developed influential concepts for adult education and "conscientization" of the urban and rural poor by engaging adults in critical analyses of the causes of their powerlessness and impoverishment (Freire, 1970/1983; 1974/1980). Similar principles of inquiry have been developed in projects in Africa and Asia (Hall, 1981), although lack of communication channels and limited opportunities for contact among investigators have delayed recognition of their common concepts and methods.

Participatory research brings outside researchers and local participants together in joint inquiry, education and action on problems of mutual interest. Ideally, all parties become learners: they share control over the research process; they commit themselves to constructive action instead of detachment; their participation promotes empowerment as well as understanding (Hall, 1981). Outside researchers who undertake participatory research projects join with local participants to define problems, design data-collection methods, analyze results and utilize research outcomes. Commitment to the interests of local participants often requires challenging oppressive political and social arrangements, so outside researchers often take political positions beside their local colleagues.

Participatory research resembles the older tradition of action research, in which efforts to solve specific social and organizational problems are combined with efforts to develop more general understanding (Passmore and Friedlander, 1982; Sanford, 1970). Participatory research, like action research, sometimes sacrifices rigorous control for pragmatic utility (Susman and Evered, 1978). However, unlike action research, participatory research focuses on actors (oppressed groups), issues (conflicts with power-holders) and values and ideology (empowerment, equity and self-reliance) that put it in opposition to dominant forces in society (Brown and Tandon, 1983). Participatory research can change the understanding of both outside researchers and local participants as well as catalyze shifts in activity by all parties. Potentially, participatory research can produce mutual education, new knowledge and solutions for specific problems.

The following example illustrates some characteristics of participatory research projects (Tandon, 1981; Tandon and Brown, 1981). A private voluntary agency committed to rural development in India had offered workshops for leaders of village farmer groups for several years. In cooperation with outside researchers, this agency sponsored several participatory research workshops which focused on organized farmers to deal with local problems in their rural Indian villages. The workshops began by posing questions (for example, Why are you poor?). Responses were initially sparse—a five-minute silence followed the first question in the initial workshop—for participants had no experience with such dialogues, and they were overawed by the status of the outsiders. The researchers were uncomfortable for different reasons: outsiders and farmers lived together on equal terms during the workshop, and researchers felt disoriented by lack of familiar facilities, such as toilets, running water and chairs.

Previous workshops had offered leaders of village farmer groups information for improving crop yields and quality, but relatively little change had resulted. Farmers seldom took advantage of the new information, and farmer groups did not work together even on projects of common interest. The participatory research differed from earlier efforts in several ways: dialogue encouraged participants to take initiatives in analysis; discussions clarified agreements and common concerns among participants; and problem-solving exercises required participants to work collectively, so they learned by experience about skills needed for joint action. Villages and outsiders together developed better understanding of village problems and discussed strategies for dealing with problems having high priority in the eyes of the group.

Outcomes of the participatory research workshops were assessed in follow-up visits to villages and through systematic analysis of journals kept by farmer group leaders. The level of problem-solving initiatives by participant groups increased dramatically over past performance, especially in comparison to groups from other villages. For example, participant groups started local schools, increased school enrollments and elected new representative to local governments. Other villagers

1927
1960
1963
1964
1967
1969
1970
1971
1972
1973
1974
1975
1976
1977
1978
1979
1980
1981
1982
1983
1984
1985
1986
1987
1988
1989
1990
1991
1992
1993
1994
1995
1996
1997
1998
1999
2000
2001
2002
2003
2004
2005
2006

observed the success of participant groups and began to emulate them. The agency decided to train the rest of its staff in participatory research skills so they could extend the impacts of the project to other villages.

This particular project required outside researchers skilled in experiential learning, organization building and participatory research. Within a few months, workshop participants had become more aware of their situations and more active about influencing them. Farmer groups had developed coalitions with neighboring villages to elect government representatives, and similar group initiatives started subsequently in other villages. The agency which sponsored the participatory experiment decided to alter its basic workshop technology to emphasize participatory research in other villages. This pattern of spreading initiatives and self-reliant activity grounded in local needs exemplifies the potential contribution of participatory research to people-centered development.

Participatory research differs in important ways from other traditions of inquiry, education and action. Some illustrative differences and their implications are identified in this section.

Participatory Research as Inquiry

This participatory research in India focused first on understanding the circumstances of local participants and then on using that understanding to plan strategies for improvement. In the course of conducting the research, outsiders learned about village life from farmers, and farmers learned skills of organization and action form the outsiders. Each learned to work effectively with the other, and each learned how village groups might take initiatives to influence their situations. The process produced both solutions to immediate problems faced by villagers (How can our village get a school?) and information relevant to theoretical questions of concern to outsiders (Can experience-based learning help small farmers organize themselves?)

This project reflects important differences in goals and procedures between participatory research and the dominant positivist tradition of U.S. social science. Positivist research seeks to build a network of general laws to explain social phenomena across all cases. Positivist researchers attempt to insure the validity of their findings by carefully controlling the design of research, the analysis of data and the impact of researcher values on phenomena, thereby reducing the ambiguity of their conclusions or the relevance of competing explanations as much as possible (Gergen, 1982; Susman and Evered, 1978).

In contrast, participatory research focuses on explaining single cases. Participants from Indian villages are less interested than outside researchers in developing general laws, particularly if those laws are not obviously relevant to understanding and improving their own situations. Shared control of the research process encourages local participants to analyze problems in terms that are intelligible to local participants. They understandably value theories that offer explanation, prediction and control of local events more than those that sacrifice local applicability to general validity. Thus, participatory research has an idiographic and pragmatic bias that violates many of the assumptions of positivist social science (Susman and Evered, 1978).

Participatory researchers often violate the procedures and constraints positivist researchers seek to validate their findings. Control over research design is frequently limited by the tolerance of local participants, the pressure of external events and the unavailability of information. … Furthermore, complex statistical analyses require expertise and resources that are often neither available nor recognized as useful by local participants. Researcher objectivity is often difficult or impossible to maintain in the face of the explicitly value-laden choices needed to establish a community of interest with local participants, to implement the participatory research tradition of explicit commitment to oppressed groups and to take constructive action on the basis of research findings. This is not to say that standards of validity are not relevant to participatory research: participatory research findings may meet the "pattern validity" criteria used by clinical and anthropological investigators (Diesing, 1978) or the "heuristic logic" appropriate to complex and uncertain systems (Sutherland, 1973). But these standards may not satisfy those strongly committed to positivist criteria.

These differences may separate participatory research irrevocably from other social-science traditions; participatory research may not be "science" by positivist criteria. But, as Susman and Evered (1978) have pointed out, there are epistemological bases other than positivism that can underpin inquiry, and positivist science has not provided a fruitful basis for developmental action in many settings. Many people-centered development theorists argue that positivist social science is part of the problem; the failure to recognize the investigation as part of the system undercuts the utility of the inquiry for promoting development (Ackoff, 1977; Dunn, 1971; Korten, 1984). Participatory research may not be good social science in positivist terms, but it may be better than positivist social science for many development purposes.

Participatory Research as Education

The powerful experiential learning process of the Indian participatory research projects reshaped the ideas and attitudes of both outside researchers and local participants. Participatory research differs significantly both in content and process from formal education.

Formal education curricula are often designed by experts in content areas, planned well in advance, standardized across regions, and adopted and disseminated through centralized bureaucracies. The "content" of learning in participatory research, however, can seldom be planned or predicted in detail across many projects. It is often negotiated between local participants and researchers to fit specific local problems. Some Indian villagers were concerned about educational resources; other wanted representation in local governments; still others wanted better services from government functionaries. Educational topics

for participatory research will vary with local interests, and standardized content training for participatory researchers/educators will rarely cover all the issues that might be considered relevant by local participants. Such diversity of interests also makes centralized organization and control of content difficult. Waiting for central agreement to curricular changes would debilitate both local interest in and researcher motivation for participatory research projects.

Participatory research also implies an education "process" different from that of formal education. Participatory research asks adults to be interdependent participants and co-learners, while most formal education assumes teacher control of young and dependent students. Successful participatory research is based on two-way discussions more often than the one-way communication from teacher to student found in traditional teaching. Both outsiders and local participants may instruct each other about topics such as research methods or local conditions. More generally, however, participatory research is an interactive process very different from the instruction patterns of formal education; it implies shared responsibility for learning rather than active teachers and passive students. The assumption of interactive learning proved difficult to introduce in the Indian workshops because the farmers expected lectures rather than discussions. But participation, once launched, unlocked the farmers' energy and laid the groundwork from which village groups later initiated independent projects.

Participatory research makes unfamiliar demands on researcher/educators. Researchers need less expertise in content areas, such as math or history, and more skills for facilitating general problem solving, such as managing meetings, getting information, organizing work or planning activity. These research strategies also call for changes in the structure and administration of educational organizations. Centralized, formalized and standardized organizations may be appropriate for communicating well-defined and routinely executed curricula, but bureaucratic organization of participatory research can rapidly strangle commitment to local problems and the emergence of local innovative problem solving (Korten, 1980).

Participatory Research as Organizational Intervention

Organizational innovations by participants and researchers can catalyze developmental changes. In the Indian villages, farmer groups initiated actions with implications for local education, political mobilization and representation, and influence over government agencies. The project created new organizational combinations that linked villagers to each other and to the outside world (Tandon and Brown, 1981). Building relations for action between participants and researchers is not easy; ordinarily, they live in very different worlds. It took courage and perseverance on the part of both outside researchers and village participants in the Indian projects to develop mutual trust and influence. Cooperative relations can combine outside resources (such as information about national and regional plans, methods for learning about local problems or organizational strategies for collective work) with local resources (such as information about local problems, commitment to understanding new options and energy and skill for solving problems). Interaction with outside researchers provides local participants with connections to the larger system by linking them with previously unexplored sources of information and outside alliances, while interaction with local participants provides researchers with access to information and insights into local collective action. Participant groups in the Indian project negotiated alliances with neighboring villages to elect representatives to local governments, but they depended on researchers for contact with larger agencies and issues.

Interventions that grow out of participatory research are locally developed, targeted and owned. The village groups defined problems, analyzed alternative solutions, chose action strategies and implemented plans in the Indian project. They learned how to organize themselves to take action, and they learned the benefits collective action could achieve. Participatory research can create new agencies for developmental intervention in the form of participant groups aware of alternative possibilities, skilled in organization and planning and experienced in successful action. These local projects can have ripple effects: there are indicators that villages which were not included in the projects in India also learned the collective action from participating groups and organized themselves to take their own initiatives. Participatory research develops organizations—not just knowledge and educated individuals—that connect participants to a larger world and empower them to act more effectively at the local level.

Summary

Participatory research offers a strategy for local education, research and organization that is consistent with the assumptions of people-centered development. It encourages inquiry that focuses on local problems and pragmatic concerns; it provides education that encourages activist attitudes and informal collective action; and it builds organizations that enable cohesive local action and that link local groups to the larger political and economic context.

Participatory research is a micro-strategy most relevant to mobilization and development at the local level, but the larger context of political, economic and cultural patterns can facilitate or impede this type of research. In politically centralized and economically concentrated systems, for example, participatory research may threaten powerful, established interests. Mobilized local groups may challenge arrangements that they perceive to illegitimately concentrate power and wealth in a few hands. Contextual events and forces may impede or even overwhelm participatory research activities. Although it provides no panacea, participatory research can offer a promising tool for promoting people-centered development in political and economic systems that encourage local empowerment.

References

Ackoff, R. L. "National Development Planning Revisited." Operations Research, 1975, 25: 212-218.

Bowles, S. "Education, Class Conflict, and Uneven Development." In J. L. Simmons, ed., The Education Dilemma. Oxford, England: Pergamon, 1980, 205-231.

Brown, C. C., and R. Tandon. "Ideology and Political Economy in Inquiry: Action Research and Participatory Research." Journal of Applied Behavioral Science, 1983, 19: 277-294.

Diesing, P. Patterns of Discovery in the Social Sciences. Chicago: Aldine-Atherton, 1971.

Dunn, D. E. Economics and Social Development: A Process of Social Learning. Baltimore: Johns Hopkins University Press, 1971.

Freire, P. Pedagogy of the Oppressed. New York: Continuum, 1983. (Original work published 1970.)

Freire, P. Education for Critical Consciousness. New York: Continuum, 1980. (Original work published 1974.)

Fry, G. W. "Schooling, Development and Inequality: Old Myths and New Realities." Harvard Educational Review, 1981, 51: 107-116.

Gran, G. Development by People: Citizen Construction of a Just World. New York: Praeger, 1983.

Gergen, K. J. Toward Transformation in Social Knowledge. New York: Springer-Verlag, 1982.

Hall, B. L. "Participatory Research, Popular Knowledge, and Power: A Personal Reflection." Convergence, 13: 6-17.

Korten, D. "Community Organization and Rural Development: A Learning Process Approach." Public Administration Review, 1980, 40: 480-510.

Korten, D. "People-Centered Development: Toward a Framework." In D. Korten and R. Klauss, eds., People-Centered Development: Contributions Toward Theory and Planning Frameworks. West Hartford, Connecticut: Kumarian, 1984.

Korten, D., and R. Klauss, eds., ibid.

Lehmann, D. Development Theory: Four Critical Studies. London: Cass, 1979.

Nugent, J. B., and P. A. Yotopoulos, P. A. (1984). "Orthodox Development Economics Versus the Dynamics of Concentration and Marginalization." In D. Korten and R. Klauss, eds., op. cit.: 107-120.

Pasmore, W., and F. Friedlander. "An Action Research Program for Increasing Employee Involvement in Problem Solving." Administrative Science Quarterly, 1982, 27: 343-362.

Sanford, N. "Whatever Happened to Action Research?" Journal of Social Issues, 1970, 26: 3-23.

Simmons, J. L., ed. (1980). "The Education Dilemma: Policy Issues for Developing Countries in the 1980s. Oxford: Pergamon Press, 1980.

Susman, G. I., and R. D. Evered. "An Assessment of the Scientific Merits of Action Research." Administrative Science Quarterly, 1978, 23: 582-603.

Tandon, R. "Dialogue as Inquiry and Intervention." In P. Reason and J. Rowan, eds., Human Inquiry: A Sourcebook of New Paradigm Research. New York: Wiley, 1981, 293-302.

Tandon, R., and L. D. Brown. "Organization-Building for Rural Development: An Experiment in India." Journal of Applied Behavioral Science, 1981, 17: 172-189.

Walters, P. B. "Educational Change and National Economic Development." Harvard Educational Review, 1981, 51: 94-106.

L. David Brown, "People-Centered Development and Participatory Research," Harvard Educational Review, volume 55:1 (February 1985), pp. 69-75. Copyright © 1985 by the President and Fellows of Harvard College. All rights reserved. Reprinted with permission.

1927
1960
1963
1964
1967
1969
1970
1971
1972
1973
1974
1975
1976
1977
1978
1979
1980
1981
1982
1983
1984
1985
1986
1987
1988
1989
1990
1991
1992
1993
1994
1995
1996
1997
1998
1999
2000
2001
2002
2003
2004
2005
2006

IS IT GOVERNMENT COMMUNICATION OR PEOPLE COMMUNICATION?

By Nora C. Quebral

1985 Providing people the means to obtain material goods and services will sustain life when they are still powerless to change oppressive conditions. National blueprints to signify where a country wants to go, and how it plans to get there, are announcements of intent. Policies can create a more a benign environment in which plans have a better chance of succeeding. But if there is anything we have learned from the past decades, it is that government and development agencies may propose but people, in the end, will dispose. No matter how poor, in matters that personally concern them, they remain active agents and, at some stage, make choices. Rightly or wrongly, according to government, they will decide to go along with public policy, repudiate or modify it, or strike off on their own.

This means that, realistically, governments have never had full control over the development progress of their citizens. Their role indeed ideally diminishes as people acquire the ability to manage their lives better. They can be supportive by providing information, resources and opportunities that individuals singly cannot muster; they can create a favorable climate within which people can unfold their wings. But in development seen as the growth of people's capacities to improve their lives and those of others with the means at hand, there is a line across which governments have neither the moral authority nor the real power to go. The bottom line in development, as so many have already said before, is that people develop themselves. Government, as the instrument of society, only can make it happen faster.

If development is so perceived, the soundest policies a government can make are those that enable its citizens to learn creatively from their experience and that of others, at the same time as policies attend to primary needs. Development then becomes lifelong learning that everyone undergoes. Participation is not a privilege granted by a tolerant government, but an inescapable element of the process. Similarly, the values of self-reliance, initiative and critical judgment are intrinsic to the outcomes. For the government of a developing country then to expect its citizen-learners to conform passively, to assent without thought or to accept without question, is to contradict itself.

With development seen as participatory learning, communication associated with it cannot be less participative or educational, in ends as or in means. This is the logic behind current projects involving village people in making slide shows or video programs that convey the essence of their situation to the world outside their communities. Properly guided, the experience enlarges their consciousness about their problems and helps them clarify their options. It also adds to their communicative skills, thereby giving them an extra measure of self-confidence. The only question is this: From which of their activities to fend for food and other necessities do they pare off the precious time to produce a slideshow that makes a statement?

References

1. Islam, Rizwanul, ed. *Strategies for Alleviating Poverty in Rural Asia*. Bangkok: International Labour Organization Asian Employment Programme, 1985.

2. Korten, David C., and Rudi Klaus, eds. *People-Centered Development: Toward a Framework*. Connecticut: Kumarian Press, 1984.

Paper presented at the BERNAMA-AMIC seminar on Communication Challenges in Asia, Kuala Lumpur, Malaysia, November 22, 1985. Reprinted with permission of the author.

COMMUNICATION AND DEVELOPMENT PARADIGMS: AN OVERVIEW

By Jan Servaes

1985

Slogans like self-reliance, basic needs, participation, decentralization and democratization of communication have been absorbed with increasing frequency in the policy and planning debate by persons and institutions with divergent backgrounds and opinions, such as the World Bank on the one hand and the Dag Hammarskjöld Foundation on the other.

…In other words, all the above terms, and many more, *mean different things to different people.* This confusion can be attributed to any aspect in the social sciences field. It is not that the social sciences purposely aim at bringing forth ambiguous products, but rather, as argued by Lederer (1980:1), that the objects of social sciences, that is, facts and processes, are more open to common experience and interest than the objects of other spheres of knowledge.

At the same time, the problematic has become even more complex, mainly due to changes in the societal and world system on the one hand, and *the interdisciplinary nature of communication and development* on the other. Let me illustrate this from two quotations from the communication research field.

The first, by Nordenstreng (1977:280), runs as follows:
> The global trends in the field of mass communication research can be expressed in terms of two interrelated tendencies on change: a tendency toward a more holistic framework and a tendency toward policy orientation. The holistic approach, for its part, may be seen to imply two sub-aspects,

a stressing of the processional approach covering simultaneously various stages of the communication process and a stressing of the contextual approach tying the particular communication phenomena into wider socio-politic economic settings.

Second, Hamelink (1981:7) observes that
> No pertinent theoretical framework for the study of international communication has yet been developed, and as a result, there is continuing dependence on: mass media theories (usually fragmentary, and based on obsolete psychological and socio-logical notions); political science theories on international relations (usually inadequate descriptions of status quo situations); imperialism dependency theories (usually too narrowly confined to the transfer of mechanisms).

Yet, in spite of the complexity, confusion and rhetoric, which have by and large resulted in a dialogue of the deaf at international forums, this paper is meant to contribute more clarity than exists at present. My departure point is very basic and simple. On the one hand, I notice that almost any publication dealing with communication policy and planning stresses the important link between the social structure and the development of communication systems. Accordingly, it is assumed that, as for example formulated by the International Commission for the Study of Communication Problems (MacBride, 1980:258): "Development strategies should incorporate communication policies as an integral part in the diagnosis of needs and in the design and implementation of selected priorities." On the other hand, looking at the real situation of national communication policies in the Third World, I learn that in nearly all nations' operational policies govern communication on an apparently *ad hoc* basis without any conceptual, organisational or structural framework.

…Most scholars agree that thinking about communication and development as a distinct discipline emerged after World War II, and they usually point out two paradigms: *Modernisation and Growth* versus *Dependency*

1927
1960
1963
1964
1967
1969
1970
1971
1972
1973
1974
1975
1976
1977
1978
1979
1980
1981
1982
1983
1984
1985
1986
1987
1988
1989
1990
1991
1992
1993
1994
1995
1996
1997
1998
1999
2000
2001
2002
2003
2004
2005
2006

and *Underdevelopment.* I perceive a new perspective, a new paradigm. This new paradigm, which can be broadly defined as *Anotherness in One World,* is gradually emerging but still is in the process of formation.

In accordance with the MacBride Commission's suggestion that each country decide what kind of development it wants prior to determining its communication policies and strategies, the main focus of attention in this paper will be on the general context of development and change in which communication takes place.

What follows is an outline:

The chronological approach has a certain bias in creating the impression that later theoretical innovations replace earlier ones. However, in the social sciences, paradigms tend to accumulate rather than to replace each other. Van Nieuwenhuijze (1982:53) has recently put it as follows: "In social change it often is the gradual shift in accent that, for its consequences, is crucial".

Therefore I conceive paradigms as *frames of meaning* mediated by others:

> The process of learning a paradigm or language game as the expression of a form of life is also a process of learning what that paradigm is not: That is to say, learning to mediate it with other, rejected alternatives, by contrast to which the claims of the paradigm in question are clarified. (Giddens, 1976:144).

Firstly, in each time period one can make a distinction between a *dominant* and an *alternative* prespective on communication and development. The modernization paradigm, for instance, continues to be influential at the political and institutional front, though it no longer enjoys the widespread theoretical endorsement which it did till the mid-sixties.

Secondly, each paradigm can be further subdivided in what can be called its *mainstream* of thinking and its various *counterpoints.* For obvious reasons, I will deal here only with the mainstream ideas of each paradigm.

Thirdly, paradigms in social sciences build on one another rather than break fundamentally with previous theories. In consequence, many theorists and researchers deepen and widen their views in an evolutionary, sometimes dialectical way. So it may occur that their early work can be seen as eloquent evidence of the modernization or dependency theory, while their later undertakings are more in line with the third paradigm.

Nevertheless...I pose some basic questions concerning communication and development...

Modernisation and Growth

During the late 1940s and early 1960s most development thinkers stated that the problem of "underdevelopment" or "backwardness" could be solved by a more or less mechanical application of the economic and political system in the West to countries in the Third World, under the assumption that the difference was one of degree rather than of kind. Therefore, the central element of this paradigm is the metaphor of *growth,* and the identification of growth with the idea of *progress.* This implies that development is assumed to be organic, immanent, directional, cumulative, purposive and irreversible.[1]

The modernisation paradigm sees development as an unilinear, evolutionary perspective, and defines the state of underdevelopment in terms of observable, quantitative differences between *"poor"* and *"rich"* countries on the one hand, and *traditional* and *modern* sectors and/or countries gradually assume the "qualities" of the modern ones. This process was initially seen as an *economic process* of capital formation determined by the level of investment. As thinking about modernization proceeded, and as the one-sided economic strategy of unbalanced growth did not solve the problem, various so-called *non-economic* factors were introduced. One started to argue that the transition from a traditional to a modern society not only presupposed economic growth indices but also changes in socio-psychological attitudes and education, as well as necessary changes in social and political institutions.

The "dualistic" nature of underdevelopment was conceived of as two stages of development, co-existing in time, and in due course the differences between them were to disappear because of an impelling force toward *consensus and equilibrium*. The problem was to remove the obstacles and barriers, which were only to be found in the traditional sector of society.

Therefore, in practice, modernization was very much the same as W*esternization*, i.e., the underdeveloped nations should follow and copy Western models.

How much and in what ways can communication contribute to this process of modernization? The basic idea is that communication stimulates and diffuses values and institutions that are favourable to achievement, mobility innovations and consumption.

The early theory of communication and modernization stems from models developed in the United States during studies in political campaign situations. Out of the Erie County study came the notion of a *two-step-flow* of communication. Two elements are involved: (1) the idea of a population divided into "active" and "passive" participants, or "opinion leaders" and "followers", according to interest and activity in relation to media and their messages; and (2) the notion of a two-step-flow of influence rather than a direct contact between "stimulus" and "respondent" (or the so-called bullet or hypodermic theory). The general conclusion of this line of research is that mass communication is less likely than personal influence to have a direct effect on social behaviour. Mass communication is important in spreading awareness of new possibilities and practices, but at the stage where decisions are being made about whether to adopt or not to adopt, personal communication is far more likely to be influential. This approach, which as been introduced in the development field by Rogers, is thus primarily concerned with the process of *diffusion and adoption of innovations* on a systematic, planned and short-term basis. Another

perspective is dealing with the *individual value and attitude change* itself. Central to this view are concepts such as "the creative personality" (Hagen), "the need for achievement" (McClelland) or "empathy" (Lerner), which are assumed to be indispensable skills for people moving out of traditional settings.

Other researchers, such as Pool, Rao and Schramm took a closer look at the connection between *mass communication and modernizing practices and institutions*. The modern mass media are the "mobility multipliers" "movers" or "innovators" for change and modernization. Their development runs parallel to the development of other institutions of modern society, such as schools and industry, and is closely related to some of the indices of general social and economic growth, such as literacy, per capita income and urbanization.

Furthermore, there is a *technological deterministic approach,* in which at least four viewpoints can be distinguished. A first is the view of technology as the driving force of development (Ogburn). A second variant views technology as an irresistible as well as an overwhelming force in development (Innis, McLuhan). A third approach posits the conviction that the development and application of technology can resolve all the varied problems of humankind. The fourth theory is a direct opposite to the third; it views technology as the source of all that goes wrong in society. All variants share the underlying assumption that technology has no history and no historical context, and that it is therefore politically neutral and value-free.

As a result of the real development in most Third World countries, the modernization paradigm became subject to strong criticism, particularly in Latin America. Undoubtedly the most influential critic has been Frank. He claimed that the modernization perspective was empirically untenable, theoretically insufficient and practically incapable of stimulating a process of development in the Third World. Afterwards, also, Western scholars joined their Latin American colleagues in the "demasque" of modernization.

1927
1960
1963
1964
1967
1969
1970
1971
1972
1973
1974
1975
1976
1977
1978
1979
1980
1981
1982
1983
1984
1985
1986
1987
1988
1989
1990
1991
1992
1993
1994
1995
1996
1997
1998
1999
2000
2001
2002
2003
2004
2005
2006

The critique concerned not only the modernization theory as such, but the whole tradition of a evolutionism and functionalism of which it forms part. Smith (1973), for instance, elaborated on four arguments:

a. *methodologically* evolutionism is based on comparative statics which neglects both the sources and the route of change;
b. from a *logical* point of view there is the mistake of equating serialism with causal explanations of transition;
c. *empirically* it is easy to prove that any effort to classify societies using indicators of tradition and modernity is groundless; and
d. the ethnocentrism of the modernization approach can be questioned from a *moral* point of view.

Also the underlying communication assumptions of the modernization paradigm came under attack. Among one of the first to attack the two-step-flow and opinion leader-theory was Klapper (1960). He stated that mass communication functions among and through mediating factors and influences. The efficiency of mass communication, either as a contributory agent or as an agent of direct effect, is affected by various aspects of communication itself or of the communication situation, including, for example, aspects of textual organization, the nature of the source and medium, the existing climate of public opinion and the like. Consequently Klapper recommends and describes a new orientation he names *phenomenistic:* "It is in essence a shift away from the tendency to regard mass communication as a necessary and sufficient cause of audience effects, toward a view of the media as influences, working amid other influences, in a total situation" (Klapper, 1960:5).

Since then the modernization and communication paradigm has been criticized, as a whole or partially, by several researchers (Elliott & Golding, 1974; Gitlin, 1978; Golding, 1974; Grossberg, 1981; McCormack, 1969; Mattelart et al., 1971; Salinas, 1982; Smythe, 1981 and Teheranian, 1977). The main points of their criticism can be summed up as follows:

a. the *empirical failings and discrepancies* in its search for specific, measurable, short-term, individual "effects;"
b. the *positivist-behaviourist assumptions,* especially in the diffusion theory, i.e., the approach is external and manipulative, and presupposes a linear, rational sequence of events, planned in advance and with criteria of rationality determined externally;
c. the *market assumptions,* i.e., by motivating individuals to aspire to mobility and higher standards of living, the media in editorial materials as well as advertising, are creating a kind of consumer demand and a Western way of life;
d. *ethnocentrism and endogenism,* i.e., one takes for granted that cultural forms and "scientific" methods, developed under specific circumstances in "modern" societies, can be equally used in Third World settings; and
e. *the static, ahistorical and structural naivete,* i.e., one assumes that mass communication takes place in a stable social system, where social harmony and integration reign, and class or group conflicts and contradictions in the social system seem to be absent.

The *principle of free flow of information* can be said to be the political translation of this modernization and communication paradigm. After a war against fascism, freedom was an appeal that drew supporters from disparate camps and, at the same time, nicely fitted the requirements of an expansionist economic system. The victors of the war, headed by the United States, defined the concept of freedom of information, according to 19th century Western ideas about press freedom, and capitalist, ways. Although more social-oriented formulations of the freedom of information were also discussed and adopted—compare, e.g., the articles 19 and 28 of the Universal Declaration of Human Rights—these rights and obligations got caught in the whirlpool of the Cold War.

This Western interpretation of the free flow principle, with its underlying values and assumptions that can be found in the Siebert, et. al. (1956) fourfold division of media theories under the heading of the *free press theory*, remained the dominant paradigm worldwide for at least two decades after 1945. At present it continues to be adopted and propagated, sometimes in slightly amended forms by *Western,* and *Western-oriented* Third World governments, communication scholars and institutions. Publications that represent its viewpoints are those by Righter (1978) and Horton (1978).

Dependency and Underdevelopment

As a result of the general intellectual "revolution" of the mid 1960s, the above Western or ethnocentric look on development was challenged by Latin American scientists, and a theory dealing with dependency and underdevelopment was born. This so-called dependency approach formed part of a general structuralistic and Marxist re-orientation in the social sciences.

Though the dependency paradigm can be said to be an indigenous Latin American creation, the "founding father" of its perspective is Baran, who is, together with Magdoff and Sweezy, spokesman for the North American Monthly Review group. He was the first to argue that development and underdevelopment had to be seen as *interrelated and continuous processes,* two aspects of a single global process, rather than as an original state of existence.

The *CEPAL development strategy* of industrialization by import substitution, planning and state interventionism in general, and regional substitution, proved the correctness of Baran's theoretical observations. This CEPAL strategy turned out to be inadequate for at least two reasons:

a. the necessary imported inputs created another kind of dependence, technological and financial;
b. the pattern of income and distribution confined the demand of goods and services to the relatively small middle class group.

Some different approaches and theoretical dimensions emerged within the field of dependency analyses. However, according to Hettne (1982), a typical dependency position in terms of methodology would *stress holism,*

external factors, *socio-political* and *economic* analysis, *regional* contradictions, *polarization* between development and underdevelopment and the role of *voluntarist* or subjective factors in history. Hence, one may state that most *dependistas* believe that the most important obstacles to development were not lack of capital or management skills but the result of the international division of labor. These obstacles were not internal but external. This meant that development in the Center somehow implied underdevelopment in the Periphery.

The dependency paradigm has influenced discussions on strategies at both national and international levels. Chile under Allende, Jamaica under Manley and Tanzania under Nyerere, are examples of governments that tried to set up a development policy within a dependency perspective. On the international level, to remove the external obstacles *dependistas* argued that each peripheral country should strive for self-reliance and search for new allies within the framework of a *New International Economic Order* (NIEO). It was assumed that, to make this operational, a more or less revolutionary political transformation would be necessary.

The communication component of the dependency paradigm is most often referred to as "media" or "cultural imperialism." While modernization scholars take the nation state as their main framework of reference do *dependistas* believe in a predominantly *international level of analysis.* They argue that the domination of the Periphery by the Center occurs through a combination of power components, that is, military, economics, politics, culture and so on. Nowadays, the cultural and communication components have become of greater importance when one wishes to perpetuate dependent relationships, because, we have a rather paradoxical situation. As the Third World begins to achieve emancipation economically and politically, cultural dominance increases.

When I adopt Boyd Barrett's (1977:117) definition of *media imperialism:* "The process whereby the ownership, structure, distribution or content of the media in any other country are single or together subject to

1927
1960
1963
1964
1967
1969
1970
1971
1972
1973
1974
1975
1976
1977
1978
1979
1980
1981
1982
1983
1984
1985
1986
1987
1988
1989
1990
1991
1992
1993
1994
1995
1996
1997
1998
1999
2000
2001
2002
2003
2004
2005
2006

substantial external pressures from the media interests of any other country or countries, without proportionate reciprocation of influence by the country so affected," I can, basing myself on Galtung (1980), distinguish between four mechanisms of imperialism: *exploitation, penetration* through a bridgehead (the peripheral elite), *fragmentation* and *marginalization*. While exploitation is seen as the *raison d' etre'* of inequality in this world, the three other mechanisms can be conceived as supporting factors, not all of them equally necessary. Their influence can be both direct and indirect, either of an objective measurable or subjective perceptible nature. Therefore, Hamelink (1978 and 1983) gives preference to the concept of *cultural synchronization,* instead of the more common cultural imperialism idea. In his opinion, cultural imperialism is the most frequent, but not exclusive, form in which cultural synchronization occurs. For cultural synchronization can take place without imperialistic relations constituting the prime causal factor or even without overt imperialistic relations. I tend to agree with this latter view.

Most studies on the cultural "bedazzlement" of Third World countries do not go far beyond *quantitative aspects.* They mainly show how much information, ideas, entertainment, advertisement, capital and hardware material flows between societies and media institutions, and therefore cause *imbalances* between Center and Periphery nations, as well as disparities within regions and countries, for example, between rural and urban areas, between linguistic or ethnic majorities and minorities, and between rich and poor groups or classes. Besides this, one needs more details on the *qualitative impact* of the Western media influences on Third World realities. How does this process affect the culture, ideology and behaviour of people in the long run? Most *dependistas* take for granted that, together with the huge volume of Western media messages, a conservative and capitalist ideology and consumptive culture will be introduced and reinforced simultaneously. Thus they question the belief of the modernization paradigm, especially the diffusion theorists that mass media can work as change agents.

Compared to the endogenism of the modernization paradigm, the dependency view in its stress on external factors appears almost as an antithesis. However, looking at the *content* of development the difference is minimal. Just as the dependency theory grew out of a dissatisfaction with the explanatory capacity of the modernization paradigm, its radical critics see it as being incapable of explaining the new realities of the post-colonial world (Berstein, 1979; Leys, 1977 and Hansen & Schulz, 1981). They argue, for instance, that the dependency theory:

a. sees the *fundamental contradiction* in the world between the Center and the Periphery and, therefore, fails to take into account the internal class and productive structures of the Periphery that inhibit development of the productive forces;

b. tends to *focus on the Center* and international capital as these are "blamed" for poverty and backwardness, instead of local class formations;

c. *fails to differentiate* capitalist from feudal, or other pre-capitalist, modes of controlling the direct producer and appropriating the surplus;

d. ignores the productivity of labour as the central point in economic development and thus locates the motor force of capitalist development and underdevelopment in the *transfer* of the economic surplus from the Periphery to the Center;

e. encourages a *Third World-oriented ideology* that undermines the potential for international class solidarity by lumping together as "enemies" the elite and masses in the Center nations;

f. is *static,* in that it is unable to explain and account for changes in underdeveloped economies over time.

Furthermore, Nwosu (1983) mentions related problems such as inadequate conceptualization, operationalisation and data gathering techniques, and the fact that the emotional, *nationalistic and ideologically-tainted debates* the dependency controversy evokes, reflect on the research data of this subject and their interpretation.

The weakest point in dependency communication research is the lack of analysis on the nature of the class *forces* and the position of the *nation state* in peripheral countries. [For an extensive literature review, see Ikonicoff, 1983]. *Dependistas* put too much emphasis on the contradictions at the international level, and accordingly, overlook the existing contradictions at national level; between the interests of the state and the media owners on the one hand, and between the government and the population on the other. The political result of the dependency view, the critics state, is to turn attention away from these internal class relations and focus on the Center. However, one has to accept that "internal" and "external" factors inhibiting development do not exist independently of each other. Thus, in order to understand and develop a proper strategy one must have an understanding of the class relationships of any particular peripheral social formation and the ways in which these structures articulate with the Center on the one hand, and the producing classes in the Third World on the other. To dismiss Third World ruling classes, for example, as mere puppets whose interests are always mechanically synonymous with those of the Center is to ignore the realities of a more complex relationship. The very unevenness and contradictory nature of the capitalist development process necessarily produces a constantly changing relationship. At the same time one has to keep in mid that all these countries *differ* vastly from one another in terms of their individual histories and cultures, size of their populations, natural resources and so on.

Peripheral countries thus have not remained static but have followed their own historical paths.

Contrary to modernization "addicts" who claim that the concept of a free flow of information should be interpreted in an individual and liberal way, *dependistas* argue that, in practice, these notions have increased the advantages of those countries and companies that possess greater communication resources. Thus, the free flow doctrine has often been used as an economic and/or ideological tool. In order to really be free,

communication flows have to be two-way, not simply in one direction, from the Center to the Periphery. Consequently, the opponents of the Western free flow concept, led by the Non-Aligned Movement, argue that communication flows should not only be *free*, but at the same time *balanced*, and that communication must be regarded as a social commodity in the hands of, or at least controlled by, sovereign *governments*.

During the 1950s and early 1960s UNESCO was in line with the then-dominant, Western ideas on free flow. However, it gradually became the platform for Third World countries to express their views and demands. Not surprisingly it also have become the target for those who see authoritarian control looming behind every critique of the status quo. The announcement by the United States to withdraw from UNESCO can be interpreted as one of the many examples of the latter. (For a Non-Aligned standpoint, see Mankekar (1981) or Masmoudi (1978.)

However, one of the still unanswered questions is: *whose new order?* Look at Latin America, the mother continent of dependency. Motta (1984: 384-385) points out that here, as elsewhere, state intervention in national affairs has increased overall. This process of capitalist state intervention has produced authoritarian, mostly military, governments that have centralized decision making. Communication policies in these states exhibit two principal tendencies:

> First, the government controls the creation, distribution, and operation of the mass media as well as the flow of messages. This control takes many forms—station licensing, broadcasting regulations, and censorship. This type of control seeks to depoliticize and demobilize society. Second, the government widely circulates official messages in order to mobilize the population towards state ends and to legitimize itself.

Motta concludes by saying,

> National communication policies have not produced the desired democratization of communication in Latin America. On the contrary, policy

1927
1960
1963
1964
1967
1969
1970
1971
1972
1973
1974
1975
1976
1977
1978
1979
1980
1981
1982
1983
1984
1985
1986
1987
1988
1989
1990
1991
1992
1993
1994
1995
1996
1997
1998
1999
2000
2001
2002
2003
2004
2005
2006

has been translated into planning and planning has meant state intervention, characterized by centralization of communication decision making, tight regulation of the media and the use of communication media and messages to legitimize authoritarian governments.

Similar situations can be easily depicted in other Third World countries; for example, two countries in Southeast Asia are known as fierce promoters of non-aligned demands. The governments of these countries hold rather *contradictory views* with regard to *external versus internal* communication policy principles. They support the demand for an expansion of the free and a balanced flow of information between and among countries, but not within the borders of their individual nations.

Therefore, Amin's remark that the NIEO strategy favours only the interests and views of the *dominant elites in the Third World* also applies to the communication sector. McQuail (1983), stating that Siebert's fourfold division of media theories is not relevant to developing countries, supplements two more normative media theories, the *development media theory* and the *democratic-participant media theory*. The principles formulated in the former are, according to McQuail, more adequate for classifying the media system in Third World countries. The latter covers the communication requirements outlined in the next paradigm.

Anotherness in One World

This new perspective has two roots: one in theory, another in practice. First, it is the result of the criticism of both the modernization and dependency theories. Secondly, one can notice the rejection of the dominant Western productivistic model by large segments of the Western so-called new generation, as well as the rising of liberation movements in the Third World against their own national elites. Even in the most authoritarian regimes that exist, alternative forms of communication exist mainly at local levels.

On a global level, one starts from the assumption that there are, in fact, no countries that are completely autonomous and self-reliant, and at the same time, no countries that develop merely as a reflection of exogenous factors. This view was strengthened as the worldwide crisis of the 1970s showed the degree to which a world economy had become a reality. Therefore the need for a more global analysis became necessary.

Contrary to the more economic and politically oriented views of the modernization and dependency paradigm, the central idea in this paradigm is that there is *no universal path* to development. Development must be conceived as an *integral, multidimensional and dialectic process* that can be different from country to country. Each society must find its own strategy.

At the same time this also implies that the problem of development is a relative one, and no part of the world can claim to be developed in all respects.

References

Amin, S., (1979), *Classe et nation dans l'histoire et la crise contemporaine*, Minuit, Paris.

Bennett, N., (1977), *Barriers and Bridges for Rural Development*, Foundation for the Promotion of Social Sciences and Humanities, Bangkok.

Bernstein, H., (1979), "Sociology of Underdevelopment vs. Sociology of Development", Lehman, D. (ed.), *Development Theory*, Frank Cass, London.

Berrigan, F., (1979), *Community Communications. The Role of Community Media in Development*, UNESCO, Paris.

Birou, A., Henry, P.M., Schlegel, J.P. (eds,), (1976), *Pour un autre developpement*, PUF, Paris.

Bordenave, J.D., (1977), *Communication and Rural Development*, UNESCO, Paris.

Boyd-Barrett, 0., (1977), "Media Imperialism: Towards an International Framework for the Analysis of Media Systems", Curran, J., Gurevitcm, M., Woollacott, J. (eds), *Mass Communication and Society*, Arnold, London.

Brandt, W. (ed.), *(1980), North-South. A Programme for Survival*, Pan Books, London.

Chapel, R., (1980), *Towards a new Strategy for Development*, Pergamon, Oxford.

Dervin, B., (1980), "Communication Gaps and Inequities: Moving toward a Reconceptualisation", Dervin, B., & Voigt, M. (eds.), *Progress in Communication Sciences*, Ablex, Norwood.

Dervin, B., (1982), "Citizen Access as an Information Equity Issue", Schement, J.R., Gutierrez, F., Sirby, M.A. (eds.), *Telecommunications Policy Handbook*, Praeger, New York.

Deutsch, K.W., (1977), *Ecosocial Systems and Ecopolitics,* UNESCO, Paris.

Elliott, P., & Golding, p (1974), "Mass Communication and Social Change. The Imagery of Development and the Development of Imagery," De Kadt, E., & Williams, G. *(eds.),Sociology and Development,* Tavistock, London.

Fisher, D., & Harms, L.S. (eds.), (1983), *The Right to Communicate: a New Human Right,* Boole Press, Dublin.

Frank, G., (1981), *Reflections on the World Economic Crisis,* Monthly Review Press, New York.

Galtung, J., (1980), *The True Worlds. A Transnational Perspective,* Free Press, New York.

Galtung, J., O'Brein, P., Preiswerk, R. (eds), *(1980), Self-reliance. A Strategy for Development,* Boyle. L' ouverture, London.

Giddens, A., (1976), *New Rules of Sociological Method,* Hutchinson, London.

Gitlin, T., (1978), "Media Sociology. The Dominant Paradigm," *Theory and Society,* 6. .

Golding, P., (1974), "Media Role in National Development: Critique of a Theoretical Orthodoxy," *Journal of Communication,* 24, 3.

Grossberg, L., (1981), "Interpreting the 'crisis' of Culture in Communication Theory," Wilhoit, G. C, & De Bock, H. (eds.), Mass *Communication Review Yearbook,* Sage, London.

Hamelink, C, (1978), *Derde Wereld en culturele emancipatie,* Wereldvenster, Baarn.

Hamelink, C (ed), (1980), *Communication in the Eighties: A Reader on the MacBride Report,* IDOC, Rome.

Hamelink, C, (1981), *New Structures of International Communication: The Role of Research,* Institute of Social Studies, The Hague.

Hamelink, C, (1983), Cultural Autonomy in Global Communications. Planning *National Information Policy,* Policy, Longman, London.

Hamelink, C, (1983), *Finance and Information: A Study of Converging Interests,* Ablex, Norwood.

Hancock, A., (1981), *Communication Planning for Development. An Operational* Framework, UNESCO, Paris.

Hansen, W., & Schulz, B. (1981), "Imperialism, Dependency and Social Class," *Africa Today,* 28, 3.

Haque, W., Mehta, N., Rahman, A., Wignaraja,P., (1977),*Towards a Theory of Rural Development,* Development Dialogue, Uppsala.

Hettne, B., (1982), *Development Theory and the Third World.* SAREC, Stockholm.

Hoogvelt, A., (1982), *The Third World in Global Development,* Macmillan, London.

Horton, P. (ed.), (1978), *The Third World and Press Freedom,* Praeger, New York.

Ikonicoff, M, (1983), "Théorie et strategie du developpement: le role de i'dtat," *Révue Tiers Monde,* 24, 93.

Katz, E., & Wedell, G., (1977), *Broadcasting in the Third World,* Harvard University Press, Cambridge.

Kay, G., (1975), *Development and Underdevelopment,* Macmillan, London.

Klapper, J.T., (1960), *The Effects of Mass Communication,* Free Press of Glencoe, Illinois.

Laclau, E. (1977), *Politics and Ideology in Marxist Theory,* New Left Books, London.

Lederer, K. (ed.), (1980), *Human Needs. A Contribution to the Current Debate.* Oelgeschlager, Konigsrein.

Lehman, D. (ed.), (1979), *Development Theory. Four Critical Studies,* Frank Cass, London.

Leys, C., (1977), "Underdevelopment and Dependency. Critical Notes", *Journal of Contemporary Asia,* 7, I.

McAnany, E. (ed.), (1980), *Communications in the Rural Thin! World. The Role of Information in Development,.* Praeger, New York.

MacBride, S.(ed.), (1980), *Many Voices, One World. Communication and Society. Today and Tomorrow,* UNESCO, Paris.

McCormack, T., (1969), "Folk Culture and the Mass Media," *European Journal of Sociology,* 10.

McQuail, D., (1983),*Mass Communication Theory,* Sage, London.

Mankekar, D.R., (1981), *Whose Freedom? Whose Order? A Plea for a New International Information Order by Third World,* Clarion Books, Delhi.

Masmoudi, M., (1978), *Call for a New International Information Order,* UNESCO, Paris.

Matta, F.R., (1981), "A Model for Democratic Communication," *Development Dialogue,* 2.

Mattelart, A., Piccini, M., & Mattelart, M., (1971), *Los medics de Comunicacion de mases: la ideologio de prensa liberal on Chile,* Signos, Buenos Aires.

Mattelart, A., (1976), *Multinationales et systemes de communication,* Anthropos, Paris.

Mattelart, A., (1979), "Introduction: A Class Analysis of Communication," Mattelart, A., & Siegelaub, S., (eds.), *Communication and Class Struggle.* Vol. I, IMMRC, Paris.

Middleton, J., (1980), "Images and Action: Theories in and of Communication Planning", Middleton, J., *Approaches to Communication Planning,* UNESCO, Paris.

Motta, G.L., (1984), "National Communication Policies: Grass Roots Alternatives," Gerbner, G., & Siefert, M (eds.), *World Communications,* Longman, New York.

Mowlana, H., (1984), "Communication for Political Change: the Iranian Revolution," Gerbner, 'G., & Sibert, M. (eds.), *ibid.*

Nerlin, M. (1977), *Another Development Approaches and Strategies,* Dag Hammarskjöld Foundation, Uppsala.

Nordenstreng, K., (1977), "From Mass Media to Mass Consciousness," Gerbner, G. (ed.), *Mass Media Policies in Changing Culture~*Wiley, New York.

Nordenstreng, K., & Schiller, H. I. (eds.), (1979), *National/ Sovereignty and International Communication,* Ablex, Norwood.

Nwosu, I., (1983), "The Role of Research in the Global Information Flow Controversy: A Critical Analysis," *Gazette,* 31.

O'Sullivan, J., & Kaplun, M., (1979), *Communication Methods to Promote Grass-roots Participations for an Endogenous Development Process.* UNESCO, Paris.

1927
1960
1963
1964
1967
1969
1970
1971
1972
1973
1974
1975
1976
1977
1978
1979
1980
1981
1982
1983
1984
1985
1986
1987
1988
1989
1990
1991
1992
1993
1994
1995
1996
1997
1998
1999
2000
2001
2002
2003
2004
2005
2006

Palloix, C., (1977),*L 'economie mondi4le capitaliste et les firmes multinationales,* Maspero, Paris.

Perroux, F., (1983), *A New Concept of Development,* UNESCO, Paris.

Petras J., (1978), *Critical Perspectives on Imperialism and Social Class in the Third World,* Monthly Review Press, New York.

PoulantzaS N., (1978), *L'etat, le pouvoir, le socialism,* PUF, Paris.

Preiswerk, R., (1980), "Identite culturelle, self-reliance et *besoins* fonda-mentaux," Spitz, P., Galtung, J. et al., *Il faut manger pour vivre ....,* PUF, Paris.

Righter, R., (1978), *Whose News? Politics, the Press and the Third World,* Burnett Books, London.

Rist, G., (197~), "Basic Questions About Basic Human Needs," Lederer, K. (eel.), *op. cit. -*

Rosario-Braid, F:, (1979), *Communication Sttategies for Productivity Improvement,* Asian Productivity Organisation, Tokyo.

Sachs, I., (1980), *Strategies de l'ecodeveloppement,* Ed. Ouvrieres, Paris.

Salama, I., & Tissier, P., *L'industrialisation dans le sous-developpement, Maspero,* Paris.

Salinas, R., (1982), *Development* Theory *and Communication Models,* Paper presented at Workshop on Communication Policy and Planning for Development, The Hague.

Schiller, HI., (1981), *Who Knows: Information in change of the Fortune 500,* Ablex, Norwood.

Servaes, J., (1980), "Het MacBride rapport: 'A Mission Impossible,'" *Communicatie.* 10.4.

Servaes, J., (1981), *Ideologic etpoU'UOir. Notespour une theorie materialiste de l'ideologic,* CeCowe, Louvain.

Servaes, J., (1983), *De nieuwsmakers. Informatie in de media,* De Nederlandse Boekhandel, AntWerpen.

Servaes, J., (1983), *Communication and Development Some Theoretical Remarks.* Acco, Louvain.

Servaes, J., (1984), "The Recent *History* of Communication Policies," *Journal of Mass Communication,* 3, 2.

Servaes, J., (1984), "Two Approaches Towards National Communication Policies for Development," *Journalism,* 5, 1.

Servaes, J., (1984), "The Context for Communication Planning: Man, Development and Technology," Kaviya, S. (ed.), *Man and Too Policy and Application Problems about New and Costly Communication Technology in Thailand,* Thammasat UniversityPress, Bangkok.

Servaes, J., (1984), *In Search of Communication and Development Paradigms,* Faculty of Journalism and Mass Communication, Thammasat University, Bangkok.

Servaes, J., (1984), *From the Global Order to the Village. Towards a Conceptual Framework /or 'Another Development' and 'Another Communication:* Unpublished working paper.

Siebert, E, Peterson, T., & Scliramm. W., (1956), *Four Theories of the Press,* University of Illinois Press, Urbana.

Singh, K., (1984), "Mass Line Communication: Liberation Movements in China and India," Cerbner, G., & Siefert, M. (eds.), World Communications, Longman, New York. - Smith, A.D., (1973), *The Concept of Social Change. A Critique of the Functionalist Theory of Social Change,* Routledge & Kegan,. London.

Smythe, D.W., (1981), *Dependency Road: Communication, Capitalism, Consciousness and Canada,* Ablex, Norwood.

Somavia, J., (1981), "The Democratisation of Communication: From Minority Social Monopoly to Majority Social Representation", *Development Dialogue,* 2.

Sunkel, O., & Fuenzalida, E., (1980), "La transnacionalizacion del capitalismoy el desarrollo nacional", Sunkel, 0., Fuenzalida, R, CardoSQ, EM. et al., *Transnacionalizaciony dependencia,* Ed. Cultura Hispania, Madrid.

Szymanski, A., (1981), *The Logic of Imperialism,* Praeger, New York.

Tehranian, M., Hakimzadeh, F., & Vidale, M. (eds.) 1977, *Communication Policy for National Development,* Routledge & Kegan, London.

Tehranian, M., (1978), *To Hold the Mirror up to Maure. Communication Policy and Planning for Development,* Iran Communication Development Institute, Teheran.

Therborn, G., (1978), *What does the Ruling Class Do When it Rules?,* New Left Books, London.

Therborn, G., (1980), *The Ideology of Power and the Power of Ideology,* Verso, London.

Todaro, M.P., (1977), *Economic Development in the Third World. An Introduction to Problems and Policies in a Global Perspective,* Longman, New York.

Timmermann, V., (1982), *Entwicklungstheorie und Entwicklungspolitik,* Vandenhoeck und Ruprecht, Gottingen.

Van Nieuwenhuijze, C., (1982), *Development Begim at Home. Problems and Prospects of the Sociology of Development,* Pergamon, Oxford.

Wallerstein, I., (1979), *The Capitalist World Economy,* Cambridge University Press, Cambridge.

Wallerstein, I., & Hopkins, T. (eds.), (1982), *World System Analysis,* Sage, London.

White, R., (1982), *Contradictions in Contemporary Policies for Democratic Communication,* paper presented at IAMCR Conference, Paris.

White, R., (1984), "Communication Strategies for Social Change: National Television versus Local Public Radio", Gerbner, G., & Siefert, M. (eds.), *World Communications,* Longman, New York.

Worsley, P. (1983), *The Three Worlds: Culture and World Development,* Weidenfeld, London.

Jan Servaes, *In Search of Communication and Development Paradigms*, mss. Bangkok: Thammasat University, 1985. Reprinted with permission of author.

ORAMEDIA IN AFRICA

Excerpt from: Mass Communication, Culture and Society in West Africa

By Frank Okwu Ugboajah

1985 One of the deterrents to socio-economic progress in Africa was colonialism. This also contributed to the destruction of African traditions. To a great extent the Europeans, particularly the British, stand guilty of extreme colonial crime to mankind.

Michael Dei-Anang of Ghana narrates his experience of an educational conference in Leiden, Holland (Dei-Anang, 1964). Chinese, Indonesian and Indian cultures were being discussed by student bodies from Britain, Africa and Asia. African representatives in attendance were asked to say something on African culture by way of comparison. Dei-Anang, being among the participants, spoke about the rich collection of African arts and crafts at the Leiden Museum of Arts and Culture:

> Whereupon, an Oxford undergraduate who had obviously fed himself fat on perversive textbooks and thrillers of the African jungle type, confounded everyone present by saying: 'What is African culture anyhow?' There was too much muddled thinking, he continued, on this question of culture. He could understand ancient people like the Indians with centuries of recorded history and tradition behind them talking culture. But for Africans, who at best lived in a sort of neo-barbarism, to talk of their culture was not only ridiculous but a serious crime against civilization. What had Africa to show the world as convincing proof of the fact that she too possessed a culture of worthy of respect? What contribution had she made to world progress? By what monument of the past could others remember her influence on the world of today? Where was the written record of her achievement? What had Africa in common with Plato, Pythagoras, Leonardo da Vinci, Mozart, Newton, and George Stephenson?

Dei-Anang sat calm under the provocative tantrums of this rhetorical effusion, pitying the education that could make a man so patently ignorant except in the materialistic nature of Western culture. Dei-Anang notes that many Westerners are guilty of this flagrant error. They always take their own culture as an infallible standard. Any other pattern is despicable or a freak of nature or the idle invention of a feeble brain...

In the circumstances of cultural domination and political and economic dependence the suppressed society loses its right to self-determination and becomes written out of history. The corollary is that societies which have cultural independence survive, continue, accommodate change and renew, in conditions of rapid social change by a selection and rejection process. This is because inbuilt regenerative facilities freely function as media for communication, participation and socialization—a process often referred to in developmental literature as informal education. This is a process of culture conscientization, a prerequisite for self-identity and cultural development.

In Africa, as well pointed out by Moore (1982), there is the usual interplay of custom and conflict, harmony and strife, fusion and fission, while interpersonal relations, social cohesion, social process and historical continuity are largely maintained through the symbolizing codes of oral tradition, which include mythology, oral literature (poetry, storytelling, proverbs), masquerades, rites of passage and other rituals expressed through oracy, music, dance, drama, use of costume, social interplay and material symbols which accompany people from womb to tomb and much beyond.

It is the purpose of this paper, therefore, to make a case for such interpersonal communication, which we have chosen to call "oramedia," especially in multi-ethnic

1927
1960
1963
1964
1967
1969
1970
1971
1972
1973
1974
1975
1976
1977
1978
1979
1980
1981
1982
1983
1984
1985
1986
1987
1988
1989
1990
1991
1992
1993
1994
1995
1996
1997
1998
1999
2000
2001
2002
2003
2004
2005
2006

societies of Africa, where messages might be blocked by linguistic, cultural or semantic obstacles. We shall attempt an explanation of oramedia and discuss their contemporary use in African communities. There will also be an attempt at describing their effectiveness as belief systems and their possible adaptability for development and use in communication both mass and modern. Suggestions will also be made in terms of their implications to research and policy.

What Are Oramedia?

Perhaps the best way to illustrate what oramedia are is to take the way the villager often makes a point (by telling a story):

A British Governor once sat on the stool of the King Ashanti as a way of communicating his authority as the representative of Queen Victoria of England. But the significance of the stool in the minds of the people of Ashanti was reverence, as being not an appurtenance of the kingly office, but of an embodiment of the nation's soul. They were insulted. They were provoked. They went home and prepared for war. Oramedia or folk media are grounded on indigenous culture produced and consumed by members of a group. They reinforce the values of the group. They are visible cultural features, often strictly conventional, by which social relationships and a world view are maintained and defined. They take on many forms and are rich in symbolism.

In the short story told above one can see an ignorant British Governor thinking about a throne signifying power and authority, whereas the people were thinking about religion and the sacredness of a stool as well as its political symbolism. What resulted was a communication gap which soon developed into hostilities.

Folk media cannot therefore be conveniently separated from folk cultures in whose context they are significant. One can perhaps look at folk media as group media, but it is better to regard them as interpersonal media speaking to the common man in his language, in his idiom, and dealing with problems of direct relevance to his situation.

Attempts are often made to delineate the characteristics of folk media. They have been described as being simple in form and generally available to all at no material cost. They are the public domain and anonymous in origin. There might be little differentiation between their producers and their consumers. But they communicate directly through any of the senses via folkways. Oramedia are made up of dialogue and verbal exchange, a feature that is provided by the almost constant presence of one or more surrounding listeners. They may be defined as functional and utilitarian. Their most important purpose is to provide teaching and initiation, with the object of imparting traditional aesthetic, historical, technical, social, ethical and religious values. They provide a legal code of sorts which rests on stories and proverbs generated through the spoken word. They also play other roles in the village society, such as mobilizing people's awareness of their own history, magnifying past events and evoking deeds of illustrious ancestors. Thus they tend to unite a people and give them cohesion by way of ideas and emotions.

An aspiring African student in this field, Desmond Wilson (1981), complaining about the word "mass" has this to say:

> To those who have come to equate the word mass with such concepts as mass audience or 'the global village,' the application may seem a bit of a misnomer given the image and picture of the large population of people that are often involved in these 'mass' concepts. But we are talking about little communities, clans, villages… numbering a few thousands in scattered settlements…whose desires are for information machinery that exists with them… For our purpose, the mass medium shall be defined as that through which large numbers of people are reached through any of our traditional mass media, namely, 'eyei,' 'nnukenin,' 'obodom,' 'ntakrok,' and others. Our definition subsumes the fact that the millions of people watching a World Cup final on television and at the arena itself [could] constitute the same kind of mass audience as the few thousand people

who hurry to the village square to listen to their elders on hearing the call of the 'obodom.' In their different [application] the two channels—'television and 'obodom'—constitute media of mass communication; their importance is not solely determined by sheer size of one but by the objective and effect of both media.

Contemporary Use of folk Media in African Communities

Traditional media have been consistently used to promote the sense of nationhood in Africa despite the low priority given to them in official circles.

One observes at once that the formal media become little used immediately after communication or information reaches the traditional authority, usually represented by a king or a chief, or in some cases a council of elders. Communication from that point takes a flow or diffusion approach and is dominated by the informal media or oral media (oramedia). These are the traditional media or folk media represented by a diffusion network of lower chiefs, age groups, the market place, market women's organizations, traditional priests, stall heads, village teachers and the indomitable village crier. Age-groups—Ogboni, Egbe, Egungun, Oro Agemo, Dagboulu—meet periodically to discuss village development affairs according to priorities set by the village authority. The age groups also teach the young villager the norms of society. Names of age-group members usually relate to spectacular events at the time of their birth. For example, the cohort or age group Obangbade is named after the fact that its members were born at the time of the installation of a chief.

The *Parakoyi* is the traditional government of a Yoruba village marketplace described as the conglomeration of all the media modes common to the village, which includes the *Ashipa* (the gong-man), the *Oluwa*, the *Iya Oja* or the village mother, the *Ifa* and *Osayin* priests. The *Parakoyi* has both a ritualistic and judicial function in the market government. It maintains law and order, offers sacrifices to the *Oloja* (the god of the market) and collects taxes for the local authority.

Marketplaces in Africa, in themselves, are veritable communication forums. In Accra, Ghana, the Queen Mothers celebrate the *Homowo* market festival annually. This is a festival to give thanks to the market goddess. Marketplaces are not just where people go to buy or sell but are diffusion forums for important social interaction (Ugboajah, 1979). Vogues are copied from marketplaces. They also constitute places of censure.

In some villages in the eastern part of Nigeria, a case of incest is censured by parading the offender adorned with a necklace of snail shells and live millipedes in the marketplace. An unmarried woman who gets pregnant while still living with her parents is censured with a song made up for her in the marketplace by her peers. Stealing farm products or livestock earns instant punishment by disgrace in the marketplace. It is no wonder that the Seminar on Motivation, Information and Communication for Development in African and Asian Countries, held in Ibadan, Nigeria (1-9 July 1974) drew attention to the fact that the marketplace "remains effective at all times because of the tremendous amount of interaction it generates."

In oriental countries, bazaars, like African marketplaces, remain powerful informal conduits in the framework of their commercial functions. The bazaar's physical and organizational set-up serves as a natural infrastructure for multidirectional dissemination of news, opinions and rumours, and it's important for the purpose of agitation.

Oramedia could be cognitive or evaluative in their orientation, composed of symbols with either empirical or super-empirical referents. In Ghana, the news of a birth is communicated to a husband by an assistant *Ogyeafo* (traditional midwife) by tying a piece of white cloth round the wrist. This symbolizes victory and proclaims that a baby has been delivered successfully. Also in Ghana, chiefs often do no speak directly to their people. They speak through a "linguist" or send their messages through the gong-man who uses a set of talking drums.

1927
1960
1963
1964
1967
1969
1970
1971
1972
1973
1974
1975
1976
1977
1978
1979
1980
1981
1982
1983
1984
1985
1986
1987
1988
1989
1990
1991
1992
1993
1994
1995
1996
1997
1998
1999
2000
2001
2002
2003
2004
2005
2006

In Nigeria, among the Yoruba, the *edan* or chief's staff is a symbol of authority for summoning an offender to the chief's court. Anyone waking up in the morning to find the *edan* at his doorstep must report to the Chief's Court first thing. The *Uhue*, among the Igbo, is used for announcing village festivities or to herald the arrival of the planting season. As a medium, it is used late at night or very early in the morning, when people can be reached. The air is soon filled with heavy rhythms. But the strange observation is that no word follows. Meaning becomes symbolically understood and shared by all.

The meaning of such cultural features has often been distorted by Westerners in the past but also sometimes imposed upon Africans to the extent of destroying cultural features. Kubik narrates:

> At Kisumu, Kenya, uniformed performers with ties and well-creased trousers were standing in a row. Afraid even to make the slightest rhythmical movement with their bodies, singing with stiff and polished voices, afraid to produce a single tone of real expression, because perhaps it might be called barbaric by the Europeans who dominate Kenya. On another platform just opposite the stage there was the jury, two fat Europeans drinking enormous quantities of beer and having each of them a pencil in his hand. These were the kinds of persons thought capable of judging the art value of the performance.

Kenya has been so colonized and thoroughly culturally destroyed by Europeans that Kipkorir (1980) has become sceptical about contemporary Kenyan national identity. He notes that Kenya, as a nation, has not seriously addressed itself to culture and that the political ideology Kenya has chosen for her national development is inimical to indigenous cultural traditions.

Oramedia are the prime disseminators of culture. In the case of the Urhobo in Mid-West Nigeria, the following features can be regarded as traditional media. The town crier is a significant village "broadcaster" who summons the elders for decision making and relays their decisions to the village masses for implementation. Body language, such as genuflecting, could convey greetings to an elder or express gratitude to a benefactor. Songs are media for moral instruction, for information about people or events, for the relief of tedium, for conveying the attributes of village deities and for lulling babies to sleep.

Drums symbolize rituals as well as dance performance. Parables convey morals and riddles and are used for sharpening of wit. Communal shrines are media for religious protection and adulation of ancestors as well as for instilling group consciousness. The kola nut is a sign of welcome, acceptance of comradeship and appreciation of company shared in mutual exchange. Aliases are used by elders to conjure rapport.

'If we are motivated by the taste of an egg, there might be no fowl to sacrifice to the gods.' This proverb advises one to apply moderation and frugality in the things we enjoy. 'A wicked man had prepared poison to harm his neighbour. He did not wash his hands after handling the preparation and suddenly scratched his vial organ. His organ died.' The lesson of this parable is that no one should plan evil for his neighbour else it might boomerang. 'I have a friend. In the morning he is tall; in the afternoon he becomes short, in the evening he is tall again. Who is my friend?' This is a riddle or a form of brainstorming often used for entertainment. The answer is 'the shadow.' Parables and proverbs are pertinent and effective in the course of discussions and during speechmaking.

Festivals are crowd pullers just as fairs or shows are, attracting town dwellers and people from outside town and from all walks of life, dialects and religious beliefs. Events are diverse in content as in audience and the heterogeneity and anonymity of characters present and indirect mass communication—people to communication not communication to people.

The *adowa* music of Ghana is an excellent example of oramedia. *Adowa* music is performed by organized female choruses. *Adowa* songs and dance are the means by which feelings about death, sympathy for the bereaved lineage, and the achievements of past chiefs and elders are expressed. Texts are communicated through the drum language of the *atumpan* drummer who, in following the speech tones and durations of the Twi language, is able to drum poems, proverbs, comments of sympathy, welcome and other instructions to dancers.

Effectiveness of Traditional Media and Belief Systems

There is a popular proverb among the Yoruba of Nigeria: '*Imale o pe kawa ma soro*' which means that "the fact we are Muslim does not forbid us from worshipping the traditional gods or performing rituals."

A man can be a Christian and might still perform traditional rituals. He might still consult the priest of the *ifa* oracle to tell him whether it's safe to go on a journey or not. He might still turn to Oshun, the god of fertility, or Obatala, the god of creation, or Yemaja, the god of the sea, when confronted with urgent personal problems. A whole village or clan in Africa could turn to the gods during a time of natural disasters such as famine, drought, epidemic and wars.

Africans, no matter the depth of their education or Christian and Islamic affiliation, have often turned to traditional belief and practice for consolation in times of crisis. This was manifested in Uganda in the case of the exile of the Kabaka of Buganda in 1953-55 and during the turbulent dictatorship of General Idi Amin. The same attitude was manifested during the Nigerian Civil War, Mau Mau oaths in the early 1950s starting as rituals, cumulated in nationalism to unite the people of Kenya against the colonial authority.

For whatever they might say, Africans have by no means abandoned their allegiances to traditional supernatural forces when the have accepted the deities of other people. Rather the new deity is added to the totality of supernatural resources on which they call for aid. Credit should therefore be given to the newly-founded Christian churches in Africa, for example,

the Aladura Church of the Lord in Nigeria, for cashing in on the failure of the older churches by adapting and providing a transfusion of the African ontological dynamism, enthusiasm, feeling for substance in ritual and recognition of the imminent and every day communal consequences of religious belief, practice and adaptation.

J.W. Fernandez (1969) has questioned the appropriateness of the Bible to African peoples. He calls the Bible "a diverse and ambitious mythological document… which provides no information except of a very expressive or non-instrumental kind and develops no skill except in the endless subtleties of exegetical interpretation." Such a strong and negative observation might not necessarily be directed at the Bible per se but more at the "hell fire" way in which it is preached to the people.

It is a relief that the Synod of African Bishops has now recognized "inculturation (socialization) to make the African Church authentically African." According to *Action Resource* of October 19980, the bishops were amazed at the strategy of "the independent churches of Africa" especially the relative ease with which these churches draw people n large numbers to their fold while expanding rapidly. The Synod recognized that the media of communication of these independent churches were often more suitable and rooted in the African mentality and culture than the media the Catholics use in their Churches and homes. In using traditional African media, the Bishops now recognize that "our people are able to develop authentic and creative art forms which are bound to bear fruit in our liturgies and forms of worship, rooting our Christian faith ever more firmly in Africa's soil…"

It should however be on record that the Roman Catholic Church and older churches in Africa have long recognized the importance of indigenous structures such as age-groups mentioned above. These village organizations have been of tremendous importance in community actions to build churches and mission schools. Even mission catechists, parish

1927
1960
1963
1964
1967
1969
1970
1971
1972
1973
1974
1975
1976
1977
1978
1979
1980
1981
1982
1983
1984
1985
1986
1987
1988
1989
1990
1991
1992
1993
1994
1995
1996
1997
1998
1999
2000
2001
2002
2003
2004
2005
2006

priests and mission teachers became a part and parcels of an extension of the community information network and they have constituted themselves as important opinion leaders and legitimizers on most topics and issues that affect the lives of villagers. What has been apparently lacking is practical recognition of the impact of other more important belief systems, such as traditional worship, folkways and rites.

The use of the rituals in oramedia for social solidarity in cases of emergency is not limited to Africa. Gandhi and Mao had little access to the modern media in mobilizing the masses for their revolution in India and China. They relied on credible secular symbols, on channels that were deeply integrated into the life of the masses and participatory exposure to their messages. Ayatollah Khomeini and his followers demonstrated the impact of indigenous networks in mobilizing popular support in which case they relied on solid institutional infrastructure and activated highly information-conductive symbols of oramedia.

Through propelled by religion or what could generally be described as the belief system, the channels of oramedia could be classified according to their ritual or mundane functions and emphases. In a situation loaded with selective and noncredible information, Khomeini's 90,000 mosques under the guidance of 20,000 mullahs (priests) provided a solid infrastructure for a revolutionary communication network, a model that could have been adapted to a successful "Green Revolution" in Nigeria. The communal component inside the context of belief systems adds to the effectiveness of communication networks.

One can also make reference to similar features such as the role of popular satire, folk songs, and "primitive" distributive technologies in the Czech uprising in 1968, in the Portuguese and Nicaraguan revolutions of the 1970s, in the Indonesian struggle against the Dutch in the 1960s, in the current Polish protest movement and more effectively in Africa's "winds of change" in which governments suffer from the ghost of rumours. There is considerable evidence in revolutions

that whoever controls alternative networks (oramedia), with or without the media of mass communication, is better equipped to mobilize and activate the masses. Belief systems constitute the basis of the villager's experience and the integral and functional part of his society. Thus, rural villages contrary to some other observations are functioning subsystems in accordance with the tenets of belief systems.

Traditional media linked to belief systems have been found effective as tools in development programmes of governments. As entertainments they can attract and hold the interest of large numbers of people. As oral media in local languages they can involve the poorest groups and classes who are often left out of development activities because of illiteracy or lack of understanding of the English or French language. As dramatic representations of local problems, they can provide a codification of reality which can be used by participants in analyzing their situation. And as collective expressions and communal activities they create the contexts for cooperative rather than individual thinking and action and the possibility for peer learning.

Adaptation of Oramedia

China has been lauded for reconstructing a village society. The village then actively moulded the kind of school it felt it needed. Rural primary education in China is directly relevant to the social and economic goals of the commune such that villagers take an active part in the operation of their learning system.

In Java, the use of folk puppetry opera (*ludruk*), comedy (*neog*) and the shadow puppet play (*evajong golek*) as the trusted media for conveying new ideas to people has been adopted by change agents. Singing poets (*cantadores*) in Brazil, cowhide characters (*nang taloogn*) in Thailand and dramatized poetry (*ngonjera*) in Tanzania are being used to the same end. "Panchatantra" has now become an effort to examine the fields of myth, legends, folklore in general by India's Space Application Centre. Experience in Botswana has shown that popular theatre can play an important role in social transformation programmes, expanding participation and self-confidence and providing a mirror for critical analysis and a stimulus for discussion and action. In Indonesia, Wayang, Pancasila was initiated by the Ministry of Information to communicate the ideological pillars of the nation. Indeed, historically, Indonesia has used the art drama forms to promote social and political transformation. In Thailand the folk-art form most successfully adapted to radio and television had been the Mau Lum, a folk opera or folk story drawn from the pool of north-eastern Thai tales and myth.

Lent (1982) point out that the mass media—particularly broadcasting, which has ironically earned most of the blame for cultural imperialism—have contributed in giving expression to indigenous art. For example the National Iranian Television has established a centre for Preservation of Traditional Music since 1971. The Iranian Television collected music from all over the country and encourages active preservation by offering grants to old musicians who could no longer earn a living by their music. The Federal Radio Corporation of Nigeria (FRCN), when it was known as the Nigerian Broadcasting Corporation (NBC), led the way among other institutions in the development of local languages for broadcasting in Nigeria.

Katz and Weddel (1978) listed the following factors as impediments to the adaptation of folk media to fit into mass media of communication:

1. Folk media tend to be eclipsed by the pace of modernization and performing arts were dying even before broadcasting made its appearance.
2. Traditional media have limited repertories while mass media demand novelty, in that case broadcasting quickly exhaust the limited classical themes.
3. The open village square settings of folk media do not adapt well to confined or tiny broadcast studios while the problem becomes confounded when broadcast stations lack outside-broadcast vans and equipment.

4. Because of the festive and occasional character of many traditional media, 'they cannot be made into just another programme on a Tuesday evening.'

Renganath (1982) agrees that some folk songs do indeed have a ritualistic base and cannot be westernized or formalized in the manner Katz and Weddel, above, expect. Such folk media are not particularly effective in conveying messages of passing importance. However Renganath's reference is too their use in the promotion of family planning which involves numerous cultural problems.

Implication to Research and Policy

In making out a case for oramedia, we are advocating a more horizontal channel of communication, more participatory communication structures and the beginning of new concepts of communication development. White (1982) hold the view that, " in so far as communication researchers are part of this historical development they may contribute an element of experienced planning and coherent direction." Also Sean MacBride and his colleagues (1980) argue that there are basic questions about the links between modern and traditional media from the viewpoint of their mutual influence or reciprocal and complimentary support. The main challenge to policymakers, communication practitioners and researchers is to find a formula that forges a relationship between traditional and modern forms of communication without damaging the traditional ways nor obstructing the necessary march towards modernity.

This challenge becomes more important when it is realized that, hitherto, few African countries have taken any serious account of culture in there development planning. Kipkorir (1980) makes the point as fare as Kenya is concerned:

> It is generally believed that a people or nation derives its unique identity not merely from political ideology but also and perhaps chiefly through its culture. National development is, therefore, conceptually not possible without cultural

1927
1960
1963
1964
1967
1969
1970
1971
1972
1973
1974
1975
1976
1977
1978
1979
1980
1981
1982
1983
1984
1985
1986
1987
1988
1989
1990
1991
1992
1993
1994
1995
1996
1997
1998
1999
2000
2001
2002
2003
2004
2005
2006

development. Culture as a subject ought therefore, to be a matter of concern at all levels of the organization of society or state. Before any development is embarked on, e.g., the construction of a trunk road, the opening of a tourist hotel, the siting of an industrial complex, etc, the effects of such a development on the culture of the people must be ascertained and provided for. If this is not done, the development, positive though its objectives may be, may not bring about adverse net results. In other words, "development" outside the context of culture can be counter productive.

Economic planners tend to leave out culture in the development model because in the industrial ideology, non-material culture has a low priority and success is measured by quantitative material progress. Moore (1982) notes that the rise of the capitalist ethos in the West has had various effects on the creative arts. The increasingly conservative taste of the nouveau rich led to a demand for mass-produced stereotyped "artistic" (cultural) work based on traditional schemes.

The non-emphasis on cultural orientation is visibly manifested in the broadcast stations of various African countries where traditional music is transmitted in non-peak hours or presented without regard to a multilingual and multi-cultural audience or classified as a specialist subject—a non-newsworthy ethic derived from Western concepts of what is relevant. Without enlisting culture and its artefacts, village people, the very soul of the African nation, may not be involved in the process of decision-making. They should be enabled to see and experience changes as bringing benefits to them within their own world view.

Whether or not development in Africa or in the Third World as a whole must be a replication of the process that earlier took place in the West is well discussed by Shinar (1982). Studies so far have predominantly exhibited a strong ethnocentricity—focused on Westernization, deterministic assumptions on development and unidimensional social perceptions that emphasize local responsibility for foreign influences.

In so far as media research is concerned, Shinar holds that communication researchers should be more concerned with the discovery of alternative networks and less subservient to the myth of the mighty media. Our researchers have so far played the role of foreign agents in the same manner that our broadcasters have represented cultural imperialism. There is an easy tendency to represent a research culture that has developed in the West and become internationalized and to take little account. ...

Development studies have for long held to a set of beliefs which has caused researchers and practitioners to focus on the technological and organizational aspects of mass-communication imported models and to underestimate the socio-cultural features in indigenous media. This set of beliefs is evident in the dominant paradigm of media sociology that prevailed in the 1930's and in subsequent orthodox modernization and diffusion theories of Weberian tradition. Such a theoretical framework that supports the diffusionist approach has necessarily led, as Shinar puts it, "to the development of the myth of the mighty media and to a frustration with their failures."

A new approach or model is now necessary in the study of the communication. Shinar suggests "a convergence approach" which will be more flexible than prevailing modernization approaches and free from their spatial, temporal, cultural and ideological constraints—the convergence of social dynamics and multi-dimensional interactions between internal and external forces. The new approach would thus consider essentialism, a set of indigenous traditions and symbols, and ephochalism, the work of ideological, technological, economic and other foreign influences.

The need for flexibility in research approaches particularly in Third World countries, notably Africa, suggests a leverage to cover more ground in terms of history and different spheres of culture. This would lead to more extensive results and a more accurate charting of communication networks based on the knowledge of institutional structures and realistic perceptions of social orders. Binod Agrawal (1982) suggest a "communication alliance" approach which manifests a cultural ethic to permit an understanding of the dynamic relationship of mutual sharing, exchange and provision of information, knowledge and wisdom overtime. Communication alliance defines relationships and is built both horizontally, vertically and diagonally of voluntary and fictive responses. The so-called right to communicate is part of it and is certainly culture-bound.

The principals of UNESCO's New World Information and Communication Order (NWICO, Section IV (e) (a), include "the removal of internal and external obstacles to free flow and wider and better balanced dissemination of information." This underscores the development and utilization of the traditional media for participation in Africa as a major way of responding to NWICO.

The challenge facing today's policymaker and communication specialist in Africa would be the need to understand clearly what results the folk media could achieve for mobilization and for development. Unfortunately there are not enough well-organized data from those countries in which oramedia have been employed in social development to strengthen a case for their wider utilization in the African region. Research calls therefore for the following tasks:

■ A comprehensive annotated worldwide bibliography on the use of traditional media.
■ An inventory of folk media systems and structures shoeing their origins and purposes, whiter mode and format, their technological adaptations and their constraints.
■ Specific case studies of major folk media structures or processes.
■ Studies which involve possible integration of folk media forms with modern mass media or group media.
■ Effectiveness studies which would compare one folk medium structure with another.
■ The development of a new communication model that will respond to a complete understanding of the potentials of folk music.

There is a need to identify systematically the symbols that exist in traditional media channels and how these symbols can be manipulated for effectiveness in communication. These challenges of research are formidable. They are challenges which need commitment and foresight in those who are genuinely convinced of the potentials and relevance of oramedia in the process of development.

1927
1960
1963
1964
1967
1969
1970
1971
1972
1973
1974
1975
1976
1977
1978
1979
1980
1981
1982
1983
1984
1985
1986
1987
1988
1989
1990
1991
1992
1993
1994
1995
1996
1997
1998
1999
2000
2001
2002
2003
2004
2005
2006

ALTERNATIVE COMMUNICATION, HORIZONTAL COMMUNICATION, ALTERNATIVE USE OF THE MEDIA, PARTICIPANT COMMUNICATION: WHICH IS THE PARADIGM?

Excerpt from: Venezuela: Communication Policy or Alternative Communication?

By Oswaldo Capriles

1986 1. There is no doubt that the topic of "another communication" is recurring in our times, both in highly industrialized countries—where the matter frequently acquires more psychological-existential traits, from group dynamics to Bergmanian metaphysics—and in dependent countries, where growing awareness of the global subjection to a *way of life* imposed and constantly reaffirmed by mass dissemination powers—a national-transnational enterprise—has clearly situated the problem in a more critical dimension, a "macro" and therefore more political dimension.

Controversy against the dominant mode of transmission–reception–massive, or mass, "communication"—is born out of questioning modernization theories, also—and not by chance—"diffusionist", first in the context of pragmatic disqualification due to their inability to offer nothing but legitimization of the incessant incorporation of technology and extension, training and education techniques; next, in the more serious framework of growing comprehension of the development model's failure to in terms of offering a greater amount of happiness to people; and finally, in the conscience of the power structure reproduced in and through communication, turning everything into a "communicational" show, evading what is really political outside the field of social intervention itself, and politicizing instead, in a negative and sad way, everything that is social; building

consensus, if not out of conflict, at least *about* conflict, and thus establishing as routine the symbolic resolution of these social contradictions.

But misunderstandings arise from the start: first, the deliberate, insistent, didactic confusion between alternative communication—as a paradigm of a "new" or "another" communication– and alternative use of the mass media; or instead the identification of the new utopia with the use of electronic artifacts for the reproduction of signs and images or programmed instruction. Second, the non-conformist left itself took care of frequently granting privileged treatment to media characteristic of turmoil—films of denouncement, agitation or protest, clandestine radio, etc.—as the alternative: poor community media, an aesthetics of violence, portability, spontaneity, pursuit of citizen participation, questioning of mediation, rescue of popular culture, and desperate search for a "language" of its own for the revolution. Certainly substantial experiences, and even more substantial study material.

The educational field is where anguish explodes first: more advanced experiences ended up revealing to the educational apparatus its own condition—analogous to that of the media in another field: it is a manipulative apparatus, a mechanism to effectively reproduce classes and their relationships. The shift in education towards communication reveals of course such an anxiety—inducing approach since the 1950s.[1] For its part, "massmediatization" reaches its greatest intensity, this time of a more radical nature, with the student and cultural rebellions of the late 1960s[2].

---

1 See particularly numbers 14, 1.5 and 23 of the *Cuadernos de Educación* journal, published monthly by *Laboratorio Educativo*, an institution that gathers many of the persons that integrate other left-wing catholic centers, such as the *Centro de Comunicación Jesus María Pollín*, which makes a newsletter –cited here– with similar dissemination monographic characteristics; or the *Centro Camilla*, which generates one of the best radical criticism magazines on society, economy and culture: SIC magazine. Ugalde, Re, Martinez Terrero, Aguirre and others, professors at the Universidad Católica, and Jesuits, are some of the facilitators of these interwoven experiences: we owe the contribution that follows to one of them, particularly Aguirre.

2 The cultural revolution, the neo-hedonist, and environmental tendencies of certain American groups, the radical contestation of the French May, with ulterior theoretical repercussions regarding the importance of Baudrillard's theses, and in general students' and youth effervescence were —since the end

2. The "other" communication, the real one, the intuitively known paradigm, is progressively defined against the background of, and in opposition to, the authoritarian model that manipulates the "massmediatization" of advertising—and also of "political" propaganda—and vis-à-vis the pyramidal structures of grouping and bureaucratic control of the media as well as its processes, be they private property or exclusive public management. The model is born as an ethics of interrelationships, as the suggestion of a primary original democracy, necessary for and prior to one that would come to express itself through decision making by all, and the allocation of goods and social benefits for all. It would be the *condittio sine qua non* of all possible democracies: permanent dialogue; participation both spontaneous and pertinent, never arbitrary or conditioned, that generates collective decisions and the socialization of production and its outcomes.

Work and experience in the educational and extension fields, especially rural, based on the two-stage flow thesis pertaining to diffusionism—interpersonal communication that "amplifies and disseminates" the media's action—founded a first type of allegedly "horizontal" communication that was sometimes designated "alternative use" of the media, or "alternative communication." The elements opposing the dominant diffusionist system were, in these cases: a predominant educational orientation, the search for a simple and efficient language; the attempt to establish a feedback relationship that would allow reorientation of the program while approaching the public. Limited participation, however, kept posing problems and causing controversy throughout such experiences.[3]

of the sixties—more inclined towards demolishing the way of life, understood as a bourgeois totality. Therefore, television came to be one of their favorite targets, as a paradigm of *mass mediatization*.

3   *Ibidem*, note (1). Of course, works such as Diaz Bordenave's are important for the critical analysis of these experiences, especially in the field of extension and rural and agricultural communication. On the other hand, many works have analyzed the important experience (of *radio schools* and *radioros* in Latin America, particularly Colombia, where radio-schools were more than 16,000 in 1965, serving an approximate number of 130,00 students, almost all of them inhabitants of rural areas. Number 23, cited from *Cuadernos de Educación* includes a long list of works: Schmelke, Roads, Piper, Martin, Ilavens. ALER's publications also incorporate some relevant data.

In socialist countries, experiences combining media/communication/the interpersonal dimension/research-study were more successful in terms of effectiveness. Such combinations were presided over and framed by a political conception of stimuli for the incorporation of specific sectors and social groups. Large national mobilization characterizes many of these experiences, of which the literacy campaign in Cuba in 1961 is an example. The fact that at least regarding the educational uses of communication processes and media, the socialist field has achieved substantial successes and strong degrees of participation—although still not granting that concept all its dialogic and spontaneous potential—well beyond the generally poor achievements in even the most "advanced" capitalist countries, cannot be denied. Likewise, the institutionalized mass media have attempted to overcome, through "culturizing" informational and educational content, their obvious structural inability to generate popular participation as a result of their massive nature, serving instead, in those countries, as a "second line" of attack that reinforces the educational apparatus.

The critical tendency that begins to advocate communication policies, from the meetings in Paris and Bogotá in the early 1960s, until the official climax at the Conference of Ministries in San José de Costa Rica, constitutes a valuable attempt to conceptualize the issue at hand, albeit within a bureaucratic-planning context. The *access-participation* dialectic dyad is useful to connect the road of policies with the alternative journey of attempts underway—some official, others unofficial, most non-conformist—aimed at seeking concrete mechanisms and methods for "another" communication.

3. But this other communication is broken up, subdivided or mixed up in a multitude of terms that use words describing …different experiences or projects, often repeating the same thing, others with small differential nuances, most of the time with a serious tendency to confuse the means, goals and processes. It is therefore advisable to offer a provisional and generic definition of a communication alternative that serves

1927
1960
1963
1964
1967
1969
1970
1971
1972
1973
1974
1975
1976
1977
1978
1979
1980
1981
1982
1983
1984
1985
1986
1987
1988
1989
1990
1991
1992
1993
1994
1995
1996
1997
1998
1999
2000
2001
2002
2003
2004
2005
2006

as a still tentative paradigm for the discussion from our point of view.

Some generic characteristics can be assigned to that "paradigm."

a. The point is to establish a dialogic interrelation, which implies a model whose relational form and structure is participants' equality in intervention, the permanent and factual possibility to reverse the transmission-reception poles (which, in order to be real, must be based on certain rules of exchange, not easy to establish for groups beyond certain sizes, or on regional or national scales). As a decisively democratic group model, it implies the reexamination of all those relationships non-reducible to the model and, therefore, some kind of confrontation with dominant diffusion modes, or the pathological, anomalous communication modes that tend to propose pseudo-dialogues or false participation. Let us not forget that this is an ethical model.

b. For this model to become fully legitimate, it is necessary to *communicate about everything*; at least about everything of a social or communitarian interest. That is where the exhaustive and globalizing claim of the model mentioned above comes from. It would only be a simulation if the model were not at the service of dialogue and management (decision making) concerning community and social affairs. Many self-called "alternative" experiences are precisely just that: a simulation of participation (group dynamics) or, even worse, a simulation of "massmediatic" relationship experiences based solely on the use of "mild" techniques in micro social environments. In any case, the point is the *social dimension* implied by what is communicated; *the meaning of production, circulation and the recreation of meaning.* The meaning of such production, circulation and recreation is the *political dimensions* of social existence in its purest form, to insist on the redundancy.

c. If an alternative (or true) communication model brings into its development the "here and now" of social existence, it must face the existing, large, institutionalized diffusion or intercommunication networks, with their predominant technical component, their bureaucratic disposition, their organizational problems, their prospective social impact, and their relational morphology; predominantly unidirectional, not dialogic, in principle intransitive and antidemocratic. Certainly, the first instinct is to constitute that "other" communication on the margins of dominant, official processes, even of the State (and sometimes *especially* apart from the State—as clandestinely as possible—at the risk of losing *life*). In any event, the primary movement aims to establish a different, lateral "here and now," an anti-system, or a set of different units opposed to predominant networks. This opposition, this marginality, becomes manifest through the search for different content to attract the same mass, but in a non-massive group and active orientation, and also through political opposition—usually radical—to the economic-political system that constantly pushes us to strive for conscientization, or overcome fetishism, through participatory action.

d. Beyond the marginal—and sometimes surreptitious—establishment of communication alternatives, a consistently repeated attempt at different social levels and spheres in Latin America since the forties (we are referring to *conscious* alternatives), the confluence of the movement advocating for policies forced us to consider—when it became embedded in the theoretical revision of these struggles—dominant diffusion apparatuses as possible targets of "alternative" action, e.g., towards a policy that would guarantee citizens' participation in their management. Thus, the point is not to seek alternatives regarding change only in the *use-goal* of media anymore, or to encompass them within a local or interpersonal support system, but instead to reconsider the wider social use of the apparatus, that so far has been manipulative. The point is to establish an access-participation balance that guarantees equality and everyone's involvement in decisions regarding the very existence, use, organization and programming of media, as deemed necessary or useful in the context of a collectively defined policy. One planned in such a way that it will not end with itself, but aim at social services, and be programmed, assessed and reprogrammed, or even reformulated at any time, through community-based participation.

This last dimension—the most ambitious of an "alternative"—has not been experimented with in its radical nature anywhere. It remains an open hypothesis: one implying complex social and political assumptions, not to mention cultural ones; and one difficult to execute on a scale that really corresponds to the level of national states and their traditional, centralized and bureaucratic policies. Certainly, this forces us to redefine the conceptualization of politics and planning, to include Waterston's and others' approach regarding planning "from the bottom up" and "from the outside in." Thus, the clash produced by "pro-political communication" theses regarding the conceptualization of alternative experiences compares only to the trauma experienced by concepts of politics and planning when attempting to include the flow of proposals derived from communication that is "participatory" in all instances.

4. For the time being, to avoid getting too deeply into this subject matter, let us point out that:

a. An "alternative" communication provisionally defined as the one described above is necessarily participatory, since this is the characteristic that defines it more in depth;

b. Not every communicational or technical "alternative", nor a simple alternative use of the media,—be they mass media or not—constitutes in part, or in totality, a form of *alternative communication* (in accordance with the participatory model);

c. "Micro" experiments, or alternative communication units without a globalizing presense at the macro-political level do not constitute true alternative political communication projects. They might in fact become alibis for the system, even if their relational morphology is participatory, the experimental value of such practices notwithstanding;

d. The term "horizontal communication" leads to confusion, since it only indicates part of what should be a set of processes, disregarding the actual existence of dominant, massive and unidirectional networks, media and processes. …On the other hand, as long as the total decentralization of social tasks and the disappearance of the social division of labor—and therefore of the State—are not achieved, it is pointless to talk about "horizontal communication" except on a small scale, at the level of simulations or experiments. It would be a paradigm, but a final one; total redemption, communism, a superior and definitive stage; in the end, a point of arrival. The type of participation proposed by a model shaped as a possible—and difficult—utopia, is an alternative communication that leads other forms of pseudo-communication in the context of encompassing a process of collective liberation, therefore absorbing and redefining the verticalist, transversal, oblique, paradoxical and other forms, to reestablish the right of all;

e. the Macluhanian "global village" is at the opposite pole of the participatory model, since it defines the new community in terms of bringing close what is distant by driving away what is close, cutting off ties with intermediaries to embrace an abstract, worldwide, superficial, vicarious, silly totality, made of pure information and zero action. Therefore, it is useless to insist on the technique's potential; even if it cannot be avoided, it can indeed be taken up again as a problem and not a solution, thought of as an object to be neutralized, inasmuch as it generates the social division of labor and reproduces social relationships and, therefore, necessarily is subject to participatory political control by the community.

Capriles, Oswaldo (1986), "Venezuela: ¿política de comunicación o comunicación alternativa?" In Simpson Gringberg, Máximo (ed.) *Comunicación alternativa y cambio social. America Latina*, Premiá, Puebla, Mexico, 1986. Reprinted with permission of Collette Capriles.

1927
1960
1963
1964
1967
1969
1970
1971
1972
1973
1974
1975
1976
1977
1978
1979
1980
1981
1982
1983
1984
1985
1986
1987
1988
1989
1990
1991
1992
1993
1994
1995
1996
1997
1998
1999
2000
2001
2002
2003
2004
2005
2006

THE CHALLENGE BEFORE US

Excerpt from: Communication and Domination: Essays to Honor Herbert I. Schiller

By George Gerbner

1986 We have moved away from the historic experience of humankind. Children used to grow up in a home where parents told most of the stories. Today, television tells most of the stories to most of the people most of the time. The electronic pulpit and faithful messenger would be the envy of every Emperor and Pope who ever lived. Children do not have five or six years of relatively protected development within the family and the neighborhood before emerging into the outside culture of schooling and reading. By the time they can speak, let alone read, they have absorbed hundreds of thousands of stories—programs, news, commercials—produced on the television assembly-line to the specifications of adult tastes and industrial needs. The pervasive mass ritual blurs, when it does not short-circuit, social distinctions rooted in subcultural and class membership, blends community consciousness into its mainstream, and bends that in the direction of its own institutional interests.

…The vast majority of stories that make up the world according to television are made to uniform specifications of institutional service and sales. Relatively attractive though it may be, the world of television acts to screen us from, rather than mediate, the changing collective requirements of morality, equity, justice and survival in a real world.

Liberation cannot be accomplished by turning it off. Television is, for most people, the most attractive thing going any time of the day or night. We live in a world in which the vast majority will not turn it off. If we don't get the message from the tube, we get it through other people.

The Strategy of Liberation

The sense of planlessness and powerlessness in the face of the television challenge is devastating and mystifying. To accept that is to accept permanent disfranchisement and the extinction of hope for authentic publics. It is a symptom of institutional inertia and political bankruptcy.

Television is the new state religion run by a private Ministry of Culture (the three networks), offering a universal curriculum for all people financed by a form of hidden taxation without representation. You pay when you wash, not when you watch. The price of every bar of soap, and of other advertised products, includes a levy of about $100 a year per household we pay for a service we do not control either by votes or by box office demand.

There is a need for organization and action led by churches, schools and citizen groups. It is not to dictate to the creative workers in television what to do; on the contrary, it is to support their efforts to free themselves from the constraints of ratings and sales and formulas placed upon them.

The strategy requires action on three fronts. Leaders of churches and schools—who else?—can spearhead the movement, as they have begun to do, to restore or build anew an independent basis for authentic publics, consciousness and philosophy. The upstream effort requires a careful assessment of the prevailing currents and their institutional directions. The skills and insights of liberal arts and classical analysis must now be applied to the everyday cultural environment from which all people learn. Media studies and critical viewing curricula must be central parts of all forms of education.

Learning to be parents and citizens in a television culture is also a part of liberation. Participation and discussion rather than proscription or prescription is the best way to put the person, and not the tube, in control of the message.

Citizenship in the television age involves the struggle for access and real participation in institutional decision making affecting the humanization of the species and the shaping of its world. That decision making is based on existing political arrangements, such as the law making advertising expenditures tax deductible and thereby shifting billions in public monies to private purposes. The democratic ways to change such arrangements are necessarily political. Every country has faced similar problems and has resolved them in ways that need to be studied to stimulate the political imagination necessary for creating viable national alternatives. Broadening the resource base under the medium is one way to free it from constraints of having to present the file in the most easily saleable packages serving media markets at the exclusion of other interests. Policy controls now effectively centralized will have to be democratized and made representative of a greater variety of public as well as private interests. Only then can a vision of authentic publics shaping their own reality come closer to realization.

Gerbner, George. "The Challenge Before Us." Jörg Becker, Göran Hedebro and Leena Paldan, *Communication and Domination: Essays to Honor Herbert I. Schiller*. Copyright © Ablex Publishing Corp., N.J. Reproduced with permission of Greenwood Publishing Group, Inc., Westport, Conn.

EXCERPT FROM:
RADIO AS A TOOL FOR DEVELOPMENT

By Daudi Mwakawago

1986 Twenty years ago the communication satellite was a technological novelty, its applications a subject of theoretical discussion and speculation. Today it is the keystone of a diverse and rapidly expanding global communications network upon which both developed and developing countries are becoming increasingly dependent. It is changing a wide array of social institutions and spawning entirely original ones.

Such is the backdrop against which the subject in question will be viewed. For raw material, we have people specifically situated in developing countries, currently called Third World countries. There is space and the intangible thing called change. The objective is to pass on carefully assembled messages which, once received, will generate in the person receiving the message a feeling of dissatisfaction with the current state of affairs and an urge to act. That is a very important initial step. Secondly, the respondent should be sufficiently motivated to act along similar lines with fellow receivers of the message, in order to alter the situation in which he finds himself. That is called change. But before going into greater detail there are a number of questions which require critical answers.

The first question centres on the group of persons who will formulate the message to be communicated. Who are they and what is their legitimacy? It is important that the group is known so that the desired change can be evaluated. In the complexities of Third World countries there are many variations. In some states the communicator is the political party in power. In others it is the multinational company owning the communication media. And a third possibility is a government department or agency. That is an important factor in discussing the media in developing countries. Once

1927
1960
1963
1964
1967
1969
1970
1971
1972
1973
1974
1975
1976
1977
1978
1979
1980
1981
1982
1983
1984
1985
1986
1987
1988
1989
1990
1991
1992
1993
1994
1995
1996
1997
1998
1999
2000
2001
2002
2003
2004
2005
2006

we identify the agency that puts out the messages we will know what kind of change is likely to be desired.

But it will not be the whole story. There is the question of how the message will be communicated. And even more critical is how widespread is the reach of the communication vehicle. The extent of the coverage of media affects the quality of change and the speed at which such change will take place.

Then there are related questions such as the clarity of the message at the receiving end, and the degree of sophistication of the receiver. An illiterate receiver, or even a semiliterate receiver of the message may distort the meaning of the message received. That is a very serious possibility.

Another question worth considering concerns the nature of the change desired. How much freedom should be granted to the listener? There is a school of thought that argues that for rapid change all avenues of communication ought to be manipulated from a single centre so that the receiver is not confused by multiple messages that call for contradictory responses. The more progressive school argues that the receiver must have freedom to choose what he wants. The onus is on the communicator of the message to make the message appealing. Yet cultural values cannot be ignored in the exercise.

Last but not least comes the important question of the interdependence of the countries of the world. The Third World is distinct only for analytical purposes. It is part of the world as a whole. As such it is influenced to varying degrees by all the forces of change, both negative and positive, that act on the world at large. Some of the influences are direct while many others are indirect. The setting has to be analysed in order to get a clear perspective of the subject.

Having set the scene we now turn to the discussion of the specific role of radio as a tool of development. It is the channel through which are communicated important messages intended to change the lifestyle of the recipients. Development in this context thus means qualitative change through the influence of externally organised messages received through the radio.

Radio and Third World Countries

But before we consider the role and place of radio in the development of new states, it is important to underscore the realities of the, so-called, developing countries. The salient features of those countries are low literacy rates, low per capita incomes and an average life expectancy of almost half that of developed states. In addition, developing countries are characterized by rampant poverty and disease. Although the death rate is high, population growth is phenomenal. It is said that the population of Africa will double by the year 2000. But food production will not match population growth. There will be more mouths to feed than food to feed them. The majority of Third World countries are producers of raw materials and consumers of finished products from the developed states. That means they are on the periphery of the world economic stage.

Such is the gloomy picture which, of necessity, has to be taken into consideration in discussing the role of radio, and indeed of the other mass media, in development. Yet in spite of this gloomy picture there are some very significant, positive aspects in developing countries. Their potential for development, especially in the agricultural field and in mineral exploitation, is tremendous. What is needed is massive capital investment and knowhow. But even before reaching out for capital and knowhow, there is the question of the total mobilization of the able-bodied population in the countries under discussion. That is where the question of the vehicle for reaching the people becomes crucial.

As far as development is concerned the new nations have, in the words of Wilbur Schramm, "the urgent requirement to change, swiftly, broadly, but as painlessly as possible."[1] In order to do this a powerful medium is

---

1   Wilbur Schramm, *Mass Media and Nation Development,* Stanford. California: Stanford University Press, 1964, p. 41.

required to make the population willing to undertake the effort involved.

Public meetings are pretty inadequate; the effectiveness of newspapers is limited by low literacy rates; while television, which could be very useful, is not only too expensive for the country, but cannot be afforded by the great majority of the people. Thus radio becomes the natural choice. Given the revolution in transistorisation, the radio is the one medium that can be afforded by the greatest number of the people in developing countries. It is therefore this medium that will receive our maximum attention in the following pages.

Development in the context of the new states has twin objectives. On the one hand there is the need for national integration. The majority of developing countries have become independent in the last 20 years. Nationhood is a new phenomenon. It cannot be taken for granted. It has to be built. Along with the building of nationhood there is the added task of raising the living standards of the people. Both objectives require the support of powerful media.

Nationhood implies the welding together of many tribes, races and ethnic groups. The cultivation of a larger consciousness requires the popularisation of concepts that cut across narrow ethnic and parochial considerations. Thus our country, our government, plus the symbolism of statehood such as the national leader, the national flag and the national anthem, need to become the focuses of loyalty in place of the tribal chief and the village headmen. Of course the international connections of a new nation state are also an important boost to the nation-building exercise. Thus it is not surprising that the radio signal is heavily loaded with nationalism. It helps in the creation and enhancement of the new identity of a people. It creates a sense of belonging, as well as a sense of participation in the achievements of the new state. In the process a nation is born, albeit by losing something that is in itself valuable. Perhaps this development of a national consciousness is a much easier exercise than of mobilizing the people to raise their living standards.

The raising of living standards is a much more complicated business, for it attacks tradition and well-tested ideas and practices. The people are called upon to change not only their attitudes but also the way they do things. Social customs are affected. This may have a very unsettling effect. But that is what change is all about. People who were self-sufficient in their villages are urged to cultivate and raise new cash crops which, in most cases, are not for their immediate use. The crops are required by the external market. In return the local people need imported goods such as radios, clothes and books, to mention but a few items. This development creates new relationships. The new crops demand new techniques of cultivation, handling and the creation of links with the wider world. The new states grow sisal, cotton, coffee, tea, pyrethrum, cashew nuts, cocoa and tobacco for the export market[2]. Thus the concepts of foreign exchange, terms of trade, world market and so on have to be understood. But even more important perhaps is that, after the sale of the crops, there is the need to learn how to use the money so obtained for purchasing new types of goods and services, which have new cultural and social and economic values, previously unknown in the small-scale life of the traditional village.

New attitudes have to be inculcated and the radio can do a very important job in this respect. It is not uncommon today in travelling around Tanzania to come across a peasant on a bicycle with his transistor radio. The radio has become a walking companion. But the radio is also a communicator of messages from all over the world. Music is the most popular item with many listeners. However, since in East Africa Kiswahili is the *lingua franca*, many radio stations of the world have developed Swahilili broadcasts. Thus the question of control of what is received by listeners in Tanzania becomes not only sensitive but crucial.

Who Controls the Radio?

As suggested earlier, the expansion of radio coverage in new states is necessary because of its role as a

---

2   I have used developing countries and new states interchangeably.

1927
1960
1963
1964
1967
1969
1970
1971
1972
1973
1974
1975
1976
1977
1978
1979
1980
1981
1982
1983
1984
1985
1986
1987
1988
1989
1990
1991
1992
1993
1994
1995
1996
1997
1998
1999
2000
2001
2002
2003
2004
2005
2006

formulator of public opinion, but other important functions are entertainment, newscasting and education. All these functions are controlled. In some states the radio is government owned and controlled; in others, although government owned, it is controlled by an autonomous body. In yet other states a mixture of public and private control prevails. Given the urge for development, whatever the mechanism for ownership and control, it is evident that there will be differences in the way the messages are formulated and then communicated to the wider public.

A government committed to rapid socioeconomic change by means of dynamic state intervention tends to wish to control all the instruments of persuasion and influence. But even a government committed to a *laissez-faire*, free enterprise system will insist on controlling the mass media. In this case the objective tends to be to control the result of events rather than to promote rapid change. One way of identifying the objective of radio in a developing country is to study its title. We have, for instance, Radio Tanzania for Socialist Tanzania, the Voice of Kenya for free-enterprise Kenya, the Voice of Revolutionary Ethiopia, the Zambia Broadcasting Service and Radio Uganda, to mention but a few. The names of the stations are indicative of the central role allotted to the mass media in the development of the countries concerned. The twin objectives of fostering nationhood and acting as the focal point of development are clearly discernible. But we need to delve deeper into the content of the programmes in order to arrive at a definitive position on the actual uses to which the media are put.

There is a growing debate in developing countries about who should control the mass media. It has already been pointed out that there are several forms and varieties of control. But what we are interested in here is to underscore the main areas of consideration in deciding the best form of control. In a country that has as its top priority the creation of nationhood, the state or the government must have control of the mass media. This proposition of necessity involves almost all developing countries. Consequently, educational programmes will be formulated and transmitted from a central authority which has as its primary objective the creation of a national consciousness.

The only area where a certain measure of decentralization could be considered is the entertainment side. But then even here a clear distinction is likely to be made. Music and drama, purely for entertainment purposes, can be decentralised. But drama intended to contribute towards nation building must be centrally directed. I know there will be cries of government manipulation and possibly indoctrination. There is no short answer to that. No programme is entirely free of manipulation. Even in free enterprise countries, there tend to be groups who try to monopolise and manipulate communication and need to be controlled by public intervention. There is no such thing as total freedom of the media. The vital questions are: who does the controlling, and what is the nature of the control?

Programme Content

Radio, like any other mass medium, performs the traditional roles of dissemination of news and information, entertainment and education. The most popular items are news and music. Invariably, Western pop music is very popular on all radio stations. However, in East Central Africa there is the added attraction of Zairean music, which has been able to provide a distinctly African alternative to Western music. Interestingly enough there are few, if any, official exchange programmes between the radio stations of the region.

In terms of distribution of time Professor Wedell's programme analysis suggests that: "Very broadly, Commonwealth countries … seem to divide their radio broadcasting schedules on a radio of 40:60 as between serious and entertainment programmes."[3] That ratio does give a clue as to the dilemma of translating wishes into reality, whatever the controllers might want. It is obvious from those figures that it is not the serious

---

3   E. G. Wedell, "Broadcasting in the Developing Commonwealth: Help or Hindrance?" *Journal of the Royal Society of Arts,* 1979, p. 219.

programmes that dominate. Rather, the lighter programmes are in the driver's seat. Consequently, in discussing the role of radio in development, broadcasters have to take note of that reality and ensure that development objectives are pursued in the output of entertainment as well as in the "serious" programming.

This leads to the need for a further look at the concept of development. Development implies change for the better. To be significant such change has to be quantitative as well as qualitative. It must benefit the majority of the people and affect their tastes and world outlook. When this happens people will become assertive and not only anxious but determined to identify with the "new look." But from this it follows that the new goods and services for which a demand has been created have to be produced or procured in much greater numbers. The acquisition of new goods and services inevitably leads to the discarding of old ways and habits. In a nonliterate society, radio can and does exert a very significant influence in stimulating this demand for new things.

As well as stimulating demand, radio therefore has the role of containing demand and of channelling it into those areas where demand can be met. There, as in Tanzania, radio advertising is used to stimulate demand as part of the development process, and the control of such advertising becomes an essential instrument of regulating the national economy. Development thus binds the commercial system to the political, social and economic systems in such a way as to restructure the fabric of society to reflect the new influences and the new modes of doing things.

The Impact of Radio

Even a small radio set can be listened to at any one moment by a group of individuals without jostling. With a newspaper even two people cannot read a single copy comfortably. The multiplier effect in radio is quite evident. Therefore, to the policymaker the radio is a very powerful instrument. Fortunately the power of radio is well known to all developing countries. It is thus understandable that radio is regarded as such a

vital instrument for the changing of attitudes and the moulding of tastes for those things considered important by the programme controllers.

Radio is used extensively in educational programmes, both for adults and children. It is a very effective teacher. It influences the listeners on the pronunciation of language, broadens their world outlook and, where the listener is helped, it can be a very potent agent for change. But given that the listener wants to be entertained, it can be quite a dilemma to decide what mix will capture the intended audience. A student of the mass media in Tanzania has put it thus: "In order to employ the broadcasting medium as a serious channel of development communication, it has to play the role of the educator a bit more. It is not easy to 'bend' the audience this way, but if the education it provides is relevant, it is likely that it could draw a lot of serious attention."[4]

The Use of Radio to Stimulate Development

Given the poor transport facilities in many developing countries, it is not possible to rely on face-to-face contacts. An alternative means of communicating with the people is essential. It has already been pointed out that literacy is low; consequently, newspapers or the written word cannot be the chief means of communication. Television would be ideal. But this medium is extremely expensive to acquire and to run. What remains therefore is the radio. Given the technological revolution that has taken place over the last 20 years, the radio is relatively cheap and because of that it can be afforded by all states.

With the relative availability of the radio, it is possible to discuss in detail the use to which it is put to stimulate development. Four areas of use are discernible. They are information, facilitating, decision making, education and entertainment. We will tackle each area in turn.

The radio is a powerful source of information on national as well as international news. It communicates

4 Nkwabi Ng'wanakilala, *Mass Communication and Development of Socialism in Tanzania,* Dar-es-Salaam: Tanzania Publishing House, 1981.

1927
1960
1963
1964
1967
1969
1970
1971
1972
1973
1974
1975
1976
1977
1978
1979
1980
1981
1982
1983
1984
1985
1986
1987
1988
1989
1990
1991
1992
1993
1994
1995
1996
1997
1998
1999
2000
2001
2002
2003
2004
2005
2006

the exhortations of the leaders and passes details of events from one corner of the country to the other. It has a dual function. On the one hand, it reports what has happened. This alerts the listener. But by the same strength it informs. Just to illustrate these twin functions by a concrete example from Tanzanian experience, we refer to a heated debate that took place in the National Assembly in 1975 during a discussion of the Ministry of Information and Broadcasting estimates for 1975/76. The issue that aroused great concern was the time allocated to death announcements. At that time, five minutes before or after the main news bulletins was made available, a total of 15 to 20 minutes a day. The Members of the National Assembly were urging the minister to allocate a block of, say, 15 minutes to one hour at a time for death announcements only. The minister was adamant that the time allocated and the way it had been distributed was ideal for reasons of effectiveness and aesthetic considerations, and the government carried the day. But the demand for an increased allocation of time showed the key role which radio plays in disseminating information and keeping families and friends in touch. Precisely because of that importance, conflicting demands and pressures on the medium are inevitable.

The second function relates to the ability of the radio, indeed of all mass media, to help the listener in decision making. It does this by clarifying issues and illustrating them with concrete data that make it relatively easy to come up with a position based on knowledge. Such techniques as commentaries, discussion groups, interviews and talks are used to help the listener grasp the concepts and issues involved in a given decision. This is a very important function of the radio. Alas, because the bulk of air-time in developing countries is used for entertainment, there tends to be little room for manoeuvre in the schedules.

In education, there is direct involvement of radio. It is used extensively as a supplement for face-to-face teaching in the classroom. Thus educational services are fairly well developed. There are specific periods for primary, secondary and adult education. In Tanzania at one time the radio was widely used in teacher training because of the critical shortage of teachers to meet the needs of universal primary education (UPE) launched in 1977. Over 43,000 teachers were required. It was evident that conventional methods of teacher training could not realise that target. In the event the use of radio along with other methods proved to be quite successful. The potential of the radio as part of a multimedia system has yet to be fully exploited in developing countries.

Last but not least, radio is a tremendous vehicle for entertainment. Music does take the lion's share of the time. But the radio is increasingly used for drama, poetry recitals, storytelling and for games and sports. Outside broadcasting is at the moment largely confined to football matches, which are very popular; and religious services, especially during religious festivals. The African people are very musical and extroverted. But this important virtue has not been exploited fully partly because of the legacy of metropolitan values and attitudes. Consequently the format used in developing countries, based on indoor studio production, continues to be used. This is of necessity very expensive and largely inappropriate to a tropical climate. The promotion of attitudes so as to develop radio styles appropriate to an African country is essential.

The Training of Radio Staff

We have already noted the crucial role of the radio in stimulating change. But the radio remains a medium. For it to be effective there must be a team of well-trained programme producers and technicians. This area is sometimes not given the importance it deserves. Most radio stations in developing countries are notable for their understaffing and inadequate provision. They are poorly equipped with inadequate funds. Consequently the full potential of radio is not fully realised. This is one area which can and must be corrected if the radio is to really act as a major agent for development in the new states.

Training has to have a policy. There is a growing debate even in Tanzania as to what category of staff should be trained. Some people argue that high-level professionals are what are required. We maintain that, given the stage of development of most of the developing countries, the training of middle-level professionals in large numbers is the immediate requirement. Once this area is satisfied then high-level and specialised training can be intensified. It is not an exaggeration to say that the effectiveness of the highly trained professional such as the engineer or programme producer is much impaired if there are insufficient middle- and lower-level technicians to support the work of the engineer. But saying that does not mean that high-level professionals should not be trained. The point is that the area of concentration should be middle-level staff. Thus certificate and diploma courses would be more appropriate than degrees and similar courses. Once there is an adequate supply of field staff, there is a basis of skilled people whom new experts, who will be promoted from the ranks, can use. Colonial experience in this field is hardly to be emulated. It was very inadequate. Training was haphazard and superficial. One gets the impression that it was done out of convenience. It lacked any conceptual framework or a planned goal. Many countries have realised this shortcoming. However, they have been slow in working out concrete ways of correcting it.

The second aspect of the training concerns the need for greater discrimination in technology and value systems from developed states, mostly in the West. There the indoor studio is the mainstay of the programme production resources. But, as has already been pointed out, developing countries are in the tropics. Open-air activity is common. It would thus be much more appropriate to use outside broadcasting techniques. The weather is very favourable and the culture is much more relaxed and adaptive. Very little of this technique has so far been utilised. It is used very sparingly when in fact it could be the main area of concentration. Indeed the impact on the population would be phenomenal. The failure to adapt techniques to suit tropical conditions has resulted in the importation of very expensive technology which requires sophisticated personnel to handle and maintain it. Given the meagre resources at the disposal of the new states, radio invariably has to complete with other demands. And radio often loses out badly in that struggle of resources. Dr. Wilbur Schramm (1964) has this to say:

> A high proportion of developing countries have now found out, from their experience, how crucial information is to their development programmes. Yet, even in many of these countries information is still a poor cousin. It is starved for operating funds, equipment, training. It has had only a tiny fraction of the support available from international organisations and bilateral loans grants.

If the radio is to be used effectively, states will have to make more funds available to facilitate training of the necessary staff and the procurement of required equipment. It is absolutely essential that new attitudes should be developed towards the radio by national decision makers, both in the government and in the ruling party. It is not good enough to recognise the importance of the medium in stimulating development, while providing too little in the way of resources to utilise it fully.

References

Wedell, E. G. "Broadcasting in the Developing Commonwealth: Help or Hindrance?" *Journal of the Royal Society of Arts,* 1979, 219.

Guttenplan, Barry. Dialogue, 1981, 52: 2.

Ng'wanakilala, Nkwabi. *Mass Communication and Development of Socialism in Tanzania.* Dar-es-Salaam: Tanzania Publishing House, 1981.

Schramm, Wilbur. *Mass Media and Nation Development.* Stanford, California: Stanford University Press, 1964.

Mwakawago, Daudi. *Radio as a Tool for Development.* Manchester, England: Manchester University Press, 1986.

1927
1960
1963
1964
1967
1969
1970
1971
1972
1973
1974
1975
1976
1977
1978
1979
1980
1981
1982
1983
1984
1985
1986
1987
1988
1989
1990
1991
1992
1993
1994
1995
1996
1997
1998
1999
2000
2001
2002
2003
2004
2005
2006

EXCERPT FROM:

COMMUNICATION AS IF PEOPLE MATTER: THE CHALLENGE OF ALTERNATIVE COMMUNICATION

By Mina Ramírez

1986 A people who have been utterly disregarded in the interests of material accumulation by national and global powers should be given the chance to articulate and express their deepest human feelings about the realities of their life. This is the challenge of alternative communication. In contrast to the one-way information flow, controlled by political and economic powers, alternative communication shifts its focus to the stories told by the marginalized and exploited sectors of society. The negative social consequences of colonialism and neocolonialism are deeply embedded in people. And the therapy to such a malady is the creation of a social climate for "storytelling." It is high time that the policy makers, including the technocrats, listen to the stories that people tell.

"Storytelling" could further be systematized. This would mean organizing and mobilizing each sector, particularly the most marginalized, towards democratic processes and leadership. These organizations may form pressure groups promoting a new self-consciousness—an awareness of the roots of their condition as well as the potential for their own liberation. Each sector could be helped by sympathetic groups among the modernized elite. Through movements such as these, the real needs of people are easily identified.

The people's stories could be channeled to a wider audience through mass media so that public opinion and positive institutional responses to people's needs may be formed and crystallized. Steps would have to be taken by valuable contributions of the various organized sectors towards a more humane life in society as a whole. In the last analysis, the establishment of a system of communication in that people matter entails the struggle of all sectors of society to obtain control of communication processes that can lead to collective understanding of human situations. Such an understanding, based on reality, action and reflection, is the basis for an alternative economic, political and communication order. Such communication would pose a challenge to the great capacities people have for personal, communal and societal transformation.

NEW INFORMATION ORDER IN LATIN AMERICA: A TAXONOMY FOR NATIONAL COMMUNICATION POLICIES

Excerpt from: Communication and Domination: Essays to Honor Herbert I. Schiller

By Rafael Roncagliolo

1986 The communication debate in the 1970s has been dominated by two topics—the New World Information and Communication Order (NWICO) and national communication policies. Both issues arose out of a common concern: democratization of communication relationships between countries was the objective of the demands for a New World Information and Communication order; democratization of communication relationships within countries was the aim of the struggle around national communication policies. Initiatives on the NWICO and national communication policies are but two sides of the same coin. The convergence of the two problems on the democratization of communication in the 1980s can therefore be seen as a natural development (Roncagliolo, 1981; 1982a, -b, -c, -d, -e).

We have stated earlier that communication media in the present transnational stage of capitalism have tended to act as ideological apparatuses and as primary socialization agencies, partially displacing the traditional apparatuses of family, church and school (Roncagliolo, 1982b, p. 28). We are living in a transnational stage of culture characterized, among other things, by a shift in the structural hierarchy of ideological apparatuses and socialization agencies towards the media. The role played by the media in socialization, as well as in ideological control and mobilization, has grown over time, while that played by the family has declined. This does not suggest that the communication media are omnipotent. Communication phenomena, being situated at the interface of transnationalization and culture, are marked by the contradiction between transnationalizing forces and national popular cultures.

National communication policies reflect the manner in which societies organize (and disorganize) their communication systems, and therefore affect national cultures. National communication policies are not a new issue in Latin America (see e.g., Beltran, 1976; Capriles, 1977; Fox, 1975; Schenkel et al., 1981). The much-publicized UNESCO (United Nations Educational, Scientific and Cultural Organization) Regional Conference on National Communication Policies held in San Jose in Costa Rica in 1976 was proof that the forces opposing even the mere discussion of these issues are present and powerful. The San Jose Conference, and the declarations made there by governments of the region, offers a benchmark against which the actual communication policies implemented by those governments within their borders can be measured. The gap between rhetoric and practice is wide, as discovered by the follow-up meeting to San Jose, convened by UNESCO at Quito in December 1981.

Work on national communication policies suffers because of the dearth of analyses of national communication systems, in toto. In Latin America, the field is characterized by too much theory (as well as rhetoric) on one side, and too many case studies on the other. Both are necessary, but what is urgently required is an emphasis on the "middle" of this continuum—on joint studies of national communication systems. Our current work, a methodological exercise that is still at a preliminary stage, is an attempt to focus attention to this area.

First, we suggest a set of taxonomies, binary for the present, to classify national communication policies. Second, we hope to initiate a discussion on what would be the necessary and significant components of a national communication policy.

1927
1960
1963
1964
1967
1969
1970
1971
1972
1973
1974
1975
1976
1977
1978
1979
1980
1981
1982
1983
1984
1985
1986
1987
1988
1989
1990
1991
1992
1993
1994
1995
1996
1997
1998
1999
2000
2001
2002
2003
2004
2005
2006

Six Classification Criteria

It is necessary at the outset to establish a set of typologies for analysis of national communication policies. Six criteria are suggested. However, the list is not all-inclusive, and the terminology is provisional. The criteria are:

1. the level of policy formulation;
2. the internal articulation and scope of the policy;
3. the degree of articulation with the extra-communicational sphere;
4. the communication objectives of the policy;
5. its national objectives; and
6. its international objectives.

1. LEVEL OF FORMULATION: IMPLICIT VS. EXPLICIT

Partisans of the transnational perspective assert that the best communication policy is no policy. However, the existence of the state presupposes the existence of policies. The absence of explicit policies merely indicates that policymaking has been moved from government agencies to the boardrooms of corporations. The starting point of this discussion is, therefore, the proposition that all states have communication policies, explicit or implicit.

Certain countries appear to have no explicit communication policies, but closer examination reveals otherwise. Even that champion of discursive liberalism, the United States of America, has a large body of normative policies relating to communication, especially in relation to new technologies, such as satellites and cable television. Indeed, the satellite policy of the United States is an excellent example of a communication policy based on collaboration between the state and the transnational interests.

Ortega and Romera (1976, p. 5) are correct in their assertion that:

> Communication policies exist in every society, although they might appear hidden and scattered, and not clearly articulated and harmonized. They might be of a very general nature, and present themselves as desirable goals and principles, or they might, in practice, be more specific and perceptive. They might exist or be formulated at many levels. They might be incorporated in the constitution or legislation of a country, in general national policies, in instructions given to administrative bodies, in codes of professional ethics and in the by-laws and regulations of certain communication institutions.

If the term "communication policies" were to be construed more restrictively, little could be said of Latin American communication policies other than a report of a few failed projects and a set of unapplied desiderata.

2. COVERAGE AND INTERNAL ARTICULATION: PARTIAL VS. COMPREHENSIVE

Most discussions of national communication policies in Latin America are limited to the legal form they should take (constitutional resolutions, organic laws, supreme decrees) and/or the composition and powers of the institutions required to administer them. Yet the mere mention of a possible regulatory regime or of a regulatory institution is enough to galvanize enough private interests into action to stifle any such initiative before it sees the light of day.

Because few explicit communication policies have ever been implemented, there is very little experience to build upon: television policy in Chile, press reform in Peru, the RATELVE project on radio and television in Venezuela and existing regulation of advertising in a number of countries. Even these limited experiments have generally failed or even resulted in retrogression. This cannot be attributed solely, or even primarily, to problems inherent in the policies themselves; rather, the main factors have been the general orientation of the state and its capacity to assume control of the overall direction of the cultural industry.

Mexico is perhaps the only country in the region that has formulated a national communication policy in the broadest sense of the term. Here, we refer to the constitutional entrenchment of the right to information and to the drafting of laws pertaining to a whole range of communication activities including the press, radio, television, films, comics, theatre and the publishing industry. This initiative of the Coordination of Social Communication of the Presidency of the Republic, undertaken during the term of Jose Lopez Portillo, gave rise to one of the most extensive debates ever to take place in Latin America on the relations between the state, democracy and communication. It was a fascinating debate that deserves wider publicity. The concern of the Mexican state over this issue can clearly be placed within the country's tradition of cultural nationalism that was earlier manifested in the establishment of the television channels 11 and 13 and Radio Education.

In summary, it is important to differentiate between partial or limited communication policies and those that encompass the entire, national communication system. The latter is practically nonexistent in present-day Latin America because of lack of coordination between decision-making bodies. Considerable time is needed to overcome this problem, even in countries undergoing revolutionary transitions, such as Nicaragua.

3. DEGREE OF EXTRA-COMMUNICATIONAL ARTICULATION: MARGINAL VS. INTEGRATED

The problem of lack of articulation can be found even in countries capable of articulating a coherent national development plan, where cultural policies tend to be formulated in isolation from that planning process. Those who form cultural policy tend to be groups of intellectuals and artists who control the most refined forms of cultural production. Communication issues can be very sensitive politically, with the result that they tend to be excluded from the board planning process. The difficulties encountered in attempting to extend nationwide changes in private property relations to the Chilean press and the printing industry during the Allende period exemplifies the problem. Another example is the case of Peru, where conservative social groups that did not dare to take to the streets to protest agrarian reform, enterprise reform, the nationalization of mines or changes in foreign relations, mounted vociferous protests as soon as newspapers were affected (Roncagliolo, 1978).

The *MacBride Report* addressed the question of separation of communication policy from the general planning process:

> Since communication is not an autonomous, separate sector, in this domain perhaps more than in others, interdependence makes it essential to develop communication policies which are not limited to information, even less to mass media—they have to take into consideration all ways and means a society needs and can utilize for its overall development purposes. We must not lose sight of the fact that communication policies go hand-in-hand with those formulated in other fields, i.e., education, culture and science, and should be designed to supplement them. Communication should interrelate with these sectors, so as to promote social, educational, scientific and other services (International Commission for the Study of Communication Problems, 1980, p. 204).

Thus, any communication policy must be articulated with the entire set of cultural, educational and technological policies, as well as with national development plans which must, in turn, take into account the important role played by the national communication system in the economy.

4. SECTORAL OBJECTIVES: MERCANTILE CONCEPTION VS. PUBLIC SERVICE

The notion that the best communication policy is no policy is derived from the mercantile conception of information. In this conception, communication is the reserved territory of private actors, forbidden to society as a whole.

The few instances of democratization of communication in Latin America, like the RATELVE project, all had their basis in the conception of communication as a public service. Concepts of public service, information as a social good and the right to information guide the design of democratic communication policies. Where communication has been considered as merchandise, and its handling a matter of profit and private power, authoritarian communication policies

1927
1960
1963
1964
1967
1969
1970
1971
1972
1973
1974
1975
1976
1977
1978
1979
1980
1981
1982
1983
1984
1985
1986
1987
1988
1989
1990
1991
1992
1993
1994
1995
1996
1997
1998
1999
2000
2001
2002
2003
2004
2005
2006

have flourished. This has been the case both where the authoritarianism has been that of the state and where it has been exercised by private monopoly corporations. Thus, the primary classification of communication phenomena is centred around the opposition between mercantile and public-service criteria. This is the touchstone and the initial *divortium aquarum*.

Real-world concerns, not abstract speculations, are at issue here. It is not possible to create a television system capable of national and cultural expression if its managers are compelled to work within the mercantile criterion of profit maximization.

5. SOCIAL OBJECTIVES: AUTHORITARIANISM VS. DEMOCRACY

If one looks beyond communication and its functions, it is obvious that communication policy is based on general social policy. In this context, the alternative is between authoritarianism and democracy.

However, it must be stressed that not all forms of authoritarianism, not even the ones most prevalent in Latin America, necessarily originate from governments.

> Freedom of expression is undoubtedly threatened when authoritarian regimes establish official censorship, but it is equally curtailed when private owners and financiers decide, in the name of their readers, what to include and what not to include in their pages. In Peru, a well-known case is that of El Comercio, which was prohibited from even mentioning in its pages the name of the main opposition party of the country, the Partido Aprista Peruano. In this manner the publisher could autocratically make decisions of power and scope comparable to those of any dictator. The concept of democratization therefore confronts two analogous types of obstacles to free expression—political authoritarianism and economic authoritarianism (Roncagliolo, 1982c, p. 4).

A valid, though inadequate, definition of democratization can be found in the *MacBride Report*:

Democratization may be defined as the process whereby: (a) the individual becomes an active partner and not a mere object of communication; (b) the variety of messages exchanged increases; and (c) the extent and quality of social representation or participation in communication are augmented (International Commission for the Study of Communication Problems, 1980, p. 166).

Therefore, it is necessary to avoid simplistic inferences from the juridical status of communication enterprises:

> Pretending that every juridical law has to be classified as being either completely in the public sphere or completely in the private sphere is an anachronism. Legislation has historically reflected the emergence and expansion of social rights. Education, labour and health are social rights that do not fit exclusively within the public sphere or the private sphere. Communications and the right to communicate belong in the same category. Communication activities must correspond to specific social and democratic circumstances in which real control of information derives from organized receivers and from social producers of messages. Many innovations are possible in this area. For instance, television stations were controlled by universities during the democratic period in Chile. In Peru, there was the unsuccessful attempt to hand over the control of national newspapers to organizations representing major social sectors (e.g., educators, professionals, intellectuals, urban workers, peasants) and to workers from each newspaper enterprise. The failure of these particular experiments does not justify ignoring the fact that these schemes were even, if only in theory, more democratic than family or government autocracies (Roncagliolo, 1982c, pp.4-5).

The democratic concept of communication is not limited to social organization as suggested by the MacBride Report definition. It corresponds to the functions of communication within societies. Proposals to democratize communications are actually proposals to democratize society. The broad objective is what matters, not communications in itself.

Over the years, there has been an interesting progression of themes and concepts: first the discussion was about "access" and "participation," terms that referred to the marginalization of parts of society in relation to communication entities; in the second stage, the nomenclature of the "right to information" recast the issue in terms of a positive right; then the call for democratization focused on the structurally oppressive nature of the existing communication system. The present stage of the discussion may be the right time to stop talking about national communication policies, to begin designing communication policies with specific democratic objectives and purposes.

This leads to the question of the subject of policy. By definition, a democratization policy cannot have the state apparatus as its only subject. Many actors must become involved in the design and implementation of policy, particularly receivers, media workers and, at a level proportionate to their importance, communication researchers.

At present, there is much talk about measures for democratization of communication. These include readers' committees, programs of critical education, effective right-of-reply provisions, consulting committees on publication policy comprising representatives of social sectors, and the incorporation of the public in the newspaper production process. However, implementation is not as easy as mere reiteration. All these measures had their Latin American test, not in any government policy, but during the flowering of the alternative press in Uruguay from 1968 to 1973. This period saw the rise and commercial success of newspapers, such as *Extra*, *DeFrente* and *Ya*, that were innovative, not only in terms of content but also in experimenting with a number of participatory measures that should be part of any democratic policy of communication (Fassano, 1973).[1]

---

1   Fassano was a former publisher of the three alternative newspapers discussed in the text. The book was banned on publication and confiscated by the Uruguayan Police. One can only hope that it will be republished.

6. NATIONAL OBJECTIVES: TRANSNATIONALIZATION VS. CULTURAL SOVEREIGNTY

Besides defining the domestic role of communication, a national communication policy affects cultural relations between the nation as a whole and external powers. It may either serve the multidimensional process of transnational expansion, or the cultural resistance of national-popular forces. In fact, the subject of democratization has become a central focus of the proposals for a New World Information and Communication Order. It was not coincidental that the NWICO was born at the same time as the New International Economic Order:

> One may consider the historical eruption of the Third World as part of the process of broadening the demand for independence and sovereignty: in the 1940s and the 1950s, the topic was political independence; in the 1960s the demand was extended to economic sovereignty; and in the 1970s, to culture and communications. As a part of this overall process, communications simply contributes to the democratization of international power.

The NWICO is a form of defence by the Third World (and not only by the Third World) against colonial expansion. Therefore it represents a democratic force that can be distinguished from the desire for government control as well as from the pervasive censorship and manipulation exercised by private monopolies over their so-called free communication media (incidentally, this latter form of control is exercised in alliance with governments—for example, the Brazilian chain, O Globo, which controls a vast portion of communication in that country, is, at the same time the official voice of the military government) (Roncagliolo, 1982, pp. 11-12).

Key Elements of Communications Policy

The taxonomies presented here tend to stress the idea that, given the existence of some form of national communication policy, the task of scientific research is to establish the criteria for discovering and

1927
1960
1963
1964
1967
1969
1970
1971
1972
1973
1974
1975
1976
1977
1978
1979
1980
1981
1982
1983
1984
1985
1986
1987
1988
1989
1990
1991
1992
1993
1994
1995
1996
1997
1998
1999
2000
2001
2002
2003
2004
2005
2006

explicating such policies. The central aspect of analysis is not a discussion of national communication councils or of the humanistic objectives of communication policies. It is, instead, a comprehensive and detailed analysis of national communication systems. It is only on the basis of this type of analysis that it would be possible to formulate specific and operative goals for the component elements of policy.

It is proposed that the following main elements must be included in any comprehensive analysis of policy:

1. *Ownership* of the means of production and distribution of communication; legislative status (public, private, social); and empirical concentrations (class monopolies, political monopolies, transnationalization of property, etc.).
2. *Financing:* advertising; sales; subsidies (state or private, concentration or dispersion of sources); transnationalization of income; political factors.
3. *Technology:* level of technological resources and their economic and sociocultural consequences; transnationalization via technology.
4. *Content:* types and semiotic analyses; role of advertising.
5. *Management and Feedback:* participation of organized social sectors and of media workers in editorial management and feedback processes (receivers' committees, right-to-reply, etc).
6. *Compatibility* with development plans and other national policies.

This preliminary list can be further developed to obtain a methodological pattern or a set of criteria for analysis of national communication systems and policies. The objective is to analyze all aspects of communications within this framework. The media should not be analyzed in isolation.

It is our hope that this preliminary methodological exercise will pave the way for a long-term Latin American research program. The objective would be to analyze, theoretically as well as empirically, the actions of states and transnational corporations in relation to our communication systems. This would necessarily involve a thorough and critical reexamination of the failures and successes of democratic communication experiences such as the RATELVE Project in Venezuela, television policies in Chile under the popular government and the Peruvian press reform.

References

Beltran, L. R. "Politicas Nacionales de Communicacion." *American Latina.* Bogotá, Colombia: CIIA, 1976.

Capriles, O. "Acciones y Reacciones Frente a la Politicia de Communicaion Promovida Dentro del Marco de Accion de la UNESCO: Analisis de la Conference de Costa Rica." Seminar on International Communication and Third World Participation: A Conceptual and Practical Framework. Amsterdam: 1977.

Fox, E. (1975). "Politicas de Comunicacion en Sociedades de Cambio." Cuadernos CEDAL, 1975, No. 4 (Costa Rica).

Fassano, F. *Paren las Rotativas.* Montevideo, Uruguay: Arca, 1973.

International Commission for the Study of Communication Problems. "One World, Many Voices." *MacBride Report.* Paris: UNESCO, 1980.

Oretga, C., and C. Romero. *Las Politicas de Comunicacion en el Peru.* Paris: UNESCO, 1976.

Roncagliolo, R. *La Reforma de la Prensa Peruana.* Mexico: ILET, 1978.

Roncagliolo, R. "The MacBride Report as a Part of a Process." In C. Hamelink, ed., *Communication in the Eighties: A Reader on the MacBride Report.* Rome: IDOC, 1981. This is an earlier version of Roncagliolo, 1982d.

Roncagliolo, R. "Comunicacion y Democracia en el Debate Internacional." Paper presented at the Conference of the International Association for Mass Communication Research. Paris: 1982a. This is another version of Roncagliolo, 1982d.

Roncagliolo, R. "Comunicacion y Cultura Transnacionales." Varios. Comunicacion Transnacional, Conflicto Political y Cultural, July 1982. Lima, Peru: DESCO-ILET, 1982b.

Roncagliolo, R. "El NOMIC: Comunicacion y Poder Interncionals." Paper presented at First International Forum on Communication and Power, Lima, Peru: 1982c. This is an earlier version of Roncagliolo, 1982d.

Roncagliolo, R. "El NOMIC: Comunicacion y Poder." Chasqui—Latin American Journal of Communication, No. 3, 1982d.

Roncagliolo, R. "A NOMIC: Contra-Informacao e Democracia a Partir do Terceiro Mundo." In L. da Silva and E. Eduardo, eds., *Comunicacao Hegemonia e Contra-Informacao.* São Paulo, Brazil: Cortez Editora—INTERCOM, 1982e. This is another version of Roncagliolo, 1982d.

Schenkel, P., et al. *Politicas Nacionales de Comunicacion.* Quito, Ecuador: CIESPAL, 1981.

Roncagliolo, Rafael. "New Information Order in Latin America: A Taxonomy for National Communication Policies." In Jörg Becker, Göran Hedebro and Leena Paldán, eds., *Communication and Domination: Essays to Honor Herbert I. Schiller.* Norwood, New Jersey: Ablex Publishing Corp., 1986. Reprinted with permission.

EXCERPT FROM:

THE APPLICATION OF
PARTICIPATORY ACTION RESEARCH
IN LATIN AMERICA

By Orlando Fals-Borda

1987 Interest in participatory action research (PAR) has grown worldwide due to its pertinence to the initiation and promotion of radical changes at the grassroots level, where unsolved economic, political and social problems have been accumulating to a dangerous potential. PAR claims to further change processes in constructive nonviolent ways due to its emphases on awareness-building processes, although it does anticipate revolutionary action in cases of collective frustrations or belligerent reactionary violence applied at base levels and groups.

Such processes of radical change include: scientific research, adult education and political action. That it can be done has been ascertained through a series of studies undertaken in many Third World countries by local scholars and activists. In Colombia, PAR studies started in the 1970s on the Atlantic Coast, where further work has been completed in recent years. Some of these studies were sponsored by Canada's International Development Research Center (IDRC) and Bogotá's Punta de Lanza Foundation. Their results are now in published under the title *Historia Doble de la Costa (The Double History of the Coast)* in four volumes (Fals-Borda, 1979-1986).

The title of this work suggests something about PAR methodology. It is a "double history" because it is written in two styles, or languages, which run simultaneously on opposite pages: one for the non-initiated reader, (presented in literary form), and the other for professional training (presented in conceptual and theoretical terms) as a sociological interpretation of the literary text. The purpose of this dual style is to assure common understanding of analytical messages and to raise levels of consciousness. The double history now used frequently by people concerned with progress and development on the Atlantic Coast and elsewhere.

Another recent attempt has involved the comparative field approach with PAR. This had never been done until 1982, when teams of researchers applied the same frame of reference in their respective countries (Nicaragua, Colombia and Mexico) among tri-racial rural communities. This effort, under the sponsorship of the International Labour Organisation Office (ILO) (Employment and Development Department, Geneva) was published in book form (Fals-Borda, 1985) with the title, *Conocimiento y poder popular: Lecciones con campesinos de Nicaragua, Colombia y Mexico (Knowledge and People's Power: Lessons with Peasants in Nicaragua, Colombia and Mexico).* (An English version is being published by The Indian Social Institute, New Delhi).

The coastal IDRC research, as well as the comparative International Labor Organisation (ILO) study with PAR, have helped in clarifying basic methodological and technical issues related to this type of work with and for grassroots units. They confirmed that PAR, as stated above, is not exclusively research oriented, nor limited only to adult education or political action. It encompasses all these aspects as three stages or emphases, not necessarily consecutive. They are combined into an experiential methodology, a process of personal and collective behaviour, occurring within a satisfying and productive cycle of life and labour. This experiential methodology for life and labour implies the acquisition of serious and reliable knowledge upon which to construct power for the poor and exploited social groups and their authentic organisations. In this connection, "people's power" may be defined as the capacity of the grassroots groups, that are exploited socially and economically, to articulate and systematise knowledge (both their own and that which comes from outside) in such a way that they can become protagonists in the advancement of their society and in defenders of their own class and group interests.

1927
1960
1963
1964
1967
1969
1970
1971
1972
1973
1974
1975
1976
1977
1978
1979
1980
1981
1982
1983
1984
1985
1986
1987
1988
1989
1990
1991
1992
1993
1994
1995
1996
1997
1998
1999
2000
2001
2002
2003
2004
2005
2006

The goals of this combination of knowledge and power are: (1) to enable the oppressed groups and classes to acquire sufficient creative and transforming leverage as expressed in specific projects, acts and struggles; and (2) to produce and develop sociopolitical thought processes with which popular bases can identity. The evaluation of these goals is done in practice by examining the results obtained in PAR projects, not by abstract reasoning or rules.

It is obvious that these goals go beyond academic traditions, which emphasize value neutrality and positivist objectivity as prerequisites for serious science. PAR does not negate the need for discipline and continuity in accumulating and systematising knowledge, and it hopes to draw such qualities from academe. However, it would promote a reorientation in theoretical terms that would lead into more integrated academic and popular, or commonsensical knowledge, so that a new type of revolutionary science (in Kuhnian terms) becomes a real possibility, not only a felt necessity. As this is still in the making, the polemical nature of such a possibility is readily granted… .

Within such polemics and limitations, the application of this methodology for productive life and labour in Mexican, Nicaraguan and Colombian rural communities in recent years has allowed progress to be made in the examination of important theoretical problems: (1) the influence that perception of reality and the contemporary world has on personal and collective everyday behaviour; (2) the effects that people's conscious struggles may have on improving existing standards of life and labour and (3) in order to accomplish, defend and promote revolutionary changes in society through internal and external mechanisms of countervailing power exercised against exploitative systems.

Obviously, distinctions must be taken into account between the revolutionary condition of Nicaragua and the representative democracies of Mexico and Colombia, even though these democratic systems are in crisis. The PAR approach has proved to be supportive of the Nicaraguan Revolution, an indication that

the latter's cultural, social and economic components have replication and projection value elsewhere on the continent.

However timely, this is not a new discovery. The recent shared experience with PAR in the three countries (and elsewhere) underlines the importance of two general issues concerning the establishment and exercise of people's power in fieldwork and adult education: (1) how to interact and organise for such purposes; and (2) how to recognise oneself and to learn in such contexts.

At first glance it may appear that there is nothing new in these issues. …

The main difference lies in their ontological conceptions. Development discourse, as is well known—Foucault's thesis of the archaeology of knowledge can help us in this respect—involves dealing with the concepts of poverty, technology, capital, growth, values and so forth, as defined from the standpoint of rich, developed countries, where in fact the concept of development was first proposed. This discourse was organised into a coherent intellectual whole for the purpose of rationalising and defending the worldwide dominance of those rich and powerful societies.

The participatory discourse, or counter-discourse, on the other hand, initiated in the Third World—quite probably as dialectical response to the actions of the developed world—postulates an organisation and structure of knowledge in such a way that the dominated, underdeveloped societies articulate their own sociopolitical position on the basis of their own values and capacities. They act accordingly to achieve liberation from the oppressive and exploitative forms of domination imposed by opulent (capitalist) foreign powers and local consular elites, and thus create a more satisfactory life for everyone. In this way, a more human…world outlook can be fashioned.

Such creative balance, or positive confrontation, may be necessary today in order to halt the destructive forces being unleashed in the world though not, of course, by the wishes of the poor and the destitute: the arrogant arms race; flagrant injustices, squandering and egotistical oligarchies; monopolistic trends; rampant abuse of nature and human excesses. PAR can make an important contribution…when knowledge and action combine for social progress.

Participation and Organisation

The first lesson—learning to interact and organise—is based on the existential concept of "vivencia" (experience or "Erlehnis") proposed by the Spanish philosopher José Ortega y Gasset. By actually experiencing something, we intuitively apprehend its essence: we feel, enjoy and understand it as reality, and we thereby place our own being in a wider, more fulfilling context. In PAR such an experience is complemented by another one: that of "authentic commitment" deriving from historical materialism and classic Marxism (Eleventh Thesis on Feuerbach: "Philosophers should not be content with just explaining the world, but should try to transform it".)

The combination of experience and commitment allows us to decide for whom knowledge is intended: the base groups themselves. Moreover, such a concept recognises that there are two types of facilitators or agents of change: those that are external, and those internal to the exploited classes and units. Both types of agents are unified in the same purpose (telos)—that of achieving the shared goals of social transformation.

Both types of facilitators (internal and external) contribute their own knowledge, techniques and experiences to the transformation process. Since elements of knowledge result from different class formations and rationalities (one Cartesian and academic, the other experiential and practical) a "dialectical tension" is created between them that can be resolved only through practical commitment, that is, through "praxis." But the sum of knowledge from both types of agents permits the acquisition of a much more accurate and correct picture of the reality that we want to transform. Academic knowledge, plus popular knowledge and

wisdom, may result in total scientific knowledge of a revolutionary nature (and perhaps another paradigm) that destroys the previous unjust class monopoly.

This dialectical tension in praxis leads to the rejection of the asymmetry implied in the subject/object relationship that characterises traditional academic research and most tasks of daily life. According to participatory theory, such a relationship must be transformed into a subject/subject one. Indeed, the destruction of the *asymmetric binomial* is the kernel of the concept of participation as understood in the present context and in other aspects of the daily routine (family, health, education, politics, etc).

Thus "to participate" means to break up voluntarily and, through experience, the asymmetrical relationship of submission and dependence implicit in the subject/object binomial. Such is its authentic essence.

Let us review one example from fieldwork related to these concepts. The Coordination Commission of El Regadio (Nicaragua), which was set up at the beginning of our research, had to become fully acquainted with the research, ensure that the census of the community was properly carried out and help in the analysis and correction of its results. The researchers noted that members of the Commission began to complain of headaches, backaches, stiff necks, etc. precisely when greater intellectual reflection was required. The latent intention was that the external facilitators should supply the "correct answers." As they did not lend themselves to such purposes, tense moments of silence arose as the members of the Commission waited for the answer, or indulged in trivial conversation and jokes.

If they had adopted other guidelines on research and action, our researchers could easily have assumed the role of indispensable leaders normally expected by the peasants of El Regadio. However, the facilitators insisted that the peasants should analyse their own patterns for dependency, authoritarianism and paternalism inherited from the traditional

1927
1960
1963
1964
1967
1969
1970
1971
1972
1973
1974
1975
1976
1977
1978
1979
1980
1981
1982
1983
1984
1985
1986
1987
1988
1989
1990
1991
1992
1993
1994
1995
1996
1997
1998
1999
2000
2001
2002
2003
2004
2005
2006

exploitation systems of the past, which continued to flourish there despite the revolution of 19 July 1979. Together with the results of the census, this historical and social self-analysis offered the community another excellent opportunity to take a look at itself. It was the first time that the inhabitants had done this, and so their history acquired a "face of its own" in a process similar to that which had occurred among the Otomis of El Mezquital (Mexico). In this way the process of change in El Regadio became more dynamic and the people could undertake new tasks for their own development with more effectiveness and confidence.

If the old habits of submission and dependency had not been broken in El Regadio, the community census would have failed because the interviewees would have given false answers. Resistance and suspicion disappeared when it was seen that the interviewers themselves were from the community and were trained "in situ" by facilitators (using socio-dramas among other techniques), thus establishing a direct subject-to-subject relationship. "If people from other places had come to do it, the investigation would have failed because there are persons here who believe that most outsiders come just to steal," the Commission rightly concluded.

In the case of Nicaragua there was no difficulty in training community cadres and interviewers in "simple methods" of registering, counting, collecting and analyzing data. Thus the concept of "research" was demystified. It was no longer seen as something magical or difficult, as if it were an exclusive monopoly of "experts" and "academics." The demystification of research and its replacement by subject-to-subject analysis also occurred in Puerto Tejada (Colombia) when the housing conditions of the poor were examined. This process strengthened the confidence of the communities to get on with the task of asserting their claims. Nevertheless, care had to be taken that the newly trained cadres did not adopt the superior attitudes of exploitation. There was resistance on the part of local groups to "founding a party," something

which they had seen fail so many times before in regional capitols, when decisions were made by intellectuals cut off from their base.

Upholding the organisational and interactive focus of PAR, the mechanisms of people's countervailing power can also reach the international level. Indeed, there already exist in several world capitols important support institutions for this type of work that respond to this special, and unexpected, challenge from the Third World. They are nongovernmental organisations, private foundations, sympathetic ministries, ecclesiastical bodies, alert United Nations agencies whose positive support calls for an awareness on the part of participatory researchers to preserve the freshness of the PAR approach as an original input from the world's periphery.

Moreover, many writers and thinkers from the dominant countries are also responding to the need to understand these new intellectual and political trends that coming from the world periphery and harmonise them with their own schemes of explanation and action. Hence the contributions of work on historical economic theory (Feder, 1976; Frank, 1978; Barraclough, 1982); the countercurrents in the sciences (Capra, 1983; Berman, 1981; Nowotny, 1978), the new emphasis on political processes from the bottom up (Gran, 1983; Wolfe, 1981; Pitt, 1976; Galtung, 1980; Castells, 1985); critical epistemology (Oquist, 1978; Moser, 1982); applied hermeneutics (Himmelstrand, 1978); radical adult education (Hall, 1977; de Schutter, 1981; Swantz, 1980); problem-oriented social science (Pearse, 1980; Taussig, 1986; Comstock, 1982; Goulet, 1977); and the convergent work on social intervention and action (Touraine, 1978), as well as on world systems versus dependence theories (Wallerstein, 1979; Seers, 1981).

Perhaps we have all been drawing closer, each in his or her own way in the face of scientific, political and moral crises facing the world today, towards the expression of a new kind of sociopolitical discourse based on revalued concepts such as participation, endogeny regionalism and power. We have tried to define them in this study, in ways that such concepts might supersede the current concepts of development, underdevelopment, integrated rural development, nationality, and growth per sales excellence. These concepts have dominated international literature since at least 1949, supporting views of rich countries, which are now in crisi.

Techniques for Knowledge and Power

The second lesson suggests the experience of learning, including of creating people's power—has a certain, phenomenological basis.

It starts with the thesis that science is not a fetish with a life of its own, or something that has an absolute value. As amply demonstrated science is a cultural product with specific human purposes and implicitly carries those class biases and values that scientists hold as a group. It favours those who produce and control it. Its present institutionalised development may, in fact, be developing into a phase that threatens humanity. It is theoretically possible to conceive of alternative ways of science, such as a people's science, to exist as an endogenous process. People's science may be formally constructed in its own terms, and perhaps it can serve as a corrective to certain destructive tendencies of the predominant inhuman forms of science. In people's science knowledge acquired and properly systematised, serves the interests of the exploited classes. This people's science would converge with the so-called "universal science" of academe to the point where a totalising paradigm would be created that would incorporate the newly acquired, systematised knowledge.

Under such conditions, it is obvious that "forms and relationships of knowledge production" should have as much, or even more, value as forms and relationships of material production. As Anisur Rahman, M.D., (1985) has pointed out, the culmination of exploitation patterns at the material or infrastructural level of a society does not assure by itself that the general system of exploitation has been destroyed or that poverty, ignorance and injustice have been overcome. It becomes necessary to also eliminate the relationship governing the production of knowledge, production that tends to give ideological support to injustice, oppression and the destructive forces that characterise the modern world. It is only in this manner that the classic Baconian axiom, "Knowledge is power" can be fully understood; when the exploited classes require such an understanding that they take a decisive step not only towards their own "liberation," but towards that of the other social classes threatened with global destruction.

This creative process of responsible all-embracing and useful knowledge-making does not take as its point of insertion the pedagogical method implied in the early Freire treatises, but dialogical research oriented to the social situation in which people live. For this reason, it begins with the question "Why is there poverty?" the answer to which may lead simultaneously to greater awareness, social research and political praxis.

Ideally, in such cases, people who live at grassroots levels should be able to participate in the research process from the very beginning, that is, from the moment it is decided what the subject of research will be. And they should remain involved at every step of the process until the publication of results and the various forms of returning the knowledge to the people are completed.

Such participatory approaches gives precedence to qualitative, rather than quantitative analysis, without losing sight of the importance of explanatory scientific schemas of cause and effect. Participatory researchers have faced the dilemmas of employing affective logic involving the heart versus dialectical logic with cold-hearted laboratory analysis. As a rule we have followed Pascal's dictum: "The heart has its reasons which the reason does not at all perceive," much as in William Bateson's ideal that scientific work can reach its highest point when it aspires to art (ed. Berman, 1981: 197). If emotion and reason have their own precise algorithms, their discovery is not beyond human understanding. Two examples of heart and reason working together include church music logic and men of letters and aesthetics who have been able to "think the heart," as

1927
1960
1963
1964
1967
1969
1970
1971
1972
1973
1974
1975
1976
1977
1978
1979
1980
1981
1982
1983
1984
1985
1986
1987
1988
1989
1990
1991
1992
1993
1994
1995
1996
1997
1998
1999
2000
2001
2002
2003
2004
2005
2006

explained by Hofmannsthal, Gide, Mann, and Einstein, Russell and Whitehead *Principia Mathematica*.

Our Mexico, Nicaragua and Colombia experiences indicated that the following *techniques* resulting from the practice of PAR are useful in the establishment of people's countervailing power and in aiding adult education.

1. ***Collective research:*** This is the systematic use of information collected and systematised on a group basis, as a source of data and objective knowledge of facts resulting from meetings, socio-dramas, public assemblies, committees, fact-finding trips, etc. This collective and dialogical method not only produces data that may be immediately corrected or verified, but also provides a social validation of objective knowledge, which cannot be achieved through individual methods based on surveys or fieldwork. In this way, confirmation is obtained of the positive values of dialogue, discussion, and consensus in the objective investigation of social realities.

Let us give some illustrations of this technique:

People's assemblies in Puerto Tejada were held at least 20 times. They became a sort of social arena in which the people discovered themselves and their history. There were several modes in such collective recognition:

■ that of individuals as acting and thinking people,
■ the past in relation to the present,
■ the legitimacy of the struggle to destroy the bourgeois values of crime and sin,
■ the causes of injustice and exploitation and the identification of those responsible,
■ the people's capacity to decide, act and transform themselves collectively.

The assemblies became a sort of "public trial" in which the people acted as judge and where the proceedings addressed the reasons for injustice. Evidence was presented to the assemblies in the form of witness accounts, documents, technical opinion from friendly experts and others, on the basis of which the sugar planters were indicted and ordered to return the land they had abusively taken. In this dynamic way the people of Puerto Tejada took over for themselves a well-known bourgeois ritual and gave it a different meaning and content.

The combination of study and practice, when done in this collective and dialogical way, implies the idea of service to the community. It is altruistic knowledge. Thus in El Mezquital, the inhabitants hoped that the outside investigators "would show the people how their training could be applied to the problems of 'real life.'" This expectation was closely connected with the Indian communal tradition. In this way, (1) the periodicity of meeting increased; (2) communal first-aid kits, maize mills, and family kitchen gardens were established; (3) defective wells were repaired; (4) buildings were roofed; (5) pine trees planted in school yards.

The same effects, at another level, were seen in the "census data socialization," meetings which took place in El Regadio. Through comments and analysis at these meetings the people not only corrected the data and filled in the gaps (they knew each other quite well) but also gave meaning to the collected information, so that the successive steps of the economic and political development of this region could then be established (see Fals-Borda, 1985 for details of this process).

The final work on the local history of El Cerrico (Colombia) was another collective experience that was indispensable for the proper completion of the task. All the inhabitants were summoned to listen to the first draft of the text. It was there—with some persons answering and others correcting—that the final orderly and polished text emerged, and was then sent to the printers as part of the local PAR experience.

2. ***Critical recovery of history***. This is an effort to discover selectively, through collective memory, those elements of the past which increased awareness. Use is made of oral tradition, in the form of interviews and witness accounts by older members of the community who possess good analytical memories; the search for

concrete information on given periods of the past kept in family coffers; data columns and popular stories; by ideological projections, imputation, personification and other techniques designed to stimulate the collective memory. In this way, folk heroes, data and facts were discovered that corrected, complemented or clarified official or academic accounts written with other class interests or biases in mind. Or, completely new and fresh information was discovered which was of major importance to regional and national history, all with the purpose of upholding the people's power.

In the case of Puerto Tejada, pertinent historical results became quickly evident. The first attempts at critical recollection during the communal forum saw the reemergence of an ideal of freedom dating back to the time of the courageous runaway black slaves who had colonised the neighbouring region of La Perezosa on the Palo River. It was a recollection that had been repressed by subsequent exploitation, when the whites established their cattle ranches and extended them by violence, destroying the free, black villages that had thrived in that region.

But the feeling of being free, which had characterised the old Palo villages, reemerged in unexpected ways during the forum. It was as if a sleeping volcano had suddenly become active. Some elders recalled the life of authentic heroes of the region like Crucito (a local Robin Hood), Fidel and José Ignacio Mina (Sinecio), Sixto and Ciro Biáfara, and Natanael Diaz. All were exceptional crusaders who had fought since the beginning of the present century for the possession of land for blacks, which the estate owners still wanted to wrest from the people. They were indeed real men who knew how to value their freedom! By comparison, the present situation of town life was hateful and incomprehensible. Critical collective memory called for something more concrete to be done to correct such injustices, because if their grandparents had been able to fight the "whites" before with relative success, why could they not also? History thus gained a new meaning from these new glimpses of truth and

power people discovered that not only could the facts be remembered, but that they could also be catapulted to improve communal life.

The notion of a free settlement for descendants of former slaves reemerged and became an ideal of freedom for the entire Northern Cauca. That was not all. As cocoa had been the principal product for trade and economic survival during that heroic period, the cocoa plant became the local symbol of freedom. At the same time, its historical counter-symbol –sugar—was positioned negatively sugar was a sign of evil, represented by the plantation owners who were destroying the traditional ways of life by taking over the land of the peasants.

In the same fashion, Don Silvestre in El Cerrito (Colombia), together with other elders, became one of the few sources of trustworthy historical facts about the region. His inimitable stories explained how the village was founded on the shores of a lagoon, with recognised legal rights to the use of the fertile plains where staple crops were grown. Formal law protected the peasants, although it was constantly ignored by the powerful landowners of Cordoba who wanted to increase their herds selfishly. They wanted the same territory as the peasants.

The struggle had begun decades ago, towards the end of the last century and the beginning of the present century. Its sparks did not spare the new hamlet of El Cerrito. It was history which had been forgotten and buried, until 1972, when a piece of participatory research was carried out with the then powerful peasant movement. Some of the heroes and heroines who had defended the interests of the working classes during the 1920s, were fortunately still alive: Juana Julia Guzman, among others, who was now old, poor and sick. She had worked shoulder-to-shoulder since 1918 with Vicente Adamo, an immigrant Italian labourer who organised the first workers' struggles in Monteria and its surrounding districts.

Juana Julia held the key to the critical, untapped historical knowledge of those years. She had not wanted

1927
1960
1963
1964
1967
1969
1970
1971
1972
1973
1974
1975
1976
1977
1978
1979
1980
1981
1982
1983
1984
1985
1986
1987
1988
1989
1990
1991
1992
1993
1994
1995
1996
1997
1998
1999
2000
2001
2002
2003
2004
2005
2006

to share it with local conservative or liberal politicians who constantly urged her to tell her story. She only relented when she saw that her own class had reemerged in the peasant movement that had inspired her in her youth she took part herself in the new struggle, attending meetings and assemblies along with the others. Juana Julia's presence at the peasant meetings was like seeing history in the flesh. In these special circumstances, her word carried the additional magic of real experience and the weight of the exciting first defeat of coastal landowners. It can be said that the rediscovery of Juana Julia (and other contemporary figures) was one of the ideological factors that most stimulated the land struggles between 1970 and 1976 in Córdoba. The legal possession of the marshes and lagoons by the people was, at last, established in El Cerrito through pressure by the peasants on the Colombia Institute of Agrarian Reform (INCORA).

Another advantage gained from the "rediscovery" of Juana Julia Guzmán was that she also opened the coffers where she kept the material souvenirs of her past struggles. In spite of the ravages of time and dampness, the coffers contained the first treasures of a genuine people's museum: silk armbands with the "three eights" (a socialist aspiration of the period); pictures of Adamo, the Monteria Workers' House, and the first public hospital; a list of members of the first organised trade unions. They were indispensable elements (we call them "data columns") to understand past events—the antecedents of the present struggle carried on by the grandchildren of those who figured in the old, yellow documents or in the faded photographs of an epoch resurrected from the past in these family coffers.

All this systematic research activity carried out in collaboration with the local people—with data columns, the recovery of popular figures and heroes, ideological projections, imputations and personifications—took place outside academic institutions. Official and academic historians had completely ignored the existence of Vicente Adamo and the socialist workers' organisations of the 1920s. But this grassroots corrector of official

history completed and illustrated it in a critical manner, putting it in the service of poor people so that they, too, could acquire a respectable identity and a collective ego through recognition of their tradition and their own history. The PAR ideal of opening new ideological and scientific perspectives of popular origin in the Atlantic coast of Colombia was thus fulfilled. The same happened in Mexico and Nicaragua, as well.

3. *Valuing and applying folk culture*. In order to mobilise the masses, this technique recognizes essential or core values among the people in each region. Values are often displayed through cultural and ethnic expression often ignored in regular political practice and allow account to be taken of cultural and ethnic elements frequently ignored in regular political practice. Art, music, drama, sports, myths, storytelling and other cultural expressions as highlighted.

Two social groups have distinguished themselves in Nicaragua by their enthusiastic and loyal dedication to the onerous revolutionary tasks: women and young teachers, that is, those young people with a minimum level of education who have only recently become literate. This is understandable. They are among the most haunted victims of the economic and social systems that dominate most of the world and who have found, in the revolutionary adventure, a genuine outlet for their creativity.... .

In El Regadio, women were considered dolls, good for making tortillas and cooking beans. Hardly anyone recognised their important role as "anchors" in society, although they were the centre and often the main support for their families. But with the revolution, women found in the educational committees a way of leaving home and kitchen. They discovered how to break their routine and organise themselves to defend their interests. They began to speak about important matters, such as how to overcome poverty. Their task was to transform the CEPs into something more productive, such as a sewing class, for example, use the proceeds to acquire sewing machine that the community would share. Debates of this kind could finish in "subversive" talk, as happened with the subject of machismo in public dances. How was it that married men, but not married women, could go alone to these dances? Armed with this dynamic and critical approach to such double moral standards, Nicaraguan peasant women became a motor for social and revolutionary change, and displayed an almost monopolistic activism in the new processes.

For their part, recently literate young Nicaraguans have experienced a spiritual elation that has made them more altruistic than before. They dedicate themselves to the educational campaigns with "body and soul." For them, there are no fixed timetables or family duties. Their spirit of sacrifice is absolute. They are the driving force of the revolutionary wheel. As they are tempted to make pupils feel the weight of their newly found knowledge—their newly acquired authority as teacher of the people—and to become somewhat domineering.

However, in this they are simply imitating the oppressive educational models they had seen applied before in the local school or nearest village. In such cases, they fail to break the subject/object binominal and prefer to bully adult pupils who cannot understand, let us say, what the stress is. But imagination can come quickly to their aid, by recourse to shared experiences. Then they can explain that the stress in any given word is like a "triple play" in baseball. Everyone can understand this and proceed to the next lesson.

Through such "feelings," it is possible to understand the primal forces of people's culture and symbols. They are like an affective logic. Ño Didacio expressed the idea: "Negro culture is not just a culture of evocation; it is not a question of memory, but of feelings." His sentiments led him to revive the old "dance of the knives," a half-dead musical folk expression the meaning of which could only be recaptured in the mobilising context of the People's Civic Movement of Northern Cauca, with its challenge to the municipal bosses. Through the importance it attached to local culture in this way, the movement experienced

the greatest political gains of its short history. It had managed to give voice to the soul of the people.

Another important activity recoverable for action through research—at least among the coastal people of Colombia—is that of storytelling tales, legends, parables, fables, anecdotes, riddles and puns. Even refined gossip, viewed as information, may be useful as a means of positive mobilization. All these elements of oral culture may be exploited as a new and dynamic political language which belongs to the people, as we saw in El Cerrito and Puerto Tejada, especially those forms that already contain an implicit protest intention. This is the case, for example, with the well-known tales of "Uncle Tiger and Uncle Rabbit". These stores narrate the impudence and skills of a defenseless little animal (the peasant) confronted with a dangerous beast (the boss) and display a powerful sense of latent resistance against the injustices characterizing the production relationship. In Colombia (as in other regions), storytelling and other expressions of oral tradition are among the most effective ways of keeping alive the people's culture and their core values. Storytelling refuses to die because, if it did, the peasant people would die with it.

The cultural processes operating within the heart of the community are an active force, allowing people's knowledge to ferment in a vast cauldron or melting pot, and building up the incredible resources of resistance characterizes the popular struggles in the three countries.

Feelings, imagination and the sense of play are apparently inexhaustible sources of strength and resistance among the people. These three elements have a common basis, which cannot be ignored in the struggle to promote mobilisation and people's power in our countries: religious beliefs. Here are some examples:

1. The death of a child during the invasion of the sugar plantations outside Puerto Tejada and the bravery of the child's mother—together with the practices and beliefs implicit during the funeral—were events that stopped the army in its tracks

1927
1960
1963
1964
1967
1969
1970
1971
1972
1973
1974
1975
1976
1977
1978
1979
1980
1981
1982
1983
1984
1985
1986
1987
1988
1989
1990
1991
1992
1993
1994
1995
1996
1997
1998
1999
2000
2001
2002
2003
2004
2005
2006

when soldiers attempted to occupy and burn the huts of the new district. The spectre of the "little angel" lying dead and the hypnotic rhythm of the "alabao" (ritual music), more than the presence of the national flag which had been hoisted there, made the troops respect the invasion.

2. A witch added secret power to the fight against a landowner who did not want to give up his excess land to the peasants of Córdoba. The witch's service must have been effective judging by the eventual success, and his support had an important moral and psychological effect among the popular masses. Another witch is still being consulted in Villapaz, not far from Puerto Tejada, to see if the course of a river can be changed so as to preserve public land and avoid floods, objectives of a new local civic movement.

…All this and much more can and should be examined and better understood with a view to establishing countervailing action. If the basic culture and values of the peasants are selectively harnessed for the popular struggle, and if negative alienation is properly contained, an unconquerable force is created which leads to the establishment of an authentic and deep-rooted people's power based on imagination and feelings, capable of transforming unjust structures of the dominant society.

4. *Production and diffusion of new knowledge*. This technique is an integral part of the research process because it is a central part of the feedback and evaluative objective of PAR. It recognises a division of labour among and within base groups. Although PAR strives to end the monopoly of the written word (which as a rule is an elitist phenomenon), it incorporates various styles and procedures for capturing new data and knowledge according to the level of political conscience and ability for understanding written, oral or visual messages by the base groups and public in general.

These four categories are useful when working with diverse people from preliterate to intellectuals. A good PAR researcher should learn to address all four levels

with the same message in the different styles required, if he or she is to be really effective.… .

Other efficient forms of communication based on a total or intentional language include: the use of image, sound, painting, gestures, mime, photographs, radio programmes, popular theatre, videotapes, audiovisual material, poetry, music, puppets and exhibitions. It is also useful to work at economic and social action organizing by community groups such as cooperatives, trade unions, leagues, cultural centres, action units, workshops, training centres, etc.

There is always an obligation to return knowledge to the communities and workers' organisations because they continue to be its owners. They may determine the priorities concerning its use and authorise and establish the conditions for its publication and dissemination.

This devolution of knowledge complies with Garmsci's objective of transforming "common sense" into "good sense," or critical knowledge ("revolutionary science" as a new paradigm) which would be the sum of experiential and theoretical knowledge. It transcends Mao Tse Tung's principle of "from the masses to the masses" in that it recognises the capacity of the masses to systematise the data discovered, that is, to participate fully in the entire process, with their own organic intellectuals from the beginning to the end.

To succeed in these endeavours requires a shared communication code between internal elements and external agents of change, leading to a common and mutually understandable conceptualisation and categorisation. The resulting plain and understandable language should be based on daily intentional expressions and be accessible to all.… .

These PAR techniques do not exclude a flexible use of other practices deriving from sociological and anthropological tradition such as: the open interview (avoiding any excessively rigid structure), census or simple survey (on rare occasions mail questionnaires), direct systematic observation (with personal participation and selective experimentations), field diaries, data filing, photography, cartography, statistics, sound recordings, primary and secondary source materials, notarial, regional and national archives. Teams ("resource persons") should not only be equipped to handle these orthodox techniques responsibly but also know how to popularise them by teaching the activists simpler, more economic and controllable methods of research, so the activists can carry on their work without being dependent on intellectuals or external agents of change with their costly equipment and procedures.

With all these ways and techniques, advancement and transformation of oppressed peoples can be made possible in several applied fields: in adult education, in political and civic action, in socioeconomic advancement and other types of fieldwork. Additional current experiences are enriching this approach and challenging academic ways in established institutions. In this manner, perhaps PAR may contribute to help build a better world for everybody with justice and peace.

References

Fals-Borda, O. "The Application of Participatory Action Research In Latin America." Sage, *International Sociology*, December 1987, Vol. 2., No. 4: 329-347.

Barraclough. *A Preliminary Analysis of the Nicaraguan Food System*. Geneva: UNRISD, 1982.

Berman, M. *The Reenchantment of the World*. Ithaca, New York: Cornell University Press, 1981.

Capra, F. *The Turning Point*. New York: Bantam, 1983.

Catells, M. "Urban Problems and Social Change." In O. Fals-Borda, ed., *The Challenge of Social Change*. London: Sage, 1985.

Comstock, D. E. *Participatory Research as Critical Theory*, The North Bonneville, U.S.A., Experience." Paper presented at Evergreen State College, Olympia, Washington, 1982.

De Schutter, A. *Investigación Participativa: Una Opción Metodológica*. Pátzcuaro, México: Crefal, 1981.

Fals-Borda, O. *Historia Doble de la Costa*. Bogotá, Colombia: Carlos Valencia Editores, 1979-1986, Vols. 1-4.

Fals-Borda, O. *Conocimiento y Poder Popular: Lecciones con Campesinos de Nicaragua, Colombia y México*. Madri, México: Siglo XXI Editores, 1985.

Feder, E. *Strawberry Imperialism*. The Hague, Netherlands: Institute of Social Studies, 1976.

Frank, A. G. *Dependent Accumulation and Underdevelopment*. London: Macmillan, 1978.

Galtung, J. *Self-Reliance: A New Development Strategy?* London: Bogle-L'Ouverture, 1980.

Goulet, D. *The Uncertain Promise*. New York: IDOC, 1977.

Gran, G. *Development by People*. New York: Praeger, 1983.

Hall, B., and A. Gillette. *Participatory Research*. Toronto: International Council for Adult Education, 1977.

Himmeltrand, U. "Action Research and Applied Social Science." In Punta de Lanza, ed., *Crítica y Política en Ciencias Sociales*. Bogotá, Colombia: Punta de Lanza, 1978, Vol. 1.

Moser, H. "The Participatory Research Approach on Village Level." Unpublished paper. Münster, Germany: University of Münster, 1982.

Nowotny, H. *Counter-Currents in the Sciences*. Dordrecht, Netherlands: Mouton, 1978.

Oquist, P. "The Epistemology of Action-Research." *Development Dialogue*, 1978, 4: 10-17.

Pearse, A., and M. Stiefel. *Inquiry Into Participation: A Research Approach*. Geneva: UNRISD, 1980.

Pitt, D. *Development From Below*. The Hague, Netherlands: Moutn, 1976.

Rahman, A. "The Theory and Practice of Participatory Action Research." In O. Fals-Borda, ed., *The Challenge of Social Change*. London: Sage, 1985.

Seers, D. *Dependency Theory: A Reassessment*. London: Frances Printer, 1981.

Swantz, M. L. *Rejoinder to Research: Methodology and the Participatory Research Approach*. Dar-es-Salaam, Tanzania: Ministry of National Culture and Youth, 1980.

Taussig. M. *Shamanism, Colonialism and the Wild Man*. Chicago: University of Chicago Press, 1986.

Touraine, A. *La Voix et le Regard*. Paris: Seuil, 1978.

Wallerstein, I. *The Capitalist World Economy*. Cambridge, England: Cambridge University Press, 1979.

Wolfe, M. *Elusive Development*. Geneva: UNRISD, 1981.

1927
1960
1963
1964
1967
1969
1970
1971
1972
1973
1974
1975
1976
1977
1978
1979
1980
1981
1982
1983
1984
1985
1986
1987
1988
1989
1990
1991
1992
1993
1994
1995
1996
1997
1998
1999
2000
2001
2002
2003
2004
2005
2006

TERMS OF THE NEGOTIATION

Excerpt from: Cultural Interaction and Popular Communication

By Alfonso Gumucio-Dagron

1987 Defending "traditionalism" excessively does not have to be the essence of popular culture, as it could be limiting, according to Nestor Garcia Canclini. This view gets to the heart of the problem that separates two tendencies, one "conservative" and the other "liberal" when discussing matters of popular cultures and interaction.

The misunderstanding among conservatives comes from a certain preconceived anthropological idea that rejects any notion of cultural interaction: One would assume, even in a world dominated by technology, that it is possible to protect the popular culture from any contact, hence, sheltering it under a glass bell. This approach stresses a lack of understanding of the problem. Today, what we know about traditional cultures is a result of permanent interaction of cultures. A prime example is the practice of the "scissors" dance in Peru. This is a ritual in which an object is to be transformed into a symbol, here a pair of scissors. Scissors were unknown the Peruvians before the arrival of the Spaniards. When sheltered, popular cultures fade away very quickly, for lack of oxygen or room to expand.

If saving traditional roots is of great importance in asserting popular culture, it should not be done with a conservative approach. "To preserve" means to revitalize, hence, reinforce the cultural identity by underlining not only the ideological aspects of expressions but also their characteristics.

The mythical way of looking at people as both initiators and players when it comes to the term "popular" can limit our thinking. What matters is recognizing in this group, and in its plurality, the legitimacy of its decision making with regards to its own cultural development. This legitimacy wouldn't exist outside crucial opposing forces.

Another extreme stand of the conservative view is to revitalize the analysis of the processes of social interaction assuming that the latter must follow its course "normally" submerged in social evolution. This suggests that the process of negotiation results from a *consensus* between the concerned parties. This position does not exclude the fact that the popular culture emerges from "conflictual result of interaction" but assumes that the conflict will be resolved by an exchange: My splendid feathers for your mirror. In reality, the exchange is even less even.

The idea of consensus is interesting because it implies the denial of paternalist approaches, which establish passive acceptance by one of the parties involved in the exchange. It also reveals a static view of history. It does not take into account the increasing inequity in the process of interaction, since mass communication occupies such an important place in cultures. Moreover, if by chance, the means of communication did not occupy this place (as it is to a certain extent the case in Bolivia, where the influence of television is minimal), one should not lose sight of the fact the trend in this direction is irreversible.

In Latin America, when going through the process of interaction, one of the interlocutors increasingly loses credibility in a significant way. The only possible consensus in these cases is to accept defeat. However, when it comes to popular culture, defeats are not assumed, although accepted. The confusion generated by a doomed negotiation jeopardizes the superstructure that guarantees the process of regeneration and revitalization.

Some researchers underestimate the role of new technologies of mass communication, which are increasingly more sophisticated. The latter tend to make Latin American countries even greater consumers of an overpowering culture, to the detriment of their ability to produce their own cultural assets. In theory,

1927
1960
1963
1964
1967
1969
1970
1971
1972
1973
1974
1975
1976
1977
1978
1979
1980
1981
1982
1983
1984
1985
1986

consumers are not inert or passive subjects, but a summary analysis of the past two last decades indicates that the transnational hegemonic project tends to strip them of critical instruments, to the benefit of cultural fusion, which easily leads to confusion.

The new technologies of communication, increasingly beyond control of the Latin American people, determine new conditions of interaction: Geometric progression of inequality, as a result of hegemonic transnational actions.

In the complex fabric of popular culture in Latin America, the *scars* resulting from the *transaction* seem to come from the war or, at the very least, from the borders that were torn down in the culture. The effect of break-dancing or "Dallas" are quite apparent here, but it is not easy to distinguish the influences of the Carnival of Oruro or the Brazilian Samba, to mention only the two most popular influences.

Gumucio-Dagron, Alfonso. "Interactions Culturelles et Formes Décentralisés de Communication." Published in *Revue Tiers Monde*, t. XXVIII N°111, July-September 1987, p. 586-594. Paris (France). Reprinted with permission of the author.

COMMUNICATION FROM THE PERSPECTIVE OF CULTURE

Excerpt from: Media to Mediation: Communication, Culture and Hegemony

By Jesus Martin-Barbero

1987 For many years in Latin America, the cultural reality of these countries was considered less important than the construction of theoretical certainties. And so we continued on, convinced that the theories had to tell us what communication is—sociological, semiotic or informational theories—for only from that perspective would it be possible to define the limits of the field and determine the specificity of its object. But something in the realities of Latin America moved with such a strong jolt that it produced a collapse of the fragile structures, erasing the boundary lines that had defined the geography of the field and that had given us a kind of psychological security. When the outlines of the "proper object of study of the field" fell apart, we found ourselves face to face with a stormy confusion of realities. But now we were not alone for along the way other people had begun to investigate, work and produce without calling it "communication." These were people from the arts and from politics, architecture and anthropology. We had to lose sight of the "proper object" in order to find the way to social movements in communication, to communication in process.

In Latin America, there have been two stages in the formation of the hegemonic paradigm of communication. The first stage came at the end of the 1960s when Lasswell's model from an epistemological background of psychological behaviourism was poured into the theoretical mould of structuralist semiology, making possible its "conversion," that is, its encounter with critical research. I call this stage "ideologist" because its objective was centred on descriptive discovery and

1987
1988
1989
1990
1991
1992
1993
1994
1995
1996
1997
1998
1999
2000
2001
2002
2003
2004
2005
2006

denunciation. It used epistemological matrices from a politically critical position to discover strategies of the dominant ideology to penetrate communication, or, in its words, to permeate the message and produce specific effects. The omnipotence that the functionalist version attributed to the media was switched over to ideology, making ideology both the object and subject of research and an all-encompassing influence on the discourse of media analysis. This led to an ambiguous reduction of the scope of the field of communication, subsuming it within the study of ideology, but ending up defining its specificity by isolation. Both the mechanism of "effects," in the psychological-behaviourist version, and analysis of the message or text in the semiotic-structuralist version, eventually reduced the meaning of the processes of communication to something inherent to the process. But it was a meaning in a vacuum. When this vacuum was filled by "ideology," we had a skeleton without any flesh—pure communicationism without any specific communication occurring. The best proof of this deficiency is that political denunciation from the perspective of communication almost never went beyond accusations of "exploitation by the system," "manipulation," etc.

The amalgam of communicationism and denunciation produced a schizophrenia that turned into an instrumentalist conception of media, depriving the media of any cultural depth or institutional structure and making the media mere tools of ideological action. To make matters worse, once reduced to an instrumental role, a moral value was attributed to media according to the direction of its use. Media was bad in the hands of reactionary oligarchies and good in the hands of the proletariat. This prevailing belief was carried to even further extremes in some militant circles where the media, because of its original sin of birth under capitalism, was seen as condemned forever to serve its masters. This apocalyptical vision was the only alternative to schizophrenia or, perhaps, it was simply its mirror image. In the end, "ideologization" made it impossible for the study of communication to be anything other than the study of the "tracks of the dominator."

Of no interest were communicative actions of the dominated, far less conflict in communication. A "theological" concept of power—because power was considered omnipotent and omnipresent—led to the belief that by studying the economic and ideological objectives of the mass media it would be possible to know the needs the media generated, and how they controlled consumers. In the analysis of broadcasters-dominators and receivers-dominated there was no suggestion of seduction or resistance, only the passivity of consumption and the alienation detected as inherent within the message-text. And in the texts themselves there was no attempt to look for conflicts or contradictions or, even less, for signs of struggle.

In the mid-1970s another line of thought began to appear, with a discourse that might be summed up with the slogan, "Enough ideology and denunciation! Let's get serious and be scientists." We entered a second stage that might be called "scientism". Now the dominant paradigm was reformed on the basis of an information model, and a positivist revival prohibited calling anything a problem to be studied if it did not have a specific method. The crisis of Latin America after the military coups in the Southern Cone region, and the confusion that followed, provided a fertile chemical culture for the "scientism" blackmail. The ensuing theoretical short-circuit can be described as follows: the processes of communication occupy an increasingly strategic place in our society because information has become a raw material input in production processes and not just an output in circulation. The study of these processes, however, is such a prisoner of scattered disciplinary and methodological approaches that it is impossible to determine with real objectivity what is happening. We are in urgent need, therefore, of a "theory" to organize the field and define the object of study. A theory of this nature is, in fact, right under our noses, but it is too far away from the ideological interests of critical researchers and goes undetected by social critics. This theory lies in the field of engineering and is called "information theory." Defined as the "transmission of information," communication finds in this theory a framework of precise concepts, clear methodological boundaries, and well-defined proposals for research operations —all strongly supported by the "seriousness" of mathematics and the prestige of cybernetics. The information model was an aesthetically pleasing model that thereafter took possession of a field already fertilized by the functionalism surviving in the structuralist proposal and in certain forms of Marxism[1].

If the semiotic model of analysis focusing on messages and codes lacked concepts to embrace the field and establish boundaries without compromising amalgams, the boundaries set by the information model were even more impoverished and left out too many things, not just questions of meaning but also the central issue of power. Untouched by information theory were issues of information as a process of collective behaviour and the conflict of interests struggling to inform, produce, accumulate and deliver information. The consequence of passing over these issues was a failure to pay attention to problems of disinformation and control. By excluding from its analysis the social conditions of the production of meaning, the information model eliminates the study of the struggle for hegemony, that is, the struggle to define the discourses that "articulate" the cultural meanings of a society.

The information model ended up excluding all of these central questions, not as an explicit proposal but because of its assumptions. And it is at the level of these presuppositions that we find the complicity between the semiotic and information models. Both assumed that the two poles of the circuit of communication—sender and receiver—are on the same level and that the message circulates between equals. This conception of communication implies not only a presupposition of the idealist tradition, which has already been questioned by Lacan posing the question of the code as a space of domination disguised as an "encounter," but also the presumptions that the greatest communication occurs with the largest amount of information, and that there is a univocal discourse used by sender and receiver[2]. The model excludes any communication that cannot be reduced or compared to the transmission and measurement of information flow. Ignored is anything that does not fit into a schema of sender, message, receiver—for example, a dance or a religious ritual—and anything that introduces an asymmetry between the codes of sender and receiver, thus challenging the linearity on which the model is based.

Furthermore, this version of the hegemonic paradigm is based on a fragmentation of communication that is sought as a guarantee of scientific rigour and sure criterion of truth. The fragmentation compares or reduces everything to the transmission of information. This makes it methodologically correct to "separate" analysis of the message—content analysis, forms of expression, textual structure, operations of discourse—from analysis of reception, with reception conceived of simply as the study of effects or, with greater sophistication, the analysis of reactions. In either case, fragmentation is a form of control that reduces the range of questions asked, limiting what is considered worthy of study and valid approaches to the analysis of problems.

But the real theoretical confines of this rationalism based on information science reside in its notion of knowledge: "accumulation of information plus classification." This looks upon social contradictions as meaningless because they are considered not as expressions of conflict, but simply as the residues of ambiguity. We find ourselves facing a rationality that dissolves and eliminates the political dimension. For politics are precisely a coming to grips with the opaqueness of social reality as a conflictive and changing process, an attempt to increase the network of mediations, and a struggle for the construction of the meaning of social solidarity. Thus, if the first model concludes with an instrumental conception of the

---

1 For a more detailed discussion of this theme see Martin-Barbero, 1982.

2 This tendency is criticized by Landi (1983), and Lechner 'Información y política: Dos formas de comunicación' (1984).

1927
1960
1963
1964
1967
1969
1970
1971
1972
1973
1974
1975
1976
1977
1978
1979
1980
1981
1982
1983
1984
1985
1986
1987
1988
1989
1990
1991
1992
1993
1994
1995
1996
1997
1998
1999
2000
2001
2002
2003
2004
2005
2006

media, this second ends up in a technocratic dissolution of the political dimension.

If social problems are transformed into technical ones, there is only one possible solution. Instead of a political decision between different possible social objectives, what occurs is a technical and scientific solution regarding the best means to achieve a pre-established end. A public debate is not necessary under these circumstances. You do not have to submit a technical question or a "scientific" truth to a vote. The citizen is replaced by the expert. (Lechner, 1981: 311)

This is where the short circuit closes: the centrality of communication in society means, for rationalistic informatics, the dissolution of political reality.

Culture and Politics:
Fundamental Mediations

It is not only the limits of the versions of the hegemonic model, however, that have made it necessary to look for a new paradigm. The events—the stubborn social processes of Latin America—have, above all, forced us to change the "object" of study in communication research. To perceive the growing pressure toward this shift, one has only to take a glance at the titles of seminars and congresses dealing with communication in Latin America over the last five years and observe the dominating presence of issues such as "transnationalization," "democratization," "culture" and "popular movements." With the introduction of the transnational question, we are not dealing simply with the old problem of imperialism. It is a new phase in the development of capitalism in which communication plays a decisive role. What is now in play is not simply the imposition of an economic model, but a "jump" to the internationalization of a political model. This change makes it necessary to abandon the old concept of the struggle against "dependency," because "the struggle for independence from a colonialist country in direct confrontation with a geographically defined power, is something very different from a struggle for identity within a transnational system that is diffuse with a complex form of global interrelations and

interpenetrations" (Garcia Canclini, 1984c). Because transnationalization is a prime influence in the field of communication technologies such as satellites or computer networks, the question of nationality is located now, to a great extent, in issues of the field of communication. And because these communication issues involving the meaning of nation are so much a part of the processes not only of class conflicts but of ethnic and regional conflicts, the nation has become the focus of increasingly intense civil conflict. These conflicts do not often enter into the framework of traditional political formulas as valid social issues, because the confrontations are giving birth to a series of new social actors whose existence questions the political cultures of both the right and the left.

To what sort of conflicts are we referring? Some of these conflicts are obvious, like high social costs borne by the increasing impoverishment of national economies and the increasing inequality of international economic relations. But we refer especially to other conflicts that new situations are producing or bringing to light, conflicts situated at the intersection of crisis between a new political culture and the new meaning of political cultures. We refer to a new perception of the problem of identity as ambiguous and dangerous as the term seems to be today—of these Latin American countries. For identities are in confrontation not only with the blatant homogenization which comes from transnational expansion, but with another more hidden process of homogenization of national identity that deforms and deactivates the complex mixtures and cultural pluralism that constitutes these countries.

The new perception of identity, in conflict with both transnationalization and the blackmail that national forces often exercise, is part of a movement for radical change in the political sphere that has brought the Latin American left not just to a tactical but also to a strategic concept of democratization, that is, democratization as the central process for social transformation[3].

---

3   Regarding this new concept of democracy, see T. Moulian, in Moulian et al., 1981: 45-61; and Moulian, 1983: 313-37.

Developments today are very different from those behind the left-wing theories and actions up to the mid-1970s—organizations built exclusively around the proletariat, politics of total transformation of society, the denunciation of bourgeois parliaments as a trap (Casullo, 1983; de Ipola and Portantiero, 1984). In the early 1980s another trend has emerged, one closely tied to the "rediscovery of the popular" and its new meaning, a re-evaluation of the articulation and mediations of civil society, and attention to the social meaning of conflicts, beyond their purely political formulation and synthesis. Most importantly, this trend recognizes the political importance of collective experiences outside the traditional parties. What has changed is the conceptualization of "political subjects." The concept of social classes as self-sufficient entities is replaced by a vision of social conflict as a manifestation of the attributes of the actors. Otherwise, the "political process in the strictest sense would not be productive and it would not generate anything substantially new" (Landi, 1983: 14). The relationships of power as they constitute each social formation, however, are not merely expressions of attributes, but products of specific conflicts and battles in the economic and symbolic field. It is here that the digressions that call into existence new subjects and collective identities are articluated. "How can you conceive of political practices," Lechner asks, "outside the ties of collective identity and belonging that we develop daily?" (1984: 26). Once the rationalist conception of social actors as self-subsisting entities is clearly revealed, we also become aware of the fatalistic vision of history that has veiled this instrumentalist conception of politics. Thus, the basic issue is that there does not exist "an objective solution" to the contradictions of capitalistic society. Therefore we have to work out possible alternatives and select the most desirable option. Development is not guided by objective solutions. There is no other way than to continually spell out and decide upon the goals of society. This is what politics is all about. (Lechner, 1984: 19)

Out of the convergence of this new interpretation of transnationalization and the new conception of politics, there has emerged in Latin America a profoundly new evaluation of culture. Some, of course, suspect that this new cultural emphasis is an evasive tactic, covering up an inability to respond to the crisis of political institutions and parties. This suspicion is probably justified in those cases where "one engages in cultural activities when it is not possible to engage in politics." Something radically different occurs, however, when culture points to new dimensions of social conflict, the formation of new sociopolitical actors around regional, religious, sexual and generational identities, and new forms of resistance and rebellion. The reconceptualization of culture brings us face to face with that alternative cultural experience, popular culture, with its multiple forms of existence and its activity not just in memories of the past, but in its conflictive and creative presence in the present. To conceive of communication from the perspective of its role in the formation of cultures implies that one cease to think of communication only in terms of particular disciplines and as a function of media. It marks the end of the security that came from reducing problems of communication to problems of technology.

We come from a field of communication research that for many years paid the price of theoretical legitimacy by being a subsidiary of other disciplines such as psychology or cybernetics. Today the danger is that communications will pay an even higher price to free itself from its subsidiary position: seeing all social and cultural change as simply the result of technological innovation. This would drain communications of all historical specificity and replace it with a radically instrumental concept. The possibility of avoiding this virtual destruction of the field of communications depends on our ability to understand that the "reconversions of the operations of the technological-institutional apparatus depend very largely on the parallel reconversion of the social uses of culture. A conflict until now thought to pertain to the superstructure will now be settled at the level of production institutions"

1927
1960
1963
1964
1967
1969
1970
1971
1972
1973
1974
1975
1976
1977
1978
1979
1980
1981
1982
1983
1984
1985
1986
1987
1988
1989
1990
1991
1992
1993
1994
1995
1996
1997
1998
1999
2000
2001
2002
2003
2004
2005
2006

(Martin Serrano, 1987: 7). Instead of a few simple "communication policies" we need a new political culture capable of addressing what is at stake today in cultural policies. We understand cultural policies not as a question of administration of institutions and the distribution of cultural goods but, rather, as the "principle of the organization of a culture, something internal to the constitution of the political sphere, the space for the production of the meaning of social order, and the principles of mutual recognition in society" (Landi, 1984: 19).

The history of the relationship between politics and culture is full of pitfalls attributable to both sides of the relationship. The problem may be a spiritualist conception of culture which sees politics as contamination or the intrusion of material interests, or it may be a mechanical conception of politics that perceives culture as simply a reflection in the superstructure of what is really happening elsewhere. In both cases, the tendency is to make the relationship an instrumental one.

The truth is that politics tends to suppress culture as a field of interest as soon as it accepts an instrumental vision of power. That is, political power is defined in terms of technical equipment, institutions, arms, control over the means and resources and organizations. Contributing to this vision of power is the inability of politics to take culture seriously, except when it finds culture in quite institutionalized forms. (Brunner, 1985a: 9; see also Brunner, 1985b; Brunner and Catalán, 1985)

From here, it is a logical step to convert cultural policy into a bureaucratic operation run by technocrats. In the last few years in Latin America, however, there is some indication of a new understanding of the relationship between politics and culture. According to Jose Joaquin Brunner, one of the Latin Americans who has contributed significantly to a new vision of cultural policies, there are three indicators of this new understanding. The first has occurred especially in countries under authoritarian regimes, where modes of resistance and opposition arise mainly from groups quite different to those studied in traditional analyses, such as small Christian communities, artistic movements and human rights groups. A second source of new awareness of the role of culture is the perception that the most repressive authoritarianism is not simply brute force and a response to the interests of capitalism. It is also the attempt to change the meaning of everyday social life by modifying the cultural imagination and symbols. A third source is the awareness that, thanks to mass education and the mass media, culture is now at the centre of political and social debate.

This debate has opened up discussion of a series of new problems which redefine the meaning of both culture and politics. The problems of communication have become part of the debate not simply from a quantitative and topical view—the enormous economic strength of the communication industries—but in a qualitative sense, namely, that the processes of redefining a culture are key to comprehending the communicative nature of culture. The importance of communication lies in its capacity to produce meanings and not simply to facilitate a circulation of information. Thus, the receiver in the communication process is not simply a decoder of what the sender has put into the message, but is also a producer of meaning.

Awareness of the profound challenge of the culture industries arises from the intersection of these two paths of advancement—that which locates the cultural question at the heart of political processes, and that which locates communication in culture. For if the return to authoritarian direction is not the answer, much less "can the expansion of plurality of voices in a process of democratization be understood as simply widening the clientele of cultural consumption" (Landi, 1985a: 11). What no longer has any meaning is to continue designating as cultural policies those activities which separate Culture, with a capital C, from what happens in mass cultural industries and the mass media. Mass culture does not demand a separate cultural policy, for what happens culturally to the masses is fundamental for democracy if democracy is going to have something to do with the people.

A Nocturnal Map to Explore a New Field

We know that struggles through cultural mediations do not yield immediate or spectacular results. But it is the only way to ensure we do not move from a sham of hegemony to a sham of democracy; to block the reappearance of a defeated domination installed by hegemony in the complicity of our thoughts and relationships (N. Garcia Canclini).

Once the frontiers of our discipline were moved and we had lost the security set up by our theoretical inertia, we have had no alternative but to follow the advice of Raymond Williams and remake the map of our "basic concepts." I do not think that this is possible, however, without changing the point from which we begin to ask questions. This is the meaning of the recent tendency to formulate questions[4] which transcend "daytime" logic and demand a reorganization of the analytic terrain that moves marginal issues to the centre of our concerns. This does not imply a "carnivalization" of theory[5], but acceptance that these are not times for synthesis and that reason is barely able to understand unexplored areas of reality that are so very near. As Laclau observes, "Today we realize that social history is deeper than our instruments allow us to conceive and beyond what our political strategies can direct" (1981: 59). Not lacking, of course, are tendencies toward an apocalyptic view of events and a return to the doctrine. A silent but even more important tendency is moving in another direction: exploring in tentative almost groping fashion without a guiding map, or with only an obscure, night-time map. This is a map which enables us to study domination, production and labour from the other side of the picture, the side of cracks in domination, the consumption dimensions of economy and the pleasures of life. It is not a map for escape but, rather, one to help us recognize our situation from the perspective of mediations and the subjects of action.

---

4   The expression is taken from Gutierrez and Munizaga, 1983: 25.
5   Used with the meaning attributed by R. Da Matta (1985: 92).

Daily Life, Consumption and an Interpretative Reading

"A market perspective permeates not only society but also the explanations of society" (Durham, 1980: 203). This explains why critical theories have privileged the image of the labourer-producer of merchandise, not only at the moment of understanding the context of production but at the moment of trying to awaken a consciousness of the exploitation in this situation. This tendency of critical theories is not unlike the tendency of most organizations of the left truly concerned with the life of the popular classes: a preoccupation with actions of vindication of rights and movements which unite people for struggle. Everything else—the practices which make up the rhythm of daily life, the ways the popular classes exist and find meaning in life—has tended to be considered an obstacle to conscientization and mobilization for political action.

> Popular conceptions of family are considered conservative; popular traditions are looked upon as fragmentary remains of a rural and precapitalist cultural past; the tastes of the popular classes are molded by the corrupting influence of the mass media; their leisure pastimes are nothing more than escapism; their religiosity, a factor of alienation; and their life plans, no more than frustrated attempts at upward social mobility (Cantor Magnani, 1984: 19).

Forms of daily existence not directly linked with structures of economic production are looked upon as depoliticized, irrelevant and insignificant. Nevertheless, the accounts which begin to describe what happens within the life of popular neighbourhoods, accounts which do not attempt to evaluate but simply to understand the functioning of popular social relations, open up to us another reality. Here - as "scandalous" as it may seem - the attachment of the working classes to family does not appear to be necessarily or, at least, only linked to conservation of the past. Rather, as E. Durham lucidly explained, "this is an attempt to overcome a generalized state of family disorganization

1927
1960
1963
1964
1967
1969
1970
1971
1972
1973
1974
1975
1976
1977
1978
1979
1980
1981
1982
1983
1984
1985
1986
1987
1988
1989
1990
1991
1992
1993
1994
1995
1996
1997
1998
1999
2000
2001
2002
2003
2004
2005
2006

associated with a much more brutal and direct exploitation of the forms of labour" (Durham, 1980: 202).

In the popular perception, the space of domestic activities is not limited to the tasks of reproduction of the labour force. On the contrary, confronted with the monotonous and uncreative workplace, the family allows a minimum of freedom and initiative. In the same way, not all consumption is merely the acceptance of the values of other classes. In the popular sectors consumption expresses just aspirations to a more human and respectful life. Not all search for social betterment is a crass social climbing. It is also a form of protest and an expression of elemental rights. For this reason, it is important to develop a concept of consumption that moves beyond culturalist and reproductionist interpretations and offers a framework for research on communication and culture from the popular perspective. Such a framework would permit comprehension of the different modes of cultural appropriation and the different social uses of communication.

In his various publications in recent years, Garcia Canclini has brought together elements for such a new theoretical perspective (1984a, 1985, 1988). These approaches are close to the concepts of Bourdieu, but broaden them to allow a consideration of praxis and forms of cultural production and transformation within the popular classes of Latin America. We must begin by identifying what we are looking for and by carefully pointing out our differences from functionalist theories of media reception. "It is not just a matter of measuring the distance between the enunciation of messages and their effects, but rather of constructing an integral analysis of consumption, understood as the overall effect of the social processes of appropriation of products" (Garcia Canclini, 1988: 493). Nor are we referring here to the much deplored "compulsive consumption," or to the repertoire of attitudes and tastes collected and classified by commercial surveys. Even less do we want to move to the airy terrain of Baudrillard's simulation. Our reflection on consumption is located in daily practices in so far as these are

an area of silent interiorization of social inequality (Garcia Canclini, 1984b: 74). This is the area of each person's relationship to his or her body, use of time, habitat and awareness of the potentialities in his or her life. It is also an area of rejection of limits to what can be legitimately hoped for, an area for the expansion of desires, a realm where one can subvert the codes and express pleasures. Consumption is not just the reproduction of forces. It is a production of meanings and the site of a struggle that does not end with possession of the object but extends to the uses, giving objects a social form in which are registered the demands and forms of action of different cultural competencies.

The proof of the new meaning of consumption is the political relevance of the "new conflicts" centring on struggles against the forms of power which penetrate daily life, and struggles over the appropriation of goods and services. The articulations between these two types of struggles become quite clear in the histories of the popular-urban culture which we have gathered.

Another theoretical stream which must be integrated into our analysis is the new conception of interpretative reading developed in Latin America, especially in the work of Beatriz Sarlo (1983b, 1985b, 1985c). Sarlo, carrying forward the analysis of H. Robert Jauss, proposes a study of the "different possible social readings" understood as the "activity by which meanings are organized in a unifying sense" (Sarlo, 1983a: 11). Thus, in an interpretative reading, as in consumption, there is not just reproduction but also production, a production which questions the centrality of the dominating text and the message understood as the source of truth which circulates in a process of communication. To bring the centrality of the text and messages into critical question implies that we assume as constitutive the asymmetry of demands and of competencies which meet and are negotiated in the text. The text is no longer the machine which unifies heterogeneity, no longer a finished product, but a comprehensive space crossed by different paths of meaning. This concept restores to reading the legitimacy of pleasure that applies not only to cultivated, erudite interpretative reading, but to any and every reading—including popular readings with their pleasure of repetition and recognition (Sarlo, 1985a: 36). This concept of reading brings together both resistance and pleasure. The stubborn popular tastes that appear in a narrative are both the raw material for advertising and an activator of cultural abilities, where commercial logics and popular demand at times conflict and at times negotiate. What follows is a nocturnal map to explore this concept at the crossroads formed in Latin America by television and melodrama.

Television Understood from the Perspective of Mediations

At a time when television is at the centre of technological transformations which emerge from informatics, satellites, optical fibre, etc., our proposal could appear to some as a bit anachronistic. We continue in this line, however, because, although the media in Latin America are experiencing many changes, the "mediations"[6] through which the media operate socially and culturally are not undergoing significant modifications. Neither the thousands of VCRs invading the market each year, nor the parabolic antennas that are sprouting from roofs everywhere, nor the new cable networks, are substantially affecting the model of production of television that we know. For most television viewers, not only in Latin America but also in other parts of the world, changes in the supply, in spite of the propaganda regarding decentralization and pluralization, appear to be in the direction of making social stratification even more sharply defined, for the differentiated video products offered to the public are linked to buying capacities of individuals[7]. Producers and programmers of video technologies are mainly interested in marketing new products, while the social application of technologies falls by the wayside (Richeri, 1985: 68). Paradoxically, the change that appears to affect

television most deeply is along the lines of our interpretation: "It is necessary to abandon mediacentrism, for the system of the media is losing its specificity and becoming an integral part of the economic, cultural and political system" (Richeri, 1985: 60).

In Latin America, however, the abdication of mediacentricism is less the result of an industrial reconversion of the media that puts the communication functions of the media in second place, behind economic and industrial considerations, but rather is influenced primarily by social movements that make visible the mediations. Therefore, instead of starting our analysis from the logic of production and reception and studying their relationships with the logic of cultural overlap and conflict, we propose to start with interventions where the social materialization and cultural expression of television are defined and configured. As hypotheses to bring together and structure converging areas of theoretical interpretation, we propose to analyse three spheres of mediation, even though some do not take television as the prime "object": the daily life of the family, social temporality, and cultural competence.

References

Brunner, J.J. (1985a) *La cultura como objeto de políticas.* Santiago: FLACSO.

Brunner, J.J. (1985b) *Políticas Culturales para la Democracia.* Santiago: FLACSO.

Brunner, J.J. and Catalan, G. (1985) *Cinco Estudios sobre Cultura y Sociedad.* Santiago: FLACSO.

Casullo, N. (1983) *Cultura Popular y Política.* Mimeo. Buenos Aires. Argentina.

Cantor Magnani, J. G. (1984) *Festa do Pedazo: Cultura Popular e Lazer na Cidade.* São Paulo: Brasiliense.

de Ipola, E. and Portantiero J.C. (1984) "Crisis Social y pacto democrático". *Punto de Vista*, 21. Buenos Aires, Argentina.

Durham, E.R. (1980) "A familia operaria: consciencia e ideología." *Dados*, 2. Rio de Janeiro. Brasil.

Garcia Canclini, N. (1984a) Desigualdad cultura y poder simbólico: La sociología de P.Bourdieu, mimeo. Mexico

Garcia Canclini, N. (1984c) Las políticas culturales en América Latina, Materiales para la Comunicación Popular, 1. Lima

Garcia Canclini, N. (1985) Cultura transnacional y cultural populares en México, (paper presented to the Congreso de Americanistas, Bogotá, 1985), mimeo. Mexico

6   The meaning given here to the term 'mediations' is that of M. Martín Serrano (1977).
7   Several of the chapters in Richeri, 1983, touch on the deepening of social differences as a result of the new video products.

1927
1960
1963
1964
1967
1969
1970
1971
1972
1973
1974
1975
1976
1977
1978
1979
1980
1981
1982
1983
1984
1985
1986
1987
1988
1989
1990
1991
1992
1993
1994
1995
1996
1997
1998
1999
2000
2001
2002
2003
2004
2005
2006

Garcia Canclini, N. (1988) Culture and power: The state of research, in Media, Cultura and Society, 10 (4): 467-97.

Laclau, E. (1981) "Teoría marxista del estado: Debates y perspectivas" in Estado y Política en América Latina. México: Siglo XXI

Landi, O. (1983) Crisis y lenguajes políticos. Buenos Aires: Cedes.

Landi, O. (1984) "Cultura Política en la Transición Democrática." Mimeo. Buenos Aires. Argentina.

Landi, O. (1985a) "Campo Cultural y Democratización Política." Mimeo. Buenos Aires.

Lechner, N. (ed.) (1981) Estado y política en América Latina. México: Siglo XXI

Lechner, N. (1984) La conflictiva y nunca acabada construcción del Orden Deseado. Santiago: FLACSO.

Martin Serrano, M. (1987) " El estructuralismo antropológico y el mito de la postmodernidad." Cuadernos del Norte, 9. Oviedo. Spain.

Richeri, G. (1985) "Nuevas Tecnologías e Investigación sobre la Comunicación de Masas," in De Moragas, M. (ed.) Sociología de la Comunicación de Masas. Barcelona: Gustavo Gili.

Sarlo, B. (1983a) "Lo popular como dimensión: tópica, Retórica y Problemática de la recepción." Mimeo. Buenos Aires.

Sarlo, B. (1983b) "Del lector." In C. Altamirano and B. Sarlo. Literatura/Sociedad. Buenos Aires: Hachette.

Sarlo, B. (1985a) El Imperio de los Sentimientos. Buenos Aires: Catálogos.

Sarlo, B. (1985b) "Los lectores: una vez más ese enigma." In El Imperio de los Sentimientos. Buenos Aires: Catálogos.

Sarlo, B. (1985c) "Crítica de la lectura. ¿Un nuevo canon?" Punto de Vista, 24. Buenos Aires.

COMMUNICATION, CULTURE AND DEVELOPMENT

By Hector Schmucler

1987 In the document accompanying the invitation to participate in this discussion the question posed is: "What is the role of mass communication systems in the configuration of national cultures and the preservation of national identities and pluralities? How do international flows of cultural messages influence?" The brevity of time assigned to each of us to speak forces us to balance between two risks: a certain degree of summarization or being brusquely interrupted by the moderator. I would rather face the first.

I am thinking, to start answering the formulated question, to support the premise: we consider it desirable that national cultures exist and cultural pluralities are preserved. This premise, this positioning, is less obvious than it looks. It is not always that declarations on the subject are harmonized with actions. Stating the will to maintain and reinforce cultural identities does not only compromise thought, but also a way of acting in the multiple fields of human action that conform what is generically called culture: the specific way men and women live in a determined time and place. In consequence, defending and reinforcing the national cultures does not simply speak about rescuing folklore (which many times hides a guilty nostalgia). It is about considering the everyday flow of individuals, that is, the way they work, the economic relationships they establish, their relationship with society, their religious beliefs, their feelings about love, their attitude toward death, their ideas about time and space.

Signaling, then, that one thinks that the maintenance and reinforcement of national cultural identities is desirable compromises the rest of the speech. In this same direction, if the idea of cultural plurality is assumed as a defensible positive concept, let us think and imagine actions in a determined sense. Looking at it backwards, if our convictions (conscious or not) shape these concepts of identity and plurality negatively, the actions promoted will be loaded with that negative outlook. It is a priority, then, to signal a starting point. Since it is not an opportunity, in this discussion, to theorize about these subjects, the statements will have to accommodate to being requests for principles: I believe it is beneficial to maintain national cultural identities as much as to support cultural priority, meaning the acknowledgment of the legitimacy of the different cultures. Let's try to link this statement with the initial questions and imagine that the "mass communication systems" and the "international flows of cultural messages" influence in the opposite sense to the configuration of "national cultures" and the "preservation of cultural identities and pluralities." The subject is no news. It has deserved, for years, the attention of scholars and international, local and regional agencies. Neither the attempt to formulate indications to neutralize or reverse those tendencies considered to be negative is original. I would like to talk about these indications briefly.

I suggest the classification of the possible answers and the distortions caused by the mass media and by the international flows of messages in two big tendencies: "statutory-coercive responses" and "organic-consensual responses." The responses of the first group, which we call statutory-coercive, the most traditional and frequent, offer two faces:

1. "Negative coercive responses" are those that pose, for example, the need of rules tending to prevent international flows from harming national cultures.
2. "Positive coercive responses:" they favor legislation imposing, for example, the compulsory nature of production and broadcast of works originated nationally.

The organic-consensual answers (please do forgive this neologism, but I don't know how to express it otherwise) indicate in the first place the need to generate sociocultural conditions so a collective will to preserve cultural identities is "possible." In turn, and linked inseparably to this possibility of collective will, it is obligatory to favor the collective "acknowledgment" pluralities. This point of view is clearly different from the statutory-coercive responses. I will try to explain this difference; at least, what this difference means for my spirit. I start from the suspicion that neither the defenses of national identities, nor the acknowledgment of pluralities, are innate or notable. Therefore, when I speak of organic-consensual response, I am suggesting the need to "create" a collective will, that is, a wished and conscious acknowledgment of these values. As you can see, it is the opposite of promulgating rules that, some times, are opposed to collective wills.

Also, some thought should be dedicated to "favoring cultural conditions for the collective acknowledgment or pluralities." I think that the current dilemma—the dilemma of the world and not the communities considered in sectors—lies in the fight between plurality and homogeneity. A deep confrontation that involves practically the whole planet. Plurality, faced with homogeneity, should be understood as the "acknowledgment" of the other and not as the "tolerance" for the other. The nuance is defining and could help to distinguish between close concepts like pluralism and plurality. Pluralism only calls for tolerance: it is admitted that in a same field of interests there are different approximations from those owned. "From" us, we accept the existence of the difference: everything else is included as part of our own world. The acknowledgment of plurality presupposes the existence of global conceptions different from ours: with senses and values that demand—to be understood—to leave our own center. The other one, in this case, is not constituted from us, but originally. It does not presuppose another look from the same reality. We have taken a step. We must recognize that plurality establishes a difficult challenge for our logoantropocentrism. A complicated and complex challenge, especially because I think that the dominant trend goes in the opposite direction, toward the realm of homogeneity.

1927
1960
1963
1964
1967
1969
1970
1971
1972
1973
1974
1975
1976
1977
1978
1979
1980
1981
1982
1983
1984
1985
1986
1987
1988
1989
1990
1991
1992
1993
1994
1995
1996
1997
1998
1999
2000
2001
2002
2003
2004
2005
2006

I would like to formulate a couple of considerations on this dominant tendency to homogeneity that have to do with our subject:

1. It seems like—by nature—the mass media tend to homogenization. If this weren't so, if the mass media were pure instruments "used" circumstantially as homogenizing elements, they would be able to play in a same social space, a non-homogenizing space. The problem is that it is not the mass media that are independently responsible for cultural homogenization processes. It is society, or rather, the specific ways of existence of men in society, that produces the homogenizing effect. In reality, the media are a part of this way of life.

2. New technologies for the handling of information accelerate this tendency to homogenization. The diffusion of some technological patterns contradicts, in many cases, the time-space conceptions in which local cultures are supported where these technological processes are installed and predominant. I emphasize the time-space variable because these are coordinates on which we recognize, at least up to now, all known cultures. The substantial change that we are undergoing in the current technological transformation affects, exactly, the long-rooted ideas about time and space.

Forty years ago some integrants of the Frankfurt School were wondering about similar aspects to those that worry us when we talk about mass media. (It is nice for me to acknowledge in public that Antonio Pasquali, my co-opponent in this opportunity, was maybe the fist to broadcast the Frankfurt studies in Latin America). The question persists: Can mass media be non-homogenizing? We already know that, in studies on mass communication, this cultural profile of the immediate postwar was substantially replaced by the functionalist approaches that were expanded by North American theorizers. Today, when we come back, with strength renewed, to feel uneasy about identities and pluralities, the field designed by functionalism feels narrow (both right and left) used to think of mass communication only linked to unique and irrefutable development models. Also some common places on what has been called "communication policies" should be revised in light of these concepts.

Let us insist on our specific subject: communication and culture. What is the semantic field cut out by the concept of communication? Also in this case certain precisions are required to advance in the search that we have embarked upon. "Communication," as well as "culture," expand their meaning so much that it ends up being impossible to cover. For our goal, we will centrally distinguish two ways to conceive communication:

1. Communication in a "technical-instrumental" sense: that is, the different ways to transmit something separable, in information units, and
2. Communication in the "ontological-moral" sense (or anthropological, constituting humanity): that is, as a way to be for the men in the world.

Our interest is fixated on this second perspective, since we are not worried about lifestyles, that is, the human living in the world. From this point of view we observe the technical-instrumental communication which, undoubtedly, is the dominant version in almost the whole planet. Technology re-dimensions its importance (we could say it is more and less insignificant at the same time); the redefinition of communication systems stops being a mere problem of technological transfer (with its virtues and its dangers for economy and self-determination of peripheral countries -, to interest for the very destiny of cultures. We should then speak about a relationship communication-culture, that is, similar spaces and not "communication and culture," since uniting these terms with an adverb presupposes a difference. If we carried on in this line of thought maybe we would arrive to suggest the convenience of thinking communication "as" culture.

Let us for a minute come back to technology to state that communication technology—like any other—is not neuter, that is, that its design and use imply more and less foreseen relationship patterns among human beings. If that is the case, the perception of the world we aspire to is also included in the technologies we use in its construction. Communication and development are mutually dependent variables. Which communication for which development could be a matter previous to any specific choice of communication policies. Nobody argues against development being a veiled concept anymore, which brings more data than simple socioeconomic statistics.

There is, however, a long way left to go for communication to be understood not only as an instrument whose positive or negative sign depends more on the user than on the relationships that it tends to implant for itself. How does technology act to ease or prevent communication in the anthropological sense we have referred to? This is the question that I consider substantial, if with development we want to talk about well-being (material and spiritual) of human beings.

The computerized world, toward which leans the impressive expansion of new technologies for the handling of information, configures a way to exist, a culture, and not a simple widening of already existing potentialities. An expression of communication in the technical-instrumental sense, it is not positive that it will favor the other also, which we consider to be a priority. The data we have available allow for the suspicion that the growing automation of the material and intellectual productive processes configure beings depending on a logic that multiplies objects, control systems, an administered human life. And the administrative planning of the existence is hardy understanding of the being of humans, which is dilated in areas that are very difficult to quantify, like wish and love. If the future is not something previously existing, where we only have to arrive—as insinuated by some speaker in this discussion—but a creation that is being germinated in our present, the decisions taken today on information technologies will pre-configure the immediate universe.

Finally, I summarize a series of wishful expressions that some may understand as an action program: a) seek plurality, not tolerate it; b) knowing there is an "other" as entitled to exist as we are ourselves and that this existence may go through cultural patterns different to ours; c) favor conditions for plurality—the cohabitation of cultures—to be possible; d) afterwards, and only afterwards, decide our technical options; e) do not accept, as the luddits two centuries ago favored in the dawn of the first industrial revolution, any machine that attempts on the happiness of the human beings.

Schmucler, Hector. "Communication Culture and Development," *Comunicación y desarrollo*, Lima, IPAL, 1987. Republished with permission of the author.

1927
1960
1963
1964
1967
1969
1970
1971
1972
1973
1974
1975
1976
1977
1978
1979
1980
1981
1982
1983
1984
1985
1986
1987
1988
1989
1990
1991
1992
1993
1994
1995
1996
1997
1998
1999
2000
2001
2002
2003
2004
2005
2006

RETHINKING DEVELOPMENT SUPPORT COMMUNICATION

Excerpt from: Development Communication Report

By Silvia Balit

1988 Communication occupies an ever more important place in development policies and programmes and is now coming into sharper focus as experience is reviewed and evaluated.

Within the United Nations (UN) System, the concept of Development Support Communication (DSC) was initially promoted by UNDP (United Nations Development Programme), UNICEF (United Nations Children's Fund) and UNFPA (United Nations Population Fund). The Food and Agricultural Organization (FAO) was quick to recognize the importance of the emerging discipline, and in 1969 the Development Support Communication Branch was formed as a field oriented unit within the Information Division. It was later incorporated as a sub-programme within the FAO Rural Development Programme with a broad mandate to service requests from Member Governments for assistance in rural communications. DSC currently is an essential component in many spheres of FAO activities including forestry, fisheries and agriculture. An integrated approach to rural development has been applied wherein communication support also has been provided to women, population, health, nutrition and literacy programmes.

FAO's mandate for communication in support of rural development was reinforced by the 1979 World Conference on Agrarian Reform and Rural Development (WCARRD), which placed special emphasis on the participation of the rural poor, not simply in sharing the benefits of development but also in sharing the responsibility of development decision making. The Conference concluded that:

Rural development strategies can realize their full potential only through the motivation, active involvement and organization at the grass-roots level of rural people with special emphasis on the least advantaged, in conceptualising and designing policies and programmes and in creating administrative, social and economic institutions, including cooperative and other voluntary forms of organization, for implementing and evaluating them.

In the light of such an approach, if development strategies are to be successful they must aim at engendering "understanding and awareness of the problems and opportunities of rural people at all levels and (a) improving the interaction between development personnel and the masses through an efficient communication system." In effect, this means that no development strategy is complete unless communication policies and activities are incorporated into the diagnosis of needs, and into the design and implementation of priorities selected for a development action.

When FAO's DSC activities began, little was known about how to use communication among largely illiterate populations in developing countries for developmental purposes. The general assumption was that the mass media could have a major impact on the problems of transferring ideas and technology to rural populations in developing countries. This assumption soon proved mistaken, and was based on an over-simplification of development problems that often overlooked people's cultures, traditions and values. Development communication is now seen more as a social process, designed to seek a common understanding or consensus among all the participants of a development initiative, leading to concerted action. The media are now seen as useful tools to help this process and to assist in learning. Their use is not an end in itself, and interpersonal communication plays a major role.

After almost 20 years of action-oriented programmes, including a number of innovative and successful experiences as well as lessons learned from failures, FAO felt that there was a wealth of experience which warranted an in-depth analysis. For this reason an Expert Consultation on DSC was organized in June 1987. For the first time, 15 rural communication specialists gathered in FAO to analyse past experience and provide guidance for future activities. They came from different backgrounds, experiences and regions, including university professors, field practitioners, DSC specialists from within the U.N. System and outside. Some were old acquaintances, having gone to the same school, while others met for the first time. Yet, notwithstanding the differences in experience and approaches, a common understanding and a consensus on the best directions to take for the future emerged during the five days of hard work and discussions. A state of the art background paper, describing the conceptual and historical development of DSC, as well as a series of case studies analysing different methodologies and approaches, as well as the impact achieved in a selected number of DSC programmes, were provided to the Expert Consultation as background material.

To begin with, the meeting analysed the role of communication in rural development today, and some of its essential features. The participants felt that:

> The essence of involving rural people in the process of their own development lies in the sharing of knowledge. Sharing is not a one-way transfer of information; it implies, rather, an exchange between communicating equals. On the one hand, technical specialists learn about peoples' needs and their techniques of production; on the other, the people learn of the techniques and proposals of the specialists.

It followed that the outcome of useful sharing of knowledge is not so much the replacement of traditional techniques by modern ones, as a merging of modern and traditional systems to produce something more appropriate that suits the economic and technical capacities of the people as well as their cultural values. The ultimate purpose of knowledge-sharing is to enable rural people to take more control over their environment, and over agriculture, health, habitat, and other elements which so critically impinge upon the quality of life.

The problem has been that sharing of knowledge has not taken place spontaneously between development agents and rural people because neither have possessed the skills necessary to overcome certain barriers. Foremost among these barriers have been socio-cultural ones; development efforts have often been undermined by incompatible communication approaches, by a clash of differing levels of education and literacy and differing use of language. Other important barriers have been the divergent interests of the parties concerned and differing perceptions of the realities of a given situation. Communication for development is a response to the need to overcome such barriers. Communication activities set out to reinforce the cultural identity, local values and knowledge of people as an avenue to their active participation in development.

The experts attempted to define DSC as follows:

> Development Support Communication (DSC) is part science, part art and part craft:
>
> ■ It is part science because is draws heavily on social science theory, methodology and general philosophy.
> ■ It is part art because it incorporates artistic talents and skills such as graphics, photography, radio, video, social marketing, instructional design and the like.
> ■ It is part craft because it employs a wide variety of aids and equipment such as cameras, projectors, type-setters, computers and broadcasting and telecommunications paraphernalia, for preparing, projecting and disseminating messages.

After analyzing the case studies and experience to date, the meeting thought the following were fundamental common factors in determining success:

1927
1960
1963
1964
1967
1969
1970
1971
1972
1973
1974
1975
1976
1977
1978
1979
1980
1981
1982
1983
1984
1985
1986
1987
1988
1989
1990
1991
1992
1993
1994
1995
1996
1997
1998
1999
2000
2001
2002
2003
2004
2005
2006

1. As in all development activities, communication—if it is to be successful—must be based on the perspectives of the rural people.

2. Communication for development must be incorporated in the planning and programming stage of projects. It helps to determine the areas of common need and interest among governments, rural people, development workers and donor agencies; this leads to projects that are viable and sustainable because of the converging interests of all sectors involved.

3. The duration of components in development projects, and of communication projects themselves, must be sufficiently long to demonstrate their value and to create an institutional base. A duration of four to five years should be considered a normal minimum for most projects.

4. For a given development activity, there will be a critical mass of communication staff, resources and equipment below which little or no impact can be expected. Hence, the dimension of the communication input must be carefully tailored to the needs of the development action. It must not be a token input, as it so often is, irrespective of the scope and importance of the communication task to be performed.

5. Particularly among the poorest of the poor, a holistic approach is essential, covering the multifaceted aspects of life in rural areas, and therefore dealing not only with agricultural production but covering also such matters as health, habitat and nutrition.

It also emerged that there are certain essentials at the national level for the successful use of communication for development. They are as follows:

1. A strategic use of communication for development requires a policy decision in its favour, followed by sustained government support.

2. A decision by government in favour of broad-based communication support for rural development, using all of the media infrastructures available to it in an orchestrated fashion, will usually give better results than concentration on one medium, such as radio broadcasting for example.

3. The issue of national staff is critical, and there are three criteria for determining the personnel requirements for carrying out communication for development—as indeed there are for the other development activities too. These are: quantity of staff; quality of staff; and the permanency of their assignments to the task.

Even when all the above factors have been taken into account, the experts believed that the common denominator that remains in successful development communication endeavours is "clear strategy and rigorous management."

The Consultation made a number of recommendations to FAO and its Member Governments to improve the planning and implementation of DSC activities. These will serve as guidelines for reorienting the work of the DSC Branch, and its assistance to Member Governments.

To Governments the Consultation recommended that they recognise more fully that development is largely based on voluntary change by people and that communication can lead to the proper situation analysis, research and participative testing necessary to ensure that activities be people-oriented, responding to real needs. Governments were requested to consider establishing functional DSC units for rural development and, in the light of the crucial role played by communication in social and economic transformation of rural societies, the Consultation recommended that governments consider allotting suitable budgets for development communication.

The recommendations to FAO included the need to provide more orientation and briefing on communication for development to field programming staff and missions, to ensure that it is incorporated into the programming cycle, from the inception of projects and throughout implementation. The DSC Branch should pay more attention to the planning and development of integrated, rural communication systems and strategies, as opposed to the individual media approaches applied in the past. The need for training in communication of national staff at all levels was underlined, and the meeting recommended that the DSC Branch reorient its activities to strengthen its training functions. National training institutions should be approached to build up their curricula in the area of development communication planning and management. In the field of research and evaluation, the Branch should continue to document successful and unsuccessful experiences, especially of an innovative nature, and make the results available to governments to assist with future planning and management of DSC activities.

Apart from serving as a basis for rethinking FAO's directions in development support communication, the Conclusions of the Expert Consultation have already aroused considerable interest on the part of governments, national institutions and international organisations concerned with rural communications. The findings of the Rome meeting are thus contributing to a better definition of the role of communication in rural development as well as providing guidelines to improve communication policies and programmes.

Annex

This article draws on the Report of the Expert Consultation on Development Support Communication, FAO, Rome, 8-11 June 1987.

Background material included seven specially prepared case studies:

1. *Perspectives on communication for rural development*. This paper outlines the conceptual and historical development of DSC, and describes its operational areas, information dissemination and motivation, participatory community development, training for rural producers and for field workers and institutional management communication. It goes on to discuss different types of media and their advantages and drawbacks, and traces the relationship between media and interpersonal communication.
2. *Rural radio in Mauritania*. This is a case study of an innovative approach to rural broadcasting carried out in Mauritania. The guiding principle of the project was to promote the maximum possible participation of the rural population in programme production. This was done through making hours of recordings with rural people in their villages. The rural radio team promoted, and participated in local festivities, and organized quizzes and competitions in eloquence on a variety of themes that are of importance to rural people.
3. *Pioneering a new approach to communication in rural areas: the Peruvian experience with video for training at grass-roots level*. Beginning in 1974, a UNDP/FAO-assisted project in Peru set up a national institution, Centro de Servicios de Pedagogia Audiovisual para la Capacitación (CESPAC), for the systematic use of video for intensified information and training among rural people. CESPAC is well known for having been the first initiative to develop such a rural training methodology based on video, backed up by simple printed materials and practical work. This case study traces the history of CESPAC until 1986, when international assistance to the project terminated.
4. *A rural communication system for development in Mexico's tropical wetlands*. Mexico's tropical wetlands hold a still largely untapped potential for agricultural and economic development. After several serious and expensive setbacks encountered by development interventions in recent decades—setbacks caused almost exclusively by failure to engage the positive participation of the local people—a new approach was adopted in the mid-1970s under a programme known as PRODERITH [Programme for Integrated Rural Development in the Tropical Wetlands], which is receiving World Bank and FAO support. The new approach incorporates intense communication activities using a variety of media, but primarily video, to assist in participatory development planning with local communities, in training and in institutional communication.
5. *The paradigm of communication in development: from knowledge transfer to community*

1927
1960
1963
1964
1967
1969
1970
1971
1972
1973
1974
1975
1976
1977
1978
1979
1980
1981
1982
1983
1984
1985
1986
1987
1988
1989
1990
1991
1992
1993
1994
1995
1996
1997
1998
1999
2000
2001
2002
2003
2004
2005
2006

participation—lessons from the Grameen Bank, Bangladesh. This case study describes in detail the planned and careful use of interpersonal communication and group work as part of the development of an outstandingly successful small farmer credit scheme in Bangladesh. It provides insights into how communication for development has been evolving, into communication as an integral part of participation and the creation of mutual trust, and into the limitations that media-based approaches have often encountered in the past.

6. *Filmstrips in extension and training—Burkina Faso*. A series of 11 filmstrips were produced in Burkina Faso by FAO/DSC on the subject of animal traction, for which there is an important development programme in the country. Some training courses for extensionists on how to use the filmstrips in the work were also organized. This case study is an enquiry of a few years later into what use is being made of the materials, how appropriate they are felt to be by field development agents, advantages and problems in using them and what farmer reaction to them has been.

7. *Education through entertainment: the British Radio drama series "The Archers, an everyday story of country folk."* "The Archers" has been running longer than any other radio series in the world. Today, many listeners do not realize that it started out as a vehicle for helping to transform the backward farming scene in post-Second World War Britain; and it played a major part in that transformation. Based on a paper by the founder of "The Archers," this case study describes the thinking behind the series, the craft and methods used in its production, and the extraordinary impact it had. Finally, the study discusses the issue of whether such an approach could be usefully tried in Third World countries today.

Balit, Silvia. "Rethinkng Developmeent Cpmmunication," *Development Communication Report (DCR)*, No. 62, 1988/3. Copyright © 1988, Academy for Educational Development. Reprinted with permission of AED.

WHY COMMUNICATION FOR DEVELOPMENT SO RARELY SUCCEEDS

Excerpt from: Development Communication: Information, Agriculture, and Nutrition in the Third World

By Robert C. Hornik

1988 There are, in the developing world, several thousand educational programs now operating that use communication technology to reach their objectives. These programs employ mass media, two-way communication technology and miscellaneous audiovisual devices in formal education, adult education, information campaigns, development administration and all manner of community development programs. Given the available data about audiences reached, practices changed, benefits achieved and long-term institutional survival, we can assume that most of them fail; they have not reached even a small part of their apparent goals. It is our purpose to understand these failures and the few successes and, insofar as we can, locate circumstances that promise success.

Following Suchman (1967), we first divide the explanations for failure into two broad categories: theory failures (resulting from an incorrect assumption that a particular development problem is amenable to a communication-based solution) and program failures (resulting from an inadequately designed or implemented project). We also add a third category: political failures. Each type of failure will be introduced and discussed at a general level; in Parts Two and Three, detailed support for these propositions will be offered in relation to particular substantive goals.

Theory Failures

Projects based on communication technology traffic in information. They throw words—ways of understanding, behaving and organizing—at development problems, problems that are substantially and contrarily defined as a lack of resources: low agricultural productivity, poor health or nutritional status or unequal shares of society's goods.

To argue that information provision alone can resolve development problems is to assume that available resources are being inefficiently used. It is to argue that substantially more benefit can be derived from what is already in place, if only individuals or groups knew better how to organize the use of those resources: additional agricultural products can result from improved farming practices without the introduction of expensive fertilizers; infants' nutritional status can be improved with better feeding and health practices, although no new food is available to the family and no new medical facilities are available in the community. In both of these examples, the assumption is that current behavior is irrational—it is not producing the maximum benefit from the available resources. People do not know, so they do not act optimally. This assumption of human deficit, of individual ignorance as to how to make the best use of the available resources, although rarely explicit, was central to much communication for development practice.

Yet most scholars who have looked closely at agricultural or nutritional practices, for example, claim that the assumption of irrationality is inappropriate. It is often inappropriate in the economic sense: it is common to find, for example, that small farmers are highly efficient users of available resources (Schultz 1964). It is also often inappropriate in the cultural sense: the benefits accrued are not limited to economic returns. For example, current weaning practices may reinforce valued social ties, even if they fail to maximize other valued goals. Indeed, if current practice fits into its economic and cultural milieu, then development strategies that depend entirely on providing information have little potential for success.

This strong statement may explain why many projects fail; let us therefore look for ways around it. If communication-based projects are essentially providers of information, under what circumstances do they have a positive developmental role? Four perspectives offer promise. The first two point to situations where current behavior is not optimum and suggest that communication can accelerate the process of adaptation to a changed environment.

The first perspective suggests that there are, in fact, important situations where current behavior is tightly linked neither to a culture nor to its economy. A rapidly changing environment can make a previously well adapted behavior no longer optimum. A growing population means that available land must be divided into parcels too small for subsistence; or it may force some people to become laborers on plantations or to migrate to cities. Changes in international commodity prices or in distribution possibilities affect which crops are sown and thus alter food prices. National upheavals—revolutions, wars, or natural disasters—dictate rapid changes in the social organization of communities. In each of these circumstances older practices no longer fit, and people may be open to newer ones that fit better with the changing environment. Provision of information under such ripe circumstances may find fertile ground for influencing the direction of change.

A second way around the assumption that current behavior is, in fact, well adapted, is to use communication in a broader program that is introducing new resources. The availability of new resources by itself implies a change in the environment that has reinforced existing behavior. Thus new programs of low-cost agricultural credit mean that farmers are making decisions according to new criteria and may value information about how to maximize benefits under these previously unknown conditions. Information is also of value when a new product or technology, whether it be a new soy milk blend or corn hybrid, becomes available. Informing people about both the

1927
1960
1963
1964
1967
1969
1970
1971
1972
1973
1974
1975
1976
1977
1978
1979
1980
1981
1982
1983
1984
1985
1986
1987
1988
1989
1990
1991
1992
1993
1994
1995
1996
1997
1998
1999
2000
2001
2002
2003
2004
2005
2006

nature and availability of a new product and the specifics of its use are potential roles.

However, if the comparative advantage of the new products or technology is very large, the need for information may be satisfied through the natural information-sharing process and no formal information campaign may be required. Thus the value of information campaigns is bounded on the one hand by an unchanging environment that does not reward new behaviors, and on the other by an environment changed by the availability of new resources whose applicability is so clear as to require no complementary information campaign.

A third way of addressing the assumption that current practices fit the environment is to argue that not all programs of information and education are means to a subsequent development end; they can be an end in themselves. Becoming politically informed or educated in basic skills is a social good, and not merely because either leads to better agricultural or nutritional practice and then higher income. This perspective assumes that education programs are in themselves new resources and their availability represents a change in the environment. People will consume the programs because the programs have intrinsic value. Their acceptance is not conditioned by the value of what is learned for other purposes.

This view of education as a social good, and thus not troubled by the irrationality problem, is, of course, not universally shared. Human capital theorists (cf. Schultz 1964; Welch 1970; Jamison and Lau 1982; Behrman and Wolfe 1984) assume that better-skilled people will use available resources more efficiently, and that education is to be valued precisely because it helps individuals rationalize their use of resources. Others argue that economic opportunity is related to educational attainment, especially when pressures on the land increase. Only if education is linked to economic advantage will it be sought. Both alternative views suggest that investments in educational programs, no less than in more obviously practice-related

information programs, will pay off only if they are related to environmental disequilibria that enhance their value.

The fourth approach to the "practice fits" obstacle is to stress the organizational value of communication as opposed to its informative value. Some would argue that information from outside a community will not affect that community unless it starts a process of autonomous development. From this perspective the value of communication programs is not in the specific practices they advocate, but in the local organization and longer-term political activism they generate. Associated with the terms "consciousness-raising" and "community development" (each from rather different political traditions), this approach accepts the notion that information delivered to, and for the use of, the individual peasant is of little value. Failure to develop is not the result of individual incapacity. Rather, even though individuals, on average, may maximize their own use of resources, communities do not. There is residual power in effective organization of the community. From the community development perspective, that means improvements in the standard of living can be achieved by adopting innovations (such as roads or a water supply) that are beyond the resources of the individual but within those of the organized community. From the consciousness-raising perspective, this means that communities can make effective demands on outside political authority for a more equitable share of national resources.

Communication programs that are designed to mobilize community organization are thus held to be free from the assumption of individual deficits in their efforts to accelerate development. They do assume a parallel "community deficit," that community failure to develop is not a reflection of true resource constraints or true lack of power, but is, at least in part, due to a failure to make use of resources and power that are potentially available. And further, it is assumed that outside stimulation of local organization is an effective means of initiating the realization of that potential.

We then have four broad classes of potential uses of communication: in the context of rapid environmental change, as a component of a program introducing new resources, as an end in itself and for purposes of community organization for development. Each recognizes that information alone is rarely a satisfactory solution to resource-based development problems. Development programs that do not use communication in one of these ways, no matter how well designed those programs are in a technical sense, have little promise of success. They fail because their theory of the role of communication in development is inadequate.

However, even programs that do make more reasonable assumptions about communication's role may not find the going easy. We turn now to our second broad category of explanation for failure: program failures due to an inadequately designed or implemented project.

Program Failures

Effective projects using communication technology are technology projects only to the naive observer. Two projects may make identical hardware purchases, and with the same intention, but produce entirely different results. What counts is what is done with the hardware. While this is commonplace wisdom to those who are experienced in media-based instructional projects, it is not always shared by the enthusiasts who are responsible for the creation of the many projects that appear each year around the world. Excited by the extraordinary reach of a medium, they may not invest sufficiently beyond the hardware to have any hope of success. Non-hardware considerations include macro- and microinstructional design, obtaining information from the field, administrative location of communication projects and internal-to-the-project staffing and organizational decisions.

Macroinstructional Design

In some schemes, providing an item of information will have its intended effect on some proportion of an intended audience, even if it is transmitted over a single channel only once. "You have the job—start Monday." "No credit available." However, such straightforward circumstances are rare, or so much of the codified experience suggests (cf. Schramm 1977; Jamison and McAnany 1978; Rogers 1983). Projects that depend on a single medium to reach their audiences may find that some part of the audience is inaccessible or does not entirely understand, or if it does understand does not use the medium as a stimulus for practice change. Projects that use multiple channels have a higher probability of success, both because different channels serve different needs and because redundancy is of intrinsic value. Support for these propositions comes from diffusion theory and instructional design theory.

Scholars of the diffusion of innovation have argued persuasively that the adoption of new behaviors should be viewed as a multistage process. The particular sequence of such stages varies (Rogers, for example, opts for knowledge, persuasion, decision and confirmation) but the proposed sequence is not important. What matters is the perception of innovation as a process, with the adopter and his or her community using information from outside to satisfy different needs at different stages in the process.

If the needs for information vary with the adoption stage, then the communication channel most appropriate for delivering that information may vary also. For example, a common diffusion model suggests that in the knowledge stage, as individuals become aware of an innovation, they rely on mass media; as individuals move toward a decision, they tend to rely on personal sources. However, one need have no faith in this particular formulation to accept the more general premise.

Indeed, it will be useful to take a broader view than is typical in diffusion research. Needs to be served by an information system can be differentiated on intra- and interindividual and intertopic dimensions. Diffusion theorists emphasize the changing cognitive and psychological context as the innovator moves toward adoption; they focus on intraindividual changes.

1927
1960
1963
1964
1967
1969
1970
1971
1972
1973
1974
1975
1976
1977
1978
1979
1980
1981
1982
1983
1984
1985
1986
1987
1988
1989
1990
1991
1992
1993
1994
1995
1996
1997
1998
1999
2000
2001
2002
2003
2004
2005
2006

A channel that can effectively provide information about what is available needs to be replaced by a channel that can assure the individual of community support for change, or one that can establish the legitimacy of the innovation for the local context. A channel that effectively supplies ideas may need to be replaced by a channel that gives the innovator the opportunity to clarify doubts, or that promises personal interaction if things go wrong.

Another dimension of needs to be considered addresses inter- rather than intraindividual variation. All channels of communication do not reach all members of the audience equally well, whether for reasons of physical access or because of differences in learned skills. Agricultural extension agents reach some farmers but not others; radio ownership is by no means universal in the rural areas of developing countries. Even when a medium physically reaches an individual, it may not serve as an effective communication channel. Literacy in a medium varies whether that involves reading pamphlets, understanding radio messages, or talking to socially distant extension agents.

A final dimension of needs looks not within or across individuals but across content areas. Some topics seem to require more or less visual support of verbal messages, or other channel capacities related to the way they are most easily presented. Sometimes a mechanism for storing information locally is required; sometimes it is essential for individuals to control the pace of their exposure to information; at other times externally paced exposure is to be valued. While many channels are feasible for satisfying each of these needs, some channels are likely to be more effective than others.

The argument for multiple channel systems has yet another support. One of the communication strategies that has proved most effective in achieving development goals is that of *mobilization*. *All* available media concentrate national attention on a particular problem. In Tanzania (Hall and Dodds 1977), China (Chu 1977) and Cuba (Fagen 1969), multiple channels (broadcast and print mass media, local groups, schools and political institutions) concentrate massive national efforts on selected social goals—whether improved health practices, the elimination of landlords or the promotion of literacy. The strength of multiple channels in these instances is not in their differentiation of roles but in their redundancy. The sense of national mobilization is communicated by the use of multiple channels per se, regardless of the content assigned to each medium.

The general argument for multiple-channel communication systems is rather easier to make than is the definition of just what communication needs a program has, and what channels are likely to serve these needs most effectively. We hold no brief for a very tight match between needs and channels. Obviously the particular sectoral, financial and institutional constraints under which a project operates will restrain its options. Also it is one thing to argue for multiple channels; no doubt more is better. It is quite another to administer and pay for them, which suggests more may not be optimum. In any case, comments about the specifics of this matter must be left to [other] chapters that address particular sectoral applications. However, one example may illustrate the argument.

An in-service teacher-training program may require (1) the transmission of information, (2) a chance to review material at one's own pace, (3) the chance to practice newly learned techniques and obtain constructive feedback, (4) motivation to maintain attention over the long haul, (5) an opportunity to clarify doubts, (6) a sense of membership in a community going through a common program, (7) an outside stimulus to maintain the pace of learning.

Daily radio broadcasts might be effective for tasks 1, 4, 5 and 7; a programmed text might serve 1 and 2; observation by supervisors or organized assistance of school principals of in-class teaching would help tasks 3 and 5; and brief periods of resident instruction might meet the need for 2, 3, 4, 5 and 6. Choosing such a combination of redundant and complementary channels matched to the information needs of a particular program addresses the macroinstructional design issue. However, choosing a useful configuration of channels is valuable only if it is followed by the effective use of the channels that are chosen.

Microinstructional Design

It is unlikely that one could find a planning document for a media-based educational project that states that there is no need to prepare good content materials once one has invested in the hardware. In fact, however, that has been the consequence of the pattern of staffing and budgeting that many projects have followed. As an extreme example, in Samoa, a single teleteacher was responsible for between 10 and 20 televised grade school programs per week, in addition to writing classroom materials! As Schramm suggests (1973, 48), such "ITV programs, are not going to win any prizes." However, that is an early example; and neither in Samoa currently nor, to our knowledge, in most other programs are such unreasonable demands made on producers. If, however, programs have moved toward greater emphasis on quality in content, that has turned out to have two quite distinct meanings.

The first, and perhaps more common, approach emphasizes aesthetic quality. It encompasses both technical accomplishments (clarity of sound reproduction, smoothness of editing) and creative accomplishment (variety of settings, quality of acting and intrinsic entertainment value). The model is commercial programming, and the standards those of the production fraternity. While certainly there is nothing wrong with achievement of aesthetic quality, it is not what we emphasize when we speak of quality. And unfortunately the emphasis on aesthetic quality has led more than one program astray.

When we speak of quality in instructional design, we refer to pedagogical quality: logical structure to the curriculum, effective building on the existing experiences of the audience and devices to make sure that audiences are actively involved in mental processing.

The quality of educational materials is not measured by the applause of colleagues and critics but by their effectiveness. Pedagogical quality is the result not merely of investment in studio facilities and talented producers, but in the support of a linked system of audience analysis, curriculum design, program production, pretesting, field utilization and feedback. In contrast to the Samoan example, the Radio Mathematics project in Nicaragua produced but five programs per week with a staff of fourteen professionals. A substantial proportion of staff time was spent maintaining links with the classroom audience, and all but two members of the staff (one Nicaraguan, one expatriate) were educators rather than broadcasters (Friend et al. 1980). It is true that the capital costs of curriculum development were high, and thus the effort is perhaps not directly replicable in many other circumstances. Nonetheless, the basic commitment to quality in instructional design is worth emulating.

Obtaining Information From the Field

Communication projects make assumptions about what is true in the environment of their intended beneficiaries, an environment that may be at a substantial geographic and cultural distance from the projects' sponsors and staff. Because of that distance, intrinsic to the use of communication technology, those assumptions will rarely serve as the basis for a successful project. The need for the confirmation of assumptions through the gathering of data is considerable both at the time a project is being planned, and at the time it is being implemented. The natural feedback cues that constrain face-to-face communication must be replaced with explicit data-gathering mechanisms in systems that rely on communication technology.

At the planning phase, a recommendation that a particular nutrition-related practice be adopted assumes that the new practice will indeed be more advantageous than the old one. A program to deliver market price information over the radio assumes that current knowledge is inadequate and farmers can act on new information. Both assumptions demand evidence.

1927
1960
1963
1964
1967
1969
1970
1971
1972
1973
1974
1975
1976
1977
1978
1979
1980
1981
1982
1983
1984
1985
1986
1987
1988
1989
1990
1991
1992
1993
1994
1995
1996
1997
1998
1999
2000
2001
2002
2003
2004
2005
2006

At the time of implementation, a message strategy that assumes that economic motivations for a particular nutritional practice are paramount may be misguided if the current behavior is largely supported by important social bonds. Similarly, market price broadcasts may be useless if the pricing unit is one the audience is unfamiliar with, or if the information is not available when they have surpluses.

Projects that operate at a distance, as communication projects do, are in constant need of information for planning and for adjusting operations. They need to know what is going well and what is not. They need both efficient data-gathering mechanisms and, no less, time and flexibility within their operational structures to define the information that can be used to take full advantage of the information that is gathered.

Administrative Locations of Communication Projects

Organizers of communication for development usually choose one of three administrative locations for their projects. The predominant mode is to locate communication projects within the substantive ministry concerned. Formal education projects like the El Salvador ITV project or the Korean Educational Development Institute are undertaken by ministries of education, for example, with secondary roles played by public or private communication institutions that help with transmission.

A second strategy is to locate projects within the communication ministry (posts and telegraphs, telecommunication or whatever its title), or national radio or TV service. This is always the strategy if rural telephone service is the object, but it also may be chosen for projects with substantive goals. These offices, it is believed, will be able to share scarce skills broadly and service the needs of a number of institutions. Indonesia and Liberia, for example, have created development communication agencies to serve different substantive agencies. Many national broadcasting operations, particularly those influenced by the British model, have rural or development

broadcasting units. Radio Gambia, for example, coordinates the production of programs for agriculture, health, schools and other governmental agencies.

A third strategy is to create a hybrid agency by drawing on two or more institutions. These include agencies created for a specific project (Colombia's INRAVISION for its primary ITV project and Guatemala's National Out-of-School Education Board are examples) and agencies of a broader gauge (integrated rural development projects like Plan Puebla in Mexico), in which a communication component will play a secondary role.

Realistically, which strategy is chosen will depend on the overall character of the project and, particularly, its political genesis and support. In that context, experience from elsewhere may be irrelevant. However, when there is some flexibility in the decision, arguments for the first mode seem to be the strongest. Placing communication within the substantive agency concerned recognizes that communication must complement a broader intervention. It serves to accelerate change, not instigate it. Success of a communication intervention will depend on joint action with field agents, or the timely distribution of resources.

Projects organized outside the agency that employs the agents or owns the resources cannot count on their long-term availability, no matter how sincere the promises of cooperation at the outset. The centrifugal, pull of institutional jealousies, rooted in competition for scarce resources, is going to be too great. In general, projects cannot succeed if they are not guaranteed the long-term support of the substantive agency, and they are not likely to achieve that support outside of that authority. The argument closely reflects our belief that communication investments must respect the existing development context, no matter how tempting it is to ignore it and rely on the power of the technology. Nonetheless, we do recognize two powerful counter arguments. One is that a substantive authority is not easily galvanized;

and while communication projects can be impressive catalysts for change, they may be insufficient to move an entrenched bureaucracy. The second is that projects organized within single agencies make rational telecommunication hardware planning difficult.

Sensible telecommunication hardware investment for a single substantive project will be very different from that for a large number of projects aggregated across agencies and over time. A radio production studio and some air time on a national radio network may make sense for an agricultural information project. No such project can justify a widespread rural telephone network. A single substantive project that proposed such an investment (or similarly costly ones involving satellites or the use of television in rural areas) would not even be considered. Yet if an existing system could be used for its marginal or average cost, different sets of considerations would come into play and such projects might be funded.

However, if projects remain under the independent control of substantive authorities, how is demand to be aggregated so as to produce a telecommunication system that is rationalized for all uses? The dilemma is real and it is not solved by letting things take their course. Under natural forces, the pattern of telecommunication investment is likely to reflect commercial—particularly urban—interests, leaving rural development concerns in second or third place. Systems inappropriate for development communication uses may be the result.

In the abstract, a hybrid agency with representatives of all communication-using institutions advising the telecommunications ministry would be ideal. However, it is not clear how this will provide funding for development telecommunication, unless the advice is accompanied by binding commitments for budget subventions. In most nations, telecommunication agencies are expected to pay their own way; a change in that policy will require some new source of funds and new political commitments.

Staffing and Organizational Decisions Internal to the Project

This is a final catch-all category. It is the tautological refuge of the planner whose parting words to those charged with implementing a project are: "Do everything else right and the project will work, but if it didn't work you didn't do everything else right." Everything else includes hiring well-trained, competent and committed staff, locating a charismatic central figure, establishing working conditions and supervisory relations that permit people to reach their potential and developing effective links between the central office and the field staff. Such circumstances are obviously ideal; the question of interest is how to realize them. Why is it that some projects employ staff who do wonders despite difficult conditions, and others, with every chance of success, flounder because of internal failures?

Three types of answers are worth considering. The first, and least helpful, credits individual judgment and luck. A given program happened to find a talented leader who chose subordinates intelligently, and together they made it work. There are real individual differences in competence, and often they are difficult to detect until people are at work on the job. By happenstance, some projects have better staff than others. How often this is a primary explanation, we do not know. However, if it is the primary explanation, short of noble pronouncements about the need for the careful selection of staff, there is little to be said that is both general and helpful.

The second type of answer looks to the character of communication technology projects per se. They have both advantages and disadvantages in the competition for talented staff and in the creation of effective organization. On the advantage side, any project that uses mass media retains a special glamor and promise of public notice and that is often an advantage in recruiting talented staff. Also, since the tasks undertaken by a media production unit, for example, have no parallel in traditional

1927
1960
1963
1964
1967
1969
1970
1971
1972
1973
1974
1975
1976
1977
1978
1979
1980
1981
1982
1983
1984
1985
1986
1987
1988
1989
1990
1991
1992
1993
1994
1995
1996
1997
1998
1999
2000
2001
2002
2003
2004
2005
2006

government bureaucracies, such units have a relatively free hand in developing an appropriate organizational structure. On the disadvantage side, it is often the case that enthusiastic young recruits do nor fit well in the traditional bureaucracy that surrounds them and is jealous of their special status. Also, both the demands of the production process, and the media tradition that rewards aesthetic rather then pedagogical success, mitigate against maintaining close links with audiences of field staff. The public visibility of media projects may mean that their staff is held more accountable than the staff of other projects, which may exaggerate the search for scapegoats at times of failure. That does not make for easy working relationships.

The special characteristics of communication technology projects thus define the second answer. The third answer suggests that failures of personnel and organization may not be technical program failures at all. The project leaders' lack of qualifications for their tasks, governmental red tape that disallows the paying of appropriate salaries and a budget insufficient to pay for vehicles and field expenses may appear to be "mere" technical failures. After all, we know about the shortage of qualified personnel, the rigidity of government bureaucracies and the shortfall of budgets. Yet in each of those cases, we are seeing the consequences of allocation decisions that are the result of a political process. If there is no money for a field operation, although it seems essential for success, if a project leader evidences more political loyalty than management competence, we are seeing not technical failures but failures of political will. The public appearance of taking action that is achieved easily by communication technology projects may satisfy the interests of project sponsors. The additional political commitments required to win adequate budget allocations and to survive bureaucratic infighting, commitments that produce successful development outcomes, may not be forthcoming. ...

References

Behrman, Jere, and B. Wolfe "More Evidence on Nutritional Demand: Income Seems Overrated and Women's Schooling Underemphasized," *Journal of Development Economics*, 14: 105-28, January/February 1984.

Chu, Godwin C., *Radical Change Through Communication in Mao's China* (Honolulu: University of Hawaii Press, 1977).

Fagen, Richard, *The Transformation of Political Culture in Cuba,* (Stanford, California: Stanford University Press, 1969).

Friend, J., B. Searle, and P. Suppes, *Radio Mathematics in Nicaragua* (Stanford, California: Institute for Mathematical Studies in the Social Sciences, 1980).

Hall, Budd L., and Tony Doods, "Voices for Development: The Tanzanian National Radio Study Campaigns," in P. Spain, D. Jamison and E. McAnany, eds., *Radio for Education and Development: Case Study* (Washington: The World Bank, 1977).

Jamison, Dean T., and Emile G. McAnany, *Radio for Education and Development* (Beverly Hills, California: SAGE Publications, 1978).

Jamison, Dean T., and Lawrence J. Lau, *Farmer Education and Farm Efficiency* (Baltimore: Johns Hopkins University Press, 1982).

Rogers, Everett M., *Diffusion of Innovations*, 3rd ed. (New York, Free Press, 1983).

Schultz, Theodore W., *Transforming Traditional Agriculture,* (New Haven: Yale University Press, 1964).

Schramm, Wilbur, *ITV in American Samoa—After Nine Years* (Stanford, California: Institute for Communication Research, 1973).

Schramm, Wilbur, *Big Media, Little Media* (Beverly Hills, California: SAGE Publications, 1977).

Suchman, Edward A., *Evaluative Research* (New York: Russell Sage Foundation, 1967).

Welch, Finis, "Education in Production," Journal of Political Economy, 78, No. 1 (1970): 35-59.

EXCERPT FROM:

COMMUNICATION TECHNOLOGY AND DEVELOPMENT; INTERNATIONAL FLOW OF NEWS

International Flows of Information: A Global Report and Analysis

By Hamid Mowlana

1988 Any discussion about communication and development should begin with a more basic analysis of not only the relationship between the two components, but more important, their separate conceptual meanings. In short, one cannot discuss the interaction of communication and development without understanding the nature of the concepts themselves.

...This is not to suggest that the area where communication and development overlap has not been critically examined. On the contrary, there are a number of highly critical and analytical essays and monographs that have examined the current literature on communication and development.[1] What is lacking

is an historical and evolutionary analysis of the concepts employed, as well as a systematic treatment of the relationship between communication and development in its sociological, epistemological and methodological context. ...

The Historical Growth of the Term Development

The role of communication in general, and the technology of mass media in particular, in the process of social change, economic growth and political upheaval in the so-called less-industrialized and developing countries was studied as early as the 19th century. In fact, examination of events in the Middle East, Latin America and Asia during the 20th century shows the direct intermingling of both old and new communication institutions with the nation-building process. It may even be said that in many of these countries, there have been direct relationships between the press and revolution, telecommunications and modernization, and traditional institutions and revolution.[2]

However, the widespread use of "development" as a conceptual framework for a number of individual,

1 Examples include Hamid Mowlana, "Towards a Theory of Communication Systems: A Developmental Approach," Gazette: *International Journal for Mass Communication Studies*, XVII, 112, 1971, pp. 17-28; and his "Mass Communication and National Development Objectives," in Albert L. Hester and Richard R. Cole, eds., *Mass Communication in Mexico* (Proceedings of the March 11-15, 1974, Seminar in Mexico), International Communication Division of the Association for Education in Journalism and the University of Iberoamericana, published by the Department of Journalism and Mass Communication, South Dakota State University, Brookings, S.D., pp. 115-120; Peter Golding, "Media Role in National Development: Critique of a Theoretical Orthodoxy," *Journal of Communication*, 243, Summer 1974, pp. 39-53; Everett M. Rogers, ed. *Communication and Development: Critical Perspectives*, Beverly Hills, California: Sage Publications, 1976; Wilbur Schramm and Daniel Lerner, eds., *Communication and Change: The Last Ten Years—and the Next*, Honolulu: University of Hawaii Press, 1976; Kaarle Nordenstreng and Herbert I. Schiller, eds., "Communication and National Development: Changing Perspectives," in *National Sovereignty and International Communication*, Norwood, N.J.: Abiex Publishing, 1979, pp. 3-8; Majid Tehranian, "Development Theory and Communication Policy; The Chang-

ing Paradigms," in Melvin J. Voigt and Gerhard J. Hanneman, eds., *Progress in Communication Sciences*, Vol. I, Nowood, N.J.: Ablex Publishing, 1979, pp. 119-166; Georg-Michael Luyken, "25 Jahre Communication and Development—Forschung in den USA: Wissenschaft oder Ideologie?" Rundfunk und Fernsehen (Hans-Bredow Institut für Rundfunk und Fernsehen an der Universität Hamburg), 28 Jahrgang 1980/1, pp. 110-122. Some of the more recent reviews include Wimal Dissanayake, "Development and Communication: Four Approaches," Media Asia, 8: 4, 1981, pp. 217-227; Maria Cornelio, "The Sociology of Development and the New World Information Order," paper presented at the Conference on Communications, Mass Media and Development, Northwestern University, Chicago, Illinois, October 1983; and Jan Servaes, "Communication and Development for Whom and for What?" Paper presented at the International Association for Mass Communication Research (IAMCR), Prague, August 27-31, 1984.
2 For examples, see Edward G. Brown, *The Persian Revolution*, Cambridge, England: Cambridge University Press, 1910; and his *The Press and Poetry in Modern Persia*, Cambridge University Press, 1914; V. I. Lenin, *What Is To Be Done?* Moscow: Progress Publishers, 1947; Hamid Mowlana, "Mass Media Systems and Communication Behaviour," in Michael Adams, ed., *The Middle East: A Handbook,* London: Anthony Blond, 1971, pp. 584-598; and his "Mass Communication, Elites, and National Systems in the Middle East," in *Der Anteil der Massenmedien bei der Herausbildung des Bewußtseins in der sich wandlen den Welt* (Proceedings of the IXth General Assembly and Scientific Conference of the International Association for Mass Communication Research, Sept. 17-21, 1974), Leipzig, DDR, pp. 55-71; and George Gerbner, ed., *Mass Media Policies in Changing Cultures*, New York: John Wiley, 1977.

1927
1960
1963
1964
1967
1969
1970
1971
1972
1973
1974
1975
1976
1977
1978
1979
1980
1981
1982
1983
1984
1985
1986
1987
1988
1989
1990
1991
1992
1993
1994
1995
1996
1997
1998
1999
2000
2001
2002
2003
2004
2005
2006

institutional, national and international changes, and for "progress," was a post-Second-World War phenomenon. In the 1940s, and especially in the 1950s and the 1960s, the term "development" became synonymous with growth, modernization, change, democracy, productivity, industrialization and a score of similar Western historical changes. Popularized first by (and among) American scholars and policy-makers, and soon introduced into Europe and the less industrialized countries of the world, the term "development" became a major issue in international organizations despite its ill-defined and less than universally recognized meaning.

"Development" was now both a legitimate and a convenient term on which a number of otherwise diversified research interests could converge. In the United States, development studies were expanded as a result of a number of scholarly projects in the areas of politics, economics, cultural anthropology, rural sociology, international relations and international communication. Indeed one study found that communication and development was the area of the greatest growth in scholarly investigation because of the number of communication-oriented studies dealing with international problems.[3]

Further, the study found that the amount of research on development and communication in specific cultural and geographical areas corresponded roughly to the level of United States political involvement in those areas, which seemed also to influence to a considerable extent what domestic studies were undertaken and what foreign works were translated. In short, by the early 1960s, development as a field of academic and social inquiry had witnessed extraordinary growth under the influence of the dominant of modernization paradigm, with a great deal of emphasis being placed on economic, technological and institutional factors.

In the context of communication and development, the popularity and diversity of the use of communication in developmental activities, especially during the last decade or so, has added to the complexity of the matter. In the early stages of convergence, the term "communication" was used to refer to communication technologies, particularly the mass media and a variety of journalistic activities.

But with the communications revolution, and especially with the expansion in communication satellites and computers, even the technological meaning of communication has been expanded to encompass everything from the use of the printing press to that of complex electronic and space equipment. At the same time, it has been recognized that there can be no communication analysis unless the complex networks of human, interpersonal and group communication are taken into account. Unlike that of earlier decades, the tendency now is to view communication as a complex whole, in which both the human and technological dimensions must be considered together.

The Meaning of Development

"Development" as a concept was introduced by Ibn Khaldun (1332-1406 A.D.), an Islamic social thinker, in his Muqaddimah (*An Introduction to History*),[4] Ibn Khaldun, who is seen by some as the founder of sociology and demography, used the term "Ilm-al-Umran" to describe a new science and development of society—that is to say—sociology. His work with this new science was, thus, basically, a paradigm and methodology of sociology. The notion of development was used to consider the basic causes of historical evolution; causes Ibn Khaldun thought to lie in the economic and social structures of societies.

For about two centuries, Ibn Khaldun's work remained the single most comprehensive analysis of social development and social organization. Beginning in the 17th century and continuing into the 19th and 20th

---

3   Hamid Mowlana, "Trends in Research on *International Communication in the United States*," Gazette: International Journal for Mass Communication Studies, XIX: 2, 1973, pp. 79-90.

4   Ibn Khaldun, *The Muqaddimah: An Introduction to History* (translated from the Arabic by Franz Rosenthal), London: Routledge and Kegan Paul, 1967.

centuries, European philosophers, social thinkers, economists and sociologists paid particular attention to the broad notion of development in terms of the transformation from rural, communal, agrarian society to the urban, rational, contractual and industrial nation-state system.

Whereas Ferdinand Toennies[5] spoke of Gemeinschaft (community relationships based on traditional association) and Gesellschaft (contracted associations based on rationally established relationships) and George Simme1[6] of rural and urban communities, Auguste Comte[7] emphasized static versus dynamic societies, and both Max Weber[8] and Emile Durkheim[9] advanced a more detailed and optimistic view of societal development, arguing that the division of labour and societal relationships are the bases of organic solidarity in modern society.

The process of societal development as economic activity was studied by Adam Smith,[10] David Ricardo[11] and Karl Marx,[12] followed by a host of other economic thinkers, such as Robert Owen[13] and Pierre Joseph Proudhon.[14] Whereas the mercantilists of the 15th and 16th centuries acted on the basis of pragmatic notions of capital formation and wealth, the classical liberals translated these notions into classical political economy, advocating the accumulation of capital as the basis for economic expansion, and consequently, societal development. It was Karl Marx who transcended the thinking of both the utopian socialists and the classical liberal economists, devising a theory of surplus value and a synthesis of economics and politics that provided an overall theory of societal development based on dialectical materialism and class struggle.

Despite the prominence of the concept of societal development in the work of these scholars, from the turn of this century until the end of the Second World War "development" as an all-encompassing concept of societal transformation and growth was not systematically used in the literature except in the discussion of economic and industrial growth and measurement. Yet, Western theories of human development, both liberal-democratic and Marxist, proceeded from a shared assumption that the development of societies requires that modern economic and social organization replace traditional structures. Firmly adopted in Europe and North America, and diffused among the elites of the less industrialized countries, this assumption included, among other things, industrialization in the economy, secularization in thought and personality and modernization modeled on some variety of capitalism, socialism, liberalism, communism, "reform" or "revolution."

In most instances, this "development" implied "Westernization" or "Europeanization." With the increased popularity of the term "development" during the early decades of the postwar era, the ethnocentric description of the majority of the world's population and societies as "backward" was gradually replaced by the more respectful adjectives "underdeveloped" and "developing."

During the last four decades, but more particularly since the 1960s, much has been written by theorists, from both orthodox and radical schools, which have used the term "development" to explain an enormous

5   Ferdinand Toennies, *Gemeinschaft and Gesellschaft* (translated by C. P. Loomis as *Fundamental Concepts of Sociology*), New York: American Books, 1940.
6   See *The Sociology of George Sirnmel*, translated and edited by Kurt Wolff, New York: Free Press, 1950.
7   *The Positive Philosophy of August Comte*, translated and condensed by Harriet Martineau, Vol. 111, London: Bell, 1896.
8   Max Weber, *The Protestant Ethic and Spirit of Capitalism*, translated by Talcott Parsons, New York: Scribner, 1930; and his *The Theory of Social and Economic Organization*, New York: Oxford University Press, 1947.
9   Emile Durkheim, *The Division of Labor in Society*, translated by G. Simpson, Glencoe, Illinois: Free Press, 1933.
10   Adam Smith, *The Wealth of Nations*," New York: The Modern Library, Random House, 1937.
11   David Ricardo, *Works and Correspondence of David Ricardo*, Vol. I, edited by Piero Sraffa, Cambridge, England: Cambridge University Press, 1951.
12   Karl Marx, *Capital*, Moscow: Foreign Languages Publishing House (three volumes), 1959.
13   For a discussion of R. Owen and P. J. Proudhon, see Louis Dupre, *The Philosophical foundation of Marxism*, New York: Harcourt, Brace and World, 1966.
14   P. J. Proudhon was the leading figure of French socialism in the 1850s and the author of *Philosophy of Poverty*. Marx attacked the political economy of Proudhon in his *The Poverty of Philosophy*, which he wrote while in exile in Paris.

1927
1960
1963
1964
1967
1969
1970
1971
1972
1973
1974
1975
1976
1977
1978
1979
1980
1981
1982
1983
1984
1985
1986
1987
1988
1989
1990
1991
1992
1993
1994
1995
1996
1997
1998
1999
2000
2001
2002
2003
2004
2005
2006

range of political, economic, social, psychological, cultural and ecological phenomena at almost all levels of human activity. This unrestricted usage has led to a certain development fetish and developmentalism, in which the term has lost both its previously identifiable meaning and specific intellectual reference. This plethora of application makes the task of analysis awesome and difficult for anyone who attempts to draw the boundaries of the field.

From 'Modernization' to 'Dependency' and Beyond

Development, both as a process, a generic notion and as a concept referring to several specific evolutionary or revolutionary phenomena, has been used since the Second World War to describe four broad types of phenomena:

1. Modernization, nationalism and political development;
2. Economic development and technological diffusion;
3. Imperialism and underdevelopment; and
4. Revolution, liberation and human development.

During the 1950s and the 1960s modernization, nationalism and political development were the dominant approaches to development and nation building, especially among the political scientists, sociologists and social psychologists in the United States.[15]

Among the early studies, Lerner's work on modernization theory is probably the most important and

influential, because it represents the first attempt to formulate a universal model of modernization through cross-national studies.[16] Lerner developed a general theory of modernization based on a "behavioral system" of an interactive lifestyle, and then tested it with survey and field work in a number of countries in the Middle East. Lerner's work primarily searches for the manner in which societies pass from traditional to transitional stages and eventually achieve modernity, and how that modernity can be communicated. Modernity is defined as a participant lifestyle: modern society is a participant society. The characteristics of participant society are those found in the West, where people attend school, read newspapers, receive monetary compensation for their work, purchase commodities, vote and have opinions on a variety of subjects. ...

Lerner's work on development and his modernization theory were highly influential on the research of American sociologists who were interested in the process of social change in developing countries. Everett M. Rogers' definition of modernization and development is an illustration. According to Rogers and F. F. Schoemaker, development is "a type of social change in which new ideas are introduced into a social system in order to produce higher per capita income levels of living through more modern production methods and improved social organization." Thus, development was defined as "modernization at the social systems level."[17]

From an economic and technological perspective, the post-Second World War period, and the decades of the 1950s and the 1960s especially, was a time when development was seen as to be synonymous with economic growth... .

One of the most influential and now a largely orthodox views of development is W.W. Rostow's theory of economic growth, which envisaged growth in

15 For examples, see Gabriel A. Almond and G. Bingham Powell, Jr., *Comparative Politics: A Developmental Approach,* Boston: Little, Brown, and Company, 1966; Gabriel A. Almond and Sidney Verba, *Civic Culture,* Boston: Little, Brown, and Company, 1963; David Apter, *The Politics of Modernization,* Chicago, The University of Chicago Press, 1965; Lucian W. Pye and Sidney Verba, eds., *Political Culture and Political Development,* Princeton, N.J.: Princeton University Press, 1965; Samuel P. Huntington, *Political Order in Changing Societies,* New Haven, Conn.: Yale University Press, 1968; Karl W. Deutsch, *Nationalism and Social Communication,* Cambridge, Massachusetts, MIT Press, 1953; Lucian W. Pye, ed., *Communication and Political Development,* Princeton University Press, 1963; Daniel Lerner, *The Passing of Traditional Society: Modernizing the Middle East,* Glencoe, Illinois: Free Press, 1958; David McClelland, *The Achieving Society,* Princeton, N.J.: Van Nostrand, 1961; Everett M. Rogers, *Modernization Among Peasants: The Impact of Communication,* New York: Holt, Rinehart, and Winston, 1969; and Leonard Binder, James C. Coleman, Joseph La Palombara, Lucian W. Pye, Sidney Verba and Myrn Weiber, *Crises and Sequences in Political Development,* Princeton University Press, 1971.

16 Daniel Lerner, *The Passing of Traditional Society,* pp. 1-99.
17 E. M. Rogers and F. F. Shoemaker, *Communication of Innovations: A Cross-Cultural Approach,* New York: Free Press, 1971, p. 11.

terms of five stages[18]: (1) traditional society, (2) the pre-condition for take-off where certain requisites were fulfilled; (3) the take-off stage; (4) the drive and climb to maturity, and finally; (5) a high level of mass consumption. This "non-communist manifesto" was based on the belief that a steady increase in per capita income, especially during the "take-off" stage, through the mechanism of savings and investment, and the emergence of a political and social framework capable of exploiting the impulse to expand would underline the "drive to maturity," resulting in development.

By the mid-1960s, many economists, political scientists, sociologists and anthropologists, while not minimizing the significance of the more obvious and generally recognized economic and political obstacles and the inadequacy of many governmental, legal, social and cultural institutions, suggested that the way people in developing countries think and their cultural and social philosophies might give different meanings to development and have a bearing on the prospects of not only economic growth but the entire realm of societal development.[19] One of the economists who discarded the economic theories of development and sought for plausible explanations of development outside his discipline was Everett Hagen. His conception of the ideal "traditional society" postulated that behaviour is governed by custom, not law and that in such a society the individual's position is normally inherited rather than achieved. Consequently, economic productivity is low.[20]

A similar theory was developed by David McClelland, whose concept of the achieving society is based on the premise that a society with a generally high level of "need achievement" will produce more entrepreneurs who, in turn, produce more rapid economic development[21]. Like Hagen, McClelland studied the sources of need achievement in child-rearing techniques. He advocated not only the modification of child socialization patterns but also the development of achievement motivation through educational techniques.

During the post-World War II period and, especially in the last two decades, the question of development has been debated within the broader framework of theories of imperialism and underdevelopment, including both Marxist and non-Marxist perspectives. Both the intellectual and policy traditions in this area were further stimulated by the fact that traditional approaches to development as applied to developing countries were not successful, and the notion of the dependency of lesser developed countries on the developed industrialized world was gaining acceptance and visibility through debate. By the 1950s and 1960s, two major propositions had been advanced concerning development and imperialism. One was the notion of neocolonialism presented by the leaders of the Third World in the mid-1950s, which claimed that the developing countries and former colonial territories were indirectly exploited by unequal trade and political relationships.[22] The second, which was rooted in the dependency school of thought advanced mostly by Latin American writers and supported by their North American counterparts in the 1960s, argued that the development and underdevelopment were interrelated and continuous processes—two sides of a single coin.[23]

18 W. W. Rostow, *The Stages of Economic Growth: A Non-Communist Manifesto*, Cambridge, England: Cambridge University Press, 1960.
19 Hamid Mowlana, "Capital Formation in the Middle East: A Study of Human Factors in Economic Development," Tennessee Survey of Business, Center for Business and Economic Research, University of Tennessee, Vol. 111, No. 1, September 1967, pp. 1-8.
20 Everett E. Hagen, *On the Theory of Social Change: How Economic Growth Begins*, Homewood, Illinois: Dorsey Press, 1962.

21 David L. McClelland, *The Achieving Society*; see also, David McClelland and David Winter, *Motivating Economic Achievement*, New York: The Free Press, 1971.
22 Paul A. Baran, *The Political Economy of Growth*, New York: Monthly Review Press, 1957; and Kwame Nkrumah, *Neo-Colonialism: The Last Stage of Capitalism*, London: 1965.
23 See Theotonio Dos Santos, "The Structure of Dependency," *American Economic Review*, LX, May 1970, pp. 231-236; Fernando Henrique Cardoso. "Dependency and Development in Latin America," *New Left Review*, July-August 1974, pp. 83-95; Celso Furtado, *Economic Growth of Brazil: A Survey From Colonial to Modern Times*, Berkeley, California: University of California Press, 1963; and his *Development and Underdevelopment*, University of California Press, 1964; Oswaldo Sernkel, "Big Business and 'Dependencia,'" Foreign Affairs, April 1972, pp. 517-531. For a review of the literature on dependency theory, see Ronald H. Chilcote, "Dependency: A Critical Synthesis of the Literature," *Latin American Perspectives* I, Fall 1974, pp. 4-29.

1927
1960
1963
1964
1967
1969
1970
1971
1972
1973
1974
1975
1976
1977
1978
1979
1980
1981
1982
1983
1984
1985
1986
1987
1988
1989
1990
1991
1992
1993
1994
1995
1996
1997
1998
1999
2000
2001
2002
2003
2004
2005
2006

Despite the enthusiasm expressed by the advocates, the theorists and the planners of the orthodox theories of development, it was clear by the 1960s and the early 1970s that the philosophies as well as the strategies had either failed to meet their desired goals, or in case of successful implementations, were becoming dysfunctional, creating sharp criticism from within and without the system. This was the beginning of what may be called a new wave, and a continuous stream of criticism, rebellion, protest, revolution, self-evaluation and a search for alternatives that reached its most crucial stage in the late 1970s.

During the last two decades, contributions to the new meaning of development have come from diverse and varied schools of thought, geographical areas and personalities. They include the Islamic response of Ayatollah Ruhollah Khomeini,[24] his disciple Murtaza Mutahhari[25] and Iranian sociologist Ali Shari'ati[26]; the Latin American discourse of such writers as Paulo Freire[27] and Gustavo Gutierrez[28]; and the African challenge of Frantz Fanon[29] and Julius K. Nyerere[30] and several others. The new notion of development not only emphasizes traditional and cultural values, but also self-reliance, grass-root initiatives and, above all, an ideology of its own, independent from traditional liberalism and Marxism.

24 Ayatollah Ruhollah al-Moosani Khomeini, *Hokumat-e Islam (Islamic Government)*, Tehran, 1979; his *Islam and Revolution: Extracts From the Writings and Declarations of Iman Khomeini* (translated by Harnid Algar), Berkeley, California: Mizan Press, 1982; and his collection of speeches, *Sahifeh Noor,* Tehran, 1983-1985, 15 volumes.

25 Murtaza Mutahhari, *Jame'a va Tarikh, (Society and History: An Introduction to Islamic World View),* Teheran: Sadra Publications, 1980 (for an English version see his three-part article, "Sociology of the Qur'an: The Islamic View of History," *Al-Tawhid: A Quarterly Journal of Islamic Thought and Culture,* Vol. 1, Nos. 3 and 4, 1983-1984, and Vol. 1, No. 1, 1984); and his *Majmoo'a Goftarha (Collection of Speeches),* Teheran: Sadra Publications, 1983.

26 Ali Shari'ati, *On the Sociology of Islam,* Berkeley, California: Mizan Press, 1979; and his *Marxism and Other Western Fallacies,* Berkeley, California: Miran Press, 1980.

27 Paulo Freire, *The Pedagogy of the Oppressed,* New York: Seabury Press, 1968; and his *Cultural Action for Freedom,* London: Penguin Books, 1970.

28 Gustavo Gutierrez Merino, "Notes for a Theology of Liberation," *Theological Studies,* 31 : 2, June 1970.

29 Frantz Fanon, *The Wretched of the Earth,* Harmondsworth, England: Penguin Books, 1967; and his *Black Skin, White Marks,* London: MacGibbon and Kee, 1968.

30 Julius K. Nyerere, *Ujamaa,* Nairobi, Kenya: Oxford University Press, 1968.

The Meaning of Communication

It is paradoxical that many of the books, monographs and articles dealing with communication and development contain chapters on the definition of development yet fail to make any attempt to define what is meant by the term "communication" or "communications" as currently used in the literature. Nevertheless, a survey of the literature shows that almost all the writers in this field continue to use the term as though they knew exactly what it meant and as though others were familiar with that meaning.[31]

It must be noted that although there have been attempts by communication scholars to arrive at a single, universally acceptable, definition of communication, such efforts have been rather unsuccessful. A number of writers have added or emphasized different dimensions of communication in their work, but it has been the technological and quantitative dimensions of communication that have received the most emphasis from both scholars and policymakers over the last few decades. The notion that communication is a means or a process of transmitting ideas or information is based on the assumption that communication is something that one does rather than something that occurs.

Challenging these somewhat orthodox views of communication, one may speak of the so-called "information age" in which individual, group, national and international communication are coming to be seen not only as hardware and software development, but more important as behavioural and social development as well. The emphasis here, then, is on communication as a process and not on communications as a means.[32]

31 James H. Platt, "What Do We Mean 'Communication'?" *Journal of Communication* 5:1, Spring 1955, p. 21; and Lee O. Thayer, "On Theory Building in Communication, Summer 1983, pp. 217-235; also, Robert L. Minter, "A Donative and Connotative Study in Communication," *Journal of Communication,* 18: 1, March 1968, p. 27.

32 See Hamid Mowlana, *Global Information and World Communication: New Frontiers in International Relations,* White Plains, N.Y.: Longman, 1985, especially chapters 1, 9, 11 and 12; also, Hamid Mowlana, International Flow of Information: A Global Report and Analysis, *Reports and Papers on Mass Communication,* No. 99, Paris, UNESCO, 1985.

In addition, we recognize a need for a shift in emphasis in the analysis of communication systems from an exclusive concern with the source and content of the messages to the analysis of the message distribution process. Communication, therefore, is defined here as social interaction by means of messages, which are both human and technological. Thus, the communication act, on societal, national or international levels, can be explained as: (1) who produces and (2) who distributes (3) what to (4) whom by (5) which channels under (6) which conditions (values) with (7) what intention (purpose) under (8) which political economy and with (9) what effect?[33]

In summary, the debate of the last two decades has made it clear that: (1) communication, although vital, is a much more complex component of "development" than it was originally thought to be, and that it cannot be removed from its social and cultural contexts; and (2) that the notion of "development" itself is still a somewhat unsettled concept that continues to have a number of less universal and more culture-bound values attached to it.

Mowlana, Hamid. "Communication Technology and Development; International Flow of News," International Flows of Information: A Global Report and Analysis, p.7-15, UNESCO, 1985. Reprinted with permission of the publisher.

33 Hamid Mowlana, *Mass Media and Culture: Toward an Integrated Theory*, p. 163.

EXCERPT FROM:

SOCIAL COMPLEXITY AND PUBLIC OPINION

By Giuseppe Richeri

1988 The complexity of contemporary social systems has been one of the most frequently examined areas of study in the social sciences in recent years. The concept of social complexity refers to society's differentiation and segmentation into an expanding number of subsystems, each of which tends to increase in autonomy. Various phenomena have been attributed to the growing complexity of contemporary society. Of particular note are the progressive loss of a common horizon of reference for the entire society—or large segments of it, for instance the social classes; and the frag-mentation of common sense and the impossibility of representing society as a whole, either cognitively or symbolically/intuitively (Rositi, 1978). Consequently, there has been a gradual weakening of the ties that bring social subgroups into relationship with universally shared and accepted norms. This has been accompanied by an enhanced autonomy on the part of those subgroups with respect to a "higher center of coordination," i.e., the State.

In short, as a result of the ever greater complexity of society, the overall social system has enjoyed increasing possibilities for action, becoming more and more open to these possibilities and providing subgroups greater autonomy. However, the burgeoning of alternatives also creates difficulty and uncertainty in decision making. If society is to survive in such an environment, a minimum level of balance and organization must be ensured, and "complexity reducers" must be established.

1927
1960
1963
1964
1967
1969
1970
1971
1972
1973
1974
1975
1976
1977
1978
1979
1980
1981
1982
1983
1984
1985
1986
1987
1988
1989
1990
1991
1992
1993
1994
1995
1996
1997
1998
1999
2000
2001
2002
2003
2004
2005
2006

According to most thinkers who have delved into the question of social complexity—notably, the German sociologist Niklas Luhmann (1978)—one of the basic complexity-reducing mechanisms is the phenomenon of public opinion, i.e., the forum in which topics of shared importance are selected and defined, serving to regulate attention and permit communication among individuals, while unifying individual and collective concerns around common problems.

This brief paper makes no attempt to summarize the vast debate in the social sciences on the issue of social complexity. It aims merely to point out the connection between the problems of social complexity and the processes of producing, distributing and consuming information that are basic to shaping public opinion.

Selection of Information

The formation of public opinion is recognized as a complex process—one, therefore, whose basic components and mechanisms for interacting with the body social are difficult to decipher (P. Bourdieu, 1973; E. Noelle-Neuman, 1974). At the most general level, the role, within this process, of agents—the mass media—that disseminate information to vast, nonspecialized audiences is universally acknowledged. In this formation process, one of the central functions of the mass media is to select the information to be disseminated. This process includes three steps:

a. The first step is choosing the subjects or events to be recognized as having the right to enter into the informational circuit.

b. The second step involves determining the hierarchy, i.e., deciding what emphasis to give to topics and events recognized as suitable for entry into the informational circuit, i.e., determining the location and amount of space to be devoted to particular news items within the repertoire of information in the print medium, and the amount of time and the sequence of particular items in the broadcast repertoire.

c. The third step entails setting an agenda, i.e., specifying the major story lines on which to focus public attention—ones that will also serve as the basis for decision making. Thus, an issue of significance to the public—one demanding a solution or decision—can be made to stand out, within an event or series of events, by devoting differing amounts of time to different events—specifically, by presenting the issue in a series of events over a prolonged period of time (Rositi, 1982).

In short, the mass media, employing these three steps of selection, present the public with the major issues and their relative weight. …

References

Bourdieu, P. 1979. La Distinction, critique sociale du jugement, Les Editions de Minuit, Paris.

Noelle-Neumann, E. (1974). "The Spiral of Silence: A Theory of Public Opinion." *Journal of Communication,* 24 (2), 43-51.

Rositi, F. Mercati di cultura, Bari, De Donato, 1982.

Luhmann N., L'opinione pubblica, in ID., Stato di diritto e sistema sociale, Guida, Naples 1978.

POPULAR VIDEO FOR RURAL DEVELOPMENT IN PERU

Excerpt from: Development Communication Report

By J. Manuel Calvelo Rios

1989 Fourteen years ago, Peru began its first effort in the systematic and massive use of video for education and training in rural areas of the country. The project was funded by the FAO [Food and Agricultural Organization] and the UNDP [United Nations Development Programme] in cooperation with the Centro de Servicios de Pedagogia Audiovisual para la Capacitacion (CESPAC), the Audiovisual Center for Educational Services—a part of the Peruvian Ministry of Agriculture. By the time the project ended in 1986, the following results had been attained:

■ Four hundred and ninety thousand peasants from the mountains of Peru had attended video-based courses lasting 5 to 20 days with three to four hours of training each day. The courses covered rural health, housing, family planning, reforestation, agriculture, animal husbandry, nutrition and water sanitation.

■ One hundred and twenty different course packages were produced. Each one included three to five audiovisual programs, as well as printed student and teacher guides. In all, 1,260 different video programs, each 10 to 18 minutes in length, were produced.

■ An additional 780 video programs were produced on institutional information, human resource development, culture and socioeconomic diagnostics.

■ One hundred and sixty audiovisual specialists completed training in video production, learned to produce audiovisual materials and to run the training programs. Seventy trainers from other countries also completed the program.

■ A total of 280 group discussion leaders learned how to use audiovisuals is the training process. Many of theses were peasants from Andean communities.

■ Considerable research on the adaptation of video technology for use in rural areas was conducted. Among several devices developed were pedal-operated electrical generators and special voltage adapters.

■ Numerous examples showed that the ideas presented in the courses were carried out in practice—domestic vegetable gardens, new adobe buildings, increased animal vaccination, restorations, reforestation, etc.

Why Use Video?

In 1975, Peru decided to support rural development through education and training. This decision was seen not only as a means to increase production and productivity, but also as a way to improve the living conditions of subsistence peasants in real terms. It was hoped that education and training would enable peasants to take better advantage of the resources that came within their reach.

Any attempt to promote rural development requires two basic elements. The first element is capital-access to affordable credit, investments and equitable pricing policies. The second important element is physical inputs—machinery, fertilizers, pesticides, improved seeds, etc. The CESPAC video project was designed to give peasants an additional input beyond these two: the skills to help them manage both capital and physical inputs more productively and the knowledge to improve their own living conditions. Knowledge and skills are intangible and unique: They do not disappear with use and, without them, other inputs can be misused and wasted.

Who Were We Trying to Reach?

The subsistence farmer who brings most of the food we consume to our markets in many developing countries is generally illiterate. He or she is likely to speak a language distinct from the official one. Farmers' activities and needs in training embrace diverse areas, from

1927
1960
1963
1964
1967
1969
1970
1971
1972
1973
1974
1975
1976
1977
1978
1979
1980
1981
1982
1983
1984
1985
1986
1987
1988
1989
1990
1991
1992
1993
1994
1995
1996
1997
1998
1999
2000
2001
2002
2003
2004
2005
2006

agriculture to business. Farmers make up a large percentage of the population and have high birth rates, high infant mortality rates and low life expectancy rates from birth. As the productive potential of farmers' surroundings disappear, under demographic pressures, and as farmers can no longer eke out an existence from the land, they are forced to use lands that may not be able to sustain agricultural activities, or migrate to the cities. To forestall the choice, entire families, including children must act as producers, artisans or salesmen.

However, farmers and their families are also well integrated with the land. For centuries, peasants in Peru have run the country's agriculture. Traditional farmers master the techniques needed to live within a habitat without destroying it. A successful training program for farmers recovers this traditional knowledge, combines it with modern science and then gives the new package back to farmers in forms that make the information both intelligible and practical.

If farmers' knowledge and culture are to be respected—even as imperfections are recognized and reduced—and if a dialogue is created to bring new knowledge to farmers, then the theoretical model of communication-speaker-medium-receiver is inadequate. A new model adapted to the need for participatory dialogue is called for, one that involves the final user of training knowledge in the communication process.

The CESPAC Approach
The CESPAC video project proposed to "recover, preserve and reproduce peasant knowledge" using multimedia. Video was used to enhance comprehension; printed guides—with many illustrations and few words—served as permanent memory aids. Interpersonal communication in group discussions served to reinforce practical learning. An old folk saying characterized the process: "If I hear it, I forget it; if I see it, I remember it; if I do it, I learn it." It is in the execution of practical tasks that knowledge is absorbed and assimilated.

The equipment chosen for the project had to be low in cost, easy to maintain and adaptable for use in rural areas. The systems were also designed to be flexible enough to accept technical modifications. We first started with black and white tape for economic reasons, then when costs went down and the personnel became more proficient, we began using color. Each editing unit—two video cassette recorders (VCRs), two monitors and an edit control unit—served three field recording units—one camera and VCR or one camcorder. For each recording unit, approximately 20 playback units were purchased—one VCR and monitor with a 16- to 20-inch screen and additional speaker. The relatively high cost of the investment in audiovisual production equipment was amortized by the widespread use of the materials produced.

Audiovisual trainers worked in production teams of two, doing every task needed to create the video programs and learning packages, including research, videotaping in the field, editing, field testing and then finally using the teaching modules. The production model guaranteed both educational quality and low cost. Forty-six percent of the audiovisual teachers were women, which helped to counteract problems of machismo. In a rural context, topics related to fertility and family planning were more easily conveyed by women teachers.

Training the Trainers
The training courses for the audiovisual trainers were selective and very intense. They included theoretical material as well as practical training experience and produced usable audiovisuals. In the final stage of training, students worked in the field. The production of reaching modules followed five stages:

- initial field investigation and consultation with the peasants to determine the themes to be taught and the best ways to convey them through video;
- academic research to develop answers to technical problems encountered;
- recording in the field;
- tape editing at the center; and

■ experimental application in the field with the same peasants who had facilitated the investigation and recording.

When the teaching video was shown to be effective, the tapes were duplicated and distributed to the training units that needed them. Once the CESPAC system became known to the peasants, demand for teaching modules exceeded production capacity.

Before each course was initiated, an agreement with the peasant group, with the community or with the cooperative was negotiated. This helped assure full participation and also ensured that the resources necessary to apply the knowledge learned from the courses would be available for the group once training was completed. Audiovisual trainers supervised activities. He or she would locate the technicians who were to be present during the sessions, organize the discussions before and after the show and evaluate the results. Courses were always given to groups of no more than 30 participants.

When, as a result of technical research, a hand-operated electric generator was introduced, it then fell to the users of the courses to pedal the machine to supply the power to charge the batteries. The participants charged the batteries if they were interested in the courses; otherwise there was no electricity to view the programs. This equipment became, in effect, a useful evaluation tool.

Total cost of the project was approximately $34 USD per peasant per course. This figure included all of the costs generated by the training activities. The amount could have been even lower if there had been more production units. The Development Support Communication Branch of the FAO has produced a case study on the project, including the feasibility study and additional documents, for anyone interested in this experience, which has been described only briefly here.

Calvelo, Manuel, "Popular Video for Rural Development in Peru," *Development Communication Report (DCR)*, Clearinghouse on Development Communication, 1989/3, No. 66, FAO. Copyright © 1989, Academy for Educational Development. Reprinted with permission of AED.

HYBRID CULTURES AND COMMUNICATIVE STRATEGIES

Excerpt from: Media Development

By Néstor García Canclini

1989 I will concentrate on two questions: a) the epistemological legitimacy and methodological fecundity of the notion of hybrid cultures; b) communication strategies in the processes of Latin American development and stagnation in the 1990s.

Hybridity as an explanatory resource

I have been asked…about the usefulness of applying the notion of hybridity, derived from biological sciences, to cultural processes. Isn't a hybrid "something infertile, like a mule?" Doesn't "cultural vitality" reside in "each culture's capacity for reproduction and renovation?" (Schmilchuk).

My biologist friends tell me that there exist several examples of hybrids that are fertile, enriching, that generate expansion and diversification. Among vegetables, since Karpeahenko's famous experiments, which crossed radishes with cabbages, there have been efforts to combine the properties of cells from different plants to improve growth, resistance and the quality of the produce. Most of the commercially grown corn in the United States is the result of hybridisation carried out by geneticists to strengthen it (Villée-Dethier, chs. 8 and 10). The hybridisation of human DNA with bacteria to produce proteins has become the principal way of producing insulin.

In any case, I see no need to get trapped in the biological dynamic from which the concept derives. The social sciences have imported many ideas from other disciplines without invalidating their uses in their original contexts. Biological concepts such as reproduction

1927
1960
1963
1964
1967
1969
1970
1971
1972
1973
1974
1975
1976
1977
1978
1979
1980
1981
1982
1983
1984
1985
1986
1987
1988
1989
1990
1991
1992
1993
1994
1995
1996
1997
1998
1999
2000
2001
2002
2003
2004
2005
2006

were reworked to speak of social, economic and cultural reproduction: the debate carried on from Marx to the present day is based on the theoretical consistency and explanatory power of that term, and does not ultimately depend on the use assigned by another science. In the same way, polemics about the metaphorical use of economic concepts to examine symbolic processes, such as that of Pierre Bourdieu, when he refers to cultural capital and linguistic markets, need not be centred on the migration of these terms from one discipline to another but on the epistemological operations that place their explanatory scope and their limits within cultural discourses: Do they or do they not permit greater understanding of something that would otherwise be inexplicable? Scientific knowledge has repeatedly advanced through carrying on with notions originating in different semantic universes in the same way that some artists have experimented with others' symbolic resources.

…My purpose has been to elaborate the notion of hybridisation as a social concept. As I explained in *Hybrid Cultures*, I found this term better suited for grasping diverse intercultural mixtures than "mestizaje," which is limited to racial mixings, or "syncretism," which almost always refers to religious combinations or to traditional symbolic movements. I thought that we needed a more versatile word to take into account those "classic" mixtures as well as the interlacing of the traditional and the modern, the educated, the popular and the mass. A characteristic of our century, which complicates the search for a more inclusive term, is that all of these types of multicultural fusion intermingle and draw strength from one another.

The notion of hybridity seemed useful for designating the mixtures of indigenous styles with Spanish and Portuguese iconography. It also served to describe processes of independence and national construction in which modernising projects have co-existed —to the present— alongside traditions that are scarcely compatible with what Europeans consider characteristic of modernity. Assembling various conceptualisations

of this process, principally those of Jürgen Habermas, Pierre Bourdieu and Howard S. Becker, I found that they could be synthesised into four concepts: emancipation, expansion, renovation and democratisation.

But the secularisation of cultural fields, the self-expressive and self-regulating production of artistic and political practices, the rationalisation of social life and growing individualism, all of which have been considered sources of modern emancipation, co-exist in Latin America with religious and ethnic fundamentalisms, illiteracy and archaic power relations. Social and cultural expansion, as well as renovation, has been manifested in the rapid industrialising development and in the growth of secondary and higher education, in artistic and literary dynamism and experimentation throughout the 20th Century and in the fluid adaptation of certain sectors to technological and social innovation.

However, these renovating impulses do not replace local traditions; at times they accompany them and at other times they conflict with them, but not destroy them. In addition, multicultural mixtures can be observed in metropolitan areas, but one characteristic that demands attention in Latin America is that heterogeneity is multitemporal. Industry does not eliminate folk art, democratisation does suppress authoritarian habits as if by evolution, nor does written culture suppress ancient forms of orality.

In some cases, the persistence of ancient customs and ways of thinking can be seen as the result of unequal access to the benefits of modernity. But at other times these hybridisations persist because they are fertile: … They have engendered happy marriages between pre-Columbian iconography and contemporary geometrism, between elite, folk and media industries' visual and musical cultures. This is evident in much Mexican, Peruvian and Guatemalan folk art that combine their own myths with transnational images, in the rock music that enlivens local festivals and is nourished with ethnic melodies that may later achieve international dissemination. Many works have taken the dialogue between the elite, the popular and the mass as their test bed: From Octavio Paz and Jorge Luis Borges to Astor Piazzola and Caetano Veloso, these testify to the fertility of liminal creations and rituals that are concerned less with the preservation of purity than with the productivity of the mix.

None of this takes place without contradictions and conflicts. Cultures do not co-exist with the serenity that we might experience in moving from one room to another in a museum. To understand this complex and often painful interaction, these experiences of hybridisation must be read as part of the conflicts of Latin American modernity. I have attempted to understand the sinuous trajectory of these interactions, discarding the thesis of a simple imposition of modernity as if it were an external force. The history of how our exuberant modernism is articulated—that is, the intellectual projects of modernity based on deficient socio-economic modernisation—is the story of how the elites, and in many cases the popular sectors, have ingeniously hybridised the desired modernity with traditions that they do not want to cast away in order to take charge of our multitemporal heterogeneity and to turn it into something productive.

Thus, the term hybridity does not take on meaning on its own, but rather is part of a constellation of concepts. Some of the principal ones are: modernity-modernisation-modernism, difference-inequality, multitemporal heterogeneity, reconversion. The latter, taken from economics, allowed me to propose a perspective that combined elite and popular classes' strategies of hybridisation. Sociocultural hybridity is not a simple mixture of discrete and pure social practices that have existed separately and which, upon combining, generate new structures and new practices. At times this occurs in an unplanned way, or is the unforeseen result of processes of migration, tourism or of economic or communications exchanges.

But often hybridity emerges from the attempt to reconvert a legacy (a factory, professional training, a set of knowledge and techniques) in order to re-insert it into new conditions of production and of the market. This is how Pierre Bourdieu used this expression to explain the strategies through which a painter becomes a designer, or national bourgeoisie acquire the languages and other competencies necessary to reinvest their economic and symbolic capital in transnational circuits (Bourdieu 1979: 155, 175, 354). But, as I analysed in *Hybrid Cultures*, strategies of economic and symbolic reconversion are also found in popular sectors: rural migrants who adapt their knowledge in order to work and consume in the city and their handicrafts in order to appeal to urban buyers; workers faced with new production technologies who reformulate their working culture; indigenous movements that reshape their demands into those of transnational politics or of an ecological discourse, and learn to communicate these through radio and television. Ultimately, for such reasons, for me the object of study is not hybridity but rather processes of hybridisation.

The empirical analysis of these processes, connected to strategies of reconversion, shows that hybridisation is of as much interest to the dominant as to the popular sectors that want to appropriate the benefits of modernity. At times, subordinate groups faced with economic and cultural policies that damage them resort to traditional political means, incorporating the modern in a hybrid or atypical way as a survival strategy. But as mixed formulas also arise from protests and negotiations, modernisation, the present globalisation and in general all hegemonic politics, cannot be understood only as imposed by the strong on the weak. Studies of hybridisation have discredited the Manichaean perspective, which radically opposes dominator and dominated, centre and periphery, sender and receiver. Instead, they demonstrate the multipolarity of social initiatives, the obliqueness with which power may be exercised and the reciprocal borrowing that take place in the midst of differences and inequalities.

Binary and polar philosophies of history are revealed to be particularly inconsistent at those intercultural borders, where there is intense hybridisation.

1927
1960
1963
1964
1967
1969
1970
1971
1972
1973
1974
1975
1976
1977
1978
1979
1980
1981
1982
1983
1984
1985
1986
1987
1988
1989
1990
1991
1992
1993
1994
1995
1996
1997
1998
1999
2000
2001
2002
2003
2004
2005
2006

But strictly speaking, in this era of globalisation we all live on borders crisscrossed by multiple diversified strategies. Those groups in which power is concentrated and which relate to subaltern groups, up to a point, must take into account their diversity and demands. In international debate, the time of extreme opposition, of binarism and unidirectional manipulative conspiracies, has passed.

Stuart Hall maintains that to understand current forms of economic and cultural power, we must face this apparent paradox: We live in a "multinational but decentred" world. Even though "global mass culture" seems to be centred in the West, "it speaks English as an international language. It speaks a variety of broken forms of English." Its expansion is achieved through an "enormously absorptive" homogenisation of local and regional particularities, "and it does not work for completeness. It is not attempting to produce little mini-versions of Englishness everywhere, or little versions of American-ness. It wants to recognise and absorb those differences within the larger, overarching framework of what is essentially an American conception of the world." In one specific reference to the ties between the United States and Latin America, Hall says that the hegemony of the United States is not understandable solely as the elimination of difference; rather, he observes, there are multiple ways that Latin American cultures can be "repenetrated, absorbed, reshaped, negotiated, without absolutely destroying what is specific and particular to them" (Hall 1991: 28-29).

Nor do recent studies of popular sectors sustain that polarity. Since many of them are interested in modernisation, they not only confront and resist, but they also transact and consent, borrow and reuse. Local cultures grow and expand by necessity to become cosmopolitan, once they discover that the pure preservation of their traditions cannot by itself reproduce and re-elaborate their situations. The prosperous artisans of Michoacán and Guerrero, in Mexico, have done this: By incorporating contemporary scenes into the devils of Ocumicho and the *amate* paintings of Ameyaltepec, by learning English and travelling by air or by using credit cards, they acquire the money that allows them to modernise their daily lives and at the same time revitalise their ancient traditions and ceremonies. The renewed rural and indigenous struggles of recent years in Chiapas and other parts of Mexico show them using the Internet and other unconventional means by which popular groups seek to integrate themselves into modernity and turn it to their advantage (Zermeño).

The aggravation of long-standing inequalities by the recent changes in Latin American society makes the confrontations seem at times like a simple opposition. There is no shortage of situations in which difference and inequality are exacerbated to the point that classes and ethnic groups act as if everything were reduced to confrontations. Or, if there are hybridisations between "our own" and "the foreign," it is because there is no choice but to accept them. In these situations, it may be useful to distinguish between dominated hybridities and hybridities of resistance, as does Homi K. Bhabha. He has made a considerable contribution towards constructing the notion of hybridity as a linguistic one, beyond biology, defining it as "a metonymy of presence" (Bhabha: 115), and situating it among power relations, not as if the hybridisation of two cultures were simply a matter of intercultural relativism.

But I find the constant polarity that he establishes between the colonial and resistance inappropriate for Latin America, because our countries ceased to be colonies almost two centuries ago, and our culture cannot be analysed "as a colonial space of intervention," but is rather a site where the meaning of modernity is contested. In this context of a relatively independent modernity (whose peripheral and subordinate characteristics cannot be captured by the term postcolonial), even the vast sectors that were damaged by the recent neoconservative restructuring interact, hybridising the hegemonic and the popular, the local, the national and the transnational. Among these entities "an interstitial intimacy" develops, an expression that Bhabha uses to challenge the "binary divisions" (13) between private and public, past and present, psychic and social, and to recognise the complex intertwining that take place "in between," in the porous boundaries of the intersections. Bhabha does not apply this subtle understanding to the relations between members of hegemonic and subaltern groups, possibly due to his subordination of the cultural to the political confrontation that governs his thinking. But in Latin America—as I have analysed in more detail elsewhere (García Canclini, 1995: ch. 9)—this perspective is indispensable for understanding the partial autonomy achieved by cultural fields in modernity, as well as the importance of transactions and negotiation in the development of hegemonic and popular identities.

Latin American Hybridities:
A Comparison with Cultural Studies

In recent years, there has been a confrontation between ways of thinking about the hybridisation of tradition and modernity, and various types of modernities, in Latin America and the United States. I would like to comment on how I see the Latin American situation in this debate and its perspectives in terms of globalisation and regional integration.

For this I find it useful to start from two criticisms of the book *Hybrid Cultures*, which also allow me to detail ideas I have been developing about the philosophy of history. George Yudice contends that my position "tends to overstate the case of hybridizations in abolishing 'the hierarchies among historical periods'." He continues:

> While I agree that the temporalities (and spatialities) have been blurred, I cannot wax so sanguine about the hierarchies. The fact is that the vast majority of traditional groups and other subaltern peoples continue to live under conditions of diminished opportunity. Cultural reconversion—that is, making cultural production marketable—is certainly an improvement over not having sufficient resources for the 'pursuit of life and happiness,' but it is to accept an economic rationale as a solution for cultural production and reception and their role in the construction of more democratic civil societies (Yudice, 1993: 151-52).

Meanwhile, Renato Rosaldo claims in his introduction to the English translation of my book that my analysis of tradition and modernity may prove difficult for readers in the United States to comprehend. The gap in comprehension derives form the absolute ideological divide between North and South, between nation-states regarded as having completed their modernisation and those that have not yet done so.

In Latin America, modernisation and development remain vital issues that are named as such in the discussions that reflect and create national self-understanding. In the United States, on the other hand, questions of modernisation do not enter the public realm of grappling with vital social issues. Such social issues as poverty and the shameful infant mortality rates among African Americans and the poor, for example, are treated neither as signs of underdevelopment nor as failures of uneven modernisation (as they conceivably could be in principle and no doubt would be in Latin America). Thus readers of this translation will need to remember that questions of modernisation may not be as alien to them as North/South ideologies would make it appear. Debate with *Hybrid Cultures* in the United States will focus not only on the tradition/modernity distinction but also on the notion that the contemporary historical period contains different temporalities (traditional, modern and postmodern), as if epochs could persist relatively unchanged into the present (Rosaldo, 1995: xiii-xi and xvi).

Two authors with much in common, theoretically, both in North American cultural studies, hold different views of my way of examining hybridity in Latin American countries. While Yudice finds that I do not sufficiently distinguish the temporalities that co-exist in the present and that I suppress the hierarchies between historical periods, Rosaldo contends that from a country that is fully modernised (United States),

1927
1960
1963
1964
1967
1969
1970
1971
1972
1973
1974
1975
1976
1977
1978
1979
1980
1981
1982
1983
1984
1985
1986
1987
1988
1989
1990
1991
1992
1993
1994
1995
1996
1997
1998
1999
2000
2001
2002
2003
2004
2005
2006

and from a discipline like anthropology that opposes evolutionism, it is difficult to accept that different eras persist separately and relatively unaltered in the contemporary world.

To try to overcome both these difficulties, I devoted many pages to examining how artisans and other traditional groups re-elaborated their cultural heritages in order to participate in modernity, which is the dominant epochal condition of Latin America. But I believe it is necessary to recognise that the historic contrivances of social, economic and cultural exclusion generated processes of dualisation and preserved marginal, "traditionalist" circuits or pockets, limiting their weak ties to, and insertions in, modern hegemonic processes.

Although the hybridisations generated by modernisation reach rural and indigenous villages through the commercialisation of their economies—the arrival of cultural industries and other movements that connect them to contemporary development—I feel it is necessary to study the scanty integration (not isolation) of traditionalist sectors into the social totality in order to understand the socio-economic and cultural bases of neo-Mexican-its, neo-Incan and other indigenous movements that attempt to re-institute idealised traditions as antimodern utopias. I share with Rosaldo the opinion that these utopias should be examined as part of modernity. But, in addition, so that they do not seem to be simply absurd ravings, we need to see them in connection with the structural conditions that make them marginal. In the context of the current selective and unjust globalisation, to which I will refer later, what I find surprising is not so much that well-rounded traditions persist into modernity but rather that the sharpening of asymmetries and forms of exclusion push ever broader sectors towards the ideological regressiveness of fundamentalism.

To my mind, the most important difference between cultural processes in the United States and in Latin America is not their ways of conceiving the ties between tradition and modernity, but rather their ways of understanding hybridity with respect to different visions of multiculturalism. Perhaps the key discrepancy between United States multiculturalism and what in Latin America has been called pluralism or cultural heterogeneity is, as various authors have observed, that in the United States "multiculturalism means separatism" (Hughes, Taylor, and Walzer). We know that, as Peter McLaren says, it is useful to distinguish between conservative, liberal and left-liberal multiculturalisms. For the first, separatism between ethnic groups is subordinated to white, Anglo Saxon Protestant (WASP) hegemony and the canon that stipulates what must be read and learned to be culturally literate.

Liberal multiculturalism postulates the natural equality and cognitive equivalence of races, while the left-liberal version attributes violations of this equality to the unequal access to resources. But only a few authors, such as McLaren, proclaim the need to "legitimate multiple traditions of knowledge" simultaneously and to emphasise building solidarity around each group's claims. Therefore, analysts like Michael Walzer express their concern that "the sharp conflict in North American life today does not oppose multiculturalism to some hegemony or singularity," to "a vigorous and independent North American identity," but rather opposes "the multitude of groups to the multitude of individuals. All the voices are loud, the intonations are varied and the result is not harmonious music—contrary to the ancient image of pluralism as a symphony in which each group plays its part (but—who wrote the music?)—but rather a cacophony" (Walzer: 109 and 105).

What could be called the canon in Latin American cultures owes much to Europe, but throughout the 20th century it has combined influences from various European countries and has linked them in a heterodox way with diverse national traditions. Writers such as Jorge Luis Borges and Carlos Fuentes cite German expressionists, French surrealists, Czech, Italian and Irish novelists: authors who do not know one another, but who write from peripheral countries "can manipulate," as Borges said, "without superstitions," with "irreverence." Although Borges and Fuentes may be extreme cases, I find in most specialists in the humanities and social sciences, and in general in Latin American cultural production, a restructured appropriation of metropolitan canons and a critical use with respect to various national needs. Furthermore, Latin American societies were not formed on a model of ethno-communal belonging, but were based upon the lay idea of the Republic and of Jacobin individualism, yet at the same time with an openness to the modulations that the French model had acquired in other European cultures and in the United States Constitution.

Since the 19th century, even in the most Westernised nations, such as Argentina and Uruguay, our reading has combined national authors and translations of European and North American literature. That variety of experiences was enriched by the Spanish and Italian orality brought by immigrants, from which emerged hybrid musical genres like the tango, the burlesque and a peculiar type of colloquialism that took on its own specific name: "the *cocoliche*." All of that was integrated into national cultures, which, while unjust and discriminatory towards the contributions of indigenous groups, tried to bring about a system based on the "melting pot" that Spanish, Italian, Jewish, Polish, French and other migrants had created in the River Plate area.

In Mexico, quite a different society, from the beginning of the 20th century, post-revolutionary modernisation programmes tried to regain possession of the 56 indigenous cultures in a unified nation-building project. Without denying the unsatisfactory scope of its achievements nor the Creole and *mestizo* society's oppression of the indigenous peoples, I would like to emphasise here that national development was guided by a multicultural conception that pursued integration and not separation. Even today, as old and new injustices erupt, it is inconceivable that these might be overcome by means of the isolated affirmation of each group. Instead, attention is focused on changing the nation as a whole.

The inclination to hybridise led those visual artists in various fields who were most reflective about national and Latin American identities, from Torres García and Antonio Berni to the informalists and geometrists of the 1960s and 1970s, simultaneously to appropriate artistic styles from different tendencies and nations. Although there were attempts to establish orthodoxies (Siqueiros, some academics and vanguardists), overall a flexible cosmopolitanism prevailed, the combination of multiple aesthetic and ethnic contributions in a multicultural patrimony.

Because of its different history, Latin America's countries tend not to resolve multicultural conflicts through affirmative action policies. This is not to say that the region has lacked nationalist and ethnic fundamentalisms. To resist hybridisation, these groups have promoted exclusionary and absolutist self-affirmations and a single cultural patrimony, which, though illusory, is believed to be pure. Analogies can be drawn between a separatist emphasis based on self-esteem as key to the demand for women's and minority rights in the United States and some Latin American nationalist and indigenous movements whose Manichaean interpretations of history assign all virtue to their own side and attribute all the defects of development to the others. Nonetheless, this has not been the prevailing tendency in our history. In this era of globalisation, in which the hybrid constitution of ethnic and national identities is more evident, as is their asymmetrical interdependence, unequal but unavoidable, each group's rights must be defended. Therefore, artistic and intellectual movements that identify with ethnic or regional demands, such as Zapatismo in Chiapas, situate this problem, as do the Zapatistas themselves, in a debate about the nation and about how to reposition it in international conflicts. That is, in a general critique of modernity.

Recent photographs and videos in Latin America provide many examples of this articulation of the local and the global. I am thinking of two in particular: (a) the series on refugees by Sebastián Salgado, exhibited

1927
1960
1963
1964
1967
1969
1970
1971
1972
1973
1974
1975
1976
1977
1978
1979
1980
1981
1982
1983
1984
1985
1986
1987
1988
1989
1990
1991
1992
1993
1994
1995
1996
1997
1998
1999
2000
2001
2002
2003
2004
2005
2006

in various capitals of Latin America and other continents with the sponsorship of the United Nations High Commission on Refugees, which organises into a single discourse the dramas of Rwanda-Burundi, Mozambique, Sudan, Bosnia and Southeast Asia; and (b) the photomural and video called "Montezuma's Foreboding" by Paolo Gasparini. This Italo-Venezuelan artist, who has recorded the continent's sociocultural contradictions for several decades, used Mexico City as a site for one of the most critical reflections on Latin American modernisation ever carried out. Based on a manuscript in which Montezuma announces the catastrophe of the Mexican capital, on Walter Benjamin's text about Paul Klee's "Angelus Novus," and on an exasperated montage of pre-Columbian, colonial and modern images of Mexico City, Gasparini indicates that the brazen multiculturalness of this metropolis is the result of a national project based on inequality. By combining the street sign that indicates Montezuma Street, folded and twisted by an anonymous inhabitant; a mask of the great fighter himself alongside other masks being sold on the street; and a photo of a Zapatista wearing a balaclava, next to indigenous and *mestizo* faces and bodies—bewildered, lovingly embracing, anguished, getting on and off buses and the metro—he offers, as he says, "a selection of post-battle images: all the civilising corpses are scattered about and the various cultural strata interweave and co-exist in the crossroads of the urban scene: from the pre-Columbian debris and the ruins of modernity to the already-decomposing pastiche of globalisation" (Gasparini: 17).

This example allows me to link the crisis of modernity in Latin America to the new forms of multicultural hybridity. The first thing I would like to suggest is that experiences such as those of Salgado, Gasparini and other Latin American artists (León Ferrari, Felipe Ehrenberg, Alfredo Jaar, Guillermo Kuitca), which I have analysed elsewhere (García Canclini 1993), indicate a new stage in the cultural functions and communicative strategies of art. In this era of audio-visual hyperreality, electronic information overload and the spectacularisation of disconnected fragments, they propose networks of meaning and sensitisation that link dispersed parts of society. Without the pretence of shaping a single totality, not even a single version of it, they contribute to problematising the given, the ordered ethnic, national or monopolistic conventions, causing diversity to emerge and making its articulations visible.

What does this have to do with relativism and affirmative action? It is easy to understand that setting quotas proportional to the demographic size of each group for university entrance and in the job market has been useful in one stage of the struggle for rights, as a way to offset prior exclusions and injustices. But, as Hughes notes, the continuing application of these quotas in museum and foundation policies ended up narrowing the distance between aesthetic pursuits and propagandistic slogans. Hughes maintains that art must again find a place between the pressures that have suffocated it in the United States in recent years: on one side, censorship and funding cuts when the National Endowment for the Arts wanted to end such irreverences as Andrés Serrano's work and Robert Mapplethorpe's nudes; on the other, the political pressures of the radicals that, in defence of racial and gender differences and in the name of political correctness, have engendered "a hotchpotch kitsch."

Even without falling into kitsch, the compartmentalised and separatist affirmation of each minority in the United States has led to the multicultural juxtaposition of aesthetics that, as Mari Carmen Ramírez wrote, do not seek to be more than "literal representations" of each identity (Ramírez: 16). Thence the monotony of the recurring stereotypes in Chicano and neo-Mexican-ist art, the overvaluing of the artesanal and naive execution as opposition to "good painting" and technical sophistication, the over-ritualising of traditional emblems and scenes. The encapsulation in these self-affirmations of "one's own" ends up blocking formal innovation and transcultural exchange, which are conditions of creativity and critical thought in a globalised society. Various unresolved dilemmas of United States multiculturalism seem to be summed up in this question: How can we move from the isolated acknowledgements of each group that in the long run perpetuate inequality and solidify differences, to the shared recognition of difference within the clashing, axial sociocultural relations of society?

The Malaise of Hybridity: Strategies and Contradictions of Globalization

Finally, let us look at some unresolved dilemmas of multiculturalism and hybridity in Latin America. This debate about the differences between multiculturalism in the United States and in our continent would be incomplete if we did not mention conditions common to both societies in the processes of contemporary hybridity, or point out that within current asymmetric globalisation, certain forms of hybridity and resistance to hybridity, present in both Americas, are results of inequality in exchange.

Recessive homogenisation. Beginning with economic conditions, we see that Latin America was never subjected to a process of continent-wide standardisation. Now, however, there is recessive homogenisation. Privatisation and transnationalisation policies were similarly applied in all Latin American economies. As a consequence, even the countries that were formerly the most dynamic (Argentina, Brazil and Mexico) produced negative indices of growth in the 'eighties, and the few societies that managed to restore their gross domestic products in the early 'nineties then suffered economic contraction again, with increased unemployment and external debt. The quality of life is deteriorating in the continent's big cities, which until a few years ago were seen both by governments and by rural migrants as the leaders of our modernisation. They have become dramatic centres of violence. Many of them are similar, insofar as their streets and plazas have become chaotic scenes of a poverty that attempts to survive through the "informal" market.

Policies of economic retreat and social decomposition create a paradoxical electoral consensus through the exacerbation of various "premodern" characteristics (populist leaders' strongman tactics, clientelism and corrupt dealings with the masses least incorporated into education and modern production), which are allied to the perverse products of modernity (drug trafficking, international financial boycotts, unpayable external debts). The most negative signs of the hybridisation of the traditional and the modern are mobilised to generate consensus for policies of de-industrialisation, unemployment and increased dependency: In sum, the national self-destruction carried out by the governments of Menem, Fujimori, Bucaram and others in the region.

This recessive homogenisation also affects the production and consumption of culture. In the last two decades the production of books, records and films in Latin America has declined; cinemas, bookshops, theatres, art museums and cultural support programmes have closed down. Many publishers and radio stations have been bought by European and United States companies that have altered their programming to follow foreign models.

Governments, overwhelmed by external debt, have reduced spending on public services, including education and culture. In every country they say that culture should be self-financing, should show a profit, and that it is better to leave it to private initiative. But the economic recession, the drop in consumption and the indiscriminate opening of national markets to international competition are strangling large private enterprises and small and medium-sized businesses. The inefficient adaptation of Latin American cultural industries and the economic recession have impoverished endogenous production and lessened the possibilities of competitive participation in globalisation. The shrinking of public spending and the weakness of private activity have brought about the following paradox: More trade is being promoted among Latin American countries and between them

1927
1960
1963
1964
1967
1969
1970
1971
1972
1973
1974
1975
1976
1977
1978
1979
1980
1981
1982
1983
1984
1985
1986
1987
1988
1989
1990
1991
1992
1993
1994
1995
1996
1997
1998
1999
2000
2001
2002
2003
2004
2005
2006

and the metropolitan centre at a time when these same countries are producing ever fewer books, fewer films and fewer records. Integration is being stimulated when there are fewer cultural goods to exchange and when falling salaries are reducing the majority's ability to consume.

Only the transnational communication companies, such as Televisa and Globo, have increased their investments, and only in the areas where they are most confident of recouping their outlay (television, video and mass magazines). As Jesús Martín-Barbero wrote in the "lost decade" of the 'eighties the only industry that developed in Latin America was communication. The number of television stations multiplied—from 205 in 1970 to 1459 in 1988; Brazil and Mexico acquired their own satellites; radio and television opened world links via satellite; computer, satellite and cable TV networks were set up; regional television channels were established. But all of that growth took place following the rhythm of the market, with little state intervention, even undermining the meaning and the possibilities for such intervention, that is, leaving public space without real support and increasing monopolistic concentrations (Martín-Barbero, 1995).

Lastly, I would like to probe the possibilities of cultural and aesthetic development that this phase of transnational integration and recessive homogenisation allows Latin Americans. The openings created by globalisation generate diverse opportunities for the hegemonic and popular sectors. For reasons of space I will limit myself to pointing out two features both sectors share.

Integration and Segregation
Free-trade agreements principally benefit peripheral countries' business and governing elites, and they reproduce these countries' subordinate position as endogenous production and international competitiveness diminish. But at the same time globalisation homogenises all sectors and brings them into the consumption process. The transnational expansion of communications, which weakens local traditions, has produced a world folklore or, as Renato Ortiz calls it, an "international-popular culture": Communities of consumers are organised less and less according to national differences, and, above all, among the younger generations, they define their cultural practices in terms of homogenised information and styles that can be received by audiences in different societies independently of their political, religious or national backgrounds. Consumers of all social classes are capable of reading the referents of a multilocalised imaginary that television and advertising bring together: Hollywood cinema idols and popular music stars, jeans and credit card logos, sporting heroes and politicians from various countries make up a constantly available repertoire of signs.

Nonetheless, the same process that integrates and hybridises also segregates. Multiculturalness and its differences are now formed not only through the co-existence and conflict of diverse historical traditions within each nation but also because of the stratification that results as countries and sectors within each society have unequal access to advanced communications media.

Inequality between central and peripheral nations, just as between economic and educational strata within each, engenders new injustices. The masses' incorporation into global culture is limited because they have access only to the first stage of audiovisual industries' offerings: entertainment and information that circulate on free radio and television. Small subsections of the middle and popular classes can receive more up-to-date and complex information by participating in the second stage of communications media use, which includes the circuits of cable TV, environmental and health education and political information disseminated on video. But it is really the entrepreneurial, political and academic elites who successfully use the most active means of communication. These form the third stage, which includes fax, electronic mail, satellite antennas and leisure pursuits, from making amateur videos to developing horizontal international electronic networks such as the Internet. The popular sectors have only limited participation in these latter circuits through the production of community periodicals, radio and videos.

It would seem difficult to develop contemporary forms of democratic citizenship without generalised access to the two last forms of communication, that is, without connections to international information and the ability to intervene significantly in global and regional agreements. The multinational dimension of such matters as pollution, drug trafficking and technological and cultural innovations requires that citizens possess information that transcends local and national spaces. Therefore, cultural policies should co-ordinate actions suited to what we may call the supranational public sphere (CEPAL 1994; UNESCO 1995).

Equalised Hybridity

What takes place in those communication circuits where symbolic goods are offered on a mass basis to all publics? The current ease of access to music from many continents, even from peripheral societies, aids composers, interpreters and audiences to become familiar with other cultures' offerings and to blend them with their own traditions. The global expansion of large communications concerns allows all of us access to multicultural repertoires. But the recording and reproduction technologies that bring us distant styles make them too easily commensurable, submitting them to standardised tastes: The percussion from a samba school or a salsa band sounds more and more like symphony orchestra kettledrums and the drumming of African or Indonesian religious music.

As José Jorge Carvalho observes, this transnational homogenisation generates misunderstandings: "The postmodern urban listener learns to receive as familiar something that is conceived by its creators and traditional cultivators as singular, original; and the typical listener from a traditional musical community has serious difficulties understanding the

fundamentally ironic, allegorical or simulacral character of musical production generated by the contemporary mass media. In other words, instead of the ideal of mutual exegesis, of the hermeneutic fusion of musical horizons, what we must analyse increasingly often are situations of communicative incompatibility" (Carvalho, 1995: 4).

However, these misunderstandings and this incompatibility are hidden by electronic artifice. A key recourse for reducing discontinuities between the variations in timbre and melodic styles implied by musical otherness is the equaliser, the device that organises the sound-balance among the instruments in a band and between instruments and voices. Applying to intercultural differences the capacity to moderate treble sounds with mid-range and bass, as well as to adjust the various channels so that everything can be heard clearly and the sonic totality is agreeable, is an intervention that transcends the aesthetic. These changes in communicative strategies imply new multicultural policies.

The search for an aesthetic of sound balance, which was first apparent in airports, restaurants, shopping centres and other places where the surroundings were "conditioned," is now expanding through industrial recording techniques that eliminate "the discordant." Carvalho has studied some of the main procedures used: a) the intensities of various musical genres and instruments—the pianissimos and fortissimos—are balanced to produce orchestral homogeneity or subordinated to the voice channel; b) the abuse of the echo or reverberation effect in shows and bars, which atrophies the listener's ability to hear subtle passages, is extended to young people's hangouts and even to those using the Walkman, for whom the best way to listen to music is to go for the highest amplification; c) the compact disc consecrates standardising paradigms of listenership by offering "cleansed" versions that are presented as if they had been produced in balanced acoustic chambers with the perfect orchestra and the spectator in the ideal listening position:

1927
1960
1963
1964
1967
1969
1970
1971
1972
1973
1974
1975
1976
1977
1978
1979
1980
1981
1982
1983
1984
1985
1986
1987
1988
1989
1990
1991
1992
1993
1994
1995
1996
1997
1998
1999
2000
2001
2002
2003
2004
2005
2006

the equalised recording, with a uniform listening subject, always in the centre.

This ethnocentric and naively modern perspective that pretends not to understand the crisis of representation that has built up over decades in literature and film disguises its erasures: Many subtle balances of intensity and rhythm eliminate vocal inflections, the displacement of energy, oscillations between moments of great sonic eloquence and significant silences.

All that remains is the sequence of chords, the meter, pure and simple, and the melodic scheme with the lyrics, all loaded with reverberation. Technical effect replaces the musical dynamic. In other words, there is execution without interpretation, without presence, without aura. The "music" is reproduced live, but it is no longer lived by the reproducer, much less by the listeners (Carvalho, 1995: 9).

Invented as an instrument of Western taste, equalisation becomes a procedure for a tranquillising hybridisation, a reduction of points of resistance to other musical aesthetics and of resistance to the challenges of diverse cultures. The sense that we can be near to others without being concerned about understanding them is hidden beneath the appearance of a friendly reconciliation of cultures. As with hurried tourism, as with so many transnational cinematic superproductions, sound equalisation is usually an attempt at a monologic conditioning, an acoustic comforting amidst the din of the world.

Certainly, equalisation has also served to re-instate the feeling of ancient, medieval and Renaissance music, to refine the recording of non-Western music and to experiment with original acoustic effects and resonances in electronic composition and interpretation, minimalism and experimental music. On the other hand, pulling the plug is always an option: Since Eric Clapton recorded "Unplugged," Sinéad O'Connor, Neil Young and Latin American musicians such as Gilberto Gil and Charly García have reminded us

that it is still possible to rediscover the modulations and subtleties of diverse styles. They have not escaped from the monopolistic transnational circuits with these "alternative" explorations, as is shown by MTV's interest in broadcasting them... .

These musical oscillations may be understood as metaphors for broader aesthetic options, which are at the same time various ways of handling multiculturalism, hybridity and those differences that do not lend themselves to hybridisation that cannot be equalised. Thus, the close of the century is opening up unprecedented opportunities for communication with many other cultures, for constructing hybrid repertoires and for recognising that which, being irreducibly distinct, does not need to be isolated in a separatist way. ...

References

Bhabha, Homi K. *The Location of Culture.* London and New York: Routledge, 1994.

Borges, Jorge Luis. Discusión. Buenos Aires: Emecé, 1957.

Bourdieu, Pierre. *La Distinction.* Paris: Minuit, 1979.

Ramírez, Mari Carmen. "Between Two Waters: Image and Identity in Latin American Art." Noreen Tomassi, Mary Jane Jacob and Ivo Mesquita, eds., *American Visions/Visiones de las Américas.* New York: American Council for the Arts, Allworth Press, 1994.

Comisión Económica para América Latina. La industria cultural en la dinámica del desarrollo y la modernidad: nuevas lecturas para América Latina y el Caribe, LC/G. 1823, 14 de junio de 1994.

Carvaldo, José Jorge de. "Hacia una Etnografía de la Sensibilidad Musicial Contemporánea." Série Antropología. Brasília: Departamento de Antropologia, Universidade de Brasília, 1995.

Campa, Román de la. "Hibridez posmoderna y transculturación: política de montaje en torno a Latinoamérica." Hispamérica, 69, 1994.

Franco, Jean. "Border Patrol." Travesía, *Journal of Latin American Cultural Studies,* London: Vol. 1, No. 2, 1992.

García Canclini, Néstor. *Culturas Híbridas: Estrategias Para Entrar y Salir de la Modernidad.* México: Grijalbo, 1990. (English edition, University of Minnesota Press, 1995).

___. "Memory and Innovation in the Theory of Art." The South Atlantic Quarterly, Duke University Press, Vol. 92, No. 3, 1993.

___. *Consumidores y Ciudadanos: Conflictos Multiculturales de la Globalización.* México: Grijalbo, 1995.

Gasparini, Paolo. Los Presagios de Moctezuma. Ciudad de México: 1994. Entrevista y presentación: Néstor Garcia Canclini, México, UAM, 1996.

Hall, Stuart. "The Local and the Global: Globalization and New Ethnicities." In Anthony D. King, ed., *Culture, Globalization and the World-System.* Binghamton: State University of New York at Binghamton, 1991.

Hughes, Robert. *Culture of Complaint: The Fraying of America*. New York: Oxford University Press, 1993.

Martín Barbero, Jesús. "Communicación e Imaginarios de la Integración." Taller de Comunicación. Cali, Colombia: 1995.

McLaren, Peter. "White Terror and Oppositional Agency: Toward a Critical Multiculturalism." In David Theo Goldberg, ed., *Multiculturalism: A Critical Reader*. Cambridge, England: Blackwell, 1994.

Ortiz, Renato. *Mundialização e Cultura*. São Paulo: Brasiliense, 1994.

Rosaldo, Renato. "Foreword." In Néstor García Canclini, *Hybrid Cultures: Strategies for Entering and Leaving Modernity*. Minneapolis: University of Minnesota Press, 1995.

Schmilchuk, Graciela. "La Fábrica de Identidades." Paper presented at the symposium, Beyond Identity, Latin American Art in the 21st Century. Austin, Texas, 21-22 April, 1995.

UNESCO. Our Creative Diversity. Report of the World Commission on Culture and Development. Paris: 1995, especially Chapters 4 and 9.

Villé, C., and V. G. Dethier. *Biological Principles and Processes*. Sanders Co., 1971.

Walzer, Michael. "Individus et Communautés, les Deux Pluralisms." *Esprit*, Paris: June 1995, pp. 103-113. Originally published in Dissent, spring 1994.
___. "Comentario." Charles Taylor, *El Multiculturalismo y "la Política del Reconocimiento."* México: FCE, 1993.

Yudice, George. "Postmodernism in the Periphery." The South Atlantic Quarterly, Duke University Press, Vol. 92, No. 3, 1993.
___. "Postmodernity and Transnational Capitalism in Latin America." In George Yudice, Jean Franco and Juan Flores, eds., *On Edge*. Minnesota: University of Minnesota Press, 1992.

Zermeño, Sergui. "La Sociedad Derrotada: El Desorden Mexicano de Fin de Siglo." México: Siglo, XXI, 1996.

García Canclini, Néstor. *Culturas Híbridas:* "Cultures and Communicative Strategies," *Media Development*, World Association for Christian Communication 1/1997. © World Association for Christian Communication.

THE HETEROPHILY GAP

Excerpt from: Development Support Communication and Popular Participation in Development Projects

By Robert Agunga

1990 Communication scholars, such as Rogers (1969, 1983) and Berlo (1960), have indicated that human communication is most effective when two individuals or parties in the communication act are alike, similar or homophilous. Homophily, says Rogers (1983), "is the degree to which pairs of individuals who interact have similar uncertain attributes, such as beliefs, education, social status and the like" (p. 18). This point is dealt with more succinctly by Berlo (1960) in his "Source-Message-Channel-Receiver" (SMCR) model of communication.

The SMCR model presents the communication process as starting with a source with ideas or information to transmit to an audience. The ideas are transformed into messages or a set of symbols, and then are conveyed to a receiver through a medium or a combination of media. Berlo focuses attention on the communicator's effectiveness and fidelity. The fidelity of communication, Berlo writes, "is the isolation of those factors within each of the ingredients of communication that determine the effectiveness of communication" (p. 41). Berlo's SMCR model specifies categories of source and receiver characteristics influencing the effectiveness of a communication exchange. These include communication skills, attitudes, knowledge, social system and cultural background. The greater the homophily that exists between source and receiver with respect to these factors the more effective the communication act becomes. The problem is that extension agents

1927
1960
1963
1964
1967
1969
1970
1971
1972
1973
1974
1975
1976
1977
1978
1979
1980
1981
1982
1983
1984
1985
1986
1987
1988
1989
1990
1991
1992
1993
1994
1995
1996
1997
1998
1999
2000
2001
2002
2003
2004
2005
2006

differ widely from their clientele, particularly in terms of their communication skills and knowledge levels.

As Rogers (1983) explains, change agents in most developing countries are more technically competent than their clients; they are highly trained, but they do not speak the same language of their "audiences." In other words, they are heterophilous. As a result, communication between change agents and their clientele is often ineffective.

Heterophily is the mirror opposite of homophily. It is the "degree to which pairs of individuals who interact are different in certain attributes" (Rogers, 1983, p. 18). The heterophily gap becomes apparent if one examines the characteristics of the participants in the project decision-making process.

Development and Decision-Making Participants

Development decision making implies two or more parties engaged in a dialogue. Dialogue is "talking together," or an "interchange and discussion of ideas, especially when open and frank, as in seeking mutual understanding or harmony" (*Webster's New World Dictionary*, 1988). Mutual understanding naturally implies some degree of commonality among the participants engaged in the dialogue (Berlo, 1960). The idea of participatory decision making, therefore, raises several questions. Who are the participants in the decision-making process? What are their characteristics? Are they compatible with each other as co-decision-making participants? If not, how can two parties of dissimilar communication characteristics be brought into dialogue?

Identification of the primary participants in development decision making depends on the level at which decisions are being made, ranging from the macro-level (i.e., government to government) to the micro-level, i.e., extension agent to farmer. The essence of aid from industrialized nations as the fuel with which to motivate and accelerate Third World development suggests a macro-level two-party nomenclature of (1) aid-giving countries, on the one hand; and (2) aid-receiving countries, on the other. Aid-giving countries are mostly the industrialized countries of the West (Hurni, 1980).

At the macro-level, decisions are made by bureaucrats and technical specialists. Significant cultural differences frequently distinguish aid givers from aid receivers, but these differences do not make communication incompatible. Government officials use professional interpreters, when necessary, and the language of science, with which technical experts communicate with each another, is designed to maximize mutual understanding.

The heterophily gap is most apparent, however, at the grassroots level. At the micro—that is, project—level, foreign-aid donors, local bureaucrats and technicians work in concert with specialists seeking to bring development to Third World people. In broad terms, the specialists are the development benefactors. Rural people and the urban poor, whose well-being the specialists seek to improve, are the beneficiaries.

Benefactors and beneficiaries both face the greatest likelihood of communication incompatibility and, therefore, the greatest danger of mutual misunderstanding. Such a misunderstanding may doom the feasibility of useful participatory decision making between the two groups (Fig. A).

The first box in Fig. A represents the benefactor system. The benefactor system comprises technical experts, often assigned to development projects. They are the agronomists, animal scientists and irrigation engineers. These technicians are, almost invariably, trained in technical areas rather than in communication.

The beneficiary system, the second box in Fig. A comprises a multitude of development clientele, among them crop and livestock farmers, women's groups and youth associations.

The dotted line represents the interface between the two systems. As a result of cultural and communication incompatibility—the heterophily gap—interaction between the two systems is often limited.

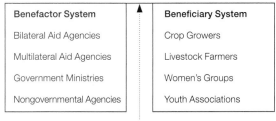

Benefactor System		Beneficiary System
Bilateral Aid Agencies		Crop Growers
Multilateral Aid Agencies		Livestock Farmers
Government Ministries		Women's Groups
Nongovernmental Agencies		Youth Associations

Interface

Limited Interaction Between
Benefactors and Beneficiaries at Interface

Figure A. Development Decision-Making Participants at
The Project Level.

An analysis of each of the parties will explain the magnitude of the heterophily gap.

The Benefactors

The term benefactor refers to someone who confers a benefit (Lionberger and Gwin, 1982). In the development context, the benefactor is the change agency. In agricultural extension, the benefactor is the change agent who carries out the development program (Lionberger and Gwin, 1982).

As shown in Fig. A, several kinds of agencies influence the innovation decisions of their intended beneficiaries. Multilateral aid agencies, such as the World Bank, FAO, [Food and Agricultural Organization] and the United Nations Children's Fund (UNICEF), exercise a great deal of influence on the innovation decision process. Bilateral change agencies, exemplified by United States Agency for International Development (USAID) and the United Kingdom Overseas Development Agency (ODA), equally influence the process. In addition, nongovernmental organizations (NGOs) serving as change agencies—Oxfam, Africare, Save the Children Fund, church-related organizations—also have a role to play in the process. These agencies are external to Third World nations. They facilitate development by providing development capital, equipment and expertise, through technical assistance.

In addition to technical assistance experts, Third World governments have their own change agencies.

Ministries of health, agriculture and specialized agencies, such as para-statal boards and corporations, exist to help bring about change. To some extent, national change agencies work with their foreign counterparts to deliver services to their common beneficiary—the Third World poor. Each foreign technician is supposed to have a local counterpart who is either a fellow expert or a trainee serving an apprenticeship with the expert (Havelock, 1973; Chambers, 1983). The relationship between foreign technicians and their local counterparts is not always smooth (Posz, Jun and Storm, 1973; Ascroft, 1974).

Technical Assistance

The basic ingredient of development aid is new ideas in the form of techniques and technologies. Under the rubric of technical assistance, experts from the industrialized economies arrive in developing societies to impart technical knowledge and skills. U.S. President Harry Truman (1951) was the first to introduce this principle of technical transfer. In his Point Four Program, Truman called on the American people (U.S. citizens), as well as [citizens] of the other industrialized nations, to make available to peace-loving peoples the benefits of their technical knowledge in order to help the poor countries realize their aspirations for a better life (Daniels, 1951, pp. 10-11).

Since then, technical assistance has remained a strong component of development-oriented agencies, such as USAID and the World Bank (Lethem and Riley, 1982). That developing countries need technical assistance from the industrialized nations cannot be denied. Technical assistance is necessary. But whether it meets its fundamental objective—helping the poor improve their quality of life—is another question.

Two broad schools of thought exist on the role of technical assistance. First, there are those who see technical assistance as contributing little to improving the lot of the people in the underdeveloped regions of the world. And second, there are those who think technical assistance works.

1927
1960
1963
1964
1967
1969
1970
1971
1972
1973
1974
1975
1976
1977
1978
1979
1980
1981
1982
1983
1984
1985
1986
1987
1988
1989
1990
1991
1992
1993
1994
1995
1996
1997
1998
1999
2000
2001
2002
2003
2004
2005
2006

TECHNICAL ASSISTANCE AS NEOCOLONIALISM

According to one school of thought, technical assistance fails to achieve its objective because it serves the needs of the benefactors rather than the needs of the beneficiaries. Ward (1970) claims that, in its present form, development benefits the industrialized countries, politically and economically, more than the less industrialized nations. Seligson (1984) has shown how the income gap between rich and poor countries has grown dramatically between 1950 and 1980, when massive infusions of technical assistance were supposed to achieve the reverse effect. The average per capita income of developing countries in 1950, Seligson points out, was $164 compared to $3,841 in the industrialized nations. By 1980, per capita income in the poor countries had risen to only $245, while in the industrialized countries per capita income had soared to $9,648.

Ndeti (1976), Goulet and Hudson (1971), Hayter (1971, 1982) and Payer (1982) maintain that the supply of technical experts, and aid in general is only a smokescreen for continued dependency. By accepting technical assistance, developing countries play into the hands of the industrialized nations.

TECHNICAL ASSISTANCE AS ALTRUISM

According to the other school of thought, technical assistance still fails to achieve intended objectives even when the motives for giving aid are altruistic. Technical assistance fails because aid givers do not understand the aid receivers and their felt needs. These scholars do not accept the view that technical assistance primarily serves the interests of the givers at the expense of the receivers. Instead, they see technical assistance as a valiant struggle to achieve the goal of development—a struggle that fails because of insurmountable constraints (Ascroft, Agunga, Gratama and Masilela, 1987).

Cardinal among these constraints is the sociocultural dimension that reveal how vastly different—literally worlds apart—foreign technicians are from their intended beneficiaries (Ascroft, 1974). Foreign technicians are different in terms of their education-based knowledge and skills. They differ from aid receivers in terms of culture, language and communication skills. A profile of foreign experts shows them to be generally highly educated (the vast majority have a college degree). They come from a monolingual environment (some are bilingual, but rarely multilingual).

Their languages are invariably word-rich, technically complex, capable of accommodating the idiom of science and each readily translatable into the other (Ascroft, Roling, Kariuki, and Chege, 1971).

A similar communication problem also exists between local technicians and technical assistance experts on the one hand, and between local technicians and the development beneficiaries, on the other.

First of all, the relationship between local technicians and counterpart foreign experts is a rocky one (Posz et al., 1973). Foreign experts generally feel themselves saddled with the incompetents of counterparts. Many of them claim that local counterparts are lazy, corrupt and show little or no sympathy toward the poor (May, 1981). Local officials, on the other hand, often find their foreign colleagues reluctant to share strategic decision making with their counterparts, eschewing collaboration in favor of assuming full control of decision making (Ascroft, 1974). In short, the inability of both local and foreign experts to interact effectively with each other creates communication problems that must be resolved before they can work together to serve their intended beneficiaries effectively.

Communication problems also exist between local technicians and their clientele. Although local technical specialists usually enjoy the advantage of cultural compatibility with their intended beneficiaries, their level of education and standard of living, are often equal to those of foreign technicians. This creates an essential incompatibility with their roots. Having assimilated one or more languages of the industrialized nations, and perhaps a foreign religion and style of life, they have lost the ability to communicate effectively among their own people. Local technical specialists may have been raised in the target area but they may no longer understand the people. They still speak the local language, but now they mix so many foreign terms into it that they are no longer understood. Such technical jargon as "grams per gallon," "centimeters," "millimeters," "hectares," "acres" and "degrees Celsius or Fahrenheit" too often have no local equivalents in the languages and dialects of the people at the grass roots. Yet they are very commonly uttered by extension agents in dialogue with small farmers (Ascroft et al., 1973; Roling, 1974).

Thus, for technical-assistance experts and local technicians to effectively communicate with one another and particularly with their beneficiaries, they would need the help of communication experts to translate technical subject matter into a simplified form that small farmers can understand. The communication expert is also needed to facilitate coordination and linkages between and among participating organizations in the Integrated Rural Development Program (IRD) complex.

Development Beneficiaries

Prominent among the lowest level beneficiaries of Third World development aid are peasant farm families. Peasants, according to Shanin (1966), are the majority of humankind, yet in spite of their numbers they are the least understood. Rogers (1969) says that peasants "constitute at least three-fourths of the population in most less-developed countries" (p. 21). Their major characteristic is that theirs is a system of survival, which almost always includes some form of participation in agriculture (Roling & de Zeeuw, 1981). Rogers (1969) describes peasants as "farmers oriented largely (but not necessarily entirely) to subsistence production" (p. 20).

Relatively, little is known about the response of peasants to the efforts of benefactors who try to change them in the name of development. The first forms of organized aid aimed specifically at Third World farmers began in the 1950s and 1960s (Schultz, 1964).

The results were discouraging in the extreme, leading to a suspicion that the local people's traditionalism rendered them resistant to change (Rogers, 1969; Inkeles and Smith, 1974).

The notion of peasant intransigence gained currency with the publication of Rogers' "subculture of peasantry" theory in 1969. Rogers characterized peasants as people who lack innovativeness, need gratification and empathy and are often hostile toward government officials.

But, in a study of Kenyan farmers, Ascroft, et al., (1973) show how peasants are neither hostile nor lacking in innovativeness. They note that to help foster the adoption of innovations, local people need information, knowledge and skills that can help them to make effective adoption decisions. Their study shows that farmers do not resist change, but they resist being forced to change, particularly when they are not being adequately informed about the wisdom of this change (Scott, 1976; Ascroft, 1974).

Gaining the confidence and understanding of farmers in a communication situation requires expertise in communication by the change agent. If a change agent interacts poorly with a small group of farmers, the news quickly spreads. Ascroft (1974) observed how news of a technology that was adopted and failed soon became common knowledge to whole regions of Zambia, making the peasants in the rest of the country wary of adopting it. Knowledge of these failures reached them via the traditional communication systems which, like their seed varieties and planting techniques, were developed over millennia into a reliable information system.

Matovu (1984) asserts that traditional communication media have been largely overlooked by change agencies as tools for reaching peasants. The missionaries of change have never really understood, let alone tapped into, these traditional communication systems. They are dismissed as primitive and non- technological and thus irrelevant. As Ascroft, Brody and Matovu

1927
1960
1963
1964
1967
1969
1970
1971
1972
1973
1974
1975
1976
1977
1978
1979
1980
1981
1982
1983
1984
1985
1986
1987
1988
1989
1990
1991
1992
1993
1994
1995
1996
1997
1998
1999
2000
2001
2002
2003
2004
2005
2006

(1982) point out, "How could they suspect that the messages pulsing from the 'talking drums' or moving along the traditional grapevines were warning others to be wary of the risks involved in following Western technological advice?" (p. 12).

Narrowing the Heterophily Gap

The analysis of the heterophily gap presented suggestions communication action at two levels: (1) promoting coordination and linkages between and among benefactor agencies; and (2) mobilizing, organizing and training beneficiary groups for active participation with the benefactor sector in development decision making. The question is whether agricultural extension workers charged with these functions have the communication skills to function effectively? Many scholars indicate that they do not.

Coombs, et al., (1976), who studied the first-generation IRD programs as they unfolded, stated that the IRD strategy was richer in rhetoric than action, insofar as lack of popular participation was concerned:

> An integrated program … is supposed to make people and their welfare its central focus, and to view programs from the people's perspectives. It is from these perspectives, based on an understanding of the people's needs, problems and development potential, that the interrelationships among programs become more meaningful (p. 82).

Also according to Coombs, et al., discovering the needs and problems of rural people and encouraging and training them for participatory decision making requires professional communication involvement, which in the IRD programs was lacking. The "training and visit" system of extension, the cornerstone of the IRD programs has been ineffective (Moore, 1984; Agunga, 1983). Indeed, the India where T & V is said to be most successful, a term has been coined for it—"Touch and Vanish." And the main reason for the failure of T & V is that the extension workers lack communication skills (Roling, 1973; Ascroft and Gleason, 1982).

Morgan (1984) pointed out that most development managers are graduates with engineering or agriculture degrees, with "virtually no management (or communication) training of any kind" (p. 6). Honadle, Morss and VanSant (1980) also noted that most IRD program managers were agricultural technicians who did not have supervisory skills. McDermott (1981) stated that agricultural development is "a function of the behavior or performance of individual persons—from the Minister of Agriculture to the person with the hoe" (p. 1). To change the behavior of people involved in agriculture, he concluded, is a social-science communication undertaking, not that of agronomists and animal scientists.

Ascroft (1985) also noted that the task of agricultural development is vested primarily in the extension agents. He pointed out, however, that these extension workers are trained first and foremost in technical agriculture and hardly at all in communication. As agriculturalists, Ascroft wrote, extension agents may be skilled in planting and nurturing hybrid corn seeds to bountiful fruition, but they lack the corresponding communication skills to plant and nurture adoption of the new seeds and allied techniques in the minds of the small farmers.

Chambers (1983), who also studied the management of rural development programs in developing countries, found that management, as a communication specialization, remains a "blind spot" in the eyes of development professionals. This sentiment is echoed by MacKenzie (1969), who decries the lack of professional communicators, given that communication constitutes the bulk of all management activity.

Development Support Communication

What the heterophily gap suggests is the need for trained professional communicators in Third World rural development. Although there are many agricultural extension workers to play the communication roles, they do not have the communication skills to be effective. For this reason, extension workers are usually more comfortable with their agricultural than with their communication know-how and, do indeed, see themselves as technical specialists who have the special task of sharing their knowledge with peasant farmers. But general communication strategists they are not and they usually shun being thought of as such. Trained mainly to show and tell, they lack the knowledge and skills, as Melkote (1984) so graphically illustrated, to prepare the necessary materials to augment, amplify or multiply their spoken words.

When it comes to diagnostics, therefore, extension agents are better prepared to help peasant farmers with their technical rather than their comprehension needs. Providing this technical assistance is indeed a singularly important function (Ascroft et al., 1987). It is one which will continue to be identified with agricultural extension workers. They will continue to identify and recommend innovations for adoption. But they will also continue to need help from more professional sources, too, with regard to the attainment of popular participation and comprehension goals of development. Who provides the communication know-how?

Starting from the early 1970s, a number of communication scholars and practitioners in Third World development have been studying the communication issues in rural development under the rubric of "development support communication." Erskine Childers (1976), now Director of Information, United Nations Development Program, who coined the term, says DSC "is a discipline in development planning and implementation in which more adequate account is taken of human behavioral factors in the design of development projects and their objectives" (p. 87). Helli Perrett (1982), a communication consultant to the World Bank, adds:

> The main role of communication support is to help create the human environment necessary for a development project or program to succeed. More specifically, such support provides the information, motivation and education activities which are needed to change any indifference toward the project that local people might have to interest and commitment, ignorance to knowledge, opposition to acceptance and support, and established attitudes or habits that militate against change to ones that actively promote it (p. 10).

Finally, Ascroft (1986), a DSC practitioner, scholar, professor and director of perhaps the first DSC graduate program in the world, explains the development problem leading to the rise of the DSC philosophy and discipline:

> Simply put, very often no appropriate message gets through. Between good intentions and final results lies a gauntlet of unexamined assumptions, inadequate information, cultural misunderstandings, inappropriate strategies and poor communication techniques which must be overcome before a suitable message can be acted upon. These social and communications factors, obvious as they are, have only recently begun to receive the attention they are due.

References

Agunga, Robert A. "A Triadic Model of Communication for Participatory Decision Making in Third World Rural Development." Ph.D. dissertation. Iowa City: University of Iowa, 1989.

Ascroft, Joseph, Niels Roling, Joseph Kariuki and Fred Chege. *Extension and the Forgotten Farmer.* Agricultural College of Wageningen, The Netherlands, Bulletin No. 37. Wageningen: Afdelingen voor Sociaal Wetenschappen aan Landbouwhogeschool Press, 1973.

Ascroft, Joseph, Robert Agunga, Ab Gratama and Sipho Masilela. "Communication in Support of Development: Lessons from Theory and Practice." Paper for Seminar on Communication and Change. Honolulu, Hawaii: University of Hawaii and the East-West Center, 1987.

Ascroft, Joseph. "A Conspiracy of Courtesy." Development Digest, 1974, Vol. XII, No. 3.

Ascroft, Joseph. Report on the Workshop on Development Communication and the Workshop for Health Education held at the University of Punjab, Lahore, Pakistan, July 1985, under the sponsorship of UNICEF, Pakistan and Iowa City, 1985.

Balit, Silvia. "Communication is the Message." *Ceres.* The FAO Review, March-April 1988, No. 122.

Berlo, David K. *The Process of Communication: An Introduction to Theory and Practice.* New York: Holt, Rinehart and Winston, 1960.

Brody, Alan M. "Development Support Communication Roles United Nations Programming: A Critical Review and Reconceptualization." Ph.D. dissertation. Iowa City: University of Iowa, 1984.

1927
1960
1963
1964
1967
1969
1970
1971
1972
1973
1974
1975
1976
1977
1978
1979
1980
1981
1982
1983
1984
1985
1986
1987
1988
1989
1990
1991
1992
1993
1994
1995
1996
1997
1998
1999
2000
2001
2002
2003
2004
2005
2006

Chambers, Robert. "No Shortcut Methods of Gathering Social Information for Rural Development Projects." Michael M. Cernea, ed., *Putting People First: Sociological Variables in Rural Development.* London: Oxford University Press, 1983.

Childers, Erskine. "Taking Humans Into Account." Media Asia, 1976, Vol. 3, No. 2, 87-89.

Coombs, Philip H., Monzoor Ahmed and Pratina Kale. "Communication and Integrated Rural Development—Is It a New Rhetoric?" Media Asia, 1976, Vol. 3, No. 2.

Daniels, Walter, ed. "The Presidents Proposal." *The Point Fourt Program.* New York: H. W. Wilson, 1956.

FAO Report of the Consultative Meeting on Development Support Communication, held in Rome, 1987.

Goulet, Denis, and Michael Hudson. *The Myth of Aid: The Hidden Agenda of the Development Reports.* Orbis Books, 1971.

Havelock, Ronald G. *Planning for Innovation Through Dissemination and Utilization of Knowledge.* Ann Arbor, Michigan: University of Michigan Press, 1971.

Hayter, Theresa. *Aid as Imperialism.* London: Penguin, 1971.

Hayter, Theresa. *The Creation of World Poverty.* London: Pluto Press in Association with Third World First, 1981.

Honadle, George, Elliot R. Morss, Jerry VanSant and David D. Gow. *Integrated Rural Development: Making It Work?* Washington, D.C.: Development Alternatives Inc., 1980.

Hurni, Bettina S. *The Lending Policy of the World Bank in the 1970s.* Boulder, Colorado.: Westview Press, 1980.

Inkeles, Alex and D. Smith. *Becoming Modern.* Cambridge, Mass.: Harvard University Press, 1974.

Lethem, Francis and Vincent Riley. "The World Bank's Technical Assistance: A Review of the Bank's Activities and the Lessons of Its Experience." Finance & Development, December 1981.

Lionberger, Herbert F., and Paul H. Gwin. *Communication Strategies: A Guide to Agricultural Change Agents.* Danville, Illinois: Interstate Printers & Publishers, 1982.

MacKenzie, R. A. "The Management Process in 3-D." Harvard Business Review, 1969, 80-87.

Matovu, Jacob. "In Search of Mass Communication Strategies to Facilitate National Unity in Uganda." Ph.D. dissertation, University of Iowa, 1984.

May, Brian. *The Third World Calamity.* London: Routledge & Kegan Paul, 1981.

McDermott, J. K. "Social Science Perspectives on Agricultural Development." Paper read at the Conference on Knowledge and Utilization: Theory and Practice. Honolulu: East-West Center, 1982.

Melkote, Srinivas Rajagopal. The Biases in Extension Communication: Revealing the Comprehension Gap. Ph.D. dissertation. Iowa City: University of Iowa, Iowa City, 1984.

Moore, Mick. "Institutional Development, the World Bank, and India's New Agricultural Extension Programme." The Journal of Developing Studies, 1984.

Morgan, E. Phillip. "Development Management and Management Development in Africa." *Rural Africana*, Winter 1984, No. 18.

Ndeti, K. "Human Factor in Rural transformation." M. E. Kempe and L. D. Smith, eds., *Strategies for Improving Rural Welfare.* Kenya: Institute of Development Studies, University of Nairobi, 1971.

Payer, C. "The World Bank: A Critical Analysis." New York: Monthly Review Press, 1982.

Perret, Heli E. "Using Communication Support in Projects: The World Bank Experience. *World Bank Staff Working Papers.* No. 551, Washington, D.C., 1982.

Posz, Gary S., Jong S. Jun and William B. Storm. *Administrative Alternatives in Development Assistantance.* Cambridge, Mass.: Ballinger Publishing Co., 1973.

Rogers, Everett M. "Communication and Development Today." Paper presented at the Seminar on Communication and Change: An Agenda for the New Age of Communication. Honolulu: July 20-Aug. 1, 1987.

Rogers, Everett M. *Diffusion of Innovations*. 3rd Edition. New York: Free Press, 1983.

Rogers, Everett M., with Lynne Svenning. *Modernization Among Peasants: The Impact of Communication.* New York: Holt, Rinehart and Winston, Inc., 1969.

Roling, Neils. "Problem Solving Research." Ceres, 1974.

Roling, Neils, and Henk de Zeeuw. "Improving the Quality of Rural Poverty Alleviation." Internationaal Agrarisch Centrum, The Netherlands, 1984.

Scott, James C. "The Erosion of the Patron-Client Bonds and Social Change in Southeast Asia." Journal of Asian Studies, November 1972, No. 33.

Scott, James C. *The Moral Economy of the Peasant.* New Haven: Yale University Press, 1976.

Seligson, Mitchell A. "Defining the Gap Between Rich and Poor." In Mitchell Seligson, ed., *The Gap Between Rich and Poor.* Boulder, Colorado: Westview Press, 1984.

Shanin, Teodor. "The Peasantry as a Political Factor." Sociological Review, 14: 5-27.

Ward, Barbara, J. D. Runnalls and Lenore D'Anjou. "The Widening Gap: Development in the 1970s." Conference on International Economic Development, Feb. 15-21, 1970. New York: Columbia University Press, 1970.

World Bank. "Rural Development." Sector Policy Paper. Washington, D.C.: February, 1975.

Agunga, Robert. "The Heterophily Gap." Excerpt from "Development Support Communication and Popular Participation in Development Projects." The Netherlands: *Gazette* 45, Kluwer Academic Publishers, 1990. Used with permission of copyright owner. Copyright © Sage Publications, 1990. Reprinted with permission of Sage Publications Ltd. and the author.

EXCERPT FROM:

COMMUNICATION IN POPULAR PARTICIPATION: EMPOWERING PEOPLE FOR THEIR OWN DEVELOPMENT

By Erskine Childers

1990 The most powerful, and yet elusive force in the world has always been communication. At every stage of human society, it has been the life-blood of news, knowledge and entertainment. Communication is the lifeblood of culture and the value systems that are the sap and the stability of society. It is the lifeblood of evolutionary change in governance and production, or of revolutionary turmoil. Communication is the substance of perceptions—what people understand about themselves and their environment and how all forces in their universe work, what they change in these understandings, and how they react to such change. Communication is the sum total of relevant information with which people can empower themselves for development in their communities.

Thus, we have in fact always lived in an incessant "age of communication," otherwise we would not have lived. Our wise ancestors in all cultures always understood this, and spoke of the primacy of "the word" and of "vision." But as professional and scientific specializations developed, they began to dominate perceptions of what moves and changes society and "the word" was submerged. Even today, when modern information technology has popularized the idea of a first-ever "age of information," or an "information revolution," attention is focused more on the gadgetry and what it does than on human communication as a stream coursing through and providing the moving force for all human endeavors, now and since the beginnings of society.

Let's look at the dominance of economics, which has acquired an almost mythical stature as a process and force of its own. Yet a moment's reflection shows that economics is only the result of particular flows of information. Money has no intrinsic value, only what given groups of human beings decide that it represents at any given moment; a piece of paper currency, backed by gold or some other exchangeable commodity, whose value rises and falls according to how much some distant group of people want something that they do not have, or more of something that they do have.

"Value" is a perception that is communicated. "Want" is a decision based on information mixed with a wish that in turn grows out of a perception, that in turn has been communicated to the one who wants. We see these constantly underlying roles of communication in economies very dramatically in today's stock exchanges, where the entire value of stocks may crumble because of the grass-fire sweep due to communication of someone's fear. Fear, in this case, is a perception that something is going to go wrong with the economy... a whole jumble of perceptions. When the news of this reaches (is communicated) across the world, in a few hours there is pandemonium in another stock exchange. Several "economies," or indeed the interdependent "world economy," are thus profoundly affected, not, necessarily, because anything physical has happened at all. Even where something physical—a drought, a war—has happened, it is the interpretation of this (perceptions that are communicated) which moves people at those stock exchanges to go into panic buying or selling.

Communication in Development

If we apply these propositions to development, we cannot avoid realizing that how it "works" and if it "works" and whether it lasts and becomes self-reliant, are heavily dependent upon human communication. Development consists of processes in which various groups are stimulated (by communication) to improve aspects of their ways of living and producing. Development is thus cultural, it is perception- and

1927
1960
1963
1964
1967
1969
1970
1971
1972
1973
1974
1975
1976
1977
1978
1979
1980
1981
1982
1983
1984
1985
1986
1987
1988
1989
1990
1991
1992
1993
1994
1995
1996
1997
1998
1999
2000
2001
2002
2003
2004
2005
2006

communication-loaded, and not at all just a matter of material "inputs." Money, material and equipment will only result in development if those supposed to use them decide that these "inputs" are safe to risk using for change that they want for themselves, and if they obtain the right new technical information. All of their decisions are functions of perception and communication; their new tools of knowledge and techniques themselves obviously arrive only with communication.

Yet human communication is the usually unwritten line between every actual written line of a development programme or project. These documents assert that, as a result of stated "inputs," a number of concrete things will happen—for example, that food production "will be" increased or disease "will be" reduced within stated timetables.

Each "will be," however, really means that whole sequences of communication must take place, with identified audiences, in the right language, in the right order, conveying innovation that they will wish to adopt because they will have been involved in planning the effort, and that they have learned how to apply through respectful and sustained information and support.

Farmers do not "increase food production" because a development planning document says that it "will be" increased—or because that document may indeed provide for injections of fertilizer and equipment, even proposed irrigation schemes. Farmers will increase their production when it makes sense for them to do so; when they are convinced that a proposed new technique will be materially safe for them to risk their very livelihoods; and when their inherited wise knowledge of their soil and their climate tells them that the new seed or method of using land is safe. And most farmers will do none of this unless they receive what they judge to be adequate information about the suggested new techniques in terms (language) they can understand, and with the questions this information will first prompt adequately answered by someone they trust (extension agents, which means local farming communicators).

Excerpt from: "Communication in Popular Participation: Empowering People for Their Own Development"
By Erskine Childers

Suddenly after several decades of [these] problems, there is a fresh chance. The development profession has been rediscovering the primacy of people over money, concrete, and machinery. No international meeting can respectably end without a serious invocation of the importance of "human resources development." And the phrase, "popular participation," which has for so long been merely tucked onto declarations and documents without anyone involved knowing what it really meant, is equally coming into vogue. With a little luck--but above all a lot of communication--the 1990s might turn out to be the decade of development by the people, of the people and for the people.

Unpublished paper. United Nations Economic Commission for Africa, Arusha (Tanzania) 1990.

People do not adopt new health practices because some distant health plan says that this "will be" done. They do so when sufficient information has been communicated to them to enable them to consider the suggested cause of illness carefully and in consultation with their own health sages, and to decide that it makes sense and merits their risking the health-state they and their children now have, to adopt the new practices. And again, they will not do this unless the new information reaches them in language they can deal with and the questions it will prompt are answered for them by someone they can trust.

For example, people do not adopt family planning because a population plan states that net fertility "will be" reduced in a country. They do so when they have carefully decided on a whole complicated web of new ideas that are offered them through communication—from male-female relationships, to lessened women's workload and family financial burdens, to perceptions that infant mortality is being reduced by new health facilities so that not only two or three children will survive, and ever deeper, how they value procreation. Everything about this is human communication before it is anything else.

The moment this is stated it is totally obvious. Yet plans for this communication cannot be found in most development documents—only the ever-present and exhaustively spelled out "will be," with "plans" for everything else. Like "economics," like "agriculture," like "health," development itself has been given a kind of mythical stature and assumed power of its own—divorced from people because its planners and administrators (national and externally assisting) have usually ignored the role of human communication.

Childers, Erskine. "Communication in Popular Participation. Empowering People for Their Own Development." Unpublished paper. United Nations Economic Commission for Africa, Arusha (Tanzania) 1990.

CULTURAL ANALYSIS IN COMMUNICATION FOR DEVELOPMENT: THE ROLE OF CULTURAL DRAMATURGY IN THE CREATION OF A PUBLIC SPHERE

By Robert A. White

1990 In the rapid growth of the development sciences following World War II, communication and media studies immediately became very central. At that time development was hastily defined as a process of extending modern technical capacities and social organization from the industrialized societies to urban centres in developing countries and from these centres out into backward rural areas.[1] This transfer was seen as a process of communication and the founders of the fledgling science of communications were called in to provide their expertise in a vast new project of social engineering.

By the mid-1940s communication research had already developed a body of knowledge based on public opinion studies, audience analysis, the impact of advertising and propaganda and other forms media-influenced attitude change. Theories of mass media effects seemed to serve well the demands of development planning which were looking for cheap, efficient and rapid forms of education and change of traditional values. The field of communication took shape with its various subfields such as interpersonal, organizational and mass communication, and development communication soon became a subfield in its own right.

With so little experience or data about the complex interaction of technology, economics, politics and

1927
1960
1963
1964
1967
1969
1970
1971
1972
1973
1974
1975
1976
1977
1978
1979
1980
1981
1982
1983
1984
1985
1986
1987
1988
1989
1990
1991
1992
1993
1994
1995
1996
1997
1998
1999
2000
2001
2002
2003
2004
2005
2006

socio-cultural organization in the developing nations, it is not surprising that there was great over simplication, failure to meet expectations and unexpected negative consequences. About every ten or 15 years, the field of development communication has been marked by agonizing reappraisals and public admission of the inadequacy of the questions posed.[2] Studies in development communication have matured, however, and this has contributed significantly to general communication theory. Most important, communication science in the developing countries is increasingly an important influence in the conceptions of development communication. This article will focus on the recent advances in thought about communication and national development coming from the developing world, especially from Latin America.

At the outset, concepts of communication and development were defined, not surprisingly, by perspectives of the industrialized countries of the North. This has been increasingly challenged by perspectives from the South.[3] In the textbook reviews which categorize approaches in terms of general paradigms[4] a first generation of theorists defined development communication as a process of incorporating developing countries into a world communication system for the diffusion of industrial technology, modern social institutions and a free market model of society. The clash of this "modernization paradigm" with the goals of national independence led to a second generation of theorists, very much influenced by dependency theory and concerned with the expansion of multinational corporations. They looked to the state, the strongest autonomous institution in many developing countries, as the foundation for independent planning, response to indigenous development needs and the focus of national culture.

Still another generation of theorists has argued that both the modernization and the disassociation paradigms end up giving a privileged role to national elites. These theorists suggest that authentic development must be based on grassroots socio-political movements and popular culture. Each of these paradigms tends to legitimate a different set of political actors and reinforces tendencies toward socio-political conflict as well as perpetuating political stalemates. Currently, a fourth generation sees the need for a model of communication policy that fosters political-economic and soci-cultural negotiation and integration. This perspective sees the formation of a common rational culture as the basis for national development and emphasizes the role of the mass media as a kind of public cultural ritual for negotiating cultural conflicts and agreeing on common values.[5]

Finding a Basis for a Public Sphere

The steady move beyond purely economic, technical and political factors to an emphasis on the cultural dimension has been driven, in large part, by the problems of the lack of a strong public sphere in many developing countries. Descriptively, the public sphere refers to that aspect of social action, cultural institutions and collective decision-making that affects all people in the society and engages the interests of all people in the national body. The definition of the public sphere and acceptance of this in the socio-political culture establishes an area of common national goals and a conception of the common welfare. It also outlines for all major social sectors obligations of contribution to the common welfare (contributive justice) and the criteria for distribution of benefits according to needs (distributive justice.)

The constitution and maintenance of a public sphere has been a perennial problem in all societies and a nation may be said to exist insofar as it has a core of social interaction that is truly common and public. However, the creation of the institutions and a culture of a public sphere has been a paramount task for new nations. As national boundaries have been drawn, this has brought together people of different regional loyalties, languages, cultures, divisions of caste and class, traditions of religious sectarianism and deep familistic, tribal identities. Suddenly, these groups found that their welfare depended on being able to work together as a united people. If, before, these societies were often broken up into small self-subsistent economic units, each with its own corporate status and historical identity, the challenge was to create a national economic system and a common political decision-making and service system. This system had to incorporate and link these subsidiary units but, at the same time, respect their particularistic interests.

The modernization approaches to development have tended to emphasize as the basis of the public sphere an infrastructure of common carrier transportation and communication technology, the neutral free market structure and the replacement of tribal, ethnic or religious divisions with the international, rationalistic conception of history. National independence movements have rejected this conception of the public sphere as a single, world-wide universal evolutionary process and have stressed, instead, the local state and state-controlled planning as the basis of a public sphere. Both of these models however, have tended to exclude lower status sectors from active participation in the public sphere…

Popular Hegemony and Popular Culture as the Public Sphere

Although national independence movements have often begun with a wide popular base and have used populist cultural symbols, the priority given to centralized planning, extension bureaucracies and industrialization has generally led to neglect of the masses of semi-subsistence peasants and the rural migrants to the cities.

Neglect or oppression of lower-status groups is certainly most obvious where rapid modernization is accentuated or where state-centred planning approaches have made concessions to the modernization model. With emphasis on a competitive market concept of the public sphere and the priority allocation of resources to commercial agriculture or other entrepreneurial sectors, the situation of semi-subsistence cultivators and unskilled labourers deteriorates rapidly.[6]

Excerpt from: *Communication in Popular Participation: Empowering People for Their Own Development*
By Erskine Childers

Once the idea of development is centered around people, an assessment of the development communication context, or environment, of a country or a region, assumes quite different starting points from the western "input" model.

In this model, an "input" is something that comes from outside—outside a country "into" it, (closely) reflected in the phrases "aid," and "technology transfer;" or from outside the rural area, where the majority of the people live, "down to" the villages (villages are always "down" in relation to cities, modern-educated folk, and central government, which are "up"). Development programmes are things which have been prepared in city offices and "arrive" in four-wheel vehicles. They contain "targets" calculated at the "macro" level (which is also "up"), and they contain references to "target groups"—the people, who "will" or "should" do the things stated in the documents.

If anyone thought of communication for these processes, it was communication to these "target groups," who supposedly do not have anything professional, or of value, to say about such development until it "arrives," already "packaged." Such communication "input" is very largely conceived as through "mass media" (print, radio, television), all of which have the same from-to characteristics; no one can ask a question of a printed document, a radio loudspeaker, or a television screen.

Unpublished paper. United Nations Economic Commission for Africa, Arusha (Tanzania) 1990.

1927
1960
1963
1964
1967
1969
1970
1971
1972
1973
1974
1975
1976
1977
1978
1979
1980
1981
1982
1983
1984
1985
1986
1987
1988
1989
1990
1991
1992
1993
1994
1995
1996
1997
1998
1999
2000
2001
2002
2003
2004
2005
2006

Establishing the transnational urban, rationalized mode of life as normative is quick to depreciate traditional folk cultures and the popular culture of the urban poor, a depreciation that is often present already in hierarchical peasant societies.

The increasing impoverishment of the peasantry and urban migrants in the midst of rising expectations leads to a desperation that is often ignited into spontaneous local protests and uprisings by sharp, brutal injustices such as expulsion from land. These local movements are often the first step toward building an alternative, horizontal communication and organization structure among the rural and urban poor. The stigmas of ethnic-racial minority status and the depreciated oral, narrative history of the underclasses become symbols of their social identity.[7] In the face of the Herodian transnationalism of the culture of the urban middle and elite classes, the unlettered leaders of the poor are quick to point to the popular classes as the source of the authentic culture and social energy in the "interior" or in the nation. The popular classes are redefined as the representatives of an adaptation to the ecology, history and indigenous tradition of the nation. In this experience, a new social actor emerges and there is the genesis of a conception of the public sphere centered on grassroots organizations and popular culture.

For political leaders and planners accustomed to think of the marginal sectors as a passive, fatalistic mass who must be awakened, educated and moulded by rationalized planning, these popular movements dramatize a new dimension of national development. The poor are now seen capable of actively resisting modernization, of articulating an alternative concept of development and building a base of socio-political organization on their own.

As was noted above, both the modernization and related planning approaches create opposition among specific sectors of urban elites as well: intellectual leaders from a literary, philosophical and socio-political background who see the richness of the national cultural tradition destroyed by shallow foreign-based technocracy and pop culture; journalists and others who resent the censorship; religious leaders at all levels who see modernization as a process of secularization: the leaders of skilled labour who are more conscious of their exploitation for the sake of capital generation; and even the upwardly mobile petit bourgeois who see that for all their technical training and the rhetoric of rationalization, the best bureaucratic jobs are still given on the basis of traditional personalistic ties.[8]

Dissidents who attempt to reform and democratize the process of development from the inside of political parties or bureaucratic structures frequently find that coalitions of politicians and modernizing elites have an almost impregnable hold on the central institutions of society. The rise of popular protest among marginal groups suggests that reform and change must build from the fringes of society to the centre until this becomes the dominant socio-political organization of the country.

Dissident elites soon build alliances with lower-status groups and bring their organizational and political skills to help build isolated protest into a national popular-based movement. This introduces a structure of communication between the rural and urban poor and national centres of decision making very much different from the traditional hierarchical structure or that of the extension bureaucracies emanating out of planning or research centres. On the one hand, when dissident social scientists or educators such as a Paulo Freire are driven out of universities or national planning offices, they bring information significant for building an opposition political organization and alternative socio-economic structure. On the other hand, they help lower-status groups articulate their culture and aspirations so that this can be projected into the sphere of national political-economic and socio-cultural debate. This dramatizes a participatory conception of the public sphere.

Dissident elites, with their alienation from modernization, reinforce the notion that the popular culture is the authentic national culture. Using their talents in education, cultural analysis and communication, elites help the poor to recognize and appropriate their culture so that lower-status groups can become actors in the formation of a national culture and history. Moreover, elites incorporate popular culture in the literature, drams and political philosophy portraying the popular classes as the real protagonists of national history.

The organizational structure of these alliances is also a factor in helping to build the patterns of alternative, horizontal interpersonal communication of scattered protest into a regional and national structure of communication by introducing new forms of communication strategy and media such as radios, audiovisuals and the inexpensive press. These movements are generally denied access to the dominant media, and their information and language are so different from the standard news and entertainment formats of the technical-economic orientation of modernization that the translation into these accepted forms destroys its original meaning. Popular media, following the participatory principle, adapt to the language, symbols and communication patterns of the poor and a quite different set of formats and organization of the media emerges from this process. The alternative, popular media are participatory, articulating popular culture, non-professional, openly critical and emphasize the indigenous, a fact that demonstrates the possibility of democratizing communication and of providing a different communication base for the public sphere. Widespread experience of popular communication in Latin America, India and the Philippines and, to some extent, parts of Asia and Africa were a significant influence in introducing the concept of democratization of communication in the later stages of the NWICO debate.

These national popular alliances have often gained sufficient strength to propose that the existing public sphere be widened to include a network of popular organization and communication. Negotiating these reforms often becomes extremely difficult politically, regardless of how reasonable and just they may seem to be, because it implies a radically different organization of society and significant re-distribution of social power. In many cases, where modernizing elites are solidly entrenched, these reforms can be implemented rapidly only through civil war. And, where popular socio-political movements do gain some degree of political power, there emerges a major administrative challenge in the task of translating more communitarian, participatory forms of socio-economic institutions and communication developed at grassroots level into national institutions articulated with an international political economy.[9]

Moreover, these reform movements are frequently based on a very idealized purist notion of popular culture that may exist only among more politicized sectors of the popular classes. Where the utopian left has been influential, popular culture has been defined interims of a rationalistic mobilization that leaves out many continuities of narrative memory, the moments of celebratory leisure, the elements of the modern that have become integral to popular culture and the normal rhythms of life in the popular classes. The rejection of the mass media as largely an imposition of dominant exploitative ideologies becomes difficult to maintain in the face of the fact that the popular classes—supposedly capable of resisting or actively interpreting mass culture—actually do gain a good deal of pleasure and self-affirmation from fictional drama, music and other forms of modern mass media.[10] Finally, if the popular culture of the poor is the only authentic national culture, then where do the more urbanized working and middle classes fit in?

The proposals for popular hegemony and participation emerging out of the new socio-political alliances have, in spite of their shortcomings, undoubtedly been a corrective to earlier conceptions of the public sphere. Most important, the debates about the role of popular culture in the formation of national cultures has brought the issue of culture to the centre of attention.

1927
1960
1963
1964
1967
1969
1970
1971
1972
1973
1974
1975
1976
1977
1978
1979
1980
1981
1982
1983
1984
1985
1986
1987
1988
1989
1990
1991
1992
1993
1994
1995
1996
1997
1998
1999
2000
2001
2002
2003
2004
2005
2006

The Public Sphere as the Common Cultural Symbols of Conflicting Groups

One of the most problematic aspects of the technical-economic, the planning and the politicized popular culture models of the public sphere is that these models tend to remain essentially the imposition of an external framework. It is assumed that the introduction of an institutional structure will force people into new social roles and that, with mass educational programmes, functioning within roles will eventually bring an acceptance of the world view, values, attitudes and emotional loyalties that re ideally associated with these roles. Some social sectors, especially modernizing elites, do attempt to take advantage of and accommodate themselves to aspects of these roles. Rarely, however, do even these groups fully recognize their personal and cultural identities in these institutions.[11] The strongest loyalties are to groups and subgroups based in traditional regional, ethnic, tribal, family, class and religious identities. In an attempt to make the external framework of a public sphere function in some degree, this framework may translate into a coercive hegemonic coalition, often depending heavily on the support of international political-economic allies. Group loyalties may be linked into this hegemonic framework by political clientelism and by alliances with new socio-political movements or with grassroots leadership and organizations.

As sociopolitical analysis has become aware of the failure of planning frameworks and rationalistic vanguard reform movements, attention has turned to more elemental levels of political culture in the seemingly non-political areas of everyday life. One fruitful line of research, especially in Latin America, has examined the political culture emerging in the popular classes and, more specifically, in the burgeoning immigrant settlements on the peripheries of metropolitan urban areas. Government planning, focusing more on industrialization and the needs of the employed working and middle classes, generally has not provided facilities for the flood of immigrants. This often means that immigrants from rural areas have had to struggle to find a living space in the cities, create their own makeshift housing and pressure city officials for schools, water supply, emergency welfare care and transportation to cities for employment. The immediate arena of political action for these millions are the local neighborhoods. The neighborhood, with its multiplying committees for obtaining facilities, is the link between the family and the larger political world of the city and the nation.

Some of the major actors in the continuity between the rural and the urban are the women who are concerned with the day-to-day integration and economic survival of the family, often providing supplementary income in the face of uncertain and unstable employment. Also important are the young people, the first generation creating a clearly modern and urban identity. Thus, the main political issues are not necessarily the controls over industrial production. Especially in contexts of political repression, some of the most important political movements are networks of community organizations, human rights groups, religious base communities and coalitions of groups working in popular communication and artistic expression in an effort to articulate and establish intercommunication among grassroots organizations.[12] The vehicles of cultural articulation are the alternative popular media of bulletins, group communication based on audio-visuals and video, popular theatre in its various forms, adaptations of popular music by local music groups, locally produced radio programmes and market-place loud speakers, posters and wall graffiti, and circulation of crude pamphlets using a graphic comic strip, cartoon style. All this is but one step away from the informal meetings on street corners, in the market places or public demonstrations and it is a direct expression of the everyday language and the symbolism emerging in these contexts.

The life in new urban settlements shows, vividly, that the operative foundation of political roles and the public sphere is not in the external planning framework but in the new cultural meanings that are being created by these or other social sectors on the basis of interests and positions within the process of modernization. These interpretations of the situation are, in part, a product of traditional identities, but more influential in a fluid situation is the daily negotiation with other groups and with the hegemonic framework. This negotiation is a complex process of confrontation, accommodation and adaptation, passive acquiescence is some areas of life but circumvention or active opposition in other areas. As groups such as rural immigrants struggle to establish neighborhoods in cities and confront urban developers or city governments, the interpretations of the city created by these people become a "discourse," that is, a systematic language organized around cultural symbols of identity which integrate immigrant communities and project a group identity within the urban field of confrontation.[13] These discourses represent a new synthesis of the traditional and the modern, regional-ethnic or class identities and national identities, local community and mass society.[14]

Thus, the real public sphere is a kind of "no man's land" of interfaces between the discourses of particularistic cultural communities and sub communities. In the context of interfacing, the discourses of each group must develop a language which simultaneously defends the internal solidarity of the group and finds some common definition of mutual rights, responsibilities and obligations. The discourse of each group becomes a kind of rhetorical dramaturgy which argues the legitimacy of the group's continued position within the field of interfacing and defends its position by extending the logic of its discourse throughout the field of meaning. Thus, each dramaturgy argues the value of the group's interpretation of the context for each other group and for the context as a whole. For example, for rural immigrants the housing built from cast-off lumber on a hillside close to the heart of the city is the logic of life-long saving of pennies and the effort to find a community of supportive friends, relatives and neighbors. It also represents a struggle with developers and city planners. For the urban developers, this is an unsightly slum which lowers property values and destroys the ideal city plan.

In the interfacing of rhetorics there is a process of mutual re-elaboration of logics in which immigrants argue to themselves and other groups that it is better for them to be close to jobs and more fully stocked food markets while the urban developers and their middle class wives looking for servants accept the fact that it is better to have a supply of cheap labour at hand. The rhetoric points toward common symbols at the areas of interfacing, symbols widely share by different groups. Such symbols, legitimating hegemonic relations, necessarily have a tense, unsatisfactory existence and there is constant pressure toward re-elaboration. The symbols have a different meaning within the internal logic of each discourse, but, precisely, because of the multifaceted nature of symbols, they hold together in tension different interpretations. In these negotiated symbols, all parties can recognize something of their identity.[15] And it is in these processes of social dramaturgy forcing the continual reinterpretation of particularistic discourses around symbols of common legitimacy that we find the formation of a public sphere.

The Role of Public Cultural Rituals

In his study of popular culture and hegemony, Mexican researcher Jorge Gonzalez has analysed in detail the cultural processes leading different "cultural fronts" to construct common, "trans-class" symbols in which all parties can recognize something in their identity.[16] Particularly important in this process are what may be called "public cultural rituals."

Gonzalez' study of the construction of meaning in the communication processes of popular culture began with the analysis of the everyday practice of *ex votos*, symbolic thank-offerings representing the favours granted by different patron saints. While official church theology tends to subordinate devotion to the saints to sacramental ritual and looks on *ex voto* practice as mostly unorthodox magic, popular religiosity puts these practices at the centre of an

1927
1960
1963
1964
1967
1969
1970
1971
1972
1973
1974
1975
1976
1977
1978
1979
1980
1981
1982
1983
1984
1985
1986
1987
1988
1989
1990
1991
1992
1993
1994
1995
1996
1997
1998
1999
2000
2001
2002
2003
2004
2005
2006

elaborate folk theology. Thus the church was forced to build its sacramental ritual around devotion to the saints, a common symbol that each social class or group can interpret as it wishes.[17]

Even more illustrative of the role of public rituals in cultural construction is Gonzalez' analysis of the communication process in community festivals typical of Mexican provincial towns and urban neighborhoods.[18] These festivals, which originally centred on patron saints and are now more of a civic-commercial event, bring together virtually all the different social classes and major institutions of power holders of the community around a common interest of the playful celebration. The bigger and merrier the crowds, the more the solidarity of the community is dramatized in rivalry with other towns and cities. In the festival, we sell all of the major dynamics of public cultural rituals. Thus:

1. The events are "ritualistic," that is, they are times and places marked off from the rhythm of more instrumentally organized "work" of society and are defined as leisure, play, freedom to think one's own thoughts and let one's imagination and emotions roam. The ritualism is often further emphasized by the basis in religious or religio-civic memory.

2. The festivals reproduce the ongoing conflict and negotiation of different cultural fronts of the community, but with an exaggerated projection of the typical symbols that represent the logic of each discourse and argue the legitimacy of this discourse for the community. The official church displays itself in the festival with its most solemn sacramental rites and ritual vestments, peasant communities don traditional costumes, political parties bring out insignia, youth dances to its loudest rock music, etc. Each cultural front dramatizes its difference interpretation of the event: the official church, with the almost exaggerated decorum of its rites expresses a hardly disguised disapproval of the degrading commercialism, the indecently clad beauty queens, the gambling, etc. Upper class patrols of the event with their tailored

clothing indicate their disdain of the smelly, sweaty crowds of people from poor barrios.

3. For the moment, however, the more dogmatic, purist, rationalistic lines of discourse are relaxed and connotative, multifaceted symbols based on the common elementarily human such as the numinous, joy, affective love and sec, physical prowess, health and sickness come to the surface. There is an emotional imaginative identity with associated memories of a patron saint, the fairest young lady elected queen, the picturesque display of regional folk culture and the home sports. No one discourse is allowed to dominate the meaning of the event.

4. Political-commercial interests may succeed in establishing a frame for the event, but in the carnival atmosphere popular culture is brought to the centre and is conceded its greatest cultural validity. The event supports the legitimacy of the major patron institutions such as the government, but also relativises and makes these subordinate to the community and the culture.

5. During this event the whole community tends to leave behind real time and enters into a kind of mythic time in the celebration of a numinous saintly patron, the historic sense of the community with its recollection of past festivals and the repetition of traditional festival rites and displays. The community then returns to ordinary time with a heightened sense of community solidarity, the re-elaboration of cultural logics at a deeper imaginative level and a new sense of interwoven community responsibilities and obligations.

Perhaps the most important public cultural ritual in many developing countries is to be found in the mass media, especially the serial dramatic fiction programmes of radio and television which consistently draw the largest audiences. Gonzalez reports that in Mexico 80 percent of the population, rural and urban, had direct to TV screens by 1986.[19] In a survey of five major cities, at least 60-80 percent of the adults, men and women, watch the serial fiction *telenovelas* and this is the common fare in the peak evening hours.

In a survey of the regional city of Colima, more than half of those interviewed considered *telenovelas* to be suitable fare for the whole family and, in the peak evening hours the whole family watches TV together as the most frequent entertainment. Some 56 percent of the Colima respondents thought that *telenovelas* help them resolve real-life problems. Most important, viewing *telenovelas* is a trans-class phenomenon with 60 percent of all social strata viewing them.[20]

Like the ferias, the popular mass media have an ancestry that can be traced back through theatre to ritual and through the entertainment traditions associate with celebratory events of the calendar to ritualistic occasions. Television audiences return from a day of work or find time during domestic activities to relax, be entertained and let their imaginations and feelings have free rein. It is also a time when deeper human problems and tensions can come to the surface of consciousness and seek a symbolic resolution of ordered meaning in the narrative structure of television's stories whether they are news, documentary or fiction.

As an essentially narrative medium, television is perfectly designed to display the conflicting, competing, negotiating social dramaturgies and rhetorical discourses of different cultural fronts in society. The folk tale structure of television (whether that is news or fiction) engages the audience's attention with an opening problem or question that touches on elementary anxieties and then follows through to an outcome or symbolic resolution.[21] The plots revolve around the timeless elementary human issues that all audience members can identify with: physical threat, romantic love, life and death, health and sickness. TV, however, is a very contemporary medium and to satisfy audiences' expectation of something new, must recast familiar issues in terms of a problem that has contemporary, realistic relevance. The success of TV is being able to carefully select highly connotative symbols of personages, geographical associations, clothing, language and argot which audiences can immediately recognize from their familiarity with the culture as

representative of the dramaturgy of different cultural discourses. The conflict of various heroes and villains is, for the audience, the conflict and rhetoric of different cultural fronts. Serial fiction such as the soap opera-*telenovela* is a genre which is able to weave together an immense number of symbolic characters, issues and subplots that represent virtually the whole gamut of familiar cultural rhetorics. Although the producer's definition of the hero may be evident, the semiotic richness of TV carries a wealth of visual irony, parody, satire and social ridicule that reveal the confrontation of discourses.[22]

Entertainment may attract because elementary human issues are, ultimately, always with us, but particular narratives engage audiences with the expectation of resolution of conflict and present an integration of meaning. This is done by the re-elaboration of the rhetoric and pretensions of universal legitimacy of a particular discourse so that commonly agreed-upon "community" symbols are accepted. In the end the young working class woman marries the son of a wealthy family and the mother of the son must give up the pretensions of purist class definitions.

Like the festival, television seeks to attract the largest possible audience and display symbols that all can somehow identify with. There is no doubt that the commercial, advertising, marketing discourse of modernizing development, allied with political and moralistic structures of power, has tried to "occupy the territory" with a hegemonic, framing discourse, but the polysemic portrayal of conflicting rhetorics has the potential for diverse, even contradictory interpretations and identifications. In spite of the attempts of various elite groups to impose a more rationalistic or a high culture agenda, the content and the tone, often criticized by elites, is distinctly popular and enables the popular classes much more than elites to recognize and affirm their identities.[23] Television is best defined as a "consensus narrative," in that it articulates the culture's central mythologies, drawing on an inheritance of shared stores, plots, character

1927
1960
1963
1964
1967
1969
1970
1971
1972
1973
1974
1975
1976
1977
1978
1979
1980
1981
1982
1983
1984
1985
1986
1987
1988
1989
1990
1991
1992
1993
1994
1995
1996
1997
1998
1999
2000
2001
2002
2003
2004
2005
2006

types, cultural symbols and narrative conventions. In contrast to the individualistic artistic expression of the "auteur," consensus narratives are a more common collective effort that involve not only teams of producers and writers but virtually every major social institution that can be associated in some way with the culture industries.[24] Martin-Barbero and others have argued that in Latin America the narrative memory of the people is best represented in the *telenovela,* a peculiarly Latin-American form of melodrama that captures the melodramatic tone of Latin-American culture and has roots far back in the entertainment history of the continent.[25] Consensus narrative speaks to people across boundaries of class, wealth, age and gender, but its status as entertainment and fiction provides a licence for expressing, at a kind of mythic level, the deepest, most persistent and wide-ranging confrontations of human cultural meaning. ...It captures the popular wisdom of the culture.

One could cite many other types of public cultural rituals. Election campaigns may be better defined as ritualistic cultural dramaturgy than as a ritualistic cultural dramaturgy than as a rationalistic process of informing the public and enabling the public to make calculated decisions on the basis of sectorial interests. National liberation movements which involve a wide cross-section of social classes in an effort to gain independence from colonial powers or to challenge concentrations of dictatorial power are, perhaps, a limit case of election campaigns. Major sports contexts, important cultural artistic festivals, counter-cultural movements or major scientific feats which involve national effort are all forms of public cultural ritual. It is important to note, however, that these events achieve a fuller dramaturgical dimension to the extent that they become part of mass media ritual.[26]

The Significance of Ritualistic Cultural Dramaturgy for Development and for the Creation of a Public Sphere

...The most important role of cultural dramaturgy in development is not to provide a new vehicle for the diffusion of technical information through bureaucratic extension systems even though cultural dramaturgy does imply an intensified circulation of information. The ritualistic dramaturgy of different cultural fronts presents a model of development communication quite distinct from the diffusion paradigm. The focus is on the grassroots construction of meaning, the generation of common cultural symbols and the projection of a public conception of historical development that evokes wide identification and participation.

Public cultural rituals defy rational planning because they exist when the public recognizes them as such. Detecting the importance of cultural dramaturgy means shifting people's attention to their initiatives for development and to the cultural definitions of the situation that emerge out of confrontation and negotiation. This implies a conception of development which is open to endogenous cultures and which accepts that development may follow multiple historical paths not easily predicted by the classical paradigms of development.[27] In instances where there has been a notable development "take-off," the processes of ritualistic cultural dramaturgy have, in fact, played a role, but conceptions of development centred on technology transfer, economic planning and directive educational campaigns often have no category for cultural dramaturgy and have treated it as a mysterious residual "x" factor. (The explanatory framework for development has no place, for example, for the cultural dramaturgy of national liberation movements or for other popular movements. ...)

Public cultural rituals are often a crucial link between the construction of meaning in everyday life and the formation of common symbols of a public sphere that people can truly identify with. Martin-Barbero points out that from 1930 to 1960 film in Mexico, the *radionovela* in Argentina, popular music in Brazil and the popular "yellow" press in Chile provided for many the first conception of nationhood. This was presented, however, not in abstract planning terminology, but in terms of melodramatic portrayals of the little crises of the changing extended family, the local neighborhood and the crises of romantic love that showed national changes in daily life.[28]

In the formation of much more complex, common symbols of cultural dramaturgy, people can find points of identification that have far reaching consequences for educational aspiration, small-scale entrepreneurial initiative, artistic expression and technological innovation. Out of the confrontation and negotiation there emerges a cultural frame work for development that may seem chaotic to planners, but it is a framework that engages the energies of the people. In the process of negotiation there is likely to be a synthesis of modernization with its free market model, conceptions of more far-reaching political and economic utopia and the expressions of popular, grassroots political movements.

Even though cultural dramaturgy and public cultural rituals cannot, in the strict sense, be planned, public policy in a broad sense does play an important role. Public cultural rituals flourish in societies which relax rationalistic, authoritarian mobilization and prize moments of leisure for more playful cultural exploration in festival and narrative fantasy. It requires a climate of less interference from political agendas, social utopianism, puritanical moral guidance, the domination of canons of high culture or the single criterion of commercial profit. Above all, it is important to re-examine the conception of culture and cultural policy which penetrates through every aspect of development policy. This means avoiding the common practice of defining culture as primarily high culture (whether this be indigenous or international high culture) or as the quaint folklore of a now passing era. The primary focus must be the contemporary processes of cultural construction exemplified in the dramaturgy of different cultural fronts and sensitivity to the public cultural rituals that are recognized and enjoyed by the people.

The main arena for cultural dramaturgy today is provided in the mass media. The culture industries in many developing countries are perfecting the capacity to produce dramatic fiction in film or television which captures well the discourses and visual symbols of different social actors and, through narrative conventions, portray the common symbols that are emerging. Unfortunately, genres of media that come under the rubric of education, culture, documentary, public information and pro-social programming are often caught in a tradition of didactic, boring styles. They miss the great opportunity of dramaturgical realism that is present in everyday life. In the area of both fiction and documentary, an opening to independent producers, who are often in closer contact with the cultural trends and sensitivities of the people, frequently brings new stories to the media that turn out to be major public cultural rituals.

Endnotes

1 Wilbur Schramm, *Mass Media and National Development,* Stanford, Calif.: Stanford University Press and Paris: UNESCO, 1964, pp. 10-57.

2 Wilbur Schramm and Daniel Lerner (Eds), *Communication and Change: The Last Ten Years – And the Next,* Honolulu, HA: The University Press of Hawaii, 1976; Jesús Martín-Barbero. *De los medios a las mediaciones,* México: Editorial Gustavo Gili, 1987, pp. 9-12.

3 Everett M. Rogers, *Communication and Development: Critical Perspectives,* Beverly Hills, Calif.: Sage Publications, 1976.

4 The contrasting typologies of communication and development appear in Göran Hedebro, *Communication and Social Change in Developing Nations.* Ames, IO: The Iowa State University Press, 1982. The explicit terminology of "paradigms" is used, for example, in the textbook of Uma Narula and W. Barnett Pearce, *Development as Communication, A Perspective on India,* Carbondale, H.: Southern Illinois University Press, 1986.

5 A major scholar in the area of communication and development who perhaps best represents some of the new lines of thinking is Jan Servaes at the institute of Mass Communication, the Catholic University of Nijmegen, The Netherlands. He has stressed the importance of cultural analysis, a dialectical process of communication among power holders, democratization of communication and the recognition of multiple patterns of development. Cf. Jan Servaes, "Communication and Development Paradigms: An Overview," *Media Asia,* Vol. 13, No 3, 1986. Jesús Martín-Barbero with his book, *De los medios a las mediaciones* and Jorge González in México are also making major contributions. Cf. Jorge González, "Los Frentes Culturales," *Estudios sobre las culturas contemporáneas,* Vol. 1, No 3, Mayo de 1987, pp. 5-44.

6 José Migdal, *Peasants, Politics and Revolution,* Princeton, NJ. Princeton University Press, 1974.

7 Robert A. White. "Mexico: The Zapata Movement and the Revolution" in *Latin American Peasant Movement.* ed. by Henry A. Landsberger, Ithaca, NY: Cornell University Press, 1969

8 Eric R. Wolf, *Peasant Wars of the Twentieth Century,* New York: Harper and Row, 1969.

1927
1960
1963
1964
1967
1969
1970
1971
1972
1973
1974
1975
1976
1977
1978
1979
1980
1981
1982
1983
1984
1985
1986
1987
1988
1989
1990
1991
1992
1993
1994
1995
1996
1997
1998
1999
2000
2001
2002
2003
2004
2005
2006

9 Fernando Reyes Matta, "La comunicación alternativa come respuesta democrática" in *Comunicación y democracia en América Latina,* Ed, by Elizabeth Fox et al, Lima, DESCO. 1982, pp. 245-264.

10 Martín-Barbero. *De los medios a las mediaciones.* pp. 229-259.

11 Binod C. Agrawal, "Dual Ethics in Indian Communication: A Cultural Crisis," in *Communication Ethics and Global Change.,* Ed. by Thomas W. Cooper with Clifford G. Christians, Frances, Forde Plude and Robert A. White. New York: Longman, Inc. 1989, pp. 147-158.

12 Martín-Barbero. *De los medios a las mediaciones.* pp. 209-220.

13 Jorge González "Frentes culturales urbanos: para comprender la construcción de hegemonía en la ciudad," *Culturas Estudios Sobre las Culturas Contemporáneas Vol. 1 No 1. pp. 135-144*

14 Martín-Barbero. *De los medios a las mediaciones.* pp. 205, 209-220.

15 González, "Semantizarás las ferias: identidad cultural y frentes cultura-les." *Culturas Estadios Sobre las Culturas Contemporáneas* Vol. 1, No 1. pp. 101-133.

16 González, "Los frentes culturales." *Estudios Sobre las Culturas Contemporáneas,* Vol. No 3. Mayo de 1987, pp. 5-44

17 Jorge González. "Ex votos y retablitos: comunicación y religión popular en México." *Culturas: Estudios Sobre culturas Contemporáneas.* Vol. 1, No 1, pp. 41-100.

18 González. "Semantizarás las ferias." pp. 101-133

19 Jorge González. "La Cofradía de las emociones (in)terminables." *Estudios Sobre las Culturas Contemporáneas.* Vol. 2, No.4-5. pp. 13-66 (in English, "The Confraternity of (Un) Finishable Emotions: Constructing Mexican Telenovelas," paper presented to the international Television vStudies Conference, London, 20-22 July, 1988.

20 Ibid, p. 48.

21 Roger Silverstone, *The Message of Television: Myth and Narrative in Contemporary Culture.* London: Heineman Educational Books, 1986. pp. 85-112.

22 John Fiske, *Television Culture,* London: Metbuen & Co., Ltd., 1987. pp. 84-107.

23 Martín-Barbero. *De los medios a las mediaciones.* pp. 237-242.

24 David Thorburn "television as an Aesthetic Medium," *Critical Studies in Mass Communication, 4,* 1987, No 2, pp. 161-173.

25 Martín-Barbero. *De los medios a las mediaciones.* pp. 242-247.

26 Elihu Katz and Daniel Dayan, "Media Events: On the Experience of Not Being There," *Religion.* Vol. 15, July 1985, pp. 305-314.

27 Jan Servaes, *One World, Multiple, Cultures: A New Paradigm for Communication for Development.* Forthcoming publication.

28 Martín-Barbero. *De los medios a las mediaciones.* pp. 180-182.

White, Robert A. "Cultural Analysis in Communication for Development—The Role of Cultural Dramaturgy in the Creation of a Public Sphere," *Journal of SID,* p 23-31, 1990:2. Copyright © 1990 Society for International Development.

AN ETHICAL PERSPECTIVE OF DEVELOPMENT

Excerpt from: Communication for Development in the Third World—Theory and Practice

By Srinivas R. Melkote

1991   Ethics is defined in the dictionary as "that branch of philosophy dealing with values relating to human conduct, with respect to rightness and wrongness of certain actions and to the goodness and badness of the motives and ends of such actions"… we have until now attempted to analyze the issues in development, noting the moral underpinnings of human actions in the theory and policymaking realms. In the course of the reader's sojourn through the saga of development, or rather underdevelopment (as outlined in this paper), a host of questions might have arisen. Let us examine a few of them:

1. What is development? This term, as denoted in the dominant paradigm, is an ethnocentric conception of what progress should be. It describes the type of modernization that has been achieved in the countries of Western Europe and North America. Also, it has looked at development from a macro level.

Most of the earlier models defined development in rather narrow terms. They viewed development as economic growth obtained through greater industrialization and accompanying urbanization. Development performance was thought to be described through measures such as the GNP [gross national product] and per capita income levels.

Missing in this definition was the need for a more broad-based definition of development. Any discussion of development must include the physical, mental, social, cultural and spiritual development of an individual in an atmosphere free from coercion or dependency. Also, greater importance would need to be given to preserving and sustaining local traditional cultures and other artifacts, as these are usually the media through which people at the grassroots structure their reality of the world around them. Local cultures in developing nations, quite contrary to some deeply held notions, are not static. The fact that they have survived centuries of hostile alien rule speaks volumes for their dynamic nature. As a development tool, these cultures can generate solutions to many of the problems at the grassroots due to their deep knowledge of the socio-cultural ethos of the people. To talk, therefore, of uprooting local cultures, is not only naive but also ethically indefensible.

2. Development at what level? Much of the work has been at the level of the nation state. Even research at the micro level has been concerned with bringing the nation, or some region as a whole into modernity.

   Missing in this was the conceptualization that different individuals and groups require different strategies for development. If development is not to create greater misery for a large body of humanity at the periphery, then we need a process by which not only the "mythical" concept of nation is developed, but the disadvantaged masses are also helped to overcome their wretched existence.

3. Who determines whether and when the definition of development—excluding or including certain problem definitions—is acceptable or unacceptable? The elites in every nation have always had the prerogative of deciding what the country needs... this is inappropriate. In many Third World countries today, economic and political power is concentrated in the hands of a small elite. In such circumstances, any definition of development by the elites will be in a direction opportune to their interests.

Missing in this approach was participation by people at the grassroots. People who are the objects of policy need to be involved in the definition, design and execution of the development process. While this idea has been raised very often, it has not been adequately operationalized. How would it be possible to bring about effective participation of the masses at the grassroots in the development process? One useful method would be to consider the creation of viable institutional structures at the interface between the agencies of the government and the "anonymous" masses, wherein they could be actively involved in all issues that concern their welfare. Participation in such a bottom-up orientation would need to be broad-based.

The concept of participation as favored by bottom-up strategies, such as participatory communication systems and intermediate technologies, was narrow: achieve the cooperation of the masses in adopting better health-care practices, increase agricultural production, etc. True participation, however, as discussed, would go beyond such goals as higher productivity and better health habits, to bringing about the conscientization of the masses on their extremely unequal social and spatial structures.

4. Who reaps the benefits of development and who bears the risks? Any policy that continues to exploit the masses at the cost of the rich and powerful is morally indefensible. What is needed in the future is a more egalitarian distribution of benefits and risks of development across all social and economic classes. Perhaps the Western model as enunciated in the dominant paradigm is inappropriate for the Third World nations. This model, which emphasised capital-intensive technology and centralized planning of development, has given an unequal advantage to the elites. An alternative model that stresses labor-intensive approaches and decentralized planning of development, with effective local people participation, would be more appropriate in the Third World.

1927
1960
1963
1964
1967
1969
1970
1971
1972
1973
1974
1975
1976
1977
1978
1979
1980
1981
1982
1983
1984
1985
1986
1987
1988
1989
1990
1991
1992
1993
1994
1995
1996
1997
1998
1999
2000
2001
2002
2003
2004
2005
2006

5. What are the moral implications at the policy-making level? Policymakers, on the basis of their own actions, should refrain from increasing human misery. The focus needs to be on humane development, i.e., to reduce human suffering and not increase it. Berger (1976: xiii) succinctly describes some of the implications at the development policymaking level: "Most political decisions must be made on the basis of inadequate knowledge. To understand this is to become very gingerly toward policy options that exact high human costs."

The most pressing human costs are in terms of physical deprivation and suffering. The most pressing moral imperative in policymaking is a calculus of pain.

What is badly needed today is such self-examination by every intellectual and policymaker concerned with development.

References

Berger, Peter L. *Pyramids of Sacrifice*. New York: Anchor Books, 1976.

EXCERPT FROM:

COMMUNITY AND TRADITIONAL BASED MEDIA APPROACHES TO POPULAR IEC: SOME EXPERIENCES IN THE AFRICAN REGION

By Onuora N. Nwuneli

1992 Nwuneli (1983) explored the conceptual approach to the use of traditional channels of communication in Africa. He indicated that traditional media are not all channels, as most earlier researchers have viewed them. The channels represent only the hardware component in the communicative process. The software component in the traditional media process often originates from an authoritative source. And the authoritative source often depends on the local political culture and leadership structure of the community.

Take for example the town crier model that is used in many West African communities as well as in a number of East and Central African communities; no matter the situation, the town crier is invariably used as the all purpose, general information disseminator. But the choice of hardware (drums, gongs, bells) for information dissemination often depends on what has been previously agreed upon by the community.

Thus, when a town crier makes an announcement, for example of the death of an important member of the community, the response or feedback of different communities to this message would invariably be the same. However, their choice of communication channels for effective participatory interaction and the ceremonies associated with the dead would vary depending on predetermined, longstanding, ethno-cultural choices and belief systems.

Records show that the concept of the town crier dates back to the Ashanti Kingdom of Ghana (Ugboajah, 1972). What is worth noting is that, after the

1927
1960
1963
1964
1967
1969
1970
1971
1972
1973
1974
1975
1976
1977
1978
1979
1980
1981
1982
1983
1984
1985
1986
1987
1988
1989
1990
1991

transmission of the primary information through the institution of the town crier, the response or feedback of the community to the information disseminated is often based on predetermined or pre-established community based response mechanism. That is, death will be responded to through specific channels designed for such response; security and war will be responded to according to predetermined interaction processes. The uses of these predetermined interactive mechanisms for responses to specific social issues vary with ethnic groups within a country and sometimes vary slightly from one community to the next.

We can thus say that in a communication process that involves the traditional channels of communication, the primary channels are invariably all purpose, general audience oriented, information-disseminating processes, while the secondary channels are often feedback channels that are mostly purpose and audience specific. These feedback channels, in responding to the initial message, are similarly converted to primary information sources, to which the people in turn react, in order to complete the communication system process. Thus, the town crier's messages are often informational and awareness-creating, rather than interactive as is often the case at the feedback or secondary level of the traditional media communication process.

Cited Reference

Ugboajah, Frank. (1972). 'Traditional-Urban Media Model: Stocktaking for Development'. Gazette, Vol. 18, No. 2

NWUNELI, ONUORA. "Community and Traditional Based Media Approaches to Popular IEC: Some Experiences in the African Region," Kenya Institute of Mass Communication (KIMC) project. 1992. Reprinted with permission of the author.

Excerpt from: Lessons for Communicators
By Neill McKee

Process Indicators for Achieving Sustainability in Social Mobilization (1)

INSTITUTIONALIZATION

1. Continued political commitment and public support
2. Increase in resource mobilization/funding
3. Increased organizational and structural support
4. Improvement in continuity of reporting and monitoring
5. Improvement in training

COORDINATION AND INTEGRATION

1. Joint planning by partners
2. Coordinated workplan and implementation schedule
3. Team approach: continuous dialogue with managers
4. Involvement of effective partners
5. Integration of accelerated efforts with routine tasks

CAPACITY BUILDING

1. Adequate budget allocation for capacity building such as training activities
2. Better understanding of the needs of end-users

3. Long-term education of community built into mobilization
4. Good prospects for expansion

SELF-RELIANCE

1. Increase in national contribution
2. Community and users' responsibility in the management of services
3. Degree of national leadership

DECENTRALIZATION

1. Participation in the programme by end-users
2. Decentralization of resource allocation and management

Note

(1) ACPR. (1990). *Assessment of EPI communication interventions in urban areas.* Associates for Community and Population Research, Dhaka.

McKee, Neill. "Lessons for Communicators," chapter five from *Social Mobilization and Social Marketing in Developing Communities: Lessons for Communicators* by Neill McKee, Southbound, Penang (Malaysia), 1992. Reprinted with permission of the author and the publisher. Arusha (Tanzania) 1990.

1992
1993
1994
1995
1996
1997
1998
1999
2000
2001
2002
2003
2004
2005
2006

EXCERPT FROM:

COMMUNICATION FOR DEVELOPMENT IN LATIN AMERICA: A FORTY-YEAR APPRAISAL

By Luis Ramiro Beltrán

1993 Excerpt 1

Three major conceptualizations of the relationship between social communication and national development have prevailed in Latin America: development communication; development support communication; and alternative communication for democratic development.

Development communication is, in essence, the notion that mass media are capable of creating a public atmosphere favorable to change, which is assumed indispensable for modernizing traditional societies through technological advancement and economic growth. Development support communication is the notion that planned and organized communication—massive or not—is a key instrument for the accomplishment of the practical goals of specific development-seeking institutions and projects.

Alternative communication for democratic development is the notion that, by expanding and balancing people's access to, and participation in, the communication process— at both mass-media and interpersonal grass-roots levels—development should secure, in addition to material gains, social justice, freedom for all and majority rule.

Excerpt 2

NOTES FOR THE 21ST CENTURY AGENDA

What can the initial practitioners of communication for development do? Not very much, perhaps, in terms of actions. They have done the best they could under changing circumstances. However, they can, and must, pass on their experiences (both good and bad) in a systematic and frank manner to those who will inherit their dreams and occupations in the very near future. They can offer notes for their 21st Century Agenda.

1. Put together the best of development support communication with alternative communication. Do not treat them as islands far apart. Blend social consciousness with a passion for planning. Put together technical abilities and political perceptions.

2. Do much more institution building than self-consuming operations. Teach people to fish; do not just hand out fishes. Persuade key schools of communication to include communication for development in their curricula. Foster in them, and in other institutions, communication research geared toward democratic development.

3. Do not support only government agencies. Put faith in the small communities themselves. Help workers' unions, peasant leagues and neighborhood groups, and work with nongovernmental organizations.

4. Place paramount emphasis on communication for health, sanitation, nutrition and population. People in Latin America must be healthy before they can afford to be well-educated, housed or employed. Plagues such as drugs, AIDS and cholera epidemics demand massive education programs that can be attained only through communication.

5. Insist on persuading political leaders and development planners to use communication rationally to attain the development they promise to the people. Help the masses press them for development.

6. Encourage basic communication training at all levels, including the universities that train health, education, housing, agriculture and development planning professionals. Communication specialists cannot cope with the massive job all by themselves. Help strengthen regional communication institutions. Our countries must expand cooperation. Not even the largest countries can do the whole job in isolation.

Beltrán, Luis Ramiro. "Communication for Development in Latin America: A Forty Years' Appraisal," paper presented during the opening of the IV Roundtable on Communication and Development, organized by the Instituto para América Latina (IPAL), February 23, 1993. Used with permission of the author.

GOING GRASSROOTS

Excerpt from: Changing Mediascapes? A Case Study in Nine Tanzanian Villages

By Ullamaija Kivikuru

1993

"Everything started from the village, but the village was soon forgotten."

Taking a new look at the U.N. and UNESCO programmes of the 1950s in the field of communication, as they are described in the UNESCO preface to Wilbur Schramm's book *Mass Media and National Development* (1964, vii-xi), what strikes one most in these "programs of concrete action" is the projection of assistance to rural communication and concern about the fact that 70 percent of the population of the world is denied effective enjoyment of the right to information. The same tendency emerges as the dominant theme of Schramm's book itself, his perspective being opened up by the presentation of two fictitious rural families, one from West Africa, the other from Asia, both representing what he calls "incompletely used resources" (ibid., 4). Other authors frequently referred to by Schramm were all village-oriented researchers, such as Daniel Lerner, who studied rural populations in the Middle East (Lerner, 1958); Y.V.L. Rao in India (Rao, 1963); and Leonard Doob in Africa (Doob, 1961).

In the early years of UNESCO activities in the field of communication, characterized more by reflection (research) than action (development assistance)—though the programmes claimed the opposite—development was predominantly equated with the transformation of rural people living in traditional societies into economic and social modernity; Julius Nyerere has called this "the terrible ascent." Soon, however, the horizon widened to whole societies on the one hand and—to some extent—personalities suffering from underdevelopment and due to undergo modernization, on the other. The small-scale, holistic village approach was pushed aside by modernization as well as by the dependency paradigms.

In this piece, the aim is to discuss the "village tendencies" both found and lost in development-communication literature in the past three or four decades, since it is the only way to place the Commedia project in its proper framework. The review makes three "rounds." It starts with more general tendencies, shifts to some predominant characteristics of development-communication literature and finally describes the literature that falls into exactly the same category as the Commedia study itself.

An indication of the ahistorical character of communication activities is the fact that the idea of directing attention to grassroots communication has been considered predominantly as a phenomenon of the 1980s, though in the field of development communication at least, efforts to reach grassroots populations have been made from the 1950s onwards, as indicated above. However, it is justified to point out that the earlier efforts were done predominantly in relation to educational activities that were most often described as developmental (e.g., Chander and Karnik, 1976; Lenglet, 1980; O'Sullivan, 1980), while the more recent projects, especially but not only in the so-called industrialized world, have aimed at increasing local level communication as such without specific educational objectives (e.g., Ugboajah, 1988a; Wilson, 1987). Recently, even highly theoretical considerations of the relationship between mass communication and the human mind in developing communities have been published (e.g., Goonasekera, 1990). These writings totally ignore the practical "how to go about it" orientation which has, so far at least, been implicitly emphasized in community-communication literature concerning developing societies.

Thus the scope has changed quite markedly within the sphere of community communication. The change has been gradual. At first communicators approached

1927
1960
1963
1964
1967
1969
1970
1971
1972
1973
1974
1975
1976
1977
1978
1979
1980
1981
1982
1983
1984
1985
1986
1987
1988
1989
1990
1991
1992
1993
1994
1995
1996
1997
1998
1999
2000
2001
2002
2003
2004
2005
2006

communities from the outside with a valuable message for a better future; at present, communication within a community is considered important enough as an objective, and empowerment comes best from the community itself defining its own problems and solutions. Francis J. Berrigan outlined the "programme" of the 1960s, while attempting to draw a borderline with the communication ideology of the 1970s:

> Because communications media can reach isolated communities, emphasis has been on the use of *mass* communications: messages flowing from capital cities to the periphery. In most cases feedback from the communities was limited. Communications media communicated one way, from the centre outward. What happened to the message, its impact and the attitude of those on the receiving end, were not taken into account. The content of programming was decided centrally, based on the opinions of a relatively small group of people as to what rural communities needed and wanted to know. In the use of media for development, emphasis has been on 'telling' and 'teaching' rather than exchange of requests and ideas between the centre and the outlying areas. (Berrigan, 1979, 7).

The dialogue model Berrigan discusses above actually refers to a challenge to the top-down model, a challenge thrown down by Paulo Freire (1972). Freire refused to view education and communication as "banking", in which the communicator "makes deposits" which the students receive, memorize and repeat. Freire suggested a liberating or problem-posing approach in which the status difference between communicator and audience is abolished. Communication functions as a dialogue in which both sides learn. Freire calls the process "conscientisation," which means a process of learning the causes of one's oppression. This understanding adds to the potential for doing something about the mistakes inflicted on one.

Freire's doctrine has not been popular among communication-policy planners, either in the West or in the South, as James Halloran has pointed out (Hartmann, et al., 1989, 29). Obviously, the setup suggested by Freire has sounded "too alternative" in its demand to ignore knowledge and power hierarchies. Still, the objective for all community communication could be called a form of conscientisation. Community communication could be considered as a programme of motivation and activation in which the final goal is improvement of the quality of life for those living in the community, thus expanding participation and minimizing marginality (e.g., O'Sullivan, 1980; Ariyaratne, 1989).

At the first phase of community communication, the main strategy for maximizing social competence, that is, the ability to cope with the world around oneself in a sensible and rewarding way, was based on linking the community more closely to the outside world, while the strategy of the latter phase seems to allow the community more of its own operational space. Subsequently, a type of loop seems to have taken place in the dominant mode of communication in communities; originally it was person-to-person communication involving dialogue, but mass communication later enabled centralized policymaking to reach entire communities simultaneously. Now, again, interpersonal communication has been given more emphasis, above all in the rediscovery of oramedia communication (Ugboajah, 1985a).

The two phases of community communication above are interlinked, however. It is quite clear that the access to communication and democratization of mass-communication movements in Europe and the United States (e.g,. Jankowski, 1992; Jakubowicz, 1988), leading to a wide-ranging debate on and gradual establishment of various civic organizations and community-radio and cable-TV institutions, basically challenges the whole idea of national media and broadcasting policies, even conventional concepts of media professionalism. Though the actual implementation of these new approaches has remained rather limited, the emergence of community media has not so far been able to change the trend toward expanding media institutions and content mainstreaming. The argument for these movements is quite revolutionary; resting on the assumption that receivers should not be considered merely as targets, or members of an audience, but rather as active participants in any communication process involving the articulation of reciprocity rather than a top-down relationship. Within the "access school," media professionalism, with its fairly fixed value systems and means of expression, has often been seen implicitly or explicitly as a hindrance rather than a promoter of spontaneous dialogue and cooperation with members of communities.

In giving new meanings to situations the media can also bring to the front region hitherto unappreciated qualities of the different communities which are close affinities among the regions and ethnic identities of the people in the Third World....

It is in this context of individual self-identity that people are ready to pick up events that 'offend' or 'hurt' their individual communities either in the media or in other sectors of society, such as education, employment, politics, etc., and use these issues to rally support for their communal causes in a way that was not possible in the past. With heightened individual self-identity every individual thinks of himself as a potential spokesman for his community, whereas in the past such roles were confined to traditionally accepted families and change was quite gradual (Goonasekera, 1990, 50).

As seen in the quotation by Anura Goonasekera and recent literature on so-called alternative communication (e.g., Saukko, 1991), the active-audience concept has "spilled over" to the literature of community communication in the so-called South also; what, in a deeper sense, happens in the community and among its members, when the "passing of traditional society" (Lerner, 1958) takes place?

Nevertheless appreciation of professionalism still runs high in development communication; the "praise of amateurism" so frequently found in Northern access

literature is fairly rare in the South (but see Stuart, 1992; Oepen, 1992). Though the distinction between professionals and lay persons is not always seen as essential (e.g., Smith de Cherif, 1992; Aguilar, 1992), emphasis on media professionalism has obviously been perceived as a means to ensure journalism's increased integrity in relation to the political decision-making system (e.g., Rural Press in Africa, 1987). Hints of a challenge to conventional perceptions of professionalism have emerged lately, however: "Why was Gandhi so effective in his communication? The answer I get is that he was not a professional communicator. Although he wrote every day like a journalist, the message came from the heart and needs of the people" (E. V. Chitnis in Stuart, 1992, 30).

In regions conventionally called "developing countries" or "the Third World," the presently applied approaches to grassroots communication still carry more resemblance to the previous attempts of development communication than to community-communication models in the industrialized world, though analysis shows that the basic tone of writings about the South has changed quite distinctly. Today, much more appreciation is given to those elements of communication already existing in these communities, than to those which are lacking there, e.g., Kunczik, 1984; Valbuena, 1986; 1987; Traber, 1988), so that it might be worthwhile to dwell on the history of development communication somewhat more systematically and to sketch some features of a profile of grassroots communication in developing countries, in order to place Commedia in its proper perspective.

It was the paradigm of diffusion of innovations and the inbuilt optimism of modernization theory that encouraged communicators to develop the variety of application models for community communication for developing countries (McAnany, 1980, xii–18), as vividly reported in literature (e.g., "An African Experiment for Radio Forums," 1968; Berrigan, 1979; Bordenave, 1976; Hall, 1978; Ng'wanakilala, 1981; Kasoma, 1992). The basic ideology of these writings

1927
1960
1963
1964
1967
1969
1970
1971
1972
1973
1974
1975
1976
1977
1978
1979
1980
1981
1982
1983
1984
1985
1986
1987
1988
1989
1990
1991
1992
1993
1994
1995
1996
1997
1998
1999
2000
2001
2002
2003
2004
2005
2006

was clear; implicitly or explicitly, they emphasized the significant role of communication in the process of "modernizing the human mind" and, through this, the developing society. Over the years, explicit notions about the empathy and mobilization effects of communication have become fewer (e.g., Kunczik, 1984, 134–154), but what this actually indicates is simply that toward the 1980s, writings on community communication became more and more specialized in the sense that they often completely lacked more general theoretical considerations and concentrated predominantly on either concrete cases or practices.

Roughly categorized, these writings suggest two distinctly different strategies. The first strategy applies to improving distribution and use of conventional mass communication in rural communities, as well as preparing the communities for mass-media use, above all via literacy programmes. The second strategy deals with communication models specially designed for rural communities in developing countries. Most frequently, the latter strategy means such approaches as combinations of mass media and interpersonal communication. Under both umbrellas, there are books and articles of a fairly practical type (guidebooks or operational kits, e.g., Kasoma, 1990), while others discuss predominantly theoretical considerations.

In the 1970s, suggestions on such setups as educational radio programmes combined with study groups were especially popular; sometimes audiocassettes were used instead of or beside radio programmes. These forms of communication were called radio fora (e.g., Hall, 1978; Ng'awanakilala, 1980, 77–97). Another fashionable and widely discussed model was educational satellite broadcasting, often combined with various forms of interpersonal communication (e.g., Chander and Karnik, 1976). Still another cherished form of community-oriented communication was the rural paper, often linked with literacy campaigns (e.g., Bashiruddin, 1979; "Rural Press in Africa," 1978). In Africa, these papers, generously sponsored from abroad, seemed to offer an opportunity to re-introduce

local mass communication in newly independent African states as a compensation for the local papers which were abolished earlier, either due to their ideological links with former colonial masters, or simply due to great efforts in unifying nation-building based on one language and one distinct power centre. Tragically, the re-introduction of local mass communication has turned out to be extremely difficult in many African and Asian countries despite foreign funding; obviously the right formula for rural communication is not easily found (e.g., "Rural Press in Africa, 1978"; "Rural Press in Africa, 1987"; Bashiruddin, 1979). Another unfortunate development is the fact that the audiocassette disappeared from the arena quickly; obviously, it sounded much less glorious than film, television, satellites and video, though in the case of rural villages, the audiocassette appears much more practical and participatory in its basic nature than expensive forms of audiovisual high tech.

The introduction of dependency theory in the field of communication research took place simultaneously with the accumulation of predominantly depressing evidence of imbalances of information flows on the macro level on the one hand and, on the other, field experiences at the micro level of communities. All these developments meant, in fact, that literature on community communication decreased radically in the late 1970s and early 1980s. It became more and more obvious that the strategies of community communication exercised so far had only rarely been successful, and even the crucial role given to communication as a catalyst for development was questioned. Simultaneously, dependency theory based its criticism on the substance of development as a concept and a socio-politico-economic configuration. The ways and means of community-based communication seemed to be of negligible significance compared with these basic questions. A glance at the titles published in the UNESCO series "Reports and Papers on Mass Communication" in the 1980s, keeping in mind that reflections on any type of changes have been gradual in the slowly moving publishing mechanism of

UNESCO, reveals much; the titles are much fewer and indicate technical or statistical orientation rather than substance orientation. Both characteristics are also direct reflections of the weakened status of UNESCO, previously an important promoter of community-communication activities in the Third World.

The second-generation "dependistas" of the so-called culturalist approach to development communication brought community communication back onto the list of favourites, and directly into focus. Summarized crudely, the culturalist approach can be viewed as favouring strongly localized "grassroots" efforts and a "small is beautiful" orientation, giving due appreciation to cultural heritage (Wang and Dissayanake, 1984; Saville-Troike, 1982); all these elements fit very well into community communication. The girl at the village well has been rediscovered, and her means of communication given due appreciation. Subsequently, a wide range of literature, predominantly theoretical and culture-bound by orientation, has been published on the grassroots aspects of communication, stressing the role of cultural elements and interpersonal communication (e.g,. Ugboajah, 1985a; 1985b; Servaes, 1986; Casmir, 1991). Furthermore, special attention has been given to what has been called "popular" or "traditional" communication (Wang and Dissayanake, 1984; Casmir, 1991), especially in Asian societies. In summary, the research has been more interested in what is and always has been there in the villages, than what the villages lack in the field of communication.

The significance of communication as a tool for change in rural and semi-rural communities has been restored, and a guidebook-type of literature has started to flourish since the late 1980s. It is surprising, however, to notice that not so much in it has actually changed; only rarely have fresh theoretical considerations of dependency and culturalist paradigms been reflected in practical literature (compare, e.g., "Rural Press in Africa," 1978, and "Rural Press in Africa," 1987).

What has frequently filtered from theoretical debates into the introductions to practical literature is a kind of "grassroots mystique," obviously a deep, almost romantic rhetoric of orality, locality, indigenity and other components of what could be called genuine culture. Unfortunately, this belief has only rarely been elaborated well enough to provide for the promotion of communication principles or practice on a community level.

It is worth noting that one form of writing on community communication has been very unpopular during both the first and the second wave of grassroots orientation in development communication, namely, actual case studies of rural communities. It might seem that both theoretical and practical achievements and constraints on grassroots communication could easily be dealt with in research focusing broadly on development and communication in the village context; however, this has been done extremely rarely for reasons which are probably practical. It is complicated, troublesome and expensive to carry out village-level field research; the subsequent empirical burden tends to overwhelm a researcher and prevent him or her from extensive theoretical considerations. The work easily ends up with a "neat" survey giving us result scores of percentage figures but hardly anything more. Communication in individual villages is rarely studied; instead, particular phenomena in village-level communication such as agricultural-extension work, puppet drama, health education and women's activities, are nowadays studied quite frequently ("Communication and the Traditional Media," 1981; "Communication and Development," 1986; Mndogo, et al., 1987).

Leonard Doob (1961) had already sought the answer to African communication needs from villages in the late 1950s, though his detailed study was not a "pure" village study in the sense that it did not concentrate on one or two particular rural communities as such, but combined village-level information on several predominantly West African communities. Though observing differences between orality and conventional mass communication sensitively and being considerate enough to acknowledge the genuine communication needs of African communities, Doob frequently became paternalistic, concluding, for example, that the majority of the population in these communities had a long way to go before reaching even the first steps to modernization; they had both the strength and the weakness of a newborn baby (Doob, 1961, 378). However, the availability of means for communication seemed to open the gate to mental mobility and modernization in the best-equipped babies:

> Only one man [in a Nigerian village] could be found who had any knowledge about world affairs, including some recent developments in the field of atomic warfare. To all the rest it seems the mass media had failed to communicate such information, but with him they had been successful, undoubtedly because he alone in the village had a radio. Under some circumstances such as a crisis, this limited success might be crucial: The man could pass on information, and—if his status were high—he could become an influential recipient-disseminator (Doob, 1961, 330–331).

Compared with the classic of development communication, Lerner's *The Passing of Traditional Society* (1958), Doob's study lacked the insight and understanding of traditional society inherent in Lerner's book. Both agreed on the objective, however: to adjust members of the traditional society to such dimensions of modern life as atomic warfare and Donald Duck (Doob, 1961, 158). Ultimately, there was no alternative to modernization.

Admittedly, one of the classics of modernization literature in the sphere of communication deals with "pure" village research. Y.V.L. Rao (1963/1966) based his argument on the relationship between development and communication, drawing his supportive data from an actual case study on two Indian villages, somewhat in the same style as Daniel Lerner in his work on Middle Eastern societies. Even more than Lerner's empathy, Rao seemed to believe in innovation diffusion and opinion leaders. He sought opinion leaders in the two villages, but he found also much more contradiction and conflict. Happily enough, Rao was alert and less

theoretical and orthodox in his considerations than Lerner, and he was more anchored in the phenomena in the villages themselves, accepting the lack of harmony in village life. His approach also allowed the coverage of many issues and sectors of life other than communication. Rao was thus able to catch a glimpse of the two villages "live," observing patterns of interaction and conflict, the role of elites as determinants of change and so on. Rao had a distinct bias toward modernization and thus his report constrains inbuilt contradictions. Rao explicitly wanted to give information a magic role in processes leading toward modernization, but his data hardly supported this kind of conclusion since the role of the media turned out to be marginal in the villages studied.

Methodologically, Rao's work was highly interesting. Fully aware of the pitfalls of structured interviews, he adopted a more anthropological approach. He lived in the villages and interviewed selected people informally over a period of months. In short, Rao proved that village-oriented communication research can be both possible and fruitful. However, not too many researchers have chosen his path.

A much more ambitious village study, also carried out in India, reveals the magnitude of the work involved in this type of approach. It took Paul Hartmann and his collaborators (Hartmann, Patil and Dighe, 1989) 11 years altogether to complete their basically three-phase research in Andhra Pradesh, West Bengal and Kerala. The idea was to approach villages with a comparatively "open" methodology, first, via participant observation in one single village in each state in order to sensitise the fieldworkers and, through them, the entire research team to significant features of local society and culture. The second phase involved a random sample of population in eight villages in Andra Pradesh and Kerala. The third phase was described as "intensive community study," comprising an extended period of six months' participant observation in each of the three areas. Numerous seminars and workshops were organized in order to avoid inconsistencies and lack of discipline, both having frequently been identified as the main weaknesses of this kind of approach.

The authors use their colorful data to emphasize first that generalizing about village life is not justified since great variation was found in communication and development in the villages studied. In Kerala, with a relatively high literacy rate, mention of media sources for new agricultural practices was comparatively frequent, while in other villages interpersonal sources were far more frequent. Still, media exposure emerged as a significant factor influencing new farming and health practices, and the media proved an important source of political and other news from the outside world. But even more important seemed to be the social learning acquired via mass communication, the media providing a reference source for urban-oriented dressing style, music and manners. New understanding of the world was generated by the penetration of urban popular culture into rural communities. However, the researchers noticed that the general run of "lighter" mass communication, such as music, drama and the news that most people with access to media attend to most of the time, had received little research attention. This was probably due to the fact that these phenomena have not been thought to have much relevance to development as defined by official development agencies. These three researchers warn that the social significance of mass communication such as film or popular music cannot be encompassed within the narrow, mechanistic model of communication adopted by advocates of "official development."

Hartmann et al. concluded that two fallacies about development and communication exist. First, the relative neglect of social structure and structural conflicts easily leads to the assumption of a harmony of interest among the rural population. There are, however, structural conflicts of interest even at village level that no development strategy can ignore if it is to make a real contribution to the lives of the poor. It is exactly such inequalities that make the problems of underdevelopment so apparently intractable. The second fallacy is rarely explicit, though it pervades development literature; that is, the tendency to regard the people who are the target of communication designed to promote development as essentially passive. The attitude has a number of unfortunate consequences. For one thing, the advertising campaign becomes the dominant model for development communication, as though development were a commodity to be sold like soap powder. Those employing communication in villages still analyse the communication process in terms of the old mechanical formula of source, message, channel, receiver and effect.

Not only the "trickle-down" but also the "two-step-flow" formula of communication was regarded as mechanistic by Hartmann, Patil and Dighe. They viewed the two-step formula as a comforting theory in the sense that it avoids the need to be overly concerned about inequalities and justifies the concentration of development effort on the comparatively advanced population, which then passes the word on further. The researchers found little evidence to support this strategy. On the contrary, poor farmers often became deeply indebted because of official development projects established in the villages. In "less severe" cases, informed people appeared to be highly selective in what and to whom they pass on information encountered in the media. The mechanistic "passive-audience formula" lurks behind the idea of two-step flow; the communication audience being seen as relatively passive, passing on information in a semi-automatic fashion rather than selecting and reinterpreting as the study suggested.

The view from an Indian village caught by the researchers in the mid-1980s surprisingly resembled the view already offered by Rao 20 years earlier — the authors stressed that changes are slow, gradual and diffuse. Media professionals have had a tendency to overestimate the expansion of mass communication, but, on the other hand, the role of entertainment-oriented mass media as a supplier of new values has grown, especially among the young, the better-educated, and the better-off. This is how the authors formulated their findings:

1927
1960
1963
1964
1967
1969
1970
1971
1972
1973
1974
1975
1976
1977
1978
1979
1980
1981
1982
1983
1984
1985
1986
1987
1988
1989
1990
1991
1992
1993
1994
1995
1996
1997
1998
1999
2000
2001
2002
2003
2004
2005
2006

Information, ideas and values originating in the media acquire currency by a process of diffusion. This process is neither automatic nor indiscriminate; diffusion tends to follow the pattern of social interaction already structured by caste, class, age and sex.

The effects of communication should not be thought of only in terms of the spread of information. One of the more important effects is to gradually alter the cultural climate and to introduce new values in a slow, diffuse way. In this, the entertainment media may play the major part by helping to promote a greater receptiveness to new values and openness to change (Hartmann, et al., 1989, 263).

Another issue clearly in contradiction with views expressed by communication optimists from previous decades was the conclusion that such development efforts as land reform in Kerala and agricultural policies did carry far-reaching change into the villages studied. These policies strongly affected village structures, which gradually showed symptoms of change. In these efforts, interpersonal communication was a far more important factor than mass communication, but basically it was the "real" value of the effort that counted, not the communication attention that it did or did not achieve. The key factor was the localised activities of political parties and factional alliances, and many important projects failed because of local-level shortcomings, corruption or dishonesty. Many administrative efforts to run community radio appeared totally unsuccessful. Official development policies had a tendency to pay insufficient attention to conflicts of interest, and government bureaucracies often identified themselves with the interests of the haves against the have-nots. Still, the authors declined to oversimplify the situation by subscribing unconditionally to nongovernmental, small-scale initiatives. According to them, reality is not as clear-cut.

Instead, the authors clearly spelled out a third fallacy, explicit in the writings of the 1960s, now predominantly implicitly expressed — the belief in the power and "wizardry" of mass communication. According to their experience, long-distance-learning education projects can never replace teachers or extension workers. Centralised solutions are systematically overrun by local-level initiative, flexibility and concern. However, this does not mean that mass communication does not have any significance in development. It only means that the time for easy equations and yes-or-no solutions is over.

It is worth dwelling on the study by Hartmann, Patil and Dighe extensively because of its insight and weight of refined thinking. It indicates both how demanding it is to carry out research of this type and how rewarding.

In Africa, West African and above all Ghanaian researchers have, more frequently than others, paid attention to village-level communication problems. Ghanaian rural-radio-forum experiments and surveys on them (Ansah, 1984) started in the early 1980s and could be considered pilot programmes of village-level development communication of the culturalist "wave." In a survey on media use, radio was rated by far the most important medium of information, the government information system was second and newspapers were third. The core of the project was consequently built around a regional radio station. On the one hand, the broadcasting policy of the radio tried to take into account the intimate character of radio broadcasting, while on the other, it made an attempt to maximize "locality" in the substance of programmes. The regional radio aimed at participation and dialogue, offering educational advice but also enjoyment without a hidden message, covering of village festivals and drama, as well as health and agricultural extension activity. The relevance of substance was found to be a crucial factor. The team working on the local radio project came to conclusions quite different from those of Leonard Doob. Where Doob accused people of backwardness, the Ghanaian team, evincing high respect for the village population and their desire to control their own environment rationally, put the blame on irrelevant content choices, when the message did not get through:

> It is clear that the lack of education excludes the citizen not only from the print media as sources of information, but from all of the mass media. The assumption that the radio leaps the barrier of illiteracy to reach all the people is unfounded. It is equally clear that the content of the mass media is not designed to serve its audience in proportion to its educational makeup. Two-thirds of radio programming in news and information campaigns is not aimed at those who have never been to school (Ansah, 1984, 5).

The fact that more than 40 percent of the population of a semi-urban settlement such as a district capital listen to the local gong-beater does not make the radio less important, but those deciding upon the content of radio broadcasting should take this fact into consideration in their planning. …

A recent limited study on two Ghanaian villages (Atarah, 1992) has an anthropological orientation, but the study concentrates almost entirely on media habits and expectations. The researcher approached people from the two villages, plus a group of urban workers and a group of urban elite, with basically the same in-depth interview format. The three different social classes were noticeably different from one another in their media preferences and news horizons. Radio was a natural choice for illiterate peasants living outside the regular distribution of newspapers; radio was for them a medium for both information and entertainment. What was interesting was the fact that the use of television seemed to follow a "Northern" formula; to most workers, television was more an entertainment medium than a source of news. The upper-middle class spent less time with television and tended to use it as a medium for serious information such as news and documentaries. Further, the preferred medium for middle- and upper-class men was print, while the consumption behaviour of upper-class women resembled that of the workers, with more time spent watching television entertainment.

Differences were also found in news criteria. To the peasants, proximity was the main criterion defining a news event. Either it was a local event or it had a direct bearing on the life situation of the interviewee; for example, the state budget was assessed as more important than district assembly elections, because its direct relevance was more obvious. A similar tendency was also quite strong among some workers. Female workers were especially insouciant about the elections as a news theme.

Foreign radio stations were assessed as the most reliable sources for foreign news. The foreign stations mentioned most frequently were BBC and the Voice of America. The middle class had access to foreign magazines also, but tended to complain about their high price. Television was an insignificant source of foreign news for all.

Disregarding social class, the respondents did not consider the mass media as being capable of contributing to improving their life situations. They all admitted the significance of the mass media, but when asked whether information from the media helped them to improve their lives, the answer was always negative. All respondents also expressed powerlessness to control the media.

All in all, literature in community communication has gradually developed into a full spectrum of approaches, starting from very practical guidebooks and ending up with thrilling combinations of well-analysed empirical compilations and good, alert theory. Maybe the most interesting recent trend is the fact that community-communication literature focusing on both the South and the North indicates more and more similarities. The questions bothering both Nick Jankowski (1992), working in urban settings in Western Europe, and Hartmann et al. (1989), studying Indian villages, are the same. Both claim that community communication as such is not crucial, but the issues and items to be communicated are. If the policies and practices exercised in the community are not participatory and people-oriented, overtly

1927
1960
1963
1964
1967
1969
1970
1971
1972
1973
1974
1975
1976
1977
1978
1979
1980
1981
1982
1983
1984
1985
1986
1987
1988
1989
1990
1991
1992
1993
1994
1995
1996
1997
1998
1999
2000
2001
2002
2003
2004
2005
2006

participatory communication mechanisms are not worth much. Still, communication carries significance, having potential for both understanding the world and channelling impulses to change it. Action by itself rarely takes the form of communication, but it is still needed for action. The key word is no longer Lerner's "empathy," because it carries an implication of "big-brother" thinking—someone else knows best what is good for the community—but, rather, Freire's liberation, because it stresses participation and partnership in change; in short, emancipation. The problem that seems to make community-communication researchers hesitant, both in the North and in the South, is whether the power structure in any community is ready for true social competence and participation, rather than merely paying lip service to themiraculous concept.

Another trend emerging from almost all recent grassroots-oriented studies is the role assigned to such previously neglected modes of mass communication as entertainment. This, in turn, finally leads to the crucial question of whether there is a need to reconsider the concept of development. People do learn new values, manners and practices through the content of cultural industries. They are able to interpret the world around them somewhat better, but the concept of development suggested by these new complexes of values often remains distant from the "official" forms of development promoted by the administrative and political machinery. On whose terms is the concept of development generally acceptable at all?

The forms of communication available for development-oriented communication are well established in the 1990s and include village reporters, village and rural papers, bulletin boards, audiocassettes, drama and dance, radio fora and other forms of interpersonal communication. All these are fairly well researched also. Existing evidence suggests that these forms of community communication are relatively inexpensive but still frequently beyond the resources of the communities to run on their own; outside assistance is needed, but close links to a strict administrative system tend to strangle the emerging new formations. There is usually a "bridgehead" of the administrative system based deeply in the community itself conditioning operational choices. Does this setup allow "real" community communication to emerge, or is it exactly the setup itself that kills the possibility of reconsidering the concept of development? The greatest problem involved in community communication is still not the form but the substance.

Bibliography

"An African Experiment in Radio Forums for Rural Development: Ghana." Reports and Papers for Mass Communication, No. 51. Paris: UNESCO, 1968.

Ansah, P.A.V. "The Community Development Approach to Human Settlements: The Ghanaian Experience." Paper prepared for the Expert Group Meeting on Information/Human Settlements. The Hague: September 5-9, 1983 (mimeo).

Ansah, P.A.V. "Communication in Third World Villages: A Ghanaian Experience." Paper presented at the Frankfurt Bookfair and Seminars. Frankfurt, West Germany: Sept. 28 to Oct. 9, 1984 (mimeo).

Ansah, P.A.V. "The Ethical Dimension of Development Communication." The Journal of Development Communication, 1990, Vol. 1, No. 2: 57-75.

Appadurai, Arjun. "Mediascapes." InterMedia, August-September 1992, Vol. 20, Nos. 4-5: 17.

Apter, David E. Rethinking Development: Modernization, Dependency, and Postmodern Politics. Newbury Park/Beverly Hills/London/New Delhi: Sage, 1987.

Ariyaratne, A. T. "Beyond Development Communication: Case Study on Sarvodaya, Sri Lanka." In Neville Jayaweera and Sarath Amunugama, eds., Rethinking Development Communication. Singapore: AMIC, 1989.

Arusha Declaration. Dar es Salaam: Tanzania Information Services, 1967.

Asante, M., and M. Appiah. "The Rhetoric of the Akan Drum." Western Journal of Black Studies, 1979, No. 2: 8-13.

Atarah, Azato Linus, "The Mass Media and Social Consciousness: The Case Study of Ghana." M.A. thesis. Finland: University of Tampere, Department of Journalism and Mass Communication (mimeo), 1992.

Bashiruddin, S. Rural Press in India. Singapore: AMIC, 1979.

Basic Education Statistics in Tanzania 1981-1985. Dar es Salaam: Ministry of Education, 1985.

The BBC in East Africa: Survey in Tanzania. London: International Broadcasting and Audience Research, 1988.

Belbase, Subhadra. "Development Communication: A Nepali Experience." In Neville Jayaweera and Sarath Amunugama, eds., Rethinking Development Communication. Singapore: AMIC, 1989.

Berrigan, Frances J. "Community Communications: The Role of Community Media in Development." Reports and Papers on Mass Communication, No. 90. Paris: UNESCO, 1981.

Bordenave, Juan D. *Communication and Rural Development*. Paris: UNESCO, 1976.

Carbaugh, Donal. "Communication and Cultural Interpretation," Quarterly Journal of Speech, 1991, 77: 336-342.

Casmir, Fred L., ed. *Communication in Development*. Norwood, N.J.: Ablex, 1991.

Communication and Development. Gabinete of Social Communication. Ministery of Information. Maputo: People's Republic of Mozambique, 1986. Maputo.

Communication and the Traditional Media. Papers and proceedings of a seminar organised by IIMC and the Film and Television Institute of India, Pune. New Delhi: IIMC, 1981.

Community Media for Rural Development Project: Terminal Report. Nairobi: UNESCO, 1990 (mimeo).

Development Communication Report, No. 177.

Doob, Leonard. *Communication in Africa: A Search for Boundaries*. New Haven: Yale University Press, 1961.

Freire, Paulo. *Cultural Action for Freedom*. Harmondsworth: Penguin, 1972.

Freire, Paulo. *Pedagogy in Process*. London: Seabury Press, 1978.

Goonasekera, Anura. "Communication, Culture and the Growth of the Individual Self in Third World Societies," Asian Journal of Communication, 1990, Vol. 1, No. 1: 34-52.

Hartmann, Paul, B. R. Patil and Anita Dighe. *The Mass Media and Village Life: An Indian Study*. New Delhi/Newbury Park/London: Sage, 1989.

Hall, Stuart. "The Rediscovery of 'Ideology': Return of the Repressed in Media Studies," In Michael Gurevich, Tony Bennet, James Curran and Janet Woollacott, eds., *Culture, Society and the Media*. London: Methuen, 1982, 59-90.

Isaacs, H. R. *Images of Asia: American Views of China and India*. New York: Capricorn Books, 1962.

Jakubowicz, Karol. "The New Information and Communication Technologies and Democratization of Communication," Paper presented at the 16th IAMCR Conference. Barcelona: July 1988 (mimeo).

Kasoma, Francis. "Rural Newspaper Forums: Another Model of Communication for Development," The Journal of Development Communication, 1990, Vol. 4, No. 3.

Katz, Elihu, and Paul Lazarsfeld. *Personal Influence: The Part Played by People in the Flow of Mass Communications*. Glencoe, Illinois: The Free Press, 1955.

Kivikuru, Ullamaija. *Tinned Novelties or Creative Culture? A Study on the Role of Mass Communication in Peripheral Nations*. Helsinki, Finland: Department of Communication, University of Helsinki, Publication No. 1 F/10, 1990.

Kunczik, Michael. *Communication and Social Change: A Summary of Theories, Policies and Experiences for Media Practitioners in the Third World*. Communication Manual. Bonn: Friedrich-Ebert-Stiftung, 1984.

Lerner, Daniel. *The Passing of Traditional Society: Modernising the Middle East*. Glencoe, Illinois: The Free Press, 1958.

Lewis, Justin. "Decoding Television News," In Phillip Drummond and Richard Paterson, eds., *Television in Transition*. London: British Film Institute, 1985.

Lippman, Walter. *Public Opinion*. New York/London: The Free Press, 1965.

MacDonald, Ian, and David Hearle. *Communication Skills for Rural Development*.

Martín-Barbero, Jesús. *Communication, Culture and Hegemony: From the Media to Mediations*. London/Newbury Park/New Delhi: Sage, 1993.

McAnany, Emile, ed. *Communications in the Rural Third World: The Role of Information in Development*. New York: Praeger, 1980.

Melkote, Shirinas R. *Communication for Development in the Third World: Theory and Practice*. Newbury Park/London/New Delhi: Sage, 1991.

Morgan, David L. *Focus Groups as Qualitative Research*. Newbury Park: Sage, 1988.

Mowlana, Hamid, and Margaret Hardt Frondorf, eds. *The Media as a Forum for Community Building: Cases from Africa, Asia, Latin America, Eastern Europe and the United States*. Washington, D.C.: The Paul H.Nitze School of Advanced International Studies, Johns Hopkins University, 1992.

Negus, Keith. "Global Scenes and Local Scenes: The Entertainment Industry and Popular Music in Europa," Paper presented for the panel, Globalization, Civil Society and the Public Sphere, at the IAMCR conference, Europe in Turmoil. Dublin: June 25, 1993 (mimeo).

Pendakur, Manjunath. "Political Economy and Ethnography: Transformations in an Indian Village," In J. Wasko, V. Mosco and M. Pendakur, eds., *Illuminating the Blindspots: Essays Honoring Dallas W. Smythe*. Norwood, New Jersey: Ablex, 1993 (82-108).

Population Census 1988: Preliminary Report. Bureau for Statistics and Ministry of Finance, Economics and Planning. Dar es Salaam, Tanzania: 1988.

Rao, Y.V.L. *Communication and Development: A Study of Two Indian Villages*. Minneapolis: 1963/1966.

Rogers, E. M. *Modernization Among Peasants: The Impact of Communication*. New York: Holt, 1969.

"Rural Press in Africa: Dialogue Between Cities and Villages," Document prepared by the Secretariat on the basis of consultant's reports for a meeting of African Council on Communication Education. Dakar: UNESCO, December 1978 (mimeo).

"Rural Press in Africa: Course Documents," Berlin: International Institute of Journalism, 1987 (mimeo).

Saville-Troike, Muriel. *The Ethnography of Communication: An Introduction*. Oxford: Basil Blackwell, 1982.

Schramm, Wilbur. *Mass Media and National Development: The Role of Information in the Developing Countries*. Stanford, California: Stanford University Press and UNESCO, 1964.

Servaes, Jan. "Cultural Identity and the Mass Media in the Third World," Third Channel, 1986, Vol. II, No. 1: 299-316.

Simpson, Michael. "How to Design and Use a Questionnaire in Evaluation and Educational Research," *Medical Teacher*, 1984, Vol. 6, No. 4.

Smith de Cherif, Teresa. "Wall Papers in the Desert: A Sahrawi Initiative for Problem Solving in Exile," In H. Mowlana and M. Hardt Frondorf, eds., *The Media as a Forum for Community Building: Cases from Africa, Asia, Latin America, Eastern Europe and the United States*. Washington, D.C.: SAIS, 1992.

Spector, Paul E. "Research Designs." In John Sullivan and Richard Niemi, eds., *Quantitative Applications in the Social Sciences*. London: Sage, 1982.

1927
1960
1963
1964
1967
1969
1970
1971
1972
1973
1974
1975
1976
1977
1978
1979
1980
1981
1982
1983
1984
1985
1986
1987
1988
1989
1990
1991
1992
1993
1994
1995
1996
1997
1998
1999
2000
2001
2002
2003
2004
2005
2006

Tehranian, Majid. *Technologies of Power: Information Machines and Democratic Prospects*. Norwood, New Jersey: Ablex, 1990.

Tomlinson, John. *Cultural Imperialism*. London: Pinter Publishers, 1992.

Traber, Michael. "The Stories People Tell: Are They Part of the Democratic Process?" *Africa Media Review*, 1988, Vol. 2, No. 2: 115-123.

Turner, Victor. "Process, System and Symbol: A New Anthropological Synthesis," *Daedalus*, Summer 1977, Vol. 1.

Ugboajah, Frank. "Oramedia," In F. Ugboajah, ed., *Communication, Culture and Society in West Africa*. Munchen/New York/London: WACC and Hans Zell Publishers, 1985a.

Ugboajah, Frank. "Media Habits of Rural and Semi-Rural (Slum) Kenya," *Gazette*, 1985(b), No. 36: 155-174.

Valbuena, Victor T. *Philippine Folk Media in Development Communication*. Singapore: AMIC, 1986.

Valbuena, Victor T. *Using Traditional Media in Environmental Communication*. Singapore: AMIC, 1989.

Vansina, Jan. *Oral Tradition as History*. London/Nairobi: James Currey and Heinemann Kenya, 1985.

Wang, Georgette, and Wimal Dissanayake, eds. *Continuity and Change in Communication Systems: An Asian Perspective*. Norwood, New Jersey: Ablex, 1984.

"Going Grassroots," in Ullamaija Kivikuru, William Lobulu and Gervas Moshiro, *Changing Mediascapes? A Case Study in Nine Tanzanian Villages*. Finland: University of Helsinki, Institute of Development Studies, 1994. Report B 28/1994, 1-12. Reprinted with permission of the author.

EXCERPT FROM:

DIFFUSION THEORY AND PARTICIPATORY DECISION MAKING

Participatory Communication Working for Change and Development

By Joseph Ascroft and Robert Agunga

1994 The concept of "diffusion," as used in social change generally refers to the process by which new ideas (called innovations) are communicated throughout a social system. A vast amount of research on diffusion of innovations has been carried out in the United States, the first studies having made their appearance in the late 1920s. But it was the 1943 Ryan and Gross study of the diffusion of hybrid seed corn in Iowa that was the watershed for diffusion research and established the foundations of a theory. The study consisted of determining when and how farmers adopted hybrid seed corn. Their rate of adoption was plotted over time, resulting in the now familiar "S" curve which was then divided on the basis of standard deviations to form adopter categories ranging from early to late adopters. The process of adoption, from first awareness of an innovation to ultimate acceptance, was also divided into stages and communication channels used in each determined.

Everett Rogers eventually came to formalize these and other findings of a similar nature first in his seminal work published in 1962 and then in subsequent updates: namely, *The Communication of Innovations* in 1971 and the *Diffusion of Innovations* in 1983. Since these works represent the best available synthesis of research in the diffusion tradition, we will subject them to particular scrutiny to determine the degree to which they include consideration of participatory decision making.

Although the three *Innovations* books each included reference to the transfer of innovations from industrialized to less developed countries, it was his

1969 book with Lynn Svenning, *Modernization among Peasants: The Impact of Communication,* which treated the notion of development support diffusion most systematically. We will, therefore, give this book special attention. What gives the works of Rogers academic strength is the Diffusion Document Center which he developed, first at Michigan State University, and later at California. Diffusion studies collected from all over the world were deposited in this centre and used as major inputs to his *Innovations* books. The 1962 book benefited from 1,126 worldwide publications, and the 1983 one from more than 2,000 empirical diffusion research reports and 3,000 publications gathered the world over. A critical review mainly of the works of Rogers, starting with his pioneering effort in 1962 is a useful exercise. Early Notions of Technical Assistance Diffusion Attention to the plight of peasant societies in what has now come to be recognized as the Third World emerged after World War II when former colonies started to get their independence. Triggered off by the now-legendary "Point Four" program promulgated by Harry S. Truman in his 1949 inaugural address, industrialized nations geared up to send platoons of international technical assistants to help diffuse innovations among peasant families. These technical assistants were an extension of a system of professional change agents that had long been a part of the diffusion of innovations in the United States.

The Role of Professional Change Agents

An important point in early diffusion theory was the role of change agents in promoting the diffusion of an innovation and thus affecting its rate. Rogers (1962, p. 254) defined a change agent as a "professional person who attempts to influence adoption decisions in a direction that change be tailored to fit the cultural values and past experiences of the clients and that the clients be enabled to perceive the need for an innovation, a necessity for it to be successfully introduced." Along these lines, Rogers advised change agents to improve their clients' competence in evaluating new ideas and to spend less energy on simply

promoting the innovations per se. The intention seemed to be to ensure that clients understood thoroughly the implications of an innovation before committing themselves to it. In other words, the basis for decision making was to be dialogue between change agent and client, the principal outcome of which is not necessarily adoption, however much the agent desires it, but a mutual understanding of the advantages and disadvantages involved.

Thus, on the face of it, Rogers' first book appeared to lay the foundation for a theory that sought to accommodate the idea of participatory decision making. Not being a controversial issue at the time, however, the book did not place any special emphasis on popular participation as an essential of decision making. One was forced rather to read between the lines in order to tease it out of the text. Let us not forget, however, that Rogers' first diffusion book was essentially about diffusion in Western countries, particularly in the United States, where the bulk of studies available in 1962 had been conducted.

From Diffusion to Communication of Innovations

It was mainly Rogers' second edition of *Diffusion of Innovations,* published in 1971 and retitled *Communication of Innovations: A Cross Cultural Approach,* that focuses more directly on the Third World. Co-authored by Floyd Shoemaker, the book strongly reflected Rogers' transition from an American rural sociologist to an international communication scholar. A major event contributed to this transition: his study of the process of diffusion in three Third World countries—Brazil, Nigeria, and India—which expanded his purview to include all three continents of the Third World. This experience, accompanied by exposure to a growing society of diffusionists, prompted Rogers to develop a philosophy of diffusion at significant variance with his 1962 view, a philosophy which conformed very well with a prevailing development model that came to be known as the "dominant paradigm."

1927
1960
1963
1964
1967
1969
1970
1971
1972
1973
1974
1975
1976
1977
1978
1979
1980
1981
1982
1983
1984
1985
1986
1987
1988
1989
1990
1991
1992
1993
1994
1995
1996
1997
1998
1999
2000
2001
2002
2003
2004
2005
2006

The dominant paradigm was mainly concerned with economic growth as measured by the rate of growth of output, i.e., gross national product (GNP). To the economists of the day, such as Rostow (1960) and Rosenstein-Rodan (1964), this meant getting the Third World to adopt innovations already common-place in the industrialized countries. This approach did not involve Third World citizens choosing between alternative sources of development. Rather, it insisted on their following inevitably in the footsteps of the industrialized nations. The essence of the dominant paradigm, therefore, was that Western technologists not only knew what was best for the development of the Third World but also how best to deliver it.

This was the view Rogers and Shoemaker adopted for their 1971 book which was in essence the second edition to Rogers' 1962 publication. The book changed little in the sections dealing with the adopter categories and their characteristics. Though it continued to emphasize that it is the receiver's perception of an innovation's attributes that affect most its rate of adoption, these perceptions, the book argues, often inhibited adoption of new practices, regardless of their relative advantage. Rather than press for greater understanding of these perceptions and the attitudes underlying them, the book took the attitude that peasant perceptions needed to be changed and replaced with attitudes more receptive to change. And the person to be charged with managing this feat was the change agent.

The Rogers and Shoemaker chapter on the change agent opens with a quotation suggesting that people naturally are afraid of new ideas and are disposed to ill-treat persons who bring them. This established an adversarial role for change agents who were now faced with the problem of doing good for clients who were disposed to be hostile to them and resistant to their overtures. This, implied the authors, was especially true of the technical-assistance worker in a less developed country, described as a person who "provides linkage between a more developed nation and clients in the less developed country in which he is introducing innovations." There was often to be found a social chasm between the system represented by the change agent and that of his or her client's system, one that may include language differences, socioeconomic status, technical competence and various beliefs and attitudes. That is, the degree of heterophile between technical assistants and their clients was particularly striking in Third World countries. (Heterophile, the mirror of opposite of homophile, is defined by Rogers and Shoemaker [1971, p. 14] as the degree to which pairs of individuals who interact are different in certain attributes.) Far from seeking ways to bridge this "chasm," Rogers and Shoemaker offer instead a subtly revised definition of a change agent, making him responsible not for influencing adoption decisions in a direction he feels desirable, but for influencing "innovation-decisions in a direction deemed desirable by the change agency" (1971, p. 35). By this statement, decision making was taken from the person in closest contact with the ultimate client and removed to a more remote point. Those now responsible for deciding the nature of change to be visited upon the peoples of the Third World could do so from the comfort of their armchairs located in Washington, D.C., Geneva or Rome, then leave it to change agents to secure the adoption of agency-selected innovations, regardless of whether targeted clients expressed or even perceived a need for them. Although never quite openly saying as much, the impression of "he who pays the piper calls the tune" is hard to escape. It is thus this authoritarian change agency orientation to development decision making that lent legitimacy to the dominant paradigm and gave it its "top-down" communication hallmark.

A One-Way Model of Diffusion Communication

As if to leave no doubt as to who was in the driver's seat in directing the development of the Third World, Rogers and Shoemaker adopted, then adapted, the Source-Message-Channel-Receiver (SMCR) communication model popularised by Berlo in his 1960 book, "The

Process of Communication." The model sought to identify the essential elements of the communication process, which, in its most elemental form, consisted of a source delivering a structured message to a receiver through the channel of the receiver's senses.

Berlo described his model as a "snapshot" of the process, rather than a "moving picture" of it. He took pains, however, to point out that as a snapshot, the model inevitably gave the impression of a unidirectional, non-iterative source-to-receiver flow of information. As a movie showing the continuous give and take interaction between source and receiver, communication would be more realistically represented as a reciprocal process, with each party taking turns as source and receiver. For pedagogic purposes, however, Berlo found it more convenient to use the snapshot notion rather than the moving picture version to abstract and display the essential elements of communication. All these explanations did not, however, prevent his SMCR from being condemned as unidirectional, and thus denigrated to the point where it is not today regarded as a particularly useful model of communication.

It is this model which Rogers and Shoemaker (1971) decided to adopt and adapt to the needs of the diffusion process. They changed Berlo's SMCR model into an effects model simply by appending an "E" for "Effect" to it and thereby rendering it as SMCRE. With this addition, any iterative reciprocity which Berlo may have originally intended was negated. The model became incontrovertibly one way and, given that the diffusion source was held to be the change agent and the receiver the peasant person, it also became "top-down." In other words, the dominant paradigm had been presented with a tailor-made model to describe its process and the world of technical assistance with a justification for foisting unilateral decision makers upon the Third World.

It did not take great imagination to interpret the SMCRE model in Third World terms. Included under "S" were such agencies of external aid as United States Agency for International Development, Germany's

Frederick Ebert Stiftung, the United Nations' World Bank and Food and Agriculture Organization, and even the U.S. Peace Corps. Included under "M" were the techniques and technologies of modernization; under "C," not channels as represented by the five senses in Berlo's original model, but the mass media, visual aids and word-of-mouth. Under "R" would, of course, be found the urban poor and rural peasantry of the Third World, who, after all, were the targeted beneficiaries of development. And under "E" was to be included the new behaviours which change agencies deemed desirable for the peasants to adopt for their own good.

Authoritative Versus Participative Approaches

The second edition contains a brief comparison between "authoritative" and "participative" approaches to

1927
1960
1963
1964
1967
1969
1970
1971
1972
1973
1974
1975
1976
1977
1978
1979
1980
1981
1982
1983
1984
1985
1986
1987
1988
1989
1990
1991
1992
1993
1994
1995
1996
1997
1998
1999
2000
2001
2002
2003
2004
2005
2006

organizational change. In the authoritative approach, "there is a very unequal distribution of power, and decisions about change are made by a centralized power position, others being required to obey the decision," whereas the participative approach consists of "wide sharing of power, and decisions about change are made in consultation with those affected by the change" (Rogers and Shoemaker, 1971, p. 314). The section ends with the intriguing generalization that "changes brought about by the authoritative approach are more likely to be discontinued than those brought about by the participative approach" (ibid., p. 314). Granted that the foregoing statements were made not in the context of Third World development but of Western organizational structure, still, it is strange that change agencies and their agents whose role of inducing the diffusion process to occur at a faster rate is represented as critical, are nevertheless, by the book's own definition, endowed with such authoritarianism that in the light of its subsequent pronouncement about the authoritative approach, must surely foredoom the effort to failure.

Non-Adoption of Development Innovations

It is not clear from their book what it is that caused Rogers and Shoemaker to swing away from the original 1962 version which seemed to favour decision making autonomy as the prerogative of the adopter. The fact is that where diffusion theory as depicted in the 1962 book appeared to favour a client-participation approach to adoption decision making, the 1971 book changed to a client-compliant approach in which there was no longer any room for peasant-participation in adoption decision making. Studies conducted by Ascroft, et al. (1973) in Kenyan farming communities, at about the same time as the publication of Rogers and Shoemaker's book produced results which were strikingly at odds with those of the United States. Diffusion rates were found to be so limited that the traditional S-curve could not be drawn. Innovations, which were being actively promoted by extension for years, still remained to be adopted by majorities ranging up to 90 percent. In the United States, non-adopters, called "laggards," seldom exceeded 15 percent.

The initial impression was that peasant farmers were for the most part like the American laggards: change-resistant, over-conformers to tradition, their attention fixed on the rear-view mirror rather than on the road ahead. This notion gained credence with the publication of the elements of the *Subculture of Peasantry* by Rogers with Svenning (1969, p. 24-41). The characteristics of this subculture were synthesized from the works of several scholars of the day, including Oscar Lewis, Daniel Lerner and David McLelland. In all, 10 elements were identified. They included: mutual distrust in interpersonal relations, perceived limited good, dependence on and hostility towards government authority, familism, lack of innovativeness, fatalism, limited aspiration, lack of deferred gratification, limited view of the world and low empathy.

However, analysis of the characteristics of the Kenyan peasants who did adopt proffered innovations revealed striking differences as compared to those who did not. Adopters were generally literate and educated to some degree. They also had considerably more change agent contact and exposure to such modernizing influences as the mass media. Non-adopters, mostly illiterate, showed lack of contact with these sources. Adopters demonstrated knowledge and skill associated with given innovations currently being promoted by extension. Non-adopters, for the most part, were unaware even of the existence of the extension campaign, let alone have any knowledge or skills of specific innovations. The conclusions were not difficult to draw: change agents were partial to some clients—while totally ignoring all others. Under the dominant paradigm, there was no communication between technical-aid assistants and illiterate peasant farmers—zero participatory decision making of any kind whatsoever.

One would have thought that if a change agency both selected the innovations to diffuse, and designed and executed the campaigns to diffuse them, and then the campaign failed to produce the desired results, that the change agency would sooner or later examine its own strategies for shortcomings. If this was done, then perhaps it would have been discovered that methods of diffusion which seemingly work well in the United States and other industrialized countries worked equally well in Third World countries, but only for that group of people endowed with the educational characteristics similar to their more developed counterparts. In most Third World countries, that group is the minority, which means that the bulk of peasant communities are left out of the diffusion process. But change agencies failed to carry out such self-analyses. And so Rogers and Svenning (1969) also wound up accusing peasants of refusing to allow themselves to be "developed."

The Policy of New Directions

When Robert McNamara pointed out that the people who needed most to benefit from development efforts, the world's "poorest of the poor," were actually benefiting the least, he offered the then novel explanation that the cause of this state of affairs might not be because they were resistant to change per se, but because they were somehow left out of processes established to be of aid to them. With change agencies taking all decisions on their behalf, little was left to them, save compliance. "No program will help small farmers if it is designed by those who have no knowledge of their problems and operated by those who have no interest in their future," said Robert McNamara (1973, p. 27).

It was, therefore, McNamara who issued the first public call for peasant farmers to participate in development decision making. Three years later, Rogers (1976) added his voice to this call by declaring the "fall of the dominant paradigm" and heralding the advent of a new approach called "self-development," which he said implied "a different role for communication than the usual top-down development approach of the past" (p. 112). This new approach envisaged village systems initiating the search for technical information about development problems, possibilities,

appropriate innovations, and through a process of "bottom-up" communication—the antithesis of "top-down" communication—transmitting their needs to change agencies. Rogers felt that this approach opened new development pathways including "popular participation in self-development planning and execution" (p. 222). But as "bottom-up" communication, the curious impression was left that in Rogers' form of popular participation, potential beneficiaries of development participated among themselves, without involvement of change agents.

Back to Diffusion of Innovations

Rogers' third edition was once more entitled *Diffusion of Innovations*. It was published in 1983, at a time when the term "dominant paradigm" had become passé, and was thus purged from the third edition. Gone too was any mention of the SMCRE model of communication. But also inexplicably missing in the third edition was any mention of authoritative versus participatory approaches to organizational change.

By way of explanation, Rogers (1983, pp. xvii-x viii) offers some self-criticism, observing that "many diffusion scholars have conceptualised the diffusion process as one-way persuasion." As such, the tendency had been to see diffusion as a linear, unidirectional, one-to-many communication activity in which the main preoccupation was selling products, actions or policies. This one-way view still described, in Rogers' perception, certain kinds of diffusion, as for example, "an individual, such as a change agent, informing a potential adopter of a new idea." However, he adds that "other types of diffusion are more accurately described by a convergence model, in which the communication is defined as a process in which the participants create and share information with one another to reach a mutual understanding."

Rogers never really clarifies what he means by this statement. The implication, however, is that diffusion managed by change agents, is necessarily one-way, and by further implication, forever married to

1927
1960
1963
1964
1967
1969
1970
1971
1972
1973
1974
1975
1976
1977
1978
1979
1980
1981
1982
1983
1984
1985
1986
1987
1988
1989
1990
1991
1992
1993
1994
1995
1996
1997
1998
1999
2000
2001
2002
2003
2004
2005
2006

a dominant paradigm orientation. This view conforms with his earlier definitions of communication, but contrasts sharply with his 1983 definition, which seemed calculated to placate (if not to accommodate) the mounting voices urging the involvement of the potential beneficiaries of the diffusion of innovations in the business of deciding their own development directions. Thus, where previous definitions seemed decidedly one- way and authoritarian, communication in the 1962 edition being the way in which influence is spread (p. 99) and in the 1971 edition as the process by which messages are transferred from source to receiver, the 1983 definition focused on participants in communication creating and sharing information to achieve mutual understanding.

Why Rogers did not deem it appropriate for change agents to participate with their clients in the creation and sharing of information with one another to reach mutual understanding is never clearly explained. In his third edition, therefore, Rogers continues to define the change agent in a top-down way as an individual who influences clients' innovation decisions in a direction deemed desirable by a change agency. So far as having participants creating and sharing information, the dice continues to be loaded in favour of the change agency, with its trained professional on hand making sure that decisions go their way. Since nowhere in Rogers' third edition is any mention made of other agents responsible for influencing policy-making decisions in directions deemed desirable by the intended beneficiaries, one is left with the disquieting feeling that the dominant paradigm did not really pass; it just got camouflaged.

Is diffusion theory, according to Rogers, inhospitable to participatory decision making? If we practiced a bit of selective perception across all of his works, a "no" can be clearly constructed. A thread of approval can be shown to link the three editions. From his 1962 dictum that change agents should be more concerned with improving their clients' competence in evaluating new ideas, and less concerned with simply promoting innovations per se, to his 1971 generalization that participatory approaches procure longer lasting innovation adoptions than those obtained through authoritative approaches, to his 1983 definition of communication as participants creating and sharing information to achieve mutual understanding, Rogers seems to demonstrate his empathy for the notion. The problem is that his depiction of change agents is in striking contradiction to this sentiment.

In the 1983 edition, Rogers did, however, abandon the SMCRE communication model. But he erred in discarding one model without replacing it with another, for it suggested that he knew what not to do, but not what to do instead. But then, as Cees Hamelink says: "Most of us have written extensively and critically about how Lerner and Schramm and Rogers have inadequately dealt with all these things ... but none of us has really come forward with a new and better model" (quoted in Servaes, 1987).

Lest we are accused of falling into the same trap, we would like to offer an alternative model, one that is not new but we hope is certainly better than Berlo's SMCR at addressing the notion of participatory decision making. In the course of explicating this model, it will also become clear that there exists a clear need for a new role player in Third World development, in addition to the traditional change agent, as described by Rogers.

References

Ascroft, Joseph, Niels Roling, Joseph Kariuki and Fred Chege. "Extension and the Forgotten Farmer," *Bulletin No. 37,* Afdelingen voor Sociale Wetenschappen aan de Landsbouwhogeschool, Wageningen, Nederlands, 1973.

Berlo, David K. *The Process of Communication: An Introduction to Theory and Practice.* New York: Holt, Rinehart and Winston, 1960.

McNamara, Robert S. "Annual Address to the Board of Governors," in *Annual Proceeding of the Board of Governors,* IBRD, 1973. Washington D.C.: World Bank.

Rogers, Everett M. *Diffusion of Innovations.* New York: The Free Press, 1962.

Rogers, Everett M., and Lynn Svenning. *Modernization Among Peasants: The Impact of Communication.* Chicago: Holt, Rinehart and Winston Inc., 1969.

Rogers, Everett M., and Floyd Shoemaker. *Communication of Innovations: A Cross-Cultural Approach.* 2nd ed. New York: The Free Press, New York, 1971.

Rogers, Everett M. "Communication and Development: the Passing of the Dominant Paradigm," *Communication Research,* 1976, 3 (2), 121-33.

Rogers, Everett M. "Rise and Fall of the Dominant Paradigm," in Whoit de Bock, ed., *Mass Communication Review Yearbook.* Thousand Oaks, California: Sage, 1980.

Rosenstein-Rodan, P. N. *Capital Formation and Economic Development.* MIT Press, Cambridge, Massachusetts: MIT Press, 1964.

Rostow, Walter W. *The Process of Economic Growth.* Oxford: Clarendon Press, 1960.

Ryan, Bruce, and Neal Gross. "The Diffusion of Hybrid Corn in Two Upper Iowa Communities," *Rural Sociology,* 1943, 8, 15-24.

Servaes, Jan. "The Last Forty Years—And the Next: Towards Another Development Communication Policy," paper presented at the 1987 Seminar on Communication and Change, University of Hawaii and the East-West Center, Honolulu: 1987.

Ashcroft, Joseph and Robert Agunga. "Diffusion Theory and Participatory Decision Making," in *Participatory Communication Working for Change and Development,* edited by Shirley White, K. Sadanandan Nair and Joseph Ascroft. Sage Publications, India, 1994. Reproduced with the permission of the copyright holders and the publishers, Sage Publications India Pvt. LtD., New Delhi, India.

EXCERPT FROM:

PARTICIPATORY DECISION MAKING IN THIRD WORLD DEVELOPMENT

Participatory Communication Working for Change and Development

By Joseph Ascroft and Sipho Masilela

1994 There are, at the moment, no new "new directions" policies in the offing to replace the old new directions policy, no fresh and invigorating concept, no mobilizing buzzword to quicken enthusiasm and rekindle development optimism. It is a time almost of despair, of a seeming bankruptcy of practical ideas, a time when the rallying point, at least for the academics, is a nonconcept called, well, "Another Development." Essentially the product of European development thinking with its epicentre located in Sweden at the Dag Hammarskjold Foundation and the International Foundation for Development Alternatives.

Another Development espouses an approach with a strong "empowerment" strain focused on securing basic needs and rights for Third World people. It promotes endogenous problem perception, problem solving and self-reliance dependent upon their own strengths and resources. It proposes decentralizing structural transformations, transferring decision making from the urban centres to the rural villages. On paper, it states all the principles that Europeans to this day are willing to fight and die for. And that is the main problem with Another Development. So far as the Third World is concerned, it lives mainly in the literature of academe, its proponents content to pontificate in turgid scholarly language rather than to enter the arena of applied development theory and put their money where their mouths are.

Perhaps the major obstacle to applying of Another Development principles are that it is just too intimidating. Bjorn Hettne (1982) laments the lack of Third World

1927
1960
1963
1964
1967
1969
1970
1971
1972
1973
1974
1975
1976
1977
1978
1979
1980
1981
1982
1983
1984
1985
1986
1987
1988
1989
1990
1991
1992
1993
1994
1995
1996
1997
1998
1999
2000
2001
2002
2003
2004
2005
2006

capacity and resolve for wholly indigenised development thinking and strategization. Third World institutions of learning and training remain dominated by neocolonial traditions decades after the acquisition of independence. Instruction is foreign and alienating and foists inappropriate schemes, models and theories upon local social scientists whose captive minds are locked in imitative, uncritical reproduction of Western values while turning a blind eye to their own.

Third World universities are the all-too-willing participants in an academic imperialism in which foreign researchers, using predesigned instruments and cheap local labour supervised by sycophantic local researchers, strip mine raw data by the crate-load for removal to their home institutions. There, the data are computer processed and the findings interpreted according to foreign theories, reported in foreign language in foreign conferences, published in foreign book packages, which become available to the institutions in the countries from which the data were mined only when foreign exchange is produced. Scholars need look no further than their own ivied halls to find thriving exemplifications of the "dependencia" theory.

Small wonder then that there is beginning to emerge almost heretical voices from the wilderness of the Third World, such as that of Elmandjira, who proposes getting rid of development aid because it discourages self-development, or Dasgupta, whose puckish "theory against development" goes one better by suggesting that it is development itself which constrains the reduction of poverty in the Third World and that the only way to get rid of poverty is to eschew development and opt for a society which opposes affluence, growth and development and sanctifies progress, happiness and liberation from poverty—a no-wealth but also no-poverty society. There may be merit in these anti-development approaches just as there probably still is in the pro-development ones.

The problem is that "we" do not know the wishes of the people on such matters. We do not know because, even though we express our earnest desire for them to participate in development planning and decision making

Excerpt from: *Participative Communication as a Part of Building the Participative Society*
By Juan Díaz Bordenave

1994

Participatory communication can be defined as that type of communication in which all the interlocutors are free and have equal access to the means to express their viewpoints, feelings and experiences. Collective action aimed at promoting their interests, solving their problems and transforming their society, is the means to an end. Participative radio has shown heroic performances in the case of the Bolivian *Radios Mineras*. For the tin miners of Bolivia, participation was a matter of life and death, and their radio was the soul of community participation in peacetime and of resistance when the army attacked them. The experience of Costa Rican community radio was also similar.

with us, we still do not know how to operationalize this idea. If it seems that our review of the development trend ends on a bleak note, it is because the trend appears to have reached this point of irresolution in its course. Understanding may be forthcoming if we take a look at trends in development communication thinking.

References

Dasgupta, Sugata. "Towards a Non-Poverty Society," *Social Development Issues*, 1982, 6 (2): 4-14

Hettne, Bjorn (1982). "Development Theory and the Third World," Swedish Agency for Research Cooperation with Developing Countries, Stockholm, Sweden: 1982.

1927
1960
1963
1964
1967
1969
1970
1971
1972
1973
1974
1975
1976
1977
1978
1979
1980
1981
1982
1983
1984
1985
1986
1987
1988
1989
1990
1991
1992
1993
1994
1995
1996
1997
1998
1999
2000
2001
2002
2003
2004
2005
2006

EXCERPT FROM:

COMMUNICATION AND PARTICIPATORY DEVELOPMENT

Participatory Evaluation

By Maria Celeste Habito-Cadiz

1994 Participatory evaluation involves beneficiaries setting the indicators, forms and methods of evaluating a development project. The people must be the ones to evaluate themselves to make it a growth process, a mechanism for self-strengthening and self-improvement in a group where the process is more important than the product. The external agent's role is to broaden the people's perspective, encourage collective behaviour and help the people formulate and articulate their thoughts more systematically and objectively (Uphoff, 1988: 43-64;Guiza, 1987:4144; Ferrer and Pagaduan, 1981: viii). Uphoff emphasized what participants can learn and conclude in participatory evaluation, towards making their organization more effective, over numerical scores. Ferrer and Pagaduan elaborated that participatory evaluation is not so much concerned with eliciting answers and arriving at a greater understanding of the subject society by the investigator, but rather with provoking people into asking more questions and obtaining a better understanding of their own socioeconomic conditions, thereby raising their collective level of consciousness and unleashing community energies for massive and organized development action.

Uphoff likewise stressed that such self-evaluation leads to: (1) informing everyone about the objectives of the people's organization, also enabling the group to re-examine and reach a consensus on them; (2) bringing shortcomings of the organization into the open, requiring everyone to speak freely without being inhibited or constrained from doing so; (3) facilitating communication within the group, allowing exchange

DISTORTIONS IN PARTICIPATION

Excerpt from: *Participative Communication as a Part of Building the Participative Society*

By Juan Díaz Bordenave

Both participation and participatory communication are not free from distortions that sometimes neutralize their contribution to building a participative society. One of the frequent distortions is manipulated participation. In the Third World, it is frequent to find invitations for the people to participate in government projects. Is it because governments have finally accepted the idea that participation is a basic human right? Or is it a ritual with little or no meaning, intended only to pacify or acknowledge the rhetoric of participation?

of ideas which is essential in building group solidarity; (4) setting of priorities for improvement; (5) helping the group identify its training needs; and (6) enabling the program proponents or sponsors to perform their own monitoring and evaluation and compare these with those of the group.

Guiza listed five major areas to be evaluated, namely: (1) change in material conditions such as ownership of the means of production, access to resources, access to credit, terms of relationships to the market, clothing and shelter and alternative economic ventures; (2) strength of the people's organization such as the number and composition of its membership, their incomes, attendance in meetings, values being promoted and their consistency with their avowed principles; (3) practice of democratic decision making; (4) individual members' personal growth such as in their self-confidence or in exercising their responsibilities and (5) impact of the project on the society at large.

As the methods in evaluation, Guiza listed small group discussions, surveys and questionnaires, focused group discussions and role-playing to bring out spontaneous reactions.

Ferrer and Pagaduan enumerated the following gains from their experience in carrying out a community-based evaluation system:

1. Group evaluation facilitated people's sharing and getting informed about the program.
2. Data collected was more accurate than if a random sample was taken, because consensus was reached and exaggerated responses were avoided.
3. People were stimulated to reflect upon their situation and experiences, assess and sum up these experiences and use them to guide future actions to advance their goals.
4. The process had a "demystifying effect" in that it erased ideas about research being difficult and beyond the capability of ordinary people.
5. The process formulated a method by which change can be studied qualitatively with workshop participants using the words "increase," "decrease" and "the same."

Meanwhile, Uphoff noted four problems that emerge in the self-evaluation process:

1. Not all groups undertaking the process may generate comparable data, because the criteria used may differ depending on what each group deems relevant.
2. The procedure raises the question of whether or not the program itself should also suggest criteria that the group may be overlooking, such as women's participation in the organization.
3. Translating questionnaire items into the vernacular can be difficult.
4. The process lacks objectivity and detachment, although this is not as important as its having an impact on the organization.

DISTORTIONS IN PARTICIPATION
Excerpt from: *Participative Communication as a Part of Building the Participative Society*
By Juan Díaz Bordenave

...We also have another dangerous distortion among people who accept participation and like it so much that it is taken to mean that everything has to be checked with everybody before any decision is made. We may call this disease "participationitis." Participation becomes equivalent to constant assemblies and meetings. The result is general inefficiency and even anarchy. Some folks get tired of wasting time in meetings and unending discussions, and after a point, they start looking for an authoritarian leader to get things done.

Now, if participation can be exaggerated and distorted, it can also be banalized. This happens when everything is called participation, from requesting a radio station to air a certain piece of music, to donating money for a campaign on AIDS. To avoid banalization we should reserve the word "participation" for the joint efforts of people for achieving a common, important objective previously defined by them.

Diaz Bordenave, Juan. "Participative Communication as a Part of Building the Participative Society," originally published in *Participatory Communication: Working for Change and Development*, edited by Shirley White, Sadanandan Nair and Joseph Ascroft. Copyright © Shirley A. White, K. Sadanandan Nair and Joseph Ascroft, 1994. All rights reserved. Reproduced with the permission of the copyright holders and the publishers, Sage Publications India Pvt. Ltd., New Delhi.

References

Ferrer, Elmer M., and Maureen C. Pagaduan. "Working as Equals? Towards a Community Based Evaluation System," unpublished master's degree thesis, College of Social Work and Community Development, University of the Philippines, Diliman, Quezon City, 1981.

Uphoff, Norman. "Participatory Evaluation of Farmer Organizations' Capacity for Development Tasks." Agricultural Administration and Extension, 1988, Vol. 30, No. 1, 43-64.

Cadiz, Maria Celeste. "Participation as Communication," *Communication and Participatory Development* by Cadiz, Maria Celeste Habito. CA Publications Program College of Agriculture, University of the Philippines, Los Baños. Laguna, Philippines, 1994. Copyright © 1994, University of the Philipines. Reprinted with permission of university of the Philippines.

EXCERPT FROM:
TOWARD COMMUNICATION THEORIES OF AND FOR PRACTICE: THE PAST/FUTURE OF LATIN AMERICAN ALTERNATIVE COMMUNICATION RESEARCH

By Robert Huesca and Brenda Dervin

1994

The three bodies of literature calling for the collapse of dualisms overlap one another yet contribute in different ways. The popular culture studies provided evidence that undercut many of the instrumentalist assumptions guiding alternative communication and revealed points of contradiction and tension in cultural practices that could be used strategically for communicative action. Transnational studies emphasized that alternative communication is not impervious to global influence, requiring it theoretically to incorporate the oppositional. Empirical projects sought to do this, primarily, by making a contextual move, binding actions across borders. Finally, the focus on praxis mandated a synthesis of local process to global referent through reflective practices. The critical contributions from these three bodies of work served to demonstrate the contradictions between the neat world of dualistic categories and the untamed terrain of practice.

The work reviewed above provided clear evidence that: a) horizontal practices at times resulted in oppressive content, b) in everyday life, people negotiated with dominant processes in liberating ways and c) liberating groups often used dominant communication modes for counterhegemonic purposes. While it successfully questioned the tidiness of early alternative communication thinking, however, this work failed to provide a coherent means of explaining—or even approaching—media, culture and praxis in a way that would lead to understanding how horizontal processes come to dominate or vertical processes come to liberate. What has been left untheorized is the central concern of how both resistance (struggle and invention) as well as acquiescence (reinscription and reification)

both emerge within structural constraints and, therefore, how media do and can play a role in processes that lead to empowerment, liberation and transformation.

Rather, the popular culture studies presented a world where communication roamed unpredictably across liberating and dominating terrains through both alternative and traditional processes. The transnational called to incorporate the dominant within the alternative, but provided no theoretical direction regarding how this could be done. Finally, the praxis literature justified both alternative and traditional processes in the interest of building transformative social movements. Theoretical guidance for how this could be accomplished, again, was never made explicit. The contribution of this work has been to jar alternative communication out of prescriptive simplicity, and in some cases, to provide useful frameworks to accompany the cultural archaeologist in the interpretation of the popular. But the literature is now adrift theoretically, inasmuch as it cannot explain the movement around the terrain of communication processes and consequences.

In essence, then, the Latin American alternative communication literature has enfolded dominant and alternative processes within both oppressive and liberating goals/content, without providing any sense of how this occurs. Whereas in the context of the legacy of dualisms, dominant processes were assumed to lead to dominant outcomes, i.e., maintaining the status quo, and alternative processes were assumed to lead to alternative outcomes, and challenging the status quo now both dominant and alternative processes are seen as potentially leading to both dominant and alternative outcomes.

This collapsing of a legacy is both a source of what can be seen as theoretical disarray and a signpost pointing to the future. To understand this, we need to restate a point made earlier; from the beginning, Latin American alternative communication research has been marked most centrally by its quest for communication theories of and for democratic practice. Latin American scholars have been struggling for more than two

1927
1960
1963
1964
1967
1969
1970
1971
1972
1973
1974
1975
1976
1977
1978
1979
1980
1981
1982
1983
1984
1985
1986
1987
1988
1989
1990
1991
1992
1993
1994
1995
1996
1997
1998
1999
2000
2001
2002
2003
2004
2005
2006

decades with concepts that only now are beginning to permeate global communication agendas, concepts that, by a variety of names, refer to diverse voices, pluralities, public spheres, democratic media and so on.

In a sense, it can be argued that the current disarray in Latin American alternative communication work is evidence of failure. Yet, at the same time, it can be argued that this disarray marks the field of communication worldwide (Dervin, 1993). The importance of the Latin American work, however, is that because of its robustness and long history, it has embedded within it lessons for the global agenda. This becomes apparent only if one re-enters the body of work, bracketing its primary narrative—the construction and collapse of dualisms—and foregrounding, instead, its secondary narrative, the quest for theories of and for practice. This search also suggests an intricate relationship between the two narratives, a hint that neither the search for dualisms nor the collapse of dualisms provides the strongest place of theoretical advance.

When one focuses on the quest for theories of, and for, practice in the Latin American work, one finds the contradiction that permeates most communication research (Dervin 1993). On the one hand, a rich body of work, as described above, skirts around communication practice but never really zeroes in on it. A marked attention focuses on the whos and whats of communicating, but little on the hows. Communication is conceptualised as messages, raw materials to be redistributed, as in dialogue; communication is seen as a tool for building social networks and popular movements as in praxis and in across-border transnational projects; and communication is seen as artifact in a nexus between the traditional and modern and postmodern, as in popular culture. At times the results point to spaces for alternative practice. But no theories of alternative practice as such have emerged. What has emerged that explicitly focuses on practice, a body of work usually subordinated to more theoretic endeavours, is an enormously rich set of descriptions of a wide variety of inventive alternative practices (Alfonso, 1983; Collyer, 1986; Kaplún,

1986; López Vigil, 1984; Lozada and Kúncar, 1983, 1986; Pareja Herrera, 1987; Reyes Matta, 1986d, 1986e; Schulein & Robina, 1983; Unidad, 1986; Valdeavellano, 1989a, 1989b). A major difficulty with these descriptions, however, is that because they are not set within a theoretical frame it is impossible to integrate them conceptually.

Yet one finds Latin American theorists opening up conceptual avenues that might allow for this integration when one re-examines the theoretic work zeroing in explicitly on moves toward theorizing practice—moves often hidden within the larger dualistic debates. García Canclini and Martin Barbero and others working in the popular culture tradition do so when they refocus attention away from the oppositions implied in the legacy of dualisms to concepts such as "mediation" and "transaction" in which consumers of media are reconceptualized as constantly struggling with walls of constraint and spaces of freedoms, the dominant and the alternative, structures and their own life worlds. Fuenzalida and Hermosilla do so when they reach out to invent practices linking popular social groups and professional media producers. In the praxis tradition, another example is provided in the reach for understanding how structural constraints are made and changed in practice (Gumucio and Cajias, 1989; Portales, 1983)

In these beginning reformulations, the dualisms are both retained and collapsed, for an implied assumption posits that both the dominant and the alternative are created, maintained and changed in communication. The focus switches from the poles to the centre; from static ends to process; from whos and whats to hows; from global process to process conceptualised as iterative steps. Clearly, the Latin American work has only begun to open up these conceptual possibilities. This is shown most clearly in Reyes Matta's call for a systematic attempt to theorize communication practice by examining "… through which methodology a self-renewing communication process can be effected …" (1986, p. 367).

More than any other body of work in the communication field worldwide, Latin American alternative communication scholarship already has struggled its way into contradictions and deadlocks, which are only beginning to characterize the communication field generally. It has grappled with issues of structure versus agency, pluralism versus order, dominant versus alternative; and it has begun to lay out, in a number of ways, both observations and logics, suggesting that it is not merely a legacy of dualistic theorizing that impedes theoretic progress. Rather, it is a legacy of theorizing communication statically that impedes progress.

When communication is reconceptualized as a process made up of many communicative procedures implemented sometimes habitually, sometimes creatively, sometimes thoughtfully, sometimes blindly by many participating actors in constant mediation, then constraints and freedoms, the dominant and the alternative are reconciled. In a sense, the dualisms remain, both in potential absence and presence—but radically reconceptualized.

References

Alfonso, C. Una experiencia de comunicación alternativa con micro-computación en Brasil [One alternative communication experience with micro-computers in Brazil]. In F. Reyes. Matta, ed., *Comunicación alternativa y búsquedas democráticas [Alternative communication and the search for democracy]*. Mexico City: Instituto Latinoamericano de Estudios Transnacionales y Fundación Friedrich Ebert, 1983, 199-208.

Collyer, P. Innovaciones y espacios: ¿Quien pone la agenda? [Spaces and innovations: Who sets the agenda?]. In F. Reyes Matta, ed., *Crítica y autocrítica en el periodismo joven [Criticism and self-criticism in new journalism]*. Santiago: Instituto Latinoamericano de Estudios Transnacionales, 1986, 91-113.

Dervin, B. (1993). "Verbing Communication: Mandate for Disciplinary Invention." Journal of Communication, 1993, Summer, 43: 3, 45-54.

Fuenzalida, V., and M. E. Hermosilla, with P. Edwards. *Visiones y ambiciones del televidente: Estudios de recepción televisiva [Visions and ambitions of the viewer: Reception studies in television]*. Santiago, Chile: CENECA, 1989.

García Canclini, N. "Culture and Power: The State of Research." Media, Culture and Society, 1988, 10, 467-497.

García Canclini, N. (1990). Culturas híbridas: Estrategias para entrar y salir de la modernidad [Hybrid cultures: Strategies for entering and exiting modernity]. Mexico City: Editorial Grijalbo.

Gumucio Dagron, A., and L. Cajías, eds. *Las radios mineras de Bolivia [The miners' radios of Bolivia]*. La Paz: CIMCA-UNESCO, 1989.

Kaplún, M. Uruguay, participación: Praxis, propuesta, problema, la experiencia del casete-foro [Uruguay, participation: Praxis, proposal, problem, the experience of the cassette forum]. In M. Simpson Grinberg, ed., *Comunicación alternativa y cambio social [Alternative communication and social change]*. Tlahuapan, Puebla, Mexico: Premiá Editora de Libros, 1986, 266-283.

López Vigil, J. I. *Una mina de coraje [An angry mine]*. Quito, Ecuador: Aler/Pío XII, 1984.

Lozada, F., and G. Kúncar. Las emisoras mineras de Bolivia: Una histórica experiencia de comunicación autogestionaria [Miners' radios in Bolivia: An historical experience in self-governed communication]. In F. Reyes Matta, ed., *Comunicación alternativa y búsquedas democráticas [Alternative communication and the search for democracy]*. Mexico City: Instituto Latinoamericano de Estudios Transnacionales y Fundación Friedrich Ebert, 1983, 105-132.

Lozada, F., and G. Kúncar. Las radios mineras, las voces del coraje [Miners' radios, the voices of wrath]. In M. Simpson Grinberg. ed., *Comunicación alternativa y cambio social [Alternative communication and social change]*. Tlahuapan, Puebla, Mexico: Premiá Editora de Libros, 1986, 186-207.

Pareja Herrera, T. "Community Radio for the Pueblos." InterMedia, 1987, 28-31.

Portales, C. D. El movimiento popular y las comunicaciones: A partir de la experiencia chilena [Popular movements and communication: The Chilean experience]. In F. Reyes Matta, ed., *Comunicación alternativa y búsquedas democráticas [Alternative communication and the search for democracy]*. Mexico City: Instituto Latinoamericano de Estudios Transnacionales y Fundación Friedrich Ebert, 1983, 59-69.

Reyes Matta, F. Análisis de las formas [Analysis of forms]. In M. Simpson Grinberg. ed., *Comunicación alternativa y cambio social [Alternative communication and social change]*. Tlahuapan, Puebla, Mexico: Premiá Editora de Libros, 1986b, 362-373.

Schulein, S., and S. Robina. Prensa alternativa y nuevas fuentes de información: La experiencia de ALTERCOM [Alternative press and new sources of information: The experience of ALTERCOM]. In F. R. Matta. ed., *Comunicación alternativa y búsquedas democráticas [Alternative communication and the search for democracy]*. Mexico City: Instituto Latinoamericano de Estudios Transnacionales, y la Fundación Friedrich Ebert, 1983, 155-169.

Unidad de Comunicación Alternativa de la Mujer (ILET). República Dominicana, Un programa para mujeres campesinas: La experiencia de "Club Mencia" en Radio Enriquillo [Dominican Republic, A program for peasant women: The experience of Radio Enriquillo's "Club Mencia"]. In M. Simpson Grinberg, ed., *Comunicación alternativa y cambio social [Alternative communication and social change]*. Puebla, Mexico: Premiá editora de libros, 1986, 208-225.

Valdeavellano, P. América Latina está construyendo su propia imagen [Latin America is constructing its own image]. In P. Valdeavellano, ed., *El video en la educación popular [Video and popular education]*. Lima: Instituto Para America Latina, 1989a, 103-130.

Valdeavellano, P., ed. El video en la educación popular [Video and popular education]. Lima: Instituto Para America Latina, 1989b.

Huesca, R., and B. Dervin. "Toward Communication Theories of and for Practice: The Past/Future of Latin American Alternative Communication Research." *Journal of Communication*, Autumn (Tardor), 1994, Vol. 44, No. 4, 53-73. Malden, Mass.: Blackwell Publishing. Reprinted with permission.

1927
1960
1963
1964
1967
1969
1970
1971
1972
1973
1974
1975
1976
1977
1978
1979
1980
1981
1982
1983
1984
1985
1986
1987
1988
1989
1990
1991
1992
1993
1994
1995
1996
1997
1998
1999
2000
2001
2002
2003
2004
2005
2006

RADIO STRATEGIES FOR COMMUNITY DEVELOPMENT: A CRITICAL ANALYSIS

By Andrew A. Moemeka

1994 We take it for granted that the reader is already aware that the concept "community" can be "correctly" defined in various ways. Basically, it stands for groupings of people, but such groupings are of many types and can be categorized in terms of common interest—the Jesuits, the Quakers, the Critical Theorists; of common ancestry—the Irish, the Eskimos, African Americans; of human society as a whole; or of political or social boundary a group of people living in the same locality and under the same government. Our concern here is with "community" as defined in the last example, but with particular reference to localities that are development-starved or underprivileged, whether in the developed or in the developing world. The thesis is that such communities need education in order to develop. By education here is meant the creation of an environment in which awareness is at its height, aspirations are rationally raised and willingness to work hard enough to "progress" becomes the rule rather than the exception (Moemeka, 1981:9). This is education not for examination and certificates but for existence and certitude. Education seen in this light finds support in Hickey et al.'s (1969) definition of community education as:

> A process that concerns itself with everything that affects the well-being of all citizens within a given community (extending its role) from one of the traditional concept of teaching children to one of identifying the needs, problems and wants of the community and then assisting in the development of facilities, programs, staff and leadership toward the end of improving the entire community.

While this type of education can be successfully carried out within communities through face-to-face communication, the pace of success and expansion of activities are generally faster if mass media communication is added. Even though it is held that interpersonal communication generally is considered more effective in inducing attitude and behavior changes, it is also true that two media are better than one in achieving desired objectives (Rogers et al, 1977: 363, Yu, 1977). This is particularly true of the combination of interpersonal and mass media communication. Unfortunately, the tendency, especially in the developing world, has been to use one or the other. What follows is a critical explanation of the different ways in which the radio has been used in community education for development.

Since the 1960s, United Nations Educational, Scientific and Cultural Organization (UNESCO) has been stressing the importance of radio broadcasting in community education, especially in the rural and/or slum areas of developing societies. The organization's faith in radio is based on that medium's unique characteristics. It is cheap to purchase and therefore is the one mass medium with which rural and slum communities are familiar; it is versatile and anyone—literate or illiterate—can learn from it. After a series of research on the use of the medium in community education, UNESCO (1968) was able to say:

> In the past few years, much attention has been given to the problems of adult education in the rural areas, and to experiments which have proved on several occasions that radio broadcasting, when skillfully used, can be a most effective medium of communication and education in such areas.

The part which radio plays in the transmission of information and culture is generally beyond question. The general impression is that the basic role of the radio (and other mass media) is to survey the environment, collect stories about everyday occurrences, transform them into news and information and transmit these back to society through dissemination. Underlying the performance of this role is the belief that the radio, as well as other media of mass communication, has the power to control our behavior fully. Hence, Sproule (1989) is convinced that the hypodermic needle theory is still largely the underlying basis of the use of mass media communication.

Much as the role of radio in information and news dissemination is seen as given, its role in the field of education is, on the face of it, not quite evident. It seems paradoxical to talk of educational broadcasting because "education" by its very nature implies exchange of ideas and dialogue or communication, while broadcasting usually involves a monologue—a "talking to" rather than a "talking with." Broadcasting is addressed to a very widely dispersed and heterogeneous audience whose members are generally unknown (an insignificant part of the audience may sometimes be just barely known). These characteristics of radio, which are very enhancing in the task of information dissemination, are a hindrance in radio's role in education or communication. The implication, therefore, is that in order to make the medium suitable for education and communication, conditions must be created that will enable it to become a channel for dialogue. This means that it must be changed from a mere information-disseminating medium to an educational medium in order to make it an effective instrument in the task of community education, which is the first step toward ensuring community development.

Radio's effectiveness depends, however, not only on its intrinsic qualities but more importantly on how it is used and for what purposes. Any use of radio as an educational medium should be based on the effects that radio is expected to have on the listening audiences, on the level of target-audience participation, on the structure of reception possible and on the amount of learning and social change that is desired or likely to occur. The success of radio as a medium for education and communication will therefore depend upon adequate clarification and understanding of these preconditions and the assumptions of the various radio utilization strategies, so that a country's needs are fitted to appropriate uses of radio.

Radio Strategies

These are concrete plans of action, in terms of infrastructural and operational arrangements, for using radio broadcasting in the task of educating communities for development. These plans generally are about what activities to perform, by whom, with what resources (human and physical), at which time, in which place, at what pace, in what order and how. They are models for action expected to yield the greatest possible benefit for the community and, subsequently, for the nation.

Five strategies of utilization of radio in rural education and development have been identified (McAnany, 1973). One or other of these strategies or a combination of them has been used in different parts of the world, especially in developing countries. Their levels of successes or failures have been determined mostly by the presence or absence of the preconditions mentioned above.

Open Broadcasting

Open broadcasting is the strategy in which broadcast messages are directed to an unorganized audience. It is based on the assumption that a "good" and relevant message is capable of being accepted by the individual on his/her own. According to Gunter and Theroux (1977), open broadcast strategy enables more people to have access to information and vicarious education. It is a strategy in which, in addition to programs such as talks, features and music, a small score of educational programs (usually in local languages) on health, agriculture, family life, sanitation and child care, among others, are broadcast. Because of the unorganized nature of the audience, there is always doubt as to whether the people are listening and, if they are, whether they are benefiting from the programs.

In Mexico (Arana, 1971) and the Philippines (Spain, 1971), it was found that even though radio stations carried information relevant to literacy, civic responsibilities, farming and health, the surveyed audience knew very little about these issues. They preferred listening to news, drama and music. In Nigeria (Moemeka, 1972), one of the findings of a survey in rural Lagos of

1927
1960
1963
1964
1967
1969
1970
1971
1972
1973
1974
1975
1976
1977
1978
1979
1980
1981
1982
1983
1984
1985
1986
1987
1988
1989
1990
1991
1992
1993
1994
1995
1996
1997
1998
1999
2000
2001
2002
2003
2004
2005
2006

the audience for programs relevant to rural improvement was that more than 70 percent of the listeners were educated young men and women, brought up away from their rural homelands, who saw the programs as "good education in the reverse." That is, for learning later in life what they would have learned as children had they been brought up in their rural villagers. They were not part of the audience of rural Lagos for whom the programs were meant. Again, in Lagos (Moemeka, 1988), a federal government-sponsored radio campaign on AIDS-prevention barely succeeded in achieving any result beyond confirming widespread knowledge of AIDS as a deadly disease. Very few respondents appreciated the fact that AIDS was incurable; still fewer had taken any preventive measures.

Open broadcast strategy is bedeviled by all the problems that affect the use of radio for the education of the rural population and in community development efforts. First, there is no interaction between producers and consumers before programs are planned, produced and broadcast. Production is usually based on the vague notion that the people would accept as relevant the studio-decided content of the program. Second, these programs are conceived in the studio, with very little or no consultation with specialist agencies, and virtually no coordination between them and the communication specialists. The result always is that such programs are generally based on perceived or assumed knowledge, both of the subject matter and the sociocultural and environmental conditions of the audience. Third and perhaps most importantly, is the fact that there is no guidance at the reception end. It is in the open broadcast strategy that a shot-in-the-dark approach to programming is most pronounced. This approach leaves the target audience forgotten while programs are being planned; remembered just before the programs go on the air; and forgotten again as soon as the programs have been broadcast. When this shortcoming is added to the lack of consultation and coordination between broadcasters and education and development agencies, and the lack of interaction between producers and the consumers of the

programs, it becomes difficult not to conclude that the best one can expect from the strategy is chance success. This, of course, is not an expectation on which a true rural community emancipation program should be predicated.

Instructional Radio

Instructional radio is the second strategy for using radio broadcasting for social change and development. Instructional radio is directed at an organized learning group, with someone able to supervise and direct as well as elicit feedback. This is the strategy used in Tanzania (Greenholm, 1975, Dodds, 1972) to teach practical skills and cooperative and civic responsibility to rural communities. It is known as Radio Study Group in that country. In Nigeria, it is known as Schools Broadcast. Using the strategy requires much more than mere broadcasting. It requires a structure for organizing listening and learning practices, provision of support materials, presence of monitors or teachers and some kind of assessment. A very important aspect of the strategy is that reception infrastructure is an integral part of its process.

Instructional radio operates on the principle of cooperation and guided listening. There is usually cooperation between broadcasters and educationists. For example, most educational programs in Nigeria are written by teachers in the field. Because of the demand for guided listening some captive audience is assured, and if the programs are sufficiently appealing and relevant to audience situations, one can expect favorable reaction—both attitudinal and behavioral. Where audience reactions are recorded, as was the case in the Tanzanian projects, such reactions may well serve as signposts to guide future programming.

The extent to which this strategy can be used on a wide scale is doubtful, because of its strong demands on factors like finance, transport and personnel. Tanzania has been able to operate the strategy fairly successfully because, first, it is a relatively compact country, and secondly and perhaps more importantly, the government places a very high priority on rural community education. Nigeria's experience in using this strategy (for formal education) has not been encouraging. For example, in a study of the use of the strategy in Lagos (Dare et al, 1973), it was found that an overwhelming majority of teachers (92 percent) do not use the broadcasts; 53 percent of students do not listen to them; and of those who do listen, less than 30 percent classified the broadcasts as "helpful." If the situation is bad in Lagos schools, then it cannot be any better in schools in rural areas that have the additional disadvantages of a shortage of radio sets and distortions of radio signals caused by distance. And if the effect of the strategy can be so minimal in formal education, it is doubtful that it can be any greater in non formal learning situations. Because instructional radio has mainly been used (except in Tanzania) for formal education, there appears to be a tacit understanding that it is not very appropriate for the non-formal, "soft-hammer-blow" type of education required for community development.

Rural Radio Forum

The rural radio forum is the strategy for using radio with discussion and decision making for rural groups. It involves the presentation of regular weekly 15- to 30-minute radio programs of a mixed nature to rural audiences formed into listening groups. Such programs usually contain news, answers to listeners' questions, family advice, a talk, discussions, etc. The groups listen and discuss under the guidance of a group leader and make decisions on the points of discussion. The strategy makes extensive use of audience reaction, where available, for subsequent programs. Because of this, there is usually a temptation for broadcasters to work on their own without cooperation with other change agents in the rural communities. However, the sense of involvement this strategy engenders in the rural communities as a result of its demand for some action-decision by the group is a great asset in development efforts.

The forum strategy has a number of advantages. First, the follow-up of a radio message with localized discussion and decisions ensures positive commitment

to agreed-upon decisions and subsequently to social change. "The combination of a message carried to many groups by a mass medium like radio, then localized by discussion in small groups and guided to a group decision, conforms closely to existing theories of communication and social change" (McAnany, 1973:10). Secondly, membership in the group helps to expose the participants to information important to the rural communities, and this turns such individuals into opinion leaders whose views would tend to be respected in the community. This is one aspect of the radiation effect of rural radio (Moemeka, 1987). That is, the effect of rural radio on non participants as a result of the impact of forum participants—an effect that leads to changes in attitudes, behaviors and practices. Thirdly, forums do send back reports and messages, thus providing the vital feedback often missing in mass media activities. And finally, the forum strategy is based on the conviction that rural community development must essentially be the duty of the rural people themselves and should not be dropped on them from above. The built-in localized discussions and decisions ensure that the people are put in a position in which they can be the subject and object of their own development.

The forum strategy also has weaknesses. There are certain obstacles in the way of successful use of this strategy. First, there is strong need for a network of supervisors, so that forums can be in contact with project leadership and do not have to depend entirely on written reports for asking questions and getting help. Unfortunately, this desired situation does not always result; supervisors or change agents—the most important factors in adoption of innovations (Rogers et al, 1970)—are always in short supply. Secondly, production centers are usually far away from most of the village groups and so cannot always benefit from contact with forums to get the feedback that is a vital factor in program content improvement.

Summing up his observations of the Indian Radio Rural Forum, Schramm (1967) said:

1927
1960
1963
1964
1967
1969
1970
1971
1972
1973
1974
1975
1976
1977
1978
1979
1980
1981
1982
1983
1984
1985
1986
1987
1988
1989
1990
1991
1992
1993
1994
1995
1996
1997
1998
1999
2000
2001
2002
2003
2004
2005
2006

Forums may have been made up of people in villages who were least likely to need them (that is, the local elite); programs needed more localness (decentralizing the programming activities); adequate materials to follow up on innovations were often lacking to villagers; more involvement by the development officers with the field experience was called for (network of supervisors to keep personal contact).

These missing links have greatly affected the successful utilization of rural radio forums. In other words, this strategy will be successful if all rural people, not just the local elite, are involved; if radio stations are near enough to the communities and program contents are relevant and fully localized; if adequate and prompt actions are taken to provide materials to implement new projects and follow up on implemented innovations; and if there are sufficient development agents around to supply the intimacy and encouragement of personal contact.

Radio Schools

Radio schools are the most widespread strategy for using radio for rural community education in Latin America. They originated in Sutatenza, Colombia, and have now permeated the life of the rural population of that country. The "schools" are small, organized (mainly illiterate adults), listening/learning groups meeting in houses or in churches under a guide. The basic aim of this strategy is to offer fundamental, integral education that goes beyond mere reading, writing and cognitive skills, and tries to change the passive and dependent attitude of the people, creating a deepening of their sense of dignity and self-worth, and turning them into "new men and women."

An organization mostly associated with this strategy is Colombia's *Accion Cultural Popular* (ACPO)—a private organization that at present has the most powerful radio transmitter in that country. ACPO also has stations all over the country, including some one-kilowatt transmitter stations in some areas. Although radio is the most important medium used, it is by no means the only one. The radio schools approach is basically multimedia, employing at least radio and printed booklets almost everywhere, but also frequently adding newspapers, charts, booklets for reading, filmstrips and actual teaching/learning methods. The schools are based on the principle of homophily, meaning that group members do not only know one another but largely have identical perceptions of the world and their own environment. Field organization usually exists in the form of a supervisor who tries to coordinate activities, distribute materials and visit groups from time to time in order to encourage them.

Like the forum strategy, radio schools have their own strengths and weaknesses. As typified by ACPO, this strategy has been successful in arousing the rural people to action. This is precisely because its orientation and identity is with the rural population and its problems. The schools foster greater knowledge of the real needs of rural areas by having a significant number of rural leaders in the organization of their activities, ensuring real contact of policymakers with the rural people and with their problems, and enabling functional feedback to flow from the audiences. Secondly, the radio schools are basically listening/learning groups. This means that the advantages of group listening and of local monitors and supervisors also accrue to this strategy. The solidarity of the group encourages perseverance in pursuing group goals, while visits from supervisors create a sense of identity. Perhaps the one peculiar aspect of this strategy as operated by ACPO is the fact that the activities are a continuing process, a factor which makes radio and the schools part of the everyday life of the people.

There are certain weaknesses, however. ACPO's efforts are almost entirely directed to literacy and basic education, in spite of the professed "integral education" ideal of the strategy. This leaves out almost completely the political, social and physical developmental aspects of rural problems. Because of this cautious stand on the part of the radio schools to engage in mobilizing the people toward community action, merely because it is political, there is no collaboration between them and rural change programs of a more developmental nature. This is "action in isolation," which does not foster concerted efforts toward total development.

Radio and Animation

Radio and animation, also known as the radio participating group, is a strategy which aims at promoting among local communities a trained cadre of decision leaders. It is used to train leaders whose role is to promote, in a nondirective way, a dialogue in which community members participate in defining their development problems, putting them in a larger social context and working out ways of mobilizing their people to take common action to overcome these problems. The strategy places emphasis on radio "defining," but not "suggesting," solutions to the people's problems. Programs are made from recorded views and responses about a definite problem are presented by some members of the listening public. The participating groups then listen to these responses and views and discuss the problem further, thus creating avenues for further responses from the public and subsequently eliciting some decisions.

The assumption of this strategy can be put into five statements:

■ There are no solutions to problems that are imposed on local communities from the outside; local communities must first arrive at the problem definition and then its solution on their own.
■ The social animator is to be as closely identified with the local community as possible.
■ He/she is to be nondirective in his/her approach.
■ Information's chief role in this approach is to help define the problem and not give the solutions.
■ Community participation and social action is the goal, and therefore feedback from the community is an essential means.

The strategy that developed from the French government's action toward rural development in its former West African territories has been used in Senegal, Benin, Togo and Niger. It started in Niger in 1963. The primary objective of the radio broadcasts and discussions here, as in the other countries, was to foster awareness of national development plans in terms of local problems, and not to provide information on a problem defined by the experts from the outside. In Senegal, the strategy was directed at inculcating new farming methods, diversifying agriculture and improving the administration and management of cooperatives. The Senegalese project known as *Radio Educative Rurale* was a cooperative venture between the Ministry of Information and Tourism, which is in charge of broadcasting, and all other ministries that have any responsibility for the rural population. Of particular importance in the Senegalese attempt was that feedback was an essential ingredient of the broadcasts. The opinions, actions and expectations of the people formed the content of the programs.

The animation strategy, in spite of its strengths, also has its weaknesses. First, to place the burden of taking initiative on the local people assumes that local control and local leadership will be forthcoming. This, however, has not easily happened in the many places where the strategy has been used. Many communities are slow to get themselves organized, and many more are not able to organize at all. There is, therefore, the temptation to try to organize them from the outside, if any positive action is to be taken. Secondly, the idea behind this strategy's local-participation principle is that people will feel that they are the ones developing themselves. But localizing development effort is not controlling that effort. There is the danger that the people may be manipulated in their sense of participating in the development of their community, and merely be given the opportunity to criticize and complain as a safety valve to forestall rural unrest, while no real policy changes may result from the local participation. The fact that this strategy has not produced significant results in the African countries where it has been used confirms this fear.

A final problem facing radio and animation strategy, just as other strategies, is the conflict between mass message and local peculiarities. Localities in the rural areas are not completely homogeneous; each local area has specific problems that can be solved better when viewed with its social, economic and political environments in context. It is therefore not possible to satisfy every locality from a central point. This is the problem of relevance and appropriateness local radio systems can help to ameliorate.

The Appropriate Strategy

All five strategies discussed above have been tried with some measure of success in different parts of the world. In Nigeria, two strategies—open broadcast and the instructional radio—are used. The former is used for rural information and education, and the latter for formal education. The Nigerian languages section of broadcasting organizations in the country use the open broadcast strategy for their non formal education activities. But the strategy is not succeeding because it is too disorganized for any purposeful and mass education of the rural population. Programs are planned and produced in the broadcasting houses with little or no consultation with other development agencies and without research to find out the best way to get to the heart of the problems of rural communities. There is no interaction between the people and the broadcasting houses because these broadcasting houses are generally too far away from the people and their communities. At the reception end, there is no direction as to how to make good use of the programs being broadcast—no structure providing a conducive atmosphere for discussions and group decision taking. The community spirit of the Nigerian rural inhabitants is not brought into play, despite the fact that it is realized all over the country that individual action, especially where long entrenched values and behaviors are concerned, is very hard to come by in the rural areas. The result is that few rural people listen to these programs, and even these do so without any intention of accepting the message content.

Instructional radio, the other strategy used in Nigeria, is too formalized and structured along the line of the teaching/learning process to be of much use in rural community education. The rural adult does not want to be a receptacle for the knowledge of "strangers" who have failed to recognize his/her own type of knowledge. He/she needs to be taken into confidence before he/she can grant his/her attention. Furthermore, if instructional radio, that is, Schools Broadcast in Nigeria, has not proved appreciably effective in formal education, it would amount to wishful thinking to believe that it can succeed in the persuasive context in which rural community education should be carried out.

The other three strategies—rural radio forum, radio schools and radio and animation—would appear to approach what one may propose as the ideal strategy. But each, as now used, has some unnecessary, self-imposed limitations. The rural radio forum strategy concentrates almost entirely on the identification of, and discussions and decisions on, local problems. As a result, it tends to attract those who least need arousal and development consciousness, that is, the local elite. Change agents are known to be mostly associated with such local elite, leaving out those for whom rural education is imperative for purposes of personal and community development, that is, the uninformed and the apathetic. It is true that rural forums can help in rural transformation, but unless the marginal rural people are brought in to play actively positive roles, the transformation will benefit only the few who are already better off than the majority.

The radio schools strategy focuses primarily on illiterate rural adults, and almost all effort is directed to literacy and basic education, in spite of the professed aim of providing fundamental, integral education. To do only this is to tackle only one aspect of the problems of rural development. Even though the marginal illiterate is the most affected by rural underdevelopment, others within the rural social milieu are also affected. In addition, education to create a "new human being" that does not lead to actions of a physical developmental nature is not likely to bring about change. It is noteworthy that ACPO, the main user of this strategy, has come to realize this fact and now has programs designed to stimulate action toward self- and community help.

The radio and animation strategy places an almost exclusive emphasis on local initiative in identifying problems and finding solutions to them. This approach assumed a strong latent capacity within the rural population, which needs only to be tickled in order to go into action. But it is only in very self-conscious communities that this capacity and willingness obtain. Most others have to be motivated from outside and continuously reinforced if any improvements are to occur. The emphasis on voluntarism may mean that many communities will, if not given direction, remain where they are. Such communities need more than sermonizing on local initiative.

The Ideal Strategy

The ideal strategy, one may venture to suggest, should be one which combines the involvement (subsequent to local group discussions and decisions) of the rural radio forum, the literacy/basic education of the radio schools and the local initiative of the radio and animation approaches. This is because rural community education and development spans the whole range of the specific areas treated in isolation by each of these strategies. The people have to be motivated to identify their problems, they have to be led to discuss these problems and to take active decisions on them and they have to be taught the techniques of reading and writing. All these are necessary to "create the new human being," without whom community development would be impossible. This strategy, which we have called "Local Radio Strategy" (Moemeka, 1981), should aim at improving the lot of the rural people in their totality—make them literate, widen their horizons, raise their aspirations realistically, point to their problems, create in them the willingness to find solutions to these problems and imbue them with a sense of dignity and self-worth.

The point about literacy is particularly important. Radio alone cannot completely handle the task of changing the rural man/woman into a development resource and rural communities into substantially productive components of the nation. To ensure some good measure of success, and a long-term effect, there must be some accompanying written materials to drive home the points made on radio and to refer to from time to time. The use of such study follow-up materials would require the employment of interpreters, unless the people have acquired the ability to read and write intelligibly enough to comprehend written communication. However, literacy should not be the prerequisite for rural community education and development. It should, instead, be the outcome of increased awareness and the thirst for more knowledge that are bound to follow effective rural educational campaigns.

This ideal strategy—the local radio strategy—combines the qualities of the rural radio forum, the radio schools and the radio and animation strategies. It utilizes their inherent and operational advantages and strengthens its position by eliminating their deficiencies. Two of the most conspicuous deficiencies are the spatial gap between production centers and the consuming rural audiences and the general nature of program contents, which treat only marginally issues of concern to many areas. If, therefore, the new strategy is to have a better chance of success, there is a strong need for proximity of radio stations to the rural audiences and for localization of program materials. This is saying, in effect, that the new strategy should be based on a local radio broadcasting system, and this means decentralization of broadcasting infrastructure and the delegation of powers concerned with programming and content materials to the local station, working in close collaboration with the rural community.

Waniewicz (1972) suggested four different models of coordination and cooperation in using radio for education and development. All four models emphasize

1927
1960
1963
1964
1967
1969
1970
1971
1972
1973
1974
1975
1976
1977
1978
1979
1980
1981
1982
1983
1984
1985
1986
1987
1988
1989
1990
1991
1992
1993
1994
1995
1996
1997
1998
1999
2000
2001
2002
2003
2004
2005
2006

the need for research (entering the socio cultural context of the people), a broad-based advisory council and a utilization service department in addition to a programs department. Moemeka (1981: 93), using elements from these models, proposed a structure of Local Radio Strategy for Community Development that calls for, among other things, local radio advisory councils with representatives from government departments and voluntary agencies that have responsibility to the community and representatives of the community and of the broadcasting organization. The council is meant to guide the station in its work, ensuring that program content and the contexts under which the programs are presented are relevant to the community's needs and expectations.

As research has shown (Katz, Blumler and Gurevitch, 1974), the relevance of mass media content to listeners' needs and aspirations is a determining factor in media message effectiveness. To achieve this relevance, not only must media personnel enter into the socio cultural contexts of the people, but media infrastructure must also be near enough to enable the people to participate actively in media activities (Moemeka, 1981). A further important factor in achieving relevance in content is working with other agencies involved in the attempt to improve the living conditions of the people. Community education and development involve the work of many agencies, e.g., health, social welfare, education, local government and various voluntary organizations. A co-ordinated approach toward relevantly educating the community for development requires concrete collaboration among all these agencies and between them and broadcasting.

To be meaningful to rural communities, such collaboration must obtain within the communities to enable the people to be part of the process. Local radio strategy appears to be the most appropriate route to reaching these goals. As Schramm (1964) rightly points out, local media are of great importance in social and economic development; not only because they are in a better position to know and serve the particular needs

of local areas, but also because they make it easier for more people to have access to the media and therefore to take part in public (community) affairs. The greater the number of people that actively participate, the broader the base of community decision making and the greater the chances of individual commitment to the community's collective decisions. It is this individual commitment to community objectives which gives expression to the aims of community education as summarized by Faure et al. (1972) as: "The complete fulfillment of man in all the richness of his personality, the variety of his forms of expression and his various commitment as an individual, as a member of a family and of a community, citizen and producer, inventor of techniques and creative dreamer."

References

Arana, E. 1971. "Informe sobre la influencia que la radio ejerce en una comunidad indigena." Xoxcotle, Morelos, Friedrich Ebert Foundation Seminar on Rural Radio, Mexico, 1971. (Memeo).

Dare, O., et al. "Consumption of Schools Broadcast in Secondary Schools in Lagos." Sessional project essay, Department of Mass Communication, University of Lagos, Portugal, 1973.

Dodds, T. "Multi-Media Approach to Rural Education: Case Studies." International Extension College, Broadsheet on Distance Learning, No. 1., London, 1972.

Faure, E., et al. "Learning to Be: The World of Education Today and Tomorrow." Paris: UNESCO, 1972.

Greenholm, L. "Radio Study Group Campaigns in the United Republic of Tanzania." Paris: UNESCO, 1975.

Gunter, J., and J. Theroux. "Open Broadcast Education Radio: Three Paradigms." In Rogers, et al., eds., *Radio for Education and Development: Case Studies Vol. I.* Washington, D.C.: World Bank, 1977.

Hickey, H., et al. *The Role of the School in Community Education.* Midland, Michigan: 1969, 36. See also C. LeTarte and J. Minzey. *Community Education: From Program to Process.* Midland, Michigan: 1975, 17.

Katz, E., J. Blumer and M. Gurevitch. "Uses of Mass Communication by the Individual." In W. P. Davidson and F. Yu, eds., *Mass Communication Research: Major Issues and Future Directions.* New York: Praeger, 1974.

McAnany, E. *Radio's Role in Development: Five Strategies of Use.* Information Center for Instructional Technology, Washington, D.C., 1973.

Moemeka, A. A. "The AIDS Epidemic: The Impact of Mass Communicated Prevention Messages." A paper presented at the Federal Ministry of Information Seminar on AIDS Prevention, Institute of International Affairs, Lagos, Portugal, 1988.

_____ . "Rural Radio Broadcasting and Community Health Practices: A Case Study of Radio O-Y-O in Nigeria." Ph.D. Dissertation, State University of New York, Albany, 1987.

_____ . "Local Radio: Community Education for Development." Ah-madu Bello University Press, 1981.

Nigerian Broadcasting Corporation's Igbo Languages Program: Audience, Preferences, Involvement and Benefits in Lagos. Unpublished bachelor's degree essay. University of Lagos, Portugal, 1972.

Rogers, E. M., et al. "Radio Forums: A Strategy for Rural Development," In *Radio for Education and Development: Case Studies, Vol. II*. Washington, D.C.: World Bank, Working Paper No. 266, 1977.

Schramm, W. "Ten Years of the Radio Forum in India," In *New Education Media in Action: Case Studies for Planners, Vol. 1*. Paris: UNESCO, 1967.

_____ . *Mass Media in National Development: The Role of Information in Developing Countries*. Stanford, California: Stanford University Press, 1964.

Spain, P. Survey of Radio Listenership in the Davao Province of Mindanao, the Philippines. Unpublished report, Stanford University, 1971.

Sproule, J. 1989. "Progressive Propaganda Critics and the Magic Bullet Myth," *Critical Studies in Mass Communication*, 1989, 6: 225-46.

UNESCO. *Reports and Papers in Mass Communication*, 1968, No. 51, Paris: 3.

Waniewicz, I. *Broadcasting for Adult Education: A Guide-Book to Worldwide Experience*. Paris: UNESCO, 1972.

Yu, E.T.C. "Communication Planning and Policy for Development: Some Research Notes," In Lerner and Nelson, eds., *Communication Research: A Half-Century Appraisal*. Honolulu: University Press of Hawaii, 1977, 185.

EXCERPT FROM:

PASSION FOR DISCOURSE: LETTERS TO STUDENTS OF COMMUNICATION

By Daniel Prieto Castillo

1994 If authoritarianism penetrates to the very roots of any society, the alternative in communication will not be at all exhausted by denunciation, by an attack on power.

A group of friends and I once did an exercise from which I learnt some things that have remained with me forever. We took four books by Latin American authors that spoke about a different society. These authors proposed a disruption of the order of that time in order to gain access to more humane conditions.

We started with some principles of analysis: An authoritarian discourse is marked by excessive use of the verbs of obligation—words related to the word "must. This language was the attempt to say it all, not leaving any chances either to doubt or for the receiver to interpret personally. There was no possibility of seeing nuances between light and shade.

Our reading led us to verify an obsessive use of these elements in works: Authoritarian discourse was something like saying: "I order you to be free".

We understood that, in communication, in addition to the content or the subject matter, what we call *alternative* is transmitted through the type of discourse used. It is not only what you say that is alternative, but it's also how you say it. The practice of discourse is as alternative as the denunciation.

I learnt then in my writings to be careful with the use of verbs of obligation, which are very common in the discourse of preachers who howl from audiovisual media—and quite frequently in classrooms.

1927
1960
1963
1964
1967
1969
1970
1971
1972
1973
1974
1975
1976
1977
1978
1979
1980
1981
1982
1983
1984
1985
1986
1987
1988
1989
1990
1991
1992
1993
1994
1995
1996
1997
1998
1999
2000
2001
2002
2003
2004
2005
2006

In time I learnt that when we speak of the alternative in communicational products, we speak of alternatives to authoritarianism … .

If there is a dominant way of producing messages, it is possible to recognize different experiences, marked by group work and by the disruption of certain hierarchical orders in order to decide on the content and form of materials. These are rare alternatives in the collective media, indeed, but very present in institutions that produce communication for educational work and relate directly to the vast majority of the population.

In the dominant forms, the trend in general is towards the formation of groups of bureaucratized producers. The structure usually consists of an editorial room or some ministerial department responsible for producing information. Although exceptions count, the system becomes vertical with the presence of censors. The producers end up becoming transmitting spokespersons, limited by controls and extreme economic dependence. The real transmitters are the owners of the companies or the politicians in power.

An alternative organization for communication is entirely made up of real transmitters, undergoes no censorship processes and does not establish economic benefits people in control.

"What comes into play here," we have written with Francisco Gutiérrez in *The Pedagogical Mediation*, "is the concept of *co-responsibility*. When you adopt an alternative process, there is no visionary with servers more or less willing to follow him".

Neither was it any great discovery to demonstrate the obviousness of the existence of an alternative distribution of messages in any society. Let's not forget, in the first place, the role still played—and will always be played—by oral communication.

And let's remember the exchange systems, through groups, associations, organizations of all kinds. I am not idealizing anything here—or anywhere else—I

hope. When a society has no space in the collective media, it finds a way to open a space in them. I recommend the works of Rosa María Alfaro on radio in Peru, published in magazines such as *Chasqui*, or *Diálogos*. [When a society has no space in the collective media, it will] generate its own systems of information circulation and exchange of experiences.

Finally, there's the use of messages. Let it be clear that I am saying *use* and not consumption. Quite a harmful terminology for understanding the scope of communication has accustomed us to naming everything in market terms. I can accept that consumption of some, or many, communication products does exist but not that all messages are consumed like hamburgers.

Dominant communication not only introduces a range of ideological elements…that imply a set of reading routines contrary to alternative proposals.

A different communication is aimed at a different reading or appropriation, a capacity to deal with the message and to be able to evaluate its content and form.

So the alternative is not as simple as it might initially appear. From the field of communication it is up to us to recognize the phases of production, the product itself, distribution and use. An ideal alternative communication would cover all four.

But very rarely do all occur in the same process. There are institutions organized in such a vertical way, and yet, they manage to produce alternative messages. There are badly distributed alternative messages, alternative readings of dominant messages, and alternative messages that are themselves the object of readings characteristic of habits of dominant perceptions.

It is not our function to dictate any model to become a reality. The measure of the alternative has always been the circumstances. If I get into evaluating a process from a framework of "pure" categories, I run the risk of becoming an "inspector of revolutions", as a friend said a few years ago. That which in the context of a university or an experience from another country appears to be a timid little reform, could represent a huge step in the circumstances in which it is produced.

What Is Alternative Communication?

I return to that question. There are some definitions I dislike, especially when, because of the subject, they seem to be preaching. But here we go:

It is a different way of

- Organizing communication, both in the content as well as in the form of discourse, for the purpose of avoiding authoritarianism at all costs;
- Organizing to produce it;
- Achieving spaces in the dominant media, or even generating separate systems, and
- Collaborating in the different use of messages by the receiver.

Be careful! I never tell anyone, "Do this," or "This is your path". I try only to recognize the range of alternative communication. …

EXCERPT FROM:
WOMEN IN GRASSROOTS COMMUNICATION: FURTHERING SOCIAL CHANGE
Women's Particiaption in Communication: Elements for a Framework

By Pilar Riaño

1994

While there have been advances in the raising of women's issues in the movement for the democratization of communications, the debate has ignored the widespread women's social movements that are building class, race and cultural alliances as well as new communication alternatives and propositions for change at the grassroots. The omission is significant: These alliances not only speak to the advances of social movements in opening democratic spaces for people's communication, but also address many of the same concerns raised by international communication agendas, such as the New World International Communications Order (NWICO) and current debates about the democratization of communications.[1]

A Typology of Women's Participation in Communication

The following typology reviews the various frameworks that address the relationships among women, participation and communication. I have placed participation at the very center of my discussion, as this concept encompasses a point of reference in the discourses and practices of states, institutions and social movements about women. The typology identifies the discourses and practices of four major frameworks:

---

1 In the 1990s, reformulating the democratization debate has become a necessity in the light of global economic, social and political changes; the shift of UNESCO's communication policies; and the critical evaluation of the previous decade's small advances toward the democratization of communications. Such a reformulation requires first and foremost that the debate be moved away from institutional agendas concerned with state-related communication policies and be situated in a grassroots perspective. Basically, what is implied by this shift is the emergence of an alternative view of communications and democracy in society, a view in which democracy is generated in the active and dynamic interaction of the people, the social movements, the institutions and the cultural industries.

1927
1960
1963
1964
1967
1969
1970
1971
1972
1973
1974
1975
1976
1977
1978
1979
1980
1981
1982
1983
1984
1985
1986
1987
1988
1989
1990
1991
1992
1993
1994
1995
1996
1997
1998
1999
2000
2001
2002
2003
2004
2005
2006

development communications, participatory communications, alternative communications and feminist communications (see Table 1.1). The order of presentation introduces critical elements developed by each framework about the others.

Sénécal (1991) argued that in every aspect of social communication—from the control of the media to public perceptions, social representations and even the definition of technological choices—each social actor possesses his or her own specific practice or discourse. For example, development communications and to some extent participatory communication frameworks respond to the logic of the State and to institutions in seeking consent and support. The logic underlying alternative communications and feminist communications is that of social movements, or the identification of a social project in which "a variety of social actors seeks to create a new social reality, a new culture, a new logic for all aspects of life, including the technology and skills of audio-visual communications" (Sénécal 1991, p. 213). Women's participation in communication initiatives constitutes a tool of struggle and a meaningful space in which to develop women's own discourses.

DEVELOPMENT COMMUNICATIONS: PARTICIPATION AS A DEVELOPMENT TOOL

Development-communication interventions are those which originated from outside the control of the community or target group and are delivered through government or international development institutions and nongovernmental organizations (NGO) (Bernard 1991). Traditionally, development communications have overlooked barriers faced by women in accessing development information and, therefore, have failed to benefit women. More recently, development communication programs have revised their approach to women.[2]

In India, Indonesia, Cameroon and Swaziland, the goal of programs directed to child survival and nutrition is to develop the mother's sense of self-confidence in child rearing and decision making. These programs rely on the use of interpersonal communication between experts or extension workers and poor urban and rural mothers. Focus groups, photo stories, photographs and radio soaps produced by professionals reinforce the educational strategy that conceives the development of the mother's self-esteem as a condition for behavioral change (Griffiths 1990). Women as farmers, mothers, wives, agents of environmental protection and managers of households constitute subjects of information in development interventions. Women's participation is encouraged in regard to three specific goals: (a) to change current critical practices, (b) to encourage active support and (c) to mobilize the community for mass campaigns.

Change current critical practices: This refers to the attempt to convince a target population to change critical practices, for example, risk behaviors such as sexual practices, smoking and drinking. *This* model implements communication strategies that encourage public awareness and consensus, including public-health campaigns for family planning, breast feeding, reduction of smoking and drinking and AIDS prevention. Participation of women is conceived as cooperation with planners, administrators and power elites and as a willingness to change critical behaviors (Deshler and Sock 1985).

Encourage active support: Communication campaigns are used to encourage the active support of women and their communities for national or regional programs of nutrition, child vaccination, agricultural extension, water supply and sanitation. International support programs are commonly concerned with disseminating development messages in a way that encourages support for specific programs. In these projects participation describes women's input or voluntary contribution of time and effort to the development program (Protz 1991); for example,

---

2   In McAnany and Storey's (1989) discussion of the guiding issues for the research and practice of development communication, they argued that participation is synthetic because it encompasses individuals and the social systems in which they live and interact with one another. In the review here, this understanding of particı pation is applied: I recognize individual and group practices as part of larger social processes not as isolated actions.

Type	Goals	Context	Participation	Empowerment	Message
Development communication (women as subjects of information)	Change critical practices Encourage support for development campaigns Mobilize the community	International/national development campaigns Development support Communication programs Extension work Social marketing	Participation as a means Public cooperation with planners Public feedback	Empowerment as acquiring information Learning new facts Engaging in discussion	One way: expert to target Diffusion of information
Participatory communication (women as participants)	Enable people to take control of their lives Reduce knowledge gap Encourage organizational and sociocultural change Influence public policies	Development of communication programs Participatory communication programs Policymaking	Participation as transaction Interaction between receivers and information source	Empowerment as enabling Acquiring knowledge and status to take control of their lives Capacity to benefit from involvement	Participatory message development Interface of top-down and bottom-up information flow Two ways
Alternative communication (women as subjects of change)	Support social struggles Advocacy and defense of rights Promote group reflection Awake consciousness of subordination	Social movements Popular communication Civil and human rights Community communication Group communication Media education	Participation as a process of control As a condition for social change As a capacity of actively producing meaning	Empowerment as developing individual and collective capacity to impact on change Increased control and ownership of process	Multidimensional flow of messages Horizontal message delivery Activity of both sender and receiver
Feminist communication (women as producers of meaning)	Naming oppressions of race, class, gender, sexual orientation and disability Negotiate fair representation and equity of access Construction of individual and collective identities Production of alternative meanings	Feminist and women's movements Advocacy Feminist communication in scholarship	Participation as ownership, inclusion and accountability Developing a sense of community Ownership of collective experiences/identities	Empowerment as transformation of social subjects and the acts of naming Coming to voice Breaking the silence	Communication as exchange Circularity of meaning of messages Horizontal messages Network of meanings

TABLE 1.1 A Typology of Women, Participation and Communication

water-supply and sanitation projects have ensured that women participate in workshops on the theme and that extension workers include women who are familiar with the local language and culture (Yacoob 1990). Participation is used as a tool to activate the acceptance of the program by the intended beneficiaries.

Mobilize the community: This seeks the participation of women in the dissemination of development messages and mobilization of the community through a variety of communicative strategies. An example of this type of program is the Facts for Life, which was launched by UNICEF, UNISON and the World Health Organization (WHO) to diffuse child-health messages to poor families in the so-called developing countries. Forms of participation include mass mobilization of information (mass media); intercultural communication (translated information and the use of religious leaders or elders

1927
1960
1963
1964
1967
1969
1970
1971
1972
1973
1974
1975
1976
1977
1978
1979
1980
1981
1982
1983
1984
1985
1986
1987
1988
1989
1990
1991
1992
1993
1994
1995
1996
1997
1998
1999
2000
2001
2002
2003
2004
2005
2006

to diffuse messages); and folk media such as traditional drama, folk songs, puppetry and indigenous dances. This approach envisions participation of the community as an instrument to further a more community-oriented development. Promotion of participation will also improve the appeal and reach of development programs and campaigns by directing their messages in a culturally appropriate language (in the local language, with actors such as popular artists, who are recognized by the local community) and by increasing the feedback from the public to the experts (Moore 1986).

These three types of participation are meant to maximize the success of a development intervention, which is designed from the principles discussed above. Participation and communication strategies are reduced to a set of techniques that are used to implement some of the stages of the development program, or to a methodological choice of doing "better development." Women constitute the target group, the subjects of the information or the active listeners, who through participation will embrace the development message.

The community's input is considered mostly in the early stages of the program design. Usually developed as a cursory consultation, it is a way to gain knowledge about the living conditions, sources of income, local hierarchies and customs of the target audience. In the final stages of dissemination and implementation, community participation is regarded as public cooperation and acceptance of the development campaign. In terms of the communication strategy, participation is seen as public feedback, i.e., filling out surveys that measure information learned) or, sometimes, interactive viewing (carrying out a discussion immediately after the program is broadcast). Participants do not formulate the message or use the communications equipment.

These programs rely on the mass media and on a growing use of indigenous communication networks such as women's informal associations, folk media (puppets, theater and dance), interpersonal communication between experts and community, and small-format media (including educational illustrations and texts displayed in areas of community gathering and photographs used as references for discussion). This use of indigenous channels reflects a belief that the interpersonal and informal levels are central when it comes to persuading people to change. Media function in this context to legitimize the centrality of the issue for public attention, to act as loudspeakers of the expert messages and to assist in reinforcing the project's messages (Hornik 1988).

Strategies aimed at empowering people to control the programs rarely appear in these discourses. Eventually, empowerment is seen as the capacity of the individual to grasp the information learned (nutritional foods, value of breast feeding and child immunization) and actively to seek more information (going to the local health clinic and talking to others).

Overall, this approach to participation in communication does not change or even question linear modes of information diffusion, or the hierarchical position between the sender/expert's and receiver/target group's approaches to this type of communication.

PARTICIPATORY COMMUNICATION: PARTICIPATION AS DEVELOPMENT

In Nepal, rural women received training in video production as part of the communication strategy of a project on credit to rural women. Video was used in community development, to engage women in assessing needs and in elaborating plans for video production and recording. Videos produced by women were shown to other women in workshops. Women responded very positively to seeing other women using this medium. They felt confident and realized they also could do it. Showing the videos to the community fostered discussion and negotiation with policymakers and government representatives (see Belbase 1988, 1989; Burkert 1989a, 1989b). ...

This approach arose out of the critique of the diffusionist and one-way tendencies of many development programs. It pointed out the importance of conceiving development communications as a participatory process (Nair and White 1987b; Servaes 1989; Williamson 1991; White 1989). In this view, participation is seen as bringing a more people-centered, rather than market-centered, perspective to development.

Media and overall development communication are used to motivate, educate and mobilize the target population to respond to planned programs (Kulakow quoted in Nair and White 1987a). The focus of participatory communication strategies is to allow an interface of information flow from the top down (institutions and development experts) and the bottom up (women and their communities). The communication message then is defined in a two-way interaction but is controlled by the information source. Participation is a transaction between grassroots receivers and information sources:

> The process is on altering communication processes and strategies. We are not talking about social movements at the grassroots, à la Freire but communication processes that take into account indigenous knowledge and self-reliance gained through increased information, access and acquisition. (Nair and White 1987c: 6)

Nair and White have applied this framework to video-production programs with village women in Poona, India, and with farmers in Washington County (New York) in the United States. Participants are trained in the use of video machines and in the production of videos around community issues. This participation is conceived as a continuum; the different levels of interaction of the group vary by the degree of activity or passivity of each member, as well as by their level of dialogue and engagement in the production of messages (Nair and White 1987a). The target group is more or less involved in the process of building a participatory message, from needs assessment through media production to final evaluation and effectiveness. People's, or popular, participation represents a driving force for the determination of development processes and the materialization of a right to participate in the decisions that affect their lives (African Charter for Popular Participation in Development and Transformation, quoted in Ansah 1992).

If information access is placed at the very center, empowerment is conceived in this approach "as the process through which individuals acquire knowledge and skills to take control of their lives" (Nair and White 1987c: 16). Empowerment is thought of as a process of enabling individuals to benefit from involvement in the development program, as a means to bring about people's control over economic and political forces (Kindervatter 1979). However, this view fails to analyze the differences in power and access to resources in the context in which people's relations with the larger social environment occur. Furthermore, in the placing of emphasis on the individual's self-reliance and capacity to deal with the problems, the larger structural condition of dependency and domination of Third World societies is disregarded.

Another missing element in this approach is the multitude of power differences hidden behind the concepts of target population and people. The question has already been posed: Who benefits from participation? Failure to account for differences of class, ethnicity, patterns of organization, age or gender can mean unequal distribution of benefits, violation of traditional practices and creation of conflict (Jurmo 1980; McKee 1988; Pigozzi 1982).

ALTERNATIVE COMMUNICATION: PARTICIPATION FOR SOCIAL CHANGE

In the *pueblos jovenes* of Lima, Peru, most market vendors are women. They are members of the association of public markets; nevertheless, until 1985, the association's executive group consisted almost entirely of men. At that time, a member of the board concerned with the weak interaction and diffusion of communication among association members invited women of the market to use the loudspeakers. A group of women, assisted by a local institution of communication, decided to use the market's loudspeakers to communicate problems such as tax payments, selling permits and legalization of land.

1927
1960
1963
1964
1967
1969
1970
1971
1972
1973
1974
1975
1976
1977
1978
1979
1980
1981
1982
1983
1984
1985
1986
1987
1988
1989
1990
1991
1992
1993
1994
1995
1996
1997
1998
1999
2000
2001
2002
2003
2004
2005
2006

Through radio soaps, which were completely created and narrated by the women, personal stories were recreated and broadcast in the market; the stories were about migration to the cities, the barrio's lack of urban facilities, working conditions and the association's internal conflicts.

The popular weekly programs began reaching many other barrios of Lima. Women's programs provided community services and support to organizational activities. Women assumed a leadership role in their communities, and by 1985, the elected board of the association consisted entirely of women (for a detailed description, see Alfaro 1988b and Chapter 18). Women in a variety of social movements (for the improvement of living conditions, reproductive rights, environmental issues, peace and human rights) have sought alternative ways of communication to support their social struggles, advocate and defend their rights, promote group reflection, awaken women's consciousness to their subordinate position in society and diffuse their own forms of representation. Women in this framework constitute subjects of struggle and change.

The framework is built around an oppositional and a proactive communication alternative that influences language, representations and communication technologies used by women. Alternative communication encourages the development of alternatives to commercial media and to the vertical, one-way, dominant communication system, while it supports the creation of local group participatory processes of solidarity and identity and the active production of cultural meanings from oppressed groups (Puntel 1992; Roncagliolo 1991). The horizontal communication model proposed in the alternative approach is based on the principles of community access to media production and decision making. It is intended to promote dialogue and a cyclical communication that does not distinguish between senders and receivers. Consequently, the communication process generates a multidirectional flow of messages.

In these approaches, participation is viewed as both a dimension of, and a condition for, social change. Women's participation in communication activities is seen as a way of empowering them to struggle and defend their rights. Participation constitutes a measure of a group's control over the process and their involvement in most, if not all, the stages of planning, design, production and diffusion. Empowerment refers to the individual and collective capacity and right to transform and affect change. The recognition of power differences in society implies that empowerment is not a matter of individuals controlling economic and political conditions, but rather of their joining social movements and struggles for the transformation of these conditions.

A common denominator that defines alternative communication practices is the struggle for democracy (Ambrosi 1991). Ambrosi defines democracy as a practice of freedom to define one's own present and future history. In the context of social movements this conception of democracy is seen as a collective project; a collective practice of freedom and government by the people. Democracy in communications involves the right to acquire and produce information (Gómez 1990) and the opening of spaces for the construction of people's (popular) cultural spaces (Alfaro 1988a).

From this understanding of democracy, alternative communication approaches see the democratization of communication as a crucial struggle that will respond to the needs of all to transmit and receive information and to see their views and groups represented in the media.

The Latin American view that the democratization of information would not succeed without a democratization of societies is particularly relevant here. Latin Americans have argued that to achieve the desired levels of democratization, communication activities would have to be implemented within those spheres of society where the control of information rests with the people and their organizations. The democratization views contained in the *MacBride Report*[3] would never be reached if systems of political repression, censorship and coercion of expression were prevalent. They emphasized that information and communication were not separate from the global social context and that their democratization was part of the struggle against oppressive structures (Kaplún 1984; Roncagliolo 1982).

There are a number of regional frameworks that can be identified here: popular communication, group communication, critical-consciousness approaches and political community action. These frameworks, besides encouraging the development of original participatory communication experiences at the regional or local level, share an assessment of the inequalities and imbalances inherent in national and international information and communication orders. The views contained in the *MacBride Report* regarding changes in the international information and communication order needed to guarantee democratic, horizontal communication and information exchange, are shared and advocated by these approaches.

POPULAR COMMUNICATION

Popular communication developed in the South and particularly in Latin America. Popular-communication initiatives aim at providing a language and an infrastructure of communication that are owned and controlled by the people.

This communicative strategy fosters women's organization and mobilization to create their own expressive channels, manifesting their nonconformity and demands (Moore 1986). The Popular Women's Union of Loja, Ecuador, is a grassroots organization working to improve the living conditions of its 1,500 members. The union promotes the organization of women to defend their rights and to develop skills and nonformal education activities. The popular communication promoted among women starts from the analysis of their own reality and leads to involvement in struggles to change their situation (Puntel 1992). Popular communication refers not only to media but to the communication that occurs among popular groups (peasants, women and workers).

Popular media are those produced, owned and operated by nonprofessionals (White 1987). Initiatives with women have used a variety of communication media, such as the cassette forum, to present material of community interest. Participants are encouraged to interact with the tape and to share their views with the forum. Other communication media used are cartoons, which provide material for reflection and discussion, and sound slides, which involve women in theme identification, research and script development, photography and editing. Radio and video production of informational programs, documentaries, dramas and forums that are concerned with women's issues (health, violence against women and human rights), local information and conflicts are widely used.

Popular-communication processes are seen as participatory processes committed to social organization and mobilization. Popular-communication methodology starts at the local level from an analysis of the individual's historical situation. Analysis of the historical reality brings and transforms individual awareness and consciousness, leading to action and, therefore, involvement in social struggles and movements. These approaches are used by grassroots organizations. ...

Group Media

The concept of group media has been actively used in Latin America, Africa and Asia, particularly in the Philippines and India. Group media refers to the use of posters, sound-slide productions, cartoons, audiocassette productions and rural newspapers developed by

---

3   In 1977, UNESCO established a commission to address problems of communication and information flow. This commission produced the *MacBride Report*, which identified the unbalanced distribution of information flow, the concentration of ownership in media industries, and the need to promote a more balanced and free flow of information. The report argued for the need to create a new world information and communication order and called on state and media institutions to enable its development by instituting democratic policies and creating national news agencies (see Puntel 1992; Roncagliolo 1992).

1927
1960
1963
1964
1967
1969
1970
1971
1972
1973
1974
1975
1976
1977
1978
1979
1980
1981
1982
1983
1984
1985
1986
1987
1988
1989
1990
1991
1992
1993
1994
1995
1996
1997
1998
1999
2000
2001
2002
2003
2004
2005
2006

small groups. The main goal of group media is to foster group interaction through media production and communication around the life situations of group members and the sharing of personal experiences. This sharing helps group media to identify common endeavors and actions (Ambroise 1987; Muller 1987). In the Philippines, for example, community and group media have been used to offer alternative systems by bringing the information disseminated by mass media several steps further, by explaining the relevance of the information to the lives of the people (Muller 1987). For this process to happen, small, cohesive and active groups need to be in place.

Group-media and critical-consciousness approaches apply similar strategies and methods, based on the goals of individual and group liberation from their oppressed condition. They evolved from the method of conscientization that is described as the bringing of the individual to critical reflection about his or her life conditions and situation. Based on the framework of Freire and liberation theology, communication and educational work is seen as awakening the individual's consciousness to his or her situation of oppression, by community animation and activation or organizational process and social change (Freire 1970; Muller 1987). The recognition of oppression leads the individual and group to become agents of change.…

Deza (1989) described this process within a Philippine fishing community. As part of a community-organizing strategy, a local communication center used group media such as posters and sound slides to support community organizing and to provide tools for reflection. The fishing community, which was facing a degeneration of its living conditions, was invited to produce the sound slides with the support of the local center. Deza (1989) described how the process of media production became a process of consciousness raising. From an initial stage of apathy, the group moved to an involvement in the identification of the community problems that would be raised by the sound slides. Participants became precritical when they identified themselves as part of the problem as well as its solution, moving then to a liberation stage, at which they expressed commitment to community organization. This growth process ran parallel to the process by which the group developed the message and final media product. …

Community Media

Participatory communication for political-community action aims to provide the means to express the claims and protests of communities and the advocacy of their rights. In 1981, residents from the small town of Cardedeu created the first local television in Catalunya. Today there are 94 television stations created by citizens' groups that act as networks linking the various community groups, providing alternative information and promoting and developing the Catalan language and cultural identity. Based on the principles of flexibility, informality and pluralism, the television stations are used by a variety of social groups: senior citizens, women, children, artists, political and environmental activists and Latin American and African immigrants (see Rodriguez 1990).

Community media have been developed mainly in North America and Europe. The concept of community media was defined by Lewis (1984) as "communication for the democratic exercise, respecting the rights of the people as subjects and participants in the actions and processes in which communication media are involved" (p. 235). Lewis also noted that the notion of community used in this approach originated in the mid-1960s in the industrialized West when capitalist states "could afford to tolerate and contain decentralized initiatives" (p. 235).

Community media offer an alternative to and an expansion of the services of the mass commercial media or state. Access and participation are the two main tenets of community-media production, and they are specifically related to the concept of citizens in the public sphere and their capacity and right to access the public resource of media systems.

So participation is largely associated with access to media and is seen as a form of democracy. Participation implies the public's involvement in the production and management of these communication systems, including decision making and planning (Kennedy 1989; Lewis 1984). However, this understanding of access and participation implies that the possible publics will have equal conditions of access to media. This assumption disregards the specific and marginal conditions of many social groups, their little knowledge of media organizations and economic and social power, and their lack of media skills and required professional competencies. Jankowski, Yos and Brouwer (1989) presented the notion of affirmative access to counterbalance this view. This notion recognizes imbalances of access and focuses on identifying, giving priority to and training marginalized groups.

The experiences reviewed here formulate a number of questions to the alternative-communications framework, identifying some gaps and limitations in addressing gender, cultural, race and class issues. For example, the enthusiasm for the empowering potential of participatory communication practices has fostered a view of participation as a salvation strategy that operationalizes communication alternatives and activates consciousness. The danger with this view is that it instrumentalizes participation and reduces empowerment to an end in itself, while disregarding the power and conflict dimensions in which processes of participation take place and are negotiated (Lozare 1989).

Another problem arises from the main goals of these approaches, which are defined in terms of non-tangible outcomes such as learning, consciousness raising and so on. These experiences tend to be weak in fostering social action for the improvement of economic conditions and for obtaining tangible changes (La Belle 1987). In light of worsening living conditions and social crises in many parts of the Third World and for poor and working-class people in the North, this disconnection between educational goals and tangible changes can reduce the trust that participants or communities have in the benefits of a participatory process. The global crisis of an increased gap between the rich and the poor, increased state repression of social movements, the inability of states to respond to their constituencies, the magnitude of the environmental and health crisis, the increase of conflicts around ethnic and territorial issues, and the rapidly changing conditions of daily life, continuously challenges simplistic associations and formulates new dilemmas for concepts such as empowerment and participation.

As group processes of media and communication production develop and evolve, uses and potentials of participation raise issues. Alfaro argues that the development of grassroots leadership skills and the appearance in the public discourse of the voices of the powerless are not necessarily indicators of effective grassroots participation. There is a need to look further to the models of leadership…for example, whether the women's movement's exercise of leadership is a democratic one, what the content of the popular discourses is, the nature of the representations held by women in their communication productions, the ways leaders and movements use and control communication media, and the ways the facilitators intervene and assume or manage their differences (of gender, race, class and status) in the process.

Feminist Communication: Gender in Participatory Communication

Gender has not been considered an analytical dimension in the frameworks mentioned above (see McAnany and Storey 1989; Nair and White 1987a, 1987b, 1987c; O'Connor 1989; Riaño 1990, 1991). References to gender are limited to identifying the gender of the participants and to describing the subordinate position of women in their communities and societies. Neither the ways gender influences the nature of participation and communication production, nor the mediation of gender in women's and men's experiences of subordination has been taken into serious consideration.

1927
1960
1963
1964
1967
1969
1970
1971
1972
1973
1974
1975
1976
1977
1978
1979
1980
1981
1982
1983
1984
1985
1986
1987
1988
1989
1990
1991
1992
1993
1994
1995
1996
1997
1998
1999
2000
2001
2002
2003
2004
2005
2006

Although much of the communication work of women's groups and feminists is inspired by the principles of alternative communications (Steiner 1992), their works are distinguished by the inclusion of a gender perspective. This perspective influences not only their goals and agendas but also their communication strategies and methodologies. …

Periodicals by women of color in the United States offer an analysis of racism, class and gender oppression from the perspective of black, Hispanic, Asian-American, American Indian, Alaska Native and Pacific Islander. Working under a collective structure and using a variety of formats such as newsletters, magazines and bulletins, the women who run these periodicals are women of color who publish for women of color (Kranich 1989). Women's participation in this framework is attached to the goal of enhancing processes of speaking about gender, race, class and other oppressions. It also involves the negotiation of fair representation and equal participation of women. …

In these approaches, participation in communication projects and media production is seen as a project of naming their own experiences and identities. Participation enhances the process of coming out, of speaking about the oppression faced as individuals and as members of a group, and the carrying out of actions designed to achieve social change (Kidd 1992). Participation also names a project of inclusion that acknowledges differences of race, gender, class and sexual orientation. Empowerment involves the transformation of women as social subjects of struggle and as active producers of meaning.

References

Alfaro, R. "Producers of Communication: What is the Proposition? *Group Media Journal*, 1988a, 7 (2): 10-15.

Alfaro, R. *De la Conquista de la Ciudad a la Apropiación de la Palabra. Una Experienca de Educación Popular y Comunicación con Mujeres*. Lima, Peru: Calandria, 1988b.

Ambroise, R. (1987). Towards a dynamic group media training strategy. *Group Media Journal*, 1987, 6 (3): 9-10.

Ambrosi, A. "Alternative Communication and Development Alternative." In N. Thede and A. Ambrosi, eds., *Video: the Changing World*. Montreal: Black Rose, 1991.

Ansah, P. "The Right to Communicate: Implications for Development." *Media Development*, 1992, 39 (1): 53-56.

Belbase, S. "Video Survey: Do Rural People Learn From Video?" *Media Asia*, 1988, 15 (2): 108-112.

Belbase, S. "Participatory Communication for Development: How Can We Achieve It?" Paper presented at the Seminar on Participation: A Key Concept for Change and Development. Pune, India: University of Poona, February 1989.

Bernard, A. "Learning and Intervention: The Informal Transmission of Knowledge and Skills of Development." *Perspectives on Education for All*. Ottawa, Ontario, Canada: IRDC, Manuscipt Report 295e, 1991, 30-766.

Burkert, C. "Videoletters in an Ancient Land." *Development Forum*, November-December 1989a: 14.

Burkert, C. "Videoletters." *Development Communication Report*, 1989b, 1 (64): 13.

Deshler, D., and D. Sock. "Community Development Participation: A Concept Review of the International Literature." Paper presented at the International League for Social Commitment in Adult Education. Sweden, 1985.

Deza, A. "Media Production and the Process of Becoming in the Context of Community-Building." Paper presented at the Seminar on Participation: A Key Concept for Change and Development, Pune, India: University of Poona, February 1989.

Freire, P. *Pedagogy of the Oppressed*. New York: Continuum, 1970.

Gómez, R. "Popular Video in the Democratization of Communication." Unpublished manuscript. University of Montreal, 1990.

Griffiths, M. "How to Improve Child Well-Being? First Increase Mother's Self-Confidence." *Development Communication Report*, 1990, 79 (3): 7-8, 18.

Hornik, R. *Development Communication.: Information, Agriculture and Nutrition in the Third World*. New York: Longman, 1988.

Jankowski, N., K. Vos, and W. Brouwer. "Training Dutch Citizen Groups in Video Production Techniques." *Media Development*, 1989 4: 22-26.

Jurmo, P. "Participation: Do Villagers Really Want It?" *Reports Magazine*, 1980, 21: 20-22.

Kaplún, M. *Comunicación Entre Grupos. El Métedo del Cassette Foro*. TS45. Ottawa, Ontario, Canada: IDRC, 1984.

Kennedy, T. "Community Animation. An Open-Ended Process." *Media Development*, 1989, 36 (3): 5-7.

Kidd, D. "Alternate Media, Critical Consciousness and Action: The Beginnings of a Conversation About Women and Grassroots Media." Unpublished manuscript. Burnaby, British Columbia, Canada: Simon Fraser University, 1992.

Kindervatter, S. "Non-Formal Education as an Empowering Process." Amherst, Mass.: Center for International Education, University of Massachusetts, 1979.

Kranich, K. "Celebrating Our Diversity. Women of Color Periodicals: 1968-1988." In M. Allen, *Directory of Women's Media*. Washington, D.C.: Women's Institute of the Freedom of the Press, 1989, 86.

La Belle, T. "From Consciousness Raising to Popular Education in Latin America and the Caribbean." *Comparative Education Review*, 1987, 31 (2): 201-217.

Lewis, P., ed. *Media for People in Cities. A Study of Community Media in the Urban Context.* Paris: UNESCO, 1984.

Lozare, B. "Power and Conflict: Hidden Dimensions of Communication, Participative Planning and Action." Paper presented at the Seminar on Participation: A Key Concept for Change and Development. Puna, India: University of Poona, February 1989.

McAnany, E., and D. Storey. "Development Communication: A Reappraisal for the 1990s." Paper presented at the International and Intercultural Division of the 39th Annual Conference of the International Communication Association. San Francisco: May 1989.

McKee, N. "Social Marketing in International Development: A Critical Review." Unpublished master's thesis. Tallassee, Fla.: Florida State University, 1988.

Moore, S. "Participatory Communication in the Development Process." *The Third Channel,* 1986, 2 (2): 587-623.

Muller, K. "The Group Media in the Next Five Years." *Group Media Journal,* 1987, 6 (3): 20-21.

Nair, K., and S. White. "Participation is the Key to Development Communication." *Media Development*, 1987a, 3: 36-40.

Nair, K., & White, S. (1987b). *Participatory message development: A conceptual framework.* Paper presented at the International Seminar of Development Communication, National Institute of Rural Development, Rajendranagar, Hyderabad, India.

Nair, K., and S. White. "A Conceptualization of Development Communication Concepts." Paper presented at Communication and Change: An Agenda for the New Age of Communication. East-West Center, Honolulu, Hawaii: East-West Center, July 1987c.

O'Connor, A. "People's Radio in Latin America—A New Assessment." *Media Development*, 1989: 47-51.

Pigozzi, M. "Participation in Non-Formal Education Projects: Some Possible Negative Outcomes." *Convergence*, 1992, 15 (3): 6-16.

Protz, M. *Seeing and Showing Ourselves: A Guide to Using Small-Format Video as a Participatory Tool for Development.* Centre for Development of Instructional Technology, 1991.

Puntel, J. "The Catholic Church and the Democratization of Communication in Latin America." Unpublished Ph.D. dissertation. Burnaby, British Columbia, Canada: Simon Fraser University, 1992.

Riaño, P. *Empowering Through Communication: Women's Experiences With Participatory Communication in Development Process.* Manuscript Report 278e. Ottawa, Ontario, Canada: IDRC, 1990.

Riaño, P. "Myths of the Silenced: Women and Grassroots Communication." *Media Development*, 1991, 38 (2): 20-22.

Rodríguez, C. "Media for Participation and Social Change: Local Television in Catalonia. *CommDev News*, 1990: 4-10.

Roncagliolo, R. "El NOMIC: Communicación y Poder." *Chasqui,* 1982, 3: 26-33.

Roncogliolo, R. "Notes on "the Alternative." In N. Thede and A. Ambrosi, eds., *Video the Changing World.* Montreal: Black Rose, 1991, 206-208.

Sénécal, M. "The Alternative Search of Its Identity." In N. Thede and A. Ambrosi, ibid., 209-218.

Servaes, J. "The Role and Place of Research in Participatory Communication Projects." Paper presented at the Seminar on Participation: A Key Concept for Change and Development. Pune, India: University of Poona, February 1989.

Steiner, L. "The History and Structure of Women's Alternative Media." In L. Rakow, ed., *Women Making Meaning. New Feminist Directions in Communications.* New York: Routledge, 1992, 121-143.

White, R. "From Group Communication to Comunicacíon Popular." Discussion paper prepared for the Board of Consultants, Sonolux. London: Centre of the Study of Communication and Culture, October 1987.

White, S. "Participation: A Key Concept in Communication for Change and Development." Background document to the Seminar on Participation. Pune, India: University of Poona, February 1989.

Williamson, H. A. "The Fogo Process: Development Support Communication in Canada and the Developing World." In F. L. Casmir, ed., *Communication in Development.* Hilldale, N.J.: Ablex, 1991, 270-288.

Yacoob, M. "Women and Water: The Bucket Starts Here." *Development Communication Report*, 1990, 70 (3): 6, 17.

1927
1960
1963
1964
1967
1969
1970
1971
1972
1973
1974
1975
1976
1977
1978
1979
1980
1981
1982
1983
1984
1985
1986
1987
1988
1989
1990
1991
1992
1993
1994
1995
1996
1997
1998
1999
2000
2001
2002
2003
2004
2005
2006

WORDS FROM THE HEART: THE POWER OF ORAL TESTIMONY

Excerpt from: Listening for a Change: Oral Testimony and Development

By Hugo Slim and Paul Thomson

1994 Words from the heart are more alive than your scribblings. When we speak, our words burn.[1] There has always been a special power in direct speech. The raw recounting of experience has an authenticity and persuasiveness which it is hard to match, and most of us would rather hear someone speak directly than read about them through another's words. Even on the printed page, passages of speech tend to attract our attention: first-person testimony is simply more engaging than impersonal commentary or interpretation.

The spoken word cuts across barriers of wealth, class and race. It is as much the prerogative of ordinary people as of those in positions of power and authority. It requires neither formal education, nor the ability to read and write, nor fluency in any national or official language. Most importantly, it gives voice to the experience of those people whose views are often overlooked or discounted. The significance of this cannot be overestimated. To ignore these voices is to ignore a formidable body of evidence and information.

This article explores ways of listening to the voice and experience of ordinary people. In so doing, it seeks to outline a variety of methods through which those involved in development—from policy makers to project workers—can gain a better understanding of the concerns and priorities, culture and experiences of the people with whom they wish to work. Above all, oral testimony can give those communities more power to set their own agenda for development.

Since much of the book from which this text is taken concentrates on the issues which arise from the collection, interpretation and preservation of oral testimony, it is vital to consider how project workers can transmit what they hear and apply what they learn. Without a thorough understanding of the issues involved in this process, listening to people and recording their words can too easily become a purely archival or voyeuristic pursuit, or an exercise in knowledge extraction.

Acting on Listening

The role of listener comes with certain obligations. A reciprocal exchange is required in which what is heard is both given back and carried forward. People's testimony must be treated with respect. The origins and ownership of the spoken word should always be honoured, either by recognising authorship or by guaranteeing anonymity.

By applying what is heard in partnership with those who voice it, collecting and communicating oral testimony can become a cooperative exercise in social action. The implications are exciting and far-reaching. It can lead to a critique of development policies, or to improved strategies for responding to famine and refugee crises. It can give rise to a more relevant school or training curriculum, the evaluation and adaptation of traditional agricultural practices or the mounting of a land rights campaign. It can encourage a more effective response to the particular circumstances of women or improved health care for children or the elderly. Whatever the outcome, it is important that the process of listening does eventually result in acknowledgement and action, and that those who have given up their time to talk know that their words have been taken seriously. This notion of "applied" oral testimony is what gives the listening process a particular relevance to development and differentiates it from a purely academic study.

---

1   H. Watson, *Women in the City of the Dead*, London: C. Hurst and Co., 1999, p. 11.

Making Development Accountable

At the heart of this principle of applied oral testimony is a challenge to the development establishment. The inclusion of direct testimony in the development debate can help to make it less of a monologue and more of a dialogue, as people's testimony begins to require answers and as their voices force the development establishment to be more accountable for their actions. In short, it is not enough for the development "expert" to summarise and interpret the views of others—the "others" must be allowed to speak for themselves.

"Accountability" and "transparency" may well be the buzzwords of development into the next decade. Bringing the voice and experience of poor people to bear on development issues will, however, be the acid test for whether these words achieve anything more than buzz status. A wide variety of development agencies from the World Bank to small non-government organisations (NGOs) are making increasing efforts to canvass the views and opinions of people in areas where they intervene. Such feedback undoubtedly highlights the immense difficulties and complexities inherent in creating sustainable patterns of development. But if these voices are ignored, then much development will continue by default to support or create further inequalities.

The concept of "listening to the people" is by no means new to the development establishment. Participation and consultation have been at the heart of most of what has been considered progressive and effective in the field to date. Similarly, the attempt to be heard is not a new one [new idea] on the part of the so-called beneficiaries of aid. Over the past three decades of development, they have tried in many ways to raise their voice above the clamour of debate that has raged around them. All too often, however, planners and policymakers hear only what they want to, and adopt methods of listening which ignore the more challenging or awkward views and testimonies. And even if people's attempts to talk and to listen are successful at field level, donors, governments and policymakers still have to be convinced.

Without the political will to take account of the results of such an exchange, people will be poorly rewarded for giving others the benefit of their time and thoughts.

A Voice in the Development Debate

Speaking out is an act of power, and the act of listening demands respect for the speaker. But listening is also an art based on certain fundamental principles which are also at the heart of any notion of just and cooperative development. Interviewing is not just a practical mechanism for gathering information. It needs the human skills of patience, humility, willingness to learn from others and to respect views and values which you may not share. As a listener, your sources are not dead documents or statistics, but living people and you have to be able to work together.

Hidden Voices

One of the reasons why poor communities are so seldom heard is because of the documentary bias—the bias of the written word—which exists at all the key stages of development planning, implementation and evaluation. People are not consulted enough because the main debates take place in documents which they do not write, or in meetings which they do not attend. Bringing together what people say and think in the form of oral testimony, and then communicating those testimonies, is one way of correcting a bias which runs through the whole development debate and dictates the majority of development initiatives. It is a way of giving volume and power to the voices of people who are outside the development establishment and of ensuring that they are heard.

If being poor means having less of a voice, then being the poorest of the poor means being the most silent of all. Even within the ranks of the disadvantaged, there are individuals and groups who—if they are remembered at all—tend to be "spoken for" and often misrepresented. The collective voice of any community tends towards generalisations, simplifications or halftruths and is dominated by the loudest voices. Like the official document, the community view will tend

1927
1960
1963
1964
1967
1969
1970
1971
1972
1973
1974
1975
1976
1977
1978
1979
1980
1981
1982
1983
1984
1985
1986
1987
1988
1989
1990
1991
1992
1993
1994
1995
1996
1997
1998
1999
2000
2001
2002
2003
2004
2005
2006

to concentrate on the concerns of the wealthy, the political elite, and social and religious leaders.

Listening to individual testimonies acts as a counterpoint to generalisations and provides important touchstones against which to review the collective version. It gives development workers access to the views and experience of more marginalised groups, such as the elderly, women, ethnic minorities, the disabled and children. Bringing in these hidden voices allows a much more subtle appreciation of the divisions and alliances within societies.

Sometimes the hidden voices are the most important of all. In many societies, it has been common for men to take the dominant role in public life, but for women to be the anchors of the household and farm economy. Yet there is an equally widespread prejudice which tends to reduce what women speak about to the realm of "gossip," while the same bias elevates men's talk to the status of serious and constructive discussion. Indeed, there are important differences in patterns of talking and listening which affect not only the way in which men and women talk, but also the times and places in which it is socially acceptable for them to speak. Men may speak out in public places, in front of people and in the centre of the town or village. Women tend to talk together "backstage"—in private places, in the home or at communal places of work. For men, talking is often a legitimate and valued activity in itself—a mark of stature and a social responsibility. For women, talking is rarely something they can make time to do for its own sake, but is more often an activity to be carried out alongside others—while working, cooking or looking after children.

Thus in many communities, men's social responsibility as the official communicators permits them to step forward and "speak for the team," as American soci linguist Deborah Tannen has pointed out.[2] This often involves them in speaking for women about things that they, as men, may know very little about, such as child-rearing, health care, women's roles in agriculture and marketing, fuel and water collection. Men may also speak for women when it is religiously or culturally unacceptable for women to talk to men or strangers.

This gender imbalance between public and private talk means that in most societies men's voices are heard over and above women's, and it makes the role of oral testimony collection even more important as a way of redressing that balance. The relative silence of women in many societies means that listening to them should be a priority. Special attention should be paid to women's oral artistry, which manifests itself most powerfully in working songs, stories and proverbs. Such artistry is particularly resonant of the reality of women's lives, a reality which can never truly be depicted, and is more likely to be distorted, when described by men. In this context—and in all attempts to listen to the hidden voices of society—the words of the American feminist Dale Spender are relevant: "Reality is constructed and sustained primarily by those who talk ... those who control the talk are also those who are able to control reality."[3]

At community level, therefore, the testimony of individual voices reveals the experience of hidden groups, and counters the bias of those who speak for or ignore them. It has the capacity to break down generalisations and misinformation about communities, their economies, needs, power structures, social organisation and goals. While this may complicate the design of relief and development projects, it may ultimately make them more equitable and effective.

Hidden Spheres

In the same way that oral testimony can give voice to hidden groups, it also provides the opportunity to describe hidden spheres of experience, particularly aspects of private and cultural life which might be missed out in a routine development analysis. Economic factors do not exist in a vacuum. Social

2 D. Tannen, *You Just Don't Understand: Women and Men in Conversation*, London: Virago, 1992, Chapter 3.

3 D. Spender, *Man-Made Language*, London: Routledge and Kegan Paul, 1980.

relationships reflect and influence economic and political ones, and an improved understanding of the former can shed light on the latter. The various forms of oral testimony give people the chance to voice their experience of family and work relationships, of friendship, love, sexuality, childbirth, parenting and leisure, culture and religion. These aspects of life, which are central to anyone's understanding of his or her world, are often overlooked in project feasibility studies, which tend to take a mechanistic view of communities, their needs and possible solutions. Yet people are more likely to take part in something they value and believe in, and are more willing to invest their time and resources in what is feasible within their current social obligations.

Hidden Connections

Individuals' own accounts of their lives and experiences usually paint a much fuller picture than most development planners and project workers look for. Above all, personal testimonies connect the various spheres of life, such as family and work, or health and income, which professionals tend to separate. Relief and development planning is often affected by a kind of intersectoral blindness, the myopia of the specialist. The various technical disciplines or professions of development workers mean that they often tackle community development in sectors: health, agriculture, economics, nutrition, law, psychology and so on. People's first-hand accounts of their lives and experiences tend to flow to and fro between sectors, and to stress the connections rather than the differences. All aspects of a life are intertwined, but it often takes direct communication, rather than a completed survey form, to remind specialists of this fact.

Such testimony obliges development workers to think across sectors and take an interdisciplinary approach. As people's experiences of famine testify, food aid is not the clear-cut solution to starvation that it seems. Survival is about much more than material relief. As women's voices have made clear, the need for supplies of clean water is not just about health, it is about time

and labour, distance and power. Personal testimonies about HIV infection and AIDS reveal that the issue is not just medical, and the consequences are not confined to illness, death and grief, but include far wider social and economic costs.

Cooperation, Confidence and Consciousness

The process of talking and listening is potentially an extremely cooperative and participatory one. If it is going well, people are involved, in the fullest sense, in the narration of their experience and the analysis of their situation. Moreover, the collection, interpretation and presentation of oral testimony can become a genuinely communal venture. In addition to the primary role of narrators, people may also become involved as interviewers, or as interpreters of information, or in the presentation and transmission of their own or others' words through publications, radio, theatre or exhibitions. The collection of oral testimony is a process that can involve a whole community.

Speaking up is a sign of confidence; being listened to increases that confidence. In many projects where people have come together to voice their ideas and experience, an increased sense of community and of social consciousness has emerged. Voicing something begins to make it concrete and therefore more possible. It also starts a process of sharing, and this pooling of experience can in turn generate or strengthen a sense of social cohesion.

The process can be not only therapeutic, but also assertive. People who begin to voice their personal or group experience can begin to understand it and to act on it. This sense of the spoken word marking the beginning of things is fundamental to many cultures where naming things is often a way of creating them in mythical and religious thought. Equally, on a purely individual and psychological level, speaking about a certain situation is often the first step towards addressing it.

For a group of Guatemalan refugee women in Mexico, narrating their life stories to one another and speaking out about the problems of their isolation was the beginning of a broader mental health programme which eventually supported a wide network of refugee families. In Egypt, a group of migrant women coming to terms with their new life in Cairo's City of the Dead found their regular storytelling sessions, based on their personal histories, played a crucial part in sustaining practical bonds of friendship and support between them and their families.[4] The case study of urban Brazilian communities illustrates how such a process can mobilise a whole community in a struggle for rights and recognition.

Equal Idioms

A central part of any attempt at listening is a commitment to accept the idiom of the people who are talking. This automatically contributes to a more equal relationship. Too often the poor and powerless are further disadvantaged by having to conform to the language and communication methods of those who hold power. Oral testimony reverses this trend. Ideally, it should take place in the speaker's mother tongue and interviewers should respect traditional ways of communicating, instead of imposing "vertical" systems, such as questionnaires and surveys, or insisting on use of the official language. In this way the collection of oral testimony shifts the burden of translation and understanding back to the listener, and begins to balance the scales in the communication process. It gives people the opportunity to express themselves in their own terms, employing their language, relating their history, their stories, traditions, songs, theatre and all that goes to make up the repertoire with which individuals communicate among themselves and with others.

Listening to people's oral testimony involves accepting this kind of "horizontal" communication, and then finding ways of preserving, translating and communicating it onwards to a wider and different audience. The latter process has its risks and pitfalls, but it is at least more equitable than any top-down or non-consultative approach.

Moreover, the process of listening reverses the roles of expert and pupil which have become all too typical of relations between development worker and so-called beneficiary. In collecting oral testimony, the interviewer sits at the feet of people who are obviously the experts on their own lives and experiences. This role reversal, and the process of listening, can generate greater mutual respect and a more equal and collaborative relationship. SOS Sahel, a development organisation which ran the three-year Sahel Oral History Project, found that:

> Not the least of the benefits of employing oral history methods in a development context is the impact on project workers, nearly all of whom have acquired valuable new insights ... [and have identified the value] of taking the time to learn, through interviews, as much as possible from individual life stories and reflections.[5]

Development is not an exact science: to date it has been riddled with misunderstandings, failed experiments and discarded theories. But it is increasingly recognised that one of the most damaging aspects of the aid industry has been the tendency of donors to impose their own theories of what constitutes development on the recipients. In this book we aim to identify some useful ways in which the voices of ordinary people may "burn" more brightly, so that it is their priorities and concerns which inform the development debate.

Hugo Slim and Paul Thomson. *Listening for a Change: Oral Testimony and Development*. London: Panos, 1994. Copyright © 1994, Panos Institute. Reprinted with permission.

---

4   H. Watson, op. cit.

5   N. Cross, and R. Baker, eds., *At the Desert's Edge: Oral Histories From the Sahel,* London: Panos Books, 1991, p. 16

VARIETIES OF ORAL EVIDENCE

Excerpt from: Listening for a Change: Oral Testimony and Development

By Hugo Slim and Paul Thomson

1994 There are many forms through which people may express their experiences and transmit interpretations of life: songs and legends, stories and plays; traditional accounts of community or family history passed down from generation to generation; simple personal life stories, recollections and memories. Oral testimonies can be collected individually or in groups. They can focus entirely on the past; or they can provide evidence about more recent events and articulate future plans and aspirations.

Broadly speaking, the different forms can be divided into three groups: oral history, oral tradition (which includes oral artistry) and life stories. For our purposes, these overlapping and closely related categories are often subsumed under the general term "oral testimony," but it is worth understanding some of the different purposes, emphases and techniques in each form of oral evidence.

Oral History

The simplest definition of oral history would be "the living memory of the past." Everyone has a story to tell of his or her own life, which offers invaluable raw material for the history of this century. These stories provide a direct account of times of unprecedented change through the men and women who experienced them. If they remain untapped, such living memories are lost forever. Since the 1940s, professional historians in the North have been recording them as archives for the future and using them as evidence to complement or counterbalance more traditional or official sources.

While in the North, oral history is in this sense one of the newest forms of historical work, it is also the oldest: in both the North and the South, its roots go back as far as can be traced.

The first great "histories" of the ancient world in Europe—by Homer, Herodotus, Tacitus—drew on both oral tradition (stories of the past handed down from generation to generation) and direct personal witness. For before the spread of writing, all social knowledge, including history, had to be handed on from memory by word of mouth.

In the North, the role of oral history in both popular culture and professional practice shrank as literacy spread. It probably reached its lowest point earlier this century, when written or printed communication was paramount. In Britain in the Victorian age, pioneers such as Henry Mayhew in his London Labour and the London Poor (1861-62) had shown the extraordinary power of directly quoting the voices of poor women and men in conveying the message of a social inquiry, but such instances remained very rare.

The revival of oral history in the North is a result of two fundamental social changes since the 1940s. The first is in the technology of communication. One hundred years ago, the news and public opinion were conveyed by printed newspaper, and personal thought by letter: even a prime minister might write two dozen letters by hand in a day. But for documenting the present, written documents cannot be enough. In the North today, television, radio and spoken and visual communication have become more powerful than the printed word. People telephone rather than write letters—and a telephone call leaves no record for the archive. Few people keep regular diaries, beyond noting appointments. Most people watch television for news and entertainment rather than read newspapers and books. And although the success of the fax machine may see some return to writing rather than phoning, the whole balance in communication has shifted back towards the oral and visual. Yet this does not mean that experiences and memories need be lost to the

1927
1960
1963
1964
1967
1969
1970
1971
1972
1973
1974
1975
1976
1977
1978
1979
1980
1981
1982
1983
1984
1985
1986
1987
1988
1989
1990
1991
1992
1993
1994
1995
1996
1997
1998
1999
2000
2001
2002
2003
2004
2005
2006

historian or social investigator. On the contrary, these new technologies have brought the tape recorder and video camera, allowing the immense variety of individual experience to be captured with a unique spontaneity and vividness.

The second fundamental change in the North was the arrival of a democratic culture: not just the extension of the right to vote to all adult men and women, but the widespread advent of popularly elected governments, and the expansion of welfare policies and of trade union influence. Working-class movements began to get at least a measure of their share of the seats of power. And because the voices of ordinary men and women now counted much more, the establishment began to take them seriously. By the 1950s, sociologists in the North were studying working-class culture in its own right, rather than simply seeing the poor as an aberration from, and threat to, "civilised" society. At the same time, historians increasingly recognised the partial nature of a discipline which concentrated on the elite and began to turn to labour history, to social history and to family history—and finally, with the women's movement, to women's history.

In many parts of the South, pressure from independence movements, combined with these shifts of attitude in the North, brought about the breakup of imperialism, and with it precisely the same shift of focus by historians from the colonial elite to the people of the newly independent nations. Independence, moreover, had often been preceded by a liberation struggle, ill-documented at the time, but now evidently crucial. The most recent countries to experience such a radical shift of focus are those of southern Africa. Mothers of the Revolution, for example, presents the story of Zimbabwe's war of liberation "from the inside"—through the first-hand accounts of the women who kept their families, homes and villages going during the fighting.[1]

Technological modernity and democratic inclusiveness are thus key characteristics of the oral history movement. It is now possible to capture the spoken word for the future, and transmit it across continents to vast audiences. In this, oral history has a power far beyond dry conventional historical writing, or the reports of statistical social surveys. It is one thing to read an academic study of Stalin; quite another to see and hear on television Russians recall their own lives as prisoners sent to the gulag, or as guards in the same camps.

Oral History and Development

By tracing the growth of oral-history practice in the North, we can see more clearly its relevance to development. Just as it helps to present a truer picture of the past by documenting the lives and feelings of all kinds of people otherwise hidden from history, so it can create a fuller understanding of the views and experience of the wide range of people too often excluded from the development debate. In addition, by allowing people to speak about any aspect of their lives, the oral-history movement opened up vital new fields of enquiry—not just hidden voices but also hidden spheres of experience. Written documentation and official records always revealed more about the concerns of the political elite than those without political influence, about landowners rather than labourers, about men rather than women, about the educated rather than the illiterate and about public rather than private life. Oral history offered new perspectives on many issues. It enabled people to examine welfare, for example, from the standpoint of those who receive it rather than those who give it out. It gave people the opportunity to talk about personal, social and cultural areas of experience. It revealed the connections between different spheres of activity, such as social and working life, and how, for example, working practices can influence patterns of family life.

A few other notable characteristics of oral history are especially relevant to development work. In the North, it has had a particular impact in the form of community history. This has been practised in a variety of

1   I. Staunton, ed., *Mothers of the Revolution*, Harare, Zimbabwe: Baobab Books, 1990.

1927
1960
1963
1964
1967
1969
1970
1971
1972
1973
1974
1975
1976
1977
1978
1979
1980
1981
1982
1983
1984
1985
1986
1987
1988
1989
1990
1991
1992
1993
1994
1995
1996
1997
1998
1999
2000
2001
2002
2003
2004
2005
2006

ways, including recording old people for the publishing of local booklets, setting up tape archives, producing cassette tapes for use in schools, making radio programmes and mounting travelling exhibitions.

The special quality in oral history that has encouraged this spread of community history is that it is fundamentally cooperative. It demands a wide range of skills, and is based on technologies—old and new—which are open to everyone, which makes it particularly suited to group work.

Oral history is also concerned with making connections between the older and younger generations, as has been most clearly shown in school projects. The most impressive educational work of this kind in the North has been the Foxfire project, which began in a small town high school in rural Georgia in the southern United States. The core to this was the interviewing of the older generation by the children, who then produced a magazine based largely on the interviews. The project caught the children's imagination and at the same time taught them skills for other purposes. But Foxfire also took off as a magazine and was soon selling well beyond the community: the magazine eventually became a best-selling book, and high schools all over the country have been trying to emulate it.

In a slightly more specialised way, oral history has been used in literacy work, both with children and adults. The clue to the success of this literacy work is closely connected with the essential nature of oral history. For it has been discovered that when people are listened to, they can gain new confidence that their experiences and their perceptions are worthwhile. This came as a surprise to the modern oral historians, who had simply set out to collect material for history. But they rather quickly discovered that most of those whom they recorded found the experience of telling their story a very positive one. Self-confidence is a key element in successful literacy teaching. By starting with the recording of the student's own life story, and then gradually transferring this into writing, the process of teaching can reinforce rather than undermine

self-esteem. In Britain, where this technique has been widely used, there was for several years a magazine in which new learners could publish their work, called *Write First Time*, which gave further encouragement to the students.

Increased self-confidence is also the key to another branch of oral history work. This focuses on the elderly, especially those who live isolated lives, cut off from families and community—an increasingly common phenomenon in the North. This is known as "reminiscence work" and was pioneered by British oral historian Joanna Bornat for the NGO (non-governmental organization) Help the Aged. By stimulating and developing the memories and recollections of old people, a sense of meaning and purpose in life can be rekindled, giving people who had become almost silent something to relate and exchange with others.[2]

Raising confidence, encouraging community action and cohesion, closing the gap between generations, providing the basis for literacy programmes, revitalising those marginalised by age or any other "disadvantage": all these qualities of oral history work can be applied to development practice.

Oral Tradition

Wherever levels of literacy remain low, oral tradition continues to play a crucial social role in transmitting information, both about present custom and past practice. Mario Vargas Llosa's novel *The Storyteller* is a brilliant evocation of how, for a scattered group of Peruvian forest Indians on the upper Amazon, the elusive travelling *hablador*—as the missionaries

---

2 In all these forms, oral history has grown rapidly in the North over the last 20 years. It now has its own societies and journals in several countries, such as *Oral History* in Britain, *Bios* in Germany, *Oral History Review* in the United States and *Historia y Fuente Oral* in Spain, and a new *International Yearbook of Oral History and Life Stories* as well as regular international conferences. These developments have certainly not been confined to the North. There are regional international oral history journals funded by UNESCO in the Spanish Caribbean and in Southern Africa, as well as academics practising oral history in many Latin American and African countries, and some in the Far East. A number of African countries have state-funded oral archives, as do Indonesia, Malaysia and, most generously of all, Singapore—a model programme for both North and South.

called him—was the lifeline of a totally nonliterate society on the edge of extinction. Always on the move, he conveyed vital information of every type, from the most sacred religious truths to mere social gossip about distant neighbours.[3]

In literate societies, too, oral tradition often remains important: in Africa, many communities have specialist narrators of local traditions. Their repertoire might include the genealogies of major families, records of land inheritance and descriptions of major events such as battles, invasions, famines and drought. African oral tradition has been divided into five categories:

1. learning formulas, rituals and slogans;
2. lists of place names and personal names;
3. official and private poetry;
4. stories (historical, didactic, artistic or personal);
5. legal and other commentaries.[4]

Since the 1950s, a major school of African historical writing has developed which draws primarily on the recording and interpretation of oral tradition. Earlier colonial administrators and missionaries had recorded oral traditions, finding them both interesting and sometimes of practical value in understanding local beliefs; but historians had made no use of them, although the only written records normally at their disposal were those of the colonisers.

The pioneer of what is now a highly specialised historical technique was Jan Vansina, a Belgian who worked in the Congo. His book *Oral Tradition*, revised as *Oral Tradition as History*, is the classic text on this method.[5] It has been used to trace the political history, migration movements and agricultural and economic developments of African societies over long periods. Traditions are of course far from fixed; but in these historians' hands, changes and divergences between sources become evidence in themselves. In some of the most striking work, such as Steven

Feierman's *The Shambaa Kingdom*, anthropology and social history are fused in an account of social change up to the present, which ranges from the material practicalities of daily living to the community's symbolic understanding of the universe.[6]

Historians of Africa thus make important uses of such oral traditions. In Europe this practice is very rare: oral history is based almost entirely on direct memory and is a form of contemporary social history, constructed from personal accounts of life experience, public and private. Nevertheless, there are some social groups in Europe in whose culture oral traditions remain important. Some are surviving rural minorities, such as the mountain Protestants in France and Italy, or the Gaelic-speaking Scottish islanders who recall—as if they had witnessed them personally—the Highland clearances over 150 years ago, when they lost their lands to make way for sheep farms. More important for recent history, however, are the new generations of urban immigrants who have carried their traditions with them from the South, such as the Bengali seafarers from Sylhet, pioneer settlers of the Bangladeshi community in Britain.[7]

Social Research

The research activity of social scientists also overlaps with oral history, but whereas oral historians interview older people about the past, social scientists interview people to obtain documents for the interpretation of contemporary social change. Sometimes this is the same as oral history, sometimes not. Life story research in social science is now strongest in Europe—especially France and Germany—but the pioneers in both sociology and anthropology in the 1920s were in the United States. While British anthropologists, perhaps too influenced by the imperial manner, would sit under a sun umbrella communicating through an interpreter, and rarely used their informants' own words

---

3   M. Vargas Llosa, *The Storyteller*, London: Faber and Faber, 1991.

4   J. Vansina, *Oral Tradition as History*, London and Heinemann, Kenya: James Currey, 1985.

5   Ibid.

6   S. Feierman, *The Shambaa Kingdom*, Madison: University of Wisconsin Press, 1974.

7   C. Adams, ed., *Across Seven Seas and Thirteen Rivers: Life Stories of Pioneer Sylheti Settlers in Britain*, London: THAP Books, 1987.

in their books, American anthropologists had already begun to publish full life story autobiographies from interviews with native Indians. This was the research approach used by Oscar Lewis for his famous studies of the culture of poverty in Mexico, such as *The Children of Sanchez*[8] and *Pedro Martinez*.[9] Latin America has a notably strong and socially committed tradition of life story research.

Finally, there is the closely related area of contemporary documentation in social research. This, too, can take the form either of in-depth interviewing, or of writing. While the immediate purpose is to understand what is happening now, the dimension of change, and so of the past, is rarely absent. And, in the long run, such material can be as valuable for future historians as oral history or life story interviews. For example, in Britain the Mass Observation project was founded in 1937 to record the culture of ordinary people. Panels of diarists and essayists were recruited to record their everyday experiences and their work was stored and catalogued: it is now a unique historical resource at the University of Sussex.

Focus on the Future

This cluster of techniques, all closely related, differ in their emphasis—past or present, oral or written, personal or collective. They also have primary attachments to different disciplines. But from our point of view, to build on these distinctions would be unhelpful. Our concern is with how these various overlapping forms of "listening" can contribute to development, the primary focus of which is the future. All offer ways of documenting the currents of change, and of discovering the meaning of change and continuity in the lives of ordinary men and women; of coming closer to understanding their social consciousness and individual identity.

It is these awkwardly individual human lives, on which enduring development ultimately depends, which have too rarely informed development practice.

Instead, this has been dominated by the views and ideas of the educated elite. Priorities have been largely dictated by those in control of financial and technical resources. But technology can now be used to narrow rather than widen the gap between "the haves and the have-nots": the tape recorder has opened up a means to capture and communicate the immense variety of individual experience, and so encourage development initiatives which more closely reflect the values and priorities of those they are meant to benefit.

Hugo Slim and Paul Thomson. *Listening for a Change: Oral Testimony and Development*. London: Panos, 1994. Copyright © 1994, Panos Institute. Reprinted with permission.

---

8   O. Lewis, *The Children of Sanchez*, New York: Random House, 1961.
9   O. Lewis, *Pedro Martinez*, New York: Random House, 1964.

1927
1960
1963
1964
1967
1969
1970
1971
1972
1973
1974
1975
1976
1977
1978
1979
1980
1981
1982
1983
1984
1985
1986
1987
1988
1989
1990
1991
1992
1993
1994
1995
1996
1997
1998
1999
2000
2001
2002
2003
2004
2005
2006

SMALL MEDIA AND REVOLUTIONARY CHANGE: A NEW MODEL

Excerpt from: Small Media, Big Revolution: Communication, Culture, and the Iranian Revolution

By Annabelle Sreberny-Mohammadi and Ali Mohammadi

1994 The particular dynamics of the Iranian revolution, and the many unexpected political experiences of the past few decades, suggest a need and give us the basis for a new model of contemporary revolutionary mobilization that is significantly different from previous dynamics of revolutionary upheaval. Mediated culture has become part of the causal sequence of revolutionary crisis, as well as central to the revolutionary process.

All revolutionary movements are creative, evolving processes that write their own scripts, even as they draw inspiration from older revolutionary movements. This is especially the case for the non-Western political movements that developed within repressive state structures since the 1970s. There was no precedent for such movements, no model that came close to the conditions existing in the Third World in the 1970s or Eastern Europe in the late 1980s. Indeed, the nature of such repressive systems—whether dominated by party, monarch or self-proclaimed dictator—was such that most opportunities for typical formally organized political activity had been blocked, so that political transformation seemed next to impossible.

Yet suddenly, at the end of the 1970s, there was revolution in Iran and Nicaragua, popular mobilization in the Philippines, and then, a decade later, the collapse of the Soviet Union and the unprecedented upheavals in Eastern Europe. All revolutionary processes are political processes, whether or not there are underlying economic causes and/or demands. Thus all revolutions are also communicative processes, including the articulation of sometimes-competing ideologies and demands, the development of leaders and followers, the circulation of information, the exhortations to participate and mobilize. Popular mythology might think of the storming of the Bastille as the revolutionary act, but, in fact, much of the politicizing and argumentation, the reading and writing, the persuading and criticizing that went before were as much if not more "political" than the final dramatic acts of violence.

Revolution has rarely been thought of in communication terms. For example, only recently, with the flourish of publishing that not only celebrates but also rethinks the French Revolution of 1789, have media forums and communicative networks been set at the center of its analysis. Darnton and Roche (1989: xii) write:

> [Historians have generally] treated the printed word as a record of what happened instead of an ingredient in the happening. But the printing press helped shape the events it recorded. It was an active force in history... we have never attempted to understand how the dominant means of communication in the most powerful country of the West contributed to the first great revolution of modern times.

In the contemporary world, media are part of the political problems and part of the solutions, essential elements of repressive political structures as well as vehicles for their overthrow. Media can be used by states to establish their definitions of the political, their versions of history; they are part of the ideological state apparatus, the forces of repression. At the same time, media can be the tools of popular mobilization, they can maintain alternative histories and promote oppositional culture. In short they constitute the resources and forms of expression of popular movements. Especially within repressive regimes, when there appears to be no public space for "political" activity, media foster the politicization of the "cultural." Media can no longer (if they ever could) be left out of analysis of the process of political transformation known as revolution. Timothy Garton Ash (1990: 94) wrote of the revolutionary year of 1989 that "in Europe at the end of the twentieth century all revolutions are tele-revolutions." At issue is how certain forms of media can function to support popular mobilization, particularly within repressive contexts.

The Problem of Defining "Small Media"

"Small media" has become a popular rubric for various kinds of mediated alternatives to state-run broadcasting systems, but the definition of nonmass media has never been very precise. From Schramm's (1972) attempts to define "big" and "little" media, to definitions of "group media" *(Media Development,* 1981), "community media" (Wade, 1981 Byram, 1981), or "radical media" (Downing, 1984), what has been crucial is a notion of these media as participatory, public phenomena controlled neither by big states nor big corporations. Thus the distinction between "big" and "small" cannot depend on particular kinds of technologies, or even on their putative audiences, but rather on the manner of use of all technologies. Even broadcast media could have a different shape, as suggested by Brecht [nearly 70] years ago:

> Radio should be converted from a distribution system to a communication system. Radio could be the most wonderful public communication, system imaginable, a gigantic system of channels; could be, that is, if it were capable not only of transmitting but of receiving, or making the listener not only hear but also speak, not of isolating him, but of connecting him. This means that radio would have to give up being a purveyor and organise the listener as purveyor.

This is an activist model for the "emancipatory use" of the media (Enzensberger, 1970), which focuses on popular involvement rather than on professional production, on horizontal rather than vertical communication, and on active participation in meaning-making rather than the passive absorption of mass-mediated culture and values. Of course, in Western democracies locally based and organized, nonprofit, participatory forms are many and various. They include free newspapers, community radio and television channels, citizens' video, community computers, and so on (Downing, 1984; Jankowski et al., 1992). Such media projects are developed by pressure groups, political organizations, counterculture aficionados and local communities and minority groups.

These alternative, participatory media forms not only satisfy demands for different contents, catering to tastes, interests and orientations not catered to by mass-media output and sometimes challenging that output, but they are also vehicles for direct participation in the mediated communications process and for the extension of the voices of groups and ideas otherwise not heard. The very existence of this non-mass media environment is a measure of the vibrancy of a democratic society. Downing (1984: 2) stresses the importance of self-managed, dissonant media, which "have posed a genuine alternative to the media patterns of both West and East."

The kind of media use described here might be covered under Fathi's (1979) rubric of "public communication." This shifts focus to an autonomous sphere of activity independent of the State, the popular production of messages, a public coming into being and voicing its own "opinion" in opposition to state-orchestrated voices; to the use of channels and technologies that are readily accessible and available; and to messages that are in the main produced and distributed freely, as opposed to private corporate production for profit or control by state organizations. Jankowski, et al. (1992) call such media "the people's voice," although "people's voices" might be more apt. Throughout this work the rubrics of "public communication" (as distinct from state or private communication), and "small media" (as a counter to the "big media" power of states or corporations), will be used interchangeably to cover the wide stock of mediated cultural resources in different

1927
1960
1963
1964
1967
1969
1970
1971
1972
1973
1974
1975
1976
1977
1978
1979
1980
1981
1982
1983
1984
1985
1986
1987
1988
1989
1990
1991
1992
1993
1994
1995
1996
1997
1998
1999
2000
2001
2002
2003
2004
2005
2006

settings that can be used to conscientize, politicize and mobilize popular revolutionary movements.

Alternate Channels and Political Challenge

The acknowledgment of the power of small media in political movements has been slow to develop, but that does not mean that this is a new phenomenon. On the contrary, an enormous range of channels has been used in a variety of historic contexts to agitate, politicize and mobilize.

The printing press has played a vital role as an agent of social change and democratic politics in the West (Eisenstein, 1979), as in the English civil war (Stone, 1972) and the American and French revolutions (Davidson, 1941; Damton, 1979). As has been well documented (Speier, 1950; Habermas 1989; Gouldner, 1978), the emergence of a "public sphere" was heavily dependent on print materials and suggests a crucial relationship between literacy, political participation and democracy. The Third World experience has been quite different, however, often because state support for electronic media has been greater than support for universal literacy.

In some 20th century revolutions, formal party organization has been the central carrier of revolutionary ideology; with strong emphasis on charismatic authority. Both the Soviet and Chinese revolutions used innovative forms to mobilize and indoctrinate; Trotsky's propaganda train and the rapid production of Soviet film, Mao's little red book and Madame Mao's operas, the use of political poetry and wall posters (tatzepao) are all well known.

In the contemporary development of popular movements against strong states, we face a new model of revolutionary mobilization. Its mode of participation is extensive-mass but low level; its ideology is populist and profoundly anti-statist. Indeed, that ingredient provides the glue for the populist solidarity that is rapidly manifest. Most groups in society become convinced that the first and necessary step in change is the removal or fundamental alteration of the existing state structure.

In Iran, because the royalist despotism of the Shah was associated with Western neocolonialism and dependency, anti-Westernism was a key ideological notion.

The forms of organization are creative and spontaneous, based on a mix of small media and traditional networks rather than on formal parties or organized unions. The dynamic is predominantly urban. Recent events saw mass demonstrations in Beijing, East Berlin, Bucharest, Budapest and Prague, not in the outlying countryside. Leading activists and major participants were students and intellectuals (as in Iran, the People's Republic of China, Czechoslovakia, and Romania), not the peasantry. In the cases of Iran, the Philippines and Poland, religious organizations and religious leadership also were significant. Although members of the urban working class participated in the mass demonstrations and rallies, their organizations were not central to the process; it was really only in Poland that an older form of political organization, a trade union, evolved into the more encompassing structure of Solidarity and came to play the crucial role in a struggle that lasted much longer than many of the more precipitous events of 1989. These movements suggest new forms of populist solidarity to achieve major political change, at least temporarily, although many of these tenuous coalitions splinter as soon as the immediate shared goal is achieved.

In all these recent movements, the distribution of various kinds of small media and the ability to produce and disseminate messages, often through electronic means, was key. Thus, these movements reflect a certain level of economic development and spread of consumer durables, even within contexts of otherwise extreme economic dislocation and shortages, as in Poland and Romania. Often, this communications hardware has been smuggled in illegally, against existing state regulations. This process may also simply involve the shift in use of ordinary media, from predominantly entertainment purposes to function as centers of political persuasion and mobilization. These situations reflected strong states with elaborate forces of coercion and persuasion, and powerful, centrally controlled mass media, with almost no possibilities for alternative political mobilization. The final dynamic of populist mobilization in these circumstances was comparatively brief yet immensely powerful, often fuelled, rather than quashed, by regime violence against the participants.

Small Media and Revolutionary Mobilization

In this section we will suggest some problems a model of small media needs to address to help elucidate and explain their crucial role in political mobilization in repressive contexts.

SMALL MEDIA AS POLITICAL PUBLIC SPACE

The wall is the voice of a people shouting.
Omar Cabezas (quoted in Mattelart, 1986: 37)

The essence of repressive societies is that political activity is severely restricted, and as part of that restriction, comes a control over public communication. Although there are important analytic differences between one-party systems and authoritarian systems, in practice the recent experience of living under each has been remarkably similar, particularly with the development of sophisticated information technologies of surveillance and large modern bureaucracies. In China and Eastern Europe, the single Communist party has dominated, defining the political sphere, operating the state-controlled mass media, and running super-efficient secret-police networks.

In Iran, a royalist dictatorship created the single political party; the mass media were state-controlled, and the secret police, SAVAK, monitored all public activity. One-party systems have sometimes been thought of as highly "mobilized," yet a more accurate analysis reveals a cadre of highly mobilized and motivated people, the party members (who often constituted not more than 15 percent of the population), and the rest of the population. In Iran, the level of political mobilization was very low until the Shah changed strategy in the mid-1970s and developed a single party and attempted a popular mobilization, which backfired. In such big-state, big-media environments, the possibilities

for more familiar elements of democratic participatory political organization, such as political groups and parties, unions and interest groups with their regular and open meetings, and independent political press or electronic media, were utterly circumscribed.

As Barrington Moore (1978: 482) argued, "for any social and moral transformation to get under way there appears to be one prerequisite that underlies all . . . *social and cultural space* within the prevailing order." In Iran, however, a public sphere of autonomous, citizen-directed, participatory debate functioning independently of the state appeared not to exist. This sphere is essentially a communicative environment in which people can freely voice opinion, gather to debate, and create politics. Yet political resistance developed, somewhere in the interstices and crevices of such systems. But where? Here the potential for small media to act as a resource of resistance, a tool of revolutionary mobilization, exists, in the carving out and occupation of such oppositional "space."

As potential sites of struggle, as carriers of already-familiar forms of communication and symbol systems, as structures that are embedded in everyday life and very hard to control, small media and cultural resistance offer fertile ground. Media function as a "virtual space" that temporarily connects people through the use of shared printed material, visual slogans, or electronic broadcasts. In situations where people are disallowed somatic solidarity—to physically assemble, demonstrate, march—small media can help to foster an imaginative social solidarity, often as the precursor *for* actual physical mobilization. Thus they are vitally important resources for mobilization (Tilly, 1978).

If the party was the means to political change in Russia in 1917, and in China in 1948, it was also the major means of political control and orthodoxy in communist regimes. Given the massive top-heavy bureaucratized structure of the party, with enormous reach into ordinary life that evolved in both societies, opposition within such systems had to be particularly subtle and creative. In the comparatively silent world of state

1927
1960
1963
1964
1967
1969
1970
1971
1972
1973
1974
1975
1976
1977
1978
1979
1980
1981
1982
1983
1984
1985
1986
1987
1988
1989
1990
1991
1992
1993
1994
1995
1996
1997
1998
1999
2000
2001
2002
2003
2004
2005
2006

socialism, small media have been crucial in the re-establishment of "horizontal linkages" against the "Soviet pyramid" (Liehm, in Downing, 1984: 310).

In Eastern Europe as in the Soviet Union, the counterpoint to state surveillance and state-run media was the powerful networks of *sarnizdat* and *magnetizdat*. Occasional, small circulation and clumsily produced materials were, in this highly censored context, of direct political significance in developing a public sphere. "Books, irregularly appearing periodicals, almost illegible newssheets, retyped lectures, 'public' gatherings of 80 people squashed inside a single apartment, 'public' lectures attended by 120 people: these are potent reconstructions of an oppositional public realm" (Downing, 1984: 308).

Sometimes the reclaiming of actual public space is more overt. As Rothschuh Villanueva and Cabezas show for Nicaragua (in Mattelart, 1986), various indigenous forms of cultural expression became part of the popular cultural opposition. Walls of city streets became the canvas of a political movement, the means of communication of the masses as well as ways for organized political groups to communicate with the masses, providing a voice for the people. There was danger if one was caught creating these public messages, but usually guards painted out slogans or poured black tar over them — and they would then be repainted. "The fundamental forms of communication of the FSLN with the masses were leaflets, flyers, 'pintas' [wall graffiti], the seizure of radio stations, its own propaganda linked to each of its battles, and the counterculture which grew throughout the war of liberation. On the walls in various cities in the country, one can still read the war slogans and the calls to insurrection. Flyers containing the denunciation of assassinations were covertly distributed on the buses, and the messages stuck to the lips of the people" (Rothschuh Villanueva in Mattelart, 1986: 34). Similarly, in Iran city walls revealed the ongoing struggle with tatters of posters, whitewash old slogans, and ever-new slogans, a public dance of speaking and silencing. Public space potentially heralded a public sphere.

In Iran no public sphere existed. The royalist dictatorship controlled directly or indirectly all forms of expression while SAVAK, the security organization, surveyed all public life. No autonomous political parties, independent labour unions or interest groups were allowed. Such control sounds like a state socialist or fascist regime, but even those regimes are typically far more politically mobilized than was Iran. The royalist dictatorship was a particularly repressive form of authoritarian system, and there appeared to be no space within which any kind of oppositional, popular movement could launch itself.

Yet the dynamics of recent movements and the role of small media suggest we have operated with a far too narrow definition of the "political public sphere," using this term in a very formalist and delimited manner and often obscuring the relationships between communication, culture, and politics. The apparent "lack" of formal organizations such as parties and unions, and the apparent "lack" of public opinion because little measurement of opinion existed, are taken as the absence of politics. But politics in Iran has always been more fluid, more informal, and more invisible than the organized politics of the established democracies, revealing another blind spot of a narrowly Western optic. There have always been informal political circles *(dowreh)* and gatherings of known individuals based on familiarity and trust developed over time (Bill, 1972; Zonis, 1971), but there was little sense in the public arena that such political groups were growing, articulate, or effective.

In Iran, as in Poland, the Philippines and elsewhere, public "space" could also be found within religious networks. The religious leadership often possessed far more extensive, and far more culturally appropriate, resources for mobilization than did the secular intelligentsia. The resources of the religious leadership in Iran included a nationwide network of physical spaces—the mosques—that were points of public assembly, the only such network not penetrated by the state.

SMALL MEDIA: TECHNOLOGIES FOR POLITICAL SURVIVAL

In Iran, new technologies of communication also helped to open up a potential public sphere of dissent. Small media such as audiotapes became electronic extensions of the religious institutions and its political discourse, and photocopied leaflets were the preferred weapon of secular groups, giving voice to what was to become an enormous popular movement.

The argument that political mobilization depends on developing political resources, usually some form of public communication, is not new. What is significant is that at certain moments, and more and more with the spread of certain technologies, control is impossible, even within the most repressive, security-oriented states. This is so for two main reasons: the nature of new communications technologies, and the development of international communications systems and international reception of messages. It is increasingly difficult, even for the most repressive regime, to control political communications. Many strong states have tried at times to control directly the importation and circulation of certain media technologies (personal computers and satellite dishes in the former Soviet Union, for example), or to impose economic barriers (such as the severe tax on videocassette players in India) (Ganley and Ganley, 1987; Boyd et al, 1989). Yet borders are leaky, smugglers adaptive and popular interest and demand for media technologies generally high.

Certain technologies carry within themselves the means for reproduction, making control an even more difficult task. Key to the success of some recent movements, or to the longevity of others, has been the technical fact that contemporary small media—particularly audio tapes and videocassettes, copy machines, personal computers, and fax machines—are the source of multiple points of production and distribution. Audiocassette systems, video recording, and Polaroid photography, for example, require no independent processing techniques but contain within the hardware the possibility of instant production and reproduction of messages. Anyone can reproduce such messages, and indeed the dynamics of movements depend precisely on each participant's making additional copies and spreading them around. Thus, Soviet *samizdat* would be typed and retyped in multiple copies to the extent of carbon-copy legibility by anyone.

In Poland, the underground network was created by KOR (Committee for Workers' Self-Defense) with signed communiqués that publicized the struggles of workers and intellectuals, and carried the exhortation that "by disseminating this bulletin you are acting within your rights, and playing a part in their defense. Read it, copy it, and pass it on" (quoted in Downing, 1984: 326). Xerography not only makes light of such tedious work but also offers an advance over various printing processes because it produces instant and virtually untraceable copy (absent the most sophisticated forensic science), from potentially multiple sources, so that the loss of one machine does not imply the demise of an entire movement. The good old days, when smashing the printing press meant the end of radical agitation, are long gone. The networking of personal computers and on-line information systems offers similar possibilities of uncontrollable multipoint production and dissemination of messages. Unfortunately, the political right has jumped to use such channels, as the use of computer networks by racist groups in the United States and the circulation of anti-Semitic computer games in Austria attest.

In Poland, the opposition movement graduated from the classic *samizdat* method of reproduction based on typewriter and carbon copies to the recycling of antiquated duplicators, photocopiers, and offset lithography, to create the technological tools of the underground network. Cassette tapes of the Gdansk negotiations circulated through factories. The political police spent a considerable part of its time trying to repress this growing underground small-media movement, and even a year after martial law had been imposed its squads seized over a million leaflets, silenced 11 radio transmitters, found 380 printing shops, and

1927
1960
1963
1964
1967
1969
1970
1971
1972
1973
1974
1975
1976
1977
1978
1979
1980
1981
1982
1983
1984
1985
1986
1987
1988
1989
1990
1991
1992
1993
1994
1995
1996
1997
1998
1999
2000
2001
2002
2003
2004
2005
2006

confiscated nearly 500 typewriters (C. Civic, quoted by Downing, 1984: 327). Independent media work still continued, however. Within the Polish context, these self-managed media created new spaces for public argument and debate, independent of the power structure, and proved to be important first steps in the giant movement that ensued. As Downing notes, "no alternative communication channel should be written off simply because it is small" (345).

The availability of certain of these technologies is in itself an indication of the level of technical modernity achieved in a society. Fax machines in Chinese cities, used to dramatic effect during the Tiananmen Square uprising, are a direct outcome of the modernization strategy adopted after the death of Mao in 1976. The widespread use of such electronic consumer durables as cassette players inside Iran is not without its irony. Technological diffusion has been at the heart of the dominant paradigm of development, and technological dependency is the lived experience for many Third World countries. The contradictions of a movement based on anti-imperialist slogans and nurturing a long-standing cultural identity that makes use of technologies delivered by Western and Japanese manufacturers, further demonstrate the complexity of the problem of development. The tension between admiration and hostility toward Western technology is frequently solved by Third World nations coming to consider the technology as neutral, as not in itself embodying values or altering mindsets. The Iranian popular movement was delighted to have an array of sophisticated technologies available for its use, and even the Islamic Republic has reflected little on the real social impacts of technological diffusion.

In Iran, it was interesting to see how the function of certain technologies shifted from one of bureaucratic control to one of political participation. Before the popular movement developed, the use of photocopy machines even for university teaching was heavily controlled. The simplest reproduction of a diagram or set of figures for classroom use was a major procedure in universities, requiring multiple signatures and often taking so long that the need had passed by the time permission was granted. Come the movement, a sea change occurred! The photocopy machine at Iran Communications and Development Institute (ICDI), for example, where Annabelle worked, became the hub of activity; its operator was a key political actor in the evolving movement, and the different fellow travelers of various political factions would vie for access to the machine. Other researchers who worked at ICDI during the revolution have noted the same phenomenon (Green, 1982).

SMALL MEDIA IN THE GLOBAL CONTEXT

Another factor that profoundly complicates the issue of "control" of the national political environment is the spread of international communications, which has collapsed global space, promoted an immense speedup of historical processes and eroded the containment effects of national boundaries (Giddens, 1990).

There are always lengthy debates about the "first moment" of revolutionary processes, but at the end of the 20th century it seems that when the will exists, popular mobilization can be astonishingly spontaneous and rapid, given the number of strong states that cracked open at the end of the 1980s. The instant dissemination around the world of information and images about political change also fosters a possible "contagion effect" of popular political upheavals that is thus stronger than ever. One of the most notable elements of the 1989 events, as with the Iranian movement, was the comparatively open access that international television and press crews had to the sites of political activity. The main televisual news agencies, Visnews and UPITN, and the television networks, such as CNN and others, sell their news footage to many other stations, so that the dramatic live coverage of the unfolding movements at Tiananmen Square, around the Brandenburg Gate, in Wenceslas Square, in Budapest and in Bucharest would be seen throughout the world. This truly was revolution while the whole world was watching. In regard to the revolutions in Eastern Europe, Ash (1990:

78, 126) had predicted that "in Poland it took 10 years, in Hungary 10 months, in East Germany 10 weeks; perhaps in Czechoslovakia it will take 10 days." The 10 days turned out to be 24, but the demonstration effects and the speedup of history appear to be real processes, partly explainable by the extensive media coverage of what had happened in the other countries.

International communications can play complex roles in domestic political upheavals. First, it has profoundly altered the nature of political exile. Exiled political activists no longer wait for events to change so that they can return home, but instead can propagandize to change conditions from outside their country, a de-territorialization of politics (Shain, 1987; Sreberny-Mohammadi and Mohammadi, 1987). There is considerable international clandestine radio broadcasting (Soley, 1987), as well as the documented beginnings of exile videography: Polish exiles in Paris smuggled videotapes *into* Poland, and Czech activists smuggled tapes of illegal demonstrations and state-orchestrated violence *out* of the country. Members of the Iranian exile community, both before and after the revolution, produced an enormous amount of political literature and broadcasting, altering the new environment in which they sojourned as much as they attempted to alter conditions back "home."

Not only do exiles send materials home, but as political actors they can try to mobilize international public opinion to take up their case in international public forums, such as the United Nations. A large part of the function of groups such as Amnesty International and Human Rights Watch is to alert international public opinion about rights violations within specific countries and to mobilize resources to effect change. The Iranian secular middle-class political groups tried hard to use various international channels to mobilize international public opinion in their favor, and achieved some modicum of success.

Occasionally, such international communication actually benefits or links political elements *within* a nation who otherwise cannot communicate or even know of each other's existence. Here, the international linkage becomes a necessary intermediate stage in what is really domestic political communication. A classic example is BBC news transmission about the activities of the anti-Hitler resistance inside Germany that was picked up by other resistance elements, a process documented by the White Rose group (Scholl, 1983). A more recent example would be the use of fax machines in the Chinese student movement in May and June 1989: because of the limited infrastructure of internal telecommunications and fear of surveillance, it was easier and faster for Chinese students in Beijing to fax messages out to their U.S. counterparts, who then faxed the message back to another city inside China, than to trust internal communication. The nightly news broadcasts of the BBC that reported demonstrations and deaths in various cities of Iran played a similar role, representing the movement back to itself as well as reinforcing the global importance of its actions.

Beyond the organization of exile communication for political purposes, international news carriers are crucial to the provision of information and imagery worldwide, made even faster with the use of satellites. Sometimes such channels provide information that is kept restricted within the society in question, and states attempt to block their penetration through jamming or preventing the purchase of shortwave receiving equipment. The detailed coverage of major stories by Western international broadcasters, such as the BBC and the Voice of America, Deutsche Welle, Radio Monte Carlo, and Israeli radio, has made them primary information sources in many political upheavals, often listened to on shortwave behind drawn curtains.

In Iran, international media attention appeared to validate the "historical importance" of the events at hand. *Time* and *Newsweek* covers on the Iranian revolution produced significant public interest at newsstands. At ICDI, the Iranian tea-boys clamored for translations of articles in these news magazines and were impressed that even American publications were writing about the Iranian revolution. Such major international channels

1927
1960
1963
1964
1967
1969
1970
1971
1972
1973
1974
1975
1976
1977
1978
1979
1980
1981
1982
1983
1984
1985
1986
1987
1988
1989
1990
1991
1992
1993
1994
1995
1996
1997
1998
1999
2000
2001
2002
2003
2004
2005
2006

are also perceived to be highly professional and "objective" in their news coverage, thus adding a great sense of veracity to their broadcasts (Gauhar, 1979). Even political activists accepted international news reports and figures, especially in preference to those of the state-run broadcasting system, and frequently quoted the BBC or other such channels in their own communiques.

SMALL MEDIA AS THE CATALYST FOR POLITICAL PARTICIPATION

The connection between communications and participation is poorly developed. The basic mass media model of vertical message transference sees the audience only as a group of message consumers (accredited with varying degrees of selectivity, and so forth). Yet the proliferation of new media, the lowering of costs, the differentiation of the audience into taste cultures, and new models of the active audience offer opportunities for communications participation so that the erstwhile "passive" audience can actively produce not only meaning but messages. Much of this is not new in the West, where community radio, local publishing ventures, and a host of pressure groups using a variety of channels exist. What certain technological developments offer, however, is the potential for developing and renewing participation in societies with state surveillance and limited possibilities for independent political participation even inside authoritarian states. In such contexts, to communicate is to act politically, with the implication that simple definitions of participation or its lack may well be outdated.

The relation between communications and politics is symbiotic, and it is impossible to separate the issue of participation in the political process from participation in the communications process. In fact, the practice of both Pahlavi shahs, particularly the last, was to discourage all forms of mass political participation, which they seemed to feel could as easily go against them as for them, a typical fear of authoritarian regimes (Perlmutter, 1981). Indeed, many theorists of political modernization, including Lerner and Huntington, have been fearful of the extremism of mass participation.

Under repressive states, the ideological and cultural spheres cannot have autonomous development but are orchestrated by the state, as is the process of economic development. Thus the "political" is not a neatly delimited sphere to which specifically political demands may be made. The very lack of development of institutions of participation encouraged the strengthening of pre-existing collective identities and the politicization of cultural practices and rituals.

Political communication has been far too preoccupied with that most visible of participatory activities, voting. But not all systems have voting procedures, and political systems have participation. Even passivity is meaningful. In Iran, the Shah promoted a strong self-deceptive tendency to believe that all was well i.e. *qui tacit, consentit*, induced by the failure of those around him to provide the full facts about social discontent to his attention, partly because he made it clear that he did not like to hear bad news (Graham, 1978). The outward appearance of submission is no proof of the inward acceptance of oppression, however. That the Shah was psychologically affected by the depth of popular hostility that became evident in 1977-78 seems to be a factor in his irresolution about responses to the political opposition.

At the popular level, once the pervasive silence was shattered by the speaking out of intellectuals and professionals who were not immediately pounced on by SAVAK, and then by the first demonstrations, the collective fear of reprisals and feelings of powerlessness were rapidly dissolved. Fear was sometimes transformed into its opposite, a desire for martyrdom. The contagion effect spread and the surveillance structure of the once-absolute state fell asunder. Communication acts were in themselves political moments of involvement and daring and the public process of communicating that such events had occurred required further involvement. In a context that had allowed no autonomous political participation for decades, the exhilaration of involvement and the visible and audible breaches in the wall of public silence were critical initial steps in the formation of the mass popular movement. Indeed, one interesting aspect of the mobilization is the shift between intellectual initiation of the process and the subsequent mass take-over and leadership, that is, the extent to which the previously mass "spectators" became even more "gladiatorial" than the secular activists (Milbrath and Goel, 1977) and were ready to encounter and battle with the military forces of the state.

The Iranian popular movement cannot be seen simply as a voluntaristic process of a developing public opinion, although there were sizable segments of the Iranian population who had been waiting for the chance to act and for whom the fracturing of state power suddenly offered undreamed-of opportunities. For most ordinary Iranians involvement was provoked by the combination of the coercive power of primordial identity, the continued social status of the *ulema*, and their political rhetoric. The Shah, on the few state occasions when it could be controlled, provoked participation through fear, fear of reprisal and of involvement with SAVAK. With the clergy and Khomeini, participation was orchestrated through the politicization of a deep-rooted cultural identity and the compulsion of religious duty, an ideology, leadership and ethos accepted as compelling by a crowd of believers in the absence of alternatives, and a deeply coercive process.

The Iranian movement, much like the movements of Poland, the Philippines, and even Nicaragua, can be characterized by massive, low-level participation that cut across clear social-class divisions, evident in such actions as participation in mass demonstrations and the shouting of anti-regime slogans from urban rooftops. The political culture of mistrust (Zonis, 1971) and private grumbling were rapidly transformed into an immensely powerful collective movement of strangers.

SMALL MEDIA AND INDIGENOUS CULTURE

One way cross-class solidarity was effected in Iran was in the repoliticizing of familiar traditional popular culture. In authoritarian systems, with severe repression of the political sphere, popular culture almost inevitably becomes the locus of political opposition, the venting of oppositional sentiments, the developing of critiques, and the playing out of alternative visions. As we have already argued, even if the existence of some delimited formal sphere called the "political" is lacking, that does not mean that politics does not exist, but rather that it is not in actuality separated from the broader sociocultural milieu in which competition for symbolic meaning occurs. Separating culture from politics is difficult, and, in processes of political change, many indigenous cultural resources may be mobilized and developed to create a cultural resistance with political impact against would-be hegemonic regimes.

Obviously these processes can take many forms by traditional channels and by combining the use of modern small-media technologies with traditional cultural forms (music, poetry and so on). In the Afghan resistance, Afghanis have woven carpets that incorporate motifs of contemporary warfare, a highly unusual example of cultural resistance. *Glasnost* revealed not only deep ethnic cleavages in the USSR but also a lively underground of punk and heavy-metal music.

The themes of indigenous cultural identity and its erosion by external cultural elements and the deleterious effects of Western culture may function as popular rhetorical tropes that help to build a mass movement against some external power. In Nicaragua, Somoza was seen as the local representative of imperialism, and resistance took the form not only of military and political resistance but of cultural resistance as well. A dynamic counterculture built on older, traditional cultural forms, substituting popular testimonial music for "disco," a poetry of revolutionary content, a revolutionary film industry and revolutionary song.

The performing arts, puppeteers, and other traditional cultural forms have also been involved with political mobilization. These forms acted as vehicles of expression of protest, dissent and reform in India, so that "these native media of 'sung communication' and

1927
1960
1963
1964
1967
1969
1970
1971
1972
1973
1974
1975
1976
1977
1978
1979
1980
1981
1982
1983
1984
1985
1986
1987
1988
1989
1990
1991
1992
1993
1994
1995
1996
1997
1998
1999
2000
2001
2002
2003
2004
2005
2006

'enacted information' proved more than a match to the Government-controlled mass media during the many political and social campaigns launched by Gandhi" (Ranganath, 1980). Bassets (in Mattelart and Seigelaub, 1983) describes the variety of clandestine communications developed under and against Franco's dictatorship, from typewritten letters to clandestine press agencies, from the underground political press to anonymous poetry, or simply the symbolic painting of letters on walls (P for protest, A for amnesty, L for liberty). Although this particular underground movement did not develop into a successful social movement, as happened in Iran, and change accrued "naturally" with the death of Franco, it is interesting to note the reduction of Spanish society and communications practices into two separate, culturally and politically antagonistic realms, very similar to the reduction of Iranian life into a "dualistic culture" of state and oppositional culture. Bassets analyzes the relationship between the clandestine culture and the exile culture, the latter serving as a historical memory bank preserving radical cultural and political expression even with internal repression. He also describes the international broadcasting and humanitarian organizations that played a vital information role as part of international public opinion, elements that were significant in the Iranian experience.

The repoliticization of popular culture as a mode of generating solidarity appears quite common, although in different contexts different media and different genres will be invoked. Popular culture takes many forms, and cultural resistance and opposition are not necessarily revolutionary. Popular culture can be highly politicized, and entertainment can be a powerful vehicle for political gathering and mobilization. The showing of an underground video in a private house in Poland or Czechoslovakia, the semipublic viewing of "critical" films, and the production and distribution of an opposition leaflet all create a symbolic space that serves to redefine the political. Participation in such events and the acceptance and reading of such material are forms of political action in and

of themselves, carried out in defiance of and at possible risk from the state. Vaclav Havel, the president of the Czech Republic, was imprisoned for a number of years as a dissident playwright, and Charter 77 in that country was comprised of many creative artists and intellectuals. Iranian poets Said Sultanpour and Golesorkhi were imprisoned by the Shah. Repressive states understand well the potential power of popular culture to undermine them, hence the widespread repression and censorship regularly reported in *Index on Censorship* and by Amnesty International.

The Discursive Reconstruction of Collective Memory/Identity

Perhaps one of the final elements in the puzzle of political change is the actual discourse of revolution, how alternative identities and political goals were constructed in language to frame revolutionary ideology. The articulation of such discourse includes a sense of collective memory, a rewriting of collective identity, and the politicization of "tradition."

Revolution is made in the historical present, building on images of the past, thrusting toward the future, albeit often looking backward, as Benjamin (1970: 262-63) described the angel of history. All nations propound a collective history; authoritarian states advocate a single authorized version of the past, with a rewriting of names and dates (and a retouching of photos, like the erasure of Trotsky from Soviet photographic records), and an authorized version of events in which they are the progressive apogee, thus creating a certain kind of collective identity of which they are the final embodiment. The breaking up of the Soviet empire has unleashed a massive retrieval and "reinvention" of nations and ethnicities throughout Eastern Europe.

Such constructions of collective remembering not only (re)create a past but perhaps more crucially (re)create a collective identity that has a past. Opposition may consist of "refusing what we are," in Foucault's (1988) terms, and reconstituting a preferred collective identity that empowers actors. This is the shift from being

1927
1960
1963
1964
1967
1969
1970
1971
1972
1973
1974
1975
1976
1977
1978
1979
1980
1981
1982
1983
1984
1985
1986
1987
1988
1989
1990
1991
1992
1993

subjects of/subject to a regime, to becoming human subjects writing our own history. Competition over memory is also competition over how current collective identities should be conceived. Here Benjamin's (1970) idea that revolution is a "tiger's leap into the past" becomes more complex; there is no single past, but rather competing definitions of how the past is to be read.

As collective memories are conjured up, the present intervenes to redefine past events and actors and functional symbols in current opposition. "Tradition" is not simply frozen memory but an active adaptation to the new, current time frame and sociopolitical context. In the politicization of memory and cultural tradition, both are changed. No longer can tradition be lived innocently and naively. In its active mobilization as a resource in an ideological struggle against an opposing cultural and political reality, tradition itself is irrevocably altered, undergoing the process of re-traditionalization.

EXCERPT FROM:
PARTICIPATORY DEVELOPMENT
COMMUNICATION:
PHILOSOPHICAL PREMISES

By Pradip Thomas

1994 Participation primarily signifies sharing in an activity or process that was traditionally organized and implemented in hierarchical or exclusive ways. Often it happens through a political choice and is therefore largely a political activity. Its logic stems from changed epistemological, political and theoretical positions that emphasize a community, dialogue, reciprocity and understanding based on mutual respect.

In this chapter I will comment briefly on the theory and practice of participation, examine the philosophical premises underlying the concept, as well as the possibilities and limits of its practice—especially in the area of communication. A brief analysis of the theoretical contributions of two scholars, Paulo Freire and Martin Buber, to the philosophy undergirding the practice of participation will be followed by an analysis of the determinants of participation, stressing the need to be realistic about its limits and possibilities.

The central point is that while participatory communication is essential for building a community, such communication needs to be based on a realistic and pragmatic understanding of the potentials and limitations of participation. As a concept, participation has brought back to discourse the accent on a praxis that has evolved from people as a mirror of their aspirations and needs rather than one imposed on them by others. It has allowed people to become the subjects of their own development and not simply objects of technology or processes. This is its strength. It is an ideal and goal toward which we need to continue working. It calls for a fuller involvement of people in their own development but not (and this is seldom pointed out) the total involvement of all people in every aspect of human development.

1994
1995
1996
1997
1998
1999
2000
2001
2002
2003
2004
2005
2006

But first let us take a look at the contributions of Paulo Freire and Martin Buber to the concept of participation.

Paulo Freire: Conscientization

Freire's pedagogy evolved from his encounter with poverty, exploitation and "domesticated" development in northeast Brazil. There he found repression in many forms—economic, political, social and cultural. Freire's views on participation grew out of his experience of living, working and reflecting, in his own words, out of a "praxis" of involvement. His ideological ascent, from the reformist, liberal-democratic stance of his early works like *Education: The Practice of Freedom* (1967), to the Marxist-humanist stance of his later works including the *Pedagogy of the Oppressed* (1970), *Pedagogy in Process* (1978) and his [recent] book *Learning to Question* in 1989 (co-authored with Antonio Faundez), becomes evident in a chronological reading of his books.

Freire was influenced by a number of thinkers: theologians such as Theilhard de Chardin who emphasized the historical vocation of the human being to be more fully human (which became a key concept in Freire's social philosophy); Reinhold Nelbuhr whose ideas on the nature of classes in society and the oppressor psyche challenged him; existentialists like Emmanuel Mounier who emphasized human authenticity; Jean Paul Sartre's critique of the dominant practice of education; Eric Fromm's observations on the ambivalent and contradictory psyche of the oppressed; Che Guevara's and Amilar Cabral's life and praxis as caring revolutionaries; and philosophers like Martin Buber whose concept of "dialogue" became a central feature of Freire's pedagogy. All these perspectives impacted on Freire's own growth as a pedagogue. Freire's entire philosophy of education and his orientation toward participation are based on the notion that the historical vocation of human beings is to be free from the shackles of material and psychological oppression and from the patterns of life that are imposed from above and do not provide for the involvement of people in the processes of change.

Freire believes that the act of liberation involves the liberation of human beings toward the fulfillment of his or her historical vocation to be free. But the liberation of both the individual and the community comes through a self-sustained effort through growth in individual awareness and community consciousness evolving through a process of learning. According to Freire, all individuals have the capacity for reflecting, the capacity for abstract thinking, for conceptualizing, taking decisions, choosing alternative and planning social change. It is not merely awareness, however, or the act of knowing or nominal involvement that is important, but it is relationship of a project to social transformation, whereby consciousness and action on consciousness are dialectically related. In Freire's pedagogy, action and reflection are not separate activities but an organic whole and it is this dialectical interplay of action and reflection that constitutes the process of "conscientizacao" [conscientization]. In other words, authentic participation leads to a "freeing"; it is an emancipatory experience, resulting in actual liberation.

Freire's orientation toward participation stems from his critique of the existing pedagogy of extension education which was both paternalistic in its philosophy and basically nonparticipatory in its modus operandi. He called it the "banking" concept of education. It was based on the premise that knowledge was a finished entity and not to be discovered in a dialogic encounter of subjects. It was a given, packaged and completed corpus. People were merely passive receivers of the body of knowledge. It was not their knowledge, but a knowledge that was exogenous and only vaguely related, if at all, to their reality.

Freire noted that people accepted content in a passive way and rarely reflected on the validity of knowledge. Therefore he proposed the act of critical reflection as a vital element in alternative participatory development. Authentic participation would then enable the subjects involved in this dialogic encounter to unveil reality for themselves. Such participation would lead to the disappearance of distinctions, the teacher acting as a catalyst, and not as the mediator of a finished body of knowledge. The teacher and the taught are jointly involved in the investigation of knowledge. The duty of the teacher, thus, is to guide the awakening of the critical faculties of the individual and to relate it to the tasks of political struggle and development.

Freire's writings have influenced an entire generation of scholars and activists involved in participatory development projects the world over. Although he never really linked his analysis to the use of a particular media, it is implicit in his writing that communication, in order to be effective, has to be participatory, dialogic and reciprocal. In fact, the entire enterprise of participatory communication projects, from the organization and production of community radio in Latin America, Australia and parts of Africa and Asia, through the practice of popular theater in countries like Brazil, Chile, Jamaica, South Africa, India and the Philippines utilize Freire's perspective. The praxis of experiential learning in progressive South African universities such as the University of Natal and various other media projects based on traditional, mass and popular media in many parts of the world owes a lot to Freire's theory and practice of participatory development.

In Freire's writings, participation is a key concept. Nowhere is it better illustrated than in what he has to say on the use of his pedagogy in the context of development in the West African state of Guinea-Bissau. In this book (1978) on actual praxis, participation is presented as a pragmatic concept. It presupposes a basic commitment based on mutuality and respect for one another. It becomes a people-based pedagogic enterprise that puts the learner and the teacher on an equal footing. Freire does believe that human beings have the capacity to control central aspects of their lives, but nowhere does he suggest that such involvement should be indiscriminately all-embracing.

Buber: Dialogue for Community

Freire's concept of "dialogue" emanated from Buber. And dialogue is central to Buber's thought. In his best known book, "I and Thou," Buber (1958) presented his basic ideas on human existence and human destiny. Buber deals with two types of relationships, the "I-Thou" and the "I-It" relationships.

The "I-Thou" encounter is one of dialogue, mutual respect, openness and give and take. It is the basis for communion, which is the key to community. It accepts and affirms the other and through such acceptance, liberates and enhances both the I, who meets, and the Thou, who is met. All life is relational, and only in terms of mutuality and meeting can human life achieve meaning and fulfillment. The dialogic encounter born of relation applies to one's life with nature, with other people, and with "the eternal Thou," who is addressed in every Thou.

In contrast, the "I-It" relationship is one of monologue, inequality, objectivity and detachment, and is at the root of the alienation of human being from one another, from nature and from God. Such estrangement is a feature of modern existence, and Buber's seminal book points to the possibility of a breakthrough, the possibility, in fact, of a new epistemology which could replace the famous basis of philosophy as formulated by Descartes: "I think, therefore I am."

The I-Thou and the I-It relationships are part of the reality that human beings experience, and neither exists in its pure form. The I-It relationships currently predominate in interpersonal contacts and in one's transactions with the nonhuman world. But there is the possibility for an I-Thou relationship to emerge, and that new relationship, based on dialogue, is to be seen not merely in terms of thought or language but it should primarily express itself in action. It is in the actual reaching out to the other, in the affirmation of the otherness of the other, that genuine dialogue takes place. And the act of dialogue is the act of making oneself whole, of freeing oneself from the shackles of individualism and emerging into full personhood in a community.

1927
1960
1963
1964
1967
1969
1970
1971
1972
1973
1974
1975
1976
1977
1978
1979
1980
1981
1982
1983
1984
1985
1986
1987
1988
1989
1990
1991
1992
1993
1994
1995
1996
1997
1998
1999
2000
2001
2002
2003
2004
2005
2006

The concept of community is also central to Buber's thought. He rejected collectivism on the one hand and individualism on the other. In both, the human being is isolated. This is true not only in totalitarian political systems but also in the industrial world where people are reduced to "hands" and life is measured in "man-hours." Of collectivity and community Buber wrote:

> Collectivity is not a binding but a bundling together; individuals packed together, armed and equipped in common, with only as much life from man to man as will inflame the marching step. But community, growing community (which is all we have known so far), is the being no longer side-by-side but with one another; a multitude of persons. … Community is where community happens. Collectivity is based on an organized atrophy of personal existence, community on its increase and confirmation in life lived toward one another. The modern zeal for collectivity is a flight from community's testing and consecration of the person, a flight from the vital dialogic, demanding the staking of the self, which is in the heart of the world (1958, p. 29).

True participation arises from dialogue. Buber's ideas on dialogue have contributed significantly to our understanding of participatory communication.

Determinants of Participatory Communication

The determinants of participatory communication are both obvious and obscure—but in any case require careful examination for both its understanding and practice. Three key determinant "arenas"—the political, epistemological and organizational—shape the possibilities and limits and merit discussion. At the outset it is important to clarify what we mean by participatory communication.

In normal communication parlance, participation means people's involvement in all stages of a communication project, be it interpersonal, mass media-based or traditional media-based. It stands in direct contrast to the philosophy and practice of the dominant paradigm with its emphasis on communication which is planned, developed, organized and implemented with outside help and in which the beneficiaries are merely passive receivers of a finished reality. This is, of course, the thrust behind most communication and development projects in India and elsewhere in the developing world. This thrust is based largely on the communication ideology of the triumvirate: Schramm, Lerner and Rogers.

The Power Equation

First of all, participatory communication is a political activity based on changed power equations. It is the means by which a scarce societal resource, i.e., the means of communication, is handed over to the people themselves so that their voices can be heard. Brecht…writing on the "inconsequentiality" of the dominant media, notes that radio can change its character from being a medium that is based on a distribution system—from being another manifestation of capitalist logic—to a communication system, a means by which two-way communications and dialogue can emerge.

> Radios could be the most wonderful public communication system imaginable, a gigantic system of channels … if it were capable not only of transmitting but of receiving, of making the listener not only hear but also speak, not of isolating him but of connecting him. This means that radios would have to give up being a purveyor and organize the listener as purveyor.

Transformation of radio to a two-way communication medium would revolutionize its role dramatically. However, this change in the organization and the goals for the media can happen only through a change in the political attitudes of the people using this type of media—a change from a fatalistic, naïve and weak mindset to a fearless and positive people-sustained vision of the future. It would also require a change of attitude on the part of those who currently control media access.

There are number of instances in India of participatory, alternative media based on a changed power equation and a clear political choice. The feminist magazine *Manushi*, brought out by a women's cooperative in New Delhi; the work of SKILLS, a Madras-based low-cost media production center; and the popular theater performances of quite a few groups working in the nongovernmental organization (NGO) sector are all examples of media activity oriented toward the fulfillment of very specific audience needs.

But it remains a fact that for every single successful alternative media enterprise, there are many others that merely project an image of being alternative and participatory, when in fact they merely reinforce some of the worst aspects of the dominant paradigm of communication. This is a very real aspect of the Indian alternative communications scenario that we have to face. A number of power-based factors come in the way of genuine communication process. These include: (a) the self-interest of the organizers and of members of the community; (b) the all-pervasive reach of populist culture; (c) the lack of trained personnel in communication skills; (d) the tendency to dogmatize and to do by the book which smothers both creativity and flexibility; (e) the influence of local and state politics; (f) patriarchy and gender discrimination; (g) the caste factor; and (h) the class factor.

Epistemological Position

Participatory communication is based on a changed epistemological position. It is based on the rhetoric and practice of liberation, of freedom, of emancipation, of struggle, of the "preferential option for the poor" and of transformation and change. It is thus diametrically opposed to the theory and practice of communication that merely reinforces the status quo, and perpetuates class, caste and gender inequalities. This changed epistemological position has been crucial to the development, organization and implementation of a changed communication practice. In fact, the redefinition and revaluation of the dominant theory, its interpretations and practices, have resulted in a new revolution in

knowledge—in a knowledge that is specifically aligned with the cause of a just world community.

However, one does get the impression that the rhetoric of participation has not been accompanied by an active, actual translation of theory into practice. Participation has definitely led to a more humanistic approach to solving the world's many problems. But what does participation mean in practice? Does it mean everybody doing everything all the time? Does it mean organizing communication activity on socialistic rather than capitalistic lines? Dogmatic positions and absolutist stances abound here as anywhere else, and are the main reasons for the failure of a number of participatory communication projects.

There are of course instances in India of landless people, of the urban oppressed, of illiterate women learning to make a video program, of tribal people producing their own popular theater and of dalits bringing out newspapers and magazines. Such examples are testimony to the fact that ordinary people can transcend their formal illiteracy and technological "ignorance" to produce alternative programs that can be understood and be close to their lives and to the lives of their people. But such examples only point to the fact that some people by their very nature possess certain gifts of expression and communication. It does not prove that all people possess such gifts. Without in any way supporting biological determinism, and fully acknowledging that people have the will and physical and psychological resources to master skills and new ways of doing and living, one can reasonably state that people have different abilities, and they are by no means shared abilities.

For example, improvisation is of course a key factor in any popular theater performance, but it is a fact that not many people can improvise well. Popular theater theorists may claim that commitment can make up for lack of skills, but in a country like India, with a highly sophisticated theater audience, skills are absolutely essential for the success of popular theater performances. I have witnessed such performances

1927
1960
1963
1964
1967
1969
1970
1971
1972
1973
1974
1975
1976
1977
1978
1979
1980
1981
1982
1983
1984
1985
1986
1987
1988
1989
1990
1991
1992
1993
1994
1995
1996
1997
1998
1999
2000
2001
2002
2003
2004
2005
2006

based on folk theater which failed primarily because the performances did not have the necessary grasp of the folk theatrical idiom. The practice of popular theater, by its very nature, is a difficult and time-consuming affair. Only a few people master the techniques of popular theater. That is not surprising. After all, out of a hundred people who learn to shoot with a video camera only a few will become highly skilled at using the camera in a creative way. Skills, techniques and the creative use of the media are vital to a participatory communication project and cannot by any means be compensated for by commitment which is, of course, vital but not sufficient for the success of participatory communication.

Organizational Aspects

Also, participatory communication is based on a changed organizational ethic and method of operation. This has been crucial for the success of participatory communication projects in many places. Their inadequate appropriation has at the same time been the reason for its failure in very many parts of the world. In the enthusiasm for a nonhierarchal, nonformal and fully democratic organizational setup, there has been a tendency for participatory projects to totally give up all previous forms of organizations and methods of work. For example, there has been an attempt by participatory groups to form unstructured organizations based on a denial of individual skills and on a totally democratic method of decision making. Common assent, individual involvement at every stage of the process, and a cooperative effort are at the very heart of this process of necessary change, but all too often this process has itself become institutionalized. The exercise of power is often masked in such a situation. In actual fact, power is often exercised by a person with a strong personality who invariably dominates proceedings. In that sense, participation is not infrequently achieved through manipulation.

Unstructured methods of organization are definitely important for motivating people, for getting their assent and cooperation; but they need to be situated within a structured movement that both directs and orients the facilitating process. The lack of clear direction has been the bane of many participatory communication projects. Added to this are the problems of leadership, the inability to terminate a project when its mandate has been fulfilled, the tendency for initially manageable media projects to grow into unwieldy proportions leading to the dilution of work methods, and of the unclear definition of objectives. There is also the temptation to absolutize the use of one medium over other, as for instance, the use of popular theater over other media like video and computers because these are of capitalist origins. One also notices a tendency to be defensive when project managers are unwilling to face up to an evaluation of the "quality" and "impact" of the work. All these and more have contributed to the demise of many participatory communication projects.

Charles Landry [et al.] (1985), in their excellent analysis of the reasons for the failure of radical media projects in England, point out the disastrous consequences of the cult of leadership, the tendency for initiators to become veritable godfathers—so true of the Indian case. They note:

It is a common experience that those originally involved in setting up a group or project find it hard to let go of the levers of control at a later stage, especially when the group has had (as it often does) one or more 'charismatic' figure(s) who have been vital to its success in the early period. Such people are usually heavily identified with the project and regard it as, in some sense, 'their baby.' Often, in this situation, progress through the deadlock which ensues is only possible by means of some kind of 'ritual slaughter' of the original 'father(s)' and 'mother(s)' of the group, to make room for the new entrants to take on some real responsibility for the direction or the project. The original people can only successfully block this at the cost of the decline of the organization itself. It should be said that voluntary 'caring,' or politically enlightened organizations can often be just as brutal in these situations as commercial companies.

Conclusion

So where are we in regard to the possibilities of participatory communication? I am convinced that we need to take a fresh look at both the concept and the practice, reappraising the contributions of people like Freire and Buber, who have provided us with an alternative pattern of living and doing. At the same time, without falling into the trap of dogmatism, there is a need to realistically evaluate projects which purport to be "participatory." No doubt participation, dialogue and communion are essential to the success of an alternative communication program, but projects based on such criteria must also recognize the danger of the rigid theoretical stance. There is a need for participatory communication projects to be open to the needs of a changed environment, and to the needs of the people, as well as be based on a non-dogmatic and flexible praxis.

The purpose of communication is to create a community. Participation is both the basis *for* and the milieu *of* community. By revolting against authoritarian structures and patriarchal styles, we have rightly stressed the need for increased participation. But we need to be on our guard lest participation itself should become a gimmick of authoritarian engineering. It is equally important to become critically aware of the limits of participation lest we should fall into the ideology of a facile egalitarianism which violates the integrity of persons in community and militates against true participation. Ultimately, the importance of any participatory communication project lies in the ability of the persons involved to internalize and "live" the logic of participation.

References

Brecht, B. "Radio as a Means of Communication: A Talk on the Function of Radios." (reprinted) *Screen,* 1979-80, Winter, 20 (2/4), 24-28. (Reprint)

Buber, Martin. *I and Thou.* Edinburgh: T. and T. Clark, 1958.
—, *Between Man and Man.* New York: Macmillan, 1965.

Freire, Paulo. *Education: The Practice of Freedom.* Rio de Janerio: Paz de Terra, 1967.
—, *Pedagogy of the Oppressed.* New York: Seabury Press, 1970.
—, *Pedagogy in Process.* New York: Continuum, 1978.

Freire, Paulo, and Antonio Faundez. *Learning to Question: A Pedagogy of Liberation.* New York: Continuum, 1989.

Landry, C., et al. *What a Way to Run a Railroad: An Analysis of Radical Failure.* London, Comedia Publishing Group, 1985.

1927
1960
1963
1964
1967
1969
1970
1971
1972
1973
1974
1975
1976
1977
1978
1979
1980
1981
1982
1983
1984
1985
1986
1987
1988
1989
1990
1991
1992
1993
1994
1995
1996
1997
1998
1999
2000
2001
2002
2003
2004
2005
2006

THE CONCEPT OF PARTICIPATION: TRANSFORMING RHETORIC TO REALITY

By Shirley A. White

1994 The notion of "power to the people" or "people power" originally did pose a threat to the hierarchical power structure of development. It connoted a revolution, a Robin Hood-like action, and "power taking"—a definite loss of status and perks connected with being in a superior power position. These reactions were linked to a power concept of "zero-sum" notions of distributive power. The idea of generative power has emerged as a less threatening, more humane and realistic approach to power issues. It is consistent with and appropriate to the concept of participation: that people, congruent with their own human potentials, inner life forces and cultural identity, can generate their own source of power—whatever power necessary to accomplish the objectives they set for themselves and their community.

Those external development catalyst/activities which aspire to lead people to develop and explore their own power sources must hold a central belief that people are also intellectually capable and have the communication competencies to organize their lives in a more liberated manner. But when this does happen, they must be prepared to back off and allow the "liberationists" to explore further on their own. If this new freedom of expression and freedom to dialogue with any other human being and to learn from this dialogue is exercised, it may be regarded as a boomerang effect by the activists. It is like waiting for one's child to grow up and be on his/her own, but disbelieving and resisting when it actually happens. If the participatory acts are genuine and the power generated is enlightened with functional knowledge, then the context wherein self-reliant development can take place becomes a reality.

Liberation

People, if given the opportunity and after acquiring the appropriate knowledge necessary to develop their own strategies, can achieve or gain the ability to determine the course of their own lives. The sense of self-confidence they develop is in itself empowering. Though empowerment is usually conceptualized as moving out of a condition or sense of deprivation or oppression, it can also be looked at as a positive, holistic outcome of self-discovery, successful human interaction and the ability to dialogue with people different from one's self. The confidence to engage in group processes is itself a liberating action.

Genuine participation is intrinsic to genuine relationships. Supportive communication behaviors characterize the truly liberated person. True liberation brings with it a solid sense of self, an active concern for one's self in relation to others and an inner life force that pushes toward meaningful human relationships, liberating and catalyzing action toward shared goals.

Conscientization

Freire's concept of *conscientization* is central to the theme of participation. To activate consciousness and critical awareness of one's situation and environment, one's identity, one's talents and one's alternatives for freedom of action is an imperative to participatory action. Freire (1973) notes "the permanent search of people together with others for their becoming more fully human in the world in which they exist." This suggests that conscientization and critical awareness alone do not inevitably lead to action. ... It does suggest that action is more likely to be an outcome when people engage in dialogue and search together.

Freire introduced the concept of "dialogic action." His recent book with Ira Shor (1989), *The Pedagogy of Liberation*, is an exciting and useful articulation of the kind of education which is necessary for liberation. Freire's dialogic action unites the concept of action with the concept of reflection—reflective thought being regarded as the core of education. He uses the concept of "praxis," which for him is a process beginning with reflection, continuing with action and returning to reflection in a spiraling, circular manner. Atucha and Crone (1982) have successfully applied this theory of conscientization and dialogic action as a communication methodology in an integrated education, health and family planning program in Honduras.

Interestingly this project is exemplary of transactional communication outlined by Nair and White (1987) as a continuous interaction of people at the grass roots and information sources over time "to arrive at shared meanings." The Atucha and Crone project cast the health institutions and their representatives in a dialogic role with the campesinos themselves, activating a conscientization process which ultimately resulted in the campesinos' investment in decisions which affected them. The researchers concluded:

> The experience of the project has been valuable in that the goals of the institutions involved have coincided with the needs and interests of the communities. In addition, the tools used in the development of the project have given rise to new knowledge which has strengthened the technical capacity of the personnel involved. By establishing close contacts with the communities through the techniques of horizontal communication, a dialogue has been generated in relation to their own reality, through which problems have been identified and alternative solutions sought.

Empowerment is achieved through conscientization. It can become specialized through participatory processes that increase understanding and a sense of control necessary for making contribution to development decisions. Having enough confidence to demand one's rights, and get them, does not rest in conscientization alone, but in generating one's own power and uniting with others in making demands that are mutually beneficial. Empowerment also rests on the integrity of people and their culture, enactment of personal values

and aspiration to preserve identity—all are necessary for sustaining the psychic energy required for human development and change.

Self-Reliance

The concept of self-reliance is an integral aspect of participation, both as an outcome and as a part of the process. Participation in and of itself is an act of self-reliance that must be accompanied by self-confidence. It is a necessary element for enabling people to move out of dependency relationships. It is an important concept for development and for participatory communication, but it can be interpreted and operationalized from a number of differing perspectives.

In development circles, the use of the term "self-reliance" often refers to conditions of economic stability and policies that, in turn, impact on "country-level" political stability. That is to say, economics and politics are often inseparable processes in development. To become self-reliant means that focus is on strengthening local economic resources and making the community more self-sufficient, at least to the point of providing indigenous employment opportunities. But local-level resources do link a broader community to clusters of small villages, and to state-, regional- and country-level economic resources.

There have been many examples of development policies pursued in the name of self-reliant economics that have had devastating effects. In some cases, the road to self-reliance has been mapped in terms of the exploitation of a particular commodity that happens to be abundant, or in the case of agriculture, a crop that grows well in a specific area. By specialization, moving away from diversity, some countries have become more, rather than less, resource dependent and are at the mercy of the world market. This interpretation of self-reliance has often been translated into a low quality of life for rural people by forcing them to change stable living patterns or to migrate to overcrowded urban settings. Additionally, it has not contributed to the autonomy and independence of countries. There are of course natural

1927
1960
1963
1964
1967
1969
1970
1971
1972
1973
1974
1975
1976
1977
1978
1979
1980
1981
1982
1983
1984
1985
1986
1987
1988
1989
1990
1991
1992
1993
1994
1995
1996
1997
1998
1999
2000
2001
2002
2003
2004
2005
2006

resource issues that do fit this interpretation of self-reliance. Oil resources are one example. Participation of the people—the masses—in the macro-level economic and political decision making, from this self-reliance perspective is necessarily limited to exercising their preferences in the political process which may only be available in democratic political systems.

But the goals for self-reliance at the local level can focus more heavily on human resource development needs, which do not necessarily negate the economic dimensions but complement them. Immediate concerns can focus on basic needs of the people, catalyzing individual and group participation. This becomes a challenging arena for making participatory communication a part of the dynamics as an important activity to develop self-reliant individuals who are confident enough to speak up with their own points of view, unite together to define community needs, and have a strong voice in setting priorities and action agendas. This includes taking control of the media, its message and ideally its ownership. Through indigenous media, the masses can be made aware of available resources and be encouraged to take advantage of useful information the media presents in a language they can understand.

When individuals become self-reliant, their behavior will change—from apathy to action, from dependence to independence, from alienation to involvement, from intolerance to tolerance, from powerlessness to assertiveness, from defensiveness to supportiveness, from manipulatable to self-determined, from other-directed to inner-directed, from ignorant to knowledgeable. A community of self-reliant people will be capable of diagnosing its own problems, of developing innovative solutions and of fostering development diversity that is relevant, culturally sensitive and ecologically sound and sustaining.

Knowledge Sharing

Knowledge systems, knowledge generation, knowledge transfer and targeted knowledge acquisition

have traditionally been the conceptual property of the academic, the well educated and the power elite. They were linked closely with the development "hardliners" who recognized only "expert, political-based or science-based" knowledge as valid and credible. In fact, they are convinced that the reason for development was the "lack of knowledge" of the masses and the "possession of knowledge" by the development bureaucracy. So designing of development projects and persuasive communication campaign strategies to sell these development projects was standard operating procedure.

But when the concept of indigenous knowledge and its informal knowledge system crept into development, concepts of knowledge generation, knowledge acquisition and knowledge sharing painted an entirely different picture of the development process. Reluctantly, the hardliners admitted that even though superior technical or scientific knowledge was valid, it might not be relevant. Gradually it was recognized that a partnership between scientist and people at the grassroots provided a stronger case for knowledge generation and application via useful and contextual research and practice. By setting up continuing dialogue, both parties of the development action modified their positions regarding knowledge and resulting knowledge bases.

But an even more important outcome of knowledge sharing and joint discovery was the feeling of worth and equality that grew out of interpersonal interaction. Participatory research innovators began using Gramsci's term "indigenous intellectual," which gave recognized status and value to the grassroots person. Simultaneously, the scientist or agent of change learned from the people, gaining a new respect for both the person and for his/her ideas and insights.

The methodologies of participatory research, or participatory action research, thus became critical in the development process itself and became an important way to operationalize the concept of participation. Recognizing the diversity and complexity of generating information—which is of immediate utility in solving immediate problems and yet has potential for expanding a widely applicable knowledge base—is a joint challenge. Collective investigation and analysis of issues and problems not only enhances understanding but also brings about both short- and long-term solutions.

But this a radical change in perspective for the creation of knowledge and what is seen as "legitimate." This was well articulated by McGuire (1987):

> Participatory research is based on a set of assumptions about the nature of society and about social science research that are directly opposed to the assumptions of the dominant, positivist-informed, social science research. Participatory research offers a critique of, and [a] challenge to, dominant positivist social science research as the only legitimate and valid source of knowledge. It provides a radical alternative to knowledge production.

Participatory researchers value useful knowledge and place a high value on developmental changes. Often adult educators as researchers put analysis within community and social structures. They conceive the world in terms of "conflict theories of society," recognizing conflict of interest, inequality and the dynamics of oppression and change. Problem definition in the participatory action research tradition is influenced by the tradition's commitment to "real" problems, for a variety of interest groups may be affected by research results. As a matter of fact, oppressed peoples often can identify their problems even when scientists or development catalyzers do not observe them (Brown and Tandon, 1983).

Uphoff (1992), the reporting on a seven-year irrigation project to improve water management and agricultural production through farmer organization and participation, admitted that his understanding of social sciences was drastically altered in the process of his research. He confessed:

> As I became immersed in efforts to establish farmer organizations so that some of the poorest families in an underdeveloped country could improve their standard of living, I found myself rethinking much of what I have previously learned as a student and as a professional social scientist. Fortunately, as the conventional explanations of individuals' motivation and collective action began to appear less satisfactory, I was able to find many helpful ideas in writings on the "cutting edge" of various disciplines ranging from physics and business management to cognitive science and philosophy.
>
> 'Rigorous' and 'analytical' approaches to problem solving, although they have their merits, can blind one to possibilities. They stereotype judgments about people and impose notions of narrow, sequential causation where more diffuse, concurrent influences and effects need to be understood and utilized with more expansive concepts of human nature and motivations.

Uphoff's comments are enlightening and represent the change of mindset required to insure genuine participation. It seems apparent that unless people can acquire knowledge and other "tools," such as confidence and ability to produce their own knowledge, they will be unable to play out their own struggles for local control and self-reliance. This is important for knowledge sharing and for the establishment of indigenous knowledge systems that will create a conducive environment and facilitate the acquisition of resources for education and training in the local context. Indeed, one of the changes of participatory communication for change and development is to catalyze and energize indigenous knowledge systems and the necessary communication systems to make them operative. ...

While rhetoric is always with us and perhaps remains just rhetoric, in the case of participation on the parameters of development circles, there is some indication that rhetoric is steadily evolving into reality. Numerous private and public foundations, nongovernment organizations, government development agencies and international development organizations are making continuous, serious efforts to

1927
1960
1963
1964
1967
1969
1970
1971
1972
1973
1974
1975
1976
1977
1978
1979
1980
1981
1982
1983
1984
1985
1986
1987
1988
1989
1990
1991
1992
1993
1994
1995
1996
1997
1998
1999
2000
2001
2002
2003
2004
2005
2006

facilitate popular participation. The positive efforts of such institutions and agencies are recognized. However, in the case of communities or countries, the vision of participation can only become reality through channeling the energy and intellect of people into human relationships and dialogue.

"Genuine participation," fortunately and unfortunately, is driven by human compassion, unselfish motives, sensitivity to the feelings and worth of others, supportive communication, openness to change, and the shifting of responsibility and power. Skeptics say it is unrealistic to have an expectation of "genuine participation." Optimists say we *can* create a new reality that honors cultural human rights and operates within a contextual environment which is tolerant of diversity and sensitive to human needs. It is possible to blend diversity and achieve common goals in the course of development.

References

Annis, Sheldon. "The Next World Bank? Financing Development From the Bottom Up," *Grassroots Development,* 1972, 11 (1).

Atucha, Luis Maria Aller, and Catherine D. Crone (1982), "A Participatory Methodology for Integrating Literacy and Health Education in Honduras," *Convergence: An International Journal of Adult Education,* 1982, 15 (2), 70-81.

Brown, L. David, and Rajesh Tandon. "Ideology and Political Economy in Inquiry: Action Research and Participatory Research." *Journal of Applied Behavioral Science,* 1983, 19 (3), 36-40.

Cohen, J. M., and Norman T. Uphoff. "Participation's Place in Rural Development: Seeking Clarity through Specificity." *World Development,* 1980, 8, 213-35.

Childers, Erskine B. "The New Age of Information: What Kind of Participation?" *Development,* 1990, 2, 11-16.

Deshler, David, and Donald Sock. "Community Development Participation: A Concept Review of the International Literature." Paper presented at the International League for Social Commitment in Adult Education, Ljungskile, Sweden, 1985.

Fals Borda, Orlando. *Knowledge and People's Power.* New Delhi: Indian Social Institute, 1988.

Freire, Paulo. *Pedagogy of the Oppressed.* New York: Seabury Press, 1970.
—. *Cultural Action for* Freedom. Harmondsworth: Penguin, 1972.
—. *Education for Critical Consciousness.* New York: Continuum, 1973.

ILEIA Staff. *Participatory Technology Development in Sustainable Agriculture.* Leusden, The Netherlands: Information Center for Low External Input and Sustainable Agriculture, 1989.

Kerr, Stephen T. "Strategies for Change: Appropriate Technology for Education in Developing Countries." PLET, 1981, 19 (3), 228-33.

Lineberry, William P., ed. *Assessing Participatory Development: Rhetoric Versus Reality.* Boulder, San Francisco: Westview Press, 1989.

McGuire, Patricia. *Doing Participatory Research: A Feminist Approach.* Amherst: University of Massachusetts-Amherst, 1987.

McNamara, Robert S. Annual address by Robert S. McNamara, President of the World Bank and its Affiliates. In the 1973 Annual Proceedings of the Board of Governors, IBRD. Washington, D.C.: World Bank, 1973.

Moore, Sylvia. "Participatory Communication in the Development Process." *The Third Channel,* 1986, 2 (2) 4, 586-623.

Nair, K. S., and Shirley A. White. "Participation is the Key to Development Communication." *Media Development,* 1987, 34 (3), 36-40.

Shor, Ira, and Paulo Freire. *Pedagogy of Liberation.* Granby, Massachusetts: Bergin and Harvey, 1989.

Uphoff, Norman, with Priti Rammamurthy and Roy Steiner. *Learning from Gal Oya: Possibilities for Participatory Development and Post-Newtonian Social Science.* Ithaca, New York: Cornell University Press, 1992.

Originally published in *Participatory Communication: Working for Change and Development,* edited by Shirley White, K. Sadanandan Nair and Joseph Ascroft. Sage Publications, India, 1994. Reproduced with permission of the publicataion, Sage Publications India Pvt. Ltd., New Delhi, India.

1984 1985 1986 1987 1988

A Handful of Pioneers That Left Too Soon

EXCERPT FROM:

THE FOGO PROCESS: AN INTERVIEW WITH DONALD SNOWDEN

By Wendy Quarry

1984 **Don:** Let's take something of relatively minor importance but worked. Paul Macleod focused on young people in the Port Au Choix area and traditional hostilities that had existed among the communities in the area. Working through the parish priest, Father Desmond McGrath, who supported this approach very strongly and understood it, Macleod spoke on film about the approach we were using. Father McGrath was able to use this film to help break down barriers among the kids in different communities. There were real hostile barriers. We used the material, as I said, to create an interest in support of a local organization, and that was effective.

Wendy: But, Don, did you know that at the beginning, or did you learn that? I mean, you went in first and learned about the community and then made decisions about what to film.

Don: First of all I should go back to our tradition in Newfoundland with the extension service. After I came we would never put an extension worker into an area unless the area asked for him or her. So that was the beginning. The field workers went into the area, spent time getting to know it well, getting to know the problems and aspirations of the people. We began to know what it was they didn't know and then were in a position to make judgments about the kinds of material and who might be good spokespeople in the area.

Wendy: So would you say that was tenet No. 1? That you must have somebody in there who is a community development worker or field worker who knows the area?

Don: Very much so.

Wendy: That was No. 1?

Don: Absolutely. I do not believe that conventional film makers can go in and make that kind of film. They can go in and make documentary films, and when they do that, they emasculate people and they pick whatever they want out of it. Good documentary film makers use that technique. But where the whole process is controlled locally, that is, the information is put on film or video, the editing rights are vested in people. One thing that Low did from the very beginning with the Fogo example was film people where they were comfortable. That is incredibly important. He did that because of his vast experience as a very, very good documentary film maker.

Wendy: But no question, Don, there must be control on the part of the film maker or film crew or community worker as to what gets filmed?

Don: Absolutely.

Wendy: Is that manipulation?

Don: No, I don't think it is manipulation at all. The community discusses the kinds of things that they think are issues. I mean it is manipulative in the sense that not every person in every community agrees. That sounds to me like a kind of spurious intellectual argument that is meaningless. I mean what the hell does manipulative mean?

Wendy: I don't know.

Don: No, I don't either, but I think I know the difference in your question. And the fact is that traditional film making can be as manipulative. But this process is far less so. Far less so. Because you have community workers who are there all the time. And who, if they are any good, know what bothers them and what potential they have, and where they are getting screwed up, and they know that because they live there and work all the time among those people.

Wendy: Well, then, what is it that film does that the community worker couldn't do without the film?

Don: Well, you can't carry people from community to community if you are a community worker. Film does that for you. It gives people a chance to see people like themselves who may have the same concerns and aspirations as they have and who seem sometimes to offer solutions that might be mutually beneficial. But it is not as effective in areas where there is not a bombardment of moving images and sound. Don't forget that in that area of Newfoundland at the time, there was almost no television. People were relatively isolated. That film under those circumstances could play a very significant role in providing information and in introducing them to possible changes in attitudes.

Wendy: Do you think that is key?

Don: Oh sure it's key. Because we subsequently were asked to go to work in the United States, Colin Low and I, and we had a massive project that took us into all the poor states of the southern United States, but it just didn't work to the same extent. One of the reasons was that, in these areas, people were used to television and had lots of access to information in ways that people didn't have in the outports of Newfoundland at that time.

Wendy: Do you think that this has anything to do with why this process might be successful in, say, the Third World, in some parts of the Third World, let's put it that way?

Don: Yes, very much so. In rural areas of the Third World particularly. I simply am not an urban worker, so I can't make any statements that are important in any sense about the way in which this might be used in urban areas. I just simply can't make any comment about how effective the techniques would be, but only in areas where people have almost no access to information. Where they are deprived of any sense of their own worth. Where they have never been able to marshall their enormous experiences in the past and to teach one another. If they have simply not had ac-

cess to the important external information, then video could do the job. There is nothing else to do. Printing for many of these people is meaningless. They can't read and write. Radio has never been designed in these places to deal with their problems and to assist them.

Wendy: It could be though?

Don: It might well be, but I would argue for the sake of argument, and from personal conviction, I would argue that it can never be as potent as video.

Wendy: Why?

Don: Because the moving image combined with sound is a far more effective device for learning, I believe. Especially when you are dealing with anything that has to do with learning manual skills. You can see things that you simply can't offer in any other way.

Wendy: Yet, one of the things that I have read about the power of the Fogo process is what happens to people when they see themselves, or they talk about the legitimatization process, people themselves are deemed worthy enough to be recorded on film. This unleashes something in individuals. Do you support that argument?

Don: I think that might be true. Although, in my experience with rural people, the thing that surprised me most of all is how easily they come to using the medium. Let's talk about video, because video is the technology that is used in this now. When people are introduced to video as a tool for them and about them only, that's how we introduce it, the novelty is high at the beginning. Everybody is excited about it. But it very soon wears off, the idea of being on video and appearing important. I don't think that that is important to most of the poor of the world. I think that what is important is what happens as a result of that. Only after something happens is it possible that they begin to think of video. But I haven't even seen that in a widespread way. I simply have not seen it. People don't have the movie star syndrome. That's not what it is about at all. They have an enormous capacity to have stimula-

1927
1960
1963
1964
1967
1969
1970
1971
1972
1973
1974
1975
1976
1977
1978
1979
1980
1981
1982
1983
1984
1985
1986
1987
1988
1989
1990
1991
1992
1993
1994
1995
1996
1997
1998
1999
2000
2001
2002
2003
2004
2005
2006

A Handful of Pioneers That Left Too Soon   **489**

tion from it based on the message they are receiving. Not on necessarily. …

Wendy: Are you telling me that it's the messages that are important?

Don: Sure it is. That's why I always resist documentary film makers introducing all kinds of fancy production values to this sort of material. I don't think it is necessary at all. I think that there is a hell of a lot of cross cultural-examination has got to go on before we know very much about that. Nobody has done it yet.

Wendy: In what sense?

Don: Well, in the sense of Andreas Fuglesang's examination of the way in which people visually perceive different things when they come from different cultures. That is a whole important area that nobody has done a lot of work in.

Wendy: You don't buy that stuff?

Don: It may work with people who are middle class urbanites. And it may work with people who are local politicians. But I don't think that it has made a lot of difference to the way people were perceived in rural communities. They may have had some importance that they didn't have. Maybe younger people too. Maybe teenagers regarded that as pretty important. But I'm not sure that it had any lasting effect on the way people were perceived. Except for those who made incredibly powerful statements, like Billy Carne on Fogo Island. Like Olga Spence in Port Au Choix. Like Ray Ward on the Labrador coast. They were seen by others as being enormously important people because of what they said. Not because they were in film. Who can say whether Billy Crane on Fogo Island was enhanced among his peers because he appeared on film, when they may have hated like hell what he had to say and disagreed, and that would be the impression they had of Billy Crane's film?

Wendy: I'm talking about the effect of seeing yourself on film.

Don: I think that's so highly subjective that I couldn't even comment on that. I don't think that it really matters. I don't think that matters very much at all. Obviously it matters if an extreme circumstance arises under which a person really despises himself for what he sees in that image. But don't forget that this process that we follow allows a person to obliterate it before anybody else ever sees it. And interestingly enough, nobody does that. So people cannot dislike that so much. They may get… I don't think that Dan Roberts on Fogo Island, for example, ever saw himself as an enhanced person because of the enormous wisdom that he imparted to people on Fogo Island, through the film material. That was just Dan Roberts. And just the way Dan Roberts thought and spoke. That film didn't change Dan Roberts, or didn't make him say anything wise or in another way, that was simply the way he was, and that's what I find. I find an enormous directness and honestly in rural people in using this medium. There is nothing slick or manipulative about it. It could be used in a manipulative way. I can see how it can be done. I don't dislike the word manipulative in examination of this process. What is manipulative is at a point where a good community animator sees some people in his community of interest beginning to pick up something and run with it. Pointing it in a direction that may lead to some kind of salvation. Some kind of solution to a problem. Then the good animator uses that material in a manipulative sense. He stops and gets people discussing it. It's how you use it. The thing about this kind of filming is that you start ass-backwards. You start with what it is you are trying to achieve. What is it you are trying to accomplish? Not what it is this marvelous person or this marvelous idea for a film is here, how do we develop it so we get a finished product? A nice documentary film. In this case you say here it is, what is it going to do?

Wendy: You set objectives at the beginning?

Don: Sure you do. What is it that people want to have happen here? Then you go backwards from that through how you use film as a tool to help that occur.

That's the kind of by-product that has come out of what Colin Low has started on Fogo Island.

Wendy: How did the film help the animator?

Don: In a number of ways. First of all, to let people see that there are other people who have ideas applicable to them. Or let them see whether those ideas are constructive or may lead to actions that could harm the community. The second thing is that the process itself allows an animator to illustrate visually things he can do in circumstances, to move tasks, projects, physical things in a way that cannot be done otherwise. The film helps an animator to focus his own thinking on where he is going. Where he is going in relation to the community he is working in. It helps the community to see different points of view. To see different techniques it can apply to itself. It also helps an animator to get into that community and into other communities that can benefit from the strength of the community on film.

Wendy: And bring it back in, you mean?

Don: Take it to other communities. Extend the learning process from the community where it has been happening into other communities where it hasn't yet happened.

Wendy: In that sense, do you see film as catalyst?

Don: Very much so. But the form itself is not very useful, I don't think. You pick a hundred people off the street and put them in front of that Fogo Island. Fogo Islanders probably last because it is about them. Collectively… if they were just used in a random fashion, it has no value. Very little. It has some historical value now, certainly. But where it is used in formal teaching situations, for example, in the Folklore Department at Memorial University, which has made extensive use of the Fogo film over the years, and does so constantly. It might well be worth somebody's going to see it. I'll tell you about him [faculty]. He uses it very much so in a classroom situation. They have used

that film as a take-off for discussion and examination of beliefs of people and so on.

Wendy: I see that as something outside of the process.

Don: Yes, very much so. It's a spin-off. There are lots of spin-offs from this. But don't forget the use of film in a direct educational sense is. You can say it's a spin-off of the process. I don't believe that. I believe it's part of the process. I believe that is not just emotion that you are attempting to stimulate, but intellect as well, and formal learning. But you use local situations and local people in that formal learning process. Labrador was the next area that had any kind of saturation coverage. Labrador was the most extreme situation in which I worked in North America.

Quarry, W. 1984. "The Fogo Process: An interview with Donald Snowden," *Interaction*. Varnasi, India: Bhargava Bhushan Press. Copyright © 1984, Wendy Quarry. Reprinted with permission of the copyright holder.

1927
1960
1963
1964
1967
1969
1970
1971
1972
1973
1974
1975
1976
1977
1978
1979
1980
1981
1982
1983
1984
1985
1986
1987
1988
1989
1990
1991
1992
1993
1994
1995
1996
1997
1998
1999
2000
2001
2002
2003
2004
2005
2006

THE FOGO PROCESS: DEVELOPMENT SUPPORT COMMUNICATION IN CANADA AND THE DEVELOPING WORLD

Excerpt from: Communication in Development: A Multinational Perspective

By H. Anthony Williamson

1990 In 1967, as part of Canada's "War on Poverty," the Challenge for Change Programme of the National Film Board (NFB) of Canada sent renowned film maker Colin Low and a film unit to Newfoundland to make a documentary on rural poverty. He teamed up with Don Snowden, then director of the Extension Service of Memorial University of Newfoundland. Snowden had been angered by a report of the Economic Council of Canada which described poverty from the point of view of an urban central Canadian, and which did not take any cognisance of the lifestyle and perceptions of rural Canadians. It was his idea to make a series of films in Newfoundland, through the Extension Service, to expose this bias and to show Canadians that the real poverty in places like rural Newfoundland was the poverty of information, of isolation from decision making, of lack of organization (Quarry, 1984). When he learned that Challenge for Change intended to make a film or films on rural poverty in Newfoundland, and that they had selected Colin Low, he was delighted, because he had been a longtime admirer of Low. Upon meeting him, he knew he was the right person in the right place at the right time.

Together they explored the province, in search of an appropriate case study. They decided upon Fogo Island, a small island in Notre Dame Bay off the northeast coast of Newfoundland, on which there were 10 communities with a total population of about 5,000 people. Like many rural areas of Newfoundland at that time, the Islanders were being encouraged to resettle to "growth areas," and redevelopment of the island did not appear likely. Fogo offered a microcosm of many rural areas in Newfoundland. Moreover, the Extension Service had Fred Earle, a field worker engaged in community development and adult education on the island. From the area, he was respected and trusted by everybody. It looked like a perfect choice, and Colin Low came to Fogo for the summer, recruited some local students to apprentice with his film crew and, with the help of Fred Earle, started interviewing and filming Fogo Islanders.

Fogo Island and rural Newfoundland twenty years ago presented a social environment so different from today that it is difficult to imagine the context in which the film project took place, but it is important to know the context, because it set the stage for a communications process that has come to be known around the world.

The Fogo Process

In the 1960s, the majority of rural "outports" were not accessible by road. Many lacked electricity, phones, television, newspapers and even reliable radio reception. With a long colonial history, Newfoundland had only become a province of Canada in 1949. The province inherited and maintained a highly centralized government, and municipal or local government only existed in the larger regional centres. A sense of isolation was exacerbated by the fact that over 50 percent of the rural population, composed in the main of descendants from pioneer settlers from Ireland and West England, in over 1,000 outports, were functionally illiterate. In these little outports authority was vested in the local merchants and clergymen, who acted as brokers in purveying information to and from the centre of decision making in St. John's, the capital of Newfoundland. The paternalism of church, state and commerce helped convince unschooled outport people that what knowledge they had was of little value. They equated knowledge with "learning" and considered themselves ignorant, despite a whole range of skills which had been passed on and accumulated for generations.

The Extension Service of Memorial University had only three field workers in 1967. They were experienced men from rural Newfoundland who were pioneering in a process of community education known as participatory development. The field workers lived in the communities and shared the lives and aspirations of the people. Thus, they established a pattern of mutual trust and growth. This kind of Extension Service work was unique among Canadian universities. The teamwork of Colin Low and Fred Earle forged a process which gave new dimension to the fledgling Challenge for Change Programme and to the Extension Service. Because it started on Fogo Island, it has come to be known as the Fogo Process.

Fogo Island

Instead of producing a single social documentary on the theme of rural poverty, Low produced a series of unscripted "modules," some 28 of them, which depicted Fogo Islanders talking about a range of concerns and interests: the fishery, location of a high school, producer cooperatives, ship building, the role of women, local government, the merchants, resettlement and so on. Modules showed the children playing with homemade toys and games, a wedding, step dancing, a house party, storytelling and singing, as well. The joys and strengths of Fogo society, as well as the problems and fears of the people, were represented. The modules focused on ordinary people and personalities rather than on issues. What emerged in the totality of the modules was a holistic view of life on Fogo Island as perceived by the people themselves. They were the subjects in the modules instead of the objects of a scriptwriter's perceptions. These film modules and the way in which they were used in the context of participatory development is what has come to be known as the Fogo Process.

In the autumn of 1967, after the 16mm black-and-white films had been developed and rough cut into modules

at the National Film Board, they were brought back to Fogo Island and shown to the people at a series of community screenings. At each meeting, the NFB utilization officer or the extension field worker, using the films as a catalyst, led a discussion on a development issue of concern to Fogo Islanders. The modular nature of the body of films facilitated utilization, because each screening could include material that was most appropriate or of most interest to each specific community or the specific group gathered at the meeting.

A number of reactions and responses, not specifically related to the subject matter of the films, took place which, at the time, were not anticipated. People viewing themselves or their friends and relatives for the first time saw themselves in a new light, as others might see them. Many saw for the first time that they in fact had knowledge, skills, strengths and a lifestyle which were of value, and which, moreover, they and their friends were expressing articulately. As Andrew Brett, of Shoal Bay, said in one module:

> We don't got to be afraid of them things anymore. What we know we got to let people know that we know it and getting out and doing something. ... By that they'll know what we can do. ... Let's let people know what we are capable of doing and what we know. Otherwise we'll never be known. (Brett, 1967)

Individuals seeing themselves in the films, and Fogo Islanders as a whole experienced an increase in self-confidence not only in the value of their own lives, but in their power to express themselves and to do something about them.

In this reinforcement process, many also saw that as islanders, they were divided one against another, community against community. Suddenly they saw that as Fogo Islanders, they were one community, and that if they pulled together for the common good of the island, they stood a better chance for development. Thus, the films became a catalyst for consensus building.

1927
1960
1963
1964
1967
1969
1970
1971
1972
1973
1974
1975
1976
1977
1978
1979
1980
1981
1982
1983
1984
1985
1986
1987
1988
1989
1990
1991
1992
1993
1994
1995
1996
1997
1998
1999
2000
2001
2002
2003
2004
2005
2006

Finally, with the newfound confidence and consensus, and with the aid of the Memorial University extension field worker and rural development agents of the provincial government, the films also acted as a catalyst for action. In meetings, people not only saw they shared common interests, but they started to create strategies for action.

It is tempting to say that the films in themselves fostered all of these things and were able to draw linear relationships between the films and subsequent action and development, but it would be incorrect to do so. The Fogo Process, as it started to emerge from the original filming and screenings on Fogo Island, was critically linked to a sustained program of community development efforts of the university and government. Although the attention Fogo Island received…helped to accelerate developments on the island, a passive viewing of the films in isolation from any constructive discussions and follow-up planning meetings would have created no more than a passing moment of excitement and interest at best.

Another element of the Fogo Process, as it emerged, was the screening of the films for Cabinet Ministers in the government of Newfoundland and Labrador. At the time, the president of Memorial University feared that criticisms of government in some of the modules would cause political problems for Memorial University. However, the Cabinet Ministers who saw the films reacted favourably and constructively. Cabinet Ministers even responded on film. More important, the government became convinced that there were development alternatives for Fogo Island other than resettlement. It entered into a partnership with the people of Fogo, one forged with at least some impetus from the films.

It is important to remember that the Fogo Process emerged as it did largely because of the isolation, lack of electronic communications and inaccessibility to the centralized decision makers. It was the widespread prevalence of these conditions which led the Extension Service of Memorial University to incorporate the Fogo Process in its community development programme elsewhere in rural Newfoundland and Labrador.

References

Brett, Anthony, 16mm black-and-white film module (13 minutes) at Shoal Bay, St. John's, Newfoundland: Educational Technology Division, School of Continuing Studies, Memorial University of Newfoundland, 1967.

Gwyn, S., "Cinema as Catalyst," Newfoundland: Extension Division, Memorial University of Newfoundland, 1972.

Iglauer, E., and Donald Snowden "Development Dialogue," 1(2), 63-71, Uppsala, Sweden: The Dag Hammarskjöld Foundation, 1964.

Kennedy, T., "Beyond Advocacy," doctoral thesis, Cornell University, Ithaca, N.Y., 1964.

Quarry, W., "The Fogo Process—an Interview with Donald Snowden," Interaction, 2(3), pp. 28-63, Varanasi, India, 1984.

Snowden, D., P. MacLeod, and L. Kusupak, "Methods and Media in Community Participation," Case Studies, Dag Hammarskjöld Foundation (forthcoming).

Williamson, H. A., The Fogo Process in Communications: Training for Agriculture and Rural Development (Rome, Italy: FAO, 1975), pp. 93-98.

From Chapter 13 in Communication in Development: A Multinational Perspective, Fred L. Casmir, ed. (Norwood, New Jersey: Ablex Publishing Corporation, 1990). Reprinted with permission.

1927
1960
1963
1964
1967
1969
1970
1971
1972
1973
1974
1975
1976
1977
1978
1979
1980
1981
1982
1983
1984
1985
1986
1987
1988
1989
1990
1991
1992
1993
1994
1995

EXCERPT FROM:

ERSKINE CHILDERS: A DEVCOM PIONEER

By Royal Colle

1996 Among the earliest pioneers in the field we now call development communication was a United Nations unit called the development support communications service (DSCS), which operated under the aegis of the United Nations Development Programme (UNDP). DSCS was based in Bangkok. It was in DSCS where the ideas began to come together to form a distinctively new approach to communication as part of development interventions and Erskine Childers was the key person in the UNDP operation.

Many knew him best for the pioneering work he did in advocating communication as an integral component of UN development projects. An example of this is the paper he and his wife, Mallica Vajrathan, directed at UN organisations in 1968 which is excerpted below.

While Childers did not write any books directly related to development communication, like those of Lerner, Rogers, Schramm and others prominent in the field, he wrote the papers and made presentations that foreshadowed some of the concepts, principles and methods that have emerged more prominently during the past several decades. ...

Perhaps the strength of his leadership in development communication is demonstrated best in Childers' own words. In "Sharing Knowledge," FAO's video program on communication for sustainable development, Childers said:

> If you want development to be rooted in the human beings who have to become the agents of it as well as the beneficiaries, who will alone decide on the kind of development they can sustain after the foreign aid has gone away, then you have got to communicate with them, you have got to enable them to communicate with each other and back to the planners in the capital city. You have got to communicate the techniques that they need in order that they will decide on their own development. If you do not do that you will continue to have weak or failing development programmes. It's as simple as that.

Although Childers spent his early career as a writer, doing scripts for radio and television, especially on topics related to international affairs and the United Nations, former United Nations Children's Fund UNICEF communication specialist Jack Ling says that Childers was a conceptualizer and a prolific writer who should be "fully recognized" for his pioneering role in development communication.

Between 1967 and 1975, Childers was based in Bangkok where, with wife Mallica Vajrathan and others, he developed the ideas and processes that became development support communication. From his post as director of the UNDP/UNICEF Regional Development Support Communication Service (Asia-Pacific), he urged the UN specialized agencies and national governments to put more resources into communication, for, as he wrote in 1968, "No innovation, however brilliantly designed and set down in a project plan of operations, becomes development until it has been communicated."

Many who had the opportunity to interact with Childers during the past decade on the Development Communication Roundtable remember the challenges he issued and the wisdom he provided in these discussions. One Roundtable member and longtime UNFPA [United Nations Population Fund] communication expert, O.J. Sikes, says:

> Erskine was a true champion of the people. He didn't invent the concept of participation, but he and Mallica breathed life into it. He drew global attention to the importance of women's rights. Today, these concepts, unpopular when he first espoused them in the 1960s, have become widely perceived as keys to development.

1996
1997
1998
1999
2000
2001
2002
2003
2004
2005
2006

Childers and Vajrathan wrote the following text in June 1968 while they were at DSCS in Bangkok. Entitled "Development Support Communications for Project Support," it was one of a collection of papers Childers was to write in the next few years advocating communication as a vital component of development planning. A major value of this piece is that it reflects lessons he and his wife learned from the field. Strikingly, with only an update of the technology mentioned, the paper is as important and relevant today as it was more than three decades ago. The careful reader can discern reference to the importance of research, to communication planning and strategy, to participation and gender issues and to the need for "bureaucratic reorientation"—all important ingredients in the practice of development communication in the 21st century. ...

Childers and Vajrathon begin their paper by noting a variety of circumstances in development that call for systematic communication support. These include the need for far greater involvement of local people in projects, confusion among farmers arising from conflicting and inaccurate information, resistance from the public due to traditional attitudes and suspicion of authority, the failure to convince key officials of the success of pilot projects, and the need to budget for their expansion. They also noted a widespread popular view that communication jobs were of inferior status compared to white-collar jobs. We join the paper after their introduction.

For the past 10 years and more, references like those set down [above] have been appearing with increasing frequency in project reports from developing countries assisted by the UN-family; or the difficulties epitomised in such phrases have been the coinage of countless discussions among UN development personnel. Each type of obstacle to project implementation encompassed by such familiar phrases is an obstacle of communication. It would be hopelessly optimistic to state that greater attention to the use of communication techniques in development projects would eliminate these recurring reports altogether.

But it can be no exaggeration on the accumulated evidence to state that perhaps no other instrument in the development process has been so grossly neglected.

There are, of course, UN-assisted projects in which there is no need for special, supporting information and communications work. But when these and a few other limited categories of projects are set apart, it must be said that virtually all others contain a very large element of communication. They are, after all, planned efforts to introduce and diffuse innovations among communities or cadres with limited funds, and to do so intensively and economically in order to telescope time-spans of growth and change that would otherwise encompass entire generations.

No innovation, however brilliantly designed and set down in a project plan of operations [PlanOps] becomes development until it has been communicated. No input or construction of material resources for development can be successful unless and until the innovations—the new techniques and surrounding changed attitudes which people will need to use those resources—have been communicated to them.

Once thus stated, the point appears to be crushingly obvious. Yet it has not been obvious in project formulation. From the moment a stranger appears in someone's field bearing government authority, a theodolite and some stakes, and drives the stakes into that ground, a long chain-reaction of communication has been launched. It begins with the first villager who sees the stake, wonders about it, speculates with a neighbour, begins asking questions that ripple out to a rapidly increasing community of profoundly concerned people. Is "Government" going to take their land? Will they get any compensation? Is it something to do with water? Will an ancestral burial ground be flooded? Is the new water for the landlord, or for us? When will "it" happen? The agricultural extension officer has been telling us to start a cooperative. Is it worth it now? "They" want us to build a new schoolhouse: will we be here, on our land, in five years' time; and if not, why put energy into a new school?

The engineers who drew up the design and specifications, the time schedule and materials—logistics for this UN-assisted project—were not asked and should not have been asked to contemplate such immediate consequences from the first act of construction. But was anyone else asked to contemplate, to draw up an accompanying information plan—a plan for purposive support communications—both to explain ... all that would follow to the surrounding community, in time, and to begin the diffusion of needed innovations among them in time?

In another entire category of projects, communication is their very raison d'etre: planned efforts to diffuse innovations among the largest possible number of ordinary people, or by training new cadres both in historically very short periods of time. The whole web of health, agricultural, vocational and other training, adult and out-of-school education, and in-school education development projects falls within this definition. All of these projects consist, first and foremost, of bodies of new information or techniques, in the hands of a relatively small number of UN and counterpart personnel, that are to be communicated to people who need them. The fundamental premise of all this assistance is that innovations can be introduced and that people will adopt them through special and accelerated effort—rather than leaving the process to "several generations of wider and better schooling," etc.

Yet the corollary of this premise in all such development work is, surely, that special and accelerative means of diffusing the innovations will be needed; every possible means that can be devised. Many, indeed most, of the innovations have been designed from experience in more developed societies. In those societies, no self-respecting planner of a training programme for a cadre of people automatically more capable of absorbing a given innovation would dream of ignoring, say, the question of advance-planning of suitable films/slides/charts and other aids to the communication process. Yet, the plain fact is that, to date, we in the UN-family have been engaged again and

again in the exercise of launching training projects for diffusion of breathtakingly "big" innovations to people far less ready to absorb them, with only the most rudimentary aids to the communication process. ...

One crucial time-factor in the communication process of development has already been mentioned—that we are trying to telescope the time-span of innovation and change from a matter of generations to a matter of years. Within this, there is a second vital time-factor—the actual phasing of a project. Whether the project-audience is a whole community or selected trainee-cadres, the innovations to be diffused are supposed to be phased over a period of perhaps five years, at most, either absolutely or per diffusion-cycle. The nature of a great many such projects leaves no margin for delay in any of the logistics. Experts are phased in by project years; newly trained cadres from one year are supposed to begin their innovation-diffusion the next; a new irrigation canal is filled with water at a date when the surrounding farmers are supposed to be ready to begin using it, first for one new kind of cultivation, then for a second crop and so on.

By the nature of what all such development projects are trying to achieve, therefore, there can be no more margin for delay in the communications-logistics than in any other, nowadays automatically, programmed element of the PlanOps. Yet this very day, all over the developing regions, there are irrigation canals filled with water not yet being used; experts and instructors for Phase-Year X of projects who can only begin to discover what communications aids they ought to have when their phase is nearly ended; and newly trained cadres of project-implementation personnel going out to their diffusion-points with no more to help them than the (quite unsuitable) texts and charts they acquired in their courses. The authors of this paper witness these problems every day of the year, in every sector of development now under UN (as other) external assistance.

In short, a great many UN-assisted projects contain, as a very precondition of efficient and effective use of the investment mode, information or communications

1927
1960
1963
1964
1967
1969
1970
1971
1972
1973
1974
1975
1976
1977
1978
1979
1980
1981
1982
1983
1984
1985
1986
1987
1988
1989
1990
1991
1992
1993
1994
1995
1996
1997
1998
1999
2000
2001
2002
2003
2004
2005
2006

"components" that ought to be advance-planned as carefully as all the other, now automatic logistics. The PlanOps of such projects should specify such a component, itemising the resources that will be required; when they will be needed relative to project phases; who will provide the resources, as between UN and government; what kinds of information materials (they may range from flip-cards and flannel graphs to films in the relevant language); and of course, the already familiar item, what communication equipment is to be supplied.

The range of development support communication in which project planners and then field executors ought to be concerned is very wide—far, far wider than is covered by considering what are called "the mass media" in the western region. Media of development support communication must be seen to include, potentially, every channel along which bodies of needed new information and ideas can be transmitted to the particular project audience. The hierarchies of government personnel in the functional or development ministries themselves are vital media. So may be a simple traditional village fair; a traditional midwife; a folk performance that may contain a potential for adaptation to a development innovation, far more powerful than a loudspeaker address by a technician from the city.

The technique of communication that may be vital in a given project need not be costly or require complicated modern equipment. We have seen communication obstacles—visibly vitiating an entire development-aid investment—that are as simple as public health education personnel not knowing how to speak to an audience. They have been well trained in the content of the health innovations they are supposed to diffuse to the people: they know the technology perfectly but they simply do not know how to address audiences of 30 or 40 village women.

It is equally important for project planners and for the new teams of specialists in development support communication—which the UN-family desperately needs—to realise that the "project-audience" for a given act of communications support varies enormously. It is by no means only "the people" en masse, whether on a national or district scale. Nor is it only the actual trainees in training projects. Echelons of government personnel who are, or who ought to be, involved in project implementation, may also need purposive, planned support communication for a variety of reasons. The moment we get away from thinking in purely Western terms, of "mass media" (publishing, radio, film, television, etc.), and consider the total network of communication that needs to be activated for a development project, the point becomes obvious. … [In this kind of communication] it may be far more important for a given project to reach, motivate and orient a precisely defined echelon of civil servants as a first phase of communications; then to devise communications programmes and materials addressed to "the people." For professionals in development support communication, "media" or channels are also considered.

It is also an axiom of this work that every act of development support communication, and the materials selected and produced for it, has to be tailored very carefully to the intended audience. Development is the deliberate introduction of a (relatively) massive disturbance in the lives, attitudes, work patterns and socioeconomic relationships of given groups of people—a disturbance deliberately telescoped, too, into unusually short periods of time. Precisely what and how much, and how quickly, and on what mental and material-incentive premises workers can ask a defined group of human beings to do is the very essence of the entire process. Consider a dairy farming film presenting electric milking machines to farmers who do not have them and have not the remotest prospect of having them. Yet the communication act of screening such a film for those farmers could involve the act of "asking" them to contemplate electric milking as an innovation. In a real case, the farmers were in fact profoundly angry about this film: they felt they were being insulted and humiliated. Development came to an angry halt at that moment.

Certain fundamental premises of development support communications follow from this. "Know your audience" … is a first precept of this development work. The need to know the "stretch potential," or the innovation-absorption capacity of given groups of people within any one phase of a project, is absolutely vital. In a great many cases, above all, for support communications directly addressed to whole communities, prior socioeconomic research and field-testing of assumptions is very important indeed.

Another crucial premise is that development support communications programmes and aids, e.g., a film, or poster, or radio broadcast, should propose only those innovations that are feasible for the audience in terms of their present actual resources (and those that a project may be injecting). Having said this, it needs hardly to be mentioned that information-communication materials made on the other side of the world, in industrialised countries for those countries depicting totally alien people doing totally alien things within alien cultures and at wholly fantastic economic and technological levels, are not only of little relevance—they may, as in the dairy film case-be counter-innovatory. And it follows inexorably from this that UN-family development projects need to have communication support materials made afresh, indigenously or within comparable situations in other (and culturally acceptable) developing countries. This is not an absolute rule: there are certain kinds of materials, on certain subjects, that can be usefully imported from advanced-technology countries; and films and other materials from such countries may be extremely useful at later phases of a project. But it may be stated as an excellent general rule of thumb that the early acts of innovation-communications in UN-assisted development projects ought to be with materials depicting the innovation in the country concerned, carried out by fellow countrymen.

Types of Development Support Communications

A broad assembly of the experience of development in the field indicates many categories of repeatedly needed support communication efforts. The following outline list is not presented in order of priority nor of action, nor are all these types of communication necessarily needed for every project. The priorities, the chronology of communication efforts within a project's time span and the combinations of programmes will vary with each project.

1. BROAD PUBLIC MOTIVATION

Every UN project is attempted, with national counterpart, in a general reservoir of public attitudes towards development in general, or the particular sector involved. The UN-family should automatically seek to assist in and encourage development support communication programmes that will motivate the public more effectively. In sectoral terms, a project may be launched at a time when, by sheer coincidence, public attention to that sector of development may be low; the national information media may never, or not for several years, present the need for development in the sector concerned. It is often true that the first support communications requirement for project implementation is simply (not necessarily easily) to "get people thinking about" the sector concerned.

2. MOTIVATION-ORIENTATION OF PROJECT IMPLEMENTERS

To date, it has almost invariably been assumed in project planning and implementation that if a given national ministry has requested the project and signed a PlanOps, all civil servants concerned will implement it automatically. Once so stated, the assumption is obviously nonsense: yet the neglect of support communications for national project-implementing personnel amounts to such an assumption.

We should assess every project to determine what help—by idea and/or material aid—the national authorities may need to ensure that the relevant echelons of civil servants, from capital city outwards, are properly informed and motivated about the project. …In our experience, one of the earliest needs may be a complete information-communications programme

1927
1960
1963
1964
1967
1969
1970
1971
1972
1973
1974
1975
1976
1977
1978
1979
1980
1981
1982
1983
1984
1985
1986
1987
1988
1989
1990
1991
1992
1993
1994
1995
1996
1997
1998
1999
2000
2001
2002
2003
2004
2005
2006

designed for these levels. ...UN-family field personnel presently have to spend grossly wasteful amounts of time simply trying to ensure that even a small number of overburdened, underpaid civil servants know even the elementary facts about a project: who is running it; what the chain of command and trouble-shooting is; where supplies come from; what the roles of possibly two or three UN agencies are; what needs to be accomplished in year one, and then and only then in year two; and so on. All of this is development support communications for project implementation. At present, we leave the whole crucial process, in the overwhelming majority of projects, to the word-of-mouth and formal-correspondence efforts of a tiny handful of UN project field officers who do have a few other things to do as well.

3. SPECIFIC ELITE AND GOVERNMENT-LEVEL INFORMATION

There are other often absolutely vital kinds of support locations at these levels, without proper attention to which, as the authors have witnessed in countless instances, an entire project runs into trouble. Among many, we would cite here:

Interdepartmental awareness of a given project and of its needs now and in the phased future is immensely important. More and more UN-assisted projects are bi- or multi-sectoral, requiring for their very functioning the coordination of several ministries at national and field levels. This simply does not happen because it is stipulated in a PlanOps. It happens only as a result of consistent, advance-planned, purposive communication—inevitably requiring special materials in one or more media.

Motivation for expansion and follow-up is another problem: At certain fairly precise dates in the forward "history" of a project, decision makers and financial controllers in Government have to authorise further steps without which the original project-investment may become largely nonsense. More counterpart personnel must be authorised, budget-allocated and recruited and trained; government has to take over

[technical assistance] costs; physical and human-resource investments of other kinds have to be implemented by government. All of this may have been foreseen and set down in the PlanOps. That does not mean that it will happen when it should happen. Once again, the first requirement is communication to the relevant decision-makers (and decision-influencers, even outside government, through press and other media) of the approaching needed actions, and of the progress of the project that justifies those actions.

.... It is [characteristic] of this problem, like so many others in development support communications, that the people who need to be reached cannot be physically brought to a place where the purpose and progress of the project can be seen by them with their own eyes. The project has to be brought to them; again, an exercise in planned communications using modern techniques and materials.

4. PROJECT CADRE-TRAINING COMMUNICATION NEEDS

The project-field where perhaps the greatest awareness of the role of planned, purposive support communications has been evident is, of course, in training. But here again, as (by now) literally thousands of UN-recruited training instructors and their counterparts could relate, we can perceive neglect in quality and quantity that is far, far more serious for training in developing countries than in industrialised ones. We have referred earlier, in the introduction, to this special phenomenon of the diffusion of innovations in developing countries inherently needing more systematic exploitation of modern techniques of communication than in the countries from which the innovations derive. Our instructors are in need of every conceivable kind of aid—films, slides, better charts and other printed aids—designed for their trainees. ...

We believe that it can be stated categorically that no project should be formulated without, there and then, its locally attuned training-aids component having been assessed, budgeted and production-planned.

This will in many cases … require prior survey and appraisal in the project-country concerned by experts in communication techniques. Only by such local assessment can any realistic appraisal be made of the extent to which the national media can produce the aids needed in time and the extent to which the UN agency concerned will have to supplement national resources. Such prior survey will cost money [but] any clinical assessment of the effectiveness of existing training projects will quickly show that the aid-investment in them has in very many cases been vitiated by neglect of this element. We believe it is entirely legitimate to assert that in training, as in all other kinds of projects under discussion in this paper, the time has come for decision to invest in communication in order to save UN assistance funds.

Communication support for training projects embraces many needs beyond the actual aids in the class of demonstration site. Among these we would mention trainee recruitment: without planned communication, no training project can possibly select the best candidates from the optimum number and level of applicants drawn from the geographical base actually envisaged for the project. We and our national partners repeatedly face the element of urbanisation in this field— the problem of training people who will stay (or at least are more likely to stay) in rural areas or at least provincial towns. …

5. APPLIED RESEARCH DISSEMINATION

Another and widespread example of the factor immediately above-referenced may be seen in the case of the numerous UN-assisted institutes for applied research in a given development sector. The PlanOps may have been only for the establishment and development of the institute itself, with the implicit assumption that government (and educational establishments) would separately see to the dissemination of the practical technology produced in the institute. In some cases, such institutes do carry a project-element of industrial-use dissemination but not, for example, extension-dissemination.

The field observations of the authors of this paper compel two suggestions about such projects. At the very least, the UN-family should plan to ensure that the work of the institute and the innovations it develops be made generally known to the public and elite through a communications document (film, brochure, as may be judged best) that can also be used in schools and colleges.

At the most, we are bound to put forward the question whether, in the appraisal of all requests for such institute projects, the family ought not to adopt the standard discipline and criterion-question to government: "Precisely how will the technology to be developed be disseminated for urgent practical use for development?" If once this question is asked as an automatic exercise, we believe that in many cases the judgment and the shaping of the project itself may alter. Accumulating practical experience indicates that it is from many such institutes themselves that the best chain of innovation-diffusion (possibly the very organisation and cadre-training of extension personnel, for example) will flow, if so planned and agreed. At the least, we believe that experience shows that it is in the early life of such institute projects, before the UN element is phased out, that concrete programming of innovation-diffusion located somewhere in very close nexus with the institute should begin. It is extremely likely that if the whole UN investment is to be maximally effective, the UN agency concerned should be prepared to assist in this innovation-diffusion as well.

In all such cases it will be obvious by now that the same kind of advance-researched, advance-planned support communications programme should be built into the project PlanOps as an outright component—the experts' permanent counterpart personnel, the materials to be produced and the appropriate share of financing needed. Institutes are ivory towers without planned communications.

6. CLOSE PROJECT-SUPPORT COMMUNICATIONS

Finally, in this necessarily broad summary of types of support needs, there is what we call "close-support"

1927
1960
1963
1964
1967
1969
1970
1971
1972
1973
1974
1975
1976
1977
1978
1979
1980
1981
1982
1983
1984
1985
1986
1987
1988
1989
1990
1991
1992
1993
1994
1995
1996
1997
1998
1999
2000
2001
2002
2003
2004
2005
2006

work for projects of all kinds. In virtually all UN-assisted projects under discussion here, there are fairly specific "project-communities" and implementing cadres. A project may be nationwide in scope, but it usually has defined sectors, and often operates either in phases or in one specific district or region entirely (i.e., a dam, a river-valley development, etc.). Assuming that the communications work at government-services level is in hand, and that there are broad national awareness and receptivity, the project still needs very considerable close-in communications support.

At this as at other levels, we and our partners in national development service have scarcely begun to use the potential of planned, project-attuned communications techniques. At very little extra cost per project-year, we could be helping to equip each such project with a properly researched and phased schedule of information-communication aids, first, to prepare the project-community for the very "arrival" of the project (for example, that matter of the "surveyors" stakes); second, to explain to the people what the project seeks to achieve for them, in their terms of reference at that time, and to answer both the easily anticipated questions they will have and (by proper prior socioeconomic research) the deeper worries which the project-disturbance will unleash; third, to motivate the people to participate for reasons that are tangible to them, and to demonstrate to them what resources of their own they can bring to bear on the effort; fourth, in careful phasing with the actual forward history of the project, to introduce to the community the specific innovations—in production, work methods, environment-exploitation and management, hygiene, whatever the sector—their adoption of which can alone make the project successful.

It needs to be heavily emphasised that, at present, the overall picture of project implementation at this level is extremely deficient in the above methods and in communication aids that are fashioned from them.

National Capability for Development Support Communications

It is, of course, fundamental in UN-family project policy that we do not, and could not ourselves alone, undertake development support communications in member-countries. But against the overall neglect of these instruments to date, and the size of the problem even strictly in terms of UN-assisted projects, the present capabilities of national media should not be overestimated. Very much more could usefully be done to provide support communications from existing national resources, given an effective communications discipline in project appraisal and formulation. But we should be under no illusions whatever as to the magnitude of extra, external assistance that ought to be brought to bear as well.

A detailed, country-by-country study of the present role and capability of national media in what we mean by development support communications is quite beyond the scope of this paper. From the aggregate experience of the authors in the several regions, however, we believe that we can make a number of legitimate general observations.

1. PROJECT LEVEL SUPPORT.

In the majority of countries receiving UN development assistance, the national authorities are constantly seeking to create a broad climate of opinion in support of development to motivate the people to participate in and contribute to economic and social progress. We have cited this kind of broad, national motivation as very important even for project implementation. But the "even" is crucial. Broad, national support communication does not by itself provide support communication at project-implementation level; it may even lose its impact if not complemented by project-level support.

A "Grow More Food Campaign," conducted across the length and breadth of a nation becomes real only when farmers in specific crop, climate and soil areas then receive the inputs and innovations they need. We must emphasise as crucial to the entire subject of this paper that this is one of the hidden "flaws" in much of the work done by national authorities today in the field of development support communications. ...

2. REACHING VILLAGES.

Among national officials who actually administer development programmes, including those receiving UN assistance, there is the universal tendency to neglect the power of communications techniques. There is a widespread assumption among governments that, since their own ministries possess infrastructures of civil servants reaching down to district and even village level, "we are in very close touch with the people already."

This view is in no way unique to the civil services of developing countries, but the reality behind the view is far more severe in them. The senior civil servant in the capital city has a picture of a nationwide network of "outlets to the people" in serried echelons below him. Those "outlets" are in fact underpaid and often overworked junior officers, usually reluctant to be working in rural or lower-status areas; operating in poor working conditions and with indifferent transport; and showered with unending and often barely legible stenciled directives about one programme and administrative problem after another.

We have studied the lines of communication of merely basic, factual information about new development projects down through these networks in many different sectors. The usual picture is that the information about the new project forms only one small element in that week's routine administrative problems, to be transmitted further down the hierarchy towards "the people." By the time transmission has experienced heat or cold, rain or dust, vehicle breakdowns or rotten overnight accommodation, and by the time the lower field echelons have coped with all the other merely routine administrative data, the new project has lost a good deal of its capital-city glory. When the news then has to be filtered through local community leadership—for example, through the village elders or council chairman, also beset by his level of

"red tape"—the new project may be lucky to enjoy two minutes of attention. Not least of the problems is that from the first moment of word-of-mouth communication, inaccuracies and omissions of vital facts that may affect community response are all too common.

3. DEVELOPMENT COMMUNICATION SPECIALISTS.

The assumption described above—that there are built-in communications for development in a country's civil service—combines in many places with a lack of awareness that modern communications techniques can be instruments of development. The view is still prevalent among many decision makers and budget controllers that media like radio, films and television are "consumer amenities that must wait for adequate economic growth"—not instruments that can virtually contribute to growth.

Apart from the deficiencies in basic infrastructure and equipment that this view perpetuates, it also produces poor morale and often indifferent calibre among government information personnel. In any country where there is any kind of private or commercial communications industry—radio, TV, feature films, privately owned newspapers—the result is that the best talent seeks the highest pay outside of government. By definition, this talent is almost entirely lost to communications for development.

The process is, of course, a vicious circle. Poorly paid and second-level information personnel, working with meagre budgets, are not very likely to stimulate new interest and respect for their development roles among decision makers and purse-controllers in Government.

4. SKILLS FOR DEVELOPMENT COMMUNICATION.

These factors mesh, in turn, with another very powerful influence currently working against the kind of development support communications we have described as so urgently needed. Existing national information personnel are still overwhelmingly urban, middle-class (or above) and Western-oriented in their concepts of communication. We discern a whole series of practical consequences that flow from this:

1927
1960
1963
1964
1967
1969
1970
1971
1972
1973
1974
1975
1976
1977
1978
1979
1980
1981
1982
1983
1984
1985
1986
1987
1988
1989
1990
1991
1992
1993
1994
1995
1996
1997
1998
1999
2000
2001
2002
2003
2004
2005
2006

a. The dominant assumption is that the job is one of disseminating "news" and/or "publicity"; and usually in press terms, since most information people have either come from the press world to government or have received print journalism training. Production of information material is widely based on the concepts of the duplicated release "for the press," as often as not with photographs of a minister or other high dignitary.

Again, there is a vicious circle. This is what most national information personnel do and are seen to do; this is what most national authorities think they are paid to do; this is what they are consequently expected to go on doing if they want next year's budget. This is all the information workers have the incentive, or often the equipment, or the time, to do. It is not at all uncommon, for example, to find a film unit with only two cameramen expected to produce up to 20 newsreel-style "documentaries on development" per year, along with a weekly newsreel proper.

b. Urban (or urbanised) themselves, working in cities, under the constant administrative influence and pressure of like people, and working in a technology that is infused with the inevitably urban outlook of Western society where it originated, these national information practitioners inevitably tend to produce for urban audiences.

c. Further consequences flow from all this. The "news release" orientation makes the content of materials very broad and generalised. The dominant notion of "national propaganda"—of needing to speak to an entire nation in a given document—has the same effect. But since the people producing the material have little real or deep contact with the overwhelming, rural majority of the nation, the generalisation becomes, in fact, urban. If a film is produced with a cinema audience in mind, it has to be very short if on a "non-entertainment" subject. If the audience in the cinemas is predominantly urban, it has to speak to them in the first instance. If the producers are not only urban but middle-class oriented, their depiction even of rural life will tend to be fleeting and somewhat romanticised, even if quite possibly infused with genuine and patriotic motives of sympathy for the rural poor.

[Yet] the villages of developing countries are filled with born, natural actors for purposes of development support communications. It is, however, very common to find a film producer transporting out to a village from the city an entire cast of actors and actresses to play bit documentary roles.

d. Development support communications, we have stated earlier as a categorical premise, must be carefully audience-attuned; it requires quite scrupulous, and optimally researched attention to the socioeconomic and socio-psychological environment of the people to whom it must speak, and to their level of absorptive capacity for innovations. The "Western" training, or Westernised social background and continuing technological orientation of information personnel, is almost bound to militate against this perspective and this creative priority.

A journalist turned government information officer who has this kind of "Western" background is trained to report "facts"; not to try to motivate readers, change their attitudes, encourage them to adopt new techniques. Indeed any such practices are traditionally frowned upon, and said to be the thin edge of the wedge towards "1984." Yet the skilled practice of development support communications calls for unceasing attention to how to reach, interest and very purposively motivate and inform people.

A documentary film producer with a "Western" orientation sees his craft at its best when he is "expressing himself" on film and sound [but] it is in no way encouraging in terms of the massive needs we have been describing. Filmmakers from developing countries when asked what they would most like to produce, respond with descriptions of film ideas suitable for the audience in their country equivalent to avant-garde enthusiasts in Paris, London, New York and Montreal.

e. Scrupulous authenticity of detail and carefully thought out choice of accurate technical information are further requirements of development support communications. It needs little elaboration that the great majority of current information workers, in whatever medium, have not had any training enabling them to translate development technology effectively into their media. Nor are they given the time or the sheer morale to have the very considerable patience that such detailed communications work requires. The reader who has had practical experience in educational television or radio, including the production of scientific or technical programmes, will appreciate these problems most readily. A film is being made about farming and requires shots of a particular kind of seed and its cultivation. That is so written in the script, with a location prescribed 30 miles outside the city. But the film unit is tired 'it is underpaid' it is thoroughly overworked and there is a college demonstration plot almost inside the city. The shot is taken there. The villagers to whom the film is screened can spot the fake at once. The utility of the film has been almost destroyed.

Among the countless examples of such problems known to us, we can discern a further cause which is the very wide "communications gap" between national information personnel and the functional development implementers. Inside the UN-family, programme and technical personnel have not always taken public information officers very seriously. This attitude also exists within national ministries and related development agencies. The development technicians often take the view that information people are largely nuisances and inaccurate, "never available when we do need them and bothering us when we don't," or "preoccupied with taking pictures of politicians." Again the causation in a vicious circle is apparent. To date, no one has asked, encouraged and equipped such information workers to reach that level of professional expertise in development support that would make development technicians regard them as serious co-professionals with skills badly needed to help programmes.

f. If the above factors militate strongly against any great optimism about national capability for support communication in project-implementation, we believe we must recognise certain other very practical problems. A key one is quite simply the size of the technical resources available within a given country receiving UN development assistance. In our experience, the existing equipment and potentially usable talent is very heavily taxed in producing what we have called broad, national development support materials, most especially in the medium of film. In countries where there are governmental film units (and that is not many countries), they are hard pressed to complete their annual quota of films required by different ministries, plus the inevitable emergency demands (a head of state visiting a disaster or war). As we have described, most of these films are very broad in content and can contribute to project implementation only in general climate-of-opinion improvement.

A further common difficulty is that the equipment and personnel resources that we need for project-level support communications are very severely diffused and dissipated within government structures. In many countries, there has been a historical tendency for each functional ministry to create its own information or public relations division—but for it to be starved of just that extra input of funds that might make it really viable. In the usual way within human authority-structures, if a central information service is then created, it may never quite get the resources it needs because the functional ministries are reluctant to support it at the expense of their own public information. For UN-family project implementation, which so often proceeds through specific sectoral ministries, this is a further difficulty.

Conclusions from the Above Appraisal

In the foregoing survey of national capabilities for this kind of communication work, we have been as realistic as our practical experience, now over many years and encompassing all regions, compels us to be.

1927
1960
1963
1964
1967
1969
1970
1971
1972
1973
1974
1975
1976
1977
1978
1979
1980
1981
1982
1983
1984
1985
1986
1987
1988
1989
1990
1991
1992
1993
1994
1995
1996
1997
1998
1999
2000
2001
2002
2003
2004
2005
2006

But we must emphasise that a great many of the problems we have described within national levels can be overcome—some quite quickly, others over a forward period of planned assistance. Broadly, there are four categories of need in improving the national resources available for development support communications as earlier defined:

1. *Expansion and improvement of communication infrastructures* is an obvious need in many countries and has, of course, been the subject of great attention by UNESCO and ITU (International Telecommunication Union) in particular. While stressing the need for this kind of assistance to continue and increase, we would add that there will be many instances where proper advance appraisal of the support communications needs of a given UN-family project would suggest a specific assistance input of equipment and possibly short-term on the-job training. This has been done, generally and to date, only in terms of supplying such basic items as cine-projectors, slide-projectors, darkroom gear and tape recorders. In specific instances, for projects with a large and relatively long-term communications element, we can envisage far more comprehensive inputs (and, far more cost effective since a cine-projector without anything to project is not very useful).

2. *Orientation of national authorities towards development support communications* is a second vital need, even for the effective implementation of UN-assisted projects (and we are assuming throughout this text that we are also collectively concerned with helping to make all development more effective). From our own concrete experience, we cannot over-emphasise the importance of outside, UN-family assistance in this respect.

3. *Training or retraining of national information personnel* in all the media in development support communications is desperately needed in almost every country. What is required is nothing less than the development of a whole new dis-

cipline and professional expertise in this kind of information work with status, standards, methodology and rational use of resources.

4. *Application of system and resources by the UN-family* to this new instrument of development support communications will be essential, in each region, if we are to begin to move towards better project implementation. Within the UN-family we must create a body of professional expertise in these particular communications techniques, a counterpart to the (numerically much larger) national resources cited earlier. We must stress that nothing in our experience in this work gives any grounds for believing that the hundreds of specific, project-tailored support communication components at this moment missing from UN-assisted projects will be supplied by national resources alone. A major UN assistance effort is required.

In earlier pages we have pointed towards the new system, methods and deployed resources which this effort will require. Work on it has already begun, both at Headquarters level and through the development support communications service in Asia now being expanded. [In section E] we offer a very compressed outline of the total system and method that are needed. ...

Many ideas in the papers of Childers and Vajrathan have relevance to us today—both inside and outside the UN-family—but several especially stand out in the 1968 piece.

First, there is the emphasis on planning. The authors note the need to give communication support to civil servants, change agents and to rural communities and that these communication efforts need to be orchestrated. They also stress the importance of research, especially for matching communication materials to communities and for knowing more about the people and the circumstances under which innovations will be proposed. This may require, they say, "organized socioeconomic research harnessing (practical,

1927
1960
1963
1964
1967
1969
1970
1971
1972
1973
1974
1975
1976
1977
1978
1979
1980
1981
1982
1983
1984
1985
1986
1987
1988
1989
1990
1991
1992
1993
1994
1995
1996
1997
1998
1999
2000
2001
2002
2003
2004
2005
2006

development-oriented) social scientists to assemble data about attitudes, motivational factors, etc." And further, Childers and Vajrathan emphasize the significant difference between publicity and development support communications. Further worth noting is their emphatic plea for "the mobilisation of properly trained communication personnel."

Underlying the overall examination of development support communications is a framework that clearly identifies the different kinds of communication in a communication plan—and a template for action in this first decade of the 21st century.

Royal D. Colle. "Erskine Childers: A Devcom Pioneer." *The Journal of Development Communication*, No. 2, Vol. VII. Kuala Lumpur, Malaysia: Asian Institute for Development Communication (AIDCOM). Copyright © 1996, AIDCOM. Used with permission of copyright holder.

UNDERSTANDING INFORMATION MEDIA IN THE AGE OF NEOLIBERALISM: THE CONTRIBUTIONS OF HERBERT SCHILLER

By Mark Hudson

1999 We live in an era of unprecedented prosperity—and staggering poverty and inequality. The combined wealth of the world's 225 richest people is now over $1 trillion, which is equivalent to the yearly income of the poorest 2.5 billion people (United Nations). Here in the United States, the wealthiest country in the world and indeed in all of history, the richest one percent of households own about 40 percent of the total wealth, the next 19 percent of households own another 45 percent, while the bottom 80 percent of households have only about 15 percent (Wolff). Entry-level wage rates for high school graduates in the United States fell by 25.4 percent between 1973 and 1991, while those of college graduates dropped 9.8 percent. The real wages of U.S. workers at almost all levels of experience and education declined between 1973 and 1991 (Yates 25-26). The top 20 percent of income earners in the United States received 48.2 percent of aggregate income in 1993, while the lowest 20 percent of earners received only 3.6 percent (U.S. Bureau of the Census). Chronic unemployment continues to plague the U.S. economy: It has been estimated that the true unemployment rate in the United States is about 3 percentage points higher than the official rate (Yates 60-64), as well as the economies of industrial Europe, Asia and Latin America. Nevertheless, governments throughout the industrialized world are curtailing or even (in the case of the United States) eliminating the social welfare programs created earlier in the [20th] century to reduce the social costs of unemployment.

The ideology that has emerged at the end of the 20th century to justify this unhappy state of affairs is neoliberalism. Neoliberalism can be defined as the belief that the unregulated free market is the essential precondition for the fair distribution of wealth and for political democracy. Thus, neoliberals oppose just about any policy or activity that might interfere with the untrammeled operation of market forces, whether it be higher taxes on the wealthy and corporations, better social welfare programs, stronger environmental regulations, or laws that make it easier for workers to organize and join labor unions. When confronted with the adverse consequences of their market-friendly policies, they usually respond by calling for patience, to give the policies more time to work their wealth-creating magic so that the benefits can "trickle down" to the rest of the population. Then, when the promised good life fails to materialize, they fall back on their ultimate defense and claim that, imperfect as the status quo may be, there is, unfortunately, no viable alternative. They point to the failed "socialist" societies of the 20th century and warn ominously that, no matter how bad things get, any attempt to remedy the situation by forthrightly interfering with the market and the prerogatives of multinational corporations only can lead to state-bureaucratic authoritarianism.[1]

Neoliberal ideas are as old as capitalism itself, but in recent decades they have seen a tremendous resurgence and have displaced the state-interventionist economic theories of the interwar and post-World War II periods to become the reigning ideology of our time. Neoliberalism emerged full force in the 1980s with the right-wing Reagan and Thatcher regimes, but its influence has since spread across the political spectrum to encompass not only centrist political parties but even much of the traditional social-democratic left. In the 1990s, neoliberal hegemony over our politics and culture has become so overwhelming that it is becoming difficult to even rationally discuss what neoliberalism is. Indeed, as Robert McChesney notes, the term "neoliberalism" is hardly known to the U.S. public outside of academia and the business community (McChesney).

The corporate stranglehold on our information and com-munications media gives neoliberal ideologues a virtually unchallenged platform from which to blast their pro-market messages into every corner of our common culture. At the same time, neoliberalism provides the ideological cover for deregulatory legislation (most recently the 1996 Telecommunications Act), that enables corporations to extend their monopoly over these media even more. For the past three decades, one of the fiercest and most coherent critics of corporate control over the information/communications sphere has been the social scientist Herbert Schiller. Although Schiller began his career before neoliberalism's ascendance, and he does not even today use the term in his writings, his work provides essential insights into the roots of neoliberal/corporate hegemony over our information media and the adverse consequences of that hegemony for our politics, economy and culture.

Born in 1919 in New York City, Schiller is now professor emeritus of communication at the University of California, San Diego. After receiving his master's degree in 1941 from Columbia University and serving in the U.S. Army in Europe during World War II, he spent 1946-48 in Germany as a civilian member of the U.S. military occupation government, an experience he recalled in a 1986 interview as his "real social science education." In Germany, Schiller came to view the occupation not as an effort to reconstruct the political economy of Germany in a genuinely democratic way—as most of his generational cohort did—but as a conscious, deliberate effort to ensure that Germany would have the same kind of monopolistic market society that it had before the war, except without the political extremes of the fascist period. The problem with this for Schiller was that, in his mind, it was the institutional structures of this type of society that had produced fascism in the first place. He came to the conclusion that there was nothing natural or inevitable about these structures, and that the "socio-economic political vacuum" that existed in Germany after the war and the defeat of fascism was being refilled with "preferred kinds of institutional arrangements that would lead to certain types of outcomes in

---

1   Of course, the fact that many of neoliberalism's opponents even today continue to use the word "socialism" in connection with these societies makes it considerably easier for neoliberals to make their case in this way.

terms of economic activity, in terms of political structure, in terms of social consciousness" (Lent 136-137).

After leaving Germany, Schiller returned to graduate school at New York University and spent the next 12 years working on a Ph.D. while teaching economics at City College of New York and the Pratt Institute in Brooklyn. He recalls his graduate school training as "poorly structured" and his completion of the Ph.D. as "almost inadvertent." This kind of graduate education, Schiller suggests, allowed him to avoid the "academic processing" that in his view plays a crucial role in shaping the way most academic scholars view the social order. Shortly after completing the Ph.D. in 1960, he took a job as a teacher and researcher in economics at the University of Illinois (ibid 137-139).

At Illinois, Schiller began to formulate the thinking that would result in the publication of his first book, *Mass Communications and American Empire,* in 1969. Around 1966-67 he began teaching a course in the College of Journalism in the "Political Economy of Communications." He recalls that he had always considered himself to be a "political economist," i.e., as someone who studies "the juncture where politics and economics come together," and around this same time he presented his first paper in the communications field on the topic of the radio spectrum considered as a natural resource. He also recalls not being given "any serious attention by the established people" in the communications field during this time, which he suggests gave him the space he needed to develop his ideas. Some of the individual chapters of *Mass Communications and American Empire* were first published in non-academic journals, such as *The Nation, The Progressive,* and *The Bulletin of the Atomic Scientists* (ibid 139-143).

The theme of *Mass Communications and American Empire* was the crucial role of modern communications media in mobilizing international support for U.S. global domination and the transnational corporate order after World War II. Schiller listed several related historical factors that contributed to the expansion of U.S. power in the postwar world: the weakening of Europe, growing U.S. industrial strength, the declining influence of the postcapitalist world due to disagreements over development policy, and the transition of most of the developing world from a condition of formal political subordination (colonialism), to one of political independence combined with economic dependence (postcolonialism) (Schiller 1992, 48).

The transition from a colonialist to a postcolonialist order, in particular, necessitated a more sophisticated approach to empire-building; unlike earlier empires founded on "blood and iron," the U.S. empire is based partly on "a marriage of economics and electronics," although Schiller noted a precedent for this kind of informal control in the 19th century British practice of "free trade imperialism." Of course, the U.S. system of informal domination is backed up by an extremely formidable military power; U.S. bases encircle the globe, ready and willing to use force when more sophisticated methods of persuasion fail. But Schiller suggested that the U.S. communications network was for the most part remarkably successful after World War II in securing, not merely grudging submission, but enthusiastic allegiance, both domestically and abroad. It did this, he argued, by identifying the U.S. presence with "freedom"—of speech, of trade and of enterprise—and offering a vision of the good life patterned on the U.S. model of individualistic consumer affluence (ibid 47-54).

Mass Communications and American Empire concluded with a call for "a democratic reconstruction of mass communications." Schiller correctly forecast that government-financed public broadcasting would not produce "the scope of change, either in outlook or allegiance, that the current social situation demands." Instead, he saw the best possibility for significant change in disaffected social groups of the time, such as black power militants, student activists, university faculty and public-sector employees, who, he hoped, would claim access to mass communications technology and put it to useful social purposes. This, he acknowledged, would require concerted political action to achieve (198-206). Thirty years later, we are no closer

1927
1960
1963
1964
1967
1969
1970
1971
1972
1973
1974
1975
1976
1977
1978
1979
1980
1981
1982
1983
1984
1985
1986
1987
1988
1989
1990
1991
1992
1993
1994
1995
1996
1997
1998
1999
2000
2001
2002
2003
2004
2005
2006

to achieving it with respect to television and radio, although the Internet now provides a means for opposition groups to create grassroots information networks that circumvent these corporate-controlled media.

In 1970, Schiller moved to the University of California, San Diego. In his second book, *The Mind Managers,* published in 1973, he turned his attention to the specific methods of mind manipulation used by the managers of U.S. communications media in the service of corporate interests. He identified five basic myths that structure the content of corporate-controlled information media. The "myth of individualism and personal choice" defines freedom in purely individualistic terms and insists that individual liberty and well-being cannot be achieved without the existence of private property in the means of production. (As we have seen, neoliberal ideology takes this a step further, with its insistence that any interference with market forces and corporate prerogatives is a threat to freedom.)

The "myth of neutrality" fosters the belief that key social institutions such as government, the education system and the scientific establishment (and of course the information media themselves) are neutral and above conflicting social interests. The "myth of unchanging human nature" keeps expectations low by emphasizing the aggressive and depraved sides of human behavior and rationalizing these as inherent and inevitable aspects of the human condition. The "myth of the absence of social conflict" presents conflict almost invariably as an individual matter, and denies its origins in the social order. The "myth of media pluralism" perpetuates the illusion of choice and diversity in information sources, when in fact there is little variety of opinion due to the common material and ideological interests of media owners (Schiller 1973).

Schiller also described two techniques used by media managers to shape consciousness. The first of these, fragmentation, is the dominant format for the communication of news information in the United States: Newspapers and magazines intentionally break up articles so that readers are forced to turn past advertisements to continue reading, while television and radio news programs are characterized by "the machine-gun-like recitation of numerous unrelated items," with frequent commercial interruptions. Advertising, Schiller argued, "disrupts concentration and renders trivial the information it interrupts," although he also thought that news information would be presented just as incoherently if advertising were eliminated or reduced; in his view, advertising, "in seeking benefits for its sponsors, is serendipitous to the system in that its utilization heightens fragmentation." The second technique, immediacy, further undermines the public's understanding of news events; the competitive pressure to provide instantaneous information, Schiller argued, generates a "false sense of urgency," with the result that "the ability to discriminate between different degrees of significance is impaired" (24-29).

Like Schiller's first book, *The Mind Managers* concluded with a call for radical change. He denounced as "cruel and deceitful" the notion that the solutions to poverty, political apathy and other social problems would come from technology itself: "It is cruel to suggest that ghetto children confronting computer consoles will magically overcome generations of deprivation." But he also found "countervailing movements stirring." He noted the growing sector of educated "knowledge workers," already somewhat critical of the status quo, with the income, leisure and expertise to allow the further development of a critical consciousness. He found reasons for hope that "the industrial working class, young and old, may be compelled for its own protection to abandon its present support for the "system" and to adopt a vigorously critical stance." He also noted the appearance of community-based "information collectives" in various U.S. urban areas, and suggested that the increasing affordability and availability of communications technology would help to "demystify the media for a significant number of people" and eventually "provide the basis for a new corps of trained individuals, capable of handling some of the now-ignored informational needs of the nation's communities" (174, 186-188). Again, one thinks of the

Internet and its alternate grassroots networks, although these online "collectives" are not based in communities bound by geography.

In 1976, Schiller returned to the theme of *Mass Communications and American Empire* with the publication of *Communications and Cultural Domination*. This book included an analysis of the media system in Chile under the Allende Popular Unity government overthrown in September 1973 by a military coup, which, it might be noted, was motivated rather explicitly by neoliberal theories of free-market competition as formulated by economists trained at the University of Chicago. In this analysis Schiller noted that, while freedom of informa-tion effectively disappeared in Chile after the coup, under the socialist Allende government there had been a remarkably free flow of information representing all points on the political spectrum. The largest number of television viewers continued to watch a commercial station that carried programs produced in the United States Most radio stations remained in the hands of conservative, antigovernment elements, and the number of conservative newspapers actually increased. Of course, socialist ideas were also disseminated more widely than before, and in Schiller's view this explained the hostility of the anti-Allende elements toward the free information flow that prevailed in 1971-73. The Chilean experience, he argued, showed that genuine pluralism becomes intolerable to property-owning classes when it leads to widespread critical thinking and social action, and he drew the conclusion that the Popular Unity government's strong adherence to the doctrine of the free flow of information was in fact a mistake. He argued that the flow of information between countries "follows the international division of labor, which itself is determined by the structure and practices of the strongest capitalist states," especially the United States Hence, the free-flow doctrine simply "legitimates and re-inforces the capability of a few dominant economies to impose their cultural definitions and perspectives on the rest of the world" (Schiller 1976, 98-103).

Invoking the principle of national sovereignty, Schiller argued that future efforts at social transformation would have to recognize the necessity of defending cultural integrity against the "external, dominating network of media information" while avoiding xenophobia and working to develop "alternate media structures and products in ways that promote widespread popular participation." It should be emphasized that in no way was Schiller calling for censorship or the closing of domestic media institutions; he merely insisted on the legitimate right of nation-states to resist the importation of "messages of domination" in media produced by multinational corporations (107-108). I am not entirely convinced by this argument, and I suspect that in practice this kind of cultural protectionism would not produce the desired result, even if it managed to avoid xenophobia. At the same time, I think Schiller's emphasis on efforts to develop popular participatory media structures is absolutely correct, and I would suggest that it might be better to focus on the teaching of media literacy as part of these efforts, so that members of oppressed groups could learn to recognize and resist "messages of domination" themselves.

As we have seen, Schiller has always emphasized the need for oppositional movements to claim access to mass communications technology and use it for their own purposes, while vehemently rejecting the notion that technology created for purposes of domination and control will in and of itself provide solutions to social problems. In the 1980s, as computerization of the economy and communications accelerated, Schiller advocated a "go-slow" computerization policy. In *Who Knows: Information in the Age of the Fortune 500* (1981), he called for "a maximum effort directed at slowing down, and postponing wherever possible, the rush to computerization," in order to allow "time to think through the enormous complexities that surround advanced communication and other technologies at this stage of unequal global power and influence" (Schiller 1981). In *Information and the Crisis Economy* (1984), he described the "deepening overall social crisis" brought about by "economic, political

1927
1960
1963
1964
1967
1969
1970
1971
1972
1973
1974
1975
1976
1977
1978
1979
1980
1981
1982
1983
1984
1985
1986
1987
1988
1989
1990
1991
1992
1993
1994
1995
1996
1997
1998
1999
2000
2001
2002
2003
2004
2005
2006

and military policies designed to maintain imperial power," and warned that "technological solutions devoid of social accountability will be terribly costly to millions of human beings" (Schiller 1984).

Schiller's most recent books are concerned with the increasing commoditization of information and corporatization of culture in the United States "*In Culture, Inc.: The Corporate Takeover of Public Expression*" (1989), Schiller lamented that "transforming information into a salable good, available only to those with the ability to pay for it, changes the goal of information access from an egalitarian to a privileged condition," with the result that "the essential underpinning of a democratic order is seriously, if not fatally, damaged." He described the absorption of the creative process and cultural production by profit-driven cultural industries that "serve as the sites for the creation, packaging, transmission and placement of cultural messages—corporate ones especially." In these industries Schiller included the information industry—database and software producers and other sellers of packaged information—as well as publishing, film, television, radio, recording, photography, sports and advertising. He also included such providers of "symbolic goods and services" as museums, galleries, shopping malls, amusement parks and corporate "public spaces." Schiller argued that, "the last 50 years have seen an acceleration in the decline of nonmarket-controlled creative work and symbolic output." The "pervasive ideological character" of the cultural industries, he contended, means that "the heavy public consumption of cultural products and services and the contexts in which most of them are provided represent a daily, if not hourly, diet of systemic values." Only the very wealthiest can afford to own information and cultural media, hence, Schiller argued, these media transmit "the thinking and the perspectives of the dominant, though tiniest, stratum of the propertied class, not only in news but also in entertainment and general cultural product" (Schiller 1989).

In *Information Inequality: The Deepening Social Crisis in America* (1996), Schiller again decries the corporate enclosure of information and cultural expression, arguing that the denial of access to information and the debasement of cultural messages is deepening the already intense social crisis brought about by corporate policies. Again rejecting technological solutions to social problems, he harshly criticizes the Clinton Adminstration's "vision of, and reliance on, high-tech communications as the ultimate answer to whatever is ailing the country." He dissects the 1993 "Agenda for Action" report issued by the task force on the National Information Infrastructure (NII), calling its promised solutions to the nation's education problems a "technological subterfuge" and suggesting that the electronic information highway's ability to carry cultural product into the nation's living rooms and facilitate "active home shopping" is the plan's primary motivation. Describing the policy of the Clinton-Gore leadership and their bipartisan supporters in Congress as "all power to the corporate communication sector," Schiller argues that private ownership and market competition are "Washington's basic prescriptions for the infrastructure that promises to carry, for business and home use, all the image and message and data flow that the country produces" (Schiller 1996).

I think one of Schiller's most important contributions to our understanding of information media is his insistence that ownership matters, that the corporate owners of mass communications media do actually use it (both consciously and unconsciously) for their own purposes, which are domination and control. Conversely, one of the great triumphs of neoliberal ideology has been to convince so many of us that it does not matter, that the media are ideologically neutral and above social conflict, and that the concentration of media ownership in a few private hands is natural, inevitable and perhaps even beneficial. Anyone who has any doubts about this matter should read Schiller's books.

Another very important contribution has been Schiller's continuing emphasis on popular agency. Although he often paints a very bleak picture, he has always stressed that significant change is possible if those of us excluded by the corporate media monopoly can find ways to create alternate media structures that resist domination and promote humane values of equality, solidarity and justice. Although Schiller is certainly right about the corporate communication sector's plans to completely commercialize the Internet, this is not inevitable if we act now. As many campus, labor and community activists have already discovered, the Internet can be a very effective organizing tool if used intelligently. Of course, we cannot afford to ignore other media; we must continue to demand access to cable television and radio frequencies, while finding ways to use print technologies more effectively as well. The work of Herbert Schiller provides a reliable guide to the obstacles we face, but it is also a goad to action.

Works Cited

Lent, John A. ed. 1995. "Interview with Herbert I. Schiller," *A Different Road Taken: Profiles in Critical Communication,* Boulder, CO: Westview Press, 136-137.

McChesney, Robert W. 1999. "Noam Chomsky and the Struggle Against Neoliberalism," *Monthly Review* 50 (April 1999), 40-47.

Schiller, Herbert I. 1976. *Communication and Cultural Domination,* Armonk, NY: M.E. Sharpe, 98-103.

Schiller, Herbert I. 1989. Culture, Inc.: *The Corporate Takeover of Public Expression,* New York: Oxford University Press, 30-33, 40, 75.

Schiller, Herbert I. 1984. *Information and the Crisis Economy,* Norwood, NJ: Ablex Publishing, xii-xiii.

Schiller, Herbert I. 1996. *Information Inequality: The Deepening Social Crisis in America,* New York: Routledge, xii, xvi, 77-82.

Schiller, Herbert I. 1973. *The Mind Managers,* Boston: Beacon Press, 8-24.

Schiller, Herbert I. 1992. *Mass Communications and American Empire,* 2nd Edition, Boulder, CO: Westview Press, 48.

Schiller, Herbert I. 1981. *Who Knows: Information in the Age of the Fortune 500,* Norwood, NJ: Ablex Publishing, 149-151.

United Nations Development Program. *Human Development Report,* New York: Oxford University Press, 1998.

U.S. Bureau of the Census. 1995. "Population Profile of the United States 1995," *Current Population Reports,* Series P23-189,

Washington, DC: U.S. Government Printing Office, 41.

Wolff, Edward N. 1995. *Top Heavy: A Study of Increasing Inequality of Wealth in America,* New York: Twentieth Century Fund Press, 7.

Yates, Michael D. *Longer Hours, Fewer Jobs: Employment and Unemployment in the United States,* New York: Monthly Review Press, 25-26, 60-64, 1994.

EXCERPT FROM:

THE WIDE ROAD OF LATIN AMERICAN COMMUNICATION

By Gabriel Kaplún

2005 Mario Kaplun's action and thinking remain an inspirational source for the debate and practice of Latin American communication to date. To revisit his journey and his thinking is to reclaim an important part of Latin American communicational and pedagogic debate, and to find in it aspects that remain fully valid, that can invigorate many of our current debates and help us face many of our current challenges.

To my understanding, this validity is due to the way Mario built theory: *from* practice and *in* practice. His personal history, the story of a communicator who became a *communicologist* but still always remained a communicator, partly explains his originality. His late—but powerful—engagement and influence in the academic field alienated him from concrete work with the masses. His critical work on Latin American communicational reality did not draw him away from his continuous work to construct concrete alternatives for that reality either.

Mass Communication: Practice and Critique

Recalling Mario's personal history can be useful to understand his praxis. As I have recounted in greater length elsewhere (G. Kaplún 1998), Mario graduated as a primary school teacher, but never practiced as such. Instead, he learned radio skills at a very young age, initially as an assistant in radio theatre productions in his hometown, Buenos Aires.

In 1942, having just turned 19, he released his first script, a program in a series on Argentinean history that was part of the so-called "*Escuela del Aire*" (School of the Air). This teacher without a classroom was a valuable find for that pioneering experience of

1927
1960
1963
1964
1967
1969
1970
1971
1972
1973
1974
1975
1976
1977
1978
1979
1980
1981
1982
1983
1984
1985
1986
1987
1988
1989
1990
1991
1992
1993
1994
1995
1996
1997
1998
1999
2000
2001
2002
2003
2004
2005
2006

educational radio, because commercial writers either had no interest, or did not adjust, and educators did not know about radio skills (1992a).[1] The teacher did not return to the classroom until much later, but educational communication had won him over forever.

It seems that those programs were quite rhetorical and grandiloquent.[2] Mario mostly took from those days the fact that he had learnt a craft: writing two scripts a week; directing a team of actors and technicians; going on air with minimum rehearsing; creating a convincing sound environment with non professional effects… and all of it directly on the air, without prerecording.

When, at the beginning of the 1950s, he emigrated… to Uruguay, which eventually became his adoptive homeland, he kept making radio and incorporated a new task: advertising. He even became co-owner of an agency and was what we would today call a very creative "creative." He ended up hating the world of advertising and becoming a critic and in-depth analyst of its mechanisms, but he knew it personally and from within.

From the 1960s, he worked with television, with a format that recaptured a youthful experience that would somehow accompany him for a long time. In fact, the "*Club del Libre Debate*" (Free Debate Club) that he facilitated in his youth was at the foundation of "*Sala Audiencias*" (The Hearing Room), his most remembered television program, where all current political and social issues were discussed using the format of an oral trial. The same format that turned into fictional but simulating live transmissions, would later be the foundation of one of his most famous radio series, "*Jurado Nº 13*" (Jury Nº 13) (1971-72). From the 1970s to the present day, this has aired on hundreds of Latin American radio broadcast stations and thousands of community-based groups use it as a trigger for their

discussions (some of his series from then have also been translated into Portuguese, Quechua and Aymara).

The genesis of these series shows in a concrete way what he would later call "*pre-alimentación*" (pre-feeding) (1985): a trip through seven Latin American countries gathering stories, hopes and dreams from people everywhere is the basis of his productions. Because addressing complex problems of Latin American social and political reality could not be done only from readings, statistics and general references: it had to be done from specific stories showing how those problems are lived, suffered, feared, avoided, dreamed of or solved by real people.

Those programs then brought together criticism and the enjoyment of a tale well told, reason and poetry, rigor and humor. Some of the many things he learned while working during that stage and previous ones, were collected in a radio handbook (1978a) which is still being used in schools and universities everywhere today.

Those radio series illustrated in practice something that he would later (1992b) theorize with clarity: rather than thinking about educational communication as a specific space, we must think about the educational nature of every communication act. Rather than a radio-school or TV-school, for example, we must think of educational radios and channels in a broader sense. Media in which all programming is envisioned from an educational perspective, but in the medium's own formats rather than using the unbearable didactics of so much educational television or radio.

The 1970s witnessed a historical turn both at a social and personal level. Dictatorships fell all over the Southern cone which led him to emigrate again, this time to Venezuela. Even before that, however, the *communicologist* was already emerging within the communicator, without denying him or drowning him in academic rhetoric. "*La Comunicación de Masas en América Latina*" (Mass Communication in Latin America, 1973) was based on a type of continental research work rare at the time. It located itself in the critical current that

---

1   From here on, the dates in parentheses refer to works by Mario himself.
2   This and other statements without reference to specific texts come from handwritten notes left by Mario and from personal and family conversations. I hope the reader will be able to forgive, in my case, the fact that I have no more "proof."

highlighted deep inequalities in terms of access to information and communication on the continent, the cultural colonization of the media, and also within the movement that would lead to the Costa Rica meeting in 1975, later on to the MacBride report (1980), and to the call for a New International Information and Communication Order fostered by UNESCO.

Even if he was part of that critical current—to which he was also connected through close personal ties[3]—early on he perceived the limits of the Latin American critique of hegemonic communication, which did not foster seeing how the media incorporated the receivers' cultural threads in their messages. Together with the reading of Donald Duck in an imperialist key,[4] he also considered it necessary to reach a deep understanding of the receiver. We were, with a group of friends that never forgot the experience, guinea pigs of his method of critical reading of the media.[5]

It was an active and deeply moving method, because it not only gave us the chance to unveil the ideological sustenance of each message, but also because of how much of ourselves and our relationship with the media it helped us to understand. Thus, for example, it rejected the insistent idea—even apparent nowadays—that advertising creates false needs, proposing that instead it uses very real needs, orienting them towards types of consumption that in general do not satisfy them. Advertising, then, tends to reveal many of our unsatisfied needs. Without using this terminology, he was distinguishing (anthropological) needs from (cultural)

satisfiers or (circumstantial) goods (Max-Neef, 1986). The continuous mention of sexuality, identity, friendship or nature, then speaks of what we lack, as much as of what we will eventually buy. As Mario remembered (1989), that was precisely the advice offered by Dichter (1970), the father of modern advertising: "What the product has to sell is not so important—and may not be important at all; what's important is the unconscious motives that the consumer has to buy." The fact that Mario had been a successful advertiser himself implied that he knew very well what he was talking about.

Community-Based Work and the Debate on Cultural Issues

This attention focused on the receiver, already present in his work on producing messages with a strong impact amongst wide audiences, would also be present later on in his analyses and teachings. In the '80s, for example, he was an early and active promoter of the analysis of popular cultures. But he was also critical of the "culturalist" currents that wanted to see resistance in mere consumption and imagined an active receiver capable of re-signifying every message.[6] He was lucid in his perception of how paralyzing the cultural approach could end up being if played in a populist key, rendering sacred any sign coming from the "people": "We cannot seize aspects peculiar to the culture of the dominated one unless their ambiguity, their ambivalence is assumed; the co-existence within it, already detected by Gramsci, of "fossilizing" and demobilizing components together with others that are dynamic, of resistance and protest, of questioning and struggle" (1984).

It is interesting to note that in this same text he cites Martin Barbero several times. It is my understanding that the intellectual distance that later on separated him

---

3   Particularly with people like Armand Mattelart and Héctor Schmucler and Hugo Assman. Mario remembered (1992a) how in a colloquium on popular communication organized by him in Montevideo in 1971, they started sketching the project that would later become the famous magazine "Communication and Culture."

4   I am referring to a series of works that have in the book by Mattelart and Dorfman (1972) their most famous representative.

5   It is a book that unfortunately has never been published due to complicated editorial reasons, which included the problem at that time of the cost of a book with slides and cassettes. There was however a mimeographed earlier version (1982). One chapter did get published as a set of materials (1989a). In addition, very recently, I have rescued the chapter on the theoretical grounding of that book for publication on the Internet (2005) and in a compilation of pioneering texts of Latin American communication forthcoming. A short description of the method can be found in Hermosilla and Kaplun (1987).

6   In the sense posed by Follari (2001:136) in his critique of the dominant current of cultural studies in Latin America, which ends up identifying itself non-critically with its objects of study: "If television dominates culture with public acceptance, we must accept it; if consumption is the sign of the times, we will praise it as a new form of citizenship; if mass culture navigates in vagueness, we must build conceptual hybrids." Follari's critique is mainly directed to the works of Nestor Garcia Canclini from the 90s onwards and –maybe even more– of those who, starting from his texts, have built many works on different "objects" of popular mass culture: shopping malls, media, music, etc.

1927
1960
1963
1964
1967
1969
1970
1971
1972
1973
1974
1975
1976
1977
1978
1979
1980
1981
1982
1983
1984
1985
1986
1987
1988
1989
1990
1991
1992
1993
1994
1995
1996
1997
1998
1999
2000
2001
2002
2003
2004
2005
2006

from Martin Barbero has more to do with his specific positioning in different debates, and above all with the use of Martin Barbero's work that started becoming generalized. The debates at the time resulted in positions such as Mario's being included—without really knowing them—in an attack against what was considered Marxist dogmatic thinking, a Leninist vanguardism that sought to substitute the "alienated conscience manipulated by the media" with the "revolutionary conscience." Mario was certainly far from this kind of thinking.

On his part, distrust in the populist uses of culture came not only from a healthy caution against intellectual oscillations, which from the hell of the media now shifted to the paradise of mediations.[7] The origin of this distrust, I think, was mostly his practice as a communicator with community-based groups that from the 1970s became particularly intense.

In fact, in the 1970s, while still in Uruguay, he created his Casete Foro method (Forum Cassette, 1978b), a pioneer experience in dialogic communication among groups, in that particular case among peasant groups. The point was no longer only to expand the audience for critical messages, but to empower emitters capable of intervening in communication processes from the bases, seeking to bring into being *interlocutors* rather than mere *announcers*[8], promoting use of the "record" key and not only the "play" key of tape recorders that had become popular at the time. For that purpose, a central team delivered tapes to all groups, recorded only on one of their two sides, with information and proposals for debate. Each group recorded their own information, opinions and proposals on the other side of the tape. The core team listened to all the tapes received, selected fragments to share with others, and produced a new program to send to the groups. In the 1980s, this method developed widely in Venezuela, at a time when Mario was actively working in the field of popular education and communication. There, he

would be renamed "*Foruco*", because "he *for*ms us; he *u*nites us; and he makes us *co*mmunicate".

The *Casete Foro* stressed the possibility of reverting one-way communication and recapturing the dialogic sense of communication, as against the dominant, informational, transmitting paradigm. To such a degree that, in assessing the first experiences, Mario declared that he was not satisfied with the participation of the peasants involved. For him, the key indicator of participation was not that they listened attentively or intervened at some points but, above all, the amount of topics for debate that they themselves proposed in that forum, versus those proposed by the program's coordinators. It would be interesting to apply such criteria to review the presumed "interactivity" with which many educational programs using new information and communication technologies are designed, mistaking such interactivity for participation. The experience of the *Casete Foro* has surely been "transcended" in the technological field, but I do not think it has been surpassed in the pedagogical and communicational terrain.

This obsession to reclaim the word, to "empower transmitters," would never leave him from then on. Venezuela was a particularly favorable field for it. After many courses and workshops with community-based groups throughout the country came the Latin American Popular Communication Workshops, attended by more than a hundred apprentices of communicators from the whole continent, myself included. One of his best known and most reprinted books is from that time: *The Popular Communicator* (1985).

There he proposes very specific methodological tools to develop messages and support participative and dialogic communication processes. He shows that there is an intimate relationship between educational and communicational conceptions. The transmission-based communication of the mechanicist classic models[9] corresponds to a traditional education ("banking", as Freire called it). The behavioralist alternative finds its

---

7   I have discussed this matter to a greater extent elsewhere (G. Kaplún 2001a)
8   Translator's note: In the original version in Spanish, the author plays with the words *interlocutores* and *locutores* respectively, stressing the importance of interaction.

9   Cf. for example Shannon and Weaver (1962)

correlation in the communication models centered on effects (Laswell 1979). For Freire's liberating education, Mario proposes a dialogic communication model as a utopian horizon, breaking the *emitter-receiver* dichotomy to develop "*emirecs*" (Cloutier 1973). A proposal as utopian—and as alive, necessary and attainable—as Freire's (1980:63), when he proposes that "men educate each other, mediated by the world."

But in order to progress towards that horizon of dialogic communication he also proposes specific and viable paths, centered on *pre-feeding* more than on *feeding back*. In fact, to start with the other, worries and hopes, context and cultural universe, is key for dialogue to be possible.

Therefore, it is not surprising that it is during this work with community-based groups and social movements that Mario's concern for cultural matters arose. The recuperation of Gramsci's thinking and Latin American cultural studies were undoubtedly useful tools to think about the challenges involved in this work. But the everyday bond with those groups and movements prevented him from mythologizing "the popular," which was frequent among many "culturalists." In direct community-based work, "the popular" appeared in all its ambiguous complexity of solidarities and individualism, resistance and passivity, rebellion and fatalism. Made of multiple mediations, yes, but also of the media. The media that Mario had been reading in a complex way, far from simplicity, for quite a while, from within and from the outside.

That is why he did not join a base-bound *alternativ-ismo* either, based only on communitarian micro-media. His long experience with the mass media, with messages with wide audiences, allowed him to also appreciate both aspects—and of their articulation—for the construction of more democratic communication alternatives. Neither did he lose sight of the fact that, together with communicational products, it was crucial to keep on reflecting upon the communication processes that frame them and that they help generate (cf. 1989b).

Together with this, he also paid constant attention to problems of reception, which were not new to him. The work that had started in the 1970s seeking a critical reading of the media that would be within everyone's reach was still surprising us in the 1990s, with sharp analyses on the use of the media. The title given to one of his latest works on the subject is thought provoking: "*Ni impuesta ni amada: la recepción televisiva y sus tierras incógnitas*" (Neither imposed nor loved: television reception and its unknown lands, 1996). There he discusses many uses of television that not only question the obsolete theories of media as a hypodermic needle, but also do not fit with the more modern—or postmodern—theories of reception and mediations. Nor are they covered by the ideological reading that he himself proposed. Television used as a remedy for anxiety or for company, for example, speaks more about generalized loneliness and anxieties in our societies than about the presumed attraction of the media and their messages.

The 'Return' to Pedagogy

In the mid 1980s, the "democratic spring" dawns in the Southern cone and Mario returns to Uruguay, from where he will not leave other than for his constant travels, now more often responding to invitations from the academic world: a world in which Uruguay also becomes a part of in contributing decisively to the creation of a university degree in communication.

It is interesting to note that the curriculum he contributed to designing is still a reference in every current discussion at my university, even if—and maybe because—it was later abandoned. Even with his long history of media experience—radio, TV—it did not occur to him or his colleagues to design a plan for graduate education oriented to different types of media, but instead one separated into professional areas. Something that by then most degrees in communication in Latin America and elsewhere had started doing.

Among the foci in that curriculum, together with the classic ones of journalism and advertising, was

1927
1960
1963
1964
1967
1969
1970
1971
1972
1973
1974
1975
1976
1977
1978
1979
1980
1981
1982
1983
1984
1985
1986
1987
1988
1989
1990
1991
1992
1993
1994
1995
1996
1997
1998
1999
2000
2001
2002
2003
2004
2005
2006

educational communication, which obviously he directed for a long time. From there, he promoted active commitment by the University to social and community-based organizations and, as early as the 1990s, to the process of participatory decentralization launched by the government of the left in Montevideo.

It is during those years that his concern for pedagogy returned, stronger than ever. He had contributed with practice and theory to develop an educational communication far from didactism, which could be integrated into ordinary people's everyday use of the media. Now, returning to his origins as a teacher, he devoted himself above all to developing a communicative education capable of understanding the complex relationship between learning and communication. "*A la educacion por la comunicacion*" (To education through communication, 1992b) is precisely the title of one of his most interesting, although probably one of his least known, books.

His reading of constructivist tendencies in terms of communication sheds light on many of the problems that had been obsessing him for quite a while. Rather than worrying about communicating for others to learn, we must facilitate their own expression because, Mario states, "to know is to communicate" (1992:35); "we learn through communicating" (1995:50). This is why it is so important to move from "the learner-listener to the speaker-learner" (1993). Language and thought are two sides of the same coin, he remembers alongside Vigotsky (1979). And since we think with words, to encourage one person's own words is to help that person to think, build knowledge. This construction is personal, but also strongly social: we learn mainly through interaction with others. This is why it is of central importance to generate spheres of interlocution in which learners truly find whom to communicate with, instead of limiting themselves to the production of words and texts read only by an educator and only of use to verify the assimilation of an alien word.

His obsession with learning is reflected even in the way in which he thought about his own work. He chose as a title for his "mini-autobiography" (1992a) "*Mis (primeros) 50 años de aprendiz de comunicador*" [My (first) 50 years as a communicator apprentice.]

This point of view—from learning rather than teaching—allowed him to analyze acutely the possibilities and limitations of the new information and communication technologies and their uses in the pedagogic field. Showing on the one hand their dialogic potential, facilitating learning processes with others, processes of collective construction of knowledge through networks of people that share knowledge and think together; and also showing how NICTs tend to be used in non-dialogic ways, perfecting the banking educational model now in its ATM version (1998). The behavioral pedagogic alternative adapts well to NICTs, which were on the horizon from the beginning. But it does so by mainly appealing to interactivity (with a machine) and not true interaction (with people), except for the "educational engineer" who designs the teaching—or rather the instruction—stimulating and then verifying compliance with desired effects. It is in this sense that I have said that what has been termed e-learning is usually a pedagogical revolution without pedagogy (G. Kaplún 2001b).

The ideal of the isolated student connected to a machine in fact denies the social nature of learning. Solitary surfing information highways cannot replace learning, which is essentially social. Of course, this also does not happen in an actual classroom where there is no dialogue, no true communication. The problem is in both cases pedagogical and communicational, and not technological, as he has been stating for years (cf. 1983).

Mario was writing about these matters when death hit him. In his last papers, the thread of live thinking capable of learning all the time, and for that reason teaching so much, is evident. Thinking about the problems of his time—as he always did—with his feet on the ground and his head looking toward a fairer social horizon, politically more liberating, more dialogic in terms of communication. Because, he said, "to define what we understand as communication is the equivalent of stating in what kind of society we want to live" (1985:67).

Speaking of Mario's "utopian thinking" can then be a fair description, as long as we do not forget that with his praxis he intended to take very concrete steps towards that horizon. For that, he had many "hours in-flight" in the media and working with social movements. He knew the limits well, but also the needs and potential. That might explain some of the differences he had with certain disenchanted viewpoints in the 1990s, which seemed to be "back" from everything… without really having gone anywhere. Views that saw with postmodern skeptic thought, such as Mario's—and many others'—that even at times of neoliberal globalization, kept on—and keep on—believing that another world is possible.

Mario liked to say that: "Communication is a wide road that I love to traverse. It interlinks with compromise and is the cornerstone of community" (1992a).

His praxis, then, was one of constructing alternatives that would serve to open two routes on the wide road of communication. To widen that street in such a way that many debates—and many people—could circulate through it and to fight for a world in which every world has space, but especially the worlds of the excluded, of the wretched of the earth.

References

Cloutier, Jean (1973) *La Communication Audio-scripto-visuelle à L'heure des Self-media.* Presse de l'Université de Montreal.

Dichter, Ernest (1970) *Las motivaciones del consumidor.* Sudamericana, Buenos Aires.

Dorfman, Ariel y Mattelart, Armand (1972) *Para leer al Pato Donald.* Ed. Universitarias de Valparaíso.

Follari, Roberto (2001) *Teorías débiles (Para una crítica de la deconstrucción y de los estudios culturales).* Homo Sapiens, Rosario (Argentina).

Freire (1980) *Pedagogia do oprimido* (8ª ed.) Paz e Terra, Rio de Janeiro. (1ª ed. 1969)

Kaplún, Gabriel (1998) "Mario Kaplún: el viajero". En *Revista Chasqui* Nº 64, CIESPAL, Quito. (otras ediciones en publicaciones en Colombia, Bolivia, Uruguay).

—, (2001a) "Facultades de comunicación: entre la crítica y el mercado". Conferencia en *Primer Encuentro de Facultades y Carreras de Comunicación del Cono Sur.* FELAFACS – UNC, Mendoza.

—, (2001b) "El e-learning: ¿una revolución pedagógica sin pedagogía?"

Ponencia *en II Seminario Regional de ALAIC.* La Plata, Argentina 2001

Kaplún, Mario (1971-72) Jurado Nº 13. Radioserie de 60 capítulos, Serpal (grabada en Montevideo, editadas en disco en Bogotá).

—, (1973) La comunicación de masas en América Latina. DEC, Bogotá.

—, (1978a) *Producción de programas de radio: el guión, la realización.* CIESPAL, Quito. Hay edición mexicana, Cromocolor 1994 y reedición de CIESPAL de 1999.

—, (1978b) *Casete-foro: un sistema de comunicación entre grupos.* IPRU, Montevideo. Hay otras ediciones. Por ejemplo, con el título *Comunicación entre grupos,* Buenos Aires, Humanitas 1989.

—, (1982) *Lectura Crítica. Un método para el desarrollo del sentido crítico de los usuarios de medios masivos.* Mimeo, CESAP, Caracas.

—, (1983) *Hacia nuevas estrategias de comunicación en la educación de adultos.* UNESCO, Santiago de Chile. (Hay otras ediciones en portugués y español.)

—, (1985) *El comunicador popular.* CIESPAL, Quito. Hay otras ediciones, como la de Humanitas (Buenos Aires 1987) y también una edición revisada y ampliada, con el título *Una pedagogía de la comunicación* (Ediciones de la Torre, Madrid 1998. Esta misma versión también en Editorial Caminos, La Habana 2002.

—, (1986) *Lectura crítica de la comunicación masiva.* Inédito.

—, (1987) *La educación para los medios en la formación del comunicador social.* En col. con Ma. Helena Hermosilla. FCU, Montevideo 1987

—, (1988) "Comunicación, democratización y hegemonía en la perspectiva del 2000". En Roncagliolo, R. (ed.) *América Latina 2000: cinco enfoques sobre el futuro de las comunicaciones.* IPAL, Lima.

—, (1989a) *Lectura crítica de la publicidad.* Ecos-UNESCO, Montevideo.

—, 1989b) "Video, comunicación y educación popular: derroteros para una búsqueda". En Valdeavellano, P. (ed.) *El video en la educación popular,* Lima, IPAL

—, (1992a) .»Mis (primeros) cincuenta años como aprendiz de comunicador" En *Boletín ALAIC* Nº.7-8, São Paulo.

—, (1992b) *A la educación por la comunicación. La práctica de la comunicación educativa.* UNESCO, Santiago de Chile 1992. Hay reedición corregida Ciespal, Quito 2001

—, (1993) "Del educando oyente al educando hablante". En *Revista Diálogos de la Comunicación Nº 37* FELAFACS, Lima

—, (1996) "Ni impuesta ni amada, la recepción televisiva y sus tierras incógnitas". En Guillermo Orozco (coord.) *Miradas latinoamericanas a la televisión,* Univ. Iberoamericana, México 1996

—, (1998) "Procesos educativos y canales de comunicación". En Rev. *Comunição e Educação.* Nº 14, São Paulo y en Rev. *Chasqui* Nº 64, Quito.

—, (2005) "Para comprender la comunicación masiva". En *La iniciativa de la comunicación.* www.comminit.com/la

Laswell, H.D. *Estructura y función de la comunicación en la sociedad.* En Moragas, M. *Sociología de la comunicación de masas,* Gustavo Gili, Barcelona 1979

Max-Neef, Manfred. et al.(1986) *Desarrollo a escala humana.* Santiago de Chile, CEPAUR.

MacBride, Sean (1980) *Un solo mundo, voces múltiples. Comunicación e información en nuestro tiempo.* Fondo de Cultura Económica, México.

Shannon, C.E. y Weaver, W. *The mathematical theory of communication.* Univ. of Illinois Press, 1962

Vygotski, Lev (1979) *Pensamiento y lenguaje.* La Pléyade, Buenos Aires.

Paper presented at CELACOM, May 2005 (UMESP: São Paulo, Brazil). Copyright © 2005, Gabriel Kaplún. Reprinted with permission of the copyright holder.

1927
1960
1963
1964
1967
1969
1970
1971
1972
1973
1974
1975
1976
1977
1978
1979
1980
1981
1982
1983
1984
1985
1986
1987
1988
1989
1990
1991
1992
1993
1994
1995
1996
1997
1998
1999
2000
2001
2002
2003
2004
2005
2006

CONTEMPORARY READINGS
VOLUME ❷
Paradigms in Communication for Development

COMMUNICATION FOR SOCIAL CHANGE: WHY DOES IT MATTER?

Excerpt from: Background Paper for Communication for Development Roundtable

By James Deane

Editors' Note: This piece was written to address some of the questions concerning CFSC as the term was used in 2001. Its purpose was to spark disclosure about key concepts during the UN Roundtable.

2001 One of the recurring criticisms levelled at communication for social change (CFSC) proponents in particular, and at CFSC advocates in general, is that what they are saying is not new. Specific criticisms tend to fall into four areas.

First, that participatory, people-centred communication has been at the core of most mainstream communication thinking and practice for many years, and most development communication initiatives aim first and foremost to empower people to make informed choices.

Second, that some of these arguments are creating artificial boundaries between different approaches and schools of thought in communication. Good communication interventions focus on an intelligent and locally appropriate mix of behaviour change, social change, advocacy and other forms of communication. In focusing on moving away from "traditional" approaches to communication, some communicators feel tension between different approaches to communication when what is needed (and, it is argued, already practised) is a synthesis of a range of interventions.

Third, that while the UNAIDS and Rockefeller (and other similar) proponents have emerged largely from practitioners on the ground, and while there is a long academic tradition of participatory communication literature, CFSC arguments should be reinforced with rigorous academic analysis, modelling and theory. Similarly, the field needs effective evaluation methodologies that can demonstrate the impact of CFSC work.

Fourth, that while many of the ideas in documents such as the UNAIDS Communication Framework are strong in terms of principle, they are difficult to translate into practice on the ground, particularly within the setting of large institutions.

Proponents of communication for social change acknowledge these criticisms. They argue, that while there is a rich and mainstream tradition of participatory communication, particularly in the field of HIV/AIDS, such approaches are often not applied. They point to a number of factors.

First, that both the UNAIDS and Rockefeller processes were centred on largely southern-based, grassroots and civil society focused and driven debates. Their convenings reveal widespread perceptions on the ground that HIV/AIDS communication initiatives in developing countries are significantly driven by institutional and external agencies operating according to their own assessment of what needs to be done, rather than supporting and working within a framework of internally driven debates and agendas. In this sense, they appear to have revealed a substantial "disconnect" between funding and some international agencies, and indigenous organisations working on the ground. Such organisations, these processes suggest, perceive that mainstream communication interventions are often highly vertical and are constructed through a process in which they are sometimes partners and sometimes involved but over which they feel they have little control.

Second, that while participatory communication is indeed mainstream thinking among communication theorists and practitioners, systematically putting these principles into practice on the ground continues to be extremely difficult. Participatory and social change communication tends to work on long-time horizons, and is difficult for donors to support. For these reasons, most financial support tends to be channelled to interventions such as social marketing programmes, with short time horizons and with quantitative evaluation mechanisms. Many proponents of Communication for Social Change argue that this type of communication is generally marginal and a peripheral add-on to otherwise vertical and behaviour-change oriented programmes. Proponents argue that CFSC can provide the core and foundation of all communication interventions.

Third, that in challenging the perceived emphasis on behaviour-change interventions, the intent is not to create a false dichotomy between the various approaches, but there is a strong argument that unless developing country societies and communities are setting and driving the underlying processes of change that are necessary to confront this epidemic, and unless support is provided for the creation of environments where that can happen, future progress in tackling HIV/AIDS is unlikely to be sustainable. They argue that developing countries, both in terms of government and civil society, still find themselves in a position where they are responding to, rather than shaping, the international response to HIV/AIDS.

Fourth, there is increasing interest in learning from the rigorous thinking that goes into much behaviour-change oriented interventions and in adapting it to communication for social change thinking.

Fifth, they argue that communication for social change is not only suggesting the incorporation of more participatory techniques in existing project programming, but also a major change in approach which involves institutions surrendering their agendas.

Sixth, they argue that many communication initiatives are overly focused on the symptoms of the HIV/AIDS pandemic, rather than the underlying causes. While high rates of sexual transmission are undeniably the principal driver for rapid spread of the virus, and changing sexual behaviour is necessary to contain the pandemic, behaviour change is unlikely to be achieved without addressing the underlying causes of these behaviours. Issues of inequality, prejudice, the status of women, the responsibility of men, marginalisation and disempowerment, community and social cohesion, poverty and many other social and political factors are fundamental drivers of the pandemic.

Addressing these issues is also fundamentally about using and fostering communication in society.

And, finally, they argue that the dispute is not necessarily an either/or issue and that clearly there is huge value in many behaviour change and social marketing interventions. Nevertheless, they argue that unless these are implemented within a broader social and political context, then there are major limitations in terms of sustainability and impact.

Deane, James. "So, Is This New and Does It Matter?" Background paper for Communication for Development Roundtable. Nicaragua, November 2001. Sponsored by UNFPA in association with the Rockefeller Foundation and UNESCO. Copyright © 2001, Communication for Social Change Consortium. Reprinted with permission of copyright holder.

1927
1960
1963
1964
1967
1969
1970
1971
1972
1973
1974
1975
1976
1977
1978
1979
1980
1981
1982
1983
1984
1985
1986
1987
1988
1989
1990
1991
1992
1993
1994
1995
1996
1997
1998
1999
2000
2001
2002
2003
2004
2005
2006

THE MULTI-DIMENSIONAL NATURE OF REALITY AND THE COMMUNICATIONAL APPROACH TO SUSTAINABLE DEVELOPMENT

By Sandra Hebe Massoni

2004 Under new scientific paradigms, social communications research is necessarily transdisciplinary (cf., among others, Morín, 1986; Deleuze and Guattari, 1994). This implies a theoretical and epistemological revision, assigning a new, situationally-defined role to communicational research on sociocultural practices. Thus, analysis, rather than residing on its own plane, apart from the world it aspires to explain, must begin by elucidating its intentions and objectives and defining its target audience.[1]

A fragment from a Sherlock Holmes story may provide an enlightening and entertaining illustration of the transdisciplinary imperative in studying communication. In the course of an investigation, Sherlock Holmes and Dr. Watson find it necessary to spend a night in the mountains. They set up their tent; after a good meal and a bottle of wine, they bid each other good night and, lying down, fall into a deep sleep. Some hours later, Holmes awakes and nudges his faithful friend. "Watson," he says, "look at the sky and tell me what you see." Watson answers that he sees millions and millions of stars. "And what," pursues Holmes, "does that tell you?" After thinking, Watson answers that, astronomically speaking, it means there are millions of galaxies, and potentially billions of planets; that, astrologically, Saturn is in Leo; that in temporal terms, it would seem to be approximately 3:30 in the morning; and that, meteorologically, a beautiful day promises to dawn. "And what," Watson asks Holmes, "does it tell you?" After appropriate reflection, Holmes answers, "Elementary, my dear Watson. It tells me some wretch has stolen our tent."

To pose a parallel, one might observe that, for a considerable period, something similar occurred in the social sciences. Disciplinary specialization was immensely beneficial in obvious ways, providing descriptions of parts, deeper knowledge of specific areas, major advances in increasingly specific fields, etc. However, it also brought with it various problems. If every question carries an implicit answer, one of the implications of specialization is a concentration on specific aspects of reality, with a correspondingly indistinct view of what surrounds them—a dilution of explanatory processes that are more comprehensive, holistic and synergistic. This is not meant to suggest that research is without value. On the contrary, its findings must be used to fuller advantage, with greater efforts at incorporating them in the social transformation process in which our peoples are immersed. The Sherlock Holmes anecdote illustrates some of the consequences of research within strictly defined traditional disciplines. They include abundant information and vast analytical intelligence, with an accompanying failure, however, to achieve operational validity, given that they lack connection to real problems.

Thus, a central postulate in the new scientific paradigms is the importance of transdisciplinary research into real problems and their underlying forces.

According to Deleuze and Guattari, the transdisciplinary approach means "a rhizomatic organization of knowledge by plateaus—these being neither end nor beginning, but rather a midpoint and, as such, a continuous zone of intensities that vibrates within itself and develops without any culminating point or external destination to guide it. The plateau, then, is a multiplicity linked to another point distinct in type. It is based on different signs, which cannot be reduced to

---

1 For treatment of this aspect, see Massoni, Sandra. "*Juegos Cruzados: comunicación y transdiciplina*" [*Juegos cruzados*: communication and transdiscipline], in La Trama de la comunicación. *Anuario del Departamento de Ciencias de la Comunicación Volumen 7* [The warp of communication. *Yearbook of the Department of Communication Sciences*, vol. 7], Laborde Editor, 2002.

1927
1960
1963
1964
1967
1969
1970
1971
1972
1973
1974
1975
1976
1977
1978
1979
1980
1981
1982
1983
1984
1985
1986
1987
1988
1989
1990
1991
1992
1993
1994
1995
1996
1997
1998
1999
2000
2001
2002
2003
2004
2005
2006

either the singular or the multiple, since it is not composed of units, but rather of changing dimensions. It has no beginning or end, but only a middle through which it grows, and which it overflows. It is made up of linear multiplicities of infinite dimensions, without subject or object, and by its nature cannot change its dimensions without changing itself. (Deleuze and Guattari, 1994.)[2]

This is the direction in which our model for strategic communication points.

A Model of Strategic Communication

Strategic communication, for the present purposes, is "a method of research and action based on two stages of understanding. The first draws on the views of whatever disciplines are germane to the problem being investigated; the second focuses on the social actors relevant to the resolution of the problem. From this perspective, communication is the relating moment of sociocultural diversity. Here, the emphasis shifts from description—the dominant objective in much communications research—to a focus on communication as a process of "making common" in relation to an objective of change defined in terms of a changing situation" (Massoni, S, 2002).

This model is based on the epistemology of complexity (Morín, 1986). It employs a transdisciplinary approach in attempting to understand what is present in terms of the included third, and focuses on the dynamic generated by the simultaneous action of the different levels of reality that exist within a development project.

As a general matter, social scientists conduct research to gain pragmatic knowledge. This means dealing with all levels of social reality, levels of

differing epistemological natures. As Orti explains (Orti, A: 1994: p. 92), at least three levels of social reality can be distinguished:

1. The first is the level or field of facts composed of the indicative or designative relationships of a proposition (Deleuze, 1989) put forth as evidence of what occurs or is done. The facts (thus configured) as individual states are evident on the level of the manifest or conscious. The facts tend to be thought of as factual processes composed of charges of energy, and hence as a quantifiable *res extensa*.

2. Entering into the simple field of facts—and in line with the meaning of the proposition (Deleuze, 1989)—is the existence of the universe of discourses. Here, meanings are not established by extension, but are, instead, part of a self-referential system of signs; the cogency of communicative propositions depends on their meaningful articulation, since they are defined by codified relationships between signifier and signified. In principle, discourses are articulated by "what is uttered," in the context of specific cultural and ideological formations. However, the institutionalization of things means that they are assigned different specific meaning in different cultures (since each culture imposes a system of codes). Along with culturemes [the significant units of a culture], discourses also imply value orientations, or ideological propositions (ideologems)—the level at which the quantitative approach (for precoded culturemes) converges with the qualitative approach (for their ideological meaning and process of symbolic production).

3. The third level is the domain of motivations—the driving forces, impulses and desires that provide answers to the "why" of social interaction. They represent, in other words, the conscious or unconscious intentionality and meaning that shape the projective process. These processes are the strategic level of the conscious and unconscious "instituent," interpretable with meaning based on hermeneutic qualitative approaches.

---

2 Massoni, Sandra. "*Estrategias de comunicación: una mirada comunicacional para la investigación sociocultural*" [Communication strategies: a communicational approach to sociocultural research], in *Recepción y mediaciones. Casos de investigación en América latina. Enciclopedia Latinoamericana de sociocultura y comunicación* [Reception and mediations. Research cases in Latin America. Latin American Encyclopedia of Socioculture and Communication], Guillermo Orozco Gómez (coord). Grupo Editorial Norma, Buenos Aires / Venezuela, 2002.

Research based on the strategic communication model takes into account the existence of these three levels as a means of dealing with the complexity of communicational phenomena.

The Dimensions of Communication

These strategies employ a transdisciplinary and multi-paradigmatic approach, one that seeks to determine—both critically and evaluatively—the various dimensions of communication within a problem situation. Such an approach is based on a recognition of the capacity of the paradigms to deal with different aspects of reality, and their specific contributions to the genealogy of the reality itself. This operation of construction/deconstruction is reprised to emphasize the transformative role of science in the field of sustainable development.

Here, the reference to dimensions, rather than levels, is intended to stress the specificity of the views provided by different disciplines, without implying a hierarchy among them or assigning them any predetermined or universal order.

Each theory operates within a specific dimension of the communicational phenomenon, imprinting upon it its individual stamp of thought and purpose. Instances of communication can be examined for marks of these modes of thinking,[3] which reflect the theoretical conceptions that organize and articulate the matrix of the encounter.

THE INFORMATIONAL DIMENSION

■ The informational dimension consists of the field of factual processes.

■ Here, communication is viewed as a process of transmitting information for a predetermined objective.

■ Theories that operate in the informational dimension describe homogeneous data and quantitative correspondences, focusing on messages and their distribution.

■ They approach communication as the dissemination of messages.

■ Marks of the thinking involved in this approach include linearity, verticality and operative communication.

Example: Communication research theories.

THE IDEOLOGICAL DIMENSION

■ The ideological dimension consists of the universe of discourse.

■ It views cultural and ideological formations from a superstructural perspective.

■ Theories that operate in the ideological dimension characterize the mechanisms and devices of alienation and manipulation, and the ways in which ideology is part of the semanticization of the social.

■ Communication is viewed as an apparatus of ideological reproduction.

■ Marks of the thinking involved in this approach include linearity, segmentation, verticality, and *denuncismo* (reportage that digs up "dirt"—whether or not based on actual fact).

Example: Theories of ideological analysis.

THE INTERACTIONAL DIMENSION

■ This consists of the field of motivations.

■ It approaches communication as a process of producing meaning, involving personal and group interactions that must be taken into account if messages are to be made more effective.

■ It approaches communication as the production of meaning based on bonds with the other.

■ Marks of the thinking involved in this approach include linearity, segmentation, horizontality and the interaction of subjects.

Example: Theories of psychodynamics (communication and group dynamics, social psychology).

THE SOCIOCULTURAL DIMENSION

■ In this field, communication is seen as social articulation, as the social phenomenon of encounter, as the "making common" of social actors or groups.

3 The category of modes of thinking set forth in Massoni, Sandra. "Estrategias de comunicación: tiempo de investigarnos vivos" Communication strategies: time for a live investigation of ourselves]. *Revista Comunicación y Sociedad [Communication and Society Journal]* N° 37. University of Guadalajara, Mexico, 2001.

- It approaches communication as the relating moment of sociocultural diversity.
- It is the field of that which is in flux.
- Theories that operate in this dimension describe sociocultural mediations as devices to articulate different dynamics.
- Here, communication is approached as the locus of the construction of the social dynamic, of the everyday production of meaning.
- Marks of the thinking involved in this approach include diversity, multiplicity, networks, communication as the articulation of social diversity, and communication as a complex, situational and historical process.

Example: Theories of communication and culture.

Communication theories and methodologies deriving from sociology, anthropology, psychology, semiology, etc. are incorporated in the strategic communication model with a recognition of both their scope and the limitations of their capacity to operate in various dimensions of the communicational situation. The researcher adopting the strategic communication approach uses these dimensions not to obtain explanations or to answer "why" questions, but rather to incorporate them as critical and evaluative elements in answering "how" questions.

Thus, the importance of a multi-paradigmatic approach in dealing with communication as a complex phenomenon is correlated with the recognition of the multiple determinants that constitute it. In the study of social reality, one finds three types of structures, and three types of different dynamics, each with its own rules: factual, signifying and motivational. Without in any way suggesting that the contributions of the mechanistic view of the social should be ignored or minimized, what is proposed here is a multiple approach based on an awareness of relationships between relationships, in which the material, the symbolic, and the affective are all included.

In addressing problems, the strategic view of the communicative dimension creates possibilities for the articulation and convergence of multiple perspectives, deriving from different disciplines and types of knowledge. A situational definition of the approach makes it possible to incorporate the distinct contributions of different disciplines, making it easier to employ different modes of thinking in considering a problem. Within the tension of the debate between science and society, the model of strategic communication as conversational social change contributes to sustainable development in precisely this way. The present research employs micro- and macro-social perspectives, and is intended to contribute to the emergence of multiple encounters around a given problem, construed in terms of demands that reflect the tensions of an evolving society.

Bibliography

Deleuze, Gilles and Guattari, Félix. *Mil mesetas. Capitalismo y esquizofrenia* [A thousand plateaus. Capitalism and schizophrenia], Valencia, Pretextos, 1994.

Massoni, Sandra. "Estrategias de comunicación: tiempo de investigarnos vivos" [Communication strategies: time for a live investigation of ourselves] *Revista Comunicación y Sociedad* [Communication and Society Journal], no. 37. University of Guadalajara, Mexico, 2001.

Massoni, Sandra. "Estrategias de comunicación: una mirada comunicacional para la investigación sociocultural" [Communication strategies: a communicational approach to sociocultural research], in *Recepción y mediaciones. Casos de investigación en América latina. Enciclopedia Latinoamericana de Sociocultura y Comunicación* [Reception and mediations. Research cases in Latin America. Latin American Encyclopedia of Socioculture and Communication], Guillermo Orozco Gómez (coord). Grupo Editorial Norma, Buenos Aires / Venezuela, 2002.

Massoni, Sandra. "Juegos Cruzados: comunicación y transdiciplina" [*Juegos cruzados*: communication and transdiscipline], in La Trama de la comunicación. Anuario del Departamento de Ciencias de la Comunicación Volumen 7 [The warp of communication. Yearbook of the Department of Communication Sciences, vol. 7], Laborde Editor, 2002

Morín, Edgard. Conocimiento del conocimiento [Knowledge of knowledge], Editorial Seuil, 1986.

Orti, A: 1994: p. 92, in Delgado, Juan and Juan Gutiérrez: Métodos y técnicas cualitativas de investigación en ciencias sociales [Qualitative techniques and methods in social sciences]. Madrid, Síntesis. 1994.

Massoni, Sandra Hebe. "The Multi-Dimensional Nature of Reality and the Communicational Approach to Sustainable Development." Published in *Comunicación, Ruralidad y Desarrollo. Mitos, paradigmas y dispositivos del cambio* [Communication, rurality and development. Myths, paradigms and devices of change] (2004), by Gustavo Cimadevilla and Edgardo Carniglia (editors). Ediciones INTA, Buenos Aires (Argentina). Reprinted with permission of copyright holder.

1927
1960
1963
1964
1967
1969
1970
1971
1972
1973
1974
1975
1976
1977
1978
1979
1980
1981
1982
1983
1984
1985
1986
1987
1988
1989
1990
1991
1992
1993
1994
1995
1996
1997
1998
1999
2000
2001
2002
2003
2004
2005
2006

EXCERPT FROM:

NAMING THE WORLD TO THEORIZING ITS RELATIONSHIPS: NEW DIRECTIONS FOR PARTICIPATORY COMMUNICATION FOR DEVELOPMENT

By Robert Huesca

1996 During the past 20 years, the communication field has seen an increased interest in participatory approaches and models for planning, implementing and theorizing development. Research of participatory communication for development has generated numerous ways of conceptualizing and implementing participation, the variety of which has been discussed usefully elsewhere (Jacobson, 1992; Nair and White, 1987). This variety has made a convincing case for the involvement of ordinary citizens in the defining of social reality, identifying of priorities and designing of media development programs. Much of this work has been inspired and justified by the theoretical and methodological contributions of Paulo Freire, whose basic premise is that researchers must privilege and learn from the experiences of ordinary people in order to begin working toward social change (in particular see Freire 1970, 1973). Of particular concern to this article is Freire's notion of "naming the world," wherein people use everyday language to unveil the complex and hidden roots of oppression. It is in the naming of the world where communication plays a central role with dialogue operating as the necessary communicative mode for participatory development.

The intention of this article is to advance this area of research by suggesting that ordinary citizens are not only capable of naming their world, but that they routinely theorize complex relationships in everyday life. Shifting the emphasis in participatory development research from encouraging people to name the world to focusing on how they theorize its relationships, would be pragmatically beneficial for projects aimed at social change. By purposively striving to uncover, identify and tease out people's theories of communication and social change, researchers can gain new insights into current media practices, generate future actions and fulfill a mandate of participatory research to recognize and honour the validity of the lived experiences of research subjects. In this article, I will demonstrate the intellectual continuity in shifting from mere naming to explicit theorizing of the world, and I will illustrate the importance of this shift with some examples from Bolivian radio practitioners.

Moving from "Naming" to "Theorizing"

Freire's advancements in literacy training laid the groundwork for a large portion of the participatory communication for development research that emerged over the past 20 years. Of central importance was his insistence on grounding pedagogical exercises in the lived experiences of the students, as both a moral imperative and a pragmatic necessity. By encouraging students to name their worlds, teachers validated their pupils' humanness while generating words and themes that resonated with everyday struggles. This sharp resonance provided students the impetus to learn to read and write, opening up the possibilities for an emergent critical consciousness that formed the basis for theoretically driven movements—praxis—for social justice.

This line of thinking has been adopted by a number of development theorists and practitioners who advocate popular participation in the identification of development goals, the determination of program structure and the evaluation of results. One of the best-known extensions of this approach in communication is Servaes' (1989) "multiplicity in one world" paradigm. The multiplicity paradigm embraces the major premises from Freire's critical pedagogy regarding popular participation in naming the world. It complicates Freire's work, however, by emphasizing that cultures are not monolithic and unified, but that they contain multiple interpretations and meanings of many notions, such as poverty and oppression. Operating under this presupposition, Servaes elevates the role of communication in exploring, cataloguing and mediating the multiplicity of meanings within a single culture.

Although this emphasis on multiplicity accentuates the role of communication for participatory development, it falls short of distinguishing that multiple meanings are made in communication. Such a distinction necessitates exploring how participants comprehend, construct and negotiate the diverse, complementary and contradictory elements of their everyday lives— how they theorize relationships of the world.

Dervin and Clark (1989) have acknowledged the capacities of ordinary people to theorize relationships in their material and symbolic environments as they adapt and adopt, resist and acquiesce, invent and change within intrusive and sometimes oppressive life conditions, including the international media context. They further posit that the theories by which people move through the world are themselves multiple and contradictory because across time they are not only explicit, conscious and invented, but are tacit, unconscious and habitual, as well. Their work suggests that progress in development can be advanced by research and practices that enable ordinary people to explain their worldviews by laying out the major propositions and relationships of the societies in which they interact. Such an approach would enrich researchers' understandings of how media can and do transform societies. Furthermore, it would provide development researchers and practitioners with new understandings of the relationship between communication and social change that would form the basis for more rele-vant and effective intervention strategies.

One approach that is consonant with the goals outlined above is Dervin's sense-making methodology (1992). Sense-making is a detailed theory of how people move communicatively through the world, which forms the basis for constructing interviews that are able to ascertain how people theorize the world. Sense-making interviews anchor questions in significant, lived experiences that respondents identify as being relevant to a given topic, such as a successful development project or a problematic media program. Sense-making then fleshes out responses by delving into circumstances that led up to the experience (e.g., histories, events, ideas, feelings, questions), thoughts and actions used to make sense of them (e.g., by ignoring, acquiescing, resisting, embellishing) and outcomes that followed them (e.g., material changes, social differences, new understandings). Because of their in-depth, iterative and cyclical nature, interviews based on sense-making's presuppositions generate rich, detailed portraits of how human agency both sustains and transforms social structures—portraits created from the perspective of the human agent, not from the gifted social theorist or development agent.

An interest in popular participation in media and a concern for privileging ordinary people as social theorists underpinned a study of radio practitioners in Bolivia's tin mining region in 1992-1993. Using participant observation and interview methods based on the theoretical directions of the sense-making approach, I lived and worked with radio practitioners in Bolivia for five months. The field sites for this study—Radio Nacional de Huanuni, Radio Pío XII and the Centro de Investigación y Servicio Popular—were selected because of their history as institutions that are highly participatory and that have achieved gains for workers and lower-class, urban dwellers. Practitioner theories drawn from interviews and field notes are offered below in abbreviated form to display the richness of this approach for scholars and workers sharing an interest in participatory development.

Participatory Communication for Social Change: Practitioner Views

Conversations with Bolivian radio practitioners produced not a unified theory of communication and social change but an amalgamation of complex and

1927
1960
1963
1964
1967
1969
1970
1971
1972
1973
1974
1975
1976
1977
1978
1979
1980
1981
1982
1983
1984
1985
1986
1987
1988
1989
1990
1991
1992
1993
1994
1995
1996
1997
1998
1999
2000
2001
2002
2003
2004
2005
2006

complementary concepts. The diversity of these theories was unexpected given both the relative homogeneity of the population and the history of the theoretically informed labor struggles that surround radio practice in Bolivia. Most academic work on the miners' radios has concluded that media have operated somewhat mechanistically in this region as tools for building networks of solidarity, mobilizing populations in resistance movements, and promoting and protecting indigenous cultures (see, for example, Lozada and Kúncar, 1986; O'Connor, 1990). Interviews with practitioners, however, generated far more complex and interesting portraits of the relationships between communication and social transformation.

Theories of Communication

Discussions of communication identified several dominant themes, including relational, political, practical and ethical aspects of communication. The most common way of describing communication focused on its relational aspect. Media practice was portrayed as work done jointly with others out of a sense of being bonded, connected, tied, linked and committed. It was not the solitary enterprise of the expert trained in documenting reality—i.e., traditional, Western journalism. The words *ligarse* (to tie, bind, link oneself) and *comprometerse* (to promise, commit, oblige oneself) were used repeatedly across interviews to explain and describe communication experiences:

> Communication is not just the sending of messages. It is getting into the masses. Getting into, well, if not the masses, getting into the life of the people, sharing with them, being there through the good and the bad. This experience has helped me as far as securing a sense of commitment with the popular sectors of society.
> —Alfredo A., director of *Radio Pío XII*

Forging committed bonds with social actors forced practitioners to take political positions regarding the specific alliances they formed in media activities. The direction of these alliances was clearest at union radio stations:

> The work of a union radio is very different from what they do in the cities (at commercial stations). Union stations are committed with the workers, with this class known as the exploited class, the dispossessed class, with the popular sectors. And this is where we can really achieve more freedom in our work than they can in the cities. Because in the cities, almost all of the radios, or almost any communication medium, is a private business. They have their owners, right? So that is a different system, a system with censorship. It would be difficult there for us to say what we think or believe or even what we see.
> —Ana L., part-time producer at *Radio Nacional de Huanuni*

The political direction provided by the union ownership structure was replicated at the other stations, which made conscious choices to align themselves with working-class people. Rather than interpreting this direction as a constraint on what they could do, however, practitioners described a sense of "freedom" and power to define reality and truth stemming from their political alliances.

Perhaps because of its highly political and committed nature, communication was often spoken of in practical terms as a tool at the disposal of unions and other popular organizations:

> One of the objectives of the institution is precisely this: to support the unions and popular organizations. This is so they can debate among themselves using elements that we offer them. They can come to their own conclusions and I believe that, indeed, they have done their own analyses. They should do their own analyses and come up with answers that respond to situations. This is the objective of CISEP (Centro de Investigación y Servicio Popular).
> —Gari E., technical producer at CISEP.

This practitioner echoed the opinions of many others when he portrayed communication as "support"; as a technical "element" that was secondary and subordinate to social movements. While beneficial in a pragmatic sense, the communication-as-tool position threatened to undermine the relational aspect of communication mentioned above.

A final aspect of communication emphasized an ethical dimension, as media practices nearly always followed and endorsed a particular agenda, one calling for the transformation of society that is more just, egalitarian, dignified and democratic:

> Most of the time, the programs that are broadcast are dead the next day because our minds are very fragile. What I believe is that one must work for this hope—if there's one thing that can't be taken away it is our right to dream—of a life where there aren't these things: injustices, social problems with consequences of alcoholism and all that. One must work for this and the radio is a medium with force and, sometimes, influence. One should work for this.
> —Pedro I., former community producer at *Radio Nacional de Huanuni.*

This vision was widespread, and, in fact, had become de facto policy at *Radio Pío XII*, whose employees received regular training from the Latin American Association of Educational Radio (ALER), which embraces a media-for-social-change agenda.

Practitioner theories of communication were not unified but functioned as amalgams that complemented one another. Often contradictory or antagonistic theories—e.g., communication-as-commitment versus communication-as-tool—were articulated by the same practitioner. Similarly, practitioner accounts of social change were diverse.

Theories of Social Change

Practitioner theories of social change clustered into two broad perspectives. The predominant perspective interpreted the process of social change as occurring in rational sequences. This sequential perspective posited that social change occurs in a somewhat predictable, controllable and evolutionary succession of steps that can be catalyzed and facilitated by communication techniques. A less prevalent perspective interpreted social change as emergent phenomena without predictable order, sequence or direction. This emergent perspective posited that social change is in the process of becoming, a process that is both enabled and hampered by communication.

Practitioners who articulated the sequential view of social change emphasized two main themes: evolution and consciousness. That is, social change followed a natural progression that began with consciousness-raising:

> The Federation of United Neighbors Organizations (The Federation of United Neighbors of El Alto (FUJUVE-El Alto) was a fairly strong organization in Llallagua. Having raised the consciousness (via the radio) of the people regarding their struggles and their organizing efforts, Llallagua now has paved streets and has achieved a certain level of progress, thanks to these efforts.
> —Loren R., director of *Radio Nacional de Huanuni* (and former director of *Radio Llallagua*).

In this instance, material accomplishments—street paving, "progress"—were attributed to raised consciousness. For some practitioners, raising consciousness was the only appropriate and long-lasting way of changing society:

> We managed to achieve a coming to consciousness of the people regarding their problems and their absolute right to make demands. Now as far as meeting specific objectives defined by their demands, we didn't achieve any of these because that is outside the nature of the radio. If we start to deal with those problems—for example, social issues—then we would become a welfare agency (*una institución asistencialista*). And the radio cannot have this sort of character. Assistancialism (welfare, handouts) in any form holds back any and all projects, any and all hopes, any and all goals of a particular group of people. It puts the brakes on their aspirations.

1927
1960
1963
1964
1967
1969
1970
1971
1972
1973
1974
1975
1976
1977
1978
1979
1980
1981
1982
1983
1984
1985
1986
1987
1988
1989
1990
1991
1992
1993
1994
1995
1996
1997
1998
1999
2000
2001
2002
2003
2004
2005
2006

Instead, what needs to be done is to motivate, so that this group will be conscious of its problems in order to achieve its particular objectives."
—Pablo J., contributor to CISEP

This practitioner further criticized media activities that took more direct, material initiatives with people as being "palliatives"; temporary solutions that actually impeded social change because they bypassed consciousness.

A final variation of the consciousness-raising theme focused on recovering memory as a way of creating a continuity of consciousness:

For example, we have seen that this district has had its essence wiped out by the movies, television and the rest. So all this memory (of the miners' movement) was being destroyed, right, and people started picking up another reality. What I mean is that I wanted my program to serve as a new experience for the young people, so that they could understand…That's the conclusion I drew. I had also seen that the union leaders failed to keep in mind the earlier struggles (for improved salaries and working conditions). Little by little the union had become the property of a political party and was no longer working for the entire working class of miners. What was happening was a distortion of what these earlier leaders had been struggling for.
—Lalo E., outreach worker with miners for *Radio Pío XII*

This practitioner fashioned a program that tapped local memories of significant events of years gone by in the struggle for better wages and working conditions. He described the historical program as both generative—a way to stimulate new interests among youth inexperienced in workers' struggles—and corrective, a manner of redirecting movements that had somehow lost their way.

In contrast to these sequential views, a number of practitioners described social change as emerging in

unpredictable ways that were shaped by contextual circumstances. This process did not always take on a recognizable form, as one practitioner explained:

Sometimes things that happen in Bolivia, and really this is the way popular movements are throughout Latin America, they are not what we could call already established or somehow inherent. They are always being created. I can't remember, for example, that there was ever a march of torches at night the way it happened here the other night. The people here have the custom of doing their marches in the day. Likewise, there had never been a crucifixion. Then there were self-crucifixions during a protest, as a form of struggle. That's the way the dynamic is.
—Alfredo A., director of *Radio Pío XII*

In addition to having multiple, manifest forms, the emergent view of social change understood popular movements as being contingent on changing circumstances. Moments of severe crisis, for example, seemed to bring out the best in people:

It is in the unfortunate moments of despair that the people are highly '*solidaria*' (in solidarity). When they try to defend against something that is going to have a great consequence on the town, it is something that is very spontaneous. They just appear, these marches of solidarity that help in creating resolve. And there is no need to drag people out. They turn out like sheep. I think this has helped me a lot.
—Marta M., outreach worker at *Radio Pío XII*

Moments of crisis also sparked the creativity of practitioners who sensed that changing circumstances demanded new communication forms. In explaining a form known as the *cadena radial*,[1] one practitioner interpreted its appearance as follows:

---

1 The "radio chain" occurs when the signal of one station is captured and retransmitted by another station, which overlaps the first. This retransmission is then captured by a more distant station and again retransmitted, creating a low technology distribution system. In addition to distributing the signal, stations take turns originating transmissions, thereby converting a limited, one-way signal into an extended multicast.

I think the chain came about as a necessity of the moment. What I mean is there was a necessity for communication, right? Because when there is a dictator who shuts down all communication—and this dictatorship of García Meza was very powerful, as I believe everyone knows. So, due to the severe censorship, I think the chains came about as a necessity for the workers to be organized. . . . If we review history, I believe—at least the events that have touched my life—the chains have functioned best in times of dictatorship. In contrast, during times like the ones we are living in now—and this is probably your experience, too, as you've been able to observe—one doesn't feel the necessity, and so only two or three stations participate. In contrast, during times of dictatorship, we all felt the need to communicate with each other.
—Ana L., part-time producer at *Radio Nacional de Huanuni*

Because the details surrounding everyday events can shift radically, movements for social change must be able to respond to new circumstances if they are to remain vital. Communication practitioners who conceptualized social change as an emergent phenomena seemed able to respond with greater programming flexibility than practitioners who conceived of social change as an evolutionary process.

Theories into Practice

The general theories of communication and social change described above functioned as important frames of reference that had a direct bearing on specific programming decisions. Practitioners who viewed social change as a sequence of evolutionary steps tended to rely on conceptions of communication as a tool or implement for raising consciousness when enacting radio programs. In contrast, practitioners who conceptualized social change as an emergent phenomena tended to rely on modes of communication that were more in flux and driven by sense, moment and relationship when at work.

Practitioners sharing the sequential, evolutionary view of social change relied on predefined, strategic notions and prescriptions of social action to direct communication responses. Predefined strategies appeared as both abstract, guiding principles (such as the Roman Catholic Church station's "option for the poor," or the union station's "solidarity with the exploited classes") and as concrete steps (such as selecting appropriate topics, interviewing leaders within organized sectors and choosing words emanating from those leaders). An example from a nongovernmental organization illustrates predefined communication strategies:

> Within our target audience, we have defined groups. To be exact, the institution, from the beginning, has been about popular support. Especially after 1985 when there were so many firings in our country. How can we alleviate this situation? By doing small studies that will be of use to the popular sector. But later, well, we had to redefine our objectives. The popular sector now, for example, is concentrated in the microregions of the mining sector. There we have, for example, Santa Fe, Cañalón, the mining sector Colquiri in La Paz department, and in the suburban poor neighborhoods around Oruro, here. We work with them. There are more than six of those poor neighborhoods. We are in Cantuta, in the neighborhood of Rosario, and it is possible that we will add more. But they have to be poor areas.
> —Gari E., technical producer at CISEP

The predefined guiding principle (option for the poor) resulted in prescribed audiences (microregions of the mining sector, new suburban neighborhoods, poor areas) with given topics (usually material conditions of wages, water, sewer, electricity) and stock interview sources (local leaders). All of the stations in this study used predefined strategies, which seemed to coincide with a sense of communication as a tool for conveying information needed to build movements for social transformation.

1927
1960
1963
1964
1967
1969
1970
1971
1972
1973
1974
1975
1976
1977
1978
1979
1980
1981
1982
1983
1984
1985
1986
1987
1988
1989
1990
1991
1992
1993
1994
1995
1996
1997
1998
1999
2000
2001
2002
2003
2004
2005
2006

In contrast, practitioners who understood social change as emergent phenomena tended to implement communication practices of an alterative nature. Alterative practices included abstract, guiding principles (monitoring, coordinating and facilitating social organization) and concrete steps (generating topics through "organic" agenda setting, seeking multiple and diverse interview sources, choosing words emanating from everyday experience at the grassroots level).

For example, one former producer at a union radio station recalled how the local housewives' committee—a common, popular organization in the mining regions—set a programming agenda. In this case, the committee voted to march from the mining town of Huanuni to the urban center of Oruro to protest the withholding of their husbands' wages. In a joint interview with her husband, the practitioner explained how this program emerged:

> This was a measure the housewives took because the workers were not being paid their salaries as they should have been. So the way things are here is that the woman places herself on the front lines and decides to march, you see, in order to demand the payment of back wages. And direct from the march, we went right on the air, using the walkie-talkies, together with Sergio (her husband).
> —Sara S., former producer at *Radio Nacional de Huanuni*

> When the housewives decided to march, since she (his wife, Sara) was integrally identified with the women and their problems, of course she had no alternative. She had to go. She had to march together with the housewives. And the whole journey was relayed to the radio station.
> —Sergio H., technician at *Radio Nacional de Huanuni*

The episode related above is a clear instance of alterative topic-selecting, wherein the practitioner never lost sight of her objectives (to monitor, facilitate and contribute to popular movements for social change),

yet she realized them without predefining her topic, sources or language. In such instances, the ability to respond flexibly is more valuable than the capacity to perform strategically.

Another example that helps to clarify the alterative approach concerns the identification of interview sources. While reporting on a labor strike where miners took over an interior section of the mine, a practitioner used multimedia forms—tape recordings, the "open microphone" and large "newspaper murals"—to connect dispersed social actors and to convert audiences into producers:

> We went into the mine to pull out the experience of the strikers: how they felt in that moment, of being exhausted, of hopelessness, of things they were living. In a small way we rescued the human experience of these people, you know. So we'd take in our newspaper murals and they themselves would draw on them. We took their drawings down to the Plaza of the Miner and we displayed them there. It was a constant coming and going, a 'permanent response' between the people on the outside and the people on strike inside.
> —Marta M., outreach worker at *Radio Pío XII*

A side effect of this sort of generation of topics and sources is the emergence of language that is closer to the lived reality of the grassroots—not the leadership—in a variety of social movements.

In this study, the most prevalent sorts of practices were those of a predefined nature based on a sequential theory of social change. This should not come as a surprise or necessarily a criticism, as predefined sources, topics and language provide efficient and pragmatic modes of moving through the demands of daily radio production. The security and stability offered by such an approach, however, brings with it a danger of stagnation, rigidification and disconnection with the social bases. On the other hand, alterative practices were difficult to conceptualize and execute due to a high degree of uncertainty and ambiguity, but they were able to respond to unanticipated exigencies and to recognize new opportunities because they were guided by principles such as monitoring, coordinating, contributing and rescuing.

Conclusion

Advocates of participatory communication for development have argued convincingly for the involvement of ordinary people in the naming of their world for program planning, design and evaluation. The research to date has failed to come to grips, however, with the full implications of "multiplicity in one world" paradigm, which suggests that ordinary people not only hold multiple understandings of their cultures, but that they posit relationships between diverse aspects of everyday life, as well.

The abbreviated account of communication and social theories from Bolivia illustrates the utility of mapping these theories of ordinary people. General theories of both communication (as commitment, as a tool) and social change (as evolutionary sequences, as emergent phenomena) guided, enabled and constrained specific media practices in the specific cases of this study. Programs that were marked by flexibility, responsiveness and facilitation of emergent social movements seemed more difficult to enact but more successful at dealing with radically shifting conditions facing labor unions. Given that much of the world is racked by the same neoliberal policies suffered in Bolivia (i.e., eliminating state subsidies, freezing wages, encouraging transnational investment), this nascent theory of communication and social change is of potentially broad application to development practitioners having to cope with constantly shifting social, political and economic contexts.

This particular contribution is less important, however, than the usefulness of understanding how broad practitioner theories guide concrete programming choices and decisions. Understanding media programs from the theoretical perspectives of ordinary people provides development workers with the basis on which to evaluate, improve and invent communication practices striving to achieve more just, egalitarian and dignified societies. Understanding everyday theories of communication and social change facilitates the construction of compatible development programs and points to fruitful, though little travelled, paths of action.

Cultivating a sensitivity to the multiple meanings within a culture is a useful first step in advancing participatory communication for development. The next logical step is to understand how multiplicity plays itself out in everyday life. This, of course, necessitates that ordinary people not only name their world, but theorize its relationships.

References

Dervin, B. "From the Mind's Eye of the User: The Sense-Making Qualitative-Quantitative Methodology." J. D. Glazier and R. R. Powell, eds., *Qualitative Research in Information Management.* 1992 (pp. 61-84).

Dervin, B., and K. Clark. "Communication as Cultural Identity: The Invention Mandate." *Media Development*, 1989, 2, 5-8.

Freire, P. *Pedagogy of the Oppressed.* Trans. M. Bergman Ramos. New York: Herder and Herder, 1970.

Freire, P. *¿Extensión o Comunicación?* Trans. L. Ronzoni. Buenos Aires: Siglo XXI, 1973.

Jacobson, T. L. "A Pragmatist Account of Participatory Communication Research for National Development." *Communication Theory*, 1993, 3, 214-230.

Lozada, F., and G. Kúncar. "Las Radios Mineras, las Voces del Coraje." M. Simpson Grinberg, ed., *Comunicación Alternativa y Cambio Social.* Tlahuapan, Puebla, Mexico: Premiá Editora de Libros, 1986.

Nair, K. S., and S. White. "Participatory Message Development: A Conceptual Framework." *Media Development*, 1987, 34 (3), 36-40.

O'Connor, A. "The Miners' Radio Stations in Bolivia: A Culture of Resistance." *Journal of Communication*, 1990, 40, 102-110.

Servaes, J. *One World, Multiple Cultures: A New Paradigm on Communication for Development.* Belgium: Acco, 1989.

Huesca, Robert. "Naming the World to Theorizing Its Relationships: New Directions for Participatory Communication for Development," *Media Development*, 1996/2. WACC, London. Copyright © 1996, World Association for Christian Communication. Reprinted with permission of author and copyright holder.

1927
1960
1963
1964
1967
1969
1970
1971
1972
1973
1974
1975
1976
1977
1978
1979
1980
1981
1982
1983
1984
1985
1986
1987
1988
1989
1990
1991
1992
1993
1994
1995
1996
1997
1998
1999
2000
2001
2002
2003
2004
2005
2006

HISTORICAL NOTES ON A POSSIBLE COMMUNICOLOGY: A HYPOTHETICAL CONFIGURATION AND TRAJECTORY

By Luis Jesús Galindo Cáceres

2004 I. First Steps Toward a Profession: Tracing the History of the Science of Communicology

A century ago, communicology did not exist; indeed, strictly speaking, there was no theory of communication. No academic field, university departments, study groups, research centers or networks of scholars were dedicated to the subject. No government funding was available to explore and develop it, no debates were devoted to it, and there were no arrangements for informing the public on it. There were no journals, bulletins, conferences, meetings or graduate programs—in short, no professional field. There were only a few ideas, notes, curiosities and visions. A hundred years later, all of this has changed. Communication is now a booming—not to say exploding—academic and professional field. It occupies the front line on political and economic agendas and is at the heart of cultural debate. Something happened over this period of time, something that changed the planet—and changed us—in a central way, and we have yet to recover from the surprise.

The attempt to trace the history of a possible communicology has two angles. One is improbably excessive in its ambition, the other timely and clearly needed. So much has happened in slightly over 60 years that trying to organize the existing information from a given perspective is, to say the least, complicated, difficult and enormously challenging. At the same time, it represents but an instant of human history—albeit an instant of tremendous importance,

which inspires efforts that are pursued with expectations of short-term impact. A great deal of material has been produced in a very few years. Moreover, there is wide variation and a diversity of voices and approaches to the topic. Much has been written and said about communication and the first task, for those with a taste for extreme detail, is to try to place the material in broad categories. At the same time, we must begin to sift what is substantive from what is not, shifting the focus from the fine weave to the overall tapestry. There will be time later to pick up any dropped threads to enrich the order.

Work has advanced on various fronts of this possible universe. This has helped in reviewing the past, understanding the present, and working toward a future. As tends to happen in the great petty world of the historian, much of what has been chronicled has turned into commonplace that invite agreement while inhibiting alternative observations. The historian of communicology, then, must trace a dual path. On the one hand, he must take up where his predecessors left off, without being blind to their defects and errors; on the other, he must attempt to look slightly beyond what is expected. Because of the limitations of our expectations (shaped by our education), it is difficult to make significant advances.

The field is still in its infancy, and there is only one text that could be called a history of communication theories—the book written by Armand Mattelart and Michèle Mattelart. Apart from this, there are only notes and scattered essays within bodies of work targeting other objectives—some closer to, others more oblique reflections of, what we think of as the profession of the history of science. Placing these texts in some sort of order is itself a task requiring concentrated energy and specialized effort. We are far from a systematic history of communicological science, and there are two reasons for this. One is the fact that the object to be studied, being barely sixty years old, is still new from the perspective of historical observation. The other is the nearly understandable lack of interest evoked by something that has yet to attain a stable form. The intention here is to glean whatever is possible from what has been lost and buried, while pointing a direction for the future.

Compiling a history of science requires that one examine different levels and peer into different dimensions. In principle, we can build on the academic work that has been carried out to date. However, its focus encompasses overall social contexts and specific scientific contexts, along with the defined arena from which the subject of communication emerges.

The subject has at least four elements. The first is historical description: registering what has been done, placing it in time and space, relating it to a chain of antecedents and consequences, and to contemporary people and events. This requires some criterion of identification, a tool for separating what *is* from what *is not* pertinent. Such a criterion may come from the world of communicology itself, or its authority may derive from another field. For present purposes, both are viable options. The academic community has been engaged in a process of proposing boundaries, determining what belongs to the field and what does not; one may also view events and records from an external, a priori, perspective.

Within the field called communication or communications, the word is used, first of all, to refer to everything related to the so-called mass media. Everything begins with the global presence of radio and television—not in the sense of the phenomenon, but in the sense of the perspective that names it. Thus, communicology begins with the study of the electronic media that emerged in the 20th century, and their effects, beginning with radio in the 1920s and continuing with television since the 1950s. Thus, the history of communicology begins in the 1920s and 1930s; from that time onward, its development can be outlined in periods of ten or twenty years, i.e., it has gone through either four or eight phases, depending on which unit is employed.

Place is the other initial parameter for communicology's "Big Bang." The study of mass communication began in the United States, acquiring formal academic status there in the course of the 1930s and 1940s. The entire endeavor began in the 1930s in the United States. The only earlier significant antecedents relate to journalism and crowd psychology. But more is involved. Communication as an interactive phenomenon, as a form of social life and as part of the world of human relations, has additional dimensions of academic and conceptual organization. Hence, we have two separate and interrelated processes of organization at work: On one hand, the history of the theoretical study of the communications media; on the other, the history of the theoretical study of human and social communication ranging from the interpersonal to the collective. Communicology, in a broad sense, includes these two vast areas—and that does not even account for the conceptual contributions of the basic sciences.

The present exercise is based in part on a broad matrix designed to facilitate the description of texts, authors and institutional factors traceable through written documents—a body of essays constituting the history of a possible communicology. The matrix is fleshed out with a series of data that offers a clearer and more precise view of events and actors. The basic structure emphasizes authors and illustrative works, leading research institutions involved in consolidating the academic field, and academic journals that have been essential to the dissemination of its ideas and programs. At the same time, these components have been characterized by content descriptors such as questions and problems. These have guided the work carried out to date, the methods used, the thematic guides, and the basic research approaches adopted. This information is presented in summary form in the following section.

II. Hypothetical Configuration and Development

The hypothetical configuration includes seven major research approaches or programs, each following its

1927
1960
1963
1964
1967
1969
1970
1971
1972
1973
1974
1975
1976
1977
1978
1979
1980
1981
1982
1983
1984
1985
1986
1987
1988
1989
1990
1991
1992
1993
1994
1995
1996
1997
1998
1999
2000
2001
2002
2003
2004
2005
2006

own path, each with close links, at certain junctures, to others. Five timeframes are involved: pre–1920, 1920–1940, 1940–1960; 1960–1980 and 1980–2000. The seven major programs are mediology, cybernetics, cultural sociology, political economics, phenomenological sociology, semiolinguistics and social psychology. The content of the hypothesis that places these seven programs in the five timeframes is set forth briefly in the following pages.

1. MEDIOLOGY

Before 1920. The little evidence that exists from this period includes speculations on the liberal press and ideas about the press's potential as a propaganda medium. There was no media research in the strict sense during this period. Mediology did not yet exist.

1920 to 1940. This is the period in which media history began. The appearance of radio had a strong impact on 19th century culture. This great phenomenon in a sense marks the beginning of the 20th century. During the 1930s research began, with Harold Laswell (in the United States) as the central figure. The *Public Opinion Quarterly* began publication in 1937. Colombia University created a research center.

1940 to 1960. It was during this key period that mediology was launched in the United States. Its central figure was Paul Lazarsfeld, and the east-coast universities played a central role. Media research accelerated under the stimulus of war propaganda and the lessons of World War II, with the survey and functionalist sociology as foundations. European thinking in the field began with a critique of Fascism.

1960 to 1980. The study of audiences led to the study of reception. Régis Debray's concept of mediology appeared in the 1970s, and, starting from that point, order was established in the field, At the same time, thinking was enriched by dialogue (between scholars) in Europe and the United States.

1980 to 2000. Mediology developed. The communicological world created associations at the global and regional levels. There were thousands of academics now, and the mass media were the central focus of their investigations. Everything changed with the advent of the Internet and so-called information and communication technologies. Pierre Lévy followed Debray's lead. Everyone had an opinion and the different approaches met.

2. CYBERNETICS

Before 1920. Here, cybernetics had antecedents only in a broad sense, e.g., Charles Babbage and the thinkers of the formal and automatized world.

1920 to 1940. Cybernetics emerged, alongside mediology, as a phenomenon of the 1930s. Norbert Wiener was the pioneering figure, but other thinkers, such as Arturo Rosenbluth, were also active in the field. A dialogue between biology, medicine and engineering ensued.

1940 to 1960. It was in the war and post-war periods that cybernetics, like mediology, found its path. The mathematical theory of information and systems theory formed a common front with cybernetics. The first application of these principles to the social sciences took place in politics, though their range of application proved wide, touching all of the sciences and all forms of engineering. This, then, is the other pillar of communicology.

1960 to 1980. Second-order cybernetics was founded by Heinz von Foerster and was in the vanguard of the cognitive sciences. The neurosciences and technosciences took a central place in academia worldwide, while the 19th century sciences underwent a postmodern crisis.

1980 to 2000. Cybernetics was universal in its approach, uniting all areas of knowledge and professional fields. The Palo Alto school granted communication a central place within the cybernetic approach, relating it to all human and social action. The development of the other communicology was now in full swing. In the world of the social sciences, the impact of Niklas Luhmann was felt.

3. CULTURAL SOCIOLOGY

Before 1920. The 19th century has numerous antecedents of cultural sociology, with the critique of the socio-cultural, the so-called thinking of the left. These socialist and Marxist currents proved to be fundamental as sources of 20th century developments. Here, too, the English-speaking world was central, though it found its inspiration in Europe.

1920 to 1940. In England, the official cradle of cultural studies, this period featured debate on culture and social class. But it was in the United States, around the so-called Chicago School, that social criticism acquired the greatest weight. The European Left was in crisis with the creation of the imperial Soviet Union. In the United States, the Left took a constructive approach, promoting democracy. With the beginning of World War II, the struggle against Fascism created a front of leftist thought.

1940 to 1960. In this period, Europe moved toward structuralism. In the United States, functionalism found its second wind in the form of structural functionalism. The cultural approach was completely obscured by the process of post-war reconstruction and the triumphs of the English-speaking nations. It was the so-called Frankfurt School in exile that brought the continents together in a framework of critical cultural thought. The critique of the culture industry appeared on the scene.

1960 to 1980. At this point, the so-called cultural studies took off. Initially Marxist, they gradually became a critique of everyday life and an ethnography of cultural particulars. The Birmingham School was the official center of the movement. The postmodern world arrived at the door of the social sciences. Now, everything was culture; the method was relativistic; everything was meaning. The qualitative ruled, and hermeneutics guided the way.

1980 to 2000. The so-called Latin American School appeared in one of its two guises: the culturalist. Martín Barbero, García Canclini and Ortiz are some of the names marking the Latin version of Anglo cultural studies, which also derived from Marxism and leftist thought, though, like its counterpart in the English-speaking world, it moved gradually toward the rhetoric of cultural detail, and into a fascination with the postmodern popular culture associated with the media. In the English-speaking world, the shift that had begun in the 1960s and 1970s continued and diversified by branching into studies of the particular: feminism, indigenous peoples, regionalism, youth.

4. POLITICAL ECONOMY

Before 1920. The antecedents of political economy, like those of critical sociology, lie in the 19th century and in leftist European thought, but the focus at the beginning of the 20th century became economic. The antecedents involved discussion of the emergence and development of capitalism, with Adam Smith and Marx the leading lights.

1920 to 1940. The discussion continued with a "second phase" of the antecedents of communicology. The Soviet Union emerged, along with Fascism.

1940 to 1960. In a peculiar way, migration from Europe to the United States also affected political economy. This represents a third phase of communicological antecedents. The Cold War served as the great backdrop; the Castro and *Cuba libre* phenomenon emerged in the Americas.

1960 to 1980. It is at this point that the program for a possible communicology emerged. It appeared in the United States among the academic Left, which gained force on both continents thanks to the power of the English-speaking academic world. Herbert Schiller and George Gerbner were a part of the movement that offered a critique of the capitalist world and of cultural imperialism as promoted by the mass media. This approach was a more orthodox Marxism than the culturalist approach of critical sociology.

1927
1960
1963
1964
1967
1969
1970
1971
1972
1973
1974
1975
1976
1977
1978
1979
1980
1981
1982
1983
1984
1985
1986
1987
1988
1989
1990
1991
1992
1993
1994
1995
1996
1997
1998
1999
2000
2001
2002
2003
2004
2005
2006

It also had a Latin American version in the form of what has been called the discourse of denunciation of imperialism, expounded by authors such as Beltrán, Pasquali, and numerous first-generation Latin American communicologists.

1980 to 2000. The process continued, with the program taking shape in the United States, Europe and Latin America.

5. PHENOMENOLOGICAL SOCIOLOGY
Before 1920. Phenomenological sociology developed within the field of academic sociology. Its relevant aspect here is its focus on social relations as interactive relations. Its antecedents were European and nineteenth century. Its action-related perspective derived from Weber, its phenomenological component from Hegel and Husserl. Simmel was its major sociological exponent.

1920 to 1940. The sociology of interaction continued, influencing the Chicago School. Alfred Schütz, a disciple of Simmel, was its major exponent. Mead was also part of this movement. Analytic philosophy also played a role, with Wittgenstein's language games and Austin's speech acts.

1940 to 1960. The movement became American. A discrete generation linked the previous to the following phase. No major authors were decisive here. The masters were training the new leading figures.

1960 to 1980. Momentum was recovered. On one side was the invisible university linking Palo Alto with Goffman and his master Birdwhistell. On the other were Berger and Luckmann, the heirs of Simmel and Schütz. The movement acquired an aspect of epistemological introspection and phenomenal exteriority. Ethno-methodology emerged.

1980 to 2000. A broad phenomenological front addressed the issues of interaction and communication. Later in the period, all of this intentionality acquired a new aspect, with a focus on networks. Interaction developed in social networks. European and American phenomenologists today are engaged in this constructive process, in dialogue with cybernetics and cognitive science. Moreno, Latour, Callon and Najmanovich are emerging figures.

6. SEMIO-LINGUISTICS
Before 1920. This approach also had its antecedents in Europe but, unlike its counterparts, continued to be essentially European. Its major predecessors were the father of structuralism, the linguist Ferdinand de Saussure, and Charles Sanders Peirce, one of the founders of American pragmatism. Semiology and semiotics found themselves face to face.

1920 to 1940. The program continued to be structuralist and linguistic in approach. The Prague Circle developed, with Russian emigrants. The Russian school arrived in Europe, then spread to the United States and the world at large. Jakobson was a central figure. In the United States, the Encyclopedia of Unified Science project emerged from the relation between the work of the logician Carnap and the semiotician Morris.

1940 to 1960. This phase was a continuation of the previous one. World War II drove research, and structuralism was developed as a universal tool for organizing knowledge in the image of language. Semiotics lost force as the Chicago School declined in importance.

1960 to 1980. In Europe, structuralism gained momentum with the semiological program of Roland Barthes and Greimas. In the United States, Morris (heir to Peirce) and Sebeok continued to advance with semiotics. Pragmatic semiotics was associated with phenomenological sociology. In France, the Center for the Study of Mass Communication was created.

1980 to 2000. Structuralism underwent reform, moved into a new phase as post-structuralism, became constructivist, associated itself with the cognitive sciences and became eclectic. Semiotic pragmatism also reshaped itself in a postmodern mould. Language and communication served as the setting for interdisciplinary merging within this reshaped program.

7. SOCIAL PSYCHOLOGY

Before 1920. Psychology was one of the founding disciplines of a possible communicology. Its antecedents can be found in the 19th century, with the beginnings of psychological thought. Here, interaction set the pace, along with social psychology—the relationship between individual and others.

1920 to 1940. Behaviorism provides the conceptual matrix for the history of psychology, and social psychology in particular. This outward approach was juxtaposed with the inward view represented by psychoanalysis, with the movement taking shape in the tension between the two. The media appeared as a focus early on, but clinical psychology and interpersonal relations also played an important role. Kurt Lewin was the great exponent of a social psychological perspective. Gestalt theory dialogued with phenomenology.

1940 to 1960. In this period, the third force appeared: the psychology of personal development, with Carl Rogers and Maslow at the head. The entire approach was interactional, seeing life in ecological terms. The world of therapies was still emerging, and to speak of therapy was to speak of interaction and communication.

1960 to 1980. The world of psychology diversified. The cybernetic perspective was still present, along with the phenomenological and the cognitive. In both the United States and Europe, the debate was structured around interaction and communication.

1980 to 2000. The constructivists spoke. Even Varela and Maturana dialogued with the post-third force psychologists. All was communication and information. Systems theory had the floor. Tomás Ibáñez was emblematic of this emerging stream of thought.

IV. Toward the Construction of a Communicological Project

The reason for reconstructing the development, over the course of a century, of a possible communicology is to produce a matrix that can throw light on today's developments and spotlight positions that may develop possible futures. This is a process of configuration and course-setting that makes the opaque evident, and that implies comprehension as it proposes clarity. Let us begin, then, by focusing on the threads that in principle have constituted the fabric of the movement, and then observe the textures that emerge.

The communicological project has been based, first of all, on the social sciences and humanities. On one hand, certain objects have taken shape; on the other, certain theoretical perspectives have addressed them. Thus, it would seem that as far as the social sciences are concerned, sociology and psychology have provided the greatest number of interesting moments from the communicological point of view.

Anthropology has been a more distant participant. The issues of communication are urban and highly modern, although a review of anthropological research on more rural, ethnic and pre-modern contexts may reveal further contributions that anthropology offers for communicology. The discipline of history has also been relatively distant from ours. The issue of communication is essentially one of the present, since its importance dates only from around World War II. The humanities contribute via linguistics and philosophy, both of which perspectives are very much present in communicological thinking. The outsider has been political economy, closely associated with sociology and economic and human geography, largely as a result of leftist thinking rooted in Marx.

New perspectives are actively making constructive contributions to communicology. Cybernetics preeminently, but also memetics, systemics, computer science and telematics are new fields contemporaneous with communicological thought.

Though many objects have attracted the conceptual visions of these very different constructive focuses, the central objects have been the mass media, new information and communication technologies, language, interpersonal relations and the political-economic contexts of socio-cultural life.

1927
1960
1963
1964
1967
1969
1970
1971
1972
1973
1974
1975
1976
1977
1978
1979
1980
1981
1982
1983
1984
1985
1986
1987
1988
1989
1990
1991
1992
1993
1994
1995
1996
1997
1998
1999
2000
2001
2002
2003
2004
2005
2006

Mediology, Debray's constructive proposal, is the closest that we have, so far, to a consolidation of the communicological project. It raises the word *media* to the level of a theoretical construct, and elevates the object *media* to the comprehensive plane of human life in all possible space and time. Thus, the center of communicology is mediology. And given the distance between the object media and other objects, perhaps what is needed before proposing a science of communicology is to confirm the notion of "sciences of communication." We would then have a conceptual space that includes the four objects in a configuration comprising four dimensions, each dimension addressing the macro-object and proposing the possible articulation of the four in a single possible perspective, the communicological perspective. The results follow.

FIRST DIMENSION: DISSEMINATION

The central place here could well be occupied by the mediological proposal. Here would be all of the phenomena associated with the reproduction and expansion of social/cultural information systems through the various media.

SECOND DIMENSION: EXPRESSION

The central place here would be occupied by a perspective that combines elements of aesthetic composition with elements of formal semiotic/linguist configuration. This would include all of the phenomena of production—of discursive and semiotic creation—including those involving the media.

THIRD DIMENSION: INTERACTION

The center here would be occupied by a perspective that combines the social psychology of interpersonal, group and collective relations with the sociology of bonds, contacts, associations and networks. Here would be all of the phenomena of intentional or non-intentional simultaneous action of human affectation—what has been called interpersonal communication.

FOURTH DIMENSION: STRUCTURING

The center here would be occupied by a combination of political economy and the sociology of socio-cultural systems. Here would be all of the elements involved in the configuration of socioeconomic structures from a communication/information perspective.

The four dimensions would form a three-dimensional, three-faceted figure composed of triangles. Each of the vertices of the figure is one of the four conceptual dimensions. This geometric figure suggests various issues and possible relationships among the four dimensions. It is a simplified representation of a complex problem. The vertices indicate the objects that obstruct the views, but the faces of the tetrahedron are the conceptual spaces of the different perspectives that construct the views of the four objects. In terms of surfaces, there are three conceptual spaces, but in three dimensions they are interwoven in the general pattern of what we have called the project of a possible communicology.

References

Aguirre, Ángel (ed.), 1982. *Conceptos clave de la Antropología cultural [Key concepts of cultural anthropology]*, DAIMON, Barcelona.

Alexander, Jeffrey C., 1989. *Las teorías sociológicas desde la segunda guerra mundial [Sociological Theories Since the Second World War]*, Gedisa, Barcelona.

Anverre, Ari, et al., 1982. *Industrias culturales: el futuro de la cultura en juego, Fondo de cultura económica [Culture Industries: The Future of Culture in Play, Economic Culture Fund]*, Mexico City.

Avila Espada, Alejandro and Joaquín Poch i Bulich (comp.), 1994. *Manual de técnicas de psicoterapia [Manual of Psychotherapeutic Techniques]*, Siglo XXI, Madrid.

Bassols, Mario et al. (comp.), 1988. *Antología de Sociología Urbana [Anthology of Urban Sociology]*, UNAM, Mexico City.

Blake, Reed H. and Edwin O. Haroldsen, 1977. *Taxonomía de conceptos de la comunicación [Taxonomy of Concepts of Communication]*, Ediciones Nuevo Mar, Mexico City.

Bollnow, Otto, 1976. *Introducción a la filosofía del conocimiento [Introduction to the Philosophy of Knowledge]*, Amorrortu, Buenos Aires.

Bottomore, Tom and Robert Nisbet (comp.), *Historia del análisis sociológico [History of Sociological Analysis]*, Amorrortu, Buenos Aires, 1988.

Bourdieu, Pierre, *Las reglas del arte [The Rules of Art]*, Anagrama, Barcelona, 1995.

Briggs, Asa and Peter Burke, 2002, From Gutenberg to Internet, Taurus, Madrid.

Brown, Robert, 1972, *La Explicación en las ciencias sociales [Explanation in the Social Sciences]*, Periferia, Buenos Aires.

Bryant, Jennings and Dolf Zillmann (comp.), 1996, Effects of the Communications Media, Paidós, Barcelona.

Buendía Eisman, Leonor et al., 1998, *Métodos de investigación en psicopedagogía [Research Methods in Psychopedagogy]*, McGraw-Hill, Madrid.

Caballo, Vicente E. (comp.), 1991, *Manual de técnicas de terapia y modificación de conducta [Manual of Therapeutic and Behavior Modification Techniques]*, Siglo XXI, Madrid.

Camps, Victoria (ed.), 1989, *Historia de la Ética [History of Ethics]*, Crítica, Barcelona.

Carozzi, María Julia et al., 1980, Conceptos de Antropología Social [Concepts of Social Anthropology], Centro editor de América Latina, Buenos Aires.

Cebrian, Juan Luis, 1998, *La red [The Web]*, Taurus, Madrid.

Cervantes, Cecilia and Enrique E. Sánchez Ruiz (coord.), 1994, *Investigar la Comunicación [Investigating Communication]*, U de G-ALAIC, Zapopan.

Cicourel, Aaron V., 1982, *Method and Measurement in Sociology*, Editorial Nacional, Madrid.

Contreras, Fernando R., 2000, *Nuevas fronteras de la Infografía [New Frontiers in Infography]*, UCAM-Mergablum, Seville.

Cordero, Valdivia, Magdalena, 1998, *Bancos de datos [Databases]*, CIS, Madrid.

Covarrubias, Karla et al., 1994, *Cuéntame en que se quedó [Let Me Know How it Turned Out]*, Trillas, Mexico City.

Curran, James et al., 1981, *Society and Mass Communication*, Fondo de Cultura Económica [Economic Culture Fund], Mexico City.

Curran, James et al. (coord.), 1998, *Cultural Studies and Communication*, Paidós, Barcelona.

Chatelet, Francois (director), 1980, *Historia de las ideologías [History of Ideologies]*, Premiá, Mexico City.

De Sola Pool, Ithiel and Wilbur Schramm (ed.), 1973, *Handbook of Communication*, Rand McNally College Publishing, Chicago.

Delgado, Juan Manuel and Juan Gutierrez (coord.), 1994, *Métodos y técnicas cualitativas de investigación en ciencia sociales [Qualitative Research Techniques and Methods in Social Science]*, Síntesis, Madrid.

Denzin, Norman K. and Yvonna S. Lincoln (ed.), 1994, *Handbook of Qualitative Research*, Sage, Thousand Oaks.

Dertouzos, Michael L., 1997, *Qué será [What Will Happen]*, Planeta, Mexico City.

Deutsch, M. and R. M. Krauss, 1984, *Teorías en psicología social [Theories in Social Psychology]*, Paidós, Mexico City.

Eco, Umberto, 1978, *Tratado de Semiótica General [General Semiotics Treatise]*, Nueva imagen-Lumen, Mexico City.

Fages, J. B. and Ch. Pagano, 1978, *Diccionario de los medios de comunicación [Dictionary of Communications Media]*, Fernando Torres editor, Valencia.

Fernandez Chistlieb, Pablo, 1994, *La psicología colectiva un fin de siglo más tarde [The Collective Psychology by the End of Another Century]*, Anthropos-Colegio de Michoacán, Bogotá.

Ferrater, José, 1984, *Diccionario de filosofía [Dictionary of Philosophy]*, Alianza, Madrid.

Festinger, L. and D. Katz, 1993, *Los métodos de investigación en las ciencias sociales [Research Methods in the Social Sciences]*, Paidós, Mexico City.

Fossaert, Robert, 1978, *La Societe [Society]*, Seuil, Paris.

Freire, Paulo, 1976, *Extension or Communication?*, Siglo XXI, Mexico City.

Fuentes Navarro, Raúl, 1988, *La investigación de comunicación en México. Sistematización documental 1956-1986 [Communication Research in Mexico. Documentary Systematization 1956-1986]*, Ediciones de comunicación, Mexico City.

Fuentes Navarro, Raúl, 1996, *La investigación de comunicación en México. Sistematización documental 1986-1994 [Communication Research in Mexico. Documentary Systematization 1986-1994]*, U de G- ITESO, Guadalajara.

Fuentes Navarro, Raúl, 1998, *La emergencia de un campo académico [The Emergence of an Academic Field]*, ITESO-U de G, Guadalajara.

Gadamer, Hans-Georg, 1991, *Verdad y Método [Truth and Method]*, Sígueme, Salamanca.

Gaitán Moya, Juan A. and José L. Piñuel Raigada, 1998, *Técnicas de investigación en comunicación social [Research Techniques in Social Communication]*, Síntesis, Madrid.

Galindo Cáceres, Jesús (coord.), 1998, *Técnicas de investigación en sociedad, cultura y comunicación [Research Techniques in Society, Culture and Communication]*, Addison Wesley-Longman, Mexico City.

Galindo, Jesús and Carlos Luna (coord.), 1995, *Campo académico de la comunicación [Academic Field of Communication]*, CNCA-ITESO, Guadalajara.

Gallino, Luciano, 1995, *Diccionario de Sociología [Dictionary of Sociology]*, Siglo XXI, Mexico City.

García Blanco, José María and Pablo Navarro Sustaeta, 2002, *¿Más allá de la modernidad? [Beyond Modernity?]*, Centro de Investigaciones Sociológicas, Madrid.

García Ferrando, Manuel et al., 1986, *El análisis de la realidad social [The Analysis of Social Reality]*, Alianza, Madrid.

García Jiménez, Antonio, 2002, *Organización y gestión del conocimiento en la comunicación [Organization and Management of Knowledge in Communication]*, Ediciones Trea, Gijón.

Gardner, Howard, 1996, *The New Science of Mind*, Paidós, Barcelona.

Geeertz, C. et al., 1991, *El surgimiento de la Antropología posmoderna [The Emergence of Postmodern Anthropology]*, Gedisa, Barcelona.

George, Pierre, 1977, *Geografía Urbana [Urban Geography]*, Ariel, Barcelona.

Giddens, Anthony et al., 1991, *La teoría social, hoy [Social Theory Today]*, CNCA-ALIANZA, Mexico City.

Goffman, Erving, 1971, *The Presentation of Self in Everyday Life*, Amorrortu, Buenos Aires.

Grandi, Roberto, 1995, *Texto y contexto en los medios de comunicación [Text and Context in the Communications Media]*, Bosh, Barcelona.

Hannerz, Ulf, 1986, *Exploración de la ciudad [Exploration of the City]*, Fondo de cultura económica [Economic culture fund], Mexico City.

Hatch, Elvin, 1975, *Theories of Man and Culture*, Prolam, Buenos Aires.

Husserl, Edmund, 1992, *An Invitation to Phenomenology*, Paidós-UAB, Barcelona.

Jensen, K. B. and N. W. Jankowski, 1993, *Metodologías cualitativas de investigación en comunicación de masas [Qualitative Research Methodologies in Mass Communication]*, Bosch, Barcelona.

Joyanes, Luis, 1997, *Cybersociety*, McGraw Hill, Madrid.

Kahn, J. S. (comp.), 1975, *El concepto de cultura: textos fundamentales [The Concept of Culture: Basic Texts]*, Anagrama, Barcelona.

Kaplan, David and Robert A. Manners, 1979, *Introducción crítica a la teoría antropológica [Critical Introduction to Anthropological Theory]*, Nueva Imagen, Mexico City.

Katz, Chaim et al., 1980, *Diccionario básico de comunicación [Basic Dictionary of Communication]*, Nueva imagen, Mexico City.

Klapper, J.T., 1974, *The Effects of Mass Communications*, Aguilar, Madrid.

Kunh, Thomas S., 1975, *La estructura de las revoluciones científicas [The Structure of Scientific Revolutions]*, Fondo de cultura económica [Economic Culture Fund], Mexico City.

1927
1960
1963
1964
1967
1969
1970
1971
1972
1973
1974
1975
1976
1977
1978
1979
1980
1981
1982
1983
1984
1985
1986
1987
1988
1989
1990
1991
1992
1993
1994
1995
1996
1997
1998
1999
2000
2001
2002
2003
2004
2005
2006

Lamo De Espinosa, Emilio and José Enrique Rodriguez Ibañez (ed.), 1993, *Problemas de teoría social contemporánea [Problems of Contemporary Social Theory]*, CIS, Madrid.

Lash, Scout, 1997, *Sociología del posmodernismo [Sociology of Postmodernism]*, Amorrortu, Buenos Aires.

Levy-Valensi, Eliane Amado, 1968, *La comunicación [Communication]*, Marfil, Valencia.

Lopez-Yarto Elizalde, Luis, 1997, Dinámica de grupos [Group dynamics], Desclée de Broker, Bilbao.

Lucas Marín, Antonio, 2000, *La nueva sociedad de la información [The New Information Society]*, Trotta, Madrid.

Ludewig, Kart, 1996, *Terapia sistémica [Systematic Therapy]*, Herder, Barcelona.

Luque, Enrique, 1990, *On Anthropological Knowledge*, CIS, Madrid.

Lyotard, Jean-Francois, 1987, *La condición postmoderna [The Postmodern Condition]*, Cátedra, Madrid.

Llobera, José R. (comp.), 1975, *La antropología como ciencia [Anthropology as Science]*, Anagrama, Barcelona.

Maingueneau, D., 1980, *Introducción a los métodos de Análisis del discurso [Introduction to Methods of Discourse Analysis]*, Hachette, Buenos Aires.

Martorell, José Luis, 1996, *Psicoterapias [Psychotherapies]*, Pirámide, Madrid.

Marx, M.H. and W. A. Hillix, 1995, *Sistemas y teorías psicológicos contemporáneos [Contemporary Psychological Theories and Systems]*, Paidós, Mexico City.

Maslow, Abraham, 1990, *La personalidad creadora [The Creative Personality]*, Kairos editora, Barcelona.

MacBride, Sean (ed.), 1980, *One World Many Voices*, Fondo de cultura económica [Economic Culture Fund], Mexico City.

McLuhan, Marshall and B. R. Powers, 1991, *The Global Village*, Gedisa, Mexico City.

Mirabito, Michael, M. A., 1998, *Las nuevas tecnologías de la comunicación [The New Communication Technologies]*, Gedisa, Barcelona.

Moles, Abraham and Claude Zeltman (direct.), 1975, *Communication and the Mass Media*, Ediciones mensajero, Bilbao.

Monteforte Toledo, Mario (ed.), 1980, *El discurso político [Political Discourse]*, UNAM-Nueva Imagen, Mexico City.

Moore, Carl M., 1994, *Group Techniques for Idea Building*, Sage, Thousand Oaks.

Morley, David, 1996, *Television, Audiences and Cultural Studies*, Amorrortu, Barcelona.

Mucchielli, Alex, 1998, *Psicología de la comunicación [Psychology of Communication]*, Paidós, Barcelona.

Nisbet, Robert, 1977, *La formación del pensamiento sociológico [The Formation of Sociological Thought]*, Amorrortu, Buenos Aires.

O´Sullivan, Tim et al., 1997, *Conceptos clave en comunicación y estudios culturales [Key Concepts in Communication and Cultural Studies]*, Amorrortu, Buenos Aires.

Paéz, D. et al., 1992, *Teoría y método en psicología social [Theory and Method in Social Psychology]*, Anthropos, Barcelona.

Quintanilla, Miguel A. (director), 1985, *Diccionario de filosofía contemporánea [Dictionary of Contemporary Philosophy]*, Sígueme, Salamanca.

Ritzer, George, 1995, *Teoría sociológica contemporánea [Contemporary Sociological Theory]*, McGraw-Hill, Madrid.

Rivadeneira Prada, Raúl, 1976, *La opinión pública [Public Opinion]*, Trillas, Mexico City.

Rogers, Everett M. and F. Floyd Shoemaker, 1974, *Communication of Innovations*, Herrero Hermanos, Mexico City.

Sabido, Miguel, 2002, *El tono [Tone]*, UNAM, Mexico City.

Schramm, Wilbur and Donald F. Roberts (ed.), 1974, *The Process and Effects of Mass Communication*, University of Illinois Press, Chicago.

Schwartz, Howard and Jerry Jacobs, 1984, *Qualitative Sociology*, Trillas, Mexico City.

Seligman, Brenda Z. (ed.), 1971, *Manual de campo del antropólogo [Anthropology Field Manual]*, UIA, Mexico City.

Sfez, Lucien, 1995, *Crítica de la comunicación [Critique of Communication]*, Amorrortu, Buenos Aires.

Sierra, Francisco, 1999, *Elementos de teoría de la información [Elements of Information Theory]*, Editorial MAD, Sevilla.

Silverstone, Roger, 1996, *Television and Everyday Life*, Amorrortu, Buenos Aires.

Smith, Alfred G. (comp.), 1966, *Communication and Culture*, Holt, Rinehart and Winston, New York.

Sowell, Thomas, 1990, *Conflict of Visions*, Gedisa, Buenos Aires.

Steinberg, Charles and A. William Bleum (comp.), 1972, *Los medios de comunicación social [Social Communications Media]*, Roble, Mexico City.

Strauss, Leo and Joseph Cropsey (comp.), 1996, History of Political Philosophy, Fondo de cultura económica [Economic Culture Fund], Mexico City.

Urmson, J.O., 1994, *Concise Encyclopedia of Western Philosophy and Philosophers*, Cátedra, Barcelona.

Vilar, Pierre, 1981, *Iniciación al vocabulario del análisis histórico [Initiation to the Vocabulary of Historical Analysis]*, Crítica, Barcelona.

Virel, André, 1985, *Vocabulario de las psicoterapias [Vocabulary of Psychotherapies]*, Gedisa, Barcelona.

Wallace, Walter L., 1976, *The Logic of Science in Sociology*, Alianza, Madrid.

Wallerstein, Immanuel, 1987, *The Modern World System*, Siglo XXI, Mexico City.

Watzlawick, Paul et al., 1971, *The Theory of Human Communication*, Tiempo contemporáneo, Buenos Aires.

Wimmer, Roger D. and Joseph R. Dominick, 1996, *La investigación científica de los medios de comunicación [Scientific Research on Communications Media]*, Bosh, Barcelona.

Wolf, Mauro, 1994, *Los efectos sociales de los media [The Social Effects of the Media]*, Paidós, Barcelona.

Wolton, Dominique, 2000, *Surviving the Internet*, Gedisa, Barcelona.

Wright, Charles R., 1978, *Mass Communication*, Paidós, Buenos Aires.

Zeitlin, Irving, 1979, *Ideología y teoría sociológica [Sociological Theory and Ideology]*, Amorrortu, Buenos Aires.

Galindo Cáceres, Luis Jesús. "Apuntes de historia de una comunicología posible: hipótesis de configuración y trayectoria." [Historical notes on a possible communicology: a hypothetical configuration and trajectory]. *Redes.Com, Revista de estudios para el desarrollo social de la comunicación, 2004.* Reprinted with permssion of author.

DEVELOPMENT SUPPORT COMMUNICATION:
A CHANGE AGENT IN SUPPORT OF POPULAR PARTICIPATION OR A DOUBLE AGENT OF DECEPTION?

By Stefan Sonderling

1997

1. Development and Salvation

Salvation is offered by a group of development practitioners and academics (Agunga 1990, 1994, 1996; Ascroft & Agunga 1994; Ascroft & Masilela 1994) who claim that they have found the missing link in the solution to Africa's and other Third (or South) World nations' development problems.

The development trend has meandered through the decades following the war, blissfully unaware that its salvation has rested in the organisation of communication forces on a scale far more systematised and complex than it has so far anticipated (Ascroft & Masilela 1994, 281).

Agunga (1996, 11) declares that "it appears that communication is the missing link" for the solution of African development. This is so because all the other ingredients for sustainable development in Africa— supportive donor agencies, abundant funding and technical experts—are already in place. All that seems to stand in the path of salvation and development is lack of popular participation in the development initiatives proposed for the people, but this, experts contend, could be gained by improving communication. According to Agunga (1990, 138), "achieving popular participation is a communication activity requiring the presence of development support communication (DSC) experts with communication skills and people know-how necessary to overcome the obstacles that constrain useful interaction between benefactors and beneficiaries." In other words, simply improving the communication skills of the developers and the developees would result in better understanding and naturally lead to popular participation. The belief that DSC offers a new and an "all-inclusive" solution to development is increasingly gaining ground in South Africa (Burton 1994, 7).

This article questions the ability of DSC to achieve popular participation and suggests that DSC provides support for the powerful development industry in its attempt to manipulate and gain compliance from the people. It is argued that the DSC theoretical position is naive and misrepresents the complex processes of development and communication. Better and more communication would not lead to popular participation because the failure of development and lack of popular participation is not due to a breakdown of communication or to the lack of understanding between developers and developees. On the contrary, international development is a conflict of domination and resistance in which developers and developees understand each other perfectly well. What is needed to achieve popular participatory development is a radically different understanding of development and communication.

2. Development Communication and Development Support Communication

The idea that communication is a major element necessary for inducing economic development and sociocultural modernisation is not new. Since the launch of the United States' Point Four Programme in 1949, social scientists and policymakers considered communication a driving force in social change.

Assuming that "it was the pressure of communications which brought about the downfall of traditional societies" (Pye 1963, 3), social scientists and development practitioners emphasised the role of the mass media in development (Schramm 1964). However, while the role of the mass media and its effects on development were the main preoccupation of most development scholars and practitioners, the role of interpersonal, face-to-face communication was considered of secondary importance but was not neglected.

1927
1960
1963
1964
1967
1969
1970
1971
1972
1973
1974
1975
1976
1977
1978
1979
1980
1981
1982
1983
1984
1985
1986
1987
1988
1989
1990
1991
1992
1993
1994
1995
1996
1997
1998
1999
2000
2001
2002
2003
2004
2005
2006

The idea of DSC is much older than the modernisation project known as the development of underdeveloped regions of the Third World. Agents of change, known as colonial officers, missionaries, educators and business people operating in cross-cultural situations, were actively seeking "to reorganise another people's way of life in terms of some ideological blueprint for personal or collective salvation" (Goodenough 1970, 11–19). Communication was considered a means to effecting such social change.

The idea of DSC already existed at the beginning of the U.S. programmes to develop the underdeveloped Third World. DSC was assumed to be the function of "point four technicians" sent on development missions. The first training programme to provide competence in intercultural communication was developed by anthropologist Edward T. Hall for the American Foreign Service Institute in 1952 (Hall 1965). Other training programmes at institutional and university levels followed. Most training programmes were designed to give change agents means to overcome resistance to development encountered throughout most of the underdeveloped Third World. Resistance to development was considered a human behavioural problem, similar to the resistance of a psychiatric patient to therapy. Thus, much of the training provided to change agents was based on an interdisciplinary blending of elements from anthropology, economics, psychology, psychiatry, sociology and other clinical helping professions (Goodenough 1970, 44). These early efforts of manipulation and persuasion were eventually formalised within the discipline of intercultural communication, while development communication became an area of study for the social sciences.

While most social scientists working in development communication were primarily interested in the role of the mass media in furthering development, a theoretical approach that focused more attention on the different roles of interpersonal communication and the mass media emerged in United States rural sociology. Elaborated by Everett M. Rogers as the diffusion of innovation theory, it was subsequently extended to the underdeveloped world. It is to this specific project that the proponents of DSC trace their intellectual lineage.

3. Development Support Communication (DSC): Applied Research and Tool for Bureaucratic Control of Development

According to Ascroft and Masilela (1994, 275), the failure of attempts of development to improve the living conditions of the poorest people in the Third World prompted Robert McNamara, former president of the World Bank (and a former United States Secretary of Defence) to announce a new direction for development initiatives in 1973. The new direction, targeting rural areas, was to include the participation of poor people in the decision-making process and implementation of development programmes. However, two decades later people's participation had not materialised owing to "an elaborate conspiracy" between the academy and the initiators of international development (Ascroft & Masilela 1994, 275). Theories of development proved ineffective, and alternative critical theorising by Latin American academics did not make an impression on the dominant paradigm. In response to the crisis, the "development industry" itself provided the appropriate alternative concept of DSC. It is claimed that the phrase "development support communication" was first coined almost *ex nihilo* by Erksine Childers, a professional information officer working for the United Nations Development Programme in Thailand in the 1960s. Soon the idea was taken up by multilateral development agencies, and training programmes for professional DSC practitioners began at the University of Iowa and other institutions around the world (Ascroft & Masilela 1994, 278).

What is apparent from Ascroft and Masilela's (1994) account of the history of DSC is that the emergence of practitioners in multilateral institutions of development led to a power struggle over the control and management of development projects. Attempting to promote their importance, DSC practitioners resented being located in the secondary levels of information and public relations departments of development institutions and removed from the planning process. In order to exert their professional importance equal to other development specialists, they felt that there was a need for specialised training (Ascroft & Masilela 1994, 277–278). Specialised academic training, qualifications and an appropriate scientific method were thought to secure a professional position for the DSC practitioner in the development industry. In other words, attempts to gain legitimisation in the professional and academic fields of development communication underlie the claim by Ascroft and Masilela (1994, 278, 292) that "academe has so far failed to cotton to the idea" of DSC "in a serious way" and meet the challenge to develop, test, package into a curriculum and market the concept to "the whole world." Indeed, the DSC concept is market driven and aims to provide a service rather than a theory. Marketing to the development industry is lucrative as well because development is big business that possibly dwarfs many multinational organisations or even the Mafia (Hobart 1993, 2).

Armed with academic legitimacy, DSC theorists now claim that "real development requires the communication scientists to be at the driver's wheel of development" (Agunga 1996). DSC is conceived as a management information function and is concerned with effective organisation of entire development programmes as a system. Taking a holistic view, DSC proposes to coordinate all aspects of communications and mobilise the masses to participate (Melkote 1991, 265-267).

However, such claims misrepresent the scope of DSC and elevate what is essentially a micro-level project into a general theory. DSC is "the application of communication strategies specifically designed for concrete development programmes ... generally in micro-situations, takes the form of campaigns and is generally terminated when the development project in question is completed" (Jayaweera 1989, 76–77). DSC is a local component and not an alternative or substitute for national development strategy for a whole society (Jayaweera 1989, 90–91). In short, DSC is a practical discipline based on applied research as against the academic-based theoretical research in development communication. It thus provides a practical tool to the bureaucracy of the development industry in solving what it believes are the real problems of development.

4. The World of Development According to the DSC

The DSC approach pretends that the whole world of development is a dialogue. Communication is simply a dialogue that involves "creating and sharing of information to achieve mutual understanding" (Ascroft & Agunga 1994, 306, 311). Likewise international development is a dialogue: In the broadest sense, the development problem is one of North–South dialogue, wherein the two parties do not usually realise that they know too little about each other's background to be able to interact meaningfully and fruitfully with each other (Ascroft & Agunga 1994, 311).

With such a statement the whole history of the West and its interaction with the Third World—colonialism, war, international power politics and the political aim of development—is eliminated and international interaction is reduced to the calmness of a Platonic dialogue. But far from not knowing each other, the Third World and the West (or North) know each other well; they are in fact "old acquaintances" (Fanon 1973, 28).

The claim that international relations is a dialogue idealises nations, communities and groups and presents them as if they were rational individuals. However, relations between nations and collectivities are not reducible to relationships between individuals. International and intergroup relationships are conflictual as they are predominantly political and determined by the proportion of power each nation possesses (Frankel 1971, 142; Niebuhr 1960, xxiii).

Significantly, the word "conflict" does not figure in the discourse of DSC, and the clue to such an omission

1927
1960
1963
1964
1967
1969
1970
1971
1972
1973
1974
1975
1976
1977
1978
1979
1980
1981
1982
1983
1984
1985
1986
1987
1988
1989
1990
1991
1992
1993
1994
1995
1996
1997
1998
1999
2000
2001
2002
2003
2004
2005
2006

could be traced to Rogers' theory of diffusion of innovations. In the preface to the first edition of *Social Change in Rural Societies*, Rogers and Burdge (1972, xiii-xiv) write that from the number of suggestions to improve the content of the textbook several suggested that the concepts of "conflict," "cooperation" and "accommodation" should be "eliminated" and that "these guidelines were used in preparing the book." This was to a large extent also reflected in Rogers' books on diffusion of innovation.

From the perspective of DSC, the problems encountered in development are basic problems of communication and misunderstanding because the participants in development should be "creating and sharing information to achieve mutual understanding" (Ascroft & Agunga 1994, 306, 311). Such a view regards development as a transaction between altruistic "benefactors" and "beneficiaries." Indeed, according to Agunga (1990, 144–145), "benefactor refers to someone who confers a benefit," such as the multilateral, unilateral and private international development agencies who "facilitate development by providing development capital, equipment and expertise, through technical assistance" to the Third World "beneficiaries." At the micro-level of development, the dialogue is between the "benefactors," foreign technical specialists and change agents who are "seeking to bring development to Third World people" (Agunga 1990, 143).

For the development dialogue to proceed, the DSC experts suggest that "popular participation implies sensitising local people to become more receptive and responsive to development programs" (Agunga 1990, 137). That is, participatory development means that nothing should be done in the rural areas without the people's approval. "It means that the people must be made aware of what is proposed as a project for the people" and "creating awareness of what governments and donor agencies have in stock for them" (Agunga 1996, 4). Implied in this view is that it is not the people who initiate the projects, but rather that they must be told what was already decided for them, and

they must be "receptive" and "responsive" and thankful for what the benefactors have in store for them. This would indicate the persistence of the top-down communication model of the 1950s with its emphasis on the sender. Regardless of the proclaimed emphasis of DSC on the receivers of communication rather than the senders, on participation, and on the exchange of meaning, such an emphasis only serves to make the sender more influential and powerful at the expense of the receivers (Servaes & Arnst 1993, 44).

The process of development decision making, which is primarily a political process, is also reduced by the DSC approach to a semblance of a peaceful Platonic dialogue. According to Agunga (1990, 142), "development decision-making implies two or more parties engaged in a dialogue." Quoting *Webster's New World Dictionary*, Agunga (1990, 142–143) elaborates that "dialogue is 'talking together,' or an interchange and discussion of ideas, especially when open and frank, as in seeking mutual understanding or harmony." Now, if development decisions between nations and the development decision-making processes are dialogues, then all problems encountered in development must be problems of communication and misunderstanding. Thus for Agunga (1990) the main problem in the decision-making "dialogue" is the misunderstanding between people because of a "heterophily gap" between the change agents and the "recipients of change": That is, there are not enough commonly shared attributes such as beliefs, education, and status among the participants as they are very different from each other (141). Such differences are particularly evident at the grassroots levels of development where "foreign donors, local bureaucrats, and technicians work in concert with specialists." Here is the greatest likelihood that both benefactors and beneficiaries will usually face "communication incompatibility" (143). The technical problems of communication demand technical solutions. The problem of development can be solved by simply improving communication skills among the various participants in the process and thus "overcome the obstacles that constrain useful interaction between benefactors and beneficiaries" (138).

The main problem is a communication breakdown. "Technical assistance fails because aid givers do not understand the aid receivers and their felt needs" (Agunga 1990, 146).

Human communication thus falls easy and constant prey to errors of transmission and understanding, of fidelity of translation and of interpretation and comprehension. All errors come to concentrate themselves in the communication situation of such singular frustration in our time: participatory knowledge sharing and decision making between technical specialists from industrialised enclaves and those they seek to help in the enclaves of peasant societies (Ascroft & Masilela 1994, 287).

According to Ascroft and Masilela (1994), the "communication problems" must be resolved before aid givers and receivers and foreign and local development experts "can work together to serve their intended beneficiaries effectively" (Agunga 1990, 147). It is here that the introduction of the technical DSC expert would improve communication and lead to greater participation in the development decision-making process by the local people (Agunga 1990, 138). According to Agunga (1990, 138), "achieving popular participation is a communication activity requiring the presence of development support communication (DSC) experts with communication skills and people know-how necessary to overcome the obstacles that constrain useful interaction between benefactors and beneficiaries." In order to gain participation, the DSC expert is concerned with constructing messages that have the appropriate effect to assist "the target group to process development information effectively" (James 1994, 322). The DSC expert will facilitate effective communication because he is able "to translate technical subject matter into simplified form that small farmers can understand" (Agunga 1990, 147). As such, the DSC specialist is "part artist, part craftsman, and part social scientist" and is

able "not only to diagnose sociocultural constraints on communication but to design strategies and materials to overcome them" (Ascroft & Masilela 1994, 278). If only this new professional "development support communicator," who first appeared somewhere in the rural areas of Thailand in the 1970s and has had an elusive existence in a number of multilateral development institutions since, if given a proper place, all "errors of human communication" will be eliminated and barriers overcome, thus facilitating dialogue and participatory communication among the people and the institutions attempting to develop them (Ascroft & Masilela 1994, 287).

Behind such a pious façade, the language of the DSC proponents betrays their intention: to "translate" and persuade the seemingly ignorant people to accept the propaganda from the powerful development industry (Freire 1974, 96–97). Arrogance is reflected in such a view as it is assumed that "lower-class people do not understand their own situation, that they are in need of enlightenment on the matter, and that this service can be provided by selected higher-class individuals" (Berger 1976, 123). The consideration of human interaction in terms of "message fidelity" and "errors of communication" is derived from a limited view of communication such as provided by cybernetics and simplistic mechanical models. The reality of these models is mistakenly assumed to be the reality of human communication. Such a view reflects the bucket theory of communication, or what Freire called the banking concept, whereby those rich in knowledge transmit information and deposit it in the minds of the poor and ignorant (Beltrán 1980, 24). These views of communication are generally underpinned by the conduit metaphor, whereby language supposedly "contains" meanings inserted by a speaker and these are "extracted" by the listener (Hobart 1993, 11). However, communication is much more complex than this would suggest. Communication is social action and is involved with social power relations. As such, communication is not aimed exclusively at reaching mutual understanding. As Bourdieu (1992, 66) puts it:

1927
1960
1963
1964
1967
1969
1970
1971
1972
1973
1974
1975
1976
1977
1978
1979
1980
1981
1982
1983
1984
1985
1986
1987
1988
1989
1990
1991
1992
1993
1994
1995
1996
1997
1998
1999
2000
2001
2002
2003
2004
2005
2006

Utterances are not only (save in exceptional circumstances) signs to be understood and deciphered; they are also signs of wealth, intended to be evaluated and appreciated, and signs of authority, intended to be believed and obeyed. Quite apart from the literary (and especially poetic) uses of language, it is rare in everyday life for language to function as pure instrument of communication.

In the reductionist DSC discourse, language is considered only as means of communication, communication as functioning only as a means for mutual understanding, and development only as a dialogue. Within such a framework, there is no place to consider other reasons for resistance to development or refusal to communicate. People's miscommunication or refusal to communicate is not simply a problem that could be solved by improved communication. International development implies a hierarchy and power relations where communication also involves giving orders and information and instructions to be obeyed. In the practice of development, "communication is not a technical question to be antiseptically dealt with in isolation from the economic, political and cultural structure of society" (Beltrán 1980, 28).

Indeed, by claiming that communication is aimed only at understanding and suggesting that people need professional help to understand each other, the DSC professional exerts political power and domination. This is clear from the use of the aggressive language of social engineers and military strategists turned rural developers, who mount a "concerted attack on all the bottlenecks at once" (Agunga 1990, 139) and devise "strategies" to "correct errors" and remove "constraints." The use of such concepts reveals that it is not mutual understanding or dialogue that is sought but means for manipulation and subordination. The manipulators have learned by now how to make the best use of "the social environment to help attain audiences' responses fitting with the purposes of communicators" and to obtain individual compliance with predetermined goals of development (Beltrán 1980, 14). For example, the claim that the "human behavioural factor" needs to be taken into consideration (Childers, in Agunga 1990, 151) implies the manipulation of attitudes by providing "information, motivation and education activities which are needed to change any indifference towards the project that local people might have to interest and commitment, ignorance to knowledge, opposition to acceptance and support" (Perrett, in Agunga 1990, 151). The use of such language creates "a disturbing analogy between an enemy village which one bombs, and a friendly villager on whom one wages a health programme or irrigation" (Vitebsky 1993, 114). As Edelman (1974, 310) would suggest, the use of such language fulfils a political function of manipulating those discontented with development into conformity and docility. Indeed, the practice of development is better understood as waging a "war against the poor" rather than against poverty (Carmen 1988, 269).

In short, the role of DSC is persuasion in the service of the project rather than dialogue with the people. It is also not the people but rather the public as a political abstraction that is considered; that is, the proposition that the people need to be educated and informed for participation means that such education is reduced to indoctrination and participation to subservience (Servaes & Arnst 1993, 46). The position of the DSC expert within the organisational structure of international development thus demands that the institutional policy be promoted, and it is doubtful whether such an expert could mediate between all parties impartially.

5. The Agent of Propaganda

Could the DSC expert who is employed by a government and who is "goal oriented, and concerns [himself or herself] with communication at the grassroots, message structure, message effects, and the ability of the target group to process development information effectively" (James 1994, 332), be an honest agent promoting the people's interest in development? According to James (1994, 333), the DSC expert could act as an honest facilitator of participation. Ascroft and Agunga (1994) and Agunga (1990) claim that the DSC agent could well operate in the interest of popular participation and elaborate their claim based on Rogers' theory of diffusion of innovations.

For Rogers, development or modernisation could be considered a diffusion of innovation. Such diffusion takes place through the use of the mass media and interpersonal, face-to-face channels of communication. According to Rogers and Shoemaker (1971, 13), "it was learned that mass media channels are often more important at creating awareness -- knowledge of new ideas, whereas interpersonal channels are more important in changing attitudes towards innovation." More specifically, Rogers and Shoemaker (1971, 24) suggest that mass communication channels are efficient means of transmitting "information" while interpersonal channels are more effective means of "persuasion." Rogers and Burdge (1972, 343) define the change agent as a government employee whose role "is to expand and explain the new ideas the farmer may have already read or heard about via mass media communication channels." Extending the role of the change agent to the Third World, Rogers and Shoemaker (1971, 227) define the change agent likewise as "a professional who influences innovation decisions in a direction deemed desirable by a change agency." This definition of the change agent is not altered in Rogers' subsequent publications, while the initial definition of the communication process is transformed from the original one-way process to a more fashionable and politically correct definition emphasising participation and "creating and sharing of information to achieve understanding" (Ascroft & Agunga 1994, 306).

Ascroft and Agunga (1994, 308) are puzzled because Rogers fails to provide the change agent with a more participatory role, as is demanded by the new definition of communication, and they suggest that the change agent could have a more independent position between representing his benefactors and acting as a representative of the people vis-à-vis the development institution (Ascroft & Agunaga 1994, 310). However, no such position is possible in the institutionalised development industry regardless of the way one may change the definition of communication. This may possibly explain why Rogers never altered his original definition of the change agent.

The role of the change agent is always determined by his position in the development institution. According to Freire (1974, 128), the change agent or the agricultural "extension" agent has no neutral position. The change agent is always in the business of persuading the "masses to accept institutional propaganda" (Freire 1974, 96–97). Of course, for the change agent to enter the field, he or she is also dependent on being accepted by the beneficiaries. But in a mediating position between the benefactors and beneficiaries the change agent represents the interest of the development bureaucracy. This position places the change agent in a conflicting situation as a double agent of deception and propaganda. Indeed, originally development was concerned mainly with propaganda, but in the 1960s the concept of communication replaced the less favourable concept of propaganda in the writings of development scholars (Delia 1987, 59). Propaganda and education are concepts that change agents (or rural extension agents) usually consider to be synonymous, and they do not consider it a contradiction in proclaiming that their fundamental educative task is to "persuade the rural masses to accept our propaganda" (Freire 1974, 96). Indeed, the concept of DSC and the entire field of development communication are biased toward normative ideology and propaganda. This is evident from the very definition of development communication. According to Rogers (1989, 73), the application of communication for development is aimed at furthering development generally by increasing mass media exposure among the population in order to strengthen the "climate for development" and support for specific development programmes. Both these aims are strongly biased towards the communication of propaganda.

1927
1960
1963
1964
1967
1969
1970
1971
1972
1973
1974
1975
1976
1977
1978
1979
1980
1981
1982
1983
1984
1985
1986
1987
1988
1989
1990
1991
1992
1993
1994
1995
1996
1997
1998
1999
2000
2001
2002
2003
2004
2005
2006

6. A Double Agent of Deception: Communication Support in the Service of Official Participatory Development Projects in the Third World

Policy research on development projects that were recognised as successfully meeting the official requirements of people's participation revealed that participation is impossible to reconcile with the existing practice of international development (Quarles van Ufford 1993).

A typical development project begins through political negotiations between a Western developer, such as a government or other donor agency and a Third World government, resulting in a bilateral cooperation agreement about the implementation of a regional rural development project. As is demanded by the new direction in development, the agreement stipulates that local participation in the decision making about actual activities of the project is essential. For such a project to survive, the allocated funds must be spent and it must appear that there is popular participation. However, these are contradictory demands because the availability of large funds means that the local peoples have limited, if any, control over spending and that their views on planning are mediated through "local organisation" in the form of an institutional representative structure set up by the developee's national government (Quarles van Ufford 1993, 136). It would appear that this "local structure" is usually controlled by the national government and local political power elites and does not represent the interests of most of the peasants (Arce & Long 1993). However, the change agents are not in a position to question the legitimacy of this structure, and, in any event, DSC experts must be or pretend to be ignorant of political matters.

Once a development project begins it takes on a life of its own, and it is essential for all parties involved to sustain the impression that the project meets the official objectives agreed upon at governmental and funding agency levels. The survival of the project and the livelihood of the change agents are dependent on their accepting the "local structures" as representative of the interest of the people and thus sustaining the impression that there is popular participation. The change agents also cannot antagonise the national government or challenge the local structure, as this would result in conflict with the local authorities and challenge the official policy assumption that there is indeed popular participation. On the other hand, admitting that there are problems at the local level would place the change agents in conflict with their own agency and result in their removal from the project and replacement by other agents more willing to sustain the official impression of popular participation, as is required by the official policy and the need for the project to proceed as planned (Arce & Long 1993, 181). The change agents are in a conflicting situation, which, in practice, makes them double agents of deception. In their communication with their sponsoring organisations they are required to engage in "careful managing of the information and images of the local scene," presenting an image of a homogeneous rural community participating in development as is required by official policy (Quarles van Ufford 1993, 136-137). Officially, the funding organisation or "benefactor" must remain ignorant of the real local political intricacies, with the result that the images of the local scene must be made to fit organisational needs, which leads to an integrated discourse in which the capabilities of the administrative "machine" and the definition of development constitute a single whole (Quarles van Ufford 1993, 140).

Indeed, such impression management provides the means for the development agencies to gain political support and access to funding, and gain their identity and legitimisation within the development industry.

At the local level of development, the change agent is placed within local political power struggles between various groups with different interests (Arce & Long 1993, 181). Conflict of interest is at the heart of any development.

Fundamental to the problem of cooperation is some kind of conflict of interest. In community development, it is the conflict between agency and community as to whose wants and interests take precedence. Practically, of course, this conflict is usually resolved in favour of whichever party holds the power advantage. But any such resolution is likely to be more apparent than real. Course of action and policies may be decided by the more powerful, but the conflict often continues, manifesting itself in noncooperation by the less powerful party (Goodenough 1970, 35).

Conflict of interest is also found among the local groups being developed because what is a desired objective of a development programme for one party may be less desirable for another (Thomas & Grindle 1990, 1163). Any directed social change (development) upsets a political and social equilibrium and will elicit response and resistance from some groups whose position would be affected by the planned change. More reaction, resistance and challenges occur as the implementation proceeds because the effects of the change become more visible (Thomas & Grindle 1990, 1166). These are not simply problems of communication but of power.

The change agent needs to take a holistic view which implies that the official agency policy is of paramount importance. In such a position the change agent would be on the side of the project, the sponsoring agency and the national government.

Whatever else resistance may indicate, it obviously serves notice that the conditions for cooperation between agents and community are in jeopardy. Because he is committed to implementing constructive change, it is the agent's professional responsibility, just as it is a psychiatrist's, to see that the necessary conditions for cooperation are meant, insofar as it is within his power (Goodenough 1970, 44).

This would imply that gaining compliance to power and devising strategies to anticipate and manipulate the "human behavioural factor" (Childers 1976, 87) that needs to be overcome, rather than communication to achieve mutual understanding, are the main objectives of the agent of change.

7. Conclusion: Towards Postdevelopment

Improved and more communication, dialogue and mutual understanding are probably not the salvation to the development problems of Africa and the Third World. Simplistic models of dialogue misrepresent the complexity and social character of communication and development. As Melkote (1993, 153) puts it: "We have learnt that communication is not the only missing link. The problems of underdevelopment or overdevelopment are rooted as much in non-communication factors as they are in information related factors."

After almost half a century of "development" and its consistent failure we need to be weary of simplistic, made-in-America, quick-fix solutions. In this sense DSC is an American semblance of participation propagated against the South American Marxist-inspired participatory paradigm. Proposing salvation through reductionist models of dialogue deflects attention from the need for effecting change in the oppressive social structures in the Third World (Beltran 1976, 19). Fanon (1973, 78) suggests that a radical global restructuring and redistribution of wealth may be required. According to Hedebro (1984, 92), the rudimentary insight gained from decades of development communication research is that:

> . . . farmers will not adopt new ideas and products if they do not have a real possibility to do so or if they will not benefit from it, no matter how cleverly the information has been designed. ... What is needed . . . is land reform . . . not information. A change in the structure is needed, not more technical know-how. This can be put another way; information can never substitute for structural changes, no matter how ambitious the effort.

The central assumption of the DSC approach that achieving "mutual understanding" would lead to desired development is an illusion. Firstly, why should communication aimed at reaching mutual understanding lead to desired social change when much of the communication that takes place in any society

1927
1960
1963
1964
1967
1969
1970
1971
1972
1973
1974
1975
1976
1977
1978
1979
1980
1981
1982
1983
1984
1985
1986
1987
1988
1989
1990
1991
1992
1993
1994
1995
1996
1997
1998
1999
2000
2001
2002
2003
2004
2005
2006

is aimed at preserving the status quo and avoiding change? Secondly, development implies a directed social change and, regardless of the benevolent and desirable objectives, it will always be met with resistance by those affected by such change because "what is a desired outcome for one may be a less optimal outcome for another" (Thomas & Grindle 1990, 1163). Such opposition and resistance are not simply problems of misunderstanding that could be solved by providing technical means for improved communication skills.

Implementation of development is a political decision and involves conflicts and battles over positions of power that are perfectly understood by those involved. It is the moralising social scientists who have no understanding of such realities. To understand development we need to use the suggestion made by Michel Foucault (1980, 114) that human history, and by implication the history of development, makes perfect sense when considered in terms of a model of war and battle rather than in terms of dialogue, meaning or mutual understanding. The concept of communication as a Platonic dialogue is static and does not capture the logic of communication as an agonistic social practice and the complexity of interaction between the actors involved in implementation of development at grassroots levels. At these "interface situations" the "interaction between actors become oriented around the problem of devising ways of bridging, accommodating to, and struggling against each other's different and cognitive worlds" (Long & Villarreal 1996, 147).

It is perhaps time to reconsider the role of communication theory in development and seriously question the purpose and interests that are promoted by the suggestion that development and communication are dialogues aimed at mutual understanding. The past 50 years have produced an immense volume of theoretical writing on development but seem to have made no impact on the problems they address. The reality of underdevelopment has moved ahead of the theories of development, with the result that most theories seem to be irrelevant to development (Edwards 1989, 116). Indeed, in the development industry (not in the academic discipline of development communication), only one theory dominates the field: the "paradigm of domination," which regards communication as top-down domination elaborated by United States scholars in the 1950s (Simpson 1994, 6).

Yet theories of development are not entirely insignificant. While changing perceptions of communication theory failed to make an impact on the development industry, they have provided tools for critical understanding of development. Many in the Third World have a good case against development. They have realised that development within the accepted international institutional framework would not benefit them as it is mostly inappropriate development projects that are carried out in the Third World. The aim of such development is to benefit the development industry, sponsoring governments, big business and local power elites rather than the people (George 1976). It is development itself that has brought popular impoverishment and misery in many Third World nations (Ekins 1993, 9-10). The poor of the Third World have realised what they already knew, that in the last resort they have only themselves to rely on to find a solution for development (Carmen 1988, 269). Therefore, the solution is not another or alternative development, but rather an alternative to development or postdevelopment (Escobar 1995, 213). It is only when scholars begin to question the whole concept and aims of development that development as practised would cease and that a space could be opened for an alternative Third World development (Esteva 1992, 20). This alternative would consist of links between grassroots movements and development scholars and of freeing the academic field of development communication from its normative bias and ideological commitment to the development industry. Alternatives to development, based on an "insurrection of subjugated knowledges" (Foucault 1980, 81), would challenge the domination of Western knowledge and articulate alternative, indigenous ways of knowing, doing and living (Apffel Marglin 1995, 880-881). Such an alternative could be relevant only if it has power to become relevant. That is, it is based primarily on the ability to propagate a political counter strategy by forging a link between grassroots movements in both the North and South worlds (Servaes 1986, 225; Rodgers & Starr 1995, 92). Such an alternative is presented by the increased postmodern modes of communication and the globalisation of communication interlinks for groups striving to establish alternatives to development within the North and the Third World, to increase their communication and information sharing (Rodgers & Starr 1995, 92). These interlinks would also contribute to freeing the academic field of development communication from its normative bias, dependence on the development industry and colonisation by American scholarship and thus open the way for a more independent theorising about development (Wiarda 1991). In this sense, as was pointed out by Foucault (1988, 208), "theory does not express, translate, or serve to apply practice: It is practice."

References

Agunga, R. 1990. "Development support communication and popular participation in development projects." *Gazette* 45:137–155.

Agunga, R. 1996. "Communication: The missing element in Africa's development struggle." Paper presented at the Symposium on Culture, Communication, Development. Human Sciences Research Council. Pretoria. August 29–31, 1996.

Apffel Marglin, F. 1995. "Development or decolonization in the Andes?" *Futures* 27:869–882.

Arce, A., and N. Long. 1993. "Bridging two worlds: An ethnography of bureaucrat–peasant relations in western Mexico." In: M. Hobart, ed. *An anthropological critique of development: The growth of ignorance*. London: Routledge.

Ascroft, J., and R. Agunga. 1994. "Diffusion theory and participatory decision making." In: S.A. White, K.S. Nair, and J. Ascroft, eds. *Participatory communication: Working for change and development*. New Delhi: Sage.

Ascroft, J., and S. Masilela. 1994. "Participatory decision making in Third World development." In: S.A. White, K.S. Nair, and J. Ascroft, eds. *Participatory communication: Working for change and development*. New Delhi: Sage.

Beltran, L.R. 1976. "Alien premises, objects, and methods in Latin American communication research." In: E.M. Rogers, ed. *Communication and development: Critical perspectives*. Beverly Hills: Sage.

Beltran, L.R. 1980. "A farewell to Aristotle: 'Horizontal' communication." *Communication* 5:5–41.

Berger, P.L. 1976. *Pyramids of sacrifice: Political ethics and social change*. New York: Anchor.

Bourdieu, P. 1992. *Language and symbolic power*. Cambridge, U.K.: Polity.

Burton, S. 1994. "Organisation and agency: Some thoughts on community videomaking as development support communication." *Communicatio* 20(2):2–8.

Carmen, R.E.R.M. 1988. "Development communication: The search for a participatory paradigm." *Community Development Journal* 24(4):264–272.

Childers, E. 1976. "Taking humans into account." *Media Asia* 3(2):87–90.

Coombs, P.H., M. Ahmed, and P. Kale. 1976. "Communication and integrated rural development—Is it a new rhetoric?" *Media Asia* 3(2):81–86.

Delia, J.G. 1987. "Communication research: A history." In: C.R. Berger and S.H. Chaffee, eds. *Handbook of communication science*. Newbury Park, Calif.: Sage.

Edelman, M. 1974. "The political language of the helping professions." *Politics and Society* 4:295–310.

Edward, M. 1989. "The irrelevance of development studies." *Third World Quarterly* 11(1):116–135.

Ekins, P. 1993. *A new world order: Grassroots movements for global change*. London: Routledge.

Escobar, A. 1995. *Encountering development: The making and unmaking of the Third World*. Princeton, N.J.: Princeton Univ. Press.

Esteva, G. 1992. "Development." In: W. Sachs, ed. *The development dictionary: A guide to knowledge as power*. London: Zed.

Fanon, F. 1973. *The wretched of the earth*. Harmondsworth, U.K.: Penguin.

Foucault, M. 1980. *Power/knowledge: Selected interviews and other writings 1972–1977*. New York: Pantheon.

Foucault, M. 1988. *Language, counter-memory, practice: Selected essays and interviews*. Ithaca, N.Y.: Cornell Univ. Press.

Frankel, J. 1971. *The making of foreign policy: An analysis of decision making*. New York: Oxford Univ. Press.

Freire, P. 1974. *Education for critical consciousness*. New York: Seabury.

George, S. 1976. *How the other half dies: The real reasons for world hunger*. Harmondsworth, U.K.: Penguin.

Goodenough, W.H. 1970. *Cooperation in change*. New York: Russell Sage Foundation.

Hall, E.T. 1965. *The silent language*. New York: Premier.

Hedebro, G. 1984. *Communication and social change in developing nations: A critical view*. Ames: Iowa State Univ. Press.

Hobart, M. 1993. "Introduction: The growth of ignorance?" M. Hobart, ed. *An anthropological critique of development: The growth of ignorance*. London: Routledge.

James, S.L. 1994. "Facilitating communication within rural and marginal communities: A model for development support." S.A. White, K.S. Nair, and J. Ascroft, eds. *Participatory communication: Working for change and development*. New Delhi: Sage.

1927
1960
1963
1964
1967
1969
1970
1971
1972
1973
1974
1975
1976
1977
1978
1979
1980
1981
1982
1983
1984
1985
1986
1987
1988
1989
1990
1991
1992
1993
1994
1995
1996
1997
1998
1999
2000
2001
2002
2003
2004
2005
2006

Jayaweera, N. 1989. "Rethinking development communication: A holistic view." N. Jayaweera and S. Amunugama, eds. *Rethinking development communication*. Singapore: Amic.

Long, N., and M. Villarreal. 1996. "Exploring development interfaces: From the transfer of knowledge to the transformation of meaning." F.J. Schuurman, ed. *Beyond the impasse: New directions in development theory*. London: Zed.

Melkote, S.R. 1991. *Communication for development in the Third World: Theory and practice*. New Delhi: Sage.

Melkote, S.R. 1993. "From Third World to First World: New roles and challenges for development communication." *Gazette* 52:145–158.

Niebuhr, R. 1960. *Moral man and immoral society*. New York: Charles Scribner.

Pye, L.W., ed. 1963. *Communication and political development*. Princeton, N.J.: Princeton Univ. Press.

Quarles van Ufford, P. 1993. "Knowledge and ignorance in the practice of development policy." In: M. Hobart, ed. *An anthropological critique of development: The growth of ignorance*. London: Routledge.

Rodgers, J., and A. Starr. 1995. "On discourse and social movements: Traversing the First World /Third World development divide." *Journal of Developing Societies* 11:74–97.

Rogers, E.M. 1989. "Inquiry in development communication." M.K. Asante and W.B. Gudykunst, eds. *Handbook of international and intercultural communication*. Newbury Park, Calif.: Sage.

Rogers, E.M., and R.J. Burdge. 1972. *Social change in rural societies*. 2nd ed. Englewood Cliffs, N.J.: Prentice Hall.

Rogers, E.M., and F.F. Shoemaker. 1971. *Communication of innovations: A cross-cultural approach*. 2nd ed. New York: Free Press.

Servaes, J. 1986. "Development theory and communication policy: Power to the people." *European Journal of Communication* 1:203–229.

Servaes, J., and R. Arnst. 1993. "First things first: Participatory communication for change." *Media Asia* 2:44–46.

Schramm, W. 1964. *Mass media and national development: The role of information in the developing countries*. Stanford, Calif.: Stanford Univ. Press.

Simpson, C. 1994. *Science of coercion: Communication research and psychological warfare 1945–1960*. New York: Oxford Univ. Press.

Thomas, J.W., and M.S. Grindle. 1990. "After the decision: Implementing policy reforms in developing countries." *World Development* 18:1163–1181.

Vitebsky, P. 1993. "Is death the same everywhere? Contexts of knowing and doubting." M. Hobart, ed. *An anthropological critique of development: The growth of ignorance*. London: Routledge.

Wiarda, H.J. 1991. "Toward a nonethnocentric theory of development: Alternative conceptions from the Third World." H.J. Wiarda, ed. *New directions in comparative politics*. Boulder, Colo.: Westview Press.

GEOMETRIES OF DEVELOPMENT

By Hemant Shah and Karin Gwinn Wilkins

2006 Geometries of development refer to ideas underlying the practice of development. This term, used in development discourse, describes the arrangement of three elements within a global system: spaces, key points and vectors. Space refers to various kinds of spatial actors such as nation states, regions and transnational configurations. Points refer to key institutional sites where development policies and programs are formulated and implemented, such as government ministries and intergovernmental organizations (IGOs). Vectors are linkages among institutional and spatial actors. The interaction among these three elements determines the overall shape of the structure of development. The overall shape of this structure is characterized by the divisions, linkages and relations of power among actors and institutions. The meaning of development is inherently unstable, and institutional actors in positions of power try to "fix" or stabilize it in ways that promote their own interests.

As an institutional practice, development began with a notion of an industrialized, modern "us" and a pastoral, traditional "them." Building from this assumption, formal development organizations based in industrialized countries (the North) initiated a planning process on behalf of traditional communities (the South). Over the years, such terminology has become dominant in development discourse.

Grounded in a cold war context, this geometry of development created spatial distinctions between South and North (poor and rich), West and East, and Third and First worlds. The underlying principle of the Cold War-era development approach, involving the transfer of financial, technical and human resources (vectors) among spatial and institutional actors, functions within a set of categories that distinguish donors from recipients with each transaction. The dominant geometry of development articulates a vision of development that compartmentalizes communities divided along various types of boundaries. In Cold War-era development circles, the world was neatly divided along political (communism in East versus democracy in West), economic (industrialized North versus agricultural South), cultural (modern versus traditional) and hierarchical (First = West; Second = East; and Third = South) lines.

We can trace the emergence of this geometry of development to the late 1940s. While preparing his 1949 inaugural address, U.S. President Harry Truman's staff agreed upon three central points regarding foreign policy: to continue support for the United Nations organization; to maintain commitment to the Marshall Plan; and to create a joint U.S.-European defense organization. Almost as an afterthought, a midlevel civil servant suggested a fourth point: to expand existing Latin American technical assistance programs to the poor countries of Asia, Africa and the Middle East, thereby expanding an existing vector between the United States and countries of the South. The suggestion was accepted and Point Four was included in the address:

> Fourth, we must embark on a bold new programme for making the benefits of our scientific advances and industrial progress available for the improvement and growth of underdeveloped areas (Rist 1997, 71).

Unexpectedly, from the perspective of the Truman administration, Point Four received massive attention from the press and policymakers around the world. As a result, government efforts in this area were intensified and over the course of several decades, new international actors were created, such as the forerunners to the United Nations Development Program (UNDP), regional development banks and United Nations Conference on Trade and Development (UNCTAD). Consequently, Point Four established in a very public, very global way the idea of underdevelopment

as a synonym for what had been called "economic backwardness," and demonstrated in a dramatic way the position of power held by the United States in defining the status of other nations.

At the time this framework emerged, the idea that development could be strategically planned and stimulated was notable for shifting away from the concept of intransitive social change (Rist 1997). Importantly, the Point Four configuration of international relations eliminated (at least rhetorically) the colonizer-colonized relationship by erasing discussions of unequal relations of power among nations. Underdevelopment was now a stage in an inevitable, linear process towards development that all nations went through. This development-underdevelopment continuum created the possibility of recognizing intervention as a humanitarian mission rather than one of colonization or imperialism. Finally, mass media were assumed to operate as an appropriate and relevant means towards inspiring people in the "underdeveloped" world to emulate those in the "developed" West (Lerner 1958). Many of these basic principles still serve as the foundations for development practice today, as international development institutions allocate resources to transfer knowledge and technologies to communities in nations with few material resources.

The geometry of development model offers a flexible analytical tool for analyzing development processes. The abstract concepts within our geometry of development are not bound by nation-states as the key unit of analysis, though it recognizes that they are important actors. Also, our geometry of development approach is not limited to viewing the flow of development aid in a "West-to-Rest" fashion. The nomenclature involving space, points and vectors allows us not only to critique various arrangements of development geometry—such as the one created by the United States after the Second World War—but also to consider alternative development arrangements that are open to incorporating a wide range of actors and in which there are no predetermined roles.

1927
1960
1963
1964
1967
1969
1970
1971
1972
1973
1974
1975
1976
1977
1978
1979
1980
1981
1982
1983
1984
1985
1986
1987
1988
1989
1990
1991
1992
1993
1994
1995
1996
1997
1998
1999
2000
2001
2002
2003
2004
2005
2006

For example, we question the morality and validity of the American Cold War-era geometry of development that has come to dominate global development policy and practice up to the present time. But also, based on an analysis of space, points and vectors in existing but less well-known development arrangements, we propose an alternative geometry of development.

We argue that the dominant geometry of development should be discarded, given the many limitations this model imposes on the idea of development and its policies and programs. As has been suggested in many other reviews of dominant development models, this approach inappropriately justifies the positioning of wealthier states as a normative model and therefore legitimizes their intervention in "underdeveloped" areas. This model has been critiqued for its ethnocentric and arrogant vision, collapsing diverse communities of the South with a wide range of cultural histories into a single monolithic space for development intervention. Even the seemingly innocuous assumption that technologies themselves are inherently "neutral" belies an ethnocentric approach (Ito 2000).

The dominant geometry of development implies a vectorial relationship whereby interventionist policies and programs, created at various institutional points in countries of the North, are posed as being in the best interests of their target communities in the South. Such views allowed many academics and policymakers in the North, without a trace of self-doubt or self-consciousness, to craft blueprints for "developing" the South in the image of the North. The dichotomization of the entire global structure of development into modern and traditional spaces (even with a transitional category in between, as evidenced in Lerner 1958) obscures the intersections between and within practices in historical contexts (Melkote 2002). These broad generalizations miss distinctions within countries (Rodgers and Starr 1995), essentialize groups into homogeneous categories (Melkote and Steeves 2001), typically at the level of nations rather than communities, and assume that

experiences of poverty (Escobar 1995), gender (Mohanty 1991) and other social conditions are similar across historical and cultural contexts. This kind of "spatial will to power," as Escobar (1995) puts it, allowed domestic elites in South countries in the postcolonial era to represent their specific self-interest as a class as equivalent to the general interest of the nation-state as a whole (Alvares 1992). More often than not, however, the interests of domestic elites in South countries actually were identical to the interests of development policymakers in the North countries. As such, the South country elites replicated the dominant international geometry of development within the boundaries of South nations. This process has, in many cases, resulted in the abuse of minority and indigenous rights.

Another problem with this dominant geometry of development is that it conceptualizes the development-underdevelopment continuum in a way that fetishizes geopolitical boundaries (Wilmer 1993). Post-development critiques have illustrated the processes through which the development industry constructs "Third World" spaces through planning and implementing strategic intervention (Escobar 1995; Nederveen Pieterse 2001). The dominant bilateral and multilateral development institutions are premised on a notion of stable geopolitical boundaries, and the development "target" becomes operationalized as the "Third World." Even in participatory models of development, despite the best intentions and dedicated work of many practitioners and scholars, "participation" serves more often to fulfill administrative needs of the industry than as an alternative to dominant development approaches (Huesca 2002).

In the geometry of development created by Point Four, since the primary unit of analysis was the nation-state, five-year plans, data gathering protocols, communication systems, infrastructure building, bureaucracy creation and other activities were all conceived as national projects. For example, the primary measure of progress was Gross National Product, and data about media production and consumption were typically reported as nation-state aggregate measures (Lerner 1938: 86). While these data may have been useful for certain large-scale planning and policy purposes, they missed recognizing the inequities in resource distribution among segments of a country's population. A tremendous amount of energy was expended on mapping territories and constructing borders of newly independent states. Again, this information may have been valuable for building infrastructure, facilitating some forms of social interaction and creating certain kinds of economic growth (all with unequally distributed benefits), but another purpose of these activities was to monitor and constrain movement of minority and indigenous communities (Radcliffe 1999).

With regard to communication issues in the dominant geometry of development, the operative assumption was that nationally based media systems were necessary to distribute information efficiently and to mobilize people to become modern in the national interest. As Lerner writes:

> Central to this change (from traditional to modern) is the shift in modes of communicating ideas and attitudes—for spreading among a large public vivid images of its own new ways is what modernization distinctly does. Not the class media of books and travel, but the mass media of tabloids, radio and movies are now the dominant mode. (Lerner 1958: 45).

Lerner and others assumed that identities fostered through national media systems would transcend other identifications within and across national boundaries, and that these larger media systems would be more efficient and sophisticated than other smaller media systems. Even current development discourse, perpetuating this geometry, seems incapable of dealing with the contemporary vectorial realities of specialized transnational media networks created by diasporic communities.

Clearly, many writers are uneasy with the vocabulary of the dominant geometry of development, employing quotations and footnotes to signal their critical use of terms such as "Third World" and "development" (Mohanty 1991; Sturgeon 1999). These scholars and practitioners are attempting to distance themselves from an ethnocentric vision of a hierarchical distinction between the Northern West as "First" and others as somehow lagging behind, in "Third" or even "Fourth" place (Melkote and Steeves 2001; Nederveen Pieterse 2001). However, even these critical usages evoke a more-or-less traditional understanding of geopolitics. For example, the term "Third World" was first posed during the 1789 French Revolution as a way to refer to a "third estate," or people in poverty lacking political power (Melkote and Steeves 2001; Payne 1999), and since then has been critically used to denote spatial actors, such as communities united through shared experiences of oppression based on race, ethnicity, class or gender hierarchies (Melkote and Steeves 2001); of economic distance from or dependency on the global capitalist economy (Glassman and Samatar 1997); or anti-colonial political struggles (Chow and Lyter 2002). Still, some of these distinctions can be misleading when considering the different political histories of many communities and nations, such as Thailand, when direct political colonization was not part of its historical experience.

Many scholars have recognized that dominant economic and political standards for categorizing countries are "hopelessly outdated and anachronistic" (Kamrava 1995), and distinctions across First, Second and Third Worlds no longer have relevance in a post-Cold War world (Kamrava 1995; Melkote and Steeves 2001). The validity of this First, Second and Third World, or North-South categorizations is indeed in question, given a rapidly shifting structure of global political-economic contexts involving changing vectors of political and economic dominance among nations and other spatial actors, the strengthening of regional institutions and identities, the globalization of economic and communication systems and the privatization of industries (Hagopian 2000; Schuurman 2000).

1927
1960
1963
1964
1967
1969
1970
1971
1972
1973
1974
1975
1976
1977
1978
1979
1980
1981
1982
1983
1984
1985
1986
1987
1988
1989
1990
1991
1992
1993
1994
1995
1996
1997
1998
1999
2000
2001
2002
2003
2004
2005
2006

In response to the limitations of the dominant geometry of development, we propose two approaches to reconceptualizing a geometry of development. First, we encourage new ways of thinking about development donors, highlighting, in effect, a set of vectors that is typically ignored in studies of the global structure of development. Little recognition has been given to the distinctions across donors, who are typically assumed to represent one monolithic approach to development work. Second, we view cultural space, territory, identities, progress and social change in ways that are not circumscribed by geopolitical boundaries that are the basis of most studies of development. Thus, we also encourage that the very idea of development be untethered from measures of Gross National Product and focus instead on notions of rights and resources for sociocultural groups, this opening up the possibility of linkages among spatial actors across geopolitical boundaries (Rist 1997).

Instead of focusing on a geometry that limits development categories to national settings within north/south and east/west references, we advocate visions of development that focus on access to resources, seen broadly as a capacity to activate power through economic, political, social and cultural means. The concept of geometry offers an abstract conceptualization enabling alternative visions of space, points and vectors. An alternative spatial configuration of development means leaving behind an emphasis on geopolitical place, and instead turning our attention to the importance of sociocultural space, where specific histories and identities are paramount (Escobar, 2000; Escobar et al., 2002). This shift moves from a discourse of development as benevolent aid to geopolitical entities, which threatens diversity, homogenizes local traditions, and encourages minorities to conform to White and western cultural practices, toward a discourse of rights and resources, which emphasizes self-determination and autonomy of minority communities and locally relevant cultural and social practices. Such a shift implies the introduction into the overall structure of development a new set of spatial actors bound to local transnational or regional territory, new points of policy formulation and implementation, and new vectors linking spatial actors and signaling decentralization.

In sum, we argue that the dominant geometry of development, rooted in historical articulations of U.S. foreign policy and grounded in current development practice, be discarded. The ethnocentric and hierarchical nature of first/third, north/south, and east/west divisions at the center of the global structure of development hold neither validity nor moral sway. Instead of essentializing diverse groups of donor and recipient nations, into broad geopolitical categories, we argue that new geometries of development consider other social groupings (i.e., new spatial and institutional actors) along local and regional lines that resonate more clearly with cultural histories within particular contexts. New geometries of development might help us better engage a central tenet of development work; the attempt to improve the human condition.

Shah, Hemant and Karin Gwinn Wilkins. "Geometries of Development." Published in *Mazi*, the electronic report of the Communication for Social Change Consortium, May 2006. *www. communicationforsocialchange.org/php.mazi* Reprinted with permission of the authors and the publisher.

EXCERPT FROM:

FAMILY TREE OF THEORIES, METHODOLOGIES AND STRATEGIES IN DEVELOPMENT COMMUNICATION

Towards a Theoretical and Empirical Convergence?

By Silvio Waisbord

2002 Can the two broad approaches that dominated the field of development communication, diffusion and participatory models converge around certain principles and strategies? Or is that unthinkable given that their underlying premises and goals are still essentially different? The following discussion reviews attempts to bring together different "branches of the family tree," agreements, and disagreements among different approaches based on lessons learned in the last decades. The fact that some coincidences can be identified does not imply that old differences have been completely bridged. This is impossible because different theoretical premises and diagnoses continue to inform approaches and strategies. The fundamental issue continues to be that definitions of the problem are different, and expectedly, theories, strategies and techniques still offer essentially opposite analyses and recommendations. To identify points of convergence does not imply that a specific value judgement is made about the desirability or necessity of the process. The intention is to map out trends and directions that attest to the richness and complexity of the field rather than to pass judgment on them.

General Remarks

Since the 1950s, the meaning of development communication has changed. Changes should not be surprising considering that "development," a concept that together with "modernisation" and "Third World" emerged and dominated academic and policy debates in the 1950s, has lost much of its past lustre. New concepts have been coined and have gained popularity but have not displaced the broad notion of development communication. Despite its multiple meanings, "development communication" remains a sort of umbrella term to designate research and interventions concerned with improving conditions among people struggling with economic, social and political problems in the non-Western world. Like "development," "communication" has also undergone important transformations in the past five decades that reflected the ebbs and flows of intellectual and political debates as well as the changing fortunes of theoretical approaches. The absence of a widespread consensus in defining "development" and "communication" reflects the larger absence of a common vocabulary in the field (Gibson n.d.). This conceptual ambiguity and confusion should not be surprising considering that different disciplines and theories have converged in the field of development communication. There has been a confluence of overlapping traditions from a variety of disciplines that imported vocabularies that had little in common. For example, do concepts such as "empowerment," "advocacy engagement of communities" and "collective community action" refer to fundamentally different ideas? Not really. The presence of different terminologies does not necessarily reflect opposite understandings but, mainly, the existence of different trunks in the family tree. In a fragmented field, diverse programmes and strategies are rooted in a myriad of intellectual fields that were rarely in fluid contact. Despite the diversity of origins, however, it is remarkable that there has been a tendency towards having a more comprehensive understanding of "development communication." The historic gap between approaches has not been bridged but, certainly, there have been visible efforts to integrate dissimilar models and strategies. Consider Jan Servaes' (1996b) definition of development as a multidimensional process that involves change in social structures, attitudes institutions, economic growth, reduction of inequality, and the eradication

1927
1960
1963
1964
1967
1969
1970
1971
1972
1973
1974
1975
1976
1977
1978
1979
1980
1981
1982
1983
1984
1985
1986
1987
1988
1989
1990
1991
1992
1993
1994
1995
1996
1997
1998
1999
2000
2001
2002
2003
2004
2005
2006

of poverty. For him, development is a "whole change for a better life." This notion comes close to the idea of "another development" that emphasises the satisfaction of needs, endogenous self-reliance, and life in harmony with the environment (Melkote 1991). We would be hard-pressed to find approaches and interventions that essentially disagree with such an encompassing idea of development.

Similarly, different approaches have gradually adopted an understanding of communication that is not reduced to the idea of information transmission, but includes the idea of process and exchange. Certainly, the persuasion model of communication maintains a towering presence in the field. Sociopsychological models of behaviour and perspectives grounded in stimulus-response communication theories continue to dominate, arguably because some premises of the "dominant paradigm" remain widely accepted. The model of top-down, sender-receiver communication has been revised, however.

The idea of "communication as process" has gained centrality in approaches informed by both behaviour change and participatory models. Moemeka's (1994, 64) words illustrate a widespread sentiment in the field: "Communication should be seen both an independent and dependent variable. It can and does affect situations, attitudes, and behaviour, and its content, context, direction, and flow are also affected by prevailing circumstances. More importantly, communication should be viewed as an integral part of development plans—a part whose major objective is to create systems, modes, and strategies that could provide opportunities for the people to have access to relevant channels, and to make use of these channels and the ensuing communication environment in improving the quality of their lives."

This perspective is somewhat akin to "ritualistic" models of communication that prioritise the Latin roots of the word (as in "making common" through the exchange of meaning) that gained currency in the field of communication in the last decades (Carey

1989). Communication is understood as communities and individuals engaging in meaning-making. It is a horizontal, deinstitutionalised, multiple process in which senders and receivers have interchangeable roles, according to participatory theorist Jan Servaes (1996a). From a perspective rooted in behaviour change models, Kincaid (1998) has similarly argued that all participants are senders and receivers. The difference lies in the fact that whereas approaches largely informed by the dominant paradigm continue to think of communication as a process that contributes to behaviour change, participatory models are not primarily concerned with "behaviour" but with transforming social conditions.

Another salient feature of recent studies in development communication is the increasing influence of theories and approaches that were originated or have been widely used in health communication. Health communication has received more attention than education or agriculture, issues that were central in early projects of development communication. Certainly, issues such as literacy, agricultural productivity and violence are included in many contemporary development plans. Behaviour change, social marketing and health promotion models have become increasingly influential in development communication, however. In a way, the growing centrality of health issues should not be surprising considering that family planning and nutrition, for example, have been dominant in the agenda of development communication since the 1960s. Additionally, attention to HIV/AIDS since the 1980s further contributed to the ascendancy of health and health-related approaches in the field.

On the one hand, this shift could be interpreted as a reflection of the priorities of funding agencies. Although further research is needed to support this finding, it seems that the presence of health issues and, consequently, the influence of health communication approaches express the agenda of development organisations. On the other hand, it can also be interpreted as a result of the emergence of a broader approach to health issues. The definition of health as "a state of well-being," widely cited in contemporary studies, allows a more comprehensive approach that includes issues such as illiteracy and poverty that were not integrated in early development communication projects.

Points of Convergence

Notwithstanding important persistent differences among theories and approaches, it is possible to identify several points of convergence that suggest possible directions in the field of international communication.

- The need of political will

One point of convergence is that political will is necessary in order to bring about change (Hornik 1988). Development communication should not only be concerned with instrumenting specific outcomes as defined in the traditional paradigm, but also with the process by which communities become empowered to intervene and transform their environment. Community empowerment should be the intended outcome of interventions. This requires coming up with a set of indicators that measure the impact of interventions in terms of empowerment.

Empowerment lacks a single definition, however. It can refer to communities making decisions for themselves and acquiring knowledge (e.g., about health issues). Whereas for participatory/advocacy approaches empowerment involves changes in power distribution, behaviour models use empowerment to represent ways for communities to change behaviour, for example, discontinuing unhealthy practices. Advocates of social marketing suggest that marketing empowers people by providing information and having constant feedback from consumers so they can be responsible for their well-being. Because understandings of empowerment are different, expectations about interventions are different too. If development requires redressing power inequalities, it conceivably takes a longer time than interventions that aim to change knowledge, attitudes and practices. The

pressures for relatively quick results and short-term impact of interventions are better suited for a particular understanding of empowerment (and thus development communication) which is more aligned with behaviour change than participatory approaches. The slowness of policy and political changes required for more equal distribution of resources and decision making, as advocated by participatory models, does not fit short-term expectations.

The problems of measuring results, however, are not unique to participatory strategies. Many observers have indicated that behaviour change models have not satisfactorily answered the question of long-term effects. The lack of longitudinal studies that document changes over time makes it difficult to know the extent of the influence of interventions and environmental factors that could help reach solid conclusions about the long-term impact of communication strategies.

The fact that the debate over "results indicators" has not concluded and that no easy resolution seem in sight, reflects the persistence of disagreements over measuring development. Answers to questions such as "What are the right results?" are expected to be different given that, notwithstanding a growing consensus on the issues of community empowerment and horizontal communication as central to development communication, behaviour change and participatory models still define the task of interventions in different terms. In other words, there continues to be a tension between approaches that are oriented to achieving results as measured in behaviour change and those that prioritise the building of sustainable resources as the goal of programmes.

- A "tool kit" conception of strategies

Another important point of convergence is the presence of a "tool kit" conception of approaches within the behaviour change tradition. Practitioners have realised that a multiplicity of strategies is needed to improve the quality of life of communities in developing countries. Rather than promoting specific

1927
1960
1963
1964
1967
1969
1970
1971
1972
1973
1974
1975
1976
1977
1978
1979
1980
1981
1982
1983
1984
1985
1986
1987
1988
1989
1990
1991
1992
1993
1994
1995
1996
1997
1998
1999
2000
2001
2002
2003
2004
2005
2006

theories and methodologies regardless of the problem at stake, there has been an emerging consensus that different techniques are appropriate in different contexts in order to deal with different problems and priorities. Theories and approaches are part of a "tool kit" that is used according to different diagnoses. There is the belief that the tools that are used to support behaviour change depend on the context in which the programme is implemented, the priorities of funders, and the needs of the communities.

For example, conventional educational interventions might be recommended in critical situations such as epidemics when large masses of people need to be reached in a short period of time. Such strategies, however, would be unlikely to solve structural, long-term health problems.

Social marketing could be useful to address certain issues (for example, increase rates of immunisation) but is inadequate to address deeper problems of community participation that are ultimately responsible for permanent changes. It also can result in the problem that interventions conclude when public information campaigns are terminated. One of the problems is that such interventions create a dependency on media programmes; the alternative, then, is focusing on self-maintaining resources that are responsible for the sustainability of programmes. Another problem is that even when social marketing strategies are successful at raising awareness, they do not last forever and, therefore, other support systems are necessary to maintain participation and communication. Because of the limitations of social marketing, other strategies are needed to address the problem of empowering and politically involving different groups. Social mobilisation, for example, offers a way to deal with certain issues such as education, sanitation, nutrition (including breastfeeding), family planning, respiratory problems, AIDS and diarrhoeal diseases. Still, while the mobilisation of a vast array of partners is necessary, this does not exclude the uses of media advocacy and social marketing to target specific problems. A breastfeeding programme in Brazil successfully integrated social mobilisation and social marketing (Fox n.d.). As a result of the programme, there was an increase in the median duration of breastfeeding and a reduction in infant mortality. Ministries and professional medical and nutrition groups participated in elaborating plans and stimulating actions at the national and state levels among their employees, members and associated institutions. At the community level, mothers' groups were formed and breastfeeding was promoted through extension workers, university students, the church and other voluntary groups.

Family planning programmes in Egypt have been another example of successful integration of different approaches (Wisensale & Khodair 1998). After the intervention, the use of contraceptives doubled and the birthrate dropped from 39.8 to 27.5 percent in 10 years. The achievements of the programme have been attributed to the fact that the Information, Education & Communication Centre of the State Information Service used multiple tools, including the mass media, interpersonal communication, and entertainment-education. The participation of the government, health organisations and religious groups was also considered to be responsible for the success of the programme.

The application of any prescriptive theory and methods might not work everywhere. Because of political and religious reasons, it is difficult to bring together a wide spectrum of forces to rally behind issues such as breastfeeding, family planning, and AIDS education in some countries. Under these circumstances, searching for a broad coalition is not recommended. In cases where governments strictly control the mass media or believe that they should be the only actors involved in public information campaigns, then, social marketing interventions confront many problems. There has been a growing sensitivity to the problems of the universal application of strategies that were successful in specific contexts. In countries where political and cultural factors limit participation and maintain hierarchical relationships, participatory approaches might be difficult to implement as they require a long-term and highly political process of transformation. This does not mean that participation should be abandoned as a desirable goal but that interventions that aim to mobilise communities necessarily adopt different characteristics in different circumstances. Public service announcements may be perceived as contradicting official power and policies. When access to national media is limited or extremely conditional, grassroots strategies such as community participation and local media could offer an alternative. But if populations are afraid of participating for fear of repression or because of past frustrations, then participatory approaches face clear obstacles and may not be advisable.

■ Integration of "top-down" and "bottom-up" approaches

Faced with different scenarios and choices, the growing consensus is that a multiple approach that combines "top-down" and "bottom-up" interventions is recommended. Here it becomes evident that development communication has gone beyond transmission models focused on implementing behaviour changes through communication activities. The Iringa Nutrition Improvement Programme in Tanzania has been mentioned as a successful example of integrating media advocacy, social mobilisation and social marketing (FPRI 1994). The programme included the mobilisation of different groups at different levels, community participation, media advocacy to popularise the goals of fighting malnutrition and child mortality, and social marketing to raise awareness among all sectors of the populations. It included "child growth monitoring, strengthening the health infrastructure, health education and women's activities." Government commitment, long-term sustainability of the programme and antipoverty efforts have been mentioned as decisive in contributing to its success in reducing malnutrition despite larger economic problems. Environmental factors such as a tradition of grassroots participation and national policies that dramatically increased literacy were crucial for the success of the programme.

■ Integration of multimedia and interpersonal communication

■ Much of the current thinking is that successful interventions combine media channels and interpersonal communication. Against arguments of powerful media effects that dominated development communication in the past, recent conclusions suggest that blending media and interpersonal channels is fundamental for effective interventions (Flay & Burton 1990; Hornik 1989).

The media are extremely important in raising awareness and knowledge about a given problem (Atkin & Wallack 1990). The media are able to expose large numbers of people to messages and generate conversation among audiences and others who were not exposed (Rogers 1998). But it would be wrong to assume that development mainly or only requires media channels. Because social learning and decision-making include considering media messages, and listening and exchanging opinions with a number of different sources, as Bandura (1994) suggested, interventions cannot solely resort to the mass media. Although television, radio and other media are important in disseminating messages, social networks are responsible for the diffusion of new ideas (Rogers & Kincaid 1981, Valente et al, 1994). Entertainment-education programming is one way, for example to activate social networks and peer communication in the diffusion of information (Rogers et al. 1999). Similarly, information given through the media is also important in raising awareness and knowledge as integrated into peer conversations and in contacts with field workers (Mita & Simmons 1995, Ogundimu 1994).

According to McKee (1992), interpersonal communication and the actions of community workers account for much of the success of several projects. Nothing can replace community involvement and education in the effective dissemination of information. Media-centred models are insufficient for behaviour change. McKee argues that the most successful strategies in family planning, HIV/AIDS, nutritional and diarrhoea programmes have involved multiple channels,

1927
1960
1963
1964
1967
1969
1970
1971
1972
1973
1974
1975
1976
1977
1978
1979
1980
1981
1982
1983
1984
1985
1986
1987
1988
1989
1990
1991
1992
1993
1994
1995
1996
1997
1998
1999
2000
2001
2002
2003
2004
2005
2006

including strong, community-based programming, networks, peer counselling, and government and NGO field workers. Successful initiatives attest to the fact that redundancy and multiple channels should be used. The media have powerful effects only indirectly by stimulating peer communication and thus making it possible for messages to enter social networks and become part of everyday interactions. Without disputing the value of interpersonal communication, McDivitt, Zimick and Hornik (1997) have stressed the importance of the mass media in behaviour change (also see Hornik 1988). In an evaluation of the impact of a vaccination campaign in the Philippines, they concluded that the media, rather than interpersonal channels, were responsible for changes in vaccination knowledge. Media exposure was sufficient to generate more knowledge about the specifics of the campaign and change in vaccinations without the intervention of social networks. It would be wrong, according to the researchers, to ignore the unmatched reach of the media, particularly among certain groups, in getting the message out. Mass media messages per se, however, do not explain the success of the campaign. The campaign provided specific information that mothers needed in order to engage in expected behaviours and other conditions (access to health centres, sufficient vaccine supplies) were also fundamental in making behaviour change possible.

■ Integration of personal and environmental approaches

The revision of traditional health promotion strategies and the integration of social marketing and social mobilisation are examples of the tendency to integrate personal and environmental approaches.

Consider the "ecological approach" as an example in that direction as used in the North Karelia Project in Finland, the Minnesota Health programme and the Stanford Three Community study (Bowes 1997). This approach espouses organisational and environmental interventions and aims to be more comprehensive than efforts directed only at individuals or social

COMMUNICATION AS PROCESS
Excerpt from: *"From Modernization to Participation: The Past and Future of Development Communication in Media Studies"*
By Robert Huesca

More than any other aspect of the Latin American critique, the observation that communication was frequently conceptualized in static, rather than process, terms constituted the greatest challenge for development practitioners. Scholars from the North had been struggling with process models of communication since Berlo's (1960) work so convincingly argued in their favor. Yet Berlo's construction of the Sender-Message-Channel-Receiver model of communication demonstrated the tenacity of static, linear models that identified components amenable to survey research and development program design. It also demonstrated the elusiveness of the dynamic process nature of communication.

Latin American scholars introduced a phenomenological orientation, which radically altered the conceptualization, study and practice of development communication. Rather than focusing on the constituent parts of communication, Latin American scholars introduced more fluid and elastic concepts that centered on how-meaning-comes-to-be in its definition. Drawing on the continent's proponents of phenomenology, Pasquali (1963) argued that knowledge of development needed to be generated phenomenologically, that is, through presuppositionless, intentional action in the world. This position undermined—on the most fundamental level—modernization approaches that assumed a separation between subject and object, researcher and development recipient. This more fluid and meaning-centered conceptualization of communication emphasized co-presence, intersubjectivity, phenomenological "being in the world," and openness of interlocutors. This view introduced a sophisticated epistemology arguing that the understanding of social reality is produced between people, in material contexts, and in communication. Freire (1973)

1927
1960
1963
1964
1967
1969
1970
1971
1972
1973
1974
1975
1976
1977
1978
1979
1980
1981
1982
1983
1984
1985
1986
1987
1988
1989
1990
1991
1992
1993
1994
1995
1996
1997
1998
1999
2000
2001
2002
2003
2004
2005
2006

action (McLeroy et al. 1988; Glanz & Rimer 1995). Nonbehavioural factors such as unemployment, poverty and lack of education are included as part of the broad view that ecological approaches encompass. Health promotion should be integrated into existing social systems such as schools, health delivery systems and community organisations. The mentioned projects required coordination among a variety of intermediate agencies that acted as liaisons between developers of health promotion innovation and potential adopters. The focus is still on behaviour change, but programmes feature environmental supports to encourage individuals to adopt and maintain changes. Similarly, community participation approaches have recognised the need to promote a "holistic approach" that integrates the contributions of both personal behaviour change and broader environmental changes in facilitating health improvement (Minkler 1999).

"Communication for Social Change" (CFSC) is another example of recent efforts to integrate different theories and approaches in development communication (Rockefeller Foundation 1999). Whereas traditional interventions were based on behaviour change models, CFSC relies on participatory approaches in emphasising the notion of dialogue as central to development. Development is conceived as involving work to "improve the lives of the politically and economically marginalised" (1998, 15). In contrast to the sender-receiver, information-based premises of the dominant paradigm, it stresses the importance of horizontal communication, the role of people as agents of change, and the need for negotiating skills and partnership. Another important contribution of CFSC is to call attention to the larger communication environment surrounding populations. In contrast to behaviour change and participatory theories

captured the sense of the phenomenological orientation toward communication writing:

> One's consciousness, intentionality toward the world, is always consciousness of, and in permanent movement toward reality. ...This relationship constitutes, with this, a dialectical unity in which knowing-in-solidarity is generated in being and vice versa. For this reason, both objectivist and subjectivist explanations that break this dialectic, dichotomizing that which is not dichotomizable (subject-object), are not capable of understanding reality. (p. 85)

In other words, traditional development approaches of "understanding reality" through the unilateral definition of problems, objectives and solutions were criticized as violating the very essence of communication.

Pasquali (1963) went as far as stating that the notion of "mass communication" was an oxymoron and that Latin American media constituted an "information oligarchy" that cultivated a social context characterized by "communicational atrophy." Though his analysis was aimed at issues of media and culture broadly, the kinds of development communication projects typical of the period were consistent with his analysis. This fundamental

criticism of static models of communication led to calls in development to abandon the "vertical" approaches of information transmission and to adopt "horizontal" projects emphasizing access, dialogue and participation (Beltrán 1980). The Latin American critique of the dominant paradigm as an extension of domination and the call for more egalitarian and responsive approaches to development were followed by a robust body of research into "participatory communication," which has emerged as the most influential concept in the subsequent decades.

References

Beltrán, L.R. 1980. "A farewell to Aristotle: 'Horizontal' Communication," *Communication* 5:5–41.

Berlo, D. 1960. *The Process of communication: An Introduction to Theory and Practice.* San Francisco: Holt, Rinehart and Winston.

Freire, P. 1973. *¿Extensión o comunicación?* L. Ronzoni, trans. Buenos Aires: Siglo XXI.

Pasquali, A. 1963. *Comunicación y cultura de masas.* Caracas: Universidad Central de Venezuela.

Huesca, R. 2003. "From Modernization to Participation: The Past and Future of Development Communication In Media Studies." In: A.N. Valdivia, ed., *A Companion to Media Studies.* Malden, Mass.: Blackwell Publishing. 50–71. Reprinted with permission of author and copyright holder.

that, for different reasons, pay little, if any, attention to the wide organisation of information and media resources, CFSC calls attention to the relevance of ongoing policy and structural changes in providing new opportunities for communication interventions. Unlike neodependency theories that negatively view worldwide changes in media and information industries as stimulating a process of power concentration, CFSC offers a mixed evaluation. It recognises that transformations open possibilities for community-based, decentralised forms of participation, but also admits that some characteristics of contemporary media are worrisome in terms of the potential for social change. CFSC views changes in health and in quality of life in general in terms of citizens' empowerment, a notion that became more relevant in behaviour change models (Hornik 1997).

But unlike participatory theories, CFSC stresses the need to define precise indicators to measure the impact of interventions. It is particularly sensitive to the expectations of funding agencies to find results of interventions, and to the needs of communities to provide feedback and actively intervene in projects. Here accountability, a concept that is also fundamental in contemporary global democratic projects, is crucial to development efforts. Projects should be accountable to participants in order to improve and change interventions and involve those who are ultimately the intended protagonists and beneficiaries. Because the intended goals are somewhat different from behaviour change approaches, then, it is necessary to develop a different set of indicators that tell us whether changes are achieved (although certainly some measurements traditionally used in health interventions are useful too). The goals are not only formulated in terms that could perfectly fit health promotion/social marketing/behaviour change theories (e.g., elimination of HIV/AIDS, lower child and maternal mortality) but also in broader social terms such as eradicating poverty and violence, and increasing employment and gender equality. These goals express a more comprehensive understanding of development that is not limited to "better health and well-being" but is aware of the need to place traditional approaches in larger social and environmental contexts.

Despite the cross-pollination of traditions and a multistrategy approach to interventions, the rift between behaviour change and participatory approaches and theories still characterises the field. The divisions are less pronounced than a few decades ago given the integration of different strategies discussed in the previous section, but are still important.

For participatory and advocacy approaches, behaviour change models are still associated with a certain scientific paradigm that is questionable on several grounds. Behaviour change models are based on premises that do not necessarily translate to developing countries (Stetson & Davis 1999). From a perspective influenced by recent theoretical developments in the social sciences, particularly postcolonial and postmodernist thinking, critics have challenged Western models of rationality and knowledge that inform behaviour change models. What is necessary is to change the traditional perspective according to which "traditional cultures" are backward and antithetical to development interventions. Because what populations know is considered wrong, local knowledge is viewed as an obstacle and unnecessary in development interventions. Overcoming ethnocentric conceptions is crucial. It requires a recognition that understandings of information and knowledge are different. Interventions also need to be sensitive to the fact that local cultures do not necessarily fit philosophical assumptions about individual rationality that are embedded in traditional models. Sense-making practices that are found in the developing world contradict key premises of behaviour change models. These models assume that individuals engage in certain actions after weighing costs and benefits of the action. Whereas individual interest and achievement are the underlying premises of those models, non-rationalistic forms of knowledge, as well community values, are central to non-Western cultures.

Critics charge behaviour change models for being focused on individual changes while underplaying (or minimising) the need to instrument larger political transformations that affect the quality of life. They call attention to the organisational structures that inhibit the successful implementation of projects for social change (Wilkins 1999). The concentration of information resources worldwide, the growing power of advertising in media systems and the intensification of inequalities that underlie the persistence of development problems require more than ever an examination of structural-political factors. Media systems have changed dramatically in the last decades. These changes, however, have been particularly revolutionary in the non-Western world as privatisation and liberalisation of media systems radically transformed the production, distribution and availability of information resources.

Behaviour change models have recognised the merits of insights from participatory approaches as well as the need to be sensitive to media access and new technologies (Piotrow et al. 1997). They continue to be mainly concerned with refining analytical and evaluation instruments and measuring the success of different intervention strategies. One of the main tasks is to identify the impact of communication/information campaigns in the context of other factors that affect behaviour (Hornik 1997). The integration of social mobilisation and social marketing strategies has been found to be successful and a positive referent for future interventions (McKee 1992).

The realisation that communities should be the main actors of development communication may constitute a starting point for further integration. Likewise, efforts to integrate theories and strategies that recognise that media campaigns are insufficient without community participation, that social marketing efforts are weak without environmental changes and that community empowerment might be the ultimate goal to guarantee sustainable development are encouraging in promoting dialogue among different theories and traditions.

Bibliography

Atkin C. & Wallack L. (Eds.) (1990) *Mass Communication and Public Health: Complexities and Conflicts*. Newbury Park: Sage Publications.

Bandura, A. (1977) *Social learning theory*. Englewood Cliffs, NJ: Prentice Hall.

Bandura, A. (1989) "Perceived self-efficacy in the exercise of control over AIDS infection. In V.M. Mays, G.W. Albee, & S.S. Schneider (Eds.), *Primary prevention of AIDS: Psychological approaches* (pp. 128-141). Newbury Park, CA: Sage.

Bowes, J.E. (1997) "Communication and community development for health information: Constructs and models for evaluation." www.nnlm.nlm.nih.gov/pnr/eval/bowes/

Carey, J.W. (1989) *Communication as culture : essays on media and society*. Boston: Unwin Hyman.

FPRI Report (1994) Seminar Series Focuses on Successful Nutrition Programs, 16, 2, www.cgiar.org/ifpri/reports/0694RPT/0694e.htm

Flay, B.R. & Burton, D. (1990) "Effective mass communication strategies for health campaigns." C. Atkin & Wallack, L. (Eds.) *Mass communication & public health* (129-145).

Fox, E. (N.D.) "Conductismo y Comunicación Social Hacia Dónde Nos Llevó?"

Gibson, Cynthia (N.D.) "Strategic communications for health and development." Typescript.

Glanz K. & Rimer B.K. (1995) *Theory at a glance*. Washington: National Institute of Health.

Hornik, R.C. (1989) "Channel effectiveness in development communication programs." Rice, R.E. & Atkin, C. K. (Eds.) *Public information campaigns*, 2nd edition, (pp. 309-330). Newbury Park: Sage.

Hornik, R.C. (1997) "Public health education and communication as policy instruments for bringing about changes in behaviour." Goldberg, M, Fishbein, M & Middlestadt S. (Eds), *Social marketing* (pp. 45-60). Mahwah, NJ: Lawrence Erlbaum.

Inkeles A. & Smith D.H. (1974) *Becoming modern*. Cambridge, MA: Harvard University Press.

Kincaid, L. (1988) "The convergence theory of communication: Its implications for intercultural communication." Y.Y. Kim (Ed.) *Theoretical perspectives on international communication*. Beverly Hills, CA: Sage.

McKee, Neill (1999) *Social Mobilization & Social Marketing in Developing Communities: Lessons for Communicators*. Southbound.

McLeroy, K.R., Bibeau, D., Steckler, A & Glanz, K. (1988) "An ecological perspective on health promotion programs," *Health education quarterly*, 15, 4, 351-377.

Melkote, S.R. (1991) *Communication for development in the Third world*. Newbury Park: Sage.

Minkler, M. (1999) "Personal responsibility for health? A review of the arguments and the evidence at century's end," *Health education & behaviour*, 26 (1), 121-140.

Mita, R. & Simmons, R. (1995) "Diffusion of the culture of contraception: Program effects on young women in rural Bangladesh," *Studies in family planning*, 26 (1), 1-13.

Moemeka, A.A. (Ed.) (1994) *Communicating for development: A new pan-disciplinary perspective*. Albany, NY: State University of New York Press.

1927
1960
1963
1964
1967
1969
1970
1971
1972
1973
1974
1975
1976
1977
1978
1979
1980
1981
1982
1983
1984
1985
1986
1987
1988
1989
1990
1991
1992
1993
1994
1995
1996
1997
1998
1999
2000
2001
2002
2003
2004
2005
2006

Ogundimu, F. (1994) "Communicating knowledge of immunization for development: A case study from Nigeria," in Moemeka, A.A. (Ed.) *Communicating for development* (219-243).

Piotrow, P.T., Kincaid, D.L., Rimon, J.G., Rinehart, W. (1997) *Health communication: Lessons from family planning and reproductive health.* Westport, CT: Praeger.

Rockefeller Foundation (1999) *Communication for social change: A position paper and conference report.* New York: Rockefeller Foundation.

Rogers, E.M. (1998) "When the mass media have strong effects: Intermedia processes." In Judith Trent (Ed.), *Communication: Views from the helm for the twenty-first century* (pp. 276-285). Boston: Allyn and Bacon.

Rogers, E.M. & Kincaid, D.L. (1981) *Communication networks: A paradigm for new research.* New York: Free Press.

Rogers, E.M., Vaughan, P.W., Swalehe, R.M.A., Rao, N., Svenkerud, P. & Sood, S. (1999) "Effects of an entertainment-education radio soap opera on family planning behaviour in Tanzania," *Studies in family planning,* 30 (3), 193-211.

Servaes, J. (1996) "Introduction: Participatory communication and research in development settings." Servaes, J., Jacobson, T. & White, S.A. (Eds.), *Participatory communication for social change.* Thousand Oaks: Sage.

Servaes, J. (1996) "Communication for Development in a Global Perspective: The Role of Governmental and Non-Governmental Agencies," *Communications,* 21 (4), 407-418.

Stetson, V. & Davis, R. (1999) *Health education in primary health care projects: A critical review of various approaches.* Core group.

Valente, T., Kim, Y.M., Lettenmaier, C., Glass, W., & Dibba, Y. (1994) "Radio Promotion of Family Planning in the Gambia," *International family planning perspectives* 20, 3, 96-104.

Wilkins, K.G. (1999) "Development discourse on gender and communication in strategies for social change," *Journal of communication,* 49(1), 46-.

Wisensale, S.K., Khodair, A.A. (1998) "The two-child family: The Egyptian model of family planning," *Journal of comparative family studies,* 29 (3), 503-516.

Zimicki S.; Hornik R.C.; Verzosa C.C.; Hernandez J.R.; de Guzman E.; Dayrit M.; Fausto A.; Lee M.B., Abad M. (1994) "Improving vaccination coverage In urban areas through a health communication campaign: The 1990 Philippine experience," *Bulletin of the World Health Organization* 72 (3), 409-22.

Waisbord, Silvio. "Towards a Theoretical and Empirical Convergence? Family Tree of Theories, Methodologies and Strategies in Development." Paper prepared for The Rockefeller Foundation, 2002. Copyright © 2002, Communication for Social Change Consortium and the Rockefeller Foundation. Used under a license agreement.

LOOKING BACKWARD/LOOKING FORWARD
Excerpt from: "From Modernization to Participation:
The Past and Future of Development Communication in Media Studies"
By Robert Huesca

2003

The history of development communication in media studies is marked by conceptual struggles and complexities that have advanced both theory and practice while leaving a number of conflicts unresolved. These struggles and complexities are not unique to development communication, but they also parallel similar issues in the larger field of media studies. Early modernization theories, followed by the Latin American critique and subsequent rise of participatory communication, reflect many of the same concerns that emerged from the effects of tradition challenged by critical theorists and leading to both political economic and cultural studies. Issues regarding individual-psychological versus cultural-contextual orientations, quantitative versus qualitative methods, and value-free versus power-laden positions have marked the conceptual advancements of both development communication and media studies. Moreover, criticisms of linear transmission models of communication have created greater sensitivity to process, meaning-centered conceptualizations of the relationship between media and society. While these struggles and contributions have reshaped communication methods, theories and practices, the future direction of research continues to be debated.

Despite a lack of consensus regarding the future of development communication, a robust interest has arisen from the notion of participatory communication. Emerging from the Latin American critique of modernization approaches to development, participatory communication has been embraced by scholars of diverse backgrounds and interests. Indeed, participatory communication appears to be an elastic notion amenable to research approaches that embrace contrasting, and even conflicting, ontological, epistemological and ethical assumptions. Proponents of entertainment education, for example, maintain empiricist and administrative methods and goals while drawing on notions of the active audience and textual openness to guide communication strategies and theoretical interpretations. Critics of this approach rightfully question its conceptual integrity, noting that social marketing approaches to texts and audiences through the use of surveys and focus groups are fundamentally inconsistent with notions of co-presence, dialogue and process that formed the basis of the critique of the dominant paradigm. Meanwhile, proponents of grassroots communication and alternative media embrace interpretive and cultural methods and goals that invest local participants with understanding and agency in the planning, execution and evaluation of development projects. Critics of this approach legitimately note its cultural relativism and social and institutional naiveté regarding local distributions of power and global arrangements of media ownership. The challenge facing scholars of development communication is to address the weaknesses and contradictions apparent in the diverse approaches to participatory communication while building on the achievements of research to date.

A major impediment to the advancement of scholarship in this area, however, is the political, economic and institutional context surrounding development efforts today. Referred to variously by terms such as "neoliberal," "postindustrial," and "globalization," this context is marked by deregulation and privatization accompanied by a retracting role of the state and traditional institutions (Huesca 2001). This contextual shift has eliminated important forms of structural support on which development efforts have relied and has identified new priorities aimed at bringing individuals and populations into alignment with postcommunist societies and economies. Participatory communication projects often threaten this alignment because they attend explicitly to the distribution of power on the local level and call for its reconfiguration. The institutional reward system surrounding development communication efforts, therefore, will pressure scholars to adopt participatory approaches that tend to exacerbate conceptual inconsistencies that have emerged over the years.

Despite its challenges, the contemporary context of globalization and neoliberalism also presents reasons for optimism for the future of participatory communication research. Worldwide structural changes that have shifted authority away from states and traditional institutions have been facilitated by a global rhetoric acknowledging universal human rights, basic environmental protections, and respect for democracy. The rhetorical veneer accompanying the retraction of the authority of states and institutions has enabled an expanding civil society in the form of new social movements organized around issues and identities concerned with development problems. Scholarship of participatory communication for development is well positioned to apply its theoretical advancements in ways that take advantage of these emerging movements, which are characterized by decentralized structures and intense local involvement. Years of experience with dialogue, praxis, and communication-as-process in research design and methods have given participatory communication scholars a head-start at working with these new movements in ways that are consistent with their characteristics. Furthermore, the moral commitment to strive for social justice explicit in early denunciations of the dominant paradigm, coupled with recent studies advocating action research methods, provides scholars with concrete strategies for responding to some of the weaknesses identified in the participatory communication research to date.

An examination of the history of development communication provides many tools for guiding future research and practice in this area. Early critics of modernization approaches noted the close relationship between development communication research and the global system of post–World War II, capitalist expansion. That relationship is equally apparent today, albeit contemporized for a postcommunist world, and it threatens to undercut the advancements of scholars of participatory communication. Future researchers would be well advised to bear in mind the relationship of development communication theory and practice to larger political and economic structures to build successfully on the accomplishments of the past 30 years of scholarship.

References

Huesca, R. 2001. "Conceptual contributions of new social movements to development communication research." *Communication Theory* 11:415–433.

Huesca, R. 2003. "From Modernization to Participation: The Past and Future of Development Communication in Media Studies." In: A.N. Valdivia, ed. *A Companion to Media Studies*. Malden, Mass.: Blackwell Publishing. 50–71. Reprinted with permission of the publisher.

1927
1960
1963
1964
1967
1969
1970
1971
1972
1973
1974
1975
1976
1977
1978
1979
1980
1981
1982
1983
1984
1985
1986
1987
1988
1989
1990
1991
1992
1993
1994
1995
1996
1997
1998
1999
2000
2001
2002
2003
2004
2005
2006

EXCERPT FROM:
WHY COMMUNICATION?

By Colin Fraser and Sonia Restrepo-Estrada

1998 After starting out in a rather unstructured and piecemeal fashion, communication for development gradually became more ordered and professional, and more strategic in its application. This was, at least in part, because it began to draw on some of the precepts of marketing. The usual definition of marketing is "identifying a need and satisfying that need, with a profit." Its relevance to development lies precisely in that principle of identifying needs and satisfying them.

In the minds of many people, marketing, promotion and advertising have negative connotations linked to selling, and so they are often thought to be vulgar and commercial. It is often forgotten that marketing theory and practice draw on a mix of elements borrowed from the respected fields of anthropology, social psychology, behavioural science and communication theory. These are then linked to skilful use of communication media. True marketing sets out to discover unfulfilled demand, not to create demand, and its theoretical basis has nothing whatsoever to do with selling soap and cigarettes.

It was logical that some marketing specialists began to promote the idea that their methods could help to achieve social objectives. They could provide valuable insights into group behaviour, people's motivations, target audiences and their characteristics and into the design of media strategies and messages. Marketing specialists were particularly interested in the areas of health and nutrition, where they believed that their concepts and practices could be powerful allies in helping people to change their attitudes and behaviour. The essence of their logic was that if useful commercial products could be promoted by marketing techniques, why could the same techniques not be applied to social aims and behaviours? This concept came to be known as "social marketing." It could be defined as "identifying a social-economic need and helping people to satisfy it, for their own profit."

The main proponent of social marketing was Richard Manoff, the head of a successful New York marketing agency. He first became involved in public health and nutrition in 1965, when he was part of a U.S. delegation to Food and Agriculture Organization. A few years later he began to apply marketing techniques to promote changes in health practices, nutrition and family planning in a number of developing countries. Manoff's proposals and his expanding experience in social marketing caught the attention of several important development agencies, including WHO, UNICEF, and USAID. Since then, USAID's numerous programmes in communication for health and for population have been based almost entirely on social marketing strategies.

The health sector, in fact, has used social marketing more than others, but communication for various development sectors has now borrowed many social marketing principles and techniques, without necessarily using the whole package.

The first of these principles is audience segmentation, which is the practical recognition of the fact that people's beliefs, attitudes, aspirations and behaviour are conditioned by their circumstances. These include education, occupation, gender, social status, income and so on. It follows that under a broad generic tide, such as "rural women" or "fishermen," there will almost always be several distinct audience segments that need to be identified and worked with, in line with the specific communication and development objective.

Qualitative research is another marketing principle that has also been increasingly adopted by communication for development. It is used to determine audiences' perceptions, attitudes and motivations about a particular issue and what they consider to be obstacles and resistance points to any necessary changes in their practices. Another function is to find out how they express themselves, what terminology they use, what information channels they prefer and the importance and credibility each one has. This provides guidance on how to formulate messages to achieve maximum comprehension and acceptability by the audiences and on what media channels would best reach them.

Such research often reveals authoritative information sources that are not media per se, but other sectors within the community, especially opinion leaders. These sectors then become relay audiences who can be reached with appropriate information that they will pass on to the primary audiences. Furthermore, it is often found that behaviour patterns are being influenced by opinion leaders, and unless they change, there will be no change by the main target audience.

In practice, audience segmentation and qualitative research might work in the following way for promoting, say, family planning in rural areas in a Muslim country where the health sector is offering the necessary services. One might begin by singling out women who already have at least three children under the age of six as the primary target audience. Qualitative research with such women might show that they are interested in spacing their children and limiting their numbers. They want to be able to bring up their children properly and are concerned about specific aspects of their own health related to frequent childbearing. They want more information about the various family planning services and methods available. They use some particular phrases when talking about different aspects of family planning and health. They listen to the radio most days while they are preparing the evening meal, and this is the only media channel they use.

The women might also say that many of their husbands are resistant to family planning, or even hostile towards it, mainly because the religious authorities in the community are against it. The women might make it clear that they need their husbands' approval before they can go to a family planning clinic. Furthermore, it might emerge that for traditional reasons many of the women's elderly mothers are also against family planning.

In such circumstances, it would be a waste of effort mounting communication activities aimed only at women with at least three children under the age of six. Communication would also have to reach husbands, religious authorities and elderly women. Therefore, further qualitative research would be needed with these other audiences to determine the most suitable content of messages and the best channels for delivering them. For mothers who already had three children under six, it would already be known that the message content should be the various family planning services and methods available, health aspects should be stressed as motivation, and a suitable channel would be radio programmes when they were preparing the evening meal.

Focus group discussions (FGDs) are a classic technique for doing qualitative research. In brief, an FGD sets out to create a situation in which a small group of 8–12 people of the same social, economic and educational level, and who share similar lifestyles and problems, discuss a particular issue of concern. An FGD has a facilitator and an observer, both playing a low-profile role. The facilitator gets the process started and guides it gently with some predetermined, open-ended questions, usually beginning with factual matters, but gradually going into increasing depth and analysis. The key to the process is to get the group participants to discuss among themselves and not with the facilitator. The observer listens, watches the body language in the group, and takes notes of what is said.

The FGD technique may be informal and loosely structured, but with a skilful facilitator, it can generate a group interaction that is uniquely effective in penetrating deep-seated attitudes and finding out how people's minds work about some specific issue. The process usually takes on aspects that are similar to group therapy.

FGDs have been used for several years for participatory analysis with people concerned with health issues. The agricultural sector has lagged behind, but we have used them in a variety of agricultural situations, from

1927
1960
1963
1964
1967
1969
1970
1971
1972
1973
1974
1975
1976
1977
1978
1979
1980
1981
1982
1983
1984
1985
1986
1987
1988
1989
1990
1991
1992
1993
1994
1995
1996
1997
1998
1999
2000
2001
2002
2003
2004
2005
2006

large-scale farmers in Argentina to bare subsistence farmers in Zambia, Uganda and Bolivia. In all cases, they have provided a wealth of useful information that can be used to help farmers to help themselves and to plan what outside assistance is needed.

Another feature of social marketing is careful message design to appeal to the concerns and perspectives of the specific audience segments. In the Muslim country of our earlier example, strategic message design for the religious leaders resisting family planning might involve selecting passages from the Koran relating to the moral obligation to preserve life and setting these against the mortality of mothers and babies during childbirth. One might also use the passages that refer to proper child care, set against the difficulties of caring for large numbers of children. This material, when woven into messages for the religious authorities, could provide legitimacy for family planning and help persuade them to support it. Real examples of communication with religious leaders will be found in Chapters 3 and 6.

Pretesting of communication materials with groups that are representative of the target audience before putting them in final form for broadcasting or distribution is another social marketing principle. It helps to ensure that the materials are comprehensible and that their messages are appropriate for the specific audience.

Other key principles of social marketing are monitoring, feedback and adjustment. Even after good qualitative research and pretesting of materials, one needs to confirm that the communication activities are on course. So, continuous monitoring and feedback are conducted to check that the messages are being received, understood and accepted by the intended audience. Any misunderstandings or undesired effects being caused by the messages and materials are corrected.

A good example of this process took place in Honduras some years ago when a USAID-supported programme for oral rehydration therapy (ORT) for infants was under way. The rehydration solution was called Litrosol and it was intensely promoted by communication media. However, ongoing monitoring with mothers revealed that most of them thought there were two different types of diarrhoea that affected their children. They had local names for each, and they were only giving their children Litrosol for what they perceived as one of these types of diarrhoea. The communicators wanted to adjust their media messages and use both the local diarrhoea names but the doctors refused to let them, on the grounds that to do so would reinforce unfounded, traditional beliefs. The compromise solution was to recast the messages to say that Litrosol was good for all sorts of diarrhoea attack.

Even if marketing has provided communicators for development with better organised and systematic approaches, there are many who abhor social marketing. They consider it to be top-down and manipulative, for they say that it uses refined social science skills and powerful mass media to try to change people's behaviour patterns to conform to criteria established by outsiders with superior knowledge. On the other hand, those who defend social marketing point out that few development interventions, even those based on community participation, do not involve manipulation of some groups by others. There may also be manipulation within peer groups. Furthermore, even in socially advanced and democratic countries, such as Denmark or Sweden, governments are constantly issuing manipulatory exhortations to their people to use car seat-belts, to eat more bread and less fat or not to drink and drive.

Those in favour of social marketing also argue that the themes to which it is applied are usually of undoubted health or social benefit, and seen in this light, some of its protagonists jokingly call it "ethical manipulation." They consider that it is morally defensible to use all the skills—and even wiles—available to us to induce behavioural change when it concerns, for example, reducing infant mortality, curbing teenage pregnancies or preventing the spread of infectious diseases such as AIDS.

The truth about the merits or otherwise of social marketing surely lies somewhere between the extreme positions for and against it. Those who state that there are certain behaviour patterns that should be changed, in the interests of people themselves and of society in general, certainly have a point. Most of these desirable changes lie in the areas of health, nutrition and safety. AIDS is a good example. Limiting the spread of HIV is undoubtedly of vital importance to individuals and to society, and this must surely justify any form of communication, manipulatory or not, to try to change behaviour. The real ethical problem with social marketing would be evident if it were used to manipulate people towards a behavioural change, or the adoption of an innovation, without the total certainty that it was in their interests and in the interests of society to do so.

As an illustration, taken from UNICEF area of work, one can hardly object to social marketing to promote the use of ORT to save infants from death. However, to use it to persuade a group of women to adopt a particular income-generating activity would be an unjustifiable imposition; and it would be dangerous too because it might fail, with long-term negative consequences. In such circumstances, a communication process without a predetermined behavioural objective should be used to help the women analyse the alternatives and make their own decision about what they want to do and can do.

Overall, marketing has provided communication for development with a number of valuable strategies and techniques, and they can be used without relation to top-down approaches or the persuasive inducing of behavioural change. Qualitative research, audience segmentation, proper message design, pretesting of communication materials and ongoing feedback are valuable tools in any communication activity.

Communication in Today's Development Strategies

Marketing certainly provided a number of approaches and techniques, but it was the notion of "bottom-up" development and the aim of achieving participation that caused the greatest evolution in the conceptual aspects of communication and its potential role. Many of the early practitioners of communication soon propounded the view that there is a direct connection between communication and true participation—in effect, that they are two sides of the same coin. Indeed, before people of a community can participate, they must have appropriate information, and they must follow a communication process to reach a collective perception of the local situation and of the options for improvement.

However, people often have difficulty in conceptualising and articulating their view of their problems, needs and possibilities, especially in poor communities of low educational levels. Nor do they have access to the information they need to form rational opinions and to take coherent decisions. Hence the usefulness of communication inputs, which may use media such as video recording and playback, or local radio broadcasts, or just group communication work with simple aids such as flip charts. In reality, when communication processes are used to inform people, enable them to contribute their points of view, reach consensus and carry out an agreed change or development action together, it can be said that communication is participation.

The need for people to acquire new knowledge and skills is as important as ever in development programmes, but information and training activities should be based on people's interests and needs, as identified in consultation with them. The traditional role of audiovisual media to improve the effectiveness of information and training programmes is obviously still as valid as ever. Great progress has been made, and experience gained, in using what were once considered delicate and sophisticated media, such as video, with local populations in harsh technical environments, as described in Chapter 4. Much has also been learned about how to structure and present information to make it accessible to people of low educational levels.

Bottom-up and participatory development approaches have introduced changes in the way mass media should be used. Bombarding people with messages

1927
1960
1963
1964
1967
1969
1970
1971
1972
1973
1974
1975
1976
1977
1978
1979
1980
1981
1982
1983
1984
1985
1986
1987
1988
1989
1990
1991
1992
1993
1994
1995
1996
1997
1998
1999
2000
2001
2002
2003
2004
2005
2006

has gone out, at least in principle. Greater access to the media by ordinary people and participation in programming, have become the aim. For example, in the area of broadcasting, more emphasis is now placed on community media, with much participation from the audience in the programming.

Similarly, improving interpersonal communication between development workers in the field and their client populations has become necessary. This is in the sense of making field workers more effective facilitators of change, listening more than they talk and helping people to help themselves, as opposed to making them better preachers of some development sermon.

Qualitative research techniques, such as focus group discussions, used originally just to investigate people's perceptions and attitudes, have been found to be a perfect technique for participatory diagnosis of problems, planning and evaluation with communities.

In general terms, for today's change and development strategies, the communication aims are, first, to stimulate debate and "conscientisation" for participatory decision making and action, and second, to help people acquire the new knowledge and skills they need. A third aim is to use communication to promote better teamwork, cooperation and coordination between various governmental, or nongovernmental, organisations involved in multidisciplinary development programmes.

Is Communication for Change and Development Utopian?

Some people may think that communication strategies for democratic decision making, change and development are too idealistic to be put into practice and that they have little relevance in the reality of today's world. Fortunately, however, there have been a number of experiences to prove that these concepts can be made to work.

The first of these noteworthy experiences took place in Canada, which has always been a leader in communication for development. As long ago as the 1930s, Canada pioneered radio programming for farmers and organised group listening, or Radio Farm Forums as they were called. These later became the model for numerous rural broadcasting projects in developing countries. Equally innovative was the setting up of a unit in the mid-1960s called Challenge for Change, as part of the Canadian National Film Board. The objective of this unit was to use film—and video when it became available later—for social development purposes. When Challenge for Change became involved in a place called Fogo Island, off the east coast of Newfoundland, the experience proved so important that it set a precedent for much communication for development in the future.

In the late 1960s, Fogo Island was in serious economic and social decline. Its people lived mainly from fishing, but their boats were small and their markets on the island were limited. Mainland-based fleets were able to roam further and had assured markets for their catch when they returned to port. This and other factors had led to such a decline in Fogo that the provincial government began working on a proposal to help the inhabitants evacuate to the mainland. At that point, the Extension Department of Memorial University of Newfoundland, in St Johns, and Challenge for Change stepped in and asked if they could carry out an experiment on the island.

On arriving on Fogo, the team told the islanders that they would like to make some films with them and show them to the community. They assured the people that no films would be taken away from the island without their permission and that anyone interviewed on camera would have a chance to see the resulting film first and have changes made before it was shown to anybody else.

They began to shoot films in pairs, usually to show both sides of an argument concerning the future of the island. For example, they made one film with a young man who explained why he was convinced that the only hope he had of making good in life was to leave for the mainland. They made the opposing film with another young man who had managed to build a long-lasting fishing boat, was content with his life and had no desire to leave.

These and many other films, and later videos, were shown to the community during evening meetings to spark off a debate. The results were striking. People argued and became emotional, but they also became involved in a serious analysis of the situation affecting their community. In addition, the filmed interviews drew attention to excellent insights and ideas held by people who would normally not have had the chance or the inclination to express them in public.

Over the months, what communicators have come to call the "Fogo Process" took hold. The people began to see themselves and their situation more clearly. The films were providing a mirror image, and the discussions that followed were opening their minds to problems and their causes and to possible courses of action. In effect, this was the same sort of process as "conscientisation," invented by Paolo Freire at about the same time.

The culmination on Fogo was that the people were able to develop a well-articulated proposal to stay on the island, but with help from the provincial government to provide certain key things to make it possible. For example, they required training facilities for young fishermen, credit to build fishing boats and so on. The authorities were able to meet the requests, and the people decided not to leave the island.

The imaginative way communication media were used to stimulate this process of participatory problem diagnosis and development planning remains a shining example of what can be done. One must raise one's hat to the team who worked in Fogo, and equally to the Canadian authorities who were willing to listen to the people and help them with development as they, the people, wanted it.

This and similar experiences in development are important because they illustrate that the essence of involving and mobilising people is the sharing of knowledge and ideas between them, and between them and development workers, through communication processes. Such sharing of knowledge implies an exchange between communication equals: On the one hand, technical specialists and the authorities learn about people's needs and possibilities, as they see them, and on the other, people learn of the ideas of the specialists and the authorities. The ultimate purpose of knowledge sharing is to help people develop the capacity to take increasing control over their environment, agriculture, health, habitat, family size and the other factors that so critically impinge on their quality of life.

The Functions of Communication for Development

In practical terms, communication for development has three separate but related components: social communication, educational communication and institutional communication.

SOCIAL COMMUNICATION

In the community, social communication promotes dialogue, reflection, participatory situation analysis, consensus building, decision making and planning of actions for change and development. In essence, it is the process of mobilising people and communities, and helping them to gain the insights and confidence needed to tackle their problems. It is also used for participatory monitoring and evaluation. It may employ audiovisual media to stimulate the process of group discussion and to record the outcome, but it may also be conducted using aids such as simple flip charts to help people visualise and keep track of the points of the discussion as they go along. Mass media services may support the process, and even become involved in it, especially when they are locally based. Traditional media, such as theatre, music and dance, can also be successfully used.

EDUCATIONAL COMMUNICATION

Educational communication is used to help people acquire the knowledge and skills they need to be able to put change and development decisions into

1927
1960
1963
1964
1967
1969
1970
1971
1972
1973
1974
1975
1976
1977
1978
1979
1980
1981
1982
1983
1984
1985
1986
1987
1988
1989
1990
1991
1992
1993
1994
1995
1996
1997
1998
1999
2000
2001
2002
2003
2004
2005
2006

action. It takes educational content from specialists and presents it in various media forms, particularly using audiovisual technology, to help people understand, learn and remember. It is an essential element in training programmes at all levels.

INSTITUTIONAL COMMUNICATION

Institutional communication creates the flows of information inside and between all the partners involved in a development action, including government departments, parastatal organisations, NGOs and the communities. The aim is to improve coordination and management by creating a common understanding among the various partners of the project's objectives, activities and progress. Such common understanding is the basis for good teamwork.

The point needs to be made that despite the increasing use of the word "communication" in many countries to cover the press and public relations functions of a corporation or institution, the concepts of communication that we present here have nothing whatsoever to do with institutional image building. That said, we might sum up with a definition:

Communication for development is the use of communication processes, techniques and media to help people towards a full awareness of their situation and their options for change, to resolve conflicts, to work towards consensus, to help people plan actions for change and sustainable development, to help people acquire the knowledge and skills they need to improve their condition and that of society, and to improve the effectiveness of institutions.

Fraser, Colin and Sonia Restrepo-Estrada. "Why Communication?" Colin Fraser and Sonia Restrepo-Estrada. 1998. *Communicating for Development: Human Change for Survival.* London and New York: I.B. Tauris. Copyright © 1998 Colin Fraser and Sonia Restrepo-Estrada. Reprinted with permission of Colin Fraser and Sonia Restrepo-Estrada.

EXCERPT FROM:

COMMUNICATION AT THE PACE OF THE PENDULUM: A HALF-CENTURY IN QUEST OF DEVELOPMENT
[LA COMUNICACIÚN AL RITMO DEL PÈNDULO: MEDIO SIGLO EN BUSCA DEL DESARROLLO]

By Carlos Eduardo Cortès S.

1997 The word "communication" derives from the Latin adjective *communis* (common), which gave rise to the verb *communicare* (to commune, in the sense of participating together or bringing into relationship), whence the nouns *commun-onis* (and our *communion*) and *communicationis* (our *communication*).

[By the 20th century], the communication field began to swell with models and paradigms that defined communication as a process of transmission, reducing the notion communication to the Procrustean bed of a model derived from mathematical physics, inspired by the telegraph and based on the functioning of the technological media. This twist of meaning proved so lasting that most definitions of communication today refer to senders, messages, channels, receivers and feedback, all within a governing context built around the technical functioning of the so-called "social communications media," whose still relatively novel appearance is now being magnified by the constant development of new data transmission technologies.

Indeed, according to the theory of economic and social modernization introduced by developmentism, the ability to introduce the common features of modern societies to traditional ones is attributable precisely to the expansion of the mass media. Thus, in the 1950s and 1960s, the work of researchers, such as Daniel Lerner, Lucien Pye, Wilbur Schramm and Everett Rogers, at MIT and Stanford, inspired profound optimism regarding the role communication would play in development. Communication-for-development models and planning for economic growth were extensively employed by government, and the professionalization of journalism emerged as a *sine qua non* of Latin American development.

Against this background, UNESCO launched its regional centers for the development of journalism in 1955, and provided support for the Ecuadorian government to create the *Centro Internacional de Estudios Superiores de Periodismo para América Latina* (the International Center for Advanced Studies in Journalism, or CIESPAL), which opened in October 1959. (The institution's self-definition and name shifted from "journalism" to "communications" in the 1970s.) From the start, CIESPAL sought to reduce the role of practical journalism and ensure that journalists had academic training. It offered hundreds of courses, and attempted to reshape the Latin American profession by proposing a curriculum model for schools of journalism within universities, with the content coming primarily from American and European UNESCO experts. This appropriation of foreign models fit perfectly with the expectations of developmentism (Cortés, 1995).

While American writers re-inforced the developmentist approach, which was organized around economic growth and built on production and consumption, a range of Latin American researchers began to consider the social consequences of these models. Paulo Freire, João Bosco Pinto, Antonio Pasquali, Juan Díaz Bordenave, Luis Ramiro Beltrán, Mario Kaplún and others turned on their own academic training, questioned the naïve assumptions under which they had begun to work in the 1950s, and produced original proposals that were to influence the future course of communications studies, not only in Latin America but worldwide. It was thanks to their efforts that the original meaning of *communicare* was recovered.

Their approach gained sufficient prestige to influence discussion within international organizations such as UNESCO, which had begun to dissect the dominant paradigm in the late 1970s. Their work led to a fruitful vein of critical thought that generated two lines of study, one based on a macro view of society, in which the communication-for-development model was replaced by a focus on national communications policies; the other based on a micro approach, in which the diffusionist model was replaced by alternative communication theory and practices that stressed self-management and participation (Fuentes, 1992; Bello et al., 1988).

Meanwhile, as the obsolescence of the dominant paradigm became clear, European and Latin American thinkers began to prefer modifications of the initial ideas of some communication-for-development experts. Everett Rogers (1976) explained that the role of mass communication in facilitating development has often been indirect and of a supporting nature, rather than direct and fundamental. Somewhat later, American thinkers adopted a number of ideas emerging from Latin America. Thus, Emile McAnany (1980) admitted a need to consider communication not as a simple independent variable, but simultaneously as a dependent and an independent variable in a complex framework of relationships with social, economic and political processes—though failing to consider one central aspect of communication research from the 1970s on, namely, the issue of culture and its relationship to communication processes.

It was in the mid-1980s, with the controversy following the Mac Bride Report *(One World, Many Voices)* and the *New World Order of Information and Communication* (NOMIC) proposal, that UNESCO experienced its greatest institutional crisis. The issues spotlighted included the right to information and expression, the need for balance in cross-border data flows and the question of the microelectronics industry and its relationship with the culture industries.

In 1985, the *Academy for Educational Development* (AED) conducted an assessment under a more suggestive title: "Beyond Flipcharts: Three Decades Of Development Communication." One of its main lines of argument related to the bias that affects a significant number of projects of this type: In general [it proposed],

1927
1960
1963
1964
1967
1969
1970
1971
1972
1973
1974
1975
1976
1977
1978
1979
1980
1981
1982
1983
1984
1985
1986
1987
1988
1989
1990
1991
1992
1993
1994
1995
1996
1997
1998
1999
2000
2001
2002
2003
2004
2005
2006

communicators group their activities around their preferred medium… Communication strategies… begin with a typical question: What can I do with radio? How can I use television to disseminate my message? The consequence of this bias was a narrow communications focus that led to promotions in the communications media, and to training programs and collective events that, on the surface, appear successful but produce no sustained change in [social] practices (Van Crowder, 1990; Rasmuson, et al., 1988: 6).

The Marketing Approach to Communication

A growing awareness of bias and of the fragmentary nature of current approaches to communication, along with the poor results of communicational developmentism, led many institutions that supported development—especially in the fields of health and nutrition—to attempt educational emulations of successful commercial and political marketing strategies. In 1969, Philip Kotler and his colleagues in the United States had begun to publish work on the application of marketing principles to non-commercial enterprises. Discussion of strategic marketing, expanded marketing, technical marketing communications, marketing of social causes and similar concepts ensued, leading to what is known today as "social marketing," the communications strategy probably most consistent with the neoliberal current of the 1980s, since it incorporated commercial market criteria and found inspiration in the success of American advertising agencies.

Social marketing somehow came to crystallize the hopes of the German geographer Friedrich Ratzel, who used the polysemic term *Verkehr* to describe the phenomenon of communication in 1897. *Verkehr* might mean commerce, relations, movement, circulation or mobility, prefiguring today's coexistence of market, information infrastructure, and economic and political power in a context of globalization (Mattelart, 1995).

The roots of social marketing lie in business's need to learn about customers' thinking, motivation and behavior, so as to convince them to buy more. The approach was driven by the development of mass industry, the appearance of supermarkets, the electronic media and advertising, and was based on work in behavioral theory (visual perception, conditioning, learning and the behavior of practical functioning). It assumes that people learn, and use products, as a result of repeated action, perceived need, imitation, assimilation of archetypal content, their need for self-affirmation, their need for a sense of belonging and the quest for security. With advertising as the starting point, this approach has been applied to education, factory work, anthropology and collective dissemination, as well as to macro projects in development (Pareja, 1988).

The marketing techniques developed in English-speaking countries are characterized by their pragmatism and their quest for short-term results. As in commercial and political advertising, heavy investments are made to create messages for large, but segmented, portions of a society and to deliver them at peak hours over long periods of time. For example, marketing campaigns are conducted in phases (expectation, launch and maintenance), with huge investments in advertising (inevitably passed on to the consumer through the price of the final goods or services), protected by the utmost care and planning.

As Rasmuson, et al. observe (1988), social marketing does not differ essentially from commercial marketing. It is based on the same analytical techniques (market research, product development, pricing, access, promotion and advertising) and can involve "selling" an idea or habit as easily as a product. Hence it is normally defined as including the design, execution and monitoring of programs aimed at increasing acceptance of a social idea or practice in a target group.

As a result, social marketing must be fundamentally oriented to the consumer, who is seen as the center of a process involving four variables: product, price, place and promotion. Thus, a good program is organized around careful analysis of each variable, with a strategy that considers the interaction of variables.

In particular, promotion requires more than just advertising. It necessitates a broader approach that educates the consumer in the proper use of products and that employs instructional design principles to teach the consumer complex attitudes. Thus, social marketing that incorporates educational components operates as a framework for selecting and segmenting consumers and for promoting products or services, though in theory it also includes behavioral analysis (research into current practices, specifying new practices and teaching them, and creating motivation for change) and anthropological methods (research into the perceptions and values behind the visible practice, since an understanding of these may help to design effective ways of introducing new practices).

To summarize these ideas from Rasmuson, et al. (1988: 9, 10, 11), communication for development requires a complex strategic vision, the ultimate object of which is to create long-term programs that produce specific sustained changes in the behavior of large populations through a process that includes phases of planning, intervention, monitoring and evaluation. The programs must be based on a solid foundation, since it is clear that:

■ Social products are often more controversial and more complex to use than commercial products;

■ Their benefits are usually less immediate;

■ Distribution channels for them are more difficult to use and control;

■ Their market is difficult to analyze;

■ Those for whom they are intended often have very limited resources;

■ The level of adoption or "sales" that they must attain is more demanding than in the case of commercial products (Rasmuson, et al., 1988: 11-20).

The Domain of the Campaigns

Social marketing, as it was introduced in Latin America, was generally crude, lacking in rigor, and without the technical and financial capacity needed to emulate successful commercial and political marketing. One reason for this was that media campaigns gained a great deal of autonomy and were employed to excess, while the strict logic of commercial marketing, with its sequence of phases, was disregarded. The understandably poor results thus reflected an entrenched and widespread planning problem in communication for development: an excessive faith in the use of media, and media alone, to achieve ostensibly educational ends.

Developmentism unfolded as a tendency to conceive of communications as a late stage in the educational process. Thus, communication became a sort of solution in search of problems. The result was intense communication activity organized according to highly deficient telegraphic models and without any attempt to become familiar with the communications issues of the environments involved—which would have required a planning process beginning with assessment.

The problem became much more visible with the boom in "educational" social marketing campaigns by Latin American governments and nongovernmental organizations. Almost always, the mass media were the chosen channel, and objectives usually involved solutions for problems that had been defined at the institutional level, without proper knowledge of communicational realities in the field. Based on insufficient study of the principles of social marketing, the campaigns were conceived as single, concentrated processes designed and targeted to inform certain segments of the population and persuade the population to adopt ideas, products or behaviors that the organizers considered desirable.

Nevertheless, the very nature of the campaigns as they were conceived obliged them to solve specific problems, so as to show results in the short term. Here they foundered, for there are no "specific problems" apart from context. Where communicating is concerned, this creates a drastic limitation, since the majority of the social problems that communications strategies aim to solve are not communications problems.

In short, communication can effectively support educational processes, as long as it does not attempt to solve problems that are beyond its means. For example, childhood malnutrition was addressed for many years through campaigns based on the belief that the malnutrition was attributable to misguided eating habits resulting from mothers' lack of dietary information. However, even well-informed mothers faced intractable problems, such as high prices, low wages, unemployment and disintegration of the family—aspects of underdevelopment that cannot be fully addressed by media campaigns (Díaz Bordenave, 1992).

The capacity of the Latin America market to change attitudes and behaviors has, in practice, always proven rather limited. Once a campaign is over, people tend to disregard the information it contained. Two main reasons for this emerge. First, there are the biases inherent in the design of communications campaigns, which fail to sufficiently consider technical and financial marketing requirements. Second is the lack of knowledge about target populations and the contexts in which the communications process is occurring.[1]

A considerable number of campaigns that regard themselves as "educational" by virtue of the fact that they use that word, though without having thought about what it implies, are (just barely) designed for the supposed value of the information their messages contain. Behind this partial understanding of the communication process lies the telegraph model with its inexplicable power to propagate and take root. Many of those responsible for communication and education programs seem to believe that the educational results of a message depend directly on its repetition in one or more media. Thus, communication planning is based on the Quixotic idea that means of dissemination are the only tool needed, making any consideration of context irrelevant.

Leaving aside the doubtful validity of the behaviorist principles behind instructional design and social marketing practices, it is a fact that the weakening of the nation state under neoliberalism has made it practically impossible for development projects (in particular, projects of government ministries), with their local reach and limited resources, to meet the requirements of a communications program conceived according to the demanding logic of social marketing.

This effectively functions as a point of no return, dooming many governmental and nongovernmental projects with communications components to conceptual and financial marginality. In assessments covering more than 10 years of training communicators, and in analyses of activities in the media and within institutions that work in the particular area of *health communication,* their problems are clear:

1. There are very few health communication experts in Latin America's educational institutions (universities, most notably), public- and private-sector organizations or collective dissemination media.
2. The great majority of those working in this field are ill-prepared for their task. As in the field of rural communications, extension workers and agronomists must generally play a role for which they become prepared only through practice or sporadic courses.
3. Few doctors are committed participants in health communication programs, which are generally run by less-educated people, or by people from other professions (public relations, nursing, social work).
4. The lack of training is manifest in a general ignorance regarding:

    4.1 The complexity of the communication process with its social actors, the content in play, institutions' responsibility for what they communicate, and the entire area of media and discourse;

    4.2 The way in which sectors of the population (especially the majorities to which a great deal of health communication programs are directed) experience and perceive health and disease;

---

1 A case study of one campaign may illustrate this weakness. During the first cholera-prevention campaign in Peru, which began in February of 1991, monitoring showed that although 85 percent of Peruvian families initially adopted the measures suggested, barely five percent continued to do so six months later (Vásquez, 1992).

4.3 The specific communications materials and activities required—and, even more important, the means of handling issues to be covered—in light of the daily life of the target population;

4.4 Appropriate formats and the general opportunities offered by the different communications media;

4.5 The real meaning of the material, which, to be understood, requires proper interpretive tools and a critical reading of the material produced;

4.6 Systems to test materials before deploying them on a mass scale;

4.7 The resources needed to monitor and assess health communication programs;

4.8 General ignorance of communications planning in health—principally as a result of the tendency to confuse communication with media campaigns, or with the sporadic production and distribution of materials (Prieto, 1994).

This latter issue represents significant risk: Cost-benefit analysis of many programs based on educational campaigns in the mass media reveals a surprising weakness in terms of medium- and long-term social consequences, despite the investment of very considerable funds and labor, which could only be justified by far more convincing results.

References

ALFONZO, Alejandro (1995). *Preparatory document for the joint UNESCO-UNFPA Program in Latin America and the Caribbean (Communication for Education in Population subprogram).* Quito: UNESCO, mimeograph.

AMSDEN, Alice H. (1997). *Corea: un proceso exitoso de industrialización tardía* [Korea: a successful process of belated industrialization]. Bogotá: Norma.

BELLO, Gilberto et al. (1988), *Concepciones de la comunicación y crisis teóricas en América Latina.* Dia-logos de la Comunicación [Theoretical concepts of communication and crisis in Latin America. Dia-logs in Communication]. (Lima: Felafacs), (20): 34-38

BELTRÁN, Luis Ramiro (1994), "La salud y la comunicación en Latinoamérica: políticas, estrategias y planes. [Health and communication in Latin America: Policies, strategies and plans]" in UNESCO/PAHO-WHO. *Por una política de comunicación para la Promoción de la Salud en América Latina* [Toward a policy on communication for health promotion in Latin America*]. Quito and Washington: UNESCO/PAHO-WHO.

—(1979), *La planificación de la comunicación para el desarrollo rural: un bosquejo histórico* [Planning in communication for rural development: an historical sketch]. Seminar on agricultural communication in rural development. Caracas, mimeograph.

CASTRO CAYCEDO, Germán (1997), *Tráfico de genes* [Traffic in genes]. Cambio 16 Colombia (187), January 13.

CHAMORRO MARÍN, Edgar and Rubén Nájera (1996), "Orígenes, evolución y perspectivas de la integración centroamericana [Origins, evolution and prospects of Central American integration]," in INCEP, *La integración como instrumento de desarrollo: sus perspectivas y desafíos para Centroamérica* [Integration as an instrument of development: its prospects and challenges for Central America]. Panorama Centroamericano (66), November-December, 29-104.

CORTÉS, Carlos Eduardo. "Educación, lenguaje y pensamiento visual [Education, language and visual thought]," in Gabriel Jaime Pérez, S.J. et al. *Comunicación, educación y cultura* [Communication, education and culture]. Bogotá: Cátedra Unesco de Comunicación Social – Pontificia Universidad Javeriana, Facultad de Comunicación y Lenguaje [UNESCO Chair in Social Communication—Pontificia Universidad Javeriana, School of Communication and Language] 1999.

—(1997a), "*No sólo de digitalizarse vive la radio* [There's more to radio than going digital]," paper presented at the "Radio and Culture" International Seminar for the working group on new technology. Asociación Latinoamericana de Educación Radiofónica [Latin American Association of Radio Education], ALER, Quito, mimeograph.

—(1997b), *Educación a distancia en el nuevo entorno tecnocultural* [Distance education in the new technocultural environment]. Chasqui (Quito: Ciespal), 58, 29-32.

—(1997c), "La prensa en la videosfera: identidad o renuncia [The press in the videosphere: preserving or relinquishing identity]," *Signo y Pensamiento* [Sign and Thought] (Bogotá: U. Javeriana), XVI, 30, 31-41.

—(1996a), *Legislación y desrregulación en el nuevo contexto* [Legislation and deregulation in the new context]. Chasqui (Quito: Ciespal), 56 (1996), 38-42.

—(1996b), "De la aldea global a la aldea corporativa: nuevos desafíos éticos a la libertad de expresión [From the global village to the corporate village: new ethical challenges to freedom of expression]," paper presented at Jornada Latinoamericana sobre los Retos a la libertad de expresión y nuevas posibilidades para su promoción y fortalecimiento en América Latina [Latin American workshop on the challenges to freedom of expression and new possibilities for its promotion in Latin America], UNESCO, Radio Netherlands Training Center (RNTC), Facultad Latinoamericana de Ciencias Sociales [Latin American School of Social Sciences] (FLACSO, Ecuador Headquarters). Quito: Servicio Conjunto de Comunicación Social [Joint Social Communication Service].

—(1996c), "Proyectos democráticos en una cultura de la desigualdad [Democratic ideals in a culture of inequality]," paper presented at the first Encuentro de Comunicación y Cultura. Procesos culturales para el desarrollo comunitario [Meeting on Communication and Culture. Cultural Processes for Community Development], Corporación para el hábitat y la autogestión comunitaria [Corporation for habitat and community self-management] (HABIT-COM) – IPDC-UNESCO, Guayaquil, Ecuador, mimeograph.

—(1995). "El campo comunicacional en América Latina. Contexto y desafíos de los estudios de comunicación social [The field of communication in Latin America. Context and challenges of social communication studies]," Quito: Servicio Conjunto de Comunicación [Joint Communication Service], mimeograph.

—(1994). "Comunicación y desarrollo: una relación sesgada por la historia [Communication and development: a historically biased relationship]," *Signo y Pensamiento* [Sign and Thought] (Bogotá, Universidad Javeriana), XIII, 24, 151-158.

1927
1960
1963
1964
1967
1969
1970
1971
1972
1973
1974
1975
1976
1977
1978
1979
1980
1981
1982
1983
1984
1985
1986
1987
1988
1989
1990
1991
1992
1993
1994
1995
1996
1997
1998
1999
2000
2001
2002
2003
2004
2005
2006

—(1993), *Culturas y destinatarios: un acceso a través de la validación de mensajes* [Cultures and recipients: access through the validation of messages]. *Signo y Pensamiento* [Sign and Thought] (Bogotá: U. Javeriana), 12 (22): 65-71.

—(1992). *Comunicación Educativa y participación: Propuestas ante los nuevos retos* [Educational communication and participation: Proposals to address the new challenges]. Paper presented at Seminario sobre promoción social de la salud [Seminar on Social Health Promotion], PAHO, Guatemala City, mimeograph.

Díaz Bordenave, Juan (1992), *La campaña como intervención social* [The campaign as social intervention]. Chasqui (Quito: Ciespal), 41, April-June.

Efe (1997), *América Latina debe USD 600 millones* [Latin America owes US$ 600 million]. El Comercio (Quito), Monday, July 21, B8.

Fuentes, Raúl (1992). *Un campo cargado de futuro. El estudio de la comunicación en América Latina* [A field suffused with future. The study of communication in Latin America]. Mexico City: CONEICC-FELAFACS.

García Canclini, Néstor (1995). *Consumidores y ciudadanos. Conflictos multiculturales de la globalización* [Consumers and citizens. Multicultural conflicts of globalization]. Mexico City: Grijalbo.

—(1992), *Los estudios sobre comunicación y consumo: el trabajo interdisciplinario en tiempos neoconservadores.* Diálogos [Studies on communication and consumption: interdisciplinary work in neoconservative times] (Lima: Felafacs), (32), 8-15.

Genro, Tarso (1996), *A síndrome FHC da intelectualidade.* * Folha de S.Paulo, October 20, cuadernillo Mais!, 3.

Gómez Mont, Carmen (1995), "*Información y sociedad mañana, el comunicador –hoy– en el ojo de la tormenta* [Information and society tomorrow; the communicator—today—in the eye of the storm]," in Alejandro Acuña Limón (Coord.) (1995). *Nuevos medios, viejos aprendizajes. Las nuevas tecnologías en la educación. Cuadernos de Comunicación y prácticas sociales 7* [New media, old lessons. New technologies in education. Notebooks of Social Practice and Communication 7]. Mexico City: Universidad Iberoamericana, pp. 49-64.

Gutiérrez, Francisco & Daniel Prieto Castillo (1991). *La mediación pedagógica. Apuntes para una Educación a Distancia alternativa* [Pedagogical mediation. Notes for an alternative distance education]. San José: RNTC.

Hathaway, David (1995), *Situação atual do Projeto de Lei sobre patentes* [Current status of the legislative bill on patents]. Boletim da CNBB (259).

His, Alan (editor) (1996). Communication and Multimedia for People. Moving into Social Empowerment over the Information Highway. Paris: La Librairie FPH.

Hobsbawm, Eric (1995). Era dos extremos. O breve século XX: 1914-1991. São Paulo: Companhia das Letras. *

Holman, Michael (1993), *New group targets the roots of corruption.* Financial Times. May 5.

Kimbrell, Andrew (1996), *Biodemocracia contra tráfico de material genético vivo* [Biodemocracy against traffic in live genetic material]. IGC News Desk – IPS/Red APC, August 15.

McChesney, Robert W. (1996), *La ley de las telecomunicaciones de 1996: Una mirada a los antecedentes históricos* [The telecommunications law of 1996: A look at the historical background*]. Clips Videazimut, (10), April.

Martín-Barbero, Jesús (1987), De los medios a las mediaciones. Comunicación, cultura y hegemonía [From media to mediations. Communication, culture and hegemony]. Mexico City: Gustavo Gili.

Mattelart, Armand (1995). *La invención de la comunicación* [The invention of communication]. Mexico City: Siglo XXI.

—(1993). *La comunicación-mundo. Historia de las ideas y de las estrategias* [The communication world. History of ideas and strategies]. Madrid: Fundesco.

Max-Neef, Manfred et al. (1986), "Desarrollo a escala humana: una opción para el futuro [Development at the human scale: an option for the future]," *Development Dialogue* (Santiago, Chile: CEPAUR/Dag Hammarskjöld Foundation) (special edition).

McAnany, Emile (1980). *Communications in the Rural Third World.* New York: Praeger Publishers.

Millán, José Antonio (1996), *La cultura en los comunales electrónicos* [Culture in the electronic communities]. El Urogallo (Madrid) (121), 27-30.

Miller, Steven E. (1996). *Civilizing cyberspace. Policy, power and the information superhighway.* New York: ACM Press.

OAS (1997). *Inter-American Convention against Corruption* http://www.oas.org/SP/CURRENT/corrupts.html.

Orozco Gómez, Guillermo (1991a), "Límites del "modelo des efectos" en la investigación del impacto de la televisión en los niños y Del acto al proceso de ver televisión [*Limitations of the "effects model" in investigating the impact of television on children* and *Television, from act to viewing*]," in *Recepción Televisiva. Tres aproximaciones y una razón para su estudio. Cuadernos de Comunicación y prácticas sociales 2* [Three approaches and one reason for studying it. Notebooks on Communication]. Mexico City: Universidad Iberoamericana.

—(1991b), *La Investigación de la Recepción y la Educación para los Medios: Hacia una articulación pedagógica de las mediaciones en el proceso comunicativo* [Research on reception and education for the media: toward a pedagogical articulation of mediations in the communicative process]. Universidad Iberoamericana, Mexico City, mimeo.

Osava, Mario (1996), *Plantas medicinales amenazadas de extinción* [Medicinal plants threatened with extinction]. IGC News Desk – IPS/Red APC, June 6.

Otchet, Amy (1995), *La ley de los genes* [The Law of the Gene*]. UNESCO Sources (Paris) (74), 18-19.

Pareja, Reinaldo (1988), "El Mercadeo Social y la Percepción de Mensajes. Perspectiva histórica y metodológica [Social marketing and the perception of messages. Historical perspective and methodology]," paper presented at the Seminario Internacional de Percepción de Mensajes [International Seminar on Perception of Messages], Quito: Ciespal, mimeograph.

Prieto Castillo, Daniel (1994). *Lineamientos para una especialización en comunicación para la salud* [Guidelines for a specialization in health communication]. Quito: PAHO/UNESCO, mimeograph.

—(1992), *La Comunicación Educativa* [Educational communication], San José de Costa Rica: RNTC, mimeograph.

—and Carlos Eduardo Cortés (1990). *El interlocutor ausente. Notas y recomendaciones sobre investigación de expectativas de comunicación y validación de mensajes en torno a la infancia* [The absent interlocutor. Notes and recommendations on research in communicational expectations and validation of messages relating to children]. San José: RNTC.

Rasmuson, Mark R. et al. (1988). Comunicación para la salud del niño [Communication for children's health*]. Washington D.C.: AED / HEALTHCOM Project / University of Pennsylvania / AID.

Reuter (1997), *Corrupción: nueva variable del FMI para dar préstamos* [Corruption: new IMF variable for granting loans]. El Comercio (Quito), Wednesday August 6, B7.

Renaud, Alain (1990), *Comprender la imagen hoy* [Understanding image today*]. In: various authors. Videoculturas de fin de siglo. Madrid: Cátedra, pp. 11-26.

Rogers, Everett (1976). "Communication and Development: The Passing of the Dominant Paradigm," in Everett Rogers (Ed.) *Communication and Development: Critical Perspectives*. Beverly Hills: Sage Publications.

Salas Nestares, María Isabel de (1995), *Percepción e interactividad a partir de los formatos de representación en la comunicación con soportes multimedia*. Comunicación y estudios universitarios [Perception and interactivity based on representational formats in communication with multimedia materials. University studies and communication] (Valencia, Spain: Centro Universitario de Ciencias de la Información), (5), 89-102.

Sánchez Ruiz, Enrique (1993), *La investigación sobre comunicación en tiempos neoliberales (Nuevos retos y posibilidades)*. Boletín ALAIC [Research on communication in neoliberal times (New challenges and possibilities). ALAIC Bulletin] (Guadalajara: ALAIC), (7-8): 99-109.

Seib, Gerald & Aura Triana (1997), "La borrosa identidad política de las filiales extranjeras. [The blurred political identity of foreign subsidiaries*]," *The Wall Street Journal Americas* (El Comercio, Quito), Thursday, July 31, B6.

SELA (Sistema Económico Latinoamericano) (1997). *Situación, políticas y perspectivas de la deuda externa latinoamericana* [Status, policies and prospects of Latin American's external debt]. Caracas: SELA.

Shiva, Vandana (1995), *Los monocultivos, los monopolios y la masculinización del conocimiento* [Monocrops, monopolies, and the masculinization of knowledge]. IDRC Reports (Ontario) (XXIII) (2), 15-17.

Unicef (1990). *Estado mundial de la infancia* [World Status of the Child*]. New York: UNICEF.

United Nations (1995). *Informe de la Conferencia Internacional sobre la Población y el Desarrollo* [Report of the International Conference on Population and Development]. Cairo, September 5-13, 1994. New York: United Nations.

Van Crowder, L. (1990). *Is There a Communication Media Bias in Development Projects?* Agricultural Communicators in Education 1990 Conference. St. Paul, Minnesota, mimeograph.

Vásquez, Jenny (1992). Datos proporcionados por esta funcionaria de OPS/Perú, durante su intervención en el *Primer Seminario Latinoamericano sobre Periodismo y Cólera* [Data presented by this official during her presentation at the *First Latin American Seminar on Journalism and Cholera*]. San José, Costa Rica, May 5 and 6.

Winkin, Yves (1982), "El telégrafo y la orquesta [The telegraph and the orchestra*]," in Yves Winkin (Ed.) (1982). *La nueva comunicación* [The New Communication]. Barcelona: Kairós.

Cortés S., Carlos Eduardo. "La Comunicación Al Ritmo Del Péndulo: Medio Siglo En Busca Del Desarrollo [Communication at the Pace of the Pendulum: A Half-Century in Quest of Development]," Mimeograph, Bogotá 1977. Reprinted with permission of the author.

SUBVERTING CONVENTIONS: CHALLENGES IN PLANNING COMMUNICATION FOR CHANGE

By Erick R. Torrico Villanueva

2004 Planning—that is, defining current and forthcoming courses of action by anticipating the future and introducing some certainty in a specific field—is ground permanently suitable for controversy.

From the debates about whether it makes sense to plan or not, to those about the actors, methods and purposes of planning, both disagreements and agreements have been constant. It is clear however, that what has predominated is a set of *pragmatic conventions* modeled by multilateral organizations or cooperation agencies, and established due to the influence or conditions such organizations exert on universal implementation.

Thus, there is some sort of "established order for planning" that is only marginally questioned and that in fact leaves no room for creativity or freedom to conceive ideas, allowing mechanical replication at best. This situation is commonly seen in the socio-economic issues of development, including communication.

From a democratizing and critical point of view, it is useful to work for *effective social profit*—increased participation and deliberation in decision-making; active consensus building; voluntary and committed incorporation in the formative processes; and involvement of the community in public policies—as a result of using planning as an organizing resource.

The reflection that follows such approaches suggests ways to create development tools that are useful, culturally situated and socially efficient for human and sustainable development planning.

The Failure Not Yet Fully Acknowledged

For nearly six decades, the issue of development has been on the agenda of multilateral and cooperation

1927
1960
1963
1964
1967
1969
1970
1971
1972
1973
1974
1975
1976
1977
1978
1979
1980
1981
1982
1983
1984
1985
1986
1987
1988
1989
1990
1991
1992
1993
1994
1995
1996
1997
1998
1999
2000
2001
2002
2003
2004
2005
2006

organizations, governments, politicians and academics. During this time, several measures designed to produce balance among economic standards of living in different countries, and within them have been tested.

In addition, the traditional way of posing and addressing the problem of the lack of development has been characterized by identifying development with economic growth, therefore basing itself on a technocratic conception that separates economy from politics, looks for results that can be expressed through statistics, and has the pretense of becoming a pattern of universal disposition and efficacy.

This way of understanding and operating does not take into account the character of the social structure and its limits, which is why it has been described as an assistance trend, which obviously will never achieve real solutions for existing inequities.

Formulas that involve opening countries to direct foreign investments; granting private or public international credit lines to cover poor nations' deficits; prioritizing the industrializing process; the increasing but unequal liberalization of international commerce; the pressure for the State to withdraw from the economic activity in the world's Southern countries; the suppression of subsidies; and the weakening of the State's attention to social needs have simply generated a higher concentration of wealth, more poverty, and more exclusion. The Latin American and the Bolivian cases are illustrative of this.

According to data from the Economic Commission for Latin America and the Caribbean (ECLAC)[1], during the last decade of the 20th century the number of poor people grew from 200.2 million to 211.4 million in Latin America. Most of them suffer serious shortages in terms of access to basic infrastructure. In addition, inequality in the distribution of income became deeper and unemployment increased, from 4.6 percent to 8.6 percent in the course of the 1990s. For 2002, ECLAC indicated that poverty increased. Real remunerations dropped 1.5 percent and, in general, the region accumulated "half a decade of low growth in an adverse international economic juncture."[2]

In this context, Bolivia is considered one of the countries in the region with the highest inequality, since the income of the wealthiest 20 percent of the population exceeds more than 30 times that of the poorer 20 percent of the population.[3] Similarly, Bolivia's economy is stagnate and its employment levels show a constant tendency to drop.[4] Moreover, the October 2003 crisis has dramatically unveiled—with the death of more than 80 people and the resignation and escape from the country of up-to-then President Gonzalo Sánchez de Lozada—the impertinence of the structural adjustment program, which never allowed the reactivation of the economy—and only deepened the contradictions and internal problems.

Facts show that the purposes outlined to favor development have not been fruitful, leading instead to new and more acute deterioration. This is not openly accepted by those responsible for such designs in recent years–fundamentally due to the work and contributions of the United Nations Development Program (UNDP) on Human Development, and the documented critiques by 2001 Nobel Prize for Economics and former World Bank official Joseph Stiglitz—a clearer focus on poverty has emerged. Concern about poverty has grown because of its growing influence on a nation's social, economic and political instability[5] that in this age of globalization may lead to imbalances of a vast reach and scope.

---

2 CEPAL (2003): *Notas de la CEPAL n. 26*. Santiago de Chile, January, special edition, p. 1

3 2. Cfr. CEPAL (2001:7)

4 See HUANCA, Efraín (2002) *"Economia boliviana: evaluación del 2001 y perspectivas para 2002"* CEDLA *Working Documents 27*, La Paz. 25 pp.

5 This concern was shown manifested in the revision of the so-called "Washington Consensus," which systematized neo-liberal recipes in the decade of the 1980s, and in the introduction of criteria to invest in productive infrastructure, education, poverty reduction and environment protection that is being supported within the World Bank and the Interamerican Development Bank.

---

1 CEPAL (2001): *Panorama social de America Latina 2000-2001.*

The Urgent Need for Another Concept for Development

The failure of conventional development models is insufficient proof. The great powers, international organizations and cooperation agencies controlled by the world powers still refuse to modify their beliefs and policies in substantial ways. This was confirmed, for example, by the International Conference on Financing for Development held in Monterrey [Mexico] in March 2002. Its delegates insisted on applying recommendations for non-developed countries while leaving the international system intact, and maintained—or even extended—the conditionalities for official assistance for development, external debt and national development plans.

Thus, facing dangerous circumstances, the concept of development must be reframed immediately. Two converging initiatives exist: one from the UNDP, (previously mentioned *human development initiatives*) and the second proposed by the Dag Hammarskjold Foundation and termed *"another development."*

The aim of both approaches is development based fully on human rights, equity, rational use of the environment, social deliberation and consensus, democratic participation and the introduction of different degrees of structural changes.

It is critical that such new visions for development, centered on human beings, nature and culture, are incorporated into the policies of multilateral organizations and cooperation agencies and also at the state level as public policies. That is to say, that they enter the field of strategic planning but with a humanizing and democratizing approach.

Planning Interdicted

To speak of changes in the underlying logic of planning is not new. Just as the prevailing concept of development has been criticized often—and quite recently in pretty realistic terms—the issue of formulating plans, programs or projects to avoid or at least diminish their technical mystification, their unilateral nature and their instrumentalizing consequences for people, so have planning changes been tested many times.

From such efforts arise, for example, proposals regarding "indicative planning" (which seeks to make flexible the traditional normative and imperative criteria), "participatory or participative planning" (oriented to opening spaces of intervention for the "beneficiaries" in some stages of the planning process), or "planning without a plan" (which aims to get rid of the document containing the plan, considered restrictive of the possibilities of decision, action and variation during the execution).

However, in practice, planning continues to be tied to formal rationality schemes that not only put an order to its phases but also determine the nature of its contents and the ways to produce them. In addition, structured planning tools have limited policies for growth.

Transferred to the communication field, planning has been defined by assuming the ethnocentric diffusionism of colonial anthropology and development economy, the causing unilateralism of mediacentrism the "scientific nature" of empiricist sociology.

What prevails is a set of "recipes" that say how to formulate a plan and which steps to follow to design a plan in technical terms. Such an approach usually does not allow for consideration of theoretical presuppositions or ideological principles or objectives from which these schemes arise.

Despite severed reflective attempts in the past, examination of the underlying meanings of the accepted forms of planning remains a pending and challenging subject.

Reopening an Incomplete Discussion

But in terms of the specialized sphere that concerns us here, it is also necessary to resume the debate regarding the notion of communication itself. Pragmatic approaches that nearly 80 years ago overrated the power of technological mediations and underestimated both the individuals and the "masses" are gaining renewed validity. This is especially due to the

1927
1960
1963
1964
1967
1969
1970
1971
1972
1973
1974
1975
1976
1977
1978
1979
1980
1981
1982
1983
1984
1985
1986
1987
1988
1989
1990
1991
1992
1993
1994
1995
1996
1997
1998
1999
2000
2001
2002
2003
2004
2005
2006

significant weakening affecting the critical intellectual positions, and the hallucinations derived from the progress reached by the wrongly termed "information society," which, in the theoretical discussion, are nurtured by *technological determinism*.[6]

Therefore, the point is to resume the questioning of an old plot that states that communication can be reduced to the act of transmitting; that the emitter is the "lord" of this process; that media and messages can determine what receivers think and do; that communication is not viable if it doesn't involve techniques and technology; that social subjects can only be seen as intervention objects; and that every communication action planned must not fail to look for a measurable impact.

These and other elements lead to a utilitarian and hardly human conception of communication that has been discussed since the 1960s, particularly in Latin America and within the then-existing Movement of Non-Aligned Countries. However, the long and rich process generated by non-conformist communication, which led to the proposals in favor of a New World Order of Information and Communication (NWOIC) and the MacBride Report [approved in 1980 by the United Nations Organization for Education, Sciences and Culture (UNESCO)], was first discredited and then rejected due to a campaign led by Western powers and transnational companies.

After that, the issue of communication's international imbalance and the demands for a New Order, with all their implications in terms of an effort to re-conceptualize and reform, were forgotten; everything went back to the old "normality." That is the reason why nowadays, when the "postmodern" discourse of the technological utopia tries to impose itself to the world, it is necessary to resume the discussion regarding communication in development.

---

6 Take into account, for example, the instrumental and free-market approach in the celebration of the World Summit on the Information Society (Geneva 2003 and Tunis 2005) where the most developed countries and global corporations are thinking of establishing the rules of the game of the business of world telecommunications.

The Necessary Triple Subversion

To follow this path towards change, it is necessary to proceed with dismantling and replacing an overall consecrated institutionality that refers to the following three instances:

- First, the *epistemological* instance; that is, the "place" as from where knowledge is produced. Up to now, knowledge regarding communication, development and planning comes from a single matrix of an empirical nature.
- Second, the *theoretical* instance; that is, the concepts that account for facts and processes, which also respond to pragmatic-instrumental points of view.
- Third, the *practical* instance; that is, the technical applications, which are apparently the *raison d'etre* of the predominant approach in these matters.

Subversion aims, as dictated by logic, at transforming what is established. In this case, its purposes are: to assume that communication is a constituting element of the social being and of society; to allow its understanding as an interacting relationship; to acknowledge it as a process of shared construction of meanings; and to think about it and turn it into participatory planning for the social intervention in social life.

We must say that the desired change will not see the light if it disregards the above-discussed triple subversion.

A Few Battlefronts

Substantial modification of the prevailing schemes, proven inadequate for communication planning, specifically requires a coherent struggle on different fronts. Among them we mention the following:

a. Self-sufficient models. The "recipes" proposed to have an automatic structuring, universal applicability and guaranteed infallibility must be subjected to critical analysis in contrast with the experience of their usage, and in particular with the development needs and objectives emanating from the social base itself.

b. The belief in "technical neutrality." The legitimacy that the above mentioned recipes have at the level of common sense based on the assumption of their presumed scientific nature, it is yet another factor that must be reverted.

c. The linguistic imposition. Considerations regarding technique are complemented by a terminology coming from the military sphere that expresses a violent conception of communication as an action against predetermined "targets;" this must be substituted with a pertinent democratic alternative.

d. The instrumentalization of democracy and interpersonal communication. The introduction of pseudo-participatory forms of planning, and resorting to face-to-face relationships with informative-persuasive ends, are already typical of the attempts to cover up the technocratic unilateral nature. The point is to seek the genuine participation of people along with technicians in the process of planning, avoiding the reduction of dialogue to the "tactic of sending messages" or a simple form of capturing feedback data.

e. The inevitability of mass-mediation. The mediacentric vision of traditional communication strategies and campaigns reinforces "technological reason" and annuls the desirable social characteristic of encounters and dialogue among subjects. It is necessary to resituate mass communication as an eligible option among others (interpersonal, group-based, institutional, communitarian, etc.) instead of assigning it a status of absolute hierarchy based on the empiric premise of its full sensationalist efficacy.

f. The discourse regarding the unfeasibility of other alternatives. The prevailing models argue that they embody the purest expression of technique, and in consequence, since they are unbeatable, they become the natural and unique way to see and do things. Thus, we need to defend pluralism and the right to think as from our own identity.

Torrico Villanueva, Erick R., "Subertir las convenciones: Desafios en la planificación de la comunicación para el cambio [Subverting Conventions: Challenges in Planning Communication for Change]," from Cimadevilla, Gustavo and Edgardo Carniglia, eds. *Comunicacion, ruralidad y desarrollo.* Ediciones INTA: Buenos Aires, 2004. Reprinted with permission of author.

EXCERPT FROM:

COMMUNICATION FOR SOCIAL CHANGE: AN INTEGRATED MODEL FOR MEASURING THE PROCESS AND ITS OUTCOMES

By Maria Elena Figueroa, D. Lawrence Kincaid, Manju Rani, and Gary Lewis

2002 The Integrated Model of Communication for Social Change (IMCFSC) describes an iterative process where "community dialogue" and "collective action" work together to produce social change in a community that improves the health and welfare of all of its members.

The development of a community can occur through a variety of change processes:

Externally generated change, such as the construction of potable water systems, roads and health clinics by outsiders that leads to a reduction in the prevalence of disease within communities affected.

Individual behavior change, such as the adoption of chlorinated water, oral rehydration solutions for diarrhea and visits to local health clinics that, when aggregated, leads to a reduction in the prevalence of disease within communities which experience sufficient individual change.

Social influence for individual behavior changes where individuals who adopt a new health behavior publicly advocate its adoption to other individuals, so that the rate of change (decline) in the prevalence of disease increases.

Community dialogue and collective action in which members of a community take action as a group to solve a common problem, such as high rates of diarrhea, lack of potable water and so forth, which leads not only to a reduction in the prevalence of disease within the community but also to social change that increases the *collective* capacity to solve new problems.

The IMCFSC was developed to describe the last type of change: community dialogue and collective action. The four types of change are not mutually exclusive. For example, externally generated, government development projects can also involve individual adoption of new behavior with social influence. A collective-action project, such as getting every household to eliminate stagnant water sources to eradicate the spread of dengue fever by mosquitoes, may require individual behavior change as a result of social pressure from neighbors. The integrated model draws from a broad literature on development communication that was developed in the early 1960s. In particular, the work of Latin American theorists and communication activists was used for its clarity and rich recommendations for a more people-inclusive, integrated approach for using communication for development. Likewise, theories of group dynamics (Cartwright and Zander 1968; Zander 1996), conflict resolution (Carpenter & Kennedy 1988; Yankelovich 1999), leadership (Scholtes 1998), quality improvement (Tenner and DeToro 1992; Walton 1986), and future search (Weisbord and Janoff 1995; Weisbord, et al. 1992), as well as the network/convergence theory of communication (Rogers & Kincaid 1981; Kincaid 1988), have been used to develop the model.

Catalyst

The model describes a dynamic, iterative process that starts with a "catalyst/stimulus" that can be external or internal to the community. This catalyst leads to a *dialogue* within the community that, when effective, leads to collective action and the resolution of a common problem.

The model identifies six potential catalysts:

1. An *internal stimulus* may be discovery of high levels of arsenic in village wells, the onset of an epidemic such as AIDS, noticeable increases in maternal mortality or, perhaps, the suggestion of a local leader that stimulates members of the community to talk to one another about a health problem.

2. A *change agent*, such as the ones used in most NGO community interventions, may visit a community to initiate a discussion of "felt needs" or of a specific health problem, in order to induce the community to take some type of collective action.

3. An *innovation*, such as a new oral rehydration solution, a new vaccine or the availability of a new type of chlorine water disinfectant, may stimulate a community to talk about its adoption.

4. *Policies* that prompt the community to act, such as a new law that requires all children to complete primary education.

5. *Availability of technology*, such as the injectable method of contraception or mechanical digging equipment, may stimulate a community to talk about family planning or to reconsider the construction of new wells.

6. *Mass media,* including messages designed to promote individual behavior or collective action, may stimulate members of a community to adopt the behavior or to emulate other communities that have achieved some common goal by working together.

The catalyst in the model represents the particular trigger that initiates community dialogue about a specific issue of concern or interest to the community. This catalyst is a missing piece in most of the literature about development communication. Much of the existing literature implies that the community *spontaneously* initiates dialogue and action, or that an external change agent visits the community to mobilize the community. Experience has shown that communities rarely initiate a dialogue about a problem spontaneously, and that some do take action on their own without being visited by external change agents.

Some authors like Juan Díaz Bordenave (1998) initiate the description of a community process with the "identification of the problem." One could ask how a problem is identified in contexts where "a problem" is seen in the community as something "normal." For example, it may be normal that children under the age of one often die, or that mothers die during pregnancy. What the model implies is that some type of *catalyst* is usually necessary to stimulate a community to consider and discuss a problem. Once this discussion is initiated it may unfold in several directions: from simply creating a greater sense of dissatisfaction, to inciting community conflict, or to cooperative action that helps solve the problem.

Bibliography

Carpenter, S.L., and W.J.D. Kennedy. 1988. *Managing Public Disputes: A Practical Guide to Handling Conflict and Reaching Agreements*. San Francisco: Jossey-Bass Publishers.

Cartwright, D., and A.F. Zander, eds. 1968. *Group dynamics*. 3rd ed. New York: Harper and Row.

Díaz Bordenave, J. 1998. "Relation of communication with community mobilization processes for health," in: L.R. Beltrán and S.F. González, comp. *Community mobilization for health: Multidisciplinary dialogue*. JHU and SAVE. 94–98.

Kincaid, D.L. 1988. "The convergence theory of communication: Its implications for intercultural communication," in: Y.Y. Kim, ed. *Theoretical Perspectives XII, International and Intercultural Annual*. Beverly Hills, Calif.: Sage. 280–298.

Rogers, E.M., and D.L. Kincaid. 1981. *Communication Networks: Toward a New Paradigm for Research*. New York: Free Press.

Scholtes, P.R. 1998. *Leader's Handbook: Making Things Happen, Getting Things Done*. New York: McGraw-Hill.

Tenner, A.R., and I.J. DeToro. 1992. *Total Quality Management: Three Steps to Continuous Improvement*. Reading, Mass.: Addison-Wesley.

Walton, M. 1986. *The Deming Management Method*. New York: Perigee Books.

Weisbord, M.R., and S. Janoff. 1995. *FuturesSearch: An Action Guide to Finding Common Ground*. San Francisco: Berrett-Koehler Publishers.

Weisbord, M.R., et al. 1992. *Common Ground: How Future Search Conferences Bring People Together to Achieve Breakthrough Innovation, Empowerment, Shared Vision and Collaborative Action*. San Francisco: Berrett-Koehler Publishers.

Yankelovich, D. 1999. *The Magic of Dialogue: Transforming Conflict into Cooperation*. New York: Simon & Schuster.

Zander, A. F. 1971/1996. *Motives and Goals in Groups*. New Brunswick, N.J.: Transaction Publishing.

Figueroa, M.E., D.L. Kincaid, M. Rani, and G. Lewis. 2002. "Communication for social change: An integrated model for measuring the process and its outcomes," *Communication for Social Change Working paper series*. The Rockefeller Foundation. New York. Copyright © 2002, Rockefeller Foundation and Johns Hopkins University. Used by permission of copyright holder via license agreement.

CONSTRUCTING AN ALTERNATIVE OPTION: HABERMAS-PASQUALI-PAOLI

Excerpt from: The Concept of Communication: The Lens We See Through [El concepto de la comunicaciûn: El cristal con que se mira]

By José Cisneros

2001 Jürgen Habermas (1993), in his *The Theory of Communicative Action,* distinguishes three types of purposive rational action, among which he places communicative action, as explained below. What is the nature of each of these types of purposive rational action defined by Habermas?

Instrumental action refers to the manipulation of bodies in motion, and is oriented to achieving an end. The rules of instrumental action serve to address technical tasks.

Strategic action, though also oriented to success, is not measured by the direct achievement of a goal, but rather by the extent to which the decisions of a rational opponent are influenced.

Communicative action is not governed by egocentric calculations of interest (success), but through understanding. In communicative action, a shared knowledge is attained and becomes the basis for agreement, representing an intersubjective recognition of validity claims—claims susceptible to criticism. When understanding is achieved, it produces among the participants an agreement based on a shared conviction. Intersubjectively shared convictions link the participants in relationships of reciprocity.

It is important to consider in greater detail social action that is goals-oriented, since by doing so the concept of communicative action can be distinguished more precisely. Let us begin with strategic action. According to Habermas, strategic action is divided into openly strategic action and covertly strategic action.

1927
1960
1963
1964
1967
1969
1970
1971
1972
1973
1974
1975
1976
1977
1978
1979
1980
1981
1982
1983
1984
1985
1986
1987
1988
1989
1990
1991
1992
1993
1994
1995
1996
1997
1998
1999
2000
2001
2002
2003
2004
2005
2006

Openly Strategic Action

Openly strategic action is that in which one of the participants (referred to here as the sender) explicitly declares the effect he hopes to bring about in his rational opponent (referred to here as the receiver). Thus, the sender openly signals the decision that he wishes the receiver to make as a result of his influence. Clear examples of openly strategic action are commercial advertising and electoral propaganda. In the former, the advertiser attempts to influence the purchasing decisions of the potential consumer; in the second, the electoral campaign strategists seek to influence the decision of the voter or elector in favor of their candidate. The goal of openly strategic action is designed by one participant to influence the other. The latter's ends or conception do not matter; what matters is influencing his decision—in short, persuading him. If, to achieve this end, the first participant must conduct research on the second, as occurs with marketing studies and political marketing in the examples cited here, the strategy—but not the goals—will be modified accordingly.

Covertly Strategic Action

In covertly strategic action, while the goal of influencing a rational opponent remains the same, it is not openly declared. Moreover, the goal of influencing the rational opponent is disguised or dissimulated so that what is actually strategic will be perceived as communicative. The stated validity of this approach pretends to be based on the intention of benefiting the rational opponent. Examples are plentiful: the woman who influences a friend to leave her husband so that she can have him; the priest who pretends to understand the pain of the wealthy old lady in order to obtain lucrative donations; the mother who influences the child to choose a cheaper toy. In all of these cases, the strategy of the first participant (sender) is predetermined and clear to the sender, but not to the second (receiver), who takes a falsely communicative relationship to be a truly communicative one.

Two types of covertly strategic action can be distinguished, according to Habermas: unconscious deception and conscious deception.

Unconscious deception is defined by Habermas as systematically distorted communication. Thus, despite the fact that the first participant has a predetermined strategy, he pretends and believes that he is carrying out a communicative action to benefit another—or more than one—participant. This case is exemplified by religious preachers (whether of a fundamentalist or other persuasion), who are convinced of the obligation to save their brothers and sisters. The same phenomenon occurs with political advocates or participants in groups of any kind, including families.

Conscious deception can be defined as the manipulation of one person by another, where the manipulator induces the manipulated to make decisions that benefit the former, but induces the manipulated person to believe that the best interest of the latter is the motive. Moreover, the manipulator's success in manipulating depends precisely on convincing his rational opponent of two false ideas: that a communicative action is taking place between them, and that its purpose is to benefit the person being manipulated, although, in reality, it is the manipulator who is benefiting. Again, examples are so abundant that there is little need to enumerate them. Habermas also describes strategic action in terms of dramatic action.

Dramatic Action

Dramatic action comprises interactions between an agent or actor in the role of self-presenter, and a social group in the role of audience. The actor evokes a certain image in the audience, a certain impression of himself, revealing his subjective reality in a more or less calculated way, based on the image he wishes to convey. Any actor or agent can control the public's access to the sphere that is his personal thoughts, feelings, attitudes, etc., to which only he is privy. The general concept of *self-representation* refers not to spontaneous expressive behavior, but to behavior that is the result of the actor's stylized experience, performed to instill in the spectators a certain image of the actor. Dramatic action is directed at an audience which, without ever becoming aware of the strategic intentions at work, believes that the representation it is witnessing is guided by the desire to achieve understanding.

Strategic action in general, then, implies an asymmetric relationship in which one of the participants establishes the goals, defines the arguments and plans the behavior so as to convince his rational opponent to make a particular decision, to the benefit of the strategizer. The dominant concept and schemes of communication as persuasion fit perfectly within Habermas's definition of strategic action, but cannot be considered communicative action.

Habermas provides a lucid analysis of the difference between strategic and communicative action. Among other things, he states that:

1. A communicative link cannot be established when one person's convictions are induced by another person. This is true even when the best of intentions are at work, as in the case of a teacher or a mother.
2. An agreement may be extracted through external influence—gratification (money), threat, suggestion, deception—rather than as a result of the person's own conviction or understanding. An example of this is the influence of the employer on the employee.
3. There may be interpersonal relations between subjects acting with a view to their own success, but regulated by relationships of economy and power: via the market or through relationships of domination. In such cases, the parties' partnership masquerades as an instrumental order. Corruption and prostitution can be examples of such instrumental relationships.

Merely exchanging messages—much less transmitting them unidirectionally—is not itself sufficient to constitute communicative action, since the purpose of an asymmetric action obviates the possibility of free agreements based on the participants' own convictions. What, then, constitutes communicative action?

Communicative Action

As explained above, communicative action is not governed by egocentric calculations of self-interest (success), but rather by an intention to produce understanding. In communicative action, shared knowledge is achieved, and validity claims susceptible to criticism are recognized. Communicative action does not mean that the parties must think the same way; rather, they are linked by shared convictions, in a relationship of reciprocity.

In Habermas' terms:

> The concept of communicative action necessarily involves actors who, as speakers and listeners, make reference to something in the objective, social and subjective world, and in this respect, they reciprocally establish validity claims that may be accepted or questioned. (Habermas: 1993, 493)

According to Habermas, each actor, guided by the desire to enhance understanding, establishes three validity claims:

- That what he says is true;
- That the claimed action is correct; and
- That the speaker's true intention is, in and fact, what he declares it to be.

The agreement of the actors, to which Habermas refers, is not based on the conclusions of the symbolic exchange (or even on the acceptance of the validity claims, which may be questioned), but on the reciprocity of the action and on the fact that it is oriented to understanding. Thus, communicative action necessarily produces shared knowledge on the basis of that agreement, even when the different actors arrive at differing conclusions and decisions.

Understanding is not to be interpreted here strictly as the decoding of signs; it goes beyond that to cover coordinated action that allows the actors to interpret their environments and actions in a new and richer way. Based on that interpretation, each can make an individual decision.

1927
1960
1963
1964
1967
1969
1970
1971
1972
1973
1974
1975
1976
1977
1978
1979
1980
1981
1982
1983
1984
1985
1986
1987
1988
1989
1990
1991
1992
1993
1994
1995
1996
1997
1998
1999
2000
2001
2002
2003
2004
2005
2006

Thus, the concept of communicative action implies a serious and deep (though not necessarily less pleasurable) relationship between actors who, as Habermas states, "are compelled or obliged to view themselves as speakers or listeners engaged in referring to something in the objective, social and subjective world." Thus, it is understandable that the thinking of many researchers and academics is based on communications theories developed through studying the functioning and operation of the mass media; that they adopt the concept of communication as persuasion; and that Habermas's notion of communicative action may seem idealistic—believing that, in real life, it does not exist: as if the only communicational reality were the one mediated by technology. However, as demonstrated by the critique of the existence or non-existence of a science of communication, an approach to communication based solely on an examination of the mass media is at best partial, if not erroneous. For this reason, it is important to continue investigating other conceptual approaches, such as Habermas's. The work of the Venezuelan researcher Antonio Pasquali (1990) adopts an approach which, in its concept of communication, is close to that of Habermas.

The Concept of Communication According to Antonio Pasquali

[C]ommunication, or communicational relationship, is used to signify that relationship which produces (and at the same time presupposes) a biunivocal interaction involving co-knowledge, this being possible only when a law of bivalence governs the two poles of the sender-receiver relational structure, such that any sender may be a receiver, and any receiver may be a sender. There is neither "communication" nor any other type of dialectical relationship with nature or raw materials, but rather some other form of monovalent relationship: utilitarian, energetic, etc.... (Pasquali: 1990,47-63)

There are striking correspondences, in this passage, between Pasquali's concept and that of Habermas.

Among the most obvious are the following:

1. Both view, as indispensable, biunivocal interaction (Pasquali) or reciprocity (Habermas) between the actors—senders and receivers—in the communicational process or communicative action.
2. Both reject the idea that there can be such a process of communication between human beings and nature or raw materials, considering that in these cases only a monovalent (Pasquali) or instrumental (Habermas) relationship is possible. Cybernetic systems, for example, even with feedback or interactive machines, fall in this category of monovalent relationships.
3. Both recognize that there is co-knowledge (Pasquali) or shared knowledge (Habermas) in the communicational action or process, which is far different from action by one person to persuade or induce agreement in another.

In this passage, the only difference (not contradiction or dissent) between Pasquali and Habermas is that Habermas explicitly considers the possibility, but not the need, of the involvement of physical or electronic media in the process. However, the possible existence of these media is subordinate to the communication process, rather than the reverse, as seems to be assumed in other conceptions of the media, such as McLuhan's (1971, 1993).

With respect to this preponderance of human actors in the communication process, Pasquali is explicit in stating that:

The only entities capable of provoking authentic communication and social forms of behavior—not mere mechanical exchange of information and stimuli—are rational beings. ... The term communication, then, applies to dialogic relationships between human beings or ethically autonomous persons. ..." (Pasquali: 1990, 49-50).

In regard to biunivocal (or, in Habermas's language, reciprocal) interaction, he adds:

Authentic communication, then, is only that which is based on a symmetric relational scheme, with parity of conditions between sender and receiver, and the possibility of one hearing or giving ear to the other (Heidegger), as a mutual will to understand one another. … (Pasquali: 1990, 51)

Further comparison of the two passages, of Pasquali and Habermas, point up the following correspondences:

4. The orientation or purpose of the communication is voluntary, free understanding.
5. The understanding is based on an agreement in principle which, among other things, makes it possible to arrive at co-knowledge or shared knowledge.
6. The agreement is between ethically autonomous persons (Pasquali), i.e., people with their own values and validity claims (Habermas) prepared to establish a link.

Based on these initial six correspondences between the two authors, it is possible to construct a concept of communication that is very different from the media concept associated with persuasion, one providing a new way of viewing communicational practices, whether mediated or not by technology. Nevertheless, it is worth considering a seventh feature common to the notions of communication proposed by Habermas and Pasquali, namely, the ethical dimension.

The Validity of Differences

Both Jürgen Habermas and Antonio Pasquali begin by underlining the validity of differences between the actors in any communication and their need to confront their own values and validity claims through mutual agreement and reciprocal, bivalent exchange. Without recognizing the validity of differences, and without mutual agreement and reciprocal exchange in any sending and receiving of messages (bidirectional but asymmetrical—i.e., qualified), although there may be instrumental or strategic action, there will never be an authentic process of communication (Pasquali) or communicative action (Habermas).

How can we expect President Fox of Mexico to understand the indigenous ethic of the Zapatistas, or President Bush the Taliban? Only with an authentic willingness to understand could one expect such understanding, not in the context of the dramatic action (and even war) to which both are inclined. Hence the importance of the ethical dimension in the concept of communication of the two authors cited here. It is precisely in this ethical dimension of the concept of communication that the observations of a third academic researcher, Antonio Paoli (1994), deserve mention.

Antonio Paoli

Paoli states:

Communication consists of establishing a deep awareness of mutual respect, and to give respect is to give value. To give value is to recognize that which is truly valuable in the human being.

True communication consists of recognizing our own value. And to give value is to engender truth.

Truth is not a datum; rather, it is when the value of the other is recognized, and when the other feels recognition of the value of his being.

When value is evoked in a mutual fashion, communication is opened. When the awareness of this mutual act of giving value is profound, we experience a moment of communication. (Paoli, 1994)

From Paoli's perspective, recognition of and respect for the value of the other, and of one's own value, are striking generators of truth and communication. Mutual giving of respect and value, and the awareness of this, become conditions for communication. Notwithstanding the exchange of words or of any type of message between the human beings involved, no communication can be conceived in which there is not respect for the other, and respect for oneself by the other. Communication implies that the participants consider each other valuable as human beings.

Of course, the bulk of so-called mass communication does not stand up to the test of either respect

1927
1960
1963
1964
1967
1969
1970
1971
1972
1973
1974
1975
1976
1977
1978
1979
1980
1981
1982
1983
1984
1985
1986
1987
1988
1989
1990
1991
1992
1993
1994
1995
1996
1997
1998
1999
2000
2001
2002
2003
2004
2005
2006

for, or recognition of, the other as a valuable human being, since the main concern within the mass communication dynamic is that the other be a consumer—of messages, merchandise, ideology—but not an ethically autonomous interlocutor, let alone a human being of value. This does not mean that mass communication is useless or unnecessary. However, it should be called something else: "mass dissemination," for example, or, more explicitly, "persuasion" or "informing" (though in the latter case, numerous other conceptual considerations would need to be taken into account). In terms of the ethical dimension described above, the fact remains that the mass media, as they are run today, do not qualify as involving a process of communication.

Paoli's contribution to the proposals of Habermas and Pasquali is perfectly consistent with their approaches. It views communication in terms of human beings, rather than vis-à-vis the media, leading us back directly to the notion that the media, like all technology at our disposal, can be used either for or against human beings. Communication, on the other hand, from the perspective of these three authors, does not admit that ambivalence.

Deliberately extracting and integrating the central ideas of Habermas, Pasquali and Paoli, one begins to see communication as something more than a simple exchange of messages that any living being—animal, plant or, in many instances, even machine—can carry out. Communication, according to these authors, is a much deeper action or process, a human prerogative in which the operational dimension of the exchange of messages occurs within other dimensions, involving numerous elements: the will to truly understand each other; mutual agreement, with the creation of knowledge and truth as outcomes; and lastly, as an ethical prerequisite, recognition of the validity of differences, reciprocal exchange, and the mutual giving of respect and value, and the awareness thereof.

Some would argue that this is a complex concept, difficult to carry out in practice. This is partially true: as

with the concepts of democracy, freedom and justice, complexity and difficulty come with the territory. And just as it is indispensable to seek democracy, freedom and justice, so it is vital—if the life of all human beings is to be valued—to seek communication as it is defined here.

As to the supposed communication of other living beings (cells, plants, animals), once communication is defined as human communication oriented to understanding, with the nature of the mass media considered in its own light, then the relationship of these other living beings will inevitably fall into another category. This is by no means to deny their importance, but simply to establish clearly the differences between these and human communication.

In summary, the concept of communication proposed here does not assume that it is a substance that can be associated with other entities (such as the media), but rather that it is an action generated by human beings with a will to understand each other, leading them to establish an agreement in principle, in which they mutually recognize each other as human beings of value, respect each other as such, value their differences and ethical autonomy, and engage in a reciprocal exchange of messages that produces new knowledge and truth, as well as a mutual commitment, with a shared awareness of all of these experiences.

References

HABERMAS, Jürgen. *Teoría de la acción comunicativa: complementos y estudios previos*. Edit. Rei. Mexico City, 1993.
—*Theory and Praxis: Studies in Social Philosophy*. Edit. Rei. Mexico City, 1993.

McLUHAN, Marshall, and POWERS, B.R. *The Global Village: Transformations in World Life and Media in the 21st Century*. Gedisa Editorial Diana. Barcelona, 1993.
—*Understanding Media: The Extensions of Man*. Editorial Diana. Mexico City, 1971.

PAOLI, Antonio. *Comunicación*. Editorial Edicol. Mexico City, 1977.

PASQUALI, Antonio. *Comunicación y cultura de masas*. Monte Avila Editores.

Cisneros, José "El concepto de comunicación: El cristal con que se mira." In the journal *Ámbitos* Nos. 7-8. Universidad de Sevilla. 2nd quarter of 2001 – 1st quarter of 2002. Seville, Spain, 2002 (pp. 49-82). Universidad de Sevilla. Reprinted with permission.

COMMUNICATION RESEARCH AND SUSTAINABLE DEVELOPMENT IN AFRICA: THE NEED FOR A DOMESTICATED PERSPECTIVE

By Francis B. Nyamnjoh

2000 Introduction

For over three decades Africa has attempted to build "nation-states" and pursue development along the path traced out by Western experience. The continent's postcolonial leaders have been persuaded by arguments that present the nation-state as the only form of political unit "recognized" and "permitted" in the modern world (Smith 1986, 230; Deutsch 1969, 171–172; Wallerstein 1964, 4), and modernisation as the unilinear route to development. Today, researchers are unanimous that the attempt by African states to build nation-states or to develop à l'européenne" has met with little success in the short term (even if the reasons advanced for this failure differ from one school of thought to another), and that from current trends, there is hardly any reason to think that things would be different in the long term. This paper will examine the workable link forward between communication research and development. But to do this properly, it tries first to answer why development has failed to occur despite multiple efforts and to evaluate the sort of communication research that has failed to inspire development in the continent.

This contribution highlights and discusses two factors responsible for the failure of both development communication research and development to make a positive and sustained impact on Africa in the last 40 years. The first factor is that the continent has relied on a notion of development and on development agendas that are foreign to most of its peoples, both in origin and objectives and that have not always addressed the right issues or done so in the right manner. The second factor is that development communication researchers have adopted research techniques designed to answer to the needs of Western societies and do not always suit African cultures or societies that are, in the main, rural and nonliterate. This means that for most of the time communication scholars have either been asking the wrong questions altogether or posing the right questions to the wrong people. This paper seeks to establish to what extent communication researchers and the media have willingly colluded in modernisation, trying to convince local people that this is good for them, the right thing to do, the central value. It contends that the communication scholars have been used most of the time, but that they have hardly had the financial and cultural independence to set their own agendas in the service of the African masses.

The external development agendas have often established an inappropriate sense of problems. Good communication has been presented as a means of being able to break through blockages (backward attitudes and practices; customs, traditions and philosophies) with knowledge. The question as to *whose* knowledge for *what* purpose has seldom been asked. The assumption has been that there can never be any such thing as the transmission of wrong (inappropriate, unwanted or unsolicited) knowledge through the media by agents of modernisation. Few ever query whether the knowledge is correct; as governments and development agencies have the same idea—that they know best the people's problems and what to prescribe as solutions. Little or no attention is paid to background or indigenous knowledge or to the need for active local participation in the conception, design and execution of development projects. Even today, when some may claim the situation is better, the attitude remains that of coming from the outside and knowing what is best in matters of local development. Nothing seems to start from the base or from grassroots research.

Thus it is hardly surprising that attempts at development have been utter and unmitigated disasters year after year for four decades and that, today, Africans are by every standard much worse off than they were in the 1950s. The pursuit of modernisation and consonant World Bank and IMF strategies for development have proved to be

1927
1960
1963
1964
1967
1969
1970
1971
1972
1973
1974
1975
1976
1977
1978
1979
1980
1981
1982
1983
1984
1985
1986
1987
1988
1989
1990
1991
1992
1993
1994
1995
1996
1997
1998
1999
2000
2001
2002
2003
2004
2005
2006

inappropriate in Africa; indeed, it has been argued that they have served to excuse Western penetration and exploitation. The idea of sustainable development is another World Bank initiative. What reason is there for optimism that things may work this time? Especially as, when examined in detail, the whole idea of sustainable development is nothing but modernisation theory in camouflage? For one thing, the agenda is still from "experts" outside, which means that the targeted populations may not have had the opportunity to scrutinise and prioritise it. Sustainable development stresses long-term effects, how to go about things in order to guarantee success and accountability, but is mute on the *why* of all this.

The basic assumption here, as in modernisation theory, is that modern or forward-looking people act in a rational and informed manner and that success inevitably results from careful planning. This "rationalist and positivist" approach, in which everything can be measured and uncertainty eliminated, is hardly a reflection of real life. These are clearly the World Bank's standards for measuring success in the battle against poverty. Not only is there the possibility that the wrong things will be measured (which has been largely the case with modernisation), but implicit is the assumption that should sustainable development fail to materialise, to blame would be the inability of a backward-looking people to free themselves of constricting customs and false beliefs and to embrace the rational culture, the best way of managing social change. For, as Summers and Thomas (1993, p. 243) argue in support of the World Bank and IMF, "nations shape their own destinies" and "poor domestic policies, more than an unfavourable external environment, are usually to blame for development failure."

Modernisation Theory and Development in Africa

As Laburthe-Tolra and Warnier (1993, pp. 6–8) have pointed out, following the Second World War, the gap between the rich, fast-growing industrialised countries and countries of the Third World buried in their poverty and underdevelopment became evident. Western sociologists saw in the success of the Western countries the result of a modernisation process. By modernisation, Western theorists understood the process of change towards the types of social, economic and political systems that developed in Western Europe and North America from the 17th to the 19th century and which subsequently spread to other regions of the world. According to this definition, modernisation touches on all aspects of existence: social and political organisation, family, kinship, belief systems, economy. It possesses an original model: that of Europe and North America. This model is placed under the sign of scientific rationality, inherited from the century of Enlightenment and perceived as universal. Consequently, it is potentially detachable from the civilisation in which it was born. It promises the only rational way, *the best way*, therefore the universal way of doing anything. The modernisation model is generally seen to be spreading beyond its area of origin through diffusion, thanks to its scientific rationality, which imposes itself on particular civilisations founded on other systems of thought, described as "prescientific," "prelogical" or simply "irrational" (Lerner 1958, 45). Modernisation is thus seen as a giant compressor determined to crush every other civilisation in order to reduce them to the model of the industrialised West. Thus Lerner's conviction that "what the West is" (Lerner 1958, 47) or "What America is" (Lerner 1958, 79), the emerging nations seek to become. That is the reason why modernisation theory is also called the theory of convergence of civilisations, since every other civilisation is considered to be moving towards the unique model—a line of reasoning very much in tune with the prevalent colonial belief that "European civilisation was the culmination of all human progress and that the new African nations could have no better pattern and should aim at nothing different" (Ajayi 1966, p. 606). Modernisation is also seen as a process of change and innovation, where what is new is perceived as progress. A modern society is one which is forward looking, not backward looking.

Thus, according to modernisation theorists, since the purely participant society is more or less utopia, it is only appropriate that the societies of the West, which happen to be the most modern, serve as models or pacesetters for the emerging nations. Westernisation is therefore their prescription for difficulties in development in Africa. By assuming a single valid path in development, such theorists imply that the problems of political instability, cultural pluralism and socio-economic underdevelopment in Africa can be overcome only through the infusion of "rationalist and positivist" Western policies, institutions and values. Africa's only chance is in seeking to become like the West, since "modernism, dynamism and stability tend to go together" (Lerner 1958, 84). The implication for African countries of taking their political, cultural and economic cues from the West, as modernisation theorists suggest, is the risk of losing any political autonomy, cultural identity and economic independence that they may have. Yet as others argue, political autonomy, cultural identity and economic independence are the necessary preconditions for genuine development.

The Illusion of Modernisation

A number of criticisms are possible of the modernisation theory of development. This theory was designed originally to account for social change in the West during the emergence of capitalism. Its assumption that "traditional" societies will (and should) converge on modern Western forms is ethnocentric. As a theory it does not correspond very well with the empirical facts, and it tends to confuse ideal types with reality (Portes 1976).

It is the belief in and quest for homogeneity, the expressed or implied assumption that other societies should reproduce Western systems and institutions regardless of feasibility or contextual variations, which proponents of the non-Western perspective have criticised in the theory of modernisation (homogenisation). By restricting the concept of the rise of nations to that of the birth of capitalism, Western researchers have developed concepts and theories that extrapolate the parochial European experience (considered as "normal") and that "reduce" the experiences of Africa, Asia and Latin America to those of the West (Abdel-Malek 1967, 250). Instead of restructuring, modifying, enriching and remodelling their concepts

and theories in order to accommodate the broader experiences and contextual variations of the contemporary world, these researchers have preferred to safeguard Western intellectual hegemony (Abdel-Malek, 1967, 259; Portes 1976, 55–56; Gareau 1987, 596–597; Riggs 1987, 607–609). As Abdel-Malek (1967, 250–264) puts it, "The European origins of the social sciences lead to Europocentrism: The world is conceived in the image of Europe," to which others are expected to conform, and where exceptions are not tolerated.

Critical of modernisation theory, some prominent scholars of Africa have explained the continent's failed or failing attempts at development with its involvement in the world capitalist system and have outlined "possible alternatives to the prevailing development models which have proved to be inadequate." Samir Amin points out that such an alternative is justified by the fact that, within the world capitalist system, Africa plays a peripheral role, with little or no access to decision making. While responsibility for Africa's tragic attempt at development might stretch back to "the brutal and primitive forms of colonial pillage," independent Africa is to blame for having pursued Westernisation policies at all, even if it did so "with the blessing and on the urgent advice of all those who, today, from the World Bank to the agencies of Western states, deplore its wretched results, foreseeable though these results were" (Amin 1987a, 1–13; Amin 1982).

In light of the weakness of Africa in relation to the centres of capitalism, and of the impossibility for democracy to exist under such circumstances, Amin advocates "delinking," or the reconstruction of the world following an alternative social system initiated and imposed by the people of Africa, who by virtue of their current subjugation are well placed to serve as the motive force of history. Africa's development problems are a challenge to be taken up only by the African people themselves, through the creation of a popular national state aimed at delinking "their development from the demands of transnationalization" (Amin 1987b, xi–xii). For "popular development can only be national and autocentred" (Amin 1980, 144; Amin 1978, 17). To ensure effective delinking, the popular national

1927
1960
1963
1964
1967
1969
1970
1971
1972
1973
1974
1975
1976
1977
1978
1979
1980
1981
1982
1983
1984
1985
1986
1987
1988
1989
1990
1991
1992
1993
1994
1995
1996
1997
1998
1999
2000
2001
2002
2003
2004
2005
2006

state would have to be strong and democratic, and capable of resisting "negative pressure" from the world capitalist system and its internal ramifications. For, "dependent capitalism … is incapable of realizing the goal of national liberation" (Amin 1980, 201). Many scholars recognise the need to form large economic, political and military units as Africa's only chance of effective intervention in the world today and of winning respect as real partners, and call for a break with "the narrow ideology of the nation" inherited from 19th century Europe (Amin 1985, 107; Doumou 1987, 57; Goulbourne 1987; Cobban 1969, 124–129; Gabou 1987, 76–85; Hadjor 1987, 139).

The issue of popular democratic participation as a prerequisite for economic development is particularly addressed by Goulbourne (1987), Hadjor (1987), Nyong'o (1987) and Soyinka (1994). They regret the little importance given this question in general discussions of Africa. The governments have given priority to "the refining of methods of control," rather than to the strengthening of active participation in national and local affairs by the population. The result has been a state that is "highly centralised, overbearing and restrictive in its operations," one with an "overwhelming presence" in almost all areas of social, economic and political life (Goulbourne 1987, 26–28). Such interventionism has given the state far more importance than is healthy for the attainment of any country's development objectives. Not only does this lead to the dispersal of energies, but division of labour, seen to be crucial in development, becomes impossible, and efficiency gets lost as the businessman increasingly becomes more of a politician and vice versa. The state becomes a menace, a major hurdle, an obstacle in nearly every walk of life (Goulbourne 1987, 30).

Goulbourne argues that African governments have often justified repression with "spurious arguments," one of which claims that to ensure "rapid development it was necessary first to put controls in place," because any political differences were likely to divert attention from development, the main national pursuit. This view gives the impression that the leaders intended to tackle the issue of national development with total seriousness and

that it was only appropriate to "consider putting aside some less pressing issues" for its sake. It was unwise for a country with limited resources "to dissipate its energies in the niceties, or luxuries, of allowing all and sundry to put their views about national matters when the task of prosecuting development is the national project over which independence was fought." But Goulbourne maintains that the very exclusion of a "high degree of popular democratic participation" is in itself an obstacle to national development. Were democracy indeed the problem, its suppression should have brought about rapid economic development (1987, 36–37). Soyinka reiterates this point by criticising the "near-mystical linkage" these leaders have tended to make between human rights and development, daring to imply that it is immoral to withhold aid from them because they withhold rights from their citizens. Soyinka compares this attitude to that of a mendicant mother who with one hand "holds out her beggar's cup to you" while "the other is busy dealing vicious blows to the head of the wretched bundle that complements her own misery." He rejects any claim to innocence by the intelligensia and accuses them of often providing the "conceptual noises which legitimate" the costly rounds of "competitive alienation" that African leaders impose on their peoples (Soyinka 1994, 7–9).

Nyong'o blames African policymakers for failing to understand the structural character of the national and international milieu in which they have operated for over three decades, and for the rigid suppression of the contending social forces in their own societies. Dependency notwithstanding, Nyong'o believes that the lack of accountability on the part of those in power has exacerbated the failure to bring about "more positive social transformation and more auto-centred processes of accumulation." He finds "a definite correlation between the lack of democratic practices in African politics and the deteriorating socioeconomic conditions" (Nyong'o 1987, 19) and stresses the need for a state capable of planning an "inward-looking, self-centred and self-sufficient development" (Nyong'o 1987, 24), but one which at the same time must be controlled by and accountable to the popular forces which have been marginalised in the contemporary political arena, despite the enormous contributions they made to "the national democratic struggles for independence" (Nyong'o 1987, 20).

Also of increasing concern to African scholars is the missing, or often inadequately stressed, link between culture and development. Writing on this issue, Ali Mazrui not only sees an inevitable link between culture and development in Africa—especially as "Africans have demonstrated that they respond more to *socio-cultural* ideologies than to *socio-economic* ideologies"—but also argues that instead of seeking the political kingdom first, as prescribed by the late Kwame Nkrumah, Africans "need to seek first the cultural kingdom—in the hope that much else will be added unto it" (Mazrui 1994, 127–136). On this subject, Nyang argues that although "the colonization of Africa was a serious challenge to African cultural autonomy," the emphasis by the post-colonial African leadership on the primacy of politics and their fascination with things foreign has meant that "cultural changes in many African societies are not always deeply rooted in the local soil or home-grown." He concludes that governments must show their commitment and seriousness "to the development of their peoples by coming to terms with local cultures" and by seeking "effective and meaningful domestication of the theory and practices of modernization" (Nyang, 1994, 429–446).

Communication Research and Sustainable Development

According to modernisation theory, for traditional Africa to develop people had to change their attitudes and ways. To achieve this, they needed vast amounts of information and persuasion, which could only be got through the mass media, "the great information multipliers" (Schramm 1964, 246–247). This conception of development gave rise to a type of communication research that focused mainly on the *effectiveness* of the techniques of persuasion, diffusion and adoption of innovations (Rogers 1962, 1973). Researchers influenced by this approach have tended to see social structure as an impediment to development and the traditional power elite as gatekeepers against modernisation. If they seek to understand the social structure of the societies they study, it is in order to determine how best this structure could be replaced by a "modern" one (Rogers 1973). Most prevailing uses of communication in development have relied heavily on this theory of "exogenously induced change," which suggests that "static societies are brought to life by outside influences, technical aid, knowledge, resources and financial assistance and (in a slightly different form) by the diffusion of ideas" (Golding 1974, 43).

Some examples of the use of communication in this connection have been analysed. In 1977, under the auspices of UNESCO, Diaz Bordenave published the results of a critical evaluation of projects in 10 countries where different mass media were used to promote rural development. The countries in question were Colombia, Brazil, India, Senegal, Peru, Iran, Tanzania, Canada, Tobago and the Philippines. Diaz Bordenave looked at the origin, background and reasons for each of the projects. He discovered that in none of the 10 case studies did the request for a rural development programme using communication originate with the rural populations most concerned. A usual pattern was for a government to decide on a development scheme and then search out a locale and a team to carry out a communication programme to promote the scheme. Another was for an international agency or group to become interested in a communication technique or a development problem currently arousing interest and then find a country willing to embark on a programme centred around this technique or problem. In the light of these inadequacies, Diaz Bordenave argues for countries and for bilateral and international organisations to take a closer look at overall priorities in rural development and at communication resources so as to determine where rural development communication efforts are most needed and will have the greatest effect. Concerning sponsorship, he remarked that communication agencies involved with development programmes were often more interested in testing and promoting new

1927
1960
1963
1964
1967
1969
1970
1971
1972
1973
1974
1975
1976
1977
1978
1979
1980
1981
1982
1983
1984
1985
1986
1987
1988
1989
1990
1991
1992
1993
1994
1995
1996
1997
1998
1999
2000
2001
2002
2003
2004
2005
2006

"hardware" than in analysing the realistic needs of the populations under study. In some of the case studies, the sponsors did not devote enough time to specify clearly what they really wanted, and why, and thus found it difficult to prevent or attenuate divergences in opinion and expectation among sponsors. Government support, in one form or another, was the norm.

Most criticisms of development communication theories (see Servaes 1983, 1986; Servaes & Arnst 1994) are similar to criticisms of modernisation theory in general. Their Western-centredness, their neglect of the international dimensions of both communication and development, and their emphasis on attitudes rather than on the structures that account for underdevelopment have been heavily criticised. Development communication studies have tended to emphasise "person blame" rather than "system blame" and have failed to recognise that "in the circumstances of many developing countries, existing patterns of power and exploitation mean that poor people have little reasonable prospect of self-betterment; and an attitude of fatalism may be the only realistic one" (Hartmann, et al. 1989, 28). The tendency by researchers has been to treat all "progressive change as unproblematic" and to assume that every innovation communicated is necessarily beneficial to the populations they affect. But as Hartmann, et al. (1989, 255–269) argue, "Changes that benefit one section of the community may leave others untouched or even damage their interests" (255).

Hartmann, et al., (1989, 256) thus advocate the inclusion of "social structure and structural conflict in discussions of development" and criticise the widespread tendency to "treat the people as an amorphous mass" and to encourage a false sense of "harmony of interests." The rural population, for example, are often credited with a harmony of interests that is more mythical than real. In their study of India, Hartmann et al., realised that not only are village societies "highly differentiated in terms of access to resources and by caste and other divisions," but that they are "characterised by competition for resources among different interest groups."

Hartmann, et al., (1989, 257–263) have also criticised the tendency in this model to consider those targeted by communication for development "as essentially passive, an audience to be manipulated into compliance with the development nostrums of those who know best." Such a tendency has made the advertising campaign the dominant model for development communication, where everything is seen in terms of "injecting" the development "message" into communications directed at the "target audience," as though development were a commodity to be sold like beer, soap or any other." Communicating development "is seen as an essentially mechanical process" in which the individual audience is treated both as passive and as detachable from his or her social context. This approach is reflected in communication studies, where the lion's share of research has been on "assessing audience response to deliberately persuasive messages of the campaign type," with emphasis on "the KAP formula— knowledge, attitude, practice—which is deemed to be the sequence in which effects occur." Yet the effects of communication are much larger than the rapid spread of information and could include the gradual socialisation into alternative ways of seeing and doing.

In view of the rising disenchantment with the fact that modernisation has encouraged an orientation of mass media and communication that "is essentially vertical, directive, aimed at manipulation and indoctrination" (Diaz Bordenave 1977, 21–22), Diaz Bordenave recommends Paulo Freire's *pedagogy of the oppressed* as a way out. Freire argues that the mere transfer of knowledge from an authoritative source to a passive receiver does not promote the receiver's growth as an autonomous person conscious of the need to contribute to and influence his or her society. He proposes a "pedagogy of the oppressed," wherein emphasis is on participation, democracy and dialogue. Freire's approach suggests that not only may Western research methods be inappropriate at certain points to African conditions but that strict adherence to dominant research models may preclude the asking of the really important questions.

This point is echoed by Halloran, using the example of comparative international research, which is quite common in development communication studies. Such research is by nature very difficult to conduct, but certain assumptions in the Western research tradition have made it even more so. "At the heart of the problem is the failure to recognize that social research is embedded in cultural values and that the fundamental differences (culture, language, demographic structure, experience, expectations, etc.) that obtain in different societies preclude the use of carbon copy survey or interview methods which assume that genuine comparability can be achieved only by administering the same questions in the same way in all participating countries. One has only to take note of the relationship between language and culture to realise that this approach is patently absurd" (Halloran 1981, 9). Thus, methods of data collection no matter how appropriate in the West, are not necessarily so in Africa. In adopting our research methods in development communication in Africa, how much attention have we paid to the continent's fundamental cultural, linguistic and demographic diversities, specificities, experiences and expectations?

The conventional techniques of data collection are not always adapted to the realities of Africa. The cultural, linguistic and social cleavages in multiethnic Africa are such that a researcher must take extra care if applying research methods developed to suit the needs and expectations of Western societies. Take the questionnaire, for example. It can only be administered selectively, given the widespread illiteracy rate in Africa. In the case of Cameroon, if the results of the 1987 census are to be believed (*Cameroon Tribune,* 21 March 1991), almost 50 percent of the entire population can neither read nor write French or English, the official languages. Of the 45 percent or so who have been to school, less than 20 percent have gone beyond primary school. Indeed less than 3 percent of the population have been educated above secondary school level. This not only seriously questions the use of questionnaires drawn up in French and English but

also its relevance as a research method in a largely oral society. Translation is arguably a way out, but given Cameroon's mosaic linguistic situation and ethnic complexities, as well as the fact that many words and concepts in French and English do not have ready equivalents in Cameroonian languages, it is hard to see of what significant use translation could be. And if one were to stubbornly insist on using the questionnaire these drawbacks notwithstanding, it would be a case of attempting to extrapolate or generalise from a most unrepresentative sample; so that any decision taken as a result of any such study is most unlikely to have grassroots support or endorsement. The elitist nature of such research methods compounds rather than alleviates the marginalisation of the African masses.

It is in this regard that as far back as 1963, Cheikh Anta Diop perceptively suggested a multimethodological approach in African sociological research. He questioned the tendency to make *a priori* distinctions between sociological and anthropological methods and to equate the latter with the study of "primitive" or "archaic" societies. Every research situation, he maintained, should determine its methods. He argued that nowhere else better than in the study of African societies can anthropology and sociology combine their methods and collaborate more effectively; for in Africa, where traditional elements co-exist with Western ones, changes are in process that are only inadequately understood with research methods exclusive to either discipline (Diop 1963, 181).

Given Africa's failure to attain development thus far, and given the methodological inadequacies in most of our communication research in the continent, I suggest that we emphasise participatory research along the Paulo Freire model. The argument here is that, if the people are understood and treated with the respect they deserve, if they are actively involved in decisions on issues that concern them and given the freedom of organisation and effective control, if the researcher and development agents can purge themselves of any superiority complex and become

1927
1960
1963
1964
1967
1969
1970
1971
1972
1973
1974
1975
1976
1977
1978
1979
1980
1981
1982
1983
1984
1985
1986
1987
1988
1989
1990
1991
1992
1993
1994
1995
1996
1997
1998
1999
2000
2001
2002
2003
2004
2005
2006

more responsive to the real needs of those whose development they claim to foster, and if the people can freely and spontaneously express themselves and engage in dialogue, without inhibition, on their problems, aspirations and visions, they are most unlikely to be reluctant partners in development and should readily recognise themselves in and endorse the recommendations that the researcher makes on the best way forward based on their collective diagnoses.

As Servaes and Arnst (1994, 2–3) have argued, it is about time the poor and the illiterate, who "have always been researched, described and interpreted by the rich and educated," became actively involved in—and why not take over—research on their predicaments, especially as often, "they best know their situation and have a perspective on problems and needs that no outsider can fully share."

This call for participatory research is in tune with the call for more representative communication systems and the need for "group and local media" in the face of increasing centralisation and synchronisation (UNESCO 1980, 55–57). In Latin America, for example, many researchers have expressed the need for an "alternative communication" system that is democratic, participatory and decentralised, and that is rooted in the masses who are currently marginalised by a communication system that serves the preponderant interests of the transnational corporations and the dominant internal economic and political power groups (White 1980; Diaz Bordenave 1977; White and McDonnell 1983; Reyes Matta 1986; Simpson Grinberg 1986). It is a type of communication that would serve the interests of "the oppressed sectors of society at the national level, and the dominated countries at the international level... a process of dialogue and widespread creativity" (Reyes Matta 1986, 190–191).

To attain this alternative communication, Simpson Grinberg, for example, reiterates Golding's call for research (Golding 1974) by stressing "the need to study the current extent and impact of native communication systems that predate the coming of the mass media"

to the Third World (Simpson Grinberg 1986, 183). The "marrow of alternative communication," he writes, "is the decentralization of communication power, which implies a decentralisation of the technological know-how" (Simpson Grinberg 1986, 184). In White's words, "comunicación popular" does not comprise merely an incorporation of "many elements of the folk culture," but must be seen, above all, as "an attempt to set up communication channels independent of the hierarchy of intermediaries" (White 1980, 3). This entails a system of communication that is managed by the people, horizontal, decentralised at every level, participatory and free from the shackles of domination by either external or internal forces. Writing about the whole of the developing world, Hamelink calls for an emancipatory science (Hamelink, 1983a) and prescribes "dissociation" as the only real alternative to the process of "cultural synchronization" perpetuated by the industrialised states and as the sole guarantor of the autonomy and self-reliance "essential for a process of independent development" (Hamelink 1983b).

The main characteristic of participatory communication is that the media arise from and are controlled by the locality. They comprise peasants or worker groups addressing themselves or other groups with similar concerns and aspirations. The media are socially horizontal in that they do not "go up" to a communication centre controlled by higher-status individuals and then back "down" again to other lower-status groups, but go directly from one lower-status group to another. The language of communication is the language of the people, freely chosen by them to communicate amongst themselves; it is not introduced or imposed by any outside leadership. If sympathetic specialists or professionals offer any expertise, it is purely technical and strictly on the terms of the locals (White 1980, 4; Criticos 1989, 36–37).

For participatory communication to take root in Africa, participatory research into how best to realise this aim is needed. For, to adapt Hadjor (1987, 38–40), only through "an intimate acquaintance with everyday life and the experience of the masses" can the communication researcher recognise "what people want and how much they want it" and so be able to recommend steps towards sustainable development. Servaes and Arnst (1994, 4–5) consider participatory research to be an educational process that is "cyclical, continuous, local and accessible," in that it comprises three interrelated facets—namely, (1) "collective definition and investigation of a problem by a group of people struggling to deal with it," (2) "group analysis of the underlying causes" of the said problem, and (3) "group action to attempt to solve the problem."

This sort of research has a lot to borrow from anthropology, noted for the long periods its practitioners take to understand, multifacetedly, and in detail, the communities or institutions they study. Laburthe-Tolra & Warnier (1993, 367) talk of "prolonged familiarity, within, in a face-to-face relationship and communication with a group, a region, a political, linguistic or residential community," as the most distinctive characteristic of anthropological studies. Unfortunately, most people and organisations who recognise and appreciate the originality of the anthropological approach have failed to recognise what accounts for that originality: the prolonged familiarity within a given community that is possible only if the researcher can get him/herself accepted into the group being studied and participate in its daily life. Only by so doing can the researcher uncover the solidarity that accounts for the dynamism of the group, or the tensions and conflicts that perpetuate underdevelopment. Findings from such research would certainly contribute towards the organisation of local or community activity that "enlists the active participation of the people most in need of better opportunities" (Hartmann et al. 1989, 268).

Doing participatory research requires resocialising ourselves and reappraising certain alternatives that we have either ignored in the past or simply never really thought of. It means that we must increasingly question certain basic assumptions, conventional wisdom, academic traditions and research practices, which we have uncritically and often unconsciously borrowed from the West,

but which remain largely ill-adapted to our context. We need to examine critically such "canned" (Ramos, quoted in Gareau 1987, 603) communication research methods imported from Europe and North America and see how they could best be harnessed or domesticated to serve Africa in its quest for sustainable development.

The bulk of communication research on the continent remains heavily coloured by the American tradition, in which the tendency has been and remains "to assume uncritically that social action can be understood mainly in terms of individual beliefs and attitudes," while largely ignoring in which ways such "attitudes may be the product rather than the cause of economic conditions and power relationships." Such "simplistic psychologism … takes insufficient account of the social and political dynamics of change and lacks an adequate conception of the relationships between ideas and actions, between culture and social structure." It has produced the false belief that "ideas may be manipulated more or less independently of structural factors" (Hartmann et al. 1989, 23).

What America has exported to Africa has been summarised by Kunczik (1993, 39) as research that emphasises the collection of "commercially and politically quickly usable, methodically unexceptionably obtained facts, without reflecting further on them." The result is usually, "a cornucopia of individual findings gained with the aid of sophisticated research instruments, findings that, because of the absence of a comprehensive theoretical framework, cannot be integrated." Focus is on "discovering short-range, quick and dependably identifiable effects," while "the consideration that the mass media are part of an over-all social framework is completely ignored. The approach deals simply with the reactions of isolated individuals or groups to specific communications." As Kunczik (1993, 40–41) further points out, the emphasis on "miniature surveys of little experiments that are quickly, routinely evaluable and usable whether for publication or for practical purposes" socialise the communication researcher in favour of "an 'atomistic'

1927
1960
1963
1964
1967
1969
1970
1971
1972
1973
1974
1975
1976
1977
1978
1979
1980
1981
1982
1983
1984
1985
1986
1987
1988
1989
1990
1991
1992
1993
1994
1995
1996
1997
1998
1999
2000
2001
2002
2003
2004
2005
2006

perspective that does not take into consideration the over-all social aspects." Questions of how the research results can contribute to progress in the field, or how they can be integrated within a comprehensive theoretical framework, are generally ignored.

Such narrowly focused and superficial studies fall within what Halloran has termed conventional research. This is a type of research that stresses efficiency and practicality, is mostly atheoretical in nature, hardly relies on well-formulated or tested hypotheses, and is usually aimed at resolving a precise policy or commercial problem. Hence, it tends to be more concerned with sampling than with conceptualisation, and with description than with analysis. It is piecemeal in approach, scarcely integrated, and does not emphasise continuity. "Irrespective of the nature of the social phenomenon under investigation, the final research report is usually confined to quantitative statements about amenable but relatively superficial aspects of a complex issue" (Halloran 1974, 8). Its "positivistic/behaviouristic" approach has tended to blind its practitioners to the "value assumptions … implicit in every research question and that … enter into the formulation of every research design" (Halloran 1983, 274). The researchers in this tradition hardly bother to redefine the research problem brought to them by governments and other agents of development; and their research tends to serve the "interests that pay for it and find it useful in optimising their security and profitability" (Smythe and Dinh, 1983, 118–121).

More critical researchers, who see themselves as having the noble duty to provide a clear idea of how existing social structures "should, could, or would be realistically changed to alternative institutional structures that research has shown as better" (Melody and Mansell 1983, 110), seek to free themselves of such positivistic/behaviouristic blindness that makes it impossible for their counterparts to realise that "real life is many sided and it needs various theories and various approaches applied together" (Nowak, quoted in Halloran 1983, 271). The mechanistic model provided by

positivistic research gives the misleading impression that social phenomena can be understood, controlled, manipulated and exploited independent of human intention and expectation. Such a "predicament-free," or social-engineering approach, Himmelstrand et al. (1994, 4–8) argue, ought to be substituted by or reconciled with a "predicament-oriented" approach which seeks first "a local understanding of the nature of given predicaments among those actually facing these predicaments in their everyday lives" and then an understanding of "the broader historical, structural and/or ecological causes generating such predicaments," with the aim of feeding such understanding "back to the local level to illuminate the understanding from below of the predicaments confronted there, and to provide guidelines for local action and struggle."

This American methodological import has survived in the continent more because it suits the purposes of the agents of modernisation than because of its relevance to understanding the African situation. Those who run international development programmes along the Western model inspired by modernisation theory "are not interested in challenge, stimulation and provocation at any level" (Halloran 1981, 18). They want their programmes to go on without disturbance, and would select as researchers or consider acceptable as research questions and findings only those that confirm their basic assumptions on development in Africa. But the development communication researcher has the responsibility to challenge such unfounded assumptions based on vested interests and hidden agendas. This is by no means an easy task, especially since we rely on these very agents of development to fund our research. As Halloran observes in general, anyone in a position of power and control would hardly accept research that is critical of them. They therefore are more likely to sponsor only research that would produce results that justify their position and/or help them in their defence when challenged (Halloran, 1981, 20). To paraphrase Susan George (quoted in Riddell 1992, 723), it matters not how many "mistakes" mainstream researchers or development theorists make for "protected and nurtured by those whose political objectives they support, package and condone; they have a licence to go on making them, whatever the consequences." Thus, "research frequently tends, in some way or other, to reflect the values and reinforce the system within which it is conceived, supported and executed. In fact, in some countries it is deliberately intended that it should do this, and it is important to look at research as a possible form of social control (Halloran, 1981, 14). As development communication researchers, we cannot afford to be partial, blind or naïve, whatever the pressures on us are and regardless of our level of misery and need for sustenance. Thus, for communication research to contribute towards a genuine, multifaceted liberation of African peoples, we ought to start not by joining the bandwagon, as we often do, but with an insightful scrutiny of the whole idea of sustainable development—its origin, form, content, assumptions and practicability; and then we will be able to decide whether to accept, reject or modify it.

This quest for methodological independence finds comfort in the research of Frederick Gareau, a leading sociologist of knowledge, who sees the social sciences in terms of competing sects and questions the tendency of the American behaviourist to claim scientific superiority over all other perspectives. To him, the social sciences are a free-for-all endeavour and not something "essentially American" (or Western) in origin, method and perspective. Social science disciplines, he argues with illustrations, cannot be explained "independent of the societies in which they are created and function" (Gareau 1987, 596); and not only are social scientists profoundly influenced by the countries in which they live, they find it difficult not to appear as "apologists for their respective establishments" (Gareau, 1987, 597).

Thus depending on the national, regional or cultural context wherein they operate, social scientists "adopt contrary research designs and methodologies" (Gareau, 1987, 598). He sees the social sciences as marked by profound ideological conflicts and their

practitioners as looking in different places for evidence and using contrasting methods to determine whether or not they have found it (1987, 598). Gareau's global view of social science thus "sees its initiates as undergoing divergent professional socialization processes, reading different bodies of literature, and often coming to contrary conclusions" (1987, 598).

Gareau further sees the social sciences within the global context of the knowledge industry, in which certain countries and regions are more advanced and expansionist, while others are underdeveloped and dependent. He remarks that American social science, in its "unrelenting one-way traffic", has thus been able to penetrate countries with cultures as different from its own as those of France, Canada, India, Japan and the Republic of Korea (Gareau 1987, 599). This has given American social science a "privileged position" with "a very favourable export balance of communications," or "talking without listening." Not only is there little importation, but American social scientists ensure that "incoming messages are in accord with American socio-cultural norms." This, Gareau observes, "betrays an ethnocentric, inward-looking fixation," with little preference for anything foreign: "if foreign, a preference for the Anglo-Saxon world; little concern for Continental Europe, and indifference or hostility towards the Second and the Third Worlds" (Gareau 1987, 598–589).

Understood in terms of the central-periphery perspective, the favourable "export balance" for American social science is explained by the spread of American political, economic and cultural values after World War II. Following the war, America, as a superpower, exported its cultural values, through educational aid and the social sciences. "In this way, the United States exported its social science sects abroad both by training social scientists in the homeland and by sending experts abroad. The expense incurred was often borne by the United States government or by private foundations" (Gareau 1987, 602). Gareau's position is in general similar to Schiller's, who argues that the

1927
1960
1963
1964
1967
1969
1970
1971
1972
1973
1974
1975
1976
1977
1978
1979
1980
1981
1982
1983
1984
1985
1986
1987
1988
1989
1990
1991
1992
1993
1994
1995
1996
1997
1998
1999
2000
2001
2002
2003
2004
2005
2006

American doctrine of free flow of information has been used as a "highly effective ideological club" by America to promote its political, economic and cultural values by whipping "alternative forms of social organization" into a ridiculous defensiveness (Schiller 1977).

Such dependence, in Africa, is compounded by the fact that the production of social-scientific knowledge "requires large capital outlays for universities, libraries, compensation for time off from teaching—and more recently computers and databanks" (Gareau 1987, 602), which not even the best scholars and institutions in the continent can easily afford. What this means in practice is that most of the time African scholars are forced to consume not books and research of their own production or choice but what their affluent and better-placed counterparts in North America and Europe choose to share with them at the peripheries. But unless we are ready to question the relevance to Africa of Western ideas of development and communication research, unless we are ready to start setting our own agendas according to the real needs of our people, sustainable development, even as seen and defined by us, will forever remain an unrealistic dream.

References

Abdel-Malek, A. 1967. "Sociologie du développement national: Problèmes de conceptualisation," *Revue de L'Institut de Sociologie* 2:249–264.

Ajayi, J.F.A. 1966. "The place of African history and culture in the process of nation-building in Africa south of the Sahara (1960)," in: I. Wallerstein, ed. *Social Change: The Colonial Situation.* John Wiley & Sons: New York. 606–616.

Amin, S. 1978. "Développement autocentré, autonomie collective et ordre economique international nouveau: Quelques réflexions," *Africa Development* 3(1):5–23.

Amin, S. 1980. *Class and Nation: Historically and in the Current Crisis.* Heinemann: London.

Amin, S. 1981. "Pour une stratégie alternative de développement en Afrique," *Africa Development* 3: 116–126.

Amin, S. 1982. "A critique of the World Bank report entitled 'Accelerated development in sub-Saharan Africa,'" *Africa Development* 7(1–2):23–30.

Amin, S. 1985. *La déconnexion: Pour sortir du système mondial.* Paris: Editions La Découverte.

Amin, S. 1987a. "Preface: The state and the question of 'development,'" In: P. A. Nyong'o, ed. *Popular struggles for democracy in Africa.* London: Zed Books. 1–13.

Amin, S. 1987b. "Preface," in M.L. Gabou. *The Crisis in African Agriculture.* London: Zed Books. ix–xii.

Cobban, A. 1969. *The Nation State and National Self-determination.* London: Collins.

Criticos, C. 1989. "Community in media," in: C. Criticos, ed. *Experiential Learning in Formal and Non-formal Education.* Durban: Media Resource Centre, Department of Education University of Natal. 35–45.

Deutsch, K.W. 1966 (1953). *Nationalism and Social Communication.* London: MIT Press.

Deutsch, K.W. 1969. *Nationalism and Its Alternatives.* New York: Alfred A. Knopf.

Diaz Bordenave, J.E. 1977. *Communication and Rural Development,* Paris: UNESCO.

Diop, C.A. 1963. "Sociologie africaine et méthodes de recherche," *Présence Africaine* 48:180–186.

Doumou, A. 1987. "The state and popular alliances: Theoretical preliminaries in the light of the Moroccan case," in: P.A. Nyong'o, ed. *Popular Struggles for Democracy in Africa.* London: Zed Books. 48–77.

Dunn, J. 1978a. "Comparing West African states," in: J. Dunn, ed. *West African States: Failure and Promise.* London: Cambridge Univ. Press. 1–21.

Dunn, J. 1978b. "Conclusion," in: J. Dunn, ed. *West African States: Failure and Promise.* London: Cambridge Univ. Press. 211–216.

Eisenstadt, S.N. 1973. *Tradition, Change and Modernity.* New York: Wiley.

Emmanuel, A. 1972. *Unequal exchange: A Study of the Imperialism of Trade.* London: Monthly Review Press.

Gabou, M.L. 1987. *The Crisis in African Agriculture.* London: Zed Books.

Gareau, F.H. 1987. "Expansion and increasing diversification of the universe of social science," *International Social Science Journal* 114: 595–606.

Gellner, E. 1983. *Nations and Nationalism.* Oxford: Basil Blackwell.

Golding, P. 1974. "Media role in national development: Critique of a theoretical orthodoxy," *Journal of Communication* 24(3):39–53.

Goulbourne, H. 1987. "The state, development and the need for participatory democracy in Africa," in: P.A. Nyong'o, ed. *Popular Struggles for Democracy in Africa.* London: Zed Books. 26–47.

Gutkind, P.C.W., and I. Wallerstein. 1976. "Introduction," in: P.C.W. Gutkind and I. Wallerstein, eds. *The Political Economy of Contemporary Africa.* London: Sage Publications. 7–29.

Hadjor, K.B. 1987. *On transforming Africa: Discourse with Africa's Leaders.* Trenton and London: Africa World Press and Third World Communications.

Halloran, J.D. 1974. *Mass Media and Society.* Leicester Univ. Press.

Halloran, J.D. 1979. *The Context of Mass Communication Research.* Paris: UNESCO.

Halloran, J.D. 1983. "A case for critical eclecticism," *Journal of Communication* 33(3):270–278.

Halloran, J.D. 1986. "Beyond development communication: The international research experience," paper presented at the AMIC-WACC-WIF Consultation. Singapore. 18–22 Nov.

Halloran, J.D. 1988. "The future in the rear-view mirror: Mass communication research: Past, present and future," paper presented at Sommatie '88 Congress Centre Koningshof, Veldhoven-Eindhoven. 13–15 Apr.

Hamelink, C.J. 1983a. "Emancipation or domination: Toward a utopian science of communication," *Journal of Communication* 33(3):74–79.

Hamelink, C.J. 1983b. *Cultural autonomy in global communications: Planning National Information Policy*. London: Longman.

Hartmann, P., B.R. Patil, and A. Dighe. 1989. *The Mass Media and Village Life: An Indian Study*. New Delhi: Sage Publications.

Kilson, Jr., M.L. 1966. "Nationalism and social classes in British West Africa (1958)," in: I. Wallerstein, ed. *Social Change: The Colonial Situation*. New York: John Wiley & Sons. 533–550.

Kothari, R. 1971. "Introduction: Variations and uniformities in nation-building," *International Social Science Journal* 23:339–354.

Kunczik, M., 1993, *Communication and Social Change*. FES: Bonn.

Laburthe-Tolra, P., and J.-P. Warnier. 1993. *Ethnologie, anthropologie*. Paris: PUF.

Lerner, D. 1958. *The Passing of Traditional Society: Modernizing the Middle East*. New York: Free Press.

Lins Da Silva, C.E. 1986. "Transnational communication and Brazilian culture," in: R. Atwood and E.G. McAnany, eds. *Communication and Latin American Society: Trends in Critical Research, 1960–1985*. Madison: Univ. of Wisconsin Press. 89–111.

Medard, J.-F. 1978. "L'etat sous-développé au Cameroun," *Année Africaine*. 35–84.

Melody, W.H., and R.E. Mansell. 1983. "The debate over critical vs. administrative research: Circularity or challenge," *Journal of Communication* 33(3):103–116.

Nyong'o, P.A. 1987. "Introduction," in: P. A. Nyong'o, ed. *Popular Struggles for Democracy in Africa*. London: Zed Books. 14–25.

Portes, A. 1973. "Modernity and development: A critique," *Studies in Comparative International Development* 8(3):251–275.

Portes, A. 1976. "On the sociology of national development: Theories and issues," *American Journal of Sociology* 82(1):55–85.

Reyes Matta, F. 1986. "Alternative communication: Solidarity and development in the face of transnational expansion," in: R. Atwood and E.G. McAnany, eds. *Communication and Latin American Society: Trends in Critical Research, 1960–1985*. Madison: Univ. of Wisconsin Press. 190–214.

Riddell, B.J. 1992. "The new face of imperialism and Africa's poverty," *Journal of Modern African Studies* 30: 721–725.

Riggs, F.W. 1987. "Indigenous concepts: A problem for social and information science," *International Social Science Journal* 114: 607–617.

Rogers, E.M. 1962. *Diffusion of Innovations*. New York: Free Press.

Rogers, E.M. 1973. "Social structure and social change," in: G. Zaltman, ed. *Processes and Phenomena of Social Change*. New York: John Wiley & Sons. 75–87.

Roncagliolo, R. 1986. "Transnational communication and culture," in: R. Atwood and E.G. McAnany, eds. *Communication and Latin American Society: Trends in Critical Research, 1960–1985*. Madison: Univ. of Wisconsin Press. 79–88.

Rotberg, R.I. 1966. "The rise of African nationalism: The case of East and Central Africa (1962)," in: I. Wallerstein, ed. *Social change: The Colonial Situation*. New York: John Wiley & Sons. 505–519.

Schiller, H.I. 1977. "The free flow of information—For whom?" in: G. Gerbner, ed. *Mass Media Policies in Changing Cultures*. London: John Wiley & Sons. 105–115.

Schramm, W. 1964. *Mass Media and National Development: The Role of Information in the Developing Countries*. Stanford, Calif.: Stanford Univ. Press.

Servaes, J. 1983. *Communication and Development*. Louvain: Acco.

Servaes, J. 1986. "Communication and development paradigms: An overview," *Media Asia* 3(3):128–136.

Servaes, J., and R. Arnst. 1994. "Participatory communication in the research process," paper for the 9th ACCE biennial conference Media and Sustainable Development in Africa. Accra, Ghana. 16–23 Oct.

Seton-Watson, H. 1977. *Nations and states: An enquiry into the origins of nations and the politics of nationalism*. London: Methuen.

Silva Michelena, J.A. 1971. "State formation and nation-building in Latin America," *International Social Science Journal* 23:384–398.

Simpson Grinberg, M. 1986. "Trends in alternative communication research in Latin America," in: R. Atwood and E.G. McAnany, eds. *Communication and Latin American Society: Trends in Critical Research, 1960–1985*. Madison: Univ. of Wisconsin Press. 165–189.

Smith, A.D. 1983. *State and Nation in the Third World: The Western State and African Nationalism*. Brighton, U.K.: Wheatsheaf Books.

Smith, A.D. 1986. "State-making and nation-building," in: J.A. Hall, ed. *States in History*. Oxford, U.K.: Basel Blackwell. 228–263.

Smythe, D.W., and T.V. Dinh. 1983. "On critical and administrative research: A new critical analysis," *Journal of Communication* 33(3):117–127.

Soyinka, W. 1994. "Democracy and the Cultural Apologia," *Afrika Spectrum* 29(1): 5–13.

Summers, L.H., and V. Thomas. 1993. "Recent lessons of development," *Research Observer* 8: 241–254.

Tipoteh, T.-N. 1987. "Foreword," in: K.B. Hadjor. *On Transforming Africa: Discourse with Africa's Leaders*. Trenton and London: Africa World Press and Third World Communications. xi–xv.

UNESCO. 1970. "Mass media in society: The need of research," *Unesco Reports and Papers on Mass Communication 59*. Paris: Unesco.

UNESCO. 1980, *Many Voices, One World: Towards a New More Just and More Efficient World Information and Communication Order*. London: Kogan Page.

Wallerstein, I. 1964. *The Road to Independence: Ghana and the Ivory Coast*. Paris: Mouton.

Wallerstein, I. 1968. *Africa: The Politics of Unity*. London: Pall Mall Press.

Wallerstein, I. 1972. "Three paths of national development in sixteenth-century Europe," *Studies in Comparative International Development* 7(2): 95–101.

Wallerstein, I. 1976. "The three stages of African involvement in the world economy," in: P.C.W. Gutkind and I. Wallerstein, eds. *The Political Economy of Contemporary Africa*. London: Sage Publications. 30–57. vol.13(1): 33–51.

Walton, J. 1972. "Political development and economic development: A regional assessment of contemporary theories," *Studies in Comparative International Development* 7(1): 39–63.

Watanuki, J. 1971. "State formation and nation-building in East Asia," *International Social Science Journal* 23:421–434.

White, R.A. 1980. "'Communicaciön popular': Language of liberation," *Media Development* 27(3): 3–9.

White, R.A., and J.M. McDonnell. 1983. "Priorities for national communication policy in the Third World," *The Information Society Journal* 2(1): 5–43.

Nyamnjoh, Francis B. "Communication Research and Sustainable Development in Africa: The Need for a Domesticated Perspective," paper presented at the conference organised by the African Council for Communication Education (ACCE) on Mass Media and Sustainable Development in Africa, at Accra, Ghana (October 15–23, 1994). Published in Jan Servaes (ed.), (2000), *Walking on the Other Side of the Information Highway: Communication, Culture and Development in the 21st Century*, Penang: Southbound, (pp.146–160). Reprinted with permission of the author and the publisher.

1927
1960
1963
1964
1967
1969
1970
1971
1972
1973
1974
1975
1976
1977
1978
1979
1980
1981
1982
1983
1984
1985
1986
1987
1988
1989
1990
1991
1992
1993
1994
1995
1996
1997
1998
1999
2000
2001
2002
2003
2004
2005
2006

EXCERPT FROM:

COMMUNICATION AS AN ESSENTIAL TOOL OF SUSTAINABLE DEVELOPMENT

Communication for Development

By Juan Díaz Bordenave

1996 The phrase "communication for development" is generally used to refer to the planned use of communication principles, media and techniques to support programs and projects in various development sectors, such as health, education, agriculture, community organization and associativism. In recent years, this field has moved beyond the vertical, top down approach to embrace an increasingly participatory paradigm. The old model, in which services provided by government or private institutions were passively received by beneficiaries, is being replaced by one emphasizing initiatives launched by organized community groups. Thus, government's vertical dissemination of development messages is being supplanted by efforts to support the people's self expression and communicational capacity. In short, *assistentialist dirigismo* (State-directed development) is giving way to community mobilization, involving sustained leadership by individuals and community groups working to achieve integral development and to promote the exercise of citizen rights, driven either by internal initiatives or outside encouragement.

Community mobilization is being developed on the basis of broad participation, rather than on the technocratic approach that until recently prevailed in all of the countries.

What form, then, does communication for development take in the context of this new participatory, self-management paradigm of community mobilization?

1. First, it helps facilitate dialogue among community members. It does this by:

■ Supporting participatory assessments of problems and by helping present these collectively-defined problems to the community.

Example: In Peru, a video helped to reveal the ways in which intermediaries were exploiting members of an agricultural cooperative. The Ministry of Agriculture, once presented with the vivid visual evidence shown in the video, was sufficiently impressed by the situation that it took immediate steps to end the exploitation.

■ Stimulating the community to think through and prioritize problems.

Example: In Jamaica, a video on female agricultural workers—including seasonal workers, small farmers and entrepreneurs—helped managers and technical personnel within government agricultural agencies to understand and value women's contribution to agricultural production, enhancing their awareness of the needs and problems of these women, and prompting them to reflect on the effects of the *machismo* prevalent in such environments.

■ Helping communities in different locations to exchange ideas and experiences.

Example: Community communication units were established in Ecuadorian communities. This involved educating young people on how simple media, such as informational murals, community newspapers, photomontage, posters, etc., can aid the community in diagnosing its own problems and formulating solutions. These community communication units transmitted news and reports from their communities to Radio Latacunga, which in turn disseminated them to other communities in the province of Cotopaxi.

■ Helping the community organize to solve problems.

Example: In the central region of Nariño, fliers and audiotapes on cholera prevention and on water use within the home—deployed following the socialization process known as cultural animation—have stimulated discussion on issues such as organizational practices and the role of certain government institutions in the region, while also eliciting clear statements on the responsibility of community and government regarding the river-basin degradation caused by intensive mining.

2. Second, communication strengthens the community's capacity to inform government, and society at large, of its aspirations, needs and problems. It does this by:

■ Providing the community with information on available services and how to access them.

Example: The Government of Mozambique has obtained international financing for the construction of

1927
1960
1963
1964
1967
1969
1970
1971
1972
1973
1974
1975
1976
1977
1978
1979
1980
1981
1982
1983
1984
1985
1986
1987
1988
1989
1990
1991
1992
1993
1994
1995
1996
1997
1998
1999
2000
2001
2002
2003
2004
2005
2006

THE CONCEPTUAL FRAMEWORK
Excerpt from: *Communication for Sustainable Development*
[La Comunicación para el Desarrollo Sostenible]
By Teresa Flores Bedregal

2002

Communication for sustainable development arises from a synthesis between communication for development, and environmental communication and education and should incorporate within its framework the great conceptual advances in human rights, social equity, plurality, respect for the differences among cultures and genders that have been agreed upon during the various world summits focused on development.

Communication for development, with a long theoretical tradition, has been complemented and enriched by environmental education and communication that, from the 1980s, has been contributing with new theoretical-methodological approaches and experiences to raise awareness not only about the need to care for the environment, but also for changing attitudes, practices and consumption habits harmful to the environment.

It should be pointed out that environmental communication and education, from the beginning, incorporates a vision that brings together communication and education as inseparable processes. It is in this sense a form of educational communication, where it is not simply about transmitting information and messages, but about educating and forming the citizen through processes that are systematically organized to influence the change in attitudes, values, practices and behaviors.

Communication for sustainable development—based on the contributions of the theory of communication, including applicable methods and techniques—intends to generate communication processes that help improve

the quality of life of the poorest people in developing countries, without destroying the environment.

In this [new] approach, it is understood that traditional cultures are not an obstacle but a means to help development. Communication becomes a tool to overcome the great inequalities, barriers and lack of opportunities in those sectors that have benefited least by economic development.

Communication for sustainable development employs mass media, middle and mini media, in separated or combined ways according to the specific objectives proposed in a communication strategy. It integrates traditional communication models with modern ones, incorporating new and old technologies, including traditional communication channels, the cybernetic space and multimedia. It also makes use of interpersonal and group communication, and indigenous channels, using them in a combined or selective manner according to their effectiveness in reaching the target [people] segment.

It tries, through communication processes, to achieve the active participation and involvement of the people so they become the main actors of their own development, participating in the design, planning and implementation of projects. It is also intended to build capacities, skills, practices and values necessary for the incorporation of all citizens in development processes.

Flores Bedregal, Teresa (2002). *Comunicación para el Desarrollo Sostenible*. La Paz: LIDEMA, Plural. Reprinted with permission of the author and the copyright holder.

21 community radio stations. One mission of the stations is to inform the population about the services provided by various institutions.

■ Training members of the community to use the media to provide government authorities, as well as the general public, with information about needs for social assistance.

Example: One mission of community radio stations is to develop the ability of the population to express itself and register complaints, while encouraging dialogue and debate on community issues.

■ Supporting communities in their demands, helping them achieve legitimacy and assisting them in gaining the support of government, opinion makers and the social communications media to implement their own solutions to the problems they face.

Example: In Brazil, the Anti-Hunger Pro-Citizen Campaign brought to the attention of the Office of the President of the Republic the people's demand for food. This led to the creation of a national committee, with a local bishop serving as its chair. Official recognition of the campaign represented a high-level form of legitimatization, resulting in organizing efforts by many governmental and private entities to obtain and distribute food.

■ Keeping the community informed on the progress of mobilization efforts aimed at achieving desired solutions.

Example: In the state of Maranhao, Brazil, the monthly newspaper *Aspiraçao*, which is published by the Maranhao Suburbs Health Association, disseminates information on successes achieved by the popular health and education movement.

3. Third, communication encourages governmental and private institutions to more fully and effectively use communications in their relationships with communities, encouraging them to:

■ respond to communities' needs and demands for assistance, and transmit them to the relevant technical sectors;
■ communicate with other organizations in coordinating community support programs;
■ develop communication strategies to support social intervention programs and community projects; and
■ prepare materials and use the media to convey messages to pertinent sectors of the population.

Bordenave, Juan Díaz (1996), "La comunicación como herramienta esencial del Desarrollo Sostenible" [Communication as an Essential Tool of Sustainable Development], in "*Población y Desarrollo*" [Population and Development], National University of Asunción, Paraguay. Used with permission of the author.

EXCERPT FROM:

COMMUNICATION AND TRANSITION IN THE MIDDLE EAST

By Karin G. Wilkins

2004 Lerner's classic work on the role of media in modernity still serves as a central foundation for subsequent scholarship on communication and transition in the Middle East. Polarizing tradition from modernity along a putatively inevitable development trajectory, Lerner declares "what America is ... the modernizing Middle East seeks to become" (Lerner 1966, 79). In order to embark on this trail towards American modernity, Lerner outlines a process through which individuals' exposure to media, particularly national and foreign sources, begets vicarious experiences leading to empathic perspectives, necessary in building democratic and entrepreneurial participants in emerging nations. The communication system that he believes will inspire this transition relies on the more "modern" media, particularly radio and film, rather than non-mediated oral traditions of communication, framed as more resonant with "traditional" culture.

Half a century later, the weaknesses in this argument are not difficult to spot and have been enumerated extensively elsewhere (Wilkins 1999, 2000). Among other issues, critics raise concerns with the ethnocentric, hierarchical and patriarchal nature of this argument, as well as its simplification of complex political, historical and cultural contexts. Still, many of Lerner's initial assumptions, concerning transition in the region and the importance of mediated communications within that process, are echoed in more recent literature on the subject.

First, Lerner believed that Middle Eastern cultures would follow a natural trajectory from more traditional towards more modern societies. This assertion builds on a notion that there is an evolutionary linear path,

leading towards a desired "modernity." One recent study (Inglehart and Baker, 2000) attempts to differentiate its approach from the modernization process ascribed by Lerner, sketching out a "postindustrial" phase, highlighting post-materialist values, communications and information processes, subsequent to the "industrial" or modern phase of development (privileging the technical, rational, materialist and secular) on the heels of a "pre-industrial" phase, grounding experience in nature. Still, the idea that development follows a linear path does not stray far from Lerner's initial vision, nor does the vision of transition within national spheres.

Other expositions on the subject of communication systems in the region similarly equate orality with tradition and media with modernity (Ayish 1999; Rawan 2002), and even new media with postmodernity (Fandy 1999). In Rawan's (2002) historical description of Afghanistan's communication systems, he not only describes oral systems, such as communication within mosques, meetings and bazaars, as traditional, and media systems, such as the press, radio and television, as modern, but also assigns these modern media systems as prerequisites for modernization: "The development and proliferation of modern mass media is not only a decisive factor in the modernization process of Afghan society, but must also be viewed as a major contributing factor for the proliferation of economic and cultural cooperation on the international level" (Rawan 2002, 168). One distinction, however, is that unlike Lerner's apparent preference for national and foreign media sources, Rawan recognizes the importance of using local information and languages in media products.

Although Ayish (1999) similarly describes oral communications as traditional or mediated communications in terms of modern modes, his argument raises important issues concerning the nature of the communication process, whether relative to context or universal across space and time. Lerner addressed this question as well, defending his position that some human processes were universal while others were

1927
1960
1963
1964
1967
1969
1970
1971
1972
1973
1974
1975
1976
1977
1978
1979
1980
1981
1982
1983
1984
1985
1986
1987
1988
1989
1990
1991
1992
1993
1994
1995
1996
1997
1998
1999
2000
2001
2002
2003
2004
2005
2006

particular. Kraidy's (1999a) work on hybridity among Lebanese youth articulates the intersections between broadly juxtaposed modern Western identities and those of traditional Arab cultures, through their consumption of media, mimicry of lifestyles and positioning within nomadic contexts. Kraidy, Ayish and others are attempting to step beyond an assumed duality of tradition and modernity that underscores much of the Western academic literature on communication and transition in the Middle East.

Lerner constructs a theoretical process he believes will lead to modernity, which he believes necessarily engages democratic reform. Whereas Lerner focused on individuals' interests in political participation, some of the more recent literature addresses structural contexts, such as legislative and judicial systems, as well as collective concerns, such as human and women's rights (Carapico 2002). Some document this transition by noting that the number of countries having elections in the Middle East/North African region almost tripled between the mid-1970s and the mid-1990s (Sreberny 2001). Explanations for this transition range from genuine internal interests to external pressures, from foreign donors such as the World Bank and the International Monetary Fund (IMF), and from historical conditions such as the collapse of the Cold War (Sreberny 2001).

A variety of perspectives depicting the role of media in promoting democratic transition are evident in recent literature. Some envision media with the power to inspire migration, facilitate markets, demarcate space for civil society, offer avenues towards expression for marginal groups, provide alternative sources of information and inculcate senses of citizenship or belonging to communities (Jamal 2000; Sreberny 2001). Carapico, for example, argues that media, migration and markets constitute "the most powerful forces for modernity at work in the world" (Sreberny 2001, 106). However, others argue that media systems may constrain democratic transition when global, regional or alternative media deflect attention from national interests, or when used as a mechanism for political

control, either through informal mechanisms, such as self-censorship, or more formal mechanisms, such as laws and arrests in the name of censorship and control (Jamal 2000, 2001).

Scholars working in political sociology have begun to theorize the dynamics between governments and news media, albeit with more attention to the official political side of this equation (Gilboa 1998; Wolfsfeld 1997; Wolfsfeld and others 2002). These theoretical models give much credence to the political environment in its ability to dominate media systems, recognizing to some extent the other pressures within the media environment and the agency of news professionals. Media scholars in political communication have a great deal to add to this discussion, but will need to concentrate more specifically on the conditions particular to this specific regional arena.

Democratic transition may be enhanced by the emergence of a civil sector separate from the state and market, allowing room for expression, critique and dialogue (Khiabany and Sreberny 2001). Whether the establishment of a "free press" system helps to foster this civil society is open to debate. While some strongly advocate a liberal press system as a way to promote political critique (Amin 2002; Khiabany and Sreberny 2001; Najjar 1998), others question the link between news systems and democratization (Ayish 2002).

Freedom of expression may be limited through formal channels, such as political regulation and policy or economic ownership and control; technical intervention; or informal dynamics extant within a political culture or professional education system (Amin 2002; Khazen 1999; Khiabany and Sreberny 2001; Najjar 1998). Governments may attempt to regulate press through imposing fines, imprisoning news professionals, regulating capital and licenses, among other means (Amin 2002; Najjar 1998).

Some argue that there may be some justification in regulating mediated expression as a form of civic responsibility or cultural preservation (Amin 2002;

Gher and Amin 1999), or as a mechanism to control chaos and opposition (Kraidy 1999b). On the other hand, global pressures towards privatization and the use of new technologies, along with political interests in maintaining particular profiles, and professional codes encouraged through Western training of Middle Eastern journalists (Amin 2002; Ayish 2002), favour the strengthening of a liberal press.

Political interests in media systems are not only used to justify attempts to control media content, but also to promote particular images of the national government within regional and global settings. Both the Lebanese (Kraidy 1999b) and Jordanian governments (Najjar 1998), for example, appear to be motivated to treat media industries in particular ways based on self-images as progressive regional leaders.

Overall, much of the research outlining political transition in the Middle East focuses on formal dimensions of democracy, whereas discussions of media's role tend to emphasize relationships between the state and media systems. There appears to be growing interest in the emergence of civil society, as an intermediary step between media systems allowing freedom of expression and subsequent democratic reform. Within this literature, we know less about social movements and opposition groups in relation to political reform, and less about strategies of resistance in relation to media systems, than we do about these more formal (government) aspects of democracy.

Although discussions of transitions towards modernity tend to highlight democratic reform, economic transitions are assumed to comprise this process towards modernity as well. The benefits of commercializing media industries are more assumed than debated within this literature. Some research has at least begun to examine the relationship between economic structure and media texts (Ayish 1997), as has been explored in other regional contexts. Some scholars praise commercial media's promotion of consumer society as a way to reflect and shape consumer interests. Gher and Amin argue, for example,

that the "Middle East passage from feudal economies to free enterprise capitalism is an absolute necessity for the ultimate survival of the Arab World" (Gher and Amin 1999, 85). Al-Makaty and others (1996) research in Saudi Arabia explores the subtle variations in approaches within Islam to advertising (some see commercial media as a threat to cultural values while others see them as an opportunity for economic gain) within this market-oriented system, arguing that advertising systems originating in the West may need to be more sensitive to other cultural contexts. These studies offer a useful beginning for more comprehensive research connecting economic with political contexts and subsequent media products with audience interpretations.

Research positioning media production within different political-economic contexts will be particularly critical to explore in this region, given that the few studies that have been conducted thus far find results contrary to those observed in similar research implemented in the West. Ayish (1997), for instance, concludes that the privately funded (through Saudi sources) Middle East Broadcasting Centre (MBC) is more likely to offer news and information programming, in contrast to the publicly run Egyptian Satellite Channel (ESC), which broadcasts more entertainment programming. Sakr's (2001) study of Egyptian satellite television confirms the importance of private transnational stations in offering political critique of national governments. As her comprehensive discussion of media industries explains, the process of privatization is propelled by support from external agents such as the U.S. Agency for International Development (USAID) and the U.S. Chamber of Commerce as well as by local businesses (Sakr 2001, 158-9). Questions of privatization and commercialization are becoming more pressing in the creation of transnational media systems (Sreberny 2001), as many television stations are producing products outside but directed towards the Middle East, such as MBC in the United Kingdom and Orbit in Rome (Franklin 1996).

1927
1960
1963
1964
1967
1969
1970
1971
1972
1973
1974
1975
1976
1977
1978
1979
1980
1981
1982
1983
1984
1985
1986
1987
1988
1989
1990
1991
1992
1993
1994
1995
1996
1997
1998
1999
2000
2001
2002
2003
2004
2005
2006

Another study describes commercial broadcasting channels as allowing "real culture" in Turkey, as opposed to the "official culture" promoted through publicly owned stations (Aksoy and Robins 1997). According to Aksoy and Robins, the "proliferation of broadcasting channels … was associated with a rapid marginalization and relativisation of the 'official' culture, and a differentiation of the Turkish audience along lines of taste, culture and identity" (Aksoy and Robins 1997, 1948). Although these multiple channels may have heralded cultural diversity in programming and content, political representation remained cautiously narrow, as new broadcasting regulation in the mid-1990s became more restrictive. Subsequent research by these authors (Aksoy and Robins 2000) further details how public Turkish television programming promotes a distinct sense of Turkish identity as a national allegiance, more so than privately run stations that appear to recognize diversity among groups of Turkish migrants across Europe.

Understanding the nature of media industries within and directed towards this region is critical in considering the potential for media in processes of social change. Instead of assuming that commercialization goes hand in hand with democratization, we need to question this link, particularly in light of recent experiences in the People's Republic of China, where privatization of industry has been decoupled from political participation. Moreover, selectively attending to private versus public distinctions may exclude recognition of critical social dimensions, such as the importance of civil institutions in social change processes (Sakr 2001).

Some studies of social transition highlight the role of media in reinscribing and fragmenting national, cultural and other identifies. Media reception may contribute to certain representations of cultural groups, which may correspond with, complement or even resist narratives of national communities. Media become the "spaces of communication in which the identity, meaning and boundaries or diasporic community are continually constructed, debated and re-imagined" (Mandaville 2001, 169). More specifically for this discussion, the area of the Middle East becomes "reconstituted and rearticulated in spaces and societies far removed from the Middle East" (Mandaville 2001, 169) through mediated representation and reception. Satellite television programmes, such as those from MBC, Egypt and Turkey, help to reinforce diasporic Muslim communities (Ghaffari-Farhangi 1998). Carter's (2001) study of Berber-language film demonstrates how Berber communities use their access to media production to counter problematic representations dominating much of the state-controlled Moroccan media. Her work articulates a critical vision of communities as not merely consumers, but as media producers, particularly important for groups marginalized from the centre of political power within societies.

Overall we know much less about the role of media, particularly alternative media, in social activism in comparison to the more formal sphere of political transition. More research should engage literature on social movements and media within the context of resistance to political oppression, from domestic and foreign governments. Anecdotal evidence of transnational television broadcasts mobilizing support for recent student protests in Iran suggests that this area warrants further investigation. Transnational television systems themselves are becoming increasingly critical agents within social, political and economic transitions.

At the time Lerner was theorizing the role of media in national development, the advent of film, radio and newspapers attracted attention. Since then many other media technologies have been considered within the context of development, including telephones, television and video, along with other communication strategies such as folk theatre and music. Information technologies, characterized as new and interactive in much of this literature, follow in this history of media technologies, first heralded for their potential in fostering social change, then critiqued for the inequities they may engender and the structural constraints of their implementation, and subsequently considered as more varied in their uses and consequences contingent upon political-economic structures and cultural contexts.

As in much of the current development literature worldwide, discussions of transition in the Middle East focus extensively on the potential promise of new information technologies, usually highlighting interactive computer technologies. Three recent studies elaborate on the contexts of Jordan, Saudi Arabia and Kuwait (Cunningham 2002; Teitelbaum 2002; Wheeler 2001). Resonant with literature described earlier on political transition, discussions of new information technologies in the Middle East tend to focus on state interests in maintaining control of information, against the technological potential to dissolve the traditional boundaries of the nation-state. Teitelbaum (2002) describes the political negotiations within Saudi Arabia as the government attempts to balance economic with Islamic interests in its attempts to shape the Internet for commercial and public uses. Similar to many others on the topic, he assumes that the "Internet, by its very nature, is a decentralized and a decentralizing medium" (Teitelbaum 2002, 225), through which government and opposition groups attempt to articulate their own perspectives.

Although most of the literature dealing with political transition and media in the Middle East tends to focus on the official government channels, an important emerging area for study engages the potential for political resistance through media. Interactive computer technologies are typically referred to within these discussions, in descriptions of Kuwaiti resistance to Iraqi occupation and Saudi opposition to official doctrine (Fandy 1999). In their attempts to control information, states may be better able to regulate broadcasting and print industries than other forms of communication, such as audio-tape production and distribution, along with telecommunication and Internet systems (Fandy 1999). Framed as postmodern technologies, Fandy suggests that current "electronic media and satellite systems virtually dissolve traditional barriers that once

separated states and nations" (Fandy 1999, 147). While Fandy takes great care in explaining opposition interests in reform, in ways that attempt to appeal to Western ideals and global structures, others focus on more revolutionary goals among opposition groups in their use of the Internet. Zanini (1999), in an article written before 9/11, details how terrorist groups are using new information technologies to mobilize constituents and wage information battles. She speculates that terrorist groups were becoming more decentralized, yet actively networked through younger, educated members able to use new technologies to coordinate their efforts without government detection. Social movement and communication scholarship could contribute to these discussions, by articulating paths through which marginal groups attempt to use mainstream and alternative media to achieve their goals, in relation to broader political and media environments.

Although studies of new information technologies have begun to explore the economic contexts of various industries within the region, the connection between privatization and global economic actors is rarely questioned. Rather, the importance of private funding for Internet providers within the Middle East tends to be assumed (Huff 2001), whether inspired by the private sector as in Jordan or governments as in Egypt and Saudi Arabia (Anderson 2000). Even in Jordan, hosting a comparatively liberalized and deregulated industry within the region, government commitment and bilateral investment encourage the information technology (IT) industry (Cunningham 2002).

Explorations of some of the social and cultural implications of new technologies in the Middle East are just beginning to gain more attention. Wheeler's (2000, 2001) research in Kuwait illustrates how youth may be replacing familial social rituals with computer interactions, particularly in terms of cross-gender interactions. Although women have not challenged political authorities directly through cyberspace, the Internet has served as a means towards mobilizing university students in opposing gender segregation

1927
1960
1963
1964
1967
1969
1970
1971
1972
1973
1974
1975
1976
1977
1978
1979
1980
1981
1982
1983
1984
1985
1986
1987
1988
1989
1990
1991
1992
1993
1994
1995
1996
1997
1998
1999
2000
2001
2002
2003
2004
2005
2006

laws. While potentially contributing to social transition within the region, new media technologies may also help to perpetuate cultural identities, particularly for Muslim (Mandaville 2001) and pan-Arab regional communities (Alterman 2000).

These discussions tend to assume that new media have the ability to transform society, yet Fandy (2000) asserts that the nature of trust changes the circumstances of this process within the Middle East. He begins by equating a modern sense of trust with television and the written word, while describing confidence in oral modes, such as those dominating communication in mosques, bazaars and coffee houses, as "premodern." Fandy cites cases in Egypt and Saudi Arabia, in which citizens failed to trust media accounts of war and other political events. However, he acknowledges that Al-Jazeera news tends to be more trusted than other sources more recently, problematizing this notion that trust is embedded within a technological system divorced from structure and context.

Several authors raise the concern that Arabs within the region are more likely to serve in the capacity of consumer rather than producer within the new communications industries (Fandy 1999; Ghareeb 2000). Anderson (2000) details instances, however, in which Arab groups are participating in these production processes, for example by creating software for use in Arabic. Ghareeb (2000) also advocates Arab participation in new media industries, such as satellite television, pan-Arab newspapers and magazines and the Internet. Despite limitations in cost, language and literacy, new media may have the potential to encourage cultural unity and to offer a space for political expression (Ghareeb 2000).

Critiques of this research resonate with concerns about the larger landscape of work conducted in the West on communication and transition in the Middle East. Alterman contests current literature on new communications technologies as confined to narrow projections based on our own cultural lens: "We need to free our studies of new media and technology in the

Middle East from the strait-jacket of Western experience" (Alterman 2000, 355). By attempting to engage the political contexts of academic research in terms of their connections to current political actions, we may pursue a mode of critique that suggests relevant areas for empirical investigation.

References

Aksoy, Asu, and Kevin Robins. "Peripheral Vision: Cultural Industries and Cultural Identities in Turkey," *Environment and Planning*, 1997, 29 (11): 1937-53.

Aksoy, Asu, and Kevin Robins. "Thinking Across Spaces: Transnational Television From Turkey," *European Journal of Cultural Studies*, 2000, 3 (3): 543-63.

Al-Makaty, Safran, G. Norman van Tubergen, S. Scott Whitlow, and Douglas A. Boyd. "Attitudes Toward Advertising in Islam," *Journal of Advertising Research*, 1996, 36(3): 16-27.

Alterman, Jon. "Counting Nodes and Counting Noses: Understanding New Media in the Middle East," *The Middle East Journal*, 2000, 54 (3): 355-63.

Amin, Hussein. "Freedom as a Value in Arab Media: Perceptions and Attitudes Among Journalists," *Political Communication*, 2002, 19 (2): 125-36.

Anderson, Jon W. "Producers and Middle East Internet Technology: Getting Beyond Impacts," *The Middle East Journal*, 2000, 54 (3): 419-34.

Ayish, Muhammad. "Arab Television Goes Commercial: A Case Study of the Middle East Broadcasting Centre," *Gazette*, 1997, 59 (6): 473-94.

Ayish, Muhammad. "Communication Research in the Arab World: A New Perspective," *The Public*, 1999, 5 (1): 33-57.

Ayish, Muhammad. "Political Communication on Arab World Television: Evolving Patterns," *Political Communication*, 2002, 19 (2): 137-54.

Carapico, Sheila. "Foreign Aid for Promoting Democracy in the Arab World," *The Middle East Journal*, 2002, 56 (3): 379-95.

Carter, Sandra Gayle. "Moroccan Berberity, Representational Power and Identity in Video Films," *Gazette*, 2001, 63 (2-3): 241-62.

Cunningham, Karla J. "Factors Influencing Jordan's Information Revolution: Implications for Democracy," *The Middle East Journal*, 2002, 56 (2): 240-56.

Fandy, Mamoun. "CyberResistance: Saudi Opposition Between Globalization and Localization," *Society for Comparative Study of Society and History*, 1999, 41 (1): 124-47.

Fandy, Mamoun. "Information Technology, Trust, and Social Change in the Arab World," *The Middle East Journal*, 2000, 54 (3): 378-94.

Franklin, Stephen. "The Kingdom and the Power (TV News in the Middle East)," *Columbia Journalism Review*, 1996, 35 (4): 49-52.

Ghaffari-Farhangi, Setareh. "The Era of Global Communication as Perceived by Muslims," *Gazette*, 1998, 60 (4): 267-80.

Ghareeb, Edmund. "New Media and the Information Revolution in the Arab World: An Assessment," *The Middle East Journal*, 2000, 54 (3): 395-418.

Gher, Leo A., and Hussein Y. Amin. "New and Old Media Access and Ownership in the Arab World," *Gazette*, 1999, 61 (1): 59-88.

Gilboa, Eytan. "Secret Diplomacy in the Television Age," *Gazette*, 1998, 60 (3): 211-25.

Inglehart, Ronald, and Wayne E. Baker. "Modernization, Cultural Change, and the Persistence of Traditional Values," *American Sociological Review*, 2000, 65 (1): 19-51.

Jamal, Amal. "The Palestinian Media: An Obedient Servant or a Vanguard of Democracy?" *Journal of Palestine Studies*, 2000, 29 (3): 45-59.

Jamal, Amal. "State-Formation, the Media, and the Prospects of Democracy in Palestine," *Media, Culture and Society*, 2001, 22: 497-505.

Khazen, Jihad. "Censorship and State Control of the Press in the Arab World," *Harvard International Journal of Press Politics*, 1999, 4(3): 87-92.

Khiabany, Gholam, and Annabelle Sreberny. "The Iranian Press and the Continuing Struggle Over Civil Society, 1998-2000," *Gazette*, 2001, 63 (2-3): 203-23.

Kraidy, Marwan. "The Global, the Local and the Hybrid: A Native Ethnography of Globalization," *Critical Studies in Mass Communication*, 1999a, 16: 456-76.

Kraidy, Marwan. "State Control of Television News in 1990s Lebanon," *Journalism and Mass Communication Quarterly*, 1999b, 76 (3): 485-98.

Lerner, Daniel. *The Passing of Traditional Society in the Middle East*. Second edition. Glencoe, Ill.: Free Press, 1966.

Mandaville, Peter. "Reimagining Islam in Diaspora: The Politics of Mediated Community," *Gazette*, 2001, 63 (2-3): 169-86.

Najjar, Orayb. "The Ebb and Flow of the Liberalization of the Jordanian Press 1985-1997," *Journalism and Mass Communication Quarterly*, 1998, 75 (1): 127-42.

Rawan, Shir Mohammad. "Modern Mass Media and Traditional Communication in Afghanistan," *Political Communication*, 2002, 19 (2): 155-70.

Sakr, Naomi. "Contested Blueprints for Egypt's Satellite Channels: Regrouping the Options by Redefining the Debate," *Gazette*, 2001, 63 (2-3): 149-67.

Sreberny, Annabelle. "Mediated Culture in the Middle East: Diffusion, Democracy, Difficulties," *Gazette*, 2001, 63 (2-3): 101-20.

Teitelbaum, Joshua. "Dueling for Da'wa: State Versus Society on the Saudi Internet," *The Middle East Journal*, 2002, 56 (2): 222-39.

Wheeler, Deborah. "The Internet and Public Culture in Kuwait," *Gazette*, 2001, 63 (2-3): 187-201.

Wheeler, Deborah. "New Media, Globalization and Kuwaiti National Identity," *The Middle East Journal*, 2000, 54 (3): 432-444.

Wilkins, Karin. "Development Discourse on Gender and Communication in Strategies for Social Change," *Journal of Communication*, 1999, 49 (1): 44-64.

Wilkins, Karin, ed. *"Redeveloping Communication for Social Change: Theory, Practice and Power*. Boulder, Colo.: Rowman and Littlefield, 2000.

Wolfsfeld, Gadi. "Fair Weather Friends: The Varying Role of the News Media in the Arab-Israeli Peace Process," *Political Communication*, 1997, 14: 29-48.

Wolfsfeld, Gadi, Rami Khouri, and Yoram Peri. "News About the Other in Jordan and Israel: Does Peace Make a Difference?" *Political Communication*, 2002, 19 (2): 189-210.

Zanini, Michele. "Middle Eastern Terrorism and Netwar," *Studies in Conflict and Terrorism*, 1999, 22: 247-56.

Wilkins, Karin G. "Communication and Transition in the Middle East." SAGE, Gazette, 2004, Vol. 66, No. 6: 483-496. Copyright © 2004 by Sage Publications. Reprinted by permission of Sage Publications, Inc.

EXCERPT FROM:

COMMUNICATION, DEVELOPMENT AND HEALTH PROMOTION. APPROACHES, BALANCES AND CHALLENGES

By José Miguel Pereira G. and Martha Cardozo B.

2003 A historical review of the intellectual field of communication in Latin America (see Benavides et al., 1998, 119–138) will show that the relationships between communication and development operate like a map: They are useful to identify the integrating role of society and the modern attitudes that would allow society to progress, and also to show the actions and struggles of different sectors of society to democratize access to communication media and to expand citizens' freedom of expression and participation. This relationship is, in turn, closely related to an old but renewed discussion about the possibilities of democracy in Latin America: How to combine economic growth with political democracy and social equity?

In fact, since it was first incorporated into government programs and social management in the late 1950s, communication has been considered a "natural partner" of the actions and promises of development, freedom and democracy made by the state and/or by some sectors of society, with the purpose of supporting and strengthening a modern public sphere capable of integrating citizens not only around a national economic market, but also around a core of shared values that promote both equal access to social welfare and the active presence of natural cultures in development processes.

What happens to communication, particularly to communication for development in this context? In general terms, some scenarios for reflection, research and intervention can be identified; they have provided the answer to this question in Latin America and have

1927
1960
1963
1964
1967
1969
1970
1971
1972
1973
1974
1975
1976
1977
1978
1979
1980
1981
1982
1983
1984
1985
1986
1987
1988
1989
1990
1991
1992
1993
1994
1995
1996
1997
1998
1999
2000
2001
2002
2003
2004
2005
2006

made possible the construction of this intellectual field in the continent.

Communication: The Infrastructure for National Integration

The links between communication and development draw a double line of actions and infrastructure. In the first place, they point at the modernizing actions undertaken by states to unite and integrate the various sectors of society into the great changes produced by industrial and technological development, especially in the second half of the 20th century. The goal is that the transition from a traditional society to a modern one be harmonious and take place within institutions; that is to say, that it be a "peaceful revolution" capable of generating economic prosperity and political stability in those nations that cannot otherwise benefit from progress. Communication has thus become a variable that depends on social change; above all, it has come to be a synonym of national integration that should accompany modernizing development.

From a technical perspective, communication has played an important role in the creation of a physical communication infrastructure—roads, railroads, ports, data and telephone systems, broadcasting, television and printing—whose purpose is to make the programs of economic transition towards capitalism feasible; this means industrial modernization, creation of internal markets and technological transfer.

Communication: Diffusion and Extension

On the other hand, communication and education for development aimed at directing —with the guidance of international experts—the minds and hearts of our men and women towards a universal discourse based on modern values about family, birth control, demographic growth, education, health, the agrarian sector, technology and culture. What was the goal? To build the institutional bases of a national public sphere and of a national public, or audience, that, by overcoming resistance to cultural change, would welcome progress and modern development in society.

With this objective in operation, illiteracy levels would decrease, family planning would improve, and peasant productivity would increase.

Communication and Information: Democracy and Citizenship

The links between communication and development have traditionally been revealed in a series of social, political and cultural conflicts that have determined what we are and what we want to be. The function of these conflicts has been to democratize the communicative system, which seems to be vertical in Latin American countries, as well as to motivate participation in the reconfiguration of our own modernity. This modernity is heterogeneous; it challenges countries not only to be incorporated into the "illustrated ideology" that would make them modern at last, but also to adjust the modernity experience to the "peripheral" conditions of existence in which history and cultural identities coexist with universal reasoning, technology and progress.

The various actors in this relationship between communication and development have been workers, peasants, indigenous peoples, women, intellectuals, artists, Christian associations and, more recently, social movements that demand the right to life, environmental preservation, local and regional autonomy, and human rights. These individuals and groups identify themselves, to a smaller or larger extent, with a concept of national public sphere modernization that is not exhausted in development and economic growth—essentially measured in terms of gross domestic product per capita—but that implies the growth of citizenship from political/cultural recognition to equitable differences among people and to equal exercise of the right to public expression by the different "voices" that make up a democracy. It is a matter of expanding freedom of expression and citizen participation.

Communication and Daily Life: The Popular Sphere

In the early 1980s, communication for development was related to a new approach to popular cultures and social movements. Taking up again the local, daily, micro and territorial dimensions, this renewed research concept went beyond the alternative current devoted to identifying the popular sphere as an un-contaminated synonym of all those system forces and to placing an insurmountable barrier between popular culture and mass culture. Instead, the type of analysis that began in the 1980s attempted to show how the popular sphere was built within mass culture through the complex processes of confrontation, negotiation, and adaptation that social majorities undergo daily when they face the standardization of their existence.

According to Jesús Martín Barbero (1987, 10–11), a pioneer researcher of this new concept of popular culture:

> In the last few years, we have discovered that the popular sphere stems not only from indigenous or peasant cultures, but also from the thick fabric of mixed races and the deformations of urban groups and masses. We have discovered that, at least in Latin America and contrary to the proph-ecies of social implosion, masses still contain the people in the double sense of controlling them and having them inside.

In fact, this conception of the popular sphere is comple-mentary to the rise of multiple social networks whose individual and collective demands go beyond purely political demands for power and locate themselves in concrete fights for the very meaning and sense of life. Social networks put in the center of public discus-sion topics related to health, sexuality, human rights, drugs, external debt, gender, racism and ecology. Such topics have been generally put aside both by the traditional spaces and agents of political represen-tation and by "the egalitarian myth of the global village and by the new communication technological order" (Mattelart 1993, 266). The latter, in turn, emerge from a "diversification" of development created by specific groups—women, young people, environmentalists, neighbors, prostitutes, and homosexuals, among others—who try to manage their own interests by fusing together their private and public roles and by

introducing expressive and symbolic dimensions into their political demands for a decent life.

Communication as Negotiation: Reception and Cultural Consumption

Communication for development is linked to a topic that, until the late 1980s, was pushed into the back-ground by Latin American communication researchers: the study of reception and cultural consumption. This line of research has come to fill the gap left by previous communication paradigms. This gap was created by a lack of analysis of the mediations and new mean-ings that intervene in the processes of appropriation and use of mass media messages, as well as by the difficulty in understanding cultural complexity in our so-cieties, particularly the mass culture phenomenon.

This type of analysis:

> aims at incorporating consumption [and recep-tion] into a broader analysis of culture. Its rele-vance goes beyond academic interest since the importance of these studies in the formulation of cultural policies has recently become apparent. Specifically, a democratic proposal in this field im-plies a creative alternative to the purely directional approach and a link between global orientations and real demands coming from a variety of popu-lation sectors" (Catalán & Sunkel 1991, 16).

From this perspective, there is a clear "return to the subject" that leads one to observe how audiences codify and give new meanings to mass media mes-sages, as well as to recognize in consumption not only an economic but also an interactive sociopolitical rationality (for more information about consumption from the perspective of cultural analysis, see Gar-cia Canclini 1995, 43). Therefore, instead of reduc-ing the problem of consumption and reception to a supply–demand equation, "the topic of the active role of receivers and users cannot be dissociated from the questions raised by organized citizens about the possibilities of exerting real democratic control over the new flows and networks of communication" (Mattelart 1993, 271).

1927
1960
1963
1964
1967
1969
1970
1971
1972
1973
1974
1975
1976
1977
1978
1979
1980
1981
1982
1983
1984
1985
1986
1987
1988
1989
1990
1991
1992
1993
1994
1995
1996
1997
1998
1999
2000
2001
2002
2003
2004
2005
2006

This reflection makes us aware of the need to refer to social actors, social movements, peasants, indigenous groups and workers, among others, to reach the objectives of development.

Communication as Interconnection: Globalization and Culture

Communication for development is also related to the new ways of inhabiting the space-world we live in. Today, the spirit of the times is strongly characterized by a double movement. On one side, there is the emergence of information, communication and knowledge networks that turn us into planetary inhabitants without leaving our homes. These networks connect us to a world agenda; without them, it is increasingly difficult to know what is going on with the world economy, human rights, drug trafficking and the environment, to mention only a few examples. On the other side, there are serious processes of privatization of our existence—processes that invite us to lock ourselves in intimate, individual spaces—and of citizen fragmentation and loss of faith in traditional certainties to use in facing the future, "playing" politics or making sense out of collective identities (Tomlinson 1999).

This space-world also undergoes very complex processes of economic globalization, cultural differentiation and life-style homogenization whose impact on popular and national cultures cannot be ignored in Latin America. As Jesús Martín Barbero (1995, 18) points out:

> We can no longer ignore that we are immersed in the world market. The way in which we have been included–excluded is our peculiarity; it is the way our policies and institutions have been historically produced. That fact is unalterable and we cannot go backwards or take refuge in a place that has not been already touched or penetrated. Like it or not, this is the way we are in this world space, and it is already part of what we are and what we do. The point is no longer deciding whether we are integrated or not, but how to integrate ourselves without being destroyed but transformed.

The Design of Communication and Cultural Policies

Communication for development is also tied to the debate about cultural policies. It is an analysis that begins with the recognition of the decisive role that culture plays in the processes of political and socioeconomic development in our societies. Cultural policies can actively influence the agreements made between the state, civil institutions and organized community groups "in order to orient symbolic development, satisfy the cultural needs of the population, and reach a consensus on a particular social order or transformation" (García Canclini 1995, 26).

The purpose of cultural policies is to foster new agreements between the state and civil society so that the public sphere can be democratically created and strengthened. The main axis of such a sphere would be "the construction of meaning and sense, the generation of cultural symbols, and the projection of a concept of historical development that stimulates citizens' participation and identification" (White 1992, 54).

References

Martín Barbero, J. 1987. "La telenovela en Colombia: Televisión, melodrama y vida cotidiana," *Diálogos de la Comunicación* 17 (June): 46–59.

Martín Barbero, J. 1995. *Pre-textos. Conversaciones sobre la comunicación y sus contextos.* Cali, Colombia: Universidad del Valle.

Benavides, J., J.I. Bonilla, and J.M. Pereira G. 1998. "Comunicación en contextos de desarrollo: Balances y perspectives," *Signo y Pensamineto* 32: 119–138.

Catalán, C., and G. Sunkel. 1991. "La tematización de las comunicaciones en América Latina," *Comunicación* 76:4–26.

Garcia Canclini, N. 1995. *Consumidores y ciudadanos.* Mexico: Grijalbo.

Mattelart, A. 1993. *The Communication-world: The History of Ideas and Strategies.* Madrid: FUNDESCO.

Tomlinson, J. 1999. *Globalization and Culture.* Mexico: Oxford Univ. Press.

White, R. 1992. "Cultural analysis in communication for development," *Diálogos de la Comunicación* 34 (September).

Pereira G., José Miguel and Martha Cardozo B. "Communication, Development and Health Promotion. Approaches, Balances and Challenges," paper presented in the 3rd National Congress on Communication and Health, and in the 1st Latin American Congress on Communication and Health held in Cochabamba, (Bolivia), September 3 to 6, 2003. Translated from Spanish by Emma Cristina Montaña R. Used with permission of copyright holder.

EXCERPT FROM:

A CRITICAL ASSESSMENT OF THEORIES/MODELS USED IN HEALTH COMMUNICATION FOR HIV/AIDS

Theories and Models of Behavior Change

Collins O. Airhihenbuwa and Rafael Obregón

2000 Models of behavior change typically used to guide health communication programs are the same ones used to inform health promotion programs. Some of the most important theories and models include the health belief model, the theory of reasoned action, social learning/cognitive theory, diffusion of innovation, and social marketing (Glanz & Rimer 1995).

The health belief model (HBM) (Becker 1974) was developed in the 1950s to predict individual response to, and utilization of, screening and other preventive health services. According to this model, the response and utilization of disease prevention programs will be predicated on an individual's perception of the seriousness of the disease, severity of the disease, perceived benefit of services, and barriers to accessing such services.

> In general, the HBM is a rational-cognitive model and assumes a 'rational' decision-maker. Most adolescents, and many adults, do not seem to approach the AIDS issue from such a logical perspective, but seem quite capable of discounting risks and optimistically perceiving themselves as invulnerable to harm (Freimuth 1992, 101).

The theory of reasoned action (Fishbein & Ajzen 1975) predicts individual behavior by examining attitudes, beliefs, behavioral intentions and observed expressed acts. In this linear progression from attitude to action, a given behavior will be determined by an individual's intention. This theory also assumes that individuals are rational in their decision-making process, "a presumption that may not be entirely relevant for AIDS-related behaviors that are heavily influenced by emotions" (Michal-Johnson & Bowen 1992, 153). Moreover, individuals evaluate information that may result in action within external constraints, which are also mediated by power relations in a society (Yoder 1997).

The social learning/cognitive theory (Bandura 1986) postulates that an individual behavior is the result of the interaction among cognition, behavior, environment and physiology. The two primary domains widely used in HIV/AIDS programs are modeling (imitation of the behavior of a role model) and self-efficacy (one's perception of one's ability to adopt a recommended behavior). Although this model is believed to be very useful in HIV/AIDS communication campaigns in the United States (Freimuth 1992; Maibach & Flora 1993), there remains the question about its relevance in cultures where individual decisions are the result of group norms whereby being individualistic is going against the grain. After all, the social learning/cognitive theory is an individual psychological model of behavior change (Yoder, Hornik & Chirwa 1996). Bandura (1998) advocates the need to focus on collective efficacy.

Diffusion of Innovations (Rogers 1983) focuses on the communication process by which a new idea or product becomes known and used by people in a given population. Two relevant principles of diffusion of innovation widely used in AIDS campaign are creating awareness of HIV and using opinion leaders to influence attitudes and behaviors (Freimuth 1992; Rogers 1983; Rogers 1995). "*Diffusion of Innovation* has been criticized for being too linear, for having a pro-innovation bias and for widening the gaps between the 'information haves' and 'have-nots' in a social system. This gap has certainly been observed in AIDS awareness and knowledge" (Freimuth 1992, 103), given the positive correlation between knowledge of HIV and level of education. In spite of its limitations, however, the use of opinion leaders in helping to shape culturally appropriate strategies is a component of

1927
1960
1963
1964
1967
1969
1970
1971
1972
1973
1974
1975
1976
1977
1978
1979
1980
1981
1982
1983
1984
1985
1986
1987
1988
1989
1990
1991
1992
1993
1994
1995
1996
1997
1998
1999
2000
2001
2002
2003
2004
2005
2006

diffusion of innovation that offers possibilities in HIV/AIDS communications. This is particularly salient since the content (focusing on a community interpretation of disease meaning rather than an imposed germ theory), context (relationships and negotiation in families and communities) and language (codes of elasticity of usage relevant) of communication will be a factor in the outcome of HIV/AIDS prevention and care. According to Soola (1991), an "African communicator need not bother with the strictly technical aspects of information on AIDS (at least not for some 80 percent of his audience) because of the non-beneficial effect of such information to a large majority of his audience" (36). Indeed, Green (1999), based on his fieldwork in Africa, has offered an African traditional healing theory of disease that is grounded in culturally defined codes and meaning similar to those in the West.

Social marketing is an organized approach to promoting acceptability of a social idea. Social maketing's four "P"s—product, price, place and promotion—have been applied extensively to HIV/AIDS prevention in condom promotion. A fifth "P" has recently been added to indicate "positioning" with regards to recognition of competing campaigns on the same subject in the same location. Among the criticisms of social marketing in HIV/AIDS are ethical concerns (Guttman 1997b), given that it sometimes utilizes manipulation, such as fear, in promoting condom use. "Fear appeals emphasize the noxious consequences that will befall message recipients if they fail to adopt the recommendations of the source" (Dillard et al. 1996, 44). Furthermore, it is also believed that social marketing employs a simple solution (such as condom distribution) to a complex problem without addressing the social conditions that cause the spread of HIV (Freimuth 1992). Social marketing targets individual behavior only, "consequently reducing public health issues to individual-level problems and defining solutions within 'information deficit' models" (Guttman, 1997a). "How AIDS is discussed, how resources are allocated, who are defined as in the 'risk groups,' and who makes the decisions about AIDS highlight the inseparable connection between AIDS and power in society" (McAllister 1992, 196). With respect to the limitations of social marketing, Smith's (1998) evaluation of social marketing indicates that product social marketing has been widely used and praised whereas relatively little effort has gone into behavior social marketing (using social marketing to change and maintain behavior change) and almost nothing has been done in the area of policy social marketing (using social marketing to influence policy to support HIV research and protection of persons living with HIV/AIDS).

The health belief model and other models and theories with similar principles were designed to address health prevention from an individual, linear and rational perspective. While these theories and models have proven effective in certain societies for addressing certain diseases, they seem to be inadequate for communicating HIV/AIDS prevention and care messages in Africa, Asia, Latin America and the Caribbean. In fact, the assumptions (such as individualism as opposed to collectivism) on which these theories and models are based are foreign to many non-Western cultures where these models/theories have been used to guide communication strategies for HIV/AIDS prevention and care. "We should not expect these models to be productive in explaining behavior in social contexts where commonsense knowledge of the world takes a quite different form" (Yoder 1997, 136).

Theories and Models Applied to HIV/AIDS Prevention Programs

Theories, models or frameworks are designed to guide the implementation and evaluation of programs along certain processes that are believed to yield an expected outcome. Even though practitioners in the field implement programs without self-expressed pathways of models and theories, they are still guided by sets of assumptions that form the foundations on which the ideas, funding and successful outcome evaluation of such projects are based. In evaluating the continuous reliance of health communication on social psychology, Lievrouw (1994) comments:

While there is no doubt that the social-psychological theory 'classics' are relevant to health communication and that they have been valuable exploratory tools, they nonetheless leave certain basic premises undisturbed. Chief among these is the presumption that communication in health is mostly a matter of interaction between institution message 'sources' (e.g. medical research, professionals, government, foundations) and individual 'receivers' (e.g. patients, their families, school children, employees) (94).

Moreover, these theories and models of health behavior change, such as social learning/cognitive theory and the hierarchy of effects, are based on individual psychology (Yoder, Hornik & Chirwa 1996) as opposed to family, group or community locus of decisions. This application of individual and psychological models in contexts where decision originates from group norms and processes led Yoder et al., (1996) to question claims made by researchers regarding the program impact on behavioral outcomes from exposure to a radio drama on HIV/AIDS education in African countries.

Theories based on the individual, which may be effective and meaningful in a Western context, have less relevance in self-effacing cultures of Asia, Africa and Latin America and the Caribbean. In these regions, family and community are more central to the construction of health and well-being than the individual, even though the individual is always recognized as an important part of the cultural context.

In these cultures, individuals are also less likely to express themselves and less likely to articulate their level of well-being from the standpoint of "ego" (the "I"). It is the state of well-being of family and community that regulates how individuals measure their state of health. Moreover, theories and models based on measuring how the individual feels about him/herself, e.g., I feel good about myself, could never capture the health locus of control in many societies because such control rests somewhere outside the self. Within this self-effacing construct, individuals are not always accustomed to expressing their attitudes and beliefs by using extreme descriptors often found on social science survey instruments such as "strongly agree" or "strongly disagree." In fact, to do so within such a cultural context is considered disrespectful. Yet instruments designed to measure health behavior, for example, self-efficacy, are often presented on such a continuum with two extremes (strongly agree to strongly disagree) in cultures where such measures are not only irrelevant but could be considered offensive. In order to capture the complexity of the context within which an individual is a part, one needs a framework that underscores the component of context which features culture as a central and organizing theme (Sue 1994; Airhihenbuwa 1995).

The professional and cultural partiality of the Westernized approach to the understanding of self renders findings from much social and behavioral science research in Africa, Asia, Latin America and the Caribbean problematic. For example, one can appreciate differences between individual-centered versus family- and community-centered cultures by examining cultural differences in daily salutations. Greetings such as "how are you doing today?" may elicit a range of self-assured responses that captures how a Westerner actually feels on a given day—from "I'm well" to "great" and "wonderful." The same greeting among the Yorubas or Ebos of Nigeria almost never elicits a state of being "great" or "wonderful" even if this is how the individual feels. Instead, a common, nondefinite response is "O.K.," "fine" or "we give thanks to the Almighty." Furthermore, such a response is consistent with cultural values and meanings that promote and reward a tempered expression about one's well being.

The corpus of social psychology is based on the behaviors of people in Western cultures (Triandis 1994). According to Triandis (1994), culture is the man-made part of the environment, and, therefore, culture is a group's attempt to control its environment. Thus, the relationship between the individual and her/his environment is unidirectional, with the individual always shaping the environment and never the reverse. As

1927
1960
1963
1964
1967
1969
1970
1971
1972
1973
1974
1975
1976
1977
1978
1979
1980
1981
1982
1983
1984
1985
1986
1987
1988
1989
1990
1991
1992
1993
1994
1995
1996
1997
1998
1999
2000
2001
2002
2003
2004
2005
2006

a result, measures of skill acquisition and self-determination are based on the individual's perception of his/her ability to control his/her environment. Thus, controlling one's environment is a central theme in Western conceptions of culture—a conception that eschews other cultural realities such as harmonizing with nature and/or adapting to one's environment. If controlling the environment is the *raison d'etre* of cultures, then the inability to control one's environment suggests retrogression, a barrier to be overcome. Hence, "cultural barriers" (never "cultural strength") becomes a common expression in this discourse.

Applied to health communication, limitations easily become self-evident. For example, the cultural complexities of adhering to media messages about STD are seldom interrogated. The call for sexual negotiation at the point of initial contact between two people who are about to begin sexual relations contradicts most culturally sanctioned behavior. Two people who are about to begin sexual relations typically avoid discussing their sexual past until they are more comfortable with each other, at which point sexual intercourse commonly has occurred (Pliskin 1997). In this case, sexual behavior precedes sexual knowledge, at least in the context of relationships, which is often the basis for most interventions on preventing HIV/AIDS. This reality of "behavior-first" renders the linear model of knowledge leading to attitude and behavior counterintuitive in the context of relationships and culture.

Cultural Contexts and HIV/AIDS

Culture, often appropriated as an exotic collective, is believed by many to exist only in Africa, Asia and Latin America and in their descendants in the Diaspora. According to Yoder (1997), beliefs are often used as a proxy for culture, such that beliefs and knowledge of illness becomes the focus of "culturally appropriate" messages and interventions. In fact, the term *belief* is often contrasted with knowledge such that "belief is used to connote ideas that are erroneous from the perspective of biomedicine and that constitute obstacles to appropriate behavior" (Peltro & Peltro

1997, 148). Therefore, when "culture" and "belief" are coupled as in cultural belief, the resulting negative biomedical appropriation of the term becomes evident. As a consequence, culture is objectified and believed to be possessed by non-Western people, only identifiable through research. An example of this is found "in health education campaigns that seek information about local idioms of expression to better communicate health messages" (Yoder 1997, 138). As a result, it is reasoned that individual practices or behaviors found in these groups could be labeled cultural and often appropriated as a barrier. Thus "barrier" often becomes the coupling metaphor with culture.

There are three major themes that characterize perceptions about these notions of culture. First, culture is a *fossilized historical artifact,* which leads to such definitions as "culture is to a society what memory is to individuals" (Kluckhohn 1954). Second, culture is the observable aspect of individual behavior which is better understood by locating behaviors (particularly those that are unfamiliar) within individual beliefs. Such beliefs are distinguished from knowledge since the KAPB model places these domains in separate locations on a parallel continuum. In fact, belief and knowledge are thus constructed as a binarism and belief invariably becomes a code for culture (Good 1994), a barrier that must be overcome. For example, if you learned from your grandmother that chicken soup is good for your common cold, it is a "cultural belief." However, if you were to learn the same health information from a physician, it is "knowledge." A third theme is that culture is people's ability to *control/dominate* their environment. Thus the onus of responsibility for adopting requisite behavior rests in the individual. The assumption is that everyone desires to change, and is capable of changing, their environment to suit their needs. Each of these domains is an aspect of culture.

In the view of some scholars, culture is what society evolves from in the process of development—a proxy for modernization. Modernization and culture are often located at two opposite ends of the spectrum.

Given this impoverished notion of culture, "it seems urgent that we concentrate on studies of the distribution of meaning in social space, and on searching social sources of diversity and heterogeneity, rather that focusing exclusively on cultural sharing, uniformity, and homogeneity" (Bibeau 1997, 248).

Western cultures, to varying degrees, tend to view the self as a production of the individual whereas many other cultures view the self as a production of the family, community and other environmental influences over which we neither have nor desire total control. Crawford (1994) believes "the heart of the cultural politics of AIDS is a contestation over the meaning of the self" (1347). A large part of this contestation involves the definition and construction of people with AIDS and those who are HIV+ as "other." In its most basic sense, health is associated with those who are not infected with HIV and unhealthy with those who are infected with HIV. "The identity signified by HIV/AIDS comes to be seen as the other who is perceived not only as a physical danger, but as an equally threatening and dangerous identity" (1348).

The cultural politics of AIDS has caused the mobilization of many of these facets of culture with varying degrees of success. The mobilization of ethnographers to study these same risk groups has served a reductive function in terms of how culture is understood and conceptualized. "Despite their intention to break with the dominant public health models, most anthropologists are not really willing to distance themselves from the methodology and theorizing of what is perceived as 'real' science in public health" (Bibeau 1997, 247). This problem is evident in the tendency to create epidemiological categories, thus reducing culture to identifications of negative individual health practices in a subgroup of the population later generalized to be the definition of the larger group's culture.

In the literature dealing with cultural sensitivity, it is rare to see "strength" coupled with the concept of culture while "cultural barrier" is commonly cited as a reason for failure in public health and health promotion and communications programs. For instance, some health communication and health promotion programs implemented in Africa have tended to undervalue the importance of oral communication as a genre. This practice is consistent with the academics' exaltation of written and visual modes of communication (slides and transparencies) as the only acceptable standard. For example, the traditional communication channel which Ugboaja (1987) terms "Oramedia," continue to maintain its potency in rural Africa (Soola 1991).

We do believe and do advocate, as have others, that cultural sensitivity be central to health communication and health promotion theory and practice. This position is evident in cultural models such as PEN-3 (Airhihenbuwa 1995), a model used in health promotion and disease prevention (Erwin & Spatz 1996; Paskett et al. 1999; Green & Kreuter 1999; Kline 1999.) In this model, cultural appropriateness in health promotion refers not only to the individual but to the context that nurtures the individual and his/her family and community. This context is evaluated for attributes that are positive, existential and negative. It is important to promote the positive, recognize and affirm the existential and contextualize the negative, such that opportunity costs and benefits for change are understood and appreciated. With regard to communication strategies for HIV prevention within the African context, for example, message segmentation is critical to reaching a population with a diverse mode of producing and acquiring information and knowledge. "In traditional societies, which most African societies are, the need for audience, message and channel segmentation is important, considering the reach and influence of the different channels of communication and the absorptive capacity of the different segments of the population" (Soola 1991, 35).

References

Airhihenbuwa, C.O. 1995. *Health and Culture: Beyond the Western Paradigm.* Thousand Oaks, Calif.: Sage Publications.

Airhihenbuwa, C.O., R.J. DiClemente, G.M. Wingood, and A. Lowe. 1992. "HIV/AIDS education and prevention among African-Americans: A focus on culture," *AIDS Education and Prevention* 4:267–276.

Bandura, A. 1986. *Social Foundations of Thought and Action: A Social Cognitive Theory.* Englewood Cliffs, N.J.: Prentice-Hall.

1927
1960
1963
1964
1967
1969
1970
1971
1972
1973
1974
1975
1976
1977
1978
1979
1980
1981
1982
1983
1984
1985
1986
1987
1988
1989
1990
1991
1992
1993
1994
1995
1996
1997
1998
1999
2000
2001
2002
2003
2004
2005
2006

Becker, M.H. 1974. "The health belief model and personal health behavior," *Health Education Monographs* 2:324–508.

Bibeau, G. 1997. "At work in the fields of public health: The abuse of rationality," *Medical Anthropology Quarterly* 11:146–155.

Bird, S.E. 1996. "CJ's Revenge: Media, folklore, and the cultural construction of AIDS," *Critical Studies in Mass Communication* 13:44–58.

Bowen, S.P., and P. Michal-Johnson. 1990. "A rhetorical perspective for HIV education with black urban adolescents," *Communication Research* 17: 848–866.

Crawford, R. 1994. "The boundaries of the self and the unhealthy other: Reflections on health, culture, and AIDS," *Soc. Sci. Med.* 38:1347–1365.

Dearing, J.W., and E.M. Rogers. 1992. "AIDS and the media agenda," in: T. Edgar, M.A. Fitzpatrick, and V.S. Freimuth, eds. *AIDS: A Communication Perspective.* Hillsdale, N.J.: Lawrence Erlbaum Associates. 173–194.

Dillard, J.P., C.A. Plotnick, L.C. Godbold, V.S. Freimuth, and T. Edgar. 1996. "The multiple affective outcomes of AIDS PSAs: Fear appeals do more than scare people," *Communication Research* 23:44–72.

Edgar, T., M.A. Fitzpatrick, and V.S. Freimuth, eds. 1992. *AIDS: A Communication Perspective.* Hillsdale, N.J.: Lawrence Erlbaum Associates.

Erwin, D.O., and T.S. Spatz. 1996. *An Implementation Guide for The Witness Project: A Culturally Sensitive, Community-Based Cancer Education Program for African American Women.* Linda Deloney, ed. Arkansas Cancer Research Center, University of Arkansas Medical Sciences. Little Rock, Ark.

Escobar, A. 1995. *Encountering Development: The Making and Unmaking of the Third World.* Princeton Univ. Press.

Fishbein, M., and I. Ajzen. 1975. *Belief, Attitude, Intention, and Behavior: An Introduction to Theory and Research.* Reading, Mass.: Addison-Wesley.

Freimuth, V.S. 1992. "Theoretical foundations of AIDS media campaigns," in: T. Edgar, M.A. Fitzpatrick, and V.S. Freimuth, eds. *AIDS: A Communication Perspective.* Hillsdale, N.J.: Lawrence Erlbaum Associates. 91–110.

Freire, P. 1994. *Pedagogy of Hope: Reliving Pedagogy of the Oppressed.* New York: Continuum.

Glanz, K., and G.K. Rimer. 1995. *Theory at a Glance. A Guide for Health Promotion Practice.* U.S. Department of Health and Human Services. PHS, NIH.

Good, B.J. 1994. *Medicine, Rationality, and Experience.* Cambridge, U.K.: Cambridge Univ. Press.

Green, E.C. 1999. *Indigenous Theories of Contagious Disease.* Thousand Oaks, Calif.: AltaMira Press.

Green, L.W., and M.W. Kreuter. 1999. *Health Promotion Planning: An Educational and Ecological Approach.* 3rd ed. Mountain View, Calif.: Mayfield Publishing.

Guttman, N. 1997a. "Beyond strategic research: A value-centered approach to health communication interventions," *Communication Theory* 7:95–124.

Guttman, N. 1997b. "Ethical dilemmas in health campaigns," *Health Communication* 9:1550–190.

Kline, M.V. 1999. "Planning health promotion and disease prevention programs in multicultural populations," in: R.M. Huff and M.V. Kline, eds. *Promoting Health in Multicultural Populations: A Handbook for Practitioners.* Thousand Oaks, Calif.: Sage Publications.

Jaccard, J., R. Turrisi, and C.K. Wan. 1990. "Implications of behavioral decision theory and social marketing for designing social action programs," in: J. Edwards, R.S. Tindale, L. Heath, and E.J. Posavac, eds. *Social Influence Processes and Prevention.* New York: Plenum Press. 103-142.

Janz, N.C., M.A. Zimmerman, P.A. Wren, B.A. Israel, N. Freudenberg, and R.J. Carter. 1996. "Evaluation of 37 AIDS prevention projects: Successful approaches and barriers to program effectiveness," *Health Education Quarterly* 23:80–97.

Kluckhohn, C. 1954. "Culture and behavior," in: G. Lindzey, ed. *Handbook of Social Psychology.* Vol. 2. Cambridge, Mass.: Addison-Wesley. 921–976.

Lievrouw, L.A. 1994. "Health communication research reconsidered: Reading the signs. A review essay," *Journal of Communication* 44:91–99.

Lupton, D. 1994. *Medicine as Culture: Illness, Disease and the Body in Western Societies.* London: Sage Publications.

Maibach, E., and J.A. Flora. 1993. "Symbolic modeling and cognitive rehearsal: Using video to promote AIDS prevention self-efficacy," *Communication Research* 20:517–545.

McAllister, M.P. 1992. "AIDS, medicalization, and the news media," in: T. Edgar, M.A. Fitzpatrick, and V.S. Freimuth, eds. *AIDS: A Communication Perspective.* Hillsdale, N.J.: Lawrence Erlbaum Associates. 195–221.

Michal-Johnson, P., and S.P. Bowen. 1992. "The place of culture in HIV education," in: T. Edgar, M.A. Fitzpatrick, and V.S. Freimuth, eds. *AIDS: A Communication Perspective.* Hillsdale, N.J.: Lawrence Erlbaum Associates. 147–172.

Paskett, E.D., C.M. Tatum, R. D'Agostino, J. Rushing, R. Velez, R. Michielutte, and M. Dignan. 1999. "Community-based interventions to improve breast and cervical cancer screening: Results of the Forsyth County Cancer Screening (FoCaS) Project," *Cancer Epidemiology, Biomarkers & Prevention* 8:453–459.

Peltro, P.J., and G.H. Peltro. 1991. "Studying knowledge, culture, and behavior in applied medical anthropology," *Medical Anthropology Quarterly* 11:147–163.

Pliskin, K.L. 1997. "Verbal intercourse and sexual communication: Impediments to STD prevention," *Medical Anthropology Quarterly* 11:89–109.

Rogers, E.M. 1983. *Diffusion of Innovations.* 3rd ed. New York: Free Press.

Rogers, E.M. 1995. *Diffusion of Innovations.* 4th ed. New York: Free Press.

Schoepf, B.G. 1991. "Ethical, Methodological and Political Issues of AIDS research in central Africa," *Soc. Sci. Med.* 33:749–763.

Seidel, G. 1993. "The competing discourses of HIV/AIDS in sub-Saharan Africa: Discourses of rights and empowerment vs discourses of control and exclusion," *Soc. Sci. Med.* 36:175–194.

Smith, W. 1998. *Social marketing: Three approaches to HIV/AIDS prevention.* Fogarty Workshop on International HIV/AIDS Prevention Research Opportunities. San Francisco. April 18.

Soola, E.O. 1991. "Communication and education as vaccine against the spread of Acquired Immune Deficiency Syndrome (AIDS) in Africa," *Africa Media Review* 5(3):33–40.

Su, S. 1994. "Instrumentation, measurement and evaluation strategies," *The Implications of Cultural Values, Beliefs, and Norms for Health Research: A Methods Conference.* University of Milwaukee. Milwaukee. September 26–28.

Triandis, H.C. 1994. *Culture and Social Behavior.* New York: McGraw-Hill.

Yoder, P.S. 1997. "Negotiating relevance: Belief, knowledge, and practice in international health projects," *Medical Anthropology Quarterly* 11:131–146.

Yoder, P.S., R. Hornik, and Chirwa. 1996. "Evaluating the program effects of a radio drama about AIDS in Zambia," *Studies in Family Planning* 27(4):188–203.

Airhihenbuwa, Collins O. and Rafael Obregón. "A Critical Assessment of Theories/Models Used in Health Communication for HIV/AIDS," *Journal of Health Communication*, Vol. 5. Supplement (2000). Taylor and Francis Ltd. Reprinted with permission.

CONTEMPORARY READINGS
VOLUME ❷
Popular Culture, Narrative and Identity

MODERNITY AT LARGE: CULTURAL DIMENSIONS OF GLOBALISM

By Arjun Appadurai

1996 Modernity belongs to that small family of theories that both declares and desires universal applicability for itself. What is new about modernity (or about the idea that its newness is a new kind of newness) follows from this duality. Whatever else the project of the Enlightenment may have created, it aspired to create persons who would, after the fact, have wished to have become modern. This self-fulfilling and self-justifying idea has provoked many criticisms and much resistance, in both theory and everyday life.

In my own early life in Bombay, the experience of modernity was notably synaesthetic and largely pre-theoretical. I saw and smelled modernity reading Life [magazine] and American college catalogues at the United States Information Service library, seeing B-grade films (and some A-grade ones) from Hollywood at the Eros Theatre, five hundred yards from my apartment building. I begged my brother at Stanford (in the early 1960s) to bring me back blue jeans and smelled America in his Right Guard when he returned. I gradually lost the England that I had earlier imbibed in my Victorian schoolbooks, in rumours of Rhodes scholars from my college and in Billy Bunter and Biggles books devoured indiscriminately with books by Richmal Crompton and Enid Blyton. Franny and Zooey, Holden Caulfield and Rabbit Angstrom slowly eroded that part of me that had been, until then, forever England. Such are the little defeats that explain how England lost the Empire in post-colonial Bombay.

I did not know then that I was drifting from one sort of postcolonial subjectivity (Anglophone diction, fantasies of debates in the Oxford Union, borrowed peeks at Encounter, a patrician interest in the humanities) to another: the harsher, sexier, more addictive New World

of Humphrey Bogart reruns, Harold Robbins, time and social science, American-style. By the time I launched myself into the pleasures of cosmopolitanism in Elphinstone College, I was equipped with the Right Stuff—an Anglophone education, an upper-class Bombay address (although a middle-class family income), social connections to the big men and women of the college, a famous (now deceased) brother as an alumnus, a sister with beautiful girlfriends already in the college. But the American bug had bit me. I found myself launched on the journey that took me to Brandeis University (in 1967, when students were an unsettling ethnic category in the United States) and then on to the University of Chicago. In 1970, I was still drifting towards a rendezvous with American social science, area studies and that triumphal form of modernization theory that was still a secure article of Americanism in a bipolar world.

What follows is as an effort to make sense of a journey that began with modernity as embodied sensation in the movies in Bombay and ended face-to-face with modernity-as-theory in my social science classes at the University of Chicago in the early 1970s. I have sought to thematize certain cultural facts and use them to open up the relationship between modernization as fact and as theory.[1] This reversal of the process through which I experienced the modern might account for what might otherwise seem like an arbitrary disciplinary privileging of the cultural, a mere professional anthropological bias.

The Global Now

All major social forces have precursors, precedents, analogues and sources in the past. It is these deep and multiple genealogies that have frustrated the aspirations of modernizers in very different societies to synchronize their historical watches. This book, too, argues for a general rupture in the tenor of intersocietal relations in the past few decades. This view of change—indeed,

---

1 The absence of specific citations in the text of this essay should not convey the impression that it was immaculately conceived. This introductory chapter, like the book that follows it, builds on many currents in the social and human sciences over the past two decades.

of rupture—needs to be explicated and distinguished from some earlier theories of radical transformation.

One of the most problematic legacies of grand Western social science (Auguste Comte, Karl Marx, Ferdinand Toennies, Max Weber, and Émile Durkheim) is that it has steadily reinforced the sense of some single moment—call it the modern moment—that by its appearance creates a dramatic and unprecedented break between past and present. Reincarnated as the break between tradition and modernity and typologized as the difference between ostensibly traditional and modern societies, this view has been shown repeatedly to distort the meanings of change and the politics of pastness. Yet the world in which we now live—in which modernity is decisively at large, irregularly self-conscious, and unevenly experienced—surely does involve a general break with all sorts of pasts. What sort of break is this, if it is not the one identified by modernization theory?

Implicit in this book is a theory of rupture that takes media and migration as its two major, and interconnected, diacritics and explores their joint effect on the work of the imagination as a constitutive feature of modern subjectivity. The first step in this argument is that electronic media decisively change the wider field of mass media and other traditional media. This is not a monocausal fetishization of the electronic. Such media transform the field of mass mediation because they offer new resources and new disciplines for the construction of imagined selves and imagined worlds. This is a relational argument. Electronic media mark and reconstitute a much wider field, in which print mediation and other forms of oral, visual and auditory mediation might continue to be important. Through such effects as the telescoping of news into audio-video bytes, through the tension between the public spaces of cinema and the more exclusive spaces of video watching, through the immediacy of their absorption into public discourse, and through their tendency to be associated with glamour, cosmopolitanism and the new, electronic media (whether associated with the news, politics, family life or spectacular entertainment) tend to interrogate, subvert and transform other contextual literacies. Below, I track some ways in which electronic mediation transforms pre-existing worlds of communication and conduct.

Electronic media give a new twist to the environment within which the modern and the global often appear as flip sides of the same coin. Always carrying the sense of distance between viewer and event, these media nevertheless compel the transformation of everyday discourse. At the same time, they are resources for experiments with self-making in all sorts of societies, for all sorts of persons. They allow scripts for possible lives to be imbricated with the glamour of film stars and fantastic film plots and yet also to be tied to the plausibility of news shows, documentaries and other black-and-white forms of telemediation and printed text. Because of the sheer multiplicity of the forms in which they appear (cinema, television, computers and telephones) and because of the rapid way in which they move through daily life routines, electronic media provide resources for self-imagining as an everyday social project.

As with mediation, so with motion. The story of mass migrations (voluntary and forced) is hardly a new feature of human history. But when it is juxtaposed with the rapid flow of mass-mediated images, scripts and sensations, we have a new order of instability in the production of modern subjectivities. As Turkish guest workers in Germany watch Turkish films in their German flats, as Koreans in Philadelphia watch the 1988 Olympics in Seoul through satellite feeds from Korea, and as Pakistani cabdrivers in Chicago listen to cassettes of sermons recorded in mosques in Pakistan or Iran, we see moving images meet deterritorialized viewers. These create diasporic public spheres, phenomena that confound theories that depend on the continued salience of the nation-state as the key arbiter of important social changes.

Thus, to put it summarily, electronic mediation and mass migration mark the world of the present not as technically new forces but as ones that seem to impel

1927
1960
1963
1964
1967
1969
1970
1971
1972
1973
1974
1975
1976
1977
1978
1979
1980
1981
1982
1983
1984
1985
1986
1987
1988
1989
1990
1991
1992
1993
1994
1995
1996
1997
1998
1999
2000
2001
2002
2003
2004
2005
2006

(and sometimes compel) the work of the imagination. Together, they create specific irregularities because both viewers and images are in simultaneous circulation. Neither images nor viewers fit into circuits or audiences that are easily bound within local, national or regional spaces. Of course, many viewers may not themselves migrate. And many mass-mediated events are highly local in scope, as with cable television in some parts of the United States. But few important films, news broadcasts or television spectacles are entirely unaffected by other media events that come from further afield. And few persons in the world today do not have a friend, relative or co-worker who is not on the road to somewhere else or already coming back home, bearing stories and possibilities. In this sense, both persons and images often meet unpredictably, outside the certainties of home and the "cordon sanitaire" of local and national media effects. This mobile and unforeseeable relationship between mass-mediated events and migratory audiences defines the core of the link between globalisation and the modern. Later, I show that the work of the imagination, viewed in this context, is neither purely emancipatory nor entirely disciplined but is a space of contestation in which individuals and groups seek to annex the global into their own practices of the modern.

The Work of the Imagination

Ever since Durkheim, and the work of the "Anneés Sociologiques" group, anthropologists have learned to regard collective representations as social facts—that is, to see them as transcending individual volition, as weighted with the force of social morality and as objective social realities. What I wish to suggest is that there has been a shift in recent decades, building on technological changes over the past century or so, in which the imagination has become a collective, social fact. This development, in turn, is the basis of the plurality of imagined worlds.

On the face of it, it seems absurd to suggest that there is anything new about the role of the imagination in the contemporary world. After all, we are now accustomed to thinking about all societies as having produced their versions of art, myth and legend, expressions that implied the potential evanescence of ordinary social life. In these expressions, all societies showed that they could both transcend and reframe ordinary social life by recourse to mythologics of various kinds in which social life was imaginatively deformed. In dreams, finally, individuals even in the most simple societies have found the space to refigure their social lives, live out proscribed emotional states and sensations, and see things that have then spilled over into their sense of ordinary life. All these expressions, further, have been the basis of a complex dialogue between the imagination and ritual in many human societies, through which the force of ordinary social norms was somehow deepened, through inversion, irony or the performative intensity and the collaborative work demanded by many kinds of ritual. All this is the surest sort of knowledge bequeathed to us by the best of canonical anthropology over the past century.

In suggesting that the imagination in the post-electronic world plays a newly significant role, I rest my case on three distinctions. First, the imagination has broken out of the special expressive space of art, myth and ritual and has now become a part of the quotidian mental work of ordinary people in many societies. It has entered the logic of ordinary life from which it had largely been successfully sequestered. Of course, this has precedents in the great revolutions, cargo cults and messianic movements of other times, in which forceful leaders implanted their visions into social life, thus creating powerful movements for social change. Now, however, it is no longer a matter of specially endowed (charismatic) individuals, injecting the imagination where it does not belong. Ordinary people have begun to deploy their imaginations in the practice of their everyday lives. This fact is exemplified in the mutual contextualizing of motion and mediation.

More people than ever before seem to imagine routinely the possibility that they or their children will live and work in places other than where they were born: this is the wellspring of the increased rates of migration at every level of social, national and global life. Others are dragged into new settings, as the refugee camps of Thailand, Ethiopia, Tamil Nadu and Palestine remind us. For these people, they move and must drag their imagination for new ways of living along with them. And then there are those who move in search of work, wealth and opportunity often because their current circumstances are intolerable. Slightly transforming and extending Albert Hirschman's important terms loyalty and exit, we may speak of Diasporas of hope, Diasporas of terror and Diasporas of despair. But in every case, these Diasporas bring the force of the imagination, as both memory and desire, into the lives of many ordinary people, into mythographies different from the disciplines of myth and ritual of the classic sort. The key difference here is that these new mythographies are charters for new social projects, and not just a counterpoint to the certainties of daily life. They move the glacial force of the habitus into the quickened beat of improvisation for large groups of people. Here the images, scripts, models and narratives that come through mass mediation (in its realistic and fictional modes) make the difference between migration today and in the past. Those who wish to move, those who have moved, those who wish to return and those who choose to stay rarely formulate their plans outside the sphere of radio and television, cassettes and videos, newsprint and telephone. For migrants, both the politics of adaptation to new environments and the stimulus to move or return are deeply affected by a mass-mediated imaginary that frequently transcends national space.

The second distinction is between imagination and fantasy. There is a large and respectable body of writing, notably by the critics of mass culture of the Frankfurt School and anticipated in the work of Max Weber, that views the modern world as growing into an iron cage and predicts that the imagination will be stunted by the forces of commoditization, industrial capitalism and the generalized regimentation and secularisation of the world. The modernization theorists of the past three decades (from Weber by way of Talcott Parsons and Edward Shils to Daniel Lerner, Alex Inkeles and

many others) largely accepted the view of the modern world as a space of shrinking religiosity (and greater scientism), less play (and increasingly regimented leisure) and inhibited spontaneity at every level. There are many strands in this view, strands that link theorists as different as Norbert Elias and Robert Bell, but there is something fundamentally wrong with it. The error works on two levels. First, it is based on a premature requiem for the death of religion and the victory of science. There is vast evidence in new religiosities of every sort that religion is not only not dead but that it may be more consequential than ever in today's highly mobile and interconnected global politics. On another level, it is wrong to assume that the electronic media are the opium of the masses. This view, which is only beginning to be corrected, is based on the notion that the mechanical arts of reproduction largely replaced ordinary people for industrial work. It is far too simple.

There is growing evidence that the consumption of the mass media throughout the world often provokes resistance, irony, selectivity and, in general, "agency." Terrorists modelling themselves on Rambo-like figures (who have themselves generated a host of non-Western counterparts); housewives reading romances and soap operas as part of their efforts to construct their own lives; Muslim family gatherings listening to speeches by Islamic leaders on cassette tapes; domestic servants in South India taking packaged tours to Kashmir: these are all examples of the active way in which media are appropriated by people throughout the world. T-shirts, billboards and graffiti as well as rap music, street dancing and slum housing all show that the images of the media are quickly moved into local repertoires of irony, anger, humour and resistance.

Nor is this just a matter of Third World people reacting to American media, but it is equally true of people throughout the world reacting to their own national, electronic media. On these grounds alone, the theory of media as the opium of the people needs to be looked at with great scepticism. This is not to

1927
1960
1963
1964
1967
1969
1970
1971
1972
1973
1974
1975
1976
1977
1978
1979
1980
1981
1982
1983
1984
1985
1986
1987
1988
1989
1990
1991
1992
1993
1994
1995
1996
1997
1998
1999
2000
2001
2002
2003
2004
2005
2006

suggest that consumers are *free* agents, living happily in a world of safe malls, free lunches and quick fixes. As I suggest below, consumption in the contemporary world is often a form of drudgery, part of the capitalist civilizing process. Nevertheless, where there is consumption there is pleasure, and where there is pleasure there is agency. Freedom, on the other hand, is a rather more elusive commodity.

Further, the idea of fantasy carries with it the inescapable connotation of thought divorced from projects and actions, and it also has a private, even individualistic sound about it. The imagination, on the other hand, has a projective sense about it, the sense of being a prelude to some sort of expression, whether aesthetic or otherwise. Fantasy can dissipate (because its logic is so often autotelic), but the imagination, especially when collective, can become the fuel for action. It is the imagination, in its collective forms, that creates ideas of neighbourhood and nationhood, of moral economies and unjust rule, of higher wages and foreign labour prospects. The imagination is today a staging ground for action, and not only for escape. The third distinction is between the individual and collective senses of the imagination. It is important to stress here that I am speaking of the imagination now as a property of collectives, and not merely as a faculty of the gifted individual (its tacit sense since the flowering of European Romanticism). Part of what the mass media make possible, because of the conditions of collective reading, criticism and pleasure, is what I have elsewhere called a "community of sentiment" (Appadurai 1990), a group that begins to imagine and feel things together. As Benedict Anderson (1983) has shown so well, print capitalism can be one important way in which groups who have never been in face-to-face contact can begin to think of themselves as Indonesian or Indian or Malaysian. But other forms of electronic capitalism can have similar and even more powerful effects, for they do not work only at the level of the nation-state. Collective experiences of the mass media, especially film and video, can create sodalities of worship and charisma, such as those that formed regionally around the Indian female deity Santoshi Ma in the 1970s and 1980s and transnationally around Ayatollah Khomeini in roughly the same period. Similar sodalities can form around sport and internationalism, as the transnational effects of the Olympics so clearly show. Tenements and buildings house video clubs in places like Kathmandu and Bombay. Fan clubs and political followings emerge from small-town media cultures, as in South India.

These sodalities resemble what Diana Crane (1972) has called "invisible colleges" in reference to the world of science, but they are more volatile, less professionalized, less subject to collectively shared criteria of pleasure, taste or mutual relevance. They are communities in themselves but always potentially communities for themselves capable of moving from shared imagination to collective action. Most important, these sodalities are often transnational, even postnational, and they frequently operate beyond the boundaries of the nation. These mass-mediated sodalities have the additional complexity that, in them, diverse local experiences of taste, pleasure and politics can crisscross with one another, thus creating the possibility of convergences in translocal social action that would otherwise be hard to imagine.

No single episode captures these realities better than the now mind-numbing Salman Rushdie affair, involving a banned book, a religiously mandated death sentence and an author committed to personal voice and aesthetic freedom. *The Satanic Verses* provoked Muslims (and others) across the world to debate the politics of reading, the cultural relevance of censorship, the dignity of religion and the freedom of some groups to judge authors without independent knowledge of the text. The Rushdie affair is about a text-in-motion, whose commoditized trajectory brought it outside the safe haven of Western norms about artistic freedom and aesthetic rights into the space of religious rage and the authority of religious scholars in their own transnational spheres. Here, the transnational worlds of liberal aesthetics and radical Islam met head-on, in the very different settings of Bradford and Karachi, New York and New Delhi. In this episode, we can also see how global processes involving mobile texts and migrant audiences create implosive events that fold global pressures into small, already politicised arenas producing locality in new, globalised ways.

This theory of a break—or rupture—with its strong emphasis on electronic mediation and mass migration, is necessarily a theory of the recent past (or the extended present) because it is only in the past two decades or so that media and migration have become so massively globalised, that is to say active, across large and irregular transnational terrains. Why do I consider this theory to be anything more than an update of older social theories of the ruptures of modernization? First, mine is not a teleological theory, with a recipe for how modernization will universally yield rationality, punctuality, democracy, the free market and a higher gross national product. Second, the pivot of my theory is not any large-scale project of social engineering (whether organized by states, international agencies or other technocratic elites) but is the everyday cultural practice through which the work of the imagination is transformed. Third, my approach leaves entirely open the question of where the experiments with modernity that electronic mediation enables might lead in terms of nationalism, violence and social justice. Put another way, I am more deeply ambivalent about prognosis than any variant of classical modernization theory of which I am aware. Fourth, and most important, my approach to the break caused by the joint force of electronic mediation and mass migration is explicitly transnational—even postnational. As such, it moves away dramatically from the architecture of classical modernization theory, which one might call fundamentally realist insofar as it assumes the salience, both methodological and ethical, of the nation-state.

We cannot simplify matters by imagining that the global is to space what the modern is to time. For many societies, modernity is an elsewhere, just as

the global is a temporal wave that must be encountered in their present. Globalisation has shrunk the distance between elites, shifted key relations between producers and consumers, broken many links between labour and family life, obscured the lines between temporary locales and imaginary national attachments. Modernity now seems more practical and less pedagogic, more experiential and less disciplinary than in the 1950s and 1960s when it was mostly experienced (especially for those outside the national elite) through the propaganda apparatuses of the newly independent nation-states and their great leaders, like Jawaharlal Nehru, Gamal Abdel Nasser, Kwame Nkrumah and Sukarno. The megarhetoric of developmental modernization (economic growth, high technology, agribusiness, schooling, and militarization) in many countries is still with us. But it is often punctuated, interrogated and domesticated by the micro-narratives of film, television, music and other expressive forms, which allow modernity to be rewritten more as vernacular globalisation and less as a concession to large-scale national and international policies. As I suggested earlier, there was something of this experiential quality for those (such as myself) born into the ruling classes of the new nations in the 1950s and 1960s, but for many working people and the poor, this experiential engagement with modernity is a relatively recent fact.

These subversive micro-narratives also fuel oppositional movements, ranging from the Shining Path in Peru to Habitat for Humanity, from green movements in Europe to Tamil nationalism in Sri Lanka, from Islamic groups in Egypt to breakaway nationalist guerrillas in Chechnya. In these movements, some of which are repressive and violent while others are democratic and peaceful, we can see that electronic mass mediation and transnational mobilization have broken the monopoly of autonomous nation-states over the project of modernization. The transformation of everyday subjectivities through electronic mediation and the work of the imagination is not only a cultural fact. It is deeply connected to politics, through the new ways

1927
1960
1963
1964
1967
1969
1970
1971
1972
1973
1974
1975
1976
1977
1978
1979
1980
1981
1982
1983
1984
1985
1986
1987
1988
1989
1990
1991
1992
1993
1994
1995
1996
1997
1998
1999
2000
2001
2002
2003
2004
2005
2006

in which individual attachments, interests and aspirations increasingly crosscut those of the nation-state.

The diasporic public spheres that such encounters create are no longer small, marginal or exceptional. They are part of the cultural dynamic of urban life in most countries and continents, in which migration and mass mediation co-constitute a new sense of the global as modern and the modern as global. Mira Nair's film "Mississippi Masala," for example, is an epic of diaspora and race redoubled, exploring how Indians transformed and displaced by race relations in Uganda deal with the intricacies of race in the American South, all the time retaining their sense of Indianness-in-motion. The viewing of cricket matches between India and Pakistan by migrants in the Gulf States from these countries is about the peculiarities of diasporic nationalism in an emergent Indian Ocean politics. The intense battles over the English language and about immigrant rights now heating up (again) in the United States are not just one more variant on the politics of pluralism; they are about the capability of American politics to contain the diasporic politics of Mexicans in Southern California, Haitians in Miami, Colombians in New York and Koreans in Los Angeles. Indeed, as I will propose in my concluding observations, it is the widespread appearance of various kinds of diasporic public spheres that constitute one special diacritic of the global modern.

So much for the global now. There is a here to these chapters as well. They are written in part out of an encounter between my postwar Anglophone upbringing and my encounter with the American social-science story of modernization as the theory of the true, the good and the inevitable. They are also written from a professional perspective shaped substantially by two American research formations within which I have had the bulk of my training and in which I have spent much of my life as an academic: these are anthropology and area studies. Although this is a book about globalisation, it is marked and constrained by the contests of the past two decades within both these American academic formations. Thus its epistemological anxieties are decidedly local, even if locality is no longer what it used to be.

The Eye of Anthropology

Anthropology is my archive of lived actualities, found in all sorts of ethnographies about peoples who have lived very different sorts of lives from my own, today and in the past. . . That is not because it is inherently better than some other disciplinary archive. Indeed, critiques of this archive have been trenchant and untiring in the past 15 years. But it is the one I best know how to read. As an archive, it also has the advantage of reminding one that every similarity hides more than one difference, and that similarities and differences conceal one another indefinitely, so that the last turtle is always a matter of methodological convenience or stamina. This archive, and the sensibility that it produces in the professional anthropologist, predisposes me strongly towards the idea that globalisation is not the story of cultural homogenisation. This latter argument is the very least that I would want the reader to take away from this book. But anthropology brings with it a professional tendency to privilege the cultural as the key diacritic in many practices (that to others might appear simply human, or stupid, or calculating, or patriotic, or something else). Because Appadurai's book claims to be about the cultural dimensions of globalisation, let me spell out the special force that this adjective carries in my usage.

I find myself frequently troubled by the word culture as a noun but centrally attached to the adjectival form of the word, that is, cultural. When I reflect on why this is so, I realize that much of the problem with the noun form has to do with its implication that culture is some kind of object, thing or substance, whether physical or metaphysical. This substantialization seems to bring culture back into the discursive space of race, the very idea it was originally designed to combat. Implying a mental substance, the noun culture appears to privilege the sort of sharing, agreeing and bounding that flies in the face of the facts of unequal knowledge and the differential prestige of lifestyles, and to discourage attention to the worldviews and agency of those who are marginalized or dominated. Viewed as a physical substance, culture begins to smack of any variety of biologisms, including race, which we have certainly outgrown as scientific categories. Alfred Kroeber's term "superorganic" nicely captures both sides of this substantialism, something with which I am not in sympathy. The efforts of the past few decades, notably in American anthropology, to escape this trap by looking at culture largely as a linguistic form (understood mainly in Saussurean structuralist terms) only partly avoids the dangers of such substantialism.

If culture as a noun seems to carry associations with some sort of substance in ways that appear to conceal more than they reveal, cultural the adjective moves one into a realm of differences, contrasts and comparisons that is more helpful. This adjectival sense of culture, which builds on the context-sensitive, contrast-centered heart of Saussurean linguistics, seems to me one of the virtues of structuralism that we have tended to forget in our haste to attack it for its ahistorical, formal, binary, mentalist and textualist associations.

The most valuable feature of the concept of culture is the concept of difference, a contrastive rather than a substantive property of certain things. Although the term difference has now taken on a vast set of associations (principally because of the special use of the term by Jacques Derrida and his followers), its main virtue is that it is a useful heuristic that can highlight points of similarity and contrast between all sorts of categories: classes, genders, roles, groups and nations. When we therefore point to a practice, a distinction, a conception, an object or an ideology as having a cultural dimension (notice the adjectival use), we stress the idea of situated difference, that is, difference in relation to something local, embodied and significant. This point can be summarized in the following form: culture is not usefully regarded as a substance but is better regarded as a dimension of phenomena, a dimension that attends to situated and embodied difference. Stressing

the dimensionality of culture rather than its substantiality permits our thinking of culture less as a property of individuals and groups and more as a heuristic device that we can use to talk about difference.

But there are many kinds of differences in the world and only some of these are cultural. And here I bring in a second component of my proposal about the adjectival form of the word culture. I suggest that we regard as cultural only those differences that either express, or set the groundwork for, the mobilization of group identities. This qualification provides a brute principle of selection that focuses us on a variety of differences having to do with group identity, both within and outside any particular social group. In putting the mobilization of group identities at the heart of the adjective cultural, I have in fact made a move that looks, at first glance, retrogressive, as it appears that I am beginning to bring the word culture uncomfortably close to the idea of ethnicity. And that gets me into some new problems that need to be unravelled.

Before I try to do the unravelling, which will allow me to move towards the idea of culturalism, let me review where we have been. Resisting ideas of culture that tempt us to think of actual social groups as cultures, I have also resisted the noun form culture and suggested an adjectival approach to culture, which stresses its contextual, heuristic and comparative dimensions and orients us to the idea of culture as difference, especially difference in the realm of group identity. I have therefore suggested that culture is a pervasive dimension of human discourse that exploits difference to generate diverse conceptions of group identity.

Having veered so close to the idea of ethnicity—the idea of naturalized group identity—it is important to be clear about the relation between culture and group identity that I seek to articulate. Culture, unmarked, can continue to be used to refer to the plethora of differences that characterize the world today, differences at various levels, with various valences and with greater and lesser degrees of social consequence. I propose, however, that we restrict the term culture

1927
1960
1963
1964
1967
1969
1970
1971
1972
1973
1974
1975
1976
1977
1978
1979
1980
1981
1982
1983
1984
1985
1986
1987
1988
1989
1990
1991
1992
1993
1994
1995
1996
1997
1998
1999
2000
2001
2002
2003
2004
2005
2006

as a marked term to the subset of these differences that has been mobilized to articulate the boundary of difference. As a boundary-maintenance question, culture then becomes a matter of group identity as constituted by some differences among others.

But is this not a way of simply equating ethnicity and culture? Yes and no. Yes, because in this usage culture would not stress simply the possession of certain attributes (material, linguistic or territorial) but the consciousness of these attributes and their naturalization as essential to group identity. That is, rather than falling prey to the assumption, at least as old as Weber, that ethnicity rests on some sort of extension of the primordial idea of kinship (which is in turn biological and genealogical), the idea of ethnicity I propose takes the conscious and imaginative construction and mobilization of differences as its core. Culture 1, constituting a virtually open-ended archive of differences is consciously shaped into Culture 2, that subset of these differences that constitutes the diacritics of group identity.

But this process of mobilizing certain differences and linking them to group identity is also unlike ethnicity—at least in an older understanding, because it does not depend on the extension of primordial sentiments to larger and larger units in some sort of unidirectional process, nor does it make the mistake of supposing that larger social units simply draw on the sentiments of family and kinship to give emotional force to large-scale group identities. Thus, below, far from drawing on the existing repertoire of emotions and moving them into a larger arena, Indian cricket is a large-scale form that comes to be inscribed on the body through a variety of practices of increasingly smaller scale. This logic is just the reverse of the old primordialist (or extensionist) idea of ethnic identity.

The idea of culture as involving the naturalized organization of certain differences in the interests of group identity, through and in the historical process, and through and in the tensions between agents and structures, comes closer to what has been called the instrumental

conception of ethnicity, as opposed to the primordial one. I have two qualifications about this convergence, qualifications that lead to my discussion of culturalism. One is that the ends to which instrumental conceptions of ethnic identity are formed may themselves be counterstructural responses to existing valorisations of difference: they may thus be value-rational rather than instrumental-rational, in Weber's sense. They may have a purely identity-oriented instrumentality rather than an instrumentality that, as is so often implied, is extracultural (economic or political or emotional). Put another way, the mobilization of markers of group difference may itself be part of a contestation of values about difference, as distinct from the consequences of difference for wealth, security or power. My second qualification about most instrumental accounts is that they do not explain the process by which certain criteria of difference, mobilized for group identity (in turn instrumental to other goals) are (re)inscribed into bodily subjects, thus to be experienced as both natural and profoundly incendiary at the same time.

We have now moved one step further, from culture as substance to culture as the dimension of difference, to culture as group identity based on difference, to culture as the process of naturalizing a subset of differences that have been mobilized to articulate group identity. We are at this point in a position to move to the question of culturalism.

We rarely encounter the word "culturalism" by itself: it is usually hitched as a noun to certain prefixes like bi, multi and inter, to name the most prominent. But it may be useful to begin to use culturalism to designate a feature of movements involving identities consciously in the making. These movements, whether in the United States or elsewhere, are usually directed at modern nation-states, which distribute various entitlements, sometimes including life and death, in accordance with classifications and policies regarding group identity. Throughout the world, faced with the activities of states that are concerned with encompassing their ethnic diversities into fixed and closed sets of cultural categories to which individuals are often assigned forcibly, many groups are consciously mobilizing themselves according to identitarian criteria. Culturalism, put simply, is identity politics mobilized at the level of the nation-state.

This sort of culturalism is my principal focus later, where I mount a sustained critique of the primordialist view of the ethnic violence of the past decade. What appears to be a worldwide rebirth of ethnic nationalisms and separatisms is not really what journalists and pundits all too frequently refer to as "tribalism," implying old histories, local rivalries and deep hatreds. Rather, the ethnic violence we see in many places is part of a wider transformation that is suggested by the term culturalism. Culturalism, as I have already suggested, is the conscious mobilization of cultural differences in the service of a larger national or transnational politics. It is frequently associated with extraterritorial histories and memories, sometimes with refugee status and exile, and almost always with struggles for stronger recognition from existing nation-states or from various transnational bodies.

Culturalist movements (for they are almost always efforts to mobilize) are the most general form of the work of the imagination and draw frequently on the fact or possibility of migration or secession. Most important, they are self-conscious about identity, culture and heritage, all of which tend to be part of the deliberate vocabulary of culturalist movements as they struggle with states and other culturalist focuses and groups. It is this deliberate, strategic and populist mobilization of cultural material that justifies calling such movements culturalist, though they may vary in many ways. Culturalist movements, whether they involve African-Americans, Pakistanis in Britain, Algerians in France, native Hawaiians, Sikhs or French speakers in Canada, tend to be counternational and metacultural. In the broadest sense, as I shall suggest in the last part of this book, culturalism is the form that cultural differences tend to take in the era of mass mediation, migration and globalisation.

How Areas Get Studied

The anthropological stress on the cultural, which is the main inflection I wish to give to the debate on globalisation, is in my case further sustained by my training and practice as a scholar of area studies, specifically of South Asian studies in the United States. There has not yet been a sustained critical analysis of the link, in the United States, between the emergence of the idea of culture areas in anthropology between the world wars and the full-fledged formation after World War II of area studies as the major way to look at the strategically significant parts of the developing world. Yet there is little doubt that both perspectives incline one to a particular sort of map in which groups and their ways of life are marked by differences of culture, and in the area-studies formation these differences slide into a topography of national cultural differences. Thus geographical divisions, cultural differences and national boundaries tended to become isomorphic, and there grew a strong tendency to refract world processes through this sort of national-cultural map of the world. Area studies add to this spatial imaginary a strong, if sometimes tacit, sense of the strategic importance of information gained in this perspective. This is the reason for the often-noted links between Cold War government funding and university expansion in the organization of area-studies centres after World War II. Nevertheless, area studies have provided the major counterpoint to the delusions of the view from nowhere that underwrites much canonical social science. It is this aspect of my training that compelled me to situate my genealogy of the global present in the area I know best: India.

There is a special anxiety that now surrounds the structures and ideologies of area studies in the United States. Recognizing that area studies is somehow deeply tied up with a strategizing world picture driven by U.S. foreign-policy needs between 1945 and 1989, leading figures in the world of universities, foundations, think tanks and even the government have made it clear that the old way of doing area studies does not make sense in the world after 1989. Thus

1927
1960
1963
1964
1967
1969
1970
1971
1972
1973
1974
1975
1976
1977
1978
1979
1980
1981
1982
1983
1984
1985
1986
1987
1988
1989
1990
1991
1992
1993
1994
1995
1996
1997
1998
1999
2000
2001
2002
2003
2004
2005
2006

left-wing critics of area studies, much influenced by the important work of Edward Said on Orientalism, have been joined by free-marketers and advocates of liberalization, who are impatient with what they deride as the narrowness and history fetish of area studies experts. Area-studies scholars are widely criticized as obstacles to the study of everything from comparison and contemporaneity to civil society and free markets. Of course, no critique that is so sweeping and so sudden could be entirely fair, and the odd mix of its critics suggests that area-studies scholarship might be taking the rap for a wider failure in the U.S. academy to deliver a broader and more prescient picture of the world after 1989.

The area-studies tradition is a double-edged sword. In a society notoriously devoted to exceptionalism, and to endless preoccupation with "America," this tradition has been a tiny refuge for the serious study of foreign languages, alternative worldviews, and large-scale perspectives on sociocultural change outside Europe and the United States. Bedevilled by a certain tendency towards philology (in the narrow, lexical sense) and a certain overidentification with the regions of its specialization, area studies has nonetheless been one of the few serious counterweights to the tireless tendency to marginalize huge parts of the world in the American academy and in American society more generally. Yet the area-studies tradition has probably grown too comfortable with its own maps of the world, too secure in its own expert practices and too insensitive to transnational processes both today and in the past. So criticism and reform are certainly in order, but how can area studies help to improve the way that world pictures are generated in the United States?

From the perspective advanced here and in the rest of this book, area studies is a salutary reminder that globalisation is itself a deeply historical, uneven and even "localizing" process. Globalisation does not necessarily or even frequently imply homogenisation or Americanisation, and to the extent that different societies appropriate the materials of modernity differently,

there is still ample room for the deep study of specific geographies, histories and languages. What I discuss in later chapters as the relationship between history and genealogy is impossible to engage without a strong sense of the actualities of the "longue durée," which always produce specific geographies, both real and imagined. If the genealogy of cultural forms is about their circulation across regions, the history of these forms is about their ongoing domestication into local practice. The very interaction of historical and genealogical forms is uneven, diverse and contingent. In this sense, history, the ruthless discipline of context (in E. P. Thompson's colourful phrase), is everything. But this recognition is not a warrant for kneejerk localism of the sort sometimes associated with area studies. In any case, area studies are a specific Western technique of research. …What does need to be recognized, if the area-studies tradition is to be revitalized, is that locality itself is a historical product and that the histories through which localities emerge are eventually subject to the dynamics of the global. …

Any book about globalisation is a mild exercise in megalomania, especially when it is produced in the relatively privileged circumstances of the American research university. It seems important to identify the knowledge forms through which any such megalomania comes to articulate itself. In my case, these forms— anthropology and area studies—predispose me by habit to the fixing of practices, spaces and countries into a map of static differences. This is, counterintuitively, a danger even in a book such as this, which is consciously shaped by a concern with diaspora, de-territorialization and the irregularity of the ties between nations, ideologies and social movements.

Social Science after Patriotism

The final part of the here and now is a fact about the modern world that has exercised some of the best contemporary thinkers in the social and human sciences: it is the issue of the nation-state, its history, its current crisis, its prospects. I did not begin to write this book with the crisis of the nation-state as my principal concern. But in the six years over which its chapters were written, I have come to be convinced that the nation-state, as a complex modern political form, is on its last legs. The evidence is by no means clear, and the returns are hardly all in. I am aware that all nation-states are not the same in respect to the national imaginary, the apparatuses of the state or the sturdiness of the hyphen between them. Yet there is some justification for what might sometimes seem like a reified view of the nation-state in this book. Nation-states, for all their important differences (and only a fool would conflate Sri Lanka with Great Britain), make sense only as parts of a system. This system (even when seen as a system of differences) appears poorly equipped to deal with the interlinked diasporas of people and images that mark the here and now. Nation-states, as units in a complex interactive system, are not very likely to be the long-term arbiters of the relationship between globality and modernity. That is why, in my title, I imply that modernity is at large.

The idea that some nation-states are in crisis is a staple of the field of comparative politics and was in some sense the justification for much of modernization theory, especially in the 1960s. The idea that some states are weak, sick, corrupt or soft has been around for several decades (remember Gunnar Myrdahl?). More recently, it has become widely acceptable to see nationalism as a disease, especially when it is somebody else's nationalism. The idea that all nation-states are to some extent bedevilled by globalised movements of arms, monies, diseases and ideologies is also hardly news in the era of the multinational corporation. But the idea that the very system of nation-states is in jeopardy is hardly popular. My persistent focus on the hyphen that links nation to state is part of an evolving argument that the very epoch of the nation-state is near its end. This view, which lies somewhere between a diagnosis and a prognosis, between an intuition and an argument, needs to be spelled out.

First, I need to distinguish between the ethical and the analytic components of my argument. On the ethical front, I am increasingly inclined to see most modern governmental apparatuses as inclined to self-perpetuation, bloat, violence and corruption. Here, I am in mixed company, from the left and from the right. The ethical question I am often faced with is, if the nation-state disappears, what mechanism will assure the protection of minorities, the minimal distribution of democratic rights and the reasonable possibility of the growth of civil society? My answer is that I do not know, but this admission is hardly an ethical recommendation for a system that seems plagued by endemic disease. As to alternative social forms and possibilities, there are actually existing social forms and arrangements that might contain the seeds of more dispersed and diverse forms of transnational allegiance and affiliation. I readily admit that the road from various transnational movements to sustainable forms of transnational governance is hardly clear. I prefer, however, the exercise of looking for—indeed, imagining—these alternative possibilities to the strategy of defining some nation-states as healthier than others and then suggesting various mechanisms of ideology transfer. This latter strategy replays modernization-cum-development policy all over again, with the same triumphalist underpinnings and the same unhealthy prospects.

If the ethical front of my argument is necessarily fuzzy, the analytic front is somewhat sharper. Even a cursory inspection of the relationships within and among the more than 150 nation-states that are now members of the United Nations shows that border wars, culture wars, runaway inflation, massive immigrant populations or serious flights of capital threaten sovereignty in many of them. Even where state sovereignty is apparently intact, state legitimacy is frequently insecure. Even in nation-states as apparently secure as the United States, Japan and Germany, debates about race and rights, membership and loyalty, citizenship and authority are no longer culturally peripheral. While one argument for the longevity of the nation-state form is based on these apparently secure and legitimate instances, the other argument is an inverse one and bases itself on the new ethno-nationalisms

1927
1960
1963
1964
1967
1969
1970
1971
1972
1973
1974
1975
1976
1977
1978
1979
1980
1981
1982
1983
1984
1985
1986
1987
1988
1989
1990
1991
1992
1993
1994
1995
1996
1997
1998
1999
2000
2001
2002
2003
2004
2005
2006

of the world, notably those of Eastern Europe. Bosnia-Herzegovina is almost always pointed to in the United States as the principal symptom of the fact that nationalism is alive and sick, while the rich democracies are simultaneously invoked to show that the nation-state is alive and well.

Given the frequency with which Eastern Europe is used to show that tribalism is deeply human, that other people's nationalism is tribalism writ large, and that territorial sovereignty is still the major goal of many large ethnic groups, let me propose an alternative interpretation. In my judgment, Eastern Europe has been singularly distorted in popular arguments about nationalism in the press and in the academy in the United States. Rather than being the modal instance of the complexities of all contemporary ethnonationalisms, Eastern Europe, and its Serbian face in particular, has been used as a demonstration of the continued vigour of nationalisms in which land, language, religion, history and blood are congruent, a textbook case of what nationalism is all about. Of course, what is fascinating about Eastern Europe is that some of its own right-wing ideologues have convinced the liberal Western press that nationalism is a politics of primordia, whereas the real question is how it has been made to appear that way. This certainly makes Eastern Europe a fascinating and urgent case from many points of view, including the fact that we need to be sceptical when experts claim to have encountered ideal types in actual cases.

In most cases of counternationalism, secession, supranationalism or ethnic revival on a large scale, the common thread is self-determination rather than territorial sovereignty as such. Even in those cases where territory seems to be a fundamental issue, such as in Palestine, it could be argued that debates about land and territory are in fact functional spin-offs of arguments that are substantially about power, justice and self-determination. In a world of people on the move, of global commoditization and states incapable of delivering basic rights even to their majority ethnic populations, territorial sovereignty is an increasingly difficult justification for those nation-states that are increasingly dependent on foreign labour, expertise, arms or soldiers. For counternationalist movements, territorial sovereignty is a plausible idiom for their aspirations, but it should not be mistaken for their founding logic or their ultimate concern. To do so is to commit what I would call the Bosnia Fallacy, an error that involves (a) misunderstanding Eastern European ethnic battles as tribalist and primordial, an error in which *The New York Times* is the leader, and (b) compounding the mistake by taking the Eastern European case to be the model case of all emergent nationalisms. To move away from the Bosnia Fallacy requires two difficult concessions: first, that the political systems of the wealthy, Northern nations may themselves be in crisis, and second, that the emergent nationalisms of many parts of the world may be founded on patriotisms that are not either exclusively or fundamentally territorial. Arguments for making these concessions animate much of this book. In making them, I have not always found it easy to maintain the distinction between the analytic and the ethical perspectives on the future of the nation-state, although I have tried to do so.

As the nation-state enters a terminal crisis (if my prognostications prove to be correct), we can certainly expect that the materials for a postnational imaginary must be around us already. Here, I think we need to pay special attention to the relation between mass mediation and migration, the two facts that underpin my sense of the cultural politics of the global modern. In particular, we need to look closely at the variety of what have emerged as "diasporic public spheres." Benedict Anderson did us a service in identifying the way in which certain forms of mass mediation, notably those involving newspapers, novels and other print media, played a key role in imagining the nation and in facilitating the spread of this form to the colonial world in Asia and elsewhere. My general argument is that there is a similar link to be found between the work of the imagination and the emergence of a postnational political world. Without the benefit of hindsight (which we

1927
1960
1963
1964
1967
1969
1970
1971
1972
1973
1974
1975
1976
1977
1978
1979
1980
1981
1982
1983
1984
1985
1986
1987
1988
1989
1990
1991
1992
1993
1994
1995
1996
1997
1998
1999
2000
2001
2002
2003
2004
2005
2006

do have with respect to the global journey of the idea of the nation), it is hard to make a clear case for the role of the imagination in a postnational order. But as mass mediation becomes increasingly dominated by electronic media (and thus de-linked from the capacity to read and write), and as such media increasingly link producers and audiences across national boundaries, and as these audiences themselves start new conversations between those who move and those who stay, we find a growing number of diasporic public spheres.

These diasporic spheres are frequently tied up with students and other intellectuals engaging in long-distance nationalism (as with activists from the People's Republic of China). The establishment of black majority rule in South Africa opens up new kinds of discourse of racial democracy in Africa as well as in the United States and the Caribbean. The Islamic world is the most familiar example of a whole range of debates and projects that have little to do with national boundaries. Religions that were in the past resolutely national now pursue global missions and diasporic clienteles with vigour: the global Hinduism of the past decade is the single best example of this process. Activist movements involved with the environment, women's issues and human rights generally have created a sphere of transnational discourse, frequently resting on the moral authority of refugees, exiles and other displaced persons. Major transnational separatist movements like the Sikhs, the Kurds and the Sri Lankan Tamils conduct their self-imagining in sites throughout the world, where they have enough members to allow for the emergence of multiple nodes in a larger diasporic public sphere.

The wave of debates about multiculturalism that has spread through the United States and Europe is surely testimony to the incapacity of states to prevent their minority populations from linking themselves to wider constituencies of religious or ethnic affiliation. These examples, and others, suggest that the era in which we could assume that viable public spheres were typically, exclusively or necessarily national could be at an end.

Diasporic public spheres, diverse among themselves, are the crucibles of a postnational political order. The engines of their discourse are mass media (both interactive and expressive) and the movement of refugees, activists, students and labourers. It may well be that the emergent postnational order proves not to be a system of homogeneous units (as with the current system of nation-states) but a system based on relations between heterogeneous units (some social movements, some interest groups, some professional bodies, some nongovernmental organizations, some armed constabularies, some judicial bodies). The challenge for this emergent order will be whether such heterogeneity is consistent with some minimal conventions of norm and value, which do not require a strict adherence to the liberal social contract of the modern West. This fateful question will be answered not by academic fiat but by the negotiations (both civil and violent) between the worlds imagined by these different interests and movements. In the short run, as we can see already, it is likely to be a world of increased incivility and violence. In the longer run, free of the constraints of the nation form, we may find that cultural freedom and sustainable justice in the world do not presuppose the uniform and general existence of the nation-state. This unsettling possibility could be the most exciting dividend of living in modernity at large.

References

Anderson, Benedict. *Imagined Communities: Reflections on the Origin and Spread of Nationalism.* London: Verso, 1983.

Appadurai, A. "Topografies of the Self: Praise and Emotion in Hindu India," in Lutz, C. A. and L. Abu-Lughod, eds., *Language and the Politics of Emotion.* Cambridge: Cambridge University Press, 1990.

Crane, D. *Invisible Colleges.* Chicago: University of Chicago Press, 1972.

EXCERPT FROM:
TELEVISION AND THE CULTURE OF PROTAGONISM

By Valerio Fuenzalida Fernández

1999 Since the decade of the 1950s and until the 1970s, for some 25 years, communication for development worked in different ways. Some approaches focused only on the multiplication of technological channels (radio and TV) as a modernizing factor *per se*. Communication was also practiced to promote the values and attitudes of "a modern personality," considered to be educational strategies fundamental to social change. A lot of work was carried out with the radio and with groups, directed specifically to the rural sector in underdeveloped countries in Latin America, Asia and Africa, to promote what was then called "extensionism," or the "diffusion of technological innovations." The aim was to modernize agriculture by extending the innovations of the times, like new and better seed [and] use of fertilizers...etc.

In the pattern of diffusionism, communicators were the technicians and experts teaching groups of farmers, or using radio programs for extensionist talks. Work was carried out under the assumption of the omnipotent effect of communication messages, that is, the contents of the messages would have a high impact on the awareness and behavior of the audience. Sánchez Ruiz (1986) highlights the incongruence in the fact that while in the United States theorists sustained the thesis of reinforcement as the most remarkable social influence of communication, in the same timeframe, American experts abroad talked about the powerful transforming efficiency of the media. ...

The 1980s witnessed an important production of reference works that systematized historically the themes of *Communication for Development* (White, 1988; *Communication Research Trends*, Vol. 9 1988/89 N° 3; Sánchez Ruiz, 1986; *Media Development*, Vol. XXXII, 4/1985; Kunczik, 1985, 1992; Pavlic-Hamelink, 1985; Hornik, 1980; Pratt C.B. &.

Manheim J.B., 1988). Many extensionist communication strategy efforts were assessed and the results often showed a lack of motivation when faced with broadcasts announcing the benefits of the use of modern technology. The diffusionist communication method was taken aback by the deep resistance, lack of interest, and lack of concern shown by sectors that would supposedly benefit from that communication. (Samarajiva-Shields, 1990; McAnany, 1980, 1984). According to Luis Ramiro Beltrán, the assessment of agricultural diffusion studies in Latin America shows that "among farmers in Latin America the influence of mass media in the adoption of innovations is minimal or nonexistent in practically all the stages of the process" (Beltrán, 1977, p. 22).

After the optimism of the 1950s and 1960s, an assessment of communication for development concludes that currently there is not a set model with ample collective acceptance for the communicational approach to issues of development, poverty and increased quality of life. Michael Kunczik (1985) in *Communication and Social Change* has carried out a thorough examination of the different concepts operating in recent decades; the book, however, offers very few positive proposals for the future, constituting evidence of the state of affairs regarding this subject. The same international agencies that specialize in this kind of communication are repeating worn-out blueprints, so their executives are cutting available funds; the brightest ones admit to the crisis and search different countries for innovative concepts. The seriousness of this conceptual and formal emptiness is that it introduces a dissuasive skepticism, and reinforces tendencies to expel from TV Broadcasting themes that relate to development and poverty.

I. Social Prominence

1. DRAMATIC PROMINENCE

The assessment of social prominence, that is, the *social group's ability to act to overcome their poverty issues*, is a factor that has been appreciated in recent years as decisive for development. ...

Firstly, the normal scenario in human, personal and social life is conceived as a dramatic conflict, with fighting energies, with internal dynamics that may alter the existing situation. The word drama, explains Aristotle himself, is derived from a verb in Doric Greek (dran), the meaning of which is to act; drama means primarily action, a transforming act.[1] …

Secondly, the conception of dramatic conflict highlights the situational transformation by the protagonist, internal actor in the dramatic scenario, who works on initiatives with activities that produce movement and alter the socio-existential condition.

The re-elaboration carried out by Greimas (1973) of the basic conception by Aristotle makes dramatic conflict more complex, enriching it with new categories of actors. For Greimas, primary action by the protagonist is focused towards the search for an object to achieve. In this active search he will face antagonistic forces and will also obtain the help of auxiliary actors.

In Greimas' outline it is clearer that the initiative by the protagonist aims primarily to obtain an object considered worth achieving. The fight and the dramatic conflict primarily unfold around a situation or a condition of adversity that has to be overcome through the action of the protagonist subject. The adversity to be faced in a transforming way can be natural, like an earthquake or drought; social, like economic or cultural deprivation; or personal, like a disability or an accident. The forces that oppose transformation are the antagonist actor; but there are also positive forces and energies in the supporting actor that the subject must articulate in his fight to obtain his object.

The theory of dramatic prominence depicts society as a dynamic scenario, in opposition to a static culture of fatalistic passivity, and resigned to the existing situation of adversity.

Consequently prominence would be an endogenous force to initiate tasks, instead of placing the fight to resolve challenges on external actors.

On the contrary, off-loading the resolution of problems onto external agents leads to an attitude of mistrust in group strengths and towards a provisory and paternalistic culture; in this culture—which exists in many countries and in specific social segments—a sentiment is generated of impotence, despair and helplessness. (Kunczik, 1992)

And it leads as well, inversely, towards fantasies about a magic power to own unlimited resources that would be enjoyed by external agents, usually authorities: political, administrative, religious, etc. In this self-perception of victimization and lack of abilities, the key to overcome poverty would not lie in prominence itself but in the proximity to the benevolence of those all-powerful agents that hold huge resources.

When highlighting social prominence, the human factor appears to be more relevant, or of at least as much relevance as another factor that has recently been considered again to be central in development processes: we are talking about information. It is common to say today that we live in a society of information and knowledge, and we are told that a high social availability of information would solve the problems of poverty and development. If this revived diffusionist information approach is accepted, the contribution of TV to development should be steered in this disseminating direction. But this approach does not include the experiences of the 1950s and 1960s, when the exact same thing was said but using expressions like "spreading technological information, "extending knowledge" etc.

…Therefore from the new perspective, rather than spread information to the wind, it is necessary to focus on the ability to be protagonists of social factors which, among other things, will also involve actively

---

1 The word "dramatic" means originally a transforming energetic action by a protagonist actor; by derivation it means the intense emotions unleashed by this action. In everyday use, this second meaning is most common and the original meaning, which is rescued in this text, tends to be diffused.

1927
1960
1963
1964
1967
1969
1970
1971
1972
1973
1974
1975
1976
1977
1978
1979
1980
1981
1982
1983
1984
1985
1986
1987
1988
1989
1990
1991
1992
1993
1994
1995
1996
1997
1998
1999
2000
2001
2002
2003
2004
2005
2006

searching, discriminating and using, in an ecologically friendly way, all useful information relating to needs.

2. NEW CONTEXT

It is necessary to stress that the revalorization of social prominence as an indispensable factor for development has arisen in new socio-cultural context.

In fact, the assessment of many a "modernizing" failure has led in the first place to increased complexity of in the conception of development (Goran, 1982; Media Development, 1985; White, 1988); it cannot be reduced to the simple dimension of technological information for greater availability of material goods anymore, but it also involves educational and cultural dimensions of social organization and the strengthening of democracy, productivity and equity.

Disenchantment with the lack of efficiency of socialist or populist states and the cruel experience with dictatorial Latin American states have also contributed to a re-valorization of the prominence and initiatives of the different groups that constitute "civil society."

In this new context, it is hardly convincing to have an ideology that justifies the expropriation of social prominence by an authoritarian leading minority, supposedly all-knowing in matters of development laws and never failing in its planning. …

This re-valorization of social prominence converges with appreciation of the social doctrines of the Church through the positive role of "intermediary groups." As well as family, at this intermediate level we find economic, social, political and cultural groups, endowed with their own space of autonomy and initiative; such an intermediate level is called by Jean Paul II "the subjectivity of society" and is basic to the building of a true democracy, since it constitutes structures that reinforce the solidarity of social networks, participation and coresponsibility (Centesimus Annus, Nº 13, 46, y 49). Delaying and, even worse, repressing the prominence of the person, in all its multiple economic, social and political dimensions, is at the root of many failures of development plans or systems, according to Centesimus Annus (Nº 24).

At the World Summit for Social Development, on March 11 1995, the President of France, François Mitterrand, expressed similar ideas:

> Finally – these will be my last words - the happiness of men cannot be built without the men themselves. Everyone's mobilization is necessary. And, in this sense, the presence in Copenhagen of 2000 NGOs looks very stimulating to me… Let us not forget that none of the most advanced countries would have known the level of development it now enjoys without the existence of a democratic life, of political parties, of union and employer's organizations, of associations; that is, of work in common, from which no social category should be excluded. This is what we have left to do. (Mitterrand, 1995)….

3. PEOPLE'S NEEDS AND STANDARDS OF LIVING

Group prominence also requires a context that pays attention to needs and motivations, the way they are perceived and felt by the social groups themselves.

> …In this new context, objective indicators of "standard of living" are combined with subjective perceptions of well-being and satisfaction: In a given time, place and society, needs are culturally defined; this is why the standard of living is very relative, and what is beneficial for one group of people can be detrimental to another... This reasoning implies that studies on the standard of living of certain persons, or a certain geographical place, must be based on their own conception of well-being (Palomar, 1994).

Thus ways of understanding standard of living are variable and tend to privilege or, on the contrary, to downgrade different indicators. The UN concept of standard of living includes nine indicators:

1. health
2. nutrition
3. education

1927
1960
1963
1964
1967
1969
1970
1971
1972
1973
1974
1975
1976
1977
1978
1979
1980
1981
1982
1983
1984
1985
1986
1987
1988
1989
1990
1991
1992
1993
1994
1995
1996
1997
1998
1999
2000
2001
2002
2003
2004
2005
2006

4. occupation and work conditions
5. housing conditions
6. social security
7. clothing
8. recreation
9. human rights.

For other authors, the standard of living has 15 components:

1. economic well-being,
2. physical well-being and health,
3. relationships with relatives,
4. having and raising sons and daughters,
5. relationships in couples,
6. close friends,
7. civic and social activities,
8. political activities,
9. personal development,
10. personal knowledge,
11. work,
12. personal expression and creativity,
13. socialization,
14. passive recreation activities,
15. active recreation activities (Palomar, 1994).

Attention to cultural perceptions and the subjective needs of people has shaped this important change in concept, according to which the final objective of development is to achieve a decent standard of living for the population. This new concept does not only take into account traditional indicators like health, nutrition, housing, work, education, social security, but also integrates indicators of a sentimental, social and aesthetic nature, like marriage, children, creativity and personal development, self-esteem, professional competition, belonging, social and civic life, pleasure and recreation, artistic and spiritual life.

4. CONDITIONS FOR SOCIAL PROMINENCE

Prominence of social groups implies the reinforcement of certain factors that increase the likelihood of its effective existence.

■ Self-reliance

A first factor is to learn an internal attitude that has been called self-reliance, which is basic to start group activities. Self-reliance is a complex attitude, very well expressed in the following text assessing an experience developed by base community groups:

Self-confidence, pride, dignity and a strong sense of their ability to achieve results, to "be able to make" was reflected in their faces, their physical posture and the conversation of community leaders, mothers and kindergarten teachers certified locally, while they walked the short distance that separates two pre-schooling centers administered by the community in the neighborhood Tres Ave María near Barranquilla (Chetley, 1990).

Self-reliance is not only motivation and determination to act with prominence; it is also self-dignity and awareness of an ability to effectively achieve results.

It is the result of education, of enabling, of a culture that dignifies and enables by transferring "knowledge and ability to make".

"Here is the wished-for culture—says Jean Paul II —that increases reliance on human potential for the poor, and therefore, in his ability to improve conditions himself through work and contribute positively to economic well-being" (Centesimus Annus, N° 52).

Self-reliance cannot be confused with self-sufficiency, isolating or excluding other groups and their initiatives. On the contrary, it forms the basis of the ability to negotiate and articulate one's own interests with other groups and with the resources of political, economic, cultural and professional agencies.

■ Ethical and cultural factors

…appreciation of ethical and spiritual factors, both personal and in groups, arises as a cultural background stimulating group prominence for development. These conditions have again been considered after failed development attempts in countries far from the Western World, like Arab, African and Asian countries.

If the social development theories and strategies are separated from the spiritual and cultural foundations of human life – as they have been in a hyper-technocratic and hyper-programmed world – we take the risk of social decadence and self-destruction. This will be manifested in totalitarian social formations, accelerating global conflicts among competitive central powers, and between centre and peripheries, leading to guaranteed mutual destruction. A common global destiny demands a global common conscience (Tehranian, 1985).

The revalorization of the social ethos is considered now as the basic condition to mobilize national development, and mere technical modernization and different structural transformations are not deemed enough: "Not only good technique and structural changes will be required, but a social ethos that values savings, efforts, responsibility, tolerance, innovation and solidarity" (Ramos, 1990).

In the words of Pope Jean Paul II during his visit to CEPAL: "The moral causes of prosperity are well known throughout history. They reside in a constellation of virtues: hard work, competition, order, honesty, initiative, frugality, savings, spirit of service, compliance with a given word, audacity; in sum, love for a work well done. No system or social structure may resolve, as if by magic, the problem of poverty outside of these virtues" (Jean Paul II, Speech to CEPAL, Santiago, April 3, 1987).

But the revalorization of spiritual goods appears not only as a factor pushing development forward, but also as a goal to achieve. According to David Gallagher (1995), the new English post-liberalism is characterized exactly by its consideration of the enjoyment of goods provided by the market as insufficient and unsatisfactory; not to be suppressed, but to be complemented with the internal richness that stems from humanist culture, religion, art, or the appreciation of nature.

…The shift in prominence from bureaucracies to social subjects and groups has brought about this new interest in subjective aspects that are the basis of socio-economic human acts, such as those expressed in culture, spiritual values, and ethical energies for action.

References

Beltrán, L. R. La Investigación en Comunicación en Latinoamérica, ¿ Indagación con Anteojeras ? Caracas, Revista Orbita, Nº 21, Oct. l977, No. 21.

Chetley, A. *El Poder de Cambiar: La Experiencia del Proyecto Costa Atlántica de Colombia (1977-1989)*. La Haya: Fundación B. van Leer, 1990, 30.

"Communication Research Trends: 1988/89." Communication and Development, Vol. 9, No. 3. London. Educational Broadcasting, Cfr. Vol. 9 (1988/89), No. 4.

"Gallaher D. Hacia el futuro posliberal." El Mercurio, Junio 9 de 1995.

Goran, H. "Communication and Social Change in Developing Nations: A Critical View." Ames, Iowa: Iowa State University Press, 1982.

Greimas, A. J. *Semántica Estructural*. Madrid: Gredos, 1973.

Hornik, R. "Communication as Complement in Development." Journal of Communication, 1980, Vol. 30, No. 2, 10-24.

Kunczik, M. *Communication and Social Change*. Bonn, Germany: Friedrich Ebert Stiftung, 1985.

Kunczik, M. *Comunicación y Desarrollo*. Bonn, Germany: Friedrich Ebert Stiftung, 1992.

McAnany, E. G. "The Role of Information in Communications With the Rural Poor: Some Reflections. In E. G. McAnany, ed., *Communications in the Rural Third World*. New York: Praeger, 1980.

McAnany, E. G. "From Modernization and Diffusion to Dependency and Beyond: Theory and Practice in Communication for Social Change in the 1980s." Conference on Development Communications in the Third World. University of Illinois at Urbana-Champaign: College of Agriculture, 1984.

"Media Development." *Communication for Development*, Vol. XXXII/4. London: WACC, 1985.

Mitterrand, F. "Nuestro Mundo Merece ser Repensado." Santiago, Chile: Revista Mensaje, Vol. XLIV, Marzo-Abril 1995, 54.

Palomar, J. "Algunas Conceptualizaciones Sobre la Calidad de Vida." México: Umbral, 1994, XXI, No. 16, 25-34.

Pavlic, B., and C. J. Hamelink. *The New International Economic Order: Links Between Economics and Communications*. Paris: UNESCO, 1985.

Pratt, C. B., and J. B. Manheim. "Communication Research and Development Policy: Agenda Dynamics in an African Setting." Journal of Communication, 1988, Vol. 38, No. 3, 75-95.

Ramos J. "La Tercera Vía de Desarrollo Hoy: ¿Conjunto Vacío, Sueño Nostálgico, o Desafío aún Vigente?" Santiago, Chile: CPU, Estudios Sociales, 1990, Vol. 4, No. 66, 44.

Samarajiva, R., and P. Shields. "Integration, Tele-Communications and Development: Power in the Paradigma." Journal of Communications, 1990, Vol. 40, No. 3, 84-105.

Sánchez Ruiz, E. *Réquiem por la Modernización*. México: Universidad de Guadalajara, 1986.

Tehranian, M. "Paradigms Lost: Development as Comunication and Learning." London: Media Development, 1985, Vol. XXXII, 4.

White, R. A. *Media, Politics and Democracy in the Developing World*. London: CSCC, 1988.

Fuenzalida Fernández, Valerio. "Televisión y Cultura del Protagonismo." *El Consumo Cultural en América Latina*. Sunkel, Guillermo compilador. Santa Fé de Bogotá, Colombia: Convenio Andrés Bello, 1999. Reprinted with permission of the author.

EXCERPT FROM:

COMMUNICATION AND CULTURE IN THE GLOBAL SOCIETY: A LATIN AMERICAN VIEW

By Jesus Martín-Barbero

2002 What we are witnessing today is the overwhelming emergence of a *communicational reason* with devices--the fragmentation that dislocates and decenters, the flow that globalizes and compresses, the connection that dematerializes and makes things hybrid.

Society is becoming a market.

…What we need to consider today is the *communicational hegemony of the market in society*: Communication has turned into the most efficient power driving the disengagement and insertion of cultures—ethnic, national or local—in the space/time of the market and in global technologies.

If the technological revolution has stopped being a *matter of means* and has become instead a matter of *ends,* it is because we are facing the configuration of a *communicative ecosystem*, comprising not only new machines or media, but also of new languages, sensibilities, knowledge and writings. We are also facing the hegemony of the audiovisual experience over typographic forms and the reinstatement of the image in the field of knowledge production. All this is influencing what we understand as communicating, as well as the forms of co-existence and the meaning of the social bond. Which is what Zigmunt Bauman aims at with his reflection when he writes, "Globalization means that we all depend on one another already. Distances are less and less important; what happens anywhere may have consequences in any other place in the world."

We have stopped being able to protect both ourselves, and those who suffer the consequences of our actions, in this worldwide network of interdependencies"[1].

Just as the nation-state implied a rupture with previous forms of political, economic and cultural organization, a crack in the line of continuity between the *traditional* organic community of local cultures and the *modern* society of the nation-state, global issues are not a continuation of international issues as proposed by the great Brazilian geographer Milton Santos. What we are facing is not a mere form of integration of nation-states but the emergence of another type of historical-social nexus, *the world*, which has become the new reality to analyze and the new central category of the social sciences[2].

Linked to its techno-economic dimensions, *globalization* sets in motion a worldwide process of interconnection that connects everything of an *instrumental* value—corporations, institutions, individuals—while it disconnects everything that, from its perspective, has no value. This inclusion/exclusion process on a worldwide scale is turning culture into a strategic space of compression of the tensions that rip apart and restore "being together," and culture has become the place where all political, economic, religious, ethnic, aesthetic and sexual crises are knotted together.

This is why it is from the cultural diversity of histories and territories, experiences and memories, that globalization is not only resisted, but also negotiated and interacted with… Today, what galvanizes identities as the force driving the struggle is inseparable from the *demand for knowledge and meaning*[3]. And neither one of them can be formulated in mere economic or political terms, since both refer to the core

1 Z. Bauman, *La globalización:consecuencias humanas*, p. 94, F.C.E., México,1999.
2 M. Santos, *Por uma outra globalizacao:do pensamiento único á consciencia universal,* Record, Rio de Janeiro,2000
3 Ch.Taylor, *Multicultualismo.Lotte per il riconoscimento,* Feltrinelli, Milan,1998; see also: N. Fraser, "Redistribución y reconocimiento" in *Justitia interrupta. Reflexiones críticas desde la posición 'postsocialista''* , Siglo del Hombre, Bogotá, 1998

1927
1960
1963
1964
1967
1969
1970
1971
1972
1973
1974
1975
1976
1977
1978
1979
1980
1981
1982
1983
1984
1985
1986
1987
1988
1989
1990
1991
1992
1993
1994
1995
1996
1997
1998
1999
2000
2001
2002
2003
2004
2005
2006

of culture itself, as a world of *belonging to* and *sharing with.* That is why, today, identity becomes the force best prepared to introduce contradictions in the hegemony of instrumental reason.

The strategic need to differentiate the unifying logics of economic globalization from those that universalize culture, no matter how intricate they might be, arises from that as well. Cultural *mundialization* does not operate from the outside in autonomous spheres, such as national or local ones. *"Mundialization* is a process done and undone incessantly, and in this sense it would be inappropriate to speak about a "global culture" with a hierarchical level situated above national or local cultures. The *mundialization* process is an overall social phenomenon, which in order to exist must be localized and take root in the everyday practices of peoples and men"[4]. *Mundialization* must not be confused with the *standardization* of different spheres of life that resulted from industrialization... We are now facing another kind of process, expressed in the *modern-world* culture*,* which constitutes a new way of being in the world, evidenced in the deep changes that have taken place in life: at work, with couples, as regards food or leisure.

The uninterrupted workday has made it impossible for millions of people to have lunch at home; every day more women work away from home; children become independent from their parents early on; the patriarchal figure has been devaluated as much as women's work has been valued; daily food, having lost its symbolism, has turned into fast food. Thus, the success of McDonald's or Pizza Hut speaks... of the profound changes in people's everyday lives, changes that these products undoubtedly cater to and turn into money. Desynchronized from the rituals of yesteryear and the places that used to symbolize family gatherings and respect for the patriarchal authority, the new nourishing modes and products "lose the rigidity of territories and customs,

becoming information adjusted to the polysemy of contexts"[5]. Acknowledging this does not mean ignoring the growing monopolization of distribution, or the decentralization that concentrates power and the uprooting that pushes cultures to hybridize. Structurally linked to economic globalization but not ending with it, phenomena universalizing images linked to different music, images and characters that represent deterritorialized styles and values, also connected to new memory figures, take place.

But in the same way local cultures did not disappear with the nation-state—even if they deeply changed their conditions of existence—globalization will not make cultural heterogeneity disappear; to the contrary, what we are observing so far is its revival and fundamentalist fight back!

Understanding this *transformation of culture* is forcing us to assume that today *identity* means and implies two diametrically different dimensions, radically opposed until now. Until recently, to speak of "identity" meant speaking about roots, tradition, territory and duration, about a symbolically dense memory. Identity was made of that and that only. Today, to say "identity" also implies—if we do not want to condemn it to the limbo of tradition disconnected from the perceptive and expressive mutations of the present—speaking of networks, flows, migrations and mobilities, instantaneity and lack of grounding.

English anthropologists have expressed that new identity through the splendid image of *moving roots*[6], mobile roots, or even better, *roots in motion*. ...As the Catalan anthropologist Eduardo Delgado states, "it is impossible to live without roots, but many roots do not allow us to walk".

This means that, to be acknowledged, we need to tell our story, since there is no identity without narration: Narration not only expresses what we are, it

---

4 R. Ortiz, *Mundializaçao e cultura,* p. 32, Brasiliense, Sao Paulo, 1994

5 Ibid, p.87; see also from the same author, *Otro territorio,* C.A.B. Bogotá, 1998

6 Translator's note: included in English in the original Spanish version.

also constitutes it[7]. For the plurality of cultures of the world to be taken into account, it is essential that the diversity of identities are told, narrated, both in their own *languages* and in the *multimedia language* that today traverses them with the double motion of *translations* –from oral to written, audiovisual, hypertextual and hybridizations. That is, it essential for there to be an interculturality in which the dynamics of economy and world culture mobilize not only the heterogeneity of groups and their readjustment to the pressures of global issues, but also co-existence within one single society with quite diverse codes and narrations

In regard to *traditional culture,* peasant, indigenous and black, we face a profound reconfiguration of those cultures in response not only to the evolution of devices of domination, but also to the intensification of their communication and interaction with other cultures in each country and the world[8]. Inside communities, those communication processes are simultaneously perceived as another threat to the survival of their particular worlds—the long and dense experience of traps through which communities have been dominated produces much suspicion to any exposure to others.

At the same time, however, communication is experienced as a possibility to break exclusion; as an experience of interaction that, while involving risks, also opens up new future possibilities. Communication allows the dynamics of traditional communities themselves to transcend the frameworks of comprehension devised by anthropologists and folklorists: In those communities, there is less nostalgic complacence with tradition and a higher consciousness of the [ability to reconstruct] the

future[9]. This is evidenced in the diversification and development of artisanal production through open interaction with modern design, and even with certain rationales belonging to cultural industries; the development of a legal framework specific to the communities; an increase in radio and television broadcasting stations programmed and managed by communities themselves. And it's evidenced in the Zapatista movement's proclaiming the utopia of Mexican indigenous peoples from Chiapas[10] through the Internet.

...Viewed from the global culture standpoint, national identity seems provincial and loaded with state-bound and paternalist liabilities. Viewed from the diversity of local cultures, national identity is the equivalent of centralist homogenization and official rigidity[11]. Therefore, it is both the idea and the social experience of *identity* that surpass the Manichaean frames of an anthropology of the traditional-native and a sociology of the modern-universal. Identity cannot continue to be considered as an expression of a single, homogeneous culture, perfectly distinguishable and coherent. The quality of being monolingual and having a single territory, which early modernization assumed from the colony, hid the dense multiculturality that comprised each nation, and the arbitrary nature of the demarcations that make up the borders of nations. Today, national identities are increasingly multilinguistic and transterritorial, and they are constituted not only by differences among cultures that have developed separately, but

7 In this regard: Homi K. Bhabha (Ed.), *Nation and narration,* Routledge,London, 1977; Jose Miguel Marinas "La identidad contada", in *Destinos del relato al fin del milenio* ps. 75-88, Archivos de la Filmoteca, Valencia, 1995
8 R.Bayardo y M.Lacarrieu (Comp.) Globalización e identidad cultural, Ciccus, Buenos Aires, 1997; D. Mato y otros, América Latina en tiempos de globalización: procesos culturales y transformaciones sociopolíticas, Unesco/U.C.V.,Caracas,1996.

9 N. Garcia Canclini, *Culturas híbridas,* ps. 280 y ss., Grijalbo, México,1990;G. Gimenez, y R. Pozas (Coord.), *Modernización e identidades sociales,* UNAM, México, 1994;W. Rowe / V. Scheling, *Memory and Modernity. Popular culture in Latin America,* Verso, London, 1991
10 In this regard: E.Sanchez Botero, *Justicia y pueblos indígenas de Colombia,* Univ.Nacional/Unijus, Bogotá,1998; A.G.Quintero Rivera, *Salsa,sabor y control,* Siglo XXI, Mexico,1998; R. Ma.Alfaro y otros, *Redes solidarias,culturas y multimedialidad,* Ocic- AL/Uclap,Quito, 1998; S. Rojo Arias, "La historia,la memoria y la identidad en los comunicados del EZLN" in *Identidades,* número especial de *Debate feminista,* México, 1996; N.García Canclini, *Las cultura populares en el capitalismo,* Nueva Imagen, México,1982
11 R. Schwarz, *Nacional por sustracción,* Rev. "Punto de vista" No. 28, Buenos Aires,1987

1927
1960
1963
1964
1967
1969
1970
1971
1972
1973
1974
1975
1976
1977
1978
1979
1980
1981
1982
1983
1984
1985
1986
1987
1988
1989
1990
1991
1992
1993
1994
1995
1996
1997
1998
1999
2000
2001
2002
2003
2004
2005
2006

also through the unequal appropriations and combinations that the different groups make of elements from different societies as well as their own. Adding to the revalorization of local aspects is the outbreak of the until recently hardly unified national history, due to ethnic, racial, regional, and gender movements' claims of *the right to their own memory*[12], that is, to the construction of their own narratives and images.

However, it is in the city, and in urban cultures much more than in the space of the State, where new identities…made up of national imaginaries, local traditions and transnational information flow. And the city is where new ways of representation and political participation, new modalities of citizenship, are configured. That is what new *ways of being together* aim at –youth gangs, Pentecostal communities, sexual ghettos; it is from them that the inhabitants of the city respond to fierce processes of urbanization, linked to the imaginaries of a modernity identified with the speed of traffic and the fragmentation of information languages. We live in cities flooded not only by computer flows, but also by other flows perpetuated by an increase in poverty and emigration of peasants that causes a great paradox. While what is urban overflows from the city, increasingly permeating the rural world, our cities experience a process of de-urbanization[13] that encompasses two facts at the same time.

The ruralization of the city gives validity again to old forms of survival that introduce markedly rural knowledge, feelings and narratives in the learning processes and appropriations of the urban modernity. The city effectively used by its citizens is progressively reduced, since once cultural references have been lost, people, insecure and distrustful, restrict the spaces in which they move, the territories in which they recognize themselves, tending to disregard most of a city that is only crossed by the inevitable paths. New urban ways of being together are produced, especially among younger generations, nowadays turned into *indigenous* representatives of cultures densely mixed in ways of speaking and dressing, the music they make or listen to, and the groups they constitute, including those fuelled by informational technology. This is what research on the night tribes in Buenos Aires, the *chavos-banda* in Guadalajara or the juvenile gangs in the northwest communes of Medellín[14] discovers throughout Latin America.

What is complicated about the narrative structure of identities is the fact that nowadays they are woven and intertwined with a diversity of languages, codes and media. On the one hand, these are hegemonized, functionalized and made profitable by market logic; on the other, they open possibilities of subverting that very same logic from the dynamics and social use of art and technique, mobilizing the contradictions that challenge new inter-media networks.

Even if proponents of the apocalyptic –from the late Popper to Sartori– thunder our weary ears with their lugubrious trumpets, neither the density of visuals, nor the resonance of the networks, are merely market and moral decadence. They are also the place from which a new social fabric, a new public space, a new web of sociality, emerge[15].

From the contradiction that turned Montesinos' evil videos into the deadliest trap for him and his followers, and a colossal tool for the struggle against corruption in Peru, to the worldwide resonance and legitimacy that the online presence of Commander Marcos generated for his Zapatista utopia. There is the World Social Forum in Porto Alegre subverting

---

12 P. Nora, *Les lieux de memoire,* Vol. III. p.1009, Gallimard, Paris,1992
13 J.Martin-Barbero, "De la ciudad mediada a la ciudad virtual",*TELOS* n° 44, Madrid.1996.

14 M. Margulis et al, *La cultura de la noche.Vida nocturna de los jóvenes en Buenos Aires* Espasa Hoy, B.A.,1994; R.Reguillo, *En la calle otra vez. Las bandas:identidad urbana y usos de la comunicación,* Iteso,Gualajara ,México,1991, A.Salazar, *No nacimos p'asemilla. La cultura delas andas juveniles en Medellín,*Cinep,Bogotá,1990.
15 VV.AA. *Redes,destión y ciudadanía,* OCLAACC/Abyayala, Quto,2002; S. Finquelevich (coord.) *Ciudadanos a la red!. Los vínculos sociales en el ciberespacio,* Ciccus/Lacrujía, Buenos Aires, 2000

the meaning that the capitalist market wants to give the Internet, and telling us through that same network about the extremes that inequality is reaching in the world, an increase in poverty, and the injustice that the neo-liberal orientation of globalization is producing, particularly in our countries. While Microsoft and others seek to monopolize the networks, lots of people, who at the same time remain a statistical minority in terms of the world's population, also constitute a dissident voice with a worldwide presence that causes more and more inconveniences to the system every day....

Thus, more than objects requiring policies, communication and culture are turned by globalization into a primordial political battlefield: the strategic scenario that requires politics to render its symbolic dimension denser, its ability to assemble and form citizens ready to face the erosion suffered by the collective order. Which is *what the market cannot do*[16] ...The market cannot *sediment traditions*, since all it produces "evaporates in the air" given its structural tendency towards an accelerated and generalized obsolescence, not only of things but also of forms and institutions. The market cannot create *societal linkages,* that is to say, true bonds *among subjects,* since these are constituted in conflictive processes of communication of meaning, and the market operates anonymously through value logic that implies purely formal exchanges, associations and quickly fading promises that only generate satisfaction or frustration, but never meaning. Ultimately, the market cannot *generate social innovation*, since this implies non-functional differences and solidarities, resistance and subversion; the only thing the market can do is what it knows best: co-opt innovation and render it profitable.

That is the framework for Arjun Appadurai's reflection. For him, financial, cultural or human rights flows take place in a movement of trends that so far have been convergent due to their articulation in the nation- state, but that in the global space become disjunctive. Namely, even though they are contemporary and of similar form in a certain way, these movements today magnify their different temporariness with the very diverse rhythms that break through them in very different directions. ...However, globalization is not a paradigm or a process: It is a multitude of processes....

For Appadurai, there is a need to build, on a worldwide scale, a *globalization from below*...an articulation already taking place in the collective imagination, acting in what he calls "emerging social patterns," from the environmental sphere to the labor arena, from civil rights to cultural citizenships. He writes:

> If it is through imagination that capitalism disciplines and controls contemporary citizens today, especially through the media, imagination is also the aptitude through which new collective patterns of dissent, disaffection and questioning of the patterns imposed on everyday life emerge. Through which we see the emergence of new social forms, not predatory like those of capital, but forms constructive of new human coexistences[17].

Martín-Barbero, Jesús. "La globalización en clave cultural: una mirada latino americana". Lecture presented at the international meeting "Bogues: Globalisme et Pluralisme", Montreal, April 22-27, 2002. Used with permission of copyright holder.

16 Brunner, "Cambio social y democracia" in *Estudios Públicos,* N°39, Santiago,1990

17 A. Appadurai, "Grassroots Globalization and the Research Imagination", *Public Culture* N° 30, p. 7, Duke University Press, 2000.

1927
1960
1963
1964
1967
1969
1970
1971
1972
1973
1974
1975
1976
1977
1978
1979
1980
1981
1982
1983
1984
1985
1986
1987
1988
1989
1990
1991
1992
1993
1994
1995
1996
1997
1998
1999
2000
2001
2002
2003
2004
2005
2006

INTRODUCTION:
CRUZANDO FRONTERAS AND THE BORDERS OF THOUGHT
The Modernity/Coloniality Research Program

By Arturo Escobar

2002 Why, one may ask, does a group of Latin Americans and Latin Americanists feel that a new understanding of modernity is needed? To fully appreciate the importance of this question, it is instructive to begin by discussing the dominant tendencies in the study of modernity from what we can call "intramodern perspectives" (the term will become clear as we move along). I am very much aware that the view of modernity to be presented below is terribly partial and contestable. I am not presenting it with the goal of "theorizing modernity," but rather in order to highlight, by way of contrast, the stark difference that the Modernity/Coloniality (MC) research program poses in relation to the dominant inquiries about modernity. In the last instance, the goal of this brief excursion into modernity is political. If, as most intramodern discussion suggests, globalization entails the universalization and radicalization of modernity, then what are we left with? How can we think about social change? Does radical alterity become impossible? … Is globalization the last stage of capitalist modernity, or the beginning of something new? As we shall see, intramodern and MC perspectives on modernity give a very different answer to these questions.

Globalization as the Radicalization of Modernity: An Intramodern View of Modernity

The idea of a relatively single globalization process emanating out of a few dominant centers remains prevalent. It is useful to review succinctly how this image arose in the most recent period and why it seems so difficult to dispel. From a philosophical and sociological perspective, the root of the idea of an increasingly overpowering globalization lies in a view of modernity as essentially a European phenomenon. Recent challenges to this view from peripheral locations have questioned the unexamined assumption—found in thinkers like Habermas, Giddens, Taylor, Touraine, Lyotard, Rorty, etc., as much as in Kant, Hegel, and the Frankfurt School philosophers before them—that modernity can be fully explained by reference to factors internal to Europe. The views of Habermas and Giddens have been particularly influential, having given rise to a veritable genre of books on modernity and globalization. From this perspective, modernity may be characterized as follows:

1. *Historically*, modernity has identifiable temporal and spatial origins: Seventeenth-century northern Europe (especially France, Germany, England), around the processes of Reformation, the Enlightenment, and the French Revolution. These processes crystallized at the end of the eighteenth century (Foucault's modern episteme) and became consolidated with the industrial revolution.

2. *Sociologically*, modernity is characterized by certain institutions, particularly the nation state, and by some basic features, such as *self-reflexivity* (the continuous feedback of expert knowledge back into society, transforming it); the *dismembedding* of social life from local context and its increasing determination by translocal forces; and *space/ time distantiation*, or the separation of space and place, since relations between "absent others" become more important than face-to-face interaction (Giddens 1990).

3. *Culturally*, modernity can be further characterized in terms of the increasing appropriation of previously taken for granted cultural backgrounds by forms of expert knowledge linked to capital and state administrative apparatuses (Habermas 1973). Habermas (1987) describes this process as the increasing rationalization of the life-world, accompanied by universalization and individuation. Modernity brings about an order on the basis of the constructs of reason, the individual, expert knowledge, and administrative mechanisms

linked to the state. Order and reason are seen as the foundation for equality and freedom and enabled by the language of rights.

4. **Philosophically**, one may see modernity in terms of the emergence of the notion of "Man" as the foundation for all knowledge and order of the world, separate from the natural and the divine (a pervasive anthropocentrism; Foucault 1973; Heidegger 1977; Panikkar 1993). On the other hand, modernity is seen in terms of the triumph of metaphysics, understood as a tendency—extending from Plato and some of the pre-Socratics to Descartes and the modern thinkers, and criticized by Nietzsche and Heidegger among others—that finds in logical truth the foundation for a rational theory of the world as made up of knowable (and hence controllable) things and beings (e.g., Vattimo 1991). For Vattimo, modernity is characterized by the idea of history and its corollary, progress and overcoming. Vattimo emphasizes the logic of development—the belief in perpetual betterment and overcoming—as crucial to the philosophical foundations of the modern order.

On the critical side, the disembeddedness of modernity is seen to cause what Paul Virilio (1999) calls global delocalization, including the marginalization of place (the here and now of social action) in the definition of social life. The underside of order and rationality is seen in various ways, from the domination and disenchantment that came about with secularization and the predominance of instrumental reason to the normalization of life and the disciplining of populations. As Foucault put it, "the Enlightenment, which discovered the liberties, also invented the disciplines" (1979, 222). Finally, modernity's anthropocentrism is related to logocentrism and phallogocentrism, defined here simply as the cultural project of ordering the world according to rational principles from the perspective of a male Eurocentric consciousness—in other words, building an allegedly ordered, rational, and predictable world. Logocentrism has reached unprecedented levels with the extreme economization and technification

of the world (Leff 2000). Modernity of course did not succeed in constituting a total reality, but enacted a totalizing project aimed at the purification of orders (separation between us and them, nature and culture), although inevitably only producing hybrids of these opposites along the way (thus Latour's dictum that "we have never been modern," 1993).

Is there a logical necessity to believe that the order so sketchily characterized above is the only one capable of becoming global? For most theorists, on all sides of the political spectrum, this is exactly the case. Giddens (1990) has made the argument most forcefully: Globalization entails the radicalization and universalization of modernity. No longer purely an affair of the West, however, since modernity is everywhere, the triumph of the modern lies precisely in its having become universal. This may be call the "Giddens effect": *From now own, it's modernity all the way down, everywhere, until the end of time.* Not only is radical alterity expelled forever from the realm of possibilities, but all world cultures and societies are reduced to being a manifestation of European history and culture. The "Giddens effect" seems to be at play, directly or indirectly, in most works on modernity and globalization at present. No matter how variously qualified, a "global modernity" is here to stay. Recent anthropological investigations of "modernity at large" (Appadurai 1996) have shown modernity to be seen as deterritorialized, hybridized, contested, uneven, heterogenous, even multiple, or in terms of conversing with, engaging, playing with, or processing modernity; nevertheless, but in the last instance these modernities end up being a reflection of a Eurocentered social order, under the assumption that modernity is now everywhere, an ubiquitous and ineluctable social fact.[1]

Could it be, however, that the power of Eurocentered modernity—as a *particular local history*—lies in the fact that is has produced *particular global designs* in such a way that it has "subalternized" other local histories and their corresponding designs? If this is the case, could one posit the hypothesis that radical alternatives

1927
1960
1963
1964
1967
1969
1970
1971
1972
1973
1974
1975
1976
1977
1978
1979
1980
1981
1982
1983
1984
1985
1986
1987
1988
1989
1990
1991
1992
1993
1994
1995
1996
1997
1998
1999
2000
2001
2002
2003
2004
2005
2006

to modernity are not a historically foreclosed possibility? If so, how can we articulate a project around this possibility? Could it be that it is possible to think about, and to think differently from, an "exteriority" to the modern world system? That one may envision alternatives to the totality imputed to modernity, and adumbrate not a different totality leading to different global designs, but a network of local/global histories constructed from the perspective of a politically enriched alterity? This is precisely the possibility that may be gleaned from the work of a group of Latin American theorists that in refracting modernity through the lens of coloniality engage in a questioning of the spatial and temporal origins of modernity, thus unfreezing the radical potential for thinking from difference and towards the constitution of alternative local and regional worlds. In what follows, I present succinctly some of the main arguments of these works.[2]

The Modernity/Coloniality Research Program

The conceptualization of modernity/coloniality is grounded in a series of operations that distinguish it from established theories of modernity. Succinctly put, these include the following: 1) an emphasis on locating the origins of modernity with the conquest of America and the control of the Atlantic after 1492, rather than in the most commonly accepted landmarks such as the Enlightenment or the end of the 18th century;[3] 2) a persistent attention to colonialism and the making of the capitalist world system as constitutive of modernity; this includes a determination not to overlook the economy and its concomitant forms of exploitation; 3) consequently, the adoption of a world perspective in the explanation of modernity, in lieu of a view of modernity as an intra-European phenomenon; 4) the identification of the domination of others outside the European core as a necessary dimension of modernity, with the concomitant subalternization of the knowledge and cultures of these other groups; 5) a conception of Eurocentrism as the knowledge form of modernity/coloniality—a hegemonic representation and mode of knowing that

claims universality for itself, and that relies on "a confusion between abstract universality and the concrete world hegemony derived from Europe's position as center" (Dussel 2000, 471; Quijano 2000, 549).

A number of alternative notions emerge from this set of positions: a) a decentering of modernity from its alleged European origins, including a debunking of the linear sequence linking Greece, Rome, Christianity and modern Europe; b) a new spatial and temporal conception of modernity in terms of the foundational role of Spain and Portugal (the so-called first modernity initiated with the Conquest) and its continuation in northern Europe with the industrial revolution and the Enlightenment (the second modernity, in Dussel's terms)—the second modernity does not replace the first, but overlaps with it, until the present; c) a focus on the peripheralization of all other world regions by this "modern Europe," with Latin America as the initial "other side" of modernity (the dominated and concealed side); and d) a rereading of the "myth of modernity," not in terms of a questioning of the emancipatory potential of modern reason, but of modernity's "underside," namely, the imputation of the superiority of European civilization, coupled with the assumption that Europe's development must be followed unilaterally by every other culture, by force if necessary—what Dussel terms "the developmentalist fallacy" (e.g., 1993, 2000). Some additional consequences include the revaluing of landmark experiences of decolonization, from the Tupac Amaru rebellion and the 1804 Haitian revolution to the 1960s anticolonial movements, as sources of visions for the future, as opposed to the conventional sources such as the French and American revolutions; and, in general, the need to take seriously the epistemic force of local histories and to think theory through from the political praxis of subaltern groups.

The main conclusions are, first, that the proper analytical unit for the analysis of modernity is modernity/coloniality—in sum, there is no modernity without coloniality, with the latter being constitutive of the former (in Asia, Africa, Latin America/Caribbean). Second, the fact that "the colonial difference" is a privileged epistemological and political space. The great majority of European theorists (particularly those "defenders of the European patent on modernity," as Quijano mockingly calls them [2000, 543]) have been blind to the colonial difference and the subalternization of knowledge and cultures it entailed. A focus on the modern/colonial world system also makes visible, besides the internal conflicts (conflicts within powers with the same world view), those that take place at the exterior borders of the modern/colonial system—i.e., the conflicts with other cultures and worldviews.[4]

Key Notions and Themes of the Modernity/Coloniality Research Program

Some of the key notions that make up the conceptual corpus of this research program are thus:

■ The *modern colonial world system* as the ensemble of processes and social formations that encompass modern colonialism and colonial modernities; although it is structurally heterogeneous, it articulates the main forms of power into a system.
■ *Coloniality of power* (Quijano), a global hegemonic model of power in place since the Conquest that articulates race and labor, space and peoples, according to the needs of capital and to the benefit of white European peoples.
■ *Colonial difference* and *global coloniality* (Mignolo), which refer to the knowledge and cultural dimensions of the subalternization processes effected by the coloniality of power; the colonial difference brings to the fore persistent cultural differences within global power structures.
■ *Coloniality of being* (more recently suggested by Nelson Maldonado-Torres in group discussions) as the ontological dimension of coloniality, on both sides of the encounter; based on Levinas, Dussel and Fanon, it points at the "ontological excess" that occurs when particular beings impose on others and, beyond that, the potential or actual effectivity of the discourses with which the other responds to the suppression as a result of the encounter (Maldonado-Torres 2003).

■ *Eurocentrism,* as the knowledge model that represents the local European historical experience and which became globally hegemonic since the 17th century (Dussel, Quijano); hence the possibility of *non-Eurocentric thinking* and epistemologies.

All of these notions are in themselves rooted in complex conceptualizations that represent decades of research; even thus, they are of course debatable. There are some other notions, more peculiar to specific authors but which are gaining currency within the group, that it is also important to introduce. These include Dussel's notion of exteriority and transmodernity and Mignolo's concepts of border thinking, pluritopic hermeneutics and pluriversality.

The question of whether there is an "exteriority" to the modern/colonial world system is somewhat peculiar to this group, and easily misunderstood. It was originally proposed and carefully elaborated by Dussel in his classic work on liberation philosophy (1976) and reworked in recent years. In no way should this exteriority be thought about as a pure outside, untouched by the modern. The notion of exteriority does not entail an ontological outside; it refers to an outside that is precisely constituted as difference by a hegemonic discourse. This notion of exteriority arises chiefly by thinking about the Other from the ethical and epistemological perspective of a liberation philosophy framework: the Other as oppressed, as woman, as racially marked, as excluded, as poor, as nature. By appealing from the exteriority in which s/he is located, the Other becomes the original source of an ethical discourse vis-à-vis a hegemonic totality. This interpellation of the Other comes from outside or beyond the system's institutional and normative frame, as an ethical challenge. This challenge might only be "quasi-intelligible" at first (Dussel 1996, 25), given the difficulties in establishing meaningful interpellation that exploited peoples have with respect to a hegemonic system (contra Habermas' notion of a communication free of domination). There are degrees of exteriority; in the last instance, the greater challenge comes from

1927
1960
1963
1964
1967
1969
1970
1971
1972
1973
1974
1975
1976
1977
1978
1979
1980
1981
1982
1983
1984
1985
1986
1987
1988
1989
1990
1991
1992
1993
1994
1995
1996
1997
1998
1999
2000
2001
2002
2003
2004
2005
2006

the interpellation which the majority of the population of the planet, located in the South, raises, demanding their right to live, their right to develop their own culture, economy, politics, etc. ... There is no liberation without rationality; but there is no *critical* rationality without accepting the interpellation of the excluded, or this would inadvertently be only the rationality of *domination*. ... From this negated Other departs the praxis of liberation as "affirmation" of the Exteriority and as origin of the movement of negation of the negation. (Dussel 1996, 31, 36, 54).[5]

This is precisely what most European and Euro-American theorists seem unwilling to consider: that it is impossible to think about transcending or overcoming modernity without approaching it from the perspective of the colonial difference. Both Mignolo and Dussel see here a strict limit to deconstruction and to the various Eurocentered critiques of Eurocentrism—in short, these continue to be thought about from within Eurocentric categories (of, say, liberalism, Marxism, poststructuralism), not from the border thinking enabled by the colonial difference. Critiques of modernity, in short, are blind to the (epistemic and cultural) colonial difference that becomes the focus of modernity/coloniality.

Dussel's notion of *transmodernity* signals the possibility of a non-Eurocentric and critical dialogue with alterity, one that fully enables "the negation of the negation" to which the subaltern others have been subjected, and one that does not see critical discourse as intrinsically European. Integral to this effort is the rescuing of nonhegemonic and silenced counterdiscourses, of the alterity that is constitutive of modernity itself. This is the ethical principle of liberation of the negated Other, for which Dussel coins the term "transmodernity," defined as a project for overcoming modernity not simply by negating it but by thinking about it from its underside, from the perspective of the excluded Other. Transmodernity is a future-oriented project that seeks the liberation of all humanity

(1996, 14, Ch. 7), "a worldwide ethical liberation project in which alterity, which was part and parcel of modernity, would be able to fulfill itself" (2000, 473), "in which both modernity and its negated alterity (the victims) co-realize themselves in a process of mutual fertilization" (1993, 76). In short, transmodernity cannot be brought about from within modernity, but requires the action—and the incorporative solidarity—of the subalternized groups, the objects of modernity's constitutive violence embedded in, among other features, the developmentalist fallacy. Rather than the rational project of a discursive ethics, transmodernity becomes the expression of an ethics of liberation.

Mignolo's notions of *border thinking*, *border epistemology*, and *pluritopic hermeneutics* are important in this regard. They point at the need "for a kind of thinking that moves along the diversity of historical processes" (Mignolo 2001, 9). There are, to be sure, no original thinking traditions to which one can go back. Rather than reproducing Western abstract universals, however, the alternative is a kind of border thinking that "engages the colonialism of Western epistemology (from the left and from the right) from the perspective of epistemic forces that have been turned into subaltern (traditional, folkloric, religious, emotional, etc.) forms of knowledge" (2001, 11). Resituating Anzaldúa's metaphor of the border into the domain of coloniality, Mignolo adumbrates the possibility of "'thinking otherwise', from the interior exteriority of the border. That is, to engage in border thinking is to move beyond the categories created and imposed by Western epistemology" (11). This is not just a question of changing the contents but the very terms of the conversation. It is not a question of replacing existing epistemologies, either; these will certainly continue to exist and as such will remain viable as spaces of, and for, critique. Instead, what he claims "is the space for an epistemology, that comes from the border and aims toward political and ethical transformations" (11). Finally, while Mignolo acknowledges the continued importance of the monotopic critique of modernity by Western critical discourse (critique from a single, unified space), he suggests that this has to be put into dialogue with the critique(s) arising from the colonial difference, which constitutes border thinking. The result is a "pluritopic hermeneutics" (a term he seemingly adapts from Pannikar's "diatopic hermeneutics"), a possibility of thinking from different spaces which finally breaks away from Eurocentrism as sole epistemological perspective. This is the double critique of modernity from the perspective of coloniality, from the exterior of the modern/colonial world system. Let it be clear, however, that border thinking entails both "displacement and departure" (2000, 308), double critique and positive affirmation of an alternative ordering of the real. To sum up, border thinking points towards a different kind of hegemony, a multiple one. As a universal project, diversity allows us to imagine alternatives to universalism (we could say that the alternative to universalism in this view is not particularism but multiplicity). "The 'West and the rest' in Huntington's phrase provides the model to overcome, as the 'rest' becomes the sites where border thinking emerges in its diversity, where 'mundialización' creates new local histories remaking and re-adapting Western global designs ….and transforming local (European) histories from where such designs emerged…. 'Interdependence' may be the word that summarizes the break away from the idea of *totality* and brings about the idea of *networks* whose articulation will require epistemological principles I called in this book 'border thinking' and 'border gnosis,' as a re-articulation of the colonial difference: 'diversality as a universal project,' which means that people and communities have the right to be different precisely because 'we' are all equals" (2000, 310, 311).

"There is no question," writes Mignolo (2000, 59), "that Quijano, Dussel and I are reacting not only to the force of a historical imaginary but also to the actuality of this imaginary today." The corollary is the need to build narratives from the perspective of modernity/coloniality "geared towards the search for a different logic" (22). This project has to do with the rearticulation of global designs by and from local histories; with

the articulation between subaltern and hegemonic knowledge from the perspective of the subaltern; and with the remapping of colonial difference towards a worldly culture—such as in the Zapatista project, which remaps Marxism, thirdworldism, and indigenism, without being any of them, in an excellent example of border thinking. While "there is nothing outside of totality … totality is always projected from a given local history," it becomes possible to think of "other local histories producing either alternative totalities or an alternative to totality" (329). These alternatives would not play on the "globalization/civilization" couplet inherent to modernity/coloniality; they would rather build on a "*mundialización*/culture" relation centered on the local histories in which colonial global designs are necessarily transformed, thus transforming also the local histories that created them. Unlike globalization, *mundialización* brings to the fore the manifold local histories that, in questioning global designs (e.g., neoliberal globalization), aim at forms of globality that arise out of "cultures of transience" that go against the cultural homogeneity fostered by such designs. The diversity of *mundialización* is contrasted here with the homogeneity of globalization, aiming at multiple and diverse social orders.

In short, the perspective of modernity/coloniality provides an alternative framework for debates on modernity, globalization and development; it is not just a change in the description of events, it is an epistemic change of perspective. By speaking of the colonial difference, this framework brings to the fore the power dimension that is often lost in relativistic discussions of cultural difference. More recent debates on interculturality, for instance in Ecuador's current political and cultural scene, deepen some of these insights (Walsh 2003). In short, the MC research program is a framework constructed from the Latin American periphery of the modern colonial world system; it helps explain the dynamics of Eurocentrism in the making of modernity and attempts to transcend it. If it reveals the dark sides of modernity, it does not do it from an intra-epistemic perspective, as in the critical

1927
1960
1963
1964
1967
1969
1970
1971
1972
1973
1974
1975
1976
1977
1978
1979
1980
1981
1982
1983
1984
1985
1986
1987
1988
1989
1990
1991
1992
1993
1994
1995
1996
1997
1998
1999
2000
2001
2002
2003
2004
2005
2006

European discourses, but from the perspective of the receivers of the alleged benefits of the modern world. Modernity/coloniality also shows that the perspective of modernity is limited and exhausted in its pretended universality. By the same token, it shows the shortcomings of the language of alternative modernities in that this latter incorporates the projects of the nonmoderns into a single project, losing the subaltern perspectives and subordinating them, for even in their hybridity subaltern perspectives are not about being only modern but are heteroglossic, networked, plural. In highlighting the developmentalist fallacy, lastly, modernity/coloniality not only refocuses our attention on the overall fact of development but also provides a context for interpreting the various challenges to development and modernity as so many projects that are potentially complementary and mutually reinforcing. Beyond Latin America, one may say, with Mignolo (2000, 309), that this approach "is certainly a theory *from/of* the Third World, *but not only for the Third World*. ... Third World theorizing is also *for* the First World in the sense that critical theory is subsumed and incorporated in a new geocultural and epistemological location."[6]

Finally, there are some consequences of this group's work for Latin American studies in the United States, Europe, and elsewhere. The MC perspective moves away from viewing "Latin America" as an object of study (in relation to which U.S.-based Latin American studies would be the "knowing subject") towards an understanding of Latin America as a geohistorical location with and within a distinct critical genealogy of thought. Modernity/coloniality suggests that globalization must be understood from a geohistorical and critical Latin American perspective. With this the MC approach proposes an alternative to the genealogy of the modern social sciences that are still the foundation of Latin American studies in the United States. In this way, *Latin American studies* in, say, North America and Europe, and *critical social thought* in Latin America (which offers the epistemic grounding for the MC group) emerge as two *complementary*

but distinct paradigms.[7] This also means that, as an epistemic perspective, the MC research program is not associated with particular nationalities or geographical locations. To occupy the locus of enunciation crafted by the MC project, in other words, one does not need to be a Latin American nor live on the continent. "Latin America" itself becomes a perspective that can be practiced from many spaces, if it is done from counterhegemonic perspectives that challenge the very assumption of Latin America as fully constituted object of study, previous to, and outside of, the often imperialistic discourses that construct it.

References

Dussel, E. 1993. Eurocentrism and Modernity. In: J. Beverly and J. Oviedo, eds. *The postmodernism debate in Latin America*. Durham: Duke Univ. Press. 65–76.

Dussel, E. 1996. *The Underside of Modernity*. Atlantic Highlands, N.J.: Humanities Press.

Dussel, E. 2000. Europe, Modernity, and Eurocentrism. *Nepantla* 1:465–478.

Giddens, A. 1990. *The Consequences of Modernity*. Stanford: Stanford Univ. Press.

Habermas, J. 1973. *Legitimation Crisis*. Boston: Beacon Press.

Habermas, J. 1987. *The Philosophical Discourse of Modernity*. Cambridge: MIT Press.

of the World Picture," In: M. Heidegger. *The Question Concerning Technology*. New York: Harper and Row. 115-154.

Leff, E. 2000. *Saber ambiental*. Mexico: Siglo XXI.

Maldonado-Torres, N. 2003. Imperio y colonialidad del ser. Presented at the XXIV International Congress, Latin American Studies Association. Dallas. March 27–29.

Mignolo, W. 2000. *Local histories/global designs*. Princeton: Princeton Univ. Press.

Mignolo, W. 2001. Local Histories and Global Designs: An interview with Walter Mignolo. *Discourse* 22(3):7–33.

Panikkar, R. 1993. *The Cosmotheandric Experience*. New York: Orbis Books.

Quijano, A. 2000. Coloniality of power, ethnocentrism, and Latin America. *Nepantla* 1:533–580.

Vattimo, G. 1991. *The End Of Modernity*. Baltimore: Johns Hopkins Univ. Press.

Virilio, P. 2000. *Politics of the Very Worst*. New York: Semitext(e).

Walsh, C. 2003. Ecuador 2003: Promises and Challenges. Presented at the UNC–Duke Latin American Studies "Burning Issues" series. April 25.

Endnotes

1. Although I have not done an exhaustive search, I believe a *Eurocentered* view of modernity is present in most conceptualizations of modernity and globalization in philosophy, geography, anthropology, and communications, and on all sides of the political spectrum. Many of these works, to be sure, are important contributions to the understanding of modernity, yet their Eurocentrism has theoretical and political consequences. Some of these works explicitly engage with Giddens' work and develop an elegant and coherent

conceptualization of globalization from this perspective (e.g., Tomlinson 1999); others follow a more ethnographic orientation (e.g., Englund & Leach 2000, and Kahn 2001 for reviews; Appadurai 1996, plus the works inspired by this author's work), or a cultural-historical orientation (e.g., Gaonkar 2001). Some assert the plurality of globalization (i.e., globalizations) yet go on to explain such plurality in political and economic terms, taking for granted a dominant cultural matrix (see the special issue of *International Sociology* on Globalizations, Vol. 15, Number 2, June 2000; e.g., Wallerstein 2002). A Eurocentered and Eurocentric notion of modernity is also at play in most of the works on the left, such as Hardt and Negri (2000). These authors' reinterpretation of the European history of sovereignty in light of current biopolitical structures of rule, as well as their elaboration of resistance in the Western philosophy of immanence, are a novel element for rethinking modernity. However, their Eurocentrism becomes particularly problematic in their identification of the potential sources for radical action, and in their belief that there is no outside to modernity (again, a la Giddens). To the view that "there is no outside," the MC perspective counterposes a notion of exteriority to modernity/coloniality not entertained by any of the authors that follow in the tradition of Eurocentered modernity.

Recent anthropological reflection on modernity has also seen major changes. In the United States, anthropology of modernity has focused again both on "modernity abroad" and on people's (largely nonexperts') engagement with it. This approach has been important in grounding the understanding of modernity in ethnographic cases. As Kahn (2001) put it in a recent review, taken as a whole these works have pluralized the accepted understanding of modernity as a homogenous process. The various ways in which modernity is "pluralized," however, need to be taken into account. Most discuss "alternative modernities" (with "hybrid," "multiple," "local," etc., as other qualifiers) as emerging from the dynamic encounter of dominant (usually Western) and nondominant (e.g., local, non-Western, regional) forms (e.g., Pred & Watts 1992; Gupta 1998; Sivaramakrishnan & Agrawal c. 1999; Arce & Long 2000). There is no unified conception in these works, however, of what exactly constitutes modernity. References range from Baudelaire to Kant, Weber, Giddens, and Habermas. Kahn is right in saying that stating that modernity is plural and then showing ethnographically the ways in which it is localized has limitations in terms of theory. However, his appeal for an anthropology of modernity based on the theories of, say, Hegel, Weber, and Habermas compounds the problem, given the Eurocentrism of most of these thinkers (see Dussel 1993 for an analysis of the deep ethnocentrism of Hegel and Habermas, whose works "take on something of the sonority of Wagner's trumpets" [71]). As Ribeiro says in his commentary to Kahn, "modernity is subject to indigenization, but this does not amount to saying that it is a native category" (2001, 669). What is lost in these debates, it seems to me, is the very notion of difference as both a primary object of anthropology and an anchoring point for theoretical construction and political action. In the last instance, the limits of pluralizing modernity lie in the fact that it ends up reducing all social practice to being a manifestation of a European experience and will, no matter how qualified. Englund and Leach (2000) make a related argument in their critique of the ethnographic accounts of multiple modernities; they argue, correctly in my mind, that these works reintroduce a metanarrative of modernity in the analysis, be it "the dialectic," a (European) core that remains invariant, or a self-serving appeal to "wider context" or "larger scale perspective." The result is a weak relativism and a pluralization of modernities that reflects the ethnographer's own assumptions. Englund and Leach's call is for a renewed attention to ethnographic knowledge as a domain for ascertaining the very contexts that are relevant to investigation, before such a context is imputed to this or that version of modernity. From this perspective, a question remains: *What other kinds of theoretical and political claims can we possibly make with the insights of the ethnographies of modernity* that are not considered by their authors? In short, it seems to me that in many

recent anthropological works modernity is, first, redefined in a way that dissolves it and deprives it of any semblance of historical coherence, let alone unitary, social and cultural logic, and then, second, found ethnographically everywhere, always plural, changing and contested. A new balance seems necessary. After all, *why are we so ready still to ascribe to capitalism powerful and systematic effects*, with a coherent and for many a totalizing logic, *while denying modernity any significant connection with a coherent cultural logic, let alone a project of domination*?

2. This is a very sketchy presentation of this group's ideas in the best of cases. Broadly speaking, this group is associated with the work of a few central figures, chiefly, the Argentinean/Mexican philosopher Enrique Dussel, the Peruvian sociologist Aníbal Quijano and, more recently, the Argentinean/U.S. semiotician and cultural theorist Walter Mignolo. There are, however, a growing number of scholars associated with the group (e.g., Edgardo Lander in Venezuela; Santiago Castro-Gómez, Oscar Guardiola and Eduardo Restrepo in Colombia; Catherine Walsh in Quito; Zulma Palermo in Argentina; Jorge Sanjinés in Bolivia; Freya Schiwy, Fernando Coronil, Ramón Grosfogel, Jorge Saldívar, Ana Margarita Cervantes-Rodríguez, Agustín Lao Montes, Nelson Maldonado-Torres, and myself in the United States. More loosely associated with members of the group are: Linda Alcoff and Eduardo Mendieta (associated with Dussel); Elina Vuola (Institute of Development Studies, Helsinki); Marisa Belausteguigoitia in Mexico City; Cristina Rojas (Canada/Colombia). A number of Ph.D. students are now working within the MC program at various universities in Quito and Mexico and at Duke/UNC. My first contact with some of the members of this group took place in Caracas in 1991 at a seminar on critical theory, where I met Lander and Quijano. This was followed by a joint session on "Alternatives to Eurocentrism" at the 1998 World Congress of Sociology in Montreal, which resulted in a collective volume (Lander 2000). In more recent years, the group has gathered around several projects and places: the Ph.D. program on *Estudios de la cultura* at the Universidad Andina Simón Bolivar in Quito, headed by Catherine Walsh; the doctoral program on *Pensamiento crítico en América Latina* at the new Universidad de la Ciudad de México in Mexico City; the geopolitics of knowledge project shared by Instituto Pensar (Universidad Javeriana, Bogotá), the Universidad Andina (Quito), and Duke University and University of North Carolina at Chapel Hill in the USA, and the ethnic studies department at Berkeley. For the main ideas presented here, see Dussel ([1975] 1983, 1992, 1993, 1996, 2000); Quijano (1988, 1993, 2000; Quijano & Wallerstein 1992); Mignolo (2000, 2001; Mignolo, ed. 2001); Lander (2000); Castro-Gómez (1996); Coronil (1996, 1997); Rojas (2001). Little of these debates has been translated into English. See Beverly and Oviedo (1993) for some of these authors' works in English. A volume in this language has been recently devoted to Dussel's work under the apposite title, *Thinking from the Underside of History* (Alcoff & Mendieta 2000). The journal *Nepantla. Views from South*, recently founded at Duke University, has a partial focus on the works of this group. See especially the Vol. 1, No. 3 issue of 2000, with contributions by Dussel and Quijano among others. Other collective volumes already produced by the group include: Castro-Gómez and Mendieta (1998); Castro-Gómez (2000); Mignolo (2001); Walsh, Schiwy and Castro-Gómez (2002). Another volume in English, by Grosfogel and Saldívar, is in preparation.

3. The choice of origin point is not a simple matter of preference. The conquest and colonization of America is the formative moment in the creation of Europe's Other; the point of origin of the capitalist world system, enabled by gold and silver from America; the origin of Europe's own concept of modernity (and of the first, Iberian, modernity, later eclipsed by the apogee of the second modernity); the initiation point of Occidentalism as the overarching imaginary and self-definition of the modern/colonial world system (which subalternized peripheral knowledge and created, in the 18th century, Orientalism as Other). The 16th century also saw crucial debates on "the rights of the people," especially the legal-theological debates in Salamanca, later

1927
1960
1963
1964
1967
1969
1970
1971
1972
1973
1974
1975
1976
1977
1978
1979
1980
1981
1982
1983
1984
1985
1986
1987
1988
1989
1990
1991
1992
1993
1994
1995
1996
1997
1998
1999
2000
2001
2002
2003
2004
2005
2006

suppressed with the discourse of the "rights of man" in the 18th century. Finally, with the Conquest and colonization, Latin America and the Caribbean emerged as "the first periphery" of European modernity.

4. Different authors emphasize different factors in the making and functioning of modernity/coloniality. For Quijano, for instance, the key process in its constitution is the colonial classification and domination in terms of race. Coloniality is at the crux of modernity precisely because of the persistence of the idea of race. The second key process is the constitution of a structure of control of labor and resources. Dussel emphasizes the original violence created by modernity/coloniality (see also Rojas 2001), the importance of the first (Iberian) modernity for the structure of coloniality, and of course the concealment of the non-European (the negation of its alterity), particularly Latin America as modernity's first periphery. Mignolo also appeals to sources outside Iberian America for his conceptualization of "border thinking," the kind of thinking that brings about the desubalternization of knowledge and rationality. Mignolo's project is that of conducting a genealogy of local histories leading to global designs, so as to enable other designs from other local histories to emerge from border thinking and the colonial difference. Some of these differences are explained by somewhat different frameworks, emphases and aims—political economy for Quijano, a philosophy of liberation for Dussel, literature and epistemology for Mignolo. For most of these authors, however, Marxism and the question of the economy remain paramount.

5. Dussel's notion of exteriority has several sources, chiefly Levinas' concept of the contradiction Totality–Exteriority caused by the ethical interpellation of the Other (say, as poor). It also finds inspiration in Marx's notion of living labor as radical Other with respect to capital. Dussel spells out his views through the use of the theory of speech acts and communication (especially Apel's but also Habermas' and Searle's). Above all, Dussel introduces the concepts of exteriority and alterity as essential to his liberation philosophy; Exteriority becomes a negativity from which the domination of the Other can be discovered. There is a clear political bent to Dussel's intervention, which can thus be seen as an original theory and a radicalization of the work of Levinas and others. For Mignolo, as for Quijano, "the modern world system looks different from its exteriority" (2000, 55). Mignolo builds on Dussel and also on other sources, from Fanon and W.E.B. Du Bois to Anzaldúa and writers from the Caribbean and the Maghreb such as Glissant, Béji and Khatibi. Theories of "double consciousness," double critique, an other thinking, creolization, and cultures of transience become equivalent to his own notion of border thinking. Mignolo's theory of exteriority is related to Dussel's but has a different emphasis. Mignolo differentiates between the "interior borders" of the modern/colonial world system (imperial conflicts, say, between Spain and England) and its "exterior borders" (imperial conflicts with cultures being colonized, e.g., between Spain and the Islamic world, between Spain and the Aztecs, or between the Britain and the India in the 19th century). The colonial difference becomes visible only from the exterior of the universal history of the modern world system; it makes possible breaking away from Eurocentrism as epistemological perspective. Without this exteriority in which subaltern knowledges dwell, "the only alternative left is a constant reading of the great thinkers of the West in search of new ways to imagine the future" (2000, 302).

Mignolo develops his notion of border thinking as "thinking from another place, imagining an other language, arguing from another logic" (313). It is a subaltern knowledge conceived from the borders of the colonial/modern world system that strives to break away from the dominance of Eurocentrism. Border thinking refers to "the moments in which the imaginary of the world system cracks" (2000, 23), "an epistemology of and from the border" (52), a kind of "double critique" (Khatibi) that is critical of both Occidentalism/ Eurocentrism and of the excluded traditions themselves; this ability stems from its location in the borderlands (Anzaldúa). Border thinking is an ethical way of thinking because, in its marginality, it has no ethnocidal dimension. Its aim is not to correct lies and tell the truth, but "to think otherwise, to move

toward `an other logic'—in sum to change the terms, not just the content of the conversation" (70). Border thinking enables a new view of the diversity and alterity of the world, one that does not fall into the traps of a culturalist (essentialist) rhetoric but rather highlights the irreducible differences that cannot be —appropriated by the monotopic critique of modernity (the radical critique of Western logocentrism understood as a universal category), and that does not conceive of difference as antithesis in search of revanchism. Border thinking is complementary to deconstruction (and to all critical discourses of modernity); it sees decolonization as a particular kind of deconstruction but moves towards a fragmented, plural project instead of reproducing the abstract universals of modernity (including democracy and rights). Border thinking, finally, is an attempt to move beyond Eurocentrism by revealing the coloniality of power embedded in the geopolitics of knowledge—a necessary step in order to "undo the subalternization of knowledge and to look for ways of thinking beyond the categories of Western thought" (326).

6. Elsewhere I have introduced the notion of *alternatives to modernity* to refer. to an explicit cultural-political project of transformation from the perspective of modernity/coloniality—more specifically, an alternative construction of the world from the perspective of the colonial difference. The dimension of alternatives to modernity contributes to a weakening of modernity as logocentrism, as some of the philosophers of end of modernity would have it (e.g., Vattimo 1991), but from a different position. We should be clear also about what this concept is not: It does not point towards a *real* pristine future where development or modernity no longer exist; it is intended, rather, to intuit the possibility of *imagining* an era where development and modernity cease to be the central organizing principles of social life—a moment when social life is no longer so permeated by the constructs of economy, individual, rationality, order, and so forth that are characteristic of Eurocentered modernity. Alternatives to modernity is a reflection of a political desire, a desire of the critical utopian imagination, not a statement about the real, present or future. Operating in the cracks of modernity/coloniality, it gives content to the Porto Alegre Global Social Forum slogan, *another world is possible.* Alternative development, alternative modernities, and alternatives to modernity are partially conflicting but potentially complementary projects. One may lead to creating conditions for the others.

7. This perspective is at the heart of the Andean Studies Working Group: Development, Modernity and Coloniality, which Walter Mignolo and I co-facilitate within the UNC–Duke Latin American Studies Consortium.

Escobar, Arturo. "Introduction: Cruzando Fronteras and the Borders of Thought." Revised from a version presented at the Tercer Congreso Internacional de Latinoamericanistas en Europa, Amsterdam, July 3–6, 2002. Published in *World and knowledge otherwise: The Latin American modernity/coloniality research programme* (2004) *CEDLA* 16:31–67. Reprinted with permission of the author and the copyright holder.

TRADITIONAL COMMUNICATION AND DEMOCRATISATION: PRACTICAL CONSIDERATIONS

By Pradip Thomas

1995 While we might occasionally use the term traditional to refer to a certain aspect or type of popular culture that comes into being through opposition to modernity, such words must be read in quotation marks...as formulas used for their functional value, to identify phenomena, not essences, that exist and that need to be given a name (García Canclini, 1993)

Typically, the traditional and the modern occupy polar ends of the continuum of civilization, development, worldview and "structures of feeling." There is a wealth of associations, understandings and assumptions related to the two concepts. Both have been used as theoretical handles, as "gatekeeping concepts," as "metonyms and surrogates" (Appadurai, 1986) to describe and account for profoundly complex, polyvariant and multidimensional life processes. The recourse to fixed, organic, dyadic constructs to make sense of life is a peculiarly Occidental "knowledge trait." However, the assumed universality of dualistic models of life based on such dyads as good and evil, the modern and the traditional, etc., is immediately called into question when confronted with the litmus test of lived experiences from around the world. For there are continuities between experiences and concepts as well as gaps, shades, blurrings and breaks. Not that dyadic categorizations are alien to the Oriental mind, but that these are, more often than not, used in a malleable, flexible sense, subordinated to common sense and context and to an "open" understanding of order.

The word "traditional" has many different connotations, in the sense that its meaning is derived in context. A traditional way of life may denote a culture—nomadic, agricultural, etc.—that is rooted in a material and normative order which is different from or only marginally conversant with the gamut of modernity. The culture of the Amish in North America and the Ibans in Sarawak, among very many others, is often called traditional. But the word also refers to a culture-specific "structure of feeling," our inherited understandings, popular memory and the means with which we negotiate identity, make sense of life, of place and space in the context of modernity. It is also often used to describe those communities that adhere to exclusivist, essentialist readings that are based more often than not on religion-derived understandings of order. Traditional ways of action are based on codes, "traditions" which are encrypted in texts as well as in the collective memories of people. All people are socialized into traditions and these are transmitted in most societies by oral means from generation to generation. Tradition, therefore, needs to be seen both as a process and as the transmission of a specific symbolic discourse through given processes.

Traditional forms of communication are inherently symbolic in content and form. Metaphor, metonymy and the use of discontinuous analogies are some of the means by which symbolic meanings are communicated in tradition. Typically, traditional forms of communication are composite, in the sense that they are expressed through the dialectic of structure and anti-structure. Both resistance and accommodation can and do occur simultaneously in traditional communication and this is often achieved through recourse to role reversals, the recombination of forms and the transformation of content. In this sense traditions are continually being reinvented. Traditional forms of communication are tremendously varied and include diverse forms of mediation— the formal as well as the informal. The formal includes all practices of communication that are organically related to the celebration of community. For example, those forms of communication that are used in the context of rituals and ceremonies associated with the life processes of community. They include theatre, dance-dramas, fairs, fiestas and carnivals, oral narratives and other means by which collective memories are re-inforced and tradition and community upheld. The informal includes all other forms of communication, for instance the use of proverbs, riddles, poetry, songs, etc., verbal and nonverbal, visual and auditory, used at times other than for ritual or ceremonial purposes.

However, the line between the formal and the informal in traditional communication may be drawn for purely descriptive rather than heuristic purposes, for it does not account for the linkages between the formal and informal media of communication. An example of this blurring is contained in the following richly evocative poem written by Basavanna, a leader of a major Hindu sect, the Virasaivites, quoted in Turner (1974). It is simultaneously a religious poem as well as an instructional one. Through making use of the dialectic of structure and anti-structure, the poet affirms the relationship between the nonmaterial, the self and the transcendental:

> The rich
> will make temples for Siva.
> What shall I,
> a poor man
> do?
> My legs are pillars,
> the body the shrine,
> the head a cupola
> of gold.
> Listen, O Lord of the meeting rivers,
> things standing shall fall
> but the moving ever shall stay [1].

Modernity's Self-Understanding of Tradition

Much has been written and said about the crisis of the traditional. Accelerated processes of modernization along with the globalization of a unilinear model of development, of science and technology and of worldview and ethos, have affected the capacity of traditional cultures to re-invent themselves in the context of change. The modernizing nation-state has contributed to this process by homogenizing tradition, often along the lines of majoritarian identities. As a result, the traditions of minority communities, of "first peoples" and of many marginalized groups are often bypassed in the making of a national tradition. This, in turn, has led to, on the one hand, the destruction of traditions or, on the other, has resulted in determined efforts by communities to assert their own traditions often through violent means of protest. The terms fundamentalism and revivalism are sometimes used to describe the actions of communities who resist modernity, secular ideals and a selectively defined global order. But these terms are used in a rather loose manner, and they rarely shed light on the complex reasons that lie behind what are seemingly intractable, exclusivist positions.

Modernity has a history of rapprochement with tradition, although its motives and reasons have not been that transparent. The science of the "other" is contained within impressive, established canons of discourse. Numerous well-meaning Western sociologists and anthropologists of both mainstream and critical persuasions, have attempted to figure out the Orient, particularly its relationship with modernity and development. While this has certainly resulted in a wealth of micro- and macro-studies on every conceivable aspect of life in traditional societies, the boundaries of discourse have inevitably been coloured by a certain way of distinguishing "them" from "us." Niranjana, et al (1993), in the introductory chapter to the volume "Interrogating Modernity: Culture and Colonialism in India," have remarked on the politics underlying this process of "othering": "The mobilization of 'Indian Culture' was as crucial to the West's construction of its identity in contrast to the Oriental other as it was to the reconstructed Orient's attempts to define itself." A sentiment reemphasized in a more specific observation of O'Hanlon's (1989) on the treatment of colonial histories of Hindu India: "The underlying assumptions

---

1 The strength of the poem lies in the dialectics of structure and anti-structure, as for instance, between making (rich) and being (poor), between standing (sthavara) and moving (jangama), God and human beings, subject and object, leading to the final obliteration of all distinctions in the confluence of the rivers—the state of Samadhi.

1927
1960
1963
1964
1967
1969
1970
1971
1972
1973
1974
1975
1976
1977
1978
1979
1980
1981
1982
1983
1984
1985
1986
1987
1988
1989
1990
1991
1992
1993
1994
1995
1996
1997
1998
1999
2000
2001
2002
2003
2004
2005
2006

… of failure, in the proper separation between state and civil society, and of static tradition counterposed to the dynamism and maturity of Western political systems, have largely determined the framework within which the Indian past has been questioned."

The question of representation has been a key element in the cultural-politics of a host of post-colonial thinkers including Edward Said (1978) and Homi Bhabha (1994), of critical traditionalists such as Ashis Nandy (1992) and Bhiku Parekh (1989), and critical modernists such as Jesús Martín Barbero (1993) and Néstor García Canclini (1993). While there is good reason not to take too seriously some of the more rabid, truculent and often ultra-exclusivist positions adopted by certain critics of modernity,[2] it is nevertheless important to reassess some of the assumptions reflected in the understanding of critical thinkers in the West. Take, for example, the German philosopher Jurgen Habermas, a critical modernist and defender (rightly so) of emancipatory traditions associated with modernity, its precious heritage of rights and freedoms and its potential for peace and justice. He has, on occasion, affirmed the need for a "fusion of horizons" if the project of rationality is to succeed. And yet, in his classic study "The Theory of Communicative Action," Vol. 1, his defence of modernity is underwritten by an inability to empathize with or understand the logic animating what he calls the "mythical worldview" (Haberman, 1981). In Habermas's words: "What irritates us members of a modern life world is that in a mythically interpreted world, we cannot, or cannot with sufficient precision, make certain differentiations that are fundamental to our understanding of the world. From Durkheim to Levi-Strauss, anthropologists have repeatedly pointed out the peculiar confusion between nature and culture."

Such a reading militates against any fusion of horizons. What we are left with is yet another understanding of "universals" that is built on a narrow conceptual base and on an inadequate dialogue with the varied particulars from around the world. These particulars are often animated by convictions based in a "unity of feeling" rather than a "unity of logic" (Fernandez, 1986), rooted in the symbolic, expressed through languages of relatedness that grasp the whole, and through a creativity that is forged in the dialectic of both "structure" and "communitas" (Turner, 1974). Gandhi, who believed in a similar self-understanding, once said that the act of liberation consists of both purifying the self as an aspect of serving the world and serving the world as a part of purifying the self, thus privileging relatedness. Johann Arnason (1991) in a critique of Habermas calls our attention to what he terms the "built-in conceptual obstacles that have to do with Habermas's vision of the distinction between the modern and pre-modern forms of thought." For if "the specific characteristics of mythical and traditional worldviews are reduced to symptoms of an inability to grasp the differences between object domains (particularly those of the natural, the social and the subjective world) as well as between the ways of relating to them, there is no scope for an authentic fusion of horizons." What is at stake here is a universal ideal of progress, inclusive of both its liberal as well as liberating variants.

There is a need to emphasize the reverse, to affirm authenticity in the particular and to come to an understanding of the universal based on a dialogue with the particular, especially with traditions whose self-understandings have evolved out of what one could term a "relational dynamic." In the Bumba-meu-Boi, a dramatic dance from Brazil, to the cult of the Candomble, also from Brazil, as well as the highly charged communicative experience of initiation during the rites of passage of the Ndembu from Zambia, to a whole host of traditions of communication from around the world, it is relational dynamics that enable meaning and the experiencing of it. The point that I have tried to make has much less to do with the particular self-understanding of a well-known social philosopher, i.e., Habermas, than with the fact that he

---

2 There are a number of instances from around the world of absolutists who have taken an uncompromisingly narrow view of matters related to ethnicity, faith and traditions. Bhargava's (1990) assertion that 'people who claim to possess rights (must) operate within a culture of rights' is an apt counter to claims of exclusivity.

is a representative of a tradition whose understanding of the "universal" stems from a myopic and narrow reading and the denial of a universe of "difference."

The Antinomies of Traditional Communication

The affirmation of relatedness is a central function of traditional communication. However, in itself, this is by no means a virtue since relatedness may be the means of legitimising a given order. The use of traditional communication in India, for instance, leads to the re-inforcement of the status quo. While conceding the fact that in the present climate characterized by an accelerated assault on anything remotely believed to be "traditional," justification of the status quo needs to be evaluated in the context of threats to the very survival of traditions, it would nevertheless be importunate for the "progressive" in the traditional to remain a yardstick, a measure of its universality. Folk theatre, in its various manifestations in India, typically affirms through content and form the system, the continuities between Sanskritic Hinduism and "folk" Hinduism, metaphysical and material order and the functional interdependence of a hierarchical, caste-based social order. Through maintaining a system of patronage (Arden, 1971; Schechner and Hess, 1977), subsidizing entire castes whose primary function is to serve as village "performers" (Jayakar, 1980) and privileging the role of Brahmin priests in key rituals during pre- and post-performance, as well as through other means, the given order is preserved[3]. Wayne Ashley, in a study of the ritual theatre of Teyyam Kettu from northern Kerala, India, has commented on the many ways in which the Teyyam performance affirms order:

> The performance serves ... to perpetuate and renew a consistent social structure and distribution of power. This has been demonstrated by several examples; the transference of Sakti (power) and the consecration of the shrine by the Brahmin; the obligatory visit of the Teyyam (consecrated idol) to the temple that houses the god of the higher caste; the allocation of special titles and gifts to the kolakarran (performers) from the king; the presence and the role of the Nair (high-caste) landowners; the calling out of the castes in order of ritual importance and the spatial delineations of the event. (Ashley, 1979)

And yet, simultaneously, Teyyam and other folk media affirm the many bases for community. While the role of power and ideology may justifiably be highlighted, it is important to assess performances in the totality of their context. Traditional communication also affirms certainty, prevents anomie, establishes the basis for a normative order, legitimises the role of the individual in society, strengthens solidarity across and between the various castes and other identity formations and reinforces traditions associated with collective memories. Clifford Geertz's observations on the role of sacred symbols in traditional societies may equally be used to describe the primary motive of traditional communication, which is to "relate an ontology and a cosmology to an aesthetics and morality: their peculiar power comes from their presumed ability to identify fact with value at the most fundamental level, to give to what is otherwise merely actual, a comprehensive normative import." (Geertz, 1973)

Towards a Critical Reading of the Traditional

It is often thought that the traditional implies something that is unchanging, fixed, static. Nothing could be further from the truth. The vitality of traditional forms of communication lies in their ability to negotiate with the current of change and to make appropriate modifications in their forms, narrative structures, characterization and content. For instance, electricity has been used to enhance both the stage setting as well as to heighten the appearance of characters in folk theatre and dance-dramas. Canclini has written about artisans from Ocumicho, Mexico, who, faced with the alienating structures of modernity, reproduced ceramics representing devils, a means

---

3 There has been a perceptible change in this situation during the last two decades. Various dislocations, economic, political and social have affected the relations of production in traditional communications. However, some of these functions are still visible in the folk traditions in different parts of the subcontinent.

by which they came to terms with the symbols of modernity within their symbolic frames of reference. There are also innumerable instances from around the world of the adaption of content to context. During the struggles for independence waged in many parts of the South, peasant uprisings, the mobilization of the marginalised, and in a variety of "social awareness" campaigns, traditional content was displaced in favour of "critical" content, often with great effect. Rowe and Schelling (1991), García Canclini (1993) and Barbero (1993), in their studies of popular culture in Latin America, have noted the trend towards the hybridisation of cultures and the increasing reality of mestizaje (mixed) identities of urban migrants living in the cities of Latin America. These communities have had to re-invent traditional crafts and cultures in order to preserve a measure of certainty in a volatile and fast-changing context. Taken in this sense, traditional forms of communication need to be seen as open texts that allow for both continuity as well as change.

Unfortunately, of late, there has been a trend towards the valorising of the traditional, particularly its more exclusivist, discriminatory aspects. Often, majority communities have been responsible for consciously cultivating exclusivist understandings of tradition and of linking these to concepts of nationhood and identity. Thus the Serbs have assiduously used traditional communication to assert their identity as a Slavic people, as a nation and as the basis for citizenship. So have the Hindu revivalist groups in India for whom Indian tradition is nothing less than Hindu tradition. To an extent, this trend has gained some legitimacy from certain developments in neo-critical discourses, post-structuralism, postmodernism and post-colonialism that have willy-nilly supported the gelatinisation of truth, objectivity and meaning. This has led conservative traditionalists to maintain that an evaluation of tradition may be conducted only from within the parameters generated by "internal value systems." The cultural critic Sarah Joseph calls our attention to some of the drawbacks of this mode of reasoning:

An approach to tradition which relies solely on internally generated standards of rationality can be questioned on a number of grounds such as how we could recognise violations of internal standards, how we could understand the causal factors which give rise to these standards of rationality and the possible conflicts and contradictions between different parts of social life. (Joseph, 1991).

But it would only be right to point out that, often, such rigid approaches are a result and consequence of history. To communities who have been the victims of modernization, the retreat to certainty in tradition is the only means of upholding community at times of great political, economic and social upheaval.

Traditional Communication and Community

The strength of traditional communication lies in its capacity to visualize/pictorialize the expression of a vision of life, bridge the gap between its deep and surface realities, and interpret this relationship in the context and idiom of the local. This is the means by which a particular vision of life is actualised and normalized. This vision is based on pragmatic, often non-dualistic understandings of life, as expressed in the following view taken by Ashis Nandy that it is often the case in Third World civilizations that, "the concept of evil can never be clearly defined, that there is always a continuity between the aggressor and his victim, and that liberation from oppression is not merely the freedom from an oppressive agency outside, but also ultimately a liberation from a part of one's own self." (Nandy, 1978)

This sense of pragmatism is deeply embedded in traditional forms of communication. Take, for example, the role of two folk theatre forms from India—the Tamasha from Maharashtra and the Terrakoothu from Tamil Nadu. Both play a role in the formation of consensus, the integration and re-integration of village traditions within the larger tradition of Hinduism; both, through their characteristic blend of satire, farce and

1927
1960
1963
1964
1967
1969
1970
1971
1972
1973
1974
1975
1976
1977
1978
1979
1980
1981
1982
1983
1984
1985
1986
1987
1988
1989
1990
1991
1992
1993
1994
1995
1996
1997
1998
1999
2000
2001
2002
2003
2004
2005
2006

ribaldry, make the connection between the sacred and the profane, the secular and the religious. Both provide the basis for the preservation of popular memory on a collective basis; both allow for an identification between the past and the present; both enable the gods to be humanized; in both cases, their closeness to the lived life of people is their greatest strength. The reinforcement of caste divisions and power relationships is also part of their overall function.

In other words, the knowledge system that provides a framework for a Tamasha or Terrakoothu performance is both extensive as well as intensive. It is extensive in that it touches aspects of lived reality that are common, and that are manifested in daily life, i.e., problems related to love and anger, jealousy, etc., and their solutions which are framed within a construct of day-to-day morality. Furthermore, it teaches the community to be responsive to the need for generosity, tolerance and mutual respect. It is intensive in that it supplies a more or less complete means of identification with a system that provides security for both the individual as well as the community. It is a vision that is eloquently expressed in the cosmological drama of life, the dance of life personified in the image of the Hindu god Siva, as creator, preserver and destroyer of life.

Pragmatism is that which gives traditional visions their particular power, a pragmatism that is often achieved through the negation of the reality that they represent. In this sense, traditional forms of communication are also a means by which life is seen in perspective, a life that is conditioned by certainty in the transcendent as well as by an indeterminate "chaos" or "fate." This dialectic is alluded to by Clifford Geertz in his description and comparison of the role of the clown in the Javanese puppet theatre tradition of Wayang with that of Falstaff in Shakespeare's *Henry IV*:

> Both figures ... provide a reminder that, despite overproud assertions to the contrary by religious fanatics and moral absolutists, no completely adequate and comprehensive human world view is possible, and behind all the pretence to absolute and ultimate knowledge, the sense for the irrationality of human life, for the fact that it is unlimitable, remains. (Geertz, 1973)

The source of strength of traditional forms of communication often stems from their use of ultra-linguistic modes of communication that privilege the imaginative over and above formally organized grammars of communication. Such modes help illumine the many ways in which society is built on mutually reciprocated relationships. The mytho-poetic heritage of traditional societies is steeped in the language of the imagination. Traditional forms of communication enable the reinforcement of historical memories and consequently are an eloquent testimony to the norm that the universal takes shape in its encounter with the many different particulars. Moral and ethical dilemmas, questions related to equity and justice and the distribution and use of power, are as much of concern to traditional societies as they are to so-called modern societies. Traditional forms of communication may not actively be used to challenge the given order or the status quo. But like the mass media that have been on occasion employed to challenge the dominant order, traditional forms of communication have been used with great effect from time immemorial to challenge authority, particularly regimes of repression (Appavoo, 1986).

Traditional forms of communication are part of a larger process related to the making and remaking of communities. They play a vital role in the process of negotiation that is itself a core element in the self-understanding and growth of traditional communities. This is an ongoing process, but one that has become increasingly complex in the light of the politics of change. It is this complexity that traditional forms of communication endeavour to decipher and to make intelligible. Nothing more and nothing less. Against the juggernaut of modernity and its tendency to homogenize difference in the name of progress, traditional forms of communication are a gentle reminder that true cultural democracy is forged in the interplay of difference, however idiosyncratic that might seem.

References

Appadurai, A. "Theory in Anthropology: Centre and Periphery." Comparative Studies in Society and History, 1986, 28: 356-61.

Appavoo, J. T. *Folk-Lore for Change*. Madurai, India: T.T.S. Publications, 1986.

Arden, J. "The Chhau Dancers of Puralia." The Drama Review, 1971, 15 (2): 64-75.

Arnason, J. "Modernity as Project and Field of Tension." A. Honneth and H. Joas, eds., *Communicative Action*. Cambridge, United Kingdom: Polity Press, 1991, 181-213.

Ashley, W. "Teyyam Kettu of Northern Kerala." The Drama Review, 1979, 23 (2): 99-112.

Barbero, Martin J. *Communication, Culture and Hegemony: From Media to Mediations*. London/Newbury Park/New Delhi: Sage, 1993.

Bhabha, H. K. *The Location of Culture*. London/Newbury Park/New Delhi: Sage, 1994.

Bhargava, It. "The Right to Culture." Social Scientist, 1990, 18 (10): 50-57.

García Canclini, N. *Transforming Modernity: Popular Culture in Mexico*. Austin, University of Texas Press, 1993.

Fernandez, J. W. "The Argument of Images and the Experience of Returning to the Whole." V. W. Turner and E. M. Bruner, eds., *The Anthropology of Experience*. Urbana and Chicago: University of Illinois Press, 1986.

Geertz, C. *The Interpretation of Cultures*. New York: Basic Books, 1973.

Habermas, J. *The Theory of Communicative Action. Vol. I: Reason and the Rationalisation of Society*. London: Heinemann, 1981.

Jayakar, P. *The Earthen Drum*. New Delhi: National Museum, 1980.

Joseph, S. "Culture and Political Analysis in India." Social Scientist, 1991, Vol. 19: 48-62.

Nandy, A. "Oppression and Human Liberation: Towards a Third World Utopia." Alternative, 1978, 4 (2): 165-480.

Nandy, A. *Traditions, Tyranny, and Utopias*. Delhi: OUR, 1992.

Niranjana, T., P. Sudhir and V. Dhareshwar, eds. *Interrogating Modernity: Culture and Colonialism in India*. Calcutta: Seagull, 1993.

O'Hanlon, ft. "Cultures of Rule, Communities of Resistance: Gender, Discourse and Tradition in Recent South Asian Historiographies." Social Analysis, September 1989, 25, 94-114.

Parekh, B. *Colonialism, Tradition and Reform: An Analysis of Gandhi's Political Discourse*. London/Newbury Park/New Delhi: Sage, 1989.

Rowe, W., and V. Schelling. *Memory and Modernity: Popular Culture in Latin America*. London and New York: Verso, 1991.

Said, F. *Orientalism*. New York: Penguin Books, 1978.

Schechner, H. and Linda Hess. "The Ramlila of Ranmagar." The Drama Review, 1977, 21 (3): 51-82.

Turner, V. *Dramas, Fields and Metaphors: Symbolic Action in Human Society*. Ithaca/London: Cornell University Press, 1974.

Thomas, Pradip 1995. "Traditional Communication and Democratisation: Practical Considerations," from Lee, Philip. Ed. Democratisation of Communication. University of Wales Press, Cardiff, 1995. Reprinted with permission.

EXCERPT FROM:

STORIES, INFORMATION AND ESSAYS

By Gustavo Cimadevilla

1997 During the 1950s, Latin America consolidated state initiatives linked to the generation and transfer of technology due to the convergence of reasons that transcended national circumstances: (1) the need of Central countries to intervene in regions that were potentially conflictive due to their state of "extreme shortage;" (2) the interest to broadcast in different markets the results of the scientific and technical advances made during the Second World War; and (3) the attempt by national states to improve their conditions by producing prime matter within the "international division of work." These reasons aligned with the diffusion orientation. So, knowledge about how attitudes and technical transfer was key. (Cimadevilla, 1990)[1]

Now, in fact, when we talk about Central countries interested in the "precarious" conditions in certain regions of the world and, in turn, about the possibility of sharing the results of their scientific-technical advances, there is no other country of reference but the United States.

During the 1950s the United States was facing a cold war, had a high technological level and enough capital to become a leader and model of intervention models for development—in this case agricultural.[2]

1 Cimadevilla, G. 1990. *A Modernização Tardia. Além do velho e do novo na extensão rural*. Dissertaço de Mestrado. CPGER-UFSM. Santa Maria. Brasil.
2 According to Argumedo—based on data by UNESCO some figures are relevant to show the "power" that the country was able to concentrate after the Second World War: "Its national income added up to near 50 percent of the overall income of capitalist nations. Its participation in world commerce was of 47 percent. Its reserves of gold corresponded to near

1927
1960
1963
1964
1967
1969
1970
1971
1972
1973
1974
1975
1976
1977
1978
1979
1980
1981
1982
1983
1984
1985
1986
1987
1988
1989
1990
1991
1992
1993
1994
1995
1996
1997
1998
1999
2000
2001
2002
2003
2004
2005
2006

In this framework, [U.S. President] Harry Truman's Point Four project (1945-53) became an antecedent of how the United States analyzed the problem and applied solutions, in the sense of considering it necessary to offer their help and external financing to facilitate the "development" of nations. The approach also was emphasized with [U.S. President] John F. Kennedy in the Alliance for Progress program.

In this context were created and/or re-inforced many of the Latin American state institutes like IBIA in Bolivia, IIA in Chile, INIPA in Peru and even INTA in Argentina[3]—as well as other organisation at the level of Departments and Secretaries like the cases of DECA in the Dominican Republic, SEEA in Ecuador, AB-CAR in Brazil and DGNA in Mexico. Organizations went on to work as coordinators of rural development actions carried out by the State. They applied policies of agricultural planning, research, circulation of technology and technical assistance and depending on the countries' Ministries of Agriculture—or similar entities. (Cimadevilla, op. cit., p. 90).

And it can be said that knowledge about how the technical transfer operated was fundamental, because in the North American model the acceleration of the economy happened hand in hand with managerial work based on research and development investments. Hunt and Sherman[4] express that principle in numbers:

> In the decades before World War I the increase in product per hour/man was of 22 percent per decade. What made these growth indexes possible were the heavy investments dedicated to research and development that (for example) were raised from $3,400 million in 1950 to $12,000 million in 1960, with a federal contribution that covered 50 percent of those assets" (Hunt & Sherman, 1985:179).

For that strategy to bring science and technology closer to economy and the interests of the State, the U.S. government supported, created and/or promoted the creation of research centers and institutes in the most diverse branches; the contribution of hard sciences. Social psychology and sociology were also relevant. Some centers dependent on the State acted with extremely close links to the problems of circulation of innovations and public attitudes vis-à-vis change, including organizations such as the Institute for Propaganda Analysis; Information and Education Division; and several institutes linked to universities, such as the Bureau of Applied Social Research of Columbia University; the Massachusetts Technological Institute (MIT) and the Department of Psychology of Yale University, among others.

Names like Paul Lazarsfeld, Kurt Lewin, Harold Lasswell and Carl Hovland (considered the founders of *Communication Research*)[5] gained international recognition for their contributions to the knowledge of

---

70 percent of world reserves. The productivity of its industry was several times higher," and in addition its military strength and atomic power were available for any region in the globe. Argumedo, A. (1985) *América Latina. Los laberintos de la crisis*. Buenos Aires, Folios Ed./ILET, p. 55).

3 The INTA considered an antecedent other minor organisms that were merged with its creation (Institute of Soil, of Microbiology, etc). In disparity with other countries, like Brazil, which counted on the support of the United States through the Rockefeller mission (Lousa, 1985), the Argentinean state did not need in the first instance any significant outside help, since it still retained a certain financing ability derived from the accumulation sustained in the war period, because of the favorable balance obtained in the decline of imports (Ferrer, A. (1973) *La economía argentina*. Buenos Aires, FCE, p. 195), a situation that, in terms of productive investments toward agriculture, was the cause of deep discussions regarding the possible misuse of this instance (Barsky, O. et. al. (1988) *La agricultura pampeana*. Buenos Aires, FCE/IICA, p. 61). However the institute also took the U.S. experience of technological generation and transfer as the model to install its own infrastructure, adding itself to what Oteiza calls a "conscious or unconscious imitation" of the experience that Europe assumed as a consequence of the application of the Marshall plan (Oteiza, E. 1992. La política de investigación científica y tecnológica argentina. *Historia y perspectivas*. Buenos Aires, CEAL.; p. 116).

---

4 Hunt, E. and H. Sherman (1985) *História do pensamento econômico*. Petrópolis, Vozes.

5 With the expression *communication research* academics refer to the studies that North American researchers carried out between 1930 and 1960 around the problem of effects or consequences generated by the media in society, generally emanating from the supposition that these effects were identifiable and possible to observe in the short term; that is, as a result of the stimulus-response relationships that were established between audiences and the media and that, although influenced by different variables, could be studied through empirical research. In this regard Mauro Wolf can be consulted *La investigación de la comunicación de masas* (1987), Barcelona, Paidós; and *Los efectos sociales de los media* (1994), Barcelona, Paidós.

communication processes and "effects"—in particular the operational ways of persuasion and the functions and limits of the mass media, the role of opinion leaders and the incidence of interpersonal relationships in the circulation of knowledge and change in attitudes. Other intellectuals, disciples or colleagues of the former, such as Elihu Katz, Leon Festinger, Robert Merton, Wilbur Schramm, Joseph Klapper, Herbert Menzel and Irving Janis will share or provide continuity to this line of work.

Within this research paradigm of "administrative" research, Everett Rogers later became one of the most outstanding intellectual exponents for his work in describing and explaining part of the game in which the circulation of innovations and the adoption of technology happen. His work *Diffusion of Innovations* (1962) was widely circulated and translated into Spanish, becoming a reference for what will be called *diffusions* among communication study currents.

Parallel to this development process and intellectual accumulation on the base of experimental and field research, an important number of North American intellectuals—and even Latin American trainees in the United States —worked on carrying out specific studies on the problem of technical transfer and modernization in the Latin American context. For the South, from this perspective, two works seem to be the key references to witness this effort to achieve knowledge. They were both published in Brazil, and maybe for that reason did not transcend enough to the Spanish-speaking countries that share the Continent. But they undoubtedly contain in a summary the most significant research that has been carried out on the subject.

The first of these is a compilation that rural sociologists Gordon Whiting—of the United States—and Lytton Guimarães—a Brazilian—carried out based on some knowledge experiences carried out in Peru, Colombia and Brazil in the 1960s, generally linked by the analysis of circulation, acceptance and refusal of innovation in agricultural, medical and social areas. The work was published in 1969 (Edições Finançeiras, Rio de Janeiro) under the wing of the *Aliança para o Progresso* and titled *Comunicação das novas idéias. Pesquisas Aplicáveis ao Brasi.* In addition to giving recognition to some works by Everett Rogers, Gustavo Quesada, Célio Nogueira da Gama, William Herzog and the organizers themselves, it offers in its last chapter—by Gordon Whiting—some interesting suggestions to differentiate the results of research in this region, as compared to those found in "developed" areas.

These research results showed (1) The great importance of the social structural variable in the determination of the adoption; (2) the importance of family ties and relationships with relatives in agricultural decisions, geographical mobility and social behavior in general; and (3) the basic importance of literacy as a variable explaining and predicting the modernization process (Whiting, G. op. cit. p. 133). Reasons that—according to the author—lead to the need to rethink the American model on the "process of innovation circulation" that comes from the supposition that the process is relatively independent from its neighbors and its surroundings when making decisions.

The general work was, undoubtedly, important to spark academic discussion and think about intervention strategies in rural areas when the welfare state seemed to still be ongoing, and in its line of thought was surpassed only a decade later with the work by José Marques de Melo (Edit. Vozes, Petrópolis, 1978) titled *Comunicação, Modernização e Difusão de inovações no Brasil.* In the book's introducion, Marques de Melo says his worry emanated from realizing that the importance of the phenomenon of communication in society at the time was not accompanied by the academic effort of universities and research centers in his country (Brazil). At the same time, it was surprising to observe the volume of knowledge that North American researchers had achieved from research in their country and others in the region. "These are facts that only find an explanation in the historical contradictions that mark the evolution of dependent countries," the author says about the paradox (Melo, 1978:5).

1927
1960
1963
1964
1967
1969
1970
1971
1972
1973
1974
1975
1976
1977
1978
1979
1980
1981
1982
1983
1984
1985
1986
1987
1988
1989
1990
1991
1992
1993
1994
1995
1996
1997
1998
1999
2000
2001
2002
2003
2004
2005
2006

The work of Marques de Melo was the result of patient research that, carried out in the main libraries of North American universities and consultation centers, allowed to gather 235 titles, including published articles and master's and Ph.D. theses, available for the university audience.[6] About the compilation, the author observes that, despite the variety of research carried out, there is a characteristic that clearly "homogenizes" most of them. And it is the fact that "they are deliberately oriented to the rural sector, evaluating the function of mass communication in the development of agriculture and cattle raising," with the main objective of finding the "communication artifices that may convince farmers to adopt certain technological innovations, like mechanization, the use of fertilizers, the diversification of cultures, etc." (Melo 1978:6)

In the first part, Marques de Melo offers a selection of texts published by North American journals that highlight different instances of field research linked to the role of communication in the circulation of technology and modernizing processes. Bostian, Fett, Herzog, Quesada, Whiting, Stanfield, Bluhm, Fliegel, Johnson, Sturm and Schneider—most of them from the United States—are the authors sharing the section. The second part of the book presents highlighted documents. These are organized according to whether they belong to thesis efforts, articles or monographic works and, lastly, research reports or other general materials. For all cases, the criterion of the author was to select works that referred to Brazil in particular, or in relation to other countries, to allow for some sort of comparison regarding the results of the research.

The work, undoubtedly, stays as current as any work without a new contribution, since there has not been any other effort to systematize using those characteristics. For this reason it is still an important point of reference….

Communicational Critics and 'Extensionist Rethinking'

The 1980s later assumes other characteristics regarding intellectual production in this field. The gradual, hard and complicated process to reclaim the state of rights in different Latin American nations[7] brought with it the possibility of a larger freedom of thought and expression, and therefore, a higher level of criticism and self-criticism about the work of institutions, co-existence and development models and the social conditions of the different regions, groups and social segments.

If the 1950s was tainted by the institutionalization of interventions in the rural sector through a strong State, which later in the 1960s received—not without self-interest—the help of international organizations and entities assuming that non-radical planning and transformation were possible, the 1970s did show serious conflicts and social struggle that finally ended with decisive military intervention processes, intellectual exodus, missing people and "gags" on the study centers and social organizations.

In the 1980s, what could not be said before started to arise as a critical instance that transcended the political arena and was deepened in the set of social and human disciplines.

But in the field of "rural communication," ignoring that there were critical antecedents already at the end of the 1960s and the decade of the 1970s would be unforgivable, even if they were not able to flow and get divulged normally, due to the changes in the various nations.

Perhaps the most important contribution, which was also the basis for many of the later reviews and a fair

---

6 The research, carried out in 1973 with the sponsorship of research financing organisms (FAPESP) covered an "ample range of matters related to communication in Brazil." The author says that while advancing in change "more than the sensation of being observed from the outside, the sensation was to perceive that Brazilian society was reduced to being a passive object, since researchers or the institutions financing them had not shown, unless with rare exceptions, the slightest interest in sharing their experiences with the members of the national academic community, to repay such a rich laboratory." The works stayed on the shelves of libraries or served "other interests" (talking, for example, about multinational corporations), the researcher added critically (Melo, 1978:6).

7 In particular most of the countries in the South Cone, among which we can mention Argentina, Brazil, Uruguay, Paraguay, Chile, Bolivia and Peru.

1927
1960
1963
1964
1967
1969
1970
1971
1972
1973
1974
1975
1976
1977
1978
1979
1980
1981
1982
1983
1984
1985
1986
1987
1988
1989
1990
1991
1992
1993
1994
1995
1996
1997
1998
1999
2000
2001
2002
2003
2004
2005
2006

part of the revisionist thought in the 1980s, is the work that Paulo Freire did to analyze the role of rural extension as "inoculating," more than liberating of farmers' consciences. His work *Extensión o Comunicación*[8] (written at the end of the 1960s and published in Spanish and Portuguese by Tierra Nueva and Siglo XXI in several countries in Latin America) was, from that perspective, some sort of "sacred word" offering a critical criterion to separate in the universe of extensionist actions those dedicated to the rural people and their increasing awareness about the world, from those to the service of manipulation, the maintenance of ignorance and the domination of farmers.

If in the linguistic analysis Freire pointed out that the term extension, in its "associative field," had a significant relation to "transmission, delivery, donation, messianism, mechanizing, cultural invasion, manipulation, etc"(Freire, 1973:21). For Freire, *communication,* however, appeared associated to "reciprocity," "co-participation," "dialogue" (pages. 75-76) and basically "education" as "freedom practice" (page. 108). Thus, his worry as an educator and his fervently humanist approach attempted to open a space of criticism so the extensionist "technician" notices the transforming role his job could assume together with the farming communities.[9]

This work certainly fed the already growing agitation of the 1970s; and in the aftermath, it worked to bring back to discussion the multidimensional problem of technical change, knowledge transfer and extensionist work. Some hurried readers confused the critical ideological value of his work. They thought that Freire was arguing there was less need of agronomists and more of communicators. Others imagined that an interdisciplinary approach would smooth down corners. The truth is that Freire never meant to attack such professional corporations or specialists but rather to highlight the value of attitudes and personal

compromises for education and the "transforming" knowledge of the impending farming realities.

Specifically, the multidimensional nature of Freire's criticism—regarding…the problem of social change in the different rural realities in the continents—caused many discussion lines to open and benefit from his thought. Communication issues found in his work an angle for analysis of dialogue in interpersonal relationships. Extensionist intervention methodologies, in part, found materials to revise the circulation and approach strategies. Educators reflected on its practice as an area for the liberation of conscience; and intellectuals, in general, about the value of knowing and acting as a possible synthesis that, in its articulation, led to what would later become research-action.

Other authors and other works, with more or less depth, continued questioning Freire's line of thought. Díaz Bordenave, for example, a Paraguayan residing in Brazil since the late 1960s and a graduate in agronomy and then in communication—oriented part of his work to rescue the role of participation for the construction of "truly democratic" relationships.[10] He analyzed the evolution that "rural communication" under way in certain development promotion organizations, such as the Inter American Cooperation Institute for Agriculture (IICA), insisted that "dialogue," "planning" and "education" will always permeate technical work linked to the transfer of knowledge in rural areas.[11]

From his extensive work, the most circulated title, linked to this field of interest, was *O que é comunicação rural*, published by Brasiliense (1983) in São

---

8   We consulted the edition by Siglo XXI/Tierra Nueva, Buenos Aires, 1973.
9   "If he weren't able to believe in farmers"—says Freire in his last thought in this work—"to join them, he would be in his work performance, in the best of cases, a cold technician. Probably a technicist or even a good reformist. Never an educator from and for radical transformations" (op. cit., page. 109).

10 In titles like *A comunicação participatória em América Latina* (1979); *Participation in communication system for development* (1979); *Democratización de la Comunicación. Teoría y Práctica* (1980); *Democratización de la comunicación, democratización de la educación* (1982); *O que é participação* (1983); *Comunicação Rural. Da Extensão à Participação* (1984); *Participação e sociedade* (1985), among others. For a bibliographical listing of Juan Diaz Bordenave's work, the master's thesis *Juan Diaz Bordenave e a comunicação para o homen rural* (1993) by Marcia Franz Amaral, Universidade Federal de Santa Maria, Santa Maria, RS, Brasil is useful.
11 Central to the works *Planificación y comunicación* (1978); *Estrategia de enseñanza-aprendizaje* (1980); *A opção pedagógica pode ter consequencias individuais e sociais importantes* (1984); and *Educar para uma sociedade participativa* (1986); among others. See Marcia Franz Amaral, op. cit.

Paulo. In this work, he argued in only a few pages to offer a fairly well-achieved sketch of the relationships around "communication," "agriculture" and the "transfer of technology" and "rural development."

…Bordenave also offers a definition of the concept "rural communication"[12] and recalls some useful pieces of advice to think about the media and messages in the field itself, using his vast experience as a consultant of agricultural organisations and institutes and the amount already written on communication models, technology diffusion and codification and decodification of messages in rural spaces.

A contemporary of Bordenave's, Luis Ramiro Beltrán is another Latin American intellectual—of Bolivian nationality—who also leaves his mark in the critical thought of the specialized field, particularly to remain alert to "foreign" thought in thoughts carried out from the continent and their weight in the "diffusionist model."

Beltrán said:

> A basic assumption of the diffusion approach is that communication by itself may generate development, independent from the socio-economic and political conditions" (Beltrán, 1985:79)— says the author and later he analyzes the arguments invalidating the fallacy of the hypothesis to finally outline a 'new science of communication' in Latin America.[13]

On the other hand, Luiz Beltrão—Brazilian—will also provide an important addition from a more anthropological approach, analyzing and thinking about rural inhabitants, the media and messages circulating in their "traditional" culture. The work, *Folkcomunicação, a comunicação dos marginalizados* (Beltrão, 1980), published by Cortez Editora (São Paulo), offers a perspective a classic for reference and a touchstone when thinking about what is left on the fringes of the dominating Western culture.

In this framework of critical compromises, not only the themes will be reviewed but also matters linked to the same act of knowing and the attitude of intellectual transformation. In that sense, one of the men who transcended the line of the so-called "research-action" is João Bosco Pinto who, after his classic *"Extensión y educación: una disyuntiva crítica"* (1973)[14], dedicated much of his work to specify and operate with the *pesquisa ação* as a "social practice project and never as a recipe book." According to Bosco Pinto, the main goal was to "raise of collective awareness for an action." [15]

In this same line, Carlos R. Brandão with his *Repensando a pesquisa participante* (1984)—by editorial Brasiliense, São Paulo—and Michel Thiollent with *Metodología da Pesquisa-ação* (1985)—by Cortez Editora, São Paulo—were, together with Bosco Pinto, a triptych for readers that used in classrooms and discussion forums in which communication and rural extension were the center of analysis. The reason was these works forced readers to think about each interventionist action from the interest of the acting parties, the sociocultural respect from individuals called to change and the methodologies and aims that could be involved in the project, as well as the level of compromise and transforming role that the participating agent should assume. "What can and must I do?" was the critical question for those who, as intervening agents, had some degree of responsibility in the transformations sought….

And in those terms, the role of universities, particularly in Brazil, was key to advance on questions without answers or on unresolved problems. From their graduate programs, the Universities Universidad Federal de Santa Maria, Viçosa and Rural de Pernambuco—the two first with master's degreees in rural extension and the latter in rural communication—allowed for the growth and production of important work,

---

12 Defined as a "group of information, dialogue and reciprocal influence flows existing among the components of the rural sector and between them and the other sectors in the nation affected by the functioning of agriculture, or interested in the improvement of rural life" (1983, op. cit., p. 7).
13 "Premises, objects and foreign methods in the communication research in Latin America" in the work organized by *Sociología de la Comunicación de Masas*, Edit. Gustavo Gilli, Barcelona, 1985.

14 In *Desarrollo Rural en las Américas*. Bogotá, 4(3): 15-25.
15 *A pesquisa ação. Detalhamento da sequência metodológica*. Recife, 1984. Universidade Federal de Pernambuco. Typed, p. 40.

undoubtedly becoming references and forefront items of the disciplinary field in the Latin American region.

In this sense, the early development of the graduate program in Brazil, continuous since the 1970s, and a strong consolidation strategy of the scientific and technological system—with lower degrees than Argentina, for example, in the conditioning factor in the ideological area—prepared the scenario for the significant evolution of the intellectual field.

Thus, in the 1980s, the trend to study with diffusionist approaches and conceptions started to favor the search of local problems and answers, trying to get distance from the "Americanophilia" that up to that point—according to Quesada (1982)[16] —conditioned Brazilian rural communication studies. And that author, professor and researcher from Universidad Federal de Santa Maria will focus intensely on the myths and fallacies that constantly surround thoughts on rural communities and their possibilities to change through technical ways. From this perspective, his book *Comunicação e Comunidade: mitos da mudança social* (Editorial Loyola, São Paulo, 1980) and the article *"Comunicação rural na integração campo-cidade"* (in *Comunicação na América Latina. Desenvolvimento e crise*. José Marques de Melo (Org.) 1989. Campinas, Papirus) will be the references of that time. Additionally, his interest in problems derived from tendencies in education, research, extensionist education and the challenges for the "post-industrial" world will be reflected in his last works and collaborations with Vivien Diesel, Antonio Costabeber or the writer of this article, among others.[17]

In Viçosa, the remaining university with a post-graduate program in rural extension in Brazil, the works of Magela Braga and Fernandez de Araújo gave continuity to the tradition in studies related to diffusion and adoption of innovations that became characteristic of the school and, in particular, to showcase the instances of technical change in Minas Gerais' rural reality.

The Universidad Federal Rural de Pernambuco, in turn, found in Maria Salett Tauk dos Santos its most projected referent, working alternatively on ideological questions of messages and speeches being transferred to the rural world, i.e., en *"A ideologia da modernização e o rádio rural"* in Revista *INTERCOM* Nro. 55, 1986 and the role of communication for "landless" persons' problems and small producers ("Comunicação e educação no mundo rural: uma experiencia libertadora com pequenos agricultores" en *Caminhos cruzados,* op. cit.).

From other universities and courses, sometimes linked to these issues from the point of view of sociology, anthropology, education or rural development itself, other works will also contribute useful approaches and insights. Among them, the work of Maria Teresa Lousa da Fonseca, *A extensão rural no Brasil, um projeto educativo para o capital* (1985, op. cit.), will be most notorious, particularly in the discussion of extensionist institutions and of the values and conditions at the center of their diffusion and transfer policies… .

All these contributions, at that time, in a framework where universities are receiving and educating many of the "technicians" and "leaders" of organisations dedicated to the transfer and diffusion of technology, undoubtedly contributed to the intervention agencies "rethinking" the *"agricultural modernization"* and the green revolution of the 1970s.[18]

---

16 *Comunicação rural? It's O.K. y hasta luego*. Speech at the *5th Congress INTERCOM*. São Paulo, 1982. Typed.
17 In the work *Pesquisa Na Era do Micro* (Edições Loyola, São Paulo, 1987) or in the works with Diesel, for example, *"Novos rumos para pesquisa e ensino da extensão rural brasileira"* (Kunsch, M. (Org.) 1986. *Caminhos cruzados,* Loyola, São Paulo.); Costabeber, particularly on energy (for example in *"Cenarios energéticos das principais culturas agrícolas do Cone Sul - ano 2000"* in *Revista de Economia e Sociologia Rural*, 31(3), 1993); or Cimadevilla (*Decada de 80: Transição paradigmâtica e crise de abertura"* in *Anais do Simposio A pesquisa Brasileira da Comunicação nos anos 80 e a contribuição da INTERCOM*, INTERCOM /CNPq, São Paulo, SP, Brasil, 1988).

18 The work of Graziano da Silva in that sense was a compulsory reference to analyze the agricultural modernization process (Graziano da Silva, José (1882) *A modernização dolorosa: estrutura agrária, fronteira agrícola e trabalhadores rurais no Brasil,* Rio de Janeiro, Zahar Editores).

1927
1960
1963
1964
1967
1969
1970
1971
1972
1973
1974
1975
1976
1977
1978
1979
1980
1981
1982
1983
1984
1985
1986
1987
1988
1989
1990
1991
1992
1993
1994
1995
1996
1997
1998
1999
2000
2001
2002
2003
2004
2005
2006

But in Brazil, that rethinking process was only a guideline for academic and discussion essays. In fact, the then so-called Technical Assistance and Rural Extension Brazilian Company, Empresa Brasileña de Asistencia Técnica y Extensión Rural (EMBRATER), particularly when led by Romeu Padilha de Figueiredo (1985-88) as president, assumed a compromise with the Nova República and gave a progressive character to its management. This implied, in Padilha's words, that:

> The execution of (our) technical functions must be backed by a political acting sense together and beside the poorest social groups, the disinherited and those excluded by the "painful modernization." This is an inalienable task of the new democratic Brazilian state.[19]

To continue to advance in this direction, an important effort using resources obtained by the International Reconstruction and Promotion Bank (Banco Internacional de Reconstrucción y Fomento (BIRF) allowed for the training of staff (with master's and Ph.D. programs) and the expansion of activities to "refresh" communicational technologies and strategies.[20]

As significant documents for communication matter, even if fairly uncommon in the rural intervention institutions, it is worth mentioning that time, by Embrater, *A Comunicação na Extensão Rural: Fundamentação e Diretrizes Operacionais* (Embrater, 1987) and *Política e diretrizes de formação extensionista* (Embrater, 1987). These documents gave context to the sense of existence of the organisation and its compromise toward society[21] and also defined the ethnical,

professional and political positions of the members of the institution, finally giving them objectives and mechanisms for their everyday action.

That stage was undoubtedly rich in posing questions, back-and-forth banter and concretion of many alternative experiences in communication, through different projects that allowed extensionists, communicators and rural subjects to share experiences with videos, educational materials, group processes and elaboration of proposals for the State and the intervention and affiliation entities.[22]

In this context, extensionists, researchers and members of companies associated witih EMBRATER, which were provincial entities required to use its guidelines, and other research and transfer organisms like Empresa Brasileña de Pesquisa Agropecuaria, Brazilian Agricultural Inquiry Company (EMBRAPA) or Empresa Bahiana de Desarrollo Agrícola, Bahian Agricultural Development Company (EBDA), who were researchers or participated in postgraduate courses, dedicated part of their intellectual efforts to support that process of questioning and thought.

Several works linked to the names of Raúl Colvara Rosinha, Carlos Roberto de Albuquerque Lima, Antonio Carneiro do Rosario, Geraldo Lobato Franco, Laércio Nunes e Nunes, Wilson Schmitt and particularly João Carlos Canuto and Miguel Angelo da Silveira (organizers of the book *Estudos de Comunicação Rural* (1988), Loyola-INTERCOM, São Paulo), multiplied the scenarios in which communication and the rural environment were linked and allowed for the consolidation of the discipline.

In that decade, entities like Sociedade Brasileira de Estudos Interdisciplinares da Comunicação (INTERCOM), Sociedade Brasileira de Economia e Sociologia Rural (SOBER) and Projeto de Intercâmbio de Pesquisa Social em Agricultura (PIPSA), among others,

---

19 In *Informe Final del I Seminario de Extensão Rural* organize by FAO/EMBRATER, Brasilia, 1986. Article by Padilha de Figueiredo entitled *"Os desafios da extensão rural brasileira: anseios democráticos numa economia rica e dubdesenvolvida"*, p. 26.

20 Aspect studied particularly in the master's essay (UFSM) bearing the title *A modernização tardia. Além do velho e do novo na extensão rural (1990)*, op. cit. There, on top of analyzing the historical context of the process, the institutional policies of EMBRATER and INTA are compared regarding the introduction of new information technologies in the extensionist strategies and activities.

21 Particularly the reediting of the text *Comunicação Rural. Proposição crítica de uma nova conceção*, by Odilo Friedrich, is in charge of explaining a humanist approach for the service (Embrater, Brasilia, 2da. edición 1988; the first is of 1978).

22 There is a vast and significant amount of materials, documents, communicational experiences reports and evaluation of projects that are minimally analyzed in *A modernização tardia* (1990), op. cit.

also gave space to the field of study that, maybe in 1988, had its peak moment when INTERCOM organized its 11th Congress to discuss the subject specifically. As a result of this, the book organized by Geraldo Magela Braga y Margarida M. Krohling Kunsch was later published under the title *Comunicação Rural: discurso e prática* (1993), edited by Universidad Federal de Viçosa.[23]

But if the 1980s in Brazil were synonymous with a good time for the field, the same cannot be said for the rest of Spanish-speaking countries on the continent, at least judging by the literature… .

Rurality, as a topic and field study, was gradually replaced by other issues that modernity turned more seductive, such the expansion of new technologies of information and communication and globalisation trends. The 1990s inherited these patterns…[24]

References

Argumedo, A. 1985. *América Latina. Los laberintos de la crisis.* Buenos Aires, Folios Ed./ILET.

Barsky, O. Et alii. 1988. *La agricultura pampeana.* Buenos Aires, FCE/IICA.

Brandão, C. 1984. *Repensando a pesquisa participante,* São Paulo, Edit. Brasiliense.

Beltrán, L.R. 1985. "Premisas, objetos y métodos foráneos en la investigación sobre comunicación en América Latina," en Moragas, M. De, *Sociología de la Comunicación de Masas,* Barcelona, Edit. Gustavo Gilli.

Beltrão, L. 1980. *Folkcomunicação, a comunicação dos marginalizados.* São Paulo, Cortez Editora.

Bosco Pinto, J. 1973. *"Extensión y educación: una disyuntiva crítica,"* en *Desarrollo Rural en las Américas.* Bogotá, 4(3): 15-25.

Canuto, J. y Miguel Angelo da Silveira (org.) 1988. *Estudos de Comunicação Rural.* São Paulo, Loyola-INTERCOM.

Cimadevilla, G. 1990. *A modernização tardía. Além do velho e do novo na extensão rural.* Dissertação de Mestrado. Universidade Federal de Santa Maria, RS. Brasil.

Cimadevilla, G. 1997. "Relatos, informes y ensayos. Un recorrido por los estudios de comunicación rural," en *La bocina que parla. Antecedentes y perspectivas de los estudios de comunicación rural* (Cimadevilla, G. et alii). Río Cuarto, INTA-UNRC.

Cimadevilla, G. y Carniglia, E. 2004. *Comunicación, ruralidad y desarrollo. Mitos, paradigmas y dispositivos del cambio.* Buenos Aires, Ediciones INTA.

Cimadevilla, G.; E. Carniglia y A. Cantú. 1997. *La bocina que parla. Antecedentes y perspectivas de los estudios de comunicación rural.* Río Cuarto, Edición conjunta INTA-UNRC.

Da Silva, J. Graziano. 1982. *A modernização dolorosa: estrutura agrária, fronteira agrícola e trabalhadores rurais no Brasil,* Rio de Janeiro, Zahar Editores.

Díaz Bordenave, J. 1983. *O que é comunicação rural.* São Paulo. Edit. Brasiliense.

Embrater. 1987. *A Comunicação na Extensão Rural: Fundamentação e Diretrizes Operacionais.* Brasilia, DF.

Embrater, 1987. *Política e diretrizes de formação extensionista.* . Brasilia, DF

Ferrer, A. 1973. *La Economía Argentina.* Buenos Aires, FCE.

Franz Amaral, M. 1993. *Juan Diaz Bordenave e a comunicação para o homen rural.* Dissertação de Mestrado, Universidade Federal de Santa Maria, Santa Maria, RS, Brasil.

Freire, P. 1973. *¿Extensión o comunicación?.* Buenos Aires, Siglo XXI/Tierra Nueva.

Friedrich, O. 1988. *Comunicação Rural. Proposição crítica de uma nova conceção.* Brasilia, 2da. Edición.

Hunt, E. & Sherman, H. 1985. *História do pensamento econômico.* Petrópolis, Vozes.

Lousa da Fonseca, M. T. 1985. *A extensão rural. Um projeto educativo para o capital.* São Paulo, Ed. Loyola.

Magela Braga, G. y Margarida M. Krohling Kunsch. 1993. *Comunicação Rural: discurso e prática.* Viçosa, Universidad Federal de Viçosa.

Marques de Melo, J. 1978. *Comunicação, Modernização e Difusão de inovações no Brasil.* Petrópolis, Ed. Vozes.

---

23 With contributions by Juan Diaz Bordenave; José Nilo Tavares; Maria Lousa da Fonseca; John Fett; Walmir de Albuquerque Barbosa; Michel Thiollent; José Marques de Melo; Eduardo Castro; Roberto Emerson Cámara Benjâmin; Antônio Luiz de Lima; Geraldo Lobato Franco; Laércio Nunes e Nunes co-authoring with Fioravante J. dos Santos and Estefania Damboariarena; Maria Salett Tauk Santos and Angelo Brás Fernandes Callou; Dilma de Melo Silva; Maria do Carmo Tafuri Paniago; José Geraldo Fernandes de Araújo with Augusto César de Queiroz and Marina Biava; and the writer of this text together with Emilio Severina.

24 A more detailed analysis can be found in Cimadevbilla's text: "Extensión y Comunicación. Antecedentes, articulaciones y contrastes" (págs. 155 a 199) in *Comunicación, ruralidad y desarrollo. Mitos, paradigmas y dispositivos del cambio* (Cimadevilla, G. y Carniglia, E. (Edit), Buenos Aires, INTA, 2004)

1927
1960
1963
1964
1967
1969
1970
1971
1972
1973
1974
1975
1976
1977
1978
1979
1980
1981
1982
1983
1984
1985
1986
1987
1988
1989
1990
1991
1992
1993
1994
1995
1996
1997
1998
1999
2000
2001
2002
2003
2004
2005
2006

Oteiza, E. 1992. *La política de investigación científica y tecnológica argentina. Historia y perspectivas*. Buenos Aires, CEAL.

Quesada, G. 1980. *Comunicação e Comunidade: mitos da mudança social*. São Paulo, Editorial Loyola.

Quesada, G. 1989. *"Comunicação rural na integração campo-cidade,"* en Marques de Melo, J. (Org.) *Comunicação na América Latina. Desenvolvimento e crise*. Campinas, Papirus.

Rogers, E. 1962. *Diffusion of innovations*. New York, The Free Press.

Tauk Santos, M.S. 1986. *"A ideologia da modernização e o rádio rural"* en Revista *INTERCOM* Nro. 55. São Paulo.

Tauk Santos, M.S. 1986. "Comunicação e educação no mundo rural: uma experiencia libertadora com pequenos agricultores," en Krohling Kunsch, M. (Org.) *Caminhos cruzados*. São Paulo, Loyola.

Whiting, G. y Lytton Guimarães. 1969. *Comunicação das novas idéias. Pesquisas Aplicáveis ao Brasil*. Rio de Janeiro. Ed. Françeiras.

Wolf, M. 1987. *La investigación de la Comunicación de Masas*. Barcelona, Paidós.

Wolf, M. 1994. *Los efectos sociales de los media*. Barcelona, Paidós.

THE FUNCTIONS OF CULTURE WITHIN A DEVELOPMENT SITUATION

Excerpt from: Development Communication as Part of the Culture

By C. W. Malan

1998 Even though the important role of culture in development is now widely recognised, development practitioners who have to deal with the concrete realities of economics, land and housing allocation, physical infrastructure, etc., often feel that the concept of culture is so vague and without boundaries that they have little use for it in their planning. The discursive decentralisation and expansion of the concept within cultural studies has done little to allay this scepticism. However, it is cultural studies that can contribute immensely to mapping out various functions and modalities of culture within development scenarios.

UNESCO's World Commission on Culture and Development (1995, 82) lists some of the uses of cultural expression at the local or grassroots level; it has been used by development agents working with communities to strengthen group identity, generate social energy, overcome feelings of inferiority and alienation, and enter the economy directly. Of particular importance to development communication is the use of culture to foster democratic discourse and social mediation, help cope with the challenges of cultural differences, teach and raise awareness, and promote creativity and innovation. (World Commission 1995, 82)

Cultural Identity

The recognition of cultural identity is a way of ensuring that receiving communities do not remain passive during development. "With the preservation of cultural identity becoming a major issue among developing societies, the acceptance of the content of communication media across international borders includes an acceptance of foreign cultural values which could, perhaps, be antithetical to the values of the receiving society" (Reddi 1987, 51). Globalisation thus remains a constant challenge to the development of local communities.

Identity is constituted by the following factors, among others, that should determine the nature and success of development. The implications of these aspects for development communication in a local context should be analysed by facilitators:

■ *Worldviews and values.* As Rajasunderam (1997) emphasises, participatory communication at the community level can only become a reality through meaningful human relations, driven by perennial values such as compassion and solidarity. Western, or First World, worldviews and values centering on modernisation theories informed the now-discredited older forms of development communication.

■ *Knowledge.* Local knowledge, ways of making sense and "naming the world" (Freire), have been recognised as essential to successful development communication. Knowledge should inform know-how.

■ *Traditions.* Traditional ways of communicating, particularly those based on oral communication, should be utilised for development communication.

■ *Customs.* Communication may break down at the first level if customs such as the recognition of hierarchy, status and social position are not recognised.

■ *Beliefs.* Beliefs in the presence and guidance of the forefathers and respect for their graves may have a considerable influence on land development.

■ *Symbols.* Carl Jung has illustrated the enormous influence of symbols that originate within the personal and collective unconscious. A single symbol within a

development communication context may say more than a thousand words.

Culture as a Facilitator of Development

Since the 1970s, culture has re-emerged as a facilitator of development and is not seen only as a backdrop to the development processes. Folk media and popular art forms can themselves very effectively be harnessed to convey messages for development projects, as has been illustrated worldwide. Since they originate from within the heart of culture, various folk media are particularly important (Ranganath 1980), including folk theatre, puppetry, storytelling, folk dances, ballads, and mime. They have served as vehicles for communication and entertainment for centuries (Melkote 1991, 211); however, locally, their potential for development support has scarcely been recognised.

Traditional media can of course also be misused for manipulation. In commenting on the use of folk media by development agents, Latin American specialist Juan Diaz Bordenave warns that the agents' "obsession with goal achievement and not with human growth may take up these folk media as another set of instruments for changing a people's way of thinking, feeling and behaving. And this is not the purpose and the function of the traditional communications media. Their purpose is expression, relationship, communion, escape, fantasy, beauty, poetry, worship" (quoted in World Commission 1995, 83).

The danger of portraying traditional media in a romantic, agrarian fashion as an *open sesame* for unscrupulous developers should be faced. For people who experience these media as a natural expression of their lives and views, there is of course no "danger."

Some of the best-known forms of cultural expression are the following:

Popular folk theatre and related forms of performance. Community theatre, often improvised, has yielded spectacular results in developing countries

1927
1960
1963
1964
1967
1969
1970
1971
1972
1973
1974
1975
1976
1977
1978
1979
1980
1981
1982
1983
1984
1985
1986
1987
1988
1989
1990
1991
1992
1993
1994
1995
1996
1997
1998
1999
2000
2001
2002
2003
2004
2005
2006

throughout the world (Reyneke, 1966). It is often combined with other forms of performance mentioned below, such as song and dance. Locally, the scandal surrounding the production of the play *Sarafina 2,* which was developed for HIV/AIDS education and caused an outcry when it was revealed that it had received state funding of 14 million ZAR (South African rand), has undoubtedly seriously harmed the concept of using theatre and dance for conveying messages. On the other hand, it has introduced the possibilities of these forms of cultural expression as communication media to the public's attention.

■ *Storytelling and other forms of narration.* Since they entertain, command attention and have an intrinsic logic, stories and other forms of narration (dramatic, poetic, mimetic and so on) have since time immemorial been some of the most effective ways of conveying a message. Development communication facilitators can learn much about communities and contribute to the preservation of "living culture" by inviting individuals to tell their own story. These stories can be recorded and transcribed to be preserved as a part of the community's heritage.

■ *Mime.* This has been perfected to an exquisite art form in the East, but "primitive" man has always had a love of mime.

■ *Puppetry.* People-sized puppets have been used with remarkable success for HIV/AIDS education in this country.

■ *Folk dances.* Again, the use of bodily movements to convey messages is probably as old as the history of *Homo sapiens.*

■ *Ballads and songs.* The combination of various forms of narration with music has always had a particular kind of appeal: It combines entertainment with an effective transmission of a message.

Intercultural Interaction

A range of intercultural relationships is part and parcel of development: Developers are often Western experts who have to interact with "Third World" people. A range of intercultural factors is relevant for development communication: worldviews, values, ethnocentrism and ethnorelativism, experience of space and time, individualism as opposed to collectivism, etc.

Creativity and Innovation

UNESCO's World Commission on Culture and Development (1995, 81–82) points out that creativity as a social force is often neglected and that its corollary, innovation, is frequently seen as being in conflict with tradition. The harnessing of the natural creativity and innovation that can be found in any community for development communication will go a long way towards ensuring success. A well-known example is direct community participation in improvised community theatre used to convey development communication messages.

Cultural Factors of Continuity and Change

Even a development communication facilitator with a sound knowledge of the community's identity, language, customs, etc., is often faced with the daunting task of systematically listing these factors in order to draw up a cultural profile of the community. When attempting to assess the extent to which culture and development are compatible, two categories of factors are distinguished by UNESCO. On the one hand, there are those that constitute the heritage and the history of a society (its continuity), and, on the other, the intrinsic creative elements and elements of change it contains (UNESCO 1995, 93).

Continuity factors (or slow variables) include modes of life, ways of thought and production, practices, customs, traditions, beliefs, value systems, events experienced as cultural in their own right, languages and other forms of nonphysical heritage.

Factors of change (or fast variables) include needs and aspirations of the people, survival strategies, knowledge (science) and know-how (technologies, modes of social, political and economic organisation), creativity, migration and changes to the environment, economic exchange and trade. Important for the purposes of development communication, these factors of change also include spoken language (in particular, ways of speaking and vocabulary), technology transfers and intercultural communications.

Indigenous Sociocultural Forms as a Basis for Development

Colletta (1980, 17) believes that there are three reasons why indigenous culture is the fabric within which development can best be woven: Indigenous elements have traditional legitimacy for participants in development programmes; these elements contain symbols that express and identify various valid perceptions of reality; and they serve multiple functions. The following social/cultural forms that he discusses, along with traditional leadership, socioeconomic processes, organisational forms, etc. (1980, 17–40), have clear implications for development communication:

- *Traditional communication systems* (social exchange, assemblies, etc.). Observers are often amazed at the effective and speedy way that notices of meetings, etc., are conveyed by word of mouth in South African townships and rural communities.
- *Indigenous knowledge systems* (farming practices, health promotion, etc.). Locally, the importance attached to traditional healing practices is well known, and it should be considered when structuring health promotion messages.
- *Traditional aetiology and belief systems* (especially cause-effect relationships, religious symbols, etc.). It could have grave consequences for land development if community bonds with burial sites and ancestors are not taken into account.
- *Indigenous technologies and transfer* (using local materials and resources, and the transfer of skills to use them).

A cultural approach is central to the participatory rural communication appraisal (PRCA) methodology explained by Anyaegbunam, Mefalopulos and Moetsabi (1997). This methodology is used by field workers and extension staff to do participatory research as a first step to prepare a communication programme. It helps field workers to understand how people perceive and define their world, to get a profile of the community, to understand the information and communication networks of the community and their interaction groups, and in general to analyse community needs, problems and solutions.

Cultural Translation

Since the development communication facilitator is the linkage between all the development agencies and the community, he/she should do "translation" in various senses of the word during the facilitation process. The term cultural translation will therefore be used here to denote the very essence of effective development communication. Basic data and information have to be translated culturally in order to have any lasting impact on development. This form of "translation" includes the following:

- *Relating basic messages and knowledge to the community's way of life and everyday experiences.* Illustrations and references to well-known situations, contexts or spaces are essential. Knowledge could mean very little *if* it is not related to the way people perceive and define their world, e.g., in a Zambian village the people did not implement most of the extension workers' recommendations because the villagers did not see themselves as farmers (Anyaegbunam et al. 1997).
- *Linguistic translation.* If the development communication facilitator cannot speak the community's language, which is of course ideal, it should be learnt. In the process of learning, the change agent accesses and appreciates indigenous knowledge and learns local norms of interaction and communication (Robinson 1997). In any case, at least essential aspects of the message should be translated. This also serves as reinforcement if most of the original message is understood.
- *Recoding writing-related messages for illiterates and even literates.* Illiteracy is without doubt one of the major challenges facing any form of development communication in this country [South Africa]. The use of indigenous cultural knowledge and oral

1927
1960
1963
1964
1967
1969
1970
1971
1972
1973
1974
1975
1976
1977
1978
1979
1980
1981
1982
1983
1984
1985
1986
1987
1988
1989
1990
1991
1992
1993
1994
1995
1996
1997
1998
1999
2000
2001
2002
2003
2004
2005
2006

and nonwritten visual communication are crucial to effective development communication in situations of illiteracy. But it should also be kept in mind that oral and visual media are generally more powerful in Africa than written media.

- *Presenting ICTs as user-friendly aids.* End users should be guided to perceive all forms of technology as non-threatening. Illiterate people will not respond to a pamphlet, but may do so to a drawing or cartoon strip; computer-illiterate persons could be fearful of a computer, but may be persuaded to type a few preprogrammed commands or use touchscreen technology.
- *Adapting development messages to the community's communication networks and systems.* This adaptation is necessary to identify and use the most effective channel, depending on the need for mass, group or interpersonal modes (Mody 1991). With multimedia technology available, messages can be conveyed in a variety of stimulating and interesting ways.
- *Channelling information of international and national networks into local networks.* Local area networks (LANs) can be linked to the Internet, with many benefits. These intranets should be adapted to be as user-friendly as possible to the community. Introductions or summaries in the local languages are one option. One skilled person can open the treasures of the entire World Wide Web to the community.
- *Negotiating the context-specific meaning of development itself.* This probably is the most crucial form of cultural mediation for the development communication facilitator. In a typical "worst-case scenario" of development, the community could be faced with the possibility that developers will move into their village with large machinery, disturb their environment and leave them with an unwanted structure. The community representatives should therefore answer the following kinds of questions put to them by the facilitator: "Given the fact that the developers have indicated that they would like to learn from you, what are your most important needs in this situation? How would you like to address them *yourselves* and how are you going to be involved as a community? In which ways are you going to take over ownership of the project?" It is equally important that this interaction should result in two-way communication and negotiation with the developers.
- *Establishing the cultural discourse within which the project will be executed.* Related to the factors listed above, the development project and process should therefore be situated within a specific discourse, a framework of meaning producing and sense making. Moreover, the general development discourse is usually an integration of discourses at the levels of technical development planning (which could be embedded in the culture of "technocratic developmentalism") and community involvement (which could be related to a culture of "politically expedient populism"). These discourses could differ considerably, and it is the job of the development communication facilitator to provide bridges between the discursive frameworks.

The list makes it clear that a variety of skills and knowledge are needed for cultural translation. Of particular importance are the areas of cross-cultural or one-way mass communication, intercultural or two-way interaction, and interpersonal communication, and even comparative communication between "cultures," as studied by an observer (Thomas 1987, 5–6).

At a participatory level, close interaction with the community is essential for good cultural translation. Since Rivera and Erlich (1995, 203) define culture as a collection of behaviours and beliefs that constitute standards for deciding what is, what can be and what to do about it, their list of a community organiser's qualities include the following: cultural and racial identification with the community, familiarity with customs and traditions, social networks and values, and an intimate knowledge of language and subgroup slang, in addition to analytical, organisational and other skills (1995, 208–221). Ideally, these qualities also apply to the development communication facilitator.

Negotiations and mediation are needed to deal with issues such as the following: (a) ownership, location and distribution of infrastructure, (b) transmitted values and the language of transmission, (c) content determination and formulation, (d) the purpose and process of skill acquisition necessary for community handling of tools, (e) programme extensiveness and effectiveness, and (f) the level of community participation in decision making regarding the operation of facilities.

A considerable range of skills and knowledge is required of the development communication facilitator who can do good cultural translation. He/she should have competence and knowledge regarding as many as possible of the areas of local languages, journalistic and communication skills, computer training and particularly the exploration of the Internet, development and literacy theory, management principles, etc. The competent development communication facilitator will certainly see this formidable list not as an obstacle, but as a challenge.

Conclusion

If anything is to be "salvaged" from the much-tainted concept of development, the lack of progress in incorporating development communication planning and research should be a cause for concern. One of the reasons for the present situation is the tendency to leave development communication research and development to communication experts only. In South Africa they are a relatively small segment of the academic community who have to cover an enormous field of communication studies. The survey above should point out the need for an interdisciplinary approach to development communication research and planning. The essentially interdisciplinary cultural and developmental studies are the obvious areas where development communication studies should be initiated, but a range of contributions from disciplines such as cultural and linguistic studies, economics, sociology, the information sciences, education, etc., are needed.

References

Anyaegbunam, C., P. Mefalopulos, and T. Moetsabi. 1997. Participatory Rural Communication Appraisal Methodology (PRCA): The application of participatory approaches to communication programme design and implementation for sustainable human development. Paper presented at virtual conference on participatory communication (ParCom 97). November 1997.

Boonzaaier, E., and J. Sharp, eds. South African keywords: The uses and abuses of political concepts Cape Town: David Philip, 1988.

Colletta, N.J. Tradition for change: Indigenous sociocultural forms as a basis for nonformal education and development. In R. Kidd and N.J. Collette, eds. Tradition for development: Indigenous structures and folk media in non formal education. Proceedings of the 1980 conference Tradition for Development. Stuttgart, Germany, 1980.

Klitgaard, R. In search of culture. Washington, D.C.: World Bank, 1991.

Klitgaard, R., ed. Assessing cultures. College Park: Center for Institutional Reform and the Informal Sector, University of Maryland, 1993.

Klitgaard, R. Taking culture into account From 'let's' to 'how'. In Serageldin, I. & Tabaroff, J. eds. Culture and development in Africa. Vol. 1. Washington: The World Bank, 1994, pp. 75-120.

Levett, A., et al., eds. Culture, power and difference: Discourse analysis in South Africa. Cape Town: Univ. of Cape Town Press, 1997.

Malan, C. The eye of the fly: Viewing development as part of culture. Paper presented at the conference of the Development Association of Southern Africa. Stellenbosch. September 25–27, 1996.

Melkote, S.R. Communication for development in the Third World: Theory and practice. New Delhi: Sage Publications, 1991.

Mody, B. Designing messages for development communication: An audience participation-based approach. New Delhi: Sage Publications, 1991.

Rajasunderam, C.V. Vision, principles and values: Some reflections. Paper presented at the virtual conference on participatory communication (ParCom 97). November 1997.

Ranganath, H.K. Folk media and communication. Bangalore: Chintana Prakashana Publishers, 1980.

Reddi, U.Y. "New communication technologies: What sort of development do they bring in their wake?" In: N. Jayaweera and S. Amunugarpa, eds. Rethinking development communication. Singapore: AMIC, 1987, pages 42–60.

Reyneke, E. The international use of popular theatre for community development. HSRC unpublished report, 1995.

Rivera, F.G., and J.L. Erlich. Organizing with people of color: A perspective. In: J.F. Tropmarni, J.L. Erlich, and J. Rothman, eds. Tactics and techniques of community intervention. Itasca, Ill.: F.E. Peacock, 1995, pages 198–213.

Robinson, C. Participatory development and language. Paper presented at the virtual conference on participatory communication (ParCom 97). November 1997.

Steyn, M., and K. Motshabi, eds. Cultural synergy in South Africa: Weaving strands of Africa and Europe. Randburg, South Africa: Knowledge Resources, 1996.

Thomas, S. Culture and communication: Methodology, behavior, artifacts and institution. Norwood, N.J.: Ablex, 1987.

Thornton, R. "Ubuntu, culture and the limits of development." Paper presented at the international symposium Culture, Communication, Development. Pretoria. August 29–31, 1996.

1927
1960
1963
1964
1967
1969
1970
1971
1972
1973
1974
1975
1976
1977
1978
1979
1980
1981
1982
1983
1984
1985
1986
1987
1988
1989
1990
1991
1992
1993
1994
1995
1996
1997
1998
1999
2000
2001
2002
2003
2004
2005
2006

Tomaselli, K.G., ed. *Rethinking culture.* Bellville, South Africa: Anthropos, 1998.

Tomaselli, K.G., and M. Aldridge. Cultural strategies in a changing development [environment]: Reassessing Paolo Freire in the information age. *Africa Media Review* 10, 1996, pages 54–72.

Tomaselli, K.G., and P.E. Louw. Communication models and struggle: From authoritarian determinism to a theory of communication as social relations in South Africa. *The Journal of African Communications* 1, 1996, pages 15–41.

Treurnicht, S.P. "Indigenous knowledge systems and participatory learning and action," In: D.A. Kotze, ed. *Development administration and management A holistic approach.* Pretoria: Van Schaik, 1997, pages 93–104.

UNESCO. *Culture and agriculture: Orientation texts on the 1995 theme.* Paris: UNESCO, 1995.

UNESCO. *The cultural dimension of development.* Paris: UNESCO, 1995.

World Commission on Culture and Development. *Our creative diversity: Report of the World Commission on Culture and Development.* Paris: World Commission on Culture and Development, 1995.

Malan, C. W. "The Functions of Culture within a Development Situation." Excerpted from: Development Communication as Part of the Culture, *Communicare,* 17 (1), 1998. Reprinted with permission.

EXCERPT FROM:
LINKING THE GLOBAL FROM WITHIN THE LOCAL

By Rico Lie

2002

A. Globalization as Development

A first perspective could be termed globalization as development. Such a perspective is grounded in a political-economic approach and the dominant part is sometimes referred to as "globalization from above" (Beck 1996). Globalization here is still regarded to be a universal applicable end point of changing societies. This end point is different from the ideal end point of the modern nation state, as it was common to pursue within the so-called modernization paradigm (Servaes 1999). Different from modernization theory—as it was promoted in the field of development and development communication by, for instance, Rostow, Rogers, Lerner and Schramm in the decades immediately following the Second World War—globalization pursues an economic change and a change in governance towards a global scale. The internationalization of national economies is regarded to be a necessary condition for development. The questions are of course: "Who is this global development for?"; "Who profits from globalization?"; "Is this kind of development creating new forms of inequality?" and "Is the global gap between the rich and the poor, the information haves and the information have-nots widening?" The protests at the summits of the WTO in Seattle (December 1999) and the IMF/World Bank summit in Prague (September 2000) made it very clear that not everybody agrees with the hypothesis that globalization is development. Development in the perspective of "globalization as development from above" is primarily seen as a structural global political, but mainly economic change. Some of the critiques of the paradigm of "modernization as development" still apply to the paradigm of "globalization as development from above." Some of these critiques concern: "the linear way of thinking," "the non-plural and homogenous way of thinking," "the positivistic and behavioristic way of thinking," "the Western/Northern way of thinking" and "the approach that development is primarily of an economic nature." Another critique is that most of the elements in the conglomerate of changes are not considered in approaching globalization as development. Aspects of interdisciplinarity, the power of culture and linking globalization with localization remain under addressed.

GLOBALIZATION FROM BELOW

"Globalization from below"—sometimes also referred to as "grassroots globalization," "governance from below" or "counterglobalization"—refers to the work done by, and the rise of, transnational communities in the field of NGOs concerned with mobilizing highly specific local, national and regional groups on matters of equity, access, justice and redistribution (Appadurai, 2000:15). Beck (1996) refers in this context to "global subpolitics," and sees "globalization from below" as pursuing globalization, "...e.g. through new transnational actors operating beyond the system of parliamentary politics and challenging established political organizations and interest groups" (Beck, 1996:16). "Globalization from below" is thus primarily oriented towards inequalities and injustice and promotes democracy and liberty. "Globalization from below" is about change for the betterment of the people, and this positive change is thought to come from below, from the grassroots, from the local. It is advocated that change should fit the local circumstances, however diverse these local circumstances might be in different localities. Communities that try to channel this quest for "grounded change" range from local NGOs to indigenous groups, women groups, peasants groups and all kinds of epistemic communities.

This globalization from below is through transnational networking among these communities, through transnational movements of all kinds of groups and the building of a transnational civil society mainly aiming at structural political change. It is collective counteraction in order to be heard within a political system and to change the system from outside by channeling

the voices of the local to the political inside. "Globalization as development from below" is thus primarily a political project and participation here is based on counteraction by all kinds of movements. Participation, in the case of "globalization from below" is in the opposition.

B. Localization as Development

A second perspective on linking globalization and development is through the intrinsic link with localization. It can therefore be termed localization as development. The interconnected processes of globalization and localization—or glocalization as some prefer—are operational at different societal levels and between different societal levels. In the case of glocalization, globalization does not refer only to contacts between the level of nations or macro international bodies (as was common in the dependency paradigm, and is mostly referred to by those who use the term globalization), but also to intercultural contacts at more grounded levels of societal organization. Globalization is a process that not only applies to nations but also to small-scale communities and individuals, including development facilitators. These interlevel contacts—also referred to as flows to emphasize more specifically the flow of cultural products and development messages—and especially the interpretations of the cultural products and messages by individuals in local communities, form the basis for a more localized perspective on globalization and see development as localization.

It is then at the local level that one can identify processes of localization. First of all, in order to be able to accept localization as a form of development, we need to ask ourselves what it entails. Localization is more or less the same as "localism." Localism might even be the more common term to use, but I prefer localization because of the processual character included in the term of localization and because of the linguistic contrast it makes with the term globalization. According to Nadel-Klein (1991), localism refers to "the representation of group identity as defined primarily

1927
1960
1963
1964
1967
1969
1970
1971
1972
1973
1974
1975
1976
1977
1978
1979
1980
1981
1982
1983
1984
1985
1986
1987
1988
1989
1990
1991
1992
1993
1994
1995
1996
1997
1998
1999
2000
2001
2002
2003
2004
2005
2006

by a sense of commitment to a particular place and to a set of cultural practices that are self-consciously articulated and to some degree separated and directed away from the surrounding social world" (Nadel-Klein, 1991:502). Localization can thus be seen as a process of articulating locally grounded cultural practices and reinforcing cultural identities at local community levels by contrasting it with other cultural localities, be these localities near (a neighboring community) or far (a television program produced in another continent). In some cases localization is explicitly seen as a reaction to the process of globalization (Van Ginkel, 1992). People deal with globalization aspects ("outgroup" messages) from their own local contexts and this interaction could lead to more emphasis on small-scale cultural processes. "In ... attempts to theorize the present phase of globalization, worldwide interconnectedness does not result in the creation of a "global society." It yields, on the one hand, a decentered set of subnational and supranational interactions—from capital transfers and population movements to the transmission of information—and these interactions help multiply, invent, and disseminate cultural differences, rather than overcome them" (Buell, 1994:10). So, even on the national level, with reference to national cultures and the nation-state, globalization does not necessarily stand for cultural integration as "the globalists" underwrite. It is instead assumed that globalization and localization are interrelated processes and that globalization can somehow stimulate processes of localization. Localization, in a development discourse, means that explicit emphasis is put on the articulation of local cultural identities and local community characteristics.

The paradigm of "localization as development" emphasizes grounded social and individual change and puts a high value on communication/culture. As such, it is very closely associated with the multiplicity paradigm (Servaes, 1999). In the sphere of communication/culture, the link between development and globalization is not so much directly concerned with globalization. The link development has with globalization

can only be established by taking the concept of localization seriously and by exploring the link between globalization and localization in-depth. This in depth exploration can start with centralizing local processes of interpretation. It is these processes of interpretation that account for world connectedness from within the local. Additionally to "globalization from below" in the political arena, we can therefore distinguish another bottom-up dimension in the specific field of communication/culture. Although all acts of (counter) action are based on processes of interpretation, this dimension has been relatively unaddressed in many discussions on globalization. "Development as localization" can thus be seen as highly associated with this power of people's interpretations.

THE POWER OF INTERPRETATION

Interpretation empowers people in the sense that the people themselves are the real actors in any kind of human (development) process. This power of interpretation is in many cases non-political, meaning it is not organized or structured in political terms. It is the people, in a nonpolitical atmosphere, who decide what to do with what is offered them. It is the people themselves, not the NGOs or the organizational movements that represent them, that this kind of localizing development is concerned with. By the act of interpretation, people localize things and make them relevant for their daily lives. This process of interpretation can be concerned with a television program like "Dallas" (Liebes and Katz, 1990), but it is also concerned with any kind of campaign or other intervention promoted by a development agency. These acts of interpretation can be interpreted as counteracts to globalization, but in a more positive perspective they can be seen as acts of localization. It is through interpretation that people empower themselves.

This nonpolitical interpretation can of course lead to political participation and can then be voiced by all kinds of organizations, but it can also lead to nonpolitical participation. Nonpolitical participation does not mean that the established relationships are without power. All human relationships have elements of power, but it refers simply to participation in non-political organizations, like (extended) families, circles of friends, formal and informal educational groups, health institutions, clubs and associations. Sometimes this distinction between political and nonpolitical is not as rigid as it seems. Media participation, for instance, can be highly politicized in one country, where it is not in another.

Development can thus be understood as accentuating these localized processes of interpretation. Interpretation is a cultural communication process. A local cultural reference frame is used to deal with everything that comes from the outside, be it a McDonald's or a population intervention program.

TOWARDS "COMMUNICATION FOR LOCALIZATION"

"Globalisation does not only concern the creation of large-scale systems, but also the transformation of the local, and even personal, context of social experience" (Giddens, 1994:4-5). What is emphasized here is that globalization not only refers to abstract changes taking place at a macro level. It also refers to how people, situated at local levels, perceive these changes. This aspect points to what Braman (1996) has termed "interpenetrated globalization." With this she means that the relationship between the parts and the whole may be understood as mutually constitutive; the global never exists except in the local. In fact, this seems to be one of the new fundamental issues in thinking about globalization. Thinking about cultural globalization is not something completely new but builds on already existing theories and ideas such as "the global village," dependency thinking, Americanization/Westernization, cultural imperialism, media imperialism and cultural synchronization. But linking it in an intrinsic way to a process of localization seems to be a breakthrough. We now recognize that globalization and localization are two polar points on a continuum and that studying globalization from a people-centered local perspective should not be the exclusive domain of fieldwork anthropologists. Globalization and localization, as far as they refer to culture, are interpretative processes. This means they are not objective processes but defined differently by different subjects, belonging to different communities, in different times and different spaces.

Building on Tomlinson (1994) and with him, reflecting on Giddens, the globalization thesis is in fact about structure, and "our day-to-day experience of locales is certainly structured by forces which are, ultimately, global" (Tomlinson 1994:153). But, it "is surely not a central figure in most people's everyday awareness" (Tomlinson 1994:154). If it is not a global structure that plays a central role in people's daily experience, what does? Building on interpretative approaches in communication studies (Carragee 1990; Evans, 1990; Servaes & Frissen, 1997), anthropology (Geertz 1973; Keesing, 1987) and sociology (Berger & Luckmann, 1967), reference frameworks, worldviews, cultures and structures that guide daily activity can, first of all, be sought in the local. An interpretative approach centers people's interpretations in a local context. In such an interpretative way, daily structure is far more local than global. So, if we return to Giddens' claim and Tomlinson's critique, I would like to state that phenomenal worlds are still truly local, instead of global. But how do we include the global level or, for that matter, everything that comes from the outside, in the locally based interpretations?

In my opinion, the cultural flow, be it local or global, is interpreted in the local context of every day life. Daily life is, as such, the primary context in which people deal, in an interpretative sense, with "outgroup"—as well as "ingroup"—messages. A (cultural) identity that is constructed (partly) based on these locally embedded interpretations is, however, derived from different societal levels, e.g., the global level, the macro-regional level, e.g., the Pacific Islands region or Europe, the national level (nation-states), the meso-regional level, e.g., provinces or counties, the local level, e.g., cities, neighborhoods, communities,

1927
1960
1963
1964
1967
1969
1970
1971
1972
1973
1974
1975
1976
1977
1978
1979
1980
1981
1982
1983
1984
1985
1986
1987
1988
1989
1990
1991
1992
1993
1994
1995
1996
1997
1998
1999
2000
2001
2002
2003
2004
2005
2006

but also (extended) families and the individual level. This is the case because the cultural flow incorporates elements, which are derived from these different levels or from bodies operating at these different levels. In this line of thought the global has indeed an influence on the construction of identity, but this influence cannot be overemphasized because the interpretations, which are local cultural interpretations, precede the construction of identity.

This process of interpreting people, institutions and products that originate from different societal levels (Servaes & Lie, 2000) can be termed cultural localization. Though, to give it a more active connotation, I would like to call it "communication for localization." With "communication for localization" I basically mean that processes of cultural change and flows of knowledge, culture or information should be interpreted and analyzed in a local context instead of trying to place them directly in a global context. The flow may have a global or outside character, but the interpretations of these flows are, first of all, local. "Communication for localization" is particularly interested in the subjective dimensions of globalization as a bottom-up process of interpretations.

A consequence of such a position is that one favors "the right to culture" from an internal point of view (from the inside out). Article 27 of the Universal Declaration of Human Rights (1948) states: "Everyone has the right freely to participate in the cultural life of the community." And one of the statements at the 1968 UNESCO conference on cultural rights as human rights was: "The rights to culture include the possibility for each man to obtain the means of developing his personality, through his direct participation in the creation of human values and of becoming, in this way, responsible for his situation, whether local or on a world scale" (Hamelink, 1994:187-188). The point that is stressed here is that the world scale or the global reference framework is not an outside force in the creation of an individual or even a collective cultural identity. The reference frame is indeed

nothing more than a framework that guides, structures, surrounds and frames the locally embedded cultural interpretations.

The other, more action-oriented dimension of "communication for localization" has already been addressed under the heading "globalization from below." The concept stands for, among other things, the activities of grass-roots social movements concerned with cultural or ethnic issues. It is these activities that try to counterbalance global cultural flows and express concern with local cultural identity. Here, the first concern is also with localization and not with globalization. When scholars talk about global grass-roots social movements, they refer to areas in which these movements have global tendencies, e.g. the environment and human rights. It is in these areas that we face common, global risks and in these cases there are no "others." But with culture there are others. Moreover, we are not even sure that our anxiety shared with others can produce the experience of, to say it with Tomlinson (1994:63), a "global we." The global warming and the rising of the sea level are for instance catastrophic for many Pacific Islands because they will literally lose their land. But in this case, there is still no "global we." This example illustrates that we might have bigger changes to add to sustainable developments by starting in the local, because even without the "problems" of ethnic diversity, fundamental religious differences and cultural variety, we have great difficulty in creating a "global we."

To sum up, "communication for localization" can be ascribed two dimensions. First, it is concerned with local interpretations and local cultural identity construction, a construction that is (partly) based on these interpretations. Interpretations of the cultural flow, be the flows global or local, are always locally contextualized using a local reference frame. However, because the flow incorporates elements from many different levels, the construction of identity also incorporates these elements. Though, because of the fact that these elements are first interpreted in a local context, they are also locally reshaped. Second, "communication for localization" is concerned with action. As an active concept it refers to supporting the voice of the local (which in some cases can also mean national or even macro-regional), or disadvantaged groups (either in a global, macro-regional, national, regional or local arena), in order to counterbalance the global communication flow and to favor positively "the right to culture" from the inside out. This dimension has now generally been termed "globalization from below."

References

Appadurai, A. (2000). "Grassroots Globalization and the Research Imagination," *Public Culture*, 12(1):1-19.

Beck, U. (1996). "Risk Society as Cosmopolitan Society?," *Theory, Culture and Society*, 13(4):1-32.

Berger, P. & Luckmann, T. (1967). *The Social Construction of Reality*, New York: Doubleday.

Braman, S. (1996). "Interpenetrated Globalisation: Scaling, Power, and the Public Sphere," in Braman, S. & Sreberny-Mohammadi, A. (eds.), *Globalisation, Communication and Transnational Civil Society*, Cresskill: Hampton Press, pp. 21-36.

Buell, F. (1994). *National Culture and the New Global System*, Baltimore: The Johns Hopkins University Press.

Carragee, K.M. (1990). "Interpretive Media Study and Interpretive Social Science," *Critical Studies in Mass Communication*, 7(2):81-96.

Evans, W.A. (1990). "The Interpretive Turn in Media Research: Innovation, Iteration, or Illusion?," *Critical Studies in Mass Communication*, 7(2):147-168.

Geertz, C. (1973). *The Interpretation of Cultures*, New York: Basic Books.

Giddens, A. (1994). *Beyond Left and Right: The Future of Radical Politics*, Cambridge: Polity Press.

Hamelink, C.J. (1994). *The Politics of World Communication; A Human Rights Perspective*, London: Sage.

Keesing, R.M. (1987). "Anthropology as Interpretive Quest," *Current Anthropology*, 28(2):161-176.

Lie, R. & Servaes, J. (2000). "Globalization: Consumption and Identity. Towards Researching Nodal Points," in Wang, G., Servaes, J. & Goonasekera, A. (eds.), *The New Communications Landscape. Demystifying Media Globalization*, London: Routledge, pp. 307-332.

Liebes, T. & Katz, E. (1990). *The Export of Meaning: Cross-Cultural Readings of "Dallas,"* New York: Oxford University Press.

Nadel-Klein, J. (1991). "Reweaving the Fringe: Localism, Tradition, and Representation in British Ethnography," *American Ethnologist*, 18(3):500-517.

Servaes, J. (1999). *Communication for Development. One World, Multiple Cultures*, Cresskill: Hampton Press.

Servaes, J. & FRISSEN, V. (1997) (eds.), *De Interpretatieve Benadering in de Communicatiewetenschap: Theorie, Methodologie en Case-studies*, Leuven: ACCO.

Tomlinson, J. (1994). "A Phenomenology of Globalization? Giddens on Global Modernity," *European Journal of Communication*, 9(2):149-72.

Van Ginkel, R. (1992). "Groen-zwart, Texels in het Hart," Over Articulatie van Identiteit op een Nederlands Waddeneiland, *Amsterdams Sociologisch Tijdschrift*, 18(4):76-99.

1927
1960
1963
1964
1967
1969
1970
1971
1972
1973
1974
1975
1976
1977
1978
1979
1980
1981
1982
1983
1984
1985
1986
1987
1988
1989
1990
1991
1992
1993
1994
1995
1996
1997
1998
1999
2000
2001
2002
2003
2004
2005
2006

ENTERTAINMENT-EDUCATION IN DEVELOPMENT COMMUNICATION:
BETWEEN MARKETING BEHAVIOURS AND EMPOWERING PEOPLE

By Thomas Tufte

2005 The use of entertainment-education (EE) as a communication strategy in development work has grown significantly over the past decade (Singhal and Rogers 2004, 1999, Sabido et al 2003, Tufte 2001, Bauman 1999). The use of EE has for decades been seen in addressing health-related issues such as blood pressure, smoking, vaccine promotion and family planning. It has also been used for the past 15 years in HIV/AIDS prevention. EE is also a communication strategy that increasingly is being applied in sectors such as environment, rural development, conflict resolution and peace-building (Skeie 2004). At the strategic level, the objectives vary: from promoting individual behaviour change to supporting social change; from enhancing social mobilization to articulating peoples' participation; and from empowering minority or marginalized groups to collective action. The main point here is that EE is increasingly being used as a strategic tool with a diversity of agendas.

The aim here is twofold: First, to provide an introduction to the history and development of the use of EE in communication for development, from the early experiences in the 1950s and 1960s to the abundance of cases seen today. Second, to attempt a categorisation of the different approaches to EE, suggesting three generations of EE communication: from the social marketing strategies which marked early experiences and continue to exist as a widespread approach, over the more interdisciplinary strategies linking diffusion and marketing with some degree of participation, to the transdisciplinary third generation of approaches which explicitly are oriented towards identification of social problems, power inequalities and their root causes, most often enhancing collection action and structural change.

The EE-communication practice we observe today is a negotiated strategy. It draws upon epistemological foundations from scholars and strategists rooted in different schools of thought. It represents varying cultural traditions of storytelling; a breadth of organisational traditions, trajectories, priorities and constraints; political agendas; and varying media infrastructures. Finally, the ad hoc tool box of communication also plays a crucial role in determining the final outcome of de facto developed strategies. In providing a brief history of the development of EE and in outlining the three core generations of EE practice, some of these synergies and characteristics will appear.

Cutting across this article is the aim to deconstruct how and where EE has managed to transcend traditional dichotomies found within both development theory and communication theory—binary thinking of either arguing for diffusion of innovations or participatory strategy; either modernisation strategies or a dependency strategy; either top-down or bottom-up, etc. Thus, in addition to providing some categorisation of the different existing EE strategies the aim is also to provide some degree of substance to conceptually developing a more critical strand of EE, the third generation of EE.

A core element of contestation has been the nature of the impact of EE. Recurrently, critical scholars have questioned the possibilities and limitations of EE, questioning the epistemological aims, theoretical foundations and working methodologies in the actual practice. Nancy Morris (in this volume) indicates that popularity is not equal to efficacy. John Sherry (1997: 93), in reviewing 20 EE soap operas, states that "the best-designed research using powerful statistical controls suggests no significant effects on knowledge, attitudes or behaviour which can be attributed to the soap operas," while Lettenmaier et al 1993

(p. 9) indicate that they found it difficult to separate out the effects of radio drama from other factors. Thus, some clarifications are needed in understanding the possibilities and limitations of the three different approaches to EE, for example:

- What aims and objectives drive EE strategies?
- At what level in society are interventions sought?
- What notion of change informs the strategy?
- What results do EE strategies seek?
- How do EE strategies work with the genre, and with the actual narratives?
- Who participates in developing the content of the strategy and narrative?
- What is the timeline in an EE strategy?
- How is the impact assessed?

There is an abundance and diversity in current EE communication practice. There is also a growing number of recent works contributing to a furthering of the thinking around EE (Bauman 1999, Fuenzalida 2005, Gao 2005, McKee et al 2004, Parker 2005, Skeie 2005, Singhal and Rogers 2004, Storey 1999). Together, this is contributing to a gradual breadth in epistemological, theoretical and methodological foundations, a breadth that can sustain the argument that EE is not just one uniform communication strategy; much like that of social marketing conceived as far back as in the days of young Popeye in the 1930s. It is much more. My suggestion for a broad definition EE is thus:

> Entertainment-education is the use of entertainment as a communicative practice crafted to strategically communicate about development issues in a manner, and with a purpose, that can range from the more narrowly defined social marketing of individual behaviours to the liberating and citizen-driven articulation of social-change agendas.

From Mexican Telenovelas to South African TV-Series

If we take a brief retrospective look at the history and development of EE as a sub-field of study within communication for development, the first characteristic to highlight is that it in many ways has followed the key theoretical and methodological trends of communication for development in general. It is reflected in the three generations of EE I discuss in this article.

One of the first modern examples of EE is "The Archers," a series produced by the BBC radio drama and broadcast in England in the early 1950s (it still runs!). It has since 1951 communicated important information to the farmers in England. In the mid-1950s, it was listened to by two out of three adult Englishmen (Fraser and Restrepo-Estrada 1998). However, from 1972 it gave up its deliberate educational perspective, becoming from then on "just" an ordinary radio soap opera. It was, however, in the 1970s that EE began to gain some more elaborate theoretical grounding. Social marketing is one of the key origins of today's EE strategies, and is still at the core of many first-generation EE communication interventions. The use of social marketing developed in the 1970s and was quickly tied up with music, drama and storytelling. Entertainment was particularly linked to mass media-based strategies, not least, television and radio. It was also in the 1970s that some of the key theories were developed, not least, Albert Bandura's theory of social learning (Bandura 1977).

One of the pioneers in the use of TV fiction for pro-social behaviour change was Mexican Miguel Sabido. Between 1975 and 1985, Sabido produced a total of seven soap operas with built-in social messages. They were broadcast at Mexico's largest television network, Televisa, and were large audience successes. In countries such as India, Kenya, Tanzania and Brazil, the use of television and radio, and the explicit use of fictional genres, gradually developed, all becoming building stones in the continuous development of EE communication strategies (Singhal and Rogers 1999, Sherry 1998, Japhet 1999, Tufte 2000).

First-Generation EE Marketing Behaviour

What characterized the growing use of telenovelas in strategic communication, with the development of EE strategies, were several issues. Firstly with the work of Miguel Sabido, a particular development of

1927
1960
1963
1964
1967
1969
1970
1971
1972
1973
1974
1975
1976
1977
1978
1979
1980
1981
1982
1983
1984
1985
1986
1987
1988
1989
1990
1991
1992
1993
1994
1995
1996
1997
1998
1999
2000
2001
2002
2003
2004
2005
2006

the genre was developed, where mass education and behaviour change via the media grew as a concern and ambition. Telenovelas, traditionally conceived of as entertainment, were increasingly ascribed an educational potential, as a tool for dissemination of information and, thus, for awareness raising and behaviour change. While social marketing, as the first generation of EE, dealt with the marketing of social behaviours, most often health related-behaviours to individuals watching the programs, the EE communication interventions have diversified in scope and aim, thereby also changing the content of the genre. Where many of the social marketing-driven radio and TV dramas have worked systematically, exploring how best and most accurately to convey messages and promote individual behaviours, more recent initiatives—reflected in the second- and third-generation EE interventions—have had a stronger focus on communicating structural inequalities, representing and working with power relations and social conflict in the everyday life of the characters and, by representation of such problems, stimulating debate and collective action. The key distinguishing feature lies in varying definitions of the problem to be addressed. Social-marketing strategies define the key challenge as a lack of information, while the second and third generation of EE define the problem as societal problems such as structural inequality and unequal power relations.

Second-Generation EE: Bridging of Paradigms

The second generation of EE was characterized by introducing new theoretical and methodological perspectives to the first-generation EE. Stated bluntly, what happened in the mid- and late-1990s was an acknowledgement of the fact that marketing of individual behaviour change often constituted a limitation in scope with, as the only focus to obtain sustainable improvement of the problem identified, be it health, as it often was, or education, rural development, etc. With a growing recognition of complexity in the social, health and other developmental problems that were addressed, a furthering of the conceptual basis

was required beyond the exclusive focus on individual behaviour change. It resulted, first and foremost, in the introduction of participatory approaches into many EE communication strategies, although in an instrumental manner.

While EE, for the first years, maintained a focus on individual behaviour change, social change agendas began in the 1990s to emerge as a key goal for many EE strategies. Alongside the individual as unit of change, there grew an increased attention towards structural elements as equally important focus. Society, as a unit of change, began to be addressed. Critical social theory has increasingly been incorporated into the theoretical debates about EE, challenging more behaviourist cause-and-effect understandings of communication. This is where both participatory communication and, also, more recent reception theory has become relevant, suggesting more nuanced and complex understandings of the process of interpretation, meaning making and change. This second generation of EE was still growing out of the historical roots of EE, not discarding social marketing as a strategy, or individual behaviour change as a goal, or social learning theory as a basis. It sought, however, to bridge this practice, originating in a modernization-oriented diffusionist paradigm of development, with elements from the participatory development paradigm.

It is not until the most recent years that a more fundamental critique of EE has grown to what I, call the third-generation EE, represented by a radical shift in definition of the key type of problem to address and, also, a changed understanding in the notion of entertainment, culture, education and of change. Where the second-generation EE marks a more interdisciplinary and inclusive furthering of the strategies known from the first-generation EE, there is now a growing voice of critique, marking the emergence of a fundamentally different way to approach EE as a communication practice. It is an approach, in line with some of the post-colonial critique of the dominating paradigms of development.

However, before engaging with the most recent third-generation EE, a key innovator in the second generation of EE communication practice should be highlighted. It is the South African NGO [nongovernmental organization] Soul City. Soul City has increasingly used multi-methodological strategies, combining several media, promoting partnerships to civil society and grassroots activities, as well as to formal educations institutions.

Soul City—A Cyclical Communication Strategy

The pioneers of the Soul City project are two medical doctors: Shereen Usdin and Garth Japhet. During the early 1990s, Garth Japhet, executive director of Soul City, worked in clinics among poor groups in the city as well as in the countryside:

> In the early 1990s I worked both in the rural areas of Zululand and in the townships of Soweto and Alexandra in Johannesburg. Here I realized that I, despite my training as a doctor, had no real influence on the basic problems. (Japhet 1999)

Japhet and his colleague, Shereen Usdin, realized the need for health training on completely basic issues such as child care, contraception and AIDS. The overall objective, according to Japhet, was to develop an ongoing vehicle that could promote social change. Seen in retrospective, the media were, from the outset, considered the vehicle whereby information had, and continued to be, made accessible, real and appropriate to the audience. Through formative research, the audiences, from the outset, played a crucial role in the overall message development process and were ultimately the agents of change, deciding themselves how, and if, to use the information provided. As such, Soul City developed an inclusive vehicle where the core agents of change were the audiences, although the unit of change transcended the individual viewers, listeners and readers, being the broad society.

The guiding communication strategy for Soul City is "edutainment," their term for EE. Japhet argues for a "cyclical communication strategy," where a number of inputs are fed into the media vehicle, which then results in a number of outputs. The overall process and the outputs, in particular, are then evaluated, which then serves as a key input into the next phase of the ongoing vehicle (Japhet 1999).

As for inputs, there are two key inputs: (1) *the audience and expert-centred research process*, the formative research, and (2) *the partnerships* established with civil society, government, private sector, international partners and others. In a very participatory process, messages are developed and worked into the creative products, the media narratives, in TV, radio and print. Soul City emphasizes that the model is generic, and that any narrative form can be applied in the media vehicle. It could also be popular theatre, music or any other form of popular cultural narrative. Soul City has had the opportunity to work in prime time, with the mass media, and believes firmly in the efficiency of this. However, the medium could well be another if this opportunity is not possible. The media vehicle results in two key types of output: (1) *the direct output*, being the changes in knowledge, attitude, social norms and intermediate and direct practices, as well as the development of a supportive environment favouring these mentioned changes. (2) The *development of potential opportunities*: These potential opportunities, made possible due to the media intervention, contain a number of interesting opportunities, some of which Soul City has come far in making use of, while others still are being developed further. These include: educational packages, advocacy at both community and national level and, the development and use of their brand name.

Soul City has been active since 1994 and has constantly and closely evaluated the outcomes of the ongoing communication interventions. It lies beyond this article to unfold the findings, except stating that the Soul City EE vehicle has obtained changes and results, both by changing individual behaviour and by influencing more profound social change processes. The heavy emphasis Soul City puts on monitoring and evaluating their communication strategy has

1927
1960
1963
1964
1967
1969
1970
1971
1972
1973
1974
1975
1976
1977
1978
1979
1980
1981
1982
1983
1984
1985
1986
1987
1988
1989
1990
1991
1992
1993
1994
1995
1996
1997
1998
1999
2000
2001
2002
2003
2004
2005
2006

contributed to making them an international show case which has inspired many other EE-focused communication strategies worldwide, such as those, in Latin America (www.soulcity.org.za, Tufte 2001).

Soul City represented a major methodological breakthrough in EE praxis when they initiated their activities in the early 1990s. They spearheaded the effort to bridge traditions of social marketing and health promotion with participatory strategies of involving the audiences in all stages of the communication strategies. The work has internationally been considered a key innovation in the 1990s EE-initiatives, spearheading what I've called the "second generation" of EE-interventions.

Third-Generation EE—Empowerment and Structural Change

In very recent years, a new wave is being seen in the field of EE. These are EE initiatives which, from the outset, have moved beyond the "either diffusion or participation" duality of previous initiatives, conceptually, discursively and in practice, including the way issues are conveyed in the mass media. From a previous focus on correct and, possibly, culture-sensitive messages conveyed via the mass media, the focus is today more on problem identification, social critique and articulation of debate, challenging power relations and advocating social change. There is a stronger recognition of the fact that lack of information is not at the core of the problem, but power imbalance, structural inequality and deeper societal problems. Solutions are sought by strengthening people's "ability to identify" the problems in everyday life, and act—collectively as well as individually—upon them. Empowerment is the keyword of the third-generation EE.

The social and structural inequality lies at the core of the problem, and consequently the EE initiative will advocate for social change—not excluding, but often in addition to, individual behaviour change—in order to find solutions. From a communications perspective, "Communication for Social Change" is emerging as the key concept (www.communicationfor socialchange.org).

The most successful case of using TV fiction for social-change purposes in Latin America is a genuine "home-grown" case from Nicaragua. It is the case of the NGO Puntos de Encuentro (Meeting Points) that has succeeded not only in producing the first Nicaraguan telenovela ever, but also in putting a broad range of social issues on the agenda for large youth populations in Nicaragua. The telenovela is called "El Sexto Sentido" (The Sixth Sense). It contained 36 episodes in the first series, transmitted in 2001 and 26 episodes in the second series, from 2004. Thus, the most innovative pro-social use of telenovelas in Latin America is currently growing in a small country with no tradition for domestic production of telenovelas. "El Sexto Sentido" was a tremendous success—the most popular TV program for the youth audience over all. Significant for this as an example of the third generation of EE is the strong community-based approach. Puntos de Encuentro had a decade-long trajectory in community-based participatory work with women from which the need grew to develop a media vehicle that could provide voice and visibility in pursuit of their social-change objectives.

Learning How: From Marketing and Persuasion to Participation and Liberating Pedagogy

Inherent in the concept of EE is that it is about using entertainment genres for educational purposes. However, what are the notions of education applied in these different EE generations? It does remain an issue of controversy and debate how, and to what degree, media audiences are influenced by what they see and, thus, a controversy to determine "how educational" such strategies end up being. This is reflected in the different approaches that exist within EE, where strategies range from media-borne social-marketing strategies to empowerment strategies such as Augusto Boal's liberating theatre (Boal 1979). Fundamentally, these different approaches are more than mere differences in communication tools. They reflect epistemological differences in how to conceive learning and education, and how to conceive audiences as either passive recipients or active participants in the communication process. They ultimately reflect different aims, objectives and understandings regarding development and change.

The epistemological differences within one or the other EE approach reflect similar differences within the overall field of communication for development. While social marketing strategies traditionally focus on individual behaviour change, there has been a growing concern for the need to develop community-based strategies as a means to involve the audiences or target groups more effectively. Thus, the traditions of participatory communication—known for many decades from the field of grass-root communication, alternative communication and citizen media initiatives—are finding their way into mass-media borne EE strategies. This has led to a resurgence of the Brazilian adult educator Paulo Freire's dialogical pedagogy as a central perspective to "second generation" EE strategies (Freire 1967, 1968). These EE strategies range from Boal's theatre for development strategies, to JHU/PCS [the John Hopkins University/Population Communication Services] more recent strategic thinking that makes at least some initial mention of Freire and his principles of community involvement, dialogue and process-orientation (Figueroa et al 2002).

Paulo Freire himself had no deep understanding of, or interest in, the mass media, as he made plain in an interview that I conducted with him in 1990 (Tufte 1990). His main orientation was to face-to-face communication and small-scale group interaction. However, Freire had a clear understanding of the need to deal with the power structures of society and the need for the marginalized sectors of society to struggle to conquer a space for their critical reflection and dialogue. A previous interview with Freire identified a clear strategic aspect required for "social change communication": the need to conquer space, challenge normative, moral and social borderlines; and to arrange a critical dialogue on pertinent issues as a pathway towards social change (Tufte et al, 1987). Freire's "conscientizacao" (consciousness-raising) could be utilized to

secure community involvement in EE strategies. This pathway, if followed consequently, offers a means through which EE interventions can be connected to the questions of power, inequality and human rights. While used only in a limited manner in the second generation EE, these are the principles guiding the third generation of EE communication practice.

Breaking the Silence: The Forces of Narratives, Emotion and Popular Culture

Having now outlined the brief history of EE and provided some notion of the characteristics of the three main lines of EE communication practices, some reflection is required as to what the main genre in EE, radio and TV soap operas, actually consist of, in terms of content, dramaturgy and other entry points. This will help explain why it has become such an attractive genre in communication for development.

One of the key issues is that the genre connects so very well—in dramaturgical rhythm and in content—with the everyday lives of many people. Thus, the format is very appropriate in order to gain access to large audiences. Secondly, it's a genre, that has a documented ability to articulate debate. People engage, identify and involve themselves strongly with the stories told in radio and TV drama. When this is explored strategically, it could well contain the potential to articulate debate around difficult-to-talk about issues. HIV/AIDS is the case in point. With Freire's thinking increasingly incorporated into the conceptual basis of the second and third generations of EE-communication practice, a conceptual approach has been applied which helps break this widespread silence around HIV/AIDS and, also, the "silence of poverty" experienced in many countries. Jesus Martin-Barbero mentions in his most recent book (2002) the "culture of silence" that characterises large sections of the marginalized segments of (Latin American) societies in their response mechanism to dominating social classes. Martin-Barbero brings this concept forward, originally developed by Paulo Freire (Freire 1967: 111). It is central to understand the need for strategies to break silence. Thus,

1927
1960
1963
1964
1967
1969
1970
1971
1972
1973
1974
1975
1976
1977
1978
1979
1980
1981
1982
1983
1984
1985
1986
1987
1988
1989
1990
1991
1992
1993
1994
1995
1996
1997
1998
1999
2000
2001
2002
2003
2004
2005
2006

it can very well be used in current discussions about HIV/AIDS and the far too widespread silence with which the epidemic is being accepted—by the victims as well as by the populations and opinion leaders of the developed countries.

The "culture of silence" can be explained in the history of some of the peoples (colonialism, the masses not having the strength and opportunity to go up against the root causes of the health problems they are faced with today) that limits the indignation and energized rage with which to demand changes and demand better conditions of life. The result is an internalized acceptance of the "status quo." However, now there are increasing numbers of minority and marginalized voices that—with the electronic media of today—gain access and make their cases visible and their voices heard. They are thus making efficient advocacy communication, articulating a strong, powerful and well-founded process of communication for social change. Although it's not always easy, and many voices also are silenced, what can be documented is the use of Freire's liberating pedagogy in the problem identification and in seeking to understand the mechanisms of the "culture of silence." Freire's liberating pedagogy becomes a communication practice in the development of solutions.

The Force of Fiction

Why then melodrama, why telenovelas, why these genres as the chosen one in entertainment-education strategies? To answer this, we must look closer at what it is this form of narrative offers the audience. Drawing on my own research into Brazilian telenovelas, and recalling the example of "Rei do Gado" which I used in the prologue to this article, there are a series of elements in the narrative construction, and in the relationship between such narratives and their audiences, that make the genre attractive for strategic communication.

The field of tension created in the quotidian mixtures of often dramatic love stories and subtle class conflicts has been, and continues to be, the main recipe stimulating what I have called socio-emotional reactions of

the viewers and, in multiple ways, articulating the cultural and social practices of everyday life among the audience (Tufte 2000). On one hand, the love drama, being central in all telenovelas, enables the identification and engagement. For example, the concern with and responsibility for the family is central. It is present in their identification with the often conflict-oriented relations between parents and children, men and women, brothers and sisters. Values, such as unity, love and mutual understanding, are the ones emphasized, when the women are asked to give résumés of favourite telenovelas and when asked to highlight positive elements. Negative elements present in their discourses pass around issues of disrespect, betrayal and personal ruptures of all sorts, reflecting—along with the positive elements—dimensions of their own social reality and personal experience.

Along with the love story, social mobility of the principal female character is often a central element in the narrative, stimulating identification among low-income women. Most of the women interviewed possessed this ambivalence between dreaming about an easier life, envying the telenovela characters their houses, cars and clothes but, on the other hand, focusing on the positive elements among themselves and their equals.

Despite a clear class discourse in the readings, the physical portraits of the lower social classes in telenovelas tend not to be as physically explicit as in real life. Slums are seldom seen, and worker's boroughs are always built almost beyond recognition, being cleaner, more beautiful and always more plentiful and richer than in real life. Nevertheless, the reader clearly comprehends who the "rich" are and who the "poor" are. So, despite a particular aesthetic that avoids the exposure of social inequality, a social interpretation of the narrative is, for example, clearly perceived in the language the women use about the characters and the narrative in general. All of them use expressions such as: "to rise in life," "up there-down here," "fight to get there," "rise-and-fall," and "ascend and descend." There are many other similar expressions, proverbs saying that "you must not give up," "keep your head up high," "there is a reason for it all," "keep going," etc. These expressions seem to reflect an understanding of the social inequality among the persons of the narrative but the expressions also reflect a reasoning and interpretation whereby social inequality can be explained, although not justified and, secondly, giving room for the hope and aspiration for social change and ascent. The struggle not to give up and to maintain their personal pride despite social misery becomes essential.

It is this fundamental struggle that telenovelas in some way recognize and, "Rei do Gado" is no exception. The poor landless woman, whose shelter is burnt to the ground, happens to get married to the rich landowner, maintaining the hope and aspiration of the audience—some would say the illusion of the audience—for social change and ascent.

However, telenovelas also make visible (Thompson 1995) and consider quotidian problems (and pleasures, I would add) as Brazilian media scholar Carlos Eduardo Lins da Silva at one moment has called them (da Silva 1985: 114), problems that everybody has and fights with in their day-to-day life: relational problems with family and friends, economic problems, personal dramas, etc. Thus, despite portraying a material world often far from the viewers' own lives, the telenovelas strike some everyday experiences which are very recognizable for the viewers, thereby sparking identification and feelings of satisfaction and pleasure, promoting a sense of social and cultural membership, counterbalancing the many processes of sociocultural and political-economic marginalization experienced by many low income citizens in the world.

In addition to the symbolic order of everyday life constructed and reconstructed in these melodramatic narratives they furthermore offer their viewers a sociocultural and often, also, a political framework of reference. Altogether, the social and cultural particularities of the constructed roles and relations in the

narrative are often very recognizable to the audience. These particularities are a product of, and referent to, a particular history, culture, and socioeconomic situation that the whole audience has in common. These processes of identification and recognition with "persons, problems and situations in common" contribute to and generate a common sense of belonging, a sense often being of national belonging (Thompson 1995). Thus, telenovelas emotionally enrich everyday life of the viewers, articulating and reinforcing particular social and cultural practices, thereby contributing to a particular symbolic construct of the country in question and, simultaneously, articulating a feeling of member of national collectivity (Tufte 1998).

Due to their narrative structures and relevant content, telenovelas can promote a high feeling of audience membership, especially into the imagined community of the nation, thereby creating the "cultural connection," a link between the stories told in the telenovela and the viewer's struggles and concerns as citizens in society. It is in this perspective that telenovelas in Latin America and, in similar entertainment and fiction genres in other countries, constantly should be revisited. The social and cultural role of television fiction in everyday life should increasingly be analysed, seeking to understand the significance the audience gives to them and trying to understand how they—along with other cultural rituals of everyday life—visualize issues and struggles of common concern. As was the case with "Rei do Gado," debates were articulated and specific social and political action promoted, thereby contributing to the sustainable development of a democratic society.

Swim in the Cultural Waters

Paulo Freire once said, "You must swim in the cultural waters of the people." I paraphrased him in an article I wrote comparing Freire, Brazil's contemporary adult educator and philosopher, Denmark's historical parallel, N.F.S Grundtvig (Tufte 1987). One of the problems in early forms of EE and, in many of the media-borne campaigns, has been the lack of connection to "the cultural

1927
1960
1963
1964
1967
1969
1970
1971
1972
1973
1974
1975
1976
1977
1978
1979
1980
1981
1982
1983
1984
1985
1986
1987
1988
1989
1990
1991
1992
1993
1994
1995
1996
1997
1998
1999
2000
2001
2002
2003
2004
2005
2006

waters"—and the life experiences—of the people. They did not achieve the cultural connection referred to above as a key feature of successful telenovelas.

Paulo Freire's ideas—developed in the 1950s, 1960s and 1970s—have, in recent years, regained momentum and force, amongst both scholars reflecting upon EE and a growing number of practitioners. Many of the ideas he launched and many of the analyses he conducted about how to articulate processes of **"conscientizacao"** have equal power today. Not least, the fight against HIV/AIDS seems to carry the potential for policy makers, organisations, social movements and ordinary people in their communities to come together and fight against this threat to humankind.

Freire's thoughts are today the epistemological centre of many of the efforts to combat HIV/AIDS, be it in the work of theatre groups where Augusto Boal's Freire-based methodology flourishes these years or large-scale mass media-heavy campaigns, such as the CADRE-run [Centre for AIDS Development, Research and Evaluation] campaign "Tsha-Tsha" in South Africa (Kelly 2002). In the academic writing around EE, Freire's thoughts are coming forth after many years away (Singhal 2004, Tufte 2003a). As Andrew Skuse points out, instead of focusing on behaviour, community dialogue is crucial (Skuse 2003). Even the ideas of theology of liberation from the church movements of Latin America in the 1980s resonate well with the type of social critique which drives this third generation of EE. The problem is not a mere problem of lacking information. The problem has to do with the structural violence in society.

What is characterising the third generation of EE strategies is a conceptual basis that moves beyond integration of diffusionist and participatory approaches. The epistemological drive is a commitment to social change, based on analysis of the structural violence and the unequal power relations and guided by commitments to human rights and social justice. These still emerging third-generation EE strategies are furthermore combined with a strong orientation towards collective action. Puntos de Encuentro with "El Sexto Sentido" is an example of that. EE communication efforts are thus increasingly seen applied to combat HIV/AIDS, poverty, conflict and thus combat what Skuse calls "the immoral of human action" (Tufte 2001, Skuse 2003).

One Strategy—Three Approaches

The growing interest in EE, seen in practice in the cases mentioned above, is confirmed in the theoretical-methodological substantiation of EE as both a theoretical and practical approach to education, development and social change. It can lead one to believe that new strategies are developing to enhance education, development and social change on the basis of competent and active involvement of the people it is about. The development of EE is seen in many elements: the increased recognition of radio and TV drama as expressions of popular culture; the increased publishing on EE; the institutionalisation of the field as seen with the global EE conferences (1989, 1997, 2000, 2004); in PCI's [Population Communication International] yearly "Soap Summit"; and in the curricular development represented in the growing number of courses offered in EE. Finally, the epistemological, theoretical and methodological diversification of EE is, not least, seen in the work of the new generation of EE scholars, which is characterized by both the critical and fundamental rethinking of EE based on the third generation conceptual basis, as well as bringing EE into new fields of practices as is, for example, conflict resolution and environmental protection.

Applying EE in accordance with post-colonial, alternative, citizen-oriented and, often, grassroots-driven development theory and practice is, as I see it, an appreciation of new languages and formats in liberating pedagogy. At the level of communication practices for social change, it is a recognition of the need to move beyond information-driven solutions and towards communication-driven solutions, beyond "logos" alone to "mythos" as well; that is beyond reason and towards emotion, not in an either-or dualism, but in

Entertainment-Education	1st Generation	2nd Generation	3rd Generation
Definition of Problem	Lack of Information	Lack of Information and Skills Inappropriate Contexts Structural Inequalities	Structural Inequalities Power Relations Social Conflict
Notion of Entertainment	Instrument: Tool for Message Conveying	Dynamic Genre: Tool for Change	Process: Popular Culture Genre as Form of Expression
Notion of Culture	Culture as Barrier	Culture as Ally	Culture as "Way of Life"
Notion of Catalyst	External Change Agent Targeting X	External Catalyst in Partnership with Community	Internal Community Member
Notion of Education	Banking Pedagogy Persuasion	Life Skills, Didactics	Liberating Pedagogy
Notion of Audience	Segments Target Groups Passive	Participants Target Groups Active	Citizens Active
What Is Communicated?	Messages	Messages and Situations	Social Issues and Problems
Notion of Change	Individual Behaviour Social Norms	Individual Behaviour Social Norms Structural Conditions	Individual Behaviour Social Norms Power Relations Structural Conditions
Expected Outcome	Change in Norms and Individual Behaviour Numerical Result	Change in Norms and Individual Behaviour Public and Private Debate	Articulation of Social and Political Process Structural Change Collective Action
Duration of Intervention	Short-Term	Short- and Long-Term	Short- and Long- Term

Figure 1: (De-) Constructing the Field of Entertainment-Education

integrated strategies where learning and awareness-raising are not just about conveying information but about involving people in changing society.

Concerns about citizenship and human rights are at the core of this matter, and when it comes to the use of radio and TV drama in EE strategies, it is also about exercising and recognizing the "cultural citizenship" of the audiences (Tufte 2000, chapter 10). EE—as an educational strategy, in the language used, content focus and notion of audience involvement as manifested in the third generation EE—is treading new ground as a strategy of "conscientizacao" that moves beyond marketing, towards empowerment, and is more in sync with the mediated and globalised world of today.

Thus, to wrap up, let me try and visualize how I see the communication practices of entertainment-education consolidate into what I have explained in this

1927
1960
1963
1964
1967
1969
1970
1971
1972
1973
1974
1975
1976
1977
1978
1979
1980
1981
1982
1983
1984
1985
1986
1987
1988
1989
1990
1991
1992
1993
1994
1995
1996
1997
1998
1999
2000
2001
2002
2003
2004
2005
2006

article as three different approaches: I call them three generations of EE because of the chronology of the development—the first generation emerging in the 1970s, the second generation emerging in the 1990s and, now, the third generation gaining voice and conceptual basis in the contemporary debate about communication for development. The first-generation EE, having existed for so long is, in many critiques of EE, the key object of criticism (Waisbord 2001, Morris 2003 and in this volume). However, some of the voices critical to EE begin now to connect the growing use of EE with the rehabilitation of popular culture as a source of power and change in everyday life (Martin-Barbero 1993, 2002), exploring the options to formulate critical, post-colonial, post-development (Escobar 1995) social-change-oriented uses of EE. This approach represents another thinking about development and change, despite drawing on the same genres as in the first and second generation EE. Figure 1 highlights—with the risk of simplification—the key differences.

The definition of the key problem is focused on structural inequalities more than on lacking a specific piece of information. This reflects that the notion of change differs—the first generation focusing on changing the behaviour and norms of individuals, while the third generation is oriented towards also addressing the underlying causes influencing and determining individual behaviour. The notion of how to catalyse a change process differs from it being seen as an externally driven change agent that targets a specific audience (first generation) to the third-generation EE understanding the change process as something catalysed from within, by the community itself, or by members of the community.

Finally, it is important to highlight the different notions of education or learning. Drawing on Freire's distinctions between the depositing of information—the "banking pedagogy" of education—and the empowering process of learning through "naming the world" in a dialectic process of action-reflection-action—the

"liberating pedagogy"—a clear parallel can be drawn to the approaches of the first- and third-generation EE. The first-generation EE seeks to convey messages and transfer information through mass media in what is like the principles of banking pedagogy. The third generation seeks to articulate a dialectic process of debate and collective action centred around social issues, conflicts, inequalities and power imbalances in societies. This is in line with the principles of Freire's liberating pedagogy.

…What I fundamentally argue is that EE is not just one communication strategy. It can be many different approaches that all have in common the use of entertainment as a communicative practice crafted to strategically communicate about development issues in a manner and, with a purpose, that can range from the more narrowly defined social marketing of individual behaviours to the liberating and citizen-driven articulation of social change agendas. At this stage, generation one and two have revealed some of the communicative potentials of using entertainment, be it storytelling, drama or music. However, in the rethinking of how to use communication for development, a rethinking of development—as reflected in post-colonial and late-modern thought as Escobar (1995), Appadurai (1996), Baumann (1998, 2003) and many others—can potentially shape a very strong epistemological basis for entertainment-education communication practice based on diversity in voice, human rights and cultural citizenship.

References

Appadurai, Arjun. *Modernity at Large. Cultural Dimensions of Globalisation.* London and Minnesota: University of Minnesota Press, 1996.

Bandura, A. *Social Learning Theory.* Englewoods Cliffs, N.J.: Prentice-Hall, 1977.

Baumann, Zygmunt. *Globalisation.* London: Routledge, 1998.

Baumann, Zygmunt. *Liquid Love.* Cambridge, England: Polity, 2003.

Biagioli, Chiara. *L'Uso Della Comunicazione Per lo Sviluppo Umano: Il Caso Soul City.* Perugia, Italy: Università per Stranieri di Perugia, 2004.

Boal, Augusto. *The Theater of the Oppressed.* New York: Theater Communications Group, Inc., 1979.

Bouman, Martine. *Collaboration for Pro-Social Change: The Turtle and the Peacock. The Entertainment-Education Strategy on Television.* Netherlands: Thesis Wageningen Agricultural University, 1999.

Cody, M., A. Singhal, M. Sabido, and E. Rogers, eds. *Entertainment-Education Worldwide: History, Research and Practice.* New York: Lawrence Erlbaum Associates, 2004.

Da Silva, C. E. Lins. *Muito Alem do Jardim Botánico: Um Estudo Sobre a Audiencia do Journal Nacional da Globo Entre Trabalhadores.* São Paulo, Brazil: Summus Editorial, 1985.

Escobar, A. *Encountering Development. The Making and Unmaking of the Third World.* Princeton, N.J.: Princeton University Press, 1995.

Figueroa, M. E., L. Kincaid, M. Rani, and G. Lewis, eds. *Guidelines for the Measurement of Process and Outcome of Social Change Interventions.* Baltimore, Md.: CCP/JHU, 2002. Prepared for the Rockefeller Foundation.

Fraser, C., and S. Restrepo-Estrada. *Communicating for Development: Human Change for Survival.* London and New York: I. B.Taurus Publishers, 1998.

Freire, Paulo. *La Educación Como Práctica de la Libertad.* Caracas, Venezuela: Nuevo Orden, 1967.

Freire, Paulo. *Pedagogy of the Oppressed.* New York: Seabury Press, 1968.

Fuenzalida, V. "Expectativas Educativas de las Audiencias Televisivas," *Colección Enciclopedia Latinoamericana de Sociocultura y Comunicación.* Bogotá, Colombia: Editorial Norma, 2005.

Gao, Melissa Yun. "Participatory Communication Research and HIV/AIDS Control: A Study among Gay Men and MSM in Chengdu, China." Unpublished Ph.D. thesis. Australia: University of Newcastle, 2005.

Japhet, Garth. *Edutainment. How to Make Edutainment Work for You: A Step by Step Guide to Designing and Managing an Edutainment Project for Social Development.* Johannesburg, South Africa: Soul City, 1999.

Kelly, Kevin. Personal conversation. Grahamstown, South Africa: October 2002.

Martin-Barbero, J. *Communication, Culture and Hegemony. From Media to Mediations.* London: Sage, 1993.

Martin-Barbero, J. *La Educación Desde la Comunicación.* Buenos Aires, Argentina: Grupo Editorial Norma, 2002.

Morris, N. "A Comparative Analysis of Diffusion and Participatory Models in Development Communication," *Journal of Communication Theory,* 2003.

Parker, Warren. "Ideology, Hegemony and HIV/AIDS: The Appropriation of Indigenous and Global Spheres," Unpublished Ph.D. thesis. South Africa: University of KwaZulu-Natal, 2005.

Sherry, John L. "Pro-Social Soap Operas for Development: A Review of Research and Theory," In *Communication and Development: Beyond Panaceas.* The Journal of International Communication, Special Issue, December 1997, 4, 2: 75-102.

Singhal, A. "Entertainment-Education Through Participatory Theatre: Freirean Strategies for Empowering the Oppressed," in M. Cody, A. Singhal, M. Sabido and E. Rogers, eds., *Entertainment-Education Worldwide: History, Research and Practice.* New York: Lawrence Erlbaum Associates, 2003.

Singhal, A., and E. Rogers. "A Theoretical Agenda for Entertainment-Education," Communication Theory, 2002, 12, 2: 117-135.

Singhal, A., and E. Rogers. *Entertainment-Education. A Communication Strategy for Social Change.* New York: Lawrence Erlbaum, 1999.

Skeie, Silje Sjøvaag. "Learning Through Entertainment. A Study of the Usage of the Entertainment-Education Strategy Among Ethnic Minorities in Vietnam," Master's thesis, Faculty of Education, Institute for Educational Research. Oslo, Norway: University of Oslo, 2003.

Skeie, Silje Sjøvaag. "Narratives for Peace—Using Entertainment-Education in the Promotion of a Culture of Peace," *Transformator* (tidsskrift for fredsforskning, 3, årgang, 2/2004). Oslo, Norway: Proion, 2005, 63-81.

Skuse, Andrew. "Communication, Education and HIV/AIDS. A Guidance Note," Prepared for the U.K. Department for International Development, 2003: 38 pages.

Thompson, John. B. *The Media and Modernity. A Social Theory of the Media.* Cambridge, England: Polity Press 1995.

Tufte, Thomas. Unpublished interview with Paulo Freire. São Paulo, Brazil: November 1990.

Tufte, Thomas. "Television Fiction, National Identity and Democracy—The Role of National Television Fiction in Modern Societies," in I. Durousseau, ed., *Réception de la Télévision.* Copenhagen, Denmark: L'Institut Français, 1998.

Tufte, Thomas. *Living with the Rubbish Queen. Telenovelas, Culture and Modernity in Brazil.* Luton, England: University of Luton Press, 2000.

Tufte, T. "Entertainment-Education and Participation—Assessing the Communication Strategy of Soul City," in *Journal of International Communication.* Sydney, Australia: IAMCR/Macquarie University, 2001, Vol. 7, No. 2, 25-51.

Tufte, T. "Soap Operas and Sense-Making: Mediations and Audience Ethnography," in M. Cody, A. Singhal, M. Sabido, and E. Rogers, eds., *Entertainment-Education Worldwide: History, Research and Practice.* New York: Lawrence Erlbaum Associates, 2003a.

Tufte, T. "Edutainment in HIV/AIDS Prevention. Building on the Soul City Experience in South Africa," in Jan Servaes, ed., *Approaches to Development. Studies on Communication for Development.* Paris: UNESCO (Communication Development Division), 2003b.

Tufte, T. "HIV/AIDS, Globalisation and Ontological Insecurity—Key Communication Challenges in HIV/AIDS Prevention," Paper Presented at the 11th FELAFACS Conference. Puerto Rico, October 4-8, 2003: 2003c.

Tufte, T., et al. Unpublished interview with Paulo Freire. São Paulo, Brazil: April 1987.

Waisbord, S. "Family Tree of Theories, Methodologies and Strategies in Development Communication: Convergences and Differences," Prepared for Rockefeller Foundation, 2001.

www.soulcity.za

Tufte, Thomas. "Entertainment-Education in Development Communication: Between Marketing Behaviors and Empowering People," chapter nine of Hemer, Oscar and Thomas Tufte, *Media and Glocal Change—Rethinking Communication for Social Change.* Buenos Aires: Clasco; and Götenora, Suleden: Ordicum, 2005. Reprinted with permission of the author and publisher.

1927
1960
1963
1964
1967
1969
1970
1971
1972
1973
1974
1975
1976
1977
1978
1979
1980
1981
1982
1983
1984
1985
1986
1987
1988
1989
1990
1991
1992
1993
1994
1995
1996
1997
1998
1999
2000
2001
2002
2003
2004
2005
2006

VOLUME 2 Popular Culture, Narrative and Identity   **701**

POPULAR-CULTURE DISCOURSE AND DEVELOPMENT: RETHINKING ENTERTAINMENT-EDUCATION FROM A PARTICIPATORY PERSPECTIVE

By J. Douglas Storey

1999 The literature on development communication is replete with compelling arguments against positivist communication. Many of these critiques portray mass media and planned communication as forms of monologue by resource-rich, politically and economically advantaged forces in society aimed at managing the trajectory of social change. Although it is true that top-down communication has been the dominant mode historically, emerging theories of popular culture and discourse—although rarely applied in the development context—suggest that the relationships among media, audiences, and social change need to be re-examined and the uses of communication for development reevaluated. In short, cultural studies and discourse theory suggest that even the most authoritatively managed communication systems are more participatory than previously conceptualized.

Entertainment-education, the use of popular forms of entertainment such as radio and television drama, popular theater, and popular music as vehicles for information, role modeling, and behavioral appeals in social change programs, is a case in point. Entertainment-education has traditionally been informed by social-scientific theories of communication and behavior change aimed at predicting and maximizing specific behavioral responses desired by program designers. Although some "enter-educate" projects employ grassroots media to foster community activism (Conquergood 1988), the majority are high profile mass-media productions with explicit attitude and behavior-change objectives defined by donor and implementing agencies, with little apparent participation by intended beneficiaries. Popular "participation" in such projects typically takes the form of audience research during the message design phase and fan mail sent to the broadcast station.

Yet, theories of popular culture and discourse suggest that entertainment-education may have a participatory dimension despite its instrumental and positivist origins. Popular culture, the domain within which entertainment-education operates by definition, is highly involving, emotionally engaging, continually evolving and inherently participatory. By attempting to operate within the sphere of popular culture, development communication—in the form of entertainment-education—becomes subject to the free play of popular discourse that reworks it in ways its producers may never have imagined. Accommodating both social science and popular-culture perspectives in the practice of development communication is possible, but will require some changes in the way we think about media, audiences, and the goals and effects of development communication.

The objectives of this article are to explore some of the opportunities presented by recent scholarship on popular culture and discourse—particularly the work of Mikhail Bakhtin—for theorizing about participatory communication, and to indicate with examples how a discourse perspective enriches analysis of entertainment-education as a form of development communication, while highlighting its participatory aspects. The discussion is illustrated with examples drawn primarily from reproductive health programs, a discursively rich domain of applied development communication, which has used entertainment-education in a variety of ways.

Popular Culture

Fiske (1994, 135) described popular culture as follows:

> Culture is the social circulation of meanings, pleasures and values, and the cultural order that results is inextricably connected with the social

order within which it circulates. Culture may secure the social order and help to hold it in place or it may destabilize it and work toward changing it, but is never either neutral or detached. The social circulation of meanings is always a maelstrom, full of conflicting currents, whirlpools, and eddies.

The interplay of commercial, political, public and individual forces generates the messages and meanings of popular culture. Public consumption of media content; individual-level feedback in the form of discussion within families and among friends; purchase and use of advertised or modeled products; and adoption or rejection of modeled behaviors; policy statements and legislation pertaining to media and public issues appearing in the media; and commercial and public service activities and investments of media organizations are all forms of pop-cultural activity. Under the rubric described by Fiske, these are all aspects of popular culture, which is, first and foremost, a *communication* phenomenon.

Theoretical approaches to popular culture had been, until the mid to late 1980s, heavily influenced by structural-materialist critiques of media institutions and mass culture that tended to paint a picture of hegemonic media manipulating a compliant audience. More recent scholarship strikes a better balance of power by recognizing that audience members actively interpret and use media content according to their own sensibilities and purposes. The interpretive acts of the audience are not completely independent of the institutional forces that shape media content and influence media behavior, but neither do media institutions operate independently of audience agendas, tastes and needs, on which the media must depend to generate interest for its programming. From this perspective, popular culture must be seen as a form of discourse or, more accurately, as a discursive system (see section on discourse).

Audience studies of the type just described provide many examples of rich multidisciplinary theorizing and research about popular culture (Ang 1991; Fiske 1994; Katz & Liebes 1987; Livingstone 1990; Morley 1993; Rosengren 1993). Audience studies like these bring together elements of the effects tradition (which typically focuses on the attitudinal and behavioral impact of messages on individuals) with the reception tradition (which typically focuses on the interpretation of texts by audiences). From this convergence emerge theories of the relationship between audiences/readers/viewers and texts/media. Within this new synthesis, mass communication is seen as an ongoing, sociocultural, and historical process, rather than as a series of discrete broadcast activities or message events. From this perspective, the communication process involves an array of interrelated elements: individuals, the communities in which they live, the social structures and institutions such as media systems that interpenetrate lives and communities, and the messages or texts generated by the various social actors. None of these elements can be studied in isolation from the others. All of these elements are posited to affect and be effected by each other through public discourse.

Discourse

The contemporary notion of discourse owes much to the work of the Russian literary theorist Mikhail Bakhtin (1895–1975). Bakhtin has become known gradually to communication theorists (far less so to communication practitioners, except novelists) through a growing number of translations of his work on a theory of the novel—his views of authorship/readership/text as a social phenomenon, in particular—and through interpretation of his work by cultural studies theorists who apply it to the analysis of media systems, media texts and audiences. His work is voluminous and complex, and an extended discussion of his theory is far beyond the scope of this article. However, certain concepts from Bakhtin and his interpreters can be introduced here to indicate how they might inform perspectives on participation and popular culture.

For Bakhtin, *dialogue is* the process by which an *utterance* (defined broadly to include speech acts

1927
1960
1963
1964
1967
1969
1970
1971
1972
1973
1974
1975
1976
1977
1978
1979
1980
1981
1982
1983
1984
1985
1986
1987
1988
1989
1990
1991
1992
1993
1994
1995
1996
1997
1998
1999
2000
2001
2002
2003
2004
2005
2006

as well as words, messages, images, texts) interacts with the greater social and ideological whole. An utterance, having taken meaning and shape at a particular historical moment in a socially specific environment, cannot fail to brush up against thousands of living dialogic threads, woven by socio-ideological consciousness around the given object of the utterance; it cannot fail to become an active participant in social dialogue. After all, the utterance arises out of this dialogue as a continuation of it and as a rejoinder to it. It does not approach the object from the sidelines (Bakhtin 1981, 277).

The pre-existence of a *language world* from which the utterance emerges ensures that the utterance will be "relativized," or juxtaposed against other competing definitions for the same things. Furthermore, the language world is *heteroglot:* It encompasses multiple languages, each of which is informed by histories of experience and socio-ideological contradiction that predate and will survive any particular users of the language. Language, as a "matrix of forces practically impossible to recoup and therefore impossible to resolve" (Bakhtin 1981, 428), causes every word, message and image to be constantly reworked through dialogue.

According to Bakhtin (Morson & Emerson 1990), dialogue is an open-ended, undominated, unfinalizable web of communicative, i.e., symbolic interaction. As Bakhtin used the term, dialogue cannot be trivialized as "mere" interaction or conversation between individuals. People (as well as social groups and social institutions) are not regarded as bounded selves or entities except in a physical sense. The historical reality of each entity is better regarded as a "cultural field" of richly intersecting temporalities and identities. People cannot be said to "enter into" dialogue because existence cannot be separated from the ongoing process of communication (Morson & Emerson 1990). Dialogue involves "the constant redefinition of its participants, develops and creates numerous potentials in each of them separately and

between them interactively and dialogically" (Morson & Emerson 1990, 52).

Bakhtin's image of the novel as an open system of interacting meanings is evocative. As his work became more widely available, cultural studies scholars were quick to pick up on its implications for the study of media systems and media "texts." Newcomb (1984) argued that dialogue can be seen among audiences, community formations, governmental bodies, and media, with each entity generating texts, e.g., conversations, behavioral norms, policy statements, program offerings, social activities, value assertions, and so on, that reveal the unfinished and unfinishable nature of social change.

However, following Hall, et al. (1980) and Morley (1980), cultural studies scholars have preferred to use the term *discourse* rather than *dialogue* to avoid some of the latter term's associations with speech and rhetorical studies. For Bakhtin, discourse had a narrower sense (meaning forms of speech—literally, "word"—including mediated and direct or unmediated, passive and active, unidirectional and varidirectional, Morson & Emerson 1990) than dialogue (meaning the process of interaction), whereas cultural studies tends to inscribe *discourse* with the broader Bakhtinian sense of *dialogue.*

For example, in his book on audience interpretation of a popular British television show, Morley (1980) referred to the locus of *dialogue* as a *discourse system,* by which he meant the system of interactions among readers (audience members), texts (words, images, utterances), and social forms (media systems, a circle of friends, one's workplace, the commercial market) of which both readers/audiences and texts are parts. A discursive system is defined "by reference to the area of social experience that it makes sense of, to the social location from which that sense is made, and to the linguistic or signifying systems by which that sense is both made and circulated" (Fiske 1987; Morley 1993; Newcomb 1984). From this perspective, mass communication begins to take on a new, more interactive, or participatory, character.

If discourse is, by definition, uncontained (Newcomb 1984), it is not, therefore, amenable to manipulation. Domination of discourse, such as occurs in persuasive attempts by authoritative media, involves the creation of boundaries or limits ("Buy this!" [Not that.] "Vote for me!" [Not for her]). To try to create such boundaries in discourse is to deny discursive opportunities. It is in the nature of discourse that when powerful voices, e.g., government media attempt to dominate, either the discourse shifts to other sites or the attempt at domination itself becomes a subject of discourse and is deconstructed and defused (Hall, et al. 1980).

Discourse informs all its participants; therefore, it is antithetical to suppose that only some participants inform the others. To achieve discourse in development communication, then, all parties to the communication must be committed to engaging (rather than dominating) each other. Popular culture (and entertainment-education as a form of popular culture) may be the ideal venue for this engagement, because it is largely beyond the control of any particular party and is the site of ongoing construction, deconstruction and reconstruction of social realities.

Entertainment-Education

The use of entertainment-education (or enter-educate) strategies to foster social change is gaining recognition as a viable option for health promotion, and applications of these strategies are growing increasingly sophisticated. Among many cases that could be cited, Piotrow, et al. (1990) reported successful uses of entertainment-education media for family-planning promotion in Africa; Singhal and Rogers (1989) documented the success of Indian soap operas at conveying family-planning themes; popular music has been used successfully to promote teenage sexual responsibility in Mexico (Coleman 1988) and in the Philippines (Rimon, et al., 1994); and Lozare, et al. (1993) reported increases in positive attitudes toward and adoption of family planning among viewers of a prosocial television drama in Pakistan.

Analyses of entertainment-education programs (Kincaid, 1993; Kincaid et al. 1988) indicate that this approach maximizes audience attention, message appeal, and message recall by using strong emotional appeals, humor, music and attractive—even sexy—role models to attract and hold an audience. Interpersonal communication, particularly between spouses, is another documented effect of entertainment-education. Interspousal communication, in turn, leads to health-clinic attendance and contraceptive adoption (Lozare, et al. 1993). Note that all of these processes and effects are of the short-term, individual-level variety. Longer-term effects are sometimes sought as well, but for the most part are also individual-level effects, e.g., confirmation of behavioral decisions and/or behavioral reinforcement.

In contrast, McAnany and Potter (1993), based on a review and reanalysis of Brazilian data, assumed an historical perspective to argue that mass communication—television soap operas, in particular—may have long-term demographic consequences by virtue of their cumulative effects on communication processes within the family and community and on social values over time. Short-term individual-level behavior change may in turn result from shifts in social values at the family level. These propositions are supported by evidence from cultivation research (Gerbner, 1973; Gerbner et al. 1980) that perceived social reality is affected by long-term exposure to the ubiquitous symbolic environment of mass media. Still, the processes by which such effects occur are little understood.

A short-term perspective results, at least in part, from the theoretical frameworks that are used to study and design entertainment-education programs. For example, message learning and persuasion perspectives (see McGuire 1987 and Petty & Cacciopo 1981 for reviews of this literature) tend to focus on messages as discrete packages of information which audiences quickly apprehend, evaluate, and respond to. Another common framework for analyzing persuasive communications programs is social learning theory.

1927
1960
1963
1964
1967
1969
1970
1971
1972
1973
1974
1975
1976
1977
1978
1979
1980
1981
1982
1983
1984
1985
1986
1987
1988
1989
1990
1991
1992
1993
1994
1995
1996
1997
1998
1999
2000
2001
2002
2003
2004
2005
2006

Social learning suggests that people learn new behaviors by observing how role models (either fictional or real) behave and what consequences occur (Bandura 1986). Classical formulations of social learning theory indicate that role models must clearly act out the steps or components of a given behavior. Only if a behavior is clearly and unambiguously modeled can a viewer learn the steps, rehearse them mentally, attempt to reproduce them, and observe whether the consequences he or she experiences match those experienced by the role model. As far as the learning process is concerned, the theory describes a largely rational process involving a linear and fairly predictable sequence of causes (enacted behaviors) and effects (consequences, good and/or bad).

Often paired in practice with social learning theory is value-expectancy theory (Fishbein & Ajzen 1980), which posits that behavioral intentions are affected by one's beliefs and attitudes toward a behavior and its consequences. These beliefs and attitudes include beliefs about and evaluations of social support for the behavior in question. Social drama or other entertainment-education formats can be used to influence perceptions of social support for a behavior and to change evaluations or expectations of the consequences of that behavior.

Although these frameworks help explain individual-level change in knowledge, attitudes, and behaviors, they do not adequately capture either the richness and complexity of entertainment-education or its potential for long-term change; neither do they deal very well with the volatility of meaning and the sense-making process engaged in by audiences who are exposed to and use entertainment-education material. For example, social dramas (especially lengthier ones that develop a narrative plot over weeks or months) cannot be single-mindedly didactic; otherwise, they lose the aesthetic, dramatic, entertaining qualities that make them interesting to audiences in the first place. Consequently, in dramas that work as entertainment, the prosocial messages are embedded in the larger structure of the narrative and may not be so easily recognized as discrete message units or appeals. Behaviors appear in context, motives are imputed, not all conflicts are neatly resolved, as in life itself. Furthermore, individuals and communities of viewers bring diverse interpretive frames to their viewing; this leads to a wide range of interpretations and uses of the already richly layered and nuanced symbolic content. So far, research and theory about entertainment and education have not dealt very effectively with how audiences identify, interpret, and use narratively structured information, or how entertainment-education operates within the larger social, cultural, and historical context of media systems and audiences.

In contrast, theories of communication that draw on semiotics (see Hawkes 1977 for a comprehensive review) and cultural studies (Foucault 1980) emphasize that messages derive much of their meaning from context and use (Fiske 1987, 1994; Newcomb 1984): Any given message has meaning *in relation to* the larger text in which it is located, the historical characteristics of the message vehicle or medium, and the experiences and social situation of receivers as they engage with symbolic material. Individuals impose shades of meaning on messages they apprehend, influenced by past experiences and present sociocultural conditions. These meanings are often socially constructed; that is, an individual makes sense of something he or she has seen or heard through subsequent interaction with others and in relation to personal history and social experience. Furthermore, the meaning that an individual derives from a message must be seen as volatile because new information or experiences will result in revised meaning. Theoretical development in entertainment-education has so far dealt very little with the issue of meaning.

Nor has there been much theoretical elaboration of the organizational and institutional aspects of entertainment—education; that is, how it operates in relation to existing media and other sociopolitical institutions. With the exception of a few studies (Singhal et al. 1994; Faria & Potter 1994), these aspects have been largely overlooked. One institutional effect of entertainment-education that has been studied is increased support for health-promotion programs in the form of political support, financing, and advocacy by opinion leaders and other influentials (Piotrow & Coleman 1992). For example, entertainment-education programs often garner support for health-promotion programs from commercial and political quarters because they are perceived to be (a) profitable—through corporate tie-ins and product endorsements; (b) cost effective—through cost sharing, through resale to commercial broadcasters and video outlets, and because of the size of the audience generated; and (c) *highly* visible—making them a politically attractive, high-profile component of a national health program.

Yet, even advocacy is underdeveloped theoretically, in part because the frameworks commonly used in entertainment-education research and practice, however insightful they are regarding individual-level psychological and behavior changes, are insufficiently elaborated regarding the larger political, cultural, and historical context of communication. Policy activity and decision making at an institutional level, and the interactions among political, economic, and cultural institutions are not typically viewed as communication phenomena. Not that the broader context has gone completely unacknowledged. Kincaid (1993, 5) noted that "[The entertainment-education approach] has the capacity to influence culture because it becomes part of a country's own popular culture (not an outside influence), competing with other sources of culture for attention and influence."

Entertainment-education, dealing as it does with popular culture, needs to be analyzed within a broader framework, provided by elements of popular culture and discourse theories.

Synthesis: Popular Culture, Discourse, and Entertainment-Education

The marriage of social-scientific and cultural-studies perspectives is in some ways an uneasy match,

not least because of the historical antipathy between critical cultural studies and positivist social-scientific theories and methods. To make this marriage work, the theories and practices need to be reevaluated in two important ways.

SYSTEMATICITY

One change will have to be an epistemic shift in the way the task is conceptualized. Fiske (1994, 195) argued that:

> Systemic theories of structure go further than do positivist ones, for systemic structures such as language are generative, whereas positivist structures are descriptive. Systemic structures generate the practices by which they are used and are, in their turn, modified by those practices. Positivist structures, however, have effects, not practices, and the relationship between structure and effect is one-way.

To illustrate this distinction in the context of mass communication, Fiske (1994) also said that television programs, the industry that makes them, and the people who watch them are all active agents in the circulation of meanings, and the relationships among them are not ones of cause and effect, in which one precedes the other, but of systematicity... . The relationships... are systemic ones of a complex of reciprocities in which contradictions and complicities struggle to gain ground over one another. (p. 196)

Yet, even projects with antipositivist goals often do seek to "intervene;" for example, to facilitate participation, to empower communities, and to conscienticize citizens as a first step toward democratic engagement. From this perspective, development communication becomes a partnership of media institutions, development agencies, donor organizations, and the audience, all of whom desire to improve the public welfare. Of course, single-minded devotion to public welfare rarely occurs. Institutions in the partnership have their own economic, political, and social priorities all of which contend discursively with

1927
1960
1963
1964
1967
1969
1970
1971
1972
1973
1974
1975
1976
1977
1978
1979
1980
1981
1982
1983
1984
1985
1986
1987
1988
1989
1990
1991
1992
1993
1994
1995
1996
1997
1998
1999
2000
2001
2002
2003
2004
2005
2006

each other and with public welfare to shape and color the goals and strategies of entertainment-education. To the extent that these contending priorities can be kept in the open, development communication programs can serve as sites of discourse. Bakhtin suggested that this is unavoidable, particularly when the format engages popular culture, as in entertainment-education programs.

PARTICIPATION

A second change, which goes to the core issue of this article, is in the way the communicator–audience relationship is conceptualized. Popular culture is not something one can readily manipulate, even with concerted effort. Instead, popular culture is something in which one can participate. This suggests a need to adopt a participatory mentality among those who would tap popular culture as a vehicle for development or social-change programs. For example, the aim of much communication in the area of reproductive health is to expand discourse (we usually speak of increasing spousal or client–provider interaction, but expanding discourse is the underlying goal) in order to open up the possibilities women and men have to control their own fertility and reproductive health. This communication takes place in the larger context of cultural imperatives and historical traditions of reproductive rights and gender relations, such as within the ethnic and nationalist politics of newly independent states, in which family size becomes an expression of awakened ethnic pride.

Campaign theory and research (Rogers & Storey 1987) tell us to select the channel or medium that is the most appropriate vehicle of the message for the audience we wish to reach. Although we usually take advantage of the visual or auditory power of television or radio to command attention, raise interest, or maximize involvement, we have yet to take advantage of the power of media as open, participatory, discursive systems. One of the most powerful effects of development communication that uses the entertainment-education approach may be the creation of discursive

space for the discussion of health and development issues. Within such a strategy, the effect of discourse is more discourse.

An added benefit of conceptualizing entertainment-education as a participatory, discursive process is that the discourse of popular culture is ongoing; that is, it is inherently—in fact, unavoidably—sustainable. The cultural-discourse perspective outlined here suggests that sustained public communication about health and development issues already exists, and that entertainment-education must merge with or participate in that discourse, rather than intervene into and change that discourse. Especially useful may be longer, serial forms of entertainment-education (television soap opera, talk radio, weekly public-affairs programming) that present more open and fluid discursive opportunities and that have the potential for interaction with audience members over time. A popular serial could become a major and ongoing part of development discourse.

Examples

Presented here are two brief examples of reproductive-health programs that used entertainment-education formats and that interpret aspects of them from the perspective of discourse and popular culture previously outlined.

Reproductive health itself is a discursively rich area of development. In the late 1950s and early 1960s, this field focused mainly on family planning and the promotion of contraceptive use as a way to reduce population pressure and to avoid food shortages. As population programs have matured, they have incorporated a wider range of interrelated issues, including child survival, maternal health, environmental quality, sexually transmitted disease and gender relationships. The International Conference on Population and Development, held in Cairo in 1994, and the Fourth United Nations World Conference on Women, held in Beijing in 1995, fostered this expanded view of reproductive health. Both conferences tried, not without controversy, to position population programs away from the narrow technological perspectives on fertility control toward broader, integrated perspectives on population growth, poverty and patterns of consumption and production as they relate to comprehensive reproductive health, reproductive rights, and the status of women and children (Garcia-Moreno & Turmen 1995). Two enter-educate projects that reflect expanded perspectives on reproductive health are the Reproductive Health Drama Project in Pakistan and the *Alang-Alang* Project in Indonesia.[1]

PAKISTAN: DISCOURSE BEGINS AT HOME

An important discursive system in its own right is spousal interaction. In health-promotion programs, the degree of interaction between husband and wife is often associated with increased health knowledge and behavior change. Especially in the area of reproductive health, husbands and wives influence each other's contraceptive behaviors (sometimes positively, sometimes negatively), so understanding the nature of this process is crucial to the study of community and family health. At the same time, interpersonal interaction is an important site of inquiry into the communication process itself. This was the focus of a series of social dramas in Pakistan supported by Johns Hopkins University/Population Communication Services (JHU/PCS) in the early 1990s.

Prior to 1990, population communication efforts in Pakistan had been limited to spot advertising campaigns promoting the small-family norm. Such indirect approaches (no explicit reference to contraception was made) were considered necessary to avoid provoking conservative religious opposition. Yet, research indicated strong latent demand for contraception. According to the Pakistan Contraceptive Prevalence Survey of 1986, 35 percent of non-using couples of reproductive age favored spacing births, whereas another 23 percent favored limiting births.

1 Both projects were funded by the United States Agency for International Development (USAID) under Cooperative Agreement DPE-3052-A-00-0014-00 with Johns Hopkins University Center for Communication Programs.

Additional research by the National Institute of Population Studies indicated that, for 63 percent of women, the spouse was the most important motivator of contraceptive adoption. Finally, a series of individual case studies revealed that the woman was most often the one to obtain family planning supplies, but her action had to be sanctioned by her husband. Many women reported fear of their husband's disapproval but lacked the skills to negotiate successfully for approval.

Between May 1990 and October 1993, the national broadcasting authority, Pakistan Television (PTV), produced and aired three television sociodramas on reproductive health. *Aahat* (An Approaching Sound) aired from October to November 1991. The six-episode drama aimed at increasing husband–wife communication regarding reproductive and family health issues, approval of spacing and family planning, clinic attendance, and adoption of family planning. *Aahat* was followed by a single-episode television film, *Aik Hi Rastha* (The Only Way), in July 1993 and the 13-part *Nijaat* (Deliverance), which aired from July to October 1993.

Public response to all three dramas was positive and press coverage extensive: More than 50 articles about *Aahat* alone appeared in the national and regional press. Thus, at the macro level, the drama entered into and influenced public discourse on family planning.

At the micro level, that of individuals and the family, research indicated substantial impact as well: Of *Aahat* viewers surveyed (n = 2,118), 12 percent said the program had prompted them to take steps to space out the births of their children, and nine percent said they had visited a family planning clinic after viewing the drama (Lozare, et al. 1993).

Consistent with the themes of the drama, spousal communication was closely linked with family-planning behavior. Of the nine percent of viewers who said they went to a clinic after watching the series, almost all of them (98 percent) had discussed family planning with his or her spouse. Put another way, 81 percent of

1927
1960
1963
1964
1967
1969
1970
1971
1972
1973
1974
1975
1976
1977
1978
1979
1980
1981
1982
1983
1984
1985
1986
1987
1988
1989
1990
1991
1992
1993
1994
1995
1996
1997
1998
1999
2000
2001
2002
2003
2004
2005
2006

those exposed to *Aahat* who discussed family-planning methods with their spouses visited a clinic.

In general, the National Family Planning Program, especially its communication component, had been historically constrained by lack of political support. Yet, public and political support for televised population information led PTV to continue its participation in public discourse around population and family planning by developing and airing *Aik Hi Rastha* and *Nijaat*.

Nijaat was launched by PTV on July 19, 1993, amid highly favorable press reports. It aired every Monday at 8:30 p.m. (prime time) through October 11. The story once more focused on husband–wife communication but was pitched more toward a rural male audience. Hazoor Baksh, a financially stressed small businessman; his wife, Sajida; their two sons, Kashi (age 7) and Tari (age 5); and a baby are the main characters. Zareena is a nurse at the understaffed hospital in their small town; she is a friend of Sajida's, having treated her through poor health and a series of miscarriages. Over time, Zareena convinces Sajida that she must talk to her husband about waiting to have another child. Hazoor, despite his softening attitude toward the adoption of family planning, fails to make a decision. Sajida discovers that she is again expecting, a condition that Zareena tells her is life threatening. When the time comes, the delivery is very difficult; the baby is lost, and Hazoor finally decides they need to practice contraception. In the concluding episodes, Sajida and Hazoor struggle to bring their family together again.

A national television ratings service in Pakistan reported 60 percent to 75 percent viewership of *Nijaat* in the major cities of Karachi, Lahore, and Islamabad/Rawalpindi, giving it the highest reach by a large margin in its time slot.

The impact of *Nijaat* was evaluated using qualitative methods (in-depth interviews with men, women and female service providers) designed to explore how discourse functioned around the drama.

Viewers clearly used the characters and situations in *Nijaat* as jumping-off points for discussion of their own concerns and experiences, as shown in the following passage from an interview with the 30-year-old wife of a welder (Aftab Associates 1994, 8):

Q. Did you talk about the drama [while you watched]?
A. My husband watched [parts of the drama]. He doesn't normally talk much. Only sometimes while watching the play he would say, "What is the A.C. doing to his wife?" or "What is Hazoor Baksh doing?" He would pass these short comments.

Q. Didn't you talk about the main subjects in the play?
A. No. We mostly talked about our own problems. Well, once he said that there is a cold war going on between the A.C. and his wife: "Two people, [when] they live under one roof, develop some kind of relationship after all." And I said, "We had the same problem, didn't we?" And he said, "That was before, not now. It's something of the past; now we understand each other."

The research on *Aahat* and *Nijaat* confirms a discursive link between the social drama, interspousal communication and visits to the clinic. Television social dramas such as *Aahat* and *Nijaat* influence ideation (Cleland & Wilson, 1987), that is, how people think and talk about reproductive health. Witnessing the experiences of a couple on the television screen and hearing what they say to each other in the intimacy of their bedroom alters the boundaries of what is thinkable, the limits of what is speakable. Viewers acquire a vocabulary of characters, dialogue and images from the drama that they subsequently incorporate into family conversations about family planning. New words, ideas and strategies for negotiation between husband and wife enter family discourse.

INDONESIA: AESTHETICS AND SOCIAL CHANGE
Alang-Alang (Wild Grass), a three-part television drama promoting the education of female children,

was a project of the Indonesian Family Planning Co-ordinating Board (BKKBN), with technical support from the JHU/PCS project. The drama was directed by Teguh Karya, one of Indonesia's and Asia's most experienced and respected film directors. Broadcast in December 1994, the drama tells the story of Ipah, the young motherless daughter of a trash scavenger living on the margins of the great garbage dumps of Jakarta. Ipah's father, Pak Rengga, fails to understand Ipah's desire for education and a better life and withholds the money she needs for her school fees, causing Ipah to seek odd jobs and to work long hours to pay for her own education. Through the help of neighbors and her own diligence, Ipah eventually sways her father's opinion, completes her schooling and becomes a teacher.

The drama was seen by 25 percent to 30 percent of the Indonesian television audience in major cities in Java and was the subject of several dozen newspaper and magazine articles in the Jakarta area. The discourse that occurred among Ipah, her father, their neighbors, and school staff, and the media coverage of the broadcast are only a few facets of the discursive quality of the entire project. Examining the effects of *Alang-Alang* from a discursive perspective indicates that numerous valuable and constructive discursive outcomes occurred as a result of this popular culture event.

Teguh Karya himself illustrates the intersection of or discourse among aesthetic priorities, commercial forces, social activism, government policy, health promotion, and foreign aid. As a renowned artist and activist—he has run a grassroots theater company, *Teater Populer,* for many years. Teguh struggled constantly with the tensions between art and delivering a message and reached accommodation between his priorities as a filmmaker and the government's wish for him to use his art in support of its family-welfare *(keluarga sejahtera)* program. He embraced the creative tension between artistic expression and social-scientific health communication by participating in focus group research used to inform the story

development process. He accommodated JHU/PCS requests for explicit population themes by adding a female character who dies as a result of repeated high-risk childbirth. And by following up an earlier collaboration with BKKBN and JHU/PCS (The Equatorial Trilogy), Teguh continues to set an example as a socially active artist.

The television industry also played a role in the discourse surrounding *Alang-Alang.* It was originally planned for broadcast on a parastatal television channel, but a major commercial television station (SCTV) bought the series instead and aired it, knowing of its prosocial content and purpose, in part because they recognized the popularity of social dramas (drama with a message) and the artistic quality of the director's work. This was the first time that SCTV had aired such a program.

BKKBN was enthusiastic about female education as a subcomponent of its *keluarga sejahtera* program and saw Teguh Karya's interest in the issue as an opportunity for collaboration. Through their involvement with and support for social dramas like The Equatorial Trilogy and *Alang-Alang,* BKKBN continues to build relations with the artistic community and to support popular culture as a site where health discourse can occur.

Reaction to the drama was also discursive: Using focus groups, a qualitative evaluation of audience response to the drama revealed multiple interpretations of what the drama's main messages were. This finding, in turn, generated discussion within JHU/PCS and between JHU/PCS and BKKBN about the specificity of and relations among BKKBN's *keluarga sejahtera* program goals and the clarity with which those goals were or could be represented in television drama. In addition, mother-daughter interaction was stimulated by the drama. References to characters in the narrative occurred in mother-daughter interactions following the broadcasts. For example, one mother reported asking her daughter, "Why can't you be more like Ipah?" The mother did not relate her

1927
1960
1963
1964
1967
1969
1970
1971
1972
1973
1974
1975
1976
1977
1978
1979
1980
1981
1982
1983
1984
1985
1986
1987
1988
1989
1990
1991
1992
1993
1994
1995
1996
1997
1998
1999
2000
2001
2002
2003
2004
2005
2006

daughter's response, but it probably reflected themes inherent in discourse among adolescent females and their parents in Indonesia.

Discourse changes the institutions as well as the audiences who participate in it. JHU/PCS, while hoping to make the family-planning and population themes as explicit as possible, supported the broad theme of girl-child education as consistent with its aims to expand reproductive-health options for women in Indonesian society. This reflects a gradual shift within JHU/PCS, and within the larger structure of United States and international population programs following the Cairo and Beijing conferences in 1994–1995, toward a broader conceptualization of population issues, in terms of reproductive health and women's rights.

A further institutional change is revealed in the choice of evaluation methodology. *Alang-Alang* impact evaluation had a qualitative component aimed at discovering what viewers had to say about their understanding of and response to the story. This is in contrast to an historical preference (within the donor community in general) for quantitative assessment of program impact. JHU/PCS has undertaken several qualitative evaluations of entertainment-education projects in the past few years.

Generalizations About Popular Culture, Discourse, and Development

Attempting to use popular culture for educational purposes, as entertainment-education proposes to do, may not be easy, although it is ripe with potential. This review of theories and entertainment-education projects suggests that we must revise the way we think about it if we would use it effectively to foster social change. Looking at entertainment-education as a manifestation of popular culture, and at popular culture as a communication process, a number of generalizations emerge.

Generalization 1: Popular Culture is Localized and Difficult to Know Very Completely or Quickly. The use of entertainment-education may require more reliance on qualitative research than has typically been the case with other types of media-based health and development projects. Furthermore, because the entertainment-education process is still little understood, more qualitative research may be needed before reliable and meaningful quantitative impact evaluation techniques can be developed.

Generalization 2. Popular Culture has its Own Dynamic that Resists External Control. This is not to say that popular culture does not change; in fact, popular culture is often highly syncretic. But it is unrealistic to expect entertainment-education to have only predictable, direct, short-term effects on individual attitudes and behavior.

Generalization 3: By Adopting a Popular-Culture Perspective, Entertainment-Education Must Take a Long-Term View of Social Change. Popular culture is an ongoing discursive process. Therefore, efforts to promote change within popular culture must recognize that historical forces have helped to shape the current forms and content of cultural expression. It also suggests that popular culture surrounding health issues, for example, will unfold over time in response to changing social, cultural, and political conditions. Entertainment-education is only one element among many that shape and are shaped by popular culture.

Generalization 4: Entertainment-Education is not Just Another Vehicle for Health and Development Messages. Entertainment-education is certainly capable of carrying discrete messages or appeals and of generating attitudinal and behavioral effects, but it is also part of the rich and dynamic discursive system of popular culture. Longer narrative and dramatic forms of entertainment-education, such as serial drama, have a particular capacity to bear sociocultural information that far exceeds the capacity of shorter forms, such as spot advertisements, print materials and other channels, which are typical of social-marketing strategies and common in development campaigns.

Generalization 5: Entertainment-Education is a Point of Engagement, a Site of Discourse, not Just Another Message. Entertainment-education can be used for more than just role modeling; it can be a powerful impetus for negotiation within families about family roles, responsibilities and priorities. It can also provide a forum for interaction between audiences, media and health institutions over social priorities and values.

Generalization 6. Entertainment-Education may be Most Useful for Initiating Discussion and Debate and Influencing the Public Agenda. Not that entertainment-education cannot motivate behavior change, but it may be best paired with advocacy efforts, public service announcements and other more focused appeals, rather than being expected to accomplish behavior change in and of itself. Because well-done serials become absorbed into the stream of popular culture, they can be a powerful means for getting issues onto the public agenda.

Generalization 7. Entertainment-Education Encourages Less Emphasis on the Message Per Se and More Emphasis on the Audience. Entertainment programming cannot be effective unless its producers respond to the sensibilities of their audience. The effective use of humor and emotion requires close attention to the origins of those narrative devices in the audience's culture.

Generalization 8: The Audience for Entertainment-Education is a Participant, Not a Target. Because entertainment-education is discursive, the audience must be regarded as a full partner in the communication process. This means that entertainment-education programs must make a special effort to involve audiences in the program development and scripting process through research and pretesting. The more participatory this research can be made, the better, as it will increase the veracity and relevance of the material for its audience. Also, as an entertainment-education program gains acceptance and becomes a part of popular discourse, health communicators must be prepared to engage with the discourse that emerges around the program, using its language and responding to it, even if that discourse diverges from the program's original objectives.

Generalization 9. The Institutions involved in Entertainment-Education Also Change because They Are Participants in the Discourse as Much as is the Audience. For example, some United States foreign assistance agencies, as exemplified by JHU/PCS and USAID, are changing in response to the discourse of which they are a part. This is indicated by shifts in terminology toward reproductive health and women's rights and away from family planning per se, increased attention to the institutions and contexts of population programs, and an increased acceptance of qualitative methods.

Conclusion

Taking a discursive approach will encourage practitioners to assume a less instrumental but more functional stance toward the people and communities they attempt to serve. That is, communication will be used less to manipulate and more to participate in what people in their communities and societies wish to achieve. By recognizing the discursively integrated nature of people and social systems, and the dynamic and unfinishable historical process of communication in which they are continuously engaged, we are forced to assume a more modest position regarding our ability to create change. Instead, we become (or, according to Bakhtin, we already are unavoidably) participants in a development dialogue that links the many individual, group, and institutional entities in a social system.

This should not render us powerless as practitioners, but we must be more modest and cautious about choosing our goals. I have argued elsewhere (Storey, 1990, 1991, 1993) that the most challenging first step in many development projects, especially projects with a strong participatory element, may be simply to start people talking to one another about

1927
1960
1963
1964
1967
1969
1970
1971
1972
1973
1974
1975
1976
1977
1978
1979
1980
1981
1982
1983
1984
1985
1986
1987
1988
1989
1990
1991
1992
1993
1994
1995
1996
1997
1998
1999
2000
2001
2002
2003
2004
2005
2006

needs, goals, resources and strategies. By entering into the ongoing process of social discourse of the people and societies we encounter in our work, we bring ourselves closer to, and perhaps into, the public space where people have been operating all along. By becoming participants, ourselves, in the discourse of those we try to serve, we meet them at their own points of engagement with their own public and private concerns. As practitioners, we cannot, any more than our clients, be disintegrated from the social and cultural environment. It is this participation in the discursive systems surrounding health that will have the most sustained impact on health behavior, and health status and development in general.

References

Aftab Associates. 1994. "A qualitative evaluation of the impact of Nijaat in the rural vicinity of Lahore, Pakistan." Unpublished research report to the International Development Research Center (IDRC). Ontario, Canada, and Karachi, Pakistan.

Ajzen, I. 1989. "Attitude structure and behavior," in A.R. Pratkanis et al., eds. *Attitude structure and function*. Hillsdale, N.J.: Lawrence Erlbaum Associates. 241–274.

Ang, I. 1991. *Desperately seeking the audience*. London: Routledge.

Bakhtin, M. 1981. *The dialogic imagination*. Austin: Univ. of Texas Press.

Bandura, A. 1986. *Social foundations of thought and action*. Englewood Cliffs, N.J.: Prentice-Hall.

Cleland, J., and C. Wilson. 1987. "Demand theories of the fertility transition: An iconoclastic view," *Population Studies* 41:5–30.

Coleman, P. 1988. "Enter-educate: A new word from Johns Hopkins," *J01CFP Review* 15:28–31.

Conquergood, D. 1988. "Health theatre in a Hmong refugee camp: Performance, communication, and culture," *TDR: The Drama Review* 38 (1):174–208.

Faria, V., and J. Potter. 1994. "Television, telenovelas, and fertility change in Northeast Brazil," paper presented to the IUSSP seminar on values and fertility change. Sion, Switzerland. February.

Fishbein, M., and I. Ajzen. 1980. *The theory of reasoned action*. Englewood Cliffs, N.J.: Prentice-Hall.

Fiske, J. 1987. "British cultural studies and television," in B. Allen, ed. *Channels of discourse: Television and contemporary criticism*. Chapel Hill: Univ. of North Carolina Press. 254–289.

Fiske, J. 1994. "Audiencing: Cultural practice and cultural studies," in N. Denzin and E. Lincoln, eds. *Handbook of qualitative research*. Newbury Park, Calif.: Sage. 189–198.

Foucault, M. 1980. *Power/knowledge: Selected interviews and other writings*. Brighton, U.K.: Harvester.

Garcia-Moreno, C., and T. Turmen. 1995. "International perspectives on women's reproductive health," *Science* 269:790–792.

Gerbner, G. 1973. "Cultural indicators—the third voice," in: G. Gerbner, L. Gross, and W. Melody, eds. *Communication technology and social policy*. New York: Wiley. 553–573.

Gerbner, G., L. Gross, M. Morgan, and N. Signorelli. 1980. "The mainstreaming of America: Violence profile no. 2," *Journal of Communication* 30:10–27.

Hall, S., P. Willis, D. Hobson, and A. Lowe, eds. 1980. *Culture, media, language*. London: Hutchinson.

Hawkes, T. 1977. *Structuralism and semiotics*. Berkeley: Univ. of California Press.

Katz, E., and T. Liebes. 1987. "Decoding Dallas: Notes from a cross-cultural study," in H. Newcomb, ed. *Television: The critical view*. New York: Oxford Univ. Press. 419–432.

Kincaid, L. 1993. "Using television dramas to accelerate social change: The enter-educate approach to family planning promotion in Turkey, Pakistan, and Egypt," paper presented at the annual conference of the International Communication Association. Washington, D.C. May.

Kincaid, L., J. Jara, P. Coleman, and F. Segura. 1988. *Getting the message: The communication for young people project* (USAID Special Study 56). Washington, D.C.: USAID.

Livingstone, S. 1990. *Making sense of television: The psychology of audience interpretation*. London: Routledge.

Lozare, B., R. Hess, S. Yun, A. Gill-Bailey, C. Valmadrid, A. Livesay, S. Khan, and N. Siddigni. 1993. "Effects of Aahat, a family planning television drama in Pakistan," paper presented at the annual conference of the American Public Health Association. Washington, D.C. October–November.

McAnany, E., and J. Potter. 1993. "Entertainment television, public policy and fertility change: Brazilian telenovelas as sites for research," paper presented at the annual conference of the International Communication Association. Washington, D.C. May.

McGuire, W. 1987. "Theoretical foundations of campaigns," in R.E. Rice and C.K. Atkin, eds. *Public communication campaigns*. Newbury Park, Calif.: Sage. 43–66.

Morley, D. 1980. *The "nationwide" audience*. London: BFI.

Morley, D. 1993. *Television, audiences and cultural studies*. London: Routledge.

Morson, G., and C. Emerson. 1990. *Mikhail Bakhtin: Creation of a prosaics*. Stanford, Calif.: Stanford Univ. Press.

Newcomb, H. 1984. "On the dialogic aspects of mass communication," *Critical Studies in Mass Communication*, 1(1):34–50.

Petty, R., and J. Cacioppo. 1981. *Attitudes and persuasion: Classic and contemporary approaches*. Dubuque, Iowa: William Brown.

Piotrow, P., and P. Coleman. 1992. "The enter-educate approach," *Integration* 31:4–6.

Piotrow, P., J. Rimon, K. Winnard, L. Kincaid, D. Huntington, and J. Conviser. 1990. "Mass media family planning promotion in three Nigerian cities," *Studies in Family Planning* 21:265–274.

Rimon, J., K. Treiman, L. Kincaid, A. Silayan-Go, M. Camacho-Reyes, A. Abejuela, and P. Coleman. 1994. *Promoting sexual responsibility in the Philippines through music: An enter-educate approach* (Occasional Paper Series #3). Baltimore: Johns Hopkins Center for Communication Programs.

Rogers, E., and D. Storey. 1987. "Communication campaigns," in C. Berger and S. Chaffee, eds. *Handbook of communication science*. Newbury Park, Calif.: Sage. 817–845.

Rosengren, K. 1993. "Audience research: Back to square one—at a higher level of insight?" *Poetics* 21:239–241.

Singhal, A., and E. Rogers. 1989. "Television soap operas for development in India," *Gazette* 41:109–126.

Singhal, A., E. Rogers, and R. Obregon. 1994. *Simplemente Mana* and the formation of the entertainment-education strategy. Paper presented at the annual conference of the American Public Health Association. Washington, D.C. October–November.

Storey, D. 1990. "Motivating participation in participatory research: Lessons from research on interpersonal communication and intragroup processes," paper presented to the Participatory Research Working Group of the International Association for Mass Communication Research. Bled, Yugoslavia. August.

Storey, D. 1991. "History and homogeneity: Effects of perceptions of membership groups on interpersonal communication," *Communication Research* 18:199–221.

Storey, D. 1993. "Mythology, narrative and discourse in Javanese wayang: Toward cross-level theories for the new development paradigm," *Asian Journal of Communication* 3(2):30–53.

Storey, J. Douglas. "Popular Culture Discourse and Development: Rethinking E-E from a Participatory Perspective," Servaes, Jan & Thomas Jacobson (1999). *Theoretical Approaches to Participatory Communication*. IAMCR book series. Hampton Press, Inc. Cresskill, New Jersey. Copyright © 1999, Hampton Press. Reprinted with permission of the copyright holder.

1927
1960
1963
1964
1967
1969
1970
1971
1972
1973
1974
1975
1976
1977
1978
1979
1980
1981
1982
1983
1984
1985
1986
1987
1988
1989
1990
1991
1992
1993
1994
1995
1996
1997
1998
1999
2000
2001
2002
2003
2004
2005
2006

ENTERTAINMENT AS A LEISURE SPACE-TIME OF DETACHMENT AND REVISION

Excerpt from: Vida cotidiana y Edu-entretenciûn en TV

By Valerio Fuenzalida

2004 While entertainment is the most basic relationship between an audience and audiovisual media, it is a scarcely studied subject in specialized literature. In the Western world, general attitudes are witnessed that value entertainment as purely positive or negative, from a macro-social point of view. The negative conception has deep roots in certain currents of Roman and Judeo-Christian ascetics, in the religious conception of Calvinist Puritanism and rationalism… . and in Marxism, all of which highlight the distracting and alienating influence related to serious and important issues in life. In this conception the valued part of life is daily production work on different tasks, to-do lists, business, studies and other activities subject to the laws of return. Entertainment is understood as unproductive leisure time, in which the law of return does not rule for important things: It's a waste of time, except for the rest that gives back energy (to continue doing something useful). Beneficial conceptions of entertainment have valued, on one hand, pleasure and humor to restore energy and, on the other hand, a free leisure sphere, different from everyday life with its laws of return, which stimulates in an affective-cognitive way creative fantasy and expands the potential of the receptor (cf, *Communication Research Trends*, 1998).

The social rulers of the Western world (politicians, religious leaders, intellectuals, businessmen, union representatives) generally share a negative conception of entertainment, as a dominant and culturally inherited perception; entertainment is understood as rest, but in the end it is a waste of time; television entertainment causes, somehow, a feeling of discomfort and uneasiness. Typically they aim to "make it productive" through three "television ideals" (a) rationalizing TV with a greater presence of the rational inheritance constituted by school, university, information of the press, social-political debate, documentaries and others; (b) intellectualize entertainment and pleasure, with the presence on TV (and with conceptual debate) of the highest and most elitist manifestations of High Culture , e.g., select music, such as opera, ballet, plastic arts, art films and others); and (c) make TV an instrument that intentionally uses entertainment as a way to enhance mass conscience (in the style of Brecht, socialist realism, political propaganda, religious education, education for health, etc.)

From the point of view of television reception, entertainment is a complex feeling that contrasts with boredom, lack of interest, of attention and of involvement; the feeling of entertainment does not oppose, and is not contradictory to, information or education; it is not a feeling that annuls cognition, which has been one of the big fears of the Western world.

From the point of view of emission, television entertainment is a production, an array of television forms and signs that may result in a feeling of entertainment on the part of the TV watcher (but which often provokes instead a feeling of boredom). Entertainment, according to the ethnography of the home, may or may not occur, as we have seen, in very different forms–of personal company–oral, rather than visual, in some cases, the narration of testimonials and personal experiences, the introduction of social problems and fiction of various types.

Entertainment as experienced by TV watchers generates a leisurely space—time with its own laws—that mixes in different proportions to the space-time of the home and the rules of return of everyday life. There are programs adapted to accompany undertaking tasks in the home to which it is possible only to pay attention as a viewer, and thus the audience journeys psychologically, continuously, between daily workspace and the leisurely space of entertainment. At times of rest for the homemaker and others at home, it is possible to view with greater attention and focus on that entertainment space–time (and attempt to rid of any distracting noises). In those situations, the greatest psychological–cultural break is produced in the daily routine and compulsory order, with its law of return and greatest income in the free sphere, different and gratifying in the leisure space.

But as we have seen about several program themes, within the leisure space-time, the audience carries out several explorations of their own everyday lives, comparing, assessing different ways to act; the fantasy of the different and possible, the search for identities. In the audience, the processes of involvement in leisure space and comparative-reflexive distance occur, individually and in groups, especially through conversations in the family and outside the home.

The ways to be involved in the leisure space–time are less analytic-conceptual and more corporeal-emotional-dramatic. Leisure space-time has its own laws of expression, among them, the law of being free and of gratification, breaking up with the cultural-everyday limits between reason/emotion, mind/body, entertainment/usefulness, and among the television genders, of education/information/entertainment. The distancing is very variable; as we have seen. It can be conceptually minimal in the case of children; in youth and adults, an important review process and anticipation of one's own life, in dialogue with oneself and with others.

From within this leisure entertainment space on the TV the audience experiences learning, where knowledge is rather reduced, comparing one's own experience with another real or imaginary person's experience, different from programs with abstract discussion on conceptual generalizations. This learning process through identification and acknowledgment is complex: It implies the emitter presenting specific models and situations, which operate to attract the exploratory interest of the TV watcher through affection; if he is attracted by a situation, he pays more concentrated attention and gets involved more actively; and he will interact with the television text, assessing and re-signifying it from his psycho-cultural situation.

From within leisure entertainment space, a way to learn arises–affective and dramatic; this learning is more through emotional identification than through conceptual reasoning. According to Western rationalism, emotion is contradictory to reason and makes the cognition of reality false. For the playwright Bertolt Brecht, the aesthetic emotion inhibits action, and it would be an alienating element of socially beneficial behavior. However, according to new conceptions that revalue emotion, this is a form of knowledge different to the rational one, and is a motivating principle of active behavior (Damasio, 2000).

This route to emotional learning through television, gratified through audiovisual language—narrative of fictional stories, testimonial apparition of reality, personalized company that takes charge of the problems of everyday life in the Home—helps us to understand the massive popularity of soap operas, fiction and other programs over television themes that are more analytic-conceptual. In the gratified relationship with those themes are cultural traces of oral expression, alive and c-existing with the analytic of reading and writing.

The route to learning through specific situations and models is not new: It has been highlighted by Werner Jaeger (1992) in *Paideia* as the oldest path to education, carried out since Homer's epics, which were used for centuries as a way to educate children and youth in Greece. This approach to learning predates the analytic route to knowledge that developed later with reading-writing, which was considered by Plato as the only way to secure valid knowledge, thus setting up Western rationalism in opposition to the narration

of experience-based stories, leisure entertainment and fantasy. …after centuries of Western rationalism, leisure-affective TV language is again making inductive learning massively popular, engaging TV watchers in the exploration of everyday situations and the assessment of experiential models, either fictional or nonfictional…. (Ford, 1994).

References

Aristotle. *The Art of Rhetoric.* Translation and Introduction by H. C. Lawson-Tancred. London: Penguin Books, 1991.

"Communication Research Trends," *Media Entertainment,* 1998, Vol. 18, No. 3. St. Louis, Missouri: CSCC, St. Louis University.

Damasio, A. R. *Sentir lo que Sucede. Cuerpo y Emoción en la Fábrica de la Consciencia.* Santiago, Chile: Andrés Bello, 2000.

Fuenzalida, V. *La Televisión Pública en América Latina. Reforma o Privatización.* Santiago, Chile: FCE, 2000.

Fuenzalida, V. *TV Abierta y Audiencia en América Latina.* Buenos Aires, Argentina: Norma, 2002.

Ford, A. *Navegaciones. Comunicación, Cultura y Crisis.* Buenos Aires, Argentina: Amorrortu Editores, 1994.

Jaeger, W. *Paideia.* México: FCE, 1992.

Parker, C. "Nuevos Enfoques Sobre Pobreza e Impacto en Programas Sociales," Santiago, Chile: CPU, *Estudios Sociales,* 1999, No. 99.

1927
1960
1963
1964
1967
1969
1970
1971
1972
1973
1974
1975
1976
1977
1978
1979
1980
1981
1982
1983
1984
1985
1986
1987
1988
1989
1990
1991
1992
1993
1994
1995
1996
1997
1998
1999
2000
2001
2002
2003
2004
2005
2006

BACK IN THE TRENCHES?
URGENT CALL TO REINVIGORATE
HIV/AIDS COMMUNICATION
FOR PREVENTION

By Thomas Tufte

2005 Slipping Off the HIV/AIDS Agenda

As the U.N. Task Force on HIV/AIDS states, treatment is dominating the AIDS agenda at all levels. Having treatment centrally on the AIDS agenda is in many ways crucial—it creates a strong incentive for people to know their status, it catalyses action on stigma and it creates the focus for political activism on HIV/AIDS. However, the point raised by the U.N. task force is that the pendulum has swung over, resulting in prevention today lacking fundamental priority amongst leaders, donors and those who fight HIV/AIDS on the ground. It seems as if we're back in the trenches of the 1990s—the prevention folks against the treatment folks—pushing aside all the accomplishments towards more integrated approaches to HIV/AIDS. Or the real question today might well be: Does prevention have a role to play in its own right?

Now, why this re-medicalisation of the HIV/AIDS agenda both at the level of political leaders, major donors and key international organisations? At the community level, prevention, care and support initiatives are mushrooming in many places with severe epidemics, but funding is tight, and political leadership focused elsewhere. The urgent call by the U.N. Millennium Project working group on HIV/AIDS to reinvigorate prevention, getting it back on to the political agenda, is very important. It is pertinent, not only to regain centrality for HIV/AIDS prevention efforts in countries that already are heavily burdened by HIV/AIDS, but also to assure that mistakes are not reproduced now in the countries of Eastern Europe, Asia and the Caribbean with rapidly growing epidemics.

Of particular concern here is that this urgent call is challenging us as, communication practitioners and scholars involved in HIV/AIDS prevention work. It sparks questions such as: Why did prevention slip off the agenda? Are we not good at making our case? Can't we prove worthy results? From the HIV/AIDS communicators' perspective: what's not working? The fact of the matter is that many successful steps have been taken. When the U.N. Communication for Development Roundtable in 2001 assembled in Managua and focused the meeting on HIV/AIDS communication, all of us present—a mix of U.N. folks, NGOs (nongovernmental organizations) and CBOs (community-based organizations) and some academics—agreed on the following achieved successes:

> HIV/AIDS communicators have been successful in broadening awareness of HIV/AIDS; increasing knowledge of how HIV/AIDS is contracted; placing HIV/AIDS in the context of human rights; increasing knowledge and demand for effective services; and mobilising political support for national HIV/AIDS plans.

However, in the same declaration, a number of limits and problems were identified. Many communication strategies had: (1) Treated people as objects of change rather than the agents of their own change; (2) Focused exclusively on a few individual behaviours rather than also addressing social norms, policies, culture and supportive environments; (3) Conveyed information from technical experts rather than sensitively placing accurate information into dialogue and debate; and (4) Tried to persuade people to do something, rather than negotiate the best way forward in a partnership process. (See the "Declaration" http://www.comminit.com/roundtable/.)

What has happened in these more recent years has been a growing acknowledgement of bridging communication approaches—more diffusionist strategies based on behavioural sciences and social marketing, mixing with strategies focused on empowerment, participation and social change. Despite this bridging,

HIV/AIDS communication for prevention is slipping off the HIV/AIDS agenda, and part of the reason for this is the lack of successful communication strategies as well as the lack of ability to learn from successful principles and practices of communication. Rather than getting back into the trenches of the 1990s, the challenge today—in times of a strong treatment agenda—is to reassess our communication science, our communication models and our communication practice when putting HIV/AIDS prevention on the agenda.

One challenge seems to be that HIV/AIDS campaigns are not achieving the participation of their audiences in problem-definition nor in problem-solving action. Research suggests that a lot of health communication does not resonate with the needs, interests, competencies and potential abilities to act that audiences may have. The Freirean strategy of "conscientization" responds to exactly this: it engages people in participatory processes of reflection, action and reflection, thereby identifying the problems of their society and seeking solutions to them (Freire 1968). Recalling the problems identified at the 2001 Roundtable, and following a Freirean strategy, I would suggest three communication-related issues whereby HIV/AIDS communication strategies for prevention could improve:

1. *Increasing Attention to the Audiences*. This includes a stronger emphasis on considering audiences as active citizens with citizen identities. They must be at the heart of developing and implementing strategies that concern them and their communities. Increased audience attention is also about improving in-depth analysis of sense-making processes when monitoring and evaluating communication interventions.

2. *Articulating Cultural Citizenship*. This implies a much stronger recognition of popular culture as a resource and ally in developing communication strategies. Inviting popular cultural genres—be it drama, music or storytelling—to be at the heart of communication strategies is a first step towards articulating a feeling of cultural citizenship and thereby articulating action and commitment (Tufte 2000: 227pp).

3. *Recognising Contexts and Communication Environments*. This is a general call for improved analysis of the broader communication environment that HIV/AIDS interventions operate within. This can improve a realistic assessment of the role one specific communication intervention may or may not have. There is far too strong a drive to flag the impact of single interventions, instead of understanding the broader contexts, the multiple mediators and the complex synergies that social communication spurs. Recognising contexts and communication environments will lead to more comprehensive and complex designs of interventions.

Communication Disconnects/ Communication Challenges

Following the above three principles, I would like to wrap up this commentary by outlining three key challenges which grow out of what I have identified in the course of my own research in recent years. Having focused on assessing HIV/AIDS communication practices mainly in sub-Saharan Africa, but also with some experiences from Central America and Eastern Europe, I have identified three key "communication disconnects." These are points, or issues, where previous HIV/AIDS communication practice does not connect with the life-worlds and real lives of the people:

A. COMMUNICATION RIGHTS, REPRESENTATION AND THE PUBLIC SPHERE

Disconnect: There is a big discrepancy between the immensity of the HIV/AIDS problems on one side and the thundering silence found in many local communities on the other side. The strong stigma associated with HIV/AIDS is at the centre of this communication disconnect. It results in an invisibility instead of visibility of people living with HIV/AIDS, and it results in the absence of their voice in the public sphere. People living with HIV/AIDS have a natural right—and need—to speak out about their experience, but they are not present.

1927
1960
1963
1964
1967
1969
1970
1971
1972
1973
1974
1975
1976
1977
1978
1979
1980
1981
1982
1983
1984
1985
1986
1987
1988
1989
1990
1991
1992
1993
1994
1995
1996
1997
1998
1999
2000
2001
2002
2003
2004
2005
2006

The first challenge is for communication practices to address issues of communication rights, especially ensuring voice and visibility to people living with HIV/AIDS. Giving voice and visibility to those that suffer the direct consequences of HIV/AIDS, provides two functions:

■ First, it allows people living with HIV/AIDS (PLWHA) to speak about their concerns. Given this voice, and also seeing the audience responding to their message, can spark empowerment, increased motivation and commitment.
■ It also allows people and communities living with HIV/AIDS the possibility of recognising the situation better and seeing the relevance of speaking out to such a degree that it may empower them to de facto speak with others about their concern.

Considering the stigma and silence surrounding HIV/AIDS, the most important element here is to conquer a space in the public sphere and create a "speech environment" where HIV/AIDS can be openly recognised and talked about.

B. POPULAR CULTURE AND CULTURAL CITIZENSHIP

Disconnect: there is a lack of connection between on one hand: (1) the content of the mediated communication; and (2) the media language used (including genre, aesthetics, format and language) and, on the other hand, the life-worlds and lived experiences of the audiences.

The second challenge is to move beyond a concern for messages and information only to communicate lessons, situations and actions rooted in popular culture and social realities. This implies moving from individual-oriented persuasion strategies towards individual and collective-oriented social communication strategies.

Focusing on audience relevance and recognition of lessons and situations is about recognising change as a process. Drama, for example, as an expression of popular culture, constitutes a space for different social groups to be recognised and to feel recognised, thereby contributing to the articulation of a

citizen identity. This can be useful in HIV/AIDS communication but also as a strategy to address many other issues.

C. POWER STRUGGLES AND CHANGE PROCESSES

Disconnect: The immense contradiction between the solutions proposed in campaign initiatives and the actual need for much more far-reaching solutions.

The final challenge is that of addressing unequal power relations in society. It is the most important of the challenges, but also the most difficult. It is an underlying condition, which is seldom put at the forefront of HIV/AIDS communication interventions. Key changes in social and economic inequalities are, however, crucial if we really want to get to the core problems of underdevelopment and HIV/AIDS. Often, it is argued to be beyond the ability of HIV/AIDS communication interventions. I would rather argue that the problems, then, have been defined too narrowly.

Reinvigorating Prevention Now

The difficulty in communicating about HIV/AIDS is that HIV/AIDS is related to love, sexuality and relationships, issues that are the most intimate of our private sphere and, yet at the core of the HIV/AIDS pandemic. Sexuality is, in many places, taboo to talk about, love is often regarded as a strictly private matter and discussing relationships is, again, dependent on cultural context. Many of us working in HIV/AIDS communication have not been good enough communicating about HIV/AIDS and, especially, sexuality in these varied contexts. As the recently published Africa Commission Report from the U.K. states:

> AIDS will not be checked until those combating it take on board cultural factors about poverty and choices, traditions and beliefs, perceptions of life and death, witchcraft and ancestral punishment, power hierarchies and gender norms, social taboos and rites of passage, control of female sexuality and the demand for male virility and pressures for widows to marry close relatives of a husband recently dead from AIDS. (http://

(www.comminit.com/redirect.cgi?r=http://www.
commissionforafrica.org page 42.)

Successful strategic communication is about articulating identification, recognition and action. It is
about establishing relations of trust. This is the case
not least in these times of insecurity, of wars against
terrorism and with transformations of society resulting in what the Indian anthropologist Arjun Appadurai
calls "a new order of instability in the production of
modern subjectivities" (Appadurai 1996). Successful
communication articulates trust, promotes feelings of
security and belonging and leads to reflection and action. No wonder that royal weddings as we saw them
in Denmark and Spain last year become the largest
media events in the history of television, not least,
here in my country, Denmark. They were the perfectly
orchestrated love stories, articulating a strong sense
of unity and belonging and social mobilisation.

HIV/AIDS communication, although communicating
about love and romance, has another objective. It
is about enhancing sustainable development processes and, about tackling the problems that enable
HIV/AIDS to keep spreading. I have in this presentation outlined some of the challenges; the aim must
be to overcome these elements of communicative
disconnect. Only by challenging our science of communication and our current communication practice can we better make the case to reinvigorate
HIV/AIDS prevention to political leaders, donors and
international organisations.

Bibliography

Appadurai, Arjun. *Modernity at Large. Cultural Dimensions of Globalisation.*
London and Minnesota: University of Minnesota Press, 1966.

Eighth Communication for Development Roundtable Web site (2001/2002).
The Communication Initiative, 2001/2002. At, http://www.comminit.com/
roundtable/.

Freire, Paulo. *Pedagogy of the Oppressed.* New York: Seabury Press, 1968.

Tufte, Thomas. *Living with the Rubbish Queen. Telenovelas, Culture and
Modernity in Brazil.* Luton, England: University of Luton Press, 2000. At,
http://www.comminit.com/materials/materials/materials-903.html.

Tufte, Thomas, 2005. "Back in the Trenches?" published in *Communication Initiative Drumbeat Commentary,* May 2, 2005, No. 297. www.comminit.com/drum_
beat_297.html. Reprinted with permission of the author and publisher.

FOCUSING ON THE FOREST, NOT JUST THE TREE: CULTURAL STRATEGIES FOR COMBATING AIDS

By Arvind Singhal

2003 Most behavior change communication interventions for HIV prevention,
care and support have focused on individuals as the
locus of change. Metaphorically-speaking, interventions have focused more on the tree, and not enough
on the forest of which the tree is a part. The present
article argues for the importance of focusing on the
forest in designing and implementing culturally-sensitive communication interventions. Culture-based approaches to HIV/AIDS communication interventions
must: (1) view culture as an ally; (2) reconstruct cultural
rites; (3) employ culturally-resonant narratives; and (4)
create a culturally based pedagogy of HIV prevention.

By early 2003, some 65 million people worldwide had
been infected with HIV, of which 25 million had died of
AIDS. Of the 40 million people who are living with HIV,
28 million are in sub-Saharan Africa, and some four
million are in India (Singhal & Rogers, 2003). In Zimbabwe, a country in Sub-Saharan Africa, 45 percent of
children under the age of five are HIV-positive, and the
epidemic has shortened life expectancy by 22 years.
Two out of three Zimbabweans, between the ages 15
to 39 are HIV-positive. A 15-year-old in Botswana or
South Africa has a one in two chance of dying with
AIDS. AIDS deaths are so widespread in South Africa that small children now play a new game called
"Funerals" (Singhal & Howard, in press). However, in
the next decade, the epicenter of HIV/AIDS is moving
from countries of Sub-Saharan Africa, to India, China
and Russia. BY 2010, India is projected to have from
15 to 20 million HIV-positive cases.

To date, most behavior change communication interventions for HIV prevention, care and support have

1927
1960
1963
1964
1967
1969
1970
1971
1972
1973
1974
1975
1976
1977
1978
1979
1980
1981
1982
1983
1984
1985
1986
1987
1988
1989
1990
1991
1992
1993
1994
1995
1996
1997
1998
1999
2000
2001
2002
2003
2004
2005
2006

focused on individuals as the locus of change. Meta-phorically-speaking, HIV/AIDS interventions have focused more on the tree, and not enough on the cultural forest of which the tree is a part. What lessons should countries like India, sitting on the cusp of HIV/AIDS explosion, glean from these past experiences? How can they more strategically employ culturally-sensitive communication strategies for HIV/AIDS prevention, care, and support?

The present article argues for the importance of incorporating locally-situated knowledge, including its constituent cultural elements, to design, develop, and implement effective HIV/AIDS interventions. The limitations of individual-directed behavior change communication strategies are discussed, and an argument is put forth for considering cultural strategies in designing and implementing campaigns for HIV/AIDS prevention, care, and support. These strategies include:

- Viewing culture as an ally;
- Reconstructing cultural rites;
- Employing culturally-resonant narratives; and
- Creating a culturally-based pedagogy of HIV prevention.

Behavior Change Communication: Focusing on the Tree

Behavior change models for HIV/AIDS communication programming—such as the diffusion of innovations (Rogers, 1995), the theory of reasoned action (Fishbein & Ajzen, 1975) and the hierarchy-of-effects (McGuire, 1981)—begin with ascertaining the knowledge, attitudes, behavioral intentions and behavioral practice of individuals regarding HIV prevention, care and support (Singhal & Rogers 2003). Gaps in knowledge, attitudes and behaviors among a target audience are identified, and communication interventions are then targeted to address these deficiencies at the individual level. However, results of behavior change communication strategies for HIV prevention that have targeted individuals have been mixed at best, and generally dismal (Airhihenbuwa, 1999; Melkote, Muppidi, & Goswami, 2000). Why? Behavior change

communication strategies, by focusing solely on individual-level changes subscribe implicitly to at least four mistaken assumptions.

- Behavior change communication strategies assume that all individuals are capable of controlling their context. However, whether or not an individual can get an HIV test, use condoms, be monogamous and/or use clean needles are all affected by cultural, economic, social and political factors over which the individual may exercise little control.
- Behavior change communication strategies assume that all persons are on an "even playing field." However, women and those of lower socio-economic status are more vulnerable to HIV/AIDS.
- Behavior change communication strategies assume that all individuals make decisions on their own free will. However, whether a woman is protected from HIV is often determined by her male partner.
- Behavior change strategies assume that all individuals make preventive health decisions rationally. Why would one logically put one's life in danger by engaging in unsafe behaviors? A Kenyan youth who the present author met in Nairobi in June, 2001 quoted a popular Kiswahili saying to justify this non-rational action: *Aliyetota hajui kutota,* which means "The one who is wet does not mind getting wetter."

Behavior change communication strategies are guilty of socially constructing HIV/AIDS as a life-threatening disease to be feared, resulting from promiscuous and deviant behaviors of the "others," the high-risk groups (Paiva, 1995). Hence, past communication approaches have mostly been anti-sex, anti-pleasure and fear-inducing. While "sexuality" involves pleasure, behavior change communication strategies have rarely viewed sex as play, as adventure, as fun, as fantasy, as giving, as sharing, as spirituality and as ritual (Bolton, 1995). Behavior change theorists, in their models and frameworks, failed to see how the social construction of "love"—which requires risk-taking, trusting and giving—contributes to unsafe sex.

Because of their focus on individual-level changes concerns, most HIV/AIDS intervention programs rarely take into account how sexuality is socially and culturally constructed in a society. Hence, HIV/AIDS intervention programs are flying blind and culturally rudderless. Here anthropologist Richard Parker's work on the social and cultural construction of sexual acts in Brazil is illustrative (Parker, 1991; Daniel & Parker, 1993). Parker argued that the "erotic experience" is often situated in acts of "sexual transgression," that is, the deliberate undermining, in private, of public norms. Common Brazilian expressions such as *Entre quarto paredes, tudo pode acontecer* (Within four walls, everything can happen) or *Por de baixo do pano, tudo pode acontecer* ("Beneath the sheets, everything can happen") signify how the erotic experience lies in the freedom of such hidden moments (Daniel & Parker, 1993). This social and cultural construction of eroticism may explain why a happily married man, with a steady home life and children, visits commercial sex workers. Within four walls, a CSW may perform a range of sexual acts that a "proper" wife would shun.

Parker's (1991) work in deconstructing "sexuality" provides social and cultural explanations for why the act of anal sex is perceived as relatively more routine in Brazil than in most Asian or African country contexts. Parker explains that anal sex is widely practiced in Brazil both between men-men and men-women, and that such sexual scripts are learned early. In the game of *troca-troca* (exchange-exchange), adolescent boys take turns inserting their penises in each other's anus (Daniel & Parker, 1993). Sexual encounters between adolescent boys and girls also routinely involve anal intercourse to avoid pregnancy and the rupturing of the girl's hymen, still viewed as an important sign of a young women's sexual "purity."

The failure to take account of such contextually-bound cultural and social constructions of sexuality has led to growing dissatisfaction with the relative ineffectiveness of individual-focused behavior-change communication interventions for HIV/AIDS. Behavior change communication interventions for HIV/AIDS rarely take into account such contextually-bound cultural and social constructions of sexuality. Hence, dissatisfaction with their relative ineffectiveness is growing. Many communication scholars believe that it is time to move away from individual-level theories of preventive health behaviors to more multi-level, cultural and contextual interventions (McKinlay & Marceau, 1999; 2000; Salmon & Kroger, 1992). Metaphorically-speaking, new voices urge communication programmers to go beyond analyzing and influencing the bobbing of individual corks on surface waters and to focus on redirecting the stronger undercurrents that determine where the cork clusters end up along the shoreline (McMichael, 1995).

At a 2000 UNAIDS meeting in Geneva (in which the present author was a participant), a representative from Kenya talked about how young school girls in Kenya rendered sexual favors to urban middle-class and affluent men (commonly known as "sugar daddies") in exchange for the 3Cs: Cash, cell phones and cars (driving in expensive cars like Mercedes-Benz and BMWs). Sugar Daddies initiate the seduction process by asking young girls: "Let me buy you chicken and chips" or "Let me give you a lift in my car." Such exchange puts these schoolgirls at risk for contracting HIV. In fact, rates of HIV infection among young girls in Kenya are five times higher than for young boys, with exploitation by sugar daddies contributing to this difference (Singhal & Rogers, 2003). Ethnographic research with school girls in Kenya showed that they were well aware of the high risks they faced in contracting HIV, but were willing to take their chances. Why say no to such glamorous adventures, when the alternative was to struggle through school and college, find a job, attend to domestic chores and reproductive roles?

In Kenya, as elsewhere, strong cultural undercurrents about masculine sexuality; beliefs in virility associated with bedding young girls (which symbolize "trophies");

1927
1960
1963
1964
1967
1969
1970
1971
1972
1973
1974
1975
1976
1977
1978
1979
1980
1981
1982
1983
1984
1985
1986
1987
1988
1989
1990
1991
1992
1993
1994
1995
1996
1997
1998
1999
2000
2001
2002
2003
2004
2005
2006

and power and prestige associated with such symbols of modernity as cash, cell phones and cars complicate the design of HIV interventions directed at young girls and Sugar Daddies. Individual-directed messages, such as "Stay away from Sugar Daddies" or "Stay away from schoolgirls," will certainly be ineffective.

Cultural Strategies: Focusing on the Forest

A cultural approach to shaping HIV/AIDS interventions represents a move away from just focusing on individuals as the main target of preventive interventions. This approach signifies that the forest is more important than the individual tree. Understanding the cultural context allows one to appreciate the ways that individuals trees are shaped and discern the order that exists between these trees, including the roles, connections and relationships that exist among them (Airhihenbuwa, 1999). Understanding the forest reveals why certain trees tower over others, which trees nurture others and other nuances.

How can the principle of "understanding the forest" be operationalized by HIV/AIDS communication interventions? Communication interventions must strive to

- View culture as an ally;
- Reconstruct cultural rites;
- Employ culturally-resonant narratives; and
- Create a culturally-based pedagogy of HIV prevention.

VIEWING CULTURE AS AN ALLY

Communication strategists often viewed culture as static and mistakenly looked upon people's health beliefs as cultural barriers. This is a predominantly negative view. Culture has often been singled out as the explanation for the failure of HIV interventions (Brummelhuis & Herdt, 1995; Parker, 1991; Moses et al., 1990). Culture can also be viewed for its strengths, and attributes of a culture that are helpful for HIV/AIDS prevention, care and support programs should be identified and harnessed (Airhihenbuwa, 1995).

Several socio-cultural and spiritual dimensions of Senegalese society strengthened the nation's effective response to HIV/AIDS: For instance, the cultural norms with respect to the universality of marriage; the rapid remarriage of widow(er)s and divorced persons; moral condemnation of all forms of sexual cohabitation not sanctioned by religious beliefs; and extended social networks of parents, cousins, relatives, neighbors and others that serve to control irresponsible sexuality (Lom, 2001). The fear of dishonoring one's family and the subsequent "What will they say?" syndrome exercises a strong check on individual behavior (Diop, 2000; UNAIDS, 1999). Thus, in Senegal, sociocultural cultural beliefs assist HIV prevention.

Similarly, the cultural attributes of the Nguni people in Southern Africa reveal points of entry for implementing HIV/AIDS behavior change communication. For instance, among the Nguni, responsibility for providing sexuality education to the young is usually delegated to an aunt or an uncle, at the onset of a youth's puberty. Cultural emphasis is placed on sexual abstinence. A strong taboo exists against bringing one's family name to disrepute. Members of an extended family take turns in caring for the sick, to avoid burdening one person. No orphans exist, as extended family members take care of children without parents. The practice of *ukusoma* (a Zulu term for non-penetrative sex) is commonly practiced by the Nguni, both to preserve virginity and to prevent pregnancy. The woman keeps her thighs closely together, while the man finds sexual release. Other groups use a bent elbow for a similar purpose. Similar non-penetrative sex practices exist among certain groups in Ethiopia (commonly referred to as "brushing"), the Kikuyu in Kenya and other groups.

In a similar vein, smoking cessation programs among Latinos identified the cultural strength of the value of *familismo* (family ties), a positive Latino cultural norm, and harnessed it to reduce smoking (Airhihenbuwa, 1995; 1999; Diaz, 1997). Similarly, close family ties are an important strength of Indian society, where the definition of the family includes neighbors and colleagues (referred to as "family friends"). This strong family bond should be harnessed by HIV prevention interventions, and by care and support initiatives (Mane & Maitra, 1992).

RECONSTRUCT CULTURAL RITES

As noted previously, existing cultural practices may often seem harmful to HIV/AIDS prevention, care and support. Under such circumstances, the metaphorical coupling of culture and harm needs to be exposed, deconstructed and reconstructed so that new, positive cultural linkages can be forged (Airhibenbuwa & Obregon, 2000)—as the following examples illustrate.

Nyanza Province in Western Kenya, the Luo ethnic heartland bordering Lake Victoria, has one of the highest rates of HIV prevalence in the world (over 40 percent of the adults are HIV-positive). HIV entered the Nyanza area in the mid-1980s and spread rapidly. Like many other East African cultures, the Luo practice widow inheritance (also called "home guardianship"). When a husband dies, one of his brothers or cousins marries the widow. This tradition guarantees that the children remain in the late husband's family and that the widow and her children are provided for. Sexual intercourse with the late husband's relative sealed the bond between the widow and her new family (Blair et al., 1997). However, this cultural practice led to the rapid transmission of HIV among the Luo.

Anthropological research in Nyanza showed that the widow-cleansing practice continues as the Luo strongly wish to avoid *chira,* a curse that befalls a person who does not perform traditional rites. However, discussions with community elders suggested possibilities for replacing the rite of "intercourse" with alternative rites, such as the male relative placing his leg on the widow's thigh, or hanging his coat in her home (Blair et al., 1997). Elders noted that such alternative rites were quite acceptable, as the Luo practiced them decades ago. The Nyanza area and the Luo culture deserve further study to derive lessons about the role of culture in HIV prevention that might apply locally and in other areas.

Cultural insights from Nyanza Province suggest that HIV/AIDS program managers should go beyond the identification of harmful cultural practices (such as "wife-cleansing"), in order to create and implement culturally-acceptable alternative rites. PATH (Program for Alternative Technology in Health) in Nairobi created an alternative ceremony for young girls in Kenya, Called "Circumcision with Words." To date, some 6,000 girls have participated in these ceremonies, thus avoiding the risk of HIV infection during circumcision ceremonies.

EMPLOY CULTURALLY-RESONANT NARRATIVES

As noted previously, communication interventions about HIV/AIDS prevention, care and support overvalue scientific and rational appeals to motivate audience members. Most HIV/AIDS prevention, care and support overvalue scientific and rational appeals to motivate audience members. Most HIV/AIDS communication campaigns in Latin American, Africa, and Asia have undervalued traditional oral communication channels and the strength of aural comprehension. In these cultures, the oral tradition is rich in visual imagery and is the basis on which learning is founded (Airhibenbuwa, 1999). Thus, proverbs, adages, riddles, folklore and storytelling are important communication messages (Singhal & Rogers, 1999). The narrative tradition offers the potential of cultural expression, particularly words of advice and encouragement, that are often couched in adage, allegory and metaphor (Airhihenbuwa, 1999).

HIV/AIDS programs fare better if scientific explanations of HIV/AIDS are couched in local contexts of understanding (Harris, 1991). Such context-based explanations are called "syncretic explanations" (Barnett & Blaikie, 1992). HIV/AIDS interventions in Africa should couch prevention messages to fit with prevailing local magico-religious myths. A diarrhea prevention campaign in northern Nigeria illustrates the importance of providing syncretic explanations. When missionaries in Nigeria were alarmed about the number of infant deaths due to diarrhea, they tried to

1927
1960
1963
1964
1967
1969
1970
1971
1972
1973
1974
1975
1976
1977
1978
1979
1980
1981
1982
1983
1984
1985
1986
1987
1988
1989
1990
1991
1992
1993
1994
1995
1996
1997
1998
1999
2000
2001
2002
2003
2004
2005
2006

teach mothers about water-boiling. The mothers were told that their children died because of little animals in the water, and that these animals could be killed by boiling the water. Talk of invisible animals in water was met with skepticism. Babies kept on dying. Finally, a visiting anthropologist suggested a solution. There were, he said, "evil spirits in the water; boil the water and you could see them going away, bubbling out to escape the heat" (Okri, 1991, p. 134-135). This message had the desired effect, and infant mortality due to diarrhea dropped sharply.

CREATE A CULTURALLY-BASED PEDAGOGY OF HIV PREVENTION

In Brazil, several HIV/AIDS prevention programs are inspired by the participatory approaches of the late Brazilian educator, Paulo Freire (1970), who argued that most political, educational and communication interventions fail because they are designed by technocrats based on their personal views of reality (Melkote & Steeves, 2001). They seldom take into account the perspectives of those to whom these programs are directed. Freire's dialogic pedagogy emphasized the role of "teacher as learner" and the "learner as teacher," with each learning from the other in a mutually transformative process. The role of the outside facilitator is viewed as working *with,* and not *for,* the oppressed to organize them in their incessant struggle to regain their humanity (Singhal, in press). True participation, according to Freire, does not involve a subject-object relationship. There is only a subject-subject relationship.

In 1990, Vera Paiva, a psychologist at the University of São Paulo and an expert in HIV/AIDS and gender issues, used Paulo Freire's participatory approach to involve students and teachers in the low-income schools of São Paulo City in HIV/AIDS prevention. Based on a deep understanding of the socio-cultural dimension of risk, the goal of the intervention was to create a generation of "sexual subjects" who could regulate their sexual life, as opposed to being objects of desire and the sexual scripts of others

(Paiva, 2000). A sexual subject is one who engages consciously in a negotiated sexual relationship based on cultural norms for gender relations; who was capable of articulating and practicing safe sexual practices with pleasure, in a consensual way; and who is capable of saying "no" to sex.

In collaboration with students, teachers and community members, Paiva developed a culturally-based pedagogy of HIV prevention, which sought to stimulate collective action and response from those directly affected by HIV, and living in a vulnerable context. Face-to-face group interaction with girls and boys pointed to the importance of understanding the role of sexual subjects in various "sexual scenes," composed of the gender-power relationship between participants, their degree of affective involvement, the nature of the moment, the place, sexual norms in the culture, racial and class mores and others (Paiva, 1995). Words such as *AIDS*, *camisinha* (little shirts or 'condoms'), and others were decoded, and participants proposed new words and codes for naming the body and gender rules, thus generating new realities.

Paiva employed a variety of creative techniques to help participants formulate a culturally-based pedagogy of HIV prevention: Group discussions, role-playing, psychodrama, team work, home work, molding flour and salt paste to shape reproductive body parts and genitals, games to make condoms erotic and art with condoms (to be comfortable in touching them with one's bare hands). To break inhibitions during role-plays, a "pillow" was placed in the middle of the room, symbolizing a sexual "subject." For example, the pillow could represent an "in-the-closet" gay or a lesbian, a virgin schoolgirl or a bisexual schoolboy. Participants could adopt the pillow to have internal discussions with the subject, experience themselves in the place of the other or understand their own fantasy. The pillow provided a vehicle to speak out through an imaginary character, while preserving their privacy (Paiva, 1995).

Group processes showed that sexual inhibitions could be broken in the context of *sacanagem* (sexual mischief), accompanied by "exaggerated" sexual talk and eroticization of the context (Paiva, 1995). Condoms became easy to discuss when both the boy and the girl were ready to "loosen the hinges of the bed," or "turnover the car," while engaging in sex. The pedagogy of prevention was based on an "eroticization" of prevention.

Conclusions

Vera Paiva's work in Brazil, and dissatisfaction with biomedical, individual-oriented behavioral change approaches, point to the importance of thinking boldly, radically and culturally about HIV prevention, care and support. Needed are more culturally-based approaches, as opposed to individual-centered rational approaches. Needed are more community-based, dialogic approaches, as opposed to individual-based "banking" approaches.

Our analysis suggests that culture can serve a positive or a negative factor in HIV prevention, care and support. Program managers must identify cultural attributes that represent an ally for HIV/AIDS initiatives, and harness them. For cultural practices that may seem like a barrier, the metaphorical coupling of culture and barriers needs to be exposed, deconstructed and reconstructed in the form of alternative cultural rites (such as, the alternative rites for female circumcision or wife-cleansing in Africa). More culturally resonant narratives, couched in local contexts of understanding, must be employed. Finally, a culturally-based pedagogy of HIV prevention must be forged to create "subjects" who can regulate their life, as opposed to being objects of desire for others.

While considering culturally-based communication strategies of HIV prevention, care and support, communication planners must be mindful about the dangers in manipulating or subverting culture (Airhibenbuwa, 1995; Melkote & Steeves, 2001). What if constructing or deconstructing culture leads to destroying culture? In focusing on the forest, one must be mindful to not subvert the underlying ecology of the forest.

References

Airhibenbuwa, C.O. (1995). *Health and culture: Beyond the western paradigm.* Thousand Oaks, CA: Sage Publications.

Airhibenbuwa, C.O. (1999). "Of culture and multiverse: Renouncing 'the universal truth' in health," *Journal of Health Education,* 30(5), 267-273.

Airhibenbuwa, C.O., & Obregon, R. (2000). "A critical assessment of theories/models used in health communication of HIV/AIDS," *Journal of Health Communication,* 5, 5-15.

Barnet, T., & Blaikie, P. (1992). *AIDS in Africa: Its present and future impact.* New York: Guildorm Press.

Blair, C., Ojakaa, D., Ochola, S.A., & Gogi, D. (1997). "Barriers to behavior change: Results of focus group discussions conducted in high HIV/AIDS incidence areas of Kenya," in D.C. Umeh (Ed.). *Confronting the AIDS epidemic: Cross-cultural perspectives on HIV/AIDS education* (pp. 47-57). Trenton, NJ: Africa World Press.

Bolton, R. (1995). "Rethinking Anthropology: The Study of AIDS," in Han ten Brummelheis and Gilbert Herdt (Eds.), *Culture and sexual risk: Anthropological perspectives on AIDS* (pp. 285-314). Amsterdam, Netherlands: Gordon & Breach.

Brummelhuis, H., & Herdt, G. (1995). *Culture and sexual risk: Anthropological perspectives on AIDS.* Amsterdam, Netherlands: Gordon and Breach.

Daniel, H., & Parker, R. (1993). *Sexuality, Politics, and AIDS in Brazil.* London: Falmer Press.

Diaz, R. M. (1997). "Latino gay men and psycho-cultural barriers to AIDS prevention," in Martine Levine, Peter M. Nardi, & John H. Gagnon (Eds.), *In Changing Times: Gay men and Lesbians encounter HIV/AIDS* (pp. 221-244). Chicago: University of Chicago Press.

Diop, W. (2000). "From government policy to community-based communication strategies in Africa: Lessons from Senegal and Uganda," *Journal of Health Communication,* 5, 113-118.

Fishbein, M., & Ajzen, I. (1975). *Belief, Attitude, Intention and Behavior.* Reading, MA: Addison-Wesley.

Freire, P. (1970). *Pedagogy of the oppressed.* New York: Continuum.

Harris, D. (1991). "AIDS and theory," *Linguafranca,* 1(5), 16-19.

Mane, P., & Maitra, S.A. (1992). *AIDS Prevention: The Socio-Cultural Context in India.* Mumbai: Tata Institute of Social Sciences.

McGuire, W. (1981). "Theoretical Foundations of Campaigns," in R. E. Rice & W. Paisley (Eds.). *Public communication campaigns* (pp. 43-65). Newbury Park, CA: Sage.

McKinlay, J. B., & Marceau, L. D. (2000). "Public health matters: To boldly go," *American Journal of Public Health,* 90(1), 25-33.

McMichael, A. J. (1995). "The health of persons, populations, and planets: Epidemiology comes full circle," *Epidemiology,* 6, 663-636.

Melkote, S. R., Muppidi, S. R., & Goswami, D. (2000). "Social and Economic Factors in an Integrated Behavioral and Societal Approach to Communications In HIV/AIDS," *Journal of Health Communication,* 5, 17-28.

Melkote, S. R., & Steeves, L. (2001). *Communication for Development in the Third World: Theory and Practice For Eempowerment.* New Delhi: Sage.

Moses, S. Bradley, J. E., Nagelkerke, N. J. D., Ronald, A. R., Ndinya-Achola, J. O., & Plummer, F. A. (1990). "Geographical patterns of male circumcision practices in Africa: Association with HIV seroprevalence," *International Journal of Epidemiology,* 19(3), 693-697.

1927
1960
1963
1964
1967
1969
1970
1971
1972
1973
1974
1975
1976
1977
1978
1979
1980
1981
1982
1983
1984
1985
1986
1987
1988
1989
1990
1991
1992
1993
1994
1995
1996
1997
1998
1999
2000
2001
2002
2003
2004
2005
2006

Okri, B. (1991). *The Famished Road*. New York: Oxford University Press.

Paiva, V. (1995). "Sexuality, AIDS, and gender norms among Brazilian teenagers," in Han ten Brummelheis and Gilbert Herdt (Eds.), *Culture and sexual risk: Anthropological perspectives on AIDS* (pp. 79-96). Amsterdam, Netherlands: Gordon & Breach.

Paiva, V. (2000). *Fazendo arte com a camisinha; Sexual-idades joverns em tempos de AID*. São Paulo: Summus Editorial.

Parker, R. (1991) *Bodies, Pleasures, And Passions: Sexual Culture in Contemporary Brazil*. Boston: Beacon Press.

Rogers, E. M. (1995). *Diffusion of Innovations*. Fourth Edition. New York: Free Press.

Salmon, C. T., & Kroger, F. (1992). "A systems approach to AIDS communication: The example of the national AIDS information and education program," in Timothy Edgar, Mary Anne Fitzpatrick, & Vicki S. Freimuth (eds.), *AIDS: A Communication Perspective* (pp. 131-146). Mahwah, NJ: Lawrence Erlbaum Associates.

Singhal A. (in press). "Entertainment-education through participatory theater: Freirean strategies for empowering the oppressed," a chapter in A. Singhal, M. J. Cody, E. M. Rogers, & M. Sabido (Eds.) *Entertainment-education and Social Change: History, Research, and Practice*. Mahwah, NJ: Lawrence Erlbum Associates.

Singhal, A., & Howard, W. S. (Eds.) (in press). *The Children of Africa Confront AIDS: From Vulnerability to Possibility*. Athens, OH: Ohio University Press.

Singhal, A., & Rogers, E. M. (1999). *Entertainment-education: A Communication Strategy for Social Change*. Mahwah, NJ: Lawrence Erlbaum Associates.

Singhal, A., & Rogers, E. M. (2003). *Combating AIDS: Communication Strategies in Action*. New Delhi: Sage.

UNAIDS (1999). *Acting Early to Prevent AIDS: The Case of Senegal*. Geneva: UNAIDS.

Singhal, Arvind. "Focusing on the Forest, Not Just the Trees: Cultural Strategies for Combating AIDS," *MICA Communications Review*, 2003. Copyright © 2003, Mudrah Institute of Communications Ahmedabad. Reprinted with permission.

EXCERPT FROM:
MISSING THE MESSAGE? 20 YEARS OF LEARNING FROM HIV/AIDS

By Thomas Scalway

2003 AIDS moves through the fracture points of society[1] targeting those whose gender means they can't negotiate safer sex, those whose economic situation means that sex is sold and those in areas where social norms push sex between men underground. It targets communities where high unemployment or low wages create environments where drug injection and sexual risk offer some of the few means of diversion or self-expression[2]. The epidemic targets communities undergoing rapid social change, conflict or displacement. Weak education systems, dilapidated or dangerous health systems and places where the media are restricted from effective reporting are all environments in which AIDS flourishes most successfully. The fact that the people most affected by HIV/AIDS are poorly represented in shaping the way in which governments and international organisations deal with the problem is of course no surprise. AIDS has always affected the poor and marginalised most, and these are the groups, almost by definition, who are outside the kinds of policy discussions that shape their societies.

The lessons of Uganda, Senegal and Thailand are that, while creating widespread public awareness and understanding of HIV/AIDS was a critical part of any effective solution, equally important was that all levels of society formulated their own responses to the epidemic. The reception of AIDS messages was complemented by people being able to speak out about it—to talk between themselves, to make demands at the national level. This debate and discussion was

---

1 Farmer, *AIDS and Accusation: Haiti and the Geography of Blame*, Oxford: University of California Press, 1992.
2 M. Foreman, *AIDS and Men*, London: Panos/Zed Books, 1999.

referenced to and informed by trusted voices in government and in the local universities. Action, whether in sexual behaviours or in the myriad social interactions that lead to social change, emerged from discussion and debate in society, a debate driven by a multitude of voices.

Communication strategies need to be redirected so that they give prominence to the creation of communication environments that encourage interpersonal communication, dialogue and debate, and that focus as much on providing a voice to those most affected by HIV as they do on educating them through messages. The evidence increasingly suggests that only when people become truly engaged in discussions and talking about HIV, does real individual and social change come about.

The logic of HIV distribution is tightly meshed within broader systems of inequality, and any attempt to overcome the health issues without tackling the underlying ones represents only a superficial fix. HIV communication is no exception. Messages about AIDS prevention, international campaigns on AIDS and men or AIDS and stigma are valuable but are insufficient when divorced from approaches that respond to the underlying structural issues. Rather, there is an urgent need for supporting interventions that facilitate communication on AIDS in a manner that adapts and responds to the inequalities within each setting. There are opportunities for enabling those most affected by the epidemic to bridge some of the communication divides that are both a cause and consequence of these inequalities. The priority is on mitigating the impact of AIDS rather than on dwelling on the process. Yet the current lack of focus on process has already had disastrous consequences.

These bridging mechanisms may take the form of a media environment in which a greater plurality of voices and world views, including those of the disenfranchised, is expressed. They may take the form of policy environments more open to the ideas and inputs of those stakeholders most affected by HIV/AIDS.

The forces of AIDS activism, fuelled by the desperation of those whose lives have been harmed by AIDS, or by the energy and anger of those working to tackle HIV/AIDS, can bridge some of these inequalities. Where local activism has caught hold, the results, as we have seen, are inspiring. But for local activism to flourish where there is not already a politicised civil society, an environment needs to be created in which dialogue and open discussion can take place, where communities of interest can emerge and where the views of those with the most at stake in public debate on AIDS can be heard.

In emphasising the importance of building enabling communication environments, we are not talking about developing new types of health messages, no matter how empowering and context sensitive. Instead we are focusing attention on the networks, channels and social infrastructure through which talk, debate, advocacy and mobilisation against HIV/AIDS can flourish. As Elizabeth Fox from USAID stated in a recent presentation, "A finely crafted message on decreasing sexual partners is useless in a world where young women have no access to the media, or, even worse, have no power over their partners." [3]

Using examples of past success, it is possible to start teasing out the different positive aspects of HIV communication environments, though at this stage, and with the resources currently available to develop this work, this is far from being an exact science. More research and analysis within this area are urgently needed.

3 Elizabeth Fox, "Managing Communication for Development," presented to the IADB Development Communication seminar, 2003.

1927
1960
1963
1964
1967
1969
1970
1971
1972
1973
1974
1975
1976
1977
1978
1979
1980
1981
1982
1983
1984
1985
1986
1987
1988
1989
1990
1991
1992
1993
1994
1995
1996
1997
1998
1999
2000
2001
2002
2003
2004
2005
2006

CULTURAL DIVERSITY: BETWEEN HISTORY AND GEOPOLITICS

By Armand Mattelart

2002 The impact of globalization on individual societies has ignited controversy over the fate of cultural diversity. Meanwhile, "cultural diversity" itself has become a catch-all term. It is used to legitimize policies formulated by states and institutions in the international community. It frames the discourse surrounding strategies for the concentration of the culture and communication industries. It inspires the organization of civil society resistance networks, dedicated to fighting the inexorable emergence of a one-dimensional model of society. Having now become a key issue in megapolitics, the vast field of culture is suffused with tensions generated by the confrontation between several different visions of the world-system. The symbolic mutability of the words used to talk about it is symptomatic of this fact.

Diversity is talked about as if it were a new issue. And yet, it is imbued with a long history. The contemporary amnesia that surrounds the idea goes hand in hand with the current severing of the term "globalization" from its roots. Ignorance of the origins of the concept explains how the mass media can pit it against social movements with internationalist leanings, labeling them as "anti-globalization," when, in fact, the "globalist" vocabulary is an inheritance from the emancipatory rhetoric of democratic internationalism. This disregard for the origin of the words is tantamount to forgetting history, and to engaging in historical revisionism.

Why It Is Important To Remember History

As the millennium ends there is an all-pervading feeling that we have entered a new era in history, the age of globalization. Yet may this not be a mere optical illusion? Even if it has spread and speeded up in recent times, the movement towards making all the world one began a long time ago (Ferro, 1999).

In refusing to add his voice to the flurry of discourse on the "new global age," this historian of the Annales School joins economists such as Robert Boyer, who, endeavoring to distinguish the truth from the "false novelty" of globalization, advocate going beyond the retrospective analysis technique favored by economists and "by most researchers in the social sciences, which looks, at best, at a period of one or to two decades" (Boyer, 2000, p.20).

The quarrel with the short-term view of history (*le temps court*) launched by Fernand Braudel in the 1950s, in opposition to anthropologists and sociologists who were proponents of the mathematical model of linear causality, remains as current today as it was then. The social sciences, noted Braudel, the historian of "the perspective of the world (*le temps du monde*)," have become slaves to the present and listen only to those who make noise. However, what Braudel called "social time" is fleeting, ephemeral. He urged a return to the "plurality of social time" and the "dialectic of the long perspective (*la longue durée*)" by "eternally reversing the hourglass." From the structure to the event. From freedom to belonging, with all the constraints that any construction of identity entails. From the universe to the place and to the diverse (Braudel, 1958). At around the same time, Maurice Merleau-Ponty was rebelling against the view of history and progress that suggests the evolution of societies took place in successive, strictly partitioned stages, the last stage necessarily setting the standard for modernity. "The sense of history," wrote Merleau-Ponty, the philosopher of phenomenology,

> is... threatened at every step with going astray and constantly needs to be reinterpreted. The main current is never without countercurrents or whirlpools. It is never even given as a fact. It reveals itself only through asymmetries, vestiges, diversions, and regressions (Merleau-Ponty, 1973, p. 39).

He replaced the compact and abstract picture of the world-system with the notion of a "baroque system," more suited to accounting for the tangle of things that make up a concrete whole, but also for discontinuities in time and space.

Pure cultures exist only as a figment of the imagination. For as long as the peoples of the world have been inter-acting with one another, cultural and institutional models introduced by hegemonic powers have met resistance from peoples and cultures who refused to be taken over, and they have been contaminated, or they have been imitated, or they have disappeared. Out of these cultural crucibles, syncretisms are born. Despite the imbalance of power, the imported culture never sweeps away all vestiges of the existing culture. The processes that historians have called Sinicization, Hellenization, Romanization and Islamization provide examples of this. Successive borrowings and branchings, inventions, compromises and concessions form the basis of composite systems. That said, however, it is wise to be wary of beatific, even religious, visions of the relations between cultures.

In the modern dialectic of cultures, the conquest of the Americas stands out as a defining moment for at least three reasons. First, because this event of worldwide scope laid the foundation for Western modernity with its global reach. The Spanish theologians justified this takeover of the world (*Weltnahme*) by Christian Europe by invoking the natural legitimacy of the exchange implicit in the *jus communicationis*, the "right to communicate," or, in other words, the right to travel and to propagate one's ideas (and one's faith), and the *jus commercii*, or the right to engage in trade.

These were two forerunners to what in the 19th century would come to be called international public law, the cement that was to hold together "the community of nations." From the very start of this takeover of the world, the facts have shown the fallacy of the abstract principle of equality of exchange.

Second, the conquest of the Americas was a defining moment because the clash between the conquerors and the conquered triggered debate among humanists on the relativity of cultures.

Finally, it was a defining moment because the new form of domination generated a new configuration of the modes of resistance, cultural intermixing (*métissage*) or rejection. The West Indian writer Edouard Glissant is not mistaken when he places among the rare precursors to the modern theory of creolization or hybridization of cultures the *Essais* [essays] of the humanist Michel de Montaigne on "the imperious work of relativization" and the *Comentarios reales* [real commentaries] of the [Spanish] Peruvian Garcilaso de la Vega, a representative of "*métissage* in defeat and alienation" (Glissant, 1996). Michel de Certeau is also right in citing the "practice of everyday life" by natives facing the coercion of conquering powers to explain the subversive "antidiscipline" tactics that have been employed by the weak and the dominated throughout history (Certeau, 1980). The corollary to the exaltation of the difference offered by the New World is the Western myth of the noble savage, by which means Europeans were able to feel a part of the faraway. "The Other" became a balm to the soul of an Old World in crisis and weary of war.

From the end of the 15th century to today, people have been dreaming of a unification of the world, whether under the banner of a religion, or of an empire, or of an economic model or of the struggles of the oppressed. The mystique of power has either coexisted or alternated with the perennial desire to regain control over the future of the world in order to free men from their state, as Bacon put it. Attempts at reorganizing the world and pacification, or peacemaking (the appropriation of this idea so dear to Erasmus by modern military doctrines speaks eloquently in and of itself) have only increased since then. All these moments in history have assigned changing meanings to "the universal" and to relations with "the Other," which have been reflected in utopias that have championed either technical networks or social networks as a means of building a universal social connection (Mattelart, 1992, 1994, 1999).

How to characterize peaceful coexistence in industrial society? It is around this question that the recurrent dilemma of homogenization vs. diversification grew up in the 19th century, starting in the early 1900s with the

1927
1960
1963
1964
1967
1969
1970
1971
1972
1973
1974
1975
1976
1977
1978
1979
1980
1981
1982
1983
1984
1985
1986
1987
1988
1989
1990
1991
1992
1993
1994
1995
1996
1997
1998
1999
2000
2001
2002
2003
2004
2005
2006

utopian quest for alternative social models. Charles Fourier, for example, attempted to reconcile in community life what centripetal industrialism had split apart: reason and passions, pleasure and work, pleasure and learning. Towards the end of the century—as the social sciences were emerging, and the dislocation of the community was being debated, and the notion of the role of sociability in the development of society, producer of the anomie and the anonymity of the masses, was taking shape—there was already ample evidence of awareness in the collective consciousness that the world was shrinking. For proof of this, one has only to look at how the biomorphic concept of interdependence took off. This analogy borrowed from the cellular world was introduced by the thinkers of world solidarity or globalism —because it was in this internationalist milieu that the term emerged early in the 20th century—to express the "new meaning of the world" resulting from the linkage of the planet through civil society networks and technical networks that spanned the globe (postal service, underwater cables, transoceanic systems). Already in the earliest days of the social sciences, Gabriel Tarde was talking about [the *analogon* of] the planet as a "brain" and had introduced the modern notion of audiences encompassing the entirety of the human race thanks to the communications media. Explorer of the infinitesimal, Tarde, the founder of social psychology, postulated that difference is the alpha and the omega of the universe. As for Spencer and Durkheim, they reasoned in terms of the organism, considering that evolution proceeded from the homogeneous to the heterogeneous, from a mechanical solidarity to an organic solidarity.

Traditional ethnology is torn between the defenders of cultural relativity and the theoreticians of diffusionism. By placing different value on different cultures, the diffusionists legitimized the civilizing policies of the colonial powers vis-à-vis so-called primitive peoples. Innovations flowed from the center to the periphery. As a counterpoint to this ethnocentric vision, a rebel geography emerged which refused to be part of a discipline that supported the explorations and other expeditions of the imperial period (roughly from 1870 to just after the Great War). A radical critic of the model of industrial development and its logic of centralization and deterritorialization prompted by the international division of labor, the anarchist geographer Piotr Kropotkin saw in the advent of the neotechnic age, heralded by the arrival of electric power, the promise of a flexible society, consisting of decentralized communities, creators of a new sociability, and the promise of reconciliation of the city and the country, industry and agriculture, manual and intellectual work, work and leisure, knowledge and pleasure (through the holistic education advocated by Fourier)—schisms which were the cause of both inequality and social injustice and which were inherent in the pre-technological age of steam, railroad networks and urban megalopolises. This critique of the multiple manifestations of concentration also ushered in a new way of looking at history, in which successive forms are adopted through the mutual help and support of the oppressed—the long-standing history of oppressed peoples, observed the Russian geographer, for which historians have found no "cure" and which "remains to be written." This movement to go beyond industrial society would, starting in the 1920s, give rise to the first socialist-oriented utopias built on the networks of post-industrial society. This revolutionary way of thinking would later influence the work of Lewis Mumford. Immersing himself in technological determinism, Marshall McLuhan would then strip it of any political significance. Social and cultural differences would vanish in a global village interconnected through the medium of television.

The controversy over the various proposals for a community of nations at the end of World War I provides a glimpse of the various ideas circulating in internationalist circles with regard to the state and the course of globalization in its relationship to diversity. Western socialist thought on the neotechnic age of post-industrialization meets the Eastern philosophy of the thinkers descended from the Indian Renaissance on the progressive expansion of humanity until the ultimate universality—"diversity in unity"—is achieved. For Sri Aurobindo or Tagore, there can be no "free, elastic and progressive global union," "a complex unit founded on diversity," without recognition of "the right of peoples to self-determination." This was obviously not the vision espoused by the League of Nations, which merely took up the evolutionist view of colonized peoples as "infant peoples" who needed guidance in order to progress into adulthood.

World War I marked yet another historical turning point. In the eyes of dependent, subjugated or dominated peoples, the slaughter of this first global conflict signified the failure of the culture of the Age of Light to make its messianic message of emancipation in harmony a reality. "Europeanism" was brought to trial during the period between the two world wars. Meanwhile, Americanism was poised on the horizon, ready to take up the mantle of global hegemony. The high culture of the Old World was being directly challenged, moreover, by the advent of a culture mediated by industrial and commercial mechanisms, of which Hollywood became the icon. As for the Communist proposal symbolized by the Soviet revolution—more Taylorist than Taylor—it did not take long for it to push the advent of another culture far into the future by making it conditional on the prior development of economic infrastructure.

The creation, in 1946, of UNESCO, the world body concerned specifically with culture, did nothing to advance the appreciation of diversity. So much was this the case, that for close to a quarter of a century, the only option that this organization held out to countries of the Third World seeking to escape underdevelopment was to follow the canonical model of evolution of the major industrial societies. The vision of the history of peoples as a general one-way movement in successive stages established the regime of truth. The sociologists of modernization extrapolated to the so-called underdeveloped countries the lessons learned from the experience of industrial marketing, which had proved its effectiveness under the strategies for disseminating new methods to American farmers between the two world wars. Accused of inertia and fatalism, the culture of the traditional societies was seen as a quagmire of impediments to development

which the diffusionist theory of social progress sought to stifle. The idealized profile of the "modern personality," said to be empathic and predisposed to psychological mobility and innovation, materializes through the models of life disseminated by the perpetual movement of the media and networks of modern societies, rooted in Euro-American modernity, the paradigm of the consumer society. In this evolutionist and numbers-oriented conception of development that proceeds in stages towards Westernization, a nation does not begin its ascent to the saving culture of modernization until it meets minimum standards of media exposure. UNESCO thus found itself torn between the technocratic ideology of social planning and advocacy in favor of the "human universal" (the central theme of the work of its then Director-General René Maheu), plans for safeguarding the heritage of humanity and the preservation of traditional music.

Diversity's Rise To Legitimacy

During the 1970s, the advent of the post-colonial era upset the balance of powers between the countries of the South and those of the North throughout the United Nations system. The revival of culture as a source of identity, of meaning, of survival, of expression and of dignity was reflected in the revolt against the *pensée unique*—"the sole way of thinking" espoused by proponents of free-market capitalism—about modernization and development. Cultural diversity was held out as an alternative to the universalism associated with the ideology of numbers (GNP) and the determinism of technical vectors. This rehabilitation of the creativeness of cultures implied greater appreciation for the value of local resources and pointed to the need for public participation and preservation of the environment. The first United Nations conference on the environment, held in Stockholm in 1972, highlighted the link between cultural diversity and biodiversity. Questioning of the dominant model of growth ended with a plea to the big industrial countries to rethink, in their own interest, their model of excessive consumption. The new philosophy of development condemned the manipulation of the notion of cultural diversity. As Galtung observed, the quest for

1927
1960
1963
1964
1967
1969
1970
1971
1972
1973
1974
1975
1976
1977
1978
1979
1980
1981
1982
1983
1984
1985
1986
1987
1988
1989
1990
1991
1992
1993
1994
1995
1996
1997
1998
1999
2000
2001
2002
2003
2004
2005
2006

cultural diversity would betray humanity if it became a retreat from shared global responsibility, a parochial isolationism, which would turn threatened cultures into fossils to be kept in a sort of social museum, a kind of mausoleum of the living dead. Certainly, its aim should never be to bring about a chaotic fragmentation without regard for the consequences it could have for national unity or international cooperation to solve vital problems. It should refuse to preserve the present iniquities stemming from systems of privilege based on caste, race, class and nationality (Galtung et al., 1980).

As the controversy stirred up by the movement of non-aligned countries escalated, UNESCO became the epicenter of the debate on the new world order of information and communication, with the so-called Third World calling for a redressing of the imbalances in the flow of information and exchange on culture. The debate was cut short, however, by the intransigence of the United States, the opportunism of the Soviet Union, the hypocrisy of the authoritative regimes among the non-aligned countries and insufficient representation of nongovernmental organizations. European ministers of culture, meanwhile, were concerned about the destabilization of public policies by the cultural industries, and the large industrial countries were grappling with the challenges posed to national identities both by the flow of information from outside and by the protest movements of minorities within their own borders.

There can be no culture without mediation and no identity without translation. During the 1980s, new questions arose concerning the processes of interaction and transaction between individual cultures and transnational flows. The monolithic vision was called into question, both with respect to the workings of power mechanisms and the formation of modernity, drawing attention to the dissociation between the globalization of the techno-productive system and the specificity of cultures and cultural practices. The hypothesis of the mestizo mind (la pensée métisse), formulated by anthropologists, highlighted the dialectics of exchanges— whether financial, scientific, religious, military or through the media; whether from permanent or seasonal migration; whether through legal or illegal channels (Appadurai, 2001; Bénat-Tachot and Gruzinski, 2001). How do negotiations occur between the individual and the universal, between the local, the national and the global? How are global signs retranscribed to fit specific contexts? How do other forms of modernity emerge alongside traditions? It is questions of this nature that have prompted the new questioning of the genealogy of the world-space. The notion of world-communication, in the Braudelian tradition, has reterritorialized the issues at stake in the contemporary phase of capitalist integration. It has replaced the return to "the subject" (the individual), to subjectivity and to cultures in the context of socio-historic determinants (Mattelart and Mattelart, 1986; Mattelart, 1992). The analysis of interactions and transactions between cultures cannot occur in isolation from the logic of geo-economics and geopolitics that governs the new structuring of hierarchies, polarization and sources of exclusion.

The merit of decentering and of adopting a view that takes into account the multiplicity of mediations and practices of ordinary culture is that it has served to dismantle an entrenched approach that examines the effects of power from the perspective of the wielder of that power, not from the perspective of those who are subject to it. But focusing on only one end of the hourglass has also opened up a Pandora's Box of ambiguity. "The ease with which current university discourse on communication bandies about the notion of mediation is suspect," writes a Mexican anthropologist. Few studies take the trouble to explain where the term comes from and how they are using it—as if the concept itself carried its own explanation or as if there had been a tacit meeting of the minds that would make any discussion superfluous (Reguillo, 1997). Enrique Guinsberg, an Argentine psychoanalyst living in Mexico, goes even further, calling such uses "perverse" and blaming them for the current disconnect between research and critical reasoning. An "anthropology lite" has in effect made the act of consuming the products of the cultural industries a forum par excellence for thought. The phenomenon of active audiences who adapt, reconstruct and reinterpret the stories portrayed in films and programs disseminated around the globe has led us to forget that, in the words of Jean-Luc Godard, "one cannot tell a story (*histoire*) without making history (*faire de l'Histoire*)." More generally, the naive interpretation of the capacity to appropriate the signs of modernity has led to a re-espousal of the idea that gave rise to the diffusionist approach, according to which American culture is an "agent of universalization" within which individual cultures can perfectly well redefine themselves without also damning themselves (Amselle, 2001). The practical effect of this evangelical theory is that it has rendered null the debate on public policy vis-à-vis the cultural industries. The liberal dogma of the sovereign consumer has thus found a powerful ally in academia. The tendency to couch the individual's accomplishment (and his supposed resistance) in terms of the consumption of cultural products has clouded the understanding of the issues involved in the reshaping of citizenship and public space. Moreover, many seem to be blind to the fact that, within the post-Fordian socioeconomic regulatory system, consumption also increasingly entails a production of information.

The ambiguous nature of the current discourse on cultural diversity has also become all the more apparent with the newfound legitimacy of the issue of identity fragmentation. The notion of multiculturalism puts a spotlight on controversies. A true-false concept, an offshoot of a "global vulgate" exported by the American academic community—the criticism leveled against the idea of multiculturalism by sociologists Pierre Bourdieu and Loïc Wacquant, is harsh. It suffers, they write, from three serious failings: *groupism* (reification of the social divisions canonized by the state-controlled bureaucracy in principles of knowledge and political protest); *populism* (or ingenuous celebration of the culture of the dominated and their point of view); and *moralism* (which results in an endless and pointless debate on the necessary cultural recognition) (Bourdieu and Wacquant, 2000).

Political pundit James Cohen, a specialist on diasporic cultures, provides insight into the political implications of applying the notions of cultural diversity and multiculturalism to the study of the Spanish-speaking community in the United States. He points out that trying too hard to cast the Latino question as a cultural diversity issue obscures the fact that tomorrow's social and political tensions will be fueled mainly by the dramatic deterioration of socioeconomic conditions among the millions of Latinos clustered in the barrios of Los Angeles and New York. In other words, the issue of how to manage cultural and linguistic diversity should be subsumed within the larger issue of the social model. Cohen also notes that the term ethnic is, by definition, a broad term, a catch-all that can be employed for myriad political purposes (Cohen, 1999).

This tendency to pass over the issue of social conflict attests to the fact that discourse on individual identities has taken precedence over discourse on the principle of equality as the primary objective of political action, which has shaped, over the last two centuries, the concept of the universal, the polemic surrounding it and the writing about it. It is, moreover, the central theme of Ernesto Laclau's book on the war of identities (*La guerre des identités*). The same panculturalism holds sway in whole areas of the field of cultural studies (Mattelart and Neveu, 1996, 2003). As the Argentine Beatriz Sarlo rightly notes, "the hodgepodge of activities that have gone on under this umbrella…has nothing to with cultural studies [as the latter emerged as a field of study in the 1960s at the University of Birmingham in England] in as much as they ceased to establish a system of linkages between the social and the symbolic dimensions. They display a theoretical laxity that causes to stumble into a morass of eclectic, typically academic references" (Sarlo, 1997).

Culture, A Public Good, A New Utopia?
The distortion of the concept of cultural diversity goes beyond the ivory towers of academia. It has occurred in particular as part of the processes of legitimizing the proposed techno-global order. Since the 1960s, the diversity argument has become the Trojan horse of an ideology fiercely opposed to the welfare nation-state.

1927
1960
1963
1964
1967
1969
1970
1971
1972
1973
1974
1975
1976
1977
1978
1979
1980
1981
1982
1983
1984
1985
1986
1987
1988
1989
1990
1991
1992
1993
1994
1995
1996
1997
1998
1999
2000
2001
2002
2003
2004
2005
2006

From Alvin Toffler to Peter Drucker, from Nicholas Negroponte to John Perry Barlow, the prophet of community libertarianism, techno-utopias, stuck at the bottom of the hourglass, have distilled a Manichaean way of thinking, contrasting the State and civil society, public policy and business self-regulation, rigidity and flexibility, centralization and de-centralization, the system and daily life, uniformity and diversity. The first part of each antinomy serves as a foil and shows the shining path to cyber-redemption, represented by the second.

In the early 1980s, marketing and management strategists began to employ cultural diversity as an operational tool, making it a principle for the transnational segmentation of target markets in consumption communities. They thus anticipated the new information stockpiling and profiling technologies which would make it possible to standardize the production of diversity.

With the processes of deregulation and privatization of audiovisual and telecommunications systems that began in the 1980s, culture has increasingly been pushed into the category of services. It is on that basis that the World Trade Organization has claimed certain prerogatives in regard to culture. Cultural diversity itself has become one of the multifarious cultural goods offered on the market. The multinationals of the culture industry have made this argument a central element in their advocacy in support of their concentration strategies. This is just one more way of refuting the need for public policies. The discourse surrounding the media concentration strategies of the communications giants has turned aggressive:

> I'll say it right from the start: my personal philosophy will always make me an enthusiastic supporter of diversity, of *métissage,* of multiculturalism (...) Whereas some may fear that the world is becoming less and less diverse, I see a world that, on the contrary, is more diverse, more open, more tolerant.

So said the CEO of Vivendi-Universal, the second largest communications group in the world, in a front-page interview with the newspaper *Le Monde* in April

2001. Title of the article: "Long Live Cultural Diversity." And, he concluded:

> there is no place within a pluralistic, colorful, multicultural globalization for doomsayers who denounce the marketing of culture and try to defend the need for a cultural exception to avoid cultural-domination. Culture cannot be forced into a uniform and made to march in rigid formation.

Down with the cultural exception! Up with diversity! The cultural exception, so roundly criticized by the head of Vivendi-Universal, is the principle that in 1993 locked the European Union in a battle of the wills with the United States during the Uruguay round of GATT, the forerunner to the World Trade Organization. Under the cultural exception doctrine, intellectual products would not be subject to the laws of free trade. The recognition of a cultural exception would mean that Europe would retain the right to set national and regional policies concerning audiovisual production. The members of the European Union have not, however, exhibited the same degree of awareness with respect to the risks posed by the imbalance of power that characterizes interchange in this area. The fact that seven years later they traded the concept of exception for that of diversity—under the pretext that the former connoted a defensive position—speaks volumes.

Since the end of the last millennium, cultural diversity has been a watchword within the United Nations system. UNESCO has introduced it into its philosophy and action plans, calling for a balance of cultural ecosystems. At the conclusion of its 31st session, held in Paris in 2001, the UNESCO General Conference unanimously adopted the Universal Declaration on Cultural Diversity. The Declaration's first article raises cultural diversity to the status of "common heritage of humanity" and deems it "as necessary for humankind as biodiversity is for nature." The main lines of the action plan for its implementation include several objectives relating specifically to the information society, notably: "encouraging digital literacy," promoting linguistic diversity in cyberspace and countering the digital divide." The same year, UNESCO added a new category to the definition of heritage of humanity: oral and intangible heritage, which includes "forms of population and traditional expression and cultural spaces." This category has been placed on the same footing with the natural and cultural sites that UNESCO seeks to protect. In 2003, the 32nd session of the General Conference endorsed the development of a new "international standard-setting instrument on cultural diversity," with the aim of giving the 2001 Declaration the force of law. This proposal for the formulation of an international convention on the protection of cultural diversity was approved unanimously, although seven countries abstained from voting. One of them was the United States, which had returned to UNESCO, having withdrawn some 18 years earlier over its disagreement with the demands for a new world information and communication order. This convention would recognize every government's right to take any legislative, regulatory or financial action needed to preserve its national cultural and linguistic heritage, as well as the need to cooperate with the countries of the South.

Additional proof of the new centrality of the issues of cultural and linguistic diversity: parallel to the process of intergovernmental negotiations, with all the uncertainties, compromises and concessions that they imply, new organizations and networks of civil society are increasingly making their voices heard. One is the Coalition for Cultural Diversity, based in Montreal, an association of writers, composers, musicians, script writers, directors, actors, independent producers, distributors and publishers, whose objective is to defend the right of countries to "adopt the policies necessary to support the diversity of cultural expression and the viability of enterprises that produce and disseminate this expression."

Nowadays, no international gathering where the future of the planet is being discussed can fail to feel the pressure exerted by nongovernmental organizations, as was exemplified by the active involvement of social networks in the preparatory discussions leading to the World Summit on the Information Society, held in Geneva in December 2003 under the auspices of the International Telecommunications Union (ITU), a specialized agency of the United Nations system. The Summit considered a number of different and contrasting visions of the information society. The nongovernmental organizations took positions on the proposals put forward by the various governments and private-sector entities, represented by the International Chamber of Commerce. They highlighted the importance of cultural and linguistic diversity in the media and information and the need to put an end to discrimination in the information and communication domains based on ethnicity, gender or disability; the priority of education and research; the need for oversight of the international institutions responsible for the infrastructure of global networks and for the new rules on intellectual property, etc. They also warned against simply repackaging the ethnocentric ideology of modernization/development in the implementation of new information and communication technologies.

Cultural diversity is today at the center of debate on what form society should take in another possible world. Far from being reduced to a conception only of the products of the cultural industries and information technologies, the idea of cultural exception or cultural diversity has become the basis for reexamining our whole way of life. Cultural diversity has become part of the debates on "public goods," which include culture, but also education, health and the environment—in short, any area in which the logic of privatization threatens to undermine the concept of public service.

Bibliography

Amselle, J. L. *Branchements. Anthropologie de l'universalité des cultures.* Paris: Flammarion, 2001.

Appadurai, A.. *Modernity at Large: Cultural Dimensions of Globalization*, Minneapolis: University of Minnesota Press, 1996.

Barlow, J. P. "The Future of Government," *Spin*, November 1995.

Bénat-Tachot, L. and S. Gruzinski (eds.). *Mécanismes de métissages.* Paris: Presses universitaires de Marne la Vallée/MSH, 2001.

Bourdieu, P. and L. Wacquant. "La nouvelle vulgate planétaire," *Le Monde diplomatique*, March 2000, pp. 6-7.

1927
1960
1963
1964
1967
1969
1970
1971
1972
1973
1974
1975
1976
1977
1978
1979
1980
1981
1982
1983
1984
1985
1986
1987
1988
1989
1990
1991
1992
1993
1994
1995
1996
1997
1998
1999
2000
2001
2002
2003
2004
2005
2006

Boyer, R. "Les mots et la réalité," in *Mondialisation au-delà des mythes*, ed. S. Cordellier. Paris: La Découverte, 2000.

Braudel, F. " Histoire et sciences sociales : la longue durée," *Annales: economies, sociétés, civilisation* 13, no. 4 (1958).

Braudel, F. *Le Temps du monde*. Vol 3, *Civilisation matérielle, économie et capitalisme XVe-XVIIIe siècle*. Paris: Armand Colin, 1979.

Certeau, M. *Arts de faire. L'invention du quotidian*. Paris: 10/18, 1980.

Cohen, J. "La latinisation des Etats-Unis: clivages sociaux et faux semblants culturels," *Actuel Marx*, 1999, no. 27.

Ferro, M. "Mirror to the future," *Le Monde Diplomatique*. English Edition. September 1999. (Originally published in French under the title "Le futur au miroir du passé," *Le Monde diplomatique* (Paris), September 1999).

Galtung, J. et al. *Self-reliance. A Strategy for Development*. London: Bogle-L'Ouverture Publications, 1980.

Glissant, E. *Introduction à une poétique du divers*. Paris: Gallimard, 1996.

Guinsberg, E. *La salud mental en el neoliberalismo*. Mexico City, Plaza y Valdés, 2001.

Laclau, E. *La guerre des identités. Grammaire de l'émancipation*. Paris: La Découverte/ MAUSS, 2000.

Mattelart, A. *La Communication-monde*. Paris: La Découverte, 1992. (Spanish translation: *La comunicación-mundo*, Madrid, Fundesco, 1992/ Siglo XXI, Mexico, 1996. English translation: *Mapping World Communication*, Minneapolis: University of Minnesota Press, 1994).

Mattelart, A. *L'Invention de la communication*. Paris: La Découverte, 1994. (Spanish translation: *La invención de la comunicación*. Mexico: Siglo XXI, 1996. English translation: *The Invention of Communication*. Minneapolis: University of Minnesota Press, 1996).

Mattelart, A. *Histoire de l'utopie planétaire: de la cité prophétique à la société globale*. Paris: La Découverte, 1999. (Spanish translation: *Historia de la utopia planetaria*. Barcelona: Paidos, 2000).

Mattelart, A. *Histoire de la société de l'information*. Paris: La Découverte, 2001. (Spanish version: *Historia de la sociedad de la información*. Barcelona: Paidos, 2002. English version: *The Information Society*. London: Sage, 2003).

Mattelart, A. and M. *Penser les medias*. Paris: La Découverte, 1986. (Spanish translation: *Pensar sobre los medios*. Madrid: Fundesco, 1987/ Santiago, Chile: Lom, 2000; English translation: *Rethinking Media Theory*. Minneapolis: University of Minnesota Press, 1992).

Mattelart, A. and E. Neveu. "Dossier: 'Cultural Studies,'" *Réseaux*, 1996, no. 80.

Mattelart, A. and E. Neveu. *Introduction aux '"Cultural Studies.'"* Paris: La Découverte, 2003.

Merleau-Ponty, M. *Adventures of the Dialectic*. trans. Joseph Bien. Evanston: Northwestern University Press, 1973. (Originally published in French under the title *Les aventures de la dialectique*. Paris: Gallimard, 1955).

Reguillo, R. "Más allá de los medios: diez años después," *Comunicación y sociedad* (University of Guadalajara, Mexico), 1997, no.30.

Sarlo, B. "Entrevista a Beatriz Sarlo," *Causas y azares* (Buenos Aires), 1997, no. 80.

UNESCO. *Rapport mondial sur la culture 2000*. Paris: UNESCO Publishing, 2000.

Mattelart, Armand. "La diversité culturelle: entre histoire et géopolitique," paper presented at the international conference "2001 Bogues: Globalisme et Pluralisme," Montreal, 22-27 April 2002. Reprinted with permission.

POPULAR CULTURES AND PARTICIPATORY COMMUNICATION: ON THE ROUTE TO REDEFINITIONS

By Rosa María Alfaro

2001 In the 1970s and 1980s, "alternative" communication, understood as "the other communication," also called popular, educational or community communication, was at its height in Latin America. It was committed to the social movements and criticism of the dominant society. It was a very fruitful period in terms of experience, commitment and reflection. The people and their importance in society were clearly understood. The vision of a coordinated, popular, democratic organization filled—and even replaced—the political utopias of this period. Actors from poor sectors became leaders, and there they were perceived as the new and authentic managers of social change.

Evidently the real context of the society was very complex, and at the same time the notions of social and political transformation were changing. The perception of class that supported these experiences was cut short with the fall of socialism, eliminating its basis and continuity. The actors of the society stopped being seen as contradictory or opposing subjects. The limits of the popular became obscure.

At the same time broader processes of globalization continued to emerge, and the hegemonic economic trend, at least in discourse, in the first place sought social integration and not precisely radical opposition. We were in a period during which the subjects were constrained to great reflexivity, falling back on themselves and on the project itself, in the midst of a process of de-territorialization (without borders) and of hybridization of the cultures. All of this led us to think about the search for new communicational utopias to guide our work and the commitment to society.

However, this process of search and redefinition is not possible without first making an exhaustive balance of the processes experienced. It is important to remember and retrieve those aspects that continue to be valid for identifying the routes of the future. Likewise, it is necessary to specify and analyze where the failures and the gaps were, all that which today has no theoretical or ethical basis or practical viability. Finally, we need to re-think a new and liberating communication, in profound dialogue with the social and political utopias starting to be discussed today.

1. Balance: Retrieval And Redefinition Towards The Future

The space we have available does not allow us to make a rigorous analysis. We will present some evaluative clues, resorting to a simplistic but valid framework on what is worth retrieving and only what continues to be valid.

The theoretical framework from which we dare to look at this set of communicational practices with social direction is that of universal and ethical values of a radical democratic view, that seeks in a profound way to bring together the individual and collective development of peoples, the interaction or merging between the notion of justice and liberty, and the dialogue between democracy and equity, as compatible and inseparable utopian directions in the new society we want to conceive.

2. Ethical Contributions To Retrieve: Against Desperation

There were years of experience and commitment all over the continent, some supported by international cooperation, others sustained by voluntary work. From that experience, one can retrieve the ethical capital that we want to emphasize and whose central element would be commitment to the oppressed and needy sectors, seeking their social and political development. Some of the lessons learned and that continue to be valid are:

A. COMMUNICATION IS A MATTER OF SUBJECTS IN RELATION TO EACH OTHER.

Emphasis was given to the existence of the subjects of communication. These should produce relations of dialogue among themselves, both among the members of a population of a specific community, or social sector, as well as among the communicators and the people. Not only was it possible to point to the importance of the communicative process, but it was also possible to see in them their problems and conflicts, their nonconformity and their weakness as victims of an unjust social order. And in spite of the simplistic structure at the cultural level, it was possible to underline that they were more or less complex cultural subjects and not only political revolutionaries. In contrast with a more structural understanding of the society, this communication put aside the human aspect—even though it was also political—from its practices, reclaiming the recreational aspects of communicational work and contact between people, both from the media as well as in the direct relation.

B. PARTICIPATION IS LEADERSHIP AND DEMOCRACY.

Communicative participation was valued and overvalued. In many cases, it was done excessively, and even extravagantly, producing stagnation at the level of the formats: many interviews, testimonies and even stories. But in other cases, people committed to the promotion of a democratic society with dialogue among peers. "It was a period in which democracy was only appreciated as an incomplete and not very satisfactory system, in which it still was not appreciated as a political societal value." This meant a positive appreciation of the popular subjects in relation to their capacities for communicating. And it assumed, furthermore, the conception of a dialogical model for communication that would convert the people into transmitters and receivers, permitting an alternative democratic exercise.

1927
1960
1963
1964
1967
1969
1970
1971
1972
1973
1974
1975
1976
1977
1978
1979
1980
1981
1982
1983
1984
1985
1986
1987
1988
1989
1990
1991
1992
1993
1994
1995
1996
1997
1998
1999
2000
2001
2002
2003
2004
2005
2006

C. THE IMPORTANCE OF THE COMMUNITY AND COLLECTIVE ACTION.

A constant and basic questioning of the individual-istic models led practices to be implemented that emphasized the importance of collective action. The existence of an organized community was highly re-spected. In many cases and times, people worked for and through the organization, or with the social move-ments. The *value-based* cohesion that sustained popular communication was located in the field of human solidarity, among subjects of the same class or social sector. It was a matter of always creating connections and commitments. These were times of "giving voice to those who have no voice," permitting them to express themselves and be leaders.

This characteristic can be retrieved today, since there does not have to be any opposition between the in-dividual and the community. We can understand that beyond the representative organizations of a territorial nature, experience of solidarity applicable to new flex-ible communities is valid. It is not possible to think of human social nature only on the individual level.

D. THE RIGHT TO COMMUNICATION: THE SIGNIFICANCE OF RADIO.

Popular and alternative communication based on criticism of the mass commercial media chose a for-mulation that was still valid in relation to the right to communication that all receivers have, especially ex-pressed for the informative field. In recent times, the cit-izen's perspective worked on in our continent has not sufficiently reflected the idea of the right to propose it as a counterpart to freedom of speech, thus conceiving of an understanding of communication as a more bal-anced relation between transmitters and the public.

If one does not openly admit the right to ownership of the media or to freedom of speech, it was empha-sized in a practical way that the vast majority could, and should, speak fairly because the *dialogical* struc-ture sustained it in this way. The independence of in-formation, but in favor of the poor, was to an extent a link to democracy.

The radio was the medium that best permitted this perspective to be explored. It was an experience that, moreover, committed the whole continent, not only using small short-range radios, but also other more powerful ones. There was a coincidence between practice and the image of the thousands of voices proposed by the MacBride report as the New Interna-tional Order of Communications[1].

E. THE EDUCATIONAL INTENTION OF COMMUNICATION.

The educational vocation of popular communication is unquestionable. It was not a case of only an adjec-tive. It was a commitment to transform the subjects in contact and participation, thus going back to the postulates of Paulo Freire. Closely linked to commu-nication as an encounter of the subject with his reality and with himself, it was important to promote pro-cesses of liberation in a pedagogical way. Education was thought to be, therefore, as a practice of trans-formation. Perhaps the most recoverable value would be that it was pointed out that the receivers educate themselves in contact with communication, both in relation to the mass media as well as to the alternative media. It was not a question of teaching or didactics, but of learning. In this context, communication could not be left to the spontaneous rhythm of an encounter with the public, but should become a whole commu-nicative work of an educational nature, a contribution not always practiced in all its implications.

F. COMMUNICATION AND DEVELOPMENT.

At the end of the 1980s and beginning of the 1990s there was a move from the exclusive and exclusionary support for popular sectors to a greater commitment to the social process of change, called *development*, which would supposedly also have results in these sectors. So the subject was related to social and po-litical action. It should have had a bearing on govern-ment systems, on ideas and social needs, to solve problems not only in the short term but also in the

---

1   MacBride, Sean, et. *al.* (1980): *Many Voices, One World.*. FCE. Mexico. 1980 (Editors' note)

long term, in a sustainable way. This perspective continues today. Some ideas on social marketing were applied in an extremely publicity-oriented way, distorting the commitment of communication to confuse it with development, to the extent that this is a more instrumental support and is external to change itself.

Communication, thus, acquired more precise thematic validity: productivity and small enterprise; gender; citizenship; health; the environment; human rights. Recent investigations into the local municipal field have given this communicative perspective a concrete commitment, which furthermore, became extremely significant, to a point that there was a proliferation of institutions and organizations devoted both to popular communication as well as to the relation between the municipal district and the community of citizens.

G. A SOCIAL COMMITMENT WITH POPULAR SOCIAL SECTORS.

In balance, we can assert that this was the most significant and retrievable value. In this way, communication took the responsibility for existing inequality. It was a case of building solidarity with the popular sectors and providing participation and dignity with educational sense. In many cases it was even possible to go from the oral commitment of the people to a more coherent and constructive proposal in relation to the use of the media, to promote dialogue among people and with other social sectors as a second priority. This led to much cultural learning and to less ideologized and more humane structures of commitment with others.

So we can speak of popular communication as a great ethical force, and of responsibility to the most dispossessed in a participatory dialogue and for their liberation. This was the retrieval of an experience that continues to be viable in some of its *value-based* principles, a kind of renewal.

Communication was not an accessory element or an instrument; it was the place where transformation processes were occurring. If this understanding sounds

romantic, we can emphasize today that it was focused on an appraisal of this field by communication itself. In other words, people were committed to the dialogues that they managed to process and the educational enrichment that emerged from that.

3. Deficiencies To Be Overcome.

We present these deficiencies for the purpose of *mapping* conflicts and identifying the gaps, work that will lead us to rethink our communicational paradigms.

3.1. A SEGMENTED LOOK AT REALITY:
A communication enclosed in an imaginary circle.

The importance acquired by the subjects weakened concern for a macro vision of society and its economic and political destiny. The changes occurring were not profoundly analyzed. The theoretical frameworks themselves—remote or in breach with previous social theories—failed to allow new situations or the future to be examined. The communicative proposal failed to mark the importance of integrating into the society, or of working on the idea of socio-communicative belonging or inclusion. Rather, this perspective generated suspicions. Therefore the idea of "non contamination" by other social sectors was emphasized and of maintaining pure and radical commitments "among the good ones" outside of society itself, whose system was in itself questionable. In other words, it was necessary to relate exclusively with "people like us," with the same way of thinking or with similar groups, in different communication frameworks. The possibility of an integration defined in critical terms and in disagreement was not foreseen. In the context of an unjust and authoritarian society, new spaces were conquered without this having an impact on the whole.

For many, communication—and the media—was the space for preferential intervention. People sought to change this, without establishing sufficient relations with the society or with the viabilities of innovation. Democratization and participation should have occurred within communicative action, almost as if on a happy island. A serious, creative and utopically based proposal was lacking regarding the democratization

1927
1960
1963
1964
1967
1969
1970
1971
1972
1973
1974
1975
1976
1977
1978
1979
1980
1981
1982
1983
1984
1985
1986
1987
1988
1989
1990
1991
1992
1993
1994
1995
1996
1997
1998
1999
2000
2001
2002
2003
2004
2005
2006

of society; rather, people doubted it. In the social and political world, paradigms focused only on justice. In communicative spaces, paradoxically, participation was sensitive and practical inside communicative action with popular sectors. Thus a certain dose of incoherence was demonstrated, since in the field of media use one appealed to democratic practices, even though socially only equality was valid. Democracy appeared to be sustained only based on communication itself. And precisely because of that, when a new radical theory was launched on democracy in the society[2], popular communication began to lose validity when it was discovered to be in opposition. Recent years, however, have represented a more consistent encounter between social and communicative theory.

This was an eminently practical movement, which made the mistake of ridiculing and distancing itself from a theoretical reflection on this deepening relationship between communication and society, built furthermore on the basis of much harmony but also on disagreement and conflict. So, the circle closed, exhausting the importance of communication for change before its time.

3.2. INTRANSIGENT MODELS ON CULTURE AND POPULAR ETHICS:

A distancing from the real and subjective subject

This stage of commitment and closeness to popular subjects had its counterpart. Although social alliances, and even political ones, were built in different communities, the understanding of the subjects went no further than just looking at the objective social problem and the organizational capacity of the people for building themselves into a collective subject. They failed to perceive cultural changes, especially in the political sphere, or the diverse processes of integration to the dominant system, including the communicative, let alone the changes in real and imaginary values presented by other models of society not consistent with those of communication and popular

education. Daily life itself and common sense in constant production and reproduction led in other coherent directions with hegemonic proposals of power.

Evidently, there are explanations that today help us understand past blindness. In the first place, we discovered the pre-eminence of a cultural orientation that saw the past not as an explanation of the present but as an almost heroic retrieval of the native side of the peoples, understanding it as real. Its dynamics of production and cultural transformation were frozen in this sense. People worked on a categorical opposition between the traditional and the modern. There was little insistence on cultural change for the present and in future projects. At the basis there was an essentialist understanding of identities, those of class, ethnic groups, gender, nationality, generation and others, perceived as fixed slots without the possibility of growth and flexibility. We were in the presence of a confrontational way of thinking that understood reality as a dichotomy, in black or white, and consequently a good and authentic communication for dealing with another alienating evil. A whole romantic ideology placed little emphasis on the complicity experienced by the people themselves in the presence of power. Social conflicts were imagined to be phenomena that were external to the oppressed subjects.

This was why so much emphasis was given to content and messages, understood as truths to be disseminated, neglecting the communicative and cultural aspects, those which build relations, dialogues, the formation of the imaginary and representations of different realities. We refer to the intrinsic relation that existed between substance and form, between reason and creativity, between responsibility and freedom. The neglect of aesthetics and the narration of many experiences were evidence of what was lacking. The forms were reduced to formats normatively consigned to be *this or that*.

To this we can add a mechanical understanding of change, understood as the emergence of a social awareness in subjects capable of making governments and ideologies collapse. People put their stakes on critical

---

2 We are referring to the movement of democratic radicals which was conceived in Europe and Latin America, presented by authors such as Adela Cortina or Chantal Mouffe.

education without giving value to the importance of a propositional and innovative awareness. For this reason, the only way to relate to reality was through denunciation and protest, idealized in our times almost as an end in itself. Nobody worked on a way out of the problems on increasing the ideology of productivity and promoting creativity as an emancipating and liberating experience.

3.3. THE COMMUNITY OVER THE INDIVIDUAL

There was an excessive emphasis on collectivism. To pay attention to the world of each subject was to fall into individualism. What was lacking was any individual proposal on the idea of change, both in the subjects, as well as in the field of reception—concentrated on more by institutions devoted to research. This perspective, which put the individual and the community in opposition to each other, brought problems and a lack of understanding about people, their tensions or conflicts and their co-ordination with the collective. And it simplified the community, understanding it as a group for presenting demands or for protest.

There was a lack of knowledge on how Western modernity and the current system of living had placed emphasis on a reflexive individual, who had to choose and decide, think, dream and imagine, formulate his own needs, solve his problems alone and with others, join the world of work and productivity, but always through the personal nuance. This implies first of all a citizen loaded with responsibilities, but also it redefines a more independent subject, more individualized, a *citizen-person*. This, which in itself is not negative, was almost ignored, and new paths for concerted action between *the person and the collective* were not sought. It is likely that a structuralist sociological explanation prevailed in this perception, in which the psychological contributed little to social theory.

So little work was done on a new idea of community that would admit very active subjects interested in by innovation and the search for progress. The collective was perceived as a renunciation of personal deliberation, the legitimation of one's own well-being. If society

can eliminate the importance of solidarity and collective work, those who seek another value proposal fail to know how to study the changes occurring in the community sense in the pragmatic definitions of popular organizations, so formal and sometime coercive. Less still did they have the capacity to think of another practical idea of modern community.

The communicative phenomenon as a pleasurable encounter was discovered in part, and in many cases only relational tactics with the public were launched, but not real encounters in the world of satisfaction, creativity and change. Perhaps for this reason an alternative aesthetic management could not be formulated in which the encounter for entertainment itself could be profoundly liberating. Curiously, many failed to understand that being a social actor in one's own territory or situation of conflict is not the same as defining oneself as the audience of the media, where there is a tendency to coincide or reject the offer without opposing figures. These are different positions require diversified strategies of appeal, even though they can be reintegrated.

3.4 COMMUNICATION WITHOUT PUBLIC CIVIC PERSPECTIVE

Finally we pose the hypothesis that the idea of community was not related to a way of understanding a broader leading role, in the structuring of nations during the phase of globalization. What predominated was the idea of the internally coherent territorial community itself, the national clearly separated from the foreign. The idea of *country* and broad *community* was lost as well as that of the localized *world*, putting fences up around the development of new ways of exercising the collective. Axiological principles tended to be defensive, even conservative, and nearly always simplistic.

Public debate and the education of citizens—which has slowly been taking shape with a great deal of conflict in our countries during the second half of the century—required a lot of support. This perspective was not adopted: The fact of seeing the subjects socially

1927
1960
1963
1964
1967
1969
1970
1971
1972
1973
1974
1975
1976
1977
1978
1979
1980
1981
1982
1983
1984
1985
1986
1987
1988
1989
1990
1991
1992
1993
1994
1995
1996
1997
1998
1999
2000
2001
2002
2003
2004
2005
2006

prevented perception of their becoming individual members of a society, that is also political and influenced by the media.

Perhaps this was why each experience tried to intervene separately without all encompassing strategies being prepared which were coordinated and exercised in different spaces in relation to mobilization and community action. Neither were some media differentiated from others. The integral nature of efforts with other areas was just methodological, incorporating or applying mechanisms of popular communication in other fields, without really building an agreed—upon educational policy.

In other words, we were inside a perspective that protected the popular sectors, and we confined ourselves to alternative experiences, isolating ourselves from the new conflicts that presented a changing reality and making use of old and intransigent oppositions. It was an attitude that was somewhat conservative in the context of new times, which sought a subconscious marginalization. However, it was and continues to be a rich experience, committed and participatory, profoundly ethical, but which requires rejuvenation. In view of this not only can we make criticisms, we can also collect contributions and begin practical searches, make reflections and seek reflective sustenance aimed at rethinking social theory with communicative theory.

4. Inconclusive Processes To Be Reflected By Committed Academic Research

To suspect or undervalue popular communication has been and is a phenomenon more or less common in the academic world, apart from a few exceptions. The university should not have related to this sphere only from a wholehearted commitment and emotional defense. The challenge is to situate oneself specifically in investigation and theoretical reflection linked to the practice from the field of current and future social communication.

It is also true that from the field of committed communicators there has been an almost absolute denial of theoretical work and an attitude contrary to the intellectual activity of the universities. And in this misencounter not only are knowledge and appraisals in competition, but also a communicative logic of mutual incomprehension, some which have been argued out and others not, since emphasis has been placed on errors and not on possibilities for mutual support. However, interesting routes of change and approaches have already been embarked upon, such as the use of research by organizations such as Latin American Association of Radio Education (ALER); a great number of university theses on some aspects of this social promotion; or the incorporation into universities of courses or professional areas such as communication and development, social marketing and popular communication itself.

It is a matter of retrieving information and converting it into knowledge. The university faculties and schools of communication have devoted preferential effort to media analysis, very little to balance and historical characteristics of alternative communication proposals, of the commitment to change in process. Questions remain that need to be answered, and there are challenges we should examine theoretically and pragmatically. Some of them could be:

■ What is the relation (similar, different and antagonistic) between mass and alternative communication? How is it received by the subjects who consume it? What operations of synthesis and application are carried out? What level of impact do both have on Latin American society?

■ What have been the points of departure and the processes of change experienced in the field of popular communication?

■ What type of communication is experienced in poor neighborhoods? How does this co-exist with national and globalized mass communication? Is there an interconnection or just an overlapping?

■ How can the senses, styles and imagination of the popular sectors be recovered in order to become a new proposal for approaching the mass media?

How can the popular media break into the mass media making it liberating?

■ With regard to the connection between participatory communication and political communication: What are the directions required for fighting against apathy and indifference in relation to politics? How can social project be related to the political project? How can development and justice be linked to democracy?

■ Education altered through training, workshops, courses or schools for popular communicators and in relation to which there has been a lot of progress at the pedagogical and participatory level: Were they worth it? How did they transform and how is it possible to attract with more structural and formal education? In reality have practices and the logic of production improved, reaching the sensitivity of people?

II. Towards New Paradigms:

The challenge is big. Such a communicative society as today's, in which economic, cultural and political life is not possible without the intervention of the media, leads us to prioritize communication as a highly strategic activity that relocates in the center the search for a different society from a new communicational paradigm. Our proposal is that popular communication be an extremely rich reference point to be incorporated into the new social and political tasks that we have ahead of us, inviting it to form part of a new search for utopian directions. In this context, we propose some thematic elements of reflection. And then we will indicate some *transitions* we should make to *arrive* at new models.

1. Citizenship Of Another Radical Democracy

If the concept of citizenship was created by traditional liberalism, today there is an interesting theoretical production occurring. From the sphere of political philosophy, democratic principles are being retrieved and the importance of the individual subject is being emphasized, recovering the idea of community as well as the importance of social justice. This production is giving rise to new sectors of commitment with

a society of change (communitarists, liberal socialists, socialists who are liberal and radical democrats). In this spirit we propose the conception of citizenship as a new horizon for communication, committed to the emancipation of our peoples.

We propose some basic definitions of citizenship for a better future, in which interest and individual leadership are balanced with the collective. Knowing that there are different (LOPEZ: 97) and classical (pre-capitalist) emphases, we rethink the idea of citizenship in the following way:

■ Citizenship is legal, social and human equality; in the first place it implies considerations and treatment of mutual respect and egalitarian consideration. But it also means taking responsibility for the existing conflict between principles and the reality. It is therefore a matter of taking responsibility for the existing social inequality in our countries, establishing prioritizations of problems, where this inequality is a determining element. It is a matter of recovering for democracy the idea of justice. This is why in this meaning, poverty is news and a subject for communication.

■ Citizenship is an active belonging. The rights and obligations that all citizens require form part of a connection with the city, the country and the world, which feels and behaves like a fundamental part of the society, deserving respect and generating responsibilities. The dynamic of rights, alone, promotes individual integrations of a defensive nature. Likewise, responsible participation demands respect for these rights. But to belong does not mean submission or being in agreement with the existing system. It is an incorporation into the society that can be uncomfortable and critical, as a minority and as dissidents who demand consideration. This commits us to a communication more closely linked to debate.

■ Citizenship involves citizen commitments with others. Take into account the importance of the common (Arendt 1993), of the building of agreements, the creation of networks, spaces and behaviors of solidarity,

1927
1960
1963
1964
1967
1969
1970
1971
1972
1973
1974
1975
1976
1977
1978
1979
1980
1981
1982
1983
1984
1985
1986
1987
1988
1989
1990
1991
1992
1993
1994
1995
1996
1997
1998
1999
2000
2001
2002
2003
2004
2005
2006

the formation of public spheres. Communication, which seeks these dialogues and promotes collective empowerment, will present the idea of community differently, linked to individual liberties and independence, in a policy of continuous *rapprochement* and collective commitments. All citizens have a knowledge and a separate truth; it is rather a case of building a collective solidarity which means efficacy and concrete productivities in local and mass management.

■ Finally, we would like to suggest there is no single model or prototype of a first-class citizen to judge each member of the population. Rather, it is a question of admitting that there are different processes for approaching citizenship, with development routes sometimes not foreseen. It is necessary to understand again concrete citizens and understand the political culture that has been forming, investigate the past, to enrich participatory educational proposals and dialogue from there. It is a case of investigating the knot of conflict of citizenship building so that from there the methods of work and citizen education can be adapted.

2. The New Public Challenges

It is communication that will deal with the promotion of public debate within a communicational model that seeks to create and maintain the "dialogue networks and symbolic production," differentiating itself from the model of publicity marketing (without denying some of its important uses) and the dissemination model, which concentrates on the transmission of information.

It is a matter of defining a communication at the center of the creation and maintenance of the public in a constructive sense, understood as common interests, spaces and images that guarantee a culturally experienced democracy, in other words, adopted as value and practice, understanding that between consumption and citizenship significant coordination is being generated, and that democracy is very much related to the media because through it power can be visualized.

Thus there are new lines of work, such as the broad and concerted production of the public agenda; the organization of a plural debate that will guarantee being heard and respected and managing to build consensus, identifying key dissent for learning and democratic exercise; the organization of symbolic accounts, which reflect life and daily history and the conflicts of the citizen today; discussions and productions that support the citizens' decision to take and open other spaces of participation; the development of a demand for quality in the media that can exercise oversight; that political problems completely change, becoming interesting and not banal. In other words, a communication that creates and recreates what is public in relation to public citizens. A communication that puts power to the *test* and helps to forge other balances, *empowering* citizens.

This involves organizing a permanent public forum and incorporating it into the popular sectors as important leaders that are not exclusionary, and whose issues will reflect their problems and aim at social inclusion. This task is not simple, since it is not only politics, but it also represents a transformation of the narratives and aesthetics of communication in such a way that will make plural and creative expression and dialogue possible. It is a matter of inducing an encounter of the society with itself and with the future being sought.

The civic educational dimensions to be incorporated should not only be present in the media, but also in the direct practices of the people, moving the society as a whole.

3. Transitions To Be Defined

The process of transforming popular communication to a more civic one is in the middle of our road. This should be from the community to its impact on power. We feel it is significant to raise some elements of change in the sense of *transition*. We point to some steps which invite collective, practical and theoretical production, such as:

- From the popular subject to the *empowered* citizen and, therefore, participating in both the society and the State.
- From the territorial community space to the generation of various public spheres, movable and interlinked: local, regional, national, open to the world. The national being the connection: internal justice, altering the location in the world.
- From the individual world to the community, renewing institutional definitions. Establish different types of community to be promoted and coordinated. The media will promote them not substitute them. These can be organizational, related to consumption, interpretation, interests, and others.
- From alternative or popular communication to the media, making the issue of communication itself part of the public agenda.
- From the production of local or educational media to citizen observation and oversight of the mass media. The right of citizens to express an opinion, to judge, propose, supervise and be informed.
- From independent and committed journalism to new models and roles of journalism in stages of transition and social transformation.
- From freedom of speech of the media to that of the consumer, ethics of balance, democratization.
- From communication for struggle to that which seeks development and justice at different levels: locally from the place where people live to the world and virtual communication; from the alternative to the media, using marketing, but going beyond this; uniting the social with the political.
- From the recovery of cultures and the popular memory to participation for universal cultural production, going through the recognition of various subjects and spaces.
- From the explanation of innovative ideas or against hegemonic ones to the furthering of a deliberative and propositional culture for change.
- From the visibility of the popular word to the conception of influences in decisions: empowerment
- From concern for the contents to requirements for ethical and aesthetic quality in communication.

And we could continue to name other transitions that would place us in the world of today, although it seems unnecessary. Hope should be represented by a search, by many searches. The new will for change will be less ambitious but more profound and demanding. Academic reflection will have to be enriched by action and the evolution that practice dictates or produces from new and old discourses. We are inaugurating another form of coexistence, which is thoughtful, democratic and inclusive, profoundly coordinating and generating a communicative society based on equity and on the daily encounter of the common.

Bibliography

ALFARO MORENO, Rosa María. "De la conquista de la ciudad a la apropiación de la palabra," *Calandria-Tarea*. Lima 1986
—"Participación para qué: un enfoque político de la participación en la comunicación popular," *Diálogos* 22. Felafacs. Lima 1988.
—"Una comunicación para otro desarrollo," *Calandria*. Lima 1993.

ARENDT, Hannah. "La condición Humana," *Paidos*. Estado y Sociedad. Barcelona 1993

BERIAIN, Josetxo. "la integración en las sociedades modernas," *Anthropos*. Barcelona 1996.

BOBBIO, Norberto. El futuro de la democracia. Fondo de cultura económica., especialmente el capítulo IV "La democracia y el poder invisible" Buenos Aires 1993.

BRAUD, Philippe. *El jardín de las delicias democráticas, FCE*. Buenos Aires 1993

CAMPS, Victoria. "El malestar de la vida pública," *Grijalbo*. Barcelona 1996.

CASULLO, Nicolás. "Comunicación: la democracia difícil," *Folios Ediciones*. ILET. Buenos Aires 1985. especialmente el capítulo de Periodistas y Medios.

CERRONI, Humberto. "Reglas y valores de la democracia," *Alianza editorial*. Consejo Nacional para la cultura y las artes. México D.F. 1991

CORTINA, Adela. "Ciudadanos del mundo. Hacia una teoría de la ciudadanía," *Alianza editorial*. Madrid 1997.
—"Razón comunicativa y responsabilidad solidaria" *Ediciones Sígueme*. Salamanca 1995.
—"El mundo de los valores. Etica y educación," *Editorial El Buho*. Bogota 1997
—CONILL, Jesús y CORTINA, Adela. "Democracia participativa y sociedad civil. Una ética empresarial". *Fundación Social*. Siglo del hombre Editores. Bogotá 1998.

DE SOUZA SANTOS, Boaventura. "De la mano de Alicia. Los social y lo político en la postmodernidad," Siglo del hombre editores. Ediciones Uniandes, Universidad de los Andes. Bogotá 1995

ESCALANTE GONZALBO, Fernando. "Ciudadanos imaginarios," Colegio de México 1993. Ver introducción: Moral pública y orden político.

FRASER, Nancy. "Iustitia Interrupta. Reflexiones críticas desde la posición *postsocialista*," *Siglo del Hombre Editores*. Universidad de los Andes. Bogotá 1997.

GARCIA, CANCLINI. "Consumidores y ciudadanos. Conflictos culturales de la globalización," *Grijalbo*. México D.F. 1995

1927
1960
1963
1964
1967
1969
1970
1971
1972
1973
1974
1975
1976
1977
1978
1979
1980
1981
1982
1983
1984
1985
1986
1987
1988
1989
1990
1991
1992
1993
1994
1995
1996
1997
1998
1999
2000
2001
2002
2003
2004
2005
2006

HERMET, Guy. "Cultura y democracia" Instituto Luis Carlos Galán," Bogotá 1995.

KAPLUN, Mario. —"El comunicador popular," *Colección Intiyan*. Quito 1985
—Educación para la Comunicación Televisiva"; Unesco-Céneca. Chjile 1986
—"Video, Comunicación y Educación Popular. Derroteros para una Búsqueda"; Ipal Lima 1989
—"A la Educación por la Comunicación," UNESCO. Chile 1983
—Producción de programas de radio. El guión, la realización," *Ciespal*. Quito 1978

LECHNER, Norbert. "Los patios interiores de la democracia. Subjetividad y política," EFE, FLACSO. Chile 1990.

LELLOUCHE, Raphael. "El fundamento de la moral y la ética del discurso de Karl Otto Apel" en "Teoría política y comunicación" ya citado

LOPEZ JIMENEZ, Sinesio. "Ciudadanos reales e imaginarios. Concepciones, desarrollo y mapas de la ciudadanía en el Perú"

MARTIN BARBERO, Jesús. "La comunicación plural: alteridad y socialidad" en "Los medios nuevas plazas para la democracia". Calandria. Lima. 1995.
—"El miedo a los medios. La nueva representación política en Colombia

MARTIN BARBERO, Jesús y REY, Germán. "El periodismo en Colombia. De los oficios y los medios". Signo y Pensamiento n.30 Sala de Redacción.

MEJIA, Marco Raúl y RESTREPO, Gabriel. "Formación y educación para la democracia en Colombia". UNESCO. Instituto Luis Carlos Galán. Bogotá 1997.

ORTIZ, Renato. "Mundialización y cultura" Alianza editorial. Buenos Aires 97.

SARTORI, Giovanni. "Ingeniería constitucional comparada," PÁGS 159-167 (lo difícil de la política. La videopolítica y la videodemocracia)

SOL, Ricardo. "medios masivos y comunicación popular," ILET. Editorial Porvenir. Costa Rica. 1984

REY, Germán, RESTREPO, Javier Darío. "Desde las dos orillas," Ministerio de Comunicaciones 1995

REY, Germán. "Deambular, entretenerse, intercambiar: medios de comunicación y expresiones ciudadanas" en "Educación ciudadana, democracia y participación", Patricia Arregui y Santiago Cueto (editores). USAID-GRADE. Lima, Junio 1998

REYES MATTA, Fernando. "Comunicación alternativa y búsquedas democráticas," ILET y F.Ebert. México 1982.

ROWE, William Y SCHELLING, Vivian. "Memoria y modernidad. Cultura popular en América Latina". Grijalbo-Consejo Nacional para la Cultura y la Paz. México 1991.

VIDAL BENEYTO, José (editor). "Alternativas populares a la comunicación de masa," *Centro de Investigaciones Sociológicas*. Madrid 1979

WHITE, Robert. "Factores sociales y políticos en el desarrollo de la ética de la comunicación," *Diálogos* n.22

Libros de varios autores:

"El nuevo espacio público". Gedis . El mamífero parlante. Barcelona 1995. Si bien todo el libro es interesante podemos destacar a:

Wolton, Dominique. "La comunicación política: construcción de un modelo"

Wolton, Dominique. "Los medios, eslabón débil de la comunicación política"

Livet, Pierre. "Medios de comunicación masiva y limitaciones de la comunicación"

Bregman, Dorine. "La función de agenda: una problemática en transformación"

Veron, Eliseo. "Interfaces sobre la democracia audiovisual avanzada"
—"Escenografías para el diálogo", CEAAL. Calandria 1997. Ver especialmente:
Rey, Germán. Otras plazas para el encuentro

Macassi, Sandro. Las agendas públicas: de lo público al espectáculo
Alfaro, Rosa María. Transiciones de época o época de transición?

Landi Oscar (compilador) "Medios, transformación cultural y política". Legasa. Buenos Aires. 1987.

"Comunicación y movimientos sociales" Carmen Caffarel, Francisco Bernete y Vicente Baca (editores) .AECI, Universidad complutense, Ayuntamiento de Almagro. Madrid 1994.

"Redes solidarias, culturas y multimedialidad" Servicio Conjunto de comunicación. Quito 1998

"La democracia de los de abajo en México" compiladores Jorge Alonso y Juan Manuel Ramírez Sáiz.

La jornada Ediciones, Consejo Electoral del estado de Jalisco, Centro de Investigaciones interdisciplinariias en Humanidades/UNAM. Jalisco 1997.

Zemelman, Hugo (coordinador). "Cultura y política en LA". Siglo XXI. Editorial de la universidad de naciones Unidas. México 1990. Ver especialmente:
—Mirko "Cultura política y democracia representativa en Perú" pág 162-176
—José Joaquín. "Chile: entre la cultura autoritaria y la cultura democrática", págs. 85-98
—"Entre públicos y ciudadanos". Calandria. Lima 1996:

Garreton. Manuel Antonio "Democracia, ciudadanía y medios de comunicación. Un marco general". Op.cit. Calandria 1995

Alfaro M. Rosa María "Descifrando paradojas ciudadanas. Una mirada cultural a la política". Op.cit Calandriia 1995.

Protzel Javier "Participación ciudadana en los medios". Op.cit. Calandria 1995

Charles Mercedes "Educación para la recepción ciudadana". Op.cit. Calandria 1995.

Empresa privada y responsabilidad social.Olga Lucío Toro y Germán Rey editores. Utópica Ediciones. Bogotá 1996:

Rey Germán "Las espaldas del vecino"

Santos Rafael "Responsabilidad social y medios de comunicación: la veeduría para la administración de justicia"

Tulande, Francisco. "Los medios de comunicación y la solidaridad ciudadana.

Herran, María Teresa. "La responsabilidad social de los medios de comunicación"

"La necesidad de información para la acción social responsable" varios autores.
—Revista iberoamericana de Educación. N.7. Madrid 1995:

Hoyos Vásquez, Guillermo. "Etica comunicativa y educación para la democracia"

Cortina, Adela. "La educación del hombre y el ciudadano"

Martinez, Martin Miquel. "La educación moral: una necesidad en las sociedades plurales y democráticas"

Calandria: varios sondeos de cultura política .

"Materiales para la Comunicación Popular", varios números desde 1983. ILET. Lima, Perú.

"Nuevos Rostros para una Comunicación Solidaria" OCIC-AL, UCLAP, UNDAAL. Quito 1994.

Alfaro, Rosa María. "Popular Cultures and Paticipatory Communication: On the Route to Redefinitions," published in Daza Hernández, Gladys (compiladora): *¿Participación social en los medios masivos?*. Fundación Konrad Adenauer y Universidad Pontificia Bolivariana, Medellín (Colombia), 1998. Reprinted with permission of the author. Originally published in Spanish.

CONTEMPORARY READINGS
VOLUME ❷
Social Movements & Community Participation

STUDYING NEW SOCIAL MOVEMENTS TO RENEW DEVELOPMENT COMMUNICATION RESEARCH

By Robert Huesca

2001 The field of development communication currently faces a critical juncture that both challenges its social relevance and offers new opportunities for practical and theoretical progress (Wilkins 2000). This juncture is characterized by changes in external, material and symbolic contexts that frame the nature of these challenges while simultaneously indicating fruitful directions for the continued progression of development communication theory.

Advancements in communication technologies occurring simultaneously with the worldwide restructuring of political, economic and social systems have reduced the legitimacy of traditional institutions, promoted the virtue of markets and questioned the pertinence of development communication theory and practice (Escobar 2000). Furthermore, the evolution of development communication theory has been marked by severe internal criticism and heated debate that—while broadening definitions, encouraging intellectual pluralism and renewing interest in the field—have clouded the direction for future conceptual advancement.

An area of recent theoretical interest that might fruitfully contribute to the directions taken by development communication scholars is offered by research of what have been called "new social movements." This growing body of research, which has emerged from sociology and political science, demonstrates the continued interest and ability of people to strive for alterations in politics, economics, and culture—relevant arenas for traditional development practice. The findings from these studies serve to inform and guide development communication research, as well as to commend its continued evolution. Moreover, the specific theoretical understandings and characteristics of new social movements converge conceptually with the advancements in participatory communication for development research.

The convergence of these two bodies of research offers directions for the continued study of development communication, while renewing conceptual interest in specific aspects of participatory approaches to development. To illustrate the directions and interests suggested by this convergence, I will first explain some key notions stemming from new social movements research. Next I will briefly sketch out the most relevant areas of conceptual affinity within the participatory communication for development research. Finally, I will trace out some of the directions for development communication that are suggested by the findings of new social movement scholarship.

Studying New Social Movements

Beginning in the late 1960s, scholars from sociology and political science began conceptualizing forces of social change as emerging from coordinated actions occurring outside of formal institutions, such as political parties and labor unions. What made these theories of social change "new" was their attention to identity formation as a locus of coordinated action and their de-emphasis of group access to institutional resources or adherence to overarching ideologies that guided mobilization. This focus on new social movements gained renewed momentum in the 1980s and 1990s, especially in Latin America, with the emergence of ethnic, gender and issue—organizing initiatives that similarly were not explained satisfactorily by liberal democratic, and/or Marxist theories of social change.

The theoretical evolution of the new social movements research parallels the intellectual transformation of the development communication field, especially in its dissatisfaction with the evaluations and prescriptions suggested by early modernization and dependency theories, which are conceptually analogous to liberal democratic and Marxist theories of social change.

Because of its focus on action, the new social movements literature has described and analyzed social contexts and action processes in a way that enriches further inquiry into development communication. Despite the outstanding descriptions and evaluations of social contexts and actions, however, the new social movements literature proceeds with little, if any, sense of communication processes and often with naive assumptions regarding the power of mass media—much as early development theories conceived of them as magic multipliers.[1] Nevertheless, the research into new social movements provides both practical and conceptual directions to developmencommunication theory.

The study of new social movements has generated literally hundreds of research projects—large and small—that would be impossible to review in this article. What follows, therefore, is a summary of the key ideas in the literature that bear directly on the contemporary study of development communication. These key ideas attend to context, basic definitions and characteristics, and the role of power as depicted in the study of new social movements. This summary will serve as a basic framework that will both inform and be informed by participatory communication approaches to development.

The Context of Globalization

Numerous scholars from distinct philosophical traditions and academic disciplines have examined broad, historical changes when analyzing the emergence of new social movements. They have noted that contemporary societies are in a period of radical transformation that is changing basic human senses of time, space, self and society (Castells 1996b; Escobar & Alvarez 1992; Hopenhayn 1993; Rodrik 1997; Touraine 1971). Referred to variously by terms such as "postmodern,"

"postindustrial," "the information society," and "globalization," this period has been accelerated by the advent of new communication technologies that have enabled the restructuring of global capitalism such that it has altered the production, distribution and consumption of material and symbolic culture significantly.

In his impressive study of the nature and consequences of this rare, historical interval, Castells (1996b) concluded that we are entering the period of the "network society,." characterized by "placeless space" and governed by "timeless time." Localities in the network society "become disembodied from their cultural, historical, geographic meaning, and reintegrated into functional networks, inducing a space of flows that substitutes for the space of places" (375). The configurations of this new space of flows are determined mostly by the organizational capacity of dominant elites and are apparent in flexible work flows, outsourced production, instantaneous global financial transactions and a homogeneous, elite, business culture linked by wired laptops and ubiquitous cellular phones.

Taking up strategic positions within the space of flows, however, is not limited to the agency of dominant elites. These transnational capital flows combined with improvements in communication and transportation have unleashed a web of processes that have facilitated migrations across the borders of underdeveloped and industrialized states, resulting in postcolonial cities and reterritorialized subcultures (Sassen 1998). Hence, the repercussions of placeless space reach asymmetrically—though not unilaterally—from the resource-rich strategic planners to the "human robots" who execute tasks that cannot be automated (Castells 1996b, 244).

The emergence of a space of flows has been accompanied by a commensurate shift in the dominant sense of temporality, which is characterized by erasure and nonlinearity. Rather than being disciplined by clock time—as occurred in modernity—space is marked by relativized time that systematically perturbs the sequential ordering of tasks performed in its context.

---

1 The work of Habermas (1981) stands as an exception, as he conceptualized new social movements early on as "sub-culturally protected communications groups" and "communicative structures" (36). The substantial body of Habermas' scholarship into constructing a theory of communicative action has been adopted widely in development communication (e.g. Jacobson 1993; Jacobson & Kolluri 1999). His research occupies an insignificant space, however, in the vast research of new social movements that has emerged from sociology and political science.

1927
1960
1963
1964
1967
1969
1970
1971
1972
1973
1974
1975
1976
1977
1978
1979
1980
1981
1982
1983
1984
1985
1986
1987
1988
1989
1990
1991
1992
1993
1994
1995
1996
1997
1998
1999
2000
2001
2002
2003
2004
2005
2006

New computing technologies enable the manipulation of time, as contingent systems can program past, present, and future to interact with one another in the same process. As with the coordination of the space of flows, time management belongs largely to elites in the network, while underprivileged actors continue to experience the time discipline of clock-run assembly lines and short life expectancies. The radical shifts in time order, together with a modified sense of space, alters "the operations and outcomes in processes of production, experience, power, and culture" in which both social order and change occur (Castells 1996b, 469).

In the context of this significant global restructuring, traditional institutions (including development agencies) charged with maintaining social order and managing change have slowly lost authority, power and credibility. The power of corporations has begun to eclipse the authority of the state, as significant policy decisions are negotiated in multilateral arenas and private associations to facilitate global restructuring.[2] The resulting relocation of significant centers of economic productivity and the shifting of work practices, from cyclical to random, flexible, and contingent schedules, has segmented and disorganized masses of people, leaving traditional institutions incapable of responding to their needs and interests. Anchoring institutions such as labor unions, political parties, churches and families are seen as incapable of reproducing culture in a manner congruous with the changes occurring at elite levels of society (Castells 1983; Touraine 1971; Hannigan 1985; Hellman 1992). This erosion of legitimacy and power forces traditional institutions—including development agencies—to rethink their organization and their approach to problems and inequities that persist in the global society.

Nevertheless, the same forces that have undermined the legitimacy, authority and power of traditional institutions and organizations also have created a symbolic space for new forms of resistance to exploitation and domination. In the timeless space of flows, neither the logic of modernization nor dependency governs political and economic policies, but an anything-goes spirit of so-called free trade guides the treaties and procedures of transnational regimes.

Bolstered by intensified, global interconnections through production and consumption activities, neoliberal policies have resulted in the partial erasure of national boundaries and a profound cultural crossing of material and symbolic products that limit the capacity of dominant ideologies to dominate, even while perpetuating relationships of subordination (García Canclini 1993; Stern 2000). From an analytic perspective, this material and symbolic restructuring coincides with the postmodern(ization) perspective that demands more concern, respect and tolerance for diverse forms of human subjectivity and identity when exploring social order and change (Beverley & Oviedo 1993; Waters 1995).

Indeed, new social movements, often diverse and focused on identity formation, have arisen in this rich, contradictory context and may pose the most significant challenge in the global struggle for democratic guarantees and the provision of social services (Melucci 1998). A number of scholars have documented how a wide variety of social movements has converged on common issues such as human rights, the environment and labor standards to affect policies in national and transnational arenas (Brecher, et al. 2000; Evans 2000; Keck & Sikkink 1998; Starr 2000). Dubbed "globalization from below," the process of coordinating social action transnationally has been enabled by the abstract contextual shifts described earlier. For example, the movement of capital, technology, equipment and commodities has created unstable identity contexts—placeless space—for workers and consumers that disturb traditional senses of self in terms of expectations and demands.

---

2 Scholars debate the extent of the decline of the role and autonomy of the nation-state and warn against discarding its importance as an analytic category in an untimely fashion. Most social scientists tend to agree, however, that contemporary forces in political, economic and cultural arenas are undermining the legitimacy and force of the nation-state with unprecedented intensity. The point here is not to argue the irrelevance of the nation-state, but merely to establish a significant shift in our understanding of the context in which development practices occur.

New social movements arising in this context have taken advantage of cheap communication and transportation technologies to create and sustain global communities that have engaged transnational regimes, such as the World Bank, International Monetary Fund and World Trade Organization. In fact, transnational regimes often provide symbolic categories and material venues that can be used by new social movements as tactics for making demands.

Studies of globalization from below ironically tend to examine the process of transnational coordination from above. That is, they emphasize and focus on the importance of networks and alliances across borders. For example, Evans (2000) explains the importance of the connections established by rubber tappers in Brazil with environmental activists in the United States in challenging Brazilian deforestation policies in the arena of the World Bank and IMF. Likewise, Brecher, et al. (2000) provide multiple accounts of how transnational networks linking small, grassroots movements were fundamental in coordinating actions to dispute, for example, water policies in Bolivia, labor negotiations in the United States and drug pricing in Africa. While these accounts are useful at documenting the consequences of new social movements, which often appear ephemeral, small and isolated, they gloss over the crucial and complex process of movement emergence and development.

Within the daunting context of a radically restructured global society, new social movements have emerged as widespread phenomena that appear to be playing a role that once was fulfilled by formal institutions, such as political parties and labor unions. Given the potential importance of new social movements in the process of social change, development communication scholars would be wise to attend to their formation, maintenance, and difficulties in order to rethink the field's practical and theoretical future. What follows is a brief review of the main characteristics of new social movements.

Understanding New Social Movements

New social movements have been conceptualized as responding effectively to the major shifts in social, political and economic relations described above. They have been understood for nearly 30 years as recognizing the decline in the importance of material relations of production and the reduction—not elimination—of the role played by unions and parties in effecting change (Touraine 1971). These early observations, which were grounded in European experiences, have been noted in Latin America as well, where new forms of organizing and acting for social change emerged in the 1980s and 1990s (Alvarez, et al. 1998; Escobar & Alvarez 1992; Fals Borda 1992; Hellman 1997; Hopenhayn 1993). Making sense of these new forms has evolved from early studies celebrating the profound impact of new social movements on political structures and policy agendas, to current research that is more circumspect and modest in assessing their consequences (Slater 1994). Despite the changing sense of the overall impact of new social movements, this theoretical framework has always maintained that these forms of organizing represented departures from the structures and practices that were situated at the heart of both modernization and dependency analyses. Hence, new social movements exist in a historical conjuncture of challenge and instability....

Defining new social movements and differentiating them from earlier theories of protest and collective mobilization has been contentious and inexact. Prior to the new social movements theories, researchers conceptualized coordinated action as resulting from unruly mobs characterized by certain psychological attributes (crowd behavior), ideological unification and direction (frame alignment processes), or access and management of material supports and organizational forms (resource mobilization).[3] What these prior

---

3 A valuable historical review of this research was published in McAdam et al. (1988). Other scholarship useful at sketching out the general patterns in social movement research and the distinctions made by new social movement theorists include Escobar & Alvarez (1992), Hannigan (1985), and Melucci (1989, 1994)

1927
1960
1963
1964
1967
1969
1970
1971
1972
1973
1974
1975
1976
1977
1978
1979
1980
1981
1982
1983
1984
1985
1986
1987
1988
1989
1990
1991
1992
1993
1994
1995
1996
1997
1998
1999
2000
2001
2002
2003
2004
2005
2006

approaches held in common was the desire to develop reductionist explanations by focusing on cognitive, structural organizational factors contributing to movement emergence and maintenance. New social movement theorists have reacted against this reductionist tendency of these earlier approaches.

Indeed, several scholars have resisted even defining new social movements, as such an external imposition would violate the self-determination, fluidity, heterogeneity, and openness that characterize them (Escobar & Alvarez 1992; Melucci 1998). And yet general characteristics have emerged that distinguish this research area from earlier approaches. New social movements are understood as small, decentralized and democratic in structure; cyclical and diffuse in their temporal arrangement; and action-driven toward identity construction in their orientation. In the most general sense, new social movements have been defined as heterogeneous groups forming outside of formal institutions and operating in discontinuous cycles to forge collective meanings and identities that direct action. Each of these dimensions—structural, temporal and identity—is outlined briefly below.

The small, decentralized and democratic structures of new social movements have been interpreted as a rejection of, alternative to and model for, traditional organizations that bridge the spheres of the institutionalized system and the everyday lifeworld (Fals Borda 1992; Habermas 1981; Hannigan 1985). Political parties, labor unions and other large bureaucracies represent ossified, unresponsive structures unable to sense changing interests, difficulties and priorities of their traditional constituents. New social movements offer structures that reflect a more human scale and rely upon member participation for their maintenance (Flacks 1994). The intense participation generated in these alternative structures means that new social movements frequently converge on highly personal and intimate issues—such as gender and sexuality—that limit their range of interest (Johnston, et al. 1994).

Ironically, such narrow interests necessitate boundary identification and maintenance, which paradoxically limit membership and participation. Lesbian feminist groups, for example, have created a space where a marginalized population could openly discuss issues relevant to its experiences, yet the group's cohesion required differentiating itself from other feminist organizations (Taylor & Whittier 1992). The practices of boundary-setting and maintaining are generally understood as axiomatic strategies of identity movements springing from participatory settings. They are mentioned here to illustrate the limits and contradictions that permeate small, democratic structures, which run the risk of dissolving into segmented, self-referential organizations incapable of forging alliances that might constitute stronger forces of social change (Hellman 1997; Johnston, et al. 1994).

Because of their small, decentralized structure, new social movements are marked temporally by sporadic, yet cyclical, orientations toward expressing collective identity and discontent (Downing 1996). The temporal ebb and flow of action is related to the deinstitutionalized contexts of new social movements, which emerge more often in the invisible laboratories and submerged networks of everyday life. Such networks are contingent upon and responsive to changing circumstances in the environment, an orientation more consistent with contemporary conditions where space organizes time, not vice versa (Castells 1996b). A sporadic temporal orientation means that new social movements, such as the early Madres de la Plaza de Mayo movement in Argentina, are difficult to document because they are often hidden from the view of social critics (Jelin 1994). They also appear to be of ephemeral, fleeting and transient consequence, but actually they constitute a "permanent reality" due to their impact on transcendent social relationships (Melucci 1994).

Finally, new social movements are oriented less toward instrumental aims of material concessions and more toward the construction of identities and meanings that give direction to collective behavior (Castells 1983;

Habermas 1981; Lowe 1986; Melucci 1998; Touraine 1981). The identity orientation of new social movements has been conceptualized in significantly different ways by scholars. One group treats identity formation as a static category that operates theoretically as a functional stand-in for ideology. Termed "experienced consciousness," "interactional accomplishments" or "identity frames," these conceptualizations of identity focus on symbolic expressions of self, antagonists, allies and audiences as the basis for interpreting social action. (Flacks 1994; Hunt, et al. 1994; Johnston, et al. 1994; Snow & Benford 1988). ...

A slightly different conceptualization of identity has emerged from scholars who have based their understanding of identity on an epistemology of action (Castells 1983; Lowe 1986; Melucci 1989; Touraine 1981). This perspective posits that new social movement participation, mobilization, intervention, reproduction and dissolution all emerge through interactions that effectively constitute collective identities and visions for the future. Rather than suggesting that identity functions as an antecedent to action, the epistemology of action perspective suggest that identity is bound up in and inseparable from action. From this perspective, empirical research of identity and new social movements must center on processes including how individuals become involved, sustained and estranged from movements; how actors construct collective identity in action; and how the unity of various elements of action is produced (Castells 1983; Hellman 1994; Melucci 1989; Stern 2000). Nevertheless, "the problem for most analysts is that we do not know enough about how this [the making of social movements] takes place" (Hellman 1994, 124). Indeed, few scholars of new social movements have actually focused on how the injustices at the heart of most movements get translated into the everyday lives and actions of collectivities and their members. "Despite the centrality of collective identity to new social movement theory, no one has dissected the way that constituencies involved in defending their rights develop politicized group identities" (Taylor & Whittier 1992, 105). An orientation toward the processes of identity construction would avoid the halls of power and examine the contexts of everyday life, given the distinctive formations of new social movements. "It is in these back alleys of society... that I have sensed the embryos of a new society" (Castells 1996a, 362).

Focusing on the contexts of everyday life, however, does not imply that scholars of new social movements ignore the force and power embedded in larger social, political and economic structures. On the contrary, adopting an epistemology of action has provided a theoretically rich framework for bridging the influences of both structure and agency on social change. Scholars have acknowledged that meanings and identities of social movements are not self-formed through collective action alone but in interaction with powerful institutions (Scott 1995). Action orientations toward new social movements acknowledge both discursive-symbolic and material-structural factors that play a part in both the reproduction and transformation of the social system (Castells 1983; Escobar & Alvarez 1992). Nevertheless, researchers of new social movements have not treated these two dimensions as independent areas of investigation and analysis, but as products of discourse and interpretation. In determining the characteristics of both symbolic and structural factors, researchers of new social movements have privileged the actual participants of collective action as sources of interpretation (Castells 1983, 1996a; Hellman 1997; Melucci 1998; Touraine 1981). This turn toward the interpretive subjectivity of movement participants is accompanied by an explicit theory of power vis-à-vis processes of social change.

Whereas power is admittedly asymmetrical in the restructured, global society, it generally is not conceptualized as either transparent or one-dimensional in the new social movements literature. Rather, power is viewed as a relationship that is diffused throughout the social system and reproduced subjectively (Alvarez, et al. 1998; Touraine 1988). "The new power lies in the codes of information and in the images of

1927
1960
1963
1964
1967
1969
1970
1971
1972
1973
1974
1975
1976
1977
1978
1979
1980
1981
1982
1983
1984
1985
1986
1987
1988
1989
1990
1991
1992
1993
1994
1995
1996
1997
1998
1999
2000
2001
2002
2003
2004
2005
2006

representation around which societies organize their institutions, and people build their lives, and decide their behavior. The sites of this power are people's minds" (Castells 1996a, 359). In understanding new social movements and their impacts, processes of identity construction and self-transformation are themselves posited as major strategies of political change (Taylor & Whittier 1992). Such a conceptualization of power not only necessitates reproduction, it is subject to modification and reinvention, which opens the way toward building strategies for social change (Fals Borda 1992). New social movements research eschews binary notions, such as powerful/powerless, and embraces more multilayered, diffuse, yet asymmetrical understandings of power that are subject to negotiation, challenge and redefinition.

The identification of the significant role played by new social movements in contemporary processes of social change offers theoretical and practical guidance to scholars of development communication. The studies of globalization and its accompanying shifts in basic time–space understandings illuminate the exigencies facing development communication researchers, even while raising new questions and difficulties. And the identification of the characteristics of new social movements provides practical and conceptual guidance to development communication scholars, while offering renewed relevance to this general area of inquiry. Moreover, the emphasis on the "hows" of social movements via the epistemology of action orientation toward identity construction invites attention to communication processes as a key dimension in understanding movement emergence, formation, maintenance and dissolution. Therefore, studies of new social movements not only provide direction to development communication scholars; they also point to areas where communication research might fruitfully contribute to understanding hese processes.

The area of participatory communication for development seems particularly compatible with continued research into new social movements. Historically,

the emergence of participatory communication approaches represents a departure from both modernization and dependency models of development, just as new social movements theory challenges liberal democratic and Marxist-structuralist accounts of social change. The focus on the dialogical processes at the heart of participatory communication for development further mirrors the attention to identity formation as a central characteristic of what's "new" about new social movements. Finally, renewed attention to power among participatory communication scholars coincides with conceptualizations of power that have been incorporated into the understandings of new social movements and their impacts.

Participatory Communication for Social Change

Since the early 1970s, the dominant paradigm of development communication has undergone significant challenge. This challenge was particularly intense from Latin American scholars who questioned the legitimacy of modernization approaches to development and called for more appropriate communication theories and practices. One of the outcomes of this intense critique of the dominant paradigm has been the emergence of a substantial body of research in the area of participatory communication for development. Despite a robust history and a rich evolution, the concept of participatory communication is subject to loose interpretation that appears at best to be variable and contested and at worst misused and distorted (Arnst 1996; Jacobson & Servaes 1999). The current state of conceptual confusion in the participatory communication field begs intervention of the sort potentially offered by the research into new social movements.

Noncommunication Models of Communication for Development

Latin American critics of the dominant paradigm of development faulted big media and diffusion projects for implementing practices that belied the dynamic essence at the heart of communication (Beltrán 1975, 1980; Freire 1970, 1973b). Modernization projects did this by relying on communication models that depicted active senders providing passive receivers with valuable information to achieve social change. Critics argued that such static, linear and transmission models violated the dynamic, interactive and meaning-centered nature of communication. Latin American scholars introduced a phenomenological and critical orientation that radically altered the conceptualization, study, and practice of development communication.

They suggested that more fluid and elastic communication models centering on how-meaning-comes-to-be form the basis for development communication interventions. These more fluid and meaning-centered conceptualizations of communication emphasized co-presence, intersubjectivity, phenomenological "being in the world" and openness of interlocutors (Pasquali 1963). This view introduced a sophisticated grounding that collective understandings of social reality are achieved between people, in material contexts, and in communication. In other words, traditional development approaches of understanding and changing reality through the unilateral definition of problems, objectives and solutions were criticized as violating the process essence of meaning making that is central to communication.

The phenomenological turn in development communication was accompanied by a commensurate introduction of critical theories of society and a concern for the role played by institutions in maintaining structures of inequality. Best known of the early critical development scholars is Freire (1970), whose experience in traditional educational structures was seen as analogous to modernization approaches to development. In contrast to oppressive, top-down pedagogies and development programs, Freire proposed a liberating, participatory approach that centered on praxis—self-reflexive, theoretically guided practice. Under this orientation, he suggested that practitioners close the distance between teacher and student, development agent and client, researcher and researched, in order to enter into a co-learning relationship guided by action and reflection. This orientation was shot through with the ethical stance on the side of the poor that was articulated by liberation theologians who influenced Freire's scholarship at the time. …

Dialogic Methods

While the critique of the dominant paradigm provided both a philosophical and an epistemological framework for scholarship, it also suggested a practical, companion method in the form of dialogue. Dialogic communication was held in stark contrast to information transmission models emerging from Lasswell's (1964) five-point question of who says what in what channel to whom with what effect. This required development researchers and practitioners to seek out the experiences, understandings and aspirations of others to construct jointly reality and formulate actions (Beltrán 1980). Freire (1970, 1973a) provided concrete exercises for initiating critical dialogues to, in effect, deconstruct social contexts, separate out their constituent parts and reconstruct a thematic universe for pursuing social transformation. This methodological approach generated a "cultural synthesis" between development collaborators to arrive at mutually identified problems, needs, and guidelines for action.

Aside from its practical contribution, dialogue was promoted as an ethical communication choice within the development context. Freire (1970) argued that true humanization emerged from one's ability "to name the world" in dialogic encounters. Grounded in Buber's notion of "I–Thou" communication, Freire argued that subject–object distinctions were impossible to maintain in true dialogue because one's sense of self and the world is elicited in interaction with others. The resulting fusion of identities and communal naming of the world did not emerge merely from an exchange of information; however; it required a moral commitment among dialogue partners. "Being dialogic is not invading, not manipulating, not imposing orders. Being dialogic is pledging oneself to the constant transformation of reality" (Freire 1973b, 46). This

1927
1960
1963
1964
1967
1969
1970
1971
1972
1973
1974
1975
1976
1977
1978
1979
1980
1981
1982
1983
1984
1985
1986
1987
1988
1989
1990
1991
1992
1993
1994
1995
1996
1997
1998
1999
2000
2001
2002
2003
2004
2005
2006

highly developed sense of dialogue—simultaneously practical and rarefied—has been adopted and refined by scholars who advocate its use in participatory development research and practice (Fals Borda 1988; Rahman 1993).

Power Revisited

Early advocates of participatory approaches to development communication recognized power dynamics as shaping both development and research projects. For the most part, however, these early critics conceptualized power through a set of binary opposites—powerful/powerless, oppressor/oppressed, authoritarian/liberatory—and naively called for its general redistribution within cultures and across nations.

More recent research has focused explicitly on power and conceptualized it in a nuanced and problematic way. For the most part, power has been theorized as both multicentered—not one dimensional—and asymmetrical (Servaes 1996b; Tehranian 1999). This multicentered and asymmetrical perspective acknowledges the force of institutions and structures, but emphasizes the role of human agency in reproducing and transforming them (Tehranian 1999). Within this generalized framework of power, participatory communication is seen by some as being a potential source of social transformation (Nair & White 1994; Riaño 1994). By virtue of the differences—ethnic, gender, sexual and the like—that multiple social actors bring to development projects, participatory communication reveals how power functions to subordinate certain groups of people (Riaño 1994). Within participatory development communication projects, individuals and groups experience "generative power" whereby they create the capacity for action, which can be harnessed to reshape and transform conditions of subordination (Nair & White 1994). Far from asserting an even distribution of power, recent participatory development communication research has attempted to be more sensitive to the multiple dimensions of power, especially as they emerge from groups marked by inherent differences.

Discussion and Conclusion

The coincidental research into new social movements and into participatory communication for development have run along parallel tracks that hold much potential for mutual enrichment. Scholars of new social movements have articulated a valuable sense of the context of globalization that must be reckoned with by development researchers. Furthermore, they have provided practical guidance regarding where communication development scholars might direct their attention. Finally, research into new social movements has included a complex interpretation of power relations in social change efforts that enriches development communication scholarship in this shared area of interest.

For the most part, scholars of new social movements have examined the importance of the contemporary transformations in social reality to a far greater degree than has the communication field. They have argued convincingly that the contemporary context of development efforts has shifted significantly in the past 20 years, altering baseline notions of time and space and diminishing the importance of traditional institutions. This refined sense of context can inform development communication scholars and practitioners who must reconsider how they conceptualize their enterprise. Many scholars and practitioners have already demonstrated sensitivity to these contextual changes by directing their attention away from state projects and big media interventions toward grassroots initiatives. But even scholars who have adopted this orientation stand to gain conceptual ground by incorporating postmodern(ization) sensibilities into their research. For example, interpreting participants themselves as multidimensional, dynamic, unstable and emergent will have a significant impact on intellectual inquiry and strategic intervention. Rather than paralyzing research and practice, as some versions of postmodern theory are wont to do, such a sensibility will open up new possibilities for intellectual and pragmatic advance. Development scholars and practitioners might be drawn to the physical junctions, hybrid zones and global cities where transnational capital intersects with reterritorialized subjects who are amenable to new notions of community, membership, expectations and entitlement. Development communication theories and practices that are responsive to the contextual shifts highlighted above will need to be far more flexible and contingent in their descriptions, explanations, and prescriptions for interventions.

Despite the unstable and diffuse nature of the contemporary context, technological and political forces driving globalization have opened up new possibilities for coordinating action through the creation of cross-border networks. A number of scholars reviewed above have documented the gains of small, grassroots organizations that have forged alliances with like-minded groups to achieve significant concessions in a process dubbed "globalization from below. "While these studies tend to neglect the complex and necessary dynamics of grassroots movement formation on which global networks rely, they are useful to development communication scholars nonetheless. Of course these studies highlight how development projects might enter the "space of flows" of global networking to extend their impacts. But they also suggest that global networks can shape and energize emergent movements by providing new symbolic categories and frames of reference that participants can access when formulating expectations and demands. Attention to such details will capture a dynamic aspect of global networking that may provide important insights to cross-border solidarity efforts.

Whereas the shifting social context noted above carries significant implications for development communication theory, the description of the characteristics of new social movements provides practical direction and guidance as well. The identification of small, decentralized, diffuse and democratic groups emerging outside of institutional structures reinforces many of the practical and theoretical directions pursued by participatory approaches to development communication. But the additional focus on the sporadic, yet cyclical, orientation of new social movements

invites development communication scholars to attend to temporal dimensions more systematically in research and practice. Most development projects, even those occurring at the grassroots level, tend to incorporate linear notions of time into their design and assessment. Incorporating the ebb and flow of action characteristic of de-institutionalized contexts into development theory and practice will necessarily change the design and study of development communication. Rather than proceeding in a linear progression, development projects themselves might become more sporadic, multifocused and cyclical in nature to align themselves to the rhythms of the lifeworld reflected in new social movements. Such development projects will build in dimensions of contingency, flux and responsiveness to anticipated exigencies that arise in the contexts of everyday life. These dimensions must also be added to the conceptual repertoire of development communication scholars as they go about the task of understanding and assessing particular development efforts. Attending to temporality in the ways suggested by the research of new social movements will achieve a coherence and consistency between development communication theory and the contemporary context marked by globalization.

Aside from raising awareness of temporality, new social movements research also emphasizes the importance of understanding the processes of identity formation in action. Several scholars of new social movements have stated that the most significant challenge facing researchers in this area regards studying how this transformation of self-in-action takes place. Participatory approaches to development are well positioned to respond to this challenge and to contribute to understandings of identity formation. With the introduction of critical theories and methods articulated by early critics of the dominant paradigm, participatory communication scholars have an established methodology based on dialogic praxis that offers a promising mode of entree into the study of how social movements emerge and develop. The philosophical foundation established by phenomenological explanations

1927
1960
1963
1964
1967
1969
1970
1971
1972
1973
1974
1975
1976
1977
1978
1979
1980
1981
1982
1983
1984
1985
1986
1987
1988
1989
1990
1991
1992
1993
1994
1995
1996
1997
1998
1999
2000
2001
2002
2003
2004
2005
2006

of collective understandings and the embrace of dialogic praxis as a methodological mandate of participatory communication research are consistent with the presuppositions and theories that describe and explain new social movements. Taking the direction indicated by the challenges noted above suggests that development communication scholars actively align themselves with popular movements as a way of gaining insights into the identity formation process that have eluded research of new social movements.

Aligning research with popular movements, or even studying them at a distance, necessitates an acknowledgment of, and accounting for, power. While scholars have noted power's complexity in its simultaneously asymmetrical and multidimensional nature, they have also identified conceptualizations of power as possibly the thorniest, problematic issue facing researchers of new social movements. Noting the tendency of small identity movements to set and maintain boundaries, scholars have warned that such groups run the risk of dissolving into self-referential organizations that undercut their democratic origins.

Moreover, movements resisting the tendencies of globalization have exercised power that is of a reactionary and oppressive nature, as in the cases of militia, skinhead and fundamentalist Christian groups. Neither new social movements research nor participatory development communication scholarship has offered a viable theoretical response for coming to terms with this empirical and conceptual challenge. Thinking through the issue of how it is that liberating processes (participation in the collective construction of identity) can generate oppressive consequences constitutes the most significant theoretical challenge currently facing both of these fields.

Participatory approaches to development communication stand to gain conceptual clarity, practical direction and renewed relevance by drawing on the contributions from scholarship of new social movements. The articulation of a changed global context, identification of shared characteristics, and elaboration of power relationships associated with new social movements provide pointers for the study and practice of development communication. But the recent emphasis on how identities emerge in action invites participatory development communication researchers to play a central role in contributing to our understanding of these groups in effecting social change. Drawing on established concepts and tools from participatory approaches with renewed direction from the new social movements research promises to give development communication theory and practice greater focus and relevance as it continues to evolve.

References

Alvarez, S.E., E. Dagnino, and A. Escobar. 1998. "Introduction: The cultural and the political in Latin American social movements," in: S.E. Alvarez, E. Dagnino, and A. Escobar, eds. *Cultures of politics/politics of cultures: Revisioning Latin American social movements*. Boulder, Colo.: Westview. 1–29.

Arnst, R. 1996. "Participation approaches to the research process," in: J. Servaes, T.L. Jacobson, and S.A. White, eds. *Participatory communication for social change*. New Delhi: Sage. 109–126.

Beltrán, L.R. 1975. "Research ideologies in conflict," *Journal of Communication* 25:187–193.

Beltrán, L.R. 1980. "A farewell to Aristotle: 'Horizontal' communication," *Communication* 5:5–41.

Beverley, J., and J. Oviedo. 1993. "Introduction: The postmodernism debate in Latin America," *Boundary 2* 20(3):1–17.

Brecher, J., T. Costello, and B. Smith. 2000. *Globalization from below: The power of solidarity*. Boston: South End Press.

Castells, M. 1983. *The city and the grassroots: A cross-cultural theory of urban social movements*. Berkeley: Univ. of California Press.

Castells, M. 1996a. *The power of identity*. Malden, Mass.: Blackwell Publishers.

Castells, M. 1996b. *The rise of the network society*. Cambridge, Mass.: Blackwell Publishers.

Dervin, B. 1993. "Verbing communication: Mandate for disciplinary invention," *Journal of Communication* 43:45–54.

Dervin, B., and K. Clark. 1993. "Communication and democracy: A mandate for procedural invention," in: S. Splichal and J. Wasko, eds. *Communication and democracy*. Norwood, N.J.: Ablex. 103–140.

Downing, J. 1996. *Internationalizing media theory: Transition, power, culture: Reflections on media in Russia, Poland and Hungary 1980-95*. London: Sage.

Escobar, A. 2000. "Place, power, and networks in globalization and postdevelopment," in: K.G. Wilkins, ed. *Redeveloping communication for social change: Theory, practice, and power*. Lanham, Md.: Rowman & Littlefield. 163–173.

Escobar, A., and S.E. Alvarez. 1992. "Introduction: Theory and protest in Latin America today," In: A. Escobar and S.E. Alvarez, eds. *The making of social movements in Latin America: Identity, strategy, and democracy*. Boulder, Colo.: Westview. 1–15.

Evans, P. 2000. "Fighting marginalization with transnational networks: Counter-hegemonic globalization," *Contemporary Sociology* 29(1):230-241.

Fals Borda, O. 1988. *Knowledge and people's power: Lessons with peasants in Nicaragua, Mexico and Colombia*. New Delhi: Indian Social Institute.

Fals Borda, O. 1992. "Social movements and political power in Latin America," in: A. Escobar and S.E. Alvarez, eds. *The making of social movements in Latin America: Identity, strategy, and democracy*. Boulder, Colo.: Westview. 303-316.

Flacks, R. 1994. "The party's over—so what is to be done?" in: E. Laraña, H. Johnston, and J.R. Gusfield, eds. *New social movements: From ideology to identity*. Philadelphia: Temple Univ. Press. 330-351.

Freire, P. 1970. *Pedagogy of the oppressed*. M. Bergman Ramos, trans. New York: Herder and Herder.

Freire, P. 1973a. *Education for critical consciousness*. New York: Seabury Press.

Freire, P. 1973b. *¿Extensión o comunicación?* L. Ronzoni, trans. Buenos Aires: Siglo XXI.

García Canclini, N. 1993. "The hybrid: A conversation with Margarita Zires, Raymundo Mier, and Mabel Piccini," *Boundary 2* 20(3): 77-92.

Habermas, J. 1981. "New social movements," *Telos* 49: 33-37.

Hannigan, J.A. 1985. "Alain Touraine, Manuel Castells and social movement theory: A critical appraisal," *The Sociological Quarterly* 26(4): 435-454.

Hellman, J.A. 1992. "The study of new social movements in Latin America and the question of autonomy," in: A. Escobar and S. Alvarez, eds. *The making of social movements in Latin America: Identity, strategy, and democracy*. Boulder, Colo.: Westview. 52-61.

Hellman, J.A. 1994. "Mexican popular movements, clientelism and the process of democratization," *Latin American Perspectives* 21(2): 124-142.

Hellman, J.A. 1997. "Social movements: Revolution, reform and reaction," *NACLA report on the Americas* 30(6): 13-18.

Hopenhayn, M. 1993. "Postmodernism and neoliberalism in Latin America," *Boundary 2* 20(3): 93-109.

Huesca, R. in press. "Participatory approaches to communication for development," in: W.B. Gudykunst and B. Mody, eds. *Handbook of international and intercultural communication*. 3rd ed. Thousand Oaks, Calif.: Sage.

Hunt, S.A., R.D. Benford, and D.A. Snow. 1994. "Identity fields: Framing processes and the social construction of movement identities," in: E. Laraña, H. Johnston, and J.R. Gusfield, eds. *New social movements: From ideology to identity*. Philadelphia: Temple Univ. Press. 185-208.

Jacobson, T.L. 1993. "A pragmatist account of participatory communication research for national development," *Communication Theory* 3:214-230.

Jacobson, T.L., and S. Kolluri. 1999. "Participatory communication as communicative action," In: T.L. Jacobson and J. Servaes, eds. *Theoretical approaches to participatory communication*. Cresskill, N.J.: Hampton Press. 265-280.

Jacobson, T.L., and J. Servaes. 1999. "Introduction," In: T.L. Jacobson and J. Servaes, eds. *Theoretical approaches to participatory communication*. Cresskill, N.J.: Hampton Press. 1-13.

Jelin, E. 1994. "The politics of memory: The human rights movement and the construction of democracy in Argentina," *Latin American Perspectives* 21(2):38-58.

Johnston, H., E. Laraña, and J.R. Gusfield. 1994. "Identities, grievances, and new social movements," in: E. Laraña, H. Johnston, and J.R. Gusfield, eds. *New social movements: From ideology to identity*. Philadelphia: Temple Univ. Press. 3-35.

Keck, M.E., and K. Sikkink. 1998. *Activists beyond borders: Advocacy networks in international politics*. Ithaca, N.Y.: Cornell Univ. Press.

Lasswell, H.D. 1964, c 1948. "The structure and function of communication in society," in: L. Bryson, ed. *The communication of ideas*. New York: Cooper Square Publishers. 37-51.

Lowe, S. 1986. *Urban social movements: The city after Castells*. New York: St. Martin's Press.

McAdam, D., J.D. McCarthy, and M.N. Zald. 1988. "Social movements," in: N.J. Smelser, ed. *The handbook of sociology*. Newbury Park, Calif.: Sage. 695-737.

Melucci, A. 1989. *Nomads of the present*. Philadelphia: Temple Univ. Press.

Melucci, A. 1994. "A strange kind of newness: What's "new" in new social movements?" in: E. Laraña, H. Johnston, & J.R. Gusfield, eds. *New social movements: From ideology to identity*. Philadelphia: Temple Univ. Press. 101-130.

Melucci, A. 1998. "Third world or planetary conflicts?" in S.E. Alvarez, E. Dagnino, and A. Escobar, eds. *Cultures of politics/politics of cultures: Re-visioning Latin American social movements*. Boulder, Colo.: Westview. 422-436.

Nair, K.S., and S.A. White. 1994. "Participatory development communication as cultural renewal," in: S.A. White, K.S. Nair, and J. Ascroft, eds. *Participatory communication: Working for change and development*. New Delhi: Sage. 138-193.

Pasquali, A. 1963. *Comunicación y cultura de masas*. Caracas: Universidad Central de Venezuela.

Rahman, M.A. 1993. *People's self development: Perspectives on participatory action research*. London: Zed Books.

Riaño, P. 1994. "Women's participation in communication: Elements of a framework," in: P. Riaño, ed. *Women in grassroots communication*. Thousand Oaks, Calif.: Sage. 3-29.

Rodrik, D. 1997. *Has globalization gone too far?* Washington, D.C.: Institute for International Economics.

Sassen, S. 1998. *Globalization and its discontents*. New York: New Press.

Scott, A. 1995. "Culture or politics? Recent literature on social movements, class and politics," *Theory, Culture & Society* 12:169-178.

Servaes, J. 1996a. "Introduction: Participatory communication and research in development settings," in: J. Servaes, T.L. Jacobson, and S.A. White, eds. *Participatory communication for social change*. New Delhi: Sage. 13-25.

Servaes, J. 1996b. "Participatory communication research with new social movements: A realistic utopia," in: J. Servaes, T.L. Jacobson, and S.A. White, eds. *Participatory communication for social change*. New Delhi: Sage. 82-108.

Slater, D. 1994. "Introduction," *Latin American Perspectives* 21(2):5-10.

Snow, D.A., and R.D. Benford. 1988. "Ideology, frame resonance, and participant mobilization," *International Social Movement Research* 1:197-217.

Starr, A. 2000. *Naming the enemy: Anti-corporate movements confront globalization*. London: Zed Books.

Stern, M.J. 2000. "Back to the future? Manuel Castells' *The information age* and the prospects for social change," *Cultural Studies* 14(1):99-116.

Taylor, V., and E. Whittier. 1992. "Collective identity in social movement communities: Lesbian feminist mobilization," In: A.D. Morris and C. McClurg Mueller, eds. *Frontiers in social movement theory*. New Haven, Conn.: Yale Univ. Press. 104-129.

Tehranian, M. 1999. *Global communication and world politics: Domination, development and discourse*. Boulder, Colo.: Lynne Rienner.

1927
1960
1963
1964
1967
1969
1970
1971
1972
1973
1974
1975
1976
1977
1978
1979
1980
1981
1982
1983
1984
1985
1986
1987
1988
1989
1990
1991
1992
1993
1994
1995
1996
1997
1998
1999
2000
2001
2002
2003
2004
2005
2006

Touraine, A. 1971. *The post-industrial society: Tomorrow's social history: Classes, conflicts and culture in the programmed society.* Leonard F.X. Mayhew, trans. New York: Random House.

Touraine, A. 1981. *The voice and the eye.* Cambridge, U.K.: Cambridge Univ. Press.

Touraine, A. 1988. *Return of the actor: Social theory in postindustrial society.* Minneapolis: Univ. of Minnesota Press.

Waters, M. 1995. *Globalization.* London: Routledge.

White, S.A. 1994. "The concept of participation: Transforming rhetoric to reality," in: S.A. White, K.S. Nair, and J. Ascroft, eds. *Participatory communication: Working for change and development.* New Delhi: Sage. 15–32.

Wilkins, K.G. 2000. "Introduction," in: K.G. Wilkins, ed. *Redeveloping communication for social change: Theory, practice, and power.* Lanham, Md.: Rowman & Littlefield. 1–4.

Huesca, R. (2001). "Conceptual contributions of new social movements to development communication research." *Communication Theory,* 11, 415-433. Copyright © Robert Huesca. Reprinted with permission.

FROM ALTERNATIVE MEDIA TO CITIZENS' MEDIA

By Clemencia Rodríguez

2001 *Ni los vientos son cuatro,
ni siete los colores;
caminante, no hay camino,
se hace camino al andar...*
—Antonio Machado

It is 1984. Somehow I find myself riding a mule that's part of an expedition, meandering up a wandering Andean trail. Our video equipment shakes and sways on the haunches of the mule ahead of me. "I hope the vibrations don't damage the camera," I mumble to myself. Claudia, my colleague, followed me on her own mule. Our journey had begun at dawn, when four men came to pick us up at the small hostel on the town's plaza. The night before, we had agreed on the time and place. They would guide us to villages and communities accessible only by foot or by mule, and we had chosen the latter. The men belong to a grassroots organization of *campesinos* (peasants), what in Latin America we call *grupos populares*. This *grupo popular* (grassroots group) struggles against the conditions of growing inequality that have fallen on the rural populations of Samaná, Caldas, a coffee-producing region hidden in the Colombian Andes.

The goal of our journey is to create a video about their work, the evolution of their movement and the escalation of military and paramilitary attempts to exterminate any organized grassroots mobilization in the country. We film all day, interviewing several group members in their homes, their fields, trying to capture their everyday life of work, family and political activity. Near day's end one of the interviewees asks me if there is any way they can see the footage, and I remember having seen an old black and white television set in one of the houses. The owner is pleased to loan his television set, and I connect it to our small camcorder; before I am finished, word has spread and the room buzzes with neighbors hoping to view the final product of our comings and goings through their day.

Pushing the play button, I sweat in beads that roll down my face; the small room has become increasingly hot and humid, as the whole community has crowded to join us; none wants to be left out; viewing the raw footage has become an important event. It was the first time that the community had the chance to look at itself on television, and this first encounter with a mediated image of itself had profound effects on each of its members. All my readings on democratic communication and unbalanced information flows never could have prepared me to understand the profundity of this experience. I was witnessing a community looking at itself and in the process, transforming its self-images. I will never forget one woman reacting to the footage taken at her house: "I never realized my kitchen could be so beautiful!" The solidified perception of her kitchen was now shaken by the new perspective she gained from the video camera.

More than 15 years later, I have participated in many alternative media experiences. I have witnessed how marginalized urban women in Colombia and poor young Latinos in Texas produce alternative video; how Catalans of different ages, genders and walks of life develop their own alternative television programming in Spain; how men and women from isolated rural areas in northern Nicaragua build their own alternative radio information system.

My initial interest in alternative media was inspired by the New World Information and Communication Order (NWICO) and its hopes to balance the flow of information and communication. This UNESCO project sought to reach this goal by putting electronic media in the hands of citizens and communities who traditionally had been denied access to the production and distribution of media messages. According to NWICO, alternative media, then, would alter the old power equation between powerful transnational media corporations and powerless audiences.

What I found during my journeys with alternative media producers was far more complex than what NWICO predicted. I saw that men and women in these projects undergo compelling transformations in which established sociological, psychological and even existential "givens" suddenly are questioned. I could see how producing alternative media messages implies much more than simply challenging the mainstream media with *campesino*-correspondents as new communication and information sources. It implies having the opportunity to create one's own images of self and environment; it implies being able to recodify one's own identity with the signs and codes that one chooses, thereby disrupting the traditional acceptance of those imposed by outside sources; it implies becoming one's own storyteller, regaining one's own voice; it implies reconstructing the self-portrait of one's own community and one's own culture; it implies exploring the infinite possibilities of one's own body, one's own face, to create facial expressions (a new codification of the face) and nonverbal languages (a new codification of the body) never seen before; it implies taking one's own languages out of their usual hiding place and throwing them out there, into the public sphere, and seeing how they do, how they defeat other languages or how they are defeated by other languages… what matters is that for the first time, one's shy languages, languages used to remain within the familiar and the private, take part in the public arena of languages and discourse.

I could also see how dramatically pre-established cultural codes and traditional power relations were disrupted. Men and women who had always and only seen themselves as audiences had to reconstruct their self-perspective and social context as they became message producers and senders. Their point of view shifted from one of passive receivers with little control to that of messengers responsible for seeking and filtering information. Women, accustomed to having men "guide" them and considering this natural, had to reframe their whole outlook on gender relations as they directed male actors for their

1927
1960
1963
1964
1967
1969
1970
1971
1972
1973
1974
1975
1976
1977
1978
1979
1980
1981
1982
1983
1984
1985
1986
1987
1988
1989
1990
1991
1992
1993
1994
1995
1996
1997
1998
1999
2000
2001
2002
2003
2004
2005
2006

own alternative soap operas. In some cases, where a woman's subordination to men is the main source of her identity, revising one's convictions about gender relationships implies a complete reformulation of one's entire worldview.

As I tried to conceptualize all these experiences, I found myself in a vacuum. I realized that the theoretical frameworks and concepts we communication scholars have used to explore and understand alternative communication and media are in a different realm. Our theorizing uses categories too narrow to encompass the lived experiences of those involved with alternative media. Communication academics and media activists began looking at alternative media as a hopeful option to counterbalance the unequal distribution of communication resources that came with the growth of big media corporations. This origin has located the debate in rigid categories of power and binary conceptions of domination and subordination that elude the fluidity and complexity of alternative media as a social, political and cultural phenomenon. It's like trying to capture the beauty of dancers' movements with one photograph. I then embarked on a journey toward finding a new route to conceptualize alternative media; my goal was to break away from the traditional static and essentialist definitions of democracy, citizenship and democratic communicative action, concepts that necessarily inform our theorizing about alternative media. Also, this new theoretical framework had to be powerful enough to capture all the richness of the lived experiences I had witnessed so closely. Although I intended to break away from static and essentialist definitions, I was also well aware of the risk of arriving at the postmodern cul-de-sac of a social reality and a social subject mutating *ad infinitum*. Consequently, I needed a theoretical proposal that while formulating nonessentialist and dynamic conceptualizations, managed to avoid the political paralysis of drastic postmodernism. My explorations in the fields of communication studies and cultural studies did not offer a satisfying answer. The communication studies perspective from which

the politics of alternative media and participatory communication are interpreted is still trapped in traditional concepts of oppositional politics; that is, politics of resistance are still thought of exclusively in terms of subversive action. Cultural studies also failed to provide a satisfying theoretical base because, as Douglas Kellner (1995, 336) has poignantly stated:

> The failure of cultural studies today to engage the issue of alternative media is more puzzling and less excusable since there are today a variety of venues for alternative film and video production, community radio, computer bulletin boards and discussion forums, and other forms of communications in which citizens and activists can readily intervene.

While cultural studies seem to be concerned with the media texts of the dominant and how audiences interact with them, the media texts of ordinary citizens have not achieved status as objects of study. My search was finally rewarded by the inspiring theorization of democracy and politics of change developed by two feminist scholars, Chantal Mouffe and Kristie McClure. From a feminist perspective, Mouffe and McClure have formulated new theoretical visions of the political subject, political action and the citizen. Mouffe's and McClure's theory of radical democracy is an attempt to develop nonessentialist and dynamic conceptualizations to rethink politics and social change. This article explains how their theory of radical democracy offers a rich and original theoretical framework to capture the lived experiences of alternative media.

Point of Departure: *The MacBride Report*
Without doubt, the 1970s was a decade of intense turmoil in the world of international communication. On the floor of the United Nations, and particularly of UNESCO, representatives from Third World countries exposed communication injustices. They protested a situation where the flow of information and communication from First World countries into Third World countries was tens of times stronger than from Third World

countries into First World countries.[1] Also, what was then called South-to-South communication—that is, communication and information traveling directly from one Third World country to another—was practically nonexistent. Of equal or more importance was the fact that most of the globe's media traffic was controlled by a few transnational communication corporations (TNCCs), all located in the United States, Western Europe and Japan (Mattelart 1974, 1977, 1983).

According to data gathered at the time by international communication scholars, most of the news media circulating around the world were produced by a handful of press agencies, mostly from First World countries: AP and UPI from the United States, Reuters from Germany, Agence France-Presse from France, and TASS from the former Soviet Union. Several negative consequences arising from this situation were emphasized. First, most information from Third World countries was gathered by First World international reporters who "objectively reported" the underdeveloped world from a very limited First World perspective; conceived in terms of its backwardness, wilderness and poverty, the Third World, as a result, became an array of images of violence, poverty and natural disasters in the world's information media.

Second, even Third World countries themselves were consuming those same one-sided images of themselves, which was particularly ironic given their geographic, social and political proximity to each other. Thus, the establishment of direct information and communication channels between Third World countries, also called South-to-South communication, became a priority.

Third, information about the Third World was not only limited in its perspective, but also restricted in its

quantity. The number of circulating news items about the First World was incomparably greater than the number of items about the Third World. Thus, almost 40 percent of all foreign reporting in American newspapers is about Western Europe and North America, while Latin America is "conspicuously under-reported" (Frederick 1993, 132).

As a way to shift this state of things, Third World communication scholars and policy makers recommended the establishment of Third World press agencies. These enterprises would favor local reporters to gather information about their own societies, from their own point of view; also, the information would be distributed directly from one Third World country to the rest, therefore bypassing the influence of First World information producers. The most salient example of a Third World press agency that resulted from all of this is InterPress Service (IPS), although many journalists and other communication professionals have invested enormous efforts in making this project a reality, IPS has never been able to compete with First World press agencies. Thus, while "the average daily news production of the world agencies ranges from an output of 17 million words a day by AP to 3.3 million words by Agence France Presse . . . InterPress Service puts out 150,000 words a day" (Hamelink 1995, 300).

The entertainment media did not fare better. The data gathered at the time exposed a situation in which a disproportionate number of television shows, films and magazine items were produced and distributed by ubiquitous communication corporations. Located in the United States, most of these corporations exported their products to the rest of the world, particularly to Third World countries, where many domestic television and film industries were still in their infancy and could not produce comparable high-technical-quality programming.[2]

As a result, Third World populations were consuming a daily ration of media products that reflected the

---

1   According to the MacBride Report, while Europe produces an average of 12,000 new book titles every year, African nations produce less than 350 (Hamelink 1995, 296); the flow of telephone, telex, and telegraph data among Third World countries is less than 10 percent of the globe's total; the flow of news from First World countries to Third World countries is 100 times more than the flow of news from the Third World to the First World; and while Europe broadcasts 855 hours of television programming to Africa annually, only 70 hours of African television reach European countries (Hamelink 1995, 298).

2   However, this is not true in all cases. In Latin America, for example, Argentina and Mexico had very strong film industries. Argentinean and Mexican films were exported and viewed in many other countries in the region.

1927
1960
1963
1964
1967
1969
1970
1971
1972
1973
1974
1975
1976
1977
1978
1979
1980
1981
1982
1983
1984
1985
1986
1987
1988
1989
1990
1991
1992
1993
1994
1995
1996
1997
1998
1999
2000
2001
2002
2003
2004
2005
2006

culture and values of the country of origin, the United States. The implications were soon voiced by Third World scholars and policy makers. The constant consumption of foreign values and cultural forms would eventually erode local cultures, undermine national identities and limit the advancement of national communication industries. Instead of strengthening its own forces in order to shape its own identities and destinies, Third World countries were becoming alienated entities without a clear idea of who they were and where they wanted to go.

In this case too the recommendations were clear: National communication policies and media regulations had to be formulated by each Third World nation in order to protect its "electronic sovereignty." Also, UNESCO stated that a more balanced (and fair) world information and communication order would require diversification of sources. A monopoly of a few TNCCs controlling the global flow of communication products should be replaced by a scenario in which many diverse social subjects could have access to the media, not only as audiences but also as producers.

Many of these issues concerning the democratization of communication were first exposed by UNESCO in the *MacBride Report* (UNESCO 1980).[3] The debate around processes of democratization of communication and redistribution of communicative power evolved around a macro and international approach to democracy. The controversy focused mainly around issues of inequality in information flows between rich countries (the North, the core, or the First World) and poor countries (the South, the periphery, or Third World). From this perspective, solutions proposed by those striving for more democratic communication practices included national communication policies, South-to-South communication and information

channels, and a code of ethics for the mass media. All these solutions were supposed to foster a New World Information and Communication Order (NWICO).[4]

Almost two decades later, however, evidence of NWICO's failure is overwhelming. Not only do the information and communication flows remain unbalanced, but the mass media are controlled by fewer and fewer owners. The late 1980s and early 1990s—the Reagan/Thatcher era—brought a climate of deregulation and privatization that resulted in the mergers of already powerful transnational corporations (Mohammadi 1997). Called by Bagdikian (1997) "the new communications cartel," fewer than 20 giants, most of them U.S. or Western European based, have gained control over the great majority of global communications.[5] Meanwhile, the developing countries control even less of the information and communication global traffic; although tightly integrated into the telecommunications flow as important markets for TNCCs, these countries possess "a mere seven percent of the existing stock of telecommunications resources" (Mohammadi 1997, 69).

In terms of the news media, the number of international press agencies has shrunk since the early 1980s. Today, most of the flow of international news is carried by only three major players: Associated Press, Reuters, and Agence France-Presse; the global flow of visual news is dominated by Reuters Television and World Television Network (WTN), and rumors of a merger between these two would lead to the world's visual news coming out of a single source (Hamelink 1997a, 92–94).

In a recent analysis of the current state of the MacBride recommendations, Cees Hamelink (1997b) finds that not only did these proposals never become realities, but also "even the acronyms NIIO [New International

---

3   In 1976, Amadou Mathar M'Bow, director of UNESCO, appointed a commission of sixteen experts; their assignment was to examine global communication problems. Chaired by Sean MacBride, the commission gathered data for two years (1977-1979) the commission's final report, which painted a shocking scenario in terms of information inequalities between First World and Third World countries, is known as the MacBride Report.

4   For a detailed history of NWICO, see Hamelink 1997b.

5   The "communications cartel" consists of world communication giants Time Warner (United States), Disney (United States), Bertelsmann (Germany), News Corp. (Australia), Capital Cities/ABC (United States), Hachette (France), CBS (United States), Gannett (United States), Fininvest (Italy), Paramount (United States), Sony (Japan), Pearson PLC (England), Qintex (Australia), Maxwell (England), Globo (Brazil) and Televisa (Mexico) (Hamelink 1997a).

Information Order], and later, NWICO have practically disappeared from the multilateral debate" (84). Under pressure to modernize their communication infrastructures, Third World countries were urged to privatize media industries in fear of being "left out" of the communication revolution. In an attempt to join the newly labeled "information society" Third World countries opened the gates to TNCCs and shifted away from national communication policies and regulation.

In view of the failure of national governments and international agencies to balance the global flows of information and communication, several scholars have suggested that the debate on the democratization of communication should take a different course. During the late 1970s and early 1980s several international conferences became forums for a novel approach to the democratization of communication; among these stand the People's Alternatives to Mass Communication, in Barcelona in 1978, and the Twelfth Conference of the International Association for Mass Communication, held in Caracas in 1980 (Reyes Matta 1986).

The new perspective visualized social movements and grassroots organizations and their alternative media as the new key players in the processes of democratization of communication. In 1981, *Comunicación Alternativa y Cambio Social,* a landmark volume on alternative communication in Latin America, was published in Mexico (Simpson Grinberg 1981b). Here, some of the most prominent Latin American communication scholars stated the potential of alternative media to counterbalance the trend toward transnational communication and cultural imperialism (Capriles 1981; Simpson Grinberg 1981a; Reyes Matta 1981; Portales 1981). The hope was now for these newly politicized social subjects (social movements, grassroots organizations, *grupos populares*) to establish their own small-scale media outlets and to spin their own communication and information networks, thereby bypassing the TNCCs (Servaes 1992).

Apart from providing their audiences with alternative information, these new media—labeled alternative media—were expected to diverge from the top-down vertical mode of communication characteristic of the mainstream mass media. While the big media function on the basis of a hierarchy of media producers and media audiences, the latter have no voice and are restricted to the passive role of receiving media messages, alternative media were thought of as a panacea consisting of horizontal communication, whereby senders and receivers have equal access to communicative power.

In their article titled "Farewell to NWICO?" Sparks and Roach (1990, 280) said: "It is not in the corridors of power that the new order will be forged but in the little experiments in which workers and peasants attempt to find new ways of communicating their ideas and their experiences to each other." In the same vein, Mattelart and Mattelart (1992, 168) called for "[t]he local dimension as opposed to centralism, the ordinary as opposed to the sensational, and experience as opposed to ideas."

Antonio Pasquali (1992, 7) favored "even modest actions, as part of a coherent plan."

Even the MacBride Round Table, held in Prague in September of 1990, concluded:

> The debate around the New World Information and Communication Order (NWICO) has thus returned to where it started. It is now in the arena of professional organizations, of communication researchers and most importantly, in the arena of grassroots movements, representing ordinary men, women and children who are directly affected by our current cultural and communication environments. (quoted in Roncagliolo 1992, 10)

Bruck and Raboy (1989, 12) advanced this approach to the NWICO debate by bringing to the fore much-needed questions concerning the alternativity of alternative media:

> [Alternative media] oblige us to ask serious political questions such as: Who is to control them? Autonomous collectives? If so, responsible to

1927
1960
1963
1964
1967
1969
1970
1971
1972
1973
1974
1975
1976
1977
1978
1979
1980
1981
1982
1983
1984
1985
1986
1987
1988
1989
1990
1991
1992
1993
1994
1995
1996
1997
1998
1999
2000
2001
2002
2003
2004
2005
2006

whom? Political organizations? If so, how can they avoid being mere propaganda sheets? The issue of media control is a microcosm of the issue of democracy in social life generally, and poses the same difficult questions. Are alternative media to produce the sender–receiver communication model of the mass media, or are they to be two-way means of communication? And how are they to be sustained? These questions have not yet been resolved, and are too rarely asked by alternative media activists.

Also, as the overwhelming power of TNCCs is perceived as a force affecting all societies and cultures; grassroots organizations and their alternative media are thought to have an important role not only in the poor countries but in all regions of the world, including postindustrial societies (Lewis 1984b; Stangelaar 1983).

In the wealthier societies of North America and Western Europe, alternative media were seen as a movement to defend a quality of life under siege by the transnational expansion of capitalism. Issues such as the arms race, nuclear war, state control of everyday life, and the creative use of free time defined "a common platform on which people from many social groups ask[ed] whether life could not be lived differently, beyond the order defined by the market and the laws of cost and benefit" (Reyes Matta 1986, 196).

Within this new framework, alternative media were conceived as the new battleground from which the new communication order would emerge. As communication scholars and activists, we were inspired with a vision, a new mediascape where alternative media would have hegemonic power; in 1986 Reyes Matta stated, "[T]hus, the alternative spiral builds a dynamic of progress toward a time when the social and popular movements that are disadvantaged today will have hegemony" (203).

It is clear that the debate around alternative media implied a relocation of the debate on the democratization of communication—a relocation from international organizations, national governments, and large media conglomerates, to citizen groups and grassroots organizations, and their attempts to use the media in their own, different way. But a relocation of the debate on democratization of communication should go beyond a mere re-accommodation of the same old concepts to a local scale. The new direction for a debate on the democratization of communication should imply finding a new conceptual framework that can capture how democratic communication *happens* within alternative media. And although the debate has shifted gears, I believe our theorizing about the democratization of communication has remained trapped within a vision of politics and democracy rooted in "grand narratives of emancipation" (Kellner 1995, 45) and essentialist concepts of power, citizenship, and political action.

Theorizing About Alternative Media

Academic literature on alternative media includes two types of works: first, descriptive pieces where a case of alternative media is explained in detail, from its origin to its funding sources and types of programming. This type of material allows us to grasp the rich complexity of alternative media as communicative phenomena.

The second type of work develops a theoretical analysis that attempts to capture the essence of alternative media and/or to explain the importance of these media as processes of communication and democracy. It is this second type of work that I address here.

Framed within the ideas of NWICO as explained above, much of the academic literature on alternative media emanates from specific concepts of power and democracy (Esteinou Madrid 1986; Fox & Schmucler 1982; Kaplún 1986; Reyes Matta 1983, 1986; Simpson Grinberg 1981a, 1986). Power is conceived as a binary opposition of the powerful versus the powerless. In this all-or-nothing conceptualization of power, social subjects are historically located on one or the other side of the power dichotomy.

Thus, mass media corporations are conceived as historically located in the camp of the powerful, while indigenous groups, ethnic minorities, Third World peoples, and other groups of ordinary people are deemed on the side of the powerless. In other words, a historical subject (a big media corporation or a grassroots organization) is thought to be either powerful or powerless; once the subject has been positioned in one of these camps, the corresponding element of the binary becomes an innate characteristic; that is, being powerful or powerless becomes an essential trait of the subject's nature. So big media corporations become essentially powerful while grassroots organizations become essentially powerless.

Framing their analyses with these types of categories, several academics study alternative media in terms of their success or their failure in balancing the power equation between TNCCs and powerless communities. In this David versus Goliath scenario, alternative media are frequently declared a failure (Portales 1983). In this line of thought Pradip Thomas (1997) maintains that alternative media initiatives are undergoing "a severe crisis of credibility," and Geoffrey Reeves (1993) points out that one of the salient characteristics of alternative media is their vulnerability. In their distinctively cynical voice and based on their study of French and Belgian alternative media, Mattelart and Piemme (1980a, 321) pronounce alternative video a failed illusion:

> Against those laggards who still believed that socialism was Soviets plus electricity, [community video activists] dreamt of a Babel-like explosion in which the cry of protest from the base, transmitted by the new technologies, would act to check the unequal linguistic distribution within society and thus its system of power. The hope was a noble one; its only failing was that it was impregnated by myth (see also Mattelart & Piemme 1980b).

Dorothy Kidd (1998) has pointed out how even the political economists of the media (Vincent Mosco, Herbert Schiller, Ben Bagdikian) have relegated alternative media to a footnote, always limited to the end of their "gloomy truth-telling" (8). Similarly, in an interesting study of diverse discourses on access television in the United States, Robert Devine (1995) has shown how communication academics[6] have marginalized access TV as nothing but an amateurish, illusory and ineffective attempt to democratize the media. Their critique, writes Devine, is based on the expectation that alternative media should deliver the same democratizing potential as the mass media, in terms of circulating professionally packaged ideas among wide audiences; against this standard, of course, alternative media are always doomed to fail.

Several authors point to the difficulty of imposing one label—alternative media—on very diverse media experiences that in some cases have little in common (Paiva 1983; Portales 1983). For example Alfredo Paiva (1983, 29) confesses that "we had to accept that what we call alternative communication is a heterogeneous set of media practices developed by very diverse groups and organizations, in specific and different contexts, and employing a great variety of media." In examining the heterogeneity of media experiments grouped under the category of alternative media, authors such as Paiva barely touch on the complexity of this communication.

For a case in point, Paiva observes that in Latin America alternative media are carried out by the most varied social groups, such as women's groups, ethnic minorities, neighborhood associations, etc. However, his assumption of a concept of power as a binary opposition forces him to overlook the rich potential of such diversity and to articulate it as a limitation. On the basis of similar analyses, alternative media have been accused of being "dispersed," "fragmented," or "shattered" (Paiva 1983; Portales 1983). Moreover, alternative media were seen as a promising political venue only as long as they succeeded in overcoming their fragmentation.

---

6 The following scholars' critiques of alternative media are included in Devine's (1995) study: Janine Marchessault, Pat Aufderheide, David Trend, David Sholle, Andrew Blau, Laurie Oullette, Nicholas Garnham, and Patricia Mellencamp.

1927
1960
1963
1964
1967
1969
1970
1971
1972
1973
1974
1975
1976
1977
1978
1979
1980
1981
1982
1983
1984
1985
1986
1987
1988
1989
1990
1991
1992
1993
1994
1995
1996
1997
1998
1999
2000
2001
2002
2003
2004
2005
2006

Alternative media's potential was recognized only if the array of small-scale and diverse media experiences could organize and join forces around a unified project for social change at a national level (Paiva 1983; Portales 1983; Schulein & Robina 1983). Following this line of thought, Paiva (1983, 52) declares that the ultimate goal of alternative media is "the construction of a new hegemony," and Portales (1983, 60) says that "alternative media are meaningful only in view of a global process of democratization." Similarly, after studying 22 participatory communication projects in Latin America, O'Sullivan-Ryan and Kaplún (1978, 88) conclude that "[they] have no real impact on the prevailing national communication system."

Confronted with such heterogeneity, communication scholars defined alternative media by what they were not, instead of by what they were. This analytic strategy entrapped these analyses in oppositional thinking and binary categories. Thus, within Latin American communication scholarship, for example, alternative media were thought as "the other media," as opposed to the big, mainstream mass media (Paiva 1983); another label frequently used is "marginal media," as opposed to, again, the "central" mass media (Portales 1983), or "confrontational media," as opposed to the complaisant mass media (Reyes Matta 1982).

Although the vast majority of academic analyses of alternative media have been framed within the binary categories explained above, a few attempts have been made to transcend this restrictive understanding.

Buried under a rigid, orthodox Marxist framework is Simpson Grinberg's (1986, 179) observation on the rich potential of alternative media to disrupt the established social order and to spin novel social processes:

> Alternative communication thus forms outposts for new social relationships and, specifically, establishes constitutive practices in a wide variety of processes that often—because of their 'heterodox' characteristics—fall outside the limits of orthodox vanguard perception and theory.

Although Simpson Grinberg insinuates here the limitations of what he calls "vanguard theory" (meaning an analysis founded on Marxist concepts of class struggle and ideology), his own exploration of alternative media remains trapped in these same categories.

In an attempt to free alternative media from the David-versus-Goliath framework, Mario Kaplún suggests that their real goal is not to correct the world's unbalanced information flows, but to strengthen popular organization and mobilization. Quoting Maria Cristina Mata, Kaplún (1983, 41) goes as far as stating that what gives meaning to alternative media is indeed "external-to-communication issues" (my translation). In the same line of thought, Ana María Nethol (1983) refers to the rich potential of alternative communication in its capacity to transform the human subject. However, Kaplún's and Nethol's voices were marginalized at the time by an overwhelming articulation of the debate in terms of the small media versus the big media.

An interesting exception to the type of analyses of alternative media based on binary categories is John Downing's *Radical Media* (1984, 17–24). Drawing on Emma Goldman's feminist anarchism and Sheila Rowbotham's Marxist feminism, Downing sketches four guiding principles to rethink media democracy. These are, first, the need to acknowledge oppression as a heterogeneous and fragmented reality; second, the need to build lateral links between fragmented movements against oppression; third, the need to visualize the struggle against oppression in terms of movements and not as institutions; and fourth, the need to think of liberation as an everyday process that disrupts immediate realities. Principles one and three are particularly poignant because they attempt to break away from a concept of oppression as a static reality with an immutable essence. While principle one suggests that as a social phenomenon oppression lacks continuity, principle three evokes the idea of resistance as movement, a phenomenon in flux that escapes our attempts to trap it within a specific social subject (a class, an ethnic minority, a gender, etc.). Downing's analysis reminds us of the urgency of revising and rescuing feminist anarchism as a potential contributor to the development of contemporary explorations of issues of power.

The second edition of *Radical Media* (forthcoming 1999) offers a still more stimulating theoretical proposal. Here, Downing integrates a wide variety of promising concepts and theories into a rich theoretical palette. Expanding way beyond anarchism, Downing brings together schools of thought as diverse as popular culture theories (Horkheimer and Adorno, Martín Barbero; audience studies (Janice Radaway, John Fiske; theories of hegemony and resistance (Antonio Gramsci, James C. Scott; Marxist class analyses, social movements theories (Alain Touraine; Paulo Freire's theory of conscientization; Mikhail Bakhtin's ideas on quotidian discourses; theories of communication and democracy (Raymond Williams, James Carey, and Michael Schudson, among others); Walter Benjamin's and Bertolt Brecht's exploration of interactive media, and Dada and surrealist vanguards. The result is a powerful conceptual "toolbox" available to scholars and media activists in our attempts to explore and understand alternative media.

Another important attempt to free the study of alternative media from binary categories is Robert Huesca and Brenda Dervin's critical examination of Latin American literature on alternative media (Dervin & Huesca 1997; Huesca & Dervin 1994). In their 1994 study, these authors identify the main dualisms that prevail in Latin American studies of alternative communication. They find that categories such as vertical communication versus horizontal communication, communication for domination versus communication for liberation, and communication as information versus communication as dialogue[7] entrap this

literature into a legacy of dualisms that "has led to theoretical confusion and truncated alternative possibilities" (Huesca & Dervin 1994, 55). Remaining within Latin American communication scholarship, Huesca and Dervin find a few convincing guideposts to liberate the study of alternative communication from rigid dualisms; particularly novel ideas such as García Canclini's "hybrid cultures," Jesús Martín Barbero's "mestizaje," and "popular culture"[8] seem to suggest a promising theoretical path. However, Huesca and Dervin conclude that "no theories of alternative practice as such have emerged" (Huesca & Dervin 1994, 66); that is, although the guideposts are there, no one has systematically used them to develop a different theory of alternative communication.

In a more recent piece, Dervin and Huesca (1997) propose a novel paradigmatic move in the study of participatory communication. Baptized as "verbing," (also known as "sense making"), this new epistemological and ontological proposal is founded on the idea that the universe inhabits some intermediate place between order and chaos. In other words, our reality, our knowing that reality, and we ourselves emerge from the continuous interaction between order and chaos. Assuming the verbing paradigm implies a new understanding of reality as something always in the making, never complete, then it follows that so will be our understandings of such reality; therefore, no theory or concept is ever final, and instead we should engage in a dialogue of knowledges. Also, if we acknowledge that a person exists in the juncture between order and chaos, we can begin to understand "that we are sometimes unconscious, sometimes decentered, sometimes disordered; that we are in a constant state of moving between order and chaos; that it is just as much a struggle to fall in line, i.e., to make ourselves fit our surroundings, our cultures, our societies, as it is to fall out of line i.e., to resist and challenge our surroundings, our cultures, our societies" (Dervin & Huesca 1997, 67).

---

7 These authors link the works of particular communication scholars with each of these three dualisms; thus, the ideas of Luis Ramiro Beltrán, Paulo Freire, Elizabeth Fox, Jesús Martín Barbero and Fernando Reyes Matta reflect the vertical/horizontal dualism; the works of Máximo Simpson Grinberg, Fernando Reyes Matta, J. Martínez Terrero, Alan O'Connor and Alfonso Paiva are linked to the domination/liberation category; and the scholarship of Antonio Pasquali, Mario Kaplún and Oswaldo Capriles is seen as building on the information/dialogue dichotomy (Huesca & Dervin 1994).

8 For an extensive historical account of these ideas, see Rodríguez and Murphy 1997.

1927
1960
1963
1964
1967
1969
1970
1971
1972
1973
1974
1975
1976
1977
1978
1979
1980
1981
1982
1983
1984
1985
1986
1987
1988
1989
1990
1991
1992
1993
1994
1995
1996
1997
1998
1999
2000
2001
2002
2003
2004
2005
2006

Drawing from ethnographic data gathered among alternative radio reporters in Bolivia, Huesca (1996; 1995) articulates how alternative communicative action moves constantly between order and chaos. Huesca (1996) describes how, in their training of Bolivian peasants, alternative radio activists act upon intuition plus a deep involvement in the trainees' social and cultural environments. That is, breaking away from "detached or predetermined positions" (Huesca 1996, 49) the trainer/teacher shapes the training sessions acting upon each specific situation, allowing for his/her preconceived notions (order) to be reshaped again and again (chaos). Further, interviewing miners' radio practitioners, Huesca (1995) detects a mode of communication that is based on the fluidity and contingency of social reality and social change and departs from traditional ideas of sequence, causality and continuity. Such mode of communication is "driven by sense, moment and relationship" (Huesca 1995, 161), in a move that pressures practitioners to seek multiple sources, to ground content in everyday life and to anchor their communication practice in a deep commitment to the community, instead of their professional *savoir faire*.

The potential of Downing's, Dervin's and Huesca's theoretical proposals is unquestionable. What follows is my own attempt to break the boundaries of binary thinking. While I try to remain in dialogue with the above-mentioned theoretical proposals, I move this exploration in a different direction, guided by the radical democracy conceptual proposal.

What would result if we shifted the angle from which we look at alternative media? What would develop from a different concept of power? What would happen if we started from a different notion of what power is, how it functions, how it affects us, and what it entails? I believe that as a consequence of our entrapment in a binary notion of power we miss seeing how multiple streams of power relationships are disrupted in the everyday lives of alternative media participants. If we were to focus on the communities that develop alternative media, we could see the myriad power equations that involve anyone and everyone in the community; we could also appreciate how these power equations are not static but constantly shifting and changing, that is, how power relationships are continually reconstituted. We could also recognize how not even at the individual level does power exist as a fixed essence. Within a community, men and women are not fixed in one power position; instead, their identities are always displaced along a continuum. Sometimes we are more powerful, other times we become powerless; access to power continually changes as people move through the landscapes of everyday life. That is, power is activated by all and each of the relationships in which we participate. Each of our everyday identities enters into games of power relationships with others' multiple identities; in some instances, identities will become identities-in-conflict. It is from these everyday movements that power emerges, more as a force than an essence. It is within the realm of the quotidian where we see the clashing of rural and urban, male and female, adult and young, local and global. However, our conceptualization of alternative media producers in terms of a homogeneous political agent has blinded our capacity to capture these power dynamics.

Exploring issues of power and democracy, two feminist scholars, Chantal Mouffe (1992c; 1992b; 1992a; 1988; Laclau & Mouffe 1985) and Kristie McKlure (1992), offer a revolutionary perspective to think about the processes of social change. Their theory of radical democracy delves into new understandings of how power is produced, who produces power, and how processes of constitution and reconstitution of power affect democratic processes. In the following pages I intend to present their most relevant ideas in light of my search for a new way to theorize about alternative media.

Power Explodes, the New Political Subject Emerges

Questioning from a feminist perspective the concept of the political subject as a unified and homogeneous identity, Mouffe (1988, 90) conceives social subjects as having heterogeneous and multiple "identities."

In the case of relations involving social subordination, for example, the same individual can be dominant in one relation and subordinate in another. Mouffe (1992c, 372) suggests:

> We can then conceive the social agent as constituted by an ensemble of 'subject positions' that can never be totally fixed in a closed system of differences, constructed by a diversity of discourses among which there is no necessary relation, but a constant movement of overdetermination and displacement.

Within this new approach, Mouffe (1988, 90) suggests that social subjects can be seen as subjectivities "to use the Lacanian term, sutured at the intersection of various discourses." Moreover, Mouffe's theory of radical democracy does not consider the social subject as constituted by an essence but by his/her historical location: "We are confronted with the emergence of a plurality of subjects, whose forms of constitution and diversity *it is only possible to think if we relinquish the category of 'subject' as a unified and unifying essence*" (Laclau and Mouffe 1985, 181; my emphasis). In other words, the fact that a human being belongs to an historically oppressed group, i.e., an indigenous community in an Anglo-dominated society, does not make him/her part of a specific "interest group" with specific needs and demands. In contrast, each social subject will experience "being indigenous" in a different way, according to other social dimensions, such as his/her gender, social class, age, etc. As political subjects, we emerge out of all this; we are located in differentiated power positions, but we are not fixed in these positions; they are historical, meaning that our location on a power continuum can be altered from within or without. McClure (1992, 122) explains:

> [S]ubjectivities are socially located, temporally specific and potentially riven within a series of other relational differences. And where social subjects are complexly constituted not only through categories of gender, but of race and sexuality, ethnicity and class, and perhaps of religion and nationality as well, a position of privilege within one frame may be simultaneously and contradictorily constructed within a position of oppression within another.

Mouffe declares that this new understanding of the social subject as a kaleidoscopic encounter of identities and differentiated "portions of power" is a necessary condition for understanding the richness of everyday political struggles. When applying this concept to alternative media, the richness of experiencing the reappropriation of mediated communication comes to life in all its exuberance. Alternative media function as environments that facilitate the fermentation of identities and power positions. In other words, alternative media spin transformative processes that alter people's sense of self, their subjective positionings, and therefore their access to power.

From Alternative Media to Citizens' Media

The concept of multiple subjectivities serves as a basis on which Mouffe (1992b) recasts the concept of citizen. The radical democratic concept of citizenship "implies seeing citizenship not as a legal status but as a form of identification, a type of political identity: something to be constructed, not empirically given" (Mouffe 1992b, 231). Thus, citizens are not born as such; citizenship is not a status granted on the basis of some *essential* characteristic. Citizens have to enact their citizenship on a day-to-day basis, through their participation in everyday political practices: "The citizen is not, as in liberalism, someone who is the passive recipient of specific rights and who enjoys the protection of the law" (Mouffe 1992b, 235).

Along with its active nature, citizenship has to do with empowerment. As citizens actively participate in actions that reshape their own identities, the identities of others and their social environment, they produce power. Contributing to the radical democracy theoretical proposal, Sheldon Wolin (1992, 250) explains the concept of power as a condition for citizenship, which is much more than simply a matter of claiming rights: "[Citizenship] is about the capacity to generate power, for that is the only way that things get

1927
1960
1963
1964
1967
1969
1970
1971
1972
1973
1974
1975
1976
1977
1978
1979
1980
1981
1982
1983
1984
1985
1986
1987
1988
1989
1990
1991
1992
1993
1994
1995
1996
1997
1998
1999
2000
2001
2002
2003
2004
2005
2006

established in the world. And it is about the capacity to share in power, to cooperate in it, for that is how institutions and practices are sustained."

Wolin (1992, 252) states the importance of empowerment and the sites where empowerment and citizenship happen:

> A political being is not to be defined as the citizen has been, as an abstract, disconnected bearer of rights, privileges and immunities, but as a person whose existence is located in a particular place and draws its sustenance from circumscribed relationships: family, friends, church, neighborhood, workplace, community, town, city. These relationships are the sources from which political beings draw power—symbolic, material, and psychological—and that enable them to act together. For true political power involves not only acting so as to effect decisive changes; it also means the capacity to receive power, to be acted upon, to change and to be changed. From a democratic perspective, power is not simply force that is generated; it is experience, sensibility, wisdom, even melancholy distilled from the diverse relations and circles we move within.

Also, the theory of radical democracy reformulates the ways in which power is enacted and citizenship is expressed. Breaking away from a modern understanding of citizenship as expressed by voting and protesting, the theory of radical democracy advances a concept of a political subject as one who expresses his/her citizenship in multiple forms, including, for example, the collective transformation of symbolic codes, historically legitimized identities, and traditionally established social relations (Wolin 1992, 251).[9]

9   On the basis of extensive ethnographic research in the AIDS community in Vancouver, Michael P. Brown (1997) explores how Mouffe's theory of radical democracy, as well as her concept of citizenship, apply to the politics of AIDS. His analysis clearly shows how practices such as "buddying" (where an AIDS volunteer pairs up with a person living with AIDS to offer practical and emotional support) and the AIDS quilt should be understood as quotidian politics, as political practices enacted by citizens. I believe Brown's theorizing about the emotional as political to be one of the most interesting ideas in his study. Such types of studies, where radical democratic theory is applied to everyday life attempts to reshape our lives and environments, constitutes a prolific source of new ways to think about social change.

In light of this novel theoretical definition of citizenship, I propose we abandon the term alternative media and coin a new term: "citizens' media." Because "alternative media" rests on the assumption that these media are alternative to something, this term easily entraps us into binary thinking: mainstream media and their alternative, that is, alternative media. Also, the label "alternative media" predetermines the type of oppositional thinking that limits the potential of these media to their ability to resist the alienating power of mainstream media. This approach blinds our understanding of all other instances of change and transformation brought about by these media.

Conversely, the term "citizens' media" implies, first, that a collectivity is *enacting* its citizenship by actively intervening and transforming the established mediascape; second, that these media are contesting social codes, legitimized identities and institutionalized social relations; and third, that these communication practices are empowering the community involved, to the point where these transformations and changes are possible.

The importance of contesting social codes, identities, and social relations—that is, the "symbolic"—is explained by Mouffe as she explores the multifaceted nature of oppression. A community can be oppressed not only by exploiting of its labor force, but also through the imposition of symbolic systems. Thus, democratic struggles have to be understood as processes of change that also include practices of dissent in the realm of the symbolic:

> [S]ome new types of struggle must be seen as resistance to the growing uniformity of social life, a uniformity that is the result of the kind of mass culture imposed by the media. This imposition of a homogenized way of life, of a uniform cultural pattern, is being challenged by different groups that reaffirm their right to their differences, their specificity, be it through the exaltation of their regional identity or their specificity in the realm of fashion, music or language. (Mouffe 1988, 93)

According to Mouffe's proposal for a radical democracy, these practices and strategies of resistance constitute the politics of the quotidian. Within the radical democracy framework, spaces for political action expand and multiply from political action of an interest group opposing the state to political action within the realms of the family, the street, the workplace or the church, growing out of economic, gender or ethnic relations (McClure 1992, 123). In other words, Mouffe's and McClure's radical democracy expands the realm of politics from "juridical demands upon the state" (McClure 1992, 123) to "quotidian politics—a politics which extends the terrain of political contestation to the everyday enactment of social practices and the routine reiteration of cultural representations" (McClure 1992, 123). The line demarcating the public/political and the private/nonpolitical blurs. In quotidian politics every dimension of everyday life becomes a potential site for social contestation.

Furthermore, the nature of political action expands to include not only demands on rights and on the quality of life, but also on the very definitions of what is culturally intelligible. That is, the transformation of legitimized cultural codes and social discourses becomes a goal of political action. With this in mind, the alteration, through everyday life practices, of socially legitimized ideas about a group's identity is conceived as political action (McClure 1992, 124). The permanent deconstruction of subordinate identities becomes an important task of democratic action. In short, cultural codes have become the "objects of political struggle" (McClure 1992, 124, 236).

These concepts provide a theoretical perspective appropriate to capture the subtle and sometimes faint (but not less important or serious) movements in which individuals and their differentiated power positions coalesce when involved in citizens' media experiences. Power happens in the realm of the quotidian, and what makes citizens' media fascinating is how they stir power in kaleidoscopic movements that fade soon after they emerge, like movements in a dance toward empowerment.

The Swamp Metaphor

Conceiving citizens' media protagonists as unified, homogeneous political actors with clear, rational agendas has led us to view many of these citizens' media experiences as chaotic and politically frail. The reason? Our understanding of how democracy is built emerges from thinking about political action and social movements as linear, continuous, and conscious processes toward a common goal. As a result, citizens' media with their often fragmented and improvised nature are dismissed for not having enough political potential to contribute significantly to the construction of democracy.

In fact, citizens' media sometimes have such short life cycles that they appear and disappear leaving—what at first glance seems to be—no signature, no accomplishments, no successes. We study citizens' media with an eye for a straight line departing from point A (state of nondemocracy) and heading toward point B (democracy). Instead what we find is a multitude of small forces that surface and burst like bubbles in a swamp. But in the same way that these bubbles are a clear sign that the swamp is alive, we should approach democratic communication as a live creature that contracts and expands with its own very vital rhythms—rhythms which often have very little to do with the linear, preplanned and rational processes that inform our scholarly inquiries. That is, instead of thinking democracy an ultimate goal, a final state-of-things to reach, we should look at how democratic and nondemocratic forces are being renegotiated constantly and how citizens' media can strengthen the former, thus contributing to the—although sometimes ephemeral—swelling of the democratic. Inspired by Mouffe's theory of radical democracy, Kristie McClure rethinks a new possibility to conceptualize political action in terms that account for this permanent movement of negotiations and renegotiations of power.

1927
1960
1963
1964
1967
1969
1970
1971
1972
1973
1974
1975
1976
1977
1978
1979
1980
1981
1982
1983
1984
1985
1986
1987
1988
1989
1990
1991
1992
1993
1994
1995
1996
1997
1998
1999
2000
2001
2002
2003
2004
2005
2006

Addressing our obsession for clinging to our theorizing that the construction of democracy is a unified and straight-line project, McClure challenges us to let go of these prefabricated notions and to learn to capture political action as a historical claim. A claim has a location in time and space.[10] A claim is relevant only within a historical context and for a situated subject, and cannot be transferred to a different positioning. A claim only lasts for as long as the dominant forces remain unmoved. As the situation changes, the claim will also change. As opposed to the "platform" or the "social project," claims are not static; they are in constant flux, following the movements of a changing social subject. Understanding political actions as historical claims, says McClure (1992, 123), does not imply the negation of their political potential but on the contrary marks the opening of a new politics:

> [T]o deny the uniqueness of the national state both as a site and as an object of political struggle, then, is not to eviscerate the potential for a transformative politics, but rather to resist its recuperation within the reductive and unifying mechanisms of interest group liberalism. And in this respect, it suggests the possibility of a politics that begins not with the object of constructing similarities to address rights claims to the state, *but opens rather with the object of addressing such claims to each other, and to each 'other,' whoever and wherever they may be.* (my emphasis)

McClure (1992, 124) recognizes that politicizing this multiple social subject, enacted in everyday life as social identities, codes, and relationships are renegotiated again and again, will have an ephemeral consistency: "It is here, then, that the possibility of direct address politicizes these postmodern subjects yet further, by recognizing their agency in such contingent reconfigurations, however local or transitory they may be."

Moreover, it is our responsibility as intellectuals trying to conceptualize the construction of democracy to assume in full force the real texture of power negotiations, their fluid consistency that escapes the traps of our ineffective essentialist and static concepts. The apparent lightweight quality of political action should not lead us into a "black hole" of political pessimism, but on the contrary, should convince us of the necessity to create new conceptual ways to capture this politics in flux.

On this basis, our explorations of citizens' media with theories and concepts that expect power struggles and the democratization of communication[11] to have a rigid consistency will systematically miss the political potential of these media experiments. As it is unlikely that the texture of political action mutates, what needs changing is our perspective as communication scholars and activists trying to understand citizens' media.

References

Bagdikian, B.H. 1997. *The Media Monopoly.* 5th ed. Boston: Beacon Press.

Bruck, P.A., and M. Raboy. 1989. "The challenge of democratic communication," in: P.A. Bruck and M. Raboy, eds. *Communication for and Against Democracy.* Montreal & New York: Black Rose Books. 3–16.

Capriles, O. 1981. "Venezuela: Política de comunicación o comunicación alternativa," in: M. Simpson Grinberg, ed. *Comunicación alternativa y cambio social: América Latina.* Mexico City: Universidad Nacional Autónoma de Mexico. 149-166.

Dervin, B., and R. Huesca. 1997. "Reaching for the communicating in participatory communication: A meta-theoretical analysis," *Journal of International Communication* 4(2):46–74.

Devine, R.H. 1995. "Discourses on Access: The Marginalization of a Medium," paper presented at the Speech Communication Association's 81st Annual Convention. San Antonio, Tex.

Downing, J. 1984. *Radical media: The Political Experience of Alternative Communication.* Boston: South End Press.

Esteinou Madrid, J. 1986. "La utopía de la comunicación alternativa en el aparato dominante de la cultura de masas," in: M. Simpson Grinberg, ed. *Comunicación alternativa y cambio social: América Latina.* 2nd ed. Mexico: Premià Editora. 72–88.

Fox, E., and H. Schmucler. 1982. *Comunicación y democracia en América Latina.* Lima, Peru: DESCO.

---

10 In a different context, Tony Bennet (1992) has intelligently articulated the concept of claims.

11 In no way am I suggesting that a struggle for more democratic communication leaves the big media off the hook. Indeed, I believe academic and activist efforts for more democratic communication should maintain multiple fronts such as political economy-type of explorations of the cultural industries, deconstruction of media texts, audiences' and consumers' organizations activism, media literacy projects, media regulation, national communication policies and support of citizens' media.

1927
1960
1963
1964
1967
1969
1970
1971
1972
1973
1974
1975
1976
1977
1978
1979
1980
1981
1982
1983
1984
1985
1986
1987
1988
1989
1990
1991
1992
1993
1994
1995
1996
1997
1998
1999
2000
2001
2002
2003
2004
2005
2006

Frederick, H.H. 1993. *Global Communication and International Relations.* Belmont, Calif.: Wadsworth Publishing.

Hamelink, C.J. 1995. "Information Imbalance Across The Globe," in: J. Downing, A. Mohammadi, and A. Sreberny-Mohammadi, eds. *Questioning the Media: A Critical Introduction.* 2nd ed. Thousand Oaks, Calif.: Sage. 293–307.

Hamelink, C.J. 1997a. "International communication: Global market and morality," in: A. Mohammadi, ed. *Internationa lCommunication and Globalization: A Critical Introduction.* Thousand Oaks, Calif.: Sage. 92–118.

Hamelink, C.J. 1997b. "MacBride with Hindsight," in: P. Golding and P. Harris, eds. *Beyond Cultural Imperialism: Globalization, Communication and the New International Order.* Thousand Oaks, Calif.: Sage. 69–93.

Huesca, R. 1995b. "Subject-authored theories of media practice: The case of Bolivian tin miners' radio," *Communication Studies* 46:149–168.

Huesca, R. 1996. "Participation for development in radio: An ethnography of the *Reporteros populares* of Bolivia," *Gazette* 57(1):29–52.

Huesca, R., and B. Dervin. 1994. "Theory and practice in Latin American alternative communication research," *Journal of Communication* 44(4):53–73.

Kaplún, M. 1983. "La comunicación popular. Alternative válida?" *Chasqui* 7:40–43.

Kaplún, M. 1986. "Uruguay: Participación, praxis, problema. La experiencia del casete-foro," in: M. Simpson Grinberg, ed. *Comunicación alternativa y cambio social: América Latina.* 2nd ed. Mexico: Premià Editora. 266–283.

Kellner, D. 1995. *Media Culture: Cultural Studies, Identity, and Politics Between The Modern and The Postmodern.* London: Routledge.

Laclau, E., and Mouffe, C. 1985. *Hegemony and socialist strategy: Towards a radical democratic politics.* London: Verso.

Lewis, P.M. 1984b. "Community radio: The Montreal conference and after," *Media, Culture and Society* 6:137–150.

Mattelart, A. 1974. *Las transnacionales y la comunicación de masas.* Quito: Editorial Universitaria.

Mattelart, A. 1977. *Multinacionales y sistemas de comunicación. Los aparatos ideológicos del imperialismo.* Mexico: Siglo XXI.

Mattelart, A. 1983. *Transnationals and the Third World.* South Hadley, Mass.: Bergin & Garvey Publishers.

Mattelart, A., and M. Mattelart. 1992. "On the new uses of media in time of crisis," in: M. Raboy and B. Dagenais, eds. *Media, Crisis, and Democracy.* London and Newbury Park, Calif.: Sage. 162–180.

Mattelart, A., and J.-M. Piemme. 1980a. "New means of communication: New questions for the left," *Media, Culture and Society* 2:321–338.

Mattelart, A., and J.-M. Piemme. 1980b. *Télévision: Enjeux sans frontières.* Grenoble: Presses Universitaires de Grenoble.

McClure, K. 1992. "On the subject of rights: Pluralism, plurality and political identity," in: C. Mouffe, ed. *Dimensions of Radical Democracy: Pluralism, Citizenship, community.* London: Verso. 108–125.

Mohammadi, A. 1997. "Communication and the globalization process in the developing world," in: A. Mohammadi, ed. *International communication and globalization: A critical introduction.* Thousand Oaks, Calif.: Sage. 67–89.

Mouffe, C. 1988. "Hegemony and new political subjects: Towards a new conception of democracy," in: L. Grossberg and C. Nelson, eds. *Marxism and the interpretation of culture.* Urbana and Chicago: Univ. of Illinois Press. 89–102.

Mouffe, C. 1992a. "Preface: Democratic politics today," in: C. Mouffe, ed. *Dimensions of radical democracy: Pluralism, Citizenship, Community.* London: Verso. 1–14.

Mouffe, C. 1992b. "Democratic citizenship and the political community," in: C. Mouffe, ed. *Dimensions of radical democracy: Pluralism, citizenship, community.* London: Verso. 225–239.

Mouffe, C. 1992c. "Feminism, Citizenship and Radical Democratic Politics," in: J. Buttler and J.W. Scott, eds. *Feminists theorize the political.* New York: Routledge. 369–384.

Nethol, A.M. 1983. "El papel de la comunicación y los procesos populares," *Comunicación y Cultura* 9:115–125.

O'Sullivan-Ryan, J., and M. Kaplún. 1978. "Communication methods to promote grass-roots participation. A summary of research findings from Latin America, and an annotated bibliography," *Documents on communication and society* 6. Paris: UNESCO.

Paiva, A. 1983. "La comunicación alternativa: Sus campos de influencia, sus limitaciones y sus perspectivas de desarrollo," in: F. Reyes Matta, ed. *Comunicación alternativa y búsquedas democráticas.* Mexico: Fundación Friedrich Ebert and ILET (Instituto Latinoamericano de Estudios Transnacionales). 29–56.

Pasquali, A. 1992. "Shifting the debate: From the academic world to the real world," *Media Development* 39(2):5–8.

Portales, D.C. 1981. "Perspectivas de la comunicación alternativa en América Latina," in: M. Simpson Grinberg, ed. *Comunicación alternativa y cambio social: América Latina.* Mexico City: Universidad Nacional Autónoma de Mexico. 61–80.

Portales, D.C. 1983. "El movimiento popular y las comunicaciones: Reflexiones a partir de la experiencia chilena," in: F.R. Matta, ed. *Comunicación alternativa y búsquedas democráticas.* Mexico: Fundación Friedrich Ebert and ILET (Instituto Latinoamericano de Estudios Transnacionales). 59–69.

Reeves, G. 1993. *Communication and the Third World.* London and New York: Routledge.

Reyes Matta, F. 1981. "La comunicación transnacional y la respuesta alternativa," in: M. Simpson Grinberg, ed. *Comunicación alternativa y cambio social: América Latina.* Mexico City: Universidad Nacional Autónoma de Mexico. 81–108.

Reyes Matta, F. 1982. "La comunicación alternativa como respuesta democrática," in: E. Fox and H. Schmucler, eds. *Comunicación y democracia en América Latina.* Lima, Peru: DESCO. 245–264.

Reyes Matta, F. 1983. *Comunicación alternativa y búsquedas democráticas.* Mexico: Fundación Friedrich Ebert and ILET (Instituto Latinoamericano de Estudios Transnacionales).

Reyes Matta, F. 1986. "Alternative communication: Solidarity and development in the face of transnational expansion," in: R. Atwood and E.G. McAnany, eds. *Communication and Latin American society: Trends in critical research,* 1960–1985. Madison: Univ. of Wisconsin Press. 190–214.

Roncagliolo, R. 1991. "The growth of the audio-visual imagescape in Latin America," in: N. Thede and A. Ambrosi, eds. *Video the changing world.* Montréal: Black Rose Books. 22–30.

Schulein, S., and S. Robina. 1983. "Prensa alternativa y nuevas fronteras de información: La experiencia de ALTERCOM," in: F. Reyes Matta, ed. *Comunicación alternativa y búsquedas democráticas.* Mexico: Fundación Friedrich Ebert and ILET (Instituto Latinoamericano de Estudios Transnacionales). 155–169.

Servaes, J. 1992. Toward a New Perspective for Communication and Development. In: F.L. Casmir, ed. *Communication in development.* Norwood, N.J.: Ablex. 51–85.

Simpson Grinberg, M. 1981a. "Comunicación alternativa: Dimensiones, límites, posibilidades," in: M. Simpson Grinberg, ed. *Comunicación alternativa y cambio social: América Latina.* Mexico City: Universidad Nacional Autónoma de Mexico. 109–129.

Simpson Grinberg, M., ed. 1981b. *Comunicación alternativa y cambio social: América Latina.* Mexico City: Universidad Nacional Autónoma de Mexico.

Simpson Grinberg, M. 1986. "Trends in alternative communication research in Latin America," in: R. Atwood and E.G. McAnany, eds. *Communication and Latin American society: Trends in critical research, 1960–1985.* Madison: Univ. of Wisconsin Press. 165–189.

Stangelaar, F. 1983. "Comunicación alternativa y video-cassette: Perspectivas en América Latina," in: F. Reyes Matta, ed. *Comunicación alternativa y búsquedas democráticas.* Mexico: Fundación Friedrich Ebert and ILET (Instituto Latinoamericano de Estudios Transnacionales). 209–236.

Thomas, P.N. 1997. "An inclusive NWICO: Cultural resistance and popular resistance," in: P. Golding and P. Harris, eds. *Beyond cultural imperialism: Globalization, communication, and the new international order.* Thousand Oaks, Calif.: Sage.

Wolin, S. 1992. "What revolutionary action means today," in: C. Mouffe, ed. *Dimensions of Radical Democracy: Pluralism, Citizenship, Community.* London: Verso. 240–253.

IF COMMUNITY MEDIA IS THE ANSWER, WHAT IS THE QUESTION?

By Alfred E. Opubor

1999 The idea of community has been problematic for Africans in the post-colonial period. In the politics and economics of nation building, attempts were made to build societies that were broad-based, with centralised political power and authority and homogenised institutions, so as to emphasise commonalties and to incorporate disparate cultures in an effort to create "national unity."

In so doing, the goal was to de-emphasise differences, ignore particularities and specificities, and minimise, or even proscribe, any tendency that was likely to question the political orthodoxy, including the expression of dissent or minority opinion. Since the 1980s, there have also been attempts to build institutions beyond the nation state, employing the notion of "community" in an expanded sense. Although the East African Community did not last, the Economic Community of West African States (ECOWAS) has passed its silver jubilee. The Southern African Development Community (SADC) is approaching a second decade, and there's talk of an African Economic Community for the 21st century. All of these processes of incorporation, of building ever larger political and economic units, have tended to bypass the ideas, opinions and direct contributions of the majority of our citizens, even in countries where they were supposedly "free" to express themselves on such matters.

But these are truly interesting and contradictory times. Most of the time, the "people" appear to have acquiesced in the decisions made by their governments and other leaders on their behalf. But from time to time, they have erupted with clear statements of disagreement or dissent, often with violent reactions to centralised instructions and arrangements. Many of the differences and specificities nation builders wanted to wish away seem to persist; and they persist just where people find themselves, where they live their daily lives, in their communities. Many Africans do not feel they live in their nation; they know they live in their communities. It is there, in their communities, that they seek to find work, to raise their families, to cure their sick, to grow old and die and be buried. Many of them from rural areas have been forced to migrate from their original communities, to seek jobs, education and fortune elsewhere, to try to become part of new urban communities. And even then, they often migrate from neighbourhood to neighbourhood in the cities where they find themselves.

Thus, in linking community and media to discuss community media, it is important that we do not marginalise the "community" in favour of the "media." …If community media is the answer, what is the question?

This is probably not the time for definitions. At the dawn of the 21st century, we all think we know what "community media" are. With the popularisation of community radios, community newspapers, magazines, newsletters and other publications, we do indeed know about "community media." Or do we? The bottom line in discussing community media is an understanding of the nature of the community which underlies media practice, access and ownership.

Today the notion of community has a strong nonphysical connotation, so that it is possible to speak about "virtual" reality and virtual communities. But in spite of the new information and communication technologies, "community" still retains a strong physical reference to people in geographic proximity, with frequent, if not continuous, contact. People who share certain cultural attributes have access to certain resources of social organisation and common institutions, resulting in common basic beliefs.

Among other things, a human community is built on the exchange of initiatives, information and meanings in the process of defining, creating and maintaining a group identity and interests for survival within a specifiable geographical and/or cultural space. A community thus creates, and is also created by, a community communication system, which includes the various communication roles (and their actors/performers), needs and resources available to the individuals and subgroups which make up the community.

Community media should be viewed then as elements of a community communication system. They serve as instrumentalities for role performance and resource utilisation, for responding to the communication needs of individuals and institutions within the community. These needs are diverse and often require different modalities of expression and satisfaction. It is within the framework of a community's communication system, therefore, that its media should properly be identified and created. It may then emerge that appropriate media are multiple channelled, rather than single, and that community media should, realistically, be multimedia.

Lessons Learned

Twentieth century approaches to community media development have been dominated by exogenous definitions of communities and the imposition of narrow, media-based solutions to the cultural, communication and survival problems communities face. For example, the general objective [here] falls within the context of several projects and activities initiated by UNESCO and other U.N. agencies and many international non-governmental organisations and donor agencies in assisting in developing such media which give different social groups, particularly the more isolated and disadvantaged, a chance to participate in development strategies and have access to communication resources at the local level (1). Driven by noble intentions to spread the benefits of "development" and, more recently, to promote indigenous development and enhance local ownership of development outcomes through "empowerment" and "participation," these "activities and initiatives" have often not been based on a conceptual or practical foundation arising from a community communication system viewpoint.

1927
1960
1963
1964
1967
1969
1970
1971
1972
1973
1974
1975
1976
1977
1978
1979
1980
1981
1982
1983
1984
1985
1986
1987
1988
1989
1990
1991
1992
1993
1994
1995
1996
1997
1998
1999
2000
2001
2002
2003
2004
2005
2006

Their inadequacies demonstrate the need for interventions based on a community communication strategy. Oepen (1990) suggested a decade ago that community communication:

> is a process of horizontal and vertical social interaction and networking through media regularly produced, managed and controlled by or in close cooperation between people at the community level and at other levels of society who share a sociopolitical commitment towards a democratic society of countervailing powers. As the people participate in this process as planners, producers and performers, the media become informing, educating and entertaining tools that would also make nonprivileged and marginalised people think and speak for themselves, not an exercise in persuasion or power. In such a process, the entry points for communication interventions have to be sought in the communities' learning methods, cultural expressions and media forms. (2)

The community media created in the 20th century have generally been single-channel media, responding to technical and instrumental orientations, favouring hardware above software, and emphasising technique over process. Their impact has usually been evaluated in terms of the achievement of standardised "improvements" in sectoral target areas such as agriculture, health, population, literacy and poverty alleviation. However, within these approaches, a number of experiences have provided lessons that should assist the development of a community communication strategy in the future, hopefully one that is more responsive to context-specific strategic communication system needs of the relevant communities, and therefore possibly resulting in the creation of "community multimedia." Oepen's (1990) list of "functions" to be ascribed to community media, "independent of the type of media or the type of people involved," provides a useful basis for the development of such a strategy.

Whose Community? Whose Media?

To move into the future with a new agenda, it is necessary to ask new questions, which may lead to new answers, or to find new answers to old questions. But the old answers are certainly not needed to new questions, as they seem to be somewhat discredited. Rather, a community communication system approach to community media development should proceed from a basic understanding of the nature and needs of the community, in communication terms. A needs assessment survey of the community should attempt to answer at least the following questions:

1. What information is needed to define the parameters and details of the community's communication system? What components need special attention? Why?
2. How are they determined?
3. What media does the community already have?
4. What media does it want?
5. What media does it need?
6. What media can it afford?
7. What media channels or combinations would meet the community's needs?
8. Who can make what media available to it, at what cost, for what purpose?

Undertaking a needs assessment of the community's communication system, through a participatory, "ethnography of communication" methodology, should provide answers to the first six questions. The last two questions should be the focus of discussions between the community and external partners interested in providing community media resources to meet identified priorities. Whether the community is physically contiguous or whether it reflects a dispersed communal group with common characteristics and interests, these questions are still valid and can yield required information. In this kind of process, participatory research becomes an important first step in the decision about whether additional media are required to meet the needs of the community communication system, and what specific media are required. This could lead to results far different from the usual situation of donors and NGOs proposing a radio station or video facilities or rural printing press or desktop publishing or Internet facilities for the community, because these facilities fit into their community media development programme.

It may well be that the community's view is that it requires more than one, even all, of the above facilities, to solve specific communication system and contextual development problems. The community and its external partners may then engage in a prioritisation process to determine how to meet the needs and perhaps involve other partners who are able to contribute some of the media components required. It may be, for example, that what is required is participatory theatre, and the strategic need becomes how to facilitate performances in particular areas of the community.

But it may also be that the area of need identified is that theatre performances, already in existence in the community, could more effectively be extended through regular radio drama, which would then be the community media input actually required by the community communications system. These answers are not always obvious without a consultative process and relevant analysis. The next steps in this process, and a possible result of ethnographic communication research, would be several strategic scenarios for developing a community's communication system. Sensitive investigation will usually reveal that a community is not necessarily homogenous, in terms of interests and points of view. An important question may then be how to have more inclusive media through providing more diverse opportunities for community communication. This may mean intervening in communication system elements, including media. Nonmedia considerations could include, for example, the notion of attracting new voices into community communication, involving more active participation of women and the elderly. This may not require creating a new medium or channel, but rather providing access for new sources of information within existing channels. But again it may require acknowledging and using new communication channels more adapted to the interests of the groups whose needs are to be addressed.

In *The Myth of Community*, Gujit and Shah (1998) have shown how participatory development models have involved flawed processes and inadequate tools from the point of view of gender analysis and the handling of gender issues and differences within communities. Their insistence that participatory methods and inventions often obscure the interests of women is a salutary *caveat* to underline the need for situation-specific research. In fact, the development of community media should be based on a community communication strategy. That strategy should seek to provide answers in support of the communication needs and objectives defined by the community.

Many existing projects for the creation of community media have indeed undertaken research to determine the various aspects and operations of the media to be established. Such studies have been usually long on sociocultural and economic background, usually related to the development "problem" to be solved, but generally short on the communication background and profile of the community that should be the basis of the choice of functional media, from an endogenous point of reference.

The argument thus far is that the choice of media is a variable to be determined with the community, rather than predetermined by exogenous interests and priorities, no matter how well meaning. It may help to clarify whether community media are media in the classic sense or whether they are techniques and technologies for responding to community communication needs.

Future Directions

The establishment and expansion of community media in African countries are still confronted with a number of problems that will need to be addressed in the 21st century. Therefore, several question areas need to be considered, including that of policy, regulation, research, training and sustainability.

1927
1960
1963
1964
1967
1969
1970
1971
1972
1973
1974
1975
1976
1977
1978
1979
1980
1981
1982
1983
1984
1985
1986
1987
1988
1989
1990
1991
1992
1993
1994
1995
1996
1997
1998
1999
2000
2001
2002
2003
2004
2005
2006

THE POLICY QUESTION

Community media are governed by the general communication/media policy environment prevailing in each country. While there has been an increase in the number of countries favouring media pluralism, and therefore more receptive to new media initiatives, including establishment of new community-level initiatives, there is still ambivalence about the regulatory and legal situation of many of these initiatives and the technologies that propel them.

In Mozambique, for example, there is ongoing discussion about the nature of community radio stations and how they should be established and run, within the liberalised media environment, where the state monopoly has been abolished. Radio stations, established by the Institute of Social Communication with funding from UNICEF and UNFPA, in Xai-Xai and Licunga, are referred to as "community" radio. But it is not clear if they are more than radio stations that cover a geographical area around these towns. In what sense are these "community" rather than "local" stations? Is it because they are nongovernmental? In what sense are they "owned" by the community? Radio Xai-Xai was founded in 1995. It was the first community radio station established after the government freed the airwaves in 1990, which, in theory, allowed anyone to broadcast. It was therefore the first radio station to be independent of the state monopoly on broadcasting that had existed until then. It has two community-based committees, one for administration, the other for programming. Some members of the committees work at the station almost daily. The general understanding is that the station is a keeper of information, which is to be transferred to the community, and that the community should be trained to take control of the station. These ideas are to be formulated into operational guidelines. It remains to be seen to what extent such guidelines can be formulated at the national level and to what extent local variations are necessary and possible.

The project is supported by the Institute of Social Communications (ISC) Delegation based in Quelimane,

some two or three hours' drive away, with funding from UNFPA. According to a recent report:

> The station participants all had an understanding of the radio station as an instrument of community development and of participation in governance and production as important principles. This vision was not written down and varied from person to person. Through a visualisation process, a mission statement and set of objectives were developed. The station has nine staff members and nine community collaborators who produce programmes. Three staff are paid by the state. The remaining staff are paid when funds are available. Everyone accepts that when there are no funds they cannot be paid.(4)

Other countries in the southern African region will also need to grapple with these definitional and policy questions, while in some countries, such as South Africa and Namibia, the realities on the ground have confirmed the mission and character of community radio stations. But even there, there are various definitional and operational procedures. David Lush (1998), quoting Guy Berger, presents some of the definitional issues posed in the South African experience, including questions related to target audiences, ownership and programme orientation.

In the context of examining the scope of community media, several attempts at organised theatre performances have been labelled "community theatre." For example, in Zimbabwe, over 200 member organisations have bonded together to form the Zimbabwe Association for Community Theatre (ZACT), which recently celebrated 10 years of existence. Its main objective is to promote and encourage indigenous culture through theatre. ZACT seeks to create employment for school leavers in the rural and urban areas. It also aims to promote indigenous culture through the electronic media. A community theatre process that involves planning, problem identification, research analysis, story, scripting, rehearsals, workshop, performance, community action and evaluation guides ZACT's work. In this process, members of the community are expected to participate. According to ZACT, community theatre groups have staged productions on conscientisation, community health, AIDS, the impact of the economic structural adjustment program and gender issues.

One common feature of community theatre is that it is participatory. It is unlike conventional theatre where people act on stage and do not talk with the audience. In community theatre, the artists talk, laugh and ask the audience questions. There is a lot of interaction between the audience and the artists. During the pretesting and evaluation stages of the production artists involve the communities. Does community theatre fall within the definition of community media? How can the development of community media include community theatre in a systematic and forward-looking manner?

REGULATION

With the introduction of the new information and communication technologies, especially E-mail and Internet services, opportunities for physical and virtual communities to communicate are enhanced. In addition to internal transactions, the community and its members can reach, and be reached by, the outside world. These opportunities also raise questions of regulation; but perhaps also transcend regulation. Regulation is, however, very relevant to the promotion of community media precisely because it deals squarely with basic principles and issues concerning ownership, control and operation of broadcasting and other media. The following issues thus need to be addressed:

1. *Ownership*. Who owns the airwaves? Do they belong to government through the people? Can individuals have private rights? If government regulates the licensing of broadcasting stations and the use of telecommunications, what considerations should be applied? How can private stations guarantee "the public interest"? Should owners of broadcast facilities be allowed to own other media

as well? Can diversity be guaranteed in the ownership of broadcasting? Will commercialisation/privatisation of telecommunications permit affordable services in impoverished rural areas?

2. *Control*. Who should control what in broadcasting and telecommunications? Does control involve only the power to issue and withdraw licenses? Who controls the content of broadcasting? What guidelines need to be established at the state level? Do local governments have a say? What is the possible role of citizen groups or civil society in the allocation of frequencies and in the operation of media institutions?

3. *Operation*. Are broadcasting stations and other community media operations to be run as purely commercial organisations? What guidelines should be provided about commercial or non-commercial approaches and the position of advertising? What technical specifications should be applied to the range of community broadcast signals? What editorial guidelines or general principles for guiding access and accountability should be established?

4. *Content*. What balance is desirable among various content categories? What percentage of programming should be entertainment, and what should be educational and developmental? What proportion of community broadcast airtime should be devoted to commercials and advertising messages? How much time should news and current affairs programmes occupy on what kinds of stations? How should special interests be catered to, e.g., those of children, women and rural dwellers? Should broadcasting stations editorialise? What categories of programme content should be proscribed?

RESEARCH

Community media operations should be sustained by continuous research about the larger social environment for defining new issues, new actors and new voices. It should also address the evolving needs of communities for new or different information about

1927
1960
1963
1964
1967
1969
1970
1971
1972
1973
1974
1975
1976
1977
1978
1979
1980
1981
1982
1983
1984
1985
1986
1987
1988
1989
1990
1991
1992
1993
1994
1995
1996
1997
1998
1999
2000
2001
2002
2003
2004
2005
2006

technical matters (health, jobs, politics, etc.) and en-quire about the feelings of community members regarding media performance. And it should assess the effect of media on the community. This is the goal of classic impact assessment; and it might be directed towards assessing:

1. the flow of communications in the community (who says what to whom, how often?);
2. community participation (what different individuals and groups are represented in media content production?);
3. expression (what are people saying through the media?), asessed through a sensitive qualitative content analysis of the feelings, moods, images, etc. conveyed through media and how they relate to community goals, etc.;
4. knowledge (what information and ideas do the media convey and what do people gain as a result of paying attention to the media?);
5. attitudes (what changes, if any, can be attributed to media and communication in the way people feel about themselves, their neighbours, their communities and the world "out there"?).

The research relating to these questions should be participatory and need not be quantitative. But the extent to which it is continuous, and involves different segments of the community as enquirers and suppliers of information, is the extent to which research as a cultural product can be demystified and indigenised for the community. It can also provide a basis for re-orienting the operational content of "community" media to make them more truly community based and owned.

TRAINING

Consideration needs to be given to whom should be trained and in what aspects. Most community media do not have, and probably cannot afford, people trained professionally in communications, journalism, marketing or other necessary skills. Often, community volunteers have little more than enthusiasm and a willingness to learn. Training in basic writing and

production skills to enable the preparation of messages that are audible, legible and communicative will be required, preferably in the short term, e.g., in weekend sessions and on the job. People already professionally trained will need help as to how to work with communities and with nonprofessional people without being condescending or permissive...[and] abandoning professional standards.

A skills profile of community media needs should be developed by communications trainers to see how new initiatives at the local level can be assisted. What information and skills are needed to be able to successfully run a community radio, a newspaper or a theatre? Case studies of ongoing community media (successful or not) are crucial for developing such profiles, which should be the joint product of community media practitioners, researchers and communications/journalism trainers. Appropriate training modules can then be developed around these case studies. Training should also involve "media literacy" for community volunteers and other community members so that the media can be truly internalised and indigenised.

SUSTAINABILITY

The cost of installing and operating community media is a basic problem for consideration. Disadvantaged and marginalised groups are defined largely by their lack of resources, and thus their inability to pay for and sustain services. Opoku-Mensah (1996) has observed: "We are all aware of the fact that "the people" have no money, and are often the poorest of the poor. So why are projects...designed to alleviate their isolation, marginalisation and voicelessness expected to become sustainable in an unrealistic time?"

Several reasons for funding community media as a social good have been advanced, with suggestions as to how various resources could be made available to sustain them. The bottom line of these suggestions is the need for communication and information policies, at the national level, which are sensitive to the plight of poorer communities, based on an understanding of the ways in which access to information can help them bridge the development gap and achieve better lives. Whether government provides the resources, or international donors and NGOs support them, community media are not likely to be sustainable from the point of view of the hosting/owning community. Is this inevitable? At the production as well as at the reception end, new technologies are beginning to introduce cost reductions that may make community communications and the media that service them more accessible and affordable.

A community communication centre might be an appropriate venue for combining the advantages of the various services with reduced costs. In this connection, Koning (1996) proposed that community media centres could serve the community by providing public education in media hardware, software and networking; public access to media tools (cameras, microphones and computers); and public access to media transmission systems (local television and FM radio). He further suggests that the local community should own the centre and that priority be given to establishing such centres in rural areas, as these are the main areas where human needs still need to be identified. Although Koning also suggests that donor funding, a public interest fund and an enabling environment from government would be necessary to support the capital-intensive community media he has in mind, he reports also on the fund-raising activities of South African community media centres, suggesting that these could be a method of providing additional resources for centres. Community broadcast receivers, telephones and reading rooms have been in operation in many countries for nearly two decades. They can now be joined by communal terminals for electronic mail. Some of the services provided by these facilities operate on a commercial basis, for people are glad to pay for a phone call and for contact with relatives through E-mail or other means. Such services can and are carried by media-related infrastructure. Might it not be possible to support "classic" media operations through them?

Within the media themselves, short personal announcements by individuals and social groups and advertising of community-level services by businesses and others, could provide modest but regular income for community media, without distorting their purpose and in fact encouraging community members to see media as sources of locally relevant vital information. Perhaps such contributions may not guarantee sustainability to community media, but they may introduce an important ingredient in concretising the notion of ownership of the media by the community.

Conclusion

The notion of community, which is central to the definition and development of "community media," is still not generally agreed upon. However, an approach to community identification from an endogenous perspective, especially through an "ethnographic" methodology, is a useful start to defining the communication profile and needs of the community, and thus identifying its communication system needs... .

References

1. UNESCO. Letter of invitation to regional seminar on promoting community media in Africa. 15 Apr. 1999.

2. Oepen, M. 1990. "Community communication: The link between the 'old' and the 'new' paradigm," *Journal of Development Communication* 1:55-66.

3. Gujit, I., and M.K. Shah. 1998. Waking up to power, conflict and process. In: I. Gujit and M.K. Shah, eds. *The myth of community*. London: Intermediate Technology Publications. 1–23.

4. *Proceedings of the 1996 MISA Annual Congress and "Community Voices Conference."* Club, Mangochi, Malawi. 6–13 Oct. 8–20.

5. Lush, D. 1998. "The role of the African media in the promotion of democracy and human rights," in: O. Adebayo and L. Wohlgemath, eds. *Towards a new partnership with Africa: Challenges and opportunities.* Uppsala: Nordiska Afrikainstitatet. 42-67.

6. Opoku-Mensah, A. 1996. "Should new communications technologies be considered as part of the new communications media?" *Proceedings of the 1996 MISA Annual Congress and "Community Voices Conference."* 6–13Oct. Club, Mangochi, Malawi. 4–6.

7. Koning, D. 1996. "The role of community media centre," *Proceedings of the 1996 MISA Annual Congress and "Community Voices Conference."* 6–13 Oct. Club, Mangochi, Malawi. 7.

Opubor, Alfred E. "If Community Media Is the Answer, What Is the Question?" Paper published as Chapter 1 in *Promoting Community Media in Africa* (2000), editor S.T. Kwame Boafo. UNESCO, Paris (France). Reprinted with permission of the copyright holder.

1927
1960
1963
1964
1967
1969
1970
1971
1972
1973
1974
1975
1976
1977
1978
1979
1980
1981
1982
1983
1984
1985
1986
1987
1988
1989
1990
1991
1992
1993
1994
1995
1996
1997
1998
1999
2000
2001
2002
2003
2004
2005
2006

INSTITUTIONS, AGENCY AND THE LIMITATIONS OF PARTICIPATORY APPROACHES TO DEVELOPMENT

By Frances Cleaver

2001 Participation in Development Discourse

Heroic claims are made for participatory approaches to development. Participation of community members is assumed to contribute to enhanced efficiency and effectiveness of investment and to promote processes of democratisation and empowerment. The conundrum of ensuring the sustainability of development interventions is assumed to be solvable by the proper involvement of beneficiaries in the supply and management of resources, services and facilities. There are even claims that participation constitutes a "new paradigm" of development (Chambers 1997).

Despite such significant claims, there is little evidence of the long-term effectiveness of participation in materially improving the conditions of the most vulnerable people or as a strategy for social change. While the evidence for efficiency receives some support on a small scale, the evidence regarding empowerment and sustainability is more partial, tenuous and reliant on assertions of the rightness of the approach and process rather than convincing evidence of outcomes. Trenchant critiques of participation approaches to development exist (Stiefel and Wolfe 1994; Biggs 1995), but these seem to have had little impact on development and policy discourses.

Participation has therefore become an act of faith in development, something we believe in and rarely question. This act of faith is based on three main tenets: that participation is intrinsically a "good thing" (especially for the participants); that a focus on

"getting the techniques right" is the principal way of ensuring the success of such approaches; and that considerations of power and politics on the whole should be avoided as divisive and obstructive.

In questioning these it is not my intention to deny the usefulness of a people-centred orientation in development, as some critics have suggested, or to dismiss all attempts at community-based development as well meaning but ineffectual. Indeed, I am not a complete pessimist about such approaches; rather I see them as promising but inevitably messy and difficult, approximate and unpredictable in outcome. Subjecting them to rigorous critical analysis is as important as constantly asserting their benefits. This article outlines some of the conceptual underpinnings of participatory approaches and illustrates how the translation of these into policy and practice is not necessarily consistent with the desired impacts. In illustrating these points I draw heavily on my research into collective action and the institutions that shape the management of common property resources (Cleaver 2000) and on my work on gender and water resource management (Cleaver 1998a).

Efficiency and Empowerment

The theorising of participatory approaches is often dichotomised into means/ends classifications (Oakley, et al. 1991; Nelson and Wright 1995). These distinguish between the efficiency arguments (participation as a tool for achieving better project outcomes) and equity and empowerment arguments (participation as a process that enhances the capacity of individuals to improve or change their own lives). The predominant discourses of development are practical and technical, concerned with project-dictated imperatives of efficiency, with visible, manageable manifestations of collective action. These, however, are commonly overlooked in the rhetoric of empowerment, which is implicitly assumed to have a greater moral value. Radical empowerment discourse (with its roots in Freirean philosophy) is associated with both individual *and* class action, with the transformation of structures of subordination through radical changes in law, property rights, the institutions of society. The model of "participation" implied is of development practitioners working with poor people to struggle actively for change (Batliwala 1994). Such ideas, associated with structural change and with collective action facilitated by and in opposition to the state, are rather out of fashion in development, although within feminist scholarship and within the Latin American participatory tradition the debate continues (e.g., Fals-Borda 1998; Jackson and Pearson 1998). As "empowerment" has become a buzzword in development, an essential objective of projects, its radical, challenging arid transformatory edge has been lost. The concept of action has become individualised, empowerment depoliticised.

A number of problems arise in analysing empowerment within projects. It is often unclear exactly *who* is to be empowered—the individual, the "community" or categories of people such as "women," "the poor" or the "socially excluded." The question of how such generalised categories of people might exercise agency is generally sidestepped. The mechanisms of such empowerment are either startlingly clear (e.g., empowerment of the individual through cash transactions in the market) or conveniently fuzzy (as in the assumed benefits to individuals of participation in management committees).The scope of and limitations on the empowering effects of any project are little explored. ...

Participation, Social Capital and Inclusion

There is a need to conceptualise participatory approaches more broadly, for more complex analyses of the linkages between intervention, participation and empowerment (Moser and Sollis 1991). We need to better understand the nonproject nature of people's lives, the complex livelihood interlinkages that make an impact in one area likely to be felt in others, and the potential for unintended consequences arising from any intended intervention or act (Giddens 1984; Long 1992).

A move away from narrow project approaches may be seen in the current concern with the role of social capital

in development. Ideas about overcoming the problem of social exclusion have linked concepts of community, democracy, the key role of nongovernmental organisations, individual responsibility and citizenship. Concepts of participation are partly subsumed within this discourse. The concept of social inclusion emphasises involvement in the structures and institutions of society—"most fundamentally, the participatory and communicative structures, including new forms of social partnership through which a shared sense of the public good is created and debated" (IILS/UNDP 1997).

The Tyranny of Techniques

Much debate about participatory approaches concerns the appropriate techniques for uncovering the "realities" of poor people and ensuring their involvement in decision making. Any cursory review of the literature on participation in development reveals a huge volume of work on techniques (PLA, PRA, etc.). As the solution to locally based development they have the advantage of being tangible, being practically achievable and fitting wel1 with project approaches. This techniques-based participatory orthodoxy is increasingly being subjected to critical analysis (Masse 1995; Goebbel 1998). Biggs (1995) suggests that such an approach to participation fails adequately to address issues of power and control of information and other resources and provides an inadequate framework for developing a critical reflective understanding of the deeper determinants of technical and social change. It is not my intention here to deal substantially with this debate except to point out that reviewing and improving participatory techniques cannot substitute for a more fundamental examination of the very concepts that inform such approaches, issues to which I now turn.

The Place of Structure and Agency

Some of the artificial dichotomies and critical paradoxes in current thinking about participation and development can be accommodated by analysing the recursive relationship between structure and agency. Considerable attempts have been made to understand the complexities, diversity and regularities of

1927
1960
1963
1964
1967
1969
1970
1971
1972
1973
1974
1975
1976
1977
1978
1979
1980
1981
1982
1983
1984
1985
1986
1987
1988
1989
1990
1991
1992
1993
1994
1995
1996
1997
1998
1999
2000
2001
2002
2003
2004
2005
2006

patterns of interaction between individuals and social structure; examples from social theory include Giddens (1984), Douglas (1987), and Granovetter (1992) and in development studies include Long and Long (1992) and Goetz (1996), among others. However, such critical reconceptualisations and analyses have little impact on the development mainstream as articulated through policy and practice. Concepts of individual action underlying participatory approaches swing widely between "rational choice" and "social being" models. The former attributes individual behaviour to calculative self-interest, the latter to culture and social norms. Social structure is variously perceived as opportunity and constraint but little analysed; the linkages between the individual and the structures and institutions of the social world the individual inhabits are ill modelled. A convenient and tangible alternative is found in the ubiquitous focus on the *organisations* of collective action; *organising the organisations* then becomes a central plank of participatory approaches to development.

It is in an attempt to highlight some of these issues and to illustrate the value of an analysis that considers the role both of social structure and of individual agency in shaping participation that the following discussion will be structured.

Institutionalism

Discourses of participation are strongly influenced by the new institutionalism, theories that suggest that institutions help to formalise mutual expectations of cooperative behaviour, allow the exercise of sanctions for noncooperation and thereby reduce the costs of individual transactions. Social institutions are perceived as clever solutions to the problems of trust and malfeasance in economic life as they can make cheating and free-riding too costly an activity to engage in (Granovetter 1992). Institutions (mostly commonly conceptualised as *organisations)* are highly attractive to theorists, development policymakers and practitioners as they help to render legible "community" and codify the translation of individual into collective

endeavour in a form that is visible, analysable and amenable to intervention and influence (Scott 1998).

In participatory approaches, institutions are seen as particularly important. Associations, committees and contracts channel participation in predictable and recognisable ways, the aim of many development interventions apparently being to establish the community structures that most clearly mirror bureaucratic structures. (A paradox, surely, when part of the justification for participatory approaches is that they avoid the shortcomings of development delivered by state bureaucracies?)

Ideas about social capital and civil society are also strongly institutionalist, although often vague. Visible, often formal, manifestations of association are attributed normative value, denoting initiative, responsibility, good citizenship and democratic engagement, as well as allegedly facilitating vibrant economic activity (IILS/UNDP 1997; Putnam 1993).

Institutional inclusion, then, has become an integral strand of participatory approaches, a process that is assumed to ensure the more efficient delivery of development, the inculcation of desirable characteristics among participants (responsibility, ownership, cooperation, collective endeavour) and therefore empowerment. Exclusion from local institutions is considered undesirable, marginalising, inefficient. Such institutional models of participation may be criticised on a number of grounds.

Formalisation and Functionalism

There is a tendency in the development literature to recognise the importance of social and "informal" institutions but nevertheless to concentrate on the analysis of "formal" institutions (Uphoff 1992a, 1992b)[1].

---

1 The terms "formal" (modern, bureaucratic, organisational) and "informal" (social, traditional) institutions are convenient but misleading. Traditional and social institutions may indeed be highly formalised, although not necessarily in the bureaucratic forms that we recognise. Much literature also exists in organisational studies about the informal dimensions of organisations. An alternative terminology might characterise institutions as "organisational" and/or "socially embedded," more nearly representing our actual usage of the terms. Obviously the two terms are not mutually exclusive; the dichotomy is a false one.

Here there is a concentration on contracts, committees and property rights as mechanisms for reducing transaction costs and institutionalising cooperative interactions (Brett 1996; Folbre 1996). Formalised institutional arrangements are considered more likely to be robust and enduring than informal ones, and desirable characteristics include a clearly specified user group and boundaries, a system of clear rules and sanctions against offenders, and public conflict-resolution mechanisms (Ostrom 1990). Such a formalisation of collective action, it is suggested, will clarify and make transparent local arrangements. Formalisation is strongly linked to evolutionism in these models. A general progression from traditional (implicitly "weak") forms of management to modern (by implication "strong") forms is considered desirable and is the focus of much "institution building" in development (INTRAC 1998). Very influential here is Elinor Ostrom's concept of the possibility of "crafting" institutions to render them more fit for the job in hand. Such crafting generally is seen to involve formalisation in the interests of functional ends (Ostrom 1990).

These models have been criticised for an over-simplistic evolutionism (Nelson 1995) and for a blindness to historical and social context. Evidence suggests more complex and fluid processes of institutional evolution, their ebb and flow according to circumstances (season, political intervention, need), and the ad hoc use of different institutional arrangements as appropriate, not necessarily conforming to project activities. An organisational model of participation ignores the fact that many interactions between people also take place outside formal organisations, that the interactions of daily life may be more important in shaping cooperation than public negotiations. This I have illustrated regarding the

LOCAL ARRANGEMENTS, "PROJECT" PERCEPTIONS: SHALLOW WELL, NYANGUGE VILLAGE, MAGU DISTRICT, TANZANIA

This well had been dug in 1989 and served the subvillage of 120 households. When we arrived, there were a number of young boys collecting water in containers they tied to the back of bicycles.

This well contains salty water and so is only used in the mornings to collect water for domestic purposes other than drinking and cooking. Another well nearby in the same subvillage is opened in the afternoons for people to collect sweet water (it was locked when we visited). There are six caretakers for the two pumps (three men and three women), and they monitor the pumps by rota for two days at a time each.

After some years of intermittent breakages and disrepair, community members decided, through their subvillages, ratified at the village council, to establish a maintenance fund. In this subvillage, households were required to pay TS500 per year and an additional TS200 every two months. The figures were decided upon at the village council after calculating the maximum amount it would cost to replace all 12 pumps in the village if they broke down. There are 720 households in the village, so revenue collection is potentially high.

This money is collected by the caretakers, and households are given receipts. One caretaker interviewed said that he collected the money by visiting the households on a twice-a-week timetable and talking to the male head of household. Of course, the woman might have to influence her husband to pay up. If people refuse to pay, then they are banned from taking water, and the caretakers regulate this. The numbers of nonpayers is small, but the community also decided to exempt old women from payment because they have few means.

Promotion staff from the HESAWA programme said that they were planning to return to this village in Phase 4 to mobilise them to set up the required Water User Groups to ensure sustainability. Without such Water User Groups, sustainable local maintenance could not be ensured, and project objectives would not be achieved.

Source: Cleaver and Kaare 1998

1927
1960
1963
1964
1967
1969
1970
1971
1972
1973
1974
1975
1976
1977
1978
1979
1980
1981
1982
1983
1984
1985
1986
1987
1988
1989
1990
1991
1992
1993
1994
1995
1996
1997
1998
1999
2000
2001
2002
2003
2004
2005
2006

use and management of water resources in Zimbabwe (Cleaver 1995, 2000). I illustrate how, despite the focus of development agencies on the promotion of community involvement through waterpoint committees, the local institutions for the management of water and grazing land are deeply embedded in social relations. Management thus depends on the maintenance of a number of grey areas and ambiguity regarding rights of access, on compliance with rules, on a continuous process of negotiation between all users, on the strong principle of conflict avoidance and on a large amount of decision making taking place through the practical adaptation of customs and norms and through the stimulus of everyday interactions.

This is not, of course, to suggest that formal institutions are irrelevant. In one project in Tanzania local management indeed took place through participation in "formal" organisations, but not those specified by programme plans. This example illustrates how a narrow project focus on establishing new functional institutional mechanisms of participation (in this case Water User Groups) may obscure the actual activities being undertaken by community members through other well-established, familiar and locally adapted channels (see Box 3.1).

Organisations, Participation and Representation

Organisational approaches to institutions contain two strong and conflicting ideas about individual participation. The focus on committee-like institutions is associated with participation through democratic representation and a concentration on the election/selection of committee members. Paradoxically, there is also a strong assumption (particularly in PLA approaches) that meaningful participation in public meetings is evidenced by individual (verbal)

PARTICIPATORY DECISION MAKING AND REPRESENTATION

Two examples raise some relevant challenges to predominant concepts of participatory decision making and representation.

For example, in one of my study villages in Zimbabwe, committees (Waterpoint, Food for Work, Pre-School, Village Development) were established according to the requirements of governments and donor agencies. However, decision making and debate rarely took place within committees; when it did it was hotly disputed and the decisions rarely complied with. Decision making was considered valid only when all those (adults) potentially affected by it were present. This, of course, resulted in lengthy decision-making processes conducted at large meetings of the people. Discussions and ideas arising from these continued to be developed through people's daily interactions. Tellingly, records were kept at village level of such multipurpose "meetings of the people," but not of the meetings of functional committees.

Reviewing a large water and sanitation programme in Tanzania, we noted the concern of project officers that at large village meetings, there was a notable disparity between the number of men speaking and the number of women speaking, and that there was a need to implement measures to ensure the greater participation of women. However, women themselves explained their participation differently. Our female informants suggested that they deputed one or two women, known for their eloquence, to speak for them. These were not formal representatives and might be decided upon during the course of the meeting, according to need. But in this way women felt they could have their voice heard and their priorities put forward in meetings most effectively. At a recent meeting villagers had debated how to spend a surplus of funds. Men were mostly in favour of buying beer and having a celebration. Women, however, insisted that the money go towards a new water source. And so it did. The triumph of water over beer illustrated, according to our female informants, the efficacy of their model of participation in decision making.

Source: Cleaver and Kaare 1998

---

contributions. Such principles are not necessarily in concurrence with local norms and practices, and an insistence on them may both exaggerate and disguise people's actual involvement (see Box 3.2).

How far do the participatory fora that we promote through development accommodate such complexities? There is a danger that unless they are taken into account, the formal manifestations of community-based approaches to development become mere empty shells, with meaningful decision making, interaction and collective action taking place elsewhere.

Socially embedded institutions are not necessarily "better" than organisational ones, as they may uphold and reproduce locally specific configurations of inequity and exclusion. However, the mere setting up of formal organisations and the specification of their membership does not necessarily overcome exclusion, subordination or vulnerability. It does not do so because the wider structural factors that shape such conditions and relations are often left untouched. Codifying the rights of the vulnerable must surely involve far more wide-reaching measures than the requirement that they sit on committees or individually speak at meetings.

Myths of Community

Ideas about local institutions are often based on problematic notions of community. The "community" in participatory approaches to development is often seen as a "natural" social entity characterised by solidaristic relations. It is assumed that these can be represented and channelled in simple organisational forms. Such assumptions are unsatisfactory for a number of reasons.

There is strong assumption in development that there is one identifiable community in any location and that there is a coterminosity between natural (resource), social and administrative boundaries. Development committees are therefore established as representative of "the community." The assumed self-evidence of "community" persists in our participatory approaches despite considerable evidence

MULTIPLE COMMUNITIES, PERMEABLE BOUNDARIES

In researching Zimbabwe it became clear to me that the idea of an administratively defined community little reflected the wealth and complexity of local networks of resource use, decision making and interaction. Thus, while water resources were managed at waterpoint and at village level, decisions about grazing land involved a wider group of people from parts of three villages. Cultural ceremonies such as rainmaking (surely an occasion for the reinforcing of community) also involved a wider and more diverse constituency than that of the village. Analysing the social networks within which my active and dynamic hostess was involved, I was hard pressed to identify a single or even dominant "community;" her life was lived through overlapping interactions between extended family (rural and urban), the physical locality, the wider cultural and resource-using locality, development-defined groups (for sewing, saving, vegetable growing), the church (a strong local and international "community") and the school where she taught, with its own networks of teachers, pupils and families. Moreover, a historical review of her family fortunes during this century revealed the constantly shifting and changing nature of such networks as people were settled and (forcibly) resettled, as government introduced new administrative structures or reformed old ones, as shifting and growing populations created different patterns of natural resource use and as marriage and migration of family members changed the extended family network.

Source: Cleaver 1996

of the overlapping, shifting and subjective nature of "communities" and the permeability of boundaries (IASCP 1998). A concentration on boundaries highlights the need in development for clear administrative arrangements, more to do with the delivery of goods and facilities than a reflection of any social arrangement (see Box 3.3).

1927
1960
1963
1964
1967
1969
1970
1971
1972
1973
1974
1975
1976
1977
1978
1979
1980
1981
1982
1983
1984
1985
1986
1987
1988
1989
1990
1991
1992
1993
1994
1995
1996
1997
1998
1999
2000
2001
2002
2003
2004
2005
2006

Participatory approaches stress solidarity within communities; processes of conflict and negotiation, inclusion and exclusion are occasionally acknowledged but little investigated. The "solidarity" models of community, upon which much development intervention is based, may acknowledge social stratification but nevertheless assume some underlying commonality of interest (Li 1996). For example, fieldworkers on a community-based water and sanitation programme in Tanzania were reluctant to publicly refer to, or even admit, socio-economic differences within the communities with which they worked. They had dropped wealth ranking from their PRA exercises, fearing that this highlighted difference, and saw the public acknowledgement of difference as incompatible with the cooperation necessary for the smooth functioning of the project (Cleaver and Kaare 1998).

More realistically, we may see the community as the site of both solidarity and conflict, shifting alliances, power and social structures. Much recent work on common property resource management recognises the role of communities in managing internal conflicts (IASCP 1998), and various authors have illustrated the shifting, historically and socially located nature of community institutions, and the power dimensions of public manifestations of collective action (Mosse 1997; Peters 1987; Goebel 1998).

Development practitioners excel at perpetuating the myth that communities are capable of anything, that all that is required is sufficient mobilisation (through institutions) and the latent capacities of the community will be unleashed in the interests of development. The evidence does little to support such claims. Even where a community appears well motivated, dynamic and well organised, severe limitations are presented by an inadequacy of material resources and by the very real structural constraints that impede the functioning of community-based institutions (see Box 3.4).

Culture and Foundationalism

Contradictory ideas about the nature of "culture" feature prominently in development discourses about community and participation. Culture is variously perceived as a constraint (for example, restricting the participation of women in development activities), the "glue" that keeps the community together (the supposed "cultural" inheritance of solidarity and cooperation from some past golden age) and a resource to be tapped in development (in terms of using the "authority" of "traditional" leaders to legitimise development interventions).

Positive views of local culture (culture as community glue, a form of social capital) tend towards a profound foundationalism about local communities and their inhabitants (Sayer and Storper 1997). There are elements of this in the writings of Robert Chambers, where a moral value is attributed to the knowledge, attitudes and practices of "the poor," the task of development being to release their potential to live these out. How, then, do we deal with situations where "local culture" is oppressive to certain people, where appeals to "tradition" run contrary to the modernising impulses of development projects? Why do we see so little debate about these tensions in the development literature? Is it for fear of criticising local practices and being seen as the professionals so roundly condemned in Chambers' work? Are we not in danger of swinging from one untenable position (we know best) to an equally untenable and damaging one (they know best)?

Model of Individuals

Participatory approaches can further be criticised for their inadequate model of individual action and the links between this and social structure. Despite the strong assumption of the links between individual participation and responsibility, there is little recognition of the varying livelihoods, motivations and impacts of development on individuals over time. Indeed, project approaches that focus strongly on institutions as a development tool often see people as "inputs," as the "human resource" (see, for example, Khan and Begum 1997). Social difference is recognised through the categorisation of people into general occupational or social roles: "women," "farmers," "leaders" and "the poor."

Paradoxically, models of individual motivation and action in participatory approaches swing between the under- and oversocialised (Granovetter 1992). The concept of the "rational economic man" is so deeply embedded in development thinking that its influence is strongly felt even where development efforts are concerned with activities that are not directly productive—with community, social action, citizenship. However, there is often a simultaneous and rather vague assumption of the "social being" whose better nature can be drawn upon in the interests of community and development. In both abstractions, the complex positions of real individuals and real groups are lost.

Incentives, Rationality and Participation

While the participatory literature is often rather vague on the incentives that will persuade people to participate, it is infected by the pervasive functionalism and economism of development thinking. It is assumed that people will find it in their rational interests to participate, due to the assurance of benefits to ensue (particularly in relation to "productive" projects) or, to a much lesser extent, because they perceive this as socially responsible and in the interests of community development as a whole (particularly in relation to public goods projects). Interestingly, many policy approaches make significant efforts to link participation with social responsibility, to characterise nonparticipation as irresponsible and, at the same time, to define benefits that may in fact be long-term, cumulative and community-wide rather than of immediate advantage to the individual. Such positions are well illustrated in the literature on women's participation in water projects, on the advantages of time savings to be obtained through improved supplies and the supposed economic benefits to individual women of paying for water (Cleaver and Lomas 1996 for a critique).

In explaining motivations to participate, social norms are seen to occupy a secondary place to economic rationality; social relations and participation are seen ultimately to serve the ends of economic development. Such perceptions allow little place for personal psychological motivations, for the needs of individuals for recognition, respect or purpose, which may be independent of other material benefits. Accounts of the involvement of young men in community activities in Zimbabwe and St. Vincent illustrate this point (Cleaver 1998b; Jobes 1998). Nor are the complexities of long-term and diffuse relationships of reciprocity occurring over lifetimes adequately recognised as shaping participation (Adams, et al. 1997; Cleaver 2000).

THE LIMITS OF PARTICIPATION

The people of Sando village in Nkayi District, Zimbabwe, had built their own school, established a variety of income-generating clubs, and had high levels of associational activity. They were in every sense a creative community, admired by district officials and neighbours for their self-reliance and resilience. And yet they were unable to ensure the functioning of their borehole or to secure adequate alternative water supplies, a problem partially explained by their location (deep in the forest, remote from the district offices, in an area where the water table is over 100 m below ground), their lack of political influence (a small population), their low incomes and the restrictions on government's ability to finance new facilities. While they had established a fund for the purchase of a windmill pump, set up a system of collection of money from households and defined those exempt from payment (newlyweds), they were unable to raise a sufficient sum to secure their new pump. Several years after initiating the Windmill Fund they still lacked adequate water supplies and were forced to travel 10 km to use a borehole in another village.

Source: Cleaver 1996

1927
1960
1963
1964
1967
1969
1970
1971
1972
1973
1974
1975
1976
1977
1978
1979
1980
1981
1982
1983
1984
1985
1986
1987
1988
1989
1990
1991
1992
1993
1994
1995
1996
1997
1998
1999
2000
2001
2002
2003
2004
2005
2006

The fragility of a conceptual model that directly relates individual motivation and participation to receipt of benefits can be illustrated with the following example. It is commonly asserted that women should participate more fully in the upgrading and management of water supplies as they are the primary carriers and users of domestic water. It is claimed that because of this role they have great incentives to participate and that the outcomes of such participation (greater sense of ownership and responsibility leading to improved supplies) will directly benefit them. However, analysis of actual water use and decision making leads us to question such assumptions. Women in a position to do so (older, richer, senior women) commonly delegate water fetching to other women and men (relatives, poor neighbours, hired workers) and, significantly, to children. The water user, decision maker, manager and beneficiary are not always, then, manifest in one individual. Do children and young people participate in public decision making about water supply improvement or management? Do those to whom water work is delegated have strong interests in reducing water-fetching times and improving supplies? Perhaps they supplement their livelihoods through water work; perhaps it is part of a complex web of reciprocal exchange upon which they depend. Are old women not to be included in participatory decision-making processes regarding water supply improvements because they no longer fetch the water directly themselves?

Located Identities, Differential Costs and Benefits

Functional project approaches to participation little recognise that in examining motivation it is helpful to see a person positioned in multiple ways, with social relations conferred by *specific* social identities (Giddens 1984), and that, in Long's words, individuals are always only partly enrolled in the projects of others (Long 1992).

According to Giddens (1984), the actions of human agents should be seen as a process rather than as an aggregate of separate intentions, reasons, motives and acts, and much of our day-to-day contact is not directly motivated. In querying the modelling of action as individual acts, Giddens draws attention to the difference between much routinised day-to-day activity, which forms part of "practical consciousness," and that about which actors may be discursively conscious and can analyse and reflect upon. Crucial to such alternative interpretations is the role of agency in processing experience and shaping action, and the role of structure in both enabling and constraining such choices.

The individual in participatory approaches is usually defined in terms of the functional nature of the project. Little recognition is made of the changing social position of individuals over life courses, of the variable costs and benefits of differently placed people, of contending and complementary concerns with production and reproduction. Age, gender, class and individual agency may all shape people's willingness and ability to participate. For example, while poor young women with small children commonly find it difficult to participate publicly in development projects due to their burden of productive and reproductive activities, some individuals find ways of doing so, while others meet their needs in differing ways, as Box 3.5 illustrates.

Contrary to the ubiquitous optimistic assertions about the benefits of public participation, there are numerous documented examples of situations where individuals find it easier, *more* beneficial or habitually familiar not to participate (Adams, et al. 1997; Zwarteveen and Neupane 1996). Nonparticipation and noncompliance may be both a "rational" strategy *and* an unconscious practice embedded in routine, social norms and the acceptance of the status quo. A fascinating study by Zwarteveen and Neupane of irrigation management in Nepal shows how some women, constrained by prevailing ideas about proper gender roles, saw it more beneficial *not to participate* in the irrigation association. Instead, they secured their water partly through the participation of male members of their own household, through other kin and neighbour networks and partly through stealing and cheating. Their absence from the formal user association made it far easier for them to do this without detection or censure.

There have recently been several calls to recognise both the costs and benefits of participation for individuals (Mayoux 1995), and yet these are little pursued, the conventional wisdom being that participation is "a good thing." If we accept that costs and benefits fall differentially and are mediated and perceived by people in differing ways, where does this leave us, for example, in terms of policies that target the participation in development of "the poor"? Also, how do we link the evaluation of such costs and benefits with a model of choice and voluntarism? It seems that where poor people are concerned, their choices may be seriously limited, the scope for variation of action narrow. They may lack the resources for effective participation and

yet remain vulnerable in their livelihood strategies based on kin and existing social structures. Participation in water supply projects, where water is scarce and it is difficult to procure enough for basic needs, is less a matter of choice (or an expression of agency), more a matter of necessity imposed by constraint.

Interpreting Inclusion and Exclusion

The recursive relationship between structure and agency is illustrated by the variability of individual participation. A recognition that the public participation of individuals may be negotiated and mediated within households and communities and shaped by prevailing social norms and structures raises critical questions about the scope of personal agency and the power of structural constraint. In the example of women irrigators in Nepal outlined above, some women chose not to participate in the irrigation association partly because they saw that in so doing they would be bound

DIFFERING STRATEGIES OF PARTICIPATION AND COMPLIANCE

Two women in similar circumstances in the same village displayed very different practices in securing their livelihood needs. They both had husbands resident but not working, small children, poor land and no livestock:

Mrs. CN participated in no community meetings, relying on her husband's very occasional attendance. She contributed to no development projects. She relied instead on kinship relations, waiting to borrow cattle for ploughing from wealthier relatives, asking for assistance from the extended family for school fees and even food during the drought months.

Mrs. Z, on the other hand, facing similar problems, had become the representative of a local NGO (ORAP), the major advantage of this being that it built on traditional concepts of communal labour and assistance but organised them in new ways. Traditionally, if a person calls communal labour to work their fields, the host must provide beer and food, a condition few poor people can meet. Under the ORAP arrangements, any member of the devel-

opment group can call on others for assistance, but without the requirement of providing refreshment.

Another example suggests that "cheating" may be a viable strategy:

In Eguqeni village I observed Mrs. PN persistently breaking community rules by using the communal water pump at closed times, apparently without incurring punishment, or even disapproval. When questioned, villagers suggested that this was acceptable in her case as she had a large number of young children and lived far from the pump. In view of her labour constraints and spatial distance, it would be difficult for her to collect sufficient water for her basic needs at the specified opening times, as, by the time she had carried one bucket home and returned for another, the pump would be closed again. Her reputation for hard work and her (distant) relationship through marriage to the pump chairman undoubtedly contributed to her ability to break the community rules without punishment.

Source: Cleaver 1996

1927
1960
1963
1964
1967
1969
1970
1971
1972
1973
1974
1975
1976
1977
1978
1979
1980
1981
1982
1983
1984
1985
1986
1987
1988
1989
1990
1991
1992
1993
1994
1995
1996
1997
1998
1999
2000
2001
2002
2003
2004
2005
2006

by rules that did not favour them. However, in drawing on ideas about the "proper" role of women to justify their nonparticipation, were they exercising agency or simply acquiescing to their structural gendered subordination, or both? Doubts among individuals about the merits of being included in development projects from the point of view of preserving individual freedom are common, suggesting a sophisticated analysis among people of the structural instruments of their subordination and a blindness among development agencies to this (Long 1992; Scott 1985).

The participatory literature in development maintains oversimplified ideas about the beneficial nature to individuals of participation, overlooking the potential links between inclusion and possible subordination. We would do well to examine issues of empowerment and subordination more critically, recognising that they are not necessarily diametrically opposed conditions (Jackson 1998) and seeking lessons from literature on participation and inclusion outside the development field (Willis 1977; Allen 1997; Croft and Beresford 1996). It is important to remember that "community" may be used as a definition of exclusion as well as inclusion, that associating concepts of responsibility, ownership and social cohesion with local entities (which may draw on religious, ethnic and locational differences in definition) is not necessarily compatible with the universalising of equality or with the rights of particular individuals. Exclusionary tendencies may be increased in locally based participatory development, as an example of changing ideas about access to water shows (see Box 3.6).

Conclusion: Reassessing Participatory Approaches

"Participation" in development activities has been translated into a managerial exercise based on "toolboxes" of procedures and techniques. It has been turned away from its radical roots: We now talk of problem solving through participation rather than problematisation, critical engagement and class

(Brown n.d.). This limited approach to participation gives rise to a number of critical tensions or paradoxes. While we emphasise the desirability of empowerment, project approaches remain largely concerned with efficiency. While we recognise the importance of institutions, we focus attention only on the highly visible, formal, local organisations, overlooking the numerous communal activities that occur through daily interactions and socially embedded arrangements. A strong emphasis on the participation of individuals and their potential empowerment is not supported by convincing analyses of individual positions, of the variability of the costs and benefits of participation, of the opportunities and constraints experienced by potential participants. The time is ripe for a critical reanalysis of "participatory approaches."

Many claims about participation, most of which assert that it is a good thing, remain unproven. We need, then, a detailed collection of empirical evidence of the effects of participation, which, despite nearly two decades of the implementation of participatory approaches, is surprisingly lacking. The well-developed tools of Participatory Rapid Appraisal /Participtory Learning in Action (PRA/PLA), which currently assume the desirability of participation and are commonly used as formulaic engagement activities in development projects, could effectively be adapted to investigate relations of power, to uncover the variability in people's perceptions of the costs and benefits of participation, and the complexity of individuals' motivations.

Further empirical evidence and analysis is needed regarding whether and *how* the structures of participatory projects include/protect/secure the interests of poor people. What *exactly* are the linkages between the participation of poor individuals and the furthering of their social and economic good? Understanding this requires analyses of "competent" communities and "successful" participatory projects that focus on process, on power dynamics, on patterns of inclusion and exclusion. These could be built up through a process documentation of the dynamics of conflict, consensus building and decision making within communities, not just the recording of project-related activities.

Understanding how participation can benefit the poor might also involve identifying the role of better, more responsive, development agencies in promoting more effective and equitable forms of involvement (Jarman and Johnson 1997; Thompson 1995) or in offering state action to substitute for or reinforce community participation where the costs of this are very high to the participants. Several studies now link meaningful societal change to state action prompted by popular political and social movements (for example, see Deere and Leon 1998), and we would do well to expand our focus away from the institutional nuts and bolts of development projects to consider the wider dynamics of economic and social change.

I have suggested that we can further our understanding of participatory processes through an approach that takes into account the relationship between social structure and individual agency. In particular, we can use this to improve our understanding of the institutions of participation and the individuals involved.

A more dynamic vision is needed of "institutions" and of "community," one that incorporates social networks and recognises dispersed and contingent power relations, the exclusionary as well as the inclusionary nature of participation. We need a much better understanding of local norms of decision making and representation, of how these change and are negotiated, of how people may indirectly affect outcomes without direct participation.

It is also necessary to develop a more complex modelling of livelihood concerns over life courses and of the negotiated nature of participation and a more honest assessment of the costs and benefits to individuals of becoming involved in agency- and state-directed development processes. In order to do this, we need to be able to analyse the resources that people need in order to be able to participate in development

INCLUSION AND EXCLUSION, PARTICIPATION AND RIGHTS OF ACCESS TO WATER

1996

In Nkayi District, in Western Zimbabwe, there were generally accepted principles by which access to water is managed.

A hierarchy of "rightful" users is apparent at waterpoints; ranging from those immediately local residents with undisputed rights of use to more distant residents whose usage is considered conditional. "Conditional" users negotiate access to waterpoints (often through kinship and appeals to custom) but remain vulnerable to exclusion. However, the deeply held idea that universal access to water is a right generally ensures that "conditional" users can meet their water needs.

Access rights are further complicated by participatory development initiatives that emphasise the concept of "ownership" of water sources, specifying that only those who have participated in implementation (through providing labour and materials) have earned the right to be considered owners. Participation in implementation in generally organised on the basis of residence close to the waterpoint. Such differentiation between users has little impact until the dry season or longer-term droughts, when the general, socially-embedded principle of allowing all to draw water contracts. In drought months the rights of "conditional" users contract severely; they have to wait until all others have collected water, and often there is not sufficient available for them. Increasingly they are seen as not "the rightful owners" of a particular water source. Often such people are poor, their residences spatially marginal and their ability to participate in community decision making limited by their poverty. Participatory development efforts may thus reinforce the marginalisation of poor and peripheral households.

Source: Cleaver 1996

1927
1960
1963
1964
1967
1969
1970
1971
1972
1973
1974
1975
1976
1977
1978
1979
1980
1981
1982
1983
1984
1985
1986
1987
1988
1989
1990
1991
1992
1993
1994
1995
1996
1997
1998
1999
2000
2001
2002
2003
2004
2005
2006

efforts, and to find ways of assessing which participatory approaches are low cost and of high benefit to poor people.

In conclusion, I see the need for a radical reassessment of the desirability, practicality and efficacy of development efforts based on community participation. This involves rethinking not just the relationship between differently placed individuals and historically and spatially specific social structure, but also the role of individuals, households, communities, development agencies and the state.

References

Adams, W., E. Watson, and S. Mutiso. 1997. *Water Rules and Gender: Water rights in an indigenous irrigation system*, Marakwet, Kenya. *Development and Change* 28:707–730.

Allen, T. 1997. "Housing renewal—Doesn't It Make You Sick?" paper presented to HSA Conference. York University. 15–16 Apr.

Batliwala, S. 1994. "The Meaning of Women's Empowerment: New Concepts Form Action," in: G. Sen, A. Germain, and L. Chen, eds. *Population policies reconsidered: Health, empowerment and rights*. Cambridge, Mass.: Harvard Univ. Press.

Biggs, S. 1995a. *Participatory Technology Development: A Critique of the New Orthodoxy*. Olive Information Service, AVOCADO series 06/95, Durban.

Biggs, S. 1995b. "Participatory technology development: Reflections on current advocacy and past technology development," paper prepared for the workshop Participatory Technology Development (PTD). Institute of Education. London. March.

Brett, E.A. 1996. "The participatory principle in development projects: The costs and benefits of participation," *Public Administration and Development* 16:5–19.

Brown, D. n.d. "Strategies of social development: Non-government organisation and the limitations of the Frierean approach," *The New Bulmershe Papers*. Department of Agricultural Extension and Rural Development, Univ. of Reading.

Chambers, R. 1997. *Whose reality counts? Putting the first last*. London: IT Publications.

Cleaver, F. 1995. "Water As A Weapon: The History of Water Supply Development In Nkayi District, Zimbabwe," *Environment and history*. vol. I. Cambridge, U.K.: White Horse Press. 313–333.

Cleaver, F. 1996. "Community Management of Rural Water Supplies In Zimbabwe," unpublished Ph.D. thesis. Univ. of East Anglia, Norwich.

Cleaver, F. 1998a. "Gendered Incentives and Institutions: Women, Men and The Management of water," *Journal of Agriculture and Human Values* 15(4).

Cleaver, F. 1998b. "There's A Right Way to Do It: Informal Arrangements for Local Resource Management," *Waterlines* 16(4).

Cleaver, F. 2000. "Moral ecological rationality: Institutions and the management of common property resources," *Development and Change* 31(2).

Cleaver, F., and B. Kaare. 1998. *Social Embeddedness and Project Practice: A Gendered Analysis of Promotion and Participation in The Hesawa Programme, Tanzania*. Univ. of Bradford for SIDA. June.

Cleaver, F., and I. Lomas. 1996. "The 5% 'Rule': Fact Or Fiction?" *Development Policy Review* 14(2):173–184.

Croft, S., and P. Beresford. 1996. "The politics of participation," in: D. Taylor, ed. *Critical Social Policy: A reader*. London: Sage.

Deere, C. and M. Leon. 1998. "Gender, Land and Water: From Reform to Counter Reform in Latin America," *Journal of Agriculture and Human Values* 15(4).

Douglas, M. 1987. *How Institutions Think*. London: Routledge and Kegan Paul.

Fals-Borda, O. 1998. *People's participation:. Challenges ahead*. London: IT Publications.

Folbre, N. 1996. "Engendering Economics: New Perspectives on Women, Work and Demographic Change," in M. Bruno and B. Pleskovic (eds), *Annual World Bank Conference on Development Economics*, World Bank, Washington, DC.

Giddens, A. 1982. *Profiles and critiques in social theory*. Berkeley: Univ. of California Press.

Giddens, A. 1984. *The constitution of society: Outline of the theory of stucturation*. Cambridge, U.K.: Polity Press.

Goebel, A. 1998. "Process, perception and power: Notes from 'participatory' research in a Zimbabwean resettlement area," *Development and Change* 29: 277–305.

Goetz, A.-M. 1996. "Local heroes: Patterns of field worker discretion in implementing GAD policy in Bangladesh," *IDS Discussion Paper* no. 358. Univ. of Sussex.

Granovetter, D. 1992. "Economic action and social structure: The problem of embeddedness," in: M. Granovetter and R. Swedburg, eds. *The sociology of economic life*. Oxford, U.K.: Westview Press.

IASCP. 1998. *Crossing boundaries: Book of abstracts*. Seventh Conference of the International Association for the Study of Common Property. Simon Fraser Univ., Vancouver. 10–14 June.

IILS/UNDP. 1997. *Social Exclusion and Anti-Poverty Strategies: Project on The Patterns and Cases of Social Exclusion and the Design of Policies to Promote Integration. A Synthesis of Findings*. International Institute for Labour Studies/United Nations Development Programme. Geneva.

INTRAC. 1998. *ONTRAC: The Newsletter Of The International NGO Training And Research Centre* No. 10. August.

Jackson, C. 1998. "Social Exclusion and Gender: Does one size fit all?" *European Journal of Development Research* 2(1):125–146.

Jackson, C., and R. Pearson, eds. 1998. *Feminist Vision of Development: Gender analysis and policy*. London: Routledge.

Jarman, J., and C. Johnson. 1997. *WAMMA: Empowerment in Practice* (a Water Aid Report). London: Water Aid.

Jobes, K. 1998. "PME under the spotlight: A Challenging Approach in St Vincent," *Waterlines* 16(4):23–25.

Khan, N.A., and S.A. Begum. 1997. "Participation in Social Forestry Re-Examined: A Case Study From Bangladesh," *Development in Practice* 7(3):260–266.

Li, T.M. 1996. "Images of Community: Discourse and Strategy in Property Relations," *Development and Change* 27:501–527.

Long, N. 1992. "From Paradigm Lost To Paradigm Regained? The Case for an Actor Orientated Sociology of Development," in: N. Long and A. Long, eds. *Battlefields of knowledge*. 16–43.

Long, N., and A. Long, eds. 1992. *Battlefields of knowledge: The Interlocking of Theory and Practice in Social Research and Development*. London: Routledge.

Mayoux, L. 1995. "Beyond Naivety: Women, Gender Inequality and Participatory Development," *Development and Change* 26:235–258.

Moser, C., and P. Sollis. 1991. "Did the Project Fail? A Community Perspective on a Participatory Primary Health Care Project in Ecuador," *Development in Practice* 1(1):19–33.

Moser, C., and P. Sollis. 1995. "Social analysis in participatory rural development," *PLA Notes* 24:27–33.

Moser, C., and P. Sollis. 1997. "History, Ecology and Locality in Tank-Irrigated South India," *Development and Change* 28:505–30.

Nelson, N. 1995. "Recent Evolutionary Theorising About Economic Change," *Journal of Economic Literature* 33:48–90.

Nelson, N., and S. Wright, eds. 1995. *Power and Participatory Development: Theory and practice.* London: IT Publications.

Oakley, P., et al. 1991. *Projects with people: The Practice of Participation in Rural Development.* Geneva: ILO.

Ostrom, E. 1990. *Governing the commons: The evolution of institutions for collective action.* New York: Cambridge Univ. Press.

Peters, P. 1987. "Embedded systems and rooted models," in: B. McCay and J.A. Acheson. *The question of the commons.* Tucson: Univ. of Arizona Press.

Putnam, R.D. 1993. *Making democracy work: Civic traditions in modern Italy.* Princeton, N.J.: Princeton Univ. Press.

Sayer, A., and M. Storper. 1997. "Ethics unbound: For a normative turn in social theory," *Environment and Planning D: Society and Space* 15:1–17.

Scott, J.C. 1985. *Weapons of the weak: Everyday Forms of Peasant Resistance.* London: Yale Univ. Press.

Scott, J.C. 1998. Address to the Seventh Annual Conference of the International Association for the Study of Common Property. Vancouver. 10–14 June.

Stiefel, M., and M. Wolfe. 1994. *A Voice for the excluded: Popular participation in development.* London: Zed Books.

Thompson, J. 1995. "Participatory Approaches in Government Bureaucracies: Facilitating the Process of Institutional Change," *World Development* 23:1521–54.

Uphoff, N. 1992a. "Local Institutions and Participation for Sustainable Development," *Gatekeeper Series* 3. London: IIED.

Uphoff, N. 1992b. "Monitoring and evaluating popular participation in World Bank–assisted projects," in: B. Bhatnagar and A. Williams, eds. *Participatory Development and the Work Bank* (Discussion Papers Series No. 183). Washington, D.C.: World Bank.

Willis, P. 1977. *Learning to labour: How working class kids get working class job.* Farnborough, U.K.: Saxon House.

Zwarteveen, M., and N. Neupane. 1996. *Free Riders or Victims: Women's Non-participation in Irrigation Management in Nepal's Chhattis Mauja Irrigation Scheme* (Research Report No.7). Colombo: International Irrigation Management Institute.

1996

"ASCENDANCY OF PARTICIPATORY APPROACHES"
Excerpt from: Participatory Communication for Development
By Chin Saik Yoon

The reaction against modernization (and to some extent the realization of global structural imbalances) gave birth to various participatory approaches. They shared the common intent of actively involving people who were the "subjects" of development in shaping the process. But in most cases this is where similarity ends and a diversity of differences begin. People's participation became defined in many different ways and this in turn led to numerous unresolved disagreements.

Generally, four different ways of participation can be observed in most development projects claiming to be participatory in nature (Uphoff: 1985). They are:

Participation in implementation: People are actively encouraged and mobilized to take part in the actualization of projects. They are given certain responsibilities and set certain tasks, are required to contribute specified resources.

Participation in evaluation: Upon completion of a project, people are invited to critique the success or failure of it.

Participation in benefit: People take part in enjoying the fruits of a project; this may be water from a hand-pump, medical care by a "barefoot doctor," a truck to transport produce to market or village meetings in the new community hall.

Participation in decision-making: People initiate, discuss, conceptualize and plan activities they will all do as a community. Some of this may be related to more common development areas, such as building schools or applying for land tenure. Others may be more political, such as removing corrupt officials, supporting parliamentary candidates or resisting pressures from the elites. Yet others may be cultural or religious in nature—organizing a traditional feast, prayers for an end to the drought and a big party just to have a good time.

1927
1960
1963
1964
1967
1969
1970
1971
1972
1973
1974
1975
1976
1977
1978
1979
1980
1981
1982
1983
1984
1985
1986
1987
1988
1989
1990
1991
1992
1993
1994
1995
1996
1997
1998
1999
2000
2001
2002
2003
2004
2005
2006

Some development initiatives provide people with opportunities to all these four ways of participation. Many do not, and restrict participation to one or two ways.

Most will agree that participation in decision making is the most important form to promote. It gives people control of their lives and environment. At the same time, the people acquire problem solving skills and acquire full ownership of projects—two important elements which will contribute towards securing the sustained development of their community.

The other three forms of participation—participation in implementation, evaluation and benefit—have been criticised as being false participation by those who believe that participation in decision making is fundamental and indispensable to the approach. They feel that people are being manipulated through these three forms of pseudo participation to accept plans made by other more powerful people.

Others who disagree argue that the three ways allow people to build up capacity to participate in decision making. They also feel that prematurely mobilizing people to make their own decisions and chart their own development can put the people at risk of conflict with powerful interests and jeopardize their safety. They sometimes go on to say that groups who mobilize people in this way are actually manipulating them towards conflict.

A number of governments of Asian countries which have met with impressive successes at economic development have articulated their reasons for not being in a hurry to promote Western-style democracy and participation:

Asian societies favour collectivism, while Western societies cherish individualism. In developing countries, national interests should take precedence over those of individuals.

Diversity of views can confuse people. People must be educated and mature before they are able to make good decisions from a diversity of views, therefore communities in developing regions require education first before diversity.

Underlining these arguments is a high preference by these governments for a consensus approach towards development. The participatory approach is not favoured because it is considered to be a conflict-based model.

Although proponents of participation appreciate more good than bad in the approach, they recognize at the same time that there are limits to the approach. An international conference of practitioners and researchers working in participatory communication announced three caveats (White: 1994) at the end of their meeting:

1. Participatory communication processes are not a panacea for development. Such processes are not suitable for solving all problems in all contexts or time frames. The mother whose child is dying of diarrhoea does not want to "participate." Short-term solutions and intervention are also needed. Participatory processes unearth "root causes" of poverty and oppression and usually involve long-term goals.
2. The apparently opposing concepts of "participation" and "manipulation" can be viewed from many perspectives. The interventionist who attempts to "sell" solutions to a "target population" may be accused of being manipulative and may also be bringing along a whole set of alien cultural premises. However the participatory social communicator may also enter a village with a particular picture of reality and set of values, hoping the people will come to perceive their oppression the way he or she sees it. This may be equally manipulative.
3. The price people have to pay for taking part in participatory processes is often overlooked. It is often assumed that the villager has nothing better to do with his or her time. For every hour spent "participating" there is an opportunity cost; that is, the fact that the villager may be foregoing more productive activity if the participatory process does not lead to benefits, either in the long or short term. The social communicator should take this into consideration when entering a village or slum.

References

Uphoff, N. "Fitting Projects to People," in M. M. Cernea, ed., *Putting people First: Sociological Variables in Rural Development*. Oxford: Oxford University Press, 1985, 369-378.

White, S. A. "The Concept of Participation: Transforming Rhetoric to Reality," in S. A. White, et al., *Participatory Communication: Working for Change and Development*. New Delhi, India: Sage Publications, 1994, 18.

EXCERPT FROM:

RIGHT TO COMMUNITY COMMUNICATION, POPULAR PARTICIPATION AND CITIZENSHIP

Popular Participation in Communication as a Strategy for Enhancing the Exercise of Citizenship

By Cicilia M. Krohling Peruzzo

2005 It is community media that most empower direct citizen participation in the sphere of public communications in contemporary Brazil. They are easily within the reach of the people, compared to the mass media. First, because they work within the people's own environment they are familiar with the locale, and they are more approachable. This process is facilitated when communication occurs through organizations in which citizens participate directly, or whose actions directly affect them. Second, community media are a form of close-range communication; their source is the reality and events of the location itself. They are also aimed at people of the community, which allows for the construction of cultural identity. Indeed, familiarity is one of the defining features of such close-range media.

There are several ways of participating in the communications media. When you call a radio broadcaster to request a song or chat with the announcer, you are participating. When you give an interview to a newspaper, you are participating. If your image is "stolen" by a photographer or filmmaker and then shown in the media, you are participating in the content of the communications media. If you answer a phone call from an employee of some magazine to which you subscribe and respond to a survey, you are participating. If you have done something noteworthy or committed a crime that resulted in an item or article in the press, you are participating, and so forth. The types of participation mentioned above are common and

important in the traditional media. However, when we speak of community communication, other forms of participation are possible and desirable.

People participate in the popular communications media in Latin America at various levels, depending upon the strategies that have been laid out, which in turn are rooted in democratic principles that have been put into practice to a greater or lesser extent. From this perspective, people may participate in the following ways:

a. As receivers of content, helping to build an audience, which is often used as a parameter to determine whether the communications medium is "popular." This is passive participation that has an effect on content only indirectly.

b. Participation in the messages: the basic level of participation, in which the person gives an interview, requests music, etc., but does not have any say in decisions concerning editing and transmission.

c. Participation in the production and dissemination of messages, materials and programs: this type of participation includes preparing, editing and transmitting content.

d. Participation in planning: involvement in setting the communication medium's policies, developing media and program format plans, developing management objectives and principles, etc.

e. Participation in management: involvement in the process of administration and control of a community communications medium (Peruzzo 2004: 140-147).[1]

In sum, people's participation may range from a role as mere listeners or readers to involvement in processes of producing, planning and managing

---

1 The levels of participation mentioned here are based on concepts developed by Merino Utreras (1988), who systematized the principles of participation in communications approved at a meeting on self-management held in Belgrade in 1977, and at a seminar sponsored by the Latin American International Center for Advanced Communications Studies (CIESPAL) and the United Nations Educational, Scientific and Cultural Organization (UNESCO) in 1978, on participation in production, planning and management.

1927
1960
1963
1964
1967
1969
1970
1971
1972
1973
1974
1975
1976
1977
1978
1979
1980
1981
1982
1983
1984
1985
1986
1987
1988
1989
1990
1991
1992
1993
1994
1995
1996
1997
1998
1999
2000
2001
2002
2003
2004
2005
2006

communications. The more advanced levels of citizen involvement assume the permeation of principles such as representiveness and co-responsibility, since they involve an exercise of power in a democratic or shared way (Perruzo 2004: 59). They also assume that popular participation is carried out freely and autonomously, i.e., independently of pressure, manipulation and other forms of interference and control by leadership and institutions.[2]

Popular participation in more advanced experiences of community communication represents a significant advance in the democratization of communications. This is essential to popular organizations, because it may be the difference that helps expand the exercise of citizenship. Community communication has the potential to contribute to the development of citizenship not only through the "content"—be it critical, accusatory, demanding or informative—of a new society, but through the very "process" of communicating. There is a dynamic relationship between communication and education that warrants further scrutiny.

Some, though obviously not all,[3] community communications media have the potential to be at once part of a process of popular organization[4]—channels loaded with information and cultural content—and to make possible the practice of direct participation in the mechanisms of planning, producing messages/programs and managing the organization of community communications. They therefore contribute in two ways to the development of citizenship: they offer educational potential both as a process and through the content of the messages they transmit.

Through their "content," they may contribute to the socialization of a historical legacy of knowledge, facilitate an understanding of social relations and the mechanisms of the power structure (enabling a better understanding of political issues) and of the country's public affairs, elucidate the rights of individuals, and foster discussion of local problems. For example, there are radio programs produced by slum dwellers, which air educational programming for children and young people to teach them the dangers of drug consumption and trafficking. They may also facilitate the embracing of cultural identities and roots by giving expression to, for example, manifestations of popular wisdom and culture: the history of a people's ancestors, from legends to natural herbs used to cure diseases. They may also serve as a channel of expression for local artists, who have difficulty penetrating the major regional and national media. Or they may provide information on how to prevent disease, on consumer rights, on access to free public services (e.g., the birth registry or access to the public defender's office) and on many other issues of social interest (Peruzzo 2002: 5-6).

They are educational from a "process" standpoint because direct participation helps people to develop their abilities. Citizens who learn to write for a small newspaper; talk on the radio; perform a role in a popular video; create, produce and broadcast a radio or television program; discuss the objectives, editorial policies and management principles of the communications medium; select content, etc., undergo a process of informal education that leads to an understanding of the media and the context in which they operate. This situation helps demystify the media, which tend to be seen by ordinary citizens as something inaccessible, something that is the exclusive domain of specialists or of "educated people."

The communications media produced by organized sectors of subordinate classes, or closely linked to them, end up creating a favorable environment for the development of citizen education. The relationships between education and communication become

---

2 The various forms of participation and their relationships with power (passive participation, controlled participation and co-management and self-management) are discussed in the book *Comunicação nos movimentos populares* [Communications in Popular Movements] (Peruzzo 2004).

3 Since many participate in reproducing, on a local or community scale, the marketing structure and objectives of the major private media, or engage in political or religious proselytizing.

4 For example, engaging in collective interest movements such as a community movement, a group home-building project, a youth group, a service to care for needy children, etc.

1927
1960
1963
1964
1967
1969
1970
1971
1972
1973
1974
1975
1976
1977
1978
1979
1980
1981
1982
1983
1984
1985
1986
1987
1988
1989
1990
1991
1992
1993
1994
1995
1996
1997
1998
1999
2000
2001
2002
2003
2004
2005
2006

1996

PARTICIPATORY DEVELOPMENT COMMUNICATION
Excerpt from: *Participatory Development Communication: A West African Agenda*
By Guy Bessette

Recognizing the importance of development communication, the International Development Research Centre (IDRC) has started to develop a research programme in that field. This programme aims to support people's participation in their development by enabling groups and communities to diagnose the problems they face, make well-informed decisions, mobilise for action and assume responsibility for their own development. We choose to use the term "participatory development communication" to draw attention to this emphasis on two-way communication processes, and to distance ourselves from one-way communication approaches that involve disseminating messages, transmitting information or persuading people to change their behaviour.

The programme wants to give preference to horizontal approaches that involve encouraging dialogue centred on problem analysis and a search for solutions, as well as bottom-up approaches that aim to raise the awareness of decision makers. These approaches are based on a process of community communication. By allowing for participation in development, participatory development communication becomes a tool for emancipating people and communities.

CIME
In terms of its overall thrust, the programme takes an interactive and participatory approach and stresses the interrelationships that exist in practice among the main lines of action. We call this concept CIME: *Communication* at the grassroots level, the exchange of *Information*, two-way *Media* and nonformal *Education*.

GRASSROOTS COMMUNICATION
The programme focuses on communication at the grassroots level in particular. Experience over the past 50 years has clearly demonstrated that if communication is really to help involve people in identifying a development problem, understanding its causes, proposing solutions and organizing themselves to take appropriate action, it must start at the community level. It must also promote "horizontal" interchange among people rather than some kind of "vertical" transmission from an expert to his audience. It follows that we must not emphasize the use of the media (which play utilitarian role), but the processes and strategies for participatory grassroots communication (feedback processes in particular).

EXCHANGE OF INFORMATION
The programme also attempts to link information to the process of communication. Information is of no use by itself, without a community communication process that allows people to grasp it and make it their own. We must also make use of proper channels of communication that will encourage the circulation and sharing of information flowing from the information source to the community, or from the community to the various levels in the decision-making process, or among groups and communities themselves.

TWO-WAY MEDIA
Under this aspect, the programme tries to promote use of various media (including interpersonal relations and traditional means of communication as much as the modern media) within systems of interactive or two-way communication that can be appropriated by groups or communities, and that are based not on the transmission of information or hortatory messages, but on facilitating the exchange of ideas. In any given context, the use of these systems must be linked to a process of community communication that will define the parameters under which they are designed or introduced, the conditions for setting them up and the ways in which they can be evaluated.

Bessette, Guy, and C. V. Rajasunderam. "Participatory Development Communication: A West African Agenda," International Development Research Centre (IDRC) Ottawa, Canada; Southbound: Penang, Malaysia, 1996. Copyright © 1996, International Development Research Centre. Reprinted with permission of IDRC.

explicit, as people involved in these processes develop their knowledge and change their way of seeing and relating to society and to the system of mass communications media itself. They take ownership of the techniques and technological instruments of communication and they acquire a more critical view, both through the information they receive and through what they learn through hands-on experience and practice. For example, the selection of news items that must be done in order to produce a community radio news program, as well as the other factors that shape the process of producing and transmitting the messages that we encounter every day, opens people's eyes to the strategies and possibilities for manipulation of messages by the major mass communications media. They become aware of opportunities for selecting messages, of the conflicts of interest that affect information or programming, of the dynamics of the advertising market and of the clout (power to give public visibility and to influence) of a communications medium, such as radio, newspaper, television, the Internet, etc. (Peruzzo 2002: 6).

The scope of engagement in the local dynamic, the content of messages and participation in all phases of the communications process are interrelated and are seen as the ideal in terms of educational communication action among community movements. However, it is known that active participation by people in all the various phases of a community communications process is still limited [5]. Still, even experiences in which not all three components occur interrelatedly also have their value. Participation in content only, for example, even in isolation, offers a certain level of educational potential. A television or radio program, even if it is not produced with the active participation of the population (through its representatives) at whom the end product is aimed, but rather by a team of local residents, or even by the staff of a nongovernmental organization or a trade association, for example, has

the potential to foster critical thinking and enhance the knowledge of both the broadcasters and the audience (Peruzzo 2002: 6).

As is known, education entails, among other things, educating oneself. As Kaplún points out (1999: 74), educating oneself involves a process of multiple flows of communication. The richer the range of communications interactions the system is able to open up and make available to those being educated, the more educational it will be.

Social movements have the potential to modify values and bring about changes in opinions. They help break through the "culture of silence" of the masses, as Paulo Freire (1981) puts it, or the culture of submission of the absent citizen, of the voiceless citizen, engendering a new citizenship. As Jesús Martín-Barbero (1999) points out:

> to a great extent, those institutions, those spaces in which citizens are formed, are diluted, just when citizenship is exercised. In that moment, there are a multiplicity of movements, albeit somewhat tentative, striving to overcome, to a certain extent, their silence. There is thus a lack of submission, a rebellion against the power of the Church, the State, the school—against many powers. Feminist movements, ecological movements, homosexual, ethnic, racial and black movements are all examples of this. These are elements of a new form of social behavior, a new agenda of issues that are important to people. When these movements, most of which are small and disconnected, begin to connect with one another and then connect to schools and to municipal and community communications media, they will create networks for the formation of citizens that will be highly effective, ensuring that those scattered voices begin to be heard in the regional sphere and even in the national sphere (Martín-Barbero 1999: 78-9).

As has been noted, in advanced participatory processes the recipients of messages from the

---

5   Broad active participation by the population is something that is built slowly within the social dynamic itself, depending on the prevailing conditions and the level of commitment of people to their own citizenship; see Peruzzo (2004).

communications media also become producers and transmitters, as well as managers of the communications process. The citizen becomes the "subject" of the communications media and tends to change his way of seeing the world and of relating to it and to the media.

For direct involvement in producing and managing community communications to occur, there must be open and unobstructed channels of participation. Indeed, participation needs to be facilitated. It is pointless to criticize nonparticipation or to issue vague invitations to participate without ensuring that real possibilities for participation exist.

There is also a need to be clear as to the importance of putting in place mechanisms that facilitate representation of the population and its organizations at the various operational levels of a communications medium or community council. To this end, local organizations need to be recognized and given real opportunities to participate in decision making. The formation of a local communications council or of representative community associations has helped to reduce a certain trend toward authoritarianism that is typical of our culture and perpetuated by the leadership.

At its root, participation implies making political decisions and employing appropriate methodologies for action.[6] If a communications strategy is limited only to the practices of the major media and traditional community action organizations, it will be difficult to avoid reproducing patronizing styles and one-way programming and seeing the communications media merely "as an end in itself" (raising awareness, convincing, educating), rather than as a "means of facilitating" a process of citizen self-emancipation.

In an instrumental conception of the media—i.e., when seen as an end in itself—media are used to indoctrinate an audience that is considered ignorant. Sometimes they are presented as democratic, but ultimately they are vertical and one-sided.

The central issue is to make the human being the subject of the process of social change, which occurs as a result of communication, but also of other mechanisms of popular organization and action. In other words, the various processes emphasized here are not limited to the action of communications "media." The media may facilitate citizen action and they do play an important role, but the local social dynamic is broader and more complex. Thus, all areas of communications (public relations, advertising, journalism, publishing, etc.) and other fields of knowledge have the potential for concrete action within their respective fields of specialization. What is most important is the coming together of principles that favor popular self-determination, respect for the broader social interest, and the involvement of people as stakeholders in popular communications and organizations.

Peruzzo, Cicilia M. Krohling. *Direito à Comunicação Comunitária, Participação Popular e Cidadania*," ["Right to Community Communication, Popular Participation and Citizenship"] in Maria José da Costa Oliveira, ed., *Comunicação pública* [Public Communication]. Campinas, Brazil: Alínea, 2004, 49-79. Reprinted with permission of the author.

6   See Peruzzo (2004).

1927
1960
1963
1964
1967
1969
1970
1971
1972
1973
1974
1975
1976
1977
1978
1979
1980
1981
1982
1983
1984
1985
1986
1987
1988
1989
1990
1991
1992
1993
1994
1995
1996
1997
1998
1999
2000
2001
2002
2003
2004
2005
2006

PARTICIPATORY COMMUNICATION AS COMMUNICATIVE ACTION

By Thomas L. Jacobson and Satish Kolluri

1999 The idea of participatory communication is central to one current formulation of the role of communication in national development. The classical paradigm in this subfield focused largely on information transfer processes from Northern sources to Southern recipients (Lemer 1958; Rogers 1962; Schramm, 1964).

The idea of participatory communication focuses, instead, chiefly on communication among local community members engaged in development efforts. It has also been used to refer to communication between community members and outside experts, academics and field workers, but in such instances information transfer is de-emphasized and the process of dialogue among participants is instead emphasized. Although the general idea of participatory communication is used increasingly often, it is used in a number of different ways, and further theoretical development is needed.

The work of Freire (1970, 1973) has been prominent in its treatment of existential, political and pedagogical elements of participatory communication, and has been widely embraced in the Third World. However, Freire's writings have not led to a body of derivative theory or research in the North, at least not one with the widespread acceptance of diffusion theory during the modernization era.

Although it has seldom been applied in this context, Habermas' (1984, 1987) work is of considerable relevance to the concerns of participatory communication. In a way that indicates sensitivity to cultural values, Habermas' thinking relies heavily on philosophical hermeneutics. In a manner that parallels struggles for political freedom, his work is explicitly democratic. And he recognizes with dependency and neodependency theorists that corporate and public interests are not entirely parallel. More importantly, at the foundation of this thinking lies a theory of communication. The *theory of communicative action* has been put forward as the centerpiece of Habermas' later work. And, notably, this formulation of communicative action strongly reflects processes that may be seen as participatory.

In this article, we argue that the theory of communicative action can be used to conceptualize participatory communication for development. A number of elements of Habermas' work can be used to this end. His analysis of the public sphere (Habermas 1989) could provide the basis for an analysis of media institutions insofar as they facilitate democratic participation through public discourse. Habermas' treatment of colonization of the lifeworld could more generally guide research into areas of the subjective lifeworld, in which normative discourse has been marginalized by instrumental or theoretical discourse.

Here we focus on the theory of communicative action and discuss one element of this theory, the *ideal speech situation.* The ideal speech situation and the communicative action it typifies underlie Habermas' project as a whole, including his analysis of the public sphere and his analysis of lifeworld colonization. This article focuses on participatory communication in interaction between aid recipients and donors, or representatives of donors, in the development setting.

Generally speaking, these relations can be thought of as being between local communities and outside development agents. But our discussion might also allude to communication among community members and among development agents as well. For the sake of practical convenience, and due to space constraints, questions related to press institutions, and a variety of relevant cultural processes, are not discussed here.

Briefly, we argue that the ideal speech situation can be used as a framework within which participatory communication can be both theoretically defined and evaluated. The definition consists of assigning various elements of participatory communication processes to their conceptual counterparts in the theory of the ideal speech situation, and in particular to one or more "validity claims." The evaluation consists of using the validity claims as a basis on which to judge ways in which particular communicative transactions are, or are not, participatory.

The argument begins with a review of participatory communication in the context of national development. It continues with an introduction to central elements of the theory of communicative action, including the ideas of lifeworld colonization, universal pragmatics, the ideal speech situation and validity claims. Participatory communication, as defined in the context of national development, is then reformulated in terms of communicative action. In the conclusion we review a number of challenges that can be raised against such an analysis, and we remark on the relevance of Habermas' work to development communication theory.

Modernization and Participation

To begin, it may be helpful to briefly review communication in both the participatory and modernization frameworks. Proceeding chronologically, recall the historical era in which modernization theory was developed. This was, of course, the era of the United States' rise, in the aftermath of World War II, as a military superpower and a dominant force in global economics. It was an era of rapid evolution in communication technologies due to the widespread emergence of television and radio. And it was an era that saw the heyday of scientific social theory. Functionalist theories advanced universalistic accounts of macrosocial processes encompassing the growth of nations. In the field, scientists both hard and soft undertook to bring the benefits of theory testing to the Third World.

Accounts of communication's role in national development accorded with these historical preoccupations. The spread of mass media led to an emphasis on the effects of mass media on the Third World, as associated with Lerner's (1958) theory of psychic mobility. The transference of expert know-how from North to South resulted in the great interest accorded to diffusion theory (Rogers 1963).

Criticisms of modernization theory became numerous during the 1970s and 1980s (Hedebro 1981; Jayaweera & Amunugama 1987; Lerner & Schramm 1976; McAnany et al. 1981; Rogers 1976), among them some that included calls for a new kind of people's participation. Rogers (1983, 121) redefined development in a general way as participatory, in considering it "a widely participatory process of social change in society intended to bring about both social and material advancement for the majority of the people through gaining greater control over their environment." Cohen and Uphoff (1980, 219) indicated a number of elements in each development program that involve participation: "participation includes people's involvement in the decision-making process, in implementing programs . . . their sharing in benefits of development and their involvement in efforts to evaluate such programs." Tilakratna (1987, 51) noted that participation is not limited to abstract principles or mere task assignments, but includes deeper levels of behavior:

> Participatory Rural Development's vision of human development as a process of unfolding the creative potential of people embodies two inter-related central elements, namely self reliance and participation. The underlying promise is that these are fundamental human values that need to be promoted in order for people to develop as creative human beings, and that objectively generated processes possess an urge for liberation of these values.

Definitions of Participatory Communication

In terms of communication, the participatory approach has tended to highlight small rather than large media, horizontal rather than vertical communication, collective self-reliance rather than dependence on outside experts, and action- rather than theory-oriented inquiry. This approach has influenced numerous project designs and field studies (Berrigan 1979;

1927
1960
1963
1964
1967
1969
1970
1971
1972
1973
1974
1975
1976
1977
1978
1979
1980
1981
1982
1983
1984
1985
1986
1987
1988
1989
1990
1991
1992
1993
1994
1995
1996
1997
1998
1999
2000
2001
2002
2003
2004
2005
2006

O'Sullivan-Ryan & Kaplan 1982) and has led to a growing body of academic theory and research (Jacobson 1993; Melkote 1991; Narula & Pearce 1986; Servaes & Arnst 1993; White et al. 1995).

Specific definitions of participatory communication are highly varied. Diverse adjectives such as "popular," "participatory," "indigenous," "self-governing" and "emancipatory" are all used to characterize it. Fuglesang and Chandler (1986, 62) argued that "recognition of shared interests, accountability, and facilitating decision-making processes in a shared milieu of interests, constitute true communication and participation." Ascroft's (1987) definition of participatory communication emphasized "knowledge sharing and creating beneficiary comprehension of benefactor intentionalities."

According to Capriles (cited in Grinberg 1986, 10), communication democratization is the *"conditio sine qua non* of all possible democracies: the permanent dialogue, the spontaneous and relevant participation, never arbitrary or conditional, generating collective decisions and the socialization of production and its fruits" (176).

Nair and White (1993) defined, from a transactional perspective, *participatory development* as a two-way, dynamic interaction between grassroots receivers and an information source mediated by the development communicators. Participatory communication is defined as, "The opening of dialogue, source and receiver interacting continuously, thinking constructively about the situation, identifying developmental needs and problems, deciding what is needed to improve the situation, and acting upon it" (Nair & White 1993, 51)

These definitions have the virtue of broadly describing a new emphasis in development communication on two-way, dialogic processes. However, they overlap one another only to varying degrees… .

The Theory of Communicative Action

Habermas' general theoretical project involves an attempt to understand the historical development of human society within the framework of a critical theory. In addition to the theory of communicative action, this has produced a theory of social evolution, a theory of ethics, and other theoretical treatments of major social processes.

Habermas' system can be entered using any of these theories as a portal. For the purposes of this article, it is convenient to begin with analysis of the colonization of the lifeworld. This has the advantage of facilitating consideration of Habermas' relevance not only to participatory communication, but also to other issues of interest in the field of national development.

Analysis of the lifeworld is founded on a selective use of the works of Max Weber, Talcott Parsons, Karl Marx and other social theorists. Similar to the manner in which Marx analytically divided society into an economic base and an ideological superstructure, Habermas also identified two major societal spheres: "system" and "lifeworld." Habermas departed from Marx, following Weber, in arguing that neither of these spheres determines the other.

The system sphere generally refers to the activities of economics and administration. Each of these activities is treated as a further subsystem and is conceptualized, using Parsonian thought, as a functionally self-regulating action context. The lifeworld sphere refers to collectively shared background convictions, to the preconscious, assumed "horizons" within which actors communicate with one another. This includes the processes in which tradition, social integration and individual identity are produced and reproduced.

The system and lifeworld play distinguishable roles in constituting society, and hence they operate differently. System maintenance is achieved by orienting human action around media, such as money and power. The mode of reasoning appropriate for such action is instrumental, technical and achievement oriented—what is sometimes called means-ends reasoning. In contrast, the lifeworld is reproduced through a different mode of reasoning and comprises ongoing communicative processes of interpretation and dialogue.

...Although Habermas made extensive use of Weber and Parsons, drawing on them to conceptualize the differentiation of spheres in society, he departed from them in an attempt to account more adequately for social "pathologies," or contradictions, that result from the imperfect integration among social spheres. Habermas' diagnosis of modem society holds that an imbalance exists between the system and the life-world. It is an imbalance in which technical system rationality dominates the lifeworld. It is this that is referred to as "colonization of the lifeworld."

Briefly, the priorities and modes of reasoning appropriate for business and administration have marginalized and fragmented the processes proper to lifeworld maintenance. In the moral sphere, ethics are marginalized in numerous ways, in the name of capital accumulation, efficiency and so on. In the aesthetic sphere, artistic appreciation is invaded by commercial priorities, to the extent that artistic expression is influenced by what is commercially viable. In the end, there is a deformation of social integration processes, a deformation that Habermas analyzed in countries of the North but may also be applicable to countries of the South.

The analysis of lifeworld colonization can be taken as a critical analysis of the effects of the commodification and bureaucratization of daily life. In order to justify this analysis, however, some kind of standard is necessary in terms of which lifeworld colonization can be negatively evaluated. This is the chief role played by the theory of communicative action. Why is this standard communicative? One way to answer this is by reference to the question of rationality. Rational assessment of what the most desirable life might be, and how to get there, has evaded philosophers. And without a basis for such rational assessment, technical, business, and bureaucratic ways of life cannot be judged better or worse than any other ways of life.

In personal terms, Habermas alluded to the Socratic credo, avowing that what is desirable is "pursuit of the good life." However, given that a rational philosophical foundation in support of this position is not possible, Habermas took a procedural approach. He argued that knowledge by which we might evaluate "the good" as a product can not be rationally assessed; however, the means by which knowledge is produced can be considered rational. In other words, knowledge is not a product that can be evaluated for truth or falsity. But, in the structure of necessary conditions for any communication, there is a basis for giving reasons with regard to knowledge claims. The "universal pragmatics" of communication constitute a communicative form of rationality.

In developing this communicative approach to reason, Habermas outlined in some detail the nature of these universal pragmatics. He also distinguished various forms of expressive, verbal and nonverbal communication. And he distinguished communication that is oriented toward reaching understanding from other forms of communication. Chiefly, this has been done to outline a program of research and to focus his own analysis on verbal communication that is oriented toward reaching understanding.

Fundamental is the position that human communication has evolved a capability that presumes the intent to reach mutual understanding. Manipulative communication itself employs forms that violate the presumption of this intent. And the intent embodied in this system can be summed up by referring to an "ideal speech situation," consisting of the assumption during communication of four "validity claims" (Habermas 1979). These include:

1. Truth: the veracity of the propositional content in the speaker's utterance.
2. Rightness: the appropriateness of the statement made by the speaker in a context-specific situation in accordance with cultural norms.
3. Sincerity: the authenticity of the speaker's good intentions in communicating.
4. Comprehensibility: whether the expression used is understood.

All parties to a communicative transaction are said to make these validity claims implicitly. And it is through adjudicating disagreements over these claims that consensus is possible. If a hearer questions the validity of an implicit claim, he or she may ask for justification, and this can then lead to discussion through which the claim can be defended, or redeemed. If a hearer is not sure whether something is comprehended, he or she might ask, "I'm not sure whether I follow you. Could you please repeat that?" If the hearer is uncertain as to the truth of a statement he or she may ask, "Are you sure? How can that be?" If a hearer feels insulted at being addressed in a way that violates social norms, he or she might respond by asking the speaker to clarify the position from which he or she is speaking. And with regard to the communicative situation as a whole, the speaker is assumed to be speaking sincerely. Disingenuousness can be called into question by suggesting, "You don't really mean that."

In any of these cases, the question involves asking the speaker to redeem a validity claim that is normally assumed. As an instance of daily behavior this may take only a momentary pause. As a kind of communication, Habermas referred to it as the discursive justification of validity claims, which involves thematizing a validity claim and explicitly making it the subject of discussion.

This also comprises a definition of "discourse." Such discourse offers both speakers the opportunity to ground action in reason. Put otherwise, it involves arriving at a rational consensus through the force of the better argument. To be fully realized it must allow all participants in a discussion a "symmetrically distributed opportunity" to ask questions with the aim of determining, truth, rightfulness and sincerity.

It is this specific form of discourse that defines communicative action. It is this process that Habermas characterized as rational and that may lead to knowledge around which action can be legitimately oriented. "It [rationality] refers to various forms of argumentation as possibilities of continuing communicative action with reflective means" (Habermas 1984, 10).

Thus defined, the ideal speech situation can be approached in two ways. First, as an analysis of the preconditions of all communication. Second, as a set of criteria in terms of which manipulative and distorted communication can be evaluated. Habermas remarked:

> The ideal speech situation is neither an empirical phenomenon nor a mere construct, but rather an unavoidable supposition reciprocally made in discourse. This supposition can, but need not be counterfactual; but even if it is made counterfactually, it is a fiction that is operatively effective in the process of communication. Therefore I prefer to speak of an anticipation of an ideal speech situation... this anticipation alone is warrant which permits us to join to an actually attained consensus the claim of a rational consensus. At the same time it is a critical standard against which every actually realized consensus can be called into question and checked. (cited in Kemp 1988, 188)

A Reconstruction of Participatory Communication

The emergence of participation as a new approach to development communication has emphasized the importance of subjective experiences of people for whom development is supposedly meant. In this line of reflection, Habermas' formulations of the ideal speech situation and of communicative action draw a parallel to recent writing on participatory communication. Gonzalez (1989) argued that the ideal speech situation is suited to studying the social relations embodied in development communication situations. To take this general argument further, we review the definitions of participatory communication presented earlier and then interpret each specifically within the framework of validity claims.

Fuglesang and Chandler (1986, 62) suggested that "recognition of shared interests, accountability and facilitating decision-making processes in a shared milieu of interests, constitute true communication and participation." In terms of the validity claims, we can say that accountability, or the willingness to be called on to redeem validity claims, suggests sincerity, as does acting in good faith. "A milieu of shared interests" implies, indirectly, rightness or appropriateness in terms of validity claims. However, validity claims related to truth and comprehensibility are not addressed.

Ascroft's (1987, 10) definition of participatory communication emphasized "knowledge sharing and creating beneficiary comprehension of benefactor intentionalities." Theoretically, Ascroft's terms seem to suggest primarily the validity claim of comprehensibility. It seems indirectly to address sincerity, and even more indirectly, normative rightness, but overlooks entirely the matter of truth.

For Capriles, participatory communication is "communication democratization characterized by permanent dialogue and participation that is never arbitrary or conditional, and collective decision making" (cited in Grinberg 1986, 176). This definition reflected his intuitive understanding of the ideal speech situation, except that in the case of ideal speech there very much is a form of conditionality. This conditionality is the implicit need for justification of the validity claims, in both directions.

Returning to Nair and White (1993), their reconceptualization of participatory communication in the form of the "transactional perspective" requires, "the opening of dialogue, source and receiver interacting continuously, thinking constructively about the situation, identifying developmental needs and problems, deciding what is needed to improve the situation, and acting upon it" (51). The term "dialogue" and the accompanying emphasis on cooperation suggest the practical spirit of communicative action, but they do not provide a framework explaining specifically what constitutes dialogue, and how one might evaluate it as a communication process.

This exercise demonstrates that definitions of participatory communication overlap considerably with the communication process treated within the framework of ideal speech. Each of them represents one or more of the validity claims. Or, in other words, each of these definitions can be interpreted as specifying that for communication to be participatory, it is necessary that one or more of the validity claims be subject to challenge. At the same time, this exercise indicates that existing definitions underspecify the participatory situation. None of them explicitly identifies all four validity claims, even though most of the definitions seem to reflect the ideal speech situation in spirit.

This suggests that communicative action may serve as a conceptualization of participatory communication, for both theoretical and practical purposes. For theoretical purposes, the theory of communicative action is comprehensive. It is clear and systematic. And it is also articulated within a larger theoretical system.

Program Formulation and Evaluation

At a practical level, the ideal speech situation provides a standard against which to evaluate practical communicative situations. Forester (1988) argued for an "applied turn" based in the theory of communicative action and illustrated it in the field of urban planning. Application is performed by restating the validity claims as questions that are relevant to policy-oriented deliberations. A similar process could be used in community participation in national development settings.

Consider a hypothetical program evaluation involving interaction between outside experts or extension agents and either an individual or a group from a local population. The questions are:

1. Is the communicator's communication correct, that is, is the information being offered undistorted and reliable? (Truth)
2. Is the communicator's role legitimate, given his or her role and the participation of other interested individuals, social groups, agencies, and nations who are party to the process of development'? (Rightness)
3. Is the communication offered sincerely, in good faith without being manipulative, on the part of

1927
1960
1963
1964
1967
1969
1970
1971
1972
1973
1974
1975
1976
1977
1978
1979
1980
1981
1982
1983
1984
1985
1986
1987
1988
1989
1990
1991
1992
1993
1994
1995
1996
1997
1998
1999
2000
2001
2002
2003
2004
2005
2006

either the individual or any organization from which the individual may have been sent? (Sincerity)

4. Is the communicator's communication comprehensible to others, that is, are idiom, cultural factors, ands message design adequately accounted for? (Comprehensibility)

In the tradition of participatory research, a negative answer to any of these questions should result in an adjustment of interpersonal relationships somehow to reflect more fully local wishes or questions. In theoretical terms, the outsiders must at least place a high priority on sensitivity to local questions, inviting challenges to any of the validity claims. As a matter of procedure in the field, the outsiders might thematize, or raise, the validity claims themselves, one by one. Of course, there are occasions in which validity claims are violated, consciously or otherwise, by locals, and in these cases the outsiders may challenge a validity claim.

The use of validity claims as a basis for evaluative questions can be illustrated with an example project. Again, the aims and statements employed in the project can be interpreted within the communicative action framework. In an agriculturally and economically backward region of rural western India, a nongovernmental organization in conjunction with outside researchers conducted several participatory research workshops. These workshops concentrated on attempts to organize farmers in dealing with localized problems in their villages (Tandon & Brown 1981). Previous workshops had adopted the diffusionist approach in disseminating to the leaders of village farmer groups information pertinent to new farm practices. Relatively little change had taken place in the level and quality of production, and this had resulted in a lack of farmer initiative. The difference between benefactor intentions and beneficiary comprehension became apparent.

A participatory research workshop then made amends in that its training principles emphasized "increasing participant awareness, improving participant skills and information bases, and developing participants' ability to operate effectively as a group" (Tandon & Brown

1981, 174). The design and implementation of the project explicitly assumed the following procedural aims:

1. Talk with participants about their situation.
2. Emphasize the concrete experience of participants as a focus for analysis and action.
3. Create a psychologically safe environment.
4. Develop the capacities of groups rather than individuals.
5. Develop concrete, well-understood steps that participants value and may realistically accomplish.

The resulting interaction between the local populace and outside researchers afforded a better understanding of problems and furthered deliberation on possible solutions to local problems.

This effort was conducted without any reference to the theory of communicative action. Nevertheless, it was conducted through a process in which some attempt was made to ensure that validity claims could at any time be called up for justification. "Create a psychologically safe environment" is a rather nebulous and encompassing phrase, but it suggests, because the researchers demonstrated interest in the participation of the villagers, sincerity and rightness in terms of the validity claims. The researchers' communication was offered in good faith, without being manipulative. Researchers dealt with local problems on local terms, which was likely to enhance comprehension and, furthermore, legitimized their own sincerity and their concrete experience. In summary, the assumptions of the design and implementation of the research project employed participatory communication or, in Habermas' phrase, communicative action.

This example illustrates how project statements and evaluations contain goal-oriented and operational guidelines that should, in the case of participatory communication, reflect ideal speech conditions. The importance of specific validity claims will vary from case to case. The theory of communicative action specifies that all four validity claims are always implicit in communication. However, one or some of them may be more problematic in a given situation, and one or some of them may be more likely to need justification.

Assuming that communicative action is a productive conceptualization of participatory communication then, it is a short step to employing validity claims explicitly in fieldwork. There is not space here to explore such a possibility in more detail, but the manner in which this would be done seems clear. The validity claims would be used as guidelines. With regard to any given project, each validity claim could form a reference point for discussion, planning, or evaluation of interaction. In any given project one validity claim may be more problematic than another, and attention to the four claims need not be addressed in equal amounts.

Conclusion

The so-called demise of modernization led to the emergence of many paradigms that, over the years, constituted the field of development studies in the West and the Third World. Participation, as a post-modernization approach, is one of them. Although participation has not assumed the status of a full-fledged theory, it has been successful in expressing a different philosophical approach to the problem of so-called underdevelopment. Participatory communication is emblematic of this new approach in that it has been realized that dialogic communication is an important part of development. At the same time, one cannot help but note the diverse meanings, connotations, and conditionalities attached to the notion of participation. Therefore, the foregoing analysis uses Habermas' theory of communicative action as a conceptual framework with which to reconstruct and systematize the notion of participatory communication.

It should be noted that the examples used here would not seem to exhaust the communicative situations to which validity claims could be applied. We have focused on interaction between outsiders and locals....

In closing, a number of difficulties involved in employing Habermas in the field of communication for national development should be raised. First, Habermas'

work does not intersect well with any one contemporary school of thought on national development processes. For example, his theory of history is lineal, suggesting affinities with modernization theory. It does not suggest the tidy march toward wealth and modernism that writers such as W. W. Rostow (1952) seemed to suggest, but it does involve stages.

On a related matter, Habermas' thinking seems to include a brand of cultural universalism. He holds that some social formations embodied in 18th Century Enlightenment values are superior to those that are organized around frameworks of religious or mythic values. Cultural sensitivity takes the form for many scholars today of a relativism holding that all social forms are of equivalent worth. Extreme skepticism regarding universals of any kind is common (Escobar 1995; Spivak 1987). Assessing these matters is not possible here due to space constraints, but Habermas' work seems too often to revisit Enlightenment values from the perspective of some postmodernist analysts.

On the other hand, the theory of communicative action is intended to comprise the foundation of a "critical theory." This aspect of Habermas' work should accord less favorably with modernization theory. For example, colonization of the lifeworld may be well suited to conceptualizing cultural imperialism.

Some additional challenges presented by Habermas are due not to schools of thought on development theory, but rather reflect common criticisms of Habermas' theory generally. One is the commonly leveled charge of idealism. Here, the ideal speech situation is seen as unrealistic, because such a considerable part of communication is not at all oriented toward attempts to reach understanding. The condition of deception is of course well recognized by Habermas, and anticipated in that the ideal speech situation does not refer to anything like intentions to reach agreement or to be honest. It refers instead to the conditions for communication, plainly speaking, of any kind, including attempts to deceive. Thus, Habermas specified various forms of action. "Strategic action" has as its aim the

1927
1960
1963
1964
1967
1969
1970
1971
1972
1973
1974
1975
1976
1977
1978
1979
1980
1981
1982
1983
1984
1985
1986
1987
1988
1989
1990
1991
1992
1993
1994
1995
1996
1997
1998
1999
2000
2001
2002
2003
2004
2005
2006

achievement of a goal without regard for the well-being of any interlocutors, and may involve deception. "Communicative action" is reserved for action whose goal is expressly oriented toward reaching understanding.

These challenges, both those related to development theory and those more general, cannot be addressed here. We are attempting primarily to outline a communicative action approach to the study of participatory communication. Details and counterarguments can be attended to in the future. For now, the question is whether participatory communication scholars cannot find in Habermas' theory something beyond a friendly critical spirit. In fact, the heart of Habermas' work concerns participatory communication.

References

Ascroft, J. 1987. "Communication in support of development: Lessons from theory and practice," paper presented at the Communication and Change: An Agenda for New Age Communication seminar. East-West Center, University of Hawaii, Honolulu.

Berrigan, F. 1979. "Community communications: The role of community media in development," *Reports and Chapters on Mass Communication* (vol. 90). Paris: UNESCO.

Escobar, A. 1995. *Encountering development: The making and unmaking of the Third World*. Princeton, N.J.: Princeton Univ. Press.

Forester, J. 1988. "Introduction: The applied turn in contemporary critical theory," in: J. Forester, ed. *Critical theory and public life*. Cambridge, Mass.: MIT Press. ix–xxvi.

Freire, P. 1970. *Pedagogy of the oppressed*. New York: Continuum.

Freire, P. 1973. *Education for critical consciousness*. New York: Continuum.

Fuglesang, A., and D. Chandler. 1986. "The Open Snuff-Box: Communication as Participation," *Media Development* 2:2–4.

Gonzalez, H. 1989. "Interactivity and Feedback in Third World Development Campaigns," *Critical Studies in Mass Communication* 6:295–314.

Grinberg, S.M. 1986. "Trends in alternative communication research in Latin America," in: R. Atwood and E.G. McAnany, eds. *Communication and Latin American society: Trends in critical research, 1960–1985*. Madison: Univ. of Wisconsin Press. 165–189.

Habermas, J. 1979. *Communication and the Evolution of Society*. Boston: Beacon.

Habermas, J. 1984. *The Theory of Communicative Action. Vol. 1: Reason and the rationalization of society*. Boston: Beacon.

Habermas, J. 1987. *The Theory of Communicative Action. Vol. 2: A critique of functionalist reason*. Boston: Beacon.

Habermas, J. 1989. *The Structural Transformation of The Public Sphere: An Inquiry Into a Category of Bourgeois Society*. Cambridge, Mass.: MIT Press.

Hedebro, G.A. 1981. *Communication and Social Change in Developing Nations: A Critical View*. Ames: Iowa State Univ. Press.

Horster, D. 1979. *Habermas: An Introduction*. Philadelphia: Pennbridge.

Jacobson, T.L. 1993."A pragmatist account of participatory communication research for national development," *Communication Theory* 3:214–230.

Jayaweera, N., and S. Amunagama. 1987. *Rethinking Development Communication*. Singapore: Asian Mass Communication Research and Information Centre.

Kemp, R. 1988. "Planning, public hearings, and the politics of discourse," in: J. Forester, ed. *Critical theory and Public Life*. Cambridge, Mass.: MIT Press. 177–202.

Lerner, D. 1958. *The Passing of Traditional Society*. Glencoe, Ill.: The Free Press.

Lerner, D., and W. Schramm. 1976. *Communication and Change: The last ten years and the next*. Honolulu: Univ. of Hawaii Press.

McAnany, E.G., J. Schnitman, and N. Janus. 1981. *Communication and Social Structure: Critical studies in mass media research*. New York: Praeger.

Melkote, S.R. 1991. *Communication for Development in the Third World: Theory and practice*. Newbury Park, Calif.: Sage.

Nair, K.S., and S.A. White. 1993. "The Development Communication Process: A Reconceptualization," in: K.S. Nair and S.A. White, eds. *Perspectives in Development Communication*. New Delhi: Sage. 47–70.

Narula, U., and B. Pearce. 1986. *Development as Communication: A Perspective on India*. Carbondale: Southern Illinois Press.

O'Sullivan-Ryan, J., and M. Kaplan. 1982. "Communication methods to promote grass-roots participation," *Communication and Society 6*.

Rogers, E.M. 1963. *Diffusion of Innovations*. Glencoe, Ill.: The Free Press.

Rogers, E.M. 1976. "Communication and development: The passing of the dominant paradigm," *Communication Research* 3(2):213–240.

Rogers, E. M. 1983. *Diffusion of innovations*. New York: The Free Press.

Rostow, W.W. 1952. *The Process of Economic Growth*. New York: Norton.

Schramm, W. 1964. *Mass Media and National Development. The Role of Information in the Developing Countries*. Stanford, Calif.: Stanford Univ. Press.

Servaes, J., & Arnst, R. 1993. "Participatory communication for social change: Reasons for optimism in the year 2000," *Development Communication Report* 79:18–20.

Spivak, G. 1987. *In other worlds: Essays in Cultural Politics*. New York: Methuen.

Tandon, R., and D.L. Brown. 1981. "Organization-building for rural development: An experiment in India," *Journal of Applied Behavioral Science* 17(2):172–189.

Tilakratna, S. 1987. *The Animator in Participatory Rural Development: Concept and Practice*. Geneva: World Employment Programme, International Labour Organization.

White, S., K.S. Nair, and J. Ascroft. 1995. *Participation: A key concept in development communication*. New Delhi: Sage.

1927
1960
1963
1964
1967
1969
1970
1971
1972
1973
1974
1975
1976
1977
1978
1979
1980
1981
1982
1983
1984
1985
1986
1987
1988
1989
1990
1991
1992
1993
1994
1995
1996
1997
1998
1999
2000
2001
2002
2003
2004
2005
2006

1996

"PEOPLE IN CHARGE"
Excerpt from: *Participatory Communication for Development*
By Chin Saik Yoon

The other form of participatory mass media places people in charge of programming decisions. They decide what to broadcast, who to do it, where and when it is done. The professionals stay in the background looking after engineering details and assisting in the creation of the programmes when called upon to do so. New technology has simplified the technicalities of radio transmitters to a point where the people can operate these independently. New technology has also led to the manufacturing of portable audio and video recorders, and desktop publishing systems which in turn have simplified technical production processes and brought down the cost of operating such media. The availability of low-cost portable power generators has also helped in the relocation of many such technologies to rural settings where people have easier access to the media. The main obstacles to the popular use of such technologies are the restrictive media laws in most developing countries which limit media ownership to government or those trusted by government.

Most of these people-managed media broadcast or print material are conceived and produced by members of the community. What they lack in professional finesse they more than make up for in credibility and feeling. Community radio stations often double up as important personal communication tools, sending personal messages to far away places not served by telephone or the post office. They also help to extend the reach of traditional and folk media by recording or broadcasting them "live." Such media also serve an important purpose of correcting the imbalance of power between the power holders and the people. When operated by fearless leaders, such media can quickly create awareness about incidents of oppression and mobilize local and external resistance to the oppression. Community radio was one of the principal "weapons" in the "people-power revolution" of the Philippines which toppled a corrupt administration.

Such dramatic events aside, most of the successes of community broadcasting are to be found in the nonformal

education sector (Beltrán: 1993). Literacy programmes have been effectively conducted via community radio and television stations. Other subjects covered by these stations include gender issues, farming, health, income-generation, workers' safety and occupational health, land tenure and religious matters.

CHALLENGES IN PRACTISE
The application of the participatory communication concept has proven to be full of challenges in actual development settings. Practitioners have been confronted with either unanticipated effects and problems of the process, or criticism of promoting undesirable types of participation. The long and loud rhetoric around the subject has generally interfered with efforts by the practitioners to bring to life this idealistic social process. Some of the challenges which practitioners have had to grapple with are discussed below:

Definitions
Disagreements on what constituted true participation have troubled practitioners right from the beginning. The disagreements stemmed partly from differences of ideology and partly from the community settings where work was attempted. The ideological debate ranged from those who felt that true participation must put people in charge of making all the decisions, against those who felt that participation at other levels was also valid, and that the process can evolve from these levels towards the ideal goal. The other debates resulted from the wide range of cultural and environmental settings to which practitioners had to respond and adapt. These adaptations created participatory communication approaches which were different enough to cause disagreements among the communicators.

Conflict
Another challenge is the conflict which participatory communication frequently causes among people. Such conflict results from the process's inadvertable effect of adjusting power relationships between those lacking

power and those holding power. By participating, people are claiming power for themselves, thereby threatening the influence of the power-holders. Conflict also frequently occurs among the people. The community is sometimes split into factions by disagreements over goals and methods of doing things, and the involvement or exclusion of certain members of the community. Participatory communication which sets out to address root causes of development tends to cause high conflict. This history of conflict has caused many practitioners to appreciate the need for equipping themselves and the people with conflict-managing skills. The most important of these are skills for negotiation and mediation.

Up-Scaling

Successes in participatory communication have proven to be difficult to replicate or upscale. This is a major obstacle to NGOs [Non Governmental Organizations] interested in extending the benefits of participatory communication to a majority of the communities they serve. The challenge appears to stem from a number of factors. The first is the people-embodied nature of participatory communication skills. Some people appear to have special attributes which make them highly effective facilitators of the process. They are the "charismatic leaders" who "make things happen." These attributes presently remain elusive and escape identification or replication through training. The attributes of the communities have also been identified as crucial to success. Certain preconditions have been thought necessary for the effective working of the process. Upscaling problems may be also traced to the special commitments and support usually given to experimental efforts by communities and organizations, but seldom available to the same degree in large-scale projects.

Governance

Among all the preconditions for success, the type of governance affecting the people may be the most important. People who live in highly controlled states may desire participation very intensely, while at the same time be very reluctant to subscribe to such approaches for fear of reprisal against them and their families and friends. This represents not only a challenge but also a risk for those setting out to promote participatory communication.

Lure of the Private Sector

Privately owned companies are starting to affect participatory processes almost to the extent that local authorities have in the past. They do so by offering money, employment opportunities and other incentives to selected members of communities in order to seek desired cooperation from communities which are not always beneficial to their long-term interests. For example, certain timber companies frequently offer jobs with high salaries to community leaders in areas to be logged, in order to secure the cooperation of these communities through the cooption of their leaders. People who set out to fight these companies must first suffer all the painful results of conflict with their own leaders. Threats from the private sector are difficult to address because their methods are subtle and usually very attractive in the short-term.

NGO Specialization

Whereas most NGOs were generalists in the past, many now work on specialized issues such as water, income-generation, agriculture, gender, etc. These organizations face difficult problems when working in the participatory mode because people often identify issues and problems outside the NGOs' areas of specialization for action. The solution here appears to be a networking of NGOs so that specialist skills may be shared in response to needs identified by the people.

Coexisting With "Other" Communication

Few communities live in total isolation from the outside world. In terms of communication they may be reached by entertainment films in cinemas; television, radio, newspapers and magazines from the cities; salespeople from companies; and others who do not practise participatory forms of communication. Facilitators need to introduce ways of coexisting with or countering components of the larger communication system, so that people may sharpen their ability to interpret the communication reaching them. One way is media education where people are sensitized to the workings of different forms of media and some of the intentions which drive their operation. The other approach is to counter competing messages with alternative information. For example, promotional campaigns for harmful chemical pesticides mounted by companies may be countered with participatory programmes on integrated pest management which require minimal use of chemicals.

Long-Term Commitment

Participation takes time. It is a process which cannot be rushed to meet deadlines or fit annual budgets. Two- or three-year funding cycles which typically govern the implementation of sponsored development projects are usually too short for real participatory communication processes to take root in communities. Such projects may actually shut down processes just as they are about ready to evolve into vibrant participatory communication. Long-term commitment is required not just of the funding agency but also of the people. Participation takes up precious time and energies (which are often the only resources) of members of the community involved. Programmes should ideally be designed to deliver sufficient short-term benefits to motivate the people in maintaining their commitment towards attaining long-term goals.

Flexibility

NGOs and their funding agencies must adopt flexible management approaches in the implementation of participatory programmes. They must structure their work plans and budgets in such a way that changes which evolve out of participatory processes may be quickly accommodated with a minimum of difficulty. The objectives, anticipated outputs and work plan described in documentation for participatory projects will probably change as people begin to take an active part in shaping project activities. Such administrative changes should be welcomed as indication of success rather than symptoms of poor project design. Funding agencies and NGOs which are run in a participatory manner are the ones which are able to operate effectively with this form of project management.

References

Beltrán, L. B. "Communication for Development in Latin America: A Forty-Year Appraisal," in D. Nostbakken and C. Morrow, eds., Cultural Expression in the Global Village. Penang, Malaysia: Southbound, 1993, 10-11.

Saik Yoon, Chin. "People in Charge," Chapter 2 of "Participatory Development Communication a West African Agenda," Guy Bessette and C. V. Rajasunderam, eds., International Development Research Centre (IDRC) Ottawa, Canada; Southbound: Penang, Malaysia, 1996. Copyright© 1996, International Development Research Centre. Reprinted with permission of IRDC.

WHO MEASURES CHANGE?

By Will Parks with Denise Gray-Felder, Jim Hunt and Ailish Byrne

2005 This article is an introduction to establishing a Participatory Monitoring and Evaluation (PM&E) process to assist in the measurement of Communication for Social Change (CFSC) initiatives. It is based on the premise that CFSC practitioners should facilitate the development of Monitoring and Evaluation (M&E) questions, measures and methods *with* those most affected and involved rather than apply pre-determined objectives, indicators and techniques to measure CFSC *on* those most affected and involved.

The primary purpose is to support communication strategies based on CFSC principles when applied to critical social issues such as HIV/AIDS prevention and care. Yet the information contained in this paper has broader applications to a variety of development concerns. It includes an explanation of how and why participatory monitoring and evaluation of CFSC is useful, as well as the steps involved in establishing a PM&E process.

Participation is not simply a fringe benefit that authorities may grant as a concession, but a human being's birthright that no authority can deny... What is a participative society? I must confess that it is easier for me to explain what a nonparticipative one is. All I have to do is point to our present society, one in which social classes live in separate worlds, in a rigid order of domination, oppression, and exploitation.[1]

Communication and Participation

Communication and participation have been described as two sides of the same development coin. When communication processes are used: *to inform people, enable them to contribute their points of view,*

1927
1960
1963
1964
1967
1969
1970
1971
1972
1973
1974
1975
1976
1977
1978
1979
1980
1981
1982
1983
1984
1985
1986
1987
1988
1989
1990
1991
1992
1993
1994
1995
1996
1997
1998
1999
2000
2001
2002
2003
2004
2005
2006

*reach consensus, and carry out an agreed change or development action together, it can be said that communication **is** participation.*[2]

Use of formalized communication approaches in development began shortly after the Second World War. Two main trends have dominated since:

1. Communication approaches based on modernisation theories and information-persuasion strategies used by Western governments and industrial sectors. Examples include: Diffusion of Innovations, Social Marketing, Information-Education-Communication (IEC), Behaviour Change Communication (BCC);

2. Communication approaches based on critical theory, collective learning, information-sharing and dialogic processes forged during social and political struggles against colonial and dictatorial powers imposed on poor communities and countries. Examples include: Participatory Communication, Communication for Social Change.[3]

Communication approaches associated with the first trend have tended to be less participatory in terms of design, implementation, and measurement.[4]

There have been frequent tensions between each trend, including:

■ Their differing developmental goals—the first set of approaches aim to tackle the immediate symptoms of poverty (e.g., promotion of discrete products and services), whereas the latter set aim to tackle the underlying causes of poverty (e.g., oppression and injustice);

■ The first set are usually owned and driven by "external" agencies (e.g., governments) whereas the second set, while often stimulated by external resources, are owned and driven by "internal" agencies (e.g., families and community groups); and

■ Practitioners of the first set accuse the latter of taking too long to achieve results, while practitioners of the second set accuse the former of promoting unsustainable approaches.

Distinctions between the two sets of approaches are not so clear in practice. For example, both can be more or less "participatory" depending on the facilitation skills of the change agents involved and the timelines of sponsoring agencies, whether government or non-government.

Over recent years, there have also been important areas of convergence between the two sets of approaches. For example, there is now fairly universal agreement that communication should focus on change at *both* individual and societal levels, and that "tangible" (e.g., service uptake) *as well as* "intangible" (e.g., community empowerment) outcomes need to be measured.

Communication for Social Change (CFSC)

Whenever participatory communication approaches are adopted, communication: *changes its role from that of a vehicle for information-persuasion to that of a tool for dialogue and interservice coordination—which is absolutely essential for participation in problem identification, problem articulation, and problem solving.*[5]

CFSC in some ways has always been around.[6] It was only in 1997, however, when the Rockefeller Foundation organised a series of meetings to discuss the role of "Communication in Social Change" that the characteristics and theoretical underpinnings of CFSC began to emerge.

CFSC can be defined as a process of public and private dialogue through which people themselves define who they are, what they need and how to get what they need in order to improve their own lives. It utilizes dialogue that leads to collective problem identification, decision-making and community-based implementation of solutions to development issues.[7] Social Change can be defined as: a positive change in peoples' lives—as they themselves define such change.

CFSC questions an approach to development that: *does not include the population that is directly affected. CFSC promotes a communication process that supports effective community participation, particularly of the most impoverished and marginalized sectors of society.*[8]

CFSC practitioners use a "bottom-up" approach by placing ownership, access and control of communication *directly in the hands of affected communities*. This shifts control of media, messages, tools and content of communication from the powerful to the traditionally powerless. Ultimately, using such skills, previously powerless communities can become "self-renewing"—able to manage their own communication processes for their own good.

Similar to other participatory communication approaches, the *process* of CFSC is a "product" in and of itself. The process helps individuals and communities build a stronger capacity to communicate in person, through the arts, or using media and other communication technologies. CFSC does not attempt to anticipate which media, messages or techniques are better. The participation of social actors, who are in turn communicators, takes places within a process of collective growth that precedes the creation of messages and products such as a radio program, a video documentary or a pamphlet. Messages and their dissemination are just additional elements of the communication process.

CFSC's focus is on *the dialogue process* through which people are able to identify obstacles and develop communication structures, policies, processes and media or other communication tools to help them achieve the goals they themselves have outlined and defined. Rather than focusing on persuasion and information dissemination, CFSC promotes dialogue, debate and negotiation *from within* communities. Rather than confining dialogue to an airing of grievances or a discussion of information, CFSC supports focused deliberation, collective decision-making and collective action.

The driving forces of CFSC can be synthesized as follows:

■ Communication is often designed around projects: specific, time-limited, often externally funded and supported, discretely targeted interventions. Too many communication projects in the context of development have failed due to lack of participation and commitment from the subjects of change. "Access" to mass media has proved insufficient and has often resulted in manipulation by vested interests. Sustainability of social change is more likely if the individuals and communities most affected *own* the process and content of communication. Communities should be the protagonists of their own change and manage their communication tools.

■ During several decades development programs were imposed on poor communities and nations in both the South and North. These communication strategies were mostly designed in the industrialised world. The same models, messages, formats and techniques were utilised—and often still are today—in widely varying cultural contexts. The communication process cannot ignore or deny the specificity of each culture and language; on the contrary, it should support them to acquire legitimacy thereby supporting "cultural renewal."[9] Cultural interaction, or the exchanges between languages and cultures, is healthy when it happens through critical dialogue within a framework of equity and respect.

■ Vertical models of communication for development take for granted that poor communities in developing nations lack "knowledge."[10] Access to information generated in industrialised countries is seen as the magic path of progress. CFSC rejects the linear model of transmission of information from a central sender to an individual receiver, and promotes instead a cyclic process of interactions focused on shared knowledge from within and outside the culture and collective action. CFSC strengthens local knowledge and promotes exchanges of information in equal terms, learning through dialogue, in a process of mutual growth. CFSC is empowering and horizontal, versus top-down, giving voice to previously unheard social actors.

1927
1960
1963
1964
1967
1969
1970
1971
1972
1973
1974
1975
1976
1977
1978
1979
1980
1981
1982
1983
1984
1985
1986
1987
1988
1989
1990
1991
1992
1993
1994
1995
1996
1997
1998
1999
2000
2001
2002
2003
2004
2005
2006

- Communication cannot be seen as an appendix, or as a set of specific tasks within an already given project. If development projects are seen as social change projects, and therefore as communication projects, they cannot begin in the headquarters of an outside organization, except as a set of questions: What happens there? Would they want us there? To do what? How? What will we leave behind that can be reused for new purposes? Every project must be planned from this communication perspective from the very beginning. This implies planning in communication with both the involved population and potential allies.[11]

- Communication means links and exchanges between different people, organizations and communities. Communication processes that "target" receivers and isolate themselves within externally defined issues often cannot help establish dialogues and are less likely to grow and be sustainable. CFSC promotes dialogue not only within the community, but also with others engaging in a similar process. Networking contributes to strengthen the process and exchanges add richness to them. CFSC is horizontal (many-to-many) and strengthens the community bonds by amplifying the voices of the poorest.[12]

- The results of the CFSC process must go beyond individual behaviour and consider social norms, current policies, culture and the general development context. CFSC strives to strengthen cultural identity, trust, commitment voice and ownership: the communication fabric of community empowerment. CFSC does not look up for answers. It is not wholly dependent on outside forces. It is hoped that CFSC approaches can be sustained and can be replicated after funding goes away.

In short, CFSC is concerned with culture and tradition; respect of local decision-making power; the mutual modification of outside information and traditional knowledge; and dialogue between development specialists and communities. CFSC is about *engaging people* to want to change, to define the change and required actions, and to carry them out. The overall goal of CFSC is *self-renewing societies*.

Communication for Social Change and HIV/AIDS

Every minute, 100 people contract HIV/AIDS. Every day, AIDS kills more than 8,000 people. Yet HIV/AIDS is a preventable and manageable condition. Global, national and sub-national communication programs designed by international agencies, governments and non-government organizations have raised awareness about HIV/AIDS, reduced stigma associated with HIV/AIDS and, to some extent, changed behaviours that if left unchanged, place people at risk of contracting the HIV virus or being unable to access services such as voluntary testing and retroviral treatment.[13]

But while mass education campaigns aimed at changing individual behaviour play an essential role in HIV/AIDS prevention and care, without deep-rooted social change, they are highly unlikely to be sustainable. Social, cultural and political factors underpin the so-called "risk behaviours". These factors include, but are not limited to: poverty, inequality, prejudice, the status of women, the responsibility of men, marginalization and disempowerment, gender-based violence, community and social cohesion, and many others.[14] Sustaining a change in behaviours or social conditions is fundamentally about fostering and supporting communication in society.[15]

Conventional approaches to HIV/AIDS communication—dependence on mass media and reliance on social marketing and behaviour change communication planning models—have been reassessed in light of the following:

- The ever-increasing scale and severity of the epidemic despite efforts to contain it. We can no longer rely only on the health sector to control HIV/AIDS.[16]
- Major international interventions have sometimes been introduced at the expense of communities and societies taking the ownership and leadership of the fights against HIV/AIDS on for themselves.[17]
- The need to address individual behaviour as well as social, political and environmental factors that influence behaviour.[18] Because sexual issues are more

sensitive for many people than other public health topics, drama and other entertaining forms of raising the issues can be particularly effective. These forms of "edutainment" can contribute to the CFSC process.[19]

■ Issues of sex and sexuality, and the intimate links between HIV and poverty, HIV and discrimination, and HIV and marginalization, require much more complex, bottom-up strategies aimed at community empowerment, horizontal forms of communication and less rigid (therefore less easily measurable) sets of interventions.[20]

■ The increasing complexity of developing country societies, prompted by greater liberalization, more complex media systems and more complex and horizontal communication patterns in society demand fresh thinking and approaches.[21]

Increased interest and debate has now focused on the field of Communication for Social Change.[22] The principles and approaches associated with CFSC can be summarized as moving communication frameworks on HIV/AIDS:

■ Away from people as the objects of change…and on to people and communities as the agents of their own change

■ Away from designing, testing and delivering messages…and on to supporting dialogue on the key issues of concern

■ Away from the conveying of information from technical experts…and on to sensitively placing that information into the dialogue

■ Away from persuading people to do something… and on to negotiating the best way forward in a partnership process

■ Away from technical experts in "outside" agencies dominating and guiding the process…and on to the people most affected by the issues of concern playing a central role.

What is PM&E?

So what exactly is PM&E? There is no single definition or methodology for PM&E due to the diverse range of field experiences and the difficulty in reaching agreement on terms such as "monitoring," "evaluation,"

"community" and "participation." As noted above, PM&E is best described as: *a set of principles and a process of engagement in the monitoring and evaluation endeavour*.[23] The *process* is at least as important as the *recommendations* and *results* contained in PM&E reports or feedback meetings.

Much literature on PM&E has emerged from the international and community-development fields.[24] Approaches such as rapid rural appraisal (RRA), Participatory Rural Appraisal (PRA), Participatory Monitoring (PM), Participatory Learning Methods (PALM) have been developed for appraising local situations in a participatory manner.[25] Training courses in PM&E are now available in several international institutions and some agencies deliver training courses "off-campus" to agencies, programs/initiatives and communities requesting PM&E support.

Participatory techniques and methods of data collection—including village mapping, transect and group walks, diagramming, seasonal calendars, matrix ranking and group discussions—have evolved as useful tools for involving local people in developing strategies for learning about their communities and for planning and evaluation.[26] A number of PM&E handbooks and assorted practical manuals have been published.[27]

Why use PM&E?

It is important to regard people as agents rather than objects; agents who are capable of analyzing their own situations and designing their own solutions.[28] Conventional M&E is often based on quantitative, non-participatory surveys designed by evaluators external to the program or project in question.[29] These processes have been increasingly criticized for being "top-down," serving only the interests of funding agencies and policy makers, and providing little if any opportunities for all stakeholders to voice their opinions and judgments.[30] Information is typically extracted from populations/communities/families/ participants and concentrated at the top of

1927
1960
1963
1964
1967
1969
1970
1971
1972
1973
1974
1975
1976
1977
1978
1979
1980
1981
1982
1983
1984
1985
1986
1987
1988
1989
1990
1991
1992
1993
1994
1995
1996
1997
1998
1999
2000
2001
2002
2003
2004
2005
2006

organizations (usually far removed from beneficiaries) where it often remains underutilized.[31] Conventional M&E has been viewed largely as a form of "policing."[32]

The idea of stakeholder participation in evaluation is now widely accepted within the evaluation community.[33] According to Estrella et al (2000), interest in PM&E has grown as a result of several factors, including: [34]

■ The trend towards "performance-based accountability," focusing results and objectives beyond financial reporting.[35]
■ The growing demand for greater accountability and demonstrable impact.
■ The move towards devolution of central government responsibilities and authority to lower levels of government, necessitating new forms of oversight to ensure transparency and to improve support to constituency-responsive initiatives.
■ Stronger capacities and experiences of Non-Government Organizations (NGOs) and Community-Based Organizations (CBOs) as decision makers and implementers in the development process.[36]
■ Mounting evidence that participatory approaches for issue identification and resolution, program design, monitoring and evaluation produce positive results.[37]

PM&E is essential if the purpose of the continuous and periodic evaluation is to understand and respond to local realities and ensure results are used for change.[38] Some of the key functions of PM&E are:

■ To facilitate mutual learning.[39]
■ To contribute to the building of local capacity for decision-making and community-centred development.[40]
■ To help participants gain the abilities to evaluate their own needs, analyze their own priorities and objectives, and undertake action-oriented planning to solve their own problems.[41]

In general, there are three main purposes of PM&E:

■ To enhance planning and management.[42]
■ To foster organizational learning.[43]
■ To shape policy.[44]

These multiple functions and purposes of PM&E often overlap. Determining core functions and purposes of PM&E in a project or program will essentially depend on different stakeholder interests and may well change over time.

In order to identify what is to be monitored and evaluated and for what purpose(s), PM&E uses a process that: *tries to offer fora (*for example, meetings and workshops) *that allow different stakeholders to articulate their needs and make collaborative decisions… PM&E requires learning about people's concerns, and how different stakeholders look at (and hence, measure) project results, outcomes, and impacts. How these differing (and often competing) stakeholder claims and perspectives are negotiated and resolved, especially when particular groups and/or individuals are powerless vis-à-vis others, remains a critical question in building a PM&E process.*[45]

Endnotes

1   Bordenave, J.D. (1994) "Participative Communication as a Part of Building the Participative Society," in White, S.A. with Nair, K.S. and Ascroft, J. (eds) *Participatory Communication: Working for change and development.* New Delhi: Sage Publications. Pp.35-59. (P.36 and P.35).

2   Fraser, C. and Restrepo-Estrada, S. (1998) *Communicating for Development: Human Change for Survival.* London: I.B. Tauris Publishers. (P.59).

3   Kumar, K.J. (1994) "Communication Approaches to Participation and Development: Challenging Assumptions and Perspectives," in White, S.A. with Nair, K.S. and Ascroft, J. (eds) *Participatory Communication: Working for change and development.* New Delhi: Sage Publications. Pp.76-92.

4   Khadka, N. B. (2000) "The participatory development communication paradigm: Communication challenges and change," Australian Journal of Communication, 27 (3), 105-122.

5   Bordenave, J.D.(1994) *op.cit.*, p.40.

6   Fraser, C. and Restrepo-Estrada, S. (1998) *op.cit.*, p.39.

7   http://www.communicationforsocialchange.org/mission.php

8   Gumucio-Dagron, A. Communication for Social Change: A key for participatory development. [Full reference information not available.]

9   Nair, K.S. and White, S.A. (1994) "Participatory Development Communication as Cultural Renewal," in White, S.A. with Nair, K.S. and Ascroft, J. (eds) *Participatory Communication: Working for change and development.* New Delhi: Sage Publications. Pp.138-193.

10   IIRR (1996) "Recording and using indigenous knowledge: A manual," International Institute of Rural Reconstruction, Silang, Cavite, Philippines.

11   Mato, D. (2002) "Communication for Social Change in Latin America: Contexts, Theories and Experiences," notes from a presentation to The

Communication Initiative Partners, November 6, 2002. Placed on The Communication Initiative site November 25, 2002.

12 Gumucio-Dagron, A. *op.cit.*

13 AIDSCAP (n.d.) *Making Prevention Work: Global Lessons from the AIDS Control and Prevention (AIDSCAP) Project* 1991-1997.

14 UNAIDS/PennState (1999) *Communications Framework for HIV/AIDS: A New Direction.* Geneva: UNAIDS.

15 Panos Institute (2001) "Background Paper for Communication Development Roundtable," sponsored by UNFPA in association with the Rockefeller Foundation and UNESCO. Nicaragua, November 2001. (Pp.6 and 9).

16 Parker, W., Dalrymple, L. and Durden, E. (1998) "Communicating Beyond AIDS Awareness: A Manual for South Africa," Department of Health, South Africa: Beyond Awareness Consortium. P.64.

17 Parker, W., Dalrymple, L. and Durden, E. (1998) *op.cit.*

18 Blake, M., and Babalola, S. (2002) *Impact of a male motivation campaign on family planning: Ideation and practice in Guinea.* Baltimore: Johns Hopkins University. Bloomberg School of Public Health, Center for Communication Programs (CPP), Field Report No 13.

19 Singhal, A. and Rogers, E. (2003) *Combating AIDS: Communication Strategies in Action.* New Delhi: Sage Publications.

20 See for example: Narayan, D., Chambers, R., Shah, M. and Petesch, P. (1999) *Global synthesis: consultations with the poor.* Washington, D.C.: World Bank; Kesby, M. (2000) "Participatory diagramming as a means to improve communication about sex in rural Zimbabwe: a pilot study," *Social Science & Medicine,* 50 (9), 1723-1741; Adeyi, O., Hecht, R., Njobvu, E. and Soucat, A. (2001) *AIDS, Poverty Reduction and Debt Relief: A Toolkit for Mainstreaming HIV/AIDS Programmes into Development Instruments.* Geneva: UNAIDS/World Bank; Volk, J. E. and Koopman, C. (2001) "Factors associated with condom use in Kenya: A test of the health belief model," *AIDS Education and Prevention,* 13 (6), 495-508; Aggleton, P. and Parker, R. (2002) World AIDS Campaign 2002-2003. *A conceptual framework and basis for action: HIV/AIDS stigma and discrimination.* Geneva: UNAIDS/02.43E; Program for Appropriate Technology in Health (PATH) (2002) *Developing Materials on HIV/AIDS/STIs for Low-Literate Audiences.* Arlington: Family Health International; Campbell, C., and MacPhail, C. (2002) "Peer education, gender and the development of critical consciousness: participatory HIV prevention by South African youth," *Social Science & Medicine,* 55 (2), 331-345; Gregson, S. Tereira, N., Mushati, P., Nyamukapa, C., and Campbell, C. (2004) "Community group participation: Can it help young women to avoid HIV? An exploratory study of social capital and school education in rural Zimbabwe," *Social Science & Medicine,* 58 (11), 2119-32.

21 UNFPA (2002) *Communication for Development Roundtable Report: Focus on HIV/AIDS communication and evaluation.* November 26-28, 2001, Managua, Nicaragua. Organized by UNFPA with The Rockefeller Foundation, UNESCO, and The Panos Institute. New York: UNFPA.

22 Panos Institute (2001) *op.cit.,* p.5.

23 Burke, B. (1998) *op.cit.*

24 See for example: Stewart, S. (1995) *Participatory Rural Appraisal: Abstracts of sources. An Annotated Bibliography. Development Bibliography Number 11.* Brighton: Institute of Development Studies; Estrella, M. and Gaventa, J., 1998. *Who counts reality? Participatory monitoring and evaluation: A literature review.* Brighton: IDS. Working Paper 70; Pasteur, K., and Blauert, J. (2000) *Participatory monitoring and evaluation in Latin America: Overview of the literature with annotated bibliography.* Brighton: Institute of Development Studies (IDS).

25 Tikare, S., Youssef, D., Donnelly-Roark, P. and Shah, P. (2001) "Chapter 7: Participation," in *Poverty Reduction Strategy Sourcebook,* Volume 1 – Core Techniques and Cross-Cutting Issues Washington D.C: World Bank; Bock, J. G., (2001) 'Towards participatory communal appraisal,' Community Development Journal, 36 (2), 146-153.

26 Cornwall, A. and Jewkes, R. (1995) 'What is participatory research?' *Social Science & Medicine,* 41 (12), 1667-1676; Roche, C. (1999) 'Methodological issues: using participatory tools.' In Impact Assessment for Development Agencies. Learning to Value Change. Oxford Publishing: Oxfam. 137-150.

27 Feuerstein, M-T. (1986) *Partners in Evaluation: Evaluating Development and Community Programmes with Participants.* London: MacMillan; Chambers, R. (1991) "Shortcut and Participatory Methods for Gaining Social Information for Projects," in *Putting People First: Sociological Variables in Rural Development.* Cernea, M.M. (ed). Pp.515-537. Oxford: Oxford University Press; Narayan-Parker, D. (1993) "Participatory evaluation: Tools for Managing Change in Water and Sanitation," World Bank Technical Paper 207. Washington, D.C.: The World Bank; MacMillan; Gajanayake, S. and Gajanayake, J. (1993) *Community Empowerment: A Participatory Training manual on Community Project Development.* Illinois: Office of International Training and Consultation, Northern Illinois University; Srinivasan, L. (1993) *Tools for Community Participation: A Manual for Training Trainers in Participatory Techniques.* Washington, DC: PROWESS/UNDP-World Bank Water and Sanitation Program; Aubel, J. (1993) *Participatory Program Evaluation: A Manual for involving program stakeholders in the evaluation process.* Dakar: Catholic Relief Services; World Bank. (1996) The World Bank participation sourcebook. Washington, D.C.: World Bank; WHO and UNDP/World Bank (1997) The PHAST Initiative. *Participatory Hygiene and Sanitation Transformation: A New approach to working with communities.* Geneva: World Health Organization; United Nations Development Program (1997) *Who are the Question Makers? A Participatory Evaluation Handbook.* New York: Office of Evaluation and Strategic Planning, United Nations Development Program; Narayan-Parker, D. and Rietbergen-McCracken, J. (1998) *Participation and social assessment: tools and techniques.* Washington, D.C.: The World Bank; Rietbergen-McCracken, J. and Narayan-Parker, D. (1998) *Participatory tools and techniques: A resource kit for participation and social assessment.* Social Policy and Resettlement Division, Environment Department. Washington, D.C.: The World Bank; UNDP-World Bank Water and Sanitation Program South Asia Region (1998) *Improving User Participation to Increase Project Effectiveness: Community Action Planning in an Adaptive Project - NWFP community infrastructure project.* UNDP – World Bank Water and Sanitation Program South Asia Region; Norton, A., Bird, B., Brock., K. Kakande., M. and Turk, C. (2001) *A rough guide to PPAs: Participatory Poverty Assessment. An introduction to theory and practice.* Brighton: Overseas Development Institute (IDS).

28 Cornwall, A. and Jewkes, R. (1995) "What is participatory research?" *Social Science and Medicine,* 41(12), pp.1667-1676.

29 Aubel, J. (2004) *Participatory Monitoring and Evaluation for Hygiene Improvement. Beyond the toolbox: What else is required for effective PM&E?* Washington, D.C.: Environmental Health Project, Strategic Report 9.

30 Cracknell, B.E. (2000) *Evaluating Development Aid: Issues, Problems and Solutions.* Pp.110-111. New Delhi: Sage Publications; Kanji, N. (2003) *Mind the Gap: Mainstreaming gender and participation in development.* London: International Institute for Environment and Development (IIED) and the Institute of Development Studies (IDS).

31 Noponen, H. (1997) "Participatory Monitoring and Evaluation – A Prototype Internal Learning System for Livelihood and Micro-Credit Programs," *Community Development Journal,* 32:1, pp.30-48 (p.47)

1927
1960
1963
1964
1967
1969
1970
1971
1972
1973
1974
1975
1976
1977
1978
1979
1980
1981
1982
1983
1984
1985
1986
1987
1988
1989
1990
1991
1992
1993
1994
1995
1996
1997
1998
1999
2000
2001
2002
2003
2004
2005
2006

32 Carden, F. (2000) "Giving Evaluation Away: Challenges in a Learning-based Approach to Institutional Assessment," in Nair, K.S. and White, S.A. (1994) "Participatory Development Communication as Cultural Renewal," in White, S.A. with Nair, K.S. and Ascroft, J. (eds) *Participatory Communication: Working for change and development*. New Delhi: Sage Publications. Pp.175-200.

33 Whitmore, E. (ed.) (1998) "Understanding and Practicing Participatory Evaluation," *New Directions for Evaluation, Number 80*. San Francisco: Jossey-Bass Publishers.

34 Estrella, M. with Blauert, J., Campilan, D., Gaventa, J. et al (eds) (2000) *Learning from Change: Issues and experiences in participatory monitoring and evaluation*. London: Intermediate Technology Publications Ltd.

35 Niven, P. (2002) *Balance Scorecard Step-by-Step: Maximizing Performance and Maintaining Results*. New York: John Wiley and Sons.

36 Guijt, I. and Gaventa, J. (1998) Participatory Monitoring and Evaluation: Learning from Change. IDS Policy Briefing 12. Brighton: Institute of Development Studies.

37 Bradley, J.E. et al (2002) "Participatory evaluation of reproductive health care quality in developing countries," *Social Science and Medicine*, 55, pp.269-282.

38 Papineau, D. and Kiely, M.C. (1996) "Participatory evaluation in a community organization: fostering stakeholder empowerment and utilization," *Evaluation and Program Planning*, 19:1, pp.79-93.

39 Rebien, C.C. (1996) 'Participatory evaluation of development assistance: dealing with power and facilitative learning.' Evaluation, 2(2), pp.151-171; Noponen, H. (1997) "Participatory Monitoring and Evaluation – A Prototype Internal Learning System for Livelihood and Micro-Credit Programs," *Community Development Journal*, 32:1, pp.30-48.

40 Nayaran,-Parker, D. (1993) "Participatory evaluation: Tools for managing change in water and sanitation," *World Bank Technical Paper, 207*. Washington, D.C.: World Bank; Papineau, D. and Kiely, M.C. (1996) "Participatory evaluation in a community organization: fostering stakeholder empowerment and utilization," *Evaluation and Program Planning*, 19:1, pp.79-93.

41 Estrella, M. and Gaventa, J. (1998) "Who counts reality? Participatory Monitoring and Evaluation: A literature review," IDS Working Paper 70.

42 MacMillan; Gajanayake, S. and Gajanayake, J. (1993) *Community Empowerment: A Participatory Training Manual on Community Project Development*. Illinois: Office of International Training and Consultation, Northern Illinois University; Bhattacharyya, K., Murray, J., Amdie, W. et al (1998) *Community Assessment and Planning for Maternal and Child Health Programs: A Participatory Approach in Ethiopia*. Arlington, Va.: Basics Support for Institutionalizing Child Survival (BASICS) project, for the US Agency for International Development; Bertoli, S. (2000) "A promising practice for increasing active collaboration and use of information by teams," *Child Survival Connections*, 1(1), 13-16; IRC. (2003) *Sustainability planning and monitoring in community water supply and sanitation: A guide on the Methodology for participatory assessment (MPA) for community driven development programs* (Eds) Mukherjee N, C Van Wijk C. [online] Available http://www.wasp.org./publications/mpa%202003.pdf. Washington D.C.: The World Bank.

43 Anon (n.d.) *Poet's user manual. Participatory organisational evaluation tool*. Education Development Centre and PACT Inc.; Cousins, J.B. and Earl, L. (Eds) (1995) *Participatory Evaluation in Education: Studies in Evaluation Use and Organizational Learning*. London: The Falmer Press; Fetterman, D.M., Kaftarian, S.J. and Wandersman, A. (1996) *Empowerment Evaluation: Knowledge and Tools for Self-Assessment and Accountability*. Thousand Oaks: Sage Publications; Bainbridge, V., Foerster., Pasteur., Pimbert., Pratt G., and

Arroyo I.Y. (2001) *Transforming Bureaucracies: Institutionalising participation and people centred processes in natural resource management—an annotated bibliography*. London: International Institute for Environment and Development (IIED) and Institute of Development Studies (IDS); Fetterman, D. and Eiler, M. (2001) *Empowerment evaluation and organisational learning: A path toward mainstreaming evaluation*. St Louis: American Evaluation Association; Fakih, M., Rahardjo, T., Pimbert, M., Sutoko, A., Wulandari, D. and Prasetyo T. (2003) *Community Integrated Pest Management in Indonesia: Institutionalising Participation and People Centred Approaches*. London: International Institute for Environment and Development (IIED) and the Institute of Development Studies (IDS).

44 Wang, C., Burris, M. A. and Ping, X. Y. (1996) "Chinese village women as visual anthropologists: A participatory approach to reaching policymakers," *Social Science & Medicine*, 42 (10), 1391-1400; Holland, J. and Blackburn, J. (1998) *Whose Voice? Participatory research and policy change*. London: Intermediate Technology Publications; McGee, R. with Norton, A. (2000) "Participation in Poverty Reduction Strategies: a synthesis of experience with participatory approaches to policy design, implementation and monitoring," Brighton: Institute of Development Studies, Working Paper 109; Robb, C.A. (2000) "How the poor can have a voice in government policy," *Finance & Development*, 37 (4), 22-25.

45 Estrella, M. (2000) 'Learning from Change.' In Estrella, M. with Blauert, J., Campilan, D., Gaventa, J. et al (eds) Learning from Change: Issues and experiences in participatory monitoring and evaluation. London: Intermediate Technology Publications Ltd. Pp.1-14. (P.8).

Parks, Will with Denise Gray-Felder, Jim Hunt and Ailish Byrne. *Who Measures Change? An Introduction to Participatory Monitoring and Evaluation of Communication for Social Change*, part of a series on measuring change published by the Communication for Social Change Consortium, Inc. Copyright © *2005* Communication for Social Change Consortium, Inc. Reprinted with permission of the publisher. www.communicationforsocialchange.org

COMMUNICATION FOR SOCIAL CHANGE

Communication Theory Should Be Adapted to the Subject Population and to the Contents of the Messages for Social Change

By Manuel Calvelo Ríos

2003 Unfortunately in the more than 300 university faculties of communication in Latin America, the model being proposed as communication theory is:

Sender - Media - Receiver.

Formulated during the Second World War, it was used for giving orders to bomber pilots and included a feedback system for making sure that the pilot had understood the orders by repeating them to the sender. It is a model from dominant to dominated, from the person giving orders to the person obeying them, from the person with power to the person without it. The model was appropriated for one of the most vertical and authoritarian structures that societies have created, the army. It is common knowledge that it is easier to militarize a civilian than to civilize a military, with exceptions that only confirm the rule. However, during the post-war period, the model was adopted, without change, by the mass media, who insisted on legitimating it by calling it theory of communication. At best they are information media, but usually they act as manipulation media.

Someone once said that there is nothing more practical than a good theory, and when we started to work in the area of communication for rural development, we used what was available. And we did fail over and over again. We began to investigate operationally, and we reached the conclusion that for a message to really be a communicational message it was essential to satisfy certain conditions:

a. instruments,
b. contents,

c. message codes,
d. processing level of the contents,
e. presentation order of the message, and
f. opportunity the messages are to be exchanged,

These should be established, agreed upon, negotiated or defined in relation to the user group of the messages produced and to some of their characteristics.

But then, the passive receiver stops being passive, begins to participate in the process of message production and use. This led us to formulate a model of communication for development, or efficient communication for improving the subjects' conditions, through the contribution of the intangible capital of "knowledge" and the recovery of their cultural values. The model is:

Interlocutor - Media - Interlocutor.

We assert that communication exists if, and only if, the messages exchanged by the interlocutors are the product of joint work, coordinated by the communicator for development.

In the mass media, the so called communicator, who usually only manages information, is under the command of, and depends on, the sender. In the proposed model, the communicator is managing the media between both universes of interlocutors: the universe of decision making interlocutors and the subjects of development.

We find very soon that the model itself attempts to approach it and generates messages with a high level of efficiency, both financial as well as pedagogical or communicative.

Of course the instruments will depend on the characteristics of the massive interlocutor, and as some of these characteristics are large-scale illiteracy and bilingualism, we chose tools that facilitate responses to these conditions: multimedia tools.

We started from something that the massive interlocutor told us: "If I hear, I forget; if I see, I remember;

1927
1960
1963
1964
1967
1969
1970
1971
1972
1973
1974
1975
1976
1977
1978
1979
1980
1981
1982
1983
1984
1985
1986
1987
1988
1989
1990
1991
1992
1993
1994
1995
1996
1997
1998
1999
2000
2001
2002
2003
2004
2005
2006

if I do, I learn." So we incorporated practical drills into the teaching process, aimed at facilitating learning, adding them to graphic literary instruments and to audiovisual ones. And as for the information, given the progress of the last two decades in developing it, we tried using the Internet.

That brought us to the other problem, that of communicators for development. The so-called communication professional who graduates from a university is prepared, at best, for producing messages with a content which is emotional, self-expressive or manipulatory. Beautiful, with their own criteria of what beauty is, but without the key elements of pedagogic aesthetics: clarity and order.

The universities are not intent on forming professionals able to manage contents and produce messages of a cognitive type, and even less do they aim at development processes, let alone rural development processes. For this reason, graduates produce "pretty," "attractive" and "zippy" messages, similar to publicity messages, with emotional contents, but they are not prepared for producing messages that are simply clear, intelligible and useful for the receiver, with cognitive contents. On all the occasions we were asked to do communication for development, the first activity was to train the communicators that were needed.

It is common to hear of new educational technologies and refer to what is called "educational television," an expression in which television is the noun and the adjective that gives it its nuance, or qualifies it, is educational. We prefer to speak of audiovisual pedagogy, so that the noun is the pedagogical process and audiovisual the instrument that is adequate and efficient for the educational process. Our choice in all kinds of instrument selection is to "prioritize neurons over electrons."

In the field of information there is a similar problem. Generally, information technology experts easily manage signals between computers but not signals between sentient beings. So the messages transmitted between computers have low levels of intelligibility, of codes, of order, of audiovisual processing and of search systems adapted to the users. It is natural, they are IT experts and have not been prepared in communication, let alone in communication for development.

The experience in Argentina of the Postgraduate Specialization in Communication for Development, had a premature end, which occurred during the generalized crisis in the country.

The experiences of the Institute of Communication and Image of the University of Chile are incipient, and it is still necessary to adapt them to the local situation in which the costs of educational processes in the market are difficult to afford.

But the experiences accumulated up to now allow us to assert that the training of these communicators should be very different from what is usually offered and is devoted to the training of journalists or manipulators. It should be a much more rigorous training and less pseudo-artistic, thinking more of a communicator committed to the subjects of change and being less concerned about appearing on the screen or being in front of the microphone.

Calvelo Ríos, Manuel (2003) "Comunicación para el Cambio Social," FAO Regional Bureau for Latin América and the Caribbean. Santiago (Chile). Reprinted with permission.

EXCERPT FROM:
THE NEW COMMUNICATOR

By Alfonso Gumucio-Dagron

1998 A new communicator is usually someone who owes at least 50 percent of his or her qualification to a wide range of experiences that have little to do with his or her own academic background. What actually makes the "new communicator" is this mixture of experience in development, a special sensibility to work with communities, and knowledge of communication tools and technologies. A new communicator has to balance a very practical approach to social reality with the capacity to elaborate and conceptualize strategies.

The academic background is somehow irrelevant, given the fact that there are no institutions that provide specific training of this type. Educators, anthropologists and agronomists often make good communicators when they add to their field experience on development and community participation the knowledge of the communication process and the skills to handle information technologies. Journalists already have this knowledge, though limited to the media, but they can also become new communicators—enriched with a holistic vision of communication—if exposed to the experience of development and community work.

This is not to say that only interpersonal communication is needed in the context of social change. The community-based approach is often a result of total lack of access to information channels. It can be the only possible strategy given the extreme process of marginalization that some communities may suffer. Nonetheless, new technologies have recently opened enormous possibilities in terms of horizontal cultural exchanges that communities and individuals can develop across the world. The meaning of *community* may broaden to groups that have common interests though from different cultures. Access is gradually being granted (or taken by assault) by social groups and individuals that were previously marginalized.

The use of electronic media for social change has already seen an impressive evolution. Since the fifties many associations, unions, community groups and NGOs have challenged the dominant radio and television networks with small stations broadcasting towards specific communities. While bigger and bigger trusts are concentrating the control of the most influential mass media in the world, alternative networks of information and communication are flourishing, often supported by use of the Internet.

The challenges of communication are constantly evolving, as new possibilities but also new needs emerge. The new communicator has the capacity to navigate from one medium to another, to choose between multiple communication tools and adapt strategies to a particular situation. His or her experience may range from helping to strengthen union organizations to covering social issues for media stations, devising participation strategies for development projects at the community level, facilitating the networking of nongovernmental organizations and/or producing educational materials. This flexibility to use communication strategies in various cultural contexts provides training that is second to none.

The following could be the main premises for the new communicator:

1. The new communicator must be equipped with the understanding that *technology is a tool* and nothing else but a tool. Technology may support the communication process, but the latter should not be totally dependent on it. Also, it is important to understand that technology doesn't only involve computers, satellites and the Internet. A pencil is an astonishing piece of technology, and communication techniques that have proved their efficacy range from popular theater to community murals.

1927
1960
1963
1964
1967
1969
1970
1971
1972
1973
1974
1975
1976
1977
1978
1979
1980
1981
1982
1983
1984
1985
1986
1987
1988
1989
1990
1991
1992
1993
1994
1995
1996
1997
1998
1999
2000
2001
2002
2003
2004
2005
2006

2. The new communicator must deeply understand that communication for social change deals essentially with culture and a very special sensitivity is needed to support the process of social change in a developing world that has nothing else to hold on to than its *cultural identity*. Development and social change must be possible within a process of horizontal and respectful cultural exchanges.

3. The new communicator must be familiar with this concept: in communication for social change *the process is more important than the products*. In journalism, the articles, the video documentaries and the radio programs are valuable results for a skilled professional. But in social change and development, the process of communication *with* the people and *within* communities is more important than printed or audiovisual aids that may emerge from that dynamic. It is in the process of communication and participation that social change starts to happen.

Gumucio-Dagron, Alfonso. "The New Communicator," presented at the Communication for Social Change seminar organized by The Rockefeller Foundation, Washington, D.C., August 1998. Reprinted with permission.

COMMUNITY, DEMOCRACY, DIALOGUE AND RADICAL MEDIA

By John Downing

2001 ▪ Radical media are quite often referred to as community media and as democratic alternatives to media monopolies. However, both "community" and "democracy" are potentially very fuzzy words, a mere heartbeat behind "motherhood," typically signifying a "generally good thing." They urgently need anchoring by definition and critique to make them in any way useful.

▪ Some significant recent writers on democracy are reviewed to underscore the frequent failure to connect media to "strong" definitions of democracy. C.B. Macpherson's work is noted because his definition of developmental, counter-hegemonic power helps ground radical media in a unifying concept.

▪ The discussion of "conversation" as the leitmotif of democratic process is resumed, reaching more closely into the everyday role of media in the United States, and to some observations of Bakhtin and Freire on the term "dialogue."

The term "community" has been widely used as a catchall. It has had a localist sense ("This community stands firm on the issue of . . ."); a world-politics rhetoric ("the international community's stance against terrorism"); a professional sense ("the scientific community"); a politics-of-sexual-frankness usage ("community standards of decency") and a nostalgic sense hearkening back to a supposed era of harmony ("We need to recover a sense of community"). "Community" also commonly turns up as a way of attributing lockstep homogeneity of opinion to minority ethnic groups ("the Black community," "the Jewish community").

The term has also been used as a populist way to refer to subordinated social classes while avoiding the use of leftist jargon. It has also been used to avoid singling out any particular grouping among the poor. Thus the designations "community radio" and "community-access television" have been ways of defining these media as institutions responsive to demands and priorities from below (the working class "plus"[1] women "plus" minority ethnic groups "plus" lesbians and gays, plus . . .). Implicit in this use of "community" is the assumption that mainstream media are at the service of power (*how* is variously conceptualized).

Often many of these latter uses imply a seamless social tissue that is local, and therefore healthy, in contradistinction to a wider governmental reality that is foreign and unhealthy. This can easily slide into a right-wing version of anarchism and even forms of xenophobia. It also makes quite idiotic assumptions about the absence of class and other serious social rifts within the local tissue. It is, therefore, exceptionally hard to give the term "community" a lucid and exact sense.[2] Yet when the word is used as convenient verbal shorthand for the spectrum of the relatively dispossessed, or local realities, it is hard to think of a replacement.

Whichever way you cut it, the term persistently raises many more questions and dilemmas than it answers. Using it in relation to radical alternative media demands that its meaning be carefully defined in order to avoid the production of endless and pointless fog. Perhaps a viable meaning, pinpointing something genuinely important in social life, can be constructed through combining the inclusive populist meaning of the word with a sense of social connectedness over at least a generation, indeed with the local communication exchange and networks that have grown up over time.[3] But we must repeat: This connectedness is but rarely egalitarian or democratic on the local level. It may only seem so relative to transnational corporate power or the national state. Terms such as "community" media or "grassroots" media may easily conceal more than they reveal. They are stronger in what they exclude—mainstream media—than in what they signify.

"Democracy," as a term, knows only highs or lows: the mellifluent highs of political theorists and the lows of shabby practice, of procedure mongering and procedure flouting, vote fixing and vote interpreting, trashcan manifestos and demagogic politicos, tens of millions spent on TV blitzkriegs and secret polling.

Yet junking actually existing democracy, rather than struggling to improve it, is self-evidently no option. So our central question for the remainder of this segment of the discussion is what roles do radical media play in democratic processes? Especially, beyond formal democratic procedures at the national or regional level, how do they strengthen democratic culture in everyday life?

If we examine the huge political science literature on democracy for guidance, we find an immediate paradox. Quite often even those in favor of struggling to improve democratic processes have little or nothing to say about communication or media, except by silent implication or occasional throwaway reference. Let us take as examples three United States contributions to debate on democracy.

Held (1987), in an exemplarily lucid dissection of ten different models of democracy that he explicitly intends to encourage a broadening of democratic process, only begins to draw near to the issues of communication and media at the close of his book (283-89) when he addresses what he argues as the pressing need for a "double democratization," i.e., of both the state and civil society. Even Barber's (1984) very searching analysis of how to strengthen democratic life that centers on communication issues barely touches upon media as such, see below.

Touraine (1994), too, underscores the urgency of extending democratic culture to rescue us from the destructive centripetal tendencies he argues are driving

---

1 The effort becomes more and more tortured, as though the working class were composed entirely of straight white males.

2 See further Downing (1999a), on "community" in cyberspace.

3 See Putnam (1993) for an extended argument in this direction, based on Italy.

1927
1960
1963
1964
1967
1969
1970
1971
1972
1973
1974
1975
1976
1977
1978
1979
1980
1981
1982
1983
1984
1985
1986
1987
1988
1989
1990
1991
1992
1993
1994
1995
1996
1997
1998
1999
2000
2001
2002
2003
2004
2005
2006

us into a technological and market-driven instrumentalism, on the one hand, and spurring retreat into a closed world of communalist[4] cultural identities, on the other. He takes on some of the most difficult problems for democratic practice, such as majority-minority rights, the status of immigrants, women's equal participation, even the ramifications of the global North-South split. He adopts, indeed, the immigrant as emblematic of modern society's acute dilemmas of inclusion and extrusion. Like Rowbotham and Husband, he insists (315-16) that the only solution to so much disparity is democracy, because that "is where dialogue and communication take place. What measures the democratic character of a society is the intensity and depth of dialogue between personal experiences and cultures different from one another that are, moreover, responses, all of them specific and limited, to the same common quests (concerning human purposes)." Yet he too has just four pages (247-50) on the need to reconstitute the public sphere, in which he nowhere suggests how this might be done in practice with actual media, mainstream or alternative.

The unfortunate aspect of the political science literature's lacuna in the area of media and communication is that it is not the worst but often, like these, the most committed to democracy who seem to wander forever in a media-free desert. Some of the worst, admittedly, do scrabble around in media and elections, to the point in some cases of offering themselves as spin merchants to career politicians, which ranks as one of the more egregious forms of academic prostitution. But most just never get to the point at all.

It is absurd. It is as though the democratic process were conceived, as I have suggested elsewhere when discussing the standard tropes of political science (Downing 1996, Chapter 1 and *passim*), as composed of astute but entirely mute chessboard pieces,

---

4   I am using the word here in the sense in which it was used in public debate in India in the later decades of the 20th century, to denote the destructive focus on the supposedly homogeneous and embattled interests of particular segments of the nation. In India it was a matter of religio-political identities (Hindu, Muslim, Sikh), but the particular labels and cues vary from nation to nation.

Excerpt from: 'Is "Empowerment" the Answer? Current Theory and Research on Development Communication'
By Robert A. White

The current research on communication for development tends to stress, rightly I would say, that empowerment means affirming the dignity and value of one's own identity and re-evaluating the local culture. It also means resignifying the cultural institutions around one so that one's own cultural capital is given greater recognition and is seen as more valuable. The resignification is also important so that the price of changing power relations is not giving up one's own identity. With the premise that all cultural identities that contribute to justice and community are valued, the world needs a rich variety of cultural identities.

The concept of empowerment, as it has been developed so far, is, at best, incomplete and possibly dangerous if it is not oriented more clearly toward social responsibilities and service within society. Empowerment needs to be explicitly located within a broader framework of commonly agreed upon parameters of human and social equity. The history of development theory is littered with paradigms, such as modernization, that have ended with the empowerment of one set of interests to the exclusion of other groups. Thus, the strong state and popular alliances of the modernization paradigm clearly favoured economic and technical entrepreneurs as the "engines" of development to the exclusion of lower-status urban and rural sectors.

One framework of public responsibility that has broad cultural and political acceptance is the language of human and collective rights. Human rights are constructs with a formulation that can be discussed, further developed, and adapted to different cultural contexts. Human rights also have a long history of legal and moral foundation. The continued strong debate about the foundations of human rights is one indicator that these are cultural symbols that can be interpreted somewhat differently by different social groups.

1927
1960
1963
1964
1967
1969
1970
1971
1972
1973
1974
1975
1976
1977
1978
1979
1980
1981
1982
1983
1984
1985
1986
1987
1988
1989
1990
1991
1992
1993
1994
1995
1996
1997
1998
1999
2000
2001
2002
2003
2004
2005
2006

The major human rights charters, beginning with the 1948 U.N. Universal Declaration of Human Rights and including the series of human rights conventions of the U.N. to the present, have made steady progress in clearly defining human rights and getting support of national governments (Linden, 1998). Increasingly, the abuses of power of governments are being critiqued in terms of the human rights agreements that these states have signed. This is providing some common framework of policy for international relations, for national development and for the defence of movements of minority groups. In many ways, human rights have proved to be a better framework for policy than the language of the "New World Orders," which was much too vague and binary for today's perception of world politics.

Most of the theory of communication and development is from the point of view of government or NGO agencies involved with an intervention to help less powerful groups. If one enters into the life situation of the rural and urban poor, there is, of course, a question of respect for identity, but their life is one long, desperate search to obtain a job or insure production and marketing of products, get children into schools, find adequate housing, get proper medical attention and the money to pay for it and meet a host of other needs. To get these resources, people build alliances with resource agencies such as government or NGO agencies providing services. Having the support of a family network or a clientelistic network of politician friends is extremely important. In rural areas or huge urban slum areas, good services simply are not available or are overwhelmed with requests that they cannot meet. These clientelistic systems survive by providing individual favours. They continue to exist because of a hierarchical structure of power. There is no such thing as the universal right to education or the right to health. It depends on who you know and your access to the "private" control of resources.

Movements to change this system seek instead to affirm a series of universal rights. That is, these various movements are attempting to resignify power from being a clientelistic response to helping a friend to being a service to citizens. This also means reorganizing the whole system of services from one in which people depend on paternalistic government agencies to one in which people have access to services because they have a right to them. Among these rights are the right to information and the right to communicate. The new movements seek to affirm this culture of universal human rights, at least within the movement, and to avoid being co-opted back into the culture of power and clientelism.

It is at this point that one may ask if "empowerment" and "power" are, in themselves, a sufficient basis for policy and for theory of communication and development. Perhaps more important are the culture of service, the culture of dialogue and community, and the culture of human rights (Hamelink, 1994: 284-316). A strategy of empowerment needs, perhaps, to be located within a broader framework of universal human rights. Too often, when movements do achieve the empowerment they are seeking, they feel that they have arrived at their goal. They have redefined their own identity and they are widely accepted. The logic of empowerment does not give them a sense of urgency to use their power to serve others in a similar situation. In contrast, the logic of a discourse of human rights or other universalistic discourse affirms that no right is secure unless it is universally respected and implemented. When one enters into the histories of responses to people's needs for services, usually an organizational structure has been created which insures that these services are provided and that those providing services are made accountable to the public. We need a kind of research that follows through the history of interventions, movements and people's organizations to see how the reforms sought have been sustained over a long period of time. Empowerment may be the answer in terms of an immediate response to a situation, but we need to see how this strategy has worked over a longer period of time. We need to see if we are arriving at universal respect for all human rights throughout the society.

References

Hamelink, Cees. *The Politics of World Communication*. London: SAGE Publications, 1994.

Linden, Ank. *Communication Policies and Human Rights in Third World Countries*. Amsterdam: University of Amsterdam, 1998.

anticipating each other's moves, and forging countermoves, in total silence. In other words, the majority of political analysts' models of democracy, because without communication, are without humans, too. Does this not risk caricaturing the simplification inherent in model construction?

I do not mean to say that such theorists have nothing at all for us. It merely means that their obsession is with structures and issues, laws and institutional procedures, all of which are certainly important but—in the absence of communicating actors and groups—resemble the machine without even its ghost. Patently unrealistic: For how, in a large-scale society, does its democracy communicate without also using media? If, however, all this quite inexorably present communication process is not discussed simply for the reason that it is automatically oiled and glistening, nonproblematic and therefore a trivial dimension for professional political scientists, why will they not tell us where lies this magic transparent land so we can all go see how it works?

There are a few voices within political science that address media seriously. Dewey and Lippmann did so,[5] though their perspective receives a needed corrective in the work of Raymond Williams.[6] The two former judged media in general as providing the necessary information and communication opportunities for effective deliberation to take place. Williams also argued that media, once freed from their overwhelming subjection to private firms or the state and opened up to mass participation, could stimulate and sustain a common culture and a lively democracy. Particularly important, he took the issue beyond straight "information," per the rather ratiocinative focus of Habermas, Dewey, Lippmann, and wrote very tellingly of the need to embrace fiction and the imaginative realms of culture, the "structures of feeling" (Williams 1977, 128-35) that are integral to a nation's or a community's public conversation.[7]

The difficulty with even these three thinkers is that while they state very attractive positions concerning communication and democracy, they do not address the messy world of actuality. They do not engage closely with the tiresome and daunting problems of trying to democratize actually existing mainstream media. So while that goal remains one of immense importance, until or unless there is substantial movement in that direction, the role of radical alternative media of all kinds will continue to be extremely significant.

This is not to say that mainstream media contribute nothing at present to democracy. That would be an ill-considered and lumpish distortion. The organized far right in the 1980s and 1990s, in the United States and elsewhere, has made great play of denouncing mainstream media as leftist pulpits, so that it would be a huge error for the left simply to contribute to a "media-attack culture" without, simultaneously, very noisily indicating fierce opposition to the extreme right's project to wipe out all expression of dissent to its left.

We still must face up to the fact that mainstream media make no pretense of offering themselves up to any form of public control, short of consumers' letters, or consumers' refusal to buy them or switch them on. As means of public leverage or democratic influence, these various responses are either feeble or indiscriminately blunt. In small communities, they may be used to some effect, but not in nations with a large population. Indeed when these levers are pulled, it seems likely to be by tightly organized extreme-right fundamentalists putting pressure on a firm to pull TV advertising from a program they hate.[8] "Consumer sovereignty," however often blazoned as a democratic fix-all, bears no relation to practical media realities.

Can we say that, by contrast, radical alternative media are the chief standard bearers of a democratic communication structure?

---

5   See Hardt (1993).

6   See Sparks (1993).

7   See similarly Edward Thompson's assertion, cited toward the close of this chapter, that "fully one-half of culture...is affective and moral consciousness."

8   The history of this tactic on the part of the extreme right goes back at least to the *Red Channels* saga of the McCarthy era (Barnouw, 1990, 121-28). .

The argument here is yes; that, while flawed, immensely varied and not necessarily oppositional, many such media do contribute in different degrees to that mission, and more truly than the mainstream, in ways that are often amazing, given their exceptionally meager resources.

It helps to support this judgment to reflect on C. B. Macpherson's (1973, Ch. 3) analysis of the basis of democracy, even though he has nothing directly to say about media at all. His concepts nonetheless provide a pivotal schema by which to interpret the roles of radical media. He has proposed, as central to our understanding of the basic purpose of power in a democracy, "developmental" power, the opportunity for members of the public "to use and develop [their] capacities" (42). Developmental power represents the positive possibilities for human achievement inherent in cooperative social life, which, up to the present, the construction of economic and political life most often sidelines.

His low-key and apparently innocuous language is actually much more momentous and challenging than it appears at first blush. It has as its ground his conviction that the public's "capacities" to create viable societal arrangements are infinitely more capacious than cynics and elitists will allow, but also that the public's ability to activate them is widely shackled. The shackles may include, most obviously, malnutrition, homelessness and illiteracy, but also lack of access to the means of production as a result of the division of power between capital and labor. They also encompass lack of protection against arbitrary attack on one's body or one's liberty. (For further explication, see Macpherson 1973, 59-70.)

He uses the term "extractive" power in the opposite direction, to denote both the power of capital over labor and also the very concepts of power customary among modern philosophers and resonant with the capital-labor relationship. These theorists almost universally define power as the ability to impose your agenda on other people. "Democracy"

in this light is then best understood as far more than a set of agreed procedural rules of debate and negotiation, important as those are; if Macpherson is correct, democracy at its best entails a cultural, political and economic setting in which developmental power flourishes. The concept of developmental power may be used to build on the notions of counterhegemony and alternative public spheres, and has an easy symbiosis with the hallmarks of many social movements.

Radical alternative media serve as developmental power agents in a number of senses. Without idealizing them, they are much more central to democracy than commentators bemused by the easily visible reach and clout of mainstream media will typically acknowledge.[9]

First, they expand the range of information, reflection and exchange from the often narrow hegemonic limits of mainstream-media discourse. This is in part by their very number. Second, they are media that frequently try to be more responsive than mainstream media to the voices and aspirations of the excluded. They often have a close relationship with an ongoing social movement and thus fairly spontaneously express views and opinions extruded from mainstream media or ridiculed in them. They are quite often in the lead in addressing issues that only later get noticed by mainstream media. Third, they do not need to censor themselves in the interests of media moguls, entrenched state power or religious authority. Fourth, their own internal organization is often much more democratic than hierarchical..... And lastly, some of these media fulfill the innovative role that Raymond Williams ascribed to what he termed

> formations; those effective movements and tendencies, in intellectual and artistic life, which have significant and sometimes decisive influence on the active development of a culture, and which have a variable and often oblique relation to formal institutions (Williams 1977, 117).

---

9   Kellner (1990, 207-222) is a notable exception.

1927
1960
1963
1964
1967
1969
1970
1971
1972
1973
1974
1975
1976
1977
1978
1979
1980
1981
1982
1983
1984
1985
1986
1987
1988
1989
1990
1991
1992
1993
1994
1995
1996
1997
1998
1999
2000
2001
2002
2003
2004
2005
2006

Putting these elements together, it makes every sense to see radical media as agents of developmental power, not simply as counterinformation institutions and certainly not as a vapid cluster of passing gnats and spats.

To be blunt, however, we are faced with a key problem still, or rather two. One is the level of abstraction of these concepts, for although they are a necessary stage in understanding the roles of radical media, they are not sufficient. We need to link these overall angles of vision with more immediate practicalities. The next two segments will address these in significant measure, but the second problem we need to re-examine more closely is equally practical, namely public conversation, dialogue, talk, communication networks, popular culture, all of which have much to do with democracy and a democratic culture.

However, the contributions we will examine to help us do this also do not address radical media but rather focus more generically on the relation between public communication and developmental power. Nonetheless it is the argument of this book that what media could be is often much better realized in alternative public spheres, so the fact that these writers do not themselves address radical media does not particularly matter.

Two major writers who directly focused on the notion of dialogue, with definite implications for the democratic roles of radical alternative media, are Freire (1970, 1972, 1974) and Bakhtin (1981). Their contributions are on quite different, but ultimately complementary, planes.

Freire, primarily concerned with literacy education for public empowerment, put oppressive structures and political engagement against them at the center of the communication process (McLaren and Lankshear 1994). In his concept of *conscientizaçao*[10] he emphasized eliciting students' intelligence and perceptions rather than delivering "superior knowledge" to empty subjects. Thus, in teaching literacy he insisted on using the everyday language and images of the students (poor farmers or city-dwellers) and rejected prepackaged language and images pulled from the scholar's authoritative shelf. This was in order to engage dialogically from the start with the learners' reality, to encourage their expression of opposition to their exploitation and material poverty. Literacy he saw, not as a technique enabling students to fit into the world as it is, but to change it, for students to challenge the history of their own shaping. He readily acknowledged, too, the opportunity for the educator to grow in this process as well as the student.

Freire solely and entirely concentrated on face-to-face interactivity and never extended his vision further to encompass media (De Lima1979, 98ff.). However, if for dialogic educator we read radical media activist, Freire's pedagogy can serve as a core philosophy within which to think through the nature of the activist producer–active audience relationship.[11] It proposes a democracy of the communication process, once more acknowledging the audience as joint-architects with the media producers, radically unlike the "they watch it, so we must be giving them what they want and need" ideology of commercial media. While Freire tended not to differentiate different groups among the

---

10 Roughly, evoking a critical perception of reality. A term Freire used in his earlier work, *mutismo*, later rendered in his writing as "the culture of silence" (of the poor), which he perceived as "rooted in the favorable spoils of Latin American land tenure" for the rich (De Lima, 117ff.), is unfortunate in that it implies still the need for

the outside intellectual to arrive in order to start people thinking. James C. Scott's work, already discussed, raises serious questions about this perception. Nonetheless, Freire maintained a mixed attitude on this score, insisting for example that clay dolls and popular songs were as much culture as internationally famous artworks (De Lima, 125). His contemporary compatriot Glauber Rocha's beautiful 1962 film *Barravento*, set in the Northeast, evinces much of the same dualism of perception. I am grateful to Dr Cacilda Rêgo for advice on interpreting Freire's work.

11 See Huesca and Dervin (1994) for a utilization of Freire's notion of "theoretically guided and self-reflective action" (63), which requires "a synthesis of local process and global referent through reflective practices" (ibid.). This untamed terrain" as they term it (65), enables, they claim, the entrenched opposition in much social theory and analysis between structure and agency to be transcended, with great benefit to the understanding of alternative media. A transition "from the conceptual to the practical world" (64) seemingly compels, or at least enables, this to happen. Yet while they correctly note (65-67) that Latin American alternative media theory, up to the date of their article, did not engage very much with the question of how communication has its effect, their own focus on praxis equally constitutes a claim, not an actuality.

oppressed (Weiler 1994), Findley (1994, 118) proposes that the learning processes Freire championed can nonetheless be an important means for social movements "in their struggle to achieve and maintain common understandings of the problems they intend to address, and thereafter to work toward continually renewed consensus on strategies, tactics and procedures." The role for radical media in this process is obvious, underscored by Rowbotham and by Husband in the public-sphere discussion above.

Bakhtin, focusing on novels[12] as a vital form of popular, even subversive, narrative communication in the modern era, particularly stressed the competing discourses and voices ("heteroglossia, raznorechie") represented in them. His observations, perhaps uncontentious to the casual reader, were penned during the depths of Stalinist repression in the Soviet Union, when enormous pressure was applied to public expression in order to force it into a deadening ideological uniformity. *Raznorechie* was a notion in deep disfavor, and indeed Bakhtin wrote his essay during a six-year political exile in an obscure little town far away from the Kremlin, in the wilds of Kazakhstan. (Some of his close intellectual associates perished in the camps.)

It was within that stifling context that Bakhtin critiqued the limitations of poetic discourse, authoritative discourse and mythological thinking (Bakhtin 1981, 297, 342-48, 369-71), in favor of "internally persuasive discourses." By this he meant the day-to-day language and voices of the general public, emerging from the public's experiences and in their great variety. His comment on the raunchy marketplace language in Rabelais's novel *Gargantua and Pantagruel*, which we shall discuss in the next chapter, is a strong example. He urges (1981, 345ff.) that the novel should always give these internally persuasive discourses pride of place over against official, uniform speech issuing from on high. He writes:

> In the history of literary language, there is a struggle constantly being waged to overcome the official line with its tendency to distance itself from the zone of contact [i.e., everyday life, JD]... The internally persuasive word is half-ours and half-someone else's. Its creativity and productiveness consist precisely in the fact that such a word awakens new and independent words...It is freely developed...It enters into interanimating relationships with new contexts.

Bakhtin's emphasis on this dialogue of voices within the novel (or the soap opera) could equally be applied to radical media as a dialogic, democratic public sphere within popular culture. Furthermore, his angle of vision on this art form underscores a recurring theme in this book's argument, already noted in the discussion of popular culture and of Iris Marion Young and Raymond Williams: the centrality of emotion and imagination in radical media, the peril of seeing their role as informative in a purely ratiocinative sense. A democratic culture cannot only subsist on rational argument … .

Both Freire and Bakhtin provide support for a dialogic vision of radical alternative media, embedded in the push and pull of everyday life, not sectarian, that at their best are engaged with "audiences" at their most active, producing as well as receiving media content.

Barber (1984) argues for a series of procedures that can be undertaken to strengthen the democratic process, and in so doing nails his colors very firmly to the mast on the subject of communication.[13] "At the heart of strong democracy is talk" (1984, 173). Indeed he is quite lyrical on the subject:

> ...Politics...would ossify completely without its (i.e. "talk's") creativity, its variety, its openness and flexibility, its inventiveness, its capac-

---

12 We perhaps tend to think of the novel as "frozen" communication, radically distinct from the unpredictable process at the heart of Freire's work, but that in turn implies that the author's intentions lock the novel's readers into a single interpretation of it. The discussion of Janice Radway's work earlier in this section suggests that to be a very inadequate understanding of how audiences operate.

13 Barber's proposals approximate Held's two final models of the democratic process, the participative and the democratic autonomy models (Held, 1987, 254-64, 289-99). .

1927
1960
1963
1964
1967
1969
1970
1971
1972
1973
1974
1975
1976
1977
1978
1979
1980
1981
1982
1983
1984
1985
1986
1987
1988
1989
1990
1991
1992
1993
1994
1995
1996
1997
1998
1999
2000
2001
2002
2003
2004
2005
2006

ity for discovery, its subtlety and complexity, its eloquence, its potential for empathy and affective expression, and its deeply paradoxical... character...[174].

In line with some of the other thinkers already cited, he stresses (*ibid*.) that "strong democratic talk" requires listening as well as uttering, that it is affective as well as cognitive and that its linkage to intentions draws it out of speculation and into the realm of real-world practice. "Listening is a mutualistic art that by its very practice enhances equality....[Talk] can build community as well as maintain rights and seek consensus as well as resolve conflict" (175, 177). He proceeds

EMPOWERMENT COMMUNICATION
Excerpt from: '*Pushing the Development Boundaries a Step Further: From Participatory to Empowerment Communication*'
By Paolo Mefalopulos

Empowerment communication is a concept that intends to draw attention on the issue of power even in those approaches more prone to be on the side of the people, such as participation. The power of words is central to maintain and strengthen other kinds of power and domination, often resulting in hegemonic realities. Communication can assist development by advocating and adopting models that genuinely require dialogue as a form of collaboration among all stakeholders and that genuinely require sharing knowledge as the best form of mutual education. However, even when paved by the best intention, communication cannot be the road to people's empowerment, unless a new paradigm will provide a plausible option for refusing or negating an external imposition to any given community or group of people. A paradigm that must break from the heritage of the positivist faith in science, which justifies the superiority of a certain perspective in the social realm.

The new paradigm must include some of the basic assumptions of constructivism that, by going beyond the question about the existence of a single verifiable reality, acknowledge that reality can be defined and interpreted in many different ways, all equally valid. This statement has led to a number of controversial issues on cultural relativism, which have been debated extensively. They will not be discussed here again, but by oversimplifying the debate, I could state that the most acceptable case for accepting an outside intervention would be when there are violations of the human rights charter as adopted by the United Nations.

Empowerment communication intends to be a step further towards a development that gives control over their own lives to the very people who have traditionally been made passive, or partially active, recipients of those efforts by those in charge of development policies. While still within the boundaries of the current paradigm, empowerment communication also advocates its demolition, basing it on the genuine application of democratic ideals, which should now pay more attention to the universal human rights regardless of other factors, e.g., nationality, religion and socio-economic status.

Participatory communication is a concept and a practice holding great potential, provided that the system within which this occurs will allow authentic democratic reforms. People's capability and opportunities to shape their own destiny is an ideal supported by virtually everybody, including the decision makers at the highest level. Still most people around the world do not have this option. Why? Trying to answer this question is not easy, and maybe not even possible, and, most of all, it is not the focus of this study. Hence, I would like to keep this as a question meant to challenge the reader's mind, planting the seed of doubt. Participatory communication and, even more, empowerment communication, is not just about decision making in the development context, but it affects every aspect of the social, economic and political sphere of life.

Mefalopulos, Paolo (2002) "Pushing the development boundaries a step further: From Participatory to Empowerment Communication". paper presented at IAMCR 2002, Barcelona, Spain. July 2002. Copyright © 2002, Paolo Mefalopulos. Reprinted with permission of the author.

(178-212) to define nine functions of what he terms strong democratic talk.

However, there are two missing items in his argument, arguably related to each other—media[14] and democracy beyond the locality. He sees media technologies as aids toward effective public debate in neighborhood assemblies. Media for him seem to be technical channels rather than social institutions. In his final chapter (273-81, 89-90), he does explore, a little gingerly, how democratic activity might deploy local television, videotex, electronic balloting and favorable postal rates for informational print media. But he does not grapple at all with national realities outside neighborhoods, let alone with the international media dimensions of a functioning democracy.

Communication theorists Carey (1995) and Schudson (1997) have presented opposing views[15] on the question of "conversation," "talk" and "democracy." For Carey, drawing heavily upon Dewey, and somewhat on Habermas, spontaneous conversation about policies and politics is the very kernel of democracy. By the close of the 20th century, however, Carey argues, a culture of political conversation is more or less extinct because mainstream media have almost ceased to prime the public's conversational pump. Political polling and manipulated television spectacle have largely replaced politics. Hence, democracy itself is withering on the vine. He does not address the question of social movements, although it seems from the music of his argument that it would naturally flow in that direction. Nor does he address alternative media.

Schudson's critique is concerned to inject a certain sour realism into Carey's impassioned call. He suggests, with corroborative evidence from both New England town meetings and the American Constitutional Convention, that while conversation in general is the very stuff of society, democratic debate is a specific form of conversation that needs to be procedurally based to work. Thus it cannot evince the quality of spontaneity that Carey sees as its soul. Furthermore, Schudson proposes, democratic debate typically issues in printed media (a petition, a notice, a law), rather than being sparked by them.

Their disagreement is apposite to this phase in our discussion of public sphere, social movements, community and democracy. It addresses exactly the intersection between the social, the political and the communicative (three conceptual categories that have heuristic value only up to the point at which they are not reified). Schudson wins the argument so long as we accept that the formal structures of democracy are its core. Yet while we certainly cannot pretend that they are not there, or are irrelevant or purely oppressive, a democratic culture is a necessary part of the democratic infrastructure. A democratically organized economy would be just as much so.[16] Without that culture, congressional proceduralism may entirely replace the rules of debate, and indeed the polling management and public relations manipulation that Carey deplores may easily be victorious. That is precisely why the energy of popularly based social movements—not manipulated Jacqueries[17]—is central to democratic culture, and why the media of such movements are at the core of the process. It is a pity Carey did not address them.

Valuable further insight is provided by Friedland (1996), who primarily discusses specific United States case studies of Internet use in the democratic process.[18] His conceptual starting point is an interesting combination of civic-engagement and social-capital theory with network theory. In the course of his argument,

---

14 His only fleeting references to media in the body of the book are slighting ones to mainstream media, to the danger of letting specialists, such as journalists, do our democratic communicating for us (193), or to the inevitable degeneration of language into an instrument of elite rule once we hand it over to "the media, the bureaucrats, the professors, and the managers" (197).
15 I am indebted to my colleague Chuck Whitney in the Journalism Department at the University of Texas for drawing my attention to this debate.

16 A serious discussion of what this might mean in practice is beyond our scope here.
17 The Rush Limbaugh phenomenon in the mid-1990s was a mediatic instance of what I mean here. I repeat, the wider question of fascist social movements and populist ultra-rightism will be addressed later.
18 The case studies on cyberdemocracy in Tsagarousianou et al. (1998) are well worth reviewing.

1927
1960
1963
1964
1967
1969
1970
1971
1972
1973
1974
1975
1976
1977
1978
1979
1980
1981
1982
1983
1984
1985
1986
1987
1988
1989
1990
1991
1992
1993
1994
1995
1996
1997
1998
1999
2000
2001
2002
2003
2004
2005
2006

Friedland underscores the very important point that the purpose of democracy is not only deliberation but also governmental action, whether on the national or the local level, or a combination.

With this in hand, he stresses that democratic conversation consists not only of people sitting around talking politics (Carey), or of legislators deliberating policy (Schudson), but of engaged citizens combining in a variety of roles to review what they may achieve with a given project—and then carrying out the project, often debating and modifying it as they go. Those combined roles may, in the United States, be those of federal, state, city or county legislators; civil-service roles at any level of government; large or small think-tank roles; academic research-institute roles; community and movement activist roles; netizen or media activist roles. There may be serendipity in debate and policy execution, or the reverse.

This conversation/deliberation is not abstract, unbundled from everyday practice; it is both national and local, and especially—Friedland stresses this point—it centrally involves ongoing relationships of reciprocity and trust.[19] This links straight back to the discussion earlier of communication networks. Thus Friedland's approach to the issues suggests a rich and complex integration of levels and aspects of talk/conversation, democratic culture, media technology and political action.

To wrap up this discussion, let us examine a very interesting argument from what Rodríguez (forthcoming) describes as a nonessentialist feminist position. She specifically takes up the question of praxis and democracy in relation to radical media. She argues that we need to break away from "a modern understanding of citizenship as expressed by voting and protesting...[and] from thinking of political actions and social movements as linear, continuous and conscious processes toward a common goal." Instead, based in part on her own research in Colombia and Nicaragua,

and partly on the theoretical work of Mouffe (1992a, b, c) and of McClure (1992), she proposes that we reconceptualize the impact of alternative media in terms of their impact on the participants' sense of themselves and their potential as human beings. She summarizes what may happen as follows:

It implies having the opportunity to create one's own images of self and environment; it implies being able to recodify one's identity with the signs and codes that one chooses, thereby disrupting the traditional acceptance of those imposed by outside sources; it implies becoming one's own story teller ... ; it implies reconstructing the self-portrait of one's own community and one's own culture; it implies exploring the infinite possibilities of one's own body, one's own face, to create facial expressions (a new codification of the face) and nonverbal languages (a new codification of the body) never seen before; it implies taking one's own languages out of their usual hiding place and throwing them out there, into the public sphere and seeing how they do, how they defeat other languages, or how they are defeated by other languages...(1996, 2).[20]

The final, very basic topic to include under the democracy heading is cost. Access to media is governed, over and above the codes mainstream media lay down for the public's participation (talk shows, game shows, opinion-poll results, establishment "experts"), by how expensive media technologies are. In early 19th century Britain, for instance, the Stamp Tax, described by its opponents as "a tax on knowledge," lifted the price of a daily newspaper to seven pence, far beyond anything a worker could afford, and was clearly designed to price workers out of the public realm.

At various periods in time, print technology has been fairly cheap. Until, for example, the outset of the 1840s,

---

19 Putnam's (1993) study of civic engagement in Italy interestingly puts this latter dimension in a long historico-cultural framework, far beyond individual lifetimes.

20 See Huesca and Dervin (1994) for a very comparable argument about the centrality of praxis in the analysis of radical media, and Huesca (1995) for an empirical study of Bolivian miners' radio stations from that perspective (although in the second piece he uses the term "process" instead of praxis).

the United States. boasted a considerable number of labor newspapers in the incipient industrial centers of Boston, New York, Philadelphia and Baltimore (Schiller 1981). The advent of the rotary technique brought with it machinery costs that mostly crushed the labor press. It would be fair to say that the spread of photocopiers since the 1970s has worked in the opposite direction (cf., Enzensberger 1974). Indeed, the very strict control of access to them within the old Soviet Union reflected rather exactly the then political elite's anxieties about the uses to which dissident communicators could put them.[21] The rise of cheap video cameras and cassette recorders had a similar trajectory, although in their earliest, most expensive phase, print was still necessarily the format of choice for low-cost radical media. Public-access television is one result. The expanding uses of the personal computer and the cheap modem since the mid-1980s are a further case in point... .

However, there are also radical formats that are not technologically driven and expensive, such as graffiti, buttons, T-shirts, song, street theater, performance art, many of which we will discuss in the Panorama section. If the public is not to be priced out of communicating via media, then low-cost formats become all the more crucial for democratic culture and process.

Summary: We have examined the rather fluffy notion of community and some approaches to expanding the democratic process. Oddly, the wing of political science that favors a deepening and strengthening of democracy rarely addresses the role of media in the cultural and procedural mesh that would be needed, including Barber, who examines communication up to a point but does not really engage with media. Even those who do, such as Williams, rarely engage with the messy world of everyday praxis, and Keane (1991), who follows Williams's basic diagnosis, similarly offers only rather implausible proposals for implementing mainstream media

change.[22] Carey and Schudson's debate about the role of "conversation" in the democratic process is resolved to a considerable extent, though he makes no specific reference to it, by Friedland when he links together deliberation, policy action and the question of ongoing reciprocity, and reviews roles that may be played by Internet communication in this linkage. Obviously, the notions of counterhegemony, alternative public sphere, dialogism, which we have already examined, are in their various ways also addressing these problems, and they ultimately all center on what Macpherson would term the expansion of developmental power.

Too often, these three are written and spoken about as though each were an entirely separate realm. The high-art/low-art distinction, which strictly segregates art from media, is really quite extraordinarily tenacious. We shall examine some approaches that do not fall into the trap of segregating information, reasoning and cognition from feeling, imagination and fantasy, and which thereby focus our attention on how media may enhance developmental power.

Dance, street theater, cartoons, posters, parody, satire, performance art, graffiti, murals, popular song and instrumental music are ... only some of the most obvious forms of radical media whose communicative thrust depends not upon closely argued logic but upon their aesthetically conceived and concentrated force. For easily understandable political reasons, tremendous weight has often been placed in the analysis of radical media on their role in transmitting to the public information that has been systematically censored, distorted or dismissed in mainstream media. This "information/counterinformation" model (cf. Baldelli 1977; Jensen 1997) is an important one but has sometimes overflowed into a purely logocentric definition of alternative media: lies/truth, cover-up/facts, ideology/reality.

We need to begin by acknowledging that part of the 19th and 20th century background to this issue is the

---

21 See the discussion on *samizdat* media in the former U.S.S.R. and Soviet bloc, not least the success of Polish oppositional movements in evading photocopier controls.

22 See, for example, the review of his book by Scannell in *Media, Culture and Society* (1992). .

1927
1960
1963
1964
1967
1969
1970
1971
1972
1973
1974
1975
1976
1977
1978
1979
1980
1981
1982
1983
1984
1985
1986
1987
1988
1989
1990
1991
1992
1993
1994
1995
1996
1997
1998
1999
2000
2001
2002
2003
2004
2005
2006

long history of ultradogmatic "alternative" media associated with leftist political currents of one stripe or another, whose rhetoric was only too often dipped in concrete and judged by its lenino-theological exactitudes, or similar pseudoreligious jargon named for some revolutionary figure (Kropotkin, Trotsky, Mao Zedong, Che Guevara, etc.). A language of lead and an incantation of enshrined phrases were the result, inordinately reassuring to the faithful and somewhere between sophomoric and soporific to those outside the magic circle: "Capitalism is in its death-agony … ." "The proletariat, under the wise guidance of the Party, … ." "Stormy applause greeted the General Secretary's speech … ." "The heroic struggles of the people …" "Imperialism, as comrade Lenin so brilliantly observed, …" "The U.S.S.R. is a degenerated workers' state … ." "The renegade revisionist clique …" "Communism will win … ." "The masses … ."

Thus the liveliness and zest that ideally should be synonymous with radical media have been conspicuous by their frailty within the highly influential Marxist and Leninist political tradition over the past 150 years.[23] For this reason alone, it is essential to recuperate the urgency of artistic flair in planning or evaluating radical media projects.

References

Baldelli, P. *Informzione e Controinformazione*. Milan, Italy: Mazzotta, 1977.

Bakhtin, M. M. *Rabelais and His World*. Bloomington, Ind.: Indiana University Press, 1981.

Barber, B. *Strong Democracy: Participatory Politics for a New Age*. Berkeley, Calif.: University of California Press, 1984.

Carey, J. "The Press, Public Opinion, and Public Discourse," in T. Glasser and C. T. Salmon, eds., *Public Opinion and the Communication of Consent*. New York: Guildford, 1995, 373-402.

De Lima, V. A. "The Ideas of Paulo Freire on Communication and Culture," Ph.D. dissertation. University of Illinois at Urbana, Institute for Communication Research, 1979.

Downing, J. *Internationalizing Media Theory: Transition, Power, Culture: Reflection on Media in Russia, Poland, and Hungary, 1980-1985*. London: Sage, 1996.

Enzensberger, H. M. "Constituents of a Theory of the Media," in H. M. Enzensberger, ed., *The Consciousness Industry*. New York: Seabury, 1974, 95-128.

Findley, P. "Conscientization and Social Movements in Canada: The Relevance of Paulo Freire's Ideas in Contemporary Politics," in P. L. McLaren and C. Lankshear, eds., *Politics of Liberation: Paths from Freire*. New York: Routledge, 1994, 108-122.

Freire, P. *Pedagogy of the Oppressed*. New York: Herder and Herder, 1970.

Freire, P. *Cultural Action for Freedom*. Harmondsworth, U.K.: Penguin, 1972.

Freire, P. *Education for Critical Consciousness*. London: Sheed &Ward, 1974.

Friedland, L. A. "Electronic Democracy and the New Citizenship," *Media, Culture*, & Society, 1996, 18 (2), 185-212.

Held, D. *Models of Democracy*. Stanford, Calif.: Stanford University Press, 1987.

Jensen, C. *20 Years of Censored News*. New York: Seven Stories Press, 1997.

Keane, J. *The Media and Democracy*. Cambridge, England: Basil Blackwell, 1991.

McCLure, K. "On the Subject of Rights: Pluralism, Plurality, and Political Identity," in C. Mouffe. Ed., *Dimensions of Radical Democracy: Pluralism, Citizenship, and Community*. London: Verso, 1992, 108-125.

McLaren , P. L., and C. Lankshear, eds. *Politics of Liberation: Paths From Freire*. New York: Routledge, 1994.

MacPershon, C. B. *Democratic Theory: Essays in Retrieval*. London: Oxford University Press, 1973.

Mouffe, C. *Dimensions of Radical Democracy: Pluralism, Citizenship, and Community*. London: Verso, 1992a.

Rodríguez, Clemencia. *Fissures in the Mediascape: A Comparative Analysis of Citizens' Media*. Creeskill, N.Y.: Hampton Press, in press.

Schiller, D. *Objectivity and the News*. Philadelphia, Pa.: University of Pennsylvania Press, 1981.

Schudson, M. "Why Conversation Is Not the Soul of Democracy," *Critical Studies in Mass Communication*, 1997, 14 (4), 297-309.

Touraine, A. *Qu'est-ce Que la Démocratie?* Paris: Fayard, 1994.

Weiler, K. "Freire and a Feminist Politics of Difference," in P. L. McLaren and C. Lankshear, eds., *Politics of Liberation: Paths from Freire*. New York: Routledge, 1994, 12-40.

Williams, R. *Marxism and Literature*. London: Oxford University Press, 1977.

23 ·

EXCERPT FROM:

REFORMULATING COMMUNITY AS A COMPLEX SOCIAL SYSTEM

Complex Systems Thinking

By David J. Connell

2001 Complex systems thinking refers to theories and concepts associated with theories of complexity. also known as "dynamical systems theory," "the theory of complexity," "non-linear dynamics," "network dynamics"; self-organisation, autopoiesis, and dissipative structures, chaotic attractors and fractals are some of its key theories and concepts (Capra 1996). Complex systems thinking is subsumed by the more general term *systems thinking*, which also includes open systems theories, soft systems methodologies and complex systems thinking.

1. The Paradigm of Complex Systems Thinking

Complex systems thinking is presented as an alternative paradigm to those presented by Jessie Bernard (1973), suggesting that this "new language" for understanding the connectedness, relationships and context of complex, highly integrative systems (Capra 1996) may also influence the study of community. Complex systems thinking may be characterised, generally, using four components: unpredictability, the nature of change, wholeness and adaptation (Turner 1997). The first key characteristic is that complex systems, by their nature, are "inherently unpredictable." In contrast, the possibility of predicting an event relies on two assumptions: "that the chain of causes is recoverable and that the universe is fundamentally deterministic in its nature" (Turner 1997, xiii). Hence, the first fundamental outcome of adopting a complex systems thinking approach is that efforts directed at prediction may be replaced by efforts directed at understanding such events in different ways. According to Turner, "unpredictable" does not necessarily mean "unintelligible," or "inaccessible to knowledge and understanding."

Turner's second key characteristic of complex systems thinking is its relevance for understanding change. What has previously been accounted for as a "margin of error" is now revealed as feedback associated with nonlinearity. This provides an alternative view of the "forces" attributed to social change such as modernisation and urbanisation. Price (1997, 13), for example, places evolution within the context of systemic global properties: "Theorists of complexity assert that local rules produce global properties, that systems move in the direction of increased variation and complexity, and there is an 'edge of chaos' that strikes a balance between stagnation and anarchy." The underlying logic is that societies reach critical stages, i.e., bifurcation points, at which new paths open up for them leading to new levels of complexity.

Complex systems thinking also changes the way the whole system is viewed, and specifically how macro-micro relations are viewed. Conventionally, a system is defined as an integrated whole whose essential properties arise from the relationships between its parts (Capra 1996, 27). However, this kind of holism, when viewed as a reduction to the whole, is just as problematic as the reductionism complexity theorists oppose. "Holism typically overlooks the interactions and the organisation, whereas complexity pays attention to them" (Price 1997, 10). In this, the third characteristic of the complex systems thinking paradigm is that society is contextualised in its own local-global relations. By emphasising the relationships that exist within the system, rather than the existence of the system as a whole, complex systems thinking downplays, to some extent, the inherent difficulty of delineating system boundaries.

The concept of adaptation, another key characteristic of complex systems thinking, derives from these local-global relations. The system adapts to perturbations arising from its environment, i.e., its "higher" layers, which give rise to another perspective of stability. "A complex adaptive system is a system in which interactions give rise dynamically to emergent phenomena

1927
1960
1963
1964
1967
1969
1970
1971
1972
1973
1974
1975
1976
1977
1978
1979
1980
1981
1982
1983
1984
1985
1986
1987
1988
1989
1990
1991
1992
1993
1994
1995
1996
1997
1998
1999
2000
2001
2002
2003
2004
2005
2006

that are resilient in the face of perturbations" (Smith 1997, 55). In this context, it is the system's ability to adapt that gives rise to stability. And the context, or environment, sets out the constraints that influence which properties of the system may emerge.

This description of complex systems thinking is sufficient to distinguish it from Bernard's paradigms of community study. In comparison, complex systems thinking complements Bernard's overarching paradigms while encompassing the four analytical frameworks. As such, complex systems thinking should be considered more than just an alternative to current frameworks; it represents a possibly new way to understand and to research community. Although an alternative to existing paradigms, complex systems thinking may be viewed as grounded within the scientific tradition (Price 1997). In recognising the need to modify reductionism, complex systems thinking responds to the limitations presented above. Premised upon nonlinearity, it reconstructs rather than deconstructs the classical scientific model.

A brief account of the principal theories of complexity lends insight to how a nonlinear approach can be pursued, and, subsequently, how such an approach may be applied to the study of community. Interaction, as will be seen, is a critical concept of complex systems thinking. Beginning with a basic definition of system as groups of *interacting*, interdependent parts (Costanza et al., 1993), the concept appears consistently throughout complex systems thinking and is the key for many disciplines that have embraced complexity (Smith 1997). Subsequently, it will be shown how interaction provides the theoretical link between complex systems theory and community.

2. Theories of Complexity
Emergence, a strong, intuitive construct central to complex systems thinking, is presented here to introduce two theories of complexity, namely, self-organisation and dissipative structures. Emergence describes the phenomenon of seeing spontaneous order *emerge*

from disorder (as opposed to "planned" change). More specifically, emergence refers to the process in which patterns of global-level structures arise from interactive, local-level processes (Mihata 1997).

> What defines such an emergent property is that it cannot be understood merely as an aggregative product of the entities or parts of the system but arises through their organisation. Interaction often yields … forms that cannot be understood through simple linear decompositions of its systems into its interacting parts. The problem of studying these complex interactions has become the focus of research on complex systems—systems in which interactions among parts are marked by nonlinear dynamics. (Smith 1997, 55)

This description of emergence encapsulates the intuitive characteristics of complex systems thinking described above. Moving forward, it gives context to theories of self-organisation and dissipative structures. Self-organisation is a theory pertaining to the characteristic ability of the whole system to respond to disorder. Dissipative structures, a more detailed aspect of self-organisation, is a theory of how the system manages the balance of order and disorder, that is, it is a theory of system self-regulation. As such, emergence, self-organisation and dissipative structures are interrelated and may be used to describe different aspects of structure, process and pattern within complex systems.

3. Self-organisation
Self-organisation is a fundamental characteristic of complex systems. The "self" part means that this ability stems from within the system, rather than from external imposition. The "organisation" part speaks to the organising of behaviours and structures, that relate to pattern. In complex systems thinking, pattern of organisation is a configuration of relationships characteristic of a particular system and systemic properties are properties of a pattern (Capra 1996). It is the spontaneous emergence of pattern is known as self-organisation.

Several important characteristics define self-organisation (Capra 1996). First, modes of behaviour, in addition to structures, may be created through the process. Second, self-organising systems operate far from equilibrium, that is, in conditions produced by continual disturbances from without or self-amplifying (via positive feedback loops) from within the system. This condition provides a constant flow of energy necessary for self-organisation to take place. Third, as per the definition of complex systems, all models include nonlinear interconnectedness of components resulting in feedback loops. Thus, self-organisation contrasts with a more conventional, mechanistic understanding of systemic change. The latter relies upon external conditions to explain the parameters of change among system components. Identifying emergent, or *global*, properties of self-organising systems marks a shift from an interest in quantity to quality, from detail to patterns. By looking at patterns of interaction, one is more interested in system behaviour than in time-specific values of variables. The phenomenon giving rise to pattern is called a strange attractor, which is produced by the repetitive iteration of very simple rules that govern interaction (Eve, et al. 1999). Most importantly, "strange attractors are not detached from the system, but very precisely *in* and defined by the process that it shapes and governs" (Eve et al. 1999, xxiii).

4. Dissipative Structures

The theory of dissipative structures is the most influential, detailed description of self-organising systems (Capra 1996). A dissipative structure is not just an outcome of a process; it is both process and structure; it is an evolving, interactive process that is temporarily manifested in globally stable structures. This notion of structure is fundamentally different from any conventional sense of the term, which may be seen as static and (literally) concrete. Dissipative *structure*, on the other hand, exists only in the context of flows that occur in system states far from equilibrium. Prigogine coined the term "dissipative structures" to describe the co-existence of continual flow and structural stability.

According to Prigogine's theory, dissipative structures not only maintain themselves in a stable state far from equilibrium, but may even evolve. When the flow of energy and matter through them increases, they may go through new instabilities and transform themselves into new structures of increased complexity.

Prigogine's detailed analysis of this striking phenomenon showed that while dissipative structures receive their energy from outside, the instabilities and jumps to new forms of organization are the result of fluctuations amplified by positive feedback loops. Thus amplifying "runaway" feedback, which had always been regarded as destructive in cybernetics, appears as a source of new order and complexity in the theory of dissipative structures. (Capra 1996, 89)

Dissipative structures are the "structural" qualities of the system. But these "structures" are openly functional structures through which energy, matter and information continually flow. In this, the term dissipative structure addresses the paradoxical co-existence of change and stability: "The pattern of organization is always embodied in the organism's structure, and the link between pattern and structure lies in the process of continual embodiment" (Capra 1996, 160). Hence, dissipative structures function as a *self-regulating* mechanism managing the balance between order and disorder. This self-regulation is what gives rise to self-organisation. According to Kay (1999, 3), "systems tend to get better and better at 'grabbing' resources and utilising them to build more structure, thus enhancing their dissipating capability." In this, the capacity and survivability of the community derives from its ability to make "ever more effective use of the resources" to build more structure.

In summary, the theories of self-organisation and dissipative structures both shape and govern complex *social* systems. Complexity, therefore, is both a theory of change (process) and a theory of structure; the two are inseparable. The whole "structure" derives from the interaction of simple rules, i.e., it emerges from the process in which patterns of global-level

1927
1960
1963
1964
1967
1969
1970
1971
1972
1973
1974
1975
1976
1977
1978
1979
1980
1981
1982
1983
1984
1985
1986
1987
1988
1989
1990
1991
1992
1993
1994
1995
1996
1997
1998
1999
2000
2001
2002
2003
2004
2005
2006

structures arise from interactive, local-level processes (Mihata 1997). In this, pattern of interaction is not a thing, but a property, simultaneously process and structure; it is precisely *in* and defined by the complexity of the system.

Community and Complex Systems Thinking

Social interaction is a significant aspect of the commonly held view of community. As early as 1915 the processes of social interaction were purported to be an essential focus of community studies (Kaufman 1955,10). Of greater significance within the field of community studies, one may look to Hillery's classic review of various definitions. He identified three common attributes of community, namely, locality, common ties and social interaction (Dasgupta 1996). However, in attempting to sort out the relative merit of each attribute (of social interaction specifically), one may ask if Hillery's tripart definition of community revealed the essence of community by searching for commonality among various definitions. Or, alternatively, was something different created as an outcome of the process?

There is reason to suggest that what Hillery derived as a common understanding of community was, in effect, a hybrid which obscures the relationship between social interaction and community. This is first revealed by distinguishing between two distinct although related concepts associated with community study: "the community" and "community." As Bernard (1973) explained, the former is associated with settlement, which places emphasis upon *locale*; the latter, "community," retains both common ties and social interaction. In effect, this distinction begins to sort out various meanings of community that may be derived from Hillery's definition. Firstly, it helps to think of community as something other than a settlement; locality, however, is never dismissed entirely. Further, in setting aside the settlement aspect of community, it is not necessary to distinguish among types of community, e.g., rural versus urban. The next step in sorting out the meaning of community is to separate common

ties from social interaction. This is to be premised upon the work of the interactional theorists, most notably within community studies by Wilkinson (1990) and Warren (1978). The following sections present this line of thinking for the purpose of isolating the relationship between social interaction and community. Subsequently, community will be conceived as a system of social interaction.

1. SOCIAL SYSTEM THEORY

A general understanding of social systems thinking begins by examining a basic definition of system. According to Hall and Fagen (1980, 75), a system is "a set of objects together with relationships between the objects and between their attributes." In this definition "objects" are the parts or components of the system; "attributes" are properties of objects; and "relationships" are those that tie the system together, that make the notion of "system" useful. Of the 94 definitions of community Hillery analysed, "community as system" appeared in only one, although it is likely that the concept was implicit in other definitions.

An early adopter of the use of "system" to denote society and social processes was the biochemist Lawrence Henderson (Lilienfeld 1978; Capra 1996). For Henderson, all factors in a social system are interactive and mutually dependent (Lilienfeld 1978,13-14). According to Buckley (1967), three types of social system models have been identified: mechanistic, organic and process. The premise of the mechanistic model is a system of elements in mutual interrelations, "which may be in a state of 'equilibrium,' such that changes in the elements are counterbalanced by changes tending to restore it" (9). The organic model, derived from biology, is characterised by a "'mutual dependence of parts' which makes society like an organism" (12). The Parsonian model, which Buckley characterised as a mix of mechanistic and organic, is presented as a conventional view of social systems. As per Bernard's frameworks, she associates Parsons' systems-based approach with the ecological analytical framework and, more generally, within the paradigm of structure-functionalism. The following draws from Talcott Parsons' *The Social System* (1951) to present the main points of his theory.

The Parsonian model underlies many approaches to the study of community, either directly or indirectly. Parsons defines a social system as processes of *interaction* between actors; the structure of the social system is a network of relations between the actors involved in the interactive process (25). The first necessary distinction to make about Parsons' theory is that the social system is but one of three aspects that complete a system of social action. The other two systems are the personality systems of the individual actors and the cultural system that is built into their action. Reducing the elementary component of the system to the actor and his situation, "it is the *participation* of an actor in a patterned interactive relationship which is for many purposes the most significant unit of the social system" (25). While there has been strong criticism of his work, e.g., it promotes the status quo and does not allow for change (Colomy 1992; Martindale 1965), Parsons' "patterned interactive relationship," as an elementary component of his theory, provides a link to complex systems thinking.

In addition to the Parsonian model, it is worthwhile to review the essential characteristics of the process model of social systems as another link between theories of community and complex systems thinking. The process model may be traced back to thinkers such as Park (Buckley 1967). Although not as well received as the other models, the process model bears similarities to principles of complex systems. Quoting Buckley:

> In essence, the process model typically views society as a complex, multifaceted, fluid interplay of widely varying degrees of intensities of association and dissociation. The "structure" is an abstract concept, not something distinct from the ongoing interactive process but rather a temporary, accommodative representation of it at any one time. These considerations lead to the fundamental insight that sociocultural systems are inherently structure-elaborating and changing; for some, the terms 'process' and 'change' were synonymous. ... societies and groups continually shift their structures as adaptations to internal or external conditions. Process, then, focuses on the actions and interactions of the components of an ongoing system, such that varying degrees of structuring arise, persist, dissolve, or change. (1967,18)

It is worth noting that for Buckley " modern" systems theory did not advance much beyond open systems theories. His views were, nevertheless, explicitly couched in complexity.

2. COMMUNITY AS A PATTERN OF CHANGE

With change, as with community, it is important to distinguish between two aspects: "changes" *within* type of social structures, which occur when processes and products in a structure become different but the basic structural type does not change; and "changes" *of type*, often marked by the emergence of new structural types that handle some or all of the function once taken care of by the older type (Colomy 1992, 50). Typologies of social systems, that is, change *of types*, are embedded in the rural-urban continuum, which is embedded in theories of social change. Modernisation, for example, illustrates this. It is described as a linear development perspective focussed on "formalisation of previously informal social control and social support structures, increased impersonality and anonymity, and the demise of *gemeinschaft*-like social relation" (Krannich & Greider 1990, 64). Along this path, society passes through types of organisational forms (Krannich & Greider, 1990) or, in other words, types of social interaction, one of which is community. Change and community, then, are linked through direction of change (e.g., market processes destroying community) and patterns of interaction (e.g., *gemeinschaft* and *gesellschaft*). Thus, community *as a pattern of interaction* is a concept that can be linked to complex systems thinking.

1927
1960
1963
1964
1967
1969
1970
1971
1972
1973
1974
1975
1976
1977
1978
1979
1980
1981
1982
1983
1984
1985
1986
1987
1988
1989
1990
1991
1992
1993
1994
1995
1996
1997
1998
1999
2000
2001
2002
2003
2004
2005
2006

3. COMMUNITY AS DIFFERENT FROM A SENSE OF COMMUNITY

The meaning of community, however, is overlaid with qualitative aspects, particularly when urban is contrasted with rural, as it is within typology-based frameworks. Roy Buck shares this view, as accounted by Bernard:

> Roy Buck was one of the few sociologists who rebuked his colleagues for looking at the rural community through inappropriate paradigms: "Traditional scholarship," he charged, "has tended to look at the American community through stereotypes growing out of European thought." He wanted to dispel "the traditional image of rural life as being wholly rooted in a European peasantry and 'elysian bliss' or an erosion of this once-upon-a-lifetime mentality." He tried to counteract the romantic idealization of the countryside. He decried the family-farm ideology that pervaded so much thinking about rural communities. (1973, 96)

Wilkinson adds, "We need to pare down the concept [of community] to its bare bones to see how much excess baggage can be shed without missing the essence of community and to get rid of the provocative ideological and normative undercurrents that give community a bad name" (1990, 153). This line of thought, as will be explained below, strengthens community as an analytical category as well as community's theoretical link with complex systems thinking.

The separation of community from the sense of community reveals the importance of social interaction as the essence of community. Building upon Schmalenbach's work, Wilkinson (1990) stated, "community arises without self-consciousness as people *interact*, and awareness of self, grounded in community and awareness of community, follows" (1990, 153; emphasis added).

> Schmalenbach (1961) nails this down even better than Toennies does by proposing an addition to Toennies' classic typology. Between *gemeinschaft* (or community) and *gesellschaft* (or

society), he says, an important category is missing. Community, as described by Toennies, is a natural and preconscious state, and society refers to rationally contrived and consciously perceived relations. What is missing, says Schmalenbach, is a category for shared responses to community. (Wilkinson 1990, 153-154)

Schmalenbach calls the part missing between community and society *communion*. "Community itself is there, as it were, before communion. It arises naturally in social interaction with or without being acknowledged or celebrated" (1990, 153). This distinction underlies Wilkinson's view that there is no good reason to equate the sense of community with community itself.

Separating communion from community effectively strengthens the theoretical link between complex systems thinking and community by isolating social interaction from common ties (as per Hillery's definition). But what of locality? Community interaction, as an important type of social interaction, occurs where people live and conduct their daily activities, and this tends to be mainly on the local scene—even in a highly mobile society (Wilkinson 1996). This, as has been shown, is consistent with the argument supporting the relevance of community, namely, that "people still live next door to others, they eat, sleep, love, hate, avoid, or seek one another in a given locale" (Bernard 1973, 187). It is also consistent with a systems perspective of locality, which either implicitly or explicitly (Bailey 1990) includes physical space-time in the definition of system (see, for example, Miller 1978). Thus, community retains locality as an implicit feature, but not as the dominant feature as it is with the settlement-based view of "the community."

4. COMMUNITY AS AN INTERACTIONAL SYSTEM

With regard to community as social interaction, Wilkinson stated: "There is more to it than interaction, and not all interaction is community; but *interaction is the essential ingredient*. Any theory of community must first be a theory of social interaction" (Wilkinson

1990, 152; emphasis added). This derives from Warren (1978, 408-422), who argued that the interactional approach, based on community as a dynamic process of social interaction, has much more to offer than does the older functional view of community as a "concrete collectivity" (i.e., the systems approach). Generally, Warren and Wilkinson's conceptions of community appear very similar to the process model described above. More specifically, they make a case for sorting out several aspects of community. First, they distinguish between community and communion, that is, between community and a sense of community. Next, they identify the community system as only one system that contributes to the sense of community. And, along the same lines, this interactional view draws upon measures of community to assess the extent to which community embraces a total society. This latter point is necessary to overcome earlier conceptions of community as concrete totalities, stemming from a criticism of functional approaches to the study of community.

What Wilkinson achieved may seem simple and reductionist (which it is), but it also strengthens a systemic conception of community in a number of ways. Surprisingly, while his argument is well grounded as a challenge to Parsonian functional analysis, he effectively revitalised Parsons' definition of a social system: *a system of processes of interaction between actors*—not to mention the earlier conceptions of process models of social systems. First and foremost, the interactional approach is a processual, systems approach; the social act is an ongoing complex of acts and responses (Lilienfeld 1978, 206). The interactional approach, having grown "out of a crisis in community theory in the wake of the passing of the long-dominant functional model" (Wilkinson 1990,154), also marked a shift away from a mechanistic worldview. By dismissing the functional model, they were marking the shift from function to organisation, which represents "a shift from mechanistic to systemic thinking, because function is essentially a mechanistic concept" (Capra 1996, 27). In this, the

relationship between the parts and the whole has been reversed, and the whole cannot be understood by analysis. This critical view of community reflects Wilkinson's concern for "wholeness" and "a functionally integrated whole," as well as Warren's concern about the "concrete collectivity." These criticisms, however, are not against a systemic view of community, as they are against the mechanistic, functional analysis of systems.

Furthermore, Wilkinson and others use the term "field" rather than system. Their concern is that "system" strictly defines a functionally integrated whole concerned with boundary maintenance and reinforcing social order (Wilkinson 1991). Such a view of system, however, runs counter to an understanding of a complex system. The definition of field, on the other hand, may be interchanged with many aspects of complex systems thinking. For example, field is variously described as "a process of interrelated actions through which residents express their common interest in the local society;" "theories [that] emphasise the dynamic, emergent aspects of community life"; "directed more to the dynamic processes that create and alter community structure;" and "an unbounded whole with a constantly changing structure" (Wilkinson 1991, 2, 33, 35). Several aspects of these descriptions relate to complex systems thinking. It appears, then, that the interactional view of community may also benefit from a reformulation of community as a complex system.

This distinction between "system" and "field" may seem trivial to those who strongly associate systems theories with structure-functionalism. For this paper, however, the distinction is significant. Primarily, it is consistent with Bernard's critique of existing paradigms of community study and substantiates her question, "is normal-science research guided by the classic [community] paradigms adequate for the purpose, or are we in need of a scientific revolution in this area to supply us with more appropriate paradigms for the postcity world of today?" (Bernard 1973:179).

1927
1960
1963
1964
1967
1969
1970
1971
1972
1973
1974
1975
1976
1977
1978
1979
1980
1981
1982
1983
1984
1985
1986
1987
1988
1989
1990
1991
1992
1993
1994
1995
1996
1997
1998
1999
2000
2001
2002
2003
2004
2005
2006

References and Suggested Further Reading

Bailey, Kenneth D. 1990. *Social Entropy Theory.* Albany: State University of New York Press.

Bernard, Jessie 1973. *The Sociology of Community.* Glenview, Illinois: Scott, Foresman and Company.

Buckley, Walter 1967. *Sociology and Modern Systems Theory.* Englewood Cliffs: Prentice-Hall, Inc.

Capra, Fritjof 1996. *The Web of Life.* New York: Doubleday.

Colomy, Paul (Editor) 1992. *The Dynamics of Social Systems.* London, UK: Sage Publications.

Costanza, Robert, Bryan G. Norton, and Benjamin D. Haskell (Eds.) 1992. *Ecosystem Health: New Goals for Environmental Management.* Washington, D.C: Island Press.

Dasgupta, S. (1996). "The Community: Definitions and Perspectives," in Satadal Dasgupta. ed. *The Community in Canada: Rural and Urban,* Landham, Maryland: University Press of America, pp. 3-86.

Eve, Raymond A., Sara Horsfall, and Mary E. Lee 1997. *Chaos, Complexity, and Sociology: Myths, Models, and Theories.* Thousand Oaks: Sage Publications.

Hall, A.D. and R.E. Fagen 1980. "Definition of a system," in Chen et al. (Eds.), *The General Theory of Systems Applied to Management and Organisation, Vol I.* Seaside, CA: Intersystems, for Society of General Systems Research.

Kay, James 1999. "An Ecosystem Approach for Sustainability: Addressing the Challenge of Complexity." http://www.fes.uwaterloo.ca/u/jjkay.

Kaufman, Harold F. 1955. "Toward an Interactional Conception of Community," *Social Forces.* 38(1):8-17.

Krannich, Richard S. and Thomas R. Greider 1990. "Rapid Growth Effects on Rural Community Relations," in Luloff, A.E. and Louis E. Swanson (Eds.), *American Rural Communities.* Boulder: Westview Press.

Lilienfeld, Robert 1978. *The Rise of Systems Theory.* Toronto, ON: John Wiley and Sons.

Martindale, Don (Ed.) 1965. *Functionalism in the Social Sciences.* Philadelphia: The American Academy of Political and Social Science.

Mihata, Kevin 1997. "The Persistence of 'Emergence,'" in Eve, Raymond A., Sara Horsfall, and Mary E. Lee, *Chaos, Complexity, and Sociology: Myths, Models, and Theories.* Thousand Oaks: Sage Publications.

Miller, James Grier 1978. *Living Systems.* McGraw-Hill, Inc.

Parsons, Talcott 1964, Fifth edition. *The Social System.* The Free Press of Glencoe.

Price, Bob 1997. "The myth of postmodern science," in Eve, Raymond A., Sara Horsfall, and Mary E. Lee, *Chaos, Complexity, and Sociology: Myths, Models, and Theories.* Thousand Oaks: Sage Publications.

Smith, Thomas S. 1997. "Nonlinear dynamics and micro-macro bridge," in Eve, Raymond A., Sara Horsfall, and Mary E. Lee, *Chaos, Complexity, and Sociology: Myths, Models, and Theories.* Thousand Oaks: Sage Publications.

Turner, Frederick 1997. "Foreword: Chaos and Social Science," in Eve, Raymond A., Sara Horsfall, and Mary E. Lee, *Chaos, Complexity, and Sociology: Myths, Models, and Theories.* Thousand Oaks: Sage Publications.

Warren, R.L. 1978. *Perspectives on the American Community.* Chicago: Rand McNally & Company.

Wilkinson, Kenneth P. 1991. *The Community in Rural America.* Westport, CT: Greenwood Publishing Group, Inc.

Wilkinson, Kenneth P. 1990. "Crime and community," in Luloff, A.E. and Louis E. Swanson (Eds.), *American Rural Communities.* Boulder: Westview Press.

Wilkinson, Kenneth P. 1979. "Social Well-being and Community." *Journal of the Community Development Society.* Vol.10(1):5-16.

Wilkinson, Kenneth P. 1970. "The Community as a Social Field." *Social Forces.* 48(3):311-322.

Connell, David J. "Reformulating Community as a Complex Social System," unpublished paper submitted as partial fulfilment of the qualifying exam, Rural Studies Ph.D. Program, University of Guelph, Ontario, Canada, February 2001. Printed with permission of the author.

EXCERPT FROM:
COMMUNITY AND COMMUNITY DEVELOPMENT
Communities as Types of Human Groups

By Donald Voth

2001 Our focus is, of course, upon groups defined by place, but there is always the residual form of community, which we refer to as "communities of interest." According to much of the literature on the community, and especially to those writing in the "eclipse" tradition of the 1960s and 1970s, the former has gradually given way in importance to the latter. One place where this distinction has been incorporated as a major conceptual device is in the literature on the "human dimension" of natural resources, and natural resource management. The term "community" itself provides a link between biological scientists and social scientists. As public lands managers increasingly realise that their responsibilities are as profoundly affected by the human communities which they serve and which surround them as by the physical environment and the biological communities, a whole field called the "human dimension" has emerged. The link has been especially easy to advocate in context of ecosystem management and comprehensive "assessments," which serve as information resources for long-range public lands planning (Voth, et al., 2000).

Communities of Place

The underlying assumption is that, in spite of all the technology of communication and transportation that has reduced the cost of space, all of the modernisation, development and globalisation that has occurred, all of Warren's "Great Change" that has transformed America's communities, place still matters, that the local community is, in fact, a very important level of social, economic and political organisation in modern society.

The term "community" is used in a generic sense and does not mean one specific form or level of geography or another. It does not necessarily mean an incorporated place, though it could. Nor does it necessarily mean a neighbourhood, though it could. Communities can be nested, that is, a neighbourhood can be considered a community, as well as the larger city or town within which that neighbourhood or community is located. The specific geographic definition is a matter of convenience, and some of these definitions are quite clear and distinct whereas others are vague and indistinct. Still, all have as their primary referent, people who share a common place, together with the infrastructure, services and institutions of that place. This is not only the preferred definition for this paper but also happens to be the one feature most common to the wide variety of existing definitions of community. As Bell and Newby summarise Hillary's comprehensive discussion of the definitions of community, "Thus a majority of definitions include, in increasing importance for each element, the following components of community: area, common ties, and social interaction" (1974, 29).

Communities of Interest

These have also been referred to as "functional communities." The term refers to those groups which share characteristics of community excluding living in a common place. As such, the term is very broad and includes such things as occupational groups, various interest groups, organisations, etc.

Webber (1963) said: "The communities in which he [a contemporary American urbanite] associates and to which he belong are no longer only the communities of place to which his ancestors were restricted; Americans are becoming more closely tied to various interest communities than to place communities, whether the interest be based on occupational activities, leisure pastimes, social relationships or intellectual pursuits. Members of interest communities within a freely communicating society need not be spatially concentrated (except, perhaps, during the formative stages of the interest community's development), for they are increasingly able to interact with each other

1927
1960
1963
1964
1967
1969
1970
1971
1972
1973
1974
1975
1976
1977
1978
1979
1980
1981
1982
1983
1984
1985
1986
1987
1988
1989
1990
1991
1992
1993
1994
1995
1996
1997
1998
1999
2000
2001
2002
2003
2004
2005
2006

wherever they may be located…spatial separation or propinquity is no longer an accurate indicator of functional relations; and, hence, mere locational pattern is no longer an adequate symbol of order."

The "Good" Community

Community Development as a field of practice is necessarily normative, as is any profession. It assumes that there is such a thing as a "good" community, or at least "good" community processes, as compared to a "bad" community or "bad" community processes. The early literature on Community Development went much further. It seemed to be based upon the assumption that democracy itself was dependent upon a "good" form of community at the local level, in the local communities and neighbourhoods. Thus, Arthur Morgan's 1942 book, "The Small Community," carried the subtitle "Foundation of Democratic Life," which was consistent with Louis Wirth's extraordinarily negative assessment of urban life (1938).

Warren's "Great Change" and the "Eclipse of Community" literature all imply that there was, once in the past, a "good" community, which has been or is being lost due to mass society and bureaucratisation. Community Development, especially that focused upon process, implies that there is, out there, a better community which can be achieved, one which has an enhanced capacity to meet the challenges confronting it as a community. Planners and architects, when they discuss the community, inevitably imply that they know something about what the good community would be like. "Sustainability" advocates imply that they know something about what the sustainable community would be. Many of the service professions which are now focusing upon the community also imply that they know something about what the good community would be when they, often very casually, use the term "community capacity."

So, what are some of these normative parameters in the literature about community? Before briefly reviewing the literature, it is important to note that we are not on slippery ground—the grounds upon which normative judgements are made demand their own, external justification. For each and every one, one may legitimately ask "why?" Upon reflection, the reader will find, though, that some may actually be justified as instrumental. They are, or seem to be, necessary to achieve some other objective. Thus, Luloff and Swanson would argue that some level of democratic decision making is essential for the community to have "agency" (1992).

Roland Warren confronted the issue directly from a philosophical framework in his 1970 essay "Toward a Non-utopian Normative Model of the Community," which has been published and reprinted in a number of different forms. After a brief discussion of social science literature dealing with the normative approach to community, he identifies, as key dimensions to consider: (1) community autonomy; (2) community viability; and (3) wide distribution of decision making, or the broad distribution of community power. In another essay published the same year under the title "The Good Community: What Would It Be?" he identified the following as the relevant dimensions to consider when thinking about the good community:

Existence of primary group relationships. Quoting from Baker Brownell's *The Human Community*, he says, "A community is a group of people who know one another well," implying, thereby, not only knowing one another in the respective, specialised relationships of the market place, but knowing each other "as persons" (1973, 168).

Autonomy. Decisions as to what goes on in the community should, as much as possible, be made by the people in the community themselves, not by outsiders or other layers of government.

Viability. By viability, Warren meant "the capacity of local people to confront their problems effectively through some type of concerted action" (1973, 470).

Power distribution. Recognising that all studies of community power find it very unequally distributed, which may not be saying any more than that leadership does exist, Warren simply notes the bias in Community Development and most community literature toward democratic structures and democratic decision making. Luloff and Swanson have much more recently dealt with the dysfunctions of unequal power distribution in their excellent essay about community agency and disaffection (1992).

Participation. Most people who concern themselves with the community believe that there should be more rather than less participation. But how much? There is, of course, no easy answer but it is certainly true that the nature and rates of participation are a key element in any consideration of the good community. Participation is simultaneously a norm or goal in its own right and instrumental in that it is necessary for effective decision making to occur.

Degree of commitment. Clearly, commitment to the community of place varies, and probably declines as communities of interest become relatively more important. Still, it is clear that there must be at least some people with at least some level of commitment to the local community for it to be a good community.

Degree of heterogeneity. This is, of course, a controversial issue. Warren pulls his punches, saying, "It has simply been accepted as a value that it is better for people to live in communities which are more or less a cross-section of the population than to live in economically or racially or ethnically segregated communities" (1973, 472).

Extent of neighbourhood control. Considering communities to be nested, with neighbourhood communities existing inside the larger communities, this simply means community control at the lowest level possible.

Extent of conflict. While it is no longer agreed that the good community should have no conflict, the key issue is the community's capacity to effectively manage the conflict which exists.

From a psychosocial point of view, Cottrell wrote an influential essay early in the formulation of the War on Poverty and its Community Action strategy. He defined the competent community as;

> here conceived as one in which the various component parts of the community: (1) are able to collaborate effectively in identifying the problems and needs of the community; (2) can achieve a working consensus on goals and priorities; (3) can agree on ways and means to implement the agreed upon goals; and (4) can collaborate effectively in the required actions" (1977, 548).

The dimensions which he identifies for consideration are commitment, self-other awareness and clarity of situational definitions, articulateness, communication, conflict containment and accommodation, participation, management of relations with the larger society, and machinery for facilitating participant interaction and decision making.

Bromley contrasts two different and somewhat incompatible conceptions of the good community, the sociological and the economic, associating such things as community autonomy and the capacity of the community to take independent action with the "sociological view," and having a viable economic base and economic development with the "economic view" (1970).

Community planners and architects do, necessarily, have a concept of what the community ought to be like. Jane Jacobs' influential book *The Death and Life of Great American Cities* (1961) is literally loaded with value statements about what the good community should be like, and what has been abandoned and lost by the forms of urban planning and management which she so thoroughly criticised. The current "new urbanism" literature is similar—cars are bad, walking is good, heterogeneity is good, living near one's work is good, the form of the European peasant community is good, the dispersed form of settlement more commonly found in the United States (sprawl) is bad, etc., etc. (Jacobs; Simonds). Indeed, it is very hard even to find, in the literature on community planning and

1927
1960
1963
1964
1967
1969
1970
1971
1972
1973
1974
1975
1976
1977
1978
1979
1980
1981
1982
1983
1984
1985
1986
1987
1988
1989
1990
1991
1992
1993
1994
1995
1996
1997
1998
1999
2000
2001
2002
2003
2004
2005
2006

community architecture treatments which even try to take a detached, objective perspective. For all of the assertions about the good community found in this literature and practice, one is always tempted to ask "Why?" "On what evidence?"

"Agency": The Essence of Community Development

WHAT IS "AGENCY"?

The one fundamental assumption of community development is that what happens at the community level is important—that it counts for something and, even more importantly, that communities might have the capacity to make decisions and take actions themselves. This assumption has both a scientific and a practical component. Scientifically it means that, in the analysis of human behaviour, communities—or "the community"—constitute a logical unit of analysis, above and beyond others, like individuals, families, institutions, firms, regions, nations or whatever. Practically it means that the community is an appropriate arena in which to try to accomplish things, also over and above the level of individuals, families, firms, etc., etc.

Bhattacharyya's somewhat dense but excellent discussion refers to agency as follows:

> Agency means the capacity of a people to order their world (de Certeau, 1986; Giddens, 1984; Inden, 1990), that is, the capacity to create, reproduce, change, and live according to their own meaning systems, the powers effectively to define themselves as opposed to being defined by others. Or, as Giddens (1984:14) observed, it is "to be able to 'act otherwise,'" that is, to be "able to intervene in the world, or to refrain from such intervention, with the effect of influencing a specific process or state of affairs." Agency is the antithesis of dependency, a condition devoid of any internal dynamic. The value premise of community development is that people have the right to agency, and the distinctive purpose of community development is to safeguard, and where impaired or lost, to reconstruct it. For any activity (be it enticing industries to a small town, organizing peasants, mobilizing for minority or gender rights, providing elderly care, agitating for environmental protection, cultural rights, or betters schools) to be called community development, then, the activity must be animated by the pursuit of solidarity and agency.

> Defining community development this way—the development of such social relations as are increasingly characterized by solidarity and agency—has the advantage of aligning community development with mainstream intellectual pursuits in the humanities and social sciences. It also opens up a vast field for community development action and research on the processes of erosion of solidarity and agency and the methods for reconstructing them. (1995, 61; see also Luloff & Swanson, 1992)

PROCESSES ESSENTIAL FOR COMMUNITY AGENCY

There are five processes that are essential for a community to act. To a certain extent, they do occur—well or poorly—in all communities anyway. These are: (1) leadership; (2) the operation of organisations; (3) the involvement and mobilisation of citizens; (4) goal setting, planning and decision making; and, finally, (5) action or implementation. This is what leads to community outcomes. Community outcomes are either content outcomes or process outcomes. Content outcomes are the concrete consequences of community development activity; community

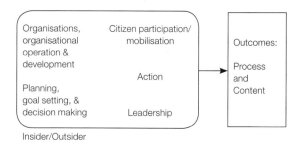

Figure 1 – The Essential Processes of the Community

facilities planned and built, jobs obtained and incomes improved, etc. Process outcomes are the more subtle consequences of community development activity, like changes in the community's capacity to act, or its "agency."

Community developers are usually outsiders to the communities with which they work. Even local community development activists, when they look at their community as an object to "develop" and improve, become outsiders in a sense. Looking at the community from the "outside," then, poses the key question of finding ways to change it. Where are the handles? Upon what should one focus? How should one try to intervene?

Handles for Intervention in Community Processes

Each of the community processes above can be the object of intervention. You could focus upon the community's leadership if you consider it to be the key and try to figure out ways that you might be able to help the community improve its leadership. An obvious example is some form of systematic leadership training. Or, you might focus upon citizen involvement, attempting to mobilise the citizens to some form of reflection, analysis and action. In this case the mechanisms used might be citizen surveys to identify community needs or community assets, community meetings, or a variety of participatory development techniques such as Participatory Appraisal, Participatory Community Mapping, etc. Thirdly, you might decide to focus upon the community's capacity to develop a vision, strategic plan and direction for itself, or help it to try to improve its decision-making capacity. Or, you might feel that what the community needs, and what could get it moving, is organisational development. So, your focus would be upon improving the existing community organisational structure or, perhaps, helping the community to establish a genuine community development organisation. And, of course, you might focus upon concrete actions by assisting the community in proposal preparation and writing, project design and implementation, etc. Finally, you

might, of course, adopt a course which focuses upon several of the community processes simultaneously. In fact, improved leadership usually does lead to greater and more effective public involvement, just as greater and more effective public involvement may lead to improved leadership. All normally lead to more effective planning and decision making and more effective action too.

It is very important to note the distinction between the general community processes on the one hand and the interventions on the other. Just because leadership training is going on (an intervention) does not mean that leadership has actually changed, not to mention improved! Thus, your own calculation of the nature and strength of the arrows going from interventions to community processes is crucial. It is in these arrows that one would find most of one's implicit theory of how community development works.

It is possible, for example, that leadership might actually be the crucial element in a community's further development but that the ability to effectively intervene in the quality of community leadership directly is judged to be very low, so one might still decide to focus upon something else, like citizen mobilisation, simply because that arrow (intervention to process) relationship is judged to be stronger and more predictable.

References

Bell, C. & Newby, H. 1974. *Community studies: An introduction to the sociology of the community.* New York, Praeger.

Bromley, D. W. 1970. "On the economic viability of rural communities," a Paper presented at Montana State University College of Agriculture Conference.

Brownell, B. 1950. *The human community.* New York: Harper and Row. de Certeau, M. 1986. *Heterologies: Discourse on the other.* Tr. B. Massoumi. Minneapolis: University of Minnesota Press.

Cottrell, W. F. 1951, June. "Death by dieselization: A case study in the reaction to technological change," *American Sociological Review*, Vol. 16, No. 3. pp. 358-365.

Giddens, A. 1984. *The constitution of society.* Berkeley: University of California Press.

Inden, R. 1990. *Imagining India.* Oxford: Basil Blackwell.

Jacobs, J. 1961. *The Death and Life of Great American Cities.* New York: Random House.

Luloff, A. E. & Swanson, L. E. 1995. "Community agency and disaffection: enhancing collective resources," in L. J. Beaulieu & D. Mulkey (Eds.),

1927
1960
1963
1964
1967
1969
1970
1971
1972
1973
1974
1975
1976
1977
1978
1979
1980
1981
1982
1983
1984
1985
1986
1987
1988
1989
1990
1991
1992
1993
1994
1995
1996
1997
1998
1999
2000
2001
2002
2003
2004
2005
2006

Investing in People: The Human Capital Needs of Rural America, (pp. 351-373). Boulder: Westview Press.

Morgan, A. E. 1942a. *The small community, foundation of democratic life: What it is and how to achieve it.* New York: Harper and Row.

Morgan, A. E. 1942b, February. The community--the seed bed of society. Atlantic Monthly, Vol. 169, No. 2.

Voth, D. E., Jardon, M. & Pell, W. F. 2000. "Chapter 3: Communities," in *USDA Forest Service, Southern Forest Experiment Station, Ozark-Ouachita Highlands Assessment: Social and Economic Conditions, Vol. 4, General Technical Report No. SRS-34,* pp. 79-98. Asheville, NC: Southern Research Station

Warren, R. L. 1970, April. "Toward a non-utopian normative model of the community," *American Sociological Review,* No. 35, pp. 219 to 228.

Warren, R. L. 1973. *The community in America,* 2nd edition, (pp. 315-20). Chicago, IL: Rand McNally.

Warren, R. L. 1973. "The good community: what would it be?" in R. L. Warren (Ed.), *Perspectives on the American Community,* (2nd ed.). (pp. 467-477). Chicago: Rand-McNally.

Wirth, L. 1938. "Urbanism as a way of life," *The American Journal of Sociology,* Vol. XLIV, pp. 1-24.

Voth, Donald. "Community and Community Development" www.uark.edu/depts/hesweb/hdfsrs/rsoc4263/cdbook6.PDF , 2000. Reprinted with permission of the author.

EXCERPT FROM:

COMMUNITY RADIO: AN IMPERFECT FUTURE

On Community Radio

By Rafael Roncagliolo

1998 What is the present landscape, and what is the immediate future? I believe this landscape has several characteristics that I will outline briefly.

In the first place, there is an absolutely objective, economic and clear fact: technology is increasingly cheaper. Therefore, there is a tendency towards expansion: creating community radio and television stations, for example, is becoming more and more accessible as regards technology costs. This sector is the only one in the economy in which the prices of final products go down, and do so more than in any other sector, be it satellite dishes, broadcast stations or computers. This is Moore's famous law: the price of the computing power is halved each year; that is to say, each year, with the same amount of money, I can buy double in terms of the value of computer technology.

In the second place, globalization coexists with the need for local reaffirmation. There is the enjoyment or habit of watching war live: first it was the Vietnam war, which inspired McLuhan's idea of the *global village*, and later the war in the Middle East, the first war broadcast live, which illustrated Baudrillard's ideas. But the need to know what happens around the corner, the village gossip—my province's, Pacasmayo, for example—and to look at oneself in the mirror coexists with this perspective.

In the third place, there is substantial modification in cultural consumption, understood in its broadest sense. Cultural consumption has increased throughout the modern era, through the transition to physical markets: cinema, theatre, political locales for political culture, and church for religious culture. We now witness the home delivery of cultural goods, which started with radio and develops further with television, video and electronic communication.

What used to require transportation now demands telecommunications. What used to imply travel can now be done over the telephone; the individual need to physically travel is decreasing. In these new conditions, the challenge is how to develop community media in this new cultural landscape.

I believe the danger is expressed in a very beautiful trilogy developed by Regis Debray, the theorist of Che Guevara's guerrilla movement in Bolivia in the 1970s, who was in prison in Camiri, Bolivia. Later on, he was President Mitterrand's adviser for many years, and has now invented a new discipline called mediology. Through his books, mainly *Courses in General Mediology*, and *Life and Death of the Image: a History of the Western Eye*, he explains that there are three stages in humanity—he does so in dialogue with Comte, since this is a dialogue between French theorists. Debray says that in the first stage, there were servants who were ordered; followed by the construction of citizens convinced by the overall democratic ideal and the ideal of modernity; and now we witness a stage in which there are no servants or citizens, but instead consumers. Just as the servant is ordered and the citizen convinced by, the consumer is seduced. If at the time of servants, influence was exerted through preaching and at the time of citizens it was exerted through publishing, now it is exerted by appearing. If the time of servants was one of pulpits and the time of citizens was one of books, in the consumers' era this preferential place is occupied by television. Thus we have gone from the logosphere to the graphosphere, and from the graphosphere to the videosphere.

The political challenge, I believe, lies not in reducing the humanity of our societies to consumers that can be seduced by stars appearing on television. We must preserve a space for citizens to defend rights and seek equality. I think this is the challenge facing community media, the reason why they get involved. I think here lies the reason that justifies our need to get involved globally, since this challenge is obviously global.

Roncagliolo, Rafael. "Radios Comunitarias: Futuro Imperfecto. [Community Radio: An Imperfect Future,]" paper presented at the Congress of Local Radio in Andalusia, 1998. Reprinted with permission of the author.

1927
1960
1963
1964
1967
1969
1970
1971
1972
1973
1974
1975
1976
1977
1978
1979
1980
1981
1982
1983
1984
1985
1986
1987
1988
1989
1990
1991
1992
1993
1994
1995
1996
1997
1998
1999
2000
2001
2002
2003
2004
2005
2006

RADIO, CONFLICT AND POLITICAL TRANSITION: THE FUTURE OF COMMUNITY RADIO IN AFRICA

Excerpt from: African Broadcast Cultures

By Aida Opoku-Mensah

2000 The phrase community radio implies a two-way process: one which entails the exchange of views from various perspectives and the adaptation of media for use by communities in light of them. In an ideal world, community radio would allow members of a community to gain access to information, education and entertainment. In its purest sense, community radio is a medium in which the community participates—as planners, producers and performers—and it is a means of expression of the community, rather than for the community (Berrigan 1979). In short, ideally it represents an alternative means of expression for the otherwise silenced majority. Until recently, media policy has not emphasised this two-way process. Instead it has focused on use of the media of mass communication to send messages from capital cities to the periphery: feedback from the communities that live there has been correspondingly limited.

The key words in community radio are "access" and "participation," but they can come to mean many different things depending on local circumstances. In India, increasing women's access to radio often means no more than that women will be permitted to listen to the radio set. The crucial issue is not whether people have access to a radio station to express their opinions or personal messages, nor even whether some local people participate on a paid or volunteer basis in radio programming. What really matters is the institutional structure of the radio station. Who is in control? Is it democratically managed? Is there a mechanism to make it accountable to those it serves (O'Connor 1990)? This article explores these issues.

Community Radio: Participation and Ownership

A community radio station, like any other community media, must encourage community participation. Community participation may be defined as the educational and empowering process in which people—in partnership with those able to assist them—identify problems and needs, so that they increasingly assume responsibility to plan, manage, control and assess the collective actions that are proved necessary.

In a community radio station, people choose what problems they should pay attention to and how they want to solve them; typically, the producers and the listeners are interchangeable. The people, guided by trained journalists, produce their own programmes. What is broadcast is the people's, rather than the journalists', agendas. The medium of community radio allows agendas to be set by the people rather than by media professionals. It may be that the people wholly or partly own a community radio station themselves through a cooperative enterprise. The cooperative movement in Zambia has been involved in relatively successful businesses, on behalf of both producers and consumers. Provided the people have the will to run such cooperatives they can run media cooperatives, such as community radio broadcasting stations and community newspapers, with equal success. Unlike community radio stations established by the government, which normally become local mouthpieces of the administration and the ruling party, such cooperative radio stations, once established, have few political strings attached to them (Kasoma 1990).

The History of Community Radio in Africa

Although community radio as we know it today has had a chequered history in Africa, the concept has always been recognised in one form or another—for instance, in the guise of rural radio (radio clubs) and/or radio forums, concepts which originated in Canada. Rural radio has existed for 30 years and came to be known as the voice of the peasants/people. Through radio forums, groups of villagers or farmers met in each other's homes in order to listen to broadcasts, study a pamphlet and discuss particular problems with a view to cooperative action in solving them. In 1964, with UNESCO and Canadian aid, 40 villages were involved in an experiment that improved the take-up of the scheme. The system was subsequently adopted widely and eventually involved some 400 groups in Ghana, Zambia, Malawi and Nigeria. Radio listening clubs are another step in the participatory direction. These involve club members' expressing views concerning their problems, which are recorded and then made into broadcast programmes.

Rural radio has been dismissed by some critics who allege it does not adequately represent the voices of the people: it is government controlled, lacks resources to ensure its continued existence and has no real political commitment behind it. However, the crisis of rural radio and farm radio forums lies equally in the overall crisis that the African continent faces: that of a stagnating resource base.

Perhaps Africa's first real community radio was the Homa Bay Community Radio Station, established in the western part of Kenya in May 1982. This station was not only an experiment in decentralisation of structures and programming but also an effort to gain experience in the utilisation of low-cost technology for broadcasting. The Homa Bay project was an initiative by the Kenyan government and UNESCO; however, in 1984, the Kenyan government closed it down. Another initiative was the establishment of three rural broadcasting stations as part of a policy to decentralise rural development in Liberia. Although these examples were attempts to decentralise broadcasting and to make it more people-centred, various pressures made it impossible for them to survive, and they failed to create the social transformation that

African societies needed for modernisation in the development process.

Early development communications theorists believed that mere exposure to radio messages was enough to cause social changes that would lead to development. This belief led to the launching of numerous radio-for-development projects. In the earlier farm forum programmes, development messages were primarily sent "down" from the government agricultural department or the extension agent to the rural people. Only the most limited feedback from farmers was invited; messages were often too prescriptive, complex and technical to be understood. These early schemes clearly revealed the limitations of "top-down" government campaigns designed to foster development (Fisher 1990).

This history of relatively ineffective initiatives demonstrates the need for interactive community radio projects to encourage grassroots development in Africa. The opening-up of the airwaves offers opportunities for the introduction of just such interactive projects, able to serve the majority of the people.

The justifications for community-led radio are as follows:

1. Given the large numbers of different local languages in African countries and communities, only community-level stations are able to ensure that people are able both to hear broadcasts and, more importantly, to understand them.
2. Community-led radio encourages media education, which the majority of citizens in Africa lack. Most Africans have been starved of information; in the contemporary information society, community radio can help create an information culture.
3. Community-led radio enhances political emancipation and creates a platform for debate, exchange of ideas and reactions to plans and projects. It can accommodate people's ideas and satisfy their spiritual and psychological well-being much better than any other form of broadcasting.

1927
1960
1963
1964
1967
1969
1970
1971
1972
1973
1974
1975
1976
1977
1978
1979
1980
1981
1982
1983
1984
1985
1986
1987
1988
1989
1990
1991
1992
1993
1994
1995
1996
1997
1998
1999
2000
2001
2002
2003
2004
2005
2006

4. With globalisation of information and the advent of satellite communications, community radio can both offer communities a cheap but vital way of projecting their language and heritage and serve as a means to standardise a local language.

Community Radio for Development and Democracy

That there exists a need to expand community radio in the interests of development and democracy in Africa seems self-evident. However, the questions that urgently arise are: What kind of development or democracy? And who is to define the types of development or democracy that are to be sought?

Used strategically, community radio may accelerate or catalyse social transformation. Handled properly, community radio can emancipate people politically by providing them with information on the political life of their country. An example of community radio strengthening democracy was given at a recent broadcasting seminar held in Zambia. In Los Baños, in the Philippines, the governor of the district goes on the air at a community radio station one day a week to answer questions that listeners raise by letters and telephone calls to the station. The government is thus held accountable locally through the community radio station (Kasoma 1997, 55).

The Future of Community Radio: The Case of Southern Africa

Since the opening-up of the airwaves in some countries in southern Africa, there has been great concern about people's access to communication and to broadcasting in particular. Community radio or broadcasting is a very popular idea in this part of the world. However, broadcasting liberalisation polices have largely ignored the existence of community broadcasting. Most new acts concerned with broadcasting have broken the monopoly of state-owned and/or controlled broadcasting entities and allowed "independent," usually commercial, broadcasting to establish their predominantly urban-based

operations. However, not all have effectively encouraged radio community. Of those that have made steps in this direction, South Africa has introduced a three tier broadcasting system—public, commercial and community; and Namibia's ground-breaking liberalisation of broadcasting granted autonomy, initially to the national broadcasting corporation, and allowed the establishment of private television and radio stations, especially community stations. Many other countries have simply developed a mix of state and commercial radio.

Strictly speaking, the community radio broadcasting landscape in this region is limited to South Africa, which has approximately 82 such stations. Community radio is still a new concept, and what it means remains subject to debate, which is often inconclusive. In South Africa, community radio stations belong to "communities;" in Mozambique and Zambia, they are owned and operated by the Roman Catholic church (although in Mozambique there are also government-owned community radio stations). In Namibia, Katura Community Radio was the brainchild of, among others, the Council of Churches, NANGOF (the umbrella body for NGOs) and the Legal Assistance Centre, which, as recognised representatives of the community, initially formed the management committee. In Zambia a commercial and independent radio station, Radio Phoenix, identifies itself as a "community" station catering to the needs of the people it serves, and so does the Roman Catholic station Radio Icengelo. How communities gain access to, and become involved in, the running of a station is quite variable. Underlying principles—concerning who controls a station, how democratic management is assured, and what if any mechanisms make managers and broadcasting accountable to those they serve—still need to be worked out everywhere, even in South Africa.

Francis Kasoma (professor of journalism and mass communication at the University of Zambia) contends that there are various viable forms of community radio

1927
1960
1963
1964
1967
1969
1970
1971
1972
1973
1974
1975
1976
1977
1978
1979
1980
1981
1982
1983
1984
1985
1986
1987
1988
1989
1990
1991
1992
1993
1994
1995
1996
1997
1998
1999
2000
2001
2002
2003
2004
2005
2006

ownership in Africa and mentions that FAO is about to set up a community radio station in Luapula Province, in Zambia (Kasoma 1997). A feasibility study for the project has already been conducted to establish the distribution of radio ownership and the listening patterns of the people in the province. The possibility of establishing a mobile community radio station is also being considered. If this system is implemented, it would use an outside broadcasting (OB) vehicle fitted with a transmitter and studio equipment. Antennae would be erected in each district, and the OB vehicle would simply be plugged into the relevant antenna in order for programmes to be broadcast in a particular district. After some weeks or months, the mobile broadcast station would move on to the next district. An NGO community radio station has also been earmarked for Solwezi, in North-Western Province.

The Community Media Movement in Southern Africa

Liberalisation of broadcasting in many countries in southern Africa has generated enormous interest from many groups, particularly from the NGO sectors. However, there is debate whether NGOs should be initiating community radio stations themselves, or whether they would not do better to stimulate local communities to own their own stations.

A movement is emerging in the southern Africa region aimed at enhancing awareness of community media issues, and in particular of community radio. For instance, the COMNESA (Community Media Network of East & Southern Africa) is made up of organisations such as MISA (Media Institute of Southern Africa); IPS (Inter Press Service??); KCOMMNET (Kenya Community Media Network); Panos Southern Africa; the National Community Radio Forum, South Africa; AMARC (World Association of Community Radio Broadcasters) Africa; and ENA (EcoNews Africa), Kenya. These organisations are committed to stimulating debate on community radio through research, workshops and seminars that bring policy-makers and other groups in civil society together

SOCIALISED MEDIA
Excerpt from: *"Media without an Audience"*
By Eric Kluitenberg

Media used in the context of a specified social group, or in a specific regional context, are best described as community media. Common forms of community media that belong to a geographically situated community are community radio and television. The use of the Internet in a geographically situated community is mostly referred to as community networking. Community networking has become very popular in the United States but also has some importance in Europe.

Special interest communities are usually organised around a topic, a theme or a shared interest. They are essentially translocal in nature, hooking up local interest groups or even scattered individuals who can be dispersed over different regions and countries.

Networked communications can be highly beneficial for the process of community building and for strengthening the cohesion of communities. It is obvious that translocal (special-interest) communities benefit most from networked communication, since it offers a low-cost and fairly effective means to stay in touch and exchange ideas. But the high degree of audience feedback and peer-to-peer interaction also makes networked communication technology an invaluable tool for social interaction within a geographically situated community.

Panos Southern Africa, for instance, has organised two major seminars in Zimbabwe and Zambia on broadcasting in general, with particular emphases on the emergence of community radio in these countries and the regulatory process. In April 1997,

Panos brought together policy-makers and media practitioners to discuss current national broadcasting policy issues and their impact on Zambian society. Specific objectives of the seminar were:

■ to bring broadcasters, development workers and members of parliament (MPs) together to debate the state of broadcasting policy in Zambia;
■ to stimulate debate about the role of broadcasting for democracy and development;
■ to sensitise Zambian MPs to developments in community and grassroots broadcasting in neighbouring countries.

Participants included representatives from the ruling party, MMD (Movement for Multiparty Democracy), and the National Party, as well as from ZAMWA (Zambia Media Women's Association), ZNBC (Zambia National Broadcasting Corporation), *The Times of Zambia* newspaper, CPU (Commonwealth Press Union), PANA (Pan African News Agency), ZUJ (Zambia Union of Journalists), Icengelo (a Roman Catholic radio station), Radio Christian Voice and Radio Phoenix. In discussing a regulatory framework, participants made the following eight recommendations (Panos 1997, 75):

COMMUNITY RADIO
1. That government puts in place a deliberate policy for the establishment of community-owned radio stations in Zambia.

REGULATOR
2. That there shall be an independent regulator who shall be answerable to an independent board of governors whose appointment and dismissal shall be ratified by parliament.

TENURE FOR REGULATOR AND INDEPENDENT BOARD
3. That the board should be funded for an initial period of three years from parliament. Thereafter the board is expected to be self-sustaining through radio and television licensing.

4. That the tenure for the regulator and the board shall be for not more than five years.

REGULATION OF BOARD PROCEDURES
5. That the board shall regulate its own procedures.

REQUIREMENTS OF THE REGULATOR
6. That the regulator should be a suitable and professionally qualified Zambian.
7. That, in effecting the legislation, the functions of licensing broadcasting may be relegated to the Communications Authority.

JURISDICTION
8. That the regulator should:

i. issue, withdraw, amend, revoke, prescribe penalties and enforce conditions,
ii. inspect and approve installations,
iii. appoint, hire and fire staff, and
iv. be responsible for preparing the regulatory report to the board for presentation to parliament.

Based on the case studies and examples of community radio in South Africa, MPs and NGOs were undoubtedly convinced of the need for similar stations in Zambia. All the MPs talked about the establishment of community radio stations in their constituencies; some, however, continued to see community radio as a tool to advance their own goals, and one MP even mentioned that if he could have a station in his constituency, it would help him during his campaign for re-election. When participants reminded him that such a station should be people driven he retorted, "I am the people."

MPs' comments included:

"This seminar was an eye opener on the impact of broadcasting and development, as well as the legal conflict in the acts of law today."

"It provided for a wider understanding on the need for the establishment of community radio."

DIGLOSSIA[1] IN THE MEDIA
Excerpt from: *Lenguas Indígenas y Medios de Comunicación*
By Xavier Albó

The mass media are currently one of the most powerful tools to rule, change or consolidate people's linguistic habits. Media reflect a global dominance with more strength and insistence than the more contained atmosphere of children's schools. They are part of the landscape, in the most intimate corner of each home, and through them, values and attitudes are moulded, like a continuous rain that—for better or for worse—penetrates all the pores of the human being.

The choice of one language over another, or the use of multiple languages in the media—in addition to transmitting explicit messages—implies implicit expressive functions. For people living in indigenous villages speaking a low-prestige language finding it or hearing in the media increases their own self-esteem, unless their language is used only in a context of delinquency or to be made fun of, with derogatory connotations. Also those who belong to the dominating groups, if they hear other, less-dominant languages used in a positive context, they may end up accepting subconsciously that they are part of a plural society. This way, autochthonous music has already come to be accepted in some countries, heard repeatedly by the high classes in their own homes, on the kitchen radio.

For this reason, the task of strengthening indigenous languages and, through them, our own identities in the national ensemble, must also go through the media. Being present in them may notably modify some attitudes not only on the part of indigenous people but also among the rest of the population. Being totally absent will accelerate the death of subordinate languages and cultures.

For many years, the mass media were restricted only to the prevailing language and culture. Until the 1950s, it was not perceived that native cultures communicated and expressed themselves routinely in these modern media, except in very specific circumstances like cases of social disturbance; information was almost always a message from whites to whites. But in more recent times there has been a partial change in that exclusionary approach. Significant gaps have been opened in the use of native languages, especially in the radio. Although in a less mass-oriented and permanent way, the achievements in cinema and video are also worth mentioning. Television is still much more unwilling, although there are indications that gains can be made there as well. The daily mass-circulating press is, up to now, the most impenetrable. So, there is a certain diglossia[1] in the different media.

Bibliography

ALER (Asociación Latinoamericana de Educación Radiofónica). 1994. "Socios activos debidamente acreditados a la IX Asamblea ALER 1994." Quito. (MS).

AMARC (Asociación Mundial de Radios Comunitarias). 1996. "Miembros latinoamericanos de AMARC. " Lima. (MS).

Archondo, Rafael. 1991. *Compadres al micrófono: La resurrección del ayllu*. La Paz: Hisbol.

Gumucio, Alfonso y Lupe Cajías. 1989. *Las radios mineras en Bolivia*. La Paz: CIMCA y UNESCO.

Instituto Indigenista Interamericano, ed. 1986. "I Seminario-taller sobre radiodifusión en regiones indígenas de América Latina, Quito 11-16 agosto 1986. Informe final." Quito: Instituto Indigenista Interamericano, UNESCO, CIESPAL, ICI, UNDA-AL, ALER.

Instituto Indigenista Interamericano, ed. 1987. "Hacer radio a diario. Memoria del II Seminario-taller sobre radiodifusión en regiones indígenas de América Latina, Tabasco, México 10-14 agosto 1987." México: Instituto Indigenista Interamericano. (Publicado también en el *Anuario Indigenista*, vol. 47, 1987.)

[Radio Shuar]. 1977. *La educación radiofónica bicultural*. Sucúa.

Reyes, Jaime. 1990. *La radiodifusión en Bolivia*. La Paz: ERBOL y OSAP.

Valderrama, Mariano. 1987. "Radio y comunicación popular en el Perú". Lima: CEPES.

Albó, Xavier. Excerpt from: "Lenguas Indígenas y Medios de Comunicación." This paper summarizes parts of a paper presented at the II International Congress of Bilingual Intercultural Education (EIB) held in Santa Cruz, Bolivia, in December 1996. Used with permission of author.

---

1 *Diglossia* refers to the use of closely-related languages used in daily life: one most often used by the upper class of society, and the other is the vernacular.

1927
1960
1963
1964
1967
1969
1970
1971
1972
1973
1974
1975
1976
1977
1978
1979
1980
1981
1982
1983
1984
1985
1986
1987
1988
1989
1990
1991
1992
1993
1994
1995
1996
1997
1998
1999
2000
2001
2002
2003
2004
2005
2006

"I didn't realise how important community radio is until after attending this seminar."

"I now understand that there can be regional/community and national broadcasting stations owned and financed by the communities themselves."

"It broadened my knowledge about technological changes and the usefulness of alternative broadcasting, like community radio."

"By explaining the wider aspects of broadcasting—which include frequency, allocation funding, etc.—I now understand that broadcasting can be possible even at the community level."

Financing Community Radio

The revenue potential of an established and well-run station is quite good; however, reaching the point at which a station is well established and has a solid advertising clientele takes time. During the intervening months, the station should be expected to operate at a loss. Taking this into account, it might be argued that potential owners and operators of stations be evaluated according to their ability to sustain an operating loss for a period of at least one year. Moreover, granting too many licences may itself inhibit the growth of the broadcasting industry.

In practice, there are two schools of thought. One believes that community radio stations should be set up as business enterprises by private individuals who will use the necessary means to make them sustainable. The second argues that community radio stations are for the poor in society, and they are therefore unlikely to make commercial profits. The second argument is most often advanced by NGOs, which feel that, for the time being, community radio stations should be financed through donor support and/or through a financial mechanism embedded in national regulatory frameworks.

Against the NGOs' arguments, it has to be noted how often stations are revealed to be unviable commercially and therefore collapse when their sponsors decide to pull out. Kasoma (1997, 54) feels the solution lies in community radio stations being "established either by co-operatives or as enterprises by government. However, since government radio stations and all government media for that matter tend to be propaganda organs rather than utilities for people's free expression, this author strongly recommends that Zambia takes the path of establishing co-operatives or privately owned community radio stations. NGOs can initiate some of the stations, but the local community should be prepared to take them over as co-operative ventures so that their sustainability is assured."

The Immediate Future

The concept of community radio in southern Africa is only now beginning to take shape, and there are many hurdles to surmount if it is to become a permanent feature of the broadcasting landscape. One major hurdle is direct or indirect political interference. Community radio represents a decentralisation of the power which has been jealously guarded in the hands of governments. Governments in the region still have overwhelming power and hold one of the keys to the future of community radio in the region.

Whilst the community radio movement in South Africa has lobbied for effective policies that can enhance this sector, for several reasons this proactive approach is still relatively new in many countries in the southern African region. South Africa's unique history ironically created the conditions whereby, in 1993–1994, there was enormous sensitivity to the control of communications once the general elections were held. Out of the political struggle came the struggle for equitable access to broadcasting channels for previously disadvantaged Africans and the creation of an Independent Broadcasting Authority. This situation is totally different from that in other countries where regulatory authorities lack the credibility and independence they need to carry out their responsibilities. …

A member of the ruling SWAPO party heads the Namibia Communications Committee (NCC), whose commissioners are appointed by the minister of information and broadcasting. For example, a year after it had gone on air, Katatura Community Radio (KCR) found it was being drowned out by test broadcasts from a new commercial radio station, Radio 100. KCR complained to the NCC, only to be told that, because the International Telecommunications Union's frequency allocation plan for Namibia made provision for a limited number of frequencies, KCR would have to move to a different frequency. The ITU denied that it could allocate frequencies within a country, a task that in Namibia is entrusted to the NCC through the NCC Act. Following an outcry, KCR was allowed to stay put at 106.2 MHz and Radio 100 was ordered to move to a different frequency, 100 MHz. It turned out that Kalahari Holdings, a company owned by the ruling political party, holds a majority shareholding in Radio 100, now known as Radio Energy. The new station was competing for the same township youth market KCR had cornered since going on air in 1995.

Zimbabwe, Mozambique and Malawi are still struggling with the creation of independent regulatory structures that can effectively regulate the broadcasting sector.

Another burning issue is how community radio stations will be financed. Indications so far suggest that many stations in South Africa are struggling to survive. No doubt, their presence has made a tremendous contribution in the short term, but it remains to be seen whether, in the longer term, they will be able to survive in the commercial world. The donor community is eager to support the establishment of community radio stations, on the grounds that such initiatives strengthen pluralism and represent the tenets of good governance. However, the self-same donors are equally keen to support initiatives that have a future and will be sustainable.

For now, the future of community radio stations in southern Africa can be assured through either government policies or willing donors. However, without a progressive political outlook—allied to a communi-

cations policy that reflects that outlook—and a vibrant civil society that can make it work, community radio stations will become yet another fashionable concept that will soon die a natural death.

References

Berrigan, F. "Community Communications: The role of Community Media in Development," *Reports and Papers on Mass Communication 90*. UNESCO, 1979.

Fisher, H. 1990. "Community Radio as a Tool for Development," *Media Development*, 1990, 4: 19–24.

Kasoma, F. P. "Media Ownership: Key to Participatory Development Communication," *Media Asia*, 1990, 17(2): 79–82.

Kasoma, F. P. "Community Broadcasting in Zambia: Prospects and Potential," in Panos Institute Southern Africa, ed., *Broadcasting and Society: Forum on Broadcasting in Zambia*. Lusaka, Zambia: Panos, 1997, 51–57.

O'Connor, A. "Radio is Fundamental to Democracy," *Media Development*, 1990, 4: 3–4.

Panos Institute Southern Africa, ed. *Broadcasting and Society: Forum on Broadcasting in Zambia*. Lusaka, Zambia: Panos, 1997.

Opoku-Mensah, Aida. "Radio, Conflict and Political Transition. The Future of Community Radio in Africa." in Fardon, Richard and Graham Furniss, eds., *African Broadcast Cultures. Radio in Transition*. Oxford: Praeger, 2000. Copyright © 2000, James Currey Publishers. Reprinted with permission of the publisher.

1927
1960
1963
1964
1967
1969
1970
1971
1972
1973
1974
1975
1976
1977
1978
1979
1980
1981
1982
1983
1984
1985
1986
1987
1988
1989
1990
1991
1992
1993
1994
1995
1996
1997
1998
1999
2000
2001
2002
2003
2004
2005
2006

SOCIAL MOVEMENTS AND COMMUNICATION

By Osvaldo León, Sally Burch and Eduardo Tamayo

2005 Communication, by its nature, is dynamic movement. Social movements are a form of live communication moving in two directions, inward and outward. Historically, social movements have opened channels of communication and established positions as key actors in advancing democracy. This historical presence has been diluted—water through the fingers—partly as a result of mistakes, or constraints, in addressing issues of communication.

The most serious mistakes in approaching the communication process are those that employ and interpose today's increasingly sophisticated complex of technologies. These technologies are more and more subsumed in an oligopolistic structure, thus aggravating the imbalance that favors the existing loci of power.

Despite this, all indications are that communication is finding a place on the agendas of social organizations. It is widely recognized that these organizations have remained trapped in the "Gutenberg" era, while radio and, supereminently, television—the mass media that became institutionalized as "culture industries" beginning in the middle of the last century—redefined the scene, appropriating a central position in the shaping of public life. Social organizations were out of step with this new scenario. First they "divorced" themselves from the media, then they disregarded them. In time, this evolved into the ambivalent position of condemnation and fascination that has ever since marked the actions of these organizations. This ambivalence, however, is giving way in light of the ever clearer influence of communication in the present world—a phenomenon reflected in the fact that the media are the principal channel through which today's neoliberal ideological hegemony (the one-dimensional mindset) has imposed itself.

The attitudes of organizations have also been affected by an awareness of the opportunities for response offered by the Internet. All of this has occurred within a context in which organizations are reshaping their internal and external dynamics, just as the social movements in which they participate are reorganizing their structures and mechanisms of interconnection.

In recent statements to the Mexican newspaper *La Jornada* (Sept. 19, 2004), Noam Chomsky commented that "the Internet, in addition to facilitating and streamlining communication within and between social movements, can be a tool to wrest some of the control from the mainstream media. These are two of the most important new factors to have emerged in the last 20 years." The relevance of this new technology to social movements is a result not merely of its low cost, but, more importantly, of its patterns and functioning. The Internet—based, in technical terms, on a web of different computer networks throughout the world (hence the term "the Web")—provides a global medium for receiving and sending data, images and sounds at any moment in either real or deferred time. It also facilitates an interrelation of the many with the many, a circumstance that has organizational implications. In short, the interactive capacity of the Internet makes it possible to receive and disseminate messages to and from anywhere without need of the mainstream media and to establish coordination mechanisms and groupings without regard to geography.

Though the Internet was originally developed by the United States military-industrial complex, its large-scale implementation and subsequent development were driven by academia and citizens' groups. This has made it an open, decentralized and ownerless forum for exchange and collaboration. It is a technology collaboratively developed and improved by its users. The most visible expression of this is the phenomenon of free/open source software. As Castells et al. (2004) observe, "The importance of free software in the spread and development of the Internet from its very inception, and of the mutual influence of these two technological areas as a contrasting fact" are clear. Though government and business tend to present the Internet as circumscribed by (if not consubstantial with) its physical or technical aspect (whence the over-emphasis on connectivity), in fact it has been, above all, a locus of social interaction on which social movements have left their mark, and by which they have in turn been shaped.

At the end of the last century, in an environment marked by organizational dismantling and dispersion resulting from neoliberal programs, a convergence of initiatives, based on relationships developed through the Net, burst onto the scene as a reaction to globalization. One of the first signs of this synchrony appeared in 1998, when a successful citizens' movement, coordinated through the Internet, was set in motion to put a brake on governments negotiating the Multilateral Agreement on Investment (MAI). One year later, in Seattle, there was a massive protest against the World Trade Organization (WTO). This was considered the baptism of the "alter-globalization" movement, in which the Net also proved key.

Writing about this event, the Canadian author Naomi Klein reports that Seattle served as a stage for the emergence of an activist organizational model that reproduces the organic, decentralized, but interconnected paths of the Internet—an Internet with its own life (Klein 2003: 31). Klein's book, *No Logo,* had in fact already pointed out this development, with one chapter devoted to social activists' campaigns against transnationals such as Nike, Shell and MacDonald's, which distinguished themselves "by a pioneering use of information technologies, an approach that continues to unnerve their corporate targets" (p. 393), Klein elaborates:

> the net is more than an organizing tool—it has become an organizing model, a blueprint for decentralized but cooperative decision-making. It

facilitates the process of information sharing to such a degree that many groups can work in concert with one another without the need to achieve monolithic consensus (which is often impossible, anyway, given the nature of activist organizations). And because it is so decentralized, these movements are still in process of forging links with their various wings around the world, continually surprising themselves with how far unreported little victories have traveled, how thoroughly bits of research have been recycled and absorbed. (Klein, 2000: 396).

After Seattle, there was a proliferation of "alter-globalization" demonstrations against the international bodies that currently regulate the globalization process (World Bank, IMF, WTO, etc.). As Donk et al. observe, "new media strategies and cyber activism played a dominant role" in these mobilizations. "Yet more and more, the Internet seems to be being developed as a new strategic platform that helps a variety of movements to mobilize and to organize protest." This platform has also been key to the architecture and public presence of the World Social Forum (WSF), which emerged in Porto Alegre, Brazil in 2001 as an alternative to the World Economic Forum in Davos, the annual meeting place of the economic and political elites that hold the reins of world power.

After the September 11 attacks on New York, the demise of the WSF was announced by the *Wall Street Journal,* which ran a headline reading, "Farewell, Porto Alegre!" Two years later, a report in the *New York Times*—in the wake of the massive worldwide demonstrations on February 15, 2003 protesting the Iraq war (then in its preparatory stage), spawned by the World Social Forum—observed that "there are two superpowers in the world: the United States and world public opinion." Once again, the Net was the key component of action. Thus, the new web of relationships fostered by the Internet has facilitated an entire course of action.

1927
1960
1963
1964
1967
1969
1970
1971
1972
1973
1974
1975
1976
1977
1978
1979
1980
1981
1982
1983
1984
1985
1986
1987
1988
1989
1990
1991
1992
1993
1994
1995
1996
1997
1998
1999
2000
2001
2002
2003
2004
2005
2006

De Wilde describes the process as follows: "The Internet is not used as a mere supplement to traditional media, it also offers new, innovative opportunities for mobilizing and organizing individuals. The new technologies, however, do not determine these innovations. The Internet fosters innovation, but this innovation has to be organized and disseminated. NGOs are especially innovative in this field. Not only has the Internet helped these organizations, NGOs were also very important for the further development of the Internet."[1]

Currently, we are witnessing an unprecedented phenomenon, for in the past the subordinate classes have had access to communications devices only when they were obsolescent, or were at best tools of secondary utility. Now, social organizations have succeeded in using the Web to propound new perspectives,[2] with little more than a trench (metaphorically speaking) from which to fight.[3]

Bibliography

Burch, Sally; León, Osvaldo; Tamayo, Eduardo (2004) *Se cayó el sistema: Enredos de la Sociedad de Información* [The System is Down: Problems of the Information Society], Quito, ALAI, July.

Campione, Daniel (2003) *Rebelión y comunicación* [Rebellion and communication], December 16. http://alainet.org/active/show_text.php3?key=5179

Castells, Manuel (1999) *La Era de la Información: Economía, Sociedad y Cultura: La sociedad Red* [The information age: economy, society and culture: the network society], Mexico City, Siglo XXI.

Castells, Manuel et al. (2004) *Declaración de Barcelona para el avance del software libre* [Declaration of Barcelona for the advance of free software], http://alainet.org/active/show_text.php3?key=6196.

Donk, Win van de et al. (2004) *Cyberprotest: New Media, Citizens and Social Movements*, London and New York, Routledge.

Elizalde, Rosa (2003) *Las redes alternativas: Una telaraña a la izquierda de Dios* [Alternative networks: a spiderweb to the left of God], www.cubasi.cu.

Hamelink, Cees J. (1999) *"Language and the Right to Communicate,"* *Media Development*, Vol. XLVI, 4/1999, London, WACC.

Klein, Naomi (2003) *Journal d'une combattante: Nouvelles du front de la-mondialisation* [Journal of a combatant: News from the globalization front], Lemeac/Actes Sud, Montreal.

Klein, Naomi (2000) *No Logo: Taking aim at the brand bullies*, Toronto, Random House of Canada.

La Jornada (2004), Mexico City, September 19.

León, Osvaldo (2004) *Exclusión social y brecha digital* [Social exclusion and digital gap], Ponencia presentada en las Jornadas Solidaridad en Red: Nuevas tecnologías, ciudadanía y cambio social [Presentation given at the Network Solidarity Workshop: New technologies, citizenship and social change], Hegoa, Vitoria-Gasteiz, November 18-19.

León, Osvaldo; Burch, Sally; Tamayo, Eduardo (2001) *Movimientos Sociales en la Red* [Social movements on the Web], Quito, ALAI, September.

Sádaba R., Igor (2004) *Del cambio tecnológico al cambio social. Conflictos y protestas globales en la red* [From technological change to social change. Global protests and conflicts on the Web]. Ponencia presentada en las Jornadas Solidaridad en Red: Nuevas tecnologías, ciudadanía y cambio social [Presentation given at the Network Solidarity Workshop: New technologies, citizenship and social change], Hegoa, Vitoria-Gasteiz, November 18-19.

Leon, Osvaldo, Sally Burch and Eduardo Tamayo. "Movimientos Sociales y Comunicación," Agencia Latinoamericana de Información, Latin American Information Agency (ALAI), 2005, Quito, Ecuador. Reprinted with permission of the author.

---

1 Quoted in Donk, et al., 2004.
2 The matter has become so serious that government is proposing to limit this "licentious" behavior through regulation and criminal sanctions. There has even been talk of "Netwar," especially since 9/11.
3 Alternative Web sites are reckoned to constitute 10 percent of the total, but only 5 percent are detected by search engines (Elizalde, R. 2003).

CONTEMPORARY READINGS
VOLUME ②
Power, Media and the Public Sphere

ACCOUNTING FOR POWER IN DEVELOPMENT COMMUNICATION

Excerpt from: Redeveloping Communication for Social Change

By Karin Gwinn Wilkins

2000 Development communication refers to the strategic application of communication technologies and processes to promote social change. Although currently the theoretical approaches and research findings of development communication are seen as applying to any community actively engaged in strategic social change, historically development discourse has been concerned with project interventions in an international setting, funded through wealthy agencies and implemented in nation-states with comparatively fewer financial resources.

In this article, I argue that future trends in development communication need to consider power more explicitly in theory and in practice. This approach builds on a reflexive stance of scholars and practitioners, who recognize the limitations of current discourse and intervention. First, I characterize how power might be conceived in frameworks of development communication. Then, I consider development as a discourse, contextualizing the representation of problems and people within power structures and dynamics. Next, I explore the production of discourse by institutions working within a global structure of dominant economic and political agencies. Finally, I illustrate assumptions made about models of social change and roles for communication processes and technologies in development communication implementation.

Accounting for Power

Power should be a central consideration in reconceptualizing the theory and practice of development communication. There are many different ways to understand and define power. Lukes reminds us that no one definition of power will serve all cases (1986, 5). There are many debates concerning the conceptualization of power, such as whether we are concerned with the production of intended effects or the capacity to produce them (Aron 1986) or the degree to which resistance might be relevant or feasible (Lukes 1986).

These differences over definitions stem from different perspectives of power. Olsen and Marger (1993) describe different approaches, beginning with a Marxist perspective, which emphasizes the economic and material foundation of society and describes social change as occurring inevitably through a dialectic process of class conflict. An elite perspective, in contrast, recognizes the ability of a small, cohesive group to control resources, but also considers social change to be more circumscribed by the very institutions, such as the government, military and media, that support this elite group. Thus, gradual change may be possible, as conflicts occur not between classes but within elite groups (Prewitt & Stone 1993).

Instead of insisting on one particular perspective, I suggest that we consider how frameworks of power help us understand this process of social change. For the purpose of this review, I consider power as an ability to shape social contexts, building on Lukes' third level of power (1986). This third level subsumes both a first level, referring to decision-making power that affects others' actions, and a second level, concerning the power to prevent activities from occurring.

Within an interactive, dynamic system, agents of powerful institutions have the capacity to shape the contexts in which problems and solutions are determined. In this framework, power is unevenly held but established through interaction (Simmel 1986) within existing networks (Foucault 1986). Moreover, power is not conceived as the property of an individual (Arendt 1986), but manifest in the institutions that offer certain high-level agents authority (Simmel 1986), functioning within political and economic systems (Habermas 1986). This structure involves a network of people and institutions, through organizationally based power in economic, political, military and ideological domains (Dumhoff 1993).

Maintaining power requires securing legitimacy among those who are governed (Arendt 1986; Skocpol 1993). This legitimation may be promoted through the ideological production of discourse (Foucault 1986). Gramsci (1971) articulates a process of hegemony, through which powerful groups attempt to maintain consent by controlling ideological institutions. Downing (1996, 200) explains that this ideological domain represents "a terrain of struggle for organized political forces ... in their attempt to claim control over the direction of society's development."

These theoretical understandings of power offer a great deal in our reconceptualization of development communication. Seeing development as a discourse, we may examine the assumptions implicit in the frameworks justifying strategic intervention. Through discourse, institutions create knowledge about groups of people, through their representation in constructed categories. Seeing development as a practice within a global economic and political system, we may illuminate the conditions through which certain problems and groups attract visibility and become reconstituted for the purpose of intervention. Seeing development as organizational intervention, we may explore the organizational contexts and project characteristics that guide implementation. Although some of the concerns raised more generally about development are relevant to a discussion of power, development communication may be seen as a special case in which institutions engage in ideological production through strategic intervention using communication processes and technologies.

Institutional Discourse

In this section, I begin by conceptualizing development as a discourse and then review how this discourse has shifted over time in offering visibility to different issues and groups. By discourse, I refer to an understanding of development as a set of interpretations that are structured through institutional statements about people, places and problems. As Crush (1995, 6) explains, development discourse becomes "constituted and reproduced within a set of material relationships, activities and powers—social, cultural and geopolitical." These relationships are manifest through the actions of development institutions, working in their global context. Discourse perpetuates the interests of the agency promoting these interpretations and therefore should be understood as political and not neutral (Escobar 1995a). The categories constructed through development discourse not only shape problems and those perceived to suffer from those problems, but also legitimize appropriate solutions (Rakow 1989; Schön 1979). Within this process, some agents hold more power than others to structure frameworks of issues and interventions.

This power to shape reality about the very nature of social change is then held by institutions acting within historical and geographical contexts (Crush 1995; Escobar 1995b). Power of this nature is rooted in ability to articulate knowledge, specifically about others. In reference to Orientalism, Said (1978, 32) suggests that to "have such knowledge ... is to dominate it, to have authority over it." Said (1978, 1993) and Escobar (1995b) agree that development has worked historically as another form of colonizing discourse.

Early approaches to development privileged economic conditions within the nation-state. President Truman's 1949 speech, suggesting that global poverty might be resolved through strategic industrialization, urbanization and technology, launched this U.S. perspective (Escobar 1995b; Melkote 1991). Schramm (1963), Lerner (1962) and others believed that communication would foster this path toward universal modernization, by encouraging individuals to act and think in more empathic ways and establishing the infrastructure needed to facilitate commercial growth and democratic governance.

As the documented conditions of many in impoverished nations did not improve despite the introduction

1927
1960
1963
1964
1967
1969
1970
1971
1972
1973
1974
1975
1976
1977
1978
1979
1980
1981
1982
1983
1984
1985
1986
1987
1988
1989
1990
1991
1992
1993
1994
1995
1996
1997
1998
1999
2000
2001
2002
2003
2004
2005
2006

of many development programs, the development model was critiqued on several grounds from the seventies on (Melkote 1991; Rogers 1976). The initial premise that all societies would evolve along similar paths was replaced with a more contextual understanding of development. In addition to moving away from a universal path or goal, equity and distribution grew in import relative to an earlier emphasis on economic growth. This was also the era of the "basic needs approach," emphasizing the fundamental resources people need for survival. Still, these new approaches did not question the very premise that development would alleviate problematic conditions.

In addition, others raised serious concerns regarding the receipt of development aid as perpetuating dependence of poorer countries on wealthier bilateral and multilateral agencies. This concern with development as a form of cultural imperialism, perpetuating dependency, moved the focus from modernization within a nation-state to concerns with an international structure of nation-states with different degrees of power. Dependency scholars reminded us then of the power structure within which developing countries work, situating power in the hands of wealthier nations (Schiller 1991).

Against the dominance of a global market system, some groups organize to promote the idea of a global civil society, recognizing the importance of postmaterialist values (Calabrese 1997). While some insist on conceptualizing the development process within a global structure, others point to local, community-level efforts as appropriate domains for examining social change (Huesca 1995; see also Escobar 2000 for discussion of global–local distinction). Recent attention to social movements complements participatory approaches, by emphasizing the ability of marginal communities to control their own social change, but also situating these processes within contexts differentiating levels of power (Gamson & Wolfsfeld 1993).

New approaches to development, referred to by some as "postdevelopment," establish social movements

as a radical alternative, promoting marginal interests against dominant development structures and ideologies (Escobar 1995b; Moore 1995). In this regard, social movements are not seen as a way to transform or improve development, but as "symbols of resistance to the dominant positions of knowledge and organization of the world … for the re-imagining of the 'Third World' and a post-development era" (Escobar 1995b, 227). This understanding of social change corresponds with Freire's (1983) approach to using communication processes, through dialogue, as a way to recognize and then resist oppression.

Several scholars are now beginning to remark upon a "crisis" in development, questioning the entire project (Moore 1995; Parpart 1995). To do so, they examine development discourse (Crush 1995), not only in terms of its historical claims, but also in terms of its current concerns, such as sustainable development, structural adjustment, and population. The latter issue, population, tends to be connected with environment degradation (Williams 1995) or limitations (Mitchell 1995), proposing a balance between demography and geography. Several authors (such as Mackenzie 1995; Moore 1995; Williams 1995) suggest that these frameworks objectify and subjugate the very people they intend to serve.

Similarly, sustainable development, as an approach that articulates the need to serve a current generation without compromising the interests of a future generation, is critiqued on several levels. First, this approach reclaims the importance of economic development, albeit with an added interest toward environmental preservation, and second, it assumes that the earth can and should be managed, by changing the irrational behavior of the poor (Escobar 1995a). This discourse legitimizes and rationalizes economic growth and efficiency within a global capitalist system, ignoring "destructive social consequences and human costs" (Ferguson 1995, 130).

Development discourse involves the institutional production of texts, justifying intervention. Through this discourse, people, as well as places and conditions, are categorized through a bureaucratization of knowledge. This process involves the creation of "techno-representations," in Escobar's words, "endowed with complex political and cultural histories" (1995a, 213) that create visual structures of groups without allowing them to be heard. Development institutions then have the ability to create knowledge about and represent others (Escobar 1995a; Said 1978, 1993).

Examining development discourse over time, one can see that groups and issues shift in their importance. The visibilities of rural poor and women, for example, grew during the seventies (Escobar 1995a). The issue of women in development (WID) became more prominent by 1975, when the U.N. launched the Year of Women. This discourse valued women's contributions as economic producers and as human reproducers (Staudt 1985). Attention to WID gradually shifted toward a concern with "gender and development" (GAD), changing the frame toward an understanding of gender as a socially constructed category (Wilkins 1997). Recent literature proposes a new shift toward "international feminisms" (Sreberny-Mohammadi 1996), recognizing differences across class, race and other social categories (Mackenzie 1995).

Despite this shift in discourse, women still dominate the focus of attention in development communication in health, population and nutrition projects, particularly in their role as reproducers (Wilkins 1999). Thus, in practice gender appears to operate in a way that essentializes women according to their biological conditions rather than account for their social, political and economic relationships. Moreover, women in these projects tend to be targeted as individual consumers, assuming that they will facilitate social change through their successful purchase of suggested services and products.

Another important trend in representation is the emergence of the "consumer" as an explicit category of beneficiary (Wilkins 1999). This implies that communication interventions are targeting those with the capacity to purchase products or services, in the process of improving their conditions. This category implies a different metaphor of social change than working with the "poorest of the poor," whose circumstances may preclude active participation in the marketplace.

Development communication projects, like many Western communication campaigns, tend to represent their beneficiaries as individuals in need of information or persuasion (Salmon 1989). This interpretation of a beneficiary is problematic, blaming individuals for the very problems the interventions claim to intend to resolve (Mody 1991). In this regard, the cause of the social problem addressed is located within an individual decision to change, rather than a problematic structure that limits the distribution of resources or even a normative climate that constrains the possibilities for change.

These categories are produced by development institutions in their production of knowledge about the people they intend to help and the problems they believe to be relevant. Formative research used in the design of these interventions, summative research used to evaluate, and managerial monitoring of planning and implementation are all used in the process of constructing communities, problems and interventions.

Institutional Practice

One may locate power within the development institutions engaged in its practice. Development communication, as a strategic intervention, is implemented by agencies working within organizational contexts, conditioning the norms of interpretation, and political-economic structures, constraining the possibilities for decision making. Situating development communication within structures of power implies that the interventions themselves need to be contextualized beyond a simplistic media-effects model. Instead of focusing on the reception of communication campaigns, this framework would ask us to consider the organizational contexts within which social problems and their solutions are articulated. Organizational

1927
1960
1963
1964
1967
1969
1970
1971
1972
1973
1974
1975
1976
1977
1978
1979
1980
1981
1982
1983
1984
1985
1986
1987
1988
1989
1990
1991
1992
1993
1994
1995
1996
1997
1998
1999
2000
2001
2002
2003
2004
2005
2006

contexts encompass both structural (in terms of interorganizational relations) and normative (in terms of shared approaches to social problems and their solutions) conditions (Putnam & Pacanowsky 1983).

A range of institutions may be involved in the process of using communication to promote strategic social change. Development projects tend to be supported through bilateral and multilateral institutions, along with national agencies and nongovernmental organizations (NGOs). Each organization may play multiple roles, as a donor distributing resources to another organization, as a recipient receiving resources, and even as a referent to other organizations engaged in similar activities. The funding relationship may be characterized in terms of the degree of concentration or control exhibited or the extent of autonomy restricted. A development agency rarely exclusively serves in either a donor or a recipient role, but acts in different capacities in relation to different organizations. An NGO, for example, may receive bilateral funding, but then in turn support other development agencies. These relationships compose a structure of institutional activity, which guides the process of implementation.

Governments, along with other agencies, create programs to promote social change within their own territorial domains. Within states, the politically powerful may be seen as holding the ability to control political, economic and ideological institutions (Olsen & Marger 1993). States must deal not only with the internal divisions of power, but also within a global system of nations with different access to resources. States with adequate resources to do so have the capacity to act as bilateral agencies, sponsoring projects in other countries. The U.S. Agency for International Development (USAID) is one of many bilateral institutions, with comparatively more resources to invest in the development project than many other agencies. Because of its prominence as a donor and as a referent, it is critical to observe trends in USAID practice, such as its movement toward the private sector in its economic and social development programs (Mitchell 1995; USAID

1993; Wilkins 1999). One might also study internal dimensions of development organizations, such as the distribution of resources and the establishment of offices devoted to particular concerns (Staudt 1997).

Multilateral agencies combine resources from two or more government institutions to support development projects. Many United Nations (U.N.) organizations, such as the U.N. Development Programme (UNDP) and the U.N. Population Fund (UNFPA), fit this category. Similar to bilateral institutions, multilateral agencies have been accused of promoting projects that do not question existing power structures, thereby serving a global elite (Escobar 1995a; Williams 1993).

Although some point to NGOs as important actors in the development sphere (such as Mody 1991), it is not easy to generalize the function of this category of agency. Some NGOs receive a high concentration of funding from government sources, while others limit or deny this source of revenue. Those that do rely on government funding may be co-opted within the process of creating and implementing strategic interventions (MacDonald 1995). Some NGOs, though, are able to resist promoting the agendas of larger agencies, either through strongly establishing their own strategic interests or through limiting the nature or proportion of received resources. Some community groups, collectively promoting social movements, do not represent formal NGO status, but merit attention given their critical role in engaging alternative visions of social change.

Development communication interventions are implemented by agencies and communities working within a global system. Recent conceptualizations of development argue that social change processes may be more adequately conceived on different spatial or local levels, in terms of social movements, connected through global rather than national parameters (see Escobar 2000). These trends toward globalization are explained through the growth of international agencies and global forms of communication and production (Schiller 1991).

This global power system appears to be dominated by a few wealthy nation-states, particularly the United States, and transnational corporations, sharing interests and practices toward markets and consumers (Schiller 1991, 21). These powerful institutions may enforce co-optation as well as control of media technologies and industries, with little consideration of inequities in use or access (Steeves 1993). While global capital may not be homogenizing communities around the world, these processes may be consolidating heterogeneous groups for the purposes of consumption and tourism (Escobar 1995b, 99).

Development discourse itself may be seen as legitimizing global capitalism as a natural and universal system (Moore 1995, 7). A trend toward privatizing development interventions (Wilkins 1999) corresponds with broader policy shifts toward deregulation and privatization within and across political boundaries (Mohammadi 1997; Moore 1995). These trends serve the interests of those agencies that benefit from the growing dominance of a global capitalist system, limiting the efforts of poorer communities and nations in their quest for capital to direct their own social change.

Strategic Intervention

In this section, I first consider models of social change embedded within development communication discourse. Then I characterize assumptions made about different communication technologies and processes in strategies for intervention.

As a strategic intervention, development communication works with communication technologies and processes to promote social change, engaging many substantive fields, such as health, nutrition, education, population, agriculture and micro-enterprise. Whether explicit or implicit, frameworks of development communication posit a source of power in their conceptualizations of the social change process. Both modernization and dependency frameworks share an assumption that media have a great deal of power to affect audiences, while participatory and social movement approaches highlight the ability of communication processes and technologies to facilitate the strategic interests of marginal communities.

Although communication interventions may be united by their assumption that information may be an appropriate means to resolve social concerns, they are divided in their approaches to intervention. Social problems, and consequently the interventions designed to resolve them, are constructed by practitioners working within organizational contexts, which are guided and constrained by normative climates and political-economic structures. Those groups and persons participating in the construction of communication campaigns have power with respect to their ability to define problems, appropriate solutions, and beneficiaries (Gergen & Gergen 1983; Salmon, 1989). Some issues are then selected over others for intervention.

Communication interventions use communication technologies and processes in many ways, for a variety of purposes. Among other functions, communication technologies may be used as low-cost loudspeakers, as motivators of demand or even as legitimators (Hornik 1988); these technologies may also be directed toward individual, social, institutional or policy change. Communication processes may be used to facilitate the planning, implementation or dissemination of an intervention. Involving beneficiaries in these communication processes may help avoid the failure of development communication interventions to account for peoples' existing knowledge and concerns (Mody 1991).

Communication interventions may fail for a variety of reasons. Hornik's (1988) review of the failure of development communication projects suggests that many fail due to inappropriate theoretical approaches, poor program implementation, inadequate resources or lack of political support. Understanding the political and economic contexts in which these projects are introduced may also allow us to have a better sense of how these interventions are interpreted. For example, one might need to assess the commercial

1927
1960
1963
1964
1967
1969
1970
1971
1972
1973
1974
1975
1976
1977
1978
1979
1980
1981
1982
1983
1984
1985
1986
1987
1988
1989
1990
1991
1992
1993
1994
1995
1996
1997
1998
1999
2000
2001
2002
2003
2004
2005
2006

context in which social messages are introduced, in order to gauge the environment in which beneficiaries are being asked to respond. Evaluations of communication projects tend to focus on the social conditions of individuals within defined groups, ignoring other salient conditions, such as other messages supported through the media in accordance with dominant political and economic agents.

An underlying issue here is who might be engaging in the production of these interventions, and for whose benefit. When strategic interventions for social change encourage individuals to consume, then the interests of the commercial and public systems do not diverge. The social marketing model (McGuire 1989) follows this trend, suggesting that individuals may improve their problematic conditions through prudent choices in the marketplace. Social marketing coincides with a broader trend toward commercializing social issues, such as public health. For example, many development agencies have devoted substantial resources to education about and distribution of oral rehydration solutions (ORS), a critical resource in alleviating devastating dehydration that accompanies diarrhea in infants. Now multinational corporations are absorbing this function, creating cereal-based ORS to market for adults as well as for infants (BASICS 1998).

Through this approach, beneficiaries of public programs are constructed as consumers, media are deemed useful to the degree they change behavior, and social change is situated within individual responses to market conditions. Characterizing social change within a commercial structure resonates with globalization trends privileging the role of multinational corporations as dominant institutions. Social marketing is quite popular among USAID projects, working within existing power structures to promote gradual change in support of a global capital system.

Other models of intervention differ from social marketing in their approaches to social change. Some efforts, for example, attempt to influence decision makers who have the capacity to change policies of key institutions,

or to foster gradual normative change about particular issues. While projects attempting structural change are implemented by a variety of institutions, projects intending to educate in the long run tend to be orchestrated through multilateral agencies or NGOs.

Another model suggests that information be offered for its own merit, as a human right, leaving aside the potential outcome of the intervention. A participatory model that conceptualizes participation as an end in itself would fit this mold (Melkote 1991). This approach to communication intervention engages a social process by which groups with common interests jointly construct messages to improve their situation or change unjust social structures (Mody 1991). Communication, then, enables people to recognize their oppressive circumstances and then perhaps act collectively to transform their situation (Freire 1983). These approaches tend to be supported by NGOs and local community organizations in their attempts to contest dominant frames and structures.

Although these interventions may seem valuable as a potential form of resistance, there are a number of concerns with their implementation. In their attempts to address local needs, some interventions may result in perpetuating inegalitarian power structures, particularly across gender, within communities. Moreover, participation, without concomitant changes in structural conditions, may not be sufficient to foster substantive social change (Escobar 1995b; Mody 1991).

Media provide critical sources of information and socialization in many of our communities. In development communication, interventions are designed to use these technologies or processes strategically to promote defined social change. As in media studies, key questions regarding strategic communication intervention include: who controls the production of knowledge, and by extension, mediated messages? Who has access to this production process? What are the constructions of people, problems, places and solutions embedded in this discourse? An assumption here is that the production of strategic communication, as in any other media industry, conveys the interests of dominant agents within a global system, becoming a site for ideology to be produced and reproduced (Mody 1991). Instead of focusing on media as isolated tools, we need to focus on the processes of power that contribute to the production of communication intervention.

The selection of channels within an intervention may rest on several concerns. At times projects may include implementation decisions based on political considerations, such as a need to legitimate or elevate a sponsoring political agency through an elite medium, such as the Internet or television. When projects have more independence from these concerns, decisions may be grounded in a concern with the access of beneficiaries to the channel, or even assumptions made about the various effects mediated and interpersonal channels might have. Some assume, for example, that people may be more persuasive than media in the process of social influence; Hornik (1989), however, recognizes the potential for mediated technologies, particularly when people both recognize intervention concerns as their own and have the capacity to act on them.

The potential for an intervention either to engage resistance or to support dominant institutions is not inherent within a channel, but contingent upon the context in which it is introduced. Melkote (1991) demonstrates how folk media may be used in many ways, as a participatory tool for community action or as a government means for disseminating information. Some groups who wish to engage in more radical visions of social change may opt for using alternative instead of dominant media systems, particularly if they believe that certain media industries will not portray their interests favorably.

Some new trends appear to do more to support the existing global economic system than to question it, positioning social change as a gradual process to facilitate at an individual level. Enter-educate strategies, for example, expand upon earlier social marketing ideas by using popular media to promote social messages. This has become an increasingly popular strategy in many countries around the world, including India and Brazil, since a Peruvian radio drama was broadcast in 1969 highlighting a young woman's advancement through her skillful use of a Singer sewing machine (Singhal & Rogers 1989). While this type of intervention is intended to influence individuals toward socially beneficial goals by attracting their attention with enticing media formats, enter-education projects may be seen as promoting social change in a way that does not question existing economic or political systems.

Similarly, new communication technologies are being used in development projects in support of global, rather than national, economic domains. Some see new communication technologies as advancing "irreversible social and political change" (Bugliarello 1994, 76). This framework assumes movement toward a global economic structure to be neutral and automatic, instead of recognizing political connections. Communication technologies then move from being constructed as tools for modernization toward being vehicles for privatization.

Current enthusiasm for new communication technologies replaces an earlier emphasis on public programs within the nation-state with a drive toward privatizing public interventions within a global context. Many emerging programs using new communication technologies for development attempt to integrate participants into a global information economy (Wilkins & Waters 1999). Like many other projects, a central tenet of this approach is that private-sector investment is necessary to build an information infrastructure. Consequently, less wealthy nations are urged to privatize their cultural industries in order to "participate" in this globalization, just as the industrialized nations have done. The potential risks from engaging in this global community include loss of control over cultural industries, loss of capital to multinational corporations, and loss of power over policy decisions.

1927
1960
1963
1964
1967
1969
1970
1971
1972
1973
1974
1975
1976
1977
1978
1979
1980
1981
1982
1983
1984
1985
1986
1987
1988
1989
1990
1991
1992
1993
1994
1995
1996
1997
1998
1999
2000
2001
2002
2003
2004
2005
2006

This integration into a global economy raises again potential concerns with dependency. As Reeves (1993) argues, the ability to produce and use new technologies is concentrated in an elite group of multinational corporations and nations (such as the United States and Japan). For a less wealthy nation to use these technologies, it would need to acquire hardware, software and maintenance from these wealthier groups, thus reinforcing structures of dependency (Schiller 1991). Such an investment would not only increase foreign debt, but also allocate resources away from needed health, education and other social services. Thus, a push from large bilateral, multilateral or even large NGOs to invest in technological infrastructure may encourage local government officials to serve commercial interests rather than meet social needs.

Another approach to understanding the role of new technologies in social change focuses on the use of these as tools for participation and empowerment, particularly among marginal groups. Research in this area is just beginning, but some studies document the use of computers to promote dialogue among women's organizations (Moseley 1995; Owen 1998), labor unions (Drew 1998) and other marginal groups (IDRC 1992).

Although projects designed to promote commercial global modernity and alternative participatory processes command substantially different levels of resources and articulate vastly divergent goals, their discourse on the importance of new technologies is remarkably similar (Wilkins & Waters 1999). These varied projects seem to concur on the benefits of this globalization through digitized information, whether as linking the global marketplace or activist communities. Neither framework appears to question the broader parameters of a system that invites poor communities to participate in a global commercial system.

Reconceptualizing Development Communication

Reconceptualizing the field in terms of power demands that we consider development communication as an intervention created and justified through institutional discourse operating within a global system. We need to reconsider what difference these structures and dynamics have made in attempts to promote social change through strategic intervention. An analysis such as this might begin with locating power sources, in order to ascribe responsibility to powerful agents and to identify potential avenues for resistance (for example, see Mody 2000). Using communication technologies and processes to promote social change need not necessarily follow a patriarchal approach. To escape this cycle, we need to recognize problematic patterns and attempt to change them.

References

Arendt, H. 1986. "Communicative Power," in: S. Lukes, ed. *Power.* Oxford, U.K.: Basil Blackwell. 59–74.

Aron, R. 1986. "Macht, power, puissance: Democratic prose or demoniacal poetry?" in: S. Lukes, ed. *Power.* Oxford, U.K.: Basil Blackwell. 253–278.

BASICS. 1998. *Social Marketing Matters* 6. Partnership for Child Health Care.

Bugliarello, G. 1995. "The global generation, transmission, and the diffusion of knowledge: How can the developing countries benefit?" *Marshaling technology for development: Proceedings of a symposium.* Washington D.C.: National Academy Press. 61–82.

Calabrese, A. 1997. "Global trade, the information society and the ambivalence of social movements," International Association of Media and Communication Research Conference.

Crush, J. 1995. "Introduction," in: J. Crush, ed. *Power of development.* New York: Routledge. 1–26.

Downing, J. 1996. *Internationalizing media theory: Transition, power, culture.* London, U.K.: Sage Publications.

Drew, J. 1998. "Global communications in the post-industrial age," Dissertation. Univ. of Texas at Austin.

Escobar, A. 1991. "Anthropology and the development encounter: The making and marketing of development anthropology," *American Ethnologist,* 18:658–682.

Escobar, A. 1995a. *Encountering development: The making and unmaking of the Third World.* Princeton, N.J.: Princeton Univ. Press.

Escobar, A. 1995b. "Imagining a post-development era," in: J. Crush, ed. *Power of development.* New York: Routledge. 211–227.

Ferguson, J. 1995. "From African socialism to scientific capitalism: Reflections on the legitimation crisis in IMF-ruled Africa," in: D.B. Moore and G.J. Schmitz, eds. *Debating development discourse: Institutional and popular perspectives.* New York: St. Martin's Press. 129–148.

Foucault, M. 1986. "Disciplinary power and subjection," in: S. Lukes, ed. *Power.* Oxford, U.K.: Basil Blackwell. 229–242.

Freire, P. 1983. *Pedagogy of the oppressed.* M.B. Ramos, trans. New York: Continuum.

Gamson, W., and G. Wolfsfeld. 1993. "Movements and media as interacting systems," *Annals, APSS* 528:114–125.

Gergen, M.M., and K.J. Gergen. 1983. "Interpretive dimensions of international aid," *New Directions in Helping* 3:329–348.

Gramsci, A. 1971. "Class consciousness," in: G. Lukacs, ed. *History and class consciousness: Studies in Marxist dialectic.* Cambridge, Mass.: MIT Press. 46–82.

Habermas, J. 1986. "Hannah Arendt's communications concept of power," in: S. Lukes, ed. *Power* Oxford, U.K.: Basil Blackwell. 5–93.

Hornik, R.C. 1988. *Development communication, information, agriculture and nutrition in the Third World.* New York: Longman.

Hornik, R.C. 1989. "The knowledge–behavior gap in public information campaigns: A development communication view," in: C.T. Salmon, ed. *Information campaigns: Balancing social values and social change.* Newbury Park, Calif.: Sage. 113–138.

Huesca, R. 1995. "A procedural view of participatory communication: Lessons from Bolivian tin miners' radio," *Media, Culture and Society* 17:101–119.

International Development Research Centre (IDRC). 1992. *101 Technologies: From the South for the South.* Ottawa: IDRC.

Lerner, D. 1962. *The passing of traditional society.* Glencoe, Ill.: Free Press.

Lukes, S. 1986. "Introduction," in: S. Lukes, ed. *Power.* Oxford, U.K.: Basil Blackwell. 1–18.

MacDonald, L. 1995. "NGOs and the problematic discourse of participation: Cases from Costa Rica," in: D.B. Moore and G.J. Schmitz, eds. *Debating development discourse: Institutional and popular perspectives.* New York: St. Martin's Press. 201–229.

Mackenzie, F. 1995. "Selective silence: A feminist encounter with environmental discourse in colonial Africa," in: J. Crush, ed., *Power of development.* New York: Routledge. 100–114.

Marger, M.N. 1993. "The mass media as a power institution," in: M.E. Olsen and M.N. Marger, eds. *Power in modern societies.* Boulder, Colo.: Westview Press. 238–250.

McGuire, W. 1989. "Theoretical foundations of campaigns," in: R.E. Rice and C.K. Atkin, eds. *Public communication campaigns.* 2nd ed. Newbury Park, Calif.: Sage. 43-66.

Melkote, S.R. 1991. *Communication for development in the Third World.* New Delhi: Sage.

Mitchell, T. 1991. "America's Egypt: Discourse of the development industry," *Middle East Report* 21(2):18–34.

Mody, B. 1991. *Designing messages for development communication: An audience participation–based approach.* New Delhi: Sage.

Mohammadi, A. 1997. "Communication and the globalization process in the Third World," in: A. Mohammadi, ed. *International communication and globalization: A critical introduction.* London: Sage. 67–89.

Moore, D.B. 1995. "Development discourse as hegemony: Towards an ideological history—1945–1995," in: D.B. Moore and G.J. Schmitz, eds. *Debating development discourse: Institutional and popular perspectives.* New York: St. Martin's Press. 1–53.

Moseley, E.S. 1995. *Women, information, and the future: Collecting and sharing resources worldwide.* Fort Atkinson, Wisc.: Highsmith Press.

Olsen, M.E., and M.N. Marger. 1993. "Theoretical perspectives on power," in: M.E. Olsen and M.N. Marger, eds. *Power in modern societies.* Boulder, Colo.: Westview Press. 75–87.

Owen, C. 1998. *New technologies and women's movements in Mexico.* M.A. thesis. Univ. of Texas at Austin.

Parpart, J. 1995. "Post-modernism, gender and development," in: J. Crush, ed. *Power of development.* New York: Routledge. 253–265.

Prewitt, K., and A. Stone. 1993. "The ruling elites," in: M.E. Olsen and M.N. Marger, eds. *Power in modern societies.* Boulder, Colo.: Westview Press. 125–136.

Putnam, L., and M.E. Pacanowsky, eds. 1983. *Communication and organizations: An interpretive approach.* Beverly Hills: Sage.

Rakow, L. 1989. "Information and power: Toward a critical theory of information campaigns," in: C. Salmon, ed. *Information campaigns: Balancing social values and social change.* Newbury Park, Calif.: Sage. 164–184.

Reeves, G. 1993. *Communications and the Third World.* London: Routledge.

Rogers, E. 1976. Communication and development: The passing of the dominant paradigm. *Communication Research* 3(2):121–133.

Said, E. 1978. *Orientalism.* New York: Pantheon Books.

Said, E. 1993. *Culture and imperialism:* New York: Alfred A. Knopf.

Salmon, C. 1989. "Campaigns for social 'improvement': An overview of values, rationales, and impacts," in C.T. Salmon, ed. *Information campaigns: balancing social values and social change.* Newbury Park, Calif.: Sage. 19–53.

Schiller, H.I. 1991. Not yet the post-imperialist era. *Critical Studies in Mass Communication* 8:13–28.

Schmitz, G.J. 1995. "Democratization and demystification: Deconstructing 'governance' as development paradigm," in D.B. Moore and G.J. Schmitz, eds. *Debating development discourse: Institutional and popular perspectives.* New York: St. Martin's Press. 54–90. Schön, D. 1979. "Generative metaphor: A perspective of problem-setting," in: A. Orthony, ed. *Metaphor and thought.* Cambridge, U.K.: Cambridge Univ. Press. 254–283.

Schramm, W. 1963. "Communication development and the development process," in L. Pye, ed. *Communications and political development.* Princeton, N.J.: Princeton Univ. Press.

Simmel, G. 1986. "Domination and freedom," in: S. Lukes, ed. *Power.* Oxford, U.K.: Basil Blackwell. 203–210.

Singhal, A., and E. Rogers. 1989. "Prosocial television for development in India," in: R. Rice and C.K. Atkin, eds. *Public communication campaigns.* 2nd ed. Newbury Park, Calif.: Sage.

Skocpol, T. 1993. "The Potential autonomy of the state," in: M.E. Olsen and M.N. Marger, eds. *Power in modern societies.* Boulder, Colo.: Westview Press. 306–313.

Sreberny-Mohammadi, A. 1996. International feminism(s): Engendering debate in international communications. *Journal of International Communication* 3(1):1–3.

Staudt, K. 1985. *Women, foreign assistance and advocacy administration.* New York: Praeger.

Staudt, K. 1997. "Gender politics in bureaucracy: Theoretical issues in comparative perspective," in: K. Staudt, ed. *Women, international development, and politics: The bureaucratic mire.* Philadelphia: Temple Univ. Press. 3–34.

Steeves, H.L. 1993. "Creating imagined communities: Development communication and the challenge of feminism," *Journal of Communication* 43(3):218–229.

U.S. Agency for International Development (USAID). 1993. *The substance behind the images: USAID and development communication.* Washington, D.C.: USAID.

Wilkins, K. 1997. "Gender, power and development," *Journal of International Communication.* December. 102–120.

1927
1960
1963
1964
1967
1969
1970
1971
1972
1973
1974
1975
1976
1977
1978
1979
1980
1981
1982
1983
1984
1985
1986
1987
1988
1989
1990
1991
1992
1993
1994
1995
1996
1997
1998
1999
2000
2001
2002
2003
2004
2005
2006

Wilkins, K. 1999. "Development discourse on gender and communication in strategies for social change," *Journal of Communication* 49(1):44-64.

Wilkins, K., and J. Waters. 1999. "New technologies in development communication," International Communication Association Conference.

Williams, G. 1993. "Modernizing Malthus: The World Bank, population control and the African environment," in: J. Crush, ed. *Power of development*. New York: Routledge. 150–175.

THE CONTEXTS OF POWER AND THE POWER OF THE MEDIA

Excerpt from: Redeveloping Communication for Social Change

By Bella Mody

2000 The contexts of power in society are economic, political, cultural and technological. Changes in the dominance of one group—be it based on gender, ethnicity, language, religion, region or economic assets—are a result of the continuous struggle over resources, material, e.g., land; and cultural, e.g., how we live, speak and behave. Dominant groups use all of the tools at their command, including power over media ownership, financing, management, professional values, equipment, programming and audiences, to influence subordinate groups' perceptions of a particular society.

Writing about communication technology in general (1983, 1988) and satellites in particular (1987; Mody & Borrego 1991), I intended to provide an alternative to the technological determinist framework for scholarly and policy discourse about media hardware. The notion that the characteristics of technology have an overwhelming influence on social effects, irrespective of who uses them and to what ends, was adopted by most communication scholars uneducated in social structural analysis or development praxis. I wanted national policy makers to analyze the power structure before they made technology adoption decisions. Little did I know that I was merely asking public policy analysts to do what those in the private sector already did: environmental analysis as the crux of strategic management of firms (Fahey & Narayanan 1986).

The purpose of this paper is historical, analytical and prospective. It describes U.S. research of the 1940s that established the limited effects of the media, shows how these findings were ignored when media were promoted as a panacea for developing countries in the 1950s and 1960s, and then documents the to-be-expected disappointment with media's contribution to national development in the subsequent decade. Shortcomings in program production and developing country dependence on foreign imports have culminated in the privatization of the ownership of domestic media systems, broadcasting from foreign satellites and cosmetic program localization. The power of entrenched developing country power structures and the impotence of media-only interventions for social change are illustrated through a devastating experience from the Kheda Communication Project, initiated by India's space technology applications program in the mid-1970s. In the current context of developing countries, more than a billion people still live on less than one dollar a day.

The major global contextual power today is private capital. Foreign aid and the nation-state are in decline. Income gaps are widening between developed and developing countries and within developing countries. Many have written about media being only a complement to other inputs for social change (e.g., Hornik 1988). This paper agrees that a communication-only strategy for social change is doomed, but for very basic reasons: continuing limited media availability, in addition to the impotence of media alone to make an impact on the multidimensional complexity of social change. A new broad-based research agenda for communication in developing countries, rooted in the experiences of particular societies, is proposed.

The Rise of the Media for Development Field

The power context that gave rise to the strategic use of print, radio and television media for "national development" in Third World countries was the Cold War (Mody 1997). The United States and the then Soviet Union were battling for global influence. While we know little about how the former Soviet Union used communication media to help it to win friends and influence nations, we do know a lot about U.S. policy and practice (Samarajiwa 1987; Simpson 1994).

During World War II, many of the U.S. founders of the field of communication worked on the design and evaluation of media campaigns in support of the Allied war effort. Daniel Lerner wrote his doctoral dissertation, entitled *Sykewar*, on psychological warfare against Germany, in 1949. Classical studies that gave birth to mass communication research in the United States (Lowery & DeFleur 1995) also influenced the conceptualization of media-for-development. These include the World War II propaganda studies, the Yale attitude change experiments, Lazarsfeld's research at Columbia University and the Iowa diffusion studies.

The U.S. War Department's Information and Education Division hired Nathan Maccoby, Carl Hovland, Irving Janis and many other psychologists to evaluate the impact of the *Why We Fight* U.S. domestic propaganda films of World War II. Their experiments showed that films could teach facts but that these were forgotten by viewers in a few weeks; their research also showed that films were even weaker at changing opinions and attitudes than they were at teaching facts.

Between 1946 and 1961, the Yale Program of Research on Communication and Attitude Change conducted more than fifty experiments with live speeches and illustrated lectures to understand how people's beliefs, attitudes and behaviors could be manipulated by modifying who said what (and how) to whom. Carl Hovland and his colleagues learned about the characteristics of an effective communicator, how to "inoculate" audiences against subsequent propaganda and how to bring about at least short-term (three-to-four-week) changes in opinions and attitudes.

In the early 1940s, surveys conducted by Lazarsfeld and his doctoral students at Columbia University found that the power of radio and print media was limited by individual differences in personality, group affiliations and interpersonal networks. Their study of the impact of the Roosevelt re-election campaign found only eight percent had changed their opinion; for the majority, the primary effect of the media campaign was reinforcement of existing opinions, not

1927
1960
1963
1964
1967
1969
1970
1971
1972
1973
1974
1975
1976
1977
1978
1979
1980
1981
1982
1983
1984
1985
1986
1987
1988
1989
1990
1991
1992
1993
1994
1995
1996
1997
1998
1999
2000
2001
2002
2003
2004
2005
2006

opinion change. The most important influence on how people voted was interpersonal; the impact of media was filtered through social and cultural power structures, such as family and friends.

In rural Iowa, Ryan and Gross also found the diffusion of hybrid corn to farmers around Ames, Iowa, did not show that print and radio media were particularly powerful in either informing farmers or persuading them to adopt innovations. These findings from classical communication studies (Lowery & DeFleur 1995), conducted around the 1940s in the United States, showed that particular media programs were not powerful manipulators of our hearts and minds in the short run. George Gerbner's significant demonstrations of the effects of media on the cultivation of social values over time were not conducted until the mid-1960s.

After World War II, some journalists and social scientists who worked for the U.S. government gravitated to the United Nations Scientific Educational and Cultural Organization (UNESCO), which the United States had helped to establish, while others went to universities. Wilbur Schramm and Daniel Lerner, who joined the faculties of U.S. universities, received funds from UNESCO, U.S. foreign aid agencies, and the Voice of America, giving the agencies old, disprove ideas about media power for use in developing countries in return. It is conceivable (but unlikely) that they had scholarly reasons to think developing country populations would be more impressionable than U.S. audiences, or power structures and agents of socialization more porous than in the United States. With hindsight, it is easy for us to identify errors, baseless optimism, naïveté or ignorance in earlier scholars, but these critiques advance scholarship.

Daniel Lerner (1958), who is credited with writing the first academic book on media and the modernization of developing societies, suggested that developing countries use the power of print, radio and TV as syringes to inject empathy into the traditional personalities of their citizens to increase their social mobility. His communication model of economic growth and increased voting specified that people would need to migrate from villages to cities and, once there, literacy and mass media automatically would lead viewers to modern ways of living. The data he used on eight Middle Eastern countries (collected for a 1950 audience research contract from the Office of International Broadcasting, which then ran the Voice of America) was not an adequate test of his media-for-modernization proposition. Nevertheless, Lerner's idea of using media for modernization acquired power in an intellectual climate and political context characterized by Walter Rostow's (1960) work on the West-to-East diffusion of modern science and technology as part of the non-Communist alternative for developing countries, and by David McClelland's (1961) work on the need for injecting achievement into fatalistic traditional personalities.

Wilbur Schramm, an alumnus of the U.S. Office of War Information, wrote *Mass Media and National Development* (1964) while a consultant to UNESCO. This very readable book diffused Lerner's unsupported notion of powerful media effects to developing countries. Young rural sociologist Everett Rogers exported Ryan and Gross's conceptualization of the process of the adoption of innovations, and the role of media in this process, to support the diffusion of Western scientific attitudes and technology as recommended by Rostow. UNESCO awarded research grants to Rogers and his doctoral students at Michigan State University, including Luis Ramiro Beltrán from Bolivia, Juan Diaz Bordenave from Paraguay, and Joseph Ascroft from Malawi, to understand how they could use media to support the process of the diffusion of innovations in their own countries.

Beyond the Hardware

When Lerner and Schramm advocated media pipelines, they did not pay attention to the following:

1. Media content
2. The high cost of program production
3. Ownership and administration of media systems (to ensure prosocial content)

4. Access to production skills (limited in many countries)
5. Middle- and upper-class preferences for entertainment programming rather than agricultural health, and educational programming,
6. The advertising industry's desire to use media to carry commercials (thus limiting educational programming in order to maximize audiences)
7. The limited diffusion of media technologies (such as radios, televisions, and Internet-ready personal computers).

Developing countries discovered that harnessing even the limited information transmission power of media required professional expertise in message design. The content of the message had to be locally usable, credible and presented in an attention-getting format for the intended audience. In the 1970s and 1980s, the U.S. Agency for International Development (USAID) sought to remedy the lack of this expertise in developing countries by funding projects in Nicaragua, Kenya and Thailand, among other sites, which focused on designing instructional content through curriculum development and systematic formative research.

External Dependency

It was only a matter of time before resource-constrained print media, radio and TV stations turned to importing Anglo-American news and entertainment. Writing only a couple of years after Schramm's advocacy of media for national development, Dizard (1966) highlighted aspects of the international context that should have been factored in, such as the unidirectional nature of television program flowing between industrialized and developing countries and the Hollywood dominance of TV program production (see Guback 1969 for a similar argument about film). Schiller (1969, 1973) drew attention to the general process of cultural imperialism, particularly in terms of satellites, while Tunstall (1977) declared the media were American. Fifteen years after Schramm's initial advocacy, Boyd-Barrett (1977) drew attention to what he called the media imperialism

process, whereby the ownership, structure, distribution and content of media in one country were subject to external pressures from more powerful media interests of other countries, without proportionate reciprocation. This focus on externally dominated communication media complemented national economic and cultural dependency perspectives on Third World development that Boyd-Barrett had encountered in his work in Latin America (e.g., Cardoso & Faletto 1979). Third World countries had less political, economic and cultural power than their former colonizers and the United States to determine and implement their own national agendas.

The Fall of Media for Development

Third World countries eagerly sought those magical multipliers of information diffusion, such as printing presses, film projectors and radio stations, from USAID and U.S.-influenced UNESCO. However, within a decade Schramm (1976) and Rogers (1976) were independently writing about the disappointing performance of media power in producing change. On a visit to India, Rogers invited my senior colleague, Prakash Shingi at the Indian Institute of Management in Ahmedabad, India, and me, to contribute to his 1976 volume. One of our findings addressed the power of the urban middle class (agricultural scientists and TV producers) over TV program topics and scripting. This resulted in the development of agricultural TV programs that did not address the information needs and vocabulary range of small and medium farmers, much less those of landless laborers. Those who could adopt the Western scientific practices featured in these agricultural TV broadcasts were those who had capital (land), education and purchasing power. U.S.-based media advocates who had ignored U.S. findings on the limited effects of the media solutions found that the populations of developing countries were not any more malleable than U.S. audiences. In addition, they had not factored in the mediating influences of distinct economic, political and social contexts of power in developing societies.

1927
1960
1963
1964
1967
1969
1970
1971
1972
1973
1974
1975
1976
1977
1978
1979
1980
1981
1982
1983
1984
1985
1986
1987
1988
1989
1990
1991
1992
1993
1994
1995
1996
1997
1998
1999
2000
2001
2002
2003
2004
2005
2006

How Context Qualifies Media Influence

In the early 1970s, I worked as a social researcher on the first major direct broadcast satellite TV project in the world, the NASA–India Satellite Instructional TV Experiment (SITE) (Mody 1979). I was appalled on my initial visits to villages when I encountered men and women telling me living conditions had not improved since the British left India some twenty-five years earlier: They said India was still someone else's *raj* (empire), not theirs. My colleagues and I were sure that television cameras used to expose violations of national laws and human rights would help villagers speak back to power sources, thus making it difficult for upper-caste people, large landlords and men to continue to exploit lower-caste folk, landless day-wage laborers and women. Most of us thought knowledge served as power under all conditions: All that was needed to dismantle caste, class and gender abuse was the harsh glare of investigative documentaries and drama on local TV. We did not think about the lack of essential fair and honest legislative, judicial and executive systems needed to support televised exposés.

The Kheda Communication Project, a federal government noncommercial unit of India's SITE project, pictured itself as an agency confronting an oppressive agricultural power structure. To illustrate this argument, I recall one of many episodes from twenty years ago. While the details may have blurred, the essence remains accurate. A producer and a writer for the local news show, called *Vaat Thumaaree* (Your News), drove to the experimental villages every morning to record incidents of injustice and exploitation as they happened, for immediate transmission that evening. The assumption was that exposing unfairness in this way would help resolve the situation promptly. Initially, the team focused on incidents of local government inefficiency, such as roads not being repaired and schools being run without teachers. The TV team interviewed victims and then responsible officials on camera to extract commitments and dates for resolving identified problems. After a reasonable amount of time, crews returned to these sites to report on whether problems had been resolved as promised. Several officials were thus shamed into efficiency.

The crew then moved on to more serious problems of exploitation, such as family agribusinesses not paying their labor the legal minimum wage. The plan was to feature daily interviews of this kind on the same topic in different villages, so the heat would be too much to bear for the offending large farmers and local district government (equivalent of a county in the United States) officials who sheltered them. As the daily coverage continued, daily laborers could not believe the government agency was standing up for them against the local economic power structure, but neither could these economic powers. The federal government agency, full of physicists, TV producers and social scientists, was dabbling in rural development. Large farmers began to protest by writing letters to the physicist-director, complaining that large farm owners were being incorrectly portrayed on their local TV station programmed by the space agency. They then marched to the TV station to protest this portrayal when nothing changed.

Televised interviews of abused labor continued as the harvest season began. Empowered by the coverage and the then Prime Minister's emergency program guaranteeing enforcement of minimum wage laws, laborers decided to strike against landlords for the legal minimum wage. The assumption was that landlords would have to negotiate at this time if they wanted their crops harvested. On the first day of the strike, the local news showed large farmers expressing shock. Disaster struck on the second day: Large farmers hired paramilitary gangs to burn down the huts of the strikers who had been interviewed on television. My TV production colleagues were safely in bed in their homes in the city two to three hours' drive away; the laborers they had interviewed saw their lives and livelihoods go up in flames. No police came, having been paid off by the large farmers. The laborers were not organized and had no political party to turn to. No villager would talk to Kheda Communication Project TV crew henceforth.

The power of TV had confronted the well-organized economic and political power structure of the village and had lost. The opposition of the formal federal political structure had no teeth in comparison to the well-orchestrated local political and economic forces. This anecdote is intended to show how the investigative journalism potential of the media can be constrained by the power structure in a society. It also indicates the need for social research at the interface of media and power structures to specify the conditions under which media power can be harnessed as a successful agent for change.

It was clear to the liberal, well-intentioned urban TV crew of the federally run Kheda Communication Project that they had been irresponsible and naive to think of taking on the village power structure alone, without a master plan or a supporting organization of landless laborers, lawyers and state government officials. We learned firsthand that development and social change through communication technology alone was impossible. Public-service activists experience confrontations like this every day in every part of the world.

Rather than openly taking sides with the exploited as in Kheda, the Western commercial journalistic tradition has radio, TV and the press playing a nonpartisan role, with the confidence that remedial action will occur through a relatively honest police and court system. This assumption is not justified, however, in that media systems in the industrialized North would not be able to sustain many investigative programs such as CBS's *60 Minutes*. Similarly, the assumption that honest government leaders will act to resolve problems in less developed societies is equally unjustified.

Privatization

In the latter half of the 1980s, as support for privatization of state activities grew in Washington, D.C., USAID grants to Johns Hopkins University's Population Communication programs focused developing country attention on private sector media formats, performers, and approaches to attract audiences for prosocial ends. Funding from the Rockefeller Foundation for entertainment-education projects followed. Early research has begun to investigate whether U.S. researchers of these current programs might be repeating possible conceptual and ethical errors made by Lerner and Schramm in promoting particular media and program formats (e.g., entertainment education) (Sherry 1997).

Investors and telecommunication operators from saturated markets in Europe and North America have expanded into the less-mined markets of Asia, Latin America and the Caribbean since the mid-1980s. This is a time when state telecommunication entities have also been looking for investment capital and new technologies. With improved audio, video and text transmission facilities, these agencies intend to meet the unmet demands of their business sectors and to compete in the increasingly global economy (Mody, Bauer & Straubhaar 1995).

The Current Contexts of Power

To understand the possible role of media in support of human welfare in developing countries in the next century, it is necessary to update constantly our environmental analysis, as do private businesses and an increasing number of nonprofit businesses. Developing countries and communities must systematically identify the national development threats and opportunities that they face within their own power structures. Although there has been more progress reducing poverty in the past fifty years than in any comparable period in human history, still more than a billion people live in extreme poverty, lacking clean water, sanitation, electricity and education (UNDP 1998). Media specialists need to specify which media conditions and discourses (if any) and which power contexts might contribute to preferential development for the poor.

The external context of developing countries has become increasingly private and corporate in the last fifteen years: Over half of the largest economies are not

1927
1960
1963
1964
1967
1969
1970
1971
1972
1973
1974
1975
1976
1977
1978
1979
1980
1981
1982
1983
1984
1985
1986
1987
1988
1989
1990
1991
1992
1993
1994
1995
1996
1997
1998
1999
2000
2001
2002
2003
2004
2005
2006

represented by countries, but by private profit-making corporations. The discourse on development in the mainstream media and in the trade press focuses on removing restrictions on private capital rather than on public service applications, such as health, education and welfare. The collapse of Communism and a weak Russia have been accompanied by Anglo-American unity and regional power blocs based on a variety of factors, including fundamentalist religious resurgence, primordial ties, personal authoritarianism and military might. As the polarizing Cold War reasons for official development assistance disappeared, rich industrialized country members of the Organization for Economic Cooperation and Development (OECD) reduced their foreign aid. In 1997, OECD countries gave less than 1/4 of one percent of their gross national product in foreign aid, with the small Nordic countries continuing to give the most (one percent of their GNP), in contrast to the United States donating only 0.08 percent (World Bank 1998).

As states become increasingly financially strapped, they tend to follow IMF advice to provide opportunities for foreign capital investment and to allow competition. In the process, states are losing their control over agriculture, health and industry. Along with the recent adoption of privatization and competition in the developing world, the United Nations Conference on Trade and Development (UNCTAD 1997) has documented a widening of resource gaps between the industrialized North and the less-developed South, as well as within developing countries. The gap between industrialized countries and Latin America has grown most quickly, but other differences, such as the level of resources between industrialized nations and those in Africa, persist. Within developing countries, the income share of the richest 20 percent has risen consistently since the introduction of privatization, deregulation and competition. Thus, most countries appear to be losing proportionately their middle classes, as discrepancies between skilled and unskilled labor grow in this age of capital-intensive, labor-eliminating technology.

Limited Media Access

Although the processes and effects of mediated communication have changed in major ways since the 1960s, there is still limited access to media technologies in many areas. Current statistics show that for every 1,000 people in developing countries, there are only 185 radio receivers, 145 TV receivers, 39 main telephone lines, 3.6 cellular subscribers, 6.5 personal computers, and 0.5 Internet users (UNDP 1998). Yet, the ownership of radio, TV and telecommunications has become less state centered and more private. The availability of foreign capital has increased the number of main telephone lines. Even when they continue to be state operated, operations of media are financed by advertising and are focused on private profit maximization. Regional satellite systems, such as STAR in Asia, provide direct-to-home systems and national cable operators with current Hollywood shows. News channels that antagonize national political regimes are willingly withdrawn from programming, so commercial interests are not hurt, as in the case of STAR dropping the BBC from its satellite feed to China.

In addition, domestic productions imitate foreign formulas and genres. The format of domestic and foreign broadcasts becomes increasingly similar to action-adventure fantasies, for example, sometimes imported and cheaply dubbed, with plots having little resemblance to everyday problems in Los Angeles or Nairobi. Where necessary, media producers use minimum "localization" of foreign formats and stories to attract the right demographic audiences for advertisers. Moreover, only three percent of Internet host computers are in developing countries, which include more than three-quarters of the world's population (Mody 1999).

Massive Development Challenge, Limited Media

One out of six people in the world still lives in poverty, most being in developing countries. The current private sector approach to development seems to be benefiting the rich rather than the poor.

As we enter the next century, communication media continue to be sparsely available. They are increasingly financed through advertising and thus are programmed with entertainment that attracts the largest audience with purchasing power. A little more than forty years ago, development communication was proposed in the United States as the strategic application of communication technology in response to an international Cold War agenda, ending up as the transmission of particular messages by states in developing countries to achieve the objectives of their ruling regimes. The reach of the ruling regime was extended, through the power of the media, to large numbers of people (hence low per-unit cost) simultaneously (hence speedily), in attempts to effect compliance through manipulation of cognitions, values and behavior. With current trends against state control, communication for public welfare and development for the poor seem to be left to nongovernmental organizations (NGOs), financed by foreign and domestic civil organizations.

Research on communication processes in developing countries must evolve beyond communication and development as a mechanistic strategy with associated tactics, to a full-blown disciplinary perspective on communication-in-society, sophisticated enough to be specific to particular developing country time-and-place conditions and universal enough to be comparable. There are lessons to be learned from communication research and praxis elsewhere; most importantly, the research agenda for communication in developing countries needs to avoid mistakes of context-free research and ungrounded theory. A new research agenda for communication in developing countries is recommended, moving beyond state initiatives to nongovernmental civic movements. Like the formal school system, media represent another input into affecting social values. It is crucial, then, that we identify the domestic and external conditions in a society's power structures, as well as the political and economic conditions in their media systems, which may positively influence both opportunities for food, shelter and education for the billion-plus poor and the awareness of human neighborly responsibility of the five billion not-poor others.

References

Boyd-Barrett, 0. 1977. "Media imperialism: Toward an international framework for the analysis of media systems," in: J. Curran, M. Gurevitch, and J. Woollacott, eds. *Mass communication and society.* London: Sage. 116–141.

Cardoso, E.H., and E. Faletto. 1979. *Dependency and development in Latin America.* Berkeley, Calif.: Univ. of California Press.

Dizard, W.P. 1966. *Television: A world view.* Syracuse, N.Y.: Syracuse Univ. Press.

Fahey, L., and V.K. Narayanan. 1986. *Macroenvironmental analysis for strategic management.* St. Paul, Minn.: West Publishing.

Guback, T.H. 1969. *The International Film Industry.* Bloomington: Indiana Univ. Press.

Hornik, R.C. 1989. "The knowledge–behavior gap in public information campaigns: A development communication view," in: C.T. Salmon, ed. *Information campaigns: Balancing social values and social change.* Newbury Park, Calif.: Sage. 113–138.

Lerner, D. 1958. *The Passing of Traditional Society.* Glencoe, Ill.: Free Press.

Lowery, S., and DeFleur, M. 1995. *Milestones in Mass Communication.* New York: Longman.

McClelland, D. 1966. *The Achieving Society* New York: Free Press.

Mody, B. 1979. "Programming in SITE," *Journal of Communication* 29(4):90–98.

Mody, B. 1983. "First World technologies in Third World contexts," in: E.M. Rogers, ed. *Communication technology in the U. S. and Western Europe.* Norwood, N.J.: Ablex. 134–149.

Mody, B. 1987. "Contextual analysis of the adoption of a communication technology: The case of satellites in India," *Telematics and Informatics* 4:151–158.

Mody, B. 1988. "From communication effects to communication contexts," *Media Development* 3:35–37.

Mody, B. 1997. "Cold War to world business system," *Journal of International Communication* 4(2):1–2.

Mody, B. 1999. "The Internet in the other three quarters of the world," *Aspen Institute of Information Studies annal.* April.

Mody, B., J.M. Bauer, and J. Straubhaar. 1995. *Telecommunication politics: Ownership and control of the information highway in developing countries.* Mahwah, N.J.: Lawrence Erlbaum.

Mody. B., and J. Borrego. 1991. "Mexico's Morelos satellite: Reaching for autonomy?" in: G. Sussman and J. Lent, eds. *Transnational communication: Wiring the Third World.* Newbury Park, Calif.: Sage. 150–164.

Rogers, E.M. 1976. *Communication and Development: Critical perspectives.* Thousand Hills, Calif.: Sage.

Rostow, W. 1960. *The Stages of Economic Growth: A Non-Communist Manifesto.* London: Cambridge Univ. Press.

Samarajiwa, R. 1987. "The murky beginnings of the communication and development field," in: N. Jayaweera and S. Amunugama, eds. *Rethinking Development Communication* Singapore: AMIC. 3–19.

Schiller, H.I. 1969. *Mass Communication and American Empire.* New York: August M. Kelly.

1927
1960
1963
1964
1967
1969
1970
1971
1972
1973
1974
1975
1976
1977
1978
1979
1980
1981
1982
1983
1984
1985
1986
1987
1988
1989
1990
1991
1992
1993
1994
1995
1996
1997
1998
1999
2000
2001
2002
2003
2004
2005
2006

Schiller, H.I. 1973. *The Mind Managers*. Boston: Beacon Press.

Schramm, W. 1964. *Mass media and National Development*. Stanford, Calif.: Stanford Univ. Press.

Schramm, W., and D. Lerner, eds. 1976. *Communication and Change: The Past Ten Years and the Next*. Honolulu: Univ. of Hawaii Press.

Sherry, J. 1997. "Prosocial soap operas for development: A review of research and theory," *Journal of International Communication* 4(2):75–101.

Simpson, C. 1994. *Science of coercion: Communication Research and Psychological Warfare 1945–1960*. New York: Oxford Univ. Press.

Tunstall, J. 1977. *The Media are American*. London: Constable.

United Nations Conference for Trade and Development (UNCTAD). 1997. *Trade and Development Report 1996*. Geneva: UNCTAD.

United Nations Development Program (UNDP). 1998. *Human Development Report 1998*. New York: Oxford Univ. Press.

World Bank. 1998. *Assessing Aid: What Works, What Doesn't and Why*. New York: Oxford Univ. Press.

EXCERPT FROM:

SET THE MEDIA FREE

The Fifth Power

By Ignacio Ramonet

2003 The media have been a recourse against abuses of power within the democratic structures of our societies. It is not unusual for the three traditional areas of power—legislative, executive and judicial—to make mistakes and operate less perfectly than they might. This is more likely to happen under authoritarian and dictatorial regimes, where the political realm is mainly responsible for violations of human rights and attacks on liberties. But there are serious abuses of power in democratic countries too, even when laws are the result of democratic votes, governments are elected through universal suffrage and justice is (at least in theory) independent of the executive.

An innocent person can be wrongly accused (as in the infamous Dreyfus affair in France); parliaments can pass laws that discriminate against sections of the population (as with the treatment of AfroAmericans over more than a century in the United States, or the current treatment of people from Muslim countries under the U.S. Patriot Act); and governments can pursue policies that damage a sector of society (as with illegal immigrants in many European countries).

In a democratic framework, the media have often seen it as a duty to denounce such violations of human rights. Sometimes journalists have paid the price—they have been physically attacked, murdered or have disappeared; this is still happening in Colombia, Guatemala, Turkey, Pakistan, the Philippines and elsewhere. This is why, in the phrase attributed to Edmund Burke, journalism is the "fourth estate." Thanks to the civic responsibility of the media and the courage of individual journalists, this fourth estate has provided a fundamental and democratic means for people to criticise, reject and reverse decisions (unfair, unjust, illegal and sometimes even criminal) against innocent people. It is the voice of those who have no voice.

Over the past 15 years, with the acceleration of globalisation, this fourth estate has been stripped of its potential and has gradually ceased to function as a counterpower. This is shockingly apparent when you look closely at the realities of globalisation. A new type of capitalism is on the rise, not just industrial but financial, based on speculation. We are witnessing a clash between the market and the state, the public services and the private sector, the individual and society, the personal and the collective, egoism and solidarity.

Real power is now in the hands of a few global economic groupings and conglomerates that appear to wield more power in world politics than most governments. These are the new masters of the world who gather annually at the World Economic Forum in Davos and lay the groundwork for policy decisions by the globalising trinity of the International Monetary Fund, the World Bank and the World Trade Organisation.

Within this geo-economic framework there has been a decisive transformation in the mass media, striking at the heart of their structure as industries. The mass-communications media (radio, newspapers, television, Internet) are being realigned to create media groups with a world vocation. Giant enterprises such as NewsCorp, Viacom, AOL Time Warner, General Electric, Microsoft, Bertelsmann, UnitedGlobalCom, Disney, Telefónica, RTL Group and France Telecom have realised that the revolution in new technology has greatly increased the possibilities for expansion. The digital revolution shattered the divisions that previously separated the three traditional forms of communication (sound, text and images) and allowed the creation and growth of the Internet. This has now become a fourth form of communication, a means of self-expression, information-access and entertainment.

Subsequently the media companies began a further stage of group restructuring by bringing into a single frame not only the classic media (press, radio and television) but also all activities in mass culture, communication and information. Previously these three spheres were independent: mass culture with its commercial logic, its emphasis on popular programming and its basically commercial objectives; communications, as advertising, marketing and propaganda; and news and information, represented by agencies, radio and television news, press, 24-hour news channels—the many-sided world of journalism.

These three spheres, previously separate, have gradually become integrated into a single sphere in which it is increasingly difficult to distinguish between the elements of mass culture, communication and news.[1] And these giant enterprises, which are assembly-line producers of symbols, now distribute their messages through a wide variety of outlets, including television, animation, film, video games, CDs, DVDs, publishing, Disneyland-type theme parks and sporting events.

The 1940 film "Citizen Kane" was Orson Welles' approach to the superpower status of a U.S. press baron, modelled on the early-20th-century newspaper tycoon William Randolph Hearst. But by today's standards even Kane's power was relatively limited. As the owner of a limited number of papers in a single country he would have been small fry in comparison to the megapower of today's corporate media giants,[2] although this is not to deny that he could have made his mark at both the national and the local level. The modern hyperenterprises have been concentrated, and have bought their way into a wide variety of media sectors in many different countries on every continent. They have acquired such economic weight and ideological importance that they are now major players in globalisation itself. Now that communications—as extended to include information technology,

---

1   See *La Tyrannie de la Communication et Propagandes Silencieuses*, Paris: Galilée, 1999 and 2002 (in paperback in the Folio series).
2   See Silvio Berlusconi's massive Fininvest media corporation in Italy, and the Lagardère and Dassault conglomerates in France.

1927
1960
1963
1964
1967
1969
1970
1971
1972
1973
1974
1975
1976
1977
1978
1979
1980
1981
1982
1983
1984
1985
1986
1987
1988
1989
1990
1991
1992
1993
1994
1995
1996
1997
1998
1999
2000
2001
2002
2003
2004
2005
2006

electronics and telephony—are the heavy industry of our time, these companies are constantly seeking to increase their scale by non-stop company acquisitions. They are also pressuring governments to break down the laws that were designed to limit concentration and prevent the creation of monopolies and duopolies.[3]

Globalisation now also means the globalisation of the mass media and the communications-information companies. These big companies are preoccupied with growth, which means that they have to develop relations with the other estates in society, so they no longer claim to act as a fourth estate with a civic objective and a commitment to denouncing human-rights abuses. They are not interested in correcting the malfunctions of democracy and creating a better political system. They have no interest in being a fourth estate and even less in acting as a countervailing power. And even when they do constitute a fourth estate, that estate is just an adjunct to the existing political and economic estates and operates as a supplementary, media power to crush people.

How do we react to all of this? How can we defend ourselves? How can we resist the offensive of this new power that has betrayed society and gone over to the enemy? The answer is simple. We have to create a new estate, a fifth estate that will let us pit a civic force against this new coalition of rulers. A fifth estate to denounce the hyperpower of the media conglomerates which are complicit in, and diffusers of, neoliberal globalisation.

In some instances the media have not only ceased to defend their citizens but have even acted against them, as in Venezuela. There the opposition swept to power in 1998 in elections that were free and democratic, but the main press, radio and television groupings launched an all-out war against the legitimacy

of President Hugo Chávez.[4] While he and his government had respected the rules of democracy, the media, in the hands of a few magnates, used manipulation, lies and brainwashing to poison minds.[5] In this ideological war they have abandoned any role as a fourth estate and instead have been determined to defend the privileges of a caste by opposing any attempt at social reform or at a slightly fairer distribution of Venezuela's wealth.[6]

Venezuela is an exemplary case of the new international situation, in which media corporations are running rampant and openly operating as guard dogs of the established economic order: a new force operating against the people and civil society. The operations of these big groups are no longer confined to the business of media; they are also, above all, the ideological arm of globalisation. Their function is to contain demands from the grassroots and, where possible, also to seize political power; Silvio Berlusconi, owner of Italy's biggest media conglomerate, has succeeded in achieving this by democratic means.

The media-based dirty war in Venezuela against Chávez is an exact copy of what was done in 1970-73 by the El Mercurio newspaper[7] in Chile, against the democratically elected government of Salvador Allende—this was the campaign that led to the coup against him. And this kind of campaign, with the media setting out to destroy democracy, could happen tomorrow in Ecuador, Brazil or Argentina, against any legal reforms that attempted to modify the social hierarchy and inequalities of wealth. The powers of the traditional oligarchy and the classical reactionaries have now been joined by the power of the media. With a single voice, claiming to speak in the name

---

3   In June, under pressure from the major U.S. media groups, the U.S. Federal Communications Commission authorised the relaxation of limits on concentration: a company is now allowed to control up to 45 percent of the national audience (35 percent previously). The decision was supposed to come into effect in September, but because some have seen it as a serious threat to democracy, it has been suspended by the Supreme Court.

4   See "The Perfect Crime," *Le Monde Diplomatique*, English language edition, June 2002.

5   See Maurice Lemoine, "Venezuela's Press Power," *Le Monde Diplomatique*, English language edition, August 2002.

6   See Maurice Lemoine, "Venezuela: the promise of land for the people," *Le Monde Diplomatique*, English language edition, October 2003.

7   Also other media, such as La Tercera, Ultimas Noticias, La Segunda, Canal 13. See Patricio Tupper, *Allende, la Cible des Médias Chiliens et de la CIA (1970-1973)*, Paris: Editions de l'Amandier, 2003.

of freedom of expression, the media attack anything that defends the interests of the majority of the people. That is the media face of globalisation, and it reveals in the clearest, caricatured way the ideology of globalisation.

Mass media and economic liberalisation are now intimately linked. This is why we think it urgent to analyse how the people of the world might demand a more ethical approach from major media, to require a commitment to truth and a respect for codes of conduct, so that journalists can operate in line with their consciences rather than the interests of the groups, companies and editors that employ them.

In the new war of ideology that globalisation has forced on us, the media are used as a weapon. Since we now face an explosive multiplication and overabundance of information, our news is being contaminated—poisoned by lies; polluted by rumours, misrepresentations, distortions and manipulation.

What is happening here has already happened in the food industry. For a long time food was a scarce commodity and it still is in many parts of the world. But when the countryside began to produce in abundance, particularly in Western Europe and North America, thanks to the revolution in agricultural technology, we found many of our foods were contaminated, poisoned by pesticides, which then caused illnesses, infections, cancers and other health problems (sometimes causing mass panics, as with madcow disease). People once died of hunger. Now they have a chance to die from eating contaminated food.

News was once a scarce commodity, and there is still, in countries run by dictatorships, an absence of reliable, comprehensive and quality news. But in democratic countries news and information overflow on all sides. They are suffocating us. The Greek philosopher Empedocles said that the world was made up of four elements: air, water, earth and fire. Information has become so abundant in our globalised world that it is now almost a fifth element.

THE CRISIS IN PUBLIC SERVICE BROADCASTING
Excerpt from: *Public Service Broadcasting: The History and Meaning of 'Public Service Broadcasting'*
By Ruth Teer-Tomaselli

By the 1980s, globally, public service broadcasting as an institutional form was suffering an historic midlife crisis—an inability to change with the requirements of changing circumstances. Historically, public service broadcasting has been very powerful, and any redirection of the organizational structure and ethos of such institutions was very difficult. The assault against public service broadcasting has come from at least five directions: market forces; new technologies; rising costs; undermining the development and nurturing of National Culture as the mainstay of public broadcasting; and the attack on the impartiality and political independence.

Published in the *South African Journalism Handbook of Excellence*. Pretoria, South Africa: Human Science Research Council, 2004. Used with permission of the author.

But at the same time, as people are now beginning to realise, news is contaminated. It poisons our minds, pollutes our brains, manipulates us, intoxicates us, and tries to instil into our subconscious ideas that are not our own. This is why we now need to establish an ecology of news, to sort real news from a flood of lies. The enormity of the situation was apparent in the invasion of Iraq.[8] We need to decontaminate our news. Just as we can now buy less-contaminated, organic foods, we need organic news. People should mobilise to demand that the media owned by the global groups show respect for the truth, because news is only legitimate when it is really engaged in a search for truth.

That is why we suggested setting up Media Watch Global (L'Observatoire international des médias). It will at last give people a peaceful civic weapon against

---

8   See "State-Sponsored Lies," Le Monde Diplomatique, English language edition, July 2003.

1927
1960
1963
1964
1967
1969
1970
1971
1972
1973
1974
1975
1976
1977
1978
1979
1980
1981
1982
1983
1984
1985
1986
1987
1988
1989
1990
1991
1992
1993
1994
1995
1996
1997
1998
1999
2000
2001
2002
2003
2004
2005
2006

the emerging superpower of the big mass media. It is an outcome of meetings of the global social movement held in Porto Alegre, Brazil, and expresses the concern of the people of the world in the face of the new arrogance of the giant communications industries at the height of their globalisation offensive.

Big media companies push their interests to the detriment of the general interest and confuse their freedom with the freedom of enterprise, held to be the first of liberties. But that freedom of enterprise cannot be permitted to override people's right to rigorously researched and verified news, nor can it serve as an alibi for the deliberate diffusion of false news and defamation.

Press freedom is no more than the extension of collective freedom of expression, which is the foundation of democracy. We cannot allow it to be hijacked by the rich and powerful. It implies a social responsibility, and its exercise must remain, in the final instance, under the control of society. That is why we propose the creation of Media Watch Global, because the media now constitute the only power without a counterweight, which creates an imbalance damaging for democracy. The strength of the organisation will be moral: It will judge media honesty on the basis of ethics, and will seek to remedy media shortcomings by reports and studies which it will prepare, publish and distribute.

Media Watch Global will act as an essential counterweight to the excessive power of the big media groups. It is needed because these groups, in providing news and information, impose the single logic of the market, and the single ideology of neoliberalism. Media Watch Global will be an international association, with the objective of exercising a collective responsibility, in the name of the higher interest of society and the right of citizens to be properly informed. We attach the greatest importance to the World Information Summit in Geneva in December. The association intends to act as a whistle-blower, warning society against the epidemic of media manipulations in recent years.

Media Watch Global will have three levels of membership, each with identical rights: professional and occasional journalists, both active and retired, from all the media, mainstream or alternative; academics and researchers from all disciplines, and particularly media specialists, because universities are now one of the few places partially protected from the totalitarian ambitions of the market; and media users, ordinary people and public figures known for their moral stance.

In all countries the existing systems for regulating the media are unsatisfactory. Since news is a common good, its quality cannot be guaranteed by organisations made up only of journalists, since they often have their own interests. The codes of conduct of individual media enterprises, insofar as they exist, are often unsuitable for judging and correcting the doctoring, suppression and censorship of news. It is vital that the codes of conduct and ethics of news are defined and defended by an impartial body that is credible, independent and objective, within which academics have a vital role. Ombudsmen, or mediators, useful in the 1980s and 1990s, have now become commercialised and degraded. They are often exploited by companies as a part of image management and as a way to help artificially reinforce the media's credibility.

One of humanity's most precious rights is the right to communicate freely our thoughts and opinions. No law should be allowed arbitrarily to restrict press freedom and the freedom of speech. But these freedoms can only be exercised by media enterprises if they do not infringe other rights that are equally sacred, such as the right of each citizen to have access to uncontaminated news. Under the pretext of freedom of expression media enterprises should not be allowed to disseminate false news or conduct campaigns of ideological propaganda.

Media Watch Global believes that the absolute media freedom that the owners of the major communications groups pursue so insistently will necessarily be detrimental to the people of the world. These big corporations need to know that a counterpower is being created, one that will bring together all who are part of the global social movement, all who are fighting against the expropriation of our right of expression. Journalists, academics, newspaper readers, radio listeners, television viewers and Internet users will come together to create a weapon of debate and democratic action. The globalisers proclaim the 21st century "the century of global enterprise." Media Watch Global says it will be the century in which communication and information at last belong to the people of the world.

(Translated by Ed Emery)

EXCERPT FROM:
INTERVIEW WITH ARMAND MATTELART: DEMOCRACY AND COMMUNICATION

By Armand Mattelart

2000 We often find ourselves perplexed and confused by the fact that the language that has been used to study and define civil and democratic society has undergone a certain semantic corruption.

A. M.: Everything becomes natural. Changes are presented from a Darwinist perspective. A declaration of solidarity is used to sell a car. This progressive subversion of the language has been in progress since 1970. The critical sectors of society have been thrown off balance. They have had to move away from a concept of communication that was entirely critical, as though communication were a demonic force, to ask what the democratic alternative to current communication and media might be.

Communication is no longer only the media. The field of communication touches all the interstices of society, which is difficult for citizens to understand.

The arrival and penetration of a single way of thinking about communication has been subtle, clandestine, such that we did not realize it was undermining society's foundations. There are sources emitting this ideology of communication, which is multi-faceted— for example, the language, concepts and notions that the European Union uses in its directives.

This quote was part of a longer interview with Armand Mattelart and was originally published in *Iniciativa Socialista*, no. 58, Autumn 2000, Madrid, Spain. Reprinted with permission of Armand Mattelart.

1927
1960
1963
1964
1967
1969
1970
1971
1972
1973
1974
1975
1976
1977
1978
1979
1980
1981
1982
1983
1984
1985
1986
1987
1988
1989
1990
1991
1992
1993
1994
1995
1996
1997
1998
1999
2000
2001
2002
2003
2004
2005
2006

Excerpt from: *Transforming State-Owned Enterprises in the Global Age: Lessons from Broadcasting and Telecommunications in South Africa*

By Ruth Teer-Tomaselli

The transformation of the information and communication sector occupies a special place in the changing milieu of the sociopolitical landscape, since it is a key location of reform and revolution in the broader society. Media and telecommunications, in common with the education sector, organised labour and the law, were dubbed "ideological state apparatuses" by modernistic structuralists (Althusser 1971). As simplistic as this position now seems, the fundamental understanding of the communication and information sector as both "sites" and "instruments" of change remains. As "sites" of transformation, they are subject to contested politico-economic tussles: the make-up of ownership and shareholdings, the control of management and production of content, the composition of the workforce employed in these industries, all of which have been found in need of overhaul. As "instruments" of transformation, information and communication networks provide essential platforms for debate, information and education around issues shaping the kind of society we are, and the kind of society we wish to become. More subtlety, but in some ways more importantly, the media in particular choose and frame the kinds of stories we read, see and hear. They provide images in which we see ourselves, and others as well, as role models to which we are able to aspire, visions of the "other" against which we rebel. All these heavily laden signifiers are the raw material through which we confirm, modify or negate our already existing sense of identity, both at the personal and at the national level. The information and communication infrastructures are thus crucial sites of contestation in the "circuit of culture" (du Gay and others 1997, 1-5) in which the production, presentation, regulation, consumption and creation of meaning are all intimately implicated in the creation of identity, at both the personal and the national levels.

Bibliography

Althusser, L. "Ideology and Ideological State Apparatuses," in *Lenin and Philosophy and Other Essays*. London, New York: New Left Books, 1971.

Gay, P. du, S. Hall, L. Janes, J. Mackay, and K. Negus. *Doing Cultural Studies: The Story of the Sony Walkman*. London: Thousand Oaks; New Delhi: Sage Publications with The Open University, 1997.

Tomaselli, Ruth Teer, 2004. "Transforming State-Owned Enterprises in the Global Age: Lessons from Broadcasting and Telecommunications in South Africa," published in *Critical Arts*, a Journal for South-North Cultural and Media Studies, June 2004, Vol. 18, No. 1. © 2004 *Critical Arts*, University of KwaZulu-Natal. Reprinted with permission of the author and publisher.

THE SINGLE THOUGHT
DOCTRINE

By Ignacio Ramonet

1997 [My] purpose is to try to describe, from an ideological perspective, the historical moment that is the occasion of this meeting. Put another way, it is an attempt to shed light on the moment, to describe the planet, as it is today, from a geostrategic, geopolitical point of view—or, simply, from an ideological and cultural point of view.

We are living in a period many describe as a transition. I think it is clear that following the 1980s and the fall of the Berlin Wall, the implosion of the Soviet Union and the Gulf War, we have entered a new period. Curiously, however, no one is able to define its specific characteristics. …History is full of transitional periods, but the one we are experiencing is, I believe, rather exceptional. My sense is that this period may be comparable to other periods of sudden and great intellectual change, shifting paradigms, and changes in civilization. One such period was the end of the eighteenth century, with the American and French Revolutions; another, probably, the end of the Middle Ages and the Renaissance.

My feeling is that we are undergoing a transition similar in scope. Like today, those periods were extremely difficult to understand from within. It is as if we were inside a conceptual edifice, the features of which we could not truly apprehend. We are at a juncture where our ways of thinking do little to help us explain the moment we are experiencing. Again, this is characteristic of periods of change.

We do possess tools that have been useful, particularly during the last 50 years—the long period, known as the Cold War, between World War II and the Gulf War. These tools, concepts, ideas, and paradigms worked, allowing us to understand the period quite thoroughly. However, they do not fit the problems we now face. Today's problems cannot be described, identified, or analyzed with the old intellectual baggage and conceptual tools—once again, a typical feature of transitional periods.

What I wish to propose is a series of elements that allow us to identify the present period, to learn what is happening, to know what we are experiencing, though we may not be able to define it in a comprehensive way. It is clear, in any case, that something strange is happening to us: Socially, politically, economically, we are experiencing things that we are unable to name. In saying that this is a period of change, I also mean to suggest that we will probably emerge from it into a long period of renewed stability. Between the two periods of stability lies the one of chaos, disorder, and uncertainty in which we are now immersed.

I believe the present period could be described by saying that we are simultaneously experiencing—or suffering—the effects of three revolutions. These three, interwoven, are affecting different aspects of our reality and environment. The most important, and the one that is partially responsible for the subsequent two, is the technological revolution.

To be more precise, we are living through a dual technological revolution. Metaphorically, it might be described as follows. Where the industrial age replaced muscle with machine (since industrialization consists essentially of transferring physical work to machines), one of the aspects of today's technological revolution is that it transfers the functions of the *brain*—or at least many of them—to machines. This generalized cerebration of the machine is an effect of, and has effects on, production in its various aspects—industrial production, intellectual production, and the production of services.

The second aspect of the technological revolution is what is referred to as the digital revolution. What is the digital revolution? To put it simply here, for the purpose of those involved in providing information and

1927
1960
1963
1964
1967
1969
1970
1971
1972
1973
1974
1975
1976
1977
1978
1979
1980
1981
1982
1983
1984
1985
1986
1987
1988
1989
1990
1991
1992
1993
1994
1995
1996
1997
1998
1999
2000
2001
2002
2003
2004
2005
2006

in working with communications, as we all are, one might summarize the digital revolution and its context in the following way. Human beings, throughout their history (until very recently) have communicated through three systems of signs: sound (words), drawing (cave paintings and other images), and text (writing of various types, ideographic and other). These three sign systems—sound, image and text—have spawned three areas of independent productive activity (though in some cases two—though not three—have joined together).

The meaning of the digital revolution is that any of the three—image, sound, or text—can now be expressed precisely with a single device. Generalized digitization makes it possible to disseminate any text, image, or sound as electronic impulses that move at the speed of light—which, as we all well know, is an absolute: there is no greater speed conceivable. This is what we call "real time."

This technological revolution, with its two aspects of generalized cerebralization and digitization, means that in principle the brains of all the machines on the planet could be joined through a system that would make it possible for them to communicate using the three systems of signs and all of the elements comprising the information and communication revolution.

This revolution of information and communication technologies has precipitated a second great revolution, which is the economic revolution we are now experiencing. It is largely shaped by the fact that certain economic activities are stimulated by the technological revolution—principally, financial activities, or what we might call the immaterial economy. This involves such intangibles as securities, and the global sale and exchange of currency. The world financial economy today, in terms of volume, is 50 times greater than the real economy, i.e., that involving the exchange of physical objects and services. Today's economy is thus dominated and shaped by the financial, or immaterial, economy.

Where the immaterial economy is concerned, the communications economy, the information economy, or the cultural economy plays a role—with the digitization and transformation of content, and worldwide circulation through the new channels that the technological revolution makes available.

This second revolution, with its financialization, or immaterialization, of the economy, has produced the dominant phenomenon of the present historical moment, which is globalization. Globalization is transforming not only all aspects of production in the different sectors, but also major political, social, and sociological concepts.

The third revolution is precisely a sociological one. It is particularly important because of the fact that one major concept for structuring society is currently in crisis: the concept of power. What is power today, and who possesses it—in the family, school, business, factory, or nation? Where is power located, and what forms does it take? Clearly, the first two revolutions represent a crisis for the concept of power, which traditionally was vertical and hierarchical. It was transmitted from person to person according to rules of authority, and was authoritarian by definition—in other words, incontestable. This concept of power no longer works. Power today is horizontal, functioning not hierarchically but in networks, or in the form of a web. Rather than authoritarian, it is consensual. Any power today that succeeds in imposing itself or in being accepted and transmitting its messages, does so consensually, with the aid of a range of burgeoning communication mechanisms.

These three revolutions are unfolding as we speak. We are living among them; they cross through our space and create havoc with the maps and systems of reference that previously helped us understand the world. Meanwhile, two fundamental paradigms—general models for thought that provide a way of structuring other aspects of reality, paradigms on which our modern societies were based—have been replaced.

Modern societies, the societies that emerged from the intellectual revolutions of the late 18th century, were built on two pillars. One was the idea of progress, the other the idea of social cohesion. Today, though the fact is unheralded and largely invisible, both of these are being replaced, such that our new society is now being constructed on a different foundation.

Progress was an idea put forth by the thinkers of the Enlightenment, the Encyclopedists, who were concerned with civilizing societies. What, one may ask, is a civilized society? In any part of the world, at any time, it is, quite simply, a society that has succeeded in excluding violence, that has found forms of organization that allow it to avoid having to live permanently with violence. In the late eighteenth century, it was believed that modern societies—the incipient industrialized societies—needed to introduce the idea of progress in order to eliminate violence. The concept of progress meant quite simply that there would not be an excessive gap between rich and poor, since too wide a gap can cause the two to collide with extreme brutality. Thus, one of the objectives for any society, in the view of the Enlightenment thinkers, was to ensure that those on the lower end of the scale would have ways of progressing so as not to be too distant from those at the top. This distance would diminish economically, socially, culturally, and educationally. Accordingly, 19th century societies featured participation, demands, and sometimes struggle, in the effort to advance toward becoming politically peaceful countries.

Today, this concept of progress is in crisis. In the new model of society under which we find ourselves living today, progress has been dethroned. This is not only a political and social process, for progress is also a scientific concept. Science incorporates the idea of progression in regard to evolution, to technique and knowledge, and to a general understanding of our surroundings. Increasingly, however, one hears that, while science is progressing, its progress is producing an opposite effect. "What is scientific progress," we hear, "but Chernobyl, nuclear dangers, the

possibility of new epidemics, contaminated blood supplies, infected beef in the most modern meat producing systems," etc. Thus, we are told that, in many areas today, progress means danger.

On the political side, we are urged to look at Albania, a "progressive" regime, or North Korea: Who would want to emulate these? We are cautioned that Stalinism represented political "progress." Thus, there is a crisis in the idea of political progress. Even at a social level, we hear that the welfare state, which represents social progress, leads to the paralysis of societies. This was the thesis of Margaret Thatcher and Ronald Reagan: that the welfare state, while pretending to stimulate social progress, actually leads, paradoxically, to its opposite.

If this idea of progress, this general paradigm that applied to many aspects of society, is being replaced, what then is replacing it? I believe that, for our societies and for their functioning, the new paradigm is communication. The 19th century saw an effort to establish the idea that progress was needed in order to achieve peace in our societies. Today, communication has assumed that role. When there are problems in the family, school, factory, firm, or nation, when things do not work and there is a threat of confrontation, we say there must be dialogue and communication, that we need to understand each other. When family members are at odds, it is because parents and children do not communicate. When there is disharmony between students and teachers, communication is considered lacking. The same applies to workers and bosses, or citizens and governments. In all aspects of everyday life today, we are urged to follow a single imperative: Communicate! Thus, communication is a central paradigm of the new society. Its mission is the same as that of its predecessor: to bring peace to societies and eliminate violence.

The second paradigm on which our modern societies rested was that of social cohesion. In the late 18th century, when the new political, democratic regimes (democracy was being reinvented) took the place of

1927
1960
1963
1964
1967
1969
1970
1971
1972
1973
1974
1975
1976
1977
1978
1979
1980
1981
1982
1983
1984
1985
1986
1987
1988
1989
1990
1991
1992
1993
1994
1995
1996
1997
1998
1999
2000
2001
2002
2003
2004
2005
2006

the *anciens régime*, the idea was that the new society must not be like the society of that *ancien régime*, which was divided into mutually exclusive groups, as if their members were biologically different. There was the aristocracy or nobility and the Third Estate on one hand, the general population on the other, and between them, creating an ideological nexus, the clergy.

The inventors of modern democracy did not conceive of a society built on these pillars. Their model was the scientific model of the late 18th century. And what was the scientific model of that time? It was mechanics, with Newton as the exponent of a universal mechanics. The theorists of modern democracy conceived of society as a perfect machine (machine in a positive sense, not as the robotization of society). The perfect machine was the clock, which articulates space and time—space without limit and absolute time. A society, then, should function like a clock.

A clock has two or three essential characteristics. None of its parts is nonessential; at the same time, none can be added. If one part is removed, the clock's functioning is impeded. Second, all of its parts are connected—or, one might say, function in solidarity. While some are more important than others, all are equally vital in the sense that without them the system does not work. Society, then, was conceived in terms of this model. There were no worthless or bad occupations or functions. Every individual was indispensable to the collective, and the collectivity felt solidarity with each of its elements. This idea that a national community must possess social cohesion, first and foremost, is one of the great constitutive paradigms of modern societies.

Today, this paradigm no longer works, because no one demands social cohesion, or even national cohesion. What paradigm is taking its place? I believe it is the market, which is not only a technique for doing business, but an idea; a paradigm that makes it possible, ideologically and philosophically, to organize today's society. The market, which is not a recent invention, but which formerly was limited to activities

such as commerce, today tends to govern all of society's activities. The market is conceived of, and presented to us as, a sort of fluid with the ability to penetrate all interstices of society. No human activity remains beyond its reach. The market legitimizes itself by having an interest in all of society's activities.

Culture was long conceived of as an activity whose purpose was to elicit feeling, to edify the spirit, to stimulate the mind and encourage sensibility. It had no direct or strong connection with the market. Today, practically all of culture is immersed in the market, with the market governing culture and cultural production. We could expand the list by adding love, death, religion, etc., all of which are increasingly guided, organized, and structured by the market. The vocation of the market is to be the law that organizes all of our activity.

Today's society, then, rests on the two pillars of communication and the market, which have replaced progress and social cohesion. What are the consequences of this? We have three revolutions (technological, economic, and sociological) and two paradigm shifts (progress and social cohesion being replaced by communication and the market). As a result, political power itself is thrown out of phase. All political power has the capacity to intervene in progress or social cohesion, and societies have been politically organized in such a way that politicians would have the capacity to affect what happened along those two basic parameters. The situation is different, however, with the new parameters of communication and the market. A politician can be one more communicator, but cannot dominate communication. That would be censorship, dictatorship, and would fall outside of democratic norms. Nor can a politician dominate the market. On the contrary, we see that as time passes, politicians remove themselves from the market by privatizing, by leaving the market to those economic sectors controlled by the government and the State.

Politicians are increasingly distanced from both fundamental areas of the new society, and consequently have less and less opportunity to affect concrete reality. In fact, this system, these revolutions, these paradigm shifts favor the emergence of a new system, a new type of sphere that I call the PPII system, for the four basic characteristics of the activities that take place within it. The PPII system fosters activities characterized by permanence, planetary scope, immediacy, and immateriality. Everything that possesses those four characteristics today is developing in an extraordinary fashion. This system, or sphere, functions, in effect, as a new divinity. Indeed, are not these four characteristics the characteristics of God? Let me clarify. Permanence refers to a quality of being present 24 hours a day; planetary scope means 'worldwide'; immediacy means that intervention in the activity is possible at any time; and immateriality is the nature of electromagnetic impulses.

What activities, one might ask, fall within the PPII sphere? First of all, the whole financial economy; the entire securities market and monetary market; all information and communication activity and a large proportion of mass culture; plus all the sectors associated with these activities, both industrial and informational. This includes, on the industrial side, everything from the production to the launching of rockets and satellites, as well as, of course, the entire software sector. All of these activities today are developing with extraordinary speed, and this four-parameter system, along with the three revolutions and two paradigm shifts, shapes the moment in which we live, which I would term the second capitalist revolution.

The capitalist revolution occurred at the end of the 18th and beginning of the 19th centuries. It brought industrialization, along with its attendant social, political, and economic consequences. The second capitalist revolution involves globalization and financialization, with *their* attendant political, economic, and social consequences.

The changes involved in the second capitalist revolution include a lessening of the importance of political power. Indeed, some believe that political power is in danger of disappearing. If this is true, it is in part because many politicians—often of their own free will—have abandoned sectors that would have allowed them to play an important role in this new historical dynamic. Another factor is that the dynamic has such energy that no politician can hold it back. It spawns what we might call the new owners of the world. Who are they? Some newspapers and magazines in recent years and months have carried features on the 10, or 30, or 40 most influential people in the world. If you look at these reports and surveys (published by serious publications), you will see that not a single one of the people featured is a politician or elected official. They are almost exclusively heads of companies or owners of large media groups. At best, they are media or cultural-media personalities. Thus, the hierarchy of power has changed. The principal power today is economic; the second most powerful sphere of power is the media; political power falls in third place. This poses a question about the very nature of democracy today.

Assuming that we agree on the existence of this new pattern, what does it mean? Simply that when we intervene, we intervene democratically. What does democratic intervention by citizens consist of? Citizens have two democratic means of influencing the debate. One, obviously, is by voting, and the other is by demonstrating or protesting, a type of action provided for by the constitutions of most democracies. So far so good. But if citizens use these two legitimate means of expressing themselves, the only thing that they will be able to change is the political configuration. Meanwhile, if politicians cannot intervene in the sectors that shape citizens' everyday lives, democracies are impotent, or at least seriously handicapped. This is extremely dangerous for democratic functioning. Indeed, we have seen the emergence of new groups that deny democracy its legitimacy as a system capable of self-regulation, self-transformation, and continual quest for social betterment. The protagonists of international political life today are the financial markets, and no one, certainly no political

1927
1960
1963
1964
1967
1969
1970
1971
1972
1973
1974
1975
1976
1977
1978
1979
1980
1981
1982
1983
1984
1985
1986
1987
1988
1989
1990
1991
1992
1993
1994
1995
1996
1997
1998
1999
2000
2001
2002
2003
2004
2005
2006

official, exercises direct influence over them. They weigh on the destiny of the peoples, without citizens having any ability to affect them. Thus, there is an imbalance between the way the world functions and the practical reality of democracy.

At the international level, what I am describing is the Single Thought doctrine. This is something we have seen repeated for years—what publications such as *Wordself Journal* (and economic publications in general), as well as television networks with stations across the globe, have ceaselessly proclaimed: that this is modernity, this is the new phase of the world, one to which we must adapt. This ideological [machacamiento note] compression, which presents itself as the only reasonable way of thinking, and which some theorists refer to as the circle of reason, becomes the only thinkable thought. To think outside of this circle (which, to make matters worse, no one identifies) is to expose oneself to accusations of abandoning reason. In other words, we are living in what is, ideologically, a totalitarian time. Curiously, those who defend these ideas termed the champions of the Soviet model "totalitarian," because of the thought monopoly that existed in the Soviet Union. However, we see the same intolerance today, the same fanaticism in defending a single way of thinking as the only possible—and only reasonable—one. Remember that in the Soviet Union those who did not accept the circle of Soviet reason were locked away in psychiatric wards. In this new single-thought world we also face the threat of psychiatric isolation for those who do not endorse this single-thought project.

What does this mean from the international perspective? Today, the main actors are unexpected ones. For example, I would say that—paradoxically—international life is essentially dominated by a single State, the United States. Not only does the United States dominate the world as never before; it dominates the world as the world has never been dominated by any State, for there has never been a state that dominated the entire planet, as the United States does today. In addition, however, the hegemony, or neo-hegemony,

of the United States covers five different areas. Politically and economically, the United States is supreme. Militarily, it towers. Technologically, it is number one—and I would remind you that while only five or six years ago Japan was spoken of as a technological power, it has now been swept aside and is out of the running, in terms of information and communication technology and the Internet. Finally, the United States dominates the world culturally. World culture is American culture. What I am attempting to say here is that, paradoxically, although the United States is dominant in all of these ways, the changes I have discussed mean that, in reality, it has very little power. President Clinton is not the most influential man in the world. He does not appear in the lists of the 10, 15, 30, or 50 most influential people. The political leader of the world's single superpower has less power than did his predecessors.

Curiously, the actors on the international stage today are not states. In fact, states are undergoing an identity crisis. No State today is capable of defining what national sovereignty means—a basic concept for the existence of a State. None can delineate its borders, because borders are now more than terrestrial—that was a 19th century concept. Borders today are climatic and spatial. Who can keep the child under control? (Not the Chilean or Peruvian armed forces, certainly.) Thus, the idea of borders and sovereignty, the idea of democracy, of political parties, the idea of unions, are ideas in crisis, because there is now a new cast of leading players.

No nation today can know who its adversary is. The United States cannot identify its enemy, and the enemy is no longer defined in geopolitical terms. For example, AIDS is an enemy of the United States, but AIDS has no nationality. It lies beyond such constructions. Drugs are an enemy of the United States, but they, too, are nationless. Threats today are cross-border, multi-national threats. Pollution is the enemy of the entire world, but it has no nationality; the cloud from Chernobyl that drifted above Europe had no passport and was not stopped at the borders.

Thus, the very identity of the State is in crisis, as is political functioning. Who, then, are the major actors on the international stage? I identify three. They are not those we are accustomed to thinking of in the leading roles—the nobility or aristocracy, the clergy and the Third Estate. The leading roles in today's globalized world are, on one hand, played by groups of States, economically integrated areas such as the European Union, NAFTA, Mercosur, and APEC. All States today are concerned about which other states they should associate with to form economic integration blocs. How different this is from the nineteenth century, when States were concerned primarily about retaining their separateness.

The second major actor today, in my view, consists of large industrial groups, large firms, large financial groups, large media groups. They are global, and are within the PPII sphere. It is they who impose and direct the globalization process at an international level. They are the central economic and ideological actors of today. As to citizens, they are, in my view, relegated to the sidelines.

The third actor, which may to a significant degree represent the feelings of the citizens, is the global nongovernmental organizations, or NGOs. They exert influence on some States. Greenpeace, for example, is an international actor today, as is Amnesty International. We have seen Greenpeace force the United Kingdom to change its position on environmental matters, and oblige Shell to change its position on ecological matters—this despite the fact that we knew Shell was in the right.

Ramonet, Ignacio. "The Single Thought Doctrine," presented at El Pensamento Unico (Conferenca Magistral) Oct. 1997. Used with permission of the author.

IMAGINING A POSTDEVELOPMENT ERA

Excerpt from: Encountering Development. The Making and Unmaking of the Third World

By Arturo Escobar

1995 Development discourse has been central and ubiquitous operator of the politics of representation and identity in much of Asia, Africa and Latin America in the post–World War II period. Asia, Africa and Latin America have witnessed a succession of regimes of representation—originating in colonialism and European modernity but often appropriated as national projects in postindependent Latin America and postcolonial Africa and Asia—each accompanied by a regime of violence.

As places of encounter and suppression of local cultures, women, identities, and histories, these regimes of representation are…sites of violence (Rojas de Ferro 1994). As a regime of representation of this sort, development has been linked to an economy of production and desire, but also of closure, difference and violence. To be sure, this violence is also mimetic violence, a source of self-formation. Terror and violence circulate and become, themselves, spaces of cultural production (Girard 1977; Taussig 1987). But the modernized violence introduced with colonialism and development is itself a source of identity. From the will to civilization in the 19th century to today, violence has been engendered through representation.

The very existence of the Third World has in fact been wagered, managed, and negotiated around this politics of representation. As an effect of the discursive

1927
1960
1963
1964
1967
1969
1970
1971
1972
1973
1974
1975
1976
1977
1978
1979
1980
1981
1982
1983
1984
1985
1986
1987
1988
1989
1990
1991
1992
1993
1994
1995
1996
1997
1998
1999
2000
2001
2002
2003
2004
2005
2006

practices of development, the Third World is a contested reality whose current status is up for scrutiny and negotiation. For some, the Third World "can be made a symbol of planetary intellectual responsibility ... it can be read as a text of survival" (Nandy 1989, 275). After the Second World War, the Third and First Worlds necessarily have to realign their places and the space of ordering themselves. Yet it is clear that the Third World has become the other of the First with even greater poignancy.[1] "To survive, 'Third World' must necessarily have negative and positive connotations: negative when viewed in a vertical ranking system ... positive when undestood sociopolitically as a subversive, 'non-aligned' force" (Trinh 1989, 97). The term will continue to have currency for quite some time, because it remains an essential construct for those in power. But it can also be made the object of different reimaginings. "The Third World is what holds in trust the rejected selves of the First and the [formerly] Second Worlds ... before envisioning the global civilization of the future, one must first own up the responsibility of creating a space at the margins of the present global civilization for a new, plural, political ecology of knowledge" (Nandy 1989, 273, 266).

...However, the Third World should in no way be seen as a reservoir of traditions. The selves of the Third World are manifold and multiple, including selves that are becoming increasingly illegible according to any known idiom of modernity, given the growing fragmentation, polarization, violence and uprootedness that are taking hold of various social groups in a number of regions.[2] It is also possible, even likely, that radically reconstituted identities might emerge from sonic of those spaces that are traversed by the most disarticulating forces and tensions. But it is too soon even to imagine the forms of representation that this process might promote. Instead, at present one seems to be led to paying attention to forms of resistance to development that are more clearly legible, and to the reconstruction of cultural orders that might be happening at the level of popular groups and social movements.

Since the middle and late 1980s, for instance, a relatively coherent body of work has emerged which highlights the role of grassroots movements, local knowledge, and popular power in transforming development. The authors representing this trend state that they are interested not in development alternatives but in alternatives to development, that is, the rejection of the entire paradigm altogether. In spite of significant differences, the members of this group share certain preoccupations and interests:[3] an interest in local culture and knowledge; a critical stance with respect to established scientific discourses; and the defense and promotion of localized, pluralistic grassroots movements. The importance and impact of these movements are far from clear; yet, to use Sheth's (1987) expression, they provide an arena for the pursuit of "alternative development as political practice." Beyond, in spite of, against development: these are metaphors that a number of Third World authors and grassroots movements use to imagine alternatives to development and to "marginalize the economy"—another metaphor that speaks of strategies to contain the Western economy as a system of production, power and signification.

The grassroots movements that emerged in opposition to development throughout the 1980s belong to the novel forms of collective action and social mobilization that characterized that decade. Some argue that the 1980s movements changed significantly the

---

1   Here I am talking primarily about the geographical Third World, or South, but also the Third World within the First. The connection between the Third World within and without can be important in terms of building a cultural politics in the West.

2   I have in mind, for instance, the profound breakdown and reconstitution of identities and social practices fostered by drug money and drug-related violence in countries like Colombia and Peru, or the social geographies of many large Third World cities, with their fortified sectors for the rich – connected with a growing number of electronic media to transnational cyberspaces- and massively pauperized and eroded sectors for the poor. These social geographies resemble more and more *Blade Runner*-type science fiction scenarios.

3   Among the most visible members of this group are Ashis Nandy (1983, 1989); Vadana Shiva (1989); D. L. Shet (1987); Shiv Visvanathan (1986, 1991); Majid Rahnema (1988a, 1988b); Orlando Fals Borda (1984, 1988; Fals Borda and Rahman (1991); Gustavo Esteva (1987); and Pramod Parajuli (1991). A more complete bibliography and treatment of the works of these authors is found in Escobar (1992b).

character of the political culture and political practice (Laclau and Mouffe 1985; Escobar and Alvarez 1992). Resistance to development was one of the ways in which Third World groups attempted to construct new identities. Far from the essentializing assumptions of previous political theory (for example, that mobilization was based on class, gender or ethnicity as fixed categories), these processes of identity construction were more flexible, modest and mobile, relying on tactical articulations arising out of the conditions and practices of daily life. To this extent, these struggles were fundamentally cultural. Some of these forms and styles of protest will continue throughout the 1990s.

Imaging the end of development as a regime of representation raises all sorts of social, political and theoretical questions. Let's start with this last aspect by recalling that discourse is not just words and that words are not "wind, an external whisper, a beating of wings that one has difficulty in hearing in the serious matter of history" (Foucault 1972, 209). Discourse is not the expression of thought; it is a practice, with conditions, rules and historical transformations to analyze development as discourse is "to show that to speak is to do something—something other than to express what one thinks; … to show that to add a statement to a pre-existing series of statements is to perform a complicated and costly gesture" (1972, 209). [Earlier], I showed how seemingly new statements about women and nature are "costly gestures" of this sort, ways of producing change without transforming the nature of the discourse as a whole.

Said differently, changing the order of discourse is a political question that entails the collective practice of social actors and the restructuring of existing political economies of truth.[4] In the case of development, this may require moving away from development sciences in particular and a partial, strategic move away from conventional Western modes of knowing in general in order to make room for other types of knowledge and experience. This transformation demands not only a change in ideas and statements but the formation of nuclei around which new forms of power and knowledge might converge. These new nuclei may come about in a serial manner.[5] Social movements and antidevelopment struggles may contribute to the formation of nuclei of problem social relations around which novel cultural productions might emerge. The central requirement for a more lasting transformation in the order of discourse is the breakdown of the basic organization of the discourse, that is, the appearance of new rules of formation of statements and visibilities. This may or may not entail new objects and concepts; it may be marked by the reappearance of concepts and practices discarded long ago (new fundamentalisms are a case in point); it may be a slow process but it may also happen with relative rapidity. This transformation will also depend on how new historical situations—such as the divisions of social labor based on high technology.

…Challenges to development are multiplying, often in dialectical relation to the fragmentary attempts at control inherent in post-Fordist regimes of representation and accumulation; post-Fordism necessarily connects or disconnects selectively regions and communities from the world economy; although always partial, disconnection often presents attractive opportunities from poor people's perspectives. Some of this is going on in the so-called informal economies of the Third World (the label is an attempt by economic culture to maintain the hold on those realities

---

4   "A change in the order of discourse," wrote Foucault in the conclusion of *The Archeology of Knowledge*, "does not presuppose 'new ideas,' a little invention and creativity, a different mentality, but transformations in a practice, perhaps also in neighboring practices, and in their common articulation. I have not denied – far from it- the possibility of changing discourse: I have deprived the sovereignty of the subject of the exclusive and instantaneous right to it" (1972, 209).

5   "The substitution of one formation by another is not necessarily carried out at the level of the most general or most easily formalized statements. Only a serial method, used today by historians, allows us to construct a series around a single point and to seek out other series which might prolong this point in different directions on the level of the points. There is always a point in space or time when series begin to diverge and become redistributed in a new space, and it is at this point that a break takes place… And when a new formation appears, with new rules and series, it never comes all at once, in a single phrase or act of creation, but emerges like a series of "building blocks", with gaps, traces and reactivations of former elements that survive under the new rules" (Deleuze, 1988, 21).

1927
1960
1963
1964
1967
1969
1970
1971
1972
1973
1974
1975
1976
1977
1978
1979
1980
1981
1982
1983
1984
1985
1986
1987
1988
1989
1990
1991
1992
1993
1994
1995
1996
1997
1998
1999
2000
2001
2002
2003
2004
2005
2006

that exist or emerge at its limits). As local communities in the West and the Third World struggle for incorporation into the world economy, they still might have to develop creative and more autonomous practices that could be more conducive to renegotiating class, gender and ethnic relations... .

The process of unmaking development, however, is slow and painful, and there are no easy solutions or prescriptions.

References

Escobar, Arturo (1992b) *Reflections on "Development": Grassroots approaches and Alternative Politics in the Third World.* Futures 24 (5): 411-36.

Escobar, Arturo and Sonia E. Alvarez (eds.) (1992) *The Making of Social Movements in Latin America: Identity, Strategy and Democracy.* Boulder: Westview Press.

Esteva, Gustavo (1987) "Regenerating People's Space," Alternatives 12 (1): 125-52.

Fals Borda, Orlando (1984) *Resistencia en el San José.* Bogotá: Carlos Valencia Editores.

Fals Borda, Orlando (1988) *Knowledge and People's Power.* Delhi: Indian Social Science Institute.

Fals Borda, Orlando and Anisur Rahman (eds.) (1991) *Action and Knowledge: Breaking the Monopoly with Participatory Action-Research.* New York: Apex Press.

Foucault, Michel (1972) *The Archeology of Knowledge.* New York: Harper Colophon Books.

Girard, René (1977) *Violence and the Sacred.* Baltimore: John Hopkins University Press.

Laclau, Ernesto and Chantal Mouffe (1985) *Hegemony and Socialist Strategy.* London: Verso.

Nandy, Ashis (1983) *The Intimate Enemy: Loss and Recovery of Self under Colonialism.* Delhi: Oxford University Press.

Nandy, Ashis (1989) *Shamans, Savages and the Wildeness:On the Audibility of Dissent and the Future of Civilizations.* Alternatives 14 (3): 263-278.

Parajuli, Pramod (1991) *Power and Knowledge in Development Discourse.* International Social Science Journal 127: 173 -90.

Rahnema, Majid (1988a) "Power and Regenerative Processes in Micro-Spaces," *International Social Science Journal* 117: 361-75.

Rahnema, Majid (1988b) "On a New Variety of AIDS and Its Pathogens: Homo Economicus, Development and Aid," *Alternatives* 13 (1): 117-36.

Rojas de Ferro, María Cristina (1994) *"A Political Economy of Violence."* Ph.D. diss., Carleton University, Ottawa.

Sheth, D.L. (1987) "Alternative Development as Political Practice." *Alternatives* 12 (2): 155-71.

Shiva, Vandana (1989) "Staying Alive. Women, Ecology and Development." *The Ecologist* 22 (1): 4-8.

Taussig, Michael (1987) *Shamanism, Colonialism and the Wild Man.* Chicago: University of Chicago Press.

Trinh T. Minh-ha (1989) *Woman, Native, Other.* Bloomington: Indiana University Press.

Visvanathan, Shiv (1986) *Bhopal: The Imagination of a Disaster.* Alternatives 11 (1): 147-65.

Visvanathan, Shiv (1991) *Mrs. Bruntland's Disenchanted Cosmos.* Alternatives 16 (3): 377-84.

EXCERPT FROM:

DEVELOPMENT DISCOURSE ON GENDER AND COMMUNICATION IN STRATEGIES FOR SOCIAL CHANGE

By Karin Gwinn Wilkins

1999 Early scholars of development communication did not explicitly address the role of gender in their discussions of media and modernity. However, an examination of their work illustrates implicit assumptions made about men's and women's roles in the development process. For example, Lerner's classic text contrasting the life of a male Turkish village chief, representing traditional values, with that of a male grocer, representing modernity, chronicles the lives of men, while diminishing women's roles. Although women do not figure in his analyses, Lerner did hire a female interviewer, who was "ordered …by the numbers: 30ish semi-trained, alert, compliant with instructions, not sexy enough to impede our relations with the men of Balgat but chic enough to provoke the women" (Lerner 1958, 29). This example is not intended to isolate Lerner's work as a specialized case but to suggest that early theorists trivialized women's roles in the development process. Valdivia's (1996) more extensive analysis of early development theorists' work confirms a pattern of discourse that minimizes women's employment and participation in development projects and constrains mediated images of gender roles. Early views of development obfuscate women's economic contributions, highlighting instead their role as vulnerable reproducers (Escobar 1995; Parpart 1995).

The mid-1970s marked a shift in attention to "women in development" (WID), along with other critical transitions in the field of development communication (Rogers 1976; Schramm and Lerner 1976). A WID strategy advocates including women as an explicit focus in order to achieve development goals (Dagenais and Piché 1994). Based on her experience implementing a WID project, Spronk (1992) explains that project documents articulate not just the intentions of the practitioners but also the institutional expectations regarding appropriate beneficiaries and practice. In 1975, WID was promoted to a global agenda when the U.N. sponsored a conference in Mexico City to launch the Year of Women, which facilitated the designation of the Decade for the Advancement of Women (1976 through 1985; Staudt 1990).

As a discourse, WID serves to organize principles for the production of knowledge about women by states, institutions and communities (Escobar 1995, 210). WID constructs women as actively contributing to society through their economic production and human reproduction (Staudt 1985). Boserup's (1970) research on the importance of women's contributions to agricultural production, which tended to be underpaid if compensated at all, inspired a focus on women's role as economic agents. WID also points to a need to improve women's access to education, employment and political participation (Parpart 1995; Valdivia 1996), conditions considered in earlier models of modernization that tended to privilege male constituents. Throughout the Decade for the Advancement of Women, several scholars recognized limits to using media to promote social change, such as problematic stereotypes of women in the media, a lack of women's employment in positions of power in media industries, and poor access to mediated technologies as a source of information, particularly among rural women.

Following the Decade for Women, attention to WID gradually shifted toward a concern with "gender and development" (GAD). This shift from "women" to

1927
1960
1963
1964
1967
1969
1970
1971
1972
1973
1974
1975
1976
1977
1978
1979
1980
1981
1982
1983
1984
1985
1986
1987
1988
1989
1990
1991
1992
1993
1994
1995
1996
1997
1998
1999
2000
2001
2002
2003
2004
2005
2006

"gender" resonates with an understanding of gender as a socially constructed category, rather than essentializing sex as a biological condition (Dagenais and Piché 1994; Parpart 1995; Riaño 1994). GAD attempts to position women as active agents of social change situated within social and structural systems of patriarchy and power (Cardinal et al. 1994; Dagenais and Piché 1994). Steeves (1993) draws our attention to critical scholarship concerning the political economy of communication and participatory approaches to development (Freire 1983), in order to propose the creation of a global, imagined feminist community that challenges power relations. As a model of social change, a GAD approach to development locates power within normative and structural conditions (Parpart 1995), in contrast to earlier development frameworks that focus on the importance of the individual in social change.

Recent literature proposes a new shift toward "international feminisms" (Sreberny-Mohammadi, 1996), recognizing differences across class, race and other social categories (Fernea 1998; Luthra 1996; Mackenzie 1995; Riaño 1994). Respecting diversity across women, a move toward international feminisms attempts to seek a collective identity across this group as an imagined community of participants seeking to change a global history of patriarchy and domination (Cardinal at al. 1994; Steeves 1987; Steeves 1993).

Existing development institutions have responded to WID and GAD by creating new structures (such as establishing WID divisions in the U.S. Agency for International Development (USAID), Canadian International Development Agency (CIDA), and United Nations Development Programme (UNDP) and strategies (articulating gender-sensitive guidelines), while new organizations (such as the United Nations Development Fund for Women (UNIFEM), Development Alternatives with Women for a New Era (DAWN), Self-Employed Women's Association (SEWA), Women's International Network (WIN), and

Women's International News Gathering Service (WINGS) have also formed to facilitate collective mobilization toward global feminist issues (Wilkins 1997). The 1995 United Nations Fourth World Conference on Women and the Non-Governmental Organization Forum in Beijing attracted more than 30,000 participants, five times as many as had the conference 20 years earlier. Despite the introduction of new structures, conferences, policies, and organizations, the emphasis on women's programs may be diminishing (Dagenais and Piché 1994, 59), limited by a lack of resources (Staudt 1990), of women in senior management positions (Parker and Friedman 1993, 117) and of appropriate gender stereotypes (Ferguson 1990).

References

Boserup, E. 1970. *Women's Role in Economic Development*. New York: St. Martin's Press.

Cardinal, L., A. Costigan, and T. Heffernan. 1994. "Working Towards a Feminist Vision of Development," in: H. Dagenais and D. Piché, eds. *Women, Feminism and Development*. Montreal: McGill-Queen's Univ. Press. 409–428.

Dagenais, H., and D. Piché, eds. 1994. *Women, Feminism and Development*. Montreal: McGill-Queen's Univ. Press.

Escobar, A. 1995. *Encountering Development: The Making and Unmaking of the Third World*. Princeton, N.J.: Princeton Univ. Press.

Ferguson, K.E. 1990. "Women, Feminism, and Development," in: K. Staudt, ed. *Women, International Development, and Politics*. Philadelphia: Temple Univ. Press. 291–303.

Fernea, E.W. 1998. *In Search of Islamic Feminism: One Woman's Global Journey*. New York: Doubleday.

Freire, P. 1983. *Pedagogy of the Oppressed*. Trans. M.B. Ramos. New York: Continuum.

Lerner, D. 1958. *The Passing of Traditional Society*. Glencoe: Free Press.

Luthra, R. 1996. International communications instruction with a focus on women. *Journalism and Mass Communication Educator* 50(4): 42–51.

Mackenzie, F. 1995. "Selective silence: A Feminist Encounter with Environmental Discourse in Colonial Africa," in: J. Crush, ed. *Power of Development*. New York: Routledge. 100–114.

Parker, A.R., and M. Friedman. 1993. "Gender and Institutional Change in International Development," in: G. Young, V. Samarasinghe, and K. Kusterer, eds. *Women at the Center: Development Issues and Practices for the 1990s*. West Hartford, Conn.: Kumarian Press. 114–126.

Parpart, J. 1995. "Post-Modernism, Gender and Development," in: J. Crush, ed. *Power of Development*. New York: Routledge. 253–265.

Riaño, P., ed. 1994. *Women in Grassroots Communication: Furthering Social Change*. Thousand Oaks, Calif.: Sage.

Rogers, E. 1976. Communication and Development: The Passing of the Dominant Paradigm. *Communication Research* 3(2):213–240.

Schramm, W., and D. Lerner, eds. 1976. *Communication and Change: The Last Ten Years—and the Next.* Honolulu: Univ. of Hawaii Press.

Spronk, B. 1992. "Wearing the WID Label: A Case Study of Unease," in: P. Van Esterik and J. Van Esterik, eds. *Gender and Development in Southeast Asia.* Montreal: Canadian Asian Studies Association. 153–162.

Sreberny-Mohammadi, A. 1996. "International Feminism(s): Engendering Debate in International Communications," *Journal of International Communication* 3(1):1–3.

Staudt, K. 1985. *Women, Foreign Assistance and Advocacy Administration.* New York: Praeger.

Staudt, K. 1990. "Gender Politics in Bureaucracy: Theoretical Issues in Comparative Perspective," in: K. Staudt, ed. *Women, International Development, and Politics.* Philadelphia: Temple Univ. Press. 3–36.

Steeves, H.L. 1987. "Feminist Theories and Media Studies," *Critical Studies in Mass Communication* 4(2):95–135.

Steeves, H.L. 1993. "Creating Imagined Communities: Development Communication and the Challenge of Feminism," *Journal of Communication* 43(3):218–229.

Valdivia, A.N. 1996. "Is Modern to Male as Traditional is to Female? Re-visioning Gender Construction in International Communications," *Journal of International Communication* 3(1):5–25.

Wilkins, K. 1997. "Gender, Power and Development," *Journal of International Communication* 4(2):102–120.

EXCERPT FROM:

STATE AND CIVIL SOCIETY: A COLLABORATION OR CAUTIONARY RELATIONSHIP?

Media and Democratic Public Sphere

By Rosa Maria Alfaro

2003 We acknowledge media's great impact on the present society and the political power system that supports it, with the primacy of television. At the same time, we have witnessed television's difficulties to produce relevant and quality information for the country and the world, the partiality in which it has resulted many times, and the acts of corruption in which it has been involved, violating the constitutional principle of freedom of expression. In other words, such a massive influence is not qualified for the advances that we require in the field of the development and democratization in the country.

However, this verification is by now recurring common sense[1] that distracts us from another, more significant discussion regarding media and their public responsibility, since we are not only facing good or bad media companies, but also a new function that the media do not know how to assume or find it difficult to visualize. In our country,[2] the connection between media and the formation of the public sphere has not been the object of much work. They are not perceived as part of a complex and creative process of construction of that collective meaning that creates bonds in a

---

1 See quantitative surveys with a qualitative emphasis and civic consultations carried out by the *Veeduría Ciudadana de la Comunicación Social* (Social Communication Citizen's Screening Office) between 2001 and 2002. The critique of the media is consensual.

2 Peru

1927
1960
1963
1964
1967
1969
1970
1971
1972
1973
1974
1975
1976
1977
1978
1979
1980
1981
1982
1983
1984
1985
1986
1987
1988
1989
1990
1991
1992
1993
1994
1995
1996
1997
1998
1999
2000
2001
2002
2003
2004
2005
2006

society, admitting ideological or other differences, individual particularities and contributions from organizations and institutions. This new practice as a political task is essential to constitute an ethically inclusive, articulate and democratic country. Unfortunately, the notion of public sphere itself, so important in modernity, is scarcely elaborated and even less assimilated, not only by the media but also by the political class and civic society. This is why the term "public opinion" is rather perceived as a homogeneity resulting from simple individual coincidences, taking the place of the voids that distinguish us in terms of social accord. Thus, political action in the media is displaced by mistaken and simplistic concepts of image and advertising, a behavior typical of populist regimes, which copy marketing strategies to seek popularity without assuming the task of engendering society and sharing power through public communication. What is public is still perceived as state or governmental, with little [or no] instruction to the public as receivers. Therefore, it is in itself subject to suspicion, a historically instituted attitude that produced anti-state political cultures, based on political mistrust, rightfully.

The Public Sphere in its Communicative Association

In the first place, I would want to reclaim Hanna Arendt's[3] contributions on this issue. Arendt outlines the importance of public-political aspects and their influences on word, persuasion, discourse and action. Political intervention or management is critical to a line of interpretation and dialogue. She highlights the importance of topics related to social interest, and establishes the boundaries between what is private and what is public. The social sphere is considered a space of harmonization between both dimensions. According to Arendt, the public sphere is the place for human affairs, the space where common interests of a society are built through the adventure of being together among the members of a modern and complex macro-community. The public sphere implies processes in which private interests circulate and are confronted in order to become public, that is to say, to become the property of all. They are not homogeneous; they are above private interests, but based on them. What is private constitutes a world in which others are absent; public matters imply the presence of various actors giving meaning to their coexistence. Thus, we are together because we have something in common. That is why some authors emphasize the importance of those images related with the identity of a national community, with the symbolic world of the future; namely, with the way in which we imagine the past, the present, and what is to come or what we wish for later. Assembling what is common turns out to be a central task of democracy, giving it a more humanistic and ethical perspective, and not only an electoral standard. For example, the issue of employment can be discussed from different perspectives and interests, yet the important thing is to discuss it beyond the expectations of one or two actors and to identify dissents and coincidences which can be mutually enriched and even transformed through dialogue to generate public employment policies that benefit many.

Another important idea of Arendt, also pointed out by Norberto Bobbio[4], defines democracy as the public power. This refers to the articulation of what is common with what is visible, since its elements would be in what can be heard, read and seen, what is advertised, and what makes itself manifest. Again, communication is associated with political action. Arendt resorts to an interesting figure, the brilliant light that blinds political power and private interests, since neither can stand the implacable brightness of the public sphere. Such light includes the society as a whole as a witness; it makes society partake in the behavior of others and be accountable for their own. She refers to public appearance, which creates perceptions of reality. In it, the subjects' presence acquires

3   Reflections included in "La Condición Humana" Paidos. Barcelona 1993. Pages 59-95

4   "El futuro de la democracia" Fondo de Cultura Económica. Mexico 1997 pages 94-118

experience and truth, because they see what we see and hear what we hear. That is to say, we face what is visible and common, not as a photograph but as video that accounts for a process and not a fixed situation. Therefore, the public sphere becomes a bright light illuminating the stage, the actors and what takes place there, with no room for secrets. For example, the *vladivideos*[5] spoke about corruption better than a theoretical dissertation or a legal accusation; they expressed, through an image, the strength that an authoritarian State can have, organized around the decomposition of its ethics. Therefore, the issue of corruption was displayed as everyone's concern, implying measures to punish the guilty and prevent its recurrence.

Thus, we are not facing an institutional notion of public sphere, but the set of visible processes that shape interests, spaces, symbolisms, values and a sense of the future, as a task taken on by the State, civil society and media in a twofold and intermingled way. We are referring to a set of public conversations that generate a tuning of subjective demands and discontent (very relevant in our country), the prioritization of objective needs through deliberation, the reconstruction of expectations and social capital for politics, that is, the politicalization of society in the extended meaning of the word. Civil society can move forward, if we make it our purpose, to review public communication policies, based on common interests. That is to say, we may promote, in the future, development of a democratic public sphere in this country, with social pressure on the mass media to commit to such a democratic public sphere.

We dare say that, in this country, neither State nor media is yet willing to build a public sphere; and civil society, influenced by an apolitical social approach, underestimates it. What we observe in the media, forums and consultations is an overlap of particular

interests, a repositioning of approaches to deny one another, a huge intransigence when it comes to generating the bonds we are suggesting. We hold an overproduction of monologues as if it was an asset. There are moments when leaders articulate issues and perspectives, but without dialogue or the search for common ground. There is no ability to listen, given the confrontational view of politics, privatized or fragmented as it is. Most do not realize that without the public sphere, permanently shaped and re-edited, human coexistence and the democratization of politics or the economy are not possible. We are still stuck in a dialogue among the deaf [those who cannot hear us]. Curiously, we can observe that, when we refer to what are political and social issues, we admit, and even support, the particularity, the specific interest and the social and political fragmentation that we are in. Are we facing a contradiction or paradox in terms of thinking? It sounds like disintegration between communicative comprehension and the politics of society.

In Peru, the search for the human collective is still a fragile and hardly settled practice. Media do not contribute to shaping common interests or cooperation perspectives; they do not help to process mutual tolerance, but rather privatize what is public and highlight intransigencies. Discrepancy necessarily leads to contention. Social problems are processed by opening spaces of opinion for each actor confined to their specific interests, including the poor. Thus, segmentation multiplies in a display of multiple interests to be observed or verified. That is to say, visibility distances itself from the generation of what is common. The preeminence of the news defines our concerns as a machinery of unconnected events ultimately impossible to categorize. It is difficult for us to set up a public agenda, an idea distorted by the notion of *"agenda setting,"* as if it were a spontaneous result of public display. We propose an agenda based on discussion and interaction, which is constantly modified.

In addition, we are not a country that indulges criticism. The political class refuses to be questioned.

---

5   Tapes where an adviser of Peru's former President Fujimori, Vladimiro Montesinos, could be seen in the act of bribing members of Parliament, entrepreneurs, key figures in the media and members of the judiciary.

1927
1960
1963
1964
1967
1969
1970
1971
1972
1973
1974
1975
1976
1977
1978
1979
1980
1981
1982
1983
1984
1985
1986
1987
1988
1989
1990
1991
1992
1993
1994
1995
1996
1997
1998
1999
2000
2001
2002
2003
2004
2005
2006

Mistrust inhabits us. We are in a process of constructing the public sphere but face a lot of obstacles and negative loads. The separation between civil society, state and market tends to remain a feature of our identity and everyday behaviors.

The State and the political class do not perceive of modernization policies in which communication can fulfill a public function while the media are managed privately. Nor do the entrepreneurial and academic world. Rather, the majority tries to ingratiate themselves with the media in order to gain greater visibility and acceptance fro them on their institutions. Few people define their communication word as needing to create a democratic public sphere, but rather focus on propaganda functions. There is limited expert knowledge in the country of political communication. Publicists get in and out of politics, leaving a trail of failures behind. Journalists acting as consultants have little imagination when it comes to this new task. Universities have not developed such a speciality, unlike in other countries. Researchers do not go beyond statistical data and do little to measure the indicators of social change. Even if, as Sinesio López said, we are quite an organized society, we are indeed when it comes to action, but not when building common interests.

Public Sphere and Opinion: Homogeneity, Difference and Conflict

Habermas[6] discovers that political life requires constructing this public sphere, and understands the notion of 'sphere' as the grand forum of modern societies, in which political participation takes place through speech. He accurately connects the public sphere to polemics, and underlines what is rational-argumentative as its specific task. He signals the importance of the set of people gathered to discuss public interest matters. We could refute his rational emphasis, the fact that this task cannot be dissociated from the expression of emotions and feelings, embedded in the political and pre-political discourses

based on discontent, especially in our stratified countries, although always in search of a more deliberative type of channeling.

Nancy Fraser[7] distances herself from Habermas in the way she understands the public sphere. She suggests that the public sphere must be rethought as from the recent capitalist societies, and not always starting from the previous existence of a public sphere, but rather assuming that it must be built. She underlines the importance that critique must have as a part of the practical exercise of elaborating what is common, being tolerant with it. According to Fraser, Habermas presents the public sphere as if it were uniform, homogeneous, a perspective that hides the inequalities that lie at the basis of the public discussion, although not always readily manifested. Thus, it is not that likely that agreements between a worker, a congressional representative, an entrepreneur or an expert will be reached, since starting points differ and difference must be assumed in the debate, opening greater opportunities for discussion for those that do not enter it equally. That is to say, the expression of difference through deliberation must be encouraged, which necessarily leads us to define other models of public sphere, post-liberal, in which the social and political conflict is always highlighted.

Among the practical uses of the public sphere, there is not only the public agenda, but also the concept of public opinion. When exploring public opinion, differentiated tendencies and tensions are exposed in the attempt to find consensus. Often, however, public pressure, in an attempt to reach consensus, requires changes that suggest adjustments within societal attitudes that are not geniune. When the "nonconformist" [displeasing] attitude is withdrawn; it is deprived of weight and visibility. Insecurity creates a spiral of silence. When it comes to speech and silence, the latter is not fought by one's own opinions, since the citizen rather tries to keep quiet and submerge [blend into]

6   Habermas J. "Historia y crítica de la opinión pública." GG MassMedia. México 1986.

7   "Iustitia Interrupta. Reflexiones críticas desde la posición postsocialista" Siglo del Hombre Editores. Universidad de Los Andes. Bogotá 1977. Pages 95-133

in the dominant position. Public opinion is connected to sanction and punishment, and to avoid being isolated each individual resorts to hiding his or her own opinions, trying to restrain themselves and submit to the dominant position (Elizabeth Noelle-Neumann.)[8] Thus, the true opinion of each individual is repressed and depoliticized, even more if the questions entangle the person polled in that spiral of silence and homogeneity. Logically, conflict dilutes and disappears from the public scene.

The public scene is shaped by hosting or suffering inequalities that must be made visible and provided space. The fact that they exist cannot be denied, and it is not possible to accept that these inequalities hide—not even for a moment—during deliberation, appearing as resolution. We would rather face competing interest groups. The public sphere should be a "structured scenario in which competition or cultural and ideological negotiation take place among a variety of publics" (Goof Eley.)[9] Thus it is important to have a plurality of perspectives, allowing counter-discourse expressing the conflicts that affect us as a society in a transparent way. This is like a new way of looking at plurality in terms of communication and public management. Multiple demands must be accommodated and they must be processed and deliberated upon. When handled this way, public opinion surveys offer critical perspectives that are useful and are not designed to eliminate differences and hide contraversies.

Therefore, the public sphere is not a structured scenario, but a space where competition, discussion, the disclosure of inequities, approaches, points of view, conflicts of interest, must take place. It recognizes publics and counter-publics. For example, the role that feminism has played as a counter-public to achieve the construction of an agenda more favorable for women and to in overcome gender discrimination is important. We need not be so tough and prevent

8   Position stated in different texts. See particularly "La espiral del silencio. Una teoría de la opinión pública," in *El nuevo espacio público*. Various authors. GEDISA. Colección El Mamífero Parlante. Barcelona 1995.
9   Cited by Nancy Fraser in the above-mentioned book. Page 117

contestation; we must establish a dialogue with differences. The point is to share information, confront discourse, allow identities to express themselves. This is why participation is key and should be facilitated. And for that purpose, it is urgent to learn to deliberate communicatively.

We are in a very fragmented society, with different cultural processes and different perspectives. Therefore, in order to develop common interests we need to think of [communication] spaces other than the media, such as networks, no longer of an alternative type, but rather of articulation, dialogue and influence, which circulate and eventually disseminate the outcome of public discussion. In this logic, I believe the Internet has a key role. However, we need to highlight the importance of dissent and civic independence against consensus. Creativity should lead us to propose innovative styles to generate what is common.

The concept of public sphere is fundamentally process-driven and, dynamic, with significance not only in terms of confrontation but also of construction of priorities; of visions of the future regarding development and democracy, which are so important for the relationship between civil society and State. Conversation and debate must be permanent practices. Those sectors that are excluded must have the right to communicate and be able to share and dialogue with those in power, empowering them as protagonists of change. In the midst of its transition process, the construction of a community of national interests agreed upon rather than dictated, created through the democratic exercise of deliberation, is a challenge for the country. This is not just a partisan exercise, but more open to civil society and its multiple approaches and interests.

According to Fraser, in the construction of the public sphere there are strong and weak publics. Strong audiences are those that decide, such as the Congress and the executive power, for example. They are strong because their opinion is always closely tied to decisions. There are also weak publics, with points of view

1927
1960
1963
1964
1967
1969
1970
1971
1972
1973
1974
1975
1976
1977
1978
1979
1980
1981
1982
1983
1984
1985
1986
1987
1988
1989
1990
1991
1992
1993
1994
1995
1996
1997
1998
1999
2000
2001
2002
2003
2004
2005
2006

and decision-making power of scarce significance. To search for a relationship between strong and weak publics is a central democratic aspect; it emphasizes the interconnection that must be established between direct and representative participative democracy. Thus, the idea of vigilance implies an acknowledgment of representation, but also exerts a form of real participation through it. Fraser adds that the public sphere crosses different scenarios. Multiple public spaces do allow disagreement: The point is to share information, discursive opinion and realization of identities. This is why participation is crucial. It is like a thread woven from multiple conversations in different spaces about public matters themselves, and those matters belong to all. Overcoming fragmentation is not the equivalent of a return to nationalist homogeneity, but a return to the networks of dialogue and rational-affective, political-cultural deliberation.

Public Space, Civil Society and State

There cannot be a radical separation between civil society and state when building a democratic public sphere: Although independence must be safeguarded, and the fields of intervention well defined, we are situated in a system of communicative interaction between both; the experiences of both have a lot to contribute. Dialogue must, therefore, be explicit. Public actors must be concerned and prepared to make proposals about the social, cultural and institutional policies the country needs, and such proposals must be available for everyone to see. We are not referring to lobbying, always hidden by its practice connected to business. We mean assuming a line of participation that looks for parities in public management from within specific space and competence, such as political action and vigilance. Since what is common and visible implies a leading role for the State and civil society in the context of a relationship between strong and weak publics, adopting Fraser's proposal in a synergistic and mutually empowering relationship.

This communication is necessary, and even more necessary when the disparity in power between one area and the other tends to be so important. In fact, the point is to democratize the relationship between them in order to achieve solid bonds with continuity. Civil society can investigate, propose, deliberate, generate opinion and exert pressure, but it does not make decisions. On the other hand, the State does, and invests in it. Sharing criticisms, disappointments, proposals and decisions is a key challenge in the construction of democracy, allowing civil society to have more influence on political life, and vice versa. In this sense, we would be democratizing politics and politicizing society. Acknowledging the fact that they are different and opposite, depending on the situation, must not inhibit agreements; on the contrary, the common good is what matters, with the State achieving more democracy, efficiency or legitimacy, and civil society achieving more power. The agreements … [would be] the result of a communicative relationship that stresses the political democratization of the State itself and of society for everyone to see. In such an interinstitutional relationship, which must be achieved, direct and representative democracy would be bound again in a same confluent line, without parallelisms. For the formation of opinion and the social capital of a nation distanced from the decision-making process does not bring together the will to transform. Drastic separation does not help the emancipating self-determination of citizens and groups in a society, since it does not include them in public management. The assumption of political responsibilities is crucial to forge participant citizenship and a democratic society.

To do this, greater articulation between development and democracy is required, as well as between social and political aspects. Democracy is legitimized when its management improves the quality of life of a society in a fairer way; that is to say, when those excluded start being included. And if this happens with the participation of civil society and citizens, democracy settles, becoming more ethical and sustainable, since humanized life conditions are the best foundation for democratic formation and organization. …

Thinking from the perspective of the State, the need arises to create communication policies and specific ways to reach civil society, to explain the objectives of the policies designed, but also to listen. In this sense, we must refuse the idea of an objective and subjective reality, understanding it as homogeneity of opinion vis-à-vis real facts. We are multiple. Civil society and universities should support more significant studies of the process of formation of what is common. They can suggest new ideas of a public sphere to be built. The market hardly ever establishes the relationship between information and opinion, for example, or the vital specificity from which a citizen makes a judgment. In this conception, tendencies and tensions cannot be seen; disagreement retreats. As a result, we Peruvians do not know ourselves much; we find it hard to identify our conflicts clearly. Public opinion studies must be much more refined in order to account for the existing richness and those levels of confrontation that must not be hidden; we need to allow them to be expressed in order to process them. To this end, we need a lot of creativity, proposing different public spaces mutually interconnected. Civil society still acts in a fragmented way, and even the State itself that organizes a forum on decentralization, then a civic consultation, then another one on the environment, without connecting themes and problems or interconnecting citizens and their institutions. I think that the main challenge for the country is to look for the articulation of interests and to build the public sphere, because an organized process, visible and subject to collective action, does not exist.

Media and Networks of Construction of the Public Sphere

Mass media and TV are relevant spaces and institutions for the construction of the public sphere. However, we must be careful not to slide towards a monotheist vision of their importance, as if they were the only place. The point is not to reiterate in any way that alternative pretense which says that the true public sphere lies in civil society and the social organizations, communitarian spaces and community-based localities. Both paths should complement each other. And mass media must improve their ability to stimulate common interests visible in society. There is also the Internet and new technologies, opening up networks as places through which public matters can circulate, favoring new senses of communicative community.

Other spaces are also relevant, such as the civic caravans organized by *Calandria*. In these forums and discussion fairs. The "street" is used not only for protest but also to talk and reach agreements, to put pressure and propose issues and make suggestions of a public nature to the State, not merely for one's own group or organization. The point is to promote a type of citizenship that does not suffocate and confront, but that connects and allows expression. The point is to conquer the fears of many people, as a group, because they are afraid to fight individually. Empowerment is also their responsibility. We must move towards a culture of conversation and deliberation... .

...Only a more integral, relational communication will achieve results: To listen and express oneself, learn from one another, accept criticism, debate and make each other better through different points of view, progressively weaving agreements that overcome private or particular interests, so that they are satisfied when majority agreements are reached. ...

Alfaro, Rosa Maria. *Relaciones entre Estado y Sociedad Civil: ¿concertación o vigilancia?* (2003), Asociación de Comunicadores Sociales Calandria, Lima (Peru). Asociación de Comunicadores Sociales Calandria. Reprinted with permission.

1927
1960
1963
1964
1967
1969
1970
1971
1972
1973
1974
1975
1976
1977
1978
1979
1980
1981
1982
1983
1984
1985
1986
1987
1988
1989
1990
1991
1992
1993
1994
1995
1996
1997
1998
1999
2000
2001
2002
2003
2004
2005
2006

COMMUNICATIONAL RECONFIGURATIONS OF THE PUBLIC SPHERE [RECONFIGURACIONES COMUNICATIVAS DE LO PÚBLICO]

Globalization and the Crisis of Representation

By Jesús Martín Barbero

2001 Perhaps politics is no longer what—until recently—we imagined it to be, and people are no longer willing to continue investing time and energy in the rites of the demonstration, the march, the parade and other acts of collective identification. The placement and direction of politics is likely to change with rising educational levels, greater dissemination of televised images, cooling of the ideological debate, expansion of individual rights, the declining importance of political parties and the diversification of people's rights.

José Joaquin Brunner

The globe, no longer simply an astronomical object, has acquired full historical meaning, according to the Brazilian sociologist O. Ianni (13). The meaning, however, is still profoundly ambiguous, even contradictory. How can we understand the changes that globalization produces in our societies without being trapped in the mercantilist ideology that guides and legitimates the process today, or in the technological fatalism that legitimates the accelerating deracination of our cultures? Identified, by some, with the only true utopia possible—that of a single shared world—and, by others, with the most horrific of nightmares, in which techniques and machines take the place of human beings, globalization plays as prominent a role in people's everyday imaginaries as it does in social processes at the macro level. Nevertheless, we are beginning to understand certain aspects of globalization—precisely those that relate to changing models and modes of communication.

Understanding these changes requires, first of all, using categories different from those we are accustomed to employing when thinking about space. By changing our sense of place in the world, information and communication technologies are making our highly intercommunicated world ever more opaque. This opacity is associated, on one hand, with the fact that the only truly global dimension of globalization so far is the market, which seeks to unify rather than unite (14); what is currently unified at the world level is not the desire to cooperate, but rather the impulse to compete. The other reason for the opacity concerns the density and compression of information accompanying the "virtual" and high-speed nature of a world space made up of networks and flows rather than encounters. A world of this sort radically weakens the boundaries of the national and the local, converting national and local spaces into access and transmission points where the meaning of communication is both activated and transformed.

Despite all of this, it remains impossible for us to live in the world without some type of territorial mooring, some insertion in the local, for it is in place, in territory, that everyday life in its corporeal nature—as well as the temporal, or historical, reality of collective action—unfolds, the two being pillars of human diversity and reciprocity, primordial features of human communication, pointing clearly to the idea that the sense of the local is not univocal. One is produced by fragmentation, which in turn is the result of the delocalization associated with globalization, while the other is the result of placing renewed value on the local as a front on which to rein in (or provide a complement to) globalization. This revaluing is a revaluing of self and self-determination, as well as of the memory of the self or group, both of which are associated with the ability to construct narratives and images of identity. This must not be confused with a regression to the various forms of racist and xenophobic particularism and fundamentalism which, though also motivated in part by globalization, are in the end the most extreme form of denial of the other, indeed of all others.

Thus, we must differentiate between the unifying dynamics of economic globalization and those that create a world culture. Cultural globalization is not something that operates on completely autonomous spheres (national or local) from outside those spheres. "It would be incorrect to speak of a 'world culture' placed hierarchically above national and local cultures. The process of globalization is a comprehensive social phenomenon and exists only insofar as it is localized and rooted in the everyday practice of human beings." (15) Globalization, then, must not be confused with the standardization of different areas of life arising out of the industrial revolution. Today, we are witnessing another process. The world culture of modernity is a new way of being in the world. It involves deep changes in ways of working, mating, dressing, eating and spending leisure time, as well as new modes of insertion in, and perception of, time and space. Also involved is the phenomenon of power-concentrating decentralization and that of the uprooting of cultures, driving them to hybridize. This is what occurs when the communications media and information technology become producers and vehicles for the globalization of imaginaries associated with music and images, representing deterritorialized styles and values, with new patterns of memory.

The globalization of culture also reshapes the sense of citizenship:

> By growing outward to such a degree, the metropolises acquire the features of multiple places. The city becomes a kaleidoscope of cultural patterns and values, languages and dialects, religions and sects, ethnic groups and races. Different ways of being are concentrated and coexist in the same place, becoming a microcosm of the world (16).

At the same time, we see the appearance of the dynamic by which world citizenship triggers new modes of social and political representation and participation (17), as the borders that once delimited the domains of politics and human rights not only have blurred but are shifting. As they do so, they are imbuing ethnic, racial and gender rights with political meaning. This must be interpreted neither over-optimistically—as the phenomenon of disappearing borders and (at last!) the emergence of a world community—nor catastrophically, as the advent of a society in which the "liberation of differences" means death to the social fabric and to the fundamental forms of social coexistence. As J. Keane has stated, (18) there is already an international public sphere that mobilizes forms of international citizenship, as evidenced by the international human rights organizations and NGOs in each country that mediate between the transnational and the local.

With globalization, the process of rationalization seems to be reaching its limit: following economic rationalization, the worlds of politics and culture are now subject to the same process. G. Marramao's genealogy of the relations between secularization and power (19) centers on the work of Weber, suggesting (along with F. Tonnies) that the constitutive rationalization of modern society would mean a break from any organic/community-based form of the social, and its reorganization as a "managed world" in which politics cannot be understood apart from bureaucracy (the "formally most rational way of exercising power"). This would imply a loss of the traditional values of respect and authority, i.e., a "rupture of the monopoly of interpretation" that was forged in the Reformation and since. This rupture and loss were to be a part of the long process of creating a secular jurisdiction, a sovereignty of the State—in short, the creation of the modern State. Only in the late eighteenth century was the idea of secularization to become the category explaining the unitary conception of historical time—the universal time of the world's history. Hegel had already used the term *mundanizacion* to refer to the formation of the mundane global sphere, which today is the intersection of secularization and globalization.

Will the world globalization system(20) prove to mark the advent of widespread disenchantment with politics, along with advances in technological

1927
1960
1963
1964
1967
1969
1970
1971
1972
1973
1974
1975
1976
1977
1978
1979
1980
1981
1982
1983
1984
1985
1986
1987
1988
1989
1990
1991
1992
1993
1994
1995
1996
1997
1998
1999
2000
2001
2002
2003
2004
2005
2006

development and rational management? Such is the view of Vázquez Montalbán, who, with accustomed irony, affirms that to engage in politics today is to create a national budget that represents as accurately as possible the overall interests of the people. For this, the politician needs two types of knowledge: legal/administrative knowledge and knowledge of communications in the advertising context. The first paradox here is that disenchantment with politics transforms public space into advertising space, making political parties into a specialized communications media apparatus, and delegitimizing any attempt to reintroduce the question of objectives. Why, after all, insist on such questions if the "ethics of power" legitimizes double standards of truth, bookkeeping and morality, and if charisma can be fabricated by media engineering? The second paradox can be summed up by the question: After the fall of the Wall, is there any sense in continuing to talk about democracy?

't is symptomatic that an agnostic like Vázquez Montalbán should introduce the question of meaning in politics. "We need an idea of purpose that, without being a transcendental proposal, resembles one, [and this means] considering the wisdom of what the obverse of those ideas of purpose has given us, whether via religion or ideology." (21) The absence of meaning in politics, however, goes beyond the corruption of power and the phenomenon of media engineering, encompassing "the disappearance of the symbolic nexus that can constitute otherness and identity," (22) an abstraction that paradoxically connects with another dimension of political "mass mediation." For while the "old" party member or political activist defined himself by his convictions and by a passionate, almost corporal, relation to "the cause," the television spectator of politics is a pure abstraction, a constituent only of a statistical percentage. And it is that abstraction that governs the televised political discourse, since what this discourse seeks is no longer adherents, but percentage-point gains among potential voters. Though the tone and rhetoric of street politics is still present in our countries, the

people/leader identification embodied in the shout of a charismatic leader's speech is almost inconceivable today. Such a shout would not only fail to resonate on the TV screen, it would be a jinx, costing many votes, since the unpredictable crowd, gathering in the plaza to form a "collectivity of belonging," has been replaced by the disaggregated, individualized experience of home-bound television viewers. The atomization of the audience disrupts not only the meaning of political discourse, but the meaning of the social bond that supported it, the "set of relations symbolized (admitted and recognized) between people."

If the audiences for politics are almost faceless—ever closer to a pure statistic—this change is one produced by society, and merely catalyzed by television. It is abstraction that underlies modernity—as well as capitalism. What we are witnessing is the disenchantment of the world by a process of rationalization—one that undermines the magical and mysterious dimensions of human existence, leaving a "steel cage" in which instrumental reasoning reigns supreme: co-opting the human power of joy, cognition and technology, and transforming the world into something predictable and subject to domination, but also something without warmth or meaning—in short, something distasteful. For Weber, a *secular* society was one in which the disappearance of traditional sources of security broke the bonds that held the city together. The socially disaggregated experience of the political, produced by television, connects with that disintegration, but the experience now involves not only a turning inward to the private, but a profound reconfiguration of the relationship between the private and the public, in which the two overlap and the separation blurs. What identifies the public stage with the television screen is not merely the insecurity and violence of the street, but the complicity of the sensorium that infuses television with the placeless city (23).

The atomization of the political public, and its conversion into statistically measurable audiences, cannot be separated from the dual crisis of representation. One facet of this crisis is the erosion of symbolic dimensions, which technological mediation catalyzes but does not explain, associated with the lack of meaning of the social. The other is the consequence of neoliberal politics, which degrades the basic mechanisms of sociopolitical cohesion. The transition, from a population that took to the streets politically, to a public that went to the theater or the movies once a week, did nothing to change the active, collective nature of people's experience. However, the transition from going to the movies to watching television marks a change of course: when social plurality is subjected to disaggregation, it radicalizes the experience of the politically unrepresentable abstraction. The fragmented citizenry then becomes grist for the market, which offers itself, via the "ratings" process, as an intermediary in the political arena.

Politics needs such intermediaries because it has become unable to create a communicative connection between the world of economics (production, market) and that of life itself (identities and the construction of meaning). This inability is closely linked to its rationalist conception, to which Alain Touraine refers when he observes that political life has been regarded as belonging to the sphere of reason and law, while private life has been seen as being governed by tradition, belonging to the same sphere as the family, feeling and passions (24). This Manichaeism becomes collective schizophrenia when globalization completes the separation between the rationality of the economy and the world of identities. This is what Castells so lucidly sets forth in analyzing the network society (25), governed, on one hand, by the world of economic rationality, with its global flows of wealth, technology, information and power and, on the other, by the intersubjective world of identities rooted in place and tradition. The breakdown of the communicative capacity of politics is aggravated when the inflammatory effects of globalization are so acute that they produce a mirage where once there were basic identities—identities with roots deep in time. Politics is left without a language that would allow it to mediate between mercantile rationalism and the passion of identity.

Another disturbance in the historical sensibility of today has an even greater effect on the crisis of representation. It involves the sense of the national, and is paradoxically the consequence, according to P. Nora, of the late-modern passion for memory: "The replacement of the national myth by memory implies a profound change: a past that has lost the organizing coherence of a history is totally transformed into a patrimonial space." (26) And a national memory built on patrimonial claims collapses, loses its center, divides and multiplies to the point of disintegration. Each region, locale and group—coastal inhabitants, indigenous peoples, women—claim the right to their memory. "Placing on stage a fragmented representation of the territorial unity of the national, the places of memory paradoxically celebrate the end of the national novel" (27)—which was the source of the legitimacy of both the intellectual's word and the politician's discourse. But in whose name do those voices speak today, when the social subject—unified in the figures and categories of "people" and "nation"—falls apart, baring the problematic and reductionist nature of the configurations of the collective and the public?

Today, one of the key scenes of the disintegration of the social bond is the workplace. Giuseppe Richeri has aptly attributed the disintegration suffered by politics in Italy to the secret connections between, on one hand, the constitutive fragmentation of the public discourse produced by television and, on the other, the disaggregation of the fabric of tradition and interaction that gave unions and mass political parties their substance (28). Today, factories are decentralized, professions are diversified and hybridized, and the spaces and occasions for interaction are reduced, while the fabric of political interests and objectives is in a state of disintegration. For political parties, the loss of opportunity for interchange with society, the disintegration of links with society, and the loss of channels of communication with it, all distance the parties from the life of the society, until they become nothing but electoral machines co-opted by

1927
1960
1963
1964
1967
1969
1970
1971
1972
1973
1974
1975
1976
1977
1978
1979
1980
1981
1982
1983
1984
1985
1986
1987
1988
1989
1990
1991
1992
1993
1994
1995
1996
1997
1998
1999
2000
2001
2002
2003
2004
2005
2006

the bureaucracies in power. The election of the Italian television magnate Silvio Berlusconi as prime minister, and the influence gained by the coalition he leads, must therefore be seen not as mere coincidence, but as a symptom of the new threads of discourse from which political representation is being woven. What is reflected here is not the dissolution of politics, but the reconfiguration of the mediations that lie at the heart of the means of questioning subjects and of representing the links that bind a society together.

Though tainted by the dynamics of the market, the communications media today are decisive for social recognition. The broadcast media have become not a substitution for, but the constitution of, the fabric of discourse and of political action itself, since their mediation gives density to the symbolic, ritual, and theatrical dimensions that politics has always contained. It is the specificity of that process of densification that remains unaddressed by, and to a degree unthinkable within, the instrumental conception of communication permeating most critical thought. For neither is the medium limited to carrying or translating existing representations, nor can it replace them: It has become a fundamental stage on which public life is played out. That which is public is not only expressed, but carried out, in the media. When a radio station hands the microphone to a poor woman so that she can personally tell the official responsible for water supply that her neighborhood has been without water for two months, and the official makes a public and personal commitment to solving the problem in two weeks, we have a reconfiguration of the public. Though it is certainly sentimentalized and "celebrity-ized," these affective and ritual dimensions, which the medium no doubt fosters, do not depoliticize action, but reintroduce into formal rationality the mediations of sensibility that the rationalism of the "social contract" pretended (in Hegelian fashion) to overcome. This brings us to the question of the changes of sensibility, which in turn are bringing about changes in sociality.

The Metamorphosis of The Public in the Information Age

In the last few years we have begun to understand the need to examine the relation between politics and the media on a map defined by three axes: the construction of the public; the constitution of media and of images in a space of social recognition; and emerging forms of citizenship and the exercise thereof.

Despite longstanding fascination for *the realm of the State*, only in recent years has *that which is public* begun to be perceived in its autonomous particularity, in its dual relationship with "civil society" and communications. In the thinking of H. Arendt and R. Sennet, the public appears as "the common, the world of all," implying that it is, at the same time, "the disseminated, that which is 'publicized' among the majority." (29) This is what Sennet emphasizes when he relates the public to that *space of the city* (from the Greek *agora*) in which people join to exchange information and opinions, to walk, listen and engage in argument (30). Germán Rey has approached the foundational articulation of the public as something that occurs between the *common interest*, the *citizens' space* and *communicative interaction*: 31 a circuit of interests and discourses in which the *common* element does not in any way exclude diversity. Indeed, it is the common that permits contrast and recognition of diversity.

One of the properties of *citizenship* today is its association with "reciprocal recognition," i.e., the right to inform and be informed, to speak and be heard, which is indispensable for participation in the decisions that concern the collectivity. One of the most flagrant ways in which citizens are excluded today is precisely by depriving them of the *right to be seen and heard*, which is equivalent to possessing social existence or importance, both individually and collectively, for both majorities and minorities—a right that has nothing to do with the star-like exhibitionism of our politicians in their perverse desire to compensate for their lost ability to represent the common by the number of minutes or hours they spend appearing on screen.

The ever-closer relationship between the public and the communicable—already present in the initial sense of the political concept of *publicity,* whose history, as noted above, has been traced by Habermas—depends, today, on the ambiguous and intensely questioned *mediation of images*. The central place occupied by a discourse involving images—from billboards to television, with a thousand forms of posters, graffiti, etc., along the way—is nearly always associated with, or reduced to, an inevitable evil, an incurable illness of modern politics, a vice emanating from America's decadent democracy, or concession to the barbarism of our times, in which a lack of ideas is concealed by images. Indeed, current society's use of images reflects this to a considerable degree. However, we must move beyond denouncing this and toward an understanding of the social product of that mediation of images—this being the only means of intervening in the process. The function of images is, first, to provide a means of channeling the crisis occurring in the *discourse on representation.* For while the growing presence of images in debate, campaigns and even political action, converts the world of current events into a spectacle—to the point that they become hard to distinguish from show business, beauty pageants and electronic churches—images remain the vehicle for a *visual construction of the social,* in which visibility represents an attempt to replace the struggle for *representation* with a demand for *recognition.* What the new social movements and minorities—ethnic groups, races, women, young people, homosexuals—demand is not so much to be represented as recognized: *to become socially visible in their differences*, giving rise to a new way of exercising their political rights. Second, images produce a profound political decentering, in terms of both the meaning of active political-party participation and party discourse. Images associated with the sectarian fundamentalism that accompanied both the right and the left (from the last century well into the present one) reflect what Norbert Lechner terms the "chilling of politics," 32 i.e., the disintegration of the rigidity of

belonging, thus paving the way for more-mobile loyalties and more-open collectivities. Insofar as *discourse* is concerned, the new social visibility of politics catalyzes the replacement of openly authoritarian and doctrinaire discourse by a democratic mode of discourse made up (though perhaps not clearly) of certain types of interactions and exchanges with other social actors. This is reflected both in political opinion polls and in the growing proliferation of citizens' oversight and watch-dog groups. At the same time, the relation between the *visibility* of the social—which makes possible the constitutive presence of images in public life—and *oversight,* which is a current form of citizen monitoring and intervention, is more than a semantic nicety.

The vacuum of utopias on the political scene has been filling up, in recent years, with a cluster of utopias from the field of technology and communication, as reflected in such phrases as "global village," "hyperspace," "digital being" and, most deceptive of all, "direct democracy," which attributes the renewal of politics to the power of information networks, replacing the "old" forms of representation with the "live expression of citizens" as they vote online from home or register personal opinions remotely. This is the most misleading of idealizations, since in its celebration of the immediacy and transparency of computer networks, it undermines the very foundations of the public sphere, namely, the processes of deliberation and criticism. While creating the illusion of a process without interpretation or hierarchy, it strengthens a belief that the individual can communicate without mediation, encouraging distrust of any form of delegation or representation. In more than a few of the proclamations and quests for "direct democracy" via the Internet, however, there is a libertarian subtext designed with an eye to the citizenry's disorientation, resulting from the absence of symbolic density in the political representation process and the failure of the representative process to be truly inclusive. The libertarian element also reflects the frustration experienced, particularly by women and young people, as

1927
1960
1963
1964
1967
1969
1970
1971
1972
1973
1974
1975
1976
1977
1978
1979
1980
1981
1982
1983
1984
1985
1986
1987
1988
1989
1990
1991
1992
1993
1994
1995
1996
1997
1998
1999
2000
2001
2002
2003
2004
2005
2006

a result of the inability of representative processes to represent their difference in anti-inequality discourse. Devaluing whatever national cultural commonality exists—due to their own inability to articulate diversity and the plurality of differences within the nation—the media and electronic networks are becoming mediators of the imaginary fabric that shapes the identity of cities, regions, localities and neighborhoods, carrying a multicultural significance that shatters the traditional referents of identity.

The *virtual* networks are not only technical, but social. In sheer factual terms, the Internet involves only one percent of the world's population. Paradoxically, telephone lines—a prerequisite to Internet access—are more numerous in just the island of Manhattan than in the entire continent of Africa. The more rapidly the user base grows in Latin America, the more radically the types of use differentiate the social meaning of being connected to the Internet. There is a vast discrepancy between the significance of the strategic information for financial decisionmaking, and the insignificance of the entranced window-shopper strolling the virtual boulevards—a discrepancy that looms even larger if one considers the increase in wealth within the Web compared to the accelerating social and psychological pauperization outside it, i.e., in the physical space from which people connect to the network. All of this has little to do with decrying, in clichéd fashion, the homogenization of life or the devalued state of book reading. The virtuality of the networks eludes the dualistic thinking we are accustomed to applying to technology, making them at once open and closed, integrating and disintegrating, totalizing and detotalizing, a niche and fold harboring logics, velocities and temporalities as diverse as those that interlink the narratives of the oral with the intertextuality of the written, and those that lurk in the intermedialities of hypertext.

Critical distance, indispensable in dealing with the vertigo in which technological innovation immerses us, begins by dissolving the mirage produced by the regime of immateriality governing the worlds of communications, culture and money, i.e., the loss of the physical substance of objects that makes us forget that our world is about to sink under the weight and freight of accumulated wastes of all varieties. At the same time, however, changing this situation requires the presence, and irreversible spread, of the technological environment in which we live. Nevertheless, the penetration and expansion of technological innovation in the everyday environment does not automatically entail submission to the demands of technological thinking, rhythm and language: the very pressure of technology is, in fact, evoking a need to find and develop other ways of thinking, other life rhythms and other relationships—with both objects and people—in which physical density and sensory presence are of primary value. Significant to those of an apocalyptic bent—currently in ample supply—are the uses many minorities and excluded communities make of the networks, introducing *noise* in them, distortions in the global discourse, distortions through which the voice of others—in large numbers—emerges. That turn of the screw is seen also in the use of electronic networks to create urban groups, which materialize in virtual space, then stake out physical space, shifting from connection to encounter, and from encounter to action. Hackneyed as they may be come the words from the mouth of Comandante Marcos, introducing—against the *background noise* of the Lacandona jungle—the gravity of utopia amidst the lightness of the interminable chatter that circulates on the Internet.

The alternative use of computer technology in constructing the public sphere will no doubt entail profound changes in mental maps, languages, and policy designs, all of which is required by the new forms of complexity that characterize the reconfigurations and hybridizations of the public and private spheres. The problem begins with the complexity of the Internet itself, a locus of private contacts, simultaneously mediated by the public space of which the Web consists. The process introduces a veritable explosion of public discourse, mobilizing the most disparate collection of communities, associations and tribes, which, as they free their narratives from the political—working from the multiple logics of the worlds of life—weaken the bureaucratic centralism promoted by most institutions, and encourage social creativity in the design of citizen participation. Technology, let there be no mistake, is not neutral: more than ever, today's technologies are enclaves for the condensation and interaction of social mediations, symbolic conflicts and economic and political interests. For that very reason, however, their starting point is the new intertwined condition of the social and the political, the formation and exercise of new forms of citizenship.

Notes

13. O. IANNI, *Teorías de la globalización* [Theories of globalization]. Mexico City: Siglo XXI, 1996, p. 3.

14. SANTOS, M. "Espaço, mundo globalizado, pos-modernidade" [Space, globalized world, post-modernity], *Margen* 2. Saõ Paulo, 1993, pp. 9-22; and, by the same author, *A natureza do espaco: técnica e tempo* [The nature of space: tecnique and time]. Saõ Paulo: Hucitec, 1996.

15. R. ORTIZ, "Cultura e modernidade-mundo" [Culture and world modernity], in *Mundializaçao e cultura* [Globalization and culture]. Saõ Paulo: Brasiliense, 1994, p. 71.

16. O. IANNI, "Naçao e globalizaçao" [Nation and globalization], in *A era do globalismo, Civilizaçao Brasileira* [The era of globalism, Brazilian civilization]. Rio de Janeiro, 1996, pp. 97-125.

17. KYMLICKA, W. *Ciudadanía multicultural* [Multicultural citizenship]. Barcelona: Paidos, 1996.

18. J. KEANE, "Structural Transformation of the Public Sphere," *The Communication Review*, vol. 1, 1, University of California, 1995.

19. G. MARRAMAO, Potere e secolarizzazione-Le categorie del tempo. Milán: Editori Reuniti, 1983; *Cielo e Terra: genealogia della secolarizzazione* [Heaven and earth: genealogy of secularizaation]. Turín: Laterza, 1994.

20. I. WALLERSTEIN, "Culture and the world system," in M. FEATHERSTONE (org.), *Cultura global. Nacionalismo, cultura e modernidade* [Global culture. Nationalism, culture and modernity]. Petrópolis: Vozes, 1999.

21. M. VAZQUEZ MONTALBÁN, *Panfleto desde el planeta de los simios* [Pamphlet from the planet of the apes]. Barcelona: Crítica-Grijalbo, 1995, p. 55 and p. 92.

22. M. AUGÉ, Hacia una antropologia de los mundos contemporáneos [Toward an anthropology of contemporary worlds]. Barcelona: Gedisa, 1995; and p. 88; also, in this vein: C. CASTORIADIS, *El mundo fragmentado* [The fragmented world]. Montevideo: Altamira, 1993.

23. M. AUGÉ, *Los "no lugares." Espacios de anonimato* ["Non-places." Spaces of anonymity]. Barcelona: Gedisa, 1993, pp. 81-119.

24. A. TOURAINE, "La decomposition de l'ordre politique" [The decomposition of the political order], in M. WIEVIORKA, *Une societé fragmenté?* [A fragmented society?] Paris: La Decouverte, 1997, p. 191.

25. M. CASTELLS, *La era de la información* [The information age], vol. 1: *La sociedad red* [The network society]. Madrid: Alianza, 1997.

26. P. NORA, *Les lieux de memoire* [Places of memory], vol. III. Paris: Gallimard, 1992, p. 1099.

27. O. MONGUIN, "Una memoria sin historia?" [A memory without history?] *Punto de vista* [Point of view], 49. Buenos Aires: 1994, p. 25.

28. G. RICHERI, "Crisis de la sociedad y crisis de la televisión" [Crisis in society and crisis in television], *Contratexto*, 4. Lima, 1989.

29. H. ARENDT, *La condición humana* [The human condition]. Barcelona: Paidos, 1993.

30. R. SENNET, Flesh and stone. The body and the city in Western civilization. Madrid: Alianza, 1997.

31. G. REY, Balsas y medusas. Visibilidad comunicativa y narrativas políticas [Rafts and medusas. Communicative visibility and political narratives]. Bogotá: Cerec/Fundación social/Fescol, 1998.

32. N. LECHNER, "Democratization in the context of a postmodern culture, in *Cultura política y democratización* [Political culture and democratization]. Santiago: Flacso/Clacso/ICI, 1987, p. 254; Bogotá, September 2000.

Martín Barbero, Jesús. "Reconfiguraciones comunicativas de lo público [Communicational Reconfigurations of the Public Sphere,]" published in *Anàlisi* 26, 2001 71-88. ITESO. Department of Socio-cultural Studies, Guadalajara, Mexico. Copyright © 2001, Jesús Martín Barbero. Reprinted with permission of the author.

1927
1960
1963
1964
1967
1969
1970
1971
1972
1973
1974
1975
1976
1977
1978
1979
1980
1981
1982
1983
1984
1985
1986
1987
1988
1989
1990
1991
1992
1993
1994
1995
1996
1997
1998
1999
2000
2001
2002
2003
2004
2005
2006

FROM FREIRE AND HABERMAS TO MULTIPLICITY: WIDENING THE THEORETICAL BORDERS OF PARTICIPATIVE COMMUNICATION FOR SOCIAL CHANGE

By Alejandro Barranquero

2005 Despite its central role in communication for development, there is no compendium comparing the contributions to the "field" (Bourdieu) of the pedagogue Paulo Freire and the German philosopher Jürgen Habermas, except some notes in the book by Richard, Thomas and Nain (2001), about the Brazilian's works and other texts that, indirectly, help link both intellectual trajectories (Servaes, 1999; Mayo and Servaes, 1994; White, Nair and Ascroft, 1994, etc.).

The most interesting comparison comes from pedagogy and education sociology. Raymond Morrow and Carlos Alberto Torres (2002), leaders in research of critical social theory, propose an approach from the point of view of "emancipating post-foundationalism," a label that defines, according to them, the most articulated meta-theoretical response to the challenge of post-modernism and post-structuralism, an emancipatory social discourse in the search for social change.

I. Divergences and Continuities

Freire's and Habermas's works are circumscribed in a very prolific theoretical continuum related to alternativity, praxis and social change. Although their departure points are different, it is easy to join lines of complementation and convergence between them.

Before getting into the analysis of the main points in common it is recommended to look at some of the most significant differences:

1. The latest bibliography in communication and development gives central role to the thoughts of Paulo Freire and Jürgen Habermas as key authors of the "participative paradigm." However, their contributions about the communication phenomenon are very different. The Brazilian contributed to clarify some of the main ontological reasons for communication: its political, educational essence or its ability to generate positive social change when used in a dialogic way (Freire, 1969, 1970). Freire´s transcendence is determined by his critique of extensionism and diffusion theories, his dialogic conception of development and his essential methodological contributions (Servaes, 1999; Waisbord, 2000; Huesca, 1994, 1996, 2002; Dervin y Huesca, 2001; Gumucio, 2001; Thomas, 1993). On the other hand, Jürgen Habermas did not write on the matter, although his communication model seeks social transformation at the end (Habermas, 1987, 1994). Nevertheless, his thinking is principal to understanding the universal emancipating potential of communication and to conceiving new development strategies based on some of the main points of the Habermas model: communicative action, consensus, discursive ethics, public sphere, (Jacobson, 2002; Jacobson and Servaes, 1999; Servaes, 1999).

2. Their contexts (space and time) and, in consequence, their inspirations are very different. Jürgen Habermas uses a sociological, philosophical and linguistic frame of reference. His perspective is in most cases Western and "Westernizer."[1] The most cited authors in the Habermasian theoretical framework come from European tradition, fundamentally, and North America: linguistics and analytics (Wittgenstein, Austin, Searle), Frankfurt

---

[1] The "academic communities" (Kuhn) where some of the most significant ruptures in communication for development have been born in Latin America or Asia, and they do not have enough projection in dominating scientific contexts, as in Europe and the United States. To revise non-Western thought in communication, consult the collective projects by Curran and Park (2000) or Atwood and McAnany (1986). To broaden the contemporary concepts of "geopolitics of knowledge," "colonial nature of power," etc., review the works by Walter Mignolo, Aníbal Quijano or Catherine Walsh.

School (Adorno, Horkheimer) or classics of social action (Durkheim, Weber, Mead, Parsons), to name just a few.

Paulo Freire integrates, on the other hand, influences from North and South, and his legacies are pedagogical and, to a lesser extent, philosophical. Among his main influences are Marxist theorists (Karl Marx himself and the Frankfurtians Fromm or Marcuse), structuralism, linguistics, existentialism (Sartre, Jaspers), etc. In opposition to Habermas, the Brazilian author gathers non Western perspectives like dependency theories and theology of liberation—both born in Latin America—as well as thinking by revolutionary leaders of the time. (Machel, Senghor, Nyerere, etc.).

3. Objectives, methodologies and actions are rather diverse. Habermas, author of the so-called "Second Generation" of the Frankfurt school, aims to revitalize the old project in epistemological and socio-political critics. He uses a predominantly theoretical perspective but oriented, at the end, to praxis. Freire, on the other hand, is inspired by his own personal experience and discoveries based on his pedagogical practice in adult and popular education.

4. Their conception of social change also differs substantially. While in Freire's dialogue, the fundamental engine for change derives from dialectic contradiction and conflict among subjects —from which knowledge and new dialogic concepts are generated—Habermasian conception is based on closed "dialogic consensus," or temporal agreements among actors in the communication scenario.

Despite the divergences, in many other aspects, Freire and Habermas pursue the same aims:

1. Both proposals could be called "dialogic theories" (Flecha, 2001)[2,] analyzing society from an emancipatory communication perspective: horizontal, bidirectional and democratic.

2. Social change is the articulating axis of their intellectual trajectories, aimed to build development through dialogical action. Against a descriptive approach (positivism, realism, etc.), Freire and Habermas seek functionality, social change and praxis. The pedagogy contributes to alphabetization and emancipation of popular and adult groups; Habermas looks for a re-reading of Western thought in the search for democratic answers in the political, ethical or legal areas.

3. They both combine rarely seen interdisciplinary theoretical constructions designed to overcome weaknesses in each discipline: Habermas combines for example, functionalism, Marxism, psychology and linguistics; Freire, existentialism, linguistics and Christian humanism. Both men's thinking crosses traditional boundaries. They agree in their reviews of Marxism, and of the less–orthodox neo-marxism. In summary, Freire and Habermas fit with precision in the transdisciplinary, holistic, dialectic and comparative research (and action) of participatory communication for development.

4. They both propose a dualistic social paradigm, based on inter-subjectivity—avoiding the traditional dichotomies of subject/object, individual/structure, etc.-. Their theories break off from the traditional monocular perspective of Western social sciences, rather partial, according to Bhabha (1994), in its understanding of individual and society[3].

5. Frequently accused of being utopian, the authors protect themselves with a strong theoretical and practical basis. Their conceptions are complex, dynamic and wide. Their proposals are open to modification in time through verification or rebuttal (Popper), precisely due to their dialogic and dialectic component. Although they both are guilty of a certain normativism, both Freire and Habermas consider,

---

2   The terms "dialogic" or "dialogical" refer to the actions taking place through dialogue and argumentation among individuals or collectives and results are accepted as valid for these, as opposed to the monologic perspective, so extended in the "field," that it determines validity by isolated "individual" reasoning and a "reproductive" or "fictitious" feedback.

3   Freire should be placed, as well as Habermas, in a meaningful theoretical "location", in a sense proposed by Homi K. Bhabha (1994): an "in-between(ness)" that overcomes the dichotomies of Western theories without denying them.

1927
1960
1963
1964
1967
1969
1970
1971
1972
1973
1974
1975
1976
1977
1978
1979
1980
1981
1982
1983
1984
1985
1986
1987
1988
1989
1990
1991
1992
1993
1994
1995
1996
1997
1998
1999
2000
2001
2002
2003
2004
2005
2006

with a higher or lesser focus, some of the obstacles to dialogic actions—power authority, conflict, structures and socio-cultural reproduction, etc.[4]

6. The Brazilian did not pay as much attention to mass media as he did to the pedagogical process of human communication and the use of popular media as educational instruments. But his thinking can also be applied to mass, group or organizational processes. Habermas does not focus specifically on mass media either, but on the process of language and social communication. Despite the differences, a more localist perspective of the pedagogue [Freire] and a global or universal one in the case of the Frankfurter, their proposals inspire equally (new) social movements, media-activism, leftist organizations and development actions: localized, endogenous, long-time/process, culturally diverse, netted, etc.

7. The conception and application of social change in both authors have received criticism recently for different reasons. The German, [criticized] for his "modernizing" perspective of cultural development (Escobar, 1995) and for the difficulty in the practical translation of some theories. However, the discipline has just discovered the significance of using Habermas in the "participatory field" (Gilder, 1988, González, 1989; Hamer, 1998; Jacobson, 2002, 2003).

Works by the Brazilian were not always well understood either. Among the main problems to putting them in practice, Jan Servaes (1999) finds Freire to pay more attention to dialogue in group than to mass media and that he doesn't concentrate on language, but on the aims of the communication actions. Rosa María Alfaro (1998) also finds problems in the indiscriminate use of Freire's method. She questions the "populist base," the "fetishization" of popular issues or the loss of a macro-social and political sense in local development actions.

II. Towards A Freire-Habermas Communication Model

Since its formulation, Habermas' and Freire's proposals have had a considerable resonance for building new social strategies, and particularly for the reactivation of a meaningful discussion in some social disciplines.

Specifically, the main contributions of the Brazilian to communication for social change are the following:

1. Freire is the "founding father" of the participatory perspective of communication for development. With his criticism of the modernizing paradigm, one of the most dominant of his era, the pedagogue helps to build the thesis of "cultural imperialism" and "communication dependence," two of the main precursors of the "paradigmatic revolution" (Kuhn).

2. On the other hand, the Brazilian helps us understand the complex network fundamental to communication and social change processes. Comparing "extension" development programs with "banking" education, he observes that they are both based on a similar concept of communication—non-dialogic and anti-democratic—that limits their ability to transform. He also discovers that the root of underdevelopment and poverty resides in communication and culture, not only in the material base, [infra] structure, typical for some orthodox marxist analysis. According to Freire, problems in the so-named Third World are, to a great extent, communication problems.

3. The pedagogue proposes new categories to build a holistic communication model for social change: dialogue and horizontal communication; access, grassroots participation and appropriation; knowledge of self and reality; diversity and cultural specificity; popular knowledge and communication; "otherness"—action directed to the "other"—praxis (action-reflexivity); awareness and emancipation; endogenous development; localization-proximity; and communication-education interactions.

---

4 The authors also understand communication as an area of conflict and symbolic negotiation, where identities, social relationships, etc. are discussed; where conflicts for hegemony are frequent; and reproduction mechanisms are parallel to those of resistance and change.

4. His conception of praxis and his instrumental contributions are a fundamental inspiration to development research methodologies; to alternative and popular communication experiences; and to design cultural strategies for development (i.e. participatory action research, participatory rural appraisal, participant observer).

On the other side, theories of communication action and public sphere, even without being examined in depth, do contribute significantly to the discipline [5]:

1. Habermas promotes social change through "communication action" and "reason." Rationality has not so much to do with knowledge, its acquisition or instrumentality as with the use made by subjects capable of language and action. Habermas recommends advancing from reason to (communicational) understanding, the only track to social change.
2. The public sphere is a homogeneous space of embodied subjects in symmetrical relations, free from State inferences, market regulations and the power of media. It pursues consensus through the critique of arguments, so public opinion emerges in its informal phase, through all kinds of civic organizations. Reconstructing public sphere, rethinking the relationship between its different components or "spheres," helps to rethink the role played by civil society in social change movements, the importance of conforming or recapturing free opinion spaces, or the different dimensions composing social change. If people have the ability to create and reproduce the [social] system, they also have ways to change it and communication is one of the main instruments, given its performance-oriented nature. Dialogue acts as a counterweight for the authoritarian potential of the system, and it

starts to be used by different protest movements. Also, we need to consider the emancipating potential of mass media themselves, as long as their actions are aimed at promoting education and [civic engagement].
3. The German proposes new categories to create a new communication model for development, some of them already mentioned: communicative reason, understanding, argumentation, consensus, ideal speech situation and public sphere(s).
4. Habermas's work contributes to clarify the debate on scale and dimensions in communication and development work (Jacobson 2002, 2003; Jacobson y Storey, 2004). Concepts like public spheres or communication action help to clarify social change can be conceived and planned at different levels: macro, intermediate and micro. On the other hand, although Habermas's work is eminently theoretical, some authors search for practical applications for analysis and evaluation of participatory components in communication processes, as well as the design and implementation of communication and development programs (Jacobson, 2002, 2003).

III. Conclusions

Despite its complexity, comparing Freire's and Habermas's thinking may help the discipline, to broaden its action and methodologies and to move toward "multiplicity" (Servaes, 1999) in the new participative proposals.

In general, the (re)construction of a model following both authors must adopt the following strategies:

■ Consolidating a firm theoretical apparatus revising concepts, theories, paradigms, approaches, and incorporating the latest findings and experiences.
■ Re-assessing the epistemological gaps and moving toward growing interdisciplinarity.
■ Making up new formats, languages, recombinations, etc. in participatory research and planning.

---

5   The Habermasian contribution to communication for development is huge, although there has not yet been enough historical distance to verifiy its validity. Habermas himself has retracted some of his first theoretical proposals. The dimensions of concepts like "ideal speech situation," "argumentation" or "public sphere" offer new clues to start a more balanced, horizontal, dialogic communication.

1927
1960
1963
1964
1967
1969
1970
1971
1972
1973
1974
1975
1976
1977
1978
1979
1980
1981
1982
1983
1984
1985
1986
1987
1988
1989
1990
1991
1992
1993
1994
1995
1996
1997
1998
1999
2000
2001
2002
2003
2004
2005
2006

References

Alfaro, Rosa María: "Participación, ¿para qué? Un enfoque político de la participación en la comunicación popular," *Diálogos de la Comunicación*. Nr. 22, 1990. 59-78.

Atwood, Rita and McAnany, Emile G. (Eds.): *Communication and Latin American Society Trends in Critical Research, 1960-1985.* Madison, Wisconsin: University of Wisconsin Press, 1986.

Bhabha, Homi K.: *The Location of Culture.* London: Routledge, 1994.

Dervin, Brenda and Huesca, Robert: "The Participatory Communication for Development Narrative: An Examination of Meta-Theoretic Assumptions and Their Impacts," Servaes (Eds.). *Theoretical Approaches to Participatory Communication.* Cresskill, NJ: Hampton Press, 2001. 169-210.
—"Theory and practice in Latin American alternative communication research," *Journal of Communication* (4), 1994. 53-73.

Flecha, Ramón, Gómez, Jesús and Puigvert, Lidia: *Teoría sociológica contemporánea.* Paidós: Barcelona, 2001.

Freire, Paulo: *Pedagogía del oprimido.* Buenos Aires: Siglo XXI, 1969.
—*Extensión y Comunicación. La concientización en el medio rural.* Montevideo: Tierra Nueva, 1970.

Gilder, Eric: "Communication for development and Habermas´ Ideal Speech Situation," *Media Development*, 35 (4), 1988.

Gumucio, Alfonso: *Haciendo Olas: Historias de Comunicación Participativa para el Cambio Social.* Fundación Rockefeller, 2001.

Habermas, Jürgen: *Historia y crítica de la opinión pública.* Barcelona: Gili, 1994.
—*Teoría de la acción comunicativa.* 2 vols. Madrid: Taurus, 1987.

Hamer, John: "The Sidama of Ethiopia and rational communication action in policy and dispute settlement," *Anthropos*, 93, 1998. 137-153.

Huesca, Robert: "Tracing the History of Participatory Communication Approaches to Development: A Critical Appraisal," en: J. Mayo & J. Servaes (eds.): *Approaches to Development Communication. An orientation and resource kit.* París: UNESCO, 1994.
—"From ´Naming the World´ to Theorizing its Relationships: New Directions for Participatory Communicaction for Development," *Media Development*, 2. 1996.

"Participatory approaches to communication for development," en B. Gudykunst y B. Mody (eds.): *Handbook of international and intercultural communication.* Thousand Oaks, CA: Sage Publications, 2002. 499-518.

Jacobson, Thomas L.: "Differentiating Kinds of Communication for social Change," *Plenipotentiary Conference of IAMCR.* Barcelona, 2002.
—"Participatory Communication for Social Change: The Relevance of the Theory of Communicative Action," en: P. Kal (ed.): *Communication Yearbook*, 27, 2003. 87-124.

Jacobson, Thomas L. & Storey, J. Douglas: "Development Communication and Participation: Applying Habermas to a Case Study of Population Programs in Nepal," *Communication Theory.* 14 (2). 99-121, 2002.

Jacobson, Thomas L. & Servaes, Jan (eds.): *Theoretical Approaches to Participatory Communication*, Cresskill: Hampton Press, 1999.

Mignolo, Walter: *Local Histories/Global Designs. Coloniality, Subaltern Knowledges and Border Thinking.* Princeton, NJ: Princeton University Press, 2000.

Morrow, Raymond A. & Torres, Carlos Alberto: *Reading Freire and Habermas: Critical Pedagogy and Transformative Change.* New York: Teacher´s Colllege Press, Columbia University, 2002.

Quijano, Aníbal: "Colonialidad del poder, cultura y conocimiento en América Latina." en: S., Castro-Gómez, O., Guardiola-Rivera y C., Millán de Benavides (Eds.): *Pensar (en) los intersticios. Teoría y práctica de la crítica poscolonial.* Santafé de Bogotá: Colección Pensar/Centro Editorial Javeriano, 1999. pp. 99-109.

Richards, Michael, Thomas, Pradip N. & Nain, Zaharom (Eds.): *Communication and Development: The Freirean Connection.* New Jersey: Hampton Press Inc., 2001.

Servaes, Jan: *One world, multiple cultures: A New Paradigm on Communication for Development.* Leuven: Acco, 1999.
—"Introduction: Participatory communication and research in development settings," en J. Servaes, T. L. Jacobson & S.A. White (Eds.), *Participatory communication for social change.* London: Sage Publications, 1996.

Thomas, Pradip N.: "Communication and development: Freirean cultural politics in a post-modern era," *PCR-Newsletter*, 1 (1) 2-3. 1993.

Waisbord, Silvio. *Family Tree of Theories, Methodologies and Strategies in Development Communication.* The Rockefeller Foundation, 2000.

White, Shirley A., Nair, K. Sadanandan & Ascroft, Joseph (Eds.): *Participatory communication: Working for change and development.* New Delhi: Sage, 1994.

Barranquero, Alejandro. "From Freire and Habermas to Multiplicity: Widening the Theoretical Borders of Participative Communication for Social Change," paper presented at IAMCR 2005 Meeting in Taipei. Used with permission of the author.

1927
1960
1963
1964
1967
1969
1970
1971
1972
1973
1974
1975
1976
1977
1978
1979
1980
1981
1982
1983
1984
1985
1986
1987
1988
1989
1990
1991
1992
1993
1994
1995
1996
1997
1998
1999
2000

POWER, KNOWLEDGE AND SOCIAL CONTROL IN PARTICIPATORY DEVELOPMENT

Excerpt from: Participation: The New Tyranny?

By Uma Kothari

2001 Since participatory research is a technique for knowing particular kinds of subjects, underlying the discussion here is an analysis of the techniques of power and the particular types of knowledge that the methodology creates and reproduces. This analysis, I argue, will challenge some of the truth claims made by participatory practitioners about the validity of the data collected and raise questions about the extent to which it represents "true" local knowledge. What is significant here is that the participative technologies used are effective in producing what is considered as "truth" or at least closer to the "truth" than other less participative, top-down methods of enquiry and knowledge accumulation. These claims to acquiring "truer" knowledge and, for some practitioners, to also empowering participants through their involvement in the process, have led to the overwhelming adoption of participatory techniques within development policy and practice. Within participatory discourse a number of binaries, or oppositions, are presented (see Chambers 1997), such as "uppers" and "lowers," North and South, professional knowledge and local knowledge, which are continuously evoked and rehearsed as popular slogans of participation and empowerment. These dichotomies set up oppositions invested with notions of the morally "good" and the morally "bad," and it then becomes the main aim of participatory approaches to development to set about reversing them, as reflected in the title of one of Chambers' books, *Rural*.

Development: Putting the Last First (1983)

Participatory methodologies, then, require the formulation and adoption of a framework in which the micro is set against the macro, the margins against the centre, the local against the elite, and the powerless against the powerful. However, the almost exclusive focus on the micro level, on people who are considered powerless and marginal, has reproduced the simplistic notion that the sites of social power and control are to be found solely at the macro and central levels. These dichotomies further strengthen the assumption that people who wield power are located at institutional centres while those who are subjugated and subjected to power are to be found at the local or regional level—hence the valorisation of "local knowledge" and the continued belief in the empowerment of "local people" through participation. Foucault, however, argues that:

> Power must be analyzed as something which circulates, or rather as something which only functions in the form of a chain. It is never localized here or there. ... Power is employed and exercised through a net-like organization. (1980, 98)

Thus Foucault's analysis of power requires us to shift our concentration from the centre and national institutions such as the state, not because this enables the powerless to speak and be heard, but because those macro spheres of authority are not necessarily the only focal conductors of power. He stresses, instead, the need to explore further the local and micro points of power because:

> Hegemonic or global forms of power rely in the first instance on those 'infinitesimal' practices, composed of their own particular techniques and tactics, which exist in those institutions on the fringes or at the micro-level of society. (99)

So power is everywhere and can be particularly analysed through the creation of social norms or customs that are practised throughout society. This disrupts the dichotomies of macro/micro, central/local, powerful/powerless, where the former are sites and holders

2001
2002
2003
2004
2005
2006

of power and the latter subjects of power. Instead, all individuals are vehicles of power. An analysis of the ways in which power extends and transforms in different micro or "everyday" contexts can further our understanding of the more readily identifiable types of social control and domination traditionally seen to be located at the "centre," be they at the level of the state or other global institutions or in the hands of local elites. Power is thus found in the creation of norms and social and cultural practices at all levels. Within much participatory development discourse, "people's knowledge" or "local knowledge" is seen as a fixed commodity that people intrinsically have and own. Instead, as is argued here, knowledge is culturally, socially and politically produced and is continuously reformulated as a powerful normative construct. Knowledge is thus accumulation of social norms, rituals and practices that, far from being constructed in isolation from power relations, is embedded in them (or against them). However, the creation of dichotomies of power within participatory discourse (the haves and the have-nots) allows the revealing of power not as a social and political discourse or as embodied practice, but only as manifest in material realities. Thus participatory approaches can unearth who gets what, when and where, but not necessarily the process by which this happens or the ways in which the knowledge produced through participatory techniques is a normalized one that reflects and articulates wider power relations in society.

The discussion here focuses on participatory techniques as methods of knowledge accumulation, and it attempts to unravel the sorts of power that are reproduced at the micro level through the use of these approaches, as well as how participants and participatory development practitioners are themselves conduits of power. The arguments presented are that participatory development can encourage a re-assertion of control and power by dominant individuals and groups, that it can lead to the reification of social norms through self-surveillance and consensus building, and that it "purifies" knowledge and the

spaces of participation through the codification, classification and control of information and its analysis and (re)presentation. The discussion also explores the limitations of participation in terms of how it demands certain kinds of performances to be enacted. It is suggested here that individuals and groups can and do subvert the methodology and, in doing so, gain control by shaping the form of their participation though their "performances" on the Participitory Ryeal Assessment (PRA) stage and in their selection of the information they conceal or choose to disclose. Thus they become social agents and actors by subverting the power of development and disrupting participatory discourses. This subversion does not always require their inclusion in processes of participation as advocated through such methodologies as PRA; indeed, they are often found through acts of self-exclusion and nonparticipation.

Reassertion of Power and Social Control

Participatory approaches to development research and planning attempt to challenge the apparent power relations in society by recognizing the control that certain individuals and groups have over others. This is based on the recognition that those who wield little power have limited opportunities to express their interest and needs and are generally excluded from key decision-making processes, and that their knowledge is considered insignificant. However, despite the aims of participatory approaches and the claims made by participatory practitioners, particularly with respect to empowering the disempowered, it is argued there that participative methods of enquiry simplify the nature of power and are thus in danger of encouraging a reassertion of power and social control not only by certain individuals and groups, but also of particular bodies of knowledge.

The very act of inclusion, of being drawn in as a participant, can symbolize an exercise of power and control over an individual. As Geof Wood suggests (1999), there are forms of "adverse incorporation," where the act or process of inclusion is not always to the benefit of those groups who have previously been excluded. Cohen (1985) similarly refers to insidious modes of inclusionary control. He suggests that programmes designed to bring the excluded in often result in forms of control that are more difficult to challenge, as they reduce spaces of conflict and are relatively benign and liberal. That is, those people who have the greatest reason to challenge and confront power relations and structures are brought, or even bought, through the promise of development assistance, into the development process in ways that disempower them to challenge the prevailing hierarchies and inequalities in society, hence inclusionary control and the inducement of conformity. ...

References

Chambers, R. (1983) *Rural Development: Putting the Last First,* Longman, London.
—(1997) *Whose Reality Counts? Putting the First Last,* IT Publications, London.

Cohen, S. (1985) *Visions of Social Control,* Polity Press, Cambridge.

Foucault, M. (1973) *The Order of Things. The Archaeology of Human Sciences,* Vintage, New York.
—(1977) *Discipline and Punish: The Birth of the Prison,* Penguin, Harmondsworth.
—(1979) *The History of Sexuality: An Introduction,* Penguin, Harmondsworth.
—(1980) *Power! Knowledge: Selected Interviews and Other Writings,* Harvester Wheat-sheaf, Brighton.

Mosse, D. (1995) "Social Analysis in Participatory Rural Development," *PLA Notes,* No. 24, IIED, London.

Wood, G. (1999) "Concepts and Themes: Landscaping Social Development," *DFID,* London.

EXCERPT FROM:

VALIDITY AND EVALUATION IN COMMUNICATION RESEARCH

Does It Make Sense?

By Jan Servaes

2001   Research in the West ... is research of social control. ... [It] tends ... to reflect the values and reinforce the system within which it is conceived, supported and executed. ... [It] is not marked by speculative and reflective approaches ... consideration of alternatives, or caution and tolerance ... but by dogma, doctrinaire statements, selective use of evidence, unsubstantiated assertions ... arrogance and hostile intolerance. ... The positions, firmly held by the new high priests, brook no contradictions, and evidence must not ... get in the way of faith. Jim Halloran (1981: 23-39)

All research begins with some set of assumptions that themselves are untested but "believed." Positivistic research, which comprises the mass of modern communication and development research, proceeds from the presupposition that all knowledge is based on an observable reality, and social phenomena can be studied on the basis of methodologies and techniques adopted from the natural sciences. In other words, "reality" *exists* apart from our interpretation of it. We can objectively perceive, understand, predict and control it. Social scientists, enamoured by the notion of a predictable universe, therefore concluded that, by applying the methods of positivistic science to study human affairs, it would be possible to predict and, ultimately, to control human social behaviour. Furthermore, its methodological premises and epistemological assumptions are based almost exclusively on the Western experience and worldview, a view that holds the world as a phenomenon to be controlled, manipulated and exploited.

Quantitative as well as qualitative researchers today increasingly recognize the weakness of a purely objectivist position. But at the same time, Jacobson (1993: 219) argues, neither can the standard response to this recognition be seen as satisfactory:

> This response holds, basically, that if we try not to assume value-based positions then we can still say we are doing social science. This does constitute recognition that complete objectivity is no longer possible, but it does not replace value freedom with anything of substance. The inadequacy of this response seems very likely to be the reason that participatory researchers feel that objectivism still resides in the practices of many social scientists.

I intend to outline the relative characteristics and merits of quantitative, qualitative and participatory approaches to research, and to emphasize some of the philosophical issues, which underpin them. However, I adopt Bryman's (1984, 1994) argument that it is *not* possible to establish a clear symmetry between epistemological positions and associated techniques of social research and, consequently, they often become confused with each other:

> It may be that at the technical level, the quantitative/qualitative distinction is a rather artificial one. … At the epistemological level, the distinction is less obviously artificial since the underlying tenets relate to fundamentally different views about the nature of the social sciences, which have resisted reconciliation for a very long time (Bryman 1984: 88).

Or, as stated by Saneh Chamarik (1993: 4): "In social science, approach and methodology are not just a matter of technique and expertise, but essentially represent an attitude of mind, that is to say, a kind of moral proposition."

Therefore, I wish to refer again to the distinction between made above the mechanistic diffusion versus organic participatory models. Contrary to the scientist who aims for an understanding of the world as it exists "out there," the participatory model takes as the fundamental focus the immediate world of the participants, their analysis of, and subsequent action in, that world. However, as has been argued, both models should be regarded as opposites on a continuum.

Moreover, it should be stated at the outset that highly rigid methodology serves to limit rather than expand humanistic understanding to the detriment of both the researcher and the "researched." The detachment, the reluctance to "contaminate" one's research design in the dynamic, holistic and human social context, while claiming to be working for the ultimate benefit of those studied, should to be challenged, if not on a methodological, then certainly on a moral, basis. Given this aloofness, many so-called quantitative, qualitative and/or participatory researchers become largely parasitical in character, and contribute little to those whom they research. Jumping from country to country, or village to village, many Western and local researchers alike conduct their "safari" and "airport research," collect the data, and return to the university to write it up, hopefully for publication in a prestigious journal. The subjects of the study do not learn of the results and obtain no benefit, except via a long, distorting cycle of traditional research and top-down social action.

However, the assertion is not that the entirety of empirical research or academic inquiry is of no value. *The intent is not to reject science but to properly define its place within human knowledge.*

Academia

Before I embark upon an assessment of the different research approaches, a few words about the social group with the greatest interest in the perpetuation of highly complex research practices, which mandate "correct" methodology above all: academia. As with bureaucracies, academic institutions strive for results that paint their activities in a concise, easily visible fashion. The reasons for this include peer status, as well as personal and organizational sustenance. The rule of "publish or perish" is known to all, and those who would go against the flow or approach their task in an unorthodox fashion are jeopardizing their personal careers. It is not the individual's place to question the prevalent paradigms or accepted methodologies. Consequently, most scholars continue to follow the intellectual fashions of the day. On the whole, their specialist knowledge prompts little divergence from the prevalent opinion of their social group or class (Long and Long, 1992). Linking this to reductionistic trends, Thayer (1983: 84) writes not only does it appear more scientific "to deal with fragments; it is also a whole lot safer. If the ends of their effort are sometimes irrelevant or trivial or equivocal, it is of no great concern, for it is not the ends but the means by which they distinguish themselves." As a result, institutions of higher education have often stayed aloof about the needs of the majority of the rural clientele.

New forms of access to and structural changes in the higher education system should be a subject of serious consideration. *The search for truth succumbs to the search for funding, which is subservient to ideology.* Therefore, while academia is supposed to be a "marketplace of ideas," and a forum for free discussion, it has often become part of the market. As a result, Simbulan (1985: 8) charges: "Many academicians have become academic prostitutes or academic profiteers who, while trying to overcome their material impoverishments by tapping the vast sources of establishment research funds have, in turn, become morally impoverished." With time, the parameters under which researchers operate can constitute, for them, a social reality. They tend to see only what their terministic screens allow them to name, and to do what the paradigmatic vocabulary predisposes. They see its limits as the limits of the world, not as a more or less arbitrary boundary between what they know and what they do not. Such trends are demeaning to the researcher as well.

Due to the widespread use and application of Western models, constructs and methodologies, intellectuals in the so-called Third World are sadly dependent for their status and acceptance on their links with the West. Juan Diaz Bordenave (1974: 208) admonishes academics to overcome this "compulsion to perceive our own reality through foreign concepts and ideologies and learn to look at communication and adoption from a new perspective." Mimicking foreign methodologies, as well as striving for more exacting standards, and tighter control, social science research is pulled farther and farther from the dynamic social context it ostensibly strives to understand.

Rajesh Tandon (1981:17) therefore argues against a situation where a research elite, be it foreign or local, dictate what is valid and what is not. "This whole game has been so much organized that everything else outside it is considered unscientific. Everything outside it is not knowledge." However, and once again, the assertion is not that the entirety of empirical research or academic inquiry is of no value. The intent is to define properly its place within human knowledge.

1. Quantitative Approaches to Research

Logic and common sense tell us that such a thing as "objectivity" exists. It also tells us the bumblebee can fly. But by the laws of physics, the bumblebee is unable to fly. "Common sense" is just that, *common sense*:

> Human progress has been achieved invariably at points where people were prepared to abandon the commonsense approach. For countless millennia, human beings hugged the coast and would not put to sea because they thought they would fall over the horizon. Similarly, commonsense tells us that matter is solid, the earth is flat and the sun goes around the earth (Jayaweera, 1986: 41).

Social research and developmental research are claimed to be objective, neutral and thus scientific. In reality, however, it often becomes an instrument in

1927
1960
1963
1964
1967
1969
1970
1971
1972
1973
1974
1975
1976
1977
1978
1979
1980
1981
1982
1983
1984
1985
1986
1987
1988
1989
1990
1991
1992
1993
1994
1995
1996
1997
1998
1999
2000
2001
2002
2003
2004
2005
2006

the hands of the powerful elite to rationalize their control of the people. Therefore, as Halloran (1981: 40) claims, "it is ideology that we are now talking about, and in mass communication research, as elsewhere, there are an increasing number of ideologists who present their work as social science ... it all depends on what one means by ideology, and what one means by social science."

OBJECTIVITY AND SUBJECTIVITY

The underlying problem of the importunate posture of "objectivity" is that in assuming that the meanings for the conditions of subjects' lives are independent of those subjects. Researchers in the human and social studies are assuming they themselves are independent of how they see those subjects or of the phenomena they are examining.

Present discussion rejects this assumption. The idol has feet of clay. Similar to the notion of relative logic, the assertion is "objectivity" is nothing more than subjectivity, which a given aggregate of individuals agree upon. It refers to what a number of subjects or judges experience, in short, to phenomena within the public domain. Therefore, as Dervin (1982: 293) observes:

> No human being is capable of making absolute observations, and since it is humans that produce that thing we call information, all information is itself constrained." And Anderson (1988: 239) adds that "the ultimate source of our knowledge is not 'out there' pressing upon us, but it is in our own consciousness.

Hence, "objectivity" is nothing more than "inter-subjectivity." For example, to ensure coder reliability, the researcher culls out those coders whose subjective coding is incongruent with the mean. The rejected coders' analysis is not "inter-subjective;" it is not "objective." Research defines the categorical constructs, then defines and refines the instruments to measure those constructs. With time (as well as painstaking research and adequate funding), "intelligence" becomes what the tests measure. Science

becomes the operationalization of concepts through the development of reliable measures, which, in turn, serve to measure and substantiate the concepts. Reliability and internal validity are perfected. However, whether this cyclical process is related with the social reality outside the lab, with external validity, remains largely unconsidered.

THE "END OF IDEOLOGY" AND "VALUE-FREE SCIENCE"

Roughly corresponding with the rise of communication models and the doctrine of modernization emerged a growing sentiment of the impending "end of ideology" in the social sciences. Superstition and ideology were to yielding to reason, positivism and science. Friberg and Hettne (1985: 209) relate the belief was that "controlled experiments and deductive reasoning guarantees an infinite growth of valid knowledge about the mechanisms of nature, and this knowledge will lay the foundation of the technological society marked by material abundance."

This new mode of inquiry was claimed to be detached, neutral and value-free. It was "the noble and final battle of 'knowledge' against 'ignorance' " (Thayer, 1983: 89). The belief was that "with just a little more data, with just a few more refined techniques of inquiry, we will indeed 'arrive.'" *Not all agree.* Some take a political stand and argue that "neutral" science has led to the dehumanizing and catastrophic utilization of knowledge, nuclear missiles, biological poisons and psychological brainwashing. Others claim, from a more methodological point of view, that no responsible social scientist would hold that the results of social science research are comprehensive, free of value premises or valid for all seasons.

Similar to the majority of efforts toward communication and participation in the development context, research most often derives from, and serves to perpetuate, dominant structures. Tying the notions of inter-subjectivity, ideology and the established order together, Addo (1985: 17) writes that "claims to scientific neutrality and objectivity come easily to the establishment [which] holds fast to a deep-seated common world view ... a theoretical structure of what the world is like and ought to be like, and what it is about and ought to be about."

POWER-BASED RESEARCH

The "dominant methodological concern is how to approach the interpretation of the modern world-system in order to make it safe for ... the perpetuation of ... this world-system" (Addo, 1985: 20). This methodology reveals its pro status quo bias in that it never considers the alternative of the creation of a new system but rather presents "functional" adjustments to the old. It facilitates the functioning of the existing system, without ever questioning its validity, however dangerous that system may be for the future of society and man's and woman's integrity. In this way the research, although often referred to as abstracted empiricism, is certainly not abstracted from the society in which it operates. In sum, science, particularly at the level of social research, is laden with ideology. It serves, and is largely intended to serve, vested power structures. As such, claims of the "end of ideology" or "value-free science" do not hold true neither in their premises, nor in their applications.

Communication is no exception. Robert White (1982: 29) argues "much of the research tradition in the field of communication—concepts, methodology and research designs—has been in the service of authoritarian communication." And Halloran (1981: 22) adds that communication research:

> has developed ... essentially as a response to the requirements of a modern, industrial, urban society for empirical, quantitative, policy-related, information about its operations. ... Research was carried out with a view to ... achieving stated aims and objectives, often of a commercial nature.

The goal of inquiry has often been to investigate how commercial or political persuasion could be effectively used. Hence, such research is an "objective" form of intelligence gathering for social control by business firms and governments. The predominant vein of social research, resting on epistemological suppositions, strives to understand reality, with the objectives of prediction and control. However, while claiming detachment and neutrality, research functions to objectify the very "reality" and assumes to be objective. This is done in a manner congruent with, and toward the benefit of, the status quo, usually those who pay the bills. In other words, it serves more to create and perpetuate a reality than to understand one.

METHODOLOGY-DRIVEN RESEARCH

In the journals and conferences, debate is more often about the method of investigation than the content. Halloran (1981: 23) argues that " 'Scientific' is defined solely or mainly in terms of method, and ... little or no attention is given to ... the nature of the relevant, substantive issues and their relationship to wider sociological concerns." This overemphasis on methodology and techniques, as well as adulation of formulae and scientific-sounding terms, exemplify the common tendency to displace value from the ends to the means. A sociologist or psychologist obsessed with frameworks, jargon and techniques resembles a carpenter who becomes so worried about keeping his or her tools clean that he or she has no time to cut the wood. Reality as experienced in the lives of people has been sacrificed to methodological rigor. Too often an emphasis upon exact measurement "precludes" the asking of "significant" questions, and the result is fragmented bits of knowledge on "researchable" topics.

As the methodology becomes increasingly complex, the questions posed become ever more trivial. The parameters of inquiry yield to increasingly sophisticated methods. It is sometimes said that modern scientists are learning so much about so little that they'll eventually know everything about nothing. Therefore, many years ago, Kuhn (1962: 35) attested that "perhaps the most striking feature of the normal research problems ... is how little they aim to produce major novelties, conceptual or phenomenal."

1927
1960
1963
1964
1967
1969
1970
1971
1972
1973
1974
1975
1976
1977
1978
1979
1980
1981
1982
1983
1984
1985
1986
1987
1988
1989
1990
1991
1992
1993
1994
1995
1996
1997
1998
1999
2000
2001
2002
2003
2004
2005
2006

With the tendency towards reductionism, the social sciences tend to "compartmentalize" the subject matter into separate parts, with only rare attempts at approaching the subject as a whole. This forces nature "into the preformed and relatively inflexible box that the paradigm supplies. No part of the aim of normal science is to call forth new sorts of phenomena, indeed those that will not fit the box are often not seen at all" (Kuhn, 1962: 24).

Categories, taxonomies, terms and their relations are largely what make a given paradigm. Yet, even though this "terminology is a reflection of reality, by its very nature it is a selection of reality and therefore also functions as a deflection of reality" (Burke, 1968: 44). The categorization is often derived from the literature rather than from "concepts that are necessarily real, meaningful and appropriate from the native point of view" (Harris, 1980: 32). This renders invisible the knowledge of the people involved in the real life activity at which the research is aimed. Consequently, Rockhill (1982: 8) asserts skewed pictures "of people result as a consequence of a research approach that seeks to interpret human behaviour using constructs derived from the perspective of the literature rather than from the perspective of the people being studied." She provides an excellent example in describing studies that conclude that participation is higher among the "educated." Rockhill (1982: 6-10) states: "Typically people are categorically defined ... as participants or nonparticipants according to whether or not they have participated in a given range of educational activities." Participation is most often defined by the researchers as "an organized educational activity." The conclusion, essentially, is that those who participate more in institutional education settings tend to participate more in institutional education settings. However, the quantum leap occurs when "nonparticipants are repeatedly categorized as non-learners [and] the false notion that people become educated only through educational programs is perpetuated." This is done empirically and "objectively." Rockhill (1982: 10) summarizes: "A difficulty in quantitative research is that constructs are often selected by the researcher to name predefined variable clusters rather than derived through the effort to understand human experience from the perspective of the subject. As in the use of 'non-learners,' typically constructs are value-laden and biased against people who do not act in ways valued by researchers who interpret data from their own, often unconscious, cultural biases."

Prevalent theories, paradigms, methodologies and taxonomies become tantamount to human understanding; they become the goal, and the reality. Adherence to the widely accepted methods produces mostly one-dimensional communication research unable to cope with complex and dynamic social realities. Analysts research isolated variables, thereby removing them from the cultural context, which gives them their meaning. But communication cannot be dissected and displaced to increase the convenience of observation without disrupting the process of meaning creation at the same time.

2. Qualitative Approaches to Research

Qualitative research almost mirrors the quantitative one and, in this sense, discussion has already addressed the qualitative approaches. However, several points require elaboration.

SUBJECTIVITY AND PHENOMENOLOGY

Qualitative research accepts subjectivity as a *given*. It does not view social science as "objective" in the ordinary and simple understanding of that term but as an active intervention in social life with claims and purposes of its own. Objectivity therefore means "seeing what an experience is for another person, not what causes it, not why it exists, not how it can be defined and classified." (Moustakas, 1974: 107). As the world is constructed inter-subjectively through processes of interpretation, the premise is that "reality does not write itself on the human consciousness, but rather, that human consciousness approaches reality with certain embedded interpretations" (Anderson, 1988: 238), and those interpretations, in turn, constitute reality. We are thus introduced to a "new principle of relativity" which holds that all observers are not led by the same physical evidence to the same picture of the universe.

As such, given the idiosyncratic nature of individuals and cultures, social reality has predominantly the character of irregularity, instead of the ordered, regular and predictable reality assumed in empirical approaches. These implications have profound impact on the manner that we look at communication and the way we strive to understand, and research, social contexts. Further confounding this subjective, idiosyncratic irregularity is the fact of its dynamism. Christians and Carey (1981: 346) assert, "To study this creative process is our first obligation, and our methodology must not reduce and dehumanize it in the very act of studying it." The emphasis should be on discovery rather than applying routinize procedures. Following the humanistic premise that people are not objects, there is no warrant for believing that the social sciences should imitate the natural sciences in form or method. The subjects of research are just that, subjects. We are not objects and cannot be objectified without losing the very humanity that is the focus of inquiry. Needed are intellectual endeavours that reach out to, rather than insulate us from, popular experience. We must therefore have the courage to underwrite contextual thinking and contextual research. "Truth" lies not in objective proof, but in the experience of existence or non-existence in the minds of men and women and their mutual affirmation. Therefore, "truth" is relative.

This brings us back to the topic of intersubjectivity. At the risk of being "irrational" and "unscientific," it is argued qualitative and phenomenological approaches, in their broadest sense, advocate a human approach toward understanding the human context. It is based on the human character of the subject matter. As a specifically human approach, it uses lived experience as acts on which to base its findings. Fuglesang (1984: 4) and Ewen (1983: 223) summarize:

If communication is difficult in today's world, it is perhaps because it is difficult to be human. Communication experts do not make it easier when they try to develop science out of something that essentially is an art. The impulse of our analysis ought to respect these voices in their own terms, not continually seek to distort them into faceless data. Such respect may mean our work will be *less* scientifically antiseptic, *less* arrogantly conclusive, *less* neatly tied up, *less* instrumental. Yet, being liberated from such constraints, our work will likely become *more* lyrical *more* speculative, *more* visionary, *more* intelligent and human.

NATURALISTIC OBSERVATION AND THE PARTICIPANT OBSERVER

To attempt an understanding of a human being or a social context, to the degree possible, we must set aside all scientific knowledge of the average man and woman and discard all theories in order to adopt a completely new and unprejudiced attitude. The researcher must set aside pre-derelictions, what he or she "already knows," because if inquiry begins with a preconceived set of interpretive templates viewpoints will be lost. Through the myopic glasses of rigid theories and constructs, other aspects that may be even more important are typically not noted because they are not looked for. This implies a re-evaluation of conceptions such as "developer," "source," "expert," "neutrality" and "objectivity." In other words, the researcher immerses herself or himself in the context not to verify hypotheses, but as sources for "understanding meaning." In a very real sense, the most important tool of inquiry becomes the researcher's attitude. Large egos are detrimental when the investigator considers herself or himself far above the group to be investigated, and refuses implicitly or explicitly the real encounter with the subject of investigation. Anderson (1988: 320) concurs in writing:

The 'us/them' character of ethnographic work and our own socialization as researchers—keepers of the truth—can lead to a sense of superiority about our social action as compared to those we

1927
1960
1963
1964
1967
1969
1970
1971
1972
1973
1974
1975
1976
1977
1978
1979
1980
1981
1982
1983
1984
1985
1986
1987
1988
1989
1990
1991
1992
1993
1994
1995
1996
1997
1998
1999
2000
2001
2002
2003
2004
2005
2006

study. Observational distancing can turn people into subjects—objects of study.

Quite the opposite of neutrality and detachment, the participant observer involves herself or himself in the natural setting in order to, to the extent possible, obtain an inside view of the social context. This involves "gaining access," but the researcher must also maintain somewhat of an aloof position to observe. The goal is to see the other objectively and, at the same time, to experience her or his difficulties subjectively. For the "outsider," participation is "a staged effort and observation is a product of routine. At the other extreme, the insider has the 'of-course-it's-true" knowledge of the member. For the insider, participation is effortless, observation difficult" (Anderson, 1988: 296).

First among the fundamental concepts of qualitative research is the axiom that the study of human life is interpretive. Anderson argues, it is the search for subjective understanding, rather than manipulative; the quest for prediction and control. Qualitative research has replaced prediction with emphatic understanding as its research aim so that social science can be freed from its exploitative uses and enlisted instead in the cause of freedom and justice. Contrary to quantitative inquiry, which accepts its premises and focuses on methodological rigor, qualitative study stresses the critical analysis of those suppositions to understand human understanding, thereby restoring the critical and liberating function to intellectual investigation.

In anthropology one usually distinguishes between an "emic" and an "etic" approach.

Emic operations have as their hallmark the elevation of the native informant to the status of the ultimate judge of the adequacy of the observer's descriptions and analyses. The test of the adequacy of emic analyses is their ability to generate statements the native accepts as real, meaningful or appropriate. In carrying out research in the emic mode, the observer attempts to acquire a knowledge of the categories and rules one must know in order to think and act as a native. ... Etic operations have as their hallmark the elevation of observers to the status of ultimate judges and concepts used in descriptions and analyses. The test of adequacy of etic accounts is simply their ability to generate scientifically productive theories about the causes of sociocultural differences and similarities. Rather than employ concepts that are necessarily real, meaningful and appropriate from the native point of view, the observer is free to use alien categories and rules derived from the date language of science. Frequently, etic operations involve the measurement and juxtaposition of activities and events that native informants may find inappropriate or meaningless (Harris, 1980: 32).

In this context I would like to plead for an "emic" position. However, as Clifford Geertz (1973: 15) warns, this is an extremely difficult approach to accomplish: "We begin with our interpretations of what our informants are up to, or think they are up to, and then systematize." Geertz, therefore, prefers the notions of "experience-near" and "experience-far" above the "emic" and "etic" concepts. The former are internal to a language or culture and are derived from the latter, which are posed as universal or scientific.

CRITICAL RESEARCH

Qualitative research has often been characterized as critical research. The reverse, that critical research is often qualitative in nature is also true, especially when that research addresses the dominant societal structures and, in particular, when the inquiry is directed toward what can be called the "academic research complex." Critical research looks at the historical, societal and dynamic context of its questions, and consequently is not amenable to rigid methodology. Hence, there exist few similarities in approaches deemed critical research. Therefore, Halloran (1981: 26), among others, argues that "the unity of the critical approach lies in its opposition to conventional work rather than in any shared, more positive approach." Lacking in "accepted" methods, critical research is often written off as unscientific or as ideological prattle. However, just as qualitative research accepts its subjectivity, critical analysis admits its ideological premises. It can also be argued the reason critical research is deemed invalid is not because of its disparate methodology, but rather because of its more populist stance. It seeks to examine social issues of importance to the generality of the people and not, to say, politicians and media managers. It is attacked "because it challenges the status quo and the vested interests and rejects the conventional wisdom of the service research that supports this establishment" (Halloran, 1981: 33). In sum, Halloran (1981: 34) asserts: "It is now suggested that research ... should be shifted away from such questions as 'the right to communicate' to 'more concrete problems.'"

But what are these "concrete problems"? They are the same as, or similar to, the safe, "value-free" micro-questions of the old-time positivists who served the system so well, whether or not they intended or understood this. All this represents a definite and not very well disguised attempt to put the clock back to the days when the function of research was to serve the system as it was—to make it more efficient rather than to question it or suggest alternatives.]

VALIDITY AND EVALUATION IN QUALITATIVE RESEARCH

Given this lack of methodological rigor, on what grounds should one accept the qualitative or critical argument? What makes the research worth recognition? Was the research "successful?" To address these questions, reference is made to the assertions above as to the premises of "value-free science" and "objectivity." If we do not accept these—*if we see the emperor is indeed naked*—then we must accept, and valuate, the conclusions of all inquiry in a different light. Unlike quantitative inquiry, qualitative research does not, as a rule, seek broad generalizability. For the qualitative researcher there is no possibility of a grand theory of social action, as theory is contextually bound. Nor does it strive for reliability in its tools

of analysis. Indeed, its basis of an interpretive, and consequently idiosyncratic, social reality precludes the strict application of such tools.

Whereas the primary concerns of quantitative research are reliability and construct validity, qualitative research seeks external validity, not through "objectivity," but rather through subjectivity. Anderson (1988: 239) writes:

> The closer the analytic effort is to the life-world, the more direct its observation; the more it uses the concepts and language of this life-world, the greater the validity. Therefore, to the degree it reflects the circumstances, inquiry is valid and reliable even though not based on randomization, repeated and controlled observation, measurement, and statistical inference. In other words, it "is more 'objective' precisely because it can bring in more of the subjective intentionality" (White, 1984: 40).

THE ROLE AND PLACE OF THE READER, VIEWER ... RECEIVER

The primary problem of validity in qualitative inquiry, then, is "of matching the researcher's conclusions and the actor's intention" (Rockhill, 1982: 12), and putting those conclusions in a form that makes sense to the reader, to go "from understanding to explanation, and from explanation to understanding" (p. 13). In light of cultural variance, indeed, the disparity of realities, this is no simple task.

Ultimately, for both quantitative and qualitative analysis, *validity ultimately rests on the acceptance or rejection of the argument by the reader him/herself*. Whether the statistical analysis was proper, the data clean, the surveyors well trained, etc., innumerable attacks can be brought against any study if the reader does not care to accept the propriety of the argument. On the other hand, if the reader (or policymaker) finds the conclusions amenable, or the author trustworthy, he or she will rarely give the methods a second glance. It comes down to the skill, the honesty and the ethics of the researcher.

1927
1960
1963
1964
1967
1969
1970
1971
1972
1973
1974
1975
1976
1977
1978
1979
1980
1981
1982
1983
1984
1985
1986
1987
1988
1989
1990
1991
1992
1993
1994
1995
1996
1997
1998
1999
2000
2001
2002
2003
2004
2005
2006

Therefore, in the final analysis, Anderson (1988: 355) writes the value of, and criticism towards, the qualitative study must

> be appropriate to its character as a personal encounter, documented by a careful record, which results in an interpretation of the social action which rises inductively to a coherent explanation of the scene. To criticize this effort for its lack of objectivity, random sampling, statistical measure of validity, deductive logic, and the like is inane. Such criticism simply established the ignorance of the critic. ... As with all research, the success of a qualitative study is dependant on reaching the knowledgeable, skeptical reader with a compelling argument. The sceptical reader will give none of these criteria away, demand an honest effort, and consider the weaknesses as well as the insights in reaching a judgement of value. That judgement of value is the bottom line of research.

3. Participatory Research

If we subscribe to the notion that social research should have a beneficial impact on society, it is imperative that we pay more attention to research philosophies that can profitably handle, and indeed stimulate, social change. Therefore, participatory research, in my opinion, borrows the concept of the interpretive, inter-subjective and human nature of social reality from qualitative research, and the inherency of an ideological stance from critical research, combines them, and goes one step further. Rather than erecting elaborate methodological facades to mask the ideological slant and purpose of inquiry, the question becomes, "Why shouldn't research have a direct, articulated social purpose?" Instead of relying on participant observation or complex techniques to gain the subjective "insider's" perspective, it is asked, "Why shouldn't the 'researched' do their own research?" Why is it: "The poor have always been researched, described and interpreted by the rich and educated, never by themselves?"

In regards to the topic at hand, why is it such a great deal of research has been conducted about participation in a nonparticipatory fashion? As in the case of participatory communication, the major obstacles to participatory research are anti-participatory, often inflexible structures and ideologies. We cannot be reductionistic about holism, static about dynamism, value-free about systematic oppression nor detached about participation. Participatory research may not be good social science in positivist terms, but it may be better than positivist social science for many development purposes.

PRINCIPLES OF PARTICIPATORY COMMUNICATION RESEARCH

That the mass of social research is largely guided by the social context in which it operates and, largely, does not function to serve those studied, has been argued at length. Participatory research was conceived in reaction to this elitist research bias. It is ideological by intent; it is the research of involvement. It is not only research with the people—it is people's research. As such, it largely rejects both the development policies of states and the "objectivity" and "universal validity claims" of many methodologies in the social sciences. Even if we momentarily assume contemporary research practices are free of ideology and do not constitute a means of oppression, the fact remains, they are of little utility to the poor.

> We have moved beyond the whole notion of some of us leading the struggles of others. This shift ... in the control over knowledge, production of knowledge and the tools of production of knowledge is equally legitimate in our continued struggles towards local control and overcoming dependency. It is here that participatory research (PR) can be an important contribution. ... PR is quite the opposite of what social science research has been meant to be. It is partisan, ideologically biased and explicitly non neutral (Tandon, 1985: 21).

It is the realization that most of the present professional approach to research is, in fact, a reproduction of our unjust society in which a few decision makers control the rest of the population that has led many to move away from the classical methods and experiment with alternative approaches. In urging participatory research, we are not speaking of the involvement of groups or classes already aligned with power. These groups already have at their disposal all the mechanisms necessary to shape and inform our explanation of the world.

Therefore, a basic tenet of participatory research is that, whoever does the research, the *results must be shared*. They must be available to the people among whom research is conducted and upon whose lives it is based. Data is not kept under lock and key or behind computer access codes, results are not cloaked in obfuscating jargon and statistical symbols.

Further, and perhaps most importantly, *the inquiry must be of benefit to the community,* and not just a means to an end set by the researcher. This benefit is contrasted to the circuitous theory-research design-data-analysis-policy-government service route, which neutralizes, standardizes, dehumanizes and ultimately functions as a means of social control: "People's voices undergo a metamorphosis into useful data, an instrument of power in the hands of another. Rather than assembling collectively for themselves, political constituencies are assembled by pollsters, collecting fragmentary data into 'public opinion'" (Ewen, 1983: 222).

Again, participatory research challenges the notion that only professional researchers can generate knowledge for meaningful social reform. Like authentic participation, it believes in the knowledge and ability of ordinary people to reflect on their oppressive situation and change it. To the contrary, in many cases, at the local community level, participants have proved to be more capable than "experts" because they know their situation best and have a perspective on problems and needs that no outsider can fully share. This perspective is quite divergent from the abstract concepts, hypothetical scenarios, and macro-level strategies, which occupy the minds and consume the budgets of development "experts" and planners.

DIFFERENCES BETWEEN PARTICIPATORY RESEARCH AND ACTION RESEARCH

Because of this nature of involvement, participatory research is often known under the rubric of social action or action-research (Argyris 1985; Fals Borda 1988, 1991; Kassam 1982; Whyte 1989, 1991). In numerous respects they are similar, and participatory research is not really new. It is a novel concept only to the extent it questions the domains of the research, as well as the economic and political elites.

However, there are fundamental differences between action and participatory research. Chantana and Wun Gaeo (1983: 37) write that action research "can be nonparticipatory and related to top-down development ... whereas participatory research must involve the people throughout the process. Action research can be intended to preserve and strengthen the status quo, whereas participatory research ... is intended to contribute to the enhancement of social power for the hitherto excluded people."

By way of example, in the realm of media production, Varma, et al. (1973: 4) define action research as a "systematic study, incorporated into the production of media, the results of which are fed back directly and immediately to the production staff to help them to improve the effectiveness of their communication."

Conversely, participatory research assumes a bias towards the "subjects" involved in the research process rather than the professional. Participatory research is related to the processes of conscientization and empowerment. It was probably Paulo Freire himself who introduced the first version of this approach in his philosophy of conscientization. Rather than agendas being defined by an academic elite and programs enacted by a bureaucratic elite for the benefit of an

1927
1960
1963
1964
1967
1969
1970
1971
1972
1973
1974
1975
1976
1977
1978
1979
1980
1981
1982
1983
1984
1985
1986
1987
1988
1989
1990
1991
1992
1993
1994
1995
1996
1997
1998
1999
2000
2001
2002
2003
2004
2005
2006

economic or political elite, participatory research involves people gaining an understanding of their situation, confidence and an ability to change that situation. White (1984: 28) writes this is quite divergent from

> the functionalist approach which starts with the scientist's own model of social and psychological behaviour and gathers data for the purpose of prediction and control of audience behaviour. The emphasis is on the awareness of the subjective meaning and organization of reality for purposes of self-determination.

Participatory research is egalitarian. Thematic investigation thus becomes a common striving towards awareness of reality and towards self-awareness. It is an educational process in which the roles of the educator and the educated are constantly reversed and the common search unites all those engaged in the endeavour. It immerses the exogenous "researcher" in the setting on an equal basis. Considering the necessary trust and attitudes as well as cultural differences, the task is not easy and makes unfamiliar demands on researchers/educators.

"INSIDERS" AND "OUTSIDERS"
Interaction fosters a pedagogical environment for all participants. The researcher, as a newcomer, contributes in that he or she requires the membership to give an account of how things are done, which fosters an atmosphere where participants may better know themselves, question themselves, and consciously reflect on the reality of their lives and their sociocultural milieu. Through such interaction, a fresh understanding, new knowledge and self-confidence may be gained. Further, awareness, confidence and cohesiveness are enhanced not only for group members, but also among and between those members and "outsiders" who may participate, thereby increasing their understanding of the context and obstacles under which the people strive. Education goes both ways. This learning process can instill confidence and ultimately empowerment. The intent of participatory research is not latent awareness. Relevant knowledge

increases self-respect and confidence, and leads to exploration of alternatives towards the attainment of goals, and to "action." Through this process, the givenness of the group is revealed, on which one can build up a superior, higher vision.

A DEFINITION OF PARTICIPATORY RESEARCH (PR)
The recent popularity of participatory research, the act of labelling it as such, may have implied that it is something special that requires a particular expertise, a particular strategy or a specific methodology. Similar to participation, there has been great effort towards definitions and models of participatory research to lend an air of "respectability." Also, similar to participation, perhaps this is no more than an attempt to claim title or credit for an approach, which by its very nature, belongs to the people involved. As one is dealing with people within changing social relations and cultural patterns, one cannot afford to be dogmatic about methods but should keep oneself open to people. This openness comes out of a trust in people and a realization that the oppressed are capable of understanding their situation, searching for alternatives and making their own decisions:

> Participatory research is an alternative social research approach in the context of development. It is alternative because, although business, government and the academic also undertake research with development in the end view, little thought and effort go as to how the research project can be used for the benefit of those researched. The central element of Participatory Research is participation. ...It is an active process whereby the expected beneficiaries of research are the main actors in the entire research process, with the researcher playing a facilitator's role (PhilDHRRA [Philippine Partnership for the Development of Human Resources in Rural Areas], 1986: 1).

Because there is no reality "out there" separate from human perception and, as put forth in the multiplicity paradigm, there is no universal path to development, it is maintained each community or grouping must proceed from its own plan in consideration of its own situation. In other words, to the extent the methodology is rigidly structured by the requisites of academia, participatory research is denied.

By its nature, this type of research does not incorporate the rigid controls of the physical scientist or the traditional models of social science researchers. Chantana and Wun Gaeo (1985: 39) state:

There is no magic formula for the methodology of such PR projects. ... However, there are common features taking place in the process:

1. It consists of continuous dialogue and discussion among research participants in all stages;
2. Knowledge must be derived from concrete situations of the people and through collaborative reflection ... return to the people, continuously and dialectically.

Therefore we would like to delineate participatory research as an educational process involving three interrelated parts:

1. Collective definition and investigation of a problem by a group of people struggling to deal with it. This involves the social investigation, which determines the concrete condition existing within the community under study, by those embedded in the social context;
2. Group analysis of the underlying causes of their problems, which is similar to the conscientization and pedagogical processes addressed above, and;
3. Group action to attempt to solve the problem.

THE PROCESS OF PARTICIPATORY RESEARCH

Therefore, the process of participatory research is cyclical, continuous, local and accessible. Study-reflection-action is the integrating process in this type of research. Kronenburg (1986: 255) gives the following characteristics of participatory research:

[It] rests on the assumption that human beings have an innate ability to create knowledge. It rejects the notion that knowledge production is a monopoly of 'professionals.' [It] is seen as an educational process for the participants ... as well as the researcher. It involves the identification of community needs, augmented awareness about obstacles to need fulfilment, an analysis of the causes of the problems and the formulation and implementation of relevant solutions. The researcher is consciously committed to the cause of the community involved in the research. This challenges the traditional principle of scientific neutrality and rejects the position of the scientist as a social engineer. Dialogue provides for a framework which guards against manipulative scientific interference and serves as a means of control by the community.

EVALUATION AND VALIDITY IN PARTICIPATORY RESEARCH

Given a continuous cycle of study-reflection-action, participatory research inherently involves formative evaluation. Indeed, the terms participatory research and participatory evaluation are often used synonymously.

Congruent with the objectives of participatory research, the purpose of evaluation is to benefit the participants themselves. It does not function to test the efficiency of an exogenous program, formulate diffusion tactics or marketing strategies for expansion to a broader level, gather hard data for publication, justify the implementing body, or collect dust on a ministry shelf. In brief, it is an ongoing process as opposed to an end product of a report for funding structures. Whether participatory research "succeeds" or "fails" is secondary to the interaction and communication processes of participating groups. The success of the research is seen no more in publications in "reputed" journals but in what happens during the process of research. Bogaert et al. (1981: 181) add that "participatory evaluation generates a lot of qualitative data which is rich in experiences of the participants. It may be ... quantitative data is sacrificed in the process. However, what is lost in statistics is more than made up by the enhanced richness of data."

1927
1960
1963
1964
1967
1969
1970
1971
1972
1973
1974
1975
1976
1977
1978
1979
1980
1981
1982
1983
1984
1985
1986
1987
1988
1989
1990
1991
1992
1993
1994
1995
1996
1997
1998
1999
2000
2001
2002
2003
2004
2005
2006

The Integration of Different Methodologies

The implication is not that quantitative or qualitative methods or exogenous collaboration in participatory evaluation are forbidden. Writing of research participants, D'Abreo (1981: 108) states:

> While they, as agents of their own programme, can understand it better and be more involved in it, the outside evaluator may bring greater objectivity and insights from other programmes that might be of great use to them. However, the main agents of evaluation, even when conducted with the help of an outside agency or individual, are they themselves.

Turning to the question of validity, Tandon (1981: 22) suggests, on a methodological level, "getting into a debate about the reliability and validity of PR is irrelevant because it is quite the opposite shift in understanding what this research is." Its focus is on authenticity as opposed to validity. However, referring to generalizability and validity addressed in relation to qualitative research, it can be argued that validity in its less esoteric sense is participatory research's hallmark. "If ordinary people define the problem of research themselves, they will ensure its relevance" (Tandon, 1981: 24), and their involvement "will provide the 'demand-pull' necessary to ensure accuracy of focus" (Farrington, 1988: 271).

Finally, the basis of participatory research, "indigenous knowledge," is inherently valid. This is not to say conditions are not changing or that this knowledge cannot benefit from adaptation. The argument is that, in most cases, this knowledge is the most valid place from which to begin.

A Word of Caution

Participatory research can all too easily be utilized as yet another tool of manipulation by vested interests. Charges are correctly made that it is often a means of political indoctrination by the right and the left alike. Often organizers have been attacked for manipulating people's minds and managing their actions towards their own ends.

While the approach strives towards empowerment, challenges existing structures and is consequently ideological, rigidly prescribed ideologies must be avoided. In addition, knowledge and perspective gained may well empower exploitative economic and authoritarian interests instead of local groups. Far from helping the process of liberation, if the researcher is not careful, he or she may only enable the traditional policymakers and vested interests to present their goods in a more attractive package without changing their substance.

Even the best-intentioned researcher/activist can inadvertently enhance dependency rather than empowerment. If he or she enters communities with ready-made tools for analyzing reality, and solving problems, the result will likely be that as far as those tools are successful, dependency will simply be moved from one tyrant to another.

In other words, overzealous researchers can easily attempt to compensate for an initial apathy by assuming the role of an advocate rather than a facilitator. "What looks like progress is all too often a return to the dependent client relationship" (Kennedy, 1984: 86). This approach is no better than more traditional researchers with hypotheses and constructs to validate, or the diffusionist with an innovation for every ill.

Synthesis

1. Most contemporary research is based on positivistic assumptions that we can objectively know the social world "out there." It is argued here that objectivity is nothing more than inter-subjectivity, principles and parameters people agree to agree upon. The danger occurs when one group assumes its constructs and methods are universally valid.

2. Qualitative and quantitative research are largely polar in orientation. The qualitative approach accepts, indeed advocates, subjectivity as a valid avenue of understanding. The emphasis is on how people perceive, understand and construct reality rather than how they mechanically react to manipulative stimuli.

3. As such, qualitative research is a human approach to the understanding of a human world. The researcher strives to see the naturalistic environment of those he or she is studying from his or her perspective. This forbids rigid, preformulated constructs and hypotheses.

4. What makes the qualitative study of value is not its construct validity or reliability, but its external validity. This validity arises from its foundations in human perception rather than rigorous methodology. In the final analysis, the relevance of any research rests on the reader's quite subjective acceptance or rejection of the argument advanced.

5. Combining aspects of qualitative and critical research, participatory research asks why the researched shouldn't do his or her own research. A further question is why is the mass of research on participation done in a nonparticipatory manner?

6. Like all research, participatory research is ideological. It is biased in the sense it holds research should be guided by, available to and of direct benefit to the "researched," rather than privileged information for a manipulative elite. It further believes research is not, nor should it be, the domain of a powerful few with the "proper" tools.

7. Participatory research is similar, but not equal, to social action research. It is research of involvement, not of detachment. It includes all parties in a process of mutual and increasing awareness and confidence. It is research of conscientization and of empowerment.

8. As has been argued for participation, and as in qualitative approaches, there can be no strict methodology for participatory research. However, it must actively and authentically involve participants throughout the process and the general flow is from study to reflection to action.

9. Evaluation is inherent in participatory research. However, it is formative rather than summative evaluation. Its purpose is not for journals, ego-boosting or to solicit further funding, but rather to monitor and reflect on the process as it unfolds.

Furthermore, people's involvement in the research assures validity of the inquiry and their own validity.

References

Addo, H. "Beyond Eurocentricity: Transformation and Transformational Responsibility," H. Addo, S. Amin, G. Asesiniero, et al., eds., *Development as Social Transformation: Reflections on the Global Problematique*. London: Hodder and Stoughton, 1985.

Anderson, J., and T. Meyer. *Mediated Communication: A Social Action Perspective*. Newbury Park, Calif.: Sage, 1988.

Argyris, C., R. Putnam, and D. Smith. *Action Science*. San Francisco: Jossey Bass, 1985.

Bogaert, M.V.D., S. Bhagat, and N. B. Bam. "Participatory Evaluation of an Adult Education Programme," in *Participatory Research in Devaluation: Experiments in Research as a Process of Liberation*. New Delhi: Indian Social Institute, 1981.

Bryman, A. "The Debate About Quantitative and Qualitative Research: A Question of Method or Epistemology," The British Journal of Sociology, 1984.

Burke, K. *Language as Symbolic Action*. Berkeley, Calif.: University of California Press, 1968.

Chamarik, S. *Democracy and Development: A Cultural Perspective*. Bangkok: Local Development Institute, 1993.

Chantana, P., and S. Wun Gaeo. *Participatory Research and Rural Development in Thailand*. Manila, Philippines: Farmer's Assistance Board, 1985.

Christians, C., and J. Carey. "The Logic and Aims of Qualitative Research," in *Research Methods in Mass Communication*. Englewood Cliffs, N.J.: Prentice Hall, 1981.

D'Abreo, D. "Training for Participatory Evaluation," in *Participatory Research and Evaluation: Experiments in Research as a Process of Liberation*. New Delhi: Indian Social Institute, 1981.

Dervin, B. "Citizen Access as an Information Equity Issue," J. R. Schement, F. Gutierrez, and M. Sirbu, eds., *Progress in Communication Sciences*. Norwood, Mass.: Ablex, 1982.

Diaz Bordenave, J., 1974

Diaz Bordenave, J. *Communication and Rural Development*. Paris: UNESCO, 1977.

Ewen, S. "The Implications of Empiricism." *Journal of Communication*, 1983, 33.

Fals Borda, O. *Knowledge and People's Power: Lessons With Peasants in Nicaragua, Mexico and Colombia*. New Delhi: Indian Social Institute, 1988.

Farrington, J. "Farmer Participatory Research: Editorial Introduction," *Experimental Agriculture*, 1988, 24.

Friberg, M., and B. Hettne. *The Greening of the World: Development as Social Transformation*. Boulder, Colo.: Westview, 1985.

Fuglesang, A. "The Myth of People's Ignorance," *Development Dialogue*, Uppsala, 1984, 1 (2).

Geertz, C. *The Interpretation of Cultures*. New York: Basic Books, 1973.

Halloran, J. D. "The Context of Mass Communication Research," in E. McAnany, J. Schnitman, and N. Janus, eds., *Communication and Social Structure: Critical Studies in Mass Media Research*. New York: Praeger, 1981.

Harris, M. *Cultural Materialism: The Struggle for a Science of Culture*. New York: Vintage, 1980.

1927
1960
1963
1964
1967
1969
1970
1971
1972
1973
1974
1975
1976
1977
1978
1979
1980
1981
1982
1983
1984
1985
1986
1987
1988
1989
1990
1991
1992
1993
1994
1995
1996
1997
1998
1999
2000
2001
2002
2003
2004
2005
2006

Jacobson, T. "A Pragmatist Account of Participatory Communication Research for National Development," *Communication Theory*, 1993, 3 (3): 214-230.

Jayaweera, N. *The Political Economy of the Communication Revolution and the Third World*. AMIC, Singapore: AMIC, 1986.

Kassam, Y., and K. Mustafa, eds. *Participatory Research: An Emerging Alternative Methodology in Social Science Research.* New Delhi: Society for Participatory in Asia, 1982.

Kennedy, T. W. "Beyond Advocacy: An Animative Approach to Public Participation," Dissertation, Cornell University, 1984,

Kronenburg, J. *Empowerment of the Poor: A Comparative Analysis of Two Development Endeavours in Kenya.* Nijmegen, Netherlands: Third World Center, 1986.

Kuhn, T. *The Structure of Scientific Revolution.* Chicago: University of Chicago Press, 1962.

Long, N., and A. Long, eds. "Battlefields of Knowledge," *The Interlocking of Theory and Practice in Social Research and Development.* London: Routledge, 1992.

Moustakas, C. E. *Individuality and Encounter.* Cambridge, Mass.: Howard A. Doyle Publishing, 1974.

Participatory Research Guide Book. Laguna: Philippine Partnership for the Development of Human Resources in Rural Areas, 1986.

Rockhill, K. "Researching Participation in Adult Education: The Potential of the Qualitative Perspective," *Adult Education*, Fall 1982, 33 (1).

Simbulan, R., ed. *Participatory Research: A Response to Asian People's Struggle for Social Transformation.* Manila, Philippines: Farmers Assistance Board, 1985.

Tandon, R. "Participatory Research: Issues and Prospects," in *Farmers Assistance Board Response to Asian People's Struggle for Social Transformation.* Manila Philippines: Farmers Assistance Board, 1985.

Thayer, L. "On 'Doing' Research and 'Explaining' Things," G. Gerbner, ed., *Ferment in the Field.* Journal of Communication, 1983, 33 (4).

Varma, R., J. Ghosal, and R. Hulls. "Action Research and the Production of Communication Media," paper, Al]l sep, Udaipur, India: India Field Workshop, 1973.

White, R. "Contradiction in Contemporary Policies for Democratic Communication," paper, Paris: IAMCR Conference, September 1982.

White, R. "The Need for Strategies of Research on the Democratization of Communication," paper, San Francisco: ICA Conference, May, 1984.

Whyte, W. F., ed. *Learning From the Field: A Guide From Experience.* Beverly Hills, Calif.: Sage, 1989.

Whyte, W. F., ed. *Participatory Action Research.* Newbury Park, Calif.: Sage, 1991.

Jan Servaes. *Communication for Development: One World, Multiple Cultures.* Cresskill, N.J.: Hampton Press, 2001, Chapter 3. Copyright © 2001 Hampton Press. Reprinted with permission of copyright holder.

EXCERPT FROM:

PUBLIC HEALTH COMMUNICATION INTERVENTIONS: VALUES AND ETHICAL DILEMMAS

By Nurit Guttman

2000

1. The Persuasion Dilemma

The persuasion dilemma incorporates two concerns that represent the flip side of each other. The first raises concerns regarding the persuasive capacities that may infringe on people's autonomy. The second is with whether the intervention fulfills the ethical imperative of doing the utmost to promote the good of its intended audience by applying the most persuasive tactics to help people adopt health-promoting messages.

To what extent is it justified to use persuasive strategies to reach the intended health-promoting effects of the intervention?

The dilemma regarding the ethics of the manipulative potential of persuasion is often shared, though less often acknowledged, by many if not all public-communication interventions (Witte 1994). Because public-health intervention goals typically aim to influence target populations' beliefs or behaviors, persuasive and social-marketing strategies are often employed. The ultimate goal of these intervention strategies, as Witte points out, is to get people to practice what the interventionists believe are health-promoting behaviors. Efforts to do good and convince the public of the benefits of adopting particular behaviors, or of avoiding others, thus often include persuasive strategies to arouse anxieties or fears and facilitate persuasion. Witte maintains that public-health communication researchers and practitioners are adept at using persuasive strategies e.g., how much and what type of information to use about a certain topic, how to order it, to manipulate people's perceptions. This raises concerns regarding the use of manipulative or persuasive tactics, which by definition infringe on individuals' rights of autonomy or self-determination. Similarly, it raises concerns regarding paternalism or the belief that certain experts or professionals know what is best for particular members of society or the public as a whole. Whereas these concerns traditionally are raised in the practitioner-patient context e.g., Bok 1978; Childress 1982; Veatch 1980, they are also highly relevant in the public-health communication-intervention context because such interventions are purposeful efforts to get people to adopt health-related practices perceived as beneficial to them, or as helping them avoid potential harm (Beauchamp 1988; Campbell 1990; Faden 1987; Pinet 1987; Doxiadis 1987). According to the principle of respect for autonomy, health promoters should honor the self-respect and dignity of each individual as an autonomous, free actor.

The use of persuasive appeals also raises concerns regarding the extent to which such appeals distort or manipulate information (as elaborated by Forester 1993), or the extent to which such manipulative strategies can undermine the development of connectedness, responsiveness and a sense of genuine care, which are important components in an ethic of care (Baier 1993). Similarly, the use of persuasion raises concerns regarding legitimacy and control: Persuasive messages that aim to affect attitude change and the adoption of the recommended behaviors succeed essentially by controlling people's perceptions and thus limiting their choices from a wider range of options (Faden and Faden 1982). As Salmon (1989) reminds us, "At the center of this conflict is the fundamental tension between social control and individual freedoms."

Social-marketing efforts, by definition, employ mechanisms of social control. Inherent in the design and implementation of public-health communication interventions, therefore, is a tension between competing values of autonomy and of doing good.

To what extent should health promoters model their persuasive messages on advertising or marketing techniques—even when these tactics are viewed as the most promising venues for affecting attitudes and behaviors? Highly persuasive messages that use emotionally charged fear-raising and guilt-raising appeals can be justified by communicators on the basis of utility, especially if they draw on research that used target audience members' perceptions. When audience members are asked what types of messages would work for them, or would help modify people's behavior and get them to adopt the recommended activity, respondents often suggest that interventionists should use scare tactics or fear appeals. But does this mean that these messages are the optimal and ethical ones? The use of persuasive strategies in the context of advertising has been criticized as being potentially unethical because they may use manipulative, misleading or deceptive messages—concerns compounded because advertising campaigns tend to target populations particularly vulnerable to their messages.

This critique can be applied to public-communication campaigns as well (Pollay 1989). The American Cancer Society, according to critics, used inflated statistics in its efforts to persuade women to engage in preventive cancer-detection behaviors. The persuasive messages they used may have unduly terrified some women, argue the critics. The American Cancer Society justified its use of these statistics by saying they believed they could serve as effective means to get women to adopt preventive measures and seek early detection (Blakeslee 1991). In contrast, Salmon and Kroger (1992) report that practitioners in the U.S. National AIDS Information and Education Programs, a government-sponsored health agency, decided to give prominence to the principle of what they considered "do no harm" and to avoid messages that could potentially frighten target populations. A different approach was revealed in a surprising announcement made by an advisory panel to the National Cancer Institute. This panel recommended that the institute

1927
1960
1963
1964
1967
1969
1970
1971
1972
1973
1974
1975
1976
1977
1978
1979
1980
1981
1982
1983
1984
1985
1986
1987
1988
1989
1990
1991
1992
1993
1994
1995
1996
1997
1998
1999
2000
2001
2002
2003
2004
2005
2006

should only provide scientific data and should not engage in persuasive appeals to get women to get mammograms at a particular age. Instead, it suggested the institute should let the public draw its own conclusions (Kolata 1993).

This approach raises ethical concerns as well: To what extent are health promoters obligated to use persuasive strategies if they believe these strategies to be the most effective method to achieve the goals of the campaign and to fulfill their mandate of maximizing the health of the target population? This concern relates to the second persuasion dilemma: The extent to which the intervention employs the most effective tactics to deliver messages that will help people or organizations adopt the recommendation of the intervention addresses several key concerns. The first is, to what extent do the interventionists have the knowledge, expertise and resources to develop appropriate messages; and second, what are the best strategies to develop such messages: Do the interventionists have the resources to develop messages and strategies that can indeed be effective? Should the interventionists employ current marketing techniques and work mainly with professionals, or adopt approaches in which intended audience members act as equal partners in message development?

2. The Coercion Dilemma

Is it justified to promote restrictive regulations or policies regarding individuals' behavior to achieve the health goals of the campaign?

The use of coercion poses the same types of concerns raised regarding persuasion:

Questions about the morality of coercion, manipulation, deception, persuasion and other methods of inducing change typically involve a conflict between the values of individual freedom and self-determination, on one hand, and such values as social welfare, economic progress or equal opportunity on the other hand (Warwick and Kelman 1973: 380).

One of the arguments in support of strategies that restrict or regulate people's or organizations' activities or control their environment is that they are relatively effective in promoting the desired health-related outcome. As McKinlay (1975: 13) states, "One stroke of effective health legislation is equal to many separate health-intervention endeavors and the cumulative efforts of innumerable health workers over long periods of time." For example, legislation for smoke-free environments is viewed as a strategy that can have a larger impact on the smoking behavior of large numbers of people than educational programs (Glantz 1996). Similarly, engineering-type solutions can also be seen as relatively effective (Schwartz, Goodman and Steckler 1995). Redesigning roadways and improving the safety engineering of cars have been shown to reduce significantly automobile accidents and fatalities, independent of the actions of the drivers. Similarly, changing lunch menus of schools or work organizations has been shown to affect the food consumption of the students or workers in these organizations (Ellison et al. 1989; Glanz and Mullis 1988). On a more macro level, regulation of the food industry and restriction on food production could increase the likelihood that consumers would buy foods relatively low in saturated fats and free of contaminants, making their food consumption healthier. This type of reasoning can be seen as applying the principle of utility, or the obligation to maximize the greatest utility from the health-promotion efforts to the greatest number of people (Hiller 1987). However, it raises concerns regarding the ethical principle of individual autonomy or the right that people have not to be restricted in their personal choices. Notwithstanding concerns for autonomy, in addition to its potential utility, an important justification for the use of restrictive strategies is based on the assumption that individuals' choices are in fact not autonomous but influenced by powerful social and market circumstances. People in our society, explain proponents of regulative strategies, are surrounded by persuasive anti-health messages and anti-health environments, and therefore, they do not freely choose unhealthy behaviors. This justifies the use of pro-health persuasive or coercive strategies, or of policies to restrict the freedom of groups, including marketers of certain products (Pinet 1987). One example of this approach is efforts to restrict the placement of cigarette-vending machines, a strategy shown as effective in curtailing cigarette sales, especially among children and adolescents (Feighery et al. 1991). Another example of policies to promote health through restrictions on public access to a product is the Japanese government's ban of birth-control pills, which was adopted in part to promote the use of condoms and justified partially by being perceived as a way to curb the spread of HIV infection (Jitsukawa and Djerassi 1994, Weisman 1992).

Coercive approaches are fraught with ethical concerns, including the infringement of individuals' free choice and free-marketplace enterprise, which are particularly prominent values in Western society. Market autonomy, according to its proponents, is the optimal method for the distribution of goods and for balancing economic contribution and economic rewards. Restricting it would impose restrictions on choices to individuals and thus impinge on individual autonomy as well (Garret et al. 1989). But the marketplace, maintain critics, does not provide free choices for individuals or communities because other socio-economic factors influence the distribution of goods, services and wealth (Beauchamp 1987; Bellah et al. 1985, 1991). Dan Beauchamp (1987) argues that, relative to other intervention approaches, enforcement strategies enhance the public good on the societal level while minimally intruding on individuals because they mainly place controls on the marketplace. Instead of placing restrictions on personal liberty, he explains, by controlling potential hazards through a collective action and sharing the burdens of protection, intervention policies can foster a sense of community responsibility for the welfare of its members. Even if we adopt this perspective, we are still left with questions regarding the extent to which individuals should be restricted from engaging in practices perceived as risky from a health-promotion perspective but nevertheless desired by some. What are the boundaries? When should society intervene? Does society have an obligation to intervene when the individual's well-being is threatened by his or her own action (Pinet 1987; Wikler 1987), or should it intervene only when a person presents a danger to others, as in the case of communicable diseases?

Regulative strategies may also be applied to the channels that disseminate intervention messages. Because broadcast media, although they may be considered a public good, are licensed to commercial or not-for-profit organizations, does this imply that interventions should be able to use these media as dissemination channels? Or more specifically, should commercial media be regulated to support messages of health interventions (Packer and Kauffman 1990), or should the interventions pay for the broadcasting of their ads through the use of excise taxes?

1927
1960
1963
1964
1967
1969
1970
1971
1972
1973
1974
1975
1976
1977
1978
1979
1980
1981
1982
1983
1984
1985
1986
1987
1988
1989
1990
1991
1992
1993
1994
1995
1996
1997
1998
1999
2000
2001
2002
2003
2004
2005
2006

POWER OF MOVEMENT

By Warren Feek

Imagine an international development funding scenario in which the following were obligatory:

1. For every dollar spent on the development of a new vaccine or drug, an equivalent dollar has to be spent in support of networking by and for a movement of people who are directly affected by the health issue that is the focus of that drug. When the [Bill and Melinda] Gates Foundation announces $130 million for malaria vaccine development, they also need to announce and provide $130 million for a network and movement of families and communities affected by malaria.

2. For every dollar spent by an international organisation on their own public and media relations (including policy advocacy), they have to contribute the same level of resources (no strings attached) in support of a high-profile voice for the people directly affected by the issues that are the focus for that organisation's work. The UNICEF [United Nations Children's Fund] budget for media relations needs to be matched by a financial contribution (no strings) to a movement of children and parents in developing countries so that their voices (which may be disparate and inconsistent) on the key issues that affect them can be heard louder and clearer.

3. No international development decision-making forum is considered legitimate unless a majority of the people making the decision are themselves directly affected by the issue in question. The majority community at every HIV/AIDS forum—from UNAIDS (the Joint United Nations Programme on HIV/AIDS) and U.N. special sessions to national coordinating mechanisms and local HIV/AIDS groups—needs to be people living with, and/or affected by, HIV/AIDS.

The chance of these proposals being adopted is of course much less than the possibility that I will become U.N. Secretary General. But posing them as proposals that touch the sharp edges of international development— technical development, funding, decision making and organisational advocacy—highlight how far international development has moved from the core elements for long-term effective change. As I argued in the most recent strategy ConunDRUMs the current, predominant model for international development based on SI = T × I × F (where SI = Sustainable Impact; T = Technical Assistance; I = a specific intervention; and F = Funding) is at best struggling and at worst has failed. But there is another model—hinted at by the proposals above.

We need to derive a change model that emanates from some of the most successful nonviolent change processes in world history. An equation drawn from those experiences might look as follows:

Degree of SI = level L × scale V × focus A, where SI is Sustainable Impact.

Level L is the level of Leadership by people most affected by a development issue in confronting that issue

Scale V is the strength of their Voices within the public debate and relevant decision-making fora

Focus A is the local resonance of priority development Agendas in any given context.

In other words, the degree of sustainable long-term impact on any development issue is directly proportionate to the level of leadership by people immediately affected by that issue multiplied by the scale of public debate and private dialogue on that issue multiplied by the extent to which the issue in question is a "local" action priority in any given context. If there is a high score on these three factors then there is a high likelihood of long-term sustainable impact. If there is a low score on these three factors then, there is a low likelihood of long-term sustainable impact.

This is very different from the predominant theory that appears to drive most development action by major international development agencies and governments as described above. So, where does degree of SI = level L × scale V × focus A come from, how is it justified and what are the implications for overall investment in development actions and specific communication interventions?

There has been no sustainable, effective social movement in which the principles of leadership from within the peoples most affected; a strong and independent voice in public debate, private dialogue and decision-making fora by people most affected; and, the people most immediately involved defining and agreeing on the development agenda, have not been core, central components of the action. I would encourage you to think of your own local and national situations. Alternatively, please reflect on these social movements: the women's movement, anti-apartheid movement, civil rights movement, anti-globalisation movement, anti-racism movement, anti-genetically modified crops movement, anti-female genital mutilation movement, Jubilee 2000 movement to reduce/eliminate the debt of developing countries, environmental movement, nonviolent independence movements in many countries and territories, gay-rights movement, the land-rights movements of many so-called ethnic minorities, peace movements and many other social movements—North and the South and crossing and joining that divide.

Successful movements have internal leadership, a powerful voice for the perspectives of those most affected in the public debate and a strong role in agenda setting and decision making as central, intrinsic components of what makes them successful ... and makes their results sustainable.

This is not to suggest that we do not develop new vaccines and other scientific solutions to some very serious development issues. Of course we should. They are vitally important. But those "solutions" will only work if they are in combination with the social movement processes.

These social movements focused change principles tend to be, "pooh-poohed" by many in international development, particularly by senior decision makers. They are often searching for the simple, hopefully low-cost, globally applicable, easy to administer, high-proven efficacy answer. Talk of people and change and movements and norms and communities and dialogue and debate and participation and other similar concepts is regarded as wishy—washy and loose and ill-formed and unable to be assessed. I challenge them to stand in front of the leaders

of the social movements that have made such significant changes in all our lives and say that to their faces: "Hey, Martin (Luther King), Te Kooti, Mahatma, Germaine ... (here fill in the leader of your own favorite social movement) ... it will never work."

The next response for why the principles of social movement are not priorities to fund and support in international development is that international development issues are technical problems requiring technical solutions. Nowhere is this perspective stronger than in health. To which I say: HIV/AIDS, northern India, northern Nigeria and tobacco. [None are just technical problems with purely technical solutions.]

HIV/AIDS is well documented. The countries/communities with the highest levels of internal leadership, public debate, private dialogue, spontaneous local action and local challenging of existing social practices and prejudices have done best—gay communities, Uganda, Thailand, etc. L, V and A (see above) are present in large quantities. Without the Treatment Action Campaign there would be no progress on substantially reduced costs for treatments. And without the People Living with AIDS network and movement there would be much less vaccine development (many pharmaceuticals having got out a long time ago). L, V and A by the bucketload.

For a negative perspective that makes the same point, take a look at what is happening to child health in northern India and northern Nigeria. We have many of the technical answers in child health. There are high efficacy, simple, low-cost, provable interventions, the most admired of which is immunisation. Case closed? Umm—no! Immunisation rates in many parts of the world are going down. In northern India and northern Nigeria, they are plummeting, with predictions of disastrous consequences for child health. Why? Because the scientific answer has come up against a movement of people. Outsiders can call these people misguided, wrong, ill-informed and any other description. But local people taking local leadership (L), voicing their perspectives (V), framing debate and dialogue on their terms and developing their own agendas (A) have inflicted severe damage on immunisation rates. We only have ourselves to blame. By ignoring those same

1927
1960
1963
1964
1967
1969
1970
1971
1972
1973
1974
1975
1976
1977
1978
1979
1980
1981
1982
1983
1984
1985
1986
1987
1988
1989
1990
1991
1992
1993
1994
1995
1996
1997
1998
1999
2000
2001
2002
2003
2004
2005
2006

principles when developing and implementing child-health programmes, we have laid a very weak foundation. [It's] a base slab that is very easily turned on its side when a group of people say, hold on. "I think those immunisations are also sterilising our girls or causing other illnesses." Such feelings, given the social and political climate, resonate and spread no matter how untrue the allegations may be. So, by all means, develop AIDS and malaria vaccines but do not expect them to work all by themselves.

In many countries, there have been very significant gains in nonsmoking rates. They were not due to quit-smoking campaigns or the patch. In most cases the changes involved a very loose coalition of organizations, large and small, working from sometimes different motivations but always with the same goal. In a coordinating group for anti-tobacco action you could find: young people angry at the ways tobacco companies market to them, cancer patients, the fire service, people concerned about second-hand smoking risks and others. It is this loose grouping, working as a movement rather than as one programmed course of action, that has moved the anti-tobacco agenda.

This perspective has important implications for those of us with communication responsibilities. Within a strategic paradigm that has technical assistance, a specific intervention and funding as its core principles, communication is reduced to a support role. Communicators are asked to help "sell" the intervention (immunisations are good—line up on Wednesday), promote the technical support (these people can help us to ...) and raise the funds (we are a great organization). These roles are important but they do not play to the real strengths we communicators can bring to more effective international development practice. Imagine (or observe where it is happening) the communication role with a social movement paradigm guiding the strategic thinking. Communication is of central importance for local leadership (L), crucial to getting the voices of those most affected into public debate and decision-making fora and (V) and indispensable for creating and shaping locally driven agendas. (A) Real, meaningful communication could take place.

This is a necessarily short analysis and explanation. The subtle textures of international development require a deeper and more nuanced approach. From my perspective, it would be great if we could move from $SI = T \times I \times F$ to Degree of $SI = $ level $L \times$ scale $V \times$ focus A. ...

CONTEMPORARY READINGS
VOLUME ❷
Information Society & Communication Rights

INFORMATION TECHNOLOGY, GLOBALISATION AND SOCIAL DEVELOPMENT

By Manuel Castells

1998 There is a raging debate in the world on the mixed record of the information technology revolution, and of globalisation, especially when we consider their social dimensions on a planetary scale. As is always the case with a fundamental debate, it is most often framed ideologically and cast in simplistic terms. For the prophets of technology, for the true believers in the magic of the market, everything will be just fine, as long as ingenuity and competition are set free. All we need are a few regulatory fixes, to prevent corruption and to remove bureaucratic impediments in the path of our flight to hypermodernity. For those around the world who are not ecstatic about surfing on the Internet, but who are affected by layoffs, lack of basic social services, crime, poverty and disruption of their lives, globalisation is nothing more than a warmed-up version of traditional capitalist ideology. In their view, information technology is a tool for renewed exploitation, destruction of jobs, environmental degradation and the invasion of privacy.

Of course, the real issues are not in between, but elsewhere. Social development today is determined by the ability to establish a synergistic interaction between technological innovation and human values, leading to a new set of organisations and institutions that create positive feedback loops between productivity, flexibility, solidarity, safety, participation and accountability, in a new model of development that could be socially and environmentally sustainable.

It is easy to agree on these goals, but difficult to develop the policies and strategies that could lead to them. Some of the disagreement comes, certainly, from conflicting interests, values and priorities. But a considerable source of current disarray in social and economic policies stems from the lack of a common understanding of the processes of transformation under way, of their origins and their implications. This paper aims to clarify the meaning of this transformation, particularly by focusing on the processes that are usually considered to be its triggers: the information technology revolution and the process of globalisation. As we shall see, in fact, these two processes interact with others, in a very complex set of actions and reactions. …

Information Technology, Globalisation and Social Development

In proceeding along the lines of this argument, I have in mind a variety of data, from reliable sources, that make somewhat plausible the analysis presented here. However, since I have just published a book that brings together many of these data, I take the liberty of referring the reader to it, in order to concentrate here on the schematic presentation (and expanded elaboration) of my argument without repeating the presentation of data sources (see Castells 1996, 1997, and 1998; as well as the synthesis of data on world poverty presented in UNDP 1997).

The New Socio-economic System: Information Technology, Networking, Globalisation

In the last quarter of this century, a new form of socio-economic organisation has emerged. After the collapse of statism, in the Soviet Union and throughout the world, it is certainly a capitalist system. Indeed, for the first time in history the entire planet is capitalist, since even the few remaining command economies are surviving or developing through their linkages to global, capitalist markets. Yet this is a brand of capitalism that is at the same time very old and fundamentally new. It is old because it appeals to relentless competition in the pursuit of profit, and individual satisfaction (deferred or immediate) as its driving engine. But it is fundamentally new because it is tooled by new information and communication technologies that are at the roots of new productivity sources, of new organisational forms, and of the formation of a global economy. ...

Information and Communication Technology as a Strategic Tool

Information technology is not the cause of the changes we are living through. But without new information and communication technologies none of what is changing our lives would be possible. In the 1990s the entire planet is organised around telecommunicated networks of computers at the heart of information systems and communication processes. The entire realm of human activity depends on the power of information, in a sequence of technological innovation that accelerates its pace by month. Genetic engineering, benefiting from this wealth of information processing capacity, is progressing by leaps and bounds, and is enabling us, for the first time, to unveil the secrets of living matter and to manipulate life, with extraordinary potential consequences. Software development is making possible user-friendly computing, so that millions of children, when provided with adequate education, can progress in their knowledge, and in their ability to create wealth and enjoy it wisely, much faster than any previous generation. The Internet, today used by about 100 million people, and doubling this number every year, is a channel of universal communication where interests and values of all sorts coexist, in a creative cacophony. Certainly, the diffusion of information and communication technology is extremely uneven. Most of Africa is being left in a technological apartheid, and the same could be said of many other regions of the world. The situation is difficult to remedy when one third of the world's population still has to survive on the equivalent of one dollar per day.

Technology per se does not solve social problems. But the availability and use of information and communication technologies are a prerequisite for economic and social development in our world. They are the functional equivalent of electricity in the industrial

era. Econometric studies show the close statistical relationship between diffusion of information technology, productivity and competitiveness for countries, regions, industries and firms (Dosi, et al. 1988). They also show that an adequate level of education, in general, and of technical education in particular, is essential for the design and productive use of new technologies (Foray and Freeman 1992). But neither the sheer number of scientists and engineers nor the acquisition of advanced technology can be a factor of development by itself (neither was enough for the Soviet Union—see Castells and Kiselyova 1995), without an appropriate organisational environment.

The crucial role of information and communication technologies in stimulating development is a two-edged sword. On the one hand, it allows countries to leapfrog stages of economic growth by being able to modernise their production systems and increase their competitiveness faster than in the past. The most critical example is that of the Asian Pacific economies, and particularly the cases of Hong Kong, Taiwan, Singapore, Malaysia and South Korea. This is so despite the current financial crisis, which is unrelated to competitive performance and may be related, in fact, to the attractiveness of booming Asian economies to global capital flows. On the other hand, for those economies that are unable to adapt to the new technological system, their retardation becomes cumulative. Furthermore, the ability to move into the information age depends on the capacity of the whole society to be educated, and to be able to assimilate and process complex information. This starts with the education system, from the bottom up, from the primary school to the university. And it relates, as well, to the overall process of cultural development, including the level of functional literacy, the content of the media, and the diffusion of information within the population as a whole.

In this regard, what is happening is that regions and firms that concentrate the most advanced production and management systems are increasingly attracting

1927
1960
1963
1964
1967
1969
1970
1971
1972
1973
1974
1975
1976
1977
1978
1979
1980
1981
1982
1983
1984
1985
1986
1987
1988
1989
1990
1991
1992
1993
1994
1995
1996
1997
1998
1999
2000
2001
2002
2003
2004
2005
2006

talent from around the world, while leaving aside a significant fraction of their own population whose educational level and cultural/technical skills do not fit the requirements of the new production system. A case in point is Silicon Valley, the most advanced information technology–producing region in the world, which can only maintain the pace of innovation by recruiting every year thousands of engineers and scientists from India, China, Taiwan, Singapore, Korea, Israel, Russia and Western Europe, to jobs that cannot be filled by Americans because they do not have proper skills (Benner in progress). Similarly, in Bangalore, Mumbai, Seoul or Campinas, engineers and scientists concentrate in high-technology hubs, connected to the "Silicon Valleys" of the world, while a large share of the population in all countries remains in low-end, low-skill jobs, when they are lucky enough to be employed at all (Carnoy 1999). Thus there is little chance for a country, or region, to develop in the new economy without its incorporation into the technological system of the information age. Although this does not necessarily imply the need to produce information technology hardware locally, it does imply the ability to use advanced information and communication technologies, which in turn requires an entire reorganisation of society (Castells and Tyson 1988, 1989).

A similar process affects the life chances of individuals. Not everybody should be a computer programmer or a financial analyst, but only people with enough education to reprogram themselves throughout the changing trajectory of their professional lives will be able to reap the benefits of the new productivity. What about "the others"?...

In sum, information and communication technology is the essential tool for economic development and material well-being in our age; it conditions power, knowledge and creativity; it is, for the time being, unevenly distributed within countries and between countries; and it requires, for the full realisation of its developmental value, an interrelated system of flexible organisations and information-oriented institutions.

In a nutshell, cultural and educational development conditions technological development, which conditions economic development, which conditions social development, and this stimulates cultural and educational development once more. This can be a virtuous circle of development or a downward spiral of underdevelopment. And the direction of the process will not be decided by technology but by society, through its conflictive dynamics.

Globalisation

There is so much ideology surrounding this notion, and its implications, that it is essential to characterise globalisation precisely, and then determine its extent and evolution in empirical terms (see Hirst and Thompson 1996). Although globalisation is multidimensional, it can be better understood starting with its economic dimension. A global economy is an economy whose core activities work as a unit in real time on a planetary scale. Thus capital markets are interconnected worldwide, so that savings and investment in all countries, even if most of them are not globally invested, depend for their performance on the evolution and behaviour of global financial markets.

In the early 1990s multinational corporations employed directly "only" about 70 million workers, but these workers produced one third of the world's total private output, and the global value of their sales in 1992 was U.S.$ 5,500 billion, which is 25 percent more than the total value of world trade in that year (Bailey et al. 1993). Therefore multinational corporations, in manufacturing, services and finance, with their ancillary networks of small and medium businesses, constitute the core of the world economy.

Furthermore, the highest tier of science and technology, the one that shapes and commands overall technological development, is concentrated in a few dozen research centres and milieus of innovation around the globe, overwhelmingly in the United States, Western Europe and Japan. Russian, Indian and Chinese engineers, usually of very high quality, when they reach a certain level of scientific development, can only pursue their research by linking up with these centres. Thus highly skilled labour is also increasingly globalised, with talent being hired around the globe…

At the same time, the overwhelming proportion of jobs, and thus of people, are not global. In fact, they are local and regional. But their fate, their jobs, their living standards ultimately depend on the globalised sector of the national economy, or on the direct connection of their economic units to global networks of capital, production and trade. This global economy is historically new, for the simple reason that only in the last two decades have we produced the technological infrastructure required for it to function as a unit on a planetary scale: telecommunications, information systems, microelectronic-based manufacturing and processing, information-based air transportation… .

However, if the new global economy reaches out to encompass the entire planet, if all people and all territories are affected by its workings, not every place, or every person, is directly included in it. In fact, most people and most lands are excluded, switched off, either as producers, or consumers, or both. The flexibility of this global economy allows the overall system to link up everything that is valuable according to dominant values and interests, while disconnecting everything that is not valuable, or becomes devalued. It is this simultaneous capacity to include and exclude people, territories and activities that characterises the new global economy as constituted in the information age.

Similar processes of selective, segmented globalisation characterise other critical instrumental dimensions of our society, including the media, science, culture and information at large.

Globalisation and liberalisation do not eliminate the nation state, but they fundamentally redefine its role and affect its operation. Central banks (including the new European Central Bank) cannot really control the trends of global flows in financial markets. And these markets are not always shaped by economic rules, but by information turbulences of various origins. National governments, in order to maintain some capacity to manage global flows of capital and information, band together, creating or adapting supranational institutions (such as the International Monetary Fund, the European Union, NAFTA or other regional cooperation agencies), to which they surrender much of their sovereignty. So they survive, but under a new form of state that links supranational institutions, national states, regional and local governments and even NGOs, in a network of interaction and shared decision making that becomes the prevalent political form of the information age: the network state.

In sum, globalisation is a new historical reality, not simply the one invented by neoliberal ideology to convince citizens to surrender to markets, but also the one inscribed in processes of capitalist restructuring, innovation and competition…

Networking

No major historical transformation has taken place in technology, or in the economy, without an interrelated organisational transformation. The large factory, dedicated to mass production, was as critical to the constitution of the industrial age as the development and diffusion of new sources of energy. In the information age, the critical organisational form is networking. A network is simply a set of interconnected nodes. It may have a hierarchy, but it has no centre. Relationships between nodes are asymmetrical, but they are all necessary for the functioning of the network, for the circulation of money, information, technology, images, goods, services or people throughout the network. The most critical distinction in this organisational logic is to be or not to be in the network. Be in the network, and you can share and, over time, increase your chances. Be out of the network, or become switched off, and your chances vanish since everything that counts is organised around a worldwide web of interacting networks.

1927
1960
1963
1964
1967
1969
1970
1971
1972
1973
1974
1975
1976
1977
1978
1979
1980
1981
1982
1983
1984
1985
1986
1987
1988
1989
1990
1991
1992
1993
1994
1995
1996
1997
1998
1999
2000
2001
2002
2003
2004
2005
2006

Networks are the appropriate organisation for the relentless adaptation and the extreme flexibility that is required by an interconnected, global economy, by changing economic demand and constantly innovating technology, and by the multiple strategies (individual, cultural, political) deployed by various actors, which create an unstable social system at an increasing level of complexity. To be sure, networks have always existed in human organisation. But only now have they become the most powerful form for organising instrumentality, rather than expressiveness. The reason is fundamentally technological. The strength of networks is their flexibility, their decentralising capacity, their variable geometry, adapting to new tasks and demands without destroying their basic organisational rules or changing their overarching goals. Nevertheless, their fundamental weakness, throughout history, has been the difficulty of coordination towards a common objective, toward a focused purpose, that requires concentration of resources in space and time within large organisations, like armies, bureaucracies, large factories and vertically organised corporations.

With new information and communication technology, the network is, at the same time, centralised and decentralised. It can be coordinated without a centre. Instead of instructions, we have interactions. Much higher levels of complexity can be handled without major disruption. It does not follow, however, that large corporations are being replaced by small and medium businesses, or that multinationals are obsolete. We observe, in fact, the opposite: there is merger mania around the world. Bigger appears to be increasingly beautiful, as Citicorp marries Travelers Insurance, Bank of America leaves its heart in San Francisco but moves its money to North Carolina, Daimler Benz swallows Chrysler, Volkswagen upgrades itself to Rolls Royce status… .

But the concentration of capital goes hand in hand with the decentralisation of organisation. Large multinational corporations function internally as decentralised networks, whose elements are given considerable autonomy. Each element of these networks is usually a part of other networks, some of them formed by ancillary small and medium businesses; other networks link up with other large corporations, around specific projects and tasks, with specific time and spatial frames.

Yes, ultimately all this complexity boils down to the need to assure a profit. But how and for whom? Once CEOs have served themselves, lavishly, there is still most of the capital to be distributed among increasing numbers of shareholders. Earnings do not remain in the firm (whether dedicated primarily to manufacturing, finance, or services): they are invested in the global casino of interrelated financial markets, whose fate is ultimately determined by a series of factors. Only some of those factors have to do with economic fundamentals. Because of this level of unpredictability and complexity, the networks in which all firms, large or small, are anchored, move along, readapt, form and reform, in an endless variation. Firms and organisations that do not follow the networking logic (be it in business, in media, or in politics) are wiped out by competition, since they are not equipped to handle the new model of management.

So, ultimately, networks, all networks, come out ahead by restructuring, even if they change their composition, their membership and even their tasks. The problem is that people, and territories, whose livelihood and fate depend on their positioning in these networks, cannot adapt so easily. Capital disinvests, software engineers migrate, tourists find another fashionable spot and global media close down in a downgraded region. Networks readapt, bypass the area (or some people), and reform elsewhere, or with someone else. But the human matter on which the network was living cannot so easily mutate. It becomes trapped, or downgraded, or wasted. And this leads to social underdevelopment…at the threshold potentially the most romising era of human fulfilment.

The Other Side of the Information Age: Inequality, Poverty, Misery and Social Exclusion

To analyse current trends of poverty and inequality in the world, we need to establish some conceptual clarity by distinguishing, first, between relationships of consumption and relationships of production, and then by differentiating four specific processes in both sets of relationships. Relationships of consumption refer to the appropriation by people of the product of their work. Here, we must differentiate between inequality, polarisation, poverty and misery. Inequality refers to the unequal appropriation of wealth (income and assets) by individuals or social groups. Polarisation is a specific process of inequality that occurs when both the top and the bottom of a scale of wealth distribution grow faster than the middle. Poverty is an institutionally defined norm establishing the level of income that a society considers necessary to live according to an accepted standard. Misery, or extreme poverty, is an institutionally defined level that establishes the lowest material standard of living, making survival problematic.

When we observe the evidence of social trends in the world, within countries and between countries, and among people, in the last two decades, the following trends can be detected. There is increasing inequality between countries in the world at large, while intra-country inequality offers a mixed record, with some countries improving their condition (e.g., India, the Asian Pacific, Spain), while others have fallen into greater inequality (United States, United Kingdom, Mexico, Brazil). Polarisation is on the rise everywhere. At a global level, the ratio of income for the top 20 percent of the population to the income of the bottom 20 percent jumped from 30 to 1 in 1960 to 78 to 1 in 1994. And the combined personal assets of 385 billionaires in the world are now higher than the annual income of countries representing 45 percent of the population of the planet.

The evolution of poverty is complex. Modernisation has contributed to reducing the proportion of poor people in some very large countries, including China, India and Brazil. Still, the proportion of the poor is growing in most countries. And the *number* of people living in poverty has significantly increased everywhere. Furthermore extreme poverty, or misery, usually defined as the proportion of people who are below 50 percent of the poverty line, is the lot of the fastest-growing segment of the poor population in almost every country (see sources cited by Castells 1998, 75–82; and UNDP 1997).

As for relationships of production, they refer to the ways and means through which people provide for their livelihood. Here I will not go into a full-fledged analysis of all relationships of production existing in our society, but I will focus on the four conditions that seem to be decisive in affecting relationships of consumption. The first process, characterising the information age as a result of its networking form of organisation, is the growing individualisation of labour: I refer to the process by which labour's contribution to production is defined specifically for each individual, with little reference to collective bargaining or regulated conditions. If the industrial era consisted, in terms of the labour process, of taking a population of peasants and craftsmen and bringing them into socialised conditions of labour, the information age is exactly the reversal. It is the desocialisation of labour and the increasing flexibility and individualisation of labour performance.

This is not necessarily either good or bad. Flexibility of labour can allow people to organise their lives better, or not. But it does transform the social relationship between capital and labour, between management and workers, and among workers themselves. And it has fundamental implications for political action.

A second characteristic of current relationships of production is overexploitation: I mean the imposition of unfavourable norms of compensation or labour conditions on certain categories of workers (e.g., immigrants, women, youth, minorities) because of their vulnerability to discrimination. Women, in particular,

1927
1960
1963
1964
1967
1969
1970
1971
1972
1973
1974
1975
1976
1977
1978
1979
1980
1981
1982
1983
1984
1985
1986
1987
1988
1989
1990
1991
1992
1993
1994
1995
1996
1997
1998
1999
2000
2001
2002
2003
2004
2005
2006

have been massively incorporated into paid work, but in many cases at miserable wages (see data in Castells 1996, chapter 4; and 1997, chapter 4).

A third characteristic is social exclusion—that is, the process by which certain individuals or groups are barred from access to social positions that would entitle them to provide for themselves adequately, in an autonomous way, within the context of prevailing institutions and values. Usually, in informational capitalism, such a position is associated with the possibility of access to relatively regular, paid labour for at least one member of a stable household, or with the right to receive sufficient long-term benefits from a non-stigmatising welfare system. There is currently an extraordinary increase in numbers of people who find themselves in situations of social exclusion in practically all countries of the world, with the exception of the Scandinavian democracies (for sources, see Castells 1998, chapter 2).

Finally, there is a fourth significant type of relationship of production that is relevant to current trends of social underdevelopment: what I call perverse integration. This refers to the labour process in the criminal economy, in other words, to income-generating activities that are normatively declared to be a crime by the state. As a significant number of people are being excluded from access to regular jobs, they are moving onto this shop floor of crime. One could say that some have little choice. People who are not needed in the information age do not vanish: they are there. And in fact, they are increasingly there, because, with the exception of Russia, many populations now have an increasing life expectancy. (For more on the explosion of the criminal economy throughout the world, see Castells 1998, chapter 3.)

Links Between Informational Capitalism and the Growing Social Crisis

These, however, are simply observations of a growing social crisis (and not exempt from controversy concerning the selection and interpretation of data). What does the analysis mean?...

First, the extreme social unevenness of the process is linked to the flexibility and global reach of informational capitalism. If everything, and everyone, who can be a source of value can be easily connected, and as soon as he/she/it ceases to be so, can be easily disconnected (because of individualisation and extreme mobility of resources), then the global system of production is populated simultaneously by extremely valuable and productive individuals and groups, and by people (or places) who are not, or are not any longer considered valuable, even if they are still physically there. Because of the dynamism and competitiveness of the dominant system, most previous forms of production become destructured, and ultimately phased out, or transformed into subdued tributaries of the highly integrated, dynamic, globalised system.

Second, education, information, science and technology become critical as sources of value creation (and reward) in the informational economy. While formal education has increased throughout the world, the quality of education becomes essential. Most public schools, both in developing countries and in the United States, are simply not up to the task of producing the new, informational labour force. But even in countries with a decent educational system, the overall cultural and technological environment that is required to exercise informational skills does not mirror the dynamism of the system. So lack of education, and lack of informational infrastructure, lead most of the world to be dependent on the performance of a few globalised segments of their economies, increasingly vulnerable to the whirlwind of global financial flows.

Third, as new technologies, new production systems and the organisation of international trade eliminate traditional agriculture (still employing two-thirds of the people in the world in this end of millennium), a rural exodus of gigantic dimensions is being propelled, particularly in Asia. Rural people are destined to be painfully absorbed into the informal economy of overcrowded megacities on the edge of ecological catastrophe. Fourth, since states are bypassed by global flows, disciplined by the enforcers of these flows (such as the IMF), or limited by the supranational institutions they have initiated to survive somehow in the midst of globalisation, welfare states come under attack, regulations break down and the social contract, wherever it has existed, is fundamentally challenged.

New technologies do not induce unemployment, as has been repeatedly demonstrated by empirical research (Carnoy 1999). Indeed, at the world level there is a massive creation of jobs, but, in most cases, under conditions of overexploitation: the most telling development is the employment of about 250 million children at the time work is supposedly ending. But there is unemployment in Western Europe when firms facing tight labour rules, high wages and generous social benefits refuse to create jobs. Those firms have the possibility of automating, subcontracting and/or investing elsewhere, while still selling goods and services in the European market. Thus, under current conditions, markets overwhelm regulations and worker protection through relying on the increased mobility of resources made possible in the new technological environment. This is why, in the midst of the most extraordinary period of human ingenuity, people around the world are taken by panic. And this is why, together with affluence and prosperity for a significant minority (about one third of the people in advanced countries, and probably about one fifth in the world at large, who have substantially improved their living standards in the last 10 years), there is the formation of a fourth world, characterised by social exclusion.

The Fourth World

This world comprises people and territories that have lost value for the dominant interests in informational capitalism. Some of them because they offer little contribution as either producers or consumers. Others because they are uneducated or functionally illiterate. Others because they become sick or mentally unfit. Others because they could not afford the rent, became homeless, and were devoured by life in the streets. Others who, unable to cope with life, became drug addicts or drunks. Others because, in order to survive, they sold their bodies and their souls, and went on to be prostitutes of every possible desire. Others because they entered the criminal economy, were caught, and became inhabitants of the growing planet of the criminal justice system (almost three percent of adult males in the United States). Others because they had an incident with a cop, or a boss, or some authority and got onto the wrong track. And places, entire places, become stigmatised, confined by police, bypassed by networks of communication and investment. Thus, while valuable people and places have been globally connected, devalued locales become disconnected and people from all countries and cultures are socially excluded by the tens of millions. This fourth world of social exclusion, beyond poverty, exists everywhere, albeit in different proportions, from the South Bronx to Mantes-la-Jolie, from Kamagasaki to Meseta de Orcasitas, and from the *favelas* of Rio to the shanties of Jakarta. And there is, as I have tried to show, a systemic relationship between the rise of informational, global capitalism, under current conditions, and the extraordinary growth of social exclusion and human despair.

Redefining Social Development in the Information Age

For millennia, social development was tantamount to social survival: The daily goal of people, with the exception of a tiny ruling minority, was to get by, make a family and steal a few moments of joy out of the harshness of the human condition. This is still the lot of many. Yet over the last two centuries, with the advent of the industrial age, social development came to involve the goal of improving people's livelihood. ...

There is something new in the information age. It can be empirically argued that at the source of productivity and competitiveness (that jointly determine the generation of wealth and its differential appropriation by economic units), there is the capacity to generate new knowledge and to process relevant information efficiently. To be sure, information and knowledge have always been essential factors in power and

1927
1960
1963
1964
1967
1969
1970
1971
1972
1973
1974
1975
1976
1977
1978
1979
1980
1981
1982
1983
1984
1985
1986
1987
1988
1989
1990
1991
1992
1993
1994
1995
1996
1997
1998
1999
2000
2001
2002
2003
2004
2005
2006

production. Yet it is only when new information and communication technologies empower humankind with the ability incessantly to feed knowledge back into knowledge, experience into experience, that there is, at the same time, unprecedented productivity potential, and an especially close link between the activity of the mind, on the one hand, and material production, be it of goods or services, on the other. The old school of thought centred on the notion of human capital is fully vindicated. To invest in education is a productive investment. An educated labour force is a source of productivity. But to be educated means nothing if labour does not enjoy good health, decent housing, psychological stability and cultural fulfilment... .

Yet the interaction between economic growth and social development in the information age is still more complex. It is the entire social organisation that becomes productive or, on the contrary, an obstacle for innovation, and thus for productivity growth. Personal freedom (and therefore liberty in its fullest sense) is a prerequisite for entrepreneurialism. Social solidarity is critical for stability and thus for predictability in investment. Family safety is essential for the willingness to take risks. Trust in one's fellow citizens, and in the institutions of governance, is the foundation for socialising ingenuity in a given space and time, thus making it possible for others to enjoy the fruits of such ingenuity. In a word...social development leads to cultural development, which leads to innovation, which leads to economic development, which fosters institutional stability and trust; and this underlies a new, synergistic model that integrates economic growth and the enhancement of quality of life.

Without social development, without institutional stability, there may still be a diffusion of economic development around the world, but it will be based upon a cost-lowering formula, rather than a productivity-enhancing model. Furthermore, both spirals (the high road to informational productivity, and the low road to economic competitiveness through cost cutting) are cumulative and contagious. If firms and countries compete on the basis of worsening the conditions of work, and concentrating as much as possible of the productivity bonanza in a few hands, they will kill incentives for most workers to invest their own mental capital in a collective undertaking, they will slow down the learning curve and they will restrict both purchasing power and the drive towards innovation. Silicon Valley will still thrive on the basis of innovation and it will still attract a substantial share of brain power in the field of information technology from around the world. But the proportion of Silicon Valley's techno-elite in relation to the population at large, even the educated population, will become so ridiculously small in comparison to its share of power and wealth, that this will be socially unsustainable. Some people's dream of a shrinking planet, made up of a highly productive, very affluent, avid consumer minority, floating on a cloud over low-skilled generic labour and ignoring the black holes into which devalued people and locales are doomed to sink, is simply untenable. It is a nightmare, shaken by the rage of fundamentalism and by the fear of desperate terrorist threats. The disassociation between economic growth and social development in the information age is not only morally wrong, but also impossible to sustain.

The reintegration of social development and economic growth through technological innovation, informational management, and shared world development will not be accomplished by simply relying on unfettered market forces. Neither will it be born only out of the individual efforts of states, engaging in defensive strategies. It will require massive technological upgrading of countries, firms, and households around the world, a strategy of the highest interest for everyone, including business, and particularly for high-technology companies. (An appropriate use of the Internet is in fact the most important feature in such an upgrading.) It will take a dramatic investment in overhauling the educational system everywhere, through cooperation between national and local governments, international institutions and lending agencies, international and local business and families ready to make sacrifices for a tangible improvement of their children's future. It will require the establishment of a worldwide network of science and technology, in which the most advanced universities will be willing to share knowledge and expertise for the common good. It must aim at reversing, slowly but surely, the marginalisation of entire countries, or cities or neighbourhoods, so that the human potential that is being wasted, and particularly that of children, can be reinvested. All people must become valued producers and consumers, and they must be recognised as human beings in a forum other than the 30-second commercials of international organisations.

All this is feasible. We have the technical know-how, the technology to do it and the economic and institutional strategies to implement it. The obstacles, of course, are political. In part, they are related to very narrow business strategies. But if we know what we want, why we want it and how to do it, we have the basic groundwork from which to try to convince business and governments. I tend to think that it is in the interest of the most enlightened business groups to support the high road of informational development, linking up productivity, quality of life and investment in technology and education throughout the world. And if there is a strong pressure of public opinion in the world in favour of this shared development strategy, with its potentially positive payoff in environmental conservation, governments may join, ultimately, or else be ousted by their citizens.

Solidarity in a globalised world means global solidarity. And it also means intergenerational solidarity. Our planet is our only home, and we would not like the grandchildren of our grandchildren to be homeless. These are basic, elementary principles of economics and policy making, as if people matter. And they are in full coherence with the productive, creative logic embedded in our information-based society. If this sounds like wishful thinking, it is only a measure of how bewildered we have become at this critical moment of historical transition.

References

Bailey, P., et al. 1993. *Multinationals and Employment: The global economy in the 1990s.* Geneva: ILO.

Benner, C. [In progress.] "The Changing Labour Market of Silicon Valley," Ph.D. diss. Department of City and Regional Planning. University of California, Berkeley.

Carnoy, M. 1999. *Sustainable Flexibility: Work, Family and Community In The Information Age.* New York: Cambridge Univ. Press.

Castells, M. 1996. *The Information Age: Economy, Society, and Culture. Vol. I: The rise of the network society.* Oxford, U.K.: Blackwell.

Castells, M. 1997. *The Information Age: Economy, Society, and Culture. Vol.III: The Power of Identity.* Oxford, U.K.: Blackwell.

Castells, M. 1998. *The Information Age: Economy, Society, and Culture. Vol. III: End of millennium.* Oxford, U.K.: Blackwell.

Castells, M., and L. d'Andrea Tyson. 1988. "High technology choices ahead: Restructuring interdependence," in: J.M. Sewell and S. Tucker, eds. *Growth, Exports and Jobs In A Changing World Economy.* New Brunswick, N.J.: Transaction Books.

Castells, M., and L. d'Andrea Tyson. 1989. "High technology and the changing international division of production: Implications for the U.S. economy," in: R. Purcell, ed. *The Newly Industrializing Countries in The World Economy.* Boulder, Colo.: Lynne Rienner.

Castells, M., and E. Kiselyova. 1995. *The Collapse of Soviet Communism: The View From The Information Society.* Berkeley: University of California, International and Area Studies Book Series.

Dosi, G., et al. 1988. *Technical Change And Economic Theory.* London: Pinter.

Foray, D., and C. Freeman. 1992. *Technologie et richesse des nations.* Paris: Economica.

Hirst, P., and G. Thompson. 1996. *Globalisation In Question.* Cambridge, U.K.: Polity Press.

United Nations Development Program (UNDP). 1997. *Human Development Report 1997.* New York: Oxford Univ. Press.

Castells, Manuel. "Information Technology, Globalisation and Social Development," United Nations Research Institute for Social Development (UNRISD) Discussion Paper No. 114, September 1999. Reprinted with permission.

1927
1960
1963
1964
1967
1969
1970
1971
1972
1973
1974
1975
1976
1977
1978
1979
1980
1981
1982
1983
1984
1985
1986
1987
1988
1989
1990
1991
1992
1993
1994
1995
1996
1997
1998
1999
2000
2001
2002
2003
2004
2005
2006

SOCIAL DEVELOPMENT, INFORMATION AND KNOWLEDGE: WHATEVER HAPPENED TO COMMUNICATION?

By Cees Hamelink

2002 There is an abundance of writings on the significance of information in processes of social development. This is understandable since in matters of population growth, hygiene and health, agriculture, finance and public policy the provision of information to those concerned is essential. Around information a whole industry of extension workers, rural media and consultants developed over the past decades. By and large, all this work has been inspired by the conviction that the acquisition and distribution of information is essential to human empowerment and that if people have better access to this basic resource this would greatly benefit their standard of living. Because of the critical importance of information, the international community has repeatedly expressed its concern about the unequal access to information and its related technologies around the world.

Already at the 1948 United Nations Conference on the Freedom of Information, the Yugoslav delegate drew attention to the wide disparities in available means of mass communication and claimed that freedom of information should be linked with the standard of equality (Hamelink 1994, 155).

In the 1950s at various UNESCO conferences even the concept of "information famine" emerged. The same problem was entitled the gap between information-poor and information-rich throughout the 1970s and 1980s and, most recently, the common buzzword is "global digital divide." As modern information-communication technologies (ICTs) developed into the key infrastructure of modern economies, the early 1980s saw the introduction of the term "information society." This turned out to be a contested notion with different meanings to different people. However, whatever its precise meaning may be, the information society has become a standard for all countries to aspire towards. In more sophisticated analyses the "information society" became even the "knowledge society." The 1999 UNDP Human Development Report presents knowledge as the new asset and states that more than half of the GDP in the major OECD countries is knowledge based. Like information, knowledge is unequally distributed across the world. Using a variety of indicators (such as enrolment in educational institutions, ownership of patents, etc.), it can be documented that there is a skewed distribution of knowledge. Research and development is shifting further away from the developing countries. In the 1980s they held six percent of the global total of R&D investments; in the 1990s this was only four percent. Industrial countries hold 97 percent of all patents worldwide. In 1995 more than half of all global royalties and licensing fees were paid to the United States, mostly from Japan, the United Kingdom, France, Germany and the Netherlands. More than 80 percent of patents granted in developing countries belong to residents of industrial countries.

The prevalent political framework presents the "knowledge society" in the following term. In modern societies knowledge is the essential resource in their economies. The mastery of knowledge determines their competitive position, and therefore they seek to invest in knowledge production and in knowledge professions. Developing countries are in general advised to become innovative knowledge societies.

Whatever development paradigm one may prefer, there is growing consensus—in current literature, policy and practice—on the thesis that social development requires information and knowledge. The forthcoming United Nations World Summit on the

Information Society (December 2003 in Geneva and end of 2005 in Tunis) will put this in the full limelight of international politics.

The irony of the matter is of course that societies have always been information and knowledge societies. Even so-called primitive societies always had access to a large volume of detailed and pertinent local information and knowledge about their environment and their resources. Knowledge, for example, about specific properties of plants and animals was and is crucial to their survival. Increasingly, however, the currently emerging global regime for the protection of intellectual property undermines this. There is growing evidence that the legal provisions of the WTO Agreement on Trade-Related Intellectual Property Rights (TRIPS, 1993) hamper the independent development of knowledge in developing societies and facilitate the plunder of their knowledge resources (e.g. their biogenetic resources). The new regime gives little attention to the knowledge of indigenous people and leaves them very vulnerable to claims from outsiders. As a result, in many poor countries local knowledge is exploited for the manufacture of very profitable drugs without the informed consent of local people.

In this article I want to draw attention to the observation that all this emphasis on information and knowledge seems to largely bypass the fundamental question as to whether information and knowledge are indeed the resources that processes of social development primarily need. This must be questioned in the light of the popular myths upon which much thinking on information and knowledge societies is based.

A very common assumption claims that whereas the access to such resources as land and capital has always been restricted, everyone can own information and knowledge. However, a number of factors defeat this expectation.

In many social sectors (health or finance, for example) information and knowledge become increasingly complex and specialist. In general, this implies that, despite an increased volume of available information and knowledge, in modern societies more people know less.

The resources information and knowledge are far more difficult to exploit than land or capital. Informational knowledge exploitation demands highly developed intellectual and managerial skills which are unevenly distributed in most, if not all, societies. With the proliferation of neoliberal economics, information and knowledge have become more than ever before private property. Its owners, primarily large transnational corporations, protect this property with strict legal measures that promote monopolistic practices and hamper broad ownership of information and knowledge. In the prevailing trend towards the commodification and commercialisation of information and knowledge, they change from public goods to saleable goods to which price tags are attached. Information and knowledge are becoming more expensive and thus less accessible for more people.

Another very popular assumption that information and knowledge equal power is very attractive but seriously flawed. Information and knowledge become sources of power only if the necessary infrastructure for their production, processing, storage, retrieval and transportation is accessible, and when people have the skills to be able to apply information to social practice and to participation in social networks through which information can be used to further one's interests. The assumption proposes that people were never able to exercise power because they were ill-informed and ignorant. However, too often people knew precisely what was wrong and unjust, and they were very well informed about the misconduct of their rulers. Yet they did not act, and their knowledge did not become a source of power, because they lacked the material and strategic means for revolt!

A very attractive line of thought proposes that once people are better informed about each other, they will know and understand each other better and be less

1927
1960
1963
1964
1967
1969
1970
1971
1972
1973
1974
1975
1976
1977
1978
1979
1980
1981
1982
1983
1984
1985
1986
1987
1988
1989
1990
1991
1992
1993
1994
1995
1996
1997
1998
1999
2000
2001
2002
2003
2004
2005
2006

inclined to conflict. However, deadly conflicts are usually not caused by a lack of information. In fact, they may be based upon very adequate information that adversaries have about each other. As a matter of fact one could equally well propound the view that social harmony is largely due to the degree of ignorance that actors have with regard to each other. Many societies maintain levels of stability because they employ rituals, customs and conventions that enable their members to engage in social interactions without having detailed information about who they really are. There may indeed be conflict situations because adversaries have so much information about each other's aims and motives.

Most assumptions about the role and effects of information and knowledge are based upon a seriously flawed cause–effect model. Information and knowledge are conceived as key variables in social processes and, dependent upon how they are manipulated, certain social effects will occur. Social science research has taught us, however, that information and knowledge sharing do not occur in the linear mode of simple stimulus/response models that propose linear, causal relations between information/knowledge inputs and social outputs.

It is important to offer these critical observations because the common thinking on the role of information and knowledge in processes of social development matches exceedingly well the prevailing development paradigm.

Following this paradigm, development is a state of affairs which exists in society A and unfortunately not in society B so that through some project of intervention in society B, resources have to be transferred from A to B. Development is thus a relationship between interventionists and subjects of intervention. The interventionists transfer such resources as information and knowledge as inputs that will lead to social development as output.

As Allan Kaplan suggests in a paper on developing capacity, the conventional development approach assumes that development can be created and engineered, that it is linear and predictable, that it has a beginning and an end, and ultimately is "the delivery of resources" (1999, 5-7).

However, if we—as Kaplan proposes—understand development differently, the transfer of information and knowledge is no longer the key issue. The core of a different notion of development is "the recognition that development is an innate and natural process found in all living beings. It is important for us to understand that as development workers we do not 'bring' or deliver development, but intervene into development processes which already exist" (11). Contrary to the conventional approach, "development is about facilitating resourcefulness" (15). This leads Kaplan to conclude that "the whole point of development is to enable people to participate in the governance of their own lives" (19).

If one accepts this position, the present emphasis on information and knowledge raises the question "whatever happened to communication?" It is disconcerting that in most of the preparatory documents for the United Nations World Summit on the Information Society (2003, Geneva) "communication" has practically disappeared. There is a real danger that the Summit commits the same mistake as the United Nations World Conference on Human Rights (Vienna, 1993) which in its Final Declaration did not refer to communication, but only mentioned information and news. Yet, the real core question is how to shape "communication societies." In fact, for the resolution of the world's most pressing problems, we do not need more information processing but the capacity to communicate. The world does not need "information/knowledge societies," but "communication societies." Ironically, as our capacity to process and distribute information and knowledge expands and improves, our capacity to communicate and to converse diminishes.

It should be the foremost priority on the development agenda to develop the capacity for social dialogue. To solve the world's most pressing problems, people do not need more volumes of information and knowledge—they need to acquire the capacity to talk to each other across boundaries of culture, religion and language.

This sounds obvious and facile. In reality, however, dialogue is an extremely difficult form of speech. In most societies people have no time and patience for dialogical communication. Dialogue requires the capacity to listen, to be silent, to suspend judgment, to critically investigate one's own assumptions, to ask reflexive questions and to be open to change.

Dialogue has no short term and certain outcome. This conflicts with the spirit of modern achievement-oriented societies. Also the requirement to listen is very hard in societies that are increasingly influenced by visual culture—listening demands an ear-centred culture!

Moreover, the mass media are not particularly helpful in teaching societies the art of conversation. Much of their content is babbling (endless talking without saying anything), hate speech, advertising blurbs, sound bites or polemical debate.

The good thing about all this is that the capacity for the dialogue is a problem for all stakeholders. No group or country is privileged over others. This is something we all need to learn!

Social dialogue is the essential approach to the conflicts around the world between people of different origins, religious values, cultural practices and languages. Such encounters all too often end in deadly conflict. In the desperate search to solve or rather prevent such conflicts, there is in the public debate a trend towards the proposal to separate those who cannot live in peace from each other by erecting walls between them. As deadly conflicts and walls of separation do not offer sustainable solutions, the only alternative is the effort to conduct dialogue. However, it needs to be realised that even if well-intended individuals master the art of dialogue and are strongly motivated to participate in cross-cultural and cross-religious encounters, the groups they belong to may not want this. We need to seriously

examine the historical possibility that the liberal dream about peaceful multiethnic, multireligious societies is a dream indeed (Dahrendorf 2002). If groups have a long history of serious rivalry, they may not be open to dialogue. It should also be realised that social groups relate to each other from different positions of power. It is questionable whether fostering dialogue among unequal parties is a serious option. The more communication takes place among unequal parties, the greater the risk of greater dependency and powerlessness for the weaker party.

This tells us we have to be careful not to adopt the dialogical form of communication as the ultimate panacea for development issues. I would like to think that dialogue is more promising than the transfer of information and knowledge in enabling people to participate in the governance of their own lives, but just like expectations about information and knowledge need to be qualified, the same holds true for the "communication society."

Conclusion

The purpose of this article is not to deny the importance of information and knowledge in development processes. The proposal to strive towards communication societies rather than information/knowledge societies should not be construed as an argument for social dialogues between people who are ignorant and ill-informed. There is abundant empirical evidence to support the importance of information and knowledge sharing. We should, however, assure that all the present emphasis on information and knowledge does not obscure the insight that at the heart of social development is communication in the form of conversation or dialogue. Since this is a complex and difficult art to master, the development community should make it its foremost challenge for the early 21st century.

This would also imply realising the following. An effective social dialogue cannot take place between people whose lives are threatened, who are not free

1927
1960
1963
1964
1967
1969
1970
1971
1972
1973
1974
1975
1976
1977
1978
1979
1980
1981
1982
1983
1984
1985
1986
1987
1988
1989
1990
1991
1992
1993
1994
1995
1996
1997
1998
1999
2000
2001
2002
2003
2004
2005
2006

to speak or to assemble, who have no means of expressing their voices, who cannot speak in confidentiality and privacy, or who are denied basic forms of education and cultural participation. There is today an urgent need for the adoption of a universal declaration on the right to communicate. This right does at present not exist as a provision of international law. As early as 1969 Jean d'Arcy introduced the right to communicate by writing, "the time will come when the Universal Declaration of Human Rights will have to encompass a more extensive right than man's right to information... This is the right of men to communicate." The motivating force for this new approach was the observation that the provisions in existing human rights law (e.g., in the Universal Declaration of Human Rights or the Covenant on Civil and Political Rights) were inadequate to deal with communication as an interactive process.

The international recognition of a right to communicate is an essential step towards the development of "communication societies" in which social development equals people's empowerment to manage and control their own lives.

References

D'Arcy, J. 1969. "Direct Broadcasting Satellites and the right to communicate," *EBU Review* 118: 14–18.

Dahrendorf, R. 2002. "Getrennt, aber gleichberechtigt," *Der Standard.* May 25: 39.

Hamelink, C.J. 1994. *The politics of world communication* London: Sage.

Kaplan, A. 1999. "The developing of capacity," *NGLS development dossier.* Geneva: UN Non-Governmental Liaison Service.

UNDP. 1999. *Human development report.* New York: Oxford University Press.

Hamelink, Cees. "Social Development, Information and Knowledge: Whatever Happened to Communication?" *Development.* Journal of the Society for International Development 45(4):5¬–9, 2002. Copyright © 2002 Palgrave Macmillan Publishers.

Excerpt from: *"Media Without an Audience"*
By Eric Kluitenberg

One of the greatest fallacies of current attempts to understand the social dynamics of networked media is the tendency to see these media as an extension of the broadcast media system. This idea has become more popular as the Internet is extended with audiovisual elements. Interactive audiovisual structures, streaming media, downloadable sound and video all contribute to the notion that the Internet is the next evolution of broadcast media. But this vision applies only partially, and is driven primarily by vested interests of the media industry. It is often not reflected in how people actually use the Net.

The predication of the conception of media on the broadcast model based on a division of roles of the active sender and passive receiver/audience relationship is the greatest barrier to understanding what goes down in a networked media environment. The networked environment should primarily be seen as a social space, in which active relationships are pursued and deployed. Activities often seem completely useless, irrational, erratic or even autistic. The active sender and the passive audience/receiver relationship seems to have been replaced by a multitude of unguided transmissions that seem to lack a designated receiver. Thus the Net is seen as an irrelevant, chaotic and useless infosphere, a waste of resources, a transitory phase of development that will soon be replaced by professional standards of quality, entertainment, information, media professionalism and, above all, respect for the audience.

Kluitenberg, Eric. "Media Without an Audience," paper presented at the Banff Centre for the Arts Interactive Screen Workshop (August 2000), and the International Festival of Streaming Media, in Amsterdam, October 2000. Published in http://www.ctrl-z.org/magazine/2001/texts/eric.htm and http://www.debalie.nl/dossierartikel.jsp?dossierid=22375&articleid=7135. Reprinted with permission of the copyright holder.

GLOBAL MEDIA GOVERNANCE AS A POTENTIAL SITE OF CIVIL SOCIETY INTERVENTION

Excerpt from: Democratising Global Media: One World, Many Struggles

By Seán Ó Siochrú

2005 A point of departure for this chapter is the increasingly globalised nature of media and communication and of their dynamics. Evidence for this abounds, for instance, in the reach of global media corporations and the proportion of national media they control, the marketing and dissemination of homogenous or routinely modified content worldwide, the widespread diffusion of a single market-based regulatory model, and the emergence of a largely uniform global regulatory regime under the World Trade Organization (WTO).

Similarly, a campaign to reform communication cannot succeed if its focus remains solely at a national level. It must, from the outset, consider global issues and build a global base. This is not to argue that civil-society intervention should be exclusively at the transnational level. The national and local remain key arenas of struggle, in their own terms, for what can be achieved there, but, also, because governments are the gatekeepers of influence in many international institutions and contexts, and activities must thus first persuade governments on their own turf. Conversely, a transnational campaign lacking local roots and direction cannot succeed in the long term. These roots can be fed through a campaign network, direct membership, alliances or by other means. But they must be present and, ultimately, must drive the transnational activity.

What are the main fears relating to media and communication, as expressed by voices of civil society that reverberate globally?

Below, these are grouped into four overlapping domains,[1] compiled from a number of sources including advocacy campaigns and literature critical of trends in media and communication.[2] Some concerns are not new—they were already raised in the debates in the United Nations Educational, Scientific and Cultural Organization (UNESCO) and elsewhere in the 1980s—but many are also peculiar to the dominant economic paradigm and to the emergence and convergence of digital technologies.

This is merely a first aggregation, and is not the result of a rigorous process. It is intended to illustrate some sense of their interdependency and suggest at least one schema by which they can be aggregated in a manner that puts the risks involved and, implicitly, the opportunities to the fore. …We argue that one of the main challenges facing a transnational media campaign is precisely to undertake a rigorous and regionally differentiated process in the context of the need to "frame" the issues for advocacy purposes.

Following a description of these domains, we extract some common dynamics and characteristics as evidence of their interdependence and, hence, of the need to address them at the transnational level. A further section takes a highly speculative look at a possible future scenario, one in which the negative aspects of the identified trends are taken to their, albeit unlikely, extreme. We conclude with a review of the main actors likely to be involved in preventing such a scenario coming into being.

1.1 Four Domains of Concern

A. THE GROWING FAILURE OF MEDIA IN THE PUBLIC SPHERE

Within the liberal democratic tradition claimed by most Western societies, the "public sphere" is the arena in which general interaction and deliberation about society and polity are practised, and where civil

1927
1960
1963
1964
1967
1969
1970
1971
1972
1973
1974
1975
1976
1977
1978
1979
1980
1981
1982
1983
1984
1985
1986
1987
1988
1989
1990
1991
1992
1993
1994
1995
1996
1997
1998
1999
2000
2001
2002
2003
2004
2005
2006

society discovers and exercises its political and social self-understanding. It encompasses the press, television, public demonstrations, discussion, e-mail lists and myriad other forms. The essence of the public sphere is that it is where people openly and transparently debate on the basis that they can be "convinced by reason," by the rationality of argumentation, and not by rhetorical appeals, or through suppression or distortion of information. A distorted public sphere, controlled by narrow interests, can obfuscate and conceal injustice, smother voices of dissent and place insurmountable barriers in the path of would-be campaigns.. The result is heightened social tensions and inequities, with all that attends these.

The idea of the public sphere is thus closely linked to that of civil society itself. Those suffering under dictatorships and repression can barely glimpse such an ideal, focusing instead on the task of constituting an autonomous civil society, free from state control. In liberal democracies, it is a partially realised ideal, the basic parameters and role achieving varying degrees of realisation and recognition. The notion must thus find distinct cultural moorings and articulation to suit the broader structures of representation and participation.

In recent decades, concern has switched somewhat from state censorship and control towards commercial and corporate control and the transformation of media into a commodity. The main underlying dynamic is the imposition of the neo-liberal model on media through, for instance:

■ Media liberalisation, one effect of which is to accelerate concentration of ownership nationally, and of cross-ownership of media, as in the United States, the United Kingdom and many other European countries.
■ The "marketisation" of the media sector, in which media corporations subsume all other goals under that of profit maximisation, in which advertising revenues play a growing role and in which subsidy of public service media comes to be regarded as a "distortion" of market forces.

■ The emergence of global media conglomerates wielding enormous, financial, marketing and even political power, and control over ever-larger slices of media markets.
■ The absence or suppression of effective international regulation of the activities of these conglomerates, and of external cross-border media such as satellite television, that can dictate to national regulators.

These all conform to the standard neo-liberal model, which is blind to the characteristics of a public sphere and holds that the market is capable of delivering on society's media needs. Even as a civil society begins to coalesce in countries emerging from feudal or modern dictatorships and the notion of the public sphere appears on the horizon, the newfound freedom is subtly spirited away under the noses of an unknowing populace. Commercially driven globalised media are undermining existing models of public-service media; are largely replacing previously state-controlled media as a low-cost, politically unthreatening option; and in the global South, are sweeping away or transforming public-minded media traditions, or filling a media vacuum and quickly becoming the norm.

A particularly dangerous hybrid is also in evidence around the world. Driven by the confluence of interests between politicians seeking to gain or retain power and media corporations, it leads to seriously worrying cases of apparent collusion, conflict of interest and covert alliances between sections of industry and politicians in countries as diverse as the United States, the United Kingdom, Russia, India, Thailand and Venezuela. From very different starting points, accommodations between neo-liberal capital and political elites are potentially hugely damaging to the public sphere since at their core is a drive to systematically distort public information in favour of specific sectoral interests.

B. THE PROPAGATION OF A SINGLE WORLDVIEW: INDIVIDUALIST CONSUMERISM

The second major concern targets the role of media in the propagation of a single worldview, consumerist capitalism and a global market economy. Fears are expressed, not only by many nongovernmental organizations (NGOs), but by many governments of the South and indeed some in the North. The focus here is not on the political health of a country per se, but on the role of media and communication in promoting a worldview—consumerism and individualism—and its economic, social and cultural counterparts, as human relationships become mediated through the market.

Several issues intertwine here: One is the role of media in the formation of individual identity, especially of young people, and how they position themselves in relation to their surroundings. Applied to a community as a whole, this can have an enormous impact on community identity and social divisiveness. In traditional societies, with the imposition of this worldview, comes the denigration and destruction of cultural traditions, which though claimed by none to be ideal, are denied the possibility of further evolution in the context of cultural continuity. Fractures introduced between social groups in this cultural reformation, especially through the exclusion of the majority of the poor as irrelevant to the media (as neither sellers nor purchasers), lead to further reinforcement of deep-seated and persisting divisions. The net effect is that an emerging consumer society in practice displaces an emerging civil society. And, at a meta-level, a fundamentally unsustainable way of life and worldview takes hold.

The underlying dynamics are driven largely by the general characteristics of neo-liberal logic outlined above. But they are manifested in specific ways. The forceful entry of global capital into new markets in the South puts a special value on advertising, particularly of international brands. This, combined with the low level of disposable income in poorer countries, means that corporate advertising budgets are the main funders of mass media, aiming to create markets and "manufacture new needs." News reporting and current affairs tend to be displaced by "lifestyle" journalism.

Facing demands from powerful governments and corporations, and outmanoeuvred by unregulated satellite, many governments acquiesce, striking a deal with the global media corporations. Mounting pressure from the World Trade Organization (WTO) aims to eliminate borders to media investment and commodification, irrespective of cultural or social implications. With its ratchet-like effect, a real concern is that room for manoeuvre will disappear, leaving media corporations free to reshape culture and society according to their imperatives.

C. THE ENCLOSURE OF KNOWLEDGE: COPYRIGHT AND THE PUBLIC DOMAIN

A third area of concern is the privatisation of information and knowledge itself, the benefits of human creativity mediated through profit-maximising strategies of the copyright industries and mass media corporations. (Ó Siochrú, Girard 2003)

Copyright has been driven for the past few decades by the "copyright" industries of film, television, radio, publishing, music and software. They significantly influence how people can appropriate and use information and, ultimately, media, and the scope and vitality of the public domain. They have a strong global dimension since the completion of the WTO's trade-related aspects of intellectual property rights (TRIPS) agreement that essentially subjugates the various treaties gathering together under the world intellectual property organization (WIPO). Over the past couple of decades, the period of copyright monopoly has been systematically extended to a total of 50 years after the author's death under TRIPS, and 70 years in the United States, which sets the trend. Furthermore, TRIPS imposes a single uniform version of copyright, irrespective of the level or nature of a country's development. Most important of all, with TRIPS the copyright industries now control the most powerful enforcement instruments available to any non-security agency, with the authority to impose massive fines on countries and prison sentences on individuals. Efforts to introduce audiovisual products into successive WTO rounds are certain to continue, in the meantime, being cumulatively imposed through bilateral and regional agreements.

1927
1960
1963
1964
1967
1969
1970
1971
1972
1973
1974
1975
1976
1977
1978
1979
1980
1981
1982
1983
1984
1985
1986
1987
1988
1989
1990
1991
1992
1993
1994
1995
1996
1997
1998
1999
2000
2001
2002
2003
2004
2005
2006

The digital age offers a further opportunity to deepen corporate control of information, starting with the Digital Millennium Copyright Act and the WIPO Copyright Treaty (WCT). Electronic distribution, encryption and digital-rights management are already severely curtailing "fair use" for educational and general social development purposes. And pressures to assert copyright and trademark on the Internet are being felt at all levels of users.

D. THE EROSION OF CIVIL RIGHTS IN ELECTRONIC COMMUNICATION

Finally, a fourth group of concerns relates to growing surveillance, censorship and direct repression, pursued both by governments and the corporate sector. Privacy International & GreenNet Educational Trust, 2003; Ó Siochrú 2003)

Government censorship of electronic information, usually at the point of the Internet service provider (ISP), is very real and growing more effective. In some places, an ongoing cat-and-mouse game is played between NGOs and governments, as each tries to outwit the other in controlling the flow of information. In a few, such as China, Vietnam and Tunisia, Internet activists are jailed.

Levels of surveillance have recently increased greatly, both in terms of technological capability and political will. Troubling legal frameworks, originating in the United States since the World Trade Centre attacks, are being replicated around the globe. A vast array of national and international laws and conventions are being set in place, giving enormous powers to governments and secretive, sometimes unaccountable, agencies to monitor the full range of communication instruments, but especially digital communication. ECHELON, Carnivore, Terrorist Information Awareness, the U.S. Patriot Act and the Council of Europe Convention on Cybercrime may be just the first wave, and the ripples are being felt throughout the world. "Purpose creep"—where the purpose is gradually extended to include other goals—is a major concern, in the context of intensified international collaboration, data retention, surveillance and monitoring of online environments in attempts to counter "cybercrime" and "terrorism."

Corporate censorship can be more insidious since it can be more difficult to identify and to grapple with. Corporations involved in Internet delivery, such as ISP and bandwidth providers, engage more extensively in "self-censorship" ultimately based on commercial priorities but with knock-on effects on a variety of actors.

1.2 Underlying and Common Features

Can common features be gleaned from this multidimensional palate of concerns? More specifically, is it possible to identify dynamics or interrelations that suggest that these domains can collectively constitute a coherent focus of a transnational campaign?

Certainly, a common underlying dynamic is easily discerned in some. The neo-liberal model of largely unregulated capitalism, open markets and private ownership is behind the first three. Wielding enormous political and economic power, its logic is forcefully impressed upon every barrier it meets, such as resistance to the destruction of the (nascent) public sphere, attempts to protect cultural diversity, or efforts to optimally deploy the fruits of human creativity for the greater social good. The need to maximise profits and to create the ideal conditions for this, endeavours to sweep aside such obstacles and transform the world in its own image and to suit its needs.

The fourth area is somewhat different. The erosion of civil and human rights in electronic communication is driven not primarily by commercial gain (though there is an indirect element of that) but by broader geopolitical forces. It is partly associated with "traditional" state repression of its own people, as in China, Tunisia, Vietnam and elsewhere. But the growing trend is not just national but international and is driven by the United States and its allies in the interests, they claim, of national and global "security." The latter work closely with the neo-liberal corporate regime, by creating a positive environment globally and in ensuring it benefits from the spoils of war. But the motivation and dynamic goes beyond corporate needs and can even enter into contradiction with them.

Yet the identification of a common dynamic behind these domains need not imply that they constitute an appropriate subject for a transnational campaign. The dominant neo-liberal paradigm of contemporary capitalism is also responsible for environmental destruction, for growing global inequity and so forth. Whilst a grand coalition may eventually emerge to counter this logic, this will happen only if in each area opposition and alternatives can be articulated and mobilised around.

A second source of coherence from a transnational campaign perspective might be that, in terms of the sub-sectoral dynamics and actors, the four domains are closely interrelated and interdependent. A high degree of apparent interconnectedness might lead those mobilising around one aspect to question what is happening in adjacent areas; concern with one has the potential to lead on to concern with another, and so forth onto the next. This, in turn, might contribute to the emergence of coherence between the domains from the perspective of affecting change. In other words, such interconnectedness means that, on the one hand, it is impossible to deal with each domain in isolation, and, on the other, it is possible to gain leverage in one domain by working on another.

A high degree of interrelatedness of actors and dependencies is indeed present, perhaps not surprisingly.

In terms of corporate actors, global media conglomerates have a strong presence especially in the first three. The same mass media corporations seeking to undermine public service media and commodify the "media market" are also busy clearing the cultural and ideological ground for global market-driven consumerism. They see it as two sides of the same coin: Clearing away "unfair competition" in the form of public media subsidies and "market constraints" in the form of regulation, and, at the same time, building up a market for themselves through promoting consumerist capitalism among the middle classes. The former has an added emphasis in the North, while the latter is to the fore in the South.

In copyright, mass media corporations also have a major stake and huge influence, but they are joined by others. The "copyright industries" include television, film and video, radio and newspapers, but they also include music, educational publishing and software. Between them, they are the major drivers of the continued extension of copyright, in depth and breadth, and in building the global enforcement regime in place today. The latter group are also especially involved in the shift to digital, and pursue encryption and the move to contractual access to information, restrictive forms of digital rights management and the erosion of fair use. Major global corporations have extensive interests and influence across many of these areas. And behind them all is a small number of powerful governments who have relentlessly pursued the interests of the copyright industries in global fora.

Electronic space is, again, exceptional but there are strong links. ISPs, Internet bandwidth retailers (who effectively operate a global oligopoly) and search engines constitute the critical intermediaries between government restrictions and end-users in electronic space. Many of these, such as American Online (AOL), are tied into the same media corporations. And the tendency of such corporations to practice self-censorship and to profit from commercial surveillance and data mining, is growing. Nevertheless, governments remain the main actors here.

At the level of international governance, examined in more depth in the next section, there are also clear linkages. At the fulcrum of many key concerns is the WTO, as the major global actor imposing a market logic across the board. It plays the lead role in copyright and in conventional publishing, defines the international regime in telecommunication and ISPs, and has potentially a major role in audiovisual media. There are others, but the role of WTO puts it far ahead as a target for advocacy in the first three domains.

1927
1960
1963
1964
1967
1969
1970
1971
1972
1973
1974
1975
1976
1977
1978
1979
1980
1981
1982
1983
1984
1985
1986
1987
1988
1989
1990
1991
1992
1993
1994
1995
1996
1997
1998
1999
2000
2001
2002
2003
2004
2005
2006

Thus there are interdependencies between the actors. First are a relatively small number of governments in pursuit of the interests of their media and copyright industries, and, a few, in geo-political strategies for global economic and military dominance. Second are the media and copyright industries themselves, sprawled across the full range of sectors after years of mega-mergers and acquisitions as well as their various associations which enable them to coordinate their considerable powers to impact on global politics. Third is a small number of intergovernmental organisations, principally but not only the WTO, which are utilised by these actors and actively collude to propagate their worldview and their communication regime.

This lends some support to our claim regarding the difficultly of tackling many issues in isolation. For instance, the copyright regime has been moving in only one direction for the past few decades, towards strengthening the rights of owners. Any attempt to change this, whether in terms of reversing the erosion of fair use, reducing the period of copyright, introducing greater flexibility or addressing the enforcement regime, is likely to meet with the full opposition of all those concerned, both corporate and government. Any breach in the copyright front is likely to be taken as an attack on the system as a whole, and on its rationale, and would thus meet concerted opposition. Ever further, copyright is seen by these interests as simply a part of the overall intellectual property rights regime, a central building block for continued corporate dominance globally. A similar argument could be made regarding attempts to regulate media at a global level—they would meet the full force of opposition for all actors.

Thus a *prima facie* case can be established that the concerns about media and communication outlined above are linked though subject matter and dynamics, and through a relatively small group of mainly transnational actors closely interacting to pursue overlapping international agendas. It is offered as a tentative basis for why these four domains (or some variation of them) can strategically be considered as a whole in terms of an international advocacy network or campaign.

2. The International Policy/Governance Context

Further consideration of the transnational governance context might inform our later consideration of how a transnational campaign might, in practice, grapple with these issues. A small set of governance institutions constitute key arenas in which these issues are played out, and in which such a campaign may operate. (Ó Siochrú, et al. 2002)

As mentioned earlier, we do not underestimate the importance of national arenas, both in their own right and as essential mediators between civil society and international change. The activities of national governments are, however, increasingly mediated through and subject to international bodies.

Chief among the institutions involved in governance of media and communication, though such a claim could not have been made even 20 years ago, is the WTO. It now straddles key areas of communication and is set to extend its mandate further.

First is copyright. The WTO, through the efforts of the United States especially, wrested copyright from WIPO with the TRIPS agreement in 1995. The set of international agreements incorporated into WIPO with its formation in 1970, the Berne and Paris Conventions reaching back nearly 120 years, comprise the baseline upon which TRIPS builds. And build it has, in a number of directions. The TRIPS agreement virtually eliminates the flexibility of intellectual property rights (IPRs) regimes that had hitherto been recognised as a necessary component of development. Under TRIPS, flexibility to tailor IPRs to national requirements is greatly reduced.[3] The duration and breadth of copyright is fixed at a very high level as compared to previous norms in most countries— the lifetime of the author plus 50 years. The copyright industries include the world's largest media corporations, and the WTO underwrites and enforces their rights in TRIPS signatory countries.

Second, under the Uruguay Round and the General Agreement on Trade and Services (GATS), the provision by governments of support for magazines, periodicals and other non-audiovisual services was deemed to be discriminatory, under threat of strong financial or trade sanctions. This was confirmed by the WTO dispute panel in a famous case taken by the United States against Canada in the mid-1990s on "split-run" magazines. Implicitly, it ruled that some media companies are less in the business of selling products to audiences than in the business of selling audiences to advertisers. An attempt was made in the Uruguay Round to lay down similar rules for film, video, television and audiovisual products, which failed due to European and other opposition. But it is back on the table at the Doha Round of negotiations and will remain so despite the breakdown in Cancun.

Third, in telecommunication, since the shift from monopoly national providers to liberalised international suppliers, the sector is governed by the trade paradigm of the WTO. An area of interest here is universal service policies, by which governments can oblige cross-subsidisation from large business users and urban areas to domestic and small users and rural areas. The WTO agreement permits this only where they do not interfere unduly with competition—a vague formulation yet to be tested. The move to trade is also leading to the redundancy of the International Telecommunication Union's (ITU) accounting rate system and to a net loss of foreign earnings for some of the poorest countries (Ó Siochrú 1997).

But what is unique about the WTO, and what makes it so attractive to the powerful countries, is "how" it governs. In usurping these activities from others and incorporating them under its various agreements, it subjects them to a new form of governance. For the WTO has at its disposal some of strongest policing and enforcement powers ever ceded to an intergovernmental body by governments, and it uses them

extensively in copyright, in media trade and in telecommunication. Furthermore, signing up to the WTO has a ratchet-like effect—it is, in practice, impossible to row back on agreements even as their full implications become clear, even when circumstances change, or even when promises of reciprocal beneficial action go unfulfilled. The contractual structure of WTO agreements is also conducive to bilateral pressures and coercion, a source of regular complaints from Southern governments.

Other organisations have not, of course, been left without influence. For instance although WIPO is largely sidelined by the WTO, the WIPO Copyright Treaty entered into force in 2002. Designed to bring copyright into the digital network era, it covers such areas as outlawing efforts to circumvent encryption of copyrighted material.[4] However, many are concerned that in extending copyright into the digital era, in practice it cuts into "fair use," the accepted means to enable limited public use of copyrighted material prior to expiration.[5] WIPO also has various responsibilities in relation to Internet domain names, including arbitrating on ownership disputes.

The International Telecommunication Union also retains responsibility for several narrow but important areas. It is the venue in which governments agree the allocation of radio spectrum across borders, terrestrially and via satellite, for the purposes of telephone (mobile and fixed), data, television, radio and others. The use of spectrum is coordinated to prevent interference and border "spillover," and slices of it are allocated to different uses and users. Since it is regarded as a scarce public resource,[6] allocating it among users is an important and contentious issue internationally. The ITU also divvies out satellite orbital slots, including the valuable and scarce geostationary orbit; another function is in standardisation for telecommunication networks and equipment, including protocols, which can be highly contentious since they are linked to struggles for market control.[7] The ITU is also concerned with extending telecommunication to

1927
1960
1963
1964
1967
1969
1970
1971
1972
1973
1974
1975
1976
1977
1978
1979
1980
1981
1982
1983
1984
1985
1986
1987
1988
1989
1990
1991
1992
1993
1994
1995
1996
1997
1998
1999
2000
2001
2002
2003
2004
2005
2006

less-industrialised countries, but has only very limited means to do so. Finally, it is worth noting that the ITU is the lead U.N. agency for the World Summit on the Information Society (WSIS), in Geneva in December 2003 and Tunis in 2005, which covers a number of areas of relevance here.

The United Nations Educational, Scientific and Cultural Organization (UNESCO), on the other hand, has much "softer" responsibilities but they extend to many areas of social concern. It is important, less for its formal powers and enforcement capacities, than as a forum for voluntary cooperation on (usually non-contentious but necessary) issues of mutual concern across a wide area. UNESCO in its early decades was instrumental in many conventions, declarations and congresses, overseeing agreements on issues, such as, the exchange of audiovisual content for educational use, cross-border direct broadcasting satellite and copyright exemptions for development purposes. In the late-1970s to the mid-1980s, it came to the fore as a debating arena for global communication issues, with the New World Information and Communication Order (NWICO).[8] Its fingers were badly burned on this, however, as Cold War politics and entrenched positions of some of the major powers eventually led to the defeat of voices calling for more open and democratic global media flows and structures. UNESCO has never fully recovered in terms of facilitating vibrant and diverse debate and, indeed, the United States announced only in 2001 its intention to rejoin after leaving in the mid-1980s.

In 1995, the UNESCO-sponsored World Commission on Culture and Development put forward some significant proposals regarding media, raising the idea of a tax on the use of spectrum, the proceeds to be utilised for noncommercial programming for international distribution, and questioning the growing concentration of media ownership. However, it is probably indicative of UNESCO's broader constraints that these failed to be ratified, or even discussed, at the follow-up inter-governmental meeting in 1998. Although it continues

to support progressive media initiatives and to sponsor debate at a lower level, current negotiations on U.S. re-entry will probably ensure that UNESCO is unlikely in the foreseeable future to become a major forum for open debate or dissenting views.

A newcomer is the Internet Corporation of Assigned Names and Numbers (ICANN). Established in 1998, its main job is to manage the process of assigning names and numbers for the Internet, an issue that has gradually taken on huge commercial and legal significance. ICANN initially saw itself as primarily technical, but its management of the ISP addresses and of the Domain Name System (DNS), which ultimately controls routing of Internet traffic, quickly moved into economic, political, social and even cultural domains. It is interesting, not just for what it does, but for how it does it. It is constituted as a nonprofit private-sector corporation under California law, designed to allow the U.S. Department of Commerce to maintain ultimate control over the DNS (which it still does). This places it in the nongovernmental sector. Its governance is still in transition, stability still eluding it. At-large membership (i.e., Internet users who registered to the process) did initially have the opportunity to elect several directors, the rest coming from the initial board and nominated by associated organisations. But this was later unceremoniously scrapped, and at-large membership is reduced to a more or less advisory capacity.

Other, less well-known organisations are also involved with the Internet.[9] The Internet Engineering Task Force (IETF), for instance, sounds highly technical. But its work in defining the new Internet protocol (called IPV6) could have significant long-term implications in terms, for instance, of surveillance and commercialisation of the Internet.

Regional level institutions are also relevant. The European Union, for instance, has its Television Without Frontiers and Database Directives, the North American Free Trade Agreement (NAFTA) encompasses cultural agreements, and the Council of Europe in 2001 oversaw the CyberCrime Treaty, all of which deeply influence media and communication. Apart from the impact in their own right, regional agreements (and indeed national legislation in powerful counties such as the United States) are often early battlegrounds for matters that are later pushed up to global governance structures. Other intergovernmental organisations, such as the Organisation for Economic Co-operation and Development (OECD) and the Group of Eight (G8), are also important loci of collaboration between governments (in these cases, of the wealthier countries) in coordinating and implementing shared policy and in providing the research and ideological backup for their shared worldviews.

But governance does not just take place in intergovernmental organisations. Corporations, for instance, take a very keen interest in how media and communications are governed, and are lobbying actively for various forms of self-governance through various associations and assemblies. There are also other forms of, what amount to, unacknowledged self-governance activities, for instance, many examples of international censorship of Internet content by bandwidth backbone providers and by global ISP.

These, then, are some of the players in global governance, and a quick glance at their areas of influence. It reveals again the reasonably coherent dynamic behind much of the trends in recent years, that of the neo-liberal interpretation of capitalism. Driven mainly by the United States but also supported in key aspects by the European Union and others, governance structures have been transformed to fulfil its needs. In media and communication, the goals are clear: Commercialisation through the elimination of government monopoly; government ownership; market "distortions" designed to achieve cultural or other social goals; the elimination of all barriers to market entry (except where they suit the dominant interests); and the annexation in perpetuity of society's knowledge into private ownership. The move to digital and growth of the Internet are regarded as an opportunity to impose these goals in electronic space; at the same time opening new opportunities for the U.S. ambitions of military and political dominance.

3. The Future: Peering Over the Edge

We conclude with a speculative glance to the future, or at least one possible future. What would happen if the trends outlined above continue unchecked for a sustained period?

The central thrust of such a scenario would be that the commercial and liberalisation logic would permeate through virtually the entire media and communication sphere, nationally and internationally, largely at the expense of social, cultural and political dimensions of that sphere. Multinational industry reigns, the U.N. system gradually displaced by an ever more powerful WTO, and closed intergovernmental clubs of powerful governments and private sector allies. It leads to the hollowing out of the public sphere, a contraction of the public domain, the severe weakening of human rights in the digital domain, and to an extension of the private sphere and the economic rights of those that can afford to exercise them.

At the macro-level, this would require the resolution of current struggles concerning for instance the WTO and Bretton Woods Institutions in favour of the neo-liberal approach, with little structural change and emerging governance needs settled in compliance with the market-driven status quo.

For the media and communication sector, structural conditions and regulation of this scenario would include:

■ Unimpeded global trade in media and cultural products, with no protection on the basis of cultural, social or environmental outcomes.
■ A fully enforceable, and all-embracing, intellectual property regime that stifles creativity and diversity and yields huge rewards for corporate owners.
■ The virtual elimination of universal service instruments in telecommunication deemed to interfere with competition and the operation of the market.

- Heightened commercialisation and looser regulation of radio, television and other mass media and public service media compelled to compete in the market place.
- The commercialisation of spectrum terrestrially and in space, sold to the highest bidder.
- The gradual extension of industry self-regulation in emerging media sub-sectors.

Were these trends to gain inexorable momentum, other global stakeholders would face stark choices. The U.N. system would be forced to choose between accommodating itself to the new world order, and, risking redundancy, being cash-strapped and lacking the internal capacity to devise and enforce an alternative development or human-rights based agenda.

Less-developed countries, similarly, would probably divide between a minority who object, and so are sidelined from the globalisation process or perhaps suffer the full rigour of what they have already signed up to and a majority who believe they have no option but to join in. A few of the larger ones would attempt, some perhaps succeeding, to gain a permanent and lucrative foothold in the industry—though paying the same price as everyone.

Civil society, realising the dangers too late to mount effective opposition, would find itself more or less excluded from this domain altogether, spectators as the global media circus rolls on.

The medium term outcomes of such a scenario might be as follows:

- The number of media channels and sources available grows, especially from international sources by direct satellite broadcast and other means.
- Within these, diversity of programme content diminishes and quality falls.
- Media ownership and content portfolios concentrate and centralise further.
- Public-service media disappears or dwindles to a niche provider.

- Support measures for local, community and people's media disappear in the clamour for market sustainability.
- Public domain information shrinks, as lucrative parts are hived off to profit-making concerns, copyright is ever more restrictive and digital-rights management deny even the right to "fair use."
- Infrastructure and new services in telecommunications grow but are confined mainly to urban and business markets, leading to an ever-growing disparities and inequities.

Brought to its (unlikely) ultimate conclusion, media and communication, in a few decades, could be expunged of all voices of dissent and criticism, an entire generation having grown up knowing little else, not just incapable of autonomous political action but unaware of the concept and practice; the gap between those with access to media and those without accentuating the already great economic inequalities; media content and information becoming the property almost exclusively of giant corporations, controlling creativity and diversity on the short rein of profit maximisation. Most insidiously, the process slowly but surely transforms the very wellspring of ideas and people's creative capacities, in the end, yielding a self-perpetuating cycle that stifles genuine diversity and is purged of all dissent and nonconformity.

The circle is complete. The endpoint feeds back to the beginning. A consistent and coherent pattern of domination impels media into a downward spiral to a new Information Age Dark Era.

4. Conclusion: A Constituency for Change

The contention here is that the issues outlined above regarding media and communications are difficult if not impossible to "pick off" on their own, through narrowly focused individual national or even international campaigns. Something broader is needed that can encompass a wide range of diverse but interconnected issues, and is capable of bringing these issues to an international and global level.

This additional element, we believe, is a transnational advocacy network pursuing a campaign in media and communication.

Where will such a campaign find its constituency? Which groups and organisation might be willing to get involved? The introduction to this book bears on these issues, and related work offers an excellent starting point (Hackett, 2000). For our purposes we will distinguish among three sets of potential actors:

The first is likely to be at the forefront of such a transnational campaign and includes those whose focus is already directly one or more aspects of media from a progressive perspective. Among them are: several international associations of community media and electronic networking, international campaigns and networks, national and transnational advocacy NGOs focusing on human-rights aspects (internet rights and communication rights), international professional associations, international trade unions and labour organisations, direct action and "activist" groups, alternative media with a global scope and a few national social movements. Despite recognisable differences between them in their specific analysis and proposals around media and communication, their general rights-based orientation and rejection of both totalitarian states and unregulated corporate dominance would suggest an alliance is, in principle, possible. Such groups are already coalescing.

A second group comprises "non-core" actors in the sense either that their horizon is currently limited to the national level, or that though transnational in focus, their interest in media and communication is secondary or only a small part of the central agenda. This would comprise similar "type" of entities as those identified above, but with a primary focus on issues, such as intellectual property rights in general, sustainable development, indigenous peoples, women's issues and so forth. If a transnational campaign is to be effective, it will be necessary to attract the support of these entities.

A third set might be considered as resource organisations, willing to provide different forms of backing to such a movement. These include: Some foundations, donor agencies, intergovernmental agencies and others whose general concern for social development might, with the emergence of a transnational network, translate into a specific concern in the domain of media.

It is through the cooperation of these three groups, gradually extending outwards from the core group, that the basis of an effective transnational campaign may be built.

References

Communication Rights in the Information Society (CRIS). "The Digital Divide and the Credibility Gap," *Issue paper No. 9*, Universal Access in Telecoms, 2004. See www.crisinfo.org.

Hackett, Robert. "Taking Back the Media: Notes on the Potential for a Communicative Democracy Movement," 2000.

Ó Siochrú, Seán. "The ITU, the WTO and Accounting Rates: Limited Prospects for the South?" *Javnost: The Public, Special Edition*, Vol. IV, No. 4. Slovenia: European Institute for Communication and Culture, 1997.

Ó Siochrú, Seán. *Global Governance of ICTs: Implications for Global Civil Society*. New York: Social Science Research Council (SSRC), 2003. http://www.ssrc.org/programs/itic/governance_report/index.page.

Ó Siochrú, Seán, Bruce Girard and Amy Mahan. *Global Media Governance: A Beginners Guide*. Boulder, Colo.: Rowman & Littlefield, 2002.

Ó Siochrú, Seán, and Bruce Girard. "Information Wants to be Free," ITU Visions Paper. Geneva: International Telecommunication Union, 2003. www.itu.int/visions/.

Privacy International and Greennet Educational Trust. "Silences: An International Report on Censorship and Control of the Internet," London: September 2003. www.privacyinternational.org/survey/censorship.

U.K. Commission on Intellectual Property Rights. *Integrating Intellectual Property Rights and Development Policy*. London: Government of the United Kingdom, 2002.

Vincent, Richard, Kaarle Nordenstreng and Michael Traber. *Towards Equity in Global Communication: MacBride Update*. New Jersey: Hampton Press, 1999.

Endnotes

1 A fifth domain could be included here although it might stretch the rationale somewhat. This is the issue of affordable access to, and the capacity to use effectively, information and communication technologies. This is sometimes referred to as the "digital divide," although the term derived from a narrow interpretation focusing mainly on infrastructure provision. A succinct argument is made in CRIS (2004). A transnational campaign should consider whether to include this, and indeed other, areas.

2 These include the CRIS Campaign, Voices 21 and others.

3 "The Paris and Berne Conventions ... allowed considerable flexibility in the design of IP regimes. With the advent of TRIPS, a large part of this flexi-

1927
1960
1963
1964
1967
1969
1970
1971
1972
1973
1974
1975
1976
1977
1978
1979
1980
1981
1982
1983
1984
1985
1986
1987
1988
1989
1990
1991
1992
1993
1994
1995
1996
1997
1998
1999
2000
2001
2002
2003
2004
2005
2006

bility has been removed. Countries can no longer follow the path adopted by Switzerland, Korea or Taiwan in their own development" (U.K. Commission on IPRs, 2002, note 6, page 23).

4   In December 1996, after the WIPO Diplomatic Conference, a new treaty was adopted: CRNR/DC/94—WIPO Copyright Treaty <http://www.wipo.org/eng/diplconf/distrib/94dc.htm>. It was ratified by a sufficient number of countries in 1992 to bring it into force.

5   The U.K. Commission on IPRs concludes: "An important concern here is that developing countries will come under pressure, for instance in the context of bilateral agreements with developed countries, to accede to the WIPO Copyright treaty, or even to adopt stricter prohibitions against circumvention of technological protection systems and effectively thereby reducing the scope of traditional 'fair use' in digital media." (U.K. Commission on IPRs, 2002, Note 6, p. 118).

6   It can be argued that "spread-spectrum" technologies are greatly reducing the element of scarcity, a fact which could have serious repercussions for spectrum governance in the future. These technologies can make much more efficient use of a given bandwidth.

7   The recent open wireless standard, IEEE 802.11b at 2.4 GHz, so-called WiFi, now being used by NGOs and communities to build autonomous wide-area networks, is a good example of a standard releasing unanticipated potential (though this was developed by the Institute of Electrical and Electronics Engineers).

8   There are many publications on this. For a retrospective review see, Vincent, et al. (1999

9   The Internet Architecture Board (IAB) oversees technical development, and formed the Internet Society (ISOC), a body of coordinating professionals. The World Intellectual Property Organisation (WIPO), by agreement with ICANN, is a key body in resolving domain name disputes.

Ó Siochrú, Seán. "Global Media Governance as a Potential Site of Civil Society Intervention," *Democratising Global Media: One World, Many Struggles.* Edited by Robert A. Hackett and Yuezhi Zhao. Boulder, Colo: Rowman & Littlefield, 2005. Copyright © 2005, Rowman & Littlefield. Reprinted with permission of the copyright holder.

TAKE FIVE:
A HANDFUL OF ESSENTIALS FOR ICTS IN DEVELOPMENT
Excerpt from: The One to Watch: Radio, New ICTs and Interactivity

By Alfonso Gumucio Dagron

2003 New information and communication technologies (ICTs), especially the Internet, have shown a very rapid development since the early 1990s. The total number of Internet users has been doubling every year since 1995. No other information and communication technology in the past has, by comparison, developed so fast. Radio took several decades to be adopted in the isolated and poor rural areas of the world until it became the most important means of communication for many marginalized communities. Television is still struggling to reach the periphery, through a combination of cable and an array of satellites, although portable video has proved its efficacy for educational purposes. Internet, in its own right, has become fashionable and it is receiving impressive support both from the private and the public sector, to become the "point of the lance" of a technological revolution that also claims to be a social revolution. We will see to what extent.

Symbiosis

The most important and interesting issue relating to the rapid expansion of new information and communication technologies in Third World countries[1] is not the Internet by itself, but the potential of its interaction with other electronic media, such as radio and eventually television. This convergence is, no doubt, the best option for the future considering that the new ICTs are here to stay. Internet-based technologies will benefit from the 50-year-long experience of community radio

1   I prefer to use "Third World" rather than "developing countries," which is a fashionable way to call many countries that have actually been going backwards in terms of economic and social development.

if they are to become the tool for social change that is hoped they might. Likewise, radio and television will certainly benefit from the speed and reach offered by the new ICTs. This symbiosis is already changing the approach to technology development in industrialized countries, but the social concepts that should be embedded are lagging behind.

Radio is largely the most impressive communication tool for development, especially in the rural context. It is not only an important mechanism for the diffusion of development information in local languages and over widespread and remote geographical areas; it is also a great tool for reinforcing and strengthening cultural expressions and ethnic identities. Moreover, it can become a platform for democratic discussion and pluralistic expression of ideas and aspirations of rural communities, as well as a means to raise awareness on social issues and to collect data on local development issues. It can contribute to build up local pride through the re-instatement of community memory and history.

Can the new ICTs do the same? They should and they must, if they are to contribute to social change and development.

ICTs Field of Dreams

The new information technologies are hailed as the long-awaited solution for the poor of the world. Some organizations, too optimistic or not very conversant with actual experience in the field, are even talking about the "dramatic opportunity to leapfrog into the future, breaking out of decades of stagnation and decline."[2] The argument is that ICTs can easily convey to marginalized, poor people the truth about development and the information that will enlighten them to take, on their own, the steps that will improve their condition.

ICTs are seen as the fire of knowledge graciously brought to the damned of the world by the wise

Prometheus of industrialized countries.[3] However, these modern Prometheus should know that their attempt is too similar to the failed "diffusion of innovations" trend that was fashionable in the 1960s especially in the world of agricultural development. The concept is the same: Provide the technological means to marginalized communities, and people will be liberated from poverty. It simply didn't work like that. As Kunda Dixit writes:

> Like the fashion business, the Third World development debate seems to go through fads and styles. Mantras come and mantras go. The latest buzzword is *knowledge*. The world is now a Knowledge Society, we are told, and the global gap between "the knows" and "know-nots" is growing. Therefore, the only way to give the poor the chance to catch up is to pump in more knowledge with computers and through the Internet.[4]

Among the risks, adds Dixit, is that "the knowledge hype may tempt us to regard only formal modern knowledge systems as worthy of attention."

A bit of historical perspective could help to avoid the same old mistakes and help us better understand the deep roots of poverty: The real causes of underdevelopment are social injustice, exploitation of poor countries by rich countries as well as the poor within each country by the rich upper classes that control government, financial institutions, services and the productive sector. Knowledge alone will not change those situations.

"If you build it they will come."[5] In the field of dreams of ICT promoters the picture is rather simple: ICTs and Internet connectivity are *per se* the solution for poverty and underdevelopment. Place computers and connectivity within reach of the poor and they will magically defeat poverty. Some international consultants

2   The World Bank: "Increasing Internet connectivity in Sub-Saharan Africa," 1996.

3   Gumucio Dagron, Alfonso: "Prometheus riding a Cadillac? Telecentres as the Promised Flame of Knowledge," *Journal of Development Communication*, Number 2, Vol 12, December 2001: 85-93.

4   Kunda Dixit: "Exiled in Cyberia."

5   Now a classic phrase from the Hollywood film "Field of Dreams."

1927
1960
1963
1964
1967
1969
1970
1971
1972
1973
1974
1975
1976
1977
1978
1979
1980
1981
1982
1983
1984
1985
1986
1987
1988
1989
1990
1991
1992
1993
1994
1995
1996
1997
1998
1999
2000
2001
2002
2003
2004
2005
2006

feel good when they arrive to the most isolated villages of Mali or Bolivia with a laptop under their arm, just to show the magic screen in action, the same way the Spaniards used shinny mirrors to subdue the Incas or the Aztecs during the conquest of America.

In the process of generating ideas—or appropriating them—academics, commercial wizards and development managers in Europe and North America love to invent new acronyms and buzz words, often to name what already exists. Now we are in the middle of a fashion of placing an "e," for "electronics," before almost every substantive word: e-commerce, e-care, e-learning, e-support, e-government, e-mail, e-forum, etc. They have gone as far as to introduce "e-development." Peter Ballantyne suggests that the "e" should stand for "effective," "empowered" and "efficient":

> Instead of thinking about e-development as something electronic—development that's digital—we should see "e-development" as a different, and a better, approach to doing development, in which e means effective. Effective development results from the use of ICTs to improve the quality and demand responsiveness of a development activity, ensuring that goals and objectives are actually achieved.[6]

Development is much more complex than planting the seeds of ICTs in poor rural areas or marginalized urban neighbourhoods. If it were so simple, we wouldn't have seen the dramatic events in Argentina early in 2002. A well-developed country, in the frontline of the adoption of ICTs and with a good telephone system and electricity service, is in the midst of a deep economic and social crisis, going backwards instead of "leapfrogging" into the future.[7] ICTs are no magic solution for anything, even less in the globalised world we are being dragged into.

This is not the first time we confront the idea that technology is the panacea for economic and social change. Those who have been active in development during the past 30 years know very well the previous wave of diffusion of innovations, by which the underdeveloped countries would magically join the industrialized world through the use of modern technology graciously provided by international agencies. Behind this recipe was the assumption that knowledge is the privilege of industrialized nations, and that countries in the South just didn't have enough of it. It could only be that simple in the field of dreams of those who know little about the reality of Third World countries, but think they know what is best for them.

At the risk of repeating something that everyone already knows, we should remind ICT pushers that when we deal with technology we are only handling instruments, and we are not affecting the social, economic or cultural environment. A knife is just a knife, a tool that can be used to hurt someone or to carve a beautiful wood sculpture. Content and patterns of utilisation make the difference. A few organisations, such as the International Development Research Centre (IDRC) recognise this and promote a *social vision* of ICTs:

> It is clear that ICTs are neither a sufficient nor a necessary condition for development. However, it is also evident that ICTs, primarily driven by commercial interests, are here to stay. It is, therefore. urgent that a social vision that puts the Internet at the service of development be strengthened. The social vision proposed rests on four central elements: 1) Going beyond connectivity, 2) Promoting enabling environments, 3) Minimizing threats and risks, and 4) Maximizing positive results. In the social vision proposed, ICTs are not inherently necessary or beneficial. The challenge is, precisely, to be able to tell when, and under what conditions, the Internet can contribute to development.[8]

---

6   Peter Ballantyne: "e-development: What's in a name?" www.iconnect-online.org, Dec. 14, 2001.

7   In the early nineties President Saul Menem decreed that Argentina was a "first world" country.

8   Ricardo Gómez and Juliana Martínez: "Internet… for what?" IDRC and Fundación Acceso, 2001. www.idrc.ca/pan

Development priorities are to be analysed, hopefully by the beneficiaries, before deciding which technology is appropriate, where and how. Communities should adapt technology to their needs and to their culture, not the opposite. As of today, the ICTs in Third World countries are only experiments with a potential.

Digital (Wars) Divide (and Rule)

Almost everyone agrees now that the so-called "digital divide" is a false problem, just a flashy manifestation of other divides that have been around for decades. Panos formulated this question back in 1995, when they asked, "Has information poverty been added to the many other gaps which separate developing countries from the rich North?"[9]

Much more thinking is needed on the topic. Thinking and research with a purpose: research as a process, in constant dialogue with the participants in the development of new ICT experiences, thus contributing to learning and timely correcting problems.

For digital wars, as for the real wars, small countries spend more money than they can afford when buying modern technology (or weapons) from industrialised countries interested in keeping the wars going forever. It's good for the economies (of industrialised countries, of course).

The World Wide Web has more than one billion pages. Eleven billion e-mails are sent every day. Impressive, isn't it? However, 60 percent to 80 percent of the world's population never made a phone call[10]. Is it a mere coincidence that 80 percent of world population lives in developing countries?

The divide has never been only a digital or technological divide. It is a social, economic and political fracture. Here's a quick review of the South:[11]

- About 20 percent of the world's population lives on less than US$ 1 per day.
- Cities occupy two percent of the world landmass, contain 50 percent of its population, consume 75 percent of its resources and produce 75 percent of its waste.
- In 1996, one U.S. citizen was responsible for producing as much greenhouse gas as 19 Indians, 30 Pakistanis, or 269 Nepalese.
- About 2.4 billion people live without basic sanitation. Two million, mostly children, die each year of diarrhoea. One million die of malaria.
- Seventy percent of the 1.2 billion people living in poverty are female. On average, women are paid 30-40 percent less than men for comparable work.
- Women produce 60 percent to 80 percent of the food in most developing countries and this percentage is growing. Women farmers receive only five percent of agricultural extension services offered worldwide.

In that context of economic, social, gender and political injustice, it is not surprising that:

- Teledensity in China is 1.7 per 100 persons, in India 0.8.
- Only six percent of world population uses Internet.
- Ninety percent of all Internet users are in industrialized countries.
- Internet users in Africa and the Middle East together account for only one percent of global Internet users.
- There are more Internet accounts in London than in the whole of Africa.
- The United States has more computers than the rest of the world combined.
- South Asia, with 23 percent of the world's people, has less than one per cent of the world's Internet users.
- Only 0.005 percent of the population of Bangladesh uses Internet.
- As many as 52 percent of Internet users worldwide are non-English speakers.
- The cost of an hour's use of the Internet in Chad is US$ 10.50 (and the Gross Domestic Product per person is US$ 187).
- A computer costs the average Bangladeshi more than eight years' income, compared with one month's wage for the average U.S. citizen.

---

9 "The Internet and the South: Superhighway or Dirty-Track?," Panos Media Briefing No. 16, October 1995.
10 As usual with worldwide statistics the percentages differ depending on the sources.
11 Main sources: The Communication Initiative: http://www.comminit.com/BaseLineArchives; UNDP Human Development Report, African Development Forum.

1927
1960
1963
1964
1967
1969
1970
1971
1972
1973
1974
1975
1976
1977
1978
1979
1980
1981
1982
1983
1984
1985
1986
1987
1988
1989
1990
1991
1992
1993
1994
1995
1996
1997
1998
1999
2000
2001
2002
2003
2004
2005
2006

Sustainability: Let's Draw the Line

The "S" word[12] is a bad word in the mouth of everyone these days and makes some very uncomfortable. I'm one of those who is tired of listening to bureaucrats demanding proof of sustainability from young ICT projects. Suddenly sustainability is an issue for hundreds of independent initiatives, while the same agencies continue to support huge development projects that have swallowed millions during several decades with very little results: White elephants giving birth to blind mice. The harshest critics of small NGOs projects often work with projects that are often not sustainable either: They exist because of the constant flow of funds from elsewhere (generally taxpayers) that support and sustain their bureaucracy. What right does anyone have to exact a certificate of sustainability from ICT projects that are only two or three years old?

I would like to suggest a completely different approach to sustainability, one that goes beyond exclusively financial criteria. The concept of financial sustainability, to the exclusion of other forms of sustainability, is being imposed on us by the same forces that push the privatisation of education and health, the pushers of neo-liberal policies who consider that no social service should be provided free of charge and be a responsibility of the State, and that all human activity should be regulated by market laws.

For many the criteria for evaluating telecentres until now seem restricted to financial success. The bottom line being if a telecentre or radio station makes money, then it is sustainable. There is usually no consideration of social sustainability or the impact on social change. Why do we measure social communication projects established to contribute to community development with the same criteria we measure commercial cyber-cafes?

That a telecentre or a community radio station is self-sustainable in terms of funding does not tell us anything about its contribution to social change and development. I do not admire a community-based communication project just because it is making money.

Sustainability deals with a wider range of issues. Let's look at ownership, for example: Community ownership is key to the sustainability of a community communication project. However, this ownership can have multiple facets. Having a legal title to the facility is one of these, but it is not sufficient to guarantee sustainability. Having managerial responsibility, control over content and a say in the project's future are equally important. Sustainable community ownership requires that the community has legal ownership, but that it is also prepared to take responsibility for the project because it has internalised the sense of ownership.

This may be a longer process, like the process of development itself. The ICT component, as any communication component, should develop along with the development process, not in isolation from it. The interaction between community participation, the technical inputs for development and the communication and knowledge tools will define the success or failure of a particular development communication effort. The understanding of this process is lacking in many of those who insist on urgent proof of economic sustainability. We need to recognize the pace of development in a particular context, instead of imposing the pace of the institutional agendas of funding agencies.

We must be coherent ourselves. If we want development and social change to be a main thrust of ICTs, then we should include them in the same category as cultural and educational institutions that are the responsibility of society as a whole and governments/states in particular. Like the roads that link places and countries, the *information highways* are also a responsibility of states. Just as governments maintain public libraries, they should support ICTs whenever these aim to provide useful knowledge for development and education. Not even the most enthusiastic proponents of privatisation insist that public libraries should be self-sustainable. Community ICT projects are our modern public libraries, so they should receive the same type of support.

---

12   Steve Cisler has been using the expression for a couple of years already.

Let's look at five non-negotiable conditions for ICTs in development:

1. Community Ownership

PROBLEMS

A large numbers of Internet-based experiences have been developed in the past five years They are called many things: telecentres, public cabins, telecottages,[13] telehuts, digital centres, information kiosks, infocentros, infoplazas, information shops, community multimedia centres[14] and village knowledge centres.[15] A quick assessment shows that most of them were initiated with little regard for community participation and ownership. The contest between organizations, both from public and private, to "connect" underdeveloped countries has resulted in the parachuting of thousands of computers into areas where safe water and electricity are not even available.

An assessment on ICTs for development conducted by FAO in 2001 revealed that most of the projects are implemented without any consultation with the community. Among the findings:

■ Only a limited number of cases of community-driven ICT initiatives were found, and these had little visibility;
■ Participatory needs assessments are rarely performed prior to the creation of telecentres;
■ The emphasis is more often on providing access than on innovative ways of applying ICTs to the specific needs of communities and local groups;
■ The priorities of many ICT projects tend to be influenced more by the interests of external organisations rather than community-based organizations;
■ The thematic sectors applied often reflect an economic, market-related focus;
■ There is a lack of local participation in the creation of content and selection of ICT tools;

■ There are many telecentres where computers are available but where a lack of awareness, ICT skills, and literacy hinder the process of local appropriation.[16]

Certain governments in Third World countries have started a crusade for establishing nationwide connectivity to the Internet, as a shortcut to modernisation. It is sad to note that the same governments conducted no crusade in the past to provide safe water or roads to the same very isolated and poor communities. However, ICTs are fashionable, and governments can capture external funding to push forward their electronic crusade, with the argument that connectivity is the key for development.

We have all heard of ICT projects that have folded after one or two years because the computers were stolen or deteriorated so quickly that they needed to be replaced. This is more likely to happen in communities that do not have the sense of ownership over the project and do not feel that the installations are essential to their social and economic development. It is not a matter of external supervision (although it may help) but rather a matter of community awareness and social appropriation of the project.

CHALLENGES

The involvement of communities in ICT projects that are set up for their benefit, or any other project aiming for social and economic development, is the first non-negotiable precondition.

In this area there is much to learn from the experience of community radio. We cannot claim social change without community participation, and this should take place from the first discussions about the potential of providing ICT support to a particular region. It is certainly not enough to discuss with government authorities and even with local authorities. This may seem a good shortcut to get things rolling, but the "shortcut syndrome" that characterizes some of the ICT pushers may do more harm than good. This is not a

13 Telecottages emerged initially during the eighties in Scandinavia. The term is currently used in some countries of Central and Eastern Europe.
14 These have been developed with support from UNESCO in Eastern and central Europe, and various countries of Asia and Africa.
15 Many of them are mere cyber-cafes, commercial ventures.

16 Michiels, Sabine and van Crowder, Loy: "Local appropriation of ICTs," FAO 2001. http://www.fao.org/sd/2001/KN0602a_en.htm

1927
1960
1963
1964
1967
1969
1970
1971
1972
1973
1974
1975
1976
1977
1978
1979
1980
1981
1982
1983
1984
1985
1986
1987
1988
1989
1990
1991
1992
1993
1994
1995
1996
1997
1998
1999
2000
2001
2002
2003
2004
2005
2006

100-meter race, in which speed is all you need. This is more like a marathon, and you will never finish if you spend all your energy in the first 100 meters. In the words of Simon Batchelor:

> It has now been recognised by many people that working from the outside towards the centre is a recipe for unsustainable programmes. Programmes that consider local capacity start at the centre and plan outwards. Yet it seems that many ICT programmes and projects start at the outer edge of the "onion," and with an acknowledged general need for information and communication, outside agencies put in significant resources. Computers are installed, infrastructure is established and some salaries are given to kickstart the cost recovery process.[17]

As for any other development program, an ICT or community radio project should be first discussed and analysed with representatives from the communities. A good start would be to ask them if they are interested or not. Many rural and even urban communities may prefer to have safe water and electricity first, rather than computers.[18] If community leaders, representing a wide range of social sectors (youth, women, traditional leaders, service providers, local authorities, etc.) believe that ICTs are important, the discussion should focus on how to develop the project and particularly, what will be the role and responsibilities of the community.

The community may donate the land and take the responsibility for building and maintaining the premises to house the computers and/or the radio station and may provide volunteers to run the project. We have seen this happen in the past with community radio stations in both rural and urban areas. If we look at the perspectives of sustainability from the point of view that is not restricted to income generation, we will find that community involvement and the development of a sense of ownership over the project will also be the best guarantee to keep the equipment safe and in running condition.

There is an opportunity to contribute to the process of community organization through an ICT and radio project or any other communication project that truly aims to ignite the process of social change. A local committee comprising representatives from the various social sectors could be formed to oversee the activities of the multimedia centre.[19] The local committee could also assume responsibility for conducting content-related tasks, as often happens with community radio stations, where the nurse is in charge of a health program, the teacher prepares a series on education issues, rural cooperative leaders arrange to find useful information for farmers, the youth leaders deal with music and topics that interest their peers, and so on.

This is not to suggest that communities are always right and their word is divine. In development we usually learn the difference between the real needs of a community and the "felt needs." For example, communities may easily identify the need of water and roads, but not of immunisation or education (let alone ICTs). The key is the dialogue between the community and the planners. Communities are seldom homogeneous or fully democratic; as any human group or society, they are fractured into groups based on economic and social interests. The challenge is to support dialogue through a democratic process of participation.

2. Local Content

PROBLEMS

It has been said many times: 90 percent of the content of the World Wide Web is totally alien to 90

---

17 Simon Batchelor: "ICT capacity development issues" at http://www.gamos.demon.co.uk/sustainable/tfoa2/tfoa2.htm.

18 In North-western Romania, CREST, a local NGO, has established as a principle not to start a new telecottage unless the community really wants it and is ready to participate with some human and/or financial investment.

19 The Community Audio Towers (CATs) in The Philippines, are managed by a Community Media Council made of representatives from the various sectors of the community: Women, youth, teachers, nurses, traditional authorities, elders, etc, and it works well. For more information see the chapter in my book: *Making Waves: Participatory Communication for Social Change*, The Rockefeller Foundation, 2001.

percent of the world's people. In terms of "providing knowledge to the poor," the purpose is defeated, unless the whole perspective changes. This contradiction is more obvious when we consider the usefulness of the Web for rural communities in the Third World. High school students, teachers or professionals in Islamabad, Rio de Janeiro or Dakar may find the Web very useful, particularly if they are fluent in English, but how about a woman who works in a factory or a poor farmer? What in the Web will interest them? Where is the knowledge they can use for their own benefit? As it is now shaped, the content that can be accessed through the Internet is irrelevant for most of those that have been recently put in front of a computer. They can play around, as any kid will do with a new toy,[20] and learn how to use the machine, but in terms of knowledge useful for their daily lives, very little is available.

One of the illusions about the Internet is that because it has no central management, everyone is free to shape it according to his or her own needs. In fact, the Internet it is very much controlled by commercial rules. The World Wide Web today looks very much like cable and satellite television, in terms of content. Years ago some thought that satellite and cable TV would bring a better choice of programmes and more diversity of information to the world. Today we know it only helped to impose mainstream points of view, one image of how life should be and a very narrow way of looking at society and reality. The rest of the world appears only as exotic images in adventure or scientific documentaries. The same corporations that regulate the flows of information from industrialized to peripheral nations have captured the Internet.

Several reports on telecentres or multimedia centres in countries of Africa, Asia and Latin America indicate that the main users are students or teachers, not the poorest in the community. They also indicate that the main services used in a multimedia centre are the telephone, the newspapers, the photocopier, the fax and the computer, not the Internet or the World Wide Web. In fact, many of Africa's telecentres do not even offer Internet access. They are actually telephone call centres, perhaps with a computer or two available for word processing. When it's available, rural students and teachers may use the Internet to chat or send e-mail messages (if they have correspondents), but other social sectors, who account for the vast majority, approach the telecentre mainly to use the other services offered.

Challenges

The development of local content is the single most important non-negotiable condition for the development of ICTs for social change and material progress in urban or rural communities. We need to invent and multiply mini-networks, small geographical Webs or local community networks to make the World Wide Web really wide and really useful for the majority of people in the planet.

Again, community radio can teach us much about local pertinence. Only the development of local content can establish a radical difference between the telecentres for social uses and the cybercafes that cater to customers who already know where and how to look for the information they need. Cybercafes only offer Internet access, while telecentres for development generate local and regional information, making it available to the community. "A telecentre may well become a key auxiliary to the school and clinic, offering continuing education for local teachers and nurses (and doctors, if any)."[21]

To cater to their users several community-based ICT projects have been producing local content,

---

20 See the interesting experiment of "The hole in the wall," in India: Children exposed to a computer screen and a joystick, with no leading information to start using it.

21 Scott Robinson: "*Rethinking Telecenters: Knowledge Demands, Marginal Markets, Microbanks and Remittance Flows*," on The Internet magazine, Vol. 6, No. 2 (Fall/Winter 2000), a publication of the Internet Society.

1927
1960
1963
1964
1967
1969
1970
1971
1972
1973
1974
1975
1976
1977
1978
1979
1980
1981
1982
1983
1984
1985
1986
1987
1988
1989
1990
1991
1992
1993
1994
1995
1996
1997
1998
1999
2000
2001
2002
2003
2004
2005
2006

appropriate to the specific population, such as the Village Knowledge Centres in Chennai, India.[22]

> The poor need access to new locally-contextualised information more than access to existing information from an alien context. The information needs of the poor will be met more by informal, 'organic' information systems than by formal, ICT-based information systems. The poor lack, and need, information of relevance to their local context. This may come more from interaction between communities and community members rather than from the typical ICT-based pattern of data transfer from North to South.[23]

3. Appropriate Technology

PROBLEMS

When we think that one in every three people globally lack electricity and that safe water is a scarce resource in large parts of the world, we are reminded that computers are still a luxury.

Fashion is always expensive, whether it be Versace or Microsoft. The fashion of planting computers all over the world is a very costly one (and is making a very few very rich). How much or how sophisticated technology do we need, for example, in a rural public telecentre? I always wonder what criteria, if any, are used to determine what hardware and software to buy. I've seen rural schools with fewer than 100 students equipped with five or six state-of-the-art computers that are only used at five percent of their capacity.

Computer equipment has a limited life span; this much more limited than radio equipment, which can last 10 or 15 years, if not more. In less than five years, computers have to be replaced, but long before that time is up their software has to be upgraded. Not because it doesn't work anymore, but because the market pressure is organized in such way that new software versions—often with very few changes, in terms of actual functionality—require more sophisticated hardware, forcing changes of computers that otherwise wouldn't be necessary. Older computers become obsolete from one year to the next just because they can't handle the new software, or they can't handle the new software or they can't communicate with other more recent models. How sophisticated should the computers [and software] be that are placed in telecentres, particularly in rural areas with very little history and experience in handling ICTs?

> The Internet is now being driven strongly by commercial forces and the Internet sector in developing countries is now highly competitive, profitable and likely to flourish, with or without the help of donors. Sufficient demand for the Internet exists even in the poorest countries to make it a viable, indeed highly profitable, venture. If the market is ensuring rapid Internet growth, donors and NGOs need to focus on ensuring access and benefits for the less advantaged.[24]

CHALLENGES

The third non-negotiable condition for ICTs aimed at social change is the use of appropriate tools. Technology should be adequate for the needs of communities, not in terms of technical standards alone, but it terms of utilization, learning and adoption.

The tools are appropriate when the community develops a sense of ownership through a continuous process of "appropriation" of the project. This appropriation should not be understood as mere adoption of technology or the development of skills to handle hardware and software. The acquisition of skills is an important step, but not enough: Management,

---

22 More information on Village Knowledge Centers in "Letters from the field" (below); Balaji.V., K.G. Rajmohan., R. Rajasekara Pandy and S. Senthilkumaran: "Toward a knowledge system for sustainable food security. The information village experiment in Pondicherry." Fall/Winter, e-OTI: On the Internet, An International Electronic Publication of the Internet Society. March- April, 2001, 32-37. http://www.isoc.org.oti, "Making Waves: Participatory Communication for Social Change," by Alfonso Gumucio Dragon; "Connecting Rural India to the World," by Celia W. Dugger, in The New York Times, 28 May 2000.
23 Heeks, Richard: "Information and Communication Technologies, Poverty and Development." Development Informatics, Working Paper #5, Institute for Development Policy and Management, 1999.

24 "The Internet and Poverty: Real help or real hype?," Panos Media Briefing No. 28, April 1998.

production of local content, research methods, training and outreach activities are also important.

Why use a four-wheel drive to get to the corner store for bread when a bicycle will do the job just as well? ICT pushers do not seem to get this concept, in spite of the fact that it has been around since the 1950s in the development world. The terminology of "appropriate technology" was born after decades of failures in huge development installations that became white elephants, useless and empty structures that were never put to work for the benefit of communities. There is a wealth of literature on the missed opportunities for development, and most has to do with top-down planning and large investments.

As a small community radio station would do, it may be reasonable to start a telecentre or a multimedia centre with the basic hardware and software and observe within the first year or two if there is a real need to upgrade either the software or the hardware, or both. One advantage of new technologies is that you get a wider range of choices. Unfortunately, very few planners or external advisors seem to look at them. Most are hooked to Microsoft and expensive Intel-based computers and do not even consider, for example, the Simputer, a computer developed in India selling for less than USD $200, or Linux and other open source software.

For community radio stations converging with Internet, the needs might be more sophisticated. Better speed and connectivity and more memory and storage capacity are needed. It is now more convenient to edit and store radio programs digitally. Computers are of enormous help for laying out program grids and for limiting the manual handling of cassettes, tapes and CDs. Many small community radio stations in the Third World have added computers to their equipment, thus improving the technical quality of their work. Others already have home pages with information on programming and even offer stored or live programs over the Web.

Appropriate training for telecentre managers is at least as important as the establishment of a new community technology hub. Looking beyond hardware, Royal Colle and Raul Román found that most training offered to telecentre staff did not address the important issues:

> Training for staffs of telecentres is, to a large extent, focused particularly on operating the hardware and software of computers and telecommunications networks. Yet training can help telecentre personnel reach out to the community and strategically build a clientele that can make a telecentre demand-driven, which may be a key to sustainability. Skills like needs analysis techniques, marketing, methods for training potential users, production of software and "value-added" practices address the kinds of access issues noted.[25]

4. Language and Culture Pertinence

PROBLEMS

Only five years ago, about 90 percent of the total Web pages accessible through the Internet were in English. Today, according to some studies, this proportion has been reduced to 50 percent. Of the six billion people in the world, only about 341 million speak English as their first language[26]. Spanish is the mother tongue of 358 million people, but is represented with only 5.62 percent of Web pages.[27] Though English is not the most spoken language in the world, it is by far the most represented among the 500 million users of Internet, to the point that Web sites in many non-English-speaking countries of Europe and the Third World are often in English.

However, the situation is quickly evolving. The Internet has been growing fast in Latin America, and, over the

---

25 Colle, Royal D, Román, Raul and Yang, Fang: "Access is more than hardware: building a constituency for telecentres." Cornell University.

26 "Ethnologue" lists 6,800 living languages in the world. Chinese Mandarin comes first with over 960 million first language speakers, Hindi is second with 366 million, Spanish is third with 358 million and English is fourth with 341 millions speakers. (2002)

27 Daniel Pimienta and Benoit Lamey: "Lengua española y culturas hispánicas en la Internet: comparación con el inglés y el francés", October 2001. At http://funredes.org

1927
1960
1963
1964
1967
1969
1970
1971
1972
1973
1974
1975
1976
1977
1978
1979
1980
1981
1982
1983
1984
1985
1986
1987
1988
1989
1990
1991
1992
1993
1994
1995
1996
1997
1998
1999
2000
2001
2002
2003
2004
2005
2006

past five years, there has been a significant growth in the amount of Spanish language content. This may be an optimistic signal for major modern languages, but what about the rest? Where on the Web are the rest of the world's more than 6,000 languages, and how many will disappear from the Earth before they appear in cyberspace?

In its present form, the Internet is a new form of apartheid and has to change.[28] When I first used the word "apartheid" for Internet around 1998 during an e-mail discussion, I received some interesting feedback. One participant bluntly asserted that anyone wanting to be part of this technological revolution had to learn English, because English was "the fluid"—the blood that made Internet possible. That was his response to my statement that "the official language of Internet has become the new skin colour of cultural supremacy, cultural domination at its best." Things are getting better since then, but not to the point of making the World Wide Web a place for dialogue among cultures. It is still a very closed club, with privileged membership.

Language is only the tip of the iceberg. Culture is the hidden mass of it. The rich diversity of cultures in our world is not represented on the Internet and the World Wide Web. Moreover, the expansion of the Internet in its current form may be contributing to the annihilation of under-represented cultures. As a report from IDRC points out:

> The content, language, class, and culture that dominate the Internet can have negative effects by generating a uniformity of ideas, preferences and world visions. The illusion of increased democracy and plurality produced by the interactive capacity of the Internet may be misleading if it, in fact, reinforces existing relationships of centralized control and domination in society.[29]

> The Third World is also inheriting a *culture* of the use of Internet. Currently, the "user culture"

remains the same that has been popularised –or globalised, through the prevailing system. The following questions—which were formulated in respect to Latin America but could apply to any other context— remain unanswered:

Beyond local content, is there anything Latin American in the way the Internet is used? Are there designs, layouts, or links indigenous to Latin America? Are there particular Latin American navigation or surfing patterns? Is there anything special in the kinds of users, their age, gender, interests, or motivations that sets them apart from the community of users worldwide? In sum, is there any indication that the style of Internet usage is different in Latin America than in the rest of the world?[30]

If culture is in the soul of development and social change, how much more beautiful would it be, for example, to witness the "Eighth Art" emerge from the Internet, something so new and innovative and culturally adaptable that can repeat the extraordinary feat of the other seven arts and truly help advance human values.

Challenges

The fourth important non-negotiable condition for ICT projects in the context of development and social change is, therefore, language and culture pertinence.

Without the presence of local cultures, including local languages, there can be no possibility of ICTs contributing to dialogue for the progress of communities. Language and cultural identity are at the core of any successful intervention with information and communication technologies.

History has taught us that it is healthy for cultures to mix and evolve through a process of dialogue and interaction. No great culture has ever remained pure and uncontaminated. Cultural interactions are

---

28 Alfonso Gumucio Dagron: "Internet: the new Apartheid?." At http://www.dev-media.org/Papers.cfm?docid=225
29 Ibid. Ricardo Gómez and Juliana Martínez: "Internet… for what?"

30 Ricardo Gómez: "The hall of mirrors: the Internet in Latin America," published in *Current History*, Vol. 99 No. 634, p.72, 2000.

responsible for some of the highlights of the advancement of humanity. However, the electronic age has made the term "cultural exchange" far too unbalanced. The rules of the game are dictated unilaterally. Cultures already weakened and divided are easily wiped out by the tidal waves of open markets. The vision of a world where everyone will have *access* to the same hamburgers and the same sweet brown bottled water is frightening, but it is also a strong trend.

To balance cultural interaction in cyberspace is not an easy task. Even if we get to a point where more Web pages are produced with contents that are representative of our cultural diversity, we will have to make them "visible." The Web is more an ocean than a library. It takes a lot to "fish" for the appropriate information, because search engines only bring up the pages that recently had many hits (or paid to appear on top of the list), not really the best pages on a particular topic.

This situation will only improve if more and better local content is produced. We need hundreds of thousands of Web pages reflecting the diversity of cultures and languages, Web pages that revive the memory of communities, their collective history, their artistic expressions, past and current. Community radio has had this role during the past decades, and that is why it is so important for new ICTs to piggyback on its experience. The convergence between radio and Internet provides useful examples on how to create local content relevant to local needs but also to local culture and provide this content in local languages.

5. Convergence and Networking

PROBLEMS

Out of the blue, ICT projects are parachuted in places where there is no previous history of local participation in development initiatives, no convergence with other programs for development and social change or with existing community organizations or local grassroots media, and no networking with other ICT projects that share similar goals. Would it not be far more reasonable to always search for institutional alliances with local organizations, with existing community media, with public libraries and schools, with projects that are already affecting the social, political and economic tissue of the society?

The establishment of ICT kiosks or telecentres as a vertical activity with no connexion with other initiatives has been questioned numerous times, but it continues to happen. "It is more beneficial to use ICTs to enhance existing practices than to promote new activities for the primary purpose of using ICTs. In this light, the creation of telecentres that are disconnected from existing community organizations and initiatives is unlikely to contribute to development."[31]

The isolation of many ICT projects from others that are similar in their aims and perspectives may be one of the reasons for so many failures. We need to challenge the Western concept of the isolated and closed relationship between the individual and the computer, and evolve towards the collective use of ICTs. Too often, telecentre projects are just reproducing the pattern of individualism. There may be several computers and people in the same room but it does not change anything. From the point of view of sustainability it is crucial to think in terms of a larger community of networks and of users with similar interests.

Various authors and organisations, including faith organizations, have evoked the risks of building networks that separate human beings and which create patterns of communication that are mediated only by technology and not by values. "Might the Web of the future turn out to be a vast, fragmented network of isolated individuals—human bees in their cells—interacting with data instead of with one another?" asks the Pontifical Council for Social Communication.[32] "We must be sure that the virtual community is at the service of real communities, not a substitute for them" adds the Anglican Archbishop of Canterbury, Dr. George Carey.

---

31 Ibid. Ricardo Gómez and Juliana Martínez: "Internet… for what?"
32 Jim McDonnell: "Virtual Communities – a comment". Cine&Media, 3/2001.

1927
1960
1963
1964
1967
1969
1970
1971
1972
1973
1974
1975
1976
1977
1978
1979
1980
1981
1982
1983
1984
1985
1986
1987
1988
1989
1990
1991
1992
1993
1994
1995
1996
1997
1998
1999
2000
2001
2002
2003
2004
2005
2006

Challenges

Convergence and networking are non-negotiable conditions for long-term sustainability. ICT projects that are converging towards other communication projects, such as community radio, have better chances to succeed, because they will be inheriting a vast experience and a whole history of development and participation.

Similarly, initiatives of information and communication technologies that complement existing social development projects, for the same reasons above, are more likely to be accepted by the community and to strengthen ongoing activities aimed at social change.

This brings to mind several important examples of convergence between ICTs and existing local institutions or media. In Peru, Intermediate Technology Development Group (ITDG) is supporting the InfoDes project, which is converging with rural public libraries.[33] Pulsar in Latin America used the Internet to feed news to hundreds of community and indigenous radio stations. We have also mentioned Kothmale Community Radio in Sri Lanka and the Indonesian network of 20 local radio stations linked via e-mail. Convergence between radio and Internet is the most promising; however it will face different challenges in the Third World than in industrialised countries. As Bruce Girard sees it:

> It is clear that convergence will impact on broadcasters in developing countries in a very different way than in Europe and North America. While in the developed world there are predictions that new media and the Internet may soon become substitutes for broadcast services and distribution systems, in the developing countries this will not happen in the foreseeable future. Radio will continue to be the most important medium for the vast majority of the world's inhabitants and television will continue to have a recognisable form in the first years of the 21st century.[34]

Schools are another important platform for ICT development, not only because they exist even in the most remote rural areas of our countries, but also because in terms of skills, teachers and students are more likely to adopt the new technologies. It is important, however, to ensure the interaction with the community as a whole, to avoid creating a closed structure for a small privileged group.

If what we are looking for is the strengthening of development for social change, the convergence between ICTs and development NGOs has enormous potential. Many have realized this and are already developing a handful of valuable experiences. We are not referring to NGOs equipping themselves with computers and connectivity to better perform their tasks; there is no major feat there. The real challenge is to use ICTs as another tool in development work, as the M.S. Swaminathan Research Foundation (MSSRF) is doing in Chennai, India. The project goes far beyond providing computers and connectivity to poor communities: It has an important component of developing local content in "value addition" centres, and giving users easy access to information that really matches their needs. The Village Knowledge Centres are a good example, both of converging tools and networking on the local level.

These networks are being called "citizen networks," though they may include much more than urban areas or citizens of a particular nation. This is how Steve Cisler defines them:

> What are citizen networks? Internet technology projects that benefit people as citizens rather than as consumers; projects that help marginalized groups have more control over their existence and even give them a stronger sense of identity. Citizen networks are about inclusion and how the technology can be used for democratic goals and for economic development."[35]

33   More information on InfoDes in "Making Waves: Participatory Communication for Social Change," by Alfonso Gumucio Dagron; and www.infodes.org.pe
34   Bruce Girard: "Converging Responsibility, Broadcasting and the Internet in Developing Countries." www.comunica.org

35   Steve Cisler: "II Global Congress of Citizen Networks, Buenos Aires, Argentina," December 2001 at home.inreach.com/cisler/ba.htm

In the same article Cisler mentions Manuel Castells, who believes that in our increasingly globalised world community networks are a key element in building social institutions; Castells is positive about the growth of community/citizen networking in the 1990s and envisions a global civil society interacting and acting through networks.

Last But Not Least

I am aware of the potential of the Internet for development because I am one of those privileged people in the world who has: Electricity, a phone line, a computer, enough money to pay for the service provider and the ability to read and write in English. However, I don't need just *any* kind of Internet, and that is precisely what we have now, any kind with little to do with the vast majority of people of the world. The same is for television: Quantity seems to reign over quality.

It is becoming increasingly crucial to define communication projects for development and social change and to prevent the reigning confusion with commercial ventures. The five non-negotiable conditions above may facilitate the task.

Gumucio-Dagron, Alfonso. "Take Five, a Handful of Essentials for ICTs in Development," chapter 2 of *The One to Watch: Radio, New ICTs and Interactivity* (2003), edited by Bruce Girard. Food and Agriculture Organization of the United Nations (FAO), Rome (Italy). Reprinted with permission.

EXCERPT FROM:

AFRICA AND THE INFORMATION SUPERHIGHWAY: SILENT MAJORITIES IN SEARCH OF A FOOTPATH

Research Issues in Indigenous Communication

By Francis B. Nyamnjoh

1996 During an African Council for Communication Education (ACCE) conference on "Traditional Communication/Oramedia and Development" held in Nairobi in November 1995, I was asked to present a research agenda for Africa in the area of indigenous communication (IC) or what the late Frank Ugboajah referred to as "oramedia." At first it sounded somehow contradictory that, in the age of the information superhighway, African scholars should be setting research agenda in IC. But a careful reflection shows that this is exactly where African communication scholars should increasingly turn their attention. These scholars who know better than their friends and colleagues in the West, that millions in Africa, elites and academics included, are yet to *know* a computer, let alone pay to hook one onto a modem and a telephone, cannot afford to ignore research aimed at informing decision making better on how best to harness the indigenous communication channels that continue to serve the bulk of their societies.

Thus my basic argument for coming up with this research agenda on indigenous communication is that Africa's attempt at development for over nearly 40 years along the lines of Western experience and with the help of the mass media has met with little success. Today there is the growing awareness that imported

1927
1960
1963
1964
1967
1969
1970
1971
1972
1973
1974
1975
1976
1977
1978
1979
1980
1981
1982
1983
1984
1985
1986
1987
1988
1989
1990
1991
1992
1993
1994
1995
1996
1997
1998
1999
2000
2001
2002
2003
2004
2005
2006

Western methods, science and technology and other Western-inspired development efforts have failed mainly because the development experts or agents have approached the exercise with a "know-best" attitude, hardly patient enough to observe, record and understand the people they have sought to help, nor modest enough to realize the importance of local knowledge and attitudes towards the attainment of development objectives. Since this overbearing we-know-best attitude has been predominant for over four decades, Africa's potential in indigenous knowledge and practices remains largely untapped. This attitude has tended to ignore systems of knowledge the indigenous communities have produced, reproduced and shared for several decades through indigenous channels of communication and have enabled them to live more harmoniously with their environment. One could safely argue that the last 40 years could have been more rewarding and less dramatic in negative outcome had steps been taken to integrate indigenous knowledge with Western science and technology.

Indigenous forms of communication or oramedia denote media that:

> are grounded on indigenous culture [sic] produced and consumed by members of a group. They reinforce the values of the group. They are visible cultural features, often strictly conventioned, by which social relationships and a world view are maintained and defined. They take on many forms and are rich in symbolism" (Ugboajah, 1985a: 167). Oramedia may be seen to be interpersonal, and as "great legitimisers," if only because "they are highly distinctive and credible, unlike the electronic media which can be elitist, mighty, vicarious and urban (Ugboajah. 1985b:32).

The distinctive feature of oramedia is their capacity to speak to the common man in his language and idioms, and in dealing with problems that are directly relevant to his situation (Ugboajah, 1985a: 167). Though oramedia are the prime disseminators of culture in Africa, Ugboajah argues, many African countries tend to pay less interest to cultural development in their plans, which is probably why their media have largely represented cultural imperialism. He writes:

> The non-emphasis on cultural orientation is visibly manifested in the broadcast stations of various African countries where traditional music is transmitted in non-peak hours or presented without regard to a multilingual and multicultural audience or classified as a specialist subject—non-newsworthy ethic derived from Western concepts of what is relevant. Without enlisting culture and its artifacts, village people, the very soul of the African nation, may not be involved in the process of decision-making. They should be enabled to see and experience changes as bringing benefits to them within their own world view (Ugboajah, 1985a: 174).

Ideas, information and knowledge can be effectively transmitted using indigenous forms of communication, which are characterized by simplicity of technology and directness of interaction. In this case, communication takes place in a very nonartificial milieu. Gestures, body language, facial expression, symbols and folklore are predominant in IC. Extensive experience shows that indigenous forms of communication can be effective in dispelling the superstitions, archaic perceptions and unscientific attitudes that people have inherited as part of tradition, and which are difficult to modify if the benefits of change are hard to demonstrate. Practitioners of the traditional media use a subtle form of persuasion by presenting the required message in locally popular artistic forms. This cannot be rivaled by any other means of communication. Examples abound where song, drama, dance groups and the like are used to promote campaigns against social evils (such as alcoholism, excessive dowries, discrimination against women, outmoded taboos) or for advances in farming, health, nutrition and family welfare, agricultural reforms, national unity and integration and other goals. In other parts of the world, experiments have been conducted on how indigenous channels could be combined with the mass media for better effect. But in Africa, the tendency is still for professional journalists, politicians and even researchers, to overlook the indigenous channels of communication and to focus predominantly on the mass media as vehicles of news, facts, ideas and information in general.

With the coming of the mass media as "magic multipliers" and their sophisticated technologies, it was widely prophesied that this would completely wipe off indigenous forms of communication. Can we argue that these forms have lost their relevance and validity? Perhaps in the West, but certainly not in Africa, where the modern mass media are limited to a privileged few. The indigenous forms of communication have lost little of their validity and importance today, despite their obvious limitations. Growth in communication networks, like changes in other areas of society, is usually cumulative, with each new form enhancing but not completely replacing the older forms. This necessarily implies that we can only appreciate the potential of the new communication technologies by using them in conjunction with indigenous forms. IC is even more relevant today not only because of the depersonalizing effects of modern technology but also because of its nonavailability or nonaffordability to most Africans. This, coupled with isolation, smallness of scale, or persistent illiteracy of most of our communities, has encouraged the survival of IC as the most common, if not the only, means of transmitting information. The majority of people in Africa, particularly the rural inhabitants, comprising as much as 60 percent to 70 per cent of the Continent's population, continues to impart, receive and accept messages through indigenous channels of communication.

In broadcasting, for example, attempts at domestication of new communication technologies in Africa, so far, have hardly meant more than the mere addition of a few "traditional" programmes to a plethora of others, conceived and produced according to the same "universal media culture" known to originate from the exclusive experiences of Western media institutions and practitioners. Popular communication, as White has argued, does not consist merely of an incorporation of "many elements of the folk culture," but must be seen above all, as "an attempt to set up communication channels independent of the hierarchy of intermediaries" (White, 1980:3). As an alternative system of communication, IC has the advantage that it is managed by the marginalised people, is horizontal, decentralized at every level, participatory and free from the shackles of domination by either external or internal forces.

The need to revalorise indigenous forms of communication is greater today than ever before. Forty years of "independence" have meant 40 years of exclusion or marginalisation for everyone but the Westernised few in Africa. If indigenous forms of communication have survived and even flourished, it has been thanks mainly to government's or the Westernised few's monopoly over the conventional, official or legitimate channels of mass communication, and the clampdown on alternative sources of information (e.g., private press, research and publications) critical of the powerful. This means that since independence, the majority of Africans, who are mainly rural, have not had any meaningful access to the mass media; radio, television and the print media have been free and accessible only in principle. Governments have seen, and continue to see, in information a weapon too powerful to be made accessible to the powerless masses. The reasoning being that, should the people know more than is necessary to keep them generally ignorant of government action and double standard, they might grow too critical and perilous for the latter. Those in power see their stay in office as contingent on public ignorance of their misdeeds. The idea has always been to feed the people not with the facts but with official options only, so that they cannot and should never think for themselves. It is hard to convince a certain opinion that radio and television in Africa are not accessible, despite their availability. This opinion mistakes the mass communication potential of these electronic media for affordability. What

1927
1960
1963
1964
1967
1969
1970
1971
1972
1973
1974
1975
1976
1977
1978
1979
1980
1981
1982
1983
1984
1985
1986
1987
1988
1989
1990
1991
1992
1993
1994
1995
1996
1997
1998
1999
2000
2001
2002
2003
2004
2005
2006

most African countries have as broadcast media means absolutely nothing in language and content to the bulk of the population that is rural or illiterate and that understands none of the Western languages that dominate broadcasts. The same argument applies to the press. The term "mass media" is therefore a misnomer; for these media, limited in language and content, have as criteria of accessibility and participation literacy in Western languages, a privilege too remote for both the rural and urban illiterate.

Thus illiteracy, and the hegemonic languages of the literate few, have for 40 years and more, made the mass media in the Continent extremely inaccessible to the majority, rural in the main. Theirs has been a chronic case of information malnourishment. So remote from McLuhan's "global village" and so peripheral to the centralized activities of their own government, are the rural masses of Africa. This makes them very open to manipulation, both by the reactionary and revolutionary forces among the power elite. All sorts of statements get made in their name, by literate elites with contending pretensions to know them best. Seldom are they invited to defend their interests or present their points of view on national issues. They are permanently eclipsed by the conventional mass media, leaving only rumour and indigenous forms of communication as their sole source of information. Their "primary channel of exchanges" on local and national affairs are, as Wete notes of the Cameroonian villagers, "gatherings of families and larger kinship groups, people engaged in cultivation and herding, religious bodies, and the numerous traditional and voluntary associations" to which most of them belong. These gatherings are supplemented by exchanges during "encounters at market places, with itinerant merchants at cultural clubs, water wells and other watering places, and with children returning home from school" (Wete, 1986:90).

The illiterate and semiliterate majority thus excluded, only the very literate few have ever stood to benefit from radio, TV and the press in most parts of Africa. It has been an information highway (never mind the

THE WAY FORWARD
Excerpt from: *Internet, Radio and Network Extension*
By Bruce Girard

The 21st century challenge is to strategise the best formulation for ensuring the benefits of the Internet reach the digital deserts, where affordable access to the technology is not available and where effective use faces a series of cultural, linguistic and content-related challenges. Knowledge for development research has highlighted the imperative of spreading access to information resources. Building and improving the United Nations Information and Communications Technologies Task Force (ICT) infrastructure will be an important element of a strategy aimed at making information "available," but a successful strategy must also focus on ensuring that information is "meaningful" within an existing knowledge infrastructure. Radio broadcasters throughout the world are becoming aware of the role they can play in this.

TECHNOLOGY IS NOT NECESSARILY THE BARRIER

Access to new ICTs need not be understood to be *the* significant barrier to participating in an information society or even to using the Internet for development. There is no need to wait until access to the Internet is universal before capitalising on the development opportunities it offers.

We should not underestimate what can be done when limited technology is combined with determination and imagination (nor should we underestimate the levels of determination and imagination available). ICTs are adaptable and if basic tools and knowledge are available, people will find a way to make the technology serve their communication needs. Adaptability and decentralisation are the fundamental characteristics that have made radio so enduring and effective because they have allowed for different approaches to its use in terms of range, interactivity and content, enabling it to integrate so effectively with existing social communication networks and practices.

Rather than convenient, one-size-fits-all type solutions, radio ICT projects should emphasise adaptability and decentralisation choosing, for example, technological solutions that are scaleable—allowing users (both radio stations and listeners) to define and refine levels of sophistication and interactivity depending on communication needs, practices and the level of access that is available to them.

TECHNOLOGY IS NOT A PANACEA

Technology can play an ambiguous role in the pursuit of goals such as pluralism, decentralisation and democratic development. The initiatives discussed here all aim at promoting these goals, but it is easy to identify uses for the technology that could efficiently deprive local communities of their autonomy and limit pluralism. In the United States, for example, the introduction of digital satellite technology that enabled relatively low-cost radio networks was accompanied by a frenzy of purchases that has seen thousands of independent stations absorbed by a handful of networks. Formerly independent stations have replaced local programming with network programming in a move that has limited the diversity of the nation's radio. The same is happening in Argentina, Brazil, Peru and many other South American countries.

Fifteen years ago, "rural radio" in Africa was not local. It was a model of state paternalism in which programs were produced by experts in the cities and beamed to "ignorant" peasants in the countryside on the state radio frequencies. This has changed and rural radio is now local and participatory. However, it will be sadly ironic if the introduction of network technologies results in the emergence of a new commercial paternalism. Similarly, while emerging models of community multimedia centres offer the promise of democratic development, it is a promise that can easily be corrupted if adequate policies and practices designed to keep them responsive to community needs are not in place.

HARNESSING KNOWLEDGE FOR DEMOCRATIC DEVELOPMENT

The injection of the Internet's digital DNA is changing the nature of radio and will undoubtedly mean that the radio's next generation will be a new species, with a different sound and a different way of relating to its community. A variety of projects worldwide offer some insight into what that might be like in the developing world, but they represent only the first few steps in the transformation of the two media. There are tremendous opportunities for broadcasters but, in order to take advantage of them, they will have to experiment and to develop visions that respond to the distinct needs and desires of their communities. Unfortunately, in many countries rigid policy and regulatory frameworks do not provide a favourable environment for experimentation and alternative visions. All too often, universal access programmes seem designed to serve national operators rather than rural communities; local entities are unable to get permission to use radio broadcast frequencies, and resources are unavailable to support innovative rural communication initiatives.[1]

It has been said that the Internet is a window to the world—offering a view that encompasses a wealth of knowledge and information. Local radio is a mirror that reflects a community's own knowledge and experience. The convergence of the two just might offer us the most effective avenue we have yet known to combine research and reflection in order to harness knowledge for democratic and sustainable development.

Endnotes

1 See Gustavo Gómez, "Estudio y Recomendaciones Sobre Radio, NTICs, y Desarrollo Rural en América Latina," paper presented at *La Onda Rural: Latin American Workshop on Radio, New ICTs and Rural Development*, Quito, Ecuador, April 20-22, 2004; www.onda-rural.net/docs/gomez.doc.

Bruce Girard, ed., *The One to Watch: Radio, New ICTs and Interactivity*. Rome: Food and Agriculture Organization of the United Nations (FAO), 2003. Reprinted with permission.

1927
1960
1963
1964
1967
1969
1970
1971
1972
1973
1974
1975
1976
1977
1978
1979
1980
1981
1982
1983
1984
1985
1986
1987
1988
1989
1990
1991
1992
1993
1994
1995
1996
1997
1998
1999
2000
2001
2002
2003
2004
2005
2006

super highway), too exclusive to be meaningful to the majority of Africans.

The reason why we as communication researchers must intensify research on indigenous channels of communication is therefore simple: If the urban-based government and Westernised few deny mass media access to the illiterate and the rural majority, they must make an effort to educate themselves in the ways, techniques, understanding and world view of this silent majority, in order even to impose themselves and their agenda more effectively. On the other hand, those interested in working at the grass roots need a thorough understanding of local cultures and symbolisms in order best to interact with the people.

We can hardly talk with any seriousness about ora-media when they have not been researched into. And by research, I mean the critical questioning of certain basic assumptions that tend to reinforce particular values and positions, much to the detriment of others. In our quest for an alternative system of communication that would serve the interests of the oppressed sectors of society through "dialogue and widespread creativity" (Reyes Matta, 1986:190-1), we need to study the current extent and impact of indigenous communication systems that predate the coming of the mass media to African countries. Through a multidisciplinary approach, research should be able to guide us on which medium to use for what purposes. Thus the following agenda:

There is need to prepare inventories of known indigenous communication practices, stating their impact in the past and present development projects or what could be done to make their impact felt in future development programmes. What role has IC played in past development programmes? With what effect? In what way could it better be integrated or serve in future development efforts? How can IC be employed in solving current development difficulties in Africa? What role could indigenous communication channels play in sustainable development? In other words, we need to document the virtues of IC in Africa.

We equally need to research into alternative forms of communication that are not necessarily indigenous but developed or invented to cope with the inaccessibility of new communication technologies for the masses or certain sections thereof, e.g., rumour, beer drinking halls, markets, hair dressers, festivals, soccer, rotatory saving associations (indigenous banking), churches, clinics, schools, etc. Also worthy of study are levels of communication closer to African indigenous communities, with the aim of theory building.

We need to identify researchers in the area of IC, especially from other disciplines, such as African literature and theatre—oral and written. The importance of folklore and oral literature cannot be overemphasized. The need to research and document more of our oral tales, rituals, myths, legends, proverbs and songs is rather acute, for popular beliefs, stereotypes and verbal performances and other forms of oral art remain the root of African literature. Although there is no controversy concerning the origin of African literature in indigenous folk performances, the distinction between indigenous festival drama and drama as it is known elsewhere should be stressed. Such research should be encouraged in the objectives of indigenous oral performances.

The growing world interest in vernacular or indigenous languages also necessitates an upsurge in research on how modern media could use local languages and oral literature. The idea is to study how best to promote alternative value systems to counteract the Western value system that is presented as universal. Indigenous cultures in general should be studied and research conducted to establish whether using IC can limit threats of cultural axphysiation of African communities through the process of cultural synchronisation with the giant compressor of the West.

We need to collect relevant literature on indigenous communication in various regions of each country, with a view to contributing towards the creation of national databases, on communication as a sharing of experiences. In addition, we should seek to know the most appropriate techniques for observing, recording and retrieving IC techniques. Knowing what economic, cultural and social value (benefit) are indigenous forms of communication is important; and studies that demonstrate these benefits should be compiled. We should establish the criteria for evaluating IC, determine how the transmission of IC best can be guaranteed and explore various approaches to IC. We also need to research into how guidelines could be developed on how best to sell IC to policymakers, development practitioners, donor agencies and university institutions. If we research into precise forms of IC, we may be able to push governments to develop communication policies that recognise and encourage the use of IC. Research on national educational policy may provide guidelines for the judicious introduction of IC into the various educational curricula in Africa. And we should be able to design programmes and courses, and prepare training manuals for researchers and practitioners, specifically for training in IC.

We should investigate women, gender and indigenous communication and establish how more positive images of women could be presented through IC. What is the role of IC in terms of women's empowerment and emancipation and the attainment of gender-balanced development? Have women developed any special skills in communication that could be tapped from by society as a whole? We may need to study communication in women's associations and movements in order to answer these questions.

Research into media awareness and appreciation would be very instructive. How do indigenous people differentiate between and/or prioritize modern systems of communication and IC? What are prevalent attitudes towards both? What could these attitudes be due to? Which channels of communication are preferred by rural or urban audiences? Or different segments of rural and urban audiences? We need to know as well the various mechanisms by which the rural and urban inhabitants could have access to our

research findings concerning them and their media uses, without necessarily having to visit a library.

It is necessary to research the preconditions and particularities of each environment to ensure effective combination of indigenous communication and modern media for sociocultural development. In other words, we should investigate the links between the conventional mass media and indigenous forms of communication in terms of their mutual influence or reciprocal and complementary support. How, for example, have policymakers and communication practitioners, negotiated the co-existence of the two forms of communication in different countries? What uses have been, or currently are, being made of indigenous modes in modern mass media productions? With what effects? What is the impact of new constraining circumstances on IC, and how elastic and adaptable is IC under pressure? What possibilities are there for adaptation of IC, the modern and postmodern technologies? We must understand the mechanisms of sustaining, adapting or perfecting indigenous modes of communication and determine the role of IC in the context of current trends in world communication technological advancements. How does Africa get onto the information superhighway?

Finally, we must understand and account for the cultural determinants and variations in nonverbal communication as an aspect of IC. How, for example, are encounters negotiated between people in different cultures? How do people generally seek to present themselves? What rules govern interpersonal relationships and how are these rules arrived at? What do we know about rules binding conversation or discourse in different cultures? What are the ethical considerations or normative aspects in IC? Understanding this would enhance our understanding of the factors that work towards the erosion of African traditions.

Conclusion
Africa is currently on the sidelines of the information superhighway, and will, for many years to come, rely

1927
1960
1963
1964
1967
1969
1970
1971
1972
1973
1974
1975
1976
1977
1978
1979
1980
1981
1982
1983
1984
1985
1986
1987
1988
1989
1990
1991
1992
1993
1994
1995
1996
1997
1998
1999
2000
2001
2002
2003
2004
2005
2006

on indigenous channels of communication to reach the majority of its people. While this research agenda recognises the importance of oramedia in the Continent, the idea is definitely not to encourage isolationism, nor to idealise a cultural heritage, but rather to see how best new information technologies could be integrated into African indigenous communication systems for more sustainable development, the benefits of which would be felt by the side-stepped and silent majorities.

References

Arriaga, P. "Toward a Critique of the Information Economy," *Media, Culture and Society*, 1985, Vol.7: 271-96.

Biagi, S. *An Introduction to Mass Media: Media Impact*. California: Wadsworth Publishing Co., California, 1996.

Elliot, P. "Intellectuals, the Information Society and the Disappearance of the Public Sphere," in: R. Collins, J. Curran, N. Garnham, P. Scannell, P. Schlesinger, C. Sparks, eds., *Media, Culture and Society: A Critical Reader*. London: Sage, 1986 (105-115).

Gandy, O. H., Jr. "The Surveillance Society: Information Technology and Bureaucratic Social Control," *Journal of Communication*, 1989, Vol. 39 (3): 61-76.

Grossman, L. K. "Reflections on Life Along the Electronic Superhighway." *Media Studies Journal*, 1994, Vol. 8 (1): 27-39.

Jussawalla, M. "The Information Revolution and its Impact on the World Economy." Dorothy I. Riddle, ed., *Information Economy and Development*. Bonn: Friedrich-Ebert Stiftung, 1988 (1133).

Lyon, D. "From 'Post-Industrialism' to 'Information Society': A New Social Transformation?" *Sociology*, 1986, Vol. 20 (4): 577-588.

Melody, W. H. "The Information Society: Implications for Economic Institutions and Market Theory," J_rg Becker, ed., *Transborder Data Flow and Development*. Bonn: Friedrich-Ebert-Stiftung, 1987 (15-28).

Nkwi, P. N. "Electronic Mail: The Experience of the Network of African Medical Anthropology," *African Anthropology*, 1995, Vol. 2 (1): 154-161.

Nyamnjoh, F. B. *The Disillusioned African*. Limbe, Cameroon: Nooremac Press, 1995.

Okigbo, C. "National Images in the Age of the Information Superhighway African Perspectives," *Africa Media Review*, 1995, Vol. 9 (2): 105-121.

Reyesmatta, F. "Alternative Communication: Solidarity and Development in the Face of Transnational Expansion," R. Atwood and E. G. McAnany, eds., *Communication and Latin American Society: Trends in Critical Research 1960-1985*. Madison: University of Wisconsin Press, 1986 (190-214).

Ritzer, G. *The McDonaldization of Society*. London: Pine Forge Press 1996.

Schiller, H. I. "The Communication Revolution: Who Benefits?" *Media Development*, 1983, 30: 18-20.

Uche, U. L. "Mass Communication and Cultural Identity: The Unresolved Issues of National Sovereignty and Cultural Autonomy in the Wake of New Communication Technologies," paper presented at the IAMCR Conference held in Barcelona, Spain, July 24-29, 1988.

Ugboajah, F. O. "'Oramedia' in Africa." F. O. Ugboajah, ed., *Mass Communication, Culture and society in West Africa*. London: Hans Zell Pub., 1985a, (165-176).

Ugboajah, F. O. "Mobilising African Resources for National Communication Strategies," *Media Development*, Vol. 32 (4): 31-33.

Wete, F. N. "Development Journalism: Philosophy and Practice in Cameroon," Ph.D. thesis, University of Missouri-Columbia, 1986.

White, R. A. "'Communication Popular': Language of Liberation," *Media Development*, Vol. 27 (3): 3-9.

Wriston, W. B. "The Inevitable Global Conversation," *Media Studies Journal*, 1994, Vol. 8 (1): 17-25.

Nyamnjoh, Francis. "Africa and the Information Superhighway: Silent Majorities in Search of a Footpath," Nairobi, Kenya: *Africa Media Review*, 1996, Vol. 10, No. 2. Reprinted with permission.

EXCERPT FROM:

COMMUNICATIONAL AND TECHNOLOGICAL CHANGES IN THE PUBLIC SPHERE

By Jesús Martín Barbero

2000 1. Communication and the Public Sphere

Since its beginnings in the 18th century, the "bourgeois public sphere," defined by J. Habermas as publicity— "through which the public interest of the private sphere in bourgeois society ceased to be perceived by the authorities as exclusive, and began to be viewed by the subjects as their own"—refers to a process of communication within which the dual traffic of merchandise and news took form. What emerged in the public sphere was a new type of non-vertical association, such as that based on the State, to which only those with education and property were originally entitled.

One century later, the public sphere was redefined by the appearance, on the social scene, of the urban masses, whose visibility was linked to a transformation in the nature of politics: from being an affair of the State to something residing within the "sphere of the community, the sphere of people's daily affairs." The political visibility of the masses was also intimately tied to the formation of a popular mass culture. The devices of mass mediation articulated the movement from the public to the technologies of the factory and the press. At the same time, the appearance of the rotary press, making possible the printing of large numbers of copies, lowered costs and reoriented the press to the public at large.

Thus, publicity, in Habermas's sense, connected two discourses: first, that of the press, which coalesces the private in the public, through ideological debate and the struggle for cultural hegemony; second, that of commercial propaganda, which dresses up private intentions and interests to look like a public good. Between the two discourses is the split that leads from that which is public to the public—consisting of readers, spectators and consumers of culture.

The other communication concept associated with the public sphere is that of public opinion. This, in principle, was the activity launched in opposition to the secrecy practiced by the absolutist State; the principle of the public's right to debate political decisions—i.e., citizen debate as an articulation between civil society and political society, between conflict and consensus. However, in a decentralized society such as today's—in which neither the State nor the Church can any longer pretend to be the central structure, a society structurally mediated by the presence of a technological environment producing an incessant flow of discourses and images—that which is public is ever more identified as that which the media present, while the public is increasingly understood as their audience. Thus, the public opinion fabricated by the media, with their polls and surveys, involves progressively less debate and criticism on the part of citizens, becoming more and more of a sham. Surveyed, civil society loses its diversity and conflictive substance and is reduced to a statistical existence. At the same time, the social vacuum of representation facilitates the assimilation of political discourse to the hegemonic model of communication promoted by television and advertising.

2. Transformation in Sociability

The new information and communication technologies are reshaping our ways of being together by transforming our perceptions of space and time. Our perception of space is affected by the progressive unmooring that modernity produces in relation to place, and by a weakening of the element of physical space in our mental maps, with concomitant changes in our way of perceiving, at both close and long range. Paradoxically, the new spatiality does not result from travel taking us out of our small worlds, but from the opposite, from domestic experience that is converted

1927
1960
1963
1964
1967
1969
1970
1971
1972
1973
1974
1975
1976
1977
1978
1979
1980
1981
1982
1983
1984
1985
1986
1987
1988
1989
1990
1991
1992
1993
1994
1995
1996
1997
1998
1999
2000
2001
2002
2003
2004
2005
2006

by the television and the computer into a virtual territory to which, as Virilio so expressively stated, everything arrives without having had to depart. As concerns time, we are faced with a media apparatus dedicated to fabricating a present—an autistic present that pretends to be sufficient unto itself. This can only come about by a weakening of the past and of historical awareness. When the mass media refer to the past, or to history, it is almost invariably out of context, reducing the past to quotations—quotations that, in most cases, are no more than a means of ornamenting or coloring the present with fads of nostalgia. The past ceases to be a part of memory, and becomes an ingredient of the pastiche that allows us to mix facts, sensibilities and styles from any period without the least connection to the contexts and background of the periods involved. This sort of past cannot shed light on the present, or put it into a relativistic perspective, since it provides no distance from our immediate experience. Thus, it contributes to submerging us in a present that has no base, bottom or horizon. The obsession with the present in turn implies a flagrant absence of future. Catalyzing the sensation of having returned from the great utopias, the media have made themselves a fundamental device for the creation of a continuous present, in a sequence of events that, as Norbert Lechner says, fails to crystallize, in any durable way (beyond the mere rhetoric of the moment), the prospect of a future—without which experience cannot be created. Thus, it becomes impossible to construct projects: There are projections, but no projects. Some individuals project themselves, but collectivities have no way of seizing onto projects. And without some minimal prospect of a future, there is no possibility of conceiving change, with society skating on a sensation of no-exit.

Increasingly unmoored, then, from spatial and temporal anchors of belonging, social ties are subject to atomization and disenchantment, and their stability and capacity to bring people together and inspire them to participate in collective projects are weakened. This instability reinforces the new techno-informational matrix of the urban order. The real concern of urban planners today is not how to make it possible for citizens to meet, but how to make it possible for them to circulate, because it is no longer considered desirable for us to be together, but rather, for us to be connected. This new communication space is a tapestry no longer of encounters and crowds, but of flows and networks, in which new ways of being together emerge, along with other perceptual phenomena mediated first by television, then by the computer and, finally, by an intertwining of the two in an accelerating alliance of audiovisual and informational velocities. In contrast to the movies, which catalyzed the experience of the crowd in the street (since it was in crowds that citizens exercised their right to the city), television today catalyzes the domestic—and domesticated—experience. It is from the home that people now exercise their connection with the city on a day-to-day basis. While the transition—from the people, who took to the street, to the public, which went to the movies—was transitive, preserving the collective character of the experience, the displacement from the public of cinema to the audience of television is a profound transformation, by which the diversity of social plurality becomes, under the logic of disaggregation, a mere occasion for ratings strategies. Unreflected by systems of political representation, the fragmentation of the citizenry becomes a matter for the market, which addresses the citizen as consumer.

Over the last several years, the fabric of tradition and interaction that gave substance to political parties and unions has begun to fall apart. Decentralization, the dispersion of the workplace, the overriding demands of urban development, the smaller family, the diversification and hybridization of professions, and the disintegration of the tapestry of traditions that gave these organizations substance converge to reduce social interaction and the places and occasions for interaction, with a resulting loosening of their moorings and the disappearance of their venues for exchange and dialogue with society. Disconnected from social life by their inability to give form to the plurality and heterogeneity of its demands, and/or by the loss of the substratum they shared with society and that connected them with it, political parties tend to become merely political machinery in the governmental apparatus, while the disconcerted unions grope for a place in the new and mobile work geography created by changing digital technology and the globalized network economy. The stage for this change is set by the new conditions associated with a capitalism of flexible accumulation (D. Harvey), which, in turn, is made possible by new productive technologies and organizational forms that lead to decentralization (vertical disintegration) of the work process—multiple offices, subcontracting, a string of assembly plants—and increasing economic concentration.

3. Reconfigurations of Visibility and Recognition

Despite longstanding fascination for the realm of the State, only in recent years has that which is public begun to be perceived in its autonomous particularity, in its dual relationship with civil society and communications. In the thinking of H. Arendt and R. Sennet, the public appears as the common, the world of all, implying that it is, at the same time, the "disseminated, that which is publicized among the majority." This is what Sennet emphasizes when he relates the public to that space of the city (from the Greek *agora*) in which people join to exchange information and opinions, to walk, listen and engage in argument. Germán Rey has approached the foundational articulation of the public as something that occurs between the common interest, the citizens' space and communicative interaction: a circuit of interests and discourses in which the common element does not in any way exclude diversity. Indeed, it is the common that permits contrast and recognition of diversity. One of the properties of citizenship today is its association with reciprocal recognition, i.e., the right to inform and be informed, to speak and be heard, which is indispensable for participation in the decisions that concern the collectivity. One of the most flagrant ways in which citizens are excluded today is precisely by depriving them of the right to be seen and heard,

which is equivalent to possessing social existence or importance, both individually and collectively, for both majorities and minorities—a right that has nothing to do with the star-like exhibitionism of our politicians in their perverse desire to compensate for their lost ability to represent the common by the number of minutes or hours they spend appearing on screen.

The ever closer relationship between the public and the communicable—already present in the initial sense of the political concept of publicity whose history, as noted above, has been traced by Habermas—depends, today, on the ambiguous and intensely questioned mediation of images. The central place occupied by a discourse involving images—from billboards to television, with a thousand forms of posters, graffiti, etc., along the way—is nearly always associated with, or reduced to, an inevitable evil, an incurable illness of modern politics, a vice emanating from America's decadent democracy, or concession to the barbarism of our times, in which a lack of ideas is concealed by images. Indeed, current society's use of images reflects this to a considerable degree. However, we must move beyond denouncing this, and toward an understanding of the social product of that mediation of images—this being the only means of intervening in the process. The function of images is, first, to provide a means of channeling the crisis occurring in the discourse on representation. For while the growing presence of images in debate, campaigns and even political action converts the world of current events into a spectacle—to the point that they become hard to distinguish from show business, beauty pageants and electronic churches—images remain the vehicle for a visual construction of the social, in which visibility represents an attempt to replace the struggle for representation with a demand for recognition. What the new social movements and minorities—ethnic groups, races, women, young people, homosexuals—demand is not so much to be represented as recognized: to become socially visible in their differences, giving rise to a new way of exercising their political rights. Second, images produce

1927
1960
1963
1964
1967
1969
1970
1971
1972
1973
1974
1975
1976
1977
1978
1979
1980
1981
1982
1983
1984
1985
1986
1987
1988
1989
1990
1991
1992
1993
1994
1995
1996
1997
1998
1999
2000
2001
2002
2003
2004
2005
2006

a profound political decentering, in terms of both the meaning of active political-party participation and party discourse. Images associated with the sectarian fundamentalism that accompanied both the right and the left (from the last century well into the present one) reflect what Norbert Lechner terms the "chilling of politics," i.e., the disintegration of the rigidity of belonging, thus paving the way for more-mobile loyalties and more-open collectivities. Insofar as discourse is concerned, the new social visibility of politics catalyzes the replacement of openly authoritarian and doctrinaire discourse by a democratic mode of discourse made up (though perhaps not clearly) of certain types of interactions and exchanges with other social actors. This is reflected both in political opinion polls and in the growing proliferation of citizens' oversight and watch-dog groups. At the same time, the relation between the visibility of the social—which makes possible the constitutive presence of images in public life—and oversight, which is a current form of citizen monitoring and intervention, is more than a semantic nicety.

4. The Metamorphosis of the Public Sphere in the Information Age

The vacuum of utopias on the political scene has been filling up, in recent years, with a cluster of utopias from the field of technology and communication, as reflected in such phrases as "global village," "hyperspace," "digital being" and, most deceptive of all, "direct democracy," which attributes the renewal of politics to the power of information networks, replacing the "old" forms of representation with the "live expression of citizens" as they vote online from home or register personal opinions remotely. This is the most misleading of idealizations, since in its celebration of the immediacy and transparency of computer networks, it undermines the very foundations of the public sphere, namely, the processes of deliberation and criticism. While creating the illusion of a process without interpretation or hierarchy, it strengthens a belief that the individual can communicate without mediation, encouraging distrust of any form of delegation or representation.

In more than a few of the proclamations and quests for direct democracy via the Internet, however, there is a libertarian subtext designed with an eye to the citizenry's disorientation, resulting from the absence of symbolic density in the political representation process and the failure of the representative process to be truly inclusive. The libertarian element also reflects the frustration experienced, particularly by women and young people, as a result of the inability of representative processes to represent their difference in inequality discourse. Devaluing whatever national cultural commonality exists—due to their own inability to articulate diversity and the plurality of differences within the nation—the media and electronic networks are becoming mediators of the imaginary fabric that shapes the identity of cities, regions, localities and neighborhoods, carrying a multicultural significance that shatters the traditional referents of identity.

What the networks put into circulation consists of both information flows and techno-economic globalization movements, the production of a new type of reticulated space that weakens the boundaries of the national and the local, while converting those physical spaces into points of access to, as well as transmission, activation and transformation of, the meaning of communicating. However, the networks must not be thought of solely in terms of communication: They play an ever more conspicuous role in the rationalization of consumption—adjusting the desires, expectations and demands of the citizens to fit the controlled pleasures of the consumer.

The virtual networks are not only technical but social. In sheer factual terms, the Internet involves only 1 percent of the world's population. Paradoxically, telephone lines—a prerequisite to Internet access—are more numerous in just the island of Manhattan than in the entire continent of Africa. The more rapidly the user base grows in Latin America, the more radically the types of use differentiate the social meaning of being connected to the Internet. There is a vast discrepancy between the significance of the strategic information for financial decision making, and the insignificance of the entranced window-shopper strolling the virtual boulevards—a discrepancy that looms even larger if one considers the increase in wealth within the Web compared to the accelerating social and psychological pauperization outside it, i.e., in the physical space from which people connect to the network. All of this has little to do with decrying, in clichéd fashion, the homogenization of life or the devalued state of book reading. The virtuality of the networks eludes the dualistic thinking we are accustomed to applying to technology, making them at once open and closed, integrating and disintegrating, totalizing and detotalizing, a niche and fold harboring logics, velocities and temporalities as diverse as those that interlink the narratives of the oral with the intertextuality of the written, and those that lurk in the intermedialities of hypertext.

Critical distance, indispensable in dealing with the vertigo in which technological innovation immerses us, begins by dissolving the mirage produced by the regime of immateriality governing the worlds of communication, culture and money, i.e., the loss of the physical substance of objects that makes us forget that our world is about to sink under the weight and freight of accumulated wastes of all varieties. At the same time, however, changing this situation requires the presence, and irreversible spread, of the technological environment in which we live. Nevertheless, the penetration and expansion of technological innovation in the everyday environment does not automatically entail submission to the demands of technological thinking, rhythm and language: the very pressure of technology is, in fact, evoking a need to find and develop other ways of thinking, other life rhythms and other relationships—with both objects and people—in which physical density and sensory presence are of primary value. Significant to those of an apocalyptic bent—currently in ample supply—are the uses many minorities and excluded communities make of the networks, introducing noise in them, distortions in the global discourse, distortions through which the voice of others—in large numbers—emerges. That turn of

the screw is seen also in the use of electronic networks to create urban groups, which materialize in virtual space, then stake out physical space, shifting from connection to encounter, and from encounter to action. Hackneyed as they may be come the words from the mouth of Comandante Marcos, introducing—against the background noise of the Lacandona jungle—the gravity of utopia amidst the lightness of the interminable chatter that circulates on the Internet.

The alternative use of computer technology in constructing the public sphere will no doubt entail profound changes in mental maps, languages, and policy designs, all of which is required by the new forms of complexity that characterize the reconfigurations and hybridizations of the public and private spheres. The problem begins with the complexity of the Internet itself, a locus of private contacts, simultaneously mediated by the public space of which the Web consists. The process introduces a veritable explosion of public discourse, mobilizing the most disparate collection of communities, associations and tribes, which, as they free their narratives from the political—working from the multiple logics of the worlds of life—weaken the bureaucratic centralism promoted by most institutions, and encourage social creativity in the design of citizen participation.

Technology, let there be no mistake, is not neutral: More than ever, today's technologies are enclaves for the condensation and interaction of social mediations, symbolic conflicts and economic and political interests. For that very reason, however, their starting point is the new intertwined condition of the social and the political, the formation and exercise of new forms of citizenship.

5. Technicity and Information: A Strategic Enclave of the Public Sphere

Public space is not only where political expression occurs, but also where access to information resides. As J. Keane has pointed out, public space goes beyond national boundaries, in an international public sphere that mobilizes new forms of world citizenship,

1927
1960
1963
1964
1967
1969
1970
1971
1972
1973
1974
1975
1976
1977
1978
1979
1980
1981
1982
1983
1984
1985
1986
1987
1988
1989
1990
1991
1992
1993
1994
1995
1996
1997
1998
1999
2000
2001
2002
2003
2004
2005
2006

as illustrated by international human rights organizations, along with NGOs in each country that mediate between the international and the local. This reality is one of the fundamental rights of today's citizen, as it is a key element in the construction of collective identity. Access to information is central in two respects: as a strategic potential for democratization in our societies; and as one of the most powerful forms of social exclusion, since that access depends on both the economic order (the cost of Internet connection) and the cultural one (knowledge, languages, habits, mental skills). All of this demands concrete commitment, and entails a number of inescapable tasks for organizations, foundations and citizens' groups:

■ to develop awareness, in the society and the State, of the strategic character of the public information space;

■ to undertake action to transform the public space into a global virtual archive in which there is access and room for all peoples;

■ to propose regulations for the public information space in a fashion that ensures respect for both private life and the confidentiality of the data required for access—in a world where such privacy and confidentiality are threatened more than ever by the market and by the State;

■ to disseminate the notion that the common good is represented, above all, in the existence of the other and, specifically, the most other, i.e., the poor;

■ to conceive of the communication and information networks as the nervous tissue of human solidarity and internationalism;

■ to promote the exchange of non-available public information, and critique and reinterpret available information;

■ to connect to the Internet the horizontal and informal organizational experiences of popular communities; and

■ to provide the technical foundation for the movements that seek to recreate democracy by expanding pluralism and multiculturalism.

Bibliography

Arendt, H., *The Human Condition*, Paidós, Barcelona, 1993.

Augé, M., *Pour une anthropologie des mondes contemporains*, Gedisa, Barcelona, 1995.

Castells, M., La sociedad red, Vol. 1 of *La era de la Información*, Alianza, Madrid, 1997.

Ferry. J-M.,/ Wolton, D., et al. *El nuevo espacio público*, Gedisa, Barcelona, 1992.

Habermas, J., *History and Critique of Public Opinion*, G. Gili, Barcelona, 1981.

Ianni, O., *Teorías de la globalización*, Siglo XXI, Mexico City, 1996.

Keane, J., "Structural Transformation of the Public Sphere," *The Communication Review*, Vol. 1, no. 1, University of California, 1995.

Kymlicka, W., *Multicultural Citizenship*, Paidós, Barcelona, 1996.

Landi, O., *Reconstrucciones: las nuevas formas de la cultura política*, Punto Sur, Buenos Aires, 1988.

Maffesoli, M., *The Time of the Tribes*, Icaria, Barcelona, 1990.

Ortiz, R., *Globalization and Culture*, Brasiliense, São Paulo, 1994.

Schmucler, S., and Mata, M.C., (Coord.) *Política y comunicación: ¿hay un lugar para la política en la cultura mediática?*, Catalogs, Córdoba, 1992.

Rey, G., *Balsas y medusas. Visibilidad comunicativa y narrativas políticas*, Cerec / Fundación Social / Fescol, Bogotá, 1998.

Sennet, R., *The Fall of Public Man*, Península, Barcelona, 1981; *Flesh and Stone: The Body and the City in Western Civilization*; Alianza, Madrid, 1997.

Virilio, P., *Un paysage d'événements*, Galilée, Paris, 1996.

Martín Barbero, Jesús (2000). "Transformaciones comunicativas y tecnológicas de lo Público," *Metapolítica* , vol. 5, Mexico City. Reprinted with permission.

1927
1960
1963
1964
1967
1969
1970
1971
1972
1973
1974
1975
1976
1977
1978
1979
1980
1981
1982
1983
1984
1985
1986
1987
1988
1989
1990
1991
1992
1993
1994
1995
1996
1997
1998
1999
2000
2001
2002
2003
2004
2005
2006

EXCERPT FROM:

INFORMATION WANTS TO BE FREE

Threats and Challenges

By Seán Ó Siochrú and Bruce Girard

2004 The last few decades have thus wrought huge changes in how society strives to achieve a balance between rewarding creativity and dissemination of ideas and information, and to build and sustain a space for public understanding and discourse on the political and social institutions by which we live. There have been positive and negative changes, though the later decades were heavily weighted towards the latter.

The dangers currently may be summarised as follows.

Copyright and That Elusive Balance

The monopoly given to copyright owners has been extended well beyond what might reasonably be regarded as offering an incentive to further intellectual creativity.[1] Under trade-related aspects of intellectual property rights (TRIPS), while patents expire 20 years after they are filed, copyright is enforced for 50 years after the death of the author, and for a total of 50 years in the case of a corporate owner—though a commission set up by the U.K. government noted that there is no clear economic rationale for copyright protection being so much longer than that for patents.[2] Indeed, the very basis of such a rationale is persuasively disputed by both left[3] and right,[4] though obviously proposing different solutions.

Yet, there is strong and sustained pressure to extend it. The United States and the European Union, who set the pace for copyright, now give 70 years protection to owners, after death. It is only a slight exaggeration that the term of copyright (always retrospectively) is extended in the United States every time Disney's hold on Mickey Mouse is about to expire.[5]

What is the practical result of these rolling extensions of copyright, apart from securing ever greater profits for the copyright holders, primarily multimedia corporations?

One issue is around the balance of trade, and the enormous sums flowing from developing countries—the copyright industries are, as indicated, hugely dominated by the United States and Europe. But, coupled with this, is the impact on efforts to develop, I think copyright industries. Some developing countries, such as India, have made huge strides in the software—in 2001-2002 worth over $10 billion, of which $7.8 billion was exported[6]—and a copyright regime equivalent to that of their major markets in developed countries is, apart from the economics of it, politically essential. Similarly, Uruguay and Brazil in 1998 had respectively 6 percent and 6.7 percent of their value-added in copyright industries.[7] But these are the exceptions, and, for the most part, developing countries lack the national infrastructure that is an essential prerequisite to developing a copyright industry. Thus, although a strong copyright regime may improve the prospects for a local industry, in the absence of other requirements, the effect may simply be to channel more copyright payments to foreign industries. There is also the issue that most smaller countries would have to look outside anyway to build an industry, since their domestic markets would be too small to sustain one. In short, most developing

1   Greg Palast's reworking of a famous remark is apt, "As Isaac Newton would say now, " 'If I see further, it is because I stand on the shoulders of giants too dumb to patent their discoveries,' " *The Best Democracy Money Can Buy,* London: Pluto Press, 2002, page 66. Used with permission by copyright holder.

2   U.K. Commission on IPRs, op. cit., note 6, page 19.

3   See for instance, Eben Mogeln, "Anarchism Triumphant: Free Software and the Death of Copyright," in *First Monday,* 1999, http://emoglen.law.columbia.edu/my_pubs/anarchism.html, or Yochi Benkler, "Coase's Penguin, or Linux and the Nature of the Firm," http://www.benkler.org/CoasesPenguin.html.

4   For a recent review of pro-market arguments see Douglas Clement "Creation Myths: Does Innovation Require Intellectual Property Rights?" in *Reason Online:*

Free Minds and Free Markets, March 2003, http://reason.com/0303/fe.dc.creation. shtml, or for a different approach William Landes and Richard A. Posner, 2002 "Indefinitely Renewable Copyright," University of Chicago Law and Economics, Working Paper No. 154, Http://papers.ssrn.com/sol3/papers.cfm?abstract_id=319321.

5   Lessig, op. cit., note 4, page 107.

6   U.K. Commission on IPRs, op. cit., note 6, page 107.

7   WIPO, op. cit., note 17, page 31.

countries are likely to end up considerably worse off with the imposition of an onerous copyright regime[8]—which is of course why so many have opposed it.

A second, related outcome is that the fruits of intellectual endeavour are more expensive than they need be. This is not just a matter of having to pay more for books, to see a video or film, or to listen to music—though for billions of poor people, this is the case.[9] Scientific and research information is also covered. There have been enormous rises in the costs of scientific journals, including online subscriptions, as these niche producers are swallowed up by the publishing giants.[10] A United Nations Educational, Scientific and Cultural Organization (UNESCO) report noted that universities in Africa, under severe financial strain due to the general economic problems, are struggling:

> Most of them can no longer afford to buy new books, and large proportions of periodical subscriptions have been cancelled. With a corresponding inability to switch to the new information technologies, African university libraries in particular and, African academics in general, face a dim future indeed.[11]

Further serious obstacles are presented, even to better-funded universities, by having to obtain copyright clearance and pay royalties for materials needed by teachers and students integrated into their work. Education is a huge and growing business, and having monopoly control over key resources represents a major asset. TRIPS has effectively eliminated much of the flexibility that, hitherto, had existed in copyright and in intellectual-property rights (IPRs) generally,[12] thereby extending the value of these assets globally.

A further effect of the electronics revolution has been to exacerbate the tension between copyright owners and reproduction for "fair dealing" and "fair use," such as education, an issue carefully circumscribed under the Berne Convention and balanced as an integral part of the copyright balance. These allow small scale, partial copying for noncommercial, research, educational and archival use. These by no means fulfil the needs of poorer countries, being far too restrictive,[13] but what is there hangs under a future threat in the digital era.

Precisely because digitalisation permits perfect, unauthorised copying at low cost, the copyright industry is increasingly using encryption technology and other means to restrict access—but without preserving the "fair use" in the move. In particular, "fair use" includes rights to browse, share and make private copies without infringing copyright, though they require access to an authorised copy in the first place. Especially where Internet access is poor and online subscriptions unaffordable, the absence of specific measures to enable fair use can represent a serious practical obstacle. The WIPO [World Intellectual Property Organization] Copyright Treaty (WCT) is also relevant here, which has been ratified by 39 counties and entered into force in 2002.[14] Article 11 spells out obligations to prevent the circumvention of encryption and other measures employed by copyright owners "in connection with the exercise of their rights under this treaty or the Berne Convention ... which are not authorised by

---

8   The U.K. Commission on IPRs (op. cit., note 6), concludes: "Many developing countries have had copyright protection for a long time but it has not proved sufficient to stimulate the growth of copyright-protected industries. Because most developing countries, particularly smaller ones, are overwhelmingly importers of copyrighted materials, and the main beneficiaries are therefore foreign rights holders, the operation of the copyright system as a whole may impose more costs than benefits for them" (page 13, Executive Summary).

9   On film, it is not only copyright on the film itself, which tends to get its greatest use within a few years or even months. It is also the additional cost of copyright that filmmakers must pay for the use of every copyrighted image appearing anywhere in the film.

10   U.K. Commission on IPRs, op. cit., note 6, page 122.

11   UNESCO, *World Information Report 1997/98*, Paris: UNESCO, 1998, Chapter 3.

12   "The Paris and Berne Conventions ... allowed considerable flexibility in the design of IP regimes. With the advent of TRIPS, a large part of this flexibility has been removed. Countries can no longer follow the path adopted by Switzerland, Korea or Taiwan in their own development," U.K. Commission on IPRs, op. cit., note 6, page 23.

13   U.K. Commission on IPRs, op. cit., note 6, page 111. See also, S. Ricketson, *The Berne Convention for the Protection of Literary and Artistic Works: 1886–1986*, London: Kluwer, 1987, page 591, cited in U.K. Commission on IPRs.

14   In December 1996, after the WIPO Diplomatic Conference, a new treaty was adopted: CRNR/DC/94—WIPO Copyright Treaty, http://www.wipo.org/eng/diplconf/distrib/94dc.htm. The 39 countries had become party to the agreement by January 15, 2003.

the authors concerned or permitted in law." Though the general principle of "fair use" is carried into the treaty, no explicit mention is made of facilitating "fair use" in practice.

WIPO raises a related concern in this area, which is the tendency in digital content to establish a contractual basis for access:

> ... increasingly, copyright works are not sold, in the way that a book or videocassette was sold in the past, but are licensed under certain terms and conditions of use. Our access to copyright works is increasingly governed by contract, which may impact on the applications of exceptions and limitations, the traditional checks and balances of the copyright system, aimed at preserving the rights of consumers and the public interest.[15]

The obstacles to establishing fair use in practice, in the context of encryption and narrow contractual access terms, could thus be insurmountable.

The U.K. Commission on IPRs notes:

> An important concern here is that developing countries will come under pressure, for instance, in the context of bilateral agreements with developed countries, to accede to the WIPO Copyright Treaty, or even to adopt stricter prohibitions against circumvention of technological protection systems and effectively thereby reducing the scope of traditional 'fair use' in digital media.[16]

Whilst the treaty permits countries to extend existing exceptions and limitations into the digital environment, or even to add new ones that "are appropriate in the digital network environment,"[17] it is not automatic. It is in that gap between what is permissible and what is acted upon by governments, that bilateral pressures are most persuasive.

The U.S. Digital Millennium Copyright Act (DMCA) of 1998, setting a powerful trend, goes even further.

Under the WCT, thwarting encryption is outlawed only where copyright is concerned. In the United States, it is illegal even where copyright is not infringed. It is also worth noting that "technological protection" is indefinite, with no stipulated time limit.

The European Union's database and copyright protection also have implications for such fair use. In both wealthy and poor countries, accessing databases—on everything from economic performance to meteorological trends to demographics statistics to research listings—are a standard part of the research process of almost every discipline. A strengthening of copyright on databases affects the cost and this, in turn, has disproportionate impact on research activities in poorer countries—especially where commercial database developers believe they can maximise profits though high-priced, low-volume packages. Although there are exceptions for educational and scientific use, these do not extend to other countries unless they reciprocate in legislation—which opens the door to database companies from outside and could restrict nationally generated information.

Then there is software. The software products for which copyright is most valuable are standard business and institutional software packages such as word-processing, spreadsheets, databases, Web-browsers and the like, since these are most easily copied and have mass markets. Unauthorised copying is barely an issue in bespoke software applications. These are also the packages of most use to the less-developed world, with smaller businesses, more limited availability of advanced information and communication technologies (ICT) skills, and less sophisticated use of ICTs. The problem of unauthorised copying is, in fact, greater in absolute terms, in developed countries where ICTs are virtually ubiquitous. But, in poorer countries, unauthorised copying is probably the only option available to many users, and weak enforcement of limited copyright laws has undoubtedly been a major factor in disseminating these technologies. Inevitably, stronger protection and enforcement as in

---

15 WIPO, op. cit., note 17, page 41.
16 U.K. Commission on IPRs, op. cit., note 6, page 118.
17 WIPO, op. cit., note 44, Article 10.

1927
1960
1963
1964
1967
1969
1970
1971
1972
1973
1974
1975
1976
1977
1978
1979
1980
1981
1982
1983
1984
1985
1986
1987
1988
1989
1990
1991
1992
1993
1994
1995
1996
1997
1998
1999
2000
2001
2002
2003
2004
2005
2006

TRIPS would reduce access and use of these, limiting participation in the "knowledge economy."

More recently, an affordable alternative has arisen, in the form of Free and Open Source Software.[18] In light of this challenge, major software firms no doubt factor in the potential of unauthorised copying and sales to create a captive market for their products for the future. Given the alternative, they may be satisfied to see the use of their software by those who can ill afford to pay, since at some time in the future, many will be able to pay. Software companies already offer special pricing and dissemination policies to bring these into the paying net, even if at a very low level, in part for fear of a widespread move to Open Source.

Overall, it seems that the practice of copyright has deviated far from its stated intentions and origins in various conventions, treaties and national constitutions. The founding idea was to temporarily grant a monopoly right, tolerated by the public in order to reward and so sustain creativity and innovation but, with the promise of imminent return to the public sphere without excessive delay. In the meantime, "fair use" and "fair trading" provide the basic minimum for scientific, educational and cultural use, essential if these areas are not to be impeded. The mood today is that copyright is an asset held in virtual perpetuity, with exceptions made in special cases as long as they do not unreasonably prejudice owners' interests.[19]

WIPO is a case in point, all the more unfortunate for being a U.N. organisation. Its authoritative report, quoted several times here on IPRs on the Internet, avoids entirely discussion of the central principle of copyright to enter the public domain even where it explicitly raises the issue of the scope of copyright in the digital environment.[20] This probably does no more than face the facts: in practice, the length of copyright protection is so extensive that it is irrelevant to the digital environment. Throughout the report, rights seem to be associated with owners, with the general public to gain access only by exception; and supporting trade seems to be the main goal. Consider the following statement on the WCT:

> ... the goal of policymakers is to achieve an appropriate balance in the law, providing strong and effective rights, but within reasonable limits and with fair exceptions. If this effort is successful, the result should be a positive impact from all perspectives. Trade in copyrighted works, performances, phonograms and other protected objects will become a major element of global e-commerce, which will grow and thrive along with the value of the material that is traded. If rights-holders are secure in their ability to sell and license their property over the Internet, they will exploit this market fully and make more valuable works available through this medium. Appropriate limitations and exceptions will continue to safeguard public interest uses. The result will be a benefit to consumers, a benefit to rights-holders, a benefit to service providers, and a benefit to national cultures and economies—a true "win-win" situation.

Thus, the public interest is to be secured by appropriate limitations and exceptions and, presumably, by trade but not by entry into the public domain. Concern for a genuine balance is entirely lacking, replaced by a sense of almost generous sacrifice on the part of copyright owners regarding control of their assets in tightly controlled circumstances. Later on, in the context of e-commerce, the report speaks of the need "to reassure intellectual-property owners and commercial enterprises that their assets will be protected in an online environment"[21]21 and the importance, in this regard, of establishing an appropriate

18 See for instance, http://www.opensource.org/ and http://www.fsf.org/. Open Source is not "cost-free," but many believe that in the long term it significantly lowers costs, can be tailored to suit local needs and raises the IT capacity nationally.
19 The language is from the Berne Convention and TRIPS Agreement, Articles 9(2) and 13 respectively. The point is that this form of access was never intended as the primary means to secure the public interest, as it appears to have become. See, WIPO site, Intellectual Property Protection Treaties, http://www.wipo.org/treaties/ip/berne/.

20 WIPO, op. cit., note 17, pages 41-42.
21 UNESCO, op.cit., note 41, page 164.

framework of intellectual property. But no mention is made of reassuring the general public that the copyrighted material will not be withheld from the public domain in perpetuity.

The last word goes to a UNESCO report, which summed up the situation overall:

> Copyright emerged as one of the most important means of regulating the international flow of ideas and knowledge-based products, and will be a central instrument for the knowledge industries of the 21st century. Those who control copyright have a significant advantage in the emerging, knowledge-based global economy. The fact is that copyright is in the hands of the major industrialised nations and of the major multimedia corporations, placing lower per capita income countries, as well as smaller economies, at a significant disadvantage.[22]

A Threatened Public Sphere

In relation to the public sphere and information rights, current trends give rise in some respects to even more serious concerns since they are at the very foundation of representative democracy.

Above, we noted that the end of the 20th century saw the growing intrusion into the public sphere of information rendered into commodities and interactions mediated by the market, and the closure of opportunities to build a renewed and vibrant public sphere. We also saw the diminishing role of governments and U.N. organisations in the governance of media and communication. The rise of organisations such as WTO and the Internet Corporation of Assigned Names and Numbers (ICANN) can only point further in this direction.

What does this mean in practice? There are a number of areas of critical concern:

Concentration and centralisation of ownership does offer the advantage of enabling economies of scale.

However, such economies are not deployed in a manner that might optimise news and current affairs, educational or generally challenging content. Rather, they are used to target the most lucrative audiences with programmes that can most easily be repackaged and disseminated to global markets—mainly entertainment of limited cultural specificity or interest. The key danger, however, is the reduction in diversity of programmes and of views available. The subjugation of content to commercial imperatives removes any incentive to challenge the status quo or to take risks. Rather, it introduces a strong bias towards the entertainment value of all content, leading to the downgrading of news quality so evident in recent years. And this applies across the board in media. Cross-ownership of media, whereby different media are owned by a single corporate entity, tends to further reduce diversity and plurality, through further reducing the number of genuinely independent outlets and the greater sharing of content.

Private sector media also put an emphasis on advertising. Its thinly veiled but deeply ideological message of consumerism in itself has a corrosive cultural impact. Equally serious, the pressure of advertisers engenders a strong bias towards audiences with disposable income, largely ignoring those without. Especially in developing countries, this leads to a media for the wealthy.

Beyond these, a further danger is in sight, quite a frightening prospect that hopefully will not proceed too far. This is the emergence, in some countries, of a more intimate convergence between the media and political and economic power. Already mentioned is apparent collusion between some government and private sector media, for instance in some former Soviet countries, often accompanied by intimidation. More worrying in some ways is the case of Italy, where the political leader is also the biggest media owner, and where, despite assurances, many believe he has used his media interests to gain power and deflect criticism. Another variation is seen in Venezuela, where even the conservative *Economist* magazine

---

22 UNESCO, op.cit., note 41, page 320, Chapter 23.

1927
1960
1963
1964
1967
1969
1970
1971
1972
1973
1974
1975
1976
1977
1978
1979
1980
1981
1982
1983
1984
1985
1986
1987
1988
1989
1990
1991
1992
1993
1994
1995
1996
1997
1998
1999
2000
2001
2002
2003
2004
2005
2006

has criticised media interests there for colluding with business in trying to overthrow the democratically elected government.[23] More subtle is the situation in the United Kingdom, where the Blair government is regularly accused by all sides of implementing a regulatory regime favouring News Corporation because of the enormous power it wields to affect public opinion there. This may be an example of where the media attains a certain threshold of power and influence at which the government can no longer regulate effectively for fear of the negative consequences on its electoral performance.

These point beyond cases of media or business influence, or even of a tacit alliance or coalescing of strategic interests. They are a much closer merging of media with political and economic interests. All are cases of an undermining of the public sphere, and of the partial or complete breakdown of the "compact" between people and government, in the sense that serious and deliberate distortions are introduced by sectional interests into public discourse.

A most tragic demonstration in recent history of the influence of the media and its hijacking by political power—though in this case the medium in question was simply an arm of political power—was Radio Milles Collines. This was the station that incited genocide in Rwanda, and is regarded as having played a significant role in spreading the killing rapidly and widely. These were exceptional circumstances in which all checks and balances were absent. But the question might nevertheless be asked, how different this is, in its impact, to media—ultimately for commercial reasons—which in a rich and powerful country incites or supports the government to go to war with another? Is the only difference that the blood is shed on another soil? This, too, is a question of ensuring a healthy public sphere.

23 In an editorial, the Economist wrote, "Devoid of a coherent programme beyond anti-Chavismo, the opposition relies too much on the newspapers and TV stations it owns to take the place of political parties." "Venezuela's Conflict: No End to the Pain," The Economist, Feb. 6, 2003. Venezuela's media is dominated by the Cisneros family, one of Latin America's richest.

In terms of information and communication rights in the digital era, the situation is also precarious and getting worse. The attacks on New York and Washington in September 2001 and the response of the United States in declaring war on a globalised terrorist threat has set in train a series of efforts at both national and international levels to enact laws claiming to defend against terrorist attacks. They include curtailing hard-won information and communication rights and greatly increasing digital surveillance. Little public debate has been the hallmark of many of these, rushed through in the context of a climate of fear, intolerance of dissent and polarisation of positions.

Growing Antagonism Between Copyright and Public Sphere

There is a further characteristic emerging in the current era, one that casts the issues in a new light and which may have major consequences for the future. It also justifies the inclusion … of these two key social sets of rules around information.

What characterises the current era is that these two pillars of social norms on information—copyright and the public sphere—are more and more coming into conflict.

Whilst there has always been tension between the two, now they are reaching a point where one is directly pitted against the other. Specifically, the depth and breadth of the copyright regime, backed up by the power of the copyright industries, their governments and the WTO-enforcement procedures, has reached the point where further expansion is not only highly questionable from an economic and development perspective, it is also in danger of undermining the public sphere, and hence the system of representative democracy. What is needed, if we are to serve the needs of less-developed countries and to build further on democratic principles, is the restoration of a reasonable balance.

Up until now, they rarely directly confronted each other. Human rights and the public sphere were slowly

1927
1960
1963
1964
1967
1969
1970
1971
1972
1973
1974
1975
1976
1977
1978
1979
1980
1981
1982
1983
1984
1985
1986
1987
1988
1989
1990
1991
1992
1993
1994
1995
1996
1997
1998
1999
2000
2001
2002
2003
2004
2005
2006

carving out their domain, built on the struggles of people nationally and a deep desire for freedom of expression and social equity, and were given a major boost in the wake of the Second World War. Copyright has continually built outwards from its initial core concern with protecting authors and publishers of books, has broadened in scope to new media (even including software) and extended to claim neighbouring rights and ever longer monopoly periods. At this point, copyright and the power of industry is such that it is eating not only into the potential future public domain in general, but into that especially sensitive and important area of the public sphere and information rights.

Put another way, a central requirement of the public sphere is that all people have equal and ready access to impartial information and analysis. This part of information, partly in the public domain but also partly within the restricted sphere of copyright information, is critical to the operation of a representative democracy and to social equity. However, copyright works in the other direction, restricting information. What is now happening is that, with the increasing commercialisation of the media and the weakening of regulation in the public interest, more and more information that is critical to grease the wheels of the public sphere is copyrighted. And the copyright industries are not slow to maximise the value to be obtained from their rights to this information. This, in turn, means that access to information is more and more determined by who can afford it; and the nature of the information itself is transformed to maximise the value and the profits to the producers.

EXCERPT FROM:

COMMUNICATION, NETWORKS AND SOCIAL CHANGE

Keys for the Creative Incorporation of Information and Communication Technologies Into Social Movements

By Víctor Manuel Marí Sáez

2004 From Flags in the Wind to Multiform Networks

The road that social movements have traveled from the 1970s to date could be reread as a paradoxical process that has come to reunite in new ways the dispersed fragments blown apart by the globalization process. An encounter takes place among different organizations, apparently unrelated, but ones which deep down, at the level of what is essential, discover common motives to get together, in unions more complex, rich and plural than the ones the *organized battalions* of the Fordist period were able to generate.

In this time of transition, it is important to pay attention to signs suggesting the birth of new solidarity and communication networks. Manuel Castells uses a very suggestive formulation to refer to this transition: He speaks of the transition from flags in the wind to multiform networks. The visual power of this expression allows us to focus on the information technology–social movement binomial from a metaphorical point of view:

> It is this decentralized and subtle character of the social change network that makes it so difficult to perceive and identify the new identity projects that are on the way. Since our historical vision is so used to organized battalions, flags in the wind and social change proclamations that follow a script, we feel lost when we face the subtle penetration of the changes of the symbols processed through multiform networks, outside the headquarters of power. It is in these back alleys of society, whether in alternative electronic networks or popular networks of community

resistance, where I have perceived the embryos of a new society, carved in the fields of history by the power of identity (Castells, 1998: 402).

From the experiences that emerged in the back alleys of informational and global capitalism we have seen how new ways of appropriation of information technology by social movements arise. The recent dates of 1994, 1999 and 2001 are significant moments for the analysis of these relationships.

In 1994, the Forum *50 años bastan* (50 Years Are Enough) takes place and helps re-focus the global resistance movement that since 1988 has been bringing together different movements opposed to the policies of supra-state institutions such as the International Monetary Fund and the World Bank. BBS (Bulletin Board System) is used to organize and develop this Forum: The incipient seeds of the Internet, which provided technological help to organizations trying to denounce the logic of these powerful institutions.[1] In that same year, on January 1, the Zapatista National Liberation Army (*Ejército Zapatista de Liberación Nacional,* EZLN) gains control of the main towns close to the Lacandona forest, in the Southern state of Chiapas (Mexico). Some have spoken of the Zapatista movement as the *first informational guerrilla,* a movement that uses weapons to make themselves heard, and that understands that in the new world order information can be much more powerful than bullets.[2] Francisco Sierra points to this as well when he indicates that communication was conceived by the EZLN as a political instrument.[3]

In November 1999, in Seattle (U.S.), when the capitalist globalization process was orchestrating the staging of what it seemed would be an inevitable additional twist in the liberalization of markets, a movement of social movements emerged vis-à-vis public opinion

that made a scream echo throughout the world: We human beings are not merchandise. Sheltered by this movement, the Indymedia Web site is born, managed by independent journalists who have faith in giving voice to the citizenship to build its discourses about reality from other points of view, different and divergent from those broadcast by the media.

In January 2001 … an alternative to this forum [World Economic Forum in Davos] is convened in the Brazilian city of Porto Alegre, bringing together social movements and those sectors among civic society which favor the construction of another possible world, different from that generated by the *globalitarian* project. In the World Social Forums (in 2001, 2002 and 2003)[4], communication networks linked to social movements from across the world get together, mainly from double origins; on the one hand, groups that have been protagonists of the birth and development of communication for development in Latin America, defined by Manuel Chaparro as a "special" G-8[5]. On the other hand, communication projects linked to movements of resistance and transformation of the neoliberal globalization get together in Porto Alegre.

The Emergence of the Network Model

After the dark 80s—the period of ferocious application of neoliberal policies—in the threshold of the 21st century a multicultural social movement has revived under the motto "another world is possible." The new solidarity and communication networks are organizational formulas that reunite important attributes, which must be reflected upon: They posses a high degree of flexibility, horizontality, interconnection capacity, and closeness between their members.[6]

1   López, Sara: *"Qué es Nodo50»* in *Foro de experiencias Nuevas Tecnologías y Movimientos Sociales.* Instituto Andaluz de la Juventud. Córdoba. 2003.

2   Martinez Torres, Maria Elena (1996): *Networking global civil society: the zapatista movement. The first informational guerrilla.* University of California.

3   Sierra Caballero, Francisco (1997): *Comunicación e insurgencia. La comunicación y la propaganda en la guerra de Chiapas.* Hiru. Bilbao.

4   A marvelous introduction to the debates and proposals of the Porto Alegre Forums can be found in the book *Justicia Global. Las alternativas de los movimientos del Foro de Porto Alegre,* by Rafael Díaz Salazar (ed.). Icaria Editorial/Intermón Oxfam. Barcelona. 2002.

5   Manuel Chaparro refers to eight communication networks in Latin America and the Caribbean that are committed to the use of the media to promote development, education and the settlement of democracy. See Chaparro, Manuel (ed.) (1999): *La democratización de los medios.* Diputación de Sevilla. Sevilla, pages 84-86.

6   To delve deeper into these matters see Burch S., Leon O. & Tamayo E. (2001): *Movimientos sociales en la red.* ALAI. Ecuador.

■ *Flexibility* because this is an organization being constructed over time and in this construction process, always open and constant, the network stretches or shrinks according to the needs of the environment, the social actors involved, or strategic alternatives. Undoubtedly, this is an essential quality for an ever-changing social context.

■ *Horizontality* between the members of a network, which results in different nodes having the same participation level, the same capacity for decision making. These are decentralized structures articulated on the principle of equality. Horizontality is at the service of the participation of the organization's members, who do not need permission from a management board to exercise this right.

■ *Interconnection* is in the network's origin and growth process. The network is strengthened in the process of incorporating new members, enhancing already existing relationships and making them more complex, establishing a great net. The network's logic leads to searching for the interconnections of everything with everything: the global and the local, ecology with politics and economy, etc.

■ *Closeness* is another important element of communication and solidarity networks. Networking is not only a more efficient form of organization; together with its functional dimension—undeniable and necessary—there is another dimension no less important: the relational and vital dimension. Networks are the way in which we visualize our "map of relationships"; networks channel our belonging to different groups, our identity, our existence.

The *relational* approach invites us to overcome excessively mechanistic views of social organizations, from which we could reach the point of designing linear action processes conceived in a lab with a rule and a set-square, as if such plans would work in the same way in the real world. Social processes of communication and social transformation are not like train stations that we pass through regularly and on time as planned; reality is always surprising; what is real resists classification; life struggles to live. This is why

Irantzu Larrañaga will say that networks, besides being useful to exchange data and information, are useful to circulate affection, encouragement, solidarity. Networks work to remind their members that they are not alone in the world, that there are people in the world just like them.

The new organizational model with its networks implies a true alternative to Fordist organizational models. When a social organization considers the incorporation of e-mail, the Internet, the design of its Web site, etc., many times only the instrument, the technological dimension, is perceived. However, along the way, in the process of incorporation, the communicational question might arise: How does this tool work to improve communication within the organization, rendering it more flexible? To what extent do new information technologies facilitate the enhancement of the creation of solidarity networks in the local and global environment?

Specific Elements of Communication Generated in Social Movements

Moving on to a more concrete level, we mention some features that allow us to identify elements specific and characteristic of communicational processes set in motion by social movements:

1. THE DENOUNCEMENT OF EXCLUSION AND SOCIAL INEQUALITY PROCESSES GENERATED BY CAPITALIST GLOBALIZATION, AND OF THE WAY IN WHICH THIS SOCIAL SYSTEM TURNS INFORMATION AND COMMUNICATION INTO YET ANOTHER MERCHANDISE.

In the era of access, the capitalist system intends to render all human actions fully commercial. Its objective is to turn the world into a grand casino where everything can be bought and sold. As pointed out by Herbert Schiller in *Aviso para Navegantes*, expectations generated by the emergence of new advances in communication technologies have been frustrated by their focus on serving economic interests. Unmasking the advertising wrapping that surrounds new information technologies is of vital

1927
1960
1963
1964
1967
1969
1970
1971
1972
1973
1974
1975
1976
1977
1978
1979
1980
1981
1982
1983
1984
1985
1986
1987
1988
1989
1990
1991
1992
1993
1994
1995
1996
1997
1998
1999
2000
2001
2002
2003
2004
2005
2006

importance, as is overcoming the seductive discourse attached to them, and discovering their real potential in local and global spheres.

Issues regarding information and communication should be posed, as indicated by Sally Burch, as a basic need for civic society. In order to really participate in public matters that affect us all, we need to be duly informed and have the ability to express different points of view vis-à-vis reality through the media.

This radical questioning of the capitalist system and its excluding and mercantile logic of life on earth is at the center of the communication discourse developed by social movements. There is a necessary correlation between communication and society, between communication technologies and social context; the communication perspective of social movements is framed in a wider project that questions the capitalist system. On a positive note, and paraphrasing Paulo Freire, these networks *teach one to read the media* as part of a more encompassing process of *teaching one to read the world*, in order to transform it. Media education, the use of communication networks, the appropriation of technology, do not have meaning if they are not set within the context of a social change process. Their communication programmes arise precisely in connection with this more encompassing process of social transformation. The process itself raises the question of how to communicate and how to build networks.

2. THE IDENTIFICATION OF INFORMATION TECHNOLOGIES AS "INFORMATIONAL CAPITAL" FOR SOCIAL ORGANIZATIONS.

It is important for social movements to acknowledge that new information and communication technologies (NICTs) are not merely instruments to be used but, rather, logics and dynamics that must be appropriated.

This perspective neglects the fact that communication is not so much a matter of media, but rather of mediation.[7] The center of communicative processes does not lie in technological instruments, but in the social processes through which people relate to NICTs, a relationship in which identities and social imaginaries are built. In other words, a criterion to discern and assess the suitability of one or another technology, and ways of incorporating it, is to look at the social processes in which a social organization is embedded, and analyze the communicative ways through which the people this organization caters to understand the world, communicate and express themselves. In this way, reflection about communication stops being merely instrumental, de *cacharreo*, and becomes a matter of culture. This allows us to rediscover communication as an ability to relate, to create bonds and construct meaning.

In this sense, Hamelink's contributions regarding the concept of *"informational capital"* allow us to move forward along paths that lead social movements to the appropriation and use of NICTs.

The concept of informational capital includes "the financial capability to pay for the use of electronic networks and information services, the technical ability to handle these networks' infrastructures, the intellectual capacity to filter and evaluate information, as well as the active motivation to seek information and the ability to apply such information to social situations."[8]

Informational capital refers to specific technical and instrumental conditions. However, the novelty does not lie there, but in the ways in which information is received, selected and appropriated as knowledge useful to transform reality. This is how logic leading to the transformation of information into knowledge, that invites us to look into processes rather than products, and discover the organizational transformations that could maximize the use of information

7   Martín Barbero, Jesús (1987): *De los medios a las mediaciones*. Gustavo Gili. Barcelona.

8   In Burch S. , Leon O. & Tamayo E. (2001): *Movimientos sociales en la red*. ALAI. Ecuador.

technologies—processes that turn information into knowledge, etc.—become more interesting.

3. DISCOVERING THAT LOGIC OF NETWORKING PRECEDES THE INTERNET AS AN INSTRUMENT.

This idea is central for technological appropriation by social movements. Organizations that already functioned based on the logic of the net have seen how the new communication tool—the Internet—which became popular at the end of the 1990s, gives new dimension to the processes of change they were involved in. In other words, it is not enough to introduce a technology such as the Internet in order to network. Organizations that tend to concentrate and monopolize information and decision making have to not only introduce new communication tools, but also to modify organizational models that conceive information as an entity to be monopolized, instead of understanding it as something that must be distributed and circulated.

Social organizations that were flexible, horizontal and interconnected with other organizations are the ones making the most of the new media. In the varied field of social movements, there are at least three traditions with ideological principles directly connected to the logics of the net: the libertarian, feminist and ecologist movements. In organizations that support a decentralized and horizontal structure based on the social being's freedom (anarchism); in those that expose the interconnection of everything with everything (ecologists); and in those that understand closeness, intuition and globality as constitutive elements of solidarity networks (feminists), we can find keys for the incorporation of NICT with models of network organization.

4. SUPPORTING FREE SOFTWARE

The creation and promotion of the use of free software has been a genuine contribution of social movements and the hacker community, understood as an ethical, technological and affordable alternative to the projects of large commercial computer software companies (Mari Saez, 2003). …

Free software has greater ethical coherence with societal projects based on participation and solidarity, in building a world community of computer programmers who freely share their knowledge for the improvement of technological support. … it meets higher quality and security standards; the danger of feared viruses virtually disappears….

5. Adoption of the key principles of popular communication inspired by Paulo Freire's ideas

Paulo Freire's contributions in the fields of education and popular communication have been put into practice by a great number of social organizations, especially in Latin American contexts. Francisco Sierra has summarized the five main characteristics of a popular edu-communication model (Sierra Caballero, 2000: 222-223):

1. Popular education is transformative education.
2. Popular education is based on reflexive praxis, in which action guides and orients the educational content.
3. The methodology of popular education must be radically democratic.
4. The action-reflection-action dynamic gives a process-oriented character to learning.
5. Popular education is part of an integral educational process, which tries to overcome the fragmentation between theory and practice, education and work, education and politics.

For social movements, conceiving communication from this perspective implies assuming a communicational state of mind and style more coherent with the objectives of social transformation. As Mario Kaplún indicated, there is a close relationship between communication, construction of the social fabric, and social transformation. Popular communication is necessarily transforming, not only in its objectives but also in the process itself, since it includes participation and the prominence of popular sectors in its development. It allows the articulation of the social fabric in solidarity networks that democratize democracy starting from its more basic levels—being

1927
1960
1963
1964
1967
1969
1970
1971
1972
1973
1974
1975
1976
1977
1978
1979
1980
1981
1982
1983
1984
1985
1986
1987
1988
1989
1990
1991
1992
1993
1994
1995
1996
1997
1998
1999
2000
2001
2002
2003
2004
2005
2006

able to speakup—to the most complex ones, such as developing new practices to manage local power.

An idea characteristic of Freire's thinking states that *the world is not; it is being.* We live in a continuous process of construction of the social order and, therefore, in the real and historical possibility of setting social processes of transformation and change in motion. Perhaps a crucial battle is at stake from this perspective, that of orchestrating the machinery of "single thinking" with the intention of preventing from the beginning any possibility of imagining other possible worlds.

Joao Pedro Stédile, leader of The Landless Workers' Movement (Brazil), claims that what gives strength to the people is not what they hold in their hands, but what they have in their heads. Starting from these fundamentals, reflecting on communication processes in the framework of social movements implies renewing existing knowledge and approaches towards communication, technologies, organizational models, and alternative projects of society, so that critical and creative processes can be developed with the information technologies at hand.

References

Castells, Manuel (1997): *La era de la información (Tres volúmenes).* Madrid. Alianza Editorial.

Chaparro, Manuel (editor) (1999): *La democratización de los medios. II Congreso de radio y televisiones locales, públicas y alternativas.* Sevilla. Diputación Provincial de Sevilla.

Mari Saez, Víctor Manuel (2002): *Globalización, nuevas tecnologías y comunicación.* Ediciones de la Torre. Madrid.

Mari Saez, Víctor Manuel: *De las banderas al viento a las redes multiformes. Globalización, nuevas tecnologías y cambio social,* en Sierra, F. y Quirós, F. (coord.) (2001): *Economía Política de la Comunicación y la Cultura.* Comunicación Social Ediciones. Sevilla.

Mari Saez, Víctor Manuel: *La información, ¿derecho o mercancía?. Democratizar las comunicaciones y radicalizar la democracia en los debates sobre la Sociedad de la Información,* en Revista Crítica (Madrid), nº 906, Junio 2003.

Sierra Caballero, Francisco (2000): *Introducción a la Teoría de la Comunicación Educativa.* Editorial MAD. Sevilla.

Marí Sáez, Victor Manuel. "Comunicación, Redes y Cambio Social," Chapter 1 in *La Red es de Todos. Cuando los Movimientos Sociales se apropian de la Red.* [*The Network is for All : When Social Movements Take Over the Net.*] Madrid, Spain: Editorial Popular, 2004. Reproduced with permission of the author.

DIGITAL GAP OR DIGITAL INCLUSION?

By Scott S. Robinson

2004 We have heard for years of the "digital gap," without knowing, in an empirical sense, what it referred to, suspecting all the while that its widespread use was just one more campaign to fashion a legend to justify the marketing and consumption of computer products and applications in "emerging markets."[1] And indeed, international organizations' concern about the "gap" coincides with a dramatic expansion of the market for new information and communications technologies (ICTs) in Latin America over the last ten years. The fact that a majority of the population in individual countries lacks Internet access equates to potential demand, and policymakers have felt pressure to address the issue of access, as well as the related issue of prices for hardware and software.

To date, however, the problem has not been addressed with any great degree of seriousness. Accompanying this process is a novel turn of magical thinking, by which a home computer becomes a ticket for admission to the information society. What this implies for the future of the democratic process, which has recently been undergoing an amorphous reconfiguration under the deceptive rubric of "e-government" and "e-governance," is far from clear at this point. The term "digital gap" is used to refer to the phenomenon of unequal access to ICTs, to people's unequal capacity to use these technologies, to differences in how they actually use them currently, and to the differing impacts of these discrepancies on personal, family and community well-being. Curiously, one seldom hears of "digital inclusion," a notably complex notion in today's context of ICT growth, largely impermeable regulatory agencies and evolving "Latin American democracies."

Digital Inclusion—A Complex and Challenging Concept

The concept of digital inclusion, as conceived here, refers to all public policies bearing on the countries' and region's construction, management and expansion of wired and wireless *public* digital networks, as well as to content offerings and the development of local capacities. It also touches on the issue of uniform privacy and security guarantees for all, as well as on the problem of training and incentives to develop new tools—open-source software, cellular telephone applications, etc. Though it represents a noble objective for national funding, progress—or even planning—toward that objective seldom goes beyond rhetoric derived from, and coordinated with, the periodic and cyclical declarations of, various international organizations.

Most importantly, the process of digital inclusion manifests itself as a continual matter of negotiation among the countries' political, financial, commercial, and sometimes, social elites.[2] "Digital inclusion" is simultaneously a process of political control,[3] a "politically correct" (indeed, impeccable) goal, a lucrative business for the few (and interrelated) providers of the technologies involved, a challenge for creative computer experts in the countries, the subject (before 9/11) of myriad speeches and international conferences,[4] and a new philanthropic vein fed by an ample supply of donors, foundations and government entities in Northern countries.

Few civil society organizations have undertaken explicit commitments to digital inclusion. Even fewer political party platforms include principles or legislative initiatives on the subject, and those that do end up serving as a sort of illusion, one that commercial interests can appropriate to justify selling equipment and software, while creating regulatory entities responsive to their interests. Nor is leadership forthcoming

from politicians and public officials. Only four countries have a functioning universal access fund—the concrete demonstration that a Latin American state is committed to making affordable Internet access available to all.[5] There is a risk of confusing government programs aimed at fostering Internet connectivity through schools, libraries and health centers, with true digital inclusion programs. In the author's view, these types of "inclusion," despite their pretensions of facilitating Web-surfing for all, are in truth moored at the wharf of the information society (another not-so-badly-named phantasm, considering the number of cybernauts in today's world, and the different activities made possible by the software developed in recent years—notwithstanding the fact that one might argue that the information "society" is, to date, little more than a club).

The Neoliberal Development Model

The speed with which these technologies have been adopted is daunting. However, resisting the temptation to swoon, one must call upon one's analytic faculties to dispel the rhetorical fog surrounding the "digital gap" and examine the particulars of the "wiring" process now occurring in each country. This is taking place within an international context, in which trade agreements and intellectual property agreements, alongside the expansion and entrenchment of interrelated digital technology multinationals,[6] permit a free flow of investment (mostly venture) capital, while the free flow of labor is precluded. International migration today is growing, as the region's economies increasingly incorporate digital services. The lack of job opportunities in many countries has created a diaspora, with thousands emigrating to the industrial countries of the North (Spain and Italy, in Europe); during the last 15 years, remittances have grown so sharply that they have become the largest source of foreign funds, outstripping foreign direct investment (FDI) and international donations.[7]

It is no secret that the remittance economy has begun to reshape various aspects of finance and politics in

1927
1960
1963
1964
1967
1969
1970
1971
1972
1973
1974
1975
1976
1977
1978
1979
1980
1981
1982
1983
1984
1985
1986
1987
1988
1989
1990
1991
1992
1993
1994
1995
1996
1997
1998
1999
2000
2001
2002
2003
2004
2005
2006

a number of countries,[8] and the still-fragmented discourses exploring the components of digital inclusion take due account of the role and needs of the region's enormous emigrant population. In short, digital inclusion today is a complex situation involving a number of factors: the incorporation of digital technology in a region whose societies are characterized by economic polarization, with dominating elites and impoverished, scattered and subservient populations; hegemonic discourse and a variety of languages of broad cultural resistance; paralysis in the process of expanding household Internet connections; private media concessions granted by the State; and projects by civil society organizations, whose mastery and constant use of emerging technologies are having a previously unimaginable, though still circumscribed, impact. Digital inclusion is now an integral part of a process touted as democratizing—a process that, in principle, is promising but, in practice, is stalled.

Digital inclusion, from this perspective, is the introduction—on different scales—of computer networks and the content available on them. One result of this is a reconfiguration of various local, national and international power structures. However, the different elites operating within the national negotiating processes of individual countries have made a point of "digitally including" themselves before concerning themselves about others.[9] They share opinions and are united in their approach to bringing ICTs into the national spheres over which they exert control. The fact that the region has not seen severe restrictions on Internet access and content (in contrast to China and some Islamic countries, for example) is.

However, any commitment to making them universally available is lacking. The Internet is, in effect, a valuable resource providing unlimited information to those able to invest in the tools needed—tools which, it should be noted, require a certain educational level, or "digital culture," to understand and manipulate. In short, while the elites have equipped and trained themselves, costs remain high for the households of those at the enormous base of the socio-economic pyramid.[10] There are indications that the different national elites have agreed upon a set of negotiating rules—an advance over an earlier time when politics was a social drama carried out between openly warring factions. Free access to online resources may now be a common value shared by the leaders of Latin America's democracies. However, the question of national commitments, and of encouraging private investment (or using public resources) to increase the number of citizens with access and incentives to effective use of the Internet and its content, has been effectively tabled.

The State, Elites and Digital Convergence

Any discussion of digital inclusion in the countries of the region must be based on an understanding of the State that takes account of the recent wave of privatizations in the telecommunications sector and of the connectivity policies implemented by governments. To date, countries within the region that have *not* privatized their telecommunications enterprises are the exception. The result is that a few multinational firms make the decisions in the different "telecom" sectors—wired and wireless telephony Internet service providers, domestic and international fiber-optics and satellite carriers, cybercafe franchises, etc., while controlling the regulatory frameworks in which rates are set and rules are made for the markets in which the firms operate. To a great extent, this privatization has occurred without competition, with long-term concessions to a small number of firms, an arrangement under which the domestic capital partners lack control over the decisions of the boards of directors. The profile of the individuals appointed to the countries' regulatory agencies, many of which are new, reflects the influence of firms that provide digital products and services over regulatory frameworks governing the concessions, as well as over the overall digital policies implemented by the State.

The rapid convergence of television, telephony, and digital content distribution over the Internet,[11] in a sort of triple play being negotiated in many countries as of the writing of this paper, is another aspect of digital inclusion. The dissemination of any content—television programming, movies, music, Web sites with Flash-type animation—now represents a swelling fortune fed by global growth in Internet use. Nearly 800 million souls are now connected, including consumers of spam, Nigerian promoters, info-addicts, the curious, scam artists, teleworkers, enthralled teenagers, providers of pornography and all manner of other products, public servants, private-sector employees, migrants, etc. This technological convergence, in which yesterday's analog products will eventually be distributed exclusively in digital formats, looms inevitable and close. It represents a landmark of ferocious competition, as the few firms with the relevant patents, licenses and concessions (not to mention the capital needed to offer different services on the international scale of the web) fight for markets. The regulatory structure governing this process is also part of the political process that invariably accompanies digital inclusion. The question of who represents what interests, as well as the balance of power between producers, distributors and consumers, is now, more than ever, linked to the democratization process.[12] Given the lack of attention focused on these issues by traditional political parties, the growing but limited power of nongovernmental organizations working in this area is not surprising. These "quasi-parties" now occupy the leadership role in technical discussions, constituting a new cast of actors on the stage on which digital services policy is enacted. However, they have little ability to maneuver effectively, due to their non representative nature, their limited power and the fact that their proposals are not widely disseminated.

The emerging information society being built on the strong infrastructure of Latin America's increasingly "wired" societies forces us to rethink the meaning—or future meaning—of democracy in this new context. Already, citizens have such an enormous fund of information at their disposal that understanding and making decisions on complex issues requires

support tools that few e-government programs appear to have considered, and that are not provided by public education systems (let alone by the region's dismal network of public libraries). There is a real danger that those responsible for online content, as it converges with analog (and soon digital) radio and television programming, will have more power and influence than the traditional politicians responsible for managing and implementing regulatory systems. This situation now appears to be pervasive in the region.

Elites and Protected Niches

It is clear that the national elites that serve are partners to the multinational firms, providing various digital technologies have found a comfortable commercial and financial niche. They receive substantial returns on their investments in protected local markets, within an international context of globalized and highly competitive markets. In other words, local capitalists who made timely investments in imported digital products and services in their respective markets (computers and accessories, Internet service, fiber-optic networks, access to satellite services, cellular telephony, digital television, etc.) have established an extremely advantageous and profitable oligopolistic position in markets operating under regulatory protection. (They are "legacy market players.")[13] These markets are designed to serve the elites themselves—those who have the purchasing power to acquire their products—and are, at this point (except for prepaid cellular telephone service), nearly saturated, judging by their slow rate of growth in many countries, where under 10 percent of the population enjoys Internet access.[14] The motivation for protecting these limited but highly profitable markets is soon. Those dominating them have every reason to want the cost of entry to their markets to be higher for other firms—firms that are either entering late or are offering new technologies that would bring down the cost of services or increase coverage at less cost than would the existing technologies. The most effective means of controlling the market is to control the regulatory entities that govern telecommunications and financial services.

1927
1960
1963
1964
1967
1969
1970
1971
1972
1973
1974
1975
1976
1977
1978
1979
1980
1981
1982
1983
1984
1985
1986
1987
1988
1989
1990
1991
1992
1993
1994
1995
1996
1997
1998
1999
2000
2001
2002
2003
2004
2005
2006

Thus, the elites in question share a further strategic point of consensus: It is to their advantage to have representatives in key positions within the downsized neoliberal State. The reshaping of the State—through the recent wave of privatizations, which placed so many national enterprises and assets in private hands—requires that greater *de facto* power be given to regulatory agencies, the ultimate locus of authority over the rules of the game of commerce in each country. Political party representatives have been notably reluctant to face the complex issues of financial and telecommunications regulation, and the region's legislatures have in recent times proven remarkably weak in this respect. The elites could hardly ask for more. They are assiduous defenders of their historical status, license and privilege, as well as of the territory they have gained in the current game. In weak democracies, they share yet an additional point of consensus: The aspiration to control a new content market in which it is to their advantage to synchronize symbolic production, to the extent possible, with the "individual and market freedom" ideology which, while close to their publicly expressed values, is not necessarily in line with their discreet but gluttonous game, or with the way they actually manage the enormous private power they possess.

Digital Services and Remittances

Return on investment is insufficient to extend service to a poor population that if it is to acquire digital products and services, requires prices far lower than the prevailing ones. In a number of the region's countries, the flow of remittances from emigrants now provides survival resources for a growing number of families whose sons and daughters work abroad, though the cost of the financial transactions continues to be usurious.[15] Two parallel patterns are evident. Not only are digital services *not* being extended at declining cost to remoter parts of the countries, but "digitally excluded" populations are receiving no relief from the high rates and commissions they must pay for remittance transactions from the United States, Canada and Europe.[16] While there is increased competition in this financial market, unlike the case of the market for digital products and services, the financial authorities (installed by the elites) are *not* taking measures to cap the rates and commissions levied on remittances. Meanwhile, the flows increase from year to year, and the families of these diasporas increasingly use digital tools for their international communications.[17] Ultimately, migrants and their families continue to pay a "poverty tax."

What is being posited here is that we are witnessing a new pattern of the neoliberal State, in which the elites dominate regulatory entities and are the masters of protected markets in at least two strategic sectors in which digital tools are increasingly predominant: telecommunications and finance. Digital services markets and, to a lesser extent, content distributed by the service providers' portals, are protected for the sake of the large firms. Meanwhile, the poor (emigrants and their families) are charged a sort of "lodging tax," with accommodations to oligopolistic markets and to unconstrained rates and commissions remittance transactions, despite the fact that these are vital elements of health and food security among increasing numbers of working class populations in many of the countries. Telecommunications and financial regulation represent bottlenecks, skillfully managed by representatives of the elites acting to secure their markets. These markets include a small number of providers of the increasingly strategic services involving communications and monetary transactions vital to family security in the countries. Both arenas are dominated by digital technologies and are overseen by a select few.

Digital Inclusion Has Arrived

Under the logic enforced by the interest groups in power in each country, digital inclusion becomes a matter of public policy, managed by individuals within this identifiable segment of society. For public consumption, however, digital inclusion is proclaimed as gospel. Perhaps even more important, it is presented as being consonant with the phantasm currently in vogue in international philanthropic discourse: the information society. Thus, though digital inclusion is *de facto* policy, the rules of negotiation used to implement it are based on the habits and customs of the elites. Rather than serving the excluded, the policy serves those very elites, which dominate the communications sector, Internet services, commercial banking, industry (insofar as it has survived) and remittance services. This *real* version of digital inclusion differs from that portrayed by the rhetoric of those advocating greater Internet connectivity through effective use of available resources. For the elites, digital inclusion is already being consolidated through their control of the various governmental structures responsible for regulating economic sectors and use of the electromagnetic spectrum. Since they are dependent on foreign technology, they do not invest in developing capacity beyond what is needed for the use of imported hardware and software. Their pattern of domination includes standards, bureaucratic procedures and concessions that serve the interests of a small number of partners. The excluded (comprising the same group as always) remain—as if it were any wonder—excluded.[18] This phenomenon is apparently invisible to the traditional political parties, as well as to the new "quasi-parties,"[19] a fragmented group of organizations which, with few exceptions, choose to deploy their limited lobbying resources to other ends. Meanwhile, though the issue is being addressed by private universities, its importance is largely disregarded by public universities.

Nor has this contradictory picture been a subject of policy debate. The orthodox version of digital inclusion points to a future in which the majority of the population will have access to the Internet's informational and educational tools and resources—a view that is, more realistically, a convenient illusion, serving as a rationalization for firms that wish to induce demand for their products while making high-profile donations to shore up the corporate image. Digital inclusion is also digital induction, a sort of self-fulfilling prophecy that supports a phantasm that stimulates demand for a range of future products and services.

For the privileged few, the happy "information society" has already arrived, and they are not about to expend their private resources or sacrifice their traditional share of the national budget by investing public funds to extend the benefits to the masses. For these elites, the discourse on digital inclusion is a useful phantasm in a number of ways. It is beneficial in international for a; it sets forth values that justify the conspicuously intense marketing efforts, and it is an example of the supposed new synergy between the State and the private sector. These powerful groups, which have already gained dominion over the digital resources of their countries, are not inclined to acknowledge the reality. Accordingly, they continue, through advertising campaigns and presidential speeches, to project the illusion of a people's digital utopia.

Impact on Democratic Processes

This situation is certain to affect the region's democratic processes. Insofar as telecommunications are concentrated in the hands of a few firms, which influence the rules of the game governing their business, there will be constraints on programming and bias in radio and television news, as well as on the Internet portals they manage and host on their servers. This does not bode well for the mass dissemination of diverse and pluralistic views on public issues, which are now relegated to the Web sites of NGOs and a very few television and radio programs broadcast at hours deemed to have no significant commercial value. A new apartheid is already evident in the media. While boasting domestically produced digital services, the political, financial and commercial elites that constitute today's hegemony determine the parameters of the content "permitted" for mass dissemination via (the public resource of) the electromagnetic spectrum. Meanwhile, a few civil society organizations are attempting to gain a foothold in the commercial Tower of Babel with messages broadcast in marginal venues, such as websites with no links on the mega-portals. Various obstacles present themselves in attempting to analyze the different issues bearing on the public policies to be negotiated in each country.

1927
1960
1963
1964
1967
1969
1970
1971
1972
1973
1974
1975
1976
1977
1978
1979
1980
1981
1982
1983
1984
1985
1986
1987
1988
1989
1990
1991
1992
1993
1994
1995
1996
1997
1998
1999
2000
2001
2002
2003
2004
2005
2006

One of the effects of the digital inclusion already implemented and serving the various elites can be seen in the government-supported connectivity programs. Most, if not all, of these programs are based on the premise that enormous numbers of computers must be acquired, installed and connected to the Internet in places such as schools and libraries (or other dedicated locations), and that "if we build it, the public will come." These programs are extremely expensive and are subject to little accountability. Often, these government-provided "telecenters" compete with a universe of pre-existing cybercafes—small digital services businesses that constitute an installed and under utilized human and technological resource, for which the government projects represent a sort of unfair competition, offering access and minimal training to their young clients. At present, many of these government-sponsored centers are languishing for lack of local commitment. Maintenance of the centers is problematic, and there are few incentives to promote their effective use or the development of capacities, while staff turnover remains high. These failures in designing such a costly public program are built in from the outset. In the author's view, the elites are not genuinely committed to training and educating their populations, let alone providing new digital technologies for the purpose.[20] This represents an enormous lost opportunity, a reality not reflected in the official reports and blissful accounts of the "ongoing digital inclusion" process.

Another factor not taken into account is the cost of delivering government services online, though economies of scale clearly provide enormous savings for the State. Even less attention is given to the quality of service offered at "virtual windows," where a wide range of administrative governmental procedures can be carried out. Nor do community telecenters (often managed by NGOs)—or the vast number of cybercafes in the various countries—reap any benefit from offering government services to their users.[21] Their clients generally lack the skills to use the procedures and informational services offered by government agencies effectively, while government makes little effort to expand its "online client base," with scant attempts to promote, and provide training for the use of, these "virtual windows," which are available at numerous access points in almost all cities and towns in the region.

This model of e-government, with its vertical focus on mandatory bureaucratic procedures, rather than on mechanisms for negotiating public policy, is also a result of the myopic (but astute) vision of the senior officials responsible for these programs. While they, of course, have already achieved digital self-inclusion, they seem incapable of recognizing the State's obligation to provide fiscal incentives to support culturally appropriate content and other instruments through efforts to consolidate and expand the network of community telecenters and cybercafes, or to invest in determining how best to address the large youth clientele in their countries.

Conclusion

The current scenario, in which the elites have effectively and audaciously "included" themselves in the information society, using the digital technologies and services available to them without investing in the wherewithal to include the rest of society, is ultimately a crisis of representativeness with respect to the interests of populations in unconsolidated democracies.[22] Recently there have been indications of change in the patterns of electoral participation,[23] a process increasingly influenced by political propaganda broadcast over radio and television. At the same time, one sees young people alienated from the parties, NGOs with no effective means of communicating with party representatives, functioning as virtual parties within national political arenas—generating proposals and initiatives in a range of public policy areas and helping build the consensus needed to write effective laws and create the regulatory structures to implement them.[24] The rapid convergence of news, entertainment, educational services, music and video on demand, telephony, etc., in digital formats transmitted wirelessly or by wire, requires massive investments. The partners in these enterprises are determined to protect and expand their business, taking advantage of the publicly-owned electromagnetic spectrum, and of their licenses, in a way made possible only by broad agreements among the elites that constitute the active force in Latin America's current states. Innovative forces in the digital policy area are largely excluded from negotiating and from the consensus-building process that occurs among the elites, a process that may prove to be the crux of a key structural contradiction within the emerging democracies.

From this perspective, traditional power groups have found the key to retaining their traditional power in today's context of national telecommunications policies, emerging digital technologies and financial rules of the game. At present, their focus is on digital content and on remittances, which are the symbolic spaces and survival resources of the poor. This has radical implications for cultural and other policy, given the elites' evident resistance to invest (or even use State resources) in expanding digital inclusion or reducing financial transaction fees. The future is not hard to foresee: A future in which the State will bear no responsibility for ensuring that strategic information is available to its citizens, in which the marginalized will be increasingly excluded, with their options limited to a self-management, social Darwinism model. Meanwhile, economies will be subsidized by the revenue from remittances, while the commercial elites exploit the markets comprising of those relatively few consumers with sufficient purchasing power to acquire the succeeding generations of digital products and services that today's inexorable technological development and marketing process generate.

Endnotes

1   Painting with a broad brush—using a common denominator to create horizontal connections—the attempt, here, is to portray a complex regional scenario. Admittedly, however, much of this derives from the author's personal view of the situation in Mexico.

2   The argument presented here is based on the thesis detailed in J. Higley and R. Gunther (compilers), *Elites and Democratic Consolidation in Latin America and Southern Europe*, Cambridge University Press, 1992. The

authors offer (p. 9) a dual description of elites. First, elites continually affect "political solutions," in the sense that their individual opinions and possible actions are perceived, and taken into consideration by, other opinion leaders, as well as by subordinates, when weighing the costs and benefits of specific policies, or even when considering major issues, such as a change of regime. Second, they affect solutions in a substantive fashion: a proposal that lacks their support has little chance of being approved or implemented.

3   A process in which those responsible for directing the various regulatory entities are not required to account directly or indirectly to the electorate, or even, in some cases, to the legislative branch.

4   There was little participation by Latin American delegations at the first World Summit on the Information Society. www.wsis.org

5   Brazil, Colombia, Chile, and Peru have such funds in operation. Mexico has authorized one, but the rules governing it are not yet transparent.

6   The convergence of radio, television and the Internet produces major movements of resources to control captive and potential markets.

7   This is a hot issue because of the extraordinary flow of remittances in the region over the last five years. See, for example, http://www.nytimes.com/2005/07/07/business/worldbusiness/07peso.html, July 7, 2005, "Study Challenges Assumptions About Money Being Remitted to Mexico."

8   There are few exceptions. Only Panama and Venezuela do not record remittance revenue in their national accounts. Southern cities, on the other hand, receive flows of labor from Bolivia, Ecuador, Paraguay and Peru; in Uruguay, remittances are important but apparently not decisive.

9   In many countries, these elites boast pedigrees rooted in their countries' history, while also incorporating a new breed of entrepreneurs. Family relationships tend to overlap, and inter-marrying reinforces class solidarity. With few exceptions (Brazil), they do not create technology, and they exhibit no scruples in protecting their privileges and markets, in which they often work in partnership with international providers.

10   This concept of the bottom of the pyramid plays a role in reshaping investment strategy, in new business alliances, in the design of digital products, in microfinance, etc., in respect to multinationals, the United States government, and some donors. See the agenda of a conference held in San Francisco, California on December 12-14, at: http://povertyprofit.wri.org/

11   In Spanish, sometimes termed "la" Internet (feminine) rather than "el" Internet (masculine)—no doubt because of its fecundity.

12   2005 saw heightened international debate on different aspects of Internet control and content. See: http://www.itu.int/wsis/newsroom/eflash/latest.html ; http://lac.derechos.apc.org ; www.wgig.org

13   However, the conditions attached to their licensing agreements with international providers inhibit the local development of technology. Thus, they are condemned to defend foreign intellectual property and discourage the development of similar national assets.

1927
1960
1963
1964
1967
1969
1970
1971
1972
1973
1974
1975
1976
1977
1978
1979
1980
1981
1982
1983
1984
1985
1986
1987
1988
1989
1990
1991
1992
1993
1994
1995
1996
1997
1998
1999
2000
2001
2002
2003
2004
2005
2006

14 In Costa Rica, which prides itself on being a leader in this field, connections are currently growing at 1.8% annually. See Ricardo Monge G. and John Hewlitt, "Tecnologías de la Información y las Comunicaciones (TICs) y el futuro desarrollo de Costa Rica: El desafío de la exclusion." ["Information and communications technologies (ICTs) and the future development of Costa Rica: the challenge of exclusion."] In all countries, there is ferocious competition in cellular telephony, a field in which new services expand the client base. www.caatec.org/publicaciones/COSTA_RICA_DIGITAL_3.pdf

15 The firms providing these transaction services at the global level admit that the marginal cost of the electronic transfers through their networks is tiny.

16 There are notable exceptions, e.g., Ecuador's Banco Solidario processes remittances without charge for emigrants in Spain. http://www.banco-solidario.com/noticias.php?id=11

17 See S. Robinson, "After Calculating Opportunity Costs, the Remittance Development Fund." See: www.ssrc.org/programs/itic/publications/knowledge_report/memos/robinsonmemo3.pdf

18 Mexico has a "small economic elite that lives like maharajas (Indian princes), and there is also a political elite that protects them. Our border becomes an escape valve for immigrants, relieving Mexican politicians and the economic elite of any obligation to provide opportunities to their own people," George Grayson, of the College of William and Mary, commenting on CNN, as documented at: http://www.jornada.unam.mx/2004/dic04/041219/023n1eco.php

19 See Israel Palma's masters thesis, Redes de Poder y Organizaciones Civiles—Antropología Política de las Organizaciones Civiles de la Ciudad de México [Power networks and civil organizations—political anthropology of Mexico City's civil organizations], Universidad Autónoma Metropolitana—Iztapalapa, 2004. www.uam-antropologia.info

20 The regional profile of government job-training programs and programs to provide training in open-source (non-proprietary) software programming is another indication of this condition.

21 The issue of the sustainability of telecenters has recently received a great deal of attention. The sociocultural, financial, technological and administrative dimensions of the issue have been largely ignored by government. Not only has this made it more difficult for them to survive, but it has also represented a lost opportunity to take a modus operandi that has proven effective in a lower-income environment and roll it out on a larger scale. It has also handicapped technical discussion of the appropriate generic model for the delivery of digital services at collective access points, by failing to provide feedback.

22 Higley and Gunther, Introduction.

23 "Grupos ciudadanos triunfan en las municipales de Bolivia en detrimento de los partidos" [Citizens groups triumph in municipal elections in Bolivia, to the detriment of the parties], see: http://www.uimunicipalistas.org/actualidad/numero42.htm

24 The comments of one respected journalist are striking in this connection: "Civil society in Mexico and Latin America has shown a notable lack of interest in the migrants' situation." Luis Hernández Navarro, "To Die a Little: Migration and Coffee in Mexico and Central America," special report, Americas Program (Silver City, NM: Interhemispheric Resource Center, December 13, 2004). http://www.americaspolicy.org/reports/2004/0412coffee.html

Robinson, Scott S. "¿Brecha o Inclusión Digital?" [Digital Gap or Digital Inclusion?] A preliminary version was published in Nueva Sociedad, No. 195, Caracas, Venezuela, 2004. Reprinted with permission.

INFORMATION SOCIETY AND SOCIAL MOVEMENTS: DEMOCRATIC ALTERNATIVES TO THE DOMINANT SOCIAL DEVELOPMENT MODEL

By Francisco Sierra

2004 In the current process of restructuring the logic of social reproduction, the intensive exploitation of communication and culture is the reference framework we must consider in order to define and understand the transformations that affect the spheres of work, education and cultural production. Consequently, it is the starting point for the construction of alternatives for progress and social emancipation. Moreover, we could also state that the way we treat the changes and the economic-political logic of communication determines social development, which is why, rather than considering this field of social activity a minor problem for social analysis and theory, we must see it as a strategic challenge as regards the alternatives and historical projection of the social change required.

In general, studies on the informational nature of contemporary society draw a contradictory scenario, governed by machines and information systems, which—far from facilitating a detailed knowledge of the development processes—favors the assumption of a fatalist way of thinking, over-determined by a "postmodern meta-narration." Such a scenario is incapable of anything other than denouncing the projects of mobilization and democratization of knowledge, the media and cultural expression.

Thereby, the de-realization of the everyday world, and the material loss of the forms of anchoring experience as an effect of the colonization of media simulations, end up blocking the political-ideological emancipating imaginary, in a process of mystification of post modernity and the new forms of flexible dominance that denies from the start every possibility of a "new cartography of late capitalism." This happens despite the pertinence and need of this intellectual exercise of historical commitment at a time like this, marked by the development of the intensive process of globalization, which translates into different ways of cultural crisis and bewilderment of the local communities, parallel to the process of decentralization of the economic, political and informative institutions.

Our work, while not in vain, attempts to discuss the conflicts and contradictions of communication in the knowledge society. For its democratic transformation, we would like to start by outlining precisely the crucial problem of informative localization and decentralization, parallel to the concentration of cultural power and symbolic capital, as a part of the social rationale of global capitalism. The principles of territoriality—and local intervention and totalization—from the theoretical perspective [remember the premise of the ecological movement "think globally and act locally"] can undoubtedly constitute strategic vectors for a transforming vision of informative social development, able to overcome the discursive inaction of postmodernism and the tautological confinement of globalization as from a research, praxis-base.

Thinking About Change, Changing the Way of Thinking

If the culture of simulation of a society like ours, in which the value of change has become generalized up to the point of deleting the traces and the memory of the original material sense, has as its image—as Guy Debord remembers—the final and most perfect form of deification of merchandise, then it seems logical to think that the project of territorializing social analysis linked to the strategies of knowledge and communitarian construction of local actors could contribute to overcome the theoretical common sense of the fetishism of merchandise. This would be achieved by

opening up the process of information and development to new rules and opportunities that favor more autonomous knowledge and social power.

The proposal outlined by this idea, in the revision of the dominant model of cultural globalization, tries in this sense to facilitate an endogenous and participative reading of development. Identifying communication, education and culture as the matrix (and driving) forces of contemporary historical change, such a reading links the social dialectics of communitarian networks to the possibility of a techno-cultural project, in which the processes of informative mediation arise from learning and from initiatives that mobilize knowledge, based on "dialogical," collective and intercultural research practices.

For this possibility to be consistent today, more than ever, it is necessary to bring together the theoretical criticism of the thinking or counter-discourse of the media's globalization, and a detailed and rigorous structural analysis of the processes of multimedia concentration in strategic sectors of the cultural industry. We start with the general considerations of globalization as the construction of the integrated world system, where the media are part of an unbalanced and oligopolic international structure clearly connected to the interests of [the sources of] a transnational and local capital. The future development of the "techno-tronic civilization" depends on the "visualization" of such processes.

Up to now, such future has been written according to the script outlined by the transnational media powers, with the consequent concentration and privatization of the power to inform and the commercialization of knowledge and learning according to the new informal conditions of production, which turn the problem of the political economy of knowledge into a crucial matter in the struggles and vindications of the left (Bolaño, 2000).

As we know, the process of appropriation and control of communication, culture and knowledge by the

1927
1960
1963
1964
1967
1969
1970
1971
1972
1973
1974
1975
1976
1977
1978
1979
1980
1981
1982
1983
1984
1985
1986
1987
1988
1989
1990
1991
1992
1993
1994
1995
1996
1997
1998
1999
2000
2001
2002
2003
2004
2005
2006

great economic empires is not only characteristic, logically, of the new global culture, nor can it be considered a recent historical problem. Since 1980, with the publication of the *MacBride Report,* UNESCO has confirmed how the inequalities in terms of access, production and circulation of information in the world have reproduced different situations of cultural colonization. This in turn has affected the economic order in favor of the interests of the great capitalist powers, for example through the influence and control of the advertising industry and the universalization of models and lifestyles alien to the socio-cultural realities of the less developed countries.

The theses of the aforementioned report indicated then in the formation of international communication:

a. The increasing privatization of world flows and processes of exchange of information and technology
b. The concentration of informational power in a few countries and transnational communication groups
c. The widening of informative and technological inequalities between countries in the North and South
d. And the isolation of regions, countries and whole continents from the process of technological circulation and transfers in the "world economy."

The dominant model of development of the world information system has progressively accentuated such tendencies in four historical periods:

1. The "diplomatic stage" (1945-1973), marked by the counter-insurgent conception of the collective media as strategic aids of U.S. foreign policy and fundamental components of the national security doctrine to defend the American interests and way of life. The media will be defined as the main agents of the new modern public diplomacy.
2. The crisis of the world system of dependency (1973-1980), also called "stage of the Third World shift," in which countries in the South will question the communication world order and its imbalances regarding the terms of social development of the less-favored nations and claim a New International Economic Order (NIEO) and a New World Information and Communication Order (NWICO) vis-à-vis the cultural dominance of the U.S. industry and some European countries; the unbalanced and oligopolic dissemination of international news by the four great press agencies (Associated Press, Agence France Presse, Reuters and UPI); the restricted access to the world radio broadcasting system controlled by the United States; and the transfer of information technologies from North to South; all of them, causes of the informative, social and cultural dependency and underdevelopment in these countries.
3. The restructuring of the U.S. hegemony (1980-1981), led by the conservative movement in England and the United States, and started with the reorganization of the international division of labor and the imposition of the doctrine of the free flow of information, against the aspirations of underdeveloped countries in their defense of a new international communications system, with support by UNESCO ultimately boycotted.
4. The era of the New World Order of capitalist globalization, ideologically sanctioned by the successful "media war" against Iraq and the passing of Vice President Al Gore's Agenda for Action for the development of the New Information Infrastructure assumed by the G7 countries as a doctrine for construction of a worldwide telecommunications network in the so called "global village."

In this last stage, the liberal ideological orientation of ongoing discussions about the role of communication and information systems in the general process of development in light of the globalization process paradoxically takes place along with the phenomenon of "planetarization of conscience," which makes possible, as well as necessary, the historical commitment of social actors vis-à-vis the set of civilizing problems faced by humanity in its more immediate vital horizon.

The problem of informational development is in fact a problem of civilization. It is that lack of conscience—the inability to think in a relational way about the set of factors and social processes that, while irreducibly complex, articulate the conditions of material development and determine the standards of living of the population—that is one of the main obstacles to the process of "community development." A radical censorship is established between the development of knowledge and material production, even if today—and this is one of the great contradictions of our times—society is defined in terms of the "economy of the mind."

Therefore it is advisable to ask what kind of reasoning feeds the current discourse of the integrated global society; what principles define the territorialization processes of global capital; and how the processes of privatization of the means of production and culture relate to the ruptures and de-territorialization of the new public space, mediated by the "industries of conscience" that today are also directly verifiable in social thinking.

Thus, if techno-informative and audiovisual globalization is the main vector of the radical changes organizing the hegemonic forms of power, to think about its territories, the space of the market, the brands and political frameworks of cultural production that organize and cross through capital, necessarily requires some sort of a pragmatic philosophy of communication, inspired, as Martin Barbero criticizes, in the technological race fostered by "market forces." The McLuhan global village, Negroponte's digital universe as a "path towards the future" of the informed society, express both discursive and theoretically, in the current historical context, the irrefutable imposition of the process of mundialization of markets and restructuring of the world system as a logical derivation and natural form of every social expectation of modernization.

As Hector Schmucler points out, the logic guiding these ideas has no cracks, and its functioning offers the world the promise of maximum freedom and the ability to choose and decide. Indeed, if information is free, everyone can have access to it; if information confers power, and since it is available for all, power can be in the hands of all; if the mundialization of information generates interdependence, there are no risks of such power being used by others to dominate us.

The current revolution of communications would be representing, in sum, the desired universalization of knowledge, and at the same time, access to world justice and peace, through the evolution and mental development of the individual, beyond the projects of collective salvation that failed in the history of modernity.

In this scenario, the doctrine of the free flow of information imposed since the 1950s by the United States is again the dominant rule in the programs of international expansion and development of new communication, and certainly of the public philosophy and post-modern theorizations of the now-trendy academic revisionism. Embedded in the populist aura of the market's competition and modernity, the old idea of *free flow of information* has become consequently the matrix idea of inspiration guiding the development of regional communication policies, favoring systematic privatization, exacerbated concentration and deregulation, under the leadership and supervision of the multimedia conglomerates at the center of the capitalist system.

The re-editing of the stale liberal principle of communication without borders questions, under the empire of financial capital, every public communication project, deregulating production processes and cultural distribution to the extent of subsuming and displacing all media policies in the commercial logic of capitalist valuation.

Cultural industries in regions like Latin America or the European Union are experiencing the progressive:

- Reduction of local production rates.
- Reduction of their own spaces of audiovisual dissemination.
- Centralization of the informative sources.
- Financial dependency from the transnational controls and advertising agencies, mainly from the United States.

1927
1960
1963
1964
1967
1969
1970
1971
1972
1973
1974
1975
1976
1977
1978
1979
1980
1981
1982
1983
1984
1985
1986
1987
1988
1989
1990
1991
1992
1993
1994
1995
1996
1997
1998
1999
2000
2001
2002
2003
2004
2005
2006

- Reduction of media diversity and creativity of content and the plurality of cultural expressions.
- Privatization of public services strategic for national economic development.
- Imposition of an audiovisual imaginary and narrative rooted in the U.S. consumption models against the needs of social and cultural development of most of the world's population.

Power and Global Control

The propagation of world networks of social communication represents not only overcoming the old idea of the right to freedom of expression but also the naturalization of new procedures of hegemonic control and dependency. Even if today the strength of technology and the power of the "technologies of the spirit" are identified as the axis for structuring what is understood to be a new social order, actually the man-machine interconnectivity constitutes an argument for the legitimacy and development of the only desirable future we can think about, certainly leaving aside the repressive and social control role with which administrative and cultural public information machines are established.

It would be appropriate to remember, in this sense, that contemporary technologies of information and cultural transmission have had their origin in the alliance of the large industrial companies with military apparatus. As Mattelart recalls, the computer, the satellite and electronics come directly from this permanent association materialized in a type of state that emerged at the end of World War II: the national security state.

Since the 1960s, the growth model of the electronic and aerospace industries, according to the rationale of war economy, has favored the centralization of international communications by the Pentagon, subordinated to the imperialist project of ideological aggression and massive penetration of the information and intelligence systems of the peripheral nations of the world system. The techniques, methods and technologies of information and collective communication have been progressively perfected during the second half of the 20th century, in a global context dominated by the economic transformations of the system and structure of production of capitalism, under the orbit of the imperialistic U.S. hegemony. Such hegemony has determined the course of the policy of transnational expansion of the Fordist system, according to the cultural patterns of North American cultural industry, in a process gradually entwining the big capitalist monopolies with the industrial-military complex of the Pentagon, following national security guidelines in the development of infrastructures and social assistance of the countries dependent in terms of information according to four lines of action:

1. Control of the satellite network and geostationary space through the expansion and support of the economic oligopoly of the telecommunications industry to control all geographical, meteorological and strategic intelligence information.
2. Development of a cooperation and technical assistance program in the framework of the exchange and economic liberalization policies that integrate the civilian and military front in programs of technological modernization.
3. Subsidizing and financing local media attuned to the geostrategic theses and interests of North American imperialism, as well as international organizations such as the Inter-American Press Society (IAPA).
4. Implementation of specific public relations, advertising and propaganda campaigns in conflictive situations of emerging insurgency or open war at a local and regional level, with the indirect participation of the Pentagon in tasks of cooperation and logistic support.

[The recent events after 9/11 do not inaugurate a new propagandistic or global control of information policy in any way, as some analysts wanted to see. The current information war to dominate minds and hearts elaborates on the experience accumulated in the Pentagon's counterinsurgency operations. That is when the need to include the use and control of telematic networks for the electronic war, using satellite telecommunications systems and the new infrastructure of information technologies to intercept and block enemy information, as well as the media and cultural information and entertainment industries to disseminate the imperialist leadership values, is observed for the first time.]

Throughout the 1960s and up to now, the successful role of the policy of disinformation and media manipulation led by the Pentagon has thus propitiated a model of development of international communications governed by violence and aggression, intensively militarizing the informational rationale of mass culture in a progressive and slow adaptation of the public sphere to informative mediation and the ways, objectives and presuppositions of the true socializing agents of the new information technologies: the industry of heavy weaponry and the political-military complex of the Pentagon.

Thus, if in the 1960s the national security doctrine was established as a ruling principle of international communications, in the 1990s the global system of political-military vigilance of the world economy started a process of renovation and perfecting of the theory of strategic defense around the "reticular" development of the new information technologies. Five fundamental premises are established; in light of the last wars against the "Empire of the Evil," these more than clarify the guidelines followed in the last years in the project to build the Global Information Society:

1. Nations' geopolitical borders have lost importance for the purposes of national security.
2. The notion of national security must be extended beyond the military sphere to include commercial and criminal law aspects.
3. The distinction between public and private spheres must be overcome.
4. Due to the ephemeral and complex nature of the defense problems, the emphasis of military policies is oriented towards gathering and processing information, as well as the development of flexible and decentralized models of organization.
5. For the same reasons, the new theory of security is firmly based on information infrastructures configuring a global surveillance system.

In this sense, we should remember that the Internet is a product of the arduous efforts of the United States to control the information sector. Already in 1989, prestigious universities such as MIT recommended that the Republican government should make a larger investment in computer industries to favor economic development, integrally automating all the production process in the industry.

[Proposing a national information infrastructure] Al Gore's reductionist technological argument is based on the fact that the development and expansion of the net indiscriminately favor all its users in an equal way, thus the transforming the "revolutionary" power of new telecommunications to accelerate social development.

Obviously, Al Gore will avoid taking into account, in the framework of the agenda for action, the real costs of this beneficial development model in technologically dependent countries. From the political economy of communication, it is no secret that technology is implanted and transferred within a system of social relationships that reproduces preexisting asymmetries and power devices.

In this sense, any informed analyst of international communication sees that in the new economy, the digital revolution responds to a capitalist tendency of concentration and accumulation of capital gain according to the objectives of transnational corporations and their need for global circulation of goods and services in the new world economy. This contrasts with the type of social and cultural democratization defended by liberal rhetoric and with promotion of the Internet as an expression of participation, equality and balanced economic development.

In his review of contemporary communication, Lucien Sfez gives a name to the logic of "sedentary"

1927
1960
1963
1964
1967
1969
1970
1971
1972
1973
1974
1975
1976
1977
1978
1979
1980
1981
1982
1983
1984
1985
1986
1987
1988
1989
1990
1991
1992
1993
1994
1995
1996
1997
1998
1999
2000
2001
2002
2003
2004
2005
2006

thinking: *tautism,* a neologism descriptive of a media culture mesmerized, tautologically and virtually autistic, incapable of looking beyond the neo-technological objects that represent it. Technology implements discourse that intends to over-determine society and subject the efficacy of all activities to its own technical criterion.

This leads to the objective of our discussion: alternatives and strategies for change of communication and culture in the information society, and its potential for the political and cultural practice of social movements.

Nodes, Links, Condensation Points

If today, as we have seen, technological development appears as the origin of globalization and the access to a post-capitalist society based on new ways of organization and sociability, this development model, based on the administrative power of the new information technologies, materializes at a political level in the identification of the New World Order with the triumph of the liberal ideology, and even farther, with the very "end of ideologies" in the process of reconstitution of the public powers.

Today, the fact that although the State continues to play an important role in international relationships, the monopoly and centralization of the sanctioning power are progressively disintegrated for the benefit of transnational entrepreneurial actors, giving way to what Hirsch terms the "national competitive state," is accepted as natural.

The current late-capitalism phase of development has not only led private companies to oversee the administration, production and consumption functions of almost all public interest goods and services. Moreover, the necessary expansion of capital's concentration and mundialization rationales is implies the hegemonic control of citizenship's socialization and civic education in the neoliberal norms of co-existence, as from the patterns of possessive appropriation of objects of consumption and radical competition between the different collective actors in the public space. And a

public speech that cultivates irresponsibility as a norm and fatalism as an attitude.

Politically, the forum *"The Other Voices of the Planet"* has identified the ideological foundations of this public speech, dominant in the New International Order, around three basic rationalization principles which are practically universal: Development, kept as a universal objective and destiny for humanity as a whole; the globalization of the economy, accepted as a historical need and the only way to manage to spread development to the whole world; competitiveness, considered as the only instrument that can regulate the functioning of the globalized economy in an optimum way.

The underlying nuclear concept common to these three principles in the discourse of the global information society is the notion of interdependency. A term that in practice, when pronounced, refers to the inevitability of the "iron law" of international economic development. "global," in this concept, expresses in a condensed way a single order, a single producing function, a single path or direction in historical development. Interdependency means, in sum, the inevitable empire of capitalist globalization, from which it is impossible to break free as a tendency— as proposed by Hamerlink years ago—except at risk of being left outside of the world production and commercialization system.

Communication in the global village would certify, in this sense, the unavoidable unification and civic participation in the planet's humanitarian problems. The local affirmation of political autonomy and cultural identities is considered, under this perspective, a restriction to the free circulation of goods and services, a "conservative reaction" to the process of totalitarian modernization. Here we find, undoubtedly, a node of the net, a critical point of condensation and social confrontation: the local affirmation of territories, identities, cultures and political wills of the citizenship, which must be taken into account as a field favorable to the articulation and construction of the communicational alternative to the dominant model of informative mediation.

The demands of production and the consumption models do not stop at the borders of the local cultures, which, driven by necessity, are forced to dilute and standardize for a more efficient and faster circulation of goods, services and capital circulating in the communication industry and other economic sectors. The ideologically mystifying nature of the public discourse on the global village is evidenced, however, when we observe that the only merchandise that sees its transfrontier circulation capacity limited is precisely the work force. Labor force is systematically marginalized in policies of trans-border liberalization and regional integration, enduring a severe disciplinary process to reterritorialize its permanent economic availability to the service of the large capital.

As Cees Hamelink rightly points out, the technological expansion of the new media has not brought about the construction of the desired global village, or the "classroom without walls" celebrated by Marshall McLuhan, but rather the opposite: A model of corporate village in which production and marketing at a planetary scale conceive the world as a great universal baseboard. Formally, we are all equal, we are all free, we all participate in the new world order. Now, [we must decide] in which way and how we participate in the immense technological net connecting us; who governs this net; who processes, transmits and classifies the strategic information circulating through these nets; and, above all, who makes decisions about the development and configuration of the new planetary cultural environment.

Strategies for Constructing the Communicational Alternative

It would be convenient to prefigure a political program and a project of cultural work in the local and regional spheres, such as within Europe, which in the medium term can support and allow the transnational organization of social movements for the transformation of world communication. The political left and social movements must seriously rethink communication as a problem not of the media or their instrumental

use for a radical political discourse, but as a space of dialogue, consensus and articulation of plural voices, diverging wills and precarious solidarities. Instead, on the contrary, the policies of the left have favored reductionist uses and conceptions of communication, which reproduce, from a progressive functionalism, the forms of conservative control and domination.

The first challenge ahead for the progressive forces is therefore to take on and set a social agenda for communication. And I underline the term *social*, because we must necessarily insist on the fact that it is not possible to outline a communication policy that advocates state ownership of communication as the only alternative to the liberal privatizing model, without the risk of incurring the same mistakes and obstacles to the democratic development of modern public communication.

Between the market and the State, it is possible and essential to consider communication and its related public policies in social terms, as from formulas of democratic planning, management and control by the citizens and their social representatives at the local and regional level. We must redefine the concept of public service as from both the breaking of the State's political power structures and the private model of cultural concentration, favoring mixed public-societal communication systems.

This aim is not viable unless the required articulation of spaces for the exchange, discussion and development of ideas between communication and citizens finds its place. For this reason, today more than ever, we need to pose, as both a challenge and an immediate practical task, a specific commitment to:

a. Raise awareness and public opinion about the need to discuss and participate actively, through political pedagogy, in the current development of information systems.

b. Articulate spaces for sectoral exchange among social collectives on the role of communication in areas such as human rights, gender perspective or attention to cultural minorities.

1927
1960
1963
1964
1967
1969
1970
1971
1972
1973
1974
1975
1976
1977
1978
1979
1980
1981
1982
1983
1984
1985
1986
1987
1988
1989
1990
1991
1992
1993
1994
1995
1996
1997
1998
1999
2000
2001
2002
2003
2004
2005
2006

c. Strengthen the integration of work platforms and civic collaboration for the defense of informative democracy and the right to access the industries of conscience.

d. Introduce on the public agenda the debate on pluralism and democracy in the media, reclaiming the legacy of international proposals such as the *MacBride Report* in the promotion of a new informative culture and the defense of the right to communicate in every sense.

e. Establish links with social movements, community media and alternative communication activists who have political and intellectual capital not yet exploited for the construction of alternatives because they are not known or politically connected.

In sum, in order to move forward we must reconstruct the forces of progress and transform social mobilization, articulating associative networks, discussion spaces, professional debate forums and cooperation and exchange platforms that in the medium-term allow the design of an alternative program for the development of the global information society. At the micro level, the development of local and regional communication public policies promote pluralism, cultural diversity, civic democracy and autonomy.

Such widening of spaces presupposes the need to go beyond the objective limits of the capitalist political economy and the communicational configuration that makes it possible, through the democratic planning of public policies adequate to social development, but always under the condition of radically renovating the discourse and emancipating practice of critical thinking in communication.

Cultural Democracy and Democratic Culture. Communication and Civic Participation

If we are to believe Raymond William's words, the growth of a large-scale organization and communication is a human achievement of capital importance, that broadly exceeds the real difficulties and confusion it has brought about, and that still needs to go even further, towards the planetary community, in the

intercultural encounter and acknowledgment of different voices converging in the planetary map. Progressive access to information in real time, with no limits in terms of time, volume or distance, is undoubtedly a great cultural revolution that, conveniently socialized, could guarantee many of the liberal utopias postponed since the dawn of modernity. But that requires a different research and social organization culture.

First, it is necessary to develop the empiric and theoretical knowledge needed to transform the structure of contemporary cultural domination. Communication research must drive this effort in part. Organizations such as CONGD[1] must support such research and support attempts to redesign its institutional culture. We find that critical thinking is often isolated or marginalized in scientific agendas and public debates about communication, leading to scarce social influence in spaces of decision and social power. Therefore, one of the urgent tasks of the social movements is to regroup and coordinate the isolated and disperse efforts of knowledge, promoting public discussion and the socialization of scientific knowledge for action against information neo-capitalism.

Without an alliance of the forces of progress with academia, communication intellectuals and scholars, in their plurality of variants and ideologies within the left, it will be hardly possible to re-orient the model of development of the information society. In addition, so far critical intelligence has not had politically propitious speakers and conditions aimed in its direction. Therefore, it seems useful, at least at the regional and national levels, to organize discussion forums and at the same time promote initiatives of articulation of local structures and platforms among unions, professional associations, users and micro companies, local and county-level entities, social organizations and public powers.

In this effort, participation must be a ruling principle of every policy and constituting strategy, favoring spaces open to social interpellation that allow access to the

---

1   Translator's note: Coordinadora de ONGs para el Desarrollo, or Development NGOs Liaison.

media and information systems, the right to replication, the dialogic articulation of local communication and pluralism. One of the most productive choices, consistent with our time, is to think about progress-oriented social change, making democracy dialogic and democratizing online communication with innovative experiences.

The politics of networks of thinking and social intervention in communication must, in this sense, constitute another way of creating culture, another way to organize communication:

■ Articulating dynamics of consensus and integration of the different social actors in the discussion of the organizational model of public communication.
■ Guaranteeing coverage and access for all users
■ Observing the principle of equality in public participation in the cultural system organized by the communication industries
■ Facilitating the multiplicity of emitters and true pluralism in the information structure, and
■ Promoting the creative and critical use of media from a pedagogy of transforming communication.

According to this logic, defense of democracy in the media must be understood as a sustained effort, open to contestation, of a political practice that widens the spaces of confrontation of discourse, "complicates" the access systems, and that distributes and groups the forms of cultural representation and expression among different social groups.

Today, the value and defense of communication for social development must be posed from new parameters: articulating whenever possible a public network of social participation resulting in communication strategies and goals based on collective criteria and methodology arising from the population's active participation in the decisions, design and benefits of public policies.

The value or the idea of development in communication would thus transcend the social-liberal logics of representation of public communication, through

a model that not only produces communication according to growth and sustained development needs but that does it by building democracy, developing links, bridging dialogue among different groups, cultures and discourses. That is to say, the choice of communication for development must go beyond the traditional centralized planning of public policies in favor of the development of organizations of interaction and self-organization, networks capable of significantly widening the cultural potential of each group, and collective mobilization of organizations committed to the democratization and transformation of the current global order.

Theorists and professionals committed to informative democracy and cultural autonomy face the challenge of putting into practice an idea that buzzes more and more strongly in our ears but that has not yet materialized in significant initiatives and action programs: *another world is possible.* Another communication is possible: a single world made of multiple voices, built dialogically, outlined by the participation and proliferation of bonds and affections. ... A single world comprising multiple voices and multiple cultures visible and acknowledged on the basis of another cultural practice ... another possible communication.

Sierra, Francisco. "Information Society and Social Movements: Democratic Alternatives to the Dominant Social Development Model," excerpt from: "Sociedad de la Información y Movimientos Sociales," In *La Red es de Todos. Cuando los Movimientos Sociales se apropian de la Red.* Coordinator: Víctor Marí Sáez. Editorial Popular, Madrid, Spain 2004. Reprinted with permission.

1927
1960
1963
1964
1967
1969
1970
1971
1972
1973
1974
1975
1976
1977
1978
1979
1980
1981
1982
1983
1984
1985
1986
1987
1988
1989
1990
1991
1992
1993
1994
1995
1996
1997
1998
1999
2000
2001
2002
2003
2004
2005
2006

BRIDGING DISCIPLINES: THE NATURAL RESOURCE MANAGEMENT KALEIDOSCOPE FOR UNDERSTANDING ICTS

By Ricardo Ramírez

2003 1. Features of Information and Communication Technologies as Development Tools

The potential of information and communication technologies (ICTs) as tools to enhance the development of rural and remote regions is difficult to grasp. A recent report suggests that observation and measurement in the field of ICTs seems to be the most neglected area of policies and projects, particularly in rural areas (OECD 2001). The initial hype about their potential was biased on a glorified technological promise, but the early advocates were apparently unaware of the underlying social, regulatory, and economic barriers that continued to constrain rural and remote societies to a continued marginalisation.

No wonder some communities could run with the new opportunities and others not; the so-called "digital divide" had precedent "divides' in all sectors, namely in health, education, jobs and economic opportunities. And yet, even the most cautious critics suggest that something is happening, that there may be benefits if the tools are appropriated carefully (Heeks 2002). Questions arise such as: What exactly is happening? And through what lenses can it be appreciated? These questions can only be addressed through an inexact science, perhaps more of an art. This article attempts to contribute some building blocks into this art, as if one were providing mirrors to assemble a new kaleidoscope.

Information and communication technologies are often defined as technologies that facilitate communication and the processing and transmission of information by electronic means. This definition encompasses a full range of ICTs, from radio and television to telephones, computers and the Internet. However, if we think more broadly about communication systems —whether they are electronic or not— they are part of the menu of media opportunities at hand: storytelling, theatre, cassettes, illustrations, local newspapers, radio, video and music, etc. There is merit in combining electronic media with other media that people already like, use and know how to control. For example, community radio stations with a link to the Internet are becoming an important option.

The need to invent a new means for assessing the potential of ICTs stems from the fact that they are essentially misplaced tools. The component technologies tend to be designed as commercial tools for industrialised settings, and the bulk of software development is meant for literate and English-speaking users. The fact that they have potential for rural and remote community development worldwide is an add-on. Those who are able to make them work in these settings are true visionaries. They are community-development workers who match-make—or mediate— among the needs of communities, the potential of the technologies, their cost and the public programmes available to subsidise their development. In many cases, they create organizations that provide computer literacy and stimulate demand for ICTs by offering public access sites where people can lose their fear of the technology, play with it and realize its potential (Ramírez 2001a).

ICTs rely on telecommunication networks that require major investments. Like with other infrastructures in the past, the intrinsic potential of the technology is often sufficient rationale to convince policy makers and regulators to invest vast amounts of capital for their expansion, even when the outcomes are difficult to predict, let alone quantify (Sawhney 2001)[1]. This leap of faith is also needed at the individual level; just think about the first time you used a computer (van Dijk 2001). Ironically, as the technology becomes more sophisticated its potential becomes less predictable (Bar et al. 2000). One reason for this is that it begins to affect multiple dimensions of everyday life of businesses, residences and public organisations; furthermore, it creates new services that were unimagined before. The notion of a single best practice begins to appear as an elusive goal (Mansell 1999). Instead, we are faced with multiple opportunities, each with the potential to be integrated into a specific context. This calls for efforts that are "… targeted at very clear activities, as simple and self-contained as possible, which are identified by stakeholders themselves as critical and representative of what can help them be better off" (Menou & Potvin 2000)[2]. So, on the one hand their impact needs case-specificity, and on the other their potential affects so many dimensions that their impact requires flexible, participatory and evolving methodologies (Stoll et al. 2002).

If what we are facing is indeed a collective journey into the unknown, then it is argued here that we need a new language to understand it. In particular, feminist writers and development communication analysts stress the needs for a new approach (Balit 1999; Jansen 1989). The kaleidoscope metaphor works well in that this tool is adjusted to each context; in addition, what we observe changes as we aim the tool to find the light that surrounds us[3].

---

1   Harmeet Sawhney mentions an anonymous quote that conveys this notion rather well: "One does not build bridges by counting the number of people who swim across the river."

2   In the midst of this multidimensional complexity, some short-term evidence of positive, short-term impact in rural areas is beginning to appear. There is growing evidence that for rural people rural phones and email communication are more cost effective relative to having access to Internet-based information (Best & Maclay 2002; Kenny 2002). The positive consumer surplus (the savings realised minus the cost of a phone call) can be significant enough to attract private investors to rural areas, as long as the regulatory environment is attractive (Richardson et al. 2000).

3   Such metaphors are not new: Kai Lee refers to the compass and the gyroscope to describe the complex relationships between science and policy-making (Lee 1993).

2. Assembling an Epistemology

The role and impact of the new technology is so vast that a multidisciplinary approach is needed to appreciate it. In the book *The Network Society*, Jan van Dijk dedicates a chapter each to the technology, the economy, politics and power, the law, the social structure, culture and psychology, before venturing into conclusions and policy perspectives (van Dijk 1999). There are a growing number of tools and diagrams in the literature to capture the multiple dimensions of ICTs (Melody 1996), to track the myriad of indicators (Mansell & Wehn 1998; Minges n.d.; Kirkman et al. 2002), to describe the phases of the Internet (Bar et al. 2000), to model the way people access technology (van Dijk 2001) and to capture the impact across every component of the industry (Houghton 1999). There is also community development literature where the impact of ICTs on enhancing communities has become a focus of research (Pigg 2001). In the end, however, we have to wonder: what is the nature of the beast we are trying to describe? Do we have an epistemology to guide us through this process?

This paper provides elements for that epistemology from the field of natural resource management (NRM). In NRM, physical scientists and social scientists have already come to realise that their particular science is too narrow and that new insights are needed to capture a complex, ever-changing context with endless variables and indicators. To complicate matters, many other stakeholders are now in the picture and their perspectives are also different and cannot be ignored.

BUILDING BLOCK NO.1:
ACKNOWLEDGING A DIVERSITY IN PARADIGMS

The overall perspective or paradigm that shapes the way we approach problem solving needs acknowledgement. The underlying appreciation of reality, the research approaches, the planning tools, and the different implementation mechanisms are not shared by all. Figure 1 shows how the modern and postmodern currents in development display significant differences (Maxwell 1996).

1927
1960
1963
1964
1967
1969
1970
1971
1972
1973
1974
1975
1976
1977
1978
1979
1980
1981
1982
1983
1984
1985
1986
1987
1988
1989
1990
1991
1992
1993
1994
1995
1996
1997
1998
1999
2000
2001
2002
2003
2004
2005
2006

	Modern	Post-modern
Underlying reality	Simple, uniform	Complex, diverse
Objectives	Growth	Development
	Preoccupation with macro	Preoccupation with micro
Research approach	Measure	Listen
	Survey	Participatory Rural Appraisal
	Reductionist	Holistic
	Deduction	Induction
	Abstract models	Complex reality
	Aggregate	Disaggregate
Planning approach	Plan	Enable
	Model	Interact
	Top-down	Bottom-up
	Centralize	Decentralize
Implementation	Blue-print	Process
	Role culture	Task culture
	Standardization	Flexibility, innovation

Figure 1. Modern and Postmodern Currents in Development (Maxwell 1996, 161)

A major challenge here is the fact that the technologies and policies behind ICTs "exist" in the modern paradigm, and their advocates thrive within this perspective. However, it is argued here that when these tools are put to work in rural and remote settings, their performance and "impact" are best appreciated in a postmodern paradigm. The settings they are embedded in are not the ones they were meant for—hence the need for the "mediators" that was mentioned earlier. Moreover, the settings are varied and the appropriation of the technologies depends to a large extent on the amount of local control and adaptation that takes place. In other words, their role and impact can only partially be predicted; indeed, much of it will emerge from local interactions and creativity. Their relevance is in fact constructed locally to fit locally perceived priorities and needs. From an analytical and research perspective, however, the postmodern paradigm can embrace components of the modern, in recognition that there are elements that best fit within that mind frame (Jiggins & Röling 1997).

Building Block No. 2: Embracing Pluralism

For the management of natural resources that include common property areas, conservation areas and watersheds, accommodating multiple interests is a necessity. Each stakeholder will defend his or her own interest and will appreciate opportunities differently.

The relationship among the parties will shift from periods of collaboration to periods of conflict (Ramírez 1999b). Understanding this complex context involves an appreciation of legal frameworks, natural sciences, social sciences and participatory planning and learning process. Not a small feat, hence the need for an epistemology that embraces pluralism (Anderson et al. 1998; Wollenberg et al. 2001). In the field of NRM, a new epistemology has emerged to grasp these features and has now evolved into a range of action-research methodologies that include, among others: collaborative management (Borrini-Feyerabend 1996), collaborative learning (Daniels & Walker 2001), adaptive collaborative management (Buck et al. 2001; Röling & Wagemakers 1998), rapid appraisal of agricultural knowledge systems (Engel & Salomon 1997), and linked local learning (Lightfoot et al. 2001b; Lightfoot et al. 2001a)[4].

In contrast, the field of ICTs for rural development is only now beginning to explore a new multidisciplinary epistemology (Stoll et al. 2002)[5]. The similarities between ICTs and NRM suggest that some of the lessons from NRM may be applied to ICTs research.

4   For a review and analysis of the different methods to accommodate multiple interests, refer to Ramírez (2001b).
5   In the broader fields of network and information systems analysis, the difficulty in predicting long-term effects of ICTs is already clearly described (van Dijk 1999; Bar et al. 2000

Characteristics	NRM context	ICT context
Epistemology	Constructivism	Constructivism
Nature of truth	Multiple perspectives, diversity	Multiple perspectives, diversity
Goals	Multiple, often contradictory	Multiple, often contradictory or competitive
Systems perspective	Acknowledging that reality is best appreciated as a system with different hierarchies and emergent properties	Soft system: learning path to reach a situation in which collective action can be taken
Planning	Interactive process	Sometimes interactive, other times top-down
Policy process	Emerges from interaction among stakeholders at different levels	Emerges from interaction among stakeholders at different levels, or is developed centrally
Role of research	Active partner in societal sense making	Active partner in societal sense making
Nature of science	Biophysical and social sciences both contribute to adaptive perspectives and action	Information and communication technologies, economic and social sciences contribute to adaptive perspectives and action
Nature of extension	Facilitation of learning processes	Facilitation of learning processes

Figure 2. The Characteristics of NRM and ICT Contexts (adapted from Ramírez 2001a).

Figure 2 describes some of the characteristics of NRM epistemology that can be brought into the field of ICT research. This bridging is based on action-research experience in Canada where multiple stakeholders were consulted in setting up a university research project on the role of ICTs in rural and remote community development[6].

Building Block No. 3: Embracing a Systems Approach

Systems theory is useful as an approach to understand the behaviour of natural resources and their complex interactions. In NRM it became evident long ago that ecosystems are complex and largely unpredictable, and systems theory embraced these features. Systems have multiple layers or hierarchies, they have feedback and communication features within them, and they have emergent properties that perplex even the best-informed forecasts (Lee 1993). Ecologists, as much as organisational researchers, use systems thinking. The properties of systems are very much part of ecosystem analysis and about how humans interact within them (Gunderson et al. 1995; Alsop & Farrington 1998; Costanza & Folke 1996; Holling & Sanderson

1996). Moreover, systems thinking is holistic; it addresses overall patterns and relationships rather than reducing issues to smaller parts, which is the tendency of engineering approaches (Bennetts et al. 2000).

Systems thinking is part of the stock of ideas by means of which we interpret the world around us (Checkland & Scholes 1990). Systems thinking is useful as a tool for learning about complex situations and for interdisciplinary research (Ackoff 1969). Since the late 1950s and early 1960s, systems thinking has also been applied to the analysis of organisations (Emery 1969; Emery & Trist 1969; Churchman 1971). Erik Trist's work with the Tavistock Institute led to the notion of sociotechnical systems (Trist 1981). Sociotechnical systems were understood at the time as a new field of inquiry where work conditions would be analysed and improved through action research and a systems perspective. What is relevant is the view that social and technological issues cannot be addressed in parallel; rather, they are to be analysed jointly as a system and with the involvement of the stakeholders.

In a variation from systems thinking, Checkland and Scholes (1990) developed soft systems methodology (SSM). One key contribution from SSM is the notion that the principal stakeholders involved in a system

---

6   For further background refer to Richardson and Ramírez (1999), Ramírez (2001a), and Ramírez (2000).

1927
1960
1963
1964
1967
1969
1970
1971
1972
1973
1974
1975
1976
1977
1978
1979
1980
1981
1982
1983
1984
1985
1986
1987
1988
1989
1990
1991
1992
1993
1994
1995
1996
1997
1998
1999
2000
2001
2002
2003
2004
2005
2006

are owners of the problem or issue. In other words, those who are directly affected "own" the problem and should be involved in understanding and addressing it. A first step in SSM is the visualisation of the problem or topic, with all the richness of stakeholders, concerns, and linkages. In SSM, these diagrams are known as "rich pictures." in that they are "rich" with information. In SSM, the "soft" refers to the human and organisational realm of relationships and interactions, e.g., social capital and trust, viewed as a component of equal importance to the "hard" system (the material objects). It is noteworthy that the inventors of SSM were hard system engineers who realised they could not solve organisational problems with attention only on the hard system. Instead, they realised they needed to address both and engage the stakeholders in the process.

The systems approach is beginning to appear in the literature on rural telecommunications and ICTs (Andrew & Petkov 2000), and to a lesser extent this is also the case with SSM (Bryden 1994; Bennetts et al. 2000).

BUILDING BLOCK NO. 4: EMPHASISING LEARNING AND PARTICIPATION

As with NRM, when ICTs are put to work towards community development goals, multiple stakeholders are involved, each with different perspectives, goals and interests. It has been argued elsewhere that for ICTs to have an impact, the users need to become involved in defining what it is they want to achieve with the technology (Mansell & Wehn 1998). They need to participate both in the design of the programmes and in defining what it is they will measure as evidence that they are achieving their goals. However, Heeks (1999) underlines that participation needs to be approached more critically and without the assumption that it will always and necessarily bring benefits. He recommends attention to: The political and cultural context, the motivation behind those who are introducing participation, and thirdly the willingness and ability to participate of those invited to contribute (Heeks 1999). This critical reflection about

participation is timely and echoes similar critiques in watershed projects (Rhoades 1998), forestry projects (van Dam 2000), and appraisal methodologies (Cornwall et al. 2001), to name a few.

Stoll et al. (2002) have begun to assemble a learning framework towards a participatory, transparent and continuous process about ICTs and development. The emphasis on learning, ongoing adjustment, and transparency—as a means of minimising conflict among stakeholders—is also a hallmark of collaborative approaches in NRM. Indeed, learning is the best way to move forward in complex, unpredictable environments where multiple stakeholders interact (Lee 1993; Woodhill & Röling 1998; Röling & Wagemakers 1998; Röling & Jiggins 1998). Learning is an active process that engages all on an equal footing to explore a complex theme where no single person has the know-how to move forward. Instead, the group is expected to negotiate and agree on visions and the means to achieve them (Lightfoot et al. 2001b; Lightfoot et al. 2001a; Ramírez 2001b; Ramírez 1999a). Learning approaches also embrace the need to experiment, make mistakes, and learn from those mistakes. This is what Sawhney (2001) refers to as "creative error."

Research into the accomplishments by Canadian community based networks that use ICTs to enhance community development suggests that a number of common steps are taken to make the technology available and relevant:

1. Make access possible, through public places.
2. Let community members experiment with the technology.
3. Allow community members to dream up how to use the technology.
4. Plan around those aspirations, aggregate demand, and develop a business and developmental case for infrastructure upgrades.
5. Organise to make the aspirations a reality in terms of infrastructure, applications, and skills (Ramírez 2001a).

This process has more learning features than predictable outcomes. ICTs create new venues and spaces for innovation that were not there before. While some of the outcomes can be predicted, many emerge as people realise how they can harness the technology. From a soft systems perspective, these are emerging properties that can only happen when people interact with the technology.

WEAVING IT ALL TOGETHER

We have now defined the pillars of a new epistemology to understand ICTs as tools for rural and remote community development:

- Acknowledging a diversity in paradigms
- Embracing pluralism
- Embracing a systems approach
- Emphasising learning and participation

Beyond an epistemology, the four pillars begin to lay the foundation for an action-research approach to ICTs in rural development. The methodological achievements in natural resource management lend a hand here, especially with visual and participatory planning tools to engage different stakeholders in the negotiation (Pretty et al. 1995; Guijt 1998; Groot & Maarleveld 2000).

3. Putting the Epistemology to Work

The first two pillars set a framework for multi-stakeholder engagement from the beginning. The cautionary pointers about participation presented by Heeks (1999) are valid. They provide a checklist that reminds one to verify that the power relations allow for a legitimate process of engagement. This is not always possible; the conditions are never ideal, and mistakes will happen. The process of stakeholder engagement is not linear or entirely predictable (Ramírez 2001b); however, as Sawhney suggests, much can be learned from "creative error." What is important is to initiate the process with an appreciation of the enabling conditions as well as the limitations[7].

Action Research

The author has had experience with action research in rural and remote communities in Ontario, Canada, that are harnessing ICTs for community development. The research documented three case studies by accomplished community-based networks. The investigation led to the formulation of a model that describes how these organisations emerge as a result of a combination of factors including: community needs, governmental policies and incentive programmes, the technology and its costs. The research began with a consultation engaging over 30 stakeholders from different sectors involved in rural and remote telecommunications. Their involvement from the start created a network of trust and led to active involvement by the case study organisations in the research and in follow-up activities beyond it (Richardson & Ramírez 1999; Ramírez 2001a; Ramírez 2000). In one setting the case study organisation used the research as the basis for a presentation on its accomplishments at an international conference (Moore et al. 2001). In another, northern network, the research partnership led to an ongoing collaboration in planning and tracking the impact of ICTs in remote communities.

Community Engagement for Collaborative Planning

The theoretical arguments made in this paper stem from on-the-ground action research work in East Africa and northern Canada[8]. Experience with multiple-stakeholder workshops for improved agro-ecosystem management in East Africa provided the foundation for action research work to harness ICTs for community development among aboriginal groups in northern Canada. Many of the facilitation and planning tools were the same: Visioning desirable futures and specifying what was needed to accomplish the goals and who needed to become involved. The subject matter was different: in Kenya we talked about restoring farms and ecosystems, whereas in

---

7   In the context of Industry Canada's Smart Communities, some best practices for community engagement have now been prepared; visit: http://smartcommunities.ic.gc.ca/best/bp-engagement_e.asp [Spaces OK in this URL?]

8   The methodological details from the African experiences are published elsewhere (Lightfoot et al. 2001b), and the Canadian work is available online at http://smart.knet.ca

1927
1960
1963
1964
1967
1969
1970
1971
1972
1973
1974
1975
1976
1977
1978
1979
1980
1981
1982
1983
1984
1985
1986
1987
1988
1989
1990
1991
1992
1993
1994
1995
1996
1997
1998
1999
2000
2001
2002
2003
2004
2005
2006

Canada we talked about improving health, education, local government and economic development using ICTs.

The main objectives of the community engagement workshops (CEWs) were: (a) To help the communities in planning for the use of ICTs; (b) to share information about the project and the progress done so far; (c) to share the results of data gathered through surveys; (d) to explore and identify how the communities would like to measure and verify the progress made in their respective communities in relation to health, education, local governance, and economic development; and (e) to provide the local centre managers with tools to assess people's training needs and track how their knowledge and skills improve using the technology. As the result of the CEWs, each of the communities identified and explored the programmes that they would like to see implemented in their communities in relation to education, health, economic development, and local governance, and identified the indicators related to each program (TeleCommons Development Group 2002).

Tracking Performance at Three Levels

The systems perspective is a useful guide in addressing the levels of analysis where change becomes evident. We approach ICTs and community development at three levels; our current work with KNet, an aboriginal network in northwestern Ontario, follows this approach[9]:

1. *Community level access*. The access to ICT across a community is tracked with standard ITU and Statistics Canada indicators about access, equipment, and expenditures. This is done through an annual survey of residences and businesses in five fly-in communities. Some of them received their first phones after our first survey and have since acquired broadband telecommunication services: a "technological poll vault" that other communities around the world will also experience.

2. *Sectors and organisations*. Capacity building and organisational strengthening for "harnessing" ICTs is assessed on the basis of the community visions in terms of better health, education and local government/economic development. The targets will be tracked on the basis of community goals, results and activities (a results-based management framework). During the engagement workshops, the community members provide the indicators of goals and results that matter to them.

3. *People's skills and knowledge*. How ICTs improve individuals' knowledge and skill. People need to play with the technology first before they can dream of possible applications. Skill is not enough to translate the opportunity into a tangible benefit, but it is a necessary foundation. We have used qualitative tools to track relative changes in knowledge and skill among students involved in Community Access Programme (CAP) sites in rural Canada. Visualising these otherwise-invisible gains is empowering to the learner (Ramírez et al. 2000).

Creating Local Capacity

A major challenge in both the Canadian and East African contexts is to create a critical mass of trained human resources that can keep the fire going. In Tanzania, a multi-stakeholder coalition has come together and has already established a track record in facilitating workshops to bring multiple stakeholders together to learn to improve natural resource management (Lightfoot & Groot 2002). Their skills have now been put to work in workshops held in Uganda during 2001. In Kenya, two farmer groups have continued the facilitation work and have adjusted the approach to address conflicts and planning in the coffee sector, meat sector, education and health. In northern Canada the work continues with community engagement efforts to ensure ICTs are put to work toward satisfying community priorities.

4. Conclusions

This paper builds a bridge between current theoretical and methodological perspectives in natural resource

---

9   Visit http://smart.knet.ca/.

management (NRM) and information and communication technology for rural and remote community development (ICTs). The two fields of study share common features: The reality they address is multi-dimensional, ever-changing, and unpredictable, and numerous stakeholders are involved. NRM enjoys a track record in terms of theoretical and methodological experiences in collaborative planning and learning approaches that respond to the major features described above. In the field of ICTs and rural development, the theoretical and methodological approaches are at an earlier stage of evolution. However, in light of the parallel circumstances, several pillars from NRM can become the foundation for a new epistemology to address ICTs and rural development. The four pillars (acknowledging diversity in paradigms; embracing pluralism; embracing a systems approach; and emphasising learning and participation) are likely not the only ones, but they do set the foundation for action research work. The ongoing action research work that underlies this paper points towards the relevance of this cross-disciplinary bridge.

The metaphor for the new epistemology is a kaleidoscope, a multiple-prism tool that provides a different view on a reality and one that changes depending on the users' perspective. The evidence thus far regarding the potential of ICTs suggests that a kaleidoscopic approach may be the most appropriate way to capture the many dimensions where the technologies may have an impact.

References

Ackoff, R. 1969. "Systems, organizations, and interdisciplinary research," in: F. Emery, ed. *Systems thinking*. Middlesex, U.K.: Penguin Books. 330–347.

Alsop, R., and J. Farrington. 1998. "Nests, nodes and niches: A system for process monitoring, information exchange and decision making for multiple stakeholders," *World Development* 26:249–260.

Anderson, J., J. Clement, and L. Crowder. 1998. "Accommodating conflicting interests in forestry: Concepts emerging from pluralism," *Unasylva* 49(194):3–10.

Andrew, T., and D. Petkov. 2000. "Towards a systems thinking approach to the planning and design of rural telecommunication infrastructure," World Congress of the Systems Sciences in conjunction with the 44th Annual Meeting of the International Society for the Systems Sciences. Toronto, Canada. July 16–22.

Balit, S. 1999. *Voices for change: Rural women and communication*. Rome: Food and Agriculture Organization.

Bar, F., S. Cohen, P. Cowhey, B. DeLong, M. Kleeman, and J. Zysman. 2000. "Access and innovation policy for the third-generation Internet," *Telecommunications Policy* 24:489–518.

Bennetts, P., A. Wood-Harper, and S. Mills. 2000. "An holistic approach to the management of information systems development: A review using soft systems approach and multiple viewpoints," *Systemic practice and action research* 13:189–205.

Best, M., and C. Maclay. 2002. "Community Internet access in rural areas: Solving the economic sustainability puzzle (Chapter 8)," in: G. Kirkman, J. Sachs, K. Schwab, and P. Cornellius, eds. *The global information technology report 2001–2002: Readiness for the networked world*. Oxford, U.K.: Oxford Univ. Press. 76-88.

Borrini-Feyerabend, G. 1996. *Collaborative management of protected areas: Tailoring the approach to the context*. Gland, Switzerland: IUCN.

Bryden, J. 1994. "Towards sustainable rural communities: From theory to action," in: J. Bryden, ed. *Towards sustainable rural communities*. The Guelph seminar series. Guelph, Canada: University of Guelph School of Rural Planning and Development. 211–233.

Buck, L., C. Geisler, J. Schelhas, and E. Wollenberg. 2001. *Biological diversity: Balancing interests through adaptive collaborative management*. Boca Raton, Fla.: CRC Press.

Checkland, P., and J. Scholes. 1990. *Soft systems methodology in action*. Chichester, U.K.: John Wiley and Sons.

Churchman, C. 1971. *The design of inquiring systems: Basic concepts of systems and organization*. New York and London: Basic Books.

Cornwall, A., S. Musyoki, and G. Pratt. 2001. "In search of a new impetus: Practitioners' reflections on PRA and participation in Kenya," *IDS working paper no. 131*. Brighton, U.K.: IDS.

Costanza, R., and C. Folke. 1996. "The structure and function of ecological systems in relation to property-rights regimes," in: S. Hanna, C. Folke, and K.-G. Mäller, eds. *Rights to nature: Ecological, economic, cultural, and political principles of institutions for the environment*. Washington, D.C., and Covelo, Calif.: Island Press. 13–34.

Daniels, S., and G. Walker. 2001. *Working through environmental conflict: The collaborative learning approach*. Westport, Conn., and London: Praeger.

Emery, F. 1969. *Systems thinking*. Middlesex, U.K.: Penguin Books.

Emery, F., and E. Trist. 1969. "The causal texture of organizational environments," in: F. Emery, ed. *Systems thinking*. Middlesex, U.K.: Penguin Books. 241–258.

Engel, P., and M. Salomon. 1997. *Facilitating innovation for development*. Amsterdam: Royal Tropical Institute.

Groot, A., and M. Maarleveld. 2000. "Demystifying facilitation in participatory development," *Gatekeeper series no. 89*. London: IIED.

Guijt, I. 1998. "Participatory monitoring and impact assessment of sustainable agriculture initiatives: An introduction to key elements," *SARL discussion paper, vol. 1*. London: IIED.

Gunderson, L., C. Holling, and S. Light. 1995. *Barriers and bridges to the renewal of ecosystems and institutions*. New York: Columbia Univ. Press.

Heeks, R. 1999. "The tyranny of participation in information systems: Learning from development projects," in: *Working paper no. 4*. http://www.man.ac.uk/idpm/diwpf4.htm.

1927
1960
1963
1964
1967
1969
1970
1971
1972
1973
1974
1975
1976
1977
1978
1979
1980
1981
1982
1983
1984
1985
1986
1987
1988
1989
1990
1991
1992
1993
1994
1995
1996
1997
1998
1999
2000
2001
2002
2003
2004
2005
2006

Heeks, R. 2002. "I-development not e-development: Special issue on ICTs and development," *Journal of International Development* 14(1):1–11.

Holling, C., and S. Sanderson. 1996. "Dynamics of (dis)harmony in ecological and social systems," in: S. Hanna, C. Folke, and K.-G. Mäller, eds. *Rights to nature: Ecological, Economic, Cultural, and Political Principles of Institutions for the Environment*. Washington, D.C., and Covelo, Calif.: Island Press. 57–86.

Houghton, J. 1999. "Mapping information industries and markets," *Telecommunications Policy* 23:689–699.

Jansen, S. 1989. "Gender and the information society: A socially constructed silence," *Journal of Communication* 39:196–215.

Jiggins, J., and N. Röling. 1997. "Action research in natural resource management: Marginal in the first paradigm, core in the second," in: C. Albadalejo and F. Casabianca, eds. *Pour une méthodologie de la recherche action*. Versailles: INRA/SAD. 151–169.

Kenny, C. 2002. "Information and communication technologies for direct poverty alleviation: Costs and benefits," *Development Policy Review* 20:141–157.

Kirkman, G., C. Osorio, and J. Sachs. 2002. "The networked readiness index: Measuring the preparedness of nations for the networked world (Chapter 1)," in: G. Kirkman, J. Sachs, K. Schwab, and P. Cornellius, eds. *The Global Information Technology Report 2001–2002: Readiness for the Networked World*. Oxford, U.K.: Oxford Univ. Press. 10–29.

Lee, K. 1993. *Compass and gyroscope: Integrating Science and Politics for the Environment*. Washington, D.C.: Island Press.

Lightfoot, C., M. Fernandez, R. Noble, R. Ramírez, A. Groot, E. Fernandez-Baca, F. Shao, G. Muro, S. Okelabo, A. Mugenyi, I. Bekalo, A. Rianga, and L. Obare. 2001a. "A learning approach to community agroecosystem management," in: C. Flora, ed. *Interactions Between Agroecosystems and Rural Communities*. Boca Raton, Fla.: CRC Press. 115–130.

Lightfoot, C., and A. Groot. 2002. "How could multi-stakeholder collaboration in ASPS contribute to poverty, gender equity, empowerment, governance, and democracy?" Development workers workshop "How to involve farmers in the implementation of the agricultural sector support programme." Tune, Denmark: F. Dolberg. April 2–6.

Lightfoot, C., R. Ramírez, A. Groot, C. Alders, F. Shao, D. Kisauzi, and I. Bekalo. 2001b. "Learning our way ahead: Navigating institutional change and agricultural decentralisation," *Gatekeeper series no. 98*. London: IIED.

Mansell, R. 1999. Information and communication technologies for development: Assessing the potential and the risks. *Telecommunications Policy* 23:35–50.

Mansell, R., and U. Wehn. 1998. *Knowledge Societies: Information Technology for Sustainable Development*. Oxford, U.K.: Oxford Univ. Press (published for and on behalf of the United Nations).

Maxwell, D. 1996. "Measuring food insecurity: The frequency and severity of 'coping strategies,'" *Food Policy* 21:291–303.

Melody, W. 1996. "Toward a framework for designing information society policies," *Telecommunications policy* 20:243–259.

Menou, M., and J. Potvin. 2000. Towards a conceptual framework for learning about ICTs and knowledge in the process of development. *GK-Leap Conceptual Framework*. Ottawa: Bellanet, IDRC.

Minges, M. (n.d.) "Counting the Net: Internet access indicators," http://www.isoc.org/isoc/conferences/inet/00/cdproceedings/8e/8e_1.htm

Moore, J., R. Ramírez, S. Coghlan, D. Oliphant, and K. Whiteford. 2001. "Community network as a learning organization: An outcome of academic and community collaboration," paper presented at the II Global Congress of Citizen Networks. Buenos Aires, Argentina. December 5–7. http://www.globalcn2001.org/abstracts/taller03/Oliphant_otros.doc

OECD. 2001. *Information and Communication Technologies and Rural Development*. Paris: OECD.

Pigg, K.E. 2001. "Applications of community informatics for building community and enhancing civic society," *Information, Communication & Society* 4:507–527.

Pretty, J., I. Guijt, I. Scoones, and J. Thompson. 1995. *A Trainer's Guide for Participatory Learning and Action*. London: IIED.

Ramírez, R. 1999a. "Participatory learning and communication approaches for managing pluralism: Implications for sustainable forestry, agriculture and rural development," *Pluralism and Sustainable Forestry and Rural Development*. Rome. December 9–12, 1997. 117–152.

Ramírez, R. 1999b. "Stakeholder analysis and conflict management," in D. Buckles, ed. *Conflict and collaboration in natural resource management*. Ottawa and Washington, D.C.: IDRC and the World Bank. 101–126.

Ramírez, R. 2000. "Rural and remote communities harnessing information and communication technology for community development," unpublished Ph.D. diss. Interdisciplinary Rural Studies, University of Guelph.

Ramírez, R. 2001a. "A model for rural and remote information and communication technologies: A Canadian exploration," *Telecommunications Policy* 25:315–330.

Ramírez, R. 2001b. "Understanding the approaches for accommodating multiple stakeholders' interests," *International Journal of Agricultural Resources, Governance and Ecology* 1:264–285.

Ramírez, R., D. Murray, G. Kora, and D. Richardson. 2000. *Evaluation report: Rural resources partnership for Oxford County Library and HRDC*. University of Guelph, Canada. www.ocl.net/rrp/evaluation/

Rhoades, R. 1998. "Participatory watershed research and management: Where the shadow falls," *Gatekeeper series no. 81*. London: IIED.

Richardson, D., and R. Ramírez. 1999. "'PACTS' for rural Ontario: Partnerships, accessibility and connectivity transformation strategies for rural Ontario," *Agri-food research in Ontario* 23(1):6–7.

Richardson, D., R. Ramírez, and M. Haq. 2000. "Grameen Telecom's Village Phone Programme: A multi-media case study," www.telecommons.com/villagephone

Röling, N., and J. Jiggins. 1998. "The ecological knowledge system," in: N. Röling & M. Wagemakers, eds. *Facilitating sustainable Agriculture: Participatory Learning and Adaptive Management in Times of Environmental Uncertainty*. Cambridge, U.K.: Cambridge Univ. Press. 283–311.

Röling, N., and M. Wagemakers. 1998. *Facilitating sustainable agriculture: Participatory Learning and Adaptive Management in Times of Environmental uncertainty*. Cambridge, U.K.: Cambridge Univ. Press.

Sawhney, H. 2001. "Dynamics of infrastructure development: The role of metaphors, political will and sunk investment," *Media, Culture & Society* 23:33–51.

Stoll, K., M. Menou, K. Camacho, and Y. Khellady. 2002. *Learning about ICTs' Role in Development: A Framework Towards a Participatory, Transparent and Continuous Process*. Ottawa: IDRC.

TeleCommons Development Group. 2002. *Kuh-Ke-Nah SMART First Nations Demonstration Project: Community Engagement Workshops*. Guelph, Ontario. November 2001–January 2002.

Trist, E. 1981. "The evolution of socio-technical Systems: A conceptual framework and an action research program," *Issues in the Quality of Working Life* 2. Toronto: Ontario Ministry of Labour & Ontario Quality of Working Life Centre.

van Dam, C. 2000. "Two decades of participatory development ... but how participatory?" *Forests, Trees and People Newlsetter* 42:11–17.

van Dijk, J. 1999. *The Network Society: Social Aspects of New Media.* London and Thousand Oaks, Calif.: Sage.

van Dijk, J. 2001. "The ideology behind 'closing digital divides': Applying static analysis to dynamic gaps," in *Statistics: Lies, Damn Lies.* IAMCR/ICA Symposium on the Digital Divide. University of Texas, Austin. November 15–17.

Wollenberg, E., D. Edmunds, and J. Anderson. 2001. "Pluralism and the less powerful: Accommodating multiple interests in local forest management" *International Journal of Agricultural Resources, Governance and Ecology* 1:199–222.

Woodhill, J., and N. Röling. 1998. "The second wing of the eagle: The human dimension in learning our way to more sustainable futures," in: N. Röling and M. Wagemakers, eds. *Facilitating sustainable agriculture: Participatory Learning and Adaptive Management in Times of Environmental Uncertainty.* Cambridge, U.K.: Cambridge Univ. Press. 46–71.

EXCERPT FROM:

MEDIA AND DEMOCRATISATION IN THE INFORMATION SOCIETY

Media, Democratisation and Regulation

By Marc Raboy

2003 The debate on media and democratisation has always had a dual focus: democratising media, as a positive value in and of itself, and fostering a role for media in the democratisation of societies. For some, the media have tended to be seen as value-free containers of information, but they are in fact contested spaces, objects of contention in their own right. Media activists have struggled with how to problematise this, how to make the media a social issue, rather than something that people merely suffer, and how to broaden the public discourse on the media's role in democracy.

Historically, media issues have not had the same resonance among social activists as other themes such as the environment, gender issues and human rights. A 1999 statement by a group of media activists, Voices 21, sought to begin building a new social movement around media and communication issues. It proposed forming an international alliance to address concerns and to work jointly on matters around media and communication. All movements that work toward social change use media and communication networks, Voices 21 pointed out; it is therefore essential that they focus on current trends such as the concentration of media ownership in fewer and fewer hands (Voices 21 1999)[1].

1 In the interest of transparency, it should be stated that the author is a member of Voices 21.

1927
1960
1963
1964
1967
1969
1970
1971
1972
1973
1974
1975
1976
1977
1978
1979
1980
1981
1982
1983
1984
1985
1986
1987
1988
1989
1990
1991
1992
1993
1994
1995
1996
1997
1998
1999
2000
2001
2002
2003
2004
2005
2006

The advent of the World Summit on the Information Society (WSIS) offers an opportunity to move in that direction. Media and communication issues are working their way onto broader social agendas (for example, through the World Social Forum). McChesney and Nichols (2002), among others, write about placing media democratisation at the centre of a social movement: they present a programme for structural media reform in the United States. Among other things, the US media reform movement has successfully lobbied Congress to roll back some of the Federal Communication Commission's (FCC's) more aggressive attempts to liberalise media ownership rules. In short, there is a need to marry mainstream and alternative media reform initiatives with policy intervention, research, and education.

Media democratisation will be based on the extent to which there can be a successful blending of five types of intervention, led by five sets of actors:

- ongoing critical analysis of media issues (researchers);
- media literacy efforts (educators);
- building and operating autonomous media (alternative media practitioners);
- progressive practices within mainstream media (journalists, editors, publishers, etc.); and
- policy intervention (media policy activists).

The WSIS presents an opportunity to work on the issues raised in this paper within an institutional framework, keeping in mind this five-pronged approach. Furthermore, at the present time, formal attempts to influence media development can take four possible pathways:

1. *The libertarian approach:* This approach does not advocate the regulation of media. With the spread of new digital technologies like the Internet, this approach is currently favoured by many national regulators (Australia is an important exception), mainly because they do not know what to do or how to do it. It is also largely favoured by many grassroots activists who are benefiting from this open communication system. But the history of older media technologies shows that, left to its own devices, this open access is not likely to last. A libertarian model of Internet governance will likely lead eventually to closed doors, restricted access, and limited communication.

2. *Self-regulation:* This is the approach most often favoured by industry players, with the encouragement of national regulators. It is currently being touted as the solution to problems such as abusive content and the protection of rights, on the argument that consumers will respond if they are not satisfied. But as we see with initiatives surrounding copyright and electronic commerce, even the promoters of self-regulation are recognising the need for a global structural framework for communication activity, within which media self-regulation would take place.

3. *The closed club, or top-down, institutional model:* This approach fills the vacuum created by the retreat of national governments from regulatory issues. Deals are negotiated in organisations such as the Organisation for Economic Co-operation and Development (OECD), the Group of Eight (G-8), and the World Trade Organisation (WTO), as well as in the new institutions emerging in the corporate sector. Here, the economically most powerful players simply dictate the rules of the game to everyone else, and the media are perceived as businesses, entertainment vehicles, and organs of tightly controlled public information.

4. *The long march through the institutions:* This is a process that is tied to the broader project of democratisation of global governance, reflected in some of the initiatives around United Nations reform and in notions such as "cosmopolitan democracy". Access to global policy making through civil society participation in processes such as the WSIS is crucial to this model, which has as a corollary the fostering of a plurality and diversity of media seen as facilitators of widespread participation in every aspect of public life.

In terms of media democratisation and a democratic role for the media, the last path is clearly the only viable one. Transparency, public participation, and a sociocultural approach to media governance are values that are now worth promoting transnationally. A global policy approach along these lines would help redefine the role of the state with respect to the media, both domestically and in its new transnational guise, while providing leverage for addressing a range of specific issues that are currently well off the agenda. In the current context of globalisation, the media can be either a locomotive of human development or an instrument of power and domination. Which it will be has not been determined, and that is why the stakes in the WSIS debates are so high.

As issues involving the regulation of broadcasting go global, then, we need to begin thinking about appropriate global regulatory mechanisms. This would make it possible to begin thinking about intervening globally on a range of issues, such as the following:

■ regulating commercial media activities in the public interest, to guarantee equitable access and basic services;

■ funding and providing institutional support for the creation and sustenance of public services and alternative media;

■ placing limits on corporate controls resulting from the transnational concentration of ownership in new and conventional media and telecommunications;

■ providing incentives (through fiscal support measures, etc.) for the production, distribution, and exhibition of media content that meets public policy objectives;

■ guaranteeing access to available media channels on the basis of public interest criteria;

■ developing universal codes and standards for curtailing the spread of abusive media content;

■ facilitating networking capacity through the use of media technologies by not-for-profit organisations; and

■ providing public media spaces for conflict resolution and democratic dialogue on global issues.

I am aware that this "regulatory approach" has important limitations. The extent to which so-called independent regulators in the liberal democracies have been captured by industry interests has been well documented[2]. Regulation, in some cases, acts as a thinly veiled justification for state interference with media independence. Alternative media activists have spent precious energy participating in meaningless consultations and meeting regulatory requirements. Yet, allow me to make the counterargument.

Take, for example, the recent highly mediated decision by the FCC loosening US restrictions on cross-media and concentration of media ownership. A close look at this situation reveals that the United States still has stronger rules than most Western countries regarding concentration of media ownership. Under the *new* FCC regulations, a network can own stations reaching up to 45 per cent of the national population and can own a limited number of other media in the same market. In neighbouring Canada, to cite an example of a country often believed to be very hands-on in regulatory measures, there are no restrictions regarding cross-media or national concentration; thus, one company (which happens to be the largest Canadian industrial corporation of all, Bell Canada Enterprises, or BCE) owns one of the country's two national newspapers as well as the leading national television network, with stations reach 99 percent of the English-speaking population[3].

In the 1980s, riding the wave of deregulatory ideology ushered in with the election of Ronald Reagan, FCC chair Mark Fowler famously stated: "Television is just another appliance, a toaster with pictures." One does not regulate toasters, so why regulate television, the argument went. However, a radio, a television set, and the Internet are not just toasters with pictures. The point is to distinguish between regulation and

---

2   See, for example, Center for Public Integrity (2003), which documents the successful lobbying activities of US media corporations vis-à-vis the FCC.
3   In fact, as this was being written, a Canadian parliamentary committee had just recommended a moratorium on further mergers until the government came up with a comprehensive policy on media ownership (Fraser 2003).

1927
1960
1963
1964
1967
1969
1970
1971
1972
1973
1974
1975
1976
1977
1978
1979
1980
1981
1982
1983
1984
1985
1986
1987
1988
1989
1990
1991
1992
1993
1994
1995
1996
1997
1998
1999
2000
2001
2002
2003
2004
2005
2006

control: regulation must be aimed at providing an enabling framework within which the media can flourish and contribute to democratic public life and human development, and at enhancing freedom of expression *and* the right to communicate. As a leading US academic, Edwin Baker (2002), has written, media regulation has to be seen as legitimate, necessary, and possible.

Independent regulatory authorities and public institutions such as public broadcasters have in fact protected the public interest from abusive state authority, be it the Richard Nixon, Ronald Reagan, or George W. Bush regimes in the United States, the Margaret Thatcher regime in the United Kingdom, or others. Despite declining audience shares (brought on by a combination of channel proliferation, cultural globalisation, and a slowness to adapt to the new context), public broadcasting still deserves widespread popular support wherever it has flourished historically. With the sole, interesting example of France, no developed country has privatised a national public broadcaster, despite the rhetoric of a generation of neoliberal political leadership.

Regulation can be even more important for promoting a third sector in the media, especially broadcasting and possibly, shortly, the Internet.

Regulation can guarantee a space in the environment for "third sector" media that cannot force their way in by commanding either great financial resources or massive audience shares. Progressive fiscal regimes and funding programmes can provide assurances that alternative voices are heard.

The issue, as suggested above, is how to transfer these values to the international sphere, guaranteeing it where it exists (in the face of challenges from regressive international trade and copyright regimes), promoting it where it does not (in the illiberal countries of the world), and refocusing it in the new context of technological convergence and globalisation.

In short, media regulation can address the following:

Excerpt from: "*Media Without an Audience*"
By Eric Kluitenberg

2000

Intimate media have a high degree of audience feedback. Typically the distance between the sender and his or her remote audience is enormous in broadcast media, if only because of the small number of active senders and the overload of passive audience. Feedback mechanisms are necessarily complicated and bureaucratic—the letter to the editors, phone-in time available for only a tiniest fraction of the audience. Intimate media instead are micro-media; there is a close relationship between sender and audience. Ideally the sender and the audience all know each other, while the relationship is still more than a one-on-one conversation (as in a telephone call).

Intimate media are spontaneous media. They emerge at the grassroots level. They cut across all available media, all available technologies. Intimate media can be low-tech; they can also be high-tech. What characterises them is an attitude. Intimate media range from micro-print to pirate radio, to hacked TV, Web casting, satellite amateurs, micro-FM or high-bandwidth networks. Intimate media can be organised in a professional way, though usually they are not. Most common is their appearance as amateur media -- their audience reach is generally economically not viable. Intimate media are generally not a good stock option. ...

Kluitenberg, Eric. "Media Without an Audience." Paper presented at the Banff Centre for the Arts Interactive Screen Workshop (August 2000), and the International Festival of Streaming Media, in Amsterdam, October 2000. Published in http://www.ctrl-z.org/magazine/2001/texts/eric.htm and http://www.debalie.nl/dossierartikel.jsp?dossierid=22375&articleid=7135. Reprinted with permission of the copyright holder.

■ licensing of public, privately owned, and community broadcasting services (goal: competition, system administration);

■ property transactions (goal: market pluralism, diversity);

■ abusive content (goal: protection of societal norms);

- content quotas (goal: protection and promotion of national culture);
- performance obligations (goal: public service, programming requirements);
- rates for free-to-air, subscriber, and pay-per-view services (goal: consumer protection);
- access provisions (goal: equal opportunity for free expression);
- relation between public and private services (goal: system balance); and
- funding requirements (goal: promotion of priority services).

The role of media regulation is to determine the public interest, on an ongoing basis and with regard to specific issues such as the ones mentioned above. This is too fine a job to be done by governments in the course of their general activities. It cannot be left to broadcasters alone, for they necessarily have vested interests (even in the case of public service broadcasters). The marketplace is too blunt an instrument.

Citizens can individually and through their collective organisations articulate their expectations but have no power for implementing them.

The success of a regulatory approach will therefore depend on the following:
- clear, but general, policy guidelines from the constituting authority;
- clearly defined powers, backed up by effective compliance mechanisms;
- the fullest possible transparency in all of its operations; and
- real, meaningful access to decision-making processes for all of the actors concerned, especially public interest organisations that are otherwise relatively removed from the centres of power.

The role of a regulatory authority would be to:
- oversee system equilibrium (balance between the public, private, and community sectors);
- guarantee the accountability of the public sector;
- specify the public service contribution of the private sector;
- facilitate the viability of the community sector;
- oversee system development (for example, introduction of new services);
- set general policy (between the macro level of broad state policy and the micromanagement of broadcasters' operations);
- oversee industry self-regulation;
- supervise licensing and renewal processes; and
- deal with complaints and content issues on the basis of established codes and standards.

Regulation can be seen as a brokering process between the interests of the state, the broadcasting industries and civil society. It is about framework structuring and enabling rather than, as is often assumed, about control. Seen in this way, WSIS can be a moment in the establishment of the new global media environment. It is an opportunity that should not be missed but whose ultimate relevance needs to be carefully weighed and placed in its proper perspective.

References

Baker, C. Edwin. *Media, Markets and Democracy.* Cambridge, England: Cambridge University Press, 2002.

McChesney, Robert W., and John Nichols. *Our Media Not Theirs: The Democratic Struggle Against Corporate Media.* New York: Seven Stories Press, 2002.

"Voices 21." A Global Movement for People's Voices in Media and Communication in the 21st Century. 1999: www.comunica.org/v21/. Accessed on 1 July 2003.

Raboy, Marc. "Media and Democratisation in the Information Society," in O'Siochru, S., and B. Girard, eds., *Communicating in the Information Society.* Geneva: UNRISD, 2003. Reprinted with permission.

1927
1960
1963
1964
1967
1969
1970
1971
1972
1973
1974
1975
1976
1977
1978
1979
1980
1981
1982
1983
1984
1985
1986
1987
1988
1989
1990
1991
1992
1993
1994
1995
1996
1997
1998
1999
2000
2001
2002
2003
2004
2005
2006

ABOUT THE AUTHORS

Robert A. Agunga is associate professor in the Department of African-American and African Studies at The Ohio State University. His areas of research include strategic communication for development; change and social transformation; institution and capacity building; communication and empowerment; and new media and distance learning.

Collins Airhihenbuwa is a professor in the Department of Biobehavioral Health, College of Health and Human Sciences at Pennsylvania State University. His area of research includes health, and culture and development.

Xavier Albó, a Jesuit priest, cofounded the Centre for the Research and Promotion of Peasantry, where he continues to work as a researcher and policy adviser. Albó is the author of numerous books and essays on rural and indigenous culture in the Andean region.

Rosa María Alfaro is an educator and communicator who founded Calandria, a Peruvian nongovernmental organization, where she has worked for the past 23 years. She is the executive director of the Veeduría Ciudadana de la Comunicación (a media observatory) and consults internationally. She taught for many years at the University of Peru, Lima. She is a member of the CFSC Practitioner and University networks.

Arjun Appadurai is a contemporary social theorist who specializes in sociocultural anthropology, globalisation and public culture. Currently, he conducts research in the internal organisation of mass media, and the historical study of state policies involving quantification.

Joseph Ascroft is an emeritus professor at the University of Iowa (United States) who worked at numerous international organizations including the United Nations Children's Fund (UNICEF) in Nigeria, Turkey, Pakistan, Rumania and Swaziland. He specializes in communications with peasants in Third World rural hinterlands.

Silvia Balit, who cofounded the Development Support Communication programme at the U.N. Food and Agriculture Organisation (FAO), has more than 30 years of experience in communication for rural development and social change. At FAO, she led many initiatives aimed at strengthening rural communication systems in Africa, Asia and Latin America to promote sustainable development and social change.

Alejandro Barranquero teaches at the Universidad de Málaga (Spain). He is the author of numerous essays on communication and social change in Latin America. He studied journalism and audiovisual communication at the Universidad de Málaga and the Universidad Complutense de Madrid. His specialties include: communication and political management, communication and arts, critical theory and historic materialism.

Luis Ramiro Beltrán is a Bolivian journalist and a writer, as well as a communication artist and a scientist. He worked for the Organization of American States in Colombia and Ecuador, at Canada's International Development Research Centre and at the United Nations Educational, Scientific and Cultural Organization (UNESCO). He is a visiting professor at several U.S. universities and the author of many articles and several books.

Luiz Beltrão de Andrade Lima (1918-1986) was a Brazilian writer, journalist, anthropologist and communication specialist. In 1961, he coordinated the first studies on journalism at the Universidade Catolica de Pernambuco (Brazil) and, in 1965, founded and edited the first specialised communication journal, *Comunicações & Problemas*. He authored many novels and studies on communication and popular cultures.

David Berlo served as head of the department of general communication arts at Michigan State University for many years. He published his main theoretical work, *The Process of Communication: Introduction to Theory and Practice*, in 1960. In this work, he introduced his model of the psychological nature of communication. The book achieved worldwide distribution and was reprinted many times.

Guy Bessette is a senior programme specialist in environment and natural resource management for Canada's International Development Research Centre. He specializes in development communication and participatory development. He has authored a number of chapters and books on development communication.

Augusto Boal began his career as art director of Teatro Arena in Sao Paulo (Brazil), and was jailed and exiled by the military regime in 1971. From 1972 to 1976, he travelled extensively around Latin America, where he developed new approaches to theatre such as, "Theatre of the Oppressed." He returned to Brazil in 1986 and created the "Popular Theatre Factory," with the objective of making theatre accessible to all. In 1992, he was elected councilman in Rio de Janeiro on a political platform that proposed to use theatre in the streets of the city to explore social problems.

Bertolt Brecht (1898–1956) was a German dramatist and poet. His brilliant wit, outspoken Marxism and revolutionary experiments in theatre made Brecht a vital and controversial force in modern drama. His early plays are examples of nihilistic expressionism and caused riots at their openings, bringing Brecht instant notoriety. In 1926, with the debut of *Mann ist Mann* (Man is Man), he began to develop his so-called "epic theatre," in which narrative, montage, self-contained scenes and rational argument are used to shock the spectator.

L. David Brown is associate director for international programmes at the Hauser Center for Nonprofit Organizations, and lecturer in public policy at the Kennedy School of Government at Harvard University. His work focuses on civil society roles in just and sustainable development and in problems of transnational governance and problem solving.

Ailish Byrne, senior associate for the Communication for Social Change Consortium, is an anthropologist, social development practitioner, researcher and communication facilitator in international contexts. She specialises in participatory communication and evaluation, learning and health in Africa, the Middle East and Europe. She has been a lecturer in social research methods at University of Bristol (United Kingdom) and a consultant to numerous NGOs, bilateral agencies and UN agencies

Sally Burch, a British journalist, is the executive director of the Latin American Information Agency with headquarters in Ecuador. She has provided technical assistance on communication and networking to various social organisations, and published numerous short essays on issues related to communication rights and democracy.

Maria Celeste H. Cadiz is associate professor and the first dean of the College of Development Communication of the University of the Philippines Los Baños (UPLB). Her career has been devoted to teaching and research and practice in development communication. She has served as project leader and coordinator for a number of nationally and internationally funded action-research programs, and written extensively on development communication. She currently serves a secretary-treasurer for the Communication for Social Change Consortium board of directors.

Manuel Calvelo has worked in Latin America since 1945. He started the educational television system at the University of Buenos Aires. As a producer and director at the University of Tucuman (Argentina), he specialised in communication for development. He has run workshops in Latin America and Spain, and has been an adviser to the United Nations Food & Agriculture Organization (FAO) for 23 years.

Osvaldo Capriles teaches and conducts research at Universidad Central de Venezuela and the Instituto de Investigaciones de la Comunicación. He founded the journal *Cine al Día,* and has authored numerous essays on communication policies and theory, and been a communication adviser to the United Nations Educational, and Scientific Organization (UNESCO).

Martha Cardozo Buitrago is an economist. As a researcher at the Centro de Investigaciones para el Desarrollo, she focuses on education and development.

Manuel Castells is a research professor at the Open University of Catalonia in Barcelona, Spain. He was formerly a professor of communication at the University of Southern California (Los Angeles), and is professor emeritus of sociology and of city and regional planning at the University of California, Berkeley. He has lectured at more than 300 academic institutions in 43 countries, is the author of 22 books, and editor of 15 books and more than 100 articles in academic journals.

Robert Chambers is a research associate in the participation group at the Institute of Development Studies at the University of Sussex (United Kingdom), specialising in east Africa and south Asia. His current

1927
1960
1963
1964
1967
1969
1970
1971
1972
1973
1974
1975
1976
1977
1978
1979
1980
1981
1982
1983
1984
1985
1986
1987
1988
1989
1990
1991
1992
1993
1994
1995
1996
1997
1998
1999
2000
2001
2002
2003
2004
2005
2006

interests include participatory methodologies, institutional learning and change, and knowledge in development.

Erskine Childers was the director of the Division of Information, Office of External Relations and Information, United Nations Development Programme, based in New York.

Gustavo Cimadevilla has taught at numerous universities in Latin America. Currently, he is coordinator of the Working Group on Technology and Development at the Asociación Latinoamericana de Investigadores de la Comunicación. He has written numerous books, among them *Dominios: Crítica de la razón intervensionista, la comunicación y el desarrollo sustentable.*

José Cisneros Espinosa is a researcher and professor at the Universidad de las Américas (Mexico). He is a member of the National Research System in Mexico and has researched and published on topics relating to communication and social participation. He has consulted on public and on educational communication for a number of institutions in Mexico.

Frances Cleaver is a senior lecturer, Bradford Centre for International Development, University of Bradford (United Kingdom). Her work is centred on three interrelated themes: water governance, institutions and participation in development. Her interests link theoretical development and practical policy application. She has pursued these themes both through academic research and consultancy work for development agencies.

Royal Colle is a professor emeritus at Cornell University (United States), where he was chair of the communication department. He has consulted for a variety of international organizations. His work focuses on institution building related to communication, and on innovative uses of information technology for development.

David J. Connell is an assistant professor, School of Environmental Planning, University of Northern British Columbia (Canada). His interest is in intentional communities, including co-housing, eco-villages and communal societies. Connell is currently researching the capacity of and potential for local food systems, including the culture of food, food security, farmers markets, industry analysis and land-use planning.

Eduardo Contreras-Budge is a Chilean consultant specializing in evaluating information and communication technologies for development strategies, programmes and projects. Since the 1970s, he has been involved in the development communication field throughout Latin America as a strategist, project evaluator and facilitator/trainer. He has worked or consulted for a number of international organisations on development of health communication strategies.

Carlos Eduardo Cortés is a researcher, producer, journalist and professor in the social communication field. For the past 20 years, he has worked in North, South and Central America with many international organisations including the United Nations Educational, Scientific and Cultural Organization (UNESCO), the United Nations Children's Fund (UNICEF) and the United Nations Development Programme (UNDP).

Karina Constantino David has been professor of community development at the University of the Philippines College of Social Work since 1975. Her career of government service spans three decades. She has held positions at the Caucus of Development Nongovernmental Organisations Networks, Women's Action Network for Development, and Independent Commission on Population and the Quality of Life.

James Deane is managing director, strategy, of the Communication for Social Change Consortium. Formerly executive director and a founding member of the Panos Institute, London, Deane has written extensively on communication issues, particularly on the role of media and communication technologies in development; on communication for social change; and on the HIV/AIDS pandemic during the last two decades.

Brenda Dervin is a professor of communication and Joan N. Huber Fellow in Social and Behavioral Sciences at The Ohio State University (United States). Her research focuses on designing research and practice-based methodology on communication rather than transmission principles.

Juan Díaz Bordenave worked as a communication specialist at the Inter-American Instituto of Cooperation for Agriculture in Costa Rica, Mexico, Brazil and Peru for

24 years. Since 1980, Díaz has been an independent consultant in communication and education for development.

Wimal Dissanayake teaches at the Academy for Creative Media in the University of Hawaii, and is an honorary professor at the University of Hong Kong. He has authored more than 30 books on cinema, communication and cultural studies. A bilingual writer, he writes many books in his mother tongue, Sinhalese. The Sri Lankan Film Festival recently honoured him with a lifetime award for his writings on Asian cinema.

John Downing is director of the Global Media Research Center, College of Mass Communication and Media Arts, Southern Illinois University (United States). He has taught at the University of Texas, Hunter College (New York) and Greenwich University (London). Downing has written and edited many books and articles on communication and social movements.

Arturo Escobar is Kenan Professor of Anthropology and Director, Institute of Latin American Studies, University of North Carolina, Chapel Hill, and is an associated researcher with the Instituto Colombiano de Antropología e Historia in Bogotá. He works with nongovernmental organisations on projects involved with globalisation, culture, women and environment.

Orlando Fals Borda, a Colombian sociologist, writer and politician, is a main proponent and theorist of participatory action-research. In 1959, he cofounded the faculty of philosophy at the Universidad Nacional de Colombia, where he became the first dean. Fals-Borda was director of research at the United Nations Institute for Social Development. He is the author of "Historia doble de la Costa" (four volumes) and many other interdisciplinary works.

Warren Feek is director of The Communication Initiative (CI). Founded in 1998, CI is a partnership of 24 development organisations which provides open access to information aimed at supporting people and organisations using communication strategies to address development issues. A New Zealander, Feek has worked at the United Nations Children's Fund (UNICEF) in health and HIV/AIDS communication.

Gloria D. Feliciano was dean of the University of the Philippines College of Mass Communication, which she founded. She authored numerous articles and several books on communication research.

María Elena Figueroa is associate faculty in the Department of Population and Family Health Sciences, and director of the Research and Evaluation Division of the Center for Communication Programs in the Johns Hopkins Bloomberg School of Public Health (the United States). Her work is in the study of health behavior in support of health communication programs in Latin America, Africa and Asia.

Teresa Flores Bedregal is a Bolivian environmentalist. She has conducted research studies at the Universidad Autónoma de Barcelona, the University of California at Davis and the University of Oregon, at Eugene (United States). Flores has written numerous articles and books on issues of sustainable development, environment, gender and communication, as well as hundreds of short essays and articles.

Elizabeth Fox is the deputy director of the Office of Health at the United States Agency for International Development (USAID). She has worked as a consultant for the Pan American Health Organization (PAHO), the World Bank and the United Nations Educational, Scientific and Cultural Organization (UNESCO) and written and edited many articles and books on development, health communications and Latin American media.

Colin Fraser was one of the earliest pioneers of communication for development, which he initiated at the United Nations Food and Agriculture Organization (FAO) in 1969 and ran for 17 years. Currently a consultant, Fraser has worked in some 75 countries for most of the major development agencies.

Paulo Freire (1921-1997), a Brazilian educator, has left a significant mark on the field of progressive practice. His book *Pedagogy of the Oppressed* is one of the most quoted educational texts in the field. Freire drew upon, and wove together, a number of strands of thinking about educational practice and liberation. His many theoretical innovations have had a considerable impact on the development of educational practice, and on informal and popular education.

1927
1960
1963
1964
1967
1969
1970
1971
1972
1973
1974
1975
1976
1977
1978
1979
1980
1981
1982
1983
1984
1985
1986
1987
1988
1989
1990
1991
1992
1993
1994
1995
1996
1997
1998
1999
2000
2001
2002
2003
2004
2005
2006

Valerio Fuenzalida Fernández is a Chilean television producer whose research focuses on audience studies and reception processes in Latin American public television. Fuenzalida is director of audience studies at the Instituto de Estudios Mediales de la Facultad de Comunicaciones en la Pontificia Universidad Católica de Chile and professor of social communication at the Universidad Diego Portales (Chile). He has published numerous essays and books.

Andreas Fuglesang was an internationally recognized authority on cross-cultural communication and adult education in Third World countries. His close connection with the African village began in 1967 in Zambia. He worked as field adviser to governments and international organizations in Africa, Latin America and Asia, and lectured throughout the world on cross-cultural communication. Fuglesang was also a freelance journalist, photographer, graphic artist and producer of educational films.

Luis Jesús Galindo Cáceres coordinates the doctoral program in communication at the Universidad Veracruzana (Mexico). Galindo is a member of the Mexican Association of Communication Researchers and coordinator of the Grupo de Acción en Cultura de Investigación (Mexico). He is the author of numerous articles and books on communication research.

Néstor García Canclini is director of studies of the Urban Culture Programme at the Universidad Autónoma Metropolitana de México, and has taught at numerous universities in Latin America, Spain and the United States. Garcia has received many awards for his writing, including the book award from the Latin American Studies Association.

Frank Gerace teaches in the department of communication skills in La Guardia Community College of the City College of New York (United States). His work, *La Comunicación Horizontal,* has been cited as seminal in the early formulation of a Latin American approach to participatory communication. Gerace worked in the United Nations Educational, Scientific and Cultural Organization (UNESCO) and the United Nations Food and Agriculture Organization (FAO) projects in Guatemala and Ecuador, and has taught in universities in Peru and Bolivia.

George Gerbner (1920-2005) was dean emeritus of the Annenberg School for Communications at the University of Pennsylvania. He founded the Cultural Indicators Research Project to track changes in television content and how those changes affect viewers' perceptions of the world. Gerbner coined the phrase "mean world syndrome," a phenomenon in which people who watch a lot of television are more likely to believe that the world is an unforgiving and frightening place. He founded the Cultural Environment Movement, an advocacy group working for greater diversity in media.

Octavio Getino is an Argentine filmmaker and researcher on issues of communication and culture. He co-authored "The Hour of the Furnaces," a documentary key to the development of the New Latin American Cinema in the 1960s. During his years of political exile in Peru and Mexico, Getino was a communication consultant for various international development organisations. He has taught in universities in Argentina, Peru, Mexico and Cuba, and published numerous books on cultural industries and film studies in Latin America.

Bruce Girard is a researcher, writer, educator and activist with extensive experience in a broad range of communication-related areas. He is a member of the executive committee of the Communication Rights in the Information Society and has published several books and articles on community radio, international communications technology for development, global media governance and communication rights. He is a member of the CFSC practitioner network.

Denise Gray-Felder, president of the Communication for Social Change Consortium, was previously a vice president of the Rockefeller Foundation. She has worked in public relations, journalism, broadcasting, audiovisual production, marketing and philanthropy, and as an adjunct communication professor at several universities. Her research areas of interest are public dialogue and community engagement.

Alfonso Gumucio-Dagron, managing director of programmes of the CFSC Consortium, is a communication specialist, photographer, filmmaker and writer with 30 years of experience working in development programmes in Africa, Asia, South Pacific, Latin America and the Caribbean. He is the author of various studies on communication, and directed dozens of documentary films on cultural and social issues.

Francisco Gutiérrez Pérez began his career in Costa Rica, where he created his concept of Pedagogy of the Total Language. He has been a researcher, professor and director of the Latin American Institute of Pedagogy of Education, and has contributed to numerous international organisations, such as Radio Netherlands. His books focus on education and communication.

Nurit Guttman is a professor at Tel Aviv University's Department of Communication, Michigan State University's College of Communication Arts and Sciences, and the University of Medicine and Dentistry of New Jersey (UMDNJ) Robert Wood Johnson Medical School. He is the author of *Public Health Communication Interventions: Values and Ethical Dilemmas.*

Cees J. Hamelink is professor of international communication at the University of Amsterdam and professor of media, religion and culture at the Free University in Amsterdam. Hamelink has worked as a journalist and consulted on media and communication policy for several international organizations and governments. He is currently the editor-in-chief of *Gazette*, an international journal for communication studies. Hamelink is a regular commentator on radio and television in the Netherlands.

Lynn M. Harter is an assistant professor at The Ohio University School of Communication Studies (the United States). Harter's writings appear in numerous communications research journals. Her teaching specialisation is organizational and health communication.

Göran Hedebro is the chargé d'affaires and head of the Embassy of Sweden to Namibia. He has consulted in communication and development for the Swedish International Development Corporation, United Nations Educational, Scientific and Cultural Organization (UNESCO), International Programme for the Development of Communication (IPDC) and other organisations.

Robert Hornik is Wilbur Schramm Professor of Communication and Health Policy at the Annenberg School for Communication, University of Pennsylvania (United States). Hornik has served as a member of four National Academy of Science Institute of Medicine committees, has won the Andreasen Scholar award in social marketing and the Fisher Mentorship award from the International Communication Association. He has published widely on development communication.

Mark Hudson is adult services librarian at the Monroeville Public Library in suburban Pittsburgh, Pennsylvania. He is a member of the American Library Association's Social Responsibilities Roundtable, the Progressive Librarians Guild and a longtime activist in the peace and global justice movements.

Jim Hunt is an educator, trainer and facilitator with more than 35 years of experience in corporate and nonprofit communication. An adviser to the Communication for Social Change Consortium from the onset, he helped develop educational and training programs for CFSC initiatives in the United States and Africa. He is a member of the CFSC practitioner network.

Robert Huesca is associate professor in the Department of Communication at Trinity University in San Antonio, Texas. His research interests include alternative media and participatory communication for social change. Huesca's research on international and development communication issues has been published in numerous books and journals.

Tom Jacobson is senior associate dean for academic affairs at Temple University's School of Communication and Theater, Philadelphia. He has numerous publications on development communication and participation.

Juan F. Jamias was professor emeritus in the College of Development Communication, University of the Philippines, Lōs Banos. He pioneered agricultural journalism in the Philippines and lectured widely on development communication.

Neville Jayaweera was Sri Lanka's ambassador to the Scandinavian countries. He was the first chairman and director general of the Ceylon Broadcasting Corporation. He has been a commentator on Sri Lankan issues on BBC 2's prestigious "Newsnight" programme, and has written and lectured on communication and technology throughout the world.

1927
1960
1963
1964
1967
1969
1970
1971
1972
1973
1974
1975
1976
1977
1978
1979
1980
1981
1982
1983
1984
1985
1986
1987
1988
1989
1990
1991
1992
1993
1994
1995
1996
1997
1998
1999
2000
2001
2002
2003
2004
2005
2006

Gabriel Kaplún is a Uruguayan communication specialist who teaches and researches at the Universidad de la República (Uruguay). He is a guest professor and communication consultant to several Latin American universities, private companies, government institutions and nongovernmental organizations.

Mario Kaplún (1923-1998) was born in Argentina, and lived in Uruguay and in Venezuela, where he developed innovative, participatory communication approaches. His experience included radio and television, popular education and communication, university teaching and consultancy work with international and national development organisations.

D. Lawrence Kincaid is an associate scientist in the Department of Health, Behavior and Society, Bloomberg School of Public Health, Johns Hopkins University (United States). Kincaid helped develop and test many methods for analysis of communication impact; helped develop a new model of communication for participatory development; and developed a drama theory to measure the impact of entertainment-education programs. He co-authored the first book in the field on communication networks.

Ullamjaja Kivikuru is professor of journalism at the Swedish School of Social Science, University of Helsinki. She has worked with eastern and southern African media for more than 25 years, most recently with community-based media in South Africa and Namibia.

Eric Kluitenberg is a theorist, writer and organiser on culture, media and technology. He is head of the media programme at De Balie Centre for Culture and Politics in Amsterdam (Netherlands), and is a lecturer on media theory at various colleges. He currently teaches at the Institute for Interactive Media at the Hogeschool van Amsterdam, and lectures and writes extensively on culture, new media and cultural politics throughout Europe.

Satish Kolluri teaches development communication, cultural studies and global cinema as an assistant professor in the department of communication studies at Pace University (New York).

Uma Kothari is a senior lecturer with the School of Environment and Development, Institute for Development Policy and Management, Manchester (the United Kingdom). Her research interests include social development, gender and development, agrarian change and rural development, processes of migration, history and theories of development, and colonialism and development. She has worked in Bangladesh, Egypt, India, Mauritius and Mexico.

Osvaldo León is director of the América Latina en Movimiento journal at the Latin American Information Agency. León has coordinated various international conferences on communication rights and published essays on alternative communication and the impact of international communication technology for development.

Daniel Lerner, who died in 1980, was a sociologist, educator and author. He taught sociology at the Massachusetts Institute of Technology (Cambridge) for 25 years. He retired as Ford Professor of Sociology and International Communications, and served as a visiting professor at numerous universities in Europe, the Middle East and Latin America.

Gary Lewis is with the Center for Communication Programs at the Johns Hopkins Bloomberg School of Public Health (United States). Since 2000, he has been the director of the Sustaining Technical Achievements in Reproductive Health/Family Planning Program, which is the United States Agency for International Development (USAID)-funded technical support program to the government of Indonesia. He has worked on family planning issues in 25 countries.

Rico Lie is a social anthropologist at the Department of Communication Science, Wageningen University (the Netherlands). He is a university lecturer in international communication specializing in the areas of development communication and intercultural communication.

Sean MacBride (1904-1988) was a journalist, barrister and politician. MacBride was a founding member of Amnesty International and president of the United Nations Educational, Scientific and Cultural Organization (UNESCO) International Commission for the Study of Communication Problems, which published his work:

Many Voices, One World: Towards a New and More Just and More Efficient World Information and Communication Order. He was awarded the Nobel Peace Prize in 1974.

Charles Malan is a research consultant and writer who heads the publishing company Hermes. For two decades, he was a chief research specialist at the Human Sciences Research Council (HSRC), Pretoria, South Africa. He has been a professor in the departments of Afrikaans and Information Science, University of Pretoria. Malan has written extensively on youth issues, cultural studies, intercultural awareness, development communication and South African literature.

Victor Manuel Mari Saez is professor of communication theory at the Universidad de Cádiz (Spain) and adviser on educational communication. His research focuses on communication, social movements and social networks in projects related to communication and local development.

José Marques de Melo teaches at the Escola de Comunicações e Artes da Universidade de São Paulo (Brazil). He is the director of the United Nations Educational, Scientific and Cultural Organization (UNESCO), chair on Communication for Regional Development at the Universidade Metodista de São Paulo and founder of the post-graduate programme on social communication.

Jesús Martín-Barbero is the founder of the Department of Communication Sciences of Valle University (Colombia). He has worked as a researcher at the Complutense University of Madrid, and taught at the Autonomous University of Barcelona, Stanford University (United States) and at the National Institute of Anthropology and History of Mexico.

Sipho (Temba) Masilela, a South African national, lived as a political refugee in Kenya for 20 years. He has been a lecturer in the School of Journalism at Rhodes University (South Africa), a director of communication in the Department of Public Service and Administration in the government of South Africa, and the chief of staff and special adviser to the Minister of Social Development.

Sandra Massoni teaches communication at the Universidad Nacional de Rosario and the Universidad Nacional de la Plata (both in Argentina). She has conducted numerous research projects in social communication strategies, communication for development, and communication and natural resources. Massoni coordinates the ALFA RED ICOD programme of communication research for academic cooperation between the European Union and Latin America.

Armand Mattelart is professor emeritus of information and communication sciences at the University of Paris. He has been professor of sociology of communication at the Catholic University of Chile, Santiago, and United Nations expert in social development. Mattelart has authored or co-authored numerous books on culture, politics, the mass media, and communications theory and history.

Emile McAnany is Schmidt Professor of Communication at Santa Clara University (California). He has taught at the University of Texas at Austin and at Stanford University (all in the United States). McAnany researches and writes on policies that promoted, or failed to promote, genuine social change.

Neill McKee has more than 37 years of experience in international development communication. He is currently the director of Healthy Russia 2020, a project of the Center for Communication Programs (CCP), Bloomberg School of Public Health, Johns Hopkins University (the United States.) McKee has held various positions in CCP, the United Nations Children's Fund (UNICEF) in Asia and Africa, International Research Centre in Canada and in Canadian University Service Overseas.

Paolo Mefalopulos is senior communications officer in the Division of Development Communication of the World Bank. He has worked at United Nations Educational, Scientific and Cultural Organization (UNESCO), United Nations Food and Agriculture Organization (FAO) and the European Union. Mefalopulos has applied and refined the principles of participatory communication in Bolivia, Colombia, Guatemala, Jordan, Namibia, Nepal, Pakistan and Zimbabwe.

Srinivas Melkote's expertise is in communication and development and international media studies. He is the author of three books and numerous articles in communication journals.

1927
1960
1963
1964
1967
1969
1970
1971
1972
1973
1974
1975
1976
1977
1978
1979
1980
1981
1982
1983
1984
1985
1986
1987
1988
1989
1990
1991
1992
1993
1994
1995
1996
1997
1998
1999
2000
2001
2002
2003
2004
2005
2006

Bella Mody is the James E. de Castro Chair in Global Media Studies at the University of Colorado in Boulder. She has consulted for U.N. agencies, national governments and nongovernmental organizations on media applications for agriculture, health and education in India, Malaysia, Singapore, Nepal, Costa Rica, Jamaica, Barbados, Ghana, Tanzania, Zimbabwe, Kenya and South Africa.

Andrew A. Moemeka is a professor of communication at the Central Connecticut State University, New Britain, Connecticut (United States). He has been involved with the theory and practice of the use of the mass media in fostering development purposes for more than two decades. He consults for international and national organizations on communication and development.

Ali Mohammadi is professor of international communication and cultural studies at Nottingham Trent University (United Kingdom). He is the author of books on Islam, globalisation, and Iran and cultural policy in the Persian Gulf region.

Luiz Gonzaga Motta is professor of communication and coordinator of the Center for Studies in Communication and Politics at the University of Brasília, Brazil. He has been a professional journalist, video and TV producer and an international adviser in communication and social change programs.

Hamid Mowlana has been a visiting professor at universities in Europe, the Middle East, Latin America and Africa, and has worked for United Nations Educational, Scientific and Cultural Organization (UNESCO) in Paris. He has written extensively on international communication, cultural and psychological aspects of international relations, and worldwide socioeconomic development.

Daudi Mwakawago is a Tanzanian politician and diplomat. He has been special representative of the U.N. Secretary-General to Sierra Leone, vice chairman of the U.N. Commission on Sustainable Development, and Permanent Representative to the United Nations for the government of Tanzania.

Kaarle Nordenstreng is professor of journalism and mass communication at the University of Tampere (Finland). He was head of research at the Finnish Broadcasting Company during an era of radical reform in the late 1960s, after which he moved to his present position. Nordenstreng has been a visiting professor at several U.S. universities, and has written and/or edited more than 400 articles and reports on communications and the media.

Onuora Nwuneli earned his doctorate in communication arts at the University of Wisconsin, Madison (United States). He taught mass communications at the University of Lagos, Nigeria, for 14 years. Nwuneli worked at the Kenya Institute of Mass Communication as United Nations Educational, Scientific and Cultural Organization (UNESCO) chief technical adviser in IEC and also as an IEC specialist/adviser under the sponsorship of the Swedish International Development Cooperation Agency (SIDA) to the government of Botswana.

Francis B. Nyamnjoh is associate professor and head of publications and dissemination with the Council for the Development of Social Science Research in Africa. He has researched and written extensively on Cameroon and Botswana, where he was awarded the Senior Arts Researcher of the Year prize for 2003.

Seán Ó Siochrú is a writer, advocate and consultant in media and communications issues. As a consultant, he works extensively with the United Nations and other international organisations in more than 40 countries. He is director of NEXUS Research, an independent not-for-profit research organisation, and chairperson of Dublin Community Television in Ireland, where he lives.

Rafael Obregón is associate professor and director of the Communication for Development Research Program at Ohio University (United States). He has been regional communication adviser in the Child and Adolescent Health Unit, Pan American Health Organization/World Health Organization and has worked and published extensively in health and development communication. He formerly taught communication at Universidad del Norte in Barranquilla, Colombia. He is a member of the CFSC Consortium practitioner network.

Aida Opoku-Mensah is team leader for the U.N. Economic Commission for Africa's Information and U.N. Information and Technologies Task Force for Development Programme, based in Addis Ababa, Ethiopia.

As regional director for the Panos Southern Africa office based in Lusaka, Zambia, she initiated a number of groundbreaking information and communication initiatives, such as supporting community-based radio for development programmes for rural women.

Alfred E. Opubor is coordinator of the Working Group on Communication for Education and Development in Cotonou, Republic of Benin. He was chairman of the Department of Mass Communication at the University of Lagos, Nigeria, where he trained several generations of journalism and communication students. Opubor was an adviser with the United Nations Population Fund in West and southern Africa for nearly 10 years.

Will Parks is a medical anthropologist who specializes in communication for international health. A former WHO staff member, he advises the World Health Organisation's Stop TB Initiative, malaria and avian influenza efforts, as well as Unicef's South Asia office. An expert in small island states, he has led numerous public health projects in such nations. He is an adjunct faculty member at University of Queensland in Australia, and a member of the CFSC Consortium's practitioner network.

Antonio Pasquali is a Venezuelan philosopher and communication researcher. He worked at the United Nations Educational, Scientific and Cultural Organization (UNESCO), during which time he was assistant director general for communication, and regional adviser for communication in Latin America. Pasquali created the audiovisual centre of the Ministry of Education of Venezuela and the Instituto de Investigaciones de la Comunicación, where he coordinated the Ratelve Project to create a new radio and television policy.

Breda Pavlic is a professor of sociology and former director of the Unit for the Promotion of the Status of Women and Gender Equality at UNESCO. She was also formerly the UNESCO Representative in Canada. She is the co-author of *The New International Economic Order: Links Between Economics and Communications* (with Cees Hamelink) and *The Challenges of South-South Cooperation.*

José Miguel Pereira is a professor in the communication department of the Universidad Javeriana de Bogotá (Colombia). He was director of the social communication

faculty at the university and academic coordinator of the United Nations Educational, Scientific and Cultural Organization (UNESCO) chair on social communication.

Cicilia Maria Krohling Peruzzo is former president of Intercom (Sociedade Brasileira de Estudos Interdisciplinares da Comunicação). She teaches in the postgraduate programme of social communication at the Universidade Metodista de São Paulo (Brazil), as well as at the Universidade Federal do Espírito Santo.

Daniel Prieto Castillo is a journalist and a professor of philosophy who specialises in Latin American studies. His focus is on the relationship between education and communication. A pioneer of alternative and participatory communication, Prieto has published 50 books on the subject.

Wendy Quarry has worked in development communication for more than 25 years. She works in Kabul, Afghanistan. She has been a communication professional with governments and nongovernmental organizations, facilitating the development of communication strategies in water and sanitation, environment, irrigation and drainage and natural resource management.

Nora C. Quebral is the former chairperson of the Department of Development Communication, College of Agriculture, University of Philippines at Los Baños. She was a professor in development communication at the Southeast Asia Regional Centre for Graduate Study and Research in Agriculture.

Marc Raboy holds the Beaverbrook Chair in Ethics, Media and Communications at McGill University, Montreal, Canada. A former journalist, he is the author or editor of numerous books and articles on media policy, as well as research reports for many international organizations. Raboy is the convenor of the Global Media Policy working group of the International Association for Media and Communication Research, and a founding member of the campaign for Communication Rights in the Information Society.

Mina Ramirez is president of the Asian Social Institute. Ramirez is widely acknowledged for her pioneering studies on Filipino families. She consults for the Geneva-based International Catholic Child Bureau and is a

1927
1960
1963
1964
1967
1969
1970
1971
1972
1973
1974
1975
1976
1977
1978
1979
1980
1981
1982
1983
1984
1985
1986
1987
1988
1989
1990
1991
1992
1993
1994
1995
1996
1997
1998
1999
2000
2001
2002
2003
2004
2005
2006

founding member of the Vatican-based Pontifical Academy for Social Sciences.

Ricardo Ramírez teaches capacity development and communication in the School of Environmental Design and Rural Development at the University of Guelph, Canada. He worked with the Communication for Development group of the Food and Agriculture Organization of the United Nations (FAO), where he integrated participatory appraisal tools with communication planning.

Ignacio Ramonet is a professor of communication theory at the University Denis Diderot in Paris, where he specializes in geopolitics, economics and the history of culture. He is the author of many books on communication issues.

Manju Rani is a scientist in the Expanded Program on Immunization at the World Health Organization (WHO), Western Pacific Region. Since 1992, she has held several senior supervisory and managerial positions dealing with rural development, health, education, and women and child development programs in rural Rajasthan, in India. The use of social mobilization techniques has been integral to her work.

Rossana Reguillo is professor in the Department of Sociocultural Studies at the Instituto de Estudios Superiores de Occidente (Western Institute of Advanced Studies), Guadalajara, Mexico. She studies the cultural relationship between fears and contemporary society.

Sonia Restrepo Estrada is a consultant in communication for rural development. She worked in several Columbian government institutions before moving to the United Nations Children's Fund (UNICEF) office in Colombia. There she planned and implemented innovative and effective communication activities targeting children.

Fernando Reyes Matta is an international communication expert and diplomat from Chile. He is one of the founders of Chile's national television. He helped draft the MacBride report, *Many Voices, One World,* for the United Nations Educational, Scientific and Cultural Organization (UNESCO). In 1983, Reyes became director of information and culture in the Chilean Ministry of Foreign Affairs and later became ambassador to New Zealand.

Pilar Riaño-Alcalá holds degrees in communications and anthropology. Her research, teaching, community/pedagogical work and writing are known throughout Latin and North America. Her research focuses on the cultural dimensions of violence and the politics of memory, witnessing and reconciliation in "unstable" societies.

Giuseppe Richeri is dean of the faculty of communication sciences at the University of Italian Switzerland (Lugano), where he teaches media economics and communication social history. He is director of the Institute of Media and Journalism and the Media Observatory in China.

Scott S. Robinson teaches at the public Universidad Metropolitana Iztapalapa campus in Mexico. He has published texts on shamanism, native rights in Ecuador, the politics of involuntary resettlement linked to hydropower dams, mobilising Internet-based information systems for rural producers in Mexico, community telecentres, community microbanks, remittance transfer for diaspora communities and rural telecommunications policy in Mexico.

Clemencia Rodríguez is associate professor at the Department of Communication, University of Oklahoma (United States). Since 1984, Rodriguez has conducted research on citizens' media in countries including Nicaragua, Colombia, Spain, Chile and in Latino communities in the United States.

Everett M. Rogers (1931-2004) was distinguished professor emeritus in the Department of Communication and Journalism at the University of New Mexico, in the United States. He was a pioneer in the field of communication for development, publishing his classic, *Diffusion of Innovations,* in 1962. He published works extensively for almost 50 years.

Niels Röling is professor emeritus at the Department of Communication Studies of Wageningen University, in the Netherlands. He specialises in social learning in integrated cachement management in Europe, and the institutional pathways of agricultural science for small-scale farmers in West Africa, especially Benin and Ghana.

Raul Roman is a research associate at the Annenberg Research Network on International Communication,

Annenberg School for Communication, University of Southern California. His research focuses on the process and consequences of diffusion and adoption of information and communication technology in communities of the developing world. He has researched and consulted on information technology and international development programs in South Asia, Latin America and sub-Saharan Africa.

Rafael Roncagliolo is a sociologist, journalist, international consultant and professor in Peru. He was vice president of the International Association of Media and Communication Research. Roncagliolo has directed radio and television programmes and published books on communication issues.

Florangel Rosario-Braid is trustee and senior adviser of the Asian Institute of Journalism and Communication. She was chairperson of the communication committee of the United Nations Educational, Scientific and Cultural Organization (UNESCO) National Commission of the Philippines and has held positions in many international organizations. Her publications include more than one dozen books on communication, information technology and continuing education.

Chin Saik Yoon is the editor-in-chief of an Orbicom – UNESCO/PAN-IDRC/ADIP-UNDP initiative to publish a regional review on the application and diffusion of international trade centres in the Asia-Pacific region.

Beatriz Sarlo is a literature professor at the University of Buenos Aires, Argentina. She has taught at Colombia University; University of California, Berkeley; University of Maryland; and University of Minnesota (all in the United States). Sarlo's research focuses on popular sentimental literature, the history of journalism and of mass media.

Thomas Scalway is an independent consultant who specialises in health communication, in particular, HIV/AIDS. He advised the World AIDS Campaign on the development of its current strategy, assisted India's Department for International Development on health communications, and redeveloped the strategy for the Nelson Mandela Foundation AIDS Programme.

Herbert Schiller (1920-2000) was a media critic and political economist. His early works, *Mass Communications*

and American Empire and *The Mind Managers,* set the stage for his lifelong attention to the imposition of U.S. cultural ideology on other countries, particularly those in the Third World and of U.S. control of worldwide media markets. Based on his critical writing, many media scholars were prompted to test his generalisations about cultural and media imperialism.

Héctor Schmucler is professor emeritus at the Universidad Nacional de Córdoba, Argentina, and has taught in many Latin American countries. He cofounded and edited the journal *Comunicación y Cultura*.

Wilbur Lang Schramm (1907-1987) was a key figure in communications research. During World War II, he served in the U.S. Office of War Information. He was director of the School of Journalism at the University of Iowa, (1943-1947) and was dean of Mass Communication Programs at the University of Illinois (1947), Stanford University (1955) and the East-West Centre, University of Hawaii (1970s).

Jan Servaes is a professor and the head of the School of Journalism and Communication at the University of Queensland in Brisbane, Australia. He has taught international communication and development communication in Belgium, the United States, the Netherlands and Thailand. Servaes has conducted research and development and advisory work around the world, and is the author of numerous journal articles and books.

Hemant Shah is a professor in the School of Journalism and Mass Communication at the University of Wisconsin, Madison. His research investigates the role of mass media in social change, such as national development, construction of cultural identities, creation of racial anxieties and social movements. Shah's most recent research is an intellectual history of mass communication and modernization theory.

Yogita Sharma is a doctoral student in communication at Texas A&M University, in the United States, with interests in feminist and social change issues. Before Texas A&M, she studied at India's Institute of Mass Communication.

Prakash M. Shingi specialises in organisational behaviour and rural communication. His research focuses on management of agricultural extension systems, social

1927
1960
1963
1964
1967
1969
1970
1971
1972
1973
1974
1975
1976
1977
1978
1979
1980
1981
1982
1983
1984
1985
1986
1987
1988
1989
1990
1991
1992
1993
1994
1995
1996
1997
1998
1999
2000
2001
2002
2003
2004
2005
2006

forestry and forestry extension, agribusiness cooperatives, large-scale irrigation systems and mass media
communication. He has been consultant to more than
20 international and national organizations.

Francisco Sierra Caballero is professor of the theory
of communication in the Department of Journalism, and
director of the master's programme in Communication
and Development, University of Seville (Spain). He is
an expert in communication policies, new technologies
and citizen participation in the European Union and has
authored numerous studies, monographs and books
on communication and development and on policies of
communication and the media.

Arvind Singhal is professor and Presidential Research
Scholar in the School of Communication Studies, Ohio
University, where he teaches and conducts research in
diffusion of innovations, mobilising for change, design
and implementation of strategic communication campaigns and entertainment-education communication
strategy. Singhal was the first recipient of the Everett
M. Rogers Award for Outstanding Contributions to
Entertainment-Education.

Hugo Slim is the senior research officer for the Save
the Children Fund, in the United Kingdom. He is the co-
founder of Rural Evaluations, a consultancy specialising in collecting oral testimony of people living in relief
and development project areas and has published widely
in journals.

Dallas Smythe was an internationally renowned communication scholar, teacher and policy adviser for more than
50 years. Several themes mark his work: the persistent
probing of the power of the mass media to restrict
independent thinking, the contradictory character of
new technologies and the tendency of people in power
to expect others to adapt to new technologies, rather
than designing technologies to serve their real needs.

Fernando Solanas was an influential figure of radical
leftist Argentine cinema in the 1960s and 1970s. In 1966,
he produced the documentary film "The Hour of the Furnaces." This four-hour film is now a classic of political
cinema. The film attempts to provoke the audience into
acting against political injustice, and it became the key
work of the movement called "Third Cinema."

Juan Somavia is director of the International Labour
Organisation as well as Chile's permanent representative
to the United Nations. He has served as an adviser to the
presidents of Mexico and Venezuela, and was awarded
the 1988 Leonidas Proano Prize of the Latin American
Human Rights Association for his contribution to peace
and human rights.

Stefan Sonderling is a senior lecturer in the Department
of Communication, University of South Africa. He lectures
in communication theory, development communication
and political communication. His areas of research and
interests include postmodern and post-colonial theory,
and language and theories of discourse.

Annabelle Sreberny is a visiting professor of global
media and communication studies in the New Media
and Film Studies Programme at SOAS, University of
London. She has held academic posts in Iran and in the
United States, and was director of the Centre for Mass
Communication Research at the University of Leicester,
in the United Kingdom, from 1992 to 1999.

J. Douglas Storey is associate director for communication science and research in the Johns Hopkins Centre
for Communication Programs, the Bloomberg School
of Public Health. His 30 years of experience in health
communication and evaluation research have taken him
to more than 20 countries. Storey has written on topics
ranging from reproductive health and HIV/AIDS prevention behaviour to community capacity strengthening
and gender equity in health care.

Eduardo Tamayo is a researcher and journalist at the
Agencia Latinoamericana de Información. He is the author
of books on communications.

Ruth Teer-Tomaselli is professor of culture, communication and media studies at the University of
KwaZulu-Natal, Durban, South Africa. Her research
interests include the political economy of broadcasting
and telecommunications in South Africa; programme
production on television and radio (in particular, community radio); and the role of media in development.

Pradip Ninan Thomas is associate professor at the School of Journalism and Communication, University of Queensland, Australia. Thomas has written widely on issues relating to communications and development and the political economy of communications. Currently, he is conducting research on Christian fundamentalism and the media in India.

Paul Thompson is a research professor at the University of Essex (United Kingdom) and director of the National Life Story Collection. A pioneer of the oral history movement in Europe, he has taught and researched (using life story interviews) for 20 years. He is founder and editor of *Oral History* and *The International Year Book of Oral History and Life Stories.*

Erick Rolando Torrico Villanueva is director of communication and journalism at Simón Bolívar Andean University in La Paz, Bolivia. He is the president of the Latin American Association of Communication Research (2005-2006), and he has been president of the Bolivian Association of Communication Research. He is member of the CFSC University Network.

Thomas Tufte is professor of communication at Roskilde University, in Denmark, where he has taught the Malmö ComDev master's course since its inception. Tufte was the United Nations Educational, Scientific and Cultural Organization (UNESCO) chair of communication at Universidad Autonoma de Barcelona (Spain), a member of an international HIV/AIDS think tank and has worked as a consultant in international health and development for many global agencies. He is a member of the CFSC university and practitioner networks.

Frank Ugboajah was a senior lecturer in mass communication and head of the Department of Mass Communication, University of Lagos. He served on the editorial boards of several communication journals and was a consultant in rural broadcasting for the U.N. Economic Commission for Africa.

Victor Valbuena is principal lecturer at the School of Film and Media Studies, Ngee Ann Polytechnic, Singapore. He has conducted development communication-related research and training programmes in the Asia-Pacific region, and he has written works on folk media, community broadcasting and family planning education.

Donald E. Voth is professor of rural sociology at the University of Arkansas (United States). He has worked extensively with the U.S. Department of Agriculture Forest Service, and is currently leader of several major research and action efforts on community-based forest management and planning. Voth has published extensively on Southeast Asian community development and rural conditions, and on forestry issues.

Silvio Waisbord is senior program officer at the Academy for Educational Development, a U.S.-based non-profit organization. He works on capacity-building projects in health communication, and he has developed and implemented activities on communication and behavior change in child health, and maternal health and infectious diseases. Waisbord writes on development communication, media and journalism and has been a professor at several universities in the United States and Latin America.

Georgette Wang is dean of the School of Communication at the Hong Kong Baptist University. Wang has worked as professor, director and dean of the College of Social Sciences, National Chung Cheng University in Chia-yi, Taiwan, and as professor at the Institute of Communication Studies at the National Chiao Tung University. Wang has been deputy director of United Daily News and managing editor of the Sinorama Monthly (both in Taiwan).

Robert A. White has been a professor of communication and development at the Gregorian University in Rome from 1990 to 2006, and the director of the Centre for Interdisciplinary Study of Communication at this university for 11 years. Founder and editor of *Communication Research Trends* and a four-book series on communication research and development, he was named director of the master's program in mass communication at University of Tanzania in September 2006. He also directs a centre on development communication.

Shirley A. White is retired from the Department of Communication, Cornell University, in the United States, where she was professor of video, development communication and organizational communication. She has undertaken extensive research in participatory communication and has written or edited numerous books.

1927
1960
1963
1964
1967
1969
1970
1971
1972
1973
1974
1975
1976
1977
1978
1979
1980
1981
1982
1983
1984
1985
1986
1987
1988
1989
1990
1991
1992
1993
1994
1995
1996
1997
1998
1999
2000
2001
2002
2003
2004
2005
2006

Karin Gwinn Wilkins is associate professor and graduate adviser with the Department of Radio-TV-Film at the University of Texas at Austin. Wilkins chairs the Intercultural/Development Division of the International Communication Association. Her research focuses on development and international communication, as well as on media and social change.

Hugh Anthony "Tony" Williamson (1935-2004) was a scholar in human geography, who used innovative techniques to help indigenous people of Labrador and the Canadian Arctic press their land claims and express their concerns to the Canadian government. He was known for his work in the use of film and videotape as a catalyst for community development. His technique, the "Fogo Process," involved villagers using these media to tell their stories, a participatory process that was unprecedented in most rural and remote areas of Canada.

Laurie J. Wilson is a professor and former chair of the Department of Communications at Brigham Young University, Utah. She consults in strategic communication planning for public, private and nonprofit organizations and associations, media relations and community relations. Wilson has co-authored numerous publications in communication and development.

Pierre de Zutter has spent 35 years working in Latin America as a journalist and an independent consultant in rural development programmes, as well as with international cooperation agencies, nongovernmental organisations, universities and other institutions. He is author or co-editor of more than 40 books dealing with participatory communication and rural development.

PERMISSIONS

The editors would like to acknowledge the publishers and the authors who granted us permission to reprint the following works:

Agunga, Robert. "The Heterophily Gap." Excerpt from: "Development Support Communication and Popular Participation in Development Projects," The Netherlands: *Gazette* 45, Kluwer Academic Publishers, Copyright © 1990 by Sage Publications. Reprinted by permission of Sage Publications, Inc.

Airhihenbuwa, Collins O. and Rafael Obregón. "A Critical Assessment of Theories/Models Used in Health Communication for HIV/AIDS," *Journal of Health Communication*, Vol. 5. Supplement (2000). Taylor and Francis Ltd. Reprinted with permission of the author and the publisher.

Albó, Xavier. Excerpt from "Lenguas Indígenas y Medios de Comunicación," This paper summarizes parts of a paper presented at the II International Congress of Bilingual Intercultural Education (EIB) held in Santa Cruz, Bolivia, in December 1996. Used with permission of the author.

Alfaro, Rosa María. "Popular Cultures and Participatory Communication: On the Route to Redefinitions," published in Daza Hernández, Gladys (compiladora): *¿Participación social en los medios masivos?* Fundación Konrad Adenauer y Universidad Pontificia Bolivariana, Medellín (Colombia), 1998. Reprinted with permission of the author.

Alfaro, Rosa Maria. *Relaciones entre Estado y Sociedad Civil: ¿concertación o vigilancia?* (2003), Asociación de Comunicadores Sociales Calandria, Lima (Peru). Asociación de Comunicadores Sociales Calandria. Reprinted with permission.

Appadurai, Arjun. "Modernity at Large," *Cultural Dimensions of Globalisation*, p 1-24. Minneapolis: University of Minnesota Press, 1996. Copyright © 1996, University of Minnesota Press. Reprinted with permission of University of Minnesota Press.

Ascroft, Joseph. From the 1974/1 issue of *Ceres, the FAO Review*, later reprinted as Ascroft, Joseph (1978). "A Conspiracy of Courtesy." International Development Review, 3, the valedictory issue. Reprinted with permission of the publisher and the author.

Ascroft, Joseph and Robert Agunga. "Diffusion Theory and Participatory Decision Making," in *Participatory Communication Working for Change and Development*, edited by White, Shirley, K. Sadanandan Nair and Joseph Ascroft, Copyright © 1994 by Sage Publications, Reprinted by permission of Sage Publications, Inc.

Ascroft, Joseph & Masilela S. "Participatory Decision Making in Third World Development," in *Participatory Communication Working for Change and Development*, edited by White, Shirley, K. Sadanandan Nair and Joseph Ascroft, Copyright © 1994 by Sage Publications, Reprinted by permission of Sage Publications, Inc.

Balit, Silvia. "Rethinking Development Support Communication," *Development Communication Report* (DCR), No. 62, 1988/3. Copyright © 1988, Academy for Educational Development. Reprinted with permission of AED.

Barranquero, Alejandro. "From Freire and Habermas to Multiplicity: Widening the Theoretical Borders of Participative Communication for Social Change," paper presented at IAMCR 2005 meeting in Taipei. Used with permission of the author.

Beltrán, Luis Ramiro. "Communication: Forgotten Tool of National Development," in *International Agricultural Development*, Communications Issue, October 1967, No. 36. Reprinted with permission of the author.

Beltrán, Luis Ramiro. "Anatomy of Incommunication," presentation at the Eleventh World Conference of the Society for International Development, New Delhi, India, November 14-17, 1969. Reprinted with permission of the author.

Beltrán, Luis Ramiro. "Rural Development and Social Communication: Relationships and Strategies," Communication Strategies for Rural Development: Proceedings of the Cornell-CIAT International Symposium; March 17-22, 1974; Cali, Colombia, S.A. Ithaca, NY : Cornell University, 1974. pp. 11-27. Reprinted with permission of the author.

Beltrán, Luis Ramiro. "A Farewell to Aristotle: 'Horizontal' Communication," published by UNESCO en el cuaderno No. 48 de su serie de documentos para la International Commission for the Study of Communication Problems, 1979, París. Copyright © 1979, UNESCO. Reprinted with permission of the author and copyright holder.

Beltrán, Luis Ramiro. "Communication for Development in Latin America: A Forty Years Appraisal," paper presented during the opening of the IV Roundtable on Communication and Development, organized by the Instituto para América Latina (IPAL), February 23, 1993. Used with permission of the author.

Beltrão, Luiz. "The Folk-Communication System," *Folkcomunicaçã a comunicação dos marginalizados o*, São Paulo (Brasil): Cortez, 1980, pp. 27-40. Reprinted with permission of Selma Beltrão.

Berlo, David. "A Model of the Communication Process," *Process of Communication*, 1st edition, pp 1-22. New York: Holt, Rinehart, and Winston, 1960. Copyright © 1960. Reprinted with permission of Wadsworth, a division of Thomson Learning. www.thomsonrights.com. Fax 800 730-2215.

Bessette, Guy, and C. V. Rajasunderam. "*Participatory Development Communication: A West African Agenda*," International Development Research Centre (IDRC) Ottawa, Canada; Southbound: Penang, Malaysia, 1996. Copyright © 1996 International Development Research Centre. Reprinted with permission of IDRC.

Boal, Augusto. *Theater of the Oppressed*. New York: Theater Communications Group, Inc., 1979. Copyright © 1979 Theater Communications Group. Reprinted with permission of TCG. Originally published as *Teatro del Oprimido y Otras Poéticas Politicas*. Buenos Aires, Argentina: Ediciones La Flor, 1974.

Brown, L. David. "People-Centered Development and Participatory Research," *Harvard Educational Review*, volume 55:1 (February 1985), pp. 69-75. Copyright © 1985 by the President and Fellows of Harvard College. All rights reserved. Reprinted with permission.

Cadiz, Maria Celeste Habito. "Participation as Communication," *Communication and Participatory Development* by Cadiz, Maria Celeste Habito. CA Publications Program, College of Agriculture, University of the Philippines-Los Baños. Laguna, Philippines, 1994. Copyright © 1994, University of the Philippines. Reprinted with permission of University of the Philippines.

Calvelo Rios, Manuel. "Popular Video for Rural Development in Peru," *Development Communication Report* (DCR), 1989/3, No. 66. Copyright © 1989, Academy for Educational Development. Reprinted with permission of AED.

Calvelo Ríos, Manuel (2003). "*Comunicación para el Cambio Social*," FAO Regional Bureau for Latin América and the Caribbean. Santiago (Chile). Reprinted with permission.

Capriles, Oswaldo. "Venezuela: ¿política de comunicación o comunicación alternativa?" In Simpson Gringberg, Máximo (ed.) *Comunicación alternativa y cambio social. America Latina*, Premiá, Puebla, Mexico, 1986. Reprinted with permission of Colette Capriles.

Castells, Manuel. "Information Technology, Globalisation and Social Development," United Nations Research Institute for Social Development (UNRISD) Discussion Paper No. 114, September 1999. Reprinted with permission.

Chambers, Robert. *Rural Development: Putting the Last First*. Essex, England: Longman Scientific & Technical, Longman Group U.K., Ltd., Longman House, 1983. Copyright © 1983, Robert Chambers. Used with permission of copyright holder.

Childers, Erskine. "Communication in Popular Participation. Empowering People for Their Own Development," unpublished paper. United Nations Economic Commission for Africa, Arusha (Tanzania) 1990.

Cimadevilla, Gustavo. "Stories, Information and Essays," in *La bocina que parla. Antecedentes y perspectivas de los estudios de comunicación rural* by Cimadevilla, Gustavo, Edgardo Carniglia y A. Cantúi. INTA-UNRC, Río Cuarto (Argentina). Reprinted with permission.

Cisneros, José. "El concepto de comunicación: El cristal con que se mira," in the journal *Ámbitos* Nos. 7-8. Universidad de Sevilla. 2nd quarter of 2001 – 1st quarter of 2002. Seville, Spain, 2002, pp. 49-82. Universidad de Sevilla. Reprinted with permission of the author.

Cleaver, Frances (2002). "Institutions, Agency and the Limitations of Participatory Approaches to Development," in *Participation: the New Tyranny?* edited by B. Cooke. and U. Kothari. London: ZED: 36-55. Copyright © 2002, Zed Books. Reprinted with permission of the publisher and the author.

Colle, Royal D. "Erskine Childers: A Devcom Pioneer," *The Journal of Development Communication*, No. 2, Vol. VII. Kuala Lumpur, Malaysia: Asian Institute for Development Communication (AIDCOM). Copyright © 1996, AIDCOM. Used with permission of copyright holder and the author.

Connell, David J. "Reformulating Community as a Complex Social System," unpublished paper submitted as partial fulfilment of the qualifying exam, Rural Studies Ph.D. Program, University of Guelph, Ontario, Canada, February 2001. Printed with permission of the author.

Cortés, Carlos Eduardo. *La comunicación al ritmo del Péndulo: Medio Siglo en busca del desarrollo*. Mimeograph, Bogotá 1977. Reprinted with permission of the author.

David, Karina C. "Community Organization and People's Participation," Lambatlaya, Third and Fourth Quarters, 1984. This paper was presented at the Conference on Methods and Media in Community Participation held in Uppsala, Sweden, on May, 1984. Reprinted with permission of the author.

Deane, James. "Communication for Social Change: Why Does it Matter?" background paper for Communication for Development Roundtable. Nicaragua, November 2001. Sponsored by UNFPA in association with the Rockefeller Foundation and UNESCO. Copyright © 2001, Communication for Social Change Consortium. Reprinted with permission of copyright holder via a license agreement.

Díaz Bordenave, Juan. "Communication of Agricultural Innovations in Latin America: The Need for New Models," SAGE, *Communication Research*, 1976, Vol. 3, No. 2: 135-154. Copyright © 1976, by Sage Publications. Reprinted with permission of Sage Publications, Inc.

Diaz Bordenave, Juan. Chapter in *Communications and Rural Development*. Paris, France: United Nations Educational, Scientific and Cultural

1927
1960
1963
1964
1967
1969
1970
1971
1972
1973
1974
1975
1976
1977
1978
1979
1980
1981
1982
1983
1984
1985
1986
1987
1988
1989
1990
1991
1992
1993
1994
1995
1996
1997
1998
1999
2000
2001
2002
2003
2004
2005
2006

Organization (UNESCO), 1977, 11-23. Copyright © 1977, UNESCO. Reprinted with permission of copyright holder.

Diaz Bordenave, Juan. "Participative Communication as Part of Building the Participative Society," originally published in *Participatory Communication Working for Change and Development*, edited by Shirley White, K. Sadanandan Nair and Joseph Ascroft. Sage Publications, India, 1994, 35-38. Reprinted by permission of the Sage Publications, Inc.

Diaz Bordenave, Juan (1996). "La comunicación como herramienta esencial del Desarrollo Sostenible" [Communication as an Essential Tool of Sustainable Development], in *"Población y Desarrollo"* [Population and Development], National University of Asunción, Paraguay. Used with permission of the author.

Dissanayake, Wimal. "A Buddhist Approach to Development: A Sri Lankan Endeavor," in Georgette Wang and Wimal Dissanayake, eds., *Continuity and Change in Communication Systems: An Asian Perspective*. Norwood, New Jersey: Ablex Publishing Corporation, Copyright © 1984, Ablex Publishing, 39-51. Reproduced with permission of Greenwood Publishing Group, Inc., Westport, Conn.

Dorfman, Ariel and Armand Mattelart. *How to Read Donald Duck: Imperialist Ideology in the Disney Comic*. New York: International General, 1971. Reprinted with permission of the author.

Downing, John. "Community, Democracy, Dialogue and Radical Media," published as Chapter 4 of *Radical Media: Rebellious Communication and Social Movements*. Edited by John Downing. Thousand Oaks, Calif.; London; New Delhi, India: Sage Publications Inc., 2001, 38-55. Copyright © 2001, Sage Publications. Reprinted by permission of Sage Publications, Inc.

Escobar, Arturo. "Imagining a Postdevelopment Era," *Encountering Development. The Making and Unmaking of the Third World* (1995), chapter 6. Princeton University Press, New Jersey (USA). Copyright © 1995, Princeton University. Reprinted with permission of Princeton University.

Escobar, Arturo. "Introduction: Cruzando Fronteras and the Borders of Thought," revised from a version presented at the Tercer Congreso Internacional de Latinoamericanistas en Europa, Amsterdam, July 3–6, 2002. Published in *World and Knowledge Otherwise: The Latin American Modernity/Coloniality Research Programme* (2004) CEDLA 16:31–67. Reprinted with permission of the author and the copyright holder.

Fals-Borda, O. "The Application of Participatory Action Research In Latin America," Sage, *International Sociology*, December 1987, Vol. 2., No. 4: 329-347. Copyright © 1986 by Sage Publications. Reprinted by permission of Sage Publications Inc.

Feek, Warren. "Power of Movement," Communication Initiative Web site, January 12, 2005. www.comminit.com. Copyright © 2005, Communication Initiative. Reprinted with permission of copyright holder.

Feliciano, Gloria D. Conference Paper. In Robert H. Crawford and William B. Ward (eds.), *Communication Strategies for Rural Development*. Proceedings of the Cornell-CIAT international symposium, Cali, Colombia, March 17-22, 1974. Cornell University, Ithaca, NY. Reprinted with permission.

Figueroa, M.E., D.L. Kincaid, M. Rani, and G. Lewis. 2002. Communication for social change: An integrated model for measuring the process and its outcomes. *Communication for Social Change Working paper series*. The Rockefeller Foundation. New York. Copyright © 2002, Rockefeller Foundation and Johns Hopkins University. Used by permission of copyright holder via license agreement with CFSC Consortium.

Flores Bedregal, Teresa (2002). *Comunicación para el Desarrollo Sostenible*. La Paz: LIDEMA, Plural. Reprinted with permission of the author and publisher.

Fox, Elizabeth. "Comunicación y Sociedad Civil: Una Temática Incipiente," *Comunicación y Sociedad* No. 7. Telemetric y Sociedad, Buenos Aires, Argentina, 1982. Reprinted with permission of the author.

Fraser, Colin & Sonia Restrepo. Why Communication? Colin Fraser and Sonia Restrepo-Estrada. 1998. *Communicating for Development: Human Change for Survival*. London and New York: I.B. Tauris. Copyright © 1998, Colin Fraser and Sonia Restrepo. Reprinted with permission of Colin Fraser and Sonia Restrepo.

Freire, Paulo. *Extensión o Comunicación*. Santiago, Chile: ICIRA, 1969. Original publication. Excerpt from Education for Critical Consciousness, Paulo Freire. Reprinted by permission of The Continuum International Publishing Group.

Freire, Paulo. *Pedagogia do Oprimido*. Rio de Janiero, Brasil: Edições Paz e Terera, 1970. Original publication. Excerpts from Chapter 3 of Pedagogy of the Oppressed, Paulo Freire, 1970, and reprinted by permission of The Continuum International Publishing Group.

Fuenzalida, Valerio. "Televisión y Cultura del Protagonismo," *El Consumo Cultural en América Latina*, Sunkel, Guillermo, compilador. Santa Fé de Bogotá, Colombia: Convenio Andrés Bello, 1999. Reprinted with permission of the author.

Fuenzalida, Valerio. "Vida cotidiana y Edu-entretención en TV," chapter 6. *Expectativas Educativas de la Audiencia Televisiva*. Buenos Aires, Argentina: Ed. Norma, 2004. Copyright © 2004, Editorial Norma. Reprinted with permission of author and copyright holder.

Fuglesang, Andreas. "Information is the Opposite of Uncertainty," *About Understanding: Ideas and Observations on Cross-Cultural Communication*, Decade Media Books, Inc., New York: 1982. Reprinted with permission of Minou Fuglesang.

Fuglesang, Andreas. "The Need for Demystifying Our Words," *About Understanding: Ideas and Observations on Cross-Cultural Communication*, Decade Media Books, Inc., New York: 1982. Reprinted with permission of Minou Fuglesang.

Galindo Cáceres, Luis Jesús. "Apuntes de historia de una comunicología posible: hipótesis de configuración y trayectoria." [Historical notes on a possible communicology: a hypothetical configuration and trajectory], *Redes. Com, Revista de estudios para el desarrollo social de la comunicación, 2004*. Reprinted with permssion of the author and the publisher.

García Canclini, Néstor. "Hybrid Cultures and Communicative Strategies," *Media Development*. World Association for Christian Communication, 1/1989. Copyright © 1989, World Association for Christian Communication. Reprinted by permission of WACC.

Gerace, Frank (1973). *Comunicación Horizontal*, Editorial Universo, Lima, Peru. Reprinted with permission of the author.

Gerbner, George. "The Challenge Before Us," in Jörg Becker, Göran Hedebro and Leena Paldán, eds., *Communication and Domination: Essays to Honor Herbert I. Schiller*. Norwood, New Jersey: Ablex Publishing Corp., 1986. Reproduced with permission of Greenwood Publishing Group, Inc., Westport, Conn.

Getino, Octavio & Solanas, Fernando. "Hacia un Tercer Cine. Apuntes y Experiencias para el Desarrollo de un Cine de Liberación en el Tercer Mundo," first published in *Tricontinental,* Paris, October 1969. Also *Cine Club,* año I, núm. 1, México, Octubre de 1970, and in Octavio Getino and Fernando Solanas, Cine, *Cultura y Descolonización*, Buenos Aires, Argentina: Siglo XXI, 1973. Reprinted with permission of author and publisher.

Girard, Bruce, ed., *The One to Watch: Radio, New ICTs and Interactivity*. Rome: Food and Agriculture Organization of the United Nations (FAO), 2003. Reprinted with permission.

Gumucio Dagron, Alfonso. "Interactions Culturelles et Formes Décentralisés de Communication," published in *Revue Tiers Monde*, t. XXVIII Nº111, July-September 1987, p. 586-594. Paris (France). Reprinted with permission.

Gumucio-Dagron, Alfonso. "The New Communicator," presented at the Communication for Social Change seminar organized by The Rockefeller Foundation, Washington, August 1998. Reprinted with permission.

Gumucio-Dagron, Alfonso. "Take Five: A Handful of Essentials for ICTs in Development," chapter 2 of *The One to Watch: Radio, New ICTs and Interactivity* (2003), edited by Bruce Girard. FAO, Rome (Italy). Reprinted with permission.

Guttman, Nurit. *Public Health Communication Interventions. Values and Ethical Dilemmas*. Thousand Oaks, London, New Delhi: Sage Publications, 2000, 175-184. Copyright © 2000, Sage Publications. Reprinted by permission of Sage Publications, Inc.

Hamelink, Cees. "Social Development, Information and Knowledge: Whatever Happened to Communication?" *Development*. Journal of the Society for International Development 45(4):5-9, 2002. Copyright © 2002 Palgrave Macmillan Publishers. Reprinted with permission.

Hedebro, Göran. "Towards A Theory of Communication and Social Change," excerpted from, "Communication and Social Change in Developing Nations: A Critical View," *Studies in Economic Psychology, 110*. Stockholm School of Economics, 1979. Reprinted with permission of the author and the publisher.

Hornik, Robert. "Why Communication for Development So Rarely Succeeds," Chapter 2 of *Development Communication: Information, Agriculture, and Nutrition in the Third World* (Longman, New York: University Press of America, 1988). Copyright ©1988, University Press of America. Reprinted with permission of the publisher.

Hudson, Mark. "Understanding Information Media in the Age of Neoliberalism: The Contributions of Herbert Schiller," *Progressive Librarian,* Issue number 16, Fall 1999. Copyright © Mark Hudson. Reprinted with permission of the author.

Huesca, Robert. "Naming the World" to Theorizing Its Relationships: New Directions for Participatory Communication for Development," *Media Development*, 1996/2. WACC, London. Copyright © 1996, World Association for Christian Communication. Reprinted with permission of author and copyright holder.

Huesca, Robert. 2001. "Conceptual contributions of new social movements to development communication research." *Communication Theory*, 11, 415-433. Copyright © Robert Huesca. Reprinted with permission.

Huesca, Robert. 2003. "From Modernization to Participation: The Past and Future of Development Communication in Media Studies," in: A.N. Valdivia, ed. *A Companion to Media Studies*. Malden, Mass: Blackwell Publishing. 50–71. Reprinted with permission of author and Blackwell Publishing.

Huesca, R., and B. Dervin. "Toward Communication Theories of and for Practice: The Past/Future of Latin American Alternative Communication Research," *Journal of Communication*, Autumn (Tardor), 1994, Vol. 44, No. 4, 53-73. Malden, Mass.: Blackwell Publishing. Reprinted with permission.

Jacobson, Thomas L. and Satish Kolluri. "Participatory Communication as Communicative Action," originally published as Chapter 9 of *Theoretical Approaches to Participatory Communication* (1999), Thomas Jacobson and Jan Servaes, eds. IAMCR, Hampton Press, Inc, Cresskill, New Jersey (USA). Copyright © 1999, Hampton Press. Reprinted with permission of the publisher.

Jamias, Juan. "The Philosophy of Development Communication," excerpt from *Readings in Development Communication*, Juan F. Jamias, ed. Department of Development Communication, College of Agriculture, University of the Philippines at Los Baños, 1975. Reprinted with permission of Estrella Jamais.

Kaplun, Gabriel. "La calle ancha de la comunicación latinoamericana" [The Wide Road of Latin American Communication,] paper presented at CELACOM, May 2005 (UNESP: Sao Paulo, Brazil). Reprinted with permission of the author.

Kaplún, Mario. Educar ¿para que? [Why Educate?] Kaplún, Mario (1978). *Producción de programas de radio. El guio--la realización*. Colección Intiyan, Ediciones CIESPAL. Quito, Ecuador. Reprinted with permission of Gabriel Kaplún.

Kivikuru, Ullamaija. "Going Grassroots," in Ullamaija Kivikuru, William Lobulu and Gervas Moshiro, *Changing Mediascapes? A Case Study in Nine Tanzanian Villages*. Finland: University of Helsinki, Institute of Development Studies, 1994. Report B 28/1994, 1-12. Reprinted with permission of the author.

Kluitenberg, Eric. "Media Without an Audience," paper presented at the Banff Centre for the Arts Interactive Screen Workshop (August 2000), and the International Festival of Streaming Media, in Amsterdam, October 2000. Published in http://www.ctrl-z.org/magazine/2001/texts/eric.htm and http://www.debalie.nl/dossierartikel.jsp?dossierid=22375&articleid=7135. Reprinted with permission of the copyright holder.

Kothari. Uma. "Power, Knowledge and Social Control in Participatory Development," excerpt from Bill Cooke and Uma Kothari (eds.) (2001) *Participation: The New Tyranny?* Zed Books, London/New York. Copyright © 2001, Zed Books. Reprinted with permission of copyright holder.

León, Osvaldo, Sally Burch and Eduardo Tamayo. "Movimientos Sociales y Comunicación," Agencia Latinoamericana de Información, Latin American Information Agency, (ALAI), 2005, Quito, Ecuador. Reprinted with permission of the author.

Lie, Rico. "Linking the Global from Within the Local," excerpt from *Spaces of Intercultural Communication: An Interdisciplinary Introduction to Communication, Culture, and Globalizing/Localizing Identities*, Hampton Press: New Jersey. Copyright © 2002, Hampton Press. Reprinted with permission of the publisher.

MacBride, Sean. "The Contemporary Dimension," *Many Voices, One World*, p15-32. UNESCO, 1980. Copyright © 1980, UNESCO. Reprinted with permission of UNESCO.

Malan, C. W. "The Functions of Culture within a Development Situation," excerpted from: "Development Communication as Part of the Culture," *Communicare*, 17 (1), 1998. Reprinted with permission.

Marí Sáez, Victor Manuel. "Comunicación, Redes y Cambio Social," Chapter 1 in *La Red es de Todos. Cuando los Movimientos Sociales se apropian de la Red. [The Network is for All: When Social Movements Take Over the Net.]* Madrid, Spain: Editorial Popular, 2004. Reproduced with permission of the author.

Marques de Melo, Jose. "A Comunicacao na Pedagogia de Paulo Freire" [Communication in the Pedagogy of Paulo Freire], excerpt from: *Pensamento Comunicacional Brasileiro*, 1979. Paper presented to the interdisciplinary seminar on communications in the thinking of Paulo Freire, 1979 at the Post-Graduate Center of the Methodist Advanced Education Institute, in São Bernardo do Campo, SP. Used with permission of the author.

1927
1960
1963
1964
1967
1969
1970
1971
1972
1973
1974
1975
1976
1977
1978
1979
1980
1981
1982
1983
1984
1985
1986
1987
1988
1989
1990
1991
1992
1993
1994
1995
1996
1997
1998
1999
2000
2001
2002
2003
2004
2005
2006

Martín-Barbero, Jesús (1979). "Lo popular y lo masivo," *Cuadernos de Comunicación* No. 62, Mexico City. Reprinted with permission of the author.

Martín-Barbero, Jesús. "Communication from the Perspective of Culture," *De los medios a las mediaciones: Comunicación, cultura y hegemonía*. Gustavo Gili, Barcelona, Spain. Copyright © 1987 by Sage Publications. Reprinted by permission of Sage Publications, Inc.

Martín-Barbero, Jesús (2000). "Transformaciones Comunicativas y Tecnológicas de lo Público." *Metapolítica*, vol. 5, Mexico City. Reprinted with permission.

Martín-Barbero, Jesús. "Reconfiguraciones comunicativas de lo público [Communicational Reconfigurations of the Public Sphere]," published in *Anàlisi* 26, 2001 71-88. ITESO. Department of Socio-cultural Studies, Guadalajara, Mexico. Copyright © 2001. Reprinted with permission of the author.

Martín-Barbero, Jesús. "La globalización en clave cultural: una mirada latinoamericana," lecture presented at the international meeting "Bogues: Globalisme et Pluralisme," Montreal, April 22-27, 2002. Used with permission of copyright holder.

Massoni, Sandra Hebe. "The Multi-Dimensional Nature of Reality and the Communicational Approach to Sustainable Development," published in *Comunicación, Ruralidad y Desarrollo. Mitos, paradigmas y dispositivos del cambio* [Communication, rurality and development. Myths, paradigms and devices of change] (2004), by Gustavo Cimadevilla and Edgardo Carniglia (editors). Ediciones INTA, Buenos Aires (Argentina). Reprinted with permission of copyright holder.

Mattelart, Armand. "Interview with Armand Mattelart : Democracy and Communication," part of a longer interview with Armand Mattelart originally published in *Iniciativa Socialista*, no. 58, Autumn 2000, Madrid, Spain. Reprinted with permission of Armand Mattelart.

Mattelart, Armand. La diversité culturelle: entre histoire et géopolitique. Paper presented at the international conference "2001 Bogues: Globalisme et Pluralisme," Montreal, 22-27 April 2002. Reprinted with permission of the author.

McAnany, Emile G. 1973. "Radio's Role in Development: Five Strategies of Use," Information Bulletin Number Four, Information Centre on Instructional Technology, Academy for Educational Development (AED), Washington D.C. Reprinted with permission of the author and the publisher.

McAnany, Emile G. "The Role of Information in Communicating with the Rural Poor: Some Reflections," excerpt from: An Alternative Pattern of Basic Education: Radio Santa Maria. *Communications In The Rural Third World: The Role of Information In Development*, edited by Emile G. McAnany, 1980. Copyright © 1980, Ablex Publishing. Reproduced with permission of Greenwood Publishing Group, Inc., Westport, Conn.

McKee, Neill. "Lessons for Communicators," Chapter five from *Social Mobilization and Social Marketing in Developing Communities: Lessons for Communicators* by Neill McKee, Southbound, Penang (Malaysia), 1992. Reprinted with permission of the author and the publisher, Southbound, http://www.southbound.com.my.

Mefalopulos, Paolo (2002). "Pushing the development boundaries a step further: From Participatory to Empowerment Communication," paper presented at IAMCR 2002, Barcelona, Spain. July 2002. Copyright © 2002, Paolo Mefalopulos. Reprinted with permission of the author.

Melkote, Srinivas R., "An Ethical Perspective of Development" from Melkote, Srinivas R. and H. Leslie Steeves. *Communication for Development in the Third World: Theory and Practice*. New Delhi: Sage Publishing India Pvt Ltd., Copyright © 2001. Reproduced with permission of the author and Sage Publishing.

Mody, Bella. "The Contexts of Power and the Power of the Media," published originally in *Redeveloping Communication for Social Change* (2000) Karin Wilkins, ed., Lanham: Rowman & Littlefield. Copyright © 2000, Rowman & Littlefield Publishers, Inc. Reprinted with permission of the publisher.

Moemeka, Andrew. "Radio Strategies for Community Development: A Critical Analysis" reprinted by permission from *Communicating for Development: A New Pan-Disciplinary Perspective* edited by Andrew A. Moemeka, the State University of New York Press © 1994 State University of New York, 124-140. All rights reserved. This is an updated version of an original (shorter) article first published in *Media Development*, Vol. 30, March 1983.

Motta, Luiz Gonzaga (1984) "Planificación de la comunicación en proyectos participativos," *Manuales didácticos* CIESPAL – 8 – Capítulo X, Quito, Ecuador. Reprinted with permission of the author.

Mowlana, Hamid. "Communication Technology and Development; International Flow of News," *International Flows of Information: A Global Report and Analysis*, p 7-15. UNESCO, 1985. © UNESCO. Reprinted with permission of the publisher.

Mwakawago, Daudi. *Radio as a Tool for Development*. Manchester, England: Manchester University Press, 1986.

Nwuneli, Onuora. "Community and Traditional Based Media Approaches to Popular IEC: Some Experiences in the African Region," Kenya Institute of Mass Communication (KIMC) project 1992. Reprinted with permission of the author.

Nyamnjoh, Francis. "Africa and the Information Superhighway: Silent Majorities in Search of a Footpath," Nairobi, Kenya: *Africa Media Review*, 1996, Vol. 10, No. 2. Reprinted with permission.

Nyamnjoh, Francis B. "Communication Research and Sustainable Development in Africa: The Need for a Domesticated Perspective," paper presented at the conference organised by the African Council for Communication Education (ACCE) on Mass Media and Sustainable Development in Africa, at Accra, Ghana (October 15–23, 1994). Published in Jan Servaes (ed.), (2000), *Walking on the Other Side of the Information Highway: Communication, Culture and Development in the 21st Century*, Penang: Southbound, (pp.146–160). Reprinted with permission of the author and the publisher, Southbound, http://www.southbound.com.my.

Ó Siochrú, Seán. "Global Media Governance as a Potential Site of Civil Society Intervention," *Democratising Global Media: One World, Many Struggles*. Edited by Robert A. Hackett and Yuezhi Zhao. Boulder, Colo: Rowman & Littlefield, 2005. Copyright © 2005, Rowman & Littlefield. Reprinted with permission of the copyright holder.

Ó Siochrú, Seán and Bruce Girard. "Information Wants to Be Free" is part of the Visions of the Information Society project, which is managed by Lara Srivastava, lara.srivastava@itu.int, policy analyst in the Strategy and Policy Unit of the International Telecommunication Union (ITU). Reprinted with permission.

Opoku-Mensah, Aida. "Radio, Conflict and Political Transition. The Future of Community Radio in Africa," in Fardon, Richard and Graham Furniss eds., *African Broadcast Cultures: Radio in Transition*. Oxford: Praeger, 2000. Copyright © 2000. James Currey Publishers. Reprinted with permission of James Currey Publishers.

Opubor, Alfred E. "If Community Media Is the Answer, What Is the Question," paper published as Chapter 1 in *Promoting Community Media in Africa* (2000), S.T. Kwame Boafo, ed. UNESCO, Paris. Reprinted with permission of the copyright holder.

Parks, Will, with Denise Gray-Felder, Jim Hunt and Ailish Byrne. *Who Measures Change? An Introduction to Participatory Monitoring and Evaluation of Communication for Social Change*, part of a series on measuring change published by the Communication for Social Change Consortium, Inc. Copyright © 2005 Communication for Social Change Consortium, Inc. Reprinted with permission of the publisher. www.communicationfor socialchange.org.

Pasquali, Antonio. "Communication Theory: The Sociological Implications of Information on Mass Culture," excerpt from: *Comunicación y Cultura de Masas*, Caracas, Venezuela: Monte Avila Editores, 1963. Reprinted with permission of the author.

Pereira G., José Miguel and Martha Cardozo B. "Communication, Development and Health Promotion. Approaches, Balances and Challenges," paper presented in the 3rd National Congress on Communication and Health, and in the First Latin American Congress on Communication and Health held in Cochabamba, (Bolivia), September 3 to 6, 2003. Translated from Spanish by Emma Cristina Montaña R. Used with permission of the author.

Peruzzo, Cicilia M. Krohling. "Direito à Comunicação Comunitária, Participaço Popular e Cidadania," ["Right to Community Communication, Popular Participation and Citizenship,"] in Maria José da Costa Oliveira, ed., *Comunicação pública* [Public Communication]. Campinas, Brazil: Alínea, 2004, 49-79. Reprinted with permission of the author.

Prieto Castillo, Daniel. "Communication and Daily Life," Vida Cotidiana y Comunicación, La Comunicación Educativa como Proceso Alternativo. From *Diseño y comunicación*, Mexico, Ed. Coyoacán, 1994. Originally circulated as "Vida cotidiana y comunicación," written for a discussion meeting at the Department of Design, Unidad Azcapotzalco, Universidad Autónoma Metropolitana, Mexico, 1979. Reprinted with permission of the author.

Prieto Castillo, Daniel. *La Pasión por el Discurso: Cartas a Estudiantes de Comunicación.* [Passion for Discourse: Letters to Students of Communication] Mexico City: Coyoacán, 1994. Copyright © 1995, Daniel Prieto Castillo. Reprinted with permission of the author.

Quarry, Wendy. "The Fogo Process: An Interview with Donald Snowden," *Interaction.* Varnasi, India: Bhargava Bhushan Press. Copyright © 1984, Wendy Quarry. Reprinted with permission of the copyright holder.

Quebral, Nora C. "Is it Government Communication or People Communication?" paper presented at the BERNAMA-AMIC seminar on Communication Challenges in Asia, Kuala Lumpur, Malaysia, November 22, 1985. Reprinted with permission of the author.

Quebral, Nora Cruz. "Development Communication in the Agricultural Context," paper presented at the symposium on the theme "In Search of Breakthroughs in Agricultural Development" held in honor of Dr. Dioscoro L. Umali, December 9–10, 1971, College, Laguna; published as "Development Communication", in *Solidarity*, 7(6), 1972, pp. 39–44 and reprinted as "What Do We Mean by Development Communication," *International Development Review*, 15(2), 1973/1972, pp. 25–28. Reprinted with permission of the author.

Raboy, Marc. "Media and Democratisation in the Information Society," in O'Siochru, S., and B. Girard, eds., *Communicating in the Information Society.* Geneva: UNRISD, 2003. Reprinted with permission.

Ramirez, Mina, "Communication as if People Matter: The Challenge of Alternative Communication," *The Myth of the Information Revolution*, ed. Traber, M. London: Sage, 1986, pp. 104-105. Copyright 1986 by Sage Publications. Reprinted by permission of Sage Publications Inc.

Ramírez, Ricardo. "Bridging Disciplines: The Natural Resource Management Kaleidoscope for Understanding ICTs," *Journal of Development Communication* 1:51–64, Kuala Lumpur, Malaysia. Copyright © 2003 Asian Institute for Development Communication. Reprinted with permission of the copyright holder.

Ramonet, Ignacio. "The Single Thought Doctrine," presented at El Pensamento Unico (Conferenca Magistral) Oct. 1997. Used with permission of the author.

Ramonet, Ignacio. "Set the Media Free," *Le Monde Diplomatique*, October 2003, No. 52. Copyright © 2003 Ignacio Ramonet. Reprinted with permission of the author and the publisher.

Reyes Matta, Fernando. Excerpt from: "Comunicación Alternativa y Cambio Social. I América Latin." Excerpt of chapter in Simpson Gringberg, Máximo (Ed.) (1981) *Comunicación Alternativa y Cambio Social. I América Latina,* Universidad Nacional Autónoma de México. Reprinted with permission of the author and the publisher.

Riaño, Pilar, ed. *Women in Grassroots Communication: Furthering Social Change.* Copyright © 1994 by Sage Publications. Reprinted by permission of Sage Publications, Inc.

Richeri, Giuseppe (1988), *Complejidad Social e Información, Dialogos de la Comunicación,* No. 21, July. Copyright © 1988, Guiseppe Richeri. Reprinted with permission of the copyright holder.

Robinson, Scott S. "¿Brecha o Inclusión Digital?" [Digital Gap or Digital Inclusion?] A preliminary version was published in *Nueva Sociedad*, No. 195, Caracas, Venezuela, 2004. Reprinted with permission.

Rodriguez, Clemencia. Chapter 1 of *Fissures in the Mediascape. An International Study of Citizens' Media* (2001) by Hampton Press, Creskill, NJ (US). Copyright © 2001, Hampton Press. Reprinted with permission of the publisher.

Rogers, E. M. "Communication and Development: The Passing of the Dominant Paradigm," *Communication Research*, April 1976: 3. Copyright 1976 by Sage Publications. Reprinted by permission of Sage Publications Inc.

Roncagliolo, Rafael. "New Information Order in Latin America: A Taxonomy for National Communication Policies," in Jörg Becker, Göran Hedebro and Leena Paldán, eds., *Communication and Domination: Essays to Honor Herbert I. Schiller.* Norwood, New Jersey: Ablex Publishing Corp., 1986. Reproduced with permission of Greenwood Publishing Group, Inc., Westport, Conn.

Roncagliolo, Rafael. "Radios Comunitarias: Futuro Imperfecto. [Community Radio: An Imperfect Future,]" paper presented at the Congress of Local Radio in Andalusia, 1998. Reprinted with permission of the author.

Rosario-Braid, Florangel. "A User-Oriented Communication Strategy" in F. Rosario-Braid, ed., *Communication Strategy for Productivity Improvement.* Tokyo: Asian Productivity Organization, 1979, 27-46. Copyright © 1979, APO. Reprinted with permission of copyright holder.

Saik Yoon, Chin. "Ascendancy of Participatory Approaches," in Chapter 2 of *Participatory Development Communication: A West African Agenda*, Guy Bessette and C. V. Rajasunderam, eds., International Development Research Centre (IDRC) Ottawa, Canada 1996. Copyright© 1996, IDRC. Reprinted with permission of the IDRC.

Saik Yoon, Chin. "People in Charge," in Chapter 2 of *Participatory Development Communication: A West African Agenda*, Guy Bessette and C. V. Rajasunderam, eds., International Development Research Centre (IDRC) Ottawa, Canada 1996. Copyright© 1996, IDRC. Reprinted with permission of IRDC.

1927
1960
1963
1964
1967
1969
1970
1971
1972
1973
1974
1975
1976
1977
1978
1979
1980
1981
1982
1983
1984
1985
1986
1987
1988
1989
1990
1991
1992
1993
1994
1995
1996
1997
1998
1999
2000
2001
2002
2003
2004
2005
2006

Sarlo, Beatriz. *Lo popular como dimensión: tópica, retórica y problemática de la recepción.* Serie Documentos. Pontificia Universidad Javeriana, Facultad de Comunicación Social, no. 842. September 1983, Bogotá, Colombia. Reprinted with permission of the author.

Scalway, Thomas. *"Missing the Message? 20 Years of Learning from HIV/AIDS."* London: Panos Institute, 2003. Copyright © 2003, Panos Institute. Reprinted with permission of the author and Panos Institute.

Schiller, Herbert I. *The Appearance of National Communication Policies: A New Arena for Social Struggle.* Vol. 21, No. 2, Gazette, Amsterdam. Copyright 1975 by Sage Publications. Reprinted by permission of Sage Publications Inc.

Schmucler, Hector. "Communication, Culture and Developments" *Comunicación y desarrollo,* Lima, IPAL, 1987. Republished with permission of the author.

Schramm, Wilbur. *Mass Media and National Development.* Stanford, Calif.: Stanford University Press, 1964. Copyright © 1964, UNESCO. Reprinted with permission of the publisher.

Servaes, Jan. "Communication and Development Paradigms: An Overview," in *Search of Communication and Development Paradigms,* mss. Bangkok: Thammasat University, 1985. Reprinted with permission of the author.

Servaes, Jan. *Communication for Development: One World, Multiple Cultures.* Cresskill, New Jersey: Hampton Press, 2001, Chapter 3. Copyright © 2001 Hampton Press. Reprinted with permission of the publisher.

Shah, Hemant and Karin Gwinn Wilkins. "Geometries of Development," published in *Mazi,* the electronic report of the Communication for Social Change Consortium, May 2006. *www.communicationforsocialchange.org/php.mazi* Reprinted with permission of the authors and the publisher.

Shingi, Prakash, and Bella Mody. "The Communication Effects Gap: A Field Experiment in TV and Agricultural Ignorance in India." *Communication Research,* Vol. 3, 2, April 1976. Copyright © 1976, Rowman and Littlefield Publishers. Reprinted with permission of the publisher.

Sierra, Francisco. "Information Society and Social Movements: Democratic Alternatives to the Dominant Social Development Model," excerpt from: "Sociedad de la Información y Movimientos Sociales" In *La Red es de Todos. Cuando los Movimientos Sociales se apropian de la Red.* Coordinator: Víctor Marí Sáez. Editorial Popular, Madrid, Spain 2004. Reprinted with permission.

Singhal, Arvind. "Focusing on the Forest, Not Just the Tree: Cultural Strategies for Combating AIDS," *MICA Communications Review,* 2003. Copyright © 2003 Mudrah Institute of Communications Ahmedabad. Reprinted with permission.

Slim, Hugo and Paul Thomson. "Varieties of Oral Evidence," excerpt from *Listening for a Change: Oral Testimony and Development.* London: Panos, 1994. Copyright © 1994, Panos Institute. Reprinted with permission.

Smythe, Dallas W. "Communications: Blindspot of Western Marxism," *Canadian Journal of Political and Social Theory/Revue Canadienne de Theorie Politique et Sociale,* Vol. 1, No. 3 (Fall/Automne 1977). Copyright © 1977 Canadian Journal of Political and Social Theory/Revue. Reprinted with permission.

Somavia, Juan, 1977. "The Transnational Power Structure and International Information," first published in: Fernando Reyes Matta (ed.) 1977. *La Información en el Nnevo Orden Iinternacional.* D. R. Instituto Latinoamericano de Estudios Transnacionales (ILET) Mexico. Reprinted with permission of F. Reyes Matta.

Sonderling, Stefan, 1997. "Development Support Communication: A Change Agent in Support of Popular Participation or a Double Agent of Deception?" paper presented at the Development, Culture and Communication Conference and Workshop, Human Sciences Research Council (HSRC), Pretoria, 56 September 1997. Copyright ©1997 Unisa Press, Pretoria, South Africa. Reprinted with permission of the author and copyright holder, Unisa Press.

Sreberny-Mohammadi, Annabelle and Ali Mohammadi. "Small Media and Revolutionary Change: A New Model," excerpt from *Small Media, Big Revolution: Communication, Culture, and the Iranian Revolution,* p. 19-39. University of Minnesota Press: Minneapolis–London, 1994. Copyright © 1994 University of Minnesota Press. Reprinted with permission of University of Minnesota Press.

Storey, J. Douglas. "Popular Culture Discourse, and Development: Rethinking E-E from a Participatory Perspective," Servaes, Jan & Thomas Jacobson (1999). *Theoretical Approaches to Participatory Communication.* IAMCR book series. Hampton Press, Inc. Cresskill, New Jersey. Copyright © 1999, Hampton Press. Reprinted with permission of the copyright holder.

Teer-Tomaselli, Ruth. "Public Service Broadcasting," *South African Journalism Handbook of Excellence.* Pretoria, South Africa: Human Science Research Council, 2004. Reprinted with permission of the author.

Teer-Tomaselli, Ruth, 2004. "Transforming State-Owned Enterprises in the Global Age: Lessons from Broadcasting and Telecommunications in South Africa," published in *Critical Arts,* a Journal for South-North Cultural and Media Studies, June 2004, Vol. 18, No. 1. Copyright © 2004 *Critical Arts,* University of KwaZulu-Natal. Reprinted with permission of the author and publisher.

Thomas, Pradip. "Participatory Development Communication: Philosophical Premises," reproduced from Shirley A. White, K. Sadanandan Nair and Joseph Ascroft: *Participatory Communication: Working for Change and Development.* Copyright © 1994 Shirley A. White, K. Sadanandan Nair and Joseph Ascroft. Reprinted by permission of Sage Publications Inc.

Thomas, Pradip. "Traditional Communication and Democratisation: Practical Considerations," from Lee, Philip, ed. *Democratisation of Communication.* University of Wales Press, Cardiff, 1995. Reprinted with permission.

Torrico Villanueva, Erick R., "Subertir las convenciones: Desafios en la planificación de la comunicación para el cambio [Subverting Conventions: Challenges in Planning Communication for Change,]" from Cimadevilla, Gustavo and Edgardo Carniglia, eds. *Comunicacion, ruralidad y desarrollo.* Ediciones INTA: Buenos Aires, 2004. Reprinted with permission of the author.

Tufte, Thomas, 2005. "Back in the Trenches?" published in *Communication Initiative Drumbeat Commentary,* May 2, 2005, No. 297. www.comminit.com/drum_beat_297.html. Reprinted with permission of the author and publisher.

Tufte, Thomas. "Entertainment-Education in Development Communication: Between Marketing Behaviours and Empowering People," chapter nine of Hemer, Oscar and Thomas Tufte, *Media and Global Change—Rethinking Communication for Social Change.* Buenos Aires, Argentina: Clasco; and Göteborg, Sweden: Nordicom, 2005. Reprinted with permission of the author and the publisher.

Ugboajah, Frank Okwu, 1985. "Oramedia in Africa," from Ugboajah, Frank Okwu, ed. *Mass Communication, Culture and Society in West Africa.* Copyright ©1985 by the World Association for Christian Communication. Reprinted with permission of the publisher and copyright holder.

Ugboajah, Frank Okwu, 1972. "Traditional-Urban Media Model: Stocktaking for African Development," from *Gazette: International Journal for Mass Communication Studies*, vol. XVIII, No. 2, 1972. Copyright © 1972 Sage Publications Ltd. Reproduced with permission of the publisher.

UNESCO. Pavlic, Breda and Cees J. Hamelink. *The New International Economic Order: Links between Economics and Communications*, UNESCO, Paris, 1985. Copyright ©1985, UNESCO. Reprinted with permission of the publisher.

Valbuena, Victor, 1980. "Philippine Theatre Arts as Development Communication," from *Continuity and Change in Communication Systems: An Asian Perspective*. Wang, Georgette and Wimal Dissanayake. Westport, Conn.: 1984. Copyright ©1984 by Ablex Publishing Corporation, New Jersey. Reproduced with permission of Greenwood Publishing Group, Inc., Westport, Connecticut and the author.

Voth, Donald. "Community and Community Development" www.uark.edu/depts/hesweb/hdfsrs/rsoc4263/cdbook6.PDF, 2000. Reprinted with permission of the author.

Waisbord, Silvio. "Towards a Theoretical and Empirical Convergence? Family Tree of Theories, Methodologies and Strategies in Development," communication paper prepared for The Rockefeller Foundation, 2002. Copyright © 2002, Communication for Social Change Consortium and the Rockefeller Foundaion. Used under a license agreement.

Wang, Georgette, and Wimal Dissanayake. "Culture, Development, and Change: Some Explorative Observations," *Continuity and Change in Communication Systems: An Asian Perspective*. Copyright © 1984 Ablex Publishing Corporation, 1984. Reproduced with permission of Greenwood Publishing Group, Inc., Westport, Conn.

White, Robert A. "Cultural Analysis in Communication for Development —The Role of Cultural Dramaturgy in the Creation of a Public Sphere," *Journal of SID*, p 23-31, 1990:2. Copyright ©1990 Society for International Development.

White, Robert A. "Is Empowerment the Answer? Current Theory and Research on Development Communication," *Gazette*, Vol. 66, No. 1, 2004, 7-24. Copyright © 2004 by Sage Publications. Reprinted by permission of Sage Publications, Inc.

White, Shirley. "The Concept of Participation: Transforming Rhetoric to Reality," *Participatory Communication: Working for Change and Development*. Copyright © 1994 Shirley A. White, K. Sadanandan Nair and Joseph Ascroft. Reprinted by permission of Sage Publications, Inc.

Wilkins, Karin Gwinn. "Communication and Transition in the Middle East," *Gazette*, 2004, Vol. 66, No. 6: 483-496. Copyright © Sage Publications, 2004. Reproduced with permission of Sage Publications Ltd.

Wilkins, Karin Gwinn. "Development Discourse on Gender and Communication in Strategies for Social Change," published in *Journal of Communication*; 1999; 49:46-68 Copyright © 1999 International Communication Association. Reprinted with permission of the copyright holder.

Wilkins, Karin Gwinn. "Accounting for Power in Development Communications," Wilkins, Karin Gwinn, ed. *Redeveloping Communication for Social Change: Theory, Practice, and Power*, Chapter 15. Copyright © 2000, Rowman & Littlefield Publishers, Inc. Boulder, CO. Used with permission of copyright holder.

Williamson, Anthony. "The Fogo Process: Development Support Communication in Canada and the Developing World," from Chapter 13 in *Communication in Development: A Multinational Perspective*, Fred L. Casmir, ed.

(Norwood, New Jersey: Ablex Publishing Corporation, 1990). Reprinted with permission of the publisher.

Zutter, Pierre de. *¿Cómo comunicarse con los campesinos?* Editorial Horizonte, Lima (Peru). Reprinted with permission of the author.

1927
1960
1963
1964
1967
1969
1970
1971
1972
1973
1974
1975
1976
1977
1978
1979
1980
1981
1982
1983
1984
1985
1986
1987
1988
1989
1990
1991
1992
1993
1994
1995
1996
1997
1998
1999
2000
2001
2002
2003
2004
2005
2006